Chambers

ANAGRAMS

for Crosswords, Scrabble®
and all other word games

Compiled by
Chaz R Pewters, Zac Wherpster
and Esther C Zwarp

Reprinted 1986
Reprinted 1987
Reprinted 1989

ISBN 0 550 19011 2

Cover design by John Marshall
Printed in Great Britain by
Martin's of Berwick

Preface

Chambers, publishers of the world-renowned Dictionary, have harnessed modern computer technology to produce this comprehensive dictionary. It contains over 100,000 clear solutions to anagrams and is, therefore, an essential addition to the reference library of every crossword puzzler, Scrabble® player and wordgame fan.

Chambers Anagrams is very easy and quick to use. Anagrams and solutions are grouped according to length and the headings indicate word length as well as providing a guide to the letter-combinations on the page. Once you have decided which letters make up the anagram, rearrange them in alphabetical order and look up the resulting letter-combination in the text. For example, if the anagram is OPEN A RIOT, arrange these letters alphabetically to give AEINOOPRT. This letter-combination can then be looked up in the nine-letter words section to give the answer: OPERATION.

Sometimes more than one solution is given under a particular letter-combination; for example, ACEEIRTV = CREATIVE OR REACTIVE. In these cases the correct answer will be obvious from the wording of the clue and the letters already in the crossword frame.

The scope of *Chambers Anagrams* can be further extended by taking into account possible word endings. It is usually clear from crossword clues whether their solutions end in -S, -ES, -ING, -D, -ED or -LY. In these cases, you should remove the expected 'ending letters' from the letter-combination and look up the 'basic' word in the dictionary.

For example, in the clue

Alas! Planet in ruins, smokes (10)

'in ruins' indicates that the anagram to be solved is 'Alas! Planet' and the plural 'smokes' indicates that the solution is a plural word. Removing the expected plural 'S' gives the letter-combination AAAELLNPT = PANATELLA. Replacing the 'S' gives the solution PANATELLAS = CIGARS = 'SMOKES'.

Similarly, in the clue

Obtained pure cord strangely (8)

'strangely' indicates an anagram of 'pure cord' and 'obtained' suggests a solution in the past tense. Removing 'D' from 'pure cord' gives the letter-combination CEOPRRU = PROCURE: replacing the 'D' gives the solution PROCURED = 'OBTAINED'.

A few minutes' practice with this ingenious book will enable you to become an expert in the subtle art of solving anagrams.

For Scrabble® players, *Chambers Anagrams* is the perfect short cut to inspiration. Simply arrange the titles on your rack into alphabetical order and look up the resulting letter-combination to see if a five- six- or bonus seven-letter word is possible. Alternatively, include one or more 'free' tiles on the board in your calculations and consult the relevant section.

With over 30,000 words listed in the seven- and eight-letter sections alone, this book is clearly a powerful aid to improved Scrabble® playing.

aaabc
  abaca
aaabk
  Kaaba
aaabr
  araba
aaaby
  abaya
aaagm
  Agama
aaakm
  kaama
aaann
  anana
aaans
  asana
aabbk
  kabab
aabcc
  bacca
aabci
  abaci
aabck
  aback
aabcl
  cabal
aabcs
  cabas
aabdl
  labda
aabem
  abeam
aaber
  abear
aabes
  abase
aabet
  abate
aabft
  abaft
aabgm
  gamba
aabhi
  Bahai
aabhs
  abash
aabil
  labia
aabin
  bania
aabjn
  bajan
aabjr
  bajra
aabks
  abask
  kasba
aabln
  Alban
  banal
aablr
  labra
aabls
  balas
  balsa
  basal
  Sabal
aablt
  tabla
aabmm
  mamba
aabmn
  amban
aabmr
  abram
aabms
  samba
aabns
  basan
aabnt
  Banat
aabnu
  abuna
aabnw
  bwana
  nawab
aabor
  aroba
aabrs
  sabra
aabrt
  rabat
aabrv
  brava
aabry
  Araby
aabrz
  bazar
  zabra
aabst
  basta
aabsu
  sauba
aabtt
  batta
aacce
  caeca
aacco
  cacao
aaccy
  yacca
aacdh
  dacha
aacei
  aecia
aacep
  apace
aacfi
  facia
aachk
  kacha
aachp
  pacha
aachr
  chara
aachy
  chaya
aacir
  acari
aackl
  alack
aacll
  calla
aacln
  canal
aaclp
  calpa
aacls
  scala
aacmn
  caman
aacms
  camas
aacmw
  macaw
aacnn
  canna
aacnt
  Tacan
aacnz
  Anzac
aacpr
  Parca
aacps
  scapa
aacrs
  sacra
aacrt
  carat
  carta
aacuv
  vacua
aaddx
  addax
aadeg
  adage
aadeh
  ahead
aadel
  aldea
aader
  Ardea
  aread
aadfl
  afald
aadfr
  daraf
  fa'ard
  farad
aadgg
  dagga
aadgr
  darga
  garda
aadin
  Diana
  naiad
aadip
  apaid
aadln
  aland
aadls
  salad
aadlt
  datal
aadmm
  madam
aadmn
  ad-man
  daman
aadmp
  padma
aadmr
  damar
  drama
aadnp
  panda
aador
  A-road
aadpt
  adapt
aadpy
  apayd
aadrr
  radar
aadrw
  award
aadsy
  adays
aadty
  adyta
aaegl
  algae
  galea
aaegp
  agape
  apage
aaegt
  agate
aaegv
  agave
aaegz
  agaze
aaehp
  aheap
aaekp
  apeak
aaekw
  awake
aaelp
  palea
aaelr
  areal
aaelt
  alate
aaelv
  avale
aaemt
  amate
aaemz
  amaze
aaenp
  apnea
  paean
aaenr
  anear
  arena
aaent
  antae
aaenv
  Avena
aaerr
  arear
aaert
  reata
aaeru
  aurae
aaerw
  aware
aaevw
  awave
aaffj
  Jaffa
aafhl
  halfa
aafim
  Mafia
aafin
  Naafi
aafit
  tafia
aafln
  fanal
aaflt
  fatal
aafnu
  fauna
aafry
  yarfa
aaghl
  galah
aagil
  agila
aagim
  agami
aagin
  again
aagis
  saiga
aagit
  taiga
aagjn
  ganja
aagkn
  kanga
aagll
  algal
aagln
  alang
  lagan
aaglr
  graal
aaglv
  vagal
aagly
  gayal
aaglz
  gazal
aagmm
  gamma
  magma
aagmr
  grama
aagnp
  pagan
  panga
aagnr
  argan
aagnt
  tanga
aagnu
  guana
aagor
  agora
aaguv
  guava
aahjr
  rajah
aahkm
  hakam
aahky
  khaya
aahll
  Allah
  halal
aahlm
  almah
  halma
  hamal
aahln
  nahal
aahlo
  aloha
aahlp
  alpha
aahlr
  lahar
aahlv
  halva
aahmo
  haoma
aahmr
  haram
  marah
aahms
  shama
aahmu
  mahua
aahmw
  mahwa
aahmz
  hamza
aahnp
  hanap
aahnt
  thana
aahps
  pasha
aahrr
  arrah
aahry
  rayah
aahsu
  Hausa
aahsw
  awash
aahsy
  shaya
aaijn
  Jaina
aaikk
  kaiak
aaikl
  laika
aaiks
  Sakai
  sakia
aailm
  lamia
aailn
  liana
aails
  alias
aailt
  Itala
aailv
  avail
aailx
  axial
aaimn
  amain
  amnia
  anima
  mania
aaimr
  maria
aaims
  Masai
aaimt
  Amati
aaimz
  zamia
aainp
  apian
aainr
  Arian
  naira
aains
  Asian
  Naias
aainv
  avian
aaips
  paisa
aairt
  atria
  riata
  taira
  tiara
aaiss
  assai

5 AAI

aaisv
  Saiva
aaitw
  await
aajlp
  jalap
aajnp
  japan
aajnv
  Javan
aajnw
  ajwan
  jawan
aajnz
  zanja
aajrt
  jarta
aakkp
  pakka
aakky
  kayak
  yakka
aaklo
  koala
aaklp
  kalpa
aaklr
  kraal
aakmr
  karma
  makar
aaknt
  tanka
aakop
  poaka
aakpp
  kappa
aakpr
  parka
aakrt
  karat
aakst
  Sakta
aallm
  llama
aalln
  nalla
aallp
  palla
aalls
  salal
aallu
  alula
aallw
  walla
aally
  allay
aalmr
  alarm
  malar
  ramal
aalmt
  Malta
  talma
  tamal
aalmv
  malva
aalmx
  malax
aalmy
  Malay
aalnn
  annal
aalns
  nasal
aalnt
  natal
aalnv
  naval
aalpp
  appal
  papal
aalps
  palas
  Salpa
aalpt
  talpa
aalpy
  palay
  playa
aalpz
  plaza
aalrt
  altar
  artal
  talar
aalru
  aural
  laura
aalrv
  arval
  larva
  lavra
aalry
  alary
aalrz
  lazar
aalst
  atlas
aalsv
  lavas
  vasal
aalwy
  alway
aammm
  mamma
aammn
  amman
aamnn
  manna
aamnt
  atman
  manta
aamny
  Mayan
aamor
  aroma
aamos
  omasa
aampp
  pampa
aampr
  praam
aamss
  amass
  massa
aamtz
  matza
aannn
  nanna
aanno
  Anona
aannt
  annat
  tanna
aanps
  sapan
aanpv
  pavan
aanpx
  panax
aanqt
  qanat
aanrs
  naras
aanrt
  antar
  ratan
aanru
  Anura
aanrv
  varan
  varna
aanrw
  awarn
aanry
  Aryan
  Nayar
aanss
  sansa
aanst
  Satan
aansu
  sauna
aantv
  avant
aaort
  aorta
aappt
  tappa
aappw
  papaw
aappy
  appay
aaprt
  apart
aapst
  pasta
aaptt
  attap
aapww
  pawaw
aarrs
  arras
aarry
  array
aarss
  sarsa
aarst
  Rasta
  tasar
aarsz
  sarza
aartt
  attar
  Tatar
aarty
  tayra
  yarta
aassy
  assay
aastv
  avast
aaswy
  asway
  aways
aatxy
  ataxy
aatzz
  tazza
abbco
  bobac
  cabob
abbcy
  cabby
abbee
  Babee
abbek
  kebab
abbel
  Babel
abber
  barbe
abbey
  abbey
abbgy
  gabby
abbir
  rabbi
abbko
  bobak
  kabob
abblu
  babul
  bubal
abbmo
  A-bomb
abbno
  nabob
abboo
  baboo
abbot
  abbot
abbty
  tabby
abbyy
  yabby
abcco
  bacco
  bocca
  caboc
abccy
  baccy
abcee
  abcee
abceh
  beach
abcel
  cable
abcer
  acerb
  brace
  caber
  cabré
abchr
  brach
abcht
  batch
abcin
  Binca®
  cabin
abcio
  cobia
abcir
  baric
  Carib
  rabic
abcis
  basic
abcjo
  Jacob
abckl
  black
abckr
  brack
abcno
  bacon
  banco
abcnu
  Cuban
abcor
  carob
  coarb
  cobra
abcrs
  scrab
abcrt
  bract
abcsu
  scuba
abdde
  bedad
abddy
  baddy
abdeg
  badge
  begad
  de-bag
abdei
  abide
abdek
  baked
abdel
  blade
abdem
  bemad
abdeo
  abode
  adobe
abder
  ardeb
  beard
  bread
  debar
abdes
  based
abdeu
  daube
abdey
  beady
abdhn
  bandh
abdil
  ad-lib
abdir
  braid
  rabid
abdit
  tabid
abdln
  bland
abdlu
  blaud
abdly
  badly
abdnr
  brand
abdny
  bandy
abdor
  abord
  board
  broad
abdoy
  a'body
abdry
  bardy
abduy
  dauby
abdwy
  bawdy
abeel
  abele
  albee
abefl
  fable
abegi
  bigae
abegl
  bagel
  belga
  gable
abegn
  began
abegr
  barge
  begar
  garbe
abegt
  begat
abehk
  bekah
abehl
  belah
  hable
abeho
  bohea
  obeah
abehs
  Sheba
abeht
  bathe
abeim
  I-beam
abeir
  erbia
abeis
  abies
abeiz
  baize
abejl
  jelab
abejm
  jambe
abekl
  bleak
abekn
  baken
abekr
  baker
  brake
  break
abell
  all-be
  be-all
  label
abelm
  amble
  blame
abelr
  baler
  blare
  blear
abels
  blaes
  blasé
  sable
abelt
  ablet
  blate
  bleat
  table

abely
bayle
belay
abelz
blaze
abemr
amber
brame
bream
embar
abemw
weamb
abemy
beamy
embay
maybe
abeno
beano
abenu
abune
abeot
E-boat
abeov
above
abept
bepat
aberr
barre
barré
abers
Saber
sabre
aberv
brave
abery
barye
beray
yerba
aberz
braze
zebra
abess
bases
basse
abest
baste
beast
Sebat
tabes
abesu
abuse
abesy
absey
abetu
beaut
Butea
taube
tubae
abeux
beaux
abeuz
buaze
abffu
buffa

abffy
baffy
abggy
baggy
abghi
bigha
abghn
bhang
abgin
ba'ing
abgno
obang
abgnu
unbag
abgor
Garbo
abhis
sahib
abhit
habit
abhls
blash
abhor
abhor
abhrs
brash
abhsu
subah
abiil
alibi
abiim
iambi
abiit
tibia
abijr
bajri
abikt
batik
abiln
blain
abilo
aboil
abilq
qibla
abilr
brail
libra
abils
basil
labis
abimr
abrim
imbar
abimt
ambit
abinr
abrin
bairn
brain
abins
basin
sabin

abinu
bunia
nubia
abinv
bavin
abiot
biota
abirr
briar
abiru
Rubia
abirv
bravi
abiss
basis
abist
absit
abiwz
bwazi
abjmo
jambo
abjmu
jambu
abjno
banjo
abjot
jabot
abkln
blank
abklu
baulk
abkly
balky
abkno
koban
abknr
brank
abkru
burka
abkry
barky
braky
abllu
bulla
ablly
bally
ablmu
album
ablmy
balmy
abloo
baloo
ablor
lobar
ablos
bolas
ablot
bloat
ablow
ablow
ablru
lubra
ablrw
brawl

ablst
blast
abltu
tubal
ablwy
bylaw
ablyy
lay-by
abmmo
mambo
abmos
ambos
sambo
abmoz
zambo
abmru
rumba
umbra
abmry
ambry
barmy
abmsy
abysm
abnns
banns
abnor
baron
abnos
bason
abnot
baton
abnru
buran
unbar
urban
abntu
Bantu
tabun
abnuy
bunya
aboot
taboo
aboqt
Q-boat
aborr
arbor
abort
abort
boart
tabor
aborv
bravo
aborx
borax
abory
boyar
aboss
basso
abost
basto
boast
sabot

abotu
about
U-boat
abotw
bowat
abouy
bayou
boyau
abqru
burqa
abqsu
squab
abrss
brass
abrst
brast
abrsu
Abrus
bursa
abrsw
braws
abrtu
tubar
abrty
rybat
abrwy
warby
abrxy
braxy
abssy
abyss
abstt
batts
abtty
batty
abuzz
abuzz
abwyy
byway
accde
Decca®
accdy
cycad
acceh
cache
accem
Mecca
acchi
chica
acchk
chack
accho
chaco
coach
accht
catch
accir
circa
accit
cacti
ticca
asckl
clack

accko
acock
acckr
crack
accoo
cocoa
accos
casco
accot
coact
accoy
accoy
accuy
yucca
acdde
decad
acddy
caddy
acdef
faced
acdeg
cadge
caged
acdel
decal
laced
acden
dance
acdep
paced
acder
acred
cadre
cedar
acdet
cadet
acdey
decay
acdgy
cadgy
acdhr
chard
acdil
calid
acdin
canid
cnida
acdir
acrid
caird
cardi
daric
acdis
Asdic
acdit
diact
dicta
acdlo
acold
acdls
scald
acdlu
cauld
ducal

acdly
yclad
acdns
scand
acdnu
adunc
acdny
candy
acdor
Draco
acdot
octad
acdry
cardy
acdsu
scaud
acdtu
ducat
aceek
ackee
aceep
peace
acees
caese
cease
acefh
chafe
acefl
fecal
acefr
facer
farce
aceft
facet
acegl
glacé
acegr
grace
acegy
cagey
acehk
cheka
acehl
chela
leach
acehn
caneh
hance
nache
acehp
chape
cheap
peach
acehr
chare
rache
reach
acehs
chase
aceht
cheat
tache
teach
theca

5 ACE

acehv
chave
aceil
Alice
ileac
aceim
amice
acein
eniac
aceip
Picea
aceir
ceria
erica
aceis
saice
aceiv
cavie
acekr
crake
creak
acekw
wacke
acell
cella
acelm
camel
macle
aceln
ancle
clean
lance
acelp
caple
place
acelr
Clare
clear
acels
claes
scale
acelt
cleat
éclat
lacet
acelv
calve
cavel
clave
acely
lacey
acemo
cameo
acemr
crame
cream
macer
acenn
nance
aceno
canoe
ocean
acenp
pance
pecan
acenr
crane
crena
nacre
rance
acens
scena
acent
enact
aceor
ocrea
acepr
caper
crape
pacer
Perca
recap
aceps
scape
space
acept
epact
acepy
pacey
acerr
crare
racer
acers
carse
scare
scrae
sérac
acert
caret
carte
cater
crate
react
recta
trace
aceru
Eruca
acerv
carve
crave
varec
acerx
carex
acerz
craze
acest
caste
cates
sceat
acesu
cause
sauce
acett
tacet
acetu
acute
acetx
exact
acetz
Aztec
acffh
chaff
acffs
scaff
acfht
chaft
acfhu
chufa
acfil
calif
acfir
Afric
farci
acfis
fasci
acfkr
frack
acflo
focal
acfnr
franc
acfny
fancy
acfrs
scarf
acfrt
craft
fract
acfry
farcy
acghn
ganch
acgim
gamic
magic
acgir
cigar
craig
acgln
clang
acgno
conga
acgor
cargo
acgot
cagot
acgou
guaco
acgrs
scrag
acguy
gaucy
acgwy
gawcy
achhn
hanch
achht
hatch
achik
haick
achin
chain
Chian
china
achio
chiao
achir
chair
achit
aitch
achkl
chalk
achkn
chank
achkr
chark
achks
shack
achkt
thack
achkw
whack
achln
lanch
achlo
loach
achlr
larch
achls
clash
achlt
latch
achlu
lauch
achlv
Vlach
achmo
macho
Mocha
achmp
champ
achmr
charm
march
achms
chasm
achmt
match
achnr
ranch
achnt
chant
natch
achnu
nucha
achop
Phoca
poach
achor
orach
roach
achos
chaos
oshac
achov
havoc
achpr
parch
achps
chaps
Pasch
achpt
patch
achrr
charr
achrs
crash
achrt
chart
ratch
achry
chary
achsu
sauch
achsw
schwa
achtw
watch
achty
yacht
aciil
iliac
aciim
amici
aciin
acini
aciis
Isiac
aciks
saick
acill
lilac
acilm
claim
malic
aciln
linac
acilp
plica
acils
salic
scail
acilt
cital
ictal
tical
acilu
aulic
acilv
cavil
acilx
calix
acimn
manic
acimr
cimar
acims
camis
acino
conia
acinp
panic
acinr
cairn
in-car
acins
Canis
Sican
acint
antic
acinv
Vinca
aciot
coati
acioz
azoic
acipr
picra
acips
aspic
scapi
spica
acirt
artic
aciru
auric
curia
acirv
vicar
vraic
acitt
attic
tacit
acitv
vatic
acjnu
cajun
ackkn
knack
ackln
clank
acklo
cloak
acklp
plack
ackls
slack
acklu
caulk
ackms
smack
ackmu
amuck
acknr
crank
ackns
snack
ackor
croak
ackpu
pucka
ackqu
quack
ackrt
track
ackrw
wrack
ackst
stack
acksw
swack
ackty
tacky
ackwy
wacky
acllo
local
aclls
scall
aclmo
cloam
comal
aclmp
clamp
aclmy
calmy
aclop
copal
aclor
carol
coral
aclot
octal
aclov
vocal
aclox
coxal
acloy
coaly
acloz
colza
aclps
clasp
scalp
aclpu
capul
aclrw
crawl
aclry
clary
aclss
class
aclsy
scaly
acltu
claut
aclxy
calyx
acmmo
comma
acmno
Maçon
acmor
carom

acmpr
cramp
acmps
scamp
acmpy
campy
acmrs
scram
acmry
cymar
acmsu
camus
Musca
sumac
acnno
ancon
canon
cañon
acnny
canny
nancy
acnop
capon
acnor
acorn
racon
acnos
Oscan
acnot
acton
canto
acnow
cowan
acnox
caxon
acnpu
uncap
acnrs
scran
acnry
carny
acnst
canst
scant
acnty
canty
acopr
copra
acops
scopa
acopt
capot
coapt
acors
Oscar
acort
actor
Croat
taroc
acory
oracy
acost
coast
costa

acott
cotta
acppu
cuppa
acprs
craps
scarp
scrap
acpry
crapy
acpsu
scaup
acpsy
spacy
acptu
caput
acrry
carry
acrss
crass
acrst
scart
scrat
acrsu
arcus
scaur
acrsw
scraw
acrsy
scary
scray
acrtt
T-cart
tract
acrtu
curat
acrvy
carvy
acryz
crazy
acssu
ascus
acstt
scatt
acstu
scuta
acsuy
saucy
actty
catty
adddy
daddy
addei
aided
addej
jaded
addel
addle
dedal
laded

adder
adder
aredd
dared
dread
addet
dated
addev
Vedda
addez
dazed
addfy
faddy
addim
madid
addio
addio
addny
dandy
addor
dorad
addos
dados
addot
add-to
addpy
paddy
addry
dryad
ydrad
addwy
waddy
adeem
adeem
edema
adeer
arede
eared
adeet
teade
adeev
deave
evade
adefg
fadge
adefm
famed
adeft
fated
adegg
gadge
adegj
gadje
adegl
glade
adegm
madge
adegr
grade
raged
adegt
gated
adegu
agued

adehj
jehad
adehk
kheda
adehl
heald
adehr
heard
adehs
Hades
shade
adeht
death
adehx
hexad
adehy
heady
adeil
eliad
ideal
adeim
amide
media
adein
Adeni
adeir
aider
irade
redia
adeis
aside
adeiu
adieu
adejw
jawed
adekl
Dalek
adekn
knead
naked
adekr
daker
drake
adekw
waked
adell
dalle
ladle
adelm
medal
adeln
eland
laden
lande
adelo
aloed
adelp
padle
pedal
plead
adelr
alder
adels
slade

adelt
dealt
delta
lated
adelw
dwale
weald
adely
delay
leady
ademm
damme
ademn
amend
maned
named
ademr
armed
derma
dream
ademu
Medau
ademw
wamed
adenn
an-end
adeno
anode
adenp
paned
adenr
dearn
redan
adens
sedan
snead
adenv
vaned
adenw
awned
dewan
waned
adeop
apode
adeor
adore
oared
oread
adepr
drape
padre
adeps
sepad
spade
adept
adept
pated
adepu
eupad
adepv
paved
adepy
payed

aderr
drear
aders
dares
rased
adert
dater
rated
trade
tread
aderw
wader
adery
deary
deray
rayed
ready
yeard
aderz
razed
zerda
adest
sated
stade
stead
adesv
saved
adesw
sawed
adetx
taxed
adevw
waved
adewy
deawy
adffr
draff
adffy
daffy
adfiv
vifda
adfno
fonda
adfrt
draft
adfru
faurd
fraud
adfrw
dwarf
adgil
algid
adgln
gland
adgly
glady
adgmo
dogma
adgno
Dagon
donga
gonad
adgnr
grand

adgoo
agood
adgop
pagod
adgos
gadso
adgot
toga'd
adgou
Gouda
adgru
guard
adgsu
Gadus
adguy
gaudy
adhij
hadji
jihad
adhik
khadi
adhim
Mahdi
adhin
ahind
adhip
aphid
adhis
Hasid
adhjo
hodja
adhlo
ahold
halo'd
adhlu
hauld
adhno
donah
adhns
shand
adhny
handy
adhor
hoard
adhrs
hards
shard
adhry
hardy
hydra
adhst
hadst
adhsu
sadhu
adhsy
shady
adiil
Iliad
adiio
iaido
oidia
adiir
radii

adiln
  Ladin
  nidal
adilo
  dolia
  Idola
adilp
  plaid
adilr
  drail
  laird
  liard
adils
  slaid
adilt
  dital
  tidal
adilu
  dulia
adilv
  valid
adily
  daily
adimn
  admin
adimr
  marid
adims
  Midas
adimt
  admit
adimx
  admix
adino
  danio
adinr
  dinar
  drain
  Indra
  nadir
adint
  idant
adinv
  divan
  viand
adinw
  diwan
adiop
  podia
adior
  aroid
  radio
adios
  adios
adiot
  diota
adiou
  audio
adiov
  avoid
adiox
  axoid
adioz
  diazo
adipr
  pardi
  rapid
adips
  sapid
adipv
  pavid
  vapid
adirr
  ard-ri
  raird
adirt
  triad
adirx
  radix
adiry
  dairy
  diary
adirz
  darzi
  izard
adist
  staid
adisy
  daisy
  sayid
aditu
  audit
aditv
  davit
adivv
  vivda
adjsu
  judas
adkko
  Kodak®
adkls
  skald
adkly
  alkyd
adkmr
  D-mark
adkmu
  dumka
adknr
  drank
adkny
  kandy
adkov
  vodka
adkry
  darky
adllo
  allod
  do-all
adlly
  dally
  laldy
adlmo
  domal
  modal
adlmw
  dwalm
adlmy
  madly
adlno
  nodal
adlnu
  laund
adlop
  L-dopa
  podal
adlot
  dotal
adlou
  aloud
adlps
  spald
adlru
  dural
adlrw
  drawl
adlry
  lardy
adlst
  stal'd
adlsy
  sadly
adltu
  adult
  dault
  tauld
adluy
  yauld
admno
  monad
  nomad
admnu
  maund
  Munda
  undam
admou
  douma
admpy
  dampy
admry
  mardy
admsu
  adsum
admtu
  datum
admuw
  dwaum
adnno
  Donna
adnnu
  nandu
adnor
  adorn
  radon
adnot
  Donat
adnow
  adown
  downa
adnoz
  zonda
adnpy
  pandy
adnrt
  drant
adnrw
  drawn
adnry
  randy
adnst
  stand
adnsu
  Sudan
adnsy
  sandy
  sdayn
adntu
  daunt
adops
  spado
adopt
  adopt
adors
  Doras
  sorda
adoru
  douar
  doura
adorw
  dowar
adoty
  toady
  today
adouy
  Douay
adprs
  sprad
adpry
  pardy
adpsy
  paysd
  spayd
adqsu
  squad
adquy
  quayd
adrru
  durra
adrst
  strad
adrsu
  rudas
  Sudra
adrsw
  sward
adrty
  tardy
adrvy
  vardy
adstu
  adust
aeefn
  neafe
aeefr
  feare
aeegl
  aglee
  eagle
aeegn
  agene
aeegr
  agree
  eager
  eagre
aeegt
  étage
aeeht
  eathe
aeehv
  heave
  hevea
aeeir
  aerie
aeekn
  akene
aeekp
  apeek
aeekr
  rakee
aeekw
  a-week
aeeln
  anele
aeelr
  leare
  leear
aeels
  easel
  easle
  lease
aeelt
  elate
  telae
aeelv
  leave
  veale
aeelw
  aweel
aeelz
  leaze
aeemn
  amene
  enema
  meane
aeemr
  ameer
  ramee
  reame
aeems
  mease
  seame
aeenr
  ranee
aeent
  eaten
  enate
aeenv
  naeve
  veena
  venae
aeeoz
  zoeae
aeeps
  pease
aeept
  étape
aeepy
  payee
aeepz
  peaze
aeerr
  arere
aeers
  erase
  saree
aeert
  arête
  eater
  reate
aeerv
  reave
aeerz
  razee
aeest
  setae
  tease
aeesv
  eaves
aeetx
  exeat
aeetz
  teaze
aeevw
  weave
aeffg
  gaffe
aefhs
  sheaf
aefir
  afire
aefkl
  flake
aefkn
  kenaf
aefkr
  faker
  freak
aefks
  fakes
aefll
  fella
aeflm
  femal
  flame
  fleam
aeflr
  farle
  feral
  flare
aefls
  false
aeflt
  aleft
  fetal
aefly
  leafy
aefmr
  frame
aefnr
  frena
aefor
  afore
aefov
  fovea
aefrs
  farse
aefrt
  after
  trefa
aefru
  feuar
aefrw
  wafer
aefry
  arefy
  faery
aefst
  feast
  festa
aeftw
  fetwa
aefuv
  Fauve
aefuw
  waefu'
aeggo
  agoge
aeggr
  agger
  eggar
aeggu
  gauge
aeghp
  phage
aeghr
  gerah
aegil
  agile
aegim
  image
aegis
  aegis
aegjr
  jäger
aegju
  gauje
aegll
  legal
aeglm
  gleam

aegln
angel
angle
genal
glean
aeglp
pagle
plage
aeglr
glare
lager
large
regal
aeglt
aglet
aeglv
gavel
aegly
agley
aeglz
gazel
glaze
aegmm
gemma
aegmn
mange
aegmo
omega
aegmr
grame
regma
aegno
agone
genoa
aegnr
anger
range
renga
aegnt
agent
aegnu
nugae
aegnv
vegan
aegny
geyan
gynae
aegos
Osage
aegpr
gaper
grape
pager
parge
aegrr
rager
regar
aegrs
sarge
segar
aegrt
grate
great
targe

aegru
argue
auger
aegrv
grave
aegrw
wager
aegry
aygre
gayer
yager
aegrz
gazer
graze
aegss
gases
aegst
stage
aegsu
usage
aegsw
swage
wages
aeguv
vague
aeguz
gauze
aehhp
ephah
aehht
heath
aehjr
hejra
aehkn
kaneh
aehks
shake
aehlm
almeh
hemal
aehlp
aleph
aehlr
haler
aehls
halse
leash
selah
shale
sheal
aehlt
ethal
lathe
aehlv
halve
aehlw
whale
wheal
aehly
hayle
aehlz
hazel

aehmn
he-man
maneh
aehmo
mahoe
aehmr
harem
herma
aehms
shame
Shema
aehmt
thema
aehnn
henna
aehns
ashen
Hanse
aehnt
neath
thane
aehnv
haven
aehny
hyena
aehot
tea-ho
aehpr
hepar
phare
raphe
aehps
heaps
Pesah
phase
shape
aehpy
heapy
aehrs
share
shear
aehrt
earth
hater
heart
rathe
thrae
aehrv
haver
aehrw
whare
aehrz
hazer
aehst
haste
aehsu
hause
aehsv
haves
shave
sheva
aehsw
hawse

aehtt
theta
aehtw
wheat
aehvy
heavy
Yahve
aehwy
Yahwe
aeikl
alike
aeilm
e-la-mi
maile
Melia
aeiln
alien
aline
anile
Elian
liane
aeilp
pilea
aeilr
ariel
aeils
aisle
aeilv
alive
aeilx
axile
aeilz
aizle
aeimn
amine
anime
aeimr
ramie
rimae
aeims
maise
aeimz
maize
aeinn
inane
aeins
anise
aeint
entia
Teian
tenia
tinea
aeinv
avine
naevi
naive
aeipr
perai
aeips
sepia
aeipt
pietà
aeirr
airer

aeirs
aesir
Aries
arise
raise
serai
aeirt
irate
terai
aeiru
aurei
aeirv
vairé
aeiry
aiery
ayrie
aeisv
avise
aeitt
tatie
aeitw
tawie
aeivw
waive
aeivz
avize
aejks
jakes
aejlp
lapje
aejlv
javel
aejms
james
aejps
jaspé
aejsy
jasey
aekln
ankle
aeklr
laker
aekls
slake
aeklw
kwela
aekly
kayle
leaky
aekmm
kamme
aekmr
maker
aekno
oaken
aeknp
pekan
aeknr
anker
Karen
naker
nerka
ranke

aekns
skean
snake
sneak
aeknt
taken
aeknv
knave
aeknw
waken
aekop
poake
aekor
oaker
aekot
atoke
aekow
awoke
aekoy
kayoe
aekps
spake
speak
aekpy
peaky
aekqu
quake
aekrr
raker
aekrs
asker
eskar
kesar
saker
aekrt
taker
aekrw
waker
wreak
aekst
skate
stake
steak
aeksu
ukase
aeksw
askew
aektw
tweak
aelll
allel
aellp
lapel
aelly
alley
aelmm
lemma
aelmn
leman
Lemna
aelmp
ample
maple
pelma

aelmr
marle
realm
aelms
mesal
samel
aelmt
metal
aelmu
ulema
aelmy
mealy
aelno
alone
aelnp
panel
penal
plane
aelnr
learn
Lerna
renal
aelns
slane
aelnt
laten
leant
aelnu
ulnae
aelnv
elvan
navel
venal
aelnw
wanle
aelny
leany
aelov
loave
volae
aelow
alowe
aeloz
zoeal
aelpp
apple
aelpr
lepra
parle
pearl
repla
aelps
Elaps
lapse
salep
sepal
spale

aelpt
  leapt
  lepta
  palet
  pelta
  petal
  plate
  pleat
aelpy
  ayelp
aelqu
  equal
aelrs
  arles
  laser
  seral
aelrt
  alert
  alter
  artel
  later
  ratel
aelru
  alure
  ureal
aelrv
  laver
  ravel
  velar
aelrw
  waler
aelrx
  relax
aelry
  early
  layer
  leary
  rayle
  relay
aelss
  salse
aelst
  least
  salet
  slate
  stale
  steal
  stela
  tales
  tesla
aelsu
  salue
aelsv
  salve
  selva
  slave
  vales
  valse
aelsw
  swale
  sweal
aeltv
  valet
aeltx
  exalt
  latex
aeluv
  uveal
  value
aelvv
  valve
aelvy
  leavy
  vealy
aemnr
  enarm
  namer
  reman
aemns
  manes
  manse
  means
  Mensa
  samen
aemnt
  ament
  manet
  meant
aemny
  meany
  yamen
aemov
  amove
aempx
  Ampex®
aemrr
  rearm
aemrs
  maser
  smear
aemrt
  armet
  mater
  tamer
  trema
aemry
  reamy
aemrz
  mazer
aemss
  massé
aemst
  steam
aemsu
  amuse
aemsy
  samey
  seamy
  ysame
aemtt
  matte
aemty
  etyma
  matey
  meaty
aemuv
  mauve
aemyz
  azyme
aennp
  panne
  penna
aenns
  senna
aennt
  anent
aennx
  annex
aenop
  paeon
aenot
  atone
  oaten
aenov
  novae
aenoz
  zonae
aenpp
  nappe
aenps
  aspen
  sneap
  spane
  spean
aenpt
  paten
  tapen
aenpv
  paven
aenqu
  quean
aenrr
  narre
aenrs
  nares
  snare
aenrt
  antre
aenru
  urena
aenrv
  raven
aenrw
  awner
aenry
  rayne
  renay
  yearn
aenst
  nates
  stane
  stean
aensu
  usnea
aensv
  avens
aensy
  sayne
aensz
  senza
aentx
  Texan
aentz
  zante
aenvw
  navew
aenwx
  waxen
aenwy
  waney
aenwz
  wanze
aenzz
  zanze
aeooz
  zooea
aeopr
  opera
aeops
  paseo
aeors
  arose
aeort
  Erato
  orate
  roate
aeoss
  oases
aeost
  stoae
aeosv
  oaves
aeotv
  ovate
aeotw
  aweto
aeotz
  azote
  toaze
aeppr
  paper
aeppu
  pupae
aeprr
  parer
  raper
aeprs
  asper
  parse
  prase
  presa
  spaer
  spare
  spear
aeprt
  apert
  pater
  peart
  petar
  prate
  taper
  trape
aeprv
  paver
aepry
  apery
  payer
  repay
aepss
  passé
aepst
  paste
  septa
  spate
  speat
aepsu
  pause
aepsv
  vespa
aeptt
  patte
  patté
  tapet
aeptu
  taupe
aepty
  peaty
aepvy
  peavy
aerrs
  serra
aerrt
  arrêt
  rater
  terra
aerrv
  raver
aerrw
  warre
aerss
  arses
  rasse
aerst
  aster
  reast
  stare
  strae
  teras
aersv
  saver
aersw
  sawer
  sware
  swear
aersy
  resay
  sayer
aertt
  arett
  tater
  tetra
  treat
aertu
  urate
aertv
  avert
  taver
aertw
  tawer
  water
  wrate
aertx
  extra
  taxer
aerty
  teary
aeruz
  azure
aervv
  varve
aervw
  waver
aerwx
  waxer
aerwy
  weary
aesss
  asses
  sasse
  sessa
aesst
  asset
  tasse
aessy
  essay
aestt
  state
  taste
  testa
aestu
  sauté
aestv
  stave
  vesta
aestw
  sweat
  tawse
  waste
aestx
  texas
aesty
  yeast
aesuv
  suave
aesvy
  savey
aetuv
  vaute
aetvw
  vawte
aetzz
  tazze
aevwy
  wavey
aevyz
  avyze
aewyy
  yawey
afffl
  flaff
affgr
  graff
affix
  affix
afflo
  offal
afflu
  luffa
affny
  nyaff
affqu
  quaff
affst
  staff
affty
  taffy
affuw
  wauff
afghu
  faugh
afgin
  Fagin
afglo
  oflag
afglu
  fugal
afgno
  fango
afgot
  fagot
afgrt
  graft
afgsu
  Fagus
afhit
  faith
afhls
  flash
afhrw
  wharf
afhst
  shaft
afikl
  kalif
afikr
  fakir
  Kafir
afill
  flail
afiln
  final
afilo
  folia
afilr
  filar
  flair
  frail
afimr
  fraim
afinr
  infra
afint
  faint
  Fanti

afirr
friar
afirs
fiars
afirt
afrit
afiry
fairy
afist
fasti
afkln
flank
afkls
flask
afkly
flaky
afknr
frank
afkrt
kraft
aflmm
flamm
aflmy
flamy
aflnw
flawn
afloo
aloof
loofa
aflor
flora
aflos
sol-fa
aflot
aloft
float
flota
aflou
afoul
aflru
fural
aflry
flary
afltu
fault
aflty
fatly
afluw
awful
aflwy
flawy
aflxy
flaxy
afmoy
foamy
afmsu
samfu
afnno
fanon
afnny
fanny
afnru
furan

afnsu
snafu
afoot
afoot
afors
sofar
afory
foray
afoss
fossa
afost
fatso
softa
afotu
fouat
afrss
frass
afrsw
swarf
afsuv
favus
aftty
fatty
aggin
aging
aggir
aggri
aggjy
jaggy
agglu
gulag
aggmo
Magog
aggms
maggs
aggny
naggy
aggor
aggro
aggry
aggry
raggy
aghhi
ahigh
aghhu
haugh
aghil
laigh
aghin
anigh
aghit
thagi
aghiz
ghazi
aghku
kaugh
aghlu
laugh
aghmo
ogham
aghno
hogan
aghns
gnash

aghnw
whang
aghpr
graph
aghrt
garth
aghst
ghast
aghsu
saugh
aghtu
aught
ghaut
aghuw
waugh
agiiv
vigia
agijr
jagir
agikl
glaik
agikn
kiang
agill
glial
agiln
algin
align
liang
ligan
linga
agilo
logia
agilr
argil
glair
grail
agils
sigla
agily
gaily
agimn
gamin
agimo
amigo
imago
agims
sigma
aginn
ingan
agino
gonia
ngaio
aginr
agrin
garni
grain
agint
giant
aginw
a-wing
wigan
aginz
zigan

agiop
igapo
agior
orgia
agipr
graip
pagri
agirt
tragi
agirv
virga
agist
agist
staig
agitu
aguti
agjlu
jugal
agkln
klang
agknr
krang
agkny
kyang
agkop
gopak
agkwy
gawky
agllo
Algol
aglly
gally
aglmu
algum
almug
glaum
mulga
aglno
Anglo
logan
longa
aglnr
gnarl
aglns
glans
slang
aglop
galop
aglor
argol
goral
largo
aglot
gloat
aglow
aglow
aglpy
pygal
aglru
glaur
gular
aglry
glary
gyral

aglss
glass
aglsu
gusla
agltu
galut
gault
aglux
Glaux
aglyz
glazy
zygal
agmmu
gumma
agmmy
gammy
agmno
among
mango
agmny
mangy
agmor
groma
agmot
magot
agmsu
magus
sagum
agmtu
gamut
agmuy
gaumy
agnno
gonna
agnnw
gnawn
agnor
argon
groan
nagor
orang
organ
agnot
tango
tonga
agnou
guano
agnow
gowan
wagon
wonga
agnoy
agony
agnoz
gazon
agnpr
prang
agnps
spang
agnrr
gnarr
agnrt
grant

agnry
angry
rangy
agnst
angst
stang
agnsw
swang
agntu
gaunt
agntw
twang
agnty
tangy
agooz
gazoo
agors
sargo
agort
argot
groat
agoru
Goura
agott
gotta
agoty
goaty
agppy
gappy
agprs
grasp
sprag
agpry
grapy
agpsy
gaspy
agrss
grass
agrst
strag
agrsu
argus
sugar
agruu
augur
agrvy
gravy
agssu
gauss
agssy
gassy
agstu
Tsuga
agsty
stagy
agsuv
vagus
agswy
gawsy
agttu
gutta
aguyz
gauzy

agyyz
azygy
ahhik
Haikh
ahhis
Shiah
ahhit
haith
ahhoo
hoo-ha
ahhpy
hypha
ahhrs
harsh
ahhss
shash
ahhsy
hashy
ahijj
hajji
ahijr
hijra
ahikk
khaki
ahikm
hakim
ahiku
haiku
ahilp
phial
ahilr
hilar
ahilt
laith
lathi
ahily
haily
ahimr
harim
ihram
ahimt
thaim
ahint
ahint
hiant
ahips
aphis
apish
spahi
ahirs
arish
ahiry
hairy
ahist
saith
taish
ahisv
Shiva
ahitu
hutia
ahjko
khoja
ahjno
Jonah

ahjtu
thuja
ahkns
shank
ahknt
thank
ahkny
hanky
ahkoo
hooka
ahkos
shako
ahkrs
shark
ahksy
shaky
ahllo
hallo
holla
ahlls
shall
ahllu
ahull
ahlmo
omlah
ahlms
shalm
ahlmu
haulm
ahlnu
uhlan
ahlor
horal
ahlos
halos
shoal
shola
solah
ahlot
loath
lotah
ahlpr
Ralph
ahlps
plash
ahlpy
haply
phyla
ahlss
slash
ahlst
shalt
ahlsw
shawl
ahlsy
shaly
ahltu
hault
ahlty
lathy
ahmmy
hammy
ahmnu
human
ahmny
mynah
ahmor
omrah
ahmps
pashm
ahmrs
marsh
ahmss
smash
ahmst
maths
ahmsu
musha
ahmsw
shawm
ahmsy
mashy
ahnos
Shona
ahnrs
harns
sharn
ahnss
snash
ahnst
shan't
snath
ahntu
haunt
unhat
ahoow
wahoo
ahooy
yahoo
ahops
sopha
ahort
Torah
ahory
hoary
ahost
hoast
hosta
shoat
ahosx
Xhosa
ahotz
azoth
ahppy
happy
ahprs
sharp
ahpru
prahu
ahpry
harpy
ahpss
shaps
ahpst
staph
ahpsw
pshaw
ahpty
Typha
ahpuw
whaup
ahqsu
quash
ahrru
hurra
ahrry
harry
ahrst
trash
ahrsu
surah
ahrtw
thraw
wrath
ahrty
rhyta
ahruw
whaur
ahrxy
hyrax
ahsst
stash
ahssw
swash
ahstw
swath
ahsty
hasty
ahswy
washy
ahttu
tuath
ahtuy
Thuya
ahtwy
thawy
ahuzz
huzza
aiiln
Ilian
aiilt
Tilia
aiimr
imari
aiipr
pirai
aiiqr
Iraqi
aijor
Rioja
aijou
ouija
aijpw
pi-jaw
aikln
lakin
aiklp
palki
aikls
skail
aiklv
vakil
aikms
kamis
smaik
aikmu
umiak
aikns
kisan
Nasik
aiknt
takin
aikop
okapi
aikpr
parki
aikrr
karri
aikrt
krait
traik
aikru
kauri
aikst
Sakti
aiktt
katti
ailln
all-in
aills
allis
aillv
villa
ailmm
limma
ailmr
armil
ailms
Islam
salmi
ailmt
Tamil
ailmu
aumil
miaul
ailmx
limax
ailnp
plain
ailns
slain
snail
ailnt
Latin
ailnu
inula
ailnv
anvil
nival
vinal
ailnw
in-law
ailny
inlay
ailop
paoli
ailov
viola
voilà
ailpp
palpi
pipal
ailpr
April
prial
ailps
lapis
spial
ailpt
plait
ailpu
pilau
ailpw
pilaw
ailqu
quail
ailrs
liras
ailrt
liart
trail
T-rail
trial
ailru
urali
urial
ailrv
rival
viral
ailry
lairy
riyal
ailss
sisal
ailsv
silva
vails
ailsx
salix
ailsy
saily
ailtt
atilt
ailtv
vital
ailty
laity
aimms
miasm
aimmu
imaum
aimmx
maxim
aimnp
panim
aimnr
inarm
minar
aimns
mains
Manis
aimnt
matin
tamin
aimnz
nizam
aimor
Maori
Moira
moria
aimow
miaow
aimox
axiom
aimpr
prima
aimps
apism
sampi
aimqu
maqui
aimrs
simar
aimrt
amrit
aimrz
Mirza
aimss
amiss
aimst
tamis
aimsv
mavis
aimsw
aswim
swami
aimty
amity
atimy
ainno
anion
ainnp
pinna
ainns
Nisan
ainnw
winna
ainop
piano
ainor
noria
ainot
Taino
ainov
avion
ainps
spain
spina
ainpt
inapt
paint
pinta
ainpv
pavin
ainqu
quina
ainrs
sarin
ainrt
riant
train
ainrv
Invar®
ravin
ainry
rainy
ainrz
nazir
ainss
sasin
ainst
saint
satin
stain
ainsv
savin
Sivan
ainsw
swain
aintt
taint
tanti
titan
aintu
Uniat
aintw
twain
witan
ainux
auxin
aiopt
patio
aiort
ariot
ratio
aiory
Oriya
aioss
oasis
ossia
aiost
ostia
stoai
aiosv
aviso
aippu
appui
aiprs
Paris
Parsi
aiprt
atrip
parti
tapir
aipru
rupia

aipss
  apsis
aipst
  stipa
  tapis
aipsv
  pavis
aiptt
  pitta
aipzz
  pizza
aiqru
  quair
aiqsu
  quasi
airrs
  arris
airru
  urari
airss
  arsis
airst
  astir
  sitar
  stair
  stria
  tarsi
  Trias
airsz
  sizar
airtt
  trait
airvx
  varix
airvy
  vairy
airwz
  wazir
airyy
  Iyyar
aisst
  saist
aistt
  Sitta
aistv
  vista
aistw
  waist
aistx
  taxis
aittv
  vitta
aitvv
  vivat
ajlru
  jarul
  jural
ajmmy
  jammy
ajmor
  joram
  major
ajmru
  jumar
ajnoy
  yojan
ajnsu
  Janus
ajntu
  jaunt
  junta
ajnty
  janty
ajoop
  pooja
ajorw
  jowar
ajosu
  sajou
ajrtu
  jurat
ajyzz
  jazzy
akklu
  kulak
akkop
  kapok
akkor
  kokra
akkpu
  pukka
aklly
  alkyl
aklnp
  plank
aklnr
  knarl
aklnu
  kulan
aklny
  lanky
aklop
  pokal
  polka
aklos
  skoal
aklpu
  pulka
aklry
  larky
aklst
  stalk
aklsw
  lawks
akltu
  taluk
akluw
  waulk
akmny
  manky
akmop
  Pomak
akmou
  oakum
akmsu
  Musak
akmuz
  Muzak®
aknor
  Koran
  krona
aknos
  sanko
aknpr
  prank
aknps
  spank
aknpu
  punka
aknrs
  krans
  skran
  snark
aknry
  narky
aknrz
  kranz
aknst
  stank
aknsu
  ankus
aknsw
  swank
aknsy
  snaky
akntw
  twank
aknuz
  kanzu
akoor
  Karoo
akooz
  kazoo
akopp
  koppa
akopy
  yapok
akort
  tarok
akorw
  awork
akoty
  Tokay
akprs
  spark
akpry
  parky
akptu
  kaput
  uptak
akpwy
  pawky
akqru
  quark
akquy
  quaky
akrst
  karst
  skart
  stark
  strak
akrsy
  sarky
akrtu
  kraut
  kurta
akssv
  kvass
aktuy
  Yakut
allly
  allyl
allmo
  molal
  molla
allms
  small
allmy
  myall
allno
  llano
allnu
  nulla
allor
  loral
allot
  allot
  all-to
  atoll
allov
  ollav
allow
  allow
alloy
  alloy
  loyal
allps
  spall
allpu
  all-up
allpy
  pally
allry
  rally
allst
  stall
allsy
  sally
allty
  tally
allwy
  wally
allxy
  laxly
almms
  smalm
almmy
  lammy
almno
  monal
almnu
  manul
almny
  manly
almoo
  moola
almor
  molar
  moral
  romal
almos
  Salmo
almot
  matlo
almoy
  loamy
almps
  plasm
  psalm
almpu
  ampul
almpy
  amply
  palmy
almqu
  qualm
almrs
  marls
almru
  larum
  mural
  rumal
almry
  marly
almst
  smalt
almty
  malty
alnnu
  annul
alnop
  nopal
alnor
  loran
alnos
  salon
  sloan
  solan
alnot
  notal
  talon
  tonal
alnox
  noxal
alnoz
  zonal
alnpt
  plant
alnrs
  snarl
alnru
  lunar
  ulnar
  urnal
alnst
  slant
alnsu
  Alnus
alnuw
  unlaw
alnuy
  unlay
  yulan
alnwy
  lawny
  wanly
aloop
  paolo
alopr
  parol
  polar
  poral
alops
  salop
alorr
  roral
alors
  solar
  soral
alort
  rotal
alorv
  orval
  volar
alory
  royal
aloss
  lasso
alost
  altos
  stola
alosv
  salvo
alott
  total
alotv
  lovat
  volta
alovv
  volva
alppu
  pupal
alppy
  apply
alpry
  parly
  pyral
alpst
  spalt
  splat
alpsu
  spaul
alpsw
  spawl
alpsy
  palsy
  splay
  spyal
alpty
  aptly
  patly
  platy
  typal
alpuy
  lay-up
  uplay
alrru
  rural
alrsu
  Larus
  sural
alrtu
  ultra
alrtw
  trawl
alrty
  lyart
alrww
  wrawl
alrwy
  rawly
alssu
  lassu
alstu
  sault
  talus
alsty
  salty
  slaty
alsuu
  usual
alsvy
  sylva
alswy
  swaly
  swayl
altty
  lytta
altuv
  vault
altwy
  walty
altwz
  waltz
aluuv
  uvula
aluvv
  vulva
ammmo
  momma
ammmy
  mammy
ammno
  ammon
ammoy
  myoma
ammrs
  smarm
ammry
  rammy
ammsu
  summa

ammsy
  Sammy
ammty
  tammy
amnno
  no-man
amnnu
  unman
amnor
  manor
  Norma
  roman
amnos
  mason
  monas
amnot
  manto
  toman
amnow
  woman
amnoy
  anomy
amnru
  Ruman
  unarm
  urman
amnsu
  manus
amnty
  manty
amopr
  pro-am
amorr
  maror
  morra
amort
  amort
  morat
amoru
  amour
amorw
  mowra
amory
  mayor
  moray
amost
  stoma
amoty
  atomy
amotz
  matzo
  motza
amprt
  tramp
ampss
  spasm
ampst
  stamp
ampsw
  swamp
amrru
  murra
amrry
  marry
amrst
  smart
amrsu
  ramus
  rusma
amrsw
  swarm
amrsy
  symar
amruv
  murva
amrwy
  awmry
amssy
  massy
amsty
  masty
  mayst
amsuw
  wamus
amtuz
  mazut
annny
  nanny
annor
  Norna
annoy
  annoy
annsu
  Sunna
anntu
  naunt
anntz
  Nantz
anoop
  napoo
anopr
  apron
anopt
  panto
anopw
  powan
anopy
  yapon
anoqr
  Qoran
anors
  arson
  sonar
anort
  orant
  toran
  trona
anorw
  rowan
anory
  rayon
anosx
  Saxon
anosy
  sayon
anotx
  taxon
anoty
  atony
  ayont
anouy
  noyau
anowy
  noway
anppy
  nappy
anprw
  prawn
anpst
  pants
anpsw
  spawn
anpsy
  pansy
anptu
  unapt
anpuy
  unpay
anpuz
  zupan
anqru
  Qurân
anqtu
  quant
anrst
  starn
anrsy
  snary
anrtt
  trant
anrtu
  arnut
anrty
  tyran
anruz
  azurn
anstu
  saunt
ansty
  nasty
  tansy
ansuy
  unsay
ansuz
  Anzus
answy
  Sawny
anttu
  taunt
antty
  natty
antuv
  vaunt
antux
  untax
antuy
  aunty
antwy
  tawny
  wanty
anvvy
  navvy
anwyy
  yawny
aoopp
  apoop
aoors
  roosa
aoppp
  poppa
aoppr
  appro
aoprs
  psora
  sapor
  sopra
aoprt
  aport
  porta
aoprv
  vapor
aopss
  psoas
aopsy
  soapy
aopty
  atopy
aoptz
  topaz
aoqtu
  quota
aorrs
  sorra
aorrw
  arrow
aorry
  roary
aorrz
  razor
aorss
  saros
aorst
  roast
aorsw
  sowar
aortt
  ottar
  tarot
  troat
aortx
  taxor
aorty
  otary
  yarto
aorvy
  ovary
aoryz
  Oryza
aosst
  assot
aossy
  say-so
aostt
  stoat
  toast
aosvy
  savoy
aottu
  tatou
aottw
  tatow
apppy
  pappy
appsy
  paspy
  sappy
appuy
  appuy
appyz
  zappy
aprry
  parry
aprst
  spart
  sprat
  strap
aprsy
  raspy
  spray
aprtu
  U-trap
aprtw
  wrapt
aprty
  party
  praty
  yrapt
apstu
  sputa
  stupa
apstw
  swapt
apsty
  pasty
  patsy
apswy
  waspy
aptty
  patty
apzzz
  pzazz
aqrtu
  quart
aqstu
  squat
aqsuw
  squaw
arrst
  starr
arrsu
  surra
arrty
  tarry
arsst
  trass
arssu
  sarus
arstt
  start
arstu
  surat
  sutra
arstw
  straw
  swart
  warst
  wrast
arsty
  satyr
  stray
arsuv
  varus
arsuy
  saury
  Surya
arsxy
  X-rays
arttu
  tuart
artty
  ratty
  tarty
artwy
  warty
aruyz
  azury
asssy
  sassy
asstw
  swats
assty
  sayst
asttt
  tatts
astty
  tasty
astux
  Taxus
astvy
  vasty
asvvy
  savvy
attty
  tatty
bbbiy
  Bibby
bbboy
  bobby
bbbuy
  bubby
bbceu
  cubeb
bbchu
  Chubb
bbcoy
  cobby
bbcuy
  cubby
bbdey
  debby
bbdoy
  dobby
bbeil
  bible
bbeir
  bribe
bbeko
  kebob
bbemo
  bombe
  bombé
bbeop
  bebop
bbesy
  sybbe
bbeuz
  zebub
bbewy
  webby
bbfuy
  fubby
bbhmo
  H-bomb
bbhoy
  hobby
bbhuy
  hubby
bbilo
  bilbo
bbiry
  ribby
bbloy
  lobby
bblru
  blurb
bblsu
  slubb
bbmou
  bumbo
bbmov
  V-bomb
bbmoy
  mobby
bbnoy
  nobby
bbnuy
  nubby
bbooy
  booby
  yobbo
bbsuy
  busby
bbtuy
  tubby
bcciu
  cubic
bceeh
  beech
bceer
  rebec
bceex
  xebec

bceez
zebec
bcehl
belch
bcehn
bench
bceho
boche
bcelo
coble
bcemo
combe
bceno
bonce
bcenu
bunce
bcesu
Cebus
bchim
chimb
bchir
birch
bchit
bitch
bchnu
bunch
bchor
broch
bchot
botch
bchtu
butch
bchuu
buchu
bcikr
brick
bcilm
climb
bcilo
cibol
bcipu
pubic
bcitu
cubit
bcklo
block
bckor
brock
bckou
bucko
bckuu
bucku
bclmo
clomb
bcloo
Cobol
bclsu
clubs
bcmoo
combo
coomb
bcmor
cromb
bcmos
combs
bcmoy
comby
bcmru
crumb
bcnou
bunco
bcoru
courb
bcrsu
scrub
bddei
bided
bddiy
biddy
bdduy
buddy
bdeel
bedel
bleed
debel
bdeem
embed
bdeen
Deneb
bdeer
brede
breed
bdeew
bedew
bdeey
bedye
Debye
bdego
bodge
bdegu
budge
debug
bdeil
bield
bdeim
bedim
imbed
bdeip
biped
bdeir
bride
rebid
bdeit
betid
bidet
debit
bdeln
blend
bdelo
bodle
lobed
bdelu
blude
bdemo
demob
bdemu
bemud
bdeno
boned
bdenu
unbed
bdeny
bendy
by-end
bdeor
borde
orbed
bdeow
bowed
bdery
derby
bdetu
début
tubed
bdfii
bifid
bdhio
dhobi
bdiln
blind
bdilu
bluid
build
bdinu
unbid
bdiop
bipod
bdlno
blond
bdloo
blood
bdloy
Dolby®
bdnou
bound
bdoor
brood
bdoos
dsobo
bdooy
boody
bdoru
bourd
bdotu
doubt
bdoxy
X-body
beeel
belee
beees
besee
beefs
beefs
beefy
beefy
beegi
beige
beegl
glebe
beegm
begem
beegr
gerbe
grebe
beegt
beget
beehn
heben
beeil
belie
beejl
jebel
beekn
nebek
beell
belle
beeln
nebel
beelp
bleep
beelr
rebel
beelt
betel
beelv
bevel
beelz
bezel
beemr
breem
breme
ember
beenn
benne
beent
benet
beeor
boree
beeos
obese
beerr
breer
beert
beret
beerv
bever
breve
beerw
weber
beery
beery
beest
beset
beetw
bewet
beeuv
bevue
beffu
buffe
befgo
befog
befir
brief
fiber
fibre
befit
befit
begil
bilge
gibel
begin
begin
being
binge
begio
bogie
begir
giber
begiw
bewig
beglo
bogle
globe
beglu
bugle
bulge
begly
gleby
begmo
embog
begmu
begum
begnu
begun
begot
begot
begou
bouge
begoy
bogey
begru
gebur
beguz
Uzbeg
behow
howbe
behrt
berth
behry
herby
beijr
jiber
beill
libel
beilo
obeli
beilr
birle
liber
beils
Eblis
beilt
blite
beimo
biome
beimu
imbue
beinn
benni
beino
Niobe
beinr
brine
beiny
inbye
beirr
brier
beirs
birse
Ribes
beirt
biter
tribe
beirz
brize
beist
besit
beisv
vibes
beitt
Tibet
beitz
zibet
beivx
vibex
bejnu
bunje
beklo
bloke
bekmo
kembo
bekor
broke
bekru
burke
bekuz
Uzbek
belly
belly
belmo
moble
belmu
umbel
belno
noble
belnt
blent
belor
blore
borel
roble
belot
botel
belou
boule
below
below
bowel
elbow
belps
plebs
belru
brûlé
ruble
belry
beryl
belss
bless
belst
blest
belsu
bulse
beluy
bluey
bemop
pombe
bemor
ombre
bemos
besom
mebos
bemow
embow
bemox
embox
bemru
brume
umber
umbre
bemsu
embus
sebum
benno
bonne
benor
boner
borne
borné
benot
béton
T-bone
benow
bowne
benox
boxen
benoy
ebony
benoz
bonze
benrt
brent
benty
benty
beoos
boose
beooz
booze
beopr
probe
beorr
borer
beors
brose
sober

beorw
  bower
beorx
  boxer
beory
  o'erby
  ybore
beost
  besot
beosu
  bouse
beosw
  bowse
beosy
  syboe
beott
  botte
beotw
  bowet
bepsu
  pubes
bepuy
  upbye
berry
  berry
bersu
  burse
  rebus
  suber
bertu
  brute
  rebut
  tuber
beruy
  buyer
bessu
  buses
bettu
  butte
betty
  betty
betuu
  U-tube
bevvy
  bevvy
bffiu
  buffi
bfflu
  bluff
bffou
  buffo
bflyy
  fly-by
bfory
  forby
bfsuy
  fubsy
bggiy
  biggy
bggoy
  boggy
bgguy
  buggy
bghit
  bight
bghor
  brogh
bghou
  bough
bghru
  burgh
bgily
  bilgy
bgino
  bingo
bginr
  bring
bgiot
  bigot
bgisu
  gibus
bgloy
  globy
bgluy
  bulgy
bgmoo
  gombo
bgmou
  gumbo
bgnoo
  bongo
  boong
bgnuy
  bungy
bgoor
  borgo
bgoru
  bourg
bgosu
  bogus
bgruy
  rugby
bhirt
  birth
bhlsu
  blush
bhmor
  rhomb
bhmpu
  bumph
bhmru
  rhumb
bhmtu
  thumb
bhoot
  booth
bhort
  broth
  throb
bhoty
  bothy
bhrsu
  brush
  shrub
bhsuy
  bushy
biiln
  blini
biils
  Iblis
biimn
  nimbi
biimz
  zimbi
biior
  oribi
bijou
  bijou
bikln
  blink
bikmo
  kimbo
biknr
  brink
bikrs
  brisk
billr
  brill
billy
  billy
bilmo
  limbo
bilmp
  blimp
bilmy
  blimy
biloo
  oboli
bilor
  broil
bilox
  bolix
bilss
  bliss
bilst
  blist
  stilb
bilsy
  sibyl
  sybil
biltu
  built
biltz
  blitz
bimot
  timbó
bimoz
  zombi
binor
  inorb
  robin
binos
  bison
binot
  biont
binru
  Bruin
  burin
  rubin
binry
  briny
binuy
  buy-in
bioot
  oobit
biort
  orbit
biott
  Tobit
biotu
  oubit
bipsu
  pubis
biqsu
  squib
birsy
  birsy
birtu
  bruit
bistu
  buist
bitty
  bitty
bivvy
  bivvy
bjmou
  jumbo
bjmuy
  jumby
bjnuy
  bunjy
bklnu
  blunk
bkluy
  bulky
bknou
  bunko
bkoor
  brook
bkooy
  booky
bkosy
  bosky
blluy
  bully
blmoo
  bloom
blmpu
  plumb
blnow
  blown
blnoy
  nobly
blntu
  blunt
bloor
  brool
blooy
  looby
blosu
  bolus
  lobus
blotu
  boult
  U-bolt
blowy
  blowy
blrsu
  slurb
blrtu
  blurt
blruy
  burly
bltuy
  butyl
bmoor
  broom
bmoos
  bosom
bmoru
  rumbo
bmoux
  buxom
bmowy
  womby
bmpuy
  bumpy
bnnoy
  bonny
bnnuy
  bunny
bnoor
  boron
bnoos
  boson
bnoru
  bourn
bnorw
  brown
bnosu
  bonus
  bosun
bnrtu
  brunt
  burnt
bntuy
  bunty
boors
  sorbo
boort
  robot
boost
  boost
  boots
bootx
  ox-bot
booty
  booty
boowx
  ox-bow
booyz
  boozy
bopuw
  up-bow
borru
  burro
bortu
  turbo
bossy
  bossy
bosuy
  bousy
boswy
  sybow
botuy
  outby
brruy
  burry
brstu
  burst
brsuu
  Rubus
bruuu
  urubu
bssuu
  bussu
bstuy
  busty
bttuy
  butty
buyzz
  buzzy
cccio
  cocci
cccoo
  cocco
cceer
  recce
ccehk
  check
ccehz
  Czech
ccekl
  cleck
ccely
  cycle
ccemu
  cumec
cceos
  cosec
  secco
ccesu
  cusec
ccfiu
  Cufic
cchhi
  chich
cchik
  chick
cchin
  cinch
cchko
  chock
cchku
  chuck
cchlu
  culch
cchno
  conch
cchou
  couch
cchru
  curch
cchtu
  cutch
cciit
  ictic
cciiv
  civic
ccikl
  click
ccikr
  crick
ccilo
  colic
ccimo
  comic
ccimu
  mucic
ccino
  conic
cciny
  cynic
ccios
  cisco
ccirs
  circs
ccisu
  succi
ccklo
  clock
ccklu
  cluck
cckor
  crock
cckoy
  cocky
cckru
  cruck
ccloy
  cyclo
ccooz
  zocco
ccoru
  occur
cddei
  Eddic
cdduy
  cuddy
cdeei
  de-ice
cdeer
  creed
cdeeu
  deuce
  educe
cdehi
  chide
cdeho
  chode
cdeim
  demic
  medic

cdeir
cider
cried
dicer
cdeis
cedis
cdeit
edict
cdeiv
Vedic
cdeiy
dicey
cdeko
decko
cdelo
dolce
cdely
ycled
cdemo
Médoc
cdens
scend
cdenu
dunce
cdeoo
cooed
cdeor
cored
credo
décor
cdeou
coudé
douce
cdeov
coved
cdeow
cowed
cdeox
codex
cdeoy
decoy
cderu
crude
cdery
cyder
decry
cdetu
educt
cdhil
child
cdhit
dicht
ditch
cdhnu
dunch
cdhny
chynd
cdhor
chord
cdhot
docht
cdhtu
dutch

cdhuy
duchy
cdiin
dinic
Indic
cdiio
iodic
cdiky
dicky
cdilu
lucid
cdimu
mucid
cdior
Doric
cdios
disco
sodic
cdipu
cupid
pudic
cdisu
scudi
cdksu
ducks
cdkuy
ducky
cdlos
scold
cdlou
cloud
could
cdnoo
codon
cdnoy
ycond
cdorw
crowd
cdosu
scudo
cdruy
crudy
curdy
ceeem
emcee
ceeep
peece
ceefn
fence
ceefs
feces
ceegr
cerge
grece
ceehk
cheek
keech
ceehl
leech
ceehn
hence
ceehp
cheep

ceehr
cheer
reech
ceein
niece
ceeip
piece
ceejt
eject
ceekl
cleek
ceekr
creek
ceelp
cleep
clepe
ceelr
creel
ceelt
elect
ceelv
cleve
ceelx
excel
ceely
lycée
ceemr
crême
ceenp
pence
ceens
cense
scene
ceent
ctene
ceeoo
cooee
ceepr
creep
crêpe
perce
ceers
Ceres
scree
ceert
erect
terce
ceerw
crewe
ceesy
sycee
ceeuv
cuvée
ceffl
F-clef
cefgl
G-clef
cefhi
chief
fiche
cefht
fecht
fetch

cefit
fecit
cefkl
fleck
ceflt
cleft
cefor
force
cegin
genic
cegio
cogie
cegir
grice
cegko
gecko
cegno
congé
cegou
cogue
cehht
hecht
cehhu
heuch
cehil
chiel
chile
elchi
cehim
chime
miche
cehin
chine
niche
cehir
Reich
cehit
ethic
theic
cehiv
chive
cehko
choke
cehkt
ketch
cehlt
letch
cehlu
leuch
cehlw
welch
cehly
chyle
cehmy
chyme
cehnt
tench
cehnw
wench
cehoo
cohoe
cehop
epoch

cehor
chore
ocher
ochre
cehos
chose
cehow
owche
cehpr
perch
cehpt
Pecht
cehrt
chert
retch
cehru
ruche
cehss
chess
cehst
chest
cehsu
chuse
cehtu
chute
teuch
cehtv
vetch
cehtw
wecht
cehty
techy
Tyche
cehvy
chevy
cehwy
chewy
ceiil
ceili
ceiju
juice
ceikr
erick
icker
ceilm
clime
melic
ceiln
cline
ceilo
Eolic
oleic
ceilp
clipe
ceilr
relic
ceils
Sicel
slice
ceilt
telic
ceimn
mince

ceimr
crime
ceims
mesic
ceimt
metic
ceimx
cimex
ceinr
crine
ceins
since
ceinw
wince
ceiny
yince
ceiov
voice
ceipr
price
ceips
spice
ceirr
crier
ricer
ceirs
cries
crise
seric
ceirt
recti
trice
ceiru
curie
ceirx
xeric
ceiry
ricey
ceitu
cutie
ceitv
civet
evict
ceitw
twice
cekks
kecks
ceklr
clerk
cekns
sneck
ceknv
V-neck
cekor
ocker
cekos
cokes
cekps
speck
cekrt
treck
cekrw
wreck

cello
cello
celmo
celom
celno
clone
celnu
uncle
celor
ceorl
celos
close
socle
celot
clote
celov
clove
celoy
coley
celoz
cloze
celpt
P-Celt
celpu
cupel
celpy
clype
celqt
Q-Celt
celru
cruel
lucre
ulcer
celsu
luces
celtu
culet
celty
cetyl
celux
culex
cemor
comer
crome
cemot
comet
cemry
mercy
cenno
conne
nonce
cenop
ponce
cenor
crone
oncer
cenos
scone
sonce
cenot
cento
conte
cenou
ounce

- cenov
  - coven
- cenoy
  - coney
- cenoz
  - cozen
- cenpu
  - punce
- censt
  - scent
- ceooy
  - cooey
- ceopr
  - coper
- ceops
  - copse
  - scope
- ceopu
  - coupe
  - coupé
- ceorr
  - corer
  - crore
- ceors
  - corse
  - score
- ceort
  - recto
- ceorv
  - cover
- ceorw
  - cower
- ceorz
  - croze
- ceost
  - coste
  - escot
  - estoc
- ceosv
  - voces
- ceott
  - octet
- ceotv
  - covet
- ceovy
  - covey
- ceprt
  - crept
- cepru
  - pruce
- cepss
  - specs
- cerru
  - curer
  - recur
- cerss
  - cress
- cerst
  - crest
- cersu
  - cruse
  - curse
  - sucre
- cersw
  - screw
- certu
  - cruet
  - eruct
  - truce
- ceruv
  - cruve
  - curve
- cessu
  - scuse
- cestu
  - scute
- cetuy
  - cutey
- cffhu
  - chuff
- cffil
  - cliff
- cfflo
  - cloff
- cffos
  - scoff
- cffou
  - cuffo
- cffsu
  - scuff
- cfhil
  - filch
- cfhin
  - finch
- cfhit
  - fitch
- cfhiu
  - fichu
- cfiis
  - sci-fi
- cfikl
  - flick
- cfiku
  - Kufic
- cfilo
  - folic
- cfilt
  - clift
- cfisu
  - Sufic
- cfklo
  - flock
- cfkor
  - frock
- cfmoy
  - comfy
- cfort
  - croft
- cfosu
  - focus
- cfrsu
  - scurf
- cfstu
  - scuft
- cfsuu
  - fucus
- cggiy
  - ciggy
- cghlu
  - gulch
- cghoo
  - cohog
- cghou
  - cough
- cgiin
  - icing
- cgiln
  - cling
- cgilo
  - logic
- cgimo
  - ogmic
- cgino
  - coign
  - incog
- cgior
  - corgi
  - orgic
- cgioy
  - yogic
- cgiru
  - Ugric
- cglnu
  - clung
- cgnoo
  - congo
- cgoos
  - scoog
- cgors
  - scrog
- cgosu
  - scoug
- chhil
  - hilch
- chhis
  - shchi
- chhit
  - hitch
- chhiw
  - which
- chhnu
  - hunch
- chhoo
  - hooch
- chhot
  - hotch
- chhtu
  - hutch
- chiil
  - chili
  - lichi
- chikn
  - chink
- chiko
  - hoick
- chikr
  - chirk
- chikt
  - thick
- chill
  - chill
- chilm
  - milch
- chiln
  - linch
- chilo
  - choli
- chilp
  - pilch
- chilr
  - chirl
- chilt
  - licht
- chily
  - hylic
- chilz
  - zilch
- chimo
  - ohmic
- chimp
  - chimp
- chimr
  - chirm
- chimu
  - humic
- chino
  - chino
- chinp
  - pinch
- chinw
  - winch
- chior
  - choir
  - ichor
- chipr
  - chirp
- chips
  - chips
- chipt
  - pitch
- chiqu
  - quich
- chirr
  - chirr
- chirt
  - chirt
  - crith
  - richt
- chist
  - stich
- chisu
  - cuish
- chitt
  - titch
- chitw
  - witch
- chity
  - itchy
  - tichy
- chivy
  - chivy
  - Vichy
- chknu
  - chunk
- chkoo
  - chook
- chkos
  - shock
- chkoy
  - choky
- chksu
  - shuck
- chktu
  - kutch
- chlmu
  - mulch
- chlnu
  - lunch
- chlny
  - lynch
- chlot
  - cloth
- chlru
  - churl
  - lurch
- chlsu
  - schul
- chmnu
  - munch
- chmoo
  - choom
  - mooch
- chmop
  - chomp
- chmos
  - schmo
- chmou
  - mouch
- chmpu
  - chump
- chmtu
  - mutch
- chnot
  - notch
- chnpu
  - punch
- chnru
  - churn
  - runch
- chnsy
  - synch
- choop
  - pooch
- chopr
  - porch
- chopt
  - potch
- chopu
  - pouch
- chort
  - rotch
  - torch
- chory
  - ochry
- chosu
  - hocus
- chotu
  - chout
  - couth
  - oucht
  - touch
- chouv
  - vouch
- choux
  - choux
- chpsy
  - psych
- chrru
  - churr
- chrsu
  - crush
- chrtw
  - crwth
- chsuy
  - cushy
- ciilt
  - licit
- ciilv
  - civil
- ciimm
  - mimic
- ciino
  - ionic
- ciinr
  - ricin
- ciins
  - Sinic
- ciipp
  - cippi
- ciirr
  - cirri
- cijuy
  - juicy
- cikln
  - clink
- cikls
  - slick
- cikmy
  - micky
- cikns
  - snick
- cikoy
  - yoick
- cikpr
  - prick
- cikps
  - spick
- cikpy
  - picky
- cikqu
  - quick
- cikrt
  - trick
- cikrw
  - wrick
- cikst
  - stick
- cikwy
  - wicky
- cilms
  - sclim
- cilno
  - colin
  - nicol
- cilor
  - loric
- cilpt
  - clipt
- cilpu
  - picul
- cilry
  - lyric
- cilsu
  - sulci
- cilxy
  - cylix
  - xylic
- cimno
  - nomic
- cimnu
  - cumin
  - mucin
- cimor
  - micro
  - Romic
- cimos
  - osmic
- cimpr
  - crimp
- cimrs
  - scrim
- cimsu
  - Musci
  - music
- cimyz
  - zymic
- cinor
  - orcin
- cinos
  - scion
  - sonic
- cinot
  - tonic
- cinov
  - covin
- cinoz
  - zinco
- cinpu
  - Punic
- cinru
  - incur
  - runic
- cinsu
  - incus
- cintt
  - tinct
- cintu
  - cut-in
  - cutin
  - incut
  - tunic
- cinyz
  - zincy

ciopt
  optic
  picot
  topic
ciorr
  roric
ciors
  siroc
ciort
  toric
  Troic
cioru
  curio
ciost
  stoic
ciotx
  toxic
ciprs
  crisp
  scrip
cipry
  pricy
cipsu
  Picus
cipsy
  spicy
cipty
  typic
cissy
  cissy
cistu
  cutis
  ictus
civvy
  civvy
cjkoo
  jocko
cjnou
  junco
ckkno
  knock
cklno
  clonk
cklnu
  clunk
cklpu
  pluck
ckluy
  lucky
ckmos
  smock
ckmuy
  mucky
cknor
  cronk
cknoy
  conky
cknsu
  snuck
ckoor
  crook
ckooy
  cooky
ckopy
  pocky
ckort
  trock
ckory
  corky
  rocky
ckoss
  socks
ckost
  stock
ckrtu
  truck
ckuyy
  yucky
clloy
  colly
cllsu
  scull
clluy
  cully
clmou
  locum
clmpu
  clump
clmtu
  mulct
clnoo
  colon
clnow
  clown
cloop
  cloop
cloot
  cloot
clooy
  cooly
cloru
  clour
closu
  locus
closw
  scowl
clotu
  clout
cloyy
  coyly
clpsu
  sculp
clruy
  curly
cmmoo
  commo
cmoop
  compo
cmooy
  coomy
cmopt
  compt
cmoru
  mucor
  mucro
cmosu
  comus
cmpru
  crump
cmrsu
  scrum
cmryy
  Cymry
cmsuu
  mucus
cnoor
  corno
  croon
cnoot
  conto
cnors
  scorn
cnort
  tronc
cnoru
  cornu
cnorw
  crown
cnory
  corny
  crony
cnosu
  oncus
cnotu
  count
cnoty
  cyton
cnruy
  curny
cnsuu
  uncus
cntuu
  uncut
coops
  scoop
coopt
  co-opt
coors
  corso
coost
  scoot
coprs
  corps
copru
  croup
copss
  Scops
copsu
  scoup
copsw
  scowp
copsy
  copsy
copuy
  coypu
corru
  cruor
corss
  cross
corst
  crost
corsu
  scour
corsw
  scrow
cortu
  court
  crout
  Turco
corwy
  cowry
cosst
  Scots
costu
  scout
cottu
  cutto
cprty
  crypt
crruy
  curry
crstu
  crust
  curst
crsuy
  crusy
cruvy
  curvy
cttuy
  cutty
dddoy
  doddy
ddeeg
  edged
ddeen
  ended
ddeey
  deedy
ddego
  dodge
ddeio
  diode
ddeir
  dried
  re-did
ddeis
  sided
ddemo
  domed
ddeny
  neddy
ddeow
  dowed
ddeoz
  dozed
dderu
  udder
ddery
  reddy
  ydred
ddety
  teddy
ddgiy
  giddy
ddgoy
  dodgy
ddiky
  kiddy
ddilo
  dildo
ddimy
  middy
ddinu
  undid
ddiru
  Druid
ddist
  didst
ddity
  tiddy
ddiwy
  widdy
ddloy
  oddly
ddmuy
  muddy
ddnoy
  noddy
ddoos
  dodos
ddopy
  poddy
ddosy
  soddy
ddoty
  toddy
ddowy
  dowdy
ddpuy
  puddy
ddruy
  ruddy
deeev
  deeve
deefr
  defer
  freed
deegh
  hedge
deegk
  kedge
deegl
  glede
  gleed
  ledge
deego
  geode
  ogee'd
deegr
  greed
deegs
  sedge
deegw
  wedge
deehw
  hewed
deeil
  edile
  elide
deeir
  eider
deekn
  kneed
deeky
  keyed
deeln
  neeld
deelr
  elder
deelu
  elude
deelv
  delve
  devel
deemn
  emend
deemt
  meted
deeno
  donee
deens
  dense
  needs
deent
  teend
deenu
  endue
  undée
deeny
  needy
deenz
  Enzed
deeop
  epode
deeor
  doree
  erode
deeox
  exode
deeps
  speed
deerr
  erred
deers
  Seder
deert
  deter
deeru
  urdee
deery
  reedy
deess
  sedes
deest
  steed
deesu
  suede
deesw
  sewed
  swede
deesx
  sexed
deesy
  seedy
deetu
  étude
deetw
  tweed
deeux
  exude
deevx
  vexed
deewy
  weedy
defgi
  fidge
defgu
  fudge
defil
  field
  filed
defin
  fiend
defir
  fired
  fried
defit
  fetid
defix
  fixed
defiy
  deify
  edify
deflt
  delft
defmr
  fremd
defnu
  unfed
defny
  fendy
defox
  foxed
degho
  Hodge
deghy
  hedgy
degik
  kidge
degil
  gelid
  glide
degim
  midge
degin
  deign
  dinge
degio
  dogie
  geoid
degir
  dirge
  gride
  ridge

degiu
guide
degju
judge
degky
kedgy
deglo
lodge
deglu
glued
degly
gyeld
ledgy
degmu
degum
degnu
nudge
degop
podge
degot
godet
toged
degow
wodge
degpu
pudge
degrs
dregs
degry
gryde
degsy
sedgy
dehir
hired
dehis
shied
dehlo
dhole
dehlp
delph
dehns
shend
dehop
ephod
dehor
horde
dehos
doseh
hosed
shoed
dehot
doeth
dehpt
depth
dehrs
sherd
shred
dehty
they'd
deiim
imide
deiiv
ivied

deiix
dixie
deijr
jerid
deikl
kidel
deikp
piked
deikr
diker
deiks
skied
deiky
dikey
deiln
eldin
lined
deilo
oldie
deilp
lepid
piel'd
plied
deilr
idler
deils
sidle
slide
deilt
tilde
tiled
deilv
devil
lived
vilde
deilw
wield
deily
yield
deimn
denim
deimr
dimer
rimed
deims
deism
disme
deimt
demit
timed
deimx
mixed
deinp
piend
deinr
diner
deins
sdein
snide
deint
teind
tined
deinu
indue

deinw
dwine
widen
deinx
index
deinz
dizen
deiov
dovie
video
deiow
dowie
deiox
oxide
deipp
piped
deipr
pride
pried
redip
deips
spied
deipt
tepid
deirr
drier
reird
rider
deirs
sider
deirt
tired
tride
tried
deirv
diver
drive
rived
deirw
weird
wired
deist
deist
stied
deisv
Dives
deisz
sized
deity
deity
deiyz
Yezdi
dejlo
jodel
dejoy
joyed
dekko
dekko
dekno
kendo
deknu
unked
dekop
poked

dekyy
dykey
dellt
tell'd
dellw
dwell
delmo
model
delmu
ledum
delno
loden
olden
delnu
unled
delor
drôle
delos
solde
delow
dowel
dowle
deloy
odyle
yodel
yodle
delps
speld
delpu
duple
upled
delry
redly
delsu
dulse
slued
deltv
veldt
deltw
dwelt
demmo
modem
demno
demon
demop
moped
demor
drome
demos
demos
demot
moted
demou
odeum
demov
moved
demow
mowed
dempt
dempt
demru
demur

demsu
mused
sedum
demtu
muted
denno
end-on
denoo
odeon
denor
drone
ronde
denos
nosed
sonde
denot
Donet
noted
toned
denow
endow
nowed
Woden
denoy
doyen
denoz
dozen
zoned
denps
spend
denpu
up-end
denrt
trend
denru
runed
under
unred
urned
denst
stend
dentu
tuned
denty
tynde
tyned
denuu
undue
denuw
unwed
deoor
rodeo
deoow
wooed
deopr
doper
pedro
roped
deops
spode
deopt
depot
deopx
podex

deopy
dopey
deorr
order
deors
dorse
rosed
deort
doter
deoru
uredo
deorv
dover
drove
deorw
dower
deorx
redox
deorz
dozer
deost
doest
deosu
douse
deosw
dowse
sowed
deotu
outed
deovw
vowed
deppu
upped
deprs
spred
depru
drupe
duper
perdu
prude
depry
perdy
predy
depsu
pseud
derry
dryer
derss
dress
derst
drest
dersu
druse
derty
tyred
deruz
Druze
desty
styed
dettu
duett
detuv
duvet

dfilu
fluid
dfinu
fundi
dfior
fiord
dfirt
drift
dfjor
fjord
dfloo
flood
dfnor
frond
dfnos
fonds
dfnou
found
dfoor
fordo
dggoo
doggo
dggoy
doggy
dghit
dight
dghou
dough
dgiir
rigid
dgiit
digit
dgilu
guild
dgino
dingo
doing
dginr
grind
dginy
dingy
dying
dgiop
pi-dog
dgiry
ridgy
dgloy
godly
goldy
dgnou
ungod
dgnuu
undug
dgnuy
dungy
gundy
dgooo
good-o
dgoos
godso
dgooy
goody
dgopy
podgy

dgoru
gourd
dgpuy
pudgy
dhiin
Hindi
dhimu
humid
dhinu
Hindu
dhiot
dhoti
dhioy
hyoid
dhirt
third
thrid
dhisy
dishy
dhitw
width
dhnou
hound
dhnsu
dunsh
dhory
hydro
dhotu
thou'd
dhowy
howdy
dhrsu
hurds
diill
dilli
diilp
lipid
diilv
livid
diimo
idiom
modii
diimt
timid
diinr
indri
diint
nitid
diiot
idiot
diirv
virid
diist
Idist
diivv
vivid
dijnn
djinn
diknr
drink
diknu
unkid
dikny
dinky
dillr
drill
dilly
dilly
idyll
dilmy
dimly
dilno
indol
dilnu
unlid
dilor
droil
dilos
silo'd
sloid
soldi
solid
dilot
doilt
diloy
doily
dilrt
trild
dilru
lurid
dilry
drily
dimos
misdo
odism
dimou
odium
dimoy
myoid
dimru
mudir
dimst
midst
dimtu
tumid
dinop
poind
dinor
nidor
dinot
on-dit
dinru
unrid
dinry
rindy
dinsu
nidus
dinsw
winds
dinwy
windy
dioov
ovoid
diooz
zooid
diops
dipso
diopy
pyoid
diorr
rorid
diors
Doris
diort
droit
diost
odist
diott
ditto
diotv
divot
dioww
widow
dippy
dippy
diptu
putid
diqsu
squid
dirst
strid
dirty
dirty
dirvy
yrivd
ditty
ditty
divvy
divvy
diyzz
dizzy
dkmuy
dumky
dknru
drunk
dkoor
drook
dkoru
drouk
dkosu
kudos
dksty
kydst
dksuy
dusky
dkuuz
kudzu
dllor
droll
dlloy
dolly
dlluy
dully
dlmou
mould
dlnou
lound
nould
dlnow
lownd
dloor
drool
loord
dloos
soldo
dloow
woold
dlorw
world
dlosy
sloyd
dlouw
would
dlpuy
duply
dlryy
dryly
dmmuy
dummy
dmnou
mound
dmoos
dooms
dsomo
Sodom
dmoou
duomo
dmooy
doomy
moody
dmory
dormy
dmosu
modus
dmpuy
dumpy
dmruu
durum
dnnou
dunno
dnnuy
dunny
dnoor
donor
doorn
rondo
dnoos
snood
dnoot
tondo
dnopu
pound
dnoru
round
dnorw
drown
dnory
drony
dnosu
nodus
sound
unsod
dnosw
sownd
dnosy
synod
dnotu
donut
dnouw
wound
dnouy
oundy
dnowy
downy
doopr
droop
doors
sordo
dooru
odour
doost
stood
dootu
outdo
doowy
woody
doprs
sprod
dopru
proud
pudor
dorss
dross
dorst
dorts
dorsu
sudor
dorsw
sword
dortu
Tudor
dorty
dorty
doruy
duroy
dorwy
dowry
rowdy
wordy
dotty
dotty
dppuy
duppy
dpsuy
pudsy
drstu
durst
drsuy
drusy
druxy
druxy
dssuy
sudsy
dstuy
dusty
study
eeefz
feeze
eeegs
geese
eeeht
tehee
eeehz
heeze
eeeir
eerie
eeekv
keeve
eeelm
mêlée
eeeln
neele
eeelp
elpee
eeelv
levee
eeemr
emeer
eeems
semée
eeemx
exeem
exeme
eeens
neese
eeent
teene
eeenz
neeze
eeept
tepee
eeerv
reeve
eeetw
etwee
weete
eefhm
fehme
eefir
fiere
eeflm
fleme
eeflr
fleer
refel
eeflt
fleet
eefrr
freer
refer
eefrt
freet
eefrv
fever
eefry
yfere
eefss
fesse
eefsu
fusee
eefsz
fezes
eeftw
wefte
eefuz
fuzee
eeggl
legge
eeggr
egger
grège
eeghn
henge
eegil
liege
eegin
eigne
genie
eegir
régie
eegis
siege
eegkl
gleek
eegkr
Greek
eeglm
gemel
eeglo
éloge
eeglr
leger
eeglt
gleet
eegly
elegy
eegmn
menge
eegmr
merge
eegnr
genre
gerne
green
eegnt
genet
eegnv
venge
eegnw
ngwee
eegrs
grees
grese
serge
eegrt
egret
greet
eegrv
greve
verge
eegss
gesse
eegst
egest
geste

5 EEG

eegsu
segue
eehkt
theek
eehls
sheel
eehlt
Lethe
eehlv
helve
eehlw
wheel
eehmt
theme
eehmv
vehme
eehnp
phene
eehns
sheen
eehnw
wheen
eehov
evhoe
eehpr
pheer
eehps
phese
sheep
eehrs
herse
sheer
shere
eehrt
ether
there
three
eehrw
hewer
where
eehry
herye
eehst
sheet
these
eehtt
teeth
thete
eeikv
kieve
eeilm
elemi
eeils
eisel
esile
eeilt
élite
eeilv
lieve
eeilx
exile
eeims
semie

eeinp
penie
eeinr
Ernie
eeins
seine
eeinv
neive
nieve
eeinx
exine
eeips
peise
eeipz
peize
eeirt
retie
eeirv
reive
revie
eeiry
eyrie
eeiss
seise
eeisv
sieve
eeisw
weise
eeisx
exies
eeisz
seize
eeitv
evite
eeity
Eyeti
Eytie
eeiwz
weize
eejlw
jewel
eejly
jeely
eejnu
jeune
eejss
Jesse
eekln
kneel
eekls
sleek
eeklv
kevel
eeknr
kerne
eekns
skene
eekop
pekoe
eekov
evoke
eekrs
esker

eekrt
terek
eekry
reeky
eekst
skeet
steek
eells
selle
eellv
level
eelmn
elmen
eelmr
merel
merle
eelms
mesel
eelnr
Lerne
eelns
lenes
eelnv
nevel
eelnw
newel
eelop
elope
eelpr
leper
repel
eelps
sleep
speel
eelpx
expel
eelrt
relet
eelrv
elver
lever
revel
eelry
leery
eelst
sleet
steel
stele
eelsv
elves
eelsw
sewel
sweel
eelsy
seely
eeltt
ettle
eeltu
elute
eeltw
tewel
tweel

eeltx
telex
Texel
eemmn
mneme
eemmr
emmer
eemmt
emmet
eemmw
emmew
eemns
mense
mesne
semen
eemnu
neume
eemnw
enmew
eemny
enemy
eemot
emote
eemov
emove
eempt
Tempe
eemqu
queme
eemrt
meter
metre
eemru
emure
eemrx
remex
eemry
emery
eemst
steem
steme
temse
eemsu
meuse
eennp
penne
eennr
renne
eennt
tenné
eenor
one-er
eenpr
neper
preen
eenps
penes
eenqu
queen
eenrs
sneer

eenrt
enter
rente
terne
treen
eenru
enure
eenrv
erven
nerve
never
eenrw
renew
eenry
reney
eenss
sense
eenst
steen
tense
eensu
ensue
eensv
evens
seven
eensw
sewen
eentt
tenet
eentu
tenue
eentv
event
eentw
'tween
eenty
teeny
eenuv
venue
eenvy
veney
yeven
eenwy
weeny
yewen
eeopt
topee
eeopy
peeoy
eeors
erose
soree
eeoxy
ox-eye
eeprs
perse
prese
speer
spree
eeprt
peter
petre

eepru
purée
rupee
eeprv
preve
eepry
peery
eepst
steep
eepsu
upsee
eepsw
sweep
eepsy
peyse
seepy
eepwy
weepy
eeqru
queer
eequu
queue
eerrs
serre
eerst
ester
reest
reset
steer
stere
terse
eersu
reuse
eersv
serve
sever
verse
eersw
sewer
sweer
eersx
Xeres
eertv
evert
revet
eertw
tweer
'twere
eertx
exert
eeruv
revue
eervv
verve
eervx
vexer
eervy
every
veery
eessy
sesey
eestt
teste

eestw
ewest
sweet
eettu
tutee
eettw
tweet
efffo
feoff
effir
fifer
effor
offer
effru
ruffe
efftu
tuffe
efgin
feign
efgir
grief
efgiu
fugie
efglo
fogle
efglu
fugle
Guelf
efgor
forge
gofer
efgoy
fogey
efguu
fugue
efhit
thief
efhlo
f-hole
efhls
flesh
shelf
efhno
foehn
efhrs
fresh
efhtt
theft
efhty
hefty
efikn
knife
efikr
kefir
efill
fille
efiln
elfin
efilo
folie

efilr
filer
flier
lifer
rifle
efils
Felis
flies
'slife
efilt
filet
flite
efimr
fermi
efimt
metif
efinr
finer
infer
efint
feint
efirr
firer
frier
efirs
fries
serif
efirt
freit
refit
efirv
fiver
efirx
fixer
efiry
fiery
reify
efirz
frize
efisv
fives
efitt
fitte
efkls
skelf
efklu
fluke
efkns
fenks
eflly
felly
eflmu
flume
eflno
felon
eflor
forel
eflot
flote
eflou
foulé
eflpy
flype

eflry
ferly
flyer
efltu
flute
eflty
flyte
lefty
efluy
fluey
efmor
forme
efmos
fomes
efmru
femur
efmtu
fumet
efnny
fenny
efnor
Freon®
efnot
often
efnry
ferny
eforr
frore
efort
fetor
forte
eforu
fuero
efory
foyer
eforz
froze
efoss
fosse
efotu
fouet
efrry
ferry
fryer
efrsw
swerf
efruz
furze
efstu
fetus
eftty
fytte
eggil
ligge
eggiu
gigue
eggly
leggy
eggnu
gunge
eggop
pogge

eggor
gorge
grego
eggou
gouge
eggpy
peggy
eggru
gurge
eghhi
heigh
eghhu
heugh
eghhw
hewgh
eghin
hinge
neigh
eghit
eight
eghiw
weigh
eghlu
leugh
eghly
hyleg
eghno
hogen
eghnt
thegn
eghpt
Peght
eghtu
teugh
egiin
genii
egijr
rejig
re-jig
egikl
glike
egikr
grike
egiln
ingle
ligne
egilo
logie
egilr
liger
Rigel
egilt
gilet
legit
egilu
guile
egimm
gimme
egimr
grime
eginp
genip

eginr
grein
Niger
reign
renig
egins
singe
egint
tinge
eginv
given
eginw
winge
eginy
eying
egiov
ogive
vogie
egipr
gripe
egirs
grise
egirt
tiger
egirv
giver
virge
egirz
grize
egist
geist
egisu
guise
egknr
kreng
egkry
gryke
eglmo
golem
eglmu
glume
eglno
longe
eglnt
glent
eglnu
lunge
eglop
golpe
eglor
ogler
eglos
segol
eglov
glove
egloy
elogy
egloz
gloze
eglru
gluer
gruel
Luger

eglsu
gules
gusle
egluy
gluey
guyle
egmmy
gemmy
egmno
emong
genom
gnome
egmot
gemot
egmru
grume
egnor
ergon
Genro
goner
grone
Negro
egnos
segno
egnpu
unpeg
egnst
gents
egnsu
genus
negus
egntu
unget
egnty
genty
egoos
goose
egooy
gooey
egopr
grope
egorr
Roger
egors
gorse
soger
egort
ergot
egoru
orgue
rogue
rouge
egorv
grove
egoss
gesso
egotu
togue
egoty
goety
egouv
vogue
vouge

egpru
purge
egpry
grype
egptu
get-up
egpty
Egypt
egrru
regur
urger
egrry
Gerry
egrsu
surge
egssu
guess
egstu
guest
egsuy
guyse
eguux
Gueux
ehhit
hithe
ehhty
hythe
ehikr
hiker
ehiks
sheik
ehikt
kithe
ehils
shiel
ehilt
lithe
ehilw
while
ehilx
helix
ehims
hiems
ehimt
meith
ehinr
rhine
ehins
shine
ehint
thine
ehinw
whine
ehios
hoise
ehirr
hirer
ehirs
shier
shire
ehirt
their
ehirv
hiver

ehist
heist
shite
sithe
ehisv
hives
shive
ehitt
tithe
ehitw
white
withe
ehklw
whelk
ehkmr
Khmer
ehkty
kythe
ehllo
hello
ehlls
shell
she'll
ehlmo
mohel
ehlmw
whelm
ehlos
she'ol
ehlot
helot
hotel
thole
ehlov
hovel
ehlow
whole
ehloy
holey
ehlps
plesh
ehlpw
whelp
ehlpy
phyle
ehlsw
welsh
ehltu
Thule
ehlty
ethyl
lythe
ehmmo
homme
ehmny
hymen
ehmor
homer
horme
ehmoy
homey
ehmpy
hempy

ehmrt
therm
ehmru
rheum
ehmry
rhyme
ehmst
meths
ehmsy
meshy
ehmty
thyme
ehnny
henny
ehnoo
ohone
ehnop
pheon
phone
ehnor
heron
rhone
ehnos
hosen
shone
ehnot
hoten
ehnov
hoven
ehnoy
honey
ehnry
henry
ehnst
shent
ehnsw
shewn
ehntt
tenth
ehntu
uneth
ehoov
hoove
ehooy
hooey
ehopr
ephor
ehopu
ouphe
ehors
horse
shoer
shore
ehort
other
throe
ehorv
hover
ehorw
howre
whore
ehoss
shoes

ehost
ethos
shote
those
ehosu
house
ehosv
shove
ehosw
whose
ehotw
theow
ehoww
ewhow
ehpry
hyper
ehrry
herry
ehrsu
usher
ehrsw
shrew
wersh
ehrsy
shyer
ehrtw
threw
ehrtz
hertz
ehstw
thews
ehsty
sythe
ehtwy
thewy
eiiln
lie-in
eiilp
pilei
eiimn
Minié
eiins
nisei
eiint
tie-in
eiinx
nixie
eiipx
pixie
eiiss
issei
eiisv
visie
eikln
inkle
liken
eiklr
liker
eikls
Sikel
eikly
kiley
kylie
ylike

eikno
eikon
Koine
eiknp
Pekin
eiknr
inker
eikns
Neski
skein
eiknv
knive
eiknz
zinke
eikoz
ozeki
eikpr
piker
eikps
spike
eikrs
skier
eikrt
trike
eikry
Kyrie
eikst
skite
eiksv
skive
eiksy
skiey
eillm
mille
eillr
rille
eills
lisle
eilmn
limen
eilmp
impel
eilmr
meril
miler
eilms
limes
slime
smile
eilmu
ileum
eilmy
limey
eilnn
linen
eilno
eloin
olein
eilnr
liner

eilns
elsin
lenis
nelis
silen
eilnt
inlet
eilnv
levin
liven
eilor
oriel
eilov
olive
voile
eilpr
peril
piler
plier
eilps
plies
slipe
spiel
spile
eilpx
pixel
eilrs
siler
eilrt
litre
tiler
eilrv
liver
livre
rivel
eilst
islet
istle
steil
stile
eilsu
ileus
eilsv
levis
lives
slive
eilsw
lewis
eilsx
silex
eilsz
sizel
eiltt
title
eiltu
utile
eiltx
ixtle
eiluy
ulyie
eiluz
ulzie
eilvy
veily

eilzz
zizel
eimmr
mimer
eimmw
immew
eimnr
inerm
miner
eimnt
meint
eimnx
mixen
eimny
meiny
eimnz
mizen
eimor
moire
moiré
eimov
movie
eimpr
prime
eimpt
tempi
eimpu
pumie
eimrr
rimer
eimrs
miser
eimrt
merit
mitre
remit
timer
eimrx
mixer
eimss
seism
semis
eimst
métis
smite
stime
Times
einnr
inner
renin
einnu
ennui
einnv
venin
einop
opine
einos
eosin
noise
einov
envoi
ovine
einpr
ripen

einps
penis
snipe
spine
einpt
inept
nepit
einpy
piney
einqu
quine
einrs
reins
resin
rinse
risen
serin
siren
einrt
inert
inter
nitre
trine
einru
inure
urine
einrv
riven
viner
einss
nisse
einst
inset
neist
sient
stein
einsv
visne
einsw
sewin
sinew
swine
eintt
ettin
eintu
unite
untie
eintw
twine
einvw
vinew
einvx
vixen
einvy
veiny
einwy
winey
einwz
winze
wizen
eioor
oorie
eiops
poise

eiopy
pioye
eiopz
piezo
eiorr
rorie
eiors
osier
eioru
ourie
eiorv
vireo
eiorw
owrie
eiost
toise
eiotz
tozie
eiowz
zowie
eippr
piper
priep
eipqu
equip
pique
eiprr
prier
riper
eiprs
épris
pries
prise
speir
spire
eiprt
piert
tripe
eiprv
viper
eiprw
wiper
eiprz
prize
eipss
spies
eipst
piste
spite
stipe
eipsw
swipe
eiptt
petit
eiptu
tie-up
uptie
eiptw
pewit
eipty
piety
eiqru
quire

eiqtu
quiet
quite
eirrs
riser
eirrt
trier
eirrv
river
eirrw
wirer
eirst
reist
resit
stire
tries
eirsv
siver
eirsw
sweir
swire
eirsx
sixer
eirsz
sizer
eirtt
titer
titre
trite
eirtu
urite
uteri
eirtv
rivet
eirtw
twier
twire
write
eirvv
viver
eirvz
vezir
eisst
sties
eissu
issue
eistu
suite
eistv
stive
eistx
exist
eisty
seity
eisvv
vives
eisvw
wives
eittw
tewit
twite
eitvx
vitex

eitzz
izzet
eivwy
viewy
ejkop
kopje
ejkor
joker
ejkoy
jokey
ejkry
jerky
ejllo
jello
ejlly
jelly
ejlou
joule
ejlpu
julep
ejmmy
jemmy
ejnny
jenny
ejnot
jeton
ejnoy
enjoy
ejptu
upjet
ejrry
jerry
ejrwy
Jewry
ejssu
Jesus
jesus
ejtty
jetty
eklln
knell
eklms
skelm
eklnt
knelt
ekloy
kyloe
yokel
eklps
skelp
spelk
eklpt
P-Kelt
eklpy
kelpy
eklqt
Q-Kelt
ekltw
welkt
eklty
kelty
eklyy
kyley

ekmos
smoke
ekmpt
kempt
eknno
ken-no
eknor
krone
eknos
snoek
snoke
soken
eknot
token
eknow
knowe
woken
eknsy
ensky
ekntu
unket
ekopr
poker
proke
ekops
spoke
ekopt
topek
ekopu
pouke
ekorr
roker
ekort
troke
ekorw
wroke
ekoss
sekos
ekost
stoke
ekpru
puker
ekpry
perky
ekpsy
pesky
ekptu
tupek
ekrru
kurre
ekrsy
skyer
skyre
syker
eksty
skyte
eksyy
skyey
ellms
smell
ellns
snell
ellny
nelly

ellor
lorel
ellos
losel
ellps
spell
ellqu
quell
ellst
stell
ellsw
swell
elltu
tulle
ellty
telly
ellwy
welly
elmmu
lumme
elmno
lemon
melon
elmnu
lumen
elmor
morel
elmot
metol
motel
elmou
oleum
elmpu
plume
elmru
lemur
elmst
smelt
elmuv
mvule
velum
elmuy
muley
elmxy
xylem
elnop
pleon
elnor
enrol
loner
elnos
solen
elnot
lento
olent
elnou
noule
elnov
novel
elnow
lowne
Nowel
elnoy
onely

elnoz
lozen
elntu
unlet
elnwy
newly
eloos
loose
soole
elopr
prole
elops
elops
slope
elopu
loupe
poule
elopy
poley
elors
loser
soler
sorel
eloru
loure
elorv
lover
elorw
lower
owler
rowel
eloss
loess
elost
stole
telos
elosu
eusol
louse
ousel
elosv
slove
solve
elosw
lowse
sowle
elosy
soyle
elotv
volet
volte
elotw
owlet
towel
elotx
extol
elouv
ovule
elouz
ouzel
elovv
volve

elovw
vowel
wolve
elovy
lovey
elpru
puler
elpry
reply
elpst
slept
spelt
elpsu
pulse
spule
elpsy
slype
elptu
let-up
elpux
Pulex
elpuz
puzel
elrru
ruler
elrsy
slyer
elrtu
luter
elrty
tyler
elrux
Lurex
elssu
sluse
elstw
swelt
elsty
style
elsux
luxes
eltux
exult
elyzz
lezzy
emnnu
numen
emnor
enorm
moner
morne
morné
emnos
meson
emnot
monte
moten
emnov
venom
emnow
women
emnoy
money

emnpt
nempt
emnru
rumen
emnty
meynt
emnuw
unmew
emoor
Romeo
emoos
moose
emopr
proem
emopt
tempo
emopy
myope
emorr
ormer
emors
mores
morse
smore
emort
metro
emorv
mover
vomer
emorw
mower
rowme
emost
mesto
smote
emosu
mouse
emosy
mosey
emott
motet
motte
totem
emoty
motey
emozz
mezzo
emprs
sperm
emprt
mpret
empsu
spume
emptt
tempt
empty
empty
emrru
murre
emrry
merry
emrsu
muser
serum

emrux
murex
Rumex
emssu
musse
emssy
messy
emstu
muset
emsty
styme
ennoo
no-one
ennos
Nones
sonne
ennot
nonet
tenon
tonne
ennox
xenon
ennpu
unpen
ennpy
penny
ennwy
wenny
enoor
roneo
enoos
noose
enooz
ozone
enopr
prone
enopy
peony
poney
enors
Norse
noser
Señor
seron
snore
enort
noter
ronte
tenor
trone
enorw
owner
rowen
enory
royne
enoss
sonse
enost
onset
seton
stone
enosw
owsen
enosy
nosey
enoty
toney
enovw
woven
enovy
envoy
enowx
woxen
enprt
prent
enpru
prune
enpst
spent
enqru
quern
enquy
queyn
enrru
rerun
enrst
stern
enrsu
nurse
enrsy
syren
enrtu
tuner
urent
enrty
entry
yrent
enrvy
nervy
enstt
stent
enstu
unset
usen't
ensuv
venus
ensuw
unsew
ensux
nexus
unsex
ensvy
senvy
enswy
newsy
entty
netty
tenty
entuw
unwet
eoopv
poove
eoors
roose
eoorw
wooer
eoost
soote
eoppt
epopt
eoppu
poupe
eoprr
porer
prore
repro
roper
eoprs
poser
prose
spore
eoprt
Porte
repot
toper
trope
eoprv
prove
eoprw
power
eopss
posse
speos
eopst
estop
stoep
stope
eopsy
poesy
poyse
sepoy
eopxy
epoxy
eoqru
roque
eoqtu
quote
toque
eorrr
error
eorrt
retro
eorrv
rover
eorrw
rower
eorst
roset
store
torse
eorsu
rouse
eorsv
servo
verso
eorsw
serow
sower
swore
worse
eorsx
sorex
eortt
otter
torte
eortu
outer
outré
route
eortv
overt
voter
eortw
tower
twoer
wrote
eortx
oxter
eorty
toyer
eortz
rozet
eoruy
you're
eorxx
Xerox®
eossu
souse
eostt
set-to
eostu
touse
eostv
stove
eostw
towse
eotuz
touze
eotwz
towze
eouvy
you've
epppy
peppy
eppru
upper
eprry
perry
pryer
ryper
eprss
press
eprst
prest
strep
eprsu
purse
sprue
super
eprsy
pryse
eprtu
erupt
eprtw
twerp
eprxy
prexy
Pyrex®
epstt
stept
epstu
set-up
stupe
upset
epstw
swept
epsuy
upsey
epswy
spewy
eptty
petty
eqruy
query
eqstu
quest
eqsuu
Equus
eqtuu
tuque
eqtuy
quyte
errsy
serry
errty
retry
terry
tryer
ersst
tress
erstt
terts
erstu
sture
erstv
verst
erstw
strew
trews
wrest
ersty
resty
styre
ersuu
Eurus
usure
ersvy
syver
erttu
utter
ertuv
vertu
ertwy
twyer
essty
styes
estty
testy
estuy
suety
estwy
stewy
estyy
yesty
estyz
zesty
ffflu
fluff
fffuy
fuffy
ffgil
gliff
ffgir
griff
ffgoo
go-off
ffgru
gruff
ffhit
fifth
ffhiw
whiff
ffhou
houff
ffhow
howff
ffhuy
huffy
ffijy
jiffy
ffiks
skiff
ffimy
miffy
ffino
in-off
ffins
sniff
ffiny
niffy
ffips
spiff
ffiqu
quiff
ffist
stiff
ffity
fifty
ffkos
skoff
fflpu
pluff
ffnoo
on-off
ffnsu
snuff
ffosw
sowff
ffoty
toffy
ffpuy
puffy
ffstu
stuff
fggoy
foggy
fgguy
fuggy
fghit
fight
fgiln
fling
fgilt
glift
fginu
fungi
fgirt
grift
fglno
flong
fglnu
flung
fgluy
gulfy
fgoor
forgo
groof
fgooy
goofy
fgoru
grouf
fhilt
filth
fhirt
firth
frith
fhist
shift
fhisy
fishy
fhitw
whift
fhlos
flosh
fhlsu
flush
fhort
forth
froth
fhott
thoft
fhotu
fouth
fhotw
fowth
fhrsu
frush
fhrtu
furth
fiins
finis
fiinx
infix

fikls
flisk
fikns
finks
fikrs
frisk
fillr
frill
filly
filly
filmp
flimp
filmy
filmy
filnt
flint
filoo
folio
filrt
flirt
filsu
fusil
filtt
flitt
filty
fitly
fimot
motif
fimtu
mufti
fimty
mifty
finny
finny
finst
snift
fintu
unfit
finty
nifty
finux
unfix
finuy
unify
fioqu
quoif
fiost
foist
fiptu
fit-up
firry
firry
first
first
frist
firtu
fruit
firzz
frizz
fissu
Sufis
fistw
swift
fisty
fisty
fiyzz
fizzy
fklnu
flunk
fkloo
kloof
fkluy
fluky
fknuy
funky
fkory
forky
flloy
folly
flluy
fully
flmpu
flump
flnou
Fluon®
flnow
flown
flnoy
fonly
floor
floor
floow
Wolof
floru
flour
fluor
furol
flory
flory
floss
floss
flotu
flout
floty
lofty
flouw
woful
flrru
flurr
fltuy
fluty
fmoor
M-roof
fmoru
forum
fmpru
frump
fnnuy
funny
fnorr
frorn
fnort
front
fnorw
frown
fnotu
fount
futon
foopr
proof
foops
spoof
foory
roofy
foost
foots
'sfoot
footy
footy
foowy
woofy
forru
furor
forry
frory
forst
frost
forty
forty
forwy
frowy
fosty
softy
fpruy
fry-up
frruy
furry
frstu
frust
frsuy
surfy
frtuy
turfy
fruyz
furzy
fssuu
Fusus
fssuy
fussy
fstuy
fusty
fttuy
tufty
fuyzz
fuzzy
ggglo
glogg
ggino
going
ggiot
gigot
ggipy
piggy
ggmoy
moggy
ggmuy
muggy
ggnuy
gungy
ggosy
soggy
ggpuy
puggy
ggruy
ruggy
gguvy
vuggy
ghhit
hight
thigh
ghhou
hough
ghikt
kight
ghilt
light
ghimt
might
ghint
night
thing
ghiny
hying
ghipt
pight
ghirt
girth
grith
right
ghist
sight
ghitt
tight
ghitw
wight
ghlly
ghyll
ghlou
ghoul
lough
ghlpy
glyph
ghnot
thong
ghoru
rough
ghost
ghost
ghosu
sough
ghotu
ought
tough
ghrsu
shrug
ghsuy
gushy
giilr
Rigil
giils
sigil
giilv
vigil
gijno
jingo
gijot
jigot
gikls
glisk
gillr
grill
gilly
gilly
gilno
lingo
gilns
sling
gilnt
glint
gilnu
lungi
gilny
lingy
lying
giloo
igloo
gilor
rigol
gilpu
pugil
gilpy
gilpy
gilru
Lurgi
gilry
girly
gilst
gilts
gilsu
gusli
giltu
guilt
giltz
glitz
gimny
mingy
gimos
gismo
misgo
gimoy
goyim
gimoz
gizmo
gimpu
guimp
gimpy
pigmy
gimry
grimy
ginor
giron
groin
ginot
ingot
tigon
ginow
owing
ginoy
yogin
ginru
ruing
unrig
ginrw
wring
ginst
sting
ginsu
suing
ginsv
V-sign
ginsw
swing
ginty
tying
ginvy
vying
ginwy
wingy
ginyz
zingy
giopp
gippo
giorr
rigor
giorv
vigor
Virgo
gippy
gippy
giprs
sprig
gipsy
gipsy
girst
grist
grits
strig
girsy
grisy
gistu
g-suit
gjmuu
jugum
gjosu
jougs
glloo
lolog
glloy
golly
glluy
gully
glmoo
gloom
glmou
mogul
glnou
gluon
glnsu
slung
gloos
Logos
glooy
gooly
glorw
growl
glory
glory
gloss
gloss
glotu
glout
glruy
gurly
gmmuy
gummy
gmnou
mungo
gmnuu
ungum
gmoor
groom
gmory
gormy
gmpyy
pygmy
gnnuy
gunny
gnoop
pongo
gnopr
prong
gnorw
grown
wrong
gnory
gyron
gnost
stong
tongs
gnotu
ungot
gnouy
young
gnoyz
zygon
gnrtu
grunt
gnruw
wrung
gnstu
stung
gnsuw
swung
goopy
goopy
goors
sorgo
goosy
goosy
gootu
outgo
goppy
gyppo
goprs
sprog

gopru
group
gopry
porgy
gorss
gross
gorsy
gorsy
gortu
grout
goruy
roguy
gostu
gusto
gosty
stogy
gotuy
gouty
guyot
gppuy
guppy
gppyy
gyppy
gprsu
sprug
gpsyy
gypsy
grruy
gurry
grsuy
gyrus
surgy
gstuy
gutsy
gttuy
gutty
hhhuu
uh-huh
hhisw
whish
hhmou
ho-hum
hhmpu
humph
hhoos
hoosh
hhott
Thoth
hhssu
shush
hhsuy
hushy
hiiln
nihil
hiims
imshi
hiiqu
qui-hi
hiirs
Irish
rishi
sirih
hijos
shoji
hiklt
thilk
hiklw
whilk
hiknt
think
hikrs
shirk
hiksw
whisk
hillo
hillo
hills
shill
hillt
illth
thill
hilly
hilly
hilmu
hilum
hilot
litho
thiol
tholi
hilrt
thirl
hilrw
whirl
hilss
slish
hilsu
hilus
hilsy
shily
hiltt
tilth
himrt
mirth
himst
smith
himsy
imshy
hinnt
ninth
hinny
hinny
hinor
rhino
hinsy
shiny
hinwy
whiny
hiopp
hippo
hiops
Sophi
hiopt
tophi
hioru
houri
hiost
hoist
hippy
hippy
hiptw
whipt
hipty
pithy
hirrs
shirr
hirrw
whirr
hirst
shirt
hissu
sushi
hissw
swish
whiss
histw
swith
whist
histx
sixth
hitwy
whity
withy
hiwzz
whizz
hkkou
hokku
hkluy
hulky
hkmou
hokum
hknoy
honky
hknsu
hunks
hknuy
hunky
hkoos
shook
hkooy
hooky
hksuy
husky
hlloo
hollo
hllou
hullo
hlloy
holly
hlluy
hully
hlmpy
lymph
hlmsu
mulsh
hloos
shool
hlooy
hooly
hlopx
phlox
hlorw
whorl
hloss
slosh
hlost
sloth
hlotw
thowl
hloty
hotly
hlpsu
plush
hlpsy
sylph
hlruy
hurly
hlssu
slush
hlsuy
lushy
hlsyy
shyly
hmnot
month
hmnpy
nymph
hmoop
oomph
hmooz
zhomo
hmopr
morph
hmorr
mhorr
hmoru
mohur
hmotu
mouth
hmoty
mothy
Y-moth
hmpsu
sumph
hmptu
thump
hmpuy
humpy
hmrry
myrrh
hmrtu
thrum
hmstu
musth
hmsuu
humus
hmsuy
mushy
hmtyy
thymy
hnoos
shoon
hnoow
nohow
hnopy
phony
hnors
shorn
hnort
north
thorn
hnory
horny
hnosw
shown
hnosy
hyson
hnssu
snush
hnstu
shunt
hoooo
hoo-oo
hoopt
photo
hoopw
whoop
hoort
ortho
hoost
shoot
sooth
Sotho
hoosw
howso
whoso
woosh
hoott
tooth
hootw
how-to
hoppy
hoppy
hoprt
thorp
hopss
sposh
hopsy
Sophy
hoqtu
quoth
horst
horst
short
horsw
shrow
horsy
horsy
hortt
troth
hortu
routh
hortw
rowth
throw
whort
worth
wroth
hostt
shott
hostu
shout
south
thous
hostw
sowth
hosty
toshy
hoswy
showy
hotuy
youth
hpsuy
pushy
hrruy
hurry
hrstu
hurst
hrsuy
rushy
hrttu
truth
hruuu
uhuru
hssuy
hussy
huyzz
huzzy
iijnn
jinni
iikln
likin
iiknn
kinin
iillv
villi
iilmt
limit
iilmu
ilium
iilnn
linin
iilnt
intil
iimmn
minim
iimmt
immit
iimmx
immix
iimnx
mix-in
iinno
inion
iinst
sit-in
iintu
Inuit
iintw
inwit
iiort
torii
iippt
pipit
iirst
Tisri
iirvz
vizir
iistv
visit
Vitis
ijkmu
mujik
ijmmy
jimmy
ijmpy
jimpy
ijnns
jinns
ijnnu
Injun
ijnot
joint
ijost
joist
ikkns
skink
ikkny
kinky
ikkos
kiosk
ikkru
kukri
ikllr
krill
iklls
skill
iklms
sklim
iklmy
milky
iklnp
plink
iklns
slink
iklny
kylin
iklpu
pikul
iklrs
skirl
iklsy
silky
iklty
kilty
iklxy
kylix
ikmps
skimp
ikmrs
smirk
ikmry
mirky
iknop
pinko

iknpr
  prink
iknps
  spink
iknpy
  pinky
iknst
  skint
  stink
iknsw
  swink
iknsy
  sinky
ikntw
  twink
iknyz
  zinky
ikpsy
  pisky
  spiky
ikptu
  tupik
ikqru
  quirk
ikrrs
  skirr
ikrst
  skirt
  stirk
ikrsy
  risky
ikrtu
  Turki
iksvy
  skivy
iktty
  kitty
illps
  spill
illqu
  quill
illrt
  trill
illst
  still
illsw
  swill
illsy
  silly
  slily
illtw
  twill
  'twill
illwy
  willy
ilmnu
  ulmin
ilmor
  milor
ilmpu
  pilum
ilmpy
  imply
ilmry
  mirly
ilmsy
  slimy
ilmtz
  miltz
ilnny
  linny
ilnos
  noils
ilnot
  Nilot
ilnpu
  lupin
ilnry
  nirly
ilnsy
  lysin
ilntu
  unlit
  until
ilnty
  linty
ilnvy
  vinyl
iloop
  polio
ilops
  spoil
ilopt
  pilot
ilopu
  poilu
ilopw
  pilow
ilopx
  oxlip
ilors
  loris
ilorv
  livor
ilory
  roily
ilorz
  zoril
ilosu
  louis
ilosy
  soily
ilppu
  pipul
  pupil
ilppy
  lippy
ilpst
  slipt
  spilt
  split
ilpsu
  pilus
ilptu
  tulip
ilqtu
  quilt
ilrsw
  swirl
ilrtw
  twirl
ilssy
  lysis
ilstt
  stilt
ilstu
  sluit
ilsty
  silty
  styli
ilttw
  twilt
immsu
  Mimus
imnor
  minor
imnot
  timon
  Timon
imnsu
  minus
imnty
  minty
imopr
  primo
imopt
  impot
imopu
  opium
imost
  moist
imosu
  Suomi
imosz
  zoism
imotv
  vomit
imppr
  primp
imprs
  prism
impru
  purim
impry
  primy
impst
  timps
impux
  mix-up
imrrs
  smirr
imssy
  missy
imstu
  muist
  musit
  tuism
imsty
  misty
  stimy
imtty
  Mitty
innno
  ninon
innny
  ninny
innoo
  onion
innop
  piñon
innot
  niton
  noint
innou
  union
innpu
  unpin
innpy
  pinny
innru
  inurn
  run-in
innsu
  Sunni
inntu
  untin
innty
  tinny
inoor
  Orion
inopr
  orpin
inopt
  pinto
  piton
  point
  potin
inopw
  powin
inopy
  piony
inoqu
  quoin
inors
  ornis
  rosin
inort
  intro
inory
  irony
inosv
  vison
inosy
  noisy
inotx
  toxin
inppu
  pin-up
inppy
  nippy
inprt
  print
inpru
  purin
  unrip
inpss
  snips
inpsy
  snipy
  spiny
inptu
  input
  put-in
inpuz
  unzip
inqtu
  quint
inrst
  snirt
inrtu
  rutin
inrty
  nitry
inssu
  nisus
  sinus
instt
  stint
  'tisn't
instu
  inust
  suint
intty
  nitty
  tinty
intuw
  unwit
intuy
  unity
intwy
  twiny
iopqu
  quipo
ioprr
  prior
iopst
  posit
iopsu
  pious
ioptv
  pivot
ioqtu
  quoit
iorrs
  orris
iorrt
  trior
iorst
  roist
  rosit
  tiros
iorsv
  visor
iortz
  rozit
iorvy
  ivory
iorvz
  vizor
iostt
  stoit
iostv
  ovist
  visto
iostz
  zoist
iosux
  Sioux
ipppy
  pippy
ipptu
  tip-up
ippty
  tippy
ippyy
  yippy
ippyz
  zippy
ipquu
  quipu
iprst
  spirt
  sprit
  stirp
  strip
iprsu
  sirup
iprsy
  spiry
iprtw
  twirp
iprvy
  privy
ipsty
  tipsy
ipstz
  spitz
ipswy
  wispy
ipsxy
  pyxis
ipttu
  putti
  titup
iqrtu
  quirt
iqstu
  quist
  quits
  squit
irssu
  risus
irstt
  trist
irstw
  wrist
irsuv
  virus
irsxy
  Xyris
irtuv
  virtu
irtyz
  ritzy
isssw
  Swiss
isssy
  sissy
isstw
  swits
isttw
  twist
istvy
  stivy
istxy
  sixty
itttu
  tutti
ittty
  titty
ittwx
  'twixt
ittwy
  witty
ityzz
  tizzy
jkloo
  jokol
jknuy
  junky
jlloy
  jolly
jloty
  jolty
jmoru
  jorum
jmpuy
  jumpy
jnopu
  jupon
jnotu
  jotun
  junto
jnoty
  jonty
jorru
  juror
jostu
  joust
jttuy
  jutty
kklsu
  skulk
kkmou
  kokum
kknsu
  skunk
kkooy
  kooky
kkuyy
  yukky

5 KLL

kllno
knoll
kllsu
skull
klnop
plonk
klnpu
plunk
klnru
knurl
klnsu
slunk
klouy
yokul
kloyy
yolky
klsuy
sulky
kmoos
smoko
kmosy
smoky
kmruy
murky
kmsuy
musky
knnow
known
knoos
snook
knooy
nooky
knops
knosp
knoqu
quonk
knost
stonk
knosu
onkus
knosw
snowk
knosy
yonks
knotu
knout
knowy
wonky
knpsu
spunk
knrru
knurr
knrtu
trunk
knstu
stunk
koops
spook
koory
rooky
koost
stook
koosz
zooks

kootw
kotow
kopry
porky
korst
stork
torsk
korsw
works
korsy
Yorks
kosty
Kotys
kouuy
Kuo-yü
kstuy
tusky
llloy
lolly
llmoy
molly
llopr
proll
llopy
polly
lloqu
quoll
llort
troll
llosy
lysol
llouy
you'll
llowy
lowly
lloxy
xylol
llrtu
trull
llstu
stull
llsuy
sully
llsyy
slyly
llxyy
xylyl
lmmuy
lummy
lmoos
mools
sloom
lmoot
molto
lmooy
mooly
lmopu
pulmo
lmost
smolt
lmosu
mouls
solum

lmotu
moult
lmoty
ymolt
lmppu
plump
lmpsu
slump
lmpuy
lumpy
plumy
lmruy
murly
rumly
lmstu
stulm
lmsuu
Ulmus
lnnoy
nylon
lnoos
snool
Solon
lnooy
loony
lnopy
pylon
lnosw
swoln
looov
ovolo
loopr
orlop
loops
sloop
spool
loopy
loopy
loost
lotos
sloot
stool
loott
lotto
loppu
poulp
loppy
polyp
lopru
proul
loprw
prowl
lopss
slops
lopsy
slopy
loptu
Pluto
poult
lorry
lorry
loruy
loury

lossu
solus
lossy
lossy
lostu
lotus
losty
stylo
losuy
lousy
lotyz
zloty
louuv
voulu
lppuy
pulpy
lprsu
slurp
lpsuu
lupus
lrruy
lurry
lrsuy
surly
lrtuy
truly
lrwyy
wryly
lstuy
lusty
mmmoy
mommy
mmmuy
mummy
mmopy
pommy
mmosu
Momus
mmoty
tommy
mmpsu
mumps
mmruy
rummy
mmtuy
tummy
mmuyy
yummy
mnoor
moron
mnoos
nomos
mnooy
moony
mnoru
mourn
Munro
mnotu
mount
muton
notum
mnouv
novum

moops
spoom
moorr
morro
moors
smoor
moort
motor
moorv
vroom
moory
moory
roomy
moost
smoot
moott
motto
moppu
mop-up
moppy
moppy
moprt
tromp
mopst
stomp
mopsu
mopus
mopsy
mopsy
myops
morru
rumor
morst
storm
morsu
Morus
mortu
tumor
morwy
wormy
mossu
smous
mossy
mossy
mostu
moust
smout
mostw
smowt
mosuy
mousy
motty
motty
mprtu
trump
mpstu
stump
mpsuy
spumy
mptuy
tumpy
umpty
mrruy
murry

mrstu
strum
mssuy
mussy
mstuy
musty
muyzz
muzzy
nnnoy
nonny
nnoru
run-on
nnost
stonn
nnosu
nouns
nnosy
sonny
nnouw
unwon
nnruy
runny
nnsuy
sunny
nntuy
tunny
noopr
porno
noops
snoop
spoon
noost
snoot
noosw
swoon
nopry
proyn
noptu
punto
put-on
ton-up
nopty
ponty
nopuy
yupon
nopwy
powny
norst
snort
norsu
urson
norsw
sworn
norty
try-on
noruy
yourn
nossy
sonsy
nostu
Notus
snout
stoun
tonus

nostw
stown
nosty
stony
nosuw
swoun
noswy
snowy
notwy
towny
nprsu
spurn
nprtu
prunt
npruu
run-up
uprun
npsuu
sun-up
nptuy
punty
nrtuu
U-turn
nrtuy
runty
nsttu
stunt
nttuy
nutty
ooppz
zoppo
ooprs
sopor
spoor
ooprt
poort
troop
ooprv
Provo
oopry
roopy
oopst
stoop
topos
oopsw
swoop
ooptt
potto
oopvy
poovy
oorrt
rotor
oorrz
zorro
oorst
roost
stoor
torso
oortw
wroot
oorty
rooty
oostt
toots

5 TTT

- oosty
  - sooty
- ootwz
  - wootz
- oowyz
  - woozy
- opppu
  - pop-up
- opppy
  - poppy
- opprs
  - props
- oppsy
  - popsy
  - psyop
  - soppy
- opptu
  - poupt
  - top-up
- oprst
  - sport
  - strop
- oprsy
  - prosy
- oprty
  - porty
- opruy
  - roupy
- oprxy
  - proxy
- opstu
  - spout
  - stoup
- opstw
  - swopt
- opsuy
  - soupy
- opttu
  - putto
- optty
  - potty
  - typto
- optuw
  - two-up
- opyzz
  - pozzy
- orrsy
  - sorry
- orrty
  - rorty
- orrwy
  - worry
- orssu
  - sorus
- orstu
  - roust
  - stour
  - sutor
  - torus
- orstw
  - strow
  - worst
- orsty
  - royst
  - story
  - stroy
- orsuy
  - yours
- orttu
  - trout
  - tutor
- ortuy
  - yourt
- oruvw
  - vrouw
- ossty
  - tossy
- osttu
  - stout
- ostty
  - ytost
- ostuy
  - tousy
- ostwy
  - towsy
- ottty
  - totty
- pppuy
  - puppy
- ppruy
  - purpy
- pptuu
  - put-up
- prstu
  - spurt
  - turps
- prsuu
  - usurp
- prsuy
  - pursy
  - Pyrus
  - syrup
- prtuy
  - purty
- pssuy
  - pussy
- pttuy
  - putty
- rsstu
  - truss
- rssuu
  - Ursus
- rsttu
  - strut
  - sturt
  - trust
- rstty
  - tryst
- rstuw
  - wurst
- rstuy
  - rusty
- rsuuy
  - usury
- rttuy
  - rutty
- tttuy
  - tutty

6 AAB

- aaabcl
  - cabala
- aaabcn
  - cabana
- aaabdh
  - bahada
- aaabdj
  - bajada
- aaabkl
  - kabala
- aaabky
  - kabaya
- aaablm
  - Balaam
- aaablt
  - albata
  - atabal
  - balata
- aaabnn
  - banana
- aaabns
  - anabas
- aaabrz
  - bazaar
- aaabtt
  - batata
- aaacci
  - acacia
- aaacdn
  - cañada
- aaacjn
  - jacana
- aaaclp
  - alpaca
- aaacmr
  - maraca
- aaacnr
  - arcana
- aaacpr
  - Carapa
- aaadgh
  - Agadah
- aaadmr
  - armada
- aaadnp
  - panada
- aaaegp
  - agapae
- aaaelz
  - azalea
- aaaenr
  - Aranea
- aaagil
  - Aglaia
- aaaglm
  - Malaga
- aaaglr
  - argala
- aaagnn
  - nagana
- aaahnv
  - Havana
- aaaill
  - alalia
- aaailr
  - aralia
- aaaitx
  - ataxia
- aaajkt
  - jataka
- aaakkn
  - kanaka
- aaakkr
  - karaka
- aaaklm
  - kamala
- aaaknr
  - anarak
- aaalmp
  - palama
- aaalms
  - salaam
- aaamnn
  - mañana
- aaamnp
  - panama
- aaamnt
  - ataman
- aaamrs
  - samara
- aaamrt
  - tamara
- aaanns
  - ananas
- aaanpr
  - Paraná
- aaantt
  - anatta
- aaappy
  - papaya
- aaarst
  - satara
- aaartv
  - avatar
- aabbbo
  - baobab
- aabbcy
  - abbacy
- aabbds
  - abdabs
- aabbhl
  - bablah
- aabbll
  - lablab
- aabblo
  - balboa
- aabbst
  - sabbat
- aabchs
  - casbah
- aabcir
  - Arabic
- aabcmn
  - cabman
- aabcnt
  - Cantab
- aabcrs
  - scarab
- aabcsu
  - abacus
- aabcuu
  - aucuba
- aabder
  - abrade
- aabdes
  - abased
- aabdet
  - abated
- aabdeu
  - aubade
- aabdgo
  - dagoba
- aabdin
  - indaba
- aabdir
  - abraid
- aabdll
  - ballad
- aabdlm
  - lambda
- aabdmn
  - badman
- aabdnr
  - bandar
- aabdor
  - aboard
  - abroad
- aabdrt
  - tabard
- aabdry
  - Bayard
- aabefn
  - befana
- aabegm
  - ambage
- aabegt
  - atabeg
  - tea-bag
- aabekt
  - atabek
- aabelr
  - arable
- aabelt
  - ablate
- aabelz
  - ablaze
- aabemo
  - amoeba
- aabens
  - Sabean
- aabent
  - Banate
- aaberz
  - zareba
- aabest
  - sea-bat
- aabetu
  - bateau
- aabetz
  - zabeta
- aabfin
  - Fabian
- aabggr
  - rag-bag
- aabggs
  - gas-bag
  - sag-bag
- aabgin
  - baaing
- aabgmn
  - bagman
- aabgrt
  - ratbag
- aabhis
  - sahiba
- aabhiw
  - Wahabi
- aabhks
  - kasbah
- aabhlr
  - bharal
- aabhmr
  - Brahma
- aabhrt
  - Bharat
- aabhsw
  - bashaw
- aabill
  - labial
- aabilm
  - Baalim
- aabilu
  - abulia
- aabilx
  - biaxal
- aabimn
  - Bimana
- aabimr
  - Bairam
- aabinn
  - banian
- aabinr
  - arabin
- aabins
  - Sabian
- aabinw
  - wabain
- aabinz
  - banzai
  - Zabian
- aabirs
  - Arabis
- aabirz
  - zariba
- aabist
  - abatis
- aabjnx
  - banjax
- aabknr
  - barkan
- aablln
  - ballan
- aabllo
  - abolla

aabllt
ballat
aablms
balsam
aablny
Albany
aablor
aboral
aablov
lavabo
aablst
basalt
aabltu
ablaut
tabula
aabmnr
barman
aabmnt
bantam
batman
aabmor
Abroma
aabmrs
sambar
aabmst
tsamba
aabnnt
Bannat
aabnny
banyan
aaborr
arroba
aabort
abator
rabato
aabrrt
barrat
aabrty
baryta
aabttu
abattu
aabzzz
bazazz
aaccdi
cicada
aaccdu
caduac
aaccel
caecal
aacchh
cha-cha
aacchm
chacma
aaccil
Alcaic
cicala
aaccim
caimac
aaccir
Carica
aacckk
ack-ack
aacckr
carack
aacclo
cloaca
aacclp
calpac
aacclr
calcar
aaccmo
macaco
aaccnn
cancan
aaccrt
caract
aacdef
facade
aacdei
acedia
aacder
arcade
aacdeu
cadeau
aacdfr
cafard
aacdhr
chadar
aacdim
Adamic
aacdir
acarid
aacdlu
caudal
aacdmp
madcap
aacdnr
canard
aacdry
Arcady
aacefl
faecal
aacefr
carafe
aacegh
achage
aacehp
apache
aacehr
areach
aaceht
chaeta
aaceln
anlace
aacelp
palace
aacels
scalae
aacelt
acetal
aacemr
camera
aacenp
canapé
aacenr
arcane
aacent
catena
aacepr
ear-cap
Parcae
aaceps
sea-cap
aacers
caesar
aacert
acater
aacest
acates
sea-cat
aacetv
caveat
vacate
aacfil
cafila
facial
aacfis
fascia
aacflu
facula
faucal
aacfnt
caftan
aacfrs
fracas
aacfrx
carfax
aacftt
fat-cat
aacghn
chagan
aacgim
agamic
aacgir
agaric
aachkn
achkan
aachkp
chapka
pachak
aachkw
kwacha
aachln
chalan
aachls
calash
aachmn
machan
aachms
camash
aachnr
anarch
aachns
ash-can
aachnt
acanth
aachrs
charas
aachrt
Cathar
charta
aachsw
cashaw
aachtt
attach
chatta
aachtw
awatch
aacill
laical
aacilm
calami
aacilp
apical
aacilr
racial
aacilt
Altaic
aacimn
caiman
maniac
aacinr
arnica
carina
crania
aacins
ascian
aaciot
atocia
coaita
aacips
capias
aacipt
capita
aacirr
air-car
aacirs
air-sac
aacirv
caviar
aaciss
cassia
aacitx
ataxic
aacjkl
jackal
aacjou
acajou
aackpz
czapka
aackrr
arrack
aackrw
awrack
aacktt
attack
aaclmu
macula
aaclnr
carnal
aaclnu
lacuna
aaclot
catalo
aaclpr
carpal
aaclps
pascal
aaclpt
cat-lap
aaclrs
lascar
rascal
sacral
scalar
aaclrw
acrawl
aaclsu
casual
causal
aacltu
actual
aacmnr
carman
aacmny
cayman
aacmoy
macoya
aacmrt
ramcat
tarmac
aacmss
camass
aacnno
Ancona
aacnor
ancora
aacnpt
captan
catnap
aacnrt
cantar
aacnrx
caranx
aacnry
canary
aacnsv
canvas
aacntv
vacant
aacppy
papacy
aacrrt
carrat
aacrru
curara
aacrsu
acarus
aacrtv
cravat
aacssv
cavass
aaddel
daedal
aadder
adread
aaddil
alidad
la-di-da
aaddnr
Dardan
aaddou
aoudad
aaddst
stadda
aadefl
aefald
aadegl
gelada
aadegm
damage
aadegn
agenda
aadegz
agazed
aadein
Idaean
aadekw
awaked
aadels
salade
aadelt
alated
aademm
madame
aademn
anadem
maenad
aadenn
Andean
aadens
Seanad
aadent
adnate
aadepr
parade
aadeps
espada
aaderv
Veadar
aadfir
afraid
aadflw
afawld
aadfnr
farand
aadfnt
fantad
aadgim
agamid
aadgio
adagio
aadgir
gardai
aadgnp
padang
pad-nag
aadgnr
argand
aadgop
pagoda
aadgrs
Asgard
aadgru
garuda
aadgty
Tagday
aadhil
dahlia
aadhmr
dharma
aadhnr
dharna
aadhrz
hazard
aadill
Dalila
aadilr
radial
aadimn
maidan
aadino
Adonai
Adonia
aadinr
radian
aadins
naiads
aadint
aidant
aadinv
navaid
aadipp
appaid
aadirt
tiara'd
aadist
stadia
aadkms
damask
aadkpu
padauk
aadlly
all-day
aadlmp
lampad
aadlmw
wadmal
aadlmy
malady
aadlno
anodal
aadlns
sandal
aadlnu
landau
aadlnv
vandal
aadlop
apodal
aadlpr
pardal

aadlru
radula
aadlwy
law-day
aadlyy
lay-day
aadmmn
madman
aadmmr
dammar
aadmny
man-day
aadmou
amadou
aadmrs
madras
aadmru
maraud
aadmrz
mazard
aadmss
admass
aadmyy
mayday
aadnnr
randan
aadnpr
pandar
aadnpu
Paduan
aadnrs
nasard
aadnrt
tarand
aadops
posada
aadppy
appayd
aadpsw
pad-saw
aadpsy
spayad
aadpyy
pay-day
aadrtu
datura
aadrty
datary
aadrvw
vaward
aaeegt
eatage
aaeelp
paleae
aaeeps
sea-ape
aaeers
sea-ear
aaeert
aerate
aaeeyy
aye-aye
aaeflm
aflame

aaeflr
rafale
aaefnr
fraena
aaefns
sea-fan
aaefnu
faunae
aaeggl
galage
aaeggr
garage
aaeggv
gavage
aaegln
alnage
anlage
galena
lagena
aaeglr
alegar
laager
aaeglt
algate
aaeglv
lavage
aaegmn
agname
manage
aaegmr
Gemara
aaegns
Ganesa
aaegnt
agnate
aaegnu
Augean
aaegor
oarage
aaegpr
parage
aaegpv
pavage
aaegrv
ravage
aaegsv
savage
aaegtu
gâteau
aaehkp
pakeha
aaehks
ashake
aaehkt
takahe
aaehlm
haemal
aaehms
ashame
aaehmt
hamate
aaehnt
aneath
Athena

aaehny
hyaena
aaehpw
awhape
aaeilm
amelia
aaeilr
aerial
realia
aaeilv
availe
aaeilx
alexia
aaeimn
anemia
aaeint
taenia
aaeirs
air-sea
araise
sea-air
aaeirt
Raetia
aaeitv
aviate
aaeklm
kamela
aaekln
alkane
aaekls
aslake
aaeknn
ananke
aaeknw
awaken
aaekrs
keasar
aaekrt
karate
aaellp
paella
pallae
aaelmp
Palmae
aaelmr
rameal
aaelms
salame
aaelmt
malate
meatal
tamale
aaelnn
anneal
aaelnt
lanate
aaelor
areola
aaelpp
appeal
aaelpr
earlap
aaelpt
palate

aaelrv
larvae
aaelrz
Azrael
aaelsw
sea-law
aaeltv
valeta
aaemmm
mammae
aaemnp
apeman
aaemnr
ramean
aaemns
seaman
aaemnt
amenta
aaemrs
asmear
aaemrt
ramate
retama
aaemst
sea-mat
aaemsw
sea-maw
aaennz
zenana
aaenop
apnoea
aaenoz
ozaena
aaenpv
pavane
aaenst
ansate
aaensu
nausea
aaeppr
appear
aaeprs
pasear
aaeprt
patera
petara
aaeprz
zarape
aaepsy
sea-pay
aaeptt
tapeta
aaerrr
arrear
aaerrt
errata
aaerst
astare
sea-rat
aaersy
arayse
aaertt
terata

aaertu
aurate
aaerwx
earwax
aaerwy
aweary
aaestv
Avesta
savate
aaeswy
seaway
aaffim
Maffia
aaffir
affair
raffia
aaffpr
affrap
aaffry
affray
aafghn
afghan
aafikl
kafila
aafinr
farina
aafirs
safari
aafknt
kaftan
aaflll
fallal
aaflnu
faunal
aaflot
afloat
aafnnt
fan-tan
aagglo
Galago
aaggqu
quagga
aaggrs
saggar
aaggrt
rag-tag
tagrag
aaghil
Alhagi
aaghkn
khanga
aaghlz
ghazal
aaghms
gamash
aaghnr
arghan
hangar
aaghst
aghast
aagiln
agnail
aagilo
alogia

aagilr
argali
garial
aagilv
gavial
aagimn
Magian
aaginn
angina
aaginr
nagari
aagint
gitana
aaginu
iguana
aaginv
vagina
aagipr
air-gap
aagirs
air-gas
aagiru
Auriga
aagjnr
garjan
aagjrs
gas-jar
aagjru
jaguar
aaglln
lalang
aagllp
plagal
aaglmm
malmag
aaglmn
mangal
aaglno
Angola
aaglnr
raglan
aaglnt
galant
aaglst
stalag
aaglxy
galaxy
aagmms
magmas
aagmnr
ragman
aagmns
gasman
aagmry
magyar
margay
aagnno
goanna
aagnnw
wangan
aagnor
angora
Onagra

aagnpr
parang
aagnrr
garran
aagnrs
sangar
aagnry
angary
aagntu
taguan
aagotu
agouta
aagppr
grappa
aagpst
gas-tap
aagrry
garrya
aagrst
gas-tar
aagrsv
Svarga
aagrsw
Swarga
aagrvy
vagary
aahhlv
halvah
aahhmz
hamzah
aahhnt
thanah
aahhpt
aphtha
aahhww
haw-haw
aahiik
haikai
aahilt
Thalia
aahims
ahimsa
aahint
tahina
aahipr
pariah
Raphia
aahirs
sharia
aahirv
vihara
aahisv
Shaiva
aahjnr
hanjar
aahjrr
jarrah
aahjrs
Jashar
aahklt
khalat
aahkst
Shakta

6 AAH

aahlll
hallal
aahlln
hallan
nallah
aahllo
halloa
aahllp
pallah
aahllw
wallah
aahlmm
hammal
mahmal
aahlmt
maltha
aahlrs
ashlar
aahlrt
hartal
aahmmm
hammam
aahmnr
harman
aahmns
shaman
aahmps
Phasma
aahmpy
mayhap
aahmrs
ashram
aahmst
asthma
aahmtz
matzah
aahnnt
tannah
thanna
aahnps
ash-pan
aahnpt
Pathan
aahnst
Sathan
aahntw
whatna
aahppr
paraph
aahpry
yarpha
aahpty
apathy
aahrss
harass
hassar
aahssy
sashay
aaiikk
kaikai
aaiimm
mia-mia
aaijnn
Janian
aaijrw
jawari
aaikll
alkali
aaiklm
kalmia
kamila
aaikln
kalian
aaikno
aikona
aaiknt
tankia
aaikor
kia-ora
aaikpt
Pitaka
aaikrs
askari
aaikrt
karait
aaillp
pallia
aaillx
axilla
aailmn
almain
animal
lamina
manila
aailmp
impala
aailms
alisma
salami
aailmu
aumail
aailnr
narial
aailns
Salian
salina
aailnt
antlia
Latian
aailny
inyala
aailpr
parial
aailqu
Aquila
aailrt
Altair
atrial
lariat
latria
aailss
assail
aailsv
saliva
salvia
aailtv
avital
aaimms
miasma
aaimmx
maxima
aaimnr
airman
Marian
marina
aaimns
Samian
aaimnt
manati
aaimnv
vimana
aaimrr
air-arm
aaimrt
amrita
tamari
aaimtt
tatami
aainno
Aonian
aainnt
naiant
aainox
anoxia
aainpp
papain
aainpr
Parian
piraña
aainpt
patina
taipan
aainrt
antiar
aainru
anuria
Urania
aaintt
attain
aaintw
atwain
aaiopr
aporia
aaiprt
pitara
aaipry
apiary
piraya
aaiptu
Tupaia
aaipzz
piazza
aairst
arista
tarsia
aairsu
Sauria
aairty
raiyat
aairvy
aviary
aairwy
airway
aairzz
razzia
aaisvy
Vaisya
aajjmr
jamjar
aajkns
sanjak
aajmnp
jampan
aajnow
ajowan
aajnoy
yojana
aajrsw
swaraj
aakklp
kalpak
aakkop
kakapo
aaklot
atokal
aakmnu
manuka
aakmru
kumara
aaknor
anorak
aaknrt
kantar
aaknst
askant
aakssv
kavass
vakass
aallln
lallan
aallls
sallal
aallor
arolla
aallpp
palpal
aallps
Pallas
aallrv
larval
vallar
aalltt
tallat
aallvv
valval
aalmmm
mammal
aalmms
Lammas
aalmnp
napalm
aalmnu
alumna
manual
aalmnw
lawman
aalmny
Almany
layman
aalmor
amoral
aalmos
omasal
aalmot
amatol
aalmpr
palmar
aalmps
lampas
plasma
aalmru
alarum
aalmsu
masula
aalnnu
annual
aalnot
atonal
aalnoz
azonal
aalnpr
planar
aalnpt
planta
platan
aalnrt
tarnal
aalnru
ranula
aalnrx
larnax
aalnst
aslant
santal
aalopr
oar-lap
aalopy
payola
aalort
aortal
aalovw
avowal
aalppu
papula
aalprr
parral
aalpry
parlay
aalpsu
pausal
aalptu
Laputa
aalrst
astral
tarsal
aalrsv
varsal
aalrsy
salary
aalrvv
valvar
aalssv
vassal
aalstt
statal
aalsux
saxaul
aalswy
always
aaltuv
valuta
aalwyy
waylay
aammnt
amtman
aammrr
marram
aammtt
tam-tam
aammuz
mazuma
aamnnu
maunna
aamnoo
manoao
aamnoz
amazon
aamnps
sampan
aamnrt
mantra
aamnrw
warman
aamntu
mantua
tamanu
aamopr
paramo
aamors
Masora
aampps
pampas
aamqsu
squama
aamrsu
asarum
aamrsw
aswarm
aamrtu
trauma
aannno
Annona
aannps
sanpan
aanntt
natant
aannyz
nyanza
aanort
torana
aanoru
Anoura
aanost
sonata
aanott
anatto
aanpps
sappan
aanppu
Papuan
aanprt
partan
tarpan
trapan
aanpru
Purana
aanpry
panary
aanqtu
quanta
aanrrs
narras
aanrrt
arrant
aanrtt
rattan
Tantra
tartan
aanrtu
Arnaut
aanrtz
Tarzan
aanruv
Varuna
aanstv
savant
aanstw
Tswana
aanstz
stanza
aansyy
nay-say
aanttv
tan-vat
aantuv
avaunt
aanwyy
anyway
aaoprt
Atropa
aaopst
sapota
aaorru
aurora
aaottv
ottava
aappww
pawpaw
aaprst
satrap
Sparta
aaprtt
attrap

aapwxx
  paxwax
aapzzz
  pazazz
aaqrsu
  quasar
aaqstu
  asquat
aarrst
  tarras
aarrtt
  tartar
aarrwy
  warray
aarsst
  assart
aarstt
  astart
  strata
aarsty
  astray
  satyra
aarttt
  rat-tat
aasttu
  statua
abbbel
  babble
abbbly
  babbly
abbcei
  cabbie
abbcir
  bicarb
abbcot
  bobcat
abbcry
  crabby
abbcsy
  scabby
abbdde
  dabbed
abbdel
  dabble
abbden
  nabbed
abbder
  barbed
  dabber
abbdet
  tabbed
  tebbad
abbdeu
  bedaub
abbdry
  drabby
abbeew
  bawbee
abbegl
  gabble
abbegr
  gabber
abbeiy
  yabbie
abbejl
  jabble
abbejr
  jabber
abbelr
  barbel
  rabble
abbelu
  bauble
abbelw
  bawble
  wabble
abbenr
  nabber
abbeor
  earbob
abberr
  barber
abbert
  barbet
  rabbet
abbery
  yabber
abbess
  abbess
abbfly
  flabby
abbghu
  gubbah
abbgor
  gabbro
abbhij
  jibbah
abbhju
  jubbah
abbhoo
  haboob
abbhsy
  shabby
abbims
  Babism
abbinr
  rabbin
abbirt
  rabbit
abbist
  Babist
abblru
  bulbar
abblsy
  slabby
abbmoo
  bamboo
abbmox
  bombax
abbnoo
  baboon
abbors
  absorb
abbrsu
  bus-bar
abcciu
  cubica
abcclu
  buccal
abcdek
  backed
abcder
  decarb
abcdeu
  abduce
abcdho
  bodach
abcdir
  bardic
abcdtu
  abduct
abceel
  belace
abceem
  became
abcegi
  ice-bag
abcego
  bocage
abcegu
  cubage
abcehl
  bleach
abcehr
  breach
abcehy
  beachy
abceir
  cabrie
  caribe
abcejt
  abject
abcekr
  reback
abcekt
  backet
abcell
  becall
abcelm
  becalm
  clambe
abcemr
  camber
  cembra
abcemx
  excamb
abceno
  beacon
abceos
  sea-cob
abcerr
  bracer
abcfir
  fabric
abcfno
  confab
abcgit
  gib-cat
abchln
  blanch
abchlu
  Baluch
abchnr
  branch
abchor
  broach
abchpu
  hub-cap
abciim
  iambic
abciir
  Cabiri
abcilt
  Baltic
abcirt
  cabrit
abcitt
  tib-cat
abckor
  barock
abckpu
  back-up
abckru
  buckra
abclmu
  bumalc
abclmy
  cymbal
abclno
  blanco
abclot
  cobalt
abcmop
  mob-cap
abcmor
  comarb
  crambo
abcmot
  combat
  tombac
abcnor
  carbon
  corban
abcorx
  box-car
abcory
  carboy
abcstu
  subact
abddee
  beaded
abddei
  abided
  baddie
abddel
  bladed
abdden
  banded
abdder
  barded
abddey
  day-bed
abddhu
  Buddha
abdeeh
  behead
abdeej
  bejade
abdeek
  beaked
abdeel
  beadle
abdees
  debase
  seabed
abdeet
  debate
abdeez
  bedaze
abdefl
  fabled
abdegg
  bagged
abdegl
  gabled
abdegn
  banged
abdego
  bodega
abdegr
  badger
abdehs
  bedash
abdeir
  air-bed
  braide
abdeis
  biased
abdekr
  debark
abdell
  balled
abdelm
  bedlam
  beldam
  blamed
abdelo
  albedo
  doable
abdelr
  bedral
abdelt
  tabled
abdelu
  belaud
abdely
  dyable
abdenp
  bedpan
abdent
  tan-bed
abderr
  barred
abders
  serdab
abderu
  dauber
abderv
  adverb
abdett
  batted
abdfor
  forbad
abdgno
  bandog
abdgor
  bodrag
abdhoy
  hobday
abdilr
  bridal
  ribald
abdinr
  riband
abdint
  bandit
abdirr
  braird
  Briard
abdirs
  disbar
abdiru
  ribaud
abdlly
  baldly
abdlry
  drably
abdnou
  abound
abdnry
  brandy
abdorr
  bordar
abdors
  adsorb
abdory
  byroad
abdoxy
  box-day
abdoyy
  day-boy
abdrru
  durbar
abdrsu
  absurd
abdrwy
  bawdry
abeees
  Seabee
abeegh
  beegah
abeegl
  beagle
abeegr
  barege
  bargee
abeehn
  beenah
abeehv
  behave
abeeil
  bailee
abeein
  beanie
abeejm
  jambee
abeejr
  bajree
abeekl
  kabele
abeekr
  beaker
abeekt
  betake
abeelm
  embale
abeeln
  baleen
  enable
abeelt
  belate
  let-a-be
abeemn
  bemean
  bename
abeemr
  beamer
abeems
  embase
abeenr
  Berean
abeent
  beaten
abeeor
  aerobe
abeerr
  bearer
  breare
abeert
  beater
  berate
  rebate
abeerv
  beaver
abeerw
  beware
abeerz
  zereba
abeest
  sebate
abeffl
  baffle
abefhl
  behalf
abefil
  faible
abefll
  befall
abeflm
  flambé
abeflr
  fabler
abefmo
  befoam

abefpr
  prefab
abefty
  tabefy
abeggr
  beggar
abeghi
  abeigh
abeglm
  gamble
abegln
  bangle
abeglr
  garble
abeglt
  gablet
abeglu
  beluga
  blague
abegmr
  bregma
abegmt
  gambet
abegnr
  banger
  graben
abegnw
  begnaw
abegor
  borage
abegoz
  gazebo
abegtu
  tubage
abehil
  habile
abehkl
  keblah
abehlm
  hamble
abehlr
  herbal
abehlu
  Beulah
abehno
  hebona
abehnt
  Theban
abehrr
  Herbar
abehrs
  basher
abehrt
  bather
  bertha
  breath
abehst
  Shebat
abeiil
  bailie
abeiit
  tibiae
abeill
  Belial
  labile
  liable
abeilm
  embail
  lambie
abeilr
  bailer
abeils
  blaise
  isabel
abeilt
  albeit
  albite
  libate
abeilv
  viable
abeilw
  bewail
abeily
  bailey
abeilz
  blaize
abeims
  imbase
abeins
  Sabine
abeint
  binate
abeirs
  braise
  rabies
abeirt
  baiter
  barite
abeirz
  braize
  zeriba
abejmn
  enjamb
abejmr
  jamber
abejnt
  bejant
abejor
  jerboa
abejrs
  jabers
abejru
  abjure
abejtu
  jubate
abeklr
  balker
abekly
  bleaky
  Kabyle
abekmn
  embank
abekmr
  embark
abeknr
  banker
  barken
abeknt
  banket
abekrr
  barker
abekry
  bakery
abekst
  basket
abellm
  emball
abellt
  ballet
abelmm
  embalm
abelmr
  ambler
  marble
  ramble
abelmu
  bemaul
abelmw
  wamble
abelmy
  belamy
abelnr
  branle
abelnu
  nebula
  unable
abelny
  by-lane
abelnz
  benzal
abelor
  boreal
abelot
  boatel
  lobate
  oblate
abelrr
  barrel
abelrt
  albert
  labret
abelrv
  verbal
abelrw
  bawler
  warble
abelry
  barely
  barley
  bleary
abelrz
  blazer
abelst
  stable
abelsu
  suable
  usable
abelsy
  basely
abelsz
  blazes
abeltt
  battel
  battle
  tablet
abeltu
  Betula
abelty
  baetyl
abelwy
  bawley
  bye-law
abelyy
  lay-bye
abemno
  bemoan
abemny
  by-name
abemrt
  tamber
abemry
  ambery
abennr
  banner
abenor
  borane
abenrr
  barren
abenru
  unbare
  unbear
  urbane
abenry
  barney
  near-by
abenrz
  brazen
abenst
  absent
  basnet
abensu
  sea-bun
abentt
  batten
abentu
  butane
abentz
  bezant
abeors
  Boreas
abeort
  boater
  borate
  rebato
abeorz
  bezoar
abeosy
  sea-boy
abeotv
  bovate
abepru
  upbear
abepst
  bespat
abeptu
  beat-up
  upbeat
abeqru
  barque
abeqsu
  basque
aberrt
  barret
  barter
aberst
  bestar
  breast
abersu
  abuser
  bursae
abertt
  batter
  tabret
abertu
  arbute
abertx
  baxter
aberty
  betray
aberuu
  bureau
aberwy
  bewray
abesst
  basset
abessu
  sub-sea
abettu
  battue
  tubate
abetuy
  beauty
abezzz
  bezazz
abfglu
  bagful
abfgow
  gowf-ba'
abfilu
  fibula
abflru
  barful
abflry
  barfly
abfotx
  fox-bat
abggit
  baggit
  gag-bit
abggiw
  bagwig
abggno
  gobang
abghtu
  hagbut
abgikn
  baking
  ink-bag
abgikt
  kit-bag
abgilm
  gimbal
abgimr
  gambir
abgimt
  gambit
abgimy
  bigamy
abgino
  bagnio
  gabion
abgins
  basing
abgint
  bating
abgios
  biogas
abgiou
  baguio
abgkno
  kobang
abgkoo
  bogoak
abgllo
  global
abglmo
  gambol
abglor
  brolga
abglou
  albugo
abglru
  Bulgar
abgmuy
  may-bug
abgnor
  brogan
abgnpu
  bang-up
abhikl
  kiblah
abhimr
  Brahmi
  mihrab
abhins
  ash-bin
  banish
abhiop
  phobia
abhirs
  barish
abhkru
  burkha
abhlsu
  ablush
abhlsy
  blashy
abhmru
  rhumba
abhmsu
  ambush
abhnot
  bothan
abhooy
  yah-boo
abhort
  athrob
abhost
  bathos
  boshta
abhotx
  hatbox
abhoxy
  haybox
abhpty
  bypath
abhrsy
  brashy
abiiln
  bilian
abiilt
  tibial
abijru
  jabiru
abikku
  kabuki
abikmo
  akimbo
abikmr
  imbark
abilmt
  timbal
abilmu
  labium
abilno
  albino
  Albion
abilns
  ablins
abilnt
  libant
abilny
  Libyan
abilot
  obital
abilrt
  tribal
abilru
  burial
abilrz
  brazil
abimmr
  mimbar
abimno
  obi-man
abimnr
  minbar
abimrs
  bismar
abimru
  barium

abimrv
Vibram®
abimsu
iambus
abinnu
bunnia
abinos
bonsai
abinot
obtain
abinry
binary
brainy
abinsu
Anubis
unbias
abiorr
barrio
abiors
isobar
abiort
orbita
abirsu
air-bus
abizzz
bizazz
abjjoo
jojoba
abjkmo
jambok
abjlmu
jambul
jumbal
abjowx
jawbox
abklny
blanky
abkmot
tombak
abknrs
branks
abknru
unbark
abknry
branky
ablllno
no-ball
abllot
ballot
ablmoo
abloom
ablmop
aplomb
ablmow
mob-law
ablmru
brumal
labrum
lumbar
umbral
ablmry
marbly
ablmty
tymbal

ablmwy
wambly
ablnoz
blazon
ablntu
tulban
abloor
robalo
abloru
labour
ablost
oblast
ablott
talbot
ablotv
abvolt
ablpru
burlap
ablpyy
by-play
ablrsu
bursal
Labrus
ablrsy
labrys
ablrtu
brutal
ablrwy
brawly
byrlaw
ablssy
byssal
ablsty
stably
ablsyy
lay-bys
abmnow
bow-man
abmnru
Burman
abmnsu
busman
subman
abmntu
numbat
abmnuy
ynambu
abmoow
waboom
abmotw
wombat
abmrsu
sambur
abmruy
aumbry
abnnry
branny
abnort
barton
abnory
barony
baryon
abnoty
botany

abnrtu
turban
abnruu
auburn
abnruy
anbury
abnrwy
brawny
abntyz
byzant
aboorw
bow-oar
abopxy
pay-box
aborru
arbour
aborrw
barrow
aborsv
bravos
abortu
outbar
rubato
tabour
abortw
towbar
abortx
tar-box
aboruy
Yoruba
abostu
Basuto
aboswwv
bow-saw
abouxy
boyaux
abprtu
abrupt
abpruy
upbray
abpssy
bypass
abpsty
by-past
abrrsu
bursar
abrssy
brassy
abrstu
aburst
abstuu
Basutu
absuwy
subway
acccil
calcic
acccl o
coccal
accdee
accede
accdel
calced
accden
accend

accdii
acidic
accdor
accord
accehn
chance
accehr
creach
acceht
cachet
acceil
celiac
acceip
ice-cap
ipecac
acceit
accite
acetic
accekl
cackle
acceln
cancel
accelr
cercal
accels
calces
accemu
caecum
accenr
cancer
accent
accent
accept
accept
accers
scarce
acceru
accrue
access
access
accesu
accuse
accgno
Cognac
acchhi
chicha
acchlt
clatch
acchno
concha
acchnr
cranch
acchny
chancy
acchou
cachou
acchoy
coachy
acchrt
cratch
acchst
scatch
acchtu
cutcha

acchty
catchy
acciir
Riccia
accilo
accoil
calico
accilt
lactic
accimm
Micmac
accins
siccan
acciny
cyanic
accipr
capric
accirr
circar
ric-rac
accirs
siccar
accirt
arctic
accitt
tactic
tic-tac
accitu
cicuta
accknu
canuck
acclou
coucal
accloy
accloy
accmoy
occamy
accnoo
cacoon
accoss
saccos
accost
accost
accruy
curacy
accstu
cactus
accsuu
caucus
acddee
decade
acddei
caddie
Eddaic
acddeu
adduce
acddii
diacid
acddin
candid
acddir
Dardic
acddis
caddis

acddit
addict
acddiy
dyadic
acddtu
adduct
acdeef
deface
acdeen
decane
acdeer
decare
acdegr
cadger
graced
acdehr
arched
chared
acdeht
detach
acdein
candie
cnidae
decani
acdeit
dacite
acdeiv
advice
acdekr
dacker
racked
acdekt
tacked
acdekv
vacked
acdelm
calmed
macled
acdeln
candle
acdelp
placed
acdelr
cradle
credal
acdels
scaled
acdelu
caudle
cedula
acdelw
clawed
acdely
lac-dye
acdemp
decamp
acdenn
canned
acdeno
deacon
acdenr
cedarn
dancer

acdens
ascend
acdent
cadent
decant
acdeop
peacod
acdepp
capped
acdepr
red-cap
acdeps
spaced
acderr
carder
acders
sacred
acdert
Dectra
redact
acderv
carved
acderz
crazed
acdest
casted
acdeux
caudex
acdhir
diarch
acdhis
Chasid
acdhmr
drachm
acdhor
chador
acdiip
adipic
acdiju
Judaic
Judica
acdill
callid
acdilp
placid
acdino
Adonic
anodic
acdinr
rancid
acdinw
windac
acdios
sodaic
acdiot
dacoit
acdioz
zodiac
acdips
capsid
acdiru
raucid
acdist
dicast

acdlnu
unclad
acdlty
dactyl
acdmtu
mud-cat
acdors
Dorcas
acdorw
coward
aceeff
efface
aceefn
enface
aceefr
reface
aceefs
faeces
aceeft
facete
aceefx
Ceefax®
aceegn
encage
aceehk
hackee
aceehn
achene
aceeht
eatche
Hecate
thecae
aceeip
apiece
aceeis
sea-ice
aceeix
ice-axe
aceejt
ejecta
aceell
cellae
aceeln
elance
enlace
aceelr
alerce
cereal
aceelv
cleave
aceemn
menace
aceemr
amerce
carème
raceme
aceems
camese
aceemz
eczema
aceenr
careen
enrace
aceens
encase
séance
Seneca
aceent
cetane
tenace
aceenv
encave
aceeor
ocreae
aceeot
coatee
aceepr
preace
aceeps
escape
aceerr
career
aceers
crease
searce
aceert
cerate
create
écarté
aceffr
Caffre
aceffт
affect
acefhr
chafer
acefil
facile
fecial
acefin
fiancé
acefir
fiacre
acefis
facies
acefls
falces
aceflu
fecula
acefly
calefy
acefss
fasces
acefsu
fauces
aceftu
faucet
aceghn
change
aceghr
charge
creagh
aceghu
gauche
acegil
Gaelic
acegin
incage
acegiu
gaucie
acegln
glance
acegly
legacy
acegnu
cangue
uncage
acegny
agency
acegos
socage
acegow
cowage
acehil
heliac
acehip
phaeic
acehir
Archie
eriach
acehis
chaise
acehkl
hackle
acehlp
chapel
pleach
acehls
laches
sealch
acehlt
chalet
thecal
Thecla
acehly
leachy
acehmn
manche
acehms
sachem
schema
acehnr
chenar
enarch
acehns
encash
acehop
epocha
phocae
acehor
chorea
ochrea
orache
acehpr
eparch
preach
acehps
Pesach
acehpt
hep-cat
acehpy
peachy
acehqu
queach
acehrr
archer
acehrs
chaser
eschar
search
acehrv
varech
acehrx
exarch
acehss
chasse
chassé
acehst
chaste
sachet
scathe
acehsw
cashew
acehtx
hexact
aceikr
eirack
aceill
allice
aceilm
maleic
malice
aceiln
ancile
inlace
aceilo
Aeolic
aceilp
epical
plaice
plicae
aceilr
éclair
aceilv
clavie
aceilx
alexic
aceimn
anemic
cinema
iceman
aceims
camise
aceimt
acmite
micate
aceimu
aecium
aceinn
canine
neanic
aceinp
ice-pan
aceins
casein
incase
aceint
anetic
aceinu
eucain
aceinv
cave-in
incave
aceips
apices
aceiqu
caique
aceirs
caries
aceisv
vesica
aceitt
tietac
aceitv
active
aceivv
vivace
acejkt
jacket
acejlo
cajole
acejnt
jacent
acejnu
jaunce
acejqu
Jacque
aceklm
mackle
aceklr
calker
lacker
aceklt
tackle
acekly
lackey
acekno
nocake
aceknr
canker
reckan
aceknt
nacket
acekpr
packer
repack
acekpt
packet
acekrr
racker
acekrs
screak
acekrt
racket
tacker
acekru
cauker
acekrw
cawker
acekry
creaky
yacker
acekst
casket
acektt
tacket
acello
locale
acellr
caller
cellar
recall
acellt
callet
acelmn
encalm
acelmp
cample
acelmr
marcel
acelms
mascle
mescal
scamel
acelmt
camlet
acelmu
macule
acelnn
cannel
acelnr
lancer
rancel
acelns
lances
acelnt
cantle
cental
lancet
acelnu
cuneal
launce
unlace
acelor
oracle
acelos
solace
acelot
Alecto
locate
acelov
alcove
coeval
acelpr
carpel
parcel
placer
acelpt
placet
acelpu
Clupea
acelqu
calque
claque
acelrr
carrel
acelrs
scaler
sclera
acelrt
cartel
claret
rectal
tarcel
acelru
raucle
acelrv
calver
carvel
claver
acelst
castle
sclate
acelsu
caules
clause
acelsv
calves
claves
acelsx
calxes
aceltt
cattle
aceltu
cautel
acelty
acetyl
acelyy
clayey
acemno
ancome
acemnp
encamp
acemnu
acumen
acemop
pomace
acemor
amorce
acemos
cameos
cosmea
acemot
comate
acempr
camper
acemrs
scream
acemrt
mercat
acemry
creamy
acemsu
muscae

acemtu
mucate
acennr
canner
acennu
nuance
acenor
cornea
acenot
octane
acenpr
prance
acenpt
catnep
acenpu
uncape
acenrs
casern
acenrt
canter
carnet
creant
Cretan
nectar
recant
tanrec
trance
acenrv
carven
cavern
craven
acenry
carney
acenrz
zarnec
acenst
ascent
secant
stance
acensu
causen
uncase
usance
acentu
uncate
acenuv
vaunce
aceopr
Pecora
aceops
scopae
aceopt
capote
toecap
aceopw
cow-pea
aceors
coarse
rosace
aceorx
coaxer
aceosw
sea-cow

aceotu
coteau
aceotv
avocet
octave
aceppr
capper
aceprr
carper
aceprs
escarp
parsec
scrape
spacer
aceprt
carpet
acepru
aperçu
race-up
acepst
aspect
acepsy
spacey
aceptu
teacup
aceqsu
casque
sacque
acerrs
scarer
scarre
acerrt
arrect
carter
crater
tracer
acerru
curare
acerrv
carver
craver
acerry
crayer
acerss
caress
crases
acerst
caster
recast
acersu
causer
cesura
saucer
acersy
creasy
scarey
scraye
acertu
cauter
curate
acestt
sceatt
stacte

acestu
cuesta
acesty
cytase
acesuy
causey
cayuse
acffhy
chaffy
acffls
sclaff
acfgin
facing
acfhln
flanch
acfhrt
fratch
acfiln
in-calf
acfils
fiscal
acfinn
finnac
acfinr
farcin
acfios
fascio
fiasco
acfipy
pacify
acflno
falcon
flacon
acflnu
canful
acflot
olfact
acflru
furcal
acfmtu
factum
acfntu
unfact
acfort
factor
forçat
acforx
carfox
acfrty
crafty
acggio
agogic
acggly
claggy
acggry
craggy
acghin
aching
acghnu
gaunch
acghou
gaucho
acghtu
caught

acgikn
caking
acgill
Gallic
acgiln
lacing
acgilo
caligo
acgilr
garlic
acgils
glacis
acgily
cagily
acgimo
ogamic
acginn
caning
acgino
agonic
angico
acginr
arcing
caring
racing
acgins
casing
acgint
acting
acginv
caving
acginw
cawing
acgirt
tragic
acglou
cagoul
acgnor
garçon
acgnos
gascon
Scogan
acgort
go-cart
acgoru
cougar
acgttu
catgut
achhin
hainch
achhis
hachis
achhnu
haunch
achhtt
thatch
achiis
ischia
achijk
hijack
achilo
lochia
achilp
caliph

achilr
archil
achilt
chital
achims
chiasm
achinr
chinar
inarch
achint
canthi
achior
choria
achips
phasic
achipt
haptic
pathic
phatic
achiqu
quaich
achirs
Charis
rachis
achist
scaith
taisch
achisu
chiaus
achkku
chukka
achkly
chalky
hackly
achkow
whacko
achkru
chukar
achktu
kutcha
achktw
thwack
achkwy
whacky
achlno
lochan
achlnp
planch
achlnu
launch
nuchal
achlor
choral
lorcha
achlry
archly
achmnu
Manchu
achmor
chroma
achmos
camsho
achmst
smatch

achmsu
sumach
achmsy
chasmy
achnor
anchor
archon
Charon
rancho
achnos
sancho
achnot
chaton
achnoy
onycha
achnpu
paunch
achnru
raunch
achnst
snatch
stanch
achntu
chaunt
nautch
achnty
chanty
achoot
cahoot
achopy
poachy
pochay
achort
orchat
achouv
avouch
achppy
chappy
achpty
patchy
achqtu
quatch
achrry
charry
achrst
scarth
starch
achstu
cushat
achtty
chatty
achtuw
waucht
aciils
sialic
silica
aciilt
italic
aciinn
niacin
aciinr
Iranic
aciirt
iatric

aciist
Iastic
acikln
calkin
aciknp
ink-cap
panick
aciknr
nickar
acikns
ink-sac
aciknt
catkin
acikop
paiock
acikps
aspick
acikrt
kit-car
aciktt
Kitcat
acills
scilla
acilmx
climax
acilno
oilcan
acilnp
caplin
acilnr
crinal
acilnt
tincal
acilnu
Lucina
uncial
acilor
lorica
acilos
social
acilot
coital
acilox
oxalic
acilpt
placit
acilrt
rictal
acilru
uracil
Uralic
acilry
racily
acilsu
caulis
clusia
acilsv
clavis
Slavic
acimno
anomic
camion
conima
manioc

acimnt
  mantic
acimoo
  oomiac
acimor
  Romaic
acimos
  mosaic
acimot
  atomic
  matico
acimov
  vomica
acimps
  scampi
acimpt
  impact
acimrs
  racism
acimrt
  matric
acimry
  Myrica
acimst
  mastic
acinnt
  tannic
  tin-can
acinny
  cyanin
acinos
  casino
acinot
  action
  atonic
  cation
acinov
  incavo
acinox
  anoxic
acinoz
  azonic
acinps
  panisc
acinpt
  catnip
acinpu
  Punica
acinrt
  criant
acinru
  uranic
acinry
  riancy
acinst
  nastic
acinsu
  acinus
acintt
  intact
acintu
  anicut
  nautic

acinuv
  vicuña
aciopt
  atopic
  copita
aciors
  scoria
aciort
  aortic
aciost
  Scotia
aciosv
  ovisac
aciotz
  azotic
acipry
  piracy
aciptt
  tip-cat
aciqtu
  acquit
acirrs
  sircar
acirrt
  tricar
acirru
  curari
acirss
  crasis
acirst
  crista
  racist
acirsy
  Syriac
acirtt
  triact
acirtu
  tauric
  urtica
acirvy
  vicary
acisss
  cassis
acituy
  acuity
acitvy
  cavity
acjkop
  pajock
ackknu
  Kanuck
ackkny
  knacky
acklop
  Polack
acklty
  talcky
acknow
  acknow
acknpr
  pranck
acknpu
  unpack

acknry
  cranky
acknst
  stanck
ackntu
  untack
ackopy
  yapock
ackory
  croaky
ackprs
  sprack
ackrst
  strack
ackrty
  Y-track
acllmy
  calmly
acllno
  clonal
acllor
  collar
acllow
  callow
acllpu
  call-up
acllsu
  callus
  sulcal
acllsy
  Scylla
aclmmy
  clammy
aclmor
  Colmar
aclmsu
  lacmus
aclmtu
  talcum
aclmuu
  lucuma
aclnuv
  vulcan
aclnuy
  lunacy
aclopu
  copula
  cupola
aclort
  carlot
  crotal
acloru
  ocular
aclorw
  owl-car
aclost
  costal
aclosy
  Lycosa
aclotw
  cotwal
aclrru
  crural

aclrsu
  cursal
aclrsw
  scrawl
aclrtu
  curtal
aclrty
  clarty
aclrwy
  crawly
aclssy
  classy
aclstu
  scutal
acmnno
  con-man
acmnor
  macron
acmnos
  mascon
  socman
acmnot
  monact
acmnow
  cowman
acmnpu
  cupman
acmnsu
  mancus
acmort
  comart
acmost
  comsat
  mascot
acmosu
  mucosa
acmott
  tom-cat
acmotu
  motuca
acmpry
  crampy
acmpsu
  campus
acmrsu
  sacrum
acmrsw
  scrawm
acmstu
  muscat
acmtuu
  mutuca
acmuuv
  vacuum
acnnno
  cannon
acnnot
  cannot
  canton
acnnoy
  canyon
acnnry
  cranny

acnoop
  poonac
acnoor
  corona
  racoon
acnopy
  canopy
acnorr
  rancor
acnort
  cantor
  carton
  contra
  craton
acnoru
  cornua
acnory
  crayon
acnost
  cantos
  Octans
acnosz
  scazon
acnott
  octant
acnotu
  noctua
  toucan
acnotw
  ant-cow
acnotx
  Caxton
acnptu
  puncta
acnrst
  crants
acnrtu
  uncart
acnstu
  cantus
  Tuscan
acnsty
  scanty
acootv
  octavo
acoprt
  captor
acoptw
  cowpat
acorrt
  carrot
  trocar
acorss
  across
acorst
  castor
  co-star
acorsu
  Acorus
acortt
  cottar
acortu
  turaco

acortv
  cavort
acorvy
  covary
acoryz
  coryza
acottu
  outact
acprsu
  carpus
acpssu
  scapus
acpstu
  catsup
  upcast
acrrsy
  scarry
acrrtu
  cratur
acrrwy
  war-cry
acrssu
  Scarus
acrstu
  crusta
acrsuy
  scaury
acstty
  scatty
adddeg
  gadded
adddel
  addled
  daddle
addden
  addend
adddep
  padded
adddew
  wadded
adddoo
  doodad
addeeh
  headed
addeei
  ideaed
addeel
  leaded
addeem
  addeem
addeen
  deaden
addeer
  deader
addefl
  faddle
addegr
  gadder
addehi
  haddie
addehk
  keddah
addehn
  handed

addehs
  shaded
addeil
  daidle
  laddie
addeim
  diadem
addeiw
  waddie
addeln
  dandle
  landed
addelo
  loaded
addelp
  paddle
addelr
  ladder
  raddle
addels
  saddle
addelw
  dawdle
  waddle
addely
  deadly
addemm
  dammed
addemn
  damned
  demand
  madden
addemr
  madder
addenr
  dander
  darned
addens
  dedans
  sadden
  sanded
addeor
  deodar
addeos
  dadoes
addeow
  woaded
addepr
  draped
  padder
  parded
adders
  sadder
addert
  traded
adderw
  warded
addgio
  gadoid
addgmo
  goddam
addgoo
  ogdoad

addhoo
  doodah
addhsu
  saddhu
addimy
  midday
addloy
  day-old
addmno
  dodman
  odd-man
addmoo
  addoom
addoor
  dorado
addort
  dotard
addswy
  swaddy
adeefl
  leafed
adeefm
  defame
adeefn
  deafen
adeefr
  feared
adeeft
  defeat
adeegg
  dégagé
adeegr
  agreed
  dragée
  geared
adeehr
  adhere
  header
  Hedera
adeeht
  heated
adeehv
  heaved
adeeil
  aedile
adeein
  Aeneid
adeeir
  dearie
  rediae
adeeit
  ideate
adeejy
  deejay
adeekp
  peaked
adeeln
  leaden
  leaned
adeelo
  Elodea
adeelp
  leaped
adeelr
  dealer
  leader
adeels
  sealed
adeelt
  delate
  tele-ad
adeelv
  leaved
adeemn
  amende
  demean
adeemo
  oedema
adeemr
  remade
  remead
adeemt
  teamed
adeenn
  ennead
adeenp
  neaped
adeenr
  deaner
  endear
adeenv
  advene
adeeps
  pesade
adeept
  pedate
adeerr
  reader
  reread
adeers
  erased
  Reseda
  seared
adeert
  derate
adeerw
  drawee
adeerx
  exedra
adeest
  seated
  sedate
adeett
  teated
adeevw
  weaved
adeffi
  affied
adefgg
  fagged
adefgn
  fag-end
  fanged
adefil
  afield
  failed
adefin
  fade-in
adefit
  daftie
adeflm
  flamed
adeflo
  feodal
adeflr
  fardel
adeflu
  feudal
adeflw
  flawed
adefly
  deafly
  flayed
adefmy
  madefy
adefnn
  fanned
adefnr
  farden
adefnu
  undeaf
adefor
  fedora
adefpu
  fade-up
adefru
  fadeur
adefry
  defray
adeftt
  fatted
adeftw
  wafted
adeggg
  gagged
adeggh
  hagged
adeggi
  gadgie
adeggj
  jagged
adeggl
  daggle
  lagged
adeggn
  nagged
adeggr
  dagger
  ragged
adeggs
  sagged
adeggt
  gadget
  tagged
adeggw
  wagged
adeghi
  hidage
adeghl
  Gadhel
adeghn
  hagden
  hanged
adegim
  mid-age
adegit
  gaited
adegln
  angled
  dangle
  lag-end
adeglr
  dargle
adegnr
  danger
  gander
  garden
adegnt
  tag-end
  tanged
adegnw
  gnawed
adegop
  dog-ape
adegor
  dog-ear
adegos
  dagoes
  dosage
  sea-dog
  sea-god
adegot
  dogate
  dotage
  togaed
adegrr
  garred
  regard
adegrs
  degras
adegrt
  grated
adegrv
  graved
adegss
  gassed
adegst
  staged
adehil
  halide
adehin
  hained
adehir
  haired
adehis
  eadish
adehkw
  hawked
adehln
  handle
adehlo
  haloed
adehlr
  hareld
  herald
adehls
  halsed
adehmr
  derham
adehms
  shamed
adehno
  head-on
adehnp
  daphne
adehnr
  hander
  harden
adehnu
  unhead
adehox
  oxhead
adehpp
  happed
adehps
  phased
  shaped
adehpt
  heptad
adehrs
  dasher
adehrt
  dearth
  hatred
  red-hat
  thread
adehst
  'sdeath
adehsv
  shaved
adehsw
  washed
adehsy
  Hyades
adehtt
  hatted
adehty
  deathy
adehyy
  heyday
adeikr
  daiker
  darkie
adeill
  allied
  laldie
adeilm
  mailed
  medial
adeiln
  Aldine
  Daniel
  Delian
  denial
  lead-in
  nailed
adeilo
  eidola
adeilp
  aliped
  paidle
  Pleiad
adeilr
  derail
  relaid
adeils
  aisled
  deasil
  ladies
  sailed
adeilt
  detail
  dilate
  tailed
adeilu
  audile
adeilw
  Dewali
adeily
  eyliad
adeimm
  maimed
adeimn
  daimen
  demain
  maiden
  median
  medina
adeimr
  admire
adeims
  mid-sea
adeimv
  vidame
adeinn
  Andine
adeinp
  pained
adeinr
  randie
adeins
  sdaine
adeint
  Danite
  detain
adeinv
  invade
adeinw
  dewani
adeior
  roadie
adeiot
  iodate
adeipr
  diaper
  paired
  pardie
  repaid
adeirr
  arride
  raider
adeirs
  resaid
adeirt
  raited
  tirade
adeirv
  varied
adeiss
  dassie
adeisu
  adieus
  Suidae
adeisv
  advise
  visaed
adeitu
  dautie
adeitv
  dative
adeitw
  dawtie
adeitx
  taxied
adeiux
  adieux
adejmm
  jammed
adejnu
  Judean
adejrr
  jarred
adejru
  adjure
adejry
  jadery
adekln
  ankled
adeklr
  darkle
adekmo
  make-do
adekmr
  demark
  marked
adekms
  masked
adeknr
  darken
  narked
  ranked
adeknt
  tanked
adekos
  soaked
adekry
  darkey
adelln
  end-all
adellp
  palled

adellr
all-red
adellu
allude
aludel
adellv
devall
adellw
walled
adelmp
palmed
adelmr
dermal
marled
medlar
adelms
damsel
adelmt
malted
adelno
enodal
loaden
adelnr
aldern
darnel
enlard
lander
adelns
sendal
adelnt
dental
adelnu
unlade
unlead
adelnw
wandle
adelop
opaled
pedalo
adelor
loader
ordeal
reload
adelos
aldose
adelpp
dapple
lapped
adelpr
pedlar
adelps
lapsed
adelpt
plated
adelpu
uplead
adelpw
dewlap
adelrr
larder
adelrs
sardel
adelrt
dartle

adelru
lauder
adelry
dearly
adelrz
drazel
adelst
desalt
salted
slated
adelsu
salued
adelsv
salve'd
adelsw
salewd
adeluv
valued
adelvv
valved
adelzz
dazzle
ademmr
dammer
rammed
ademnn
manned
ademno
daemon
modena
nomade
ademnp
dampen
ademnr
manred
randem
red-man
remand
ademns
amends
desman
ademnt
tandem
ademnu
unmade
ademop
apedom
pomade
ademor
radome
ademos
Samoed
ademot
moated
ademow
meadow
adempp
mapped
adempr
damper
ademrr
marred
ademrt
dreamt

ademru
remuda
ademrw
warmed
ademry
dreamy
ademst
masted
ademsu
amused
medusa
ademtt
matted
ademwy
may-dew
adennt
tanned
adennu
duenna
adennv
vanned
adennw
wanned
adenot
donate
adenoy
noyade
adenpp
append
napped
adenpr
pander
repand
adenpt
pedant
pentad
adenpx
expand
adenrr
darner
errand
adenrs
sander
adenrt
ardent
endart
adenru
dauner
undear
unread
adenrw
dawner
wander
warden
adenry
denary
adenrz
zander
adensu
sundae
adensw
new-sad
adentt
attend

adentu
undate
adentv
advent
adentw
wanted
adenuw
unawed
adenwx
wax-end
adeopp
pea-pod
adeorr
adorer
adeort
doater
adeorw
redowa
adeovw
avowed
adeoyz
azodye
adeppr
dapper
rapped
adepps
sapped
adeppt
tapped
adeprr
draper
adeprs
spread
adeprt
depart
drapet
parted
petard
adeprw
warped
adepry
prayed
adepss
passed
adeptt
patted
adeptu
update
aderrt
darter
dartre
retard
tarred
trader
aderrw
drawer
redraw
reward
warder
warred
aderry
dreary

adersw
sawder
sweard
adertt
ratted
tetrad
adertv
advert
adertw
warted
adervv
varved
aderwx
wax-red
adestt
stated
tasted
adestu
sudate
adestv
staved
adestw
stawed
wadset
adesty
stayed
steady
adeswy
swayed
adffor
afford
adffoy
off-day
adffry
draffy
adfgin
fading
adfgly
gadfly
adfhsu
shaduf
adfilu
aidful
adfily
ladify
adfirt
adrift
adfiry
Friday
adflos
sol-fa'd
adflty
daftly
adflyy
day-fly
ladyfy
adfmno
fandom
adfmou
fumado
adfnot
fantod
adforr
forrad

adfrst
drafts
adghno
hagdon
adgiin
aiding
adgiln
lading
ligand
adgilo
algoid
dialog
adgimy
digamy
adgino
ganoid
adginr
daring
gradin
adginw
wading
adgirv
gravid
adglly
gladly
adglnu
unglad
adglop
lapdog
adgnor
dragon
adgnru
durgan
adgorw
wardog
war-god
adgpru
updrag
adgrsu
gradus
adgrtu
Utgard
adhhit
hadith
adhhou
houdah
adhhow
howdah
adhijs
jadish
adhiku
haiduk
adhill
all-hid
adhilo
haloid
adhimr
dirham
adhinn
hand-in
adhins
Danish
sandhi

adhior
hair-do
adhips
aphids
adhirs
radish
adhiry
hydria
adhiss
Hassid
adhisw
dawish
adhjko
khodja
adhlry
hardly
adhmno
hodman
adhmnu
numdah
adhmru
Durham
adhnnu
unhand
adhnor
hadron
adhnou
houdan
adhnpu
uphand
adhnsy
shandy
adhosw
shadow
adhpru
hard-up
purdah
adhpuu
uphaud
adhrru
dhurra
adhuzz
huzza'd
adiiko
aikido
adiill
illiad
adiilm
miladi
adiiln
inlaid
adiilr
iridal
adiilv
Divali
adiilw
Diwali
adiimo
daimio
adiimr
mid-air
adiinn
Indian

adiinz
dizain
adiios
Isodia
adiipr
diapir
adijms
masjid
adijno
adjoin
adikmo
mikado
adiknp
kidnap
adikot
dakoit
adikst
dikast
adiktt
diktat
adillp
pallid
adilly
laidly
adilms
dismal
adilmy
diamyl
milady
adilnn
inland
adilno
Ladino
adilnr
aldrin
adilns
island
adilnt
tindal
adilnu
dualin
unlaid
adilny
Lydian
adiloo
ooidal
adilop
podial
adilor
laroid
adiloz
Ozalid®
adilry
aridly
adilrz
lizard
adilst
distal
adilsu
Lusiad
adiluv
vidual
adilvy
avidly

adimmt
dammit
adimno
domain
adimnr
mandir
adimns
disman
adimnt
mantid
adimot
diatom
adimqu
quidam
adimrs
disarm
adimru
radium
adimry
myriad
adimss
sadism
adimst
amidst
adimsy
dismay
adimwy
midway
adinnu
induna
adinor
Dorian
inroad
ordain
adinos
Adonis
sodain
adinox
diaxon
dioxan
adinpt
pandit
adinpu
unpaid
adinrt
indart
adinru
durian
adinrw
inward
adinsu
unsaid
adinsw
windas
adinty
dainty
adiort
adroit
adippu
paid-up
adiprs
sparid
spraid

adipss
dipsas
adipsx
spadix
adirrs
sirdar
adirrz
rizard
adirsu
radius
adirsw
wisard
adirvz
vizard
adirwz
wizard
adirzz
izzard
adisst
sadist
saidst
adistv
vista'd
adisxy
six-day
adisyy
sayyid
aditty
dittay
adjkou
judoka
adjnor
Jordan
adjstu
adjust
adklry
darkly
adkopu
padouk
adllop
dallop
adllor
dollar
adlluy
dually
adlmno
almond
dolman
adlmow
wadmol
adlmpy
damply
adlmtu
Talmud
adlnop
Poland
adlnor
lardon
Roland
adlnos
soland
soldan
adlnou
unload

adlnox
oxland
adlnpu
upland
adlnru
lurdan
adlors
dorsal
adloss
dossal
adlosw
dowlas
adlpsu
spauld
admmno
mandom
admnor
random
rodman
admnos
damson
admnow
woman'd
admnoy
dynamo
Monday
admnuy
maundy
admorr
ramrod
admorz
Ormazd
admtuy
adytum
adnnoo
nandoo
adnnor
randon
adnnot
danton
donnat
adnoor
nardoo
adnopr
pardon
adnopt
dopant
adnoru
around
adnorw
onward
adnory
donary
adnosu
Soudan
adnott
dotant
adnrst
strand
adnrsu
sundra

adnrtu
draunt
durant
tundra
adnruw
undraw
adnsty
dynast
adnsuy
Sunday
adoors
adoors
adoouv
vaudoo
adopru
Podura
adopry
parody
adorru
ardour
adortw
toward
adppry
drappy
adpruw
updraw
upward
adrsuw
usward
adrsuy
sudary
adrswy
swardy
adrtwy
tawdry
aeeels
sea-eel
aeeffr
affeer
aeefgu
feague
aeefir
faerie
aeeflm
female
aeefnt
Fantee
aeefov
foveae
aeefrt
afreet
terefa
aeeggn
engage
engagé
aeeggr
agrégé
raggee
reggae
aeeggs
sea-egg
aeegir
Egeria

aeegjr
jaeger
aeegll
allege
aeeglp
pelage
aeeglr
galère
regale
aeeglt
eaglet
legate
teagle
telega
aeeglu
league
aeegmm
gemmae
aeegmn
manège
ménage
aeegmr
meagre
aeegmt
gamete
metage
aeegnr
enrage
enragé
genera
aeegns
sagene
senega
aeegnt
negate
aeegnv
avenge
geneva
aeegop
apogee
aeegot
goatee
aeegrs
grease
aeegrt
ergate
aeegrv
greave
aeegst
egesta
aeegsw
sewage
aeegtu
Teague
aeehhw
heehaw
aeehir
hearie
aeehlr
healer
aeehlt
lathee
aeehlw
awheel

aeehlx
exhale
aeehmr
hareem
hermae
aeehmu
heaume
aeehnp
pea-hen
aeehnt
Athene
ethane
aeehnv
heaven
aeehnx
hexane
aeehps
spahee
aeehrr
hearer
rehear
aeehrs
hearse
aeehrt
aether
heater
hereat
reheat
aeehrv
heaver
aeehrw
a'where
aeehsv
sheave
aeehtv
theave
aeeilm
mealie
aeeils
Elaeis
laesie
aeeimn
meanie
aeeims
semeia
aeeint
teniae
aeeipr
epeira
pereia
aeeips
sea-pie
aeejms
Jeames
aeejnt
jantee
aeejrv
evejar
aeeklp
palkee
aeeklr
leaker
aeeklv
vakeel

aeekmr
remake
aeekms
kamees
aeeknw
weaken
aeekny
Yankee
aeekpr
parkee
aeekrt
retake
aeekru
eureka
aeelll
allele
aeellm
mallee
aeells
sallee
aeellv
A-level
aeelmn
enamel
aeelmp
empale
aeelmr
mealer
aeelms
measle
aeelmz
meazel
aeelnp
alpeen
aeelns
enseal
aeelnt
elanet
lateen
aeelnv
leaven
aeelnw
weanel
aeelor
areole
aeelot
oleate
aeelpr
leaper
repeal
aeelps
asleep
elapse
please
sapele
aeelpu
epaule
aeelqu
quelea
aeelrs
leaser
resale
sealer

aeelrt
elater
relate
aeelrv
laveer
reveal
aeelry
E-layer
aeelss
eassel
aeelst
steale
stelae
teasel
aeelsv
leaves
sleave
aeelsw
weasel
aeeltu
eluate
aeeltv
velate
veleta
aeeltw
atweel
aeelty
eyalet
aeeltz
teazel
teazle
aeelwy
leeway
aeemmm
mammee
aeemnn
Nemean
aeemnr
rename
aeemns
enseam
aeemnt
entame
aeemnx
examen
aeempr
ampere
empare
aeempw
wampee
aeemrr
reamer
aeemrs
seamer
aeemrt
teamer
aeemss
sesame
aeemsw
sea-mew
aeennp
pennae

aeennt
Etnean
neaten
aeennx
annexe
aeenps
sea-pen
aeenpw
pawnee
aeenrr
earner
nearer
aeenrs
ensear
aeenrt
entera
aeenst
ensate
sateen
senate
steane
aeensu
unease
aeentw
atween
aeenuv
avenue
aeenwz
weazen
aeeooz
zooeae
aeeouu
euouae
aeeovv
evovae
aeeppr
rappee
aeeprr
reaper
aeeprs
a-per-se
Parsee
prease
serape
aeeprt
repeat
aeepst
peseta
aeepsw
pesewa
aeepsx
apexes
aeeptt
pattée
aeepvy
peavey
aeeqru
quaere
aeeqtu
equate
aeerrr
rearer

aeerrs
eraser
serrae
aeerrt
tearer
terrae
aeerrv
reaver
aeerrw
wearer
aeerst
easter
reseat
saeter
steare
teaser
aeersu
réseau
aeersv
averse
aeerty
eatery
aeervw
weaver
aeessw
seesaw
aeestt
estate
tea-set
aeffgr
gaffer
aeffht
haffet
aeffin
affine
aeffip
piaffe
aeffkr
Kaffer
aefflr
raffle
aefflw
waffle
aeffly
yaffle
aeffrt
affret
aeffrz
zaffer
zaffre
aefgln
fangle
flange
aefgmu
fumage
aefgor
forage
aefgos
sea-fog
aefgru
gaufer
gaufre
aefgry
fegary

aefhll
fellah
aefhln
halfen
aefhnt
fat-hen
aefhrs
afresh
aefhrt
father
aefhsy
sheafy
aefiks
faikes
aefill
faille
aefiln
finale
aefilr
ferial
aefils
falsie
aefilt
fetial
aefimn
famine
infame
aefinn
Fenian
aefinr
infare
aefirs
fraise
sea-fir
aefist
fiesta
aefitx
fixate
aefjnt
fan-jet
aefkln
fankle
aefkry
freaky
aeflln
fallen
aeflmn
flamen
aeflnn
fannel
aeflnu
flaune
aeflnx
flaxen
aeflor
florae
loafer
aeflot
foetal
aeflov
foveal
aeflrs
falser
flaser

aeflrt
falter
aeflru
earful
ferula
aeflry
flayer
aeflst
festal
aeflsy
safely
aefltu
fluate
aeflty
fealty
featly
aefluw
waeful
aefmnn
fenman
aefmno
foeman
aefmor
femora
aefmrr
farmer
framer
aefnnr
fanner
aefnor
forane
aefnru
furane
aefnrw
fawner
aefnst
fasten
nefast
aefnsu
unsafe
aefntt
fatten
aefosv
favose
aefosx
sea-fox
aefppr
frappé
aefpry
perfay
aefrrt
frater
rafter
aefrry
rarefy
aefrst
afters
faster
strafe
aefrtt
fatter
aefrtw
wafter

aefrwy
wafery
aefsty
safety
aegggl
gaggle
aegggr
gagger
aegghl
haggle
aeggin
ageing
aeggjr
jagger
aeggln
laggen
aegglr
gargle
lagger
raggle
aegglw
waggle
aeggnr
ganger
grange
nagger
aeggnu
gangue
aeggrs
sagger
seggar
aeggrt
garget
tagger
aeggru
gauger
aeggry
yagger
aeggww
gewgaw
aeghir
hegira
aeghis
geisha
aeghiw
a-weigh
aeghls
sealgh
aeghlt
haglet
aeghlz
ghazel
aeghmo
homage
aeghnr
hanger
aeghos
sea-hog
aeghpt
hatpeg
aeghrt
gather
aegilm
milage

aegiln
  genial
  linage
aegilo
  goalie
aegilp
  paigle
aegilr
  lea-rig
aegils
  silage
aegilt
  aiglet
  ligate
  taigle
aegilv
  glaive
  vagile
aegimn
  enigma
  gamine
aegimp
  magpie
aegimr
  maigre
  mirage
aegims
  ageism
aeginr
  earing
  gainer
  graine
  regain
  regina
aegins
  agnise
aegint
  eating
  ingate
  tangie
aeginu
  guinea
aegipp
  pipage
aegips
  sea-pig
aegirs
  agrise
aegirt
  gaiter
  triage
aegirv
  Argive
  garvie
  rivage
aegirw
  earwig
aegirz
  agrize
aegist
  ageist
aegisu
  aguise
aegisv
  visage
aegitu
  augite
aegity
  gaiety
aegiuz
  aguize
aegjln
  jangle
aegjst
  gas-jet
aegjtu
  jugate
aegklr
  grakle
aegkst
  gasket
aeglln
  leglan
aegllt
  gallet
aegllu
  ullage
aeglly
  egally
  galley
aeglmn
  leg-man
  mangel
  mangle
aeglmr
  malgre
aeglmy
  gamely
  gleamy
  mygale
aeglno
  engaol
aeglnr
  angler
  largen
  regnal
aeglnt
  tangle
aeglnu
  lagune
  langue
aeglnw
  wangle
aeglny
  lynage
aeglnz
  glazen
aeglor
  galore
  gaoler
aeglot
  legato
aeglov
  lovage
  volage
aeglpu
  plague
aeglrt
  tergal
aeglru
  regula
aeglrv
  gravel
aeglry
  argyle
aeglrz
  glazer
aeglsu
  saulge
aeglsy
  sagely
aegltu
  tegula
aegltw
  talweg
aegmmn
  gemman
aegmmr
  gammer
  gramme
aegmms
  smegma
aegmno
  gnomae
aegmnr
  engram
  german
  manger
aegmns
  magnes
aegmnt
  magnet
aegmny
  mangey
aegmor
  romage
aegmru
  maugre
  murage
aegmss
  megass
aegmsy
  gamesy
aegmuy
  maguey
aegmuz
  zeugma
aegnno
  nonage
aegnnp
  pangen
aegnnt
  gannet
aegnor
  onager
  orange
aegnos
  geason
aegnrr
  garner
  ranger
aegnrs
  serang
aegnrt
  argent
  garnet
aegnru
  ungear
aegnrv
  graven
aegnrw
  gnawer
aegops
  sapego
aegopt
  potage
aegors
  sorage
aegort
  orgeat
  toe-rag
aegott
  togate
aegotu
  outage
aegotw
  towage
aegotx
  oxgate
aegovy
  voyage
aegprs
  gasper
  sparge
aegprt
  parget
aegpty
  Aegypt
aegpuz
  upgaze
aegrrt
  garret
  garter
  grater
aegrru
  arguer
aegrrv
  graver
aegrrz
  grazer
aegrst
  Greats
  stager
aegrsu
  sauger
  usager
aegrsv
  graves
aegrsw
  Swerga
aegrsy
  greasy
aegrtt
  target
aegrtu
  argute
  rugate
  Tuareg
aegrty
  gyrate
aegryz
  agryze
aegsty
  gayest
  stagey
aegttu
  guttae
aehhjv
  Jahveh
aehhlt
  health
aehhpy
  hyphae
aehhrs
  rehash
aehhrt
  hearth
aehhst
  sheath
aehhty
  heathy
aehhvy
  Yahveh
aehhwy
  Yahweh
aehijr
  hejira
aehikn
  hankie
aehiks
  sakieh
aehikw
  hawkie
aehilm
  hiemal
aehiln
  Hielan'
  inhale
aehils
  sheila
aehilt
  halite
aehilw
  awhile
aehimn
  haemin
aehims
  mashie
aehimt
  hamite
aehinr
  hernia
aehins
  ashine
aehinw
  wahine
aehiqu
  haique
aehirs
  sheria
aehist
  saithe
aehisv
  shavie
aehjrs
  Jasher
aehknr
  hanker
  harken
aehkns
  shaken
aehkos
  she-oak
aehkrs
  shaker
aehkrw
  hawker
aehksy
  ash-key
aehkwy
  hawkey
aehllt
  lethal
aehlmp
  pelham
aehlmr
  harmel
aehlmt
  hamlet
aehlno
  enhalo
aehlns
  hansel
aehlnt
  hantle
  lathen
aehlnu
  unheal
aehlos
  haloes
aehlot
  loathe
aehlrs
  ashler
  halser
  lasher
aehlrt
  halter
  lather
  thaler
aehlru
  hauler
aehlrv
  halver
aehlrw
  whaler
aehlss
  hassle
aehlst
  haslet
  Shelta
aehlsv
  halves
aehlsy
  haysel
aehltw
  wealth
aehlty
  eathly
  hyetal
aehmmr
  hammer
aehmmy
  mayhem
aehmnt
  anthem
  hetman
aehmnu
  humane
  Humean
aehmos
  hamose
aehmot
  at-home
aehmpr
  hamper
aehmrs
  masher
  shamer
aehmst
  smeath
aehnov
  have-on
aehnpp
  happen
aehnps
  shapen
aehnrt
  anther
  thenar
aehnst
  hasten
  snathe
  sneath
aehnsv
  Hesvan
  shaven
aehnsw
  washen
  whenas
aehnsz
  sazhen
aehntu
  uneath
aehntw
  whaten
aehnuy
  haüyne
aehors
  ahorse
  ashore
  hoarse
aehorx
  hoaxer

aehppu
upheap
aehprr
harper
aehprs
phrase
seraph
shaper
sherpa
sphaer
aehprt
teraph
threap
aehpss
phases
aehpst
spathe
aehpsw
peshwa
aehpty
hypate
aehrrs
rasher
sharer
aehrrt
rather
aehrss
shears
aehrst
'sheart
aehrsv
shaver
aehrsw
hawser
washer
aehrsy
ashery
hearsy
aehrtt
hatter
threat
aehrtv
thrave
aehrtw
thawer
wreath
aehrty
earthy
hearty
aehrvw
wharve
aehsss
she-ass
aehstw
swathe
aeiils
liaise
aeijlr
jailer
aeijlz
jezail
aeijmm
jemima
aeikls
alsike
aeiklt
talkie
aeikmn
kinema
aeikns
kinase
aeiknt
intake
take-in
aeikny
yankie
aeikrs
kaiser
aeikrt
arkite
karite
aeilln
lienal
lineal
aeills
allies
aeilmm
lammie
aeilmn
menial
aeilmp
impale
aeilmr
mailer
aeilms
mesail
mesial
samiel
aeilmz
mezail
aeilno
Eolian
aeilnp
alpine
penial
pineal
aeilnr
larine
linear
nailer
aeilns
saline
silane
aeilnt
entail
tenail
aeilnv
alevin
alvine
valine
venial
aeilnx
alexin
xenial
aeilop
leipoa
aeilpp
lappie
aeilps
espial
lipase
aeilrr
railer
rerail
aeilrs
sailer
serail
serial
aeilrt
retail
retial
aeilrw
wailer
aeilss
eassil
laisse
lassie
aeilsu
saulie
aeilsv
silvae
valise
aeilsw
walise
aeilsy
easily
aeilty
tailye
aeimmn
immane
aeimno
anomie
aeimnp
pieman
aeimnr
marine
remain
aeimns
inseam
mesian
aeimnt
inmate
tamine
aeimpr
premia
aeimpv
impave
aeimpy
pyemia
aeimru
uremia
aeimrw
awmrie
aeimst
samite
tamise
aeimxx
maxixe
aeinnp
pinnae
aeinnr
narine
ranine
aeinns
insane
sienna
aeinnt
innate
aeinnz
enzian
aeinoz
azione
aeinpr
rapine
aeinpt
pineta
aeinpv
Evipan®
aeinrs
arisen
arsine
sarnie
aeinrt
Nerita
ratine
retain
retina
aeinrv
ravine
aeinss
sanies
sasine
aeinst
tisane
aeinsv
savine
aeintu
auntie
Uniate
aeintv
native
aeiopt
opiate
aeiopz
epizoa
aeiorr
roarie
aeiprr
rapier
repair
aeiprs
aspire
praise
spirea
aeiprt
pirate
pratie
pteria
aeiprv
Vipera
aeipsv
pavise
aeiptt
tapeti
aeiptu
taupie
aeiptw
tawpie
aeipzz
Peziza
aeiqsu
saique
aeirrs
raiser
sierra
aeirrt
'Arriet
aeirrv
arrive
varier
aeirst
satire
striae
aeirtt
attire
ratite
tertia
aeirtv
taiver
aeirtw
waiter
aeirvw
waiver
aeisst
siesta
tassie
aeissu
Aussie
aeissz
assize
aeistv
sative
aeisty
aseity
aeittt
tattie
aeittv
vittae
aeittw
tawtie
twaite
aejknr
janker
aejmrt
ram-jet
aejmst
jetsam
aejnst
sejant
aejnsu
jaunse
aejprs
jasper
aejrvy
jarvey
aekknr
kraken
aekkry
yakker
aeklno
Ankole
aeklnr
rankle
aeklnt
anklet
aeklnw
knawel
wankle
aeklrr
larker
aeklrt
talker
aeklrw
walker
aeklst
lasket
sklate
aekltu
auklet
aeklwy
weakly
aekmnu
unmake
aekmpu
make-up
upmake
aekmrr
marker
remark
aekmrs
masker
aekmrt
market
aeknnr
enrank
aeknnt
kanten
aeknos
soaken
aeknow
awoken
aeknrr
ranker
aeknrt
tanker
aeknru
unrake
aeknrw
wanker
aeknry
yanker
aeknsy
sneaky
aekors
arkose
soaker
aekprr
parker
aekprs
sparke
aekptu
take-up
uptake
aekqru
Quaker
aekqsu
squeak
aekrry
rakery
aekrst
skater
strake
streak
tasker
aekrwy
ywrake
aekwyy
key-way
aellmt
mallet
aellmy
lamely
mellay
aellnu
unleal
aellnw
enwall
aellny
leanly
aellpt
pallet
aellpy
palely
aellrt
tellar
aellru
allure
laurel
aellrw
waller
aellry
re-ally
really
aellst
sallet
aellsy
alleys
aelltt
tallet
aelltu
luteal
aelltw
wallet
aellty
lately
lealty
aellvy
valley
aelmmr
lammer
aelmno
melano

aelmns
lemans
mensal
aelmnt
lament
mantel
mantle
mental
aelmny
meanly
namely
aelmor
morale
aelmpr
palmer
aelmps
sample
aelmpu
ampule
aelmrt
armlet
martel
aelmrv
marvel
aelmry
almery
aelmst
samlet
aelmsy
measly
samely
aelmtu
amulet
aelmty
tamely
aelnnp
pennal
aelnnr
lanner
aelnnw
wannel
aelnos
lanose
aelnot
etalon
lean-to
aelnpp
pen-pal
aelnpr
planer
replan
aelnpt
planet
platen
aelnpu
uplean
aelnrs
ransel
aelnrt
altern
antler
learnt
rental
ternal

aelnru
neural
ulnare
unreal
aelnrv
nerval
vernal
aelnry
anerly
nearly
aelnrz
ranzel
aelnsu
unseal
aelnsy
sanely
aelntt
latent
latten
talent
aelntu
eluant
lunate
aelntv
levant
aelnty
neatly
aelntz
zelant
aelnuw
unweal
aelooz
zooeal
aelopr
parole
aelops
aslope
aelopt
pelota
pot-ale
aelopx
pole-ax
aelors
roseal
aelort
lorate
aelory
o'erlay
aelost
osteal
aelosv
loaves
aelosw
leasow
sea-owl
aelotz
zealot
aelppr
lapper
rappel
aelppt
lappet

aelppu
papule
upleap
aelpqu
plaque
aelprr
parrel
aelprt
palter
plater
aelpru
pleura
aelprw
prawle
aelpry
parley
pearly
player
replay
aelpst
pastel
septal
staple
aelptt
pattle
T-plate
aelptu
puteal
aelqsu
squeal
aelrrt
retral
aelrry
rarely
rearly
aelrst
laster
salter
slater
stelar
tarsel
aelrsu
saurel
aelrsv
salver
serval
slaver
versal
aelrsw
warsle
aelrsy
slayer
aelrtt
latter
rattle
tatler
aelrtv
travel
varlet

aelrty
elytra
lyrate
raylet
realty
telary
aelruv
valuer
aelrvv
varvel
aelrwx
wraxle
aelrwy
lawyer
aelryy
yarely
yearly
aelrzz
razzle
aelsst
tassel
aelstt
latest
stealt
taslet
aelstu
salute
aelstv
vestal
aelstw
wastel
aelsty
astely
aelsuv
avulse
aelsux
sexual
aelsvy
slavey
aelsyz
sleazy
aelttt
tattle
aelttw
wattle
aeltux
luxate
aeluuv
uvulae
aemmmr
mammer
aemmmt
mammet
aemmnr
merman
aemmnt
met-man
aemmrr
rammer
aemmry
yammer
aemmst
stemma

aemmtu
maumet
aemmtw
mawmet
aemnno
one-man
aemnnp
penman
aemnnr
manner
aemnor
enamor
monera
aemnot
omenta
to-name
aemnoy
yeoman
aemnpu
pneuma
aemnqu
manqué
aemnrt
marten
aemnru
manure
murena
aemnss
messan
aemnst
stamen
aemnsu
unseam
aemnsy
yes-man
aemntu
untame
unteam
aemopz
apozem
aemorr
remora
roamer
aemors
ramose
aemort
amoret
aemorw
womera
aemost
osmate
aemosv
vamose
aemosw
awsome
aemppr
mapper
pamper
aemprr
ramper
aemprt
tamper

aemprv
revamp
vamper
aempsu
empusa
aemqru
marque
aemqsu
masque
squame
aemrru
armure
aemrrw
warmer
aemrst
master
stream
aemrsu
amuser
Mauser
aemrsy
smeary
aemrtt
matter
aemrtu
mature
aemssu
assume
aemstu
meatus
aemsty
mayest
steamy
aemsyz
zymase
aemttu
mutate
aemuzz
mezuza
aennno
nonane
aennos
nosean
aennov
novena
aennoy
anyone
aennrt
tanner
aennrv
vanner
aenntt
tenant
aenops
peason
aenopv
pavone
aenopw
weapon
aenopy
paeony
aenors
reason
Señora

aenort
atoner
ornate
aenoss
season
aenott
notate
aenotz
zonate
aenowy
one-way
aenppr
napper
parpen
aenprt
arpent
enrapt
entrap
panter
parent
trepan
aenprw
enwrap
pawner
aenpry
napery
aenprz
panzer
aenpst
pesant
aenptt
patent
patten
aenptu
peanut
aenptz
pezant
aenrrs
serran
snarer
aenrrt
errant
ranter
Terran
aenrrw
warner
warren
aenrss
sarsen
aenrst
astern
transe
aenrsw
answer
aenrsy
sarney
senary
aenrtt
natter
ratten
aenrtu
aunter
nature
tea-urn

aenrtv
tavern
aenrtw
wanter
aenrty
trayne
aenruw
unware
aensst
assent
snaste
aenstu
nasute
unseat
aenstx
sextan
aenstz
stanze
aensuv
naevus
aensuy
uneasy
aenswy
sawney
aenttt
attent
aenttu
attune
nutate
tauten
aenttx
extant
aentty
tetany
aeopps
appose
aeopqu
opaque
aeoprt
protea
aeoptt
aptote
tea-pot
aeopty
teapoy
aeorrr
roarer
aeorss
serosa
aeorst
Ostrea
aeorsu
arouse
aeortt
rotate
to-tear
aeoruv
avoure
aeostv
avoset
aeottu
outeat
aeouvz
Zouave

aepprr
rapper
aepprs
sapper
aepprt
tapper
aeppru
pauper
aepprw
wapper
aeppry
papery
prepay
yapper
aeppsy
apepsy
aepptt
tappet
aepptu
pupate
aeprrs
parser
rasper
sparer
aeprrt
parter
prater
aeprru
parure
uprear
aeprrw
rewrap
warper
aeprry
prayer
aeprss
passer
repass
sparse
aeprst
paster
repast
trapes
aeprsu
pauser
aeprsy
speary
aeprtt
patter
aeprtu
uprate
uptear
aeprtx
pre-tax
aeprty
petary
aepruv
rave-up
aeprwy
yawper
aepsst
stapes
aeqrsu
square

aeqrtu
quarte
aeqruv
quaver
aeqsuy
queasy
aequyz
queazy
aerrss
serras
aerrst
arrest
raster
starer
terras
aerrsu
rasure
aerrtt
ratter
aerrty
artery
aerruz
razure
aerrwy
warrey
aersst
assert
aerssu
assure
aerssw
wrasse
aerstt
astert
taster
aerstu
Auster
aerstv
starve
aerstw
waster
aerstx
astrex
aersty
estray
reasty
stayer
aerstz
ersatz
aersuu
aureus
uraeus
aersvw
swarve
aerswy
sawyer
swayer
aerttt
tatter
aerttv
tavert
aerttw
tewart

aertty
treaty
yatter
aertuu
auteur
aertwy
tawery
watery
aervwy
wavery
aessss
assess
aessst
assets
aesstt
tasset
aesstv
staves
vestas
aesstw
saw-set
aessty
sayest
aesttt
attest
aesttu
astute
statue
aestwy
sweaty
aestxy
extasy
aestyy
yeasty
aesvvy
savvey
aetuxy
eutaxy
afffor
far-off
affguw
guffaw
affhit
haffit
affikr
Kaffir
affilp
pilaff
affimr
affirm
affirt
tariff
affloy
lay-off
afflux
afflux
affopy
pay-off
affrst
straff
afggly
flaggy
afggot
faggot

afghos
fogash
afginn
fingan
afginr
Gräfin
afgisy
gasify
afglno
flagon
afglnu
fungal
afglru
frugal
afgmno
fogman
afgmor
fogram
afgnpu
pangfu'
afgorr
fragor
afgort
forgat
afgotu
fugato
afgruy
argufy
afhikl
khalif
afhikr
kharif
afhiku
kufiah
afhims
famish
afhios
oafish
afhlmu
fulham
afhloo
loofah
afhlsy
flashy
afhltu
hatful
afhmot
fathom
afhors
shofar
afiill
filial
afiiln
finial
afijnn
finjan
afiknu
funkia
afikrs
friska
afikuy
kufiya

afilln
fall-in
infall
afilmy
family
afilno
in-foal
afilnu
infula
afilnv
flavin
afilny
fainly
afilor
foliar
afilry
fairly
afilrz
frazil
afilsy
salify
afimnr
firman
afimny
infamy
afimry
ramify
afimss
massif
afimsv
favism
afinnn
finnan
afinno
fanion
afinnt
infant
afinru
unfair
afinry
fin-ray
afinst
faints
afinsu
fusain
afinsy
sanify
afinty
fainty
afinyz
Nazify
afiort
faitor
afiqru
faquir
afirry
friary
afirty
ratify
afiruy
aurify
afjlru
jarful

afllmu
fullam
afllno
onfall
afllnu
fullan
afllor
floral
afllot
to-fall
afllow
fallow
afllpu
lapful
afllty
flatly
aflluw
lawful
aflmnu
manful
aflmny
fly-man
aflmor
formal
aflmru
armful
fulmar
aflmyy
mayfly
aflnot
fontal
aflnpu
panful
aflntu
flaunt
afloty
floaty
aflpsu
sapful
aflrtu
artful
aflstu
flatus
aflsty
fastly
aflswy
saw-fly
afltuv
vatful
afltuy
faulty
afmnot
fantom
afmoos
samfoo
afmort
format
afmosu
famous
afnort
afront
afnryz
franzy

afoort
footra
aforrw
farrow
aforry
forray
aforsy
forsay
afortu
far-out
fautor
foutra
aforuv
favour
afossu
foussa
afosuv
favous
afptuw
upwaft
afrrty
fratry
afrstu
frusta
agghis
haggis
agghsy
shaggy
aggiil
gilgai
aggiln
gingal
laggin
aggilo
loggia
aggimn
gaming
gigman
aggino
agoing
agginp
gaping
paging
agginr
raging
aggint
gating
aggiww
wigwag
aggizz
zigzag
aggkny
knaggy
agglny
gangly
agglot
loggat
agglsy
slaggy
agglwy
waggly
aggmno
moggan

aggmot
maggot
aggnow
waggon
aggnox
oxgang
aggnpu
upgang
aggnru
nuggar
aggnsy
snaggy
aggpry
pygarg
aggquy
quaggy
aghhtu
haught
aghijr
jaghir
aghiku
kiaugh
aghilt
alight
aghint
anight
a'thing
aghinv
having
aghiny
haying
aghinz
hazing
aghiqu
quaigh
aghirr
gharri
aghirs
garish
aghirt
aright
graith
aghisu
aguish
aghkru
Gurkha
aghllu
Gullah
aghlos
galosh
aghlsy
gashly
aghltu
galuth
aghluy
laughy
aghnnu
unhang
aghnpu
hang-up
uphang
aghnrt
Granth
thrang

aghnru
nurhag
aghntu
naught
aghnuy
gunyah
aghoqu
quahog
aghort
hog-rat
aghrru
gurrah
aghrry
gharry
aghrtu
raught
aghttu
taught
aghtuw
waught
agiiln
ailing
nilgai
agiinr
airing
agijln
jingal
agijnw
jawing
agijsw
jigsaw
agikmn
making
agiknr
raking
agikns
gaskin
agiknt
taking
agiknw
waking
agillo
Gallio
agillu
ligula
agilmm
gimmal
agilmn
lingam
malign
agilmo
glioma
agilmp
magilp
agilnp
paling
agilns
signal
agilnu
lingua
nilgau
agilnw
lawing

agilny
gainly
laying
agilor
gloria
agilos
golias
oil-gas
agilot
galiot
agilov
ogival
agilry
glairy
agilst
gas-lit
agimms
Magism
agimnn
naming
agimnp
pig-man
agimnr
ingram
margin
agimnt
taming
agimny
maying
agimos
imagos
agimru
gurami
agimst
stigma
agimww
wigwam
aginno
ganoin
aginnt
anting
aginnu
guanin
ungain
aginnw
awning
waning
aginor
ignaro
origan
aginos
sagoin
aginot
gitano
aginpr
paring
raping
aginpv
paving
aginpy
paying
aginrr
raring

aginrt
rating
aginru
air-gun
Ugrian
aginrv
raving
aginrw
rawing
aginry
grainy
aginss
assign
aginsu
Anguis
saguin
aginsv
saving
aginsw
aswing
sawing
aginsy
saying
agintw
tawing
agintx
taxing
aginvw
waving
aginwx
waxing
agioru
giaour
agiorv
virago
agiotu
agouti
agiprt
pig-rat
agiqru
Griqua
agirst
gratis
striga
agirtu
guitar
agjlmo
log-jam
agjlny
jangly
agjnor
jargon
agklno
kalong
agkloo
kagool
agklot
kgotla
agklou
kagoul
agknru
kurgan
agkort
go-kart

agllno
gallon
gollan
agllop
gallop
agllor
gollar
agllow
gallow
agllry
Argyll
agllsu
gallus
aglmmy
gymmal
aglmno
log-man
aglnno
longan
aglnoo
lagoon
aglnos
slogan
aglnou
lanugo
aglnru
langur
aglnry
gnarly
aglnsy
slangy
aglnty
tangly
aglnuu
ungual
ungula
agloot
galoot
agloss
glossa
aglosw
log-saw
agloty
otalgy
aglpuy
plaguy
aglrsu
guslar
aglruv
vulgar
aglruy
glaury
raguly
aglssy
glassy
aglsuv
valgus
agmmno
gammon
agmmnu
magnum
agmmry
Grammy

agmnnu
gunman
agmnox
magnox
agmnsu
musang
agmooy
oogamy
agmors
orgasm
agmorv
vagrom
agmory
goramy
morgay
agmoyz
zygoma
agmpuz
gazump
agmrtu
Targum
agnnot
tonnag
agnnry
granny
agnntu
tangun
agnnuw
wangun
agnooz
gazoon
agnoqu
quango
agnorr
garron
agnors
sarong
agnorw
awrong
agnoss
gossan
agnost
sontag
agnotu
nougat
agnowy
gowany
agnozz
gozzan
agnprs
sprang
agnrsu
sungar
agnrty
gantry
gyrant
agntwy
twangy
agoort
agorot
agoorv
vorago
agopru
gopura

agorrt
garrot
agorst
groats
agorsy
argosy
agortu
ragout
agostu
outgas
agottu
tautog
agouyy
gay-you
agpsuu
gaupus
agpsuw
gawpus
agrssu
sargus
agrssy
grassy
agrstu
tragus
agrsuy
sugary
agruuy
augury
agstuu
august
ahhijr
hijrah
ahhirs
harish
ahhkoo
hookah
ahhlpy
hyphal
ahhort
Thorah
ahhrru
hurrah
ahhrst
thrash
ahiilt
lithia
ahiint
tahini
ahikls
lakish
ahiklt
khilat
ahikns
Naskhi
ahikow
kowhai
ahikrs
rakish
shikar
ahikss
shiksa
ahikst
Shakti
skaith

ahiktw
hawkit
ahillp
phalli
ahills
shalli
ahillt
thalli
ahillz
zillah
ahilmo
holmia
ahilms
lamish
ahilnr
rhinal
ahilny
linhay
ahilps
palish
ahilpt
Lapith
ahilry
Hilary
ahilst
latish
tahsil
ahilsv
lavish
ahiltu
thulia
ahiltw
withal
ahilyz
hazily
ahimnr
harmin
ahimns
Mishna
ahimnt
hit-man
ahimnu
Humian
ahimor
mohair
ahimps
mishap
pashim
ahimrs
mahsir
marish
ahimrt
Mithra
thairm
ahinpt
hatpin
ahinrs
arshin
shairn
ahinru
unhair
ahinsv
vanish

ahinsw
wash-in
ahiops
sophia
ahiort
hot-air
ahipps
papish
ahiprs
parish
raphis
ahipru
rupiah
ahipss
phasis
ahipst
ash-pit
ahipty
Pythia
ahirrs
arrish
shirra
sirrah
ahirst
hairst
ahirsv
ravish
ahirsw
rawish
ahirtw
wraith
ahissw
siwash
ahistt
staith
ahistu
hiatus
ahjoop
poojah
ahkloo
koolah
ahklpu
pulkha
ahkmnu
khanum
ahkmow
mohawk
ahknpu
punkah
ahknrs
shrank
ahkopt
Pakhto
ahkptu
Pakhtu
ahkrst
skarth
ahkrtu
khurta
ahllmo
mollah
ollamh
ahllmu
mullah

ahllnu
nullah
ahlloo
halloo
holloa
ahllow
hallow
ahllrt
thrall
ahllux
hallux
ahllwy
whally
ahlmny
hymnal
ahlmoo
moolah
ahlmtu
lum-hat
ahlnop
phonal
ahlnsu
unlash
ahloop
hoop-la
ahlops
pholas
ahlort
harlot
ahlost
shalot
ahlosy
shoaly
ahloty
loathy
ahlpss
splash
ahlpsu
lash-up
sulpha
ahlpsy
plashy
ahlrsy
rashly
ahlstu
haulst
ahmmsy
shammy
ahmnnu
numnah
ahmnos
hansom
ahmnou
Mahoun
ahmoop
oompah
ahmorz
mahzor
ahmosu
hamous
ahmosv
moshav
ahmosy
shamoy

ahmotu
mahout
ahmotz
matzoh
ahmowy
haymow
ahmrru
murrha
ahmrsy
marshy
ahmrtw
warmth
ahmssu
samshu
shamus
ahnnsy
shanny
ahnopr
orphan
ahnopy
aphony
ahnors
shoran
ahnosx
Xhosan
ahnowy
anyhow
ahnpru
Nuphar
ahnpsu
unhasp
ahnrsy
sharny
ahnrtw
thrawn
ahnstu
sunhat
ahnsty
shanty
ahntuw
unthaw
ahopps
Sappho
ahoprs
pharos
ahopst
Pashto
pathos
potash
ahoptt
pot-hat
top-hat
ahoqtu
quotha
ahorrw
harrow
ahorry
horary
ahortt
throat
ahortu
author
ahortw
wroath

ahortx
thorax
ahostw
whatso
ahprst
sparth
ahprsy
phrasy
ahpstu
Pashtu
ahpsuw
wash-up
ahqssu
squash
ahrruy
hurray
ahrssu
hussar
ahrstt
strath
ahrstw
swarth
ahrsty
trashy
ahrttw
thwart
ahrtwy
wrathy
ahsstu
tussah
ahsswy
swashy
ahstwy
swathy
aiikkw
wakiki
aiillr
arilli
aiilms
simial
aiilnp
Alpini
aiilry
airily
aiimmn
minima
aiimms
misaim
aiimnp
painim
aiimns
simian
aiimnt
intima
aiimor
Moirai
aiimpr
impair
aiimps
simpai
aiinno
Ionian
aiinnz
zinnia

aiinrs
raisin
Sirian
aiinst
isatin
aiintt
titian
aiiptw
wapiti
aiirtv
trivia
aiisst
Isatis
aijjmm
jimjam
aijlms
Majlis
aijlnu
Julian
aijlor
jailor
aijlov
jovial
aijnov
Jovian
aijorw
jowari
aijpss
jaspis
aijptu
jupati
aiklls
killas
aiklmn
malkin
aiklmu
kalium
aiklno
kaolin
aiklnw
walk-in
aiklos
skolia
aiklps
kalpis
aiklsu
saluki
aikmms
immask
aikmns
kamsin
aikmnw
mawkin
aikmoo
oomiak
aikmpr
impark
aikmru
kumari
aiknnn
nankin
aiknnp
napkin

aiknot
kation
aiknpr
parkin
aiknps
panisk
aikort
troika
aikost
Ostiak
aikrrs
sirkar
aikrst
straik
aillmu
Allium
aillnv
villan
aillnw
inwall
aillpr
pillar
aillpu
pillau
pilula
aillrv
villar
aillry
railly
aillyz
lazily
ailmno
monial
oil-man
ailmnr
marlin
ailmns
maslin
ailmnu
alumni
lumina
ailmny
mainly
ailmop
lipoma
ailmot
tomial
ailmpr
imparl
primal
ailmrt
mitral
ailmru
ramuli
ailmss
missal
salmis
ailmst
malist
ailmsx
laxism
smilax
ailmsy
mislay

ailmtu
ultima
ailmuv
Valium®
ailmyz
mazily
ailnnu
annuli
unnail
ailnop
Alpino
ailnot
talion
ailnov
Novial
ailnps
spinal
ailnpt
plaint
pliant
ailnrt
ratlin
trinal
ailnru
urinal
ailnss
'snails
ailnst
instal
ailnsu
insula
ailnsv
silvan
ailnsw
in-laws
ailnsy
snaily
ailntu
unital
ailnty
litany
ailnuv
unvail
ailnvy
vainly
ailoor
oorial
ailors
sailor
ailort
Rialto
tailor
ailoru
ourali
ailoss
assoil
ailost
ostial
ailosx
oxalis
ailotx
oxtail
ailprs
spiral

ailpst
pastil
spital
ailptu
tail-up
tipula
Tulipa
ailqsu
squail
ailrsw
aswirl
ailrtu
ritual
ailrwy
warily
ailstu
situla
ailstv
vistal
vitals
ailstx
laxist
ailsuv
visual
ailsvy
sylvia
ailsvz
vizsla
ailtxy
laxity
aimmmu
mummia
aimmos
Maoism
mimosa
aimmrs
Ramism
aimmss
miasms
aimnno
amnion
Minoan
aimnnp
pin-man
aimnns
nanism
aimnnt
tinman
aimnnu
numina
aimnny
Minyan
aimnor
mainor
aimnot
manito
aimnpt
pitman
aimnpw
impawn
aimnpy
paynim
aimnrt
martin

aimnru
rumina
aimnst
mantis
matins
aimnsu
animus
aimnsz
Nazism
aimnuv
mauvin
aimopt
optima
aimopy
myopia
aimost
Maoist
Samiot
Taoism
aimpps
papism
aimprt
armpit
impart
partim
aimpss
passim
aimpsu
Sapium
aimqsu
maquis
aimrst
Marist
Ramist
aimrtu
atrium
aimrtx
matrix
aimssy
missay
aimstu
autism
ainnnt
tannin
ainnos
nasion
ainnot
anoint
nation
ainnow
wanion
ainnps
inspan
ainnru
uranin
ainnuz
Zuñian
ainooz
Aizoon
ainopp
Popian
ainoqu
quinoa

ainort
aroint
ration
ainoss
Ossian
ainosu
Siouan
ainprs
spinar
sprain
ainpru
pruina
ainprw
inwrap
ainpst
ptisan
ainptt
tan-pit
ainptu
Tupian
ainpty
painty
ainqrt
qintar
ainqtu
quaint
quinta
ainrst
instar
santir
strain
ainrsy
Syrian
ainrtu
nutria
ainrty
in-tray
Tyrian
ainstt
tanist
ainstu
Austin
ainsty
sanity
satiny
stay-in
aintvy
vanity
aioors
arioso
aioprv
pavior
aiopst
patois
aioptu
utopia
aiorru
ourari
aiorst
aorist
aristo
satori
aiorsu
souari

aiortv
viator
aiostt
Taoist
aipprr
riprap
aippry
papyri
aippst
papist
aipptt
pit-pat
tappit
aiprst
rapist
aiprsv
parvis
aiprsw
rip-saw
aiprsx
praxis
aiprtt
rat-pit
aiprty
parity
aipruy
pyuria
aipsst
pastis
aipstt
tapist
aipstw
pit-saw
sawpit
aipzzz
pizazz
airrty
rarity
airrzz
rizzar
airsst
sistra
airssu
russia
airstt
artist
sittar
strait
airstu
aurist
airstv
travis
airtty
yttria
airvvy
vivary
aissst
assist
stasis
aitttu
tautit
aittwx
atwixt

ajloor
jarool
ajlopy
jalopy
ajmopt
jampot
ajmrtu
jumart
ajnort
Trojan
ajnrtu
jurant
ajntuy
jaunty
ajprtu
Rajput
akknru
kunkar
akkoqu
quokka
akkoss
sakkos
akllny
lankly
aklnou
koulan
aklnow
walk-on
aklnox
klaxon
aklnry
rankly
aklost
stalko
aklosv
Slovak
aklotw
kotwal
aklpry
parkly
aklsty
stalky
akmnsu
unmask
akmnsy
skyman
akmpru
mark-up
aknoru
koruna
aknotu
oak-nut
aknpry
pranky
aknrtz
krantz
aknswy
swanky
akoorr
Karroo
korora
akorss
kaross

akostu
 out-ask
akosty
 Ostyak
akpttu
 kaputt
akqsuw
 squawk
akrstu
 tuskar
akswyy
 skyway
allmos
 slalom
allmow
 mallow
allmuv
 vallum
allnop
 pollan
allnos
 llanos
allnuu
 lunula
alloop
 apollo
 palolo
allopr
 pallor
allopw
 wallop
allors
 sollar
allory
 orally
allosw
 sallow
allott
 tallot
allotu
 all-out
allotv
 lavolt
allotw
 tallow
allouy
 you-all
allovy
 ovally
alloww
 wallow
alloyy
 Y-alloy
allpru
 plural
allqsu
 squall
allrsu
 Rallus
allsty
 lastly
 saltly
alluuz
 Luzula

alluvv
 vulval
almmsy
 smalmy
almmuy
 amylum
almnor
 normal
almnos
 salmon
almnou
 monaul
almnru
 murlan
almors
 morsal
almort
 mortal
almoru
 morula
almost
 almost
 smalto
almotw
 matlow
almoxy
 xyloma
almquy
 qualmy
almrwy
 warmly
almsuy
 asylum
almtuu
 mutual
 umlaut
alnnor
 norlan'
alnnou
 nounal
alnoos
 alsoon
 saloon
 solano
alnooz
 zoonal
alnopt
 pontal
alnort
 latron
alnosv
 Volans
alnotv
 volant
alnouz
 zonula
alnptu
 pultan
alnrsy
 snarly
alnruy
 lunary
 uranyl

alnrxy
 larynx
alnstu
 sultan
alnsvy
 sylvan
alntuw
 walnut
aloops
 saloop
aloppr
 poplar
aloprt
 patrol
 portal
aloprv
 vorpal
alopry
 Pyrola
alopst
 postal
aloqtu
 loquat
alorrw
 worral
alorsu
 rosula
alorsv
 salvor
alortu
 rotula
 Torula
alortw
 low-tar
aloruv
 ovular
 valour
alorvy
 volary
alosss
 lassos
alotuw
 outlaw
alotuy
 lay-out
 outlay
alppsu
 palpus
 slap-up
alprru
 larrup
alprsu
 pulsar
alprsw
 sprawl
alprty
 paltry
 partly
alpruw
 pulwar
alpsty
 yplast
alrstu
 lustra

alrsty
 stylar
alrsuu
 Laurus
alrsuw
 walrus
alrtty
 tartly
alrtuw
 tulwar
alruuv
 uvular
alruvv
 vulvar
alsstu
 saltus
 tussal
alstvy
 vastly
altuvy
 vaulty
ammmno
 mammon
ammmou
 amomum
ammort
 marmot
ammosu
 omasum
ammoxy
 myxoma
ammpuw
 wampum
ammrru
 marrum
 murram
ammrsu
 summar
ammrsy
 smarmy
ammstu
 summat
ammsuw
 wammus
ammtuz
 Tammuz
amnnor
 norman
amnnoy
 anonym
amnoop
 Pomona
amnoor
 maroon
amnopt
 pot-man
 tampon
 topman
amnors
 ramson
 ransom
amnort
 matron

amnoru
 Rouman
amnory
 mornay
 Romany
amnoss
 Samson
amnotu
 amount
 moutan
 outman
amnoty
 toyman
amnpty
 tympan
amnrtu
 antrum
amnttu
 mutant
 tutman
amntuu
 autumn
amoopt
 pomato
amoorv
 moorva
amoott
 tomato
amorrt
 mortar
amorru
 armour
amorrw
 marrow
amorry
 armory
amorss
 morass
amorst
 stroam
 stroma
amorsu
 ramous
amosuw
 awmous
amotuz
 mazout
amprst
 stramp
ampruw
 warm-up
ampsuw
 mawpus
 wampus
ampswy
 swampy
amrrty
 martyr
amrruy
 murray
amrstu
 struma
amrsty
 smarty

annoox
 xoanon
annopr
 napron
annopt
 panton
annort
 natron
annory
 nonary
annost
 santon
 sonant
annott
 tonant
annotw
 wanton
annoty
 Tannoy®
annpsu
 sannup
annptu
 pantun
annrty
 tranny
annstu
 suntan
annsty
 syntan
annswy
 swanny
annttu
 nutant
anoort
 ratoon
anoosw
 aswoon
anoprs
 parson
anoprt
 parton
 patron
 tarpon
anoptt
 optant
anopuy
 yaupon
anorrw
 narrow
anorsv
 sovran
anortt
 attorn
 ratton
 rottan
anortv
 vorant
anorty
 aroynt
 notary
 Troyan
anorwy
 Norway

anoryz
 zonary
anossw
 sowans
anostz
 stanzo
anoswy
 noways
anosxy
 saxony
anppsy
 snappy
anprsu
 unspar
anprty
 pantry
anpruw
 unwrap
anpruy
 unpray
anpsuw
 supawn
anrstu
 santur
 Saturn
anrsuu
 Uranus
anrsuy
 sunray
anrttu
 truant
anrtty
 tyrant
anruwy
 runway
 unwary
ansttu
 tutsan
anstxy
 syntax
ansyzz
 snazzy
aoopst
 astoop
aooptt
 potato
aoorrt
 orator
aoorry
 arroyo
aoortt
 tooart
aoortv
 ovator
aoottt
 tattoo
aopprt
 apport
aoprrt
 parrot
 raptor
aoprru
 uproar

aoprst
asport
pastor
portas
sap-rot
aopruv
vapour
aopsst
potass
aopstu
aspout
aoptuy
pay-out
aopwww
powwaw
aoqrtu
quarto
aorrst
rostra
sartor
aorrsy
rosary
aorrtw
tarrow
aorrty
rotary
aorrwy
arrowy
yarrow
aorsst
assort
aorstt
stator
aorstu
soutar
aorstx
storax
aorsuu
aurous
aorsuv
savour
aorsvy
savory
aortuy
yaourt
aortvy
votary
aorvwy
avowry
aosstt
assott
aotuwy
way-out
aotwwy
two-way
apppsu
pappus
apprty
trappy
aprrsy
sparry
aprsty
pastry

aprswy
psywar
apsssu
passus
apstuy
upstay
apsuwy
upsway
aqrruy
quarry
aqrtuz
quartz
arrsty
starry
arssst
strass
arsstu
tarsus
arsttu
astrut
arstuu
Taurus
arstuw
waurst
arstux
surtax
arstwy
strawy
swarty
wastry
arstxy
styrax
assttu
status
bbbdeo
bobbed
bbbeir
bibber
bbbelo
bobble
bbbelu
bubble
bbbhuu
hubbub
bbbino
bobbin
bbbluy
bubbly
bbcdeu
cubbed
bbcelo
cobble
bbceor
cobber
bbceow
cobweb
bbchuy
chubby
bbddei
dibbed
bbddeu
dubbed
bbdeen
nebbed

bbdeew
webbed
bbdefi
fibbed
bbdegu
bedbug
bbdeij
jibbed
bbdeil
dibble
bbdein
nibbed
bbdeio
dobbie
bbdeir
dibber
ribbed
bbdejo
jobbed
bbdelo
lobbed
bbdelu
bulbed
bbdemo
mobbed
bbdeor
dobber
robbed
bbdeos
sobbed
bbdeox
box-bed
bbderu
rubbed
bbdesu
subbed
bbdgiu
big-bud
bbdino
dobbin
bbdinu
dubbin
bbdkuy
dybbuk
bbeeik
kebbie
bbeekl
lebbek
bbeelp
pebble
bbeemu
bum-bee
bbeemx
Bembex
bbeenn
neb-neb
bbeerr
Berber
bbeeyy
bye-bye
bbefir
fibber
bbegir
gibber

bbegit
gibbet
bbeglo
gobble
bbegnu
bebung
bbegot
gobbet
bbehlo
hobble
bbeiim
imbibe
bbeiir
ribibe
bbeijr
jibber
bbeikl
kibble
bbeiln
nibble
bbeilr
libber
bbeimo
mobbie
bbeirr
briber
bbejor
jobber
bbeknu
nebbuk
bbelmo
mobble
bbelmu
bumble
bbelno
nobble
bbelnu
nubble
bbelow
wobble
bbelpy
pebbly
plebby
bbelru
burble
lubber
rubble
bbemnu
benumb
bbemor
bomber
bbeorr
robber
bberru
rubber
bbertu
rubbet
tubber
bbfloy
bob-fly
bbgino
gibbon
bbgiow
bobwig

bbgruy
grubby
bbhjoo
hobjob
bbhnoo
hobnob
bbikos
ski-bob
bbillu
bulbil
bbinor
ribbon
bbirtu
rubbit
bbknoy
knobby
bbknuy
knubby
bbkoos
bosbok
bblluu
bulbul
bblnuy
nubbly
bblosy
slobby
bblowy
by-blow
wobbly
bblruy
rubbly
bblsuy
slubby
bbmoxy
Bombyx
bbmruy
brumby
bbnnoo
bonbon
bbnosy
snobby
bbnotu
nobbut
bbnsuy
snubby
bboooo
booboo
bboowy
bow-boy
bbortu
burbot
bbosuy
busboy
bbrsuu
suburb
bbstuy
stubby
bccior
cobric
bcdeek
bedeck
bcdeio
bodice

bcdeku
beduck
bcdemo
combed
bcdiou
cuboid
bcdnou
bonduc
bceeho
obeche
bceehr
breech
bceekn
nebeck
bceekr
rebeck
bceekt
becket
bceekz
zebeck
bceelo
ecbole
bceely
Cybele
bceemo
become
bcegil
Belgic
bcehln
blench
bcehor
broché
bcehos
bosche
bcehou
bouche
bcehru
cherub
bceiis
ibices
bceikr
bicker
bceiku
buckie
bceilm
emblic
bceilr
criblé
bceior
corbie
bceiox
icebox
bceips
biceps
bceirs
scribe
bceirt
terbic
bceist
bisect
bcejot
object
bceklu
buckle

bcekmo
bemock
bcekno
beckon
bcekru
bucker
bcektu
bucket
bcelor
corbel
bcelou
bouclé
bcelru
becurl
bcemor
comber
bcemru
cumber
bcenou
bounce
bceors
scrobe
bceott
obtect
bcgoru
coburg
bchilo
chibol
bchiop
phobic
bchity
bitchy
bchlot
blotch
bchnru
brunch
bchnuy
bunchy
bchoor
brooch
bchors
borsch
bchoty
botchy
bchrsu
Bursch
bciino
bionic
niobic
bciinu
incubi
bciiop
biopic
bciiot
biotic
bcikno
kincob
bcikry
bricky
bciloo
colobi
bcilpu
public

bcilru
lubric
bcimor
bromic
bcimot
tombic
bcimsu
cubism
bcirru
rubric
bcistu
cubist
bcmoot
tomboc
bcmory
corymb
bcmrsu
crumbs
bcmruy
crumby
bcnoor
bronco
bcnotu
cobnut
bcnouy
bouncy
bcoowy
cowboy
bdddee
bedded
bdddeu
budded
bddeei
bedide
bddeen
bended
bddeer
bedder
bddeet
debted
bddeey
bedyde
bedyed
bddein
bidden
bddeio
bodied
bddeir
bidder
bddelo
boddle
bddelu
buddle
bddeno
bonded
bdderu
red-bud
bddisu
disbud
bddjoo
odd-job
bdeeen
need-be

bdeeet
debtee
bdeegg
begged
bdeego
dog-bee
bdeehl
beheld
bdeeil
belied
debile
edible
bdeeis
beside
bdeeit
betide
bdeejl
djebel
bdeeky
bed-key
bdeell
bedell
bdeeln
blende
bdeelt
belted
bdeenr
bender
bdeeps
besped
bdeett
betted
bdefir
fibred
bdeggu
bugged
bdegil
begild
bdegio
bodgie
bdegip
pig-bed
bdegir
begird
bridge
bdegiu
budgie
bdeglo
globed
bdeglu
bludge
bdegnu
bedung
bdegor
bodger
bdegru
budger
bdegtu
budget
bdehin
behind
bdehir
Hebrid

bdehlo
behold
bdehos
debosh
bdehot
hotbed
bdehsu
bushed
bdeiim
ibidem
bdeiir
birdie
bridie
bdeill
billed
bdeilm
dimble
limbed
bdeilo
boiled
bolide
bdeilr
bridle
bdeilu
bludie
bdeily
bieldy
bdeimn
nimbed
bdeinr
binder
inbred
rebind
bdeint
bident
bdeinu
beduin
bdeioo
boodie
bdeior
boride
bdeios
bodies
bdeirs
debris
bdeiru
burdie
buried
rubied
bdeist
bed-sit
bdeisu
busied
bdeitt
bitted
bdeknu
debunk
bdeksu
busked
bdello
bolled
bdelmo
mobled

bdelno
blonde
bolden
bdelnu
bundle
bdeloo
boodle
bdelor
bordel
bdelou
double
bdelow
blowed
bdemmu
bummed
bdemnu
numbed
bdemoy
embody
bdennu
unbend
bdenor
bonder
bdenot
obtend
bdenoy
beyond
bdenru
burden
burned
unbred
bdensu
sunbed
bdentu
bunted
but-end
bdeoot
booted
bdeooz
boozed
bdeopr
bedrop
bdeorr
border
bdeors
desorb
bdeort
betrod
debtor
bdeoru
obdure
bdeorx
red-box
bdeoss
bossed
bdeoww
dew-bow
bdersu
surbed
bdestu
bedust
bestud
busted

bdesuu
subdue
bdesuw
subdew
bdettu
butted
bdfilo
bifold
bdfior
forbid
bdgiin
biding
bdgino
boding
bdgoru
dor-bug
bdhiry
hybrid
bdiilo
libido
bdiimr
midrib
bdiitt
tidbit
bdikno
bodkin
bdiloy
bodily
bdiluy
bluidy
bdimor
morbid
bdimoy
imbody
bdinnu
unbind
bdinpu
upbind
bdiorx
ox-bird
bdiotu
outbid
bdirtu
turbid
bdkloo
kobold
bdlloy
boldly
bdlmuy
dumbly
bdloos
'sblood
bdlooy
bloody
bdlouy
doubly
bdmruu
rum-bud
bdnooy
nobody
bdnotu
obtund
bdnouy
ybound

bdoory
broody
bdorwy
byword
beeefl
feeble
beeehp
ephebe
beeekl
kebele
beeelt
beetle
beeems
beseem
beeemt
bemete
beteem
beeens
beseen
beeepw
beweep
beeers
breese
beeerz
breeze
beeesv
beeves
beefil
belief
beefll
befell
beefly
feebly
beefor
before
beefrt
bereft
beeghr
Gheber
Ghebre
beegil
beigel
beegly
leg-bye
beegno
begone
beegnu
bungee
beegru
burgee
Gueber
Guebre
beehip
ephebi
beehlt
bethel
beehop
phoebe
beehot
behote
beehov
behove
beehrt
berthe

beehrw
Hebrew
beehry
hereby
beehst
behest
Thebes
beehtt
Tebeth
beeikl
belike
beeilv
belive
beeimr
bemire
bireme
beeimt
betime
beeirt
rebite
beeisx
ibexes
beejnu
bunjee
beekor
reebok
beekrs
breeks
beekru
rebuke
beelmm
emblem
beelmr
remble
beelms
semble
beelno
Belone
beelnu
nebule
nebulé
beelov
belove
beelpt
bepelt
beelrt
treble
beelzz
bezzle
beemmr
member
beemru
embrue
beemsu
bemuse
beennr
brenne
beennt
bennet
beenor
boreen
enrobe
beentu
butene

beeoot
bootee
beeopp
bo-peep
beeorr
rebore
beeort
bo-tree
beeory
obeyer
beeptw
bewept
beerrt
berret
beerru
beurré
beerrv
reverb
beerrw
brewer
beersu
Erebus
beertt
better
beertv
brevet
beeryz
breezy
beestu
bustee
beffpu
bepuff
beffru
buffer
rebuff
befftu
buffet
befgit
begift
befhoo
behoof
befilm
fimble
befilo
foible
beflmu
beflum
fumble
befloo
befool
beflou
befoul
beflry
belfry
befory
forbye
befruy
rubefy
befsuu
subfeu
beggii
biggie
beggir
bigger
begglo
boggle
beggox
egg-box
beggru
bugger
beghis
besigh
begiil
Liebig
begiln
bingle
begilo
oblige
begilr
gerbil
begilt
giblet
beginn
benign
begino
biogen
begins
besing
beginu
beguin
bungie
begioo
boogie
begios
bogies
begiou
bougie
begirt
begirt
begiru
brigue
begknu
begunk
beglno
belong
beglnu
blunge
bungle
beglot
goblet
beglow
bow-leg
beglru
bugler
bulger
burgle
begltu
buglet
begnoy
bygone
begnsu
besung
begoor
bog-ore
goober
begopx
peg-box
begoru
brogue
begosy
bogeys
begrru
burger
behikr
kirbeh
behilt
blithe
thible
behins
nebish
behint
hen-bit
behiot
bothie
behitt
thibet
behlmu
humble
behlow
behowl
behlru
burhel
behlsu
bushel
behnor
brehon
behoos
hoboes
behort
bother
beiikr
birkie
beiill
billie
beiirs
Iberis
beiitt
bittie
beijlr
jerbil
jirble
beijmu
jumbie
beijnu
bunjie
beikln
libken
beiklr
bilker
beiknr
birken
beikoo
bookie
beikss
bekiss
beillt
billet
beilmn
nimble
beilmo
bemoil
emboil
mobile
beilmr
limber
beilmw
wimble
beilmy
blimey
beilno
ben-oil
beilnr
berlin
beilnu
nubile
beilny
byline
beilnz
benzil
beilor
boiler
reboil
beilot
betoil
beilrr
birler
beilrs
birsle
beimos
obeism
beimoz
zombie
beimrt
betrim
timber
timbre
beimru
erbium
imbrue
beimrx
imbrex
beimty
by-time
beinno
bonnie
beinnp
pen-nib
beinnt
inbent
beinov
bovine
beinox
bonxie
beinoz
bizone
beinrs
nebris
beinru
rubine
beinry
byrnie
beintt
bitten
beiors
ribose
beioru
ourebi
beiost
sobeit
beipst
bespit
beipty
bepity
beiqsu
bisque
beirry
briery
beirst
bestir
bister
bistre
beirsu
bruise
beirsw
brewis
beirtt
bitter
Tibert
beituy
ubiety
bejjuu
jujube
bejlmu
jumble
bejoru
objure
beklru
bulker
beknor
broken
beknru
bunker
bekoot
betook
bekorr
broker
bekors
bosker
bekost
bosket
bekrsu
busker
bekstu
busket
bellno
bollen
bellou
boulle
lobule
bellow
bellow
bellru
buller
belltu
bullet
belmmu
bummle
mumble
belmoy
emboly
belmru
lumber
rumble
umbrel
belmsu
umbles
belmtu
tumble
belnny
blenny
belnoz
benzol
belntu
unbelt
belnty
yblent
belnuy
nebuly
belnyz
benzyl
beloor
bolero
beloos
lobose
sobole
belopu
pueblo
belorr
borrel
belort
bolter
beloru
rouble
belorw
blower
bowler
belosu
blouse
boules
obelus
belosw
blowse
belott
bottle
belowz
blowze
belrru
burler
burrel
belrtu
butler
belrty
trebly
belstu
bustle
sublet
subtle
belttu
buttle
beltuu
tubule
bemmru
bummer
bemnot
entomb
bemnow
enwomb
bemnru
number
bemoor
boomer
bemors
sombre
bemory
embryo
bemoss
emboss
bempru
bumper
bemruy
umbery
bemstu
besmut
bemsuy
embusy
bennot
bonnet
bennou
unbone
bennsu
Bunsen
benntu
ben-nut
unbent
benoor
Oberon
benoot
botone
benorr
reborn
benort
breton
benoru
bourne
unrobe
benorz
bonzer
bronze
benoty
betony
benrru
burner
benrtu
brunet
bunter
burnet
benrty
ybrent
beoors
broose
beoorz
boozer

beoost
Boötes
beooyz
boozey
beoppr
bopper
beopst
bespot
beorrs
resorb
beorst
besort
sorbet
strobe
beorsu
bourse
beorsw
bowser
browse
beortt
bettor
beortv
obvert
beorvy
overby
beorwy
bowery
bowyer
owerby
beosss
obsess
beosst
betoss
beostt
obtest
beostu
obtuse
beostw
bestow
beotuy
outbye
beprsu
superb
berruy
rebury
berstu
buster
surbet
berttu
butter
bertuy
uberty
beruzz
buzzer
besstu
subset
bffiin
biffin
bffino
boffin
bfgoow
fog-bow
bfiilr
fibril
bfiinr
fibrin
bfimor
biform
bfinow
bowfin
bfiruy
rubify
bfloty
botfly
bfloux
boxful
bfltuu
tubful
bfmory
by-form
bggiin
biggin
bggiiw
bigwig
bggluy
bluggy
bggnoo
bogong
bggnou
bugong
bghilt
blight
bghirt
bright
bghmuu
humbug
bghoru
brough
bghotu
bought
bgiint
biting
bgilly
glibly
bgilno
globin
goblin
lobing
bgilnu
bluing
bginno
boning
bginor
boring
robing
bginos
obsign
bginox
boxing
bginsu
busing
bgintu
tubing
bginuy
buying
bglnoo
oblong
bgmoor
gombro
bgnooy
gobony
bgooru
burgoo
bgosuw
sow-bug
bgotuu
bug-out
bhhikt
k'thibh
bhiist
bhisti
bhikos
kibosh
bhiksu
bukshi
bhilsu
bluish
bhimor
rhombi
bhiops
bishop
bhiosy
boyish
bhirsu
hubris
bhirsy
hybris
bhknou
bohunk
bhkosy
kybosh
bhlmuy
humbly
bhlosy
bolshy
bhmtuy
thumby
bhoooo
boo-hoo
bhrsuy
brushy
biiikn
bikini
biiktz
kibitz
biimos
obiism
biimuv
bivium
biinot
biotin
biiorv
vibrio
biirrs
sbirri
biirtu
buriti
biistv
vibist
biittt
titbit
bijoux
bijoux
biklns
blinks
bikmnu
bumkin
bikmos
imbosk
biknsu
buskin
bikrsy
brisky
billno
billon
billou
lobuli
billow
billow
billox
bollix
billoy
billy-o
bilmny
nimbly
bilmru
umbril
bilmsu
Limbus
bilmuy
bulimy
bilnos
Lisbon
bilntz
blintz
bilopu
upboil
bilrty
trilby
bilstu
subtil
bilsuy
busily
bimnos
bonism
bimnsu
nimbus
bimoss
imboss
bimstu
submit
binnor
inborn
binnou
bunion
binoot
bonito
binort
Briton
binory
briony
binoss
bisson
binost
bonist
binpuy
bunyip
binttu
unbitt
bioorz
borzoi
bioost
oboist
bioosv
ovibos
biopsy
biopsy
biorrs
sbirro
biorst
bistro
biorty
orbity
biostu
subito
biottw
two-bit
biotuw
woubit
birttu
turbit
bjlmuy
jumbly
bjloot
job-lot
bkmnuu
bunkum
bkoosy
booksy
bkorwy
bywork
bllory
brolly
blmooy
bloomy
blmosy
symbol
blnotu
unbolt
bloosu
obolus
bloott
blotto
bloowy
lowboy
blopty
by-plot
blopuw
blow-up
upblow
bloswy
blowsy
blotty
blotty
blowyz
blowzy
blstuy
subtly
bmnotu
untomb
bmoory
broomy
byroom
bmoosy
bosomy
bmoott
bottom
bmooty
tomboy
bmorst
stromb
bmorsu
morbus
bnnoru
unborn
bnoost
boston
bnootu
bouton
unboot
bnorsu
suborn
bnortu
burton
bnorwy
browny
bnoryy
bryony
bnoryz
bronzy
bnosuw
sunbow
bnottu
button
bnotuy
bounty
bnpruu
burn-up
bnrtuy
Tyburn
bnruuy
unbury
bnsuuy
unbusy
booptw
bowpot
boopty
pot-boy
boorrw
borrow
bootuw
woobut
bootux
outbox
boowww
bowwow
borruw
burrow
borstu
robust
borstw
browst
borttu
turbot
botuuy
buy-out
bpstuu
bust-up
brstuu
Brutus
bsssuy
byssus
cccdio
coccid
cccily
cyclic
cccosu
coccus
cccoxy
coccyx
ccdeko
cocked
ccdeot
decoct
cceehl
cleché
cceehr
crèche
cceeor
coerce
ccehil
chicle
cliché
ccehim
chemic
ccehio
choice
echoic
ccehit
hectic
ccehky
checky
ccehln
clench
ccehlo
cloche
ccehlu
cleuch
ccehor
croche
ccehos
cosech
ccehou
couché
cceiil
cilice
icicle
cceilr
circle
cleric
cceils
cecils
cceilt
Celtic
cceily
cicely

cceins scenic
cceior cicero
cceipt pectic
cceirt cretic
cceity cecity
cceklo cockle
ccekop copeck
ccekor cocker
ccekot cocket
ccelry cycler
ccenos sconce
cceors escroc soccer
ccepsy speccy
ccersu cercus cruces
ccfilo flocci
cchhii chichi
cchhin chinch
cchhru church
cchikt tchick
cchiln clinch
cchilo cholic
cchily chicly
cchino chicon Cochin
cchior choric
cchipu hiccup
cchlnu clunch
cchltu clutch cultch
cchnoy conchy
cchnru crunch
cchors scorch
cchort crotch
cchoru crouch
cchost scotch
cchrtu crutch
cchstu scutch
cciiln clinic
cciino iconic
cciinp picnic
cciipr picric
cciirt citric critic
cciist cistic
cciisv civics
ccikry cricky
ccilno clonic
cciltu cultic
ccimos cosmic
ccimry Cymric
ccinos conics
ccinpy pycnic
ccinsu Cnicus
cciopt Coptic
cciors sciroc
cciost Scotic
ccipru cupric
ccirsu circus
ccisty cystic
cckloo o'clock
cckmoo mocock
cckmou mocuck
ccknou uncock
cckoou cuckoo
cckopu cock-up
cckosy cocksy
cclmuu mucluc
cclotu occult
cclsuy cyclus
ccnooo cocoon
ccnoru concur
ccooor rococo
ccopuy occupy
ccorsu crocus succor
ccostu stucco
ccssuu cuscus succus
cdddeo codded
cddeei decide
cddeek decked
cddeeo decode
cddeeu deduce deuced
cddehi chided
cddeiu cuddie
cddelo coddle
cddelu cuddle
cddeor corded
cddetu deduct
cddloy cloddy
cddluy cuddly
cddruy cruddy
cdeeer decree recede
cdeees secede
cdeeex exceed
cdeefn fenced
cdeeft defect
cdeeho echoed
cdeeil delice
cdeeim décime
cdeein Edenic incede
cdeeir de-icer
cdeeit deceit
cdeeiv device
cdeeix excide
cdeejt deject
cdeekl deckle
cdeekn necked
cdeeko decoke
cdeekr decker recked
cdeell celled
cdeelu Culdee
cdeeno encode
cdeenr decern
cdeent decent
cdeeot Docete
cdeers screed
cdeeru reduce
cdeesu seduce
cdeett detect
cdefii deific
cdefku fucked
cdefnu fecund
cdefor forced
cdeggo cogged
cdegio geodic
cdeglu cudgel
cdegor codger
cdehil chield
cdehin inched niched
cdehir chider dreich herdic
cdehko choked
cdehnr drench
cdehou douche
cdeikm medick
cdeikp picked
cdeikr dicker
cdeikt ticked
cdeikw wicked
cdeiky dickey
cdeilo docile
cdeilt delict
cdeimn minced
cdeimo medico
cdeimr dermic
cdeinr cinder
cdeinu induce
cdeinw Wendic
cdeinz zinced
cdeiop copied epodic
cdeiov voiced
cdeiox exodic
cdeipr priced
cdeips spiced
cdeipt depict
cdeirs scried
cdeirt credit direct
cdeiry cidery
cdeist cisted
cdekno docken
cdeknu undeck
cdekop pocked
cdekor corked docker
cdekot docket
cdekru ducker
cdeksu sucked
cdeloo locoed
cdelos closed
cdelow cowled
cdeloy cloyed
cdelru curdle curled
cdeltu dulcet
cdemoo comedo
cdemoy comedy
cdenno conned
cdenor conder corned
cdenos second
cdensu secund
cdeopp copped
cdeopu couped
cdeorr record
cdeorw crowed
cdeosu escudo
cdeott cotted
cdeotu doucet
cdeoty cytode
cdeppu cupped
cdepsu cusped
cdersu cursed
cdersy descry
cderuv curved
cderuy decury
cdessu cussed
cdfiou fucoid
cdfioy codify
cdgiin dicing
cdhior droich orchid rhodic
cdhiry hydric
cdiiir iridic
cdiint indict
cdiioy idiocy
cdiisv viscid
cdilno codlin
cdimnu mundic
cdimor dromic
cdimou mucoid
cdimoy cymoid
cdimsu muscid
cdimtu dictum
cdinoo conoid
cdinor Nordic
cdinsy syndic
cdintu induct
cdiors roscid
cdiorv corvid
cdiost codist
cdioty cytoid

cdipry
cyprid
cdipsu
cuspid
cdissu
discus
cdisty
cystid
cdjnou
jocund
cdknou
undock
cdlloy
clodly
coldly
cdlouy
cloudy
cdmnoo
condom
cdnoor
condor
cordon
cdnoru
uncord
cdnouw
dun-cow
cdooot
doocot
cdoort
doctor
cdoory
corody
ceeefl
fleece
ceeegn
egence
ceeegr
greece
ceeehl
elchee
ceeehs
cheese
ceeeno
Eocene
ceeers
creese
ceeffo
coffee
ceefft
effect
ceefhl
flèche
fleech
ceefir
fierce
ceefly
fleecy
ceefnn
fennec
ceefnr
fencer
ceefrt
refect
ceefsu
fescue
ceegir
cierge
griece
ceegno
congee
ceegny
egency
ceehil
lichee
ceehis
seiche
ceehkl
heckle
ceehky
cheeky
ceehln
elench
ceehlr
lecher
ceehls
sleech
ceehly
lychee
ceehms
scheme
smeech
ceehnt
chenet
thence
ceehnv
cheven
ceehnw
whence
ceehor
cheero
choree
cohere
echoer
re-echo
ceehos
echoes
ceehps
speech
ceehqu
cheque
ceehrs
cheers
creesh
ceehrt
etcher
ceehru
euchre
ceehry
cheery
reechy
ceehss
secesh
ceehsw
eschew
ceehsy
cheesy
ceehtw
chewet
ceeimr
eremic
ceeimt
emetic
ceeinn
Nicene
ceeinp
picene
piecen
ceeint
entice
ceeinv
evince
Venice
ceeipr
piecer
pierce
recipe
ceeips
specie
ceeirs
cerise
ceeirt
cerite
recite
tierce
ceeiru
écurie
ceeisx
excise
ceeitx
excite
ceejno
conjee
ceejrt
reject
ceekkl
keckle
ceekls
seckel
ceeklt
teckel
ceekpr
pecker
ceekry
creeky
ceelnp
pencel
ceelnr
crenel
ceelor
creole
ceelos
eclose
ceelou
coulée
ceelov
veloce
ceelrs
sclere
ceelrt
tercel
ceelrv
clever
ceelrw
crewel
ceelry
celery
ceelst
select
ceemnt
cement
ceemrr
mercer
ceemrt
cermet
ceenor
encore
ceenps
spence
ceenpt
pecten
ceenrs
censer
scerne
screen
secern
ceenrt
center
centre
recent
tenrec
ceensy
esnecy
ceeopu
coupee
ceeorv
corvée
ceeprt
recept
ceepry
creepy
ceeptx
except
expect
ceepty
ectype
ceerru
recure
ceerss
recess
ceerst
certes
resect
secret
ceersu
Cereus
ceruse
cesure
recuse
rescue
secure
ceertt
tercet
ceessx
excess
ceestx
exsect
ceesux
excuse
ceffio
office
cefflo
coffle
cefflu
cuffle
ceffor
coffer
cefhim
fehmic
cefhit
fetich
fitché
cefhln
flench
cefhlt
fletch
cefhnr
french
cefikl
fickle
cefint
infect
cefirr
ferric
cefkly
feckly
cefkru
fucker
ceflos
fo'c'sle
cefnor
confer
ceforr
forcer
cefors
fresco
cefruw
curfew
ceggii
ciggie
ceggio
coggie
cegglo
coggle
ceggor
cogger
ceggpu
eggcup
ceghio
chigoe
ceghir
chigre
ceghlu
cleugh
cegino
coigne
ceginr
cringe
cegirs
grices
cegist
gestic
ceglry
clergy
cegnor
conger
cegnot
cogent
cegnty
cygnet
cegorr
grocer
cehhsu
sheuch
cehhtt
thetch
cehiln
lichen
cehils
chesil
chisel
cehilt
eltchi
cehimr
chimer
micher
cehimv
vehmic
cehinp
phenic
cehinr
enrich
nicher
richen
cehint
ethnic
cehinv
chevin
cehinx
chenix
cehior
co-heir
heroic
cehipr
ceriph
cipher
cehiqu
quiche
cehirs
riches
cehirt
cither
thrice
cehist
ethics
cehitt
thetic
cehklu
huckle
cehknu
Kuchen
cehkor
choker
hocker
cehkoy
chokey
hockey
cehkst
sketch
cehktv
kvetch
cehlmo
Molech
cehlms
schelm
cehlmu
muchel
cehlno
nochel
cehlor
choler
orchel
cehlot
clothe
cehlou
louche
cehlps
schlep
cehlpu
pleuch
cehlqu
quelch
cehmmy
chemmy
cehmor
chrome
cehmos
schmoe
cehmtu
humect
cehnoo
ochone
cehnos
chosen
cehnou
cohune
cehnqu
quench
cehnrt
trench
cehnrw
wrench
cehnst
stench
cehnuu
eunuch
cehoos
choose
cehopt
potche
cehors
cosher

cehort
hector
rochet
rotche
tocher
troche
cehory
ochery
ochrey
cehosu
chouse
cehotu
touché
cehpru
cherup
cehpry
chypre
cypher
cehpst
spetch
cehpsy
psyche
cehqtu
quetch
cehquy
chequy
cehrry
cherry
cehrtw
wretch
cehrty
cherty
cehstu
tusche
cehsty
chesty
scythe
cehtty
tetchy
cehtvy
vetchy
ceiiks
sickie
ceiils
ilices
ceiilt
elicit
ceiilx
exilic
ceiimr
cimier
ceiinp
picine
ceiinr
irenic
ceiins
incise
ceiint
incite
ceijnt
inject
ceijru
juicer
ceikkr
kicker
ceiklm
mickle
ceikln
nickel
ceiklp
pickle
ceiklr
licker
rickle
ceikls
sickle
ceiklt
Keltic
tickle
ceiklu
luckie
ceikmy
mickey
ceiknr
nicker
ceikns
sicken
ceiknt
ticken
ceiknw
wicken
ceikoo
cookie
ceikpr
picker
ripeck
ceikpt
picket
ceikrr
ricker
ceikrs
scrike
sicker
ceikrt
ticker
ceikrw
wicker
ceikry
crikey
ceiktt
ticket
ceiktw
wicket
ceikty
tickey
ceillo
collie
ocelli
ceilno
cineol
ceilnp
pencil
ceilnt
client
lentic
ceilnu
leucin
nuclei
ceilny
nicely
ceiloo
coolie
ceilop
police
ceilor
recoil
ceilot
citole
ceilps
splice
ceilpv
pelvic
ceilqu
clique
ceilrs
slicer
ceilrt
relict
ceilsu
sluice
ceilsv
clevis
ceiltt
Lettic
ceiltu
luetic
ceimmn
mnemic
ceimmo
commie
ceimno
income
ceimnr
mincer
ceimpu
pumice
ceimrt
metric
ceimru
cerium
uremic
ceimsu
miscue
ceimty
etymic
ceinno
conine
ceinor
coiner
orcein
orcine
ceinos
cosine
oscine
ceinot
noetic
notice
ceinov
novice
ceinpr
pincer
prince
ceinpt
incept
pectin
peinct
ceinqu
cinque
quince
ceinrs
scrine
ceinrt
cretin
ceinru
ice-run
ceinrw
wincer
ceinst
incest
insect
scient
ceinsu
incuse
ceinty
nicety
ceinwy
wincey
ceiooz
Eozoic
ceiopr
copier
ceiopt
picoté
poetic
ceiorr
corrie
ceiors
cosier
ceiort
erotic
tercio
ceiorv
voicer
ceiorw
cowrie
ceiorz
cozier
ceioss
cossie
ceiost
cotise
oecist
ceiotx
exotic
ceiotz
zoetic
ceippt
peptic
ceiprs
cripes
Persic
précis
spicer
ceipry
pricey
ceipss
Pisces
ceipst
septic
ceiptu
cup-tie
ceipty
etypic
ceiqru
cirque
ceirrs
cerris
ceirss
crises
ceirst
steric
ceirsu
cruise
crusie
ceirsv
scrive
ceirsz
cizers
ceirtu
cuiter
curiet
uretic
ceirtw
twicer
ceiruv
cruive
ceirvx
cervix
ceisst
citess
ceissu
cuisse
ceissy
cyesis
ceistu
cestui
cueist
cejkoy
jockey
cejnou
jounce
cejoos
jocose
cekkop
kopeck
cekksy
kecksy
ceklmu
muckle
ceklno
enlock
ceklnu
lucken
ceklor
locker
ceklot
locket
ceklru
ruckle
ceklsu
suckle
cekmor
mocker
cekmru
mucker
ceknor
conker
reckon
ceknot
nocket
ceknsu
sucken
cekoor
cooker
cekopt
pocket
cekorr
corker
rocker
cekors
socker
cekort
rocket
cekost
socket
cekpru
pucker
cekpry
rypeck
cekpss
specks
cekpsy
specky
cekrsu
sucker
cekrtu
tucker
cekruy
yucker
cekstu
sucket
cekttu
tucket
cellot
collet
cellou
locule
cellru
culler
celltu
cullet
celmnu
culmen
celmoo
coelom
celmop
compel
celmoy
comely
celmsu
muscle
celmuy
lyceum
celnnu
nuncle
celnor
cornel
celnov
cloven
celnoy
Ceylon
celnru
lucern
celntu
lucent
celnuu
nucule
celnuw
unclew
celoor
cooler
celoot
ocelot
celopp
copple
celopu
couple
celoqu
cloqué
celors
closer
cresol
escrol
celort
colter
lector
celoru
colure
celorv
clover
Velcro®
celost
closet
celosu
coleus
oscule
celosx
scolex
celoty
cotyle
celouv
vocule
celpru
curpel
celpty
yclept
celpuu
cupule
celrru
curler
celrsu
cruels

celrtu
culter
cutler
reluct
celruu
curule
celruv
culver
celruw
curlew
celttu
cutlet
cuttle
cemmru
cummer
cemnoo
come-on
oncome
cemnru
crumen
cemntu
centum
cemoos
comose
cemopu
upcome
cemorr
cremor
cemosy
cymose
cemrtu
rectum
cennor
conner
cennot
nocent
cennru
cunner
cenoor
ceroon
cenoos
coosen
cenopr
crepon
cenopu
pounce
uncope
cenorr
corner
cenors
censor
cenort
cornet
cronet
cenoru
rounce
cenost
centos
cenotu
econut
cenovx
convex

cenovy
convey
covyne
cenrsy
scryne
cenrty
centry
cenruy
curney
censsu
census
censty
encyst
ceoopr
cooper
ceoors
cooser
ceooty
coyote
oocyte
ceoppr
copper
ceoprs
corpse
ceopru
couper
croupe
recoup
ceopty
ectopy
ceoqtu
coquet
ceorrs
scorer
ceorrt
rector
ceorss
crosse
scorse
ceorst
corset
Cortes
coster
escort
scoter
sector
ceorsu
course
crouse
source
ceorsv
corves
ceorsw
escrow
ceortt
cotter
ceortu
couter
croûte
ceortv
corvet
covert
vector

ceortx
cortex
ceosst
cosset
ceossu
scouse
ceottt
octett
ceottu
cuttoe
ceppru
cupper
ceprsu
spruce
cerrsu
curser
cerrsy
scryer
cerssu
cusser
cerssy
cressy
cerstu
cruset
rectus
cersux
cruxes
cersuz
scruze
cerswy
screwy
certtu
cutter
certuv
curvet
cesstu
cestus
cffhuy
chuffy
cffily
cliffy
cffino
coffin
cffinu
cuffin
cffotu
cut-off
offcut
cffrsu
scruff
cffsuy
scuffy
cfhilt
flitch
cfhirt
fricht
cfhity
fitchy
cfhlsy
Flysch
cfiilm
filmic
cfiinn
Finnic

cfiinu
unific
cfiist
fistic
cfilor
frolic
cfilty
clifty
cfimor
formic
cfimot
comfit
cfinot
confit
cfinox
confix
cfiort
fictor
cfistu
fustic
cfkpuu
fuck-up
cflpuu
cupful
cfostu
fustoc
cfrsuy
scurfy
cggloy
cloggy
coggly
cghhou
chough
cghilt
glitch
cghiot
Gothic
cghlou
clough
cghoru
grouch
cghrtu
grutch
cgilny
clingy
glycin
cgilpu
gilcup
cgimno
coming
gnomic
cgimny
gymnic
cginoo
cooing
cginop
coping
cginov
coving
cginry
crying
cglloy
glycol

cglnou
unclog
cgloou
colugo
cgnoou
congou
chhior
chi-rho
chhist
shtchi
chhity
hitchy
chhoot
hootch
chiill
chilli
chiilt
litchi
lithic
chiint
chitin
chiipp
hippic
chiirz
rhizic
chikns
chinks
chiknt
knitch
chikny
chinky
chikor
chikor
chikos
hoicks
chikrs
kirsch
chikst
kitsch
schtik
shtick
chikty
thicky
chilly
chilly
chilmo
holmic
chilnu
unlich
chilor
orchil
chilry
richly
chimnu
Munich
chimny
hymnic
chimrs
chrism
smirch
chimss
schism
chimty
mythic

chinnu
Hunnic
chinop
chopin
phonic
chinot
chiton
chinpy
hypnic
chinru
urchin
chinst
snitch
chintz
chintz
chiopr
Orphic
chiops
sophic
chiopt
photic
chiors
orchis
chiort
rhotic
chiorw
chowri
chiost
Sothic
chiosw
cowish
chiosy
coyish
chiosz
schizo
chippy
chippy
chipry
chirpy
chipsy
physic
scyphi
chipty
pitchy
Pythic
chiqtu
quitch
chirst
Christ
strich
chisst
schist
chistt
stitch
chistu
schuit
chistw
switch
chittw
twitch
chitty
chitty
chivvy
chivvy

chkmoo
Mohock
chknuy
chunky
chkoru
chukor
chkssu
shucks
chlmoo
moloch
chlmuy
muchly
chloos
school
chloot
Clotho
coolth
chlors
schorl
chlost
cloths
chlosu
slouch
chlott
T-cloth
chmmuy
chummy
chmoor
chromo
chmoos
smooch
chmosu
smouch
chmstu
smutch
chnoop
poncho
chnoor
cohorn
chntuu
tuchun
choort
cohort
choosy
choosy
choppy
choppy
chopsy
psycho
chopuy
pouchy
chorsu
chorus
chorwy
chowry
chostu
schout
scouth
chostw
scowth
chotuy
couthy
touchy

chpstu
putsch
chsssu
schuss
chstuy
schuyt
ciiirt
iritic
ciiknw
inwick
ciikst
tisick
ciilmu
cilium
ciilnp
inclip
ciimsv
civism
ciimtv
victim
ciinnu
uncini
ciinor
ironic
oniric
ciinqu
quinic
ciinrt
citrin
nitric
ciinsv
viscin
ciiprs
spiric
ciirss
crisis
ciirtv
vitric
ciisty
cytisi
cijnoo
cojoin
cikkns
knicks
cikkpu
kick-up
ciklno
inlock
ciklry
rickly
ciklsy
sickly
ciklty
tickly
cikmnu
nickum
ciknpu
unpick
ciknpy
pyknic
ciknsu
suck-in
cikntu
tuck-in

ciknyz
zincky
cikorr
corkir
cikosy
yoicks
cikppu
pick-up
cikrtu
Turkic
cikrty
tricky
ciksty
sticky
cillou
loculi
cillsu
cullis
cilmuu
cumuli
cilnou
ulicon
uncoil
cilntu
incult
cilopu
upcoil
cilopy
policy
cilort
lictor
cilosy
cosily
cilotu
coutil
toluic
cilquy
cliquy
cilsuy
sluicy
cimmnu
cummin
cimmos
commis
cimmot
commit
cimmox
commix
cimnno
nincom
cimnnu
nincum
cimnor
micron
cimnou
muonic
cimopy
myopic
cimoru
corium
cimost
sitcom
cimosu
Suomic

cimoty
comity
myotic
cimprs
scrimp
cimpry
crimpy
cimruu
curium
cimsty
mystic
cimsuv
viscum
cinnou
nuncio
cinnoy
incony
cinoos
coosin
cinooz
zoonic
cinopp
coppin
cinopt
pontic
cinort
citron
cinorz
zircon
cinoss
sonics
cinost
tocsin
cinosu
cousin
cinpsy
Cynips
cioort
octroi
cioprs
psoric
cioprt
tropic
ciopst
optics
ciorsu
curios
ciortt
tricot
ciortv
victor
ciostu
coitus
cippsu
cippus
ciprst
script
ciprsy
crispy
cypris
cirrsu
cirrus
cirstt
strict

cirstu
citrus
rictus
rustic
cirtty
yttric
cisstu
cistus
cissuv
viscus
cjnsuu
juncus
cklnou
unlock
cklopu
lock-up
uplock
cklpuy
plucky
ckmopu
mock-up
cknoru
uncork
ckntuu
untuck
ckosty
stocky
ckrstu
struck
ckrsuu
ruckus
clloop
collop
cllooy
coolly
cllors
scroll
clmnou
column
clmopy
comply
clmouu
lucumo
clmpsu
clumps
clmpuy
clumpy
clmsuy
clumsy
clnoou
uncool
clnooy
colony
clnosu
clonus
consul
clnotu
uncolt
clnouw
uncowl
clnruu
uncurl
clooru
colour

cloost
Cloots
clostu
locust
closty
costly
clotty
clotty
clpruu
upcurl
clpstu
sculpt
clrtuy
curtly
clssuu
sulcus
clstuu
cultus
cmmnoo
common
cmmoot
commot
cmmruy
crummy
cmmsuy
scummy
cmnnoo
non-com
cmoopt
compot
cmooss
cosmos
cmoosu
comous
cmorsu
cormus
cmostu
custom
cmosuu
mucous
cmosuy
cymous
cmprsu
scrump
cmpruy
crumpy
cmstuu
scutum
cnnnoo
non-con
cnnopy
pycnon
cnoopu
coupon
cnoort
croton
cnoost
nostoc
oncost
cnoott
cotton
cnooty
coonty
tycoon

cnoovy
convoy
cnoptu
puncto
cnorsu
Cornus
cnoruy
rouncy
cnotuy
county
cnrstu
scrunt
cooorz
corozo
cooprs
scroop
cooptu
cop-out
coopwx
cowpox
coortu
octuor
cooruu
roucou
coppry
croppy
coprsu
corpus
coprty
crypto
copruy
croupy
corrsu
cursor
corsst
T-cross
corstu
scruto
corsuv
corvus
cortuy
outcry
cosstu
costus
custos
costtu
Cottus
costty
Scotty
cottuu
cut-out
cprsuy
cyprus
crrsuy
scurry
crssuu
cursus
ruscus
crstuy
crusty
curtsy
crsuvy
scurvy

ddddeo
dodded
dddeei
eddied
dddeet
tedded
dddeew
wedded
dddego
godded
dddeik
kidded
dddeil
diddle
lidded
dddeir
didder
ridded
dddeiu
duddie
dddeno
nodded
dddeop
podded
dddeor
dodder
ddderu
dudder
ddeeem
deemed
ddeeer
reeded
ddeees
seeded
ddeeew
weeded
ddeefi
defied
ddeefn
defend
ddeegl
gelded
ddeegr
dredge
ddeegs
sedged
ddeegw
wedged
ddeehl
heddle
ddeein
denied
indeed
ddeeir
deride
dièdre
ddeelm
meddle
ddeeln
ledden
ddeelp
peddle
ddeelr
reddle

ddeels
sleded
ddeelu
delude
ddeenp
depend
ddeenr
redden
ddeens
sended
ddeent
tended
ddeenu
denude
dudeen
ddeenw
wended
ddeeor
eroded
ddeeos
eddoes
ddeepr
pedder
ddeerr
redder
ddeert
tedder
ddefil
fiddle
ddeflu
fuddle
ddefnu
funded
ddefor
fodder
ddeggi
digged
ddeggo
dogged
ddegil
gilded
ddegin
dinged
ddegir
girded
ridged
ddeglu
guddle
ddegmo
dodgem
ddegno
dog-end
god-den
ddegor
dodger
red-dog
ddegru
drudge
ddehin
hidden
ddehir
hidder

ddehis
dished
eddish
ddehlo
hoddle
ddehlu
huddle
ddehno
hodden
ddehnu
hudden
ddehoo
hooded
ddeiio
iodide
ddeiit
tidied
ddeiiv
divide
ddeikl
kiddle
ddeikr
kidder
ddeilm
middle
ddeiln
dindle
ddeilo
dildoe
doiled
ddeilp
piddle
ddeilr
riddle
ddeils
slided
ddeilt
tiddle
ddeimm
dimmed
ddeimn
midden
minded
ddeims
desmid
ddeinn
dinned
ddeinr
ridden
rinded
ddeint
tinded
ddeinw
winded
ddeiot
doited
ddeiov
devoid
voided
ddeipp
dipped
ddeitt
ditted

ddeitu
dutied
ddejru
judder
ddelmu
muddle
ddelno
noddle
ddeloo
doodle
ddelot
toddle
ddelpu
puddle
ddelru
ruddle
ddemoo
doomed
ddenno
donned
ddennu
dunned
ddenor
nodder
ddenos
sodden
ddenow
downed
ddenoy
dynode
ddenpu
pudden
ddenru
dunder
ddensu
sudden
ddenuy
undyed
ddeoos
dodoes
ddeoow
wooded
ddeorw
worded
ddeott
dotted
dderru
rudder
ddersu
sudder
dderuw
redwud
ddfily
fiddly
ddfior
fordid
ddhios
oddish
ddhisu
dudish
ddhosy
shoddy
ddhpuu
huddup

ddiikk
dik-dik
ddiims
misdid
ddikno
dodkin
ddilnr
dirndl
ddilty
tiddly
ddimru
dirdum
ddimsu
dudism
ddimsy
smiddy
ddinno
nid-nod
ddinoo
Diodon
ddioos
dosi-do
ddiopy
dipody
ddiors
sordid
ddioty
oddity
ddlpuy
puddly
ddmmuu
dumdum
ddmruu
durdum
ddnoos
odds-on
ddpsuy
spuddy
deeefr
feeder
deeegr
degree
deeehl
heeled
deeeip
deepie
deeejr
jereed
deeekl
keeled
deeeln
needle
deeelp
peeled
deeelt
delete
deeemr
meered
redeem
remede
deeenp
deepen

deeenr
needer
reeden
deeenv
vendee
deeepv
peeved
deeerr
reeder
deeers
seeder
deeerv
reeved
deeerw
weeder
deeery
redeye
deefgl
fledge
deefil
defile
deefin
define
deefir
defier
deeflw
flewed
deeflx
deflex
deefnr
fender
deefnu
unfeed
deefsu
defuse
deefuz
defuze
deefzz
fezzed
deeggi
gidgee
deeggl
gledge
legged
deeggp
pegged
deeghr
hedger
deegij
gidjee
deegiw
wedgie
deegkr
kedger
deegll
gelled
deegln
legend
deeglp
pledge
deeglr
gelder
ledger
redleg

deegls
sledge
deeglu
deluge
deegly
gleyed
deegmm
gemmed
deegmn
menged
deegnn
genned
deegnr
gender
deegnu
dengue
unedge
deegry
greedy
deehlm
helmed
deehlp
helped
deehmm
hemmed
deehnr
herden
deehrs
hersed
deehtw
thewed
deeilr
lieder
relide
relied
deeils
diesel
sedile
deeilv
levied
veiled
deeily
eyelid
deeimp
impede
deeimr
remeid
deeims
demise
Medise
deeinn
indene
deeinr
denier
nereid
renied
deeint
eident
deeinv
endive
veined
deeior
oreide

deeiov
voidee
deeipr
perdie
deeips
espied
deeirs
desire
reside
deeirt
dieter
re-edit
deeirv
derive
deeiss
dieses
seised
deeisv
devise
viséed
deeitx
exited
deejss
jessed
deeknn
kenned
deeksw
skewed
deelmt
melted
deelmy
medley
deelnr
lender
deelnt
dentel
deelnw
wedeln
deelny
needly
deelpp
lepped
deelpy
deeply
deelrv
delver
deelrw
welder
deelst
eldest
steeld
deelsv
delves
deelsw
slewed
deeltt
letted
deeltu
teledu
deelvv
devvel
deemno
omened

deemnr
mender
deemnt
dement
deemot
demote
deempr
premed
deemrt
metred
deemru
demure
deemry
remedy
deemsy
emydes
deenno
donnée
deennp
penned
deennt
dennet
deenop
depone
deenor
re-done
deenot
denote
deenpx
expend
deenrr
render
deenrs
sender
deenrt
tender
tendre
deenru
endure
deenrv
nerved
vender
deenrz
dzeren
deenss
sensed
deenst
sedent
deensu
ensued
deensy
desyne
deentt
detent
netted
tented
deentu
détenu
deentv
vented
deentx
dentex
extend

deenuv
vendue
deenuy
uneyed
deeops
depose
speedo
deeort
teredo
deeotv
devote
deeoxy
ox-eyed
deeppr
repped
deepru
perdue
deepsy
speedy
deeptt
petted
deeptu
depute
deequu
queued
deerrw
redrew
deerst
desert
deersv
versed
deertt
retted
deertv
verdet
deertx
dexter
deervv
revved
deestt
detest
deestv
devest
vested
deestw
stewed
deettv
vetted
deettw
wetted
deffir
differ
defflu
duffel
duffle
deffno
offend
deffor
doffer
deffpu
puffed
deffru
duffer
ruffed

defggi
figged
defggo
fogged
defgir
fridge
defgit
fidget
gifted
defgly
fledgy
defhoo
hoofed
defilo
foiled
definn
finned
definr
finder
friend
defiot
foetid
defirv
fervid
defisx
sexfid
defitt
fitted
defizz
fizzed
defkor
forked
deflno
enfold
fondle
deflor
folder
deflou
defoul
deflow
flowed
deflty
deftly
defluu
dueful
defmor
deform
formed
defnor
Fronde
defnou
fondue
defnru
refund
defoor
roofed
defoot
footed
defoow
woofed
defopu
poufed
defoss
fossed

defrru
furder
furred
defrtu
turfed
defttu
tufted
deggho
hogged
degghu
hugged
deggij
jigged
deggin
edging
deggip
pigged
deggir
digger
rigged
deggiw
wigged
deggjo
jogged
deggju
jugged
degglo
dog-leg
logged
degglu
lugged
deggor
dogger
gorged
deggos
sogged
deggru
grudge
rugged
deggry
dreggy
deggtu
tugged
deghin
hinged
deghop
dog-hep
degiir
dirige
degilm
mid-leg
degiln
dingle
elding
engild
gilden
degilo
goidel
degilr
gilder
girdle
glider
lidger
ridgel

degilu
guiled
degimn
minged
degimt
midget
deginn
ending
ginned
deginr
dinger
engird
ringed
degins
design
dinges
singed
degint
nidget
deginw
winged
deginy
dingey
dyeing
degiop
pie-dog
degirr
girder
degiru
guider
degist
digest
degitw
widget
deglno
golden
deglnu
gulden
lunged
deglny
gylden
deglor
lodger
deglov
gloved
deglsu
sludge
degmmu
gummed
degmru
red-gum
degmsu
smudge
degnow
gowned
degnru
gerund
degnsu
snudge
degopy
pye-dog
degorr
droger

degors
sodger
degoru
drogue
gourde
degost
stodge
degppy
gypped
degrtu
trudge
degstu
degust
degttu
gutted
dehhsu
hushed
dehill
hilled
dehils
shield
dehimr
dirhem
dehino
hoiden
honied
dehinr
hinder
dehins
shined
dehios
hoised
dehiow
howdie
dehipp
hipped
dehirt
dither
dehitt
tithed
dehkoo
hooked
dehksu
husked
dehlno
holden
dehlor
holder
dehlow
howled
dehlps
delphs
dehlpu
upheld
dehlru
hurdle
dehmmu
hummed
dehmny
hymned
dehmot
method
mothed

dehmpu
humped
dehmry
rhymed
dehnor
dehorn
horned
dehnoy
hoyden
dehnru
hurden
dehnsu
unshed
dehnsy
yshend
dehnyy
hydyne
dehopp
hopped
dehors
Rhodes
shoder
dehort
dehort
red-hot
dehosw
showed
dehpsu
pushed
dehrsw
shrewd
dehttu
hutted
deiill
lilied
deiilp
lipide
deiino
iodine
deiins
inside
deiint
indite
deiinv
divine
deiios
iodise
deiipr
pierid
deiipt
pitied
deiirs
irides
irised
deiiss
diesis
deiisx
deixis
deiiyz
Yezidi
deijnx
jinxed
deikln
kindle

deiklo
keloid
deiklt
kilted
deiknp
pinked
deikny
kidney
deiknz
zendik
zinked
deikps
spiked
deikpu
duikep
deillm
milled
deilln
nilled
deillu
illude
deilmn
milden
Mindel
deilmp
dimple
deilms
misled
deilmw
mildew
deilnn
dinnle
linden
deilno
indole
Leonid
deilnr
nirled
deilnt
dentil
deilnw
windle
deiloo
doolie
deilop
diploe
dipole
peloid
deilos
siloed
soiled
deilot
toiled
deilpp
lipped
deilps
dispel
deilpx
diplex
deilrs
slider
deilrv
drivel
deilrw
wilder
deilst
listed
deilsv
slived
deiltt
tilted
titled
deiltu
dilute
deilwy
dewily
widely
wieldy
deimmn
nimmed
deimmr
dimmer
rimmed
deimms
Medism
deimmu
medium
deimno
monied
deimnp
impend
deimnr
minder
remind
deimor
dormie
moider
deimpu
mud-pie
deimrs
dermis
deimss
demiss
deimst
demist
deimsu
medius
deimsv
Vedism
deimtu
tedium
deinno
ondine
deinnp
pinned
deinnr
dinner
deinns
sinned
deinnt
dentin
indent
intend
tinned
deinnu
undine
deinnw
enwind
deinop
pioned
deinos
donsie
no-side
onside
side-on
deinot
ditone
intoed
deinow
Downie®
deinpp
nipped
deinpr
pinder
deinps
spined
deinpt
dip-net
deinpu
uniped
deinrt
rident
tinder
deinru
ruined
deinrv
driven
deinrw
rewind
winder
deinsu
undies
deinsv
vendis
deintu
dunite
united
untied
deintw
twined
deioor
oroide
deioow
woodie
deiopp
doppie
deiopr
period
deiops
poised
deiopt
pioted
podite
deiors
dorise
deiort
editor
tie-rod
triode
deiorv
devoir
voider
deiorw
weirdo
deippp
pipped
deippr
dipper
ripped
deipps
sipped
deippt
tipped
deiprs
spider
spired
deiprt
trepid
deiprz
prized
deipss
pissed
deipsu
upside
deiptt
pitted
deiqtu
quited
deirrs
derris
deirru
durrie
deirrv
driver
deirst
driest
stride
deirsv
divers
deirtu
reduit
deirtv
divert
verdit
deisst
desist
deissu
disuse
deistu
suited
deistv
divest
stived
Vedist
deittw
dewitt
witted
dejlow
jowled
dejmpu
jumped
dejott
jotted
dejttu
jutted
dekloy
yolked
dekmos
smoked
dekmsu
musked
deknot
token'd
deknoy
donkey
deknoz
zonked
deknru
Dunker
deknsu
dusken
dekoot
dooket
dekorw
worked
dekruy
dukery
duyker
dekstu
tusked
dellmu
mulled
dellop
polled
dellor
rolled
dellou
duello
dellwy
lewdly
delmno
dolmen
delmos
seldom
delmou
module
delmoy
melody
delmpu
dumple
plumed
delnno
on-lend
delnoo
noodle
delnor
rondel
delnot
dolent
delnou
louden
nodule
delnow
new-old
delnoz
donzel
delnru
lurden
rundle
delnry
dernly
delnuv
vulned
delnuy
nudely
deloop
looped
poodle
deloos
oodles
deloot
Toledo
delopp
lopped
delopr
polder
delopy
deploy
podley
delors
dorsel
resold
solder
delort
retold
delorw
weldor
delory
yodler
deloss
dossel
delost
oldest
stoled
delosu
souled
delott
dottle
lotted
delotx
extold
deloyy
doyley
delpru
drupel
delpsu
pulsed
delptu
duplet
delpux
duplex
delruy
rudely
demmmu
mummed
demmsu
summed
demnoo
mooned
demnor
moder
morne
demoor
droom
roome
demopp
moppe
demorr
dorme
demoru
remou
demorw
worme
demost
modest
demosu
dumose
demott
domett
demppu
pumped
dempru
dumper
demrru
murder
dennot
tendon
dennou
undone
dennpu
punned
dennru
undern
dennsu
sunned
denoos
nodose
denoow
wooden
denopr
Pernod®
ponder
denort
rodent
to-rend
denoru
undoer
denorv
vendor
denorw
downer
wonder
denory
yonder
denoss
endoss
denost
stoned
denotu
deuton
denotw
wonted

denouw
unowed
denpsu
send-up
unsped
upsend
denptu
pudent
denrsu
sunder
denrtu
retund
runted
turned
denrty
trendy
denruu
unrude
densty
syndet
densuu
unused
densuw
sun-dew
denttu
nutted
deoopp
pooped
deoopx
exopod
deoort
rooted
deoorv
overdo
deoppp
popped
deoppr
dopper
deopps
sopped
deoppt
topped
deoprt
deport
redtop
deoprv
proved
deoprw
powder
deopst
despot
deopsu
pseudo
deoptt
potted
deorrs
dorser
deorrt
dorter
retrod
deorru
ordure
deorrv
drover

deorrw
reword
deorss
dosser
sordes
deorst
strode
deorsu
douser
deorsw
dowser
drowse
deortt
detort
rotted
deortu
detour
douter
outred
deoruv
devour
deorvy
verdoy
deosst
tossed
deossu
soused
deostt
sotted
deostw
dowset
deosux
exodus
deottu
duetto
deotuv
devout
deotux
tuxedo
depppu
pupped
deppsu
supped
depruy
dupery
depsuu
used-up
depsuy
pudsey
depttu
putted
deptuy
deputy
derruy
rudery
derssu
duress
derstu
duster
rusted
derttu
rutted
dffimo
mid-off

dfggoo
fog-dog
dfgiir
frigid
dfgilu
fulgid
dfgoox
dogfox
dfiiny
nidify
dfiirt
trifid
dfikox
kid-fox
dfilno
infold
dfilnu
dinful
dfilor
florid
dfiluv
fulvid
dfimoy
modify
dfirty
drifty
dflnou
unfold
dflnoy
fondly
dflory
dor-fly
dflryy
dry-fly
dfnsuu
fundus
dfoorx
Oxford
dggnou
dugong
dggopu
pug-dog
dghiin
hiding
dghiny
dinghy
dghiop
dog-hip
dghooo
good-oh
dghoop
hopdog
dghotu
dought
dghouy
doughy
dgiilr
ridgil
dgiinn
indign
niding
dgiino
indigo

dgiinp
pidgin
dgiinr
riding
dgiins
siding
dgiinv
diving
dgijou
judogi
dgilnu
ungild
dgilot
diglot
dgimtu
mid-gut
dginno
onding
dginop
doping
pongid
dginor
roding
dginot
doting
dginou
guidon
dginoz
dozing
dginru
during
ungird
dginry
drying
dginsu
dingus
dgiotw
godwit
dgirtu
turgid
dglooy
goodly
dglsuy
sludgy
dgmsuy
smudgy
dgnoor
drongo
dgnoos
godson
dgnoow
go-down
godown
dgnoru
ground
dgnosu
sun-dog
sungod
dgorsu
gourds
dgoruy
gourdy
dgosty
stodgy

dgotuu
dugout
dhiips
hispid
dhilos
oldish
dhilpu
uphild
dhimos
modish
dhinoo
Hindoo
dhinsy
shindy
dhioot
dhooti
dhiopy
hypoid
dhiorr
horrid
dhiost
dotish
dhiosv
dovish
dhirsu
rudish
dhirsy
dryish
dhlooy
dhooly
dhlopu
hold-up
uphold
dhlosu
should
dhnoou
unhood
dhnosu
unshod
dhoooo
hoodoo
dhorsu
shroud
dhortu
drouth
diijnn
djinni
diilmp
limpid
diilop
lipoid
diilos
solidi
diilqu
liquid
diilst
distil
diilty
tidily
diimnu
indium
diimos
iodism

diimou
oidium
diimty
dimity
diinnw
inwind
diinop
Dipnoi
diinox
dioxin
diinrs
indris
diinsv
invis'd
diiost
Idoist
diiott
doitit
diittt
dittit
diklny
kindly
dikmnu
dinkum
dikmsy
mid-sky
diknnu
unkind
dillmy
mildly
dillvy
vildly
dilmor
milord
dilmou
dolium
Idolum
moduli
dilmpy
dimply
dilnnu
dunlin
dilnoo
Idolon
dilnop
diplon
dilntu
indult
dilopt
pot-lid
diloss
dossil
dilost
stolid
diloxy
xyloid
dimnoo
domino
dimnor
Nimrod
dimnsu
nudism
dimoor
dromoi

dimopu
podium
dimors
Dorism
dimost
modist
dimosu
modius
sodium
dimosw
wisdom
dimotu
dim-out
dimoyz
zymoid
dinnos
sindon
dinnuw
unwind
dinoor
indoor
dinooz
zonoid
dinopu
dupion
unipod
dinoru
durion
dinorw
in-word
dinosw
disown
dinoww
window
dinptu
pundit
dinpuw
upwind
wind-up
dinrsu
sundri
dinstu
nudist
dintuy
nudity
untidy
dioops
isopod
dioort
toroid
dioosu
iodous
odious
diootx
toxoid
dioprt
torpid
tripod
diorrt
torrid
diostt
dittos
diostu
studio

diotvy
ivy-tod
dippry
drippy
diprtu
putrid
dipstu
stupid
djlmoy
jymold
djnnoo
donjon
dklsuy
duskly
dknopu
Podunk
dkoooo
koodoo
dkorsy
drosky
dlloop
dollop
dllory
drolly
lordly
dllouy
loudly
dlmoou
modulo
dlmouy
mouldy
dlmruy
drumly
dlnopu
Dunlop
dlnoru
unlord
dlnosu
unsold
dlnotu
untold
dlnuuy
unduly
dloops
podsol
dloopz
podzol
dlooru
dolour
dmnoor
dromon
dmnooy
monody
dmnosu
osmund
dmoors
dromos
dmoosy
sodomy
dmoott
motto'd
dmorsu
dorsum

dmoruz
Ormuzd
dmosuu
dumous
dnnoot
donnot
dnntuu
tundun
dnoors
rondos
dnoosu
nodous
dnortu
rotund
untrod
dnostu
stound
dnostw
stownd
dnosuw
swound
dnosuz
zounds
dnosww
swownd
dnouwy
woundy
dnrsuy
sundry
doooov
voodoo
doopru
uropod
doopry
droopy
doorrs
sordor
doorww
row-dow
dooswy
woodsy
doouuv
voudou
doprsy
dropsy
dorrty
dry-rot
dorssy
drossy
dorstu
stroud
dorswy
drowsy
doruvy
dyvour
dpstuu
dust-up
drstuu
Turdus
drstuy
sturdy
drsuyy
dysury

eeeegg
gee-gee
eeeeht
teehee
eeeept
teepee
eeeepw
peewee
eeeett
tee-tee
eeeeww
wee-wee
eeeffr
effere
eeefft
effete
eeefir
féerie
eeeflr
feeler
eeefnr
enfree
eeefrr
reefer
eeefrz
freeze
eeegmr
emerge
eeegnp
peenge
eeegnr
renege
eeegrs
greese
eeegrz
geezer
eeegtv
'vegete
eeehiz
heezie
eeehlr
heeler
reheel
eeehlt
lethee
eeehnt
ethene
eeehnx
hexene
eeehpr
pheere
eeehps
pheese
eeehpz
pheeze
eeehst
seethe
eeehwz
wheeze
eeeijl
jeelie
eeeikl
keelie

eeeikr
reekie
eeeilr
Leerie
eeeipr
peerie
eeeipw
weepie
eeeity
Eyetie
eeejrr
jeerer
eeejst
jestee
eeekkr
keeker
eeeklr
keeler
eeekmn
meeken
eeeknr
keener
eeekpr
keeper
eeekrs
kreese
seeker
eeellt
leetle
eeelns
Selene
eeelnv
eleven
enlevé
eeelpr
peeler
eeelrr
reeler
eeelss
lessee
eeelst
eel-set
eeelsv
sleeve
eeelty
eyelet
eeemms
sememe
eeemnr
meneer
eeemrs
seemer
eeemst
esteem
mestee
eeemtu
émeute
eeenrs
serene
eeenrt
entrée
eterne
retene

eeenrv
enerve
veneer
eeenss
Essene
eeensz
sneeze
eeentw
weeten
eeeopp
epopee
eeeppr
peeper
eeeprv
peever
preeve
eeeprw
weeper
eeerrt
retree
eeerrv
revere
eeersv
severe
eeertt
teeter
terete
eeervw
weever
eeestt
settee
testee
eeestv
steeve
eeffir
effeir
eeffkl
keffel
eeffot
toffee
eeffsu
effuse
eefgru
refuge
eefhir
heifer
eefhor
hereof
eefiln
feline
eefilr
liefer
relief
eefilt
leftie
eefinr
enfire
ferine
fineer
infere
refine
eefipr
priefe

eefirz
frieze
eefllo
felloe
eefllr
feller
eeflnn
fennel
eeflns
flense
eeflrr
ferrel
eeflrt
felter
reflet
eeflru
ferule
refuel
eeflrx
reflex
eeflry
freely
eefltt
fettle
eefluy
eyeful
eefmno
foemen
eefmtw
fewmet
eefnnr
frenne
eefnru
unfree
eefprr
prefer
eefprt
perfet
eefpty
tepefy
eefqrv
Q-fever
eefrrt
ferret
eefrst
fester
freest
eefrsu
refuse
eefrtt
fetter
eefrtu
feutre
refute
eefrtw
fewter
eefrty
freety
eefstt
eftest
eefszz
fezzes
eeggir
greige

eegglp
peg-leg
eegglr
eggler
legger
eeggor
George
eeggry
eggery
eeghnu
eughen
eeghnw
ewghen
eeghss
ghesse
eegilr
leiger
lieger
eegimr
émigré
régime
eeginn
engine
eegins
seeing
eegint
teeing
eeginy
eyeing
eegirs
sieger
eegirv
grieve
regive
eeglln
leglen
eegllt
leglet
eeglmu
emulge
legume
eeglnr
lenger
eeglnt
gentle
eeglrt
reglet
eeglty
gleety
eegmmn
gemmen
eegmno
genome
eegmnr
germen
eegmnt
tegmen
eegmnu
emunge
eegmrr
merger
eegmuw
mug-ewe

eegnnt
gennet
eegnop
pongee
eegnor
engore
eegnox
exogen
eegnrt
erg-ten
gerent
regent
eegnrv
venger
eegnry
energy
greeny
eegnst
gentes
eegrrt
regret
eegrru
reurge
eegrrv
verger
eegrss
egress
eegrst
regest
eegrsy
geyser
eegrtt
getter
eehinr
herein
inhere
eehint
theine
eehirt
either
eehitv
thieve
eehkls
shekel
eehllr
heller
eehlmt
helmet
eehlnu
unhele
eehlpr
helper
eehlsv
shelve
eehlsw
shewel
eehlwy
wheely
eehmms
emmesh
eehmnp
hempen
eehmns
enmesh
eehmrs
Hermes
eehmst
smeeth
eehmux
exhume
eehnnp
hen-pen
eehnnr
henner
eehnor
hereon
eehnot
eothen
eehnps
sephen
sphene
eehnpw
nephew
eehnrr
Herren
eehnrt
nether
threne
eehnss
sneesh
eehnsy
sheeny
eehorr
Herero
eehors
heroes
eehort
hereto
eehorw
howe'er
eehosx
hexose
eehotw
towhee
eehprs
herpes
Hesper
sphere
eehprt
pether
threep
eehpsy
sheepy
eehrss
sheers
eehrsy
heresy
eehrtt
tether
eehrtw
wether
eehrty
they're
eehsst
theses
eehstw
thewes
eehsty
sheety
eehtvy
they've
eehwyy
wheyey
eehwyz
wheezy
eeiikk
kie-kie
eeiikr
kierie
eeiimn
meinie
eeijnn
jinnee
eeijss
jessie
eeiklp
kelpie
eeikls
selkie
eeiklt
keltie
eeills
eisell
eeillv
vielle
eeillw
wellie
eeilnp
penile
eeilnr
lierne
reline
eeilns
enisle
ensile
nelies
senile
silene
eeilpt
pelite
eeilrr
relier
eeilrs
resile
eeilrv
liever
relive
revile
eeilry
eerily
eeilss
seseli
eeilsx
ilexes
eeiltv
levite
eeilvw
weevil
eeimnr
ermine
eeimns
inseem
eeimnt
emetin
eeimny
meiney
eeimpr
empire
epimer
eeimrs
misère
remise
eeimrt
métier
trémie
eeimss
emesis
missee
eeimst
Semite
eeinnr
nerine
eeinpr
repine
eeinqu
equine
eeinrs
seiner
serein
sirene
eeinrt
entire
nerite
eeinrv
envier
venire
Verein
eeintt
tentie
eeintv
venite
eeintx
extine
eeiors
soirée
eeippy
yippee
eeipqu
équipe
eeiprv
prieve
eeiprx
expire
eeiptt
petite
eeiptw
peewit
eeipty
eye-pit
eeirrs
sirree
eeirrt
étrier
reiter
retire
eeirrv
reiver
verier
eeirrw
rewire
eeirss
series
eeirst
re-site
eeirsv
revise
eeirsz
seizer
eeirtt
ti-tree
eeirvv
revive
eeirvw
review
viewer
eeissv
essive
eeistv
stieve
eejjnu
jejune
eejkrr
jerker
eejnnt
jennet
eejqru
jerque
eejrst
jester
eejrsy
jersey
eejssw
Jewess
eekksy
keksye
eeklmp
kemple
eeklmy
meekly
eeklnn
kennel
eeklnr
kernel
eeklny
keenly
eeklrt
kelter
eeklsy
skeely
sleeky
eekltt
kettle
eeklwy
weekly
eekmnu
unmeek
eekmpr
kemper
eekmrs
kermes
eeknnr
kenner
eeknnt
kennet
eeknot
ketone
eeknrs
skreen
eekorv
revoke
eekppu
upkeep
eekpru
Keuper
peruke
eekrst
streek
eekrsw
skewer
eekrsy
kersey
eellmr
merell
eellnw
newell
eellov
O-level
eellpt
pellet
eellrs
resell
seller
eellrt
retell
teller
eellru
ruelle
eelltv
vellet
eellvy
Y-level
eelmot
omelet
eelmps
semple
eelmpt
pelmet
temple
eelmru
relume
eelmry
merely
eelmst
telesm
eelmsy
seemly
eelmtt
mettle
eelmty
meetly
eelnnt
lenten
eelnnv
vennel
eelnov
elevon
eelnps
pensel
spleen
eelnrt
relent
eelnru
unreel
eelnss
lenses
lessen
eelnst
nestle
eelnsu
unseel
eelntt
nettle
eelnuv
venule
eelnvy
evenly
eelnxy
xylene
eelopp
people
eelopr
eloper
eelors
resole
eelouv
évolué
eelovv
evolve
eelppu
peepul
eelprt
pelter
petrel
eelpry
yelper
eelpst
pestle
eelpsv
pelves
eelpsy
sleepy
eelptt
pettle
eelqsu
sequel
eelrrv
verrel
eelrss
lesser
eelrst
streel

eelrtt
letter
eelrtw
welter
eelruv
velure
eelrvv
vervel
eelssv
selves
vessel
eelstt
settle
eelstv
svelte
eelsty
sleety
steely
eelsuv
evulse
eelsyz
sleezy
eeltvv
velvet
eeltvw
twelve
eemmor
merome
eemmss
semsem
eemmst
stemme
eemnor
moreen
eemnot
toneme
eemnov
enmove
eemnoy
yeomen
eemnss
menses
eemntu
unmeet
eemnyz
enzyme
eemopt
metope
eemorr
roemer
eemort
meteor
remote
eemorv
remove
eemprs
semper
sempre
eemprt
temper
eempry
empery
eempsu
empuse

eemptx
exempt
eemrrt
termer
eemrst
restem
Termes
eemrsu
resume
résumé
eemrsv
vermes
eemssw
mewses
eemstu
mustee
eennoz
enzone
eennpr
penner
eennrt
rennet
tenner
eennst
sennet
eennsu
unseen
eennuv
uneven
eennuy
ennuyé
eenopr
opener
perone
reopen
repone
eenopt
poteen
eenorw
erenow
eenosv
venose
eenotv
voteen
eenotw
townee
eenovz
evzone
eenprt
repent
eenpry
pyrene
eenptu
puntee
eenrrt
renter
eenrrv
nerver
eenrst
resent
eenrsu
ensure
eenrsy
sneery

eenrtt
tenter
eenrtu
neuter
tenure
tureen
eenrtv
venter
ventre
eenrtx
extern
eenrvv
verven
eenrvy
venery
eenstu
tenues
eenstv
steven
eensty
teensy
eensvw
sweven
eenswy
sweeny
eensyz
sneezy
eenttx
extent
eentty
teenty
eentux
exeunt
eentwy
tweeny
eeoppy
pop-eye
eeoprs
repose
eeopsx
expose
exposé
eeoptu
toupee
eeopty
peyote
eeorst
stereo
eeorsv
soever
eeoruv
oeuvre
eeosst
setose
eeostv
vetoes
eepppr
pepper
eeppst
steppe
eeprrs
sperre
eeprru
repure

eeprss
preses
sperse
eeprst
pester
eeprsu
persue
peruse
eeprsv
vesper
eeprsw
spewer
eeprtt
petter
eeprtu
repute
eeprtw
pewter
eeprtx
expert
eeprty
re-type
eepstt
septet
eepsty
steepy
eepswy
sweepy
eepttu
puttee
eeqstu
queest
eequxy
exequy
eerrst
rester
eerrsv
revers
server
verser
eerrtt
terret
eerrtu
ureter
eerrtv
revert
eerrvy
revery
verrey
eerssv
Sèvres
eerstt
setter
street
tester
eerstu
retuse
Sûreté
eerstv
revest
verset

eerstw
stewer
sweert
wester
eerstx
exsert
eersty
reesty
steery
yester
eersvw
swerve
eersvy
severy
eerttt
tetter
eertuv
vertue
eertuy
tuyère
eertvv
vervet
eertvx
vertex
eertwy
twyere
eesstt
sestet
testes
tsetse
eesttu
suttee
eesttx
sextet
eestwy
sweety
effgin
effing
effgir
griffe
effgiy
effigy
effgor
goffer
effilp
piffle
effilr
riffle
effils
siffle
effinr
niffer
effint
infeft
effkoy
off-key
efflmu
muffle
efflop
poffle
efflot
let-off
efflru
ruffle

efflux
efflux
effnoo
one-off
effopu
pouffe
effort
effort
efforx
forfex
effost
offset
set-off
effpru
puffer
effrsu
suffer
effttu
tuffet
efggor
fogger
efginr
finger
fringe
efgiru
figure
efglnu
engulf
efglor
golfer
efgoor
forego
efgorr
forger
efgort
forget
efgorw
gowfer
efhils
elfish
efhirs
fisher
sherif
efhiss
fishes
efhist
fetish
efhlsy
fleshy
shelfy
efhmuy
humefy
efhort
fother
efhrru
Führer
efiint
finite
efiivx
fixive
efikry
fikery

efillr
filler
refill
efillt
fillet
efilmt
flemit
efilno
olefin
efilnt
infelt
efilny
finely
lenify
efilos
filose
efilpp
fipple
efilpr
pilfer
efilrr
rifler
efilrt
filter
lifter
trifle
efilru
ireful
efilry
rifely
efilss
fissle
efilst
itself
stifle
efilsu
fusile
efiltu
futile
efilwy
wifely
efilzz
fizzle
efimrt
fremit
efinnr
finner
efinnu
unfine
efinry
finery
efinst
feints
infest
efinsu
infuse
efinzz
fizzen
efiors
froise
efiorx
orifex
efiost
softie

efiprx
prefix
efirst
sifter
strife
efirtt
fitter
titfer
efirty
ferity
freity
efirux
fixure
efirvy
verify
efirzz
fizzer
efisty
feisty
efkorr
forker
efllot
flotel
efllow
fellow
efllru
fuller
eflmsy
myself
eflnnu
funnel
eflnoy
felony
eflnpu
penful
eflnsu
unself
eflntu
fluent
netful
unfelt
efloot
footle
eflooz
foozle
eflort
floret
lofter
efloru
furole
eflorw
flower
fowler
reflow
wolfer
eflorx
flexor
eflosu
flouse
eflouw
woeful
eflppu
pepful
eflpru
purfle
eflrtu
fluter
eflruu
rueful
eflrux
reflux
eflruy
fleury
eflsuu
useful
efltwy
wet-fly
efluzz
fuzzle
efmnor
enform
efmnot
foment
efmnru
frenum
efmorr
former
reform
efmtuy
tumefy
efnorr
froren
frorne
efnorz
frozen
efnost
soften
efnrtu
turfen
efnryz
frenzy
efnstu
funest
efoorr
roofer
efoort
foetor
footer
refoot
tofore
efoorw
woofer
efoprt
forpet
eforru
furore
eforst
forest
foster
efortu
fouter
foutre
efostu
foetus
efrrsu
surfer
efrrtu
returf
efrruu
fureur
efrssu
fusser
efrttu
tufter
efrtty
fretty
efrtuu
future
efrtux
frutex
efsttu
fustet
egggil
giggle
eggglo
goggle
eggglu
guggle
egggno
eggnog
egghil
higgle
egghor
hogger
egghot
hogget
eggiil
gilgie
eggiip
piggie
eggijl
jiggle
eggijr
jigger
eggiln
gingle
liggen
niggle
eggilo
loggie
eggilr
ligger
eggilt
giglet
eggilu
luggie
eggilw
wiggle
egginr
ginger
nigger
eggirr
rigger
eggjlo
joggle
eggjlu
juggle
eggjor
jogger
eggloo
google
egglor
logger
egglot
goglet
toggle
egglow
woggle
egglru
gurgle
lugger
eggmru
mugger
eggntu
nugget
eggort
gorget
eggrru
rugger
eggrtu
tugger
eghhir
higher
eghhit
eighth
height
eghhsu
sheugh
eghhuw
wheugh
eghiin
hieing
eghiks
skeigh
eghikt
keight
eghils
sleigh
eghinw
hewing
whinge
eghinx
hexing
eghiot
hogtie
eghitw
weight
eghity
eighty
eghlmp
phlegm
eghlnt
length
eghlos
seghol
eghlpu
Guelph
pleugh
eghluy
hugely
eghmmo
megohm
eghnop
hog-pen
eghnos
Goshen
eghnou
enough
eghnru
hunger
eghopr
gopher
eghott
ghetto
eghrsu
gusher
egiiill
gillie
egiilr
girlie
egiimn
gemini
egiinn
ingine
egiinp
pieing
egiinr
girnie
egiint
ignite
egiitw
tie-wig
egijln
jingle
egikln
kingle
egiklr
kilerg
egilln
leglin
lingel
lingle
egillr
grille
egillt
gillet
egillu
ligule
egilmn
mingle
egilmp
megilp
egilmt
gimlet
egilnn
ginnel
egilno
eloign
legion
egilnp
pingle
pin-leg
egilnr
girnel
linger
egilns
single
egilnt
tingle
egilnu
lungie
egilnz
zingel
egilpt
piglet
egilpy
gilpey
egilrs
Glires
grilse
egilru
guiler
ligure
egilst
legist
egiltu
glutei
egimmr
gimmer
megrim
egimnr
germin
egimny
geminy
egimos
egoism
egimpu
guimpe
egimst
stigme
eginnr
enring
ginner
eginns
ensign
eginnu
ingénu
eginop
epigon
pigeon
eginor
ignore
region
eginos
ingoes
soigné
eginow
wigeon
eginpp
pigpen
eginpr
pinger
eginps
gipsen
eginpy
pyeing
eginrr
erring
ringer
eginrs
resign
signer
singer
eginrt
engirt
eginru
rueing
eginrw
winger
eginss
gneiss
eginst
ingest
signet
eginsu
genius
eginsw
sewing
swinge
egintu
gunite
egintw
twinge
eginvx
vexing
eginzz
gizzen
egiopr
porgie
egiors
orgies
egiort
goiter
goitre
egiost
egoist
stogie
egioty
egoity
egippr
grippe
egippy
gyppie
egiprr
griper
egirrv
virger
egirsu
guiser
regius
egirsy
griesy
grysie
egirtv
grivet
egirty
tigery
egjlnu
jungle
egkmsu
muskeg
egllru
guller

eglltu
gullet
eglluy
gulley
eglnnu
gunnel
eglnor
longer
eglnou
lounge
eglnpu
plunge
eglnsu
gunsel
eglntu
englut
gluten
eglnty
gently
eglnuu
unglue
eglooy
gooley
eglopr
proleg
eglops
gospel
eglorv
glover
grovel
eglorw
glower
eglost
goslet
eglosy
gelosy
eglouv
voulge
eglouy
eulogy
eglrtu
gurlet
eglruy
guyler
eglryy
greyly
egltttu
guttle
egltuu
Telugu
egluzz
guzzle
egmnor
monger
morgen
egmnoy
gemony
myogen
egmntu
Gnetum
nutmeg
egmort
gromet

egmoru
morgue
egmosu
ugsome
egmosy
Geomys
egmrtu
tergum
egnnoo
non-ego
egnnou
guenon
egnnpu
pen-gun
egnnru
gunner
egnoor
orgone
egnoot
gentoo
egnooy
gooney
oogeny
egnopr
Progne
egnops
sponge
egnopw
gowpen
egnorv
govern
egnory
eryngo
groyne
egnott
gotten
egnotu
tongue
egnoxy
oxygen
egnpru
repugn
egnpsu
spunge
egnpux
expugn
egnrtu
gunter
gurnet
urgent
egnrty
gentry
egnsuu
ungues
egnuvy
ungyve
egoorv
groove
overgo
egooss
gooses
egoost
stooge

egoosy
goosey
egoppt
peg-top
egoprr
groper
egorrs
groser
egorrw
grower
egorss
ogress
egorst
groset
storge
egorsu
grouse
rugose
egorsy
gyrose
egosty
stogey
egosyz
zygose
egottu
get-out
egotyz
zygote
egouvy
voguey
egprru
purger
egprsu
spurge
egpruw
upgrew
egrttu
gutter
egsstu
gusset
ehhiks
sheikh
ehhirt
hither
ehhnpy
hyphen
ehhrst
thresh
ehhrsu
husher
ehiist
histie
Shiite
ehijsw
Jewish
ehikno
honkie
ehikns
Neskhi
ehikpr
kephir
ehikrs
shriek
shrike

ehilmo
Elohim
ehilmu
helium
humlie
ehilns
elshin
ehilos
isohel
ehilot
eolith
ehilpr
hirple
ehilrs
hirsel
hirsle
relish
ehilrt
lither
ehilsv
elvish
ehilsw
whiles
ehiltv
thivel
ehimms
immesh
ehimnr
menhir
ehimnu
inhume
ehimrt
hermit
mither
ehimru
humeri
ehimst
theism
Themis
ehimtu
humite
ehinor
heroin
Hornie
ehinrs
shiner
shrine
ehinrw
whiner
ehinst
sithen
ehinsw
newish
ehintw
whiten
ehinty
thyine
ehintz
zenith
ehinuv
unhive
ehiopt
Ethiop
ophite

ehiors
hosier
ehiort
heriot
ehiott
hottie
ehiprs
perish
reship
seriph
ehiquy
qui-hye
ehirst
theirs
ehirsv
shiver
shrive
ehirsw
wisher
ehirsx
rhexis
ehirtt
hitter
tither
ehirtv
thrive
ehirtw
wither
writhe
ehirtz
zither
ehisst
shiest
sithes
thesis
ehistt
theist
ehistw
whites
ehittw
tewhit
ehitwy
whitey
ehjops
joseph
ehjors
josher
ehklpt
klepht
ehklwy
whelky
ehknru
hunker
ehkoor
hooker
ehkooy
hookey
ehkors
kosher
ehkorw
howker
ehkory
horkey

ehkrsu
husker
ehllor
holler
ehllsy
shelly
ehllty
they'll
ehlmmu
hummel
ehlmnu
unhelm
ehlmop
phloem
ehlmoy
homely
ehlmpu
Phleum
ehlmty
methyl
ehlnop
holpen
phenol
ehlnpy
phenyl
ehlooy
hooley
ehlopp
hopple
ehlorw
howler
ehlost
hostel
ehlosu
housel
ehlosv
shovel
ehlotw
howlet
thowel
ehlrru
hurler
ehlrsu
lusher
ehlrtu
hurtle
ehlruy
hurley
ehlstt
shtetl
ehlstu
hustle
sleuth
ehlsty
shelty
ehlsvy
shelvy
ehmmru
hummer
ehmnot
moneth
ehmort
mother

ehmrry
rhymer
ehmrsu
musher
ehmruy
rheumy
ehnnru
hen-run
ehnnuw
unhewn
ehnoor
heroon
ehnoov
hooven
ehnopu
euphon
ehnopy
phoney
ehnorr
horner
ehnors
Senhor
ehnort
hornet
throne
ehnost
honest
ehnosu
unshoe
ehnrsu
rushen
ehnrtu
hunter
ehooop
hoopoe
ehoopr
hooper
ehoopy
phooey
ehoort
hooter
ehoorv
hoover
ehoost
soothe
ehoosv
hooves
ehoppr
hopper
ehoprt
pother
thorpe
ehopru
uphroe
ehoptt
Tophet
ehorrs
shorer
ehorrt
rhetor
rother
ehorst
tosher

ehorsv
shover
shrove
ehorsw
shower
ehortt
hotter
tother
ehortv
throve
ehortx
exhort
ehorty
theory
ehortz
zeroth
ehprsu
pusher
ehprsy
sphery
ehpryz
zephyr
ehrrsu
rusher
ehrrsy
sherry
ehrrtu
hurter
ehrrwy
wherry
ehrssu
rhesus
ehrsty
thyrse
ehrtuw
wuther
ehsstu
tusseh
ehssty
shyest
ehstty
Tethys
eiikls
silkie
eiiklt
kiltie
eiiknp
pinkie
eiiksv
skivie
eiilln
nielli
eiillp
illipe
eiilms
simile
eiilmu
milieu
eiilnr
inlier
nirlie
eiilns
inisle

eiilnt
lintie
eiilnv
live-in
eiilot
iolite
eiilpp
lippie
eiilrv
virile
eiilrx
elixir
eiilsv
visile
eiimnn
minnie
eiimnt
intime
eiimst
stimie
eiinnp
pinnie
eiinnt
intine
tinnie
eiinnx
nix-nie
eiinos
ionise
eiinpr
pirnie
eiinpt
pinite
tie-pin
eiinqu
quinie
eiinrt
intire
tinier
eiinss
seisin
eiinsz
seizin
eiintv
invite
eiiprs
Pieris
eiiprt
pitier
eiirss
irises
eiirsv
visier
eiirvz
vizier
eiirwz
wizier
eiistv
visite
eiisvv
visive
eiivzz
vizzie

eijkno
in-joke
eijknr
jerkin
eijknu
junkie
eijllt
jillet
eijlms
Mejlis
eijnno
enjoin
eijnor
joiner
rejoin
eijnru
injure
eijnty
jitney
eijrtt
jitter
eijstu
Jesuit
eikkln
kinkle
eikkoo
kookie
eikllr
killer
eiklly
likely
eiklmn
milken
eiklmr
milker
eiklnn
enlink
eiklns
silken
eiklnt
tinkle
eiklnu
unlike
eiklnv
kelvin
eiklnw
welkin
winkle
eiklrt
kilter
kirtle
eiklsu
Kisleu
eiklsv
Kislev
eikltt
kittle
eikmmr
kimmer
eikmnr
merkin
eikmns
misken

eikmos
Eskimo
eikmrs
kermis
eikmss
kiss-me
eikmst
kismet
eiknno
kinone
eiknoo
nookie
eiknov
invoke
eiknpr
perkin
eiknpy
key-pin
eiknrs
sinker
eiknrt
tinker
eiknrw
winker
eiknsu
sunkie
eiknsv
knives
eikntt
kitten
eikoor
rookie
eikopp
koppie
eikouy
ukiyo-e
eikppr
kipper
eikppt
keppit
eikrrs
risker
eikrss
kisser
krises
eikrst
strike
eikrsv
skiver
eikstw
wisket
eillmo
mollie
eillmr
miller
eillmt
millet
eillmu
illume
eillno
lionel
niello

eillnt
lentil
lintel
eillot
oillet
eillpu
pilule
eillrs
siller
eillrt
rillet
tiller
eillrw
willer
eillst
listel
eillsu
ill-use
eilltt
little
eilltu
tuille
eilltw
willet
eillvy
evilly
lively
vilely
eillwy
willey
eilmmr
limmer
eilmno
moline
eilmnr
limner
merlin
eilmns
simnel
eilmnu
lumine
unlime
eilmny
myelin
eilmor
moiler
eilmot
motile
eilmpp
pimple
eilmpr
prelim
eilmps
simple
eilmpt
limpet
eilmpu
pileum
eilmpw
wimple
eilmpx
implex
eilmrs
smiler

eilmrt
milter
eilmrv
vermil
eilmss
missel
eilmst
mistle
smilet
eilmsu
muesli
eilmsy
milsey
eilmty
timely
eilmzz
mizzle
eilnno
on-line
eilnnt
linnet
eilnnu
unline
eilnoo
loonie
eilnop
pinole
eilnor
neroli
eilnos
esloin
insole
lesion
eilnot
entoil
lionet
Nilote
eilnpp
lippen
nipple
eilnps
pensil
spinel
spline
eilnpt
pintle
eilnpu
line-up
lupine
up-line
eilnrt
linter
eilnst
enlist
listen
silent
tinsel
eilnsv
sliven
snivel
eilnsy
linsey
lysine

eilntt
litten
eilntu
luiten
lutein
untile
eilntv
ventil
eilntw
wintle
eilnty
lenity
eilnuv
unlive
unveil
eilnuy
lunyie
eiloor
oriole
eiloot
oolite
eilops
pilose
eilopt
piolet
polite
eilort
loiter
toiler
eilorv
oliver
violer
eilorw
Lowrie
eilory
oilery
eilosv
solive
eilott
toilet
eilotu
outlie
eilotv
olivet
violet
eilppr
ripple
eilpps
sipple
eilppt
tipple
eilppu
pile-up
eilprs
lisper
pliers
eilprt
triple
eilpry
ripely
eilpss
plissé
eilpst
stipel

6 EIL

eilpsu
  epulis
  eus
  sv
  pelvis
eilptu
  puteli
eilpzz
  pizzle
eilrst
  lister
eilrsv
  silver
  sliver
eilrtt
  litter
  tilter
  titler
eilrtu
  rutile
eilrty
  tilery
eilrvy
  livery
  verily
eilsss
  lisses
eilstt
  stilet
eilstu
  sutile
eilsvw
  swivel
eilswy
  wisely
eilszz
  sizzle
eilttt
  tittle
eilttu
  titule
eilttv
  vittle
eiltty
  titely
eiltvy
  levity
eilvvy
  vively
eilvwy
  viewly
eimmnr
  nimmer
eimmnu
  immune
eimmor
  memoir
eimmrs
  merism
  simmer
eimmru
  immure
eimmrz
  zimmer
eimmst
  semmit
eimnnx
  meninx
eimnoo
  Moonie
eimnop
  impone
eimnor
  merino
eimnos
  eonism
  monies
eimnpt
  piment
eimnrt
  minter
eimnru
  murine
  Nerium
eimnrv
  vermin
eimntt
  mitten
eimntu
  minuet
  minute
  munite
  mutine
eimnty
  enmity
eimnux
  xenium
eimnzz
  mizzen
eimops
  impose
eimopt
  optime
eimors
  isomer
  rimose
eimoss
  mossie
eimost
  somite
eimosu
  mousie
eimosv
  movies
eimosx
  exomis
eimotv
  motive
eimoty
  moiety
eimozz
  mozzie
eimprr
  primer
eimprs
  simper
eimprt
  permit
eimpru
  impure
  umpire
eimpsu
  sepium
eimptu
  impute
eimrrt
  retrim
  trimer
eimrss
  remiss
eimrst
  mister
  smiter
eimrsv
  verism
  vermis
eimrsy
  misery
eimsss
  misses
eimsst
  misset
  tmesis
eimssu
  misuse
eimssx
  sexism
eimsty
  stymie
eimsuv
  musive
eimtyz
  zymite
einnnr
  rennin
einnoo
  ionone
einnot
  intone
einnpr
  pinner
einnpt
  pinnet
einnrs
  sinner
einnrt
  intern
  tinner
einnru
  unrein
einnrw
  winner
einnss
  Nissen
einnst
  sennit
  sinnet
  tennis
einntt
  intent
einntv
  invent
einnty
  ninety
einopr
  orpine
  pioner
einopt
  pointe
  pontie
einopw
  pownie
einopy
  pioney
einorr
  ironer
einors
  senior
  soneri
einort
  norite
  orient
einorv
  renvoi
einoss
  enosis
  essoin
  noesis
  ossein
  sonsie
einost
  Nesiot
einosv
  Nivôse
einosw
  nowise
einott
  tonite
einotw
  townie
einovw
  inwove
einppr
  nipper
einpps
  pepsin
einprs
  sniper
einprt
  nipter
  pterin
einpru
  punier
  purine
  unripe
einpry
  pinery
einpst
  instep
  spinet
  step-in
einpsu
  puisne
  supine
einptt
  pitten
einqsu
  sequin
einqtu
  quinte
einquu
  unique
einquz
  quinze
einrrs
  rinser
einrru
  ruiner
einrst
  insert
  sinter
  Strine
einrsu
  insure
  rusine
  ursine
einrsv
  versin
einrsy
  Erinys
einrtt
  tinter
einrtu
  triune
  uniter
einrtv
  invert
  virent
einrtw
  twiner
  winter
einrty
  nitery
einruw
  unwire
einrvw
  wivern
einrvy
  vinery
einrwy
  winery
einstu
  intuse
  tenuis
einstv
  invest
einstw
  wisent
einsty
  tinsey
einsuw
  unwise
einsux
  unisex
einswy
  sinewy
  winsey
eintty
  entity
einuvw
  unwive
eioort
  toorie
eioost
  otiose
eioprs
  poiser
eiopru
  pourie
eiopss
  possie
eiopst
  postie
  sopite
eioptt
  tiptoe
eiorrs
  rosier
eiorrt
  rioter
eiorst
  sortie
  tiroes
eiorsv
  virose
eiorsx
  orexis
eiorsy
  osiery
eiostv
  soviet
eiottt
  tottie
eiottu
  toutie
eiotuv
  outvie
eiotvv
  votive
eipprr
  ripper
eipprs
  sipper
eipprt
  tipper
eippru
  purpie
eipprz
  zipper
eippst
  sippet
eipptt
  tippet
eipqtu
  piquet
eiprrz
  prizer
eiprst
  esprit
  priest
  Pteris
  sitrep
  sprite
  stripe
eiprsu
  uprise
eiprsw
  swiper
eiprtt
  pitter
eiprtv
  privet
eiprtx
  extirp
eiprty
  pyrite
eiprxy
  expiry
eipsss
  sepsis
  speiss
eipsst
  stipes
eipssw
  swipes
eipswy
  swipey
eipttu
  puttie
eiqrsu
  risque
  risqué
  squier
  squire
eiqrtu
  requit
eiqruv
  quiver
eiqtuy
  equity
eirrtt
  ritter
  territ
eirrtw
  writer
eirrvy
  rivery
eirrzz
  rizzer
eirsst
  resist
  sister
eirssu
  issuer
  uresis
eirstt
  sitter
  triste

eirstv
stiver
strive
trevis
verist
eirstw
sweirt
eirsvv
vivers
vivres
eirttt
titter
eirttv
trivet
eirttw
witter
eirtuv
virtue
eirtvy
verity
eisstt
testis
eisstu
tissue
eisstx
sexist
eistty
tystie
eisuvz
suivez
eitttx
tettix
ejklsu
Seljuk
ejknru
junker
ejkntu
junket
ejlort
jolter
ejlorw
jowler
ejlost
jostle
ejlstu
justle
ejmost
jetsom
ejmpru
jumper
ejnost
jetson
ejnott
jetton
ejorss
josser
ejortt
jotter
ejottu
outjet
ekllsy
skelly
eklmmu
kümmel
eklmsu
muskle
eklnos
kelson
sloken
eklnru
runkle
ekloor
looker
eklowy
low-key
eklrru
lurker
ekmnoy
monkey
ekmnru
murken
ekmoop
mopoke
ekmors
smoker
ekmstu
musket
eknnor
kronen
eknnot
nekton
eknnsu
sunken
eknntu
unkent
eknops
spoken
eknorr
kroner
eknorw
knower
wroken
eknory
yonker
eknouy
unyoke
eknptu
unkept
eknrtu
Tunker
eknstu
sunket
ekoort
retook
ekoprr
porker
proker
ekorrw
rework
worker
ekorry
yorker
ekorst
stoker
stroke
ekortx
trek-ox
ekorwy
ywroke
ekosst
stokes
ekrrsy
skerry
skryer
ekrstu
tusker
ekrtuy
turkey
ekruvy
kurvey
elllor
loller
ellloz
lozell
ellmow
mellow
ellmru
muller
ellmsy
smelly
ellmtu
mullet
ellmuv
vellum
ellmuy
mulley
ellnop
pollen
ellnor
enroll
ellnov
vellon
ellnow
Nowell
ellnoy
lonely
ellnsu
sullen
ellnsy
snelly
ellnuu
lunule
ellnuw
unwell
ellopr
poller
ellops
ellops
ellopx
pollex
ellorr
roller
ellors
soller
sorell
ellort
toller
ellost
tolsel
ellosy
solely
ellovy
lovely
volley
ellowy
yellow
ellpru
puller
ellptu
pullet
ellpuw
upwell
ellpuy
pulley
ellstu
Tellus
elmmop
pommel
elmmos
Moslem
elmmpu
pummel
elmnor
merlon
elmnos
solemn
elmnot
loment
melton
elmnoy
lemony
myelon
elmnpu
lumpen
plenum
elmoop
pomelo
elmopu
pumelo
elmopy
employ
elmors
morsel
elmost
molest
elmosu
mousle
elmosy
smoyle
elmott
mottle
elmoty
motley
elmouv
volume
elmoxy
oxymel
elmppu
peplum
elmpru
lumper
replum
rumple
elmrty
myrtle
termly
elmssu
mussel
elmtuu
mutule
elmtuy
mutely
elmuzz
muzzle
elnnos
nelson
elnnru
runnel
elnntu
tunnel
elnoos
loosen
elnoot
looten
elnopt
lepton
elnopu
loupen
elnopy
openly
poleyn
elnort
lentor
elnoss
lesson
elnost
stolen
telson
elnosu
ensoul
nousle
Olenus
elnosv
sloven
elnouv
unlove
elnouz
zonule
elnovy
lenvoy
elnozz
nozzle
elnppu
luppen
elnpst
splent
elnptu
penult
elnpty
plenty
elnrsu
nursle
elnrtu
runlet
elnruu
unrule
elnruz
luzern
elnssu
unless
elnsxy
lynxes
elnttu
lutten
nutlet
elntxy
nextly
elnuzz
nuzzle
eloopr
looper
eloort
looter
retool
rootle
eloosv
looves
eloosw
woosel
eloosz
zeloso
eloott
tootle
eloppp
popple
eloppr
lopper
propel
elopps
peplos
eloppt
topple
eloppu
poulpe
eloppy
polype
eloprr
proler
eloprs
splore
eloprt
petrol
eloprv
plover
eloprx
plexor
elopry
pelory
elopsu
souple
eloptt
pottle
eloptu
tupelo
elorrs
sorrel
elorrw
worrel
elorss
lessor
elorst
ostler
sterol
torsel
elorsv
solver
elorsy
sorely
elortt
tolter
elortu
elutor
outler
elortv
revolt
elortw
trowel
wortle
elorty
troely
eloruv
louver
louvre
velour
elorvw
wolver
elorvy
overly
volery
elorwy
lowery
owlery
elossu
louses
soleus
elostu
solute
tousle
elostw
lowest
elosty
tolsey
elosvw
wolves
elosxy
xylose
eloszz
sozzle
elottu
let-out
outlet
elotty
tylote
elotuv
volute
elotuz
touzle
elotwy
owelty
elotyz
tolzey
elowyy
yowley

elppru
pulper
purple
repulp
elppsu
peplus
supple
elpquu
pulque
elprru
purler
elprty
peltry
pertly
elpruv
pulver
elpruy
purely
elpssu
pussel
elpsuv
Vulpes
elpsux
plexus
elpsuy
spulye
elpuzz
puzzel
puzzle
elrssu
russel
elrstu
luster
lustre
result
rustle
sutler
ulster
elrsuy
surely
elrttu
turtle
elrtty
tetryl
elruwy
wurley
elsstu
tussle
elssty
slyest
elsttu
suttle
elstty
stylet
eluwzz
wuzzle
emmmot
mommet
emmmru
mummer
emmnno
Memnon
mnemon
emmnot
moment
montem
emmntu
mentum
emmory
memory
emmosu
mousmé
emmoyz
zymome
emmpru
mumper
emmrru
rummer
emmrsu
summer
emmsuu
museum
emnoor
mooner
emnopy
eponym
emnors
sermon
emnort
mentor
montre
emnost
Ostmen
emnoty
etymon
emnoxy
exonym
emnpsu
pensum
emnrsu
Mensur
emnssu
sensum
emoorr
roomer
emoors
morose
emoort
mooter
emooss
osmose
emoppr
mopper
emoppt
moppet
emoppy
pompey
emoprr
romper
emoprs
Merops
emoprt
trompe
emoqsu
mosque
emorrt
termor
tremor
emorrw
wormer
emorst
motser
emorsu
mouser
emortu
mouter
emossu
mousse
smouse
emosuy
mousey
emottt
motett
emppru
pumper
emprru
Rumper
empssu
mess-up
empstu
septum
emrruy
murrey
emrsss
Messrs
emrstu
muster
stumer
emrttu
mutter
emssty
system
ennnop
pennon
ennopt
ponent
ennoru
neuron
ennorw
renown
ennost
sonnet
stonen
tenson
ennosv
ven'son
ennotw
newton
ennotz
tenzon
ennpru
punner
ennptu
punnet
unpent
ennrru
runner
ennrst
Nernst
ennrtu
runnet
unrent
ennruw
wunner
ennstu
unnest
unsent
ennsuw
unsewn
ennttu
untent
enntuu
untune
enoooz
Eozoon
enoors
seroon
enoort
enroot
enoosz
snooze
enootw
one-two
enoppu
unpope
enoprr
perron
enoprs
person
enopru
unrope
enoprv
proven
enopry
pyoner
enopst
pontes
posnet
enoptt
potent
enopwy
powney
enorrs
snorer
sorner
enorry
ornery
enorss
sensor
enorst
Nestor
stoner
tensor
enorsw
worsen
enortt
rotten
to-rent
enorvy
renvoy
enosst
seston
tossen
enossw
sowens
enostt
ostent
teston
enostx
sexton
enosuv
venous
enottu
tenuto
Teuton
enottw
tow-net
enpptu
pent-up
enprru
pruner
enprst
sprent
enprsu
spurne
enprtu
punter
enpruy
penury
enpstu
unstep
enpttu
putten
enptuw
unwept
enrrsu
nurser
enrrtu
return
turner
enrstu
unrest
enrstw
strewn
enrsty
sentry
enrsuu
unsure
enrttu
nutter
enrtuu
untrue
enruzz
nuzzer
enrvwy
wyvern
ensstu
sunset
enttwy
twenty
eoopps
oppose
eooprs
porose
eooprt
Pooter
eoopst
stoope
eoorrt
rooter
torero
eoortt
tooter
eopppr
popper
eopppt
poppet
eopprr
proper
eopprt
topper
eoppry
popery
pyrope
eoprrs
proser
eoprrt
porter
report
eoprru
pourer
eoprrv
prover
eoprry
ropery
eoprst
poster
presto
repost
eoprsu
poseur
souper
uprose
eoprsy
osprey
eoprtt
potter
eoprtu
pouter
troupe
eoprtw
powter
eoprtx
export
eoprty
poetry
eopruv
up-over
eopsst
posset
eopssu
spouse
eopstx
sexpot
eopttu
toupet
eoqrtu
quoter
roquet
torque
eoqstu
quotes
eorrrt
rorter
terror
eorrry
orrery
eorrss
rosser
eorrst
resort
roster
sorter
storer
eorrsu
rouser
eorrsw
worser
eorrsy
rosery
eorrtt
retort
rotter
torret
eorrtu
retour
router
tourer
eorrtv
trover
eorrzz
rozzer
eorsst
sortes
tosser
eorssu
serous
eorstu
ouster
souter
touser
trouse
eorstv
stover
strove
eorstw
sowter
stower
stowre
towser
eorsty
oyster
rosety
storey
tyroes
eorstz
zoster
eorsww
wowser
eorttt
totter
eorttu
touter

eorttw
wet-rot
eorttx
extort
eortvx
vortex
eortwy
towery
eoruvy
voyeur
eosssu
souses
eosstt
set-tos
eossvw
vowess
eosttu
outset
set-out
epppry
preppy
eppptu
puppet
epprsu
supper
eppstu
step-up
eprrsu
purser
eprrsy
spryer
eprsst
sperst
eprstu
uprest
eprsuu
pursue
eprttu
putter
eprtty
pretty
eprtuu
puture
epruvy
purvey
errstu
rustre
errsuu
usurer
errsuy
surrey
errttu
rutter
turret
ersset
stress
ersstu
russet
tusser
erssty
syrtes
tressy
erssuv
versus

erstuu
suture
uterus
erstuv
turves
erstuy
surety
erstvy
vestry
erstxy
xyster
ersuvy
survey
esttuy
suetty
fffluy
fluffy
ffgino
offing
ffhiis
Fifish
ffhios
offish
ffhiwy
whiffy
ffhoop
hop-off
ffhors
shroff
ffiint
tiffin
ffillo
ill-off
ffillu
fulfil
ffilot
filfot
ffiltu
fitful
ffimnu
muffin
ffinpu
puffin
ffinru
ruffin
ffinsy
sniffy
ffiopr
rip-off
ffiopt
tip-off
ffiost
soffit
ffipsy
spiffy
ffiqsu
squiff
ffisux
suffix
ffloty
fylfot
fflpuy
pluffy

ffnoru
run-off
ffnsuy
snuffy
ffopsy
spoffy
ffoptu
offput
put-off
ffrruu
furfur
ffstuy
stuffy
fggiis
fisgig
fggiiz
fizgig
fggory
froggy
fghilt
flight
fghirt
fright
fghotu
fought
fgiiln
filing
fgiinn
fining
fgiinr
firing
fgiinx
fixing
fgilnu
ingulf
fgilny
flying
fgiluy
uglify
fginox
foxing
fginry
frying
fgjluu
jugful
fglmuu
mugful
fgloru
fulgor
fgnory
gryfon
fgnsuu
fungus
fgoort
forgot
fhiiks
fikish
fhiins
finish
fhilty
filthy
fhimuy
humify

fhirst
shrift
fhirtt
thrift
fhissu
hussif
fhisty
shifty
fhlopy
hop-fly
fhlosu
floush
fhlsuy
flushy
fhooor
forhoo
fhoorw
forhow
fhortu
fourth
fhorty
forthy
frothy
fhorwy
forwhy
fhpruy
furphy
fiiknr
firkin
fiilln
infill
fiillp
fillip
fiilvy
vilify
fiimnr
infirm
fiimny
minify
fiimst
misfit
fiinor
fiorin
fiitxy
fixity
fiivvy
vivify
fijlor
frijol
fiklsy
flisky
fiknos
finsko
fikrsy
frisky
fillpu
upfill
fillry
frilly
filluw
wilful
filmou
folium

filmry
firmly
filmsy
flimsy
filnor
florin
filnow
inflow
filnsu
sinful
filntu
tinful
filnty
flinty
filnux
influx
filort
firlot
filorv
frivol
filoss
fossil
filptu
uplift
fimnor
inform
fimnoy
omnify
fimnru
unfirm
fimnuy
munify
fimoss
Sofism
fimssu
Sufism
finoos
foison
finort
forint
finorx
fornix
finosu
fusion
finoty
notify
finsty
snifty
fioprt
forpit
profit
fiorrt
forrit
fiorst
fortis
fiorty
Torify
fiossy
ossify
fiottu
fit-out
outfit
fipruy
purify

fiptyy
typify
firstt
strift
firtuy
fruity
firyzz
frizzy
fjlouy
joyful
fklosy
folksy
fknoty
konfyt
flloow
follow
fllouy
foully
flmnou
muflon
flmoor
formol
flnoou
unfool
flnoow
flow-on
flnruu
unfurl
urnful
floosy
floosy
floouz
zufolo
flooyz
floozy
floppy
floppy
floptu
potful
flopuu
foul-up
flopuw
upflow
floruy
floury
flossy
flossy
flosty
softly
flotuy
outfly
flpruu
upfurl
flpruy
purfly
flrruy
flurry
fmnoru
unform
fmosuu
fumous
fmpruy
frumpy

fnooru
unroof
fnostu
unsoft
fnrtuu
unturf
fooprs
proofs
foorss
fossor
footux
outfox
forruw
furrow
forstw
frowst
forsty
frosty
forsuu
rufous
forswy
frowsy
fortyy
Toryfy
forwyz
frowzy
gggiit
Giggit
gggily
giggly
gggloy
goggly
gggory
groggy
gghino
hoggin
gghnou
gung-ho
ggiijj
jigjig
ggiinp
piggin
ggiinv
giving
ggiirr
gri-gri
ggijjo
jig-jog
ggikno
gingko
ginkgo
ggilno
ogling
ggilnu
luging
ggilny
niggly
ggiloo
gigolo
ggilot
giglot
ggilwy
wiggly

gginno
  nig-nog
  noggin
gginor
  goring
  gringo
gginru
  urging
ggioor
  gorgio
ggitwy
  twiggy
ggjjuu
  jug-jug
gglloo
  loglog
gglooo
  googol
gglooy
  googly
ggmosy
  smoggy
ggnoor
  gorgon
ggorst
  troggs
ggrruu
  gru-gru
ggstuy
  stuggy
ghhhit
  highth
ghhily
  highly
ghhipu
  high-up
ghhosu
  shough
ghhotu
  though
ghiinr
  hiring
ghiknt
  knight
ghilno
  holing
ghilny
  nighly
ghilpt
  plight
ghilst
  lights
  slight
ghilsu
  gluish
ghimno
  homing
ghimty
  mighty
ghinst
  nights
ghinty
  nighty
  thingy
ghiopz
  phizog
ghiors
  ogrish
ghiort
  righto
ghiosy
  goyish
ghipty
  ypight
ghiqtu
  quight
ghirtw
  wright
ghistt
  tights
ghittw
  twight
ghloos
  golosh
ghlopu
  plough
ghlosu
  slough
ghlotu
  log-hut
ghmotu
  mought
ghmpru
  grumph
ghnnuu
  unhung
ghnort
  throng
ghnosu
  shogun
ghnotu
  nought
ghnruy
  hungry
ghnsuy
  gun-shy
ghoors
  sorgho
ghortu
  trough
ghortw
  growth
ghoruy
  roughy
ghostu
  sought
ghosty
  ghosty
ghpsuu
  upgush
giikln
  liking
giiknr
  girkin
giikns
  skiing
giiknv
  viking
giilmn
  liming
giilnn
  lignin
  lining
giilnr
  riglin
giilnt
  tiling
giilnv
  living
giilor
  oil-rig
giimnn
  mining
giimnt
  timing
giinnn
  inning
giinor
  origin
giinpp
  piping
giinpw
  wiping
giinrs
  rising
giinrt
  tiring
giinrv
  virgin
giinrw
  wiring
giinsz
  sizing
gijlnu
  jungli
gijlny
  jingly
giklny
  kingly
giknnu
  unking
giknop
  poking
giknoy
  yoking
gillnu
  ulling
gilloo
  Loligo
gillor
  rigoll
gillot
  ill-got
gilluy
  uglily
gilmnu
  lignum
gilmry
  grimly
gilnoo
  logion
gilnop
  poling
gilnor
  loring
gilnos
  losing
gilnot
  lingot
  tiglon
  toling
gilnov
  loving
gilnow
  lowing
gilnpu
  plug-in
  puling
gilnpy
  plying
gilnru
  ruling
gilnsy
  singly
gilntu
  luting
  ungilt
gilnty
  tingly
gilory
  gorily
gilrsy
  grisly
gilrty
  trigly
giltuy
  guilty
giltyz
  glitzy
gimnov
  moving
gimnow
  mowing
gimnoy
  ignomy
gimnpu
  impugn
gimnru
  ingrum
gimnsu
  musing
gimors
  simorg
gimosy
  yogism
gimotu
  gomuti
gimrsu
  simurg
ginnoo
  gonion
ginnos
  nosing
ginnow
  woning
ginnoz
  zoning
ginnru
  urning
ginntu
  tuning
ginoos
  isogon
ginoow
  wooing
ginopr
  proign
  roping
ginops
  posing
ginors
  grison
  signor
ginort
  trigon
ginorv
  roving
ginoss
  gnosis
ginost
  stingo
ginosw
  sowing
ginotu
  outing
ginotw
  towing
ginoty
  toying
ginppu
  upping
ginprs
  spring
ginpry
  prying
ginpsy
  pigsny
  spying
ginptu
  pig-nut
ginpty
  typing
ginrru
  runrig
ginrst
  string
ginrtu
  ungirt
ginrty
  trying
  tyring
ginsty
  stingy
ginsuu
  unguis
ginsux
  six-gun
giopss
  gossip
giopst
  spigot
giorru
  rigour
giortu
  rig-out
gioruv
  vigour
giostu
  giusto
gippry
  grippy
gipsty
  pigsty
girtty
  gritty
gjlnuy
  jungly
gjnruu
  gurjun
gkmoou
  gomoku
gllmuy
  glumly
gllnoy
  longly
glloop
  gollop
glmnoo
  mongol
glmooy
  gloomy
glmpsu
  glumps
glmpuy
  glumpy
glmruy
  grumly
glmsuy
  smugly
glnnoo
  long-on
glnooo
  oolong
glnoos
  so-long
glnoou
  oulong
glnpuu
  unplug
glnsuy
  snugly
glooоy
  oology
gloory
  grooly
gloosw
  go-slow
gloptu
  putlog
glorwy
  growly
glossy
  glossy
glsuuv
  vulgus
gmnnoo
  gnomon
gmnost
  'mongst
gmoopr
  pogrom
gmootu
  gomuto
gmpruy
  grumpy
gmpsuy
  gypsum
gnnouw
  ungown
gnnsuu
  unsung
gnoort
  trogon
gnoppu
  oppugn
  pop-gun
gnopsy
  spongy
gnoptu
  pot-gun
gnorst
  strong
gnorty
  Trygon
gnotuu
  outgun
gnprsu
  sprung
gnrstu
  strung
gnstuu
  Tungus
goooor
  gooroo
goopst
  stop-go
goortt
  grotto
goorvy
  groovy
gopruw
  upgrow
gopruy
  groupy
gorrtu
  turgor
gorsuu
  rugous
gorsuy
  gyrous
gorttu
  rotgut
gortty
  grotty
gortuy
  grouty

gostuy
gousty
gsyyyz
syzygy
hhissy
shyish
hhistw
whisht
hhmmuu
humhum
hhmrty
rhythm
hhoooy
yo-ho-ho
hhoosw
whoosh
hhrstu
thrush
hiimms
mishmi
hiimns
minish
hiimps
impish
hiimss
Shiism
hiimst
mishit
hiinps
inship
hiintw
inwith
within
hiirst
Tishri
hikmuz
muzhik
hiknrs
shrink
hikssy
skyish
hikswy
whisky
hilloy
holily
hillpu
uphill
hillrs
shrill
hillrt
thrill
hillwy
whilly
hilmos
holism
hilmow
whilom
hilmoy
homily
hilmsu
mulish
hilmsy
hylism

hilnpt
plinth
hilnty
thinly
hiloot
tholoi
hilops
polish
hilost
holist
hilosw
owlish
hilpst
spilth
hilssy
slyish
hilstw
whilst
hilsty
hylist
himmsu
Humism
himmsy
shimmy
himmwy
whimmy
himnoy
hominy
himnsu
munshi
himops
mopish
Ophism
himors
morish
Romish
himprs
shrimp
himstu
Humist
himsty
smithy
himswy
whimsy
hinnsy
shinny
hinntu
thin'un
hinnwy
whinny
hinoop
inhoop
hinops
siphon
hinost
Shinto
tonish
hinpsu
punish
unship
hinpsx
sphinx
hinrsu
inrush

hinstu
shut-in
hinsty
shinty
hinsuv
Vishnu
hinsuw
unwish
hioosv
shivoo
hiopps
popish
shippo
hioprt
trophi
hiopst
pithos
hiopsy
physio
hiosty
toyish
hiottu
outhit
hippsu
hippus
uppish
hippwy
whippy
hiprst
thrips
hiqssu
squish
hirrwy
whirry
hirstt
thirst
T-shirt
hirsty
shirty
thyrsi
hirtty
thirty
hisswy
swishy
histty
stithy
hjnnoy
johnny
hknoou
unhook
hknrsu
shrunk
hknsuu
unhusk
hkoopu
hook-up
hkossy
Hyksos
hlloow
hollow
hllowy
wholly
hllsuy
lushly

hlmoty
thymol
hlmpuy
phylum
hlnouy
unholy
hloost
tholos
hlopss
splosh
hlopsy
poshly
hloruy
hourly
hlossy
sloshy
hlostu
tholus
hlpruu
uphurl
hlpsuy
plushy
hlssuy
slushy
hmmmuu
hummum
hmmsuu
hummus
hmnopy
nympho
hmnpuy
hypnum
hmoopr
morpho
hmoost
smooth
hmoruu
humour
hmosty
mythos
hmosuu
humous
hmotuy
mouthy
hmpruy
murphy
hmptuy
humpty
tumphy
hmstuy
mythus
thymus
hmtuyz
zythum
hnnoop
phonon
hnoopt
photon
hnoopu
unhoop
hnoort
thoron
hnooru
honour

hnopsu
nosh-up
hnopsy
Hypnos
syphon
hnopty
phyton
python
Typhon
hnorsu
onrush
hnortw
thrown
hnorty
rhyton
thorny
hnostu
unshot
hnotwy
why-not
hnrtuu
unhurt
hnstuu
unshut
hooooy
yoo-hoo
hooptt
hotpot
hoorrr
horror
hooruz
huzoor
hoossw
swoosh
hootty
toothy
hootuw
tu-whoo
hoppsy
shoppy
hoprty
trophy
hopssy
hyssop
sposhy
hopstu
Pushto
tophus
upshot
horsty
hostry
shorty
hortwy
worthy
hosttu
stouth
hotuyy
youthy
hprssu
sprush
hprsuu
uprush
hpstuu
Pushtu

hpstuy
typhus
hrsttu
thrust
hrttuy
truthy
iiimrt
miriti
iiirst
iritis
iijmny
jiminy
iikknr
kirkin'
iikmns
simkin
iiknpp
pipkin
iiknss
siskin
iikost
oikist
iikott
titoki
iillmu
Lilium
iillot
til-oil
iilloy
oilily
iillpu
illupi
iillwy
wilily
iilmno
nim-oil
iilnnu
inulin
iilnov
violin
iilnrt
nirlit
iilnst
instil
iilpst
pistil
iilrwy
wirily
iilstu
ulitis
iilttw
twilit
iimmnu
minium
iimnno
minion
iimnos
Ionism
iimnou
ionium
iimoss
miosis
iimsss
missis

iimstt
timist
iinnop
pinion
iinnpy
Pinyin
iinntu
Innuit
iinorv
virion
iinost
Ionist
iinosv
vision
iinppp
pippin
iinprt
pirnit
iinptx
pinxit
iinsst
insist
iinttu
intuit
iinttw
nitwit
iiorss
Osiris
iiostt
otitis
iiprst
spirit
iiprtu
pituri
iirrtt
tirrit
iirssu
Sirius
ijkmou
moujik
ijknos
joskin
ijlmpy
jimply
ijnoru
junior
ijnruy
injury
ijrstu
jurist
ikkorr
korkir
ikkuuy
kikuyu
ikllsy
skilly
iklltu
killut
iklnnu
unlink
iklnoo
look-in
iklnou
ulikon

6 IKL

iklnpu
link-up
iklnsy
slinky
iklnty
tinkly
iklssu
suslik
iklttu
kittul
ikltty
kittly
ikmnoo
kimono
ikmnor
mikron
morkin
ikmnru
rumkin
ikmors
Morisk
ikmprs
skrimp
ikmpsy
skimpy
ikmrsy
smirky
ikmssu
kumiss
iknnsy
skinny
ikkntu
unknit
iknopt
inkpot
iknorw
inwork
work-in
iknptu
upknit
iknrsu
ski-run
iknssu
unkiss
ikoopt
pookit
ikoptu
poukit
ikqruy
quirky
ikrssu
Russki
ikrstu
turkis
iksvvy
skivvy
illmou
Lolium
illmsy
slimly
illnoy
lionly
illnpu
pull-in

illnuw
unwill
illopw
pillow
illort
trillo
illoww
willow
illptu
up-till
illpuv
pulvil
illqsu
squill
illsty
stilly
illsuv
villus
illtwy
twilly
ilmmsu
Muslim
ilmnou
moulin
ilmnru
murlin
ilmnsu
muslin
ilmoss
lissom
ilmosu
limous
ilmotu
ultimo
ilmppy
pimply
ilmpry
primly
ilmpsy
simply
ilmrsy
lyrism
ilmrty
trimly
ilmssy
slimsy
ilmstu
litmus
ilmsuv
Milvus
ilmtuu
tumuli
ilmyzz
mizzly
ilnoot
lotion
ilnopp
poplin
ilnops
slip-on
ilnopt
pontil
ilnoqu
quinol

ilnost
tonsil
ilnosu
insoul
ilnotu
nut-oil
oil-nut
ultion
ilnotw
Wilton
ilnpru
purlin
ilnpst
splint
ilnpuy
punily
ilnrty
nitryl
ilnstu
insult
sunlit
iloort
loriot
iloost
solito
ilooyz
oozily
iloppy
polypi
iloprx
prolix
ilopry
ropily
ilopst
pistol
postil
spoilt
ilopsu
pilous
ilopsx
oxslip
iloptu
loupit
ilopty
polity
iloqru
liquor
ilorsy
rosily
ilossu
ulosis
ilostw
lowsit
ilottw
wittol
ilppry
ripply
ilppsu
slip-up
ilppsy
slippy
ilpptu
pulpit

ilprty
triply
ilpttu
uptilt
ilrstu
trisul
ilrsty
lyrist
ilrswy
swirly
ilrtwy
twirly
ilsttu
lutist
ilstty
stilty
ilstuu
lituus
ilstwy
wistly
immnos
monism
nomism
'simmon
immnou
omnium
immoos
simoom
immosu
osmium
immotu
tomium
immstu
mutism
summit
immswy
swimmy
imnnow
minnow
imnntu
muntin
imnoor
morion
imnoos
simoon
imnoot
motion
imnost
inmost
monist
imnosy
myosin
simony
imnrtu
untrim
imnruy
unmiry
imntuy
mutiny
imootv
vomito
imoprs
porism

imoprt
import
imopst
impost
imorrr
mirror
imorrs
morris
imorsu
rimous
imossy
myosis
imostu
ostium
timous
imottt
tomtit
imprsu
primus
purism
imprsy
prismy
impstu
sumpit
imqrsu
squirm
imrrsy
smirry
imrstu
truism
imrsuu
miurus
imsssu
missus
innoot
notion
innooy
oniony
innopp
Nippon
innorw
inworn
innosu
unison
innotw
intown
innoww
winnow
innpsy
spinny
inoops
poison
inoopt
option
potion
inoors
orison
inoorz
zorino
inoppr
Rippon
inoprs
prison

inopst
piston
inoptt
tinpot
inorsy
rosiny
inortt
triton
inortu
turion
inostu
ustion
inosuv
vinous
inotuw
outwin
inotvy
novity
inppsy
snippy
inprst
sprint
inprtu
turnip
inpsuy
puisny
inqstu
squint
inqsuy
quinsy
squiny
inrsxy
syrinx
inrtvy
vintry
inrtwy
wintry
instty
stinty
instuu
unsuit
instuw
unwist
iooprt
roopit
ioosss
sissoo
iopptt
tiptop
ioprry
priory
ioprst
prosit
tripos
ioprtu
roupit
iopsst
ptosis
iopstu
putois
ioqstu
quoist
iorrtw
worrit

iorrty
riotry
iorrzz
rizzor
iorssu
urosis
iorstu
suitor
iorsuv
virous
iosstt
tsotsi
iosttu
outsit
iottuw
outwit
ipptuy
uppity
iprrtu
irrupt
iprsst
stirps
iprssy
prissy
iprstu
purist
spruit
uprist
iprsty
stripy
iprtuy
purity
ipstty
typist
ipstxy
ptyxis
ipsvvy
spivvy
iptttu
tittup
ipttuy
titupy
iqrrsu
squirr
iqrstu
squirt
irssty
syrtis
irstwy
wristy
irttux
tutrix
issstu
tussis
isttwy
twisty
jnnotu
jötunn
jnstuu
unjust
jooppy
popjoy
joosuy
joyous

6 TTT

jottuu
outjut
kklmuu
mukluk
kknruu
kunkur
kkostu
Sukkot
klnruy
knurly
kloopu
uplook
klrtuu
Kultur
kmooss
kosmos
kmosux
musk-ox
kmprsu
skrump
knnotu
unknot
knoorr
kronor
knoors
Kronos
knooss
snooks
knoruw
unwork
knotty
knotty
knpsuy
spunky
koopsy
spooky
kootww
kowtow
krrsuy
skurry
krssuy
Russky
llloop
lollop
llloot
tol-lol
llnoor
roll-on
llnopu
pull-on
llnoru
unroll

llootu
toluol
lloowy
woolly
llopru
roll-up
uproll
llopux
Pollux
llorst
stroll
llorty
trolly
lloswy
slowly
llppuu
pull-up
lmmoux
lummox
lmmpuy
plummy
lmmsuy
slummy
lmmtuu
multum
lmooru
ormolu
lmoosy
sloomy
lmorsu
musrol
lmosty
mostly
lmppuy
plumpy
lmpsuy
slumpy
lmttuu
tumult
lnoopy
polony
lnoost
stolon
lnopsy
pylons
lnoptu
pluton
pulton
lnostu
unlost
lnosuu
unsoul

lnotwy
townly
lnptuu
pultun
lnruuy
unruly
looort
rotolo
loopry
poorly
loostv
volost
loovvx
Volvox
lopppy
popply
loppry
propyl
loppsy
polyps
sloppy
loprty
portly
protyl
lopsuu
opulus
loptty
plotty
loptwy
two-ply
lorsuy
sourly
lortty
trotyl
lostyz
zlotys
losyzz
sozzly
lppruy
purply
lppsuy
supply
lprsyy
spryly
lpstuu
Plutus
lrrsuy
slurry
lrstuy
sultry
lruuxy
luxury

lsstuy
stylus
mmnoor
Mormon
mmnosu
musmon
summon
mmoopp
pompom
mmoott
motmot
tom-tom
mmrruu
murmur
mmttuu
tum-tum
mmtuuu
mutuum
mmuuuu
muu-muu
mmuuyy
yum-yum
mnnouw
unmown
mnoopp
pompon
mnoopt
tompon
mnooru
unmoor
mnoosy
monosy
mnootw
towmon
mnossu
Somnus
mnottu
mutton
mnotuy
mounty
moopry
pomroy
moorrw
morrow
moorty
motory
moossu
osmous
mopprt
prompt
mopssu
possum

mopstu
upmost
moqruu
quorum
moqtuu
quotum
morruu
rumour
morsty
stormy
mortuu
tumour
mosttu
utmost
mostuu
outsum
mprsuu
rumpus
mpstuu
sputum
mpstuy
stumpy
mrrsuy
smurry
mrstuy
Myrtus
msttuy
smutty
nnoopt
ponton
nnoory
ronyon
nnortu
untorn
nnoruw
unworn
nnosuw
unsown
nnotuw
unwont
nnpsuu
unspun
nnrtuu
unturn
nooprt
pronto
proton
noopst
spot-on
noopsy
spoony

noorry
Norroy
noorst
tonsor
noortu
notour
unroot
noosst
nostos
noosty
snooty
noosuy
noyous
noottu
not-out
noppru
unprop
noprtu
uptorn
nopstu
unstop
noptuw
uptown
norstw
strown
norsty
snorty
nortuu
outrun
nostty
snotty
nostuw
unstow
nostuy
snouty
nprtuu
turn-up
upturn
nrsttu
strunt
oooott
too-too
ooozz
zoozoo
oopprt
troppo
ooprrt
torpor
ooprsu
porous
ooprtu
uproot

oopttu
outtop
oopwww
powwow
oorrsw
sorrow
oostty
tootsy
oouuww
wou-wou
oowwww
wow-wow
oprsst
sports
oprstu
sprout
stroup
stupor
oprsty
sporty
opsstu
toss-up
opstty
spotty
opstuy
spouty
opttuu
output
orsttu
strout
orstuy
stoury
orttuy
trouty
try-out
osstxy
xystos
ppttuu
put-put
prrsuy
spurry
prsuyy
syrupy
rsttuy
trusty
sstuxy
xystus
ttttuu
tut-tut

7 AAA

aaaalty
atalaya
aaabbcl
cabbala

aaabbkl
Kabbala
aaabccr
baccara

aaabclv
baclava
aaabcnr
baracan

aaabctw
catawba
aaabdnn
bandana

aaabegl
galabea
aaabens
Sabaean

aaabfll
falbala
aaabgil
galabia

7 AAA

aaabilx
abaxial
aaabinr
Arabian
aaabllw
wallaba
aaabmst
mastaba
aaabnnr
rabanna
aaabnpr
Pan-Arab
aaaborr
araroba
aaabrsx
abraxas
aaacclr
caracal
aaaccrs
cascara
aaacdin
Acadian
aaacdir
Acarida
aaacdlu
acaudal
aaacdmm
macadam
aaaceer
araceae
aaacehn
Achaean
aaacenp
panacea
aaachhl
Halacha
aaachin
Achaian
aaachlz
chalaza
aaachnt
acantha
aaacijm
Jamaica
aaacilm
malacia
aaacimr
Aramaic
cariama
aaacinp
acapnia
aaacinr
acarian
Acarina
aaacint
Cataian
aaacjmr
jacamar
aaacllv
cavalla
aaaclmn
almanac
aaaclnt
Catalan

aaaclpt
catalpa
aaacmnp
campana
aaacmrs
mascara
aaacnnr
caranna
aaacnpt
catapan
aaacnrt
nacarat
aaacnru
carauna
aaacnrv
caravan
aaacnst
canasta
aaacntt
cantata
aaacnty
Catayan
aaacrwy
caraway
aaacssv
cassava
aaacstt
catasta
aaadelm
alameda
aaadfry
faraday
aaadggh
Haggada
aaadhmr
adharma
aaadilx
adaxial
aaadirt
dataria
Radiata
aaadjmr
jamadar
aaadknn
Kannada
aaadlmn
mandala
aaadlmw
wadmaal
aaadmnr
Ramadan
aaadmnt
adamant
aaadmrs
madrasa
aaadnrt
tanadar
aaaeenr
Araneae
aaaeglt
galatea
aaaegnp
apanage

aaaehkt
takahea
aaaehlt
althaea
aaaehrs
sea-haar
aaaeimn
anaemia
aaaelmp
palamae
aaaenst
anatase
aaaffll
alfalfa
aaafirt
ratafia
aaafnrs
sarafan
aaafrwy
faraway
aaaggln
galanga
aaaghip
aphagia
aaaghln
langaha
aaaghnt
ataghan
aaaghpr
agrapha
aaaginp
Panagia
aaagipt
patagia
aaagiss
assagai
aaaglmm
amalgam
aaaglmn
nagmaal
aaaglns
lasagna
aaagmmt
magmata
aaagmnr
anagram
aaagmns
sagaman
aaagnpr
pargana
aaagnrt
Tanagra
aaagnru
guaraná
aaagnty
yatagan
aaahhkl
Halakah
aaahhlv
halavah
aaahips
aphasia
aaahjkw
kajawah

aaahlmr
harmala
aaahlnn
alannah
aaahmmt
mahatma
aaahmrs
ashrama
aaahmrt
Maratha
aaahmst
tamasha
aaahnrs
Saharan
aaahprt
paratha
aaahrtw
waratah
aaaiklt
Latakia
aaailmr
malaria
aaailps
aplasia
aaailrt
talaria
aaailst
Alsatia
aaaimnt
amanita
aaainns
Ananias
aaaiprx
apraxia
aaaipss
Aspasia
aaaiqru
aquaria
aaajmps
pajamas
aaallpt
palatal
aaalmny
Malayan
aaalmrs
Marsala
aaalnnt
lantana
aaalwyy
layaway
aaamnrt
amarant
Maranta
aaamnst
atamans
aaamprt
patamar
aaamrrz
zamarra
aaannsv
savanna
aaanntt
annatta

aaanrtt
tantara
tartana
aaansst
Satanas
aaaoprz
parazoa
aaapprt
apparat
aaarttt
rat-a-tat
aaarttu
tuatara
aaartxy
ataraxy
aabbceg
cabbage
aabbcgy
cabbagy
aabbdgr
gabbard
aabbdhs
habdabs
aabbdis
Abbasid
aabbegn
bean-bag
aabbelt
batable
aabbert
barbate
aabbggr
grab-bag
aabbgrt
gabbart
aabbgry
rag-baby
aabbhst
Sabbath
aabblor
barbola
aabbnry
Barnaby
aabbrry
Barbary
aabbrss
bass-bar
aabbssu
babassu
aabccer
baccare
aabccet
baccate
aabccir
braccia
aabcekr
backare
aabceln
balance
aabcelp
capable
pacable
aabcemr
macabre

aabcems
ambs-ace
aabcepr
pea-crab
aabcerr
barrace
aabcert
abreact
bear-cat
cabaret
aabchmt
ambatch
aabchnr
barchan
aabchor
abroach
aabcilm
cambial
aabciln
Caliban
aabciop
copaiba
aabcitx
taxicab
aabckly
layback
aabcknr
cab-rank
aabckpy
backpay
aabckrr
barrack
aabcksw
backsaw
aabclmu
calumba
aabclsy
scybala
aabcmsu
sambuca
aabcort
abactor
acrobat
aabcost
Tabasco®
aabcott
catboat
aabcrsu
Carabus
aabcttu
cattabu
aabddno
Abaddon
aabdefl
fadable
aabdegn
bandage
aabdehs
abashed
aabdeis
diabase
aabdell
ballade

aabdelt
datable
aabdenu
bandeau
aabdghn
handbag
aabdgmo
gambado
aabdgns
sandbag
aabdgrr
drag-bar
aabdhms
badmash
aabdhnt
hatband
aabdhny
hayband
aabdhru
Bahadur
aabdiis
basidia
aabdiln
baladin
aabdimr
barmaid
aabdint
tabanid
aabdiot
biodata
aabdlns
salband
aabdlrw
bradawl
aabdmnr
armband
aabdnno
abandon
aabdnrs
sand-bar
aabdnsw
band-saw
aabdorv
bravado
aabdrrw
draw-bar
aabdrst
bastard
aabdrsu
subadar
aabeehw
Wahabee
aabeelt
eatable
aabeemo
amoebae
aabeens
sea-bean
aabeers
sea-bear
aabeerz
zareeba
aabeest
sea-beat

aabeffl
affable
aabeffn
beffana
aabefgl
flea-bag
aabefgu
aufgabe
aabeggg
baggage
aabeggm
game-bag
aabeggr
garbage
aabeglr
algebra
aabegmr
bergama
megabar
aabegms
ambages
aabegrr
barrage
aabegrt
tear-bag
aabegss
bagasse
aabegsu
abusage
aabehit
Bahaite
aabehlt
hatable
aabehnt
abthane
aabehrs
earbash
aabeikn
ikebana
aabeilm
amiable
aabeilt
Baalite
labiate
aabeirs
air-base
arabise
aabejll
jellaba
aabejmu
jambeau
aabeklm
makable
aabeklt
takable
aabekns
sea-bank
aabelll
labella
aabellm
lamb-ale
aabelln
balneal

aabells
sabella
salable
aabelmn
namable
aabelmt
tamable
aabelno
abalone
aabelpp
papable
aabelpr
parable
aabelpy
payable
aabelrt
ratable
aabelst
astable
aabelsv
savable
aabelsy
sayable
aabeltu
tableau
tabulae
aabeltx
taxable
aabemns
baseman
aabenrt
ant-bear
aabeost
sea-boat
aaberst
abreast
aabertt
rabatte
tabaret
aabertu
abature
aabesss
sea-bass
aabetux
bateaux
aabffly
affably
aabfilu
fabliau
aabflru
fabular
aabghns
gabnash
nashgab
aabghpu
Buphaga
aabghsw
bagwash
aabgiil
abigail
aabgilm
mail-bag
aabginr
bargain

aabhhis
sahibah
aabhhru
bruhaha
aabhims
Bahaism
aabhirt
air-bath
Bharati
aabhist
Bahaist
aabhitt
habitat
aabhknr
barkhan
aabhlty
bathyal
aabhmnr
Brahman
aabhost
Sabaoth
aabhsuu
Bauhaus
aabiilx
biaxial
aabijmy
jambiya
aabijnp
Panjabi
aabikns
banksia
aabillr
barilla
aabilmn
bimanal
aabilms
Baalism
aabilmy
amiably
aabilou
aboulia
aabilrs
basilar
aabilst
balista
aabimmr
marimba
aabimrs
Arabism
aabimss
Sabaism
aabinou
ouabian
aabinrt
atabrin
aabinst
abstain
Tsabian
aabipux
paxiuba
aabirst
Arabist
aabistt
abattis

aabknrt
tan-bark
aabkooz
bazooka
aabllnt
ballant
aabllny
banally
aabllpt
patball
aabllst
ballast
aabllsy
salably
aabllwy
wallaby
aablmru
labarum
aablmst
lambast
aablmsy
abysmal
balsamy
aablnsu
Balanus
aablntt
blatant
aablort
ablator
aablpru
pabular
aablrst
arblast
aablrty
ratably
aablssy
abyssal
aablttu
abuttal
aabltxy
taxably
aabmnot
boatman
aabmnst
batsman
aabmoru
marabou
aabmorz
Mozarab
aabmssy
ambassy
aabnnoz
bonanza
aabnost
sabaton
aabnstu
Tabanus
aaboppt
pap-boat
aabotty
attaboy
aabqsuu
subaqua

aabrrsu
saburra
aabrruv
bravura
aabsssy
sassaby
aabtttu
battuta
aabzzzz
bazzazz
aaccdes
cascade
aaccdir
cardiac
aacceet
Cetacea
aacceir
Circaea
aaccekr
carcake
aaccelo
cloacae
aaccenv
vacance
aacceps
cap-case
aaccers
carcase
aaccest
saccate
aacchhk
kachcha
aacchir
archaic
aacchln
clachan
aacchmp
champac
aacchnn
cannach
aaccilm
acclaim
aaccior
carioca
aaccitt
atactic
aaccklp
calpack
aacckrr
carrack
aaccllo
cloacal
aaccllt
catcall
aacclop
polacca
aacclor
caracol
aacclpt
placcat
aacclru
accrual
caracul

aacclsu
  accusal
aaccltu
  Lactuca
aaccnvy
  vacancy
aaccort
  car-coat
aaccoru
  curaçao
  curaçoa
aaccost
  accoast
aaccott
  toccata
aaccrrt
  carract
aaccrss
  carcass
aacddel
  decadal
aacdder
  arcaded
aacddhr
  chaddar
aacddin
  candida
aacdeem
  academe
aacdees
  sea-dace
aacdefl
  falcade
aacdehm
  chamade
aacdehr
  charade
aacdeht
  cathead
aacdeii
  aecidia
aacdein
  aidance
  Canidae
aacdeln
  candela
  decanal
aacdelr
  caldera
aacdels
  scalade
aacdemn
  Cadmean
aacdemy
  academy
aacdenv
  advance
aacdenz
  cadenza
aacders
  sea-card
aacderv
  cadaver
aacdetu
  caudate
aacdfir
  faradic
aacdhmr
  drachma
aacdhnr
  handcar
aacdiis
  ascidia
aacdilr
  radical
aacdint
  antacid
aacdinv
  vanadic
aacdior
  acaroid
aacdirs
  ascarid
aacdjkw
  jackdaw
aacdlno
  calando
aacdlns
  scandal
aacdlos
  scalado
aacdloy
  day-coal
aacdlpr
  placard
aacdnrs
  cadrans
aacdoov
  avocado
aacdrss
  csárdás
aacdrst
  dart-sac
aacdrsz
  czardas
aaceegr
  acreage
aaceehr
  earache
aaceeht
  chaetae
aaceekt
  tea-cake
aaceelm
  mace-ale
aaceeln
  anelace
aaceems
  ames-ace
aaceent
  catenae
aaceett
  acetate
aacefft
  fat-face
aacefls
  sea-calf
aaceflt
  falcate
aaceflu
  faculae
aacefmn
  faceman
aaceggr
  aggrace
aacegkp
  package
aacegks
  sackage
aacegnr
  carnage
  cranage
aacegrt
  cartage
aacegsv
  scavage
aacehlp
  acaleph
aacehnp
  panache
aacehnr
  acharné
aacehpp
  appeach
aacehpu
  chapeau
aacehrt
  trachea
aacehst
  Achates
aacehtt
  attaché
aacehtu
  château
aacehty
  Cyathea
aacehwy
  each-way
aaceimn
  anaemic
aaceimu
  camaieu
aaceinn
  Nicaean
aaceinr
  acarine
aaceins
  Sciaena
aaceipp
  cap-à-pie
aaceirv
  avarice
  caviare
aacekll
  lac-lake
aacekmm
  ack-emma
aaceknp
  pancake
aacekns
  askance
aacekot
  oatcake
aacelln
  canella
aacellp
  Capella
aacells
  sacella
aacellt
  lacteal
aacelmn
  lace-man
  manacle
aacelmr
  cameral
  caramel
aacelmu
  maculae
aacelnu
  lacunae
aacelnv
  valance
aacelny
  Lycaena
aacelos
  sea-coal
aacelpt
  placate
aacelrt
  Lacerta
aacelrv
  caravel
aacelst
  lactase
aacelsw
  case-law
aaceltt
  lactate
aaceltv
  clavate
aacemmr
  macramé
aacemns
  caseman
aacemnv
  caveman
aacempr
  paracme
aacemqu
  macaque
aacenot
  Actaeon
aacenrs
  Saracen
aacenrt
  cateran
aacentt
  cantate
aacenty
  cyanate
aaceopt
  pea-coat
aaceors
  rosacea
aaceprt
  caprate
aacerst
  cat's-ear
aacersu
  caesura
aacertu
  arcuate
aacerwy
  raceway
aacettu
  actuate
aacetuv
  vacuate
aacffil
  caffila
aacfhlp
  half-cap
aacfils
  fascial
aacfilu
  faucial
aacfinr
  African
aacfint
  fanatic
aacfllu
  falcula
aacfllw
  law-calf
aacflly
  fallacy
aacflpt
  flat-cap
aacflru
  facular
aacfltu
  factual
aacfrru
  farruca
aacgill
  glacial
aacgilm
  magical
aacgils
  scaglia
aacgint
  agnatic
aacgirv
  agravic
aacglos
  coal-gas
  gas-coal
aacgnou
  guanaco
aachikr
  chikara
aachilr
  rachial
aachimr
  Amharic
  machair
aachims
  chiasma
aachips
  aphasic
aachipt
  chapati
aachirs
  arachis
aachirt
  cithara
aachkmp
  champak
aachkrt
  hatrack
aachksw
  hack-saw
aachlln
  challan
aachlps
  paschal
aachlsu
  acushla
aachmnp
  chapman
aachnop
  panocha
aachnou
  huanaco
aachnpx
  panchax
aachnrv
  navarch
aachnry
  anarchy
aachrrt
  catarrh
aachrsw
  car-wash
aachrwy
  archway
aaciiln
  lacinia
aaciils
  Isiacal
aaciilt
  Ciliata
aaciinp
  Apician
aaciinr
  Arician
  Icarian
aaciins
  Asianic
aaciint
  actinia
aaciist
  Asiatic
aacijlp
  jalapic
aaciklr
  clarkia
aaciknn
  canakin
aacilmr
  mail-car

aacilnr
cranial
aacilnt
actinal
alicant
aacilnz
Zincala
aacilos
asocial
aacilox
coaxial
aacilps
spacial
aacilpt
capital
placita
aacilrr
rail-car
aaciluv
Avicula
aacimmr
macrami
aacimpr
Campari
picamar
aacinnt
cantina
aacinor
Aaronic
conaria
ocarina
aacinps
Capsian
aacinpt
capitan
captain
aacinrz
czarina
aacinst
satanic
aacintv
Vatican
aaciopt
tapioca
aaciopv
copaiva
aaciprs
Sarapic
aaciqtu
aquatic
aacirss
ascaris
aacirst
caritas
aacirtt
Tataric
aacistt
astatic
aacjkmn
jackman
manjack
aacjkss
jackass
aacklll
lack-all
aackltw
cat-walk
aackmnp
packman
aackmrt
amtrack
aacknrs
ransack
aacknrt
tank-car
aackprr
carpark
aackprt
pack-rat
aackpwy
packway
aacllnt
callant
aacllnu
Calluna
lacunal
aacllor
coralla
aacllsu
clausal
aacllvy
cavally
aaclmno
coalman
aaclmnt
calmant
clamant
aaclmpr
arc-lamp
aaclmpt
palm-cat
aaclmru
macular
aaclmsu
calamus
aaclnnu
cannula
aaclnor
Alcoran
aaclnru
lacunar
aaclnsu
Calanus
aaclopr
caporal
aaclopt
octapla
aaclort
coal-tar
aaclorz
alcorza
aaclost
coastal
aaclott
cattalo
aaclotv
octaval
aaclprt
caltrap
aaclpsu
scapula
aaclpty
play-act
aaclrst
castral
aaclrvy
Calvary
cavalry
aaclssu
casuals
aaclstt
salt-cat
aaclsuv
vascula
aaclttu
tactual
aacmnru
arcanum
aacmnsy
caymans
aacmorr
Camorra
aacmors
sarcoma
aacmort
marcato
aacmrrt
tram-car
aacmrru
Macrura
aacmrss
sarcasm
aacnnoz
canzona
aacnpst
capstan
aacnrtu
curtana
aacnssv
canvass
aacorst
ostraca
aacortu
acatour
autocar
aacotuv
autovac
aacpstw
cat's-paw
aacrttt
attract
aacrttx
tax-cart
aacrtuv
vacatur
aacrtuy
actuary
aacrtwy
cartway
aactuwy
cutaway
aaddden
addenda
aaddeel
daedale
aaddefi
deaf-aid
aaddegi
Gadidae
aaddeil
alidade
aaddenp
dead-pan
aaddept
adapted
aaddepy
dead-pay
aaddgnr
graddan
grandad
aaddhkr
khaddar
aaddhrs
sraddha
aaddiik
didakai
aaddims
Dadaism
aaddist
Dadaist
aaddnvv
dvandva
aaddrst
dastard
aadeelt
tea-lead
aadeffr
affear'd
aadefgl
faldage
aadefgr
fardage
aadefht
fat-head
aadefis
fadaise
aadeflu
aefauld
aadeggr
aggrade
aadegho
go-ahead
aadegmn
agnamed
aadegmr
megarad
aadegrt
gradate
aadegry
drayage
yardage
aadehmn
headman
aadehms
ashamed
aadehps
saphead
aadehrw
rawhead
warhead
aadehwy
headway
aadeilr
Laridae
radiale
aadeilv
vedalia
aadeimr
madeira
aadeims
sea-maid
aadeimt
Adamite
aadeino
Dionaea
aadeinr
araneid
Ranidae
aadeins
naiades
aadeips
diapase
aadeirt
radiate
tiaraed
aadeiwy
die-away
aadejmr
jemadar
aadejnu
Judaean
aadekmr
kamerad
aadellp
padella
aadelmo
alamode
aadelmr
alarmed
aadelnr
adrenal
aadelnw
danelaw
aadelpy
leap-day
aadelru
radulae
aadelry
already
aadeltu
adulate
aademmn
man-made
aademno
adenoma
aademnt
mandate
aademny
name-day
aademnz
Mazdean
aadennp
Pandean
aadennt
andante
Dantean
aadenrv
veranda
aadenss
sea-sand
aadenst
ansated
aadensw
weasand
aadentv
Vedanta
aadenwz
weazand
aadeors
sea-road
aadeprr
para-red
aadeprs
aspread
aadeprt
adapter
readapt
aadepss
passade
aaderrs
arrased
aadersw
seaward
aadertu
aurated
aadfgly
flag-day
aadfhly
half-day
aadfiry
fair-day
aadfltw
twafald
aadfnrr
farrand
aadfsty
fast-day
aadgghr
haggard
aadgglr
laggard
aadggrs
saggard
aadghil
hidalga
aadgimm
digamma
aadgimo
agamoid
aadgimr
diagram
aadgios
adagios

7 AAD

aadgllw
gadwall
aadglmy
amygdal
aadglnr
garland
aadglns
sladang
aadglnt
Landtag
aadglru
gradual
aadgmnr
drag-man
grandam
grandma
aadgmns
gadsman
aadgnpr
grandpa
aadgnrt
gardant
aadgnry
yardang
aadgopr
podagra
aadhill
Dalilah
aadhjnr
handjar
aadhkny
yakhdan
aadhlry
halyard
aadhnpr
hard-pan
aadhnrs
darshan
Hansard
aadhnsw
handsaw
aadhrwy
hayward
aadhswy
wash-day
aadiiln
idalian
aadiilr
diarial
aadiinr
diarian
aadiips
aspidia
aadiirr
air-raid
aadijmn
jamdani
aadikly
ilkaday
aadillo
alodial
aadilmr
admiral
amildar

aadilmt
Matilda
aadilnp
paladin
aadilnr
laniard
aadilps
apsidal
aadilrt
tailard
aadiltv
datival
aadimnr
mandira
aadimor
diorama
aadimot
domatia
aadinrr
darrain
aadinrt
radiant
aadinrv
viranda
aadinrw
Wardian
aadirrw
airward
aadjmpy
pyjama'd
aadkmry
daymark
aadknrt
tankard
aadkrww
awkward
aadllmr
mallard
aadllnw
land-law
lawland
aadllpu
paludal
aadlmnn
landman
aadlmno
mandola
aadlmnu
ladanum
aadlmuv
mud-lava
aadlmyy
May-lady
aadlnrt
land-rat
aadlnry
lanyard
aadlntx
land-tax
aadlopy
pay-load
aadlppu
applaud

aadlpyy
play-day
aadlrru
radular
aadmnno
Madonna
aadmnns
sandman
aadmnnw
dawn-man
aadmnor
madroña
mandora
monarda
roadman
aadmnrs
mansard
aadmnry
drayman
yardman
aadmnsy
daysman
man-days
aadmntu
mutanda
aadmopr
road-map
aadmoqu
madoqua
aadmort
matador
aadmosy
Asmoday
aadmrry
yard-arm
aadmrzz
mazzard
aadnnot
notanda
aadnoot
Odonata
aadnopr
pandora
aadnort
ondatra
aadnory
anyroad
aadnpru
pandura
aadnrry
darrayn
aadnrst
astrand
tar-sand
aadnrty
tanyard
aadnrvw
vanward
aadnrwy
nayward
aadoprs
parados
aadoprt
adaptor

aadoprx
paradox
aadopss
passado
aadorwy
roadway
aadqrtu
quadrat
aadrsty
daystar
aadrwwy
wayward
aaeefgl
leafage
aaeeflt
tea-leaf
aaeegkl
leakage
aaeeglt
galeate
aaeegmn
amenage
aaeegmr
Megaera
aaeegno
Neogaea
aaeegrv
average
aaeegst
sage-tea
sea-gate
aaeehrs
sea-hare
aaeehrt
hetaera
aaeeint
taeniae
aaeekls
sea-kale
aaeekrw
reawake
aaeelmt
maleate
aaeelns
sea-lane
aaeelor
areolae
aaeelrt
laetare
aaeemnt
emanate
enemata
manatee
aaeemtt
meat-tea
aaeennt
Aetnean
aaeepps
appease
aaeeprt
paterae
aaeersw
sea-ware

aaeertu
aureate
aaeertx
exarate
aaeesvw
sea-wave
aaeffgr
agraffe
aaeffir
affaire
aaeffll
falafel
aaeffnr
fanfare
aaefftt
taffeta
aaefgln
Falange
aaefgtw
waftage
aaefhlp
half-ape
aaeflpr
earflap
parafle
aaeflrt
rat-flea
aaefmos
sea-foam
aaefmrt
fermata
aaefqru
aquafer
aaefrrw
warfare
aaefrwy
wayfare
aaeggno
anagoge
aaeggop
apagoge
aaeggrt
aggrate
aaeghlu
haulage
aaeghnt
thanage
aaeghpt
peat-hag
aaegilr
lairage
regalia
aaegils
algesia
aaeginv
vaginae
aaeginw
wainage
aaegipr
igarapé
aaegirr
arriage
aaegiss
assegai

aaegitt
agitate
aaegjtu
ajutage
aaegknt
tankage
aaegkos
soakage
aaegkrw
Gaekwar
aaegllr
glareal
Grallae
aaegllt
gallate
tallage
aaeglmn
gamelan
aaeglmt
gametal
aaeglnr
alnager
aaeglns
lasagne
aaeglop
apogeal
aaeglrr
realgar
aaeglst
algates
lastage
aaeglsv
salvage
aaegmmy
May-game
aaegmnr
manager
aaegmnt
gateman
magenta
magnate
aaegmpr
rampage
aaegmrt
regmata
aaegmrw
war-game
aaegmss
massage
aaegnnp
pannage
aaegnnt
tannage
aaegnop
apogean
aaegnpt
pageant
aaegnrr
arrange
aaegnrt
tanager
aaegnst
sea-tang

aaegntv
 vantage
aaegntw
 wantage
aaegnyz
 Zygaena
aaegprr
 parerga
aaegpss
 passage
aaegpsy
 paysage
aaegquy
 quayage
aaegrrv
 ravager
aaegrst
 tear-gas
aaegrtt
 regatta
aaegssu
 assuage
 sausage
aaegstw
 saw-gate
 wastage
aaegttw
 wattage
aaegtwy
 gateway
 getaway
aaehhps
 ash-heap
aaehhpt
 aphthae
aaehilp
 aphelia
aaehirt
 hetaira
 Rhaetia
aaehknt
 khanate
aaehksw
 sea-hawk
aaehlll
 allheal
 heal-all
aaehlpx
 hexapla
aaehlrt
 trehala
aaehltt
 athleta
aaehmtt
 themata
aaehnpr
 hanaper
aaehprz
 pheazar
aaehpst
 sea-path
aaehrsy
 hearsay

aaehstt
 hastate
aaeikrt
 Karaite
aaeillx
 axillae
aaeilmn
 Almaine
 laminae
 Limnaea
aaeilms
 malaise
aaeilno
 aeolian
aaeilnr
 air-lane
aaeilnt
 antliae
aaeilpx
 epaxial
aaeilru
 aurelia
aaeilrv
 velaria
aaeilss
 aliases
aaeimmt
 imamate
aaeimns
 amnesia
aaeimnt
 amentia
 animate
aaeimpy
 pyaemia
aaeimru
 uraemia
aaeimtv
 amative
aaeinno
 aeonian
aaeinns
 Sinaean
aaeinrt
 Raetian
aaeinrz
 Zairean
aaeipps
 apepsia
aaeiprr
 pareira
aaeiprs
 spiraea
aaeiprt
 apteria
aaeiptt
 apatite
aaeirst
 asteria
 atresia
aaeirsx
 xerasia

aaeirtt
 arietta
 Ratitae
aaeirtv
 variate
aaeirvw
 airwave
aaeistt
 satiate
aaejnrt
 naartje
aaeklmr
 meal-ark
aaeklnt
 alkanet
aaeklrs
 sea-lark
aaekmnw
 wakeman
aaekmrr
 earmark
aaekmrs
 seamark
aaekprt
 partake
aaellm
 lamella
aaellnz
 zanella
aaellpr
 parella
aaellpt
 patella
aaellrt
 lateral
aaellry
 allayer
aaellsv
 save-all
aaellsw
 sea-wall
aaelmmn
 meal-man
aaelmmt
 lemmata
aaelmns
 Ameslan
aaelmnt
 amental
aaelmnu
 alumnae
aaelmny
 Lymnaea
aaelmot
 oatmeal
aaelmpt
 palmate
aaelmst
 maltase
aaelmsy
 amylase
aaelnov
 valonea

aaelnpt
 platane
aaelnpu
 paenula
aaelnrs
 arsenal
aaelnrt
 Lateran
aaelnst
 sealant
aaelnsy
 analyse
aaelntt
 tetanal
aaelntz
 zealant
aaelorr
 areolar
aaeloru
 aureola
aaelotx
 oxalate
aaelppr
 apparel
aaelppt
 palpate
aaelppu
 papulae
aaelprt
 apteral
aaelprv
 palaver
aaelptt
 tapetal
aaelptu
 plateau
aaelpty
 apetaly
aaelrst
 tar-seal
aaelrtv
 larvate
aaelrtz
 lazaret
aaelrvy
 alveary
aaelsst
 atlases
 sea-salt
aaelstt
 saltate
aaelsux
 asexual
aaelswx
 seal-wax
aaeltuv
 valuate
aaeltvv
 valvate
aaelwwy
 welaway
aaemmmr
 maremma

aaemmmt
 mammate
aaemmnt
 meat-man
aaemmot
 ommatea
aaemnnt
 emanant
aaemnpp
 pampean
aaemnps
 spaeman
aaemnpt
 peatman
aaemnrt
 ramenta
aaemnru
 muraena
aaemnry
 man-year
aaemntu
 manteau
aaemotz
 metazoa
aaemppt
 pap-meat
aaemqsu
 squamae
aaemrtu
 amateur
aaennnt
 antenna
aaennst
 annates
aaenntt
 tannate
aaenntv
 ventana
aaenppr
 parpane
aaenpst
 anapest
 peasant
aaenrrt
 narrate
aaenrst
 Antares
aaenrtt
 tartane
aaenrtu
 taurean
aaenrtv
 taverna
aaenruw
 unaware
aaenruz
 azurean
aaenssv
 vanessa
aaenstv
 Avestan
aaeorrt
 aerator

aaepprt
 parapet
aaepprv
 Papaver
aaeprty
 peatary
aaepsss
 sea-pass
aaerrtt
 tartare
aaersst
 sea-star
aaerssy
 assayer
aaerstt
 Astarte
aaerttu
 tuatera
aaertty
 tea-tray
aaettuw
 Watteau
aaffins
 saffian
aafgirr
 rag-fair
aafgorr
 farrago
aafhikl
 khalifa
aafhlpy
 half-pay
aafhlwy
 halfway
aafiilr
 Filaria
aafilnt
 fantail
aafilnv
 Flavian
aafilqu
 alfaquí
aafimru
 Fumaria
aafimry
 Mayfair
aafinnt
 infanta
aafiprt
 parfait
aafirwy
 fairway
aafjllw
 jawfall
aafllty
 fatally
aaflmpr
 frampal
aaflnor
 forlana
aaflnru
 furlana
aaflssy
 salsafy

aaflstt
salt-fat
aaflwyy
flyaway
aafmnrt
raftman
aafmnst
fantasm
aafnrrt
farrant
aafnstt
fantast
aafnsty
fantasy
aaggiln
ganglia
aagglot
Tagalog
aaggnoy
anagogy
aaghilr
gharial
aaghlnt
gnathal
aaghlos
gasahol
aaghmnn
hangman
aaghmnw
whangam
aaghquu
quahaug
aaghsty
sagathy
aagiknw
awaking
aagiknz
ziganka
aagikrw
Gaikwar
aagilmy
myalgia
aagilnn
anginal
Anglian
aagilno
Logania
aagilnp
paginal
aagilnv
vaginal
aagilot
otalgia
aagiltt
tag-tail
aagiltw
wagtail
aagimno
angioma
aagimns
gas-main
siamang
aagimnz
amazing

aaginnw
wanigan
aaginnz
Zingana
aaginrr
arraign
aaginrs
sangria
sarangi
aaginru
guarani
Guaraní
aaginrz
Zingara
aaginst
against
aaginsv
vaginas
aaginsy
gainsay
aagiott
agitato
aagipru
piragua
aagirry
argyria
aagistt
sagitta
aagkllo
oak-gall
aagkmss
gas-mask
aagknst
gas-tank
aagkooz
gazooka
aagllnt
gallant
aaglmps
gas-lamp
aaglnoy
analogy
aaglnru
angular
aaglruu
augural
aagmmns
magsman
aagmmrr
grammar
aagmmtu
gummata
aagmnnr
grannam
aagmnpr
pangram
aagmnpy
pangamy
aagmnrt
tangram
trangam
aagmnsw
swagman

aagmopy
apogamy
aagmors
margosa
smarago
aagmosu
agamous
aagmrry
gramary
aagnopr
paragon
aagnorz
organza
aagnrry
granary
aagnrtv
vagrant
aagopss
sapsago
aagorsu
saguaro
aagprst
gas-trap
aahhnnt
thannah
aahhnpt
naphtha
aahhopr
Pharaoh
aahijnr
Harijan
aahikrt
kithara
aahilll
all-hail
hallali
aahilln
hallian
aahilmr
almirah
aahilmt
thalami
aahilns
Sinhala
aahilnt
thalian
aahilpv
Pahlavi
aahimno
mahonia
aahimnr
Ahriman
aahimrt
Marathi
aahinop
aphonia
aahinpp
Paphian
aahinpr
piranha
aahinst
shaitan
aahinsv
Shavian

aahiprt
pitarah
aahiptz
zaptiah
aahirst
shariat
aahisvy
Vaishya
aahklrs
lashkar
aahkmsy
yashmak
aahknsy
Sankhya
aahkrss
rakshas
aahllwy
hallway
aahlmms
mashlam
aahlmrs
marshal
aahlmru
hamular
aahlnpx
phalanx
aahlnrw
narwhal
aahlntu
Nahuatl
aahlprs
phrasal
aahlpst
asphalt
taplash
aahmnnu
hanuman
aahmopr
amphora
aahmors
Masorah
aahmqsu
quamash
aahmstv
mash-vat
aahnnos
hosanna
aahnnpr
harn-pan
aahnort
athanor
aahnorv
navarho
aahnrtx
anthrax
aahnrty
rhatany
aahprtw
warpath
aahptwy
pathway
aahrsst
shastra

aahrsty
ash-tray
aahrttw
athwart
aaiillp
Palilia
aaiilmr
air-mail
aaiilnt
Italian
aaiilnv
Vinalia
aaiilnz
Azilian
aaiilpr
pairial
aaiilrr
air-rail
aaiilrz
alizari
aaiinnr
Iranian
aaiinnz
anziani
aaiintt
Titania
aaiinzz
Zizania
aaiirvv
vivaria
aaijlnp
jalapin
aaijmnp
jampani
aaijnrz
janizar
aaikllm
Kallima
aaiklls
alkalis
aaiklpt
kail-pat
aaikmnn
manakin
aaikmnr
ramakin
aaikmor
romaika
aaiknnt
Kantian
aaikppr
paprika
aaikstt
astatki
aaiktvv
akvavit
aaillp
pallial
aaillmm
mamilla
aaillmn
manilla
aaillmr
armilla

aaillmx
maxilla
aaillnv
vanilla
aaillpp
papilla
aaillrx
axillar
aaillsv
salival
aailluv
alluvia
aaillxy
axially
aailmmn
mailman
aailmms
Lamaism
miasmal
aailmmx
maximal
aailmnr
laminar
railman
aailmnt
matinal
aailmnu
alumina
aailmnv
mail-van
aailmrt
marital
martial
aailmst
Lamaist
aailnop
Pianola®
aailnot
ailanto
Laotian
aailnov
novalia
valonia
aailnps
salpian
aailnpt
platina
aailnpu
Paulian
aailnru
ulnaria
Uralian
aailnry
laniary
aailnss
Nasalis
aailntv
Latvian
valiant
aailors
rosalia
aailorv
variola

aailprt
partial
patrial
aailpst
spatial
aailptt
talipat
aailrrv
arrival
aailrtt
rat-tail
aailrtv
travail
aailrwy
railway
aailssv
vassail
aailssw
wassail
aailttt
latitat
aaimmno
ammonia
aaimmss
miasmas
aaimnno
omniana
aaimnos
anosmia
aaimnrt
Martian
tamarin
aaimnrx
Marxian
aaimnst
stamina
aaimntx
taximan
aaimprs
Arimasp
aaimrsu
samurai
aaimsst
stasima
aaimstv
atavism
aainnru
Uranian
aainnrv
navarin
nirvana
aainops
paisano
aainorr
orarian
aainorv
ovarian
aainprt
Patarin
aainrst
artisan
tsarina
aainrsu
saurian
aainrsv
savarin
aainrtv
variant
aainttt
attaint
aainttu
tutania
aaioprr
pair-oar
aaioprt
atropia
aaiorsu
saouari
aaiortv
aviator
aaippru
puparia
aaipptt
pitapat
aaiprrt
air-trap
aaiprss
Sarapis
aaiprtt
partita
aaiqssu
quassia
aaiqtuv
aquavit
aajklwy
jaywalk
aajkmnr
jarkman
aajmnzz
jazzman
aajmort
majorat
aajmpsy
pyjamas
aajnruy
January
aajopsu
sapajou
aakklru
karakul
aakkmot
tokamak
aakksuz
zakuska
aaklmry
malarky
aaklmuy
yamulka
aaklnoo
oolakan
aaklnor
Alkoran
aaklnou
oulakan
aakloop
palooka
aaklrsu
kursaal
rusalka
aaklssu
saksaul
aaklwwy
walkway
aakmmnr
markman
aakmost
oak-mast
aakmosu
mousaka
aakmruz
mazurka
aakmrwy
waymark
aaknntu
nunatak
aakntwy
twankay
aakorst
ostraka
aakprwy
parkway
aakrtuy
autarky
aallins
Lallans
aallmpu
ampulla
aallnpu
planula
aallnsy
nasally
aalloss
Salsola
aallotv
lavolta
aallppy
papally
aallrst
all-star
aallruy
aurally
aallrvy
vallary
aalltwy
ally-taw
aalluvv
valvula
aalmmno
ammonal
aalmmns
alms-man
aalmmnt
maltman
aalmnos
salamon
aalmnoy
anomaly
aalmort
alamort
aalmory
mayoral
aalmpry
palmary
palmyra
aalmpwx
wax-palm
aalmrru
ramular
aalmttu
mulatta
aalnnru
annular
aalnors
also-ran
aalnprt
plantar
aalnpst
salt-pan
aalnpsv
Pan-Slav
aalnptu
Laputan
aalnpuu
punalua
aalnqtu
quantal
aalnrtu
natural
aalnstt
saltant
aalnstu
sultana
aalnsty
analyst
aaloppt
Appalto
aaloprs
parasol
aalopvv
pavlova
aalorru
auroral
aalorsu
arousal
aalortx
laxator
aalotty
talayot
aalppru
papular
aalprsw
asprawl
aalpstu
spatula
aalpwyy
play-way
aalrstu
austral
aalrsty
astylar
satyral
aalrwyy
lyra-way
aalsstu
assault
aammmry
mammary
aammnnx
Manxman
aammnrt
mantram
aammnty
Tammany
aammrst
ramstam
aamnnoy
anonyma
aamnntu
Mantuan
aamnorr
Marrano
aamnors
oarsman
aamnorw
man-o'-war
aamnoty
anatomy
aamnprt
mantrap
rampant
aamnpss
passman
aamnpst
tapsman
aamnpty
tympana
aamnrst
artsman
star-man
aamoors
amorosa
aamorrz
zamarro
aamorss
Massora
aamorsv
samovar
aamorty
amatory
aamostt
stomata
aamottu
automat
aamprrt
rampart
aamprst
star-map
aampssy
ampassy
aamrsst
matrass
aamrstu
sumatra
aamrtwy
tramway
aamsstu
satsuma
aannott
annatto
aanortu
Arnaout
aanprst
Spartan
aanpsst
passant
aanqrtu
quartan
aanrrtw
warrant
aanrsuv
Varanus
aanruwy
runaway
aansttt
statant
aanswyy
anyways
aaoorrw
woorara
aaopsst
potassa
aaprrtt
rat-trap
aaprsty
satrapy
aapzzzz
pazzazz
aarrtty
Tartary
abbbdel
blabbed
abbbelr
babbler
blabber
brabble
abbbitt
babbitt
abbcder
crabbed
abbcdes
scabbed
abbcehu
babuche
abbcelr
clabber
abbcels
scabble
abbcryy
cry-baby
abbdegr
grabbed
abbdeit
tabbied
abbdekr
bark-bed
abbdelr
dabbler
drabble
abbdels
slabbed

abbderr
drabber
abbdert
drabbet
abbdest
stabbed
abbdesw
swabbed
abbdgin
dabbing
abbdhij
djibbah
abbdilo
Bobadil
abbdilr
libbard
abbdinr
ribband
abbdlru
lubbard
abbdmor
bombard
abbdmou
babudom
abbdnox
band-box
abbdnyy
by-and-by
abbdruu
rub-a-dub
abbeglr
gabbler
grabble
abbegno
bogbean
abbegnu
bugbane
abbegrr
grabber
abbegru
bugbear
abbehls
shabble
abbellr
bar-bell
abbelmr
bramble
abbelns
snabble
abbelpr
prabble
abbelrr
rabbler
abbelrs
slabber
abbelru
barbule
abbelrw
wabbler
abbelsu
basbleu
abbeluy
buyable

abbemuz
bumbaze
abberst
stabber
abbersw
swabber
abbfirt
frabbit
abbginn
nabbing
abbginu
bubinga
abbgoou
bugaboo
abbhino
Hobbian
abbhisy
babyish
abbhnoo
hob-a-nob
abbhoos
baboosh
abbhrru
rhubarb
abbhttu
bathtub
abbiims
Babiism
abbilor
bilobar
abbilot
bobtail
abbilsu
bubalis
abbimno
bambino
abbimsu
babuism
abbinor
rabboni
abbirty
rabbity
abbisty
baby-sit
abbklou
blaubok
abblltu
bullbat
abblmry
brambly
abblsuu
Bubalus
abbmost
bombast
abbmotu
bum-boat
abbnrtu
bran-tub
abbqsuy
squabby
abccchi
Bacchic
abcceer
Rebecca

abcceir
acerbic
breccia
abcceis
sebacic
abcchii
bacchii
abcchor
choc-bar
abcchsu
Bacchus
abcchty
bycatch
abcciir
Cabiric
abccilu
cubical
abccimr
cambric
abccinu
buccina
abccior
boracic
braccio
abcckow
bawcock
abccktu
cutback
abccoor
barocco
abccoot
tobacco
abccsuu
succuba
abcdeeh
beached
abcdeei
Cebidae
abcdeel
débâcle
abcdehu
debauch
abcdeik
dieback
abcdeip
pedicab
abcdeir
carbide
abcdekn
back-end
abcdelo
coal-bed
abcdemp
camp-bed
abcdeor
brocade
abcderu
cudbear
abcdgor
dog-crab
abcdhio
ichabod
abcdhor
chobdar

abcdiis
dibasic
abcdilr
baldric
abcdins
abscind
abcdirs
scabrid
abcdirt
catbird
abcdiru
baudric
abcdisu
subacid
abcdnos
abscond
abcdoor
córdoba
abcdorr
brocard
abceemr
embrace
abceens
absence
abceerr
rebrace
abceesu
because
abcegir
ribcage
abcegmo
camboge
abcegor
brocage
abcegos
boscage
abcehir
Hebraic
abcehit
Thebaic
abcehko
backhoe
abcehlu
bauchle
abcehmr
becharm
brecham
chamber
chambré
abcehos
basoche
abcehrt
brachet
abceiir
Cabeiri
abceilm
alembic
abceilr
caliber
calibre
abceilt
citable
abceimo
amoebic

abceinr
carbine
abceint
cabinet
abceior
aerobic
abceiot
ice-boat
abceirs
ascribe
abceiss
scabies
abceitt
tabetic
abcekln
blacken
abceknr
bracken
abcekrt
bracket
abcekst
backset
setback
abceksy
backsey
abcektw
wetback
abcellu
bullace
cue-ball
abcelmo
cembalo
abcelmr
cambrel
clamber
abcelms
scamble
abcelop
placebo
abcelov
vocable
abcelpu
bluecap
abcelpy
byplace
abcelru
curable
abcelsu
bascule
abcenow
cowbane
abcenru
unbrace
abceoos
caboose
abceoru
corbeau
abcesss
abscess
abcfikn
finback
abcfilo
bifocal

abcfloo
cobloaf
abcflox
box-calf
abcghko
hogback
abcgikn
backing
abcgiln
cabling
abcginr
bracing
abcgklo
backlog
abchils
Chablis
abchilu
Baluchi
abchimt
bathmic
abchiot
cohabit
abchkou
chabouk
abchktu
hackbut
abchkuw
hawbuck
abchnor
brochan
abchnry
branchy
abchstu
bush-cat
abciill
bacilli
abciimn
minicab
abciior
ciboria
abciiot
abiotic
abcijno
Jacobin
abciksy
sick-bay
abcilor
crab-oil
abcilrs
scribal
abciltu
cubital
abcimms
cambism
abcimmu
cambium
abcimst
cambist
abcinot
botanic
abciorr
barrico
abcioru
caribou

abciouv
  bivouac
abcirty
  barytic
abcisss
  absciss
abcjosu
  jacobus
abckmru
  buckram
abcknno
  bannock
abckotu
  outback
abckstu
  sackbut
  subtack
abcksuw
  buck-saw
  saw-buck
abcllow
  cob-wall
abcllox
  call-box
abclloy
  call-boy
abclluw
  club-law
abclmnu
  clubman
abclmou
  Columba
abclmoy
  cymbalo
abclnoy
  balcony
abcloox
  coal-box
abcnosw
  cob-swan
abcnrtu
  crab-nut
abcootx
  box-coat
abcorrw
  crow-bar
abcottu
  cab-tout
abddeer
  bearded
  breaded
abddees
  debased
abddeez
  bedazed
abddein
  abidden
  bandied
abddeir
  braided
abddelr
  bladder
abddemr
  mad-bred

abddenr
  branded
abddens
  sand-bed
abddeor
  road-bed
abdderw
  bedward
abddhis
  baddish
abddins
  disband
abddllo
  oddball
abddmor
  dambrod
abdeehv
  behaved
abdeeil
  lie-abed
abdeelm
  beldame
  bemedal
abdeelr
  bederal
  bleared
abdeelt
  belated
abdeely
  dyeable
abdeemn
  benamed
abdeemr
  ambered
abdeems
  embased
abdeemz
  bemazed
abdeept
  peat-bed
abdeers
  debaser
abdeert
  betread
  debater
abdeest
  bestead
abdeett
  abetted
abdeflu
  leafbud
abdefor
  forbade
abdefos
  sofa-bed
abdefrw
  bedwarf
abdefst
  bedfast
abdeggr
  bragged
abdeghi
  bighead

abdeghr
  beghard
abdegin
  beading
abdegir
  abridge
  brigade
abdegiw
  wide-gab
abdegln
  bangled
abdeglr
  belgard
abdegno
  bondage
  dogbane
abdehit
  Thebaid
abdehlr
  halberd
abdehow
  bowhead
abdehrt
  breadth
abdehsu
  sub-head
abdeiln
  nail-bed
abdeilp
  bipedal
  piebald
abdeilr
  ridable
abdeils
  disable
abdeilu
  audible
abdeimr
  embraid
abdeinr
  brained
abdeinw
  bedawin
abdeirr
  briared
abdeirs
  darbies
  sea-bird
abdeirt
  tribade
abdeiss
  biassed
abdejou
  j'adoube
abdeknu
  unbaked
abdelmr
  marbled
abdelot
  bloated
abdelow
  dowable
abdelpu
  dupable

abdelpy
  pyebald
abdelrr
  drabler
abdelru
  durable
abdelst
  blasted
abdelyz
  lazy-bed
abdemno
  abdomen
abdenor
  bandore
  broaden
abdenoy
  naebody
abdenrr
  brander
abdenrw
  brawned
abdenss
  badness
abdensu
  subdean
abdentu
  unbated
abdeoot
  tabooed
abdeorr
  boarder
abdeotu
  boutade
abdeqsu
  basqued
abderst
  dabster
abdersu
  subedar
abderty
  drybeat
abderuy
  daubery
abdettu
  abutted
abdggor
  boggard
abdgiin
  abiding
abdgiln
  balding
abdginn
  banding
abdginr
  brigand
abdgint
  dingbat
abdginu
  daubing
abdginw
  wind-bag
abdglno
  bogland

abdgluy
  ladybug
abdhhos
  dobhash
abdhiit
  adhibit
abdhils
  baldish
abdhmor
  rhabdom
abdhmsu
  budmash
abdhmtu
  mud-bath
abdhnow
  bow-hand
abdhnsu
  husband
abdhrsu
  burdash
  rhabdus
abdiknw
  bawdkin
abdikrs
  disbark
abdilnw
  Baldwin
abdiloo
  diabolo
abdilor
  labroid
abdilot
  tabloid
abdilrw
  awlbird
abdilry
  rabidly
abdiluy
  audibly
abdilwy
  bawdily
abdimor
  ambroid
abdimry
  may-bird
abdinor
  inboard
abdinrt
  ant-bird
abdinst
  bandits
abdiosu
  badious
abdipru
  upbraid
abdirsu
  subarid
abdirty
  tribady
abdknoo
  bandook
abdkooy
  day-book

abdllny
  blandly
abdllor
  bollard
abdlmor
  lombard
abdlnor
  bandrol
abdlory
  broadly
abdlruy
  durably
abdlryy
  byrlady
abdlsuu
  subdual
abdmnno
  bondman
abdmnoy
  man-body
abdmotu
  mud-boat
abdmruy
  marybud
abdnopr
  proband
abdnosu
  bausond
abdnosx
  sand-box
abdnosy
  sand-boy
abdnoyy
  anybody
abdnsty
  stand-by
abdoorw
  barwood
abdorwy
  draw-boy
abdrstu
  bustard
abdruzz
  buzzard
abeeeft
  beeftea
abeeels
  seeable
abeeemy
  eye-beam
abeeerv
  bereave
abeeest
  sea-beet
abeeffl
  effable
abeefgr
  Fabergé
abeefhm
  beef-ham
abeeflo
  beefalo
abeeftu
  beaufet

7 ABE

abeeghr
herbage
abeegll
gabelle
abeeglr
beagler
abeegrr
gerbera
abeegru
auberge
abeegrw
brewage
abeehms
beshame
abeehmt
embathe
abeehnn
henbane
abeehns
banshee
has-been
abeehnt
beneath
abeehrs
she-bear
abeehrt
breathe
herb-tea
abeehty
eye-bath
abeeimt
tie-beam
abeeirt
ebriate
abeeist
beastie
abeeknt
betaken
abeeknv
beknave
abeekop
peekabo
abeekps
bespake
bespeak
abeekrr
breaker
abeelly
eyeball
abeelmm
emblema
abeelmw
ewe-lamb
abeelmz
emblaze
abeelnt
Beltane
tenable
abeelnu
nebulae
abeelpr
bepearl
abeelqu
equable

abeelrr
errable
abeelrt
retable
abeelsu
sea-blue
sueable
abeelsv
beslave
abeemrs
besmear
abeemrv
embrave
abeenor
ear-bone
abeenrv
verbena
abeerrt
rebater
terebra
abeertt
abetter
abeervy
beavery
abeeswx
beeswax
abefflr
baffler
abeffot
offbeat
abefgil
filabeg
abefgst
gabfest
abefiln
finable
abefilr
friable
abefilx
fixable
abefinu
beaufin
abefirr
fire-bar
abefirv
five-bar
abefity
beatify
abefllu
baleful
abeflly
flyable
abeflnu
baneful
abeflny
flybane
abeforr
forbear
abefrsu
bus-fare
abeggmo
gamboge
abeggny
gang-bye

abeggru
burgage
abeggry
beggary
abeghns
shebang
abegiln
Belgian
Bengali
abegimn
beaming
abegimr
gambier
abegimt
megabit
abegino
begonia
abeginr
bearing
abegint
beating
abeginw
wine-bag
abegipp
bagpipe
abegkor
brokage
abeglmr
gambler
gambrel
abeglnr
brangle
abeglor
albergo
abeglot
globate
abeglrr
garbler
abegmor
embargo
abegmru
umbrage
abegnnt
banteng
abegnos
nosebag
abegopt
peat-bog
abegopy
page-boy
abegorr
begorra
abegorx
gearbox
abegott
bottega
abegouy
buoyage
abegrst
bargest
abehilr
hirable
abehims
beamish

abehimt
imbathe
abehirs
bearish
abehisu
beauish
abehitu
habitué
abehitz
zabtieh
abehkru
hauberk
abehlms
shamble
abehlrt
blather
halbert
abehlsu
ale-bush
abehnos
bone-ash
abehoty
hay-bote
abehrry
herbary
abehrty
breathy
abeiill
baillie
abeiinr
Iberian
abeijmr
jambier
abeijns
basenji
abeikll
likable
abeikls
skiable
abeiknr
break-in
inbreak
abeiknt
beatnik
abeillo
lobelia
abeillp
pliable
abeillr
air-bell
Braille
liberal
abeillv
livable
abeilmr
mirable
remblai
abeilmt
limbate
timbale
abeilmy
beamily
abeilnp
biplane

abeilns
lesbian
abeilny
bay-line
abeilps
ba'spiel
abeilpt
patible
abeilrt
librate
triable
abeilst
bestial
stabile
abeilsz
sizable
abeilvv
bivalve
abeimnr
mirbane
abeimnt
ambient
abeimot
Moabite
abeinno
Niobean
abeinpr
bran-pie
abeinpt
bepaint
abeinrs
Serbian
abeinrt
atebrin
abeinst
basinet
besaint
bestain
abeintt
tabinet
Tibetan
abeinty
bay-tine
abeiors
isobare
abeioss
isobase
abeiotv
obviate
abeipst
baptise
abeirrr
barrier
abeirrs
brasier
abeirrt
arbiter
rarebit
abeirrz
bizarre
brazier
abeirss
brassie

abeirtt
biretta
abeirtv
vibrate
abeirux
exurbia
abeistt
batiste
abeisuv
abusive
abeitux
bauxite
abejllr
bell-jar
abejmno
jambone
abejmux
jambeux
abejnow
jawbone
abejrru
abjurer
abeklly
bleakly
abeklnt
blanket
abekoor
abrooke
abekort
to-brake
to-break
abekpru
break-up
upbreak
abellmn
bellman
abellno
Bellona
abellnt
netball
abellos
losable
abellov
lovable
volable
abellru
rubella
rulable
abelltu
bullate
abelmmr
membral
abelmnt
lambent
abelmnu
albumen
abelmov
movable
abelmrr
marbler
rambler
abelmrt
lambert

abelmtu
mutable
abelnot
notable
abelnoy
baloney
abelnrs
bransle
abelnrt
brantle
abelnru
nebular
abelnry
blarney
abelntu
tunable
abelopr
ropable
abelopt
potable
abelors
labrose
abelort
bloater
abeloru
rubeola
abelosv
absolve
abeloxx
axle-box
abelpru
puberal
abelquy
equably
abelrrw
brawler
warbler
abelrss
braless
abelrst
blaster
stabler
abelrtt
battler
blatter
brattle
abelrtw
blewart
abelruz
zebrula
abelrvy
bravely
abelstt
battels
abelstu
sublate
abelsty
beastly
abemnos
ambones
abemnry
byreman
myrbane

abemnsu
sun-beam
abemort
bromate
abemssy
embassy
abemttu
meat-tub
abennrw
bran-new
abenors
sea-born
abenort
baronet
reboant
abenorw
rawbone
abenoty
bayonet
abenqtu
banquet
abenrsu
sun-bear
abenrux
exurban
abenstu
sun-beat
abeootv
obovate
abeoprs
saprobe
abeoprt
probate
abeoqru
baroque
abeorrs
brasero
abeorrt
arboret
taborer
abeorst
boaster
sorbate
abeorsu
aerobus
abeorsv
bravoes
abeorsy
rose-bay
abeortt
abettor
taboret
abeostx
box-seat
abeprty
type-bar
aberrsu
Bursera
aberrvy
bravery
abersst
brasset
aberssu
surbase

aberssz
zebrass
aberstu
surbate
aberstw
wabster
abersty
barytes
abersuu
bureaus
aberttu
abutter
abertty
battery
aberuux
bureaux
abezzzz
bezzazz
abffiil
bailiff
abfflou
buffalo
abfgglo
golf-bag
abfgiln
fabling
abfgkno
fog-bank
abfglsu
bagfuls
abfhlsu
bashful
abfiilr
bifilar
abfiimr
fimbria
abfilru
fibular
abfimor
fibroma
abfloty
boat-fly
flyboat
abfoort
footbar
abfsttu
tubfast
abgggin
bagging
abggily
baggily
abgginn
banging
abggorw
grow-bag
abghins
bashing
abghlot
hagbolt
abghlru
burghal
abghmru
Hamburg

abghotu
abought
abghrsu
rag-bush
abgiins
biasing
abgiint
baiting
abgikln
balking
abgilln
balling
abgilmn
ambling
abgilnt
tabling
abgilnw
bawling
abgilor
garboil
abgimst
gambist
abginnt
banting
abginor
Grobian
abginot
boating
abginrr
barring
abginst
basting
abgintt
batting
abgiopt
pigboat
abgkmsu
musk-bag
abgkoor
rag-book
abgkorw
work-bag
abglmmu
mug-lamb
abglmnu
lumbang
abglmou
lumbago
abglnoo
Bologna
abgloot
toolbag
abglort
ragbolt
abglrru
burglar
abgmnoy
bogy-man
abgnopr
probang
abgnotu
gunboat
abgoort
botargo

abgopst
post-bag
abgorru
goburra
abgortu
outbrag
abgosuy
gas-buoy
abgottu
tug-boat
abhhipt
hip-bath
abhhkot
khotbah
abhhktu
khutbah
abhhoop
Pooh-Bah
abhhsuy
hushaby
abhiint
inhabit
abhiktw
hawkbit
abhilno
hobnail
abhilos
abolish
abhilot
oil-bath
abhiltu
halibut
abhimnr
Brahmin
abhinst
absinth
abhiors
boarish
abhiost
isobath
abhklsy
bashlyk
abhkoru
bourkha
abhkrsu
kurbash
abhloux
box-haul
abhlrtu
hurl-bat
abhmnsu
bushman
abhmstu
mash-tub
abhnstu
sun-bath
abhorru
harbour
abhotuy
hautboy
abhrstu
tarbush
abhstuw
wash-tub

abiikkt
kibitka
abiilmu
bulimia
abiilnq
inqilab
abiilns
aiblins
abiilry
biliary
abiilst
stibial
abiilty
ability
abiimst
iambist
abiinor
robinia
abiinry
biryani
abiioss
abiosis
abijlnr
brinjal
abijnot
abjoint
abijnpu
Punjabi
abiklmn
lambkin
abiklmr
milk-bar
abiklor
kilobar
abikmnr
barmkin
abikott
kit-boat
abikrst
britska
abikrtz
britzka
abillmn
billman
abillmu
ballium
abillnp
pinball
abillpy
pay-bill
pliably
abillsw
saw-bill
abillsy
syllabi
abillwx
wax-bill
abillwy
way-bill
abilmnu
albumin
abilmox
mail-box

abilnos
albinos
abilnot
bitonal
abilnoz
bizonal
abilnry
bairnly
abilopr
bipolar
parboil
abilort
orbital
abilorv
bolivar
abilotu
obitual
abilrry
library
abilrsu
railbus
abimnru
Umbrian
abimoss
biomass
abimpst
baptism
abimtty
ambitty
abinoor
boronia
abinorr
bar-iron
abinors
Sorbian
abinort
taborin
abinorw
rainbow
abinost
bastion
abinosu
abusion
abinrtv
vibrant
abiortv
vibrato
abiprtt
bit-part
abipstt
baptist
abirtty
traybit
abizzzz
bizzazz
abjkmos
sjambok
abjlmoo
jambool
abkllny
blankly
abkloow
law-book
abklruw
bulwark
abkmnoo
bookman
abknopt
pot-bank
abknruu
bunraku
ablllluy
lullaby
abllnoo
balloon
abllopr
proball
abllorr
roll-bar
abllort
toll-bar
ablloru
lobular
ablloty
tallboy
abllpsu
balls-up
abllruy
bullary
ablmmou
bummalo
ablmnou
umbonal
ablmoot
tombola
ablmosy
lamboys
ablmovy
movably
ablmpuu
pabulum
ablmtuy
mutably
ablnoty
notably
ablntuy
tunably
abloory
obolary
abloptt
tap-bolt
ablopxy
play-box
ablopyy
playboy
ablorst
borstal
ablortw
blawort
abloruw
bourlaw
ablostx
salt-box
ablrtuu
tubular
abmmnos
mobsman
abmoorr
bar-room
abmortu
tambour
abmostu
subatom
abnoors
soroban
abnoorz
borazon
abnooss
bassoon
abnorty
baryton
abnoruy
Yoruban
abnossu
bonasus
abnotuy
buoyant
aboopsx
soapbox
aboortw
rowboat
abooryz
Bryozoa
abostuu
autobus
abprstu
upbrast
abrrsuy
bursary
abrrtuy
turbary
abrstuu
arbutus
absuwzz
buzz-saw
acccily
acyclic
accddei
caddice
accdeen
cadence
accdeer
acceder
accdeii
accidie
accdeiu
caducei
accdeko
cockade
accdekr
cracked
accdeny
cadency
accderu
cardecu
accdesu
accused
succade
accdfil
flaccid
accdils
scaldic
accdins
Scandic
accdiot
octadic
accdkno
candock
accdkow
dawcock
accdloy
cacodyl
acceeho
coachee
acceeln
cenacle
acceenr
creance
acceert
accrete
acceflu
felucca
accegin
accinge
accegno
Cocagne
accegos
soccage
accegpu
cage-cup
accehhi
chéchia
accehil
caliche
chalice
accehim
macchie
accehin
chicane
accehln
chancel
accehlo
cochlea
accehnr
chancer
chancre
accehnu
chaunce
accehor
caroche
coacher
accehpu
capuche
accehrt
catcher
accehtu
catechu
accehxy
cachexy
acceikp
icepack
pack-ice
acceiln
calcine
acceilo
coeliac
acceilt
calcite
acceimr
ceramic
racemic
acceino
cocaine
oceanic
acceinr
Circean
acceinv
vaccine
acceipr
caprice
acceiqu
cacique
acceirs
carices
acceirt
creatic
acceist
ascetic
acceklr
cackler
clacker
crackle
accekmo
meacock
accekop
peacock
accekos
sea-cock
accekrr
cracker
accelly
calycle
accelno
conceal
accelor
coracle
accelot
cacolet
accelsu
saccule
accelsy
calyces
accemno
Meccano®
accemnu
cacumen
accenor
conacre
accenos
asconce
accenov
concave
accenpt
peccant
acceopy
cacoepy
acceorw
cracowe
accepry
peccary
accerrt
carrect
accersu
accurse
accuser
accfiip
pacific
accfily
calcify
accflow
cow-calf
accghio
Chicago
acchhku
kuchcha
acchims
chasmic
acchino
chicano
Noachic
acchiot
chaotic
acchirs
scraich
acchjsu
jacchus
acchkoy
haycock
acchltu
claucht
acchnrs
scranch
acchnru
craunch
acchotw
choctaw
acchouy
acouchy
acchptu
catchup
upcatch
acchrru
currach
acchrst
scratch
acchrsu
scrauch
acciiln
aclinic
acciint
actinic
acciist
sciatic
accikrs
car-sick
accillu
calculi
accilmo
comical
accilmu
calcium

accilno
conical
laconic
accilnu
Cluniac
accilny
cynical
accilor
caloric
accilov
vocalic
accilru
crucial
accilry
acrylic
accilss
classic
accilst
clastic
accilsu
sacculi
accimoz
zimocca
accinno
canonic
accinop
Canopic
accinot
cantico
accinru
crucian
acciopr
caproic
acciors
scoriac
acciprt
practic
accistt
tactics
accistu
caustic
accklmu
Calmuck
accklor
carlock
acckl ry
crackly
acckmor
cromack
acckoss
cassock
Cossack
acckost
castock
accmopt
accompt
compact
accmruu
curcuma
accnnoo
coon-can
accnoor
raccoon

accnott
contact
accnotu
account
accopty
copy-cat
accoqsu
squacco
accorss
corcass
accortu
accourt
accrstu
accurst
acdddko
daddock
acddeer
cedared
acddeey
decayed
acddehr
Cheddar
acddein
candied
acddeiu
decidua
acddelo
cladode
acddemu
ducdame
acddeop
decapod
acdderu
adducer
acddhhu
chuddah
acddhis
caddish
acddhko
haddock
acddhru
chuddar
acddinu
Dunciad
acddirs
discard
acddkop
paddock
acddssy
caddyss
acdeees
decease
acdeefr
defacer
acdeeft
faceted
acdeehl
Chaldee
acdeehr
reached
acdeeir
deciare
acdeejt
dejecta

acdeelr
Cedrela
creedal
declare
acdeels
seed-lac
acdeelv
cleaved
acdeemr
racemed
acdeenv
vendace
acdeeot
Docetae
acdeert
cedrate
acdeest
tedesca
acdeetu
educate
acdeety
cat-eyed
acdefin
fancied
acdefir
farcied
acdefop
po-faced
acdefrs
scarfed
acdefrt
fracted
acdeggr
cragged
acdegis
discage
acdegko
dockage
acdegno
decagon
acdegor
cordage
acdehin
chained
echidna
acdehip
edaphic
acdehix
hexadic
acdehkw
whacked
acdehlr
chalder
acdehmr
charmed
acdehms
chasmed
acdehmt
matched
acdehnr
endarch
acdehot
cathode

acdehpp
chapped
acdehpr
parched
acdehpt
patched
acdehpu
cuphead
acdehrr
charred
acdehtt
chatted
acdeiio
Dioecia
acdeill
cedilla
acdeilm
decimal
declaim
medical
acdeiln
Iceland
acdeilr
decrial
radicel
radicle
acdeils
Alcides
acdeilt
citadel
deltaic
dialect
edictal
acdeimy
mediacy
acdeino
oceanid
acdeins
candies
acdeiny
cyanide
acdeipr
epacrid
acdeips
dispace
acdeirr
carried
acdeirs
radices
sidecar
acdeiru
decuria
acdeiss
discase
acdeist
die-cast
acdeitt
dictate
acdeity
edacity
acdeklt
tackled
acdekrt
tracked

acdekst
stacked
acdeksu
sea-duck
acdells
scalled
acdelmm
clammed
acdelms
mascled
acdelno
celadon
acdelns
calends
acdelpp
clapped
acdelpy
ycleap'd
acdelrs
scalder
acdelss
classed
declass
acdelst
castled
acdelww
dew-claw
acdemmr
crammed
acdemnu
decuman
acdemor
comrade
acdempr
cramped
acdenns
scanned
acdennt
candent
acdenor
acorned
acdenpt
pandect
acdenrt
cantred
tranced
acdenru
durance
unraced
acdenry
ardency
acdenst
descant
acdentu
unacted
acdeops
peascod
acdeorr
corrade
acdeors
sarcode
acdeort
cordate
redcoat

acdeouv
couvade
acdeprs
scarped
acderrs
scarred
acdersu
crusade
acdertt
detract
acdertu
traduce
acdfiiy
acidify
acdginn
dancing
acdgino
gonadic
acdgklo
daglock
acdgnot
cantdog
acdgort
dogcart
acdhiil
chiliad
acdhiis
Hasidic
acdhiop
phacoid
acdhiry
diarchy
acdhiss
Chassid
acdhkoy
Hock-day
acdhlor
chordal
dorlach
acdhnow
cowhand
acdhoot
cathood
acdhopr
pochard
acdhorr
orchard
acdhruy
duarchy
acdhryy
dyarchy
acdiinn
indican
acdiino
conidia
acdiinr
acridin
acdiirs
cidaris
sciarid
acdiirt
triacid
triadic

acdiity
acidity
acdikls
skaldic
acdillo
codilla
acdilmo
domical
acdilno
nodical
acdilop
placoid
podalic
acdilor
cordial
acdilot
co-tidal
acdilpu
paludic
acdiltw
wild-cat
acdimmu
cadmium
acdimno
mandioc
monacid
monadic
nomadic
acdimny
dynamic
acdinru
iracund
acdinst
discant
acdinsu
sudanic
acdinsx
Scandix
acdiopr
parodic
picador
acdiors
sarcoid
acdiort
arctoid
carotid
acdiost
Sotadic
acdioty
dacoity
acdioxy
oxy-acid
acdiqru
quadric
acdirst
drastic
acdituv
viaduct
acdjntu
adjunct
acdklop
padlock
acdklsy
skyclad

acdkmoo
mockado
acdkmpu
mudpack
acdkntu
duck-ant
acdkopr
pockard
acdllor
collard
acdlluy
ducally
acdlnor
caldron
acdlnot
cotland
acdlnsu
sun-clad
acdlopu
cupola'd
acdlowy
ladycow
acdmmno
command
acdmoow
cam-wood
acdmorz
czardom
acdnoor
cardoon
acdnoru
candour
caudron
acdorst
costard
acdorsu
crusado
acdrstu
custard
acdrsuu
carduus
aceeeps
escapee
aceeeuv
evacuee
aceefft
A-effect
aceefhn
enchafe
aceefin
faience
fiancée
aceefny
fayence
aceefpr
preface
aceeggs
egg-case
aceegil
elegiac
aceegnr
engrace
aceegnt
centage

aceegsu
escuage
aceehht
cheetah
aceehit
hicatee
teachie
aceehiv
achieve
aceehko
hoe-cake
aceehlr
relâche
aceehls
Chelsea
aceehlt
chelate
aceehmr
machree
aceehmt
machete
aceehnn
enhance
aceehnp
cheapen
ha'pence
aceehns
enchase
aceehpp
échappé
aceehpr
peacher
aceehrr
reacher
aceehrt
cheater
hectare
rechate
recheat
teacher
aceehst
escheat
aceehtt
thecate
aceeilp
calipee
aceeilt
Eleatic
aceeimt
emicate
aceeinr
Cairene
cinerea
aceeinu
eucaine
aceeisv
vesicae
aceeknp
knee-cap
aceelln
nacelle
aceelmp
emplace

aceelmr
réclame
aceelnr
cleaner
aceelns
cleanse
scalene
aceelnt
latence
aceelnv
enclave
valence
aceelpr
percale
replace
aceelrr
clearer
aceelrs
rescale
aceelrt
treacle
aceelru
caerule
aceelrv
cleaver
aceelst
celesta
aceelsu
euclase
aceelvx
exclave
aceemrr
creamer
aceemrt
ceramet
cremate
meercat
aceennp
penance
aceenns
Senecan
aceennt
canteen
aceenny
cayenne
aceenot
acetone
aceenps
pen-case
aceenrs
caserne
aceenrt
crenate
re-enact
aceentu
cuneate
aceeors
acerose
aceeort
ocreate
aceeost
acetose
aceeotv
evocate

aceeprr
caperer
aceeprs
escaper
percase
aceerrt
caterer
retrace
terrace
aceerst
secreta
aceertx
exacter
excreta
aceesty
cat's-eye
acefffo
face-off
aceffhr
chaffer
aceffis
scaffie
aceffor
afforce
acefhmr
chamfer
acefhor
arch-foe
acefill
ice-fall
acefilm
malefic
acefilr
filacer
acefinn
finance
acefinr
fancier
acefins
fascine
acefitv
factive
acefity
acetify
acefklr
flacker
acefklt
flacket
aceflru
careful
acefnno
façonné
acefnrt
cantref
acefnru
furnace
acefopr
proface
aceforr
forecar
acefotu
outface
acefrrt
refract

acefrru
farceur
acefrsu
surface
acefrtu
facture
furcate
aceghlo
galoche
aceghnr
changer
aceghnu
chaunge
aceghou
gouache
aceghow
cowhage
aceghrr
charger
acegill
ellagic
Gallice
acegiln
angelic
anglice
Galenic
acegilp
pelagic
acegilr
glacier
gracile
acegimr
grimace
acegimt
gametic
acegino
coinage
aceginr
Grecian
acegins
ceasing
aceginv
veganic
acegklo
lockage
acegklr
grackle
acegkmo
mockage
acegkor
corkage
acegkos
gas-coke
acegllo
collage
acegino
congeal
aceglnr
clanger
aceglot
catelog
aceglou
cagoule

acegmop
compage
acegnor
acrogen
cornage
acegnot
co-agent
cognate
acegors
cargoes
corsage
acegoru
courage
acegott
cottage
acegrtu
trucage
acegstu
scutage
acehhlt
hatchel
acehhrt
hatcher
acehhru
hachure
acehhrx
hexarch
acehhtt
hatchet
acehikr
kacheri
acehill
helical
acehilp
aphelic
acehilr
Charlie
acehilt
ethical
acehimn
machine
acehimp
impeach
acehimr
chimera
acehims
chamise
acehinn
cain-hen
enchain
acehins
inchase
acehint
chantie
teach-in
acehiny
hyacine
acehipp
chappie
acehipr
charpie
acehipt
aphetic
hepatic

acehirs
cashier
acehirt
Rhaetic
theriac
acehirv
archive
acehklr
hackler
acehkls
shackle
acehklt
hacklet
acehkny
hackney
acehkrw
whacker
acehkry
hackery
acehllp
pellach
acehlls
shellac
acehllt
hell-cat
acehlmt
chamlet
acehlmy
alchemy
acehlnn
channel
acehlno
chalone
acehlnr
charnel
larchen
acehlop
epochal
acehlor
cholera
chorale
acehlos
oscheal
sea-loch
acehlot
cat-hole
acehlpt
chaplet
acehlpy
cheaply
acehlrt
archlet
acehlry
Charley
acehlst
satchel
acehltt
chattel
latchet
acehmnr
encharm
Märchen
acehmnt
manchet

acehmrr
charmer
marcher
acehmrs
marches
mesarch
acehmrt
matcher
rematch
acehmty
ecthyma
acehnnt
enchant
acehnor
Acheron
acehnrr
rancher
acehnrt
chanter
tranche
acehnst
chasten
acehnsv
Chesvan
acehntt
etchant
acehntu
unteach
acehnty
chantey
acehopr
poacher
acehpps
schappe
acehprt
chapter
patcher
acehpry
eparchy
preachy
acehquu
quechua
acehquy
queachy
acehrrt
charter
acehrrx
xerarch
acehrry
archery
acehrsu
archeus
acehrsy
hyraces
acehrtt
chatter
ratchet
acehrtw
watcher
acehrty
yachter
acehrxy
exarchy

acehttw
watchet
aceiilm
cimelia
aceiils
laicise
aceiilt
ciliate
aceiint
Cainite
aceiitv
caitive
aceiklo
oil-cake
aceiklt
cat-like
aceikmr
keramic
aceikop
paiocke
aceikpr
earpick
aceikpx
pickaxe
aceikss
seasick
aceiktt
tietack
aceillm
limacel
micella
aceillr
air-cell
aceillx
lexical
aceilmn
melanic
aceilmr
claimer
miracle
reclaim
aceilms
limaces
aceilmt
climate
aceilmx
exclaim
aceilmy
mycelia
aceilnp
capelin
panicle
pelican
aceilnr
carline
aceilns
sanicle
aceilnu
cauline
aceilor
calorie
cariole
loricae

aceilos
coalise
aceilot
aloetic
Coalite®
aceilpr
replica
aceilps
special
aceilpt
plicate
aceilrr
cerrial
aceilrt
article
recital
aceilru
auricle
aceilrv
caliver
clavier
velaric
aceilss
salices
aceilst
elastic
latices
salicet
aceilsv
vesical
aceiltt
lattice
tactile
aceimno
encomia
aceimnp
pemican
aceimnr
carmine
aceimns
amnesic
aceimnt
emicant
nematic
aceimnx
Mexican
aceimpy
pyaemic
aceimrt
matrice
aceimru
uraemic
aceimst
etacism
sematic
aceimsu
caesium
aceinnp
pinnace
aceinnt
ancient
aceinny
cyanine

aceinop
paeonic
aceinot
aconite
anoetic
aceinpr
caprine
aceinps
inscape
pincase
aceinrs
arsenic
cerasin
aceinrt
certain
crinate
nacrite
aceinst
Insecta
aceinsy
cyanise
aceintt
nictate
tetanic
aceintv
venatic
aceintx
inexact
aceinty
cyanite
aceiooz
zooecia
aceiopt
ectopia
aceiors
scoriae
aceiort
erotica
aceiost
sociate
aceiotx
exotica
aceippr
epicarp
aceippt
tappice
aceiprs
epacris
ice-spar
scrapie
Serapic
aceiprt
paretic
picrate
aceipst
aseptic
spicate
aceipsu
auspice
aceipsz
capsize
aceiptv
captive

aceiqru
  acquire
aceiquz
  cazique
aceirrr
  carrier
aceirrt
  cirrate
  erratic
aceirrw
  air-crew
aceirst
  stearic
aceirsu
  saucier
  uricase
aceirsv
  varices
  viscera
aceirtt
  citrate
aceisss
  ascesis
aceisst
  ascites
  ectasis
aceistt
  statice
aceistv
  Avestic
aceittx
  extatic
aceitux
  auxetic
acejkop
  pajocke
acejlor
  cajoler
acejnot
  jaconet
acejnoy
  joyance
  Joycean
acejntu
  juncate
acejptu
  cajeput
acejrtt
  traject
acekknr
  knacker
acekllp
  pellack
aceklnr
  crankle
aceklor
  earlock
aceklpt
  placket
aceklqu
  quackle
aceklrs
  slacker
aceklrt
  tackler
aceklru
  caulker
acekmrs
  smacker
aceknpr
  prancke
aceknry
  cankery
acekoos
  sea-cook
acekorr
  croaker
acekppr
  prepack
acekrrt
  tracker
acekrtt
  rackett
acekrty
  rackety
acekstt
  stacket
acektty
  tackety
acellmo
  calomel
acellnu
  nucleal
acellny
  cleanly
acellor
  corella
  ocellar
acellot
  collate
acellps
  scalpel
acellpy
  clypeal
acellrr
  carrell
acellrs
  scleral
acellru
  cure-all
acellry
  clearly
acelmor
  caromel
acelmot
  camelot
acelmou
  caulome
  leucoma
acelmpr
  clamper
acelmry
  camelry
acelmtu
  calumet
acelnnu
  unclean
acelnny
  lyncean
acelnor
  corneal
acelnps
  enclasp
  spancel
acelnpt
  clapnet
acelnpu
  clean-up
  unplace
acelnrt
  central
acelnru
  lucarne
  nuclear
  unclear
acelnry
  larceny
acelnst
  scantle
acelnsu
  censual
  unscale
acelntt
  cantlet
acelnty
  latency
acelnvy
  valency
acelopr
  polacre
acelops
  escalop
acelopt
  polecat
aceloqu
  coequal
acelors
  escolar
acelory
  caloyer
acelost
  alecost
  lactose
  scatole
  talcose
acelott
  calotte
acelotu
  oculate
aceloty
  acolyte
  cotylae
acelouv
  vacuole
acelppr
  clapper
acelpps
  scapple
acelprs
  clasper
  scalper
acelprt
  plectra
acelpry
  prelacy
acelpsu
  capsule
  lace-ups
  specula
acelpty
  ectypal
acelqru
  lacquer
acelquy
  lacquey
acelrrw
  crawler
acelrst
  scarlet
acelrsu
  secular
acelrtt
  clatter
acelrty
  treacly
acelsss
  sacless
acelstu
  sulcate
acelsty
  scytale
acelsux
  excusal
acelsxy
  calyxes
aceltuy
  acutely
aceltxy
  exactly
acemmrr
  crammer
acemnor
  cremona
  romance
acemopr
  compare
  compear
acemoru
  morceau
acemprs
  scamper
acemprt
  crampet
acemrsy
  cramesy
acemstt
  metcast
acennos
  ancones
  sonance
acennot
  connate
acennoy
  noyance
acennoz
  canzone
acennrs
  scanner
acennry
  cannery
acennst
  nascent
acennty
  tenancy
acenoor
  coronae
acenopt
  patonce
acenopu
  ponceau
acenors
  carnose
  coarsen
acenort
  enactor
acenoss
  cassone
acenost
  costean
acenotv
  centavo
acenprr
  prancer
acenptt
  pentact
acenpty
  patency
acenrss
  ancress
acenrsu
  surance
acenrsy
  scenary
acenrtt
  tranect
acenrtu
  centaur
  untrace
acenrty
  encraty
  nectary
acenstu
  nutcase
acenstw
  stew-can
aceoopp
  apocope
aceootz
  ectozoa
aceoprr
  crop-ear
aceoprx
  exocarp
aceopst
  scopate
aceoptu
  outpace
aceorrt
  acroter
  creator
  reactor
aceorst
  coaster
aceorsu
  acerous
  carouse
aceorsw
  sea-crow
aceortu
  outrace
aceortv
  overact
aceortx
  exactor
aceossu
  caseous
aceostt
  costate
aceostu
  acetous
aceosty
  tea-cosy
aceottv
  cavetto
aceotuu
  autocue
aceotux
  coteaux
aceprrs
  scarper
  scraper
aceprst
  precast
  spectra
aceprsu
  scauper
aceprtu
  capture
acepruv
  carve-up
acepstu
  cuspate
aceqrtu
  racquet
aceqstu
  acquest
acerrtt
  retract
acerrty
  tracery
acerruv
  verruca
acersst
  actress
acerssu
  sucrase
acerssv
  scarves
acerstt
  scatter

acerstu
crustae
acersty
sectary
acerttt
tetract
acerttu
curtate
acerttx
extract
acertty
cattery
acertuv
curvate
acertux
curtaxe
acertuy
cautery
acesstu
caestus
acessty
ecstasy
acesttu
scutate
acestty
testacy
acestuy
eustacy
acffhpu
huff-cap
acffiit
caitiff
acffikm
maffick
acffilt
afflict
acffirt
traffic
acffiry
farcify
acffost
cast-off
acfginr
farcing
acfhist
catfish
acfhisu
fuchsia
acfhrty
fratchy
acfiiln
finical
acfiknn
finnack
acfilry
clarify
acfimor
aciform
Formica
acfimss
fascism
acfinny
infancy

acfinot
faction
acfinrt
frantic
infarct
infract
acfipry
caprify
acfirsy
scarify
acfisst
fascist
acfklsu
sackful
acflruu
furcula
acflttu
tactful
acfltuy
faculty
acfortx
X-factor
acforty
factory
acggios
agogics
acggrsy
scraggy
acghikn
hacking
acghimo
oghamic
acghinr
chagrin
charing
acghint
gnathic
acghinw
chinwag
acghipr
graphic
acghirs
scraigh
acghklo
hack-log
acghltu
claught
acghrru
curragh
acghrsu
scraugh
acgiiln
alginic
acgiitu
augitic
acgikln
lacking
acgiknp
packing
acgiknr
arcking
carking
racking

acgikns
sacking
acgiknt
tacking
acgiknv
vacking
acgilln
calling
acgillo
logical
acgilmy
myalgic
acgilns
scaling
acgilnt
catling
acgilnu
glucina
acginnn
canning
acginnt
canting
acginor
organic
acginot
coating
cotinga
acginpp
capping
acginpr
carping
acginps
spacing
acginrs
sacring
acginrt
tracing
acginrv
carving
craving
acginst
casting
acgirst
gastric
acgkmmo
gammock
acgkorv
garvock
acgllpu
cupgall
acglsuu
Glaucus
acgnnor
crannog
acgnoot
octagon
acgorry
gyrocar
acgoruu
couguar
achhipt
chip-hat
achhirs
rhachis

achhost
toshach
achhttt
thatcht
achiikm
kamichi
achiils
ischial
achiimt
Hamitic
achiint
Chianti
achiips
pachisi
achijnt
jacinth
achikrs
ricksha
achikry
hayrick
achikss
shicksa
achillo
lochial
achillp
phallic
achills
challis
achillt
thallic
achilmo
malicho
achilos
scholia
achilrs
carlish
achilry
charily
achilsy
clayish
achilwy
lichway
achimno
manihoc
Mohican
achimos
chamiso
chamois
achimrs
charism
achimss
schisma
achimst
mastich
tachism
achinnu
unchain
achinop
aphonic
achinoy
onychia
achinps
spinach

achinrz
zarnich
achintx
xanthic
achinuv
chauvin
achiopt
aphotic
achiort
chariot
haricot
achipps
Sapphic
achipst
haptics
spathic
achiptu
chupati
achiptw
whipcat
achiqru
charqui
achiquu
Quichua
achirrt
triarch
achirtu
haircut
achirty
charity
achisss
chassis
achistt
cattish
tachist
achkmmo
hammock
achkops
hopsack
achkoss
hassock
achkott
hattock
achlloo
alcohol
achllor
chloral
achlmsy
chlamys
achlmyy
alchymy
achlnoy
halcyon
achlntu
tulchan
unlatch
achlopr
raploch
achlors
scholar
achlort
trochal
achlosw
salchow

achloty
acolyth
achlpst
splatch
achmnoo
manchoo
achmnor
monarch
nomarch
achmnru
uncharm
achmopr
camphor
achmorz
machzor
achmost
stomach
achmsuw
cumshaw
achnnos
chanson
achnort
chantor
achnoty
tachyon
achnouy
chanoyu
achnovy
anchovy
achnpss
schnaps
achnpuy
paunchy
achnrty
chantry
achnruy
raunchy
unchary
achnstu
canthus
staunch
achnsty
snatchy
achoprt
toparch
achopry
charpoy
Corypha
achorsu
aurochs
achpptu
patch-up
achrsty
starchy
achrsuu
urachus
achstuy
cyathus
aciiknn
canikin
aciikrs
airsick
aciilmm
mimical

aciilms
Islamic
aciilmt
Tamilic
aciilns
salicin
aciilnv
vicinal
aciilnz
Zincali
aciilov
viliaco
aciilry
ciliary
aciilss
Liassic
aciimms
miasmic
aciimnr
minicar
aciimot
comitia
aciimst
ismatic
itacism
aciinno
anionic
aciinov
avionic
aciinps
piscina
aciintt
titanic
aciippr
priapic
aciiprt
piratic
aciirst
satiric
aciirtt
triatic
acijnop
Japonic
acijuzz
Jacuzzi®
aciklno
Lockian
aciklor
air-lock
acikmns
sick-man
acikmoo
oomiack
acikmpr
rampick
acikmpw
pickmaw
aciknnp
pannick
aciknor
Koranic
aciknpy
panicky

aciknst
catskin
acikntt
tin-tack
acikprt
patrick
acikpsx
six-pack
acillms
miscall
acilloo
coal-oil
acillry
lyrical
acilmno
limaçon
acilmot
comital
acilmps
plasmic
acilmrs
Carlism
acilmsu
musical
acilmtu
Tamulic
acilnny
cannily
acilnor
clarion
Locrian
acilnoz
Zincalo
acilnps
inclasp
acilnpy
pliancy
acilntu
lunatic
acilnuv
vincula
acilopt
Capitol
coal-pit
optical
pit-coal
topical
acilorr
racloir
acilorv
co-rival
acilost
stoical
acilott
coal-tit
acilotv
volatic
voltaic
acilotx
toxical
acilpst
plastic
acilpsu
spicula

acilpty
clay-pit
typical
acilrst
Carlist
acilrtu
curtail
trucial
acilrty
clarity
acilryz
crazily
acilsss
classis
acilsuy
saucily
aciltty
tacitly
aciltuv
victual
acimnop
campion
acimnor
Marconi
Minorca
Romanic
acimnos
masonic
acimnot
Comtian
acimnpu
Panicum
acimnru
cranium
cumarin
acimntt
catmint
acimopt
potamic
Tampico
acimorr
Armoric
acimost
somatic
acimprt
crampit
ptarmic
acimpry
primacy
acimpss
spasmic
acimrsz
czarism
acimsst
miscast
acimstt
tactism
acinnot
actinon
cantion
contain
acinnoz
canzoni

acinnst
stannic
acinntu
annicut
acinopt
caption
paction
acinorr
carrion
acinors
Roscian
acinort
carotin
acinoss
caisson
cassino
acinost
Scotian
acinosx
Saxonic
acinott
taction
acinotu
auction
caution
acinprt
cantrip
acinpru
Puranic
acinpry
cyprian
acinqtu
quantic
acinrsu
crusian
acinrtt
Tantric
acinrtu
curtain
turacin
acinstu
nautics
acioprs
prosaic
acioprt
apricot
parotic
patrico
acioptt
aptotic
aciopty
opacity
aciorrs
corsair
aciorsu
carious
curiosa
aciortt
ricotta
aciprsy
piscary
aciprtt
tip-cart

aciprvy
privacy
acipsst
spastic
aciptuy
paucity
aciqrtu
quartic
acirsst
sacrist
acirssu
cuirass
acirstt
astrict
acirstu
Austric
acirstw
twiscar
acirsty
satyric
acirstz
czarist
acisstt
statics
acisstu
casuist
acisttu
catsuit
acistuv
vacuist
acituvy
vacuity
acjkksy
skyjack
acjklow
lock-jaw
acjknno
jannock
acjkopt
jackpot
acjloru
jocular
acjmntu
muntjac
acjptuu
cajuput
ackklmu
Kalmuck
ackkoor
cork-oak
ackllop
pollack
acklloy
laylock
ackllsy
slackly
acklmno
lockman
acklmor
lockram
acklnou
uncloak
ackloor
oar-lock

acklorw
warlock
acklory
rocklay
ackloss
lassock
acklosy
yolk-sac
ackmmmo
mammock
ackmnoo
man-cook
ackmort
cork-mat
ackmott
mattock
ackmpru
cup-mark
ackmssu
musk-sac
ackmstu
musk-cat
acknstu
unstack
ackorrt
rock-tar
tarrock
aclllоy
locally
aclloor
corolla
acllops
scallop
aclloru
locular
acllosu
callous
acllovy
vocally
aclmnoo
locoman
aclmnuy
calumny
aclmoru
clamour
aclmsuy
masculy
aclnoor
coronal
aclnoot
coolant
aclnoov
volcano
aclnoru
cornual
courlan
aclnorw
corn-law
aclnouv
unvocal
aclnpsu
unclasp
aclnrtu
truncal

aclnsty
scantly
acloprt
caltrop
proctal
aclopru
copular
cupolar
aclopsu
scopula
aclopsy
calypso
aclopty
polyact
aclorsu
Carolus
oscular
acloruv
vocular
aclostu
locusta
talcous
aclprty
cryptal
aclpruu
cupular
aclrssy
crassly
aclrstu
crustal
aclrsty
crystal
aclrswy
scrawly
aclsstu
cutlass
acmnopr
crampon
acmnopy
company
acmnory
acronym
acmnstu
sanctum
acmoost
scotoma
acmoprt
compart
acmopss
compass
acmqtuu
cumquat
acnnnuy
uncanny
acnnorv
corn-van
acnnory
canonry
acnnosy
sonancy
acnnrsy
scranny
acnoors
coronas
acnoort
cartoon
coranto
acnopsu
Canopus
acnopsw
snowcap
acnorru
rancour
acnorry
carry-on
acnorsu
nacrous
acnortu
courant
acnostu
conatus
acnprsy
syncarp
acnrrtu
currant
acnrswy
scrawny
acnrtuy
truancy
acnsstu
Sanctus
acooprr
corpora
acooprt
root-cap
acoopsu
opacous
acooptt
top-coat
acoortu
touraco
acoprrt
carport
acopstu
upcoast
acorrtt
tractor
acorrtu
curator
acorrty
carroty
acorssu
sarcous
acorstu
surcoat
acorsty
castory
acorsuu
raucous
acosttu
outcast
acosuuv
vacuous
acpprsy
scrappy
acprttu
trap-cut
acpstuu
usucapt
acrsttu
tractus
addddor
doddard
adddeen
dead-end
adddegl
gladded
adddelr
raddled
adddeno
deodand
addeeey
dead-eye
addeegr
degrade
addeehr
red-head
addeeln
delenda
addeelp
pleaded
addeely
delayed
addeemn
dead-men
addeemr
dreamed
addeeot
deodate
addeerr
dreader
addeest
dead-set
steaded
addeesy
sad-eyed
addefly
fadedly
addefnu
unfaded
addefru
defraud
addefrw
dwarfed
addeggr
dragged
addegho
dog-head
godhead
addegju
adjudge
addegln
gladden
addegru
guarded
addehir
die-hard
addehln
handled
addehnr
red-hand
addehrs
sharded
addeiik
didakei
addeiis
daisied
addeill
dallied
dialled
addeilp
plaided
addeilr
diedral
addeilt
dilated
addeino
adenoid
addeinu
unaided
unidea'd
addeinv
videnda
addeiot
toadied
addeisv
advised
addejly
jadedly
addejnu
unjaded
addejrt
Jeddart
addelpp
dappled
addelpr
paddler
addelrs
saddler
addelrw
dawdler
addelry
dreadly
laddery
addelst
staddle
addelsw
swaddle
addeltw
twaddle
addelyz
dazedly
addemst
maddest
addenor
road-end
addenot
nodated
addenou
duodena
addenpu
pudenda
addenru
daunder
addensu
asudden
addentu
undated
addeopt
adopted
adderss
address
addersw
swarded
addersy
dryades
addertt
dratted
addfhis
faddish
addfims
faddism
addfiny
dandify
addfist
faddist
addggin
gadding
addgiir
diagrid
addgimn
madding
addgimr
Midgard
addginp
padding
addginw
wadding
addglno
gladdon
addgmno
goddamn
addgoow
dagwood
addgooy
good-day
addgorw
godward
addgosy
dogdays
addhiks
Kaddish
addhiqs
Qaddish
addhiss
saddish
addhity
hydatid
addiins
disdain
addikty
katydid
addilmn
midland
addilny
dandily
addilos
disload
addimno
diamond
addimor
diadrom
addinor
android
addinry
diandry
addirzz
dizzard
addllru
dullard
addloos
soldado
addltwy
twaddly
addmnos
oddsman
addnnor
donnard
addnoow
downa-do
addooss
dos-à-dos
addopsy
dasypod
addqsuy
squaddy
adeeefy
fedayee
adeeemn
demeane
adeeeps
deep-sea
adeeerr
arreede
adeeers
sea-reed
adeeerx
exedrae
adeeesw
seaweed
adeefil
Felidae
adeefir
fedarie
adeeflr
federal
adeeflt
deflate
adeefpr
prefade
adeefrt
draftee
adeeggh
egghead
adeeggn
engaged
adeeghs
hag-seed
adeeghw
hag-weed
adeegll
alleged

adeegmn
endgame
adeegnr
derange
enraged
grandee
grenade
adeegnv
vendage
adeegot
dogeate
goateed
adeegrr
regrade
adeegrw
ragweed
adeegsw
saw-edge
adeehlo
Helodea
adeehlr
hederal
adeehnn
hennaed
adeehnv
havened
adeehpr
ephedra
adeehrr
adherer
adeehrs
sheared
adeehrt
hearted
red-heat
adeehrx
exhedra
adeehst
headset
adeehsv
sheaved
adeehsy
hayseed
adeeiir
Irideae
adeeijt
jadeite
adeeiln
aliened
delaine
adeeilp
Pleiade
adeeils
deiseal
adeeily
eyeliad
adeeimn
demaine
adeeimt
mediate
adeeinn
adenine
adeeins
aniseed

adeeiqu
Equidae
adeeirr
readier
adeeirw
wearied
adeeiss
disease
seaside
adeeitv
deviate
adeeknr
kneader
adeeknw
wakened
adeekrw
wreaked
adeekwy
weekday
adeells
allseed
adeelly
alleyed
adeelmr
emerald
adeelms
measled
adeelmt
medalet
adeelnr
learned
adeelns
sand-eel
adeelnt
edental
adeelnw
Wealden
adeelpr
pearled
pleader
adeelps
delapse
pleased
adeelrt
related
treadle
adeelrw
leeward
adeelry
delayer
layered
relayed
adeelst
stealed
adeelsv
sleaved
adeeltv
velated
adeeltx
exalted
adeeluv
devalue

adeemnr
amender
enarmed
meander
reamend
adeemnw
new-made
adeemny
demayne
adeemrr
dreamer
adeemst
steamed
adeemsu
medusae
adeemsw
mawseed
adeemtw
matweed
adeemwy
mayweed
adeennv
Vendean
adeenru
uneared
adeenry
deanery
ne'erday
renayed
adeentt
dentate
adeeors
oreades
adeeorw
oarweed
adeeosv
sea-dove
adeeppy
day-peep
adeeprs
speared
adeeprt
pad-tree
predate
red-tape
tapered
adeeprv
deprave
pervade
adeerrs
redsear
adeerrt
retread
treader
adeerrv
averred
adeerst
estrade
adeersv
adverse
adeertv
averted

adeertw
tarweed
watered
adeessy
essayed
adeestw
sweated
adeetux
exudate
adeffin
affined
adefflm
maffled
adefggl
flagged
adefgln
fangled
flanged
adefgou
fougade
adefhst
shafted
adefils
disleaf
adefims
disfame
adefint
defiant
fainted
adeflln
elfland
adefllw
dew-fall
adeflnn
fenland
adeflos
sol-faed
adeflpp
flapped
adeflru
dareful
adefltt
flatted
adefltu
default
adefmnu
unfamed
adefmst
mast-fed
adefnuz
unfazed
adefoos
sea-food
adefory
feodary
foreday
adefotu
fade-out
adefrrt
drafter
redraft
adefruy
feudary

adegghs
shagged
adeggiu
gaudgie
guidage
adegglr
draggle
adeggns
snagged
adeggry
raggedy
adeggsw
swagged
adeghin
heading
adeghir
hag-ride
headrig
adeghlo
log-head
adegiln
dealing
leading
adegilo
geoidal
adegilp
pig-lead
adegilv
glaived
adeginr
deraign
gradine
grained
reading
adeginw
windage
adeginy
yeading
adegiot
godetia
adegirs
agrised
adegirv
Rigveda
adegisv
visaged
adegiuv
viduage
adeglnn
endlang
adeglnr
dangler
gnarled
adeglnt
tangled
adeglnu
langued
adeglru
raguled
adeglry
gradely
adegmnu
gude-man

adegnno
nonaged
adegnnu
dunnage
adegnop
pondage
adegnos
sondage
adegnot
tangoed
adegnov
dogvane
adegnow
gowaned
adegnpu
unpaged
adegnrr
gnarred
adegnrt
drag-net
adegnru
enguard
adegnuz
ungazed
adegors
dog's-ear
adegorw
dowager
wordage
adegott
togated
adegprs
spadger
adegpru
upgrade
adegrsu
sugared
adegrty
tragedy
adegruy
gaudery
adegssu
degauss
adehhop
hop-head
adehhot
hothead
adehikv
khediva
adehill
Delilah
adehiln
Hieland
adehilp
helipad
adehily
headily
adehinp
pinhead
adehipr
raphide
adehips
aphides

adehipt
pithead
adehirr
harried
adehirw
rawhide
adehist
tea-dish
adehkns
shanked
adehkor
hardoke
adehkot
kathode
adehlmu
lum-head
adehlnr
handler
adehlns
handsel
adehlot
loathed
adehlss
slashed
adehlty
deathly
adehmms
shammed
adehmnr
herdman
adehmor
hadrome
adehnru
unheard
adehnst
handset
adehntu
haunted
adehoop
apehood
adehopt
pot-head
adehopx
hexapod
adehorr
hoarder
adehotw
tow-head
adehpst
spathed
T-shaped
adehpsu
U-shaped
adehpsv
V-shaped
adehrst
hard-set
adehrty
hydrate
thready
adehuzz
huzzaed

adeiilr
deliria
irideal
adeiils
sedilia
adeiirs
diarise
adeijmr
jemidar
adeijsu
Judaise
adeiklz
Zadkiel
adeillr
dallier
dialler
rallied
adeills
disleal
sallied
adeillt
tallied
adeillv
vialled
adeilly
ideally
adeilmm
dilemma
adeilmp
implead
adeilms
misdeal
mislead
adeilnn
annelid
lindane
adeilnt
tail-end
adeilnu
aliunde
unideal
adeilnw
new-laid
adeilop
Oedipal
adeilor
dariole
adeilos
deasoil
adeilou
douleia
adeilpp
applied
adeilpr
lip-read
pedrail
predial
adeilps
palsied
Pleiads
adeilpt
plaited
taliped

adeilrs
sideral
adeilrt
dilater
adeilry
readily
adeilss
aidless
adeilsu
deasiul
adeilsv
devisal
adeilsy
dialyse
adeimmr
mermaid
adeimms
mismade
adeimnr
adermin
Amerind
adeimnt
mediant
adeimnu
unaimed
adeimrr
admirer
married
adeimrs
misread
adeimrt
readmit
adeimru
Muridae
adeimry
mid-year
adeimst
misdate
adeimtu
taedium
adeimty
daytime
adeinnn
nandine
adeinor
aneroid
adeinos
adonise
anodise
Diasone
sodaine
adeinov
naevoid
adeinox
dioxane
adeinpr
pardine
adeinps
pansied
adeinpt
depaint
painted
patined

adeinrr
drainer
adeinrs
sardine
adeinrt
detrain
tan-ride
trade-in
trained
adeinru
unaired
uranide
adeinrv
invader
ravined
adeinst
instead
sainted
stained
adeinsw
sea-wind
adeintt
tainted
adeintu
audient
adeintv
deviant
adeinvv
navvied
adeiops
adipose
adeiopt
opiated
adeiors
soredia
adeiorx
exordia
adeiosx
oxidase
adeiotx
oxidate
adeiovv
vaivode
adeiovw
waivode
adeippr
drappie
prepaid
adeippu
appuied
adeiprr
drapier
parried
adeiprs
despair
adeiprt
Diptera
adeipss
apsides
adeirrt
tarried

adeirst
asterid
astride
disrate
staired
adeirsu
residua
adeirsv
adviser
adeirtv
tardive
adeirty
dietary
adeisst
disseat
saidest
adeistv
vistaed
adeistw
waisted
adeiswy
sideway
wayside
adeituz
Deutzia
adeitwy
tide-way
adejopr
jeopard
adeklns
kalends
adeklny
nakedly
adeklst
stalked
adeklsy
yslaked
adekmuy
may-duke
adeknpp
knapped
adeknrr
knarred
adeknru
unraked
adeknsu
unasked
adeknuw
unwaked
adeknvy
Vandyke
adekpsy
pay-desk
adellmu
medulla
adellnr
ländler
adellnw
ellwand
adellor
odaller
adellow
allowed

adellru
udaller
adellst
stalled
adelmms
slammed
adelmnr
mandrel
adelmor
earldom
adelmos
damosel
adelmoz
damozel
adelnnp
planned
adelnnu
unladen
adelnor
ladrone
adelnot
taloned
adelnoy
yealdon
adelnrs
slander
snarled
adelnru
launder
lurdane
rundale
adelnry
dearnly
adelnst
slanted
adelntu
lunated
adelntw
wetland
adelopr
leopard
adelops
deposal
adelopt
tadpole
adelors
sea-lord
adelort
delator
leotard
adeloru
roulade
Urodela
adeloss
lassoed
adelotu
lead-out
adelovy
love-day
adelpps
slapped
adelpry
pedlary

adelptt
platted
adelptw
dewlapt
adelrru
ruderal
adelrrw
drawler
adelrst
star-led
adelrtx
dextral
adelrty
lyrated
adelrzz
dazzler
adelstt
slatted
adelttw
wattled
adeltuv
vaulted
ademnnu
mundane
unnamed
ademnru
duramen
maunder
unarmed
ademnss
madness
ademnsu
medusan
sudamen
ademntu
unmated
untamed
ademosy
Samoyed
someday
ademowy
meadowy
ademrru
eardrum
ademrty
term-day
ademssu
assumed
adennoy
annoyed
anodyne
adennps
spanned
adennpt
pendant
adennst
standen
adennwy
dewanny
adenooz
endozoa

adenopr
operand
padrone
pandore
adenops
dapsone
adenopt
notepad
adenort
tornade
adenoru
rondeau
adenost
onstead
adenotz
zonated
adenppr
parpend
adenpps
snapped
adenppw
wappend
adenprr
pardner
adenpru
unpared
adenpsy
dyspnea
adenpuv
unpaved
adenrry
reynard
adenrss
sanders
sarsden
adenrst
stander
adenrsu
asunder
danseur
adenrtu
natured
untread
adenrtv
verdant
adenrtw
draw-net
adenrtx
dextran
adenrty
dentary
rent-day
adenruy
unready
adensss
sadness
adenstu
unsated
adensuv
unsaved
adenswy
endways
adentuv
vaunted

adentux
untaxed
adenuwy
unwayed
adeoort
odorate
adeoprr
eardrop
padrero
adeoprt
readopt
adeopss
spadoes
adeopst
podesta
adeorrs
drosera
rear-dos
adeorst
torsade
adeortu
outdare
read-out
adeoryz
zedoary
adeostt
toasted
adeottu
outdate
adepprt
trapped
adepprw
wrapped
adeppsw
swapped
adeppuy
appuyed
adeprrs
sparred
adeprry
drapery
adeprss
adpress
adeprsy
sprayed
adeqrsu
squared
aderrst
starred
aderssu
assured
aderstv
starved
aderstw
steward
strawed
adersty
rest-day
strayed
adersuy
dasyure
adesstu
sea-dust

adesttu
statued
adesttw
wadsett
adestuy
Tuesday
adffgin
daffing
adffhno
hand-off
offhand
adffist
distaff
adffloo
offload
adfforw
off-ward
adfginr
farding
adfhisy
fish-day
adfhlnu
handful
adfhoos
shadoof
adfiimt
Fatimid
adfillu
fluidal
adfimnr
findram
adfimny
damnify
adfinrt
indraft
adfllyy
ladyfly
adflmoo
damfool
adflmpu
mud-flap
adflmtu
mud-flat
adflnop
plafond
adflnsy
sand-fly
adfloru
foulard
adfnnot
fondant
adfoopt
footpad
adforrw
forward
froward
adfortx
draft-ox
adgghno
hangdog
adggiln
gadling
adggilr
riggald

adgginr
niggard
adggirs
Rigsdag
adggoot
goat-god
adghilo
hidalgo
adghins
dashing
shading
adghipr
digraph
adghirr
ard-righ
adghirs
dish-rag
adghnnu
hand-gun
adghnos
sand-hog
adghnow
hagdown
adghoor
road-hog
adghort
hard-got
adghorw
hogward
adghrtu
draught
adgiiln
gliadin
adgiilt
digital
adgiino
gonidia
adgiinw
gwiniad
adgiiny
Digynia
adgikrs
Riksdag
adgilmn
madling
adgilnn
landing
adgilno
digonal
loading
adgilnr
darling
adgilnu
languid
adgilor
goliard
adgilry
day-girl
adgilsu
gladius
adgiluy
gaudily
adgimmn
damming

adgimnn
damning
adginnr
darning
adginns
sanding
adginnw
dawning
adginor
Gordian
gradino
roading
adginot
doating
adginrt
darting
trading
adginrw
drawing
warding
adginwy
gwyniad
adgirsu
guisard
adgirzz
gizzard
adgllno
golland
adglloo
all-good
adgllor
rag-doll
adglmno
mangold
adglnoo
gondola
adglnow
gowland
adglnoy
daylong
adglnry
grandly
adgmnoo
goodman
adgmnor
gormand
adgnoor
dragoon
gadroon
adgnoru
aground
adgnrru
gurnard
adgnruu
unguard
adgorst
Dogstar
adgrstu
rag-dust
adhhirs
hardish
adhhirt
hard-hit

adhiims
maidish
adhiiop
Ophidia
adhikns
dankish
adhikrs
darkish
adhilmo
halidom
adhilny
handily
adhilop
haploid
adhiloy
holiday
hyaloid
adhilry
hardily
adhilsy
ladyish
shadily
adhimms
Mahdism
adhimps
dampish
phasmid
adhimrs
Midrash
adhimst
Mahdist
adhinor
Rhodian
adhinot
anthoid
adhinpu
dauphin
adhkorw
dorhawk
adhlllo
hold-all
adhllno
holland
adhlmoy
holydam
adhlmpy
lymphad
adhmnoo
hoodman
manhood
adhmnor
horn-mad
adhmnou
Mahound
adhnnuy
unhandy
adhnoru
unhoard
adhnorw
hard-won
adhnotu
handout
adhnotw
two-hand

adhnrru
hard-run
adhnrsy
shandry
adhnrty
hydrant
adhnruy
unhardy
adhoorr
rhodora
adhoosw
wood-ash
adhopru
uphoard
adhopry
hop-yard
adhopst
dash-pot
adhoswy
shadowy
adhrswy
dry-wash
adiiilr
iridial
adiiinr
iridian
adiiklo
dika-oil
adiikot
dakoiti
adiilms
mislaid
adiilnv
invalid
adiilos
sialoid
adiilst
dialist
adiimms
maidism
adiimpv
impavid
adiimru
mudiria
adiimss
missaid
adiinnn
in-and-in
adiinov
Ovidian
adiinpr
pindari
pridian
adiinst
distain
adiinsu
indusia
suidian
adiipxy
pyxidia
adiirst
diarist
adiirty
aridity

adiitvy
avidity
adijmsu
Judaism
adijnot
adjoint
adijstu
Judaist
adiklny
ladykin
adiklos
odalisk
adiklps
klipdas
adikmnn
mankind
adikmss
dismask
adiknps
skidpan
adiknrs
disrank
adikprs
dispark
adillmm
milldam
adillsy
disally
adillvy
validly
adillyy
day-lily
adilmno
mondial
adilmnr
mandril
adilmnu
maudlin
adilmoo
Modiola
adilmop
diploma
adilmou
alodium
adilmoy
amyloid
adilmps
plasmid
adilmsu
dualism
adilmsy
dismayl
ladyism
adilnor
nail-rod
ordinal
adilnru
diurnal
adilnsu
sundial
adiloov
ovoidal
adilopr
dipolar

adilopw
low-paid
adilort
dilator
adilotw
wildoat
adilpry
pyralid
rapidly
adilpst
plastid
adilpsy
display
adilptu
plaudit
adilpvy
vapidly
adilqsu
squalid
adilrty
tardily
adilssu
Lusiads
adilssw
wild-ass
adilstu
dualist
adilsty
staidly
adiltuy
duality
adimoos
isodoma
adimorr
mirador
adimost
mastoid
adimott
mattoid
adimpry
pyramid
adimrsw
misdraw
adimsst
dismast
adimstu
dumaist
stadium
adinnop
dipnoan
Pandion
adinnor
andiron
adinnrs
innards
adinnrw
indrawn
adinnry
innyard
adinnst
stand-in
adinopp
oppidan

adinopr
padroni
poniard
adinopt
pintado
adinorr
ordinar
adinors
sad-iron
adinorv
virando
adinotx
oxidant
adinpst
sand-pit
adinrrt
tridarn
adinrsu
Drusian
sundari
adinrsw
inwards
adinrtu
triduan
adinstt
Dantist
distant
adinstu
unstaid
adintty
dittany
adioops
Isopoda
adioprr
air-drop
adioprs
sparoid
adioprt
parotid
adioprv
privado
adiorst
astroid
adiorsu
sauroid
adiorsv
advisor
adiortu
auditor
adiosuv
Vaudois
adiosvw
disavow
adipprt
dip-trap
adiprst
dispart
adiprty
pay-dirt
adirssu
sardius
adirsty
satyrid

adirsuy
dysuria
adjnoru
adjourn
adkkloy
kakodyl
adklmru
mudlark
adkooow
oak-wood
adkorwy
day-work
work-day
adkrswy
skyward
adlllor
lollard
adllmow
wadmoll
adllmoy
modally
adllnow
lowland
adllopr
pollard
adllowx
wax-doll
adlmmpu
dum-palm
adlmoru
modular
adlmory
May-lord
adlmosv
Slavdom
adlnnor
norland
adlnoor
lardoon
adlnopu
poundal
adlnoru
nodular
adlnosu
souldan
adlnosy
synodal
adlnotu
outland
adlnruy
laundry
adlntwy
Tynwald
adlopru
poulard
adlorrw
warlord
adlorsu
sudoral
adlrsty
dry-salt
admmnsu
summand

admnoor
door-man
madroño
admnoow
woodman
admnooz
madzoon
admnoqu
quondam
admnors
rodsman
admnort
dormant
mordant
admnosu
osmunda
admnstu
dustman
admoort
doormat
admoppu
popadum
admorst
stardom
tsardom
admortw
madwort
admrruw
war-drum
admrstu
durmast
mustard
adnnooy
noonday
adnnort
donnart
adnnotu
daunton
adnnsuw
sun-dawn
adnoopr
pandoor
adnoort
donator
odorant
tornado
adnooss
so-and-so
adnootw
wood-ant
adnopru
pandour
adnoprv
provand
adnorrw
norward
adnorsw
onwards
adnortu
rotunda
adnorwy
nayword
adnostt
stand-to

adnostu
astound
adnpruw
updrawn
adnpstu
dust-pan
stand-up
upstand
adnrsuw
sunward
adnstyy
dynasty
adoopsu
apodous
adoopsw
sap-wood
adoortw
wood-tar
adoorwy
doorway
adoowwx
wood-wax
adoprrw
wardrop
adopsty
post-day
adorstw
towards
adorsuu
arduous
adortuw
outward
adouuvx
vaudoux
adprsuw
upwards
adpssuy
Dasypus
adsstuw
sawdust
aeeeflr
eelfare
aeeeggl
lee-gage
aeeegkl
keelage
aeeeglt
legatee
aeeegnt
teenage
aeeegpr
peerage
aeeegps
seepage
aeeeiln
alienee
aeeelln
lee-lane
aeeelrs
release
aeeeltv
elevate
aeeertt
tea-tree

aeeffll
felafel
aeeffmr
fee-farm
aeefgnt
fanteeg
aeefgrs
serfage
aeefgtw
weftage
aeefhrt
feather
terefah
aeefiln
Felinae
aeefilw
alewife
aeefirs
freesia
sea-fire
aeefisw
sea-wife
aeeflltt
fellate
leaflet
aeeflms
alms-fee
aeeflpy
eye-flap
aeeflrt
reflate
aeeflrw
welfare
aeeflsu
easeful
aeefmnr
enframe
freeman
aeefmrr
free-arm
reframe
aeefotv
foveate
aeefppr
frappée
aeefrrt
ferrate
aeefrst
feaster
sea-fret
aeefrtu
feature
aeefrtx
tax-free
aeefrwy
freeway
aeegglr
gregale
aeegglt
gateleg
aeeggnr
Engager
aeeggop
epagoge

aeeghnn
Gehenna
aeeghnw
whangee
aeegill
galilee
aeegilm
mileage
aeegiln
lineage
aeegilp
epigeal
aeeginp
epigean
aeeginu
Eugenia
aeegipr
pierage
aeegiss
assiege
aeegllz
gazelle
aeeglmn
gleeman
mélange
aeeglnr
enlarge
general
gleaner
aeeglnt
elegant
aeeglnu
Euglena
aeeglnv
evangel
aeeglpr
peregal
aeeglru
leaguer
regulae
aeeglry
eagerly
aeeglss
ageless
sea-legs
aeeglsv
selvage
aeegltu
tegulae
aeegltv
vegetal
aeegmmt
gemmate
aeegmnr
germane
aeegmss
megasse
message
aeegnnp
pangene
aeegnnr
enrange
aeegnnv
Genevan

aeegnop
peonage
aeegnpp
genappe
aeegnrt
grantee
greaten
reagent
aeegnru
renague
aeegnrv
avenger
engrave
aeegntt
tentage
aeegntv
ventage
aeegntw
Newgate
aeegorv
over-age
aeegprs
asperge
presage
aeegrrs
greaser
aeegrrt
greater
regrate
aeegrrw
wagerer
aeegrst
ergates
restage
aeegrsv
greaves
aeegrtu
treague
aeegruz
guereza
aeegstt
gestate
tagetes
aeegttz
gazette
aeehhnt
heathen
aeehhrt
heather
aeehhst
sheathe
aeehilr
hair-eel
aeehirv
heavier
aeehist
atheise
aeehknr
hearken
aeehknt
thankee
aeehkru
heureka

aeehlnt
lethean
aeehlor
ear-hole
aeehlpt
heel-tap
aeehlrt
leather
tar-heel
aeehlrv
haverel
aeehlsy
eyelash
aeehltt
athlete
aeehmnt
methane
aeehmrs
mahseer
aeehmrt
thermae
aeehnpt
heptane
phenate
aeehnrs
arsheen
aeehnrt
earthen
hearten
aeehnsw
Shawnee
aeehntw
wheaten
aeehprs
reshape
sphaere
aeehprt
preheat
aeehpuv
upheave
aeehqsu
Quashee
aeehrrs
shearer
aeehrsw
whereas
aeehrtt
theater
theatre
thereat
aeehrtv
threave
aeehrtw
weather
whate'er
whereat
wreathe
aeehssv
sheaves
aeehswy
eye-wash
aeeijnt
Janeite

aeeikls
  sea-like
aeeikps
  sea-pike
aeeilms
  sea-mile
aeeilnp
  alepine
aeeilns
  sea-line
aeeilnt
  lineate
aeeilpt
  epilate
  pileate
aeeilrr
  earlier
aeeilrs
  realise
aeeilrt
  atelier
  realtie
aeeiltt
  ailette
aeeiltv
  elative
aeeimnr
  remanié
aeeimns
  nemesia
aeeimnx
  examine
aeeimpt
  meat-pie
aeeimrs
  seriema
aeeimrt
  emirate
aeeimss
  misease
  siamese
aeeimst
  steamie
aeeimtt
  tea-time
aeeinnp
  Peneian
aeeinrt
  retinae
  trainee
aeeinst
  etesian
aeeintt
  teniate
aeeintv
  naïveté
aeeinvw
  inweave
aeeiort
  etaerio
aeeiprr
  pereira
aeeiptx
  expiate

aeeirrs
  rearise
aeeirst
  seriate
aeeirtt
  ariette
  iterate
aeeirtv
  evirate
aeeisvv
  evasive
aeeisvw
  sea-view
aeeittv
  aviette
  evitate
aeeitux
  eutexia
aeeiuvx
  exuviae
aeejnst
  sejeant
aeejntu
  jauntee
aeejrsw
  Jew's-ear
aeekllt
  lakelet
aeeklmn
  keelman
aeekmns
  kamseen
aeekmnw
  man-week
aeekmrt
  meerkat
aeeknnn
  nankeen
aeeknnp
  knee-pan
aeeknrs
  sneaker
aeeknrt
  retaken
aeeknrw
  wakener
aeekort
  oak-tree
aeekprs
  respeak
  speaker
aeekprt
  pertake
aeekrrt
  retaker
aeekrrw
  wreaker
aeekrst
  sakeret
aeeksty
  key-seat
aeellop
  ale-pole

aeellov
  alveole
aeellpr
  parelle
aeellrs
  all-seer
aeellwy
  wall-eye
aeelmnp
  empanel
  emplane
aeelmnt
  manteel
aeelmnv
  velamen
aeelmny
  amylene
aeelmpx
  example
  exempla
aeelmrt
  lameter
aeelmss
  measles
aeelmst
  Maltese
aeelmtu
  emulate
aeelnnr
  lernean
aeelnps
  spelean
aeelnrr
  learner
aeelnrt
  alterne
  enteral
  eternal
aeelnrw
  renewal
aeelnsv
  enslave
aeelnty
  entayle
aeelopx
  pole-axe
aeeloru
  aureole
aeelosw
  leasowe
aeelprr
  pearler
aeelprs
  pleaser
  relapse
aeelprt
  prelate
aeelpru
  pleurae
aeelptt
  palette
  peltate
aeelptu
  epaulet

aeelqsu
  sequela
aeelrrt
  re-alter
  relater
aeelrss
  earless
aeelrst
  stealer
aeelrsv
  several
aeelrsy
  sealery
aeelruv
  revalue
aeelssu
  Auslese
aeelssw
  aweless
aeelstu
  setuale
aeeltty
  layette
aeeltvw
  wavelet
aeemmpy
  empyema
aeemmrt
  ammeter
  metamer
aeemnno
  anemone
aeemnnp
  pen-name
aeemnrt
  remanet
aeemort
  erotema
aeemosw
  awesome
  waesome
aeemprt
  tempera
aeempry
  empayre
aeemptu
  amputee
aeemqru
  marquee
aeemrst
  sea-term
  steamer
aeemrsu
  measure
aeemrty
  métayer
aeemsst
  seam-set
aeennot
  neonate
aeennpt
  pennate
  pentane

aeennrs
  ensnare
aeennrx
  reannex
aeenntu
  uneaten
aeenopr
  peraeon
aeenpst
  penates
  pesante
aeenpsx
  expanse
aeenrst
  earnest
  eastern
  nearest
aeenrtt
  entreat
  ratteen
  ternate
aeenrtv
  nervate
  veteran
aeenruv
  unreave
aeenssw
  waeness
aeenttv
  navette
aeenuvw
  unweave
aeeoprt
  operate
aeeorss
  serosae
aeeorst
  roseate
  tea-rose
aeeorsv
  oversea
aeeortv
  overeat
aeeorvw
  overawe
aeepprr
  prepare
  repaper
aeeprrt
  taperer
aeeprss
  asperse
  praeses
  preasse
aeeprsz
  spreaze
aeeprtu
  epurate
aeeprty
  peatery
aeeprtz
  trapeze

aeepstt
  septate
  spattee
aeerrst
  serrate
aeerrsu
  erasure
aeerrsw
  swearer
aeerrtt
  retrate
  retreat
  treater
aeerrtw
  waterer
aeerrvw
  waverer
aeersst
  tessera
aeerssu
  seasure
aeerssv
  assever
aeerssy
  essayer
aeerstt
  estreat
  restate
aeerstu
  austere
aeerstw
  sweater
aeersuv
  vareuse
aeersux
  réseaux
aeerttx
  extreat
aeertwx
  wax-tree
aeesttt
  testate
aeffflr
  flaffer
aeffgil
  fig-leaf
aeffgir
  giraffe
aeffgnr
  engraff
aeffipr
  piaffer
aeffkop
  offpeak
aeffkor
  rake-off
aeffkot
  offtake
  take-off
aefflly
  flyleaf
aefflmw
  flamfew

7 AEF

aefflns
  snaffle
aefflrr
  raffler
aefflru
  fearful
aeffltu
  fateful
aeffqru
  quaffer
aeffrst
  restaff
  staffer
aefftty
  taffety
aefgggo
  foggage
aefggmo
  megafog
aefggry
  faggery
aefgiln
  finagle
  leafing
aefgilo
  foliage
aefgilr
  fragile
aefgirs
  gas-fire
aefgirt
  frigate
aefgiru
  refugia
aefgitu
  ague-fit
  fatigue
aefgllu
  fullage
aefglot
  flotage
aefglow
  flowage
aefglru
  rageful
aefgluz
  gazeful
aefgnrr
  granfer
aefgnrt
  engraft
aefgoot
  footage
aefgorr
  forager
aefgorv
  forgave
aefgrrt
  grafter
aefhiss
  sea-fish
aefhlno
  half-one

aefhloo
  ale-hoof
aefhlop
  hop-flea
aefhlor
  fahlore
aefhlrs
  flasher
aefhlrt
  farthel
aefhlrz
  fahlerz
aefhltu
  hateful
aefhrrt
  farther
aefhrst
  shafter
aefhrsy
  fashery
aefiilt
  filiate
aefijlo
  jeofail
aefillm
  ill-fame
aefilmn
  feminal
  inflame
aefilnt
  inflate
aefilnu
  infulae
aefilnv
  flavine
aefilot
  foliate
aefilpt
  flea-pit
aefilru
  failure
aefilrz
  filazer
aefilss
  falsies
  filasse
aefimnr
  fireman
aefimrr
  fire-arm
aefimrs
  misfare
aefinnt
  infante
aefinnz
  fanzine
aefinpr
  firepan
aefinrr
  refrain
aefinrt
  fenitar
aefinrx
  xerafin

aefintw
  wine-fat
aefintx
  antefix
aefiqru
  aquifer
aefirrr
  farrier
aefklnr
  flanker
aefklos
  sea-folk
aefklst
  flasket
aefkluw
  wakeful
aefknor
  oak-fern
aefkors
  forsake
aefkrsw
  saw-kerf
aefllnn
  fannell
  flannel
aefllor
  Floréal
aefllot
  floatel
aefllsy
  falsely
aeflltt
  flatlet
aeflltu
  taleful
aeflluz
  zealful
aeflmor
  femoral
aeflmty
  meat-fly
aeflmuw
  wameful
aeflmuz
  mazeful
aeflnnn
  flannen
aeflnov
  flavone
aeflnrs
  salfern
aeflnru
  flâneur
  funeral
aeflntt
  flatten
aefloov
  foveola
aeflopw
  pea-fowl
aeflors
  safrole

aeflort
  floater
  floreat
aefloru
  four-ale
aeflory
  forelay
aeflosw
  sea-fowl
  sea-wolf
aeflppr
  flapper
aeflprs
  felspar
aeflpru
  flare-up
aeflpry
  palfrey
aeflrsu
  fur-seal
  refusal
aeflrtt
  flatter
aeflrtu
  refutal
  tearful
aeflrzz
  frazzle
aeflttu
  fat-lute
aefmnor
  foramen
  foreman
aefmnru
  fraenum
aefmorr
  forearm
aefmort
  formate
aefmpru
  frame-up
aefmrry
  farmery
aefnopr
  profane
aefnorr
  foreran
aefnrss
  farness
aefnsst
  Fastens
  fatness
aefoprw
  forepaw
aeforrv
  overfar
aeforry
  forayer
aeforsw
  foresaw
aeforsy
  foresay
aefostu
  featous

aefrrty
  fratery
aefrstw
  fretsaw
aefrttu
  Tartufe
aefrtuw
  wafture
aefsttt
  fattest
aeggglu
  luggage
aegghlr
  haggler
aeggiln
  lignage
aeggios
  isagoge
aeggisw
  swaggie
aeggjry
  jaggery
aegglno
  agelong
aegglnr
  gangrel
aegglry
  grey-lag
aeggmny
  yeggman
aeggmss
  eggmass
aeggnnu
  gunnage
aeggnor
  o'ergang
aeggnst
  ant-eggs
  G-agents
aeggrry
  raggery
aeggrss
  aggress
aeggrst
  gagster
  stagger
  taggers
aeggrsw
  swagger
aeggrwy
  waggery
aeghhit
  aheight
aeghijr
  jaghire
aeghiln
  healing
aeghinp
  heaping
aeghinr
  hearing
aeghint
  gahnite

aeghinv
  heaving
aeghiny
  Hygeian
aeghinz
  genizah
aeghlno
  halogen
aeghlnt
  alength
aeghlru
  laugher
aeghltw
  thalweg
aeghmno
  hog-mane
  Mohegan
aeghmor
  homager
aeghmsu
  meshuga
aeghnox
  hexagon
aeghnru
  nuraghe
aeghnst
  stengah
aeghopy
  hypogea
aeghost
  hostage
aeghprs
  spreagh
aegiimn
  imagine
aegikln
  linkage
aegiklt
  glaiket
aegiknp
  peaking
aegikns
  sea-king
  sinkage
aegikpp
  kippage
aegikpr
  garpike
aegilll
  illegal
aegilln
  nigella
aegillp
  pillage
aegills
  gallise
aegillt
  tillage
aegillv
  village
aegilly
  agilely

aegilmr
gremial
lamiger
aegilms
gas-lime
aegilmt
time-lag
aegilnn
eanling
leaning
aegilnp
leaping
aegilnr
engrail
nargile
realign
reginal
aegilns
leasing
sealing
aegilnt
atingle
gelatin
genital
aegilnv
leaving
aegilou
eulogia
aegilrz
glazier
aegilss
algesis
aegiltu
glutaei
aegilty
egality
aegimnn
meaning
aegimnp
pigmean
aegimnr
germain
reaming
aegimnt
mintage
teaming
tegmina
aegimpr
epigram
primage
aegimpt
pigmeat
aegimrr
armiger
aegimrs
gisarme
aegimrt
migrate
ragtime
aegimry
imagery
aegimst
sigmate

aegimsv
misgave
aeginnr
earning
engrain
grannie
aeginnt
antigen
gentian
aeginnu
anguine
guanine
aeginnv
Angevin
aeginnz
Zingane
aeginor
origane
aeginos
agonise
aeginpp
genipap
aeginps
spinage
aeginrr
earring
grainer
aeginrs
searing
seringa
aeginrt
granite
ingrate
tearing
aeginrv
vinegar
aeginrw
wearing
aeginrz
Zingare
aeginst
easting
genista
ingesta
seating
teasing
tsigane
aeginsw
sea-wing
aegintv
vintage
aeginvw
weaving
aegipps
gas-pipe
aegiprs
prisage
spairge
aegirrz
grazier
aegirst
agister
sea-girt
strigae

aegirtv
virgate
vitrage
aegisty
gaseity
aegjlnr
jangler
aegkkno
angekok
aegklou
kagoule
aegkmry
kerygma
aeglllly
legally
aegllno
allonge
galleon
aegllnr
langrel
aegllor
allegro
aegllot
tollage
aegllry
allergy
gallery
largely
regally
aegllsu
seagull
sullage
aegllsw
gas-well
aeglltu
gluteal
aeglmnr
mangler
aeglmor
gomeral
aeglmpu
plumage
aeglmru
maulgre
aeglnot
tangelo
aeglnpr
grapnel
aeglnps
spangle
aeglnrt
tangler
trangle
aeglnru
granule
aeglnrw
wangler
wrangle
aeglnry
angerly
aeglnss
glassen
aeglnsu
angelus

aeglntt
gantlet
aeglntu
languet
aeglntw
twangle
aeglnuu
ungulae
aeglnuw
gunwale
aeglopr
pergola
aeglort
legator
aeglorw
low-gear
aeglotv
voltage
aeglppr
grapple
aeglpru
earplug
graupel
aeglpsu
plusage
aeglpuy
plaguey
aeglrru
regular
aeglrss
largess
aeglrsv
verglas
aeglrtu
gaulter
tegular
tragule
aeglrty
greatly
aeglrvy
gravely
aeglssu
sea-slug
aeglstt
gestalt
aegltuv
vulgate
aegluuy
guayule
aegluvy
vaguely
aegmmru
rummage
aegmnno
agnomen
aegmnor
megaron
aegmnos
mangoes
aegmnot
magneto
megaton
montage

aegmnpy
pygmean
aegmnrt
garment
margent
ragment
aegmntu
augment
mutagen
aegmoor
moorage
aegmosy
gaysome
aegmoxy
exogamy
aegnnot
tonnage
aegnnrt
regnant
aegnnru
gunnera
aegnntt
tangent
aegnntu
tunnage
aegnoor
oregano
aegnopt
pontage
aegnors
nose-rag
aegnorw
wagoner
aegnosv
Vosgean
aegnosw
sea-gown
aegnosy
nosegay
aegnotw
tea-gown
aegnowy
waygone
aegnprs
engrasp
aegnprt
trepang
aegnrrt
granter
regrant
aegnrst
strange
aegnssy
gayness
aegnstt
gestant
aegnstv
V-agents
aegnttu
tutenag
aegoort
rootage
aegoppr
propage

aegoprt
portage
aegopst
Gestapo
postage
aegoptt
pottage
aegorst
storage
aegortt
garotte
aegortu
outrage
aegorvy
voyager
aegossu
gaseous
aegostw
stowage
aegottu
outgate
aegottv
gavotte
aegprrs
grasper
sparger
aegprry
grapery
aegpssu
pegasus
aegpstu
upstage
aegrrss
grasser
aegrruu
augurer
aegrruv
gravure
verruga
aegrsty
stagery
aegstuu
auguste
aegtttu
guttate
aehhjov
Jehovah
aehhlos
ash-hole
aehhlty
healthy
aehhnrs
harshen
aehhnsv
Heshvan
aehhsty
sheathy
aehiksy
sakiyeh
aehilmn
heliman
aehilmo
hemiola

aehilms
Ishmael
aehilnr
hernial
inhaler
aehilnt
Hielant
aehilny
hyaline
aehilor
airhole
aehilpr
hare-lip
aehilru
haulier
aehilsw
whaisle
aehiltt
lithate
tile-hat
aehilty
hyalite
aehiluv
vihuela
aehilvy
heavily
aehilwz
whaizle
aehimnr
harmine
aehimps
phaeism
aehimrs
mishear
aehimss
Messiah
aehimst
atheism
aehinpr
heparin
aehinps
inphase
aehinpt
penthia
aehinrs
arshine
aehinrt
hair-net
inearth
aehinss
hessian
aehinsv
evanish
aehippt
epitaph
aehipss
aphesis
aehipsw
peishwa
aehiptz
zaptieh
aehiqsu
Quashie

aehirrr
harrier
aehirst
sheriat
aehirsv
ashiver
aehirsw
wearish
aehirwy
haywire
aehistt
atheist
staithe
aehittw
thwaite
aehjlow
jawhole
aehjrtt
Jethart
aehknrt
thanker
aehkpsu
shake-up
aehkrrs
sharker
aehllov
hellova
aehlloy
holy-ale
aehllrs
hersall
aehlluv
helluva
aehllyz
hazelly
aehlmno
manhole
aehlmny
hymenal
aehlmor
armhole
aehlmpw
whample
aehlmrt
thermal
aehlmru
humeral
aehlnot
ethanol
aehlnrt
enthral
aehlnsu
Hulsean
unleash
unshale
aehlort
loather
rat-hole
aehlprs
spheral
aehlpss
hapless
aehlpst
plashet

aehlpsy
shapely
aehlrss
slasher
aehlrst
harslet
slather
aehlrsv
halvers
aehlrty
earthly
heartly
lathery
aehlrwy
whalery
aehlsst
hatless
aehlstt
stealth
aehltwy
wealthy
aehmmrs
shammer
aehmnor
menorah
aehmnos
hoseman
aehmnot
nathemo
aehmnoy
haemony
aehmnpy
nymphae
aehmnst
hetmans
aehmott
moth-eat
aehmpty
empathy
aehmrss
smasher
aehmrst
hamster
aehmrtu
mauther
aehmrtw
mawther
aehmuzz
mezuzah
aehnnpy
ha'penny
aehnntu
unneath
aehnnwy
anywhen
aehnopr
Orphean
aehnopt
phaeton
phonate
aehnopw
wanhope

aehnors
hoarsen
Senhora
aehnort
another
aehnotv
have-not
aehnprs
sharpen
aehnprt
panther
aehnpsu
unshape
aehnrss
harness
aehnrtu
haunter
unearth
unheart
urethan
aehnrtx
narthex
aehnstu
shea-nut
aehnttw
whatten
aehoort
toheroa
aehopst
tap-shoe
tea-shop
aehorst
asthore
ear-shot
aehoruv
haveour
aehostu
atheous
aehpprs
perhaps
aehprrs
phraser
sharper
aehprss
seraphs
aehprst
sparthe
aehprty
therapy
aehpssy
hey-pass
aehrrtu
urethra
aehrsst
shaster
aehrssw
swasher
aehrstt
rathest
shatter
aehrstv
harvest
aehrstw
wreaths

aehrsvw
wharves
aehrtuu
hauteur
aehrtwy
wreathy
aehstux
exhaust
aeiiknt
kainite
aeiillt
taillie
aeiilmr
Ramilie
aeiilnn
aniline
aeiilrs
Israeli
aeiilss
silesia
aeiiltz
tailzie
aeiimnt
intimae
miniate
aeiimrt
airtime
aeiimtt
imitate
aeiinns
asinine
insanie
aeiinpr
Pierian
aeiinqu
equinia
aeiinrs
Sirenia
aeiinrt
inertia
aeiinst
isatine
aeiinsx
sixaine
aeiintx
axinite
aeiiprr
prairie
aeiirrv
riviera
aeiirst
irisate
aeiistv
Saivite
Sivaite
aeiittv
vitiate
aeijlnv
javelin
aeijmns
jasmine
aeijnrs
Jersian

aeijnrt
nartjie
aeijntu
jauntie
aeiklmn
manlike
aeiklno
kaoline
aeiklnu
unalike
aeiklot
keitloa
aeiklov
live-oak
aeiklrs
serkali
aeiklrv
klavier
aeiklrw
warlike
aeikmms
mismake
aeikmnp
pikeman
aeikmnr
ramekin
aeikmpr
rampike
aeikmst
mistake
aeiknnr
Karenni
Rankine
aeiknps
sea-pink
aeiknrt
keratin
aeiknsy
kyanise
aeiknty
kyanite
aeikrss
sea-risk
aeiksss
askesis
aeillmn
manille
aeillmt
all-time
aeillnr
ralline
aeillov
alveoli
aeillps
illapse
aeillrr
rallier
aeillrt
literal
aeillru
ruellia
aeillst
tallies

aeillsy
sea-lily

aeilluv
eluvial

aeillvx
vexilla

aeilmms
melisma

aeilmnn
Lemnian
lineman
melanin

aeilmno
mineola

aeilmnp
impanel
maniple

aeilmnr
marline
mineral

aeilmns
isleman
Malines
seminal

aeilmnt
ailment
aliment

aeilmpr
impearl

aeilmpt
implate
palmiet

aeilmrr
larmier

aeilmrs
realism

aeilmrt
lamiter

aeilmru
Lemuria

aeilmss
aimless
seismal

aeilmty
laytime

aeilnnn
Linnean

aeilnns
nainsel'

aeilnop
opaline

aeilnor
aileron
alerion
alienor

aeilnos
sea-lion

aeilnot
elation
toe-nail

aeilnoz
Zoilean

aeilnpr
pearlin
praline

aeilnps
spaniel

aeilnpt
pantile

aeilnpu
Pauline

aeilnpx
explain

aeilnqu
equinal

aeilnrt
entrail
Latiner
latrine
reliant
retinal
trenail

aeilnrv
ravelin

aeilnrx
relaxin

aeilnry
inlayer
nailery

aeilnst
eastlin
elastin
salient
slàinte
staniel

aeilnsu
inulase

aeilnsy
Elysian

aeilntu
alunite

aeilnuv
unalive

aeilnuw
lauwine

aeilnvy
naïvely

aeilopr
peloria
rape-oil

aeilorv
variole

aeilost
isolate

aeilotv
violate

aeilppr
aripple

aeilprt
plaiter

aeilprv
prevail

aeilpst
talipes

aeilpsy
paisley

aeilqsu
Salique

aeilqtu
liquate
tequila

aeilrrt
retiral
retrial
trailer

aeilrss
airless

aeilrst
realist
saltier
saltire

aeilrsv
revisal

aeilrtt
tertial

aeilrtu
uralite

aeilrty
irately
reality

aeilrvv
revival

aeilrvy
virelay

aeilrwy
wearily

aeilssv
vessail

aeilstu
situlae

aeiltvy
vilayet

aeiluvx
exuvial

aeimmns
misname

aeimmrt
marmite

aeimmst
mismate

aeimmty
May-time

aeimmzz
mizmaze

aeimnnt
mannite

aeimnor
moraine

aeimnou
moineau

aeimnpr
Permian

aeimnrr
mariner
rein-arm

aeimnrs
remains
seminar
sirname

aeimnrt
minaret
raiment

aeimnrv
Minerva
vermian

aeimnrw
wire-man

aeimnss
samisen

aeimnst
mista'en
Samnite

aeimnsz
man-size

aeimnty
amenity
anytime

aeimoop
ipomoea

aeimopr
emporia

aeimorr
armoire

aeimost
atomise
osmiate
Samiote

aeimprr
rampire

aeimprs
impresa
sampire

aeimprt
primate

aeimprv
vampire

aeimpss
impasse

aeimpst
impaste
pastime

aeimpsw
mapwise

aeimrrr
marrier

ae[illegible]rs
simarre

aeimrst
maister
misrate
semitar
smartie

aeimrtu
muriate

aeimrtw
wartime

aeimsss
Messias

aeimsst
asteism

aeimssv
massive

aeimstz
mestiza

aeimsuv
amusive

aeimtyz
azymite

aeinnot
enation
Etonian
Noetian

aeinnow
Owenian

aeinnoz
neo-Nazi

aeinnpr
pannier

aeinnpt
pantine
pinnate

aeinnrs
insnare

aeinnrt
entrain
trannie

aeinnru
aneurin

aeinopr
open-air
pea-iron

aeinopz
epizoan

aeinors
erasion

aeinort
otarine

aeinoss
anoesis

aeinosv
evasion

aeinprs
Persian

aeinprt
painter
pertain
repaint

aeinpst
panties
sapient
spinate

aeinpsw
wine-sap

aeinptt
patient

aeinptu
petunia

aeinpty
paneity

aeinqtu
antique
quinate

aeinrrs
sierran

aeinrrt
retrain
terrain
trainer

aeinrst
resiant
retsina
stainer
starnie
stearin

aeinrsv
Servian

aeinrtt
iterant
nitrate
tartine
tertian

aeinrtu
ruinate
taurine
uranite
urinate

aeinrtw
tinware

aeinruz
azurine

aeinrvv
vervain

aeinsst
entasis
sestina

aeinssv
vinasse

aeinstt
instate
satinet

aeinstu
sinuate

aeinswy
anywise

aeintvw
wine-vat

aeintvy
naïvety

aeintxy
anxiety

aeinuxz
Zeuxian

aeioqsu
sequoia

aeiorrr
arriero

aeiorst
otaries

aeiostt
ostiate

aeiostz
azotise

aeipprs
apprise

aeipprt
periapt
Rappite

aeiprrs
praiser
aeiprss
paresis
Serapis
aeiprst
piastre
traipse
aeiprsu
spuriae
upraise
aeiprsv
parvise
aeiprtt
partite
tear-pit
aeiprtv
private
aeiprtw
wiretap
aeiprxy
pyrexia
aeipsss
asepsis
aeipssv
passive
aeiptxy
epitaxy
aeirrrt
tarrier
aeirrst
tarsier
aeirrtu
Etruria
aeirrty
retiary
aeirrvv
Viverra
aeirsst
tirasse
aeirssz
assizer
aeirstt
artiste
striate
aeirstw
waister
aeirttt
attrite
titrate
aeirttv
taivert
aeirttx
extrait
aeirtuy
aureity
aeirtuz
azurite
aeirtvy
variety
aeirwwy
wire-way
aeissuv
suasive

aeissux
auxesis
aeisttu
situate
aeisttv
stative
aeistty
satiety
aeitttu
attuite
aeitttv
vittate
aejknrs
jankers
aejlnuv
juvenal
aejlosu
jalouse
jealous
aejlouz
azulejo
aejmssy
jessamy
aejmsty
majesty
aejnnos
joannes
aejnorz
zanjero
aejnsst
jessant
aejprsy
jaspery
aekkrsy
skreaky
aekllrt
Kartell
aeklltu
kellaut
aeklnpp
knapple
aeklnpr
prankle
aeklnst
asklent
aeklory
rokelay
aeklost
skatole
aeklprs
sparkle
aeklrst
stalker
aekmnos
sokeman
aekmpru
upmaker
aeknntu
untaken
aeknppr
knapper
aeknprs
spanker

aeknpsu
sneak-up
unspeak
aeknrst
starken
aeknrsw
swanker
aeknrvy
knavery
aeknswy
swankey
aekorrs
rosaker
aekottu
outtake
take-out
aekppsu
upspake
upspeak
aekpssy
passkey
aekqsuy
squeaky
aekrsty
streaky
aellmnu
lumenal
aellmsu
malleus
aellmsy
mesally
aellmty
metally
aellmwx
maxwell
aellnop
pallone
aellnor
llanero
aellnov
novella
aellnpy
penally
aellntt
tallent
aellnvy
venally
aellopx
poll-axe
aellors
rosella
aellort
reallot
aellorv
all-over
overall
aellpru
pleural
aellpsw
spa-well
aellptu
pluteal
aellpty
playlet

aellquy
equally
aellrst
stellar
aellrty
alertly
elytral
aellruw
wall-rue
aellsst
tassell
aellssw
lawless
aellstw
setwall
swallet
aellsty
stalely
aelltuu
ululate
aelluvv
valvule
aelmmno
mamelon
aelmmoy
myeloma
aelmmrs
slammer
aelmmrt
trammel
aelmmst
stammel
aelmmsy
malmsey
aelmnor
almoner
nemoral
aelmnot
lomenta
omental
telamon
aelmnpr
lampern
aelmnru
numeral
aelmnsu
mensual
aelmntt
mantlet
aelmntu
nut-meal
aelmopr
pleroma
aelmopu
ampoule
aelmopy
maypole
aelmort
molerat
aelmorv
removal
aelmoss
Molasse

aelmost
maltose
aelmott
matelot
aelmprs
sampler
aelmprt
templar
trample
aelmpry
lamprey
aelmptu
plumate
aelmrrs
marrels
aelmrss
armless
aelmrtt
martlet
aelmssu
Musales
aelmstu
Mustela
aelnnpr
planner
aelnnpu
unpanel
aelnnrs
ensnarl
aelnnrt
lantern
aelnnru
unlearn
aelnnst
stannel
aelnntu
annulet
aelnoos
alsoone
aelnopt
polenta
aelnors
orleans
aelnotv
volante
aelnppy
play-pen
aelnprt
pantler
planter
replant
aelnpry
plenary
aelnpss
napless
aelnptx
explant
aelnpty
aplenty
net-play
penalty
aelnquu
unequal

aelnrrs
snarler
aelnrst
saltern
sternal
aelnrtt
trental
aelnrtu
neutral
aelnrtv
ventral
aelnruv
unravel
aelnssu
sensual
aelnssw
awnless
aelnssx
laxness
aelnsty
stanyel
aelntuv
envault
aeloors
aerosol
roseola
aeloppr
propale
aeloppx
apoplex
aeloprr
preoral
aeloprs
reposal
aeloprt
prolate
aeloprv
overlap
aelopst
apostle
aelopsx
exposal
aeloptt
paletot
aeloptu
outleap
aelorrt
Realtor®
relator
aelorss
oarless
aelorst
oestral
aelortv
levator
aelorty
royalet
aeloruu
rouleau
aelorvy
overlay
aelosss
lassoes

aelossv
salvoes
aelostv
solvate
aelosuz
zealous
aelosvy
saveloy
aelotuv
ovulate
aelpprs
slapper
aelppry
reapply
aelppss
sapples
aelppst
stapple
aelppsu
appulse
papules
aelprst
plaster
Psalter
stapler
aelprsu
perusal
serpula
aelprsy
parsley
sparely
aelprtt
partlet
platter
prattle
aelprty
peartly
prelaty
pteryla
aelpsss
sapless
aelpstt
peltast
aelpstu
pulsate
spatule
aelpuuv
upvalue
aelqrru
quarrel
aelqtuz
quetzal
aelrrsu
surreal
aelrrtt
rattler
aelrrtw
trawler
aelrsst
artless
aelrssy
rayless
aelrstt
slatter
starlet
startle
Telstar
aelrstu
saluter
aelrstv
vestral
aelrstw
wastrel
aelrsvy
slavery
aelrttt
tartlet
tattler
aelrttu
tutelar
aelrtuv
vaulter
aelrtwz
waltzer
aelsswy
wayless
aelstty
stately
stylate
aelsuvy
suavely
aeltttw
twattle
aelttux
textual
aeltuvv
vulvate
aemmnot
momenta
aemmntu
amentum
aemmors
marmose
aemmrst
stammer
aemnnos
mannose
name-son
aemnnot
montane
aemnnou
noumena
aemnnrt
manrent
remnant
aemnnsw
newsman
aemnntu
unmeant
aemnors
Romanes
aemnort
tone-arm
aemnoru
enamour
neuroma
aemnorv
overman
aemnory
romneya
aemnotu
notaeum
outname
aemnpst
enstamp
aemnptu
putamen
aemnpty
payment
aemnrru
manurer
aemnrst
sarment
smarten
aemnrsu
surname
aemnrtu
trueman
aemnrtv
varment
aemnsty
amnesty
aemnttx
text-man
aemntwy
wayment
aemoors
sea-room
aemoort
tea-room
aemoorw
woomera
aemoost
osteoma
aemoosv
vamoose
aemoosz
Mesozoa
aemoppr
pampero
aemorrv
overarm
aemorst
maestro
aemorsu
rameous
aemorsw
sea-worm
aemortu
Euratom
aemosss
sea-moss
aemostw
twasome
aemosuz
zamouse
aemoswy
someway
aemottz
mozetta
aempnry
mappery
aemprrt
tramper
aemprst
stamper
aemprsw
swamper
aemprtu
tempura
aempttt
attempt
aempttu
tapetum
aemqrsu
masquer
aemrrry
remarry
aemrrsw
swarmer
aemrrtu
erratum
aemrruu
Réaumur
aemrssu
masseur
aemrstt
smatter
aemrstu
strumae
aemrsty
mastery
streamy
aemrttx
mar-text
aemrtty
mattery
aemrtuu
trumeau
aennnpt
pennant
aennops
pannose
aennotu
tonneau
aennprs
spanner
aennpsw
span-new
aennqtu
quannet
aennrtt
entrant
aennrtv
vernant
aennrty
tannery
tyranne
aennssw
wanness
aenootz
entozoa
tan-ooze
aenoppr
propane
aenoprs
persona
aenoprt
operant
pronate
protean
aenopsu
posaune
aenorrv
overran
aenorst
nor'-east
senator
treason
aenorsw
sea-worn
aenortv
venator
aenorxy
anorexy
aenostu
soutane
aenosvw
waveson
aenpprs
parsnep
snapper
aenpprt
parpent
aenppru
unpaper
aenprrt
partner
aenprst
pastern
aenprsw
spawner
aenprtt
pattern
reptant
aenpruv
parvenu
aenpsst
aptness
patness
aenpssy
synapse
aenpstw
stewpan
aenpsty
synapte
aenrrtt
tranter
aenrrty
ternary
aenrsst
sarsnet
aenrssw
rawness
aenrstu
saunter
sea-turn
aenrstv
servant
versant
aenrstw
strawen
aenrsuv
Avernus
aenrsuw
unswear
unwares
aenrttu
taunter
aenrtty
nattery
aenrtuv
vaunter
aenrtuw
unwater
aenruwy
unweary
aensstx
sextans
aensttu
tetanus
unstate
aensttx
sextant
aentttu
attuent
aeoopps
papoose
aeooprs
oropesa
aeoppps
pappose
aeopprs
apposer
aeopprv
approve
aeoppsu
pea-soup
aeoprrt
patrero
praetor
prorate
aeoprst
esparto
seaport
aeoprtt
portate
aeoprvy
overpay
aeoprwy
ropeway
aeoqrtu
equator
aeoqruv
vaquero
aeoqsuu
aqueous
aeorrss
Rasores
aeorrst
roaster

aeorrsu
  arouser
aeorstt
  toaster
aeorstz
  Zostera
aeortuw
  outwear
aeortvx
  overtax
aeosstt
  sea-tost
aeossyy
  easy-osy
aepprrt
  trapper
aepprrw
  wrapper
aepprss
  appress
aepprsu
  upspear
aepprsw
  swapper
aeppstu
  paste-up
aepqrtu
  parquet
aeprrrs
  sparrer
aeprrsy
  respray
  sprayer
aeprrtu
  rapture
aeprrty
  petrary
aeprssy
  pessary
aeprstt
  spatter
  tapster
aeprstu
  pasture
  upstare
aeprsty
  yapster
aeprsyy
  sprayey
aeprtxy
  apteryx
aepsstu
  petasus
aepsttu
  upstate
aeqrrsu
  squarer
aeqrrtu
  quarter
aeqrstu
  T-square
aeqrttu
  quartet
aeqruvy
  quavery
aerrssu
  assurer
aerrstt
  restart
  starter
aerrsty
  strayer
aerrtty
  rattery
aersstt
  starets
aersttt
  stretta
aersttu
  stature
aersttw
  swatter
aersttz
  staretz
aerstuy
  estuary
aerstwy
  wastery
aerttty
  tattery
aerttuv
  vettura
aesstuy
  eustasy
aestttu
  statute
affggin
  gaffing
affghis
  fish-fag
affginy
  affying
affhiln
  hafflin
affhirs
  raffish
affhlly
  fly-half
affilmn
  mafflin
affilsy
  falsify
affimst
  mastiff
affinru
  funfair
  ruffian
affinty
  tiffany
affiorr
  forfair
affirru
  furfair
affllpy
  fly-flap
afflopy
  play-off
affnors
  saffron
affnort
  affront
affnosw
  sawn-off
afgggin
  fagging
afggiot
  goat-fig
afghhis
  hagfish
afghirs
  garfish
afghlsu
  gashful
afghltu
  flaught
afghost
  Gasthof
afghrtu
  fraught
afgiiln
  failing
afgiinr
  fairing
afgilln
  falling
afgilmn
  flaming
afgilno
  loafing
afgilnr
  flaring
afgilnt
  fatling
afgilnu
  gainful
afgilny
  anglify
  flaying
afgilru
  figural
afgimno
  foaming
afgimnr
  farming
  framing
afgimny
  magnify
afginnn
  fanning
afginnw
  fawning
afginry
  fraying
afginst
  fasting
afgintt
  fatting
afgintw
  wafting
afgirty
  gratify
afgknop
  pakfong
afgkort
  koftgar
afgllly
  gall-fly
afglluy
  fall-guy
  fugally
afglmop
  fog-lamp
afglryy
  grayfly
afgmnor
  frogman
afgoott
  fagotto
afhiirs
  fairish
afhikuy
  kufiyah
afhilln
  halflin
afhilss
  falsish
afhiltu
  laithfu'
afhiltw
  half-wit
afhimnu
  hafnium
afhinos
  fashion
afhintu
  unfaith
afhiors
  oar-fish
afhisst
  fastish
afhissw
  saw-fish
afhistt
  fattish
afhiswy
  fish-way
afhkory
  hayfork
afhkrtu
  futhark
afhlmru
  harmful
afhlotu
  out-half
afhloty
  hayloft
afhlstu
  hatfuls
afhoopt
  pooftah
afhoptu
  pouftah
afiilrt
  airlift
afiilry
  fairily
afiknrt
  ratfink
afillms
  misfall
afillny
  finally
afillpt
  pitfall
afillpu
  pailful
afillry
  frailly
afillty
  tail-fly
afilluv
  fluvial
  vialful
afilluw
  wailful
afilmpy
  amplify
afilnow
  Wolfian
afilnpu
  painful
afilntu
  flutina
afilnty
  faintly
afilotx
  fox-tail
afilquy
  qualify
afilrry
  friarly
afilrty
  frailty
afilssy
  salsify
afilstu
  fistula
afilstw
  fist-law
afilsty
  falsity
afilsvy
  Slavify
afimoos
  mafioso
afimorv
  aviform
afimsuv
  Fauvism
afinnor
  franion
afinors
  insofar
afinstu
  faunist
  fustian
  infaust
afiortu
  faitour
afisstt
  sitfast
afissty
  satisfy
afistuv
  Fauvist
afittuy
  fatuity
afjlrsu
  jarfuls
afjootw
  foot-jaw
  jaw-foot
afklnry
  frankly
afklntu
  tankful
afklort
  folk-art
afklowy
  folkway
afklrsu
  sarkful
afkrrtu
  Fraktur
afllmpu
  palmful
afllmpy
  lamp-fly
afllooy
  aloofly
afllotu
  fall-out
  outfall
afllpuy
  playful
aflluwy
  awfully
aflmnou
  moanful
aflmoru
  formula
aflmorw
  wolfram
aflmost
  flotsam
aflmstu
  mastful
aflmsuu
  famulus
aflnort
  frontal
aflnott
  flotant
aflnpsu
  panfuls
aflnrtu
  runflat
aflntuy
  flaunty
aflootw
  woolfat

aflorsu
fusarol
afloruv
flavour
aflorww
warwolf
aflossu
fossula
aflprty
fly-trap
aflrstu
Flustra
aflrtuy
trayful
afmnoot
footman
afmnort
formant
afmnrsu
surfman
afmnrtu
turfman
afmorst
farmost
afmortu
foumart
afmostt
aftmost
afmostu
sfumato
afnorrt
Fortran
afnorrw
forwarn
afnsstu
sunfast
afooppr
approof
afoorru
four-oar
afoortz
forzato
afootwy
footway
afoprtx
fox-trap
afostuu
fatuous
aggggin
gagging
agggijn
jagging
agggiln
lagging
aggginn
ganging
aggginr
ragging
agggins
sagging
aggging
tagging
aggginu
gauging

aggginw
wagging
agghhis
haggish
agghiil
ghilgai
agghimn
gingham
agghinn
hanging
agghisw
waggish
aggiijj
jigajig
aggiilm
mail-gig
aggijjo
jigajog
aggilln
galling
gingall
aggilnn
angling
aggilnr
glaring
aggilnt
Lagting
aggilnz
glazing
agginnp
panging
agginoy
Ogygian
agginps
gasping
agginrs
gas-ring
sirgang
agginrt
grating
agginrv
graving
agginrz
grazing
agginss
gassing
agginst
staging
agglnoo
long-ago
aggmorr
grogram
aggmoty
maggoty
aghhhit
high-hat
aghhimn
highman
aghhiwy
highway
aghhosw
hogwash
aghhtuy
haughty

aghiinn
haining
aghikns
shaking
aghiknw
hawking
aghilln
halling
aghilnr
harling
aghilns
lashing
aghilnt
Althing
halting
lathing
aghilnw
whaling
aghilot
Goliath
aghilrs
largish
aghilrt
alright
aghilsu
Gaulish
aghimns
mashing
aghimps
gampish
aghinnt
tanghin
aghinpp
happing
aghinps
shaping
aghinrs
garnish
sharing
aghinru
nuraghi
aghinsu
anguish
aghinsv
shaving
aghinsw
washing
aghintt
hatting
aghintw
thawing
aghiost
goatish
aghiprs
Graphis
aghipsw
pigwash
aghirsu
guarish
aghjmno
mah-jong
aghkoor
Goorkha

aghkosw
goshawk
aghlmpu
galumph
aghlnuy
nylghau
aghloos
gasohol
aghlosu
goulash
aghlptu
plug-hat
aghlsty
ghastly
aghmoss
moss-hag
aghnotu
hangout
aghnruy
ahungry
Hungary
aghntuy
naughty
aghortw
wart-hog
aghpsuw
Pugwash
aghptuy
paughty
aghrsty
gytrash
agiiklt
glaikit
agiilmn
mailing
agiilnn
nailing
agiilnr
glairin
railing
agiilns
sailing
agiilnt
tailing
agiilnw
wailing
agiilov
viliago
agiilpt
pigtail
agiilty
agility
agiimmn
maiming
agiimms
imagism
agiimor
origami
agiimst
imagist
agiinnr
ingrain
agiinnz
Zingani

agiinpr
pairing
agiinpt
T'ai-p'ing
agiinrs
raising
agiinrt
raiting
agiinrz
Zingari
agiintw
waiting
agijmmn
jamming
agijnnu
Jungian
agijnrr
jarring
agiklno
oakling
agiklnr
Karling
agiklnt
talking
agiklnw
walking
agikmnr
marking
agiknnr
ranking
agiknnt
tanking
agiknnu
unaking
agiknny
yanking
agiknos
soaking
agiknqu
quaking
agiknrs
sarking
agiknrt
karting
agiknss
gaskins
agiknst
skating
tasking
agillln
lalling
agillmu
gallium
agillnp
palling
agillnu
lingual
lingula
agillnw
walling
agillny
allying
agillor
gorilla

agillot
galliot
agillru
ligular
agillsu
lugsail
agilmmn
lamming
agilmnp
lamping
agilmnr
marling
agilmnt
malting
agilmpu
plagium
agilnno
loaning
agilnns
linsang
agilnnt
tanling
agilnop
galopin
agilnot
antilog
agilnpp
lapping
agilnps
sapling
agilnpt
plating
agilnpw
lapwing
agilnrw
warling
agilnry
angrily
nargily
agilnst
anglist
lasting
salting
slating
agilnsv
salving
agilnsw
swaling
agilnty
giantly
agilnuw
wauling
agilnww
wawling
agilopt
galipot
agilors
girasol
agilost
saligot
agilsty
stagily
agilsyz
syzgial

agimmnr
ramming
agimnnn
manning
agimnnr
ringman
agimnor
Moringa
agimnpp
mapping
agimnpt
tamping
agimnpv
vamping
agimnrr
marring
agimnrt
migrant
agimnrw
warming
agimnry
myringa
agimnsu
amusing
agimntt
matting
agimors
isogram
agimoru
gourami
agimosy
isogamy
agimrrt
trigram
agimrty
trigamy
aginnnp
panning
aginnnt
tanning
aginnnv
vanning
aginnoz
Zingano
aginnpp
napping
aginnpt
panting
aginnrs
snaring
aginnrw
warning
aginntw
wanting
aginnuz
Günzian
aginnwy
yawning
aginooo
oogonia
aginorr
roaring
aginors
Signora
soaring
aginort
Grotian
aginorz
Zingaro
aginost
agonist
aginosu
sagouin
aginosv
Vosgian
aginppr
rapping
aginpps
sapping
aginppt
tapping
aginprs
parsing
rasping
sparing
aginprt
parting
prating
aginprw
warping
aginpry
praying
aginpss
passing
aginpsu
pausing
aginptt
patting
aginrrt
tarring
aginrrw
warring
aginrst
staring
aginrsy
signary
syringa
aginrtt
ratting
aginrtw
ring-taw
aginrty
giantry
aginrvy
varying
aginrwy
ringway
aginstt
tasting
aginstw
wasting
aginsty
staying
Stygian
aginswy
swaying
aginttt
tatting
agintxy
taxying
agintyz
tzigany
aginwwx
waxwing
agiorst
agistor
orgiast
agirtvy
gravity
agjlnsu
Juglans
agjlruu
jugular
agjnoor
jargoon
agkmnop
kampong
agknopt
paktong
agkorrw
ragwork
agllnoo
galloon
agllntu
gall-nut
nut-gall
aglloss
glossal
agllosw
gallows
agllott
glottal
agllryy
gyrally
aglmopy
polygam
aglmoru
glamour
aglmory
Morglay
aglnops
Gosplan
aglnopu
up-along
aglnoru
languor
aglnost
alongst
aglnpsy
spangly
aglnpuy
gunplay
aglntuy
gauntly
agloopy
apology
agloorw
rag-wool
aglopsu
Solpuga
agmmory
myogram
agmnnos
songman
agmnnow
gownman
agmnoru
organum
agmnost
amongst
agmnstu
mustang
agmnsty
gymnast
agmnsyy
syngamy
agmooyz
zoogamy
agmoprr
program
agmopru
gopuram
agmorrw
ragworm
agmprsu
grampus
agmrssu
grassum
agnnnoo
nonagon
agnnoor
organon
agnorrt
grantor
agnorst
art-song
agnorsw
war-song
agnrtuy
gauntry
agoppst
stop-gap
agorrtw
ragwort
agosuyz
azygous
ahhhiss
hashish
ahhiksw
hawkish
ahhimns
Mishnah
ahhiprs
rhaphis
ahhiptt
pith-hat
ahhistt
shittah
ahhlloo
hollaho
ahhlrsy
harshly
ahhoops
hoop-ash
ahhoprs
shophar
ahhoprt
hap'orth
ahiikrs
shikari
ahiilor
hair-oil
ahiilps
silphia
ahiilsw
Swahili
ahiimnt
thiamin
ahiinpr
hairpin
ahiintu
huitain
ahiiprs
airship
ahiipsx
Xiphias
ahijnno
Johnian
ahiklms
Lakshmi
ahiklrs
larkish
ahiklst
silk-hat
ahiklsy
shakily
ahikmns
khamsin
ahikmrs
Kashmir
ahikmsw
mawkish
ahiknrs
Krishna
ahiknss
snakish
ahiknsv
knavish
ahikprs
parkish
ahillno
hallion
ahillnp
phallin
ahillnt
ant-hill
ahillrt
athrill
ahilltt
tallith
ahilmms
mashlim
ahilmns
mashlin
ahilmot
halimot
ahilmsu
alumish
ahilnps
planish
ahilnrs
shrinal
ahilory
hoarily
ahilpps
Lappish
shiplap
ahilppy
happily
ahilpsy
apishly
ahilsst
saltish
ahilssv
slavish
ahilstu
halitus
ahilsty
hastily
ahimmrs
rammish
ahimnns
mannish
ahimnnu
inhuman
ahimnot
Manihot
ahimnps
shipman
ahimopr
morphia
ahimpsv
vampish
ahimpsw
wampish
ahimrst
Mithras
ahimtuz
azimuth
ahimtvz
mitzvah
ahinnsw
wannish
ahinntx
xanthin
ahinort
orthian
ahinotz
hoatzin
ahinpss
Spanish
ahinpty
Pythian
ahinrst
tarnish
ahinrsv
varnish
ahinrty
rhytina
ahinstu
inhaust

ahiopru
Ophiura
ahiopxy
hypoxia
ahioruv
haviour
ahiprst
harpist
ahiprsw
warship
ahipssw
waspish
ahipsww
whip-saw
ahipswy
ship-way
ahirrsy
'Arryish
ahirstt
athirst
rattish
tartish
ahirstw
trishaw
ahisstu
thiasus
ahisstw
whatsis
ahisttw
whatsit
ahistvy
Yahvist
ahistwy
Yahwist
ahittww
whittaw
ahjmnos
Mas-John
ahklmoo
holm-oak
ahkmorr
markhor
ahkmrtu
mukhtar
ahkrsuu
Kurhaus
ahllnos
shallon
ahllnoy
hallyon
ahllops
shallop
ahllost
shallot
ahllosw
shallow
ahlloty
loathly
tally-ho
ahllpsu
phallus
ahllpyy
aphylly

ahllstu
thallus
ahlmmsu
mashlum
ahlmnpy
nymphal
ahlmnuy
humanly
ahlmoru
humoral
ahlmsuu
hamulus
ahlnopr
alphorn
ahlnort
althorn
ahlostu
outlash
ahlotuu
outhaul
ahlprsy
sharply
ahlpruy
hypural
ahlpssy
splashy
ahmmmot
mammoth
ahmmmuu
hummaum
ahmmtuz
thammuz
ahmnntu
manhunt
ahmnnuu
unhuman
ahmnops
shopman
ahmnopt
phantom
ahmnors
Romansh
ahmnoru
man-hour
ahmnory
harmony
ahmnosw
showman
ahmnrsu
Rhamnus
ahmnryy
hymnary
ahmnstu
mash-tun
ahmoops
shampoo
ahmooss
samshoo
ahmorru
morrhua
ahmorst
harmost
ahmottz
matzoth

ahmotwx
wax-moth
ahmpssu
smash-up
ahnnoty
Anthony
ahnoopr
harpoon
ahnorsx
saxhorn
ahnottw
whatnot
ahnppuu
pupunha
ahnppuy
unhappy
ahnprxy
pharynx
ahnstuy
unhasty
ahoopst
hop-oast
ahoprty
atrophy
ahopstw
wash-pot
ahopttw
towpath
ahortty
throaty
ahostuw
wash-out
ahprrty
phratry
ahpsxyy
asphyxy
ahqssuy
squashy
ahrstwy
swarthy
ahrtuwy
thruway
aiiilms
Ismaili
aiiilmt
militia
aiiilnt
initial
aiiimrs
saimiri
aiijmns
Jainism
aiikmms
skimmia
aiikmnn
manikin
aiikrtt
traikit
aiilllp
lapilli
aiillmn
liminal
aiillnv
villain

aiillqu
quillai
aiilmmn
minimal
aiilmno
monilia
aiilmrs
similar
aiilmry
miliary
aiilnos
liaison
aiilnpt
pintail
aiilnpu
nauplii
aiilntu
nautili
aiilnty
anility
aiilopp
papilio
aiilorv
ravioli
aiilott
Italiot
aiilqsu
siliqua
aiilrtv
trivial
vitrail
aiimmns
animism
aiimnor
amorini
aiimnps
pianism
aiimnpt
impaint
timpani
aiimnrt
martini
aiimnst
animist
aiimnsz
Naziism
aiimntt
imitant
aiimntu
minutia
aiimntv
vitamin
aiimrss
air-miss
aiimrst
simitar
aiimssv
Saivism
Sivaism
aiimssy
myiasis
aiinnop
pianino

aiinnrt
Nitrian
aiinnty
inanity
aiinops
sinopia
aiinott
notitia
aiinprs
aspirin
aiinpst
pianist
aiinrss
Rissian
aiinrtv
vitrain
Vitrina
aiiprst
piarist
aiipttu
pituita
aiissvv
vis-à-vis
aijklps
jap-silk
aijlyzz
jazzily
aijnort
janitor
aikksuz
zakuski
aiklmmn
milkman
aiklmnn
linkman
aiklmns
silk-man
aiklnsy
snakily
aiklopt
kail-pot
aiklpwy
pawkily
aiklrtt
titlark
aiklssy
skysail
aikmnns
kinsman
aikmnst
Kantism
aikmsst
Saktism
aiknstt
Kantist
aikprrt
Prakrit
ailllot
tall-oil
aillmnu
luminal
aillmop
oil-palm
palm-oil

aillmot
maillot
aillmpu
pallium
aillmsw
saw-mill
aillmyy
may-lily
aillnno
lanolin
aillnop
paillon
aillnpy
plainly
aillnst
install
aillntu
Tullian
aillnvy
villany
aillpru
pilular
aillpuv
pluvial
aillrsu
arillus
aillstw
law-list
aillsty
saltily
ailltvy
vitally
ailltww
witwall
ailmmor
immoral
ailmmsy
myalism
ailmmuu
alumium
ailmnno
nominal
ailmnop
lampion
ailmnos
malison
Osmanli
somnial
ailmnoy
alimony
ailmnps
plasmin
ailmnpt
implant
ailmnru
murlain
ailmopt
optimal
ailmopy
Olympia
ailmost
somital
ailmosz
Zolaism

ailmprt
marl-pit
ailmpru
primula
ailmpst
palmist
ailmpsy
misplay
ailmrst
mistral
ailmrsu
simular
ailmssv
Slavism
ailnnot
ant-lion
ailnnpu
pinnula
ailnnsu
unslain
ailnoop
Polonia
ailnopy
polynia
ailnoqu
Aquilon
ailnprw
prawlin
ailnpsx
salpinx
ailnptu
nuptial
patulin
unplait
ailnpty
inaptly
ptyalin
ailnqtu
quintal
ailnrsu
insular
ailnrtt
rattlin
ailnstu
unalist
ailnsty
nastily
saintly
ailnsvy
Sylvian
ailntty
nattily
ailntuv
unvital
ailoorw
woorali
ailoprs
Polaris
ailopst
apostil
topsail
ailopsy
soapily

ailoptt
talipot
ailoptv
pivotal
ailopxy
Xylopia
ailoqtu
aliquot
ailoruw
wourali
ailorux
uxorial
ailorvy
olivary
ailostu
outsail
ailppsy
pay-slip
ailpqsu
Pasquil
ailprsu
parulis
uprisal
ailprsy
Pyralis
ailpstt
salt-pit
ailpsty
pay-list
ailpswy
slipway
ailqttu
quittal
ailqtuy
quality
ailrrvy
rivalry
ailrstt
starlit
ailrstu
trisula
ailrsty
trysail
ailrttu
titular
ailrtuv
virtual
vitular
ailstty
tastily
ailstuw
lawsuit
ailttty
tattily
aimmmux
maximum
aimmnnt
mint-man
aimmntu
manumit
aimmors
amorism
aimmoss
Mosaism

aimmost
atomism
aimmrsx
Marxism
aimnnos
mansion
onanism
aimnoor
amorino
aimnopr
rampion
aimnopt
maintop
tampion
timpano
aimnort
tormina
aimnoru
mainour
aimnorw
Wormian
aimnotu
manitou
tinamou
aimnrru
murrain
aimnrsu
Surinam
uranism
aimnrtu
natrium
aimnrtv
varmint
aimnruu
uranium
aimnruw
Würmian
aimnstt
mattins
aimnstu
tsunami
aimnsyz
zanyism
aimopst
impasto
aimorru
orarium
aimorst
amorist
aimortt
Tritoma
aimoruz
zoarium
aimostt
atomist
aimppru
air-pump
aimppst
mappist
aimprry
primary
aimprss
Parsism

aimqrsu
marquis
aimrsst
tsarism
aimrssy
Syriasm
aimrstu
Maurist
aimrstx
Marxist
aimsstt
statism
ainnnow
wannion
ainnoox
Oxonian
ainnopr
iron-pan
ainnops
saponin
ainnptu
unpaint
ainnqtu
quinnat
quintan
ainnrtt
intrant
ainnrtu
urinant
ainnstt
instant
ainnstu
unsaint
ainntuy
annuity
ainoopr
pronaoi
ainoorr
orarion
ainoort
oration
ainootv
ovation
ainoppt
appoint
ainoprs
parison
soprani
ainoprt
atropin
ainopss
passion
ainoptu
opuntia
utopian
ainorsw
warison
ainortx
triaxon
ainossu
suasion
ainostt
station

ainosux
anxious
ainosvy
synovia
ainottz
Zantiot
ainpprs
parsnip
ainpqsu
Pasquin
ainpqtu
piquant
ainprst
spirant
spraint
ainprtu
puritan
uptrain
up-train
ainqruy
quinary
ainqstu
asquint
ainrrty
trinary
ainrruy
urinary
ainrssu
Russian
ainrstt
straint
transit
ainrtuy
unitary
ainsstu
issuant
sustain
ainssxy
synaxis
ainttvy
tantivy
ainttww
want-wit
aioprrt
airport
paritor
aioprst
airstop
parotis
aioprtt
patriot
aioprtw
two-pair
aioprty
topiary
aiopruv
paviour
aiorrrw
warrior
aiorrtt
traitor
aiorrtx
oratrix

aiorstu
sautoir
aiorstv
travois
aiorsty
ostiary
aiorsuv
saviour
various
aipprst
Rappist
aipprsu
Priapus
aiprtvy
pravity
aipzzzz
pizzazz
airrtzz
rizzart
airsstt
tsarist
airsstu
Tarsius
airsttt
attrist
airstvy
varsity
airsuuv
uva-ursi
airtuvx
vitraux
aissttt
statist
aisttvy
vastity
aistuvy
suavity
ajkmnnu
junkman
ajkmntu
muntjak
ajllruy
jurally
ajlnoru
journal
ajloppy
jaloppy
ajmnruy
juryman
ajooprt
Rajpoot
akklrsy
skylark
akllnow
know-all
akllorw
all-work
aklmopu
oak-lump
akloprw
lapwork
aklopuv
Volapük

aklottu
outtalk
aklotuw
outwalk
walk-out
aklrsty
starkly
akmnoor
kroo-man
akmnorw
workman
akmnrtu
trankum
Turkman
akmoort
mooktar
akmqtuu
kumquat
akmrstu
musk-rat
aknortu
outrank
akooprt
partook
akoostu
atokous
akorrtw
artwork
akorwwx
waxwork
akqsuwy
squawky
allloyy
loyally
allmnop
pollman
allmnot
tollman
allmnpu
Pullman
allmory
morally
allmpuu
plumula
allnoow
Walloon
allnrtu
Trullan
allnruu
lunular
allnsty
slantly
allntuu
ululant
allootx
axolotl
allopry
pay-roll
alloptx
poll-tax
allorty
ally-tor
alloryy
royally
allosww
swallow
alloswy
sallowy
allotty
totally
allotuw
out-wall
allotwy
tallowy
allotyy
loyalty
allqsuy
squally
allrruy
rurally
allrstu
lustral
allsuuy
usually
almnnuy
unmanly
almnoop
lampoon
almnoow
woolman
almnoru
unmoral
almnory
almonry
almnosu
solanum
almnowy
womanly
almnpsu
sun-lamp
almnsuu
alumnus
almoprt
marplot
almorru
morular
almottu
mulatto
almrsty
smartly
almrsuu
ramulus
almrtuu
tumular
almssuy
alyssum
asylums
alnnrsu
unsnarl
alnnsuu
annulus
alnoopt
platoon
alnoort
ortolan
alnoppy
panoply
alnopss
sponsal
alnopyy
polynya
alnoruy
unroyal
alnoruz
zonular
alnprsu
snarl-up
alnpruy
planury
alnptuy
unaptly
alnptxy
planxty
alnsuuu
unusual
aloopnrw
poor-law
aloopyz
Polyzoa
aloorrs
sororal
aloppru
popular
aloppry
propyla
aloprru
parlour
aloprsu
parlous
alopssu
spousal
alopsuv
voluspa
aloptuy
outplay
aloqrru
rorqual
aloqrsu
squalor
alorrst
rostral
alortyy
royalty
alosttu
outlast
alostxy
oxy-salt
alprsuu
pursual
alprswy
sprawly
alrstty
startly
alrstuu
sutural
ammnoor
moorman
ammnoot
mootman
ammnory
May-morn
Rommany
ammnruy
nummary
ammoorr
mormaor
ammoptu
pomatum
ammorww
maw-worm
ammrsuy
summary
amnnoox
monaxon
amnnosw
snowman
amnnott
montant
amnnoty
antonym
amnnouw
unwoman
amnoopp
pompano
amnoopr
moor-pan
amnoott
Ottoman
amnootz
matzoon
amnoprt
portman
amnopry
paronym
amnopst
postman
topsman
amnoptu
pantoum
amnopty
tympano
amnorst
transom
amnorsy
masonry
amnortu
romaunt
amnosst
stamnos
amnotuy
autonym
amnptyy
tympany
amnqtuu
quantum
amnrruy
unmarry
amnrstu
unsmart
amnrttu
tantrum
amooors
amoroso
amooprt
taproom
amoorsu
amorous
amopstt
topmast
amorruy
armoury
amorrwy
marrowy
amorsst
matross
amorssy
morassy
amosuyz
azymous
amprsuw
upswarm
amrrstu
rastrum
amrrtyy
martyry
amrsttu
stratum
annotty
tantony
annrtyy
tyranny
anooprs
pronaos
soprano
anooprt
patroon
pronota
anoortt
arnotto
anoprrs
sporran
anoprsy
spray-on
anoprtv
provant
anopstu
outspan
anorrww
war-worn
anorstu
rousant
santour
anorsuu
anurous
uranous
anorwwy
wayworn
anosttu
Totanus
anppsuw
suppawn
anprstu
suntrap
unstrap
aoopprs
apropos
aooprst
Atropos
aooprtt
taproot
aoorrtt
rotator
aoorrtu
outroar
aoorrty
oratory
aoorstu
outsoar
aoostuz
azotous
aootxyz
zootaxy
aopppsu
pappous
aopprrt
rapport
aoprrsw
sparrow
aoprrty
parroty
portray
aoprstt
tar-spot
aoprstu
asprout
aoprstw
post-war
aoprttu
outpart
aoprttw
two-part
aoprtuy
outpray
aopruvy
vapoury
aopsstu
passout
aopstuy
autopsy
aopstwy
way-post
aorrswy
sowarry
aorssuy
ossuary
suasory
aorstww
saw-wort
aorsuvy
savoury
aorttuy
out-tray
aortuvy
avoutry
aosttuy
outstay
apprruu
Purpura
apprsty
strappy

apprsuy
  papyrus
aprsssu
  surpass
aprsttu
  start-up
  upstart
aprsuwy
  spur-way
aqrtuyz
  quartzy
aqsttuy
  squatty
arssttu
  stratus
bbbelru
  blubber
bbbeory
  bobbery
bbbgino
  bobbing
bbbhios
  bobbish
bbcciko
  bibcock
bbcdehu
  chubbed
bbcdeir
  cribbed
bbcdelu
  clubbed
bbcehin
  nebbich
bbceilr
  cribble
bbcekko
  kebbock
bbcekku
  kebbuck
bbcelor
  clobber
  cobbler
bbcginu
  cubbing
bbchisu
  cubbish
bbcinou
  bubonic
bbcrsuy
  scrubby
bbdderu
  drubbed
bbdeeit
  ebb-tide
bbdeelp
  pebbled
bbdeeno
  bone-bed
bbdegru
  grubbed
bbdeilo
  bilobed

bbdeilr
  dibbler
  dribble
bbdeirr
  dribber
bbdekno
  knobbed
bbdelos
  bobsled
bbdelsu
  slubbed
bbdensu
  snubbed
bbdeosw
  swobbed
bbdestu
  stubbed
bbdgiin
  dibbing
bbdginu
  dubbing
bbdilry
  dribbly
bbdooss
  od's-bobs
bbeeeru
  bebeeru
bbeelss
  ebbless
bbefilr
  fribble
bbefiry
  fibbery
bbefruy
  fubbery
bbegilr
  gribble
bbeginw
  webbing
bbegios
  gibbose
bbeglor
  gobbler
bbeglru
  grubble
bbegrru
  grubber
bbehins
  nebbish
bbehlor
  hobbler
bbehmtu
  bethumb
bbeiiilr
  ribible
bbeiimr
  imbiber
bbeilnr
  nibbler
bbeilos
  bilboes
bbeilot
  bibelot

bbeilpr
  pribble
bbeilqu
  quibble
bbeilrt
  tribble
bbeilst
  stibble
bbeilsy
  yibbles
bbeinor
  rib-bone
bbeirry
  bribery
bbejory
  jobbery
bbeklno
  knobble
bbeklnu
  knubble
bbeklos
  blesbok
bbekluu
  bubukle
bbeknor
  knobber
bbelloy
  bell-boy
bbelnor
  nobbler
bbelors
  slobber
bbelorw
  wobbler
bbelrsu
  slubber
bbelstu
  stubble
bbenotw
  bowbent
bbenrsu
  snubber
bbeorry
  robbery
bbeorsw
  swobber
bberruy
  rubbery
bbfgiin
  fibbing
bbgiijn
  jibbing
bbgiinr
  ribbing
bbgijno
  jobbing
bbgimno
  mobbing
bbginor
  robbing
bbginos
  sobbing
bbginru
  rubbing

bbginsu
  gubbins
  subbing
bbgintu
  tubbing
bbgiosu
  gibbous
bbhhios
  hobbish
bbhimos
  Hobbism
  mobbish
bbhiost
  Hobbist
bbhirsu
  rubbish
bbhistu
  tubbish
bbhoouw
  whoobub
bbhrsuy
  shrubby
bbiiilm
  bilimbi
bbiilst
  biblist
bbijmoo
  jib-boom
bbikoss
  ski-bobs
bbiktuz
  kibbutz
bbilnoy
  nobbily
bbinory
  ribbony
bbklnoy
  knobbly
bbklnuy
  knubbly
bbkloou
  bloubok
bbkoooo
  boobook
bblosuu
  bulbous
bblstuy
  stubbly
bbnooru
  bourbon
bcceeiu
  ice-cube
bcceilo
  ecbolic
bcceilu
  cubicle
bcceily
  bicycle
bccilou
  bucolic
bccinoo
  obconic
bccisuu
  succubi

bccmoox
  coxcomb
bccmsuu
  succumb
bccnoor
  corn-cob
bcdeeil
  decibel
bcdehnu
  bunched
bcdehou
  debouch
bcdeiio
  biocide
bcdeiir
  ice-bird
bcdeiks
  sick-bed
bcdeikt
  bedtick
bcdeilm
  climbed
bcdeiox
  dice-box
bcdeklo
  blocked
bcdekor
  bedrock
  brocked
bcdelou
  becloud
bcdesuu
  subduce
bcdhoou
  cubhood
bcdiorw
  cowbird
bcdkoru
  burdock
bcdstuu
  subduct
bceeehn
  beechen
bceeehs
  beseech
bceefin
  benefic
bceegir
  iceberg
bceehip
  ephebic
bceehlr
  belcher
bceehnr
  bencher
bceeilt
  ice-belt
bceeilu
  ice-blue
bceeips
  bespice
bceeirs
  escribe

bceeknu
  buckeen
bceekuy
  buck-eye
bceenos
  obscene
bceenru
  crubeen
bcefiis
  sebific
bcehinr
  birchen
bcehint
  benthic
bcehior
  brioche
bcehitw
  bewitch
bcehlru
  blucher
bcehort
  botcher
bcehrsu
  cherubs
bcehrtu
  butcher
bceiisv
  vibices
bceiklr
  brickle
bceiknr
  bricken
bceikst
  bestick
bceilmo
  embolic
bceilmr
  climber
  reclimb
bceilno
  binocle
bceilor
  bricole
  corbeil
bceimno
  combine
bceimor
  microbe
bceinoz
  benzoic
bceinru
  brucine
bceiopp
  cob-pipe
bceirrs
  scriber
bceirsu
  suberic
bceirtu
  brucite
bcejstu
  subject
bceklor
  blocker

bceklru
bruckle
buckler
bcekort
brocket
bcekoru
roebuck
bcekoty
bycoket
bcekpru
Purbeck
bcekstu
bestuck
bcellow
cowbell
bcelmru
clumber
crumble
bcelmsu
scumble
bceloru
coluber
bcelssu
cubless
bcemntu
cumbent
bcemors
Scomber
bcemrsu
scumber
bcenoru
bouncer
bceoort
October
bceorsu
obscure
bceortt
Corbett
bcfssuu
subfusc
bcgiknu
bucking
bchiiot
cohibit
bchikou
chibouk
bchiksu
buckish
bchimor
rhombic
bchinor
bronchi
bchiopr
pibroch
bchloty
blotchy
bchnoor
broncho
bchorst
borscht
bortsch
bciikln
niblick

bciilor
colibri
bciinos
bionics
bciinot
biontic
bciistu
biscuit
bcikort
brockit
bcikott
bittock
bcilmpu
plumbic
upclimb
bcilnou
lion-cub
bcinnor
corn-bin
bcinoox
coin-box
bcinoru
rubicon
bcinory
Byronic
bcinsuu
incubus
bcioort
robotic
bciorst
strobic
bciosty
sybotic
bcirtuy
butyric
bcistuu
cubitus
bcjkmuu
jumbuck
bckllou
bullock
bcklnou
unblock
bckmmou
bummock
bckottu
buttock
bckotux
tuck-box
bclmoou
coulomb
bclmruy
crumbly
bcloosu
colobus
bclortu
clotbur
bcmootu
comb-out
bcmostu
combust
bcootty
boycott

bdddeir
bedridd
bddeeer
reed-bed
bddeees
seedbed
bddeeis
bedside
bddeeit
betided
bddeeln
blended
bddegin
bedding
bddeiln
blinded
bddeilr
bridled
bddeinr
brinded
bddeirt
dirt-bed
bddeloo
blooded
bddenou
bounded
bddenow
down-bed
bddeotu
doubted
bddesuu
subdued
bddgiin
bidding
bddginu
budding
bddgior
bird-dog
bddinru
dun-bird
bdeeell
deleble
bdeeelr
bleeder
bdeeeps
bespeed
bdeeerr
breeder
bdeefir
debrief
bdeegor
begored
bdeeguy
bug-eyed
bdeeikn
beinked
bdeeill
bellied
delible
bdeeilv
bedevil
bdeeimr
bemired

bdeeimt
bedtime
bdeeinr
inbreed
bdeeinz
bedizen
bdeeirr
berried
briered
bdeeirt
bedrite
bdeeiss
besides
bdeeivv
bevvied
bdeelnr
blender
bdeelnt
bendlet
bdeelov
beloved
bdeelss
blessed
bdeeltt
bletted
bdeemow
embowed
bdeemru
umbered
bdeenpr
prebend
bdeentt
tent-bed
bdeeors
bedsore
bdeeosx
seedbox
bdeeotw
web-toed
bdeerru
bur-reed
bdeertt
Debrett
bdeeruw
burweed
bdeestt
test-bed
bdeflou
bodeful
bdefoor
forbode
bdeggir
egg-bird
bdeghit
bedight
bdeginn
bending
bdegiot
bigoted
bdeglot
dog-belt
bdeglru
bludger

bdegooy
good-bye
bdegoru
budgero
bdehmtu
thumbed
bdehory
herdboy
bdehrsu
brushed
bdeikln
blinked
bdeikmo
kimboed
bdeillr
ill-bred
bdeillu
bullied
bdeilnr
blinder
brindle
bdeilop
lobiped
bdeilrr
bridler
bdeilrt
driblet
bdeilru
builder
rebuild
bdeimmr
brimmed
bdeimor
bromide
bdeimtu
bitumed
bdeinou
bedouin
bdeinry
bindery
bdeiopr
poe-bird
bdeiorr
broider
bdeiors
disrobe
bdeiorv
overbid
bdeiorz
zebroid
bdeiosx
side-box
bdeiosy
disobey
bdeiowy
wide-boy
bdeirst
bestrid
bistred
bdeissu
subside
bdeistu
subedit

bdeituy
dubiety
bdeknoo
book-end
bdekoor
red-book
bdekorw
bedwork
bdekrsy
sky-bred
bdellor
bed-roll
bdelmru
drumble
bdelnru
blunder
bdeloru
boulder
doubler
bdelorw
bowlder
low-bred
bdelosw
blowsed
bdelott
blotted
bottled
bdelotu
doublet
bdelouu
double-u
bdelouw
would-be
bdelowz
blowzed
bdelrru
blurred
bdelssu
budless
bdelswy
lewdsby
bdemnou
embound
bdemoor
bedroom
boredom
bdemoos
bosomed
bdennou
bounden
bdenoru
bounder
rebound
bdenory
bone-dry
bdenorz
bronzed
bdenouw
unbowed
bdenstu
subtend
bdensuy
sebundy

bdenttu
butt-end
bdeoorr
brooder
bdeoprt
bedropt
bdeopst
bedpost
bdeorru
bordure
bourder
bdeorsu
rose-bud
bdeortu
doubter
obtrude
outbred
redoubt
bderruy
ruby-red
bderstu
bursted
bdersuu
subduer
bdersuy
rudesby
bdfgiir
fig-bird
bdfiior
fibroid
bdfiisu
fidibus
bdgglou
gold-bug
bdgiinn
binding
bdgiinr
birding
bdgiloo
globoid
bdginno
bonding
bdginoy
bodying
bdgllou
bulldog
bdgloot
dogbolt
bdgoruw
bug-word
bdhinop
hopbind
bdhiosu
bushido
bdhmooo
hobodom
bdhoooy
boyhood
bdiikno
bodikin
bdiilms
dislimb
bdiilor
oil-bird

bdijoor
jib-door
bdiknor
brodkin
bdillny
blindly
bdilnnu
unblind
bdilnuu
unbuild
bdilpuu
build-up
upbuild
bdilruy
buirdly
bdiltuy
dibutyl
bdinoor
bridoon
bdinrsu
sun-bird
bdinstu
dust-bin
bdiooov
obovoid
bdiooru
boudoir
bdiopry
poy-bird
bdiorsw
wosbird
bdiossy
byssoid
bdiosuu
dubious
bdirstu
disturb
bdissuy
subsidy
bdknoou
bundook
bdlooox
oxblood
bdlorwy
blow-dry
bdnnouu
unbound
bdnooru
bourdon
bdnooww
downbow
bdnopuu
upbound
bdnortu
turbond
bdnoruw
rubdown
bdooowx
boxwood
beeeemt
beteeme
beeefir
freebie

beeegis
besiege
beeeglu
bee-glue
beeehiv
beehive
hive-bee
beeehns
shebeen
beeeikt
bee-kite
beeeilv
believe
beeejlw
bejewel
beeejlz
Jezebel
beeekps
bee-skep
beeelpr
bleeper
beeeluy
blue-eye
beeemos
beesome
beeennz
benzene
beeentw
between
beefilr
febrile
Félibre
beefint
benefit
beefirs
Frisbee
beeflty
beet-fly
beeggnu
geebung
beegill
legible
beegilo
obligee
beegilu
beguile
beegimr
begrime
beeginn
beginne
beeginr
bigener
beeginu
beguine
beeglno
englobe
beegmno
gombeen
beegmou
embogue
beegntu
unbeget
beehins
beshine

beehist
bhistee
beehksu
bukshee
beehlrt
blether
herblet
beehmot
bee-moth
beehnno
hebenon
beehnos
beshone
beehoov
behoove
beehors
herbose
beehorw
bewhore
beehpsu
ephebus
beehrst
sherbet
beehrsw
beshrew
beehrty
thereby
beehrwy
whereby
beehsty
bheesty
beeijlu
jubilee
beeilnr
berline
beeilos
obelise
beeiltt
betitle
beeimst
betimes
beeinnz
benzine
beeinos
ebonise
beeinot
ebonite
beeinpr
pébrine
beeinrz
zebrine
beeintz
bez-tine
beeiors
ebriose
beeiquz
bezique
beeirrs
berries
beeirrv
brevier
beeirty
ebriety

beeknot
betoken
beekops
bespoke
beekrrs
berserk
beekrru
rebuker
beellot
lobelet
beelmow
embowel
beelmrt
tremble
beelnno
ennoble
beelnoz
benzole
beelnux
Benelux
beeloty
eyebolt
beelruz
zebrule
beelttu
bluette
beemnpt
benempt
beemorw
embower
beemrru
umbrere
beemrsu
Burmese
beemrtu
embrute
beenost
boneset
beeoprs
beprose
beeorru
bourrée
beeorsv
observe
obverse
verbose
beeortx
box-tree
beeorwy
eyebrow
beeqstu
bequest
beerrwy
brewery
beerssu
rebuses
beerstw
bestrew
webster
beerttu
burette
befflru
bluffer

befgiil
filibeg
befgiru
firebug
befgllo
fog-bell
befilpy
plebify
befilrt
filbert
befilry
briefly
befilsu
fusible
befinor
bonfire
befiors
fibrose
befiorx
firebox
befirst
fibster
befllot
elf-bolt
befllty
flybelt
beflmru
fumbler
befltuu
tubeful
befmnru
f-number
befoorr
forbore
befootw
web-foot
begggin
begging
beggist
biggest
begglor
boggler
beggruy
buggery
beghhit
behight
beghint
benight
beghrru
burgher
begiimt
big-time
begiinn
inbeing
begilly
legibly
begilno
Gobelin
ignoble
inglobe
begilnt
belting
begilnu
blueing

begilny
belying
begilrt
gilbert
begilst
giblets
beginnu
unbeing
beginoy
biogeny
beginrr
bringer
beginrw
brewing
beginss
bigness
begintt
betting
begkmos
gemsbok
begllou
globule
beglmoo
begloom
beglmru
grumble
beglnru
blunger
bungler
begloos
globose
begloot
bootleg
beglosu
glebous
beglrty
bergylt
begnnuu
unbegun
begnoru
burgeon
begnosy
bygones
begnotu
unbegot
begorsu
rose-bug
begrssu
burgess
behhkot
khotbeh
behiitx
exhibit
behiknt
bethink
behilms
blemish
behilmt
thimble
behilos
bolshie
behilpt
hip-belt
behilrt
blither
behilsu
helibus
behinop
hip-bone
hopbine
behiotw
howbeit
behirrt
rebirth
behirst
herbist
behllop
bellhop
behllox
hell-box
behlmow
whomble
behlmsu
humbles
behloot
bothole
behlort
brothel
behlrru
burrhel
behlrsu
blusher
behlstu
blushet
behmotu
bemouth
behmptu
bethump
behnost
benthos
behnrtu
burthen
behoort
theorbo
behoprt
pot-herb
behopsu
Phoebus
behorrt
brother
behorst
boshter
behorsu
herbous
behortt
betroth
behrrsu
brusher
behtuwy
whey-tub
beiiklr
riblike
beiills
billies
beiilrs
risible
beiilsv
visible
beiinot
niobite
beiinst
stibine
beiiott
biotite
beiklnr
blinker
beiklos
obelisk
beiknrs
brisken
beikoos
booksie
beikotx
box-kite
beikrst
brisket
beillot
oil-belt
beillst
bestill
beilmor
embroil
beilmrt
timbrel
beilmrw
wimbrel
beilmsu
sublime
beilnoo
bone-oil
obelion
beilnow
bowline
beilntz
blintze
beiloqu
oblique
beilorr
broiler
beilort
trilobe
beilory
boilery
beilovx
live-box
beilrss
ribless
beilrst
blister
bristle
beilrtt
brittle
triblet
beilrty
liberty
beilruy
brulyie
beilruz
brulzie
beilstu
subtile
beilstw
blewits
beimmrr
brimmer
beimmru
Brummie
beimnor
bromine
beimntu
bitumen
beimorw
imbower
beimrsu
imburse
beimrtu
imbrute
terbium
beinnos
benison
beinnoz
benzoin
beinort
bornite
beinorw
brownie
beinost
ebonist
beinott
bottine
beinrsu
suberin
beinrtt
bittern
beinrtu
tribune
turbine
beinssy
byssine
beiorrt
orbiter
beiossu
soubise
beiosty
obesity
beipssu
pubises
beiqrtu
briquet
beirrsu
brisure
bruiser
beirstt
bitters
beirttu
tribute
beirtty
treybit
beirtvy
brevity
beittwx
betwixt
bejkoux
juke-box
bejlmru
jumbler
bejloss
jobless
beklnru
blunker
bekloot
booklet
beklsuy
sky-blue
bekmost
stembok
beknnow
beknown
beknors
bonkers
beknoru
unbroke
bekorry
brokery
belllow
low-bell
bellnpu
bull-pen
bellorr
borrell
bellosu
soluble
bellosw
bellows
bellouv
voluble
bellrru
burrell
belmmoo
embloom
belmmru
mumbler
belmnou
nelumbo
belmnsu
numbles
belmoor
bloomer
rebloom
belmopr
problem
belmosu
embolus
belmpru
plumber
belmrru
rumbler
belmrsu
slumber
belmrtu
tumbler
tumbrel
belmstu
stumble
belnnou
unnoble
belnntu
unblent
belnooy
boloney
belnoyz
benzoyl
belnssu
unbless
belnstu
unblest
belooss
soboles
belorst
bolster
lobster
belorsy
soberly
belortt
blotter
bottler
belortu
blue-rot
boulter
trouble
belostu
Boletus
belrstu
bluster
bustler
belrtuy
butlery
bemmoos
embosom
bemmorr
brommer
bemmrru
brummer
bemnorw
embrown
bemnory
embryon
bemnosu
umbones
bemnttu
butment
bemorst
bestorm
mobster
bemorsu
umbrose
bemorsy
embryos
bemorww
webworm
bemotuy
myotube
bemssuu
subsume
bennorw
newborn
bennorz
bronzen
benorst
sorbent

benorwy
bywoner
benosuz
subzone
benoswy
newsboy
benrstu
bursten
beoopuz
booze-up
beoorst
booster
beoprrv
proverb
beoprst
besport
beopstu
bespout
beoqsuy
obsequy
beoqtuu
bouquet
beorsuu
uberous
beorsuz
subzero
beoruvy
overbuy
beprrtu
perturb
beprtuy
puberty
bepstuy
subtype
beqrsuu
brusque
berrstu
burster
berstuv
subvert
berttuy
buttery
besttux
subtext
bfflluy
bluffly
bffnoou
buffoon
bffopux
puff-box
bfgiort
frogbit
bfhilsu
lubfish
bfhirsu
furbish
bfhistu
tubfish
bfiinor
fibroin
bfilmru
brimful
bfiorsu
fibrous
bfirtuy
brutify
bfkloou
bookful
bfklooy
flybook
bfkssuu
subfusk
bfllowy
blowfly
flyblow
bflosux
boxfuls
bfoooty
footboy
bggginu
bugging
bgghiis
biggish
bggilnu
bulging
bgginoy
bygoing
bghhioy
highboy
bghilty
blighty
bghinor
bighorn
bghinty
by-thing
bghmoru
Homburg
bghnoru
hornbug
bghooru
borough
bghortu
brought
bgiilln
billing
bgiilno
boiling
bgiilnr
birling
bgiilns
sibling
bgiimnr
briming
bgiinnr
inbring
bgiinrt
ringbit
bgiknoo
booking
bgiknsu
busking
bgillpu
pill-bug
bgilmou
gumboil
bgilnot
biltong
bolting
bgilnow
bowling
bgilnoy
ignobly
bgiloor
obligor
bgilooy
biology
bgilrsu
busgirl
bgimnnu
numbing
bgimnoo
booming
bgimosy
bogyism
bginnru
burning
bginntu
bunting
bginoor
bog-iron
bginooz
boozing
bginosu
bousing
bginpru
upbring
bginruy
burying
rubying
bginssu
bussing
bginsuy
busying
bginswy
swing-by
bginuzz
buzzing
bgiorty
bigotry
bgiuwzz
buzz-wig
bgjotuy
toby-jug
bgklooo
log-book
bgkorsy
grysbok
bglmruy
grumbly
bglnoow
longbow
bglnouw
blowgun
bgloosu
globous
bglossu
bugloss
bgmooss
bog-moss
bgmootu
gumboot
bgnoowy
gownboy
bgortuw
bugwort
bhiiint
inhibit
bhiinrs
brinish
bhiipss
sibship
bhiirst
British
bhiknop
hip-knob
bhikoos
bookish
bhilloy
billy-oh
bhillsu
bullish
bhilotu
holibut
bhilpsu
publish
bhimoor
rhomboi
bhimoos
hoboism
bhimops
phobism
bhimort
thrombi
bhimstu
bismuth
bhinrsu
burnish
bhioopr
biophor
bhioors
boorish
bhiopst
phobist
bhiopsy
ship-boy
bhiorss
Sorbish
bhioswz
showbiz
bhirstu
brutish
bhirttu
turbith
bhisttu
bush-tit
bhisuvy
ivy-bush
bhlrsuu
bulrush
bhmoors
rhombos
bhmorsu
rhombus
bhmuuzz
humbuzz
bhnorty
Brython
bhoopsy
shop-boy
bhoostw
bowshot
bhooswx
show-box
bhprsuu
brush-up
biiklot
kilobit
biillno
billion
biillou
bouilli
biilltw
twibill
biilmru
Librium®
biilnnr
birlinn
biilnqu
quiblin
biilntu
built-in
in-built
biilosu
bilious
biilsvy
visibly
biimnou
niobium
biimnsu
minibus
mini-sub
biimstu
stibium
biiosuv
bivious
bijnosu
subjoin
biklluy
bulkily
biklnoy
linkboy
biklrsy
briskly
bikmnpu
bumpkin
bikorrw
ribwork
billnou
bullion
billooy
loobily
billopx
pill-box
billowy
billowy
billrwy
wrybill
bilmnor
nombril
bilmosu
limbous
bilmrtu
tumbril
bilmsuu
bulimus
bilnnoy
bonnily
bilntuu
unbuilt
bilooyz
boozily
bilorst
Bristol
bilossu
subsoil
bilptuu
built-up
bilrsty
bristly
bilrtuy
tilbury
bimmoos
imbosom
bimnors
misborn
bimnorw
imbrown
bimnosu
omnibus
bimnosy
symbion
bimrsux
bruxism
bimsssu
submiss
binoorx
box-iron
binorst
ribston
binrstu
inburst
binstuu
subunit
bioosuv
obvious
bioprtw
pit-brow
bioprty
probity
biopstx
spit-box
biorrtw
ribwort
biorstt
bistort
biorsuu
rubious
bissstu
subsist
bjoruxy
jury-box
bknorsy
skyborn

bkooory
kroo-boy
bkoorwx
work-box
bllntuy
bluntly
bllosuu
lobulus
bllouvy
volubly
bllppuu
bull-pup
blmmpuu
plumbum
blmnpuu
unplumb
blmooot
tombolo
blmoorw
lobworm
blmooss
blossom
blmrsuy
slumbry
blmstuy
stumbly
blnnouw
unblown
blnoorw
low-born
blnoosu
blouson
blnopuw
upblown
bloootx
toolbox
blooquy
obloquy
bloorww
low-brow
blootuw
blow-out
blopstu
subplot
bmnooow
moon-bow
bmnoosu
unbosom
bmnoruw
mowburn
bmooorx
boxroom
bmorsuu
brumous
umbrous
bnnouuy
nun-buoy
bnnrsuu
sunburn
bnnrtuu
unburnt
bnooswx
snow-box

bnootty
bottony
bnorsuu
burnous
bnortuu
burn-out
outburn
bnosttu
buttons
bnottuy
buttony
boooprx
poor-box
boooptt
top-boot
boopstx
post-box
bopsstu
bus-stop
post-bus
borstxy
bostryx
bprstuu
burst-up
upburst
cccdioo
coccoid
cccehio
choc-ice
cccehiz
Czechic
cccnoot
concoct
ccdeeio
ecocide
ccdeeno
concede
ccdeeny
decency
ccdeesu
succeed
ccdehil
clichéd
ccdeiit
deictic
ccdeilo
ice-cold
ccdeilr
circled
ccdeios
codices
ccdeiot
Docetic
ccdeklo
cockled
ccdelou
occlude
ccdenou
conduce
ccdhiil
cichlid
ccdiilo
codicil

ccdiilu
culicid
ccdiior
cricoid
ccdiloy
cycloid
ccdklou
cuckold
ccdkoor
rock-cod
ccdnoor
concord
ccdnotu
conduct
ccdostu
stucco'd
cceegno
cogence
cceehkr
checker
recheck
cceehor
écorché
cceehou
couchee
cceehrs
screech
cceeiln
licence
cceeinr
eccrine
cceeins
science
cceeirv
crevice
cceekoy
cockeye
cceelry
recycle
cceenry
recency
cceersy
secrecy
ccefnot
confect
ccegnoy
cogency
ccehikn
chicken
ccehiku
chuckie
ccehino
conchie
ccehint
technic
ccehirs
screich
scriech
ccehklu
chuckle
ccehknu
uncheck
ccehkor
chocker

ccehkpu
check-up
ccehlru
cleruch
ccehort
crochet
cceiikp
ice-pick
cceiims
cimices
cceiirt
icteric
cceiklr
clicker
cceiklt
clicket
cceikrt
cricket
cceikry
crickey
cceilmo
celomic
cceilot
coctile
cceilpt
P-Celtic
cceilqt
Q-Celtic
cceilrr
circler
cceilrt
circlet
cceilsu
culices
cceilsy
cylices
cceiltu
cuticle
cceimno
meconic
cceimot
cometic
cceimst
smectic
cceinor
cornice
cceinos
concise
cceinot
conceit
cceinrt
centric
cceiopp
coppice
cceiopt
ectopic
cceiort
orectic
cceiost
Scotice
cceipst
sceptic
ccejnot
conject

cceklor
clocker
cceknot
conteck
cceknoy
cockney
ccekopt
petcock
ccekort
crocket
ccellot
collect
ccelnoy
cyclone
ccelnuy
lucency
ccemnoo
Comecon
ccennor
concern
ccennot
concent
connect
ccenopt
concept
ccenort
concert
cceoott
cocotte
cceoprt
percoct
cceorrt
correct
cceossu
succose
ccesssu
success
ccfiruy
crucify
ccflosu
floccus
ccghino
gnocchi
ccgkoor
gorcock
cchhiit
ichthic
cchhils
schlich
cchhruy
churchy
cchiist
stichic
cchikst
schtick
cchilny
Lychnic
cchilor
chloric
cchimor
chromic
cchinor
chronic

cchiory
chicory
cchiotw
cowitch
cchipsy
psychic
cchipuy
hiccupy
cchirst
scritch
cchklos
schlock
cchkmos
schmock
cchkmsu
schmuck
cchkosy
cockshy
shy-cock
cchnrsu
scrunch
cchnruy
crunchy
cchostu
Succoth
cchosty
Scotchy
cciiils
silicic
cciirtu
circuit
cciisty
siccity
cciklow
cowlick
ccikloy
cockily
colicky
ccikopt
cockpit
ccilnoo
colonic
ccilnou
council
cciloop
piccolo
ccilsty
cyclist
ccimoty
mycotic
ccinoot
coction
ccinotv
convict
ccioors
sirocco
ccioptu
occiput
cciprty
cryptic
ccirsuy
circusy
cckostu
custock

ccloooz
zoccolo
cclopsy
cyclops
ccmooor
morocco
ccnoopu
puccoon
ccnootu
coconut
ccnopuy
concupy
ccnossu
concuss
ccorsuu
succour
ccorsuy
succory
ccosstu
stuccos
ccossuu
succous
ccsssuu
succuss
cdddeei
decided
cdddelo
clodded
cdddesu
scudded
cddeeer
decreed
cddeeii
deicide
cddeeir
decider
decried
cddeekl
deckled
cddeens
descend
cddeeor
decoder
cddeeru
reduced
cddeeuw
cudweed
cddehil
childed
cddehin
chidden
cddeiis
discide
cddelou
clouded
cddelru
cruddle
cddelsu
scuddle
cddeorw
crowded
cddersu
scudder
cddgino
codding
cddhior
dichord
cddiiio
didicoi
cddiios
discoid
cddiioy
didicoy
cddiiru
druidic
cddikop
piddock
cddiors
discord
cddkopu
puddock
cddkoru
ruddock
cddkory
dry-dock
cdeeefl
fleeced
cdeeefn
defence
cdeeehs
cheesed
cdeeeip
epicede
cdeeeiv
deceive
cdeeekl
cleeked
cdeeepr
precede
cdeeers
seceder
cdeeert
decreet
erected
cdeefii
edifice
cdeefkl
flecked
cdeeflt
deflect
cdeefor
deforce
cdeegir
grieced
cdeehip
cepheid
cdeehis
dehisce
cdeehpr
perched
cdeehst
chested
cdeeiit
eidetic
cdeeiln
decline
cdeeilp
pedicel
pedicle
cdeeimn
endemic
cdeeino
codeine
cdeeinr
cedrine
cdeeios
diocese
cdeeiov
devoice
cdeeipr
pierced
cdeeipt
pedetic
cdeeirr
decrier
cdeeitx
excited
cdeeknr
redneck
cdeeknv
V-necked
cdeelpu
decuple
cdeelpy
ycleped
cdeelru
ulcered
cdeelsu
seclude
cdeelux
exclude
cdeenos
seconde
cdeenrt
centred
credent
cdeenst
descent
scented
cdeeopr
proceed
cdeeorv
covered
cdeeost
cestode
tedesco
cdeeotv
coveted
cdeeoww
cow-weed
cdeerru
reducer
cdeerst
crested
cdeersu
rescued
seducer
cdeersw
screwed
cdeffhu
chuffed
cdeffil
cliffed
cdefhin
finched
cdefiit
deficit
cdefilt
clifted
cdefino
confide
cdefkor
defrock
frocked
cdefnor
corn-fed
cdefntu
defunct
cdefoor
od-force
cdefosu
focused
cdefrtu
fructed
cdefsuu
fucused
cdegglo
clogged
cdegikn
decking
cdegior
ergodic
cdehiil
ceilidh
cdehill
chilled
cdehilo
cheloid
helcoid
cdehilp
Delphic
cdehino
hedonic
cdehinp
pinched
cdehiow
cowhide
cdehipp
chipped
cdehipt
pitched
cdehirt
ditcher
cdehkos
shocked
cdehkuy
heyduck
cdehlot
clothed
cdehnor
chondre
cdehnot
notched
cdehnru
chunder
cdehopu
pouched
cdehorw
chowder
cowherd
cdehosu
hocused
cdehosw
cowshed
cdehotu
touched
cdehrsu
crushed
cdehssu
duchess
cdehsty
scythed
cdeiimr
dimeric
cdeiins
incised
indices
cdeiint
identic
cdeiior
ericoid
cdeiiov
ovicide
cdeiist
deistic
cdeiisu
suicide
cdeijst
disject
cdeiklp
pickled
cdeikls
sickled
cdeikns
dickens
cdeiknz
zincked
cdeikos
dockise
cdeikrr
derrick
cdeikst
sticked
cdeillo
codille
collide
collied
cdeillu
cullied
cdeilmo
melodic
cdeilnu
include
nuclide
cdeiloo
oceloid
cdeilpp
clipped
cdeilpu
clupeid
cdeiltu
ductile
dulcite
cdeimno
demonic
cdeimor
dormice
cdeimot
demotic
cdeinot
ctenoid
deontic
D-notice
cdeinou
doucine
cdeinoz
zincode
cdeinrs
discern
rescind
cdeinru
inducer
cdeinry
cindery
cdeinsu
incudes
cdeinsx
exscind
cdeiopr
percoid
cdeiort
cordite
cdeiorv
divorce
cdeiorw
crowdie
cdeiost
. cestoid
cdeiprs
discerp
cdeiprt
predict
cdeipst
discept
cdeirru
curried
cdeirtv
verdict
cdeisst
dissect
cdeissy
ecdysis
cdeitux
excudit
cdeklow
wedlock
cdekloy
key-cold
cdeklpu
plucked

cdeknru
drucken
cdeknsu
sun-deck
cdekoor
crooked
cdekotw
wet-dock
cdellou
collude
cdellry
dry-cell
cdelmsu
muscled
cdelmtu
mulcted
cdelnoo
condole
cdelnou
encloud
cdelnoy
condyle
cdeloor
croodle
decolor
cdelors
scolder
cdelorw
red-cowl
cdelosu
dulcose
cdelott
clotted
cdelotu
clouted
cdelouy
doucely
cdelpuu
clued-up
cdelrsu
scudler
cdelruy
crudely
cdemmno
commend
cdemmoo
commode
cdemmsu
scummed
cdemnno
condemn
cdemnop
compend
cdemnou
mud-cone
cdemoru
decorum
cdennoo
condone
cdennot
contend
cdenoos
secondo

cdenopu
pounced
cdenors
corsned
cdenort
net-cord
cdenorw
crowned
decrown
cdenotu
counted
cdenpuy
pudency
cdenruu
uncured
cdenruy
duncery
cdeoopp
copepod
cdeoops
scooped
cdeoorr
corrode
cdeootv
dovecot
cdeoppr
cropped
cdeopru
produce
cdeoqtu
docquet
cdeorrw
crowder
cdeorss
crossed
cdeorsw
scowder
cdeortu
eductor
cdeoruu
douceur
cdeostu
custode
cdeprty
decrypt
cderruy
dry-cure
cdfhios
codfish
cdfiilu
fluidic
cdfiluy
dulcify
cdfioot
octofid
cdghiin
chiding
cdgiino
gonidic
cdgikno
docking
cdgiknu
ducking

cdgikos
dogsick
cdgikot
dog-tick
cdgilno
codling
cdginno
condign
cdginor
cording
cdgnouw
cow-dung
cdhiint
chindit
cdhiist
distich
cdhilly
childly
cdhilnu
unchild
cdhilos
coldish
cdhinor
chondri
cdhioor
choroid
ochroid
cdhiory
droichy
cdhipty
diptych
cdhkoor
hordock
cdiiiot
idiotic
cdiijru
juridic
cdiilly
idyllic
cdiilmo
domicil
cdiinor
crinoid
cdiinot
diction
cdiinov
Vidicon®
cdiinoz
zincoid
cdiioss
cissoid
cdiioty
idiotcy
cdiknor
dornick
cdiknow
windock
cdilloo
colloid
cdilluy
lucidly
cdilotu
dulotic

cdimmou
modicum
cdimnoo
monodic
cdimosu
muscoid
cdinoot
odontic
cdinosy
synodic
cdinotu
conduit
noctuid
cdioott
cottoid
cdioprr
rip-cord
cdiosty
cystoid
cdiotuv
oviduct
cdirsuy
dysuric
cdirtuy
crudity
cdisssu
discuss
cdistuy
Dyticus
cdkmosu
musk-cod
cdknnou
dunnock
cdlnouu
uncloud
cdloopy
lycopod
cdmosuw
mudscow
cdnnotu
contund
cdnoory
Corydon
cdooopt
octopod
cdoorry
corrody
cdootuw
woodcut
cdoprtu
product
cdostuy
custody
ceeeehl
leechee
ceeefir
ice-free
ceeeflr
fleecer
ceeegnr
regence
ceeehnr
encheer

ceeehpr
cheeper
ceeehrr
cheerer
ceeeinp
epicene
ceeeipr
creepie
ceeeirv
receive
ceeeknw
ewe-neck
ceeellu
écuelle
ceeelpy
ycleepe
ceeelrt
re-elect
ceeelst
celeste
ceeempr
emperce
ceeenrs
recense
ceeenss
essence
ceeeprr
creeper
ceeerrt
erecter
re-erect
ceeerst
secrete
ceeersv
screeve
ceeertx
excrete
ceeetux
execute
ceeffno
offence
ceeffor
efforce
ceefhir
chiefer
ceefhit
fetiche
fitchée
ceefilo
ice-floe
ceefinr
ice-fern
ceefinv
venefic
ceefklr
flecker
freckle
ceeflrt
reflect
ceefnor
enforce
ceefnox
ox-fence

ceefprt
perfect
prefect
ceeggll
egg-cell
ceeginr
energic
generic
ceegint
genetic
ceeginu
eugenic
ceegirs
Grecise
ceegllo
college
ceeglnt
neglect
ceeglou
eclogue
ceegnor
congree
ceegnru
urgence
ceegnry
regency
ceegort
cortège
ceegqru
grecque
ceehiln
elenchi
ceehils
helices
ceehilv
vehicle
ceehimr
chimere
ceehims
chemise
ceehinr
inherce
ceehins
Chinese
ceehior
cheerio
ceehios
echoise
ceehirt
etheric
heretic
ceehklr
heckler
ceehknp
henpeck
ceehlno
echelon
ceehlnu
leuchen
ceehlow
cowheel
ceehlrw
welcher

ceehlry
  cheerly
  lechery
ceehlss
  chessel
ceehlsy
  sleechy
ceehmrs
  schemer
ceehmrt
  merchet
ceehnrw
  wencher
ceehorr
  coherer
ceehort
  trochee
ceehouv
  vouchee
ceehprr
  percher
ceehpru
  upcheer
ceehpsu
  Cepheus
ceehqru
  chequer
ceehquy
  queechy
ceehrsy
  creeshy
ceeiinr
  eirenic
ceeijor
  rejoice
ceeiklt
  cleekit
ceeiknt
  necktie
ceeikpr
  pickeer
ceeillm
  micelle
ceeilno
  cineole
ceeilnr
  recline
ceeilns
  license
  selenic
  silence
ceeilnu
  leucine
ceeilps
  eclipse
ceeilrt
  reticle
  tiercel
ceeilst
  sectile
ceeilsv
  vesicle
ceeiltu
  leucite
ceeimno
  Miocene
ceeimnt
  centime
ceeinns
  incense
ceeinos
  senecio
ceeinpr
  percine
ceeinpt
  pentice
ceeinrs
  ceresin
  sincere
ceeinrt
  enteric
  enticer
ceeinrv
  cervine
ceeiopt
  picotee
ceeiort
  coterie
ceeiprr
  piercer
ceeiprs
  precise
ceeiprt
  receipt
ceeipru
  epicure
ceeipss
  species
ceeipst
  pectise
ceeiqsu
  quiesce
ceeirrt
  reciter
ceeirsv
  scrieve
  service
ceeirtu
  eucrite
ceeirtx
  exciter
ceeittz
  zetetic
ceejort
  ejector
ceeklnt
  necklet
ceeklps
  speckle
ceekosy
  sockeye
ceekpry
  rye-peck
ceekrrw
  wrecker
ceelllu
  cellule
ceellno
  colleen
ceellpu
  pucelle
ceellsx
  sex-cell
ceelltw
  wet-cell
ceelmnt
  clement
ceelmoo
  coelome
ceelmow
  welcome
ceelnos
  enclose
ceelnrt
  lectern
ceelnru
  lucerne
ceelors
  reclose
ceelort
  elector
  electro
ceelotu
  elocute
ceelotv
  covelet
ceelprt
  plectre
  prelect
ceelrsu
  recluse
ceelrsw
  crewels
ceelrtu
  lecture
ceelrty
  erectly
ceelttu
  lettuce
ceemmor
  commère
ceemnow
  newcome
ceemnru
  cerumen
ceemoor
  o'ercome
ceemopr
  compeer
  compere
ceemopt
  compete
ceemrry
  mercery
  remercy
ceemstu
  tumesce
ceemsty
  mycetes
ceennou
  enounce
ceennov
  convene
ceennrt
  centner
ceenopt
  potence
  potencé
ceenors
  necrose
ceenorz
  cozener
ceenprs
  spencer
ceenrsu
  censure
ceenrsy
  scenery
ceenttu
  cunette
ceeopst
  pectose
ceeopty
  ecotype
ceeorrs
  rescore
ceeorrt
  erector
ceeorru
  recoure
ceeorrv
  recover
ceeorrw
  recower
ceeorsu
  cereous
ceeortw
  cow-tree
ceeottt
  octette
ceepprt
  percept
  precept
ceeppru
  prepuce
ceeprss
  precess
ceeprst
  respect
  sceptre
  specter
  spectre
ceeprtx
  excerpt
ceerrsu
  rescuer
  securer
ceerrsw
  screwer
ceerruv
  recurve
ceersst
  cresset
ceersux
  excurse
ceerttu
  curette
ceettuv
  cuvette
ceffior
  officer
ceffisu
  suffice
cefflsu
  scuffle
ceffmoo
  come-off
  off-come
ceffors
  scoffer
ceffort
  coffret
cefgilu
  Guelfic
cefginn
  fencing
cefhiis
  ice-fish
cefhilr
  filcher
cefhily
  chiefly
cefhiry
  chiefry
cefhitt
  fitchet
cefhitw
  fitchew
cefhltu
  futchel
cefhnry
  Frenchy
cefiils
  Filices
cefiilt
  fictile
cefiior
  orifice
cefiirs
  Friesic
cefiitv
  fictive
cefiklr
  flicker
cefilnt
  inflect
cefilnu
  funicle
cefilru
  lucifer
cefimry
  mercify
cefinno
  confine
cefinor
  conifer
  fir-cone
  inforce
cefioot
  ice-foot
cefipsy
  specify
cefirss
  sferics
cefirty
  certify
  rectify
cefklot
  fetlock
cefklry
  freckly
ceflnou
  flounce
ceflnuy
  fluency
cefmory
  comfrey
cefnoru
  frounce
cefnoss
  confess
cefnost
  confest
cefnosu
  confuse
cefnotu
  confute
cefoprs
  forceps
ceforrt
  crofter
cefossu
  focuses
cefssuu
  fucuses
cegghir
  chigger
ceggior
  georgic
cegglor
  clogger
ceggosy
  egg-cosy
ceghino
  echoing
ceghint
  etching
ceghirs
  screigh
ceghitu
  guichet
ceghoru
  cougher
ceghrtu
  gutcher
cegiiln
  ceiling
cegiknn
  necking
cegiknp
  pecking

cegilnr
 cringle
cegilnu
 lucigen
cegilny
 glycine
cegimnu
 mucigen
cegimrs
 Grecism
ceginos
 cognise
ceginrr
 cringer
cegklor
 cork-leg
 grockle
ceglooy
 ecology
ceglosu
 glucose
ceglosy
 glycose
cegnoru
 congrue
cegnory
 congery
 cryogen
cegnost
 congest
cegnruy
 urgency
cegoors
 scrooge
cegorry
 grocery
cegorsu
 scourge
 scrouge
cehhirs
 cherish
cehhirt
 hitcher
cehiikn
 Chinkie
cehiill
 ice-hill
cehiinr
 hircine
cehiins
 niceish
cehiint
 ichnite
cehijor
 Jericho
cehiknt
 kitchen
 thicken
cehiknw
 chewink
cehikoo
 chookie
cehikps
 peckish

cehikrs
 shicker
 skriech
cehikrw
 whicker
cehikst
 chekist
cehiktt
 thicket
cehilmn
 Mechlin
cehilno
 choline
cehilnt
 linchet
 tinchel
cehilpr
 pilcher
cehilrv
 chervil
cehilsv
 Chislev
cehimms
 chemism
cehimny
 chimney
cehimor
 Homeric
 moriche
cehimos
 echoism
cehimrt
 thermic
cehimst
 chemist
cehinop
 chopine
 phocine
cehinor
 chorine
cehinot
 henotic
cehinox
 choenix
cehinpr
 nephric
 phrenic
 pincher
cehinps
 sphenic
cehinqu
 quinche
cehinrt
 cithern
cehinst
 sthenic
cehinsu
 echinus
cehintw
 witchen
cehiops
 hospice
cehiopt
 potiche

cehiort
 rotchie
 theoric
cehiost
 echoist
 toisech
cehiosw
 ice-show
cehiotu
 couthie
cehiotv
 Cheviot
cehippr
 chipper
cehiprr
 chirper
cehiprs
 spheric
cehiprt
 pitcher
cehirst
 estrich
cehirtt
 chitter
cehistu
 Cushite
cehkkru
 chukker
cehklmo
 hemlock
cehkors
 shocker
cehkptu
 ketchup
cehkrsu
 shucker
cehksty
 sketchy
cehlloy
 yelloch
cehlmsz
 schmelz
cehlmwy
 wych-elm
cehlnnu
 chunnel
cehlnot
 notchel
cehlnru
 luncher
cehlnty
 lynchet
cehloos
 schoole
cehlort
 chortle
cehlost
 clothes
cehlpps
 schlepp
cehlqsu
 squelch
cehlrru
 lurcher

cehmnru
 muncher
cehmoor
 moocher
cehmoru
 moucher
cehmoss
 schmoes
cehnnru
 chunner
cehnoop
 hen-coop
cehnoor
 coehorn
cehnorv
 chevron
cehnpru
 puncher
 unperch
cehnrtu
 chunter
cehnsty
 stenchy
cehntuy
 chutney
cehoors
 chooser
 soroche
cehoort
 cheroot
cehoosy
 choosey
cehoppr
 chopper
cehoprt
 potcher
cehopry
 coryphe
cehorrt
 torcher
cehorsu
 choreus
cehorsy
 coshery
cehorsz
 scherzo
cehortu
 retouch
 toucher
cehortw
 wotcher
cehoruv
 voucher
cehqstu
 quetsch
cehrrsu
 crusher
cehrstt
 stretch
cehrsty
 scyther
ceiikls
 siclike

ceiiknr
 ice-rink
ceiiknt
 kinetic
ceiikqu
 quickie
ceiikst
 ekistic
ceiills
 silicle
ceiilnn
 incline
ceiilpp
 clippie
ceiilpt
 pelitic
 tie-clip
ceiiltv
 levitic
ceiimmt
 mimetic
ceiimnr
 crimine
ceiimns
 menisci
ceiimot
 meiotic
ceiimpr
 empiric
ceiimps
 epicism
ceiimss
 seismic
ceiimst
 Semitic
ceiimtt
 titmice
ceiinno
 coniine
 inconie
ceiinor
 oneiric
ceiinos
 iconise
ceiinov
 invoice
ceiinps
 piscine
ceiinrs
 irenics
 sericin
 sirenic
ceiinrt
 citrine
 crinite
 inciter
 neritic
ceiinss
 iciness
ceiinsu
 cuisine
ceiintz
 citizen
 zincite

ceiiopz
 epizoic
ceiippr
 piperic
ceiiprt
 picrite
ceiipst
 epicist
ceiirst
 eristic
ceiirsu
 cruisie
ceiisvv
 civvies
ceijstu
 justice
ceikknn
 Kennick
ceikknr
 knicker
ceiklnr
 clinker
 crinkle
ceiklns
 slicken
ceiklpr
 pickler
 prickle
ceiklpt
 P-Keltic
ceiklqt
 Q-Keltic
ceiklrs
 slicker
ceiklrt
 tickler
 trickle
ceiklst
 stickle
ceikmrs
 smicker
ceikmst
 smicket
ceiknot
 kenotic
ceiknqu
 quicken
ceiknrs
 snicker
ceikorr
 rockier
ceikprr
 pricker
ceikprt
 pricket
ceikpry
 pickery
ceikpst
 skeptic
ceikrrt
 tricker
ceikrst
 rickets
 sticker

ceikrty
rickety
ceillno
lioncel
ceillor
collier
ceillst
cellist
ceilmop
compile
polemic
ceilmpr
crimple
ceilnnu
nuclein
ceilnop
pinocle
ceilnos
conseil
inclose
ceilnot
lection
ceilnox
lexicon
ceilnps
splenic
ceilnst
stencil
ceilntu
tunicle
ceiloot
Clootie
ceilopr
peloric
ceilopt
toeclip
ceilort
cortile
ceiloss
ossicle
ceilott
cole-tit
ceilppr
clipper
cripple
ceilpsu
spicule
ceilquy
cliquey
ceilrsv
clivers
ceilrsy
clerisy
ceilrtt
clitter
ceilrtu
utricle
ceilsss
scissel
ceilssu
Celsius
ceilttu
cuittle

ceimmrr
crimmer
ceimnno
meconin
ceimnos
mesonic
ceimnot
entomic
metonic
tonemic
ceimnru
numeric
ceimnyz
enzymic
ceimopt
metopic
ceimoqu
comique
ceimorr
morrice
ceimort
mortice
ceimorw
ice-worm
ceimosu
Couéism
ceimott
totemic
ceimotv
vicomte
ceimprr
crimper
ceimprs
spermic
ceimrst
cretism
ceimrsu
murices
ceinnor
Neronic
ceinnov
connive
ceinoot
coontie
ceinooz
Neozoic
ceinopr
porcine
ceinopt
entopic
nepotic
ceinors
crinose
sericon
ceinort
rection
ceinoru
nourice
ceinorv
corvine
ceinory
oriency

ceinoss
cession
Oscines
ceinost
section
ceinosw
snow-ice
ceinott
entotic
tonetic
ceinotx
exciton
ceinouv
unvoice
ceinpry
cyprine
ceinpst
inspect
ceinpty
pycnite
ceinrst
cistern
ceinrsv
crivens
ceinrtt
cittern
ceinruv
incurve
ceinsty
insecty
ceinttx
extinct
ceinvvy
vivency
ceioopr
oporice
ceioprs
persico
ceiopsu
piceous
ceiorrs
cirrose
crosier
ceiorru
courier
ceiorrz
crozier
ceiorsu
scourie
ceiorsv
corsive
ceiorsw
scowrie
ceiortt
cottier
ceiortv
evictor
ceiortx
excitor
xerotic
ceiorvy
viceroy
ceiossv
viscose

ceiostt
cottise
Scottie
ceiostu
Couéist
ceiostv
costive
ceiostx
co-exist
ceiosty
society
ceippst
peptics
ceipqtu
picquet
ceiprrs
crisper
ceiprst
triceps
ceiprsy
spicery
ceiprtu
cuprite
picture
ceiprty
pyretic
ceiprxy
pyrexic
ceipsss
scepsis
ceipsst
cesspit
ceirrru
currier
ceirrsu
cruiser
sucrier
ceirrtt
critter
ceirrtu
recruit
ceirrtx
rectrix
ceirssu
cuisser
ceirstt
trisect
ceirstu
icterus
ceirsuv
cursive
ceirttx
tectrix
ceisstu
ictuses
cejnoru
conjure
cejoprt
project
cekklnu
knuckle
cekknor
knocker

ceklop
pellock
ceklry
clerkly
ceklmor
rock-elm
ceklnos
slocken
ceklnow
Wenlock
ceklnru
crunkle
ceklpru
plucker
ceklrsu
suckler
ceklrtu
truckle
cekmory
mockery
ceknoov
convoke
ceknors
conkers
ceknrwy
wryneck
cekoopr
precook
cekoopw
cowpoke
cekoory
cookery
cekorry
rockery
cekorst
restock
cekpruy
puckery
cekrrtu
trucker
cellmou
columel
cellnoo
colonel
cellors
escroll
cellosu
ocellus
cellosy
closely
cellrru
cruller
cellrsu
cruells
sculler
cellruy
cruelly
celmnoo
monocle
celmopx
complex
celmpru
crumple

celmsuu
seculum
celmsuy
lyceums
celnnou
nucleon
celnoos
console
celnosu
counsel
unclose
celnotu
noctule
celnsuu
nucleus
celopru
coupler
celopsu
close-up
opuscle
upclose
celoptu
couplet
octuple
celorst
corslet
costrel
celorsu
closure
celorsy
scroyle
celortt
clotter
crottle
celortu
cloture
coulter
celorvy
clovery
celosty
cotyles
celottu
culotte
celprsu
scruple
celpsuy
clypeus
celrstu
cluster
custrel
celrsty
clyster
celrttu
clutter
celrtuu
culture
celrtuv
culvert
celrtuy
cruelty
cutlery
celsttu
scuttle

cemmnot
comment
cemmnou
commune
cemmoov
commove
cemmotu
commute
cemmrsu
scummer
cemnnoo
non-come
cemnnot
contemn
cemnoop
componé
cemnooy
economy
cemnosu
consume
cemnrtu
centrum
cemoops
compose
cemoopt
compote
cemoors
Moresco
cemootu
outcome
cemoprt
compter
cemoptu
compute
cemossu
muscose
cemostu
costume
cemprtu
crumpet
cemrruy
mercury
cennoot
connote
cennost
consent
cennott
content
cennotv
convent
cennrsu
scunner
cenoorr
coroner
crooner
cenoort
coronet
cenopsy
syncope
cenoptu
pouncet
cenopty
potency
cenoqru
conquer
cenorrs
scorner
cenorrw
crowner
cenorry
rye-corn
cenorst
conster
cenortt
cornett
cenortu
cornute
counter
recount
trounce
cenortv
convert
cenortw
crownet
cenoruv
uncover
cenossy
coyness
cenostt
contest
cenostu
contuse
cenottx
context
cenptux
expunct
cenrrtu
current
cenrstu
encrust
cenrsuu
uncurse
cenrsuw
unscrew
cenrtuy
century
ceooprs
scooper
ceoopry
coopery
ceoorst
scooter
ceoortw
crow-toe
ceopprr
cropper
ceoppry
coppery
ceoprrs
scorper
ceoprrt
porrect
ceoprru
procure
ceoprss
process
ceoprtt
protect
ceopruu
coupure
ceopruv
cover-up
ceoqrtu
croquet
rocquet
ceorrss
recross
scorser
ceorrsu
courser
scourer
ceorrsy
sorcery
ceorrty
rectory
ceorssu
Croesus
scourse
sucrose
ceorstu
rose-cut
scouter
ceortuu
couture
cepprru
crupper
cepprsu
scupper
ceprssu
percuss
ceprssy
cypress
ceprsty
sceptry
ceprsuy
Cyperus
cepsstu
suspect
ceqrsuu
Quercus
cersttu
scutter
cerstuy
curtsey
cffhino
chiffon
cffikko
kick-off
cffmosu
offscum
cffrsuy
scruffy
cfgiknu
fucking
cfhimyy
chymify
cfhiosw
cowfish
cfhortu
futhorc
cfiiimr
mirific
cfiiivv
vivific
cfiikny
finicky
cfiilnt
inflict
cfiimno
omnific
cfiinot
fiction
cfiinyz
zincify
cfiioss
ossific
cfikkly
fly-kick
cfiknno
finnock
cfikoss
fossick
cfiloru
fluoric
cfimnor
confirm
cfiorsy
scorify
cfiosty
Scotify
cfkllou
lockful
cfkloot
cot-folk
cfknoru
unfrock
cfkottu
futtock
cflmruu
fulcrum
cflnory
cornfly
cflnoux
conflux
cflopru
cropful
cflpsuu
cupfuls
cfmnoor
conform
cfmoort
comfort
cfossuu
fuscous
cggino
cogging
cgginos
Scoggin
cggorsy
scroggy
cghiimn
miching
cghikot
Gothick
cghilpy
glyphic
cghinno
chignon
cghinru
ruching
cghiosy
goyisch
cghoort
torgoch
cghoruy
grouchy
cgiikln
licking
cgiikmm
gimmick
cgiiknp
picking
cgiiknt
ticking
cgiilns
slicing
cgiimnn
mincing
cgiinno
coining
cgiinnw
wincing
cgiinnz
zincing
cgiinov
voicing
cgikmno
mocking
cgiknor
corking
rocking
cgiknpu
kingcup
cgiknsu
sucking
cgillno
colling
cgillnu
culling
cgilnos
closing
cgilnow
cowling
cgilnoy
cloying
cgilnru
curling
cgilntu
cutling
cgilorw
cowgirl
cgiloss
Glossic
cgilott
glottic
cgilptu
giltcup
cgilpty
glyptic
cginnno
conning
cginnnu
cunning
cginnos
consign
cginopy
copying
cginorr
corn-rig
cginors
scoring
cginost
gnostic
cginppu
cupping
cginprs
c-spring
cginrsu
cursing
cginrsy
scrying
cginruv
curving
cgiooos
giocoso
cgiotyz
zygotic
cgklnou
gun-lock
cgoorrw
gorcrow
chhikor
chikhor
chhinor
rhonchi
chhintu
unhitch
chhirst
shritch
chhisty
ichthys
chhrttu
thrutch
chiiist
Shiitic
chiiknn
kinchin
chiikss
sickish
chiimns
Mishnic
chiimsu
ischium
chiinnp
inchpin
chiiopt
ophitic
chiiost
stichoi
chiipst
Pictish

chikllo
hillock
chiklop
hip-lock
chiklty
thickly
chiknoo
chinook
chikntu
thick'un
chikory
hickory
chikpsu
puckish
chiksty
kitschy
chillmu
chillum
chillow
lich-owl
chillty
lichtly
chilnou
ulichon
chilnsy
lychnis
chiloos
coolish
chilost
coltish
chimmor
microhm
chimnpy
nymphic
chimopr
morphic
chimors
chrisom
chimrry
myrrhic
chimsty
tychism
chinoor
chorion
chinops
phonics
chinors
Cornish
chinort
Corinth
chinosu
cushion
chinotw
two-inch
chinqsu
squinch
chintuw
unwitch
chintyz
chintzy
chioopr
pochoir
chioors
isochor

chioprt
trophic
chiopst
photics
chiopxy
hypoxic
chiorst
chorist
ostrich
chiosst
stichos
chiprru
chirrup
chiprry
pyrrhic
chipssy
physics
chiqstu
squitch
chirrsu
currish
chirsty
Christy
chistwy
switchy
chittwy
twitchy
chklooo
hoolock
chklosy
Shylock
chkmmoo
hommock
chkmmou
hummock
chknoos
schnook
chkptuu
putchuk
chlopst
splotch
chlorty
choltry
chlosss
schloss
chlosuy
slouchy
chmosuy
chymous
chnnoor
chronon
chnnosu
nonsuch
chnoops
ponchos
chnoort
torchon
chnorrs
schnorr
chnortu
cothurn
chnotuu
uncouth

chnppuu
punch-up
choopps
cop-shop
choorsu
ochrous
chorstu
trochus
chpssuy
scyphus
chrrsuu
churrus
ciiillt
illicit
ciiimnr
crimini
ciikkll
killick
ciikmmm
mimmick
ciikmnn
minnick
ciiknpt
nit-pick
ciikntu
cutikin
ciikstt
stickit
ciillty
licitly
ciillvy
civilly
ciilnop
cipolin
ciilnos
silicon
ciilnot
Nilotic
ciilnuv
uncivil
ciiloot
oolitic
ciilopt
politic
ciilost
colitis
solicit
ciilpsy
spicily
ciilsss
scissil
ciimmry
mimicry
ciimnno
nimonic
ciimnot
miction
ciimost
mistico
somitic
ciimott
mitotic
ciimotv
motivic

ciinntu
tunicin
ciinoot
coition
ciinops
psionic
ciinors
incisor
ciinprs
crispin
ciinqtu
quintic
ciinrsu
Ricinus
ciintuy
unicity
ciiorst
soritic
ciiosuv
vicious
ciiprty
pyritic
ciirstv
vitrics
ciirtvx
victrix
cijmorw
jim-crow
cijnnoo
conjoin
cijnntu
injunct
cikkllo
killock
ciklllu
ill-luck
cikllor
rollick
cikllos
sillock
cikllow
killcow
cikllsy
slickly
ciklluy
luckily
ciklmow
milk-cow
ciklmsu
misluck
ciklmsy
smickly
ciklnry
crinkly
cikloor
rock-oil
ciklory
rockily
ciklost
Lockist
ciklpry
prickly
ciklquy
quickly

ciklrty
trickly
ciklstu
lustick
cikmnno
minnock
ciknnop
pinnock
ciknnow
winnock
ciknpsu
snick-up
ciknptu
pin-tuck
ciknstu
unstick
cikoppt
pockpit
cikopst
pot-sick
cikotuw
outwick
cikpstu
stickup
cikrsty
tricksy
cillnos
Collins
cillnou
cullion
cilloor
criollo
cilmnop
complin
cilmopy
Olympic
cilmstu
cultism
cilnoor
orcinol
cilnoos
cloison
cilnopr
pilcorn
cilnotu
linocut
cilnoxy
xylonic
cilnpsu
insculp
sculpin
cilnptu
unclipt
cilnstu
linctus
ciloopt
copilot
ciloorụ
couloir
ciloost
sciolto
ciloprw
pilcrow

cilopry
pyloric
cilopsw
cowslip
cilostu
oculist
cilprsy
crisply
cilprtu
culprit
cilrrsu
scurril
cilsttu
cultist
cimmoss
cosmism
cimmost
Comtism
cimnoor
moronic
omicron
cimnors
crimson
cimoors
Morisco
cimoost
osmotic
cimopsy
copyism
miscopy
cimosst
cosmist
Scotism
cimossy
mycosis
cimostt
Comtist
cimotyz
zymotic
cimprsy
scrimpy
cinnnou
inconnu
cinnoru
unicorn
cinnotu
unction
cinnsuu
uncinus
cinoops
opsonic
cinoors
coronis
cinoprt
corn-pit
cinoprx
princox
cinorrt
tricorn
cinorst
cornist
cinortu
ruction

cinosst
consist
cinossu
Oniscus
cinostu
suction
cinosuz
zincous
cinrstu
incrust
ciooprs
scorpio
ciooprt
portico
prootic
cioopsu
copious
ciooqtu
coquito
cioorsu
corious
cioprty
Cypriot
ciopsty
copyist
ciorrsu
cirrous
ciorsss
scissor
ciorssu
Roscius
ciorstu
citrous
ciorsuu
curious
ciortvy
victory
ciosssy
sycosis
ciosstt
Scotist
ciossuv
viscous
ciprssu
prussic
Scirpus
ciprtty
tryptic
cipstty
styptic
cirrttu
crittur
cirssuu
Sciurus
cirtuvy
curvity
cisstuy
cytisus
cjnoruy
conjury
ckknnoo
knock-on
ckknopu
knock-up

ckllmou
mullock
cklloop
pollock
cklloor
rollock
cklloru
rullock
cklnotu
lock-nut
cklnuuy
unlucky
cklooy
olycook
ckloorw
rowlock
cklootu
lockout
ckloptu
pot-luck
putlock
ckmmmou
mummock
cknostu
unstock
cknstuu
unstuck
ckoorsu
sourock
ckopttu
puttock
ckosstu
tussock
ckottuu
tuck-out
ckpstuu
stuck-up
cllmosu
mollusc
clloops
scollop
cllosuu
loculus
clmoopt
complot
clmoptu
plumcot
clmosuu
osculum
clmsuuu
cumulus
clnoort
control
clnooss
consols
clnostu
consult
clnstuu
sun-cult
clooruy
coloury
cloostw
low-cost

clorssy
crossly
clorsuy
Corylus
clortuy
courtly
cmmnoos
commons
cmmrsuy
scrummy
cmnooot
monocot
cmnoopy
compony
cmnptuu
punctum
cmooprt
comport
cmoopst
compost
cmoosty
scotomy
cmopssu
cup-moss
cmorstu
scrotum
cmortuw
cutworm
cmosuvy
Muscovy
cmprsuy
scrumpy
cnnortu
nocturn
cnnoruw
uncrown
cnooppr
popcorn
cnoopru
croupon
cnoopry
Procyon
cnoopsu
soupçon
cnoorst
consort
cnoortt
contort
cnoortu
contour
cornuto
croûton
cnoosuu
nocuous
cnoottw
cottown
cnootty
cottony
cnoprty
crypton
cnorssu
uncross
cnortuy
country

cnrstuy
scrunty
cooprrt
proctor
cooprtu
outcrop
coopstu
octopus
coostty
otocyst
coprrtu
corrupt
coprsuu
cuprous
corrsuy
cursory
dddeels
sledded
dddeelu
deluded
dddeemo
demoded
dddeeru
uddered
dddeflu
fuddled
dddehlu
huddled
dddeilr
diddler
dddeilt
tiddled
dddeimu
muddied
dddeiov
Veddoid
dddeiru
ruddied
dddelop
plodded
dddenos
snodded
dddeopr
prodded
dddeory
doddery
ddderuy
duddery
dddestu
studded
ddeeeoy
doe-eyed
ddeeeps
speeded
ddeeers
red-seed
ddeefgl
fledged
ddeefii
deified
edified
ddeefil
fielded

ddeeflu
deedful
ddeegis
disedge
ddeegrr
dredger
ddeehrs
shedder
ddeeils
sleided
ddeeily
deedily
ddeeims
misdeed
ddeeirr
derider
ridered
ddeellu
duelled
ddeellw
dwelled
ddeelmr
meddler
ddeelpr
peddler
ddeelrt
treddle
ddeelru
deluder
ddeenov
odd-even
ddeenow
endowed
ddeenrs
Dresden
ddeeotv
devoted
ddeerss
dressed
ddeerst
reddest
ddeertu
detrude
ddeeryy
dry-eyed
ddefilr
fiddler
ddefily
fiddley
ddefloo
flooded
ddeflru
fuddler
ddefnor
fronded
ddeggru
drugged
ddegilr
girdled
glidder
griddle
ddegimo
demigod

ddeginr
redding
ddegint
tedding
ddeginw
wedding
ddeginy
eddying
ddegmos
Dodgems
ddegnoo
good-den
ddegnos
godsend
ddegnou
dudgeon
ddegors
gorsedd
ddegory
dodgery
ddegoss
goddess
ddegrru
drudger
ddehirs
reddish
shidder
ddehirw
whidder
ddehiry
hydride
ddehnru
hundred
ddehrsu
shudder
ddehrsy
shreddy
ddeiikr
kiddier
ddeiiks
kiddies
ddeiiox
dioxide
ddeiirt
dirtied
ddeiirv
divider
ddeiist
stiddie
ddeiklo
odd-like
ddeiknr
kindred
ddeillo
dollied
ddeilmp
dimpled
ddeilns
slidden
ddeilnw
dwindle
ddeilot
deltoid

7 DDE

ddeilpr
piddler
ddeilqu
quiddle
ddeilrr
riddler
ddeilrs
slidder
ddeilrt
tiddler
ddeiltu
Luddite
ddeiltw
twiddle
ddeilty
lyddite
tiddley
ddeimnu
mueddin
ddeimos
desmoid
ddeimst
middest
ddeimsu
dedimus
ddeinot
dentoid
ddeinps
dispend
ddeinru
undried
ddeinst
distend
ddeippr
dripped
ddeirru
ruddier
ddeistu
studied
ddekmou
dukedom
ddelmru
muddler
ddelnou
noduled
ddelnru
rundled
ddeloor
doodler
ddeloow
woolded
ddelopr
plodder
ddelort
toddler
ddelorw
worlded
ddelott
dottled
ddelpru
puddler
ddelstu
studdle

ddemmru
drummed
ddemmsu
smeddum
ddemnot
oddment
ddennor
dendron
ddenoos
snooded
ddenops
despond
ddenopw
dew-pond
ddenort
trodden
ddenoru
redound
rounded
underdo
ddenorw
drowned
wondred
ddenoss
oddness
ddenstu
studden
ddeooru
odoured
ddeoorw
redwood
ddeoowy
dye-wood
ddeoppr
dropped
ddeoprw
dew-drop
ddghooo
godhood
ddgiikn
kidding
ddgiily
giddily
ddgiinr
ridding
ddgilow
wild-dog
ddginno
nodding
ddginop
podding
ddginos
sodding
ddginpu
pudding
ddgooow
dogwood
ddhiisy
Yiddish
ddhiory
hydroid
ddhoowy
howdy-do

ddhorsy
dry-shod
ddiikls
skid-lid
ddiikny
dinky-di
ddiilop
diploid
ddiiqtu
quiddit
ddilmsu
Luddism
ddilmuy
muddily
ddilosy
dysodil
ddilowy
dowdily
ddilruy
ruddily
ddiltwy
twiddly
ddinost
snoddit
ddiprry
drip-dry
ddllmoo
dolldom
ddmnoor
dromond
deeefns
defense
deeefpt
deep-fet
deeefrv
fevered
deeeglp
pledgee
deeegmr
demerge
deeegrr
regrede
deeegrt
deterge
greeted
deeehlw
wheedle
wheeled
deeehst
seethed
sheeted
deeeipy
pie-eyed
deeeisv
devisee
deeeiyz
Yezidee
deeeizz
Zezidee
deeejnu
dejeune
deeekln
kneeled

deeeknw
weekend
deeelms
meseled
deeelnr
needler
deeelpt
deplete
deeelrt
deerlet
deeelst
steeled
deeelsv
sleeved
deeeltw
tweedle
deeemns
demesne
deeemrs
demerse
emersed
deeenoy
one-eyed
deeentt
détente
deeentu
détenue
deeeorr
roe-deer
deeeorw
oreweed
deeeotv
devotee
deeeprs
speeder
deeersv
deserve
deeersw
sweered
deeerwy
weedery
deeettv
vedette
deeffin
effendi
deeffls
self-fed
deeffor
offered
deefgin
feeding
feigned
deefgip
pigfeed
deefhls
fleshed
deefhlu
heedful
deefiir
deifier
edifier
deefikn
ink-feed

deefiln
enfiled
deefilr
defiler
fielder
deefinr
refined
deefirr
ferried
deefiry
re-edify
deefirz
friezed
deefllu
fuelled
deefllw
well-fed
deeflns
self-end
deeflnu
needful
deefmor
freedom
deefnor
fore-end
deefnuu
unfeued
deeforv
overfed
deefpry
deep-fry
deefrtt
fretted
deeghiw
weighed
deeghor
hog-deer
deeghow
hog-weed
deegilr
leidger
deeginr
energid
reeding
deegins
sdeigne
seeding
deeginw
weeding
deegior
geordie
deegipr
pig-deer
deegipw
pigweed
deegipy
pig-eyed
deegirv
diverge
deegjru
rejudge
deegloy
goldeye

deeglpr
pledger
deeglpt
pledget
deeglrs
sledger
deegnno
endogen
deegnoo
good-e'en
deegosy
geodesy
deegotu
outedge
deehikv
khedive
deehilt
lethied
deehklw
whelked
deehlls
shelled
deehmru
rheumed
deehnot
hen-toed
deehnoy
honeyed
deehnpr
prehend
deehnuy
unheedy
deehprs
sphered
deehrss
herdess
deehttw
whetted
deeiint
dietine
deeiipr
epeirid
deeiirw
weirdie
deeijll
jellied
deeikll
killdee
deeikmw
mid-week
deeiknn
in-kneed
deeikov
dovekie
deeilns
linseed
deeilny
dyeline
needily
deeilos
oil-seed
seed-oil
deeilpp
lip-deep

deeilpr
replied
deeilps
seedlip
deeilrt
tile-red
deeilrv
deliver
livered
deeilrw
wielder
deeilry
yielder
deeilss
idlesse
deeilst
til-seed
deeilsy
seedily
deeiltu
dilutee
deeiltv
devilet
deeimms
misdeem
deeimnr
ermined
deeimns
desmine
deeimnt
démenti
deeimpr
demirep
deeimps
semiped
deeimpt
emptied
deeimrt
demerit
dimeter
deeimtt
emitted
deeinnp
pennied
deeinnt
dentine
deeinnz
denizen
deeinor
ordinee
deeinpy
pin-eyed
deeinru
uredine
deeinrw
widener
deeinrx
indexer
deeinst
destine
deeinsw
endwise
sinewed

deeinsx
indexes
deeintt
dinette
deeintu
detinue
deeintv
evident
deeinvw
vinewed
deeinvx
invexed
deeinwz
wizened
deeiops
episode
deeiopt
epidote
deeiopx
epoxide
deeiors
osiered
deeippt
peptide
deeiprs
Perseid
preside
deeiprv
deprive
deeiprx
expired
deeipss
despise
pedesis
deeipst
despite
deeiqru
queried
deeirrs
desirer
serried
deeirrt
retired
retried
deeirrv
redrive
rivered
deeirsu
residue
deeirsv
deviser
diverse
deeirtu
erudite
deeirtv
riveted
deeissu
diseuse
deeittv
vidette
deekkrt
trekked
deekksy
key-desk

deeklrs
skelder
deellps
spelled
deellru
dueller
deellrw
dweller
deellry
elderly
deellst
stelled
deellsw
swelled
deelmor
remodel
deelmpt
templed
deelmpu
deplume
deelmtt
mettled
deelnos
nose-led
deelnrs
slender
deelnss
endless
deelopr
deplore
deelopv
develop
deelopx
explode
deeloru
urodele
deelorv
lovered
deelosu
delouse
deelotv
dovelet
deelovv
devolve
deelowy
owl-eyed
deelprs
spelder
deelpru
prelude
deelstt
settled
deelstw
swelted
deelvxy
vexedly
deemmst
stemmed
deemnov
venomed
deemnoy
moneyed
deemntu
unmeted

deemors
emerods
deemorv
removed
deemorx
exoderm
deennop
open-end
deennor
enderon
deennos
données
deennoy
doyenne
deennpt
pendent
deenntz
tendenz
deenops
spondee
deenopt
pentode
deenors
endorse
deenort
erodent
deenorw
endower
re-endow
deenppr
perpend
deenprs
spender
deenprt
pretend
deenrru
endurer
deenrss
redness
deenrst
sterned
deenrsu
end-user
deenrtu
denture
deensuw
unsewed
deensux
unsexed
deenuvx
unvexed
deeoppw
pop-weed
deeoppy
pop-eyed
deeoprr
pedrero
deeoprs
deposer
reposed
deeoprw
powered
deeopry
eye-drop

deeopsx
exposed
deeorrr
orderer
reorder
deeorrs
reredos
rose-red
deeorrv
overred
deeorst
oersted
deeortt
tetrode
deeortw
towered
deeoruv
overdue
deeorvy
overdye
deeotuw
outweed
deeotwy
two-eyed
deeppst
stepped
deeppsu
speed-up
deeprru
perdure
deeprss
depress
spersed
deeprtu
reputed
deerrss
dresser
redress
deerruv
verdure
deersst
dessert
tressed
deerssu
duresse
deerstw
strewed
deersty
dyester
deertux
extrude
deesttt
stetted
deffios
offside
deffisu
diffuse
deffllu
full-fed
defflmu
muffled
defflru
ruffled

deffnor
forfend
deffnos
send-off
deffstu
stuffed
defgglo
flogged
defggor
frogged
defghhi
high-fed
defginr
fringed
defginu
feuding
defginy
defying
defgior
firedog
defgiru
figured
defgity
fidgety
defhirs
redfish
defhist
shifted
defhloo
elfhood
defhlsu
flushed
defiiln
infidel
infield
defiims
fideism
defiimw
midwife
defiinu
unified
defilnr
flinder
defilnu
unfiled
defilos
od's-life
defilru
direful
defilst
stifled
defiltt
flitted
defilxy
fixedly
defimor
deiform
definot
fin-toed
definru
unfired
definux
unfixed

definuy
  undeify
defioru
  foudrie
defipry
  perfidy
defirrt
  drifter
defirtt
  fritted
defirtu
  fruited
defirzz
  frizzed
defistu
  feudist
defllou
  doleful
deflluw
  dewfull
deflnoo
  onefold
deflnop
  penfold
deflnor
  fondler
  forlend
deflnot
  tenfold
deflnru
  dernful
defloor
  floored
defloru
  foulder
deflpru
  purfled
deflruu
  dureful
defmnuu
  unfumed
defmors
  serfdom
defmpru
  rump-fed
defnoor
  fordone
defnort
  fronted
defnoru
  founder
  refound
defnosw
  snow-fed
deforst
  defrost
  frosted
deftuuy
  feu-duty
deggglo
  goggled
degghin
  hedging
degghos
  shogged
deggiln
  gelding
degginw
  wedging
  wind-egg
deggjlo
  joggled
degglor
  doggrel
degglpu
  plugged
deggnoo
  doggone
deggnou
  gudgeon
deggnsu
  snugged
deggory
  doggery
deggoss
  doggess
deggrru
  drugger
deggrtu
  drugget
deghiln
  hindleg
deghilt
  delight
  lighted
deghint
  nighted
deghipr
  pig-herd
deghist
  sighted
deghloo
  doghole
deghnot
  thonged
deghorr
  drogher
degiiln
  eilding
degiimn
  Geminid
degiklo
  godlike
degillr
  grilled
degillu
  gullied
degilly
  gelidly
degilnn
  lending
degilno
  glenoid
degilnu
  indulge
degilnv
  devling
degilnw
  welding
  wing-led
degilor
  gloried
degilrr
  girdler
degilru
  guilder
degilrw
  wergild
degiluv
  divulge
degimnn
  mending
degimns
  smidgen
deginnp
  pending
deginnr
  grinned
deginns
  sending
deginny
  denying
deginop
  pidgeon
deginor
  groined
  negroid
deginos
  dingoes
deginow
  widgeon
deginrr
  grinder
  regrind
deginrw
  wringed
deginst
  stinged
deginsw
  swindge
degiort
  goitred
degippr
  gripped
degirss
  digress
degisst
  disgest
deglnno
  endlong
deglopr
  pledgor
deglops
  splodge
degloss
  godless
deglttu
  glutted
degmrsu
  smudger
degnnou
  dungeon
degnopr
  pronged
degnoru
  guerdon
  undergo
  ungored
degnotu
  tongued
degnrtu
  trudgen
degnruu
  unurged
degnuvy
  ungyved
degoors
  dog-rose
degorst
  stodger
degortu
  droguet
degrrtu
  trudger
dehiips
  piedish
dehilms
  dishelm
dehilnp
  delphin
dehilty
  diethyl
dehimor
  heirdom
  Homerid
dehimos
  dishome
dehimot
  ethmoid
dehinnt
  thinned
dehinop
  diphone
dehinor
  hordein
dehinps
  end-ship
dehinpt
  in-depth
dehinru
  unhired
dehinsw
  Wendish
dehiort
  theroid
dehiosu
  hideous
dehiosv
  doveish
dehiotu
  hideout
dehipps
  shipped
dehippw
  whipped
dehirrs
  shirred
dehirru
  dhurrie
  hurried
dehirrw
  whirred
dehirsu
  hurdies
dehirsv
  dervish
  shrived
dehirtv
  thrived
dehissw
  Swedish
dehiwzz
  whizzed
dehlmou
  mud-hole
dehloot
  toe-hold
dehlorw
  whorled
dehloss
  sloshed
dehlrru
  hurdler
dehmoru
  Hordeum
dehmotu
  mouthed
dehmoty
  Methody
dehnnsu
  shunned
dehnoow
  hoedown
dehnopu
  unhoped
dehnort
  thonder
  thorned
  throned
dehnotz
  dozenth
dehnrtu
  thunder
dehoott
  toothed
dehopps
  shopped
dehostt
  shotted
dehostw
  wet-shod
deiiirs
  iridise
deiikls
  dislike
deiilmp
  implied
deiilmt
  delimit
  limited
deiilos
  idolise
deiimno
  dominie
deiimst
  misdiet
deiimvw
  midwive
deiinot
  edition
  tenioid
deiinrs
  insider
deiinrt
  inditer
  nitride
deiinrv
  diviner
  drive-in
deiiort
  diorite
deiiorv
  ivoried
deiiosx
  oxidise
deiippp
  dip-pipe
deiiprt
  dirt-pie
  riptide
  tide-rip
deiistt
  dietist
deijnor
  joinder
deijnot
  jointed
deijnsu
  disjune
deijory
  joy-ride
deiklls
  skilled
deiklnr
  kindler
deiklor
  rodlike
deiklrt
  kirtled
deikmms
  skimmed
deiknns
  skinned
deiknos
  doe-skin
deiknrr
  drinker
deiknrs
  redskin
deiknsw
  swinked

deikntt
knitted
deikorw
die-work
deikosy
disyoke
deikpps
skipped
deikrst
skirted
deillnw
indwell
deillor
dollier
deillps
spilled
deillqu
quilled
deillrt
trilled
deillrv
drevill
deillss
lidless
deillsu
ill-used
sullied
deilltw
twilled
deilmms
slimmed
deilmnt
mid-Lent
deilmnu
unlimed
deilmop
implode
deilmot
old-time
deilmoy
myeloid
deilmpp
pimpled
deilmwy
mildewy
deilmxy
mixedly
deilnnu
unlined
deilnoo
eidolon
deilnos
sondeli
deilnot
lentoid
deilnou
unoiled
deilnow
lie-down
deilnps
speldin
spindle

deilnrt
tendril
trindle
deilnsw
swindle
deilnsy
snidely
deilntu
diluent
untiled
deilntw
indwelt
deilopp
Pelopid
deilops
despoil
soliped
spoiled
deilors
soldier
deilpps
slipped
deilppu
uppiled
deilpxy
pixy-led
deilqtu
quilted
deilrtu
diluter
deilrvy
devilry
deilrwy
weirdly
deilrwz
wrizled
deilrzz
drizzle
deilstt
stilted
deilsty
distyle
deimmmu
mummied
deimmpr
primmed
deimmrt
mid-term
trimmed
deimnnu
minuend
deimnos
misdone
deimnru
unrimed
deimnss
dimness
missend
deimnsw
miswend
deimnux
unmixed
deimoor
moidore

deimors
misdoer
deimoru
erodium
deimost
modiste
deimott
omitted
deimotv
vomited
deimprt
dirempt
deimpux
mixed-up
deimruu
uredium
deimstw
Midwest
deinnnu
nundine
deinnop
pinnoed
deinnor
endiron
deinntw
twinned
deinopr
poinder
deinops
dispone
spinode
deinopt
pointed
deinors
indorse
rosined
sordine
deinoru
dourine
deinorv
on-drive
vine-rod
deinorw
windore
deinpps
snipped
deinpst
stipend
deinpsu
unspied
deinpuw
unwiped
deinrtt
trident
deinrtu
intrude
turdine
untired
untried
deinrtx
dextrin
deinrty
tindery

deinsst
disnest
dissent
deinssv
vendiss
deinstt
dentist
distent
stinted
deinstu
distune
deinsty
density
destiny
deinsuz
unsized
deinuvw
unwived
deioost
osteoid
deioovv
voivode
deiooww
woiwode
deioppp
poppied
deioprt
diopter
dioptre
peridot
proteid
deioprv
provide
deiopss
dispose
deiopst
deposit
posited
topside
deiopsu
Oedipus
deiopsv
vespoid
deioptt
tiptoed
deioptv
pivoted
deiorrw
worried
deiorss
dossier
deiorst
steroid
storied
deiorsv
devisor
visored
deiortu
étourdi
ioduret
outride
deiorvz
vizored

deiorww
widower
deiostu
outside
tedious
deiostx
exodist
deiosuv
devious
deipprt
tripped
deiprst
striped
deiprsy
spidery
deipssu
upsides
deipstt
spitted
deipstu
dispute
deipsxy
pyxides
deipttu
puttied
deiqttu
quitted
deiquzz
quizzed
deirrst
stirred
deirstu
studier
deisttw
twisted
deitttw
twitted
deklnru
knurled
deklrsu
skudler
deknnru
drunken
deknosy
donkeys
deknott
knotted
deknouy
unyoked
deknrtu
trunked
dekorwy
dye-work
delloow
woolled
dellopr
redpoll
delmors
smolder
delmoru
moulder
remould
delmott
mottled

delmouv
volumed
delnoru
lounder
roundel
roundle
delnory
Reynold
delnoss
oldness
delnotw
let-down
delnoty
notedly
delnouv
unloved
delnpru
plunder
delnrtu
rundlet
trundle
delnruu
unruled
delnssu
dulness
deloopp
pleopod
deloorw
woolder
deloppp
plopped
deloppr
dropple
delopps
slopped
deloprt
droplet
deloptt
plotted
delorry
orderly
delorss
rodless
delorst
oldster
strodle
delortt
dottrel
deloruv
louvred
deloszz
sozzled
delotuv
voluted
delrrsu
slurred
delrstu
strudel
demmrru
drummer
demmstu
stummed
demnoor
morendo

demnort
mordent
demnory
demonry
demnost
endmost
demnotu
demount
mounted
demnouv
unmoved
demnpru
rump-end
demoopp
popedom
demoopr
predoom
demoott
mottoed
demootu
outmode
demorww
dew-worm
demosty
modesty
demsttu
smutted
dennort
tendron
dennoru
enround
dennotu
unnoted
untoned
dennotw
town-end
dennouw
unowned
dennouz
unzoned
dennstu
stunned
denntuu
untuned
denoost
stooden
denoosw
swooned
denootu
duotone
denoouw
unwooed
denoppr
propend
denoprs
respond
denoprt
drop-net
portend
protend
denopru
pounder
denoprv
provend
denopsu
unposed
denopux
expound
denorru
rounder
unorder
denorrw
drowner
denorsu
resound
sounder
denoruw
wounder
denostu
snouted
denostw
set-down
denprtu
prudent
prunted
uptrend
denpssu
suspend
denrssu
undress
denrssy
dryness
denrsuu
unsured
densttu
student
stunted
deooprt
torpedo
deoopst
stooped
deoorrt
red-root
deoorrw
o'erword
deopppr
propped
deopprr
dropper
deoppst
stopped
deoppsw
swopped
deoprwy
powdery
deopstt
spotted
deoqrtu
torqued
deorrst
rodster
deorrsw
sworder
deorstw
strowed
worsted
deorsty
destroy
deorttt
trotted
deortuu
outdure
deossyy
odyssey
deosttu
testudo
deostuu
duteous
deprrsu
spurred
deprruy
prudery
deprsuu
usurped
derrstu
rustred
dersstu
trussed
derstuu
sutured
dffiimr
midriff
dffiirt
triffid
dffimor
difform
dffloou
foodful
dffotuy
off-duty
dfghios
dogfish
fish-god
dfgiinn
finding
dfgiiny
dignify
dfgilno
folding
dfgilop
flip-dog
dfginnu
funding
dfginou
fungoid
dfglnuy
dung-fly
dfgloow
wolf-dog
dfgmooy
fogydom
dfhilsu
dishful
dfhimsu
mud-fish
dfhinsu
dun-fish
dfilmmo
filmdom
dfilmnu
mindful
dfilnop
pinfold
dfilosx
sixfold
dfilotw
twifold
dfiltuu
dutiful
dfimnuy
mundify
dfimors
disform
dfioorw
fir-wood
dfirsty
dry-fist
dflmoou
doomful
dflootu
fold-out
dflootw
twofold
dflopry
dropfly
dflotwy
twyfold
dfnnouu
unfound
dfnoruy
foundry
dfoorty
dry-foot
dgggiin
digging
dgggino
dogging
dgghios
doggish
dggiiln
gilding
gliding
dggiinr
girding
ridging
dggiinu
guiding
dggilno
godling
lodging
dghhooo
hoghood
dghiiln
hidling
hilding
dghiins
dishing
shindig
dghilno
holding
dghilos
goldish
dghilpy
diglyph
dghintu
hind-gut
undight
dghioos
goodish
dghiops
dogship
godship
dghortu
drought
dghotuy
doughty
dgiikln
kidling
dgiilln
dilling
dgiilns
sliding
dgiilnw
wilding
dgiilry
rigidly
dgiimmn
dimming
dgiimns
smidgin
dgiimos
sigmoid
dgiinnn
dinning
dgiinnw
winding
dgiinov
voiding
dgiinpp
dipping
dgiinpu
pinguid
dgiinrv
driving
dgiinst
tidings
dgiinty
dignity
tidying
dgiiort
tigroid
dgikmno
kingdom
dgiknor
Dorking
king-rod
dgiknos
dogskin
dgilloy
godlily
dgilnor
lording
dgilnyy
dyingly
dgilruy
guildry
dgimnoo
dooming
dgimopy
pygmoid
dginnno
donning
dginnnu
dunning
dginnou
undoing
dginnuw
wind-gun
dginnuy
undying
dginopp
dopping
dginorw
wording
dginosw
disgown
dginott
dotting
dgiopry
prodigy
dgiorsu
Gordius
dgisstu
disgust
dglnouy
ungodly
dglooow
logwood
dglopsy
splodgy
dglosyy
dyslogy
dgmnooo
moon-god
dgmopru
gumdrop
dgnooor
godroon
dgnooos
good-son
dgnooow
good-now
dgnootw
dogtown
dgoortt
dogtrot
dhiilns
hidlins
dhiilot
lithoid
dhiilsw
wildish
dhiimms
dimmish
dhiimno
hominid
dhiimps
midship
dhiinru
hirudin
dhiiopx
xiphoid

dhiiorz
rhizoid
dhiiost
histoid
dhikrsu
Kurdish
dhikssu
duskish
dhillos
dollish
dhillsu
dullish
dhilmuy
humidly
dhilnop
dolphin
dhilost
doltish
dhilosu
loudish
dhilpsu
ludship
dhilpsy
sylphid
dhilrty
thirdly
dhimopr
dimorph
dhimoru
humidor
mid-hour
rhodium
dhimpsu
dumpish
dhinnos
donnish
dhinnsu
dunnish
dhinops
donship
dhinopy
hypnoid
dhinors
dishorn
dronish
dhinstu
tun-dish
dhiopty
typhoid
dhiorsw
wordish
dhiorty
thyroid
dhiprsu
prudish
dhiprsy
syrphid
dhkmoou
mud-hook
dhkorsy
droshky
dhlmoou
hoodlum

dhmmruu
humdrum
dhmnoyy
hymnody
dhnnoou
nunhood
dhoorsu
rhodous
dhoortt
hot-trod
dhorsuy
hydrous
shroudy
dhortuy
drouthy
dhorxyy
hydroxy
diiimru
iridium
diiinps
insipid
diijnos
disjoin
diikkns
kid-skin
diiklns
dislink
diiknot
doitkin
diillst
distill
diilmns
dislimn
diilmos
idolism
diilmty
timidly
diilnwy
windily
diilost
idolist
diilrty
dirtily
diilvvy
vividly
diilyzz
dizzily
diimors
diorism
diimsss
dismiss
diimsuv
vidimus
diinors
sordini
diioprs
spiroid
diiorsv
divisor
diipprt
drip-tip
diituvy
viduity

dijostu
judoist
dikknru
Dunkirk
diklnor
lordkin
diklnry
kiln-dry
diklsuy
duskily
diknnos
non-skid
diknorv
dvornik
diknssu
sun-disk
dikoort
drookit
dikortu
droukit
dillosy
solidly
dillruy
luridly
dilmnru
drumlin
dilmooy
moodily
dilmost
mistold
dilmosu
solidum
dilmosy
odylism
dilmtuy
tumidly
dilnoos
oodlins
dilnopt
diplont
dilnoqu
quodlin
dilnosu
unsolid
dilnpsu
lispund
dilnpsy
spindly
dilooow
wood-oil
dilortu
dilutor
dilorwy
rowdily
wordily
dilossu
dulosis
solidus
dilosty
styloid
dilryzz
drizzly
dilstuy
dustily

dimmmou
mim-mou'd
dimmost
midmost
dimnnoo
midnoon
dimnnos
donnism
dimnnot
dinmont
dimnopu
impound
dimopsu
spodium
dimorsw
misword
dimrtuu
triduum
dimruuv
duumvir
dinnoor
rondino
dinnoot
tondino
dinnopr
non-drip
dinoors
indoors
sordino
dinoost
isodont
dinootw
wood-tin
dinorsw
Windsor
dinorww
windrow
dinostw
sitdown
dinotuw
outwind
dinprsy
spin-dry
dinpstu
pin-dust
dioorst
disroot
dioortt
ridotto
dioprst
disport
dioprty
tripody
diopsst
dispost
diorrst
stridor
diorstt
distort
diosuuv
viduous
diprstu
disrupt

dirstuy
surdity
dkmopsu
musk-pod
dknnruu
undrunk
dkooosz
odzooks
dllorwy
worldly
dlmmpuu
mud-lump
dlmnooy
mylodon
dlmnouu
unmould
dlmosuu
modulus
dlnnooy
Londony
dlnooww
low-down
dlnopru
puldron
dlnopsy
spondyl
dlnoruy
roundly
dlnosuy
soundly
dloooww
wood-owl
dlooppy
polypod
dloopty
tylopod
dloopuy
duopoly
dloopwy
plywood
dlopruy
proudly
dmnnooo
Monodon
dmnootw
towmond
dmortuw
mudwort
dnnoruu
unround
dnnoruw
run-down
dnnosuu
unsound
dnnosuw
sundown
dnnouuw
unwound
dnnrtuu
turndun
dnoortu
orotund
dnopruu
round-up

dnoptuw
put-down
dnopuuw
upwound
dooorsu
odorous
dooortu
outdoor
dooprsy
prosody
dooprtu
drop-out
doopstu
upstood
doorrtu
dortour
doruvyy
dyvoury
eeeefrr
referee
eeeegtx
exegete
eeefffo
feoffee
eeefgru
refugee
eeefhrs
shereef
eeeflrr
fleerer
eeefmnr
freemen
eeefors
foresee
eeefrrz
freezer
eeeghnw
wheenge
eeegils
elegise
eeeginp
epigene
eeegipr
perigee
eeeglnt
genteel
eeegmrr
remerge
eeegnno
Neogene
eeegnos
Genoese
eeegnpr
epergne
eeegnrr
reneger
eeegnru
renegue
eeegnrv
revenge
eeegnss
geneses
eeegntt
genette

7 EEE

eeegrrt
regreet
eeegrux
exergue
eeehilw
wheelie
eeehlln
Hellene
eeehlnw
enwheel
eeehloy
eye-hole
eeehlpw
wheeple
eeehlrw
wheeler
eeehlwz
wheezle
eeehnrw
whene'er
eeehrrw
where'er
eeehrst
seether
eeeilpt
Peelite
eeeilrv
relieve
eeeimnt
emetine
eeeimrt
eremite
eeeinss
Sienese
eeeirrt
retiree
eeeirrv
reverie
eeeirsz
reseize
eeeistw
sweetie
eeejprs
jeepers
eeekllu
ukelele
eeeklnr
kneeler
eeeklns
sleeken
eeeklrs
sleeker
eeeknpt
keepnet
eeekrst
skeeter
eeelmnt
element
eeelnst
stelene
eeelnsv
elevens

eeelprs
sleeper
speeler
eeelprt
replete
eeelpst
steeple
eeelrtv
leveret
eeelssy
eyeless
eeemmss
meseems
eeemort
eroteme
eeemrtx
extreme
eeennpt
pentene
eeenntt
entente
eeenprt
terpene
eeenprv
prevene
eeenpst
ensteep
steepen
eeenpsw
ensweep
eeenpsx
expense
eeenrrs
sneerer
eeenrrt
enterer
re-enter
terreen
terrene
eeenrrv
venerer
eeenrrw
renewer
eeenrsz
sneezer
eeenrtv
eventer
eeenrtx
externe
eeenruv
revenue
unreeve
eeenstw
sweeten
eeenstx
extense
eeeoppt
peep-toe
eeeorsv
oversee
eeeorsy
eyesore
eeeorvy
overeye

eeeprss
peeress
eeeprst
estrepe
steeper
eeeprsw
sweeper
eeeprsz
spreeze
eeeprtu
Euterpe
eeeqsuz
squeeze
eeerrrv
reverer
eeerrst
steerer
eeerrsv
reserve
reverse
eeerstv
Everest
eeersvw
servewe
eeerttw
tweeter
eeertwy
yew-tree
eefffno
enfeoff
eefffor
feoffer
eeffglu
effulge
eeffinr
fen-fire
eeffint
fifteen
eeffnos
offense
eefforr
offerer
eeffstu
suffete
eefgiln
feeling
fleeing
eefginr
freeing
reefing
eefgirt
fig-tree
eefgllu
gleeful
eefglor
foreleg
eefhinw
hen-wife
eefhisy
fisheye
eefhlns
enflesh

eefhlrs
flesher
herself
eefhnrs
freshen
eefhort
thereof
eefhorw
whereof
eefhrrs
fresher
refresh
eefhrru
Fuehrer
eefhrst
freshet
eefillx
flexile
eefilno
olefine
eefilor
forelie
eefilrt
fertile
eefilst
felsite
liefest
eefimrt
femiter
eefinrr
refiner
eefinrw
fire-new
eefinss
finesse
eefirrt
ferrite
fir-tree
eefistv
festive
eefllru
fueller
eefllty
fleetly
eeflmtu
teemful
eeflnno
enfelon
eeflnos
oneself
eefloov
foveole
eeflrru
ferrule
eeflrtt
fettler
eeflrtu
fleuret
eeflrux
flexure
eefmnor
foremen
eefmnrt
ferment

eefmott
mofette
eefmpru
perfume
eefmttu
fumette
eefnrry
fernery
eefnrtv
fervent
eefnssw
fewness
eeforrv
forever
eefottu
fouetté
eefprsu
perfuse
eefrrsu
refuser
eefrrtu
refuter
eefrrty
ferrety
eegghtu
thuggee
eeggiln
négligé
eeggkrs
skegger
eeggnor
engorge
eeggnoy
geogeny
eeggnst
nest-egg
eeggorr
regorge
eeggpru
puggree
eeghiln
heeling
eeghiny
hygiene
eeghirw
reweigh
weigher
eeghlnu
leughen
eeghnrt
greenth
eeghnry
greyhen
eeghops
shoe-peg
eegijnr
jeering
eegikln
keeling
eegiknp
keeping
eegiknr
reeking

eegilnp
peeling
eegilnr
leering
reeling
eegilnt
gentile
eegilrv
veliger
eegilst
elegist
eegimmr
immerge
eegimnr
regimen
eegimns
seeming
eegimnt
meeting
teeming
eegimrs
remiges
eeginnr
enginer
erg-nine
ingener
eeginnu
genuine
ingénue
eeginnv
evening
eeginop
epigone
eeginor
E-region
eeginos
soignée
eeginpw
weeping
eeginrs
greisen
eeginrt
integer
eeginrv
veering
eeginss
genesis
eegintv
ventige
eegintw
weeting
eegintx
exigent
eegiost
egotise
eegirrv
griever
eegirtt
tergite
eegistv
vestige
eegknor
kerogen

eegllor
log-reel
eegllss
legless
eeglmmu
gemmule
eeglnor
erelong
eeglnoz
lozenge
eeglnry
greenly
eeglnst
lengest
eeglrst
leg-rest
eeglrty
telergy
eegmmry
gemmery
eegmnos
emonges
eegmnst
segment
eegnors
Negroes
eegnptt
tent-peg
eegnptv
vent-peg
eegnpux
expunge
eegnrss
Negress
eegnstu
guesten
eegoprt
protégé
eegortv
overget
eegprux
expurge
eegrrss
regress
eegrrsu
resurge
eegrruy
Gruyère
eegrssu
guesser
eegrstu
gesture
eehhrtt
thether
eehhrtw
whether
eehhstw
wheesht
eehillr
hellier
eehilmn
hem-line
eehilpv
Pehlevi

eehilst
sheltie
eehilsx
helixes
eehimms
mishmee
eehimno
hemione
eehimpt
epithem
eehimst
Shemite
eehinor
heroine
eehinrr
errhine
eehinrt
neither
therein
eehinrw
wherein
eehiors
heroise
eehiost
shoe-tie
eehiprt
prithee
eehipsv
peevish
eehiptt
epithet
eehirss
heiress
hérisse
eehirst
heister
eehirsv
shrieve
eehistv
thieves
eehkloy
keyhole
eehkooy
eyehook
eehllmp
phellem
eehllns
enshell
eehllrs
sheller
eehlmmw
whemmle
eehlprt
telpher
eehlrst
shelter
eehlrsw
welsher
eehlrsy
sheerly
eehlssu
hueless
eehlssv
shelves

eehmnop
phoneme
eehmnry
mynheer
eehmort
theorem
eehmrux
exhumer
eehnnry
hennery
eehnopt
potheen
eehnort
thereon
eehnorw
Erewhon
nowhere
whereon
eehnost
hose-net
eehnosw
wheeson
eehnrtu
Ruthene
eehnstu
enthuse
eehnstv
seventh
eehoopw
whoopee
eehoprt
hop-tree
eehopru
euphroe
eehorsu
rehouse
eehorsw
whereso
eehortt
thereto
eehortw
whereto
eehorvw
however
whoever
eehosty
eye-shot
eehprst
hepster
sperthe
eehprty
prythee
eehrrtw
wherret
eehrttw
whetter
eehrvwy
whyever
eehstuy
shut-eye
eeiimpr
riempie
eeiimrt
emeriti

eeiimst
itemise
eeiinrt
erinite
niterie
eeiirrv
rivière
eeiistv
visitee
eeiklmw
ewe-milk
eeiklpt
pikelet
eeiklst
sleekit
eeiknpy
pink-eye
eeiknrt
kernite
eeiknwy
eye-wink
eeikppy
pipe-key
eeikstt
steekit
eeikttt
tektite
eeillmt
mellite
eeillmy
mill-eye
eeillps
ellipse
eeillrt
treille
eeilmnr
ermelin
eeilmpt
implete
eeilmrv
vermeil
eeilnno
leonine
eeilnnt
lenient
eeilnnv
enliven
eeilnps
pensile
eeilnrt
Trilene®
eeilnss
sensile
eeilnst
set-line
tensile
eeilntt
entitle
eeilopt
petiole
eeilort
oil-tree
troelie

eeilorv
overlie
relievo
eeilost
estoile
eeilotz
zeolite
eeilprr
replier
eeilprs
spieler
eeilprt
perlite
reptile
eeilpru
puerile
eeilpss
pelisse
eeilpst
epistle
eeilqru
relique
eeilrrv
reliver
reviler
eeilrst
leister
sterile
eeilrsu
leisure
eeilrsv
servile
eeilrvz
Elzevir
eeilsss
sessile
eeilsst
telesis
tieless
eeilstv
lievest
eeilstx
sextile
eeilsuv
elusive
eeilttx
textile
eeilvwy
weevily
eeimmns
immense
eeimmrs
immerse
eeimmss
misseem
eeimnno
nominee
eeimnnt
eminent
eeimnos
semeion
eeimnrv
minever

eeimnss
Meissen
nemesis
siemens
eeimnsw
misween
eeimntt
minette
eeimopt
epitome
eeimors
isomere
eeimotv
emotive
eeimprr
premier
reprime
eeimprs
emprise
imprese
premise
spireme
eeimprt
emptier
eeimpst
empties
septime
eeimqru
requiem
eeimrrt
trireme
eeimrst
triseme
eeimrtt
termite
eeimsst
métisse
eeinnnp
pennine
eeinnps
pennies
eeinnrt
interne
eeinnru
neurine
eeinnrv
enriven
innerve
nervine
eeinnst
intense
eeinntw
entwine
eeinopr
pereion
pioneer
eeinotw
Owenite
eeinpps
pepsine
eeinprr
repiner
eeinprs
erepsin

eeinprt
Petrine
eeinprz
prenzie
eeinpst
pentise
eeinpsv
pensive
vespine
eeinqru
enquire
eeinqtu
quieten
eeinquy
queynie
eeinrrs
resiner
eeinrrt
reinter
rentier
terrine
eeinrrv
vernier
eeinrst
trenise
eeinrsv
inverse
versine
eeinrsy
Erinyes
eeinrtu
retinue
reunite
uterine
eeinsst
sestine
eeinstv
tensive
eeinstx
sixteen
eeinsty
syenite
eeiopst
poetise
eeiorsv
erosive
eeiosst
isoetes
eeippst
peptise
eeipptt
pipette
eeipqru
perique
re-equip
repique
eeiprrr
perrier
eeiprrs
reprise
respire
eeiprst
respite

eeiprsv
previse
eeiprvw
preview
eeiprzz
prezzie
eeiqrru
require
eeiqrsu
esquire
eeiqrtu
quieter
requite
eeirrrt
terrier
eeirrsv
reversi
reviser
eeirrtv
riveret
riveter
eeirrtw
rewrite
eeirrvv
reviver
eeirssu
reissue
eeirstv
restive
Servite
veriest
eeirstx
re-exist
eeirsuz
seizure
eeirtvv
vetiver
eeituxz
zeuxite
eejllmu
jumelle
eejlrwy
jewelry
eejnory
enjoyer
eejprru
perjure
eejqrru
jerquer
eekkrrt
trekker
eekllnv
knevell
eekllsy
sleekly
eeklluu
ukulele
eeklnos
keelson
eekloos
look-see
eeklrst
kestrel
skelter

eeklrsz
Szekler
eeklssy
keyless
eekmrss
kermess
eeknoty
keynote
eeknpsu
knees-up
eeknsst
Knesset
eeknstu
netsuke
eellmos
Moselle
eellmrs
smeller
eellnov
novelle
eellors
roselle
eellorz
rozelle
eellprs
respell
speller
eellqru
queller
eellrsw
sweller
eellstw
well-set
eelmmop
pommele
eelmmpu
emplume
eelmnoo
oenomel
eelmopr
plerome
eelmopt
leptome
eelmorw
eelworm
eelmpst
stempel
stemple
eelmptt
templet
eelmrst
smelter
eelmrsu
lemures
eelnopv
envelop
eelnosv
Slovene
eelnosy
esloyne
eelnott
notelet
eelnotu
toluene

eelnpsy
spleeny
eelnquy
queenly
eelnruv
nervule
eelnstu
unsteel
eelnsty
enstyle
tensely
eelnttu
lunette
eeloprs
leprose
eeloprx
explore
eeloptu
eelpout
eelorsv
resolve
eelortt
lorette
eelorvv
revolve
eelosst
osselet
eelostt
teleost
eelotuv
evolute
velouté
eelpprx
perplex
eelpqru
prequel
eelprst
Prestel®
spelter
eelprsu
repulse
eelprsy
sleepry
eelprtz
pretzel
eelprux
plexure
eelprvy
replevy
eelpsty
steeply
eelpsux
expulse
eelqruy
queerly
eelrrvy
revelry
eelrsst
tressel
eelrstt
settler
sterlet
trestle

eelrstw
swelter
wrestle
eelrsty
restyle
tersely
eelrstz
seltzer
eelsssu
useless
eelsssx
sexless
eelstuy
eustyle
eelstwy
sweetly
eeltvvy
velvety
eemmnot
memento
eemmosu
mousmee
eemnnov
envenom
eemnoos
someone
eemnooy
moon-eye
eemnory
moneyer
eemnost
temenos
eemnptu
umpteen
eemoosw
woesome
eemoprr
emperor
eemoprv
premove
eemoprw
empower
eemorrs
remorse
eemorru
uromere
eemorrv
remover
eempprt
pre-empt
eemprrt
preterm
eemprss
empress
eemprsu
presume
supreme
eemprtt
tempter
eemprtu
permute
eempstt
tempest

eemrsux
murexes
eemsttu
musette
eennort
enteron
tenoner
eennoru
neurone
eennoss
oneness
eennott
nonette
eennoty
neoteny
eennptu
Neptune
eennquu
unqueen
eennruv
unnerve
eennssu
unsense
eennssw
newness
eenoppr
propene
eenoppt
peptone
eenopst
onestep
pentose
posteen
eenortu
Euronet
eenortv
overnet
eenossy
essoyne
eenostv
ventose
Ventôse
eenpprt
perpent
eenprst
present
serpent
eenprtv
prevent
eenprtw
pew-rent
eenpsty
stepney
eenqstu
sequent
eenrrty
re-entry
eenrruv
nervure
eenrstt
testern
eenrstw
western

eenrsty
styrene
yestern
eenrttu
nut-tree
eenrtuv
venture
eenssst
setness
eensstw
wetness
eenstty
teentsy
eenstuw
unsweet
eenstvy
seventy
eeooprs
operose
eeopptu
outpeep
eeoprrv
reprove
eeoprsx
exposer
eeoprtt
treetop
eeoprtu
outpeer
eeopsst
poetess
eeopssu
espouse
poseuse
eeopstt
steep-to
eeopsty
eye-spot
eeoptuw
outweep
eeorrst
restore
eeorrsv
reverso
eeorrtw
rewrote
eeorsst
osseter
eeorstt
rosette
eeorstv
estover
overset
eeorstx
xerotes
eeorsty
esotery
eeorsuv
oeuvres
overuse
eeorsvw
oversew
eepppry
peppery

eepprst
stepper
eeppstu
steep-up
eeppsuw
upsweep
eeppsuy
eupepsy
eeprrss
presser
repress
eeprrsu
peruser
eeprrtv
pervert
eeprssu
Perseus
eeprssx
express
eeprstu
pertuse
eeprttx
pretext
eepsttt
septett
eeqrruy
equerry
eeqrstu
quester
request
eeqsuyz
squeezy
eerrstw
strewer
wrester
eerrsvw
swerver
eerrsvy
servery
eerrttu
reutter
utterer
eerrtty
rettery
eersttu
trustee
eerstty
streety
eerstuv
versute
vesture
eersuvw
survewe
eerttux
texture
eessttt
sestett
eestttx
sextett
effflot
left-off
efffoor
feoffor

effhilw
whiffle
effhirs
sheriff
effhirw
whiffer
effhitw
whiffet
effhlsu
shuffle
effiist
fifties
effikls
skiffle
effillu
lifeful
effilno
off-line
effilns
sniffle
effilpr
piffler
effilrr
riffler
effilry
firefly
effinrs
sniffer
effinst
stiffen
effiopr
piffero
effiort
forfeit
effllos
sell-off
effllow
well-off
efflmru
muffler
efflnsu
snuffle
efflosu
souffle
soufflé
efflrru
ruffler
efflrtu
fretful
truffle
effnrsu
snuffer
effnruu
unruffe
effoprr
proffer
effpruy
puffery
effrstu
stuffer
effssuu
suffuse
efggilp
egg-flip

efggirr
frigger
efggiry
figgery
efghirt
fighter
freight
efgilmn
Fleming
efgilnt
felting
efgimnt
figment
efginnp
pfennig
efginor
foreign
efginru
gunfire
efgiorv
forgive
efgirrt
grifter
efglntu
fulgent
efglort
froglet
efgloss
fogless
efgnoor
forgone
efgorru
ferrugo
efgorry
forgery
efgortu
foregut
efhiins
fineish
efhijsw
jewfish
efhilms
Flemish
himself
efhilss
selfish
efhinns
fennish
efhinst
fish-net
net-fish
efhirss
serfish
efhirst
shifter
efhirsy
fishery
efhisuw
huswife
efhllpu
helpful
efhllsy
fleshly

efhlnsu
unflesh
efhloox
foxhole
efhlopu
hopeful
efhlost
elf-shot
efhlrsu
flusher
efhlrsy
freshly
efhlsty
thyself
efhlttw
twelfth
efhnort
forhent
efhrrtu
further
efiilms
misfile
efiilrt
fitlier
efiilry
fierily
efiilss
fissile
efiimrs
misfire
efiinpr
pin-fire
efiinpv
fivepin
efiinru
unifier
efiissv
fissive
efijlly
jellify
efijlor
frijole
efijlot
jetfoil
efikrrs
frisker
efikrst
frisket
efillms
misfell
efilloo
foliole
efillow
low-life
efilluw
wileful
efilmnu
fulmine
efilmot
filemot
efilmss
selfism
efilmst
leftism

efilnox
flexion
efilnss
finless
efiloos
floosie
foliose
efilooz
floozie
efilopr
profile
efilort
trefoil
efilosx
sexfoil
efilovx
fox-evil
efilppr
flipper
efilppu
pipeful
efilpry
pilfery
efilquy
liquefy
efilrrt
trifler
efilrst
stifler
efilrtt
flitter
efilrvv
flivver
efilrzz
frizzle
efilsst
selfist
efilstt
leftist
efiluvx
fluxive
efimmru
fermium
efimnor
fermion
efimntt
fitment
efimost
fomites
efinnor
inferno
efinnos
no-fines
efinnsu
funnies
efinopr
forpine
efinrst
snifter
efinrsu
infuser
efinruy
reunify

efinsst
fitness
efioprr
porifer
efioprt
firepot
efiorrt
rotifer
efiorst
foister
forties
efipprr
fripper
efiprty
petrify
efirrru
furrier
efirrtt
fritter
efirrty
terrify
efirssu
fissure
efirstu
surfeit
efirstw
swifter
efirsvy
versify
efirttu
turfite
efirtuv
furtive
efirtux
fixture
efistty
testify
efjlstu
jestful
efklmno
menfolk
efklmor
merfolk
efklnuy
flunkey
efklopu
pokeful
efklpsu
skepful
efllstu
fullest
eflmosu
fulsome
eflmpru
frumple
eflmsuu
museful
eflnort
forlent
eflnoru
fleuron
eflnorw
fern-owl
eflnory
felonry
eflnott
fletton
fontlet
eflnssu
fulness
eflnttu
tentful
eflntuu
tuneful
efloorr
floorer
efloors
forsloe
efloory
foolery
efloorz
foozler
eflorsu
ourself
eflortt
fortlet
eflortw
felwort
eflorvy
flyover
overfly
eflorww
werwolf
eflorwy
flowery
rye-wolf
eflpruy
preyful
eflpstu
pestful
eflrstu
fluster
restful
eflrttu
flutter
eflstty
test-fly
eflstuz
zestful
efmnoot
footmen
efmoorz
zoeform
efmoprr
perform
preform
efmoprt
pomfret
efmpruy
perfumy
efmrtuy
furmety
efnnort
fornent
efnnotu
unoften
efnoost
festoon
efnoott
ten-foot
efnorru
forerun
efnortu
fortune
efnortw
forwent
efooprr
reproof
efooprs
spoofer
efooprt
foretop
poofter
efoppry
foppery
efoprss
profess
efoprsu
profuse
efoprtu
poufter
efoprty
torpefy
eforrsu
ferrous
eforrty
torrefy
eforruv
fervour
eforssu
fourses
efprtuy
putrefy
efpstuy
stupefy
eggsiln
legging
egggilr
giggler
eggginp
pegging
eggglor
goggler
egghilr
higgler
egghirt
thigger
egghory
hoggery
eggiips
piggies
eggilln
gelling
eggilms
leggism
eggilnr
niggler
eggilns
sniggle
eggilnu
lugeing
eggilrw
wiggler
wriggle
eggimmn
gemming
egginns
ginseng
egginrs
snigger
egginry
gingery
niggery
eggintt
getting
eggintw
twiggen
eggiprr
prigger
eggipry
piggery
eggirrt
trigger
eggirsw
swigger
eggirtw
twigger
eggirwy
wiggery
eggjlru
juggler
eggllno
long-leg
egglmpu
egg-plum
egglmsu
smuggle
egglnsu
snuggle
egglooy
geology
egglors
slogger
egglpru
plugger
egglrsu
slugger
eggnooy
geogony
eggntuy
nuggety
eggorry
gregory
eggorty
toggery
eggpruy
puggery
eggsstu
suggest
eghhhio
heigh-ho
eghhimn
highmen
eghhirs
Highers
eghhist
highest
high-set
eghiill
ghillie
eghiint
nightie
eghiinv
inveigh
eghiinw
weigh-in
eghiknr
gherkin
eghikrs
skreigh
skriegh
eghilnp
helping
eghilnr
herling
eghilns
English
shingle
eghilnt
enlight
lighten
eghilpt
pightle
eghilrt
lighter
relight
eghilst
sleight
eghimmn
hemming
eghimns
meshing
eghimpt
empight
eghinnu
unhinge
eghinos
shoeing
eghinrr
herring
eghinrt
righten
eghinrw
whinger
eghintt
tighten
eghiors
ogreish
eghioru
roughie
eghiott
göthite
eghiotu
toughie
eghiotv
eightvo
eghirrt
righter
eghirst
sighter
eghirsy
greyish
eghitwy
weighty
eghlmpy
phlegmy
eghlnor
leghorn
eghlnty
lengthy
eghloos
shoogle
eghlosw
leg-show
eghmnou
humogen
eghmosu
gumshoe
eghnoos
hog-nose
eghnoru
enrough
roughen
eghnotu
toughen
eghorru
rougher
eghosuu
hugeous
eghrtuy
theurgy
egiilmt
legitim
egiilnt
lignite
egiilnv
veiling
egiimnp
impinge
egiimrs
Isegrim
egiimsv
misgive
egiinns
insigne
seining
egiinnv
veining
egiinop
epigoni
egiinps
pigsnie
egiinrt
igniter
tigrine
egiinsz
seizing
egiinuv
Iguvine

egiinvw
viewing
egiiprw
periwig
egijknr
jerking
egijlnr
jingler
egijlnt
jinglet
egijnst
jesting
egikllm
milk-leg
egiklnr
erl-king
egiklnt
kinglet
egikmnp
kemping
egiknnn
kenning
egiknry
key-ring
egillno
logline
egillnt
telling
egillnw
welling
egillny
yelling
egillps
leg-slip
egillsu
gullies
egilmmn
lemming
egilmmr
glimmer
egilmnr
gremlin
merling
mingler
egilmnt
melting
egilmnu
legumin
egilmor
gomeril
egilmos
semilog
egilmou
elogium
egilmps
glimpse
egilnor
leg-iron
egilnos
sloe-gin
egilnot
lentigo
egilnpr
pingler

egilnps
leg-spin
spignel
egilnpt
pelting
egilnpy
yelping
egilnrs
slinger
egilnrt
ringlet
tingler
tringle
egilnry
relying
egilnst
glisten
singlet
egilnsw
swingle
egilntt
letting
egilntw
winglet
egilnvy
levying
egiloos
goolies
egilorr
Grolier
egilost
elogist
egilppr
gripple
egilrst
glister
gristle
egilrtt
glitter
egilrty
tigerly
egilruv
virgule
egilrzz
grizzle
egilssw
wigless
egimmtu
gummite
egimnos
misgone
egimnpr
impregn
egimnpt
pigment
egimntu
time-gun
egimost
egotism
eginnnp
penning
eginnop
opening

eginnpu
penguin
eginnrt
ringent
eginnry
ginnery
renying
eginnss
sensing
eginnsu
ensuing
eginntt
netting
tenting
eginntv
venting
eginnvy
envying
eginopr
perigon
eginops
epigons
eginorr
ignorer
eginors
Signore
eginort
genitor
Negrito
eginosu
igneous
eginosw
ingowes
eginosy
isogeny
eginott
tentigo
eginprs
springe
eginpsy
espying
pigsney
eginptt
petting
eginpyy
epigyny
eginquu
queuing
eginrrw
wringer
eginrss
ingress
eginrst
resting
stinger
eginrsu
signeur
eginrsv
serving
versing
eginrsw
swinger
eginrsy
syringe

eginrtt
gittern
retting
eginrvv
revving
eginrvy
revying
eginstt
setting
testing
eginstv
vesting
eginstw
stewing
westing
eginttv
vetting
eginttw
wetting
egioprs
serpigo
egioprt
ego-trip
egiopru
groupie
egiortv
vertigo
egiortz
zorgite
egiostt
egotist
egiotuv
outgive
egipprr
gripper
egipruu
guipure
egirsst
Striges
tigress
egklorw
legwork
eglllpu
leg-pull
egllruy
gullery
egllsuy
gulleys
eglmnoo
engloom
eglmnor
mongrel
eglmoor
legroom
eglnooy
neology
eglnoru
lounger
eglnost
longest
eglnouv
unglove

eglnoxy
loxygen
xylogen
eglnoyz
lozengy
eglnpru
plunger
eglnrtu
gruntle
egloosy
gooleys
egloptu
glue-pot
eglorrw
growler
eglorss
glosser
eglprsu
splurge
eglrsuu
regulus
eglrsyy
grysely
eglsstu
gutless
eglstuu
gluteus
egmmort
grommet
egmmrtu
grummet
egmnoru
murgeon
egmnory
mongery
egmnost
emongst
egmnoyz
zymogen
egmorsu
grumose
egmortu
gourmet
egnnort
röntgen
egnnptu
pungent
egnnruy
gunnery
egnntuu
unguent
egnoory
orogeny
egnootu
outgone
egnooyz
zoogeny
egnoprs
sponger
egnopry
progeny
pyrogen
egnopsu
pug-nose

egnorrw
wronger
egnorss
engross
egnorsu
surgeon
egnrrtu
grunter
egnrstu
surgent
egnrsyy
synergy
egnrttu
grutten
turgent
egoorsy
goosery
egoortu
outgoer
egoprru
grouper
regroup
egopruy
guy-rope
egorrst
grosert
egorrsu
grouser
egorruy
roguery
egprsuu
upsurge
egrrsuy
surgery
ehhills
hellish
ehhimrs
Rhemish
ehhinrs
Rhenish
ehhiprs
hership
ehhirtt
thither
ehhirtw
whither
ehhiswy
wheyish
ehiiltt
lithite
ehiinrt
inherit
ehiinrz
rhizine
ehiirrs
Irisher
ehiirst
hirstie
ehiittt
Hittite
ehijnno
johnnie
ehikmnt
methink

ehiknrs
 kernish
ehiknrt
 rethink
 thinker
ehiknst
 Kentish
ehikrrs
 shirker
ehikrsw
 whisker
ehikstw
 whisket
ehikswy
 whiskey
ehillmn
 hillmen
ehillno
 hellion
ehillns
 inshell
ehillrs
 rellish
ehillrt
 thiller
ehillty
 lithely
ehilmpw
 whimple
ehilmtt
 meltith
ehilmuw
 umwhile
ehilnop
 pinhole
ehilnot
 neolith
ehilnps
 plenish
ehilopt
 hoplite
ehilost
 Elohist
 hostile
ehilprt
 philter
 philtre
ehilrrw
 whirler
ehilrst
 slither
ehilrsv
 shrivel
ehilrtu
 luthier
ehilrtw
 whirtle
ehilstt
 Lettish
 listeth
 thistle
ehilstw
 whistle

ehilttu
 thulite
ehilttw
 whittle
ehiltwy
 whitely
ehimnps
 shipmen
ehimnru
 rhenium
ehimnty
 thymine
ehimors
 heroism
 moreish
ehimorz
 rhizome
ehimprw
 whimper
ehimrst
 Rhemist
ehimrsu
 heurism
ehimrtt
 Thermit®
ehimsty
 mythise
ehimswy
 whimsey
ehinnop
 phone-in
ehinnrt
 thinner
ehinnsw
 wennish
ehinopv
 hop-vine
ehinopx
 Phoenix
ehinors
 inshore
ehinost
 histone
ehinosu
 heinous
 in-house
ehinpps
 shippen
ehinrsv
 shriven
ehinrtv
 thriven
ehinrtw
 writhen
ehinrtz
 zithern
ehinsss
 shiness
ehinsst
 sithens
ehiopps
 pie-shop
ehioprs
 rose-hip

ehiopst
 ethiops
 Peshito
ehiorrt
 heritor
ehiorst
 shortie
ehiorsy
 hosiery
ehiortt
 thorite
ehiortu
 outhire
 routhie
ehiortv
 overhit
ehiosty
 isohyet
ehipprs
 shipper
ehipprw
 whipper
ehipptw
 whippet
ehiprst
 hipster
ehiprsw
 whisper
ehipstt
 pettish
ehirrss
 sherris
ehirrsv
 shriver
ehirrtv
 thriver
ehirrtw
 whirret
ehirssw
 swisher
ehirstu
 hirsute
ehirstw
 swither
 withers
ehirsvy
 shivery
ehirttw
 whitret
ehirwzz
 whizzer
ehisstu
 Hussite
ehisttw
 wettish
ehjmnos
 Mes-John
ehkmoos
 smoke-ho
ehknrsu
 hunkers
ehllnsu
 unshell

ehlmmow
 whommle
ehlmmuw
 whummle
ehlmnot
 menthol
ehlmnoy
 homelyn
ehlnort
 hornlet
ehlntty
 tenthly
ehloopp
 hop-pole
ehloopt
 pothole
 top-hole
ehlopsy
 spy-hole
ehlorst
 holster
 hostler
ehlorty
 helotry
ehlostt
 shottle
ehlosty
 thylose
ehlrstu
 hustler
ehlsttu
 shuttle
ehmnoor
 hormone
 moorhen
ehmnpty
 nymphet
ehmnttu
 hutment
ehmooss
 shmoose
ehmoost
 smoothe
ehmoosw
 somehow
ehmoprw
 morphew
ehmorst
 smother
 thermos
ehmortu
 mouther
ehmorty
 mothery
ehmoswy
 somewhy
ehmprtu
 thumper
ehmrrtu
 murther
ehmrsuu
 humerus
ehnnoor
 non-hero

ehnnopr
 nephron
ehnnopy
 hypnone
ehnnstu
 unshent
ehnnsuw
 unshewn
ehnoopr
 no-hoper
ehnoors
 onshore
 sorehon
ehnoost
 one-shot
ehnopry
 hyperon
ehnopuy
 euphony
ehnorrt
 horrent
 norther
ehnorry
 heronry
ehnorst
 shorten
 threnos
ehnorsu
 unhorse
ehnosst
 hotness
ehnostt
 shotten
ehnosty
 honesty
ehnosuu
 unhouse
ehnrstu
 shunter
ehnrtwy
 wrythen
ehnsssy
 shyness
ehooprw
 whooper
ehoopty
 oophyte
ehoorst
 shooter
 soother
ehopprs
 shopper
ehopprt
 prophet
ehopprw
 whopper
ehoprry
 orphrey
ehoprst
 strophe
ehoprsu
 Orpheus
ehoprtu
 pouther

ehoprty
 pothery
ehopruy
 euphory
ehorrtw
 thrower
ehorstu
 shouter
 souther
ehorswy
 showery
ehossst
 hostess
ehotttw
 wotteth
ehprttu
 turpeth
ehrssty
 shyster
ehrsttu
 shutter
ehrsttw
 'strewth
ehrstuy
 tushery
ehrttty
 thretty
eiiilst
 ileitis
eiiklms
 mislike
eiiklps
 pliskie
eiiknns
 niks-nie
eiiknss
 kinesis
eiillmm
 millime
eiillnv
 villein
eiillsw
 willies
eiilltt
 tillite
eiilltv
 vitelli
eiilmnv
 milvine
eiilmpr
 imperil
eiilmrs
 milreis
eiilmrt
 limiter
eiilmss
 missile
eiilmst
 elitism
 limites
eiilmsv
 mislive
eiilmux
 milieux

eiilnos
elision
isoline
lionise
eiilnot
etiolin
eiilnov
olivine
eiilnrt
nitrile
eiilorv
rilievo
eiilpst
spilite
eiilqsu
silique
eiilstt
elitist
eiilstu
utilise
eiiltuy
tuilyie
eiiltuz
tuilzie
eiiltxy
exility
eiimmss
mimesis
eiimmst
mistime
eiimnpr
primine
eiimnrt
interim
termini
eiimnrv
miniver
eiimntv
minivet
eiimnty
nimiety
eiimoss
meiosis
eiimprs
pismire
primsie
eiimpst
pietism
eiimpty
impiety
eiimssv
missive
eiinnnp
nine-pin
eiinnqu
quinine
eiinnsw
insinew
eiinntv
invenit
eiinntw
intwine
eiinopr
ripieno

eiinops
pionies
eiinors
ironise
eiinprs
inspire
eiinqru
inquire
eiinqtu
inquiet
eiinrtt
nitrite
eiinrtv
inviter
vitrine
eiinrtw
write-in
eiinsst
Sistine
eiinstt
sittine
tiniest
eiinstu
unitise
eiintuv
unitive
eiiorst
riotise
eiiostz
zoisite
eiipprr
rippier
eiipstt
pietist
eiipttt
pittite
eiipttu
pituite
eiirstv
revisit
eiisstx
sixties
eiistuv
uveitis
eijknns
Jenkins
eijknpr
perjink
prejink
eijllny
injelly
eijnort
jointer
eijnory
joinery
eijnpru
juniper
eijnrru
injurer
eijprtu
Jupiter
eijrstt
jitters

eijrtty
jittery
eijssuv
jussive
eikklnr
klinker
eikknrs
skinker
eikllnw
inkwell
eikllst
skillet
eiklmnr
kremlin
eiklnrs
slinker
eiklnrt
tinkler
eiklnrw
wrinkle
eiklnss
kinless
eiklnst
lentisk
eiklnsu
sunlike
eiklnsy
skyline
eiklntt
knittle
eiklntw
twinkle
eiklpry
perkily
eiklpsy
peskily
eiklstt
skittle
eikmmrr
krimmer
eikmmrs
skimmer
eikmnor
moniker
eikmors
irksome
eikmosy
misyoke
eikmrss
kirmess
eiknnrs
skinner
eiknoor
rooinek
eiknoss
kenosis
eiknpsu
spunkie
eiknrst
stinker
eiknrtt
knitter
trinket

eikntty
kitteny
eikoppr
pork-pie
eikosst
ketosis
eikpprs
skipper
eikppst
skippet
eikpsss
skepsis
eikrrst
skirret
skirter
striker
eikrstt
skitter
eikrstu
turkies
eilllow
oil-well
eillmnu
mullein
eillmot
melilot
eillmou
mouillé
eillmst
mistell
eillnnp
pennill
eillnss
illness
eillorz
zorille
eillosv
villose
eillprs
spiller
eillpss
lipless
eillqtu
quillet
eillrst
stiller
trellis
eillrsw
swiller
eillrsy
Sillery
eillstw
willest
eilmmno
molimen
eilmmrs
slimmer
eilmnsu
emulsin
eilmopr
implore
eilmorr
lorimer

eilmory
Lyomeri
eilmoss
lissome
eilmppu
plumpie
eilmprs
prelims
simpler
eilmpry
primely
eilmpsu
impulse
eilmpsx
simplex
eilmrry
merrily
eilmrss
rimless
eilmrsu
misrule
eilmrsy
miserly
eilmssy
messily
eilmsuy
Elysium
eilmuuv
eluvium
eilnnpu
pinnule
eilnoop
polonie
eilnoov
violone
eilnopp
plenipo
eilnops
epsilon
eilnopt
pointel
pontile
top-line
eilnorr
loriner
eilnort
retinol
eilnoss
lioness
eilnosu
elusion
eilnotu
elution
line-out
outline
eilnotv
violent
eilnotw
towline
two-line
eilnovv
involve
eilnprs
Pilsner

eilnpru
purline
eilnpst
plenist
eilnpsu
spinule
eilnpty
ineptly
eilnpuv
vulpine
eilnrst
snirtle
eilnrsv
silvern
eilnrty
inertly
eilnsss
sinless
eilnssu
insulse
silenus
eilnstu
utensil
eilnstw
westlin
eilnsvy
sylvine
eilnvxy
vixenly
eiloort
troolie
eiloost
ostiole
stoolie
eilootz
zoolite
eiloprs
spoiler
eiloprt
poitrel
eilopst
pistole
eilopsv
plosive
eiloptt
plottie
eiloptx
exploit
eilorss
rissole
eilorsu
soilure
eilorsw
low-rise
eilortt
tortile
triolet
eilortu
outlier
eilostt
litotes
eilotuv
outlive

eilpprr
rippler
eilpprs
slipper
eilpprt
ripplet
tippler
tripple
eilppss
pipless
eilppst
stipple
eilppsw
swipple
eilprst
spirtle
eilprtt
triplet
eilprtx
triplex
eilpruu
purlieu
eilpstt
spittle
eilpstu
stipule
eilpsuy
spulyie
eilpsuz
spulzie
eilptty
pettily
eilqrtu
quilter
eilqruu
liqueur
eilqtuy
quietly
eilrrtw
twirler
eilrstt
slitter
stilter
testril
eilrsuw
wurlies
eilrsvy
silvery
eilrszz
sizzler
eilrtty
littery
tritely
eilrtuv
rivulet
eilsstw
witless
eilssty
stylise
eilstty
stylite
testily
eilstvy
sylvite

eilswzz
swizzle
eimmpru
premium
eimmrrt
trimmer
eimmrst
misterm
eimmrsw
swimmer
eimmstz
tzimmes
eimnnot
mention
eimnoor
ionomer
eimnoos
Moonies
noisome
eimnoot
emotion
eimnoox
exomion
eimnops
peonism
pi-meson
eimnopt
emption
pimento
eimnors
merinos
mersion
eimnost
moisten
eimnosw
Owenism
winsome
eimnotu
mountie
eimnoty
omneity
omniety
eimnptu
pinetum
eimnrru
murrine
eimnrst
entrism
minster
eimnrvy
verminy
eimnsss
sensism
eimnsst
mess-tin
missent
eimnstu
mistune
eimnstw
miswent
eimnuzz
muezzin
eimoppr
pompier

eimoprr
primero
eimoprs
imposer
promise
eimoprv
improve
eimorst
erotism
mortise
eimorsv
verismo
eimortt
omitter
eimostu
timeous
eimostz
mestizo
eimottu
time-out
eimottw
two-time
eimprru
primeur
eimprss
impress
Persism
premiss
eimprst
imprest
eimprtu
imputer
eimpsst
misstep
eimpstu
impetus
eimqstu
mesquit
eimrssu
misuser
surmise
eimrstt
metrist
eimrsty
mistery
smytrie
eimrttu
rut-time
eimrtuv
vitreum
eimrtux
mixture
einnops
pension
einnoqu
quinone
einnort
intoner
ternion
einnoru
reunion
einnorv
environ

einnost
Sonnite
tension
einnosv
venison
einnott
tontine
einnovw
inwoven
einnprs
spinner
einnprt
enprint
einnpst
spinnet
tenpins
einnpsy
spinney
einnptt
tent-pin
einnptu
nut-pine
einnrsu
unrisen
einnrtv
vintner
einnruv
unriven
einnssy
sinsyne
einnstu
Sunnite
einnsuw
unsinew
einntuw
untwine
einoopz
epizoon
einoorr
iron-ore
einoors
erosion
einoost
isotone
einoosz
ozonise
einootz
zoonite
einoppr
poperin
propine
einoprr
roper-in
einoprt
pointer
protein
pterion
repoint
einoprv
provine
einopss
spinose
einoqux
equinox

einorst
tersion
triones
einorsv
version
einortt
tritone
einortu
routine
einortz
trizone
einosss
session
einosst
sonties
einossu
sinuose
einostw
Owenist
einosuv
envious
niveous
veinous
einottt
totient
einottv
oven-tit
einpprs
snipper
einppst
snippet
einprrt
printer
reprint
einprsu
uprisen
einprtx
Pinxter
einpstt
spitten
einpstu
puniest
einptty
tintype
einqruy
enquiry
einqstu
inquest
einqttu
quintet
einqtuu
unquiet
einrrsu
insurer
einrssu
sunrise
einrstt
entrist
stinter
einrstv
striven
einrsty
sintery

einrswy
swinery
einrttw
twinter
wren-tit
written
einrtuv
unrivet
venturi
einrtuw
unwrite
einrtwy
wintery
einssst
sensist
einsssu
Senussi
einsssy
synesis
einsstw
witness
einssuw
sunwise
einsttw
entwist
twin-set
einstty
tensity
eintttw
twitten
einttuy
tenuity
eioopst
isotope
eioortv
Orvieto
eioostt
tootsie
eioprrt
pierrot
eioprst
periost
reposit
riposte
eioprsx
Siporex
eioprtv
pivoter
eiopsst
sepiost
eiopstu
piteous
eiopsty
isotype
eioqrtu
quoiter
eiorrrs
sorrier
eiorrrw
worrier
eiorrst
roister
eiorrsv
revisor

eiorrvv
revivor
eiorsst
sorites
eiorssu
serious
eiorssx
xerosis
eiorstt
stoiter
eiorstv
torsive
eiorttv
tortive
viretot
eiortuv
voiture
eiosstv
stovies
eiosttu
toustie
eiostuz
outsize
eipprrt
tripper
eipprtt
trippet
eiprrty
tripery
eiprruv
upriver
eiprsst
persist
stirpes
stripes
eiprssu
suspire
eiprstt
spitter
tipster
eiprsty
pyrites
stripey
eiprsuu
euripus
eiprttu
puttier
eiprtuw
write-up
eipruvw
purview
eiqrstu
querist
eiqrttu
quitter
eiqruzz
quizzer
eiqstuu
quietus
eiqsuzz
quizzes
eirrrst
stirrer

eirrstv
striver
eirsstv
treviss
eirsttw
twister
eirstwz
Switzer
eirsuvv
survive
eirsuvw
surview
eirtttw
twitter
eisstuv
tussive
ejjmnuu
jejunum
ejjmptu
jump-jet
ejkoory
jookery
ejkoruy
joukery
ejlossy
joyless
ejmnruy
jurymen
ejnorru
rejourn
ejnoruy
journey
ejoorvy
overjoy
ejopprt
prop-jet
ejosttu
outjest
ejprruy
perjury
ekklooy
olykoek
ekklrsu
skulker
ekllmsu
skellum
eklnopr
plonker
eklnors
snorkel
eklnpru
plunker
eklootw
wet-look
eklsttu
skuttle
ekmmors
Kommers
ekmmrsu
skummer
ekmnory
monkery
ekmnptu
unkempt

eknoors
snooker
eknopsu
unspoke
eknorst
stonker
eknortt
knotter
eknortw
network
eknoruy
younker
eknorwy
ywroken
eknrtuy
turnkey
ekooprv
provoke
ekoorry
rookery
ekoorst
stooker
ekoppsu
upspoke
ekorrst
stroker
ekppsuu
seppuku
ekpstuw
skew-put
ekrsstu
Turkess
elllorr
lorrell
ellmnoo
moellon
ellmoor
morello
ellmowy
mellowy
ellmpuu
plumule
ellnoow
woollen
ellnopt
pollent
ellnosu
nousell
ellnosw
swollen
ellnoww
well-won
ellnoxy
xylenol
ellnpsu
unspell
elloosw
woosell
elloosy
loosely
elloprr
proller
elloptu
pollute

ellorrt
troller
ellorry
rye-roll
ellorty
trolley
ellorvy
loverly
ellostu
outsell
sell-out
ellottu
outtell
ellotuw
outwell
ellovwy
vowelly
ellowyy
yellowy
ellpsuw
upswell
elmmort
trommel
elmmptu
plummet
elmmrsu
slummer
elmmstu
stummel
elmnotu
moulten
elmnppu
plumpen
elmnpuu
unplume
elmoopp
pompelo
elmoort
tremolo
elmopry
polymer
elmopsu
plumose
elmorsu
emulsor
elmosuu
emulous
elmppru
plumper
elmpruy
plumery
elmrtuu
multure
elmrtuy
elytrum
elmruzz
muzzler
elmsssu
sumless
elnoosu
unloose
elnoosz
snoozle

elnopru
pleuron
elnopry
pronely
elnoptu
opulent
elnorsu
noursle
elnorty
elytron
elnosss
sonless
elnossw
lowness
elnostu
lentous
elnostv
solvent
elnotuz
zonulet
elnotvy
novelty
elnrsty
sternly
elnsssu
sunless
elnsssy
slyness
elnsuzz
snuzzle
elooprs
spooler
eloortt
rootlet
eloostu
outsole
elooswy
woolsey
eloppst
stopple
eloppsy
polypes
elopprru
prouler
eloprrw
prowler
eloprss
plessor
eloprsu
leprous
pelorus
perlous
sporule
eloprsy
leprosy
eloprtt
plotter
eloprtu
plouter
poulter
eloprtw
plowter
eloprty
protyle

eloprvy
overply
plovery
elopsst
topless
elorstt
settlor
slotter
elorsuv
velours
elorsuy
elusory
elortty
lottery
elortvy
overtly
elossty
systole
tyloses
elostuu
luteous
elprstu
spurtle
elprtuu
pulture
elpruzz
puzzler
elpstuu
pluteus
pustule
elrrstu
rustler
elrrttu
turtler
elrsstu
lustres
elrstuy
sutlery
elrstwy
sweltry
elrttuy
utterly
elrtuuv
vulture
elsstyy
systyle
emmmruy
mummery
emmnoor
monomer
emmnosu
mu-meson
emmnotu
omentum
emmnoty
metonym
emmoprr
prommer
emnnoor
moneron
emnnort
non-term
emnnoww
new-mown

emnoopt
  metopon
emnoort
  montero
emnoost
  moonset
emnoosy
  noysome
emnooty
  enomoty
emnorru
  mourner
emnorst
  monster
emnortt
  torment
emnortu
  monture
  mounter
  remount
emnosst
  stemson
emnostu
  unsmote
emnrstu
  sternum
emooprt
  promote
emoopry
  pomeroy
emoorry
  Moorery
emoorss
  Mooress
emoorsu
  urosome
emoostt
  mottoes
emoostw
  twosome
emoosty
  myosote
  toysome
emootuv
  outmove
emopptu
  up-tempo
emoprsu
  supremo
emorrsu
  morsure
emorrwy
  wormery
emorssu
  smouser
emorstu
  oestrum
emorsuy
  mousery
emostvz
  zemstvo
emprstu
  stumper
  sumpter
emprttu
  trumpet
emrstyy
  mystery
ennnruy
  nunnery
ennoott
  nonetto
ennorst
  stonern
ennorsu
  non-user
ennortu
  neutron
ennostu
  neuston
ennouvw
  unwoven
ennpstu
  unspent
ennrstu
  stunner
ennttuy
  untenty
enooppr
  propone
enooprs
  snooper
enoopsy
  spooney
enoorsu
  onerous
enoorsz
  snoozer
enoortt
  to-torne
enoortw
  to-worne
enoorww
  woeworn
enoostt
  testoon
enoostu
  unsoote
enoottw
  two-tone
enootxy
  oxytone
enoprru
  proneur
enoprst
  postern
enoprtt
  portent
enoprty
  entropy
enopsst
  stepson
enopsux
  Xenopus
enoqtuu
  unquote
enorrst
  snorter
enorrtt
  torrent
enorruv
  overrun
enorssy
  sensory
enorstt
  snotter
  stentor
enorstu
  tonsure
enorstw
  nor'-west
enorsty
  tyrones
enorsuv
  nervous
enortuy
  tourney
enosstt
  Stetson
enosstu
  outness
enosstw
  twoness
enosttu
  stouten
enostuu
  tenuous
enostuy
  yu-stone
enottuw
  outwent
enprrsu
  spurner
enprstu
  punster
enprsuu
  unpurse
enpsttu
  stupent
enpstuw
  unswept
enrrsuy
  nursery
enrrtuu
  nurture
enrrtuy
  turnery
enrsswy
  wryness
enrsttu
  entrust
enrsuux
  Xenurus
eoooprs
  oospore
eoopprs
  opposer
  propose
eoopprv
  popover
eooprrs
  spoorer
eooprrt
  trooper
eooprst
  stooper
eooprtu
  outrope
eooprtv
  overtop
eooprtw
  towrope
eooprvy
  poovery
eoopryz
  zoopery
eooptyz
  zootype
eoorrst
  rooster
eoorsvw
  oversow
eoortuv
  out-over
eoortuw
  out-owre
eoosssu
  osseous
eoottuv
  outvote
eopprrs
  prosper
eopprss
  oppress
eopprst
  stopper
eopprsu
  purpose
eopprsw
  swopper
eoppssu
  suppose
eoprrst
  sporter
eoprrtu
  trouper
eoprsst
  portess
eoprssw
  prowess
eoprstt
  protest
  spotter
eoprstu
  petrous
  posture
  proteus
  septuor
  spouter
eoprstw
  prowest
eoprsuu
  uprouse
eoprtty
  pottery
eoprtuy
  eutropy
eoprtvy
  poverty
eopssss
  possess
eopsttu
  outstep
eopsttw
  stewpot
  two-step
eoqrstu
  questor
eorrstu
  rouster
eorrstw
  strower
eorrsty
  royster
eorrttt
  trotter
eorrttu
  torture
  trouter
eorsstu
  oestrus
  tussore
eorsttt
  stotter
  stretto
eorsttw
  swotter
eorstty
  rosetty
eorstux
  sextuor
eorttty
  tottery
eostttw
  wottest
epprrtu
  prerupt
epprruu
  purpure
epprssu
  press-up
eppstuw
  upswept
eprrrsu
  spurrer
eprrsuu
  pursuer
  usurper
eprrsuy
  spurrey
eprrtuu
  rupture
eprssty
  spryest
eprsttu
  sputter
errsstu
  trusser
errsttu
  truster
errstty
  tryster
ersssuu
  usuress
erssttu
  tutress
ersstuy
  russety
erstttu
  stutter
fffilot
  lift-off
ffgiinr
  griffin
ffgiint
  tiffing
ffginor
  griffon
ffginpu
  puffing
ffglnoo
  long-off
ffglruy
  gruffly
ffhhisu
  huffish
ffhiisy
  fishify
ffhilsu
  fishful
ffhilty
  fifthly
ffhiluy
  huffily
ffhiost
  toffish
ffhoosw
  show-off
ffhopsu
  push-off
ffiisuz
  ziffius
ffilpuy
  puffily
ffilrty
  frit-fly
ffilstu
  fistful
ffilsty
  stiffly
ffinops
  spin-off
ffinopt
  pontiff
ffiorty
  fortify
ffiqsuy
  squiffy
ffjmopu
  jump-off
fflloou
  loofful

fflloouz
zuffolo
ffnortu
turnoff
turn-off
ffoopst
stop-off
fgggiin
figging
fgghiis
fishgig
fggiizz
fizzgig
fggilno
golfing
fggiloy
foggily
fgginor
forging
fghhios
hog-fish
fghiins
fishing
fghiips
pig-fish
fghilsu
sighful
fghilty
flighty
fghiosy
fogyish
fghnoor
foghorn
fghoruy
froughy
fghotuy
foughty
fgiilln
filling
fgiilno
foiling
fgiilnr
rifling
fgiilny
lignify
fgiinrr
firring
fgiinry
nigrify
fgiinst
sifting
fgiinsy
signify
fgiintt
fitting
fgiinzz
fizzing
gin-fizz
fgilnoo
fooling
fgilnop
fopling

fgilnow
flowing
fowling
wolfing
fgilntu
fluting
fgilnty
flyting
fgilooy
goofily
fgilory
glorify
fgimnor
forming
fgimosy
fogyism
fginnnu
funning
fginoor
roofing
fginoot
footing
fginrru
furring
fginrsu
surfing
fginrtu
turfing
fginttu
tufting
fgiortw
figwort
fgistuu
fuguist
fgjlsuu
jugfuls
fglmsuu
mugfuls
fglnoru
furlong
fglnosu
songful
fglnpuu
upflung
fgloouy
ufology
fgloruu
fulgour
fglotuy
goutfly
fglstuu
gustful
fgnooru
fourgon
fgnosuu
fungous
fhiilms
filmish
fhiilos
fish-oil
fhiinns
Finnish
fhiinps
pinfish

fhillsu
fullish
fhiloos
foolish
fhilosw
wolfish
fhilpsu
shipful
fhilptu
pithful
fhilsuw
wishful
fhinosu
fushion
fhinrsu
furnish
fhinssu
sun-fish
fhioopr
hip-roof
fhioost
ooftish
fhiopps
foppish
fhiopsx
foxship
fhiorry
horrify
fhiosst
softish
fhippsu
pupfish
fhirtty
thrifty
fhirtuy
thurify
fhkortu
futhork
fhllotu
full-hot
fhlnoru
hornful
fhlnsuu
unflush
fhlopsu
shopful
fhlpsuu
pushful
fhlrtuu
hurtful
ruthful
fhnotux
fox-hunt
fhooort
hoof-rot
fhooott
hotfoot
fiiiknn
finikin
fiiklst
ski-lift
fiiknyz
zinkify

fiillmo
milfoil
fiilnot
tinfoil
fiilptu
pitiful
fiimssu
Sufiism
fiinoss
fission
fiinrty
nitrify
fiipsty
tipsify
fiirtvy
vitrify
fijlloy
jollify
fijstuy
justify
fikklno
kinfolk
fikllsu
skilful
fiklnow
wolfkin
fiklnsu
skinful
fiklrsu
riskful
fiknnos
finnsko
fillmoy
mollify
fillnuy
nullify
fillotu
toilful
filloty
loftily
fillstu
listful
filmnoo
monofil
filmstu
mistful
filnnuy
funnily
filnoux
fluxion
filnstu
tinfuls
filntuy
unfitly
filootw
witloof
filorst
florist
filortu
floruit
filorty
trifoly
filppuy
pulpify

filrsty
firstly
filryzz
frizzly
filssuy
fussily
filsttu
flutist
filstuw
wistful
filstwy
swiftly
filuyzz
fuzzily
fimmmuy
mummify
fimmors
misform
fimnoru
uniform
fimoorv
oviform
fimorrt
triform
fimorty
mortify
fimrtuy
furmity
fimstyy
mystify
finopty
pontify
finorss
frisson
fioorsu
furioso
fioostx
six-foot
fiopstx
postfix
fiorsuu
furious
firrsty
stir-fry
firssuy
Russify
fklnoor
Norfolk
fkloruw
workful
fkooors
forsook
flloptu
plotful
topfull
fllosuu
soulful
flloswy
fly-slow
fllotuu
full-out
fllouwy
wofully

fllstuu
lustful
flmmoux
flummox
flmnoou
mouflon
flmooot
tomfool
flmooru
roomful
flnoorr
forlorn
flnoswy
snow-fly
floorsw
forslow
flootuw
outflow
flopstu
potfuls
flosuuv
fulvous
fmrstuu
frustum
fnnnuuy
unfunny
fnnoort
fronton
fnooott
foot-ton
fnoorrw
forworn
fnoorsu
sun-roof
fooprt
roof-top
fooortt
footrot
foootttu
outfoot
foottw
two-foot
foorttx
fox-trot
foortuw
two-four
fopsstu
fuss-pot
forruwy
furrowy
forstwy
frowsty
ggghino
hogging
ggghinu
hugging
gggiijn
jigging
gggiinp
pigging
gggiinr
rigging
gggiinw
wigging

7 GGG

gggijno
jogging
gggijnu
jugging
gggilno
logging
gggilnu
lugging
gggimnu
mugging
ggginno
nogging
ggginos
sogging
ggginpu
pugging
ggginru
rugging
gggintu
tugging
gghhios
hoggish
gghiijs
jiggish
gghiinn
hinging
gghiins
sighing
gghiips
piggish
gghiirs
riggish
gghiitt
thiggit
gghimsu
muggish
gghinsu
gushing
gghipsu
puggish
ggiiiln
gingili
ggiilnp
pigling
ggiilnr
rigling
ggiinnn
ginning
ggiinno
ingoing
ggiinnr
ringing
ggiinns
singing
ggiinnt
tinging
ggiinpr
griping
ggiinrt
ringgit
ggijnsu
juggins
ggilnno
longing
ggilnnu
lunging
ggilnop
long-pig
ggilnos
gosling
ggilnou
Guignol
ggilnow
glowing
ggilnoz
glozing
ggilosy
soggily
ggimmnu
gumming
ggimnsu
muggins
gginnnu
gunning
gginnoo
ongoing
gginopu
upgoing
gginoru
roguing
gginorw
growing
gginpru
purging
gginrst
G-string
gginrsu
surging
gginttu
gutting
ggiprsy
spriggy
ggnoruw
rug-gown
ghhhiis
highish
ghhiksy
sky-high
ghhilow
high-low
ghhiopt
high-top
ghhiort
right-oh
ghhirst
shright
ghhortu
through
ghhottu
thought
ghiiknt
king-hit
ghiilnr
hirling
ghiilrs
girlish
ghiinns
shining
ghiinnt
in-thing
nithing
ghiinnw
whining
ghiinpp
hipping
ghiinss
hissing
ghiinst
insight
ghiinsw
wishing
ghiintt
hitting
tithing
ghiintw
whiting
ghiirst
tigrish
ghiklnu
hulking
ghiknos
hog-skin
ghiknsu
husking
ghillsu
gullish
ghillty
lightly
ghilnos
longish
ghilnow
howling
ghilnru
hurling
ghilnsy
shingly
ghilnty
nightly
ghilops
log-ship
ghilpty
yplight
ghilrty
rightly
ghilsty
sightly
ghiltty
tightly
ghiltwy
wightly
ghimmnu
humming
ghimnny
hymning
ghimnos
gnomish
ghimrsu
simurgh
ghimstt
mightst
ghinnor
horning
ghinnot
nothing
ghinntu
hunting
ghinopp
hopping
ghinops
ginshop
ghinors
horsing
shoring
ghinost
song-hit
ghinosu
housing
ghinosw
showing
ghinott
tonight
ghinpsu
gunship
pushing
ghinrtu
ungirth
unright
ghinstu
unsight
ghinttu
hutting
ghioptu
hip-gout
ghiorsu
roguish
ghiosuv
voguish
ghiprst
spright
ghiprtu
upright
ghipttu
uptight
ghlmooo
homolog
ghlmopu
hog-plum
ghloruy
roughly
ghlosty
ghostly
ghlosuy
sloughy
ghlotuy
toughly
ghmoptu
pug-moth
ghmorsu
sorghum
ghmostu
mugshot
ghnopry
gryphon
ghnoruu
unrough
ghnostu
gunshot
shotgun
ghnotuy
youngth
ghooosw
hoosgow
ghortuw
wrought
ghortuy
yoghurt
ghostuu
outgush
giijnno
joining
giikknr
kirking
giiklln
killing
giiklmn
milking
giiklnn
inkling
giiklnt
kitling
giiknnp
king-pin
pinking
giiknns
sinking
giiknnw
winking
giiknnz
zinking
giiknps
pigskin
giiknrs
griskin
giiknsv
skiving
giillmn
milling
giillno
gillion
giillnt
tilling
giillnw
willing
giillpy
pig-lily
giilmnn
limning
giilmnp
limping
giilmns
smiling
giilmpr
pilgrim
giilmry
grimily
giilnny
inlying
lying-in
giilnor
ligroin
giilnos
soiling
giilnot
toiling
giilnpp
lipping
giilnps
lisping
spiling
giilnst
listing
giilntt
tilting
titling
giilntw
witling
giilost
oligist
giilrst
strigil
giimmnr
rimming
giimnpp
pimping
giimnpr
priming
giimnss
missing
giimnst
misting
giinnnp
pinning
giinnns
innings
sinning
giinnnt
tinning
giinnnw
winning
giinnop
pioning
giinnor
ironing
giinnpp
nipping
giinnps
sniping
giinnpu
pinguin
giinnrs
rinsing
giinnru
ruining
giinnsw
inswing
giinntt
tinting
giinntu
uniting
giinntw
twining

giinopr
pig-iron
giinors
Signior
giinort
rioting
giinppp
pipping
giinppr
ripping
giinpps
sipping
giinppt
tipping
giinptt
pitting
giinpty
pitying
giinqtu
quiting
giinrtw
writing
giinstt
sitting
giinstu
suiting
giinttw
witting
gijmnpu
jumping
gijmppu
pig-jump
gijnott
jotting
gijnttu
jutting
giklnoo
looking
giklnru
lurking
gikmnos
smoking
giknnow
knowing
giknorw
working
giknssy
sky-sign
gillmpu
pug-mill
gillnnu
nulling
gillnoo
long-oil
gillnop
polling
gillnor
rolling
gillnot
tolling
gillnyy
lyingly
gilmnor
morling
gilmnpu
lumping
gilnnoo
looning
gilnnsu
unsling
gilnoop
looping
gilnoot
tooling
gilnopp
lopping
gilnops
sloping
gilnoru
louring
gilnosw
slowing
gilnott
lotting
gilnotu
tung-oil
gilnovw
wolving
gilnowy
yowling
gilnpru
purling
gilnpuy
uplying
gilnstu
singult
gilnvyy
vyingly
giloors
girosol
gilortt
triglot
gilorty
trilogy
gilostt
glottis
gilrsty
gristly
gilrtuy
liturgy
gilryzz
grizzly
gimmmnu
mumming
gimmnsu
summing
gimnnor
morning
gimnntu
munting
gimnoor
mooring
gimnoot
mooting
gimnopp
mopping
gimnoru
rouming
gimnosu
mousing
souming
ginnnoo
nooning
ginnnpu
punning
ginnnru
running
ginnnsu
sunning
ginnntu
tunning
ginnops
spongin
ginnors
snoring
sorning
ginnoru
grunion
ginnorw
ingrown
ginnpru
pruning
ginnrtu
turning
ginnttu
nutting
ginntuv
vingt-un
ginntuy
untying
ginoort
rooting
ginoppp
popping
ginopps
sopping
ginoppt
topping
ginoprs
prosing
ginopru
ingroup
pouring
ginoprv
proving
ginopst
posting
stoping
ginoptt
potting
ginoptu
pouting
ginorst
sorting
ginorsu
rousing
souring
ginorsy
signory
ginortt
rotting
ginortu
routing
touring
ginosss
sossing
ginosst
tossing
ginossu
sousing
ginostt
sotting
ginostu
tousing
ginostv
stoving
ginostw
stowing
ginottt
totting
ginottw
wotting
ginotuw
outwing
ginpppu
pupping
ginppsu
supping
ginprru
purring
ginprsy
springy
ginpsuw
upswing
ginpttu
putting
ginrstu
rusting
ginrsty
stringy
ginrsuu
usuring
ginrttu
rutting
giooprr
porrigo
gioprru
prurigo
giopssy
gossipy
giossyz
zygosis
gjoortt
jog-trot
gllloor
log-roll
glmooor
moorlog
glmooyy
myology
glmoruw
lugworm
glnnoor
lorgnon
glnnsuu
unslung
glnoooy
noology
glnoopr
prolong
glnoopy
polygon
glnorwy
wrongly
glnosuw
sunglow
glnottu
glutton
glnouyy
youngly
glooory
orology
gloooty
otology
glooruy
urology
glorssy
grossly
glprsuy
splurgy
gmmosuu
gummous
gmmpuuw
mugwump
gmnooru
gunroom
gmnoorw
morwong
gmorsuu
grumous
gmortuw
mugwort
gmruyyz
zymurgy
gnnoruw
ungrown
gnnoryy
gyronny
gnnptuu
punt-gun
gnnruuw
unwrung
gnooors
gorsoon
gnoooss
gossoon
gnoooyz
zoogony
gnoopps
pop-song
gnoprtu
gunport
gnopruw
grown-up
upgrown
goortuw
outgrow
hhiipps
hippish
hhiistw
whitish
hhinnsu
Hunnish
hhinors
hornish
hhiopst
hip-shot
hhiorsw
whorish
hhiostt
hottish
hhknoru
Kuh-horn
hhoostt
hotshot
hiijkns
hijinks
hiikmss
Sikhism
hiiknps
kinship
pinkish
hiilmtu
lithium
hiilpst
shilpit
hiilpty
pithily
hiilrtt
trilith
hiimsss
missish
hiimstt
shittim
hiinors
roinish
hiinssw
swinish
hiiorst
histrio
hiipsuz
Ziphius
hiirrsy
Irishry
hiklssu
luskish
hiklsuy
huskily
hikmnos
monkish
hikmrsu
murkish
hiknnor
inkhorn
hikntu
unthink
hiknoop
hook-pin
hikoors
rookish

hikopps
kip-shop
hikorsy
Yorkish
hikrstu
Turkish
hillopt
hilltop
hillopy
lyophil
hillrsy
shrilly
hillrty
thrilly
hilmmou
holmium
hilmosw
wholism
hilmpsu
lumpish
hilmsuy
mushily
hilmtuu
thulium
hilnnty
ninthly
hiloott
otolith
hilootz
zoolith
hilortu
urolith
hilossw
slowish
hilostu
loutish
hilosty
hyloist
hilosvw
wolvish
hiloswy
showily
hilotww
whitlow
hilpruw
upwhirl
hilssty
stylish
hilstty
thistly
hilstxy
sixthly
himmmtu
Thummim
himmost
Thomism
himmpsu
mumpish
himmrsu
rummish
himmsty
mythism
himnoos
moonish

himnsty
hymnist
himoors
moorish
himoprs
Orphism
rompish
himopss
sophism
himopst
photism
himortu
thorium
himossu
Suomish
himostt
Thomist
himotty
timothy
himprtu
triumph
himptuy
pythium
himrsty
rhymist
himsstu
isthmus
himstty
mythist
hinnnsu
nunnish
hinnoot
Honiton
hinnost
tonnish
hinnpsu
nunship
hinoort
hornito
hinoorz
horizon
hinoost
insooth
hinopps
shippon
hinopss
sonship
hinorst
hornist
hinorsu
nourish
hinorsy
roynish
hinortw
throw-in
hinossw
snowish
hinostw
townish
hinppsu
push-pin
hinptuw
unwhipt

hinrstu
runtish
hinstuw
Whitsun
hiooprs
poorish
hiopptw
whip-top
hioprsw
worship
hiopsst
sophist
hiopstu
uphoist
hiorssu
sourish
hiorsty
history
hiosstt
sottish
hiottuw
outwith
without
hiqssuy
squishy
hirsttu
ruttish
hirstty
thirsty
hkklooz
kolkhoz
hkkostu
Sukkoth
hknootu
nut-hook
hknooww
know-how
hkooopt
pothook
hkorswy
work-shy
hlmnoty
monthly
hlmnpyy
nymphly
hlmootw
owl-moth
hlmorry
myrrhol
hlmrtuy
Lythrum
hloosty
soothly
hloprty
prothyl
hlorsty
shortly
hlotuyy
youthly
hlprsuu
sulphur
hmmnooy
homonym

hmmrtuy
thrummy
hmnstuy
sun-myth
hmoprsu
rum-shop
hnnorsu
unshorn
hnnortu
horn-nut
hnnosuw
unshown
hnoopty
typhoon
hnortuw
unworth
hnostuu
unshout
hnpstuu
hunt's-up
hnrttuu
untruth
hooppps
pop-shop
hooppst
pot-shop
hooprst
porthos
hoopstt
pot-shot
hoopstu
Pushtoo
upshoot
hoopsty
toyshop
hoorrst
orthros
hoosttu
outshot
hoprstu
Hotspur
hoprtuw
upthrow
hopsttu
shot-put
hopstuy
typhous
horstuu
outrush
hosttuu
shut-out
hprssuy
Syrphus
hrsstuy
thyrsus
iiijjln
jinjili
iiikmnn
minikin
iiisttw
wistiti
iijmnos
misjoin

iijnnot
injoint
iikknps
kip-skin
iikllmy
milkily
iikllos
oil-silk
iikllsy
silkily
iiklmru
Krilium®
iiklnos
oilskin
iiklpsy
spikily
iiklrsy
riskily
iikmnor
kirimon
iikmnps
simpkin
iikmprt
pit-mirk
iillllw
ill-will
iilllmo
oil-mill
iilllsy
sillily
iillmno
million
iillmsy
slimily
iillnop
pillion
iillnoz
zillion
iillnst
instill
iillntt
littlin
iilmnos
lionism
iilmors
similor
iilmoss
limosis
iilmosz
Zoilism
iilmstu
stimuli
iilmsty
mistily
iilnnsu
insulin
iilnors
sirloin
iilnosy
noisily
iilnptu
pili-nut
iilnpuv
pulvini

iiloprt
tripoli
iilortv
vitriol
iilostv
violist
iilostz
Zoilist
iilprvy
privily
iilpsty
tipsily
iilttuy
utility
iilttwy
wittily
iimmmnu
minimum
iimmnsu
minimus
iimnoss
mission
iimnosu
nimious
iimnosz
Zionism
iimnotx
mixtion
iimnprt
imprint
iimopsu
impious
iimosst
mitosis
iimossu
simious
iimostt
Titoism
iimpstt
Pittism
iimrttu
tritium
iimrtuv
trivium
iimsstu
missuit
iinnoop
opinion
iinnotu
unition
iinopss
sinopis
iinorst
ironist
iinortt
introit
iinostz
Zionist
iinosuv
invious
iinottu
tuition
iinqruy
inquiry

iinrtty
  trinity
iinsttw
  intwist
iioprss
  pissoir
iiorssv
  virosis
iiorstv
  ivorist
  visitor
iiosttt
  Titoist
iiosttu
  oustiti
iiprsst
  tripsis
iiprsty
  spirity
iiprtvy
  privity
ijjstuu
  ju-jitsu
ijklloy
  killjoy
ijllloy
  jollily
ijlloty
  jollity
ijlmnor
  Mjölnir
ijlmpuy
  jumpily
ijlnoqu
  jonquil
ijlnoty
  jointly
ijnnotu
  unjoint
ikkmnou
  kikumon
ikknort
  kirkton
ikllsuy
  sulkily
iklmnpu
  lumpkin
iklmnru
  milk-run
iklmops
  milk-sop
iklmosy
  smokily
iklmruy
  murkily
iklmsuy
  muskily
iklnoos
  skolion
iklnpsu
  skulpin
iklnrwy
  wrinkly
ikloott
  toolkit
iklossu
  souslik
ikmnoos
  mono-ski
ikmnosw
  misknow
ikmnppu
  pumpkin
ikmnrtu
  trinkum
ikmoost
  mistook
ikmossu
  koumiss
iknnptu
  unpinkt
iknoost
  isokont
iknossw
  sow-skin
iknpstu
  sputnik
ikorsty
  Yorkist
ikprssy
  krypsis
illlowy
  lowlily
illmnou
  mullion
illmoor
  moor-ill
illmpuy
  lumpily
illmsuu
  limulus
illnoqu
  quillon
illnoru
  rullion
illnpuu
  lupulin
illnrtu
  ill-turn
illntuy
  nullity
illooow
  wool-oil
illoorz
  zorillo
illopry
  pillory
illopwy
  pillowy
illosuv
  villous
illosuy
  lousily
illowwy
  willowy
illrsuy
  surlily
illstuy
  lustily
ilmmruy
  rummily
ilmmsuu
  mimulus
ilmnoot
  moonlit
ilmnotw
  Miltown
ilmoory
  roomily
ilmooss
  molossi
ilmortu
  turmoil
ilmosty
  moistly
ilmpstu
  plumist
ilmstuy
  Mytilus
ilmuyzz
  muzzily
ilnnops
  non-slip
ilnnsuy
  sunnily
ilnooop
  poon-oil
ilnoops
  plosion
ilnoopv
  volpino
ilnopru
  purloin
ilnopsu
  upsilon
ilnopsy
  ypsilon
ilnorst
  nostril
ilnorsu
  surloin
ilnortu
  torulin
ilnostt
  Stilton
ilnosty
  stonily
ilnoswy
  snowily
ilnotuv
  volutin
ilnpstu
  unspilt
ilooors
  rosolio
iloopst
  poloist
  top-soil
iloorty
  olitory
iloosst
  soloist
iloosty
  sootily
iloowyz
  woozily
iloppsy
  soppily
iloprsy
  prosily
ilopsuy
  piously
ilorrsy
  sorrily
ilossty
  tossily
  tylosis
ilrssuu
  Silurus
ilrstuy
  rustily
ilsstty
  stylist
immnosu
  musimon
immnouu
  muonium
immoptu
  optimum
immsstu
  summist
imnnnou
  munnion
imnnoor
  norimon
imnoopp
  pompion
imnoopt
  tompion
imnoorr
  morrion
imnoort
  monitor
imnooss
  monosis
imnoosu
  ominous
imnoosy
  isonomy
imnooux
  oxonium
imnoppu
  pumpion
imnorty
  trionym
imnosvy
  visnomy
imooprx
  proximo
imoosss
  osmosis
imoossu
  osmious
imoprst
  tropism
imoprtu
  protium
imopstu
  utopism
imorstu
  tourism
imorsty
  Toryism
imossyz
  zymosis
imrsstu
  sistrum
  trismus
imrttuy
  yttrium
innnoru
  runnion
innoops
  opsonin
innostu
  nonsuit
innqsuy
  squinny
inooprt
  portion
inoopst
  positon
inoorst
  isotron
  torsion
inoortw
  tow-iron
inoosux
  noxious
inoppst
  topspin
inopptt
  pint-pot
inoppty
  pit-pony
inopssu
  poussin
  spinous
inopstu
  sit-upon
  spinout
inorstu
  nitrous
inorsuu
  ruinous
  urinous
inorsuv
  unvisor
inossuu
  sinuous
inprstu
  unstrip
inprsty
  trypsin
insstuu
  sunsuit
insttuw
  untwist
inttuwy
  unwitty
iooprss
  porosis
iooprsv
  proviso
ioopsty
  isotopy
ioorsss
  sorosis
ioorstt
  risotto
ioorstu
  riotous
ioppprt
  pit-prop
ioppsst
  piss-pot
ioppstt
  pit-stop
ioprssy
  pyrosis
ioprstt
  protist
  tropist
iopsttu
  utopist
ioqrttu
  quittor
iorrttx
  tortrix
iorsttu
  tourist
iprrstu
  stirrup
iprstuu
  pursuit
ipsssty
  stypsis
iptttuy
  tittupy
jmoptuu
  outjump
jnoorsu
  sojourn
kllmosu
  mollusk
kloootu
  lookout
  outlook
knnnouw
  unknown
knooptt
  top-knot
knoprty
  krypton
kooprtw
  worktop
koortuw
  outwork
  work-out

7 KOO

koottty
Kotytto
korttuw
tutwork
llmoopr
rollmop
llmppuy
plumply
llooprt
roll-top
trollop
lloortu
roll-out
lloptuu
pull-out
lmnooos
Solomon
lmopsuu
plumous
lmopsuy
Olympus
lmrstuu
lustrum
lmstuuu
tumulus
lnnopsu
nonplus
lnooptu
pultoon
lnrtuuv
vulturn
lnrtuuy
untruly
loooors
oloroso
loppsuu
pulpous
loppsuy
polypus
loprsuy
pylorus
loprtuy
poultry
lorstuu
torulus
losttuy
stoutly
lprssuu
surplus
mmnossu
summons
mmooprs
Mormops
mmopsty
symptom
mnnooos
monsoon
mnnosyy
synonym
mnnotuu
unmount
mnooopp
pompoon
mnoooyz
zoonomy
mnoopty
toponym
mnoosuy
onymous
mnoottw
towmont
mnoprtu
no-trump
mnorstu
nostrum
mnottuy
muttony
moootyz
zootomy
mooppsu
pompous
moopssu
opossum
moopstt
topmost
moorttt
tom-trot
moosttu
outmost
mopssuu
spumous
morrstu
rostrum
nnnsuuy
unsunny
nnooopt
pontoon
nnoopru
pronoun
nnoopss
sponson
nnoopst
non-stop
nnorsuw
unsworn
nnossuy
unsonsy
nnostyy
syntony
nooprss
sponsor
noorstu
unroost
noortuw
outworn
worn-out
nopsstu
sunspot
nopstuu
spun-out
norsuuz
Zonurus
norttuu
outturn
turn-out
nrsstuu
Sturnus
untruss
nrsttuu
untrust
ooooprt
potoroo
oooprtu
outroop
ooorttu
outroot
ooprrtw
row-port
ooprssu
sour-sop
ooprstu
portous
ooprstv
provost
ooprttu
outport
ooprtuu
outpour
oopsstt
tosspot
oopsttu
outpost
oorstuu
routous
opprrtu
purport
opprstu
support
opprsty
stroppy
opprsuy
pyropus
orssuuu
usurous
orsttuu
surtout

8 AAA

aaaaccrr
caracara
aaaacjrr
jararaca
aaaacnrs
anasarca
aaaadmtv
amadavat
aaaadtvv
avadavat
aaaaemnr
Aramaean
aaaaggrr
agar-agar
aaaahjmr
maharaja
aaaaimpr
arapaima
aaaairtx
ataraxia
aaaajkrr
jararaka
aaaakkmt
takamaka
aaaakknt
katakana
aaaaklrz
kala-azar
aaaallvv
lava-lava
aaaalntt
Atalanta
aaaammtt
matamata
aaaamnry
Ramayana
aaaarrss
sasarara
aaabbelt
abatable
aaabbhkl
Kabbalah
aaabbilt
abbatial
aaabccrt
baccarat
aaabchls
calabash
aaabchmu
macahuba
aaabcint
anabatic
aaabcnrr
barracan
barranca
aaabcnru
carnauba
aaabcpry
capybara
aaabdest
database
aaabdknt
databank
aaabdnnn
bandanna
aaabdnrs
saraband
aaabdnrt
abradant
aaabeghl
galabeah
aaabegll
gallabea
aaabehnr
habanera
aaabehrt
barathea
aaabeilt
Labiatae
aaabekkk
kaka-beak
aaabempr
parabema
aaabghil
galabiah
aaabgill
gallabia
aaabgily
galabiya
aaabglor
algaroba
aaabgrtu
rutabaga
aaabhlmr
Alhambra
aaabilnn
Albanian
aaabiltt
battalia
aaabinss
anabasis
aaabintv
Batavian
aaabipss
piassaba
aaabkpss
baasskap
aaablopr
parabola
aaabmmnr
abram-man
aaabnstu
sauba-ant
aaaccdin
Accadian
aaaccepr
carapace
aaaccimm
caimacam
aaaccrtt
cataract
aaaccttu
tac-au-tac
aaacdeim
academia
aaacdenr
Dracaena
aaacdequ
aquacade
aaacdetu
acaudate
aaacdilm
Adamical
aaacdinn
Canadian
aaacdinr
acaridan
Arcadian
aaacdkly
lackaday
aaacdnno
anaconda
aaacdnrs
sandarac
aaacdotv
advocaat
aaaceefg
Fagaceae
aaaceetx
Taxaceae
aaacegtu
aguacate
aaacehlp
acalepha
aaacehnr
Archaean
aaacelnt
analecta
aaacelst
catalase
aaacennp
panacean
aaacenst
Castanea
aaacgint
caatinga

aaacglsw
scalawag
aaacgmnp
campagna
aaacgmnr
Armagnac
aaachhhl
Halachah
aaachint
Cathaian
aaachips
aphasiac
aaachlnr
anarchal
aaachnty
Cathayan
aaacijmn
Jamaican
aaacilmn
maniacal
aaacilrs
Scalaria
aaacilsy
calisaya
aaacinrt
Craniata
aaacintv
cavatina
aaacipsu
sapucaia
aaacirrs
sacraria
aaacirtx
ataraxic
aaacisvx
Saxicava
aaackmrt
tamarack
aaaclmry
calamary
aaaclrst
alcatras
aaacmrsu
amaracus
aaacnosv
Casanova
aaacrrwy
carraway
aaacstwy
castaway
aaadefwy
fade-away
aaadegim
Agamidae
aaadegnp
apanaged
aaadehmv
Mahadeva
aaadeinr
Araneida
Aranidae
aaadekmv
Kamadeva

aaademnn
Mandaean
aaademsv
Samaveda
aaadentv
vanadate
aaadeprt
tapadera
aaadgghh
Haggadah
aaadglmy
amygdala
aaadhmnr
Ramadhan
aaadhmrs
madrasah
aaadhnrt
thanadar
aaadiilr
radialia
aaadikkn
Akkadian
aaadilru
adularia
aaadimny
adynamia
aaadklmn
kalamdan
aaadkrrv
aardvark
aaadlmnq
qalamdan
aaadmntu
tamandua
aaaeglmx
malaxage
aaaeglrt
altarage
aaaegnpp
appanage
aaaegrst
gastraea
aaaehmnt
anathemá
aaaehnps
anaphase
aaaeinrr
Arenaria
aaaekllv
Kalevala
aaaektwy
take-away
aaaelmpt
palamate
aaaelmtx
malaxate
aaaennrz
Nazarean
aaaenopr
paranoea
aaaenprv
paravane
aaaenpst
anapaest

aaaertwy
tearaway
aaafginr
Graafian
aaafgirr
Fragaria
aaafinst
fantasia
aaafinuv
avifauna
aaaggl ln
galangal
aaagglop
galapago
aaaghinn
Ghanaian
aaaghinp
Panhagia
aaaghipr
agraphia
aaaghlms
Malagash
aaaghnty
yataghan
aaagilpt
patagial
aaaginrr
agrarian
aaaglmst
stalagma
aaaglmsy
Malagasy
aaaglnrs
Sangraal
aaaglrrw
warragal
aaaglrst
astragal
aaagmprr
paragram
aaagnopr
araponga
aaagnprs
parasang
aaagnpru
arapunga
aaagorst
Saratoga
aaagpruy
Paraguay
aaahiinw
Hawaiian
aaahilmy
Himalaya
aaahimnr
maharani
aaahimns
shamiana
aaahimrt
hamartia
aaahinpr
raphania
aaahkrss
rakshasa

aaahlllv
Valhalla
aaahlllw
Walhalla
aaahmnns
manna-ash
aaahmnrt
amaranth
aaahmrtt
Mahratta
aaahnnsv
savannah
aaahnopr
anaphora
aaahnsst
Sathanas
aaahnsty
athanasy
aaahswwy
wash-away
aaahttwy
thataway
aaaiinpr
apiarian
aaaikkmm
kaimakam
aaaillmr
malarial
aaaillpt
palatial
aaailmmm
Mammalia
aaailmnr
malarian
aaailmsv
malvasia
aaailnru
aularian
aaailnst
Alsatian
aaailprv
paravail
aaailrst
salariat
aaailrsu
Laurasia
aaaimmrs
Aramaism
aaaimmst
miasmata
aaaimrst
Sarmatia
aaaimrtt
Marattia
aaainnrr
ranarian
aaainopr
paranoia
aaainqru
aquarian
aaainrtt
Tatarian
aaaipssv
piassava

aaaklwwy
walk-away
aaakoswy
soakaway
aaallprx
parallax
aaalnnpt
platanna
aaalnntu
Annulata
aaalnprt
rataplan
aaalnrtt
tarlatan
aaalprst
satrapal
aaamnopr
panorama
aaamnrst
Rastaman
aaamottu
automata
aaamqstu
Squamata
aaamrttu
traumata
aaamrtzz
razmataz
aaanoprz
parazoan
aaanorsy
sayonara
aaanprtv
paravant
aaanqtuu
aquanaut
aaanrstt
tarantas
aaapqrtu
paraquat
aabbcdkn
backband
aabbcdrs
scabbard
aabbcekr
bareback
aabbcinr
barbican
aabbcirr
barbaric
aabbcist
sabbatic
aabbctty
tabby-cat
aabbdeis
Abbaside
aabbdert
barbated
aabbdors
Barbados
aabbeelr
bearable
aabbeelt
beatable

aabbeill
bailable
aabbekln
bankable
aabbellm
blamable
aabbells
baseball
aabbelry
bearably
aabbhhll
blah-blah
aabbhksu
babushka
aabbiill
bilabial
aabbilll
bail-ball
aabbilrt
barbital
aabbklty
baby-talk
aabbllmy
blamably
aabblssu
subbasal
aabbmmoz
zambomba
aabbnoor
bona-roba
aabcchi
bacchiac
aabccehk
backache
aabccelr
cable-car
aabccels
cascabel
aabccert
braccate
aabcchin
bacchian
aabcchis
biscacha
aabcchiz
bizcacha
aabcchkt
backchat
aabcchnt
bacchant
aabccinn
cannabic
aabcckkp
backpack
aabccklp
blackcap
aabcck lt
black-cat
aabccklw
clawback
aabccmot
catacomb
aabcdein
abidance

aabcdeit
abdicate
aabcdekt
back-date
aabcdell
caballed
aabcdeln
balanced
aabcdhkn
backhand
aabcdhkr
hardback
aabcdiis
diabasic
aabcdikl
laid-back
aabcdint
abdicant
aabcdkrw
backward
drawback
aabcdkry
backyard
aabcdlnr
land-crab
aabcdnrr
brancard
aabcdnst
cab-stand
aabceehs
sea-beach
aabceeix
Bixaceae
aabceeny
abeyance
aabceers
scarabee
aabceert
acerbate
aabceerv
cave-bear
aabcegot
cabotage
aabcehnr
barchane
aabceilm
amicable
aabceimn
ambiance
aabceinr
carabine
aabceirt
bacteria
aabcejno
Jacobean
aabceklm
clambake
aabceklr
lacebark
aabcellp
placable
aabcellr
caballer
race-ball

aabcells
scalable
aabcelnr
balancer
barnacle
aabcelor
albacore
aabcelrt
bracteal
aabcelwy
cableway
aabcemrv
vambrace
aabcenyy
abeyancy
aabceort
boatrace
aabceprs
space-bar
aabcfhkl
half-back
aabcfiil
bifacial
aabcfkll
backfall
fall-back
aabcfkst
fastback
aabcgklo
cloak-bag
aabchikr
back-hair
aabchilr
brachial
aabchinr
branchia
aabchkkr
hark-back
aabchkls
backlash
aabchkrs
shabrack
aabchksw
backwash
aabchloo
coolabah
aabchrrt
bar-chart
aabciils
basilica
aabciinr
Cabirian
aabcijno
Bajocian
Jacobian
aabciklt
tailback
aabcillr
bacillar
aabcilms
balsamic
cabalism
aabcilmy
amicably

aabcilnn
cannibal
aabcilno
anabolic
aabcilst
basaltic
cabalist
aabcimnr
Cambrian
aabcinnn
cannabin
aabcinno
Baconian
aabcinnr
cinnabar
aabcinns
cannabis
aabcinrt
Bactrian
aabcinsu
banausic
aabcinsy
Biscayan
aabcioss
Scabiosa
aabcirss
brassica
aabcisss
abscissa
aabckklt
talk-back
aabcklny
clay-bank
aabcklpy
playback
aabcknrs
snack-bar
aabckswy
sway-back
aabclllo
coalball
aabcllpy
placably
aabclnuu
cunabula
aabclrry
carbaryl
aabcnorr
barranco
aabcrstt
abstract
aabcrswy
crab-yaws
aabddeet
dead-beat
aabddehl
bald-head
aabddehn
headband
aabddlns
badlands
aabddmor
damboard

aabdeehl
beheadal
aabdeelr
readable
aabdeelt
dealbate
aabdeelv
evadable
aabdeert
tea-bread
aabdeery
bayadère
aabdegin
badinage
aabdeglr
gradable
aabdegnt
T-bandage
aabdehhi
dahabieh
aabdehkr
hardbake
aabdehmr
hardbeam
aabdeiln
baladine
aabdeilr
Labridae
aabdeinr
Abderian
aabdeiou
aboideau
aabdejll
djellaba
aabdekry
daybreak
aabdellu
laudable
aabdelmn
damnable
aabdelor
adorable
aabdelpt
baldpate
aabdelrs
baselard
aabdelrw
drawable
aabdelry
readably
aabdelsw
saw-blade
aabdemns
beadsman
aabdemrs
smear-dab
aabdentu
unabated
aabdenux
bandeaux
aabdenvw
waveband
aabdeors
seaboard

aabdeort
tea-board
aabderrt
taberdar
aabderrw
bearward
aabdertv
vartabed
aabderwy
waybread
aabdfhln
fahlband
aabdfrrt
draft-bar
aabdgnov
vagabond
aabdgorr
garboard
aabdgotu
gadabout
aabdhinr
hair-band
aabdhlln
handball
hand-ball
aabdhnst
sand-bath
aabdhrsu
subahdar
aabdhrsw
Bradshaw
aabdiils
basidial
aabdimnr
madbrain
aabdinnr
rain-band
aabdknns
sand-bank
aabdllry
balladry
aabdlluy
laudably
aabdlmnu
labdanum
aabdlmny
damnably
aabdlnpt
platband
aabdloot
boat-load
aabdlopr
lap-board
aabdlorr
Labrador
larboard
aabdlory
adorably
aabdmnns
bandsman
aabdmnny
bandyman
aabdnntu
abundant

aabdnrry
barnyard
aabdoprx
pax-board
aabdorsv
bravados
aabdorwy
broadway
way-board
aabdrrss
brassard
aabdrsty
bastardy
aabeefln
flea-bane
aabeefls
leaf-base
aabeegkr
breakage
aabeegnt
abnegate
aabeehll
healable
aabeehlt
hateable
aabeeklm
makeable
aabeeklt
takeable
aabeekmt
bakemeat
makebate
aabeekrt
tea-break
aabeells
leasable
saleable
aabeelmn
amenable
nameable
aabeelmt
tameable
aabeelrs
erasable
aabeelrt
rateable
aabeelrw
wearable
aabeeltt
tea-table
aabeempr
abampere
aabeemrs
sea-bream
aabeenor
anaerobe
aabeerrs
bear's-ear
aabeerrt
aberrate
aabeertt
trabeate
aabeesst
sea-beast

aabefhkl
half-beak
aabeflmu
flambeau
aabeghil
galabieh
aabeghks
shake-bag
aabeghln
hangable
aabeghnr
berghaan
aabeghrt
earth-bag
aabegiln
gainable
aabeglll
glabella
aabegllm
ball-game
aabeglrt
glabrate
aabeglru
arguable
aabegmnr
bargeman
aabegmny
mangabey
aabegmrt
bregmata
aabegnor
baronage
aabegort
abrogate
aabegost
sabotage
aabegrtw
water-bag
aabehirr
herbaria
aabehitw
Wahabite
aabehkls
shakable
aabehlny
Hyblaean
aabehlot
oathable
aabehlps
shapable
aabehlpt
alphabet
aabehlrw
warhable
aabehlsw
washable
aabeikrr
air-brake
aabeillm
mailable
aabeills
isabella
sailable
aabeilnr
inarable
aabeilrs
raisable
aabeilrv
variable
aabeilst
satiable
aabeiltv
ablative
aabeinoz
zabaione
aabeinrr
Briarean
aabeinst
basanite
aabeiotu
aboiteau
aabeirsv
abrasive
aabejkrw
break-jaw
aabejmux
jambeaux
aabekllt
talkable
aabekllw
walkable
aabeknpt
peat-bank
aabeknrt
bank-rate
aabeknrv
brake-van
aabekprr
parbreak
aabellmt
meat-ball
aabellno
loanable
aabellpp
palpable
aabellps
lapsable
aabellpy
playable
aabellsv
salvable
aabellsy
saleably
aabelluv
valuable
aabelmny
amenably
aabelmot
metabola
aabelmst
blastema
lambaste
aabelmsu
amusable
aabelmtt
table-mat
aabelmtu
ambulate
aabelnnt
tannable
aabelnps
anableps
aabelnpt
pantable
aabelnry
balneary
aabelopr
parabole
aabelorr
arboreal
aabelovw
avowable
aabelprs
sparable
aabelpss
passable
aabelrst
arbalest
aabelrty
betrayal
rateably
aabelstt
statable
tastable
aabelttu
tabulate
aabelttx
battle-ax
aabeltux
tableaux
aabenrrt
aberrant
aabenrst
ratsbane
aabeorrt
arboreta
aabeortw
water-boa
aabfilux
fabliaux
aabflott
faltboat
flatboat
aabgggnn
gang-bang
aabggnot
taboggan
aabggrrt
braggart
aabghkrs
shag-bark
aabghprr
bar-graph
aabgilnt
bang-tail
aabgirst
bargaist
aabgllry
ballyrag
aabglmnu
galbanum
aabglnps
slap-bang
aabglruy
arguably
aabgmorr
barogram
aabhhoru
brouhaha
aabhiimp
Amphibia
aabhijmy
jambiyah
aabhillr
hair-ball
aabhiltu
habitual
aabhimst
Baathism
aabhimsw
Wahabism
aabhinst
habitans
aabhintt
habitant
aabhirst
tabashir
aabhistt
Baathist
aabhllsw
wash-ball
aabhmnrs
bran-mash
aabhnotu
Autobahn
aabhqssu
squabash
aabiilns
Basilian
aabiittw
wait-a-bit
aabikkll
kaka-bill
aabillly
labially
aabillst
ballista
aabilmns
bailsman
aabilmot
mail-boat
aabilnnu
biannual
aabilnop
Polabian
aabilnor
baronial
aabilnot
ablation
aabilnru
binaural
aabilnty
banality
aabilost
sail-boat
aabilott
boattail
aabilrrt
arbitral
aabilrst
arbalist
aabilrvy
variably
aabimnru
manubria
aabimors
ambrosia
aabimrsu
simaruba
aabinnpr
brainpan
aabinors
abrasion
aabinrst
bartisan
aabinrtz
bartizan
aabiortt
abattoir
aabirtuy
rubaiyat
aabjlmno
jambolan
aabkmnns
banksman
aabkoprs
soap-bark
aabllmor
balmoral
aabllnst
tan-balls
aabllops
soap-ball
aabllppy
palpably
aabllprt
trap-ball
aabllstu
blastula
aablluvy
valuably
aablmnor
abnormal
aablmntu
ambulant
aablotuy
layabout
aablpssy
passably
aablrrsu
saburral
aabmmosu
abomasum
aabmnotw
batwoman
aabmnrtu
rambutan
aabmortu
marabout
tamboura
aabmossu
abomasus
aabnnost
absonant
aaborrrt
barrator
aaborstt
barostat
aabrrrty
barratry
aabrrsst
brassart
aaccchhu
cachucha
aacccloo
Coca-Cola®
aacccruy
accuracy
aaccdefr
face-card
aaccdeim
academic
aaccdelo
accolade
aaccdenu
caducean
aaccderr
race-card
aaccders
card-case
aaccdhil
Chaldaic
aaccdort
coat-card
aaccdovy
advocacy
aacceefh
face-ache
aacceelt
calceate
aacceent
cetacean
aacceflo
coal-face
aaccegru
carucage
aaccehix
cachexia
aacceiil
Caecilia
aacceinr
Circaean
aacceirr
cercaria
aaccekrs
sack-race
aaccelor
caracole
aaccenrt
carcanet

aaccertu
accurate
carucate
aaccfgoo
cacafogo
aaccfilr
farcical
aaccfoot
cocoa-fat
aaccgilt
galactic
aacchhil
Halachic
aacchill
caillach
aacchilp
pachalic
aacchinr
anarchic
aacchisv
viscacha
aacchivz
vizcacha
aacchllt
catch-all
aacchlor
charcoal
aacchlot
cachalot
aacchlrs
clarsach
aacchmno
coachman
aacchnor
coranach
aacchowy
coach-way
aacciinv
vaccinia
aacciist
sciatica
aaccilnu
Canicula
aaccilnv
vaccinal
aaccilru
acicular
aacciltt
tactical
aaccioru
cariacou
aaccipty
capacity
aaccirty
caryatic
aaccjkrw
crackjaw
aaccjoru
carcajou
carjacou
aacckort
coatrack
aacckost
sack-coat
aaccllru
calcular
aacclmny
clamancy
aacclprs
calcspar
aacclrsu
saccular
aaccorry
Caryocar
aaccostt
staccato
stoccata
aacddefs
sad-faced
aacddehi
acid-head
aacddeil
daedalic
aacddenv
advanced
aacddeop
Decapoda
aacddert
dead-cart
aacddetu
caudated
aacddety
tea-caddy
aacdeehh
headache
aacdeehr
headrace
aacdeels
escalade
aacdeeps
escapade
aacdeest
estacade
aacdeetu
ecaudate
aacdefft
fat-faced
aacdefhr
hardface
aacdeflt
falcated
aacdegkp
packaged
aacdegmr
card-game
decagram
aacdehhy
headachy
aacdehin
hacienda
aacdehln
Chaldean
aacdehmr
drachmae
aacdehpt
death-cap
aacdehrt
cathedra
aacdehtt
attached
aacdeimn
maenadic
aacdeims
camisade
aacdeinr
radiance
aacdeirs
Scaridae
aacdeirt
radicate
aacdejnt
adjacent
aacdelnr
calendar
landrace
aacdelnv
valanced
aacdelos
case-load
escalado
aacdeltv
clavated
aacdemop
Campodea
aacdenpt
tap-dance
aacdenrw
war-dance
aacdentu
aduncate
aacdentv
tadvance
aacdeops
escapado
aacdeotu
autocade
aacdeotv
advocate
aacdequy
adequacy
aacderst
cadastre
aacdgghi
Haggadic
aacdginr
arcading
cardigan
aacdhhkr
hardhack
aacdhiis
dichasia
aacdhilr
diarchal
aacdhimr
drachmai
aacdhinp
handicap
aacdhinr
arachnid
aacdhkrt
hardtack
aacdhlnp
handclap
aacdhlot
cathodal
aacdhlry
charlady
aacdhmmr
drammach
aacdhmrs
drachmas
aacdhnrt
hand-cart
aacdhort
Chordata
aacdhprs
crashpad
aacdiimt
Adamitic
aacdiinr
cnidaria
aacdiins
ascidian
aacdijlu
Judaical
aacdillm
mail-clad
aacdillp
palladic
aacdilmt
dalmatic
aacdilmu
Caladium
aacdilno
diaconal
aacdilnr
cardinal
aacdilnu
Claudian
dulciana
aacdilnv
Vandalic
aacdiloz
zodiacal
aacdilrr
railcard
aacdimno
mandioca
aacdimny
adynamic
aacdimos
camisado
aacdimrs
camisard
aacdimrt
dramatic
aacdinns
Scandian
aacdinor
Orcadian
aacdinrt
radicant
tridacna
aacdinry
radiancy
aacdiotu
autacoid
aacdirty
caryatid
aacdituy
audacity
aacdjqru
jacquard
aacdklln
lackland
aacdklop
pack-load
aacdlort
cartload
aacdlosv
Calvados
aacdlrty
dactylar
aacdmmor
cardamom
aacdmnno
mancando
aacdmnor
cardamon
aacdnsst
sand-cast
aacdorrt
cart-road
aaceeeht
Theaceae
aaceeelo
Oleaceae
aaceefit
facetiae
aaceefll
lace-leaf
aaceeflp
pale-face
aaceegir
acierage
aaceegku
ague-cake
aaceeglr
clearage
aaceeglv
cleavage
aaceegrs
gear-case
aaceehlp
acalephe
aaceehlt
leachate
aaceehrt
tracheae
aaceeilm
Limaceae
aaceeimt
emaciate
aaceeinn
encaenia
aaceeirt
acierate
aaceeitv
Vitaceae
aaceekpr
rape-cake
aaceelmu
Ulmaceae
aaceelrt
lacerate
aaceelst
escalate
aaceeltu
aculeate
aaceemns
Maecenas
aaceemor
Moraceae
aaceemrt
macerate
racemate
aaceemst
casemate
aaceemsu
Musaceae
aaceenrs
Canarese
Cesarean
aaceentt
catenate
aaceeors
Rosaceae
aaceeprt
caper-tea
aaceepss
seascape
aaceersy
easy-care
aaceertu
Rutaceae
aaceertv
acervate
aaceetuv
evacuate
aaceetvx
excavate
aaceffhl
half-face
aaceffin
affiance
aacefhlp
halfpace
aacefist
fasciate
aacefklo
loaf-cake
aaceflrs
leaf-scar
aaceflrt
flat-race
aacefrru
Furcraea
aacefrst
seacraft
aacefrtt
artefact
aaceghnt
chantage

aacegiln
angelica
aacegilt
glaciate
aaceginr
canaigre
aacegiop
apogaeic
aacegirr
carriage
aacegirv
vicarage
aacegkrt
trackage
aaceglny
lancegay
aacegrsv
scavager
aacehhls
ash-leach
aacehill
heliacal
aacehiln
achenial
aacehimr
chimaera
aacehimt
haematic
aacehipt
Hepatica
aacehirs
archaise
aacehirt
theriaca
aacehisz
Schizaea
aacehlos
sea-loach
aacehlrt
tracheal
aacehlst
alcahest
aacehmnp
camphane
aacehmrs
marchesa
aacehmst
schemata
aacehnop
Phocaena
aacehnrr
Achernar
aacehors
sea-orach
aacehprt
race-path
aacehrrr
rear-arch
aacehrst
sea-chart
aacehrsu
archaeus
aacehrtt
reattach

aacehtux
châteaux
aaceiiln
laciniae
aaceiint
actiniae
aaceiipr
Picariae
aaceillm
camellia
aaceilln
alliance
canaille
aaceilmn
analcime
calamine
aaceilmt
calamite
aaceilns
canalise
aaceilnt
analcite
aaceilnv
valiance
aaceilop
alopecia
aaceilrt
tail-race
aaceilrv
cavalier
aaceilst
saliceta
aaceimnr
American
Cinerama®
aaceimns
amnesiac
aaceimrs
macarise
mesaraic
aaceimrz
macarize
aaceimtt
catamite
aaceinno
Oceanian
aaceinrt
carinate
aaceinrv
variance
aaceinst
estancia
aaceiprs
airspace
aaceiprt
apricate
aaceiptt
apatetic
capitate
aaceirtv
vicarate
aaceittv
activate

aacejltu
jaculate
aacekklw
cakewalk
aaceklst
salt-cake
aacekmty
kamacyte
aacekrsw
sea-wrack
aacekrtt
attacker
aacelllr
all-clear
aacellmr
marcella
aacellot
allocate
aacelmnp
placeman
aacelmtu
maculate
aacelnnu
cannulae
aacelnor
Carolean
lecanora
aacelnpr
parlance
aacelnpt
placenta
aacelnrt
lacerant
aacelnry
arcanely
aacelnst
analects
aacelntu
lacunate
aacelrsu
caesural
aacelrwy
clearway
aacelsty
catalyse
stay-lace
aacemnps
spaceman
aacemnst
camstane
aacemnsu
sauceman
aacemrss
massacre
aacemrst
steam-car
aacemstt
cat's-meat
aacenors
sea-acorn
aacenotu
oceanaut
aacenprs
pancreas

aacenpst
pastance
aacenpsu
saucepan
aacenrst
canaster
aacenrtt
reactant
aacenrtu
areca-nut
aacenrty
catenary
aacenrvz
czarevna
aacentuv
evacuant
aaceoprt
caproate
aaceorsu
araceous
aaceosst
sea-coast
aacepppr
cap-paper
aaceppsu
pupa-case
aacerstt
castrate
aacerttt
tractate
aacesstt
sceattas
aacesuwy
causeway
aacffhll
half-calf
aacfgrst
cragfast
aacfhmst
camshaft
aacfilly
facially
aacfilos
fasciola
aacfirrt
aircraft
aacfirtt
artifact
aacfisst
Fascista
aacfjklp
flapjack
aacfllop
coal-flap
aacggino
anagogic
aacggiop
apagogic
aacghipr
agraphic
aacghirr
chiragra
aacghllo
agalloch

aacghopz
gazpacho
aacghoru
guacharo
aacgiimn
magician
aacgiinr
Garcinia
aacgilln
Gallican
aacgillo
alogical
aacgillu
alguacil
aacgilnn
Anglican
aacgilno
analogic
aacgilnv
galvanic
aacgilox
coxalgia
aacgilrt
tragical
aacgimmt
magmatic
aacgimnn
manganic
aacgimnp
campaign
pangamic
aacgimrr
margaric
aacgimuu
guaiacum
aacgisty
sagacity
aacglmou
glaucoma
aacgmnrs
cragsman
aacgnrvy
vagrancy
aachhikr
kachahri
aachhtwy
hatchway
aachiimr
mariachi
aachiknr
chinkara
aachillr
rachilla
aachilms
chamisal
aachilmt
thalamic
aachilnp
chaplain
aachilps
calipash
aachilrv
archival

aachimnn
Chinaman
aachimnp
chinampa
aachimnr
chairman
aachimns
shamanic
aachimnt
matachin
aachimrr
armchair
aachimrs
archaism
charisma
aachimst
cathisma
aachinno
Noachian
aachinnt
acanthin
aachinrt
canthari
aachinsw
chainsaw
aachiptt
chapatti
aachirst
archaist
aachirtx
taxiarch
aachkpss
schapska
aachksty
haystack
aachlmno
monachal
aachlmos
chloasma
aachmmnr
marchman
aachmnnr
ranchman
aachmntw
watchman
aachmnuy
naumachy
aachmort
trachoma
aachmprt
champart
aachmpry
pharmacy
aachnrst
trash-can
aachnrvy
navarchy
aachnstu
acanthus
aachoppr
approach
aachortu
racahout

aachottu
tacahout
aachrtuy
autarchy
aaciilmo
maiolica
aaciilrt
iatrical
aaciilrv
vicarial
aaciinns
Sicanian
aaciinnt
actinian
aaciinpr
picarian
aacijlmo
majolica
aacijnop
japonica
aaciklrr
rack-rail
aacikmnw
mackinaw
aacikrtu
autarkic
aacillmr
lacrimal
aacillmt
climatal
aacillpy
apically
aacilmnt
calamint
claimant
aacilmor
acromial
aacilmot
atomical
aacilmrt
mail-cart
aacilmty
calamity
aacilnno
Laconian
aacilnor
Carolina
conarial
aacilnrt
cant-rail
aacilnrv
carnival
aacilntt
Atlantic
tantalic
aacilntu
nautical
aacilnty
analytic
aacilnuv
navicula
aacilnvy
valiancy

aacilopr
carap-oil
aacilorv
Arvicola
aacilosx
Saxicola
aacilott
tail-coat
aacilpru
piacular
aacilpst
aplastic
aacilpsz
capsizal
aacilptu
capitula
aacilpty
atypical
aacilqru
acquiral
aacilrty
alacrity
aacilruu
auricula
aacilstt
cat's-tail
statical
aacilsty
salacity
aacimmno
ammoniac
aacimmrs
macarism
marasmic
aacimnor
macaroni
marocain
aacimnot
anatomic
aacimort
aromatic
aacimotx
maxi-coat
aacimrst
Sarmatic
aacinnot
Catonian
aacinopr
paranoic
aacinopt
capitano
pacation
aacinort
Croatian
raincoat
aacinorv
Racovian
aacinotv
vacation
aacinqtu
acquaint
aacinrst
arcanist

aacinstz
stanzaic
aacinttu
Tunicata
aacipprs
Capparis
aaciprst
satrapic
aaciprty
rapacity
aacirrtt
tartaric
aacirstt
castrati
aacirtzz
czaritza
aacjklps
slapjack
aacjklsw
slack-jaw
aacjklyz
lazy-jack
aacjkoor
jackaroo
aackknps
knapsack
aacklnps
knapscal
aackmnrt
trackman
aackmnst
tacksman
aackorwy
rockaway
aackrtwy
trackway
aaclllno
call-loan
aacllmry
clay-marl
lacrymal
aacllnry
carnally
aacllrry
carry-all
aacllrsy
rascally
aacllsuu
clausula
aacllsuy
casually
causally
aaclltuy
actually
aaclmnns
clansman
aaclmnss
classman
aaclmrru
macrural
aaclnnot
cantonal
aaclnott
octantal

aaclnrsu
lacunars
aaclnruy
lacunary
aaclntvy
vacantly
aacloopt
tapacolo
aacloptu
tapaculo
aaclorru
oracular
aaclorsu
carousal
aacloruv
vacuolar
aaclpprt
claptrap
aaclprsu
capsular
scapular
aaclprty
calyptra
aaclpttu
catapult
aaclrssw
class-war
aaclrstu
claustra
aaclrsuv
vascular
aaclrtux
curtal-ax
aaclstty
catalyst
aaclstuy
casualty
aacmnoor
macaroon
aacmnors
mascaron
aacmnprs
scrap-man
aacmnpry
rampancy
aacnotty
catatony
aacnprtu
carap-nut
aacnrstt
transact
aacoortx
toxocara
aacoprsu
acarpous
aacoprtu
autocarp
aacorrtv
varactor
aacorstt
castrato
aacorttu
actuator
autocrat

aadddeeh
dead-head
aadddeel
dead-deal
aadddehn
dead-hand
aadddgnr
granddad
aaddeeht
dead-heat
aaddeelp
pale-dead
aaddeemt
dead-meat
aaddeers
sea-adder
aaddefhl
half-dead
aaddefll
dead-fall
aaddehhr
hardhead
aaddehln
headland
aaddehmn
handmade
aaddeiln
dedalian
aaddeirt
radiated
aaddellw
dead-wall
aaddemry
daydream
aaddenrv
veranda'd
aaddgnru
graduand
aaddguyy
gaudy-day
aaddhhil
lah-di-dah
aaddhhrs
shraddha
aaddhimn
handmaid
aaddiinr
Diandria
aaddilno
dianodal
aaddkmmo
mokaddam
aaddllny
landlady
aaddlnrw
landward
aaddlnry
yardland
aaddmmqu
muqaddam
aaddnrst
sand-dart
standard

aaddnrwy
yardwand
aaddotyy
day-to-day
aaddrsty
dastardy
aadeeghr
headgear
aadeeglt
galeated
aadeegmn
endamage
aadeegnr
Gadarene
aadeehlr
hard-a-lee
aadeeilr
Airedale
aadeeirt
eradiate
aadeeirw
awearied
aadeeltv
alveated
aadeemrr
demerara
aadeentt
antedate
Edentata
aadeeqtu
adequate
aadefflt
afflated
aadeffry
affrayed
aadefhlt
flathead
aadefhst
headfast
aadefilr
fair-lead
aadefirs
faradise
aadefllr
falderal
aadeflns
sand-flea
aadeflry
defrayal
aadefltt
faldetta
aadefotu
auto-da-fé
aadefsty
feast-day
aadeggru
guardage
aadeghln
danelagh
aadeghst
stag-head
aadegill
diallage

aadegilt
gladiate
aadeginr
drainage
gardenia
aadegint
indagate
aadegitt
agitated
aadegitv
divagate
aadegjtu
adjutage
aadeglmn
Magdalen
aadeglmy
amygdale
aadeglns
seladang
aadegrrw
draw-gear
aadegrsv
savegard
aadegrtu
graduate
aadehhor
hoarhead
aadehiln
nail-head
aadehilr
headrail
railhead
aadehirr
diarrhea
aadehiwy
hideaway
aadehkmr
headmark
aadehlmp
headlamp
aadehmns
headsman
aadehmst
masthead
aadehnnr
near-hand
aadehnns
Shandean
aadehnps
sand-heap
aadehnrv
verandah
aadehopx
Hexapoda
aadehrrw
hardware
aadehrss
harassed
aadehrty
death-ray
aadehstt
hastated
aadeillr
Rallidae

aadeilmp
maid-pale
aadeilnn
Annelida
aadeilnt
dentalia
aadeilpr
praedial
aadeilps
palisade
aadeilpt
lapidate
Talpidae
aadeilrs
salaried
aadeilrt
Araldite®
aadeiltv
validate
aadeimnn
amandine
aadeimnp
pandemia
aadeimnr
marinade
aadeimnt
animated
diamanté
aadeimpz
diazepam
aadeimrv
maravedi
aadeimst
diastema
aadeinrr
darraine
aadeinrt
dentaria
aadeiprs
paradise
Sparidae
aadeipsu
diapause
aadeiptv
adaptive
aadeisst
diastase
aadeitvw
viewdata
aadejmpy
pyjamaed
aadejnnp
japanned
aadeklnr
kalendar
aadeklop
peak-load
aadeklos
soda-lake
aadekmnr
mandrake
aadellpp
appalled

aadellwy
welladay
aadelmnr
alderman
malander
aadelmns
dalesman
leadsman
aadelmpp
mad-apple
aadelmpt
date-palm
palmated
aadelmyz
amazedly
aadelnst
eastland
aadelrtu
radulate
aadelrtv
larvated
aademnnw
manna-dew
aademnot
Nematoda
aademnps
spademan
aademort
matadore
aademrru
marauder
aadenost
Sotadean
aadenrtt
tartaned
aadeoprt
tapadero
aadeopst
adespota
aadeorrt
aerodart
aadeppry
paper-day
aadeqrtu
quadrate
aaderrrw
rearward
aaderrst
star-read
aaderssw
seawards
aaderstw
eastward
aadfglns
sand-flag
aadfgnno
fandango
aadfhmnr
farm-hand
aadfhnst
handfast
aadfimrs
faradism

aadfinru
unafraid
aadfllln
landfall
aadflorw
aardwolf
aadflotx
toadflax
aadfmrry
farmyard
aadgglnn
gangland
aadggrst
staggard
aadghils
hidalgas
aadghipr
diagraph
aadghrtu
hatguard
aadgiins
gainsaid
aadgillr
gaillard
galliard
aadgilmr
madrigal
mail-drag
aadgilno
diagonal
gonadial
aadgilns
salading
aadgimpr
paradigm
aadgimrt
gradatim
aadginrr
darraign
aadginru
guardian
aadgiqru
quadriga
aadglmor
malgrado
aadglopr
podagral
aadgmnor
dragoman
Garamond
aadgmnos
goadsman
aadgmnrs
dragsman
aadgnnqu
quandang
aadgnors
Sangrado
aadgnrru
radar-gun
aadgnrtu
guardant
aadgnruv
vanguard

aadgrrtu
rat-guard
aadgrruw
gurdwara
aadhhips
padishah
aadhiinp
aphidian
aadhillr
halliard
aadhilnr
handrail
aadhilrv
havildar
aadhinrr
harridan
aadhlmoy
dalmahoy
aadhlnpy
handplay
aadhlpss
slap-dash
aadhmnny
handyman
aadhmnou
omadhaun
aadhnsst
ash-stand
aadhnstt
hatstand
aadhrrtw
thraward
aadhrryz
hazardry
aadiimnn
Indiaman
aadiinrr
air-drain
aadiiqru
daiquari
aadikllo
alkaloid
aadikllr
killadar
aadiklry
kailyard
aadikmns
damaskin
aadillllo
allodial
aadillnr
landrail
aadillrs
silladar
aadillry
radially
aadilmnn
mainland
aadilmno
domainal
domanial
aadilmnp
plaidman

aadilnor
ordalian
aadilnpr
prandial
aadilntt
dilatant
aadilops
palisado
aadilorr
railroad
aadilprs
pardalis
aadilpry
lapidary
aadilrrs
risaldar
aadilrsy
sail-yard
aadilrty
trial-day
aadimmsz
Mazdaism
aadimnnr
mandarin
aadimnrt
tamarind
aadimnry
dairyman
mainyard
aadimnrz
zamindar
aadimnss
damassin
aadimnsu
sudamina
aadimntu
Adiantum
aadimnuv
vanadium
aadimstz
samizdat
aadinnot
adnation
aadinopr
paranoid
aadinops
diapason
aadinopt
adaption
aadinprs
Spaniard
aadinpsu
Upanisad
aadinrrw
air-drawn
aadinsss
Sassanid
aadioprs
diaspora
aadiorrt
radiator
aadipsuy
upadaisy

aadirrsw
airwards
aadirrsy
disarray
aadjnttu
adjutant
aadjntuv
adjuvant
aadklmnr
landmark
aadklnpr
parkland
aadklnrs
sand-lark
aadklrtu
talukdar
aadkmnrs
darkmans
aadkorwy
workaday
aadkprrw
parkward
aadllmns
Landsmål
aadlmnns
landsman
aadlmnor
mandorla
aadlmnry
land-army
aadlmnss
landmass
aadlmnuu
laudanum
aadlmpvy
Davy-lamp
aadlnopr
parlando
aadlnost
saltando
aadlorst
loadstar
aadlortu
adulator
aadmmnow
madwoman
aadmmnsu
mandamus
aadmnors
roadsman
aadmnort
mandator
aadmnowy
day-woman
aadmoppp
pappadom
aadmorrt
tram-road
aadnnpsu
Pandanus
aadnorty
donatary
aadnosuv
vanadous

aadnoswy
nowadays
aadnprst
sand-trap
aadnpssw
sand-wasp
aadnqrsu
quadrans
aadnqrtu
quadrant
aadnqruy
quandary
aadnrsst
sand-star
aadnrvyy
navy-yard
aadopprr
paradrop
aadoprxy
paradoxy
aadopsuy
paduasoy
aadorsvy
Savoyard
aadprstv
star-pav'd
aadrstuy
Saturday
aaeeegls
sea-eagle
aaeefmst
meat-safe
aaeefrrs
seafarer
aaeegiln
alienage
aaeegilp
epigaeal
aaeeginp
epigaean
aaeeglln
enallage
aaeeglry
eagle-ray
aaeegmpr
amperage
aaeegmrs
sea-marge
aaeegmty
métayage
aaeegnno
Neogaean
aaeegnps
Pegasean
aaeegnrs
sangaree
aaeegprs
sea-grape
aaeegrtw
waterage
aaeehhst
sea-heath
aaeehirt
hetaeria

aaeehprt
earth-pea
heartpea
aaeehrrs
hare's-ear
aaeehrtw
a-weather
wheatear
wheat-ear
aaeehrwy
hereaway
aaeeilmn
Alemaine
aaeeilnt
alienate
aaeeintt
taeniate
aaeejmnp
jampanee
aaeejnps
Japanese
aaeejnsv
Javanese
aaeeklst
ale-stake
aaeekltw
latewake
aaeekmns
namesake
aaeeknrs
Kanarese
aaeeknrw
reawaken
aaeeknss
sea-snake
aaeekprt
parakeet
aaeekqsu
seaquake
aaeellm
lamellae
aaeellmt
malleate
aaeellpt
patellae
aaeelnnr
annealer
lernaean
aaeelnps
seaplane
spelaean
aaeelort
areolate
aaeelpry
leap-year
aaeelrtu
laureate
aaeelstx
slate-axe
aaeeltuv
evaluate
aaeelvwy
way-leave

aaeemmtt
team-mate
aaeemnpt
name-tape
aaeemnrt
man-eater
aaeemprs
paramese
aaeennnt
antennae
aaeennrz
Nazarene
aaeenopr
Pareoean
aaeenprt
paranete
aaeenrrs
arrasene
aaeenrst
arsenate
serenata
aaeenrtt
ant-eater
aaeenstu
nauseate
aaeepprr
appearer
rapparee
reappear
aaeeprst
asperate
separate
aaeepstt
aseptate
aaeerstt
stearate
aaeerstw
sea-water
aaeffgst
staffage
aaeffils
fail-safe
aaeffllll
leaf-fall
aaefflpr
paraffle
aaeffstt
taffetas
aaefghrw
wharfage
aaefgitt
fatigate
aaefglll
flagella
aaefglot
floatage
aaefhlry
half-year
aaefilty
fayalite
aaefimrr
airframe
aaefinnt
fainéant

aaefintx
antefixa
aaeflmtt
flatmate
aaeflrtw
flatware
aaefmrsw
frame-saw
saw-frame
aaefnrrt
tara-fern
aaefrrrw
warfarer
aaefrrwy
wayfarer
aaegghpt
peat-hagg
aaegginr
grainage
aaeggiot
agiotage
aaegglnr
langrage
aaegglnu
language
aaeggnow
wagonage
aaeggnry
garganey
aaeggopr
paragoge
aaeghkrs
shake-rag
aaeghlnp
phalange
aaeghmrx
hexagram
aaeghnru
harangue
aaeghopy
hypogaea
aaeghprt
hag-taper
aaegilln
Galilean
aaegillt
alligate
aaegilnp
Pelagian
aaegilnr
Algerian
regalian
aaegilnt
agential
alginate
aaegilrs
gasalier
aaegiltt
tail-gate
aaegimno
egomania
aaegimns
magnesia

aaegimnz
magazine
aaegimrr
marriage
aaegimrt
gematria
maritage
aaeginpp
Aganippe
aaeginps
paganise
aaeginpt
paginate
aaeginst
saginate
aaegintv
navigate
vaginate
aaegipru
periagua
aaegirsv
vagaries
aaegivwy
giveaway
aaegllms
smallage
aaegllmw
wall-game
aaegllpr
pellagra
aaegllss
galleass
aaegllst
stallage
aaeglltu
glutaeal
aaeglmnv
gavelman
aaeglmst
Almagest
aaeglnou
analogue
aaeglnpt
plantage
aaeglnrs
Sangreal
aaeglntw
law-agent
aaeglosv
aasvogel
aaeglrrs
resalgar
aaeglrst
agrestal
aaeglrty
legatary
aaeglsvy
savagely
aaegltuv
vaultage
aaegmmnr
engramma
aaegmnpy
pygmaean

aaegmnrv
gravamen
aaegmorr
aerogram
aaegmors
sagamore
aaegmpru
rampauge
aaegmrrv
margrave
aaegmrry
gramarye
aaegmttw
megawatt
aaegnnop
neopagan
aaegnnru
near-gaun
aaegnoot
Notogaea
aaegnrst
staragen
aaegnrtu
runagate
aaegnstt
stagnate
aaegntuv
vauntage
aaegorrt
arrogate
aaegortt
aegrotat
aaegpprr
rag-paper
aaegpprw
wrappage
aaegprtw
water-gap
aaegrsss
sea-grass
aaegrstw
gas-water
water-gas
aaegrstz
star-gaze
aaegrsvy
savagery
aaegrvwx
grave-wax
aaegsstw
tasswage
aaehiirt
hetairai
hetairia
aaehilmn
hielaman
aaehilnp
aphelian
aaehilnr
Harleian
aaehilns
Sahelian
aaehilnt
anthelia

aaehilpr
parhelia
aaehilrs
hair-seal
aaehimnt
anthemia
haematin
aaehimrt
Mithraea
aaehinnt
Athenian
aaehinpt
aphanite
aaehinrt
Atherina
Rhaetian
aaehinst
asthenia
aaehirtt
Hatteria
aaehirvw
hair-wave
aaehklst
alkahest
aaehkmry
haymaker
aaehlmnw
whale-man
aaehlmsy
sealyham
aaehlmtu
hamulate
aaehlntx
exhalant
aaehlprs
harp-seal
pearl-ash
aaehlprx
hexaplar
aaehlpuv
upheaval
aaehlrtt
theatral
aaehmnpy
Nymphaea
aaehmnrs
shareman
shearman
aaehmopr
amphorae
aaehmort
atheroma
aaehnpst
pheasant
aaehnpsy
synaphea
aaehnttx
xanthate
aaehoprt
opera-hat
aaehrrss
harasser
aaehrtwx
earthwax

aaeiikns
akinesia
aaeiinrs
Arianise
aaeijmns
Jamesian
aaeikkmz
kamikaze
aaeiklln
alkaline
aaeiklls
alkalies
alkalise
aaeikmrr
krameria
aaeilllu
alleluia
aaeillmm
mamillae
aaeillmx
maxillae
aaeillpp
papillae
aaeillpt
palliate
aaeillrt
arillate
aaeillry
aerially
aaeilltt
talliate
aaeilmnt
laminate
aaeilmnv
velamina
aaeilmrs
Marsilea
aaeilmrt
material
aaeilnnn
Linnaean
aaeilnns
annalise
aaeilnnz
Zelanian
aaeilnpr
airplane
aaeilnpt
palatine
aaeilnru
aurelian
aaeilnrv
valerian
aaeilnss
nasalise
Salesian
sea-snail
aaeilntt
antliate
Latinate
aaeilntv
aventail
aaeilpps
papalise

aaeilprt
parietal
aaeilpst
stapelia
aaeilrrt
arterial
aaeilrtv
varietal
aaeilstv
aestival
salivate
aaeilstx
saxatile
aaeiltvx
laxative
aaeimnno
Maeonian
aaeimnnr
Armenian
aaeimnot
metanoia
aaeimnpr
pearmain
aaeimnpt
impanate
aaeimnrt
marinate
aaeimnrz
mazarine
aaeimopr
paroemia
aaeimotx
toxaemia
aaeinnpr
Naperian
aaeinntt
antenati
aaeinort
aeration
aaeinorx
anorexia
aaeinppr
Priapean
aaeinprt
Patarine
Tarpeian
aaeinrst
antisera
Artesian
Erastian
resinata
aaeinrsu
Eurasian
aaeinrsy
Aryanise
aaeinrtt
reattain
aaeinrtu
inaurate
aaeinrtz
Nazarite

aaeinstt
astatine
sanitate
tanaiste
aaeinstv
sanative
aaeinttt
titanate
aaeipprs
appraise
aaeiprst
aspirate
parasite
septaria
aaeiprtt
patriate
aaeiprtz
trapezia
aaeiprxy
apyrexia
aaeirrrt
terraria
aaeirrtt
Tartarie
aaeirsst
Asterias
aaeirstt
aristate
aaeirttz
zaratite
aaeittvx
taxative
aaejnnpr
japanner
aaejnpsy
Japanesy
aaekllst
salt-lake
aaeklmrw
law-maker
aaeklmry
malarkey
aaeklnrs
larnakes
aaeklopp
oak-apple
aaekmrwy
way-maker
aaeknprt
partaken
aaeknrrr
rear-rank
aaekprrt
partaker
aaelllmr
lamellar
aaelllms
small-ale
aaelllpr
parallel
aaellmpu
ampullae
aaellnpu
planulae

aaellorv
alveolar
aaellprt
patellar
aaelltwy
alley-taw
aaellwwy
wellaway
aaellwyy
alleyway
aaelmmno
melanoma
aaelmmtu
malamute
aaelmnpt
plateman
aaelmnrt
maternal
aaelmnss
salesman
aaelmnst
talesman
aaelmnsw
wealsman
aaelmnsy
seamanly
aaelmppy
may-apple
aaelmprr
rear-lamp
aaelmprt
malapert
aaelmprx
examplar
aaelmpry
play-mare
aaelmpss
lampasse
aaelmpst
plateasm
aaelmptv
vamplate
aaelmpty
playmate
aaelmrsy
lamasery
aaelmrtt
maltreat
aaelnnnt
antennal
aaelnnot
neonatal
aaelnntu
annulate
aaelnoss
seasonal
aaelnppt
pea-plant
aaelnprs
prenasal
aaelnprt
parental
paternal
prenatal

aaelnprw
warplane
aaelnpst
pleasant
aaelnptt
tea-plant
aaelnrsy
analyser
aaelnrtt
alterant
alternat
aaelnrtx
relaxant
aaelnssv
envassal
aaelnssy
analyses
aaelnstt
Atlantes
aaelnstv
slave-ant
aaelorty
aleatory
aaelppsu
applause
aaelprst
palestra
aaelprsy
paralyse
aaelprtt
tetrapla
aaelpstv
palstave
aaelptuv
vapulate
aaelptux
plateaux
aaelrtuv
velatura
aaelruzz
zarzuela
aaelrwyy
waylayer
aaelsstx
sales-tax
aaemmnrt
armament
aaemmstt
stemmata
aaemnosw
sea-woman
aaemnotz
metazoan
aaemnprs
Parmesan
spearman
aaemnprt
name-part
parament
aaemnrst
sarmenta
semantra
aaemnrtt
atrament
aaemnrtw
waterman
aaemntux
manteaux
aaemortt
teratoma
aaemostt
steatoma
aaemottu
automate
aaempttu
amputate
aaemqstu
squamate
aaemrrtu
armature
aaemrrtw
water-ram
aaemrttu
maturate
aaemrtwy
water-yam
aaennnst
antennas
aaennott
annotate
aaennstt
stannate
aaennstu
nauseant
aaenorru
aurorean
aaenorsu
araneous
aaenortu
aeronaut
aaenosst
assonate
aaenpprt
apparent
trappean
aaenprty
prytanea
aaenpstt
antepast
aaenrstv
tsarevna
aaenrsuw
unawares
aaenrtty
Tyrtaean
aaeopstt
apostate
aaeorstt
aerostat
aaepprrt
tar-paper
aaepprwx
wax-paper
aaeppstt
appestat
aaeprstw
pea-straw
aaeprttw
tap-water
water-tap
aaeprtty
tea-party
aaeprtxy
tax-payer
aaepstty
stay-tape
aaerrsuu
Saururae
aaerrttt
tartrate
aaerrttw
tar-water
water-rat
aaerrwwy
war-weary
aaersttu
saturate
aaertwwy
waterway
aaffgils
gaff-sail
aaffhllo
half-loaf
aaffilrt
taffrail
aaffinpr
paraffin
aafflpst
palstaff
aafflstu
afflatus
aaffnnor
fanfaron
aaffsttu
tau-staff
aafgllnu
langlauf
aafglnrt
flagrant
aafgnrrt
fragrant
aafhhikl
khalifah
aafhiklt
khalifat
khilafat
aafhirst
airshaft
aafhlmst
half-mast
aafhlsty
lay-shaft
aafhrrtw
wharf-rat
aafhrsuu
hausfrau
aafiillm
familial
aafiillr
filarial
aafiilmr
familiar
aafiinst
fistiana
aafiklly
alkalify
aafillnr
rainfall
aafilmst
fatalism
aafilopr
parafoil
aafilptx
pita-flax
aafilstt
fatalist
aafiltty
fatality
aafimnor
foramina
aafinnov
Favonian
aafinnrs
safranin
aafinort
Fanariot
aafinrrw
warfarin
aafinstu
faustian
aafllprt
fall-trap
pratfall
trap-fall
aaflmorv
lavaform
aaflnott
floatant
aaflstwy
flatways
aafmnorw
man-of-war
aafmnrst
raftsman
aaggginr
garaging
aaggilnr
gangliar
aaggimnn
managing
aaggimnr
maraging
aaggittw
gigawatt
aaggllly
lallygag
aaggmnns
gangsman
aaghhins
shanghai
aaghilnn
hangnail
aaghilpy
hypalgia
aaghilrs
harigals
aaghimns
ashaming
aaghimrt
taghairm
aaghinps
paganish
aaghiprr
airgraph
aaghirsv
vagarish
aaghkmny
gymkhana
aaghlnns
Langshan
aaghlnpy
anaglyph
aaghmnoy
Hogmanay
mahogany
aaghmrss
marsh-gas
aaghnopr
agraphon
aaghoopz
Zoophaga
aaghoppr
apograph
aaghrrtu
arraught
aaghsstu
Gasthaus
aagiilmn
imaginal
aagiilnv
availing
aagiimst
astigmia
aagiinnt
Ignatian
aagijrtu
Gujarati
aagiklno
kaoliang
aagikluy
kaliyuga
aagikmrs
skiagram
aagillnu
Anguilla
aagillny
allaying
aagillss
galliass
aagilltv
gallivat
aagilluz
alguazil
aagilmno
magnolia
aagilmnr
alarming
marginal
aagilmot
gliomata
aagilnrr
larrigan
aagilnrs
Sangrail
aagilnuv
vaginula
aagiloop
apologia
aagilpry
plagiary
aagilrrw
warrigal
aagilstt
sagittal
aagimmrr
marigram
aagimnnn
manganin
aagimnps
paganism
aagimnrr
margarin
aagimnsy
gymnasia
aagimptu
patagium
aagimstt
stigmata
aaginnot
agnation
aaginntv
vaginant
aaginntw
awanting
aaginsst
assignat
aaginssu
gaussian
aaginssy
assaying
aagiortt
agitator
aagirstv
gravitas
stravaig
aagknoor
kangaroo
aagknorr
Ragnarök
aagkpprs
spark-gap
aagllmoy
allogamy
aagllnry
laryngal
aagllopy
polygala
aagllowy
Galloway
aagllpsw
gall-wasp

aaglmnss
glassman
aaglmops
sago-palm
aaglnnoo
analogon
aaglnopt
Plantago
aaglnpst
gas-plant
aaglnquu
aqualung
aaglnrru
granular
aaglntuu
Ungulata
aaglopry
paralogy
aaglrstu
gastrula
aagmmort
gram-atom
aagmnnor
nanogram
aagmnopz
zampogna
aagmnort
martagon
aagmnorw
ragwoman
aagmnssw
swagsman
aagmnsty
syntagma
aagmotuy
autogamy
aagmrsst
matgrass
aagnnstt
stagnant
aagnoprt
tragopan
aagnorrt
arrogant
tarragon
aagnortu
argonaut
aagnrtuy
guaranty
aagnstuu
Augustan
aagorsss
sargasso
aagorsst
oat-grass
aagrsstu
sastruga
aagrstuz
zastruga
aahhlloo
holla-hoa
aahhlluu
hula-hula

aahiikrr
hara-kiri
hari-kari
aahiilrt
hair-tail
aahijprs
rajaship
aahiklps
pashalik
aahilmnr
harmalin
aahilnnt
inhalant
aahilnot
halation
aahilnst
Stahlian
aahilpsy
physalia
aahimnps
pashmina
aahinntx
xanthian
aahinort
Horatian
aahinprt
Parthian
aahinrsw
rain-wash
aahinrtu
hauriant
aahipsxy
asphyxia
aahjnnot
Jonathan
aahkllmr
hallmark
aahkmotw
tomahawk
aahkprsw
spar-hawk
aahkrssw
saw-shark
aahllloo
hallaloo
aahllopt
allopath
aahlmoos
masoolah
aahlmstu
thalamus
aahlnpst
ash-plant
aahlnptt
hat-plant
aahmmnrs
marshman
aahmmorr
Moharram
aahmmrru
Muharram
aahmnort
marathon

aahmnost
hoastman
aahmnotx
xanthoma
aahmnpst
phantasm
aahmorss
Massorah
aahmrsst
stramash
aahnootz
Anthozoa
aahnprsu
Raphanus
aahnpsty
phantasy
aahnrtux
Xanthura
aahoprtu
autoharp
aahrrttw
thrawart
aahrsttw
straw-hat
aaiikknn
kinakina
aaiillqu
quillaia
aaiilmns
mainsail
aaiilmnt
Tamilian
aaiilmrs
Marsilia
aaiilnpr
Aprilian
aaiilnrz
alizarin
aaiilnsv
Salvinia
aaiilnux
uniaxial
aaiilprr
prairial
riparial
aaiilrtx
triaxial
aaiilrux
auxiliar
aaiimnnr
Arminian
aaiimnnt
maintain
aaiimnpx
panmixia
aaiimnrs
Arianism
aaiinntt
Titanian
aaiinotv
aviation
aaiinprr
riparian

aaiinprs
Parisian
aaiinpzz
piazzian
aaiinrst
intarsia
aaiiopst
apositia
aaiiorrt
air-to-air
aaiiortz
zoiatria
aaiiprst
apiarist
aaiirstv
aviarist
aaiirstw
wistaria
aaiirtvx
aviatrix
aaijllqu
quillaja
aaijnryz
janizary
aaiklnor
Kolarian
aaiklnst
nastalik
aaiklrst
sark-tail
aaikmnst
antimask
aaikmrst
tamarisk
aaiksstv
svastika
aaiksstw
swastika
aaillluv
alluvial
aaillmmm
mammilla
aaillmmr
mamillar
aaillmnt
mantilla
aaillmny
animally
aaillnov
vallonia
aaillppr
papillar
aaillrry
arillary
aaillrxy
axillary
aailmnnt
lamantin
aailmnop
palamino
aailmnor
manorial
morainal

aailmnox
monaxial
aailmnps
panislam
aailmnru
manurial
aailmnry
laminary
aailmnst
staminal
talisman
aailmnsv
navalism
aailmopt
lipomata
aailmorr
armorial
aailmpps
papalism
aailmprt
primatal
aailmrst
alarmist
alastrim
aailmttu
ultimata
aailnnot
national
aailnnpt
plainant
plantain
aailnnru
lunarian
aailnnst
annalist
santalin
aailnops
salopian
aailnopt
talapoin
aailnort
notarial
rational
aailnosv
Slavonia
aailnotv
lavation
aailnprt
air-plant
aailnpru
planuria
aailnptu
Laputian
aailnqtu
aliquant
aailnssy
analysis
aailnstt
Atlantis
aailnsty
nasality
aailnttt
latitant

aailntty
natality
aailorrs
rasorial
aailorrv
variolar
aailppru
puparial
aailppst
papalist
aailprst
triapsal
aailrstt
rat's-tail
aailrstz
Lazarist
aailrsvy
salivary
aailssty
staysail
aaimmnrr
arm-in-arm
aaimmnst
mainmast
aaimmrsu
samarium
aaimnnor
Maronian
Romanian
aaimnnru
Rumanian
aaimnort
animator
montaria
tamanoir
aaimnorv
Moravian
aaimnorw
airwoman
aaimnprz
marzipan
aaimnptu
putamina
aaimnrrt
trimaran
aaimnrru
ranarium
aaimnsst
mantissa
satanism
aaimnstu
amiantus
aaimnsty
mainstay
aaimoprs
mariposa
aaimprst
pastrami
aaimqruu
aquarium
aaimrrsy
misarray
aainnopv
pavonian

aainnost
sonatina
aainnosu
Ausonian
aainnott
natation
aainnotv
Novatian
aainnrtu
nutarian
Turanian
aainnsst
naissant
aainnssy
sannyasi
aainorrs
rosarian
aainorrt
Rotarian
aainottx
taxation
aainprst
aspirant
partisan
aainprtz
partizan
aainpstu
sapi-utan
aainqrtu
quatrain
aainqttu
aquatint
aainrrss
sarrasin
aainrrst
Sartrian
aainrrsz
sarrazin
aainrssy
Assyrian
aainrstu
Austrian
Saturnia
aainrsty
sanitary
aainrtwy
way-train
aainssss
assassin
aainsstt
satanist
aainsttt
antistat
aainstty
satanity
aaioprrt
troparia
aaioprsu
parousia
aaiopstu
autopsia
aaiqrstu
aquarist

aaiqrsuu
Aquarius
aairsstt
tsaritsa
aairstwy
stairway
aajmmorr
marjoram
aakkmmoo
makomako
aaklmnns
Klansman
aaklmruy
yarmulka
aaklprty
kalyptra
aakmmnrs
marksman
aakmnrsw
swan-mark
aakmossu
moussaka
aaknprtt
tank-trap
aallllmp
pall-mall
aalllsty
lay-stall
aallmmrs
small-arm
aallmnst
stallman
aallmnsy
sally-man
aallmnty
tallyman
aallmnuy
manually
aallmppy
palm-play
aallnnuy
annually
aallnpru
planular
aalloorw
wallaroo
aallorsu
allosaur
aallprst
plastral
aallruvv
valvular
aalmnort
matronal
aalmnoru
monaural
aalmnpsu
Paul's-man
aalmnpty
tympanal
aalmnstu
Santalum
aalmnttu
tantalum

aalmntuu
autumnal
aalmooss
massoola
aalmostt
stomatal
aalmppsu
paspalum
aalmpsty
platysma
aalmqsuu
squamula
aalnnopt
pantalon
aalnnpuu
punaluan
aalnoprt
patronal
aalnopru
Anoplura
aalnpstu
Platanus
aalnsttu
tantalus
aalopprv
approval
aaloprst
pastoral
aalortuv
valuator
aalortvy
lavatory
aalprstu
pastural
spatular
aalrrtty
tartarly
aalrssvy
vassalry
aalrsttw
stalwart
aalrstuy
salutary
aammnprs
rampsman
aammotxy
myxomata
aammrssu
marasmus
aamnnopr
apron-man
aamnprty
party-man
aamnqsuw
squawman
aamoprru
paramour
aamorstt
stromata
aannosst
assonant
aannrsty
stannary

aanooppx
opopanax
aanooprz
parazoon
aanoprty
anatropy
aanorrrt
narrator
aanorsty
sanatory
aanortty
natatory
aanrrtwy
warranty
aanrsttu
saturant
aaopssty
apostasy
aaorsstt
starosta
aaorsuvv
vavasour
aaorsvvy
vavasory
aaostwwy
stowaway
aaprrstt
star-trap
aarrsttu
Tartarus
aarsttuy
statuary
abbbdeel
bedabble
abbbgiln
babbling
blabbing
abbbhsuy
bush-baby
abbbirty
Babbitry
abbcckmo
back-comb
abbcdkno
backbond
abbceeir
Caribbee
abbceeru
barbecue
abbcegir
cribbage
abbcehou
babouche
abbcehtu
bathcube
abbceikt
backbite
abbceilr
barbicel
abbcekln
black-neb
abbceklu
blueback

abbcekno
backbone
abbceknu
buckbean
abbcellu
clubable
abbcelrs
scrabble
abbcelru
curbable
abbcgior
gabbroic
abbciill
biblical
abbciinr
rabbinic
abbcikrt
brickbat
abbcinoy
cabin-boy
abbckloy
blackboy
abbcnory
corn-baby
abbddeel
beddable
abbddeil
biddable
abbdeeer
bee-bread
abbdeelt
bed-table
abbdeert
rabbeted
abbdeilr
ad-libber
abbdelmo
babeldom
abbdelrr
drabbler
abbdenru
unbarbed
abbdeors
absorbed
abbdfooy
babyfood
abbdgiln
dabbling
abbdgior
gabbroid
abbdhirs
drabbish
abbdhirt
birdbath
abbdhooy
babyhood
abbdilno
bail-bond
abbdnorw
bawd-born
abbeeims
Babeeism
abbeeinr
bearbine

abbeejrr
jabberer
abbeejrs
bejabers
abbeenor
barebone
abbeertt
barbette
abbefgir
brief-bag
abbehils
babelish
abbehkru
hub-brake
abbehort
bathrobe
abbeilms
babelism
abbeilnu
bubaline
abbeilot
bilobate
abbeilst
bistable
abbeintt
tabbinet
abbeirrt
rabbiter
abbelopr
probable
abbeloru
belabour
abbelqsu
squabble
abbelrsy
slabbery
abbemoor
aerobomb
abbenors
base-born
abbeorrs
absorber
reabsorb
abbeortw
browbeat
abberrry
barberry
abberryy
bayberry
abbggiln
gabbling
abbgginr
grabbing
abbgilnr
rabbling
abbgilnu
baubling
abbgilnw
wabbling
abbginst
stabbing
abbginsw
swabbing

abbginty tabbying
abbhiims bimbashi
abbhilsy shabbily
abbhrruy rhubarby
abbiinot bibation
abbiklln bank-bill
abbiknry kirn-baby
abbillot boatbill
abbillsu sillabub
abbilmno nail-bomb
abbilost bioblast
abbirrty rabbitry
abbirsuu suburbia
abbkknoo bank-book
abblllow blowball
abbllsuy syllabub
abblopry probably
abbnrsuu suburban
abbossty bobstays
abccdeho caboched
abccdhik dabchick
abcceehn bechance
abcceelp peccable
abcceeor caboceer
abcceflu club-face
abcceily celibacy
abcceirt bacteric
abccekmo come-back
abccesuu succubae
abcchisu bacchius
abcchnoo cabochon
abcchoox coach-box
abccikkk kickback
abccikkp pickback
abccikor abricock
abccilor carbolic
abccilot cobaltic
abccinor carbonic
abcciors ascorbic
abcckllo ballcock
abccklox clack-box
abcckoot cockboat
abcckrtu buckcart
abccssuu succubas
abcddeor brocaded
abcdeefk feed-back
abcdeelm becalmed
abcdeelu educable
abcdeemr embraced
abcdegir birdcage cagebird
abcdehir chair-bed
abcdehlu club-head
abcdehnr branched
abcdehos caboshed
abcdeiit diabetic
abcdeiks backside
abcdeilr calibred
abcdeklo bale-dock blockade
abcdeklv backveld
abcdeknn neck-band
abcdeknu unbacked
abcdekot boat-deck
abcdeloo caboodle
abcdelsu bud-scale
abcdemnu dumb-cane
abcdemot combated
abcdenru unbraced
abcdentu abducent
abcdfruy farcy-bud
abcdhklo holdback
abcdiilo biocidal diabolic
abcdiimy cymbidia
abcdiklo bail-dock
abcdiklr baldrick
abcdikru baudrick
abcdillr birdcall call-bird
abcdilou cuboidal
abcdirsu subacrid
abcdknow backdown
abcdkoor back-door
abcdkopr backdrop
abcdkorw backword
abcdloot bald-coot
abcdnruw cub-drawn
abcdoorw crab-wood
abcdopru cupboard
abcdortu abductor
abcdoruy obduracy
abceeefk beefcake
abceefnt benefact
abceehlm béchamel
abceehln alebench
abceehlr bleacher
abceehno bone-ache
abceeilt celibate
abceeimn ambience
abceelno bone-lace
abceelrr cerebral
abceelrt bracelet
abceemrr embracer
abceenov bone-cave
abceerrt crab-tree
abcefiit beatific
abcefikr backfire fire-back
abcefino boniface
abcegkll blackleg
abcegklo blockage
abcegnor bongrace
abcegnst scent-bag
abcehitt bathetic
abcehktw bethwack
abcehlor bachelor
abcehlsu chasuble
abcehltu leach-tub
abcehmot hecatomb
abcehnrr brancher
abcehopu pabouche
abcehorr broacher
abcehoru barouche
abcehrtt bratchet
abceijnr jib-crane
abceijot Jacobite
abceikkl kickable
abceiklr crablike
abceikrt brick-tea
abceikwz Zwieback
abceillr cribella
abceillt balletic
abceilnn binnacle
abceilnu baculine
abceilor albicore cabriole
abceilos sociable
abceiltt bittacle
abceiltu baculite
abceimst betacism
abceinoo coenobia
abceintu incubate
abceiors aerobics
abceiort boracite
abceirrt cribrate
abceirsw crabwise
abceirtt brattice
abceirty acerbity
abceisss abscisse
abceisst asbestic
abcejklt jet-black
abcejlty abjectly
abcekksw skew-back
abceklmo mockable
abceklpu palebuck
abcekoos bookcase casebook
abcekopr back-rope
abcellpu culpable
abcellsu bucellas
abcelmny lambency
abcelmrs scambler scramble
abcelnot balconet
abcelnuu nubecula
abceloot bootlace lace-boot
abcelort brocatel
abcelost obstacle
abcelotu bluecoat
abcelrsw bescrawl
abcelrtt bractlet
abcelttu table-cut
abcemnru cream-bun
abcenouy buoyance
abcentux excubant
abceosux sauce-box
abcerrtu carburet
abcerstu sabre-cut
abcertuu cubature
abcestuu subacute
abcffotu buff-coat
abcfikll backfill
abcfilos bifocals
abcfklox black-fox
abcfkost softback
abcflllu bull-calf
abcflmox flax-comb
abcggimo gambogic
abcghint batching
abcghkos hog's-back
abcgikln blacking
abcgiknr king-crab
abcgilno log-cabin

abcgilru
Bulgaric
abcgkluy
lucky-bag
abchikls
blackish
abchikrs
brackish
abchilmo
choliamb
abchimor
choriamb
abchinor
bronchia
abchioor
borachio
abchirrt
tribrach
abchklot
hackbolt
abchkmpu
humpback
abchkoop
chapbook
abchkoos
cash-book
abchksuw
buck-wash
abchlluu
club-haul
abchmotx
matchbox
abchoptx
patch-box
abchotwx
watch-box
abciikrr
air-brick
abciinot
cibation
abciiors
isobaric
abciirst
tribasic
abciisty
basicity
abciitux
bauxitic
abciklll
back-lill
abciknps
backspin
abcillny
billy-can
abcillru
lubrical
abcillsu
bacillus
abcillsy
syllabic
abcilnpu
publican
abcilosy
sociably

abcilrru
rubrical
abcimorr
microbar
abcimrtu
umbratic
abcinoru
conurbia
abcinpuy
panic-buy
abcinrvy
vibrancy
abciossu
scabious
abcirstt
abstrict
abcjkoot
boot-jack
jackboot
abckkorw
backwork
abckllos
ballocks
abckllpu
pull-back
abcklopt
blacktop
abcklosw
slowback
abcklotu
blackout
abckmoor
backroom
abckmorr
brockram
abckmoss
moss-back
abckmost
backmost
abcknrtu
turnback
abckooru
buckaroo
abckopst
backstop
abcllnor
corn-ball
abcllpuy
culpably
abclmnou
Columban
abclmsuy
scybalum
abclnory
carbonyl
abclorxy
carboxyl
abclpruw
pub-crawl
abclsssu
subclass
abclsuuu
subucula

abcmoort
mobocrat
abcnnoru
conurban
abcnnoyy
nancy-boy
abcnorty
corybant
abcnouyy
buoyancy
abcorrss
crossbar
abcorrtu
turbocar
abcorssu
scabrous
abcosstu
subcosta
abcosttu
cottabus
abcrsttu
subtract
abddeeht
death-bed
abddeenr
reed-band
abddeerr
debarred
abddeest
bedstead
abddehmo
hebdomad
abddehoy
hobdayed
abddeils
disabled
abddeilu
buddleia
abddeinr
brandied
abddeins
side-band
abddeinv
divan-bed
abddelot
dead-bolt
abddelry
bladdery
abddennu
unbanded
abddenor
dead-born
abddersw
bedwards
abddhior
rhabdoid
abddilmo
lambdoid
abddilry
ladybird
abddimno
bondmaid
abdeeefn
bedeafen

abdeeenr
Aberdeen
abdeeerv
beavered
bereaved
abdeeflm
flambéed
abdeefnr
reef-band
abdeeggl
bedaggle
abdeeghr
herbaged
abdeegln
gable-end
abdeegru
bedeguar
abdeehno
bonehead
abdeehrt
breathed
abdeehst
Bethesda
abdeeiln
deniable
abdeeilr
bride-ale
rideable
abdeeilt
delibate
abdeeilw
bewailed
abdeeirt
Abderite
ebriated
abdeeist
diabetes
abdeekmr
bedmaker
embarked
abdeeknr
bedarken
abdeelll
labelled
abdeellw
weldable
abdeelno
Denebola
abdeelnt
bandelet
abdeelor
lee-board
abdeelpt
bed-plate
abdeelzz
bedazzle
abdeemns
beam-ends
bedesman
abdeemrr
embarred
abdeennr
bannered

abdeeprs
bespread
abdeeprx
pax-brede
abdeerry
rye-bread
abdeerst
breasted
abdeertt
drabette
abdeertw
water-bed
abdeffst
bed-staff
abdefhlr
half-bred
abdeflnu
fundable
unfabled
abdeflor
fordable
abdefnru
faburden
abdeggil
diggable
abdegiio
Gobiidae
abdegiln
blindage
abdegilu
guidable
abdegimr
game-bird
abdegino
gabioned
abdegins
debasing
abdegirr
abridger
abdeglot
globated
abdeglry
badgerly
abdeglsu
slug-a-bed
abdegnor
bondager
abdegnos
dog'sbane
abdegnow
wagon-bed
abdegopr
pegboard
abdehill
billhead
abdehitu
habitude
abdehklu
bulkhead
abdehlln
handbell
abdehllu
bullhead

abdehlot
bolt-head
abdehmoo
head-boom
abdehntu
unbathed
abdehorr
abhorred
abdehosw
beshadow
abdeiirt
diatribe
abdeiknu
baudekin
abdeilmn
mandible
abdeilnr
bilander
abdeilnt
bidental
abdeilny
deniably
abdeilov
voidable
abdeilry
diablery
abdeiltu
dutiable
abdeimnr
brideman
abdeimoo
amoeboid
abdeimor
amberoid
abdeinor
debonair
abdeinrs
air-bends
brandise
abdeinsu
unbiased
abdeintu
unbaited
abdeipss
piss-a-bed
abdeirty
Darbyite
abdeissu
disabuse
abdeittu
dubitate
abdeklnp
plank-bed
abdeklsw
skewbald
abdeknnu
unbanked
abdeknru
unbarked
abdeknsu
sun-baked
abdekory
keyboard

abdellor
bead-roll
abdellot
balloted
abdellpu
balled-up
abdelmno
lemon-dab
abdelmnu
unblamed
abdelnor
banderol
abdelnry
bylander
abdelnss
baldness
abdeloru
laboured
abdelpty
play-debt
abdemoor
rood-beam
abdemrsu
Bermudas
abdemrtu
drumbeat
umbrated
abdennos
nose-band
abdennrw
brand-new
abdenorw
rawboned
abdenory
boneyard
abdenotw
downbeat
abdenrru
unbarred
abdenrss
drabness
abdenrst
bandster
abdenrtu
breadnut
turbaned
abdenttu
débutant
abdeorru
arboured
abdeorrw
wardrobe
abdeorsw
sow-bread
abdeortu
obdurate
abdeorux
Bordeaux
abderssu
surbased
abderstu
surbated
abderstw
bedstraw

abdertuw
draw-tube
abdesttu
taste-bud
abdffloy
badly-off
abdffoor
off-board
abdfhins
band-fish
abdfloot
foldboat
abdgggoy
doggy-bag
abdghinr
hangbird
abdgiinr
braiding
abdgilly
dilly-bag
abdgilnr
bardling
abdgilor
gaol-bird
abdgimru
guimbard
abdginny
bandying
abdginor
boarding
abdgitty
ditty-bag
abdgloor
logboard
abdhhssu
shadbush
abdhiist
dishabit
abdhilln
handbill
abdhilns
blandish
abdhinrs
brandish
abdhiors
broadish
abdhiprs
bardship
abdhirty
birthday
abdhknoo
handbook
abdhlnos
ash-blond
abdhmotu
badmouth
abdhsttu
dust-bath
abdiijlr
jail-bird
abdiillr
billiard
abdiimnr
mid-brain

abdiimrs
Braidism
abdiimsu
basidium
abdiinos
obsidian
abdiinrr
rain-bird
abdiintt
banditti
abdiirty
rabidity
abdiklnr
blinkard
abdilorw
wild-boar
abdilost
blastoid
abdilrry
ribaldry
abdilrzz
blizzard
abdinopr
pair-bond
abdinoty
antibody
abdinrty
banditry
abdirruy
ribaudry
abdklnoo
bookland
abdkooor
road-book
abdllnos
slobland
abdllstu
dust-ball
abdlootx
blood-tax
abdlrsuy
absurdly
abdmnnos
bondsman
abdmnoor
moor-band
abdmnouw
mawbound
abdmoopr
mopboard
abdnoorr
barndoor
abdnorsu
Baudrons
sound-bar
abdnoruy
boundary
abdoortu
outboard
abdoossw
basswood
abeeeert
bee-eater

abeeegrv
beverage
abeeehtt
hebetate
abeeenrr
near-beer
abeeenrt
tenebrae
abeeenrv
bereaven
abeeenst
absentee
abeeepru
beau-pere
abeefilr
bale-fire
abeefils
feasible
abeefilt
flea-bite
abeefirs
sea-brief
abeeflll
fellable
abeeflln
befallen
abeeforr
forebear
abeeggnr
green-bag
abeeginr
baregine
abeegirv
verbiage
abeegklr
leg-break
abeegllr
gabeller
abeegmry
emery-bag
abeegmty
megabyte
abeegrst
absterge
abeegttu
baguette
abeehilr
hireable
abeehint
thebaine
abeehirs
Hebraise
abeehlll
heel-ball
abeehllr
harebell
abeehnop
Phoebean
abeehnpp
behappen
abeehnss
has-beens
abeehntt
hebetant

abeehqtu
bequeath
abeehrrt
breather
abeehrst
hartbees
abeeikll
likeable
abeeiklt
Bakelite®
abeeikrt
tie-break
abeeillr
reliable
abeeillv
leviable
liveable
abeeilnp
plebeian
abeeilns
Balinese
base-line
abeeilnv
enviable
abeeilpx
expiable
abeeilrt
liberate
abeeilst
sea-blite
abeeilsv
evasible
abeeilsz
seizable
sizeable
abeeiltv
evitable
abeeilvw
viewable
abeeimrt
amberite
abeeinsu
Eusebian
abeeinty
ayenbite
abeeiprs
bepraise
abeeirtv
breviate
abeeitux
beauxite
abeejmor
jamboree
abeejnpu
Punjabee
abeeklot
keelboat
abeekmnr
embanker
abeekmrr
re-embark
abeekoop
peekaboo

abeekrst
bestreak
abeellls
sellable
abeelllt
tellable
abeellot
ballotee
abeellov
loveable
abeelmmr
embalmer
emmarble
abeelmno
bone-meal
abeelmov
moveable
abeelmpr
preamble
abeelmrt
atremble
abeelmss
assemble
assemblé
beamless
abeelmtt
embattle
abeelnop
beanpole
openable
abeelnrt
rentable
abeelntu
tuneable
abeelopr
operable
ropeable
abeelorx
exorable
abeelrry
ale-berry
abeelrsu
reusable
abeelrsv
beslaver
abeelrtt
batteler
abeelrtu
bateleur
abeelsss
baseless
abeelsst
bateless
abeelssu
sublease
abeelstt
seat-belt
testable
abeemmnr
membrane
abeemmru
bummaree
abeemnor
bemoaner

abeemnst
basement
abeemntt
abetment
batement
abeennrt
banneret
abeennru
eburnean
abeenntu
unbeaten
abeenors
seaborne
abeenotz
benzoate
abeenrrt
banterer
abeenrss
bareness
abeensss
baseness
abeeorrv
overbear
abeeortv
overbeat
abeeprry
peaberry
abeerrrt
barterer
abeerrsy
seaberry
abeerrtt
barrette
abeerrtv
vertebra
abeerrty
betrayer
teaberry
abeerstu
suberate
abeestwy
sweet-bay
abeffkor
off-break
abefgllr
bergfall
abefhils
fishable
abefhllu
half-blue
abefilll
fallible
abefillm
filmable
abefillr
fire-ball
abefillt
liftable
abefilot
lifeboat
abefilsu
fabulise
abefilsy
feasibly
abefirrt
firebrat
abefituy
beautify
abefklnt
left-bank
abefllmu
blameful
abeflltu
tableful
abeflnru
funebral
abefoort
barefoot
abefortu
Beaufort
abefrruy
February
abegghlu
huggable
abeggiln
beagling
abegglos
gas-globe
abegglry
beggarly
abeghilp
philabeg
abeghorr
begorrah
abeghrry
hagberry
abeghrst
barghest
abegiknn
bean-king
abegiknr
breaking
abegilns
singable
abegilnt
bleating
tangible
abegilot
obligate
abeginor
aborigen
abegintt
abetting
abegintw
wingbeat
abegippr
bagpiper
abegipps
bagpipes
abegirtu
auger-bit
abegkors
grosbeak
abeglllu
gullable
abegllor
bargello
abeglmuy
mealy-bug
abeglstu
gustable
abegmnos
gambeson
abegmnoy
bogey-man
money-bag
abegmort
bergamot
abegnrst
bangster
abegnrtu
burganet
abegnstu
subagent
abegoors
bargoose
abegorrw
row-barge
abegostx
stage-box
abegrruv
burgrave
abegrtuw
water-bug
abegsstu
substage
abehillr
hairbell
abehilnr
hibernal
abehiltt
tithable
abehimms
mem-sahib
abehimno
Bohemian
abehimos
obeahism
abehinnt
Banthine®
abehinst
absinthe
abehirst
Hebraist
abehkllw
hawkbell
abehknor
hornbeak
abehllrt
bethrall
abehlnot
benthoal
abehloty
hylobate
abehlsss
bashless
abehmnor
hornbeam
abehmoor
rehoboam
abehmopt
Baphomet
abehnstu
sunbathe
abehorrr
abhorrer
abehorst
bathorse
abehrssu
sea-shrub
abeiilmt
imitable
abeiilnn
biennial
abeiilnv
inviable
abeiilpt
pitiable
abeiilrs
biserial
abeiilst
albitise
sibilate
abeiiltv
live-bait
vitiable
abeijltu
jubilate
abeijmnn
benjamin
abeikllm
lamblike
abeiklln
balkline
abeikmrr
rim-brake
abeiknor
beak-iron
abeiknrs
bearskin
abeikrst
breaskit
abeillllt
tillable
abeillmm
limbmeal
abeillmt
time-ball
abeillos
isolable
abeillov
violable
abeillqu
liquable
abeillry
beryllia
reliably
abeillst
bastille
abeilmnt
bailment
abeilmor
bromelia
abeilnnw
winnable
abeilnop
opinable
abeilnpt
pintable
abeilnrs
rinsable
abeilnru
ruinable
abeilnss
albiness
abeilnst
instable
abeilntv
bivalent
abeilnuv
unviable
abeilnvy
enviably
abeilprt
partible
abeilprz
prizable
abeilpss
passible
abeilpst
epiblast
abeilrru
reburial
abeilrtw
writable
abeilssu
issuable
suasible
abeilstu
suitable
abeilsux
bisexual
abeimrru
Brumaire
abeimrtv
ambivert
verbatim
abeimssu
iambuses
abeinnoz
bezonian
abeinnpr
brine-pan
abeinnru
inurbane
abeinoot
Boeotian
abeinorr
airborne
abeinors
sea-robin
abeinort
baritone
obtainer
abeinost
botanise
obeisant
abeinqsu
basquine
abeinrst
banister
abeinrsu
urbanise
abeinrtu
urbanite
abeinsst
bassinet
abeinttu
intubate
abeiorst
sabotier
abeiortt
Taborite
abeiortv
abortive
abeipqsu
squab-pie
abeirrvy
breviary
abeirsty
bestiary
sybarite
abeirtty
ytterbia
abeitttu
titubate
abejklou
kabeljou
abejmoor
jeroboam
abejnors
Sobranje
abeklmos
smokable
abeklnow
knowable
abeklnty
blankety
abeklorw
workable
abeklrss
barkless
abekmoot
book-mate
abeknnot
bank-note
abeknssy
sneaksby
abekoory
year-book
abekortu
break-out
outbreak
abekorvw
break-vow
abekrsty
basketry
abelllmu
labellum
abelllor
rollable

abelllot
tollable
abelllsy
syllable
abellmor
ombrella
abellmru
umbrella
abellmss
mass-bell
abellnot
ballonet
abellnru
Brunella
rubellan
abelloot
loo-table
abellosv
solvable
abellotu
lobulate
abellotw
well-boat
abellrvy
verbally
abelmnno
nobleman
abelmnoz
emblazon
abelmnst
semblant
abelmoot
mootable
abelmosv
movables
abelmovy
moveably
abelmptu
plumbate
abelmrty
Bartlemy
abelmssy
assembly
abelnnor
bannerol
abelnnru
runnable
abelnorz
blazoner
abelnruy
urbanely
abelnryz
brazenly
abelnstu
unstable
abelnsty
absently
abelnsuu
unusable
abelnuvy
navy-blue
abeloprt
portable
abeloprv
provable
abeloptt
table-top
abeloptx
box-pleat
abeloqtu
quotable
abelorru
labourer
abelorst
sortable
storable
abelorsv
absolver
abelorwx
ox-warble
abelossu
sabulose
abelostu
absolute
abelostw
bestowal
abelprtu
pubertal
abelqsuu
subequal
abelrstu
baluster
abelrttu
burletta
rebuttal
abelstuu
subulate
abelttuu
tubulate
abemmnoo
moonbeam
abemnnor
mean-born
abemnort
rent-a-mob
abemnotu
umbonate
abemnpru
penumbra
abemnsuy
sunbeamy
abemnttu
abutment
abemorrs
embrasor
abemorsu
amberous
abemortz
barometz
abenopsu
subpoena
abenorss
baroness
abenorsy
Sobranye
abenortt
betatron
abenortv
bevatron
abenorty
barytone
abenossw
saw-bones
abenrrtu
burnt-ear
abenrryz
brazenry
abeoosst
sea-boots
abeoppry
paper-boy
abeorstu
saboteur
abeorttu
obturate
tabouret
abeortuv
outbrave
abeortwx
water-box
abeossst
asbestos
abeostuv
subovate
abeprssy
passer-by
abeqrsuu
arquebus
aberrwxy
waxberry
abersstu
abstruse
aberstuw
water-bus
aberttuy
butyrate
abffgijy
Jiffybag
abffgiln
baffling
abffllpu
puffball
abfflost
blast-off
abffnotu
bouffant
abfglllo
golf-ball
abfglloo
goofball
abfgoruu
faubourg
abfhiist
baitfish
abfhills
fishball
abfhiors
boarfish
abfhloot
half-boot
abfhlsux
flax-bush
abfhoott
foot-bath
abfiillr
fibrilla
abfillly
fallibly
abfilnsu
basinful
abfilstu
fabulist
abfirttu
fruit-bat
abfjorsu
frabjous
abfkllor
korfball
abflloot
football
abflloru
four-ball
abfllost
softball
abfllssu
fuss-ball
abflluzz
fuzz-ball
abflostu
boastful
abflosuu
fabulous
abfnortu
turbofan
abforstu
surf-boat
abggginr
bragging
abggijnn
jingbang
abggilnr
garbling
abggnoot
toboggan
abghhikn
bank-high
abghhill
highball
abghhmru
Hamburgh
abghiopr
biograph
abghmoru
brougham
abgiilns
saibling
abgiimst
bigamist
abgiinno
Bignonia
abgiinor
aborigin
abgiinss
biassing
abgiknrr
ring-bark
abgillmn
lambling
abgilmnr
marbling
rambling
abgilmnw
wambling
abgilnnt
bantling
abgilnot
bloating
bog-Latin
obligant
abgilnrt
bratling
abgilnrw
brawling
warbling
abgilnst
blasting
stabling
abgilnty
tangibly
abgimosu
bigamous
subimago
abginnrx
banxring
abginoot
tabooing
abginost
boasting
bostangi
abginstw
batswing
abginttu
abutting
abgirrss
rib-grass
abgllloy
globally
abglloru
globular
abgllruy
bullyrag
abglmopu
plumbago
abglnoot
longboat
abglnouw
bungalow
abglooty
batology
abglorsu
glabrous
abglrruy
burglary
abgmnoor
gambroon
abgnoost
boat-song
abgnoowx
box-wagon
wagon-box
abgnorsu
osnaburg
abgorssx
grass-box
abhhostu
hush-boat
abhhrstu
hatbrush
abhiinrs
brainish
abhiiorz
rhizobia
abhiklor
kohlrabi
abhillpt
pithball
abhilnot
biathlon
abhilrtw
whirl-bat
abhilsst
stablish
abhimmst
bathmism
abhinort
hot-brain
abhiostu
hautbois
abhirrsu
air-brush
abhirstt
brattish
abhisttz
sitz-bath
abhkooot
boat-hook
book-oath
abhkorsu
kourbash
abhllmot
moth-ball
abhllooy
ballyhoo
abhllpsu
push-ball
abhlortw
whorl-bat
abhlosww
wash-bowl
abhlsstu
salt-bush
abhmnoty
bothyman
abhmnsuu
subhuman
abhmoort
bathroom
abhoorst
tarboosh
abhoostw
show-boat

abhopstt
stop-bath
abhorstu
tarboush
abhrrstu
tar-brush
abiiinry
biriyani
abiiklss
basilisk
abiillmr
millibar
abiilmno
binomial
abiilmns
albinism
abiilnot
libation
abiilnst
sibilant
abiilpty
pitiably
abiilrtu
air-built
abiimnot
ambition
abiirssv
vibrissa
abijlntu
jubilant
abijnoot
jobation
abijnost
banjoist
abiklmns
lambskin
abiklnry
byrlakin
abikmnnr
brinkman
abiknorr
ironbark
abikrstz
britzska
abillpy
play-bill
abillott
toll-bait
abillovy
violably
abillrty
tribally
abilmnou
olibanum
abilmoot
tail-boom
abilmops
bioplasm
abilnoot
lobation
oblation
abilnoru
unilobar
abilnotu
ablution
abutilon
abilnrtu
tribunal
turbinal
abilnstu
stub-nail
abilopst
bioplast
abilorst
strobila
abilorty
libatory
abilottt
tilt-boat
abilpssy
passibly
abilrssy
brassily
abilrtuy
ruby-tail
abilssuy
issuably
abilstuy
suitably
abimmnoo
mainboom
abimnoow
obi-woman
abimnosu
bimanous
abimnprs
snap-brim
abimrsst
strabism
abinnorw
Brownian
abinnrsu
Burnsian
abinoort
abortion
abinoptx
paint-box
abinortu
tabourin
abinorwy
rainbowy
abinostt
botanist
abinrtuy
urbanity
abintttu
titubant
abioprsu
biparous
abiopstu
subtopia
abiorrst
arborist
rib-roast
abiorrtv
vibrator
abiortuy
obituary
abirrstu
airburst
abirssuz
subsizar
abkkmoor
bookmark
abkllmsu
musk-ball
abkllnor
bankroll
abkloopy
playbook
abkmooss
mass-book
abknprtu
bankrupt
abkoopss
pass-book
abkoortw
workboat
abkoostt
kottabos
ablllow
wool-ball
abllmoor
ball-room
abllmopw
blowlamp
abllnosw
snowball
abllorst
borstall
abllrtuy
brutally
abllssuy
syllabus
ablmmooy
may-bloom
ablmnruu
alburnum
laburnum
ablmosty
myoblast
ablnoryz
blazonry
ablnosuz
subzonal
ablnrsuu
sublunar
ablnsuuy
unusably
abloostt
bootlast
abloostz
zooblast
abloprvy
provably
ablopsuu
pabulous
abloqtuy
quotably
ablorssu
subsolar
ablossuu
sabulous
ablosttu
subtotal
ablostty
stay-bolt
ablprtuy
abruptly
abmmorty
tommy-bar
abnoorrt
roborant
abnortuu
runabout
abnosssu
bonassus
aboorrsu
arborous
accedeio
Coccidae
acccdiio
coccidia
accelry
cycle-car
acccenpy
peccancy
acccfiil
calcific
accciipr
capricci
acccilly
cyclical
accddeen
cadenced
accddiit
didactic
accdeeeu
deuce-ace
accdeeru
cardecue
accdehil
chaliced
accdeilo
dice-coal
accdeilu
caudicle
accdeily
delicacy
accdeint
accident
accdeirt
accredit
accdeisu
caudices
accdelly
calycled
accdelsu
cul-de-sac
accdeorr
accorder
accdersu
accursed
accdesuu
caduceus
accdghoo
coachdog
accdhiir
diarchic
accdhiis
Chasidic
accdhimo
dochmiac
accdhiot
cathodic
accdiist
dicastic
accdiity
dicacity
accdiloy
calycoid
accdilty
dactylic
accdinor
cancroid
draconic
accdioor
coracoid
accdiors
sarcodic
accdiost
sticcado
accdituy
caducity
accdlloy
clay-cold
accdoost
stoccado
accdooxy
cacodoxy
accdosuu
caducous
acceehit
hiccatee
acceehrt
ceterach
acceehst
seecatch
acceeilr
celeriac
acceeils
ecclesia
acceeimr
ice-cream
acceekln
necklace
acceelnr
clarence
acceelos
coalesce
acceenns
nascence
acceenpr
crepance
acceenst
acescent
acceeort
croceate
acceeprt
accepter
acceffiy
efficacy
accefils
fascicle
accefirt
ice-craft
accegino
Cocaigne
accegkmo
game-cock
accegkos
sage-cock
accegnoy
co-agency
accehhko
chechako
accehikp
chick-pea
pea-chick
accehilm
alchemic
chemical
accehilp
cephalic
accehilt
hectical
accehimn
mechanic
accehino
anechoic
accehinr
chicaner
accehity
ice-yacht
accehlor
cochlear
accehlot
catechol
accehnno
chaconne
accehnny
cynanche
accehnor
charneco
encroach
accehnot
conchate
accehnry
Chancery
accehopt
cache-pot
accehrst
cratches
acceilln
cancelli
acceillr
clerical
acceillu
caulicle

acceillv
clavicle
acceilns
scenical
acceilnt
canticle
acceilnv
clavecin
acceilny
calycine
acceilos
calicoes
acceilrv
cervical
acceinrt
Nearctic
acceinry
Cyrenaic
acceintu
cuneatic
acceiopr
Cecropia
acceiotv
coactive
acceiprt
practice
acceirrr
ricercar
acceirtu
cruciate
acceistt
ecstatic
accekkor
rock-cake
acceklnr
cracknel
acceknor
corn-cake
acceknoy
Cockayne
accekopy
peacocky
accekrrs
crackers
accellor
Roccella
accelluy
calycule
accelmny
cyclamen
accelnov
conclave
accelnru
caruncle
accelntu
clean-cut
accelrsy
scarcely
accelrtu
clear-cut
accelssu
saccules
accelwyy
cycleway
accennsy
nascency
accenorr
cornacre
accenort
accentor
accenost
cosecant
accenosu
concause
acceoprt
acceptor
acceoptu
occupate
acceorst
ectosarc
acceortu
accoutre
acceprsw
screw-cap
accesstu
cactuses
accffltu
calc-tuff
accfhklo
half-cock
accfhlty
catchfly
accfiilt
lactific
accfikll
calf-lick
accghino
coaching
accghint
catching
accghior
choragic
accgikmr
gimcrack
accgiknr
cracking
accglooy
cacology
acchhitt
chitchat
acchhmos
camshoch
acchiirt
rachitic
acchiist
chiastic
acchilmy
chymical
acchilno
chalonic
acchilor
orichalc
acchilot
catholic
acchinno
Cinchona
acchinpu
capuchin
acchiort
thoracic
trochaic
acchiptt
catch-pit
acchirrt
carritch
acchklor
charlock
acchkort
hock-cart
acchloot
cacholot
acchlopt
cloth-cap
acchmors
caschrom
acchnnuy
unchancy
acchnoor
coronach
acchnotu
couchant
acchortu
cartouch
acchrsty
scratchy
acciiiot
oiticica
acciilln
clinical
acciilmt
climatic
acciilpp
Calippic
acciilrt
critical
acciimnn
cinnamic
acciinno
aniconic
acciinot
aconitic
acciinps
capsicin
acciinpu
Puccinia
acciipst
pasticci
acciirtx
cicatrix
accijkmr
jimcrack
accikkrr
rick-rack
accikktt
tick-tack
acciklot
cocktail
acciklst
stick-lac
accikmst
canstick
accikopr
apricock
accikstt
cat-stick
accilmos
cosmical
accilmox
cacomixl
accilnot
ciclaton
accilnov
volcanic
accilnuv
vulcanic
accilort
cortical
accilpry
caprylic
accilrru
circular
accimmos
Occamism
accimnos
moccasin
accimntu
canticum
accimoru
coumaric
accimost
Occamist
accimpsu
capsicum
accinoos
occasion
accinoot
coaction
accinort
narcotic
accinorv
cavicorn
accinost
Scotican
accinoty
canticoy
cyanotic
acciopst
spiccato
acciorst
acrostic
Socratic
acciorsy
isocracy
acciostt
sticcato
acciostu
acoustic
accirrtt
tric-trac
accirsty
scarcity
acckkrsu
rucksack
acckmmru
crummack
accknrsu
sun-crack
acckooot
cockatoo
acckoprt
crackpot
accllosu
occlusal
accllsuu
calculus
acclmoop
coco-palm
acclopru
cup-coral
acclssuu
sacculus
accmostu
accustom
accnootu
cocoanut
accnopru
acorn-cup
accnoprw
crown-cap
accnoptu
occupant
accnortt
contract
accorrty
carrycot
acdddeit
addicted
acddeees
deceased
acddeefr
red-faced
acddeeht
detached
acddeeit
dedicate
acddeelr
declared
acddeenr
credenda
acddeent
decadent
acddeesu
Sadducee
acddefgo
dog-faced
acddehkn
deck-hand
acddeiil
deicidal
acddeiim
medicaid
acddeilu
decidual
acddeinr
cider-and
riddance
acddeint
dedicant
acddeklo
deadlock
deck-load
acddentu
adducent
acddfoor
food-card
acddgiln
cladding
acddhiio
diadochi
acddhimr
didrachm
acddhkos
shaddock
acddiior
cardioid
acddilny
candidly
acddilty
didactyl
acddinnu
uncandid
acddinsy
discandy
acddioow
wood-acid
acddklno
dockland
acddkory
dockyard
acddortu
adductor
acddotty
toddy-cat
acdeeeft
defecate
acdeeeks
seedcake
acdeeemr
reed-mace
acdeeent
antecede
acdeeers
decrease
acdeefft
affected
acdeefin
defiance
acdeefis
side-face
acdeefrs
frescade
acdeefry
federacy
acdeeggn
egg-dance
acdeegkm
deck-game
acdeegly
delegacy
acdeehnr
enarched

acdeehns
enchased
acdeeiip
epicedia
acdeeilt
delicate
acdeeimn
Medicean
acdeeimr
medicare
acdeeimt
decimate
medicate
acdeeinn
enneadic
acdeeinr
déraciné
acdeeinu
audience
acdeeinv
deviance
vice-dean
acdeeipr
Percidae
acdeeips
dispeace
acdeeirt
tide-race
acdeejkt
jacketed
acdeeknr
cankered
acdeekrt
racketed
acdeelnr
calender
encradle
acdeelnt
lanceted
acdeelrr
declarer
acdeelrt
decretal
acdeelrv
calvered
acdeelss
déclassé
acdeemno
code-name
acdeennt
tendance
acdeenny
cayenned
acdeenot
anecdote
toe-dance
acdeenrs
ascender
reascend
acdeenrt
crenated
decanter
nectared

acdeenrv
caverned
acdeenrz
credenza
acdeentt
dancette
dancetté
acdeeops
pease-cod
acdeeort
decorate
acdeeost
seed-coat
acdeeprt
carpeted
acdeerrt
terraced
acdeesux
caudexes
acdeesuy
causeyed
acdefgip
pig-faced
acdefgpu
pug-faced
acdefhln
flanched
acdefiil
deifical
acdefill
ill-faced
acdefotw
two-faced
acdefrsu
surfaced
acdefrtu
furcated
acdeggrs
scragged
acdeghil
Gadhelic
acdeghop
dog-cheap
acdegiil
algicide
acdegimr
decigram
acdeginu
guidance
acdegirs
disgrace
acdegllo
gold-lace
acdeglou
cloudage
acdegnrs
scrag-end
acdegnru
ungraced
acdegott
cottaged
acdehhtt
thatched

acdehiip
aphicide
acdehill
Helladic
acdehilr
Heraclid
heraldic
acdehilt
dithecal
acdehims
schiedam
acdehiop
Phocidae
acdehirs
rachides
acdehirt
thridace
tracheid
acdehknu
unhacked
acdehkov
havocked
acdehkru
archduke
acdehlnp
planched
acdehlnr
chandler
acdehnor
rondache
acdehnsu
uncashed
acdehorr
hardcore
acdehort
chordate
acdehpst
despatch
acdehptu
death-cup
acdehrst
starched
acdeiilt
ciliated
acdeiimu
aecidium
acdeiinr
acridine
acdeiins
sciaenid
acdeiint
actinide
diactine
indicate
acdeiinu
induciae
acdeiitv
cavitied
vaticide
acdeijnu
jaundice
acdeikmn
main-deck

acdeiknp
panicked
acdeillm
medallic
acdeilln
declinal
acdeillv
cavilled
acdeilmo
cameloid
acdeilmt
maledict
acdeilnp
panicled
acdeilnu
Dulcinea
acdeilnv
vine-clad
acdeilps
displace
acdeilpt
plicated
acdeilpy
dice-play
acdeilrt
articled
acdeilru
auricled
radicule
acdeimno
comedian
daemonic
demoniac
mid-ocean
acdeimnp
pandemic
acdeimrt
dermatic
time-card
acdeimsu
Muscidae
acdeinnr
crannied
acdeinop
canopied
acdeinos
diocesan
acdeinov
voidance
acdeinpt
pedantic
pentadic
acdeinrt
crinated
dicentra
acdeinst
distance
acdeintv
Vedantic
acdeinvy
deviancy
acdeiors
idocrase

acdeiort
ceratoid
acdeiorv
Corvidae
acdeiosu
edacious
acdeipss
spadices
acdeipst
spicated
acdeiqru
acquired
acdeirtt
tetracid
tetradic
acdeknot
tacked-on
acdeknpu
unpacked
acdeknru
unracked
acdekost
stockade
acdellnu
uncalled
acdellor
carolled
collared
acdellos
so-called
acdelmsu
muscadel
acdelnoo
canoodle
acdelnor
colander
acdelnpu
unplaced
acdelnry
calendry
dry-clean
acdelnsu
unscaled
acdelopt
clodpate
acdelopu
cupolaed
acdelorv
overclad
acdelotu
oculated
acdelrsy
sacredly
acdelstu
sulcated
acdemort
democrat
acdennor
ordnance
acdennot
cantoned
acdennst
scandent

acdenopr
endocarp
acdenors
endosarc
acdenory
deaconry
acdenosy
cyanosed
acdenotu
outdance
acdenrtu
cedar-nut
underact
untraced
acdenrvy
verdancy
acdensuu
uncaused
acdentty
dancetty
acdeoopp
Copepoda
acdeoors
door-case
acdeopru
croupade
acdeorrt
redactor
acdeorss
Sarcodes
acdeortu
educator
acdeortv
card-vote
acdeostt
costated
acdepprs
scrapped
acdeqtuu
aqueduct
acderrsu
crusader
acderrtu
traducer
acderttu
tear-duct
acdertuv
curvated
acdffhnu
handcuff
acdffirt
diffract
acdfflos
scaffold
acdfiilu
fiducial
acdfilou
fucoidal
acdflrtu
turf-clad
acdghotw
dog-watch
watch-dog

acdgiilo
dialogic
acdgilnr
cradling
acdgilns
scalding
acdgimot
dogmatic
acdgiopr
podagric
acdgkloo
good-lack
acdglltu
gall-duct
acdglnoo
Golconda
acdgnrtu
dung-cart
acdhiiot
thio-acid
acdhiiss
Hassidic
acdhiknp
hand-pick
acdhikor
chokidar
acdhilmn
man-child
acdhilpr
pilchard
acdhilps
clapdish
acdhinor
hadronic
rhodanic
acdhinry
dinarchy
acdhinsw
sandwich
acdhiops
scaphoid
acdhiory
hyracoid
acdhipst
dispatch
acdhkkuw
duck-hawk
acdhlnor
chaldron
chondral
acdhlopt
pad-cloth
acdhmntu
Dutchman
acdhnorw
chawdron
acdhootw
wood-chat
acdhorss
sash-cord
acdhorsw
show-card
acdhorsy
dyschroa

acdiiipr
diapiric
acdiijlu
judicial
acdiilms
disclaim
acdiilno
conidial
acdiilns
scaldini
acdiilsu
suicidal
acdiilty
calidity
dialytic
acdiimor
dioramic
acdiimot
diatomic
acdiimsu
ascidium
acdiinnt
indicant
acdiinop
pinacoid
acdiinot
actinoid
diatonic
acdiinpr
Pindaric
acdiioss
acidosis
acdiirst
carditis
acdiirty
acridity
acdiisst
sadistic
acdikltu
duck-tail
acdikmoo
cookmaid
acdikrry
rickyard
acdillou
caudillo
lodicula
acdillpy
placidly
acdilmor
dromical
acdilmtu
Talmudic
acdilnoo
conoidal
acdilnor
iron-clad
acdilnos
scaldino
acdilnsy
syndical
acdilnuu
nudicaul

acdilopy
polyacid
acdilouv
oviducal
acdilpsu
cuspidal
acdilsty
Dactylis
acdimnoo
monoacid
acdimnsu
muscadin
scandium
acdimnsy
dynamics
acdimosy
docimasy
acdinops
spondaic
acdinors
sardonic
acdinort
tornadic
acdinorw
cordwain
acdinsty
dynastic
acdintuy
aduncity
acdioprs
sporadic
acdiortt
dictator
acdiprst
adscript
acdipssu
Dipsacus
acdirstt
distract
acdkmmor
drammock
acdlnnor
cornland
acdlnoru
cauldron
acdlnory
condylar
acdlnost
Scotland
acdlooow
wood-coal
acdloort
doctoral
acdloorw
wool-card
acdlorwy
cowardly
acdlostu
coal-dust
acdmmnoo
commando
acdmnory
dormancy
mordancy

acdnoorr
roncador
acdnoorv
cordovan
acdnootu
ducatoon
acdnorrw
ward-corn
acdnostw
downcast
acdnosuu
aduncous
acdooopt
Octopoda
acdoopty
octapody
acdoorst
ostracod
scordato
acdoprst
postcard
acdorrwy
cowardry
acdortuy
court-day
acdosttu
dust-coat
acdrsttu
dust-cart
aceeegln
elegance
aceeegrs
cargeese
aceeeipr
earpiece
aceeeips
sea-piece
aceeeknt
neckatee
aceeelmr
cameleer
aceeensv
evanesce
aceeerrt
recreate
aceeertx
execrate
aceeffin
caffeine
aceeffrt
affecter
aceefhwy
whey-face
aceefilm
malefice
aceefkor
ecofreak
aceeflpu
peaceful
aceeflrt
tree-calf
aceeflss
faceless

aceefprt
praefect
aceefpty
type-face
aceefrsu
farceuse
aceeghnr
encharge
aceeghnx
exchange
aceeghrr
recharge
aceegins
Genesiac
aceegirs
Graecise
aceegknr
neck-gear
aceegkrw
wreckage
aceeglny
elegancy
aceeglpu
pucelage
aceegnoz
cozenage
aceegnry
reagency
aceegnsv
scavenge
aceegorr
racegoer
aceegorv
coverage
aceehimn
Manichee
aceehint
echinate
aceehipt
petechia
aceehlln
Chellean
aceehlmw
cam-wheel
aceehlos
shoe-lace
aceehltv
chevalet
aceehmnp
camphene
aceehmnr
menarche
aceehmrs
cashmere
marchese
aceehnrv
revanche
aceehort
ochreate
aceehprr
preacher
aceehprs
sea-perch

aceehprt
ethercap
aceehrrr
rere-arch
aceehrrs
research
searcher
aceehrrt
treacher
aceehrtt
catheter
aceehrty
cheatery
aceehsst
sea-chest
aceehstt
tea-chest
aceeikst
ice-skate
aceeilmn
cameline
aceeilmt
emetical
aceeilnp
capeline
aceeilnr
cinereal
reliance
aceeilns
salience
aceeilps
especial
aceeilrv
receival
aceeimot
acoemeti
aceeimrr
rearmice
aceeimrs
racemise
aceeimrz
racemize
aceeinps
sapience
aceeinpt
patience
aceeinrs
increase
resiance
aceeinrt
centiare
creatine
increate
iterance
aceeinst
cinéaste
aceeintv
enactive
aceeintx
exitance
aceeipps
pipe-case
aceeipst
speciate

8 ACE

aceeipsy
say-piece
aceeirsu
causerie
aceeirsw
wiseacre
aceeirtv
creative
reactive
aceeirtw
ice-water
water-ice
aceeistv
vesicate
aceejkrt
jack-tree
aceeklmr
mackerel
aceeklrw
eelwrack
aceekmpt
empacket
aceeknrw
neckwear
aceekrrt
racketer
aceekrst
sack-tree
aceellnt
lancelet
aceellot
ocellate
aceellov
Lovelace
aceellpt
capellet
aceellrr
cellarer
aceellrt
cellaret
aceelmno
cameleon
aceelmrs
sclerema
aceelnpt
pentacle
aceelnrr
larcener
aceelnrs
cleanser
aceelnru
cerulean
aceelnsu
nuclease
aceelntt
tentacle
aceelntu
nucleate
aceelops
escalope
aceelors
escarole
aceelort
relocate

aceelprr
replacer
aceelptu
peculate
aceelpty
clypeate
aceelrss
careless
aceelrst
scelerat
aceelrsv
cleavers
aceelrtu
ulcerate
aceelrtv
cervelat
aceelstt
telecast
aceemnns
scene-man
aceemnot
meconate
aceemnst
casement
aceemors
racemose
aceemrrs
screamer
aceemrry
creamery
aceennrt
entrance
aceenort
carotene
aceenost
note-case
aceenprr
parcener
aceenrrt
recanter
recreant
aceenrst
reascent
sarcenet
aceenrtt
entr'acte
aceenrtu
enacture
uncreate
aceeorst
creasote
aceeostt
ecostate
aceeprtt
ettercap
aceeprtu
peracute
aceepstt
spectate
aceerrsu
écraseur
aceerrtu
creature

aceerruv
verrucae
aceersst
cateress
cerastes
aceerssu
surcease
aceerssv
crevasse
aceerstu
secateur
aceerttu
eructate
aceesstt
cassette
aceffhru
chauffer
aceffhry
chaffery
aceffils
sea-cliff
aceffilt
face-lift
aceffims
caffeism
aceffllu
full-face
acefglru
graceful
acefhiks
fishcake
acefhoru
farouche
acefiipr
pacifier
acefiirt
artifice
acefilly
facilely
acefilmt
calf-time
acefilop
epifocal
acefilos
fasciole
focalise
acefilry
fire-clay
acefimpr
camp-fire
acefinrx
carnifex
acefirty
feracity
acefklry
cly-faker
acefllov
calf-love
acefllru
leaf-curl
aceflss
calfless
aceflmno
flamenco

aceflnor
falconer
aceflnot
conflate
falconet
aceflnry
crane-fly
aceflors
alfresco
aceflrtu
fulcrate
acefmnoo
moon-face
acefnorv
conferva
acefnprt
pencraft
acefoopt
footpace
acefoort
foot-race
acefopst
postface
aceforst
forecast
acefrrsu
surfacer
acefrrtu
fracture
acegghps
pasch-egg
aceggiln
cageling
aceggiop
epagogic
aceghiln
leaching
aceghilt
lichgate
aceghinr
reaching
aceghint
teaching
aceghlrs
schläger
aceghlty
lychgate
aceghmmu
chummage
aceghmor
echogram
aceghnru
uncharge
acegiimp
epigamic
acegiinv
vicinage
acegillr
allergic
acegilmu
mucilage
acegilnn
cleaning

acegilnr
clearing
acegilnv
cleaving
acegilnw
lace-wing
acegilps
Pelasgic
acegilrv
claviger
acegilss
glacises
acegilst
gelastic
acegimnn
menacing
acegimnr
Germanic
acegimnt
magnetic
acegimox
exogamic
acegimrs
Graecism
aceginno
canoeing
aceginnt
enacting
aceginrt
catering
citrange
aceginss
caginess
aceginsw
wing-case
acegintx
exacting
acegiott
cogitate
acegiprs
spageric
acegiprt
price-tag
acegirst
agrestic
acegirtt
tiger-cat
acegklot
lock-gate
acegklov
gavelock
acegkorw
cagework
acegkrtu
truckage
acegllno
collagen
acegllsy
scaly-leg
aceglnoo
log-canoe
acegmmpu
gemma-cup

acegmnoy
geomancy
acegmops
compages
acegmors
scarmoge
acegmrry
gramercy
acegnnoy
cyanogen
acegnnty
tangency
acegnssy
cagyness
acegoops
goose-cap
acegoors
cargoose
acegopry
geocarpy
acegorst
escargot
acegortt
cottager
acegorty
category
grey-coat
acehhirr
hierarch
acehhlsu
shauchle
acehhmnn
henchman
acehhnrt
ethnarch
acehhnsv
Cheshvan
acehhprt
heptarch
acehhrtt
thatcher
acehhrty
hatchery
thearchy
acehhtty
hatchety
acehiims
ischemia
acehiirt
hieratic
acehijkr
hijacker
acehijpt
Japhetic
acehiklp
kephalic
acehiklw
lichwake
acehillt
hellicat
acehilmn
inchmeal
acehilmp
impleach

acehilms
camelish
acehilno
Chelonia
acehilnt
chainlet
ethnical
acehilor
halicore
heroical
acehilpr
parhelic
acehilss
Lachesis
acehiltt
athletic
thetical
acehimnu
achenium
acehimpr
camphire
acehimpt
empathic
emphatic
acehimrt
rhematic
acehimst
misteach
tachisme
acehimtt
thematic
acehinot
inchoate
acehinpt
inch-tape
acehinst
asthenic
acehinsy
synechia
acehiops
po'chaise
acehiost
toiseach
acehiprs
seraphic
acehiprt
chapiter
phreatic
acehiprw
pew-chair
acehipst
pastiche
acehiptt
pathetic
acehiptw
whitecap
acehirst
Charites
acehirsw
archwise
acehirtt
theatric
acehisst
chastise

acehistt
tachiste
acehistx
cathexis
acehklov
havelock
acehklpr
kreplach
acehklty
latchkey
acehkmpu
muck-heap
acehkotu
tuckahoe
acehkrtw
thwacker
acehktwy
watch-key
acehllls
shell-lac
acehllmo
mallecho
acehlloo
coal-hole
acehllor
orchella
acehllsu
halluces
acehlmpr
carl-hemp
acehlnou
eulachon
acehlnpt
planchet
acehlnru
launcher
acehlnst
stanchel
acehlort
chelator
chlorate
trochlea
acehlost
eschalot
acehlott
tea-cloth
acehlprt
chaptrel
acehlpry
chapelry
acehlpss
chapless
acehlrtu
archlute
trauchle
acehlsty
chastely
acehmnrt
merchant
acehmnss
chessman
acehmort
chromate

acehmprs
champers
acehmstu
mustache
acehnnop
pancheon
acehnnpt
penchant
acehnopr
canephor
chaperon
acehnopt
cenotaph
acehnorr
ranchero
acehnort
anchoret
acehnprt
pentarch
acehnpru
unpreach
acehnquu
Quechuan
acehnrss
archness
acehnrst
snatcher
stancher
acehnrtu
chaunter
acehnstu
unchaste
acehoprr
reproach
acehoprt
arch-poet
acehorrs
horsecar
acehorrv
hover-car
overarch
acehorst
thoraces
acehortt
theocrat
acehortu
outreach
acehosst
case-shot
acehossw
showcase
acehostu
cathouse
soutache
acehotww
cow-wheat
acehprsu
purchase
acehprty
patchery
petchary
acehrrst
starcher

acehrrtt
tetrarch
acehrssu
chasseur
acehrtty
trachyte
acehsssu
chausses
acehsttu
cathetus
acehttuz
zuchetta
aceiilmn
limacine
aceiilnr
irenical
aceiilns
salicine
Sicelain
silicane
aceiilnt
Catiline
aceiilst
silicate
aceiimtu
maieutic
aceiinps
piscinae
aceiinst
canities
aceiintv
inactive
aceiintz
anticize
aceiirrt
criteria
aceiistt
Atticise
aceijknp
jack-pine
aceijmst
majestic
aceijnrr
jerrican
aceiklry
creakily
aceikmnn
nickname
aceikmrv
maverick
aceiknsw
wine-cask
aceikppr
pipe-rack
aceikrrv
vraicker
aceiksst
sea-stick
aceillt
clitella
aceillmn
cane-mill

aceillmr
micellar
millrace
aceillmt
metallic
aceillmy
mycelial
aceillnt
cliental
aceillop
Calliope
aceillor
rocaille
aceillos
localise
aceillot
teocalli
aceillpr
calliper
aceillps
allspice
aceillpy
epically
aceillrv
caviller
aceilmmo
camomile
aceilmnn
clinamen
aceilmno
coal-mine
aceilmnp
manciple
aceilmns
mescalin
aceilmos
camisole
aceilmps
misplace
aceilmpt
pelmatic
aceilmrt
metrical
aceilmst
clematis
aceilmsu
musicale
aceilmtu
amuletic
aceilnnp
pannicle
pinnacle
aceilnnr
encrinal
aceilnor
acrolein
Caroline
creolian
aceilnpt
ice-plant
pectinal
planetic
aceilnrt
clarinet

aceilnsu
aesculin
aceilnsy
saliency
aceilopr
capriole
aceilopt
poetical
aceilorr
carriole
aceilort
erotical
loricate
aceilost
societal
aceilosv
vocalise
aceilotv
locative
aceilppy
clay-pipe
pipeclay
aceilprs
calipers
spiracle
aceilprt
particle
prelatic
aceilpru
peculiar
aceilpss
slip-case
aceilpty
etypical
aceilpxy
epicalyx
aceilrst
altrices
selictar
aceilrsv
visceral
aceilrtt
tractile
aceilrtv
vertical
aceilrty
literacy
aceilsuv
vesicula
aceiltvy
actively
aceimmnp
pemmican
aceimmos
semicoma
aceimmrs
racemism
aceimnoo
Monoecia
aceimnor
coramine
aceimnru
manicure

8 ACE

aceimnst
semantic
aceimnsu
semuncia
aceimnsy
sycamine
aceimopt
poematic
aceimotx
toxaemic
aceimotz
metazoic
aceimprr
mericarp
aceimpss
escapism
aceimpst
campsite
aceimptu
pumicate
aceimrst
ceramist
matrices
aceimrtt
trematic
aceimrtu
muricate
aceinnos
canonise
aceinnot
enaction
aceinnst
instance
aceinnsu
nuisance
aceinntu
uncinate
aceinopr
caponier
ice-apron
procaine
aceinops
caponise
aceinors
scenario
aceinort
anoretic
creation
reaction
aceinorv
Corvinae
veronica
aceinorx
anorexic
aceinost
canoeist
aceinotv
conative
invocate
aceinotx
exaction
aceinptt
pittance

aceinpuy
picayune
aceinrru
curarine
aceinrry
cinerary
aceinrss
raciness
aceinrst
canister
aceinrtt
interact
aceinrtu
Teucrian
aceinrtv
navicert
aceinrtx
xerantic
aceinrvy
vicenary
aceinssu
issuance
aceinstv
cistvaen
vesicant
aceinttu
tunicate
aceinttx
excitant
aceintty
tenacity
aceintuv
unactive
aceioprt
operatic
aceiorrv
air-cover
aceiorsv
varicose
aceiossu
caesious
aceiostt
oscitate
aceiotvv
vocative
aceipprr
pericarp
aceiprrs
perisarc
aceiprst
crispate
practise
aceiprtv
practive
aceiprty
apyretic
aceipsst
escapist
aceirrsu
curarise
aceirrsw
airscrew
aceirrtx
creatrix

aceirrty
retiracy
aceirssv
vicaress
aceirstt
cristate
aceirstu
suricate
aceirttu
urticate
aceirttv
tractive
aceirtuv
curative
aceirtvy
veracity
aceissst
ecstasis
aceisssu
saucisse
aceisstu
sauciest
suit-case
aceisttu
eustatic
acejkoor
jackeroo
acejlory
cajolery
acejnrry
jerrycan
acekkmru
muck-rake
acekknry
knackery
acekllov
lack-love
aceklmpu
pack-mule
plum-cake
aceklntu
untackle
aceklorv
laverock
aceklprs
sprackle
aceklsss
sackless
aceknnow
acknowne
aceknnsw
swan-neck
aceknort
one-track
aceknpru
unpacker
aceknpsu
sneak-cup
aceknrrt
rack-rent
acekorrv
overrack
acekorsw
case-work

acekortu
rout-cake
acekosst
sea-stock
acekpssy
skyscape
acekqruy
quackery
acekssuw
waesucks
acelllru
cellular
acellmsu
sacellum
acellnot
call-note
acellnru
nucellar
acellops
collapse
escallop
acellorr
caroller
acellorv
coverall
overcall
acellosw
cole-slaw
acellotu
loculate
acellpru
Lupercal
acellrty
rectally
acellssw
clawless
acellstu
scutella
acelltwy
cetywall
acelmmou
mameluco
acelmnor
amelcorn
acelmnru
crumenal
acelmnss
calmness
acelmopt
compleat
acelmors
scleroma
acelmory
claymore
acelmost
molecast
acelmosu
maculose
acelmpsy
eclampsy
acelmstu
muscatel
acelmsuu
saeculum

acelmtuu
cumulate
acelnnrs
scrannel
acelnorv
noverca l
acelnosu
lacunose
acelnotv
covalent
acelnovy
conveyal
acelnruy
nucleary
acelnrvy
cravenly
aceloppu
populace
aceloprs
parclose
aceloprt
pectoral
acelopru
opercula
aceloptu
copulate
acelopty
calotype
acelorrt
rectoral
acelorss
lacrosse
acelorst
sectoral
acelorsu
carousel
acelorsy
coarsely
acelortu
colature
acelosst
coatless
acelostt
salt-cote
acelostu
lacteous
locustae
osculate
acelprst
sceptral
spectral
acelprsu
specular
acelptuu
cupulate
acelptuy
eucalypt
acelqruu
claqueur
acelrrsw
scrawler
acelrsss
scarless

acelrstt
scrattle
acelrttu
cultrate
acelsstt
tactless
acelssuu
Aesculus
acemmoty
mycetoma
acemnorr
romancer
acemnost
camstone
acemnrtu
cream-nut
acemnruy
numeracy
acemoost
comatose
acemoprs
mesocarp
acemorrt
cremator
Mercator
acemorsw
case-worm
acemorsy
sycamore
acemorty
cometary
acemorux
morceaux
acennnou
announce
acennoss
canoness
acennott
co-tenant
acennotv
covenant
acennotz
canzonet
acennpry
pernancy
acennptu
pecan-nut
acennsuy
seacunny
acenoort
coronate
acenootz
ectozoan
acenoprt
portance
acenopst
capstone
open-cast
acenopux
ponceaux
acenoqtu
cotquean
acenorrw
careworn

acenorss
narcoses
acenorst
ancestor
sortance
acenorsu
carneous
nacreous
acenortt
contrate
acenortu
courante
outrance
acenoruy
eucaryon
acenossv
cavesson
acenostt
constate
acenottu
toucanet
acenprsu
encarpus
acenpttu
punctate
acenrstt
transect
acenrstu
Etruscan
recusant
acenrsty
ancestry
acenrttu
truncate
acenrtuy
centaury
cyanuret
acensstw
newscast
aceoopsu
poaceous
aceoortv
overcoat
aceopprs
copperas
aceoprrt
recaptor
aceoprtt
attercop
aceorrsu
carouser
aceorrtt
retroact
aceorstt
sectator
aceorstv
overcast
aceortuy
eucaryot
aceortww
water-cow
aceosstu
sea-scout

aceosttu
outcaste
acepstty
typecast
acersttu
crustate
acerstty
scattery
acerttuw
cut-water
acffghin
chaffing
acffhnor
chaffron
acffiilo
official
acffilnu
fanciful
acfghins
Fasching
acfgiimn
magnific
acfgiipr
caprifig
acfgikls
sick-flag
acfginny
fancying
acfginrs
scarfing
acfgituy
fugacity
acfgknop
packfong
acfglnor
corn-flag
acfhhinw
hawfinch
acfhilno
falchion
acfhilnu
faulchin
acfhilos
coalfish
acfhirss
scarfish
acfhirsw
crawfish
acfhirsy
crayfish
acfhlmru
charmful
acfhltuw
watchful
acfhorrt
Rh-factor
acfiilst
fistical
acfiilsv
salvific
acfiilty
facility
acfiimps
pacifism

acfiipst
pacifist
acfiisst
Fascisti
acfiklns
calfskin
acfilort
trifocal
acfilrty
craftily
acfilssy
classify
acfimnru
francium
acfimoss
Fascismo
acfinort
fraction
acfinprs
scarf-pin
acfinsty
sanctify
acfiostu
factious
acfirtuy
furacity
acfissst
Fascists
acfjkloo
jack-fool
acfkllor
rock-fall
acfklopw
wolf-pack
acfklors
forslack
acfklost
lockfast
acfklruw
wrackful
acfklssu
sackfuls
acfkoorr
roof-rack
acfllmru
cram-full
acflmnoo
mooncalf
acflnory
falconry
acfloops
foolscap
acflorsu
scrofula
acflrruu
furcular
acfmottu
factotum
acfoostt
cat's-foot
acggiint
gigantic
acggiios
isagogic

acggilnn
clanging
glancing
acggioor
coraggio
acgglnou
glucagon
acgglrsy
scraggly
acghhijk
highjack
jack-high
acghhint
hatching
acghiknw
whacking
acghilns
clashing
acghilor
oligarch
acghilrt
arc-light
acghilru
lug-chair
acghimnr
charming
acghimnt
matching
acghinnr
ranching
acghinnu
unaching
acghinop
poaching
acghinpt
nightcap
patching
acghinrr
charring
acghinrs
crashing
acghinru
churinga
acghinst
scathing
acghintt
chatting
acghinty
yachting
acghiprs
graphics
acghllor
gralloch
acghntuu
uncaught
acghorsu
choragus
acghptuu
upcaught
acgiilno
logician
acgiimos
isogamic

acgiimst
sigmatic
acgiinrt
granitic
acgiiprs
spagiric
acgijjko
jickajog
acgikklo
goal-kick
acgiklnn
clanking
acgiklnt
tackling
acgiklnu
caulking
acgiklry
garlicky
acgikmns
smacking
acgiknor
croaking
acgiknrt
tracking
acgiknst
stacking
acgikprs
gripsack
acgilllr
call-girl
acgilmmn
clamming
acgilnpp
clapping
acgilnps
clasping
acgilnrw
crawling
acgilrsu
surgical
acgimmnr
cramming
acgimnos
coamings
acgimnps
scamping
acgimnsy
gymnasic
syngamic
acgimors
orgasmic
acgimrtu
Targumic
acginnns
scanning
acginnpr
prancing
acginnru
uncaring
acginnuv
vauncing
acginory
congiary

acginost
agnostic
coasting
acginprs
scarping
scraping
acginrrs
scarring
acginrry
carrying
acgioors
gracioso
acgiorst
orgastic
acgiorsu
gracious
acgioruw
Guicowar
acgiprsy
spagyric
acgjlnou
conjugal
acglmouu
coagulum
acglnoru
clangour
acglosuu
glaucous
acgnnoot
contango
acgorssw
cowgrass
acgppsuu
scuppaug
achhilpt
phthalic
achhintw
whinchat
achhinty
hyacinth
achhippr
hipparch
achhlmos
mashloch
achhlnor
rhonchal
achhlpry
phylarch
achhlsuy
shauchly
achhnttu
nuthatch
unthatch
achhostw
chat-show
achhptuz
chutzpah
achhrstu
crush-hat
achiilms
chiliasm
achiilst
chiliast

8 ACH

achiimns Mishnaic
achiimrt Mithraic
achiinps Hispanic
achiinrt trichina
achiirst rachitis
achiirsu ischuria
achijkpw whipjack
achikkns knackish
achikksw kickshaw
achikllw hickwall
achiklpt chalkpit
achikrsw rickshaw
achillor orchilla
achillrt clithral
achilmop omphalic
achilmrs chrismal
achilmty mythical
achilnns clannish
achilnoo hoolican
achilnos lichanos
achilnps clanship
achilopr rhopalic
achilops sophical
achilort acrolith
achilpsy physical
achilpty patchily
achilruy chyluria
achilrvy chivalry
achimmos machismo
achimmst mismatch
achimnnw winchman
achimnop champion
achimnor choirman harmonic
achimnsu inasmuch
achimopr amphoric
achimoss isochasm
achimpss scampish
achimrst chartism
achimssu chiasmus
achimtuy cyathium
achinnop panchion
achinopr parochin
achinort anorthic
achinotz hoactzin
achinquu Quichuan
achinsty Scythian
achiorss coarsish
achiprrt parritch
achipttu chupatti
achirrsy Syriarch
achirrty triarchy
achirstt chartist straicht
achistty chastity
achkkorw hack-work
achkmors shamrock
achknoot canthook
achkossy hassocky
achllnwy lynch-law
achllory chorally
achlmstz schmaltz
achlnoou oulachon
achlnsty stanchly
achloprt calthrop
achlopry polyarch
achloptt potlatch
achlotwx wax-cloth
achmnoor Monarcho
achmnors Romansch
achmnory monarchy nomarchy
achmnosu Monachus
achmnrsu Rumansch
achmnrtu truchman
achmopst camp-shot
achmortu outmarch
achmosty stomachy
achmottu outmatch
achmprtu thrum-cap
achnnoru unanchor
achnooot Ochotona
achnopru up-anchor
achnppss schnapps
achnrstu unstarch
achnrsyy synarchy
achnrtuy chauntry
achoortu co-author
achoorty chay-root
achoprty toparchy
achottuw outwatch watch-out
achprstu push-cart sharp-cut
achrsttu straucht
aciiilmn inimical
aciiilns Sicilian
aciiilnv civilian
aciiinst Sinaitic
aciiknnn cannikin
aciikprt paitrick
aciillsu silicula
aciilltv villatic
aciilmnr criminal
aciilmpt palmitic
aciilnor ironical
aciilnpt platinic
aciilnsu Siculian
aciilntx Calixtin
aciilrtt tritical
aciilrtu uralitic
aciilstv silvatic
aciimnor morainic
aciimnos simoniac
aciimnot amniotic
aciimnst actinism
aciimnsu musician
aciimntu actinium
aciimnty imitancy intimacy minacity
aciimost iotacism
aciimott amitotic
aciimprt primatic
aciimprv vampiric
aciimrst scimitar
aciimrtu muriatic
aciimstt Atticism
aciimstv activism
aciimtuv viaticum
aciinnop Panionic
aciinnos Socinian
aciinnot inaction nicotian
aciinnqu cinquain
aciinntt incitant
aciinnty caninity
aciinopt optician
aciinorz zirconia
aciinoss Ossianic
aciinosv avionics
aciinott citation
aciinrss narcissi
aciinrtu uranitic
aciiortv victoria
aciiostt Taoistic
aciippst papistic
aciirsst Triassic
aciirstt artistic
aciisttu autistic
aciisttv activist
aciittvy activity
aciitvvy vivacity
acijkkps skipjack
acijkstw stickjaw
acijrssu Jurassic
acikllst salt-lick
aciklmst malstick
aciklnry crankily
aciklory croakily
acikmnty nicky-tam
acikmpst mapstick
acilllmy clay-mill
acilllop pollical
acilllps clap-sill
acillmmy clammily
acillmos localism
acillnoo colonial
acillnor carillon
acillnos scallion
acillooz colza-oil
acilloqu coquilla
acillort clitoral
acillosy socially
acilloty locality
acilmnno non-claim
acilmnop complain
acilmnos laconism
acilmopr proclaim
acilmopt compital
acilmosv vocalism
acilmptu placitum
acilmsty mystical
acilmtuy ultimacy
acilnoot colation location
acilnoov vocalion
acilnops salpicon
acilnopt platonic
acilnort contrail
acilnory iron-clay
acilnosu unsocial
acilnosv Slavonic Volscian
acilnouv univocal
acilnrsu cislunar

acilnruy
culinary
acilnstu
sultanic
acilnsty
scantily
aciloops
Scopolia
aciloprt
tropical
acilorst
calorist
acilortv
vortical
acilostv
vocalist
acilotvy
vocality
acilprsu
spicular
acilprtu
pictural
acilpsst
plastics
acilrstu
rustical
acilrtuv
cultivar
curvital
acilstvy
sylvatic
acimmoss
acosmism
acimmtuy
cymatium
acimnnno
cinnamon
acimnoor
acromion
acimnort
romantic
acimnoru
conarium
coumarin
acimnory
acrimony
acimnoss
mocassin
acimnost
monastic
acimnosu
un-mosaic
acimnotu
aconitum
acimnpty
tympanic
acimorst
acrotism
acimorsy
cramoisy
acimosst
acosmist
massicot

acimostt
masticot
stomatic
acimrrsy
miscarry
acinnoot
conation
acinnorr
naricorn
acinnoss
scansion
acinnost
canonist
sanction
acinnotu
continua
acinnrty
tyrannic
acinnsty
instancy
acinoopr
picaroon
acinootv
vocation
acinoppt
panoptic
acinoprs
parsonic
acinorss
narcosis
acinorst
cantoris
cast-iron
acinortt
traction
acinossy
cyanosis
acinostt
oscitant
acinostu
anticous
acinostw
wainscot
acinoswx
coxswain
acinottx
toxicant
acinpquy
piquancy
acinpsty
synaptic
acinrsst
Sanscrit
acinrstu
saturnic
acinrttu
taciturn
urticant
acinstty
sanctity
scantity
acioopst
scotopia

aciootyz
zoocytia
acioprst
piscator
acioprtt
protatic
acioprty
poticary
aciopsst
potassic
aciopssu
spacious
aciopstu
captious
aciopttu
autoptic
aciorssu
scarious
aciorstu
Suctoria
aciortty
atrocity
citatory
aciortvy
voracity
aciostuu
cautious
aciprruu
pirarucu
acirrttx
tractrix
acirrtux
curatrix
acirssty
sacristy
acisttuy
astucity
ackklorr
rock-lark
ackkmopr
pockmark
ackkorrw
rackwork
ackllpsu
skull-cap
acklmnos
locksman
acklmoru
rock-alum
ackloopw
wool-pack
ackloosw
woolsack
acklorst
rock-salt
ackmnost
stockman
ackmnrtu
truckman
ackmsuvy
musk-cavy
ackoprrt
trap-rock

aclllor
roll-call
aclllot
toll-call
aclllnuu
Lucullan
acllmnou
columnal
acllmoru
corallum
acllmosu
Mollusca
aclloort
collator
aclloss
colossal
aclloruy
ocularly
acllrtuu
cultural
aclmmnou
communal
aclmnoru
columnar
aclmnory
normalcy
aclmortu
crotalum
aclmprsu
scalprum
aclmrsuu
muscular
aclmsuuv
vasculum
aclnoort
colorant
aclnopsy
syncopal
aclnoptw
cow-plant
aclnorsu
consular
aclnostu
osculant
aclnptuu
punctual
aclooprr
corporal
acloopt
Coalport
acloopsx
Scolopax
acloprxy
xylocarp
aclopsuu
opuscula
aclorrtu
torcular
aclorstu
Crotalus
aclortuw
law-court

aclosstu
outclass
soul-scat
aclostuw
scout-law
acmmnosy
scammony
acmmnoyy
myomancy
acmnoopr
monocarp
acmnoorr
cromorna
acmnoort
monocrat
acmnooyz
zoomancy
acmnopuy
Apocynum
acmnortu
Turcoman
acmnosst
Scotsman
acmoorrt
motor-car
acmorstw
worm-cast
acmorsty
costmary
acmsuvvy
cum-savvy
acnnnory
cannonry
acnnostt
constant
acnooort
octaroon
acnoorry
coronary
acnoorst
ostracon
acnoorsu
canorous
acnoorty
octonary
acnopstw
snow-capt
acnorrty
contrary
acnorstt
contrast
acnorsww
crown-saw
acnorttu
turncoat
acnortuy
noctuary
acnprsyy
syncarpy
acnrrtuy
curranty
acooprrs
corporas

acoprrtt
protract
acorrtuy
carry-out
curatory
acorsstu
tau-cross
acorssuw
curassow
acorsswy
crossway
acorstty
cryostat
acpsstuy
pussy-cat
acrrstuu
Arcturus
adddeegr
degraded
adddeeim
diademed
adddeelr
laddered
adddeenr
reddenda
adddeinw
dead-wind
adddemnu
addendum
adddeoow
dead-wood
adddeors
addorsed
addeeefh
feed-head
addeeenr
deadener
endeared
addeeepr
deep-read
addeefil
defilade
addeefir
dead-fire
addeefry
defrayed
addeegln
danegeld
addeegmu
gude-dame
addeegnr
deranged
addeegor
dog-eared
addeegsw
saw-edged
addeehly
aldehyde
addeehnr
hardened
addeeiln
deadline
addeeilp
deep-laid

addeeilt
detailed
addeeiss
diseased
addeeist
steadied
addeellm
medalled
addeellp
pedalled
addeelms
alms-deed
addeemnr
demander
addeenrr
reed-rand
addeenrw
wandered
addeenss
deadness
addeentu
denudate
addeeopr
dead-rope
addeeprv
depraved
addeerrt
retarded
addefiil
ladified
addefilt
dead-lift
addefily
ladyfied
addeflru
dreadful
addefnow
fade-down
addegirs
disgrade
addegmoo
good-dame
addegnru
ungraded
addehhin
hindhead
addehhln
hand-held
addehilr
dihedral
addehlnr
land-herd
addehmru
drumhead
addehnny
dandy-hen
addehnsu
undashed
unshaded
addehorw
headword
addehost
dead-shot

addeiitv
additive
addeimos
sodamide
addeimrs
misdread
addeimtt
admitted
addeinos
adenoids
addeiopr
parodied
addeiors
roadside
side-road
addeippr
didapper
addeiprs
dispread
addeipss
dipsades
addeirsw
sideward
addeirvz
vizarded
addeissu
dissuade
addeknvy
vandyked
addekorw
dead-work
addellor
dollared
addellpu
dead-pull
addelnou
duodenal
unloaded
addelnpu
pudendal
addelnsu
unsaddle
addeloor
Eldorado
addelrst
straddle
addelrsw
swaddler
addelrsy
saddlery
addelrtw
twaddler
addemmnu
undammed
addemnnu
undamned
addemnpu
undamped
addennsu
sand-dune
addenoru
unadored
addenpru
undraped

addenrst
stranded
addenrtu
untraded
addenruw
unwarded
addeottu
outdated
addeprsu
superadd
addffilo
daffodil
addffinr
dandriff
addffnru
dandruff
addggiln
gladding
addgiiln
daidling
addgilnp
paddling
addgilnw
waddling
addginor
daring-do
addgiosy
dog-daisy
addgmruu
mud-guard
addgorsw
godwards
addhhlno
handhold
addhimoo
maidhood
addhinrw
hindward
addhinsy
dandyish
addhioty
hydatoid
addhlooy
ladyhood
addhoorw
hardwood
addiiluv
dividual
addiinot
addition
addillnw
wild-land
addilnnw
landwind
addimnsy
dandyism
addimpsy
Paddyism
addinnoo
Dodonian
addinnor
ordinand
addinors
disadorn

addinquy
quiddany
addinrww
windward
addiorrt
dirt-road
addiptuy
duty-paid
addknrru
drunkard
addllnor
landlord
addlnnow
downland
addlnoow
woodland
addlnors
landdros
addmmooy
moody-mad
addmoosy
doomsday
addnopuy
pound-day
addnopwy
pandowdy
addnorww
downward
addoorry
door-yard
addoorww
woodward
adeeeffr
affeered
adeeefls
seed-leaf
adeeefny
fedayeen
adeeefrt
federate
adeeeglt
delegate
adeeegnr
renegade
adeeegnt
teen-aged
adeeegps
gapeseed
adeeegrs
degrease
adeeehrx
exhedrae
adeeehsy
eyeshade
adeeeint
detainee
adeeekwy
weak-eyed
adeeelpy
pale-eyed
adeeelst
teaseled
adeeeltv
elevated

adeeemnt
emendate
adeeenrs
serenade
adeeentt
edentate
adeeenwz
weazened
adeeeprs
rape-seed
adeeeprt
repeated
adeeertt
date-tree
adeefhnr
free-hand
adeefhor
forehead
adeefhrt
earth-fed
adeefiln
enfilade
adeefior
foedarie
adeefirr
rarefied
adeefiry
reaedify
adeeflms
self-made
adeeflor
freeload
adeeflrr
deferral
adeeflrt
deflater
adeeflss
fadeless
adeeflsx
flax-seed
adeefmnr
freedman
adeefmtu
deaf-mute
adeefnot
tone-deaf
adeefnru
unfeared
adeefnss
deafness
adeeforr
foreread
adeefort
foredate
adeefrrt
raftered
adeefrry
defrayer
federary
adeefrtu
featured
adeegirs
disagree

adeegitt
tide-gate
adeeglnr
enlarged
adeeglnt
danegelt
adeegmnr
gendarme
adeegmny
Ganymede
megadyne
adeegmop
megapode
adeegnnr
endanger
adeegnor
renegado
adeegnrr
gardener
adeegnru
dungaree
under-age
ungeared
adeegnrv
engraved
adeegnss
agedness
adeegort
derogate
adeegotw
goatweed
adeegprt
pargeted
adeegrrr
regarder
adeegrrt
garreted
adeegrru
redargue
adeegrss
dressage
adeegrtt
targeted
adeegswy
edgeways
adeegttz
gazetted
adeehhst
sheathed
adeehikp
pike-head
adeehiln
headline
adeehils
deisheal
adeehipr
pier-head
adeehirr
deer-hair
adeehirt
head-tire
adeehisv
adhesive

adeehkww
hawkweed
adeehkwy
hawk-eyed
adeehllw
well-head
adeehlno
dane-hole
adeehlnp
hen-padle
adeehlnr
rehandle
adeehlnu
unhealed
adeehlss
headless
adeehmmo
home-made
adeehmnn
menhaden
adeehnot
headnote
adeehnrr
hardener
adeehnrt
adherent
neat-herd
threaden
adeehntu
unheated
adeehopr
headrope
adeehors
sorehead
adeehorv
overhead
adeehrrs
redshare
adeehrrt
threader
adeehrst
headrest
adeehrtw
wreathed
adeeiils
idealise
adeeiint
Tineidae
adeeiipr
Pieridae
adeeiitv
ideative
adeeijmr
jeremiad
adeeilln
lead-line
adeeillo
oeillade
adeeilmn
endemial
adeeilmr
remedial
adeeilmt
meal-tide

adeeilmv
medieval
adeeilnt
date-line
lineated
adeeilpr
pedalier
adeeilps
Pleiades
adeeilpt
depilate
pileated
adeeilrr
derailer
adeeilrs
sidereal
adeeilss
idealess
adeeilsv
disleave
sea-devil
adeeimnt
dementia
adeeimrs
maderise
adeeimrt
diameter
remediat
adeeimtt
meditate
adeeinns
andesine
adeeinop
Oedipean
adeeinpr
pindaree
adeeinpt
diapente
neaptide
adeeinrs
arsenide
nearside
adeeinrt
detainer
adeeinst
andesite
adeeipss
speisade
adeeipsv
Vespidae
adeeiptt
tape-tied
adeeirst
readiest
steadier
adeeirsv
readvise
adeeirtv
derivate
adeeistv
sedative
adeeitvw
tide-wave

adeekmrr
remarked
adeekmrt
marketed
adeeknpw
knapweed
adeekprr
deer-park
adeekrst
streaked
adeelllp
lapelled
adeellmt
metalled
adeellmu
medullae
adeellmw
well-made
adeellnp
panelled
adeellny
leadenly
adeellpr
pedaller
predella
adeellpt
palleted
petalled
adeellqu
equalled
adeellrs
sardelle
adeellrv
ravelled
adeellrw
well-read
adeellss
leadless
adeellty
elatedly
adeellvy
day-level
adeellwy
wall-eyed
adeelmno
lemonade
adeelmns
emendals
adeelmnt
lamented
adeelmos
somedeal
adeelmrs
demersal
adeelnnu
unaneled
adeelnor
oleander
adeelnrt
antlered
adeelnrv
lavender
adeelnry
Alderney

adeelnsu
unleased
unsealed
adeelnsv
enslaved
adeelntt
talented
adeelntu
unelated
adeelopr
lop-eared
adeelors
lease-rod
adeeloru
aureoled
adeelorv
overlade
adeelost
desolate
adeelppt
lappeted
adeelprs
relapsed
adeelpst
pedestal
adeelpty
pedately
adeelrrr
larderer
adeelrrt
treadler
adeelsst
dateless
adeelsty
sedately
adeemmss
mesdames
adeemmxy
myxedema
adeemnnr
mannered
adeemnor
demeanor
adeemnot
nematode
adeemnss
seedsman
adeemnst
stamened
adeemnsu
unseamed
adeemntw
metewand
adeemnyy
many-eyed
adeemors
seadrome
adeemort
moderate
adeemosy
Samoyede
adeempst
stampede
stepdame

adeemrry
dreamery
adeemrsu
measured
adeemrty
meteyard
adeennru
unearned
adeennuw
unweaned
adeennuy
unyeaned
adeenopw
weaponed
adeenors
reasoned
adeenory
aerodyne
adeenoss
seasoned
adeenott
denotate
detonate
adeenppr
end-paper
adeenpps
sand-peep
adeenpru
unreaped
adeenprx
expander
re-expand
adeenptt
pattened
adeenrrw
wanderer
adeenrss
dearness
adeenrsu
undersea
adeenrtt
attender
nattered
adeenrtu
denature
adeenssu
danseuse
Sudanese
adeenstu
unseated
adeensvy
seven-day
adeenttv
vendetta
adeeoprr
paderero
adeeorrv
overread
adeepprr
prepared
adeeprrs
spreader
adeeprrt
departer

adeeprru
upreared
adeeprsu
persuade
adeeprtu
depurate
adeepswy
speedway
adeerrrt
retarder
adeerrrw
rereward
rewarder
adeerrst
serrated
adeerrtw
red-water
adeerttt
tattered
adeertww
wartweed
adeervyy
everyday
adeesttt
attested
adeffort
trade-off
adefgilo
foliaged
adefgils
gas-field
adefgimn
defaming
adefgirs
gas-fired
adefgirt
driftage
adefgitu
fatigued
adefgllo
gold-leaf
adefgllu
full-aged
adefglot
gatefold
adefglru
feldgrau
adefgnor
frondage
adefgnuw
wage-fund
adefhils
dealfish
adefhilt
half-tide
adefhily
hayfield
adefhkor
forkhead
adefhlno
half-done
adefhlnt
left-hand

adefhltu
  deathful
adefhnor
  forehand
adefhnrr
  hard-fern
adefhost
  softhead
adefiikl
  fail-dike
adefiilr
  airfield
adefiils
  salified
adefiimr
  ramified
adefiirt
  ratified
adefillr
  all-fired
adefillt
  ill-fated
adefilmn
  inflamed
adefilnr
  filander
adefilnt
  inflated
adefilot
  foliated
adefimpr
  firedamp
adefinrr
  infra-red
adefinru
  Freudian
adefinrw
  fine-draw
adefiors
  foresaid
adeflllu
  ladleful
adefllrw
  well-far'd
adefllry
  alder-fly
adefllst
  stall-fed
adeflluy
  feudally
adeflmru
  dreamful
adeflnor
  foreland
adeflnru
  dearnful
adeflnry
  lady-fern
adeflnuu
  unfeudal
adeflnuw
  unflawed
adeflort
  deflator

adeflprs
  feldspar
adeflpsu
  spadeful
adeflrtu
  tradeful
adeflrtw
  leftward
adefmnru
  unframed
adefnnnu
  unfanned
adefnsst
  daftness
adeforrr
  forrader
adeforrw
  foreward
adeforuv
  favoured
adeggjly
  jaggedly
adegglru
  leg-guard
adegglry
  raggedly
adeggmoy
  demagogy
adeggnuu
  ungauged
adeggopy
  pedagogy
adeggprs
  spragged
adeggrty
  gadgetry
adeghhos
  hogshead
adeghilt
  alighted
  gilt-head
adeghinr
  headring
adeghins
  sheading
adeghity
  eight-day
adeghlno
  headlong
  long-head
adeghmno
  hog-maned
adeghmoy
  hey-go-mad
adeghnnu
  unhanged
adeghnpu
  dung-heap
adeghoop
  pagehood
adeghort
  goatherd
adeghotw
  dog-wheat

adeghrtu
  daughter
adeghuyy
  hay-de-guy
adegiino
  Ganoidei
adegiitt
  digitate
adegillo
  gladiole
adegillr
  grillade
adegilno
  galenoid
adegilnp
  pleading
adegilnr
  dearling
  dragline
adegilny
  delaying
adegilou
  dialogue
adegilrs
  Griselda
adegilss
  glissade
adegilsv
  disgavel
adegimnr
  dreaming
  margined
adegimor
  ideogram
adeginor
  organdie
adeginos
  agonised
  diagnose
adeginpu
  anguiped
adeginrr
  drearing
adeginrt
  derating
  gradient
  treading
adeginst
  steading
adeginyz
  zygaenid
adegiort
  ergatoid
adegirwy
  ridgeway
adegissu
  disusage
adegllnu
  glandule
  ungalled
adeglmos
  gladsome
adeglmpu
  plumaged

adeglmuy
  amygdule
adeglnps
  spangled
adeglnrs
  glanders
adeglnss
  gladness
adeglnuz
  unglazed
adegmnoy
  endogamy
adegmost
  dog's-meat
adegnnor
  androgen
  dragonné
adegnnpu
  unpanged
adegnopu
  poundage
adegnort
  dragonet
adegnpuy
  pyengadu
adegnrru
  grandeur
adegnruu
  unargued
adegoory
  goodyear
adegoosw
  wood-sage
adegorst
  goadster
adegortt
  garotted
adegortw
  water-dog
  water-god
adegorwy
  dog-weary
adegrrst
  dragster
adegtttu
  guttated
adehhipr
  rhaphide
adehhips
  headship
adehhntu
  headhunt
adehiklv
  khedival
adehikns
  skinhead
adehillp
  phialled
adehilnn
  hand-line
adehilnp
  Delphian
adehilnr
  hardline

adehilnu
  unhailed
adehimry
  hydremia
adehinnr
  rein-hand
adehinop
  diaphone
adehinos
  adhesion
adehinps
  deanship
adehinpu
  dauphine
adehinru
  unhaired
adehiors
  Rhodesia
adehiott
  athetoid
adehiprs
  raphides
adehipst
  side-path
adehirvw
  hiveward
adehissw
  Swadeshi
adehjlot
  jolthead
adehknrs
  red-shank
adehknsu
  skean-dhu
  unshaked
adehkorw
  headwork
adehllpy
  lady-help
adehllrw
  hellward
adehlmno
  homeland
adehlmoy
  holydame
adehlnos
  sand-hole
adehlnrw
  Landwehr
adehlnss
  handless
adehlnst
  shetland
adehlnsu
  unhalsed
adehlops
  asphodel
  pholades
adehlrry
  heraldry
adehmnos
  handsome

adehmnot
  methadon
  thanedom
adehmnrs
  herdsman
adehmnru
  unharmed
adehmnsu
  unshamed
adehmoor
  headroom
adehmort
  mort-head
adehmorw
  homeward
adehmost
  headmost
adehmosu
  madhouse
adehmppu
  pump-head
adehnnsw
  hand-sewn
adehnorv
  handover
  overhand
adehnoss
  sand-shoe
adehnosu
  sea-hound
adehnpsu
  unshaped
adehnptu
  unpathed
adehnrss
  hardness
adehnrsu
  unshared
adehnrsw
  swanherd
adehnrtu
  unthread
adehnssu
  sun-shade
  unsashed
adehnsuv
  unshaved
adehnsuw
  unwashed
adehnttu
  unhatted
adehnttx
  text-hand
adehntuw
  unthawed
adehoprs
  rhapsode
adehopxy
  hexapody
adehorsw
  shadower
adehortt
  throated

adehpsuw
washed-up
adehrttw
thwarted
adeiilmn
limnaeid
adeiilms
idealism
adeiilpr
peridial
adeiilst
idealist
adeiiltv
dilative
adeiilty
ideality
adeiimnr
meridian
adeiinns
sanidine
adeiinot
ideation
taenioid
adeiinst
adenitis
adeiinuv
induviae
adeiiprr
perradii
prairied
adeiiprs
presidia
adeiirst
irisated
adeiittv
tidivate
adeiituv
auditive
adeijrsu
Judaiser
adeikllo
keloidal
adeikllp
pikadell
adeiklly
ladylike
adeiklsw
sidewalk
adeikmrt
tidemark
adeikort
keratoid
adeillmy
medially
adeillnn
land-line
adeillno
load-line
adeillnu
unallied
adeillor
arillode
adeillps
spadille
adeillrv
rivalled
adeilmnn
land-mine
adeilmnu
unmailed
adeilmny
maidenly
adeilmos
soda-lime
adeilmpp
palmiped
adeilmps
misplead
adeilmry
dreamily
adeilmss
maidless
adeilmst
misdealt
adeilmsy
dysmelia
adeilnnr
inlander
adeilnop
palinode
adeilnos
nodalise
adeilnot
delation
adeilnpt
pantiled
adeilnpu
paludine
adeilnrs
islander
adeilnsu
unsailed
adeilntv
divalent
adeilops
episodal
opalised
sepaloid
adeilopt
petaloid
adeiloqu
odalique
adeilors
solidare
sordial
adeilort
idolater
adeilorv
overlaid
adeilorx
exordial
adeilost
diastole
sodalite
solidate
adeilott
datolite
adeilotv
dovetail
adeilppp
pedipalp
adeilprt
dipteral
tripedal
adeilpru
epidural
adeilprv
deprival
adeilpss
despisal
adeilptu
plaudite
adeilrry
drearily
adeilrsu
residual
adeilrsy
dialyser
adeilrtt
detrital
adeilrty
dielytra
adeilrvy
variedly
adeilssy
dialyses
adeilsty
diastyle
steadily
adeilsuv
disvalue
adeilsxy
dyslexia
adeilttu
altitude
latitude
adeimmnu
unmaimed
adeimmst
mismated
adeimmsz
Mazdeism
adeimnno
Demonian
adeimnop
dopamine
adeimnor
Armenoid
adeimnos
nomadise
adeimnot
dominate
nematoid
adeimnrz
zemindar
adeimnss
sidesman
adeimnst
tides-man
adeimnsz
man-sized
adeimnty
dynamite
adeimorr
airdrome
adeimort
mediator
adeimoss
sesamoid
adeimpst
impasted
adeimrss
sidearms
adeimrtu
muriated
adeimrxy
ready-mix
adeinnot
antinode
adeinnov
Devonian
adeinnpt
pinnated
adeinnpu
unpained
adeinnsu
unsained
adeinnsx
disannex
adeinntu
inundate
adeinopt
antipode
adeinorr
ordainer
reordain
adeinort
deration
ordinate
Rodentia
adeinost
sedation
adeinott
antidote
tetanoid
adeinotv
donative
adeinpps
sand-pipe
adeinppx
appendix
adeinprt
dipteran
adeinpru
unpaired
unrepaid
adeinpsv
spavined
adeinrrs
serranid
adeinrss
aridness
adeinrst
strained
adeinrsu
denarius
unraised
adeinrsv
sandiver
adeinrsy
synedria
adeinrtu
daturine
indurate
adeinruv
unvaried
adeinrvy
vineyard
adeinstu
sinuated
adeinsty
desyatin
adeioprs
diaspore
adeiopst
dioptase
adeioptv
adoptive
adeiorst
asteroid
adeiortt
teratoid
adeiortv
deviator
adeiprst
spirated
adeiprsu
upraised
adeiprtu
eupatrid
adeipttu
aptitude
adeiqrru
quarried
adeiqsuy
quayside
adeirrww
wire-draw
adeirsst
disaster
adeirstt
striated
adeirvwy
driveway
adeissst
assisted
adeisstt
distaste
adeisswy
sideways
adeisttu
situated
adeitttu
attitude
adejnruw
under-jaw
adejopry
jeopardy
adejrstu
adjuster
readjust
adeklmry
markedly
adeklnsu
unslaked
adekmnru
unmarked
adekmnsu
unmasked
adekmors
darksome
adeknnss
dankness
adeknotw
take-down
adeknrss
darkness
adellmru
medullar
adellnnu
annulled
adellnps
spendall
adellnss
landless
adellnsw
wallsend
adellntt
Lettland
adellnuw
unwalled
adellott
allotted
totalled
adellovy
lady-love
adelloww
wallowed
adellrww
draw-well
adelmnos
lodesman
sand-mole
adelmoow
wood-meal
adelmotu
modulate
adelmptu
date-plum
adelmrru
demurral
adelmsuy
amusedly
adelnnot
lentando
adelnopr
Polander
ponderal
adelnors
solander

adelnoru
  unloader
  urodelan
adelnorv
  overland
  rondavel
adelnprs
  spandrel
adelnpru
  pendular
  underlap
  uplander
adelnpry
  panderly
adelnpsy
  dyspneal
adelnrty
  ardently
adelnruy
  underlay
adelnstu
  unsalted
adelntuu
  undulate
adelnuuv
  unvalued
adelnuzz
  undazzle
adeloorv
  overload
adeloowm
  woodwale
adelopsu
  paludose
adelopsy
  sepalody
adelopty
  petalody
adelorrv
  overlard
adelorst
  lodestar
adelovwy
  avowedly
adelppry
  dapperly
adelprty
  dry-plate
adelrrtu
  ultrared
adelrstt
  startled
adelrtuy
  adultery
adelstty
  statedly
ademnnnu
  unmanned
ademnnou
  unmoaned
ademnnru
  underman

ademnopr
  name-drop
  pomander
ademnowy
  dey-woman
ademnpss
  dampness
ademnrru
  underarm
  unmarred
ademnrtu
  undreamt
ademnruw
  unwarmed
ademnsuu
  unamused
ademoort
  moderato
ademopst
  stampedo
ademorru
  armoured
ademorrw
  Romeward
ademortw
  ward-mote
ademossu
  Asmodeus
adempruw
  warmed-up
adennntu
  untanned
adennors
  Anderson
adennotu
  unatoned
adennruw
  unwarned
adenntuw
  unwanted
adenoops
  epanodos
adenoorw
  wanderoo
adenoprr
  pardoner
adenoprx
  expandor
adenopss
  spadones
adenopsu
  unsoaped
adenopsy
  dyspnoea
adenoptt
  not-pated
adenorux
  rondeaux
adenossy
  Odyssean
adenotuy
  autodyne
adenouvw
  unavowed

adenppsu
  unsapped
adenpptu
  untapped
adenprsu
  unspared
adenprtu
  depurant
adenprty
  pedantry
adenpruw
  unwarped
adenpruy
  underpay
adenqrsu
  squander
adenrrtu
  untarred
adenrrwy
  wardenry
adenrstu
  transude
adenrsty
  dry-stane
adenrsuy
  undersay
adensttu
  unstated
  untasted
adenstuw
  unwasted
adenstuy
  unstayed
  unsteady
adensuwy
  unswayed
adeoorrt
  toreador
adeoottt
  tattooed
adeopprr
  pear-drop
adeoprrt
  parroted
  predator
  tear-drop
adeoprtt
  tetrapod
adeopruv
  vapoured
adeopstt
  despotat
  postdate
adeopttu
  up-to-date
adeorrst
  roadster
adeorrvw
  overdraw
adeorsst
  assorted
adeorstx
  extrados

adeorsuv
  savoured
adeosstt
  assotted
adepprst
  strapped
adeprrtu
  raptured
adeprttu
  tarted-up
adeqsttu
  squatted
aderrssw
  wardress
aderrstt
  red-start
adersttu
  statured
aderstww
  westward
adffhirs
  draffish
adfflruu
  fraudful
adffnnoo
  off-and-on
adffnost
  stand-off
adfforsw
  offwards
adfginnu
  unfading
adfglouw
  god-awful
adfhilns
  land-fish
adfhiost
  toad-fish
adfhirsw
  dwarfish
adfhisty
  day-shift
adfhlnsu
  handfuls
adfhloor
  half-door
adfhlost
  hold-fast
adfiilpy
  lapidify
adfiirst
  first-aid
adfillln
  landfill
adfillmn
  filmland
adfillnw
  windfall
adfillru
  ill-faurd
adfilmno
  manifold
adfimory
  fairydom

adfiorsv
  disfavor
adfirsty
  first-day
adfirtwy
  drift-way
adfkllno
  folkland
adfllnow
  downfall
adflmopr
  frampold
adfloowy
  floodway
adfmrstu
  stud-farm
adfnoorz
  forzando
adforrsw
  forwards
  frowards
adggginr
  dragging
adggilnn
  dangling
adgglrsu
  sluggard
adggorss
  dog-grass
adghhiln
  highland
adghhinn
  nigh-hand
adghhior
  highroad
adghilnn
  handling
adghilos
  hidalgos
adghilpy
  diaglyph
adghilty
  daylight
adghinpr
  handgrip
adghisty
  day-sight
adghittw
  tightwad
adghlnno
  longhand
adghnotu
  do-naught
adghnrtu
  drag-hunt
adghoopr
  odograph
adghorst
  drag-shot
adghpsyy
  dysphagy
adghrtuy
  draughty

adgiilln
  dialling
adgiillo
  gladioli
adgiilno
  gonidial
adgiilnp
  plaiding
adgiilnr
  ring-dial
adgiilpy
  pygidial
adgiilty
  algidity
adgiimst
  digamist
adgiinny
  digynian
adgiinry
  dairying
adgiinsv
  advising
adgijnru
  adjuring
adgiklnr
  darkling
adgillno
  oil-gland
adgillnr
  landgirl
adgillnw
  wind-gall
adgillny
  dallying
adgilmor
  marigold
adgilnns
  sandling
adgilnnu
  unlading
adgilnot
  dog-Latin
adgilnry
  daringly
adgilnzz
  dazzling
adgilopr
  prodigal
adgilory
  goliardy
  gyroidal
adgilrsy
  Ygdrasil
adgimnno
  Mandingo
adgimosu
  digamous
adginnst
  standing
adginoor
  rigadoon
adginorr
  ring-road

adginoty
toadying
adgkoosz
gadzooks
adgloopr
drop-goal
adgloory
gardyloo
adglopsw
gold-wasp
adgmnoru
gourmand
adgnnoqu
quandong
adgnnors
grandson
adgnnryy
gynandry
adgnooop
Podogona
adgooprs
gospodar
adgoprsu
Podargus
adgortuu
outguard
adhhinpw
whip-hand
adhhiprs
hardship
adhhnnor
hand-horn
adhhnoru
hour-hand
adhhnrty
hydranth
adhiimms
Mahdiism
adhiimss
Hasidism
adhiimst
Mahdiist
adhiinop
ophidian
adhiinrw
whiniard
adhiisst
Hasidist
adhiistw
had-I-wist
adhijnno
join-hand
adhillmn
hand-mill
mill-hand
adhillmo
hollidam
adhillns
sand-hill
adhillop
phalloid
adhillot
thalloid
adhilmoo
homaloid
adhilmss
alms-dish
adhilnps
land-ship
adhilnst
hand-list
adhilops
ship-load
adhilopy
haploidy
adhilpsy
ladyship
adhimnos
admonish
adhimnou
humanoid
adhimopp
amphipod
adhimrty
myriadth
adhinrwy
whinyard
adhinsst
standish
adhinssy
sandyish
adhinstu
dianthus
adhiopss
soap-dish
adhiosty
toadyish
adhiprsw
wardship
adhiprsy
shipyard
adhirstw
wash-dirt
adhirtww
withdraw
adhknorw
handwork
adhllnos
hollands
adhlloor
hall-door
adhlmnoo
hand-loom
adhlmort
thraldom
adhlnorw
waldhorn
adhlnouw
down-haul
adhmoops
shampoo'd
adhmoprs
dram-shop
adhmortt
dart-moth
adhnopst
hand-post
adhnostu
thousand
adhnosuw
unshadow
adhooprs
hospodar
adhoorss
sash-door
adhoorsw
roadshow
adhooryz
Hydrozoa
adhoprsy
rhapsody
adhorstu
toad-rush
adhorswy
show-yard
adhpstyy
dyspathy
adhrstuy
Thursday
adiiinrv
viridian
adiiklmm
milkmaid
adiiklst
tailskid
adiiknop
pinakoid
adiillmr
milliard
adiillny
idyllian
adiilluv
diluvial
adiilnot
dilation
adiilnsu
indusial
adiilnsw
wind-sail
adiilnty
daintily
Ladinity
adiilnuv
diluvian
induvial
adiilopp
diplopia
adiilssy
dialysis
adiiltvy
validity
adiimpsu
aspidium
adiinnot
nidation
adiinosy
Dionysia
adiinotu
audition
adiinrst
distrain
adiioprs
sporidia
adiioprt
tapiroid
adiiorst
tarsioid
adiiprty
rapidity
adiipsty
sapidity
adiiptvy
vapidity
adiirstt
distrait
triadist
adikkrrw
kirkward
adikkrry
kirkyard
adiklnps
landskip
adiknnnu
dunnakin
adiknnst
inkstand
adiknrst
stinkard
adilllpy
pallidly
adillmnr
mandrill
adillmou
allodium
adillmov
villadom
adillmsy
dismally
adillnps
landslip
adillops
spadillo
adillosw
disallow
adillosy
disloyal
adillrwy
willyard
adillsty
distally
adilmmos
modalism
adilmnno
mandolin
adilmnos
salmonid
adilmoor
modiolar
adilmoow
lima-wood
adilmopt
diplomat
adilmopy
Olympiad
adilmoru
ordalium
adilmost
modalist
adilmoty
modality
adilmpsu
paludism
adilnnnu
nundinal
adilnnsu
disannul
adilnoor
doornail
adilnoov
vindaloo
adilnopy
palinody
adilnoty
nodality
adilnprs
spandril
adilnpst
displant
adilnrwy
inwardly
adilnssw
windlass
adiloopr
Polaroid
adiloort
toroidal
adiloprt
tripodal
adilopss
disposal
adilorsy
solidary
adilorty
adroitly
dilatory
idolatry
adilosty
sodality
adilppsy
disapply
adilrtty
tilt-yard
adilrtwy
tawdrily
adilrwyz
wizardly
adimmnos
monadism
nomadism
adimmnsy
dynamism
adimmost
amidmost
adimmotu
domatium
adimnnot
dominant
adimnoor
main-door
adimnost
donatism
saintdom
adimnoww
widow-man
adimnrsy
misandry
adimnsty
dynamist
adimopry
myriapod
adimopst
impasto'd
adimopsy
sympodia
adimosty
toadyism
adimotux
Taxodium
adimrsuu
sudarium
adinnntu
inundant
adinnoot
donation
nodation
adinnors
iron-sand
adinnort
ordinant
adinnotu
in-and-out
nudation
adinoops
isopodan
adinoopt
adoption
adinoort
tandoori
adinoott
dotation
adinoprr
raindrop
adinopst
pintados
adinorry
ordinary
adinorst
intrados
adinorsu
dinosaur
adinortu
duration
adinorwz
Zionward
adinostt
Donatist
adinostu
sudation
adinpssu
Sapindus

adinruvz
  unvizard
adioopss
  apodosis
adioppst
  post-paid
adioprst
  parodist
adioprty
  podiatry
adiopstt
  toad-spit
adiopsty
  dystopia
adiorrst
  stair-rod
adiorrtt
  traditor
adiorstt
  stradiot
adiorsvy
  advisory
adiortuy
  auditory
adirrwyz
  wizardry
adjknruy
  junk-yard
adjorstu
  adjustor
adkloopt
  polka-dot
adkloorw
  wood-lark
  workload
adkmnorw
  mark-down
adkmoorr
  dark-room
adknrstu
  stunkard
adkorwyy
  worky-day
adkrsswy
  skywards
adlllnor
  land-roll
adlllory
  Lollardy
adllnoru
  all-round
adllorsy
  dorsally
adlmmoop
  doom-palm
adlmmopu
  doum-palm
adlmnoor
  moorland
adlmnory
  randomly
adlmnoss
  mossland
adlmooru
  malodour
adlmoprw
  moldwarp
adlmopsy
  psalmody
adlmsttu
  malt-dust
adlnnotw
  townland
adlnntuu
  undulant
adlnoopr
  land-poor
adlnoorw
  loan-word
adlnoprt
  portland
adlnopru
  pauldron
adlnorwy
  onwardly
adlooopw
  wood-opal
adloopty
  Tylopoda
adloorww
  woolward
adlopsuu
  paludous
adloqsuw
  oldsquaw
adlorsww
  sword-law
adlortwy
  towardly
adlpruwy
  upwardly
admmnoos
  doomsman
admmntuu
  mutandum
admnnory
  monandry
admnnotu
  notandum
admnooot
  odontoma
admnoors
  door's-man
admnoost
  mastodon
admnoosw
  woodsman
admnoosx
  Saxondom
admnorru
  round-arm
admnorsw
  sand-worm
  swordman
admnppsu
  sand-pump
admoorrw
  ward-room
admopppu
  poppadum
admorrsw
  sword-arm
adnnorty
  dynatron
adnooprs
  spadroon
adnooqru
  quadroon
adnoorty
  donatory
adnoosvw
  advowson
adnoqrsu
  squadron
adnorstw
  sandwort
adnorsxy
  sardonyx
adnortuw
  untoward
adnorwwy
  wanwordy
adnosttu
  outstand
adnostwy
  stay-down
adnrssuw
  sunwards
adooprrt
  trap-door
adooprst
  post-road
adooprsu
  sauropod
adoopsww
  wood-wasp
adoprssw
  password
adopsssu
  soap-suds
adorrstu
  dartrous
adorstuw
  outwards
adorstuy
  sudatory
adortuvy
  advoutry
adrssttu
  star-dust
adrssuuy
  Dasyurus
adsstuwy
  sawdusty
aeeeelrs
  releasee
aeeefrty
  aftereye
aeeegglu
  lee-gauge
aeeeggnr
  re-engage
aeeeglnr
  generale
aeeeglrt
  eglatere
  regelate
  relegate
aeeeglrv
  leverage
aeeegnpr
  pea-green
aeeegnrs
  sea-green
aeeegnrt
  generate
  renegate
  teenager
aeeegrst
  steerage
aeeegrsw
  sewerage
aeeegttv
  vegetate
aeeehlrt
  ethereal
aeeehltw
  wheat-eel
aeeehmpr
  ephemera
aeeehnrs
  enhearse
aeeehrrs
  rehearse
aeeehrrt
  reheater
aeeehrst
  shea-tree
aeeehstt
  aesthete
aeeeimnx
  examinee
aeeekkps
  keepsake
aeeeklns
  snake-eel
aeeeknrw
  weakener
aeeekprt
  peat-reek
aeeellsv
  sea-level
aeeelmrt
  meal-tree
aeeelnrv
  venereal
aeeelnst
  selenate
aeeelprr
  repealer
aeeelprs
  eel-spear
aeeelpry
  pearl-eye
aeeelpst
  paste-eel
aeeelqsu
  sequelae
aeeelrrs
  releaser
aeeelrrv
  revealer
aeeelrst
  teaseler
aeeelrsw
  weaseler
aeeelrtx
  axle-tree
aeeelsvy
  eye-salve
aeeemmrt
  metamere
aeeemnrt
  Nemertea
aeeemnst
  easement
aeeemprt
  permeate
aeeennrv
  venerean
aeeenptt
  patentee
aeeenrtt
  enterate
aeeenrtv
  enervate
  venerate
aeeeprrt
  pear-tree
  repartee
  repeater
aeeepstw
  sweetpea
aeeerrst
  arrestee
aeeersst
  tesserae
aeeertwy
  eye-water
aeeffknr
  frank-fee
aeefffllr
  free-fall
aeefflrt
  tafferel
aeeffnrt
  afferent
aeefgilr
  filagree
aeefginr
  Faringee
aeefgint
  gate-fine
aeefgirr
  ferriage
aeefglsu
  fuselage
aeefhlls
  self-heal
aeefhlst
  self-hate
aeefhrty
  feathery
aeefikll
  leaf-like
aeefikrw
  wakerife
aeefilnr
  flânerie
aeefilnv
  vine-leaf
aeefilpr
  pea-rifle
aeefilrs
  serafile
aeefilrt
  frailtee
aeefipsw
  spaewife
aeefkmnt
  fakement
aeefkopr
  forepeak
aeefllmr
  femerall
aeefllmt
  flamelet
aeefllnv
  evenfall
aeefllrw
  farewell
aeefllss
  leafless
aeeflmnr
  male-fern
aeeflmos
  fleasome
aeeflmss
  fameless
aeeflnos
  nose-leaf
aeeflnru
  funereal
aeeflors
  rose-leaf
aeeflorv
  overleaf
aeeflotv
  love-feat
aeeflrrr
  referral
aeeflrss
  fearless
aeefmnor
  foremean
  forename
aeefmors
  fearsome
aeefmrty
  femetary

aeefnrst
fastener
fenestra
aeefnrtt
fattener
aeefnsss
safeness
aeefostu
feateous
aeefttuv
fauvette
aeegghiw
weighage
aeeggirv
aggrieve
aeeggkor
oak-egger
aeegglou
aeglogue
aeegglpp
egg-apple
aeeggnnr
gangrene
aeeggnos
gasogene
aeeggnoz
gazogene
aeeggpru
puggaree
aeeghiln
Hegelian
aeeghirt
heritage
aeeghllt
hell-gate
aeeghlot
helotage
aeeghlrs
shear-leg
aeeghlrw
ragwheel
aeeghmpr
grapheme
aeeghnrs
shagreen
aeeghrrt
gatherer
regather
aeegiinr
aegirine
aeegiirt
aegirite
aeegills
legalise
aeegilmn
liegeman
aeegilnr
algerine
aeegilns
ensilage
aeegilnt
galenite
gelatine
legatine

aeegilnv
inveagle
aeegilpr
perigeal
aeegilrs
gaselier
aeegilst
elegiast
aeegiltv
levigate
aeegimnr
germaine
aeegimnt
geminate
aeegimrt
emigrate
remigate
aeeginpr
perigean
aeeginrr
regainer
aeeginrs
gesneria
aeeginss
assignee
aeeginst
sagenite
aeeginsv
envisage
aeegintv
gate-vein
negative
aeegipqu
equipage
aeegirtt
aigrette
aeegllnr
allergen
aeegllow
eagle-owl
aeeglmov
love-game
aeeglmrt
telegram
aeeglmry
meagrely
aeeglnnt
entangle
aeeglnos
gasolene
aeeglnot
elongate
aeeglnrr
enlarger
aeeglnst
Gnetales
aeeglnvy
evangely
aeeglost
segolate
aeeglrss
eelgrass
largesse

aeeglrtu
regulate
aeeglrux
exergual
aeeglsst
gateless
aeeglssy
eyeglass
aeeglttu
tutelage
aeegltuv
evulgate
aeegmmos
gamesome
aeegmnor
argemone
aeegmnrs
agrémens
aeegmnrt
agrément
aeegmnss
gameness
aeegmntz
gazement
aeegmost
somegate
aeegmrst
gamester
gas-meter
aeegmssu
messuage
aeegnnno
enneagon
aeegnnrt
generant
aeegnnru
enraunge
aeegnnrv
engraven
aeegnprs
sap-green
aeegnrrv
engraver
aeegnrst
estrange
segreant
sergeant
sternage
aeegnrtu
gauntree
aeegnsss
sageness
aeegnttv
vegetant
aeegoprv
overpage
aeegprrs
asperger
presager
aeegprrt
pargeter
aeegprss
asperges

aeegrrrt
regrater
aeegrsst
Argestes
aeegrssw
sewer-gas
aeegrstw
strewage
aeehhhnt
heath-hen
aeehhhss
hasheesh
aeehhnst
ensheath
aeehhrty
heathery
aeehijmr
Jeremiah
aeehikrs
shikaree
aeehilnp
elaphine
aeehilrs
shiralee
aeehilrt
etherial
aeehiltw
white-ale
aeehimpt
epithema
aeehimtt
hematite
aeehinps
Ephesian
aeehinrs
inhearse
aeehinrt
atherine
aeehintt
Theatine
aeehiprs
Pharisee
aeehipst
aphetise
hepatise
aeehiptt
hepatite
aeehirsv
shivaree
aeehirtu
Eutheria
aeehistt
athetise
hesitate
aeehistv
heaviest
aeehkllr
rakehell
aeehkllu
keelhaul
aeehllrs
ear-shell
aeehllss
seashell

aeehlmnw
wheelman
aeehlmny
hymeneal
aeehlmos
healsome
aeehlmpt
helpmate
aeehlnpt
elephant
aeehlnrt
leathern
aeehlnss
haleness
aeehlnvy
heavenly
aeehlopt
peat-hole
aeehlors
arsehole
aeehlorv
overhale
aeehlosu
ale-house
aeehlptt
telepath
aeehlrst
halteres
aeehlrtt
heartlet
aeehlrty
leathery
aeehlsst
hateless
aeehltty
ethylate
aeehmnny
hymenean
aeehmnrt
three-man
aeehmntx
exanthem
aeehmpss
emphases
aeehmrty
erythema
aeehmtux
exhumate
aeehnnss
sneeshan
aeehnntx
xanthene
aeehnopr
earphone
aeehnpst
stephane
aeehnrst
hastener
aeehnrsu
unhearse
aeehnrtt
haterent
threaten

aeehnrtu
urethane
aeehnrtw
water-hen
wreathen
aeehnrwy
anywhere
aeehnstu
uneathes
aeehnstw
enswathe
aeehorrv
overhear
aeehorss
sea-horse
seashore
aeehortv
overheat
aeehostu
tea-house
aeehprrs
rephrase
aeehprst
spreathe
aeehpsty
pay-sheet
aeehrrtu
urethrae
aeehrrtw
wreather
aeehrtvw
whatever
aeehrtwy
three-way
aeeiimrt
métairie
aeeikklw
likewake
aeeiklvw
wavelike
aeeikmmr
Merimake
aeeiknrt
ankerite
kreatine
aeeillnt
tenaille
aeeillvx
live-axle
aeeilmmn
melamine
aeeilmmt
meal-time
aeeilmnt
melanite
aeeilmrt
eremital
matériel
realtime
aeeilmsv
malvesie
aeeilnpr
perineal

aeeilnps
penalise
sepaline
aeeilnpt
petaline
tapeline
aeeilnrt
elaterin
entailer
treenail
aeeilntv
elvanite
ventaile
aeeilort
aerolite
aeeilott
etiolate
aeeilppp
apple-pie
aeeilpps
seal-pipe
aeeilprs
espalier
pearlies
aeeilprt
pearlite
aeeilpsw
palewise
aeeilqsu
equalise
aeeilqux
exequial
aeeilrrs
realiser
aeeilrrt
retailer
aeeilrst
earliest
aeeilrsv
velarise
aeeilrtt
laterite
literate
aeeilrtv
levirate
relative
aeeilrvw
liveware
reviewal
aeeilsvw
alewives
aeeilttv
levitate
aeeimmnt
meantime
aeeimnnv
Menevian
aeeimnrx
examiner
aeeimnst
seminate
aeeimnuv
mauveine
aeeimrtv
viameter
aeeimstt
estimate
étatisme
aeeimstw
teamwise
aeeinnrs
anserine
aeeinntv
Venetian
aeeinprt
aperient
aeeinpss
sea-snipe
aeeinptt
pianette
aeeinrrt
rain-tree
retainer
aeeinrst
arsenite
resinate
sin-eater
stearine
aeeinsss
easiness
aeeinssv
vainesse
aeeinssw
sea-swine
aeeinstt
anisette
tetanise
aeeioopp
epopoeia
aeeippst
appetise
aeeippsu
eupepsia
aeeipptt
appetite
aeeiprrr
repairer
aeeiprtv
perviate
aeeirstt
treatise
aeeirsvv
aversive
aeeisttt
steatite
aeeittux
eutaxite
aeeituvx
exuviate
aeejllsy
sea-jelly
aeejlnpt
jetplane
aeejlosu
jealouse
aeejnrst
serjeant
aeejoprt
pejorate
aeejrttw
water-jet
aeekklwy
lykewake
aeekkpsy
keepsaky
aeekllst
skeletal
aeeklmmu
Mameluke
aeeklmop
meal-poke
aeeklmrt
telemark
aeeklmss
makeless
aeeklpty
key-plate
aeeklssw
wakeless
aeeklsty
eyestalk
aeekmoty
yoke-mate
aeekmrrr
remarker
aeekmrrt
marketer
aeeknpsw
newspeak
aeeknssw
weakness
aeeknstt
stake-net
aeekorrv
overrake
aeekorst
keratose
kreasote
aeekortv
overtake
take-over
aeekqrsu
squeaker
aeekrrst
streaker
aeellltt
telltale
tell-tale
aeellmms
mamselle
aeellmrt
Tremella
aeellnot
let-alone
aeellnov
novellae
aeellptt
platelet
aeellrrt
terrella
aeellrtw
wall-tree
aeellsst
satelles
tessella
aeellssz
zealless
aeellstt
stellate
aeellswy
weaselly
aeelltvv
valvelet
aeelmmnt
Emmental
aeelmmnu
Emmanuel
aeelmmtu
malemute
aeelmnos
sea-lemon
aeelmnps
ensample
aeelmnss
lameness
maneless
nameless
aeelmntt
mantelet
aeelmntv
lavement
aeelmott
matelote
aeelmprt
palm-tree
aeelmprx
exemplar
aeelmpry
empyreal
aeelmptt
palmette
template
aeelmsss
seamless
aeelmsst
mateless
meatless
tameless
aeelnnrt
lanneret
aeelnnss
leanness
aeelnopr
peroneal
aeelnopt
antelope
aeelnoru
aleurone
aeelnpps
spalpeen
aeelnpss
paleness
aeelnrss
realness
aeelnrsv
enslaver
aeelnrtv
Levanter
relevant
aeelnrtx
external
aeelnsst
lateness
aeelnssv
vaneless
aeelnswy
Wesleyan
aeelntuv
eventual
aeelntvy
ventayle
aeeloprv
overleap
aeelorrs
releasor
aeelorst
oleaster
aeelortt
tolerate
aeelortv
elevator
aeelostv
love-seat
aeelottt
teetotal
aeelottw
tea-towel
aeelprrs
relapser
aeelprrt
palterer
aeelprsu
pleasure
serpulae
aeelprsv
vesperal
aeelprty
pterylae
aeelpsst
tapeless
aeelpstv
septleva
aeelqrsu
squealer
aeelrrsv
reversal
slaverer
aeelrrtu
ureteral
aeelrsst
tearless
tesseral
aeelrssw
wareless
aeelrstu
resalute
aeelrsty
easterly
aeelrsvy
aversely
aeelssst
sateless
seatless
aeelssvw
waveless
aeemmnrs
meresman
aeemmntz
mazement
aeemmsst
messmate
aeemnnot
mean-tone
aeemnnrt
remanent
aeemnnss
meanness
aeemnorv
overname
aeemnorz
armozeen
aeemnprt
peter-man
aeemnpry
empyrean
aeemnptv
pavement
aeemnquy
may-queen
aeemnrst
seam-rent
aeemnrsv
verse-man
aeemnrtu
numerate
aeemnrtv
averment
aeemnrvy
Everyman
aeemnsss
sameness
aeemnsst
tameness
aeemnstu
mansuete
aeemorst
Masorete
aeemorsu
mouse-ear
aeemossu
sea-mouse
aeempprr
pamperer
aeemprrt
tamperer
aeemprsu
Serapeum
aeemprtt
attemper
aeemqrru
remarqué

aeemqttu
maquette
aeemrrst
streamer
aeemrrsu
measurer
aeemrsst
masseter
seamster
aeemrssu
reassume
aeemrstt
teamster
aeemsssu
masseuse
aeemsstu
meatuses
aeemsttu
amusette
aeennpry
Pyrenean
aeennrss
nearness
aeennrtu
enaunter
aeennrtv
revenant
aeennrux
annexure
aeennsss
saneness
aeennsst
neatness
aeenopru
European
aeenopst
pea-stone
aeenorrs
reasoner
aeenorss
seasoner
aeenorst
resonate
aeenortv
overneat
renovate
aeenorvw
ovenware
aeenostx
axe-stone
aeenpptt
appetent
aeenpqtu
petanque
aeenrrrw
warrener
aeenrrss
rareness
aeenrrsw
answerer
reanswer
aeenrrtv
taverner

aeenrsss
searness
aeenrsst
assenter
sarsenet
aeenrstt
seat-rent
aeenrstu
Sauterne
aeenrsvw
never-was
aeenrttv
antevert
aeenrttx
externat
aeenrtty
entreaty
aeeoprrt
paterero
perorate
aeeoprst
protease
soap-tree
aeeoprsw
sea-power
aeeoprtt
operetta
aeeorrst
ore-stare
aeeorrsv
sea-rover
aeeorrsw
sowarree
aeeorrtv
overrate
aeeorrvw
overwear
aeeorrvy
overyear
aeeorssv
overseas
aeeorstt
sea-otter
aeepprrr
preparer
aeeprrrt
parterre
aeeprrtt
patterer
aeeprrtu
aperture
aeeprsss
Passeres
aeeprssu
sea-purse
aeeprstu
superate
upas-tree
aeepssww
sweep-saw
aeeqrruv
quaverer

aeerrrst
arrester
rearrest
aeerrsst
asserter
reassert
aeerrssu
reassure
aeerrstu
treasure
aeerrstv
traverse
aeerrstw
sewer-rat
aeerssss
reassess
aeersttt
attester
aeertttz
terzetta
aeervwyy
everyway
aeffgilr
fire-flag
aeffgost
off-stage
aeffgrsu
suffrage
aeffhiky
kaffiyeh
aeffhill
half-life
aeffhkos
off-shake
aeffiluv
effluvia
aeffimrr
affirmer
reaffirm
aeffklru
freakful
aefflntu
affluent
aeffloru
four-leaf
aefflstu
feastful
sufflate
aeffmrsu
earmuffs
aeffnort
affronté
aefforst
afforest
aeffrttu
Tartuffe
aefghinr
hangfire
aefghist
sea-fight
aefghitt
tea-fight
aefghmor
hog-frame

aefghttu
fughetta
aefgiirs
gasifier
aefgimtu
fumigate
aefginst
feasting
aefgintu
fantigue
aefgirtu
figurate
fruitage
aefgllop
flagpole
aefgllpu
full-page
aefglmnu
fugleman
aefglnss
fangless
aefglopr
leap-frog
aefglorw
garefowl
aefglrtu
grateful
aefgmnor
forgeman
aefgmnrt
fragment
aefgnnot
fontange
aefgnort
frontage
aefgoopt
footpage
aefgoort
footgear
aefgoprx
fox-grape
aefgortt
frottage
aefgossu
fougasse
aefhiist
Shafiite
aefhiklp
half-pike
aefhikrs
freakish
aefhiksw
weakfish
aefhilln
fellahin
aefhilms
fish-meal
aefhilmt
half-time
aefhilnw
fin-whale
aefhilor
forhaile

aefhlmrt
half-term
aefhlmsu
shameful
aefhlnot
half-note
half-tone
aefhlpst
half-step
aefhlrty
fatherly
aefhlttx
half-text
aefhltwy
wheat-fly
aefhmmor
home-farm
aefhmnrs
freshman
aefhnrsw
fernshaw
aefhoort
hare-foot
aefhorst
sea-froth
aefhortx
fox-earth
aefhrstt
farthest
aefiilln
nail-file
aefiilns
finalise
aefiimns
infamise
aefiimrr
Frimaire
aefiinrs
Friesian
aefiiprt
aperitif
aefiirrt
ratifier
aefiitvx
fixative
aefiklrw
fire-walk
aefikmrr
fire-mark
aefikruw
waukrife
aefillot
fellatio
aefillsv
all-fives
aefilmnr
inflamer
rifleman
aefilmnt
filament
aefilmty
femality
aefilnnr
infernal

aefilnot
olefiant
aefilnps
lifespan
aefilnru
fräulein
aefiloor
aerofoil
aefilopr
fire-opal
aefilors
foresail
aefilrtt
filtrate
aefilrtu
filature
aefilruw
weariful
aefilstu
fistulae
aefilstv
festival
aefilstw
flatwise
aefiltuu
fauteuil
aefimmmr
mammifer
aefimnst
manifest
aefimorr
aeriform
aefimort
formiate
aefimrrw
firmware
aefinnss
fainness
aefinopr
pinafore
aefinors
farinose
aefinrss
fairness
sanserif
aefioprr
Porifera
aefiorrt
Rotifera
aefirrry
farriery
aefirtux
fixature
aefkllot
folk-tale
aefklmry
fly-maker
aefklnsy
snake-fly
aefklruw
wreakful
aefklstt
talkfest

aefknorr
fore-rank
aefknors
forsaken
aefkoprs
forspeak
aefkortu
freak-out
aefllor
leaf-roll
aefllmmu
flammule
aefllnnu
unfallen
aefllnry
fern-ally
aefllorv
overfall
aefllptu
plateful
aefllrux
flexural
aefllssw
flawless
aefllsty
festally
aeflmnot
matfelon
aeflmoru
formulae
fumarole
aeflmoss
foamless
aeflmprr
frampler
aeflnnot
fontanel
aeflnopr
foreplan
aeflnopt
pantofle
aeflnosw
snow-flea
aeflnrtu
flaunter
aeflnsst
flatness
aeflnsuy
unsafely
aefloors
sea-floor
aeflopry
foreplay
aeflorrw
elf-arrow
aeflorst
forestal
aeflorsu
fusarole
aeflostt
falsetto
aeflppry
flypaper
aeflpsuu
pauseful
aeflrstt
fattrels
aeflrtty
flattery
aeflrtwy
water-fly
aeflsttu
tasteful
aeflstuw
wasteful
aefmnrry
ferryman
aefmorst
foremast
mort-safe
aefmorvw
waveform
aefnnstu
unfasten
aefnoprr
profaner
aefnorrw
forewarn
aefnorst
sea-front
aefnostw
feast-won
aefnprst
far-spent
aefnrrst
transfer
aefnrruy
funerary
aefnssst
fastness
aefnstuy
unsafety
aefoortw
footwear
aefoprrt
forepart
raft-rope
aefoptuu
pot-au-feu
aeforrsw
forswear
aeforruv
favourer
aeforrwy
forweary
aeforstw
forwaste
software
aeforsty
forestay
aefosswy
Fosseway
aefostuu
featuous
aefprsst
pressfat
aeggginn
engaging
aeggglss
egg-glass
aegghhir
high-gear
aegghmsu
meshugga
aegghopy
geophagy
aegghoru
roughage
aeggillr
grillage
aeggilmn
gleaming
aeggilnn
gleaning
aeggilou
oil-gauge
aegginnv
avenging
aegginor
Georgian
aegginos
sea-going
aeggiopr
arpeggio
geropiga
aeggirwy
earwiggy
aegglnpt
egg-plant
aegglory
gargoyle
aeggmorr
ergogram
aeggmort
mortgage
aeggnorv
overgang
aeggnorw
waggoner
aeggnrst
gangster
aeggnsst
ants'-eggs
aeggopru
groupage
aeghhors
shear-hog
aeghhort
earth-hog
aeghills
shigella
aeghilmt
megalith
aeghilnr
narghile
nargileh
aeghilns
shealing
aeghilnt
atheling
aeghilrt
litharge
thirlage
aeghimps
mageship
aeghinnt
naething
aeghinpt
night-ape
aeghinrs
shearing
aeghintt
gnathite
aeghiort
eight-oar
aeghippr
epigraph
aeghiprt
graphite
aeghllss
gas-shell
aeghlopy
hypogeal
aeghlotx
hexaglot
aeghlrtu
laughter
aeghlrty
lethargy
aeghmnop
phenogam
aeghmopt
apothegm
aeghnnor
hanger-on
aeghnnst
hangnest
aeghnopt
heptagon
pathogen
aeghnopy
hypogean
aeghnorv
hangover
overhang
aeghoppy
apophyge
aeghopxy
exophagy
aeghorst
shortage
aeghprtu
upgather
aeghrsyy
ashy-grey
aegiillu
aiguille
aegiilmr
remigial
aegiilps
Spigelia
aegiiltt
litigate
aegiimnr
imaginer
migraine
aegiimns
imagines
aegiimtt
mitigate
aegiinnr
arginine
aegiirrt
irrigate
aegiistv
vestigia
aegijrtu
Gujerati
aegiklnw
weakling
aegikmns
skin-game
aegikmrw
wig-maker
aegiknns
sneaking
aegiknnw
wakening
aegiknps
speaking
aegiknrt
retaking
aegillms
legalism
aegillno
goal-line
aegillnv
vine-gall
aegillny
genially
aegillpr
pillager
aegillps
spillage
aegillru
guerilla
aegillrv
all-giver
villager
aegillst
legalist
stillage
aegillsu
ill-usage
aegilltu
ligulate
aegillty
legality
aegilmmr
aglimmer
lammiger
aegilmnr
germinal
maligner
malinger
aegilmns
Galenism
aegilmnt
ligament
aegilmrs
regalism
aegilmrx
lexigram
aegilnnr
learning
aegilnnt
gantline
aegilnnu
ungenial
aegilnnw
weanling
aegilnny
yeanling
aegilnor
geraniol
regional
aegilnos
gasoline
aegilnot
gelation
legation
aegilnpr
pearling
aegilnps
pleasing
aegilnrs
sanglier
seal-ring
aegilnrt
integral
triangle
aegilnrx
relaxing
aegilnry
layering
yearling
aegilnss
gainless
glassine
aegilnst
eastling
Galenist
genitals
stealing
aegilnsv
leavings
aegilnsw
swealing
aegilntv
valeting
aegilnuv
vaginule
aegilops
spoilage
aegilopt
pilotage
aegilors
gasolier
girasole
seraglio

aegilpps
slippage
aegilrst
regalist
aegilrsy
greasily
aegilrtt
aglitter
aegilrtu
ligature
aegilrty
regality
aegilrvw
law-giver
aegilsst
Glassite
aegimnrt
emigrant
aegimnru
geranium
aegimnst
steaming
aegimnsv
veganism
aegimopt
magot-pie
aegimorw
wagmoire
aegimpru
umpirage
aegimqru
quagmire
aegimrrt
ragtimer
aegimrst
magister
sterigma
aegimssu
misusage
aeginnot
negation
aeginnps
sneaping
aeginnrs
earnings
aeginnrv
ravening
aeginnry
renaying
yearning
aeginnst
steaning
aeginnsu
sanguine
aeginors
organise
aeginppr
papering
aeginprt
tapering
aeginpry
repaying
aeginpty
Egyptian

aeginrrv
averring
aeginrss
reassign
aeginrst
astringe
ganister
aeginrsw
swearing
aeginrtt
treating
aeginrtv
vintager
aeginrtw
watering
aeginrvw
wavering
aeginrvy
vinegary
aeginsst
giantess
aeginssy
essaying
aeginstw
sweating
aegioprr
progeria
aegiostx
geotaxis
aegiprty
pterygia
aegiqrsu
squirage
aegirrty
argyrite
geriatry
aegirstt
strigate
aegjltuu
jugulate
aegkkkno
angekkok
aegkmnru
gunmaker
aegkoprs
gas-poker
aegkorww
wage-work
aeglllmu
glumella
aeglllss
gall-less
aegllnps
langspel
aegllopr
galloper
aegllorv
overgall
aegllory
allegory
aegllost
log-slate
aegllott
tollgate

aegllrvy
gravelly
aegllssu
galluses
aeglmnno
mangonel
aeglmntu
gunmetal
aeglmotv
megavolt
aeglmssu
gaumless
aeglnnpt
plangent
aeglnntu
untangle
aeglnopt
gantlope
aeglnory
yearlong
aeglnovw
long-wave
aeglnprs
spangler
sprangle
aeglnpss
pangless
aeglnpst
spanglet
aeglnrrw
wrangler
aeglnrst
strangle
aeglnrsy
larynges
aeglnruy
gunlayer
aeglnssu
sea-lungs
aeglnttu
gauntlet
aeglntuu
ungulate
aegloooz
zoogloea
aegloopu
apologue
aegloory
aerology
aeglopry
glory-pea
play-goer
aeglorsu
glareous
aeglortu
outglare
aeglortw
waterlog
aeglorty
geolatry
aeglossw
galowses
aeglprsu
Spergula

aeglpssu
plussage
aeglrstu
gestural
aeglrtuy
argutely
aeglstuu
glutaeus
aegmmnor
gammoner
aegmmrru
rummager
aegmnnot
magneton
aegmnorv
mangrove
aegmnory
rag-money
aegmnoxy
xenogamy
aegmnrtu
argument
aegmoprw
gapeworm
aegmorrw
worm-gear
aegmorss
gossamer
aegmpstu
stumpage
aegmsttu
steam-tug
aegnnopt
pentagon
aegnnort
negatron
aegnnprt
pregnant
aegnnrty
gannetry
aegnoprr
parergon
aegnorry
orangery
aegnorst
ragstone
stone-rag
aegnortt
tetragon
aegnorty
negatory
aegnoruv
vargueño
aegnotuy
autogeny
aegnpryy
panegyry
aegnrrst
stranger
aegnrstu
straunge
aegooswy
waygoose

aegoppst
stoppage
aegoppsu
suppeago
aegoprtu
portague
aegopssu
spousage
aegopstt
gate-post
aegorrrt
regrator
aegorrtt
garotter
garrotte
aegorstu
goat's-rue
aegorttu
tutorage
aegoruvy
voyageur
aegosstv
gas-stove
aegprrsu
spur-gear
aegqrtuu
truquage
aegrrssy
rye-grass
aegrrsuv
verrugas
aegrstty
strategy
aehhikns
Shekinah
aehhimtw
hamewith
aehhipsw
peishwah
aehhlntu
unhealth
aehhnopt
Phaethon
aehhnrsw
hernshaw
aehhrrst
thrasher
aehiilmo
hemiolia
aehiilnr
hairline
aehiimnt
thiamine
aehiimop
hemiopia
aehiinnt
ianthine
aehiirrw
wire-hair
aehiistv
Shaivite
Shivaite
aehikltw
what-like

aehiknss
sneakish
aehillno
nail-hole
aehillnt
thalline
aehillos
oil-shale
shale-oil
aehillow
whale-oil
aehilmny
hymenial
aehilmot
halimote
aehilmsw
limewash
aehilnop
aphelion
aehilnos
shoe-nail
aehilntx
anthelix
aehilntz
zenithal
aehilooz
Heliozoa
aehilort
aerolith
aehilrss
hairless
aehilrsv
shrieval
aehilrty
heartily
aehimmnp
Memphian
aehimnnu
inhumane
aehimnrs
shireman
aehimnss
shamisen
aehimnsu
humanise
aehimntu
inhumate
aehimppt
pita-hemp
aehimprs
samphire
seraphim
aehimprt
teraphim
aehimprx
xeraphim
aehimpss
emphasis
misshape
aehimpst
shipmate
aehimrtw
white-arm

aehimsst
  mathesis
aehinntx
  xanthein
  xanthine
aehinopu
  euphonia
aehinort
  anti-hero
aehinppy
  Epiphany
aehinprs
  parishen
  seraphin
aehinprt
  perianth
aehinpst
  thespian
aehinrsv
  enravish
  vanisher
aehinrtu
  haurient
aehinrtw
  tarwhine
aehinrtz
  Hertzian
aehinsst
  anthesis
aehinssz
  haziness
aehinstt
  hesitant
aehinstw
  inswathe
aehinttt
  antithet
aehinttw
  white-ant
aehioprs
  aphorise
aehiopru
  euphoria
aehiorrv
  overhair
aehiorsu
  air-house
aehipprs
  papisher
  sapphire
aehippst
  peatship
aehiprrt
  rathripe
aehiprtt
  threapit
aehipstt
  Peshitta
aehirrsv
  ravisher
aehirrsy
  Ayrshire
aehirstw
  waterish
aehirsty
  hysteria
aehisssy
  essayish
aehisstu
  hiatuses
aehitwwx
  white-wax
aehjnnos
  johannes
aehjprsw
  Jew's-harp
aehkllrs
  ark-shell
aehkmopw
  mopehawk
aehknnsu
  unshaken
aehknsww
  newshawk
aehkorsw
  sore-hawk
aehkostu
  shake-out
aehllmop
  lamphole
aehllnrt
  enthrall
aehllosy
  sea-holly
aehlmmns
  helmsman
aehlmmpp
  hemp-palm
aehlmnot
  methanol
aehlmnsw
  Welshman
aehlmnuy
  humanely
aehlmppt
  pamphlet
aehlmrss
  harmless
aehlnprs
  shrapnel
aehlnpty
  enthalpy
aehlnrtu
  Lutheran
aehlnsst
  nathless
aehlnsty
  naythles
aehlntuz
  hazelnut
aehloprt
  plethora
aehlorsy
  hoarsely
aehloruv
  overhaul
aehlpprt
  thrapple
aehlprss
  splasher
aehlpsst
  pathless
aehlpstu
  sulphate
aehlpsty
  staphyle
aehlrrtu
  urethral
aehlsstw
  thawless
aehlstty
  stealthy
aehmmrru
  Muharrem
aehmnnpy
  nymphean
aehmnopr
  morphean
aehmnors
  horseman
  shoreman
aehmnosu
  houseman
aehmnpru
  prehuman
aehmnpsy
  sea-nymph
aehmoprt
  metaphor
aehmorst
  Masoreth
aehmostw
  somewhat
aehmprst
  hampster
aehmrrty
  rat-rhyme
aehmstty
  amethyst
aehmsuzz
  mezuzahs
aehnnopt
  Pantheon
aehnnoty
  honey-ant
aehnnpru
  nenuphar
aehnnpsu
  unshapen
aehnnsuv
  unshaven
aehnoopt
  hanepoot
aehnoppy
  pay-phone
aehnoprt
  hapteron
aehnopst
  stanhope
aehnopty
  Typhoean
aehnopxy
  xenophya
aehnoqtu
  haqueton
aehnorst
  Sheraton
aehnostv
  have-nots
aehnprty
  hen-party
aehnrsss
  rashness
aehnrttu
  earth-nut
aehnsstt
  thatness
aehnsstw
  whatness
aehnstuw
  unswathe
aehopprs
  prophase
aehopsst
  potashes
  spathose
aehopstt
  heatspot
aehopstu
  tap-house
aehoptvy
  top-heavy
aehorrss
  rose-rash
aehorrsv
  overrash
aehorrsw
  war-horse
aehorrtt
  heart-rot
aehorssw
  saw-horse
aehorstt
  rheostat
aehorstu
  share-out
aehorsvw
  overwash
aehorswy
  horseway
aehpprsu
  pear-push
aehprsst
  sharp-set
aehprsux
  haruspex
aehprsuy
  euphrasy
aehqrssu
  squasher
aehrrsty
  trashery
aehrrttw
  thwarter
aehrstty
  shattery
aeiiintt
  initiate
aeiiklns
  Sikelian
aeiiklnt
  kalinite
aeiiknss
  akinesis
aeiillmr
  milliare
  Ramillie
aeiillrv
  live-rail
aeiilmnn
  mainline
aeiilmns
  alienism
  Milesian
aeiilmpr
  imperial
aeiilmrs
  Ramilies
aeiilmss
  Islamise
aeiilmst
  Islamite
aeiilmtt
  militate
aeiilnpr
  plein-air
aeiilnqu
  aquiline
aeiilnrr
  airliner
aeiilnrt
  inertial
aeiilnst
  alienist
  Latinise
aeiilnsw
  Lewisian
aeiilott
  Italiote
aeiilppt
  tail-pipe
aeiilprt
  liparite
  Reptilia
aeiilrsv
  rivalise
aeiilrtt
  literati
aeiilstv
  vitalise
aeiimmrt
  maritime
aeiimmsx
  maximise
aeiimntt
  intimate
aeiimntu
  minutiae
aeiimrst
  seriatim
aeiimssx
  semi-axis
aeiinnrs
  sirenian
aeiinnrt
  Neritina
aeiinntv
  innative
aeiinpst
  pianiste
aeiinrrv
  riverain
aeiinrss
  airiness
aeiinrtz
  Nazirite
aeiinsst
  sanitise
  teniasis
aeiinsvv
  invasive
aeiinttt
  titanite
aeiinttu
  uintaite
aeiiprsw
  pairwise
aeiiprzz
  pizzeria
aeiipsst
  epitasis
aeiirrtt
  irritate
aeiirsst
  satirise
aeiirstw
  wisteria
aeiirttt
  tritiate
aeiirtvz
  vizirate
aeiitttv
  titivate
aeiittvv
  vitative
aeijlosu
  jalousie
aeijorst
  jarosite
aeikkllw
  likewalk
aeikklpr
  parklike
aeikkmrt
  kite-mark
aeiklnnp
  pannikel
aeiklnos
  snake-oil
aeiklnrs
  near-silk

aeiklnss
sealskin
aeiklnsw
swanlike
aeiklnsy
sneakily
aeiklrst
starlike
aeiklrvy
Valkyrie
aeiklrwy
Walkyrie
aeiklsss
saikless
aeikmnpr
pin-maker
aeikmnst
mistaken
aeikmpss
misspeak
aeiknpst
snake-pit
aeiknrtw
knitwear
aeiknstv
kistvaen
aeikprss
après-ski
aeikrsst
asterisk
aeikrstw
water-ski
aeilllny
lineally
aeillmsy
mesially
aeillnno
lanoline
aeillnns
nainsell
aeillnnu
unlineal
aeillnop
apolline
aeillnor
allerion
aeillnps
splenial
aeillnry
linearly
aeillnss
sensilla
aeillnsw
Wellsian
aeillnvy
venially
aeillotv
volatile
aeillovz
Vellozia
aeillpst
pastille
aeillpsv
lipsalve

aeillqtu
tequilla
aeillrry
raillery
aeillrss
railless
aeillrsy
serially
aeillrtt
ill-treat
aeillsss
sailless
aeillsst
tailless
aeillsuv
allusive
aeillsyz
sleazily
aeilltuz
lazulite
aeilmmns
melanism
aeilmmnt
immantle
aeilmmnu
Immanuel
aeilmmny
immanely
aeilmmor
memorial
aeilmmot
immolate
aeilmmrt
trilemma
aeilmnno
minneola
aeilmnnp
impannel
aeilmnns
linesman
aeilmnos
semolina
aeilmnpr
Palmerin
aeilmnpw
palm-wine
wine-palm
aeilmnrt
terminal
tram-line
aeilmnru
lemurian
aeilmnss
islesman
aeilmnst
salt-mine
aeilmopr
proemial
aeilmops
semi-opal
aeilmors
moralise
aeilmprv
primeval

aeilmpst
petalism
septimal
aeilmpty
playtime
aeilmrsy
smearily
aeilmrtt
remittal
aeilmruv
velarium
aeilmstt
smaltite
aeilmstu
simulate
aeilmsty
steamily
aeilmttu
mutilate
ultimate
aeilnnos
solanine
aeilnnot
neo-Latin
aeilnnrt
internal
aeilnnsy
insanely
aeilnnty
innately
aeilnopt
Antilope
antipole
aeilnopu
poulaine
aeilnort
oriental
relation
aeilnorv
overlain
aeilnost
insolate
aeilnott
tonalite
aeilnotv
Olivetan
aeilnppt
pie-plant
aeilnprt
triplane
aeilnpss
painless
aeilnptt
tin-plate
aeilnrss
rainless
aeilnrst
entrails
aeilnrsy
snailery
aeilnrtt
rattline
trail-net

aeilnrtu
retinula
tenurial
aeilnrtv
interval
aeilnrty
interlay
aeilnsst
eastlins
aeilnssz
laziness
aeilnstt
Intelsat
aeilnstu
insulate
aeilnsuy
uneasily
aeilnttu
Lutetian
aeilntvy
natively
venality
aeilnuvv
univalve
aeiloorv
ovariole
aeiloppt
oppilate
aeiloprs
polarise
aeiloprt
epilator
petiolar
tail-rope
aeilopst
spoliate
aeilorss
solarise
aeilorst
soterial
aeilorsv
oversail
valorise
aeilorsy
royalise
aeilortt
literato
aeilostt
totalise
aeilottv
volitate
aeilppqu
appliqué
aeilpptu
pupilate
aeilprrs
reprisal
aeilprst
pilaster
plaister
aeilprsw
slipware
aeilprxy
pyrexial

aeilpsty
ptyalise
aeilpsuv
plausive
aeilqrsu
squailer
aeilqrtu
quartile
requital
aeilqsuy
queasily
aeilqtuy
equality
aeilrrsu
ruralise
aeilrrty
literary
aeilrsst
slaister
aeilrssv
rivaless
aeilrswy
lyra-wise
aeilrtty
alterity
aeilrtuz
lazurite
aeilrtvv
trivalve
aeimmnnt
immanent
aeimmnot
ammonite
aeimmpst
psammite
aeimmrtu
immature
aeimnnot
nominate
aeimnnrs
reinsman
aeimnopp
Pompeian
aeimnopt
ptomaine
aeimnors
Romanise
aeimnort
Maronite
aeimnorz
armozine
aeimnosw
womanise
aeimnotz
monazite
aeimnprt
tripeman
aeimnprz
prize-man
aeimnqru
ramequin
aeimnrrv
riverman

aeimnrsu
aneurism
Sumerian
aeimnrsy
seminary
aeimnrtt
martinet
aeimnrtu
ruminate
aeimnrtw
wariment
aeimnssz
maziness
aeimnttu
matutine
aeimoptt
optimate
aeimorst
amortise
atomiser
aeimortt
amoretti
aeimottt
Ottamite
aeimottv
motivate
aeimprrt
imparter
aeimprst
Primates
aeimprtt
part-time
aeimprtu
apterium
aeimqrsu
marquise
aeimqsuu
Esquimau
aeimrsst
asterism
aeimrssy
emissary
aeimrstt
mistreat
teratism
aeimrstu
semitaur
aeimrstx
matrixes
aeimrsww
swimwear
aeimsstt
misstate
aeimsstz
mestizas
aeimttuv
mutative
aeinnnor
Neronian
aeinnnos
Senonian
aeinnnox
annexion

aeinnoos
sea-onion
aeinnopv
pavonine
aeinnors
raisonné
aeinnort
inornate
aeinnost
Estonian
aeinnott
intonate
aeinnotv
innovate
venation
aeinnrrt
inerrant
aeinnrsu
unarisen
aeinnssv
vainness
aeinnstt
stannite
aeinnsuv
Venusian
aeinntuv
unnative
Venutian
aeinoppt
antipope
aeinoprt
atropine
aeinopst
saponite
aeinoptz
topazine
aeinoqtu
equation
aeinorrt
anterior
aeinorrw
ironware
wear-iron
aeinorst
arsonite
notarise
rosinate
Señorita
aeinorsv
aversion
aeinortv
Orvietan
aeinosst
assiento
aeinossx
Saxonise
aeinostv
stovaine
aeinostx
saxonite
aeinottz
Zantiote
aeinotvx
vexation

aeinppps
Pan-pipes
aeinppsy
Pepysian
aeinpptx
Xantippe
aeinpptz
Zantippe
aeinprrt
terrapin
aeinprru
unrepair
aeinprst
pinaster
aeinprsu
unpraise
aeinprtt
triptane
aeinprtu
painture
aeinprtx
expirant
aeinpruv
Peruvian
aeinpstu
supinate
aeinpsty
epinasty
aeinptty
antitype
aeinqstu
quantise
aeinqttu
equitant
aeinrrst
restrain
strainer
transire
aeinrrtu
Etrurian
aeinrrtv
veratrin
aeinrrtw
interwar
aeinrssu
senarius
aeinrssw
wariness
aeinrssx
xeransis
aeinrstt
straiten
aeinrsuz
suzerain
aeinrttu
tainture
aeinssst
saintess
aeinsstt
Titaness
aeinssvw
waviness
aeinsswx
waxiness

aeinsuvv
Vesuvian
aeinttuu
autunite
aeioppst
apposite
aeioprrt
priorate
aeioprrw
air-power
aeioprst
isoptera
aeioprsv
vaporise
aeioprtx
expiator
aeiopttv
optative
aeiorttv
rotative
aeipprrz
apprizer
aeipqrtu
pratique
aeiprsst
Tarsipes
aeiprsty
asperity
aeiprsvy
vespiary
aeipttuv
putative
aeiqrrru
quarrier
aeiqrrtu
quartier
aeirrrtv
river-rat
aeirrssy
siserary
aeirrttt
retraitt
aeirrtty
tertiary
aeirrvwy
riverway
aeirsstw
waitress
aeirstvy
vestiary
aeirswwy
waywiser
aeisssty
essayist
aejllnpy
jelly-pan
aejlosuy
jealousy
aejmpstu
jump-seat
aekkmnoo
kakemono
aeklmnos
monk-seal

aeklmruw
lukewarm
aeklmruy
yarmulke
aeklnnss
lankness
aeklnorw
walker-on
aeklnosy
ankylose
aekloprw
rope-walk
aeklopty
kalotype
aeklorsw
salework
aeklortv
overtalk
aeklorvw
walk-over
aeklprrs
sparkler
aeklprst
sparklet
aeklqruy
quakerly
aekmnrsu
unmasker
aekmoprt
topmaker
aekmortw
team-work
work-mate
aekmprsu
musk-pear
aekmprtu
up-market
aeknnrss
rankness
aeknorrv
overrank
aeknoruy
eukaryon
aeknottu
outtaken
aekopstu
outspeak
aekorrww
workwear
aekorstv
overtask
aekortuy
eukaryot
aekqrsuw
squawker
aekrrsst
starkers
aelllrtu
tellural
aelllssw
wall-less
aelllsuv
vulsella

aellmnty
mentally
aellmorr
moraller
aellmort
martello
aellmoty
tomalley
aellmpuu
plumulae
aellmrsy
mersalyl
aellnopv
volplane
aellnoww
enwallow
aellnpru
prunella
aellnpss
planless
aellnptt
plantlet
aellnptu
plantule
aellnruy
unreally
aellnrvy
vernally
aellnsst
tallness
aellntty
latently
aellntuu
lunulate
aellntww
wall-newt
aelloprw
walloper
aellopry
role-play
aellorty
alley-tor
aellorww
wallower
aellosuv
alveolus
aellqrsu
squaller
aellrrty
retrally
aellrtty
latterly
aellrtvy
trevally
aellrwyy
lawyerly
aellssst
saltless
aellssty
tasselly
aellsuxy
sexually
aelmmorw
meal-worm

aelmmrst
strammel
aelmnnot
non-metal
aelmnnou
noumenal
aelmnnry
mannerly
aelmnntu
unmantle
aelmnops
neoplasm
pleonasm
aelmnost
salmonet
aelmnosu
melanous
aelmnoyy
yeomanly
aelmnrsu
mensural
aelmoopt
omoplate
aelmoors
sale-room
aelmoprr
premolar
aelmoprt
prometal
temporal
aelmopsx
exoplasm
aelmopsy
playsome
aelmoptt
palmetto
pot-metal
aelmorsu
ramulose
aelmortu
emulator
aelmosss
molasses
aelmosty
atmolyse
aelmprrt
trampler
aelmprsy
lampreys
samplery
aelmqsuu
squamule
aelmrstt
maltster
aelmrsty
masterly
aelmrtuy
maturely
aelmssst
mastless
aelnnnpu
unpannel
aelnnoop
napoleon

aelnnoox
naloxone
aelnnopp
open-plan
aelnnoru
neuronal
aelnnosu
annulose
aelnnrtu
unlearnt
aelnootz
entozoal
aelnoprs
personal
aelnopst
lapstone
pleonast
aelnoptw
tow-plane
aelnortt
tetronal
tolerant
aelnortu
outlearn
aelnorty
ornately
Tyrolean
aelnprsu
purslane
supernal
aelnprty
plenarty
aelnpsss
spanless
aelnpssu
spansule
aelnpttu
petulant
aelnrrty
errantly
aelnrruv
nervular
aelnrstt
slattern
aelnrsxy
larynxes
aelnrttw
trawl-net
aelnruwy
unwarely
aelnssst
saltness
aelnsuux
unsexual
aelnttux
exultant
aeloopr z
zooperal
aeloortw
Waterloo
aeloortz
zoolater

aeloppr s
prolapse
sapropel
aeloppsu
papulose
aelopptu
populate
aeloppxy
apoplexy
aelopquy
opaquely
aeloprrv
reproval
aeloprst
petrosal
aeloprvy
overplay
aelopsss
soapless
aelopssu
espousal
sepalous
aelopstu
petalous
aelorstu
rosulate
aelorttv
varletto
aelorttw
water-lot
aelortyz
zealotry
aeloruux
rouleaux
aelossty
asystole
aelostuy
autolyse
aelotuuv
outvalue
aelprrsw
sprawler
aelprrtt
prattler
aelprssy
sparsely
aelprstt
splatter
sprattle
aelprstu
aplustre
aelprsty
plastery
psaltery
aelpssss
passless
aelqrsuy
squarely
aelqsttu
squattle
aelrrstt
startler
aelrrtvy
varletry

aelrssst
starless
aelrsstw
wartless
aelrsttu
lustrate
aelrstty
slattery
aelrstuv
vestural
aelrsuvy
surveyal
aelrtttw
twattler
aelrttux
textural
aelrttuy
tutelary
aelsssty
stayless
aelsttuy
astutely
aemmmotu
ommateum
aemmmrty
mammetry
aemmnrry
merryman
aemmnrtu
ramentum
aemmoort
room-mate
aemmorst
marmoset
aemmrtuy
maumetry
aemmrtwy
mawmetry
aemnnopw
penwoman
aemnnors
Norseman
aemnnort
ornament
aemnoorr
marooner
aemnoort
anteroom
aemnoory
aeronomy
aemnootz
metazoon
aemnoprs
proseman
aemnoprt
empatron
aemnoprw
manpower
aemnorrs
ransomer
aemnorst
on-stream
aemnorsv
oversman

aemnortt
martenot
aemnorty
monetary
aemnoryy
yeomanry
aemnostu
sea-mount
aemnprss
pressman
aemnprsu
superman
aemnpsst
passment
aemnrruy
numerary
aemnrssw
warmness
aemnrstu
menstrua
transume
aemnrstw
transmew
trewsman
aemnrsuy
aneurysm
aemooprt
peat-moor
aemoortt
amoretto
aemoosst
maestoso
aemoostt
tomatoes
aemoostu
autosome
aemoprtw
pomwater
tapeworm
aemopsst
peat-moss
aemoqssu
squamose
aemorrru
armourer
aemorrst
rearmost
aemorrsy
rosemary
aemorrtu
Euromart
aemorsst
sea-storm
aemorssy
mayoress
aemorstv
overmast
aemorttu
tautomer
aemosstt
eastmost
aemosswy
someways

aemottzz
mozzetta
aemprrsy
spermary
aemprstu
upstream
aemqrssu
marquess
aemrrtuv
veratrum
aemrsstt
mattress
aemrsttu
testamur
aemrtuux
trumeaux
aemstttu
testatum
aennnttu
untenant
aennopst
pentosan
aennopuw
unweapon
aennorst
resonant
aennorsu
unreason
aennorvy
novenary
aennossu
unseason
aennostw
tenon-saw
aennrswy
swannery
aennrtty
tenantry
aenoopst
teaspoon
aenoorrt
ratooner
aenoprry
rope-yarn
aenoprss
Responsa
aenoprtt
patentor
aenoprwy
weaponry
aenopstt
ante-post
aenorrst
antrorse
aenorsst
assentor
star-nose
aenorstw
stone-raw
aenorsuv
ravenous
aenorttx
tetraxon

aenortty
attorney
aenosstw
saw-tones
aenossuu
nauseous
aenprstt
transept
aenprsty
Strepyan
aenqrrtu
quartern
aenqsttu
questant
aenrrrty
errantry
aenrrssu
Serranus
aenrsstt
tartness
aenrstwy
sternway
aenrtuvy
vauntery
aenrtuwy
unwatery
aensssttv
vastness
aenssttu
tautness
aeooppps
pappoose
aeooprrt
operator
poor-rate
aeoopstt
potatoes
aeoorrst
sororate
aeoorttt
tattooer
aeopprrv
approver
aeoppsuy
pea-soupy
aeopqrtu
paroquet
aeoprrrt
parroter
aeoprrst
Raptores
aeoprrtv
overpart
aeoprruv
vapourer
aeoprrvw
wrapover
aeoprssu
asperous
aeoprssv
overpass
Passover
aeoprstt
prostate

aeoprstu
apterous
aeoprstv
overpast
aeoprttw
water-pot
aeoprtwx
water-pox
aeopsstt
soap-test
aeopttuy
autotype
aeoqrstu
quaestor
aeoqrttu
torquate
aeoqrtuz
quatorze
aeorrrst
arrestor
aeorrsst
assertor
assorter
oratress
aeorrstt
rostrate
aeorrtzz
terrazzo
aeorssss
assessor
aeorsstt
stratose
aeorsstv
votaress
aeorsttt
attestor
testator
aeorsttu
outstare
rout-seat
sea-trout
aeorstuw
outswear
aeorstvy
overstay
aeorsuvw
waverous
aeorsvwy
oversway
aeortuwy
outweary
aeortvxy
vexatory
aeossstt
seas-tost
aepprrst
strapper
aeprssst
trespass
aeprsttu
stuprate
aeprstty
tapestry

aeprstux
supertax
aeqrsttu
squatter
aeqrtttu
quartett
aerrsstu
serratus
aerrstuy
treasury
aerrstwy
rye-straw
aersssty
satyress
aersttvy
travesty
aerttuxy
textuary
affffggi
giff-gaff
affffinn
niffnaff
affffirr
riff-raff
affghirt
affright
affgiirt
graffiti
affgilmn
maffling
affgimrs
misgraff
affgiort
graffito
affglnru
far-flung
affhilst
flatfish
affhiltu
faithful
affhimrs
fish-farm
affhorrt
far-forth
affiinty
affinity
affillmm
flim-flam
affillpp
flip-flap
affilnow
Wolffian
affilsux
suffixal
affinorr
forfairn
affinosu
affusion
affipstt
tipstaff
afflloot
footfall
afflltuu
faultful

afflooot
foalfoot
affloott
flat-foot
afflrruu
furfural
affnorsy
saffrony
affnrruu
furfuran
afgggiln
flagging
afgginot
fagoting
afgginrt
grafting
afghilln
halfling
afghilns
flashing
afghilnt
fanlight
afghilps
flagship
afghinrt
farthing
afghinrw
wharfing
afghinst
shafting
afghiost
goat-fish
afghlluu
laughful
afghlnsu
flash-gun
afghlstu
ghastful
afgiinnt
fainting
afgikort
koftgari
afgillnt
flatling
afgilmno
flamingo
afgilnos
sol-faing
afgilnot
floating
afgilnpp
flapping
afgilntt
flatting
afgilorw
gairfowl
afgilssy
glassify
afgimntu
fumigant
afgimors
gasiform
afgimrst
misgraft

afginrtu
figurant
afginsuy
sanguify
afgiprtw
gift-wrap
afgllnot
flatlong
afgllnpu
pang-full
afgllruu
fulgural
afgllruy
frugally
afgllssu
glassful
afglmorw
flag-worm
afglnnoo
gonfalon
afglnoru
groanful
afglnouw
wagonful
afgnnnoo
gonfanon
afgoortz
zoograft
afgortuw
tug-of-war
afhhiksw
fish-hawk
afhhloru
half-hour
afhiilrs
frailish
afhiilss
sail-fish
afhiilst
fish-tail
afhiimst
misfaith
afhiinst
faintish
afhiklps
hip-flask
afhiknrs
Frankish
afhillsw
wallfish
afhillsy
flashily
afhilnpt
half-pint
afhilntt
half-tint
afhilstt
flattish
afhimnst
manshift
afhinstu
tuna-fish
afhiossu
fashious

afhirsst
starfish
afhklntu
thankful
afhkmoor
hoof-mark
afhkorsx
fox-shark
afhllotu
loathful
afhlmnoo
half-moon
afhlostu
outflash
afhlrtuw
wrathful
afhooptt
footpath
afiiilnp
Filipina
afiikmrs
fakirism
afiillly
filially
afiillnu
unfilial
afiilmms
familism
afiilmns
finalism
afiilmst
Familist
afiilnru
unifilar
afiilnst
finalist
afiilnty
finality
afiimrsy
fairyism
afiinnos
sainfoin
sinfonia
afiinotx
fixation
afiinstw
Swiftian
afiiorrt
triforia
afijmnor
janiform
afikllmo
milk-loaf
afiklnnr
franklin
afiklort
fork-tail
afilllmx
flax-mill
afilllot
flotilla
afilllsu
full-sail

afilllxy
flax-lily
afillnpu
plainful
afillost
sail-loft
afilltuy
faultily
afilmnor
formalin
informal
afilmopr
paliform
afilmoss
sol-faism
afilnort
flatiron
inflator
afilnppt
flippant
afilnruy
unfairly
afilnstu
inflatus
afilorty
filatory
afilosst
sol-faist
afilrstu
fistular
afilsttu
flautist
afimmnor
maniform
afimnopr
napiform
afimnorr
raniform
afimnort
natiform
afimnosu
infamous
afimntuu
Funtumia
afimorru
auriform
afimorrv
variform
afimorsv
vasiform
afinnotu
fountain
afinnrty
infantry
afinopsy
saponify
afinqtuy
quantify
afinrstx
transfix
afinrsux
Fraxinus
afirstty
stratify

afjmnoru
Januform
afkllmos
alms-folk
afklnotu
outflank
afklnpru
prankful
afkmoort
footmark
aflllory
florally
aflllluwy
lawfully
afllmnuy
manfully
afllmory
formally
afllnosw
snowfall
afllnuuw
unlawful
afllopuy
foul-play
afllorsu
all-fours
afllrtuy
artfully
aflmnoru
unformal
aflmoprt
platform
aflmorru
formular
aflmortu
foulmart
aflmortw
flat-worm
aflmosuy
famously
aflnrtuu
unartful
aflntuuv
vauntful
aflntuuy
unfaulty
afloostt
salt-foot
aflostuu
flatuous
aflprsyy
fly-spray
aflrsttu
startful
afmnnort
frontman
afmnortu
farm-toun
afmooprr
pro-forma
afmortuy
fumatory
afnooprs
span-roof

afooprrt
ratproof
afooprrw
war-proof
afoopsst
soft-soap
afoorstt
root-fast
afoorstz
sforzato
afoprrtt
raft-port
afoprrtu
four-part
aforsttw
forswatt
afosstuu
fastuous
afppptuy
puppy-fat
aggggiln
gaggling
agggilnn
gangling
agggiyzz
zigzaggy
agghhint
night-hag
agghilnt
Lagthing
agghilnu
laughing
agghilst
gaslight
agghilsy
shaggily
agghistt
gas-tight
agghjmno
mah-jongg
agghloot
Golgotha
agghmoss
moss-hagg
agghoott
gag-tooth
aggiilnv
gingival
aggiinnr
graining
aggiinns
gainings
aggijlnn
jangling
aggilmno
gloaming
aggilmps
gig-lamps
aggilnno
ganglion
aggilnns
slanging

aggilnnt
gnatling
tangling
aggilnnw
wangling
aggilnot
goatling
aggilnpy
gapingly
aggilnry
grayling
ragingly
agginnor
groaning
agginntw
twanging
agginoor
Gorgonia
agginowy
way-going
agginprs
grasping
agginrss
grassing
agginrsu
sugaring
aggirtuz
ziggurat
aggllloy
lollygag
aggllooy
algology
aggllоss
log-glass
agglmoor
logogram
aggloory
agrology
agglrsty
straggly
aggmrsuu
sugar-gum
aggnuwzz
zugzwang
aghhiilt
hightail
aghhlotu
although
aghiiprr
hair-grip
aghiirtt
airtight
aghijnrt
nightjar
aghiknnt
thanking
aghiknrs
sharking
aghillnt
all-night
aghilmty
almighty
aghilnoo
hooligan

aghilnor
long-hair
aghilnos
shoaling
aghilnot
loathing
aghilnps
plashing
aghilnrs
ringhals
aghilnss
slangish
slashing
aghilnsu
languish
aghilnsw
shawling
aghilrsy
garishly
aghilrty
graithly
aghilsuy
aguishly
aghiltwx
wax-light
aghimmns
shamming
aghimnnt
night-man
aghimnss
smashing
aghimnty
thingamy
aghimpru
graphium
aghinntu
haunting
aghinnty
anything
aghinprs
harpings
phrasing
sharping
aghinpry
Phrygian
aghinrry
harrying
aghinsst
hastings
aghinssw
swashing
aghinuzz
huzzaing
aghiprrt
trigraph
aghipssw
pig's-wash
aghirstt
straight
aghllmpu
gallumph
aghllnou
long-haul

aghlmoor
hologram
aghlnosu
shogunal
aghmmooy
homogamy
aghmnpsu
Sphagnum
aghmoopy
omophagy
aghmoott
goat-moth
aghmopry
myograph
aghnnstu
shantung
aghnoors
shagroon
aghnorst
staghorn
aghnprsy
syngraph
aghnsttu
stag-hunt
aghnttuu
untaught
aghopssw
swagshop
aghrsttu
straught
agiiinns
insignia
agiiinrv
Virginia
agiillov
villagio
villiago
agiilltt
gilt-tail
agiilnnp
plaining
agiilnnu
inguinal
agiilnny
inlaying
agiilnor
original
agiilnot
intaglio
ligation
taglioni
agiilnox
gloxinia
agiilnpt
plaiting
agiilnqu
quailing
agiilnrt
ring-tail
agiilnrv
virginal
agiilntt
litigant

agiilntv
vigilant
agiiltvy
vagility
agiimnss
amissing
agiimnst
giantism
agiimntt
mitigant
agiinnpt
painting
agiinnrt
training
agiinnst
staining
agiinnsw
swaining
agiinors
Signoria
agiinprs
aspiring
praising
agiinrtt
attiring
agiinrty
Trigynia
agijnntu
jaunting
agiklmor
kilogram
agiklnno
Algonkin
agiklnnp
planking
agiklnrw
ring-walk
agiklnst
stalking
agiklnty
takingly
agikmnns
kings-man
agikmnnu
unmaking
agikmnpu
upmaking
agikmruu
kauri-gum
agiknnpp
knapping
agiknnpr
pranking
agiknnps
spanking
agiknnsw
swanking
agiknost
goatskin
agillmny
malignly
agillmsu
Gaullism

agillnot
long-tail
agillnru
alluring
lingular
agillnrw
ring-wall
agillnry
rallying
agillnst
stalling
agillnsy
sallying
signally
slangily
agillnty
tallying
agilloor
gillaroo
agillopt
gallipot
agillpry
playgirl
agillpuy
plaguily
agillssy
glassily
agillstu
Gaullist
agilmmns
slamming
agilmnnt
mantling
agilmnps
sampling
agilmnqu
qualming
agilmopr
lipogram
agilmors
algorism
agilnnnp
planning
agilnnop
pangolin
agilnnpt
planting
agilnnrs
snarling
agilnnst
slanting
agilnnuy
ungainly
agilnooo
oogonial
agilnoos
isogonal
agilnort
trigonal
agilnoss
glossina
lassoing
agilnotw
wagon-lit

agilnoty
antilogy
agilnpps
slapping
agilnppy
applying
agilnprs
sparling
springal
agilnptt
platting
agilnrst
starling
agilnrsu
singular
agilnrtt
rattling
agilnrtw
trawling
agilnrvy
ravingly
agilnrwx
wraxling
agilnsvy
savingly
agilnswy
swayling
agilnttt
tattling
agilnttw
wattling
agilntuv
vaulting
agilntwz
waltzing
agiloors
gloriosa
agilooxy
axiology
agilorss
grass-oil
agilostu
Ustilago
agimmosy
misogamy
agimnnru
manuring
agimnopw
pig-woman
agimnors
Orangism
organism
agimnoru
origanum
agimnory
agrimony
agimnpst
stamping
agimnrry
marrying
agimnrsw
swarming
agimnssu
assuming

agimorrt
migrator
agimqruy
quagmiry
aginnnps
spanning
aginnopt
poignant
aginnort
ignorant
aginnpps
snapping
aginnpsw
spawning
wingspan
aginnrtu
naturing
aginnstu
unsating
aginnttu
taunting
aginntuv
vaunting
aginnvvy
navvying
aginoort
rogation
aginorrs
garrison
aginorry
iron-gray
aginorss
assignor
aginorst
organist
roasting
aginortv
graviton
aginorty
gyration
organity
aginostt
tangoist
toasting
aginpprt
trapping
aginpprw
wrapping
aginppsw
swapping
aginppuy
appuying
aginprrs
sparring
aginprry
parrying
aginqrsu
squaring
aginrrst
starring
aginrrty
tarrying
aginrsst
nit-grass

aginrstt
starting
aginrstv
starving
aginrsty
sting-ray
straying
agioorsu
oragious
agioortu
autogiro
agiopprt
agitprop
agiorrtt
grattoir
agirttuy
gratuity
agjlosuv
Jugoslav
agkkosyz
kok-sagyz
agkllsuu
skua-gull
agkorssw
gas-works
aglllnow
longwall
agllmopw
glowlamp
aglloosw
slag-wool
agllossw
owl-glass
agllprsu
spur-gall
agllruvy
vulgarly
aglmooty
atmology
aglmooyy
Mayology
aglmopyy
polygamy
aglnnops
span-long
aglnosty
long-stay
aglnoswy
longways
aglnruuv
unvulgar
aglnstuy
yglaunst
agloopst
goalpost
aglootuy
autology
agloprss
lopgrass
aglorssy
glossary
aglosuvy
Yugoslav

aglpsssy
spyglass
aglrttuu
guttural
aglstuuy
augustly
agmmnoor
monogram
nomogram
agmmnooy
monogamy
agmmoort
tomogram
agmnnosw
gownsman
agmnoory
agronomy
agmnorst
angstrom
agmooosu
oogamous
agmoopry
porogamy
agmoorst
gas-motor
agnnoqtu
quantong
agnnossw
swan-song
agnoprst
part-song
agnortuy
nugatory
agnpprsu
upsprang
agnprsuy
spray-gun
agnrsstu
nut-grass
agoorrty
rogatory
agoortuy
autogyro
agorrsst
grossart
rotgrass
agorrtyy
gyratory
agorstty
gyrostat
ahhhooow
whoa-ho-ho
ahhilnpt
phthalin
ahhilost
hailshot
ahhilpsw
whiplash
ahhimmss
mishmash
ahhimmww
whim-wham
ahhimsst
smash-hit

ahhiprss
sharpish
ahhissww
wish-wash
ahhkmotw
hawk-moth
ahhlmrty
rhythmal
ahhlnopt
naphthol
ahhloopu
hula-hoop
ahhmprru
harrumph
ahhnortw
hawthorn
ahhopstu
aphthous
ahiilnps
plainish
ahiilost
haliotis
ahiilprs
Aprilish
ahiilptw
whip-tail
ahiilrty
hilarity
ahiimnot
himation
ahiimnrs
Irishman
ahiimnst
isthmian
ahiimssv
Shaivism
Shivaism
ahiinsst
saintish
ahiinssw
swainish
ahiiopst
hospitia
ahiklnrs
rinkhals
ahiklors
shark-oil
ahiklrsy
rakishly
ahikmsst
Shaktism
ahiknprs
prankish
ahikorrw
hair-work
ahikprss
sparkish
ahillmps
phallism
ahillmss
smallish
ahillmtu
thallium

ahillntw
wanthill
ahillsvy
lavishly
ahilmopt
philamot
ahilmqsu
qualmish
ahilmsst
Stahlism
ahilnops
siphonal
ahilnopt
oliphant
ahilnort
horntail
ahiloort
Lothario
ahilopst
hospital
ahilostt
thio-salt
ahilostu
halitous
ahilpssy
physalis
ahilrsty
trashily
ahilrtwy
wrathily
ahimmnsu
humanism
ahimmorz
mahzorim
ahimmosv
moshavim
ahimnors
Romanish
ahimnost
hoistman
ahimnosw
womanish
ahimnrtu
Mathurin
ahimnstu
humanist
ahimntux
xanthium
ahimntuy
humanity
ahimoprs
aphorism
ahimopst
opsimath
ahimorrw
hair-worm
ahimppss
sapphism
ahimrsty
Rhytisma
ahinnopt
antiphon
ahinnoru
Huronian

ahinopru
ophiuran
ahinosst
astonish
ahinppss
snappish
ahinprst
tranship
ahinqsuv
vanquish
ahiooppt
photopia
ahioorrt
root-hair
ahioprst
aphorist
ahiorstv
tovarish
ahiostwy
hoistway
ahippsst
sapphist
ahiqrssu
squarish
ahirsstt
startish
ahjmnoss
mass-john
ahjoottw
jaw-tooth
ahkllooy
holly-oak
ahklostw
talk-show
ahllmoot
hall-moot
moot-hall
ahllnoos
shalloon
ahllnouw
unhallow
ahllostu
thallous
ahllpryy
phyllary
ahlmmopy
lymphoma
ahlmnoor
hormonal
ahlmoops
omphalos
ahlmopru
lamp-hour
ahlmopty
polymath
ahlmpsyy
Symphyla
ahlnnort
lanthorn
ahloosst
sash-tool
ahlopsuz
Zalophus

ahlorrty
harlotry
ahlrstuy
lathyrus
ahlrttwy
thwartly
ahmnnort
Northman
ahmnnstu
huntsman
ahmnopty
phantomy
ahmnorrs
ram's-horn
ahmnorsu
man-hours
ahmoorsw
washroom
ahmorsty
harmosty
ahmosttw
mostwhat
ahmpstyy
sympathy
ahmqssuu
musquash
ahnnstyy
synanthy
ahnoopsu
aphonous
ahnoorry
honorary
ahnoppsw
pawnshop
ahnoppsy
pansophy
ahnopsst
snapshot
ahnortww
wanworth
ahnosstw
swan-shot
ahnostux
xanthous
ahnostuz
Zoanthus
ahooprww
war-whoop
ahooptyz
zoopathy
Zoophyta
ahoossty
soothsay
ahoosttw
saw-tooth
ahopprry
Porphyra
ahoppssw
swap-shop
ahopstuw
southpaw
ahorttuw
watt-hour

ahosstuy
southsay
aiiillvx
lixivial
aiiilrvz
vizirial
aiiirsss
siriasis
aiijkmot
komitaji
aiijnrtx
janitrix
aiikksuy
sukiyaki
aiikllst
silktail
aiiklnrr
larrikin
aiikmnnn
mannikin
aiiknnnp
pannikin
aiilllmt
mill-tail
aiillmry
milliary
aiillnnv
vanillin
aiillnop
pollinia
aiillnot
illation
aiillnry
Illyrian
aiillnvy
villainy
aiillprs
sliprail
spirilla
aiillwww
williwaw
aiilmmss
Islamism
aiilmnor
iron-mail
aiilmnot
limation
miltonia
aiilmnps
alpinism
aiilmnpt
palmitin
aiilmnst
Latinism
aiilmntt
militant
aiilmpuv
impluvia
aiilmrst
mistrial
trialism
aiilmrty
limitary
military

aiilmstv
vitalism
aiilnopt
oil-paint
aiilnopv
pavilion
aiilnort
train-oil
aiilnosv
visional
aiilnpst
alpinist
tail-spin
aiilnqru
Quirinal
aiilnrsu
Silurian
aiilnstt
Latinist
aiilnsty
salinity
aiilntty
Latinity
aiilrstt
trialist
aiilrtty
triality
aiilrtvy
rivality
aiilsttv
vitalist
aiilsttw
wait-list
aiilttvy
vitality
aiimmnrs
Marinism
aiimmnty
immanity
aiimmstx
maximist
aiimnnos
insomnia
aiimnpss
sinapism
aiimnpsx
panmixis
aiimnrst
Marinist
aiimnsst
saintism
samnitis
aiimnstt
Titanism
aiimnstv
nativism
aiimnttu
titanium
aiimopsx
apomixis
aiimortt
imitator
timariot

aiimosst
amitosis
aiimpprs
priapism
aiimprss
Parsiism
aiimprty
imparity
aiimruvv
vivarium
aiimsstt
mastitis
aiinnort
Tironian
aiinnosv
invasion
aiinnqtu
quintain
aiinnsty
insanity
aiinorst
intarsio
aiinortt
tritonia
aiinrrtt
irritant
aiinsttv
nativist
visitant
aiinstwx
twin-axis
aiinttvy
nativity
aiiorstt
aortitis
aiiorstv
ovaritis
aiiorttv
vitiator
aiiprrst
airstrip
aiiprvvy
vivipary
aiirsstt
satirist
aiisssty
syssitia
aijkknou
kinkajou
aijlloor
jillaroo
aijllovy
jovially
aijlntuy
jauntily
aijmorty
majority
aijnnnou
Junonian
aijnnrtu
injurant
aijnoppy
popinjay

aikkllmw
milk-walk
aikknoty
kantikoy
aikkrtuz
zikkurat
aiklllmw
walk-mill
aikllmnt
malt-kiln
aikllmrr
rillmark
aikllmuw
wauk-mill
aikllrss
all-risks
aiklmmrw
milk-warm
aiklmptu
kalumpit
aiklnnps
snap-link
aiklnpst
lantskip
aiklnrtu
kail-runt
aiklottw
kilowatt
aikmmnoo
makimono
aikmmnrt
mint-mark
aikmorss
komissar
aiknnoos
nainsook
aiknnssw
swan-skin
aiknorst
skiatron
aiknrsst
Sanskrit
aiknrssu
Russniak
aikrssty
satyrisk
ailllmmt
malt-mill
aillmmsy
smalmily
aillmnqu
quillman
aillmost
misallot
aillmoty
molality
aillmpry
primally
aillmuuv
alluvium
aillnopp
papillon
aillnost
stallion
aillnosu
allusion
aillnouv
alluvion
aillnpty
pliantly
aillopps
slop-pail
aillopuz
pulza-oil
aillorsy
sailorly
aillortt
littoral
tortilla
aillorvy
lyra-viol
aillosty
loyalist
aillppsu
supplial
aillprsy
spirally
aillprty
paltrily
aillpswy
spillway
aillrtuy
ritually
aillrtwy
willyart
aillsuvy
visually
ailmmnoo
monomial
ailmmnuu
aluminum
ailmmors
moralism
ailmmort
immortal
ailmmrsy
smarmily
ailmnnot
mannitol
ailmnntu
luminant
ailmnoop
palomino
ailmnoor
monorail
ailmnoos
moonsail
ailmnoot
motional
ailmnopr
prolamin
ailmnopy
Olympian
palimony
Polymnia
ailmnort
torminal
ailmnptu
platinum
ailmnruy
luminary
ailmnstu
simulant
ailmoors
sail-room
ailmoort
motorail
motorial
ailmoprx
proximal
ailmorss
solarism
ailmorst
moralist
ailmorsu
solarium
ailmorsy
royalism
ailmorty
molarity
morality
ailmostu
solatium
ailmostv
voltaism
ailmppsy
misapply
ailmpsst
psalmist
ailmpsty
ptyalism
ailmrrsu
ruralism
ailmrssu
surmisal
ailmrstu
altruism
ultraism
ailnnoop
Polonian
ailnnoot
notional
ailnnosu
unisonal
ailnnosw
son-in-law
ailnnotu
lunation
Ultonian
ailnnptu
unpliant
ailnnstu
insulant
ailnoopt
optional
ailnoost
solation
ailnopru
unipolar
ailnopty
pony-tail
ailnorst
tonsilar
ailnortw
owl-train
ailnortz
trizonal
ailnosss
sassolin
ailnosuv
avulsion
ailnosvy
synovial
ailnottv
volitant
ailnotty
tonality
ailnotux
luxation
ailnppsy
snappily
ailnprsu
purslain
ailnpruv
pulvinar
ailnpsuu
nauplius
ailnpttu
tulipant
ailnqrtu
tranquil
ailnqtuy
quaintly
ailnrstu
lunarist
ailnrttu
rutilant
ailnruwy
unwarily
ailnsstu
stunsail
ailnsttu
lutanist
ailnstuu
nautilus
ailnstvy
navy-list
ailooprt
troopial
ailoorrs
sororial
ailoorst
isolator
ailoortv
violator
ailoprst
strap-oil
ailoprtu
troupial
ailoprty
polarity
ailopruy
polyuria
ailorsst
solarist
ailorstu
sutorial
ailorsty
royalist
solitary
ailorttu
tutorial
ailortuv
outrival
ailottty
totality
ailppruy
pupilary
ailprrsu
spur-rial
ailprstu
stipular
ailpstuy
playsuit
ailrrstu
ruralist
ailrrsty
starrily
ailrrtuy
rurality
ailrsttu
altruist
ultraist
ailrstty
straitly
ailrsuvv
survival
aimmmnou
ammonium
aimmnors
Romanism
aimmnort
mortmain
aimmosst
somatism
aimmossu
miasmous
aimmrrsy
mismarry
aimmrsuu
masurium
aimmxxyy
mixy-maxy
aimnnotu
mountain
aimnnoty
antimony
antinomy
aimnnrtu
ruminant
aimnoooz
zoonomia
aimnoptv
pivot-man
aimnoqru
maroquin
aimnorst
Romanist
aimnortu
Minotaur
aimnorty
minatory
aimnosst
stasimon
aimnossx
Saxonism
aimnottu
mutation
aimnpryy
paynimry
aimnpstu
sumpitan
aimnrstt
Tantrism
transmit
aimnrstu
naturism
aimoprss
prosaism
aimoprst
atropism
aimopssy
symposia
aimorrst
armorist
aimorrsu
rosarium
aimorruv
variorum
aimorssu
ossarium
aimosstt
somatist
aimppruu
puparium
aimprsty
partyism
aimrsttu
striatum
aimrttuy
maturity
ainnnost
santonin
ainnoott
notation
ainnootv
novation
ainnootz
zonation
ainnottu
nutation
ainnppss
snip-snap
ainnrstu
insurant
ainnrsty
tyrannis
ainooptt
potation
ainoortt
rotation

ainoostt
ostinato
ainoottv
ottavino
ainopprt
parpoint
ainopptu
pupation
ainoprtv
proviant
ainopstt
post-nati
ainorrsw
warrison
ainorrtu
urinator
ainorsst
arsonist
ainorstt
strontia
ainorstu
sutorian
ainortvy
vanitory
ainosstx
Saxonist
ainosttu
titanous
ainpprtt
trippant
ainprssu
Prussian
ainpsssy
synapsis
ainpsstu
puissant
ainqttuy
quantity
ainrsttt
Tantrist
ainrsttu
naturist
ainrstty
tanistry
aiooorrt
oratorio
aioorsuv
ovarious
aioprrtt
portrait
aioprsst
prosaist
protasis
aioprstt
Protista
aiopsttu
utopiast
aiorrstv
varistor
aiorrtwy
ryotwari
aiorsttv
votarist

aiorstuv
virtuosa
aiosssty
isostasy
aipprstt
Trappist
aipprsty
papistry
aippttty
pitty-pat
aiprrruu
pirrauru
aiprrttu
partitur
aiprsstu
upstairs
aiprssty
sparsity
airrstty
artistry
ajklnstu
salt-junk
ajlmpuwy
lumpy-jaw
ajmrstuy
jurymast
ajorrtuy
juratory
akkorstw
taskwork
akllnotw
wall-knot
aklnnopt
plankton
aklnottw
town-talk
aklorstw
salt-work
aklprrsu
larkspur
akmmnoor
monomark
akmnortu
Turkoman
akmoprst
postmark
aknoorst
ostrakon
akooprsw
soap-work
akoprrtw
partwork
alllpruy
plurally
allmnory
normally
allmopsx
smallpox
allmorty
mortally
allmossw
wall-moss
allmpruu
plumular

allmtuuy
mutually
allnoopy
Apollyon
allnorss
lasslorn
allortww
wall-wort
wallwort
allruuvy
uvularly
almmnruu
nummular
almmnsuu
Musulman
almmortw
maltworm
almnnoor
non-moral
almnorty
matronly
almoopry
playroom
almoortu
alum-root
almoppst
lamppost
almorsuu
ramulous
alnnotwy
wantonly
alnooprt
portolan
pronotal
alnoopxy
polyaxon
alnoopyz
polyzoan
alnopptt
plant-pot
pot-plant
alnoprst
plastron
alnorrwy
narrowly
alnppstu
supplant
alnrrtuu
nurtural
aloopprs
proposal
aloooprtu
uprootal
aloorsuv
valorous
aloortyz
zoolatry
alopprryy
polypary
aloppssu
supposal
aloppsuu
papulous

aloprrsu
sporular
aloprstt
portlast
aloprstu
postural
pulsator
aloprsty
pastorly
alopstuu
patulous
alorrsuy
surroyal
alorsttw
salt-wort
alorsuvy
savourly
alortuwy
outlawry
alppstuy
platypus
alprrsuy
spur-ryal
alprstuu
pustular
ammnoort
motorman
ammnptuy
tympanum
amnnorsw
mansworn
amnnostw
townsman
amnnottu
mountant
amnnpstu
puntsman
amnnsttu
stuntman
amnoorty
many-root
amnootuy
autonomy
amnootwy
toywoman
amnootxy
taxonomy
amnopryy
paronymy
amnottuy
tautonym
amooprsy
Pyrosoma
amoorrty
moratory
amoorstz
smorzato
amoortwy
motorway
amoosstu
astomous
amoottuy
autotomy

amoprrst
mar-sport
amoprstt
tram-stop
amoprsxy
paroxysm
amoqssuu
squamous
amorrtuy
mortuary
amorsttu
outsmart
amorttuy
mutatory
annooqtu
non-quota
annoorst
sonorant
annoprty
non-party
annosstu
stannous
annprsuy
spun-yarn
anooppps
pap-spoon
anooprrt
pronator
anoorsuu
anourous
anoqrssu
squarson
anorstvy
sovranty
anprstuu
pursuant
anrrsttu
star-turn
anrrttuy
truantry
anrsstyy
synastry
aoooprst
soap-root
aoooprsz
Sporozoa
aoooprtz
protozoa
aoopprsy
apospory
aooprssu
saporous
aooprstt
pot-roast
aooprstu
atropous
aooprstw
soapwort
aooprsuv
vaporous
aooprtty
potatory
aoorrtty
rotatory

aoorssuv
savorous
aopprsst
passport
aopqrttu
quart-pot
aoprrrty
parrotry
aoprsstt
starspot
aoprstty
pyrostat
aorrsttw
starwort
aorrttww
wartwort
aorssttu
stratous
aorsstty
starosty
bbbceowy
cobwebby
bbbeinot
bobbinet
bbbeootu
boob-tube
bbbhnooy
hobnobby
bbbhoouu
hubbuboo
bbbinopy
bobby-pin
bbblmopu
plumb-bob
bbblooxy
box-lobby
bbcdeilr
cribbled
bbcdersu
scrubbed
bbcdimoy
bombycid
bbceilrs
scribble
bbceklu
blue-buck
bbcelory
cobblery
bbcemnou
buncombe
bbcerrsu
scrubber
bbcgiinr
cribbing
bbcgilno
cobbling
bbcgilnu
clubbing
bbchilsu
clubbish
bbchkoos
boschbok
bbchksuu
bush-buck

8 BBC

bbcilmsu
clubbism
bbcilrsy
scribbly
bbcilstu
clubbist
bbddeeir
bride-bed
bbddeemo
demobbed
bbddenuu
undubbed
bbdeemnu
benumbed
bbdeenuw
unwebbed
bbdeersu
subbreed
bbdehort
throbbed
bbdeilln
bellbind
bbdeillr
bell-bird
bbdeilrr
dribbler
bbdeilrt
dribblet
bbdeilru
bluebird
bbdeilry
dry-bible
bbdeimov
dive-bomb
bbdeinor
dobber-in
bbdeinru
unribbed
bbdekoot
book-debt
bbdellmu
dumb-bell
bbdelstu
stubbled
bbdenruu
unrubbed
bbdginru
drubbing
bbdilort
bird-bolt
bbdosuyy
busybody
bbeeehrr
herb-beer
bbeefllu
bull-beef
bbeehins
nebbishe
bbeehlow
bobwheel
bbeeiirr
beriberi
bbeeirrs
berberis

bbeellllu
bluebell
bbefilrr
fribbler
bbefimor
fire-bomb
bbegiist
gibbsite
bbegilnp
pebbling
bbegilry
glibbery
bbehiotw
bob-white
bbeillno
bonibell
bbeilqru
quibbler
bbeilrry
bilberry
bbeilrst
stibbler
bbeimmot
time-bomb
bbeimost
bomb-site
bbeirstu
subtribe
bbeknoot
bontebok
bbellouy
bell-buoy
bbellruy
lubberly
bbelorsy
slobbery
bbenorsy
snobbery
bberrruy
Burberry
bbgginru
grubbing
bbghilno
hobbling
bbgiijns
jibbings
bbgiilmn
blimbing
bbgiilnn
nibbling
bbgilnow
wobbling
bbgilnoy
lobbying
bbgilnru
burbling
bbgilnsu
slubbing
bbginnsu
snubbing
bbginosw
swobbing
bbginstu
stubbing

bbhimosy
hobbyism
bbhinoss
snobbish
bbhinssu
snubbish
bbhioosy
boobyish
bbhiosty
hobbyist
bbhirsuy
rubbishy
bbhrssuu
subshrub
bbiklloo
billbook
bbiklnoo
bobolink
bbilloyy
billyboy
bbilosty
lobbyist
bbilosuu
bibulous
bbimnoss
snobbism
bbimoosy
boobyism
bbinorry
ribbonry
bbllouyy
bully-boy
bbnorstu
stubborn
bccdhiko
dobchick
bccdikor
cockbird
bcceeirr
cerebric
bccehiru
cherubic
bcceiiis
cicisbei
bcceiilo
libeccio
bcceiios
cicisbeo
bcceilru
crucible
bccemruu
cucumber
bcciimor
microbic
bccilmou
Columbic
bcciloor
broccoli
bccimnuu
Buccinum
bccirtuu
cucurbit
bccklmou
bum-clock

bccssuuu
succubus
bcddehil
childbed
bcdeeehr
breeched
bcdeeemr
December
bcdeehnr
bedrench
bcdeehou
débouché
bcdeeikn
Benedick
bcdeeilr
credible
bcdeeilu
educible
bcdeeint
Benedict
bcdeeirs
describe
bcdeemru
cumbered
bcdeeorv
bedcover
bcdeeott
obtected
bcdefklo
flock-bed
bcdehins
disbench
bcdehlot
blotched
bcdeiilr
bird-lice
bcdeiirr
rice-bird
bcdeikrr
brick-red
redbrick
bcdeilry
credibly
bcdeiltu
bile-duct
bcdeimno
combined
bcdeimos
side-comb
bcdeinou
ice-bound
bcdeirsu
curbside
bcdekoss
bedsocks
bcdemnou
uncombed
bcdenruu
uncurbed
bcdiipsu
bicuspid
bcdikllu
duckbill

bcdikorr
rock-bird
bcdilmoy
molybdic
bcdinruu
rubicund
bceeefin
benefice
bceeefkn
neck-beef
bceeehrs
breeches
bceeeirr
rice-beer
bceeenrs
bescreen
bceeeqru
Quebecer
bceeersu
berceuse
bceefiln
fencible
bceefnor
corn-beef
bceehilo
beech-oil
bceehnru
unbreech
bceehpsy
by-speech
bceeiilm
imbecile
bceeinot
cenobite
bceeirtt
brettice
bceeknno
neck-bone
bceellot
bellcote
bceeloor
borecole
bceelrtu
tubercle
bceemnru
encumber
bceemrru
cerebrum
cumberer
bceerrsu
Cerberus
bceerstu
suberect
bceffiir
febrific
bcefilor
forcible
bcegiino
biogenic
bcegimno
becoming
bceglnoo
conglobe

bcehilpu
blue-chip
bcehimrs
besmirch
bcehimru
cherubim
bcehinru
cherubin
bcehirst
britches
bcehirty
bitchery
bcehmstu
besmutch
bcehnrsu
burschen
bcehorru
brochure
bcehorty
botchery
bcehrstu
butcher's
bcehrttu
Cuthbert
bcehrtuy
butchery
bceiikln
iceblink
bceiilms
miscible
bceiilnv
vincible
bceiimrs
imbrices
bceiinrs
inscribe
bceikloo
booklice
bceiknor
beck-iron
bceillnu
club-line
bceilmru
Mulciber
bceilnru
runcible
bceilotu
tubicole
bceilpru
republic
bceimosw
comb-wise
bceinovx
biconvex
bceioops
bioscope
bceioovx
voice-box
bceiopsx
spice-box
bceiorrs
cribrose
bceiorst
bisector

bcejoort
objector
bceklnot
bloncket
bceklnuu
unbuckle
bcekmstu
stembuck
bcellruw
well-curb
bcelmoss
combless
bcelortu
clotebur
bceloruv
over-club
bcelrssu
curbless
bcemoors
rose-comb
bcenorry
by-corner
bcenostx
scent-box
bceorrsu
obscurer
bceorrwy
cowberry
bcfgllou
golf-club
bcfiimor
morbific
bcfiiort
fibrotic
bcfilory
forcibly
bcfimoru
cubiform
bcflootu
club-foot
bcfoorru
curb-roof
bcghinnu
bunching
bcghinot
botching
bcghintu
butching
bcgiiknr
bricking
bcgiilmn
climbing
bcgiinrs
scribing
bcgikkru
grub-kick
bcgiklno
blocking
bcgiklnu
buckling
bcgiklow
wig-block
bcgiknor
brick-nog

bcgimnos
combings
bcginnou
bouncing
bchiissu
Hibiscus
bchiklos
blockish
bchioory
choirboy
bchknoru
buckhorn
bchkostu
buckshot
bchlootx
box-cloth
bchlrsuu
club-rush
bchnorsu
bronchus
bchootux
touch-box
bciiknor
bick-iron
bciimnoo
bionomic
bciimoru
ciborium
bciimrss
scribism
bciinorv
vibronic
bcikknsu
buckskin
bciklnot
block-tin
bcikloot
bootlick
bcikorrw
cribwork
bcillorw
crow-bill
bcillpuy
publicly
bcilmosy
symbolic
bcilnouy
bouncily
bcimosux
music-box
bcinossu
subsonic
bcinostu
subtonic
bcinosuu
incubous
bcioorst
robotics
bciorrss
cross-rib
bckkoooo
cook-book
bckllоos
bollocks

bckooopy
copybook
bclmooow
wool-comb
bclmooru
clubroom
bclmossu
club-moss
bcloortu
clubroot
bcmorsuu
cumbrous
bcnorssu
cross-bun
bcoorssw
crossbow
bcorsttu
obstruct
bdddeenu
unbedded
bdddenuu
unbudded
bddeeell
debelled
bddeeflu
befuddle
bddeegir
begirded
bddeegtu
budgeted
bddeeimm
bedimmed
bddeeimo
embodied
bddeeint
indebted
bddeeinw
bindweed
bddeeirr
reed-bird
bddeeirs
birdseed
bddeeiry
bird-eyed
bddeelmu
bemuddle
bddeennu
unbended
bddeeorr
bordered
bddeilnr
brindled
bddeinnu
unbidden
bddeinou
unbodied
bddeinru
underbid
bddeiors
disorbed
bddeiowy
wide-body
bddeloor
blood-red

bddgoosy
dog's-body
bddhiiry
dihybrid
bddhimsu
Buddhism
bddhistu
Buddhist
bddinoow
woodbind
bddinpuu
pudibund
bdeeegno
edgebone
bdeeegru
budgeree
bdeeehtu
hebetude
bdeeeins
beniseed
bdeeellr
rebelled
bdeeellv
bevelled
bdeeelos
seed-lobe
bdeeeluw
blueweed
bdeeemmr
membered
bdeeertt
bettered
bdeeertv
breveted
bdeeettw
bewetted
bdeeffru
buffered
bdeefilr
belfried
bdeefinr
befriend
bdeefitt
befitted
bdeefoor
forebode
bdeefoow
beef-wood
bdeeggiw
bewigged
bdeeggru
begrudge
bdeegiln
bleeding
bdeeginr
breeding
bdeehllr
hell-bred
bdeehlno
beholden
bdeehlor
beholder
bdeehmor
home-bred

bdeehorv
hover-bed
bdeeiiln
inedible
bdeeiiny
bindi-eye
bdeeikrs
kerb-side
bdeeilll
libelled
bdeeillt
billeted
bdeeillu
eludible
bdeeilnn
bed-linen
bdeeilno
bone-idle
bdeeilnv
vendible
bdeeilrw
bewilder
bdeeimrt
timbered
bdeeinot
obedient
bdeeinsw
bendwise
bdeeiors
osier-bed
bdeeirrv
river-bed
bdeeirst
bestride
bdeeirsy
bird's-eye
bdeeknru
bunkered
bdeellow
bowelled
bdeellrw
well-bred
bdeellry
red-belly
bdeelmno
embolden
bdeelmor
rebeldom
bdeelmpu
beplumed
bdeelntu
unbelted
bdeeloru
redouble
bdeelosu
besouled
bdeemnot
bodement
bdeemorr
emborder
bdeemory
re-embody
bdeemoss
embossed

bdeemssu
embussed
bdeennot
bonneted
bdeenouy
unobeyed
bdeeoprw
bepowder
bdeeorrr
borderer
bdeeorst
bestrode
bdeeortu
outbreed
bdeeossy
boss-eyed
bdeeostt
besotted
bdeeprru
pure-bred
bdeeprss
press-bed
bdeerrtu
true-bred
bdeerrwy
dew-berry
bdeerttu
rebutted
bdefiirr
fire-bird
bdefoory
fore-body
bdeggnou
egg-bound
bdeghhir
high-bred
bdeghilt
blighted
bdeghirt
bedright
bdegilnn
blending
bdegiorx
Oxbridge
bdeglloy
belly-god
bdeglnou
bludgeon
bdegorry
dogberry
bdegoruw
budgerow
bdehkoor
herd-book
bdehlsuv
bushveld
bdeiilmr
bird-lime
bdeiilty
debility
bdeiirrw
wire-bird
bdeiknor
brodekin

8 BDE

bdeiknsu
  buskined
bdeillmu
  bdellium
bdeillow
  billowed
bdeilmsu
  sublimed
bdeilnou
  unilobed
bdeilnru
  unbridle
bdeilnvy
  vendibly
bdeilort
  trilobed
bdeilorv
  lovebird
bdeiloss
  bodiless
bdeilosw
  disbowel
bdeilrry
  lyre-bird
bdeilrst
  bristled
bdeimnsu
  nimbused
bdeimnuu
  unimbued
bdeimorr
  imborder
bdeinoow
  woodbine
bdeinorv
  oven-bird
bdeinrsu
  burnside
bdeinrtu
  turbined
bdeinruu
  unburied
bdeinttu
  unbitted
bdeiorry
  broidery
bdeiosux
  suboxide
bdeirssu
  disburse
bdeknoou
  unbooked
bdekoopu
  booked-up
bdelloor
  bordello
  doorbell
bdellouz
  bulldoze
bdelmruu
  delubrum
bdelnnuu
  unbundle
bdelnoss
  boldness
bdelnotu
  unbolted
bdelnouu
  undouble
bdelnouw
  unblowed
bdeloorv
  overbold
bdelortu
  troubled
bdelpsuu
  subduple
bdemnotu
  untombed
bdemnssu
  dumbness
bdemoosy
  somebody
bdemoott
  bottomed
bdennouy
  ybounden
bdennruu
  unburden
  unburned
bdenooru
  Eurobond
bdenootw
  bentwood
bdenoruy
  under-boy
bdenostu
  bone-dust
bdenruuy
  underbuy
bdeoorrw
  borrowed
bdeoptyy
  type-body
bdeorrsu
  suborder
bdeorrtu
  obtruder
bderstuu
  subtrude
bdffipru
  puff-bird
bdfgnoou
  fogbound
bdfilllo
  billfold
bdfinoru
  unforbid
bdfinruu
  furibund
bdfirrsu
  surf-bird
bdfirtuu
  fruit-bud
bdflotuu
  doubtful
bdggiinr
  bridging
bdghoouy
  dough-boy
bdgiiknr
  king-bird
bdgiilnn
  blinding
bdgiilnu
  building
bdgilnnu
  bundling
bdgilnou
  doubling
bdgilntu
  blind-gut
bdginnou
  bounding
  unboding
bdginors
  songbird
bdginotu
  doubting
bdgnruuy
  burgundy
bdhiiprw
  whipbird
bdhimoor
  rhomboid
bdhimort
  birthdom
bdhiorst
  birdshot
bdhkooru
  Dukhobor
bdhlooot
  blood-hot
bdhmosuw
  dumb-show
bdiiloqu
  obliquid
bdiimruu
  rubidium
bdiioosw
  wood-ibis
bdillloo
  ill-blood
bdillooy
  bloodily
bdilmory
  morbidly
bdilnnsu
  sun-blind
bdilnorw
  wild-born
bdilnpru
  purblind
bdilootw
  blood-wit
bdilrtuy
  turbidly
bdimnoru
  moribund
bdimooss
  disbosom
bdimostu
  misdoubt
bdinnruw
  windburn
bdinorsw
  snow-bird
bdinrtuu
  unturbid
bdioorty
  botryoid
bdiottxy
  ditty-box
bdknooor
  doorknob
bdkooorw
  wordbook
bdkoorwy
  bodywork
bdkoostu
  stud-book
bdllotuy
  dolly-tub
bdlnooou
  doubloon
bdlnoouy
  unbloody
bdlnooww
  blowdown
bdlosttu
  stud-bolt
bdlostuw
  dust-bowl
bdmoorrs
  smørbrød
bdnnootu
  bunodont
bdnooorw
  wood-born
bdnooptu
  pot-bound
bdnoosuw
  sound-bow
bdnoosux
  sound-box
bdnootuu
  outbound
beeeefln
  enfeeble
beeeenqu
  queen-bee
beeeenrt
  terebene
beeeenrz
  ebenezer
beeegirs
  besieger
beeegrtt
  begetter
beeehist
  bheestie
beeehlrt
  herbelet
beeehlww
  webwheel
beeehnoy
  honey-bee
beeehosu
  bee-house
beeeilrv
  believer
beeeinrt
  bien-être
beeeinst
  ébéniste
beeellrr
  rebeller
beeellrt
  belleter
beeellrv
  beveller
beeelmns
  ensemble
beeelmrs
  resemble
beeelmsy
  beseemly
beeelmzz
  embezzle
beeemmrr
  remember
beeemnsu
  unbeseem
beeemrss
  Bessemer
beeensst
  sebesten
beeepppr
  bepepper
beeeprst
  bepester
beeersst
  bretesse
beeerstt
  besetter
beefflmu
  bemuffle
beefghnu
  hung-beef
beefginr
  befringe
beefhils
  feeblish
beefillt
  lifebelt
beefillx
  flexible
beefilnu
  unbelief
beefiort
  fire-bote
beefirtu
  fire-tube
beeflorw
  beflower
beefnorr
  freeborn
beefnrry
  fen-berry
beefnrtu
  unbereft
beeghlmr
  bergmehl
beegiill
  eligible
beegiilx
  exigible
beegillr
  gerbille
beegilnt
  beetling
beegilru
  beguiler
beeginnr
  beginner
beeginsw
  beeswing
beeginuu
  Eugubine
beegkluy
  keybugle
beeglruy
  blue-grey
beegmrsu
  submerge
beegnoow
  wobegone
beegnott
  begotten
beehhmot
  behemoth
beehilmn
  Blenheim
beehllnt
  hell-bent
beehloor
  borehole
beehlovy
  behovely
beehlrss
  herbless
beehmorw
  home-brew
beehnors
  nose-herb
beehnrrt
  brethren
beeiilnz
  zibeline
beeiilst
  Tebilise
beeiinos
  ebionise
beeiinot
  Ebionite
beeiinrt
  bénitier
beeiinst
  Ibsenite

beeijstu
bejesuit
Jebusite
beeiklwy
bi-weekly
beeilllr
libeller
beeillno
lobeline
beeilltt
belittle
beeilmpr
periblem
beeilmpu
umble-pie
beeilnss
sensible
beeilnst
stilbene
tensible
beeilnsu
nebulise
beeilrrt
terrible
beeilryz
breezily
beeimrru
umbriere
beeimrtt
embitter
beeinnss
beinness
beeinort
tenebrio
beeiorss
soberise
beeiortv
overbite
beeirssu
suberise
beekmopr
pembroke
beeknops
bespoken
beeknorz
Brezonek
beeknost
steenbok
beellntt
bell-tent
beellopr
bell-rope
beellorw
bellower
rebellow
beellsst
bestsell
beellsuy
bull's-eye
beelltuw
tube-well
beelmmop
bepommel
beelmnno
noblemen
beelmrrt
trembler
beelmrru
lumberer
beelnoss
boneless
noblesse
beelnosu
bluenose
beelnssu
blueness
beelnttu
betel-nut
beelntuy
butylene
beeloost
obsolete
beeloqru
breloque
beelostw
steelbow
beelpruv
buplever
beelrssv
verbless
beelsstu
tubeless
beemnorv
November
beemnrru
numberer
renumber
beemoprt
obtemper
beemorss
embosser
beemppru
beer-pump
beemqsuu
embusqué
beemrssu
submerse
beemrttu
umbrette
beemrtuz
zerumbet
beenortu
bountree
beenprst
besprent
beenrstw
bestrewn
beenrttu
brunette
beensstu
subtense
beeoorrt
root-beer
beeoortt
beetroot
boottree
beeorrsv
observer
beeorrtu
bourtree
beeorssu
suberose
beeorstu
tuberose
beeorstw
bestower
beeprsty
presbyte
beerrstw
brewster
beerrttu
rebutter
beerssuv
subserve
subverse
beerstty
by-street
beestttu
test-tube
befgiill
fillibeg
befgiinr
briefing
befhilsu
bluefish
befhinos
fish-bone
befiknox
knife-box
befiknoy
knife-boy
befillxy
flexibly
befilmor
forelimb
befilouy
life-buoy
befiortt
forebitt
befllluy
bellyful
beflnors
self-born
beflooot
lobe-foot
befloruw
furbelow
befnoorr
forborne
befoottu
tube-foot
beforrxy
foxberry
beggooos
goosegob
beghiilp
philibeg
beghilrt
blighter
beghinrt
brighten
beghlnou
bung-hole
beghnotu
boughten
beghostu
besought
beghosuu
bughouse
begiiiln
ill-being
begiiily
eligibly
begiinrz
zingiber
begiioss
sigisbeo
begilllu
gullible
begillny
bellying
begilnnu
Nibelung
begilnny
benignly
begilnos
Gobelins
begilnov
beloving
begilnss
blessing
glibness
begilnuw
bluewing
begimost
misbegot
begimosy
bogeyism
beginnnu
unbenign
beginnor
ringbone
beginnot
not-being
beginoos
besognio
beginors
sobering
beginrry
berrying
begllory
gor-belly
begllotu
globulet
beglmrru
grumbler
beglnouw
bluegown
begnntuv
bung-vent
begnooru
bourgeon
begnortu
burgonet
begnssuu
subgenus
behhmpsu
hempbush
behikpsu
push-bike
behillos
shoe-bill
behillty
blithely
behilmrw
whimbrel
behilorr
horrible
behilrtu
thurible
behimnoo
bonhomie
behinnos
shin-bone
behinosw
wishbone
behioopr
biophore
behiotwy
Whiteboy
behllnor
hell-born
behlloot
bolthole
behlloow
blowhole
behllops
shop-bell
behllpsu
bellpush
behloopy
hypobole
lyophobe
behlossu
sloebush
behmnoor
home-born
behnnouy
honeybun
behooost
boothose
behoorsy
horse-boy
behoosuy
houseboy
behoprsu
bush-rope
behorssu
rose-bush
behorsuv
hover-bus
beiikrtz
kibitzer
beiillmt
time-bill
beiilmmo
immobile
beiilmos
mobilise
beiilnrs
rinsible
beiilrsx
ex-libris
beiilrtt
libretti
beiilruz
bruilzie
beiilstt
stilbite
beiimnos
ebionism
beiimnss
Ibsenism
beiimrtt
imbitter
beiinprt
brine-pit
beiinstt
stibnite
beijmosu
jumboise
beijnorw
bijwoner
beikoort
brookite
beillmno
bone-mill
beillmss
limbless
beillmsu
semibull
beillntu
bulletin
beilmmos
embolism
beilmnou
nobelium
beilmnru
unlimber
beilmnuu
nebulium
beilmptu
plumbite
beilmrss
brimless
beilnnsu
Blennius
beilnntu
buntline
beilnops
bonspiel
beilnorv
live-born
beilnssy
sensibly
beiloorv
overboil
beiloppw
blowpipe

beilopss
possible
beilorst
strobile
beilortt
libretto
beilrrty
terribly
beilrsty
blistery
beilrtty
bitterly
beilsttu
subtitle
beimnssu
nimbuses
beimoors
ribosome
beimorty
biometry
beimotvy
by-motive
beimrstu
resubmit
beinnoss
boniness
beinnryz
zebrinny
beinorst
ribstone
beinortw
brow-tine
beinortz
bronzite
beinrrsy
nisberry
beinrstu
Burnsite
turbines
beinsssu
business
beioqtuu
boutique
beiorrtu
roburite
beiorstu
to-bruise
beiorsty
sobriety
beirrttu
tributer
bejkoost
jestbook
bejorttu
turbo-jet
beklnory
brokenly
beklooor
booklore
bekloort
brooklet
beklooss
bookless

bekloruv
overbulk
bekmoops
spekboom
bekmoosx
smoke-box
beknnoru
unbroken
beknooot
notebook
beknoort
to-broken
bekooorv
overbook
bekoorst
bookrest
bekoottx
text-book
textbook
bellllpu
bellpull
belllosu
soul-bell
bellmort
mortbell
bellmoru
umbrello
bellmosw
swell-mob
bellmruy
lumberly
bellnorw
well-born
bellntuy
tunbelly
bellopty
pot-belly
bellortw
bellwort
belmoors
bloomers
belmoory
bloomery
belmorsy
sombrely
belmoruw
rumbelow
belmosst
tombless
belmpruy
plumbery
belmrruy
mulberry
belmrstu
stumbler
belmrsuy
slumbery
belnnoww
new-blown
belnosuu
nebulous
belnstuu
unsubtle

belooosx
loose-box
belooprt
bolt-rope
beloorsw
rose-bowl
beloorvw
overblow
beloosst
bootless
belootuv
obvolute
belorrtu
troubler
belorssw
browless
belostuy
obtusely
belprsuy
superbly
belrsssu
Brussels
belrstuy
blustery
belsstuy
substyle
belsttuy
subtlety
bemnoort
trombone
bemnooxy
money-box
bemnopru
rump-bone
bemnorsy
embryons
bemoorrs
sombrero
bemortuw
tube-worm
worm-tube
bennnotu
unbonnet
bennoors
Sorbonne
bennootu
boutonné
benoostw
stone-bow
benorrsu
suborner
benorrtu
true-born
benorruv
overburn
benorstu
rubstone
benorstw
bestrown
benorsuu
burnouse
benorttu
rebutton

bensssuy
busyness
beoorrrw
borrower
beoorrvw
overbrow
beoorsty
botryose
beoottzz
bozzetto
beoprssx
press-box
beorssuu
suberous
beorstuu
tuberous
beorsuvy
overbusy
beosstuu
souse-tub
berrstuu
surrebut
berssttu
buttress
bffhorsu
brush-off
bffiistt
stiff-bit
bffllouy
bully-off
bffnosux
snuffbox
bffosstu
sob-stuff
bfghintu
bun-fight
bfgikoot
gift-book
bfglloru
bullfrog
bfhlloou
bull-hoof
bfhllsuu
blushful
bfhlosux
flush-box
bfhorsux
fox-brush
bfiiorss
fibrosis
bfillmru
brim-full
bfillssu
blissful
bfiloost
soft-boil
bfimnoru
nubiform
bfimortu
tubiform
bfinoryz
bronzify
bfllnowy
fly-blown

bflnooor
fool-born
bfloorsu
subfloor
bggiilno
obliging
bggiilny
gibingly
bggiinnr
bringing
bggiinru
briguing
bggilnnu
bungling
bgginoot
toboggin
bghhinor
high-born
bghhiorw
highbrow
bghilmnu
humbling
bghilnsu
blushing
bghilrty
brightly
bghinrsu
brushing
bghnnuuy
bunny-hug
bghnotuu
unbought
bghooptu
boughpot
bgiijlny
jibingly
bgiiklnn
blinking
bgiilnrs
brisling
bgiimmnr
brimming
bgiinrsu
bruising
bgiklnot
king-bolt
bgillnou
globulin
bgillnru
bull-ring
bgillnuy
bullying
bgilmmnu
mumbling
bgilmnoo
blooming
bgilmnpu
plumbing
bgilmnru
rumbling
bgilmntu
tumbling
bgilmory
gorblimy

bgilnnos
snobling
bgilnort
ring-bolt
bgilnott
blotting
bgilnotu
boulting
bgilnrru
blurring
bgilnrtu
blurting
bginnorw
browning
bginnorz
bronzing
bginorsw
browsing
bgklnoou
lung-book
bgknooos
songbook
bgloorxy
glorybox
bglooryy
bryology
bgoprsuu
subgroup
bhiikrss
briskish
bhiilmps
blimpish
bhiimrst
misbirth
bhiioprt
prohibit
bhiklloo
billhook
bhillnor
hornbill
bhillosw
show-bill
bhillstu
bullshit
bhilnstu
bluntish
bhilorry
horribly
bhilosyy
boyishly
bhimnort
thrombin
bhimoopr
biomorph
bhinopsu
unbishop
bhinorsw
brownish
bhiorrst
short-rib
bhknooor
hornbook
bhkoooot
boot-hook

bhkooops
bookshop
bhllnoru
bull-horn
bhlooott
tolbooth
bhlrsuuy
bulrushy
bhmopttu
thumbpot
bhmorstu
thrombus
bhmrrsuu
rum-shrub
biiknoot
bootikin
biillmor
morbilli
biillnqu
quill-nib
biilmoty
mobility
biilnoov
oblivion
biilnoty
nobility
biilntuy
nubility
biilorst
strobili
biilorsu
Orbilius
biilossu
sibilous
biimmosz
zombiism
biinrstu
burinist
biirsstu
bursitis
biklnnsu
sun-blink
bikoouuz
bouzouki
billmsuy
bullyism
billnoou
bouillon
billstuw
swill-tub
billstuy
subtilly
bilmmpsu
plumbism
bilmostu
botulism
bilnosuu
nubilous
biloorst
sorbitol
bilopssy
possibly
bilorsst
bristols

bilssttu
subtlist
bilsttuy
subtilty
bimnooor
boom-iron
bimnorsw
Brownism
bimnorsy
Byronism
bimnosty
symbiont
bimnruuv
viburnum
bimossty
sybotism
binnortw
twin-born
binoorst
isobront
binorstw
Brownist
bioopstt
post-obit
bioprrsu
subprior
bioprstw
bowsprit
biorstuy
bistoury
biosttuy
obtusity
birssttu
subtrist
bkkooorw
bookwork
workbook
bkmooorw
bookworm
bkmooruz
zomboruk
bkooopst
book-post
bllllooy
loblolly
bllmoorw
boll-worm
blloopsw
slop-bowl
blmoooty
lobotomy
blmoossy
blossomy
blmopsuu
plumbous
bloossty
slyboots
blorstuy
robustly
blostuuu
tubulous
bmnortuw
mowburnt

bmoorssu
sombrous
bmoorstu
motor-bus
bmorsstu
strombus
bnnortuw
nut-brown
bnnottuu
unbutton
bnnrstuu
sunburnt
bnooostw
snow-boot
bnooosuy
sonobuoy
bnorruuw
unburrow
bnrsstuu
sunburst
boooprsx
poor's-box
boorssty
sob-story
borsttuu
outburst
cccdiily
dicyclic
cccegosy
coccyges
ccceiirt
eccritic
ccceilny
encyclic
ccceiluy
eucyclic
cchiory
chiccory
ccciinsu
succinic
cccilnoy
cyclonic
cccilopy
cyclopic
cccinstu
succinct
cccioors
scirocco
ccckoorw
cock-crow
ccclosuu
Cocculus
ccdeeenr
credence
ccdeeins
scienced
ccdeeiop
cod-piece
ccdeekoy
cockeyed
ccdeenor
conceder
ccdehipu
hiccuped

ccdehltu
declutch
ccdehors
scorched
ccdehort
crotched
ccdehrtu
crutched
ccdeiino
coincide
ccdeilos
scolecid
ccdeinor
corniced
ccdeinot
occident
ccdeiopu
occupied
ccdeipru
cider-cup
ccdelnou
conclude
ccdelotu
occulted
ccdeorru
occurred
ccdeostu
stuccoed
ccdhiikp
dipchick
ccdhiilo
cichloid
ccdhiior
dichroic
ccdhinoo
conchoid
ccdiinoo
conoidic
ccdiinos
scincoid
ccdiinst
discinct
ccdiiort
dicrotic
ccdklouy
cuckoldy
ccdkooow
woodcock
ccdoooow
coco-wood
cceeeehh
chee-chee
cceeelmn
clemence
cceehinz
zecchine
cceehkky
check-key
cceehlow
cow-leech
cceehrsy
screechy
cceeilnr
encircle

cceeilnt
elenctic
cceeilpy
epicycle
cceeilrt
electric
cceeilst
eclestic
cceeimnu
ecumenic
cceeinor
cicerone
cceeinov
conceive
cceeiorv
coercive
cceeirsv
crescive
cceeittu
eutectic
cceeklor
cockerel
cceelmny
clemency
cceeloss
scoleces
cceemmno
commence
cceemmor
commerce
cceemops
compesce
cceennos
ensconce
cceenort
concrete
cceenrst
crescent
cceeoort
coco-tree
cceffhko
check-off
ccefiips
specific
ccefirru
crucifer
ccefllou
floccule
ccefloos
floccose
cceghior
choregic
ccegikln
clecking
ccegiloo
ecologic
ccegilry
glyceric
ccegnoos
cognosce
ccehiimr
chimeric
ccehiims
ischemic

ccehiksu
chuckies
ccehilnr
clincher
ccehilor
choleric
ccehiloy
choicely
ccehinor
corniche
enchoric
ccehinoz
zecchino
ccehinst
technics
ccehiort
ricochet
ccehlmor
cromlech
ccehlnnu
unclench
ccehlruy
cleruchy
ccehorrs
scorcher
ccehortt
crotchet
ccehrstu
scutcher
ccehrtuy
cutchery
cceiikln
nickelic
cceiilnt
enclitic
cceiilnu
culicine
cceiilor
licorice
cceiilpt
ecliptic
cceiilst
scilicet
cceiiltu
leucitic
cceiinnr
encrinic
cceiinor
ciceroni
cceiirrt
circiter
cceiirss
eccrisis
cceiirtt
rectitic
cceiirtu
eucritic
cceilmoo
coelomic
cceilmop
complice
cceilnor
cornicle

cceilnuy
unicycle
cceilrru
curricle
cceilrty
tricycle
cceilruu
curlicue
cceimnoo
economic
cceimost
cosmetic
cceimrru
mercuric
cceinnos
insconce
cceinnov
convince
cceinoor
coercion
cceinooz
Cenozoic
cceinort
necrotic
cceinost
C-section
cceinott
concetti
tectonic
cceinoty
conceity
cceinprt
precinct
cceinrtu
cincture
cceinsty
synectic
cceioort
crocoite
cceiootz
ectozoic
cceioprt
ectropic
cceiopru
occupier
cceiorst
cortices
cceiostt
Scottice
cceiprtu
cut-price
cceirstu
Cricetus
ccekorry
crockery
ccekorsu
cocksure
ccelmopt
complect
ccelopsy
cyclopes
ccenoort
concerto
ccenoott
concetto
ccenorru
corn-cure
ccenorty
cornetcy
ccenrruy
currency
cceooorr
corocore
cceoorsu
croceous
cceopruy
reoccupy
cceorstu
stuccoer
ccfiinor
cornific
ccfiirux
crucifix
ccfillou
flocculi
ccfilnot
conflict
ccfkllou
full-cock
ccfkloot
cockloft
ccfloooo
locofoco
ccghhiou
hiccough
ccghinou
couching
ccgiikln
clicking
ccgiilnr
circling
ccgilnoy
glyconic
cchhiinn
chin-chin
cchhinot
chthonic
cchhlruy
churchly
cchhnruu
unchurch
cchhoooo
choo-choo
cchhoopp
chop-chop
cchhooww
chow-chow
cchiinuz
zucchini
cchiiort
orchitic
cchiistu
Cushitic
cchikmpu
chipmuck
cchilmow
milch-cow
cchinoty
Tychonic
cchipssy
psychics
cchkoost
cockshot
cchkoptu
putchock
cchkostu
cockshut
cchlntuu
unclutch
cchnrsuy
scrunchy
cciikktt
tick-tick
cciiknpy
picnicky
cciillry
Cyrillic
cciimnsy
cynicism
cciinnsu
cicinnus
cciinorz
zirconic
cciirtuy
circuity
ccikklop
picklock
ccikkott
tick-tock
cciknopr
princock
ccikoprs
cropsick
ccillluu
Lucullic
ccillopp
clip-clop
cciloruu
curculio
ccilossy
cyclosis
ccimnsuu
succinum
ccinoprt
procinct
ccinopsy
syncopic
ccinorsy
cryonics
ccioopst
scotopic
ccirssuy
circussy
ccjnnotu
conjunct
cckklmuu
muckluck
cckkooor
rock-cook
cckkoorr
rock-cork
cckmmoru
crummock
cckmooor
moorcock
ccknortu
turncock
cckoopst
stop-cock
cckoprsu
cockspur
cclloopp
clop-clop
ccllotuy
occultly
cclmoopu
cocoplum
cclnooor
concolor
ccloorsu
occlusor
ccoooorr
corocoro
ccoossuu
couscous
ccoottuu
tucotuco
ccorsstu
crosscut
ccottuuu
tucutuco
ccrsuuuu
surucucu
cdddiiio
diddicoi
cdddioyy
diddycoy
cddeeefn
defenced
cddeeejt
dejected
cddeeent
decedent
cddeeilp
pedicled
cddeeirs
descried
cddeeknu
undecked
cddeekot
docketed
cddeekuw
duckweed
cddeelmo
co-meddle
cddeelsu
secluded
cddeelux
excluded
cddeeluy
deucedly
cddefiio
codified
cddeilnu
included
cddeknou
undocked
cddekosu
dock-dues
cddemnou
duncedom
cddghilo
godchild
cddghiot
ditch-dog
cddgilno
clodding
cddginsu
scudding
cddhilos
cloddish
cddhiryy
dyhydric
cddiisty
dytiscid
cddknopu
duck-pond
cddmmouu
mocuddum
cddooorw
cord-wood
cdeeegil
ice-ledge
cdeeehst
tedesche
cdeeeinv
evidence
cdeeeirv
deceiver
received
cdeeeknr
deer-neck
cdeeeknw
neckweed
cdeeellx
excelled
cdeeelos
cole-seed
cdeeelst
selected
cdeeennt
tendence
cdeeenrt
centered
cdeeeptx
expected
cdeeerrs
screeder
cdeeerss
recessed
cdeeffor
coffered
cdeefiil
ice-field
cdeefiit
feticide
cdeefklr
freckled
cdeefkor
foredeck
cdeefnnu
unfenced
cdeefors
frescoed
cdeefort
defector
cdeeghlo
dog-leech
cdeegiir
regicide
cdeegino
genocide
cdeeginr
receding
cdeegios
geodesic
cdeegiot
geodetic
cdeehiln
lichened
cdeehilp
cheliped
cdeehipr
decipher
cdeehist
tedeschi
cdeehitw
itchweed
cdeehlmo
leechdom
cdeehlsu
schedule
cdeehnrr
drencher
cdeehnuw
unchewed
cdeehrtw
wretched
cdeehssu
duchesse
cdeeiimn
medicine
cdeeiimp
epidemic
cdeeiint
indictee
cdeeiisv
decisive
cdeeiitt
dietetic
cdeeiklr
deer-lick
cdeeiknv
invecked
cdeeikpt
picketed
cdeeikrw
wickered
cdeeilnp
pendicle
cdeeilnr
reclined

cdeeilns
licensed
silenced
cdeeilnt
denticle
cdeeilnu
nucleide
cdeeilrs
sclereid
cdeeilrt
derelict
cdeeilsu
Seleucid
cdeeimnr
endermic
cdeeimor
mediocre
cdeeimpr
premedic
cdeeimrs
miscreed
cdeeimrv
decemvir
cdeeinnt
indecent
cdeeinps
dispence
cdeeintv
invected
cdeeiorv
divorcee
cdeeiprt
decrepit
depicter
cdeeipru
pedicure
cdeeirrt
redirect
cdeeirst
discreet
discrete
cdeekllw
well-deck
cdeeklps
speckled
cdeeknru
unrecked
cdeekopt
pocketed
cdeekorw
rockweed
cdeekost
socketed
cdeekrsu
suckered
cdeellpu
cupelled
cdeelnpu
peduncle
cdeelnty
decently
cdeeloow
loco-weed

cdeelorv
clovered
cdeelost
closeted
cdeelpru
preclude
cdeemort
ectoderm
cdeennos
condense
cdeennou
denounce
cdeennpy
pendency
cdeenntu
undecent
cdeennty
tendency
cdeenorr
cornered
cdeenors
seconder
seed-corn
cdeenort
centrode
cdeenotx
co-extend
cdeenovx
convexed
cdeenpru
prudence
cdeenruv
verecund
cdeensty
encysted
cdeeootv
dovecote
cdeeopps
speed-cop
cdeeorrr
recorder
cdeeorst
corseted
cdeeortt
detector
cdeeosst
cosseted
cdeeprst
sceptred
cdeerrru
recurred
cdeerruv
recurved
cdeertuv
curveted
cdefhill
elf-child
cdefhimo
chiefdom
cdefiiil
filicide
cdefiior
codifier

cdefiirt
drift-ice
cdefinno
confined
cdefinnu
infecund
cdefinor
confider
cdeflory
forcedly
cdefnoru
unforced
cdefnosu
confused
cdegiilo
Goidelic
cdegiino
Diogenic
cdeginru
reducing
cdeginry
decrying
cdeginsu
seducing
cdeginsy
dysgenic
cdegorsw
scrowdge
cdehiilo
helicoid
cdehiimo
homicide
cdehiino
echinoid
cdehikot
hock-tide
cdehikrw
herdwick
cdehilmr
merchild
cdehilnr
children
cdehilor
chloride
cdehilrt
eldritch
cdehimot
methodic
cdehinnr
indrench
cdehinos
hedonics
cdehioor
ochidore
cdehioty
theodicy
cdehistt
stitched
cdehklsu
shelduck
cdehloos
schooled
cdehmntu
Dutchmen

cdehoorr
rheocord
cdehorsu
chorused
cdehossu
hocussed
cdeiiils
silicide
cdeiiirv
viricide
cdeiiitv
viticide
cdeiikks
side-kick
cdeiikls
sicklied
cdeiikmm
mimicked
cdeiiknr
ciderkin
cdeiikrs
dricksie
cdeiilmo
domicile
cdeiilnn
inclined
cdeiilno
indocile
cdeiilot
idiolect
cdeiilps
disciple
cdeiilru
ridicule
cdeiimos
dioecism
cdeiimrt
dimetric
cdeiinnt
incident
cdeiinos
decision
cdeiinrt
indirect
cdeiiopr
periodic
cdeiiops
episodic
cdeiiopt
epidotic
cdeiirtu
diuretic
cdeiklnu
unlicked
cdeiklos
sidelock
cdeiklot
tide-lock
cdeiklwy
wickedly
cdeiknpu
unpicked
cdeikntu
tunicked

cdeikost
die-stock
cdeillou
lodicule
cdeillpu
pellucid
cdeilmop
complied
cdeilmos
melodics
cdeilmru
dulcimer
cdeilmsy
dysmelic
cdeilnry
cylinder
cdeiloow
woodlice
cdeilopu
clupeoid
cdeilors
scleroid
cdeilorv
coverlid
cdeiloss
disclose
cdeilrty
directly
cdeilsxy
dyslexic
cdeimnru
mind-cure
cdeimoow
woodmice
cdeimost
Docetism
domestic
cdeimprs
scrimped
cdeinnou
uncoined
cdeinnow
wind-cone
cdeinooz
endozoic
cdeinorr
cordiner
cdeinors
consider
cdeinort
centroid
doctrine
cdeinoru
decurion
cdeinost
deontics
cdeinotu
eduction
cdeinouv
unvoiced
cdeinprs
prescind
cdeinpru
unpriced

cdeinpsy
dyspneic
cdeinrru
incurred
cdeinruv
incurved
cdeinsty
syndetic
cdeioprt
depictor
cdeiopst
despotic
cdeiorrt
creditor
director
cdeiorrv
divorcer
cdeiorsv
discover
cdeiorsy
decisory
cdeiostt
Docetist
cdeiprsy
cyprides
cdeklmor
clerkdom
cdeklmru
mud-clerk
cdeklnou
unlocked
cdeklopu
uplocked
cdeklory
yeldrock
cdeknoou
uncooked
cdeknsuu
unsucked
cdekntuu
untucked
cdekoorv
rock-dove
cdellnuu
unculled
cdelloop
clodpole
cdellors
scrolled
cdelloru
colluder
cdellotu
cloudlet
cdelmnou
columned
cdelmpru
crumpled
cdelnoss
coldness
cdelnosu
unclosed
cdelnosy
secondly

cdelnouw
uncowled
cdelnruu
uncurled
cdelooru
coloured
decolour
cdelorss
cordless
cdelrsuy
cursedly
cdelrtuu
cultured
cdelsstu
ductless
cdemnoow
comedown
down-come
cdemnotu
document
cdemoops
composed
cdemostu
costumed
customed
cdennouy
uncoyned
cdenoort
creodont
cdenoost
secodont
cdenortu
cornuted
cdenrsuu
sun-cured
cdenrtuu
undercut
cdeoopst
Postcode
cdeoorsu
decorous
cdeoprru
producer
cdeorsst
doctress
cdeorstu
seductor
cdepruuv
upcurved
cdersttu
destruct
cdfiilsu
fluidics
cdfikors
disfrock
cdfkrsuu
surf-duck
cdfnnoou
confound
cdghiiln
childing
cdghkoos
shock-dog

cdgiklnu
duckling
cdgiklor
gridlock
cdgikort
dog-trick
cdgilnos
scolding
cdgilnou
clouding
cdhhiils
childish
cdhiiltw
twichild
cdhiioor
chorioid
cdhiiort
hidrotic
trichoid
cdhiiosz
schizoid
cdhiisst
distichs
cdhiloos
dolichos
cdhimosu
dochmius
cdhinnor
chondrin
cdhioort
trochoid
cdhioprw
whipcord
cdhiopry
hydropic
cdhiopsy
psychoid
cdhiorrt
trichord
cdhiosuv
disvouch
cdhkostu
duck-shot
cdhloopy
copyhold
cdhnorsu
chondrus
cdhoorru
urochord
cdiiiort
dioritic
cdiikpst
dip-stick
cdiiloty
docility
cdiiltuy
lucidity
cdiimnou
conidium
oncidium
cdiimors
Doricism
cdiinoos
isodicon

cdiinstt
distinct
cdiioors
soricoid
cdiioprt
dioptric
cdiiorsu
Dioscuri
sciuroid
cdiiptuy
cupidity
pudicity
cdiirstt
district
cdijnstu
disjunct
cdikknow
kickdown
cdikkopr
drop-kick
cdiklops
slip-dock
cdiklpuy
lucky-dip
cdiknosw
wind-sock
cdikootw
wood-tick
cdillotu
dulcitol
cdillouy
cloudily
cdiloort
lordotic
cdilooty
cotyloid
cdilosst
disclost
cdimoort
microdot
cdinnquu
quidnunc
cdinooor
coronoid
cdinorsw
discrown
cdinortu
inductor
cdinostu
discount
cdiooprs
prosodic
cdioorrr
corridor
cdioprsu
cuspidor
cdisstuy
Dytiscus
cdjlnouy
jocundly
cdkkmsuu
musk-duck
cdkloorw
cold-work

cdkmmoru
drummock
cdkooorw
corkwood
rock-wood
cdllloop
clodpoll
cdlnoosw
snow-cold
cdlnouuy
uncloudy
cdlootw
coltwood
cdloorsu
sour-cold
cdloorty
doctorly
cdloostu
outscold
cdloostw
Cotswold
cdmnoopu
compound
cdmnoruu
corundum
cdoorruy
corduroy
cdorssuw
cuss-word
cdorstuw
sword-cut
ceeeeipy
eye-piece
ceeeeprs
preceese
ceeeffir
effierce
ceeeffrt
effecter
ceeefinr
enfierce
ceeefnor
conferee
ceeeginx
exigence
ceeegitx
exegetic
ceeegmnr
mergence
ceeehist
ice-sheet
ceeehkor
Cherokee
ceeehlrv
cheverel
ceeehnnp
penneech
ceeehrss
secesher
ceeeijtv
ejective
ceeeilnn
lenience

ceeeilns
licensee
ceeeilnt
telecine
ceeeilrt
erectile
ceeeiltv
cleveite
elective
ceeeimnn
eminence
ceeeimpr
empierce
ceeeimrr
reremice
ceeeinnt
enceinte
ceeeinop
one-piece
ceeeinpr
piecener
ceeeinrs
ceresine
ceeeiopt
toe-piece
ceeeiprv
perceive
ceeeirrv
receiver
ceeeirsx
exercise
ceeeirtv
erective
ceeejrrt
rejecter
ceeeknnp
penneeck
ceeelprt
pre-elect
ceeelrst
reselect
ceeelrtt
electret
tercelet
ceeemnrt
cerement
ceeemrty
cemetery
ceeemsux
excuse-me
ceeennpt
tenpence
ceeennst
sentence
ceeenprs
presence
ceeenprt
pretence
ceeenqsu
sequence
ceeenrrs
screener
ceeenrrt
recentre

ceeeprtx
expecter
ceeerrsv
screever
ceeersst
sesterce
ceeertux
executer
ceeffort
effector
ceefhikr
kerchief
ceefhilr
Chelifer
ceefhiry
chiefery
ceefhiss
chiefess
ceefhist
chiefest
ceefhlrt
fletcher
ceefhlru
cheerful
ceefiint
inficete
ceefilry
fiercely
ceefinpp
fippence
ceefinrt
frenetic
ceefiprt
perfecti
ceefirty
free-city
ceefklss
feckless
ceeflllu
fuel-cell
ceeflnor
florence
ceeflntu
feculent
ceefnorr
confrère
renforce
ceefnrvy
fervency
ceefoprr
perforce
ceefoprt
perfecto
ceeforrs
frescoer
ceeforss
frescoes
ceeforst
cost-free
free-cost
scot-free
ceeggils
egg-slice

ceeghlow
cog-wheel
ceegilot
eclogite
ceegilrt
telergic
ceegilru
rice-glue
ceegimns
miscegen
ceeginor
erogenic
ceeginpr
creeping
ceeginrt
gentrice
ceeginst
genetics
ceeginsu
eugenics
ceeginxy
exigency
ceegknos
Geckones
ceegllmr
germ-cell
ceegllor
colleger
ceegmmor
commerge
ceegnnor
congener
ceegnnpu
pungence
ceegnoos
Congoese
ceegnort
congreet
co-regent
ceegnorv
Congreve
converge
ceegnoty
ectogeny
ceegnrvy
vergency
ceehhmnn
henchmen
ceehiist
ethicise
ceehikly
cheekily
ceehiknw
cheewink
ceehilln
chenille
Hellenic
ceehills
shell-ice
ceehillv
cheville
ceehilrv
cheveril

ceehilrw
clerihew
ceehilry
cheerily
ceehilsw
swelchie
ceehiltv
Helvetic
ceehimrt
hermetic
ceehinor
co-inhere
ceehinpr
encipher
ceehinst
sithence
ceehintt
enthetic
ceehiosu
ice-house
ceehiosv
cohesive
ceehiprt
herpetic
ceehirss
richesse
ceehirtu
heuretic
ceehklor
cork-heel
ceehkrst
sketcher
ceehkrtv
kvetcher
ceehllor
Rochelle
ceehlnoo
Holocene
ceehlnot
enclothe
ceehlnsu
elenchus
ceehlort
reclothe
ceehloss
echoless
ceehltuw
wheel-cut
ceehmort
comether
ceehnnow
nowhence
ceehnnrt
entrench
ceehnort
coherent
ceehnorv
cheveron
ceehnqru
quencher
ceehnrrt
retrench
trencher

ceehopry
coryphee
ceehoptt
pochette
ceehorrs
cosherer
ceehorrt
hectorer
torchère
ceehrttu
teuchter
ceeiimnp
mince-pie
ceeiimpr
epimeric
ceeiimrt
eremitic
ceeiinrt
icterine
ceeiinvv
evincive
ceeiirst
sericite
ceeijnot
ejection
ceeijorr
rejoicer
ceeijruv
verjuice
ceeiklnn
neckline
ceeiklpr
pickerel
ceeiknrs
sickener
ceeikprt
picketer
ceeilllp
pellicle
ceeillnt
lenticel
lenticle
ceeilmps
semplice
ceeilnny
leniency
ceeilnop
Pliocene
ceeilnot
coteline
election
ceeilnov
violence
ceeilnpt
Pentelic
ceeilnrr
recliner
ceeilnrs
licenser
silencer
ceeilnru
cerulein
ceeilnrv
vernicle

ceeiloss
solecise
ceeilqsu
liquesce
ceeilrst
sclerite
ceeilrsu
ciseleur
ciselure
ceeilrsv
versicle
ceeilrtu
reticule
ceeilrty
celerity
ceeilstt
telestic
testicle
ceeimmrs
mesmeric
ceeimnny
eminency
ceeimnps
specimen
ceeimort
meteoric
ceeinnop
pine-cone
ceeinnot
neotenic
ceeinnpz
pince-nez
ceeinnrs
incenser
ceeinnrt
incentre
ceeinnss
niceness
ceeinnst
nescient
ceeinort
erection
neoteric
ceeinorv
overnice
ceeinorx
exocrine
ceeinost
ice-stone
seicento
ceeinotv
evection
ceeinprt
prentice
ceeinpst
pectines
ceeinpsx
sixpence
ceeinrst
scienter
secretin
ceeinrsu
insecure
sinecure

ceeinrtt
reticent
ceeinrtu
enuretic
ceeinsst
centesis
ceeioppr
pericope
ceeiopps
episcope
ceeioptw
two-piece
ceeiorst
esoteric
ceeiorsx
exorcise
ceeiortt
erotetic
ceeiortx
exoteric
ceeiostv
covetise
ceeipprt
precepit
ceeipptu
eupeptic
ceeirrtu
ureteric
ceeirstu
cerusite
ceeirstv
vertices
ceeisuvx
excusive
ceejkott
jockette
ceejorrt
rejector
ceekknps
kenspeck
ceeklrss
clerkess
reckless
ceeknorr
reckoner
ceeknrsu
suckener
ceekoprx
ox-pecker
ceekorrt
cork-tree
rocketer
ceellmou
molecule
ceellnou
nucleole
ceellort
récollet
ceellrvy
cleverly
ceellssu
clueless
ceelmopt
complete

ceelmorw
welcomer
ceelmrtu
electrum
ceelnnop
penoncel
ceelnnot
non-elect
ceelnopu
opulence
ceelnors
encloser
ceelnort
electron
ceelnoru
encolure
ceelnptu
centuple
ceelnrtu
relucent
ceelnrty
recently
ceelnstu
esculent
ceelorss
coreless
sclerose
ceelorst
corselet
selector
ceelortv
coverlet
ceelrrtu
lecturer
ceelrsst
lectress
ceelrssu
cureless
ceelrsty
secretly
ceelrsuy
securely
ceemnorr
cremorne
ceemnorw
newcomer
ceemnory
ceremony
ceemnoyz
coenzyme
ceemoorv
overcome
ceemoorw
owrecome
ceennoos
nose-cone
ceennort
cretonne
ceennoru
renounce
ceennorv
convener
ceenoorv
once-over

ceenoptw
twopence
ceenorst
ten-score
ceenorsv
conserve
converse
ceenortt
trecento
ceenorvy
conveyer
reconvey
ceenpptu
tuppence
ceenrstu
unsecret
ceeoorst
creosote
ceeoprrt
receptor
ceeoprtx
exceptor
ceeoqttu
coquette
ceeorrrs
sorcerer
ceeorrsu
recourse
resource
ceeorrvy
recovery
ceeorttv
corvette
ceeortux
executor
ceeprrsu
precurse
ceerrsst
rectress
ceerrstu
rest-cure
ceerrtuz
creutzer
ceersstw
set-screw
ceertuxy
executry
ceffioru
coiffeur
coiffure
cefforu
forceful
cefflrsu
scuffler
cefghint
fetching
cefglnuy
fulgency
cefhiims
mischief
cefhilnr
flincher
cefhilrt
flichter
rich-left
cefhinsu
fuchsine
cefhistu
fuchsite
cefhlstu
chestful
cefiilst
felsitic
cefiilty
felicity
cefiiopr
opificer
cefiiprt
petrific
cefiirrt
ferritic
terrific
cefiklor
fire-lock
cefilllo
follicle
cefilmru
crimeful
merciful
cefilouv
voiceful
cefinnor
confiner
cefinors
forensic
forinsec
cefinort
ice-front
infector
cefinott
confetti
cefioprs
forcipes
cefiorty
ferocity
cefirstu
frutices
cefkllos
elflocks
cefkloor
forelock
cefklruw
wreckful
cefllosu
floscule
ceflnruu
furuncle
ceflnstu
scentful
cefoorst
soft-core
ceforstu
fructose
ceggiloo
geologic
ceggilrs
scriggle
cegginoo
geogonic
ceggiors
scroggie
cegglnoy
glycogen
ceghiiny
hygienic
ceghimns
scheming
ceghinpr
perching
ceghirtu
theurgic
ceghmruy
chemurgy
ceghnors
groschen
ceghoors
hog-score
ceghorsu
choregus
cegiiknv
vice-king
cegiilnt
gentilic
cegiilop
epilogic
cegiilos
logicise
cegiinnt
enticing
cegiinpr
piercing
cegiinss
gneissic
cegiintx
exciting
cegiiost
egoistic
cegijlou
log-juice
cegikkln
keckling
cegiklnr
reckling
cegiknrw
wrecking
cegilnoo
neologic
cegilnry
glycerin
cegilntu
cultigen
cegimnoy
myogenic
ceginnrt
centring
ceginnst
scenting
ceginnsy
ensigncy
ceginoop
geoponic
ceginoor
orogenic
ceginooz
zoogenic
ceginopy
pyogenic
ceginort
gerontic
ceginorv
covering
ceginotv
coveting
ceginrsu
rescuing
ceginrsw
screwing
ceginrsy
synergic
cegirstu
scutiger
cegllloou
collogue
ceglllory
glycerol
cegllryy
glyceryl
ceglnoty
cogently
ceglooty
cetology
cegmnnoo
cognomen
cegnnpuy
pungency
cegnooty
gonocyte
cegnorss
congress
cegnorsu
scrounge
cegnoryy
cryogeny
cegorrsu
scourger
scrouger
cehhhiow
heich-how
cehhinpy
hyphenic
cehhnoru
hurcheon
cehhopty
hypothec
cehiilmo
hemiolic
cehiilnn
lichenin
cehiilnt
lecithin
cehiilot
eolithic
cehiimop
hemiopic
cehiimos
isocheim
isochime
cehiimpt
mephitic
cehiimst
ethicism
cehiimtt
itch-mite
cehiinnn
nine-inch
cehiiopt
Ethiopic
cehiirst
Christie
cehiirtt
trichite
cehiistt
ethicist
theistic
cehiitvy
Vichyite
cehiklpt
klephtic
cehiklrs
clerkish
cehiklsu
suchlike
cehikmos
homesick
cehikstt
thickset
cehiktty
thickety
cehillrs
schiller
cehilmms
schimmel
cehilmtw
witch-elm
cehilmty
methylic
cehilnop
phenolic
pinochle
cehilnor
chlorine
cehilnpy
phenylic
cehilnss
chinless
cehilort
chlorite
clothier
cehilory
heroicly
cehilpty
phyletic
cehilstw
switchel
cehilsty
lecythis
cehiltty
tetchily
cehimnop
phonemic
cehimnow
chow-mein
cehimort
chromite
trichome
cehinoos
cohesion
cehinops
Echinops
cehinopt
phonetic
cehinopu
euphonic
cehinoru
unheroic
cehinosy
hyoscine
cehinoty
onychite
cehinpru
uncipher
cehinrss
richness
cehinrst
christen
snitcher
cehinrtu
ruthenic
cehioors
isochore
cehioprs
sopheric
cehiopru
euphoric
cehiopst
postiche
cehiorrt
rhetoric
cehiortt
trochite
cehiprss
spherics
cehiprst
spitcher
cehirstt
stitcher
cehirsty
hysteric
cehirttw
twitcher
cehirtwy
witchery
cehissuw
suchwise
cehkllos
skelloch
cehknorw
rock-hewn
cehkrstu
huckster

cehllmsu
schellum
cehllouy
louchely
cehlmnou
homuncle
cehlnnou
luncheon
cehlnotu
unclothe
cehlorsu
sloucher
cehlorty
hectorly
cehlostu
selcouth
cehlppsy
schleppy
cehlqsuy
squelchy
cehlstuy
Lecythus
cehmnssu
muchness
cehmoosz
schmooze
cehmoruv
overmuch
cehnnnou
nuncheon
cehnnopu
puncheon
cehnnosu
nonesuch
unchosen
cehnoors
schooner
cehnortu
hen-court
cehnorvy
chevrony
cehnsssu
suchness
cehnsttu
chestnut
cehooorz
zoochore
cehoorsu
ocherous
ochreous
cehoostu
cot-house
cehoosuw
cowhouse
cehoppry
prophecy
cehopsuy
chop-suey
cehorstu
scouther
cehorstw
scowther
cehottuz
zuchetto

cehrstty
stretchy
ceiiilsv
civilise
ceiiimnt
ciminite
ceiiinos
Ionicise
ceiiinss
sinicise
ceiiinsv
incisive
ceiijstu
Jesuitic
ceiiklmr
limerick
rice-milk
ceiiklnr
licker-in
ceiikmmr
mimicker
ceiiknss
kinesics
ceiiknst
kinetics
ceiiksst
ekistics
ceiillmt
mellitic
ceiillpt
elliptic
ceiillsu
silicule
ceiilmnt
limnetic
ceiilmot
cimolite
ceiilnos
isocline
silicone
ceiilnqu
clinique
ceiilnss
enclisis
ceiilopp
epiploic
epipolic
ceiilort
elicitor
ceiilost
Siceliot
ceiilotz
zeolitic
ceiilprt
perlitic
ceiilpru
pirlicue
ceiilptx
explicit
ceiilpty
pyelitic
ceiilrtv
verticil

ceiilsss
scissile
ceiimnot
emiction
ceiimopt
epitomic
ceiimors
isomeric
ceiimost
semiotic
ceiimrrt
trimeric
ceiimrst
meristic
trisemic
ceiimsst
Semitics
ceiinnop
nepionic
ceiinnor
irenicon
ceiinnos
oscinine
ceiinnot
nicotine
ceiinnrt
intrince
ceiinnst
inscient
ceiinops
epinosic
ceiinopt
epitonic
ceiinors
recision
soricine
ceiinosx
excision
ceiinotv
eviction
ceiinrsu
incisure
sciurine
ceiinrtu
neuritic
ceiinstu
cutinise
ceiinsty
cytisine
syenitic
ceiioprs
iriscope
ceiioprt
periotic
ceiioptt
picotite
ceiiostv
sovietic
ceiiqrtu
critique
ceiirstt
rectitis
ceiirstv
veristic

ceiistvv
vivisect
ceijnort
injector
ceijnouv
cunjevoi
ceijrstu
justicer
ceikknrs
knickers
ceiklnps
spicknel
ceiklosv
lovesick
ceiklrst
stickler
strickle
ceiklrsy
sickerly
ceiklrtt
tricklet
ceikmnor
monicker
ceikmopt
impocket
ceikmppu
pick-me-up
ceikmrsu
musicker
ceiknnsu
insucken
ceiknrst
stricken
ceiknrsu
unsicker
ceiknsss
sickness
ceikqstu
quickset
ceikrrty
trickery
ceikrtty
ricketty
ceillloy
ice-lolly
ceillnou
nucleoli
ceillops
pollices
ceillors
orsellic
ceillory
colliery
ceillotu
coutille
ceillrtu
telluric
ceilmmuy
mycelium
ceilmnop
compline
ceilmnot
monticle

ceilmopr
compiler
complier
ceilmops
polemics
ceilmoss
solecism
ceilmosu
coliseum
ceilmpuu
peculium
ceilmtuu
lutecium
ceilnnot
contline
ceilnnsy
syncline
ceilnoos
colonise
eclosion
ceilnopr
percolin
ceilnors
incloser
licensor
ceilnpry
princely
ceilnrtu
lincture
ceilnruv
culverin
ceilnsuu
unsluice
ceiloprt
petrolic
ceiloprv
proclive
ceiloptu
epulotic
poultice
ceilopty
epicotyl
ceilorst
cloister
coistrel
ceilorty
cryolite
ceilosst
solecist
solstice
ceilossu
coulisse
ceilotvy
velocity
ceilprsu
surplice
ceilpruu
purlicue
ceilrrsu
scurrile
ceimmnou
encomium
meconium

ceimmort
recommit
ceimmrsy
merycism
ceimnnoo
encomion
ceimnnoy
neomycin
ceimnors
sermonic
ceimnort
intercom
ceimnpsu
music-pen
ceimnrst
centrism
ceimnssu
meniscus
ceimoosz
Mesozoic
ceimoouz
zooecium
ceimoprs
comprise
ceimorsx
exorcism
ceimorsy
isocryme
ceimorty
emictory
ceimosss
cosmesis
ceimrrsu
scrimure
ceimrrtu
turmeric
ceimssty
systemic
ceinnnot
innocent
ceinnnou
inconnue
ceinnors
incensor
ceinnorv
conniver
ceinnotu
continue
ceinnotw
Newtonic
ceinootz
entozoic
enzootic
ceinoppr
cornpipe
ceinoprs
conspire
incorpse
ceinoprt
inceptor
ceinoprv
province
ceinoptt
entoptic

ceinoptu
unpoetic
ceinorrs
resorcin
ceinorrt
tricorne
ceinorss
necrosis
ceinortt
contrite
ceinortu
neurotic
ceinortv
contrive
ceinosss
cosiness
ceinossx
coxiness
ceinostt
centoist
ceinosty
cytosine
ceinottu
Teutonic
ceinprss
princess
ceinrstt
centrist
ceinrsvv
crivvens
ceinrttu
intercut
tincture
ceiooptv
co-optive
ceiootuv
outvoice
ceioppsy
episcopy
ceioprru
croupier
ceioprst
persicot
ceioprsu
precious
rice-soup
ceioprtu
eutropic
ceioprty
Cypriote
ceiopssu
specious
ceiorrtu
courtier
ceiorruz
cruzeiro
ceiorsst
cross-tie
ceiorssx
sixscore
ceiorstu
citreous
ceiorstv
vortices

ceiorstx
exorcist
ceiorttu
toreutic
ceiprrst
rescript
ceiprstu
crepitus
piecrust
ceirrrsu
scurrier
ceirrstt
restrict
ceirsssu
scissure
ceirsstv
victress
ceirstuy
security
cejlmouu
Leucojum
cejloosy
jocosely
cejnorru
conjurer
cejnrtuu
juncture
cekllnor
roll-neck
ceklloov
lovelock
cekllssu
luckless
ceklnost
stenlock
cekloors
cork-sole
ceklopst
lockstep
ceklrssu
sucklers
ceknopst
penstock
ceknortu
cokernut
ceknostu
unsocket
cekoorrs
rock-rose
cekoorrw
co-worker
cekoprst
sprocket
cekorrty
rocketry
cellnsuu
nucellus
cellntuu
luculent
cellooqu
colloque
cellossy
cloyless

cellrsuy
scullery
celmnoty
cloyment
celmnouy
uncomely
celmntuu
muculent
celmooot
locomote
celmoosy
cloysome
celmopsy
symploce
celmosuu
cumulose
celmprtu
plectrum
celmpsuu
speculum
celnnoty
nocently
celnnouv
uncloven
celnoors
consoler
celnooru
encolour
celnooss
coolness
celnoovv
convolve
celnoprt
plectron
celnopuu
uncouple
celnortw
crownlet
celnorwy
clownery
celnosuv
convulse
celnosvy
solvency
celnovxy
convexly
celnptuu
punctule
celooorv
over-cool
celoopss
cesspool
celoortw
cole-wort
celoorvy
overcloy
celopssu
Scopelus
celopsuu
opuscule
celopttu
octuplet
celorsst
crosslet

celorssu
sclerous
celorsty
coystrel
celorsuu
ulcerous
urceolus
celorsuy
crousely
celorttu
courtlet
celortvy
covertly
celosttu
culottes
celprrsu
scrupler
celprsuy
sprucely
celrsttu
scuttler
celrstuy
clustery
cemmnoor
commoner
cemmnoos
consommé
cemmnooy
commoney
cemmortu
commuter
cemnoorr
cromorne
cemnoptt
contempt
cemnorsu
consumer
cemooprs
composer
cemoorst
Rome-scot
cemoorsy
sycomore
cemoprss
compress
cemoprtu
computer
cemorstu
costumer
customer
cemprstu
spectrum
cennoopr
corn-pone
cennoorv
convenor
cennorrt
corn-rent
cennortu
nocturne
cenoootz
ectozoon
cenoopst
scoop-net

cenoorsu
corneous
cenoortt
cornetto
cenoorvy
conveyor
cenoprsy
necropsy
cenoqstu
conquest
cenorrtu
trouncer
cenorstu
construe
cenorsuu
cernuous
cenorsuy
cynosure
cenortvy
Coventry
cenosstu
countess
cenprtuu
puncture
cenrsstu
curtness
ceooopst
otoscope
ceooprrv
overcrop
ceoorrvw
overcrow
ceoorstw
two-score
ceoostuv
covetous
ceopprst
prospect
ceoprrru
procurer
ceoprstw
screwtop
ceoprsuu
cupreous
ceoqrtuy
coquetry
ceorrssu
cursores
ceorstuy
courtesy
ceprstuu
cutpurse
cerssuux
excursus
cffginos
scoffing
cffirtuy
fructify
cfghiiln
filching
cfgiknor
frocking
cfginort
crofting

cfginosu
focusing
cfhiinoo
finochio
cfhiiorr
horrific
cfhikors
rock-fish
cfhimoss
scomfish
cfhimssu
scumfish
cfhlopuu
pouchful
cfiiilsy
silicify
cfiiknyz
zinckify
cfiilopr
prolific
cfiilpsu
pulsific
cfiimnos
somnific
cfiimort
mortific
cfiinopt
pontific
cfiinort
friction
cfiisstu
Sufistic
cfiklstu
stickful
cfikpstu
puckfist
cfilmoor
coliform
cfimnoor
coniform
cfimnoru
unciform
cfinnotu
function
cfiostty
Scottify
cfkkloor
folkrock
cflnoort
cornloft
cflnorsu
scornful
cfloopsu
scoopful
cfloprsu
cropfuls
cfnnoort
confront
cfooortw
crowfoot
cfrstuuu
usufruct
cggghinu
chugging

cgghinou
coughing
cggiinnr
cringing
cggilrsy
scriggly
cghiilln
chilling
cghiinnp
pinching
cghiinpp
chipping
cghiinpr
chirping
cghiinpt
pitching
cghiintw
witching
cghiknos
shocking
cghiknsu
shucking
cghilnot
clothing
cghimpsy
sphygmic
cghinnot
notching
cghinnru
churning
cghinopp
chopping
cghinosu
hocusing
cghinotu
touching
cghinptu
pinchgut
cghinrsu
crushing
cghloost
shot-clog
cghnoosu
souchong
cgiiilnt
lignitic
cgiiklnn
clinking
cgiiklns
slicking
cgiiklnt
tickling
cgiikmmy
gimmicky
cgiiknnz
zincking
cgiiknpr
pricking
cgiiknrt
tricking
cgiiknst
sticking
cgiilnpp
clipping

cgiilost
logistic
cgiilrtu
liturgic
cgiimnno
incoming
cgiinoos
isogonic
cgiinort
trigonic
cgikknno
knocking
cgiklnor
rockling
cgiklnsu
suckling
cgikmnos
smocking
cgiknorw
corkwing
king-crow
cgiknost
stocking
cgiknrtu
trucking
cgiknstu
gunstick
cgillnsu
sculling
cgillnuy
cullying
cgilmnoo
Mongolic
cgilmnpu
clumping
cgilmnsu
muscling
cgilmnuu
cingulum
glucinum
cgilnnow
clowning
cgilnooy
cooingly
cgilnopu
coupling
cgilnosw
scowling
cgilnott
clotting
cgilooru
urologic
cgilpsty
glyptics
cgimmnsu
scumming
cgimnnoo
gnomonic
oncoming
cgimrruy
micrurgy
cginnoor
crooning

cginnors
scorning
cginnorw
crowning
cginoops
scooping
cginootv
cognovit
cginoppr
cropping
cginorss
crossing
cginorsu
coursing
scouring
cginortu
courting
cginostu
scouting
cginrruy
currying
cginsttu
tungstic
cginstuu
Tungusic
cgknostu
gunstock
cglmooyy
mycology
cglnoooy
oncology
cgloooty
tocology
cglootyy
cytology
cgmnnoor
mongcorn
cgmnnoru
mungcorn
cgnnooos
coon-song
chhiikst
thickish
chhiilty
hitchily
chhiinpt
pinch-hit
chhiipst
phthisic
chhilrsu
churlish
chhimrty
rhythmic
chhiopst
chip-shot
chhnorsu
rhonchus
chhooptt
hotchpot
chiiklst
ticklish
chiikrst
trickish

chiikstu
Kushitic
chiillly
chillily
chiilmsy
hylicism
chiilnnp
linchpin
chiilost
holistic
chiilpry
chirpily
chiilqsu
cliquish
chiilsty
hylicist
chiimpru
pichurim
chiinops
siphonic
chiinort
ornithic
chiiorss
chorisis
chiiorst
historic
orchitis
chiippru
hippuric
chiirstt
tristich
chiklloy
hillocky
chikloop
clip-hook
chiklsty
kitschly
chikmnpu
chipmunk
chikmntu
mutchkin
chiknnop
phinnock
chikopst
tick-shop
chikopty
kyphotic
chikorst
trochisk
chikosst
stockish
chikpsyy
physicky
chilloot
oilcloth
chilmosu
scholium
chilnoos
scholion
chilnosw
clownish
chilooz
holozoic

chiloopt
holoptic
chilosyy
coyishly
chilotuy
touchily
chilrsty
Christly
chimmoru
chromium
chimnoor
hormonic
chimnorw
inch-worm
chimnosu
insomuch
chimorst
christom
chimpssy
psychism
chinoort
orthicon
chinopty
hypnotic
pythonic
typhonic
chinortu
cothurni
chinostz
schizont
chinosuy
cushiony
chinsttu
unstitch
chiooppt
photopic
chioorsu
ichorous
chioortt
orthotic
chioprst
strophic
chiopsty
hypocist
chiorsss
crossish
chiosstt
Scottish
chiprruy
chirrupy
chiprtty
triptych
chipssty
psychist
chirrssu
scirrhus
chkmmouy
hummocky
chknorsu
cornhusk
chkooops
cookshop
chkooppr
pork-chop

chkopstu
tuck-shop
chlnooop
colophon
chlnoruw
churn-owl
chloorsu
chlorous
chlopsty
splotchy
chlortuy
choultry
chmnoort
corn-moth
chmnorru
crumhorn
chmnorsu
Rumonsch
chmnpruu
rum-punch
chnooptt
top-notch
chooorty
choy-root
choooryz
zoochory
chorsttu
shortcut
ciiikntu
cuitikin
ciiilmpt
implicit
ciiilmsu
silicium
ciiilpst
spilitic
ciiilstv
civilist
ciiiltvy
civility
ciiimnss
Sinicism
ciiimnsv
incivism
ciiinnos
incision
ciiintvy
vicinity
ciijrstu
juristic
ciikksst
ski-stick
ciikllsy
sicklily
ciiklopt
politick
ciiklpst
lipstick
ciiklrty
trickily
ciiklsst
sick-list
ciiklsty
stickily

ciiknoot
cootikin
ciiknors
iron-sick
ciiknppr
pin-prick
ciillnop
pollinic
ciilmnot
Miltonic
ciilmopy
impolicy
ciilmoss
sciolism
ciilmqsu
cliquism
ciilmrsy
lyricism
ciilnoot
Noctilio
ciiloopt
politico
ciilootz
zoolitic
ciiloppt
poplitic
ciilopst
politics
psilotic
ciilorst
clitoris
coistril
ciilosst
sciolist
ciilosty
solicity
ciilosvv
slivovic
ciilrtuu
utriculi
ciimnoos
isonomic
ciimnost
monistic
nomistic
ciimorst
trisomic
ciimosst
stoicism
ciimosty
myositic
ciimrsty
myristic
ciimrttu
Triticum
ciinnstt
instinct
ciinoost
isotonic
ciinootz
zoonitic
ciinopsu
opinicus

ciinosss
scission
ciinotty
tonicity
ciinpstu
sinciput
ciioopst
isotopic
ciioprst
poristic
ciioqtux
quixotic
ciiorrww
wirricow
ciiottxy
toxicity
ciiprrtu
pruritic
ciiprstu
puristic
ciirsttu
truistic
ciisstty
cystitis
cijkosty
joy-stick
cijnnoot
conjoint
cijnnotu
junction
cijoosty
jocosity
cikllmtu
tuck-mill
cikllopr
killcrop
cikllpuy
pluckily
ciklnost
linstock
ciklossu
soul-sick
ciklosty
stockily
ciklrssu
kiss-curl
cikmopst
mopstick
ciknorst
corn-kist
cikopstt
pot-stick
cikosstt
stockist
cillmnor
corn-mill
cillmsuy
clumsily
cullysim
cillnoot
cotillon
cillnors
inscroll

cillnosu
scullion
cilloopw
wool-clip
cilmnopu
pulmonic
cilmnouu
inoculum
cilmnuuv
vinculum
cilmopsy
olympics
cilmorux
microlux
cilmprsy
scrimply
cilmpsuu
spiculum
cilnooru
unicolor
cilnoost
colonist
cilnootu
locution
cilnoptu
plutonic
cilnosuy
cousinly
cilnpstu
insculpt
cilooptw
cow-pilot
ciloopyz
polyzoic
ciloorrt
tricolor
ciloorst
cortisol
ciloossu
sciolous
cilopPry
propylic
cilorsty
coystril
cilossty
systolic
cilossuu
luscious
cilprstu
spit-curl
cilpsstu
sculpsit
cilrstty
strictly
cilrstuy
crustily
cilrsuvy
scurvily
cimnoooz
zoonomic
cimnooru
coronium
cimnoprt
comprint

cimnostu
miscount
cimnosuy
syconium
cimoootz
zootomic
cimoppsu
pop-music
cimostuu
muticous
cimostuy
mucosity
cinnooss
scoinson
cinnoost
scontion
cinnootu
continuo
cinnosty
syntonic
cinnquux
quincunx
cinooopt
co-option
cinooprs
scorpion
cinooprt
protonic
cinoosuv
covinous
cinootxy
oxytocin
cinopsty
synoptic
cinorstt
contrist
cinorsuy
cousinry
cinostuv
viscount
cinprsuy
Cyprinus
cinrsttu
instruct
cinrstuy
scrutiny
ciooptyz
zootypic
cioorrww
worricow
cioorssu
scorious
cioprssu
Scorpius
ciorrstu
cursitor
ciorssss
scissors
cipprruu
purpuric
cjnoorru
conjuror
cjooorsu
jocorous

cjrsuuuu
sucurujú
ckknootu
knockout
ckkoorrw
rock-work
cklmmosu
slummock
ckmmoruw
muck-worm
ckmoooor
cookroom
cknnoost
non-stock
cknrstuu
unstruck
ckoopstt
stock-pot
ckosstuy
tussocky
clllоopt
clotpoll
cllooquy
colloquy
clmmnooy
commonly
clmmooos
Comsomol
clmoooty
colotomy
clnooowy
cony-wool
clnostuy
uncostly
cloooprt
protocol
cloortuy
locutory
cloosssu
colossus
cloosstu
soul-scot
cloprssy
cross-ply
cloprstu
sculptor
clopsstu
cost-plus
closstuy
Scolytus
clrssuuu
surculus
cmmnnoou
uncommon
cmnoorrw
cornworm
cmnopstu
consumpt
cmooprss
moss-crop
cnnooort
contorno
cnnoorsw
corn-snow

cnoooort
octoroon
cnoorrty
cryotron
cnoorstu
outscorn
cnoottuu
count-out
cnostuuu
unctuous
coooprrt
root-crop
cooopsyz
zooscopy
cooprsuu
croupous
cooprsuy
uroscopy
coorrssw
cross-row
coorrwwy
worrycow
coorsstu
outcross
coorttyz
trot-cozy
ddddeeor
doddered
dddeeefn
defended
dddeeenu
undeeded
dddeeepy
deep-dyed
dddeehrs
shredded
dddeenor
reddendo
dddeenuw
unwedded
dddeeorr
dodderer
dddeiinv
dividend
dddeilnu
unlidded
dddeimos
dismoded
dddeinor
dendroid
dddeinru
underdid
dddiioor
doridoid
ddeeeflx
deflexed
ddeeefnr
defender
ddeeefrr
deferred
ddeeehnu
unheeded
ddeeeimr
remedied

ddeeeiwy
wide-eyed
ddeeelss
deedless
ddeeemnt
demented
ddeeemrs
demersed
ddeeennu
unneeded
ddeeenrz
Enzedder
ddeeensu
unseeded
ddeeentx
extended
ddeeenuw
unweeded
ddeeeovy
dove-eyed
ddeeerrt
deterred
ddeeersv
deserved
ddeeewyy
dewy-eyed
ddeefgit
fidgeted
ddeefilw
field-dew
ddeefinr
friended
ddeefinu
undefied
ddeefipr
drip-feed
ddeefmor
deformed
ddeefnru
underfed
ddeeforr
fodderer
ddeeghnu
unhedged
ddeeginr
enridged
ddeegops
godspeed
ddeegotw
two-edged
ddeehrrs
shredder
ddeeiijm
Medjidie
ddeeiint
inedited
ddeeiirv
redivide
ddeeillv
devilled
ddeeilly
ill-deedy
ddeeilrw
wildered

ddeeinnt
indented
intended
ddeeinos
one-sided
ddeeinrt
dendrite
ddeeintu
unedited
ddeeiprv
deprived
ddeellmo
modelled
ddeelluy
dull-eyed
ddeelopx
exploded
ddeemnor
endoderm
ddeemrru
demurred
ddeennoy
endodyne
ddeenntu
untended
ddeenopr
perdendo
ddeenopw
pondweed
ddeenorr
reed-rond
ddeenors
endorsed
ddeenorw
wondered
ddeenrsu
sundered
ddeeoprw
powdered
ddeerruv
verdured
ddeffisu
diffused
ddefiilm
midfield
ddefiimo
modified
ddefiimw
midwifed
ddeflnou
unfolded
ddeflruu
udderful
ddefnnuu
unfunded
ddeggloy
doggedly
ddeggnoo
doggoned
ddeghins
shedding
ddegilmn
meddling

ddegilnp
peddling
ddegilns
sledding
ddegilnu
ungilded
ddegilos
dislodge
ddegilry
gliddery
ddeginor
der-doing
ddeginru
ungirded
ddeginuu
unguided
ddegiort
dog-tired
ddeglnos
gold-ends
ddegnoru
grounded
underdog
ddegooor
do-gooder
ddegooww
Wedgwood
ddegrruy
drudgery
ddehiiss
side-dish
ddehilny
hiddenly
ddehiloo
idlehood
ddehinnu
unhidden
ddehinor
dihedron
ddehnoou
unhooded
ddehoosw
woodshed
ddehoowy
how-d'ye-do
ddehorsu
shrouded
ddehrsuy
shuddery
ddeiikny
dinky-die
ddeiimvw
midwived
ddeiinsw
side-wind
wind-side
ddeiiops
diopside
ddeilmov
devildom
ddeilnps
splendid
ddeilnru
unriddle

ddeilops
displode
lop-sided
ddeilosy
dysodile
ddeilqru
quiddler
ddeilrst
striddle
ddeilrsy
sliddery
ddeilrtw
twiddler
ddeimmnu
undimmed
ddeimnnu
unminded
ddeimnuv
videndum
ddeimosu
medusoid
ddeimrsu
side-drum
ddeinnru
unridden
ddeinntu
undinted
ddeinorw
wind-rode
ddeinosw
disendow
ddeinoww
windowed
ddeinppu
undipped
ddeinrst
stridden
ddeinrsu
sun-dried
ddeinruv
dun-diver
ddeioors
side-door
ddeioprs
dropsied
ddeioprv
provided
ddeiopss
disposed
ddeiorrs
disorder
ddeiostw
two-sided
ddeirssu
Druidess
ddeirstu
ruddiest
sturdied
ddellnuu
undulled
ddelnoru
unlorded
ddelnsuy
suddenly

ddeloorw
dowel-rod
ddeloowy
wool-dyed
ddelorst
stroddle
ddelosyy
dysodyle
ddemnoou
undoomed
ddemnouu
duodenum
ddemnpuu
pudendum
ddemootu
outmoded
ddennosu
unsodden
ddenoouw
unwooded
ddenoruw
unworded
ddenstuy
suddenty
ddeoorww
rowdedow
ddfgiiln
fiddling
ddfgilnu
fuddling
ddfiiosu
fiddious
ddfmnouu
dumfound
ddgginno
ding-dong
ddgiiinv
dividing
ddgiilmn
middling
ddgiilnp
piddling
ddgiilnr
riddling
ddgilnop
plodding
ddgilnot
toddling
ddgilnpu
puddling
ddgimnuy
muddying
ddgimrsu
drudgism
ddginopr
prodding
ddginpuy
puddingy
ddginruy
ruddying
ddginstu
studding
ddglostu
gold-dust

ddgoorsy
dry-goods
ddhilosy
shoddily
ddhioswy
dowdyish
ddhllooo
dollhood
ddiiiivv
dividivi
ddiilopy
diploidy
ddiimmuy
didymium
ddiimrsu
druidism
ddiiqtuy
quiddity
ddilooww
wild-wood
ddilorsy
sordidly
ddimosuy
didymous
ddimoswy
dowdyism
ddinnoww
downwind
ddinooot
odontoid
ddinooww
woodwind
ddlloorw
old-world
world-old
ddlmorsu
doldrums
ddmnooty
tom-noddy
ddnoortw
down-trod
ddoorwwy
rowdydow
deeeefrr
free-reed
deeeefrz
defreeze
deeeegkr
kedgeree
deeeeknp
knee-deep
deeeemms
meseemed
deeeemrr
redeemer
deeeemst
esteemed
deeefgir
fire-edge
deeefgor
fore-edge
deeefinr
need-fire

deeefipp
feed-pipe
deeefirw
fireweed
deeefiry
fire-eyed
deeefllr
refelled
deeeflpt
deep-felt
deeeflrx
reflexed
deeefnrs
fern-seed
deeefnrt
deferent
deeefnst
enfested
deeeforv
overfeed
deeefrrr
deferrer
referred
deeefrrt
ferreted
deeegipr
pedigree
deeegisw
edgewise
deeeglss
edgeless
deeeglsv
selvedge
deeegnnr
engender
deeegryy
grey-eyed
deeehkps
sheep-ked
deeehlmt
helmeted
deeehlno
dene-hole
deeehlrw
wheedler
deeehlss
heedless
deeehmps
hemp-seed
deeeikls
seed-like
deeeilns
selenide
deeeiltv
deletive
deeeilvw
weeviled
deeeimst
seed-time
deeeinrr
reindeer
deeeintv
eventide
deeeippr
reed-pipe
deeeiptx
expedite
deeeirss
diereses
deeejllw
jewelled
deeekopw
pokeweed
deeelllv
levelled
deeellnt
dentelle
deeellnw
newelled
deeellpr
repelled
deeellpx
expelled
deeellrv
revelled
deeelmos
somedele
deeelmoy
mole-eyed
deeelmru
mule-deer
deeelnpu
unpeeled
deeelnss
needless
seldseen
deeelosy
sloe-eyed
deeelpst
steepled
deeelrss
redeless
deeelrtt
lettered
deeelrtu
dule-tree
deeelsss
seedless
deeelssw
weedless
deeeltvv
velveted
deeemnnt
needment
deeemprt
tempered
deeemrst
deemster
deeennrt
entender
deeennrv
nerve-end
deeennuw
unweened
deeenopy
open-eyed
deeenors
endorsee
deeenprt
repetend
deeenpru
unpeered
deeenprx
expender
deeenpss
deepness
deeenrrr
renderer
deeenrrt
tenderer
deeenrrv
reverend
deeenrrw
reed-wren
deeenrtx
extender
deeenruv
revenued
deeensss
seedness
deeensuv
vendeuse
deeeoprr
pederero
deeeoprt
deportee
deeeosty
seedy-toe
deeerrrv
verderer
deeerrst
deserter
deeerrsv
reserved
reversed
deeerrtv
reverted
deeerstt
streeted
deeerstx
exserted
deeerttv
revetted
deeesttu
suedette
deeffglu
effulged
deeffint
infefted
deeffnor
offender
reoffend
deefginr
fingered
deefgluw
gulfweed
deefhiss
seed-fish
deefhlor
freehold
deefhlrs
feldsher
deefhorr
Hereford
deefiiln
fedelini
deefiint
definite
deefiirs
fireside
deefiirv
verified
deefillt
filleted
deefilnx
inflexed
deefilwx
flix-weed
deefimtu
tumefied
deefinrr
inferred
deefinrz
frenzied
deefiors
foreside
deefllnu
unfelled
deeflluy
full-eyed
deeflnor
forelend
deeflntu
defluent
deeflorw
deflower
flowered
deeflpsu
speedful
deefmorr
deformer
reformed
deefmppu
feed-pump
deefmpru
perfumed
deefnrru
refunder
deefnsst
deftness
deeforst
deforest
forested
deefrtuy
duty-free
deegghho
hedgehog
deegghip
hedgepig
deeggijr
jiggered
deegglor
doggerel
deeggnor
engorged
deeghhop
hedge-hop
deeghops
sheepdog
deeghorw
hedgerow
deegiinn
indigene
deegiiss
diegesis
deegilmo
liegedom
deegilmp
impledge
deegilno
legioned
deegilnr
engirdle
reedling
deegilns
seedling
deegilrw
weregild
deegilry
greedily
deegimru
demiurge
deeginps
speeding
deeginrs
designer
redesign
resigned
deeginss
edginess
deeginst
signeted
deegirst
digester
Erdgeist
estridge
deegirsu
gudesire
deegjpru
prejudge
deegkmor
Greekdom
deeglnou
engouled
deeglnoz
lozenged
deeglnru
elder-gun
deeglnry
legendry
deeglopr
pledgeor
deeglops
dog-sleep
deegmnru
dungmere
deegnnoy
endogeny
deegnoov
good-even
deegotuw
goutweed
deehhprs
shepherd
deehilns
enshield
deehilrs
shielder
deehilsv
dishevel
she-devil
deehinrr
hinderer
deehinst
disthene
deehipps
sheep-dip
deehiprs
hesperid
perished
shred-pie
deehirrs
redshire
deehirrt
ditherer
deehirsv
shrieved
deehirtw
withered
deehirty
heredity
deehknos
keeshond
deehknsu
skene-dhu
deehlmnu
unhelmed
deehlnpu
unhelped
deehnorr
deer-horn
dehorner
deehnort
dethrone
threnode
deehnowy
honey-dew
deehopss
seed-shop
deehorrt
dehorter
deehorsu
rose-hued
shore-due
deehosuy
dye-house
deeiilns
side-line
deeiilrv
liveried

deeiimrs
dimerise
deeiinsx
endeixis
deeiiprs
Pierides
deeiipru
prie-dieu
deeiirss
dieresis
deeiirst
siderite
deeiirsv
derisive
deeiisss
disseise
deeiissw
sidewise
deeiissz
disseize
deeiisvw
side-view
deeijrtv
jet-drive
deeikllr
killdeer
deeiklmw
milk-weed
deeiklnn
enkindle
deeiklnr
rekindle
deeiklov
dovelike
deeiknps
skin-deep
deeiknpy
pink-eyed
deeiknrs
deerskin
deeikstt
diskette
deeillmp
impelled
milleped
deeillno
nielloed
deeillor
orielled
deeillpr
perilled
deeillrt
tredille
deeillrv
rivelled
deeilmnu
demi-lune
deeilmos
melodise
deeilnot
deletion
deeilnru
underlie

deeilnss
idleness
deeilnst
lintseed
deeilnuv
unveiled
deeilopt
lepidote
petioled
deeilort
dolerite
deeilorv
evil-doer
deeilott
toileted
deeilpsy
speedily
deeilrsu
leisured
deeilrsv
desilver
deeilrtt
littered
deeilrvy
delivery
deeilsst
tideless
deeilssv
deviless
deeilsuv
delusive
deeiltuy
yuletide
deeimmns
endemism
deeimmos
semi-dome
deeimmrs
immersed
deeimnor
domineer
deeimnos
demonise
deeimnpt
pediment
deeimnrr
reminder
deeimnrv
vermined
deeimnst
sediment
deeimnsu
semi-nude
deeimntt
mittened
deeimost
tedisome
deeimprr
periderm
deeimprs
premised
deeimrst
demister

deeimrtt
remitted
deeinnrt
indenter
intender
deeinnru
unreined
deeinnst
desinent
deeinnuv
unenvied
deeinops
disponee
deeinopw
wide-open
deeinort
oriented
deeinost
side-note
deeinosv
nose-dive
deeinpss
dispense
piedness
deeinpsu
unespied
deeinrrt
interred
deeinrst
inserted
resident
deeinrsu
uredines
deeinrtv
inverted
deeinrtw
wintered
deeinrtx
dextrine
deeinssw
dewiness
wideness
deeinsuz
unseized
deeinuvw
unviewed
deeioprt
peridote
deeioprx
peroxide
deeiorrv
override
deeiorsv
overside
deeiotvx
videotex
deeippqu
equipped
deeiprss
despiser
disperse
deeipsst
side-step

deeipstu
deputise
deeiqrru
required
deeiqrtu
requited
deeiqruv
quivered
deeiqtuu
quietude
deeirrst
destrier
deeirrtv
verditer
deeirsst
dress-tie
editress
deeirssv
disserve
dissever
deeirttv
rivetted
deejkntu
junketed
deejprru
perjured
deekmrsu
musk-deer
deeknnnu
unkenned
deeknotw
knotweed
deekooty
yoke-toed
deellmor
modeller
deellnor
enrolled
deellorw
rowelled
well-doer
deellory
yodeller
deellotw
towelled
deellotx
extolled
deellovw
vowelled
deellovy
volleyed
deellssw
weldless
deelmnoo
melodeon
deelmnow
new-model
deelmntu
unmelted
deelmntw
weldment
deelmoos
dolesome

deelmopr
empolder
deelmopy
employed
deelmosu
duelsome
deelmruy
demurely
deelnort
redolent
deelnprs
resplend
deelnrtu
underlet
deelnrty
tenderly
deelnssw
lewdness
deelnwwy
newly-wed
deelnxyy
lynx-eyed
deeloprx
exploder
deelopry
redeploy
deelopst
seed-plot
deelorrs
solderer
deelorsv
resolved
deelortt
dotterel
deelortv
revolted
deelorty
deletory
deeloruv
louvered
deelprtu
drupelet
deelptty
pettedly
deelrstu
ulstered
deelrstw
lewdster
deemmors
mesoderm
deemmrru
dummerer
deemnntu
tenendum
deemnoos
moonseed
deemnooy
moon-eyed
deemnoqu
queendom
deemnort
entoderm

deemnoss
demoness
enmossed
deemnouy
eudemony
deemoort
odometer
deemopst
deepmost
deemoqru
queerdom
deemorsw
worm-seed
deemortu
udometer
deemprst
dempster
deemrrru
demurrer
murderer
deemssty
systemed
deennnop
pennoned
deennnpu
unpenned
deennopt
deponent
deennopu
unopened
deennorw
renowned
deennoss
doneness
deennovw
even-down
deennrtu
untender
deennruv
unnerved
deennssu
nudeness
unsensed
deennttu
unnetted
untented
deenntuv
unvented
deenoorv
overdone
deenoprr
ponderer
deenoprs
rope's-end
deenorrs
endorser
deenorrw
wonderer
deenortu
deuteron
deenosst
stenosed
deenrrsu
sunderer

deenrssu
rudeness
deenrstu
sederunt
underset
undesert
deenrsuu
underuse
deenrsuv
unversed
deensttu
untested
deenttuw
unwetted
deeoorrt
rood-tree
deeoorrv
overdoer
deeoorsv
overdose
deeoppst
estopped
deeoprrr
preorder
deeoprst
reed-stop
deeopruz
douzeper
deeorrtt
retorted
deeorruv
devourer
deeorstt
rosetted
deeorstx
dextrose
deeorsty
storeyed
deeorsuy
sour-eyed
deeorttt
tottered
deeprstu
pertused
deeprsuy
pseudery
deerrttu
turreted
deerrtux
extruder
deerssst
stressed
deerssuv
suversed
deerstuv
vestured
deerttux
textured
deffilov
fivefold
deffiors
offsider
deffiorv
off-drive

deffirsu
diffuser
defflrtu
truffled
deffstuy
dyestuff
defghilt
flighted
defgiiln
fielding
defgiiny
deifying
edifying
defgilty
giftedly
defgintu
ungifted
defgioow
goodwife
defgjoru
forjudge
defgnoru
unforged
defhiins
fiendish
finished
defhiisv
fish-dive
defhillo
lifehold
defhilss
disflesh
defhinsu
unfished
defhioow
wifehood
defhloos
selfhood
defhoors
serfhood
defiiilv
vilified
defiillo
oil-field
defiillp
filliped
defiillw
wildlife
defiilor
oil-fired
defiilps
flip-side
defiilrw
wildfire
defiilsu
fluidise
defiilty
fidelity
defiimor
modifier
defiinot
notified
defiintu
finitude

defiinty
identify
defiioss
ossified
defiipru
purified
defiipss
fissiped
defiipty
typified
defillnu
unfilled
defilmnu
unfilmed
defilmow
demi-wolf
defilnno
ninefold
defilnop
pond-life
defilnru
unrifled
urnfield
defilnry
friendly
defiloru
fluoride
defilotu
outfield
defilpru
prideful
defilptu
uplifted
defilrru
flurried
defilrvy
fervidly
defimnor
informed
defimory
remodify
defimrru
drumfire
definnru
reinfund
unfriend
definorw
forewind
definrtt
drift-net
definstu
unsifted
definttu
unfitted
defioorw
firewood
defiotxy
detoxify
defirssu
fissured
defklory
forkedly
deflloor
folderol

deflnoru
flounder
unfolder
deflnruy
fly-under
deflnssu
fundless
defloort
foretold
defloorv
overfold
deflooss
foodless
defmnoru
unformed
defmooor
foredoom
defnnort
frondent
defnnoss
fondness
defnnouw
new-found
defnoops
spoon-fed
defnoors
frondose
defnooru
unroofed
defnoorv
overfond
defnootu
unfooted
defnoprs
forspend
defnorru
frondeur
defnortu
fortuned
defnossw
dowfness
defnrruu
underfur
unfurred
defoorrw
foreword
degghrsu
shrugged
deggilns
sledging
degginov
God-given
degginru
unrigged
degginuw
unwigged
deggiors
disgorge
deggiprs
sprigged
degglmsu
smuggled
degglruy
ruggedly

deggnoru
ungorged
deghilns
shingled
deghilpt
plighted
deghilrt
red-light
deghinnu
unhinged
deghiops
dogeship
deghklow
dog-whelk
deghlnor
horngeld
deghlosu
sloughed
deghnort
thronged
deghnory
hydrogen
deghoosu
dog-house
house-dog
degiiirs
rigidise
degiiist
digitise
degiilnr
gridelin
degiilns
sideling
degiilnt
diligent
degiilnv
deviling
degiilny
yielding
degiilty
gelidity
degiimsu
misguide
degiinnr
nidering
degiinnt
indigent
degiinnx
indexing
degiinrs
ringside
degiinrt
dirigent
degiinst
indigest
degiissu
disguise
degijmsu
misjudge
degiklnu
dukeling
degiklov
kid-glove

degiknry
ring-dyke
degillnu
duelling
degillnw
dwelling
degilmno
gold-mine
degilnop
diplogen
degilnos
sidelong
degilnps
spelding
degilnru
indulger
degilnry
yeldring
degilnwy
wingedly
degiloor
goodlier
degilooy
ideology
degilorw
gold-wire
degilosz
gold-size
degilpsu
pulsidge
degilrzz
grizzled
degimnos
smidgeon
degimoot
goodtime
degimooy
geomyoid
deginnnu
unending
deginnps
spending
deginnru
enduring
unringed
deginnsu
unsigned
deginntu
untinged
deginnuw
unwinged
deginops
disponge
deginorr
ordering
deginoru
guéridon
deginorv
ring-dove
deginpsu
dispunge
deginrry
grindery

deginrss
  dressing
deginrst
  stringed
deginrsy
  synergid
degioors
  goodsire
degioprr
  porridge
degiorrv
  river-god
degjmntu
  judgment
degllnoy
  goldenly
deglloss
  goldless
deglmnot
  lodgment
deglmooy
  demology
deglnouv
  ungloved
deglnrtu
  gruntled
degloopy
  pedology
degloosu
  dog-louse
deglooou
  duologue
degloruv
  love-drug
degmmnuu
  ungummed
degnnopy
  penny-dog
degnnoru
  grounden
degnnouw
  ungowned
degnooss
  dog's-nose
  goodness
degnoost
  stegodon
degnopsu
  pug-nosed
degnorru
  grounder
degnoruu
  unrouged
degnoryy
  gyrodyne
degnpruu
  unpurged
dehhiloy
  hidy-hole
dehhiltw
  withheld
dehhmrty
  rhythmed
dehiills
  hillside
dehiilsv
  devilish
dehiimru
  mudirieh
dehiimst
  ditheism
dehiinnw
  whinnied
dehiinsu
  Hinduise
dehiirst
  disherit
dehiistt
  ditheist
dehijmno
  demijohn
dehikmos
  sheikdom
dehikpsu
  dukeship
dehillop
  phelloid
dehilmos
  demolish
dehilmty
  dimethyl
dehilnor
  inholder
dehilnpy
  diphenyl
dehiloor
  heliodor
dehilops
  polished
dehilpsu
  sulphide
dehilpsy
  sylphide
dehilrtw
  writhled
dehimnos
  hedonism
dehimpsy
  demyship
dehinopr
  nephroid
dehinops
  sphenoid
dehinost
  hedonist
dehioovw
  wivehood
dehioprs
  spheroid
dehioprt
  trophied
dehiorss
  dishorse
dehiorst
  Rhodites
dehiorty
  thyreoid
dehiossu
  dishouse
dehiossw
  side-show
dehirrst
  red-shirt
dehirtww
  withdrew
dehklnou
  elkhound
dehllopy
  phyllode
dehlmory
  hydromel
dehlooow
  wood-hole
dehloorv
  overhold
dehlooss
  hoodless
dehloost
  tool-shed
dehlopru
  upholder
dehlorsu
  shoulder
dehlostu
  dust-hole
dehlrswy
  shrewdly
dehmmrtu
  thrummed
dehmnooy
  homodyne
dehmnruy
  unrhymed
dehmoorw
  whoredom
dehmopry
  hypoderm
dehmoruu
  humoured
dehnntuu
  unhunted
dehnooru
  honoured
dehnorsu
  enshroud
dehnorsy
  enhydros
dehnortw
  nowt-herd
dehnorty
  threnody
dehnosuu
  unhoused
dehnrtuy
  thundery
dehooopp
  popehood
dehooprt
  theropod
dehoortu
  out-Herod
dehopppu
  hopped-up
dehoprst
  potsherd
dehopttu
  hotted-up
dehorrst
  redshort
deiiinsv
  divinise
deiiirtv
  viridite
deiiisvv
  divisive
deiiklnv
  devilkin
deiillmp
  milliped
deiillmt
  ill-timed
  tidemill
deiilmru
  delirium
deiilmsv
  devilism
deiilnnu
  induline
deiilnpv
  vilipend
deiilnvy
  divinely
deiilors
  idoliser
deiilpss
  side-slip
deiilrst
  redistil
deiilstz
  Seidlitz
deiimmrs
  dimerism
deiimmst
  mistimed
deiimmtt
  immitted
deiimnrt
  diriment
deiimntu
  mutinied
deiimpru
  peridium
deiimsvw
  midwives
deiinnpp
  pinniped
deiinnuv
  undivine
deiinors
  derision
  Ironside
deiinost
  sedition
deiinosv
  visioned
deiinppw
  windpipe
deiinprs
  inspired
deiinprt
  intrepid
deiinpry
  pyridine
deiinptu
  unpitied
deiinrst
  disinter
deiinrsu
  disinure
deiinsst
  tidiness
deiinstu
  disunite
  nudities
deiinttu
  intuited
deiintty
  identity
deiioprs
  presidio
deiiopzz
  pezizoid
deiiorsx
  oxidiser
deiiortx
  trioxide
deiiorty
  iodyrite
deiiprst
  spirited
deiiprsz
  disprize
deiiptty
  tepidity
deiiqstu
  disquiet
deiirssu
  diuresis
deijorry
  joy-rider
deikklno
  klondike
deiklmnu
  unmilked
deiklnnu
  unlinked
deiklnrw
  wrinkled
deiklnss
  kindless
deiknnpu
  unpinked
deiknnss
  kindness
deiknorv
  overkind
deiknssu
  unkissed
deikrsvy
  sky-diver
deillmnu
  unmilled
deillntu
  untilled
deillnuw
  unwilled
deillopw
  pillowed
deillovw
  low-lived
deilloww
  willowed
deillstu
  duellist
deilmnoo
  melodion
deilmnss
  mildness
  mindless
deilmnsu
  muslined
deilmoot
  dolomite
deilmoow
  lime-wood
deilmopr
  impolder
deilmort
  old-timer
deilmoru
  lemuroid
deilmost
  melodist
deilmosu
  emulsoid
deilmotv
  demi-volt
deilmppu
  plumiped
deilmpsu
  displume
deilmptu
  multiped
deilmssy
  demissly
deilnnot
  indolent
deilnnow
  down-line
deilnoos
  solenoid
deilnopw
  dowel-pin
deilnors
  disenrol
deilnosu
  delusion
  unsoiled
deilnprs
  speldrin
deilnpru
  underlip

8 DEI

deilnrss
rindless
deilnrsw
swindler
deilnssv
vildness
deilnssw
wildness
windless
deilnstu
unlisted
deilnttu
untitled
deilntuy
unitedly
deilnuwy
unwieldy
deiloopw
wood-pile
deiloovw
wood-evil
deilopps
dip-slope
deiloppy
polypide
deilopru
preludio
deiloqru
liquored
deilorsy
soldiery
deilossv
dissolve
deilostu
solitude
deilppst
stippled
deilppsu
supplied
deilpptu
pulpited
deilpstt
splitted
deilpstu
stipuled
deilpttu
uptilted
deilrsvy
diversly
deilrtvy
deviltry
deilstuy
sedulity
deimmnos
demonism
deimmost
immodest
deimmrru
mire-drum
deimnoos
dominoes
deimnoot
demotion

deimnoox
monoxide
deimnopt
Piedmont
deimnort
dormient
deimnost
demonist
deimnosw
Wodenism
deimnotw
downtime
deimnpss
misspend
deimnptu
impudent
deimnrtu
rudiment
deimnssu
unmissed
deimooss
sodomise
deimoost
Sodomite
deimootw
wood-mite
deimorrr
mirrored
deimorrs
misorder
deimorss
Messidor
deimorsu
dimerous
soredium
deimorux
exordium
deimostt
demotist
deimrsuu
residuum
deinnnou
innuendo
deinnnpu
unpinned
deinnntu
untinned
deinnoot
noontide
deinnoru
unironed
deinnoww
winnowed
deinnpru
underpin
deinnruu
uninured
deinnruv
undriven
deinoops
Poseidon
deinoopw
pine-wood

deinootv
devotion
deinoppw
downpipe
deinoprs
disponer
deinopry
pyrenoid
deinopsu
unpoised
deinoptw
dewpoint
deinorsu
sourdine
deinorsw
windrose
deinortt
intorted
deinorvw
overwind
deinossv
voidness
deinossz
doziness
deinottu
duettino
deinppru
unripped
deinpruz
unprized
deinrrtu
intruder
deinrssu
sundries
deinrstt
strident
deinrtuw
underwit
deinsssy
syndesis
deinstuu
unsuited
deiopprr
drop-ripe
deioprrv
provider
deioprss
disposer
deioprst
dipteros
deioprsv
disprove
deioprsw
dropwise
deiopsst
side-post
deiorrsy
derisory
deiorrtu
outrider
deiorssu
desirous
deiorstu
outsider

deiortuv
outdrive
deiostuz
outsized
deipprst
stripped
deiprssu
dispurse
deiprstu
disputer
deipstuv
stived-up
deirssst
distress
deirsstu
diestrus
deirsttu
detritus
deistttu
duettist
dejlooor
jordeloo
dejmppuu
jumped-up
dekklnoy
klondyke
dekkorsw
desk-work
deklnoou
unlooked
dekmorsy
smoke-dry
deknoruw
unworked
deknrsuy
undersky
deknsssu
duskness
dekorswy
dye-works
dellmosw
swelldom
dellnopu
unpolled
dellnorw
rowndell
dellnpuu
unpulled
dellnssu
dullness
dellootw
well-to-do
delloptu
polluted
dellorry
drollery
dellorss
lordless
dellotuw
outdwell
delmnoov
noveldom
delmnory
modernly

delmnosu
unseldom
delmnotw
meltdown
delmnpuu
pendulum
delmorsu
smoulder
delmosty
modestly
delnnoor
Londoner
delnoosu
nodulose
delnoowy
woodenly
delnoppu
unlopped
delnoprs
splendor
delnorsu
unsolder
delnortu
roundlet
delnossu
loudness
delnosuu
undulose
unsouled
delnosuv
unsolved
deloooot
toodle-oo
deloorrv
overlord
deloorrw
word-lore
deloorsv
oversold
deloorty
rootedly
deloossw
woodless
delopstu
postlude
delopstw
spot-weld
delorssw
wordless
delorsuy
delusory
delossuu
sedulous
delotuvy
devoutly
delssstu
dustless
demmnsuu
unsummed
demmrstu
strummed
demnooop
monopode

demnorsy
syndrome
demnoruw
unwormed
demnostu
mudstone
demnosuu
mouse-dun
demooprr
prodrome
demoorst
doomster
demoorsu
dormouse
demoorty
odometry
demopprt
prompted
dennnsuu
unsunned
dennoooz
endozoon
dennoptu
pound-net
ten-pound
dennotuw
unwonted
dennpruu
unpruned
dennrruu
underrun
dennrtuu
unturned
denooopr
open-door
denoootw
wood-note
denooovw
ovenwood
denoortu
unrooted
denoortx
next-door
denoorww
wood-wren
denopruv
unproved
denopstu
unposted
denopstw
step-down
stewpond
denorruu
roundure
denorssu
dourness
denorstu
tonsured
unsorted
denorsty
dry-stone
denorsuu
unsoured

denorttu
unrotted
denortuw
undertow
denostuu
unsued-to
denotuuv
undevout
denprtuu
upturned
denrrsuy
dry-nurse
denrsssu
sun-dress
deooorsw
rosewood
deooosww
woodwose
deoopprt
pteropod
deooprrs
rose-drop
deooprrv
provedor
deooprst
doorstep
deoorrsw
sorrowed
deoorrvw
overword
deoorrww
owreword
deopprst
stropped
deopprsu
purposed
deoppssu
supposed
deoppsuu
souped-up
deoprrtu
protrude
deoprsst
top-dress
deoprstu
sprouted
deorstuv
overdust
deorstux
dextrous
deorstvy
dry-stove
deppssyy
dyspepsy
deqrsuuy
surquedy
derstttu
strutted
dffiiluy
fluidify
dfflmpuu
plum-duff
dfflooru
fourfold

dffooruw
woodruff
dfgghiot
dog-fight
dfghilos
goldfish
dfgiiiry
rigidify
dfgiilry
frigidly
dfgilloo
gold-foil
dfgilnno
fondling
dfgilnoo
flooding
dfginnou
founding
dfginoor
fordoing
dfgknoru
dung-fork
dfhiimuy
humidify
dfhimrsu
drumfish
dfhinoot
hind-foot
dfhinops
fishpond
dfhlooot
foothold
dfhnooux
foxhound
dfiiinvy
divinify
dfiilmtu
multifid
dfiilosy
solidify
dfiiltuy
fluidity
dfiinprt
driftpin
dfilloot
floodlit
dfillory
floridly
dfilloww
wild-fowl
dfimooor
iodoform
dfiooprs
disproof
dflnooww
downflow
dflooort
rood-loft
dfnoopru
profound
dfooorw
wood-roof
dfooostw
softwood

dgggiins
diggings
dggginru
drugging
grudging
dgghinot
night-dog
dggiilnr
ridgling
dggiinnr
grinding
dggiinnw
wingding
dgginrtu
trudging
dggirstu
druggist
dghiilns
hidlings
dghiimnt
midnight
dghiimst
misdight
dghiinnw
hind-wing
dghiinps
sphingid
dghiinrt
thirding
dghiisst
dissight
dghiknoo
kinghood
dghillnu
dung-hill
dghilnru
hurdling
dghiloor
girlhood
dghimost
god-smith
dghlorsu
gold-rush
dghnootu
do-nought
dghnotuu
doughnut
dghooott
dogtooth
dghorruy
rough-dry
dghortuy
droughty
dgiiimrs
dirigism
dgiiirty
rigidity
dgiiklnn
kindling
dgiiknnr
drinking
dgiiillnr
drilling

dgiillou
liguloid
dgiilnos
disloign
dgiimnos
misdoing
dgiimnou
gonidium
dgiimpuy
pygidium
dgiinnop
poinding
dgiinnor
Girondin
non-rigid
dgiinnss
sindings
dgiinorr
gridiron
dgiinppr
dripping
dgiinrty
dirtying
dgiinyzz
dizzying
dgiiottw
two-digit
dgiklooy
kidology
dgiknoor
drooking
dgiknoow
kingwood
dgiknoru
drouking
dgillnor
drolling
lordling
dgilloow
goodwill
dgilmnou
moulding
dgilmnpu
dumpling
dgilmsuy
smudgily
dgilnoow
woolding
dgilnory
yoldring
dgilootw
giltwood
dgilosty
stodgily
dgilrtuy
turgidly
dgimmnru
drumming
dginnoru
rounding
dginnorw
drowning
dginnosu
sounding

dginnouw
wounding
dginnssy
syndings
dginoops
spongoid
dginoppr
dropping
dginosuy
digynous
dginstuy
studying
dglooopy
podology
dglooosy
dosology
dgloooxy
doxology
dgmopsyy
gypsydom
dgnnoruu
unground
dgnootyz
zygodont
dgopppuy
puppy-dog
dhhilotw
withhold
dhiiimns
diminish
dhiiiost
histioid
idiotish
dhiikwzz
whizz-kid
dhiiloss
solidish
dhiimnoo
hominoid
dhiimnsu
Hinduism
dhiimpss
midships
dhiimtuy
humidity
dhiintww
withwind
dhiiopru
ophiurid
dhiiorss
hidrosis
dhiknoow
hoodwink
dhikorsy
hydroski
dhillnow
downhill
dhillopy
phylloid
dhillors
drollish
dhillost
tolldish

dhilmosy
modishly
dhiloprs
lordship
dhilopss
slipshod
dhilorry
horridly
dhimnost
hindmost
dhimnosu
unmodish
dhimoooy
omohyoid
dhimooss
misshood
dhinnoor
Rhinodon
dhinoors
dishonor
dhinorsu
roundish
dhinotuw
who-dun-it
dhiooprz
rhizopod
dhioprsu
proudish
dhiorsty
thyrsoid
dhiorswy
rowdyish
dhjoprsu
jodphurs
dhkmnooo
monkhood
dhllnouw
hull-down
dhllopyy
phyllody
dhlooort
roothold
dhlooory
holy-rood
dhlorxyy
hydroxyl
dhlosstu
shouldst
dhmnooot
homodont
dhmooppu
pump-hood
dhmorsyy
Hydromys
dhnoosww
show-down
dhnorsuu
unshroud
dhnorsuw
downrush
dhnostuw
shut-down
dhooprs
shop-door

dhoooprt
orthopod
dhooortx
orthodox
dhooprst
drop-shot
dhoorsuw
wood-rush
dhoprsyy
hydropsy
dhossttu
dust-shot
diiillqu
illiquid
diiiltvy
lividity
diiimost
idiotism
diiimtty
timidity
diiinosv
division
diiintvy
divinity
diiiprst
dispirit
diiirtvy
viridity
diiitvvy
vividity
diijnost
disjoint
diikllny
kindlily
diillmnw
windmill
diillmpy
limpidly
diillquy
liquidly
diillsty
idyllist
diilmoss
solidism
diilmoty
mytiloid
diilmuuv
diluvium
diilnotu
dilution
diilnouv
diluvion
diilnoxy
xyloidin
diilntuy
untidily
diiloprt
triploid
diilopsy
ypsiloid
diilorsu
siluroid
diilosst
solidist

diilosty
solidity
diimnnoo
dominion
diimnsuu
indusium
diimoprs
prismoid
diimpuxy
pyxidium
diimruuv
duumviri
diimttuy
tumidity
diinnors
Dinornis
diinnosu
disunion
diinoort
Triodion
diinossu
sinusoid
diinstuy
disunity
diioprty
pityroid
diklmoow
milkwood
diklnnuy
unkindly
diklruuu
durukuli
diknoosw
wood-skin
diknortu
outdrink
dikoostu
ditokous
dillmnop
millpond
dillnopy
pond-lily
dilloors
door-sill
dillosty
stolidly
dilmnorw
lindworm
dilmoosu
modiolus
dilnopsu
lispound
dilnouwy
woundily
dilooppy
polypoid
dilooprу
droopily
diloorss
lordosis
diloorsu
louis-d'or
diloosuy
odiously

dilootuv
volutoid
diloprty
torpidly
dilprtuy
putridly
dilpstuy
stupidly
dilrstuy
sturdily
dimmnory
myrmidon
dimmoosu
isodomum
dimnooos
isodomon
dimnoost
monodist
dimnostu
dismount
dimnosuw
unwisdom
dimnsstu
Stundism
dimooprr
prodromi
dimoopry
myriopod
dimoortw
modiwort
dimoprsu
misproud
dimorswy
rowdyism
dimostuy
dumosity
dimrsuuv
duumvirs
dinooorw
ironwood
dinoopsu
dipnoous
dinoorsu
nidorous
dinoostt
odontist
dinoosty
nodosity
dinoprty
dry-point
dinorstu
sturnoid
dinprtuy
punditry
dinrstuy
industry
dinssttu
Stundist
diooprrt
proditor
diooprrv
providor
diosstuu
studious

dirssttu
distrust
dknnootw
don't-know
dknorsuw
sow-drunk
dkooorww
woodwork
dkorstuw
studwork
dllmoopy
dolly-mop
dllnoruy
unlordly
dlmnooty
mylodont
dlmorsuy
smouldry
dlnoopru
pouldron
dlnoosuu
nodulous
dlnooswW
slow-down
dlnortuy
rotundly
dlnosuuu
undulous
dloooors
doloroso
dloooowW
wood-wool
dlooorsu
dolorous
dlooppuw
pulpwood
wood-pulp
dlooppyy
polypody
dmnnooot
monodont
dmnoostw
downmost
dmooorww
wood-worm
wormwood
dmopppuu
puppodum
dmopppuy
puppydom
dmpppuuy
mud-puppy
dnnoopru
pundonor
dnnoortw
torn-down
dnnootww
down-town
dnnortuw
downturn
turn-down
dnoooopw
poon-wood

dnooppru
propound
dnooprsw
snowdrop
dnooprtu
round-top
dnoopruw
downpour
dnoorsuw
wondrous
dnoostww
stowdown
dnoprssu
sun-drops
dnorrsuu
surround
dnorssuy
undrossy
doooprst
doorpost
dooorstu
outdoors
doopprtu
top-proud
dooprrsy
rosy-drop
dooprrtw
drop-wort
doopswwy
powsowdy
doorrsuu
ordurous
doorrttu
trout-rod
doorssuu
sudorous
eeeefnrz
enfreeze
eeeefrrz
refreeze
eeeeggrr
greegree
eeeegmrr
re-emerge
eeeegnsv
Genevese
eeeegqsu
squeegee
eeeellpx
expellee
eeeelmst
teleseme
eeeenrrv
veneerer
eeeeppsw
peesweep
eeeepttw
peetweet
eeeffgir
fee-grief
eeefflor
forefeel
eeefflty
effetely

eeeffnrt
efferent
eeeffort
forefeet
eeeffrvw
feverfew
eeefilpr
life-peer
eeefiprr
repriefe
eeefnnpy
penny-fee
eeefnors
foreseen
eeefnrrt
referent
rent-free
tree-fern
eeefnrss
freeness
eeefnrtt
enfetter
eeefnruz
unfreeze
eeeforrv
overfree
eeefpruz
freeze-up
eeefrrrt
ferreter
eeeggiln
negligee
eeeghint
eighteen
eeeghorv
hog-reeve
eeegilnv
enveigle
eeegilps
espiègle
eeeginnr
engineer
eeeginrs
energise
eeeginrv
engrieve
eeegirty
tiger-eye
eeegissx
exegesis
eeegistv
egestive
eeegitvv
vegetive
eeeglmos
gleesome
eeeglnrt
greenlet
eeegmnrt
emergent
eeegmort
geometer
eeegnnrs
sengreen

eeegnosv
Genovese
eeegnrru
reneguer
eeegnrrv
revenger
eeegnrry
greenery
eeegoprt
protégée
eeehilrw
erewhile
while-ere
wire-heel
eeehirst
etherise
eeehitwy
white-eye
eeehklno
kneehole
eeehlmpt
helpmeet
eeehlntv
eleventh
eeehlnty
ethylene
eeehlnxy
hexylene
eeehlopp
peep-hole
eeehlopw
weephole
eeehlors
hose-reel
eeehmntv
vehement
eeehmrss
herseems
eeehmryy
eye-rhyme
eeehnnpt
nepenthe
eeehnnqu
henequen
eeehnpps
sheep-pen
eeehnprs
ensphere
eeehnrss
hereness
eeehnrvw
whenever
eeehorrs
Hereroes
eeehorst
shoe-tree
eeehprst
spreethe
eeehrrvw
wherever
eeeiknps
Pekinese
eeeillrv
reveille
eeeilmrs
seemlier
eeeilmrt
lime-tree
eeeilnno
éolienne
eeeilnpr
pelerine
eeeilnrt
tree-line
eeeilnry
eyeliner
eeeilnst
selenite
eeeilrrv
reliever
eeeilssw
elsewise
eeeilstv
televise
eeeiltvw
teleview
eeeimnru
meunière
eeeimprr
première
eeeimprs
emperise
eeeimrrs
Miserere
eeeimrtt
remittee
eeeinnnt
nineteen
eeeinnrt
internee
eeeinnss
Siennese
eeeinnst
seine-net
eeeinnsv
Viennese
eeeinnsy
nine-eyes
eeeinprt
pine-tree
eeeinqtu
queenite
eeeinrss
eeriness
eeeinrst
eternise
eeeinrtt
reinette
eeeintux
euxenite
eeeipprt
pipe-tree
eeeiprrv
reprieve
eeeiqsux
exequies
eeeirrsv
rerevise
eeeirrtv
retrieve
eeeirrvw
reviewer
eeeirtvx
exertive
eeejkknr
knee-jerk
eeejllrw
jeweller
eeeklnnr
enkernel
eeekmnss
meekness
eeeknnss
keenness
eeeknors
kerosene
eeeknorv
overknee
eeekoprv
overkeep
eeelllrv
leveller
eeellllsw
sewellel
eeellnqu
quenelle
eeellnsw
well-seen
eeellprr
repeller
eeellrrt
reteller
eeellrrv
reveller
eeellvwy
wye-level
eeelmopp
empeople
eeelmopy
employee
eeelmott
omelette
eeelmrtu
muleteer
eeelmsss
seemless
eeelmsst
teemless
eeelnopv
envelope
eeelnpst
steel-pen
eeelnqtu
queenlet
eeelnrsw
newsreel
eeelnrsy
serenely
eeelnrtv
nervelet
eeelnrty
Terylene®
eeeloppr
repeople
eeelorst
sloetree
eeelprss
peerless
eeelprsy
sleepery
eeelrrtt
letterer
eeelrsst
treeless
eeelrstt
resettle
eeelrstv
verselet
eeelrsvy
severely
eeelrtvv
velveret
eeelsstw
weetless
eeelstvy
steevely
eeeltttx
teletext
eeemmruz
mezereum
eeemnntt
tenement
eeemnorz
mezereon
eeemnrst
entremes
eeemnsst
meetness
eeemorrv
evermore
eeemorst
stereome
eeemortv
overteem
eeemprrt
temperer
eeemrrtx
extremer
eeemrsst
semester
eeennopr
neoprene
eeennssv
evenness
eeenoprr
reopener
eeenorsv
overseen
eeenorvw
overween
eeenorvy
everyone
eeenpprs
prepense
eeenprrt
repenter
eeenpstw
sweep-net
eeenrrst
resenter
eeenrrsv
renverse
eeenrrtv
reverent
eeenrsss
sereness
eeenrsty
yestreen
eeeoprrv
overpeer
eeeorrst
rose-tree
eeeorrsv
overseer
eeeppprr
pepperer
eeeppstu
steepe-up
eeeprrst
pesterer
eeeprrsu
reperuse
eeeprrsv
perverse
preserve
eeeprrtw
pewterer
eeepsttt
septette
eeeqrruv
verquere
eeeqrsuz
squeezer
eeerrrsv
reverser
eeerrstt
resetter
eeerstwz
tweezers
eeesstt
sestette
eeestttx
sextette
eefffglu
gefuffle
eefffklu
kefuffle
eeffgiis
effigies
eeffgirr
greffier
eeffhiky
keffiyeh
eeffills
self-life
eeffisuv
effusive
eeffklor
folk-free
eeffllst
self-left
eefflntu
effluent
eefflort
forefelt
eeffrrsu
sufferer
eefgiilr
filigree
eefgilnr
fleering
eefgilnt
fleeting
eefginrr
refringe
eefginrz
freezing
eefgirru
refigure
eefglnry
greenfly
eefglnuv
vengeful
eefgnoor
foregone
eefgoorr
foregoer
eefgorrt
tree-frog
eefhhlns
hen-flesh
eefhillr
hell-fire
eefhilmo
home-life
eefhimor
home-fire
eefhiors
fire-hose
eefhirsv
feverish
eefhllps
self-help
eefhllwy
flywheel
eefhlmot
home-felt
eefhlsty
fly-sheet
eefhmorr
here-from
eefhnort
forehent
eefhnrsw
fresh-new
eefhorrt
therefor
eefhorrw
wherefor
eefhorst
free-shot
shot-free

eefhorsw
foreshew
eefiikll
lifelike
eefiiklw
wife-like
eefiilln
life-line
eefiilmt
lifetime
eefiilsz
life-size
eefiimnn
feminine
eefiimns
feminise
eefiirrv
verifier
eefiklls
self-like
eefiknnp
penknife
eefillmt
telefilm
eefillrw
free-will
eefillss
lifeless
eefilmos
lifesome
eefilmtx
Flextime®
eefilnrt
life-rent
eefilnss
fineless
eefilnuv
nieveful
eefilors
free-soil
eefilprr
pilferer
eefilrss
fireless
eefilrsu
fusileer
eefilssw
wifeless
eefimort
foretime
eefimstu
time-fuse
eefinnss
fineness
eefinntu
fine-tune
eefinorv
overfine
eefinrry
refinery
eefinrss
finesser
rifeness
eefinrsu
reinfuse
eefiorrv
overfire
eefiprst
fire-step
eefirrsu
sure-fire
eefirsty
esterify
eefknort
reef-knot
eefllnss
fellness
eefllort
foretell
toll-free
eefllosv
self-love
eefllrxy
reflexly
eefllsss
selfless
eeflmnsu
menseful
eeflnort
forelent
eeflnorw
enflower
eeflnost
felstone
eeflnrtu
refluent
eeflnsss
selfness
eeflnssu
senseful
eeflntuv
eventful
eeflorrw
flowerer
eeflortv
left-over
eeflortw
floweret
eeflorww
werewolf
eeflosux
flexuose
eefmnort
fomenter
eefmorrr
reformer
eefmprru
perfumer
eefnnors
enfrosen
eefnorst
enforest
softener
eefnortu
fourteen
eefnortw
forewent
eefnqrtu
frequent
eefnrttu
unfetter
eefoorrt
roof-tree
eefoprst
post-free
eeforrst
forester
fosterer
eeforrsu
ferreous
eeforrty
feretory
eeforsuv
feverous
eeforsuy
four-eyes
eefosstt
fossette
eegggoos
goose-egg
eegghlls
eggshell
shell-egg
eegghlor
hoggerel
eegghmsu
meshugge
eeggijrr
rejigger
eeggilnr
legering
eeggimnr
emerging
eeggimrt
egg-timer
eegginnr
greening
eegginrs
greesing
eegginrt
greeting
eegginsu
siege-gun
eeggloor
geologer
eeggortt
go-getter
eeggprrs
preggers
eeggprsu
egg-purse
eeghhikn
knee-high
eeghhint
heighten
eeghiist
eighties
eeghikrs
Greekish
eeghilns
sheeling
eeghilnw
wheeling
eeghiltw
white-leg
eeghinpt
phengite
eeghinrs
greenish
eeghinst
seething
sheeting
eeghintt
teething
eeghinwz
wheezing
eeghisst
sightsee
eeghisty
eyesight
eeghlnnt
lengthen
eeghmnoy
hegemony
eeghmpsu
mug-sheep
eeghnnru
enhunger
eeghnoop
geophone
eeghnops
phosgene
eeghnopy
hypogene
eeghnssu
hugeness
eeghopty
geophyte
eeghortt
together
eegiiktw
Ewigkeit
eegiilnr
lingerie
eegiilnv
inveigle
eegiinrt
re-ignite
eegiintv
genitive
eegiklns
sleeking
eegiklot
eklogite
eegilnps
sleeping
eegilnrr
lingerer
eegilnru
reguline
eegilnst
steeling
eegilopu
epilogue
eegilosu
eulogise
eegilqsu
squilgee
eegilrsu
regulise
eegilrtv
verligte
eegilrty
legerity
eegimnns
meninges
eegimnrt
regiment
eegimnru
meringue
eegimnsu
eugenism
eeginnqu
queening
eeginnrs
sneering
eeginnrt
entering
eeginnrw
renewing
eeginnry
enginery
eeginnst
steening
eeginnsu
unseeing
eeginnsz
sneezing
eeginntv
eventing
eeginopr
perigone
eeginops
epigones
eeginorr
erigeron
eeginorv
virogene
eeginost
egestion
eeginpsw
sweeping
eeginquu
queueing
eeginrrs
resigner
eeginrst
steering
eeginrsu
seigneur
eeginrsw
sewering
eeginrtu
geniture
eeginrtx
genetrix
eeginruz
Zigeuner
eeginssu
geniuses
eeginstu
eugenist
eeginstv
steeving
eeginstw
sweeting
eeginttv
vignette
eegintux
teguexin
eegiopsu
epigeous
eegiorst
ergotise
eegiorvv
overgive
eegiprst
prestige
eegirrst
register
eegirstt
grisette
eeglmntu
emulgent
eeglmoss
glosseme
eeglnntu
ungentle
eeglnopy
polygene
eeglnoty
telegony
eegmmosu
gemmeous
eegmnost
emongest
gemstone
eegmnttu
tegument
eegmorsu
gruesome
eegmorty
geometry
eegnnort
roentgen
eegnnoss
goneness
eegnnosv
evensong
eegnoorv
engroove
eegnopty
genotype
eegnorsu
generous
eegnprux
expunger
eegnrssy
greyness
eegnrsuy
guernsey

eegnrttu
tung-tree
eegoprsu
super-ego
eegoprtu
Portugee
eegorrst
ostreger
eegorstu
urostege
eehhipss
sheepish
eehhirtw
herewith
eehhlllo
hell-hole
eehhlrst
threshel
eehhnosu
hen-house
eehhrrst
thresher
eehiiklv
hivelike
eehikllt
hell-kite
eehiklmo
homelike
eehikrrs
shrieker
eehiktww
Whitweek
eehillms
shlemiel
eehilnno
nine-hole
eehilnpw
pin-wheel
eehilort
hotelier
eehilrss
heirless
eehilssv
hiveless
eehilwyz
wheezily
eehimmpt
Memphite
eehimmss
himseems
eehimprs
emperish
eehimquv
vehmique
eehimrst
erethism
etherism
eehimrtt
thermite
eehinnqu
henequin
eehinnrs
enshrine

eehinnrt
inherent
eehinnss
sneeshin
eehinort
etherion
eehinprs
insphere
eehinprt
nephrite
prehnite
trephine
eehinrtt
thirteen
eehinrtw
whitener
eehinstt
sheet-tin
eehinstv
hive-nest
eehiopps
hosepipe
eehiorst
isothere
theorise
eehippst
psephite
eehippty
epiphyte
eehiprrs
perisher
eehiprss
Hesperis
eehiprst
treeship
eehiprtt
perthite
pith-tree
tephrite
threepit
eehipsst
steepish
eehipsuu
euphuise
eehiqrsu
queerish
eehirrsw
wherries
eehirstt
etherist
tee-shirt
eehirtvy
thievery
eehisstw
sweetish
eehjlowy
joy-wheel
eehlllow
well-hole
eehllmss
helmless
eehllorv
hoveller

eehllpss
helpless
eehlmoss
homeless
eehlnott
telethon
eehlnotv
vent-hole
eehlopss
hopeless
eehlorst
hosteler
eehlosss
shoeless
eehlprsu
spherule
eehlprty
three-ply
eehlrsty
sheltery
eehlsstw
thewless
eehmmopr
morpheme
eehmmort
ohmmeter
eehmnoos
moonshee
eehmnosw
somewhen
eehmoort
rheotome
eehmorst
rest-home
eehmorvw
whomever
eehnnort
enthrone
eehnnppu
unheppen
eehnnsss
neshness
eehnnstu
unnethes
eehnoors
one-horse
eehnopru
hereupon
eehnopst
poshteen
eehnopty
neophyte
eehnorsw
heronsew
eehnortu
hereunto
eehnortv
overhent
eehnprsu
sheep-run
unsphere
eehnrrty
Tyrrhene

eehnrttu
untether
eehooprs
oosphere
eehoorss
shoe-rose
eehoorsv
overshoe
eehootty
eye-tooth
eehoppsw
peep-show
eehoppsx
sheep-pox
eehoprst
sheep-rot
eehorrtx
exhorter
eehorsvw
whosever
eehorttu
thereout
eehortuw
whereout
eehprssu
Hesperus
eehprstu
superhet
eehprsty
physeter
eehrsssu
usheress
eeiiklpp
pipelike
eeiiklsw
likewise
wise-like
eeiillmm
millième
eeiillmt
melilite
eeiillop
eolipile
eeiilmnn
nine-mile
eeiilmnt
ilmenite
melinite
eeiilmss
emissile
eeiilnnt
Leninite
eeiilnpp
pipeline
eeiilnrw
wire-line
eeiilntv
lenitive
eeiilrvw
live-wire
eeiilstw
lewisite
eeiimmtt
mimetite

eeiimnot
meionite
eeiimsst
Semitise
eeiimssv
emissive
eeiinnst
nineties
eeiinppr
piperine
eeiinppw
pipe-wine
eeiinprv
viperine
eeiinrrv
riverine
eeiinrss
resinise
eeiinrtt
intertie
retinite
eeiinssv
inessive
eeiiprtt
epitrite
eeiiqtuv
quietive
eeiirrtv
tirrivee
eeiirstv
verities
eeijlnnu
julienne
eeijlnrt
jetliner
eeijlnuv
juvenile
eeijnnor
enjoiner
eeijnotv
vee-joint
eeikllry
kyrielle
eeiklmrt
milk-tree
eeiklnss
likeness
eeiklors
roselike
eeiklort
lorikeet
eeiklpst
spikelet
eeiklrst
triskele
eeiknors
kerosine
eeikoquv
equivoke
eeikpprr
kipperer
eeilllvw
live-well

eeillmpr
impeller
eeillmru
reillume
eeillors
orseille
eeillpss
ellipses
eeillpsy
sleepily
eeillrty
tree-lily
eeillssv
veilless
eeilltvy
velleity
eeillvwy
weevilly
eeilmnnu
enlumine
eeilmnos
Seminole
eeilmnru
lemurine
relumine
eeilmnsu
selenium
semilune
eeilmops
polemise
eeilmort
motelier
eeilmost
mesolite
eeilmsst
timeless
eeilmsuv
emulsive
eeilnnor
one-liner
eeilnnst
sentinel
eeilnopr
leporine
eeilnost
noselite
eeilnosv
novelise
eeilnppz
zeppelin
eeilnprs
Pilsener
eeilnpru
perilune
eeilnprv
replevin
eeilnrss
reinless
eeilnrst
listener
re-enlist
eeilnrty
entirely
lientery

eeilnruv
unveiler
eeilnssv
evilness
vileness
eeilorrt
loiterer
eeilorrv
overlier
eeilorst
literose
eeilorvv
overlive
overveil
eeilostw
sweet-oil
eeilosvw
vowelise
eeilottt
toilette
eeilppss
pipeless
eeilppsy
epilepsy
eeilprst
epistler
eeilpsty
epistyle
eeilrsst
tireless
eeilrssw
wireless
eeilsstw
witeless
eeilssvw
viewless
eeilstvy
stievely
eeimmors
memorise
eeimmost
sometime
eeimmrst
meristem
mimester
mismetre
eeimmrsu
eumerism
eeimmrtt
term-time
eeimmstu
semi-mute
eeimnops
episemon
eeimnors
emersion
eeimnort
timoneer
eeimnorv
vomerine
eeimnost
monetise
semitone
eeimnotx
xenotime
eeimnotz
time-zone
eeimnpru
perineum
eeimnpst
sepiment
eeimnrrt
terminer
eeimnrtu
mutineer
eeimnrtv
virement
eeimnsss
Essenism
eeimoprs
promisee
reimpose
eeimopst
epsomite
eeimorst
tiresome
eeimortv
overtime
eeimortx
oximeter
eeimossw
somewise
eeimpprs
episperm
eeimppst
pipe-stem
eeimprrs
simperer
eeimprss
impresse
premises
eeimpssy
empyesis
eeimqstu
mesquite
eeimrrtt
remitter
trimeter
eeimrstu
emeritus
eeimrtty
temerity
eeinnptt
penitent
eeinnrsw
new-risen
eeinnrtt
renitent
tin-terne
eeinnrux
xenurine
eeinnstt
sentient
eeinoppr
peperino
eeinoprs
isoprene
eeinorrt
reorient
eeinorss
essoiner
eeinorst
serotine
eeinorsv
eversion
eeinortt
tenorite
eeinortx
exertion
eeinosst
essonite
eeinostt
noisette
eeinpprw
pen-wiper
eeinpptv
vent-pipe
eeinpptz
Zentippe
eeinprss
ripeness
eeinprsu
resupine
eeinprtx
inexpert
eeinpstt
spinette
eeinqrru
enquirer
eeinqrsu
squireen
eeinrrst
inserter
reinsert
eeinrrsu
reinsure
eeinrrtv
inverter
eeinrrtx
interrex
eeinrsst
interess
eeinrssu
enuresis
eeinrstt
interest
sternite
eeinrstu
esurient
eeinrstv
reinvest
servient
sirvente
eeinrstx
intersex
eeinrsty
serenity
eeinrsuv
universe
eeinrtty
entirety
eternity
trey-tine
eeinsssw
wiseness
eeinsssx
sexiness
eeinsttw
tentwise
eeinsttx
existent
eeiopprr
rope-ripe
eeiopprs
epispore
eeioprrt
portière
eeioprrv
overripe
eeioprrw
wire-rope
eeiorrtv
overtire
eeiorrtx
exterior
eeiorsst
erotesis
eeiorsvw
overwise
eeiorsvz
oversize
eeiorvvw
overview
eeiorvww
wirewove
eeipprrs
perspire
eeipprty
peripety
eeiprrtt
preterit
eeiprstx
pre-exist
eeiprsty
perseity
eeiprtuv
eruptive
eeipsstw
stepwise
eeipstuy
Puseyite
eeiqrrru
requirer
eeiqrrtu
requiter
eeiqrruv
verquire
eeiqrtuy
queerity
eeirrssv
reversis
eeirrstv
reverist
eeirrttt
titterer
eeirstvy
severity
eejjlnuy
jejunely
eejkmoos
jokesome
eejlpstu
pulsejet
eejprrru
perjurer
eejprstu
super-jet
eekllnry
kernelly
eeklnnnu
unkennel
eeklnost
skeleton
eeklnosv
velskoen
eeknopst
knee-stop
eeknosty
keystone
eekoorst
kreosote
eekrrtuz
kreutzer
eellllmp
pell-mell
eellmptu
plumelet
eellnorr
enroller
eellnpru
prunelle
eellnstu
entellus
eelloptv
top-level
eellorst
solleret
eellorsv
oversell
eellossv
loveless
eellosuv
levulose
eellrssu
ruleless
eelmmpux
exemplum
eelmnoos
lonesome
eelmnsuy
unseemly
eelmnttu
temulent
eelmntuy
unmeetly
eelmoosv
lovesome
eelmopry
employer
eelmopsy
polyseme
eelmorst
molester
eelmorty
remotely
eelmossv
moveless
eelmotvw
twelvemo
eelmppru
empurple
eelmprtu
plum-tree
eelmrrtu
murrelet
eelmrsst
termless
eelmrsty
smeltery
eelmrtux
luxmeter
eelmssst
stemless
eelnnoss
loneness
eelnnuvy
unevenly
eelnoors
loosener
eelnoppu
unpeople
eelnoprt
petronel
eelnoptt
tent-pole
eelnoqtu
eloquent
eelnorst
entresol
eelnortt
teletron
eelnosss
noseless
soleness
eelnosst
noteless
toneless
eelnossu
selenous
eelnossz
zoneless
eelnostv
love-nest
eelnotvv
evolvent
eelnsstu
tuneless
eelnsttu
unsettle
eeloppst
estoppel

eeloprrx
explorer
eelopstu
outsleep
eelorrsv
resolver
eelorrtv
revolter
eelorruv
overrule
eelorrvv
revolver
eelorsss
roseless
eelorstu
resolute
eelorsty
Tyrolese
eelorttu
roulette
eelortuv
revolute
true-love
eelosstv
voteless
eelosttx
sextolet
eelppstu
septuple
eelprtxy
expertly
eelpssux
plexuses
eelpstux
sextuple
eelrrstw
wrestler
eelrssst
restless
eelrssty
tyreless
eelrstwy
westerly
eemmnoop
menopome
eemmnotv
movement
eemmoors
merosome
eemnnrsu
mensuren
eemnorrs
sermoner
eemnorst
sermonet
eemnorsu
mounseer
eemnprtu
untemper
eemnsstu
muteness
tenesmus
eemnsttv
vestment

eemoorrv
moreover
eemoossx
exosmose
eemoprrs
premorse
eemoqrsu
Moresque
eemoqttu
moquette
eemorrtu
mouterer
outremer
eemorsst
somerset
tree-moss
eemorstu
temerous
eemotttu
teetotum
eemprrsu
presumer
eemprsst
sempster
eemrrttu
mutterer
eennnoss
nonsense
eennnotv
non-event
eennnpty
tenpenny
eennooot
one-to-one
eennoort
rotenone
eennopss
openness
eennoptx
exponent
eennorrw
renowner
eennsstx
nextness
eenoorst
roestone
eenoortv
overtone
eenopprs
propense
eenoprss
response
eenoprst
protense
eenoprsu
peroneus
eenoprtt
entrepot
tent-rope
eenoprxy
pyroxene
eenorsss
soreness

eenorssu
neuroses
eenorstt
onsetter
setter-on
eenorstx
extensor
eenortvw
overwent
eenosswy
snow-eyes
eenprsst
pertness
eenprssu
pureness
eenprstt
strepent
eenprstu
purse-net
eenpsssu
suspense
eenpsttu
petuntse
eenpttuz
petuntze
eenrrstv
renverst
eenrrtuv
venturer
eenrsssu
sureness
eenrsstu
trueness
eenrstuw
wet-nurse
eeooprsx
exospore
eeooprtz
zoetrope
eeoorrvv
rove-over
eeoorrvw
overwore
eeopprss
porpesse
eeoprrrt
reporter
eeoprrrv
reprover
eeoprrsu
reposure
eeoprrtt
potterer
eeoprrtx
exporter
re-export
eeoprsss
espresso
eeoprsst
portesse
eeoprssu
espouser
repoussé

eeoprstv
overstep
eeoprsty
serotype
eeoprsux
exposure
eeopsstw
sweet-sop
eeoqrttu
roquette
eeorrrst
resorter
restorer
retrorse
eeorrrtt
retorter
eeorrstx
extrorse
eeorrttt
totterer
eeorrttu
teru-tero
eeorrtuv
overture
trouvère
eeorstvx
vortexes
eeortttz
terzetto
eeossttt
sestetto
eepqrruu
perruque
eeprrssu
pressure
eeprsttu
setter-up
upsetter
eerrsstu
tressure
eerrstuv
vesturer
eerrstvy
revestry
eerrsuvy
resurvey
eersttu
utterest
effgilru
griefful
effginor
offering
effhiils
file-fish
effhiisw
fishwife
effhiitt
fiftieth
effhikuy
kuffiyeh
effhilrw
whiffler
effhiotw
off-white

effhllsu
shelf-ful
effhllsy
flesh-fly
effhlrsu
shuffler
effhoors
offshore
effilnrs
sniffler
effilort
forelift
effinosu
effusion
effiortw
write-off
effiqrsu
squiffer
efflmnuu
unmuffle
efflnrsu
snuffler
efflnruu
unruffle
effnrssu
snuffers
effooort
forefoot
efforruv
overruff
efggiinn
feigning
efggilos
solfeggi
efggirtu
egg-fruit
efggorry
froggery
efghiinr
Feringhi
efghilsu
fish-glue
efghinot
night-foe
efghinrt
frighten
efghirsy
grey-fish
efghnotu
foughten
efgiilnu
figuline
efgiimns
misfeign
efgiinnr
infringe
refining
efgiinru
figurine
efgiituv
fugitive
efgiknor
foreking

efgillno
lifelong
long-life
efgillnu
fuelling
efgilluu
guileful
efgilmor
filmgoer
efgilnor
florigen
efgilntt
fettling
efgilntw
left-wing
efgilpru
fire-plug
efgimruu
refugium
efginnnp
pfenning
efginorv
forgiven
efginorw
forewing
efginpuy
pinguefy
efginrry
ferrying
efginrtt
fretting
efginrty
gentrify
efgioptt
pettifog
efgkmoos
fog-smoke
efgloovx
foxglove
efglrsuu
surgeful
efglsstu
slugfest
efgnssuu
funguses
efhhirss
freshish
efhiilmn
Niflheim
efhiilns
line-fish
efhiilst
tilefish
efhiinrs
finisher
efhiipps
pipe-fish
efhiiprs
fireship
efhiirss
Friesish
efhiirsw
fish-weir

8 EFH

efhikoor
fire-hook
efhiksty
shift-key
efhiltwy
white-fly
efhiooor
forhooie
efhioprs
foreship
efhiorss
rosefish
efhiorsv
overfish
efhiortt
fortieth
efhiprss
serfship
efhirrtu
thurifer
efhisstw
fish-stew
efhklnou
funkhole
efhlllsu
shellful
efhlnors
hornfels
efhlooss
hoofless
efhloost
elf-shoot
efhlopst
flesh-pot
efhlorsy
horsefly
efhlorvy
hover-fly
efhlosuu
houseful
efhlosuy
house-fly
efhnrrsu
fresh-run
efhoorsw
foreshow
efhoosst
soft-shoe
efhorrty
frothery
efhrsttu
furthest
efiiilrv
vilifier
efiiinnt
infinite
efiiirvv
vivifier
efiikrrs
fire-risk
efiillrs
frillies
efiilnrt
infilter
efiilnty
felinity
finitely
efiiloqu
filioque
efiilprt
rifle-pit
efiilrsu
fusilier
efiilstt
fitliest
efiimmns
feminism
efiimnst
feminist
efiimnty
feminity
efiinorr
inferior
efiinort
notifier
efiinpsv
fivepins
efiinpsx
spinifex
efiinrsy
resinify
efiinsuv
infusive
efiiprrs
Spirifer
efiiprru
purifier
efiiprst
spit-fire
efiiprty
typifier
efiirtuv
fruitive
efiirvvy
revivify
efijlors
frijoles
efikloor
roof-like
efiklorw
life-work
efiknnos
finnesko
efiknors
foreskin
efiknrsu
refusnik
efikorrw
firework
efikrtuy
key-fruit
efilllnu
fluellin
efilllsw
self-will
efillmsu
smileful
efillmtu
full-time
efillorv
overfill
efillosu
fusel-oil
efillruy
irefully
efillsty
stellify
efilltuy
futilely
efilmrss
firmless
efilmsuy
emulsify
efilnntu
influent
efilnoru
fluorine
efilnosu
noiseful
efilnrtt
flittern
efilnuwy
unwifely
efiloprr
profiler
efilopst
sept-foil
efilortu
fluorite
efilprtu
uplifter
efilpstu
spiteful
efilpsty
self-pity
efilrstw
fewtrils
efilsttw
swiftlet
efimnorr
informer
reinform
reniform
efimnors
ensiform
efimnrss
firmness
efimorrt
retiform
efimorrw
fireworm
efimosst
semi-soft
efimostt
oft-times
efimrstu
fremitus
efinnoot
nine-foot
efinnpsu
fine-spun
efinoptx
pontifex
efinorrt
frontier
efinorsu
refusion
efinossx
foxiness
efinossz
foziness
efioprrt
port-fire
profiter
efiorrtt
retrofit
efipprry
frippery
efiprruy
repurify
efiprtty
prettify
efirrruy
furriery
efirrtuy
fruitery
efklloor
folklore
efklmnos
menfolks
efklnotu
folk-tune
efkloruw
fluework
efknoorw
foreknow
efkorrtw
fretwork
efllloow
woolfell
eflllowy
fellowly
eflllpsu
spellful
eflllptu
full-pelt
efllnssu
fullness
efllntuy
fluently
eflloorw
follower
eflloruv
overfull
efllosst
self-lost
soft-sell
efllouwy
woefully
efllruuy
ruefully
efllsuuy
usefully
eflmmruy
flummery
eflmorry
formerly
eflmorss
formless
eflnootw
wolf-note
eflnortt
frontlet
eflnossu
foulness
eflnossw
self-sown
eflnosty
stone-fly
eflnsuuu
unuseful
efloorss
roofless
efloorsw
foreslow
efloortu
footrule
efloorvw
overflow
eflopruw
powerful
eflopstw
fowl-pest
eflorruy
rye-flour
eflorsuy
yourself
eflosuux
flexuous
eflprssu
pressful
eflprsuu
purseful
eflrstuu
frustule
eflrstuy
flustery
efmmorst
stem-form
efmnorty
fromenty
efmnrtuy
frumenty
furmenty
efmoorst
foremost
efmoorsu
foursome
efnnooor
forenoon
efnnorst
fornenst
efnnoruz
unfrozen
efnooott
footnote
efnooprt
pentroof
efnoosst
eftsoons
efnoprst
forspent
efnossst
softness
efoooprt
foot-rope
efooorst
footsore
efooprsy
spoofery
efoopstt
footstep
efoorrsw
forswore
efoorstt
footrest
efoprrsu
profuser
eforrsst
fortress
eforrstw
frowster
eforrsty
forestry
eforrttu
frotteur
eforssst
fostress
egggooos
goosegog
egggorry
groggery
egghiinw
weighing
egghiksw
egg-whisk
egghirwy
Whiggery
egghoott
egg-tooth
egghrtuy
thuggery
eggiinns
singeing
eggillny
gingelly
eggilnnu
lungeing
eggilnrs
sniggler
eggilnry
gingerly
eggilqsu
squiggle
eggilrrw
wriggler
egginorr
gorgerin
egginrss
gressing
egginssu
guessing

eggiprry
priggery
eggjlruy
jugglery
eggllnos
long-legs
egglmooy
gemology
egglmrsu
smuggler
eggloruy
gurgoyle
egglrstu
struggle
eggnoops
egg-spoon
eggnoost
geognost
eggnoosy
geognosy
eggnorst
gongster
eggnrsuy
snuggery
eggoorsu
gorgeous
eghhiirs
high-rise
eghhilno
high-lone
eghhilty
eighthly
eghhinss
highness
eghhipru
higher-up
eghhipty
type-high
eghhistt
high-test
eghhloow
whole-hog
eghhoruw
rough-hew
eghiilnr
hireling
eghiilns
sheiling
shieling
eghiintv
thieving
eghiiptt
tithe-pig
eghiirst
tigerish
eghillns
shelling
eghillnw
well-nigh
eghilnpt
penlight
eghilnrs
shingler

eghilnss
shingles
eghilnsv
shelving
eghilntu
tile-hung
eghilort
regolith
eghilprt
plighter
eghimpru
grumphie
eghimstt
mightest
eghinnoy
honeying
eghinnss
nighness
eghinnst
sennight
eghinost
histogen
eghinosu
ginhouse
eghinpss
sphinges
eghinrsu
ushering
eghinttw
whetting
eghiopsu
pishogue
eghiorrv
river-hog
eghiotuw
outweigh
weigh-out
eghirruy
hierurgy
eghllnuw
well-hung
eghlmnop
phlegmon
eghlnruy
hungerly
eghlooor
horologe
eghloory
rheology
eghloosu
log-house
eghlooty
ethology
theology
eghlopru
plougher
eghlorst
short-leg
eghmnooy
homogeny
eghmopuy
hypogeum
eghmosuu
mug-house

eghnoopr
prong-hoe
eghnoopt
photogen
eghnooty
theogony
eghnoruv
hung-over
overhung
eghnotuu
Huguenot
eghnrstt
strength
eghooosw
hoosegow
eghorrtw
regrowth
egiikkln
kinglike
egiikllo
killogie
egiiknsz
king-size
egiilmmn
immingle
egiilmtw
lime-twig
egiilnor
niger-oil
religion
egiilnrs
Riesling
egiilnrt
girtline
tireling
egiilnrv
reviling
egiilnsw
wiseling
egiimnnu
ingenium
egiimnrs
Isengrim
semi-ring
egiimnrt
ring-time
egiimnsv
misgiven
egiimntt
emitting
egiimopt
impetigo
egiimorr
grimoire
egiimrst
tigerism
egiinnpr
repining
egiinnst
steining
egiinopr
peignoir
egiinors
seignior

egiinprx
expiring
egiinqtu
quieting
egiinrrt
retiring
egiinrst
strigine
egiinrsu
signieur
egiinrsw
ringwise
egiinrtu
intrigue
egiinrtv
riveting
egiinrtx
genitrix
egiinrvv
reviving
egiituxy
exiguity
egijnqru
jerquing
egikknrt
trekking
egiklnos
song-like
egiklnps
skelping
egiklnss
kingless
egiknorv
overking
egillmns
smelling
egillnor
Negrillo
egillnov
livelong
egillnps
spelling
egillnsw
swelling
egillntu
glutelin
egilloor
gloriole
egilmmry
glimmery
egilmnpu
implunge
egilmnst
smelting
egilmouu
eulogium
egilnnno
long-nine
egilnnst
nestling
egilnopp
popeling
egilnorw
lowering

egilnosu
ligneous
egilnosw
longwise
egilnprs
sperling
springle
egilnpry
replying
egilnrry
erringly
egilnrss
ringless
egilnrst
lingster
sterling
egilnrsw
newsgirl
egilnsss
signless
egilnssu
ugliness
egilnssw
wingless
egilnstt
settling
egilnvxy
vexingly
egiloosu
isologue
egilostu
eulogist
egilrrzz
grizzler
egilrtty
glittery
egimmnst
stemming
egimnors
negroism
egimnosu
geminous
egimnpru
impugner
egimnptt
tempting
egimnpty
emptying
egimnrss
grimness
egimnruy
eryngium
egimorst
ergotism
egimostw
twigsome
eginnors
nose-ring
eginnort
nitrogen
eginnorv
vigneron
eginnppy
penny-pig

eginnrru
unerring
eginoorv
ingroove
eginopry
pigeonry
eginorry
iron-grey
eginorst
Negritos
eginorsy
seignory
eginortu
outreign
eginortw
towering
eginorvw
overwing
eginppst
stepping
eginprrs
springer
eginprss
pressing
eginprtu
reputing
eginpryy
perigyny
eginqruy
querying
eginqstu
questing
eginrrst
restring
ringster
stringer
eginrrty
retrying
eginrsst
trigness
eginrssy
syringes
eginrstw
strewing
eginrsvw
swerving
eginrttu
tiger-nut
uttering
eginsttt
stetting
egioprtu
portigue
egiorsst
strigose
egiorssu
griseous
egiorsuv
grievous
egiosuux
exiguous
egirrsty
registry

egissyyz
syzygies
egjlnoru
jongleur
egjlnotu
jelutong
egllmorw
gromwell
eglloopy
pelology
eglmnoos
longsome
eglmnooy
menology
eglmnort
long-term
eglmnssu
glumness
eglmopru
promulge
eglmorss
gormless
eglnnoor
longeron
eglnnoss
longness
eglnntuy
ungently
eglnoooy
oenology
eglnoopr
prolonge
eglnoopy
penology
eglnoors
slogorne
eglnoorv
overlong
eglnoosv
love-song
eglnopyy
polygeny
eglnoruu
longueur
eglnosss
songless
eglnptuv
vent-plug
eglnrtuy
urgently
eglooory
oreology
egloopru
prologue
egloopty
logotype
egloorsy
serology
egloosxy
sexology
eglorrwy
growlery
eglorsuu
rugulose

eglorsuy
rugosely
egmnnooy
monogeny
nomogeny
egmnooos
mongoose
egmnoory
merogony
egmnoosu
mungoose
egmnrssu
grumness
egmnsssu
smugness
egnnooty
ontogeny
egnnostu
gunstone
egnnottu
ungotten
egnnsssu
snugness
egnnsttu
tungsten
egnoorrv
governor
egnootux
ox-tongue
egnoppru
oppugner
egnorrst
stronger
egnorsst
songster
egnorstu
sturgeon
egnorsty
sentry-go
egnsstuu
Tunguses
egooprru
prorogue
egoorrvw
overgrow
egoprrss
progress
egopssuy
gypseous
ehhiiprs
heirship
ehhiistv
thievish
ehhilmnt
helminth
ehhioprs
heroship
ehhiortt
hitherto
ehhiottw
white-hot
ehhirssw
shrewish

ehhloost
shot-hole
ehhnoors
shoehorn
ehhnssuy
hen-hussy
ehhoopss
shoe-shop
ehhoopst
theosoph
ehhoostu
hothouse
ehhorstu
shouther
ehiiklpt
pithlike
ehiiloss
heliosis
ehiilrsv
liverish
ehiimnnt
Nethinim
ehiimpst
mephitis
ehiinnos
inhesion
ehiinnrs
inshrine
ehiinrrt
hirrient
ehiinsvx
vixenish
ehiiprst
ship-tire
ehiiprsv
viperish
ehiirrtx
heritrix
ehiirssu
huissier
ehiisttx
sixtieth
ehijlswy
Jewishly
ehijostv
Jehovist
ehikllno
kiln-hole
ehiklnos
sink-hole
ehiklosy
yokelish
ehiklrsu
rush-like
ehikmnst
methinks
ehiknrrs
shrinker
ehikoprs
pokerish
ehikrswy
whiskery
ehilllmo
mole-hill

ehillmop
Philomel
ehillmot
mote-hill
ehillmoy
homelily
ehillopy
lyophile
ehillpty
phyllite
ehillrrt
thriller
ehillrty
litherly
ehillssw
swellish
ehillsww
well-wish
ehilmoor
heirloom
ehilmost
helotism
ehilmpsy
symphile
ehilmquu
umquhile
ehilnoop
oenophil
ehilnopt
thole-pin
ehilnoss
holiness
ehilnosv
novelish
ehilnotx
xenolith
ehilnpsy
sylphine
ehiloopz
zoophile
ehiloost
Holostei
ehiloprs
pilhorse
polisher
ehiloprt
heliport
ehilopss
slip-shoe
ehilopst
helistop
isopleth
ehilorty
rhyolite
ehilpsss
shipless
ehilpsst
pithless
ehilpstu
sulphite
ehilrsst
thrissel
ehilrstt
thristle

ehilrstw
whistler
ehilrsty
slithery
ehilrtty
triethyl
ehimmnuy
hymenium
ehimmrsy
shimmery
ehimnopr
morphine
ehimnort
thermion
ehimnosu
hemionus
ehimnott
monteith
ehimnpst
shipment
ehimnrru
murrhine
ehimnrry
myrrhine
ehimooss
homeosis
ehimoost
smoothie
ehimoprs
sopherim
ehimopst
Mephisto
ehimorst
isotherm
ehimppss
psephism
ehimprrs
shrimper
ehimprsu
murphies
ehimpsuu
euphuism
ehimpttu
umptieth
ehimrsst
smithers
ehimrsty
smithery
ehimssty
methysis
ehinnopr
phoner-in
ehinnopu
huon-pine
ehinnotw
non-white
ehinnsst
thinness
ehinnssu
sunshine
ehinnstt
thinnest
ehinoppr
hornpipe

ehinoprt
triphone
ehinopry
Hyperion
ehinopst
siphonet
ehinorss
herisson
ehinostu
outshine
ehinprsu
punisher
ehinssst
thisness
ehioppps
popeship
ehioppst
poetship
ehioppsu
Eohippus
ehiopstt
Peshitto
ehiopttw
white-pot
ehiorstt
theorist
ehiorstw
worthies
ehiortwz
howitzer
ehiottuw
white-out
ehipqsuy
physique
ehiprsst
hipsters
thripses
ehiprstw
whipster
ehiprswy
whispery
ehipstuu
euphuist
ehirrstt
thirster
ehirtttw
whittret
ehisstuw
thuswise
ehjmnoss
mess-john
ehklnoot
knot-hole
ehklosty
lekythos
ehkmmnor
mon-khmer
ehkmoorw
homework
ehkmorsu
humoresk
ehkmorsw
mesh-work

ehknnrsu
shrunken
ehllmopy
phyllome
ehllnstu
nutshell
ehllooop
loophole
ehllopst
top-shell
ehlmnouy
unhomely
ehlmoorw
worm-hole
ehlmorty
motherly
ehlnnopu
unholpen
ehlnopsu
sulphone
ehlnorss
hornless
ehlnosty
honestly
ehlnsssu
lushness
shunless
ehlooprt
porthole
ehloopst
post-hole
ehloopty
holotype
ehlopprt
thropple
ehloprty
prothyle
ehlorstt
throstle
ehlorsty
hostelry
ehlorttt
throttle
ehlosstw
thowless
ehlossty
thyloses
ehlrsstu
hurtless
ruthless
ehmmrrtu
thrummer
ehmnnpsu
sunn-hemp
ehmnoost
smoothen
ehmnootw
home-town
ehmnooty
theonomy
ehmnopsu
homespun
ehmoootz
zoothome

ehmoopty
homotype
ehmoorst
smoother
ehmoprsu
Morpheus
ehmorsty
smothery
ehmortuv
vermouth
ehmotuzz
mezuzoth
ehmrtuyy
eurythmy
ehnnoprt
penn'orth
ehnnorrt
northern
ehnnortu
unthrone
ehnnostu
unhonest
ehnoopty
honeypot
ehnoorru
honourer
ehnoorst
hen-roost
ehnoorsw
whoreson
ehnoossw
snow-shoe
ehnoprst
Strephon
ehnopsss
poshness
ehnorstt
thornset
ehnorstu
southern
ehnostuu
nut-house
ehnrrsuw
shrew-run
ehnrsstu
huntress
ehnssstu
thusness
ehooprty
orthoepy
ehoopstu
housetop
pothouse
ehooptyz
zoophyte
ehoorstv
overshot
ehoorstw
two-horse
ehoostuu
outhouse
ehopprsy
prophesy

ehoprsst
hot-press
ehoprsty
trophesy
ehoprsuv
push-over
ehoprtuy
eutrophy
ehopstuy
Typhoeus
ehorstuy
try-house
ehrrsttu
thruster
eiiilmss
similise
eiiilppr
liripipe
eiiimmns
minimise
eiiirrtv
tirrivie
eiijknrt
jirkinet
eiikkllm
milklike
eiikllmn
limekiln
eiikllno
lion-like
eiiklmrs
misliker
eiiklnps
spelikin
eiiklops
spike-oil
eiiklost
Sikeliot
eiiknnss
inkiness
eiiknnsw
wine-skin
eiiilllvy
livelily
eiillmnr
milliner
eiillmns
slimline
eiillmnu
illumine
eiillnst
niellist
eiillnsu
suilline
eiillntv
vitellin
eiilloov
olive-oil
eiillpss
ellipsis
eiillsuv
illusive
eiilmnns
Leninism

eiilmnnt
liniment
eiilmnot
limonite
eiilmnss
liminess
eiilmopt
impolite
eiilmpst
slime-pit
eiilmstt
mistitle
eiilmsty
myelitis
eiilnnot
lenition
eiilnnst
Leninist
eiilnoss
oiliness
eiilnott
toilinet
eiilnqtu
quintile
eiilnssw
wiliness
eiilnstw
wine-list
eiilnsty
senility
eiilnsvy
sylviine
eiilnttu
intitule
eiilntuv
vituline
eiilopps
soil-pipe
eiilopst
pisolite
eiilortt
troilite
eiilotvv
volitive
eiilprsu
plurisie
eiilpsst
pitiless
eiilpsty
pyelitis
eiilpsuz
spuilzie
eiilrstu
utiliser
eiimmnnt
imminent
miniment
eiimmnsu
immunise
eiimmpru
imperium
eiimmsss
seismism

eiimmsst
Semitism
eiimnnor
iron-mine
eiimnopt
pimiento
eiimnort
minorite
eiimnoss
emission
eiimnost
Timonise
eiimnosv
visnomie
eiimnotv
monitive
eiimnrss
miriness
eiimnrst
minister
eiimnrtt
intermit
eiimnrtx
intermix
eiimnttu
time-unit
eiimoprx
mirepoix
eiimopst
optimise
eiimossv
omissive
eiimosux
eximious
eiimotvv
vomitive
eiimprss
misprise
eiimprsz
misprize
eiimqstu
quietism
eiimrstt
metritis
eiimrstw
miswrite
eiimsstt
Semitist
eiinnnps
ninepins
eiinnosu
unionise
eiinnosv
envision
eiinnpss
spinnies
eiinnrtv
invertin
eiinnsst
tininess
eiinopst
sinopite
eiinoptt
petition

eiinorrt
interior
eiinorsv
revision
visioner
eiinprrs
inspirer
eiinprst
pristine
eiinptuv
punitive
eiinqrru
inquirer
eiinqtuy
equinity
inequity
eiinrsst
sinister
eiinrssw
wiriness
eiinrstt
sitter-in
eiinrstu
neuritis
eiinsssz
siziness
eiiopstv
positive
eiiosstt
osteitis
eiiotttv
totitive
eiipprtv
pit-viper
eiiprrtw
trip-wire
eiiprsty
pyritise
eiipsstt
stipites
eiiqrstu
Quirites
eiiqsttu
quietist
eiirsttu
uteritis
eijjntuy
jejunity
eijmnpss
jimpness
eijnortu
jointure
eijnostt
jettison
eijrstuy
Jesuitry
eikllmss
milkless
eikllntw
well-knit
eikllnuy
unlikely
eikllorv
overkill

eikllsss
skilless
eiklmnos
moleskin
eiklnoor
looker-in
oerlikon
eiklnosw
snowlike
eiklnprs
sprinkle
eiklnrst
linkster
strinkle
eiklnrtw
twinkler
eiklnsss
skinless
eikloprw
pilework
eiklopss
ski-slope
eiklsstt
skittles
eikmmors
mirksome
eikmnost
tokenism
eikmnosu
mousekin
eikmortw
time-work
eiknnost
inkstone
eiknnpss
pinkness
eiknoprs
rose-pink
eiknprst
Pinkster
eiknprtu
turnpike
eikopprw
pipework
eikoprsv
overskip
eikorrww
wirework
eikpstyy
tipsy-key
eillnty
lent-lily
eilllovy
lovelily
eilllpuv
pulville
eillmnou
linoleum
eillmops
plimsole
eillmpss
misspell
psellism
eillmptu
multiple
eillmuvx
vexillum
eillnoop
loop-line
eillnopy
epyllion
eillnost
stellion
eillnotu
luteolin
eillnpqu
quill-pen
eillnpst
ill-spent
eillnpuu
lupuline
eillnsty
silently
tinselly
eillnsvy
snivelly
eillnuvy
unlively
eilloosw
woollies
eillopty
politely
eillosss
soilless
eillosst
toilless
eillrstt
testrill
eillrsvy
silverly
eillssst
listless
eillstuv
vitellus
eilmmnos
Moslemin
eilmmsst
slimmest
eilmnoor
iron-mole
eilmnosu
emulsion
eilmnosv
novelism
eilmnotu
moulinet
eilmnoty
mylonite
eilmnpsu
splenium
eilmnptu
tump-line
eilmnrst
minstrel
eilmnsss
slimness
eilmnstu
muslinet
eilmntuy
minutely
untimely
eilmoops
liposome
eilmoost
toilsome
eilmoprr
implorer
eilmoprs
pelorism
sperm-oil
eilmoprw
pile-worm
eilmopst
polemist
eilmppru
impurple
eilmpruy
impurely
eilmpsst
misspelt
eilmrssy
remissly
eilmrsuu
Merulius
eilmttuu
lutetium
eilmttuy
multeity
eilnnost
insolent
eilnnosw
snowline
eilnnotv
vinolent
eilnntty
intently
eilnoopp
epiploon
eilnoops
polonise
eilnoopw
pine-wool
eilnoost
oilstone
stone-oil
eilnoppy
polypine
eilnoprt
Interpol
top-liner
eilnoptu
unpolite
eilnopty
Linotype®
eilnorrt
ritornel
eilnortt
trotline
eilnossw
lewisson
eilnostv
novelist
eilnosuv
evulsion
eilnotuv
involute
eilnotxy
Xylonite®
eilnotyz
zylonite
eilnprst
splinter
eilnpssu
splenius
eilnpstw
split-new
eilnpsuy
supinely
eilnquuy
uniquely
eilnrstu
insulter
lustrine
eilnrsty
tinselry
eilnrsuu
Ursuline
eilnrtuv
virulent
eilnrtwy
winterly
eilnsstt
tintless
eilnsttu
lutenist
eilnsuwy
unwisely
eilooptz
zopilote
eiloortv
overtoil
eiloppty
polypite
eiloprss
oil-press
eiloprsu
perilous
eiloprsv
overslip
slip-over
eiloprtw
pilewort
eilopstt
pistolet
eilopsuv
pluviose
eilorrtu
ulterior
eilorrtv
liver-rot
eilortty
toiletry
eilosttt
stiletto
eilostuv
love-suit
solutive
eilpprrt
trippler
eilpprst
stippler
eilpprsu
periplus
supplier
eilpprsy
slippery
eilpprtu
pulpiter
eilprstt
splitter
eilprsty
priestly
spritely
eilprsuy
pleurisy
eilprtty
prettily
eilqrrsu
squirrel
eilqrsuy
squirely
eilqstuu
lustique
eilrssst
stirless
eilrssty
sisterly
eilrsttw
wristlet
eilrsttz
strelitz
streltzi
eimmmnot
immoment
eimmnntu
muniment
eimmnors
misnomer
eimmopru
emporium
eimmopst
metopism
eimmostt
totemism
eimmrsuy
Erysimum
eimnnopt
imponent
eimnnopy
pin-money
eimnnott
ointment
eimnnouy
euonymin
eimnoops
empoison
eimnoors
moonrise
eimnoort
remotion
eimnoorv
omnivore
eimnoprt
orpiment
eimnoptt
impotent
eimnorss
minoress
eimnorsu
monsieur
eimnortw
time-worn
eimnorty
enormity
eimnprss
primness
eimnpsst
misspent
eimnrsst
trimness
eimnrstu
terminus
eimnrsty
misentry
eimnsssu
sensuism
eimoorst
motorise
eimoottt
Ottomite
eimopprr
improper
eimoprrs
primrose
promiser
eimoprrt
importer
reimport
eimoprrv
improver
eimoprst
imposter
eimopruu
europium
eimopstt
post-time
eimoqstu
misquote
eimorrtt
remittor
eimorrww
wire-worm
eimorstu
moisture
eimorsty
isometry
eimorsvw
overswim
eimorttw
two-timer
eimosstz
mestizos

eimosttt
totemist
eimosttu
titmouse
eimpssty
emptysis
eimpssuy
Puseyism
eimqstuy
mystique
eimrrssu
surmiser
eimrssst
mistress
einnorsv
environs
einnortt
tontiner
einnortu
neutrino
einnortv
noverint
einnorww
winnower
einnosss
nosiness
einnostt
tinstone
einnprsy
spinnery
einnpssu
puniness
einnpssy
spinneys
einnpsxy
sixpenny
einnrstu
sturnine
einnrttu
nutrient
einooprs
poisoner
einoorsz
ozoniser
einoossz
ooziness
einopprv
vine-prop
einoprrs
prisoner
einoprss
poriness
pression
ropiness
einoprsu
pruinose
einoprsv
overspin
einoprsy
Epyornis
einoprtu
eruption
einoprtw
port-wine
einopstt
nepotist
stone-pit
einopswx
swine-pox
einoqstu
question
einoqttu
quotient
einorrst
introrse
einorrtv
invertor
einorsss
rosiness
einorssu
neurosis
resinous
einorstt
tenorist
einorstv
investor
einorsty
tyrosine
einorsuv
souvenir
einorttu
ritenuto
einossst
stenosis
einosssu
Senoussi
einostuu
tenuious
einostvy
venosity
einpprrt
pre-print
einppsty
snippety
einprrst
sprinter
einprrtu
prurient
einprsst
spinster
einprstu
unpriest
einprstw
wrest-pin
einpsttx
spintext
einqrstu
squinter
einqrttu
quit-rent
einqtttu
quintett
einrssst
instress
einrssxy
syrinxes
einrtuuv
unvirtue
einssstu
sensuist
einsstwy
swine-sty
einsstxy
syntexis
eiooppr s
porpoise
eiooppst
opposite
eiooprst
portoise
eioorrss
sororise
eioorstt
tortoise
eiopprtw
pipewort
eioprrss
prioress
eioprrsu
superior
eioprrtv
overtrip
eioprstt
rispetto
eioprstv
sportive
eioprsuv
pervious
previous
viperous
eioprttt
triptote
eioprtty
petitory
eioprtuz
outprize
eiorrrst
errorist
eiorrrtu
roturier
eiorrsst
resistor
sorriest
eiorrstv
servitor
eiorrsvy
revisory
eiorssty
serosity
eiorsttu
tutorise
eiorstuv
virtuose
vitreous
eipprrst
stripper
eipprrty
trippery
eipqrstu
quipster
eiprrrsu
spurrier
eiprrssu
surprise
eiprsvvy
spivvery
eiqrrstu
squirter
eiqrsssu
squiress
eiqruyzz
quizzery
eirrsttu
trustier
eirssstu
suitress
eirtttuy
tityre-tu
eirtttwy
twittery
eirttuwz
wurtzite
ejlopstu
pulsojet
ejmoortt
motor-jet
ejmopruv
overjump
ejnssstu
justness
ekkmorsy
kromesky
eklnooor
looker-on
onlooker
eklnootv
love-knot
eklnosst
knotless
eklooorv
overlook
ekloopsw
slowpoke
eklorssw
workless
eklssstu
tuskless
ekmmorsu
murksome
ekmooprr
more-pork
ekmoorsw
worksome
ekmorssu
musk-rose
ekmrstuy
musketry
eknnopsu
unspoken
eknoorst
rose-knot
eknorttw
tent-work
ekooprrv
provoker
ekooprrw
ropework
ekooprsy
spookery
ekoorrvw
overwork
work-over
ekoprstu
upstroke
ekorruvy
kurveyor
elllmowy
mellowly
elllnsuy
sullenly
ellmnosy
solemnly
ellmnoty
moltenly
ellmnpuy
lumpenly
ellmoorw
well-room
ellmppuw
pump-well
ellnnssu
nullness
ellnoorv
lovelorn
ellnopru
prunello
ellnorrt
rent-roll
ellnorww
well-worn
ellnosvy
slovenly
ellnouvy
unlovely
elloprst
pollster
elloprtu
polluter
ellopruv
pullover
ellopsst
plotless
ellorrst
stroller
ellosssu
soulless
ellostuw
outswell
ellssstu
lustless
elmmnotu
lomentum
elmmnoty
momently
elmmrstu
strummel
elmmrsuy
summerly
elmnnosu
unsolemn
elmnooss
moonless
elmnopsu
pulmones
elmnuuzz
unmuzzle
elmoopsy
polysome
elmoorsy
morosely
elmoprty
metopryl
elmopryy
polymery
elmopsyy
polysemy
elmosyyz
lysozyme
elmprssu
rumpless
elmrrtuu
multurer
elnnoosu
unloosen
elnnoptu
nonuplet
elnopptu
punt-pole
elnoptty
potently
elnorstu
turnsole
elnorsvy
slovenry
elnortty
rottenly
elnosssw
slowness
snowless
elnosstw
wontless
elnprtuu
purulent
eloopruw
owerloup
eloopsss
sesspool
eloorsst
rootless
eloorstu
torulose
eloorsuv
oversoul
eloossst
sootless
elopprry
properly
eloprrty
porterly
eloprsty
prostyle

eloprsuv
overplus
eloprsyy
pyrolyse
eloprxyy
pyroxyle
elopssst
spotless
stopless
elorstuy
souterly
urostyle
elorttttu
troutlet
elprsssu
spurless
elprsttu
splutter
elrssstu
rustless
elrsttuy
sluttery
emmmnotu
momentum
emmnnotu
monument
emmnorsu
summoner
emmnottu
tomentum
emmnotyy
metonymy
emmooors
roomsome
emmoorss
mess-room
emmoptty
pommetty
emmrrruu
murmurer
remurmur
emmrstyy
symmetry
emnnnoou
noumenon
emnnooot
monotone
emnoopty
monotype
moon-type
emnoorst
mesotron
emnoorsu
enormous
nemorous
emnoorsw
newsroom
emnoorty
noometry
emnoosuv
venomous
emnootty
tenotomy

emnootuv
outvenom
emnopsyy
spy-money
emnorstt
sortment
emnorsuu
numerous
emnosuuy
euonymus
emooprrt
promoter
emooprsy
pyrosome
emooprsz
zoosperm
emoorrst
rest-room
emoorsss
moss-rose
emoortyz
zoometry
emopprrt
prompter
emoprssu
spermous
emorrruu
rumourer
emorsstu
strumose
emossttw
westmost
emprrtuy
trumpery
emprsttu
strumpet
ennnorty
non-entry
ennooort
tenoroon
ennoootz
entozoon
ennooppt
opponent
ennoprsu
unperson
ennopruv
unproven
ennoptwy
twopenny
ennorsst
sternson
ennorsty
sonnetry
ennorttu
unrotten
ennosstu
sunstone
ennpptuy
tuppenny
ennprruu
runner-up
enooossz
zoonoses

enooppst
postpone
enooprss
poorness
enoopstt
potstone
top-stone
enoorrvw
overworn
enoorstt
rot-stone
enopprru
unproper
enoprttu
putter-on
enopsssy
synopses
enorrtuu
tournure
enorrtuv
overturn
turnover
enorsssu
sourness
enorsttu
stentour
enorstty
snottery
enosssuu
sensuous
enprsssy
spryness
enprttuy
unpretty
enrrrtuu
nurturer
eoooprss
soporose
eoooprsz
zoospore
eoooprtz
zootrope
eooorrst
rose-root
eoopprrs
proposer
eooprrtu
outroper
uprooter
eooprstu
porteous
eooprstv
overpost
stop-over
eooprtuw
outpower
eoorrrsw
sorrower
eoorsstu
oestrous
eoorttuv
outvoter
eopprrty
property

eopprssu
supposer
eoppsssu
supposes
eoprrsst
portress
eoprrstu
posturer
eoprruvy
purveyor
eorrrttu
torturer
eorrssst
trossers
eorrsstu
trousers
eorrsuvy
surveyor
eorrtuuv
trouveur
eorssttu
tutoress
eorsttuw
outwrest
eorstuuv
vertuous
eppprtuy
puppetry
epprsssu
suppress
eprsttuy
sputtery
eqrrtuuu
truqueur
errstttu
strutter
ffffppuu
puff-puff
fffmootu
footmuff
ffggiiln
gliffing
ffghiinw
whiffing
ffghiors
frogfish
ffghirsu
gruffish
ffgiilnp
piffling
ffgiinns
sniffing
ffgiinps
spiffing
ffgilnru
ruffling
ffginnsu
snuffing
ffginstu
stuffing
ffhiisst
stiffish
ffhiisty
fiftyish

ffhilosu
foul-fish
ffhilosw
wolf-fish
ffhiopss
spoffish
ffhirssu
surf-fish
ffhlorty
froth-fly
ffhooost
offshoot
ffiilmor
filiform
ffiilnsy
sniffily
ffiilnty
flintify
ffiinoos
soffioni
ffiklrsu
friskful
ffillopp
flip-flop
ffilltuy
fitfully
ffilrtuu
fruitful
ffilrtuy
fruit-fly
ffilstuy
stuffily
ffimorsu
fusiform
ffinoprt
offprint
fflmnoou
moufflon
fflnotuu
fountful
fflorruu
furfurol
ffnstuuy
unstuffy
ffooortu
four-foot
ffoorruu
frou-frou
ffoorsst
off-sorts
fgggiinr
frigging
fgggilno
flogging
fgghiint
fighting
fgghintu
gunfight
fggiilnn
flinging
fggilnor
frogling
fgginoor
forgoing

fghiikns
kingfish
fghiilnt
in-flight
fghiinst
shifting
fghilltu
lightful
fghilmtu
mightful
fghilnsu
flushing
lung-fish
fghilnty
night-fly
fghilrtu
rightful
fghiopst
gift-shop
fghiottu
outfight
fghisstu
fish-guts
fghloruu
furlough
fghnotuu
unfought
fgiiknrs
frisking
fgiillnr
frilling
fgiilnpp
flipping
fgiilnrt
flirting
trifling
fgiilnst
stifling
fgiilntt
flitting
fgiinnuy
unifying
fgiinrtt
fritting
fgiinrtu
fruiting
fgiirstu
figurist
fgillnow
wolfling
fgilmnor
long-firm
fgilnntu
gunflint
fgilnoor
flooring
fgilnoot
footling
fgilnooz
foozling
fgilnost
softling
fgilnotu
outfling

fgilnpru
purfling
fgilntyy
fly-tying
fginnorw
frowning
fginoopr
proofing
fginorst
frosting
fgioprst
frog-spit
fgklnoos
folk-song
fgllmoou
gloomful
fglnoruw
wrongful
fglooost
footslog
fgnoortu
unforgot
fhhikoos
fish-hook
fhhoorst
shofroth
fhiiklms
milkfish
fhiiknss
fishskin
fhiillty
filthily
fhiilrst
flirtish
fhiilsty
shiftily
fhiklllo
hillfolk
fhikmnos
monk-fish
fhiknort
forthink
fhilloot
foothill
fhillort
hill-fort
fhilmpsu
lumpfish
fhilmrtu
mirthful
fhilorsu
flourish
fhilorty
frothily
fhimnoos
moon-fish
fhimprsu
frumpish
fhinrttu
unthrift
fhiooptt
photo-fit
fhiorsty
fortyish

fhllostu
slothful
fhlmotuu
mouthful
fhloostu
soothful
fhloottu
toothful
fhlorttu
trothful
fhlortuw
worthful
fhlortuy
fourthly
fhlostuu
outflush
fhlotuuy
youthful
fhlrttuu
truthful
fhooorst
forsooth
fiiilnop
Filipino
fiiinnty
infinity
fiijnort
joint-fir
fiiklrsy
friskily
fiillmsy
flimsily
fiillmtu
multifil
fiillnty
flintily
fiilmnry
infirmly
fiilmopr
piliform
fiilmpsy
simplify
fiilttuy
futility
fiimoprs
pisiform
fiimosty
moistify
fiinnosu
infusion
fiinortu
fruition
fiintuxy
unfixity
fiiquyzz
quizzify
fikklnos
kinsfolk
fiklnosw
wolf-skin
fiknorsw
forswink
filllttu
full-tilt

fillluwy
wilfully
fillnuuw
unwilful
filloppy
floppily
fillopsu
spoilful
filmoprs
slipform
filmorry
lyriform
filmossu
mofussil
filmpptu
lift-pump
filorsty
frostily
filrsttu
tristful
filsttuy
stultify
fimmnoor
omniform
fimmorru
muriform
fimoprry
pyriform
fimortuy
fumitory
fimostuy
fumosity
fimrstuu
futurism
finorsuy
infusory
fiorttuy
fortuity
fiprssuy
Prussify
firsttuu
futurist
firttuuy
futurity
fjllouyy
joyfully
fjlnouuy
unjoyful
fkkloorw
workfolk
fkkoortw
koftwork
fklmooot
folkmoot
fklnrtuu
trunkful
fkmoorrw
formwork
fknorsuw
forswunk
fkooortw
footwork
fllnooow
follow-on

flloopuw
follow-up
upfollow
flmnoruu
mournful
flmooorw
moorfowl
flmoossw
moss-flow
flmorstu
stormful
flnoopsu
spoonful
flnoostu
snootful
floooptt
poltfoot
flooostw
slow-foot
flooptty
toplofty
floosstw
soft-slow
floprstu
sportful
florttuu
troutful
flrsttuu
trustful
fmoopptu
foot-pump
fnnooort
frontoon
fnooortw
footworn
fnooprsu
sunproof
fnoorrsw
forsworn
fnoortuw
outfrown
fooopstt
footpost
ggggiiln
giggling
ggggilno
goggling
ggghiiln
higgling
ggghiint
thigging
ggghinos
shogging
gggiilnn
niggling
gggiinpr
prigging
gggijlno
joggling
gggijlnu
juggling
gggilnpu
plugging

ggginnsu
snugging
gghhiisw
Whiggish
gghiilnt
lighting
gghiimsw
Whiggism
gghiinrt
righting
gghiiprs
priggish
gghilssu
sluggish
gghimstu
thuggism
gghooprs
grog-shop
ggiijlnn
jingling
ggiiklnn
kingling
ggiillnr
grilling
ggiilmnn
mingling
ggiilmny
ginglymi
ggiilnnp
pingling
ggiilnns
gin-sling
singling
ggiimprs
priggism
ggiinnnr
grinning
ggiinnor
groining
ggiinnrw
wringing
ggiinnst
stinging
ggiinnsw
swinging
ggiinnuv
ungiving
ggiinppr
gripping
ggiirrss
grisgris
ggillnuw
gull-wing
ggilloow
golliwog
ggilmnoo
glooming
ggilnnou
lounging
ggilnnpu
plunging
ggilnorw
growling

ggilnory
glorying
ggilnttu
glutting
ggilqsuy
squiggly
gginnoos
goings-on
gginnopp
ping-pong
gginnoss
singsong
gginnotu
tonguing
gginnrtu
grunting
gginootu
outgoing
gginoprs
proggins
gginopru
grouping
gginortu
grouting
gglloowy
gollywog
gglpuuy
plug-ugly
gglnoost
long-togs
ggoooorr
groo-groo
ghhiilst
lightish
ghhiipsw
Whigship
ghhiistt
tightish
ghhilosu
ghoulish
ghhimost
highmost
ghhiorsu
roughish
ghhiostu
toughish
ghhoortu
thorough
ghiijnos
jingoish
ghiiknnt
thinking
ghiiknps
kingship
ghiiknsw
whisking
ghiillns
shilling
ghiilmst
mislight
ghiilmty
mightily
ghiilnrw
whirling

ghiilnst
tinglish
ghiilntw
whitling
ghiilttw
twilight
ghiinnnt
thinning
ghiinost
hoisting
ghiinpps
shipping
ghiinppw
whipping
ghiinrrs
shirring
ghiinrrw
whirring
ghiinrst
shirting
ghiinrsv
shriving
ghiinrtv
thriving
ghiinrtw
writhing
ghiinssw
swishing
ghiinwzz
whizzing
ghiiostv
Visigoth
ghiirstt
rightist
ghiklnty
knightly
ghiklsty
skylight
ghikmruu
Gurmukhi
ghiknntu
unknight
ghillotw
owl-light
ghillsty
slightly
ghilmpsu
glumpish
ghilnops
longship
ghilnopy
hopingly
ghilnosu
housling
ghilnotw
night-owl
ghilnruy
hungrily
ghilnstu
hustling
sunlight
ghiloprs
shop-girl

ghilorsw
showgirl
ghilprty
triglyph
ghimnopu
gumphion
ghimnptu
thumping
ghimnstu
gunsmith
ghinnnot
non-thing
ghinnnsu
shunning
ghinnort
northing
ghinnstu
shunting
ghinoopw
whooping
ghinoost
shooting
soothing
ghinopps
shopping
ghinoppw
whopping
ghinopss
shop-sign
ghinortw
ingrowth
throwing
ghinostt
shotting
ghinostu
shouting
southing
ghinostw
wing-shot
ghinosuy
youngish
ghinottu
outnight
ghinrrsu
rush-ring
ghinrruy
hurrying
ghinsstu
hustings
ghinsttu
shutting
ghiorttu
outright
ghiosttu
outsight
ghlmoooy
homology
ghlnnoor
longhorn
ghlnooru
hourlong
ghlnorsu
slughorn

ghlnotyy
yongthly
ghlooory
horology
ghlortuu
turlough
ghmpssuy
sphygmus
ghnopyyy
hypogyny
ghnostuu
unsought
ghoortuy
yoghourt
ghoprtuw
upgrowth
giiilmnt
limiting
giiilotv
vitiligo
giiinnot
ignition
giiinntv
inviting
giiinstv
visiting
giijmnos
jingoism
giijnnow
jowing-in
giijnost
jingoist
giikknns
skinking
giikllns
skilling
giiklnnt
tinkling
giiklnrs
skirling
giikmmns
skimming
giikmnps
skimping
giiknnns
skinning
giiknnst
stinking
giiknntt
knitting
giiknpps
skipping
giiknrst
skirting
striking
giillmr
mill-girl
giillnps
spilling
giillnqu
quilling
giillnrt
trilling

giillnst
stilling
giillnsw
swilling
giillntt
littling
giillopw
polliwig
giillpsw
pigswill
giilltuy
guiltily
giilmmns
slimming
giilmnps
simpling
giilmnpy
implying
giilmnzz
mizzling
giilmpsu
pugilism
giilnntw
twinling
giilnnuv
unliving
giilnppr
rippling
giilnpps
slipping
giilnprt
tripling
giilnqsu
quisling
giilnqtu
quilting
giilnrvy
virginly
giilnstt
slitting
stilting
giilnstu
linguist
giilnsty
stingily
giilnszz
sizzling
giilpstu
pugilist
giimmnpr
primming
giimmnrt
trimming
giimmnsw
swimming
giimnnoy
ignominy
giimnops
imposing
giimnott
omitting
giimnotv
vomiting

giimnssw
swingism
giimorrs
rigorism
giinnnot
intoning
giinnnps
spinning
giinnntw
twinning
giinnopt
pointing
giinnort
ignitron
giinnpps
snipping
giinnprt
printing
giinnrss
rinsings
giinnrtu
untiring
giinnstt
stinting
giinopst
positing
giinoptv
pivoting
giinorst
roisting
giinpprt
tripping
giinprss
rispings
giinprst
striping
giinprsu
uprising
giinprxy
pixy-ring
giinpstt
spitting
giinqttu
quitting
giinquzz
quizzing
giinrrst
stirring
giinrstv
striving
giinsssw
swissing
giinsttw
twisting
giintttw
twitting
giiorrst
rigorist
gijklnoy
jokingly
gijknnru
junk-ring
gijlnost
jostling

gikklnsu
skulking
giklnnop
plonking
giklnnru
knurling
giklnnuy
unkingly
giklnopr
porkling
giklorrw
work-girl
giknnott
knotting
giknnrtu
trunking
giknopst
kingpost
giknorrw
ringwork
giknorst
stroking
gillmooy
gloomily
gillnops
long-slip
gillnort
trolling
gillnosy
losingly
gillnovy
lovingly
gillnpuy
pulingly
gillnsuy
sullying
gilloopw
polliwog
gillopss
lipgloss
gillopwy
pollywig
gillorvy
gillyvor
gillossy
glossily
gilmmnsu
slumming
gilmnopy
mopingly
gilmnort
mortling
gilmnoss
moslings
gilmnott
mottling
gilmnotu
moulting
gilmnovy
movingly
gilmnsuy
musingly
gilmoosy
misology

gilmpruy
grumpily
gilnnotw
townling
gilnnouv
unloving
gilnnrsu
nursling
gilnoosy
Sinology
gilnoovy
vinology
gilnoppp
plopping
gilnopps
slopping
gilnoprw
prowling
gilnopsy
posingly
spongily
gilnoptt
plotting
gilnorvy
rovingly
gilnotuy
outlying
gilnprsu
spurling
gilnpryy
pryingly
gilnpuzz
puzzling
gilnrrsu
slurring
gilnrstu
lustring
rustling
gilnrttu
turtling
gilnrtyy
tryingly
gilntuuy
unguilty
gilooors
rosoglio
gilooost
oologist
giloorsu
glorious
giloorvy
virology
giloosss
isogloss
giloosty
sitology
gilostuy
gulosity
gimmmnuy
mummying
gimmnstu
stumming
gimmossu
gummosis

gimnnors
mornings
gimnnoru
mourning
gimnnotu
mounting
gimnnouv
unmoving
gimnooou
oogonium
gimnoops
spooming
gimnoptu
gumption
gimnorrw
ringworm
gimnorst
storming
gimnosyy
misogyny
gimpssyy
gypsyism
ginnnstu
stunning
ginnoosw
swooning
ginnopss
sponsing
ginnopsy
pyonings
ginnorst
snorting
ginnprsu
spurning
ginnrstu
unstring
ginoopps
opposing
ginoopst
stooping
ginopppr
propping
ginoppst
stopping
ginoppsw
swopping
ginoprst
sporting
ginopsst
signpost
ginopstt
spotting
ginorrwy
worrying
ginorstt
Storting
ginorstw
strowing
ginorsty
roysting
storying
ginorttt
trotting

ginorttu
trouting
tutoring
ginosttw
swotting
ginostuw
outswing
ginpprsu
upspring
ginprrsu
spurring
ginprsuu
pursuing
usurping
ginpttuy
puttying
ginrsstu
trussing
ginrsttu
trusting
gioorrsu
rigorous
gioorstu
goitrous
gioorsuv
vigorous
gioprsst
Strigops
gioprssy
gossipry
gioprstu
groupist
giorstuy
rugosity
gkloooty
tokology
gllnosuw
low-slung
glloopty
polyglot
glloopwy
pollywog
gllooxyy
xylology
glmnooot
monoglot
glmnoooy
monology
nomology
glmooopy
pomology
glmoorww
glow-worm
glmooyyz
zymology
glnnopsu
long-spun
glnooosy
nosology
glnoooty
ontology
glnoopst
long-stop

glnoopyy
polygony
glnopyyy
polygyny
glnorsty
strongly
glnortuw
lungwort
glnossuv
Volsungs
glnottuy
gluttony
glooopsy
posology
glooopty
optology
topology
gloooruy
ourology
gloopssy
gossypol
glooptyy
typology
gloorsuu
orgulous
gmmnotuy
tommy-gun
gmnnoooy
monogony
gmnnooyy
monogyny
gnnprsuu
unsprung
gnnrstuu
unstrung
gnoorsuw
wrongous
gnpprsuu
upsprung
gooppru
pop-group
goorttuw
goutwort
hhhhssuu
hush-hush
hhiinnst
thinnish
hhiipsst
phthisis
hhilpssy
sylphish
hhimnpsy
nymphish
hhimpssu
sumphish
hhinoosw
nohowish
hhiorsst
shortish
hhkkssuu
khuskhus
hhmrstuy
rhythmus

hhoooopp
pooh-pooh
hhoopprs
phosphor
hhoorstt
hot-short
hiiilmns
nihilism
hiiilnst
nihilist
hiiilnty
nihility
hiiimrss
Irishism
hiiinrst
rhinitis
hiijnopt
hip-joint
hiikmnst
misthink
hiikmrss
skirmish
hiikoprs
piroshki
hiikoprz
pirozhki
hiikqrsu
quirkish
hiiksstt
skittish
hiilmmss
slimmish
hiilmost
homilist
hiilmpsu
silphium
hiilmpsy
impishly
hiilmswy
whimsily
hiilmtuy
humility
hiilnops
Sinophil
hiilpsst
thlipsis
hiilpssy
syphilis
hiilsstt
stiltish
hiimnstt
tinsmith
hiimopss
phimosis
hiimopst
Ophitism
hiinorst
histrion
hiinprst
shirt-pin
hiinpstw
twinship
hiippqsu
quippish

hiipprsu
Hippuris
hikknost
kink-host
hiknottu
outthink
hikooprt
trip-hook
hikoopss
spookish
hikoorsu
Kuroshio
hikopssy
kyphosis
hillmoot
moot-hill
hillmsuy
mulishly
hillnouy
unholily
hilloswy
silly-how
hilmnoot
monolith
hilmoopt
philomot
hilmopsy
mopishly
hilmppsu
plumpish
hilmpsyy
symphily
hilnopsu
unpolish
hilnosty
tonishly
hiloorst
short-oil
hiloppsy
popishly
hilortux
Ulothrix
hilortwy
worthily
hilossty
thylosis
hilostyy
toyishly
hilpprsu
purplish
hilppsuy
uppishly
hilssttu
sluttish
himmopru
phormium
himnoprx
phorminx
himnopsy
phisnomy
himnorrs
horn-rims
himooprs
isomorph

himoprsw
ship-worm
himoprww
whipworm
himorstu
humorist
himottvz
mitzvoth
hinnostw
thin-sown
hinnpstu
thin-spun
hinnssuy
sunshiny
hinopssy
hypnosis
hinopstw
township
hinortxy
thyroxin
hiooprtt
poortith
hioprsuz
rhizopus
hiopssty
phytosis
hiorrssy
sorryish
hiorsttu
Struthio
hiossttu
stoutish
hipppsuy
puppyish
hipsuyzz
Zizyphus
hjknopsu
junk-shop
hjnooopr
poor-john
hkkoopyy
hoky-poky
hkmnorru
krumhorn
hkmooorw
hook-worm
hknoorrw
hornwork
hkooprsw
workshop
hllloowy
hollowly
hllmnoou
monohull
hlloppry
prophyll
hllppsuu
push-pull
hlmoosty
smoothly
hlmoptuy
Plymouth
hlnooppy
polyphon

hlooppss
slop-shop
hlooprry
lorry-hop
hloosstu
soul-shot
hlprsuuy
sulphury
hmmnooyy
homonymy
hmmoorsu
mushroom
hmmrstuu
humstrum
hmnooost
moonshot
hmnoooty
homotony
hmnoorrw
hornworm
hmnoostu
unsmooth
hmnopsyy
symphony
hmoooprz
zoomorph
hmooorsw
showroom
hmooptyy
homotypy
hmoorsuu
humorous
hmopsstu
puss-moth
hnoooopr
oophoron
hnooprst
post-horn
hnooprsw
shopworn
hnoorrtw
hornwort
hnoorstu
southron
hnortuwy
unworthy
hoooottt
hoot-toot
hooosttu
outshoot
shoot-out
hooppsty
photopsy
hooprrst
porthors
hoorttuw
outworth
throw-out
hootttuu
hout-tout
hopprryy
porphyry
hoprrsuy
pyrrhous

hprsttuu
upthrust
iiiklnps
spilikin
iiikmnss
miniskis
iiillmnp
minipill
iiillmnu
illinium
iiillnos
illision
iiilmrsv
virilism
iiilmuvx
lixivium
iiilrtvy
virility
iiimmmns
minimism
iiimmnst
intimism
minimist
iiimmprs
imprimis
iiimnstt
intimist
iiimntty
intimity
iiinorrs
irrision
iiinprst
inspirit
iiinqtuy
iniquity
iiinsstu
sinuitis
iiiosttu
ouistiti
iijjstuu
jiu-jitsu
iijlnoot
joint-oil
iikklmms
skim-milk
iikklmnr
kirn-milk
iikllnos
skillion
iiklmpsy
skimpily
iillllptu
Lilliput
iilllpuv
pulvilli
iillmrtu
trillium
iillnoor
orillion
iillnort
trillion
iillnost
stillion

iillnosu
illusion
iillopuv
pulvilio
iilmmnos
Molinism
iilmmpss
simplism
iilmnort
mirliton
iilmnost
Molinist
iilmnosu
Limousin
iilmnstu
luminist
iilmorst
troilism
iilmotty
motility
iilmpsst
simplist
iilmrssy
missilry
iilnnoot
nolition
iilnoors
rosin-oil
iilnoost
inositol
iilnootv
volition
iilooppr
liripoop
iilopsss
psilosis
iilopsst
ptilosis
iilopsty
pilosity
iilrsstu
silurist
iilstuuv
uvulitis
iilstuvv
vulvitis
iimmnost
Timonism
iimmntuy
immunity
iimmopst
optimism
iimmsttu
mittimus
iimnnoot
monition
iimnnosu
unionism
iimnnotu
munition
iimnooss
omission
iimnoprs
imprison

iimnopst
mispoint
iimnortt
intromit
iimnorty
minority
iimnosst
simonist
iimnostt
Timonist
iimnprst
misprint
iimnptuy
impunity
iimnrsty
ministry
iimopstt
optimist
iimossty
myositis
iimottvy
motivity
iimprtuy
impurity
iimrrttu
Trimurti
iimrrtuv
triumvir
iimsstuw
swimsuit
iinnoppt
pinpoint
iinnoptu
punition
iinnostu
inustion
unionist
iinnsttu
tinnitus
iinoopst
position
iinostvy
vinosity
iinprstw
wrist-pin
iinqrsuu
Quirinus
iinrttuy
triunity
iiooppuu
piou-piou
iioopstv
oviposit
iioostty
otiosity
iioppstv
pop-visit
iioprrty
priority
iiorrrsy
irrisory
iiorstuv
virtuosi

iiprsstu
spiritus
ijllmnor
Mjōllnir
ikklnorw
linkwork
ikklnosy
kolinsky
ikknortw
kirktown
ikllmorw
mill-work
iklootv
kilovolt
ikllossy
kyllosis
iklmorsw
silkworm
iklmortw
milkwort
iklnoosw
skin-wool
iklnopst
slip-knot
ikloopsy
spookily
iklopsty
sky-pilot
iknnopsy
pony-skin
iknnrstu
turnskin
iknooprt
pinkroot
iknoorrw
ironwork
iknopstt
stink-pot
iknopstw
townskip
ikorsstu
kurtosis
ikorsttu
outskirt
illlmoow
wool-mill
illlmops
plimsoll
illlmppu
pulpmill
illloopp
lollipop
illmoprw
pill-worm
illmopst
post-mill
illmptuy
multiply
illooprw
poorwill
illoppss
slipslop
illoppsy
sloppily

illoprtw
pillwort
illoprxy
prolixly
illopstt
pot-still
illorsuy
illusory
illottwy
wittolly
illrstuy
sultrily
ilmnoops
polonism
ilmnoopu
polonium
ilmnosuu
luminous
ilmoppsu
populism
ilmopstu
Psilotum
ilmorsty
stormily
ilmostuv
volumist
ilmostuy
timously
ilmpptuu
pulpitum
ilmpstuy
stumpily
ilmsstuu
stimulus
ilmsttuy
smuttily
ilnoopsy
spoonily
ilnoortw
toil-worn
ilnoostu
solution
ilnoottt
tint-tool
ilnootuv
volution
ilnopstu
unspoilt
ilnortxy
nitroxyl
ilnosstw
stowlins
ilnostty
snottily
ilnpsuuv
pulvinus
iloopppy
poppy-oil
iloopprs
propolis
iloorstu
risoluto
iloppstu
populist
iloprsty
sportily
ilopstty
spottily
ilopsuuv
pluvious
iloqrtuu
loquitur
ilpprtuy
pulpitry
ilrsttuy
trustily
ilrstuux
luxurist
immoortu
motorium
immrstuy
summitry
immrttuu
rum-ti-tum
imnnoott
monotint
imnnosuu
numinous
imnoopsu
opsonium
imnoorty
monitory
imnostuu
mutinous
imnrstuu
untruism
imooprrs
promisor
imooprst
impostor
imooprtu
muir-poot
imooqstu
mosquito
imoorstt
motorist
imoorstu
timorous
imoorsty
morosity
imoortvy
vomitory
imoossty
myosotis
imoprrsy
primrosy
imoprtuu
muir-pout
imorsttu
tutorism
impppsuy
puppyism
imrssttu
mistrust
imrsstty
mistryst
innnnoou
non-union
innnortu
trunnion
innnosty
syntonin
innoopss
sponsion
innoopsu
unpoison
innoorst
notornis
innoprsu
unprison
innprrtu
print-run
innprstu
sun-print
inooossz
zoonosis
inoootxz
zootoxin
inooprst
positron
sorption
inoopstt
spittoon
inoopttu
outpoint
inoorsty
sonority
inoprttu
print-out
inoprtuy
punitory
inoprtwy
port-winy
inopsssy
synopsis
inorssuv
sun-visor
inortuvy
ivory-nut
inpprruu
purpurin
inprsttu
turnspit
iooprrsv
provisor
iooprssy
isospory
iooprsty
isotropy
porosity
ioorrsty
sorority
ioorrttt
trottoir
ioorssuv
voussoir
ioorsttu
tortious
ioorstuv
virtuoso
ioorsuux
uxorious
ioossttu
stotious
ioprssuu
spurious
ioprsttu
outstrip
ioprstuy
pyritous
ioqrtuxy
quixotry
iorrsuvv
survivor
iorssuuu
usurious
iorsttuy
touristy
yttrious
iorstuuv
virtuous
iprrstuu
pruritus
jlnstuuy
unjustly
jloosuyy
joyously
jnnoorru
nonjuror
jnoosuuy
unjoyous
kknoortw
knotwork
kkoossuu
kouskous
kllmnsuu
numskull
klmmooos
Komsomol
klmmpsuu
musk-plum
klnorsty
klystron
kloooorww
woolwork
klooprsw
slopwork
kmooorrw
workroom
knooortt
root-knot
llooprty
trollopy
lloopryy
roly-poly
llosuuvv
volvulus
lmnooopy
monopoly
lmnoopyy
polyonym
lmoooort
toolroom
lmoopsyy
polysomy
lmoorsww
slow-worm
lmoosssu
molossus
lmopprty
promptly
lnoooprt
poltroon
lnooopyz
polyzoon
lnoopprу
propylon
looppsuu
populous
looppsuy
polypous
lorsstuu
lustrous
mmooppru
pump-room
mmoortty
tommy-rot
mnnoooty
monotony
mnnosyyy
synonymy
mnooortw
moonwort
mnooorxy
oxymoron
mnooprtu
pronotum
mnooptyy
toponymy
mnoprstu
no-trumps
mnorstuu
surmount
moooprrt
promotor
moooprtu
moor-pout
mooorrtw
tomorrow
moorrsuu
rumorous
moorstuu
tumorous
mopprstu
rump-post
morsstuu
strumous
nnooopst
spontoon
nooorssu
sonorous
noopsttw
post-town
nrsttuuy
untrusty
ooopprrt
prop-root
oooprssu
soporous
ooprsttu
outsport
oorsttuu
tortuous
oprsssuu
sourpuss
rrsssuuu
susurrus

9 AAA

aaaabcllv
Balaclava
aaaabennt
Nabataean
aaaabikll
balalaika
aaaacchmt
tacamahac
aaaacchrr
arracacha
aaaacdjnr
jacaranda
aaaacdkly
alack-a-day
aaaacgilt
agalactia
aaaacirru
araucaria
aaaacmnrt
catamaran
aaaaglprt
alpargata
aaaahhjmr
maharajah
aaaaillpr
paralalia
aaaallmmy
Malayalam
aaaamprtt
paramatta
aaaanrrtt
tantarara
tarantara
aaaarrsss
sassarara
aaabbdinr
Barbadian
aaabbinrr
barbarian
aaabblmox
balaam-box
aaabccemn
Maccabean
aaabcchhr
bacharach
aaabcchln
bacchanal
aaabcchnr
charabanc
char-à-banc
aaabcdeir
Carabidae
aaabcdiit
adiabatic
aaabcdrru
barracuda
aaabceltu
acetabula
aaabcemrt
carbamate
aaabcenrs
sarbacane
aaabchirt
batrachia

aaabchnnr
anabranch
aaabchnru
carnahuba
aaabciktt
katabatic
aaabcilnt
abactinal
aaabcinpr
Pan-Arabic
aaabciqtu
aquabatic
aaabcknnt
cantabank
aaabclmor
carambola
aaabclmru
ambulacra
aaabclnot
canal-boat
aaabdeehh
dahabeeah
aaabdegrv
bavardage
aaabdeint
Tabanidae
aaabdelnr
Aldebaran
aaabdelpt
adaptable
aaabdhhiy
dahabiyah
aaabdills
sabadilla
aaabdoqru
aquaboard
aaabeemno
amoebaean
aaabeghll
gallabeah
aaabegmss
ambassage
aaabeillv
available
aaabeilmn
alabamine
aaabeilmt
Balaamite
aaabekprr
parabrake
aaabekrwy
breakaway
aaabellpt
palatable
aaabelmot
Ametabola
aaabelmss
amassable
aaabelrst
alabaster
aaabelssy
assayable
aaabghill
gallabiah

aaabghily
galabiyah
aaabgilly
gallabiya
aaabglorr
algarroba
aaabhlrst
balthasar
aaabhlrtz
balthazar
aaabiksst
katabasis
aaabilltv
ablatival
aaabillvy
availably
aaabilmns
Balsamina
aaabinnsu
banausian
aaabiprss
parabasis
aaabjlmno
jambolana
aaabknott
tanka-boat
aaabllpty
palatably
aaabloprs
parabolas
aaaccceet
Cactaceae
aaaccchhh
cha-cha-cha
aaaccdelv
cavalcade
aaaccdhmn
camanachd
aaaccdilr
cardiacal
aaacceeer
Aceraceae
aaacceehr
Characeae
aaaccehim
cachaemia
aaaccelln
calcaneal
aaaccelnn
calcanean
aaaccelnv
calavance
aaaccelpr
palace-car
aaaccelrt
calcarate
aaaccenrv
caravance
aaaccflot
catafalco
aaaccinsu
Caucasian
aaaccirtt
ataractic

aaacclmno
calamanco
aaacclmst
cataclasm
aaacddiln
dandiacal
aaacdehln
Chaldaean
aaacdeinr
acaridean
aaacdeirs
Ascaridae
aaacdenrv
caravaned
aaacdhinr
Arachnida
aaacdhnrs
sandarach
aaacdiinr
acaridian
aaacdilnr
calandria
aaacdlmru
dulcamara
aaacdlrst
cadastral
aaacdnrss
Cassandra
aaaceeioz
Aizoaceae
aaaceelmv
Malvaceae
aaaceelru
Lauraceae
aaaceenno
Anonaceae
aaaceenrs
Caesarean
aaacegort
Arctogaea
aaacehlnp
acalephan
aaacehlnv
avalanche
aaacehrtt
Tracheata
aaaceimnr
Americana
aaaceimnt
catamenia
aaaceimpr
paramecia
aaaceimtt
atacamite
aaaceinrs
Caesarian
aaacemmnr
cameraman
aaacenrrv
caravaner
aaacenrsy
sea-canary
aaacfilnt
fanatical

aaacgilnt
agnatical
aaacgllsw
scallawag
aaachilnr
anarchial
aaachilnw
Walachian
aaachimnu
naumachia
aaachinrs
anacharis
aaachlmnt
nachtmaal
aaachlnrt
charlatan
aaachlprr
chaparral
aaachlrrt
catarrhal
aaachnpty
panchayat
aaachosuy
Ayahuasco
aaaciirss
acariasis
aaacillmr
camarilla
aaacilnor
Aaronical
aaacilnpt
aplanatic
aaacilnru
lacunaria
aaacilnst
Castalian
satanical
aaacilrtu
actuarial
aaacinopr
paranoiac
aaacinott
catatonia
aaacinrsu
Casuarina
aaacinstt
anastatic
aaaclmmpw
macaw-palm
aaaclmnpu
Campanula
aaaclmpst
cataplasm
aaaclnrsy
canal-rays
aaacmorst
sarcomata
aaacmrsst
camass-rat
aaacmrtux
Taraxacum
aaaddeiln
Daedalian

aaaddhmry
hamadryad
aaaddilnr
Dalradian
aaaddinnr
Dardanian
aaadeffnr
fanfarade
aaadefgmr
megafarad
aaadefist
asafetida
aaadegnpp
appanaged
aaadegntv
advantage
aaadeinrv
Varanidae
aaadelmmr
marmalade
aaademnot
adenomata
aaadeoptz
zapateado
aaadgnppr
grandpapa
aaadhhprz
haphazard
aaadhiopr
adiaphora
aaadhlmrs
dharmsala
aaadhmrss
madrassah
aaadillnp
Palladian
aaadilmnt
Dalmatian
aaadilprs
paradisal
aaadinnos
Adansonia
aaadioppr
parapodia
aaadllmns
Landsmaal
aaadlmmnn
landamman
aaadlmnqu
qualamdan
aaadlmpry
lampadary
aaadloprx
paradoxal
aaadmnrty
mandatary
aaaeegrrr
arrearage
aaaeehmnr
maharanee
aaaeeknrs
area-sneak
aaaegglrv
galravage

aaaeggrtv
aggravate
aaaegilns
analgesia
aaaegiqru
aqua-regia
aaaeglllt
talegalla
aaaeglmnu
malagueña
aaaeglnns
salangane
aaaeglssv
vassalage
aaaegmnnt
manganate
aaaehmmot
haematoma
aaaehmnst
anathemas
aaaeilmrs
lamaserai
aaaeilprx
paralexia
aaaeimnps
spanaemia
aaaeimprs
sapraemia
aaaeiqtuv
aqua-vitae
aaaellnpt
panatella
aaaelnntt
antenatal
Atlantean
Tantalean
aaaelnpqu
aquaplane
aaaelnttt
tantalate
aaaelprst
palaestra
aaaemrrrt
terramara
aaaenrrtt
Tartarean
aaaffnnor
fanfarona
aaafgirsx
Saxifraga
aaafiknrs
Afrikaans
aaafinors
Afro-Asian
aaafirrst
Rastafari
aaaflorst
solfatara
aaafrssss
sassafras
aaaggmrss
gama-grass
aaaghjnnt
Jagannath

aaaghllnp
phalangal
aaaghpprr
paragraph
aaagilopr
paralogia
aaagilrst
tarsalgia
aaagimnot
angiomata
aaaginnrv
Varangian
aaaglnpty
anaglypta
aaagmnpty
pantagamy
aaagnorrt
Tarragona
aaagprssu
asparagus
aaahhimns
shamianah
aaahhllms
mashallah
aaahikklt
kathakali
aaahilmny
Himalayan
aaahimnru
marihuana
aaahinsvv
Vaishnava
aaahknrst
astrakhan
aaahlloty
ayatollah
aaahmnntt
Manhattan
aaahmnpst
phantasma
aaahmnrtt
harmattan
aaaiilmnr
Laminaria
aaaiinrst
sanitaria
aaaijmnru
marijuana
aaaikklmr
kalamkari
aaailmmmn
mammalian
aaailmnpr
palmarian
aaailmnsy
Malaysian
aaailmort
amatorial
aaailnnot
Anatolian
aaailnnpr
planarian
aaailnntt
Tantalian

aaailnppt
antipapal
aaailnrsu
Laurasian
aaailnsst
assailant
aaailpprs
appraisal
aaaimnnoz
amazonian
aaaimnnst
Tasmanian
aaaimnntz
manzanita
aaaimnort
amatorian
inamorata
aaaimnrst
Samaritan
Sarmatian
aaainnsss
Sassanian
aaainoprs
Saponaria
aaainqttu
aquatinta
aaainrrtt
Tartarian
aaainrstt
Astrantia
aaainssst
anastasis
aaaiprstx
parataxis
aaalmortx
malaxator
aaalnpsty
anaplasty
aaalnrssv
salvarsan
aaalnrttu
tarantula
aaaloopps
Appaloosa
aaammnrst
man-at-arms
aaamnnotz
amazon-ant
aaamnrstu
Amarantus
aaanprtuv
paravaunt
aaanrsstt
tarantass
aaaopprzz
paparazzo
aaapprstu
apparatus
aaarrsssu
sussarara
aabbccirr
bric-à-brac
aabbcdeil
abdicable

aabbcdkln
blackband
aabbcehll
beach-ball
aabbceinr
Caribbean
aabbcekkr
breakback
aabbceoot
babacoote
aabbcilms
cabbalism
aabbcilst
cabbalist
aabbcklll
blackball
aabbckmrr
barmbrack
aabbddnor
broadband
aabbdeelt
debatable
aabbdeknr
band-brake
aabbdekor
bakeboard
aabbdenor
broad-bean
aabbdeors
Barbadoes
baseboard
aabbdllny
bandy-ball
aabbdnost
bandobast
aabbeeklr
breakable
aabbehill
habilable
aabbehilt
habitable
aabbeiilt
bilabiate
aabbeinrt
Barnabite
rabbinate
aabbeinst
sabbatine
aabbeirrs
barbarise
aabbeisst
sabbatise
aabbelrst
barbastel
aabbhilty
habitably
aabbimrrs
barbarism
aabbimsst
sabbatism
aabbirrty
barbarity
aabbirssu
babirussa

aabborrsu
barbarous
aabccccei
beccaccia
aabccdefr
crab-faced
aabccehlt
catchable
aabccehnt
bacchante
aabcceklm
camelback
aabccelsu
accusable
aabcchhkt
hatchback
aabcchikn
back-chain
aabcchkku
huckaback
aabcchnow
chaw-bacon
aabccikkp
pickaback
aabcciort
acrobatic
aabccjkkl
blackjack
aabcckkrt
backtrack
aabcckllo
coal-black
aabcck1rw
back-crawl
aabcddefl
bald-faced
aabcddenn
dance-band
aabcddorr
cardboard
aabcdeefr
barefaced
aabcdeehh
beachhead
aabcdehkl
blackhead
aabcdeill
cable-laid
cebadilla
aabcdeimr
carbamide
aabcdeirr
barricade
aabcdekll
blacklead
aabcdeklp
back-pedal
aabcdeklr
lack-beard
aabcdelnr
barnacled
aabcdelpr
clapbread
aabcdelrt
card-table
aabcdemrv
vambraced
aabcdemsu
ambuscade
aabcdenno
abondance
aabcdennu
abundance
aabcdenor
carbonade
aabcdenps
space-band
aabcdfrrt
bard-craft
aabcdhiln
baldachin
aabcdhilr
Archibald
aabcdilms
labdacism
aabcdiorr
barricado
aabcdiors
scaraboid
aabcdkrsw
backwards
aabcdlopr
clapboard
aabcdlsuu
subcaudal
aabcdmosu
ambuscado
aabcdnnuy
abundancy
aabcdnoor
carbonado
aabcdnort
cant-board
aabcdorst
broadcast
aabceeeen
Ebenaceae
aabceeelp
peaceable
aabceehlr
reachable
aabceehlt
teachable
aabceehrs
sea-breach
aabceeiru
Rubiaceae
aabceekls
leaseback
aabceeknr
cane-brake
aabceellr
lacerable
aabceellv
cleavable
aabceelms
scale-beam
aabceelps
escapable
aabceelpy
peaceably
aabceelrs
calabrese
aabceelrt
creatable
traceable
aabceenrr
aberrance
aabceerrt
crab-eater
aabceertt
bracteate
aabcefirt
fabricate
aabcefosu
fabaceous
aabcefotu
about-face
aabcegilr
algebraic
aabcegklm
blackgame
aabcegkst
backstage
aabceglmr
cablegram
aabcegprt
carpet-bag
aabcehilr
Hebraical
aabcehinr
branchiae
aabcehitz
chabazite
aabcehklw
whale-back
aabcehlmt
matchable
aabcehlny
Chalybean
aabcehlpt
patchable
aabceillm
claimable
aabceilln
caballine
aabceilmn
imbalance
aabceilmp
impacable
aabceilmr
bicameral
aabceilnp
incapable
aabceilnt
cantabile
aabceilrt
bacterial
calibrate
aabceimnr
mainbrace
aabceimtt
metabatic
aabceinor
anaerobic
aabceinrs
braincase
aabceinrt
bacterian
aabceisss
abscissae
aabcekkls
slack-bake
aabceklpt
backplate
aabcekppr
paperback
aabcekrrr
barracker
aabcekrtw
backwater
aabcelllo
allocable
aabcellor
caballero
aabcellss
classable
aabcelmmr
crammable
aabcelmnu
ambulance
aabcelmor
carambole
aabcelnnu
unbalance
aabcelnpu
uncapable
aabcelntu
unactable
aabceloos
calaboose
aabcelorr
barcarole
aabcelppr
crab-apple
aabcelrtt
tractable
aabcelrtu
trabecula
aabcelrty
traceably
aabcemorx
box-camera
aabcemost
emboscata
aabcenort
carbonate
aabcenrry
aberrancy
aabcenrtv
vantbrace
aabceorst
ascorbate
aabceostu
sauce-boat
aabceprrt
barret-cap
aabcerrtu
carburate
aabcfhkls
flash-back
aabcfinrt
fabricant
aabcgilln
caballing
aabcgklns
back-slang
aabcglrss
glass-crab
aabcgnors
gas-carbon
aabchilnr
branchial
aabchimnr
Brahmanic
aabchklsw
black-wash
aabchmnos
hansom-cab
aabchrruy
Brachyura
aabciills
basilical
aabciilns
basilican
aabciinot
anabiotic
aabcikllm
blackmail
aabciklnr
lack-brain
aabciklot
katabolic
aabcillry
bacillary
aabcillsy
basically
aabcilnot
botanical
aabcilnpy
incapably
aabcilopr
parabolic
aabcilruv
vibracula
aabcimnor
macrobian
aabcimorz
Mozarabic
aabcinorr
Carbonari
aabcissss
abscissas
aabckllmp
lamp-black
aabckllst
backstall
aabcklpsu
backspaul

aabcklrsy
scaly-bark
aabckmprr
cramp-bark
aabckorrz
razor-back
aabckortt
track-boat
aabckrstw
swart-back
aabckssty
backstays
aabclorss
coal-brass
aabcloruv
vocabular
aabclrssu
subsacral
aabcmnott
combatant
aabcnoorr
barracoon
aabddegls
saddle-bag
aabddehor
headboard
aabddeikr
dika-bread
aabddeinr
brain-dead
aabddelpt
baldpated
aabddelrs
saddle-bar
aabddenno
abandoned
aabddhorr
hardboard
aabddhors
dashboard
aabddnnst
bandstand
aabddorrt
dart-board
aabdeegll
bald-eagle
aabdeeilu
beau-ideal
aabdeellp
pleadable
aabdeellr
balladeer
aabdeelmn
amendable
aabdeelns
lease-band
aabdeemno
endamoeba
aabdeemss
embassade
aabdeenno
abandonee
aabdeertt
trabeated

aabdefglr
fardel-bag
aabdefhkl
half-baked
aabdeflnu
unfadable
aabdeflor
broad-leaf
loaf-bread
aabdegino
gabionade
aabdeginr
gabardine
aabdeglru
guardable
aabdegmor
board-game
aabdegnrr
bargander
aabdehhiy
dahabiyeh
aabdehjll
djellabah
aabdehknr
hand-brake
aabdehlnr
handlebar
aabdehnsu
unabashed
aabdeiiln
inaidable
aabdeillt
dilatable
aabdeilmr
admirable
aabdeilmt
table-maid
aabdeilnr
bird-alane
drainable
aabdeilnu
unaidable
aabdeilov
avoidable
aabdeilrv
adverbial
aabdeilsv
advisable
aabdeinst
bastinade
aabdeknrs
sand-break
aabdellnt
tableland
aabdellst
ballasted
aabdelnor
bandalore
aabdelnru
burd-alane
aabdelnst
sand-table
aabdelppy
dapple-bay

aabdelrtw
Bretwalda
aabdeltwy
tway-blade
aabdemnnr
brand-name
aabdemort
dreamboat
aabdemrtu
adumbrate
aabdeorst
adsorbate
aabdeorsv
bravadoes
aabderrss
debarrass
aabdfhlor
half-board
aabdggnor
gangboard
aabdgiilr
garibaldi
aabdglnor
Langobard
aabdgnnow
bandwagon
aabdhiorz
biohazard
aabdhorsw
wash-board
aabdhrsuy
subahdary
aabdijnor
jaborandi
aabdillst
balladist
aabdilmno
abdominal
aabdilmry
admirably
aabdilnqu
baldaquin
aabdilors
sailboard
sail-broad
aabdilort
broadtail
tail-board
aabdilsvy
advisably
aabdinnrt
train-band
aabdinost
bastinado
aabdinstw
waistband
aabdklorw
boardwalk
aabdllorw
wall-board
aabdlnsst
sand-blast
aabdloruy
day-labour

aabdlrsty
bastardly
aabdorrst
starboard
aabdorswy
broadways
aabeeeglr
agreeable
aabeeenst
sea-beaten
aabeefllt
table-leaf
aabeefnst
beanfeast
aabeegglu
gaugeable
aabeegilm
imageable
aabeeglll
glabellae
aabeeglt
bagatelle
aabeeglrr
barrelage
aabeeglry
agreeably
aabeegltt
get-at-able
aabeegmss
embassage
aabeehkls
shakeable
aabeehllx
exhalable
aabeehlps
shapeable
aabeehnsu
hause-bane
aabeehrst
sea-bather
tabasheer
aabeehrtt
heart-beat
aabeeilln
alienable
aabeeilrs
raiseable
aabeeinrs
béarnaise
aabeeklpp
bakeapple
aabeeklps
speakable
aabeellm
malleable
aabeellnr
learnable
aabeellrt
alterable
aabeelmmt
emblemata
aabeelntu
uneatable

aabeelort
elaborate
aabeelprr
reparable
aabeelprs
separable
aabeelpry
repayable
aabeelpst
baseplate
aabeelrtt
treatable
aabeelrtv
avertable
aabeelrtw
table-ware
aabeelttx
battle-axe
aabeemnot
entamoeba
aabeemnst
abasement
aabeemntt
abatement
aabeeqrsu
arabesque
aabeerrtv
beaver-rat
aabefgilt
fatigable
aabefkrst
breakfast
aabefllmm
flammable
aabefllmu
album-leaf
aabefllot
floatable
aabeflmux
flambeaux
aabeflost
sofa-table
aabeggino
gabionage
aabeggmnr
beggar-man
aabeghill
gallabieh
aabeghllu
laughable
aabegilnv
navigable
aabeginrr
bargainer
aabegirrt
arbitrage
aabegklor
gaol-break
aabegkmrs
bergamask
aabegknnt
bank-agent
aabeglllr
glabellar

aabeglnrt
grantable
aabeglprs
graspable
aabeglrtt
rattlebag
aabegmnrt
bar-magnet
aabegnnot
tonga-bean
aabegnort
abnegator
aabegnrsu
sugar-bean
aabegortw
wager-boat
aabegpssy
by-passage
aabehhrtt
earth-bath
aabehiitw
Wahabiite
aabehinrr
herbarian
aabehittu
habituate
aabehlotw
whale-boat
aabehlsss
abashless
aabehmnst
abashment
aabehrttw
water-bath
aabeiills
labialise
aabeiimnr
bain-marie
aabeiimns
baisemain
aabeiirtu
aubrietia
aabeiirtv
bivariate
aabeijklr
jail-break
aabeijmns
semi-bajan
aabeiklns
Balkanise
lake-basin
aabeiknrr
karabiner
aabeilllt
talliable
aabeillmn
laminable
aabeillnr
ballerina
aabeillns
Sabellian
aabeillpp
appliable

aabeillrt
bilateral
aabeilmnu
unamiable
aabeilnpt
paintable
aabeilnrt
trainable
aabeilnrz
balzarine
aabeilpst
basipetal
aabeilrsu
subaerial
aabeimnot
abominate
aabeimnrt
bairn-team
aabeimsst
metabasis
aabeinors
arabinose
aabeinrrv
verbarian
aabeinrst
abstainer
aabeinrvw
brainwave
aabeirrtt
arbitrate
aabeklltt
table-talk
aabeklmnu
unmakable
aabeklnst
beanstalk
aabekmnrs
brakes-man
aabeknnot
tonka-bean
aabeknppr
bank-paper
aabelllmr
alarm-bell
aabelllor
albarello
aabelllow
allowable
aabellnpt
plantable
aabellnsu
unsalable
aabellppr
palpebral
aabelmnnu
unnamable
aabelmnst
stable-man
aabelmntu
untamable
aabelmrtu
maturable
aabelmssu
assumable

aabelnpuy
unpayable
aabelnrty
bay-antler
aabelnstu
unsatable
aabelnsuy
unsayable
aabeloprv
vaporable
aabelorrz
razorable
aabelorst
astrolabe
aabelortt
rotatable
aabelprry
reparably
aabelprsy
separably
aabelrrst
arblaster
aabelrssu
assurable
aabelrstu
saturable
aabelrttu
tablature
aabemnrtt
rabatment
aabemostt
steamboat
aabemrrss
embarrass
aabeopprt
approbate
aabeoprrs
boar-spear
aabfgilsu
basifugal
aabfiimns
Fabianism
aabfiinst
Fabianist
aabfimort
fibromata
aabggimno
gambogian
aabggrryy
argy-bargy
aabghlluy
laughably
aabghoprr
barograph
aabgilnru
Bulgarian
aabgimosu
ambagious
aabginoru
baragouin
aabginrtt
rabatting
aabgintvy
vanity-bag

aabgloorr
algarrobo
aabgoorrt
abrogator
aabgortvy
gravy-boat
aabhiilrz
bilharzia
aabhiimnp
amphibian
aabhiimsw
Wahabiism
aabhimrvz
barmizvah
aabhimssw
bashawism
aabhimsvz
basmizvah
aabhimtvz
batmizvah
aabhinnot
Bathonian
aabhinrsw
brainwash
aabhinssw
wash-basin
aabhiprrv
vibraharp
aabhllowx
boxwallah
aabhlsstt
bath-salts
aabhmrrtu
barathrum
aabiiilmr
mirabilia
aabiillms
labialism
aabiilnot
notabilia
aabiilnrr
librarian
aabiilnrz
Brazilian
aabiilnst
balanitis
aabiimnss
Sabianism
aabiinnrt
Britannia
aabiinoss
anabiosis
aabiinrtv
bivariant
aabiinrzz
Zanzibari
aabijnotw
jawbation
aabillors
isallobar
aabilmnos
anabolism
aabilmnru
manubrial

aabilmopy
amblyopia
aabilmors
ambrosial
aabilmpst
baptismal
aabilnott
battalion
aabilrrsu
bursarial
aabilrtuu
Tubularia
aabimnors
ambrosian
aabinortt
boat-train
aabinostw
boatswain
aabiosttw
waistboat
aabirrrty
arbitrary
aabirtttu
ribattuta
aabklotuw
walkabout
aabkmoorz
zamboorak
aablllowy
allowably
aabllmsyy
abysmally
aabllntty
blatantly
aabllorsy
aryballos
aabllostv
Baltoslav
aabllrstu
blastular
aabllrsyy
syllabary
aabllrtuy
tabularly
aablmnory
myrobalan
aablmnrwy
byrlaw-man
aablmntuy
untamably
aablmoops
opobalsam
aablmortt
altar-tomb
aablmortu
ambulator
aablmssuy
assumably
aablnoors
saloon-bar
aablorsst
albatross
aablorttu
tabulator

aablrsstu
subastral
aablsssuv
subvassal
aabnnsttu
Bantustan
aabnrsstv
vant-brass
aabrssttu
substrata
aacccehim
cachaemic
aaccchirs
saccharic
aaccddeir
caddie-car
aaccddiny
candidacy
aaccdeelt
calceated
aaccdeiir
acaricide
aaccdeirv
cadaveric
aaccdejny
adjacency
aaccdhlru
archducal
aaccdhoor
coach-road
aaccdiinr
circadian
aaccdimno
mandiocca
aaccdknrs
sand-crack
aaccdnort
accordant
aacceeeir
Ericaceae
aacceeist
Cistaceae
aacceejnu
Juncaceae
aacceekmr
cream-cake
aacceelnr
clearance
aacceenor
Cornaceae
aacceenrt
cancerate
reactance
aaccefgou
cacafuego
aaccehill
cailleach
aaccehinr
cane-chair
aaccehjkp
cheap-jack
aaccehrrt
character

aaccehstw
watch-case
aacceiiln
caecilian
aacceilmt
acclimate
aacceilnr
calcarine
aacceilnt
analectic
aacceilst
ascetical
aacceiltu
aciculate
aacceinrr
cercarian
aacceinrs
Saracenic
aacceintv
vaccinate
aacceirrt
ricercata
aaccejkln
lance-jack
aaccejksu
jack-sauce
aacceknrs
crankcase
aaccekrrt
racetrack
aaccellln
canal-cell
aaccelltu
calculate
aaccelmnu
calcaneum
aaccelmty
cyclamate
aacceIntu
accentual
aaccenptt
acceptant
aacceortt
coarctate
aaccerssy
accessary
aaccerstu
Crustacea
aaccfiilp
pacifical
aaccginrr
racing-car
aacchiiill
cailliach
aacchilmo
mail-coach
aacchimpr
camp-chair
aacchimsy
sciamachy
aacchinrs
saccharin
aacchinrt
anthracic

aacchirtt
cathartic
aacchirtu
autarchic
aacchmrsu
Saccharum
aacchnnwy
wanchancy
aacchortu
raccahout
aacciilnv
vaccinial
aacciilst
ascitical
sciatical
aacciinps
capsaicin
aacciintt
tactician
aaccikkpp
pickapack
aaccillno
cloacalin
cloacinal
laconical
aaccillny
calycinal
aaccillss
classical
aaccilluv
clavicula
aaccilmnu
cacuminal
aaccilnno
canonical
aaccilnru
canicular
aacciloos
Colocasia
aaccilprt
practical
aaccilstt
stalactic
aacciltty
catalytic
aaccimnor
carcinoma
macaronic
aaccinorv
Cracovian
aaccinott
catatonic
toccatina
aaccinprt
pancratic
aaccinpty
captaincy
aaccinrtt
Antarctic
aaccioopt
cacotopia
aaccioprt
capacitor

aacciopsu
capacious
aaccirsst
sarcastic
aacckmnrs
cracksman
aacckrrtt
cart-track
aaccllruy
calculary
aacclmory
cyclorama
aacclmsty
cataclysm
aacclorrv
carvacrol
aaccmnopy
accompany
aaccoprrs
sarcocarp
aaccortuy
autocracy
aacddeetu
decaudate
aacddehls
scald-head
aacddehmr
dead-march
aacddeinr
Decandria
aacddeint
candidate
aacddeirt
radicated
aacddelop
decapodal
aacddenns
sand-dance
aacddenop
decapodan
aacddensu
Sadducean
aacddentu
aduncated
aacddgnot
cat-and-dog
aacddhimr
didrachma
aacddiist
Dadaistic
aacddnrty
dandy-cart
aacdeeeft
defaecate
aacdeefln
lean-faced
aacdeeflt
defalcate
aacdeehhr
headreach
aacdeehrs
scare-head
aacdeeiir
Iridaceae

aacdeeimt
acetamide
emaciated
aacdeeirt
eradicate
aacdeelrt
lacerated
aacdeeltu
aculeated
aacdeemns
damascene
aacdeemrt
camerated
demarcate
aacdeemst
casemated
aacdeenrv
readvance
aacdeentt
decantate
aacdeetux
excaudate
aacdeffhl
half-faced
aacdeffin
affianced
aacdeffir
fair-faced
aacdefgru
face-guard
aacdefist
fasciated
aacdeflrs
false-card
aacdeginy
Decagynia
aacdegiot
dacoitage
aacdeglno
decagonal
aacdegnos
Gasconade
aacdegnst
stag-dance
aacdehhir
headchair
aacdehiln
enchilada
aacdehlln
dance-hall
aacdehlrt
cathedral
aacdehmmt
cat-hammed
aacdehort
octahedra
aacdeiirs
Sciaridae
aacdeiirt
Arctiidae
aacdeilln
dalliance
aacdeillt
dialectal

aacdeillv
cevadilla
aacdeilmr
cream-laid
aacdeilno
Laodicean
aacdeilnt
cadential
aacdeilps
asclepiad
aacdeiltu
acidulate
aacdeimnr
cardamine
aacdeimny
cyanamide
aacdeimpr
paramedic
pre-adamic
aacdeimst
academist
aacdeinot
diaconate
aacdeinov
avoidance
aacdeinps
Cispadane
aacdeirss
ascarides
aacdejkll
jackalled
aacdejkmp
jam-packed
aacdeklry
lardy-cake
aacdellnu
calendula
aacdelmno
Damoclean
aacdelmns
Candlemas
aacdelnot
anecdotal
aacdelnps
landscape
aacdelnrt
declarant
aacdemntu
manducate
aacdemopr
campeador
aacdennno
cannonade
aacdennst
adnascent
ascendant
aacdenorr
carronade
aacdenoss
cassonade
aacdenotu
coadunate
aacdenprt
tap-dancer

aacderstt
castrated
aacderttx
taxed-cart
aacdfhnrt
handcraft
aacdfiilt
fatidical
aacdforrt
road-craft
aacdghinr
drag-chain
aacdgiill
diallagic
aacdgilry
cardialgy
aacdginor
carangoid
aacdhiilp
aphidical
aacdhiilr
rachidial
aacdhiils
dichasial
aacdhiinr
rachidian
aacdhiirr
Richardia
aacdhilms
chaldaism
aacdhilop
phacoidal
aacdhinor
arachnoid
aacdhinot
acanthoid
aacdhinrt
cantharid
aacdhirsy
chair-days
aacdhlnps
hand-clasp
aacdhlnrs
crash-land
aacdhlnty
land-yacht
aacdhnsty
sand-yacht
aacdhprrs
card-sharp
aacdiilnt
diactinal
aacdiimno
amino-acid
aacdiinrr
Ricardian
aacdiiprs
paradisic
aacdiisst
diastasic
aacdiistt
diastatic
aacdillry
radically

aacdilmno
monadical
aacdilmny
dynamical
aacdilmru
caldarium
aacdilnty
dilatancy
aacdilopr
parodical
aacdilrru
radicular
aacdimrst
dramatics
aacdinnor
draconian
aacdinnot
contadina
aacdinors
Sarcodina
aacdinort
Octandria
aacdinrtu
Traducian
aacdiosuu
audacious
aacdiprty
cryptadia
aacdiqrtu
quadratic
aacdirssy
dyscrasia
aacdirsty
caryatids
aacdjntuy
adjutancy
aacdjnuvy
adjuvancy
aacdknsst
cask-stand
aacdkorrt
trackroad
aacdkrsty
stackyard
aacdlmors
rascaldom
aacdlnors
corn-salad
aacdnostt
coatstand
aacdooprw
carap-wood
aacdoorst
Ostracoda
aacdoortv
advocator
aacdorstw
coastward
aacdprrsy
scrap-yard
aaceeegnr
careenage
aaceeegnt
Gnetaceae

aaceeeilm
Meliaceae
aaceeekmp
make-peace
aaceeelmn
Lemnaceae
aaceefinn
fainéance
aaceefirt
cafeteria
aaceefkrw
wafer-cake
aaceeflls
scale-leaf
aaceeflmr
lace-frame
aaceeflpt
face-plate
aaceeflrt
leaf-trace
aaceefrrt
aftercare
aaceefrsv
face-saver
aaceeghns
sea-change
aaceegill
elegiacal
aaceegkln
angel-cake
aaceegllr
cellarage
aaceegnrr
carrageen
aaceegpss
gas-escape
aaceehhrt
heartache
aaceehipt
Hepaticae
aaceehlnr
Heraclean
aaceehlnu
Acheulean
aaceehlpt
cephalate
aaceehors
sea-orache
aaceehprt
eparchate
aaceehpty
Typhaceae
aaceehrtt
tracheate
aaceehrtv
cave-earth
aaceehrtx
exarchate
aaceeiill
Liliaceae
aaceeiilt
Tiliaceae
aaceeilmu
leucaemia

aaceeilov
Violaceae
aaceejkpt
pea-jacket
aaceejltu
ejaculate
aaceeklry
layer-cake
aaceekmpr
pacemaker
aaceekmrs
casemaker
aaceekrrt
caretaker
aaceelnps
pleasance
aaceelnpt
placentae
aaceelnrt
nectareal
aaceelnru
caerulean
aaceelnst
elastance
aaceelntu
anucleate
aaceelppr
lace-paper
aaceelprt
paraclete
aaceelrry
relay-race
aaceelrtt
altercate
aaceelrty
clay-eater
aaceelstw
weasel-cat
aaceemnny
Mycenaean
aaceemrtw
macaw-tree
aaceemrty
Myrtaceae
aaceennrt
nectarean
aaceenrsv
cesarevna
aaceeoprs
aerospace
aaceepprs
paper-case
aaceeprss
cassareep
aaceeprsv
parasceve
aaceerstt
estate-car
aaceerttu
reactuate
aaceffirt
affricate
aacefglnr
flagrance

aacefgnrr
fragrance
aacefgopr
forage-cap
aacefgort
factorage
aacefgosu
fagaceous
aacefhllw
whale-calf
aacefhlst
half-caste
aacefilpr
prefacial
aacefinny
fainéancy
aacefinrr
Africaner
aacefinst
fascinate
aaceflltu
falculate
aaceflmpr
farm-place
aaceflprt
after-clap
aaceghimr
archimage
aaceghinr
chain-gear
aaceghlnr
archangel
aaceghltt
Gaeltacht
aaceghmnp
champagne
aaceghmnr
charge-man
aaceghnor
anchorage
aaceghrst
gatecrash
aacegilln
angelical
Galenical
aacegilnp
gin-palace
aacegilns
analgesic
aacegilrt
cartilage
aacegimno
egomaniac
aacegistt
castigate
aacegkrwy
graywacke
aaceglmou
guacamole
aaceglort
cataloger
aaceglost
galactose
aaceglotu
catalogue
coagulate
aacegnorr
arrogance
aacegnort
cartonage
aacegnrsu
cane-sugar
sugar-cane
aacegopst
scapegoat
aacegortt
greatcoat
aacegrstu
Crataegus
aacehhins
shanachie
aacehiims
ischaemia
aacehiirt
hieratica
aacehilln
Achillean
aacehillo
echolalia
aacehilmo
cholaemia
aacehilmt
malachite
aacehilns
selachian
aacehilnt
châtelain
aacehilnu
Acheulian
aacehilpt
caliphate
hepatical
aacehilrt
theriacal
aacehimnn
Manichean
aacehimnt
machinate
aacehimnu
achaenium
aacehimtt
athematic
aacehinnt
acanthine
aacehinrr
rancheria
aacehinrs
anarchise
aacehinrt
catarhine
aacehinrw
China-ware
aacehinst
Hanseatic
aacehiopt
apothecia
aacehiost
taoiseach
aacehiprs
hair-space
aacehiptt
apathetic
aacehirrs
archaiser
aacehirst
catharise
aacehirsy
easy-chair
aacehkmor
hackamore
aacehkrsv
haversack
aacehlmpp
peach-palm
aacehlmrs
mareschal
aacehlmuu
chalumeau
aacehlrtt
clathrate
aacehmnpr
marchpane
aacehmrsy
camera-shy
aacehnnps
snaphance
aacehnnsy
seannachy
aacehnopr
canephora
aacehnors
sea-anchor
aacehnrst
cane-trash
aacehnsss
Sassenach
aacehpprs
scrap-heap
aacehprtu
parachute
aacehrrty
tracheary
aaceiilnt
laciniate
aaceiinrr
cineraria
aaceiirtv
vicariate
aaceijkrt
air-jacket
aaceiknps
sink-a-pace
aaceillpt
capitella
aaceillrs
rascaille
aaceillrv
varicella
aaceilltv
laticlave
vacillate
aaceilmmn
immanacle
aaceilmnn
Alemannic
aaceilmnp
campanile
aaceilmps
eclampsia
aaceilmst
mica-slate
aaceilmtv
calmative
aaceilnnr
carnelian
aaceilnnt
cantilena
lancinate
aaceilnpp
appliance
aaceilnpt
analeptic
aaceilnrs
arsenical
carnalise
aaceilnrt
lacertian
nectarial
aaceilntv
venatical
aaceilort
aleatoric
aaceilorv
cavaliero
aaceilppt
applicate
aaceilpss
asclepias
aaceilptu
apiculate
aaceilrrt
erratical
aaceilrst
sectarial
aaceilssu
casualise
aaceilstu
actualise
aaceilstx
catalexis
aaceimnps
spanaemic
aaceimnpt
mancipate
aaceimntu
acuminate
aaceimopr
paroemiac
aaceimprs
sapraemic
aaceimrss
Caesarism
aaceimrst
marcasite
aaceimstt
masticate
aaceinnrt
incarnate
aaceinopr
paranoeic
aaceinopt
capotaine
copataine
aaceinost
caseation
aaceinrrt
tarriance
aaceinrrv
arrivance
aaceinrst
ascertain
Cartesian
sectarian
aaceiorrt
acroteria
aaceiosst
associate
aaceiprss
cassaripe
aaceipstu
auspicate
aaceipttv
captivate
aaceirsst
Caesarist
staircase
aaceistuv
causative
aacejkkln
ankle-jack
aacejklnp
jack-plane
aacejklnt
Jack-a-Lent
aacejklpp
apple-jack
aacejklsv
Jack-slave
aaceklprt
plate-rack
aacekmrst
caste-mark
aaceknpsw
spawn-cake
aaceknrrs
ransacker
aacekppty
pay-packet
aacekpstt
peat-stack
aacekrstw
water-cask
aacelllru
acellular
aacellluv
vallecula

aacellmnr
cellarman
aacellnor
lanceolar
olecranal
aacellnow
allowance
aacellnpt
placental
aacellnry
Carlylean
aacellnst
castellan
aacellopt
coal-plate
aacellpsw
wall-space
aacellsty
clay-slate
aacellsuu
clausulae
aacelltuv
clavulate
aacelmnnu
unmanacle
aacelmnst
calmstane
aacelmntt
cattleman
aacelmoot
Coelomata
aacelmost
steam-coal
aacelmrst
smart-alec
aacelmsst
classmate
aacelnntu
antelucan
cannulate
aacelnrst
ancestral
aacelnttu
tentacula
aaceloppr
paper-coal
aaceloprt
acropetal
aacelorst
escalator
aacelotuv
autoclave
vacuolate
aacelpprt
apple-cart
aacelprty
caprylate
aacelpstu
aspectual
capsulate
aacelpsty
catalepsy
aacelptxy
cataplexy

aacelrrtu
creatural
aacelrrty
carrytale
aacelrsty
catalyser
aacelrtuw
caterwaul
aacemnnru
manurance
aacemnopr
campanero
aacemnory
aeromancy
aacemnprt
mercaptan
aacemnrst
sacrament
aacemnstu
caumstane
aacemoprt
cameo-part
aacemorrt
macerator
aacemrsty
camsteary
aacennnoy
annoyance
aacennoss
assonance
aacenoprs
Scorpaena
aacenppry
apparency
aacenprry
parcenary
aacenrssu
anacruses
assurance
aacenrssv
canvasser
aacenrttu
cauterant
aacensstt
castanets
aaceooppt
apocopate
aaceortuv
evacuator
aaceortvx
excavator
aacerrttw
water-cart
aacffffrs
scaff-raff
aacffjkst
jack-staff
aacffkpst
packstaff
aacfglnry
flagrancy
aacfgnrry
fragrancy

aacfhimnr
chamfrain
aacfhklrt
half-track
aacfiilnn
financial
aacfiilrt
trifacial
aacfilnot
factional
falcation
aacfilort
factorial
aacfinstt
fantastic
aacfmnrst
craftsman
aacgghinn
chain-gang
aacggiknp
packaging
aacggiopr
paragogic
aacghhiry
hagiarchy
aacghilpr
graphical
aacghimnp
champaign
aacghmort
tachogram
aacghmpry
cymagraph
aacgillmr
calligram
aacgillmy
magically
aacgillos
scagliola
aacgillrt
Largactil®
aacgilnnr
ring-canal
aacgilnor
organical
aacgimmrt
grammatic
aacgimotu
autogamic
aacgimprt
pragmatic
aacgiossu
sagacious
aacgllswy
scallywag
aacglnoot
octagonal
aacglnotu
coagulant
aacgloory
acarology
aacgmorrt
cartogram

aacgnnsty
stagnancy
aacgnorry
arrogancy
aachhhiuu
chihuahua
aachhlnoo
hoolachan
aachiilmn
chain-mail
aachiilpt
aliphatic
aachiiprs
pharisaic
aachiirrv
charivari
aachikmsy
skiamachy
aachilmrs
marischal
aachilnps
ship-canal
aachilopr
parochial
aachilopt
chipolata
aachilors
Charolais
aachilpst
asphaltic
aachilsst
thalassic
aachimnor
harmonica
aachimnrs
anarchism
aachimnru
Manchuria
aachimrrt
matriarch
aachimrst
Catharism
aachimstt
asthmatic
aachinopr
anaphoric
pharaonic
aachinort
Tocharian
aachinprs
parischan
aachinrst
anarchist
cantharis
aachioppt
apophatic
aachiprrt
patriarch
aachiprss
chaprassi
aachirrst
Aristarch
aachirsst
catharsis

aachirstt
Catharist
aachllmry
lachrymal
aachllpty
cataphyll
aachlmnor
monarchal
aachlmost
stomachal
aachlmpty
match-play
aachlmrsy
marshalcy
aachmnnor
anchorman
aachmnorw
charwoman
aachmnsty
yachtsman
aachnnoty
anthocyan
aachnoprt
anthocarp
aachnostu
acanthous
aachnotty
chatoyant
aachnprty
pyracanth
aachnrstu
cantharus
aachoppry
apocrypha
aachqsstu
sasquatch
aaciiilns
siciliana
aaciillrt
altricial
aaciilmnp
campanili
aaciilmrs
racialism
aaciilmst
ismatical
lamaistic
aaciilnpt
ancipital
aaciilnpu
Paulician
aaciilnst
Castilian
aaciilntv
vaticinal
aaciilprt
piratical
aaciilrst
racialist
satirical
aaciilstv
viaticals
aaciimmst
miasmatic

aaciimotx
axiomatic
aaciinnop
poinciana
aaciinnot
nicotiana
aaciinnst
antiscian
aaciinort
raciation
aaciinprt
patrician
aaciinrtz
Nazaritic
aaciiprst
parasitic
aaciirrtu
urticaria
aaciirtvy
air-cavity
aaciisttv
atavistic
aacijnott
jactation
aacikllnt
lack-Latin
aaciknprt
pack-train
aacilllqu
quail-call
aacillmny
manically
aacillnor
Corallian
aacillnot
allantoic
aacillnry
ancillary
aacillntv
vacillant
aacilloxy
coaxially
aacillpry
capillary
aacillpty
capitally
aacilmnrs
carnalism
aacilmpst
plasmatic
aacilmrry
lacrimary
aacilmrss
rascalism
aacilmrsu
simulacra
aacilmrtu
matricula
aacilmssu
casualism
aacilnnov
volcanian
aacilnnuv
vulcanian

aacilnopt
pactional
placation
aacilnort
cantorial
aacilnott
lactation
aacilnotv
clavation
aacilnppt
applicant
aacilnpsv
Pan-Slavic
aacilnqtu
quantical
aacilnrst
carnalist
aacilnrty
carnality
aacilnruv
navicular
aacilnruy
caulinary
aacilntty
latitancy
aaciloprs
prosaical
aacilortu
auctorial
caliatour
aacilossu
salacious
aacilprsu
spiracula
aacilprtu
capitular
aacilprty
paralytic
aacilqttu
acquittal
aacilrrtu
articular
aacilrruu
auricular
aacilrstt
cart's-tail
aacilrsty
rascality
satyrical
aacilssty
catalysis
aacilsttu
actualist
aacilstuy
causality
aacilttuy
actuality
aacimnnnu
Mancunian
aacimnopr
panoramic
aacimnorr
Armorican

aacimnors
macaronis
aacimnort
manticora
aacimnott
mactation
aacimnpst
campanist
aacimorsx
macroaxis
aacimortu
amaurotic
aacimottu
automatic
aacimpsst
spasmatic
aacimrrsu
sacrarium
aacimrsty
camstairy
aacimrttu
traumatic
aacinnopt
pontianac
aacinnort
carnation
aacinnost
santonica
aacinootv
avocation
aacinootz
Actinozoa
aacinoprs
caparison
aacinoprt
paratonic
aacinorrv
Carnivora
aacinortu
arcuation
aacinortv
covariant
aacinosst
cassation
aacinostu
causation
aacinottu
actuation
aacinotuv
vacuation
aacinprty
captainry
aacinrrvy
arrivancy
aacinrsst
sacristan
aacinrssu
anacrusis
aacioprsu
rapacious
aaciopstt
apostatic
aaciorttv
activator

aaciosttw
waistcoat
aaciprssu
paracusis
aacjkrstw
jack-straw
aacjkssty
jack-stays
aacjlortu
jaculator
aackorstt
toast-rack
aaclllmos
small-coal
aacllnopt
coal-plant
aacllopry
allocarpy
aacllprty
party-call
aacllrstu
claustral
aacllrsuu
clausular
aacllttuy
tactually
aaclmorrz
razor-clam
aaclmrryy
lacrymary
aaclnoors
saloon-car
aaclnoptu
cantaloup
aaclnruuv
avuncular
aacloprtu
portulaca
aacloprty
placatory
play-actor
aaclorstv
slavocrat
aaclprsuy
capsulary
scapulary
aaclrrtuy
cartulary
aacmmoors
cosmorama
aacmnorst
stramaçon
aacmnottu
catamount
aacmoostt
scotomata
aacnprstu
carap-nuts
aacnrstuy
sanctuary
aacoopstt
capotasto

aacorrttt
attractor
tractator
aacorsswy
cassowary
aadddelps
pad-saddle
aadddgnry
grandaddy
aaddeefht
fat-headed
aaddeehps
sapheaded
aaddeeilv
dead-alive
aaddeemry
ready-made
aaddeertw
dead-water
aaddegmnu
undamaged
aaddegrtu
graduated
aaddehhir
hardihead
aaddehhmn
ham-handed
aaddehmnr
hermandad
aaddehmpt
death-damp
aaddehrtw
deathward
aaddeilno
adenoidal
aaddeinrw
Edwardian
aaddeiopz
Zapodidae
aaddellns
sandalled
aaddellps
saddle-lap
aaddelmnn
landdamne
aaddelmnr
dreamland
raddleman
aaddelrst
astraddle
aaddemnnt
demandant
aaddemnor
andromeda
aaddennoo
Dodonaean
aaddenptu
unadapted
aaddeorst
roadstead
aaddhnnst
handstand
aaddhnrrw
hard-drawn

aaddiimny
Didynamia
aaddiimry
dairymaid
aaddiinrv
Dravidian
aaddilmsy
lady's-maid
aaddinprt
dandiprat
aaddiorst
stadia-rod
aaddllruw
auld-warld
aaddlnrsw
landwards
aaddlrsty
dastardly
aaddnprty
dandyprat
aadeefhmr
headframe
aadeeflpr
flap-eared
aadeeghmt
megadeath
aadeeghrs
shageared
aadeeglmn
magdalene
aadeegnor
orangeade
aadeegnpp
appendage
aadeegnrt
tea-garden
aadeehhks
headshake
aadeehhlw
whale-head
aadeehiny
Hyaenidae
aadeehlsw
alewashed
aadeehprs
spearhead
aadeehpst
heapstead
aadeehrrt
heart-dear
aadeehrtt
death-rate
aadeehrtw
head-water
water-head
aadeeikww
wide-awake
aadeeilmv
mediaeval
aadeeirrt
reradiate
aadeekmns
damaskeen

aadeekmry
make-ready
aadeellmn
allemande
aadeellsw
sea-walled
aadeelnps
esplanade
aadeelort
areolated
aadeelprr
ale-draper
aadeeltuv
devaluate
aadeemnrt
tradename
aadeemrsu
admeasure
aadeemrtw
medaewart
aadeeortt
toad-eater
aadeepprt
parapeted
aadeeppst
peat-spade
aadeeprst
estrapade
paederast
aadeerrtt
retardate
aadeesttv
devastate
aadefglnn
fandangle
aadefgrsu
safeguard
aadefhnor
aforehand
aadefhnps
fan-shaped
aadefilnt
fantailed
aadefiltt
fat-tailed
aadefinnr
farandine
aadefinst
fantasied
aadefiors
aforesaid
aadeflnor
farandole
aadefmprt
after-damp
aadefmrst
farmstead
aadefostu
autos-da-fé
aadefrrtw
afterward
aadefsstt
steadfast

aadegglnu
languaged
aadeghnru
harangued
aadeghnry
hydrangea
aadeghnst
stage-hand
aadegiinu
Iguanidae
aadegimnt
diamagnet
aadeginrr
darraigne
aadeginrt
tragedian
aadegintv
vaginated
aadegiprs
disparage
aadegiqru
quadrigae
aadegllop
gallopade
aadeglnnr
engarland
aadeglnnt
land-agent
aadeglnrt
tear-gland
aadeglnrv
landgrave
aadeglnst
standgale
aadeglntu
angulated
aadeglrss
gala-dress
aadeglrux
axle-guard
aadeglrvw
waldgrave
aadegmnnu
unmanaged
aadegmosv
savagedom
aadegmsuu
gaudeamus
aadegnors
sea-dragon
aadegnort
road-agent
aadegnrrt
regardant
aadegorss
dogaressa
aadegrrru
rear-guard
aadegrrvy
graveyard
aadegrstu
date-sugar
aadehhkns
handshake

aadehilrr
diarrheal
aadehimot
haematoid
aadehimps
Phasmidae
aadehimry
hydraemia
aadehinrx
Hexandria
aadehiorr
diarrhoea
aadehiprt
apartheid
hit-parade
aadehirst
stairhead
aadehirzz
hazardize
aadehkmst
death-mask
aadehllst
headstall
aadehlmnn
manhandle
aadehlmps
lampshade
aadehlmrt
hard-metal
aadehlmsy
ashamedly
aadehlnnp
panhandle
aadehlnrt
heartland
aadehmnst
deathsman
aadehmnsu
unashamed
aadehnort
rhodanate
aadehnppr
hand-paper
aadehorrw
arrow-head
aadehprst
hard-paste
aadehprtt
death-trap
aadehrrtw
earthward
aadeiilrs
radialise
aadeiinrt
dietarian
aadeiiprs
praesidia
aadeiiptu
Tupaiidae
aadeiirrt
irradiate
aadeiirtv
radiative

aadeijnps
jaspidean
aadeiknrs
sneak-raid
aadeillpt
dial-plate
aadeillrt
arillated
lardalite
aadeilmnn
almandine
aadeilmnt
laminated
aadeilmrt
diametral
aadeilnnr
Adrenalin®
aadeilnpt
lead-paint
aadeilnss
sea-island
aadeilnsv
vandalise
aadeilprr
perradial
aadeilpry
Pyralidae
aadeilpst
stapedial
aadeilrtv
travailed
aadeilrty
radiately
aadeiltuv
laudative
aadeimnnp
pandemian
aadeimnnr
mandarine
meandrian
aadeimrst
dramatise
aadeinptt
patinated
aadeinrst
steradian
aadeinrtt
antitrade
attainder
aadeipprs
disappear
aadeiprst
disparate
aadeiprty
paediatry
aadeirsty
Satyridae
aadejruvy
Yajurveda
aadekmorr
road-maker
aadekmrrt
trademark

aadekmrty
market-day
aadeknnss
sand-snake
aadellmnr
mallander
aadellmry
alarmedly
aadellnnp
land-plane
aadellnpr
Laplander
aadellntu
landaulet
aadellnuv
land-value
aadellnuy
unallayed
aadellssy
saleslady
aadelmmor
melodrama
aadelmnor
ealdorman
aadelmort
road-metal
aadelnntu
annulated
aadelnrsu
Ausländer
aadelnstw
wasteland
aadelppru
applauder
aadelprtw
draw-plate
aadelrrss
ressaldar
aadelrswy
seawardly
aadelrtty
latter-day
aademmnor
memoranda
aademnoor
enamorado
aademnopt
tamponade
aademnprs
ampersand
aademnprz
amperzand
aademnpss
spadesman
aademnrst
tradesman
aademoqru
aquadrome
aademortt
Trematoda
aadennppt
appendant
aadennttt
attendant

aadenpprs
sandpaper
aadenprtu
pandurate
aadenrrtt
retardant
aadenrrtw
warranted
aadenrsst
sea-strand
aadenrwwy
way-warden
aadenssuy
unassayed
aadeoprrx
paradoxer
aadeorstw
soda-water
aaderrsvy
adversary
aadersstw
eastwards
aadersttu
saturated
aaderstww
war-wasted
aadffhnst
handstaff
aadffiitv
affidavit
aadfhhlry
half-hardy
aadfilnry
fairyland
aadfimrry
dairy-farm
aadfmnrst
draftsman
aadgghist
Haggadist
aadgghlry
haggardly
aadgglnor
galdragon
aadghhins
shanghai'd
aadghijrr
jaghirdar
aadghilnp
phalangid
aadghilrs
harigalds
aadghimpr
diaphragm
aadghipsy
dysphagia
aadghlnss
hand-glass
aadghnnor
hand-organ
aadghrrss
hardgrass
aadgilmny
amygdalin

aadgilnor
girandola
aadgilort
gladiator
aadgilrru
guard-rail
aadgimmno
gammadion
aadgimorr
radiogram
aadgimoru
audiogram
aadginnrs
sand-grain
aadginort
gradation
indagator
aadgllnru
glandular
aadgllruy
gradually
aadgllrwy
wallydrag
aadglmsuy
Amygdalus
aadglnoow
wagon-load
aadglnrry
garlandry
aadglnrss
grassland
aadglnsss
sand-glass
aadgmnors
dragomans
aadgmnrsu
guardsman
aadgmrrtu
dramaturg
aadgnnrtu
grand-aunt
aadgnrsss
sand-grass
aadgorrtu
graduator
aadgorsst
toad-grass
aadhilrst
tahsildar
aadhimopp
Amphipoda
aadhinott
thanatoid
aadhinpsu
Upanishad
aadhipssy
dysphasia
aadhklnrs
land-shark
aadhllmns
small-hand
aadhllnst
hallstand

aadhlmnrs
marshland
aadhnsstw
wash-stand
aadhorrsu
hadrosaur
aadhorsuz
hazardous
aadiiklry
kailyaird
aadiilrrt
triradial
aadiilrty
radiality
aadiimmot
ommatidia
aadiimmst
Adamitism
aadiimnry
dimyarian
aadiimnrz
zamindari
aadiinnnt
Dinantian
aadiinnrs
Sardinian
aadiinnrw
Darwinian
aadiinort
radiation
aadiinrrt
irradiant
Triandria
aadiiortu
auditoria
aadiissst
diastasis
aadijnnor
Jordanian
aadillmor
armadillo
aadillmoy
amyloidal
aadillmpu
palladium
aadillmry
amaryllid
aadillnot
allantoid
aadillnpu
paludinal
aadillops
sapodilla
aadillpry
radial-ply
aadilmnsu
sudaminal
aadilmnsv
vandalism
aadilmops
plasmodia
aadilmort
maladroit

aadilmost
mastoidal
aadilmpry
pyramidal
aadilmpst
lampadist
aadilmrty
Admiralty
aadilnnot
antinodal
Daltonian
aadilnnpr
plain-darn
aadilnopt
antipodal
aadilnott
antidotal
aadilnotu
adulation
laudation
aadilnrty
radiantly
aadilortt
dilatator
aadilosvw
disavowal
aadimnnor
Monandria
aadimnnot
damnation
aadimnqsu
damasquin
aadimnsuv
avisandum
aadimnuvz
avizandum
aadimopry
Myriapoda
aadimorss
madarosis
aadimqrsu
maquisard
aadimrstt
dramatist
aadinnnot
andantino
aadinnopt
pandation
aadinnors
sardonian
aadinoort
adoration
aadinorrt
road-train
aadinprrt
drain-trap
aadinpsss
spadassin
aadiorrty
radiatory
aadipssuy
ups-a-daisy
aadklnprs
parklands

aadklorsv
  volksraad
aadklrwwy
  awkwardly
aadkprrsw
  parkwards
aadllopsu
  palladous
aadlmmpsu
  plumdamas
aadlmnpsw
  swampland
aadlortuy
  adulatory
  laudatory
aadlrwwyy
  waywardly
aadmmnoor
  monodrama
aadmnnoss
  sand-mason
aadmnorty
  damnatory
  mandatory
aadmnqruu
  quadruman
aadnnorsu
  anandrous
aadnoopsw
  sapan-wood
aadooprsu
  Sauropoda
aadopprst
  strappado
aadqrstuu
  quadratus
aadrrstwy
  straw-yard
aaeeekltv
  take-leave
aaeeelmps
  pease-meal
aaeeemrtt
  meat-eater
aaeeffllm
  flame-leaf
aaeefgmrt
  aftergame
aaeefinns
  feiseanna
aaeefllmt
  leaf-metal
aaeeflotv
  faveolate
aaeeflrsw
  self-aware
aaeeflrtw
  water-flea
  water-leaf
aaeegggrt
  aggregate
aaeegglln
  galengale

aaeeggrtw
  water-gage
aaeeghklw
  eagle-hawk
aaeeghrst
  gas-heater
aaeegijmr
  jigamaree
aaeegilnr
  generalia
aaeegimnr
  Gramineae
aaeegintv
  evaginate
aaeegirtv
  variegate
aaeegirtw
  waiterage
aaeeglnst
  sea-tangle
aaeeglnsu
  Elaeagnus
aaeeglors
  soar-eagle
aaeeglpps
  sage-apple
aaeegmnns
  manganese
aaeegmnop
  Agapemone
aaeegmnst
  stage-name
aaeegnors
  sea-orange
aaeegnprt
  parentage
aaeegnrrr
  rearrange
aaeegnrrs
  sea-ranger
aaeegnrrt
  ergataner
aaeegnrtu
  guarantee
aaeegprss
  repassage
aaeegprsu
  gaspereau
aaeegrttw
  Watergate
  water-gate
aaeegsttw
  waste-gate
aaeehimtt
  haematite
aaeehisst
  aesthesia
aaeehkmrs
  rakeshame
aaeehlmtw
  wheat-meal
aaeehlrrs
  rehearsal

aaeehmntt
  hetmanate
aaeehmntu
  Athenaeum
aaeehmntx
  exanthema
aaeehmpst
  metaphase
aaeehnrst
  hare-stane
aaeehpsvw
  waveshape
aaeehrrrt
  rare-earth
aaeehrtwy
  thereaway
aaeeiklmu
  leukaemia
aaeeillrv
  lavaliere
aaeeilltv
  alleviate
aaeeilnpr
  perinaeal
aaeeilntv
  aventaile
aaeeilrtt
  retaliate
aaeeimnrt
  reanimate
aaeeimntv
  emanative
aaeeimntx
  examinate
  exanimate
aaeeinrst
  arseniate
aaeeipttx
  expatiate
aaeeisttv
  aestivate
aaeejnpss
  Japaneses
aaeeklnnp
  palankeen
aaeeknptw
  wapentake
aaeekprrt
  parrakeet
aaeekpssy
  speak-easy
aaeelllmt
  lamellate
aaeellmns
  sallee-man
aaeellnrw
  wellanear
aaeellotv
  alveolate
aaeellppt
  appellate
aaeellptt
  patellate

aaeellqru
  aquarelle
aaeelmnps
  pleaseman
aaeelmnpt
  name-plate
aaeelmptt
  meat-plate
aaeelmsst
  matelassé
aaeelmstt
  stalemate
aaeelnopr
  aeroplane
aaeelnrtt
  alternate
aaeelnrtv
  ervalenta
  revalenta
aaeelpprr
  reapparel
aaeelppsx
  sex-appeal
aaeelprrv
  palaverer
aaeelrstw
  water-seal
aaeelrswy
  sea-lawyer
aaeemmntz
  amazement
aaeemprrt
  parameter
aaeempstt
  meat-paste
aaeemrrrt
  terramare
aaeemrstt
  masterate
aaeennpry
  Pyrenaean
aaeenrrtw
  warrantee
aaeenrssw
  awareness
aaeentttu
  attenuate
aaeeoprtv
  evaporate
aaeeprrty
  ratepayer
aaeerrttw
  water-rate
aaeerssty
  sea-satyre
aaeersttt
  tea-taster
aaeertvww
  water-wave
aaeffiilt
  affiliate
aaeffilrs
  Rafflesia

aaeffinpr
  paraffine
aaeffinrt
  raffinate
aaefgiltt
  flagitate
aaefginrs
  seafaring
aaefgirsx
  saxifrage
aaefglrtw
  water-flag
aaefglrvw
  flag-waver
aaefhiklt
  khalifate
aaefhllpt
  half-plate
aaefhllrt
  all-father
  earthfall
aaefhlprt
  flare-path
aaefhlrtx
  earthflax
aaefhmrss
  sash-frame
aaefhmrtt
  aftermath
  hamfatter
aaefhmsst
  shamefast
aaefhrstt
  earthfast
aaefiknnr
  Frankenia
aaefiknrr
  Afrikaner
aaefilmrr
  fire-alarm
aaefilnnr
  Falernian
aaefilntx
  antefixal
aaefilptt
  palafitte
aaefilrty
  fairy-tale
aaefimmnr
  mainframe
aaefinnrs
  safranine
aaefinsst
  fantasise
aaefinttu
  infatuate
aaefjllnw
  jaw-fallen
aaefkllst
  leaf-stalk
aaeflllry
  fallalery
aaefllrtw
  waterfall

aaeflnrrt
fraternal
aaeflortu
autoflare
aaefnqstu
fantasque
aaeggilln
galingale
aaeggilnt
gangliate
aaeggilnw
Galwegian
aaeggilrv
gilravage
aaegginnt
gigantean
aaegginrr
gregarian
Gregarina
aaegginru
rain-gauge
aaeggirrs
gargarise
aaeggllno
gallonage
aaeggmssu
megagauss
aaeggopru
paragogue
aaeghilrt
Thargelia
aaeghinxy
Hexagynia
aaeghllpy
hypallage
aaeghlnox
hexagonal
aaeghlnpr
phalanger
aaeghlnps
phalanges
aaeghlopy
hypogaeal
aaeghlprt
tragelaph
aaeghlrtw
waghalter
aaeghmnop
phaenogam
aaeghnopr
orphanage
aaeghnopy
hypogaean
aaeghnrru
haranguer
aaeghoprr
aerograph
aaegiilnt
genitalia
aaegiilqu
aquilegia
aaegiittv
agitative

aaegiknnw
awakening
aaegillnt
allegiant
aaegillnv
villanage
aaegilmrr
armigeral
aaegilnnn
annealing
aaegilnnt
galantine
aaegilnos
analogise
aaegilnpp
appealing
lagniappe
aaegilnps
Pelasgian
aaegilnru
neuralgia
aaegilnsv
galvanise
aaegilnuv
vaginulae
aaegilrst
agrestial
aaegimmns
mismanage
aaegimnns
magnesian
aaegimnnt
manganite
aaegimnrr
margarine
aaegimnrs
sea-margin
aaegimnrt
marginate
aaegimrrt
margarite
aaegimrsy
Magyarise
aaeginnrt
tanagrine
aaeginnrw
Wagnerian
aaeginort
aragonite
aaeginotv
evagation
aaeginrrr
arraigner
aaeginrsu
guaranies
aaeginrsy
asynergia
gainsayer
aaegiorrt
gear-ratio
aaegiprst
pargasite
aaegirttv
gravitate

aaegisttt
sagittate
aaegllnov
longaeval
aaegllnry
laryngeal
aaegllrtw
water-gall
aaegllstz
salt-glaze
aaeglmnst
gas-mantle
aaeglmttu
glutamate
aaeglnrtu
granulate
aaegloprs
pearl-sago
aaeglprry
pearl-gray
aaeglprsv
palsgrave
aaeglprvy
pay-gravel
aaeglpsty
stage-play
aaeglrssw
glassware
aaeglrsty
slate-gray
aaeglrttu
gratulate
aaegmmnno
Agamemnon
aaegmmnor
anemogram
aaegmnnor
Orangeman
aaegmnnpr
Pan-German
aaegmnopt
tamponage
aaegmnort
matronage
aaegmnprt
pentagram
aaegmnpsu
sagapenum
aaegmnrtt
termagant
aaegmosst
moss-agate
aaegmprst
strap-game
aaegmrrtt
tetragram
aaegmrstt
stratagem
aaegmrstu
gastraeum
aaegnnoot
Notogaean
aaegnoprs
parsonage

aaegnoprt
patronage
aaegnprty
pageantry
aaegnrttu
great-aunt
aaegopprt
propagate
aaegoprsu
Areopagus
aaegprsst
tape-grass
aaegprstu
pasturage
aaegrrstz
star-gazer
aaehhimtv
have-at-him
aaehhlnot
halothane
aaehhlptt
phthalate
aaehhrttx
hearth-tax
aaehilllu
alleluiah
aaehilmms
Hamamelis
aaehilmnr
harmaline
aaehilntv
leviathan
aaehilort
hariolate
aaehilrtw
heir-at-law
aaehimnot
theomania
aaehinpsy
synapheia
aaehiprrs
parrhesia
aaehirrvw
hair-waver
aaehjnnno
Johannean
aaehklnrs
ranshakle
aaehknosw
oakenshaw
aaehllmsu
alum-shale
aaehllstu
haustella
aaehlmnoy
hyalonema
aaehlmstu
steam-haul
aaehlnppt
pentalpha
aaehlnpsx
phalanxes
aaehloppr
phalarope

aaehlpsty
Staphylea
aaehmmmnr
hammerman
aaehmmnot
Mahometan
aaehmnprs
phraseman
aaehmnrss
sharesman
aaehmnrsw
washerman
aaehmostt
haemostat
aaehmrstu
shamateur
aaehnnops
Ansaphone®
aaehnoopt
haanepoot
aaehnpsww
wapenshaw
aaehnrrtx
Xenarthra
aaehnrttt
attrahent
aaehnstuy
euthanasy
aaehpprty
parhypate
aaehrrstt
earth-star
aaeiilmns
animalise
aaeiilmrt
marialite
aaeiilnrz
alizarine
aaeiilnst
Salientia
aaeiilptx
epitaxial
aaeiilrst
aerialist
aaeiilrty
aeriality
aaeiimnnt
inanimate
aaeiimnrs
semi-Arian
aaeiimrst
artemisia
aaeiinnpr
Napierian
aaeiinnrt
Aretinian
aaeiinsst
taeniasis
aaeiinstt
insatiate
aaeiirtvv
variative
aaeikllrz
lazar-like

aaeiklttv
talkative
aaeikmnrr
rain-maker
aaeiknrsu
Euskarian
aaeillmmt
mamillate
aaeillmnp
mail-plane
aaeillmnt
alimental
aaeillnps
sailplane
aaeillnpt
tailplane
aaeillppt
papillate
aaeillprt
plate-rail
prelatial
aaeillpss
paillasse
palliasse
aaeillrst
Stellaria
aaeillrtv
relatival
aaeilmmno
melomania
aaeilmmst
melismata
aaeilmnru
melanuria
aaeilmnst
stamineal
aaeilmntu
aluminate
aaeilmopr
paroemial
aaeilmprv
primaeval
aaeilmptt
palmitate
aaeilmrst
mare's-tail
aaeilmrtu
tularemia
aaeilnnsu
annualise
aaeilnort
alienator
rationale
aaeilnprt
perinatal
aaeilnstt
tantalise
aaeilnttt
tantalite
aaeilortv
variolate
aaeilpptt
palpitate

aaeilprst
psalteria
aaeilprtz
trapezial
aaeilrrtw
water-rail
aaeilrssw
wassailer
aaeilrstu
estuarial
aaeilrstw
altarwise
aaeimmrrs
marmarise
aaeimnnoo
oenomania
aaeimnnot
emanation
aaeimnnox
xenomania
aaeimnnss
anamnesis
aaeimnntx
examinant
aaeimnost
anatomise
aaeimnotz
amazonite
aaeimnprr
repairman
aaeimnrtw
water-main
aaeimnstt
emanatist
staminate
aaeimorst
aromatise
aaeimprrs
spermaria
aaeimprst
spermatia
aaeimrrtz
terza-rima
aaeinnort
arenation
aaeinnott
Totaninae
aaeinorrt
aerotrain
aaeinortx
exaration
aaeinpprt
appertain
aaeinprst
septarian
aaeinqttu
antiquate
aaeinrrtv
narrative
aaeinrrtw
rain-water
aaeinrsst
star-anise

aaeinrstu
estuarian
aaeinrsty
Satyrinae
aaeinsttt
satinetta
aaeinsttu
unsatiate
aaeiorstx
aerotaxis
aaeipprrs
appraiser
aaeirrstt
tartarise
aaeisssuv
assuasive
aaejklrwy
jaywalker
aaejmortt
état-major
aaejpprww
wapper-jaw
aaejrtttu
jettatura
aaekktyyy
yakety-yak
aaekllsst
sales-talk
aaeklmprt
plate-mark
aaeklprst
lapstreak
aaekmmnrt
market-man
aaekmrrtw
watermark
aaekmrsty
stay-maker
aaeknnrtu
nunataker
aaelllmor
malleolar
aaelllnry
allenarly
aaelllptw
wall-plate
aaelllrty
laterally
aaellmntt
maltalent
aaellmnty
allayment
aaellmpty
palmately
aaellmqsu
squamella
aaellmstu
alum-slate
aaellnppt
appellant
aaellnstt
neat-stall
aaellpprw
wallpaper

aaellsuxy
asexually
aaelmmorr
marmoreal
aaelmmost
Melastoma
aaelmmpst
metaplasm
aaelmnnrz
ranzelman
aaelmnoss
sea-salmon
aaelmnosu
mausolean
aaelmnrsy
man-slayer
aaelmoppr
palampore
aaelnnopt
pantaleon
aaelnnptu
pennatula
aaelnnrtt
alternant
aaelnoprt
rotaplane
aaelnorzz
lazzarone
aaelnppru
unapparel
aaelnppss
sans-appel
aaelnprty
planetary
aaelnpstt
pantalets
aaelnpsux
pansexual
aaelnrstt
translate
aaelnsttu
sultanate
aaelnsttx
sextantal
aaeloppry
propylaea
aaeloprst
pastorale
aaelopssu
asepalous
aaelopstu
apetalous
aaelorrsu
rearousal
aaelorttz
lazaretto
aaelpprrs
pearl-spar
aaelpprst
star-apple
aaelpprtt
apple-tart
aaelprrsy
paralyser

aaelpsttu
spatulate
aaelrsstu
assaulter
saleratus
aaelrsttw
salt-water
aaelssssv
vassaless
aaelsstwy
leastways
aaemmnsst
amassment
aaemmortt
mattamore
aaemnorst
manor-seat
aaemnorty
emanatory
aaemnprtt
apartment
aaemnpsst
passament
aaemnrrty
arrayment
aaemnrssw
wasserman
aaemnsstt
statesman
aaemorstt
roast-meat
aaemprstt
steam-trap
aaemprstu
separatum
aaemprsty
paymaster
aaemrssty
say-master
aaennnrst
transenna
aaennnrty
antennary
aaennttu
attenuant
aaenprsst
apartness
aaenprsty
peasantry
aaenpssty
synaptase
aaenrrrtw
warranter
aaeoprrst
sea-parrot
separator
aaeoprstt
pastorate
aafffglst
flagstaff
aaffgnrsu
suffragan
aaffilnot
afflation

aaffimnrt
affirmant
aaffinpry
paraffiny
aafgilmns
falangism
aafgilnrs
Franglais
aafgilnst
falangist
aafginrrw
warfaring
aafginrwy
wayfaring
aafgiorss
ossifraga
aafglorsu
loaf-sugar
sugar-loaf
aafgorttu
autograft
aafhllory
half-royal
aafhlmotu
Fomalhaut
aafiirryy
airy-fairy
aafillnop
Fallopian
aafilmnor
foraminal
aafiloruw
Rauwolfia
aafimortu
fumatoria
aafinrttu
Tartufian
aafinsstt
fantasist
aafmorrtw
marrowfat
aafnrstty
fantastry
aaggimnor
angiogram
aaggimrrs
gargarism
aagginssu
assuaging
aaggklnnp
gangplank
aaggllls
glass-gall
aagglnosy
synagogal
aaghiilmp
Malpighia
aaghijrtu
Gujarathi
aaghikmny
haymaking
aaghikprs
skiagraph

aaghilnrs
ashlaring
Shangri-la
aaghilors
Haloragis
aaghimoop
omophagia
aaghimprr
marigraph
aaghinnru
Hungarian
aaghinrss
harassing
aaghiorst
goat's-hair
aaghirrss
hair-grass
aaghllopr
allograph
aaghlnpry
pharyngal
aaghlopxy
Xylophaga
aaghnoopz
zoophagan
aaghnprst
strap-hang
aaghoprtu
autograph
aaghoptuy
autophagy
aagiimmns
Magianism
aagiimnnt
animating
aagiimnry
imaginary
aagiimrst
Stigmaria
aagiinott
agitation
aagijnnnp
japanning
aagiklnno
Algonkian
aagiknprt
partaking
aagillnoz
gallinazo
aagillnpp
appalling
aagillntv
gallivant
aagillort
alligator
aagillpsw
galliwasp
aagilmmnu
magnalium
aagilmnns
signalman
aagilmnnt
malignant

aagilmnsv
galvanism
aagilmnsy
gymnasial
aagilmnyz
amazingly
aagilmopy
Polygamia
aagilmors
sialogram
aagilmrst
magistral
aagilnoru
urolagnia
aagilnost
analogist
nostalgia
aagilnruu
inaugural
aagilnruv
vulgarian
aagilnstv
galvanist
aagimmnot
gammation
aagimmrsy
Magyarism
aagimnprt
ptarmigan
aagimssst
massagist
aaginnrtu
turnagain
aaginoprs
sporangia
aaginortv
navigator
aagiorsuv
vagarious
aagipssty
paysagist
aagirstty
sagittary
aagknnotw
tank-wagon
aaglllnty
gallantly
aagllmpss
lamp-glass
aagllnntu
ungallant
aagllnrsu
slangular
aagllnrty
gallantry
aagllopss
opal-glass
aagllrsuy
sugar-ally
aaglmmmoy
mammalogy
aaglmnoru
granuloma

aaglmprsu
palm-sugar
sugar-palm
aaglnoosu
analogous
aaglnoouz
guanazolo
aaglnrruy
granulary
aaglnrttu
gratulant
aaglopsss
glass-soap
aagmnnost
mangostan
aagmnnosu
manganous
aagmnrttu
turmagant
aagmoopsu
apogamous
aagnnnoty
nanny-goat
aagnnortu
orang-utan
aagnorrtu
guarantor
aagnorstu
Angostura
aagnpsstu
Spatangus
aagprstty
stag-party
aagrrssst
star-grass
aahhhooow
whoa-ho-hoa
aahhiimrs
maharishi
aahhijprs
rajahship
aahhillns
inshallah
aahhimrty
arhythmia
aahhorstt
Ashtaroth
aahiknort
Tokharian
aahikrsst
katharsis
aahikrsty
Kshatriya
aahilmnot
Malathion®
aahilmtuz
azimuthal
aahilnort
inhalator
aahilnstu
ailanthus
aahilorst
sailor-hat

aahilortu
authorial
aahimmnss
shamanism
aahimnopy
hypomania
aahimnpst
phantasim
aahimnsst
shamanist
aahimnstt
thanatism
aahimnstu
amianthus
aahinoprt
Phanariot
aahinorrv
Harrovian
aahinpsww
wapinshaw
aahinptty
antipathy
aahinrrtu
Arthurian
aahinsttt
thanatist
aahiorstu
haustoria
aahiprrsy
hair-spray
aahklmors
shoal-mark
aahklnors
loan-shark
aahllmosw
Hallowmas
aahllopty
allopathy
aahllsttt
Hallstatt
aahlmnntu
lanthanum
aahlmpstu
asphaltum
aahlmrsst
salt-marsh
aahlpppsy
slap-happy
aahmnnsty
shantyman
aahmnppry
paranymph
aahmnpsst
phantasms
aahmopprr
paramorph
aahnnostu
ananthous
aahnortux
Xanthoura
aahnrstuy
Thysanura
aahortwwy
throw-away

aaiiilmns
Ismailian
aaiiilmrt
militaria
aaiiknnru
Ukrainian
aaiiknpst
Pakistani
aaiikprtt
Tripitaka
aaiilmmns
animalism
aaiilmnrt
mail-train
aaiilmnst
animalist
aaiilmnty
animality
aaiilmprt
impartial
primatial
aaiilnnpu
Paulinian
aaiilnppz
Lippizana
aaiilnrtv
antiviral
aaiilortv
viatorial
aaiilruxy
auxiliary
aaiimmnst
animatism
aaiimnnot
animation
aaiimpprr
primipara
aaiinnrtu
Unitarian
aaiinnrtv
invariant
aaiinoprt
topiarian
aaiinortv
variation
aaiinostt
satiation
aaiinprru
Ripuarian
aaiinrrtu
Ruritania
aaiiqrstu
aquariist
aaijmrssw
swarajism
aaijnrssy
janissary
aaijrsstw
swarajist
aaikkkorw
krakowiak
aaikktyyy
yakity-yak

aaiklloss
alkalosis
aaiklmmns
slammakin
aaiklnosv
Slovakian
aaiknnopt
pontianak
aaiknqrtu
antiquark
aaikrsttu
autarkist
aailllmux
maxillula
aailllnot
lallation
aaillmmry
mamillary
aaillmmxy
maximally
aaillmopp
papilloma
aaillmrry
armillary
aaillmrsy
amaryllis
aaillmrty
maritally
martially
aaillmrxy
maxillary
aaillnost
allantois
aaillnpru
nullipara
aaillntvy
valiantly
aailloptz
zapotilla
aaillopxy
polyaxial
aaillppry
papillary
aaillprty
partially
aaillpsty
spatially
aaillrrty
artillary
aailmmors
amoralism
aailmnnps
plainsman
aailmnopt
palmation
aailmnors
sailor-man
aailmnort
laminator
aailmnost
atonalism
aailmnpru
manipular

aailmnstt
tantalism
aailmnttu
matutinal
aailmorst
amoralist
aailmorsu
malarious
aailmprsu
marsupial
aailmprtu
multipara
aailnnopt
planation
aailnnost
santolina
aailnnosv
Slavonian
aailnnotw
Waltonian
aailnnpqu
palanquin
aailnnpru
uniplanar
aailnoppt
palpation
aailnopss
passional
sponsalia
aailnopuw
paulownia
aailnopvv
Pavlovian
aailnortt
latration
aailnorzz
lazzaroni
aailnostt
saltation
stational
aailnostv
salvation
aailnotty
atonality
aailnotuv
valuation
aailnpptt
palpitant
aailnprtu
tarpaulin
unpartial
aailnptty
antitypal
aailoorrt
oratorial
aailoortz
zoolatria
aailoprrt
raptorial
aailoprry
pair-royal
aailorrst
sartorial

aailpprru
pluripara
aailprssy
paralysis
aailrrrty
tirra-lyra
aailrsswy
wassailry
aaimmnnoo
monomania
aaimmnrst
Martinmas
aaimmorry
myriorama
aaimmrssu
Marasmius
aaimnnoru
Roumanian
aaimnoops
opsomania
aaimnoort
inamorato
aaimnopry
pyromania
aaimnopty
typomania
aaimnortz
Mozartian
aaimnostt
anatomist
aaimnrstt
tarantism
aaimoorrt
moratoria
aaimorssu
amaurosis
aaimqrsuu
aquariums
aainnnssy
sannyasin
aainnnttu
annuitant
aainnorrt
narration
aainnortt
tarnation
aainnrstu
Saturnian
aainoorrt
oratorian
aainopstt
antipasto
aainopstu
sapi-outan
aainorrst
sartorian
aainprsst
satin-spar
aainpsstt
antispast
aainpstxy
anaptyxis
aainqrtuy
antiquary

aainssstt
assistant
aaiopprrt
apparitor
aaiopqrtu
paraquito
aaioprrst
aspirator
aaiopsttu
autopista
aaiorrttt
trattoria
aaiprrstt
trap-stair
aaiprrttu
partitura
aajoprrtw
parrot-jaw
aaklllmst
small-talk
aaknoosst
saskatoon
aalllmops
alloplasm
aallmmrss
small-arms
aallnrtuy
naturally
aallorruy
aurorally
aallprstu
palustral
plaustral
aallprtwy
party-wall
aalmmnosw
alms-woman
aalmnoosu
anomalous
aalmnoprt
patrolman
aalmnoptu
Pulmonata
aalmnorst
Monastral
aalmnprty
rampantly
aalmoostu
autosomal
aalmoqssu
squamosal
aalmortyy
mayoralty
aalnnoopt
Pantaloon
aalnnrtuu
unnatural
aalnoopzz
pozzolana
aalnopsst
post-nasal
aalnopstt
post-natal

aalnopuzz
puzzolana
aalnprsty
spartanly
aalnprtwy
lawn-party
aalnsstwy
slantways
aaloprrty
portrayal
aalorssvv
valvassor
aalorstty
saltatory
aalorstvy
salvatory
aalorttuy
autolatry
aammnnowx
Manxwoman
aamnnprty
pantryman
aamnoorsw
oarswoman
aamnoottu
automaton
aamnoprtu
paramount
aamnorstz
stramazon
aamnqrruy
quarryman
aamoprttu
amputator
aannoortt
annotator
aannorstt
stannator
aanorrrtw
warrantor
aanorrrty
narratory
aanorsttu
astronaut
aanprsssu
Parnassus
aaoorrttv
rotavator
aaoprrsty
raspatory
aaorrsttu
saturator
aapqrrsuy
quarry-sap
abbbcellu
clubbable
abbbcelru
bubble-car
abbbeilru
air-bubble
abbbiimst
Babbitism
abbccehkn
back-bench

abbcckklo
back-block
abbcckklu
blackbuck
abbcdekow
bow-backed
abbcdelry
crabbedly
abbcdiklr
blackbird
abbcdkoru
buckboard
abbceikrt
backbiter
abbceillm
climbable
abbceilrs
scribable
abbcekllu
blue-black
abbceklno
bone-black
abbcelrrs
scrabbler
abbchikrt
bath-brick
abbchnrsu
subbranch
abbciiosu
bibacious
abbcimost
bombastic
abbckloot
bootblack
abbdeeert
breed-bate
abbdeelno
blade-bone
abbdeglnu
bugle-band
abbdeilot
bobtailed
abbdeilrt
bird-table
abbdeiltu
dubitable
abbdellny
belly-band
abbdeloru
double-bar
abbdelotu
doubtable
abbdelsuu
subduable
abbdgiiln
ad-libbing
abbdgilnr
drabbling
abbdhloot
blood-bath
abbdhnnoo
hob-and-nob
abbdhooty
tabbyhood

abbdillor
billboard
abbdiltuy
dubitably
abbdimorr
broad-brim
abbdknoru
bark-bound
abbdlloru
bull-board
abbdmnoor
bombardon
abbeeelrt
table-beer
abbeeklru
rebukable
abbeellms
semblable
abbeelrrs
slabberer
abbeelrry
blaeberry
abbeenrry
baneberry
abbeeorrs
sea-robber
abbeerrry
bear-berry
abbegijnr
jabbering
abbeginrt
rabbeting
abbehinos
Hobbesian
abbeiinrt
rabbinite
abbeilmot
bombilate
abbeilmuy
bum-baylie
abbeilost
biostable
abbeimnos
bombasine
abbeimnot
bombinate
abbeimnoz
bombazine
abbeinort
barbitone
abbekloot
table-book
abbellmsy
semblably
abbelmooz
bamboozle
abbelosty
stable-boy
abbelqrsu
squabbler
abbelsttu
taste-bulb
abbemortu
obumbrate

abbenoory
baboonery
abbenorst
absorbent
abbfhllsu
flash-bulb
abbgillno
billabong
abbgilmnr
brambling
abbgiloot
obbligato
abbginors
absorbing
abbhinoos
baboonish
abbhiopst
abbotship
abbhiqssu
squabbish
abbhistuy
bathybius
abbhmoppy
bomb-happy
abbiimnrs
rabbinism
abbiinrst
rabbinist
abbilloru
bilobular
abbimnnor
ribbon-man
abbllootx
ballot-box
abbooprty
booby-trap
abboorrwy
barrow-boy
abcccefio
beccafico
abccckklo
blackcock
abccdefhu
chub-faced
abcceeikp
backpiece
abcceenru
buccaneer
abcceinov
biconcave
abcceinru
buccanier
abcceinrw
cabin-crew
abccelnru
carbuncle
abccemnru
cumbrance
abccfhiks
backfisch
abccfimor
bacciform
abcchhknu
hunchback

abcchklot
back-cloth
abcchknot
notchback
abcchkotu
touch-back
abcchltuy
yacht-club
abcciijno
Jacobinic
abcciijot
Jacobitic
abccikllo
acock-bill
abcciklry
brick-clay
abccikrst
crabstick
abccillou
bucolical
abccilluy
cubically
abccilnoo
obconical
abcciloru
corbicula
abccinoos
cocoa-nibs
abccirstu
subarctic
abccjkklo
jack-block
abcckkoor
crookback
abccklloo
block-coal
abcckorss
backcross
abccmoory
mobocracy
abcddeehu
debauched
abcddeeil
decidable
abcddeflo
bold-faced
abcddeilu
adducible
abcddeirr
cedar-bird
abcddkoru
duck-board
abcdeeehu
debauchee
abcdeegrr
berg-cedar
abcdeehmr
chambered
abcdeehpt
bepatched
abcdeehru
debaucher
abcdeeikr
bridecake

abcdeeilm
medicable
abcdeeilr
calibered
abcdeeimr
Barmecide
abcdeejkt
bed-jacket
abcdeeprt
carpet-bed
abcdefoot
boot-faced
abcdegikr
ridgeback
abcdegimr
Cambridge
abcdehklo
blockhead
abcdeijlu
judicable
abcdeikls
backslide
abcdeikru
rudbeckia
abcdeilno
balconied
abcdeilrs
crab-sidle
abcdeilrv
devil-crab
abcdeiort
bacteroid
abcdeiorz
bezoardic
abcdellno
blond-lace
abcdellnu
bull-dance
abcdenorr
bread-corn
corn-bread
abcdenors
absconder
abcdenosu
case-bound
subdeacon
abcdeoort
obcordate
abcdflnou
calf-bound
abcdhinrs
disbranch
abcdhiopr
chipboard
abcdhirsy
Charybdis
abcdikrry
brickyard
abcdillno
blind-coal
abcdilmor
Lombardic
abcdiloot
baldi-coot
abcdilopr
clip-board
abcdiloru
colubriad
abcdinoot
bandicoot
abcdinotu
abduction
abcdintuy
dubitancy
abcdkloor
roadblock
abcdkloow
blackwood
abcdkoosw
backwoods
abcdkorsw
backsword
abcdlnrsu
scrubland
abcdnorss
crossband
abceeelrt
celebrate
abceeelrx
execrable
abceeerrr
rerebrace
abceeerrt
cerebrate
abceefirs
brief-case
abceefklt
Blackfeet
abceefltu
flûte-à-bec
abceeforr
fore-brace
abceeghrr
herb-grace
abceegknr
back-green
greenback
abceehiot
cohabitee
abceehirt
Rechabite
abceehlly
bellyache
abceehlrs
bleachers
abceehlry
bleachery
abceehmrr
chamberer
abceehmst
beech-mast
abceehpss
sheep-scab
abceehrst
bretasche
abceeilmr
merciable
abceeilnv
bivalence
abceeilsx
excisable
abceeiltx
excitable
abceeimrv
embracive
abceeinos
obeisance
abceeinrr
cerberian
abceeirst
bacterise
abceekknr
breakneck
abceekprs
backspeer
abceekpsw
sweepback
abceelmns
semblance
abceelnrt
celebrant
abceelnst
albescent
abceelnuu
nubeculae
abceelort
bracteole
abceelorv
revocable
abceelosu
leuco-base
abceelotv
covetable
abceelrsu
rescuable
securable
abceelrxy
execrably
abceelsux
excusable
abceemmrt
Camembert
abceemorr
embraceor
abceemort
embrocate
abceemrry
embracery
abceenstt
tabescent
abceeorst
obsecrate
abceeossu
sebaceous
abceeprru
cupbearer
abceerssy
crab's-eyes
abceerstt
bescatter
abcefhitu
faith-cube
abcefhlsu
flashcube
abcefilru
febricula
abcefinor
forecabin
abcefirtu
bifurcate
abcefostu
obfuscate
abceghiln
bleaching
abcegilot
cogitable
abcegimnr
embracing
abcegimrt
bregmatic
abceglllu
bugle-call
abcegnopu
pounce-bag
abcegnsuy
subagency
abcegrsuu
sugar-cube
abcehilty
chalybite
abcehinot
aitchbone
abcehinrt
Brechtian
abcehioop
ecophobia
abcehklll
hell-black
abcehklls
shellback
abcehklos
shoeblack
abcehkmnr
bench-mark
abcehkors
horseback
abcehkrry
hackberry
abcehkstu
ash-bucket
abcehktuw
buckwheat
abcehlnrt
branchlet
abcehlopw
peach-blow
abcehlotu
touchable
abcehlrsu
crushable
abcehnoor
Orobanche
abcehnrry
branchery
abcehoqru
quebracho
abcehorrs
shore-crab
abcehprsu
caper-bush
abceiilns
sibilance
abceiilrs
irascible
abceiimrt
imbricate
abceijlnu
jubilance
abceijnot
abjection
abceikmqu
quickbeam
abceikprs
backspeir
abceikrtw
write-back
abceillos
obeliscal
abceillrr
cribellar
abceillss
classible
abceilmot
metabolic
abceilmst
cembalist
abceilnnu
incunable
abceilnot
balection
abceilnru
incurable
abceilnvy
bivalency
abceilort
cabriolet
abceilott
cobaltite
abceilrtu
lubricate
abceilrux
Excalibur
abceilstu
Baculites
bisulcate
abceimmux
excambium
abceimnot
combinate
abceimnox
excambion
abceimotv
combative
abceimrtu
bacterium
abceinors
carbonise
escribano

abceirrsu
carburise
abceirrtu
rubricate
abceissss
abscisses
abcejnstu
subjacent
abcekkorr
rock-brake
abceklnss
blackness
abceklpru
parbuckle
abceknorr
corn-brake
abcekortu
outbacker
abcekpstw
swept-back
abcekrtuw
water-buck
abcellrsw
screwball
abcellstu
slate-club
abcelmnoy
belomancy
abcelmoor
rocambole
abcelmopt
comptable
abcelmotu
columbate
abcelmrrs
scrambler
abcelmrtu
tumble-car
abcelnost
constable
abcelnotu
countable
abcelnruu
uncurable
abcelorsu
crab-louse
abcelorvy
revocably
abcelostt
ectoblast
abcelrsst
bractless
abcelrstu
scrutable
abcelrtty
battle-cry
abcelrtuu
lucubrate
abcelssuu
subclause
abcelsuxy
excusably
abcemnopr
cramp-bone
abcemorss
crossbeam
abcemorsy
embryo-sac
abcemrsuv
Verbascum
abcennrru
cab-runner
abcenorty
baronetcy
abcenrrry
cranberry
abcenrtuu
Bucentaur
abcensstu
substance
abceooprs
baroscope
abceoprry
reprobacy
abceorstu
basecourt
abceostuv
suboctave
abcfghikt
fight-back
fightback
abcfhikls
blackfish
abcfhiksy
fishyback
abcfhrstu
bushcraft
abcfimmor
cambiform
abcfkloot
Blackfoot
abcggikpy
piggyback
abcghikst
backsight
abcghinnr
branching
abcghloos
schoolbag
abcgiinrt
racing-bit
abcgiklns
sling-back
abcgiknor
king-cobra
abcgiknsw
swing-back
abcgilmns
scambling
abcgimnot
combating
abcgknouw
buck-wagon
abchhikss
backshish
abchhksuw
bushwhack
abchiilln
chilblain
abchiimnr
Brahminic
abchiiost
isobathic
abchikrst
britschka
abchilltw
watch-bill
abchilmos
shambolic
abchilnor
bronchial
abchilnot
chain-bolt
abchklluw
bullwhack
abchkmttu
thumb-tack
abchknort
thornback
abchllnpu
punch-ball
abchlmort
barm-cloth
abchnorrs
cornbrash
abciiiklw
bailiwick
abciiilpt
bicipital
abciiknrs
brainsick
abciillmu
umbilical
abciillst
ballistic
abciilmor
microbial
abciilnos
basilicon
abciilnot
albinotic
abciilnsy
sibilancy
abciilrsy
irascibly
abciimnor
microbian
abciinnrt
Britannic
abciinrru
rubrician
abciirsty
sybaritic
abcijlnuy
jubilancy
abcikllrw
brickwall
abcikllst
blacklist
abciknors
rock-basin
abcillmru
lumbrical
abcilloru
bilocular
abcillssy
syllabics
abcilmnou
Columbian
abcilmsty
cymbalist
abcilnnou
connubial
abcilnopt
panic-bolt
abcilnoru
binocular
abcilnrtu
lubricant
abcilnruy
incurably
abcilopsy
polybasic
abcilorru
courbaril
orbicular
abcilortu
tubicolar
abcimnoos
monobasic
abcimostu
subatomic
abcimrsty
cambistry
abcinortu
incubator
abcinostu
subaction
abcinosty
obstinacy
abcinttuy
titubancy
abckknost
bank-stock
abcklooss
class-book
abcknorrw
crown-bark
abckooprs
scrap-book
abckrstuy
rusty-back
abclmnouw
clubwoman
abclmoruy
columbary
abclorsuu
subocular
abclosstu
subcostal
abclossuy
scybalous
abcmrrtuy
crumb-tray
abcnorstu
obscurant
subcantor
abcnorsty
corybants
abcrssttu
substract
abdddeelr
bladdered
abdddipry
paddy-bird
abddeeest
besteaded
abddeeghi
big-headed
abddeegrr
berg-adder
abddeeirt
diet-bread
abddeellu
deludable
abddeelmo
beadledom
abddeelzz
bedazzled
abddeenrr
brandered
abddeenru
unbearded
abddeensu
undebased
abddeeprs
bedspread
abddeerty
teddy-bear
abddeggor
badger-dog
abddehmno
mob-handed
abddeiilv
dividable
abddeiimr
bridemaid
abddeilss
slab-sided
abddeinru
unbraided
abddeiors
broadside
sideboard
abddeirru
ribaudred
abddelopx
paddle-box
abddelosw
saddle-bow
abddfilor
forbiddal
abddgoruy
bodyguard
abddilnns
sand-blind
abddjmnoo
odd-jobman

abddnrstu
dust-brand
abdeeeflr
deferable
abdeeegll
delegable
abdeeelmn
emendable
abdeeelry
blear-eyed
abdeeerrt
bread-tree
abdeefhlr
half-breed
abdeefiln
definable
abdeeforr
free-board
abdeegglr
bedraggle
abdeeghin
beheading
abdeeginr
gaberdine
abdeegmor
embargoed
abdeegnrr
bergander
abdeegorr
garderobe
abdeegrry
greybeard
abdeehinr
haberdine
Hebridean
abdeehllt
death-bell
abdeehlnw
band-wheel
abdeehmos
besom-head
abdeehosu
bead-house
abdeehrrt
earth-bred
abdeehrsw
shewbread
abdeeiilr
diablerie
abdeeillr
ebrillade
abdeeillw
wieldable
abdeeilly
yieldable
abdeeilms
demisable
abdeeilmt
bedlamite
abdeeilno
Belonidae
abdeeilnr
bandelier
breadline

abdeeilns
disenable
abdeeilrs
desirable
abdeeilrv
derivable
abdeeilst
side-table
abdeeilsv
devisable
abdeeiltt
tide-table
abdeeinnr
Bernadine
abdeeinst
besainted
abdeeintt
bidentate
abdeeintu
butadiene
abdeeittu
beatitude
abdeellps
speed-ball
abdeellrr
barrelled
abdeelmtt
embattled
abdeelnop
pedal-bone
abdeelnor
banderole
bandoleer
abdeelnot
denotable
abdeelnpr
prebendal
abdeelnps
spendable
abdeelnru
endurable
abdeelops
deposable
abdeeloux
double-axe
abdeelrss
beardless
abdeemnot
abodement
abdeemnrt
debarment
abdeemnsu
sunbeamed
abdeemrsy
Ember-days
abdeenops
spade-bone
abdeenoty
bayoneted
abdeenqtu
banqueted
abdeenrrt
bartender

abdeenrru
underbear
abdeenrtu
unrebated
abdeenttu
debutante
abdeeopst
speed-boat
abdeerrst
redbreast
abdefflnu
unbaffled
abdefiisx
basifixed
abdefilny
definably
abdefinrr
firebrand
abdefoopr
bead-proof
abdegggin
de-bagging
abdegglsu
sluggabed
abdeggmor
beggardom
abdegiirr
air-bridge
brigadier
abdeginrr
debarring
abdegllmo
gambolled
abdeglnru
ungarbled
abdegnnor
dannebrog
abdegrtuy
budgetary
abdehhirt
heath-bird
abdehiinr
Hebridian
abdehilno
hobnailed
abdehirtw
wheat-bird
abdehlnos
ash-blonde
abdehloot
bloodheat
abdehlort
holderbat
abdehlotw
death-blow
abdehnort
heart-bond
abdehnrrt
brandreth
abdehoost
beasthood
abdehorsw
showbread

abdehrrsy
shadberry
abdeiilnu
inaudible
abdeiilos
diabolise
abdeiinsw
basin-wide
abdeiklnr
drinkable
abdeikmrs
disembark
abdeiknrs
snakebird
abdeiknrw
break-wind
wind-break
abdeikrst
Dekabrist
abdeilllo
labelloid
abdeilmms
bedlamism
abdeilmor
bromeliad
abdeilnno
bandoline
abdeilnor
bandolier
bird-alone
abdeilnru
unridable
abdeilrsy
desirably
abdeilrvy
derivably
abdeimnrs
bridesman
abdeinorw
rainbowed
abdeinost
bastioned
abdeinrss
rabidness
abdeinssu
unbiassed
abdeinssw
bawdiness
abdeioort
boodie-rat
abdeiorsw
broadwise
abdeipru
upbraider
abdeirrtw
water-bird
abdeknorw
breakdown
abdelllsy
syllabled
abdellmou
mouldable
abdellmst
small-debt

abdellotu
lobulated
abdellpsu
ballsed-up
abdellrss
ball-dress
abdelmnoy
baldmoney
abdelmoty
molybdate
abdelnnss
blandness
abdelnoor
bandolero
abdelnost
endoblast
abdelnosv
bond-slave
abdelnouw
woundable
abdelnruy
endurably
abdelnstu
Dunstable
abdelnsuy
unbasedly
abdeloruv
boulevard
abdelttuu
tubulated
abdemnnor
Dobermann
abdemoorr
breadroom
abdennost
band-stone
abdenoorr
road-borne
abdenopsu
subpoena'd
abdenorry
errand-boy
abdenorss
broadness
abdenorst
adsorbent
abdenorsw
sword-bean
abdenrsty
bystander
stander-by
abdenrsuw
subwarden
abdeoorrt
breadroot
abdeoorrv
overboard
abdeoorwz
zebra-wood
abdeorrrw
wardrober
abderruyy
rybaudrye

abdfhlloo
half-blood
abdfhlnou
half-bound
abdfiirrr
friarbird
abdfooorr
roof-board
abdfooort
board-foot
footboard
abdforrsu
surf-board
abdghinsu
sgian-dubh
abdghllou
dough-ball
abdgiilny
abidingly
abdgilnnr
brandling
abdgilnou
bungaloid
abdgilooy
diabology
abdginnou
abounding
abdginors
signboard
abdginrry
brigandry
abdgkooru
guard-book
abdglnoor
Longobard
abdhiinnr
hind-brain
abdhimrty
dithyramb
abdhinrst
shirt-band
abdhioprs
shipboard
abdhlnsuy
husbandly
abdhnooru
boarhound
abdhnrsuy
husbandry
abdhooprs
shopboard
abdiiilln
libidinal
abdiillrs
billiards
abdiilmos
diabolism
abdiilnuy
inaudibly
abdiilost
idioblast
abdiimpry
bipyramid
abdiimrst
tribadism
abdiinrst
satin-bird
abdillmor
mill-board
abdilnoor
blood-rain
abdiloprs
slip-board
abdilrssu
disbursal
abdimnnot
badminton
abdimnopu
dumb-piano
abdinnorr
brand-iron
abdinnoru
rain-bound
abdinorry
by-ordinar
abdinorww
window-bar
abdinrstw
wristband
abdirstuy
absurdity
abdknoost
bookstand
abdlmooor
broadloom
abdloppru
pulpboard
abdmmnosu
ombudsman
abdmnnoow
bond-woman
abdmnoowy
woman-body
abdmooorr
boardroom
abeeeefrt
beefeater
abeeeersz
sea-breeze
abeeefkst
beefsteak
abeeeflrr
referable
abeeeflrz
freezable
abeeeggrt
egg-beater
abeeegllr
relegable
abeeeglnr
generable
abeeeglnv
vengeable
abeeeglru
beleaguer
abeeeglrv
bevel-gear
abeeegltv
vegetable
abeeehlsw
wheelbase
abeeehmrt
embreathe
abeeeklst
eel-basket
abeeeknrv
break-even
abeeekprr
barkeeper
abeeelmpr
permeable
abeeelmty
may-beetle
abeeelnrt
enterable
abeeelnrv
venerable
abeeelnrw
renewable
abeeelnsu
unseeable
abeeelrrv
reverable
abeeelrsv
severable
abeeemrst
beemaster
abeeerrtt
terebrate
abeeerrtv
verberate
vertebrae
abeeertux
exuberate
abeeffiln
ineffable
abeefflor
offerable
abeefglor
forgeable
abeefikrr
fire-break
abeefillt
life-table
abeefilnr
inferable
abeefilrs
bas-relief
abeeflrsu
refusable
abeeflrtu
refutable
abeeflssu
self-abuse
abeeforst
roast-beef
abeegginu
beguinage
abeeghilw
weighable
abeeghnor
habergeon
abeegillv
levigable
abeegilnn
bengaline
abeeginru
aubergine
abeegkorr
brokerage
abeegllmo
Malebolge
abeeglmnr
embrangle
abeeglnpr
pregnable
abeeglnps
bespangle
abeeglnvy
vengeably
abeeglopr
bargepole
porbeagle
abeeglrtu
butlerage
abeeglssu
guessable
abeegltvy
vegetably
abeegmors
embargoes
abeegnnrt
rennet-bag
abeegnors
Boanerges
abeegnrsu
subgenera
abeegrstu
sugar-beet
abeehhkss
baksheesh
abeehilrt
heritable
abeehimnr
Brahminee
abeehimsv
misbehave
abeehimtw
whitebeam
abeehinrt
hibernate
inbreathe
abeehirrs
Hebraiser
abeehirtw
white-bear
abeehkors
brake-shoe
abeehkosu
bakehouse
abeehlmps
blaspheme
abeehlnow
whalebone
abeehnort
bone-earth
abeehnory
honey-bear
abeehortu
hereabout
abeeiinrt
inebriate
abeeiklst
beastlike
abeeiknst
snakebite
abeeillmr
mirabelle
abeeillnr
ballerine
abeeilmno
Meliboean
abeeilmrs
miserable
abeeilmst
estimable
abeeilmtt
timetable
abeeilnnt
intenable
abeeilnps
albespine
abeeilnqu
inequable
abeeilnrr
inerrable
abeeilppt
appetible
abeeilprt
pier-table
abeeilprx
expirable
abeeilqtu
equitable
abeeilrsv
revisable
verbalise
abeeilrtt
albertite
abeeilrtv
avertible
veritable
abeeilrvv
revivable
abeeilstw
tablewise
abeeimnss
beaminess
abeeinost
seine-boat
abeeinrtv
binervate
abeeinsst
asbestine
abeeiprst
rebaptise

abeeirrss
brasserie
brassière
abeeirrst
biserrate
abeejllnu
banjulele
abeejllny
jellybean
abeejlnoy
enjoyable
abeejnpuu
Punjaubee
abeeklnss
bleakness
abeeklrss
brakeless
abeeklstw
skew-table
abeekmorr
robe-maker
abeeknost
bakestone
abeeknpsu
unbespeak
abeellllmt
bell-metal
abeellllps
spellable
abeellmss
blameless
abeellmtu
umbellate
abeellort
tolerable
abeellovv
evolvable
abeelmmor
memorable
abeelmnru
numerable
abeelmoru
belamoure
abeelmorv
removable
abeelmosv
moveables
abeelmpry
permeably
abeelmptt
temptable
abeelmrss
assembler
abeelmrsu
resumable
abeelmrtw
Bartlemew
abeelnntu
untenable
abeelnops
speal-bone
abeelnpsu
spulebane
abeelnpsy
albespyne
abeelnquu
unequable
abeelnrtz
bez-antler
abeelnrvy
venerably
abeelostt
sea-bottle
abeelprrv
preverbal
abeelprst
beplaster
abeelprsu
superable
abeelprtu
reputable
abeelrrtv
vertebral
abeelrssz
brazeless
abeelrttu
utterable
abeemmnty
embayment
abeemorrt
barometer
abeemrrsu
embrasure
abeemrruz
embrazure
abeennorv
raven-bone
abeennstu
sun-beaten
abeenorwy
bone-weary
abeenqrtu
banqueter
abeenqttu
banquette
abeenrrst
sternebra
abeenrrsy
naseberry
abeenrrtt
terebrant
abeenrtux
exuberant
abeeoprrt
reprobate
abeeoprtt
peter-boat
abeeostuu
beauteous
abeeprstt
bespatter
abeeqrsuu
arquebuse
abeffilny
ineffably
abefflosu
buffaloes
abefgilln
befalling
abefgilnr
frangible
abefgilru
figurable
abefhimrs
amber-fish
abefhlrtu
breathful
abefiiillr
fibrillae
abefiilnu
unifiable
abefiilot
bifoliate
abefiimrt
fimbriate
abefillrt
filtrable
abefilnru
funebrial
abefilrst
fire-blast
abefiltuu
beautiful
abefinorr
fore-brain
abefklstu
basketful
abeflllmu
flabellum
abeflllluy
balefully
abefllnuy
banefully
abefllrru
barrelful
abefllrwy
warble-fly
abeflnosw
wolfsbane
abeflrtuy
refutably
abefoorst
bear's-foot
abeforrty
ferry-boat
abefrtttu
butter-fat
abeggnops
sponge-bag
abeghiknw
weigh-bank
abeghillp
phillabeg
abeghilrt
rightable
abeghinrr
harbinger
abeghinrt
breathing
abeghmrru
hamburger
abeghrssu
sagebrush
abegiillt
litigable
abegiilmt
mitigable
abegiilns
abseiling
abegiilnt
ignitable
abegiilnw
bewailing
abegiilrr
irrigable
abegiinor
aborigine
baignoire
abegikmnr
embarking
abegillln
labelling
abegillmn
emballing
abegillos
globalise
abegilmmn
embalming
abegilmnr
imbrangle
abegilmny
beamingly
abegilnor
ignorable
abegimnno
bemoaning
abegimnrr
embarring
abegimrrs
ambergris
gris-amber
abeginnnt
benignant
abeginnrt
bantering
abeginnru
unbearing
abeginntt
battening
abeginost
obsignate
abeginrsw
sabre-wing
abeginsst
beastings
abegjortu
objurgate
abegjstuu
subjugate
abegkmnoy
monkey-bag
abegkmors
bergomask
abegkrstu
grub-stake
abeglllss
bell-glass
abegllswy
swag-belly
abeglmuzz
muzzle-bag
abeglnoru
lounge-bar
abeglostt
bottle-gas
gas-bottle
abeglrssu
bluegrass
abegmmmru
Brummagem
abegmnoor
boomerang
abegmnoow
wagenboom
abegnrrsu
gas-burner
abegnrsst
bent-grass
abegorstu
subrogate
abehhostu
bathhouse
abehiinnr
Hibernian
abehiinrt
reinhabit
abehiittw
whitebait
abehiklnt
thinkable
abehikntt
bethankit
abehilmop
amphibole
abehilott
batholite
abehilrst
herbalist
abehilrty
breathily
heritably
abehilsst
establish
abehiltty
bathylite
abehimrru
herbarium
abehinoop
neophobia
abehinrtt
tithe-barn
abehiopru
euphorbia
abehiorrv
herbivora
abehioruv
behaviour
abehiprrs
herb-Paris

abehirrtt
birth-rate
abehisstw
whitebass
abehkllrs
shellbark
abehknnos
shank-bone
abehllost
blast-hole
abehllstu
sublethal
abehlmnsu
bushel-man
abehlmort
alembroth
abehlmotu
mouthable
abehlmpsy
blasphemy
abehlmstu
bush-metal
abehloost
shootable
abehloott
tholobate
abehlopry
hyperbola
abehlorst
sloth-bear
abehlortt
betrothal
abehlortw
bowler-hat
abehlosty
Hylobates
abehmoort
Theobroma
abehnorrt
abhorrent
earthborn
abehnottu
thenabout
abehnrrtu
heartburn
abehnrstu
sunbather
abehoorst
shore-boat
abehoostu
boathouse
house-boat
abehorrru
harbourer
abehqrsuu
harquebus
abeiiklnr
bairnlike
abeiilllr
illiberal
abeiillmt
limitable
abeiillrt
biliteral

abeiilmnr
birlieman
abeiilmss
amissible
abeiilmtv
lambitive
abeiilrrt
irritable
abeiilrtv
vibratile
abeiilsst
stabilise
abeiilstv
visitable
abeiimnrt
bairn-time
abeiinnpt
bipinnate
abeiinnrt
inebriant
abeiiprtt
bipartite
abeiirssv
vibrissae
abeiirtvv
vibrative
abeikllnu
unlikable
abeiknnrt
interbank
abeiknorw
wake-robin
abeiknrrv
river-bank
abeilllnt
libellant
abeilllry
liberally
abeillnot
tabellion
abeillnpu
unpliable
abeillnuv
unlivable
abeillpsu
plausible
abeillrtx
Bellatrix
abeillssu
subsellia
abeillssy
syllabise
abeilmmov
immovable
abeilmmsw
swimmable
abeilmmtu
immutable
abeilmnno
nominable
abeilmnss
balminess
abeilmops
imposable

abeilmort
Baltimore
abeilmptu
imputable
abeilmrsv
verbalism
abeilmrsy
miserably
abeilmrtu
umbratile
abeilmstu
sublimate
abeilmsty
estimably
abeilnorr
rail-borne
abeilnors
sail-borne
abeilnprt
printable
abeilnpsu
subalpine
abeilnrry
inerrably
abeilnrss
brainless
abeilnrsu
insurable
sublinear
abeilnrtu
untirable
abeilnsuv
subniveal
abeilnsuz
unsizable
abeiloqsu
obsequial
abeilorrt
liberator
abeilorst
strobilae
abeilortt
trilobate
abeilortu
Labourite
abeilppst
blast-pipe
abeilqtuy
equitably
abeilrstu
brutalise
abeilrstv
verbalist
abeilrtvy
verbality
veritably
abeilrvvy
revivably
abeilsttw
twistable
waistbelt
abeilsuvy
abusively

abeiltttt
tittlebat
abeimmnrt
timber-man
abeimnrss
barminess
abeimnrst
tribesman
abeimnrsu
submarine
abeimnrtu
inumbrate
abeimprst
rebaptism
abeinnors
Serbonian
abeinnost
sanbenito
abeinnstt
abstinent
abeinnsuv
subnivean
abeinntyz
Byzantine
abeinoort
aerobiont
reboation
abeinoprt
bioparent
abeinortt
torbanite
abeinostt
obstinate
abeinprst
breastpin
stepbairn
abeinpstu
unbaptise
abeinrttu
tribunate
turbinate
abeioprtv
probative
abeiorrtv
river-boat
abeipsstt
se-baptist
abeirrrst
barrister
abeirrsst
arbitress
abeirtttu
attribute
abejklouw
kabeljouw
abejlnoyy
enjoyably
abejmorst
job-master
abekkmoor
bookmaker
abekllmos
smoke-ball

abeklnnss
blankness
abeklnoot
ankle-boot
abekloopt
bookplate
abeklortw
table-work
work-table
abekmoort
bootmaker
abeknnnpy
penny-bank
abeknorsw
snow-break
abekoostw
waste-book
abelllmru
larum-bell
abellmnty
lambently
abellmors
small-bore
abellnosu
unlosable
abellnouv
unlovable
abellorty
tolerably
abellovvw
blowvalve
abellrtuw
water-bull
abelmmnru
lumberman
abelmmory
memorably
abelmnory
embryonal
abelmnouv
unmovable
abelmnpru
penumbral
abelmnrtt
tremblant
abelmnruy
numerably
abelmnstt
blastment
abelmnstu
submental
abelmoort
motorable
abelmorvy
removably
abelmosst
mesoblast
abelnntuu
untunable
abelnoptu
unpotable
abelnorsv
slave-born

abelnosst
slabstone
abelnostt
entoblast
abelnosyz
lazy-bones
abelnrstu
subaltern
abelnrsuu
subneural
abelnrttu
turntable
abelnstuu
sublunate
abeloopps
opposable
abelootvy
obovately
abeloppars
sorb-apple
abeloprst
sportable
abeloprty
pot-barley
abeloprvy
proveably
abeloptty
talbotype
abelossst
boastless
abelostty
stylobate
abelprsuu
pursuable
abelprsuy
superably
abelprtuy
reputably
abelrssuv
subversal
abelrsuyy
Aylesbury
abemnorwy
byrewoman
abemooprr
broomrape
abemoostt
sea-bottom
abemoprty
ambrotype
abemorrtu
arboretum
abemorrty
barometry
abemorstt
storm-beat
abemrsstu
truss-beam
abennsttu
subtenant
abenoprrs
barperson
abenorstv
observant

abeooprtw
powerboat
abeoorrsu
arboreous
abeoprrsy
soapberry
abeoqrsuu
bourasque
abeossstu
asbestous
abeosttuw
west-about
abeprrrsy
raspberry
abeprsssy
passers-by
abeprtttu
butter-pat
abersstu
substrate
aberttuw
water-butt
abfhllsuy
bashfully
abfhlnsuu
unbashful
abfhstttu
butt-shaft
abfiillrr
fibrillar
abfiiorsu
bifarious
abfillsyy
syllabify
abfilmsuy
subfamily
abfilnssu
basinfuls
abflllstu
full-blast
abflloopr
ball-proof
abggiinpp
bagpiping
abggiknpy
piggy-bank
abggilnnr
brangling
abgginnrs
bangsring
abgginort
tarboggin
abgginrst
string-bag
abggnttuy
butty-gang
abghiknrt
right-bank
abghillt
light-ball
abghilmns
shambling
abghinorr
abhorring

abghinwzz
whizz-bang
abghiopry
biography
abgiillnu
bilingual
abgiimtuy
ambiguity
abgijnnow
jawboning
abgikllny
balkingly
abgillnot
balloting
abgilloty
billy-goat
abgilnosx
signal-box
abgilnrtt
brattling
abgimosuu
ambiguous
abginopsv
bog-spavin
abginostw
swingboat
abglmnoos
boom-slang
abglnsuuu
subungual
abglootty
battology
abhhhikss
bakhshish
abhhiiruv
bahuvrihi
abhhilott
batholith
abhhiltty
bathylith
abhhipssu
subahship
abhhirrsu
hair-brush
abhiillms
bismillah
abhiinort
inhabitor
abhikllsw
hawksbill
abhikmrrt
birthmark
abhilmntu
thumbnail
abhilmopy
amphiboly
abhilnoot
halobiont
abhilnrsu
nail-brush
abhilnrty
labyrinth
abhiooopz
zoophobia

abhiopstu
about-ship
abhkmmrtu
thumb-mark
abhlopsty
hypoblast
abhnorruu
unharbour
abhooptuy
autophoby
abhoprtyy
Bryophyta
abiiillty
liability
abiiilmrs
mirabilis
abiiilnty
inability
abiiiltvy
viability
abiiillnrt
brilliant
abiilmnno
binominal
abiilmnos
albinoism
abiilmrst
tribalism
abiilnoot
abolition
abiilnoov
boliviano
abiilnort
libration
abiilnory
nobiliary
abiilortt
Trilobita
abiilrrty
irritably
abiilrstt
tribalist
abiilstty
stability
abiilstuy
suability
abiimostu
ambitious
abiinootv
obviation
abiinortv
vibration
abijnrrry
brinjarry
abikllnst
stink-ball
abikloprs
spoil-bark
abillmssy
syllabism
abillnopt
ball-point
abillnpuy
unpliably

abilloprx
pillar-box
abillorrz
razor-bill
abillpsuy
plausibly
abilmmotu
bummaloti
abilmmovy
immovably
abilmmtuy
immutably
abilmnouv
ovalbumin
abilmorsu
labourism
abilmptuy
imputably
abilnoprs
Planorbis
abilnopss
slop-basin
abilnostu
sublation
abilooptt
pilot-boat
abiloorsu
laborious
abilorrty
libratory
abilorstu
labourist
abilrstuy
salubrity
abilrttuy
brutality
abimmnruu
manubrium
abimnortu
tambourin
abimnorty
abnormity
abinnnoru
Brunonian
abinooprt
probation
abinoopst
spoon-bait
abinoprtu
abruption
abinopstu
subtopian
abinotvxy
vanity-box
abiorrtvy
vibratory
abiorsttu
stirabout
abiprstty
baptistry
abirrttuy
tributary
abjllooty
jollyboat

abklloost
bookstall
abkllooty
book-tally
abklmoops
psalm-book
ablllloost
stoolball
abllmoosw
lamb's-wool
ablloortu
roll-about
ablmnorsu
subnormal
ablmnouvy
unmovably
ablnntuuy
untunably
ablnorsuu
alburnous
ablnrsuuy
sublunary
ablrsstuy
substylar
abmnnoorw
woman-born
abmnoorsu
abnormous
abmnorrst
barnstorm
abmooortt
motor-boat
abmprsttu
bump-start
abnorttuu
about-turn
turnabout
abooprrty
probatory
aboorrttu
obturator
abrrsttuw
bratwurst
accccehit
cachectic
acccdeeen
accedence
acccdeein
accidence
accceeens
acescence
accceensy
acescency
acccegloy
coccygeal
acccehhho
chechacho
acccehitt
cathectic
accceiirt
cicatrice
accceillo
calcicole
accceiopt
copacetic
acccenopu
occupance
acccginoy
coccygian
accchiknp
pack-cinch
accchkmot
cockmatch
accchkoor
cockroach
accchnoty
cony-catch
accchoprt
catch-crop
acccíilly
alicyclic
accciilmt
climactic
accciiopr
capriccio
acccnopuy
occupancy
accddeeen
decadence
accddeeny
decadency
accddehor
decachord
accddeils
discalced
accddiist
didactics
accddiors
disaccord
accddknoy
dandy-cock
accdeehik
chickadee
accdeehtw
catchweed
accdeeist
desiccate
accdefils
fascicled
accdefily
decalcify
accdegkor
deck-cargo
accdeglno
clogdance
accdehiil
Cichlidae
accdehikr
deck-chair
accdehist
decastich
accdeiiim
Cimicidae
accdeiiln
Cicindela
Icelandic
accdeiilt
dialectic
accdeiilu
Culicidae
accdeinst
desiccant
accdeiorw
cowardice
accdeklop
cock-padle
accdekoss
cassocked
accdelnoy
calcedony
accdemnoo
cacodemon
accdemopt
compacted
accdemory
democracy
accdensuu
unaccused
accdeorrs
score-card
accdeortu
accoutred
accdfilly
flaccidly
accdginor
according
accdhhruy
archduchy
accdhiiis
ischiadic
accdhiiss
Chassidic
accdhikls
clackdish
accdhinor
chancroid
accdhmort
match-cord
accdhnpru
card-punch
punch-card
accdhoort
octachord
accdhortw
catchword
accdiiint
diactinic
accdiiirt
diacritic
accdiillp
piccadill
accdiiopt
apodictic
accdiiosu
dicacious
accdiklor
cocklaird
accdilloy
cycloidal
accdimorr
microcard
accdinoor
accordion
accdinort
dracontic
accdioopt
octapodic
accdknorw
crackdown
accdkpsuu
scaup-duck
accdlorsw
scald-crow
accdloruy
dulocracy
accdnoort
concordat
accdoooow
cocoa-wood
accdorrtu
court-card
acceeehsx
cache-sexe
acceeelnr
canceleer
acceeelrs
recalesce
acceeenrr
recreance
acceeglmy
megacycle
acceehhko
cheechako
acceehikr
chickaree
acceehilr
chelicera
acceehist
catechise
acceehity
haecceity
acceehkmt
checkmate
acceehlot
cochleate
acceehnpr
perchance
acceehost
cacoethes
acceeikps
spice-cake
acceeills
ecclesial
acceeilnr
arc-en-ciel
cancelier
acceeilrt
clericate
acceeiptv
acceptive
acceeirrr
ricercare
acceeirtv
accretive
acceeistx
exsiccate
acceeklor
ear-cockle
acceeklot
cockateel
acceellor
clearcole
acceelnpr
pre-cancel
acceelpst
spectacle
acceennst
canescent
acceenort
concreate
acceenrry
recreancy
acceenrsu
recusance
securance
acceeoprs
praecoces
acceeorsu
ceraceous
acceeostu
cetaceous
accefffil
cliff-face
acceffhno
off-chance
accefgilu
calcifuge
accefhlnu
chanceful
accefhlot
face-cloth
accefiirs
sacrifice
accefilsu
fascicule
acceghosu
gauchesco
accegikno
Cockaigne
accegiopr
geocarpic
accegiott
geotactic
accehhior
coach-hire
accehhirt
thearchic
accehhkot
heathcock
accehhlru
church-ale
accehhoqu
chechaquo
accehiims
ischaemic

accehiknr
raincheck
accehilmo
cholaemic
accehilno
cochineal
accehilnt
technical
accehilor
choleraic
accehilru
cleruchia
accehimns
mechanics
mischance
accehimst
catechism
schematic
accehinor
anchor-ice
ice-anchor
accehinry
chicanery
accehirtt
architect
accehirvz
czarevich
accehistt
catechist
accehklot
cockle-hat
accehkmpr
crack-hemp
accehkopt
patchocke
accehkpss
pass-check
accehlnor
chloracne
accehloot
chocolate
accehlopt
catchpole
accehmmnu
mumchance
accehmntt
catchment
accehnrru
cranreuch
accehorrt
torch-race
accehortu
cartouche
accehortv
overcatch
accehorty
theocracy
accehrrst
scratcher
acceiilrt
icterical
acceiimnr
cineramic
acceiimnt
cinematic
acceiimtv
cevitamic
acceiinos
cocainise
acceiinot
ice-action
acceiinrt
circinate
acceiirst
cicatrise
acceiistv
siccative
acceikklp
place-kick
acceiklot
cockatiel
acceikrsw
wisecrack
acceillot
laccolite
acceillrs
clericals
acceilmot
celomatic
acceilmpt
eclamptic
acceilnrt
centrical
acceilntu
inculcate
acceilopr
precocial
acceilpst
sceptical
acceilrtu
circulate
acceimnpt
impeccant
acceimosu
micaceous
acceimssu
music-case
acceinnos
accension
acceinooz
Caenozoic
acceinort
accretion
anorectic
acceinoss
accession
acceinstu
encaustic
succinate
acceinstx
exsiccant
acceintxy
excitancy
acceiortt
corticate
acceiprvy
pervicacy
acceipsty
cityscape
accekmors
smock-race
acceknorr
corncrake
accekoprr
crack-rope
accekortw
water-cock
accelloot
collocate
accellosu
calculose
accelltuu
cucullate
accelnopy
cyclopean
accelnovy
concavely
covalency
accelnpty
peccantly
accelotuy
autocycle
accelprtu
claret-cup
accemnory
ceromancy
accemoprr
cremocarp
accemoprt
recompact
accemorty
macrocyte
accennoss
non-access
accennoty
co-tenancy
accenoors
coenosarc
accenootv
convocate
accenorsu
cancerous
acceorrsw
scarecrow
acceorruy
Eurocracy
acceorssy
accessory
acceorstu
coruscate
accffhhin
chaffinch
accfiilor
calorific
accfiilss
classific
accfiilsu
fasciculi
accfiisst
fascistic
accfiknsy
fancy-sick
accfimors
sacciform
accfimort
cactiform
accfinnou
Confucian
accfkoort
coat-frock
frock-coat
accflloru
floccular
accghiinn
chicaning
accghiirr
chiragric
accghlnoo
cacholong
accgiklnr
crackling
acchhiilr
chiliarch
acchhiopw
coachwhip
acchhlors
scholarch
acchhmnru
churchman
acchhnoor
coach-horn
acchhruwy
churchway
acchiiist
ischiatic
acchiilrv
chivalric
acchiinnp
chincapin
acchiklno
lock-chain
acchilloo
alcoholic
acchillot
laccolith
acchilnor
chronical
acchilops
slip-coach
acchilort
Holarctic
acchilotu
acoluthic
acchilpsy
psychical
acchimnor
monarchic
acchimnsy
mischancy
acchimopr
camphoric
acchimort
chromatic
acchimost
stomachic
acchinort
archontic
acchiostt
octastich
acchirtty
trachytic
acchklmot
matchlock
acchklopt
pack-cloth
acchklost
sackcloth
acchknpru
rack-punch
acchkooop
cock-a-hoop
acchkoorw
coachwork
acchllopt
catchpoll
acchloort
colcothar
ochlocrat
acchloosw
slowcoach
acchmnost
Scotchman
acchnoopy
cacophony
acchnopyy
phycocyan
acchnorsu
chancrous
acchosstu
succotash
acciiilnn
clinician
acciiintv
anticivic
acciillpp
Callippic
acciillsy
salicylic
acciillvy
civically
acciilnor
conciliar
acciilopt
occipital
acciiltvy
acclivity
acciimnos
cocainism
acciimnuv
vaccinium
acciimopt
apomictic
acciinooz
Cainozoic
acciinost
cocainist

acciinrty
intricacy
acciiopst
pasticcio
acciiorst
isocratic
acciiostt
isotactic
acciisstu
casuistic
acciittty
tacticity
accikknny
nick-nacky
accikmrsu
music-rack
acciknosw
cockswain
accillmoy
comically
accillnoy
conically
accillnyy
cynically
accilnopy
cyclopian
accilnorv
clavicorn
accilnotu
ciclatoun
noctiluca
accilortu
coticular
accilosuv
acclivous
accilprty
cryptical
accilrruu
curricula
accilrtuu
cuticular
accimnops
pancosmic
accimnory
acronymic
accimorty
timocracy
accimprtu
practicum
accinnnou
uncanonic
accinoprr
Capricorn
accinosty
oscitancy
accinostz
scazontic
accinotvy
concavity
accinstty
syntactic
accioprst
sarcoptic
accioprtt
catoptric
accioprty
procacity
acciosstu
acoustics
accjkorss
crossjack
accklllops
scalp-lock
acckloorr
coral-rock
accllosuu
calculous
acclmopty
compactly
acclnnnoo
colcannon
acclortuy
clay-court
acclrssuu
succursal
accmmoors
macrocosm
accmnoory
monocracy
nomocracy
accmnotuy
contumacy
accmooprt
compactor
accmoopry
macrocopy
accmoorst
cosmocrat
accnnootu
no-account
accnnosty
constancy
accnoortt
contactor
accnorstu
coruscant
accnorttu
cunctator
accoprruy
procuracy
accoprsty
cystocarp
acdddeeit
dedicated
acddeeeit
dedicatee
acddeefnu
undefaced
acddeeimt
medicated
acddeeitu
deciduate
acddeelnn
candle-end
acddeemno
code-named
acddeenuy
undecayed
acddeeort
decorated
acddefgoo
good-faced
acddefhis
dish-faced
acddefiii
acidified
acddeflpu
fuddle-cap
acddefory
fore-caddy
acddegllo
gold-laced
acddegnoo
dodecagon
acddehrru
hard-cured
acddeiins
discandie
acddeiitv
addictive
acddeijnu
jaundiced
acddeiklu
luckie-dad
acddeinrx
card-index
acddeiort
dedicator
acddeituv
adductive
acddelnru
underclad
acddelopt
clodpated
acddelrsu
scuddaler
acddenosy
second-day
acddeoorw
cedarwood
acddfilsy
caddis-fly
acddhhnsu
dachshund
acddhiilm
maid-child
acddhirru
arch-druid
acddiilos
discoidal
acddiilru
druidical
acddiimou
diacodium
acddiinoo
diacodion
acddiinot
addiction
acddilnpu
duplicand
acddimssu
Sadducism
acddinotu
adduction
acddllnou
cloudland
acddlnorw
cold-drawn
acddmoort
mad-doctor
acddnoort
doctorand
acdeeehip
headpiece
acdeeehnr
adherence
acdeeelry
clear-eyed
acdeeelss
déclassée
acdeeemrt
decametre
acdeeentt
dancettee
acdeeeprt
deprecate
acdeeerst
decastere
desecrate
acdeeertu
re-educate
acdeeffls
self-faced
acdeeffnu
uneffaced
acdeefhmr
chamfered
acdeefhwy
whey-faced
acdeefikr
friedcake
acdeefntu
fecundate
acdeefort
defecator
acdeefrrt
redecraft
refracted
acdeeglou
decalogue
acdeegnno
endecagon
acdeegopu
decoupage
acdeehiil
Helicidae
acdeehint
echinated
acdeehior
Orchideae
acdeehipp
epedaphic
acdeehirt
tracheide
acdeehkny
hackneyed
acdeehllt
death-cell
acdeehlpt
chapleted
acdeehnnt
enchanted
acdeehnru
unreached
acdeehnrv
chavender
acdeehnst
chastened
acdeehrrt
chartered
three-card
acdeeiilp
epicedial
acdeeiinp
epicedian
acdeeiirt
Icteridae
acdeeijtv
adjective
acdeeilmn
demi-lance
endemical
acdeeilmr
declaimer
acdeeilnn
celandine
decennial
acdeeilnr
Icelander
acdeeilnt
declinate
acdeeilnu
Euclidean
acdeeilpu
Clupeidae
acdeeilrt
decalitre
acdeeiltu
elucidate
acdeeimno
macedoine
acdeeimnp
impedance
acdeeinos
oceanides
acdeeinrs
Ecardines
acdeeiopr
adipocere
acdeeiprt
predicate
acdeeiptu
paedeutic
acdeeirrt
traceried
acdeeisst
ecstasied

acdeeituv
educative
acdeekknr
knackered
acdeekppr
prepacked
acdeekrtw
water-deck
acdeellmr
marcelled
acdeellot
decollate
ocellated
acdeellpr
parcelled
acdeellst
steel-clad
acdeelnnu
uncleaned
acdeelnrr
calendrer
acdeelnrs
esclandre
acdeelnru
uncleared
acdeelntt
tentacled
acdeelntu
nucleated
acdeelors
seed-coral
acdeelsty
decastyle
acdeeltuv
cut-leaved
acdeemmuv
vade-mecum
acdeemnor
Decameron
acdeemnru
unamerced
acdeennru
endurance
acdeennry
decennary
acdeennst
ascendent
acdeenntu
dance-tune
acdeenopr
rope-dance
acdeenoss
deaconess
acdeenpst
step-dance
acdeenrtu
uncreated
acdeeoprr
crop-eared
acdeeprrt
red-carpet
acdeerrtt
retracted

acdeerstt
scattered
acdeerstu
reductase
acdeesstu
decussate
acdeffilt
afflicted
acdeffist
disaffect
acdefflu
full-faced
acdeffmor
coffer-dam
acdefglno
long-faced
acdefgmsu
smug-faced
acdefhinr
arch-fiend
acdefhint
thin-faced
acdefiiil
edificial
acdefiilr
clarified
acdefiilt
feticidal
acdefiirs
scarified
acdefillo
coalfield
acdefilor
coal-fired
acdefilru
cauld-rife
acdefiluv
adviceful
acdefinrt
infracted
acdefklno
folk-dance
acdefllor
called-for
acdeflmor
cold-frame
acdeflnor
force-land
land-force
acdeflorz
calfdozer
acdefmnoo
moon-faced
acdeforss
cross-fade
acdeggimo
demagogic
acdeggiop
pedagogic
acdeggirt
cat-rigged
acdeghinr
chagrined

acdeghirs
discharge
acdeghnnu
unchanged
acdeghnru
uncharged
acdeghoop
good-cheap
acdegiilr
regicidal
acdegiirt
citigrade
acdegilno
genocidal
acdegiloo
logaoedic
acdegimno
endogamic
acdeginnr
ring-dance
acdeginns
ascending
acdeginoy
gynaecoid
acdegirrs
disgracer
acdegirrt
cartridge
acdegllru
guard-cell
acdegloos
gas-cooled
acdegmnoo
come-and-go
acdegmory
God-a-mercy
acdehhikt
thickhead
acdehhirs
rhachides
acdehhkos
shock-head
acdehhlot
headcloth
acdehhntu
unhatched
acdehhorx
hexachord
acdehiins
side-chain
acdehiirr
diarrheic
acdehiitt
diathetic
acdehikmr
march-dike
acdehikst
headstick
acdehillo
cheloidal
acdehilmn
name-child
acdehinnr
hindrance

acdehinnu
unchained
acdehinrt
theandric
acdehinsv
cavendish
acdehiort
Trochidae
acdehiprs
Sephardic
acdehiprt
dirt-cheap
acdehipst
cadetship
acdehirsv
crash-dive
acdehkmop
chokedamp
acdehkmry
march-dyke
acdehkost
headstock
acdehllrt
dratchell
acdehlmsy
chlamydes
acdehlnot
decathlon
acdehlnry
chandlery
acdehlpry
parchedly
acdehmmos
sachemdom
acdehmnru
uncharmed
acdehmntu
unmatched
acdehmost
stomached
acdehmpry
pachyderm
acdehnnrt
trenchand
acdehnoot
chaetodon
acdehnorw
crown-head
acdehnrrt
trenchard
acdehnrsw
hand-screw
acdehnrtu
uncharted
acdehnstu
unscathed
acdehntuw
unwatched
acdehoopt
chaetopod
acdehoopw
peach-wood
acdehorss
cross-head

acdeiiint
dietician
acdeiilmn
adminicle
medicinal
acdeiilnt
identical
acdeiilnx
indexical
acdeiilpu
Pulicidae
acdeiilrv
larvicide
veridical
acdeiilst
deistical
acdeiiltw
twice-laid
acdeiimmy
immediacy
acdeiimrt
diametric
matricide
acdeiinor
Crinoidea
acdeiinos
sciaenoid
acdeiinot
dianoetic
acdeiinpy
Cynipidae
acdeiinrs
inside-car
acdeiinst
andesitic
dianetics®
acdeiintv
vindicate
acdeiiopr
aperiodic
acdeiiors
Soricidae
acdeiiprr
parricide
acdeiiprt
patricide
acdeiiptu
paideutic
acdeiipty
diapyetic
acdeiirsu
Sciuridae
acdeikmpr
rampicked
acdeikrst
side-track
acdeiktty
ticket-day
acdeillmy
decimally
medically
acdeillou
lodiculae

acdeillty
edictally
acdeilmnu
unclaimed
undecimal
acdeilnnp
pinnacled
acdeilnnt
declinant
acdeiloor
air-cooled
acdeilost
dislocate
acdeilosy
Lycosidae
acdeiloty
Dicotylae
acdeilpru
pedicular
acdeilptu
duplicate
acdeimnno
dominance
acdeimnnt
mendicant
acdeimnop
companied
compendia
acdeimnsu
muscadine
acdeimnty
mendacity
acdeimort
decimator
acdeimosy
Samoyedic
acdeimrtu
muricated
acdeinnor
ordinance
acdeinnot
contadine
acdeinntu
uncinated
acdeinorr
coriander
acdeinors
Dinoceras
iron-cased
acdeinort
redaction
acdeinotu
education
Noctuidae
acdeinotv
advection
acdeinprt
predicant
tap-cinder
acdeinrty
Antrycide

acdeinsty
asyndetic
cystidean
syndicate
acdeinttu
tunicated
acdeioors
Dioscorea
acdeiorst
Cordaites
acdeiosty
Cystoidea
acdeiprst
crispated
practised
acdeiprty
predacity
acdeipstu
cuspidate
acdeiqttu
acquitted
acdeirsty
dicastery
acdeirttu
dictature
acdeissty
ecdysiast
acdeitttw
cat-witted
acdekmstu
duck's-meat
acdeknopu
pound-cake
acdeknrsw
sneck-draw
acdeknrtu
untracked
acdeknruv
raven-duck
acdellops
scalloped
acdelmopr
placoderm
acdelmory
comradely
acdelmtuu
cumulated
acdelnnoo
colonnade
acdelnnor
clarendon
acdelnntu
candle-nut
acdelnoow
lance-wood
acdelnosu
unsolaced
acdelnotu
unlocated
acdelnrty
trancedly
acdelnruy
underclay

acdelnssu
unclassed
acdelopsw
slow-paced
acdeloptu
cupolated
acdelprsy
clepsydra
acdelrttu
cultrated
acdemmmno
commendam
acdemmnor
commander
acdemmoor
macrodome
acdemnopr
compander
acdemoort
motorcade
acdennnsu
unscanned
acdennrst
transcend
acdenoort
coronated
acdenooss
soda-scone
acdenoott
cottonade
acdenorsw
sword-cane
acdenorsy
secondary
acdenortu
undercoat
acdenpttu
punctated
acdenrrsu
unscarred
acdenrssw
sand-screw
acdenrstu
undercast
acdenrttu
reductant
truncated
acdeoorrt
decorator
acdeoortt
doctorate
acdeoprrt
carpet-rod
acdeorrsw
score-draw
acdeorrtt
detractor
acdeorsst
coat-dress
dress-coat
acdeorstu
ceratodus
croustade

acdeortuy
educatory
acdersttu
crustated
acdesstuy
case-study
acdfhilss
scald-fish
acdfiiilp
lapidific
acdfiiruy
fiduciary
acdfinnot
confidant
acdfintuy
facundity
acdfnttuy
candytuft
acdfoortw
woodcraft
acdghimoy
dichogamy
acdghipsy
dysphagic
acdgiilor
goliardic
acdgiinnr
dining-car
acdgiinny
cyaniding
acdgiirst
digastric
acdgilnss
scaldings
acdgimost
dogmatics
acdginrtu
traducing
acdglloor
dog-collar
acdgorrss
cord-grass
acdhhnnpu
hand-punch
acdhiiist
stichidia
acdhiilmo
homicidal
acdhiilst
distichal
acdhiimor
chromidia
acdhiimss
Chasidism
acdhiimsu
dichasium
acdhikorw
chowkidar
acdhikprt
pitch-dark
acdhilmuy
diachylum
acdhilnoy
diachylon

acdhiloop
Chilopoda
acdhilrsy
chrysalid
acdhilruy
hydraulic
acdhilstt
last-ditch
acdhimort
dichromat
acdhinors
disanchor
acdhinrtw
wind-chart
acdhioprs
rhapsodic
acdhiorsy
dyschroia
acdhiosuv
disavouch
acdhloosy
day-school
school-day
acdhlorty
cloth-yard
acdhmootw
doomwatch
matchwood
acdhnorru
roundarch
acdhnortu
court-hand
acdhoopps
scaphopod
acdhoorru
Urochorda
acdhortww
watchword
acdiiilot
idiotical
acdiiimot
idiomatic
acdiijlru
juridical
acdiijmot
comitadji
acdiijruy
judiciary
acdiijstu
Judaistic
acdiiknos
Dicksonia
acdiillty
callidity
acdiilmno
dominical
acdiilnor
crinoidal
acdiiloss
dissocial
acdiilost
diastolic
acdiilpty
placidity

acdiilstu
dualistic
acdiimnno
Dominican
acdiimpry
pyramidic
acdiimrty
mydriatic
acdiinnot
contadini
acdiinors
radionics
acdiinort
indicator
acdiinosy
Dionysiac
acdiinott
dictation
acdiinrty
rancidity
acdiioprt
diatropic
acdiirttx
dictatrix
acdijortu
judicator
acdikllpr
pack-drill
acdiknqsu
quicksand
acdiknrst
rickstand
acdikrrtt
dirt-track
acdikrsty
yardstick
acdillloo
colloidal
acdilloor
coralloid
acdillory
cordially
acdilmnoo
monodical
acdilmops
psalmodic
acdilmopy
diplomacy
acdilnort
doctrinal
acdilnoru
rain-cloud
uncordial
acdilnosy
synodical
acdilnprs
land-scrip
acdiloopt
octaploid
acdiloort
doctorial
acdiloprs
dropsical
acdilorsy
Corydalis
acdilostu
custodial
acdilosuu
acidulous
acdilotuv
oviductal
acdilrtty
tridactyl
acdilstty
dactylist
acdimnnoy
dominancy
acdimnors
draconism
acdimopss
spasmodic
acdimorty
mordacity
acdinnoot
contadino
acdinostu
custodian
acdiortty
dictatory
acdjlntuy
adjunctly
acdjoortu
coadjutor
acdklmosy
lady-smock
acdklortu
truck-load
acdkorrsw
sword-rack
acdkorsty
stockyard
acdlmnooy
condyloma
acdlmnopw
clampdown
acdlnnorw
crown-land
acdlnnuuy
undulancy
acdlnstyy
syndactyl
acdmmnoru
communard
acdmnoopr
compandor
acdmooprr
comprador
acdmoosuv
muscovado
acdmprrtu
trump-card
acdnnoruu
uncandour
acdoorrss
crossroad
acdorrtuy
courtyard
aceeefirs
cease-fire
aceeeflnr
free-lance
aceeefprs
free-space
aceeeghpr
repechage
aceeeglny
eye-glance
aceeegnnv
vengeance
aceeegrst
secretage
aceeehipt
petechiae
aceeehlrw
wheel-race
aceeehnpr
cheapener
aceeehprt
peach-tree
aceeehstv
cheese-vat
aceeeilmp
piecemeal
aceeeimpt
peacetime
aceeeinpt
epaenetic
aceeeippp
peace-pipe
aceeeiprt
piece-rate
aceeejlsw
jewel-case
aceeeknqu
queen-cake
aceeekrrt
racketeer
aceeelnrv
relevance
aceeelntu
enucleate
aceeelnty
acetylene
aceeelprt
peat-creel
aceeelpss
peaceless
aceeelrst
scelerate
aceeelsss
ceaseless
aceeemnnr
remanence
aceeemnpr
permeance
aceeenppt
appetence
aceeenprs
esperance
aceeenprt
pecan-tree
aceeenrsv
severance
aceeenrtw
new-create
aceeersuy
saucer-eye
aceeffhrr
chafferer
aceeffhru
réchauffé
aceeffitv
affective
aceefflnu
affluence
aceeffltu
effectual
aceeffnry
fancy-free
aceefhhkl
half-cheek
aceefhitw
white-face
aceefhlnp
halfpence
aceefhlpr
parfleche
aceefhorr
forereach
aceefhort
foreteach
aceefikns
case-knife
aceefilnr
rail-fence
aceefilnv
venefical
aceefilpr
fireplace
aceefinor
Coniferae
aceefinrt
interface
aceefirss
fricassee
aceefkopr
poker-face
aceeflnrs
scale-fern
aceeflorr
coral-reef
aceeflotv
volte-face
aceefmort
forcemeat
aceefmprv
camp-fever
aceefnorv
confervae
aceefrrst
scart-free
aceeghiru
gaucherie
aceeghlln
challenge
aceeghnrx
exchanger
aceeghnsx
sex-change
aceegiils
gaelicise
aceegilnr
generical
aceegilns
Cingalese
aceegilnt
clientage
genetical
aceegilnv
evangelic
aceegilrs
sacrilege
aceegilrv
vice-regal
aceegimru
megacurie
aceeginor
recoinage
aceeginrv
grievance
aceegirrt
cigar-tree
aceegirtt
cigarette
aceegkrwy
greywacke
aceegllou
colleague
aceeglnrt
rectangle
aceeglrss
graceless
aceegmnor
geomancer
aceegmnuy
gynaeceum
aceegmops
megascope
aceegnnpr
pregnance
aceegnoru
encourage
aceegnrsv
scavenger
aceegnrsy
sergeancy
aceegoopr
cooperage
aceegorst
escortage
aceegrttu
curettage
aceehhtux
Hexateuch
aceehiipr
hair-piece
aceehilpt
petechial

aceehilrt
cheralite
etherical
heretical
aceehilrv
chevalier
aceehimns
mechanise
aceehimpr
impeacher
aceehinns
sennachie
aceehinnv
enhancive
aceehinpt
phenacite
aceehinst
hesitance
aceehirrs
cashierer
aceehistt
aesthetic
aceehkopr
choke-pear
aceehkpst
packsheet
aceehlmno
chameleon
aceehlmpv
champlevé
aceehlnru
Herculean
aceehlnss
seneschal
aceehlpss
chapeless
aceehlrss
reachless
aceehlrtw
cartwheel
aceehlsst
teachless
aceehmmrt
machmeter
aceehmnry
arch-enemy
aceehmoty
haemocyte
aceehmrsu
charmeuse
aceehmttu
humectate
aceehnnos
encheason
aceehnnrt
enchanter
aceehnopr
canephore
chaperone
aceehnpss
cheapness
aceehnrst
chastener

aceehnrtt
entrechat
aceehnrty
Cytherean
aceehnstu
chanteuse
aceehorrs
racehorse
aceehorrv
overreach
aceehorst
escheator
aceehostu
theaceous
aceehprty
archetype
aceehrrrt
charterer
aceehrrss
archeress
aceehrrtt
chatterer
aceehrrty
treachery
aceeiilpt
tailpiece
aceeiinpt
epainetic
aceeijqru
Jacquerie
aceeiklls
scalelike
aceeiklsv
sick-leave
aceeillnp
capelline
aceeillst
celestial
aceeilltv
vellicate
aceeilmrr
reclaimer
aceeilmrt
Carmelite
aceeilmst
timescale
aceeilnpr
percaline
Periclean
aceeilnpt
pectineal
aceeilnrs
scare-line
aceeilnrt
interlace
lacertine
reclinate
aceeilnty
ceylanite
aceeilopv
piacevole
aceeilprs
periclase
sale-price

aceeilprt
replicate
aceeilptx
explicate
aceeilrst
cartelise
cerealist
aceeimmnn
immanence
aceeimmnt
mincemeat
aceeimmrt
metameric
aceeimnpr
mepacrine
aceeimnrt
incremate
aceeimnsx
exciseman
aceeimprt
imprecate
aceeimpst
empaestic
space-time
aceeimrrs
careerism
aceeimrss
cassimere
aceeimrst
miscreate
stream-ice
aceeimrtt
metricate
aceeinnrt
nectarine
aceeinntu
enunciate
aceeinopr
caponiere
aceeinpru
Epicurean
aceeinptt
pectinate
aceeinrrs
increaser
aceeinrss
scenarise
aceeinrtt
Encratite
aceeinssv
ascensive
aceeiortx
excoriate
aceeiosss
écossaise
aceeiotvv
evocative
aceeipprr
rice-paper
aceeiprtt
crepitate
aceeiprtv
precative

aceeipstx
expiscate
aceeiqrru
reacquire
aceeirrst
careerist
aceeirrtw
rice-water
aceeirstu
cauterise
aceeirstv
viscerate
aceeirttx
extricate
aceeissst
ecstasise
aceejnrsy
serjeancy
aceeklnnr
enranckle
aceekorst
sea-rocket
aceelllot
locellate
aceellort
electoral
aceellpss
placeless
aceellrsy
Carlylese
aceellrtw
water-cell
aceellsss
scaleless
aceelmnpt
placement
aceelmnrt
recalment
aceelmnst
select-man
aceelmoor
cameo-rôle
aceelmoot
coelomate
aceelmops
someplace
aceelmort
late-comer
aceelnnor
ale-conner
aceelnnru
cannelure
aceelnnss
cleanness
aceelnort
coeternal
tolerance
aceelnprt
percental
aceelnptu
petulance
aceelnrss
clearness

aceelnrtu
calenture
crenulate
aceelnrvy
relevancy
aceelnstt
latescent
aceelntux
exultance
aceeloosu
oleaceous
aceeloprt
percolate
aceelorrt
coral-tree
correlate
aceelorss
casserole
aceelorsw
lower-case
aceelortt
lectorate
aceelortu
urceolate
aceelpsss
scapeless
spaceless
aceelpstu
speculate
aceelptux
exculpate
aceelqrru
lacquerer
aceelrrtt
clatterer
aceelrsst
traceless
aceelrttu
reluctate
aceelrtuy
electuary
aceelsssu
causeless
aceelsstt
cast-steel
aceemnnry
remanency
aceemnntt
enactment
aceemnpst
scapement
aceemnrry
mercenary
aceemnttx
exactment
aceemoprt
Mecoptera
aceemopst
copes-mate
aceemortt
octameter
aceemorvw
cream-wove

aceemrrst
cremaster
aceemrsty
mercy-seat
aceennnor
cannoneer
aceennopr
can-opener
aceennors
resonance
aceennost
caen-stone
Cantonese
aceennosv
sovenance
aceennott
centonate
aceennrst
renascent
aceennrty
centenary
aceenppty
appetency
aceenprrt
carpenter
aceenpttx
exceptant
expectant
aceenrrtu
crenature
aceenrssy
necessary
aceenrttu
utterance
aceensstu
acuteness
aceensstx
exactness
aceenttux
executant
aceeooprt
co-operate
cooperate
aceeoprrt
procreate
aceeoprss
spore-case
aceeoprtv
patercove
aceeorrtt
rectorate
aceeorrtv
overreact
aceeorrtw
water-core
aceeortuy
eucaryote
aceeortvx
over-exact
aceeosstu
setaceous
aceepprsu
upper-case

aceeprrtu
recapture
aceerrsst
creatress
aceerrstt
scatterer
street-car
aceerrsty
secretary
aceerrtuw
water-cure
aceersstu
secateurs
aceersstx
exactress
aceffflru
carfuffle
aceffgint
affecting
aceffhlss
chaffless
aceffhruu
chauffeur
aceffiiot
officiate
aceffikmr
mafficker
aceffinot
affection
aceffiopy
pay-office
aceffiort
forficate
aceffostu
suffocate
acefghlnu
changeful
acefghlru
chargeful
acefglnor
gerfalcon
acefhiint
chieftain
acefhilpr
half-price
acefhilss
scale-fish
acefhinrs
franchise
acefhipry
preachify
acefhirtw
watch-fire
acefhissu
fish-sauce
acefhllos
half-close
acefhlnor
arch-felon
acefhlnwx
flax-wench
acefhlstu
scatheful

acefhmort
homecraft
acefhosuv
vouchsafe
acefhrtty
fratchety
acefiills
Filicales
acefiilms
facsimile
acefiilrr
clarifier
acefiinnr
financier
acefiirrs
scarifier
acefiirrt
artificer
acefiirtv
fricative
acefiittv
factitive
acefijkkn
jack-knife
acefikrtu
fruit-cake
acefilnno
falconine
acefilnrz
frenzical
acefilnss
fanciless
acefilopr
caprifole
acefilort
fortalice
acefilosu
filaceous
acefilotv
olfactive
acefimort
formicate
acefinort
fornicate
acefinrtu
canefruit
acefinstt
fatiscent
acefinstu
infuscate
acefinttv
ventifact
acefiorst
factorise
acefiorsu
feracious
acefiostu
facetious
acefirssw
scarfwise
acefjlnor
jerfalcon
acefklors
foreslack

acefkorst
task-force
aceflllsu
full-scale
acefllmru
full-cream
acefllruy
carefully
aceflmopy
pomace-fly
aceflmotu
camouflet
aceflnruu
uncareful
aceflptuu
teacupful
aceflrruy
curry-leaf
aceflrsst
craftless
aceflrsuu
saucerful
acefltttuu
fluctuate
acefnorsu
surf-canoe
acefnrrtu
rune-craft
acefoprrt
after-crop
aceforrrt
refractor
acefostuu
tufaceous
acefrttuu
fructuate
acegginor
race-going
aceghhilp
high-place
aceghhmsu
camsheugh
aceghilrt
lethargic
aceghilsu
Ausgleich
aceghiltt
tight-lace
aceghimpr
graphemic
aceghimrs
mischarge
aceghinpr
preaching
aceghinrs
searching
aceghirst
Reichstag
aceghloos
school-age
aceghıort
cole-garth
aceghmnos
cheong-sam

aceghmort
hectogram
aceghmory
hercogamy
aceghoprr
cerograph
aceghopty
phagocyte
aceghrrsu
surcharge
acegiills
gallicise
acegiilms
gaelicism
acegiilns
anglicise
acegiilnv
vigilance
acegiimnt
enigmatic
acegiinnt
antigenic
acegiinrr
rice-grain
acegiinst
sagenitic
acegiirrt
geriatric
acegiknrt
racketing
acegikprr
rag-picker
acegikrst
gear-stick
acegilllo
collegial
acegillno
collegian
acegillor
allegoric
acegillot
colligate
acegilnno
congenial
acegilnns
cleansing
acegilnru
neuralgic
acegilnrw
clearwing
acegilrtu
curtilage
graticule
acegimmrs
scrimmage
acegimnot
geomantic
acegimnrs
screaming
acegimnrt
centigram
acegimnst
magnetics

acegimntu
mutagenic
acegimtuz
zeugmatic
aceginnor
ignorance
aceginnot
négociant
aceginnsu
unceasing
aceginoot
Notogaeic
aceginosu
cousinage
aceginprt
carpeting
aceginpry
panegyric
aceginrrt
terracing
aceginrss
caressing
acegioprr
paregoric
acegiostt
geostatic
acegipprs
scrippage
acegirrss
rice-grass
acegirstt
strategic
acegjlrtu
claret-jug
acegjnotu
conjugate
acegkoors
gas-cooker
aceglmnry
clergyman
aceglnnou
uncongeal
aceglnnpy
plangency
aceglnosu
consulage
acegmmnoo
commonage
acegmmrsu
scrummage
acegnnott
cotangent
acegnnpry
pregnancy
acegorrtu
corrugate
acegprstu
scrape-gut
acehhhins
Shechinah
acehhilps
chelaship
acehhirry
hierarchy

acehhistx
hexastich
acehhlwyz
wych-hazel
acehhmntt
hatchment
acehhmoty
theomachy
acehhmrtw
Wehrmacht
acehhmssy
Hesychasm
acehhnrty
ethnarchy
acehhoott
toothache
acehhprty
heptarchy
acehhssty
Hesychast
acehiiltu
halieutic
acehiimru
Hieracium
acehiinnp
Phenician
acehiinpp
epiphanic
acehiinpr
chain-pier
acehiinrt
trichinae
acehiippt
epitaphic
acehiistt
atheistic
acehikort
artichoke
acehikrst
heart-sick
acehillly
helically
acehillrt
cleithral
acehillty
ethically
acehilmmo
chamomile
acehilmrt
thermical
acehilmst
alchemist
acehilmtw
witch-meal
acehilnno
chelonian
acehilnor
enchorial
acehilnot
chelation
acehilnru
chain-rule
acehilnss
chainless

acehilntu
unethical
acehilnty
thylacine
acehilopt
phacolite
acehilorw
archilowe
acehilprs
spherical
acehilpry
preachily
acehilruv
vehicular
acehilstt
athletics
acehiltty
tachylite
acehimmns
mechanism
acehimnry
machinery
acehimnst
mechanist
acehimopt
omphacite
acehimory
cherimoya
acehimrtu
rheumatic
acehinnop
open-chain
acehinnot
oenanthic
acehinnry
Hercynian
acehinnst
encanthis
acehinopr
parochine
acehinort
anchorite
antechoir
acehinosv
schiavone
acehinprt
nephratic
acehinrru
hurricane
acehinrss
chariness
acehinrsu
sea-urchin
acehinsty
hesitancy
acehinttu
authentic
acehintuy
Eutychian
acehiootz
zoothecia
acehiopry
coryphaei

acehiorrt
hierocrat
acehiorst
rhotacise
acehippss
spaceship
acehirrrt
trierarch
acehirrst
Reichsrat
acehirstt
theatrics
acehirstu
Eucharist
acehirstv
tsarevich
acehirstx
exarchist
acehklnsu
unshackle
acehklosu
hause-lock
acehkoprs
pack-horse
acehkorst
shortcake
acehlllms
clam-shell
acehlllor
Chlorella
acehlmopr
polemarch
acehlmorv
love-charm
acehlmost
moschatel
acehlmotv
love-match
acehlmrss
charmless
acehlmsst
matchless
acehlnnpu
up-Channel
acehlnnru
uncharnel
acehlnosy
anchylose
acehlnpsu
spleuchan
acehloosu
coal-house
acehlopsu
cephalous
acehlopsw
show-place
acehlorrt
trochlear
acehlorsu
house-carl
acehlortt
charlotte
acehlprsu
sprauchle

acehlpssu
sphacelus
acehlrsst
chartless
acehlttyy
tachylyte
acehmnopy
cymophane
acehmnoty
theomancy
acehmnprt
parchment
acehmnsty
scytheman
acehmnttu
humectant
acehmorst
stomacher
acehmortv
overmatch
acehmostt
chemostat
acehmostu
moustache
acehmprty
champerty
acehmsttt
test-match
acehnnrtt
trenchant
acehnoqtu
hacqueton
acehnorss
anchoress
acehnorst
arch-stone
acehnortw
wheat-corn
acehnorty
honey-cart
acehnostt
stonechat
acehnostu
Ceanothus
acehnpprs
schnapper
acehnprty
pentarchy
acehnrsst
chantress
acehnrsuz
schnauzer
acehoostu
house-coat
acehoprrs
share-crop
acehoprst
chase-port
acehoprsu
proseucha
acehoprtw
wheat-crop
acehoprty
pothecary

acehopsst
Chassepot
acehorrst
cart-horse
orchestra
acehorrtu
treachour
acehorstu
cart-house
acehorsty
theocrasy
acehorsxy
xerochasy
acehortty
athrocyte
acehortvw
overwatch
acehprrsu
purchaser
acehrrtty
tetrarchy
acehrrtux
Chartreux
acehrssuu
chaussure
aceiiilst
italicise
aceiiinnp
epinician
aceiiklnt
kinetical
aceiikmnt
kinematic
aceiillot
ciliolate
aceiilltv
levitical
aceiilmmt
mimetical
aceiilmpr
empirical
aceiilmpt
implicate
aceiilmss
seismical
aceiilmst
climatise
aceiilmsv
vicesimal
aceiilnnt
anticline
aceiilnnv
vicennial
aceiilnps
Cisalpine
aceiilnst
inelastic
sciential
aceiilntx
Calixtine
aceiilort
aerolitic
aceiiloss
socialise
aceiilost
socialite
aceiilprt
pearlitic
aceiilrst
eristical
realistic
aceiilrtt
triticale
aceiilstv
calvities
aceiimmnr
Cimmerian
aceiimmru
americium
aceiimnot
emication
aceiimnrt
criminate
metrician
aceiimnss
Messianic
aceiimptt
impactite
aceiimrst
armistice
aceiimstu
maieutics
aceiinnot
aconitine
aceiinotv
noviciate
aceiinprs
periscian
precisian
aceiinprt
pictarnie
aceiinpst
epinastic
aceiinrtt
intricate
triactine
aceiinrty
itineracy
aceiinttt
nictitate
aceiiostv
sociative
aceiiprst
peirastic
aceiipstt
epistatic
aceiirstt
ceratitis
aceiirstv
variscite
aceiisttt
steatitic
aceiittux
eutaxitic
aceijknps
jack-snipe
aceijkrrv
river-jack
aceikllnn
lack-linen
aceiklmns
sickleman
aceiklnpt
tan-pickle
aceiklnrs
clear-skin
aceiklprs
spraickle
aceiknptw
pack-twine
aceiknsst
tackiness
aceiknssw
wackiness
aceikoprt
air-pocket
aceikpprt
pipe-track
aceikpsty
tipsy-cake
aceiksstt
seat-stick
aceilllrt
clitellar
aceilllxy
lexically
aceillmop
polemical
aceillmot
collimate
aceillnor
collinear
coralline
aceillnps
spellican
aceillnpt
plant-lice
aceillors
localiser
aceillort
corallite
aceillost
oscillate
aceillotv
collative
aceillprs
callipers
aceillpsy
specially
aceillpty
plicately
aceillrst
cellarist
aceillssu
sulcalise
aceilmmno
Commelina
melomanic
aceilmmss
mescalism
aceilmnnu
luminance
aceilmnop
policeman
aceilmnor
coal-miner
aceilmnot
melanotic
aceilmnru
melanuric
numerical
aceilmnsu
masculine
semuncial
aceilmntu
culminate
aceilmopt
Ptolemaic
aceilmors
lacrimose
aceilmoss
coseismal
aceilmosu
limaceous
aceilmpst
emplastic
aceilmptv
palm-civet
aceilmrru
mercurial
aceilmrsu
simulacre
aceilmrtu
climature
tularemic
aceilmstu
salicetum
aceilnnor
cornelian
aceilnnot
octennial
aceilnnsu
insulance
aceilnnty
anciently
aceilnopr
porcelain
aceilnopt
point-lace
aceilnors
censorial
aceilnort
clarionet
crotaline
aceilnost
coastline
sectional
aceilnosv
volcanise
aceilnotu
inoculate
aceilnptu
inculpate
aceilnrst
larcenist
aceilnrsw
screw-nail
aceilnrtu
centurial
aceilnrty
certainly
aceilnsss
scaliness
aceilnsuv
vulcanise
aceilntuv
vulcanite
aceilntxy
inexactly
aceilopps
episcopal
aceilopss
Asclepios
aceilopst
scapolite
aceiloquv
equivocal
aceilorrt
rectorial
aceilorst
sclerotia
sectorial
aceilorsv
vocaliser
aceilortt
tectorial
aceilortv
vectorial
aceilottu
autotelic
aceilotwy
wylie-coat
aceilpppr
paper-clip
aceilprtu
plicature
aceilprtx
X-particle
aceilpssu
Asclepius
capsulise
aceilpstu
spiculate
aceilpsty
specialty
aceilptuy
eucalypti
aceilrrtu
recruital
reticular
aceilrstu
sterculia
aceilrstv
cat-silver
aceilrsuv
vesicular
aceilrtuv
lucrative
revictual

aceilttuv
cultivate
aceimmnny
immanency
aceimmnot
comminate
aceimnnoo
Neocomian
aceimnnot
monactine
aceimnops
campesino
aceimnort
cremation
manticore
aceimnost
encomiast
aceimnott
omittance
aceimnptu
pneumatic
aceimnrst
Encratism
miscreant
aceimnrsu
muscarine
aceimnsst
semantics
aceimnstu
mint-sauce
aceimntyz
enzymatic
aceimoprs
premosaic
aceimorst
Masoretic
aceimorvw
microwave
aceimprst
spermatic
aceimrstu
cauterism
Cerastium
aceimrttu
micturate
aceinnnor
cannonier
aceinnnss
canniness
aceinnoov
Novocaine®
aceinnors
censorian
aceinnort
container
crenation
narcotine
aceinnoss
ascension
aceinnrry
inerrancy
aceinnrsu
insurance
nuisancer

aceinnrtu
encurtain
runcinate
uncertain
aceinnrty
ancientry
aceinnsst
cantiness
incessant
aceinoost
iso-octane
aceinootv
evocation
aceinoprt
recaption
aceinopst
stenopaic
aceinorrt
cinerator
aceinorrv
carnivore
aceinorst
narcotise
aceinortt
carnotite
aceinortu
cautioner
Cointreau®
aceinosst
cessation
aceinostu
tenacious
aceinosuv
vinaceous
aceinprry
pericrany
aceinprss
scarpines
aceinprtt
crepitant
aceinpruy
pecuniary
aceinpssu
puissance
aceinqttu
quittance
aceinrsst
scenarist
aceinrssz
craziness
aceinrstu
securitan
aceinrsty
insectary
aceinrtty
certainty
aceinrtuv
incurvate
aceinsssu
sauciness
aceinsstt
tacitness
aceinstty
intestacy

aceinstwx
wax-insect
aceioprrs
acrospire
aceioprsu
auriscope
parecious
aceiopstv
vitascope
aceiopttt
petticoat
aceiorsst
ostracise
Socratise
aceiorsty
societary
aceiorsuv
veracious
aceiosstw
coastwise
aceiprrst
practiser
aceiprstt
scarpetti
aceipsstu
space-suit
aceiqstuy
sequacity
aceirsttu
rusticate
aceirsuwy
cruiseway
aceirtuvv
curvative
aceissttu
suscitate
acejkkmos
smoke-jack
acejkkrsy
skyjacker
acejlmsuu
majuscule
acekkmrru
muck-raker
acekknors
rock-snake
acekllmmu
mallemuck
acekllmsw
well-smack
acekllnss
clankless
acekllpss
plackless
aceklnsss
slackness
aceklnstu
snake-cult
aceklopr s
slack-rope
acekloprw
workplace
aceklorsw
scale-work

aceklortw
towel-rack
aceklrsst
trackless
acekmstuw
muck-sweat
aceknnrss
crankness
aceknorsu
cankerous
acekorrtw
rockwater
acekprssu
sapsucker
acekrstuw
awe-struck
acellLmou
columella
acelllnuu
Lucullean
acellmnoy
call-money
acellmoru
molecular
acellmstu
castellum
acellnnuy
uncleanly
acellnops
pollen-sac
acellnoru
nucleolar
acellnrty
centrally
acellnruy
unclearly
acelloquy
coequally
acellorst
sclerotal
acellorsu
cellarous
acellpsss
scalpless
acellrssw
wall-cress
acellrstu
scutellar
acellrsuy
secularly
acellssss
classless
acelmmnos
commensal
acelmmnsu
muscle-man
acelmnost
calmstone
acelmntuu
tenaculum
acelmoosu
coal-mouse
acelmopst
ectoplasm

acelmorru
clamourer
acelmorsu
Mucorales
acelmorsy
lacrymose
acelmosss
scale-moss
acelmosuu
ulmaceous
acelnnoor
olecranon
acelnoorw
coal-owner
acelnoost
consolate
stone-coal
acelnoosv
volcanoes
acelnoprv
Provençal
acelnorsu
larcenous
acelnoruv
rounceval
acelnossv
vocalness
acelnostu
consulate
acelnprtu
crapulent
acelnptuy
petulancy
acelnrsuu
unsecular
acelnrttu
reluctant
acelntuxy
exultancy
acelooprr
corporeal
aceloortw
water-cool
aceloostt
coelostat
acelopr ru
opercular
aceloprtu
peculator
acelopstu
scopulate
acelorrst
stercoral
acelosstu
cassoulet
acelostty
coat-style
octastyle
acelostuu
cautelous
acelpprru
curl-paper
acemmmsuy
mummy-case

acemmottu
commutate
acemnnooy
oenomancy
acemnnorr
corner-man
acemnoops
moonscape
acemnopss
encompass
acemnortu
mucronate
acemnostu
caumstone
acemoopss
somascope
acemoopsu
pomaceous
acemoorsu
moraceous
acemootyz
Mycetozoa
acemorrty
crematory
acemorstu
castoreum
acemossuu
musaceous
acemostvy
vasectomy
acemprsuy
supremacy
acennnoru
announcer
acennoopr
cornopean
acennoott
connotate
Notonecta
acennortu
connature
acennptuu
nuncupate
acennssst
scantness
acennsstu
uncessant
acenooprt
cooperant
co-operant
acenootty
tycoonate
acenoprrt
copartner
procreant
acenoprst
sportance
acenopssw
snowscape
acenopstw
townscape
acenopsty
syncopate

acenoptyy
cyanotype
acenorrtu
raconteur
acenorsss
Scansores
acenorstu
courtesan
nectarous
acenorsuv
cavernous
acenortuz
courtezan
acenosstt
stone-cast
acenosttu
En-Tout-Cas®
acenostuu
cutaneous
acenprsuu
pursuance
acenpttuu
punctuate
acenrssss
crassness
acenrstuu
Centaurus
aceooprrt
corporate
aceooprss
ascospore
aceoorssu
rosaceous
aceoorstu
root-cause
aceoortvy
evocatory
aceoprrty
precatory
aceoprsst
Sarcoptes
aceoprstt
scarpetto
spectator
aceorrrtt
retractor
aceorrrvy
overcarry
aceorrstu
craterous
aceorrttx
extractor
aceorstuu
rutaceous
acerrsstw
wart-cress
acerrtuuv
curvature
acffghiln
cliffhang
acffiilno
officinal
acffiinot
officiant

acffilmor
falciform
acffiloru
Forficula
acffimnpu
muffin-cap
acffklort
folk-craft
acffloost
calf's-foot
acfflostw
cowl-staff
acfghilnn
flanching
acfghinrt
fratching
acfghmorr
frogmarch
acfgiimno
magnifico
acfgiklny
cly-faking
acfgiklst
flagstick
acfgiknrt
kingcraft
acfginort
factoring
acfginrrs
scarf-ring
acfginrsu
surfacing
acfgiosuu
fugacious
acfglnory
gyrfalcon
acfgnorst
songcraft
acfhhhilt
half-hitch
acfhiilrt
chairlift
acfhilnou
faulchion
acfhilors
coral-fish
acfhimprs
cramp-fish
acfhiprss
fish-scrap
acfhkorst
rock-shaft
acfhlmrsu
scrum-half
acfhlnorw
half-crown
acfhmorsu
forasmuch
acfiiilmr
mirifical
acfiiilor
orificial
acfiillny
finically

acfiilnot
fictional
acfiilrsu
surficial
acfiiltuv
fluviatic
acfiimnor
aciniform
acfiinstu
faunistic
acfiioprv
vaporific
acfijkrtu
jack-fruit
acfiknrss
scarfskin
acfilmnor
lanciform
acfilmoru
cauliform
acfilmorv
claviform
acfilnnor
francolin
acfilnoot
olfaction
acfilnppy
flippancy
acfilnruu
funicular
acfilorst
trifocals
acfimnort
formicant
acfimoprr
capriform
acfimorry
formicary
acfinorrt
infractor
acfinortu
furcation
acfiorstu
fractious
acfiorsuu
furacious
acfkmrrtu
truck-farm
acfknorwy
fancywork
acfllorss
crossfall
acfllorsu
floscular
acflloswww
wolf's-claw
aclltttuy
tactfully
acflmnoor
conformal
acflnttuu
fluctuant
acfloorty
olfactory

acfmosttu
factotums
acfoorruy
Fourcroya
acforttuy
outcrafty
acfrrtuuy
fructuary
acggiioss
isagogics
acggiloor
agrologic
acggilrsy
scraggily
acghhhiir
high-chair
acghhilnt
hatchling
acghhilss
high-class
acghhintt
thatching
acghiilno
chiliagon
acghiiprt
graphitic
acghiknov
havocking
acghikntw
thwacking
acghilnno
long-chain
acghilory
oligarchy
acghimmoo
homogamic
acghimoop
omophagic
acghinnot
gnathonic
acghinnst
stanching
acghinrtt
night-cart
acghlmooy
logomachy
acghloory
archology
acghmopry
cymograph
acghmopyy
mycophagy
acghopssy
psychogas
acghorstu
roughcast
acgiiimst
imagistic
acgiiknnp
panicking
acgiiknrv
vraicking
acgiilllo
illogical

acgiillms
gallicism
acgiillnv
cavilling
acgiillor
cigarillo
acgiilmns
anglicism
acgiilnst
anglicist
acgiilrty
gracility
acgiimstt
stigmatic
acgiinnor
inorganic
acgiinnot
incognita
acgiinnrt
nigricant
acgiinost
agonistic
acgiiorst
orgiastic
acgiknnpu
unpacking
acgillloy
logically
acgillnor
carolling
acgillnou
unlogical
acgillooy
caliology
acgillorw
galli-crow
acgilmopy
polygamic
acgilnnst
scantling
acgilnost
gnostical
nostalgic
acgilnoxy
coaxingly
acgilnpry
carpingly
acgilnrsw
scrawling
acgimmnoo
monogamic
acgimmorr
microgram
acgimnnor
romancing
acgimnoor
agronomic
acgimnorr
cairngorm
acgimnoss
Gasconism
acgimnotu
contagium

acgimnprr
cramp-ring
acgimnsty
gymnastic
nystagmic
acgimoopr
porogamic
acgimoors
sociogram
acgimoprt
pictogram
acgimotyz
zygomatic
acginnoot
cognation
contagion
acginnopy
canopying
poignancy
acginnost
cognisant
acginooty
Octogynia
acginopsw
coping-saw
acginpprs
scrapping
acginptuy
pugnacity
acgjnorru
currajong
acgklnoow
wagon-lock
acgknooru
rock-guano
acgllnorw
crown-gall
acgllorwy
gally-crow
acglmoory
macrology
acglnoost
long-coats
acgloorsy
sarcology
acgloorty
cartology
acgloosty
scatology
acgmnnoor
Cro-Magnon
acgmnoryy
gyromancy
acgmoprty
cryptogam
acgnnoost
contangos
acgnorruw
currawong
achhiirst
rhachitis
achhilnor
rhonchial

achhilopt
phacolith
achhilort
haircloth
achhimrty
arhythmic
achhinnot
chthonian
achhinost
chain-shot
achhiorst
Tocharish
achhiprsu
push-chair
achhlllot
cloth-hall
achhlostu
slouch-hat
achhlostw
wash-cloth
achhlpryy
phylarchy
achhnorty
Rhynchota
achhnrsty
chrysanth
achiiknnp
chinkapin
achiilmos
isochimal
achiilmsw
whimsical
achiimnst
machinist
achiimory
chirimoya
achiinpsy
physician
achiinrst
Christian
achiiopst
pistachio
achiiprsv
vicarship
achiiprtu
upaithric
achiirrtt
arthritic
achiirstt
citharist
trachitis
achiirstv
archivist
achijkmst
jacksmith
achikknpt
pick-thank
achikkssw
kickshaws
achiklmst
mahlstick
achikmmos
Ockhamism

achikmost
Ockhamist
achiknorw
chainwork
achikpruy
Puck-hairy
achillloy
allicholy
achillmsu
music-hall
achillnty
Chantilly
achillost
sail-cloth
achilmnpy
nymphical
achilmpty
lymphatic
achilnopt
piña-cloth
achilnort
antichlor
achilnstu
clianthus
achilnsty
snatchily
achiloptu
patchouli
achilortv
archivolt
achiloruz
rhizocaul
achilosst
scholiast
achilpstu
sulphatic
achilrssy
chrysalis
achilrsty
starchily
achimmnos
monachism
achimmorz
machzorim
achimmoss
masochism
achimnopy
hypomanic
achimnors
harmonics
man-orchis
achimnort
chromatin
achimnost
macintosh
monachist
achimnppu
chain-pump
achimnstw
switchman
achimootx
homotaxic
achimorst
rhotacism

achimoryz
mycorhiza
achimosst
masochist
achimostu
mustachio
achimrsst
Christmas
achimrssw
scrimshaw
achinnost
stanchion
achinnotw
Chinatown
achinnsty
synanthic
achinoort
chinaroot
achinopps
pansophic
achinoprt
anthropic
rhapontic
achinorru
hurricano
achinorst
thrasonic
achinprst
chinstrap
achinrstu
Trachinus
achinrsty
strychnia
achinrtuy
uncharity
achioopst
sociopath
achiopprs
hippocras
achioprrz
rhizocarp
achiosstu
astichous
achiprsuy
haruspicy
achiqrrsu
squirarch
achkmortu
touch-mark
achknorrw
hornwrack
achkoprtw
patchwork
achlloopt
photocall
achllorsy
scholarly
achlmnoos
schoolman
achlmorsw
slow-march
achlmostw
slow-match

achlmstyz
schmaltzy
achlnotuu
outlaunch
achlnsssu
Anschluss
achlnstuy
staunchly
achloostu
holocaust
achlopryy
polyarchy
achloptuy
patchouly
achlortty
tray-cloth
achmmnooy
monomachy
achmnorsu
Roumansch
achmooprs
promachos
achmoorrt
chartroom
achnoopry
acrophony
achnopsty
sycophant
achoopsyz
Scyphozoa
achoorstt
short-coat
achopsttw
stop-watch
achopstuy
hypocaust
achortttu
cut-throat
achprssuy
chuprassy
aciiilmst
Islamitic
italicism
aciiilnos
siciliano
aciiimnst
animistic
aciiinppr
principia
aciiinpst
pianistic
aciiisstv
Sivaistic
aciijrstu
justiciar
aciikmnrt
Minitrack®
aciiknooz
Kainozoic
aciikprrt
Prakritic
aciillnos
isoclinal
aciillnst
scintilla
aciillopt
political
aciilmnpu
municipal
aciilmnsv
Calvinism
aciilmnty
militancy
aciilmoss
socialism
aciilmosu
malicious
aciilmqtu
quit-claim
aciilmrsu
curialism
aciilnoot
coalition
aciilnopt
plication
aciilnosx
clinoaxis
aciilnovv
convivial
aciilnppr
principal
aciilnstv
Calvinist
aciiloprt
pictorial
aciilorst
soritical
aciilosst
socialist
aciilosty
sociality
aciilosvv
slivovica
aciilprty
pyritical
aciilquzz
quizzical
aciilrstu
curialist
rusticial
aciilsttt
tactilist
aciilttty
tactility
aciimmoss
mosaicism
aciimmpst
psammitic
aciimnnos
aniconism
insomniac
aciimnnot
antimonic
antinomic
aciimnopt
impaction
aciimnort
mortician
aciimnosu
minacious
aciimoprs
micropsia
aciimopst
simpatico
aciimortt
triatomic
aciimosst
mosaicist
aciimostt
atomistic
aciimotty
atomicity
aciimprst
prismatic
aciimrssy
Syriacism
aciimrsty
Myristica
aciinnoru
Uriconian
aciinnost
aniconist
onanistic
aciinnott
nictation
aciinnotu
incaution
aciinoort
octonarii
aciinopst
panoistic
aciinortv
Victorian
aciinostt
actionist
aciinottx
antitoxic
aciinotty
atonicity
aciinprtu
puritanic
aciinptty
antitypic
aciinrrty
irritancy
aciioprst
psoriatic
aciioprtt
patriotic
aciioptzz
pizzicato
aciiorstz
zoiatrics
aciiorsuv
vicarious
aciiosstt
isostatic
aciiosuvv
vivacious
aciiprstt
patristic
aciiprstx
piscatrix
aciipttvy
captivity
aciissttt
statistic
acijklopt
pilot-jack
acikknnot
antiknock
acikkrstt
kick-start
aciklmstu
maulstick
aciklnoop
plain-cook
acikloprs
spark-coil
aciklpsst
slapstick
acikopssy
skiascopy
acikprstt
trap-stick
acilllnuu
Lucullian
acilllryy
lyrically
acillmort
millocrat
acillmrsy
Carlylism
acillmsuy
musically
acillnnsy
synclinal
acillnoot
collation
acillnotu
clout-nail
acillooqu
colloquia
acillopty
optically
topically
acillorst
cloistral
acilloryz
zircalloy
acillosty
callosity
stoically
acillotxy
toxically
acillptyy
typically
acilmmott
committal
acilmnntu
culminant
acilmnoos
Salomonic
acilmnopt
complaint
compliant
acilmnosv
volcanism
acilmnouy
Alcyonium
acilmnsuu
unmusical
acilmnsuv
vulcanism
acilmoprs
comprisal
acilmorst
crotalism
acilmorsy
isocrymal
acilmptuu
capitulum
acilmsstu
simulcast
acilnnnuy
uncannily
acilnnotu
continual
acilnnqtu
clinquant
acilnnruu
ranunculi
acilnoprt
prolactin
acilnortt
contralti
acilnorty
latrociny
acilnostu
sulcation
acilnostv
volcanist
acilnottu
luctation
acilnptuy
untypical
acilnstuv
vulcanist
acilnstyy
syncytial
acilooprs
acropolis
aciloopst
apostolic
aciloorst
castor-oil
aciloossu
solacious
aciloprty
placitory
aciloqtuy
loquacity
acilorrsu
cursorial
acilorrvy
co-rivalry

acilorssu
ossicular
acilorstu
suctorial
acilottuy
autolytic
acilpprsy
scrappily
acilppstu
supplicat
acilpstty
styptical
acilrrtuu
utricular
acilsstty
systaltic
acimmnoot
monatomic
acimmnoty
myomantic
acimmorrs
Camorrism
acimmorss
commissar
acimnnoop
companion
acimnnoox
monaxonic
acimnoost
onomastic
acimnootu
autonomic
acimnootx
taxonomic
acimnootz
zoomantic
acimnoprr
cramp-iron
acimnorst
narcotism
acimnosuv
Muscovian
acimopssy
symposiac
acimorrst
Camorrist
acimorsst
ostracism
acimorstt
stromatic
acimorttw
microwatt
acimosttu
comitatus
acimrsttu
strumatic
acinnnoot
connation
acinnorst
constrain
transonic
acinnqsuy
squinancy

acinnrtuu
uncurtain
acinoorrs
corrasion
acinoorst
consortia
Ostracion
acinoosst
iconostas
acinoprrs
scrap-iron
acinopsuu
usucapion
acinorsst
croissant
acinorstt
narcotist
stratonic
acinorsty
carnosity
acinorttu
curtation
ructation
acinortuv
curvation
acinortuy
cautionry
acinosssu
saucisson
acinrsssu
narcissus
acinrssuu
uraniscus
aciooprsu
paroicous
aciooprsz
saprozoic
aciooprtt
copatriot
acioorstu
atrocious
acioorsuv
voracious
acioprssy
caryopsis
acioprstt
prostatic
acioprsty
piscatory
aciosstuu
astucious
acipssttu
Psittacus
acirsstuy
casuistry
acjkoprst
jockstrap
acjlloruy
jocularly
acjloortu
joculator
ackkmnopy
pockmanky

ackllnpsu
knapscull
ackllnrtu
trunk-call
acklmooor
cloakroom
acklnoprt
rock-plant
acklnorst
cornstalk
acklorrwy
warlockry
acklorsst
cross-talk
acklorssw
crosswalk
ackmoorst
stack-room
ackmoprrs
crop-marks
ackmoprsw
scamp-work
ackrsttuy
cutty-sark
aclllosuy
callously
acllmnosu
molluscan
acllnoopt
loco-plant
aclloorry
corollary
acllorssw
scroll-saw
aclmmotuu
commutual
aclmnooru
colourman
monocular
aclmoopst
camp-stool
aclmoorss
classroom
aclmoorsu
clamorous
aclmopsty
cytoplasm
aclmrstuu
claustrum
aclnnortu
nocturnal
aclnoortt
contralto
aclnoortu
colourant
aclnopsty
nyctalops
aclooorrt
coral-root
acloorrtw
coral-wort
acloorsuu
oraculous

acloprsuu
crapulous
acloprttu
plutocrat
acloprtuy
culpatory
aclorsuuy
raucously
aclostuuy
Autolycus
aclosuuvy
vacuously
acmmnoort
commorant
acmnoorrt
cormorant
acmnoostu
cosmonaut
acmnopryy
pyromancy
acmnopttu
computant
acmorrsuu
macrurous
acmorstuy
customary
acmrstuuy
custumary
acnnnoost
consonant
acnooprry
procaryon
acnooprst
corposant
acnooprtv
provocant
acnoorrsu
rancorous
acnoprttu
punctator
acoopprrs
sporocarp
acooprrty
procaryot
acoopstuy
autoscopy
acoorsstu
autocross
acoprrrty
parrot-cry
acorrsstt
star-crost
acorrsttu
scrutator
acossttty
statocyst
adddeehnr
redhanded
adddeekls
skedaddle
adddeenru
undreaded
adddeerss
addressed

adddefiin
dandified
adddeglop
dog-paddle
adddegmno
goddamned
adddeiins
disdained
adddeiior
Dorididae
adddeimno
diamonded
adddeknru
dead-drunk
adddelnsu
unsaddled
adddhmnoo
hodmandod
addeeegry
degree-day
addeeehrt
hederated
addeeellv
dead-level
addeeemnr
meandered
addeeenrr
end-reader
addeeeprt
depredate
addeeerrt
retreaded
addeeerss
addressee
addeefnnt
defendant
addeefnss
fadedness
addeefrru
defrauder
addeeghip
pigheaded
addeeghru
rug-headed
addeegilm
middle-age
addeeginn
deadening
addeegjmu
judge-made
addeeglnr
glandered
addeeglns
sedgeland
addeehhot
hotheaded
addeehill
ill-headed
addeehirr
red-haired
addeehlnp
hen-paddle
addeehmop
mop-headed

addeehnno
one-handed
addeehnot
not-headed
addeehosu
dead-house
addeehotw
tow-headed
two-headed
addeehrss
head-dress
addeehrty
dehydrate
addeeilrv
dare-devil
addeeimtt
meditated
addeeinty
tie-and-dye
addeeiotx
deoxidate
addeeiprr
draperied
addeelmnr
reddleman
addeelmnt
addlement
addeelnuy
undelayed
addeelppw
dewlapped
addeelrss
dreadless
addeemnnu
unamended
addeemnru
undreamed
addeemorr
dromedare
addeennpt
dependant
addeenoru
Oudenarde
addeenost
stone-dead
addeenprw
deep-drawn
addeenswy
Wednesday
addeeoprs
desperado
addeeortv
overdated
addeeprss
adpressed
addeerrss
addresser
readdress
addeffhno
offhanded
addefflos
offsaddle
addeffpru
puff-adder

addefiipt
pedatifid
addefilrw
fieldward
addefinss
faddiness
addegginr
degrading
addeggoot
dog-eat-dog
addeghinr
hag-ridden
addegiitt
digitated
addegimnn
demanding
maddening
addegirrs
disregard
addeglnot
long-dated
addeglruy
guardedly
addegnoor
gadrooned
addegnorw
downgrade
addegnrru
undergrad
addegnruu
unguarded
addehhoty
hydathode
addehiilp
Didelphia
addehinry
anhydride
addehinsy
hendiadys
addehirtw
deid-thraw
addehlnnu
unhandled
addehlrru
hard-ruled
addehnnru
underhand
addehnors
hardnosed
addehnoru
Roundhead
addehnotw
two-handed
addehttuy
death-duty
addeiiimt
dimidiate
addeiilnx
Dixieland
addeiimnr
air-minded
addeiknpp
kidnapped

addeillns
landslide
addeilmmn
middleman
addeilmno
Domdaniel
addeilnno
dandelion
addeilnps
saddle-pin
addeilnru
underlaid
addeilnsv
sand-devil
addeilpsy
displayed
addeilsvy
advisedly
addeimmnn
man-minded
addeimnru
unadmired
addeimnsy
many-sided
addeimort
dermatoid
addeinnru
undrained
addeinopt
dead-point
addeinouv
unavoided
addeinprs
sand-pride
addeinpru
underpaid
addeinrtt
dittander
addeinsuv
unadvised
addeirssu
dissuader
addeirssw
sidewards
addelmnru
ruddleman
addelnotu
nodulated
addelnsuw
unswaddle
addelntuu
undulated
addelnuzz
undazzled
addemorry
dromedary
addennoru
unadorned
addennrtu
redundant
addenntuu
undaunted
addenoort
deodorant

addenoptu
unadopted
addenoruy
duodenary
addenostu
astounded
addenrruw
underdraw
addenrruy
Dundreary
addeoorrv
drove-road
addeoorst
door-stead
addeorrss
addressor
addeorrtw
adderwort
addepqruu
quadruped
addfiiqru
quadrifid
addfilnrt
drift-land
addfknnuy
dandyfunk
addfllnoo
land-flood
addgginrr
Gradgrind
addghnoru
drag-hound
addgilmny
maddingly
addgilntw
twaddling
addhhinrt
third-hand
addhhioor
hardihood
addhiknsw
wind-shak'd
addhlootu
adulthood
addhnnoru
roundhand
addhnorsw
sword-hand
addiiiops
aspidioid
addinorsu
diandrous
addinrsww
windwards
addllnory
dandy-roll
addlmopty
toddy-palm
addlnorst
landdrost
addmnootu
odd-man-out
addnnopuw
up-and-down

addnorsww
downwards
addrsstuy
Dryasdust
adeeeegly
eagle-eyed
adeeefhrt
feathered
adeeefirr
federarie
adeeefnrr
referenda
adeeefrrt
free-trade
adeeefrtu
defeature
adeeefrtw
feed-water
adeeeggrt
gadgeteer
adeeeglpr
pearl-edge
adeeeglrv
everglade
adeeegprs
grapeseed
adeeegttv
vegetated
adeeehlst
sheet-lead
adeeehrst
heartseed
shade-tree
adeeehrtw
weathered
adeeeiipr
Epeiridae
adeeeilmn
madeleine
adeeeilnt
delineate
adeeeimrt
remediate
adeeeinru
Uredineae
adeeeirss
diaereses
adeeekknw
weak-kneed
adeeeknsw
snakeweed
adeeellmn
enamelled
adeeellns
lease-lend
lend-lease
adeeellst
teaselled
adeeelnrv
land-reeve
adeeelntt
dae-nettle
adeeelprs
seed-pearl

adeeelpry
pearl-eyed
adeeelruv
rue-leaved
adeeemntt
dementate
adeeemost
edematose
adeeenrrs
serenader
adeeenrst
Eastender
adeeepprr
paper-reed
adeeeprst
desperate
adeeeqrtu
détraquée
adeeerrtw
water-deer
adeeerttu
deuterate
adeeertww
water-weed
adeeffilr
fieldfare
adeefginn
deafening
adeefhirt
death-fire
adeefiisv
five-a-side
adeefikrr
fire-drake
adeefilor
Florideae
adeefilot
defoliate
adeefilrs
feralised
adeefilrw
weel-faird
adeefilsu
feudalise
adeefimst
defeatism
adeefiort
foederati
adeefistt
defeatist
adeefllmw
well-famed
adeefllst
stall-feed
adeeflnos
leaf-nosed
adeeflort
deflorate
floreated
adeeflotw
two-leafed
adeeflpry
palfreyed

adeeflrtu
defaulter
adeeflrtw
Delftware
adeeflruw
weel-faur'd
adeefmnor
forenamed
adeefmorr
reformade
adeefnost
stone-deaf
adeegginr
gingerade
adeeggins
disengage
adeeggirv
aggrieved
adeegglot
lodge-gate
adeeggmou
demagogue
adeeggnnu
unengaged
adeeggopu
pedagogue
adeeggrst
staggered
adeeghnnr
greenhand
adeeghnor
negrohead
adeeghnru
ahungered
adeegillr
galleried
adeegilnw
wide-angle
adeegilou
idealogue
adeegilrs
sea-girdle
adeegimoy
Geomyidae
adeeginnr
endearing
engrained
grenadine
adeeginpu
anguipede
adeeginrr
grenadier
adeeginrt
denigrate
adeeginst
designate
adeegiuvw
waveguide
adeeglllly
allegedly
adeegllrv
gravelled
adeeglnnr
Englander

adeeglnor
long-eared
adeeglnot
elongated
adeeglnry
legendary
adeegloow
eaglewood
adeeglpru
red-plague
adeeglttu
tegulated
adeegmnrr
germander
adeegmnrt
garmented
adeegmntu
augmented
adeegmrru
demurrage
adeegnnrs
greensand
adeegnnuv
unavenged
adeegnorr
reed-organ
adeegnrst
estranged
adeegorrz
razor-edge
adeegrrss
reed-grass
adeegrsuy
argus-eyed
adeegsttu
degustate
adeehhitw
White-head
adeehhllt
hell-hated
adeehhlsw
dash-wheel
adeehhnop
headphone
adeehhnpy
hedyphane
adeehiklt
deathlike
adeehiktv
khedivate
adeehilnp
hen-paidle
adeehilnr
headliner
adeehimnv
mid-heaven
adeehimor
Homeridae
adeehinor
rhoeadine
adeehinrt
herniated
adeehinss
headiness

adeehirrv
river-head
adeehirtv
rivet-head
adeehklrs
sheldrake
adeehllns
hanselled
adeehllos
leasehold
adeehllst
date-shell
adeehlmor
dreamhole
adeehlorw
rowel-head
adeehlsss
shadeless
adeehlsst
deathless
adeehmnot
methadone
adeehmost
homestead
adeehnost
headstone
adeehnppr
apprehend
adeehnrsu
unhearsed
adeehnrtu
unearthed
adeehorsv
overshade
adeehoswy
eye-shadow
adeehprsy
sharp-eyed
adeehrstt
shattered
adeehrstw
draw-sheet
watershed
adeehstux
exhausted
adeeiilrs
idealiser
adeeiimmt
immediate
adeeiimst
mediatise
adeeiimtv
mediative
adeeiinrt
Neritidae
adeeiiprv
Viperidae
adeeiirss
diaeresis
adeeillmw
well-aimed
adeeillnt
niellated

adeeillss
idealless
adeeilmnn
Mendelian
adeeilmpp
palmipede
adeeilmpr
epidermal
impleader
adeeilmrs
misleader
misleared
adeeilmty
mediately
adeeilnrt
interdeal
tail-ender
adeeilprr
lip-reader
adeeilpss
displease
adeeilrrt
irrelated
adeeilrsv
velarised
adeeiltuy
eudialyte
adeeilvvy
ivy-leaved
adeeimmnr
mermaiden
adeeimmns
misdemean
adeeimnno
menadione
adeeimnos
Maeonides
adeeimnou
eudemonia
adeeimnrr
remainder
adeeimopr
Meropidae
adeeimppr
pipe-dream
adeeimsst
demitasse
adeeimssy
seamy-side
adeeinnpr
panniered
adeeinpst
pedantise
adeeinrss
readiness
adeeinrtt
denitrate
adeeinruw
unwearied
adeeinstt
destinate
adeeintvv
adventive

adeeioprt
periodate
adeeioptv
videotape
adeeiorst
sorediate
adeeippss
passepied
adeeiprrs
draperies
adeeiprss
sea-spider
spear-side
adeeiprsv
eavesdrip
adeeiprtu
repudiate
adeeiprtv
predative
adeeipstw
waist-deep
adeeirstv
advertise
adeeirstw
waterside
adeeirttt
tetradite
adeeirttw
tide-water
adeeirttx
extradite
adeeisstt
stateside
steadiest
adeeisttw
statewide
adeeituvx
exudative
adeejoprr
jeoparder
adeejrstu
Judas-tree
adeeklsst
seed-stalk
adeeklsty
stalk-eyed
adeekmnoy
Yankeedom
adeeknnss
nakedness
adeeknnuw
unwakened
adeeknrtu
undertake
adeeknruw
unwreaked
adeekrrst
redstreak
adeelllru
laurelled
adeellmnr
mallender
adeellmrt
martelled

adeellmrv
marvelled
adeellmtu
medullate
adeellnry
learnedly
adeellorv
overalled
adeellrtv
travelled
adeellrvv
varvelled
adeellsst
tasselled
adeellstt
stellated
adeelmmop
melampode
adeelmmor
melodrame
adeelmnop
pademelon
adeelmops
mole-spade
adeelmoru
remoulade
adeelmorx
exodermal
adeelmrss
dreamless
adeelnnru
unlearned
adeelnorv
overladen
adeelnost
endosteal
adeelnpst
seed-plant
adeelnpsu
unpleased
adeelnptu
pendulate
unpleated
adeelnrrs
slanderer
adeelnrru
launderer
adeelnrsu
underseal
adeelnrtu
unaltered
unrelated
adeelnrux
unrelaxed
adeelnssv
Valdenses
adeelnssw
Waldenses
adeelnsty
slant-eyed
adeelntty
day-nettle
adeelntux
unexalted

adeelorst
desolater
adeelotvw
two-leaved
adeelprst
plastered
adeelrrtt
red-rattle
adeelrrtu
adulterer
adeelrsst
tradeless
adeelrsty
steelyard
adeelrsvy
adversely
adeelrtvy
avertedly
adeemmnnt
amendment
adeemmost
steam-dome
adeemmoxy
myxoedema
adeemnopr
open-armed
promenade
adeemnort
emendator
Notre-Dame
adeemnoru
demeanour
enamoured
adeemnouy
eudaemony
adeemnrru
maunderer
adeemoorr
aerodrome
adeemoprr
madrepore
adeemorrx
xeroderma
adeemortt
trematode
adeemoruw
meadow-rue
adeemostu
edematous
adeempstu
despumate
adeemqrru
remarqued
adeemrstw
smart-weed
adeennprt
trepanned
adeennqru
quarenden
adeennttx
extendant
adeenoprt
ponderate

adeenorss
road-sense
adeenoruv
endeavour
adeenorvy
oven-ready
adeenossu
Soudanese
adeenppru
unpapered
adeenprss
panderess
adeenqrru
quarender
adeenqstu
Dantesque
adeenrrtu
underrate
adeenrruw
underwear
adeenrsty
sedentary
adeenrttu
untreated
adeenrttv
advertent
adeenrtuv
adventure
adeenrtuw
unwatered
adeenssst
satedness
adeenssuy
unessayed
adeeooppr
peraeopod
adeeoprsv
eavesdrop
adeeopstt
despotate
adeeorrrs
rear-dorse
adeeorrtv
overtrade
adeeorrtz
zero-rated
adeepqrtu
parqueted
adeeprrsu
persuader
adeeprrtu
departure
adeeprstu
depasture
adeeqrrtu
quartered
adeerrstv
traversed
adeersttw
wadsetter
adeerstyy
yesterday
adeesstuu
assuetude

adeffiils
falsified
adeffnors
saffroned
adeffnort
affronted
adefghort
godfather
adefgiimn
magnified
adefgiirt
gratified
adefgills
gas-filled
adefgilru
lifeguard
adefginry
defraying
adefgirru
fireguard
adefglnoo
angel-food
adefgloot
floodgate
adefglrru
regardful
adefgnsuw
wages-fund
adefhimst
ham-fisted
adefhlnoz
half-dozen
adefhloor
floorhead
adefhloos
falsehood
adefhlpst
feldspath
adefhnoru
unheard-of
adefiilmp
amplified
adefiilqu
qualified
adefiiprr
rapid-fire
adefiisst
satisfied
adefillsu
fusillade
adefilmns
fieldsman
adefilmsu
feudalism
adefilnnr
Finlander
adefilnor
floridean
adefilnot
deflation
defoliant
adefilnty
defiantly

adefilort
floriated
adefilstu
feudalist
adefiltuy
feudality
adefinnrw
fine-drawn
adefinopr
pinafored
adefitttw
fat-witted
adefknnru
unfranked
adeflllsu
ladlefuls
adefllmou
leaf-mould
adeflltuw
waldflute
adeflmmor
malformed
adeflopst
soft-pedal
adeflottw
twa-lofted
adeflrruw
rewardful
adeflrstw
leftwards
adefmnntu
fundament
adefmoorr
reformado
adefnnosu
nefandous
adefnorrw
forwander
adefooort
oar-footed
adefooprr
proof-read
adefoopst
spade-foot
adefoottu
out-of-date
adeforrrw
forwarder
adeforrtv
overdraft
adeforrtw
afterword
adefortuy
feudatory
adefprstu
turf-spade
adefrrstu
fraudster
adegggizz
zigzagged
adegghhir
high-grade
adeggiitz
dziggetai
adeggillm
gall-midge
adeggilnr
langridge
adegginnr
gardening
adegginrr
regarding
adegginuw
wind-gauge
adeggmnor
doggerman
adeggnoru
groundage
adeghhilt
headlight
adeghinrs
degarnish
adeghinsu
anguished
adeghiopr
eidograph
ideograph
adeghirst
sight-read
adeghlnoo
angelhood
adeghlors
gas-holder
adeghmoru
home-guard
adeghnopr
hop-garden
adeghnopy
endophagy
adeghnost
death-song
adeghnouz
gaze-hound
adeghrrtu
draughter
adegiilos
dialogise
adegiilot
dialogite
adegiilru
guide-rail
adegiinnr
ingrained
adegiinpr
diapering
adegiklnv
gavelkind
adegillmm
gimmalled
adegillmn
medalling
adegillnn
all-ending
adegillno
glenoidal
adegillnp
pedalling
adegillns
signalled
adegilnor
girandole
negroidal
adegilnos
alongside
adegilnrt
treadling
triangled
adegilnru
gerundial
adegilnst
desalting
adegilntw
delta-wing
adegilprw
wild-grape
adegilrvw
wildgrave
adegiltuv
divulgate
adegimnrs
ganderism
semigrand
adegimntu
magnitude
adegimost
dogmatise
adegimrrs
misregard
adeginnrt
integrand
adeginnrw
wandering
adeginors
dragonise
grandiose
organised
adeginoss
diagnoses
adeginoyz
zygaenoid
adeginprs
spreading
adeginprt
departing
adeginrrs
grandsire
adeginrrw
rewarding
adeginrtu
giant-rude
adeginssu
gaudiness
adeginsty
steadying
adegiprrt
partridge
adegirruw
wire-guard
adegirttu
gratitude
adegllnoo
gallooned
adegllopt
gold-plate
adeglmnoo
moon-glade
adeglnntu
untangled
adeglnpuu
unplagued
adegloopy
paedology
adeglrssu
guardless
adegmoprr
deprogram
adegnnopr
pendragon
adegnnrss
grandness
adegnoors
goosander
adegnoprt
godparent
adegnorss
dragoness
adegnorsu
dangerous
adegnortu
nature-god
adegnostw
downstage
adegoorst
stage-door
adegoorsy
goodyears
adegorrtt
garrotted
adehhiprs
rhaphides
adehhllrs
hardshell
adehhnoot
thanehood
adehhnory
hornyhead
adehhotuy
youthhead
adehiiipx
Xiphiidae
adehiiipz
Ziphiidae
adehiiklv
khedivial
adehiillr
ill-haired
adehiilnp
delphinia
adehiilrs
hair-slide
adehiimno
Hominidae
adehiimns
maidenish
adehiinru
Hirudinea
adehiiprt
rhipidate
adehiirrr
hair-drier
adehiisst
diathesis
adehiknps
handspike
adehillow
lowlihead
adehillst
still-head
adehilmns
mishandle
adehilmot
ethmoidal
adehilmsy
shield-may
adehilnor
hodiernal
adehilnpr
philander
adehilnrr
hardliner
adehilnst
Nithsdale
adehilopx
hexaploid
adehiloxy
oxy-halide
adehilrrt
trihedral
adehilstu
lustihead
adehiltwy
white-lady
adehimnor
rhodamine
adehimnrs
Sanhedrim
adehimnrt
hardiment
adehimopp
hippodame
adehimosu
housemaid
adehimprs
Sephardim
adehimpss
misshaped
adehimrty
diathermy
adehinnrs
Sanhedrin
adehinnss
handiness
adehinopu
audiphone
adehinors
rhodanise
Rhodesian

adehinrss
hardiness
adehinrst
interdash
tarnished
adehinrty
anhydrite
adehinryz
hydrazine
adehinsss
shadiness
adehioprt
atrophied
adehipprs
sapphired
adehiprst
therapsid
adehiprsy
Syrphidae
adehirrry
hair-dryer
adehirrtt
third-rate
adehirstw
dish-water
adehirsvw
hivewards
adehirsvy
yravished
adehissty
dysthesia
adehjlloy
jollyhead
adehjlosu
Judas-hole
adehknntu
unthanked
adehknosw
hawk-nosed
shake-down
adehkorsu
dark-house
adehllnor
Hollander
adehllnss
shell-sand
adehllort
death-roll
adehllrsw
hellwards
adehlnotw
handtowel
adehlopry
polyhedra
adehmmotu
mouth-made
adehmoops
shampooed
adehmopry
hypoderma
adehmorsw
homewards
adehnntuu
unhaunted
adehnorst
stone-hard
adehnortw
two-hander
adehnorvy
hydrovane
adehnprss
hand-press
adehnprsu
urn-shaped
adehoorsu
roadhouse
adehoortw
heartwood
adehoostt
statehood
adehopppy
poppy-head
adehoppty
heptapody
adehorrsw
shoreward
adehorrsy
dray-horse
adehostuw
washed-out
adeiiinns
Indianise
adeiiinpr
peridinia
adeiiintt
dietitian
adeiillms
misallied
adeiilmnn
Mindelian
adeiilmnv
vindemial
adeiilmty
Mytilidae
adeiilnpt
pintailed
adeiilnrt
deliriant
drain-tile
adeiilnru
uredinial
adeiilnst
disentail
adeiiloor
Oriolidae
adeiilops
apsidiole
episodial
adeiilort
editorial
adeiilppp
Pedipalpi
adeiilprs
presidial
adeiilptu
Tipulidae
adeiilptx
pixilated
adeiilqtu
liquidate
qualitied
adeiilrsu
Siluridae
adeiilsvy
Sylviidae
adeiimnot
mediation
adeiimnrz
zemindari
adeiimott
diatomite
adeiimrtx
mediatrix
adeiimssv
admissive
misadvise
misavised
adeiinnou
Unionidae
adeiinotv
deviation
adeiinppr
drain-pipe
adeiinprs
Pindarise
adeiinrvv
vivandier
adeiinstu
indusiate
adeiintuv
induviate
adeiiprrs
disrepair
adeiiprss
dispraise
adeiipsst
dissipate
adeiipssy
diapyesis
adeiirsst
Aristides
adeiirstt
disattire
adeiirttv
traditive
adeiisuxz
diazeuxis
adeijlosu
jalousied
adeiklnpu
plaid-neuk
adeikmors
kaiserdom
adeiknnnp
pen-and-ink
adeiknppr
kidnapper
adeiknprs
spikenard
adeiknprt
predikant
adeiknrrr
rank-rider
adeilllmo
lamelloid
adeillmnn
ill-manned
adeillmno
medallion
adeillmot
metalloid
adeillmrt
treadmill
adeillmst
medallist
adeillnrw
well-drain
adeillnst
installed
adeillpru
preludial
adeillqru
quadrille
adeillrtw
dill-water
adeilmnno
mandoline
adeilmnst
dismantle
adeilmntu
datum-line
dentalium
adeilmopt
diplomate
adeilmopy
polyamide
adeilmorr
mail-order
adeilmptu
amplitude
adeilmstu
simulated
adeilmttu
mutilated
adeilnnpu
unplained
adeilnnru
underlain
adeilnopp
panoplied
adeilnops
delapsion
adeilnopt
planetoid
adeilnppu
unapplied
adeilnpru
Paludrine
adeilnpsu
unpalsied
adeilnptu
unplaited
adeilnrrt
interlard
adeilnrsy
synedrial
adeilnrtt
tridental
adeilnrtu
uitlander
adeilnruy
unreadily
adeilnssv
validness
adeiloprs
polarised
adeiloprt
depilator
adeilopsu
lapideous
adeiloqsu
odalisque
adeilorvy
olive-yard
adeilprss
dispersal
adeilprsy
displayer
adeilpsss
sapidless
adeilpttu
platitude
adeilrsxy
Xyridales
adeilrttu
rutilated
adeilrtvv
trivalved
adeilrtww
wild-water
adeilsstu
lassitude
adeimmrst
midstream
adeimmrtu
immatured
adeimnopr
meropidan
adeimnopt
ademption
adeimnors
masonried
randomise
adeimnoss
mid-season
adeimnost
staminode
adeimnprr
reprimand
adeimnprs
panderism
spider-man
adeimnpru
drepanium
adeimnpst
pedantism

adeimnrru
murrained
unmarried
adeimnrsu
nursemaid
adeimnrty
dynamiter
adeimnryz
zemindary
adeimopst
impastoed
adeimortt
trematoid
adeimorty
mediatory
adeimprst
red-tapism
spermatid
adeimprsy
pyramides
adeimrssx
maxi-dress
adeimrttu
diatretum
adeimrtux
admixture
adeimrtxy
taxidermy
adeinnnps
inspanned
adeinnntt
intendant
adeinnott
dentation
adeinnptu
unpainted
adeinnrtu
untrained
adeinnsss
sandiness
adeinnstu
unstained
adeinnttu
untainted
adeinoppt
appointed
adeinoprr
preordain
adeinoprt
predation
adeinopss
passioned
adeinopst
antipodes
adeinorrs
serranoid
adeinorsu
deinosaur
adeinorty
arytenoid
adeinoruz
Zonuridae
adeinotux
exudation

adeinpprs
sandpiper
adeinppst
stand-pipe
adeinprss
rapidness
adeinprsu
unpraised
adeinprtt
trepidant
adeinpssv
vapidness
adeinrrsv
river-sand
adeinrrww
wiredrawn
adeinrsst
tardiness
adeinrstu
Sturnidae
adeinrttu
unattired
adeinssst
staidness
adeinsstu
sustained
adeinsttu
disattune
adeinsttv
Adventist
adeioprsu
deiparous
adeioprtt
dioptrate
adeioprtz
trapezoid
adeiorstt
storiated
adeiortvy
deviatory
adeipprsu
dispauper
adeippssy
dyspepsia
adeiprrsu
perradius
adeiprstt
red-tapist
adeiprtvy
depravity
adeipsstu
stapedius
adeipssux
pseudaxis
adeirrsuy
residuary
adeirsstu
auditress
adeirstvy
adversity
adeisttuv
vastitude
adeklnnpu
unplanked

adeklnosy
ankylosed
adekmnnoy
donkey-man
adekmoqru
Quakerdom
adeknoosw
snakewood
adekoprsw
spadework
adelllowy
allowedly
adellmruy
medullary
adellnopr
landloper
adellnorw
lowlander
adellnouy
unalloyed
adellntuu
lunulated
adelloorw
low-loader
adelloprt
patrolled
adellrrwy
dry-waller
adellrtxy
dextrally
adelmnnuy
mundanely
adelmnops
endoplasm
adelmnopy
padymelon
adelmorsu
asmoulder
adelmssuy
assumedly
adelnnnpu
unplanned
adelnnnpy
pennyland
adelnnorw
landowner
adelnnptu
unplanted
adelnoost
loadstone
adelnopsy
dyspnoeal
adelnorrv
Land-rover®
adelnortu
outlander
adelnoruy
roundelay
adelnpruy
underplay
adelnrssu
laundress
adelnrtvy
verdantly

adelnsstu
dauntless
adelnstuu
unsaluted
adelooosw
aloeswood
adelooprt
door-plate
adeloorst
desolator
adeloptuy
played-out
adelpqruu
quadruple
adelprssy
sparsedly
adelrrsty
drysalter
adelrssuy
assuredly
ademmnopp
mappemond
ademmorst
masterdom
ademnnort
adornment
ademnnruu
unmanured
ademnorsu
meandrous
ademnpstu
unstamped
ademnrrsu
snare-drum
ademnrtuu
unmatured
ademnssuu
unassumed
ademoorrt
moderator
ademoorst
astrodome
ademoorsy
mooseyard
ademorrsw
Romewards
ademosttw
two-masted
adennnstu
suntanned
adennosst
sandstone
adennosty
asyndeton
adennsstw
news-stand
adenoorst
tornadoes
adenoortt
detonator
adenoostt
toad-stone
adenootwz
zante-wood

adenoowwx
wood-waxen
adenoppty
pentapody
adenoprsu
panderous
adenoprtv
davenport
adenopruv
up-and-over
adenoqrsu
squadrone
adenorruy
year-round
adenorruz
unrazored
adenorsst
star-nosed
adenorstv
overstand
adenorttu
rotundate
adenosuvw
sound-wave
adenottwy
wyandotte
adenprssu
underpass
adenqrsuu
unsquared
adenrrstw
sternward
adenrrtuy
day-return
adenrssuu
unassured
adeoopprt
Pteropoda
adeoopprw
wood-paper
adeooprsw
spear-wood
adeoprrtu
depurator
adeoprrtw
top-drawer
water-drop
adeoprrty
predatory
adeoprstu
outspread
adeoprttw
two-parted
adeoprtty
tetrapody
adeoqrttu
torquated
adeorrstt
rostrated
adeorrsww
swear-word
adeorrtuv
advoutrer

aderrstwy
stewardry
adersstww
westwards
adffffruu
ruff-a-duff
adffiimrs
disaffirm
adffilntu
find-fault
adffsttuy
staff-duty
adfgilnou
fungoidal
adfginors
sangfroid
adfglnory
dragonfly
adfgoorru
roof-guard
adfhinrst
first-hand
adfhioory
fairyhood
adfhlnopu
half-pound
adfhlnoru
half-round
adfhloory
foolhardy
adfhlorsw
half-sword
adfiilnot
latifondi
adfiilrst
drift-sail
adfilmsuy
dismayful
adfinoorx
Oxfordian
adfinrrtu
turf-drain
adfiorsuv
disfavour
adfirrstt
star-drift
adfklmoor
floodmark
adflloost
faldstool
adflorrwy
forwardly
frowardly
adfmooppr
damp-proof
adfnoorsz
sforzando
adfnorrtw
frontward
adggilnry
niggardly
adggilrsy
Yggdrasil

adgginrru
guard-ring
adghhilns
highlands
adghhinrt
right-hand
adghhoopr
hodograph
adghiiopr
idiograph
adghikoow
gawkihood
adghilllu
guildhall
adghilnsy
dashingly
adghimnor
harm-doing
adghinoot
gianthood
adghinors
dragonish
adghinosw
shadowing
adghinrtu
indraught
adghinrtw
nightward
adghiprsu
guard-ship
adghirrtw
rightward
adghnorsu
ground-ash
adghnostu
staghound
adghorruw
rough-draw
adghortux
draught-ox
adghprtuu
up-draught
adgiiilnt
digitalin
adgiiilst
Digitalis
adgiijnno
adjoining
adgiilmos
sigmoidal
adgiilost
dialogist
adgiimnrs
disarming
adgiimntt
admitting
adgiinnnt
indignant
adgiinort
granitoid
adgiinoss
diagnosis
adgiinrty
dignitary

adgiirtvy
gravidity
adgikllmn
milk-gland
adgiklln s
silk-gland
adgiklnrs
darklings
adgillnuy
languidly
adgillosu
gladiolus
adgilnnou
unloading
adgilnnst
Landsting
adgilnory
adoringly
adgilnoss
glissando
adgilnprs
springald
adgilnrty
dartingly
adgiloory
radiology
adgiloouy
audiology
adgimmost
dogmatism
adgimnors
dragonism
adgimostt
dogmatist
adginnnuw
undawning
adginnoou
Iguanodon
adginnopr
pardoning
adginnrst
ringstand
adginopry
parodying
adginprsy
dayspring
adgklmnsu
musk-gland
adgknooru
ground-oak
adglmnoos
dog-salmon
adglnnorw
long-drawn
adglnoory
andrology
adglnooty
odontalgy
adgmnnoru
groundman
adgmoorru
guard-room
adgmoorty
dogmatory

adgnnoryy
androgyny
adgnorsuw
snow-guard
adgooprst
gastropod
adgooprsu
podagrous
adgoorsuw
wood-sugar
adhhimopr
rhamphoid
adhhnooru
hoarhound
adhhnoott
hot-and-hot
adhhnorst
shorthand
adhhoprss
sharp-shod
adhiiklnr
drink-hail
adhiillot
lithoidal
adhiilopu
audiophil
adhiilopx
xiphoidal
adhiilorz
rhizoidal
adhiilprs
lairdship
adhiimmrs
Midrashim
adhiimpss
amidships
adhiimsss
Hassidism
adhiiopru
Ophiurida
adhiiopty
idiopathy
adhiipssy
diaphysis
adhikmnnu
humankind
adhiknorw
handiwork
adhillosw
dishallow
adhilmnpy
nymphalid
adhilmoop
omphaloid
adhilnnuy
unhandily
adhilnopy
hypnoidal
adhilnpsu
uplandish
adhilopty
typhoidal
adhimnosy
Mondayish

adhimnrst
thirdsman
adhimstyy
dysthymia
adhinnrtu
hit-and-run
adhinoost
sainthood
adhinopsy
dysphonia
adhinorty
hydration
adhinrtww
withdrawn
adhinsttw
withstand
adhiooprz
Rhizopoda
adhioprsy
dysphoria
adhknorwy
handywork
adhllmort
thralldom
adhlmnouy
lyam-hound
adhlnnort
northland
adhlnostu
southland
adhmnooow
womanhood
adhmoorsy
hydrosoma
adhnnrstu
handsturn
adhnooryz
hydrozoan
adhnorrtw
northward
adhnorsuy
anhydrous
adhnortuy
hydronaut
adhooprrt
arthropod
adhorstty
hydrostat
adhorstuw
southward
adiiinnst
Indianist
adiiinors
Isidorian
adiiinosz
isoniazid
adiijksst
disjaskit
adiikkrry
kirkyaird
adiillnvy
invalidly
adiillops
spadillio

adiillpty
pallidity
adiilmnno
mandilion
adiilmops
idioplasm
adiilmpvy
impavidly
adiilmsss
dismissal
adiilmsty
dismality
adiilnopt
platinoid
adiilnopu
nauplioid
adiiloorv
varioloid
adiiloprs
sporidial
adiilowww
widow-wail
adiimnoss
admission
adiimnost
staminoid
adiimnprs
Pindarism
adiimnrsw
Darwinism
adiimrssy
mydriasis
adiinnost
disanoint
adiinnosy
Dionysian
adiinootx
oxidation
adiinoqtu
quotidian
adiinortt
tradition
adiinortv
divinator
adiinosst
soi-disant
stasidion
adiinprst
Pindarist
adiinrstt
distraint
adiiopsty
adiposity
adiiprsty
disparity
adiisstuy
assiduity
adiisttvy
vastidity
adijksssu
Judas-kiss
adijmopsu
Poujadism

adijopstu
Poujadist
adiklmnrs
alms-drink
adikmnnow
womankind
adilllpsu
spauld-ill
adillmnoo
almond-oil
adillnopt
land-pilot
adillnopu
planuloid
adillnruy
diurnally
adilloptw
tallow-dip
adillorrx
rix-dollar
adillqsuy
squalidly
adilmnnoy
mandylion
adilmnoos
salmonoid
adilmnost
Daltonism
adilmnruu
duralumin
adilmopsy
sympodial
adilmruuv
duumviral
adilmsttu
Talmudist
adilnnnoo
Londonian
adilnnops
pond-snail
adilnoost
isodontal
adilnrtuu
diuturnal
adilnstty
distantly
adilooprs
prosodial
adiloprsv
disproval
adilorstw
sword-tail
adimnntuy
mundanity
adimnoort
admonitor
dominator
adimnopry
pyramidon
adimnosty
staminody
adimooqsu
Quasimodo

adimortuw
moudiwart
adimortww
mowdiwart
adinnortw
down-train
adinnosst
dissonant
adinnprtu
tip-and-run
adinooprs
prosodian
adinoostw
satinwood
adinopsty
dystopian
adinorstw
downstair
adinotwwx
window-tax
adinpsttu
disputant
adioopstu
adoptious
adiosssuu
assiduous
adipssuyy
upsy-daisy
adjmmooor
major-domo
adjmmorru
drum-major
adknorrtu
trunk-road
adknorrww
drawn-work
adlllorry
Lollardry
adllnostu
Lotus-land
adlloprwy
play-world
adlmnorty
mordantly
adlmnrstu
Landsturm
adlmooprr
prodromal
adlmoortu
modulator
adlmopruw
mouldwarp
adlnopryy
polyandry
adlooostt
toadstool
adloprswy
swordplay
adlorsuuy
arduously
adlortuwy
outwardly
admmorrty
martyrdom

admnnorsu
roundsman
admnnossy
synodsman
admnoorsz
smorzando
admnoorty
dynamotor
admnoosuv
novodamus
admnorsst
sand-storm
admnorssw
swordsman
admooppru
pompadour
admoopstw
wood-stamp
admpsttuy
stamp-duty
adnnooott
Notodonta
adnnossww
swansdown
swans-down
adnoottuu
out-and-out
adnoprrty
protandry
adnoprruw
wrapround
adnopsstu
sand-spout
aeeeehmpr
ephemerae
aeeeelrtv
re-elevate
aeeeelssv
sea-sleeve
aeeeeppsw
peaseweep
aeeeetttt
tête-à-tête
aeeefglnr
leaf-green
aeeefgnrr
free-range
aeeefhrrt
heart-free
hereafter
aeeefhrtv
fever-heat
aeeefirrt
fire-eater
aeeeflmrt
flame-tree
aeeeflmrz
ramfeezle
aeeefnnst
fasten-e'en
aeeefsttt
estafette
aeeegggnr
greengage

aeeeggilr
gier-eagle
aeeeggnnr
engrenage
aeeeggnpr
pre-engage
aeeeggnrs
sage-green
aeeeggrst
segregate
aeeeghlrw
gear-wheel
aeeegimnr
menagerie
aeeeglors
sore-eagle
aeeeglrrv
gear-lever
aeeeglrtt
letter-gae
aeeeglstw
sweet-gale
aeeegmnnp
empennage
aeeegmnrt
agreement
aeeegnrss
eagerness
aeeegprrt
grapetree
aeeegrrrt
garreteer
aeeegrrtt
targeteer
aeeegrstt
streetage
aeeegrttz
gazetteer
aeeegrtuz
gauze-tree
aeeehhnst
ensheathe
aeeehknrr
hearkener
aeeehllmn
mallee-hen
aeeehlmpr
ephemeral
aeeehmnst
mane-sheet
aeeehmpst
sheepmeat
aeeehmrtx
hexameter
aeeehnnrt
enhearten
aeeehnrtw
enwreathe
aeeehrrrs
rehearser
aeeehrstt
tear-sheet
aeeeillot
elaeolite

aeeeilrtt
elaterite
aeeeimnrx
re-examine
aeeeipprt
papeterie
aeeeirrtt
reiterate
aeeejnntt
jeannette
aeeeklttt
tea-kettle
aeeekmrrt
marketeer
aeeeknrst
tree-snake
aeeeknrtt
entertake
aeeellmnr
enameller
aeeellmnt
elemental
aeeellrst
teaseller
aeeellrsw
weaseller
aeeellsst
tessellae
aeeelmstw
sweetmeal
aeeelnnpp
peneplane
aeeelnprt
plane-tree
aeeelnstt
sea-nettle
aeeelpprt
apple-tree
aeeelpttu
epaulette
aeeelrstt
sea-letter
aeeelrstw
steel-ware
aeeemmnst
semanteme
aeeemnnrt
nemertean
aeeemnrst
erasement
aeeemnrtu
enumerate
aeeemorrt
aerometer
areometer
aeeemprtt
temperate
aeeemrrsu
remeasure
aeeemrtvw
wavemeter
aeeemsttw
sweetmeat

aeeennprt
perennate
aeeenortx
exonerate
aeeenprtt
penetrate
aeeenprtu
Euterpean
aeeenrrst
easterner
aeeenttuv
eventuate
aeeenttux
extenuate
aeeeqrstu
tee-square
aeeersttw
Teeswater
aeeessttty
essayette
aeefffmuw
fee-faw-fum
aeeffilrt
after-life
aeeffnort
affrontée
aeeffrstt
staff-tree
aeefgilms
self-image
aeefgilpr
pilferage
aeefginrs
far-seeing
aeefgirrt
fire-grate
aeefgllot
flageolet
aeefglmor
foregleam
aeefglnnw
newfangle
aeefglnuv
avengeful
aeefglorv
gaol-fever
aeefglorw
flowerage
aeefglstw
sweet-flag
aeefgorrt
frog-eater
aeefgorst
forestage
fosterage
aeefhirss
sea-fisher
aeefhlmst
flesh-meat
aeefijlrv
jail-fever
aeefilltt
title-leaf

aeefilnrt
interleaf
aeefilnss
leafiness
aeefilotx
exfoliate
aeefilppr
paper-file
aeefilppw
apple-wife
aeefilrsv
life-saver
aeefilrwy
life-weary
aeefimort
aforetime
aeefimrtt
aftertime
aeefinstt
festinate
aeefinstx
antefixes
aeefirrtw
fire-water
aeefirstt
feast-rite
aeefirstw
wasterife
aeefklovw
folk-weave
aeefkoprs
forespeak
aeefllmss
flameless
aeefllnnw
new-fallen
aeeflloos
loose-leaf
aeeflnrst
fenestral
aeeflnsss
falseness
aeeflorst
foresteal
aeeflostv
love-feast
aeeflrrtt
flatterer
aeeflrtuy
featurely
aeefmnnru
unfreeman
aeefmnors
freemason
aeefmnorw
freewoman
aeefmrrss
farmeress
aeefnnort
foreanent
aeefnrrtw
water-fern
aeefnstty
safety-net

aeefoprrt
perforate
aeeforstt
foretaste
aeeggilno
galiongee
aeegginns
gas-engine
aeegginrr
gregarine
aeegginrs
sea-ginger
aeegglnoy
genealogy
aeeggmort
mortgagee
aeeggnrsu
grease-gun
aeeggorrt
toe-ragger
aeeggrrst
staggerer
aeeggrrsw
swaggerer
aeeghimrt
hermitage
aeeghinnu
guinea-hen
aeeghinrr
rehearing
aeeghinrs
garnishee
aeeghlmst
gas-helmet
aeeghloru
auger-hole
aeeghlost
segholate
aeeghlprt
telegraph
aeeghmnop
megaphone
aeeghmrtw
wheat-germ
aeeghmrtz
megahertz
aeeghnrsy
ashen-grey
aeeghostu
gate-house
aeegiilns
genialise
aeegiimnr
gaminerie
aeegiinnr
air-engine
aeegillms
misallege
aeegillns
all-seeing
aeegillnv
villenage
aeegillrt
treillage

aeegillst
legislate
aeegilmnn
malengine
meningeal
aeegilmns
semi-angle
aeegilmss
imageless
aeegilnnt
eglantine
inelegant
aeegilnnv
leavening
aeegilnrv
revealing
aeegilnst
anglesite
teaseling
aeegilnsw
anglewise
aeegilptt
title-page
aeegilrtu
gauleiter
aeegimmtv
gemmative
aeegimnnn
engine-man
aeegimnrs
Germanise
aeegimnrt
germinate
aeegimnst
magnesite
magnetise
aeegimntt
magnetite
aeegimost
isogamete
aeegimptt
pegmatite
aeegimrrt
remigrate
aeegimrtu
mugearite
aeeginnrr
engrainer
aeeginnrt
argentine
tangerine
aeeginnyz
zygaenine
aeeginopp
pigeon-pea
aeeginops
espionage
aeeginott
negotiate
aeeginprt
interpage
pignerate
repeating

aeeginprv
grapevine
aeeginrst
stingaree
aeeginrtt
argentite
integrate
aeeginrtw
Wagnerite
aeegiopsu
epigaeous
aeegiqrsu
squireage
aeegiruwz
wire-gauze
aeegisttv
gestative
aeegjlmou
megajoule
aeegjnorr
jargoneer
aeegllnor
organelle
aeegllnry
generally
aeegllnty
elegantly
aeeglmnnt
gentleman
aeeglmnry
germanely
aeeglmnst
segmental
aeeglmntt
tegmental
aeeglmoos
mesogloea
aeeglmort
glomerate
aeeglmrry
germ-layer
aeeglnnpt
pentangle
aeeglnrss
angerless
largeness
aeeglnttu
languette
aeegloprt
petrolage
aeeglorvz
overglaze
aeeglprry
pearl-grey
aeeglprss
grapeless
aeeglqrsu
square-leg
aeeglrssv
graveless
aeeglrsty
slate-grey
steel-gray

aeegmnoty
gate-money
aeegmnrrs
merganser
aeegmnrtu
augmenter
aeegmootz
zoogamete
aeegmoprs
megaspore
aeegmorst
gasometer
aeegnnstw
newsagent
aeegnoprs
personage
aeegnorrt
generator
aeegnortt
teratogen
aeegnortu
entourage
aeegnottw
wagonette
aeegnotxy
oxygenate
aeegnprss
passenger
aeegnrrst
estranger
aeegnrrvy
engravery
aeegnrsst
greatness
aeegnrssv
graveness
aeegnssuv
vagueness
aeegoossw
wase-goose
aeegoppst
estoppage
aeegoprrt
porterage
reportage
aeegorrtv
overgreat
aeegorrvz
overgraze
aeegorttw
gate-tower
aeegprtux
expurgate
aeegrrsst
grass-tree
aeehhinst
insheathe
aeehhllps
shell-heap
aeehhlosw
hawsehole
aeehhnpty
hyphenate

aeehhnrty
heathenry
aeehhnstu
unsheathe
aeehhoovy
yo-heave-ho
aeehhpssw
sheep-wash
aeehiknpt
phenakite
aeehillnw
whale-line
aeehilmns
shale-mine
aeehilmnw
meanwhile
aeehilnss
Sinhalese
aeehilntv
Helvetian
aeehilorv
overhaile
aeehilpst
ephialtes
aeehilrtt
theralite
aeehimnst
mainsheet
aeehimprr
epirrhema
aeehimprt
Hemiptera
aeehimpss
emphasise
aeehimpst
empathise
aeehimrst
hetaerism
aeehimstw
white-seam
aeehinprs
Hesperian
inspheare
seraphine
aeehinrsv
haversine
aeehinrtw
inwreathe
near-white
aeehinssv
heaviness
aeehipprt
epitapher
aeehippsw
hawsepipe
aeehiprrt
ratheripe
three-pair
aeehiprss
apheresis
aeehiprst
sphaerite
aeehirstt
hetaerist

aeehirtww
whiteware
aeehissst
aesthesis
aeehisstt
athetesis
aeehkllrs
lark's-heel
aeehkllry
rakehelly
aeehklpsw
sheepwalk
aeehkmmor
homemaker
aeehkmors
shoemaker
aeehllmow
whole-meal
aeehllnow
Hallowe'en
aeehllors
aeroshell
aeehllosw
wholesale
aeehllrst
tear-shell
aeehlmmnt
Emmenthal
aeehlmpry
melaphyre
aeehlmrty
erythemal
aeehlmsss
shameless
aeehlmtty
methylate
aeehlnops
anopheles
aeehlnopt
phenolate
aeehlnrst
hesternal
aeehlnsst
natheless
aeehlopst
telophase
aeehlortw
water-hole
aeehlpsss
phaseless
shapeless
aeehlptty
telepathy
aeehlrsst
heartless
aeehlrstw
star-wheel
aeehlrtwy
weatherly
aeehlsttw
whet-slate
aeehlstxy
hexastyle

aeehmmort
hammer-toe
aeehmmpsy
emphysema
aeehmnnop
phenomena
aeehmnorr
menorrhea
aeehmnort
nathemore
aeehmnott
moth-eaten
aeehmoprs
semaphore
aeehmorst
heartsome
horsemeat
aeehmostu
house-mate
aeehmprst
petersham
aeehnoopr
aerophone
aeehnoort
Oenothera
aeehnoptx
toxaphene
aeehnostu
neat-house
aeehnprrs
sharpener
aeehnrtuw
unwreathe
aeehnstty
Thyestean
aeehoprty
aerophyte
aeehorrrs
rearhorse
aeehorrst
heart-sore
aeehorrsw
raree-show
aeehorstv
overhaste
aeehorstw
whatsoe'er
aeehorsuw
warehouse
aeehprrtt
three-part
aeehprstu
superheat
aeehrrstt
ratherest
aeehrrstv
harvester
aeehrstux
exhauster
aeeiillop
aeolipile
aeeiilmnt
eliminate

aeeiilqru
reliquiae
aeeiilrss
serialise
aeeiilrst
Israelite
aeeiinnot
neoteinia
aeeiinrtt
itinerate
aeeiipprt
peripetia
aeeiiprtv
aperitive
aeeiirstv
varieties
aeeiirttv
iterative
aeeiirtvz
vizierate
aeeijlrss
jaileress
aeeijmnss
jessamine
aeeijprss
jasperise
aeeikklns
snakelike
aeeiklnpr
Keplerian
aeeiklnps
aspen-like
aeeiklnss
leakiness
aeeikmnsy
Yankeeism
aeeiknnsy
Keynesian
aeeiknppw
wink-a-peep
aeeiknrrs
ink-eraser
aeeiknssw
snakewise
aeeikrrss
seraskier
aeeikrstw
awestrike
aeeillmnt
metalline
aeeillmot
emolliate
aeeillmst
metallise
aeeillnot
lineolate
aeeillnst
sea-lentil
aeeillntt
littleane
aeeillopy
aeolipyle
aeeillpst
palletise
aeeillptt
paillette
aeeillstt
satellite
aeeilltvw
wavellite
aeeilmmst
semi-metal
aeeilmnnt
alinement
lineament
aeeilmnnu
eumelanin
aeeilmnry
mine-layer
aeeilmnss
mealiness
aeeilmort
meliorate
aeeilmpss
misplease
aeeilmpst
time-lapse
aeeilmrst
misrelate
salimeter
aeeilmrtt
altimeter
aeeilmrtu
elaterium
aeeilmrtw
limewater
aeeilmtuv
emulative
aeeilnnpp
peneplain
aeeilnnpr
perennial
aeeilnnsx
sexennial
aeeilnntv
Levantine
valentine
aeeilnotv
elevation
aeeilnppp
pineapple
aeeilnprx
explainer
aeeilnpsx
expansile
aeeilnrss
earliness
aeeilnrsu
unrealise
aeeilnrsv
vernalise
aeeilnrtu
retinulae
aeeilnrtv
eviternal
intervale
aeeilnrtw
water-line
aeeilnsst
essential
aeeilnttv
ventilate
aeeiloptt
petiolate
aeeilorrt
arteriole
aeeilppry
pipe-layer
aeeilprrv
reprieval
aeeilprst
prelatise
aeeilqrsu
equaliser
aeeilquvv
equivalve
aeeilrrtv
retrieval
aeeilrssw
weariless
aeeilrstu
Aleurites
aeeilrstv
versatile
aeeilrsty
seriately
aeeilrttu
elutriate
aeeilsstw
leastwise
aeeilssux
sexualise
aeeilsvvy
evasively
aeeimnnox
xenomenia
aeeimnnpp
Menippean
aeeimnnrt
nemertian
aeeimnnrv
venireman
aeeimnnzz
mezzanine
aeeimnpru
perinaeum
aeeimnrru
numeraire
aeeimnrtt
terminate
aeeimnrtv
verminate
aeeimnsss
seaminess
aeeimnsst
meatiness
aeeimnstt
estaminet
aeeimnstv
avisement
aeeimntvv
vivamente
aeeimorst
osmeteria
aeeimorsw
wearisome
aeeimppst
steam-pipe
aeeimprss
Parseeism
aeeimprst
spare-time
aeeimprtt
impetrate
aeeimrstt
tasimeter
aeeimrttx
taximeter
aeeinnpst
septennia
aeeinnrrw
Wernerian
aeeinnrtt
entertain
Terentian
aeeinnrtv
innervate
aeeinnsst
insensate
aeeinnstt
intensate
aeeinoppt
appointee
aeeinortt
orientate
aeeinprss
parenesis
passerine
aeeinprst
pistareen
sparteine
aeeinprtu
petaurine
aeeinpsvx
expansive
aeeinrrtt
reiterant
aeeinrrtv
veratrine
aeeinrssw
weariness
aeeinrstt
reinstate
aeeinrstu
estuarine
aeeinrstv
invertase
aeeinrsty
eyestrain
aeeinrtvw
water-vine
aeeinsstv
assentive
aeeinsttt
enstatite
intestate
satinette
aeeinsttu
austenite
aeeintttv
attentive
tentative
aeeioprtv
operative
aeeipprst
appetiser
aeeipprsu
pauperise
aeeipprtw
water-pipe
aeeippstw
waste-pipe
aeeiprrst
sparterie
aeeiprrtv
privateer
aeeiprssv
aspersive
aeeiprstw
taperwise
aeeiprsvv
pervasive
aeeiprttx
extirpate
aeeirrstv
arrestive
aeeirsstt
sestertia
aeeirsstv
assertive
aeejlmrsu
Jerusalem
aeejmortt
majorette
aeejmrstt
jetstream
aeejnrsst
jesserant
aeejnrsty
serjeanty
aeekllsss
slakeless
aeeklmnnn
kennel-man
aeeklmorv
love-maker
aeeklrssw
wreakless
aeeklsttw
sweet-talk
aeekmmrry
merrymake
aeekmnrtt
tent-maker
aeekmnrtw
newmarket

aeekmoprr
rope-maker
aeekmopst
peat-smoke
aeekmrsty
master-key
aeeknortv
overtaken
aeekortuy
eukaryote
aeekqrssu
Quakeress
aeekqrsuy
squeakery
aeelllmos
lamellose
aeelllsuv
vulsellae
aeellmntw
well-meant
aeellmrss
realmless
aeellnprt
repellant
aeellnptx
expellant
aeellnrrt
rentaller
aeellnrty
eternally
aeelloppv
love-apple
aeellopst
Sellotape®
sole-plate
aeellosuv
laevulose
aeellrrtv
traveller
aeellrsst
tessellar
aeellrsvy
severally
aeellrttu
tellurate
aeellssuv
valueless
aeellssvv
valveless
aeelmmnrt
entrammel
aeelmnost
Telamones
aeelmnpss
ampleness
aeelmnrtv
ravelment
aeelmoppr
palempore
aeelmorst
elastomer
aeelmortw
water-mole

aeelmoswy
awesomely
aeelmprst
emplaster
aeelmprxy
exemplary
aeelmpssy
esemplasy
aeelmptty
type-metal
aeelmrsst
semestral
aeelmrstt
streamlet
aeelmrttu
tremulate
aeelmrttw
melt-water
aeelnnntu
antennule
aeelnnoss
aloneness
aeelnnpry
arle-penny
aeelnopst
pleonaste
aeelnosuv
leavenous
aeelnprrv
pre-vernal
aeelnprtv
prevalent
aeelnprty
net-player
aeelnqssu
equalness
aeelnrsst
alertness
aeelnrstw
water-lens
aeelnrsty
earnestly
aeelnrttv
tervalent
aeelnrtty
ternately
aeelnrtuv
vulnerate
aeelnssst
staleness
aeelnstvx
sexvalent
aeelnsuvw
news-value
aeelopprs
rose-apple
aeeloprty
epeolatry
aeelopstt
salopette
aeelorrtv
revelator
aeelorstu
teleosaur

aeelorsty
areostyle
aeelortvw
water-vole
aeelortvy
elevatory
aeeloruvv
overvalue
aeelpprru
puerperal
aeelpprtu
perpetual
aeelpqttu
plaquette
aeelprrst
plasterer
aeelprrsu
pleasurer
reperusal
aeelprrtu
prelature
aeelprsss
spareless
aeelprsst
prelatess
aeelprstt
saltpetre
steel-trap
aeelprstu
pulse-rate
aeelprtuy
eutrapely
aeelpsssu
pauseless
aeelpsuvw
pulse-wave
aeelrrstu
serrulate
aeelrsstv
varletess
aeelrsstw
waterless
aeelrsttu
sea-turtle
aeelrstuy
austerely
aeelrstvy
severalty
aeelssstt
stateless
tasteless
aeemmnort
manometer
aeemmnstu
amusement
aeemmortt
atmometer
aeemmpruy
empyreuma
aeemmrrst
stammerer
aeemnnntx
annexment

aeemnnopr
praenomen
aeemnnort
nanometre
aeemnnott
atonement
aeemnnprt
permanent
aeemnoprt
treponema
aeemnopsu
menopause
aeemnopyz
apoenzyme
aeemnortw
worm-eaten
aeemnoruv
manoeuvre
aeemnprty
pentamery
repayment
aeemnpsst
passement
aeemnqrsu
queen's-arm
aeemnrsst
mare's-nest
steersman
aeemnrttt
treatment
aeemnsstt
means-test
aeemnsttt
statement
testament
aeemoprtw
pome-water
aeemorrsu
rearmouse
aeemorrty
aerometry
aeemorsst
Massorete
aeemorttu
amourette
aeemortux
auxometer
aeemprrtu
premature
aeemprttt
attempter
aeemprttu
permutate
aeemrrstt
smatterer
aeemrtttw
wattmeter
aeennopst
pentosane
aeennprrt
trepanner
aeennprtt
penetrant
repentant

aeennrrtt
re-entrant
aeenopprt
notepaper
aeenoprst
Esperanto
personate
aeenopttt
potentate
aeenorrst
nor'-easter
aeenorrtv
venerator
aeenorrtw
rowan-tree
aeenorstw
stoneware
aeenpprrt
entrapper
aeenpprru
unprepare
aeenpprsw
newspaper
aeenprrtu
enrapture
aeenprsss
spareness
aeenprsst
apertness
taperness
aeenprsty
septenary
aeenprtty
Pernettya
aeenrrstu
saunterer
aeenrrtuv
nervature
aeenrsstu
Sauternes
aeenrstuv
rune-stave
aeensssstw
wasteness
aeeooprtz
azeotrope
aeeoorrtt
root-eater
aeeopprsu
pea-souper
aeeoppssu
pease-soup
aeeoprrtw
water-pore
aeeoprstt
poetaster
aeeoprttw
water-poet
aeeorrstt
erostrate
aeeorrstv
overstare
aeeorrstw
rose-water

aeeorrsvw
overswear
aeeorrtuv
avouterer
aeeorrtuw
outerware
aeeorrvwy
overweary
aeeorsttv
overstate
aeeorsttw
twoseater
aeepprssu
pauperess
aeepprstt
test-paper
aeeprrstu
repasture
aeeprsttu
pertusate
aeeqrtttu
quartette
aeeqrtuux
exequatur
aeerrrssu
reassurer
aeerrrstt
restarter
aeerrrstu
serrature
treasurer
aeerrrstv
traverser
aeerrttvx
extravert
aeersttwy
streetway
aeesttttu
statuette
aeffghors
shroffage
aeffgiinr
giraffine
aeffiilrs
falsifier
aeffiiprr
pifferari
aeffijmor
fife-major
aeffikpst
pikestaff
aeffilluv
effluvial
aeffilort
firefloat
aeffinors
raffinose
aeffioprr
pifferaro
aeffllruy
fearfully
aefflltuy
fatefully
aefflnopt
pantoffle
aefflnruu
unfearful
aefflorsw
safflower
aeffmorst
off-stream
aeffnooss
offseason
aefforstv
overstaff
aeffppstu
puff-paste
aefghilns
angel-fish
aefghirst
gear-shift
aefghlosu
house-flag
aefghlrtu
flaughter
aefghorrt
forgather
aefgiilnr
filigrane
aefgiimnr
magnifier
aefgiirrt
gratifier
aefgillry
fragilely
aefgilnrt
faltering
aefgilort
fortilage
aefgilosu
Solifugae
aefgilruy
lay-figure
aefgimort
fogramite
aefginnru
unfearing
aefginnst
fastening
aefginntt
fattening
aefginrrt
raftering
aefginrry
rarefying
aefginrst
afterings
aefginrtu
figurante
aefgiorss
ossifrage
aefgirstt
gas-fitter
aefgisttu
fustigate
aefglllmu
flagellum
aefgllmnu
flugelman
aefglnost
flagstone
aefglortw
afterglow
aefglrtuu
fulgurate
aefgmorrr
ferrogram
aefgnoprt
front-page
aefgnorrt
frontager
aefgnortx
xenograft
aefgooppr
page-proof
aefgoopru
ague-proof
aefhhisst
sheat-fish
aefhhllls
half-shell
aefhhlltu
healthful
aefhhlotw
heath-fowl
aefhiinrs
sherifian
aefhikmst
makeshift
aefhillmr
half-miler
aefhilltt
half-title
aefhilmrt
half-timer
aefhilors
loaferish
aefhilpst
fish-plate
aefhilsst
faithless
aefhimnrs
fisherman
aefhinors
fashioner
refashion
aefhiprss
fish-spear
spearfish
aefhklmrs
shelf-mark
aefhlltuy
hatefully
aefhlnnpy
halfpenny
aefhlnssw
news-flash
aefhlortw
earthwolf
aefhlostv
love-shaft
aefhlrttu
threatful
aefhlssst
shaftless
aefhmorsu
farmhouse
aefhoorst
hare's-foot
aefiiklry
fairylike
aefiilmns
semifinal
aefiilmpr
amplifier
aefiilnnt
infantile
aefiilntv
inflative
aefiilqru
qualifier
aefiilrrt
trial-fire
aefiimnns
Fenianism
aefiinnnt
infantine
aefiinrtu
infuriate
aefiirsst
satisfier
aefikllsu
sail-fluke
aefiklnss
flakiness
aefillmns
misfallen
aefillnot
fellation
aefillnss
self-slain
aefilloot
foliolate
aefilluvz
avizefull
aefilmmor
oriflamme
aefilmntu
fulminate
aefilmors
formalise
aefilmrsw
welfarism
aefilnnuz
influenza
aefilnort
reflation
aefilnrss
frailness
aefiloprr
poriferal
aefilorrt
rotiferal
aefilortu
foliature
aefilprst
strip-leaf
aefilprsu
praiseful
aefilrrtv
river-flat
aefilrstw
welfarist
aefimmnrt
firmament
aefimnost
manifesto
aefimorss
misfeasor
aefimortv
formative
aefinnsst
faintness
aefinoprr
poriferan
aefinorss
Sanforise
aefinorsu
nefarious
aefinpsty
safety-pin
aefinsstt
fattiness
aefiorrrw
fire-arrow
aefiorrst
forestair
aefiortuv
favourite
aefirrstt
first-rate
aefklluwy
wakefully
aefklnosw
snowflake
aefkloost
sootflake
aefklorsv
slave-fork
aefklorsw
falsework
aefkmorrw
framework
aefknnrss
frankness
aefkoorst
forest-oak
aeflllnny
flannelly
aefllmnow
fellow-man
aefllnttu
flatulent
aefllorst
astrofell
forestall
aefllrtuw
well-faurt

aefllrtuy
tearfully
aefllsstu
faultless
aeflmortu
formulate
aeflmorwy
mayflower
aeflmrstu
masterful
aeflmrttu
matterful
aeflnooss
aloofness
aeflnopry
profanely
aeflnoptu
pantoufle
aeflnssuw
awfulness
aeflooprt
roof-plate
aeflooptt
footplate
aeflortww
water-flow
water-fowl
aeflorwwx
wax-flower
aeflosstu
fossulate
aeflprruy
prayerful
aeflpsttu
step-fault
aeflrsttu
flustrate
aeflrstuw
wasterful
aefmnoorw
forewoman
aefmorrst
store-farm
aefmorstt
aftermost
aefnnoort
afternoon
aefnoprrs
perforans
aefnoprrt
perforant
aefnorttu
fortunate
aefnortvw
wavefront
aefnrsstt
stern-fast
aefnrsstu
transfuse
aefoprrty
prefatory
aefopsstt
soft-paste

aefrrsttu
frustrate
aeggginru
ring-gauge
aegghiknt
knightage
aegghinrt
gathering
night-gear
aegghirtz
gigahertz
aegghoprr
ergograph
aegghopry
geography
aeggiinpu
guinea-pig
aeggimopt
maggot-pie
aegginnrv
engraving
aegginoor
gorgoneia
aegginorr
Gregorian
aegginosy
easy-going
aegginprt
pargeting
aegginrrt
regrating
aegginttz
gazetting
aegglnnor
long-range
aegglnrry
glengarry
aegglrrst
straggler
aeggmorrt
mortgager
aeggnosuy
synagogue
aeggnprss
press-gang
aeggorrss
aggressor
aeggoruvy
gyrovague
aeghhinst
sheathing
aeghhiprt
high-taper
aeghhopty
theophagy
aeghhrrtu
hearth-rug
aeghijrtu
Gujerathi
aeghiknnr
hankering
aeghiknrs
ring-shake
shrinkage

aeghillny
healingly
aeghilnox
holing-axe
aeghilnrs
ashlering
shearling
aeghilnrt
earthling
heartling
aeghilnsv
shaveling
aeghilrrt
rear-light
aeghilrty
light-year
aeghimmnr
hammering
aeghimnrs
Germanish
aeghimnrt
nightmare
aeghimnst
eightsman
aeghimorr
hierogram
aeghimott
Gothamite
aeghimppr
epiphragm
aeghimprt
tephigram
aeghinnpp
happening
aeghinops
siphonage
aeghinppu
upheaping
aeghinrrs
garnisher
aeghinrsv
haverings
aeghinrtw
nightwear
aeghinstt
tea-things
aeghiopst
hospitage
aeghippry
epigraphy
aeghiprrs
serigraph
aeghipstt
spaghetti
aeghkmory
herkogamy
aeghlmosu
laughsome
aeghlmosy
moygashel
aeghlnoru
hour-angle
aeghlnpry
nephralgy

aeghloopr
oleograph
aeghloorr
logorrhea
aeghlooty
atheology
aeghloptt
heptaglot
aeghlopxy
xylophage
aeghlortt
larghetto
aeghlrstu
slaughter
aeghmnopr
nephogram
aeghmopuy
hypogaeum
aeghmpryy
hypergamy
aeghnnpru
pergunnah
aeghnoorr
gonorrhea
aeghnoprt
pot-hanger
aeghnopty
pathogeny
aeghnostu
shogunate
aeghnprsy
pharynges
aeghnssst
ghastness
aeghoprst
grapeshot
aeghoprxy
xerophagy
aeghopssu
esophagus
aeghorrtu
ore-raught
aegiillrs
grisaille
aegiillrt
argillite
aegiillss
Gallisise
aegiillst
sigillate
aegiilmnr
regiminal
aegiilmsv
vigesimal
aegiilnps
Spigelian
aegiilnrs
realising
aegiilnrv
Vergilian
aegiilnss
signalise

aegiilntv
genitival
vigilante
aegiilnty
geniality
aegiilrtt
tiger-tail
aegiilstv
vestigial
aegiimmrt
immigrate
aegiimnnx
examining
aegiinnrt
retaining
aegiinnst
sin-eating
aegiinort
originate
aegiinosv
voisinage
aegiinott
goniatite
aegiinrst
granitise
aegiinrtt
granitite
aegiinrtw
waitering
aegiinstt
instigate
aegiinttu
tinguaite
aegiirstt
Stagirite
aegiisstv
visagiste
aegijnors
jargonise
aegikkmnr
king-maker
aegikllss
glasslike
aegiklnpp
king-apple
aegikmmrs
skrimmage
aegikmnrt
marketing
aegiknnrs
ring-snake
aegiknqsu
squeaking
aegiknrst
streaking
aegiknssw
gawkiness
aegillly
illegally
aegilllnu
gallinule
aegillmnt
metalling

aegillnnp
panelling
aegillnos
lignaloes
aegillnpr
Pellagrin
aegillnps
langspiel
aegillnqu
equalling
aegillnrs
signaller
aegillnrv
ravelling
aegillntu
lingulate
aegillppu
pupillage
aegillprs
aspergill
aegillrru
guerrilla
aegillrss
salesgirl
aegillrvy
villagery
aegilmnnt
alignment
lamenting
aegilmnny
meaningly
aegilmnpt
pigmental
aegilmnry
malingery
aegilmntu
glutamine
aegilmorr
rigmarole
aegilmors
glamorise
aegilnnoo
neologian
aegilnors
seignoral
aegilnoru
neuroglia
aegilnory
legionary
aegilnoss
sloganise
aegilnprs
relapsing
aegilnqsu
squealing
aegilnrsv
slavering
aegilnrsy
syringeal
aegilnrtu
granulite
traguline
aegilnsst
eastlings
aegilnssw
wine-glass
aegilnsty
teasingly
aegiloops
apologise
aegilooty
aetiology
aegilorst
goslarite
aegilorsu
glaireous
aegilortu
trialogue
aegilpprr
paper-girl
aegilpptu
plague-pit
aegilprss
pier-glass
aegilprtv
gravel-pit
aegilprty
pterygial
aegilrrru
irregular
aegilrsuv
vulgarise
aegilrtuv
virgulate
aegimmnot
gemmation
aegimmnrs
Germanism
aegimmnru
germanium
aegimmnry
yammering
aegimmnst
magnetism
aegimmnsu
magnesium
aegimnnno
no-meaning
aegimnnnu
unmeaning
aegimnnrt
germinant
aegimnnss
manginess
aegimnnsy
gymnasien
aegimnops
panegoism
aegimnors
Orangeism
aegimnort
morganite
aegimnprt
tampering
aegimnrst
Germanist
mastering
streaming
aegimnrsu
measuring
aegimnrsw
Wagnerism
aegimnstt
agistment
magnetist
aegimosty
stegomyia
aegimrstu
sugar-mite
aegimrsty
magistery
aeginnors
reasoning
aeginnort
Argentino
aeginnorw
Norwegian
aeginnorz
organzine
aeginnoss
seasoning
aeginnprt
parenting
aeginnrss
angriness
ranginess
aeginnrst
gannister
aeginnrtt
integrant
rattening
aeginoppr
organ-pipe
pipe-organ
aeginoprt
operating
orange-tip
pignorate
aeginorrs
organiser
aeginorrv
overgrain
aeginorry
regionary
aeginorsv
sea-roving
aeginorty
iatrogeny
aeginosst
agonistes
aeginostt
gestation
aeginprst
string-pea
trapesing
aeginprsu
sugar-pine
aeginpsss
gaspiness
aeginqruv
quavering
aeginrrtu
garniture
aeginrstu
signature
aeginrstw
Wagnerist
aeginrtty
yattering
aeginrwzz
Zwanziger
aeginssst
staginess
aeginssuz
gauziness
aeginstuu
Augustine
aegiortvy
ivory-gate
aegiprsst
spagerist
aegiprtuv
purgative
aegirrrst
registrar
aegirrssw
wire-grass
aegirstty
Stagyrite
aegisttuv
gustative
aegkoprrw
parge-work
aegllnorv
governall
aegllnost
gall-stone
aegllossw
gallowses
owle-glass
aegllrruy
regularly
aegllrtuy
tegularly
aeglmmprs
germ-plasm
aeglmnooy
anemology
aeglmnorw
angle-worm
lawmonger
aeglmopry
pyelogram
aeglmrssy
lyme-grass
aeglnopry
gyroplane
aeglnorsu
granulose
aeglnostu
langouste
aeglnrrst
strangler
aeglnrsst
strangles
aeglnrsty
strangely
aeglnruvy
ungravely
aegloosuv
volageous
aegloppru
propagule
aegloprss
glass-rope
aeglorrtu
regulator
aeglortty
tetralogy
aeglprsss
graspless
aeglrsssu
sugarless
aegmmoprr
programme
aegmnnort
magnetron
aegmnoorw
woomerang
aegmnorru
neurogram
aegmnorrw
warmonger
aegmnortu
augmentor
aegmnostu
mangouste
aegmnottu
mangetout
aegmnrttu
gutter-man
aegmoosux
exogamous
aegmorruw
auger-worm
aegmorssy
gossamery
aegmorsty
gasometry
aegnnorsu
non-usager
aegnnprtu
repugnant
aegnnsstu
gauntness
aegnoossw
swan-goose
aegnorrwy
garryowen
aegnrsstu
assurgent
aegnstttu
tungstate
aegooprrt
prorogate
aegooswyz
wayzgoose
aegorrrtt
garrotter

aegorrssv
overgrass
aegorrstt
gas-retort
aegorrstu
surrogate
aegorsstu
stegosaur
aegorstty
gestatory
aegprrruy
prayer-rug
aehhillls
shillelah
aehhillop
halophile
aehhilltw
Whitehall
aehhillty
healthily
aehhilnpt
phthalein
aehhinpst
thaneship
aehhiorrs
horsehair
aehhippss
shipshape
aehhirrst
ratherish
aehhisstw
white-hass
aehhistww
whitewash
aehhklrsu
shear-hulk
aehhllmst
Stahlhelm
aehhllprs
harp-shell
aehhlntuy
unhealthy
aehhlopty
halophyte
aehhlostv
shovel-hat
aehhmoopt
homeopath
aehhmottw
wheat-moth
aehhnopty
theophany
aehhnorsw
heronshaw
aehhnrsss
harshness
aehhoppst
phosphate
aehhoptty
theopathy
aehhorstt
Ashtoreth
aehhossuw
wash-house

aehiiknrt
heartikin
aehiilmtu
humiliate
aehiilnsy
hyalinise
aehiilntx
antihelix
aehiimnst
histamine
aehiimops
hemiopsia
aehiimrst
hetairism
aehiimrty
Himyarite
aehiinopt
Ethiopian
aehiinrss
hairiness
aehiinttu
uintahite
aehiipstt
hepatitis
aehiirstt
hetairist
aehijlosu
jailhouse
aehijnnno
Johannine
aehikklms
milk-shake
aehiklmnu
humanlike
aehikmnps
phenakism
aehikmrss
shakerism
aehikmrtw
mark-white
aehiknpsv
knaveship
aehiknpsw
whip-snake
aehiknsss
shakiness
aehikqrsu
Quakerish
aehillmop
Philomela
aehillmsz
shlimazel
aehillpry
Phillyrea
aehillpty
philately
aehilltty
lethality
aehilltwy
wealthily
aehilmnop
nemophila
aehilmnps
nephalism

aehilmpss
sisal-hemp
aehilnnot
anthelion
aehilnooz
heliozoan
aehilnopp
philopena
aehilnopr
parhelion
aehilnort
lion-heart
aehilnost
hailstone
aehilnprs
planisher
aehilnpst
nephalist
aehilnqru
harlequin
aehilopps
spoil-heap
aehilopst
hospitale
aehilorst
horsetail
isotheral
aehilossw
shoalwise
aehilostt
heliostat
aehilosty
isohyetal
aehilppst
plate-ship
aehilppty
epiphytal
aehilprst
prelatish
aehilpssv
slave-ship
aehilrsty
hairstyle
aehilsttw
white-salt
aehimmrtu
Mithraeum
aehimnnot
anthemion
aehimnors
harmonise
aehimnort
Harmonite
aehimnpps
mishappen
aehimnpss
misshapen
aehimnpst
pantheism
aehimnrst
mishanter
aehimnrtu
Mathurine

aehimopxy
hypoxemia
aehimprss
seraphims
aehimpsst
steamship
aehimqssu
squeamish
aehimrtuz
rheumatiz
aehinnost
Esthonian
aehinnrtu
Hunterian
Ruthenian
aehinopst
pantihose
siphonate
aehinorss
hoariness
aehinorst
Senhorita
aehinortt
anorthite
aehinppss
happiness
aehinpptt
tappit-hen
aehinpptx
Xanthippe
aehinprss
seraphins
aehinpsss
apishness
aehinpssy
Sisyphean
aehinpstt
pantheist
aehinrrst
tarnisher
aehinrrsv
varnisher
aehinrrty
erythrina
aehinrsst
starshine
aehinssst
hastiness
aehinsssw
washiness
aehiopprry
hyperopia
aehioprrs
aphoriser
pair-horse
aehiorstt
hesitator
aehiorstu
authorise
aehiorstx
rheotaxis
aehiorttv
hortative

aehiosstt
athetosis
aehiprstt
therapist
aehirrstt
trashtrie
aehirttww
whittawer
aehjlnopp
apple-john
John-apple
aehklnsst
thankless
aehkmmopr
hammerkop
aehkmnorr
horn-maker
aehknoops
hoop-snake
aehknostw
stone-hawk
aehkorrtw
earthwork
aehlllmps
lamp-shell
aehlllmrs
shell-marl
aehllmost
homestall
aehllmrty
thermally
aehllnoop
allophone
aehlloorw
holloware
aehllprux
prehallux
aehllpssy
haplessly
aehllrsst
star-shell
aehllsssw
shawlless
aehlmnopy
palm-honey
aehlmoost
loathsome
aehlmopsu
palmhouse
aehlmopty
ampholyte
aehlmorst
malt-horse
aehlmossu
alms-house
aehlmostu
malt-house
aehlmrstu
salt-rheum
aehlnnopr
alpenhorn
aehlnnopt
panthenol

aehlnosss
shoalness
aehlnpsuy
unshapely
aehlnrtuy
unearthly
aehlnstuv
slave-hunt
aehloppsy
polyphase
aehloprst
astrophel
aehloprsy
horseplay
aehloprtu
hourplate
aehloprty
ephoralty
aehlopsuy
playhouse
aehlorsst
salt-horse
aehlortuu
outhauler
aehlprrsu
spherular
aehlrsstw
wrathless
aehmmnpuy
nymphaeum
aehmmoort
harmotome
aehmnnssu
humanness
aehmnoops
monophase
aehmnorss
shoresman
aehmnrrwy
wherryman
aehmnrstu
transhume
aehmooprs
shampooer
aehmooprt
Homoptera
aehmoorss
smasheroo
aehmopprt
top-hamper
aehmorrtw
earthworm
aehmortww
wheat-worm
aehmosstu
masthouse
aehnnoprt
Parthenon
aehnnrssu
unharness
aehnnstuw
whunstane
aehnooprr
harpooner

aehnoopsx
saxophone
aehnoorst
hoar-stone
aehnoprtu
neuropath
aehnorstt
north-east
aehnprsss
sharpness
aehnprsxy
pharynxes
aehooorrt
otorrhoea
aehooprry
pyorrhoea
aehoopstt
osteopath
aehoosstu
oast-house
aehopprvy
overhappy
aehoppssy
apophyses
aehoprssu
rasp-house
aehopsstt
post-haste
aehorsstu
authoress
aehorsttw
water-shot
aehorstvw
short-wave
aehorstvy
overhasty
aehorstwy
seaworthy
aehossttu
south-east
aehrsstuu
thesaurus
aeiiiknnp
epinikian
aeiiilrvz
vizierial
aeiiiltvx
lixiviate
aeiiimprt
primitiae
aeiiimttv
imitative
aeiiintvv
vivianite
aeiijlnuv
juvenilia
aeiikkttw
kittiwake
aeiikllns
snail-like
aeiiklnos
kaolinise
aeiiklnot
kaolinite

aeiiklnps
spike-nail
aeiiklnst
saintlike
aeiiklrst
triskelia
aeiiklrtv
larvikite
aeiikmrss
kaiserism
aeiiknpru
kauri-pine
aeiikrrst
air-strike
aeiikrstt
keratitis
aeiillmnn
millennia
aeiillmnr
Millerian
aeiillmrs
Ramillies
aeiillmrt
mitraille
aeiillnty
lineality
aeiillttt
titillate
aeiilmnnr
mainliner
aeiilmnnt
eliminant
aeiilmnps
maniplies
aeiilmnru
luminaire
aeiilmnsu
aluminise
aeiilmosv
malvoisie
aeiilmrss
serialism
aeiilmrtt
literatim
aeiilnnop
Neopilina
aeiilnnot
lineation
aeiilnnrt
triennial
aeiilnopt
epilation
polianite
aeiilnorv
Oliverian
aeiilnotv
inviolate
aeiilnprt
reptilian
aeiilnpst
platinise
aeiilnptv
plaintive

aeiilnrrt
trilinear
aeiilnrst
Listerian
aeiilnrsu
uniserial
aeiilnrty
linearity
aeiilnstw
waistline
aeiilnsvy
Sylviinae
aeiilntvy
veniality
aeiilorst
solitaire
aeiilortv
variolite
aeiilossz
assoilzie
aeiilostv
isolative
aeiilotvv
violative
aeiilppqu
quail-pipe
aeiilrrty
irreality
aeiilrsst
serialist
aeiilrstu
ritualise
uralitise
aeiilrstv
vitaliser
aeiilrsty
seriality
aeiilssuv
visualise
aeiimnprs
mainprise
aeiimnpst
impatiens
aeiimnptt
impatient
aeiimnrtu
miniature
aeiimprrs
impresari
aeiimprss
mispraise
aeiimprsv
vampirise
aeiimpssv
impassive
aeiimrrsv
arrivisme
aeiinnopt
inopinate
aeiinnotv
evanition
aeiinnptt
in-patient

aeiinnqtu
inquinate
aeiinnrss
raininess
aeiinnrtt
itinerant
nitratine
aeiinnrtu
uraninite
aeiinnstu
insinuate
aeiinoprw
piano-wire
aeiinoptx
expiation
aeiinorst
seriation
aeiinortt
iteration
aeiinottv
evitation
novitiate
aeiinrrty
itinerary
aeiinrtuv
urinative
aeiinsttu
inusitate
aeiinstty
insatiety
aeiiprstv
privatise
aeiiprttv
partitive
aeiiprtvv
privative
aeiipssst
epistasis
aeiipsstx
epistaxis
aeiipsttt
stipitate
aeiirrstt
arteritis
aeiirrstu
retiarius
aeiirrstv
arriviste
aeiirsstw
stairwise
aeiirttvw
writative
aeiittttv
tittivate
aeiitttuv
attuitive
aeijklnsu
Seljukian
aeijmnnss
Jansenism
aeijnnsst
Jansenist
aeijnrsst
janitress

aeijnsszz
jazziness
aeikklloo
look-alike
aeikllnnp
pannikell
aeikllnpt
plant-like
aeikllpty
kallitype
aeiklmnnu
unmanlike
aeiklmnow
woman-like
aeiklmnwy
milken-way
aeiklmoss
smoke-sail
aeiklnnss
lankiness
aeiklnort
oil-tanker
aeiklnrss
larkiness
aeiklnruw
unwarlike
aeiklqsuy
squeakily
aeiklrsty
streakily
aeikmqrsu
Quakerism
aeiknnprs
spinnaker
aeiknnsss
snakiness
aeiknoost
Isokontae
aeiknpssw
pawkiness
aeiknqssu
quakiness
aeikoprst
periaktos
aeikorsst
keratosis
aeikppqsu
pipsqueak
aeikprsty
strike-pay
aeilllppu
papillule
aeilllrty
literally
aeillmmst
small-time
aeillmnry
millenary
aeillmnsy
seminally
aeillmppr
paper-mill
aeillmrtw
water-mill

aeillmssy
aimlessly
aeillmstt
metallist
aeillnnot
tenaillon
aeillnopt
pollinate
aeillnorw
Orwellian
aeillnpry
plenarily
aeillnpst
panellist
aeillnptt
pétillant
aeillnrst
reinstall
aeillnrtu
ill-nature
tellurian
aeillnrtw
trawl-line
aeillnsty
saliently
aeillopps
papillose
aeilloppt
papillote
popliteal
aeillopst
apostille
aeillortw
towel-rail
aeillpptu
pupillate
aeillprsu
pluralise
aeillpstu
pulsatile
aeillqssu
sea-squill
aeillrrvw
river-wall
aeillrssv
rivalless
aeillrstw
stair-well
aeillrtvy
vitellary
aeillrtwy
waterlily
aeillrvxy
vexillary
aeillstty
statelily
aeilmmnps
pelmanism
aeilmmnst
mentalism
Simmental
aeilmnnps
pennalism

aeilmnnss
manliness
aeilmnoot
emotional
aeilmnopr
prolamine
aeilmnopt
emptional
aeilmnors
normalise
Orleanism
aeilmnort
lion-tamer
mentorial
aeilmnoss
loaminess
melanosis
aeilmnotu
emulation
aeilmnpsu
Asplenium
aeilmnpsy
manyplies
aeilmnptu
penultima
aeilmnrsu
semi-lunar
unrealism
aeilmnrvy
liveryman
aeilmnstt
mentalist
aeilmntty
mentality
aeilmorrs
moraliser
aeilmorst
mortalise
aeilmostu
mouse-tail
aeilmostz
zealotism
aeilmprst
prelatism
aeilmsstu
semilatus
aeilmssux
sexualism
aeilmssvy
massively
aeilmsttu
stimulate
aeilmstuu
mutualise
aeilnnnor
non-linear
aeilnnnov
novennial
aeilnnopr
nonpareil
aeilnnosv
Slovenian
aeilnnotv
anti-novel

aeilnnpss
plainness
aeilnnpsu
peninsula
aeilnnptu
pinnulate
aeilnnptw
twin-plane
aeilnnpty
pinnately
aeilnntuv
univalent
aeilnoops
polonaise
aeilnoppr
piperonal
aeilnoprt
prelation
rantipole
aeilnopst
Platonise
seal-point
aeilnoptt
potential
aeilnoptu
epulation
aeilnorss
sensorial
aeilnorst
Orleanist
aeilnorsv
versional
aeilnortt
natrolite
tentorial
aeilnortu
outlinear
aeilnosss
sessional
aeilnossv
Slavonise
aeilnprty
interplay
painterly
party-line
aeilnpstu
spinulate
aeilnpsty
sapiently
aeilnptty
patiently
aeilnptuv
pulvinate
aeilnqtuy
antiquely
aeilnrrtu
retinular
aeilnrsuv
universal
aeilnrttv
trivalent
aeilnrtuy
unreality

aeilnrtvy
vernality
aeilnssst
saltiness
slatiness
stainless
aeilnsstt
taintless
aeilnsstw
slantwise
aeilnstuy
sinuately
aeilnstvy
sylvanite
aeilnsuux
unisexual
aeilntuvw
wine-vault
aeiloostt
ostiolate
aeiloprrs
polariser
aeiloprst
saprolite
aeiloprtt
portatile
aeiloprtv
prolative
aeiloptyz
zelotypia
aeiloqruu
Euraquilo
aeilorrtt
literator
aeilorsst
tailoress
aeilorstt
totaliser
aeilorttx
textorial
aeilossst
sassolite
aeilpprst
periplast
aeilpprtu
preputial
aeilpqrsu
pasquiler
aeilprstt
prelatist
aeilprtvy
privately
aeilpssvy
passively
aeilpsttu
stipulate
aeilpstuv
pulsative
aeilqrruy
reliquary
aeilrrtww
law-writer
aeilrssty
slaistery

aeilrsttu
literatus
aeilrtttw
latter-wit
aeilrtuux
luxuriate
aeilssstv
vistaless
aeilsstux
sexualist
aeilssuvy
suasively
aeilstuxy
sexuality
aeimmmnot
mammonite
aeimmnnno
Memnonian
aeimmnnoo
monoamine
aeimmnnrs
mannerism
aeimmnntu
minuteman
aeimmnopt
pantomime
aeimmrssu
summarise
aeimmstuv
summative
aeimnnnoo
neonomian
aeimnnnqu
mannequin
aeimnnopu
pneumonia
aeimnnosz
neo-Nazism
aeimnnott
mentation
aeimnnpty
inpayment
aeimnnrst
mannerist
aeimnoprt
protamine
aeimnorrs
romaniser
rosmarine
aeimnorst
matronise
aeimnorsw
womaniser
aeimnortv
normative
aeimnortw
tire-woman
aeimnossx
Semi-Saxon
aeimnprst
spearmint
aeimnrrst
ranterism
aeimnrstt
stream-tin
aeimnrstu
antiserum
misaunter
aeimnrstx
Axminster
aeimnrtty
maternity
aeimnssss
massiness
aeimoprrt
imperator
aeimoprtx
proximate
aeimopstt
optimates
aeimorrsv
Averroism
aeimorstt
estimator
aeimorttu
autotimer
aeimpprsu
pauperism
aeimprrtt
part-timer
aeimprstu
septarium
aeimprtuz
trapezium
aeimqstuu
quaesitum
aeimqsuux
Esquimaux
aeimrrrtu
terrarium
aeimrrsty
martyrise
aeimrrtty
termitary
aeimssttu
mussitate
aeinnnotw
Newtonian
aeinnnptu
Neptunian
aeinnopsx
expansion
aeinnorst
Nestorian
rain-stone
Rosinante
aeinnortu
neuration
aeinnortv
nervation
vernation
aeinnortz
Rozinante
aeinnosst
sensation
aeinnostw
wantonise
aeinnottt
attention
tentation
aeinnppss
nappiness
aeinnpsst
inaptness
aeinnrrtu
Turnerian
aeinnrstt
instanter
transient
aeinnrstu
saturnine
aeinnrsty
tyrannise
aeinnssst
nastiness
aeinnsstt
nattiness
aeinnsstw
tawniness
aeinooprt
operation
aeinoopsu
ionopause
aeinoortx
exoration
aeinopppr
Popperian
aeinopprt
reappoint
aeinoprss
aspersion
aeinoprst
patronise
aeinoprsv
pervasion
aeinoprsy
Aepyornis
aeinoprtt
reptation
aeinoprtu
epuration
aeinoprtv
overpaint
aeinopsss
soapiness
aeinopstt
septation
aeinoqrtu
ortanique
aeinorrst
serration
aeinorrtv
overtrain
aeinorsst
assertion
aeinorssu
arsenious
aeinorstt
stationer
aeinorstv
overstain
aeinosttt
testation
aeinppsss
sappiness
aeinprrst
transpire
aeinprsst
paintress
aeinprtty
paternity
aeinprtwy
wine-party
aeinpssst
pastiness
aeinrrsst
tarriness
aeinrrstt
inter-arts
restraint
aeinrrttv
travertin
aeinrsstt
resistant
aeinrsstu
sustainer
aeinssttt
tattiness
aeioorrst
oratories
aeioprrss
aspersoir
aeioprrsv
vaporiser
aeioprttv
portative
aeioprtxy
expiatory
aeioqttuv
quotative
aeiorrstv
Averroist
aeiortuvv
uvarovite
aeiossstt
steatosis
aeiostuvx
vexatious
aeipprstu
peripatus
aeiprrsst
spiraster
aeiprrstu
rapturise
aeiprrtvy
Varityper®
aeiprsstu
prussiate
aeiprsttu
petaurist
aeiprstuz
trapezius
aeiprstwy
pit-sawyer
aeipssttv
tipstaves
aeiqrrttu
triquetra
aeiqrrtuu
quaeritur
aeiqrsstu
sea-squirt
aeiqrttuz
quartzite
aeirrsssy
sisserary
aeirrsstt
traitress
aeirrsttu
striature
aeirrtttu
triturate
aeirssttu
tessitura
aeirstttx
testatrix
aeirsttuy
austerity
aejkmnory
monkey-jar
aejllosuy
jealously
aejllrsty
star-jelly
aejlnosuu
unjealous
aejmprtuw
water-jump
aejoprssu
jasperous
aejopstux
juxtapose
aekklosty
yoke-stalk
aekllssst
stalkless
aeklmoort
toolmaker
aeklmortw
metal-work
aeklprsss
sparkless
aekmmnoss
monk's-seam
aekmnooqu
moonquake
aekmnoorr
moonraker
aekmnoprs
pranksome
aekmnopss
spokesman
aekmnorsy
sokemanry
aekmprrss
press-mark
aeknoorst
snakeroot

aeknprrst
prankster
aeknrssst
starkness
aekoopsst
soopstake
aekoorrst
stroke-oar
aekorrtww
water-work
aekorrwwx
waxworker
aelllmosu
malleolus
aellloprr
lap-roller
aelllppsy
play-spell
aelllptuu
pullulate
aelllrstu
stellular
aelllsswy
lawlessly
aellmnott
allotment
aellmnruy
numerally
aellmnsss
smallness
aellmopry
permalloy
aellmprst
smell-trap
aellmptuu
plumulate
aellmqssu
qualmless
aellnoort
lanterloo
aellnoprt
plant-lore
aellnostw
stonewall
aellnottt
attollent
aellnpsst
plantless
aellnquuy
unequally
aellnrtuy
neutrally
aellnrtvy
ventrally
aellnssuy
sensually
aelloorprt
allotrope
aelloprrt
patroller
aelloprry
preorally
aelloprtw
pot-waller

aelloprty
prolately
aelloptuv
pole-vault
aellorrst
rostellar
aellorsww
swallower
aellosuyz
zealously
aellrssty
artlessly
aellttuxy
textually
aelmmoops
amplosome
aelmmorst
maelstrom
aelmmosuu
mausoleum
aelmmrsty
symmetral
aelmnnntu
annulment
aelmnnoop
monoplane
aelmnoopr
lampooner
aelmnoort
monolater
aelmnoppy
empanoply
aelmnoptu
pulmonate
aelmnorst
marlstone
aelmnortt
tremolant
aelmnorww
lawn-mower
aelmnostu
alum-stone
aelmnosty
salt-money
aelmnottu
outmantle
aelmnpstu
psalm-tune
aelmnrstu
menstrual
aelmnrttu
tremulant
aelmooprt
plate-room
aelmrtwxy
myrtle-wax
aelnnptwy
twalpenny
aelnoprsy
layperson
aelnorstu
Solutrean
aelnortvw
navelwort

aelnosuuz
unzealous
aelnotuvv
vol-au-vent
aelnrrssu
ruralness
aelnrruvy
vulnerary
aelnrsttu
resultant
aelnssstu
sultaness
aelnsssuu
usualness
aelooprsx
exosporal
aelooprtw
water-polo
aelooprvy
parleyvoo
aeloorrtt
tolerator
aeloorrvw
love-arrow
aeloppstu
soup-plate
aeloprrtw
pearl-wort
aeloprrty
proletary
pyrolater
aeloprstu
sporulate
aeloprtwy
polywater
aelopsttu
postulate
aelorrstw
laserwort
aelorttuv
outtravel
aelppppru
paper-pulp
aelpprruu
purpureal
aelprssst
psaltress
strapless
aelprsstu
pertussal
supersalt
aelpsttuu
pustulate
aelqrrtuy
quarterly
aelrssstw
strawless
aemmnnoty
momentany
aemmnorrw
marrow-men
aemmnorty
momentary

aemmnrstu
sarmentum
aemmorssy
massymore
aemmrstyy
asymmetry
aemnnorst
semantron
aemnnortt
remontant
aemnnosww
newswoman
aemnooprt
protonema
aemnoopst
spoonmeat
aemnoortt
Nototrema
aemnoortx
taxonomer
aemnopstt
stamp-note
aemnorrtu
numerator
aemnorstv
transmove
aemnorsty
monastery
aemnpprsy
panspermy
aemnprtuy
prytaneum
aemnrssst
smartness
aemnrsttu
transmute
aemnrstvy
vestryman
aemooorrt
aeromotor
aemoorstt
stateroom
aemoprrty
temporary
aemoprstt
steam-port
aemoprstu
mouse-trap
aemopstty
asymptote
aemorsttw
two-master
aempprtuw
pump-water
water-pump
aemprrstu
supermart
aemprssty
spymaster
aemqrrtuy
marquetry
aemrrsstu
surmaster

aemrssttw
straw-stem
aennorrst
resnatron
aennorsty
sonnetary
aennpsstu
unaptness
aennrssty
tyranness
aenoopsst
soapstone
aenoorrst
resonator
aenoorrtv
renovator
aenoprrtw
part-owner
aenoprsst
patroness
transpose
aenoprsuv
supernova
aenorrtww
water-worn
aenorsstt
star-stone
aenorstww
snow-water
aenppprsu
snapper-up
aenqssstu
squatness
aenrrstvy
servantry
aenrssstw
swartness
aenrssttv
transvest
aeoopprrt
porporate
aeooprstz
rose-topaz
aeooprttv
vaporetto
aeoorrssw
sea-sorrow
aeoorrstv
overroast
aeoorttuu
autoroute
aeopqrrtu
parroquet
aeoprrrty
portrayer
aeoprrssy
aspersory
aeoprrstt
prostrate
aeoprrstu
pterosaur
aeoprrstw
spearwort
straw-rope

aeoprstty
poetastry
aeoprstwy
top-sawyer
aeoqrrssu
squarrose
aeoqrstuz
quartzose
aeoqrtttu
quartetto
aeorrssty
assertory
aeorsstuu
trousseau
aepprstuu
suppurate
aepqrrtuy
parquetry
aeprrsstu
superstar
aerrssvyy
arsy-versy
aerrsttwy
stewartry
affffinny
niff-naffy
affgiirst
sgraffiti
affgiknot
taking-off
affgiorst
sgraffito
affhhilst
half-shift
affhilrsy
raffishly
affhipstw
whipstaff
affiilnpt
plaintiff
affillnty
flay-flint
affilnoux
affluxion
affilnruy
ruffianly
affimmnnu
muffin-man
affipsstt
tipstaffs
afflootttu
footfault
affmoorst
staffroom
afggginot
faggoting
afggiintu
fatiguing
afggilnos
fog-signal
afghhillt
half-light
afghhirst
fish-garth
afghillnt
nightfall
afghinosu
fish-guano
afghiprtw
whip-graft
afghmoort
homograft
afghnrtuu
unfraught
afghorstu
far-sought
afgiiilnr
filigrain
afgiilnnu
unfailing
afgiilnsy
salifying
afgiilrty
fragility
afgiimnrs
misfaring
afgiimnry
ramifying
afgiimstu
fastigium
afgiinrry
fairy-ring
afgiinrty
ratifying
afgiknors
forsaking
afgillmny
flamingly
afgillnry
flaringly
afgillnst
flatlings
afgillnuy
gainfully
afgillopt
pilot-flag
afgilmnos
flamingos
afgilmnoy
foamingly
afgilnntu
flaunting
afgilnnuu
ungainful
afgilnnwy
fawningly
afgilrstu
frugalist
afgilrtuy
frugality
afgimnoru
anguiform
afgimortu
fumigator
afgimorty
fogramity
afginnpry
frying-pan
afginoort
frigatoon
afgiosttt
fagottist
afglnrtuu
fulgurant
afgnooorw
wagon-roof
afgnrsuuy
ray-fungus
afgorssst
soft-grass
afhhlrttu
half-truth
afhiiknop
Kniphofia
afhiilnss
snail-fish
afhiilprs
April-fish
afhilrstw
trawl-fish
afhimnosw
fish-woman
afhiorrsz
razor-fish
afhiorsty
forsythia
afhirsttu
Tartufish
afhllmruy
harmfully
afhllorst
shortfall
afhlmnruu
unharmful
afhlooppy
fool-happy
afhoorrst
hoar-frost
afhoosstt
soothfast
afiiilnot
filiation
afiilnnot
inflation
afiilnoot
foliation
afiimnrry
infirmary
afiinnost
saintfoin
afiinorsu
infusoria
afiiorrtu
fioritura
afijkorst
forjaskit
afikllmot
milk-float
afiklorty
forky-tail
afillnoux
fluxional
afillnptu
plaintful
afillnpuy
painfully
afillrtuw
wall-fruit
afilmmors
formalism
afilmnntu
fulminant
afilmoprs
salpiform
afilmorrv
larviform
afilmorst
formalist
afilmorty
formality
afilnnpuu
unpainful
afilnoott
flotation
afilnorst
frost-nail
afilnquuy
unqualify
afiloorss
fossorial
afimmmmor
mammiform
afimnnort
informant
afimnoort
formation
afimorrtu
tauriform
afimrsttu
Tartufism
afinooprr
rainproof
afinoprty
profanity
afioorstt
stairfoot
afiosttuu
fatuitous
afkloostt
footstalk
afkmooprr
proof-mark
afknnorrt
front-rank
aflllpuyy
playfully
afllmnosy
salmon-fly
afllmnouy
moanfully
afllmoort
malt-floor
aflloostt
foot-stall
aflmnorsy
salmon-fry
aflmorruy
formulary
afloopsty
splay-foot
afloorsuv
flavorous
afloorsuy
soya-flour
afloprrsu
fluorspar
afmnorrst
transform
afmorrttu
trout-farm
afnorstwy
frontways
afooprrst
star-proof
agggillny
laggingly
aggginprs
spragging
agghhilsy
haggishly
agghilooy
hagiology
agghilswy
waggishly
agghloopr
logograph
aggiiimnn
imagining
aggiilnnt
ting-a-ling
aggiilnvw
law-giving
aggiimnst
gigantism
aggiimnty
gigmanity
aggiinnos
agonising
aggiinntv
vintaging
aggillny
gallingly
aggillnop
galloping
aggillnry
glaringly
aggilnnos
ganglions
sing-along
aggilnnps
spangling
aggilnnrw
wrangling
aggilnntw
twangling
aggilnopy
play-going
aggilnpsy
gaspingly

aggilnrty
gratingly
aggiloory
agriology
aggimmnno
gammoning
agginnoor
gorgonian
agginorrs
grosgrain
agginortt
garotting
aggmoorrt
mortgagor
aggmostyy
mystagogy
aghhiistw
waist-high
aghhikntw
night-hawk
aghhilrtu
ultra-high
aghhiltuy
haughtily
aghhinrst
thrashing
aghhloopr
holograph
aghhmoopr
homograph
aghiillnp
phialling
aghiilltt
tail-light
aghiilnrt
night-rail
aghiinnnt
tanghinin
aghiinnsv
vanishing
aghiinpst
giantship
aghiinrsv
ravishing
aghiinrtt
raintight
aghiiorsv
viragoish
aghiirrst
hairst-rig
aghiklntw
night-walk
aghilllop
gallophil
aghillmpt
lamplight
aghillnop
anglophil
aghillnry
narghilly
aghillnty
haltingly

aghilmort
algorithm
logarithm
aghilnpss
splashing
aghilnpty
plaything
aghilntuy
naughtily
aghiloopt
Lotophagi
aghilrstt
starlight
aghimnnru
unharming
aghimnrst
hamstring
aghimnrty
nightmary
aghimopry
amphigory
aghimorst
histogram
aghimostt
Gothamist
aghimsttu
mistaught
aghinnstu
unhasting
aghinnttu
unhatting
aghinorrw
harrowing
aghinortu
authoring
aghinpsuw
washing-up
aghinrrsy
garnishry
aghinrttw
thwarting
aghiprsuu
augurship
aghkmopry
kymograph
aghkoorss
grasshook
aghlloopy
haplology
aghlmnopu
ploughman
aghlmoopr
lagomorph
aghlmootu
goalmouth
aghlnooty
anthology
aghlnostu
onslaught
aghloopty
pathology
aghloppry
polygraph

aghloppyy
polyphagy
aghloprxy
xylograph
aghlorssu
hour-glass
aghmnoopr
monograph
nomograph
phonogram
aghmnoopy
monophagy
aghmnrstu
hamstrung
aghmooprt
photogram
tomograph
aghmopryy
myography
aghmorsst
grass-moth
aghnoottw
wang-tooth
aghnopssu
sphagnous
aghnprsuw
spur-whang
aghooprrt
rotograph
aghooprry
orography
aghoopryz
zoography
aghoprruy
urography
aghorstty
hygrostat
agiiilnrv
Virgilian
agiiimnst
imaginist
agiiinnns
Sinningia
agiiinnrt
Nigritian
agiiinnrv
Virginian
agiiinstv
vaginitis
agiiklmnr
grimalkin
agiikmnnp
pin-making
agiikmnst
mistaking
agiillnor
gorillian
agiillnrv
rivalling
agiillnry
railingly
agiillnuv
ingluvial

agiillnwy
wailingly
agiillrsy
sigillary
agiilmnty
malignity
agiilnnpt
pantiling
agiilnnst
saintling
agiilnnsw
wing-snail
agiilnnwz
Zwinglian
agiilnors
sailoring
signorial
agiilnort
largition
tailoring
agiilnoru
Liguorian
agiilnqsu
squailing
agiilnsss
isinglass
agiilntwy
waitingly
agiimmnrt
immigrant
agiimmsst
sigmatism
agiimnort
migration
agiimnost
sigmation
agiimnrst
maistring
agiimnsss
misassign
agiimnssy
missaying
agiimortt
mitigator
agiimrstt
trigamist
agiinnors
Signorina
agiinnrst
straining
agiinnrtt
intrigant
agiinnrty
trigynian
agiinorst
trisagion
agiinpprz
apprizing
agiinprst
traipsing
agiiorrrt
irrigator
agiiprsst
spagirist

agiirsstt
gastritis
agiirsttu
guitarist
agijlnrry
jarringly
agijnorst
jargonist
agiklmrsu
milk-sugar
agiklnosy
soakingly
agiklnott
talking-to
agiklnprs
sparkling
agiklnquy
quakingly
agiklrsss
silk-grass
agikmnnsu
unmasking
agikmnopt
topmaking
agiknqsuw
squawking
agilllnru
all-ruling
agilllnuy
lingually
agilllopy
palillogy
agillmnrs
ring-small
agillmrsu
sugar-mill
agillnnnu
annulling
agillnnpt
plantling
agillnopw
walloping
agillnott
allotting
totalling
agillnoww
wallowing
agillnqsu
squalling
agillnsty
lastingly
agilmnnoo
Mongolian
agilmnnot
lamington
agilmnops
panlogism
agilmnprt
trampling
agilmnsuy
amusingly
agilmoors
lagrimoso

agilmoory
Mariology
agilmrsuv
vulgarism
agilnnops
plainsong
agilnnoqu
Algonquin
agilnnoty
atoningly
agilnnpty
pantingly
agilnnrty
rantingly
agilnnrwy
warningly
agilnnwyy
yawningly
agilnopyy
Polygynia
agilnorry
roaringly
agilnorsy
soaringly
agilnorvy
vainglory
agilnostw
wagons-lit
agilnprsw
sprawling
agilnprsy
raspingly
sparingly
agilnprty
pratingly
agilnpryy
prayingly
agilnpsuy
pausingly
agilnrstt
startling
agilnrsty
staringly
strayling
agilntttw
twattling
agiloopst
apologist
agilopruy
uropygial
agiloqrsu
gas-liquor
agilrrtuy
garrulity
agilrtuvy
vulgarity
agimmnsuy
gymnasium
agimnnoor
marooning
agimnnooy
Monogynia
agimnnors
amornings

agimnnsuu
unamusing
agimnnsuy
synangium
agimnorst
sigmatron
agimnorsu
ignoramus
agimoossu
isogamous
agimorrty
migratory
agimorstu
trigamous
agimrsttu
Targumist
aginnorrw
narrowing
aginnprsu
unsparing
aginnruvy
unvarying
aginnstuu
Tungusian
aginnstuw
unwasting
aginnstuy
unstaying
aginoopss
poison-gas
aginoprtt
pottingar
aginoprtu
purgation
aginopruv
vapouring
aginorsty
signatory
aginosttu
gustation
aginotttu
guttation
aginpprst
strapping
trappings
aginprstu
upstaring
aginqrruy
quarrying
aginqsttu
squatting
agioprrsy
Spirogyra
agiprssty
spagyrist
agjknorru
kurrajong
agklmnooy
golomynka
agkloosty
skatology
agklorssw
glasswork

agklpprsu
spark-plug
agknorsst
knotgrass
agkoprstu
task-group
agllnoopy
polygonal
aglmoorsu
glamorous
aglmooryy
Maryology
aglmprsuu
lump-sugar
sugar-lump
sugar-plum
aglnooruy
uranology
aglnorsuu
granulous
aglnostyz
lazy-tongs
aglooprty
patrology
agloorsst
glossator
agloorsty
astrology
agloottuy
tautology
agloppruy
playgroup
agloprsst
grass-plot
aglorrssu
grossular
aglorrsuu
garrulous
aglorsstw
glasswort
agmmnoors
groomsman
agmmostuu
gummatous
agmnnorst
strongman
agmnorrst
strongarm
agmnossuy
syngamous
agmnrtuyz
zygantrum
agmnsstuy
nystagmus
agmooosuz
zoogamous
agmorrssw
worm-grass
agnnopptu
oppugnant
agnpsstuw
wasp-stung
agnrrstuy
strangury

agoprrtuy
purgatory
agorsttuy
gustatory
ahhiirrst
hair-shirt
ahhiklswy
hawkishly
ahhikorst
Tokharish
ahhillopy
halophily
ahhillwwy
whillywha
ahhilmopt
philomath
ahhilttuw
withhault
ahhiorstu
authorish
ahhmoprtu
mouth-harp
ahhmostuw
mouthwash
ahhnorrst
hartshorn
ahhnrsttu
ant-thrush
ahhoosttw
toothwash
ahiiilsst
lithiasis
ahiillost
sialolith
ahiilmntu
humiliant
ahiiloopz
zoophilia
ahiilorsu
hilarious
ahiilosst
halitosis
ahiilprsv
rivalship
ahiilrstt
shirt-tail
ahiimmrst
Mithraism
ahiimrstt
Mithraist
ahiinoppr
Hipparion
ahiinorst
historian
ahiinpsst
saintship
ahiipprty
hippiatry
ahiiprssz
sizarship
ahiirrstt
arthritis
ahijmoprs
majorship

ahikknntt
think-tank
ahikknost
kink-hoast
ahikknrss
sharkskin
ahiklmswy
mawkishly
ahiklnsvy
knavishly
ahiklossv
Slovakish
ahillnrtt
thrillant
ahilloprt
prothalli
ahillopsv
Slavophil
ahillossw
sallowish
ahillostw
tallowish
ahillpssy
splashily
ahillpstw
whipstall
ahillssty
saltishly
ahillssvy
slavishly
ahilmnnuy
inhumanly
ahilmoprs
rhopalism
ahilmopsy
syphiloma
ahilmorst
hail-storm
ahilmprtu
triumphal
ahilmrsty
lathyrism
ahilnopty
notaphily
ahilnppuy
unhappily
ahilortty
throatily
ahilosttt
statolith
ahilpsswy
waspishly
ahilqssuy
squashily
ahilrsstt
startlish
ahimmmnos
mammonish
ahimmnoru
harmonium
ahimmoprs
amorphism
ahimnnory
inharmony

ahimnoosu
homousian
ahimnoprs
orphanism
ahimnorst
harmonist
ahimnrtuu
anthurium
ahimoostx
homotaxis
ahimoprsy
mayorship
ahimopsty
opsimathy
ahimopsux
amphioxus
ahimorrsw
marrowish
ahimorstu
authorism
ahinnoopt
phonation
ahinnopty
antiphony
Typhonian
ahinnottu
Huttonian
ahinooprr
orpharion
ahinoortt
hortation
ahinoprss
parsonish
ahinprsst
transship
ahiooppst
photopsia
ahioorstx
orthoaxis
ahiopprry
porphyria
ahioppssy
apophysis
ahioprstu
outparish
ahioprsuv
vapourish
ahioprsux
Xiphosura
ahiopstxy
hypotaxis
ahiorrsst
arthrosis
ahiorrtwy
airworthy
ahiorttuy
authority
ahjnnorwy
Johnny-raw
ahjopsswy
phossy-jaw
ahkloostu
akoluthos

ahkorssww
swashwork
ahllloswy
shallowly
ahllmoopr
allomorph
ahllopsty
tallyshop
ahllopsuy
aphyllous
ahlmnoswy
showmanly
ahlmooopr
homopolar
ahlmoopsy
homoplasy
ahlmoopty
homotypal
ahlmoptyy
polymathy
ahlorsttw
stalworth
ahlorstuw
twalhours
ahmmnottu
mutton-ham
ahmnoopsw
shopwoman
ahmooprsu
amorphous
ahmorrstw
marshwort
ahnnnooty
hootnanny
ahnooprty
phonatory
ahnooptuy
autophony
ahnopstyy
hyponasty
ahnorrtty
thyratron
ahooprrtx
prothorax
ahooprttu
autotroph
ahoorrstw
arrow-shot
ahoorrtty
hortatory
ahoortwwx
thorow-wax
ahprssttu
push-start
aiiillnty
initially
aiiilmmss
Ismailism
aiiilmnst
laminitis
aiiilmprt
primitial
aiiimnnot
miniation

aiiimnott
imitation
aiiimprst
primitias
aiiinnnot
inanition
aiiinnsty
asininity
aiiinorst
irisation
aiiinortt
initiator
aiiinottv
vitiation
aiijlotvy
joviality
aiikmrstx
maxi-skirt
aiillmrsy
similarly
aiillprrs
spirillar
aiillprst
pillarist
aiillrtvy
trivially
aiilmmnuu
aluminium
aiilmnnot
Miltonian
aiilmnort
trinomial
aiilmnpsu
Paulinism
aiilmnrty
matriliny
aiilmnsst
Stalinism
aiilmosst
altissimo
aiilmprry
primarily
aiilmprty
primality
aiilmrstu
ritualism
aiilnoost
isolation
aiilnootv
violation
aiilnoqtu
liquation
aiilnorsv
livraison
aiilnostt
siltation
aiilnottu
tuitional
aiilnprst
air-splint
aiilnpstu
Paulinist
aiilnrsst
sinistral

aiilprsst
spritsail
aiilprstu
spiritual
aiilprsty
spirality
aiilrsttu
ritualist
aiilsstuv
visualist
aiilstuvy
visuality
aiimmprsv
vampirism
aiimnnors
Rosminian
aiimnntuy
unanimity
aiimnoprs
prosimian
aiimnopss
impassion
aiimnosty
animosity
aiimnpstt
timpanist
aiimnrssy
Syrianism
aiimoprrs
apriorism
aiimpsssv
passivism
aiimrstuu
Mauritius
aiinnortt
nitration
aiinnortu
ruination
urination
aiinnostu
sinuation
aiinnottx
antitoxin
aiinnprrt
rain-print
aiinnqquu
quinquina
aiinooqru
Iroquoian
aiinoprst
spiration
aiinoprtt
partition
aiinoprtv
privation
aiinorstt
striation
aiinorsvy
visionary
aiinorttt
attrition
titration
aiinosttu
situation

aiinotttu
attuition
aiinqttuy
antiquity
aiinrtuvv
Vitruvian
aiioprrst
apriorist
aiioprrty
apriority
aiioprsss
psoriasis
aiioprstt
parotitis
topiarist
aiioprtvy
oviparity
aiiorrrtt
irritator
aiiorsttv
visitator
aiiprttuy
pituitary
aiipssstv
passivist
aiipsstvy
passivity
aikklnors
Raskolnik
aiklllmuw
waulk-mill
aikllmmor
milk-molar
aiklmnrtu
trunk-mail
aiklnoprw
plainwork
aiklnossy
ankylosis
aiklnostt
klinostat
aiklrruvy
Valkyriur
aikmnnosw
kinswoman
aikmorssv
visor-mask
aiknnoost
isokontan
aiknooops
poison-oak
aiknprstt
stink-trap
aikorrstw
stair-work
ailllmtuw
multi-wall
ailllpruv
pulvillar
aillmmory
immorally
aillmmpst
stamp-mill

aillmnnoy
nominally
aillmnouv
voluminal
aillmoops
liposomal
aillmprsu
pluralism
aillnorst
tonsillar
aillnorsu
lunisolar
aillnossw
snail-slow
aillnosuv
villanous
aillnotuu
ululation
aillnrsuy
insularly
ailloppsu
papillous
ailloptvy
pivotally
aillppruy
pupillary
aillprstu
pluralist
aillprtuy
plurality
aillrttuy
titularly
aillrtuvy
virtually
ailmmoort
immolator
ailmmrsuy
summarily
ailmmstuu
mutualism
ailmmttuu
ultimatum
ailmnooss
Molossian
ailmnoprt
trampolin
ailmnopss
spoilsman
ailmnopst
Platonism
ailmnorty
normality
trionymal
ailmnosuu
aluminous
ailmnsttu
stimulant
ailmoorrt
rail-motor
ailmoprvy
ivory-palm
ailmopssy
symposial
ailmorsst
storm-sail
ailmorstu
simulator
ailmorttu
mutilator
ailmortty
mortality
ailmossty
atmolysis
ailmprsty
palmistry
ailmttuuy
mutuality
ailnnoptu
Plutonian
ailnnossw
sons-in-law
ailnnsttu
insultant
ailnnstty
instantly
ailnnstuy
unsaintly
ailnooprt
prolation
ailnoorst
tonsorial
torsional
ailnoosst
saloonist
ailnoostv
solvation
ailnootuv
ovulation
ailnopstt
Platonist
ailnopstu
platinous
pulsation
ailnoqrtu
tan-liquor
ailnorstu
insulator
Solutrian
ailnosuxy
anxiously
ailnppstu
suppliant
ailnpqtuy
piquantly
ailnrtuux
luxuriant
ailooprst
spoliator
ailoopttu
autopilot
ailoorsss
rosa-solis
ailoorsuv
variolous
ailorrtty
traitorly
ailorsuvy
savourily
variously
ailosstuy
autolysis
ailprrssu
surprisal
ailprstuy
stipulary
ailqrstuy
squiralty
aimmmmnos
mammonism
aimmmnost
mammonist
aimmnnoot
motion-man
aimmnnost
Montanism
aimmnorty
matrimony
aimmnostu
summation
aimmprsuu
marsupium
aimmrsstu
summarist
aimnnoort
nominator
aimnnopst
pointsman
aimnnorsy
mansionry
aimnnostt
Montanist
aimnnosuu
unanimous
aimnnotyy
anonymity
aimnoprsy
parsimony
aimnoprtt
important
aimnoprty
patrimony
aimnorrst
rainstorm
aimnorrtu
ruminator
aimnorttw
taint-worm
aimnpstty
tympanist
aimnrsstu
saturnism
aimoorsty
amorosity
aimopsstu
potassium
aimpssstu
assumpsit
aimqrstuu
Utraquism
ainnnnotu
nunnation
ainnnostu
unisonant
ainnoootz
ozonation
ainnooprs
sopranino
ainnooprt
pronation
ainnoortt
intonator
ainnoortv
innovator
ainnoprsv
prison-van
ainnosuux
unanxious
ainnottww
witwanton
ainoopprt
appointor
apportion
ainooprrt
proration
troparion
ainooprst
rat-poison
ainoopttu
autopoint
ainooqttu
quotation
ainoorstt
sortation
ainoottux
autotoxin
ainoprsst
sopranist
ainoprstu
Proustian
supinator
ainoprsuu
uniparous
ainorsttu
outstrain
ainorstuu
souari-nut
ainpsstuu
puissaunt
ainrssttu
saturnist
ainrstttu
anti-trust
aiooppttt
potato-pit
aiooprsuv
apivorous
oviparous
aioostttt
tattooist
aiorrsstu
sartorius
aiorrstuv
rotavirus
aiprrsttu
rapturist
aiqrsttuu
Utraquist
ajmnoruwy
jurywoman
ajmprsttu
jump-start
ajprrtuyy
party-jury
akkllnpsu
knapskull
akllmmowy
mollymawk
aklmnorwy
workmanly
aklmnpstu
musk-plant
aklorsstw
salt-works
akmnoorww
work-woman
akmorrswy
marrowsky
aknooprry
prokaryon
akooprrty
prokaryot
akooprssw
soapworks
akoprrstw
strap-work
allnoopty
polytonal
allnoopyz
polyzonal
allnopttu
pollutant
allnoruyy
unroyally
allnsuuuy
unusually
alloprty
allotropy
alloppruy
popularly
alloprsty
sallyport
allrstuuy
suturally
almmnruuy
nummulary
almmnssuu
Mussulman
almnnooos
monsoonal
almnnouwy
unwomanly
almnoopty
toponymal
almnoorty
monolatry
almnopruy
pulmonary

almnopsst
moss-plant
almoorsuy
amorously
almopstyy
polymasty
alnnopstw
snow-plant
alnooprt
portolano
alnoopsst
salt-spoon
alnoppruu
unpopular
alnoprrsu
sun-parlor
alnopsttu
postulant
alnortuvy
voluntary
alnpsttuu
pustulant
aloorrtw
owl-parrot
aloorrtuv
pot-valour
aloopryyz
polyzoary
aloopstyz
zooplasty
alopprssu
prolapsus
aloprrsuy
spur-royal
aloprrtyy
pyrolatry
aloprstuy
pulsatory
amnnoosuy
anonymous
amnoooprt
Monotropa
amnoopstw
post-woman
woman-post
amnoorsty
astronomy
amnoprsst
sportsman
amnorsstt
snort-mast
amnprsttu
transumpt
amooorstv
vasomotor
amorrstww
straw-worm
amorssttу
storm-stay
amprstuuy
sumptuary
annooprsu
nonparous

annorstuy
tyrannous
annrrttuu
nurturant
anoooprtz
protozoan
anoopsswy
spoonways
anoprrstt
transport
anorsuuvy
unsavoury
anrrsstuu
susurrant
aoooprttt
potato-rot
aooorrrtw
arrowroot
aooorrttv
rotovator
aoprrsttw
strapwort
aoprrstuu
rapturous
aorstttuy
statutory
bbbckoosy
bobbysock
bbbdeelru
blubbered
bbbeeelmu
bumble-bee
bbbeeeluz
Beelzebub
bbbeelors
beslobber
bbbeelrsu
beslubber
bbbeglmuu
bubble-gum
bbbehjoor
hobjobber
bbbeinnot
bobbin-net
bbcchklou
chubb-lock
bbcdirrsu
scrub-bird
bbcehkmot
bomb-ketch
bbcehlouy
cubby-hole
bbcehorry
bob-cherry
cherry-bob
bbceilrrs
scribbler
bbceirssu
subscribe
bbcginrsu
scrubbing
bbciiilms
biblicism

bbciiilst
biblicist
bbckklooo
block-book
bbddejoor
odd-jobber
bbddiloor
blood-bird
bbdeehmtu
bethumbed
bbdeelmtu
betumbled
bbdegimno
demobbing
bbdehmopt
depth-bomb
bbdeimrru
umber-bird
bbdeiorrw
bower-bird
bbdelmmou
Bumbledom
bbdnooruw
brow-bound
bbdnostuu
bundobust
bbeeeeinr
bebeerine
bbeeegglr
beglerbeg
bbeeehlmu
humble-bee
bbeeeinrr
berberine
bbeefhort
beef-broth
bbeeflluy
bully-beef
bbeehinrs
nebbisher
bbeeillno
bellibone
bbeeirrsu
rubberise
bbeelrruy
blueberry
bbeflorry
robber-fly
bbeggnoow
wobbegong
bbeghiirs
gibberish
bbeghilos
bobsleigh
bbeglmtuu
tumble-bug
bbegorttu
bog-butter
bbehllmos
bombshell
bbehlnooy
honey-blob
bbehlossy
hobbyless

bbehrrsuy
shrubbery
bbeillnno
bonnibell
bbeinnoss
nobbiness
bbeinsstu
tubbiness
bbejnortu
nutjobber
bbekmmoos
smoke-bomb
bbeorttux
butter-box
bberrttuu
butterbur
bbfgiilnr
fribbling
bbfhiilrs
fribblish
bbfmooopr
bombproof
bbggijmou
jiggumbob
bbghilnoo
hobgoblin
bbghinort
throbbing
bbgiiilmn
bilimbing
bbgiilnqu
quibbling
bbgiinqsu
squibbing
bbgiiosty
gibbosity
bbgilnosy
sobbingly
bbgilosuy
gibbously
bbhillnoo
Hobbinoll
bbhilrsuy
rubbishly
bbiiilnru
bilirubin
bbiikmtuz
kibbutzim
bbiimnors
Ribbonism
bbikmnost
stink-bomb
bcccimoox
coxcombic
bccckmoos
cockscomb
bccdklmuu
dumb-cluck
bccdkoouu
cuckoo-bud
bcceeiktu
ice-bucket
bcceeilor
coercible

bccehiilo
libecchio
bccehiknp
pinchbeck
bcceilory
coercibly
bcceinnou
concubine
bcceinors
conscribe
bcceinsuu
succubine
bccekloru
cockle-bur
bcchkoort
cock-broth
bcciilsty
bicyclist
bcciklloy
billycock
bcciknoor
cock-robin
bcciorstu
scorbutic
bccmoorxy
coxcombry
bccmorruy
curry-comb
bccossuuu
succubous
bcddeeilu
deducible
bcddiikry
dicky-bird
bcdeeeehs
beseeched
bcdeeefin
beneficed
bcdeeeino
obedience
bcdeehiir
herbicide
bcdeehoow
beech-wood
bcdeeiirv
verbicide
bcdeeilru
reducible
bcdeeinot
Cobdenite
bcdeeirrs
describer
bcdeejstu
subjected
bcdeellor
corbelled
bcdeelost
bed-closet
bcdeelrtu
tubercled
bcdeemntu
decumbent
bcdehlosv
boschveld

bcdeiilno
indocible
bcdeiilnu
inducible
bcdeilstu
bile-ducts
bcdeimnos
Cobdenism
bcdeimrsu
discumber
bcdeistuu
decubitus
bcdelnruu
underclub
bcdeorrss
crossbred
bcdeorruy
body-curer
bcdgiklor
gold-brick
bcdhknouu
buckhound
bcdiimmuy
cymbidium
bcdikrstu
brick-dust
bcdilmnow
climb-down
bcdimoors
scombroid
bcdklooow
woodblock
bcdknooos
boondocks
bcdknooru
rock-bound
bcdnoopru
cropbound
bcdoprtuy
by-product
bceeeehrs
beseecher
bceeeehtt
tête-bêche
bceeefhnr
beech-fern
free-bench
bceeehkno
cheek-bone
bceeeklps
bespeckle
bceeekqru
Quebecker
bceeffgou
coffee-bug
bceefilru
febricule
bceeghinr
breeching
bceegiinr
bigeneric
bceehhlno
bench-hole
bceehilos
cohesible
bceehiors
bee-orchis
bceehkoor
chokebore
bceehpruy
hypercube
bceehrttu
trebuchet
bceeiiknn
Nickie-ben
bceeiilnv
evincible
bceeijotv
objective
bceeillor
corbeille
bceeillos
bellicose
bceeillru
rubicelle
bceeilrty
celebrity
bceeimmos
misbecome
bceeimnor
recombine
bceeinoot
coenobite
bceeinrtt
centre-bit
bceeioqsu
Québecois
bceeiprrs
prescribe
bceeissuv
subsecive
bceejnort
jobcentre
bceeknorz
Zernebock
bceelnosy
obscenely
bceelooss
obsolesce
bceelrtuu
tubercule
bceemnrtu
recumbent
bceenpstu
pubescent
bceenrstu
rubescent
bceffioox
box-office
bceffiooy
office-boy
bceffiosu
suboffice
bcefiikrr
firebrick
bcefiirty
febricity
bcefijoty
objectify
bcefiorty
fibrocyte
bcefkltuu
bucketful
bcegikntu
bucketing
bcegkttuu
gutbucket
bcegloosu
goose-club
bcegrrsuw
grub-screw
bcehiiost
bioethics
bcehikrst
sick-berth
bcehimrsu
cherubims
bcehinnot
benthonic
bcehioquu
chibouque
bcehipssu
spice-bush
bcehllnpu
bell-punch
bcehlosuu
clubhouse
bcehlrtuy
butcherly
bcehmnooy
honeycomb
bceiiinot
ebionitic
bceiiirst
Briticise
bceiijstu
Jebusitic
bceiilnvy
evincibly
bceiilpsu
publicise
bceiimort
biometric
bceiinost
bisection
bceiinrrs
inscriber
bceiinssu
subincise
bceiioprt
prebiotic
bceijnoot
objection
bceiknost
steinbock
bceillmru
cribellum
bceilmnou
columbine
bceilmopt
comptible
bceilmotu
columbite
bceilnoot
bolection
bceilnoru
colubrine
bceimnnou
uncombine
bceimnntu
incumbent
bceimnoou
coenobium
bceimnory
embryonic
bceimorty
embryotic
bceinortw
twice-born
bceinosty
obscenity
bceinssuu
incubuses
bceioprrs
proscribe
bceiorsst
crossbite
bceiorstt
obstetric
bcejnstuu
unsubject
bcekoorrr
cork-borer
rock-borer
bcelmooty
lobectomy
bceloossu
lobscouse
bcelorstw
screw-bolt
bcelorsuy
obscurely
bcemmortu
combretum
bcemoorsy
corymbose
bcemottuy
tubectomy
bcenoopux
pounce-box
bcenoorrr
corn-borer
bcenoorry
corner-boy
bcenorstu
curbstone
bceorrrwy
crow-berry
bceprttuu
buttercup
bcffikstu
buff-stick
bcfhillnu
bullfinch
bcfimmory
cymbiform
bcfimoorr
cobriform
bcflorsuw
scrub-fowl
bcghilnot
blotching
bcghilntu
night-club
bcghorssu
scrog-bush
bcgiimnno
combining
bcgilmnsu
scumbling
bcgknopru
prongbuck
bcgorsssu
scrog-buss
bchhikssu
buckshish
bchiioprs
bishopric
bchiirstu
hubristic
bchiklops
block-ship
bchiloopy
lyophobic
bchinorty
Brythonic
bchknorsu
buck's-horn
bchknortu
buckthorn
bchkoottu
bucktooth
bchlnopuw
punch-bowl
bchlooosy
schoolboy
bchloortw
blowtorch
bchmooott
toothcomb
bciiimrst
Briticism
bciikklnr
brick-kiln
bciilmsuu
umbilicus
bciilpstu
publicist
bciilptuy
publicity
bciimnoos
bionomics
bciimosty
symbiotic
bciiootz
zoobiotic
bcikknost
knob-stick

bcikkorrw
brickwork
bciklnott
tint-block
bciknoqru
quick-born
bcillorss
crossbill
bcillorsw
crow's-bill
bcilmmouu
columbium
bcilmnooz
zinc-bloom
bcilmossy
symbolics
bcilmrsuu
lumbricus
bcilorsuu
lubricous
bcimnorsu
submicron
bciooprss
proboscis
bcioorstt
Octobrist
bcioprstu
subtropic
bciorstuy
obscurity
bciprsstu
subscript
bcjklooss
joss-block
bcknorrtu
burnt-cork
bcmnooorr
broom-corn
bcrssttuu
substruct
bdddeeinr
bedridden
bdddeiios
disbodied
bddeeeinz
bedizened
bddeegirs
sedge-bird
bddeegorx
dredge-box
bddeeirsu
debruised
bddeelnnu
unblended
bddeenort
betrodden
bddeenrru
underbred
bddeeoppr
bedropped
bddeeortu
redoubted
bddefilow
fiddle-bow
bddefinor
forbidden
bddefloou
blood-feud
bddeginru
unbridged
bddegloou
doodlebug
bddehinou
hide-bound
bddehloos
bloodshed
bddeiilns
blind-side
bddeiisuv
subdivide
bddeilnnu
unblinded
bddeilnru
unbridled
bddeimosy
disembody
bddeinrsu
disburden
bddeirstu
disturbed
bddelnoou
unblooded
bddelsuuy
subduedly
bddennouu
unbounded
bddenotuu
undoubted
bddensuuu
unsubdued
bddfillno
blindfold
bddfmnouu
dumbfound
bddiiorww
widow-bird
bddilnorw
word-blind
bddimnoru
mound-bird
bddinnouw
wind-bound
bddloooow
bloodwood
bddloostu
blood-dust
bddnooruw
wordbound
bddnoosuy
sound-body
bddnotuuy
duty-bound
bdeeeelrv
belvedere
bdeeeenns
benne-seed
bdeeefint
benefited
bdeeeghot
hedge-bote
bdeeehnst
sheet-bend
bdeeeinns
benni-seed
bdeeelnos
nose-bleed
bdeeelort
dor-beetle
bdeeelstt
settle-bed
bdeeemmnt
embedment
bdeeenrtu
debenture
bdeeerrry
deerberry
bdeeerstw
bestrewed
bdeeerttv
brevetted
bdeefiils
disbelief
bdeefilrt
filter-bed
bdeefiorr
fire-robed
bdeefllow
bedfellow
bdeeflorw
flower-bed
bdeefoorr
foreboder
bdeefootw
web-footed
bdeegglow
bow-legged
bdeeghill
hedgebill
bdeeghint
benedight
benighted
bdeeghnor
hedge-born
bdeegilln
debelling
bdeeginor
ridge-bone
bdeegmrsu
submerged
bdeehilps
bedelship
bdeehortt
betrothed
bdeeiiiln
indelible
bdeeiilrs
derisible
bdeeiinnz
benzidine
bdeeillrw
bridewell
bdeeilmss
dissemble
bdeeimmrs
dismember
bdeeimorr
embroider
bdeeinoss
side-bones
bdeeinrrt
interbred
bdeeinrtu
underbite
bdeeiorrr
broiderer
bdeeiprsw
spider-web
bdeeirstt
bed-sitter
bdeeknruu
unrebuked
bdeekoorw
brookweed
bdeellssy
blessedly
bdeelnouv
unbeloved
bdeelnrru
blunderer
bdeelnssu
unblessed
bdeelorst
bolstered
bdeemrssu
submersed
bdeemsttu
besmutted
bdeeopstt
bespotted
bdeeorsty
oyster-bed
bdeeorvyy
everybody
bdeeprrtu
perturbed
bdefiilrr
rifle-bird
bdefiirtu
brutified
bdefilloo
life-blood
bdefilrtu
flute-bird
bdefinory
boyfriend
bdefioorw
wood-fibre
bdeflloru
full-orbed
bdefloruw
flower-bud
bdeflostu
self-doubt
bdegghmuu
humbugged
bdeggintu
budgeting
bdeggnuuy
dune-buggy
bdeghilno
beholding
bdeghilsu
shield-bug
bdegiiilr
dirigible
bdegiilos
disoblige
bdegiimmn
bedimming
bdegikoou
guide-book
bdegilnny
bendingly
bdegimnoy
embodying
bdeginnnu
unbending
bdeginprs
spring-bed
bdegiorrx
box-girder
bdeglooor
gore-blood
bdegmmtuu
mum-budget
bdehiirsy
hybridise
bdehinory
honey-bird
bdehinrry
hindberry
bdehllosy
bodyshell
bdehlmnuu
unhumbled
bdehmnoou
homebound
bdehnrsuu
unbrushed
underbush
bdeiiilsv
divisible
bdeiiilty
edibility
bdeiillny
indelibly
bdeiilstv
devil's-bi
bdeiisssu
subsidise
bdeillnps
spellbind
bdeillnss
blindless
bdeilmpru
plume-bird
bdeilmssy
dissembly

bdeilnnss
blindness
bdeilootw
blood-wite
bdeilorsu
bird-louse
bdeiloruv
overbuild
bdeimnost
disentomb
bdeimsttu
submitted
bdeinortx
tinder-box
bdeinosst
dib-stones
bdeinrsst
bird's-nest
bdeinrssu
side-burns
bdeinrsuu
unbruised
bdeinrtuw
winter-bud
bdeinruzz
unbrizzed
bdeioorrw
brier-wood
bdeiorstu
subeditor
bdeirrstu
disturber
bdekooorr
order-book
bdekootu
booked-out
bdellmosy
symbolled
bdellnosu
bull-nosed
bdellooss
bloodless
bdelloruz
bulldozer
bdelmnpuu
unplumbed
bdelmntuu
untumbled
bdelnntuu
unblunted
bdelnootu
doubleton
bdelnossu
boundless
bdelnottu
unblotted
bdeloopru
pure-blood
bdelootuv
obvoluted
bdelouuy
double-you
bdelorstw
sword-belt
bdelosstu
doubtless
bdennoost
bondstone
bdennopuu
upbounden
bdennossu
snub-nosed
bdennottu
obtundent
bdennrsuu
sunburned
bdenooruv
overbound
bdenorsuu
burdenous
bdenostuw
westbound
bdeoooptt
top-booted
bdeooorrw
wood-borer
bdeooprwx
powder-box
bdfhiilns
blindfish
bdfhnooou
hoof-bound
bdfilortt
drift-bolt
bdfioorst
bird's-foot
bdflllou
full-blood
bdfllnouu
full-bound
bdflooru
foul-brood
bdghiinrt
night-bird
bdgiillno
ill-boding
bdgiinnnu
unbinding
bdginnoor
boning-rod
bdginortu
obtruding
bdhiimrsy
hybridism
bdhiirrty
trihybrid
bdhiirtyy
hybridity
bdhimoops
bishopdom
bdhiorsuy
hybridous
bdhkoooru
Doukhobor
bdhlooost
bloodshot
bdhoorsuw
brushwood
bdhrsstuu
dust-brush
bdiiilsvy
divisibly
bdiiinnru
indirubin
bdiiknoss
'sbodikins
bdiiknrst
stink-bird
bdiilrstt
stilt-bird
bdiimorty
morbidity
bdiinosuu
indubious
bdiiostuy
dubiosity
bdiirttuy
turbidity
bdikknrsu
skunk-bird
bdillorsw
sword-bill
bdilmnnoo
moon-blind
bdilmnorw
blindworm
bdilnnosw
snow-blind
bdilnoosu
soil-bound
bdilosuuy
dubiously
bdimorrst
storm-bird
bdinnooru
iron-bound
bdinoowww
bow-window
bdinoowwx
window-box
bdlloostu
bloodlust
bdlmooorw
blood-worm
bdlmoosuy
molybdous
bdloooort
bloodroot
bdloossuu
subdolous
bdmnoooor
doorn-boom
bdnnoosuw
snow-bound
bdnooortu
root-bound
bdnoostuu
outbounds
beeeeekpr
beekeeper
beeeehnrs
shebeener
beeeekmrw
Ember-week
beeeflorw
bee-flower
beeegikll
bilge-keel
beeegimns
beseeming
beeeglnru
blue-green
beeegnnor
green-bone
beeegnoow
woebegone
beeegnotw
go-between
beeehllor
hellebore
beeehorsu
beer-house
beeehprrt
herb-Peter
beeehrssw
Hebrewess
beeeikllr
rebel-like
beeeillot
oil-beetle
beeeilmms
emblemise
beeeilmnt
belemnite
beeeilnuv
unbelieve
beeeilrsv
eversible
beeeimmss
misbeseem
beeeimrsv
semibreve
beeeinntw
in-between
beeeinrss
beeriness
beeeistuv
sieve-tube
beeekoprx
boxkeeper
beeekrrrs
berserker
beeellstu
steel-blue
beeelmntv
bevelment
beeelmrrs
resembler
beeelmrzz
embezzler
beeelsssu
sublessee
beeemnory
beer-money
beeemnstt
besetment
beeemprst
September
beeenorst
tenebrose
beeenosss
obeseness
beeenosxz
sneeze-box
beeenrrsy
neesberry
beeffgiru
febrifuge
beeffhluw
buff-wheel
beefgiilr
Félibrige
beefglost
self-begot
beefhlouv
behoveful
beefhottt
theftbote
beefiilms
misbelief
beefilrss
briefless
fibreless
beefklruu
rebukeful
beeflnors
self-borne
beefnortu
befortune
beefoorty
freebooty
beeggiins
besieging
beeggintt
begetting
beeghiiln
Ghibeline
beeghinnt
benighten
beeghinrt
benighter
beeghirty
eyebright
beegiiill
illegible
beegiilnv
believing
beegiinot
Gibeonite
beegillnr
rebelling
beegillnv
bevelling
beegillnw
well-being
beegilnrs
inselberg
beegilnss
beingless

beegilnuu
unbeguile
beeginnss
beingness
beeginrtt
bettering
beeginrtv
breveting
beeginsst
beestings
beeginstt
besetting
beegklntu
kent-bugle
beeglnoos
Bolognese
beehiinrs
hibernise
beehiirtx
exhibiter
beehillms
embellish
beehilmpu
humble-pie
beehimrsw
Hebrewism
beehinrtt
terebinth
beehioprs
biosphere
beehiorrv
herbivore
beehipsst
sheep's-bit
beehllrsu
busheller
beehlmssu
humblesse
beehlopry
hyperbole
beehnoopx
xenophobe
beehoostu
house-bote
beehorsuw
brew-house
beeiillnz
zibelline
beeiilnnt
intenible
beeiilnrt
libertine
beeiinrty
inebriety
beeiklmru
berkelium
beeillnor
rebellion
beeillntu
ebullient
beeillort
bolletrie

beeillrtu
bulletrie
rubellite
beeilmnpu
numble-pie
beeilmpru
lumber-pie
beeilnnoz
benzoline
beeilnopx
exponible
beeilnpru
prenubile
beeilnrsu
nebuliser
beeilottu
oubliette
beeilrsst
tribeless
beeilstuv
vestibule
beeimnrst
tenebrism
beeimrrsu
reimburse
beeinnott
bentonite
beeinrrwy
wine-berry
beeinrstt
tenebrist
beeinrstu
subentire
Trubenise®
beeinrttu
butterine
beeinrtty
tenebrity
beeioqssu
obsequies
beeiosssv
obsessive
beeiqrttu
briquette
beeirrttu
retribute
beeirsssu
subseries
beejnrruy
Juneberry
beeklrrsy
berserkly
beeknorst
kerbstone
beekoprry
pokeberry
beelllmuu
umbellule
beellorrw
well-borer
beellorsu
resoluble
beellortw
bell-tower

beellrtuy
bully-tree
beelmoort
bolometer
beelmrrsu
slumberer
beelnnoss
nobleness
beelnoors
rose-noble
beelnopsu
spulebone
beelnostu
bluestone
beelorsvy
obversely
verbosely
beelorttx
letter-box
beelqrsuu
burlesque
beelrsttu
subletter
beemmnnor
non-member
beemnorst
bemonster
beennootu
boutonnée
beenoqstu
obsequent
beenorrst
resorbent
beenorsss
soberness
beenorstu
tenebrous
beenorsuu
eburneous
beenrsstu
bruteness
beeoppprx
pepper-box
beeopprsy
presbyope
beeorsttu
soubrette
beeorstty
street-boy
beeprrrtu
perturber
beeprrsty
presbyter
beerrstuv
subverter
beffgintu
buffeting
befflnssu
bluffness
befghilos
globe-fish
befgiintt
befitting

befgilnsu
fungibles
befhirrsu
brush-fire
furbisher
refurbish
befhkloos
bookshelf
befhoottt
theftboot
befiilnor
fibroline
befiilnsu
infusible
befiilort
fibrolite
befiilrty
febrility
befilntty
fly-bitten
befiorstt
frostbite
beflllopy
belly-flop
befllottu
bottleful
beflrttuy
butterfly
begggilny
beggingly
beggglook
goggle-box
begghmruu
humbugger
beggiinnn
beginning
begginoss
bogginess
beghhilst
high-blest
beghhinot
thigh-bone
beghhottu
bethought
beghiillp
phillibeg
beghillnt
night-bell
beghinort
night-robe
beghinoru
neighbour
beghlnoru
bugle-horn
beghnrtuu
bug-hunter
beghoortt
borghetto
beghorrux
Roxburghe
begiiilnt
ignitible
begiillln
libelling

begiillly
illegibly
begiillnt
billeting
begiimnrt
timbering
begiinnty
benignity
begiinsst
biestings
begiinstt
besitting
begijrttu
jitterbug
begillnow
bowelling
begillotu
globulite
begilmnrt
trembling
begilmnru
lumbering
begilmoor
embroglio
begilmory
gorblimey
begilmppu
bilge-pump
begilmrru
limburger
begilnssu
bulginess
begilrttu
litter-bug
begimnssu
embussing
beginoosu
biogenous
beginorsu
subregion
beginorsv
observing
beginostt
besotting
beginrttu
rebutting
begioorsu
bourgeois
behhllort
hell-broth
behhlmotu
thumb-hole
behhorssu
shoe-brush
behiilpst
phlebitis
behiilrtv
live-birth
behiimnoy
yohimbine
behiiortx
exhibitor
behiirrst
Britisher

behiirstt
bitterish
behiklosv
Bolshevik
behillnty
thin-belly
behilmnru
rhumb-line
behilnorw
whirl-bone
behilprsu
publisher
republish
behimmnoo
bonhommie
behinrrsu
burnisher
behinsssu
bushiness
behiopsss
bishopess
behiorrst
herborist
behiorstt
theorbist
behkmossu
smoke-bush
behllsssu
blushless
behlmsstu
thumbless
behlorrty
brotherly
behlorsst
throbless
behlorssu
blush-rose
behlrsssu
shrubless
behmoorst
thrombose
behnnrtuu
unburthen
behnoopxy
xenophoby
behnorstu
buhrstone
behoprtyy
bryophyte
beiiilnsv
invisible
beiillnsy
Sibylline
beiilmopu
epilobium
beiilmoss
omissible
beiilmrsx
ex-librism
beiilmssu
sublimise
beiilnrtt
litter-bin
beiilortt
trilobite
beiilrstx
ex-librist
beiilsstu
subtilise
beiinoovv
ovibovine
beiinrttu
tribunite
beiiorsty
ebriosity
beiiprttt
bitter-pit
beiklmoor
brooklime
beiklnott
ink-bottle
beiklnssu
bulkiness
beikmoort
motor-bike
beiknosss
boskiness
beiknrsss
briskness
beikrsttu
tube-skirt
beilllosu
libellous
beilll tuw
well-built
beillmnoy
money-bill
beillmnpu
plumb-line
beillmruy
beryllium
beillmsuy
sublimely
beillnosu
insoluble
beilloquy
obliquely
beillssss
blissless
beillstuy
subtilely
beilmmnuu
nelumbium
beilmoptt
bottle-imp
beilmossy
symbolise
beilnopss
sponsible
beilnorru
oil-burner
beilnprtu
blueprint
beilnrssu
burliness
beiloopr s
peribolos
beilooprt
pot-boiler
beiloprsu
peribolus
beilorssu
subsoiler
beilsttuy
subtilety
beimnorst
brimstone
beimnossu
omnibuses
beimnpssu
bumpiness
beimosstw
misbestow
beimrsttu
submitter
beimrttuy
ytterbium
beinnnoss
bonniness
beinnoott
obtention
beinnootv
obvention
beinooprt
obreption
beinoorsv
obversion
beinoosss
obsession
beinorsst
Britoness
beinorsuu
rubineous
beinossss
bossiness
beinottwy
bytownite
beinrssuu
subursine
beiooprru
pourboire
beioorrrt
brier-root
beioqrstu
sobriquet
beiorssst
sob-sister
beiorstuv
obtrusive
beiorstvy
verbosity
beiprsstu
Buprestis
beiprstuy
superbity
bejlnoorw
jobernowl
bekknooot
book-token
beklooosu
booklouse
bekloosty
style-book
beknnnouw
unbeknown
bekooorst
bookstore
bekooprss
press-book
bellmooss
bloomless
bellmpruu
plumb-rule
bellmpssu
plumbless
bellootwy
welly-boot
belloowyy
yellow-boy
belmmooss
emblossom
belmooorw
elbow-room
belmoorss
reblossom
belmoorty
bolometry
belmopsuu
plumbeous
belmorstt
storm-belt
belnnsstu
bluntness
belnoorvw
overblown
belnootvv
obvolvent
belnrttuu
turbulent
belootttw
two-bottle
belorsssu
sublessor
belqrsuuy
brusquely
bemmnstuu
submentum
bemnoorsu
unbosomer
bemnoostt
tombstone
bemnortuu
outnumber
bemnossux
buxomness
bemooprry
proembryo
bemrrttuu
rum-butter
bennnostu
sun-bonnet
bennorssw
brownness
benoostuu
bounteous
benorrstu
burrstone
benorrswy
snow-berry
benorsttu
obstruent
benorstxy
sentry-box
benrtttuu
butternut
nut-butter
beopprsyy
presbyopy
bffiimorr
fibriform
bfghilltu
bullfight
bfhhiorrt
frithborh
bfhirstuu
bush-fruit
bfiinorsu
fibrinous
bfilnotuu
bountiful
bfimorrsu
bursiform
bfinorrst
first-born
bflllnouw
full-blown
bfmmooorr
bromoform
bfoortuwy
four-by-two
two-by-four
bgghiilnt
blighting
bggilmnru
grumbling
bghhilnow
high-blown
bghilmntu
thumbling
bghilopru
rib-plough
bghimnrtu
thumb-ring
bghinortu
inbrought
bghinrstu
sun-bright
bghloopuy
ploughboy
bghoprtuu
upbrought
bgiiikprr
kirbigrip
bgiikprry
kirby-grip
bgiillnow
billowing
bgiilmnsu
subliming

bgiilmoor
imbroglio
bgiilnrst
bristling
bgiiloost
biologist
bgiinnnru
inburning
bgiknoprs
springbok
bgillnstu
sting-bull
bgilmnooy
myoglobin
bgilnnruy
bunny-girl
bgilnortu
troubling
bgilnortw
wring-bolt
bgilnuyzz
buzzingly
bgiloorty
tribology
bgiloosty
globosity
bginnortu
binturong
bginnpruu
upburning
bginoorrw
borrowing
bginoprsx
spring-box
bginorstw
bowstring
bglloosuu
globulous
bglmoopuy
bumpology
bglmoosyy
symbology
bgnoorstx
strong-box
bgnorstuw
bowstrung
bhhnorstu
thorn-bush
bhiiinort
inhibitor
bhiilllly
hill-billy
bhiillnot
billionth
bhiimoruz
rhizobium
bhiinrstu
un-British
bhiinrttw
twin-birth
bhikmnstu
thumbkins
bhiknoosu
unbookish

bhilllsuy
bullishly
bhilmnoty
bimonthly
bhilmoopr
ombrophil
bhiloorsy
boorishly
bhilrstuy
brutishly
bhiorrttw
birthwort
bhkmnottu
thumb-knot
bhkorrsuw
brushwork
bhllloors
loll-shrob
bhllooott
tollbooth
bhlmpsuuy
subphylum
bhmnooosu
bonhomous
bhnoorstw
snow-broth
biiilnsvy
invisibly
biillosuy
biliously
biillssty
Sibyllist
biilmstuy
sublimity
biilnoovw
violin-bow
biiloosuv
oblivious
biiloqtuy
obliquity
biilssttu
subtilist
biilsttuy
subtility
biimoprty
improbity
biimosssy
symbiosis
biissttyy
itsy-bitsy
biklnnosw
snow-blink
billnoops
spoonbill
billnorst
still-born
billnosuy
insolubly
billopstu
slop-built
bilmmossy
symbolism
bilmossty
symbolist

bilmsssuy
submissly
bilnnotuu
unbuilt-on
bilooprtu
Politburo
biloosuvy
obviously
bilorsstu
strobilus
bimnorsty
brimstony
bimopstuu
bumptious
binooosux
obnoxious
binoorsst
Sorbonist
binoorstu
obtrusion
binoosuuv
unobvious
bkllmnsuu
numbskull
bklloooruy
bully-rook
bkmooruuz
zumbooruk
bkooorsty
story-book
bllorttuu
bull-trout
blmorssuu
slumbrous
bloorstuu
troublous
blrsttuuw
blutwurst
blssstuuu
subsultus
boopprrtu
turboprop
ccccilnoy
concyclic
cccdiimou
coccidium
ccceeilst
eclectics
ccceeinrt
eccentric
ccceiilpy
epicyclic
ccceiinor
Ciceronic
ccceiloot
coccolite
cccenoort
concocter
cccginooo
gonococci
cchiinno
cinchonic
ccchiknop
pinchcock

ccchilmou
colchicum
ccchiloot
coccolith
ccciilmsy
cyclicism
ccciilnoz
zinc-colic
ccciilosy
isocyclic
ccciilrty
tricyclic
ccciiltyy
cyclicity
cccnooort
concoctor
ccddekouy
decoy-duck
ccddelnou
concluded
ccdeeehkr
checkered
ccdeeersu
succeeder
ccdeehikm
chemicked
ccdeehikw
chickweed
ccdeehknu
unchecked
ccdeehort
crocheted
ccdeeiinn
incidence
ccdeeiint
endeictic
ccdeeinny
indecency
ccdeeinot
conceited
ccdeeiotv
decoctive
ccdeellot
collected
ccdeemoor
coco-de-mer
ccdeennor
concerned
ccdeennot
connected
ccdeenors
crescendo
ccdeenort
concerted
ccdeeortu
decocture
ccdefiiru
crucified
ccdeiiknp
picnicked
ccdeiilpr
dip-circle
ccdeiloor
crocodile

ccdeiloos
scolecoid
ccdeilsty
dyslectic
ccdeinoot
decoction
ccdeinouv
conducive
ccdeinrtu
cinctured
ccdeistty
dystectic
ccdekorss
dock-cress
ccdelnotu
occludent
ccdenorru
concurred
ccdhhirsu
dischurch
ccdhiimor
dichromic
ccdhkoouw
woodchuck
ccdiilnry
cylindric
ccdiioort
corticoid
ccdkllouy
cuckoldly
ccdklmoou
cuckoldom
ccdkloruy
cuckoldry
ccdnoortu
conductor
ccdooosuw
cocus-wood
cceeeflnu
feculence
cceeehhrr
recherché
cceeehnor
coherence
cceeehrrs
screecher
cceeeiknp
neck-piece
cceeeinns
nescience
cceeeinrt
reticence
cceeellor
clerecole
cceeffopu
coffee-cup
cceefilly
life-cycle
cceeflnuy
feculency
cceeginor
concierge
cceeginot
ectogenic

cceeginty
cynegetic
cceehiknr
check-rein
cceehikoy
ice-hockey
cceehkorv
overcheck
cceehlort
cere-cloth
cceehnory
coherency
cceehottu
couchette
cceeiinns
inscience
cceeiippr
precipice
cceeikrrt
cricketer
cceeilnno
on-licence
cceeilnor
reconcile
cceeilost
scolecite
cceeilpry
pericycle
cceeimnou
oecumenic
cceeimnsu
ecumenics
cceeinnno
innocence
cceeinort
ectocrine
cceeinrtx
excentric
cceeinrty
reticency
cceeirrst
rectrices
cceeirstt
tectrices
cceellort
recollect
cceelosty
cystocele
cceelotuy
leucocyte
cceennort
concenter
concentre
connecter
reconnect
cceffiiil
felicific
ccefhilou
choiceful
ccefiirru
crucifier
ccefknoyy
cockneyfy

cceghimru
chemurgic
cceginnoo
oncogenic
cceginops
pigsconce
cceginory
cryogenic
cceglnosy
song-cycle
ccehiklit
check-till
ccehiklst
checklist
ccehilnor
chronicle
ccehilnpu
cup-lichen
ccehiloru
euchloric
ccehilrtu
hut-circle
ccehiorst
orchestic
ccehklnot
neck-cloth
ccehkmoor
checkroom
ccehkoors
cockhorse
ccehkoprr
rock-perch
ccehkopst
spot-check
ccehlosty
cholecyst
ccehlpsuy
push-cycle
ccehnnoos
sconcheon
ccehnnosu
scuncheon
ccehnostu
scutcheon
ccehortty
crotchety
ccehottuz
zucchetto
ccehrrtuy
cutcherry
cceiiiprt
epicritic
cceiiirst
criticise
sericitic
cceiiknpr
picnicker
cceiilmst
Celticism
cceiilnot
niccolite
cceiilrty
clericity

cceiimoss
coseismic
cceiinstu
succinite
cceiklloy
kilocycle
cceiklmot
time-clock
cceiklosw
clockwise
cceiknoss
cockiness
cceilnosy
concisely
cceilorst
sclerotic
cceilosuv
occlusive
cceilrrty
tricycler
cceilssuu
Leuciscus
cceimnoos
economics
cceimnruu
curcumine
cceimorty
microcyte
cceinnnoy
innocency
cceinnost
conscient
cceinnott
conticent
cceinorrt
incorrect
cceinostt
tectonics
cceinrsty
syncretic
cceinssty
synectics
cceioprty
precocity
ccekloouz
ouzel-cock
ccekorrss
rockcress
ccekorrsw
cork-screw
ccellnooy
colonelcy
ccelloort
collector
ccelnstuu
succulent
cceloprsu
corpuscle
ccelopssy
cyclopses
ccelorrty
correctly
ccennnoru
unconcern

ccennoort
connector
ccenooory
cocoonery
ccenoorst
concertos
ccenoorsu
concourse
ccenoortv
convector
ccenorrtu
occurrent
ccenorstu
succentor
ccensssuu
unsuccess
cceooprsy
cryoscope
cceoorrrt
corrector
cceoppruy
preoccupy
cceorrsuu
succourer
cceorsssu
successor
cceossuux
exsuccous
ccfghikot
cockfight
ccfgklloo
clock-golf
ccfhiinoo
finocchio
ccfhkkoru
fork-chuck
ccfhkllou
chock-full
ccfhklluu
chuck-full
ccfiiloor
colorific
ccfimorru
cruciform
ccfkloouy
cuckoo-fly
ccfkooost
cocksfoot
ccfllosuu
flocculus
ccghhinou
chincough
ccghhinru
churching
ccghiikln
chickling
ccghiinpu
hiccuping
ccghiklnu
chuckling
ccghiloop
chop-logic
ccghinors
scorching

ccghinstu
scutching
ccgilmooy
mycologic
ccgilnotu
occulting
ccginopuy
occupying
ccginorru
occurring
ccgllooy
glycocoll
cchhimrsu
churchism
cchhoopst
hop-scotch
cchiiirtt
trichitic
cchiilort
chloritic
trochilic
cchiimopr
microchip
cchiimoru
Cichorium
cchiinost
conchitis
cchiioors
isochoric
cchiiorrt
trichroic
cchilloty
cyclolith
cchiloort
chlorotic
cchinrsty
strychnic
cchiopsty
psychotic
cchknorsu
corn-shuck
cchkooost
cockshoot
cchlnooty
colocynth
cchoorrsu
Corchorus
cciiilnos
isoclinic
cciiilnrt
triclinic
cciiilost
silicotic
cciiilosu
cilicious
cciiimrst
criticism
cciiinnot
nicotinic
cciikknst
nickstick
cciikkrst
rickstick

cciikllop
pillicock
cciiloost
scoliotic
cciiloprt
proclitic
cciinnnsu
cincinnus
cciinnoos
concision
cciiorrtt
tricrotic
cciiosstt
Scotistic
cciirrtuy
circuitry
ccilmostu
occultism
ccilnooru
councilor
ccilnoosu
occlusion
cciloorst
colostric
ccilosttu
occultist
ccimmoors
microcosm
ccimoopry
microcopy
ccinoossu
conscious
ccinoprst
conscript
ccinopsty
syncoptic
ccinorstt
constrict
cciooopsz
zooscopic
ccioottxy
cytotoxic
cckkloorw
clockwork
cckkloost
stock-lock
ckklooyy
cockyolly
cckmoorst
storm-cock
cckoopppy
poppycock
cclnoorty
cyclotron
ccnorsttu
construct
ccooprsyy
cryoscopy
cdddeeens
descended
cdddeeily
decidedly
cdddeeinu
undecided
cdddeilno
condiddle
cdddelors
scroddled
cdddenruu
uncrudded
cddeeeflt
deflected
cddeeeiiw
weedicide
cddeeenrs
descender
redescend
cddeegllu
cudgelled
cddeehhiu
cuddeehih
cddeehlsu
scheduled
cddeeikru
eider-duck
cddeeisst
dissected
cddeeituv
deductive
cddeeknru
underdeck
cddeemnno
condemned
cddeemnru
credendum
cddeenruu
unreduced
cddeensuu
unseduced
cddefiilu
dulcified
cddehiilp
didelphic
cddehklsu
sheldduck
cddeiilmo
domiciled
cddeiinrt
dendritic
cddeiirst
discredit
cddeiltuu
dulcitude
cddeimoou
duodecimo
cddeinotu
deduction
cddeiosuu
deciduous
cddelnouu
unclouded
cddelnruu
uncurdled
cddelooop
opodeldoc
cddenoruw
uncrowded
cddhhiloo
childhood
cddhiiory
hydriodic
cddhinoor
chondroid
cddilnooy
condyloid
cdeeeefnr
deer-fence
deference
cdeeeeknw
ewe-necked
cdeeeeprr
creepered
cdeeeffor
force-feed
cdeeefitv
defective
cdeeeflrt
reflected
cdeeeforw
cowfeeder
cdeeeginr
decreeing
cdeeeginx
exceeding
cdeeehkrt
three-deck
cdeeehnru
uncheered
cdeeehorr
decoherer
cdeeehpru
upcheered
cdeeehqru
chequered
cdeeeilrs
sclereide
cdeeeimrr
remercied
cdeeeimrt
decimetre
cdeeeinns
desinence
cdeeeinpt
centipede
cdeeeinrs
residence
cdeeeinrt
intercede
cdeeeinuv
undeceive
cdeeeiptv
deceptive
cdeeeirst
decistere
cdeeeirtv
decretive
cdeeeittv
detective
cdeeekntw
'tween-deck
cdeeellnr
crenelled
cdeeellot
décolleté
cdeeelnor
redolence
cdeeelntu
unelected
cdeeelort
electrode
cdeeemnrt
decrement
cdeeemntu
educement
cdeeenprt
precedent
cdeeeoprr
proceeder
cdeeeopru
doucepere
cdeeeorrt
retrocede
cdeefiilr
rice-field
cdeefiint
deficient
cdeefiiot
foeticide
cdeefiips
specified
cdeefiirt
certified
rectified
cdeefiltu
deceitful
cdeefiluv
deviceful
cdeefinot
defection
cdeefiort
fore-cited
cdeefklot
fetlocked
cdeefknsu
fen-sucked
cdeefkost
feedstock
cdeeflort
deflector
cdeefnorr
conferred
cdeefnoss
confessed
cdeegiiln
ceilinged
diligence
cdeegiimr
germicide
cdeegiinn
indigence
cdeegilry
glyceride
cdeeginno
endogenic
cdeeginpr
preceding
cdeeginrs
screeding
cdeegiost
geodetics
cdeegllru
cudgeller
cdeegnost
congested
decongest
cdeehhirs
cherished
cdeehiinn
echidnine
cdeehikrs
shickered
cdeehiktt
thicketed
cdeehikty
thick-eyed
cdeehills
chiselled
cdeehinot
ethnocide
cdeehinst
dehiscent
cdeehiort
ditrochee
cdeehkoor
door-cheek
cdeehkosu
deck-house
cdeehlory
hydrocele
cdeehnorv
chevroned
cdeehoprs
co-sphered
cdeehppru
up-perched
cdeehrstt
stretched
cdeeiilrt
decilitre
cdeeiiltv
videlicet
cdeeiimnr
mediciner
cdeeiimnt
menticide
cdeeiimpr
epidermic
cdeeiimpu
epicedium
cdeeiimrv
decemviri
vermicide
cdeeiiprr
cirripede
cdeeiipst
pesticide
cdeeiiptv
depictive

cdeeirtv
directive
cdeeistt
dietetics
cdeeijnot
dejection
cdeeijpru
prejudice
cdeeijruv
verjuiced
cdeeikknr
knickered
cdeeiklln
nickelled
cdeeikquy
quick-eyed
cdeeillnp
pencilled
cdeeilnno
indolence
cdeeilnpr
pendicler
cdeeilorr
Cordelier
cdeeilors
creolised
cdeeilprt
predilect
cdeeilstu
celsitude
cdeeimnnu
decennium
cdeeimnou
eudemonic
cdeeimnpu
impudence
cdeeimrsv
decemvirs
cdeeinnor
endocrine
cdeeinnsu
secundine
cdeeinopt
deception
cdeeinort
recondite
cdeeinoss
decession
cdeeinott
detection
cdeeinpru
unpierced
cdeeinrrs
discerner
cdeeinrst
stridence
cdeeinrsy
residency
cdeeintux
unexcited
cdeeiorrs
crosiered
cdeeiottu
eutectoid

cdeeiprtu
depicture
cdeeirstt
decretist
cdeeirsuv
decursive
cdeeirttu
certitude
rectitude
cdeeirtuv
reductive
cdeeistuv
seductive
cdeejorty
dejectory
cdeeklnow
low-necked
cdeeklorw
lower-deck
cdeeklprs
spreckled
cdeekmnru
muckender
cdeeknors
knee-cords
cdeeknrwy
wry-necked
cdeekortw
two-decker
cdeellmop
compelled
cdeellnru
cullender
cdeelmntu
demulcent
cdeelmopt
completed
cdeelmopx
decomplex
cdeelnory
redolency
cdeelorss
sclerosed
cdeelorst
corsleted
cdeelrstu
clustered
cdeemmnor
recommend
cdeemnnot
contemned
cdeemoops
decompose
cdeennors
condenser
cdeennort
contender
cdeennoru
denouncer
cdeennott
contented
cdeennstu
unscented

cdeenoops
endoscope
cdeenoort
coroneted
cdeenoprs
drop-scene
cdeenoruv
uncovered
cdeenossu
douceness
cdeenostt
contested
cdeenprty
encrypted
cdeenrrtu
decurrent
cdeenrssu
crudeness
cdeenrsuu
unsecured
cdeeoprru
procedure
reproduce
cdeeoprss
processed
cdeeoprtt
protected
cdeeoprty
deceptory
cdeeoqttu
coquetted
cdeeorrty
decretory
cdeeorssy
cross-eyed
cdeeprssu
percussed
cdeepsstu
suspected
cdeerttuv
curvetted
cdefgiinu
fungicide
cdefhiilw
child-wife
cdefhiors
cod-fisher
cdefiinst
disinfect
cdefiiost
Scotified
cdefiklor
frolicked
cdefilnor
cornfield
cdefimnor
confirmed
cdefinnot
confident
cdefintuy
fecundity
cdefknoru
unfrocked

cdefloruu
cul-de-four
cdefnosuu
unfocused
cdegglnou
unclogged
cdeghhiiv
high-viced
cdegiiloo
ideologic
cdegiimru
demiurgic
cdegiinny
indigency
cdegiknot
docketing
cdegiloop
police-dog
cdegilosu
glucoside
cdegimouw
cowdie-gum
cdeginnos
consigned
cdeginorr
recording
cdeginoty
dictyogen
cdeginrsy
descrying
cdeginssy
dysgenics
cdeglorst
goldcrest
cdehhoorr
rheochord
cdehiikll
childlike
cdehiilno
lichenoid
cdehiiopt
pithecoid
cdehiiort
dichroite
cdehiklsu
shielduck
cdehikpsy
physicked
cdehillov
love-child
cdehillss
childless
cdehilnss
childness
cdehilpst
stepchild
cdehinort
chondrite
threnodic
cdehinosu
cushioned
cdehinouu
eunuchoid

cdehinstw
wind-chest
cdehiorsv
dish-cover
cdehiostu
dithecous
cdehistty
dysthetic
cdehkllsu
shellduck
cdehkmmou
hummocked
cdehknosu
unshocked
cdehlnoru
chondrule
cdehlnotu
unclothed
cdehloosu
coldhouse
cdehnotuu
untouched
cdehnstuy
unscythed
cdehooops
hodoscope
cdeiiilsv
civilised
cdeiiirst
sideritic
cdeiikmtw
mid-wicket
cdeiikrst
sick-tired
cdeiillno
decillion
cdeiilntu
inductile
cdeiilopr
prolicide
cdeiilort
doleritic
cdeiilosu
delicious
cdeiilpuv
vulpicide
cdeiilrru
ridiculer
cdeiiltvy
declivity
cdeiimnos
meniscoid
cdeiimnty
mendicity
cdeiimrst
miscredit
misdirect
cdeiinnot
incondite
cdeiinntu
unincited
cdeiinopt
depiction

cdeiinort
  cretinoid
  direction
cdeiinrtt
  interdict
cdeiintuv
  inductive
cdeiioosu
  dioecious
cdeiioprt
  peridotic
cdeiiorux
  uxoricide
cdeiiorvv
  divorcive
cdeiirrtx
  directrix
cdeijnnoo
  conjoined
cdeiklnsu
  klendusic
  unsickled
cdeikppru
  up-pricked
cdeilllou
  celluloid
cdeilnnoy
  indolency
cdeilnopu
  unpoliced
cdeilnory
  cordyline
cdeilnotu
  Dulcitone
cdeilnppu
  unclipped
cdeilnssu
  lucidness
cdeilosuv
  declivous
cdeilottw
  twice-told
cdeilprsu
  surpliced
cdeilpsuu
  Pediculus
cdeilrtuy
  credulity
cdeimmnoo
  incommode
cdeimmory
  myrmecoid
cdeimmott
  committed
cdeimmsuy
  music-demy
cdeimnnot
  condiment
cdeimnopr
  princedom
cdeimnoru
  indecorum
cdeimnrru
  mind-curer

cdeimortu
  udometric
cdeinnotu
  continued
  unnoticed
cdeinoprt
  procident
cdeinopsy
  dyspnoeic
cdeinorsu
  decursion
cdeinortu
  introduce
  reduction
cdeinostu
  seduction
cdeinprtu
  unpredict
cdeinrssu
  curdiness
cdeinrsty
  stridency
cdeinttuv
  ventiduct
cdeiooprt
  porticoed
cdeioorst
  scorodite
cdeioprrt
  predictor
cdeioprst
  dip-sector
cdeioprsu
  cuspidore
cdeiorrty
  directory
cdeiorsst
  dissector
cdeiorssu
  discourse
cdeiorstu
  custodier
cdeiorstv
  discovert
cdeiorsvy
  discovery
cdeippsty
  dyspeptic
cdeklnpuu
  unplucked
cdekloory
  crookedly
cdeknooru
  undercook
cdeknostu
  unstocked
cdekoostv
  stock-dove
cdellossu
  cloudless
cdelnnoot
  condolent
cdelnoort
  decontrol

cdelnooru
  undercool
cdelnoost
  stone-cold
cdelnoosw
  close-down
cdelnooty
  cotyledon
cdelnopuu
  uncoupled
cdelnorsu
  scoundrel
cdelooruv
  overcloud
cdeloprsu
  supercold
cdelorsuu
  credulous
cdemmooor
  commodore
cdennoorw
  nonce-word
cdennoruw
  uncrowned
cdennotuu
  uncounted
cdenooprs
  drop-scone
cdenoopsy
  endoscopy
cdenoorrt
  corrodent
cdenoorst
  consorted
cdenoortt
  contorted
cdenoortu
  contoured
cdenoppru
  uncropped
cdenorssu
  uncrossed
cdenorsuu
  unscoured
cdenorsww
  screw-down
cdenprtuu
  punctured
cdeooopst
  octopodes
cdeooopsw
  copsewood
cdeoopprr
  pop-record
cdeoorrvw
  overcrowd
cdeoorsst
  doctoress
cdeoorsww
  wood-screw
cdeorstuv
  dust-cover
cdffiiltu
  difficult

cdfghilno
  goldfinch
cdfgiinno
  confiding
cdfgiinoy
  codifying
cdfhinory
  chondrify
cdfiiloor
  dolorific
cdfiimost
  discomfit
cdfiiorsu
  sudorific
cdfimoorr
  cordiform
cdfiorrtu
  Fructidor
cdfkoostu
  duck's-foot
cdghlloot
  gold-cloth
cdghoopru
  cough-drop
cdgiiotyz
  dizygotic
cdgiklost
  goldstick
cdgilnnoy
  condignly
cdhhiioty
  ichthyoid
cdhhilost
  dish-cloth
cdhiimopr
  dimorphic
cdhiimors
  dichroism
cdhiiorrs
  scirrhoid
cdhiiorst
  orchidist
cdhiipstw
  dip-switch
cdhiirrty
  trihydric
cdhilostu
  dish-clout
cdhimnoor
  monorchid
cdhimooty
  dichotomy
cdhimstyy
  dysthymic
cdhinopsy
  dysphonic
cdhiooprr
  cirrhopod
cdhioopry
  chiropody
cdhioopsz
  schizopod
cdhioprsy
  dysphoric

cdhioprty
  hydroptic
cdhioprwy
  whipcordy
cdhkooosw
  wood-shock
cdhloorst
  cold-short
cdhmnooor
  monochord
cdhnooort
  notochord
cdhnootuw
  touch-down
cdhoootuw
  touchwood
cdiiilmns
  diclinism
cdiiinnot
  indiction
cdiiinoot
  idioticon
cdiiiorst
  dioristic
cdiiistvy
  viscidity
cdiijosuu
  judicious
cdiilmoot
  dolomitic
cdiilnosu
  diclinous
cdiilptuy
  duplicity
cdiilttuy
  ductility
cdiimnpuy
  pycnidium
cdiimoost
  sodomitic
cdiimorst
  dicrotism
cdiinnoot
  condition
cdiinnotu
  induction
cdiinopry
  cyprinoid
cdiiooprs
  scorpioid
cdiioprst
  dioptrics
cdiiorrtt
  tortricid
cdiiprstu
  tricuspid
cdijnotuy
  jocundity
cdikllorr
  rock-drill
cdikloors
  rock-solid
cdikmrstu
  drumstick

cdikooprw
prickwood
cdillnooo
collodion
cdilooopt
octoploid
cdiloorsu
discolour
cdiloosty
scolytoid
cdilorsuu
ludicrous
cdimmnoos
discommon
cdimmooty
commodity
cdimnorsy
syndromic
cdimooprr
prodromic
cdinorssw
crosswind
cdioorstu
dicrotous
cdirsssuu
discursus
cdkknnoow
knock-down
cdmnnoruu
conundrum
cdmooorty
cordotomy
cdnnootuw
count-down
cdoorrssw
crossword
ceeeeehsw
ewe-cheese
ceeeeffnr
efference
ceeeefnrr
reference
ceeeegmnr
emergence
ceeeehilp
heel-piece
ceeeehmnv
vehemence
ceeeenrrv
reverence
ceeeeorrv
recoveree
ceeeffitv
effective
ceeefflnu
effluence
ceeeffory
rye-coffee
ceeefilnn
line-fence
ceeefinnr
inference
ceeefinpv
fivepence
ceeeflnru
refluence
ceeeflnss
fenceless
ceeeflrrt
reflecter
ceeefnorr
re-enforce
ceeefnqru
frequence
ceeefprrt
perfecter
ceeegilnt
telegenic
ceeegimns
miscegene
ceeeginrt
energetic
ceeegistx
exegetics
ceeeglmnu
emulgence
ceeeglnor
conger-eel
ceeeglnrt
neglecter
ceeegmnry
emergency
ceeehilps
sheep-lice
ceeehilst
scheelite
ceeehinnr
inherence
ceeehinps
nip-cheese
ceeehipst
tip-cheese
ceeehlnty
entelechy
ceeehlopr
creep-hole
ceeehlrss
cheerless
ceeehlruv
chevelure
ceeehmnvy
vehemency
ceeehnrvw
whencever
ceeehoprs
ecosphere
ceeehopst
sheep-cote
ceeehqrux
exchequer
ceeehrttv
chevrette
ceeeiimpt
timepiece
ceeeiinrv
vicereine
ceeeikprr
pickeerer
ceeeillnt
clientèle
ceeeilnop
Pleiocene
ceeeilnst
Celestine
ceeeilpss
pieceless
ceeeilpsy
eye-splice
ceeeilrst
electrise
Leicester
ceeeilrtt
tiercelet
ceeeilstv
selective
ceeeimntt
cementite
ceeeimrrs
mercerise
ceeeinnnp
ninepence
ceeeinnpt
penitence
ceeeinnrt
centenier
ceeeinnst
sentience
ceeeinops
nose-piece
ceeeinprt
epicentre
ceeeinquv
vice-queen
ceeeinrsu
esurience
ceeeinstx
existence
ceeeiprrv
perceiver
ceeeiprsu
précieuse
ceeeiprtv
receptive
ceeeiptvx
exceptive
ceeeirrsx
exerciser
ceeeirssv
recessive
ceeeirstv
secretive
ceeeirsvx
ex-service
ceeeirtvx
excretive
ceeeissvx
excessive
ceeeituvx
executive
ceeejmntt
ejectment
ceeeknrsv
neckverse
ceeekorrt
rocketeer
ceeellnrv
nerve-cell
ceeellntx
excellent
ceeelmntu
temulence
ceeelnoqu
eloquence
ceeelnosy
Ceylonese
ceeelopst
telescope
ceeelortv
clove-tree
ceeelottt
côtelette
ceeelprst
preselect
ceeelrsst
electress
ceeemnrrt
recrement
ceeemnrtx
excrement
ceeemstuy
Eumycetes
ceeennorv
reconvene
ceeennrst
secernent
sentencer
ceeennsst
senescent
ceeennssu
unessence
ceeenortt
entrecôte
ceeenosty
synoecete
ceeenrsst
erectness
ceeeopstt
escopette
ceeeorrrv
recoverer
ceeeprrst
respecter
ceeeprstu
persecute
ceeffiint
efficient
ceeffilor
life-force
ceeffiosu
coiffeuse
ceeffnort
off-centre
ceeffoopt
coffee-pot
ceefghiln
fleeching
ceefgikpr
fig-pecker
ceefginnr
ring-fence
ceefglntu
genuflect
ceefhilrs
fish-creel
ceefhilss
chiefless
ceefhipsy
speechify
ceefhlpsu
speechful
ceefiintv
infective
ceefiirrt
certifier
rectifier
ceefilnnu
influence
ceefilnrt
fernticle
ceefilrty
electrify
ceefimnor
confirmee
ceefimort
focimeter
ceefimprt
imperfect
ceefinorr
confrérie
reinforce
ceefinort
refection
ceefinttu
fettucine
ceefirrst
firecrest
ceefkllss
fleckless
ceeflnort
tenor-clef
ceefloors
foreclose
ceeflorrt
reflector
ceeflorss
forceless
ceeflorsu
fluoresce
ceeflprty
perfectly
ceefmnorw
worm-fence
ceefnopru
fourpence
ceefnorrr
conferrer
ceefnprtu
unperfect

ceefnqruy
frequency
ceefnrstu
rufescent
ceefoprrt
perfector
ceefoprss
forcepses
ceeforrty
refectory
ceeghimno
hegemonic
ceeghinno
hecogenin
ceeghinrw
Greenwich
ceegiilps
spicilege
ceegiimns
miscegine
ceegiinrs
isenergic
ceegiinst
Genesitic
ceegillnx
excelling
ceegilnoo
Oligocene
ceegilnry
glycerine
ceegimort
geometric
ceeginnos
consignee
ceeginnrs
screening
ceeginnrt
centering
centreing
ceeginnst
ignescent
ceeginoot
oogenetic
ceeginops
engiscope
ceeginors
congeries
recognise
ceeginprs
cee-spring
ceeginptx
excepting
expecting
ceeginrsv
screeving
ceegjklot
jockteleg
ceegknoos
goose-neck
ceeglnoos
Congolese
ceegnopsy
engyscope

ceegorttu
courgette
ceehhirvw
whichever
ceehhopst
hope-chest
ceehiiptt
epithetic
ceehiirtt
erethitic
ceehikknt
thick-knee
ceehiknrt
kitchener
thickener
ceehikppr
pike-perch
ceehikpry
cipher-key
ceehikpst
sheep-tick
ceehillms
schlemiel
ceehilnos
lichenose
ceehilnrs
schlieren
ceehilrsv
cleverish
ceehilstt
telestich
ceehimpty
chemitype
ceehimrst
hermetics
ceehimrsw
shrew-mice
ceehimtuv
humective
ceehinnry
inherency
ceehinprt
phrenetic
ceehinqtu
technique
ceehinrtt
threnetic
ceehinrty
hercynite
ceehinstu
euthenics
ceehinstz
Zechstein
ceehiopsw
showpiece
ceehiorss
coheiress
ceehiortt
theoretic
ceehiprry
cherry-pie
ceehiprtt
pitch-tree

ceehkllow
wheel-lock
ceehlorsu
lecherous
ceehlprsu
sepulchre
ceehlqrsu
squelcher
ceehmmoor
home-comer
ceehmnorz
chernozem
ceehmoorz
zoechrome
ceehmortt
ectotherm
ceehnoprr
percheron
ceehnopry
coryphene
ceehnostt
chest-note
chest-tone
ceehoprrv
overperch
ceehoprsu
proseuche
ceehoptty
ectophyte
ceehorrtu
retoucher
ceehprrsy
sprechery
ceehrrstt
stretcher
ceeiijlmu
lime-juice
ceeiiklnn
nickeline
ceeiiklns
nickelise
ceeiilnpr
pericline
ceeiilnrt
lienteric
ceeiilnst
insectile
selenitic
ceeiilppt
epileptic
ceeiilprx
pre-exilic
ceeiilpss
epiclesis
ceeiimmnn
imminence
ceeiimnrs
reminisce
ceeiimost
semeiotic
ceeiimprs
imprecise
ceeiimpst
epistemic

ceeiimrst
metricise
ceeiinnor
eirenicon
ceeiinnot
neoteinic
ceeiinnrs
insincere
ceeiinnrt
encrinite
ceeiinntv
incentive
ceeiinprt
recipient
ceeiinptv
inceptive
ceeiinptx
excipient
ceeiinrsv
in-service
ceeiintvv
invective
ceeiiopst
poeticise
ceeiiorrt
écritoire
ceeiiprss
Persicise
ceeiiprsu
epicurise
ceeiiprsv
precisive
ceeiiqstu
equisetic
ceeiirrtt
trieteric
ceeijlouv
love-juice
ceeijlssu
juiceless
ceeijnort
rejection
ceeijnrtt
interject
ceeikkllr
clerk-like
ceeikksss
skeesicks
ceeikmstt
metestick
ceeiknqru
quickener
requicken
ceeikoprw
piece-work
workpiece
ceeilllno
lioncelle
ceeilllov
level-coil
ceeillltu
cellulite
ceeillnpr
penciller

ceeillnsw
clew-lines
ceeillntt
intellect
ceeillotv
covellite
ceeilmnnt
inclement
ceeilmnsu
luminesce
ceeilmors
misoclere
ceeilmrss
crimeless
merciless
ceeilmruv
vermicule
ceeilnnos
insolence
ceeilnopr
crepoline
pencil-ore
ceeilnost
selection
ceeilnoty
ceylonite
ceeilnprt
princelet
ceeilnpst
splenetic
ceeilnrsu
licensure
ceeilnrsy
sincerely
ceeilnrtv
ventricle
ceeilnruv
virulence
ceeiloptt
pectolite
ceeiloptu
poeticule
ceeilorrt
terricole
ceeilorsx
excelsior
ceeilosss
isosceles
ceeilossv
voiceless
ceeilprss
priceless
ceeilprsw
screw-pile
ceeilprsy
precisely
ceeilrstw
crewelist
ceeilrsuv
reclusive
ceeilssuv
seclusive
ceeilsuvx
exclusive

ceeimmnsu
ecumenism
ceeimmott
committee
ceeimnnrt
increment
ceeimnoos
economise
ceeimnopt
impotence
ceeimnstu
intumesce
ceeimttuv
vitecetum
ceeinnors
nine-score
recension
ceeinnovx
connexive
ceeinnpty
penitency
ceeinnrty
renitency
ceeinnstt
insect-net
ceeinnsty
sentiency
ceeinoprs
preconise
ceeinoprt
reception
ceeinoptx
exception
ceeinorrt
tierceron
ceeinorss
recession
ceeinorst
necrotise
resection
secretion
ceeinorsu
cinereous
ceeinortv
covin-tree
ceeinortx
excretion
ceeinosss
secession
ceeinossy
synoecise
ceeinostx
exsection
ceeinotux
execution
ceeinprru
prurience
ceeinprss
princesse
ceeinprst
prescient
reinspect
ceeinprsu
unprecise

ceeinprsw
screw-pine
ceeinprtt
intercept
ceeinqstu
quiescent
ceeinrrsv
scrivener
ceeinrstt
intersect
ceeinrstv
virescent
ceeinrsuy
esuriency
ceeinssty
necessity
ceeioortz
ozocerite
ceeioorvv
voice-over
ceeiopprs
periscope
ceeiopsst
cespitose
ceeiorrst
corsetier
ceeiorrsx
exorciser
ceeiorssu
sericeous
ceeiprrwz
prize-crew
ceeirrrtu
recruiter
ceeirrsuv
recursive
ceeirsstu
cerussite
ceeirssww
screw-wise
ceeirsuvx
excursive
ceeirtuxx
executrix
ceejorrtt
retroject
ceekkknno
knock-knee
ceekllrss
clerkless
ceeklpsss
speckless
ceeklruvy
culver-key
ceeknprtu
nutpecker
ceelllosu
cellulose
ceellmnty
clemently
ceellmprs
sperm-cell
ceellnors
ensorcell

ceellnost
stone-cell
ceelloptu
locuplete
ceellrsuy
reclusely
ceelmmptu
emplectum
ceelmnopt
emplecton
ceelmnouw
unwelcome
ceelmntuy
temulency
ceelmoosu
cole-mouse
ceelmootu
leucotome
ceelnnnop
pennoncel
ceelnorsu
enclosure
ceelnosss
closeness
ceelnostu
consultee
ceelnpruu
purulence
ceelnrssu
cruelness
ceelnssst
scentless
ceelnsttu
lutescent
ceeloprrt
prelector
ceelopsty
telescopy
ceelorsuu
ceruleous
ceelorsux
exclosure
ceelorttu
court-leet
ceelrssst
crestless
ceelrsstu
truceless
ceemmnort
commenter
ceemnnort
contemner
ceemnoort
oncometer
ceemnoprt
contemper
ceemnoptt
competent
ceemnorsu
cornemuse
ceemnsttu
tumescent
ceemooprs
recompose

ceemorrty
cryometer
ceemorsuv
curvesome
ceemossty
ecosystem
ceemqrtuu
quercetum
ceennorrt
rencontre
ceennorru
renouncer
ceennortu
encounter
ceenoopst
cope-stone
ceenoprrt
precentor
ceenoprst
co-present
ceenopstt
Pentecost
ceenoqrru
reconquer
ceenorrsv
conserver
ceenorrtv
converter
reconvert
ceenorstw
sweet-corn
ceenrrrtu
recurrent
ceenrrtux
excurrent
ceeoorrrv
recoveror
ceeoorrsv
overscore
ceeoorrvv
overcover
ceeopprrt
preceptor
ceeoprrss
reprocess
ceeoprrtx
excerptor
ceeoprstu
prosecute
ceeoqrttu
croquette
ceeorrsss
sorceress
ceeorrsst
crosstree
rectoress
ceeorrstw
worcester
ceeorrsty
secretory
ceeorrsuv
verrucose
ceeorrtuv
coverture

ceeorrtxy
excretory
ceeorsstt
crossette
ceeortuxy
executory
ceeprrrru
precurrer
ceeprrssu
repercuss
ceerrrstu
resurrect
cefflruu
curfuffle
ceffhinry
Frenchify
ceffiinot
coffinite
ceffiknst
stiff-neck
cefghiiln
chiefling
cefgiklnr
freckling
cefginors
frescoing
cefginoru
configure
cefhhiips
chiefship
cefhiilss
fish-slice
cefhiimst
fetichism
cefhiinnp
pine-finch
cefhiistt
fetichist
cefhiitww
witch-wife
cefhkllou
choke-full
cefhkoors
foreshock
cefhloort
forecloth
cefhmoort
forthcome
home-croft
cefhoorsu
corf-house
cefiikqru
quick-fire
cefiikrst
fire-stick
cefiilnru
luciferin
cefiiltwy
Wyclifite
cefiinnot
infection
cefiinopt
pontifice

cefiinttu
fettucini
cefiiorrs
scorifier
cefikorss
fossicker
cefilorru
rice-flour
cefimnorr
confirmer
reconfirm
cefimnort
cteniform
cefimnoru
cuneiform
cefimoprr
perciform
cefimorru
eruciform
cefimortt
tectiform
cefimortu
comfiture
cefinnnou
unconfine
cefinoort
confiteor
cefinorss
forensics
cefinortu
confiture
cefioorsu
ferocious
cefiorrss
crossfire
cefiorsst
frescoist
cefiorstu
fruticose
cefiprrsu
spruce-fir
cefklnosw
snowfleck
cefkloptu
pocketful
cefklorss
frockless
cefkoorrw
workforce
ceflnnotu
confluent
ceflnosty
confestly
cefmnoorr
conformer
cefmoorrt
comforter
recomfort
cefmoppru
force-pump
cefnnoort
confronté
cefnoorss
confessor

cefoorrsu
fourscore
cefoorrtu
forecourt
ceghiilop
geophilic
ceghiinpr
ciphering
ceghiinsy
hygienics
ceghiiost
gothicise
ceghillou
guilloche
ceghilntv
vetchling
ceghiloor
rheologic
ceghiloot
ethologic
theologic
ceghinnqu
quenching
ceghinnrw
wrenching
ceghinoot
Neo-Gothic
theogonic
ceghinors
coshering
ceghiopty
geophytic
ceghknoru
rough-neck
ceghloouy
euchology
cegiijnor
rejoicing
cegiiknns
sickening
cegiiknpt
picketing
cegiilnnr
reclining
cegiilnsy
lysigenic
cegiinotv
cognitive
cegiiostt
egotistic
cegikllnr
clerkling
cegiknnor
reckoning
cegiknopt
pocketing
cegiknost
socketing
cegillmou
collegium
cegillnpu
cupelling
cegilmmno
commingle

cegilnopy
polygenic
cegilnost
closeting
cegilnrsu
surcingle
cegilooz
zoogloeic
cegiloost
ecologist
cegimnoor
ergonomic
cegimnouy
gynoecium
cegimnoyz
zymogenic
ceginnoot
ontogenic
ceginnors
consigner
ceginoopr
coopering
ceginoops
geoponics
ceginoppr
coppering
ceginopry
pyrogenic
ceginopty
genotypic
ceginorrt
corrigent
ceginorst
corseting
ceginosst
cosseting
ceginostt
stegnotic
ceginrrru
recurring
ceginrtuv
curveting
cegiooprt
geotropic
ceglnoory
necrology
cegmnoosy
cosmogeny
cegnnoorr
negro-corn
cegnnortu
congruent
cegnoorsu
Coregonus
cegnorrsu
scrounger
cegnorsuy
surgeoncy
cegooprsy
gyroscope
cehhhiikt
hitch-hike
cehhiimst
hemistich

cehhillms
schlemihl
cehhillot
cholelith
cehhimstt
hem-stitch
cehhlootu
touch-hole
cehhoopsu
chop-house
cehiiklrs
lickerish
cehiillop
olephilic
cehiilmns
lichenism
cehiilmot
homiletic
cehiilnot
ichnolite
Neolithic
cehiilnst
lichenist
cehiilooz
heliozoic
cehiilost
Elohistic
cehiimmpt
Memphitic
cehiimnst
ethnicism
cehiimsty
mythicise
cehiinppt
pitchpine
cehiinprt
nephritic
phrenitic
cehiinsst
itchiness
cehiintty
ethnicity
cehiintwz
zinc-white
cehiipppt
pitchpipe
cehiippty
epiphytic
cehiiprtt
perthitic
tephritic
cehiirstt
Thersitic
cehiirstu
heuristic
cehijpstw
Jew's-pitch
cehiklmtv
milk-vetch
cehiklprs
clerkship
cehiklsty
sketchily

cehiknsst
thickness
cehikoppr
hop-picker
cehikoppt
hip-pocket
cehikossu
sick-house
cehikprsw
shipwreck
cehillnss
chillness
cehilmntu
lunch-time
cehilmoos
molochise
cehilnoor
holocrine
cehilnosu
lichenous
cehilnotu
touch-line
cehilnpsu
siphuncle
uncleship
cehiloops
heliscoop
cehiloprt
plethoric
cehimmopr
morphemic
cehimnnou
ichneumon
cehimnops
phonemics
cehimnsuu
eunuchism
cehimoprt
morphetic
cehimopxy
hypoxemic
cehimorrt
trichrome
cehimorst
hectorism
cehimortt
thermotic
cehimpruy
Hypericum
cehimptyy
chemitypy
cehimrsty
chemistry
cehimstty
methystic
cehinoors
isochrone
cehinopst
Ctesiphon
phonetics
cehinopty
neophytic
cehinorst
sticheron

cehinostu
cushionet
cehinprst
sphincter
cehinstty
synthetic
cehiooprt
orthoepic
cehioorrt
coheritor
cehiopprs
copperish
cehiopprt
prophetic
cehioprtt
prothetic
cehioprtu
eutrophic
cehioprtv
overpitch
cehioprty
hypocrite
cehiorrst
chorister
cehiossst
schistose
cehiprrty
cherry-pit
cehirssty
hysterics
cehirstty
stitchery
cehitttwy
witchetty
cehklnors
schnorkel
cehklooov
clove-hook
cehkloosu
lockhouse
cehkooosu
cookhouse
cehkooppt
hop-pocket
cehkrstuy
huckstery
cehlloopt
photocell
cehlloruy
holy-cruel
cehlmnouu
homuncule
cehlnoszz
schnozzle
cehlnottt
tent-cloth
cehlooosu
cool-house
cehlooprs
preschool
cehloorsy
schoolery
cehloostu
clout-shoe

cehlosstu
touchless
cehmooprt
ectomorph
cehmoorru
urochrome
cehmottyy
thymocyte
cehnnortu
truncheon
cehnnrtuw
nut-wrench
cehnoottu
touch-tone
cehnootyz
zootechny
cehnorrrs
schnorrer
cehoooprs
horoscope
cehopsssy
psychoses
cehopttuy
touch-type
cehorstuy
scouthery
ceiiilnru
Ricinulei
ceiiilrsv
civiliser
ceiiimnrs
irenicism
ceiiimstv
victimise
ceiiinnop
epinicion
ceiiinnpt
incipient
ceiiinrsu
cuisinier
ceiiipstt
pietistic
ceiijnnot
injection
ceiijnssu
juiciness
ceiijnstu
injustice
ceiiklmps
mispickel
ceiiklmqu
quicklime
ceiiklmst
Kelticism
ceiiklrty
ricketily
ceiiknnpr
princekin
ceiilmort
microlite
ceiilmpss
simplices
ceiilnnor
crinoline

ceiilnppr
principle
ceiilnsuv
inclusive
ceiilopst
epistolic
ceiiloqru
liquorice
ceiilossu
siliceous
ceiilprst
price-list
ceiilprtu
pleuritic
ceiilrsst
scleritis
ceiilstty
sectility
ceiilstuv
Leviticus
ceiimmnny
imminency
ceiimnost
semitonic
ceiimnrst
cretinism
ceiimnsst
scientism
ceiimopst
impeticos
poeticism
ceiimorrw
microwire
ceiimorst
eroticism
isometric
meroistic
ceiimosst
semiotics
ceiimostx
exoticism
ceiimprsu
epicurism
ceiimrstt
metricist
ceiinnopt
inception
ceiinnost
insection
ceiinoppw
wincopipe
ceiinoprs
precision
ceiinoprt
proteinic
ceiinorrt
criterion
tricerion
ceiinortv
victorine
ceiinprss
priciness
ceiinpsss
spiciness

ceiinrstt
sternitic
ceiinrstx
extrinsic
ceiinrsty
sincerity
ceiinrsuv
incursive
ceiinrtty
intercity
ceiinrtyz
citizenry
ceiinsstt
scientist
ceiiooptz
epizootic
ceiiorsst
isosteric
ceiiorstt
eroticist
ceiiorstu
triecious
ceiipptty
pepticity
ceiipstty
septicity
ceiirsstu
rusticise
ceiirttvy
verticity
ceijkmosy
jockeyism
ceijnortt
introject
ceiklnnpy
lickpenny
ceiklnopv
clove-pink
ceiklnort
interlock
ceiklnost
close-knit
ceiklnosu
nickelous
ceiklnsss
slickness
ceiklnssu
luckiness
ceiklopst
stockpile
ceiklortu
courtlike
ceiklostv
livestock
ceikmnors
misreckon
ceikmnssu
muckiness
ceikmorst
tricksome
ceiknoops
koniscope

ceiknorss
corkiness
rockiness
ceiknostt
stockinet
ceiknostv
vine-stock
ceiknqssu
quickness
ceiknrssu
sick-nurse
ceikoprrt
rock-tripe
rope-trick
ceikorrtv
overtrick
ceikpprsu
pick-purse
ceikpqstu
quickstep
ceikrrstt
trickster
ceilllmtu
clitellum
ceillmoow
come-o'-will
ceillnoor
corolline
ceillnouv
involucel
ceilloppt
pole-clipt
ceillosuv
colluvies
ceillpsty
sylleptic
ceilmnnoo
monocline
ceilmnoos
semicolon
ceilmnopu
encolpium
ceilmnotu
monticule
ceilmnsuu
minuscule
ceilmopry
micropyle
polymeric
ceilmopty
lipectomy
ceilmrtuu
reticulum
ceilnnoop
encolpion
ceilnnoos
cloisonné
ceilnootu
elocution
ceilnopru
pronuclei
ceilnorsu
inclosure
reclusion

ceilnoruv
involucre
volucrine
ceilnossu
seclusion
ceilnosux
exclusion
ceilnrssu
curliness
ceilnruvy
virulency
ceilnsstu
linctuses
ceilooprt
coprolite
ceilopprt
proleptic
ceiloprsv
coverslip
ceilorsss
sclerosis
ceilostvy
costively
ceilrsuvy
cursively
ceimmnoor
monomeric
ceimmnoos
monoecism
ceimmnosu
communise
ceimmnotu
comminute
ceimmnoty
metonymic
ceimmoors
microsome
ceimmoort
microtome
ceimmrsty
symmetric
ceimnnopu
pneumonic
ceimnnors
encrimson
ceimnnort
Comintern
ceimnoopt
coemption
ceimnoort
microtone
ceimnoost
economist
ceimnoosu
monecious
ceimnopty
impotency
ceimnossy
synoecism
ceimnrtuv
centumvir
ceimooprr
poromeric

ceimooprt
compotier
ceimoopst
composite
ceimoortz
zoometric
ceimoostx
exosmotic
ceimoprtu
ectropium
ceimopsuu
pumiceous
ceimorstu
costumier
ceimosstu
customise
ceimostuv
Muscovite
muscovite
ceinnnoox
connexion
ceinnnott
continent
ceinnnotv
connivent
ceinnootv
connotive
ceinnorsy
incensory
ceinnortu
centurion
continuer
ceinnostt
centonist
ceinnrrtu
incurrent
ceinnttux
unextinct
ceinooprt
ectropion
ceinoorst
cortisone
ceinoppru
porcupine
ceinoprrs
conspirer
ceinoprrt
intercrop
ceinoprst
inspector
ceinoprtt
cotter-pin
ceinoprxy
pyroxenic
ceinopstt
entoptics
ceinopsuu
pecunious
ceinorrrs
serricorn
ceinorrsu
recursion
ceinorrtv
contriver

ceinorrtw
town-crier
ceinorstt
cornetist
ceinorstu
cretinous
ceinorsux
excursion
ceinostuv
contusive
ceinotvxy
convexity
ceinprruy
pruriency
ceinprsss
crispness
ceinrstww
twin-screw
ceiooprst
porticoes
ceiooprtz
zoetropic
ceioorrsv
corrosive
ceioorstv
vorticose
ceiopprrt
periproct
ceioprrty
procerity
ceioprssu
prescious
ceiorrsss
scissorer
ceiorrstt
tortrices
trisector
ceiorrstu
scrutoire
ceiorrtuu
couturier
ceiorsssw
crosswise
ceiorsstv
victoress
ceiorsttu
toreutics
ceipprrst
prescript
ceiprrstu
scripture
ceirrsttu
stricture
cejooprrt
projector
cekknopru
knocker-up
cekkorsty
sky-rocket
ceklnnpuy
luck-penny
ceklossst
stockless

cekmnortu
mocker-nut
cekoorstv
overstock
cellmopxy
complexly
cellmstuu
scutellum
cellnosuu
nucleolus
celloopty
collotype
cellorrsy
scrollery
cellortuy
clouterly
celmnooot
melocoton
celmnotuy
contumely
celmoopry
co-polymer
celmoossu
colosseum
celmootuy
leucotomy
celmopruu
operculum
celmopsux
complexus
celnootuv
convolute
celnoprtu
corpulent
celnorssw
crownless
celnorstu
consulter
celnosstu
countless
celnpruuy
purulency
celnrrtuy
currently
celnrttuu
truculent
celooprsu
supercool
celooprtu
turcopole
celoortuy
elocutory
celoostty
octostyle
celorrsuu
soul-curer
celorrsuy
reclusory
celorssuu
surculose
celorsuxy
exclusory
celprstuu
sculpture

celrssstu
crustless
cemmnoort
commentor
cemnnoopt
component
cemnnoort
contemnor
cemnoooqu
monocoque
cemnooors
monoceros
cemnoorst
storm-cone
cemnoorty
necrotomy
cemnortuy
emunctory
cemooprsu
composure
cemoopstu
mutoscope
cemooptty
topectomy
cemorrsuu
mercurous
cemorrsww
screw-worm
cemprstuu
prescutum
cennooppy
opponency
cennoopru
pronounce
cennoorst
cornstone
cennosssu
consensus
cennrrtuu
uncurrent
cenooprst
stonecrop
cenooqrru
conqueror
cenoorrst
consorter
cenoorrtv
convertor
cenoortuv
overcount
cenoortyy
tycoonery
cenorrstu
construer
cenorssss
crossness
cenorsstw
crow's-nest
cenorstxy
xenocryst
cenprrtuu
up-current
cenpsstuu
unsuspect

cenrrstuw
turn-screw
cenrssstu
curstness
ceooopprs
poroscope
ceoopprsy
pyroscope
ceooprrrt
prorector
ceooprrss
processor
ceooprrst
prosector
ceooprrtt
protector
ceoopsstu
octopuses
ceoorrsss
rose-cross
ceoorrssu
sorcerous
ceoorrssv
crossover
ceoorstty
trot-cosey
ceoorstuu
courteous
ceoprrrsu
precursor
ceoprrrtu
corrupter
ceoprrssu
percussor
procuress
ceoprsstu
susceptor
ceoprsstw
crow-steps
ceorrsuuv
verrucous
ceprsssuu
Cupressus
cerrsttuu
structure
cfffiistu
fisticuff
cffgiinsu
sufficing
cffiioosu
officious
cfflooru
off-colour
cfforrssu
cross-ruff
cfgiiiknn
finicking
cfgiiinss
significs
cfgiinnno
confining
cfgilnnou
flouncing
cfhiinnoo
finnochio
cfhiinoor
honorific
cfhiinpst
pinchfist
cfhikoprt
pitchfork
cfhikosst
stockfish
cfhinnosw
snow-finch
cfhiorsss
crossfish
cfhloootf
footcloth
cfhlopsuu
pouchfuls
cfiiisstu
Sufiistic
cfiikklns
skinflick
cfiilmmor
microfilm
cfiilorst
floristic
cfiimoprs
pisciform
cfiimorrr
cirriform
cfiiooprs
soporific
cfikllnot
flintlock
cfiklloor
folkloric
cfiklmosu
folk-music
cfiklnosw
snowflick
cfilnsuuu
funiculus
cfimmnoor
Cominform
cfimmoorr
microform
cfimnoorr
confirmor
corniform
cfimorruv
curviform
cfimorstu
scutiform
cfimorsty
cystiform
cfinnoosu
confusion
cfiooprry
corporify
cfkloorru
rock-flour
cflloorruu
colourful
cflnoorru
corn-flour
cflooortu
court-fool
cflooostt
coltsfoot
cfmnnooru
unconform
cfooorstw
crowfoots
crow's-foot
cforstuuu
fructuous
cggiknost
gong-stick
cghiillns
schilling
cghiilorr
choir-girl
cghiimost
Gothicism
cghiinstt
stitching
cghiinstw
switching
cghiinttw
twitching
cghikknou
kink-cough
cghilnoos
schooling
cghilnooy
ichnology
cghilnosu
slouching
cghilooor
horologic
cghiloory
chirology
cghiloruy
grouchily
cghinorsu
chorusing
cghinortw
night-crow
cghinossu
hocussing
cghioprty
copyright
cghllnoot
long-cloth
cghlooory
chorology
cghloopyy
phycology
cghnoorst
torch-song
cgiiikmmn
mimicking
cgiiilnnn
inclining
cgiiklnpr
prickling
cgiiklnrt
trickling
cgiikmmry
gimmickry
cgiikmnsu
musicking
cgiilmnny
mincingly
cgiilmnuu
glucinium
cgiilnppr
crippling
cgiilosst
logistics
cgiilrstu
liturgics
cgiimnnos
comings-in
cgiinnoot
cognition
incognito
cgiinnouv
unvoicing
cgiinnrru
incurring
cgijnnoru
conjuring
cgiklmnoy
mockingly
cgiklnrtu
truckling
cgiknoprs
prick-song
cgikoopst
pogo-stick
cgilmnooo
monologic
cgilmnopy
complying
cgilmnpru
crumpling
cgilmoory
micrology
cgilmooyz
zymologic
cgilnnnuy
cunningly
cgilnnoor
longicorn
cgilnnruu
uncurling
cgilnooot
ontologic
cgilnoooy
iconology
cgilnooru
colouring
cgilnopuv
loving-cup
cgilnortu
courtling
cgiloooopt
topologic
cgiloosy
sociology
cgimmnnou
communing
cgimmnssu
scummings
cgimnnoos
gnomonics
cgimnnosu
consuming
cginnoors
consignor
cginnoott
cotton-gin
cginnortu
trouncing
cginorrss
ring-cross
cginortuy
congruity
cglmooosy
cosmology
cglmoosuy
muscology
cglooopry
coprology
cgmnooosy
cosmogony
cgnnoottu
guncotton
cgnoorsuu
congruous
chhiloost
soothlich
chhimrsty
rhythmics
chhiopsuu
Ophiuchus
chhklooy
hollyhock
chhlnoruu
lunch-hour
chiiilppp
philippic
chiiilrtt
trilithic
chiikknst
thickskin
chiiklpst
thick-lips
chiiklssy
sickishly
chiiknnov
chinovnik
chiillopy
lyophilic
chiilmort
microlith
chiilootz
zoolithic
chiilorty
rhyolitic
chiilostw
wholistic

chiilptty
typhlitic
chiimmnsu
Munichism
chiimmsty
mythicism
chiimostt
Thomistic
chiimpssy
physicism
chiimstty
mythicist
chiinostu
chitinous
chiinosty
onychitis
chiiopsst
sophistic
chiiorrss
cirrhosis
chiiorsst
trichosis
chiiorsty
hircosity
chiipssty
physicist
chiirsstt
strictish
chiklmnpu
milk-punch
chiklmnru
churn-milk
chiklmost
locksmith
chiklooss
ski-school
chiknostw
thick-sown
chiknottw
witch-knot
chikooptt
pick-tooth
toothpick
chikopstw
stock-whip
whip-stock
chillnoot
loin-cloth
chillorty
torch-lily
chilmnouu
homunculi
chilnopsu
sulphonic
chilnopsw
clownship
chiloopty
holotypic
chiloorss
chlorosis
chiloprtu
Turcophil
chilorstu
trochilus
chilortuy
ulotrichy
chilostty
cystolith
lithocyst
chilprsuu
sulphuric
chilrrsuy
currishly
chimmnooy
homonymic
chimnooot
homotonic
chimnoory
chironomy
chimnoost
monostich
chimnopsy
symphonic
chimnorsu
unchrisom
chimooprt
morphotic
chimoopty
homotypic
chimpstyy
symphytic
chimrstyy
chymistry
chinoopty
hypotonic
chinoortz
chorizont
chinoprry
Pyrrhonic
chinopstu
countship
chinpstuy
physic-nut
chinsssyy
synchysis
chioooprz
zoophoric
chiooprtt
orthoptic
chioopssy
sciosophy
chiooptyz
zoophytic
chioorstt
orthotics
chioprstu
courtship
chioprsyy
hypocrisy
chiopsssy
psychosis
chiorrssu
scirrhous
chiossstu
schistous
chkmopsuu
musk-pouch
chkoprstu
truck-shop
chlmoortt
mortcloth
chlnooopy
colophony
chlnotuuy
uncouthly
chlooppsu
slop-pouch
chlooptyy
hypocotyl
chlopptyy
polyptych
chmnooort
monotroch
chmoorrsu
crush-room
chmorrruw
churr-worm
chnnorsyy
synchrony
chnopppru
punch-prop
chnorstuu
cothurnus
choooppty
photocopy
choooprsy
horoscopy
ciiillty
illicitly
ciiilmnot
limonitic
ciiilmopt
impolitic
ciiilopst
pisolitic
ciiilortv
vitriolic
ciiilosss
silicosis
ciiilossu
silicious
ciiimrstt
triticism
ciiimsttw
witticism
ciiinnrst
intrinsic
ciiiostvy
viciosity
ciijlnopt
clip-joint
ciiknnoty
cytokinin
ciikopprt
rock-pipit
ciillnoop
cipollino
ciillnoos
collision
ciillnoot
cotillion
octillion
ciillnpuu
lupulinic
ciillnuvy
uncivilly
ciillopty
politicly
ciilmnoty
mylonitic
ciilmotyz
zymolitic
ciilmprsy
scrimpily
ciilnnosu
inclusion
ciilnoptu
punctilio
unpolitic
ciiloorst
solicitor
ciiloosss
scoliosis
ciilosuvy
viciously
ciilsstty
stylistic
ciimmssty
mysticism
ciimnorsu
criminous
ciimnoruz
zirconium
ciimorstv
vorticism
ciinnnotu
inunction
ciinnorsu
incursion
ciinnotuy
innocuity
ciinooprt
inotropic
ciinopssu
suspicion
ciinorsuu
incurious
ciinrtuvy
incurvity
ciiooprst
isotropic
ciioprstt
proctitis
protistic
tropistic
ciiorsttu
touristic
ciiorsttv
vorticist
ciiorstuv
virtuosic
ciiorstuy
curiosity
ciiosstvy
viscosity
ciirsttuy
rusticity
cijkossst
joss-stick
cijnnottu
T-junction
cikllnuuy
unluckily
ciklnostt
lintstock
ciklosstt
stock-list
cikpprrsu
prick-spur
cilllnouy
cullionly
cillmorsu
music-roll
cillmoruy
collyrium
cillnoosu
collusion
cilloooru
oil-colour
cilloppuw
pillow-cup
cilloqruw
crow-quill
cillorsss
cross-sill
cilmnooos
Solomonic
cilmnostu
columnist
cilmoorsu
miscolour
cilnooruu
unicolour
ciloopsuy
copiously
ciloorrtu
tricolour
ciloorstu
colourist
cilopptyy
polytypic
ciloprtyy
pyrolytic
ciloprxyy
pyroxylic
cilorrsuy
cursorily
cilorsttu
cultorist
cilorsuuy
curiously
cilosstyy
cytolysis
cilrsttuu
culturist
cilrstuuu
utriculus

cimmmnosu
communism
cimmnnoou
communion
cimmnooot
commotion
cimmnostu
communist
cimmnotuy
community
cimmoorsu
music-room
cimmoorty
microtomy
cimnnooot
monotonic
cimnnosyy
synonymic
cimnnotuu
continuum
cimnooopp
nicompoop
cimnoopty
monotypic
toponymic
cimnootxy
mycotoxin
cimnstuyy
syncytium
cimootuyz
zoocytium
cimoprssu
promuscis
cimopsttu
computist
cimopstty
symptotic
cinnoostu
contusion
cinnoosuu
innocuous
cinoooprt
co-portion
cinooorrs
corrosion
cinoossuy
synoicous
cinoottxy
cytotoxin
cinoprrtu
incorrupt
cinorsuuu
uncurious
cinostuvy
viscounty
ciooprsz
zoosporic
cioooprtz
protozoic
cioopsstu
posticous
ciopprrst
proscript

cioprrsty
scriptory
ciorrrsuu
scurriour
ckkoorstw
stockwork
ckllnoorr
rock-'n'-roll
ckloorsuy
sky-colour
ckmooorst
stock-room
cknoorrww
crownwork
cknrsstuu
sunstruck
ckooorstt
rootstock
cllmooprt
comptroll
clloorrtu
court-roll
clmoooort
locomotor
clmooosty
colostomy
clmoorstu
colostrum
clmopsuuu
opusculum
clmossuuu
musculous
clnooprsu
proconsul
clnoorstu
consultor
clnoosuuy
nocuously
clnortuuy
uncourtly
cloprrtuy
corruptly
cmnooorst
cosmotron
cmnoprtyy
cryptonym
cmooorsst
motocross
cmooorttu
moot-court
cmoosttyy
cystotomy
cnnooossu
consonous
cnooprstw
crown-post
cnoprrtuu
uncorrupt
cnoprtuuy
up-country
cnorssuuy
Cynosurus
coooopprsy
poroscopy

cooooprsuy
ouroscopy
cooprssty
sporocyst
coorrsstw
crosswort
coorrstuu
sour-crout
ddddegios
disgodded
dddeelnuu
undeluded
dddeemnru
reddendum
dddeginor
doddering
dddeiilvy
dividedly
dddeiinuv
undivided
dddilloop
doddipoll
dddlloopy
doddypoll
ddeeeehlr
red-heeled
ddeeeehly
heddle-eye
ddeeefils
seed-field
ddeeefnru
underfeed
ddeeegglr
red-legged
ddeeegipr
pedigreed
ddeeehnpr
deprehend
ddeeeiltt
title-deed
ddeeeimms
misdeemed
ddeeelopv
developed
ddeeennop
open-ended
ddeeennpt
dependent
ddeeenopt
deep-toned
ddeeenprt
pretended
ddeeeprss
depressed
ddeeerswy
dyer's-weed
ddeeestuu
desuetude
ddeefglnu
unfledged
ddeefiimy
demi-deify
ddeefilnu
undefiled

ddeefinnu
undefined
ddeefinop
dope-fiend
ddeefirtw
drift-weed
ddeeggglo
dog-legged
ddeeggilt
gilt-edged
ddeeghilt
delighted
ddeeginnp
depending
ddeeglnpu
unpledged
ddeegoops
good-speed
ddeehiint
hiddenite
ddeehinnr
hinder-end
ddeehnooy
needy-hood
ddeehnoru
deer-hound
ddeehnrru
hundreder
ddeeiilmv
demi-devil
ddeeiiosx
deoxidise
ddeeiklnn
enkindled
ddeeillps
dispelled
ddeeillrs
seed-drill
ddeeillrv
drivelled
ddeeimmno
demi-monde
ddeeimnpu
unimpeded
ddeeinnux
unindexed
ddeeinops
dispondee
ddeeinorw
eiderdown
ddeeinpss
dispensed
ddeeinrsu
underside
undesired
ddeeinrtt
tridented
ddeeioors
deodorise
ddeekloor
red-looked
ddeellopr
red-polled

ddeelotvy
devotedly
ddeelrssu
udderless
ddeelrswy
dyer's-weld
ddeennoru
underdone
ddeennouw
unendowed
ddeenorrt
retrodden
ddeenorru
underdoer
unordered
ddeenortu
outredden
ddeenoruy
round-eyed
ddeenpssu
suspended
ddeenrssu
undressed
ddeeorsty
destroyed
ddeersttu
trust-deed
ddeffiint
diffident
ddeffmoru
dufferdom
ddefggiot
god-gifted
ddefgiiin
dignified
ddefgillo
goldfield
ddefginor
foddering
ddefginru
drug-fiend
ddefiloot
floodtide
ddefirsty
dry-fisted
ddeflloow
oddfellow
ddefnnouu
unfounded
ddeggnruu
ungrudged
ddeghhiir
high-dried
ddeghinrs
shredding
ddegiiirw
rigwiddie
ddegiimsu
misguided
ddegiinnr
niddering
ddegiinss
giddiness

ddegiissu
disguised
ddegijllu
ill-judged
ddegikmno
kingdomed
ddeginnpu
puddening
ddeginorr
derring-do
ddeginpru
redding-up
ddeginrru
undergird
ddegioosz
good-sized
ddegisstu
disgusted
ddeglnnuu
delundung
ddeglnoor
golden-rod
ddeglooop
poodle-dog
ddegnovwy
down-gyved
ddegooory
do-goodery
ddehhnrtu
hundredth
ddehiirsy
Yiddisher
ddehilpsy
Didelphys
ddehiorxy
hydroxide
ddehnorru
hundredor
ddeiiklnr
kiln-dried
ddeiiknrt
diet-drink
ddeiillst
distilled
ddeiillsu
disillude
ddeiinors
iron-sided
ddeiinsst
dissident
ddeiiooxy
oxy-iodide
ddeiklnnu
unkindled
ddeillnru
undrilled
ddeilmnow
low-minded
ddeilnrru
unriddler
ddeilntuu
undiluted
ddeilorww
worldwide

ddeilstuv
dust-devil
ddeilstuy
studiedly
ddeimmosu
desmodium
ddeimnssu
muddiness
ddeinossw
dowdiness
ddeinrssu
dissunder
ruddiness
ddeinstuu
unstudied
ddeioppru
proud-pied
ddeioprsv
disproved
ddeiorstt
distorted
ddelmnooo
noodledom
ddelmnouu
unmoulded
ddennortu
untrodden
ddennoruu
unrounded
ddennoruw
undrowned
ddennosuu
unsounded
ddennouuw
unwounded
ddenooruw
underwood
ddenopsuu
pudendous
ddeooppsu
pseudopod
ddfioortw
drift-wood
ddgiilnrs
riddlings
ddgiilntw
twiddling
ddgiinorr
riding-rod
ddgimooos
do-goodism
ddhioooww
widowhood
ddhlmooou
hood-mould
ddiikknwy
kiddywink
ddiiosuuv
dividuous
ddilloprr
drop-drill
ddinopsuu
dupondius

ddooorwww
row-dow-dow
deeeegnrw
greenweed
deeeegnry
green-eyed
deeeejlww
jewel-weed
deeeeknrw
week-ender
deeefgikn
knife-edge
deeefiirr
re-edifier
deeefiknr
reed-knife
deeefinpr
predefine
deeefinsv
defensive
deeefirrr
free-rider
deeefirrv
free-diver
deeefllnu
needleful
deeeflrux
deflexure
deeefmnor
enfreedom
deeefmnrt
deferment
fermented
deeefprrr
preferred
deeefrryz
freeze-dry
deeegglno
one-legged
deeegilsw
wild-geese
deeegimnr
redeeming
deeegisww
wedgewise
deeegklnt
kentledge
deeeglnnu
needle-gun
deeeglnoy
golden-eye
deeeglosv
sleeve-dog
deeegmnst
segmented
deeegnnru
engendure
deeegnrsw
sedge-wren
deeegnrtt
detergent
deeegrrtt
regretted

deeehillw
idle-wheel
deeehilms
seemlihed
deeehilsw
side-wheel
deeehiltt
dithelete
deeehimms
himseemed
deeehimpr
ephemerid
deeehinpr
ephedrine
deeehinss
heediness
deeehlrst
sheltered
deeehmrss
medresseh
deeehnprr
reprehend
deeehnrru
hereunder
deeehorsw
shore-weed
deeeiilss
dieselise
deeeillmp
millepede
deeeillvw
weevilled
deeeilnnt
needle-tin
deeeilnrt
tree-lined
deeeilptv
depletive
deeeilrrv
deliverer
redeliver
deeeilssw
edelweiss
deeeimnrt
determine
deeeimnsu
Eumenides
deeeimsst
disesteem
deeeinnnz
endenizen
deeeinnss
neediness
deeeinntv
net-veined
deeeinptx
expedient
deeeinrss
reediness
deeeinrst
tenderise
teredines
deeeinsss
seediness

deeeinssw
weediness
deeeirrvw
riverweed
deeeirstv
detersive
deeeirsww
wire-sewed
deeekllnn
kennelled
deeeknpru
underkeep
deeellpsw
speedwell
deeellrvv
vervelled
deeelmnow
lemon-weed
deeelnopv
enveloped
deeeloprv
developer
redevelop
deeelorrs
rose-elder
deeelpsss
speedless
deeelrrtt
red-letter
deeelrstw
sweltered
deeemnrtt
determent
deeemoprt
pedometer
deeemorst
dose-meter
deeemorsu
deer-mouse
mouse-deer
deeemprst
destemper
deeennquu
unqueened
deeennrtu
unentered
deeennruw
unrenewed
deeennsss
denseness
deeenppru
underpeep
deeenprrt
pretender
deeenrrsv
renversed
deeenrrtt
deterrent
deeenrsuv
undeserve
unsevered
deeenssvx
vexedness

deeeoorvw
wood-reeve
deeeoprtv
predevote
deeeorrrs
reredorse
deeeorrss
reredosse
deeeorrst
ore-rested
deeeorstv
stevedore
deeeorsvx
oversexed
deeeprsst
speedster
deeeprssu
supersede
deeerrrss
redresser
deefffstu
feedstuff
deeffinrt
different
deeffnoru
unoffered
deeffoprr
proffered
deefgiiln
Englified
deefgiilr
filigreed
deefgilny
feignedly
deefginnr
finger-end
deefginnu
unfeigned
deefginrr
deferring
deefgjoru
forejudge
deefglorv
gold-fever
deefhlluy
heedfully
deefhlnsu
unfleshed
deefhlnuu
unheedful
deefhlops
sheepfold
deefhlort
threefold
deefiikln
fiend-like
deefiilmn
mine-field
deefiilnr
infielder
deefiilqu
liquefied
deefiilsz
life-sized
deefiiprt
petrified
deefiipss
fissipede
deefiirrt
terrified
deefiirsv
versified
deefiistt
testified
deefilnop
open-field
deefilnox
deflexion
deefilnry
refinedly
deefilort
trefoiled
deefilrsv
self-drive
deefimpst
septemfid
deefinnpr
pen-friend
deefinnru
unrefined
deefinrru
underfire
deefinsst
fetidness
deefinssx
fixedness
deefiorrt
torrefied
deefiprrv
perfervid
deefiprtu
putrefied
deefipstu
stupefied
deefirstu
surfeited
deefllnnu
funnelled
deefllnuu
unfuelled
deefllnuy
needfully
deefllpsu
full-speed
deeflmosv
self-moved
deeflnnuu
unneedful
deeflnosv
sevenfold
deeflnrsu
underself
deeflnrtu
underfelt
deefnoops
spoon-feed
deefnoprs
forespend
deefnorru
refounder
deefnrttu
unfretted
deefnrtuu
unrefuted
deefoprss
professed
deeforrst
defroster
deeggimor
demi-gorge
deegglotw
two-legged
deeggmntu
nutmegged
deeggoprw
egg-powder
deeghhips
high-speed
deeghilnw
wheedling
deeghinnu
unheeding
deeghinuw
unweighed
deeghoors
goose-herd
deegiilns
ingle-side
deegiilnu
guideline
deegiilrt
ridge-tile
deegiinty
tie-dyeing
deegiistv
digestive
deegiklnt
kintledge
deegillor
liege-lord
deegilnns
single-end
deegilnrt
ringleted
deegilnss
gelidness
deegilnst
legendist
deegiloou
ideologue
deegilopr
ridge-pole
deegilprs
spider-leg
deegilrsy
lysergide
deegilssu
guideless
deegimnpt
pigmented
deegimnry
remedying
deegimort
geometrid
deeginnrr
rendering
deeginnrt
tendering
deeginntw
net-winged
deeginort
redingote
deeginprs
predesign
deeginrrr
derringer
deeginrrt
deterring
deeginrsv
deserving
deeginrtu
negritude
deeginrtv
divergent
deeginruv
gerundive
deegioprr
ridge-rope
deegiopru
guide-rope
deegiosst
geodesist
deegiprst
predigest
deegjmntu
judgement
deegklnno
dog-kennel
deegklnow
knowledge
deeglloop
lodgepole
deegllorv
grovelled
deeglmnot
lodgement
deeglorsw
sow-gelder
deeglortt
dog-letter
deegnnnou
endungeon
deegnnoru
dungeoner
deegnoorw
greenwood
deegnorru
reguerdon
deegnorss
engrossed
deegnorww
weed-grown
deegnouyy
young-eyed
deegnssuu
unguessed
deehhilnw
hind-wheel
deehhiloy
hidey-hole
deehhimry
hemihedry
deehhiors
horsehide
deehiinpt
pethidine
deehikrsw
whiskered
deehilmor
helidrome
deehilnuy
unheedily
deehiloru
hierodule
deehilprs
eldership
deehimost
methodise
deehinrrv
hen-driver
deehinrsw
swineherd
deehinrty
enhydrite
deehinttw
hen-witted
deehioprt
herpetoid
deehiorss
shore-side
deehllosu
houselled
deehllosv
shovelled
deehlnopr
penholder
deehloprw
pew-holder
deehlorst
holstered
deehlpsst
depthless
deehlrsss
shredless
deehmoort
hodometer
deehmorst
smothered
deehmrtuy
thrum-eyed
deehnnops
sphendone
deehnooqu
queenhood
deehnopty
endophyte
deehnorrt
dethroner
deehnrrtu
thunderer

deehnrsuu
unushered
deehooprt
heteropod
deehoortx
heterodox
deehoosuv
dove-house
deehrsttu
shuttered
deehssttu
dust-sheet
deeiiinpr
pieridine
deeiiknrs
die-sinker
deeiillmp
millipede
deeiimntt
midinette
deeiimpqu
demipique
deeiimprs
epidermis
deeiimssv
demissive
deeiinnpp
pinnipede
deeiinnrt
interdine
deeiinpst
desipient
deeiinrtu
inerudite
deeiiopst
epidosite
deeiipssw
sideswipe
deeiirrsv
riverside
deeiirrtv
river-tide
deeiirtvv
divertive
deeiisssu
side-issue
deeijnorr
rejoinder
deeijnrtv
jet-driven
deeikllnr
knee-drill
deeiklnsw
slinkweed
deeiklnsx
sex-linked
deeiklovy
yoke-devil
deeiknorv
overinked
deeiknory
kidney-ore
deeillInt
lintelled

deeilllnw
well-lined
deeilllow
well-oiled
deeillmno
ill-omened
deeillmtw
well-timed
deeillnrw
indweller
deeillnst
tinselled
deeillnsv
snivelled
deeillnsw
Willesden
deeillntv
divellent
deeillrrt
tredrille
deeillrrv
driveller
deeillrst
trellised
deeillrsu
slide-rule
deeillrsv
ill-versed
deeillrtu
telluride
deeillrvy
deliverly
deeillssw
wieldless
deeilmmns
Mendelism
deeilmntv
devilment
deeilmptu
multipede
deeilnnpu
penduline
deeilnnru
underline
deeilnopt
depletion
deeilnptu
plenitude
deeilnrtu
interlude
deeilnssx
indexless
deeilntvy
evidently
deeilopps
dispeople
deeiloprs
despoiler
pelorised
deeilpprs
slippered
deeilprss
prideless

deeilrrss
riderless
deeilrrty
retiredly
deeilrsst
slide-rest
deeilrsvy
diversely
deeilrtuy
eruditely
deeimnnpt
impendent
deeimnnru
undermine
deeimnors
demersion
modernise
deeimnptu
unemptied
deeimnrtt
detriment
deeimnrtu
undertime
unmerited
deeimnssx
mixedness
deeimoort
meteoroid
deeimoprr
peridrome
deeimorst
dosimeter
deeimorsx
exodermis
deeimprst
distemper
deeimprtt
permitted
deeimrsst
misdesert
deeimrtuu
deuterium
deeinnnpu
unpennied
deeinnooy
onion-eyed
deeinnort
internode
deeinnott
detention
deeinnpru
unripened
deeinnrst
dinner-set
deeinnrtu
indenture
deeinnsss
snideness
deeinnsuw
unsinewed
deeinoppr
drone-pipe
deeinoptx
pentoxide

deeinorst
desertion
detersion
deeinorsw
rosin-weed
deeinprru
under-ripe
deeinprrv
pen-driver
deeinprss
dispenser
deeinprst
president
deeinprux
unexpired
deeinpsst
tepidness
deeinrrsu
surreined
deeinrsst
dissenter
tiredness
deeinrssw
weirdness
deeinrsuv
unrevised
deeiooppr
pereiopod
deeiooptx
exopodite
deeiopprw
piepowder
deeioprvw
power-dive
deeiorrrv
overrider
deeiorrvv
overdrive
deeiorsvz
oversized
deeiorttx
tetroxide
deeiprrss
disperser
deeiprstu
disrepute
deeirsttv
test-drive
deeirstuv
servitude
deeirttxy
dexterity
deeistttu
destitute
deejnoruy
journeyed
deekkooyy
okey-dokey
deekllnnu
unknelled
deeklnosv
veldskoen
deeknoruv
unrevoked

deellmmop
pommelled
deellmmpu
pummelled
deellmssu
musselled
deellnntu
tunnelled
deellnquu
unquelled
deellnrsu
undersell
deellnrsy
slenderly
deellnssy
endlessly
deelloppr
propelled
deelloprt
petrolled
deellortw
trowelled
deelmoorv
velodrome
deelnnoos
Londonese
deelnnpst
splendent
deelnnpty
pendently
deelnoost
lodestone
deelnoppu
unpeopled
deelnprru
plunderer
deelnsttu
unsettled
deeloprs
rope-soled
deeloprsy
reposedly
deeloprty
depletory
deelorrss
orderless
deelorssw
dowerless
deelprtuy
reputedly
deemnnotw
endowment
deemnnouy
unmoneyed
deemnooss
endosmose
deemnoprs
endosperm
deemnopsu
spodumene
deemnortt
tormented
deemnoruv
unremoved

deemnostu
endosteum
deemnpttu
untempted
deemoorst
osteoderm
deemprttu
trumpeted
deemrrssu
murderess
deennortu
undernote
undertone
deennosst
notedness
deennrstu
nurse-tend
deenooprs
endospore
deenoprrs
responder
deenoprrv
provender
deenoprsv
overspend
deenoprux
expounder
deenopstw
steep-down
deenopsux
unexposed
deenprssu
suspender
unpressed
deenrrrsu
surrender
deenrrstu
unredrest
deenrsstu
untressed
deenrstuv
undervest
deenrstyy
dysentery
deenrttuu
unuttered
deeooprrt
torpedoer
deeooprrv
provedore
deeooprst
torpedoes
deeoostww
sweetwood
deeopppsy
poppy-seed
deeoprrss
depressor
deeoprssw
prowessed
deeoprsuz
douzepers
deeopssss
possessed

deeorrssv
overdress
deeorrstu
trousered
deeorrstx
dextrorse
deeorrsty
destroyer
deeorstux
dexterous
deerrsstu
tressured
deffiiort
fortified
deffiisuv
diffusive
deffilllu
fulfilled
deffilntu
diffluent
deffilsuy
diffusely
deffimrsu
dufferism
deffinoot
fin-footed
defflnruu
unruffled
defflortu
toruffled
deffnnsuu
unsnuffed
deffnstuu
unstuffed
defggiint
fidgeting
defggilln
fledgling
defgglruu
grudgeful
defghilot
eightfold
defgiiiln
lignified
defgiiins
signified
defgiilor
glorified
defgiinnr
friending
defgiirsu
disfigure
defgillno
long-field
defgilnsu
designful
defginruu
unfigured
defgnnoru
underfong
defhhloos
flesh-hood
defhiilsv
devil-fish

defhiiorr
horrified
defhinrsu
furnished
defhiorrs
rodfisher
defhlooow
wholefood
defiiilqu
liquified
defiiinrt
nitrified
defiiirtv
vitrified
defiijstu
justified
defiillmo
mollified
defiillnu
nullified
defiillrr
fire-drill
defiilmsu
semifluid
defiimmmu
mummified
defiimnny
indemnify
defiimort
mortified
defiimrwy
midwifery
defiimsty
mystified
defiinrty
denitrify
defiinsst
disinfest
defiirsvy
diversify
defiirtvy
devitrify
fervidity
defiklorw
fieldwork
defikortw
twiforked
defillnno
linen-fold
defillruy
direfully
defilmnru
remindful
defilmsuy
demulsify
defilnort
interfold
defilnosw
snowfield
defilnoux
defluxion
defilnssu
fluidness

defilnstu
unstifled
defilorsx
dorsiflex
defilrsst
driftless
defimnort
dentiform
defimnoru
uniformed
defimorrt
triformed
defimortw
twiformed
defimorty
deformity
defiorsst
disforest
defiorttu
fortitude
defiosttw
two-fisted
defkoortw
two-forked
defkortwy
twyforked
deflllouy
dolefully
defllnouw
well-found
defllrssu
full-dress
deflnooru
unfloored
deflnoruw
underflow
wonderful
deflsstuy
self-study
defmorrss
dress-form
defmortwy
twyformed
defnoorru
under-roof
defnoortu
underfoot
defnoosst
soft-nosed
defnorssu
foundress
defnorsuu
unsued-for
defooostv
dove's-foot
defoootttw
two-footed
deggiinns
designing
deggiinrv
diverging
deggimnor
niggerdom

degginoss
dogginess
degglnpuu
unplugged
deghhinot
high-toned
deghhottu
thoughted
deghiilpr
hip-girdle
deghiilst
sidelight
deghiinst
night-side
deghiintt
night-tide
deghiipsu
guideship
deghijpsu
judgeship
deghikory
hygrodeik
deghilmsu
gumshield
deghilntu
undelight
unlighted
deghilptu
uplighted
deghilstu
light-dues
deghimnru
humdinger
deghinrtu
ungirthed
deghinstu
unsighted
deghiortv
overdight
deghmoorr
herd-groom
deghmoort
godmother
deghnnruu
underhung
deghnoruw
grewhound
deghnoruy
greyhound
deghoorss
dogshores
degiiimrs
dirigisme
semi-rigid
degiiirst
digitiser
dirigiste
degiiknsz
king-sized
degiillnv
devilling
degiilnnr
niderling

degiilnrw
wildering
degiimnnp
impending
degiimrsu
misguider
degiinnos
diosgenin
degiinnss
dinginess
degiinoss
gneissoid
degiinost
digestion
degiinrrs
ringsider
degiinrss
rigidness
degiinrtu
nigritude
degiinrtv
diverting
degiinstu
distingué
degiioorw
rigwoodie
degiirrsv
verdigris
degiirssu
disguiser
degiklnou
ungodlike
degiknnru
underking
degillmno
modelling
degillnov
long-lived
degillnow
well-doing
degilmnnu
unmingled
degilmnor
goldminer
degilnnru
underling
degilnntu
indulgent
degilnnyy
denyingly
degilnoor
gondolier
degilnors
soldering
degilnoss
godliness
degilnost
Odelsting
degilnotu
longitude
degilnprs
speldring
degiloost
goodliest

degiloosw
wild-goose
degilootv
dog-violet
degilostt
glottides
degimnrru
demurring
degimrsuu
demiurgus
deginnorw
wondering
deginnrsu
sundering
undersign
deginnruw
underwing
deginnssy
dyingness
deginooss
goodiness
deginopss
podginess
deginoruv
devouring
deginpssu
pudginess
degioortw
tiger-wood
degioprty
pterygoid
degiopstu
guide-post
deglloowy
yellow-dog
degllossy
godlessly
deglnoost
goldstone
deglnoouz
Zeuglodon
deglnorsu
groundsel
deglnossu
unglossed
degmnooru
ungroomed
degnnorsu
undersong
degnnoruw
undergown
degnoorrw
wrong-doer
degnoostt
stegodont
degnopruw
gunpowder
degorrstu
drug-store
dehhikmos
sheikhdom
dehhinosy
hoydenish

dehhiopps
phosphide
dehhllnou
hellhound
dehhloosu
household
dehhlorst
threshold
dehhnooru
horehound
dehiiinst
histidine
dehiilmst
dithelism
dehiiloop
iodophile
dehiilpsv
devilship
dehiilrss
disrelish
dehiimnsu
disinhume
dehiimnty
thymidine
dehiinnru
hirundine
dehiinoop
idiophone
dehiioopx
pixie-hood
dehiiosty
hideosity
dehiipsty
diphysite
dehiklnor
inkholder
dehilmnou
lime-hound
dehilnnor
innholder
dehilnopt
dolphinet
dehilnowy
wild-honey
dehilnpsu
Delphinus
dehiloort
rhodolite
dehilostw
dish-towel
dehilosuy
hideously
dehilrruy
hurriedly
dehimmost
methodism
dehimnosy
hoydenism
dehimnssu
humidness
dehimorrt
Thermidor
dehimostt
methodist

dehinnoor
Rhineodon
dehinnopr
endorphin
dehinoort
rhodonite
dehinoosw
swinehood
dehinorrt
trihedron
dehinorst
disthrone
dehinorvw
wind-hover
dehinosst
dishonest
dehinppuw
unwhipped
dehinrruu
unhurried
dehinrsuv
unshrived
dehiootww
howtowdie
whitewood
dehiorsty
hysteroid
dehiorsuy
yird-house
dehkloost
stokehold
dehknooos
hook-nosed
dehlmnopy
endolymph
dehlmnouy
lyme-hound
dehlmooru
hordeolum
dehlmoorw
worm-holed
dehlnoosu
sound-hole
dehlnossw
seldshown
dehlorsyy
hydrolyse
dehlortyy
hydrolyte
dehlosstu
shouldest
dehlprsuu
desulphur
dehmmopru
prudhomme
dehmnoopr
endomorph
dehmoorsy
hydrosome
dehmoorty
hodometry
dehmorrwy
rhyme-word

dehnnnsuu
unshunned
dehnnoops
sphenodon
dehnnosuw
newshound
dehnooowy
wood-honey
dehnooprs
horse-pond
dehnorstu
undershot
dehnorsuy
enhydrous
dehnprtuu
upthunder
dehoooppt
hooped-pot
dehooorsw
wood-horse
dehooosuw
woodhouse
dehooprty
orthopedy
dehoosssu
doss-house
dehorsstu
stud-horse
dehostuuy
house-duty
deiiikntt
identikit
deiiillmt
illimited
deiiilmss
dissimile
deiiilqsu
liquidise
deiiinnqu
quinidine
deiiinsss
disseisin
deiiinssz
disseizin
deiikklnr
kilderkin
deiiklnnx
index-link
deiiknrsv
skin-diver
deiillmpy
impliedly
deiillmty
limitedly
deiillnst
instilled
deiillopr
pilloried
deiillops
ellipsoid
deiillovw
wild-olive
deiillrst
distiller

deiilmntu
unlimited
deiilmquu
deliquium
deiilmttu
multitide
deiilnnuv
unlived-in
deiilnotu
toluidine
deiilnoxy
xyloidine
deiilnssv
lividness
deiiloprt
reptiloid
deiilorsu
delirious
deiilpptu
lippitude
deiilpttt
tip-tilted
deiilsuvv
divulsive
deiimmrsu
disimmure
deiimnnos
dimension
deiimnnst
misintend
deiimnnty
indemnity
deiimnoss
demission
deiimnosx
endomixis
deiimnrss
mini-dress
minidress
deiimnrtw
mid-winter
deiimnruu
uredinium
deiimnsst
timidness
deiimortv
dormitive
deiimprss
misprised
deiimprsu
presidium
deiimprtu
Pteridium
deiimrtty
tridymite
deiinnnot
indention
deiinnoop
opinioned
deiinnors
Deinornis
deiinnort
rendition

deiinnosu
unionised
deiinnott
dentition
deiinnotv
vendition
deiinnrtw
interwind
deiinnssw
windiness
deiinntuv
uninvited
deiinoprt
perdition
deiinopss
indispose
deiinorss
Ironsides
deiinorst
disorient
deiinorsv
diversion
deiinortt
detrition
deiinortu
erudition
deiinprrs
spin-drier
deiinpstz
pint-sized
deiinrsst
dirtiness
deiinsstv
disinvest
deiinssvv
vividness
deiinsszz
dizziness
deiinstuv
unvisited
deiintttw
nitwitted
deiiorsss
disseisor
siderosis
deiiorssz
disseizor
deiiosstu
seditious
deiiostty
tediosity
deiiprrst
priest-rid
deiiprstt
dipterist
deiirstvy
diversity
deiirsuvv
redivivus
deijnnotu
unjointed
deijnnruu
uninjured

deikllnsu
unskilled
deikllosv
Volkslied
deiklnstu
Kunstlied
deiklorsw
swordlike
deikmmnsu
unskimmed
deikmnnow
womenkind
deiknnnsu
unskinned
deiknsssu
duskiness
deilllpuv
pulvilled
deillmnou
mullioned
deillmnuu
unillumed
deillnoss
dolliness
deillnpsu
unspilled
deillnstu
unstilled
deillnsuu
unsullied
deillopst
pistolled
deillorsy
soldierly
deillprtu
uptrilled
deillstty
stiltedly
deilmnopt
implodent
deilmnuxy
unmixedly
deilmoosu
melodious
deilmopsy
disemploy
deilmorsw
idle-worms
deilnnoos
Londonise
deilnopsu
unspoiled
deilnoptu
unpiloted
deilnopty
pointedly
deilnorsu
undersoil
deilnosss
solidness
deilnotuv
involuted
deilnrssu
luridness

deilnstty
stintedly
deilooppt
toodle-pip
deiloortw
lowrie-tod
Tod-lowrie
deilopptw
two-lipped
deilosstu
dissolute
deilostuy
tediously
deilosuvy
deviously
deilrsstu
dislustre
deimmmrsu
midsummer
deimmnors
modernism
deimmnouy
neodymium
deimmnrtu
untrimmed
deimmnssu
dumminess
deimmosty
immodesty
deimnooss
moodiness
deimnopru
impounder
deimnopsu
unimposed
deimnorst
modernist
deimnorty
modernity
deimnotuv
unmotived
deimnprtu
imprudent
deimnpssu
dumpiness
deimnrsuy
synedrium
deimnsstu
tumidness
deimoprrs
primrosed
deimoprss
sporidesm
deimopsst
despotism
deimoqrsu
squiredom
deimorsty
dosimetry
deinnnosu
innuendos
deinnoptu
unpointed

deinnorsu
unrosined
deinnorsy
synedrion
deinnossw
downiness
deinnostu
tendinous
deinnprtu
unprinted
deinnrsuu
uninsured
deinnrttu
undertint
deinnsttu
unstinted
deinooprt
portioned
deinoorst
detorsion
deinoortt
detortion
deinoossw
woodiness
deinopprr
properdin
deinoprst
drip-stone
deinoprsv
disproven
deinoprtv
provident
deinorruw
unworried
deinorssw
rowdiness
wordiness
deinorstu
detrusion
deinorsuu
uredinous
deinortww
write-down
deinosstt
dottiness
deinprrsy
spin-dryer
deinprstu
unstriped
deinpstww
windswept
deinrstty
dentistry
deinssstu
dustiness
deinsttuw
untwisted
deiooprst
depositor
deiooprtx
protoxide
deioopstw
wood-spite

deioopsuw
pousowdie
deioprssu
disposure
deioprstu
dipterous
deioprttu
torpitude
deiorsstu
dioestrus
deiorssuu
residuous
deiotttuw
outwitted
deiprrssu
surprised
deiprrstu
disrupter
deiprsuvy
dispurvey
deiprttuu
turpitude
deirssstu
dress-suit
dejkmnoru
junkerdom
deklnnruy
drunkenly
deknoortu
undertook
deknorruw
underwork
dellnopsw
spelldown
dellnorss
drollness
delmnooov
moon-loved
delmnouvy
unmovedly
delmnpruu
unrumpled
delmnuuzz
unmuzzled
delmooorx
loxodrome
delmopuzz
puzzledom
delnoorww
low-downer
delnoprsu
splendour
delnoprtu
underplot
delnopsuu
pendulous
delnorruy
unorderly
delnosssu
soundless
delnossuw
woundless
delnprtuy
prudently

delooosuw
woodlouse
deloorssu
odourless
deloorsuu
urodelous
delorsssw
swordless
delorstuy
desultory
delostuuy
duteously
delprsuuy
usurpedly
demnnoruu
unmourned
demnnotuu
unmounted
demnopsuy
pseudonym
demnorstu
undermost
demooortw
two-roomed
demooosuw
woodmouse
demooppru
propodeum
demorrsuu
murderous
dempprtuu
trumped-up
dennorssu
roundness
dennorsuw
sun-downer
dennosssu
soundness
denoooppr
propodeon
denooorst
door-stone
denooostw
wood-stone
denooppsu
unopposed
denooprst
drop-stone
denooprsu
ponderous
denooprtv
devonport
denoorstu
tournedos
denoorsuw
wonderous
denooruvw
overwound
denoppppru
unpropped
denopprru
underprop
denoppstu
unstopped

denoprssu
proudness
denopsttu
unspotted
denorttuu
untutored
denostuuu
unduteous
denprsuuu
unpursued
denrrrsuy
surrendry
denrsstuu
untrussed
denrsttuy
studentry
deooorrtw
rood-tower
deooprruv
overproud
deopprrss
drop-press
deorrsuuv
verdurous
deorstuvy
overstudy
deprssstu
press-stud
deqrrsuuy
surquedry
dfffoostu
food-stuff
dffhinssu
snuff-dish
dffiinosu
diffusion
dfghiilrt
frithgild
dfgiiimnw
midwifing
dfgiiinny
indignify
dfgiiirty
frigidity
dfgiimnoy
modifying
dfgiinnuy
undignify
dfgilnnou
foundling
unfolding
dfgilnnoy
goldfinny
dfgooosst
soft-goods
dfhhinosu
hound-fish
dfhiloory
hydrofoil
dfhinorsu
round-fish
dfhiorssw
swordfish

dfhlnoouw
wolf-hound
dfiilorty
floridity
dfiinprst
spindrift
dfiinstww
wind-swift
dfiioprst
disprofit
dfillmnuy
mindfully
dfilltuuy
dutifully
dfilmnnuu
unmindful
dfilmnosu
sound-film
dfilntuuu
undutiful
dfinorstw
snowdrift
dfioortuw
fruitwood
dfllmootu
mould-loft
dfloooruw
wood-flour
dfnoooops
spoon-food
dfnoooptu
foot-pound
dfooprstu
dustproof
dfoosttuy
dusty-foot
dgghilosy
doggishly
dgghinoot
good-night
dgghnooru
ground-hog
dggiillny
glidingly
dgginnoow
down-going
dgginnoru
grounding
dghhiinst
hindsight
dghhinoot
thinghood
dghhinopt
diphthong
dghhoorsu
rough-shod
dghiinttw
wind-tight
dghiknoos
king's-hood
dghilmost
goldsmith
dghilnopu
upholding

dghilotuy
doughtily
dghimopsy
sphygmoid
dghinnoot
do-nothing
dghinorsu
shrouding
dghinortw
downright
right-down
dghlooryy
hydrology
dghooostt
dog's-tooth
dghoorstw
ghost-word
dghoorsuu
sour-dough
dgiiimnvw
midwiving
dgiiinnot
indigotin
dgiiinnrt
nitriding
dgiiinnty
indignity
dgiijnory
joy-riding
dgiiknsvy
sky-diving
dgiillnsy
slidingly
dgiilnnps
spindling
dgiilnnsw
swindling
dgiilnnwy
windingly
dgiilnrst
stridling
dgiimnors
Girondism
dgiinnnuw
unwinding
dgiinopss
disposing
dgiinorst
Girondist
dgiirttuy
turgidity
dgiklnops
goldspink
dgiknopsw
gowdspink
dgillnorw
worldling
dgillnouy
ungodlily
dgilmnooo
mongoloid
dgilnnory
droningly

dgilnnosy
goldsinny
dgilnnowy
down-lying
dgilnnuyy
undyingly
dgiloooosy
dosiology
dgilootty
dittology
dgimnrsuy
Grundyism
dginnosww
downswing
dginoorsw
swing-door
dginorstu
strouding
dginoruvy
ground-ivy
dglnoopty
Glyptodon
dgmnnsuuu
mundungus
dgmoorruw
gourd-worm
dgmoorstu
stud-groom
dgnnortuu
ground-nut
dgoorrsuu
sour-gourd
dhhoootuy
youthhood
dhiiilstt
lithistid
dhiiimpru
rhipidium
dhiiinopr
rhipidion
dhiiipsty
hispidity
dhiilnrww
whirlwind
dhiilopsy
syphiloid
dhiinoort
ornithoid
dhiintwwy
withywind
dhiioopru
ophiuroid
dhiklssuy
duskishly
dhillosty
doltishly
dhilmooyy
mylohyoid
dhilmpsuy
dumpishly
dhilnnoos
Londonish
dhilnorsy
dronishly

dhiloostu
lustihood
dhilprsuy
prudishly
dhimnosty
hymnodist
dhimorstw
wordsmith
dhimorsuu
dishumour
dhinnotuw
whodunnit
dhinooprs
rhodopsin
dhinoopty
hypnotoid
dhinoorsu
dishonour
dhinoppsu
ship-pound
dhinopruw
whip-round
dhioosttw
withstood
dhirssttu
shirt-stud
dhkmnooos
monkshood
dhknoruyy
hunky-dory
dhllooowy
Hollywood
dhllooppy
phyllopod
dhlloopsy
dolly-shop
dhlmootuu
loudmouth
dhlnooopt
lophodont
dhlnoosuw
slow-hound
dhloprtuy
hydropult
dhmnoopwy
wood-nymph
dhnoooryz
hydrozoon
dhnoortww
down-throw
throw-down
dhnoostuw
Southdown
dhnorstuu
thundrous
dhooortxy
orthodoxy
dhoopppuy
puppyhood
dhoprstyy
dystrophy
diiikmrst
midi-skirt

diiilmpty
limpidity
diiilnpsy
insipidly
diiilqtuy
liquidity
diiinossu
insidious
diiinosuv
invidious
diillmnoo
modillion
diilnosuv
divulsion
diiloprty
triploidy
diilostty
stolidity
diimnoort
dormition
diimoorty
iridotomy
diimoprsu
sporidium
diimorssy
dimissory
diimprtuu
tripudium
diinoprss
disprison
diinoprxy
pyridoxin
diioprtty
torpidity
diiorrtty
torridity
diiprttuy
putridity
diipsttuy
stupidity
dijnotuww
jut-window
diknoostw
stink-wood
dillnosuy
unsolidly
dillooppy
polyploid
dillooptt
dottipoll
dilmnnoos
Londonism
dilmnooru
iron-mould
dilmooppy
polypidom
dilnooopz
Diplozoon
dilnopsux
spondulix
dilnoqtuw
down-quilt
dilooopyz
polyzooid

dilooptuw
tulip-wood
dimmnnouw
mud-minnow
dimmopsuy
sympodium
dimnopruu
purdonium
dimnorstw
storm-wind
dimoooosv
voodooism
dimooossu
isodomous
dimoorrty
dormitory
dimoortuw
moudiwort
dimoortww
mowdiwort
dinooorsu
inodorous
dinooprst
piston-rod
dinoprrtu
round-trip
dinopttuy
point-duty
dinorttuy
rotundity
diooostv
voodooist
diooopssu
isopodous
diooprrty
proditory
diooprsst
prosodist
dioprrstu
disruptor
dioprrstw
wrist-drop
dklnoooru
look-round
dknoorstw
sword-knot
dllnoruwy
unworldly
dlmooorxy
loxodromy
dlnnosuuy
unsoundly
dlooorsuy
odorously
dmmorrstu
storm-drum
dmnoorruw
round-worm
dmooprrsu
prodromus
dmorssttu
dust-storm
dnnorrtuu
turnround

dnooorrtu
ororotund
dnoopsstu
sound-post
dnoortuww
woundwort
dooorstuy
outdoorsy
eeeefhlrw
free-wheel
eeeefhrst
freesheet
eeeegnrrv
evergreen
eeeehlmpt
telepheme
eeeehlrsw
elsewhere
eeeehpssy
sheep's-eye
eeeelmrtt
telemeter
eeeelnssv
elevenses
eeeelntvv
velveteen
eeeemnntv
événement
eeeennstv
seventeen
eeeenopry
eye-opener
eeeenprst
presentee
eeeenrstw
sweetener
eeeeprrsv
persevere
eeeerstvy
yestereve
eeeffinrt
fifteener
eeeffmttu
muffettee
eeefghinr
Feringhee
eeefgknru
fenugreek
eeefhirtt
tithe-free
eeefhlorw
fore-wheel
eeefhnrrs
freshener
refreshen
eeefhorrt
therefore
eeefhorrw
wherefore
eeefhortt
foreteeth
eeefhrrrs
refresher

eeefilrrs
  serrefile
eeefilrrv
  free-liver
eeefilrvx
  reflexive
eeefinrrt
  interfere
eeefisssw
  fesse-wise
eeeflnsst
  fleetness
eeeflrsty
  free-style
eeeflrttu
  fleurette
eeefmnorw
  freewomen
eeefnorst
  freestone
eeefprrrr
  preferrer
eeeggortt
  georgette
eeeghoprs
  geosphere
eeegiknps
  Pekingese
eeegillnr
  leger-line
eeegillss
  liegeless
eeegilmns
  gelsemine
eeeginnot
  eigentone
eeeginnrv
  veneering
eeeginprr
  peregrine
eeeginrvv
  revengive
eeegirsty
  geyserite
  tiger's-eye
eeegisttx
  exegetist
eeegklrss
  Greekless
eeegllnty
  genteelly
eeeglmnnt
  gentlemen
eeeglnntu
  ungenteel
eeeglrsty
  steel-grey
eeegmnnru
  energumen
eeegmnntv
  vengement
eeegmnrss
  messenger

eeegmorrt
  ergometer
eeegnnrss
  greenness
eeegnorrv
  overgreen
eeegrttuv
  vee-gutter
eeehillns
  hellenise
eeehilmtt
  Thelemite
eeehilnnp
  nepheline
eeehilnpt
  nephelite
eeehilprt
  three-pile
eeehilrtu
  eleutheri
eeehimprs
  ephemeris
eeehimpsu
  euphemise
eeehimstt
  time-sheet
eeehklosu
  house-leek
eeehlmnty
  methylene
eeehlnopt
  telephone
eeehlnosw
  nose-wheel
eeehlnrst
  enshelter
eeehlnsst
  netheless
eeehlopsu
  peel-house
eeehlrrst
  shelterer
eeehmmnty
  enthymeme
eeehmnopr
  ephemeron
eeehmorrt
  rheometer
eeehmorst
  threesome
eeehmorsw
  somewhere
eeehnnpst
  nepenthes
eeehnrsst
  thereness
  threeness
eeehnrssw
  whereness
eeehnrvwy
  everywhen
eeehnsstw
  news-sheet

eeehoprsx
  exosphere
eeehorstu
  ethereous
eeehprsst
  Herpestes
eeehrrstw
  tree-shrew
eeehrsttu
  usherette
eeeiiklnv
  keelivine
eeeiikrst
  kieserite
eeeiklnqu
  queen-like
eeeiklnvy
  keelyvine
eeeikmrst
  kermesite
eeeiknnpr
  innkeeper
eeeiknost
  sinoekete
eeeillmrv
  vermeille
eeeillpst
  pelletise
eeeillsuv
  veilleuse
eeeilmnrv
  envermeil
eeeilmntx
  exilement
eeeilmsst
  seemliest
eeeilnnrv
  enlivener
eeeilnstx
  extensile
eeeilostt
  Teleostei
eeeilptvx
  expletive
eeeilrstx
  exsertile
eeeilsvwy
  swivel-eye
eeeimmnno
  menominee
eeeimmrss
  mesmerise
eeeimmsst
  misesteem
eeeimnnrt
  nemertine
eeeimnrtx
  extermine
eeeimorrt
  eriometer
eeeimortt
  meteorite
eeeimprrt
  perimeter

eeeinnprs
  persienne
eeeinnrtv
  intervene
eeeinorst
  neoterise
eeeinprrs
  reserpine
eeeinprty
  pyreneite
eeeinpsvx
  expensive
eeeinqsuz
  queen-size
eeeinrrtw
  wernerite
eeeinrstt
  serinette
eeeinrstv
  resentive
eeeinrstx
  sixteener
eeeinrttv
  retentive
eeeinsstv
  seventies
eeeinstvx
  extensive
eeeiprrtt
  Pierrette
  preterite
eeeiprstx
  expertise
eeeiqtttu
  etiquette
eeeirrrtv
  retriever
eeeirrtvv
  revertive
eeeirsttv
  serviette
eeejllrwy
  jewellery
eeejrsttt
  jet-setter
eeekllnsw
  knee-swell
eeeklnsss
  sleekness
eeekmmort
  mekometer
eeekmorst
  smoke-tree
eeekmrstu
  musketeer
eeeknopst
  open-steek
eeellnprt
  repellent
eeellnptx
  expellent
eeellpsss
  sleepless

eeelmmnop
  Melpomene
eeelmnopt
  elopement
eeelmnsss
  menseless
eeelmoppr
  merpeople
eeelmrtty
  telemetry
eeelmrtxy
  extremely
eeelnnpty
  pentylene
eeelnorvw
  wolverene
eeelnostt
  solenette
eeelnottv
  novelette
eeelnqssu
  queenless
eeelnrrty
  terrenely
eeelnrssv
  nerveless
eeelnssss
  senseless
eeelnstuv
  sleeve-nut
eeeloprsv
  oversleep
eeeloprtw
  peel-tower
eeelrrsvy
  reversely
eeemmoprt
  emmetrope
eeemnoort
  oenometer
eeemnorrs
  sermoneer
eeemnorrv
  nevermore
eeemnorst
  merestone
eeemnrstt
  entremets
eeemnrsty
  mesentery
eeemnrttv
  revetment
eeemoprtx
  extempore
eeemorrsu
  reremouse
eeennorst
  sonneteer
eeennssst
  tenseness
eeenopprw
  pew-opener
eeenorsuv
  venereous

eeenprrst
presenter
represent
eeenprrtv
preventer
eeenprsuv
supervene
eeenpssst
steepness
eeenqrssu
queerness
eeenrrstw
westerner
eeenrrsuv
unreserve
eeenrssst
terseness
eeensssstw
sweetness
eeeoprrtv
portreeve
eeeoprsst
poetresse
eeeorrstv
oversteer
eeeorrtvx
overexert
eeeppprtu
puppeteer
eeeprrrsv
preserver
eeeprrrtv
perverter
eeeqrrstu
requester
eeeqrsstu
sequester
eeerrttux
retexture
eefffklru
kerfuffle
eefffmnot
feoffment
eeffghopt
off-the-peg
eeffglntu
effulgent
eeffhills
shelf-life
eeffhintt
fifteenth
eeffhlrsu
reshuffle
eeffimnru
muffineer
eeffinosv
offensive
eeffinrst
stiffener
eeffiorrt
forfeiter
eefflaott
fleet-foot

eeffoprrr
profferer
eefforsstt
off-street
setter-off
eefghiorw
foreweigh
eefghirrt
freighter
eefgillnr
refelling
eefgillny
feelingly
eefgilnnu
unfeeling
eefgilrss
griefless
eefgimruv
vermifuge
eefginorr
foreigner
eefginrrr
referring
eefginrrt
ferreting
eefgiortv
forgetive
eefgiprru
prefigure
eefglnrtu
refulgent
eefglrrtu
regretful
eefgorrtt
forgetter
eefhiiklt
thief-like
eefhijlsw
jewelfish
eefhillrs
shellfire
eefhiorsu
firehouse
eefhiosuw
housewife
eefhiprsv
ship-fever
eefhisstw
sweetfish
eefhllsss
fleshless
eefhlmnst
fleshment
eefhloruw
four-wheel
eefhmorrt
therefrom
eefhmorrw
wherefrom
eefhnorsw
foreshewn
eefhnrsss
freshness

eefhoorrs
fore-horse
foreshore
eefhoortt
three-foot
eefhorrtu
three-four
eefhrrrtu
furtherer
eefiillnp
fillipeen
eefiilmtx
flexitime
eefiilnrt
infertile
eefiilqru
liquefier
eefiilrst
fertilise
eefiimnty
femineity
eefiimrrt
metrifier
eefiinrss
fieriness
eefiiprtw
tripewife
eefiirrsv
versifier
eefiirstt
testifier
eefiklmrv
milk-fever
eefiklnss
knifeless
eefiknrst
knife-rest
eefiknrsu
refusenik
eefilllos
filoselle
eefillpty
pelletify
eefillrty
fertilely
eefilmpxy
exemplify
eefilnorx
reflexion
eefilnrux
inflexure
eefilntuw
wulfenite
eefilortu
outrelief
eefilstvy
festively
eefimnrtt
refitment
eefinnpvy
fivepenny
eefinoprt
reef-point

eefinorst
firestone
forestine
eefinprsu
superfine
eefinrrst
renfierst
eefinrstu
interfuse
eefioprrt
profiteer
eefioprrw
fire-power
eefiossuw
sousewife
eefipprrr
fripperer
eefiprstu
stupefier
eefiprsuv
perfusive
eefirrrtt
fritterer
eefirrrtu
fruiterer
eefirrstu
surfeiter
eefirrttu
fruit-tree
eefklltu
kettleful
eefknoort
foretoken
eefllnpsu
spleenful
eefllopww
pew-fellow
eeflmortw
flowmeter
eeflnnntu
funnel-net
eeflnostu
nose-flute
eeflnrstu
resentful
eeflnrtvy
fervently
eefloprsu
reposeful
eeflorrtx
retroflex
eeflrsttu
streetful
eefmnoorw
forewomen
eefmoprrr
performer
eefmorrvw
worm-fever
eefmprruy
perfumery
eefnnosst
oftenness

eefoprrrv
perfervor
eefoprrty
ferrotype
eefprssuu
superfuse
eegghorsw
whore's-egg
eeggiilnt
gelignite
eeggiklnr
Greekling
eeggilmnr
gemel-ring
eeggilnnt
negligent
eeggilnss
legginess
eeggiloos
geologise
eegginnpu
pug-engine
eegginnrv
revenging
eegginrrs
sniggerer
eegginrst
gee-string
eegginrtt
gettering
eeggiorsu
egregious
eeggoorrv
overgorge
eeggoorsy
grey-goose
eeggrsstu
suggester
eeghhiitt
eightieth
eeghhillv
high-level
eeghhirtt
thegither
eeghikntw
weeknight
eeghilmnt
metheglin
eeghilnnt
enlighten
eeghilnrs
Englisher
eeghimost
egotheism
eightsome
eeghinnss
sneeshing
eeghinpst
phengites
eeghinrrr
herringer
eeghinrtt
tightener

eeghiorvw
overweigh
eeghippst
peep-sight
eeghirsst
sightseer
eeghllnop
phellogen
eeghloort
theologer
eeghloott
logothete
eeghlootu
theologue
eeghnnorr
greenhorn
eeghnoopt
photogene
eeghnortu
toughener
eegiilmnt
gmelinite
eegiilnno
oil-engine
eegiilnrv
inveigler
relieving
eegiilnst
gentilise
eegiilops
epilogise
eegiilors
religiose
eegiilprv
privilege
eegiinrsu
signeurie
eegiinstv
ingestive
eegiisttz
zeitgeist
eegijllnw
jewelling
eegijlnry
jeeringly
eegijnnnt
jenneting
eegillllnv
levelling
eegillnpr
repelling
eegillnpx
expelling
eegillnrv
revelling
eegillnry
leeringly
reelingly
eegillntv
Glenlivet
eegillnvw
well-given
eegillssu
guileless

eegilmmsu
Gelsemium
eegilmnsy
seemingly
eegilnnrt
relenting
eegilnnuy
genuinely
eegilnoos
neologise
eegilnorv
line-grove
eegilnpwy
weepingly
eegilnrst
steerling
eegilnrtt
lettering
eegilnrtw
weltering
eegilnrvy
veeringly
eegilntvv
velveting
eegilntwy
weetingly
eegilopss
gospelise
eegilorst
sortilege
eegilsttw
Weltgeist
eegimnnsu
unseeming
eegimnprt
tempering
eeginnnuu
ungenuine
eeginnssv
givenness
eeginntuw
unweeting
eeginooss
oogenesis
eeginorss
egression
eeginorsv
sovereign
eeginosss
gneissose
eeginosxy
oxygenise
eeginpppr
peppering
eeginprss
speerings
eeginqsuz
squeezing
eeginrrst
restringe
eeginrrsv
reversing

eeginrstw
swingtree
westering
eeginrsty
eye-string
eeginrttv
revetting
vignetter
eegisstuw
guestwise
eeglllpru
leg-puller
eegllmoru
glomerule
eegllooty
teleology
eeglloprs
gospeller
eegllorrv
groveller
eeglnortt
lorgnette
eeglnottu
tonguelet
eeglnssuy
glueyness
eeglppuzz
puzzle-peg
eeglrsssu
surgeless
eegmmnttu
tegmentum
eegmnnotu
engoûment
eegmnoorr
greenroom
eegnoorst
oestrogen
eegnoorsu
erogenous
eegnoosty
osteogeny
eegnoosux
exogenous
eegnoprrr
porrenger
eegnorrss
engrosser
eegnorssv
governess
eegnpstuy
type-genus
eegnrrstu
resurgent
eegoopsst
goose-step
eegoprstu
guest-rope
eegoprtuu
Portuguee
eegoqrstu
grotesque
eegorrttu
tregetour

eehhinoss
shoeshine
eehhinovy
hive-honey
eehhinpsy
hyphenise
eehhirttw
therewith
eehhirtww
wherewith
eehhklrsu
sheer-hulk
eehhkoops
sheep-hook
eehhlllos
shell-hole
eehhnopps
phosphene
eehhoorss
horseshoe
eehiilmtw
white-lime
eehiilrtt
Hitlerite
eehiinnrw
Rhinewine
eehiinntt
ninetieth
eehiipsst
epithesis
eehiirttw
witherite
eehiklllls
shell-like
eehikmnsv
Menshevik
eehiknpss
sheepskin
eehillllms
shell-lime
eehillllmw
mill-wheel
eehillmns
Hellenism
eehillnst
Hellenist
eehilmnop
Philomene
eehilmost
lithesome
eehilmosw
somewhile
eehilmtuv
helvetium
eehilnnos
nine-holes
eehilnoop
oenophile
eehilnopx
xenophile
eehilnors
shoreline
eehilnosu
house-line

eehilnprs
replenish
eehilnpss
spleenish
eehilnpsw
wheel-spin
eehilnrst
inshelter
eehilnsss
shineless
eehilnsst
litheness
eehilopty
heliotype
eehilortv
rivet-hole
eehilpsvy
peevishly
eehilrstw
erstwhile
eehimmpsu
euphemism
eehimnrrt
herriment
eehimoprt
hemitrope
eehimprrw
whimperer
eehimrsst
hermitess
eehinopsu
euphonise
pine-house
eehinoptt
epitheton
eehinopvw
viewphone
eehinorst
sheet-iron
eehinorsv
overshine
eehinortt
thereinto
eehinortw
whereinto
eehinosst
hessonite
eehinpqsu
queenship
eehinprss
phrenesis
eehinrttw
white-rent
eehinsstw
whiteness
eehinsttu
euthenist
eehinsttx
sixteenth
eehintttw
twentieth
eehioprtt
tephroite

eehioqrtu
theorique
eehiorrst
rhetorise
theoriser
eehiorsst
heterosis
eehiorstw
otherwise
eehipprry
periphery
eehippssy
epiphyses
eehiprrsw
whisperer
eehiprsuv
superhive
eehirrsst
heritress
eehirrtty
erythrite
eehkllnoy
knee-holly
eehkloost
stoke-hole
eehklorww
wheelwork
eehkmpssu
musk-sheep
eehknrtuy
turkey-hen
eehlllsss
shell-less
eehllmmru
hummeller
eehllorst
hosteller
eehllorsv
shoveller
eehllosuw
well-house
eehlmnstu
sun-helmet
eehlmoosu
mouse-hole
eehlmoosw
wholesome
eehlmorru
home-ruler
eehlmorty
mother-lye
eehlmorvw
overwhelm
eehlmorww
worm-wheel
eehlmoszz
shemozzle
eehlmrssy
rhymeless
eehlnopty
polythene
telephony
eehlnossw
wholeness
eehlnossy
honeyless
eehlnstvy
seventhly
eehlooptt
telephoto
eehlorsss
horseless
shoreless
eehlossst
hostlesse
eehlosssu
houseless
eehlprsuw
spur-wheel
eehmmoory
homeomery
eehmnoopr
pheromone
eehmnoott
nomothete
eehmnoprt
phonmeter
eehmnorty
heteronym
eehmnpttu
umpteenth
eehmnrrty
herryment
eehmopsty
mesophyte
eehmorrst
smotherer
eehmrrrtu
murtherer
eehmrrsty
rhymester
eehmrrtuy
eurytherm
eehnnoost
hone-stone
eehnooprs
noosphere
eehnoppty
phenotype
eehnoprrs
prehensor
eehnoprtu
thereupon
eehnopruw
whereupon
eehnopstu
penthouse
eehnoptty
entophyte
eehnorrst
shortener
eehnorrtt
thorntree
eehnorsst
otherness
eehnorttu
thereunto
eehnortuw
whereunto
eehnosttw
whetstone
eehnpprsu
pen-pusher
eehnssssty
syntheses
eehooprrt
rheotrope
eehooprsu
rope-house
eehoorsvw
howsoever
whosoever
eehoprsty
hey-presto
eehoprtxy
xerophyte
eehopsstu
pesthouse
eehorsstu
rest-house
eeiiklrrv
riverlike
eeiiknntz
zinkenite
eeiillmrt
millerite
eeiillmtw
willemite
eeiillntv
vitelline
eeiilnnrt
interline
eeiilnotv
olivenite
eeiilnrst
resilient
eeiilnstu
luteinise
eeiilopst
sepiolite
eeiilrsst
Listerise
sterilise
eeiilrssv
silverise
eeiimmrst
eremitism
eeiimnost
Simeonite
eeiimnprs
mire-snipe
eeiimopst
epitomise
eeiimorss
isomerise
eeiimrssv
remissive
eeiinnnpt
penninite
eeiinnrtv
intervein
eeiinnstt
intestine
eeiinnstv
intensive
eeiinnttv
intentive
eeiinntvv
inventive
eeiinprrs
reinspire
eeiinrrvv
viverrine
eeiinrstt
enteritis
eeiinrstw
winterise
eeiinrsvv
inversive
eeiinrtvw
interview
eeiinssst
sensitise
eeiinsstv
sensitive
eeiinssvw
viewiness
eeiiopqsu
equipoise
eeiiosstv
sovietise
eeiiprssw
spirewise
eeiipsuxz
epizeuxis
eeiiqrstu
requisite
eeiiqstux
exquisite
eeiirsstv
resistive
eeijknnot
knee-joint
eeijknrss
jerkiness
eeijmmnss
jemminess
eeijnsstt
jettiness
eeikknrst
steenkirk
eeiklmort
kilometre
eeiklnrsu
nurselike
eeiklrtwy
tri-weekly
eeikmnort
konimeter
eeiknprss
perkiness
eeiknrrtt
trinketer
eeiknsttx
sex-kitten
eeikoortz
ozokerite
eeikopssw
spokewise
eeillmnot
emollient
eeillmnpt
impellent
eeillmopr
millepore
eeillmprt
ill-temper
eeillmsss
smileless
eeillnnpu
plenilune
eeillnnty
leniently
eeillnrsv
sniveller
eeillopsw
powellise
eeilloptu
petiolule
eeilloptw
powellite
eeillortt
title-role
eeillrstu
tellurise
eeillrsuv
surveille
eeillrsuy
leisurely
eeillrsvy
servilely
eeillrttu
tellurite
eeillsstt
titleless
eeillsuvy
elusively
eeillttttu
tuillette
eeilmmnpt
implement
eeilmmnsy
immensely
eeilmmors
sommelier
eeilmmort
milometer
eeilmmpsu
semiplume
eeilmnnot
eloinment
eeilmnnty
eminently
eeilmnort
Nilometer
eeilmnoss
solemnise

eeilmnost
limestone
milestone
eeilmnppr
pimpernel
eeilmnstu
musteline
eeilmopry
pleiomery
eeilmopst
septimole
eeilmoptt
title-poem
eeilmortt
tremolite
eeilmostt
mistletoe
eeilmosvw
semivowel
eeilmrsty
lysimeter
eeilnnpss
penniless
eeilnnsty
intensely
eeilnoors
oleo-resin
eeilnoprt
interlope
repletion
terpineol
eeilnoprv
polverine
eeilnorsv
noveliser
eeilnorvv
reinvolve
eeilnorvw
wolverine
eeilnosss
noiseless
eeilnossu
selenious
eeilnostt
tile-stone
eeilnostv
novelties
eeilnotuv
veloutine
eeilnpruv
pulverine
eeilnpsss
spineless
eeilnpstt
pestilent
eeilnpsvy
pensively
eeilnrstu
unsterile
eeilnrsvy
inversely
eeilnsssw
sinewless

eeilntuvw
nut-weevil
eeiloprst
epistoler
pistoleer
eeiloprtx
exploiter
eeilopssw
slopewise
eeilopstt
epistolet
eeilopsvx
explosive
eeilorstv
televisor
eeilorttt
ottrelite
eeilosttt
toilet-set
eeilotuvv
evolutive
eeilpprtu
pulpiteer
eeilprsss
spireless
eeilprstu
serpulite
eeilprsty
peristyle
eeilprsuv
prelusive
pulverise
repulsive
eeilprttu
tulip-tree
eeilpsuvx
expulsive
eeilrrssv
riverless
eeilrstvy
restively
eeilrsuvv
revulsive
eeilssssu
issueless
eeimmmrss
mesmerism
eeimmnrrt
merriment
eeimmnrtt
remitment
eeimmorrt
memoriter
eeimmorst
meteorism
eeimmosst
sometimes
eeimmprst
mistemper
eeimmrsst
mesmerist
eeimmrstw
swimmeret

eeimmrstx
extremism
eeimnnnot
Mennonite
eeimnnorw
mine-owner
eeimnnrtt
interment
eeimnnrtu
inurement
eeimnnstt
sentiment
eeimnoptx
exemption
eeimnorss
sermonise
eeimnorst
neoterism
eeimnostx
sixteenmo
eeimnoswy
money-wise
eeimnpqtu
equipment
eeimnprss
primeness
eeimnprst
sempitern
eeimnpsst
emptiness
eeimnrrss
merriness
eeimnrrtu
intermure
eeimnrttt
remittent
eeimnssss
messiness
eeimnsttv
vestiment
eeimoortz
merozoite
eeimoprst
peristome
temporise
eeimoqstu
quietsome
eeimorrtv
overtimer
eeimorsst
esoterism
eeimorstt
meteorist
eeimpprrs
perisperm
eeimprrtt
permitter
pretermit
eeimprrty
perimetry
eeimprstv
septemvir
eeimpsstu
impetuses

eeimqstuu
equisetum
eeimrrstt
trimester
eeimrsssu
messieurs
eeimrssty
mysteries
eeimrsttx
extremist
eeimrttxy
extremity
eeimsssty
systemise
eeimssttu
sutteeism
eeinnnnpy
ninepenny
eeinnoort
tree-onion
eeinnopps
Nipponese
eeinnoprs
pensioner
eeinnoprt
interpone
tin-opener
eeinnopst
penistone
stone-pine
eeinnortt
retention
eeinnortz
interzone
eeinnosst
sonnetise
eeinnostv
veinstone
eeinnostw
wine-stone
eeinnostx
extension
eeinnprst
spinneret
eeinnprtt
pertinent
eeinnprty
perennity
eeinnpsst
ineptness
eeinnpswy
penny-wise
eeinnrsst
inertness
eeinnrssv
Inverness
nerviness
eeinnsssw
newsiness
eeinoppst
peptonise
pipestone
eeinoprrv
overripen

eeinoprss
personise
eeinoprst
interpose
eeinoqruv
véronique
eeinorrsv
reversion
versioner
eeinorrtu
routineer
eeinorstt
neoterist
eeinorstx
exsertion
eeinosstv
ostensive
eeinosttu
Teutonise
eeinprrtt
interpret
eeinprssw
wine-press
eeinpsssw
spewiness
eeinpsstt
pettiness
eeinqsstu
quietness
eeinqstuy
squint-eye
eeinqtttu
quintette
eeinrrrsu
reinsurer
eeinrrstt
intersert
eeinrrttw
rewritten
eeinrsssw
sweirness
eeinrsssy
syneresis
eeinrsstt
resistent
triteness
eeinrsstw
witnesser
eeinssstt
testiness
eeinsttxy
extensity
eeiooprsv
overpoise
eeioppstv
stove-pipe
eeioprrvz
overprize
eeioprttu
pirouette
eeiopsttt
pettitoes
eeioqquuv
equivoque

eeiorrrst
roisterer
terrorise
eeiorrrsv
reservoir
eeiorrttv
retortive
eeiorrtvw
overwrite
eeiorrtvy
ivory-tree
eeiorssuv
overissue
eeiorsttt
storiette
eeiorstvx
extorsive
eeiorttvx
extortive
eeiprrstt
preterist
eeiprssst
priestess
eeiprssuv
supervise
eeiprttwy
typewrite
eeirrsstv
reservist
eeirrsstw
writeress
eeirrtttw
twitterer
eeirstttu
restitute
eeirsttuv
vestiture
eeirsttux
texturise
eeirstuvx
extrusive
eejmnnoty
enjoyment
eejmpquuu
queue-jump
eejnnnrwy
jenny-wren
eejnoqsuu
Junoesque
eejnorruy
journeyer
eejnosstw
Jew's-stone
eekkorsty
keystroke
eeklmosss
smokeless
eeklnootv
love-token
eeklorstw
steelwork
eekmorrty
kryometer

eeknrrttu
tree-trunk
eelllmsss
smell-less
eelllnosu
Olenellus
eellmnoos
lemon-sole
eellmpssu
plumeless
eellnnrtu
tunneller
eellnpstw
well-spent
eellooprt
trollopee
eelloostw
steel-wool
eelloppr
propeller
eellopprx
prepollex
eellorrtw
troweller
eellorssv
loverless
eellorsvw
overswell
eellossvw
vowelless
eellpsssu
pulseless
eellpsssy
syllepses
eellpstuw
well-set-up
eellsssty
styleless
eellsssuy
uselessly
eelmmnotu
emolument
eelmnnort
enrolment
eelmnooty
teleonomy
eelmnosss
solemness
eelmnossy
moneyless
eelmnottx
extolment
eelmoopst
leptosome
eelmoppry
pre-employ
eelmoprtu
petroleum
eelmorstt
slot-meter
eelmorttv
voltmeter
eelmortuv
volumeter

eelmortxy
xylometer
eelmprsuy
supremely
eelnnnttu
tunnel-net
eelnnoprs
personnel
eelnnquuy
unqueenly
eelnoosss
looseness
eelnoppry
propylene
eelnopstu
plenteous
eelnorssw
ownerless
eelnorstv
resolvent
eelnortuv
volunteer
eelnossst
stoneless
eelnppurx
unperplex
eelnprsty
presently
eelooprsy
operosely
eeloppprss
prolepses
eeloprrsy
leprosery
eeloprrtu
poulterer
eeloprssw
powerless
eeloprsty
polyester
proselyte
eeloprtxy
expletory
eelorrruv
overruler
eelorrtuv
revel-rout
eelorssst
ostleress
eelorsstw
towerless
eelorssuv
ourselves
eelppsttu
septuplet
eelprssxy
expressly
eelprstuu
sepulture
eelpsttux
sextuplet
eelrssttu
utterless

eemmnnosy
Mnemosyne
eemmnoort
metronome
monometer
monotreme
eemmoorst
osmometer
eemmortyz
zymometer
eemmrsstu
summerset
eemnnopry
Rome-penny
eemnnopst
penstemon
eemnoortt
tonometer
eemnoostt
tomentose
eemnopryz
proenzyme
eemnorstu
rousement
eemnrsttw
strewment
eemooostt
osteotome
eemoopprs
prose-poem
eemooprtt
optometer
potometer
eemoorstu
meteorous
eemopprrt
pre-emptor
eemoprrty
pyrometer
eemorrrvy
overmerry
eemprrttu
trumpeter
eemprsstt
temptress
eennnprty
penny-rent
eennooprt
pontoneer
eennoostu
neotenous
eennoprss
proneness
eennprtuy
truepenny
eennrssst
sternness
eenoorrsu
erroneous
eenopprtt
prepotent
eenopqstu
queen-post

eenoprrss
responser
eenoprstv
overspent
eenopsstt
step-stone
eenopstty
stenotype
eenorrstw
nor'-wester
eenorrtuy
tourneyer
eenorsssw
worseness
eenorstuu
souteneur
eenortttu
neutretto
eenossstx
sextoness
eenprrsty
serpentry
eenprrtuv
unpervert
eenrssttu
utterness
eeooprrvw
overpower
eeoorrtvw
overtower
eeoppprt
pepper-pot
eeopprssu
superpose
eeoprrrss
repressor
eeoprrrty
repertory
eeoprrsst
porteress
eeoprrssv
overpress
eeoprrstt
protester
eeoprssss
repossess
eeoprsstu
pesterous
eeoprsttu
route-step
eeoprstux
exposture
eeopssttu
poussette
eeorrrsty
roysterer
eeorrrttv
retrovert
eeorrsstu
retroussé
eeorrstvw
overstrew
overwrest

eeorrttvx
extrovert
eeorssttu
roussette
eeorsstuw
sou'-wester
eeorstttu
setter-out
tetterous
eeorsttty
storyette
eeorsttww
sweetwort
eeprrsttu
sputterer
eerrstttu
stutterer
effggilnu
effulging
effgginor
goffering
effginrsu
suffering
effglortu
forgetful
effgnrssu
gruffness
effhikswww
skew-whiff
effhilrsy
fly-fisher
effhilrwy
whifflery
effhinssu
huffiness
effiimnss
miffiness
effiiorrt
fortifier
effilllru
fulfiller
effilmuuv
effluvium
effilnoux
effluxion
effilrstu
strifeful
effinpssu
puffiness
effinssst
stiffness
effinstuv
veinstuff
effiooprr
fireproof
effiorrty
refortify
effiortvy
forty-five
effllrtuy
fretfully
efflorruu
furfurole

efflorsty
forest-fly
effnoorrt
forefront
effoorrty
offertory
effoprttu
off-putter
efforstuv
overstuff
efggiinnr
fingering
efggiloos
solfeggio
efgginoor
foregoing
efgginoss
fogginess
efghhiilr
high-flier
efghhilry
high-flyer
efghiilot
eight-foil
efghiilrt
firelight
efghiinrt
nightfire
efghillns
fleshling
efghilnss
fleshings
efghiltwy
flyweight
efghinort
forenight
efghiooss
goose-fish
efghiott
eight-foot
efghiorst
foresight
grief-shot
efghllntu
lengthful
efghlnruu
hungerful
efgiiinrs
signifier
efgiillnt
filleting
efgiilnpr
pilfering
efgiinnrr
inferring
efgiinnss
finessing
efgiinprt
fingertip
efgiinrtt
refitting
efgiinrvy
verifying

efgiklnot
Folketing
efgilnorw
flowering
reflowing
efgilortw
tiger-wolf
efgilosty
festilogy
efgilrtuu
fulgurite
efgimntuy
tumefying
efginnost
softening
efginooss
goofiness
efginorst
fostering
efgllntuy
fulgently
efglnopuw
gowpenful
efglnorsw
self-wrong
efgloosty
festology
efglootuv
tug-of-love
efgnoortt
forgotten
efgoooost
goosefoot
efhhiistw
whitefish
efhhillss
shellfish
efhhkloos
flesh-hook
efhiikpss
spike-fish
efhiimsst
fetishism
efhiinpss
snipe-fish
efhiinsss
fishiness
efhiinssw
swine-fish
efhiirrtt
thriftier
efhiisstt
fetishist
efhijllsy
jellyfish
efhiknort
forethink
efhillors
fill-horse
efhillssy
selfishly
efhilnssu
unselfish

efhilnstt
flesh-tint
efhilorst
rifle-shot
short-life
efhilossu
fish-louse
efhilssst
shiftless
efhinosst
stonefish
efhinrrsu
furnisher
refurnish
efhiorrst
shotfirer
efhllnory
holly-fern
efhllnpuu
unhelpful
efhllnsuy
unfleshly
efhllopuy
hopefully
efhllosst
soft-shell
efhllosuv
shovelful
efhllttwy
twelfthly
efhlmoors
shelfroom
efhlmorsw
fleshworm
efhlnnssu
nun's-flesh
efhlnopuu
unhopeful
efhlnsssu
flushness
efhloopsu
flophouse
efhlorsst
frothless
efhlorsuv
overflush
efhlorsuw
showerful
efhlossuu
housefuls
efhnoorsw
foreshown
efhnortux
fox-hunter
efhooorst
horse-foot
efhooortt
foretooth
efhoorrsu
four-horse
efhosttuu
theftuous
efiijrstu
justifier

efiilllst
still-life
efiillmor
mollifier
efiillnru
nullifier
efiillrst
fillister
efiilmnss
filminess
efiilmott
leitmotif
efiilnnox
inflexion
efiilopsv
spoil-five
efiilosss
fossilise
efiilprtt
filter-tip
efiilrrsv
silver-fir
efiilrtty
fertility
efiimorrt
mortifier
efiimrstt
first-time
efiimrsty
mystifier
efiinnsst
niftiness
efiinnsty
intensify
efiinoprx
prefixion
efiinorrs
fire-irons
efiiorrtu
fioriture
efiisttvy
festivity
efijkorst
forjeskit
efijllmor
jelliform
efikmnnoo
moon-knife
efiknnssu
funkiness
efiknorss
forkiness
efikorrst
foreskirt
efillmopu
filoplume
efillmrtu
full-timer
efillnptu
plentiful
efillooos
foliolose
efilmnort
lentiform

efilmnosy
solemnify
efilmoprv
pelviform
efilmoprx
plexiform
efilmorsu
formulise
efilnnort
front-line
efilnoors
solferino
efilnoosu
felonious
efilnortw
interflow
efilnosst
loftiness
efilopssu
self-pious
efilorsvx
silver-fox
efilosstu
fistulose
efilprstu
spriteful
efilqruuv
quiverful
efilrsstu
fruitless
efilrtuvy
furtively
efimmorrs
reformism
efimmorrv
vermiform
efimnnopr
penniform
efimoprst
septiform
efimorrst
fire-storm
reformist
restiform
efimorrsv
versiform
efinnnssu
funniness
efinnortu
infortune
efinnsstu
unfitness
efinooprt
forepoint
efinoprsu
perfusion
efinoprsy
personify
efinorstw
frontwise
efinortuz
fortunize
efinrrtuu
furniture

efinrsstu
turfiness
efinsssu
fussiness
efinssstu
fustiness
efinssstw
swiftness
efinssuzz
fuzziness
efioorstx
six-footer
efioorsuv
oviferous
efiortttu
outfitter
efiosstuv
festivous
efklmnoow
womenfolk
efklmoruw
flukeworm
efknnoorw
foreknown
efllmostu
molestful
efllmosuy
fulsomely
efllmsuuy
musefully
efllntuuy
tunefully
efllоovww
vow-fellow
efllrstuu
resultful
efllrstuy
restfully
efllstuyz
zestfully
eflnntuuu
untuneful
eflnoorvw
overflown
eflnoprtu
profluent
eflnorsst
frontless
eflnorsuw
sunflower
eflnossuw
wofulness
eflnrstuu
unrestful
eflooost
foot-loose
efloоprss
proofless
eflooprtw
flowerpot
efloprsuy
profusely
eflorssst
frostless

eflprsuux
superflux
eflrssstu
stressful
eflrssttu
self-trust
efnnoostt
font-stone
efnnopruy
fourpenny
efnnortuu
unfortune
efnoorsst
foster-son
efoooprrv
overproof
efooprrss
professor
efooprttx
proof-text
efooqrrtu
Roquefort
efoorrsuv
fervorous
egggilmsu
misguggle
eggginott
go-getting
egghiilns
sleighing
egghiinnw
whingeing
egghiinrs
niggerish
egghiintw
weighting
egghinorr
hog-ringer
eggiilnnr
lingering
eggiimnrs
niggerism
eggiinnsw
swingeing
eggillnru
gruelling
eggiloors
goose-girl
eggiloost
geologist
eggiloprw
porwiggle
eggimnnor
mongering
egginnorv
governing
egginnptu
tuning-peg
egginoors
gorgonise
egginoorv
going-over
overgoing

egginooss
geognosis
egginoosw
goose-wing
egginorsu
gingerous
egginosss
sogginess
eggiorrtu
outrigger
egglmmooy
gemmology
egglnoors
sloggorne
egglrrstu
struggler
eghhilost
sight-hole
eghhinrst
threshing
eghhiortu
eight-hour
eghhmottu
methought
eghhnoruw
rough-hewn
eghhnottu
thoughten
eghiiknrs
shrieking
eghiillmt
limelight
eghiilnnt
night-line
eghiilnrt
girthline
eghiilnst
gentilish
sight-line
eghiilppt
pipe-light
eghiiltwy
weightily
eghiimntt
night-time
eghiinntw
whitening
eghiinprs
perishing
eghiinrsv
shivering
eghiinrtw
withering
eghiinsty
hygienist
eghiintww
whitewing
eghiklost
ghost-like
eghillnsw
wing-shell
eghillnty
lengthily

eghillooy
heliology
eghillosu
gill-house
eghillotv
lovelight
eghillsst
lightless
eghilmost
lightsome
eghilnnsu
un-English
eghilnopr
negrophil
eghilnrsy
Englishry
eghilnrtu
night-rule
eghilnsst
lightness
nightless
eghiloory
hierology
eghilrsst
rightless
eghilssst
sightless
eghimnort
mothering
eghimnost
something
eghimortt
tiger-moth
eghimppsu
pemphigus
eghinnsst
thingness
eghinorsu
rehousing
eghinorsw
showering
eghinortv
overnight
eghinosty
histogeny
eghinrsst
rightness
eghinrstt
night-rest
eghinrtuw
wuthering
eghinsstt
tightness
eghioprsu
rogueship
eghioprtt
tight-rope
eghiorstu
righteous
eghiorstv
oversight
eghirsttu
theurgist

eghlllouy
gully-hole
eghlloory
glory-hole
eghlmnopu
ploughmen
eghlmooou
homologue
eghlnoopy
nephology
phenology
eghlnoors
longshore
sloghorne
eghlnoosu
long-house
eghlnooty
ethnology
eghlnopyy
phylogeny
eghlnorsu
slughorne
eghlooorr
horologer
eghloorty
therology
eghlootyy
hyetology
eghlosuuy
hugeously
eghmnoorw
home-grown
eghmnrtuu
mug-hunter
eghnnopyy
hypnogeny
eghnooopr
gonophore
eghnoopry
gynophore
eghnoopty
photogeny
eghnoptyy
phytogeny
eghnorssu
roughness
eghnosstu
oughtness
toughness
eghoopsuy
hypogeous
eghoptyyz
zygophyte
egiiinrtv
Irvingite
egiiklnsv
king's-evil
egiiknnrt
tinkering
egiikrstz
sitzkrieg
egiillmnp
impelling

egiillnno
nielloing
egiillnor
gorilline
egiillnpr
perilling
egiillrty
tiger-lily
egiilmnst
gentilism
egiilmors
mirligoes
egiilmprr
pilgrimer
egiilnnpp
lippening
egiilnnuv
unveiling
egiilnort
loitering
egiilnpss
singspiel
egiilnrsv
silvering
egiilnrvw
liver-wing
egiilnsuv
ingluvies
egiilntty
gentility
egiilorsu
religious
egiimnnpt
impingent
egiimnnss
minginess
egiimnors
Origenism
egiimnprs
simpering
egiimnrss
griminess
egiimnrtt
remitting
egiimstuv
vestigium
egiinnors
nigrosine
egiinnost
ingestion
egiinnosu
ingenious
egiinnrrt
interring
egiinnrsw
inswinger
egiinntuy
ingenuity
egiinoptt
tiptoeing
egiinorst
Origenist
egiinorsy
seigniory

egiinppqu
equipping
egiinprrz
prize-ring
egiinprss
speirings
egiinqrru
requiring
egiinrrtu
intriguer
egiinrsst
sistering
egiinrstt
string-tie
egiinrttt
tittering
egiinrttv
rivetting
egiinrtty
integrity
egijknntu
junketing
egijlnsty
jestingly
egiklnnoo
ingle-nook
egiknntuy
tuning-key
egilllnty
tellingly
egillmnty
meltingly
egillmoru
glomeruli
egillmotu
guillemot
egillnnor
enrolling
egillnors
Negrillos
egillnorw
rowelling
egillnott
ill-gotten
egillnotw
towelling
egillnotx
extolling
egillnpty
peltingly
egillnpuw
upwelling
egillossy
syllogise
egillsstu
guiltless
egilmnoos
Mongolise
neologism
egilmoosy
semiology
egilnnoss
lessoning

egilnnost
singleton
egilnnrsu
nurseling
egilnoory
irenology
egilnoost
neologist
egilnoosu
Sinologue
egilnoprx
exploring
egilnorsu
ring-ousel
egilnortv
revolting
egilnoruz
ring-ouzel
egilnorvv
revolving
egilnorvy
overlying
egilnossx
long-sixes
egilnotvy
longevity
egilnprst
springlet
egilnrstu
resulting
egilnrstw
wrestling
egilnssst
stingless
egilnsuvw
swivel-gun
egiloprs
prologise
egilorsty
sortilegy
egilortuv
voltigeur
egimmnors
monergism
egimmnrsu
summering
egimmnssu
gumminess
egimnnory
ring-money
egimnntuu
minute-gun
egimnorsv
misgovern
egimnortw
wit-monger
egimnostt
misgotten
egimnotuy
timenoguy
egimnprsu
presuming
egimnrssy
synergism

egimnrttu
muttering
egimprtuy
pterygium
eginnnost
sonneting
eginnnruv
unnerving
eginnnuvy
unenvying
eginnostt
onsetting
eginnosuu
ingenuous
eginnottw
towing-net
eginnpruy
penguinry
eginnrstt
stringent
eginnrstu
insurgent
unresting
eginnrtuv
venturing
eginnttuv
vingt-et-un
eginooprt
protogine
eginoopss
spongiose
eginoossu
isogenous
eginopppr
poppering
eginopprs
pop-singer
eginoppst
estopping
eginoprrr
porringer
eginoprrt
reporting
eginoprrv
reproving
eginoprst
progestin
eginoprtt
pottering
pottinger
repotting
eginopssy
gossypine
eginopsuy
epigynous
eginorrst
rostering
eginorrtw
intergrow
eginorstt
gritstone
eginorttt
tottering

eginossst
stegnosis
eginosstu
goutiness
eginpsttu
upsetting
eginrsstu
russeting
eginrssty
synergist
eginrsuvy
surveying
eginssstu
gustiness
gutsiness
egioorsuv
ovigerous
egkorssuw
guesswork
eglllloorr
log-roller
egllmnory
mongrelly
eglmnooou
monologue
eglmooorv
overgloom
eglmoosuy
museology
eglmootyy
etymology
eglnnosuu
sun-lounge
eglnnptuy
pungently
eglnooopy
poenology
eglnooprr
prolonger
eglnooruy
neurology
eglnoosuv
longevous
eglnorsty
strongyle
eglnostuu
glutenous
eglnrttuy
turgently
eglooosty
osteology
eglooprty
petrology
egloopsty
pestology
eglopstyy
pygostyle
egmnoooss
mongooses
egmoorstu
guest-room
egmoprsyz
zygosperm

egnnnrruu
gunrunner
egnnorssw
wrongness
egnnossuy
youngness
egnooossw
snow-goose
egnooosuz
zoogenous
egnooprss
prognoses
egnooprsy
sporogeny
egnoopssu
spongeous
egnoorrvw
overgrown
egnoosuxy
oxygenous
egnoottuu
outtongue
egnorssss
grossness
egnorsstt
strongest
egnorstuy
youngster
egnprssuu
sun-spurge
egnrrttuu
turret-gun
egooprsyz
zygospore
egopprttu
gruppetto
ehhiirttt
thirtieth
ehhilllsy
hellishly
ehhilmoop
homophile
ehhiloprs
philhorse
ehhimnpsy
hyphenism
ehhimrsty
rhythmise
ehhinopps
phosphine
ehhinortw
nowhither
ehhioppst
phosphite
ehhioprsw
horsewhip
ehhiprssu
ushership
ehhlooopt
holophote
ehhloopty
holophyte
ehhloptyy
hylophyte

ehhlossuu
lush-house
ehhmnooop
homophone
ehhmorttu
home-truth
ehhmrtuyy
eurhythmy
ehhoopsty
theosophy
ehhorsttu
thrust-hoe
ehiijnort
joint-heir
ehiiklmtw
milk-white
ehiiknstt
kittenish
ehiillnss
hilliness
ehiillopt
helipilot
ehiillrsw
ill-wisher
ehiilltwy
lily-white
ehiilmrst
Hitlerism
ehiilnops
Sinophile
ehiilnttw
lintwhite
ehiilprst
Philister
ehiilpssy
syphilise
ehiilrstt
Hitlerist
ehiimmpst
mephitism
ehiimrstt
tritheism
ehiinnssw
whininess
ehiinopst
Tisiphone
ehiinorrt
inheritor
ehiinpprw
whipper-in
ehiinprst
nephritis
phrenitis
ehiinpsst
pithiness
ehiipprtu
hippurite
ehiippssy
epiphysis
ehiiqrsuv
quiverish
ehiirsttt
tritheist

ehijkmost
jokesmith
ehikllpsy
sylph-like
ehiklmnpy
nymph-like
ehiklmosu
milk-house
ehiklmpst
klephtism
ehiklorsw
shriek-owl
ehiklortz
kilohertz
ehiklrttu
truthlike
ehikmnosy
monkeyish
ehiknprrs
pre-shrink
ehiknsssu
huskiness
ehikorrsy
Yorkshire
ehikprssu
spike-rush
ehikrswyy
rye-whisky
ehillmors
mill-horse
ehillosty
hostilely
ehilloswy
yellowish
ehilmoott
lithotome
ehilmoszz
shimozzle
ehilmppry
perilymph
ehilmpssy
emphlysis
ehilmrsst
mirthless
ehilmrstu
Lutherism
ehilmrtty
trimethyl
ehilnnoop
phelonion
ehilnoopt
lithopone
phonolite
ehilnoopy
oenophily
ehilnosuy
heinously
ehiloprxy
xerophily
ehilprrsu
rulership
ehilpstty
pettishly

ehilrssst
shirtless
ehilrsttu
Lutherist
ehimnnoor
monorhine
ehimnnoos
moonshine
ehimnoprs
premonish
ehimnopst
phonetism
ehimnopsy
ship-money
ehimnopuu
euphonium
ehimnorss
sermonish
ehimnorst
horsemint
ehimnprst
shrimp-net
ehimnrtuu
ruthenium
ehimnsssu
mushiness
ehimnsttu
tunesmith
ehimoooss
homoeosis
ehimoorst
shire-moot
ehimoostz
zootheism
ehimopprr
perimorph
ehimorstt
short-time
ehimorttw
mother-wit
ehimprrtu
triumpher
ehimrrsty
erythrism
ehinnopss
phoniness
ehinnorss
horniness
ehinnostw
whinstone
ehinnrsuv
unshriven
ehinoprss
nephrosis
ehinoprsw
ownership
ship-owner
ehinopstt
phonetist
ehinopsty
hypnotise
ehinopsvy
envoyship

ehinorrsu
nourisher
ehinorsss
horsiness
ehinortxy
thyroxine
ehinosssw
showiness
ehinostww
snow-white
ehinottuw
withouten
ehinprrty
pyrethrin
ehinrsssu
rushiness
ehinsssty
synthesis
ehinsttwy
twentyish
ehiooprtw
wire-photo
ehiopprst
tripe-shop
ehioprsst
prothesis
sophister
store-ship
ehiorrstv
overshirt
ehiorsttu
stouthrie
ehiprstty
prettyish
ehjoosssu
joss-house
ehjoprrsy
jerry-shop
ehkllorsw
shellwork
ehkllsstu
tusk-shell
ehklottyy
thelytoky
ehkmrssuw
musk-shrew
ehknorstu
trunk-hose
ehkooostt
theotokos
ehkoorrsw
workhorse
ehkoorsuw
housework
workhouse
ehllmopsy
mesophyll
ehlloostu
toll-house
ehlmmoptu
plume-moth
ehlmosstu
mouthless

ehlnooppy
polyphone
ehlnoopxy
xylophone
ehlnoorst
sloethorn
ehlnoosty
holystone
ehlnorrty
northerly
ehlnorsst
thornless
ehlooostu
toolhouse
ehloopstu
spout-hole
ehloopstv
hovel-post
ehloosstt
toothless
ehloprstu
upholster
ehlopstyy
hypostyle
ehlorrttt
throttler
ehlorsstt
trothless
ehlorsstw
worthless
ehlorstuy
southerly
ehlprstuu
sulphuret
ehlrssttu
truthless
ehmmnoory
monorhyme
ehmmooprs
mesomorph
ehmnnoooy
honeymoon
ehmnostuu
mouse-hunt
ehmooooprs
sophomore
ehmooorsu
house-room
ehmooostt
toothsome
ehmooostu
moothouse
ehmooprrx
xeromorph
ehmooptty
mythopoet
ehmoorrty
horometry
ehmoostuy
youthsome
ehmorrstt
short-term
ehmprrtuy
pyrethrum

ehnnoorst
hornstone
ehnoooppr
phonopore
ehnoooppt
optophone
ehnooortt
orthotone
ehnoopppry
pyrophone
ehnoopppty
phonotype
ehnoopstt
on-the-spot
ehnoosstt
stoneshot
ehnoostuw
townhouse
ehnootttt
hottentot
Hottentot
ehnoprttu
pot-hunter
ehnopssty
pythoness
ehnorssst
shortness
ehnorsttw
north-west
ehnrsttuu
unshutter
ehoooprsu
poorhouse
ehooorstu
root-house
ehooorstv
overshoot
ehoopptty
phototype
ehooprrtv
hoverport
ehooprsst
post-horse
ehooprstu
porthouse
ehoopsstu
posthouse
ehoorrtvw
overthrow
ehoorsttw
shot-tower
ehorrsttw
throwster
ehossttuw
south-west
eiiiknnop
epinikion
eiiilmmtt
time-limit
eiiilnnqu
inquiline
eiiimprtv
primitive

eiiinnpst
insipient
eiiinprst
ripienist
eiiinrstt
retinitis
eiiinttuv
intuitive
eiijmsstu
Jesuitism
eiijnnort
interjoin
eiijqrtuy
jequirity
eiikllnps
spellikin
eiikllort
kilolitre
eiiklmnss
milkiness
eiiklnnrt
interlink
eiiklnsss
silkiness
eiiknnppr
nipperkin
eiiknnpss
pinkiness
eiiknnrtt
interknit
eiiknpsss
spikiness
eiiknrsss
riskiness
eiillmnru
illuminer
eiillmnry
millinery
eiillmost
mollities
eiillmsst
limitless
eiillnopt
pointillé
eiillnsss
silliness
eiilloprs
pillorise
eiilmmors
meliorism
eiilmnops
moniplies
eiilmnopt
impletion
eiilmnopx
implexion
eiilmnorv
vermilion
eiilmnosu
limousine
eiilmnpps
mislippen
eiilmnpru
primuline

eiilmnsss
sliminess
eiilmopps
epipolism
eiilmopsv
implosive
eiilmorst
meliorist
eiilmorty
meliority
eiilmottv
leitmotiv
eiilmprsu
puerilism
eiilmpsst
simpliste
eiilmpsuv
impulsive
eiilmrsst
Listerism
eiilmrssv
servilism
eiilmrssy
missilery
eiilnnoqu
quinoline
eiilnosss
soiliness
eiilnottv
volitient
eiilnpsst
splenitis
eiilnpsty
pensility
eiilnptuv
vulpinite
eiilnqtuy
inquietly
eiilnrtuy
neurility
eiilnstty
tensility
eiilnstvy
sylvinite
eiilntuvy
unitively
eiilopqtu
politique
eiilopsst
spilosite
eiiloqssu
siliquose
eiilprstu
pleuritis
spirituel
eiilprstz
prize-list
eiilprtuy
puerility
eiilrstty
sterility
eiilrstvy
servility

eiimmmors
memoirism
eiimmnors
immersion
eiimmnoss
misoneism
eiimmnrst
terminism
eiimmnsty
immensity
eiimmorss
isomerism
eiimmorst
memoirist
eiimmpsss
pessimism
eiimnnorr
iron-miner
eiimnorss
missioner
remission
eiimnosst
misoneist
eiimnostu
minutiose
eiimnosuv
vimineous
eiimnotzz
mizzonite
eiimnprst
Petrinism
strip-mine
eiimnrstt
terminist
eiimnssst
mistiness
eiimoprsu
imperious
eiimoprsv
improvise
eiimopstt
epitomist
eiimosstv
sovietism
eiimpssst
pessimist
eiinnnost
intension
eiinnnott
intention
eiinnnotv
invention
eiinnorst
insertion
eiinnorsv
inversion
eiinnosss
noisiness
eiinnpsss
spininess
eiinnrstt
internist
eiinnsstt
insistent
tintiness
eiinnstty
intensity
eiinoprsv
prevision
eiinoptvw
viewpoint
eiinorsss
resinosis
eiinorsty
seniority
eiinpprst
pin-stripe
eiinpssst
tipsiness
eiinrsstu
insisture
eiinrstuv
intrusive
eiinrttuv
nutritive
vetturini
eiinsssyz
synizesis
eiinssttw
wittiness
eiinstttu
institute
eiiorrtuv
voiturier
eiiorsstt
sottisier
eiiprrtuv
irruptive
eiiqrrstu
quirister
eiirssstv
visitress
eijjknotu
juke-joint
eijkmnrsu
junkerism
eijllmnot
jolliment
eijllnoss
jolliness
eijlmnptu
mint-julep
eijlnosst
jointless
eijmnpssu
jumpiness
eijnnosst
jointness
eijnorrsu
surrejoin
eijnorsst
jointress
eijnprsuu
Juniperus
eiklllsss
skill-less
eiklmorsy
irksomely
eiklnnrtu
trunk-line
eiklnnruw
unwrinkle
eiklnprrs
sprinkler
eiklnsssu
sulkiness
eiklrssst
skirtless
eikmmnosy
monkeyism
eikmnnort
Komintern
eikmnnost
minkstone
eikmnoors
mono-skier
eikmnorsy
risk-money
eikmnosss
smokiness
eikmnrssu
murkiness
eikmnsssu
muskiness
eiknnoprt
Pinkerton
eiknnpssu
punkiness
eiknoorst
sooterkin
eiknorrtw
interwork
eiknorstv
overstink
eiknrrtty
trinketry
eikorrstv
overskirt
eikorsttu
outstrike
strikeout
eillmnorw
mill-owner
eillmnost
millstone
stone-mill
eillmnssu
sensillum
eillmopsw
Powellism
eillmpttu
multiplet
eillmptux
multiplex
eillmrtuu
tellurium
eillnorrt
ritornell
eillnorst
stornelli
eillnortu
tellurion
eillnossw
lowliness
eillnosty
stone-lily
eillnotvy
violently
eillnpuuv
pulvinule
eillnssst
stillness
eillnsssy
sinlessly
eilloprst
postiller
eilloprsv
overspill
spillover
eilloprty
pellitory
eillopsst
pilotless
eilloptuv
pollutive
eillpsssy
syllepsis
eillsstwy
witlessly
eilmmmoss
Moslemism
eilmmnnuu
nummuline
eilmmntuu
nummulite
eilmmopsy
misemploy
eilmnoosy
noisomely
eilmnopst
simpleton
eilmnopsy
monyplies
eilmnorst
line-storm
eilmnortt
tormentil
eilmnosty
solemnity
eilmnoswy
winsomely
eilmnpssu
lumpiness
eilmostuy
timeously
eilnnostv
insolvent
eilnnpstu
unslept-in
eilnoopsx
explosion
eilnootuv
evolution
eilnoprru
purloiner
eilnoprsu
prelusion
repulsion
eilnopsst
pointless
eilnopssu
spinulose
eilnopstv
pontlevis
eilnopsux
expulsion
eilnorsuv
revulsion
eilnosssu
lousiness
eilnosstt
siltstone
eilnosuvy
enviously
eilnppssu
pulpiness
eilnpqtuu
quintuple
eilnprsst
printless
eilnprsty
splintery
eilnqtuuy
unquietly
eilnrsssu
surliness
eilnrsttu
turnstile
eilnrtuuv
vulturine
eilnssstt
stintless
eilnssstu
lustiness
eiloprrss
prolepsis
eilopprty
propylite
eiloprsty
leprosity
eilopstuy
piteously
eilorrtvw
liverwort
eilorssuy
seriously
eimmnnost
mnemonist
eimmnoors
Monroeism
eimmnoort
Mormonite
eimmnoprs
persimmon
eimmnrssu
rumminess

eimmoopru
pomoerium
prooemium
eimmoorst
timorsome
eimmopstu
impostume
eimnnootz
monzonite
eimnnoprt
prominent
eimnnorst
innermost
eimnnptuu
neptunium
eimnnrttu
nutriment
eimnnsttu
unsmitten
eimnooopr
prooemion
eimnooprt
premotion
eimnoorss
roominess
eimnoprsu
simon-pure
eimnoprtu
entropium
importune
eimnoqruy
querimony
eimnorrtw
worriment
eimnorsst
monitress
eimnorssu
sensorium
eimnorsuv
verminous
eimnorttu
tentorium
eimnossss
mossiness
eimnossst
moistness
eimnosttu
Teutonism
eimnostty
testimony
eimnostuu
untimeous
eimnottzz
mezzotint
eimnssssu
mussiness
eimnssuzz
muzziness
eimooprst
Pooterism
eimooprtv
promotive
eimoorrsw
worrisome
eimoorssu
isomerous
eimoosssx
exosmosis
eimoprrst
misreport
eimoprstu
imposture
eimoprtyz
prozymite
eimopstuu
impetuous
eimorrrst
terrorism
eimorrssy
remissory
eimorrstu
trimerous
eimorrttw
mitre-wort
eimorsuvy
voyeurism
eimostttt
motettist
eimprstty
prettyism
eimprstuy
supremity
einnnotty
nonentity
einnnsssu
sunniness
einnooprt
entropion
pontonier
prenotion
einnoorst
ironstone
serotonin
einnortvy
inventory
einnossst
stoniness
einnossw
snowiness
einnosstt
sonnetist
einnosuuv
unenvious
einnprstw
newsprint
einnpsttu
Neptunist
einnrttuw
unwritten
einnssttu
nuttiness
sustinent
einoopprt
preoption
einooprrs
prerosion
einooprrt
portioner
einoopssw
spoonwise
einoorrst
retorsion
einoorrtt
retortion
einoorttx
extortion
einoortty
notoriety
einoossst
sootiness
einoosswz
wooziness
einoppsss
soppiness
einoprrtv
overprint
einoprsss
prosiness
einoprstu
pertusion
einoprsuu
penurious
einoqtttu
quintetto
einorrsss
sorriness
einorrttv
introvert
einorrtuu
nouriture
einorssuu
unserious
einorstux
extrusion
einorttuv
vetturino
einostttu
Teutonist
einosttvy
ventosity
einprrttu
interrupt
einrssstu
rustiness
einrsttuy
strenuity
eiooprrst
posterior
repositor
eiooprstx
expositor
eiooprsty
operosity
eiooprstz
zooperist
eioossstx
exostosis
eioossttv
ovotestis
eiopprrty
propriety
eiopprsuv
purposive
eioprrttv
vertiport
eioprsttu
proustite
eioprstty
posterity
eioqrstuu
turquoise
eiorrrstt
terrorist
eiorrrtty
territory
eipqrttuy
triptyque
eiprrrssu
surpriser
eiprssstu
pertussis
eiqrssttu
questrist
eirsstttu
trustiest
ejllossyy
joylessly
ejmnoruwy
jurywomen
ejmprstuw
Jew's-trump
ejnoorrsu
sojourner
ejoprrsuu
perjurous
ekkooprrw
poker-work
ekllnnoww
well-known
eklmmnosu
musk-melon
ekmmooors
smoke-room
ekmnnoors
non-smoker
ekmnnoruy
monkey-run
ekmnnotyy
teknonymy
ekmnoopty
monkey-pot
ekmnoostu
musketoon
eknoopruv
unprovoke
eknoopstu
outspoken
eknoorstw
stonework
eknorsstu
sunstroke
eknorstuv
overstunk
ekooprrsw
ropeworks
ekoorrtuw
outworker
ekoorsttw
twostroke
ekoprrssw
press-work
ekorrttuw
tutworker
elllmsuuv
vulsellum
ellmnoopy
poll-money
ellmopsuu
plumulose
ellmorstu
rostellum
ellmosuuy
emulously
ellmrstuu
surmullet
ellnoorst
stornello
ellnoprsu
prunellos
ellnoptuy
opulently
elloostuu
luteolous
ellopstyy
polystyle
ellorstuu
tellurous
elmmnssuu
Mussulmen
elmnnoost
somnolent
elmnoosty
monostyle
elmnopstu
plum-stone
elmnppssu
plumpness
elmoooprw
power-loom
elmoorstw
lowermost
elmoorsuy
lyomerous
elmorssst
stormless
elmorstuu
tremulous
elnoorsuy
onerously
elnoppstu
pulpstone
elnorsuvy
nervously
elnostuuy
tenuously
eloopptttt
pottle-pot
eloorstuw
lousewort

eloorstvy
love-story
elopprsuy
purposely
eloprrsuw
rowel-spur
spur-rowel
eloprrsuy
prelusory
eloprssst
sportless
eloprsuuv
pulverous
elopssstu
spoutless
eloqrsuuu
querulous
elorssttu
troutless
elorsttuu
outlustre
elorstuvy
overlusty
elpprssuu
superplus
elprsttuy
spluttery
elrssstu
trustless
emmnoostu
momentous
emmnorttu
tormentum
emmnrstuu
menstruum
emnnooost
moonstone
emnnrrruu
rum-runner
emnoooptt
monoptote
emnoopsuy
eponymous
emnoorrtt
tormentor
emnoorstt
mort-stone
emnoortuv
overmount
emnoortuy
neurotomy
emnoortwy
moneywort
emnoosttu
tomentous
emnoprrtu
no-trumper
emnoprssu
responsum
emnorsstt
sternmost
emooorrst
storeroom

emooostty
osteotomy
emooprrss
press-room
emooprtty
optometry
emoorsttu
outermost
emoorttuy
uterotomy
emopprrtu
prompture
emopprstu
uppermost
emoprrtuv
overtrump
emoprrtyy
pyrometry
emorstttu
uttermost
ennnooprs
non-person
ennnprtuy
turn-penny
ennoooprt
pontooner
ennoopprt
proponent
ennoppsty
penny-post
ennoprtwy
pennywort
ennorrtuu
outrunner
ennorsttu
turnstone
enoopprst
postponer
enoopprtu
opportune
enooprrss
responsor
enooprrtu
root-prune
enoorssty
ostensory
enoorsttw
stonewort
enoossttu
sostenuto
enopprstu
unstopper
enoprrstt
sternport
enoprsssu
suspensor
enoprsstt
stern-post
enoprstty
post-entry
enopsttyy
stenotypy
enorsstuu
strenuous

enorsttuy
out-sentry
enorstuuv
venturous
enosssttu
stoutness
enotttwwy
twenty-two
enrrsstuu
untrusser
eoooprrtu
outrooper
eoopprrss
oppressor
eoopprtty
prototype
eooprrstt
protestor
eooprrttu
out-porter
eooprrtuu
outpourer
eooprssss
possessor
eooprstuu
eutropous
eoorsttwy
two-storey
eopprrstu
supporter
eopprssst
stop-press
eoprtttuu
putter-out
eorrsssst
strossers
eorrsttuv
overtrust
eorrstuxy
extrusory
ffghiilnw
whiffling
ffghilnsu
shuffling
ffghilrtu
frightful
ffgilnnsu
snuffling
ffgilnpuy
puffingly
ffgimnoru
fungiform
ffginoprs
offspring
ffgnostuw
stuff-gown
ffhhilsuy
huffishly
ffhlorsuu
four-flush
ffhmoorty
froth-fomy
ffillmnsu
snuff-mill

ffilmoorr
floriform
ffinossuu
suffusion
ffioorstt
first-foot
ffioosttw
swift-foot
ffllmnsuu
snuff-mull
ffllnortu
full-front
fflooopr
foolproof
fflooostw
wolf's-foot
fforrsuuu
furfurous
fggiinorv
forgiving
fghhilnow
high-flown
fghhioopr
high-proof
fghiiinns
finishing
fghiillty
flightily
fghiinsst
sting-fish
fghiklort
folk-right
fghillptu
plightful
fghilnotw
night-fowl
fghilottt
footlight
light-foot
fghiloptt
top-flight
fghinortt
fortnight
fghlnortu
throngful
fghmoortu
frogmouth
fgiiillnn
infilling
fgiiillnp
filliping
fgiiilnvy
vilifying
fgiilllrt
flirt-gill
gillflirt
fgiillnpu
upfilling
fgiilnnow
inflowing
fgiilnnoy
foiningly
fgiilnptu
uplifting

fgiilnrst
firstling
fgiilnsty
siftingly
fgiilntty
fittingly
fgiinnopt
fining-pot
fgiinnoty
notifying
fgiinnttu
unfitting
fgiinoprt
profiting
fgiinossy
ossifying
fgiinpruy
purifying
fgiinptyy
typifying
fgikllnos
golf-links
fgillnoow
following
fgillnowy
flowingly
fgilnrruy
flurrying
fgiloostu
ufologist
fgilsstuu
fustilugs
fgimnoruu
unguiform
fginostuy
fungosity
fgllnoruw
full-grown
fgllnosuy
songfully
fgloorsuu
fulgorous
fglorsuuu
fulgurous
fgnooortw
wrong-foot
fhhiorttw
forthwith
fhiijnost
fish-joint
fhiilopst
pilot-fish
fhiilrtty
thriftily
fhiiorsty
historify
fhiknrstu
trunkfish
fhikorstw
shift-work
fhilloosy
foolishly
fhilloswy
wolfishly

fhillsuwy
wishfully
fhilnsuuw
unwishful
fhiloppsy
foppishly
fhilorsuy
flourishy
fhilrsttu
thirstful
fhinnrsuu
unfurnish
fhinnstuy
tunny-fish
fhinooprt
hoofprint
fhinrttuy
unthrifty
fhllpsuuy
pushfully
fhllrtuuy
hurtfully
ruthfully
fhlmostuu
mouthfuls
fhlnrtuuu
unhurtful
fhloooprs
shop-floor
fhloottw
wolf-tooth
fhmoooprt
moth-proof
fhnooprst
shop-front
fhoooprst
shot-proof
fhoorrsuu
four-hours
fiiilssty
fissility
fiiimnrty
infirmity
fiijlllrt
jillflirt
fiiklnnst
skinflint
fiillmorv
villiform
fiillmotu
multifoil
fiillptuy
pitifully
fiilmortu
trifolium
fiilnnoux
influxion
fiilnptuu
unpitiful
fiiloprst
profilist
fiilortvy
frivolity

fiilprstu
spiritful
fiimmnors
misinform
fiimmorrt
mitriform
fiimnoprs
spiniform
fiimnossu
fusionism
fiimorrtu
triforium
fiimorrtv
vitriform
fiinosstu
fusionist
fiiorstuy
furiosity
fikklnoss
kinsfolks
fiklllsuy
skilfully
fikllnsuu
unskilful
fikmmnoor
Kominform
filllpstu
full-split
fillstuwy
wistfully
filmmortu
multiform
filmnoruy
uniformly
filmnosuu
fulminous
filmorsty
styliform
filmoruvv
vulviform
filnprtuy
turnip-fly
filoooprt
portfolio
filoorssu
fluorosis
filoorsuv
frivolous
filorrsty
floristry
filorsuuy
furiously
filosstuu
fistulous
fimmmmoru
mummiform
finooprsu
profusion
finooprtt
footprint
fkkloorsw
workfolks
fklnoostw
townsfolk

fkooortuw
out-of-work
fkoorrstw
frostwork
flllosuuy
soulfully
flllstuuy
lustfully
fllnoorry
forlornly
floooostt
footstool
floooprrt
plot-proof
floooptu
poult-foot
floorrsuw
sorrowful
floprssuu
plus-fours
fooprrstu
rust-proof
foopsstuy
pussyfoot
gggiilnns
sniggling
gggiilnrw
wriggling
gggiinprs
sprigging
gggiinrst
strigging
gggilmnsu
smuggling
gggilntuy
tuggingly
gghhhiilt
highlight
gghhilosy
hoggishly
gghhinorw
high-grown
gghiiilrw
whirligig
gghiilnns
shingling
gghiilnnt
lightning
gghiilnsy
sighingly
gghiilpsy
piggishly
gghiinnsu
unsighing
gghiinrtw
right-wing
gghiinsst
sight-sing
gghilnnot
nightlong
gghilnopu
ploughing
gghilnsuy
gushingly

gghiloopr
logogriph
gghinnotw
nightgown
gghinpsuu
upgushing
gghlooryy
hygrology
ggiiimnnp
impinging
ggiiimnsv
misgiving
ggiijnnor
jingo-ring
ggiilnnry
ringingly
ggiilnnsw
swingling
ggiilnnsy
singingly
ggiilnpry
gripingly
ggiinnorw
ingrowing
ggiinnprs
springing
ggiinnrst
stringing
ggiinnsww
swing-wing
ggiinopss
gossiping
ggiinotuv
outgiving
ggillnnoy
longingly
ggillnowy
glowingly
ggilmnsuy
ginglymus
ggilnnouy
youngling
ggilnopry
gropingly
ggimnoors
Gongorism
gginnprsu
spring-gun
gginoorst
Gongorist
gginoostu
goings-out
gginopruw
upgrowing
gglnnoruw
lung-grown
ghhiilpst
lightship
ghhiilsst
slightish
ghhilopry
hygrophil
ghhilrstu
rushlight

ghhlortuy
throughly
ghhmoostt
ghost-moth
ghiiknstt
skin-tight
ghiiknttt
tight-knit
ghiilllmt
light-mill
ghiillnrs
shrilling
ghiillnrt
thrilling
ghiillrsy
girlishly
ghiilnnsy
shiningly
ghiilnnty
hintingly
ghiilnnwy
whiningly
ghiilnost
night-soil
ghiilnssy
hissingly
ghiilnstw
whistling
ghiimnprs
shrimping
ghiinnnwy
whinnying
ghiinnpsu
punishing
ghiinnrsu
inrushing
ghiinnsuw
unwishing
ghiknortw
night-work
ghilloopt
loop-light
ghilloopy
philology
ghillooty
lithology
ghilmnnot
monthling
ghilmnoot
moonlight
ghilnoopt
potholing
ghilnoory
rhinology
ghilnopyy
philogyny
ghilnosst
sling-shot
ghilnpsuy
pushingly
ghilnstuy
unsightly
ghilooopy
ophiology

ghilooppy
hippology
ghiloosty
histology
ghilopstt
spotlight
ghilorsuy
roguishly
ghilprsty
sprightly
ghilprtuy
uprightly
ghimmnrtu
thrumming
ghimmntuy
thingummy
ghimnoost
smoothing
ghimnosst
songsmith
ghimoopss
gomphosis
ghimorstw
misgrowth
ghinopstt
nightspot
ghinorrtt
troth-ring
ghinorsst
strongish
ghinorstt
Storthing
ghinortuw
inwrought
ghinrsttu
thrusting
ghiorrsty
hygristor
ghllooopy
hoplology
ghlmnooyy
hymnology
ghlmootyy
mythology
ghlnooopy
phonology
ghlnoopyy
hypnology
ghlnosstu
slung-shot
ghlnostuy
unghostly
ghlnotuyy
youngthly
ghlooptyy
phytology
ghmnoopsy
gymnosoph
ghnnooprr
pronghorn
ghnoorstw
shortgown
ghnorrsuw
rush-grown
ghnortuuw
unwrought
ghooorstt
Ostrogoth
ghoorttuw
outgrowth
ghoprtuuw
upwrought
wrought-up
giiikknst
ski-kiting
giiiklmns
misliking
giiikmnsv
vikingism
giiilostu
litigious
giiimmntt
immitting
giiimnrsv
Irvingism
giiimnruv
virginium
giiimrsst
mistigris
giiinnosv
visioning
giiinnqru
inquiring
giiinprst
spiriting
giiinrtvy
virginity
giijknors
skijoring
giiklnntw
twinkling
giiklnnwy
winkingly
giiknnnuw
unwinking
giiknnorw
inworking
giilllnwy
willingly
giillmnpy
limpingly
giillmnsy
smilingly
giillmrst
grist-mill
giillnnuw
unwilling
giillnpsy
lispingly
giilmnnsu
unsmiling
giilmnssy
missingly
giilnnnwy
winningly
giilnnotu
untoiling
giilnnppy
nippingly
giilnnstu
insulting
giilnntwy
twiningly
giilnosuu
uliginous
giilnppry
rippingly
giilnppst
stippling
giilnprst
stripling
giilnprsy
springily
giilnpstt
splitting
giilnptyy
pityingly
giilnrsty
stringily
giilnttwy
wittingly
giiloosty
sitiology
giilossst
glossitis
giilrsttu
liturgist
giimnntuy
mutinying
giimnoprs
promising
giimnoprv
improving
giimnorrr
mirroring
giimnottw
two-timing
giimnrssu
surmising
giimprstu
spirit-gum
giinnnoww
winnowing
giinnnptu
tuning-pin
giinnopru
inpouring
giinnppru
unripping
giinnprst
sprinting
giinnptuy
unpitying
giinnqstu
squinting
giinnrssu
sunrising
giinnrtuw
unwriting
giinnsstu
unsisting
giinnstuu
unsuiting
giinnttuw
unwitting
giinpprst
stripping
giinpsttu
upsitting
giinqrstu
squirting
giinrsuvv
surviving
giiorrsuu
irriguous
gijllnoty
joltingly
gijlnttuy
juttingly
gijnnnoru
non-juring
giklnnooo
onlooking
giklnnowy
knowingly
giklnoooy
koniology
giknnnouw
unknowing
giknnoruw
unworking
giknooprv
provoking
gillllnoy
lollingly
gillmnooy
limnology
gillmoorr
grill-room
gillmossy
syllogism
gillnopsy
slopingly
gillnorst
strolling
gillnoruy
louringly
gillooopy
oligopoly
gilloorsu
orgillous
gilmmnoos
mongolism
gilmnopry
rompingly
gilmoosty
myologist
gilnnnruy
runningly
gilnooory
onirology
gilnooruy
urinology
gilnoppty
toppingly
gilnoptuy
poutingly
gilnorsuy
rousingly
gilnorttu
troutling
gilnostuu
glutinous
gilnppsuy
supplying
gilnprruy
purringly
gilooorst
orologist
gilooossu
isologous
gilooostt
otologist
gilooostz
zoologist
giloorstu
urologist
gimmnpsuu
summing-up
gimmnrruu
murmuring
gimmnrstu
strumming
gimmostuy
gummosity
gimnnoors
Monsignor
gimnopprt
prompting
gimopruuy
uropygium
gimopssuy
Gossypium
gimopstuu
gumptious
ginnnootv
non-voting
ginnnrtuu
unturning
ginnooprt
Orpington
ginnprtuu
upturning
ginooprss
prognosis
ginooprtu
uprooting
ginoopssu
spongious
ginoorrsw
sorrowing
ginoorstu
trigonous
ginoppptu
topping-up
ginopprst
stropping
ginoppssu
supposing

ginoprsst
  Stringops
ginoprstu
  outspring
  sprouting
ginopttu
  totting-up
ginopttuw
  tuptowing
ginorrttu
  torturing
ginorstuy
  trigynous
ginppttuu
  up-putting
ginrstttu
  strutting
gllooptty
  polyglott
gllooptuy
  plutology
glmnoopuy
  polygonum
glnooosty
  nostology
glooopryt
  tropology
gmnoorssw
  moss-grown
gnoooosuz
  zoogonous
gnooprtyy
  protogyny
goorsstuu
  goustrous
goprstwyy
  gypsywort
hhhmnnouy
  Houyhnhnm
hhhooprst
  shophroth
hhiilnort
  rhinolith
hhiirstty
  thirtyish
hhilooppt
  photophil
hhilorswy
  whorishly
hhimoosst
  smoothish
hhimrstty
  rhythmist
hhmmooopr
  homomorph
hhmnooopy
  homophony
hhnoorrst
  short-horn
hiiiprsvz
  vizirship
hiikmstwy
  tim-whisky

hiillmnot
  millionth
hiillosww
  willowish
hiilnopsy
  Sinophily
hiilnortt
  trilithon
hiilnsswy
  swinishly
hiiloqrsu
  liquorish
hiilostty
  hostility
hiilpstty
  typhlitis
hiilrstty
  thirstily
hiimnoprs
  minorship
hiimnorst
  ironsmith
hiimnosst
  Shintoism
hiimopstu
  hospitium
hiimorsst
  historism
  hit-or-miss
hiinopssy
  hypinosis
hiinosstt
  Shintoist
hiiopprrs
  priorship
hiklmoott
  milk-tooth
hiknnorst
  stinkhorn
hiknnossy
  hyson-skin
hilllmtuu
  multihull
hillloost
  tol-lolish
hillmoott
  mill-tooth
hillmoruu
  ill-humour
hillmpsuy
  lumpishly
hillnsttu
  still-hunt
hilloprw
  whirlpool
hillostuy
  loutishly
hillosvwy
  wolvishly
hillsstyy
  stylishly
hilmmpsuy
  mumpishly

hilmoosyz
  hylozoism
hilmootty
  lithotomy
hilmoprsy
  rompishly
hilnnosty
  tonnishly
hilooptxy
  toxophily
hiloostyz
  hylozoist
hiloprsst
  short-slip
hiloprssu
  Russophil
hilorsstt
  short-list
hilorssuy
  sourishly
hilosstty
  sottishly
hilrstuuv
  vulturish
himnnoosy
  moonshiny
himnopsty
  hypnotism
himooprss
  morphosis
himooprst
  motor-ship
himpsssyy
  symphysis
hinopprst
  print-shop
hinopstty
  hypnotist
hioopprry
  porphyrio
hiooppmst
  troop-ship
hiooprrst
  rotor-ship
hioorsttt
  orthotist
hioprssty
  sophistry
hioprsttu
  tutorship
hiorrstty
  thyristor
hiorssttw
  wrist-shot
hkknnooty
  honky-tonk
hkmmnorru
  krummhorn
hknoooops
  spoon-hook
hlmoopry
  polymorph
hlmooppxy
  pompholyx

hlnooppyy
  polyphony
hmmoopsty
  tommy-shop
hmmpstuyy
  Symphytum
hmnnooopy
  monophony
hmnoorstt
  northmost
hmooopryz
  zoomorphy
hmoopttyy
  phytotomy
hmoossttu
  southmost
hnoopptyy
  phonotypy
hnooprtty
  phytotron
hnoorstuu
  Southroun
hoooprsuz
  zoophorus
hoooprtyz
  zootrophy
hooortttw
  toothwort
hoopttyy
  phototypy
hooprsstt
  short-stop
iiikllnps
  spillikin
iiikmnrst
  miniskirt
  mini-skirt
iiilnostv
  violinist
iiilnttuy
  inutility
iiilosuvx
  lixivious
iiimmnoss
  immission
iiimprsst
  spiritism
iiimrrtuv
  triumviri
iiinnottu
  intuition
iiinosstv
  visionist
iiinprttu
  pituitrin
iiinsssstu
  sinusitis
iiiosttvy
  vitiosity
iiiprsstt
  spiritist
iijnorsuu
  injurious

iijnortuy
  juniority
iikklnnss
  slinkskin
iiklnorst
  nitro-silk
iiknnnoos
  onion-skin
iilllopuv
  pulvillio
iillmnopu
  pollinium
iillmprsu
  spirillum
iillnnnoo
  nonillion
iillostvy
  villosity
iilmmmssu
  Muslimism
iilmmnost
  Miltonism
iilmmpuuv
  impluvium
iilmnoops
  implosion
iilmnopsu
  impulsion
iilmnostv
  voltinism
iilmnpsuv
  vulpinism
iilmopsss
  solipsism
iilnoopst
  postilion
iilnsstuy
  insulsity
iilnttuwy
  unwittily
iiloopsty
  isopolity
iiloprtxy
  prolixity
iilopssst
  solipsist
iilortty
  tortility
iilostvvz
  slivovitz
iilostvwz
  slivowitz
iimnoossu
  simonious
iimnoostt
  motionist
iimnopssz
  Spinozism
iimnorstu
  routinism
iimoprtxy
  proximity
iimoqstux
  quixotism

9 IIM

iimorsttu
tutiorism
iimrrtuvy
triumviry
iimrssttu
strumitis
iinnoorst
intorsion
iinnoortt
intortion
iinnoostt
notionist
iinnoosux
innoxious
iinnorstu
intrusion
iinnorttu
nutrition
iinooprsv
provision
iinoopsvy
poison-ivy
iinooqttu
quotition
iinoorstt
sortition
iinoprrtu
irruption
iinopssty
spinosity
iinopsstz
Spinozist
iinorsttu
introitus
routinist
iinosstuy
sinuosity
iinosstvy
synovitis
iiooprsst
spiritoso
iioprsstu
spiritous

iiorstttu
tutiorist
ijmnoortw
joint-worm
illlpsuuv
pulvillus
illmoorst
still-room
illnooptu
pollution
illnopvyy
polyvinyl
illooqsuy
soliloquy
illoqrtuw
quillwort
ilmnoosuy
ominously
ilmnopstu
Plutonism
ilmnoptuu
plutonium
ilmoprsuy
impulsory
ilmossyyz
zymolysis
ilmrstuuv
vulturism
ilnnosstw
stownlins
ilnooprsu
prolusion
ilnoosuxy
noxiously
ilnoprxyy
pyroxylin
ilnopssuu
spinulous
ilnopsttu
Plutonist
ilnorsuuy
ruinously

ilnossuuy
sinuously
iloopprsy
isopropyl
ilooppssy
polyposis
iloopqrtu
pot-liquor
ilooprttu
tulip-root
iloopstxy
pixy-stool
iloorsstu
torulosis
iloorstuy
riotously
iloprssyy
pyrolysis
ilorsuuux
luxurious
immmnoors
Mormonism
immmpssuu
mumpsimus
immopprtu
impromptu
immopssuy
symposium
immpsssuu
sumpsimus
imnoooprt
promotion
imnooossu
isonomous
imnooostz
zoonomist
imnoorstu
torminous
imnorsttu
strontium
imooosttz
zootomist

imooppsty
pomposity
imooprrss
promissor
imopsssty
symptosis
imorsuvxy
myxovirus
innoopstu
poison-nut
innooqrtu
quintroon
innoossuu
unisonous
inooopssu
poisonous
inooorstu
notorious
inoopprtu
pourpoint
inooprssu
prisonous
inopprttu
turnip-top
inoppsttu
pint-stoup
iooorrrst
orris-root
ioopprrtu
pot-pourri
ioopprsst
proptosis
iooprrsvy
provisory
ioprssttu
posturist
kknorrtuw
trunk-work
kmoprstuw
stump-work
kooprssty
sky-troops

lloooprrs
poor's-roll
lmnnoooxy
monoxylon
lmnooptuy
plutonomy
lmnoopyyy
polyonymy
lmooppsuy
pompously
loopprsuy
Polyporus
looprrsuy
prolusory
loorstuuy
routously
lopsstuuu
pustulous
lorstuuuv
vulturous
mmorrsuuu
murmurous
mnnooopsy
monopsony
mnoorsstu
monstrous
mnoorsstw
snowstorm
mopsstuuu
sumptuous
nnoosstuy
syntonous
nooooprtz
protozoon
noooppssu
soupspoon
ooprrstvy
provostry
ooprsstuu
stuporous
oorrsttuu
torturous

10 AAA

aaaaabccrs
asarabacca
aaaabccemn
Maccabaean
aaaabehnnt
Nabathaean
aaaabemprt
parabemata
aaaabhmmnr
Abraham-man
aaaabilmrv
Ambarvalia

aaaablmrrt
malabar-rat
aaaaccilpr
carapacial
aaaacdeein
Naiadaceae
aaaacdmmrt
tarmacadam
aaaaceeilr
Araliaceae
aaaaclmnrt
almacantar

aaaademnnt
adamantean
aaaadglnnr
Angaraland
aaaadhmruz
Ahuramazda
aaaaeeglop
palaeogaea
aaaaeglmmt
amalgamate
aaaaelmnqu
aquamanale

aaaaggllnn
alang-alang
aaaaghrsty
satyagraha
aaaahinnst
Athanasian
aaaahipprs
paraphasia
aaaaimnnnp
Panamanian
aaaamprrtt
parramatta

aaabbcilst
sabbatical
aaabbdhsty
Sabbath-day
aaabbdrrst
bastard-bar
aaabcchlns
bacchanals
aaabcchnrs
charabancs
aaabccknsv
canvas-back

aaabcclmtu
catacumbal
aaabcdeirs
scarabaeid
aaabcdelnr
candelabra
aaabcegggr
baggage-car
aaabcehlmr
beach-la-mar
aaabcehltt
attachable
aaabcekltt
attackable
aaabcelllr
clarabella
aaabcelrtu
acetabular
aaabcerssu
Scarabaeus
aaabchinrt
batrachian
aaabcikrss
cassia-bark
aaabciqstu
aquabatics
aaabcllmru
ambulacral
aaabcoorrt
barracoota
aaabcorrtu
barracouta
aaabdeeglm
damageable
aaabdehlrz
hazardable
aaabdeilnn
alabandine
aaabdeilnt
alabandite
aaabdmnrru
barramunda
aaabdmorss
ambassador
aaabdorrst
astarboard
aaabeeglmn
manageable
aaabeellpp
appealable
aaabeelpps
appeasable
aaabegggwy
way-baggage
aaabeggmnr
garbageman
aaabegimnr
mangabeira
aaabeglmny
manageably
aaabehlnpt
analphabet
aaabeillss
assailable

aaabeilntt
attainable
aaabeinpst
anabaptise
aaabellnsy
analysable
aaabelnrrt
narratable
aaabghilly
gallabiyah
aaabimnprs
Pan-Arabism
aaabimnpst
anabaptism
aaabinpstt
anabaptist
aaaccceeir
Caricaceae
aaacccjkkr
crackajack
aaaccdeilm
academical
aaacceeils
Salicaceae
aaaccehrss
saccharase
aaaccehrst
saccharate
aaacceiptt
capacitate
aaaccenosu
acanaceous
aaacchilnr
anarchical
aaacchkkmt
hackmatack
aaacchprtt
cataphract
aaaccillrs
cascarilla
aaaccilnst
anaclastic
aaaccimort
acroamatic
aaacciprtt
paratactic
aaaccirrtu
caricatura
aaacddensu
Sadducaean
aaacddjkny
jack-a-dandy
aaacdeimms
macadamise
aaacdelmnr
calamander
aaacdennrv
caravanned
aaacdgiilr
cardialgia
aaacdhinnr
arachnidan
aaacdiilmt
Adamitical

aaacdiiprs
paradisaic
paradisiac
aaacdiklsy
lackadaisy
aaacdilmrt
dramatical
aaacdilrty
caryatidal
aaacdimnru
anacardium
aaaceegnor
Onagraceae
aaaceehmnr
Rhamnaceae
aaaceeilms
Alismaceae
aaaceelnos
Solanaceae
aaaceenppr
appearance
aaaceenrrv
caravaneer
aaaceeopst
Sapotaceae
aaaceflqtu
catafalque
aaaceghlpr
cephalagra
aaacegnort
Arctogaean
aaacehimnn
Manichaean
aaacehirrt
Trachearia
aaaceilmnt
catamenial
aaaceinnrt
catenarian
aaaceinprs
parascenia
aaaceinpst
anapaestic
sea-captain
aaaceinrrs
sarracenia
aaacejknps
jackanapes
aaacellnpt
aplacental
aaacelmprt
metacarpal
aaacelpsty
acatalepsy
aaacennrrv
caravanner
aaacfinnpr
Pan-African
aaacggilno
anagogical
aaacggilop
apagogical
aaacghnrtt
tragacanth

aaacghoprs
Sarcophaga
aaacgillno
analogical
aaacgilmrt
ragmatical
aaacgimrrv
Marcgravia
aaacginnrv
caravaning
aaachillnw
Wallachian
aaachimnrt
marchantia
aaachipprs
paraphasic
aaachjoprs
chaparajos
aaachlmnnr
manna-larch
aaachlnotu
anacolutha
aaachnprty
pyracantha
aaachqtuuu
Chautauqua
aaaciilruv
Avicularia
aaaciirsss
ascariasis
aaaciklmnp
pack-animal
aaaciklmnr
Lamarckian
aaaciklrtu
autarkical
aaacillmnu
animalcula
aaacillmny
maniacally
aaacillnty
analytical
aaacillnuv
Vulcanalia
aaacillrtu
Ural-Altaic
aaacilmmno
ammoniacal
aaacilmnot
anatomical
aaacilnory
Alcyonaria
aaacilnpst
anaplastic
aaacilnrss
carnassial
aaacilnrst
scarlatina
aaacilorrt
crotalaria
aaacilprst
satrapical
aaacilrttu
Articulata

aaacinnprt
pancratian
aaacinnrtu
Cantuarian
aaacinrrtt
tractarian
aaacissstt
catastasis
aaaclmnpru
campanular
aaaclmnrtu
almucantar
aaaclmnrvy
cavalryman
aaaclprrsw
wrap-rascal
aaacmnnrtt
marcantant
aaacmrrtwy
tramway-car
aaacnrtttt
attractant
aaaddelmpt
maladapted
aaaddelnot
adelantado
aaaddgirrt
Tardigrada
aaadeeghnp
phagedaena
aaadefiost
asafoetida
aaadefisst
assafetida
aaadeggl nr
garlandage
aaadeginrt
Tanagridae
aaadeginrv
devanagari
aaadegnrtv
avant-garde
aaadeimnnt
adamantine
aaadeimnrz
mazarinade
aaadeimstt
diastemata
aaadeinprs
paradisean
aaadeipttv
adaptative
aaadeirrsv
adversaria
aaadelmnrs
salamander
aaadgillnr
granadilla
aaadgmmmnr
grandmamma
aaadgmnorr
mandragora
aaadgnoppr
propaganda

aaadhhlmrs
dharmshala
aaadhmmmnu
Muhammadan
aaadiilnpr
lapidarian
aaadiilorr
Radiolaria
aaadiilprs
paradisial
aaadiinprs
paradisian
aaadilmorr
alarm-radio
aaadilnnsu
Andalusian
aaadilnopr
paranoidal
aaadiloppr
parapodial
aaadimnott
datamation
aaadinoptt
adaptation
aaadlmmnnn
landammann
aaadlnqrtu
quadrantal
aaadmnqruu
Quadrumana
aaadorsttu
autostrada
aaaeegpsss
sea-passage
aaaeeilmmn
melanaemia
aaaefglllt
Flagellata
aaaeflmnst
malfeasant
aaaeggimnt
gametangia
aaaeghllnp
phalangeal
aaaeghttww
wag-at-the-wa'
aaaegilmnr
managerial
aaaegilppr
paraplegia
aaaeginprs
asparagine
aaaeglmttu
malaguetta
aaaeglmtxy
metagalaxy
aaaegmrrtv
margravate
aaaegpsswy
passageway
aaaehimrtu
haematuria
aaaehinstu
euthanasia

aaaehjnprt
japan-earth
aaaehlmrss
Marshalsea
aaaehnoppr
epanaphora
aaaehpprrs
paraphrase
aaaeiilntt
Italianate
aaaeillpst
palatalise
aaaeilmnqu
aquamanile
aaaeilmpst
metaplasia
aaaeilmrtu
tularaemia
aaaeilnppr
parapineal
aaaeilnprt
planetaria
aaaeilnptt
palatinate
aaaeimnnrt
amarantine
aaaeimnprs
paramnesia
aaaeimnqru
aquamarine
aaaellnrrz
Ranzellaar
aaaellnrtt
tarantella
aaaellprst
palaestral
aaaelmmnot
melanomata
aaaelmnrtt
atramental
aaaelmprrt
parametral
aaaelmrstt
metatarsal
aaaelnpqru
aquaplaner
aaaelsstwy
leastaways
aaaemorttt
teratomata
aaafginnuu
anguifauna
aaaggillno
algolagnia
aaaggilrst
gastralgia
aaaggnnrtu
gargantuan
aaaghilrrt
arthralgia
aaaghllmop
Mallophaga
aaaghnpstu
agapanthus

aaagiilmnr
marginalia
aaagiilmst
galimatias
aaagiirstt
Sagittaria
aaagillmno
gallomania
aaagilmnno
anglomania
aaagimmnrr
grammarian
aaagimnstt
anastigmat
aaaginnopt
Patagonian
aaagloprss
paraglossa
aaaglrsstu
astragalus
aaagmnnrss
manna-grass
aaagmnstty
syntagmata
aaahiilppr
paraphilia
aaahikmnrt
Karmathian
aaahilmrrs
air-marshal
aaahilnsst
thalassian
aaahimnnot
anthomania
aaahinoppr
paraphonia
aaahinortz
Zoantharia
aaahinrrtu
Arthuriana
aaahiprrrt
pararthria
aaahlmnpst
phantasmal
aaahlnpxyy
anaphylaxy
aaahmnrstu
Amaranthus
aaahpprrst
paraphrast
aaaiijnnrz
janizarian
aaaiillntt
natalitial
aaaiilmnnr
laminarian
aaaiimnprs
Arimaspian
aaaiinnrst
sanitarian
aaaiirrtwy
raiyatwari
aaaillmnnz
manzanilla

aaaillmnpr
rampallian
aaaillortv
lavatorial
aaaillrrst
altar-rails
aaailmnotx
malaxation
aaailmnpst
aplanatism
aaailnortt
natatorial
aaailnrstu
Australian
Saturnalia
aaaimrtttv
amritattva
aaainnprss
Parnassian
aaalmnoprr
paranormal
aaalnnosst
assonantal
aaamnnortt
tramontana
aaamrtzzzz
razzmatazz
aabbbeiltv
babblative
aabbbelors
absorbable
aabbcdeekr
barebacked
aabbcdklor
blackboard
aabbcdnrsu
unscabbard
aabbcefgly
cabbage-fly
aabbceilrs
ascribable
aabbcelmot
combatable
aabbciilnr
rabbinical
aabbcijkrt
jack-rabbit
aabbddeorr
bread-board
aabbddeors
broad-based
aabbdeeelt
debateable
aabbdegorr
barge-board
aabbdeilry
abbey-laird
aabbdeoorv
above-board
aabbdllnry
brandy-ball
aabbeeirtv
abbreviate

aabbeellrs
baseballer
aabbeellrt
barbellate
aabbeelnru
unbearable
aabbeelntu
unbeatable
aabbefmrry
baby-farmer
aabbegirst
sage-rabbit
aabbeillnu
unbailable
aabbeilmno
abominable
aabbeilnot
obtainable
aabbeilrrt
arbitrable
aabbeimnwz
Zimbabwean
aabbekllst
basketball
aabbeklrwy
baby-walker
aabbellmnu
unblamable
aabbelnruy
unbearably
aabbggilnr
Balbriggan
aabbhorrru
harbour-bar
aabbillntu
balibuntal
aabbilmnoy
abominably
aabbilnnoy
Babylonian
aabbiorssu
babiroussa
aabbllmnuy
unblamably
aabbmmnpyy
namby-pamby
aabccdefkl
blackfaced
aabccdelor
accordable
aabcceelpt
acceptable
aabccehiln
chain-cable
aabcceilln
calcinable
aabccekkpr
backpacker
aabccelllu
calculable
aabccelost
accostable
aabccelpty
acceptably

aabccenoos
cocoa-beans
aabcchinst
catch-basin
aabcciilst
cabalistic
aabcciinnr
cinnabaric
aabcciinrt
bacitracin
aabcciknrr
crackbrain
aabccimort
imbroccata
aabccinotu
accubation
aabcciorst
acrobatics
aabcclluy
calculably
aabcddehkn
backhanded
aabcddekls
saddleback
aabcdeehlt
detachable
aabcdeeilr
eradicable
aabcdeellr
declarable
aabcdeelns
ascendable
aabcdegknr
back-garden
aabcdehknr
backhander
aabcdeiilt
diabetical
aabcdeilmr
Barmecidal
aabcdeiotv
advice-boat
aabcdelmnu
manducable
aabcdelnnu
unbalanced
aabcdelnsu
subdecanal
aabcdelors
scale-board
aabcdelprw
parcel-bawd
aabcdennor
carbonnade
aabcderstt
abstracted
aabcdgklru
blackguard
aabcdhiinr
Dibranchia
aabcdhklor
chalkboard
aabcdhmort
matchboard
aabcdhoprt
patchboard
aabcdiillo
diabolical
aabcdiinot
abdication
aabcdilmms
lambdacism
aabcdinrry
canary-bird
aabcdklpsu
backspauld
aabcdklrwy
backwardly
aabcdllnpu
cup-and-ball
aabcdmossu
ambuscados
aabcdnnort
contraband
aabceeeffl
effaceable
aabceeeltu
Betulaceae
aabceeemrr
mace-bearer
aabceeertt
ebracteate
aabceeertu
Tuberaceae
aabceeertx
exacerbate
aabceefnrz
brazen-face
aabceeghln
changeable
aabceeghlr
chargeable
aabceegkrt
age-bracket
aabceehilv
achievable
aabceehlrs
searchable
aabceehlty
chalybeate
aabceehrst
sabretache
aabceeilmr
amerciable
aabceeinrr
carabineer
aabceeirtu
eubacteria
aabceelllr
recallable
aabceellns
cleansable
aabceelmot
come-at-able
aabceelnrt
tabernacle
aabceelpst
aspectable
aabceelrtu
trabeculae
aabcefiilp
pacifiable
aabcefiilt
beatifical
aabceflort
factorable
aabceghlny
changeably
aabceghlry
chargeably
aabcegkrst
gas-bracket
aabcegllou
coagulable
aabceglmnn
blancmange
aabcehilpt
alphabetic
aabcehilrt
charitable
aabcehinrt
branchiate
aabcehintu
habitaunce
aabcehklrt
blackheart
aabcehkmnr
harman-beck
aabcehkors
ahorseback
aabcehlouv
avouchable
aabceiinrr
carabinier
aabceiintu
beautician
aabceillmp
implacable
aabceillpp
applicable
aabceilmot
ametabolic
aabceilmst
masticable
aabceilnot
actionable
aabceiloss
associable
aabceilpsz
capsizable
aabceilqru
acquirable
aabceinnos
ocean-basin
aabceinort
abreaction
aabceinstt
state-cabin
aabceiorst
aerobatics
aabceirstt
tetrabasic
aabcekkmrr
backmarker
aabceklrtw
blackwater
aabceknors
rackabones
aabcekoptt
packet-boat
aabcelllot
collatable
aabcellmor
collar-beam
aabcellnsu
unscalable
aabcellorr
barcarolle
aabcelmopr
comparable
aabcelmtuu
acetabulum
aabcelnotu
outbalance
aabcelrrtu
trabecular
aabcerrstt
abstracter
aabcerrtuu
bureaucrat
aabcerstuu
subarcuate
aabcfiorrt
fabricator
aabcflnoru
confabular
aabcgiillm
galliambic
aabcgiknrr
barracking
aabcgillsu
subglacial
aabcginort
boat-racing
aabcgkmmno
backgammon
aabcglrrtu
cat-burglar
aabchhimpr
amphibrach
aabchhpsty
bathyscaph
aabchilrty
charitably
aabchinoop
canophobia
aabchinott
cohabitant
aabchioopr
acrophobia
aabchirsxy
brachyaxis
aabchklmor
Bramah-lock
aabchklpss
splash-back
aabchlmnpr
palm-branch
aabchlrruy
brachyural
aabchmoruy
moucharaby
aabciillmy
iambically
aabciilpty
capability
aabciiltty
actability
aabciioprt
parabiotic
aabcikrsst
backstairs
aabcilllsy
syllabical
aabcillmpy
implacably
aabcillnny
cannibally
aabcillppy
applicably
aabcilmost
catabolism
aabcilmrtu
umbratical
aabcilnnno
cannabinol
aabcilnnuu
incunabula
aabcilnrsu
subcranial
aabcilnsuv
subclavian
aabcilorrt
calibrator
aabcilrstu
arcubalist
ultrabasic
aabcimoort
macrobiota
aabcimorst
acrobatism
aabciqstuu
subaquatic
aabcklmoor
blackamoor
aabcllnnno
cannonball
aabclmmruu
ambulacrum
aabclmopry
comparably
aabcloruvy
vocabulary
aabclrstty
abstractly
aabcnorsst
contrabass
aabcorrstt
abstractor

aabdddeehl
bald-headed
aabddeeehr
bareheaded
aabddeeglr
degradable
aabddeelmn
demandable
aabddeeprs
spade-beard
aabddeggns
sandbagged
aabddehlmo
hebdomadal
aabddehlrs
balderdash
aabddehmor
hebdomadar
aabddeilrr
air-bladder
aabddeimnr
mad-brained
aabddeinst
bastinaded
aabddelopr
pedal-board
aabddelopt
paddle-boat
aabddeorry
day-boarder
aabddillmo
lambdoidal
aabdeeelms
sealed-beam
aabdeeelrr
bear-leader
aabdeeemno
endamoebae
aabdeeflry
defrayable
aabdeeglrr
regardable
aabdeehkkw
hawk-beaked
aabdeehrrt
threadbare
aabdeekprr
parbreaked
aabdeelnru
unreadable
aabdeelrrv
laverbread
aabdeelrrw
rewardable
aabdeemnov
above-named
aabdeeprry
prayer-bead
aabdeeqrsu
arabesqued
aabdefinrt
fat-brained
aabdefirsy
fairy-beads

aabdegginr
brigandage
aabdeggnrs
sandbagger
aabdeggoru
broad-gauge
aabdeghnsu
husbandage
aabdegimrr
Bridgerama
aabdegimrs
bragadisme
aabdegmnnr
German-band
aabdegorst
goat's-beard
aabdegorsw
board-wages
aabdegrrss
beard-grass
aabdehknst
hand-basket
aabdehkrsw
hawksbeard
aabdehnstw
sweathband
aabdehorrt
earth-board
aabdeilllu
illaudable
aabdeillnr
banderilla
aabdeillsy
dialysable
aabdeilmtt
admittable
aabdeilnor
ordainable
aabdeilnot
dealbation
aabdeilost
Blastoidea
aabdeinnor
Aberdonian
aabdeinrst
bartisaned
aabdeirsst
bastardise
aabdejlstu
adjustable
aabdekllms
masked-ball
aabdekllnr
randle-balk
aabdekorst
skateboard
aabdellnno
belladonna
aabdelnopr
pardonable
aabdelorrz
razor-blade
aabdelrstu
balustrade

aabdemnosw
beadswoman
aabdemnrst
bandmaster
aabdemorss
embassador
aabdeopprr
paperboard
aabdeoprst
pasteboard
aabdfhlors
flash-board
aabdfloort
float-board
aabdghrrtu
draught-bar
aabdgiilnw
law-abiding
aabdgiknos
baking-soda
aabdhmnnsu
husbandman
aabdhnorrw
hand-barrow
aabdhnortt
throat-band
aabdillluy
illaudably
aabdillory
aryballoid
aabdilmnru
mandibular
aabdiloopr
paraboloid
aabdimnrru
barramundi
aabdimrsst
bastardism
aabdlnntuy
abundantly
aabdlnopry
pardonably
aabdlorrty
bardolatry
aabdnnprsy
brandy-snap
aabdoorrrw
broad-arrow
aabdorrstw
strawboard
aabeeellpr
repealable
aabeeellrs
releasable
aabeeellrv
revealable
aabeeelprt
repeatable
aabeeelrrt
tale-bearer
aabeeemnot
entamoebae
aabeefilrr
rarefiable

aabeeflllt
flabellate
aabeegilnr
regainable
aabeeglmss
assemblage
aabeeglovy
voyageable
aabeeglrtt
targetable
aabeegnnru
near-begaun
aabeegnort
baronetage
aabeehkrrt
heartbreak
aabeehllnu
unhealable
aabeehlqtu
bequeathal
aabeehlrtt
earth-table
aabeehmmmr
hammer-beam
aabeeillrs
realisable
aabeeilmnx
examinable
aabeeilnrs
inerasable
aabeeilnrt
retainable
aabeeilprr
repairable
aabeeinrrr
arrière-ban
aabeejkrrw
jaw-breaker
aabeeklmrr
remarkable
aabeeklmrt
marketable
aabeeklrrw
law-breaker
aabeekrrtw
breakwater
water-break
aabeellmnt
lamentable
aabeellnpt
plane-table
aabeellnsu
unsaleable
aabeellprr
pall-bearer
aabeelmnnu
unamenable
unnameable
aabeelmntu
untameable
aabeelmrsu
measurable

aabeelmstt
metastable
stablemate
aabeelnntt
tenantable
aabeelnors
reasonable
aabeelnoss
seasonable
aabeelnptt
patentable
aabeelnrsu
unerasable
aabeelnrsw
answerable
aabeelnrtu
untearable
aabeelnruw
unwearable
aabeeloprv
evaporable
aabeelppry
prepayable
aabeelrrst
arbalester
arrestable
aabeelrsst
assertable
aabeelrttw
table-water
water-table
aabeelssss
assessable
aabeelsttt
attestable
aabeerrttv
Vertebrata
aabeffiill
affiliable
aabeffilmr
affirmable
aabefgiltu
fatiguable
aabefgklnr
klangfarbe
aabefgklst
flag-basket
aabefhlmot
fathomable
aabefiills
salifiable
aabefillmn
inflamable
aabefillnt
inflatable
aabefimors
framboesia
aabefloruv
favourable
aabefnorrt
forbearant
aabeghinst
sea-bathing

aabeghorru
  harbourage
aabegiilmn
  imaginable
aabegilnoz
  zabaglione
aabegilnrv
  Belgravian
aabegilnss
  assignable
aabegilrst
  algebraist
aabeginnot
  abnegation
aabeginrru
  rue-bargain
aabegiortv
  abrogative
aabegkrrsu
  sugar-baker
aabeglnruu
  unarguable
aabegloppr
  propagable
aabehiiltt
  habilitate
aabehikmrt
  habit-maker
aabehinrrt
  Herbartian
aabehioopr
  aerophobia
aabehklnsu
  unshakable
aabehlrszz
  belshazzar
aabehqrssu
  squabasher
aabehrrstw
  water-brash
aabeiilnrv
  invariable
aabeiilnst
  insatiable
aabeiilntu
  unilabiate
aabeiilsst
  assibilate
aabeijlosu
  Beaujolais
aabeiklmst
  mistakable
aabeiknnrv
  knave-bairn
aabeillmnu
  unmailable
aabeillmpp
  impalpable
aabeillnrs
  ballerinas
aabeillnuv
  invaluable
aabeilmntu
  albuminate
aabeilmntv
  ambivalent
aabeilmpss
  impassable
aabeilnnot
  balneation
aabeilnrsy
  inerasably
aabeilnruv
  unvariable
aabeilnstu
  unsatiable
aabeilopr s
  parabolise
aabeilqrru
  quarriable
aabeilrrst
  arbalister
  breastrail
aabeilrstu
  tabularise
aabeimprtv
  vampire-bat
aabeinorrt
  aberration
aabeinortt
  trabeation
aabeinrrtw
  water-brain
aabekkmnrr
  banker-mark
aabeklmrry
  remarkably
aabeklrttw
  wattlebark
aabekoprrt
  parrot-beak
aabellmnty
  lamentably
aabellnpuy
  unplayable
aabellnuuv
  unvaluable
aabellrrsy
  salal-berry
aabelmnors
  ransomable
aabelmnsuu
  unamusable
aabelmntuy
  untameably
aabelmrsuy
  measurably
aabelnnotu
  unatonable
aabelnorsy
  reasonably
aabelnossy
  seasonably
aabelnpssu
  unpassable
aabelnrswy
  answerably
aabelnsuwy
  unswayable
aabeloorrt
  elaborator
aabelopprv
  approvable
aabeloprrt
  proratable
aabelpprsy
  parablepsy
aabelprstu
  pasturable
aabelstttu
  statutable
aabemrsttu
  masturbate
aabffiilty
  affability
aabflmnoty
  flamboyant
aabfloruvy
  favourably
aabghiloop
  algophobia
aabgiilmny
  imaginably
aabgiilnor
  aboriginal
aabgimnptw
  gambit-pawn
aabgimorty
  ambagitory
aabginnotw
  angwantibo
aabginoort
  abrogation
aabginortu
  outbargain
aabgiossss
  bagassosis
aabglnrsuu
  subangular
aabhhimtvz
  bathmizvah
aabhhipssw
  bashawship
aabhiinntt
  inhabitant
aabhiinott
  habitation
aabhilltuy
  habitually
aabhilorty
  habilatory
aabhimmnrs
  Brahmanism
aabhimrstv
  barmitsvah
aabhimrtvz
  barmitzvah
aabhimsstv
  basmitsvah
aabhimsttv
  batmitsvah
aabhimstvz
  basmitzvah
aabhimttvz
  batmitzvah
aabhinoopp
  panophobia
aabhklnsuy
  unshakably
aabhllloou
  hullabaloo
aabhlpssyy
  hypabyssal
aabhoprtuv
  vapour-bath
aabhosttuw
  whatabouts
aabiiilmty
  amiability
aabiiinnpr
  bipinnaria
aabiillsty
  salability
aabiilmtty
  tamability
aabiilnrvy
  invariably
aabiilnsty
  insatiably
aabiilrtty
  ratability
aabiilttxy
  taxability
aabiinnssy
  Abyssinian
aabiinprst
  bipartisan
aabiinqruu
  ubiquarian
aabiioprss
  parabiosis
aabijnortu
  abjuration
aabiklmost
  katabolism
aabiknoprt
  Portakabin®
aabillmppy
  impalpably
aabillmsst
  lamb's-tails
aabillnoot
  oblational
aabillnruy
  binaurally
aabillnuvy
  invaluably
aabillruvv
  bivalvular
aabilmnotu
  ambulation
aabilmpssy
  impassably
aabilmrsst
  strabismal
aabilnottu
  tabulation
aabilnrtuu
  tubularian
aabiloprst
  parabolist
aabilprtuy
  patibulary
aabimnoort
  abominator
aabinnrrtu
  intra-urban
aabinprrst
  bairn's-part
aabiorrrtt
  arbitrator
aabkkoorru
  kookaburra
aabllmnory
  abnormally
aabllnopst
  planoblast
aablmmosty
  Amblystoma
aablmmpstu
  stamp-album
aablmortuy
  ambulatory
aablnrstuu
  subnatural
aabloorrty
  laboratory
aabloprrru
  bar-parlour
aablorttuy
  tabulatory
aablrssttu
  substratal
aablstttuy
  statutably
aabmorrrtw
  barrow-tram
aabnoorrtw
  narrow-boat
aaborrrstu
  barratrous
aacccdenor
  accordance
aacccdnory
  accordancy
aaccceenpt
  acceptance
aaccceiltt
  catalectic
aacccekrrt
  cat-cracker
aacccenpty
  acceptancy
aaccceostu
  cactaceous
aacccinruy
  inaccuracy
aaccddehkn
  cack-handed

aaccddeiss
caddis-case
aaccddiils
didascalic
aaccddiilt
didactical
aaccdeefmr
cream-faced
aaccdeenns
ascendance
aaccdeerrz
care-crazed
aaccdehirs
saccharide
aaccdehnor
archdeacon
aaccdeilnt
accidental
aaccdeimnu
unacademic
aaccdeiort
coradicate
aaccdejnot
coadjacent
aaccdellno
candle-coal
aaccdelltu
calculated
aaccdelrst
card-castle
cat's-cradle
aaccdelstu
sacculated
aaccdemmoo
cacodaemom
aaccdennsy
ascendancy
aaccdhiiln
Chalcidian
aaccdhilmo
dochmiacal
aaccdhinrt
catch-drain
aaccdhiors
saccharoid
aaccdhnost
coach-stand
aaccdiirty
caryatidic
aaccdiistu
diacaustic
aacceeelrt
accelerate
aacceeepry
Cyperaceae
aacceeffot
face-to-face
aacceefhss
chasse-café
aacceegprs
scapegrace
aacceeilsu
Clusiaceae
aacceeimnr
cine-camera
aacceeimry
Myricaceae
aacceeinpu
Punicaceae
aacceeirtu
Urticaceae
aacceellnt
cancellate
aacceellot
calceolate
aacceelnrt
accelerant
aacceenttu
accentuate
aacceeorsu
aceraceous
aacceeortv
coacervate
aacceeprsu
caper-sauce
aaccefiipt
pacificate
aacceflort
calefactor
aaccefprst
spacecraft
aacceghost
stagecoach
aaccegiort
Arctogaeic
aaccegllno
glance-coal
aaccehillm
alchemical
aaccehilmn
mechanical
aaccehilor
Cochlearia
aaccehinnt
cachinnate
aaccehinnw
wanchancie
aaccehinrs
saccharine
aaccehinru
Chaucerian
aaccehirst
chaise-cart
aaccehirsv
viscachera
aaccehlnot
coelacanth
aaccehnoty
chatoyance
aaccehorss
saccharose
aaccehrrtt
rat-catcher
aaccehrrty
charactery
aacceillno
cloacaline
aacceilopr
praecocial
aacceilptt
cataleptic
aacceinorv
covariance
aacceinosu
acinaceous
aacceinprt
pancreatic
aacceinrtt
cantatrice
aacceinrtu
inaccurate
aacceiortt
aerotactic
aacceirrtu
caricature
aacceistuv
accusative
aacceKllvv
clack-valve
aaccelllor
coal-cellar
aaccellnno
cannel-coal
aaccellott
toccatella
aaccelmtuu
accumulate
aaccelorsu
calcareous
aaccelrtuy
accurately
aaccenrstu
crustacean
aaccfhirsy
saccharify
aaccfillry
farcically
aaccfilrsu
fascicular
aaccfinnrs
Franciscan
aaccghhlns
Nachschlag
aaccghiory
hagiocracy
aaccghloss
glass-coach
aaccghopry
cacography
aacchhiinn
chinachina
aacchhintw
watch-chain
aacchiimrs
archaicism
aacchiirst
archaistic
aacchilnpy
chaplaincy
aacchimort
achromatic
aacchinnor
anachronic
aacchinopt
cataphonic
aacchlnory
acronychal
aacchlopty
Phytolacca
aacchmorsu
scaramouch
aacciillmt
climatical
aacciillnu
canaliculi
aacciilors
sacroiliac
aacciinorv
Cavicornia
aacciinprt
practician
aacciinpty
incapacity
aacciinrss
Circassian
aaccillruv
clavicular
aaccilltty
tactically
aaccilmmuy
immaculacy
aaccilmnor
romancical
aaccilnnos
canonicals
aaccilnoos
occasional
aaccilorst
Socratical
aaccilostu
acoustical
aaccilpttu
catapultic
aaccinnrsz
cancrizans
aaccinoopt
cacotopian
aaccinortv
vaccinator
aaccinostu
accusation
aaccinptty
anaptyctic
aaccinrstu
anacrustic
aaccinstty
asyntactic
aacciorttu
autocratic
aacckllmor
alarm-clock
aaccllioors
sarcocolla
aaccllortu
calculator
aaccllrtuu
accultural
aacclnottu
contactual
aacclnrruu
caruncular
aacclorsvy
slavocracy
aaccmnnopy
capnomancy
aaccmnoptt
accomptant
aaccmnorty
cartomancy
aaccnnottu
accountant
aaccnorsst
sacrosanct
aacddeehlr
decahedral
aacddeeimp
aide-de-camp
aacddeeirt
eradicated
aacddehkkn
kack-handed
aacddeijtu
adjudicate
aacddeinnr
decandrian
aacddeinsv
disadvance
aacddeklps
pack-saddle
aacddellns
scandalled
aacddglnru
grand-ducal
aacddhkpwy
paddy-whack
aacddiottu
autodidact
aacdeeeers
Resedaceae
aacdeeefns
defeasance
aacdeeemns
damasceene
aacdeeffls
false-faced
aacdeefhms
shamefaced
aacdeefppr
paper-faced
aacdeeglln
lead-glance
aacdeegmmr
decagramme
aacdeegnot
anecdotage
aacdeehnrs
case-harden
aacdeehrrt
race-hatred

aacdeehrtt
tracheated
aacdeeiins
Sciaenidae
aacdeeiint
taeniacide
aacdeeilny
Lycaenidae
aacdeeilrt
dilacerate
aacdeeinrt
deracinate
ecardinate
aacdeeiptt
decapitate
aacdeeirxy
Xyridaceae
aacdeeittv
deactivate
aacdeeknns
snake-dance
aacdeelnrr
calendarer
aacdeelntu
anucleated
aacdeennrr
ance-errand
aacdeenntt
attendance
aacdeenrsy
canary-seed
aacdeesuwy
causewayed
aacdeffirt
affricated
aacdefglss
glass-faced
aacdefinrr
Africander
aacdefinru
fricandeau
aacdefjnsu
Janus-faced
aacdeflnno
flanconade
aacdeflort
defalcator
aacdefpsty
pasty-faced
aacdeggiop
paedagogic
aacdeghhnr
charge-hand
aacdeginny
decagynian
aacdegnors
Gasconader
aacdehhttw
death-watch
aacdehilnr
Heraclidan
aacdehinrs
sedan-chair

aacdehiors
icosahedra
aacdehiory
Hyracoidea
aacdehkprt
pack-thread
aacdehlmty
chlamydate
aacdehlort
octahedral
aacdehnttu
unattached
aacdehoopt
Chaetopoda
aacdehorty
cathode-ray
aacdeiilnt
laciniated
aacdeiilrs
radicalise
aacdeiiluv
Aviculidae
aacdeiinrr
irradiance
aacdeiiprt
paediatric
aacdeiirrt
irradicate
aacdeiirtv
divaricate
aacdeijltv
adjectival
aacdeillln
candelilla
aacdeilmno
demoniacal
aacdeilmnr
aldermanic
aacdeilmnt
declaimant
aacdeilnno
Caledonian
aacdeilnps
snail-paced
aacdeilnpt
pedantical
aacdeilnss
scandalise
aacdeilort
Crotalidae
aacdeimntt
admittance
aacdeimntu
acuminated
aacdeimopr
paramedico
aacdeinqtu
acquainted
aacdeinquy
inadequacy
aacdeinrrw
warrandice
aacdeinrtx
taxi-dancer

aacdeinsuv
disavaunce
aacdeiorrt
Cortaderia
eradicator
aacdeirsty
caryatides
aacdejlnty
adjacently
aacdekllrw
cradlewalk
aacdelmnnu
unmanacled
aacdelmopr
camelopard
aacdelnnsu
sand-launce
aacdelnsst
sand-castle
aacdeloprt
leopard-cat
aacdelorrt
declarator
aacdelorst
sacerdotal
aacdelorsu
lardaceous
aacdelotuv
vacuolated
aacdelpstu
scapulated
aacdelrtwy
tawdry-lace
aacdemrrst
master-card
aacdenntty
attendancy
aacdenrssu
sand-saucer
aacdenttuu
unactuated
aacdeoprrs
radarscope
aacdeorsuv
cadaverous
aacdfhinrt
handicraft
aacdfiills
falsidical
aacdfiinoo
aficionado
aacdfiinor
Africanoid
aacdfimnrt
frantic-mad
aacdfimorr
microfarad
aacdgginrr
drag-racing
aacdghiipr
diagraphic
aacdghrtuw
watch-guard

aacdgilopr
podagrical
aacdgimorr
cardiogram
aacdginnpt
tap-dancing
aacdgnrsuy
sugar-candy
aacdgorstu
coastguard
aacdhiinsy
daisy-chain
aacdhinort
anthracoid
aacdhirrsu
Charadrius
aacdhlorsy
day-scholar
aacdhmnorr
orchard-man
aacdhoopps
Scaphopoda
aacdhosstw
shadowcast
aacdiiillrv
larvicidal
aacdiilmrs
radicalism
aacdiilmrt
matricidal
aacdiilnop
pinacoidal
aacdiilprr
parricidal
aacdiilprt
patricidal
aacdiilrty
radicality
aacdiilstt
diastaltic
aacdiinors
Icosandria
aacdiinort
radication
aacdiinrry
irradiancy
aacdijlluy
Judaically
aacdillmtu
Talmudical
aacdillnry
cardinally
aacdilmory
myocardial
aacdilnops
spondaical
aacdilnors
sardonical
aacdilnsty
dynastical
aacdiloprs
sporadical
aacdimmrsu
music-drama

aacdimnrtu
undramatic
aacdinnort
octandrian
aacdinnost
contadinas
aacdinootv
advocation
aacdinorrt
ration-card
aacdinrrsw
Drawcansir
aacdjnottu
coadjutant
aacdlmorru
armour-clad
aacdlnossu
scandalous
aacdloprst
postal-card
aacdmmnnot
commandant
aacdnoorwy
canary-wood
aacdooprrt
paradoctor
aacdooprst
capodastro
aacdoortvy
advocatory
aacdorrstu
scordatura
aacdorsstw
coastwards
aaceeeghst
escheatage
aaceeeglln
allegeance
aaceeeiost
Isoetaceae
aaceeeippr
Piperaceae
aaceeekmpr
peacemaker
aaceeelmnp
elecampane
aaceeelmrt
telecamera
aaceeelnop
Palaeocene
aaceeeoprt
proteaceae
aaceefgsty
safety-cage
aaceefqrsu
square-face
aaceeghnrr
carragheen
aaceegilln
allegiance
aaceegilns
Genesiacal
aaceegkptw
wage-packet

aaceeglnuy
launcegaye
aaceegmprs
megaparsec
aaceehilmu
leuchaemia
aaceehilnr
Heracleian
aaceehilnt
châtelaine
aaceehinns
seannachie
aaceehinry
Rhyniaceae
aaceehkpst
cheapskate
aaceehlmno
chamaeleon
aaceehlnpt
antechapel
aaceehlorv
coal-heaver
aaceehlpst
sphacelate
aaceehlrtt
trachelate
aaceehlrty
Lythraceae
aaceehmnry
aerenchyma
aaceehnnrt
anthracene
aaceehoprs
sea-poacher
aaceehpprs
paper-chase
aaceehprtw
peach-water
aaceeiknps
sinke-a-pace
aaceeilmrs
caramelise
aaceeilprt
altarpiece
aaceeilrtv
lacerative
aaceeilstt
elasticate
aaceeimmos
Mimosaceae
aaceeimnpt
emancipate
aaceeinprt
Capernaite
paraenetic
aaceeipprt
appreciate
aaceeipssy
assay-piece
aaceeirttv
reactivate
aaceeituvv
evacuative

aaceeklrrw
race-walker
aaceellluv
valleculae
aaceellnot
lanceolate
aaceellort
reallocate
aaceelmstu
emasculate
aaceelnnrt
alternance
aaceelnosu
sauce-alone
aaceelnttt
neat-cattle
aaceeloprt
capreolate
aaceelopry
Pyrolaceae
aaceelopsu
paleaceous
aaceemnrst
steam-crane
aaceennrss
arcaneness
aaceenorsu
arenaceous
aaceenosuv
avenaceous
aaceenrrtw
water-crane
aaceepprty
peace-party
aaceeprstt
peat-caster
aaceersstv
stavesacre
aaceffginy
faying-face
aaceffimnr
affirmance
aacefginsv
face-saving
aacefglmou
camouflage
aacefgnrsu
gas-furnace
aacefgrstt
stagecraft
aacefhllnp
chapfallen
aacefhlmnr
arch-flamen
aacefhrsty
safety-arch
aacefiillm
maleficial
aacefiiltt
facilitate
aacefiinrs
Africanise
aacefiinst
fanaticise

aacefilmos
leaf-mosaic
aacefinort
arefaction
aacefinrru
Eurafrican
aacefjkrrt
jack-rafter
aaceflllpr
cellar-flap
aacefllotw
tallow-face
aaceflmort
malefactor
aaceflrrtu
Fratercula
aacefmnrsu
surfaceman
aacefrrttw
water-craft
aacefrsttt
statecraft
aaceghilnw
ca'ing-whale
aaceghinor
archegonia
aaceghlrsw
scrag-whale
aaceghmopr
macrophage
aaceghnort
coat-hanger
aacegillmn
Magellanic
aacegillpr
pre-glacial
aacegilmnn
malignance
aacegilmnt
magnetical
aacegilort
categorial
aacegilotz
catalogize
aacegilppr
paraplegic
aacegilprs
spagerical
aacegimnpr
campaigner
aaceginrss
Cassegrain
aacegipprr
paper-cigar
aacegjnotu
Conjugatae
aaceglmnor
carmagnole
aaceglmory
acromegaly
aaceglortu
cataloguer
aacegmnnno
cannon-game

aacegmnrty
termagancy
aacegnnort
cartonnage
aacehhilrr
hierarchal
aacehhklms
hamshackle
aacehiimnt
haematinic
aacehiiprr
hiera-picra
aacehillly
heliacally
aacehilmms
Michaelmas
aacehilmpr
alphameric
aacehilmpt
alphametic
emphatical
aacehilntx
hexactinal
aacehilopt
apothecial
aacehilprs
seraphical
aacehilprx
hexaplaric
aacehilpst
chaptalise
aacehilptt
pathetical
aacehilrtt
theatrical
aacehimmnn
machineman
aacehimmpr
amphimacer
aacehimmtt
mathematic
aacehimnoo
haemoconia
aacehimnot
theomaniac
aacehimnrt
carthamine
aacehinprs
parischane
aacehinrrt
catarrhine
aacehinrtt
anthracite
aacehinstu
Eustachian
aacehioprx
echopraxia
aacehiorst
Oireachtas
aacehiprrt
arch-pirate
aacehiprss
Caesarship

aacehirrtv
architrave
aacehjkmmr
jackhammer
aacehjoprs
chaparejos
aacehklmrs
ramshackle
aacehklnrs
ranshackle
aacehkmmrt
matchmaker
aacehkmnny
hackneyman
aacehkmrtw
watchmaker
aacehlmmrw
claw-hammer
aacehlmuux
chalumeaux
aacehlopsu
acephalous
aacehlopty
Polychaeta
aacehlprrt
Petrarchal
aacehlprty
archetypal
aacehlrstt
scarlet-hat
aacehmnpry
parenchyma
aacehmnrty
athermancy
aacehmnttt
attachment
aacehmoprs
Chamaerops
aacehmoprt
camphorate
aacehmstty
steam-yacht
aacehnnpsu
snaphaunce
aacehnopty
tachypnoea
aacehnortt
archontate
aacehnprrt
Petrarchan
aacehnpsww
wapenschaw
aacehoprty
apothecary
aacehpprtw
watch-paper
aaceiillpr
capillaire
aaceiillrt
Lacertilia
aaceiilpst
capitalise
aaceiimnot
emaciation

aaceimprt
parmacitie
aaceiinnrv
invariance
aaceiinptt
anticipate
aaceiinttv
inactivate
vaticinate
aaceiiopss
Cassiopeia
aaceiiprrs
persicaria
aaceiiprtt
patriciate
aaceijlmst
majestical
aaceikllrs
rascal-like
aaceiklrtt
racket-tail
aaceillmnu
animalcule
aaceillnos
escallonia
aaceillnpt
planetical
aaceillnrt
carnallite
aaceillntt
cantillate
aaceillosu
alliaceous
aaceillprt
prelatical
aaceillpru
Lupercalia
aaceillrrv
varicellar
aaceillrtu
calliature
aaceillrvy
cavalierly
aaceillsty
salicylate
aaceilmmno
melomaniac
aaceilmmtu
immaculate
aaceilmnot
Celtomania
noematical
aaceilmnpr
imparlance
aaceilmnrt
reclaimant
aaceilmnru
unicameral
aaceilmntu
calumniate
aaceilmrtu
tularaemic

aaceilnort
creational
laceration
aaceilnost
escalation
aaceilnptu
paniculate
aaceilnrrt
intercalar
aaceilnrtu
retinacula
aaceiloopz
Palaeozoic
aaceilorrt
acroterial
aaceilprst
palaestric
aaceilpttu
capitulate
aaceilrsst
scale-stair
aaceilrstt
strait-lace
aaceilrttu
articulate
aaceilrtuu
auriculate
aaceilsttt
stalactite
aaceilsttu
actualités
aaceiltttw
tattie-claw
aaceimmpru
paramecium
aaceimnnor
Cameronian
aaceimnnru
un-American
aaceimnnst
anamnestic
aaceimnors
macaronies
aaceimnort
cameration
maceration
racemation
aaceimnoru
oceanarium
aaceimnrss
Saracenism
aaceimopst
aposematic
aaceimprrt
parametric
aaceimsttt
metastatic
aaceinnntu
annunciate
aaceinnott
catenation
aaceinnprt
pancreatin

aaceinnrtu
centaurian
aaceinortu
aeronautic
aaceinortv
acervation
aaceinotuv
evacuation
aaceinotvx
excavation
aaceinqrtu
reacquaint
aaceinrsst
incrassate
aaceinssst
assistance
aaceinstvy
vanity-case
aaceiorstt
aerostatic
aaceirtttv
attractive
aacejknrtt
natterjack
aacekktyyy
yackety-yak
aaceklmrst
smart-Aleck
aaceklnors
coral-snake
aacekloopr
opera-cloak
aaceklrstw
slack-water
aaceklstty
stay-tackle
aacelllort
collateral
aacelllrst
salt-cellar
aacelllruv
vallecular
aacellprry
carpellary
aacelmmors
sarcolemma
aacelmnopt
complanate
aacelmopsu
palmaceous
aacelmorst
coalmaster
aacelmosuv
malvaceous
aacelmosuy
amylaceous
aacelmprst
campestral
scrap-metal
aacelmrtuu
maculature
aacelnnost
stone-canal

aacelnoptu
cantaloupe
aacelnpstu
pulsatance
aacelnrruv
vernacular
aacelnrttu
tentacular
aacelnsssu
casualness
aaceloppsy
apocalypse
aacelorsty
escalatory
aacelorsuu
lauraceous
aacelprtty
calyptrate
aacelsttuu
auscultate
aacemnoprt
compearant
aacemnopsw
spacewoman
aacemprstu
metacarpus
aacennoosu
anonaceous
aacennottz
canzonetta
aacenopprv
approvance
aacenrtttx
extractant
aaceorrttt
terracotta
aacepstttu
statute-cap
aacffiinpr
paraffinic
aacffiirrt
air-traffic
aacffirtwy
way-traffic
aacfgiilmn
magnifical
aacfgiimnt
Magnificat
aacfgillnw
wall-facing
aacfhknrst
crankshaft
aacfhllotw
fallow-chat
aacfhlnorw
half-a-crown
aacfiiilrt
artificial
aacfiillmn
flaminical
aacfiillsv
salvifical
aacfiilnrv
acriflavin

aacfiilstt
fatalistic
aacfiimnrs
Africanism
aacfiimnst
fanaticism
aacfiimorr
formicaria
aacfiinost
fasciation
aacfiinpsu
piscifauna
aacfiinrst
Africanist
aacfillosu
fallacious
aacfilmort
matrifocal
aacfilnort
fractional
aacfiloprt
patrifocal
aacfilorst
solfataric
aacfilttuy
factuality
aacfinorst
fascinator
aacfinorty
factionary
aacfinostt
fantastico
aacfllmrst
small-craft
aacfmoorst
coat-of-arms
aacfnrsttu
surfactant
aacfrrttyy
arty-crafty
aacggiilos
sialagogic
aacggilrst
gastralgic
aacghhoprt
tachograph
aacghhprty
tachygraph
aacghillor
oligarchal
aacghilnpy
anaglyphic
aacghilrrt
arthralgic
aacghilrtv
galravitch
aacghinorr
chair-organ
aacghioprs
sarcophagi
aacghlmruu
chaulmugra
aacghlsstw
watch-glass

aacghmmosy
chasmogamy
aacghnnsuu
Anschauung
aacghoprsy
sarcophagy
aacghopsty
scatophagy
aacgiillst
glacialist
aacgiilnot
glaciation
aacgiilprs
spagirical
aacgiimrrt
margaritic
aacgiimstt
astigmatic
aacgillrty
tragically
aacgilmnny
malignancy
aacgilnpty
anaglyptic
play-acting
aacgiloprt
proctalgia
aacgimnort
morganatic
aacgimrsty
magistracy
aacginortu
argonautic
aacginprss
panic-grass
aacgiorstt
castigator
aacgkrrssw
grasswrack
aacgkrrsuw
sugar-wrack
aacgllmooy
malacology
aacglnortu
octangular
aacgloortu
coagulator
aachhilnpt
naphthalic
aachhiortz
chota-hazri
aachhnnpsu
snaphaunch
aachiillor
allochiria
aachiilnop
canophilia
aachiimnps
amphiscian
aachiinnot
Antiochian
aachiinptt
antipathic
aachiinrst
Christiana
aachiirssu
Saurischia
aachillopt
allopathic
aachillors
Charollais
aachilmnor
harmonical
monarchial
aachilnnpt
plain-chant
aachilnpry
chaplainry
aachilnpsy
Lychnapsia
aachilopry
acarophily
aachilprsu
haruspical
aachimmnoo
monomachia
aachimmnrs
Rachmanism
aachimnnor
anharmonic
Monarchian
aachimnnru
Manchurian
aachimnoos
monochasia
aachimnopr
anamorphic
aachimnors
maraschino
aachimnort
achromatin
machinator
aachimnorw
chairwoman
aachimnpst
phantasmic
aachimprst
pharmacist
aachimrrty
matriarchy
aachinoppr
paraphonic
aachinopry
paronychia
aachinpstt
phantastic
aachinpsww
wapinschaw
aachinrstu
Carthusian
aachiprrty
patriarchy
aachiprsty
parastichy
aachirsttu
autarchist
aachllortt
altar-cloth
aachlmmoos
schoolma'am
aachlmrryy
lachrymary
aachlnnnot
nonchalant
aachloppry
apocryphal
aachlrrtuy
chartulary
aachmooprt
apochromat
aachmortuy
tauromachy
aachorrstu
catarrhous
aachprsttw
watch-strap
aaciiimsst
Asiaticism
aaciillnnt
anticlinal
aaciillnos
salicional
aaciillopt
apolitical
aaciilmnos
simoniacal
aaciilmnps
panislamic
aaciilmnst
talismanic
aaciilmntx
anticlimax
aaciilmprt
primatical
aaciilmpst
capitalism
aaciilnnor
Carolinian
aaciilnnst
annalistic
aaciilnopt
capitolian
aaciilnors
salicornia
aaciilnost
antisocial
aaciilnrtt
triactinal
aaciilppst
papistical
aaciilpstt
capitalist
aaciilrrtu
urticarial
aaciilrstt
artistical
aaciimnstv
Vaticanism
aaciimostx
axiomatics
aaciinnptt
anticipant
aaciinnrrt
Trinacrian
aaciinoprt
aprication
aaciinoptt
capitation
aaciinortv
victoriana
aaciinottv
activation
cavitation
aaciinsttt
antistatic
aaciinsttv
Vaticanist
aaciiorsuv
avaricious
aacijlnotu
jaculation
aaciklmmrs
Lamarckism
aaciklmrst
smart-Alick
aacillmort
matrilocal
aacillmosy
mosaically
aacillnoot
allocation
aacillnopt
Platonical
aacillnors
rascallion
aacillntuy
nautically
aacilloopr
coprolalia
aacilloprt
patrilocal
aacillstty
statically
aacilmnnot
monactinal
aacilmnort
romantical
aacilmnost
monastical
aacilmnotu
maculation
aacilmorrt
lacrimator
aacilmostu
calamitous
aacilmrrtu
matricular
aacilnntuy
unanalytic
aacilnootv
vocational
aacilnoppt
panoptical
aacilnoprs
parsonical
aacilnopty
nyctalopia
aacilnorss
scansorial
aacilnortt
tractional
aacilnpttu
capitulant
aaciloorrt
oratorical
aacilopprt
applicator
aacilopstu
apolaustic
aacilopttu
autoptical
aacilprrsu
spiracular
aacilprrtu
particular
aacilprtuy
capitulary
aacilpssuw
wassail-cup
aaciltttuy
tactuality
aacimmmnou
ammoniacum
aacimmnnoo
monomaniac
aacimnnoxy
axinomancy
aacimnoops
opsomaniac
aacimnopry
pyromaniac
aacimnprtu
pancratium
aacimoprsu
rampacious
aacimorrst
Camorrista
aacimorstt
masticator
aacinnoort
octonarian
aacinnortt
incantator
aacinnostt
Constantia
aacinooptt
coaptation
aacinorstt
castration
aacinorttt
attraction
aacinortuy
auctionary
cautionary
aacinprstt
pancratist
practisant

aaciopprt
apotropaic
aaciorrstt
aristocrat
aaciossuvx
saxicavous
aaciprsstt
Spartacist
aacjlortuy
jaculatory
aacknorsvw
canvas-work
aacllorruy
oracularly
aacllrsuvy
vascularly
aaclmmopsy
mycoplasma
aaclmnnosw
clanswoman
aaclmoprss
sarcoplasm
aaclmorrty
lacrymator
aaclnnortu
connatural
aaclooprrt
parrot-coal
aacloorrtu
coloratura
aacloprrru
parlour-car
aacmnnopru
manna-croup
aacmnopruy
paramouncy
aacmnrssuu
cassumunar
aacmooprrt
comparator
aacmoorrtu
coat-armour
aacmopsssw
compass-saw
aacnnnostt
constantan
aacnorrstt
transactor
aacnorrstw
narrowcast
aacoopprsu
apocarpous
aacoprrstu
artocarpus
aacorrsttt
stratocrat
aadddgnry
granddaddy
aadddeehhr
hard-headed
aadddeehrt
death-adder
aadddeellr
all-dreaded

aadddeelpt
addle-pated
aadddeeluv
value-added
aadddehhnr
hard-handed
aadddeilpr
paradiddle
aadddeilrt
taradiddle
aadddgrsuy
sugar-daddy
aadddhnnyy
handy-dandy
aaddeeehkw
weak-headed
aaddeefhir
fair-headed
aaddeeghst
stag-headed
aaddeehhor
hoar-headed
aaddeehhst
death's-head
aaddeehiln
nail-headed
aaddeehimn
maidenhead
aaddeehirr
drearihead
aaddeehknw
weak-handed
aaddeehmny
many-headed
aaddeehnnt
neat-handed
aaddeehnrr
hard-earned
aaddeehnrv
verandahed
aaddeehrst
sad-hearted
aaddeeirst
desiderata
aaddeeirwy
day-wearied
aaddeeistt
state-aided
aaddeeklmr
madder-lake
aaddeemrry
daydreamer
aaddefhnst
fast-handed
aaddeflsst
saddle-fast
aaddegglry
ragged-lady
aaddeggnrt
egg-and-dart
aaddeghlnr
glad-hander
aaddeghnor
dragonhead

aaddegiilt
digladiate
aaddegirrt
tardigrade
aaddegmnor
Armageddon
aaddegnnor
dragonnade
aaddehiilp
Diadelphia
aaddehimnn
handmaiden
aaddehnruz
unhazarded
aaddeiilpt
dilapidate
aaddeimntt
additament
aaddeirsuy
Dasyuridae
aaddelmrss
maladdress
aaddelprrt
trap-ladder
aaddenprtu
pandurated
aaddgiillo
diallagoid
aaddgilmoy
amygdaloid
aaddgnnrst
grandstand
aaddhhinnn
hand-in-hand
aaddhnnrsy
shandrydan
aaddiilnot
additional
aaddiimnny
didynamian
aaddilnrsz
sand-lizard
aaddimnrty
dynamitard
aaddinorrt
ritardando
aaddllnors
sand-dollar
aaddlnoosw
sandalwood
aadeeeglmr
game-dealer
aadeeelnpt
peel-and-eat
aadeeelrsy
day-release
aadeefglrt
deflagrate
aadeefilrr
fair-leader
aadeeflnrt
trade-falne
aadeeggopu
paedagogue

aadeeginyz
Zygaenidae
aadeegirtv
variegated
aadeegnrru
daguerrean
aadeegnrst
degreasant
aadeegnrtu
guaranteed
aadeegoprt
pagoda-tree
aadeehhlrx
hexahedral
aadeehhmmr
hammerhead
aadeehknss
snake's-head
aadeehlnvy
heavy-laden
aadeehlors
Rhoeadales
aadeehlppt
lappet-head
aadeehlrtt
rattle-head
aadeehmrst
headmaster
head-stream
aadeehmrvy
heavy-armed
aadeehnprt
pentahedra
aadeehnrvw
heavenward
aadeehqrsu
headsquare
square-head
aadeeiilmn
Limnaeidae
aadeeilmnn
Madelenian
aadeeilmnt
delaminate
aadeeilnst
desalinate
aadeeilrtv
revalidate
aadeeimnot
Nematoidea
aadeeimnou
eudaemonia
aadeeimnru
Muraenidae
aadeeimprs
emparadise
aadeeimprt
pre-Adamite
aadeeinnnr
Enneandria
aadeeinqtu
inadequate
aadeeinrrs
Serranidae

aadeeiorst
Asteroidea
aadeeiprst
deaspirate
aadeeiqtuv
adequative
aadeeirrww
war-wearied
aadeeirstt
asteriated
aadeeknnuw
unawakened
aadeelllmt
lamellated
aadeelllpr
paralleled
aadeellppr
apparelled
aadeellpry
playleader
aadeellrrs
serradella
aadeelnnnu
unannealed
aadeelnrsx
alexanders
aadeeloprs
sea-leopard
aadeelqtuy
adequately
aadeelrssw
easselward
aadeelrstv
slave-trade
aadeelrttu
adulterate
aadeemnnoy
anadyomene
aadeemnssz
amazedness
aadeemprrt
Dermaptera
aadeemqrsu
masquerade
aadeemqstu
desquamate
aadeenppsu
unappeased
aadeenrrwy
wander-year
aadeenstvz
Zend-Avesta
aadeentttu
attenuated
aadeeortty
ready-to-eat
aadeeprsty
paederasty
aadeffnort
fore-and-aft
aadefgrrtu
after-guard
aadefhiirr
fair-haired

aadefhlnoz
half-a-dozen
aadefhlnrt
fatherland
aadefiknrr
Afrikander
aadefimnot
defamation
aadefinnrr
farrandine
aadefinttu
infatuated
aadefklrsw
Dewar-flask
aadefmorty
defamatory
aadefrrstw
afterwards
aadeggillt
daggle-tail
aadeggilnt
gangliated
aadegginrs
aggrandise
aadeggossu
sausage-dog
aadeghhins
shanghaied
aadeghhirs
shag-haired
aadeghiinr
hearing-aid
aadeghnoty
death-agony
aadegiintv
indagative
aadegillnr
grenadilla
aadegilmnr
lead-arming
aadegilnsy
sealing-day
aadegilprr
paraglider
aadegilrst
saltigrade
aadegiltty
agitatedly
aadegimnpr
map-reading
aadegimnrs
smaragdine
aadegimnrt
marginated
aadegimrst
smaragdite
aadeginott
toad-eating
aadeginrrs
disarrange
aadegiprrs
disparager
aadegknprt
peg-tankard

aadegllnru
eglandular
aadeglnopr
pedal-organ
aadeglnqru
quadrangle
aadegmrrtu
dramaturge
aadegnnrru
unarranged
aadegnssuu
unassuaged
aadegrrtuw
water-guard
aadehiilot
Haliotidae
aadehiimnr
maidenhair
aadehiinrt
antheridia
aadehiiprs
sphaeridia
aadehilmrt
diathermal
aadehilnrt
Thailander
aadehilorr
diarrhoeal
aadehilrsw
hawser-laid
aadehinnrx
hexandrian
aadehinotz
Zoanthidae
aadehinprt
Heptandria
aadehinrss
hansardise
aadehiopst
Hitopadesa
aadehllmrs
marshalled
aadehlnnpr
panhandler
aadehlnpst
shade-plant
aadehlrssy
harassedly
aadehmmmno
Mahommedan
Mohammedan
aadehmmmnu
Muhammedan
aadehmnrst
master-hand
aadehprsst
star-shaped
aadeiilnot
ideational
aadeiilntv
invalidate
aadeiimnnr
Amerindian

aadeiimnnt
diamantine
inanimated
maintained
aadeiimnst
disanimate
aadeiimprs
imparadise
aadeiimrtv
admirative
aadeiinntv
vanadinite
aadeiinort
eradiation
aadeiinptv
inadaptive
aadeiirrtt
triradiate
aadeiksstu
diaskeuast
aadeillmmt
mamillated
aadeillmtu
Adullamite
aadeillppt
papillated
aadeillrrs
serradilla
aadeillrtu
laurdalite
aadeilmmst
Lammas-tide
aadeilmnnr
mainlander
aadeilmnnt
nidamental
aadeilmnos
Salmonidae
aadeilmnty
animatedly
aadeilmort
tailor-made
aadeilmrtx
taxidermal
aadeilnnsw
Waldensian
aadeilnprs
palisander
aadeilnprt
land-pirate
aadeilnrsu
unsalaried
aadeilnrtw
land-waiter
aadeilnssu
unassailed
aadeilnstu
andalusite
aadeilopss
palisadoes
aadeilorrr
railroader
aadeilorst
asteroidal

aadeilpprs
disapparel
aadeilptvy
adaptively
aadeimmnot
ammoniated
aadeimnnsw
swan-maiden
aadeimnntu
unanimated
aadeimnrtv
animadvert
aadeinnopt
antipodean
aadeinnprt
Pentandria
aadeinnqru
quadrennia
aadeinnrty
Tyrannidae
aadeinnttu
unattained
aadeinorty
arytaenoid
aadeinpqsu
pasquinade
aadeinprsu
unparadise
aadeinqttu
antiquated
aadeinrrtt
Tetrandria
aadeinsttu
unsatiated
aadeiorstv
advisorate
aadeiprrtu
pietra-dura
aadeiprsst
disparates
aadekknrst
stark-naked
aadeklmorw
meadow-lark
aadeknpttu
put-and-take
aadeknrstt
start-naked
aadellmnry
aldermanly
aadellnppu
unappalled
aadellrtty
tally-trade
aadelmnptu
datum-plane
paludament
aadelmnrry
aldermanry
aadelnnsuy
unanalysed
aadelnrttu
adulterant

aademmnssu
mandamuses
aademmortu
trou-madame
aademnorty
amendatory
aademnqruu
quadrumane
aademrrsty
yard-master
aadennrttu
denaturant
aadenqrstu
quadrantes
aadenrsttu
transudate
aadeoprrux
paradoxure
aadeorsttv
devastator
aadeqrrtuu
quadrature
aadeqrrtuy
quarter-day
aadffghnsy
shandygaff
aadfglnopr
flap-dragon
aadfhlllor
half-dollar
aadfiilmpt
palmatifid
aadfiilntu
latifundia
aadghinswy
washing-day
aadghioprr
radiograph
aadghiopru
audiograph
aadghiprsy
dysgraphia
aadghllnop
hand-gallop
aadghmnrtu
draughtman
aadgiinnot
indagation
aadgiinnrt
grant-in-aid
aadgiinnsu
ungainsaid
aadgiinotv
divagation
aadgijnoru
jaguarondi
aadgijnruu
jaguarundi
aadgikmnor
road-making
aadgillnoy
diagonally
aadgilmnsu
salmagundi

aadgilmrsu
gradualism
aadgilnoot
odontalgia
aadgilnppu
applauding
aadgilorty
gladiatory
aadgilrstu
gradualist
aadgilrtuy
graduality
aadgimnrst
magistrand
aadginopst
spatangoid
aadginortu
graduation
aadginorty
indagatory
aadglmnsuy
salmagundy
aadgmnnort
Montagnard
aadgmrrtuy
dramaturgy
aadgmrsstu
mustard-gas
aadgnnoprs
snapdragon
aadgooprst
Gastropoda
aadhiioprs
aphrodisia
aadhikrsww
awkwardish
aadhillmoo
homaloidal
aadhillnps
Laplandish
aadhilrtww
withdrawal
aadhimnnos
madonnaish
aadhimnory
hydromania
aadhinoopr
adiaphoron
aadhinopsu
diaphanous
aadhinorsw
rain-shadow
aadhkmorsw
shadow-mark
aadhlopswy
shadow-play
aadhooprrt
Arthropoda
aadiiinstt
antiaditis
aadiiklnop
pinakoidal
aadiillnst
tillandsia

aadiilnopt
lapidation
aadiilnott
dilatation
aadiilnotv
validation
aadiilprst
lapidarist
triapsidal
aadiilqruv
quadrivial
aadiimnops
dipsomania
aadiimnort
admiration
aadiinnrrt
triandrian
aadiinorsu
Dinosauria
aadiioprst
parasitoid
aadiiprsst
aspidistra
aadiirrstv
Stradivari
aadijnortu
adjuration
aadikmrsvz
vizard-mask
aadilllrwz
wall-lizard
aadillopsu
palladious
aadilnopry
Polyandria
aadilnortu
durational
aadilnssuw
duniwassal
aadilprrtu
ultra-rapid
aadimnnoox
Monaxonida
aadimnnrst
sand-martin
aadimnprty
pantrymaid
aadimoppru
parapodium
aadinorruv
ouvirandra
aadioprssu
Sauropsida
aadioprstx
paradoxist
aadiorstvy
advisatory
aadiqrrtux
quadratrix
aadjmnnpru
panjandrum
aadjorrtuy
adjuratory

aadklnoruw
walk-around
aadlmnnnos
no-man's-land
aadlmnnruy
laundry-man
aadlmnortu
Laundromat
aadlnoqrsu
squadronal
aadmnooott
odontomata
aadmnoorsu
anadromous
aadmnpssuy
ampussy-and
aadnooppsw
sappan-wood
aadnoprruw
wraparound
aaeeefhrst
sea-feather
aaeeeggrtx
exaggerate
aaeeeglnop
Palaeogene
aaeeeglsst
easselgate
aaeeehlmny
hymeneaeal
aaeeehmnny
hymeneaean
aaeeehrsst
heart's-ease
aaeeelnprs
paraselene
aaeeelrstt
real-estate
aaeeemnnos
sea-anemone
aaeeemorrt
araeometer
aaeeeprstx
exasperate
aaeeersstv
asseverate
aaeefgimrt
after-image
aaeefglllt
flagellate
aaeefgmrsw
sewage-farm
aaeefhhlst
leaf-sheath
aaeefhhstw
wheatsheaf
aaeefhrstv
aftershave
aaeefkkqsu
Kafkaesque
aaeefkmmrr
frame-maker
aaeefmrrtw
water-frame

aaeefrsttt
aftertaste
aaeeggiprt
arpeggiate
aaeeggmstu
steam-gauge
aaeeggppru
paper-gauge
aaeeggrtuw
water-gauge
aaeeghlnot
halogenate
aaeeghlpry
harpy-eagle
aaeeghmnop
Phenogamae
aaeeghrtww
weather-gaw
aaeegilnrv
evangeliar
aaeegilntt
gelatinate
aaeegimnrt
emarginate
aaeegimrrr
remarriage
aaeegimssx
Sexagesima
aaeeginrtv
vegetarian
aaeegioprt
Areopagite
aaeegkmrrv
grave-maker
aaeeglmnop
epagomenal
aaeeglmprs
palm-grease
aaeeglnnno
enneagonal
aaeeglnrtw
angel-water
aaeegmmnnt
management
aaeegmmorr
aerogramme
aaeegmnrss
manageress
aaeegnprrr
prearrange
aaeegnrsxy
sexagenary
aaeegnsssv
savageness
aaeegqrrtu
quarterage
aaeehhilrt
hartie-hale
aaeehilrtx
exhilarate
aaeehimpry
hyperaemia
aaeehimptt
epithemata

aaeehimrtt
Metatheria
aaeehiprss
aphaeresis
aaeehklort
oak-leather
aaeehkqrtu
earthquake
heart-quake
aaeehlprtt
earth-plate
aaeehmnrtw
weatherman
aaeehmprst
metaphrase
aaeehmprtw
weather-map
aaeehrrstw
shearwater
aaeeiklmns
seamanlike
aaeeilllrv
lavallière
aaeeillqtu
illaqueate
aaeeillrtt
alliterate
aaeeilmnns
Melanesian
aaeeilmort
ameliorate
aaeeilnprt
penetralia
aaeeilprtu
eutrapelia
aaeeilrttv
alterative
aaeeilrtvx
relaxative
aaeeiltuvv
evaluative
aaeeimnrrw
Weimaraner
aaeeimprsv
sea-vampire
aaeeinpprv
papaverine
aaeeinprrt
pea-trainer
aaeeinprss
paraenesis
aaeeinstuv
nauseative
aaeeipprrs
reappraise
aaeeiprrtt
repatriate
aaeeiprrtv
reparative
aaeeiprstv
separative
aaeeiprttx
expatriate

aaeejnpqsu
Japanesque
aaeejnprsy
Japanesery
aaeejprrsw
jasperware
aaeekllrwy
lake-lawyer
aaeeklprsv
parkleaves
aaeekmmrtt
meat-market
aaeekmpprr
paper-maker
aaeeknrstw
water-snake
aaeekqrtuw
waterquake
aaeellmsst
matellasse
aaeellprty
plate-layer
aaeelltttt
tattle-tale
aaeelmnopt
Ptolemaean
aaeelmnrst
man-stealer
aaeelmprrt
marprelate
aaeelmpsty
Sympetalae
aaeelmrrtt
tetrameral
aaeelnnptu
pennatulae
aaeelnprrt
parenteral
aaeelnprtt
tea-planter
aaeelnprtw
water-plane
aaeeloppty
palaeotype
aaeelorsty
araeostyle
aaeelprsty
separately
aaeelprttt
rattle-pate
aaeelprttw
water-plate
aaeemmnrrt
rearmament
aaeemnnssu
amanuenses
aaeemnsstt
estatesman
aaeemorrty
araeometry
aaeemssstt
metastases
aaeenqrttu
quaternate

aaeenrsstv
tsesarevna
aaeenrstty
asynartete
aaeepprstt
state-paper
aaeeprsstw
pease-straw
aaeffftttu
tuftaffeta
aaeffgilny
yaffingale
aaeffhrstt
aftershaft
aaeffilorv
love-affair
aaefgghrtu
fraughtage
aaefgiistt
fastigiate
aaefginnpr
frangipane
aaefgklmrr
marker-flag
aaefglllnt
flagellant
aaefglmnrt
fragmental
aaefgrrsst
aftergrass
aaefhinrtt
faint-heart
aaefhllryy
half-yearly
aaefhprsst
spear-shaft
aaefillnrx
Fraxinella
aaefimrrrt
terra-firma
aaefinprst
afterpains
aaefkmnrrt
tank-farmer
aaefllnstu
fustanella
aaegggglnuv
luggage-van
aaegggglssu
gauge-glass
aaeggillrv
gillravage
aaeggilnsw
Glaswegian
aaeggilosu
sialagogue
aaeggilrrv
gilravager
aaeggnostw
stage-wagon
aaeghhinrs
shanghaier
aaeghilmps
phlegmasia

aaeghilnpr
nephralgia
aaeghilort
hagiolater
aaeghilpsy
hypalgesia
aaeghilrtu
gaultheria
aaeghinnns
shenanigan
aaeghinnxy
hexagynian
aaeghinpty
Heptagynia
aaeghlnopt
heptagonal
aaeghlnpry
pharyngeal
aaeghmnopr
anemograph
phanerogam
aaeghnpprt
pentagraph
aaeghoprry
aerography
areography
aaeghrsssv
shave-grass
aaeghsstux
exhaust-gas
aaegiillnv
villainage
aaegiilprs
plagiarise
aaegiinntv
invaginate
aaegiinrtt
ingratiate
aaegillmnt
ligamental
aaegillmqu
maquillage
aaegillnot
allegation
aaegillprs
aspergilla
aaegilmnrt
martingale
aaegilmstt
stalagmite
aaegilnntt
tangential
aaegilnopt
palagonite
aaegilnrsv
galvaniser
aaegilnswx
sealing-wax
aaegiloprs
paralogise
aaegilprty
apterygial
aaegimnrrs
misarrange

aaegimnrrv
margravine
aaegimprst
pragmatise
aaegimrstt
magistrate
sterigmata
aaeginnost
antagonise
aaeginnpty
Pentagynia
aaeginnstu
nauseating
aaeginoprt
paragonite
aaeginorrt
arragonite
aaeginprst
paste-grain
aaeginrttv
Gravettian
aaeginrtty
Tetragynia
aaeginrtuu
inaugurate
aaeginsttt
tea-tasting
aaegiorrtv
variegator
aaegirrstv
stravaiger
aaegkllrvw
gravel-walk
aaegklmnos
maskalonge
aaegklnsss
glass-snake
aaegkmnnos
maskanonge
aaegknrsss
grass-snake
aaegllpsst
plate-glass
aaeglmorsu
megalosaur
aaeglmprsu
sugar-maple
aaeglnnopt
pentagonal
aaeglnortt
tetragonal
aaeglnrrtu
granulater
aaegloprss
opera-glass
aaeglpprss
glass-paper
aaeglpprsu
sugar-apple
aaeglrsstw
water-glass
aaegmmppuw
wampumpeag

aaegmoprsu
rampageous
aaegnoprst
apron-stage
aaegnortww
water-wagon
aaegoprtty
Apterygota
aaegprrsss
spear-grass
aaehhilllu
halleluiah
aaehhjlllu
hallelujah
aaehhklrsw
whale-shark
aaehhlnopy
hyalophane
aaehhlprty
hypaethral
aaehhmnstu
Haemanthus
aaehiilmns
leishmania
aaehiilnnt
annihilate
aaehiiltww
wait-a-while
aaehiimnop
hemianopia
aaehiinopt
Aethiopian
aaehiinppt
epitaphian
aaehiirrrs
hair-raiser
aaehikmnsz
Ashkenazim
aaehikrrst
hairstreak
aaehillopt
palaeolith
aaehilnnot
anhelation
aaehilnotx
exhalation
aaehilnrtx
exhilarant
aaehimmnot
methomania
aaehimnpru
Amphineura
aaehimnpss
seamanship
aaehimnpst
phantasime
aaehimnsty
myasthenia
aaehimopxy
hypoxaemia
aaehimosst
haematosis
aaehimrstu
amateurish

aaehimsttu
thaumasite
aaehinnorv
Hanoverian
aaehiprsst
parathesis
aaehipstxy
asphyxiate
aaehistttw
tattie-shaw
aaehisttuw
Watteauish
aaehkllmrt
market-hall
aaehllmnoy
hyalomelan
aaehllmrrs
marshaller
aaehlmrttt
lattermath
aaehlnopsy
synaloepha
aaehlnrrtx
xenarthral
aaehlorstw
shoal-water
aaehlpsttu
spathulate
aaehmnorrt
marathoner
aaehmnortw
woman-hater
aaehmnrsst
harassment
aaehmnrstv
harvestman
aaehmorttx
metathorax
aaehmostty
stay-at-home
aaehmprstt
metaphrast
aaehnoprst
anastrophe
aaehnopsww
weapon-shaw
aaehnppsww
wappenshaw
aaehnprsst
trans-shape
aaehnprsty
pheasantry
aaehpprssy
paraphyses
aaeiiilnst
Italianise
aaeiillptv
palliative
aaeiilmmrt
immaterial
aaeiilmnrs
laminarise
seminarial

aaeiilmnrt
Terminalia
aaeiilmptv
ampliative
aaeiilmsst
assimilate
aaeiilnnot
alienation
alineation
aaeiilnpst
sapiential
aaeiilnstv
insalivate
aaeiilprst
patrialise
aaeiilprtz
partialize
aaeiimnnnr
Riemannian
aaeiimnnrs
seminarian
aaeiimnnrt
maintainer
aaeiimpprr
primiparae
aaeiinrtuv
univariate
aaeiiprsst
parasitise
aaeijlmnnv
javelin-man
aaeijlnnuv
Juvenalian
aaeiklmnot
Keltomania
aaeiklmnoz
Amazon-like
aaeikmrsst
samarskite
aaeiknnnot
Neo-Kantian
aaeiknprst
painstaker
aaeilllmux
maxillulae
aaeillmnot
malleation
aaeillmnpt
palliament
aaeillmprx
premaxilla
aaeillmrty
materially
aaeillnort
relational
aaeillnrtu
unilateral
aaeillnstw
Eatanswill
aaeillortv
alleviator
aaeillrrtt
trilateral

aaeillrtty
laterality
aaeillrtvy
varietally
aaeilmmnnt
immanental
aaeilmnnsu
semi-annual
aaeilmnprt
parliament
aaeilmnptu
manipulate
aaeilmnrrt
interramal
aaeilmnrsu
aneurismal
aaeilmnrtt
alternatim
aaeilmnrtu
unmaterial
aaeilmnrty
alimentary
aaeilmnruv
Verulamian
aaeilmnsst
assailment
aaeilmorrt
Mariolater
aaeilmprrt
premarital
aaeilmpsst
metaplasis
aaeilnnopt
Neapolitan
aaeilnnrtu
Laurentian
aaeilnoort
areolation
aaeilnoprs
personalia
aaeilnopst
spaniolate
aaeilnorst
senatorial
aaeilnortt
alteration
aaeilnortu
laureation
aaeilnortv
venatorial
Voltairean
aaeilnortx
relaxation
aaeilnottx
exaltation
aaeilnotuv
evaluation
aaeilnprst
psalterian
aaeilnrstt
tantaliser
aaeilnrstu
naturalise

aaeiloqrtu
equatorial
aaeilorrtt
retaliator
aaeilpprst
epiplastra
aaeilppsuv
applausive
aaeilqrssu
square-sail
aaeilrrstu
Sertularia
aaeilrsttt
state-trial
aaeilrsttu
australite
aaeilstuxy
asexuality
aaeimmnort
metromania
aaeimmnrst
mainstream
aaeimmrstu
amateurism
aaeimnnopr
Pomeranian
aaeimnnosy
mayonnaise
aaeimnnott
antimonate
aaeimnnssu
amanuensis
aaeimnnttt
attainment
aaeimnoort
erotomania
aaeimnortx
examinator
aaeimnqstu
antimasque
aaeimnrttt
anti-matter
aaeimprsst
separatism
aaeimqrstu
marquisate
aaeimqrsuu
seaquarium
aaeimrsttu
traumatise
aaeimrttuv
maturative
aaeimssstt
metastasis
aaeinnnotx
annexation
aaeinnnttu
annuntiate
aaeinnorrt
enarration
aaeinnqrtu
quarantine
aaeinnrsst
Stannaries

aaeinnrtuv
avanturine
aaeinoprrt
praetorian
reparation
aaeinoprst
separation
aaeinopsst
passionate
aaeinpprst
satin-paper
aaeinprstu
Pasteurian
aaeinrrstw
warrantise
aaeinrrttz
tartrazine
aaeinrtttu
attainture
aaeioprttx
expatiator
aaeiopsstt
apostatise
aaeiprrstx
separatrix
aaeiprsstt
separatist
aaekmrsstt
taskmaster
aaekrrstuu
sauerkraut
aaelllllpry
parallelly
aaelllmnos
salmonella
aaelllnpru
unparallel
aaelllorst
saltarello
aaelllpstt
stall-plate
aaellmnops
salmon-leap
aaellmnrty
maternally
aaellmortt
martellato
aaellmorzz
mozzarella
aaellmprty
malapertly
aaellmrssw
small-wares
aaellnossy
seasonally
aaellnpprw
parpen-wall
aaellnprty
parentally
paternally
aaellnpsty
pleasantly
aaellosssww
sea-swallow

aaellrsttt
Tattersall
aaelmnnort
ornamental
aaelmnnrtu
unmaternal
aaelmnoppw
apple-woman
aaelmnopsu
menopausal
aaelmnossw
saleswoman
aaelmnrsuy
aneurysmal
aaelmooptz
Pelmatozoa
aaelmorrss
serrasalmo
aaelmorrty
Maryolater
aaelmrrtux
extra-mural
aaelnnnpru
penannular
aaelnnprtu
unparental
aaelnnpstu
unpleasant
aaelnorrtt
alternator
aaelnorstt
altar-stone
aaelnpprty
apparently
aaelnprrsu
suprarenal
aaelnprstt
transeptal
aaelnprsty
pleasantry
aaelnprttw
water-plant
aaelnpstty
yeast-plant
aaelnrstuv
transvalue
aaeloopstt
apostolate
aaelorrstx
extra-solar
aaelorrttv
travelator
aaelprrstu
superaltar
aaelprrttt
rattle-trap
aaelsttuw
statute-law
aaemnnortt
tramontane
aaemnnrrty
rent-an-army

aaemnnrstv
man-servant
servant-man
aaemnoosst
anastomose
aaemnstvvy
steam-navvy
aaemopsszz
passamezzo
aaempppprst
stamp-paper
aaemrssttu
metatarsus
aaennpprtu
unapparent
aaenorsstt
assentator
aaenortttu
attenuator
aaenqrrtuy
quaternary
aaenrrsttu
restaurant
aaeooprrtv
evaporator
aaeopprrrt
preparator
aaeopprsuv
papaverous
aaeoprrrty
reparatory
aaeoprrsty
separatory
aaeorrrsst
terra-rossa
aaeorrsttu
tartareous
aaeqrstuuy
quaestuary
aaffgimnru
ragamuffin
aaffinrttu
Tartuffian
aafggilnvw
flag-waving
aafgiinnpr
frangipani
aafgilmnnt
Flamingant
aafginnrrt
infragrant
aafgklnruu
Aufklärung
aafgllnrty
flagrantly
aafglnrrty
fragrantly
aafhimnnru
infrahuman
aafiiilrss
filariasis
aafiillmry
familiarly

aafiilmnru
unfamiliar
aafiinrrtu
fruitarian
aafilnoott
floatation
aafiloprss
passiflora
aafimoorrs
afrormosia
aafioqrstu
aquafortis
aagghinnru
haranguing
aagghlnnsw
slang-whang
aaggiiilnn
ilang-ilang
aaggiinnrr
arraigning
aaggiinnsy
gainsaying
aaggiinrrt
air-grating
aagginrstz
star-gazing
aagglllloss
galloglass
aaggllnnyy
ylang-ylang
aaggmnoorr
organogram
aaggnnooww
wonga-wonga
aaggrrsssu
sugar-grass
aaghhimnwy
highwayman
aaghiilmnp
Malpighian
aaghiinrvw
hair-waving
aaghilmnpu
Gnaphalium
aaghilnppr
planigraph
aaghilnpst
phalangist
aaghiloppy
polyphagia
aaghilorty
hagiolatry
aaghinprss
spring-haas
aaghipprsy
pasigraphy
aaghlnopxy
xylophagan
aaghnopprt
pantograph
aaghnoppty
pantophagy
aaghoprtuy
autography

aagiiillrs
Sigillaria
aagiiinnrv
viraginian
aagiillnot
alligation
aagiillnvy
availingly
aagiilmprs
plagiarism
aagiilnnps
salpingian
aagiilnnuv
unavailing
aagiilnssw
wassailing
aagiilprst
plagiarist
aagiimnrst
stigmarian
aagiinnopt
pagination
aagiinnost
sagination
aagiinnotv
navigation
aagijklnwy
jaywalking
aagikmnrst
king-at-arms
aagilllnuu
Anguillula
aagillmnry
alarmingly
marginally
aagillorss
glossarial
aagillstty
sagittally
aagilmnnsu
sign-manual
aagilmnoor
agronomial
aagilmnors
organismal
aagilmoprs
paralogism
aagilnnoqu
Algonquian
aagilnoprs
sporangial
aagilnorty
gyrational
aagilnostv
solivagant
aagilnprtu
tarpauling
aagilnrrtu
triangular
aagilnrtuy
angularity
aagilrssss
sisal-grass

aagimmprst
pragmatism
aagimmrstt
grammatist
aagimnnost
antagonism
aagimnnprw
warming-pan
aagimnprsu
sparganium
aagimnssty
gymnasiast
aagimprstt
pragmatist
aaginnoopr
piano-organ
aaginnortw
wagon-train
aaginnostt
antagonist
stagnation
aaginnrrtw
warranting
aaginnrsuy
sanguinary
aaginooprz
Zaporogian
aaginoorrt
arrogation
aaginoprss
paragnosis
aaginrsttu
antitragus
aagllmoosu
allogamous
aagllnoptt
top-gallant
aagllnrruy
granularly
aaglloostw
goat-sallow
aaglmmopsy
plasmogamy
aaglmopsty
plastogamy
aaglnnoosx
Anglo-Saxon
aaglnnstty
stagnantly
aaglnoosty
satanology
aaglnorrtu
granulator
aaglnorrty
arrogantly
aaglnotuvw
wagon-vault
aagmmmnowy
mammy-wagon
aagmoostuu
autogamous
aagoopprrt
propagator

aagorrrssw
arrow-grass
aagrrrssst
starr-grass
aahhilmopt
ophthalmia
aahhimrrty
arrhythmia
aahiillnor
rhinolalia
aahiilnnot
inhalation
aahiilnntu
Lithuanian
aahiimnprs
airmanship
aahiimprss
pharisaism
aahilloprt
prothallia
aahilloptw
topi-wallah
aahilmnstu
Malthusian
aahilmootx
homotaxial
aahilmttuz
altazimuth
aahilnnopt
antiphonal
aahimmnoty
mythomania
aahimooppr
apomorphia
aahinopstx
xanthopsia
aahinosstt
thanatosis
aahinpstxy
asphyxiant
aahipprssy
paraphysis
aahjkmprru
rajpramukh
aahkknnpyy
hanky-panky
aahklorrsw
ashlar-work
aahllllosw
All-Hallows
aahllmopsy
hyaloplasm
aahlmopsty
staphyloma
aahloprsty
hyoplastra
aahmoprsst
Ramphastos
aahnnnooty
hootananny
aahnoprttu
naturopath
aahnorrstu
anarthrous
aahnprstty
phantastry
aahprsttuu
tatpurusha
aahrsttwwy
thwartways
aaiiiilmmnt
militiaman
aaiiilmnrt
limitarian
aaiiilmnst
Italianism
aaiiilnqru
Quirinalia
aaiiilnstt
Italianist
aaiijlnort
janitorial
aaiikllnty
alkalinity
aaiikmnnst
Kantianism
aaiillnopt
palliation
aaiillnpst
plastilina
aaiillnuxy
uniaxially
aaiilmmrst
martialism
aaiilmmstx
maximalist
aaiilmnnot
antimonial
lamination
aaiilmnopt
ampliation
aaiilmprst
partialism
patrialism
aaiilmrstt
martialist
aaiilnnstt
instantial
aaiilnnstu
Lusitanian
aaiilnorrt
irrational
aaiilnorst
solitarian
aaiilnortv
Voltairian
aaiilnostv
salivation
aaiilnottt
latitation
aaiilnppzz
Lippizzana
aaiilnpstu
Paulianist
aaiilnrsty
sanitarily
aaiilpprss
paralipsis
aaiilprstt
partialist
aaiilprtty
partiality
aaiilpstty
spatiality
aaiilrrrrt
tirra-lirra
aaiimmnnot
immanation
aaiimmnrsx
Marxianism
aaiimnnnot
antinomian
aaiimnnopt
impanation
aaiimnnrtu
Ruminantia
aaiimnprtu
panaritium
aaiimnrstu
sanitarium
aaiimnrstz
Nazaritism
aaiimprsst
parasitism
aaiinnnost
nanisation
aaiinnoptt
patination
aaiinnostt
sanitation
aaiinnqquu
quinaquina
aaiinnrrtu
Ruritanian
aaiinnrsty
insanitary
aaiinnrtuv
univariant
aaiinopprt
apparition
aaiinoprst
aspiration
aaiinoprtt
patriation
tritanopia
aaiinpttvy
Patavinity
aaiinrsstt
sanitarist
aaiirsssty
satyriasis
aaikorrstw
tarsia-work
aailllopvw
pillow-lava
aailllpstu
Pulsatilla
aaillmpruu
Plumularia
aaillnnoop
Apollonian
aaillnnoty
nationally
aaillnnovv
Villanovan
aaillnnstt
installant
aaillnopst
spallation
aaillnorty
notarially
rationally
aailloprty
palliatory
aaillrstuy
salutarily
aailmnopru
Pulmonaria
aailmnpssv
Pan-Slavism
aailmnrrtu
intramural
aailmnrstu
naturalism
aailmopprx
approximal
aailmopsty
polymastia
aailmorrty
Mariolatry
aailnnnotu
annulation
aailnnoott
notational
aailnnoptt
plantation
aailnnorrv
non-arrival
aailnnostt
altisonant
aailnnottt
altitonant
aailnnottu
nutational
aailnnrtuy
annularity
aailnoortt
rotational
aailnopptu
papulation
aailnopttv
pot-valiant
aailnoptuv
vapulation
aailnosttu
salutation
aailnpqstu
pasquilant
aailnprstu
palustrian
aailnpsstv
Pan-Slavist
aailnrssuy
uranalysis
aailnrsttu
naturalist
aailnrstuy
insalutary
aailoorrtv
variolator
aailprsttw
straw-plait
aaimmmnsty
Tammanyism
aaimmorrss
marmarosis
aaimmosstu
miasmatous
aaimmosttu
automatism
aaimmrsttu
traumatism
aaimnnoost
nostomania
aaimnoottu
automation
aaimnopttu
amputation
aaimnoqstu
squamation
aaimnorstu
sanatorium
aaimnorttu
maturation
natatorium
aaimoorstu
amatorious
aaimostttu
automatist
aainnnoott
annotation
aainnorsxy
synaxarion
aainnrstuy
unsanitary
aainoopprt
protanopia
aainoprssy
passionary
aainopstty
pay-station
aainoqrttu
quartation
aainoqrtuz
quatorzain
aainorsttu
saturation
aainorsttv
starvation
aainorstty
stationary
aainorstuu
saouari-nut
aainosttwy
way-station
aainpsttwy
panty-waist

aaioprrsty
aspiratory
aakkllttyy
talky-talky
aakklltwyy
walky-talky
aaklmoprsy
karyoplasm
aaklnorsuy
ankylosaur
aakmmnorsw
markswoman
aakorrtttu
Turko-Tatar
aalllnnuu
nulla-nulla
aallllotww
wall-to-wall
aallmnotwy
tally-woman
aallmntuuy
autumnally
aalloprsty
pastorally
aallorssuu
Allosaurus
aallpsswyy
palsy-walsy
aallrsttwy
stalwartly
aalmmoopss
plasmosoma
aalmoopprs
malapropos
aalmooprty
laparotomy
aalmoprsxy
paroxysmal
aalmorrtyy
Maryolatry
aalnnnortu
non-natural
aalnnoopst
pantaloons
aalnnprstt
transplant
aalnnrrstu
translunar
aalnoopuzz
pozzuolana
aalnoprsst
transposal
aalnoprstu
unpastoral
aalnorrstt
translator
aalnprrsuu
supralunar
aaloorrttv
travolator
aaloprrstu
Australorp
aalopsttuy
autoplasty

aalorrstty
astrolatry
aalorsttuy
salutatory
aamnnotttu
tantamount
aamnooprsy
paronomasy
aamnoosttu
automatons
aamnoprttu
portmantua
aamoorsssu
Mosasauros
aamoossttu
astomatous
aanooprstu
anatropous
aaoopprrst
paratroops
aaoopprttt
potato-trap
abbbbinory
baby-ribbon
abbbceilno
bobbin-lace
abbbceorrr
robber-crab
abbbcikrtu
buck-rabbit
abbbddruuu
rub-a-dub-dub
abbbeelmnt
babblement
abbbeelrsu
sea-blubber
abbbeilnru
unbribable
abbbelopsu
soap-bubble
abbcckklos
back-blocks
abbcdeehmr
bedchamber
abbcdeimoy
Bombycidae
abbcdelmno
candle-bomb
abbcdemrru
bread-crumb
abbceeeipy
abbey-piece
abbceinsss
scabbiness
abbcejkorw
jabberwock
abbcejllot
object-ball
abbcekklor
brake-block
abbcekkstu
buck-basket
abbceklrry
blackberry

abbcekmnru
back-number
abbcellnuu
unclubable
abbcellotu
cobalt-blue
abbcelnruu
uncurbable
abbcenorsy
absorbency
abbcgiiknt
backbiting
abbcgiiort
gabbroitic
abbciiilly
biblically
abbciillnu
unbiblical
abbciirrtu
barbituric
abbcikorrt
rock-rabbit
abbcklllluy
black-bully
abbddeeilo
able-bodied
abbdeeirrw
barbed-wire
abbdeenrru
unbarbered
abbdeerrry
breadberry
abbdefiorr
fibreboard
abbdeimnry
baby-minder
abbdeimorr
bombardier
abbdeinrss
drabbiness
abbdejlnor
land-jobber
abbdellnru
land-lubber
abbdelorsy
absorbedly
abbdelossu
double-bass
abbdgginor
Brobdignag
abbdgillny
dabblingly
abbeeeillv
believable
abbeeeklrt
bark-beetle
abbeeelprw
pebble-ware
abbeeelrrr
beer-barrel
abbeeelrry
barley-bree
abbeegillr
Gibberella

abbeeglmnt
gabblement
abbeegnrtt
Battenberg
abbeekrttu
butter-bake
abbeelmnrt
rabblement
abbeelorsv
observable
abbeelrstu
bluebreast
abbeelrttu
rebuttable
abbeenorst
breastbone
abbeenrttu
butter-bean
abbefilnss
flabbiness
abbeggllru
bull-beggar
abbehilort
rabbit-hole
abbehinsss
shabbiness
abbehoprrs
barber-shop
abbeiilmno
bibliomane
abbeillmsu
sublimable
abbeilmopr
improbable
abbeilnors
ribbon-seal
abbeilnotu
obnubilate
abbeilnsss
slabbiness
abbeilnssw
wabbliness
abbeilnttu
balbutient
abbeirstty
baby-sitter
abbejmpruy
baby-jumper
abbekllrru
barrel-bulk
abbekmmorr
marker-bomb
abbeloorry
barley-broo
abbeloprtw
pot-wabbler
abbelorsvy
observably
abbeortttu
butter-boat
abberrttuy
buttery-bar
abbffiilmu
bumbailiff

abbfhiirst
rabbit-fish
abbfilorst
fibroblast
abbghinotx
bathing-box
abbgilnsty
stabbingly
abbhiimnos
Hobbianism
abbhilnosy
Babylonish
abbilmopry
improbably
abbilorstu
suborbital
abbllnottu
button-ball
abcccefios
beccaficos
abccdeeirt
brecciated
abccdelnru
carbuncled
abccdhlntu
band-clutch
abccdknooy
cock-a-bondy
abcceeeirt
Rebeccaite
abcceeelns
albescence
abcceeenst
tabescence
abcceeilmp
impeccable
abcceeilss
accessible
abcceeimrs
Rebeccaism
abcceeknrt
centre-back
abcceelloy
bel-accoyle
abcceellry
recyclable
abccehilru
cherubical
abcceillru
circulable
abcceilmpy
impeccably
abcceiloru
corbiculae
abcceilssy
accessibly
abcceinosu
suboceanic
abcchiilmo
choliambic
abcchiimor
choriambic
abcchiirrt
tribrachic

abcchiklno
block-chain
abcchiklpt
pitch-black
abcchikstt
backstitch
abcchikstw
switchback
abcchilosu
calico-bush
abcchilotu
coach-built
abccikksty
sticky-back
abccilrtuu
cucurbital
abccimoort
mobocratic
abccinortu
buccinator
abccinorty
corybantic
abccnoopry
carbon-copy
abccnoorsy
snobocracy
abcddeehlu
club-headed
abcddefikl
fiddle-back
abcddeklor
badderlock
abcdeeeelr
decreeable
abcdeeeilv
deceivable
abcdeeellt
delectable
abcdeeelpr
deprecable
abcdeeelrt
celebrated
abcdeeeltt
detectable
abcdeehlnu
unbleached
abcdeehnru
unbreached
abcdeehruy
debauchery
abcdeeikrs
bride's-cake
abcdeeilln
declinable
abcdeeilns
ascendible
abcdeeilnu
ineducable
abcdeeilpr
predicable
abcdeeilps
despicable
abcdeeilrt
creditable

abcdeeilvy
deceivably
abcdeeiopr
broadpiece
abcdeeklrv
backvelder
abcdeellno
blonde-lace
abcdeellny
belly-dance
abcdeellty
delectably
abcdeelnuu
uneducable
abcdeelorr
recordable
abcdefiknr
back-friend
abcdefirtu
bifurcated
abcdefostu
obfuscated
abcdegkorr
rock-badger
abcdehiilr
herbicidal
abcdehkmpu
humpbacked
abcdehmory
brachydome
abcdehnnru
unbranched
abcdehorss
chessboard
abcdeiilmo
biomedical
abcdeiilnt
indictable
abcdeiilnv
vindicable
abcdeiiort
aborticide
bacterioid
abcdeiklrs
backslider
abcdeikouv
bivouacked
abcdeikrst
bread-stick
abcdeiloru
Colubridae
abcdeilpsy
despicably
abcdeilrty
creditably
abcdeimors
Scombridae
abcdeiprrs
crispbread
spider-crab
abcdekorsu
sea-burdock
abcdelrrsy
scald-berry

abcdeoorrs
score-board
abcdeorstu
subcordate
abcderrrtu
curb-trader
abcdgknoru
background
abcdhiilnr
brainchild
abcdhinnru
nudibranch
abcdhioopr
brachiopod
abcdhloort
broadcloth
abcdhnoort
notch-board
abcdiillsy
disyllabic
abcdiimnoy
biodynamic
abcdiirsty
scabridity
abcdiistuy
subacidity
abcdilnost
cnidoblast
abcdnnorry
corn-brandy
abceeeffno
coffee-bean
abceeeikrr
ice-breaker
abceeeilnt
enticeable
abceeeilpr
pierceable
abceeeilrv
receivable
abceeejlrt
rejectable
abceeellrr
cerebellar
abceeeltux
executable
abceeenrux
exuberance
abceefiiln
beneficial
abceefnort
benefactor
abceegillr
clergiable
abceegllry
clergyable
abceehhkss
backsheesh
abceehilnr
hibernacle
abceehklst
sketchable
abceehknqu
bank-cheque

abceehkrtu
hackbuteer
abceehlmry
Chamber-lye
abceehlnqu
quenchable
abceehnorr
abhorrence
abceehnrry
cherry-bean
abceehorsu
herbaceous
abceeillnr
reclinable
abceeillns
licensable
abceeillpx
explicable
abceeilmmt
emblematic
abceeilnnu
enunciable
abceeilnot
noticeable
abceeilrtx
extricable
abceeinnoz
benzocaine
abceeinnst
abstinence
abceejkltu
bluejacket
abceejnsst
abjectness
abceekrrry
crake-berry
abceellmrw
Camberwell
abceellort
brocatelle
abceellpux
exculpable
abceelnnov
convenable
abceelnott
balconette
abceelnovy
conveyable
abceelnrsu
censurable
abceelorrt
celebrator
abceelortv
table-cover
abceelostt
case-bottle
abceelrtvv
velvet-crab
abceenoprr
reprobance
abceenorsv
observance
abceenruxy
exuberancy

abceeprstt
spectre-bat
abcefhinor
chief-baron
abcefhinrz
zebra-finch
abcefillot
olfactible
abcefilnno
confinable
abceflnotu
confutable
abcefrssuu
subsurface
abceghimnr
chambering
abcegilnos
cognisable
abceginnny
benignancy
abceglnoot
conglobate
abcehiimrs
Hebraicism
abcehiirst
Hebraistic
abcehiknrs
Reichsbank
abcehikpst
chip-basket
abcehikrrt
brick-earth
abcehilorw
elbow-chair
abcehilprt
birthplace
abcehimnrt
Chambertin
abcehimntu
Buchmanite
abcehimopt
baphometic
abcehimort
bichromate
abcehimrrt
hermit-crab
abcehinnrv
vine-branch
abcehioopr
aerophobic
abcehipprr
paper-birch
abcehiprry
hyperbaric
abcehiprty
hyperbatic
abcehklort
heart-block
abcehllott
table-cloth
abcehlmoop
peach-bloom
abcehlnrss
branchless

abcehlpsuu
Bucephalus
abcehmoprt
chamberpot
abcehnorry
abhorrency
abcehnrstu
subchanter
abcehopsty
bathyscope
abcehorttx
chatterbox
abceiijnos
Jacobinise
abceiillmt
bimetallic
abceiillnn
inclinable
abceiillnr
brilliance
abceiilmtu
umbilicate
abceiilnos
insociable
abceiilpst
epiblastic
abceiintuv
incubative
abceiioort
aerobiotic
abceiisstu
sea-biscuit
abceikkmrr
brickmaker
abceiklnpu
unpickable
abceiklrry
bricklayer
abceiknpru
Purbeckian
abceillmop
compliable
abceillnou
inoculable
abceillnpu
inculpable
abceillnrs
cranesbill
abceilltuv
cultivable
abceilmopt
compatible
abceilmruy
embryulcia
abceilmstu
table-music
abceilnosu
unsociable
abceilnoty
noticeably
abceilnpru
republican
abceilnrru
incurrable

abceimnrtt
mitten-crab
abceimoort
macrobiote
abceimorrt
barometric
abceinnsty
abstinency
abceinrrst
transcribe
abceiorsuu
rubiaceous
abcejklmru
lumber-jack
abcekklmos
smoke-black
abcekkorrw
backworker
abcekkorst
backstroke
abceklloor
cellar-book
abcekllowy
yellowback
abceklnoru
coal-bunker
abceklrttu
turtleback
abcekmrrtu
curb-market
abcelllmoo
Collembola
abcellloru
blue-collar
abcellnoor
collar-bone
abcellnoos
consolable
abcellooru
colourable
abcellrtuu
culturable
abcelmmnoo
commonable
abcelmmotu
commutable
abcelmmpru
lumber-camp
abcelmnosu
consumable
abcelmnrsu
unscramble
abcelmoptu
computable
abcelmostu
customable
abcelmrstu
clubmaster
abcelmrttu
tumble-cart
abcelnorry
barleycorn
abcelnostu
locust-bean

abcelnrstu
subcentral
abcelnrsuy
censurably
abcelooprv
provocable
abceloppry
clapperboy
abceloprru
procurable
abcelorrry
coral-berry
abcelrrtuu
tubercular
abcemtuuuv
vacuum-tube
abcennsstu
subnascent
abcennstuy
subtenancy
abcenopuuy
upbuoyance
abcenorsst
crab-stones
abcenorsty
corybantes
abcenorsvy
observancy
abcenorttu
obtruncate
abcenrrtuy
canterbury
abceoorrst
Serbo-Croat
abceosssuy
byssaceous
abcghiiopr
biographic
abcghloryy
brachylogy
abcghnoryz
zygobranch
abcghnrssu
bunch-grass
abcgiilloo
biological
abcgiinrtt
bratticing
abcgiknopx
packing-box
abcgilmnrs
scrambling
abcgilnosy
cognisably
abchhilott
habit-cloth
abchhioprs
archbishop
abchhlmttu
thumb-latch
abchiilmop
amphibolic
abchiiloot
halobiotic

abchiilott
batholitic
abchiiltty
bathylitic
abchiklmst
blacksmith
abchiklrst
Blackshirt
abchilttuy
yacht-built
abchimmnsu
Buchmanism
abchinoopy
cynophobia
abchiortyy
charity-boy
abchklnort
blackthorn
abchknorrw
branch-work
abchnorrtu
turnbroach
abciiinott
antibiotic
abciijmnos
Jacobinism
abciijmost
Jacobitism
abciillnry
brilliancy
abciillsst
ballistics
abciilnoot
bilocation
abciilrtuy
curability
abciimnoss
ambisonics
abciimoort
microbiota
abciimrsst
strabismic
abciinnotu
incubation
abciinorrt
cribration
abciinosss
abscission
abciinrstu
urbanistic
abcijnnotu
abjunction
abcikllory
rockabilly
abciklorvy
ivory-black
abciknorrt
rick-barton
abciknprsw
spawn-brick
abcillmosy
symbolical
abcillnpuy
inculpably

abcillrruy
rubrically
abcilmopty
compatibly
abcilmosty
myoblastic
abcilmruuv
vibraculum
abcilnoors
Sorbonical
abcilnosuy
unsociably
abcilorrtu
lubricator
abcilostuv
vocabulist
abcimosstu
subatomics
abcinortuy
incubatory
abciorrrtu
rubricator
abckknootu
knockabout
abcknprtuy
bankruptcy
abcllooruy
colourably
abclmmruuu
umbraculum
abclorrtuu
lucubrator
abclosstty
blastocyst
abcnnrrtuu
currant-bun
abcnoorrtu
court-baron
abcorrsttu
subtractor
abddeeefln
defendable
abddeeelnp
dependable
abddeegglr
bedraggled
abddeeghir
bridgehead
abddeehllu
bull-headed
abddeehloo
beadlehood
abddeeimns
base-minded
abddeeintt
bidentated
abddeelnpy
dependably
abddeelrst
bestraddle
abddeenrru
undebarred
abddefilss
bass-fiddle

abddeghkou
dough-baked
abddegilnr
land-bridge
abddeginru
unabridged
abddegiorr
road-bridge
abddegirrw
drawbridge
abddehhinn
behind-hand
abddehillr
hard-billed
abddehilnr
bridle-hand
abddehilor
hard-boiled
abddeiimrs
bridesmaid
abddeilorr
bridle-road
abddeinnrs
sand-binder
abddelnorr
borderland
abddelnrtu
bladder-nut
abddelorsw
sword-blade
abddenorru
underboard
abddgginpu
pudding-bag
abddhhiirw
whidah-bird
abddhhirwy
whydah-bird
abddhnrsuy
dandy-brush
abddlmooru
mould-board
abddnoorsu
sound-board
abddoorrsw
broadsword
abdeeeehlt
beetlehead
abdeeeelmr
redeemable
abdeeefhrt
feather-bed
abdeeefils
defeasible
abdeeeflrr
deferrable
abdeeefrst
breast-feed
abdeeegglr
barelegged
abdeeegllp
pledgeable
abdeeegnrr
beer-garden

abdeeehlnt
needle-bath
abdeeehnrv
heaven-bred
abdeeeilln
delineable
abdeeeilmr
remediable
abdeeeilrt
deliberate
abdeeeinrv
aberdevine
abdeeelnpx
expendable
abdeeelnrr
renderable
abdeeelnrz
land-breeze
abdeeelntx
extendable
abdeeelryy
bleary-eyed
abdeeelstt
detestable
abdeeemnst
debasement
abdeeenruv
unbeavered
abdeeeprst
breast-deep
abdeeerstw
sweetbread
abdeeffhlu
bufflehead
abdeefgilr
leaf-bridge
abdeefhnor
beforehand
abdeeflmor
deformable
abdeefoort
barefooted
abdeeghnrr
herb-garden
abdeegilns
designable
abdeegilrt
ledger-bait
abdeeglort
gold-beater
abdeegorrv
verge-board
abdeehills
déshabillé
abdeehillt
billet-head
abdeehillv
ill-behaved
abdeehilps
beadleship
abdeehilrr
halberdier
abdeehimsv
misbehaved

abdeehirtw
white-beard
abdeehllps
bell-shaped
abdeehlltu
bullet-head
abdeehlott
bottle-head
table-d'hôte
abdeehmmru
head-bummer
abdeehnrtu
unbreathed
abdeehorrs
horse-bread
abdeehorst
broadsheet
abdeeiiltt
debilitate
abdeeiknny
kidney-bean
abdeeillmr
mallee-bird
abdeeilmry
remediably
abdeeilnnu
undeniable
abdeeilnru
unrideable
abdeeilnuw
unbewailed
abdeeilorr
rear-boiled
abdeeilpru
repudiable
abdeeilprv
deprivable
abdeeilpss
despisable
abdeeimrtx
ambidexter
abdeeinnor
debonnaire
abdeeioprt
paedotribe
abdeeirrvw
weaver-bird
abdeeklotu
double-take
abdeekrrrt
kerb-trader
abdeelllnu
unlabelled
abdeellmru
umbrellaed
abdeellmtu
umbellated
abdeellopr
deplorable
abdeellpsu
spuleblade
abdeelmrru
demurrable

abdeelnopr
ponderable
abdeelnors
endorsable
abdeelortt
battledore
abdeelprru
perdurable
abdeelrstu
balustered
abdeelstty
detestably
abdeemorry
emery-board
abdeenprry
prebendary
abdeenrsuy
subdeanery
abdeenrttu
unbattered
abdeenrtuy
unbetrayed
abdeeoorvw
beaver-wood
abdeffrstu
breadstuff
abdefgirrt
raft-bridge
abdefiilmo
modifiable
abdefiimrt
fimbriated
abdefiknor
knife-board
abdefilmor
formidable
abdefirrrt
rafter-bird
abdefirrtu
breadfruit
abdefllotu
double-flat
abdeflnoru
unfordable
abdeggirru
budgerigar
abdeghinsu
subheading
abdeghiorw
weigh-board
abdeghortu
dearbought
abdegiinnr
brigandine
abdegilnsy
debasingly
abdegilnty
debatingly
abdegimnrt
abridgment
abdeginnrr
brandering
abdeginory
reading-boy

abdegnorsu
ground-base
abdehiills
dishabille
abdehikllw
hawk-billed
abdehilprt
bridle-path
abdehinort
hot-brained
abdehinrtt
hard-bitten
abdehloort
heart-blood
abdehnorrs
shard-borne
abdehnortu
earthbound
abdehnrstu
subtrahend
abdehorrst
shortbread
abdehosuwy
bawdy-house
abdeiiklls
dislikable
abdeiilmps
bipedalism
abdeiilmss
admissible
abdeiilnot
delibation
abdeiilosx
oxidisable
abdeiilpss
dissipable
abdeiittuv
dubitative
abdeikqrru
Quaker-bird
abdeikrttu
dika-butter
abdeilllny
blind-alley
abdeilllsy
disyllable
abdeilmstu
sublimated
abdeilnnuy
undeniably
abdeilnory
debonairly
abdeiloprv
providable
abdeilopss
disposable
abdeilortt
trilobated
abdeilpstu
disputable
abdeilrttw
wattle-bird
abdeimnrst
disbarment

abdeimnstu
submediant
abdeimorzz
morbidezza
abdeimrrty
timber-yard
abdeimrssy
bradyseism
abdeimrtuw
dumb-waiter
abdeinnotu
unobtained
abdeinpstu
unbaptised
abdeinrttu
turbinated
abdekllotu
double-talk
abdeklopru
double-park
abdekmoors
smoke-board
abdeknnrsu
sand-bunker
abdelloopt
blood-plate
abdellopry
deplorably
abdelmorst
blastoderm
abdelmrruy
lumber-yard
abdelnopsu
spauld-bone
abdelnortu
round-table
abdelnoruu
unlaboured
abdelnosuv
unabsolved
abdeloortt
battledoor
abdelortuy
obdurately
abdelprruy
perdurably
abdemnorrs
roberdsman
abdenooruv
overabound
abdenorrst
sternboard
abdenortuw
water-bound
abdenrsssu
absurdness
abdenrssty
standers-by
abdeoorrtt
otter-board
abdeoprrst
spot-barred
abdfgiinor
fair-boding
abdfilmory
formidably
abdfilnoru
floribunda
abdflooorr
floorboard
abdgginorr
bordraging
abdgiinpru
upbraiding
abdginnrst
band-string
string-band
abdginortu
groundbait
abdglnooow
blood-wagon
abdhhilort
rhabdolith
abdhiiinot
adhibition
abdhilmoor
rhomboidal
abdhinrtuy
unbirthday
abdiiilrty
ridability
abdiiilsty
disability
abdiiiltuy
audibility
abdiiirstt
diatribist
abdiilmnou
albuminoid
abdiilnoos
obsidional
abdiilorrt
tailor-bird
abdiilptuy
dupability
abdiilrtuy
durability
abdiinottu
dubitation
abdiirssuy
subsidiary
abdiknnrst
stink-brand
abdillnost
Bollandist
abdillryzz
blizzardly
abdilnoost
bloodstain
abdilnorsu
subordinal
abdiloorty
botryoidal
abdiloorwz
brazil-wood
abdilpstuy
disputably
abdimnoosu
abdominous
abdimnrruu
burramundi
abdinoortu
obduration
abdinoprrs
parson-bird
abdinrrtty
tyrant-bird
abdinrsttu
disturbant
abdllooory
blood-royal
abdlmnoott
bottom-land
abdmnnoosw
bondswoman
abdnoortuu
roundabout
abdoorrtuu
troubadour
abeeeefllt
flea-beetle
abeeeerrtv
beaver-tree
abeeefiklm
make-belief
abeeeflprr
preferable
abeeegglrs
segregable
abeeegimnn
beam-engine
abeeeglstt
stag-beetle
abeeehklrw
brake-wheel
abeeehrstt
hartebeest
abeeeiklnr
Berkeleian
abeeeikrrt
tie-breaker
abeeeillrv
relievable
abeeeilmrr
irremeable
abeeeilrvw
reviewable
abeeelmprt
temperable
abeeelmrss
reassemble
abeeelnprt
penetrable
abeeelnpru
unpeerable
abeeelqsuz
squeezable
abeeelrrsv
reservable
abeeemmnst
embasement
abeeemnrtt
rebatement
abeeennozz
azobenzene
abeeenqrtu
banqueteer
abeeeoprss
pease-brose
abeeeorstt
stereobate
abeeerrttv
vertebrate
abeefflrsu
sufferable
abeefhlrst
self-breath
abeefiilns
infeasible
abeefiilrv
verifiable
abeefiirtu
beautifier
abeefiklnt
table-knife
abeefikrst
fire-basket
abeefillrt
filterable
abeefilnor
Froebelian
abeefilnrr
inferrable
abeefilnsu
unfeasible
abeefilntt
flea-bitten
abeefllnsu
self-unable
abeeflmorr
reformable
abeefloprr
perforable
abeeflorru
free-labour
abeeflorsw
safe-blower
abeeflprry
preferably
abeeflrssu
self-abuser
abeeflstty
safety-belt
abeeghllnr
bellhanger
abeegiinrs
raising-bee
abeegilmnr
germinable
abeegilnot
negotiable
abeegilnrt
integrable
abeegilnss
Albigenses
abeegilrtu
glauberite
abeegilrtw
bilge-water
abeegirstu
aubergiste
abeeglnorv
governable
abeeglnpux
expugnable
abeegmmnno
gombeen-man
abeegmossy
message-boy
abeegnrstt
abstergent
abeehillrs
relishable
abeehilort
heriotable
abeehilprs
perishable
abeehimntt
Benthamite
abeehinott
hebetation
abeehknors
boneshaker
abeehlmprs
blasphemer
abeehlrsst
breathless
abeehmortt
bathometer
abeehmrtty
bathymeter
abeehnnorv
heaven-born
abeehoorrs
seborrhoea
abeehorstu
hereabouts
abeehorttu
outbreathe
thereabout
abeehortuw
whereabout
abeehortww
weather-bow
abeehortwx
weather-box
abeehprrsy
barysphere
abeehqrsuu
harquebuse
abeehrrtwy
wheat-berry
abeehrsttt
breath-test
abeehrsttu
shea-butter
abeeiillmn
eliminable

abeeiillns
isabelline
abeeiillrs
liberalise
abeeiilnpx
inexpiable
abeeiilnrs
inerasible
abeeiilntv
inevitable
abeeiilsst
bestialise
abeeiirrrz
bizarrerie
abeeikllnu
unlikeable
abeeiknnrt
barkentine
abeeillmnr
bellarmine
abeeillnnt
table-linen
abeeillnru
unreliable
abeeillnst
listenable
abeeillntv
ventilable
abeeillnuv
unliveable
abeeillrsu
leisurable
abeeilmmov
immoveable
abeeilmnrt
terminable
abeeilmnsu
albumenise
abeeilmost
metabolise
abeeilmott
metabolite
abeeilmrry
irremeably
abeeilmstv
semblative
abeeilnnuv
unenviable
abeeilnopr
inoperable
abeeilnorv
verbena-oil
abeeilnorx
inexorable
abeeilnpsx
expansible
abeeilnrss
bleariness
abeeilnrst
insertable
abeeilnsuz
unseizable
unsizeable

abeeilortt
obliterate
abeeilprrs
respirable
abeeilprtx
extirpable
abeeilqrru
requirable
abeeilqrtu
requitable
abeeilrrtu
tree-burial
abeeilrssu
reissuable
abeeimmrrt
timber-mare
abeeinnprr
pine-barren
abeeinptuy
pine-beauty
abeeinrtux
exurbanite
abeeiorttx
exorbitate
abeeirrstw
sweet-briar
abeeirsstv
abstersive
abeejllmsu
jumble-sale
abeejmmnnt
enjambment
abeekkmrrt
kerb-market
abeekllmrt
market-bell
abeekmmnnt
embankment
abeekmmnrt
embarkment
abeeknorst
stone-break
abeellntu
untellable
abeellmntu
ante-bellum
abeellmopy
employable
abeellmoru
bellamoure
abeellnouv
unloveable
abeellnruv
vulnerable
abeellorsv
resolvable
abeellpruv
pulverable
abeelmmmnt
embalmment
abeelmnorz
emblazoner
abeelmnoty
table-money

abeelmnouv
unmoveable
abeelmnpru
rumple-bane
abeelmnrst
resemblant
abeelmnrsu
Lebensraum
mensurable
abeelmnttt
battlement
abeelmorst
blastomere
abeelmprsu
presumable
abeelmprtu
permutable
abeelmrssy
reassembly
abeelnntuu
untuneable
abeelnoprs
personable
abeelnosst
oblateness
abeelnprty
penetrably
abeelnqttu
blanquette
abeelnrrtu
returnable
abeelnssst
stableness
abeeloprrt
reportable
abeeloprtx
exportable
abeelorrst
restorable
abeelorttt
tear-bottle
abeemnorty
embryonate
abeennnrru
runner-bean
abeennorsv
raven's-bone
abeennrrss
barrenness
abeennrrsu
baserunner
abeennrssz
brazenness
abeenorrtw
water-borne
abeenorsst
baronetess
abeeoprrtx
exprobrate
abeeorrstw
water-brose
abeeprrttu
perturbate

abeffgilru
febrifugal
abeffilnst
snaffle-bit
abefflnruu
unruffable
abefflrsuy
sufferably
abefgilorv
forgivable
abefgilrss
fibreglass
abefginorr
forbearing
abefhirrtt
afterbirth
abefhrrstu
surf-bather
abefiillln
infallible
abefiillrt
fibrillate
abefiilnot
notifiable
abefiilntu
infibulate
abefilllnu
unfallible
unfillable
abefiloprt
profitable
abefimmoor
amoebiform
abefklsstu
basketfuls
abefknorrt
break-front
abeflllmuy
blamefully
abeflllorw
ball-flower
abeflloort
footballer
abefllrrsu
barrelfuls
abeggimnor
embargoing
abeggnoort
tobogganer
abeghhirst
breast-high
abeghhmrru
Hamburgher
abeghioopr
ergophobia
abeghioprr
biographer
abeghllluy
belly-laugh
abeghlloop
gallophobe
abeghllopu
ploughable

abeghlnoop
anglophobe
abeghnopst
sponge-bath
abeghnrrsu
bushranger
abeghqsuuu
usquebaugh
abeghrsttu
bestraught
abeghrstuv
harvest-bug
abegiijntw
Jew-baiting
abegiilnnt
intangible
abegiilnrt
Gilbertian
abegiimnrt
reaming-bit
abegiinnrt
brigantine
abegiinors
aborigines
abegiinost
abiogenist
abegiklnnt
blanketing
abegillrt
ballet-girl
abegilmnpu
impugnable
abegilnntu
untangible
abegilnrsw
swingle-bar
abegilrrsu
burglarise
abeginnors
Bergsonian
abeginnqtu
banqueting
abeginnrst
string-bean
abeginrssu
ear-bussing
abeginrstu
gas-turbine
abegllnooy
balneology
abeglnorry
loganberry
abegmorrss
brome-grass
abegmorsuu
umbrageous
abegnnsttu
subtangent
abegnoorst
brant-goose
abegnorrtu
gubernator
abehhillst
sheath-bill

abehhioopt
theophobia
abehhorrtt
heart-throb
abehhorstw
shower-bath
abehiiilps
bailieship
abehiilmnt
habiliment
abehiklnrs
shrinkable
abehiklstt
basket-hilt
abehiknrrs
shin-barker
abehillops
polishable
abehilmprs
blepharism
abehilnpsu
punishable
abehilopst
hospitable
abehilprsy
perishably
abehilpstt
battleship
abehilpstu
bisulphate
abehilrstv
silver-bath
abehimmnst
Benthamism
abehimnnst
banishment
abehinoopx
xenophobia
abehinoprv
vibraphone
abehirsstw
white-brass
abehkooprs
phrase-book
abehlmortw
Bartholmew
abehlmottu
ethambutol
abehlnooru
honourable
abehloopsv
Slavophobe
abehlorttu
bluethroat
abehlosttw
wash-bottle
abehmmnstu
ambushment
abehmnorrt
brother-man
abehmrsstu
bushmaster
abehmrttyy
bathymetry

abehnoprty
hyperbaton
abehnorsst
basset-horn
stone-brash
abehnosttu
thenabouts
abehoorstt
sabre-tooth
abehqrssuu
harquebuss
abeiiilmnt
inimitable
abeiiilnnz
Leibnizian
abeiillmrs
liberalism
abeiillnny
biennially
abeiillnov
inviolable
abeiillrst
liberalist
abeiillrty
liberality
abeiillstt
ballistite
abeiillstu
utilisable
abeiilmnss
lesbianism
abeiilmnsu
albuminise
abeiilmprt
impartible
abeiilmpss
impassible
abeiilmrst
bimestrial
abeiilmsst
bestialism
abeiilnort
liberation
abeiilnott
nobilitate
abeiilnprs
inspirable
abeiilnpxy
inexpiably
abeiilnrsy
inerasibly
abeiilntty
tenability
abeiilntvy
inevitably
abeiilqtuy
equability
abeiilrsst
stabiliser
abeiilstty
bestiality
abeiilstuy
sueability

abeiimnttu
bituminate
abeiinnrss
braininess
abeiinrrsv
river-basin
abeiinrttu
abiturient
abeiioorss
aerobiosis
abeiklnnsu
unsinkable
abeiklnrtw
water-blink
abeilllntu
untillable
abeillmmos
embolismal
abeillmstu
stimulable
abeillnnst
tennis-ball
abeillnosv
insolvable
abeillnosw
Boswellian
abeillnstu
insultable
abeilloprw
pillow-bear
abeillrsuy
leisurably
abeilmmost
metabolism
abeilmnqru
lambrequin
abeilmnrty
liberty-man
terminably
abeilmnssw
wambliness
abeilmootu
automobile
abeilmoprt
importable
abeilmoprv
improvable
abeilmrssu
surmisable
abeilnnors
Selbornian
abeilnnruy
inurbanely
abeilnnuvy
unenviably
abeilnoops
poisonable
abeilnopry
inoperably
abeilnorxy
inexorably
abeilnpruz
unprizable

abeilnpsxy
expansibly
abeilnstuu
unsuitable
abeilooprs
soap-boiler
abeiloprrv
proverbial
abeilopstu
bipetalous
abeilorrty
liberatory
abeilorstt
strobilate
abeilortvy
abortively
abeilrstuv
vestibular
abeimnnott
obtainment
abeimnortt
montbretia
abeimnortu
tambourine
abeimnrrsu
submariner
abeimosstu
abstemious
abeinnopsv
bone-spavin
abeinnortu
eburnation
abeinnortv
native-born
abeinnostt
abstention
abeinnrrtu
interurban
abeinnrssw
brawniness
abeinorsst
abstersion
abeinorttx
exorbitant
abeinrssss
brassiness
abeiopprsy
presbyopia
abeioprstv
absorptive
abeiorrrst
rib-roaster
abeiorrstt
birostrate
abeiossst
asbestosis
abeiprrstt
bitter-spar
abeiprstty
baptistery
abeirstuvy
subvariety
abekkmoorr
bookmarker

abekkorstw
basketwork
work-basket
abeklnnouw
unknowable
abeklnoruw
unworkable
abeklnottt
knat-bottle
abekloopr v
provokable
abekmnnotu
mountebank
abekmnooty
monkey-boat
abeknoprrw
pawnbroker
abeknorstt
breast-knot
abeknorsty
oyster-bank
abekooprry
prayer-book
abekorrstw
breastwork
abelllloy v
volley-ball
abellnosuv
unsolvable
abelloorwy
woolly-bear
abellorrru
bull-roarer
abellostuy
absolutely
abellrsstu
substellar
abellsssuy
syllabuses
abelmmnosu
somnambule
summonable
abelmmptuw
wampum-belt
abelmnnoow
noblewoman
abelmnorxy
onyx-marble
abelmnoryz
emblazonry
abelmnouvy
unmoveably
abelmnprru
lamp-burner
abelmoorst
stable-room
abelmoorsu
laboursome
abelmoortw
water-bloom
abelmprsuy
presumably
abelmprttu
palm-butter

abelnnrtuu
unturnable
abelnoopst
table-spoon
abelnopruv
unprovable
abelnoqtuu
unquotable
abelnorrtt
latter-born
abelnorrtw
brow-antler
abelnorstu
neuroblast
abelnrsstu
substernal
abeloopprs
proposable
abelooprst
blastopore
abeloorruv
overlabour
abeloosstt
osteoblast
abeloppssu
supposable
abeloprstt
table-sport
abeloprttx
prattlebox
abelrsstuy
abstrusely
abelrstttu
salt-butter
abelrttuuu
tubulature
abemmnorsu
membranous
abemnnostu
submontane
abemnoorrw
marrow-bone
abemnoorww
bowerwoman
abemnorrst
robertsman
abenorrrtw
barrenwort
abenorrrwy
rowan-berry
abenprrttu
perturbant
abenprsstu
abruptness
abeooprrrt
reprobator
abeoorrstv
observator
abeoorstuu
rouseabout
abeopsttuy
beauty-spot
abeoqrrtuy
quarter-boy
abeoqssuuu
subaqueous
aberrrstwy
strawberry
abffgillny
bafflingly
abffikmoor
kaffir-boom
abfflnotuu
buffalo-nut
abffmoorst
broomstaff
abfgilnotw
batfowling
abfiiilrty
friability
abfiilllny
infallibly
abfiillrry
fibrillary
abfiilnorv
riboflavin
abfiloprty
profitably
abfilostuy
fabulosity
abfjlorsuy
frabjously
abfllostuy
boastfully
abfllosuuy
fabulously
abflnostuu
unboastful
abgggilnry
braggingly
abggginorw
growing-bag
abggillmno
gambolling
abghhinttu
bathing-hut
abghhmortu
Homburg-hat
abghimnstu
mashing-tub
abghinnstu
sunbathing
abghioprrv
vibrograph
abghiorttu
right-about
abghirrstt
star-bright
abghoorruy
Yarborough
abgiiilnnt
nail-biting
abgiilnnty
intangibly
abgiilnoot
obligation
abgiimnnoo
Mabinogion
abgiimnnst
bantingism
abgiimnors
Grobianism
abgiinnoru
Bourignian
abgikkmnoo
bookmaking
abgikmnoot
bootmaking
abgillmnou
lumbang-oil
abgillmnry
ramblingly
abgillmnwy
wamblingly
abgillnnoo
ballooning
abgillnrwy
warblingly
abgillnsuu
sublingual
abgilmosuy
bigamously
abgiloorty
obligatory
abgiloostt
batologist
abginoortw
rowing-boat
abginorrtu
barring-out
abgjorstuu
subjugator
abglllorуy
globularly
abglnooruy
urbanology
abhhorrsuw
bush-harrow
abhiimmnrs
Brahminism
abhiimopsu
amphibious
abhiioopst
sitophobia
abhiiooptx
toxiphobia
abhiirssty
sybaritish
abhillrstw
whirl-blast
abhilopsty
hospitably
abhilortuw
whirl-about
abhilosstt
histoblast
abhimnooop
monophobia
abhimnorrs
marsh-robin
abhimoopsy
mysophobia
abhinooops
nosophobia
abhinprstu
paint-brush
abhiprrssu
bursarship
abhlllorsu
loll-shraub
abhllmsttu
thumb-stall
abhlmoosty
homoblasty
abhlnooruy
honourably
abhlorrruw
hurl-barrow
abhorrttuy
ruby-throat
abiiillpty
pliability
abiiilmnty
inimitably
abiiilmsst
stibialism
abiiilnost
sibilation
abiiinosst
antibiosis
abiiiorstt
tibiotarsi
abiijlnotu
jubilation
abiillmnsu
subliminal
abiillnovy
inviolably
abiilmotvy
movability
abiilmpssy
impassibly
abiilmttuy
mutability
abiilnnoty
non-ability
abiilnotty
bitonality
notability
abiiloprty
bipolarity
abiilorsty
sibilatory
abiimrssty
sybaritism
abiinnottu
intubation
abiinnrtuy
inurbanity
abiinotttu
titubation
abiiorsttu
obituarist
abiiqrtuuy
ubiquitary
abijllntuy
jubilantly
abijnoortu
objuration
abiklnnopt
point-blank
abiknooort
ration-book
abillnoost
balloonist
abillnootu
lobulation
abillnoruu
unilobular
abillnosvy
insolvably
abilloprrt
parrot-bill
abilmnosuu
albuminous
abilmnotuw
woman-built
abilmoprvy
improvably
abilmopssy
Amblyopsis
abilmosstu
absolutism
abilnoostu
absolution
abilnottuu
tubulation
abilnstuuy
unsuitably
abiloorstv
absolvitor
abilorssuu
salubrious
abilossttu
absolutist
abilrttuuy
tubularity
abimnnootu
umbonation
abimnorrst
brainstorm
abimrssstu
strabismus
abinnorstw
town's-bairn
abinnrsttu
subintrant
abinooprst
absorption
abinoorttu
obturation
abinoossst
bassoonist
abinoprrss
prison-bars
abinossttu
substation
abjlnoorux
journal-box

ablmmoossy
may-blossom
ablnrrtuuw
burr-walnut
abloorstuy
absolutory
abloppssuy
supposably
ablorrsuww
law-burrows
ablorrttuu
turbulator
abmoorstty
strabotomy
abmrssttuu
substratum
abnoorrstu
brontosaur
aboorsttuu
roustabout
accccikkll
click-clack
accceeelns
calescence
accceeenns
canescence
accceehitt
catechetic
accceenrst
accrescent
acccefhkor
cockchafer
accceginos
cacogenics
accceh iprt
ecphractic
acccehkopt
patchcocke
acccehortw
cowcatcher
acccehoruu
accoucheur
accceiirst
cicatrices
accceikort
cockatrice
accceillny
encyclical
accceilmop
accomplice
accceimnpy
impeccancy
acccglnooo
gonococcal
accchhiimr
arch-chimic
accchinoop
cacophonic
accchklotw
watch-clock
accchkopst
spatchcock
accchloory
ochlocracy

accchootuu
caoutchouc
acccii llot
laccolitic
accciilllyy
cyclically
acccilmoox
coxcomical
acccilmopy
complicacy
acccilmory
cycloramic
acccinoppu
cappuccino
accddeeint
accidented
accddeeirt
accredited
accddeklop
cock-paddle
accdeeenns
ascendence
accdeehlot
cochleated
accdeeinns
incandesce
accdeelpst
spectacled
accdeennst
candescent
accdeennsy
ascendency
accdeenntu
unaccented
accdefhklo
half-cocked
accdefkmos
smock-faced
accdehirst
cash-credit
accdehlnoy
chalcedony
accdehnort
torch-dance
accdeiilny
indelicacy
accdeiilst
dialectics
accdeiimoy
Cecidomyia
accdeiiopt
apodeictic
accdeiituz
diazeuctic
accdeiklnw
candlewick
accdeiklop
cock-paidle
accdeiklot
cocktailed
accdeillop
peccadillo
accdeilnot
occidental

accdeilopy
cyclopedia
accdeimnny
mendicancy
accdeimnsu
dance-music
accdeimort
democratic
accdeinntu
inductance
accdeiorst
desiccator
accdeiortt
corticated
accdelltuu
cucullated
accdemostu
accustomed
accdenortt
contracted
accdfiilty
flaccidity
accdgnooor
raccoon-dog
accdhhrruw
churchward
accdhhrruy
churchyard
accdhiinor
diachronic
accdhilnoo
conchoidal
accdhilorr
clarichord
accdhilorv
clavichord
accdiillop
piccadillo
accdiillpy
piccadilly
accdiilnoo
conoidical
accdiilnoy
cycloidian
accdiiloor
Crocodilia
accdiimost
docimastic
accdiinnoo
diaconicon
accdiiostu
diacoustic
accdikloor
clock-radio
accdilnoor
concordial
accdilooow
calico-wood
accdilorsu
sdrucciola
accdinortt
contradict
accdlooruy
doulocracy

accdnnoort
concordant
acceeeehks
cheesecake
acceeehilr
chelicerae
acceeehist
seecatchie
acceeehrty
eye-catcher
acceeelnst
latescence
acceeelprt
receptacle
acceeennrs
renascence
acceeenptx
expectance
acceefhlrt
leechcraft
acceefinst
fatiscence
acceefirru
Cruciferae
acceehhklo
cheechalko
acceehhlow
coach-wheel
acceehiimn
ice-machine
acceehilnp
encephalic
acceehinsv
chevisance
acceehirst
catechiser
acceehisst
catechesis
acceehkkrt
check-taker
acceehlnss
chanceless
acceehmntu
catechumen
acceehnorr
encroacher
acceeillrt
electrical
acceeilmnu
ecumenical
acceeilmrs
cream-slice
acceeilnps
pencil-case
acceeilort
calico-tree
acceeilorv
varicocele
acceeilsst
ecclesiast
acceeimnrs
miscreance
acceeinpqu
cinque-pace

acceeiorsu
ericaceous
acceeirtux
excruciate
acceekoopr
peacock-ore
acceekopry
peacockery
acceekorst
cockteaser
acceelnost
coalescent
acceelnosv
convalesce
acceelnpru
crapulence
acceelnrtu
reluctance
acceelnrux
Clarenceux
acceelnsst
scent-scale
acceelnstt
lactescent
acceelnstu
caulescent
acceelpsst
spectacles
acceemnopu
come-upance
comeupance
acceemnrst
marcescent
scarcement
acceemnstu
accusement
acceemosty
ascomycete
acceennnov
convenance
acceennovy
conveyance
acceenoprr
coparcener
acceenorst
consecrate
acceenptxy
expectancy
acceenrsss
scarceness
acceentuxy
executancy
acceeorrsu
racecourse
acceeorstu
cretaceous
acceffiiny
inefficacy
acceffiity
efficacity
accefhlrty
fly-catcher
accefiilps
specifical

accefiirrs
sacrificer
accefiknrt
fan-cricket
accefillor
calciferol
accefilmor
calceiform
accefilrsu
flea-circus
accefilryy
fairy-cycle
accefinost
confiscate
accefllotu
flocculate
accegiinor
cariogenic
accegillnn
cancelling
accegilloo
ecological
accegilnot
lactogenic
accegimops
megascopic
acceginnor
carcinogen
acceginnos
cognisance
accehhiirr
hierarchic
accehhiprt
heptarchic
accehhoors
coach-horse
accehhoosu
coach-house
accehhrrtu
church-rate
accehiilmr
chimerical
accehiimrt
chemiatric
accehiinnt
technician
accehiinpt
epicanthic
accehikops
peacockish
accehillmy
chemically
accehillty
hectically
accehimnnu
unmechanic
accehimnny
chimney-can
accehimnoo
maconochie
accehimprt
emphractic
accehimrsu
Chaucerism
accehinort
Acherontic
anchoretic
accehiorry
hierocracy
accehiorst
escharotic
accehiortt
theocratic
accehirtvz
czarevitch
accehklnot
checklaton
accehllnor
chancellor
accehlmoor
homocercal
accehlorry
cherry-coal
accehmnoor
comanchero
accehnnpty
catchpenny
accehnnrty
trenchancy
accehnortt
technocrat
trench-coat
accehoorsu
ochraceous
accehorruw
crouch-ware
acceiilnot
conciliate
acceiilrrt
rectricial
acceiilrtt
tectricial
acceiimrst
ceramicist
acceiimsst
asceticism
acceiinnnt
cincinnate
acceiinnor
Ciceronian
acceiinnrs
circensian
acceiinrst
Cistercian
acceiirstx
cicatrixes
acceikknnt
nick-nacket
acceikrrtw
wit-cracker
acceilllor
claircolle
acceillnru
unclerical
acceillnsy
scenically
acceilmmor
commercial
acceilmnoo
economical
acceilmnop
compliance
acceilmoot
coelomatic
acceilmopt
complicate
acceilmost
cacomistle
cosmetical
acceilnoss
neoclassic
acceilnrst
calc-sinter
acceiloppt
apoplectic
acceiloprr
reciprocal
acceimnors
conacreism
acceimnrsy
miscreancy
acceinnnov
connivance
acceinnoor
cancionero
acceinnopr
Copernican
acceinnort
concertina
acceinoors
occasioner
acceinoost
consociate
acceinorst
Cestracion
acceinttuv
cunctative
acceioorsu
coriaceous
acceioppsy
episcopacy
acceioprty
pyro-acetic
acceioptuv
occupative
acceiorrtu
Eurocratic
acceiorstx
exsiccator
acceiortuy
eucaryotic
accejkkort
cork-jacket
accejnosuu
juncaceous
accekklmor
clockmaker
acceklortw
water-clock
acceknrrtu
nutcracker
accekoprrt
cork-carpet
accellnosu
cancellous
accellssuu
calculuses
accelmnopt
complacent
accelmnory
cleromancy
accelmoprs
camel-corps
accelnoptu
conceptual
accelnotxy
nectocalyx
accelnrtuy
reluctancy
acceloopst
lactoscope
accelorttu
coal-cutter
accelrssuu
succursale
accemnnory
necromancy
accemoprtu
compacture
accemorstu
reaccustom
accennnoos
consonance
accennnost
connascent
accenoorrt
cancer-root
accenorsty
consectary
accenorttu
counteract
acceorsuuv
curvaceous
accffffhhi
chiff-chaff
accfhirttw
witchcraft
accfiiimps
pacificism
accfiiipst
pacificist
accfiinnot
fantoccini
accfilmory
calyciform
accfilssuu
fasciculus
accfimnorr
cancriform
accfnoorrt
corn-factor
accforrttu
courtcraft
accforsttu
scoutcraft
accgghiloo
cholagogic
accghiiiop
pichiciago
accghiilor
oligarchic
accghinrst
scratching
accghiopty
phagocytic
accghirstw
scratch-wig
accghknouw
chuck-wagon
accghlopry
cyclograph
accghorssu
couch-grass
accgiimort
tragi-comic
accginnotu
accounting
accginortu
accoutring
acchhiilln
chinchilla
acchhiilry
chiliarchy
acchhillss
clish-clash
acchiiilst
chiliastic
acchiimoss
isochasmic
acchiimsst
mica-schist
schismatic
acchiinort
anchoritic
acchiinoty
thiocyanic
acchikmqtu
quick-match
acchikmstt
matchstick
acchilmops
accomplish
acchilnnps
splanchnic
acchilnoot
catholicon
acchiloost
catholicos
acchilootu
acolouthic
acchilosst
scholastic
acchilrsty
scratchily
acchilsstt
talc-schist
acchilttyy
tachylytic

acchimnooy
iconomachy
acchimnory
chiromancy
acchimorst
chromatics
acchinoopr
acrophonic
acchinorst
stracchino
acchioprsz
schizocarp
acchioptty
hypotactic
acchiosstt
stochastic
acchmooort
motor-coach
acchmorsst
cross-match
acchnopsyy
sycophancy
acchnorrst
cornstarch
acchooprty
cacotrophy
acchoprsst
crosspatch
acciiilllp
piccalilli
acciilllny
clinically
acciillrty
critically
acciilmnos
laconicism
acciilmoru
coumarilic
acciilmoty
comicality
acciilmsss
classicism
acciilnory
conciliary
acciilnrtu
uncritical
acciiloprt
pictorical
acciilssst
classicist
acciimnnno
cinnamonic
acciimnoot
iconomatic
acciimnops
misocapnic
acciimortt
timocratic
acciinnnpy
piccaninny
acciinnost
canonistic
acciinnoty
canonicity
acciinorss
carcinosis
acciioprsu
capricious
acciiottvy
coactivity
acciisttuy
causticity
accikkkknn
knick-knack
accikkrrtt
trick-track
accillmory
millocracy
accillmosy
cosmically
accillrruy
circularly
accillsuuu
cauliculus
accilmnnou
councilman
accilmnoos
iconoclasm
accilmnopt
complicant
accilmnopy
compliancy
accilmorss
cross-claim
accilnoost
iconoclast
accilnopty
nyctalopic
accilnortu
inculcator
accilnostv
conclavist
accilnssty
synclastic
acciloppry
polycarpic
accilorrtu
circulator
accilrrruu
curricular
accimmoors
cosmoramic
accimnoopr
monocarpic
accimnoopt
compaction
accimnoort
monocratic
accimnosuu
cacuminous
accinnnovy
connivancy
accinnottu
cunctation
accinoopru
cornucopia
accinooptu
occupation
accinoprsy
conspiracy
acciooprsu
procacious
accioopstu
autoscopic
accioprstt
catoptrics
acciorsuuv
curvacious
accklmooru
cockalorum
acckorsttu
track-scout
acckrrstty
crack-tryst
accloprtuy
plutocracy
accnnnoosy
consonancy
accnooprry
pornocracy
accnoorrtt
contractor
accnorttuy
cunctatory
acdddegipy
giddy-paced
acdddgirtu
drug-addict
acddeeeirt
rededicate
acddeehloo
cool-headed
acddeehlty
detachedly
acddeehnor
decahedron
acddeeiipt
diapedetic
acddeeiitv
dedicative
acddeellot
decollated
acddeellry
declaredly
acddeellsy
Clydesdale
acddeelnru
undeclared
acddeelnty
decadently
acddeennru
redundance
acddeennst
descendant
acddeennsu
unascended
acddeentuu
uneducated
acddeesstu
decussated
acddefghou
doughfaced
acddefnoru
round-faced
acddegilno
Iceland-dog
acddeginot
date-coding
acddehiiip
aphidicide
acddehklru
herald-duck
acddehlorr
card-holder
acddehnnos
second-hand
acddehnooo
deaconhood
acddeiijtu
dijudicate
acddeiiltu
dilucidate
acddeiinot
dedication
acddeiklss
saddle-sick
acddeiknrs
crank-sided
acddeilmou
duodecimal
acddeinnss
candidness
acddeiopsu
pseudo-acid
acddeiorty
dedicatory
acddeipstu
cuspidated
acddeirstt
distracted
acddekllno
land-locked
acddeklors
dreadlocks
acddelnnoo
colonnaded
acddelnoow
candle-wood
acddelnopu
candle-doup
acddennruy
redundancy
acddenorsu
decandrous
acddenorsw
sword-dance
acddeoopsu
decapodous
acddfhioru
chaudfroid
acddghilnr
grandchild
acddiinops
dispondaic
acddilnnuy
uncandidly
acddinorst
discordant
acdeeeehhs
head-cheese
acdeeeelns
needle-case
acdeeeelrt
decelerate
acdeeeeprs
predecease
acdeeefhps
sheep-faced
acdeeeflnr
fer-de-lance
acdeeefmnt
defacement
acdeeegnry
degeneracy
acdeeehltt
decathlete
acdeeehnrt
head-centre
acdeeeilsu
Seleucidae
acdeeeiprt
depreciate
acdeeelnrt
candle-tree
acdeeemnst
casemented
acdeeenntt
antecedent
acdeeenrtv
advertence
acdeeeorrt
redecorate
acdeeerrst
desecrater
acdeeersuy
saucer-eyed
acdeeffhrt
far-fetched
acdeefflty
affectedly
acdeeffntu
unaffected
acdeefhitw
white-faced
acdeefhors
horse-faced
acdeefinot
defecation
acdeefinwz
wizen-faced
acdeefirss
fricasseed
acdeefkopr
poker-faced
acdeeflnor
confederal
acdeeflnoy
falcon-eyed
acdeefoprw
face-powder

acdeeforst
forecasted
acdeeghinp
phagedenic
acdeeghnno
hendecagon
acdeegiint
diagenetic
acdeegilmo
geomedical
acdeegilns
side-glance
acdeegilos
geodesical
acdeegilot
geodetical
acdeegimmr
decigramme
acdeeginnr
grand-niece
acdeeginrt
centigrade
acdeegllou
colleagued
acdeegllrw
well-graced
acdeeglnrt
rectangled
acdeegorty
grey-coated
acdeehiino
Echinoidea
acdeehilnr
chandelier
acdeehinnr
hinderance
acdeehinot
theodicean
acdeehiort
cote-hardie
acdeehklls
shellacked
acdeehllmu
chaud-mellé
acdeehllnn
channelled
acdeehllrt
thread-cell
acdeehllst
satchelled
acdeehlort
cloth-eared
acdeehlrru
hurdle-race
acdeehmntt
detachment
acdeehnnrs
hand-screen
acdeehnrsu
unsearched
acdeehoppr
copperhead
acdeeiilmp
epidemical
acdeeiilms
decimalise
acdeeiilnt
indelicate
acdeeiiltt
dietetical
acdeeiimrt
acidimeter
acdeeiimtv
medicative
acdeeikprr
prick-eared
acdeeillnp
lead-pencil
pencil-lead
acdeeillnr
Cinderella
acdeeillrs
escadrille
acdeeillty
delicately
acdeeilmnr
endermical
acdeeilmnt
maledicent
acdeeilmpr
premedical
acdeeilmrv
decemviral
acdeeilnrt
credential
interlaced
acdeeilnsu
Seleucidan
acdeeilops
Scopelidae
acdeeilosv
devocalise
acdeeilpry
dice-player
icy-pearled
acdeeilptu
pediculate
acdeeilrtt
red-lattice
acdeeimmnt
medicament
acdeeimnou
eudaemonic
acdeeimnrt
endermatic
acdeeimott
comedietta
acdeeimprt
mercaptide
acdeeimrst
medicaster
miscreated
acdeeinntu
denunciate
acdeeinors
Deinoceras
acdeeinost
cestoidean
acdeeinpps
appendices
acdeeinptt
pectinated
acdeeinrrw
wire-dancer
acdeeinsst
desistance
acdeeiortv
decorative
acdeeiottx
detoxicate
acdeeipstu
paedeutics
acdeeirttv
detractive
acdeeittux
exactitude
acdeeklnry
cankeredly
acdeelllpw
well-placed
acdeellltu
cellulated
acdeellmpu
cul-de-lampe
acdeellnps
spancelled
acdeellnru
unrecalled
acdeellops
escalloped
acdeelmort
ectodermal
acdeelmrtu
emerald-cut
acdeelnnov
decennoval
acdeelnnsu
uncleansed
acdeelnorr
corn-dealer
acdeelnost
adolescent
acdeelnrtu
crenulated
acdeeloort
decolorate
acdeeloppy
Pelecypoda
acdeeloprv
overplaced
acdeelortu
edulcorate
acdeelprtu
curled-pate
acdeelrrtt
letter-card
acdeemmnor
commandeer
acdeemmnpt
decampment
acdeemnoty
adenectomy
acdeemorsu
decamerous
acdeennopr
ponderance
acdeennorr
once-errand
acdeennost
condensate
acdeennotv
covenanted
acdeennrsu
sunderance
acdeenoprr
rope-dancer
acdeenorst
second-rate
acdeenprru
perdurance
acdeenprst
step-dancer
acdeenprtu
uncarpeted
acdeenrsss
sacredness
acdeenrttu
detruncate
acdeenrtvy
advertency
acdeeoprrt
deprecator
tape-record
acdeeoprsu
predaceous
acdeeorrst
desecrator
acdeffikrt
trafficked
acdefflors
scaffolder
acdefghilt
light-faced
acdefgilny
defacingly
acdefginor
dog-fancier
acdefhilns
candle-fish
acdefhosuv
vouchsafed
acdefiiint
nidificate
acdefiilot
foeticidal
acdefiilss
classified
acdefiinpu
unpacified
acdefiinst
sanctified
acdefiirrt
fratricide
acdefilmtu
multifaced
acdefilssy
declassify
acdefinnot
confidante
acdefinort
deforciant
acdefioprt
forcipated
acdefirssy
decrassify
acdeflnoot
foot-candle
acdefnorru
uncared-for
acdefnrrtu
under-craft
acdefpttuy
putty-faced
acdeggiops
pedagogics
acdeghhilp
high-placed
acdeghiltt
tight-laced
acdeghirrs
discharger
acdeghrrsu
surcharged
acdegiilmn
declaiming
acdegiilmr
germicidal
acdegiinnn
indignance
acdegiinor
radiogenic
acdegiinot
Cotingidae
acdegiinst
die-casting
acdegiirrr
cirrigrade
acdegilnrw
arc-welding
acdegilost
decalogist
acdegilrtt
cattle-grid
acdegimnoy
geodynamic
acdeginnor
androgenic
acdeginorr
corrigenda
acdeginrtt
detracting
acdegiorsu
discourage
acdegjnotu
conjugated
acdegknorr
rock-garden
acdegllopr
placer-gold

acdegllpuy
cudgel-play
acdeglnnru
grand-uncle
acdeglnnst
scent-gland
acdegloors
socdolager
acdegnosuy
decagynous
acdegooprs
scrape-good
acdegorrtu
corrugated
acdehhimor
hemichorda
acdehhnttu
unthatched
acdehhoprt
heptachord
acdehhorty
hydrotheca
acdehiillo
helicoidal
acdehiimrt
diathermic
acdehiinns
disenchain
acdehiinrv
chain-drive
acdehiiorr
diarrhoeic
acdehilmot
methodical
acdehilmrs
Childermas
acdehilnrs
Reichsland
acdehilort
chloridate
acdehilrtw
witch-alder
acdehimort
dichromate
acdehinnst
disenchant
acdehinops
deaconship
acdehinopt
dictaphone
acdehinort
ditrochean
acdehinprt
cinder-path
acdehioppt
heptapodic
acdehiprst
dispatcher
acdehirttw
ditch-water
acdehklnsu
unshackled
acdehllnpu
punch-ladle
acdehllnry
chandlerly
acdehlmoos
dame-school
school-dame
acdehlnosy
anchylosed
acdehlnrsu
rush-candle
acdehloopp
cephalopod
acdehlrsty
starchedly
acdehmostu
moustached
acdehnnoru
unanchored
acdehnnstu
unstanched
acdehnoort
octahedron
acdehnoprt
pentachord
acdehnorsz
scherzando
acdehnrrsy
sand-cherry
acdehnrstu
unstarched
acdehoprsy
hydrospace
acdehorrtt
tetrachord
acdeiiilst
idealistic
acdeiiintv
indicative
acdeiiiprr
Cirripedia
acdeiijtuv
judicative
acdeiiknns
Dickensian
acdeiillot
idiolectal
acdeiilmms
decimalism
acdeiilmmt
dilemmatic
acdeiilmrs
disclaimer
acdeiilmrv
vermicidal
acdeiilmst
decimalist
acdeiilnnt
incidental
acdeiilopr
periodical
acdeiilops
episodical
acdeiilors
cordialise
acdeiilpst
pesticidal
septicidal
acdeiilptu
Pediculati
acdeiimnot
decimation
medication
acdeiimrtx
taxidermic
acdeiimrty
acidimetry
acdeiinnor
crinoidean
acdeiinnry
incendiary
acdeiinosy
isocyanide
acdeiinpry
Cyprinidae
acdeiiorsu
iridaceous
acdeiiosst
dissociate
acdeiippry
cypripedia
acdeiipstu
paideutics
acdeijntuv
adjunctive
acdeijrtuu
judicature
acdeillorr
cordillera
acdeilltuv
victualled
acdeilmnor
decinormal
acdeilmost
domestical
acdeilnnor
endocrinal
acdeilnort
declinator
acdeilnory
corydaline
acdeilnosv
volcanised
acdeilnpss
placidness
acdeilnrtw
winter-clad
acdeilnsty
syndetical
acdeiloprr
precordial
acdeilopst
despotical
acdeilorsu
radiculose
acdeilortu
elucidator
acdeilostu
Locustidae
acdeilosty
Scolytidae
acdeilosuy
edaciously
acdeilottu
colatitude
acdeilpstu
disculpate
acdeilrttw
wildcatter
acdeimmory
immoderacy
acdeimnnno
demi-cannon
acdeimnnop
Pandemonic
acdeimnnor
corn-maiden
acdeimnopr
incompared
acdeimnoru
androecium
acdeimnosu
mendacious
acdeimnrsu
muscardine
acdeimoprr
madreporic
acdeinnnty
intendancy
acdeinnoss
dissonance
acdeinnrss
rancidness
acdeinoort
carotenoid
coordinate
co-ordinate
decoration
acdeinoppt
pentapodic
acdeinoqru
quadricone
acdeinorrw
cordwainer
acdeinorst
draconites
acdeinortt
detraction
acdeinostt
anecdotist
acdeinostw
wainscoted
acdeinottx
detoxicant
acdeinprst
discrepant
acdeinpstt
pandectist
acdeinrtuv
incurvated
acdeinsttu
sanctitude
acdeiooprs
radioscope
acdeioprsu
predacious
acdeiopssu
spadiceous
acdeiorstu
outside-car
acdeiosstt
tossicated
acdeiosttt
tosticated
acdeipqrsu
quadriceps
acdeiprstu
custard-pie
acdeiqrstu
quadrisect
acdeirsstt
dictatress
acdeirsstu
crassitude
acdeirssty
dyscrasite
acdeirttuv
traductive
acdejksttu
dust-jacket
acdekkmopr
pockmarked
acdeklnoos
saloon-deck
acdekmnors
second-mark
acdekmorst
dock-master
acdeknrssu
sand-sucker
acdeknrsuv
raven's-duck
acdellorsw
worldscale
acdelmnoor
coromandel
acdelmnotu
columnated
documental
acdelnoort
decolorant
acdelnooty
acotyledon
acdelnortu
edulcorant
acdelnpruu
peduncular
acdelnrssu
underclass
acdeloorrw
wool-carder
acdeloopptu
clapped-out
acdeloprru
procedural

acdelosstu
outclassed
acdemmnory
commandery
acdemmostu
custom-made
acdemnortu
mucronated
acdemooprr
compradore
acdemoprsu
damp-course
acdemorrss
cross-armed
acdemprstu
spermaduct
acdennnoor
ordonnance
acdennnoos
nanosecond
acdennopry
ponderancy
acdenoppsw
snow-capped
acdenopsty
syncopated
acdenorrtu
underactor
acdenorrtw
rent-a-crowd
acdenrrrtu
redcurrant
acdenrrstu
transducer
acdenrsttu
cruet-stand
acdeoorrvw
wood-carver
acdeopprsu
pseudocarp
acdeoprrtt
protracted
acdeoprsuu
drupaceous
acdeorrtty
detractory
acdffhinsu
handicuffs
acdfgiiiny
acidifying
acdfgiilnu
fungicidal
acdfgilrtu
craft-guild
acdfglnoru
calf-ground
acdfiilluy
fiducially
acdfiimorr
radiciform
acdfimnnor
confirmand
acdflnossy
candy-floss

acdforrstw
swordcraft
acdghinorr
orcharding
acdghioprt
Dictograph
acdghiprsy
dysgraphic
acdghnootu
touch-and-go
acdgiiimnr
gramicidin
acdgiiloor
radiologic
acdgiinors
disorganic
acdgiinort
riding-coat
acdgiinost
diagnostic
acdgilnoot
odontalgic
acdgiloory
cardiology
acdgimmnno
commanding
acdginnpru
cup-and-ring
acdglnoruy
clay-ground
acdglotyyz
zygodactyl
acdhhlnoor
anchor-hold
acdhiiiopt
idiopathic
acdhiilosz
schizoidal
acdhiimsss
Chassidism
acdhillryy
hydrically
acdhilmnow
woman-child
acdhilmoos
schoolmaid
acdhiloort
trochoidal
acdhilrsst
third-class
acdhilrssy
chrysalids
acdhilrsuy
hydraulics
acdhimstyy
dysthymiac
acdhinooox
chionodoxa
acdhiooprr
Cirrhopoda
acdhiooprs
Discophora
acdhioopsz
Schizopoda

acdhioprsw
cowardship
acdhiorrst
orchardist
acdhiorrsw
disc-harrow
acdhiortty
trachytoid
acdhloorru
urochordal
acdhloorsw
schoolward
acdhmnoryy
hydromancy
acdhmnotuw
Dutchwoman
acdiiijlnu
injudicial
acdiiinnot
indication
acdiijlluy
judicially
acdiijnotu
judication
acdiillopr
prolicidal
acdiillsuy
suicidally
acdiilmopt
diplomatic
acdiilmost
modalistic
acdiiloprt
dioptrical
acdiilorst
clostridia
acdiilorty
cordiality
acdiimnoot
coati-mondi
acdiimnort
antidromic
acdiimnosy
isodynamic
acdiimnotu
coati-mundi
acdiimnsty
dynamicist
dynamistic
acdiinnory
inordinacy
acdiinoort
carotinoid
acdiinoorv
Ordovician
acdiinoost
scotodinia
acdiinortv
vindicator
acdiinorty
dictionary
indicatory
acdiinostt
donatistic

acdiinrtuy
iracundity
acdiioortx
radiotoxic
acdiioprst
parodistic
acdijnnotu
adjunction
acdijortux
coadjutrix
acdijortuy
judicatory
acdiklorrz
rock-lizard
acdiknqsuy
quick-sandy
acdilloost
idoloclast
acdilnrstu
translucid
acdilooprs
prosodical
acdiloopty
octaploidy
acdiloprtu
duplicator
acdimmoruy
myocardium
acdimnortu
Dracontium
acdimnsstu
music-stand
acdimoorsu
mordacious
acdinnossy
dissonancy
acdinoorrt
rain-doctor
acdinorsty
syndicator
acdinorttu
traduction
acdiooprsy
radioscopy
acdklmossy
lady's-smock
acdknorstu
sound-track
acdlloopsw
codswallop
acdlloptyy
polydactyl
acdllorstu
collar-stud
acdlmnoouv
mud-volcano
acdlnstyyy
syndactyly
acdmnoopsy
spodomancy
acdnoorstu
octandrous
acdoopprsu
Podocarpus

acdoorrsss
crossroads
aceeeeghss
sage-cheese
aceeeffmnt
effacement
aceeefftu
effectuate
aceeefiprs
fire-escape
aceeefiprt
afterpiece
aceeefknns
snake-fence
aceeeflnrr
freelancer
aceeefmnnt
enfacement
aceeegilnn
inelegance
aceeegiltx
exegetical
aceeeginrt
great-niece
aceeegnprt
percentage
aceeegnrry
regeneracy
aceeehilsv
chevesaile
aceeehirtt
hereticate
aceeehkprs
cash-keeper
aceeehlpsw
scape-wheel
aceeehorrt
Heterocera
aceeehrrrs
researcher
aceeehrrrt
treacherer
aceeeimrst
camsteerie
aceeeinnnt
ante-Nicene
aceeeinrrs
reincrease
aceeeinrrt
reiterance
aceeeinrss
nécessaire
aceeeipprv
apperceive
aceeeirrst
secretaire
aceeeirrtv
recreative
aceeeirssv
sea-service
aceeeirstv
eviscerate
tea-service

aceeeirtvx
execrative
aceeekpppr
pepper-cake
aceeellnpr
repellance
aceeellnrt
crenellate
aceeelmnnt
enlacement
aceeelnprv
prevalence
aceeelortt
electorate
aceeelostt
steatocele
aceeelprvy
everyplace
aceeelpsss
escapeless
aceeelrrtw
welter-race
aceeelrstt
telecaster
aceeelrtux
exulcerate
aceeelsttu
sea-lettuce
aceeemmnrt
amercement
aceeemnnpr
permanence
aceeemnnst
encasement
aceeemnprt
temperance
aceeemnpst
escapement
aceeemnrst
meatscreen
aceeemnrtt
metacentre
aceeemnrtx
excrementa
aceeennotv
covenantee
aceeennprt
penetrance
repentance
aceeennrrt
re-entrance
aceeennstv
evanescent
aceeeprrtu
recuperate
aceeeprstt
pace-setter
aceeffhsuu
chauffeuse
aceeffimny
effeminacy
aceeffnrsu
sufferance

aceefgirst
siegecraft
aceefhinpr
pine-chafer
aceefhlnrt
centre-half
aceefhorrs
rose-chafer
aceefiiiln
Filicineae
aceefiiltt
felicitate
aceefijklt
life-jacket
aceefilmnt
maleficent
aceefilnrt
frenetical
aceefilnss
facileness
aceefilnst
leaf-insect
aceefilrsu
luciferase
aceefiortv
vociferate
aceefirrtv
refractive
aceefkorrw
faceworker
aceefllntu
flatulence
aceefllorv
cloverleaf
aceefllpuy
peacefully
aceeflnpuu
unpeaceful
aceeflnstv
flavescent
aceeflorst
forecastle
aceeflrttu
leaf-cutter
aceefnqrtu
queencraft
aceefopssu
pousse-café
aceeforrst
forecaster
aceefrrrtu
refracture
aceeggilno
genealogic
aceegglpsu
egg-capsule
aceeggnort
congregate
aceeghilnt
genethliac
aceeghllnr
challenger
aceeghlnss
changeless

aceeghlrss
chargeless
aceeghnorv
change-over
aceeghnrrt
rent-charge
aceeghorrv
overcharge
aceegikttw
wicket-gate
aceegillnr
allergenic
aceegillot
collegiate
aceegillpr
peelgarlic
aceegilnny
inelegancy
aceegilntu
geniculate
aceegilstu
sluice-gate
aceeginnpt
pangenetic
aceegiorrt
groceteria
aceegiorst
categories
categorise
aceegiottx
excogitate
aceegknops
sponge-cake
aceeglmnor
camerlengo
aceeglnorv
overglance
aceeglnrtu
great-uncle
aceeglnrtw
clew-garnet
aceeglrtuv
culvertage
aceegmmosu
gemmaceous
aceegnnorv
governance
aceegnnpru
repugnance
aceegnorru
encourager
aceegnrsty
sergeantcy
aceegnrsvy
scavengery
aceegoprst
corpse-gate
aceehhilrw
wheel-chair
aceehhirrs
heresiarch
aceehhpttu
Heptateuch

aceehiiprt
perithecia
aceehilmnn
manchineel
aceehilmrt
hermetical
aceehilnnp
encephalin
aceehilnst
anthelices
aceehilptt
telepathic
aceehilsss
chaiseless
aceehimnpz
chimpanzee
aceehimpry
hyperaemic
aceehimptt
empathetic
aceehimrtx
hexametric
aceehimsst
schematise
aceehimttt
metathetic
aceehinnot
Antiochene
aceehinnpt
phenacetin
aceehinopr
peacherino
aceehinprs
phrenesiac
aceehiorrt
charioteer
aceehisstt
aesthetics
aceehkmnsu
hamesucken
aceehkprst
sheep-track
aceehllmos
cameo-shell
aceehllnop
cellophane®
aceehlnnop
encephalon
aceehlnpru
leprechaun
aceehlnprw
leprechawn
aceehlnptt
planchette
aceehlopty
polychaete
aceehlrsss
searchless
aceehlrsst
thale-cress
aceehlrtvw
lever-watch
aceehlssst
scatheless

aceehmmrsu
meerschaum
aceehmnnst
encashment
aceehmnprt
preachment
aceehmnrst
Manchester
aceehmopss
mesoscaphe
aceehmortt
tachometer
aceehmprty
pachymeter
aceehmrtty
tachymeter
aceehmsstt
steam-chest
aceehnopst
peach-stone
aceehnpttu
Pentateuch
aceehnrsst
stern-chase
aceehnssst
chasteness
aceehoprrr
reproacher
aceehoprsu
proseuchae
aceehorrst
trace-horse
aceehpprsy
hyperspace
aceehprrsu
repurchase
aceehprtuy
hyperacute
aceehrrstu
Chartreuse
aceehrttuw
water-chute
aceeiilmrt
eremitical
aceeiilntt
licentiate
aceeiilpss
specialise
aceeiilsst
elasticise
aceeiimnpt
impatience
aceeiimpst
episematic
aceeiinnrt
creatinine
incinerate
aceeiipsst
asepticise
aceeiirttv
recitative
aceeiittvx
excitative

aceeiklmns
simnel-cake
aceeiklmtt
meal-ticket
aceeiklrrs
arse-licker
aceeiknnss
snick-a-snee
aceeikprtt
ticker-tape
aceeillmst
mile-castle
aceeillmty
emetically
aceeillnrw
wine-cellar
aceeillort
electorial
aceeillpsy
especially
aceeilmmrs
mesmerical
aceeilmnor
ceremonial
aceeilmnot
melaconite
aceeilmnrt
mercantile
aceeilmnst
centesimal
lemniscate
aceeilmosu
meliaceous
aceeilmptt
metaleptic
aceeilmstt
telesmatic
aceeilnnnt
centennial
aceeilnnpt
Pentelican
aceeilnnuv
univalence
aceeilnopu
leucopenia
aceeilnort
neoterical
aceeilnprt
epicentral
aceeilnrrt
centre-rail
aceeilnrst
centralise
aceeilnrtv
cantilever
trivalence
aceeilortv
co-relative
aceeilortx
exoterical
aceeilpprt
preceptial
tea-clipper

aceeilprsw
parcelwise
aceeilrrtt
retractile
aceeilrssu
secularise
aceeilrttu
reticulate
aceeilrtuv
ulcerative
aceeilrtvy
creatively
reactively
aceeilstuv
vesiculate
aceeimnnst
incasement
aceeimnoru
Mucorineae
aceeimnrss
creaminess
aceeimnrsv
serviceman
aceeimnrtt
remittance
aceeimorrt
aerometric
aceeimprst
spermaceti
aceeimrstt
tetrasemic
aceeinnprs
Spencerian
aceeinnrst
transience
aceeinopst
stenpoaeic
aceeinorrt
recreation
aceeinorst
estanciero
aceeinortu
auctioneer
aceeinortx
execration
aceeinpprt
apprentice
pine-carpet
aceeinprst
interspace
aceeinrsst
resistance
aceeinrttt
tetractine
aceeinrtvy
inveteracy
aceeinsstv
activeness
aceeiooprs
aeciospore
aceeioppst
episcopate
aceeiopsst
caespitose

aceeioqtuv
equivocate
aceeipqrsu
picaresque
aceeiprrsv
riverscape
aceeiqrstu
requiescat
aceeirrttv
retractive
aceeirttvx
extractive
aceejlmnot
cajolement
aceejnrsty
serjeantcy
aceekllnno
kennel-coal
aceekllrss
sales-clerk
aceeknoptt
packet-note
aceeknrrrt
rack-renter
aceekorrsw
case-worker
aceellmnrt
recallment
aceellnotu
nucleolate
aceellnpry
repellancy
aceellnpst
pallescent
aceellortt
collarette
aceellrssy
carelessly
aceellsttu
scutellate
aceelmnost
solacement
aceelmortt
lactometer
aceelnoprv
Provençale
aceelnopst
opalescent
aceelnorrt
necrolater
aceelnprsy
screenplay
aceelnprvy
prevalency
aceelnrrty
recreantly
aceelooprt
Coleoptera
aceeloorsu
oleraceous
aceeloostw
weasel-coot
aceelopprt
Plecoptera

aceeloprtu
operculate
aceelosstt
cassolette
aceelpprtu
perceptual
aceelprstw
screw-plate
aceelqrruu
craquelure
aceelrrtuy
creaturely
aceemmnnpt
encampment
aceemmnott
commentate
aceemmorsu
commeasure
aceemnnpry
permanency
aceemnopst
compensate
aceemnorty
cyanometer
aceemnprst
escarpment
aceemostuz
eczematous
aceennoprv
provenance
aceennopsu
pennaceous
aceennortv
contravene
covenanter
aceennosuv
sovenaunce
aceennottz
canzonette
aceennprty
penetrancy
aceennprvy
prevenancy
aceennrrty
re-entrancy
aceennrssv
cravenness
aceennsstu
sustenance
aceenoostu
coetaneous
aceenorsss
coarseness
aceenorsst
antecessor
aceenorstu
nectareous
raconteuse
aceenprstt
respectant
aceenpruvy
purveyance
aceenrrtuu
nature-cure

aceenrssst
ancestress
aceenrsstw
newscaster
aceenrsuvy
surveyance
aceeorrstt
stercorate
aceeorrtxy
execratory
aceeossttu
testaceous
aceeprrrtu
recapturer
aceeprstuu
superacute
aceerrsstw
watercress
aceffginsu
suffigance
aceffhlpsu
shuffle-cap
aceffiiltv
afflictive
aceffiimns
caffeinism
aceffiiorr
air-officer
aceffikrrt
trafficker
aceffilnoo
loan-office
aceffilorw
law-officer
aceffinssu
suffisance
aceffostuu
tuffaceous
acefghirrt
freight-car
acefgiklru
craigfluke
acefgilnst
self-acting
acefginrrt
refracting
acefgllruy
gracefully
acefglnruu
ungraceful
acefgloruu
courageful
acefhhirrs
archer-fish
acefhilpst
felspathic
acefhilrtu
ultrafiche
acefhinott
fianchetto
acefhinrrs
franchiser
acefhirrsv
fish-carver

acefhllnop
chopfallen
acefhlopry
hyperfocal
acefhlopsw
wolf's-peach
acefhorrtv
hovercraft
acefhorstu
housecraft
acefiiilnn
filicinean
acefiiilst
facilities
acefiilnru
Luciferian
acefiilorr
calorifier
acefiilpst
spiflicate
acefiilrss
classifier
acefiinrst
sanctifier
acefikllns
sick-fallen
acefiklnps
clasp-knife
acefilnors
forinsecal
acefilnost
self-action
acefilntuu
funiculate
acefiloosu
foliaceous
acefilrssy
reclassify
acefimnoss
Neofascism
acefinorrt
refraction
acefinortv
vociferant
acefinosst
Neofascist
acefinrsst
craftiness
acefirrrtv
river-craft
acefirrttu
trifurcate
acefklnors
cornflakes
acefkloppr
flock-paper
acefllnoor
once-for-all
acefllntuy
flatulency
aceflnoors
sore-falcon
acefloostv
calves'-foot
aceflrssuu
saucerfuls
acefnoprtt
Pontefract
aceforrrty
refractory
acegghilnn
changeling
acegghiopr
geographic
acegghloou
cholagogue
aceggilloo
geological
acegginnoo
ocean-going
acegginnsv
scavenging
acegginrss
cragginess
aceggnnort
congregant
aceghhijkr
highjacker
aceghhinot
high-octane
aceghhloor
hog-cholera
aceghhoprt
hectograph
aceghiilmt
megalithic
aceghiinrs
cashiering
aceghiippr
epigraphic
aceghilmpt
phlegmatic
aceghilpsy
hypalgesic
aceghilrtt
tight-lacer
aceghilrtu
theurgical
aceghimnnu
machine-gun
aceghimnop
phenogamic
aceghimprs
graphemics
aceghinnnt
enchanting
aceghinopt
pathogenic
aceghinrtt
chattering
aceghioops
hagioscope
aceghirstw
switchgear
aceghloory
archeology
aceghoprry
cerography
aceghoprtv
vectograph
aceghortuv
overcaught
aceghrrrsu
surcharger
acegiillst
legalistic
acegiilmty
legitimacy
acegiilnno
lignocaine
acegiimost
isogametic
acegiimptt
pegmatitic
acegiinnrs
increasing
acegiinort
iatrogenic
acegiiottv
cogitative
acegiiprst
epigastric
acegiirrst
geriatrics
acegiklnns
slackening
acegikmrty
kerygmatic
acegillnoo
neological
acegillnpr
parcelling
acegilloos
oligoclase
acegillprt
parcel-gilt
acegilmnny
menacingly
acegilmnor
camerlingo
acegilmrss
melic-grass
acegilnnor
iron-glance
acegilnnot
congenital
acegilnoop
geoponical
acegilnopy
clay-pigeon
acegilnotu
glauconite
acegilnppr
clappering
acegilnqru
lacquering
acegilnrry
gyre-carlin
acegiloopt
apologetic
acegimmmno
mammogenic
acegimmrrs
scrimmager
acegimorst
gasometric
aceginnnrt
entrancing
aceginnoru
guinea-corn
aceginnost
costeaning
aceginnrtu
uncreating
aceginnstt
casting-net
aceginntux
unexacting
aceginoprs
saprogenic
aceginrstt
scattering
acegiorstt
categorist
acegiosstt
geostatics
acegirsstt
strategics
acegkmnoor
mock-orange
acegknorrt
garnet-rock
acegkorstu
goatsucker
aceglmosuu
glumaceous
aceglnoooy
oceanology
acegloprt
colportage
acegloopsy
escapology
aceglootuy
autecology
acegloprs
scrog-apple
acegmmrrsu
scrummager
acegmnoorr
Greco-Roman
acegnnorst
scent-organ
acegnnortw
crown-agent
acegnnpruy
repugnancy
acegnoorsu
acrogenous
acegnoorty
octogenary
acegnrssuy
assurgency
acegnrsttu
scatter-gun
acegooprrt
proctorage
acegoorsuu
courageous
acegoprrsu
supercargo
acegprrstu
gut-scraper
acehhilopt
Achitophel
acehhiltwz
witch-hazel
acehhimpss
sachemship
acehhinopt
theophanic
acehhinort
rhinotheca
acehhirrst
Reichsrath
acehhkllns
chank-shell
acehhlsstt
thatchless
acehhorstu
charthouse
acehhostuw
watch-house
acehiillpt
philatelic
acehiilmos
isocheimal
acehiilmpt
mephitical
acehiilmrt
hermitical
acehiilnno
Heliconian
acehiilnpr
hair-pencil
acehiilnst
Cisleithan
acehiilpst
cephalitis
acehiilstt
theistical
acehiilstu
halieutics
acehiimmns
Manicheism
acehiimrtt
arithmetic
acehiinnop
Phoenician
acehiinnrt
Cerinthian
interchain
acehiinort
anti-heroic
acehiinotv
inchoative
acehiinttt
antithetic
acehiiopst
teichopsia

acehiirstt
tracheitis
acehiklnss
chalkiness
acehikmnos
chain-smoke
acehikmrrs
reichsmark
acehikppst
packet-ship
acehillmsz
schlimazel
acehillnty
ethnically
acehilloos
alcoholise
acehillory
heroically
acehilltty
thetically
acehilmmst
mischmetal
acehilmoop
phocomelia
acehilmoty
haemolytic
acehilnopt
phonetical
acehilnopu
euphonical
acehilnort
chlorinate
acehilnoru
unheroical
acehilnoty
inchoately
acehilnsst
schalstein
acehiloorz
coleorhiza
acehilootz
zoothecial
acehiloprt
arctophile
cartophile
acehilorrt
rhetorical
acehilrsty
hysterical
acehilssst
scaithless
acehimmsst
schematism
acehimnnor
enharmonic
acehimnopt
phonematic
acehimnors
monarchise
acehimnoru
euharmonic
acehimnory
hieromancy

acehimnott
theomantic
acehimnptu
unemphatic
acehimnrst
mischanter
acehimnrsv
revanchism
acehimnsty
myasthenic
acehimoprt
amphoteric
metaphoric
acehimoptu
apothecium
acehimopxy
hypoxaemic
acehimostx
chemotaxis
acehimpsty
metaphysic
acehimrstt
chrematist
acehimsstt
schematist
acehinoort
orthocaine
acehinopss
poachiness
acehinoptt
heptatonic
acehinorrt
chitarrone
acehinorst
chain-store
acehinortv
chevrotain
acehinpstt
pentastich
acehinpstu
epicanthus
acehinpttu
unpathetic
acehinrstv
revanchist
acehioprrt
Chiroptera
acehioprsx
echopraxis
acehiopsst
postchaise
acehippstt
pettichaps
acehiprrst
arch-priest
acehiprssu
haruspices
acehiprstu
curateship
pasticheur
acehiprstw
pear-switch
acehiprsty
psychiater

acehiprttu
picture-hat
acehiqrrsu
squirearch
acehirrrty
trierarchy
acehirsttt
tetrastich
acehirsttv
tsarevitch
acehirttww
water-witch
acehjknnoy
Johnny-cake
acehjrrsuw
jaw-crusher
acehklmmor
hammerlock
acehklnntz
lanzknecht
acehklnost
chalkstone
shecklaton
acehllmnoy
melancholy
acehllnors
acorn-shell
acehllosty
shellycoat
acehllprsu
sepulchral
acehlmmoru
chrome-alum
acehlmnoot
monothecal
acehlmoost
school-mate
acehlmorsy
lachrymose
acehlnoops
Sophoclean
acehlnorss
anchorless
acehlnorst
Charleston
acehlnoruv
overlaunch
acehlnssst
stanchless
acehlnstuy
unchastely
acehloorst
orthoclase
acehlopprt
paper-cloth
acehlopttu
touch-plate
acehlorrst
orchestral
acehlprtyy
phylactery
acehmnnsuu
Munchausen

acehmnorst
march-stone
acehmnosty
chemonasty
acehmnotuv
avouchment
acehmnprty
parchmenty
acehmnrrty
merchantry
acehmoprtt
carpet-moth
acehmoprty
chromatype
acehmorrtu
route-march
acehmortty
tachometry
acehmrttyy
tachymetry
acehnnortt
contrahent
acehnnssst
stanchness
acehnooprt
Ctenophora
acehnoprsu
canephorus
acehnorrtt
trochanter
acehnprstt
stench-trap
acehnrsstu
chauntress
acehnsstuw
cashew-nuts
acehoopprr
carpophore
acehoopstu
tophaceous
acehoorrst
Orthoceras
acehopprtu
touch-paper
acehoprsuy
coryphaeus
acehopstuy
typhaceous
acehorttww
watch-tower
acehppstty
pettychaps
aceiiiknst
ekistician
aceiiilmss
Islamicise
aceiiilrst
Israelitic
aceiiinttv
incitative
aceiijlstu
Jesuitical
aceiikmnst
kinematics

aceiikrstt
rickettsia
aceiilllpt
elliptical
aceiillnpr
periclinal
aceiillnry
irenically
aceiillosu
liliaceous
aceiillrty
illiteracy
aceiillstt
satellitic
aceiilmmst
melismatic
aceiilmnst
melanistic
aceiilmnsu
semi-uncial
aceiilmopt
epitomical
aceiilmpss
specialism
aceiilnnrt
encrinital
aceiilnopt
capitoline
aceiilnorv
arvicoline
aceiilnosx
saxicoline
aceiilnott
actinolite
aceiilnpst
Plasticine
aceiilntvy
inactively
aceiilostu
tiliaceous
aceiilpprt
participle
aceiilprtt
triplicate
aceiilpsst
plasticise
specialist
aceiilpsty
speciality
aceiilrsss
scleriasis
aceiilstty
elasticity
aceiimnort
Marcionite
aceiimnpst
emancipist
aceiimnrru
cinerarium
aceiimnrsu
musicianer
aceiimottv
comitative

aceiimpsst
  asepticism
aceiinnntv
  Vincentian
aceiinnort
  cineration
aceiinnqru
  quinacrine
aceiinnrty
  itinerancy
aceiinopst
  speciation
aceiinortt
  recitation
aceiinostv
  vesication
aceiinottx
  excitation
  intoxicate
aceiinpprt
  principate
aceiinpstt
  antiseptic
  psittacine
aceiinrtvy
  inveracity
aceiinsttu
  austenitic
aceiiorrrt
  certiorari
aceiiorttv
  recitativo
aceiippsst
  epispastic
aceiirrssu
  cuirassier
aceiirsttv
  astrictive
aceiirttvy
  creativity
  reactivity
aceiisssty
  essayistic
aceijkmntu
  minute-jack
aceijkprst
  jack-priest
aceijnortt
  trajection
aceikknnss
  knackiness
aceiklrstv
  travel-sick
aceikmnopt
  pockmantie
aceiknnrss
  crankiness
aceiknpttw
  pawnticket
aceikortuy
  eukaryotic
aceikqrtuw
  quick-water

aceilllopw
  lace-pillow
  pillow-lace
aceilllpru
  pellicular
aceillmnsy
  miscellany
aceillmptu
  capitellum
aceillmrty
  metrically
aceillnnno
  cannelloni
aceillnoot
  ocellation
aceillnort
  citronella
aceillnrtu
  lenticular
aceillopsw
  pillowcase
aceillopty
  poetically
aceilloqtu
  colliquate
aceillorst
  sclerotial
aceillortv
  vorticella
aceillosty
  societally
aceillpruy
  peculiarly
aceillpsty
  septically
aceillrtuv
  victualler
aceillrtvy
  vertically
aceilmmnno
  mnemonical
aceilmmnss
  clamminess
aceilmnopr
  complainer
aceilmnors
  sermonical
aceilmnrst
  centralism
aceilmnrtu
  unmetrical
aceilmnruw
  lawrencium
aceilmoprr
  proclaimer
aceilmoprt
  pleromatic
aceilmrruv
  vermicular
aceilmrssu
  secularism
aceilmtuuv
  cumulative

aceilnnoop
  Napoleonic
aceilnnotu
  nucleation
aceilnnrtu
  unicentral
aceilnnruu
  uninuclear
aceilnoort
  co-relation
  iconolater
  relocation
aceilnooru
  Eriocaulon
aceilnoprt
  pratincole
aceilnopst
  neoplastic
  pleonastic
aceilnoptu
  peculation
  unpoetical
aceilnopty
  polyactine
aceilnortu
  ulceration
aceilnorty
  lectionary
aceilnosss
  socialness
aceilnostu
  inosculate
aceilnotuv
  novaculite
aceilnppsu
  suppliance
aceilnrstt
  centralist
aceilnrstu
  lacustrine
aceilnrtty
  centrality
aceilnrtvy
  trivalency
aceilnruux
  luxuriance
aceilooprt
  laeotropic
aceiloosuv
  olivaceous
  violaceous
aceiloppr s
  sapropelic
aceilopprt
  police-trap
aceiloprtx
  explicator
aceiloptuv
  copulative
aceiloqtuy
  coequality
aceilppstu
  supplicate

aceilprtuu
  apiculture
aceilrrsuv
  versicular
aceilrrtuy
  reticulary
aceilrsstu
  secularist
aceilrsttu
  testicular
  trisulcate
aceilrstuy
  secularity
aceilrtuuv
  aviculture
aceimmnort
  manometric
aceimmrsty
  asymmetric
aceimnnost
  cismontane
aceimnnruy
  innumeracy
aceimnoprt
  importance
aceimnoptt
  Camptonite
  pentatomic
aceimnorsu
  main-course
aceimnoruy
  aureomycin
aceimnpprs
  panspermic
aceimnpstu
  pneumatics
aceimnqttu
  acquitment
aceimoopst
  Compositae
aceimopppt
  apopemptic
aceimorrst
  miscreator
aceimorrtt
  meritocrat
aceimorrtu
  acroterium
aceimorsst
  Massoretic
aceimorttu
  tautomeric
aceimosttt
  totemastic
aceimpprsu
  music-paper
aceimrstuw
  water-music
aceimsstty
  systematic
aceinnnosu
  uncanonise
  unisonance

aceinnoort
  incoronate
  nero-antico
aceinnoptt
  pentatonic
aceinnorsu
  sea-unicorn
aceinnortu
  enunciator
aceinnottu
  continuate
aceinnrrsu
  insurancer
aceinnrsty
  transiency
aceinnrtuu
  nunciature
aceinnssst
  scantiness
aceinnsstt
  intactness
aceinoorrt
  acroterion
aceinoortv
  revocation
aceinoppst
  episcopant
aceinoprtu
  precaution
aceinoprty
  capernoity
aceinopssu
  spinaceous
aceinopstt
  constipate
  costean-pit
aceinorrtt
  retraction
  triaconter
aceinorssy
  cessionary
aceinorstu
  recusation
aceinorttu
  eructation
aceinorttx
  extraction
aceinosttu
  unicostate
aceinosttv
  constative
aceinpssuu
  puissaunce
aceinpstuu
  usucapient
aceinrsttu
  scaturient
aceinrsuvv
  survivance
aceinrtuvy
  unveracity
aceinssstt
  scattiness

aceiooprrt
aerotropic
aceiooprtz
azeotropic
aceiooptv
co-optative
aceioorttu
autoerotic
aceioprrsu
precarious
aceioqssuu
sequacious
aceiorsttt
tricostate
aceiorstvy
vesicatory
aceiorttxy
excitatory
aceipprstt
tapescript
aceiprrstu
crispature
aceiprsttu
tricuspate
aceiprsttx
spectatrix
aceirrstuw
rustic-ware
acejorrtty
trajectory
acekkmosst
smoke-stack
acekllortw
wall-rocket
acekllrstu
lack-lustre
aceklnopst
alpenstock
acekloprw
wool-packer
acekmnorrw
canker-worm
acekopssst
sack-posset
acekprrssy
skyscraper
acellmnotu
loculament
acelloost
osteocolla
acelloprty
pectorally
acellopstu
leucoplast
acellopsty
closet-play
acelloptuy
eucalyptol
acellorrty
trolley-car
acellorssw
lower-class
acellorsux
sexlocular

acellprsty
spectrally
acellssty
tactlessly
acelmmnoow
commonweal
acelmnnott
malcontent
acelmnttuu
tentaculum
acelnnoott
notonectal
acelnnossu
consensual
acelnnotuv
conventual
acelnoprru
pronuclear
acelnoprsy
narcolepsy
acelnoprtx
contraplex
acelnopsty
nyctalopes
acelnorrty
necrolatry
acelnottux
contextual
acelnpttuu
punctulate
acelnrttuy
truncately
acelooprrt
coal-porter
percolator
aceloosstt
osteoclast
aceloprstu
speculator
aceloprswy
cow-parsley
acelopstuu
pultaceous
acelorrsty
clear-story
acelpprssu
upper-class
acelprsssu
superclass
acelpstuuy
eucalyptus
acemmnorty
commentary
acemmnostu
consummate
acemmostty
mastectomy
acemnnnott
cantonment
acemnnorst
monstrance
acemnooprt
montero-cap

acemnootyz
mycetozoan
acemnostty
nematocyst
acemooprrs
macrospore
acemoorstu
octamerous
acemorstuy
myrtaceous
acennoortu
onocentaur
acennoortv
covenantor
acennorstv
conservant
conversant
acennosttt
contestant
acenooppst
pantoscope
acenooprvy
overcanopy
acenoorrsz
scorzonera
acenopprry
pyrenocarp
acenoprrty
copartnery
acenprsstu
percussant
acenrssttu
tersanctus
aceoooprrt
co-operator
cooperator
aceoopprst
Psocoptera
aceooprrrt
procreator
aceooprrsu
porraceous
aceooprrty
procaryote
aceoopsstt
statoscope
aceoorrtvy
revocatory
aceoorsstu
ostraceous
aceorrrsty
stercorary
aceorstuxy
excusatory
acffghilny
chaffingly
acffgiikmn
mafficking
acffgiilnt
afflicting
acffhnrstu
churn-staff
acffhorstt
torch-staff

acffiilloy
officially
acffiilnno
coffin-nail
acffiilnot
affliction
acffiilnou
unofficial
acffiiloty
officialty
acffiioort
officiator
acffillnuy
fancifully
acffoprsst
staff-corps
acfforssst
cross-staff
acfghilnnu
flaunching
acfghmorrs
frog's-march
acfgiilnry
clarifying
acfgiinrsy
scarifying
acfgilopry
profligacy
acfginoort
foot-racing
acfgnorrtw
crown-graft
acfhilnopr
francophil
acfhimorty
cyathiform
acfhimrstt
smithcraft
acfhioprst
factorship
acfhlltuwy
watchfully
acfhlmostu
stomachful
acfhlntuuw
unwatchful
acfhooprrs
crash-proof
acfiiilmst
familistic
acfiiilnty
finicality
acfiillopr
prolifical
acfiilmmor
limaciform
acfiilnopt
pontifical
acfiinnors
infrasonic
acfiinnort
infarction
infraction

acfiinostt
factionist
acfiiosttu
factitious
acfijnorst
scarf-joint
acfillloru
follicular
acfilloruy
cauliflory
acfilnnoot
conflation
acfilnnotu
functional
acfilostuy
factiously
acfilrssst
first-class
acfinnstuy
unsanctify
acfinoorrt
fornicator
acfinoorsu
facinorous
acflnrruuu
furuncular
acfloorstu
colour-fast
acggilnrs
scraggling
acgghhirwy
Whiggarchy
acgghiiloo
hagiologic
acgghinnnu
unchanging
acgghinopy
hypnagogic
acgghinott
chittagong
acggiillot
Glagolitic
acggiilnno
ganglionic
acggillnny
glancingly
acggillooy
glaciology
acggimosty
mystagogic
acghhiinrt
night-chair
acghhilntt
night-latch
acghhilttw
watch-light
acghhinttw
night-watch
watch-night
acghhioprr
chirograph
acghhorsyy
hygrochasy

acghiiknrs
king's-chair
acghiinpsw
wishing-cap
acghiioppx
xiphopagic
acghiknnor
king-archon
acghiknops
hopsacking
acghilmnry
charmingly
acghilnsty
scathingly
acghiloopt
pathologic
acghimnnop
champignon
acghimnnru
uncharming
acghimoprr
micrograph
acghimopry
myographic
acghinnorr
anchor-ring
acghinnptu
hunting-cap
acghinnttu
hunting-cat
acghinoorr
choir-organ
acghinoprt
prognathic
acghinoprz
zincograph
acghiooprr
orographic
acghiooprz
zoographic
acghiopprt
pictograph
acghioprru
urographic
acghirrttw
cartwright
acghllosst
glass-cloth
acghloopry
carphology
acghmmoorr
chromogram
acghmnoorr
chronogram
acghmoprsy
psychogram
acghnoopyy
onychopagy
acghoopprу
coprophagy
acgiikkmns
sick-making
acgiikllpr
pilgarlick

acgiillost
logistical
acgiilloty
logicality
acgiillrtu
liturgical
acgiilnoor
air-cooling
acgiilnosu
caliginous
acgiilnpuu
Pinguicula
acgiilnrtu
granulitic
acgiilnrty
laryngitic
acgiimmrrt
trigrammic
acgiimnors
organicism
acgiimnrst
scintigram
acgiinnott
incogitant
acgiinoott
cogitation
acgiinorst
organicist
acgiinosst
agonistics
acgiinprst
practising
acgiinqttu
acquitting
acgiiorsty
graciosity
acgijkknsy
skyjacking
acgikkmnru
muck-raking
acgikqrssu
quick-grass
acgillmooy
myological
acgillooor
orological
acgilloooz
zoological
acgillooru
urological
acgillopry
pyrogallic
acgillrsuy
surgically
acgilmnnoo
cognominal
gnomonical
acgilmosty
clistogamy
acgilnnpry
prancingly
acgilnoory
craniology

acgilnopss
Panglossic
acgilnppsu
sapling-cup
acgiloorst
astrologic
acgiloottu
tautologic
acgilorsuu
glucosuria
acgilorsuy
glycosuria
graciously
acgilosuvy
Yugoslavic
acgimnnopy
companying
acgimnnory
nigromancy
acgimnopss
compassing
acgimooprt
gamotropic
acginnorry
carrying-on
acginoostu
contagious
acginopsuu
pugnacious
acginorrtu
touring-car
acginorsuu
ungracious
acginpprtu
parting-cup
acginprrst
spring-cart
acgiorstty
gyrostatic
acgjllnouy
conjugally
acgjlnnouu
unconjugal
acglnoorsu
clangorous
acglnorssw
crown-glass
acgmoprrty
cryptogram
acgmoprtyy
cryptogamy
acgnnoppuy
oppugnancy
acgoorrrtu
corrugator
achhiilpst
phthisical
achhiiprtu
hupaithric
achhilmopt
ophthalmic
achhilmrty
rhythmical

achhilopty
halophytic
achhimrrty
arrhythmic
achhinnott
Antichthon
achhinoprs
archonship
achhioppst
phosphatic
achhnoottu
autochthon
achhnoprsy
chrysophan
achhoppsty
psychopath
achiiimrty
Himyaritic
achiiipprt
hippiatric
achiiirsst
trichiasis
achiiisstv
Shivaistic
achiijknrs
jinricksha
achiiklnny
kinchin-lay
achiillmps
phallicism
achiilnopt
notaphilic
achiiloopr
ciliophora
achiilorst
historical
achiimnnor
inharmonic
achiimnstu
humanistic
achiimnsuv
chauvinism
achiimoppp
hippocampi
achiinnoot
inchoation
achiinnopt
antiphonic
achiinnort
Corinthian
achiinnpqu
chinquapin
achiinorst
sticharion
achiinorsu
air-cushion
achiinpsuy
picayunish
achiinrstt
Antichrist
achiinstuv
chauvinist
achiioprst
aphoristic

achijkkswy
whisky-jack
achijmnott
match-joint
achikknprs
shrinkpack
achikloorw
workaholic
achiklprsy
prickly-ash
achikmnost
mackintosh
achikmnrss
scrimshank
achillmoos
alcoholism
achillmors
chloralism
achillmtyy
mythically
achillnnsy
clannishly
achillnoop
allophonic
achillooyz
hylozoical
achilloprt
prothallic
achillopsy
sophically
achillostt
lithoclast
achillpsyy
physically
achilmnoty
lithomancy
achilmopty
polymathic
achilmoryz
mycorhizal
achilmpssy
scampishly
achilmrttu
thalictrum
achilnoors
isochronal
achilnossy
anchylosis
achiloppsy
polyphasic
achiloprty
cartophily
achilorsuv
chivalrous
achilosttw
waistcloth
achimmnors
monarchism
achimmoopr
Commiphora
achimnnoor
harmonicon
achimnoops
monophasic

achimnopty
Amphictyon
achimnorst
monarchist
achimorrtt
trichromat
achimorryz
mycorrhiza
achimrssty
Christmasy
achinsttuy
unchastity
achioopsty
sociopathy
achioprsty
physiocrat
achiopstty
hypostatic
achiprstyy
psychiatry
achiqrrsuy
squirarchy
achirsttww
wrist-watch
achklmorss
marshlocks
achlllloyy
allycholly
achlloopsy
playschool
achlmmoors
school-marm
achlmnoruu
homuncular
achlnnorsy
synchronal
achlooostu
acolouthos
achloorsuw
colour-wash
achmoosstu
stomachous
achmossuyy
Hyoscyamus
achnnnoost
cannon-shot
achnnorsyy
asynchrony
achnoooprv
onychopora
achnoopprv
apocryphon
achoorsstt
short-coats
aciiiilmst
Ismailitic
aciiillmnp
Ampicillin®
aciiillmny
inimically
aciiilmort
miarolitic
aciiilmsst
Islamicist

aciiilnopt
politician
aciiilnors
incisorial
aciiilnppr
principial
aciiilnpst
sincipital
aciiilsttv
vitalistic
aciiimnstv
anticivism
aciiinnott
incitation
aciiinrstt
inartistic
aciiinsttv
nativistic
aciiinttvy
inactivity
aciijlrstu
juristical
aciijrstuy
justiciary
aciiknnnpy
pickaninny
aciiknrsst
Sanskritic
aciiillmnry
criminally
aciiillnnos
Scillonian
aciiillnors
nicrosilal
aciiillnory
ironically
aciiillrtty
tritically
aciiilmnors
consimilar
aciiilmnost
monistical
aciiilmnrty
matricliny
aciiilmnsuy
musicianly
aciiilmorst
moralistic
aciiilmstuy
musicality
aciiilnoort
lorication
aciiilnoprv
provincial
aciiilnortt
tinctorial
aciiilnostt
solicitant
aciiilnotxy
anxiolytic
aciiilnprty
patricliny
aciiiloortv
variolotic

aciiloprst
poristical
aciiloptty
topicality
aciilossuv
lascivious
aciilprstu
puristical
aciilpstty
plasticity
aciilpttyy
typicality
aciilrsttu
altruistic
aciilrttty
tractility
aciimmnopt
pantomimic
aciimmnstu
numismatic
aciimnorst
Marcionist
Romanistic
aciimnptty
tympanitic
aciimnrsss
narcissism
aciimnrstu
manicurist
aciimoprss
prosaicism
aciimoprst
porismatic
aciinnootv
invocation
aciinnostu
insouciant
aciinnottx
intoxicant
aciinoostt
oscitation
aciinoottx
toxication
aciinoprst
ascription
crispation
aciinoprtt
tritanopic
aciinopstu
ancipitous
aciinorstt
astriction
aciinorttu
urtication
aciinostuu
incautious
aciinrssst
narcissist
aciinrsttu
naturistic
unartistic
aciioprrst
scriptoria

aciiopssuu
auspicious
aciiorstvy
varicosity
aciiprsstt
patristics
aciipsstty
spasticity
aciiqrttuz
quartzitic
acijlortuy
jocularity
acikklmnor
Kilmarnock
aciklmrttu
multi-track
aciklnnopt
planktonic
acilllnooy
colonially
acilllooqu
colloquial
acillmnnoo
monoclinal
acillmoort
collimator
acillmotuv
multivocal
acillmstyy
mystically
acillnootu
allocution
acillnopst
splint-coal
acillnoqtu
colliquant
acillnoruu
unilocular
acillnoruv
involucral
acillnosuy
unsocially
acillnouvy
univocally
acillooprt
allotropic
acilloorst
oscillator
acilloorux
uxorilocal
acilloprty
tropically
acillorrtu
trilocular
acillortvy
vortically
acillrstuy
rustically
acilmmoors
microsomal
acilmmrsuu
simulacrum
acilmnooos
nosocomial

acilmnorty
matrocliny
acilmnosuu
calumnious
acilmnotuu
cumulation
acilmnrsuu
minuscular
acilmnstuy
stimulancy
acilmoootz
zootomical
acilmooprt
compilator
acilmoopty
polyatomic
acilmoprry
micropylar
acilmopsty
polymastic
acilmorsuu
miraculous
acilmprsuu
spiraculum
acilnnpsuu
panniculus
acilnooort
coloration
acilnooprr
incorporal
acilnooptu
copulation
acilnoopxy
polyaxonic
acilnoopzz
pozzolanic
acilnoortu
inoculator
acilnoorty
iconolatry
acilnoostu
osculation
acilnoottt
cottontail
acilnoprty
patrocliny
acilnopsty
synoptical
acilnorrty
contrarily
acilnorstu
ultrasonic
acilnostty
oscitantly
acilnppstu
supplicant
acilnrttuy
taciturnly
acilnruuxy
luxuriancy
aciloopprrt
proctorial
aciloopstz
zooplastic

acilooqsuu
loquacious
aciloossux
saxicolous
acilopprsu
Pilocarpus
acilopssuy
spaciously
acilopstty
calotypist
acilopstuy
captiously
acilorrtuv
vorticular
acilorttuv
cultivator
acilostuuy
cautiously
acilpptuvy
pulp-cavity
acilprrstu
scriptural
acimmnopss
pancosmism
acimmnorty
matronymic
acimmoprrs
macroprism
acimmorssy
commissary
acimnnoory
oniromancy
acimnnortu
unromantic
acimnnosty
sanctimony
acimnooprs
comparison
acimnoopss
compassion
acimnoorst
astronomic
acimnoorty
craniotomy
acimnoosst
onomastics
acimnoostu
autonomics
acimnoprty
importancy
patronymic
pyromantic
acimnprstu
manuscript
acimooprtt
compatriot
acimoortvy
varicotomy
acimopstty
asymptotic
acinnnostt
inconstant
acinnnottu
continuant

acinnooort
coronation
acinnooppt
panopticon
acinnoprst
conspirant
acinnopttu
punctation
acinnorsst
transonics
trans-sonic
acinnorstt
constraint
acinnorttu
truncation
acinnsttyy
nyctinasty
acinoooptt
co-optation
acinoopprt
protanopic
acinoorstt
cartoonist
acinoorstu
octonarius
acinoortvy
invocatory
acinopprsw
cow-parsnip
acinopstuu
usucaption
acinorsttu
crustation
acinprrstt
transcript
acioorrsst
cross-ratio
acioprstty
pyrostatic
aciorrsttu
rusticator
acjnoorrtu
conjurator
ackknrstuw
knackwurst
acklloorrw
collar-work
acklmnoors
rock-salmon
ackmorrstt
storm-track
ackooprsty
pastrycook
ackoqrrtuz
quartz-rock
aclllloorr
rollcollar
aclllrtuuy
culturally
acllmmnouy
communally
acllmrsuuy
muscularly

acllnptuuy
punctually
aclloopr ry
corporally
acllprstuu
sculptural
aclmmnooty
commonalty
aclmoorsty
cosmolatry
aclnnosttu
consultant
aclnnostty
constantly
aclnnostuv
convulsant
aclnnptuuu
unpunctual
aclnnrsuuu
ranunculus
aclnoorstt
contraltos
aclnoorsuy
canorously
aclnopstuy
postulancy
aclooprtuy
copulatory
acloorstuy
osculatory
acloorsuwy
colour-ways
aclrrsttuu
structural
acmmoorttu
commutator
acmnnortuy
countryman
acmnoorsuy
acronymous
acmnoosstw
Scotswoman
acmoooprtt
compotator
acmooprttu
computator
acnnnosttu
unconstant
acnoopprrt
contraprop
acnooprsty
syncopator
acnoprssuy
syncarpous
acnoprttuu
punctuator
acoooprrrt
corporator
acoooprrtv
provocator
acooprrrtt
protractor
acooprrrtu
procurator

adddeeehil
idle-headed
adddeeehnw
hand-weeded
adddeefhil
fiddlehead
adddeegilm
middle-aged
adddeehlmu
muddlehead
adddeehnru
dunderhead
adddeeilss
side-saddle
adddefilpy
paddy-field
adddeginwy
wedding-day
adddegnoru
dead-ground
adddeilnor
dendroidal
adddelloty
toddy-ladle
adddeloopw
paddle-wood
addeeeepst
deep-seated
addeeefhnr
free-handed
addeeefntu
undefeated
addeeeghry
grey-headed
addeeehnnv
even-handed
addeeehors
sore-headed
addeeeimnw
maidenweed
addeeeirst
desiderate
addeeelntt
dead-nettle
addeeelrst
saddle-tree
addeeelrtt
dead-letter
addeeennru
unendeared
addeefhlnt
left-handed
addeefhnor
forehanded
addeefhost
soft-headed
addeefmnor
fore-damned
addeefnrvy
dandy-fever
addeegghlu
head-lugged
addeeggins
disengaged

addeeghitw
dead-weight
addeeghlno
long-headed
addeeghprs
sharp-edged
addeegnrru
unregarded
addeegosss
sea-goddess
addeehllns
handselled
addeehlnru
unheralded
addeehnnop
open-handed
addeehnnru
unhardened
addeehnnss
handedness
addeehnoow
wooden-head
addeehnorv
overhanded
addeehnrtu
unthreaded
addeehrrty
dehydrater
addeeiimmx
mixed-media
addeeiinnr
dinanderie
addeeiinrt
ride-and-tie
addeeiipss
diapedesis
addeeikmnw
weak-minded
addeeilnss
deadliness
addeeilpss
displeased
addeeinnru
unindeared
addeeipprv
dive-dapper
addeeiprsw
widespread
addeejnruw
underjawed
addeekorst
dead-stroke
addeellsss
saddleless
addeelmnor
endodermal
addeelmnoy
almond-eyed
addeeloprr
rope-ladder
addeelorss
saddle-sore
addeelprst
step-ladder

addeelprvy
depravedly
addeemnnru
undernamed
addeemnorr
road-mender
addeennpux
unexpanded
addeennttu
unattended
addeenorru
round-eared
addeenorst
adderstone
addeenprtu
dunderpate
addeenpruv
undepraved
addeenqrsu
squandered
addeenrrss
red-sanders
addeenrrtu
unretarded
addeenrruw
unrewarded
addeeoprrt
depredator
addeeoprss
desperados
addeeprssy
pressed-day
addefhiins
dead-finish
addefhilrs
fish-ladder
addefhirst
hard-fisted
addefhllnu
full-handed
addefhnoru
four-handed
addefiiilp
lapidified
addefiimnr
fair-minded
addefilrsw
fieldwards
addeflloop
flapdoodle
addefllruy
dreadfully
addeflmnoy
many-folded
addefloors
saddle-roof
addeghhhin
high-handed
addeghiloo
goodlihead
addeghilst
dead-lights
addeghlooy
goodlyhead
addeghlort
gold-thread
addegiknnp
padding-ken
addeginnru
undreading
addegiorrs
dorsigrade
addegjmntu
adjudgment
addeglmnno
gold-end-man
addegmnorr
dendrogram
addegorssw
war-goddess
addegrrssu
dressguard
addehhilns
shield-hand
addehhprsu
hard-pushed
addehiilms
shield-maid
addehiilnp
didelphian
addehilnnr
hinderland
addehimnoo
maidenhood
addehinnor
iron-handed
addehioorr
drearihood
addehirsyz
hydrazides
addehknorw
handworked
addehllnor
landholder
addehlorst
stadholder
addehmnnow
hand-me-down
addehnorsy
dandy-horse
addehnosuw
unshadowed
addehnotuw
death-wound
addehorrty
dehydrator
addehorstt
short-dated
addeiiillsv
ill-advised
addeiiltvy
additively
addeiimssv
misadvised
addeiipsst
dissipated
addeilmtty
admittedly
addeimnrsw
miswandred
addeimnsuy
undismayed
addeimnttu
unadmitted
addeinnoru
unordained
addeinnotu
denudation
addeinnrru
underdrain
addeinoors
radiosonde
addeinrstu
disnatured
addeiprrsy
spray-dried
addejnstuu
unadjusted
addelmnopy
paddymelon
addelmoors
saddle-room
addelmorrw
dream-world
addelnnorw
wonderland
addelnoorw
woodlander
addennopru
unpardoned
addennpruu
up-and-under
addennrstu
understand
addenoqrsu
squadroned
addeorrstw
adder's-wort
addffilloy
daffodilly
addfiilnsu
disdainful
addfilmory
myriadfold
addghiinrr
hard-riding
addgillnwy
dawdlingly
addgilloss
dildo-glass
addgorrsuw
sword-guard
addhiilmos
old-maidish
addiiilnuv
individual
addiillnst
distilland
addiilmmos
old-maidism
addilllyy
dilly-dally
addimnosuy
didynamous
addlnorwwy
downwardly
addnnootuw
down-and-out
adeeeefhrt
feed-heater
adeeeegnrt
degenerate
adeeeehrtx
exheredate
adeeeelrtt
leaderette
adeeefikny
Yankeefied
adeeefillr
file-leader
adeeefilrs
federalise
adeeefirtv
federative
adeeeflorr
freeloader
adeeefrrrt
free-trader
adeeeggglt
gate-legged
adeeegglnr
near-legged
adeeeghnrs
shagreened
adeeegilmn
gleemaiden
adeeegknrr
green-drake
adeeeglrsv
Everglades
adeeegnnrr
endangerer
adeeehhnrt
hen-hearted
adeeehhpss
sheep's-head
adeeehilms
seemlihead
adeeehkllr
lark-heeled
adeeehlnsv
sleeve-hand
adeeehlpsy
sleepy-head
adeeehlrtt
letterhead
adeeehlrtw
tread-wheel
adeeehnrtt
threatened
adeeeikmmn
maiden-meek
adeeeinntv
Venetianed
adeeeinssv
seven-a-side
adeeeiorww
woewearied
adeeeiprrt
pied-à-terre
adeeeipttx
expeditate
adeeeirrtt
reiterated
adeeeirstt
Eastertide
adeeejkmrt
jerked-meat
adeeeknnuw
unweakened
adeeellmnp
empanelled
adeeellnrw
well-earned
adeeelnnss
leadenness
adeeelnnuv
unleavened
adeeelnpru
unrepealed
adeeelnrrt
randle-tree
adeeelnrsu
underlease
adeeelnrsw
newsdealer
adeeelnruv
unrevealed
adeeelnsst
elatedness
adeeelprty
repeatedly
adeeelrrtw
water-elder
adeeemnnrt
endearment
man-entered
adeeemoost
oedematose
adeeemprtt
attempered
adeeemrrst
streamered
adeeenprtt
predentate
adeeenprtu
unrepeated
adeeenrrsw
news-reader
adeeenrsss
searedness
adeeensst
sedateness
adeeepprwy
wapper-eyed
adeefflorru
four-leafed
adeefghiru
figurehead

adeefgllsz
self-glazed
adeefglnnw
newfangled
adeefglnrs
self-danger
adeefgmnrt
fragmented
adeefhiltw
wheat-field
adeefhlnrt
left-hander
adeefhlorw
flower-head
adeefhlrst
self-hatred
adeefhnrtu
unfathered
adeefillns
self-denial
adeefilmrs
federalism
adeefilrst
federalist
adeefilssu
diseaseful
adeefinnrr
ferrandine
adeefinort
federation
adeefinrrw
fire-warden
adeefiorsv
fore-advise
adeefiprtv
five-parted
adeefirstu
disfeature
adeeflllnn
flannelled
adeefllssy
fadelessly
adeefloruv
four-leaved
adeefmnorw
freedwoman
adeefmnrty
defrayment
adeefnnstu
unfastened
adeefnrtuu
unfeatured
adeefoprrt
perforated
adeeforstu
foederatus
adeegghhru
head-hugger
adeegghinr
nigger-head
adeegghlor
loggerhead
adeeggjnss
jaggedness

adeeggnrss
raggedness
adeeggnruy
gaudy-green
adeeghhirr
high-reared
adeeghiknw
weak-hinged
adeeghilrt
lethargied
adeeghimtw
wheat-midge
adeeghirry
grey-haired
adeeghnrru
eard-hunger
adeeghnrtu
ungathered
adeegiinss
diagenesis
adeegillrt
treillaged
adeegilnot
delegation
adeegilnrr
ringleader
adeegimnnr
meandering
adeegimort
diagometer
adeeginnot
denegation
adeeginrrt
gradienter
intergrade
adeegiortv
derogative
adeegllnos
golden-seal
adeegllnry
enlargedly
adeeglnort
goal-tender
adeeglnpru
plunderage
adeeglnruz
underglaze
adeeglnttu
gauntleted
adeeglorty
derogately
adeeglppry
dapple-grey
adeeglrrss
regardless
adeegmnort
dermatogen
adeegmnrss
gensdarmes
adeegnnrru
ungarnered
adeegnnrtu
underagent

adeegnorrs
rose-garden
adeegnorrt
dragon-tree
adeegnrrsw
greensward
adeegnrrtu
ungartered
adeegoorsv
overdosage
adeegoorsw
greasewood
adeegorrrt
retrograde
adeegorstu
uredo-stage
adeehhilmr
hemihedral
adeehhisst
dissheathe
adeehhlosv
shovel-head
adeehhmnot
heathendom
adeehhnorx
hexahedron
adeehhnpty
hyphenated
adeehhnrtu
headhunter
adeehhnstu
unsheathed
adeehhortt
death-throe
adeehiiktv
khediviate
adeehiillv
livelihead
adeehiilps
aedileship
adeehiirrw
wire-haired
adeehijknr
jerkinhead
adeehiklrs
shieldrake
adeehillov
lovelihead
adeehilmnr
mind-healer
adeehilmrw
dreamwhile
adeehilntu
heulandite
adeehilopp
paedophile
adeehilppr
hare-lipped
adeehilprs
dealership
leadership
adeehilsvy
adhesively

adeehilswy
daisy-wheel
adeehimnsu
dehumanise
adeehinrst
dishearten
adeehiprrs
readership
adeehirrss
sherardise
adeehirrty
hereditary
adeehjlort
jolterhead
adeehkllnt
death-knell
adeehkllrs
shelldrake
adeehknott
death-token
adeehkorrw
headworker
adeehllnrt
enthralled
adeehlnotw
down-at-heel
adeehlpuzz
puzzle-head
adeehmnpru
unhampered
adeehnnrtu
underneath
adeehnrrtu
underearth
adeehnrrtw
netherward
adeehnstvy
seventh-day
adeehooprt
Heteropoda
adeeiijnrr
jardinière
adeeiiklmn
maidenlike
adeeiilmtt
delimitate
adeeiilntv
evidential
adeeiilstv
devitalise
adeeiimnru
minauderie
adeeiimntv
vindemiate
adeeiimttv
meditative
adeeiinorv
Vireonidae
adeeiinrst
distrainee
adeeiinrvv
vivandière
adeeiinsst
dessiatine

adeeiirrvv
Viverridae
adeeiirttw
tide-waiter
adeeiirtvv
derivative
adeeijoprs
jeopardise
adeeiklmnn
kennel-maid
adeeiknrrt
dreikanter
tea-drinker
adeeikrsst
asterisked
adeeillmry
remedially
adeeillmvy
medievally
adeeillprs
espadrille
adeeillrru
dérailleur
adeeillsvv
slide-valve
adeeilluvv
vaudeville
adeeilmnpt
pedimental
adeeilmnrt
derailment
adeeilmors
demoralise
adeeilmoru
Lemuroidea
adeeilmprr
peridermal
adeeilmstu
Mustelidae
adeeilnntt
tendential
adeeilnntu
unentailed
adeeilnort
delineator
adeeilnprt
interplead
adeeilnrsu
unrealised
Uredinales
adeeilnrtu
adulterine
adeeilnssv
disenslave
adeeilnttt
dilettante
adeeilnttw
lean-witted
adeeiloppt
deoppilate
adeeiloprs
depolarise
adeeiloptt
petiolated

adeeilorss
sea-soldier
adeeilorsv
devalorise
adeeilprrv
pearl-diver
adeeilprst
pilastered
adeeilprtu
tulip-eared
adeeilrstu
adulterise
adeeimmnss
maimedness
adeeimmort
immoderate
adeeimmrsu
immeasured
adeeimnnot
denominate
emendation
adeeimnntt
detainment
adeeimnnux
unexamined
adeeimnprt
pandermite
adeeimnrrt
dreariment
adeeimnrrw
new-married
adeeimnrss
dreaminess
adeeimnstv
advisement
adeeimnstw
tandemwise
adeeimorrs
drearisome
adeeimorrt
radiometer
adeeimorrx
xerodermia
adeeimortu
audiometer
adeeimqrru
quadrireme
adeeimrsst
mediatress
adeeinoprt
Pontederia
adeeinortt
orientated
adeeinottv
denotative
adeeinppsx
appendixes
adeeinprru
unrepaired
adeeinprst
pedestrian
adeeinptux
unexpiated
adeeinrrss
dreariness
adeeinrrst
restrained
adeeinrstt
straitened
adeeinrstu
denaturise
adeeinrttt
tridentate
adeeinssst
steadiness
adeeinssty
dessyatine
adeeioprsx
peroxidase
adeeiprstt
tapestried
adeeiprtuv
depurative
adeeirrstv
advertiser
adeeirsstt
dissertate
adeejklnru
junk-dealer
adeekllmrw
well-marked
adeekmnrru
unremarked
adeekmrrss
dressmaker
adeeknnrtu
undertaken
adeeknorst
drakestone
adeeknrrtu
undertaker
adeellmmrt
trammelled
adeellmntu
unmetalled
adeellmtuv
datum-level
adeellnnpu
unpanelled
adeellnquu
unequalled
adeellnrss
sallenders
adeellnruv
unravelled
adeellorss
loss-leader
adeellosty
desolately
adeellqrru
quarrelled
adeelmnntu
unlamented
adeelmnort
almond-tree
adeelmnpux
unexampled
adeelmntzz
dazzlement
adeelmorty
moderately
adeelmrsuy
measuredly
adeelnnsuv
unenslaved
adeelnnttu
untalented
adeelnopru
endopleura
adeelnorrv
overlander
adeelnrruy
underlayer
adeelnruuv
undervalue
adeelopptu
depopulate
adeeloprss
leopardess
adeelorsww
weasel-word
adeelpprry
preparedly
adeelrrssw
rewardless
adeelrrstu
serrulated
adeelrsstu
adulteress
adeemnnnru
unmannered
adeemnnttt
attendment
adeemnoprr
promenader
adeemnorst
sordamente
adeemnorty
emendatory
adeemnoryy
ready-money
adeemnppru
unpampered
adeemnprtt
department
adeemnrrtt
retardment
adeemnrstu
unmastered
unstreamed
adeemnrsuu
unmeasured
adeemnsstu
sense-datum
adeemnstuu
mansuetude
adeemoostu
oedematous
adeemoprrt
Dermoptera
adeemorrvw
warmed-over
adeennnttu
untenanted
adeennopuw
unweaponed
adeennorsu
unreasoned
adeennossu
unseasoned
adeennprtt
pretendant
adeennprtu
unparented
adeennrsuw
unanswered
adeenoprst
personated
adeenorstw
down-easter
adeenpprru
unprepared
adeenpprss
dapperness
adeenprrtu
enraptured
adeenprsst
depressant
adeenprsty
present-day
adeenqrrru
quarrender
adeenqrrsu
squanderer
adeenrrtuv
adventurer
adeenrrtuw
underwater
adeenrsttu
understate
adeensttu
unattested
adeeoopstt
seed-potato
adeeoprrsv
overspread
spread-over
adeeoqrstu
square-toed
adeeorrrrt
rear-dorter
adeeorstwy
ready-to-sew
adeepqrttu
parquetted
adeerrsttw
street-ward
adeerrstyy
starry-eyed
adeerssstw
stewardess
adeffgggir
gaff-rigged
adeffghirt
affrighted
adeffloott
flat-footed
adefgginor
God-fearing
adefghirst
far-sighted
adefghoort
good-father
adefgiinor
Indigofera
adefgnoorr
roof-garden
adefhhoort
fatherhood
adefhilttw
half-witted
adefhinprt
pathfinder
adefhlttwy
twelfth-day
adefhmnotu
unfathomed
adefhoorsw
foreshadow
adefhorrst
draft-horse
adefiilnrs
flindersia
adefiinops
saponified
adefiinrtu
unratified
adefiirrst
first-aider
adefiirstt
stratified
adefiklort
fork-tailed
adefillry
all-firedly
adefilllsu
full-sailed
adefillnnw
windfallen
adefilmnnu
uninflamed
adefilmnor
manifolder
adefilnntu
uninflated
adefiloort
defoliator
adefilortu
fluoridate
adefilprsu
despairful
adefimmstu
deaf-mutism
adefinoorr
foreordain
adefklnotu
untalked-of

adefklorst
tradesfolk
adefllnnow
downfallen
adefllrtwy
leftwardly
adeflnrtuu
fraudulent
adefloortw
floodwater
water-flood
adefloprsy
self-parody
adeflorrtw
afterworld
adefnnopru
unprofaned
adefoprrtu
four-parted
adeforsstw
soft-sawder
adefrrsttu
frustrated
adegggilnr
laggen-gird
adegghilnr
hang-glider
adegghoott
gag-toothed
adegghoruy
hydragogue
adeggiinrs
niggardise
adeggimmos
demagogism
adeggimops
pedagogism
adeggiprsw
digger-wasp
adeggloors
sogdolager
adeggnoptu
get-up-and-go
adeghhiirs
high-raised
adeghhilnr
Highlander
adeghhinst
nightshade
adeghhistt
high-tasted
adeghiinps
Sphingidae
adeghilmrt
light-armed
adeghilnnr
rehandling
adeghilnor
long-haired
adeghilnsu
languished
adeghinprs
springhead
adeghiopry
ideography
adeghlnnru
land-hunger
adeghloopy
edaphology
adeghlorsw
gold-washer
adeghlrtuy
daughterly
adeghmopry
demography
adeghnorst
headstrong
adeghnortt
hard-gotten
adeghnrruy
eard-hungry
adeghnrttu
draught-net
adeghooptt
gap-toothed
adeghorsuu
guard-house
adegiiimns
disimagine
adegiillsu
seguidilla
adegiilmns
misleading
adegiilnot
deligation
gadolinite
gelatinoid
adegiilnpr
lip-reading
adegiilnrt
ring-tailed
adegiiltty
digitately
adegiimnnu
unimagined
adegiimnrs
misreading
adegiinprs
despairing
spinigrade
adegiinrtt
dirt-eating
adegiioprr
prairie-dog
adegiklnor
dragonlike
adegillnpy
pleadingly
adegillnyy
delayingly
adegilmnry
dreamingly
adegilnnno
non-aligned
adegilnnnt
landing-net
adegilnnrs
sanderling
adegilnnuy
undelaying
adegilnosy
agonisedly
adegilnppr
dapperling
adegilnrrr
errand-girl
adegilnrtt
glitterand
adegilnruv
gerundival
adegilorry
goliardery
adegilostw
slow-gaited
adegilrssw
wired-glass
adegimnnos
Mandingoes
adegimnnru
maundering
undreaming
adegimnopu
impoundage
adegimnors
gormandise
adegimopsu
pseudimago
adegimorst
dogmatiser
adeginnprw
drawing-pen
adeginnssu
unassigned
adeginoort
derogation
Trogonidae
adeginorrt
denigrator
adeginorrv
overdaring
adeginorst
designator
adeginprsw
wing-spread
adegiorrty
argyrodite
adegknrrru
Krugerrand
adegllmosy
gladsomely
adeglmorst
stream-gold
adeglnorsu
glanderous
adegloprsy
dog-parsley
adegmmoprr
programmed
adegmnnoor
gander-moon
adegmnnoyy
dynamogeny
adegmnoosu
endogamous
adegnooorw
orange-wood
adegnoopst
steganopod
adegnoortu
good-nature
adegnoprrs
sandgroper
adegnorssu
sand-grouse
adegooprst
gasteropod
adegoorrty
derogatory
adehhiiprt
diphtheria
adehhilnpw
whip-handle
adehhilprs
heraldship
adehhirrtw
hitherward
adehhirssw
dish-washer
adehhlloor
holohedral
adehhnoopr
rhodophane
adehhnopry
hydrophane
adehiilopu
audiophile
adehiilptw
whip-tailed
adehiimrtt
mithridate
adehiinnru
hirudinean
adehiinott
dithionate
adehiknnsw
wind-shaken
adehilllsw
shieldwall
adehillntw
thin-walled
adehilloru
loudhailer
adehilnnrs
hinderlans
adehilnnrt
hinterland
adehilnops
sphenoidal
adehilnort
threnodial
adehilnorz
endorhizal
adehilnrst
disenthral
adehiloprs
spheroidal
adehilpruy
hyperdulia
adehilpstu
disulphate
adehimnntu
minute-hand
adehimnory
Rhodymenia
adehimortu
rheumatoid
adehimsssw
Swadeshism
adehinoopr
radiophone
adehinosst
astonished
adehinprsw
wardenship
adehinpssu
dauphiness
adehinrsst
Sanhedrist
adehinrsuv
unravished
adehiooprt
orthopedia
adehioortw
waiterhood
adehioprrw
hair-powder
adehioprss
rhapsodise
adehirrtww
withdrawer
adehllmopr
lampholder
adehllnoor
loan-holder
adehllnouw
unhallowed
adehllopry
polyhedral
adehlmnort
enthraldom
mother-land
adehlmnosy
handsomely
adehlmnppu
pump-handle
adehlmopry
hypodermal
adehlnopry
hydroplane
adehlosssw
shadowless
adehlrttwy
thwartedly
adehmmnopr
hammer-pond
adehmmoprr
drop-hammer

adehmnnosu
unhandsome
adehmnottu
mutton-head
adehmoorst
masterhood
adehmorrtw
thread-worm
adehnooprr
androphore
adehnooprt
parenthood
adehnopprs
sand-hopper
adehnoprss
sharp-nosed
adehnorsux
hexandrous
adehooprty
orthopaedy
adehoorsvw
overshadow
adehoosttw
saw-toothed
adehorrssw
shorewards
adeiiillnt
initialled
adeiiimntt
intimidate
adeiiinnpp
Pinnipedia
adeiiinnpr
peridinian
adeiiinosz
isoniazide
adeiillmpx
maxilliped
adeiillptx
pixillated
adeiillrtv
vitrailled
adeiillstt
distillate
adeiilmmtu
multimedia
adeiilmnor
meridional
adeiilmnsu
unidealism
adeiilnnpr
dinner-pail
adeiilnopt
depilation
adeiilnort
deliration
adeiilnotv
inviolated
adeiilnrtt
intertidal
adeiilnttt
dilettanti
adeiilorst
idolatrise

adeiimnnot
antimonide
adeiimnott
meditation
adeiimnotv
admonitive
dominative
adeiimnpru
unimpaired
adeiimnrst
administer
adeiimprsu
praesidium
adeiimprtu
tepidarium
adeiimrstt
dermatitis
adeiinnnos
Indonesian
adeiinnort
inordinate
adeiinnotx
indexation
adeiinnotz
denization
adeiinnppt
pinnatiped
adeiinnrst
disentrain
adeiinnsst
daintiness
adeiinorst
sideration
adeiinortv
derivation
adeiinpttu
inaptitude
adeiinrrst
distrainer
adeiinrtuv
indurative
adeiinttuv
unvitiated
adeiiprrss
dispraiser
adeiiprrsy
presidiary
adeiiprttu
tripudiate
adeiirrtvx
taxi-driver
adeiisssuv
dissuasive
adeiisttvv
devastivit
adeijlnopt
lap-jointed
adeijmmnrw
windjammer
adeijopssu
jaspideous
adeiklllry
lady-killer

adeikllnuy
unladylike
adeiklnsty
litany-desk
adeillnoos
solenoidal
adeillnosu
delusional
adeillnpru
unpillared
adeillnpss
pallidness
adeillnrrt
tendrillar
adeillnrtu
ill-natured
adeillnruv
unrivalled
adeillpstu
plastidule
adeillqrru
quadriller
adeillrrst
ill-starred
adeilmnnor
molendinar
adeilmnnuy
unmaidenly
adeilmnopr
palindrome
adeilmnrtu
rudimental
adeilmnsss
dismalness
adeilmntvy
ivy-mantled
adeilmopss
psalmodise
adeilmpruu
praeludium
adeilnnort
internodal
adeilnnptu
pinnulated
adeilnoost
desolation
adeilnootv
devotional
adeilnoppt
pedal-point
pentaploid
adeilnorty
ordinately
adeilnotuv
unviolated
adeilnprtu
prudential
adeilnptuv
pulvinated
adeilnqtuu
unqualited
adeilnrsty
strainedly

adeilnsttu
testudinal
adeilnstuy
unsteadily
adeiloprtt
tetraploid
adeiloprty
depilatory
adeilopssu
disepalous
adeilopstu
dipetalous
adeilorsst
idolatress
adeilosstt
solid-state
adeilpppsu
pedipalpus
adeilrsttu
stridulate
adeilrttxy
dextrality
adeimmnntu
nidamentum
adeimmnrst
mastermind
adeimmnttu
manumitted
adeimmorst
moderatism
adeimnnort
ordainment
adeimnnotu
mountained
adeimnoors
moon-raised
adeimnoort
moderation
adeimnorrs
randomiser
adeimnorsw
randomwise
adeimnortw
woman-tired
adeimnprtu
unimparted
adeimnrrru
red-murrain
adeimnrsty
mistrayned
adeimorrtx
moderatrix
adeimorsst
dermatosis
adeimortuw
moudiewart
adeimortww
mowdiewart
adeimrtuuv
duumvirate
adeinnoott
denotation
detonation

adeinnopww
window-pane
adeinnortu
trade-union
adeinnrssw
inwardness
adeinnrstu
unstrained
adeinooprt
readoption
adeinoprtu
depuration
adeinopttu
deputation
adeinorsst
adroitness
adeinostww
window-seat
adeinpprsu
unapprised
adeinprsst
dispersant
adeinprssy
dispensary
adeinqrruu
unquarried
adeinrsstw
tawdriness
adeinrsttu
unstriated
adeinrttuw
twi-natured
adeinssstu
unassisted
adeiopprsv
disapprove
adeioprrtu
repudiator
adeioprsty
depositary
adeiorsstt
siderostat
adeipprrty
day-tripper
adeirsstwy
strideways
adejmnsttu
adjustment
adejooprsu
jeopardous
adeklnpsty
sky-planted
adekmnortw
down-market
adelllorss
dollarless
adellnopru
land-louper
adellnorru
all-rounder
adellnottu
unallotted
adellntuuy
undulately

adelloorrr
road-roller
adelmmntuu
nummulated
adelmmopss
plasmodesm
adelmnoort
tremolando
adelmnprtu
untrampled
adelmopstu
deutoplasm
adelnoprss
pardonless
adelnorssu
slanderous
adelnouvwy
unavowedly
adelnrstuw
wanderlust
adeloorsty
desolatory
adeloortwy
two-year-old
adelorrwwy
world-weary
adelorstuu
adulterous
adelpqrtuu
quadruplet
adelpqruux
quadruplex
adelrrstyy
drysaltery
adelrstwwy
westwardly
ademmmnoru
memorandum
ademmoostu
stomodaeum
ademnnorsu
unransomed
ademnoprst
pond-master
ademnorruu
unarmoured
ademnorstw
downstream
adennooprt
pteranodon
adennorrru
road-runner
adennprstu
underpants
adenoppruv
unapproved
adenorsstw
towardness
adenpprstu
unstrapped
adenprssuw
upwardness
adenprstuu
unpastured

adenrrsstw
sternwards
adenrttuwy
twy-natured
adeoprrtuy
depuratory
adeoqrrsuw
word-square
adffgimnop
damping-off
adffllruuy
fraudfully
adfghhortu
hard-fought
adfghinors
dragon-fish
adfghorrtu
rough-draft
adfgilmnor
glandiform
adfgilnnuy
unfadingly
adfginorru
fair-ground
adfginorrw
forwarding
adfgoorstu
foot-guards
adfhilrswy
dwarfishly
adfhinnoru
four-in-hand
adfiiilnos
solifidian
adfiiinnpt
pinnatifid
adfiilqsuy
disqualify
adfiiosstu
fastidious
adfiisssty
dissatisfy
adfillmnoy
manifoldly
adfilmorru
raduliform
adfilorsty
faldistory
adfimmnoor
monadiform
adfimoqrru
quadriform
adfinnootu
foundation
adfnoortuy
foudroyant
adfnorrstw
frontwards
adggginoru
gauging-rod
adgghintuy
gaudy-night
adggillrsy
Yggdrasill

adgginnoor
gadrooning
adghhiilos
hidalgoish
adghhoprry
hydrograph
adghiiillnn
dining-hall
adghiilmos
hidalgoism
adghiinrss
disgarnish
adghiioprt
graphitoid
adghikmrtu
khidmutgar
adghilnnst
Landsthing
adghimnopp
hopping-mad
adghinnprs
handspring
adghinrrtw
right-drawn
adghirrstw
rightwards
adghirsttu
distraught
adghllnopu
ploughland
adghlopruy
dray-plough
adghooprxy
doxography
adgiiilnnv
invaliding
adgiiinott
digitation
adgiiknnpp
kidnapping
adgiiknnrr
rank-riding
adgiilmnnn
land-mining
adgiilmnou
gadolinium
adgiilmnry
admiringly
adgiimnnru
unadmiring
adgiimnrsw
misdrawing
adgiinnprw
drawing-pin
adgiinrsst
distringas
adgiknorwy
working-day
adgillnrwy
drawlingly
adgillnyzz
dazzlingly
adgillopry
prodigally

adgilnnnow
land-owning
adgilnnprs
land-spring
adgilnntuu
undulating
adgimmnors
gormandism
adgimmnpuy
mumping-day
adgimnnrsy
gynandrism
adgimnosty
nystagmoid
adgimoopru
amido-group
adginnostu
astounding
adginnpstu
upstanding
adginoorst
goods-train
adginrrstw
draw-string
adgiorssww
grass-widow
adgllnosuu
glandulous
adglmnoooy
monadology
adglnnopru
groundplan
adglnopruy
playground
adgmnnorsu
groundsman
adgmnorssu
groundmass
adgnnorsuy
gynandrous
adgnooorrt
dragon-root
adgorrsssw
sword-grass
adhhillnos
Hollandish
adhhnooopr
orphanhood
adhhnosttu
thousandth
adhhoprtyy
hydropathy
adhiiilnsv
invalidish
adhiiilstt
Lithistida
adhiiillnop
phalloidin
adhiilnrst
disinthral
adhiimmnps
midshipman
adhiimnsst
hit-and-miss

adhiimsttu
humidistat
adhiinnstu
Hindustani
adhilloprs
dollarship
adhillpruw
uphillward
adhilnnoot
hand-lotion
adhilnopyy
hypolydian
adhilnostu
outlandish
adhiloprs
drosophila
adhilorsty
thyrsoidal
adhimnorsy
disharmony
adhimnotwy
Whit-Monday
adhinnooot
nationhood
adhinooprt
anthropoid
adhinoopry
hypodorian
radiophony
adhinoopss
soda-siphon
adhinossww
sash-window
window-sash
adhinstuwy
Whitsunday
adhioprsst
rhapsodist
adhioprsty
dystrophia
adhiorstxy
hydrotaxis
adhiprrtty
third-party
adhllnoowy
woolly-hand
adhllooppy
Phyllopoda
adhlmoorsy
hydrosomal
adhlnopssw
splashdown
adhmnooort
matronhood
adhnorrstw
northwards
adhoorrtwy
roadworthy
adhorsstuw
southwards
adiiilmnsv
invalidism
adiiilmrss
dissimilar

adiiilnosv
divisional
adiiilntvy
invalidity
adiiinnotv
divination
adiiinottv
tidivation
adiillorty
dilatorily
adiilmmnsu
maudlinism
adiilmnoxy
mixolydian
adiilmoprr
primordial
adiilmoprs
prismoidal
adiilmorss
solidarism
adiilnnotu
nidulation
adiilnorry
ordinarily
adiilnossu
sinusoidal
adiilnrstu
diurnalist
industrial
adiiloppsy
polydipsia
adiiloqrtu
liquidator
adiilorsst
solidarist
adiilorssy
radiolysis
adiilorsty
solidarity
adiilqstuy
squalidity
adiimmmotu
ommatidium
adiimnnoot
admonition
domination
adiimnopry
pyramidion
adiimnrsst
misandrist
adiimoprst
diatropism
adiimortuu
auditorium
adiimprsty
pyramidist
adiimqruuv
quadrivium
adiinnnotu
inundation
adiinnoort
ordination
adiinnoory
onirodynia

adiinnortu
induration
adiinoppst
disappoint
adiinopsss
dispassion
adiinorrst
distrainor
adiinortvy
divinatory
adiinosssu
dissuasion
adiioprstt
podiatrist
adiiprrtuy
tripudiary
adilllmors
Lollardism
adilllosyy
disloyally
adillnsstt
standstill
still-stand
adillostyy
disloyalty
adilmmopsu
plasmodium
adilmnnoty
dominantly
adilmnooop
monopodial
adilmnootu
modulation
adilmopsst
psalmodist
adilmorstu
mustard-oil
adilnnootu
nodulation
adilnnotuu
undulation
adilnopsuu
paludinous
adilnrsttu
stridulant
adiloorstu
idolatrous
adiloprtuy
plauditory
adimnnrsuy
synandrium
adimnoorty
admonitory
adimopssst
spasmodist
adimorstuu
sudatorium
adimqrruuv
quadrumvir
adinnopstt
standpoint
adinnorruy
unordinary

adinooprst
adsorption
adinorrstu
triandrous
adinorsstw
downstairs
adiorssstu
disastrous
adiorsssuy
dissuasory
adllmorssw
small-sword
adlloorrty
lordolatry
adlmooorsu
malodorous
adlnootuww
walnutwood
adlnorstuu
ultrasound
adlnortuuy
undulatory
adlnortuwy
untowardly
admnnoorsu
monandrous
admooopstt
stomatopod
adnnorrtuu
turnaround
adnnorssuy
synandrous
aeeeefgrwz
wage-freeze
aeeeefllrt
leafleteer
aeeeegkmpr
gamekeeper
aeeeegkprt
gate-keeper
aeeeegnrrt
regenerate
aeeeehrtwy
weather-eye
aeeeekprrt
peat-reeker
aeeeelprrs
prerelease
aeeeenrttx
exenterate
aeeeffglru
effleurage
aeeeffimnt
effeminate
aeeeffmnrt
affeerment
aeeefgrstv
stage-fever
aeeefhinrs
shereefian
aeeefhlrst
flesh-eater
aeeefhnprt
pen-feather

aeeefhrrtt
thereafter
aeeefilstt
life-estate
aeeefinrtz
antifreeze
aeeefllnst
fenestella
aeeefllptt
plate-fleet
aeeeflltvv
velvet-leaf
aeeeflmnss
femaleness
aeeefnrrst
transferee
aeeefnrstt
fenestrate
aeeefnsstv
Fastens-eve
aeeeggmnnt
engagement
aeeeghlprt
telpherage
aeeeghnrrt
greenheart
aeeegilnrs
generalise
aeeegilnrv
vinegar-eel
aeeegilnsv
evangelise
aeeegilnuv
eigenvalue
aeeegimntt
tea-meeting
aeeeginnor
aeroengine
aeeeginnrt
ingenerate
aeeeginrtv
generative
aeeegittvv
vegetative
aeeegklopr
goal-keeper
aeeegllnsu
Euglenales
aeeeglmnrt
regalement
aeeeglnopr
orange-peel
aeeeglnost
eagle-stone
aeeegmnnrt
enragement
aeeegmnntv
avengement
aeeegmnrss
meagreness
aeeegmnstt
segmentate
aeeegnorrt
orange-tree

aeeegnrssv
avengeress
aeeegprssx
expressage
aeeegqstuu
squeteague
aeeehhinst
heathenise
aeeehiklrs
hearse-like
aeeehirstw
weatherise
aeeehllrty
ethereally
aeeehlmstt
sheet-metal
aeeehlnsst
nathelesse
aeeehlorsv
shore-leave
aeeehlpstt
steeple-hat
aeeehlrsst
shear-steel
aeeehlrtww
water-wheel
aeeehmnorx
hexaemeron
aeeehmprtt
heptameter
aeeehmsstt
metatheses
aeeehnnnpt
nepenthean
aeeehnnrtt
thereanent
aeeehnnstv
heaven-sent
aeeehnorty
honey-eater
aeeehnrrtt
threatener
aeeehrsttw
sweetheart
aeeeiilrrs
earlierise
aeeeiipprt
peripeteia
aeeeillstt
little-ease
aeeeilnrst
eternalise
aeeeilnrtv
interleave
aeeeilpstv
sieve-plate
aeeeilrtvv
revelative
aeeeimnnrt
Nemertinea
aeeeimnrtt
intemerate
aeeeimnstv
Vietnamese

aeeeimprtv
permeative
aeeeimrstt
Eastertime
aeeeinnrtt
intenerate
aeeeinrttv
entreative
inveterate
aeeeinrtvv
enervative
aeeeinrtvw
interweave
aeeejkrrrt
tear-jerker
aeeejnrtuv
rejuvenate
aeeekkpprr
parkkeeper
aeeekmrrsv
verse-maker
aeeekpsstw
sweepstake
aeeelllrtt
tale-teller
aeeellpstt
steel-plate
aeeellrtvw
water-level
aeeellsstt
tessellate
aeeelmmnrt
Emmentaler
aeeelmnntt
lentamente
tenemental
aeeelmnptu
epaulement
aeeelmnrtt
manteltree
aeeelmnrtv
revealment
aeeelmnrty
elementary
aeeelnnsty
enneastyle
aeeelnorvv
overleaven
aeeelnostt
teleostean
aeeelnprtt
terneplate
aeeemmnort
anemometer
aeeemnprtt
pentameter
aeeemnrrtu
remunerate
aeeemorstt
taseometer
aeeempprry
emery-paper
aeeemrrttt
tetrameter

aeeemrrttw
water-meter
aeeemrsstt
steersmate
aeeemrsttw
watersmeet
aeeennpstt
septennate
aeeenorstt
stone-eater
aeeenprsst
sea-serpent
aeeenrrstu
entreasure
aeeenrsssv
averseness
aeeenrstvy
eye-servant
aeeeoprrst
patereroes
aeeepprrtt
perpetrate
aeeepprttu
perpetuate
aeeerrstyy
yesteryear
aeeersttww
sweet-water
aeeffgirtu
effigurate
aeeffhorrt
forefather
aeeffllorr
free-for-all
aeefflstux
exsufflate
aeefforrst
reafforest
aeefgghirt
freightage
aeefghinrt
feathering
aeefghirrt
heart-grief
aeefghorrt
foregather
aeefgilnrr
rifle-range
aeefgilprs
persiflage
aeefginorw
orange-wife
aeefgirttu
Guttiferae
aeefglprsu
presageful
aeefhhinrt
Fahrenheit
aeefhikltw
flake-white
aeefhiknst
sneak-thief
aeefhikrtt
thief-taker

aeefhilrss
seal-fisher
aeefhinprt
pin-feather
aeefhirttw
water-thief
aeefhloppr
leaf-hopper
aeefhlrsst
fatherless
aeefhmmorr
fore-hammer
aeefhmorsu
frame-house
aeefhmortt
fathometer
aeefhmrrsv
marsh-fever
aeefhprstt
stepfather
aeefhrrstw
freshwater
aeefiirrrs
fire-raiser
aeefiklrrw
fire-walker
aeefiknppr
paper-knife
aeefiknrss
freakiness
aeefillrsv
silver-leaf
aeefilnntt
life-tenant
aeefilnprr
palfrenier
aeefiloprt
perfoliate
aeefimnrrt
freemartin
aeefimrrst
fire-master
aeefimrstu
misfeature
aeefinrrst
fraternise
aeefinrsty
safety-rein
aeefiqrsuv
five-square
aeefklllrw
fell-walker
aeeflllmow
mallee-fowl
aeefllmsst
smell-feast
aeefllnnot
fontanelle
aeefllrssy
fearlessly
self-slayer
aeeflmorsy
fearsomely

aeeflostuy
feateously
aeefmnrrst
stern-frame
aeefnnsssu
unsafeness
aeefnrrrst
retransfer
aeeforrstu
four-seater
aeegghilrt
lighterage
aeegghoprr
geographer
aeegginopr
arpeggione
aeegginors
seignorage
aeegginrrs
grangerise
aeeggintty
vegetating
aeeggirssv
aggressive
aeeggirttu
egurgitate
aeeggmorrt
remortgage
aeeggnortv
voetganger
aeeggnorty
ergatogyne
aeeggnrrss
grass-green
aeeggorssu
sage-grouse
aeeghiilmp
hemiplegia
aeeghikmtw
make-weight
aeeghilmno
hegemonial
aeeghilnrt
leathering
aeeghilnss
Singhalese
aeeghilpst
legateship
aeeghilrst
lethargise
aeeghinpsw
weeping-ash
aeeghinrrs
rehearsing
aeeghinrrv
Rhinegrave
aeeghinrtv
Rh-negative
aeeghinrtw
weathering
aeeghipprr
epigrapher
aeeghknnrs
greenshank

aeeghllrsu
auger-shell
aeeghlmort
geothermal
aeeghlntvw
wavelength
aeeghloott
theologate
aeeghlortt
altogether
aeeghlprty
telegraphy
aeeghlssst
sheet-glass
aeeghmnoot
homogenate
aeeghmnort
thereamong
aeeghmorty
heterogamy
aeeghnostu
house-agent
aeeghorsst
stage-horse
aeeghorstt
othergates
aeeghprrsy
spreaghery
aeegiillls
illegalise
aeegiillnv
villeinage
aeegiilmtt
legitimate
aeegiilnst
gelatinise
aeegiimnnt
ingeminate
aeegiimnst
enigmatise
aeegiinrrt
garnierite
aeegiinrst
siege-train
aeegiknnnt
tank-engine
aeegiknrst
tiger-snake
aeegillmnn
enamelling
aeegillnst
teaselling
aeegillors
allegorise
aeegillrty
galleryite
aeegilmnrr
malingerer
aeegilmnrt
regimental
aeegilmnsv
evangelism
aeegilnnss
genialness

aegilnort
regelation
relegation
aeegilnrrt
interregal
aeegilnrst
easterling
generalist
aeegilnrty
generality
aeegilnstv
evangelist
aeegilntvy
negatively
aeegiloptx
exploitage
aeegilrrsu
regularise
aeegilrtuv
regulative
aeegimnnrt
regainment
aeegimnnsv
Genevanism
aeegimnprt
impregnate
aeegimnrst
magnetiser
aeegimnstu
mutagenise
aeegimorrt
morigerate
aeegimrrtu
marguerite
aeegimrrtv
gravimeter
aeeginnnsu
ensanguine
aeeginnort
generation
renegation
aeeginnpss
pangenesis
aeeginnrrt
interregna
aeeginnrtt
entreating
aeeginnrtv
enervating
aeeginnssy
Syngenesia
aeeginnsux
exsanguine
aeeginorrs
reorganise
aeeginottv
vegetation
aeeginprsy
panegyrise
aeeginrrtx
generatrix
aeeginrsss
greasiness

aeeginrssv
vernissage
aeegiprrtw
gripe-water
aeegiprsst
petrissage
aeegjllnor
jargonelle
aeeglllosw
gallows-lee
aeegllnrst
stallenger
aeegllortt
allegretto
aeegllstwy
galley-west
aeeglmmnor
meal-monger
aeeglmnntt
tanglement
aeeglmnost
tanglesome
aeeglmnprt
graplement
aeeglmnttu
tegumental
aeeglmopsu
plaguesome
aeeglmrrsw
leg-warmers
aeeglnorst
estrangelo
aeeglnortu
outgeneral
aeeglnortv
graveolent
lovat-green
aeeglnsstt
tassel-gent
aeegloprsu
grape-louse
plague-sore
aeeglortuv
travelogue
aeegmnnost
mangosteen
aeegmnnotw
meganewton
aeegmnoprr
pearmonger
aeegmnrrtu
garmenture
aeegmnrsty
segmentary
aeegmoprsu
soup-meagre
aeegmorrst
stereogram
aeegnnorss
sense-organ
aeegnnortv
governante
aeegnoprst
grapestone

aeegnorssu
sea-surgeon
aeegnorstv
gravestone
aeegnortty
teratogeny
aeegnprsst
press-agent
aeegnrsstu
arguteness
aeegoprssu
repoussage
aeehhhinst
heathenish
aeehhimnst
heathenism
aeehhinrrr
hen-harrier
aeehhinrst
earth-shine
aeehhirttw
white-heart
aeehhistww
white-hawse
aeehhknpss
sheepshank
aeehhllsst
healthless
aeehhlmost
healthsome
aeehhlmstu
Methuselah
aeehhlortw
heart-whole
aeehhlotww
whole-wheat
aeehhlssst
sheathless
aeehhnoprt
open-hearth
aeehhorstu
earth-house
aeehiillpt
epithelial
aeehiilmst
Ishmaelite
aeehiinprr
prairie-hen
aeehiisttv
hesitative
aeehiklnnp
enkephalin
aeehillnsw
snail-wheel
aeehillort
heliolater
aeehilmnrs
shale-miner
aeehilmnty
ethylamine
aeehilmprt
epithermal
hemipteral

aeehilmrtt
Thermalite®
aeehilnnop
anopheline
aeehilpprr
peripheral
aeehilprst
sphalerite
aeehilprtw
pearl-white
aeehilsstw
sea-whistle
aeehimnopp
epiphonema
aeehimnprt
hemipteran
aeehimnstw
anthemwise
aeehimrstu
rheumatise
aeehimrtuz
rheumatize
aeehimsstt
metathesis
aeehinnorw
Erewhonian
aeehinnprt
pantherine
aeehinprst
interphase
aeehinpstt
stephanite
aeehinrrtw
Wertherian
aeehinrsst
earthiness
heartiness
aeehinrttu
uintathere
aeehinsstt
antitheses
aeehipprrs
periphrase
aeehirttww
white-water
aeehistuvx
exhaustive
aeehkknruz
Hakenkreuz
aeehkmorst
earth-smoke
aeehknossu
snake-house
aeehkopssv
spokeshave
aeehkorstt
heatstroke
aeehkosstu
steakhouse
aeehlllprs
pearl-shell
aeehlloptw
whole-plate

aeehllorsw
wholesaler
aeehllosuw
whale-louse
aeehlmmrss
hammerless
aeehlmnnop
phenomenal
aeehlmnprt
telpherman
aeehlmortx
exothermal
aeehlmprsw
sperm-whale
aeehlnppst
sheep-plant
aeehlnrstt
nettlerash
aeehloprtw
power-lathe
aeehlprsss
phraseless
aeehlprtwy
telpherway
aeehlrsstw
wreathless
aeehlrttty
tetraethyl
aeehmnnssu
humaneness
aeehmnoorr
menorrhoea
aeehmnoprt
Heptameron
promethean
aeehmoostt
Etheostoma
aeehmoprst
atmosphere
aeehmorrrt
arthromere
aeehmorrst
horse-tamer
aeehmorsux
hexamerous
aeehnooprr
harpooneer
aeehnoppty
phaenotype
aeehnorsss
hoarseness
aeehnorstv
note-shaver
aeehnprsst
pantheress
aeehnrtuuy
Euthyneura
aeehooprst
peashooter
aeehooprsu
opera-house
aeehoopsst
apotheoses

aeehorrstw
water-horse
aeehorstvw
whatsoever
aeehorttxy
heterotaxy
aeehossttu
state-house
aeehprrstt
three-parts
aeehprsuvy
superheavy
aeeiiknrst
keratinise
aeeiillrst
literalise
aeeiillrtt
illiterate
aeeiilmnnt
eminential
aeeiilmnrs
mineralise
aeeiilnnsu
Eleusinian
aeeiilnprx
pre-exilian
aeeiilnrtt
retinalite
trilineate
aeeiilosst
ateleiosis
aeeiilqrru
reliquaire
aeeiilrrtv
irrelative
aeeiilrstv
relativise
revitalise
aeeiimnnst
inseminate
aeeiimnstt
anti-Semite
aeeiimprtv
imperative
aeeiimsttv
estimative
aeeiinnprs
Parisienne
aeeiinpprt
peripetian
aeeiinpprz
piperazine
aeeiinprss
Persianise
aeeiinrrvv
Viverrinae
aeeiinrstu
uniseriate
aeeiinrtwx
water-nixie
aeeiippttv
appetitive
aeeiiprssv
vespiaries

aeeijmnost
Jamesonite
aeeijoprtv
pejorative
aeeiklnssw
weakliness
aeeiklrrww
wire-walker
aeeikmnnrr
reim-kennar
aeeiknnsss
sneakiness
aeeiknrstt
kersantite
aeeilllllnv
villanelle
aeeillmnst
enamellist
aeeillnprt
Parnellite
aeeillpstt
stipellate
aeeillrtvy
relatively
aeeillsstt
satellites
aeeillstuv
televisual
aeeilmmnpt
impalement
aeeilmmnru
neurilemma
aeeilmnntt
entailment
aeeilmnprt
planimeter
aeeilmnrst
streamline
aeeilmnrtt
retailment
aeeilmnsss
measliness
aeeilmnstu
Mustelinae
semi-lunate
aeeilmortt
meteorital
aeeilmpsst
metalepsis
aeeilmrsst
semestrial
aeeilnnnpy
penny-a-line
aeeilnnpst
septennial
aeeilnnstt
sentential
aeeilnnttu
lieutenant
aeeilnoprt
peritoneal
aeeilnortv
revelation

aeeilnprru
perineural
aeeilnprss
pearliness
aeeilnprst
episternal
presential
aeeilnpstv
splenative
aeeilnqstu
sequential
aeeilnqtuv
equivalent
aeeilnrrtv
irrelevant
aeeilnrstt
eternalist
aeeilnrstu
neutralise
aeeilnrtuv
unrelative
aeeilnsssu
sensualise
aeeilnsssz
sleaziness
aeeilnstvx
sexivalent
aeeiloprst
periosteal
aeeilorrsv
revalorise
aeeilpprrt
peripteral
aeeilprrsv
reap-silver
aeeilprsss
praiseless
aeeilprssy
erysipelas
aeeilpsttu
estipulate
aeeilrrttu
literature
aeeimmmrst
metamerism
aeeimmoprt
emmetropia
aeeimmortv
memorative
aeeimmrssu
mismeasure
aeeimnnprt
pine-marten
aeeimnnrtt
retainment
aeeimnnrtu
innumerate
aeeimnoprt
permeation
aeeimnortt
marionette
aeeimnostt
maisonette

aeeimnprru
praemunire
aeeimnrsss
smeariness
aeeimnrstt
martensite
misentreat
aeeimnrttt
attirement
aeeimnssst
steaminess
aeeimopqsu
semi-opaque
aeeimoprtu
opium-eater
aeeimorrtv
variometer
aeeimprsst
passimeter
aeeimqrsuv
semiquaver
aeeinnnsss
insaneness
aeeinnnsst
innateness
aeeinnnttt
tennantite
aeeinnortv
enervation
veneration
aeeinnpptt
inappetent
aeeinnprss
Spenserian
aeeinnrtuv
aventurine
aeeinnsssu
uneasiness
aeeinnsstt
assentient
aeeinnsstv
nativeness
aeeinopttt
potentiate
aeeinprstu
resupinate
aeeinqrstu
equestrian
aeeinqsssu
queasiness
aeeinqsttu
Titanesque
aeeinrrrst
restrainer
aeeinrrttt
triternate
aeeinrrttv
travertine
aeeinrrtvy
veterinary
aeeinrssst
reastiness
aeeinrsssy
synaeresis

aeeinrsstw
ear-witness
wateriness
aeeinrsttt
interstate
aeeinrsttw
wine-taster
aeeinrttxy
extraneity
aeeinssstw
sweatiness
aeeinsssty
yeastiness
aeeioprrsv
overpraise
aeeipprrst
perspirate
aeeiprsstt
strip-tease
aeeiprsstu
pasteurise
aeeiprssuv
persuasive
aeeiprsttx
sexpartite
aeeiprttuv
reputative
vituperate
aeeiqrssuw
squarewise
aeeirrrtvw
river-water
aeeirrstvy
revestiary
aeejlnorsu
journalese
aeejnrrsty
serjeantry
aeekllmnpr
palm-kernel
aeekloprrw
rope-walker
aeekmmnory
money-maker
aeekmmnpry
kempery-man
aeekmmrrry
merrymaker
aeekmnorty
money-taker
aeekmorrtu
Euromarket
aeekmorstw
water-smoke
aeekmprrtv
verkrampte
aeekmrsttt
test-market
aeekmsstuy
eyas-musket
aeeknnosst
snakestone
aeellllsttu
stellulate

aeelllstty
stellately
aeellmmrrt
trammeller
aeellmnotv
malevolent
aeellmnqru
man-queller
aeellmnrtu
allurement
aeellmnssy
namelessly
aeellmortw
tree-mallow
aeellnoprt
petronella
aeellnrruv
unraveller
aeellnrtvy
relevantly
aeellnrtxy
externally
aeellnsstt
talentless
aeellntuvy
eventually
aeellorrsu
rose-laurel
aeellorstt
rostellate
aeellorttw
tallow-tree
aeellortty
tea-trolley
aeellottty
teetotally
aeellppprw
wall-pepper
aeellqrrru
quarreller
aeelmmnoru
neurolemma
aeelmmnrtt
trammel-net
aeelmnoprt
planometer
aeelmnortv
overmantel
aeelmnortw
water-lemon
water-melon
aeelmoprsy
polymerase
aeelmoprtx
extemporal
aeelmorttv
voltameter
aeelmprstt
streetlamp
aeelmrssst
masterless
streamless
aeelmrsstt
matterless

aeelmrsstu
emulatress
aeelnnprsy
arles-penny
aeelnnpttu
antepenult
aeelnnqstu
lansquenet
aeelnnsstt
tenantless
aeelnooptx
ox-antelope
aeelnoprst
pearl-stone
aeelnopssw
weaponless
aeelnorsss
reasonless
aeelnorsvw
slave-owner
aeelnortvz
zero-valent
aeelnossss
seasonless
aeelnostuv
suaveolent
aeelnprsst
parentless
aeelnprttw
wentletrap
aeelnpstty
pentastyle
aeelnrrtty
trey-antler
aeelnrsssw
answerless
aeelopprtu
repopulate
aeeloqrruu
roquelaure
aeelorrtvy
revelatory
aeelorsttu
lotus-eater
aeelortuwz
water-ouzel
aeelpprrru
paper-ruler
aeelprrssy
prayerless
aeelprstux
superexalt
aeelrrstuw
lustreware
aeelrsttty
tetrastyle
aeemmnorty
anemometry
aeemnnoprt
Pentameron
aeemnnorrt
ornamenter
aeemnnoruv
mavourneen

aeemnnprtt
entrapment
aeemnnprtw
enwrapment
aeemnntttu
attunement
aeemnopttt
tapotement
aeemnoqrsu
Romanesque
aeemnorrtu
enumerator
aeemnorruv
manoeuvrer
aeemnorsst
sarmentose
sea-monster
aeemnorsww
womenswear
aeemnpprst
sapperment
aeemnpprty
prepayment
aeemnprssx
expressman
aeemnrrstt
arrestment
aeemnrsstu
matureness
aeemnrsttu
menstruate
aeemnsssst
assessment
aeemoorttt
tree-tomato
aeemoprstw
steam-power
aeemorrstv
overmaster
aeemorrttv
overmatter
aeemorsstt
eastermost
aeemorstuu
outmeasure
aeemorstuw
water-mouse
aeemprrttu
ear-trumpet
aeemrsssst
seamstress
aeennnpsty
penny-stane
aeennorsst
ornateness
aeennrssuw
unwareness
aeenopqssu
opaqueness
aeenoprrtt
penetrator
aeenoprrtu
Neuroptera

aeenorstux
extraneous
aeenorttux
extenuator
aeenpprstt
step-parent
aeenprssss
sparseness
aeenqrsssu
squareness
aeenrrsstv
transverse
aeenrrstuu
untreasure
aeensssttu
astuteness
aeenssttu
sustentate
aeeoprrstt
tetraspore
aeeoprrtww
water-power
aeeoprstty
poetastery
aeeoprtttt
tetraptote
aeeoqrsstu
square-toes
aeeorrttww
water-tower
aeeprrssst
trespasser
aeeprssttu
super-state
aeeprsswxy
expressway
aeeqrsstuy
satyresque
aeeqssttuu
statuesque
aefffttuy
tuftaffety
aeffghinrt
affrighten
aeffgkmnoy
monkey-gaff
aeffhimrrs
fish-farmer
aeffiiintv
affinitive
aeffilnorw
waffle-iron
aeffilnstu
insufflate
aeffinortv
affrontive
aeffknrstu
snuff-taker
aeffllntuy
affluently
aefflppry
fly-flapper
aeffnpprsu
snuff-paper

aeffoosttu
affettuoso
aefggilnss
flagginess
aefghhllnt
half-length
aefghiinss
sea-fishing
aefghilrtt
after-light
aefghinrrw
wharfinger
aefghirtwy
way-freight
aefghlsttu
self-taught
aefghnortu
fearnought
aefghorttu
foretaught
aefgiillor
florilegia
aefgiilmst
smifligate
aefgiilnnr
fingernail
aefgiilnsv
life-saving
aefgiirtuv
figurative
aefgikmnrr
fingermark
aefgilmnnu
meaningful
aefgilmnos
flamingoes
aefgilmnry
ley-farming
aefgilmruv
vermifugal
aefgilnouw
guinea-fowl
aefgilnrtt
flattering
aefgilnrtu
ingrateful
aefgilnrvy
vinegar-fly
aefgiloprt
profligate
aefgiprrtu
grapefruit
aefgllopuw
fowl-plague
aefgllrtuy
gratefully
aefglnoott
tanglefoot
aefglnrtuu
ungrateful
aefglpstuy
safety-plug
aefgnorstw
wafer-tongs

aefhhhisst
sheath-fish
aefhhimmrs
hammer-fish
aefhhiprst
fathership
aefhhlorsy
halfe-horsy
aefhhlossu
flash-house
aefhhorsst
shaft-horse
aefhikllrt
half-kirtle
aefhiklrsy
freakishly
aefhilllow
hail-fellow
aefhilmnot
fathom-line
aefhilnrtt
flint-heart
aefhilnsss
flashiness
aefhilpprs
flapperish
aefhilrsst
half-sister
aefhimmnst
famishment
aefhimnrsu
fish-manure
aefhlllovy
half-volley
aefhllmsuy
shamefully
aefhlmosst
fathomless
aefhlnrtuy
unfatherly
aefhlrstvy
harvest-fly
aefhmooprs
shame-proof
aefhorrttu
fourth-rate
aefiiinntt
infinitate
aefiilltuv
fluviatile
aefiilmnty
feminality
aefiilnrtt
infiltrate
aefiilortt
trifoliate
aefiilprst
spirit-leaf
aefiimnnos
infamonise
aefiinqrtu
quantifier
aefiinsstu
fustianise
aefiknoprs
fair-spoken
aefillmmor
malleiform
aefillnnry
infernally
aefillnnuz
influenzal
aefillruwy
wearifully
aefilmnsty
manifestly
aefilmorrt
life-mortar
aefilmortw
wolframite
aefilnorsu
laniferous
aefilnortu
fluorinate
aefilnprtu
turnip-flea
aefilnsstu
faultiness
aefiloqrtu
quatrefoil
aefilorssu
saliferous
aefilpqruy
pre-qualify
aefimnoryy
fairy-money
aefimrsstu
mutessarif
aefinnrssu
unfairness
aefinooprt
fortepiano
pianoforte
aefinorrst
rain-forest
aefinorrsw
wafer-irons
aefinorsty
fairy-stone
aefinorttu
refutation
aefinrrtty
fraternity
aefiorrsuu
auriferous
aefklnorsy
forsakenly
aefknnorsu
unforsaken
aeflllopwy
playfellow
aeflllorww
wallflower
aefllnoort
root-fallen
aefllnossw
fallowness
aefllnssuw
lawfulness
aeflloorry
ferro-alloy
aefllpsuuy
pausefully
aefllsttuy
tastefully
aefllstuwy
wastefully
aeflmnnssu
manfulness
aeflmorrsv
salverform
aeflnoostt
float-stone
aeflnoprrt
prefrontal
aeflnrsstu
artfulness
aeflnrstuw
wanrestful
aeflnsttuu
untasteful
aeflopprt
plate-proof
aeflooruvv
love-favour
aeflorssuv
favourless
aefmnosssu
famousness
aefmoorrtw
foot-warmer
aefmoprrst
permafrost
aefmorrsty
oyster-farm
aefnorrrst
transferor
aefnorrttw
waterfront
aefnrrsstu
transfuser
aefooprrrt
perforator
aefooprrtw
waterproof
aefoorrstt
tortfeasor
aefoprrstu
perforatus
aefopsstty
safety-stop
aefoqrrsuu
foursquare
aegggilnny
engagingly
aeggginrst
staggering
aeggginrsw
swaggering
aegggiryzz
zigzaggery
aegghimops
geophagism
aegghimorw
whiggamore
aegghinsss
shagginess
aegghiopst
geophagist
aegghloptu
ploughgate
aegghoopsu
geophagous
aeggiilmpr
pilgrimage
aeggijmrst
jigger-mast
aeggiklnos
Ginkgoales
aeggiknnss
knagginess
aeggillnrv
gravelling
aeggiloosu
sialogogue
aeggimnrrs
Grangerism
aeggimnrrt
triggerman
aegginnprs
gingersnap
aegginorss
aggression
aegginprtt
pargetting
aegginqssu
quagginess
aeggiorrsu
gregarious
aeggjnrtuu
juggernaut
aeggllnooy
angelology
aeggmostuy
mystagogue
aeggnnoory
organogeny
aeggnnorsu
gangrenous
aeggoorsss
goose-grass
aeghhiknrr
high-ranker
aeghhillls
shillelagh
aeghhilopr
heliograph
aeghhilrtt
earth-light
aeghhinstw
wing-sheath
aeghhioprr
hierograph
aeghhlorsu
horselaugh
aeghhmoppt
apophthegm
aeghhnoppr
nephograph
aeghhoprty
hyetograph
aeghiilost
goliathise
aeghiinrsv
vinegarish
aeghiiprst
graphitise
aeghikmnos
shoemaking
aeghiknrst
Kentish-rag
aeghikrrst
tiger-shark
aeghilllop
gallophile
aeghillnns
hanselling
aeghilmnns
Englishman
aeghilmnos
home-signal
aeghilmnrt
lighterman
aeghilmort
lithomarge
aeghilnoot
theologian
aeghilnrsu
languisher
aeghilnsss
gashliness
aeghilprxy
lexigraphy
aeghimmopr
mimeograph
aeghimnpst
stamp-hinge
aeghimsttt
steamtight
aeghinnrtv
night-raven
aeghinprrs
rangership
spring-hare
aeghinprst
strap-hinge
aeghinprtt
night-taper
aeghinrsss
garishness
aeghinrstt
straighten
aeghiprrsy
serigraphy
aeghirtttw
watertight
aeghjllpry
jellygraph

aeghllossw
Howleglass
aeghlmooot
homologate
aeghlmoptu
plough-team
aeghlnnoop
anglophone
aeghlnoopy
phaenology
aeghlnoorr
gonorrheal
aeghlnoors
alongshore
aeghlnoosu
halogenous
aeghlnstwy
lengthways
aeghlooorr
logorrhoea
aeghloopry
oleography
aeghloopty
hepatology
aeghlorsuv
overslaugh
aeghlosssu
glasshouse
aeghlrstuy
slaughtery
aeghmmorrt
thermogram
aeghmnoopr
gramophone
aeghmnoprs
sphenogram
aeghnnoowy
honey-wagon
aeghnooorr
gonorrhoea
aeghnoorsw
horse-gowan
aeghnoprry
granophyre
aeghnoprst
stenograph
aeghnorrst
short-range
aeghnosuxy
hexagynous
aeghooprry
oreography
aeghooprrz
zoographer
aeghoopssu
oesophagus
aeghoopsux
exophagous
aeghoopsuy
hypogaeous
aeghoorstv
shove-groat
aeghoprrxy
xerography

aeghorrtuv
overraught
aeghorssuu
sugar-house
aegiiilntv
invigilate
aegiiilttv
vitiligate
aegiiimttv
mitigative
aegiiirrtv
irrigative
aegiiknrss
ear-kissing
aegiilllty
illegality
aegiillptv
pit-village
aegiilmnrt
trigeminal
aegiilmnst
time-signal
aegiilmnsx
maxi-single
aegiilnopr
perigonial
aegiilnotv
levigation
aegiilnppy
pipe-laying
aegiilnprv
prevailing
aegiilnsst
tasseiling
aegiimmnno
meningioma
aegiimnnot
gemination
aegiimnort
emigration
remigation
aegiimnstt
enigmatist
aegiimnstv
negativism
time-saving
aegiimsstt
stigmatise
aegiinnprt
repainting
aegiinnrtt
intrigante
aegiinoppr
pigeon-pair
aegiinortv
invigorate
aegiinppst
appetising
aegiinrstv
gainstrive
aegiinttvy
negativity
aegiirrstt
geriatrist

aegiklmmor
kilogramme
aegiklmnov
love-making
aegiklnnsy
sneakingly
aegiklnpsy
speakingly
aegikmnnos
maskinonge
aegikmnopr
rope-making
aegiknnpsu
unspeaking
aegiknnsst
takingness
aegiknprss
king's-spear
aegikprsss
spike-grass
aegillllnu
Lingulella
aegillmnrv
marvelling
aegillnory
orange-lily
regionally
aegillnpru
prelingual
aegillnpsy
pleasingly
aegillnrst
stallinger
aegillnrtv
travelling
aegillnrty
integrally
aegillnsty
stealingly
aegillorst
allegorist
legislator
aegillpssx
plexiglass
aegilmmnnt
malignment
aegilmnnnr
Ringelmann
aegilmnnor
non-gremial
aegilmnoop
monoplegia
aegilmnory
mineralogy
aegilmnrst
streamling
aegilmsttu
multi-stage
aegilnnoot
elongation
aegilnnosu
lanuginose
aegilnnpsu
unpleasing

aegilnnrtu
unaltering
aegilnnryy
yearningly
aegilnnsss
slanginess
aegilnnsuy
sanguinely
aegilnoosu
oleaginous
aegilnorsu
lanigerous
aegilnortu
regulation
urogenital
aegilnorvy
overlaying
aegilnostu
gelatinous
aegilnprst
plastering
aegilnprty
taperingly
aegilnrstv
starveling
aegilnrvwy
waveringly
aegilnssss
glassiness
aegiloorst
aerologist
aegiloprtt
graptolite
aegilorrss
gressorial
aegilrrtuy
regularity
aegimmnrst
stammering
aegimmorss
seismogram
aegimnnoru
enamouring
aegimnnprt
impregnant
aegimnnrsv
serving-man
aegimnnsst
assignment
aegimnoprs
angiosperm
aegimnorsu
gramineous
aegimnortw
worm-eating
aegimnoruw
guinea-worm
aegimnprty
pigmentary
aegimnrrst
ring-master
aegimnrstt
smattering

aegimoprsu
soup-maigre
aegimorrsu
armigerous
aegimorrty
emigratory
aegimrrtvy
gravimetry
aeginnnprt
trepanning
aeginnorrs
engarrison
aeginnpprw
enwrapping
aeginnrstt
astringent
aeginnrstu
sauntering
aeginnrsuw
unswearing
aeginnruvw
unwavering
aeginnruwy
unwearying
aeginnsssv
savingness
aeginoortt
negotiator
aeginorrtt
integrator
aeginorsuu
aeruginous
aeginprstu
supergiant
aeginprsty
panegyrist
aeginpsttu
Septuagint
aeginqrrtu
quartering
aeginrrssu
reassuring
aeginrrstt
registrant
aeginrrstu
austringer
aeginrrstv
traversing
aeginrssss
grassiness
aeginrsssu
sugariness
aeginrstww
water-wings
aegirrrsty
registrary
aegirssttt
strategist
aegllmorru
glomerular
aegllmorwy
galley-worm
aegllmrtuy
metallurgy

aegllnnpty
plangently
aegllnopst
long-staple
aeglloprsu
pellagrous
aeglmnooty
nematology
aeglmnorss
lemon-grass
aeglmoprtu
promulgate
aeglmprssu
plume-grass
aeglnnoost
logan-stone
aeglnnprty
pregnantly
aeglnooprt
prolongate
aeglnoosuv
longaevous
aeglnorsvw
slave-grown
aeglnssssu
sunglasses
aegloorrst
astrologer
aegloortty
teratology
aegloppstu
plague-spot
aeglorrtuy
regulatory
aeglprssuu
surplusage
aegmmnrtuu
argumentum
aegmmoprrr
programmer
aegmnoorst
gastronome
aegmnorrst
starmonger
aegnnnprtu
unpregnant
aegnnrtuuy
unguentary
aegnooorrt
orange-root
aegnoortxy
oxygenator
aegnoostuu
autogenous
aegnoprstt
patter-song
aegnopstuw
wasp-tongue
aegnrrssst
transgress
aegnssstuu
augustness
aegoorstuu
outrageous
aegoprrtux
expurgator
aegprrsssu
supergrass
aehhhilopt
Ahithophel
aehhilnopt
lithophane
aehhilnstu
Helianthus
aehhimnpst
hetmanship
aehhinoprt
hierophant
aehhinprst
pantherish
aehhinrtwy
anywhither
aehhloorps
holophrase
aehhlopttu
heath-poult
aehhmooopt
homoeopath
aehhmoopty
homeopathy
aehhnooprt
anthophore
aehhnoprty
hypaethron
aehhoorstt
root-sheath
aehhorttwy
hateworthy
aehiiknpst
kinesipath
aehiikprss
kaisership
aehiilnpst
Philistean
aehiiloprz
pileorhiza
aehiilostx
heliotaxis
aehiimnstt
antitheism
aehiinostt
hesitation
aehiinpprs
sapphirine
aehiinsstt
antithesis
aehiinsttt
antitheist
aehiipprrt
Rhipiptera
aehiippstt
epitaphist
aehikknopt
pinakothek
aehiklnssy
sneakishly
aehiklssst
skaithless
aehikmnnst
Kentish-man
aehikmstwy
Wykehamist
aehiknrsss
rakishness
aehikorrst
hair-stroke
aehilllnss
snail-shell
aehilloovw
view-halloo
aehillopsv
Slavophile
aehilloptw
pilot-whale
aehillopty
polyhalite
aehillorsv
all-overish
aehillorty
heliolatry
aehillosty
halloysite
aehillstty
stealthily
aehilmmnst
Simmenthal
aehilmmrtt
tilt-hammer
aehilmnopy
anemophily
aehilmnstv
lavishment
aehilmoprt
hemitropal
aehilmorst
isothermal
aehilmossy
haemolysis
aehilmpstu
multiphase
aehilnnoop
phaelonion
aehilnnops
Alphonsine
aehilnoopp
philopoena
aehilnoprz
rhizoplane
aehilnopst
Polianthes
aehilnoptt
thiopental
aehilnpsty
staphyline
aehilnsssv
lavishness
aehilnstuw
Whitsun-ale
aehilooprt
ophiolater
aehiloprst
trophesial
aehilorrty
hierolatry
aehilrstvy
shrievalty
aehimmprrt
trip-hammer
aehimmrstu
rheumatism
aehimnnpps
penmanship
aehimnnstv
vanishment
aehimnnsuu
unhumanise
aehimnopps
hippomanes
aehimnorrs
harmoniser
aehimnotux
exhumation
aehimnrsss
marshiness
aehimnrstv
ravishment
aehimnsstu
enthusiasm
aehimorrsv
Averrhoism
aehimosttu
autotheism
aehimprsst
mastership
ship-master
aehimpssty
sympathise
aehinnnoot
hootnannie
aehinnoprt
antiphoner
aehinnpstt
tenantship
aehinnrrty
Tyrrhenian
aehinnrtvw
wanthriven
aehinoprtu
euphoriant
aehinorrtv
hover-train
aehinostux
exhaustion
aehinqrsuv
vanquisher
aehinrssst
trashiness
aehinrsstw
wrathiness
aehinssttu
enthusiast
aehioopsst
apotheosis
aehiopprrs
repair-shop
aehiorrstv
Averrhoist
aehiorssst
air-hostess
aehiorstty
hesitatory
aehiostttu
autotheist
aehirssttw
sweat-shirt
aehirsttww
thwartwise
aehklmrtuw
lukewarmth
aehklnnsuy
unshakenly
aehklnosty
honey-stalk
aehkloprsw
shop-walker
aehllmrssy
harmlessly
aehllmstuu
haustellum
aehlloorww
hollow-ware
aehlloprxy
phylloxera
aehllorrsz
razor-shell
aehlloswwy
yellow-wash
aehlmnortt
antler-moth
aehlmnpttu
pentathlum
aehlmooprs
Homorelaps
aehlmoosux
homosexual
aehlmorryy
rhyme-royal
aehlmpssyy
symphyseal
aehlnnoptt
pentathlon
aehlnopprt
thorn-apple
aehlnopstu
plant-house
sulphonate
aehlnoptty
entophytal
aehlnorttt
tetrathlon
aehlooprry
pyorrhoeal
aehloorssw
wool-shears
aehlorrsvy
overrashly
aehlorsstu
authorless

aehlprstuu
sulphurate
aehlrttuuv
truth-value
aehmmmtuwy
mummy-wheat
aehmnoorsu
manor-house
aehmnoorsw
horse-woman
aehmnortwy
nameworthy
aehmnprsuu
superhuman
aehmnprtwy
water-nymph
aehmnrttuy
nature-myth
aehmnsstty
assythment
aehmoorstx
mesothorax
aehmoprrtt
Tetramorph
aehmorsttt
thermostat
aehnnnooty
hootenanny
aehnnoopst
panton-shoe
aehnoooprt
orthopnoea
aehnooprst
heart-spoon
aehnoopssu
sousaphone
aehnoprtuy
neuropathy
aehnorstww
snow-wreath
aehoopprst
apostrophe
aehoopprty
opotherapy
aehooprrtt
orthoptera
aehooprtyz
zootherapy
aehoopsttt
toothpaste
aehoopstty
osteopathy
aehoorssty
soothsayer
aehoorsttw
water-shoot
aehopprsty
saprophyte
aehoprstuy
house-party
aehorrrstw
rest-harrow
aehorrttvw
overthwart

aehorsstuy
southsayer
aehprsstty
strathspey
aeiiiilnst
initialise
aeiiinttv
initiative
aeiiilmrst
militarise
aeiiilmstv
similative
aeiiilmttv
limitative
aeiiilrstv
trivialise
aeiiilsttv
vitalities
aeiiimnrst
ministeria
aeiiimnstv
vitaminise
aeiiirrttv
irritative
aeiiisttvv
visitative
aeiikllnpr
pain-killer
aeiikllors
sailor-like
aeiiklrtuv
laurvikite
aeiiillmms
millesimal
aeiiillmnn
millennial
aeiiilltvy
illatively
aeiiillmnpp
Pimpinella
aeiiillmntu
illuminate
aeiiillmpry
imperially
aeiiillmrst
literalism
aeiiillnrtu
uniliteral
aeiiillnssv
villainess
aeiiillostv
volatilise
aeiiillpstt
pistillate
aeiiillrrtt
triliteral
aeiiillrrtu
tirailleur
aeiiillrrty
literarily
aeiiillrstt
literalist
aeiiillrtty
literality

aeiilmmmor
immemorial
aeiilmnort
eliminator
aeiilmnrst
mineralist
aeiilmnsty
seminality
aeiilmnszz
mizzen-sail
aeiilmntty
intimately
aeiilmopst
optimalise
aeiilmosss
isoseismal
aeiilmrstv
relativism
aeiilmrsvv
revivalism
aeiilmstuv
simulative
aeiilnnopt
antilopine
aeiilnnors
rosaniline
aeiilnnstt
intestinal
aeiilnoott
etiolation
aeiilnopss
spaniolise
aeiilnorrt
irrelation
aeiilnorsv
revisional
aeiilnortt
literation
aeiilnortv
leviration
aeiilnosst
leontiasis
aeiilnottv
levitation
tonalitive
velitation
aeiilnpprz
Lippizaner
aeiilnprzz
Lipizzaner
aeiilnqtuy
inequality
aeiilnrsty
silentiary
aeiilnrttv
intervital
aeiilopptv
oppilative
aeiilopstv
spoliative
aeiilorttv
vitriolate
aeiilrssuv
visualiser

aeiilrsttv
relativist
aeiilrsttz
strelitzia
aeiilrstvv
revivalist
aeiilrttvy
relativity
aeiimmnprt
impairment
aeiimmnsss
Messianism
aeiimnnnot
innominate
aeiimnnost
Noetianism
semination
aeiimnnott
antimonite
aeiimnnotv
nominative
aeiimnostt
estimation
aeiimnqtuy
equanimity
aeiimnrsst
seminarist
aeiimnrtuv
ruminative
aeiimnssst
Messianist
aeiimoprrs
impresario
aeiimprstt
team-spirit
aeiimpttuv
imputative
aeiinnoqtu
inequation
aeiinnosst
enantiosis
aeiinnotvv
innovative
aeiinnprtt
tripinnate
aeiinnpsst
paintiness
aeiinoppst
inapposite
aeiinopptt
appetition
aeiinopptv
appointive
aeiinoprtx
expiration
aeiinopstt
poinsettia
aeiinopstu
utopianise
aeiinoqttu
equitation
aeiinotuvx
exuviation

aeiinprstu
puritanise
aeiinprttu
unipartite
aeiinpssst
antisepsis
inspissate
aeiinqttuv
quantitive
aeiinrrttt
trinitrate
aeiinrsssu
Russianise
aeiinrsttv
revisitant
transitive
aeiiopprtt
propitiate
aeiioppstv
appositive
aeiioprrss
proairesis
aeiiprrttt
tripartite
aeijlnorsu
journalise
aeijlnossv
jovialness
aeijnnsstu
jauntiness
aeijnooprt
pejoration
aeijnorttw
water-joint
aeijrsttww
jaw-twister
aeikllmnsu
muslin-kale
aeikllmppr
lapper-milk
aeiklmmnrs
slammerkin
aeiklmnort
matron-like
aeiklmnory
monkey-rail
aeiklmnoty
monkey-tail
aeiklmnsty
mistakenly
aeiklmpprr
ripple-mark
aeiknorstu
keratinous
aeilllnqsu
line-squall
aeilllsuvy
allusively
aeillmmrst
mill-stream
aeillmnprs
Parnellism
aeillmnptu
multiplane

aeillmnrty
terminally
aeillmppss
small-pipes
aeillmttuy
ultimately
aeillnnpru
plenilunar
aeillnnrty
internally
aeillnoptt
Potentilla
aeillnorty
orientally
aeillnpsst
plaintless
aeillnpssy
painlessly
aeillopstt
postillate
aeillorsss
sailorless
aeillortuv
trouvaille
aeillqrrtu
quarter-ill
aeillrrttu
Turritella
aeillrsttu
illustrate
aeilmmnsss
smalminess
aeilmmrtuy
immaturely
aeilmnnoty
nominately
aeilmnnstt
instalment
aeilmnoprs
impersonal
aeilmnoprt
trampoline
aeilmnortu
tourmaline
aeilmnosst
assoilment
aeilmnprty
planimetry
aeilmnrstu
neutralism
aeilmnrttt
latter-mint
aeilmnsssu
sensualism
aeilmnsttu
last-minute
aeilmoorrt
meliorator
aeilmoppss
ampelopsis
aeilmoprst
peristomal
aeilmopstt
Ptolemaist

aeilmppsst
palimpsest
aeilmprsst
slipstream
aeilmprssu
plumassier
aeilmprstu
psalterium
aeilmprtuu
pari-mutuel
aeilmrrssu
surrealism
aeilmsttux
textualism
aeilnnnppy
penny-plain
aeilnnopsy
Polynesian
aeilnnortt
intolerant
aeilnnortz
interzonal
aeilnnosst
nationless
aeilnnprsu
peninsular
aeilnnprtt
interplant
aeilnnpsst
pliantness
aeilnnrrtu
interlunar
aeilnnrstt
lanternist
aeilnoortt
toleration
aeilnoppst
pentapolis
aeilnoprrt
interpolar
aeilnoprrv
rain-plover
aeilnoprst
interposal
aeilnoprtu
eruptional
aeilnorrtt
torrential
aeilnorrty
anteriorly
aeilnorttv
ventilator
aeilnottux
exultation
aeilnprsst
paltriness
aeilnprstu
palustrine
aeilnpsuuv
unplausive
aeilnrrtuy
unliterary
aeilnrsttu
neutralist

aeilnrstuu
laurustine
aeilnrttuy
neutrality
aeilnssstu
sensualist
aeilnsstuu
nautiluses
aeilnsstuy
sensuality
aeilnstuvw
wine-vaults
aeiloopstt
toilet-soap
aeiloopttz
topazolite
aeilopprst
Leptospira
aeiloppru
popularise
aeiloppsty
appositely
aeiloprssu
plesiosaur
aeiloprstt
tetrapolis
aeiloprsty
epistolary
aeilopttvy
optatively
aeilorrttu
elutriator
aeilorsttu
staurolite
aeilprrsty
peristylar
aeilprrtwy
play-writer
aeilprssuv
supervisal
aeilqrrttu
triquetral
aeilrrsstu
surrealist
aeilstttux
textualist
aeimmnnrss
mismanners
aeimmnorst
monetarism
aeimmnotuu
auto-immune
aeimmnprtt
impartment
aeimmnrsss
smarminess
aeimmnrstt
mint-master
aeimmnrsty
symmetrian
aeimmnstzz
mizzen-mast
aeimmprrsu
spermarium

aeimmprstu
spermatium
aeimnnoprr
mainpernor
aeimnnortu
numeration
aeimnoorst
aeronomist
aeimnootvw
wave-motion
aeimnoprtt
armipotent
aeimnoprtw
tripewoman
aeimnopttt
temptation
aeimnoqsuu
equanimous
aeimnorrst
iron-master
aeimnorrtt
terminator
aeimnorstt
monetarist
aeimnorstu
Mousterian
aeimnosstu
stamineous
aeimnpprst
pentaprism
aeimnpstty
tympanites
aeimnrrrty
intermarry
aeimnrrstt
retransmit
aeimoorstx
xerostomia
aeimoottuv
automotive
aeimoprrtu
praetorium
aeimprssst
mass-priest
aeimprsstt
spermatist
aeimprsstu
pasteurism
aeimpsstuv
assumptive
aeimqrstuz
quiz-master
aeimrrsttt
ritt-master
aeinnoortv
renovation
aeinnoprsy
pensionary
aeinnoqrtu
quaternion
aeinnorstt
stentorian
aeinnosstt
satin-stone

aeinnqsstu
quaintness
aeinnrssuw
unwariness
aeinoopprt
propionate
aeinooprrt
peroration
aeinooprst
operations
aeinoorrtt
orientator
aeinoppprt
preappoint
aeinopprst
spear-point
aeinoprrst
patroniser
aeinoprssu
persuasion
aeinoprstt
prestation
aeinoprstu
superation
aeinoprttu
reputation
aeinoprtty
potentiary
aeinopttu
out-patient
aeinorrstu
souterrain
aeinorrstv
overstrain
aeinorstty
stationery
aeinpprsst
trappiness
aeinpprstw
wit-snapper
aeinprrstu
rupestrian
aeinprrttu
parturient
aeinprsttt
strepitant
aeinqrttuy
quaternity
aeinrrssst
starriness
aeinrssstt
straitness
aeinrstuyz
suzerainty
aeioprrrst
respirator
aeioprrttx
extirpator
aeioprrtxy
expiratory
aeiorrrssw
warrioress
aeiorrsttw
stair-tower

aeiorssttt
Stratiotes
aeirssstuu
saussurite
aeirsttttww
water-twist
aejllmosww
Jew's-mallow
aejmnnoruy
journeyman
aekkmnrrtu
trunk-maker
aekllmruwy
lukewarmly
aekloprsty
stroke-play
strokeplay
aeklorttww
wattle-work
aekmnorsst
strokesman
aekmnorttw
market-town
aekmorrstw
master-work
workmaster
aekooprrty
prokaryote
aekoprrsty
oyster-park
aellmnorty
trolley-man
aellmoorsw
rose-mallow
aellmoprty
temporally
aellmopssy
plasmolyse
aellmorsuv
marvellous
aellnooprt
Trollopean
aellnopprt
propellant
aellnoprsy
personally
aellnopstu
plant-louse
aellnoptvy
polyvalent
aellnortty
tolerantly
aellnosssw
sallowness
aellnprsuy
supernally
aellnpttuy
petulantly
aellnrstty
slatternly
aellnttuxy
exultantly
aelloopstw
wool-staple

aelloopswy
yellow-soap
aellopprsu
all-purpose
aelloprsuy
superalloy
aellprstuu
sepultural
aellrttuxy
texturally
aelmmnnotu
monumental
aelmmoopss
plasmosome
aelmmoprrw
palmer-worm
aelmmprstu
emplastrum
aelmnnnruy
unmannerly
aelmnnootv
monovalent
aelmnooprt
monopteral
aelmnoopry
lampoonery
aelmnoprst
emplastron
aelmnoprsu
neuroplasm
aelmnoprtt
portmantle
aelmnopsty
polysemant
aelmnorsss
ransomless
aelmnsssuw
swan-mussel
aelmoopptt
tappet-loom
aelmooprtu
tropaeolum
aelmoppruy
propylaeum
aelmoprttu
petrolatum
aelmoprtty
temporalty
aelmoqssuu
squamulose
aelmorrssu
armourless
aelmorrssw
marrowless
aelmorsstu
somersault
aelmorsttt
lattermost
aelmrssttu
mulattress
aelmtttuuu
tumultuate
aelnnopryy
pennyroyal

aelnnorsty
resonantly
aelnooprrt
rotor-plane
aelnopprtw
power-plant
aelnoprsst
patronless
aelnoprsty
personalty
aelnopsttv
stove-plant
aelnorsuvy
ravenously
aelnossuuy
nauseously
aelnpprstu
supplanter
aelnprrsuu
superlunar
aeloooprty
aeolotropy
aeloppprru
pourparler
aeloprrsuy
super-royal
aelorrtttw
otter-trawl
aelorsssuv
savourless
aelppptuy
puppet-play
aelppsstuy
platypuses
aemmnoprtu
map-mounter
aemmnorsty
smart-money
aemmnrstyy
mystery-man
aemmossttu
stemmatous
aemnnnopty
non-payment
aemnnoosst
stone-mason
aemnnorttt
attornment
aemnnorttu
tournament
aemnnrrsuy
nurseryman
aemnooprtt
portamento
aemnoorrst
astronomer
aemnorrtuy
uranometry
aemnorsstt
assortment
aemnorsstu
sarmentous
aemnrrsttu
transmuter

aemoopstty
somatotype
aemoorrttw
water-motor
aemoprrssw
swarm-spore
aemoprsstt
postmaster
aemorrsttw
masterwort
storm-water
aennnosstw
wantonness
aennopstty
stannotype
aennorrssw
narrowness
aennorrstt
non-starter
aenooprrst
personator
aenooprtxy
paroxytone
aenooqrrtu
quarteroon
aenoorsstu
treasonous
aenoprrsst
transposer
aenoprsttt
protestant
aeoopprrrt
propraetor
aeoopprrst
praepostor
aeoopprstu
tropopause
aeooqrrstu
square-root
aeopprrrtu
rapporteur
aeoprrsstw
sportswear
aeoprrssuy
persuasory
aeoprsttuw
water-spout
aeoqrrstuz
rose-quartz
aeorsstuux
trousseaux
aeprrstuuu
usurpature
affffinnyy
niffy-naffy
afffgillno
falling-off
affgiilnsy
falsifying
affgimrssu
suffragism
affginnort
affronting

affginrstw
wring-staff
affgirsstu
suffragist
affgnoorst
stroganoff
affhiinrsu
ruffianish
affhilltuy
faithfully
affhilntuu
unfaithful
affhirsttu
Tartuffish
affiimnrsu
ruffianism
affilnostu
sufflation
affimrsttu
Tartuffism
affpprstuy
puff-pastry
afgggilnnu
unflagging
afggiimnny
magnifying
afggiinrty
gratifying
afggilmnor
gangliform
afghhillst
flashlight
afghilnpsu
upflashing
afghiortwy
right-of-way
afghllstuy
ghastfully
afgiillnsy
sail-flying
afgiilmnpy
amplifying
afgiilnquy
qualifying
afgiilostu
flagitious
afgiimnotu
fumigation
afgiinortu
figuration
afgiinottu
fugitation
afgiinssty
satisfying
afgikmnors
king-of-arms
afgillnoty
floatingly
afgillnsst
flint-glass
afgilnoruv
flavouring
afgimortuy
fumigatory

afginnoops
poison-fang
afglllsssu
glassfulls
afhhlloruy
half-hourly
afhiilmopr
phialiform
afhiinosst
fashionist
afhillmort
thalliform
afhilnopst
flash-point
afhioprrst
parrot-fish
afhkllntuy
thankfully
afhklnntuu
unthankful
afhllorttu
throat-full
afhllrtuwy
wrathfully
afiiinnntt
infinitant
afiiinnrty
infinitary
afiiklortt
forkit-tail
afiilllnuy
unfilially
afiillrrty
fritillary
afiillstuv
fluvialist
afiilmnosw
Wolfianism
afiilnnost
fontinalis
afiilnorsu
infusorial
afiilnortt
filtration
flirtation
afiinnorsu
infusorian
afiinssttu
fustianist
afiiorrstu
trifarious
afilllltyy
tilly-fally
afillmnory
informally
afillnppty
flippantly
afilmnosuy
infamously
afilnoruxy
fluxionary
afimmoqrsu
squamiform

afimmortuu
fumatorium
afimnoorsu
foraminous
afimnrstuu
rumfustian
afimooprrv
vaporiform
afimorrstt
stratiform
aflllnuuwy
unlawfully
afllmnnuuy
unmanfully
afllmnouwy
womanfully
afllnrtuuy
unartfully
afloooprsw
sloop-of-war
aggggiinzz
zigzagging
agggiiinnv
gaingiving
agggilnntu
gatling-gun
agggilnrst
straggling
agghhoprry
hygrograph
agghiinnrs
garnishing
agghillnuy
laughingly
agghilnnsy
gnashingly
agghilnnuw
whaling-gun
agghilnort
light-organ
agghilnsst
night-glass
agghloopry
graphology
logography
aggiillnns
signalling
aggiilnntu
agglutinin
aggiimnnns
singing-man
aggillnnsy
slangingly
aggillnnty
tanglingly
aggillnoty
gloatingly
aggilloost
algologist
aggilmorsy
gargoylism
aggilnntwy
twangingly

aggilnprsy
graspingly
aggiloorst
agrologist
agginnssww
swing-swang
agginorrtt
garrotting
agginosstu
outgassing
agglnooorz
Gorgonzola
aggloorsty
gastrology
aggmosstuy
mystagogus
aggnorrssw
grass-grown
aghhiloprt
lithograph
aghhiopppy
hippophagy
aghhloopry
holography
aghhnooppr
phonograph
aghhoopprt
photograph
aghhooprrt
orthograph
aghhooprry
horography
aghhortuwy
throughway
aghiilnors
Anglo-Irish
aghiimnntt
tithing-man
aghiinnrsv
varnishing
aghiinprrs
hairspring
aghiinrtww
wainwright
aghikmrttu
khitmutgar
aghillnosw
shallowing
aghillnoty
loathingly
aghilloptu
plough-tail
aghilnntuy
hauntingly
aghilnprst
spring-halt
aghilnpsty
night-palsy
aghilnrstt
stringhalt
aghiloppry
lipography
aghiloppsy
gypsophila

aghilprtwy
playwright
aghilrstty
straightly
aghimmopry
mimography
aghimnoops
siphonogam
aghimnprtu
upright-man
aghinnrttu
rat-hunting
aghinopttw
towing-path
aghiopprrs
spirograph
aghioppsux
xiphopagus
aghlmmopry
lymphogram
aghlnooort
orthogonal
aghloppryy
polygraphy
aghloprsty
stylograph
aghloprxyy
xylography
aghmmooosu
homogamous
aghmnoopry
gramophony
monography
nomography
aghmnoopty
pathognomy
aghmnoortu
mouth-organ
aghmooopsu
omophagous
aghmooprty
tomography
aghnnoopru
harpoon-gun
aghnooprsy
nosography
aghnoorstt
goat's-thorn
aghooopsuz
zoophagous
aghoopprty
topography
aghooprsst
gastrosoph
aghopprryy
pyrography
aghopprtyy
typography
agiiilmnnn
mainlining
agiiilnott
litigation
agiiilnstv
vitalising

agiiimnott
mitigation
agiiinorrt
irrigation
agiikkmnnr
marking-ink
agiiknnnpr
napkin-ring
agiillnnst
installing
agiillnnuu
unilingual
agiillnory
originally
agiillnrtu
trilingual
agiillnrvy
virginally
agiillntvy
vigilantly
agiillrtty
gratillity
agiilnnoru
unoriginal
agiilnprst
springtail
agiilnprsy
aspiringly
praisingly
agiilnrsty
laryngitis
agiiloostx
axiologist
agiimmosst
misogamist
agiimmsstt
stigmatism
agiimnnprs
mainspring
agiimnssuv
vaginismus
agiimortty
mitigatory
agiimssttt
stigmatist
agiinnnnps
inspanning
agiinnnttu
untainting
agiinnoort
ignoration
agiinnortv
invigorant
agiinnprsu
unaspiring
agiinnrttu
intriguant
agiinnsstu
sustaining
agiinnstuy
sanguinity
agiinoorrt
originator

agiinoprrr
rip-roaring
agiinorstt
instigator
agiinorsuv
viraginous
agiinpprsw
ripping-saw
agikklnrsy
skylarking
agiklmnnos
king-salmon
agiklnnpry
prankingly
agiklnnpsy
spankingly
agikmnnoor
moonraking
agikmnnotu
Kuomintang
agikmnnrtu
marking-nut
agilllnruy
alluringly
agilllnryy
rallyingly
agillnnsty
slantingly
agillnoprt
patrolling
agillnrsuy
singularly
agillntity
tattlingly
agilloosss
isoglossal
agilloostt
isoglottal
agillootww
goat-willow
agilmnssuy
assumingly
agilmoostt
atmologist
agilmoostu
gliomatous
agilmoosty
Mayologist
agilmopsty
polygamist
agilnnnopy
non-playing
agilnnnoyy
annoyingly
agilnnopty
poignantly
agilnnopyy
polygynian
agilnnorty
ignorantly
agilnnosuu
lanuginous
agilnnppsy
snappingly

agilnnttuy
tauntingly
agilnntuvy
vauntingly
agilnoostu
antilogous
agilnprsst
salt-spring
agilnrstty
startingly
agiloorsty
aristology
agilorssst
glossarist
agimmnnory
May-morning
agimmnoost
monogamist
agimnnnooy
monogynian
agimnnssuu
unassuming
agimnoopru
amino-group
agimnoorst
agronomist
agimnoprsu
sporangium
aginnooprt
organ-point
aginnppsuw
swan-upping
aginnrstuw
turning-saw
aginoorsuv
voraginous
aginprsssu
surpassing
agiorsttuu
gratuitous
aglllooprry
pyrogallol
agllnoopyy
palynology
agllrttuuy
gutturally
aglmooopty
potamology
aglmooosty
somatology
aglmoopsuy
polygamous
aglmoppruu
propagulum
aglmorssst
storm-glass
aglnoorsuu
languorous
aglooppryy
papyrology
agmmnooosu
monogamous
agmnnoorww
woman-grown

agmnoorsty
gastronomy
agmoorstty
gastrotomy
agmorrstuu
surrogatum
agoorrssst
grass-roots
ahhillwwwy
whillywhaw
ahhilmopty
philomathy
ahhilopsty
lithophysa
ahhimnopry
rhinophyma
ahhimnopst
phantomish
ahhimnosty
Mishnayoth
ahhimnptuy
hypanthium
ahhiooprrz
Rhizophora
ahhioprstu
authorship
ahhiprsttw
thwartship
ahhisswwyy
wishy-washy
ahhllmooty
homothally
ahhllooopt
holophotal
ahiiijknrs
jinrikisha
ahiiilnppp
Philippian
philippina
ahiiilnpst
Philistian
ahiiimmpsx
amphimixis
ahiikmnrss
Krishnaism
ahiilmortu
humiliator
ahiimnnotu
inhumation
ahiimnntuy
inhumanity
ahiimnorsw
Irishwoman
ahiirssttw
shirtwaist
ahijnnnoos
Johnsonian
ahikkmnrss
skrimshank
ahiklprssy
sparkishly
ahiknprrsw
shrinkwrap

ahiknpsstu
Skupshtina
ahillmqsuy
qualmishly
ahillortty
litholatry
ahilmmopps
psammophil
ahilmmorsu
humoralism
ahilmnnoor
monorhinal
ahilmnopyy
Polyhymnia
ahilmnoswy
womanishly
ahilmorstu
humoralist
ahilmpssyy
symphysial
ahilnoortz
horizontal
ahilnppssy
snappishly
ahilnpsstu
sultanship
ahilooprty
ophiolatry
ahimnooosu
homoousian
ahimnoorru
honorarium
ahimnoorsu
harmonious
ahimnoppss
pansophism
ahimnoprst
matronship
ahimnoprty
Amphitryon
ahimnprttu
triumphant
ahimorstuu
haustorium
ahinnooprt
Trophonian
ahinnoprry
pyrrhonian
ahinoppsst
pansophist
ahinoprsux
xiphosuran
ahinprsttu
truantship
ahioopsstz
zoothapsis
ahioopsttx
phototaxis
ahiopprsst
pastorship
ahiopsssty
hypostasis
ahklooostu
akolouthos

ahllmoostt
small-tooth
ahllmorssu
small-hours
ahlloprstu
prothallus
ahlloptxyy
phyllotaxy
ahlmmoopsy
homoplasmy
ahlnopstuy
polyanthus
ahlooprstu
south-polar
ahlorrsttu
ultrashort
ahmnnoorsu
honours-man
ahmnnoostu
Anthonomus
ahmnpstuyy
unsympathy
ahnnosstuy
synanthous
ahnooprtyz
zoanthropy
ahnoopstty
nostopathy
photonasty
ahnoopttuy
tautophony
ahnopprtty
tryptophan
ahoopprtty
Protophyta
ahooprrtxy
orthopraxy
ahoorrtttw
throatwort
aiiiinnott
initiation
aiiillmntu
illuminati
aiiillmrty
militarily
aiiillppst
papillitis
aiiilmmmns
minimalism
aiiilmmnst
minimalist
aiiilmmrst
militarism
aiiilmnoss
moniliasis
aiiilmnott
limitation
aiiilmrstt
militarist
aiiilmrstv
trivialism
aiiilmrsty
similarity

aiiilorstv
visitorial
aiiimnnott
intimation
aiiimnopss
pianissimo
aiiimprsvv
viviparism
aiiinnoost
ionisation
aiiinnottv
invitation
aiiinorrtt
irritation
aiiinorttt
tritiation
aiiinortty
initiatory
aiiinosttv
visitation
aiiinotttv
titivation
aiiiprssty
pityriasis
aiiiprtvvy
viviparity
aiillmnntu
illuminant
aiillmnory
millionary
aiillmnotu
illuminato
aiillmntty
militantly
aiillnootv
volitional
aiillnosuv
villainous
aiillnosvy
visionally
aiillnotuv
outvillain
aiilloortv
volitorial
aiillorsty
solitarily
aiillorttt
titillator
aiillosstt
solstitial
aiillottvy
volatility
aiillprsty
pistillary
aiillstuvv
valvulitis
aiilmmmors
immoralism
aiilmmnnos
nominalism
aiilmmnoot
immolation
aiilmmnrsu
luminarism

aiilmmorst
immoralist
aiilmmorty
immorality
aiilmnnost
nominalist
aiilmnnotu
lumination
aiilmnoort
monitorial
aiilmnostu
simulation
aiilmnottu
mutilation
aiilmnrssu
insularism
aiilmnrstu
luminarist
aiilmnrtuy
unmilitary
aiilmorstv
Voltairism
aiilmpprst
spirit-lamp
aiilmrrtuv
triumviral
aiilmrstuv
virtualism
aiilnnoost
insolation
aiilnnostu
insulation
aiilnooppt
oppilation
aiilnoopst
positional
spoliation
aiilnoottv
volitation
aiilnpttuy
nuptiality
aiilnrssuy
urinalysis
aiilnrstuy
insularity
aiilorsstu
sailor-suit
aiilqrstuy
squirality
aiilrsttuv
virtualist
aiilrtttuy
titularity
aiilrttuvy
virtuality
aiimmnnotu
ammunition
aiimmprrtu
imprimatur
aiimmrttuy
immaturity
aiimnnnoot
nomination

aiimnnoors
Morisonian
aiimnnortu
rumination
aiimnnrstt
ministrant
aiimnoottv
motivation
aiimnoprtv
provitamin
aiimnoprty
omniparity
aiimnopstu
utopianism
aiimnopttu
imputation
aiimnorssy
missionary
aiimnprstu
puritanism
aiimnpsstu
impuissant
aiimnpstty
tympanitis
aiimnrsssu
Russianism
aiimoprstt
patriotism
aiimorrstt
traitorism
aiimossttt
stomatitis
aiinnnoott
intonation
aiinnnootv
innovation
aiinnopstu
supination
aiinnorstt
transition
aiinnorstu
insinuator
aiinooppst
apposition
aiinoprrst
inspirator
aiinopssst
Passionist
aiinorttuy
tuitionary
aiinorttvy
invitatory
aiinrssstu
Russianist
aiioprsuvv
viviparous
aiipprsstu
Aristippus
aiiprsttvy
varitypist
aijlmnorsu
journalism
aijlnorstu
journalist

aijmnoqrtu
quint-major
aiklopstuv
Volapükist
aiknoprstw
paintworks
ailllltvyy
tilly-vally
aillmmorty
immortally
aillmnoopy
polynomial
aillmoprtu
multipolar
aillmoprxy
proximally
aillmqrtuz
quartz-mill
aillnnooty
notionally
aillnnosuy
unisonally
aillnooprt
pollinator
Trollopian
aillnoopty
optionally
aillnoostu
solutional
aillnopptt
pilot-plant
aillnqrtuy
tranquilly
ailloooprrt
pillar-root
ailloorrsy
serorially
aillorstty
stillatory
aillorttuy
tutorially
ailmmnortu
unimmortal
ailmnnooos
Solomonian
ailmnnoopr
pronominal
ailmnnorsu
surnominal
ailmnnrtuy
ruminantly
ailmnoopst
lampoonist
ailmnortuy
unmorality
ailmooprrt
implorator
ailmooprst
prostomial
ailmoopstu
lipomatous
ailmorsttu
stimulator

ailmorstuy
simulatory
ailmosssty
asystolism
ailnnoopss
sponsional
ailnnoprst
rosin-plant
ailnnqrtuu
untranquil
ailnooopst
piano-stool
ailnoopptu
population
ailnooprss
sponsorial
ailnoottuv
volutation
ailnorsttu
lustration
ailnosttuu
ustulation
ailnpsstuy
puissantly
ailooprsty
spoliatory
ailopprtuy
popularity
ailoprsttu
stipulator
aimmnorstu
stramonium
aimmoorrtu
moratorium
aimmttxxyy
mixty-maxty
aimnooprsu
omniparous
aimnoosttu
autonomist
aimnoosttx
taxonomist
aimnopsstu
assumption
aimnrsttuu
nasturtium
aimooortvy
ovariotomy
aimoprsstt
prostatism
aimoqsstuy
squamosity
ainnooprtt
antiproton
ainnoortvy
innovatory
ainooprsty
anisotropy
ainoopsstu
outpassion
ainoorrsuv
ranivorous
ainoprsttu
stupration

ainoprstuu
usurpation
ainorrsstt
transistor
ainorrstty
transitory
ainorsttuu
suturation
ainprstuuv
pursuivant
aiooprrsuu
uproarious
aiooprstvy
vaporosity
aiooqsttuu
quotatious
aioorrsttu
traitorous
aiopprrsuu
pupiparous
aioprrsuvv
parvovirus
aiorrrtttu
triturator
akllmmosuw
musk-mallow
akloprrsuy
sky-parlour
akmnorttuw
tutworkman
alloopprrt
poll-parrot
alloorsuvy
valorously
alloprstyy
polystylar
alloprttuy
plutolatry
almmnsssuu
Mussulmans
almnoorsty
monostylar
almoopprst
protoplasm
almopsttuu
postulatum
almrttuuuy
tumultuary
alnprstuuy
pursuantly
alooorstuz
zoolatrous
aloopprstt
protoplast
aloopprtty
prototypal
alooprsuvy
vaporously
aloprtuuvy
voluptuary
ammoostuxy
myxomatous
amnnoostww
townswoman

amnooostuu
autonomous
amnooprsuy
paronymous
amoorssttu
stromatous
amopprrtuy
promptuary
amopprsttu
post-partum
aooopprssu
aposporous
aooopprstu
apotropous
aooprrrstz
razor-strop
aoprrstuuy
usurpatory
bbbceeilrs
bescribble
bbbceeorwy
cobwebbery
bbbcjklouy
bubbly-jock
bbbdeeinor
beribboned
bbbeeiinrw
wine-bibber
bbbehhlosu
hobble-bush
bbbeoorsxy
bobbysoxer
bbbghijnoo
hobjobbing
bbbghinnoo
hobnobbing
bbbgiiknos
ski-bobbing
bbbhrssuuy
subshrubby
bbblloowwy
blow-by-blow
bbcdeikorr
rock-ribbed
bbcdeirssu
subscribed
bbceeknrru
rubber-neck
bbceelnoou
bubonocele
bbcehinssu
chubbiness
bbceirrssu
subscriber
bbcgiiinrt
crib-biting
bbcgiilnrs
scribbling
bbchmrrsuu
crumb-brush
bbdeeflstu
stubble-fed
bbdeegiill
big-bellied

bbdeeimorv
dive-bomber
bbdeeinorw
ribbon-weed
bbdehnrsuu
unshrubbed
bbdeiknoor
bookbinder
bbdeimnort
bond-timber
bbdeirrttu
butter-bird
bbdelopsuu
pseudobulb
bbdhiioprs
bishop-bird
bbeeefgrru
beefburger
bbeeefirsw
beef-brewis
bbeeehnnrt
herb-bennet
bbeeellsuv
bull-beeves
bbeeelortt
beer-bottle
bbeehorrrt
herb-robert
bbeellottu
bluebottle
bbeelmortt
letter-bomb
bbeelmossv
bomb-vessel
bbeelnnotu
blue-bonnet
bbeemmnntu
benumbment
bbeflmootu
bumble-foot
bbegiilopy
bibliopegy
bbegilnrsu
slubbering
bbegloossu
subglobose
bbehhilost
shibboleth
bbehhoorsy
hobby-horse
bbehmooopr
ombrophobe
bbeiilloop
bibliopole
bbeikllorr
bill-broker
bbeiknnoss
knobbiness
bbeilnossw
wobbliness
bbeinssstu
stubbiness
bbeiooprуz
booby-prize

bbeklorruw
rubble-work
bbelooprtw
pot-wobbler
bbemprttuu
butter-bump
bbeoorrrtu
root-rubber
bbfhiinors
ribbon-fish
bbghiinrsu
rubbishing
bbghillnoy
hobblingly
bbghimnotu
thingumbob
bbgiillnny
nibblingly
bbgiillooy
bibliology
bbgiklnuuy
bulk-buying
bbgilnnsuy
snubbingly
bbhiiillop
bibliophil
bbhilnossy
snobbishly
bbhnosttuu
button-bush
bbiiiimnot
imbibition
bbiikkntuz
kibbutznik
bbiilloopy
bibliopoly
bbimnoorrw
ribbon-worm
bbimnoorsu
Bourbonism
bbinoorstu
Bourbonist
bbjmmmoouu
mumbo-jumbo
bblmoorsuy
Bloomsbury
bblnorstuy
stubbornly
bccdeeemnu
decumbence
bccdeeilot
decoctible
bccdeemnuy
decumbency
bccdeilnou
conducible
bcceeemnru
recumbence
bcceeenpsu
pubescence
bcceeiinos
bioscience
bcceeinrty
cybernetic

bcceemnruy
recumbency
bccehiimru
cherubimic
bccehnorss
crossbench
bcceiiimss
cicisbeism
bcceiinoot
coenobitic
bcceimnnuy
incumbency
bccekmoopt
pocket-comb
bccesssuuu
succubuses
bcchiinort
bronchitic
bcchlmortu
crumb-cloth
bcddeegikr
deck-bridge
bcddeeiltu
deductible
bcddeikllu
duck-billed
bcddhiistu
Buddhistic
bcdeeeehmr
bêche-de-mer
bcdeeefilt
defectible
bcdeeehnru
unbreeched
bcdeeeiint
benedicite
bcdeeeilpt
deceptible
bcdeeeiltt
detectible
bcdeeeirrs
redescribe
bcdeeelmry
Decemberly
bcdeehlnnu
unblenched
bcdeehlost
bedclothes
bcdeehoprs
beech-drops
bcdeehoruu
debouchure
bcdeeiilnr
incredible
bcdeeilnnz
zinc-blende
bcdeeilnru
uncredible
bcdeeimrst
Decembrist
bcdeeinssu
subsidence
bcdeeinstu
Benedictus

bcdeekllnu
bull-necked
bcdeeklrtu
truckle-bed
bcdeemnoru
code-number
bcdeemnruu
uncumbered
bcdeemoors
rose-combed
bcdeenosst
second-best
bcdeeorrss
crossbreed
bcdefiiklr
brickfield
bcdeflootu
club-footed
bcdehilnou
double-chin
bcdehirrry
bird-cherry
bcdehloors
school-bred
bcdeiillnu
includible
bcdeiilnry
incredibly
bcdeiiloos
obeliscoid
bcdeiloorr
corrodible
bcdeilopru
producible
bcdeinssuy
subsidency
bcdeirrrsu
scrub-rider
bcdekorttu
butterdock
bcdelorruy
cloudberry
bcdemmnruu
cummerbund
bcdenorruv
curb-vendor
bcdenorsuu
unobscured
bcdenrrsuu
underscrub
bcdgiiostu
dog-biscuit
bcdhhiilrt
childbirth
bcdhooopru
brood-pouch
bcdiiiloty
docibility
bcdiilmoru
lumbricoid
bcdiioprrt
tropic-bird
bcdillotuu
cloud-built
bcdiloossu
discobolus
bcdinostuu
subduction
bcdkloost
bloodstock
bcdkmrstuu
dumbstruck
bcdkorruuw
burrow-duck
bcdlorstuu
cloudburst
bceeeehlsu
blue-cheese
bceeeffilt
effectible
bceeefinnt
beneficent
bceeeghins
beseeching
bceeehlrss
breechless
bceeeiikrt
riebeckite
bceeeijlrt
rejectible
bceeeillnu
ebullience
bceeeilprt
receptible
bceeeirstu
erubescite
bceeellmru
cerebellum
bceeenrstu
erubescent
bceeeprrsu
spruce-beer
bceefiinrt
tenebrific
bceefikrtu
fire-bucket
bceefllruw
curfew-bell
bceefprstu
subprefect
bceegiinot
biogenetic
bceeginrsu
subgeneric
bceehimptu
thumbpiece
bceehirtwy
bewitchery
bceehklnou
huckle-bone
bceehklosu
shoebuckle
bceehkooqu
cheque-book
bceehkorry
chokeberry
bceehmnrsu
Ubermensch
bceehmoruu
embouchure
bceeiilpst
plebiscite
bceeiirrst
cerebritis
bceeijstuv
subjective
bceeiklmnr
limber-neck
bceeillmru
Illecebrum
bceeillnpu
blue-pencil
bceeillnuy
ebulliency
bceeilmost
comestible
bceeilnort
Colbertine
bceeilnoty
by-election
bceeiprrrs
prescriber
bceeipsssu
subspecies
bceejlosst
objectless
bceeklnott
bottle-neck
bceeklorsw
skew-corbel
bceelmrssu
cumberless
bceelnottu
cuttle-bone
bceelnrtuu
turbulence
bceemmnrtu
cumberment
bceemmorsu
cumbersome
bceeooorrr
corroboree
bceffinnoo
coffin-bone
bcefhnnort
front-bench
bcefijstuy
subjectify
bcefilnoru
unforcible
bcefklstuu
bucketfuls
bceghiintw
bewitching
bceghinrtu
butchering
bcegiilorr
corrigible
bcegillnor
corbelling
bcegilmnoy
becomingly
bcegiloooy
bioecology
bcegimnnou
unbecoming
bcegmorssu
comburgess
bcehhnnouy
honeybunch
bcehiiiotv
cohibitive
bcehiimost
biochemist
bcehiinsst
bitchiness
bcehilnoor
bronchiole
bcehilopry
hyperbolic
bcehinnssu
bunchiness
bcehkkoost
sketch-book
bcehkloosu
blockhouse
bcehllloos
school-bell
bcehmrstuw
thumbscrew
bcehooprtu
Turcophobe
bceiiilmms
immiscible
bceiiilmty
imbecility
bceiiilnnv
invincible
bceiikllls
sickle-bill
bceiilmmos
embolismic
bceiimoqtu
coquimbite
bceiimorst
biometrics
bceijnostu
subjection
bceikloort
bootlicker
bceiknrrru
rick-burner
bceikootty
tickety-boo
bceillmooo
locomobile
bceilmoort
bolometric
bceilnpssu
publicness
bceilnrtuu
tuberculin
bceiloorrs
corrosible
bceimostuv
combustive
bceinnossu
bounciness
bceinorttu
contribute
bceinosstu
subsection
bceiopprsy
presbyopic
bceioprrrs
proscriber
bceiorsstt
obstetrics
bcejkmpruu
buck-jumper
bcejloostu
object-soul
bcekklnouw
knuckle-bow
bcekkooopt
pocket-book
bceklnrtuu
turnbuckle
bcekoorsu
source-book
bcekorrttu
rock-butter
bcelmooorw
wool-comber
bcelmrtuuu
tuberculum
bcelnrtuuy
turbulency
bcelooorst
boot-closer
bcelopstuu
suboctuple
bcelrstuuu
subculture
bcemnoprtu
procumbent
bcemoorssx
Scombresox
bcenooptux
pouncet-box
bcenoorsss
crossbones
bceoorrssw
crossbower
bceorrsttu
obstructer
bcfiimorrr
cribriform
bcfosssuuu
subfuscous
bcghinntuu
cub-hunting
bcgiknprsu
springbuck
bchiiinoot
cohibition
bchiimoopr
biomorphic
bchiinorst
bronchitis

bchiiopssy
  biophysics
bchimnooop
  monophobic
bchimoortt
  thrombotic
bchiooorrt
  orthoboric
bchiorrsst
  cross-birth
bchkloooos
  school-book
bciiilnnvy
  invincibly
bciiilortt
  trilobitic
bciilnopsy
  psilocybin
bciilorsuu
  lubricious
bcikmoorst
  broomstick
bciknopttu
  pin-buttock
bciloostuu
  tubicolous
bcimnoostu
  combustion
bcinossstu
  consubsist
bcioprsstu
  subtropics
bckmooortt
  rock-bottom
bckmooruuz
  zumbooruck
bckoorrttu
  rock-turbot
bcllnooott
  cotton-boll
bclmorsuuy
  cumbrously
bcnoorruwy
  cony-burrow
bcnoortuxy
  country-box
bcoorrsttu
  obstructor
bdddeeginw
  wedding-bed
bdddeeloor
  red-blooded
bdddeelouy
  double-dyed
bddeeeillv
  bedevilled
bddeeeilrw
  bewildered
bddeeelouy
  double-eyed
bddeeenrtu
  debentured
bddeeeoprw
  deep-browed

bddeegntuu
  unbudgeted
bddeeimmnu
  unbedimmed
bddeeimnnr
  mind-bender
bddeeimnou
  unembodied
bddeeinnnu
  unbedinned
bddeeinrst
  bestridden
bddeeiorrv
  overbidder
bddeelmoru
  dumbledore
bddeelnrtu
  trundle-bed
bddeelooyy
  bloody-eyed
bddeennruu
  unburdened
bddefillou
  full-bodied
bddefioost
  soft-bodied
bddegillou
  double-gild
bddehiippr
  bird-hipped
bddehinoor
  behind-door
bddehlnoor
  bond-holder
bddehlooot
  hot-blooded
bddeiiprrs
  bird-spider
bddeiirsuv
  subdivider
bddeiirttw
  bird-witted
bddeilmorw
  middlebrow
bddeilnoou
  unbloodied
bddeilnruu
  underbuild
bddeiloosz
  blood-sized
bddeimnoru
  dendrobium
bddelloruw
  dull-browed
bddelmorru
  drumbledor
bddfgiinor
  forbidding
bddhlnooou
  bloodhound
bddiiknssu
  'sbuddikins
bddiklnnru
  blind-drunk

bdeeeeelty
  beetle-eyed
bdeeeelrtw
  beweltered
bdeeefilns
  defensible
bdeeefittw
  beef-witted
bdeeeflott
  bottle-feed
bdeeeginsw
  beeswinged
bdeeegllot
  gold-beetle
bdeeeglntu
  dung-beetle
bdeeehllnr
  hellbender
bdeeehmorw
  home-brewed
bdeeeiilsv
  disbelieve
bdeeeilnss
  edibleness
bdeeeilntx
  extendible
bdeeeilnuv
  unbelieved
bdeeeilstw
  wildebeest
bdeeeimrtt
  embittered
bdeeeinnrz
  Benzedrine
bdeeeinrrt
  interbreed
bdeeellmow
  embowelled
bdeeelmnor
  emboldener
bdeeelmtuw
  tumble-weed
bdeeelortu
  doubletree
bdeeelrrry
  elderberry
bdeeenrttu
  unbettered
bdeeeprrss
  bedpresser
bdeeerrsvw
  bed-swerver
bdeefggloo
  fool-begged
bdeefilnrs
  self-binder
bdeefilnsy
  defensibly
bdeeflooot
  lobe-footed
bdeeforrst
  forest-bred
bdeegiilst
  digestible

bdeegiinnr
  inbreeding
bdeegiirrw
  wire-bridge
bdeegikrsw
  skew-bridge
bdeegillor
  gor-bellied
bdeegilnuu
  unbeguiled
bdeegilrss
  bridgeless
bdeegimosu
  disembogue
bdeeginrrt
  regent-bird
bdeeginttw
  bed-wetting
bdeegiorrv
  overbridge
bdeehillps
  bedellship
bdeehlnnor
  hornblende
bdeehlnnou
  unbeholden
bdeeiilmos
  demobilise
bdeeiilnnv
  invendible
bdeeiilnrr
  bridle-rein
bdeeiilrtv
  divertible
bdeeiilstv
  divestible
bdeeiinnot
  inobedient
bdeeillntu
  tunbellied
bdeeillopt
  pot-bellied
bdeeilmosu
  semi-double
bdeeilmosw
  disembowel
bdeeilmrss
  dissembler
bdeeilnnos
  disennoble
bdeeilnnuv
  unvendible
bdeeilnorr
  borderline
bdeeilnoty
  obediently
bdeeilorsw
  bowdlerise
bdeeimmnot
  embodiment
bdeeimnntt
  indebtment
bdeeimnrtu
  untimbered

bdeeimooss
  somebodies
bdeeimorrs
  besom-rider
bdeeimorry
  embroidery
bdeeinnotu
  unobedient
bdeeiorsss
  sobersides
bdeeipppr
  bird-pepper
bdeeirrssu
  redisburse
bdeeknorrv
  kerb-vendor
bdeellnruy
  underbelly
bdeelnossu
  doubleness
bdeelorrss
  borderless
bdeelostty
  besottedly
bdeemnnruu
  unnumbered
bdeemnorsu
  burdensome
bdeemnstuu
  subduement
bdeennnotu
  unbonneted
bdeennorru
  underborne
bdeenorruv
  overburden
bdeenorsuv
  unobserved
bdeenostuw
  unbestowed
bdeenrttuu
  unbuttered
bdeffiilsu
  diffusible
bdefginoor
  foreboding
bdefgioort
  footbridge
bdefgsstuu
  fuss-budget
bdefillost
  soft-billed
bdefiloost
  fieldboots
  soft-boiled
bdefnoortw
  bow-fronted
bdegggiinn
  egg-binding
bdegglnooo
  boondoggle
bdeghhiinr
  highbinder

bdeghimotu
big-mouthed
bdeghinnou
hinge-bound
bdeghlnouu
double-hung
bdeghnoruu
underbough
bdegiillmr
limb-girdle
bdegiillnv
diving-bell
bdegiilnou
indigo-blue
bdegiimntu
mini-budget
bdegiinorr
broidering
riding-robe
bdegillort
tollbridge
bdegilnnot
Bedlington
bdegilnnru
blundering
bdegimoorr
bridegroom
bdeginoory
gooney-bird
bdeglmntuu
tumble-dung
bdehiilpsu
bisulphide
bdehiirrsy
hybridiser
bdehimntux
thumb-index
bdehimoors
rhomboides
bdehinrstu
disburthen
bdehiorrsw
whore's-bird
bdehirsttu
butter-dish
bdehklooor
book-holder
bdehllnosu
shellbound
bdehlooors
blood-horse
bdehnoosuu
housebound
bdehnortux
thunder-box
bdehnrrsuu
underbrush
undershrub
bdeiiilnrv
biliverdin
bdeiikrrst
bird-strike
bdeiilmors
disembroil
bdeiilmrss
missel-bird
bdeiirsttu
distribute
bdeijnorsu
subjoinder
bdeiknnorw
wind-broken
bdeillmotu
multilobed
bdeillorwy
yellow-bird
bdeillossu
dissoluble
bdeillotux
billet-doux
bdeilmnsuu
unsublimed
bdeilmorsw
bowdlerism
bdeilnnost
stone-blind
bdeilnooww
window-bole
bdeilorstu
distrouble
bdeimmooss
disembosom
bdeimnorss
morbidness
bdeimoorxy
oxy-bromide
bdeinoorss
broodiness
bdeinrsstu
turbidness
bdeioorttw
bitterwood
bdeknnoorw
broken-down
bdellnopsu
spellbound
bdelloorvy
overboldly
bdellortuy
troubledly
bdelmmnouy
molybdenum
bdelmnoooy
blood-money
bdelmnotuw
tumbledown
bdelnooost
bloodstone
bdelnortuu
untroubled
bdemnnoouy
money-bound
bdemnoottu
unbottomed
bdemoorrrs
smorrebrød
bdemoorrsy
dyer's-broom
bdennottuu
unbuttoned
bdenoorruw
unborrowed
bdenopttuu
buttoned-up
bdfllotuuy
doubtfully
bdflnotuuu
undoubtful
bdfnoorstu
frostbound
bdgiiiknrs
bird-skiing
bdgiiknnry
by-drinking
bdgiilnpuu
upbuilding
bdgiinoort
riding-boot
bdgiinorvx
driving-box
bdgikmnosu
subkingdom
bdgillootu
blood-guilt
bdgilnnnuu
unbundling
bdgilnoory
broodingly
bdgilnotuy
doubtingly
bdginnotuu
undoubting
bdginooorw
wood-boring
bdglooopru
blood-group
bdglrrstuu
Struldbrug
bdhiiiinst
disinhibit
bdhiilrrwy
whirlybird
bdhilopryy
polyhybrid
bdhimnoory
monohybrid
bdhinoootu
bountihood
bdhlnoottu
button-hold
bdhnnoortu
north-bound
bdhnoostuu
south-bound
bdiiiilnst
libidinist
bdiiilnosu
libidinous
bdiiloorst
strobiloid
bdillnpruy
purblindly
bdilmoossy
molybdosis
bdimnorttu
mutton-bird
bdknnooory
Donnybrook
bdmnoorstu
stormbound
bdnooottuw
button-wood
beeeeflnss
feebleness
beeeegiknp
beekeeping
beeeegilly
eye-legible
beeeeginnr
beer-engine
beeeeglstu
Betelgeuse
beeeegltuz
Betelgeuze
beeeeilnpt
pine-beetle
beeeellnsw
well-beseen
beeeelorst
rose-beetle
beeeelortv
rove-beetle
beeeelrssz
breezeless
beeeemmrrr
rememberer
beeefillrx
reflexible
beeefillss
beliefless
beeefilrrr
referrible
beeefimort
beforetime
beeefinrrv
nerve-fibre
beeefmrruz
bumfreezer
beeefoorrt
freebooter
beeeghinns
shebeening
beeeghlosu
glebe-house
beeegiillr
re-eligible
beeegilnrs
inselberge
beeeglnruy
bluey-green
beeegmoors
ember-goose
beeehiprst
sheep-biter
beeehllrtw
bell-wether
beeeiilmsv
misbelieve
beeeikllrr
bierkeller
beeeikmnrt
knee-timber
beeeilnruv
unbeliever
beeeilnstx
extensible
beeeilrrsv
reversible
beeeilrrtv
revertible
beeeimrrtt
embitterer
timber-tree
beeeimrstt
beetmister
beeeinrssz
breeziness
beeeinttwy
betweenity
beeeirrstw
sweet-brier
beeekkoopr
bookkeeper
beeeklmstu
musk-beetle
beeellprsv
vesper-bell
beeellrsst
bestseller
beeellrttu
bullet-tree
beeelmmnst
emblements
beeelmnotu
éboulement
beeelnnotv
benevolent
beeelnrsst
trebleness
beeelorttt
bottle-tree
beeemnrttt
betterment
beeennpryz
benzpyrene
beeenorstt
bonesetter
beeenrrstu
subterrene
beeenrsstt
betterness
beeeoqsuxz
squeeze-box
beeerrtttu
butter-tree
beefgiinnt
benefiting
beefgrstuu
subterfuge

beefiillnx
inflexible
beefiilnrr
inferrible
beefillmru
umbellifer
beefilmors
Froebelism
beefilnost
stifle-bone
beefilrstu
subfertile
beefiorssu
sebiferous
beefirttuw
butter-wife
beeflllorw
bell-flower
flower-bell
beeggiilln
negligible
beeggloort
bootlegger
beeghiilln
Ghibelline
beeghiknsu
husking-bee
beeghillls
sleigh-bell
beeghilnrt
blethering
beeghnoopr
negrophobe
beegiiilln
ineligible
beegiilnrt
Gilbertine
beegiilnst
ingestible
beegiinoss
biogenesis
beegillnrr
bell-ringer
beegilmnot
obligement
beegilmnrs
resembling
beegilnnnu
Nibelungen
beeginrttv
brevetting
beeglnotuu
blue-tongue
beegmnoryy
embryogeny
beegnnottu
unbegotten
beegnoorst
brent-goose
beegoorrsy
gooseberry
beehhlrsuw
brushwheel

beehiiitvx
exhibitive
beehillopt
phlebolite
beehilmost
blithesome
beehilnsst
blitheness
beehilossv
bolshevise
beehimmprs
membership
beehinrrry
Rheinberry
Rhineberry
beehlmnssu
humbleness
beehmoorst
bothersome
beehmoortt
mother-to-be
beehnoprrs
sphere-born
beeiijortu
bijouterie
beeiiklmrt
kimberlite
beeiilmnrt
timber-line
beeiilmrss
remissible
beeiilnnss
insensible
beeiilnntv
inventible
beeiilrsst
resistible
beeiilsstx
bissextile
beeikknorr
knobkerrie
beeiklnprs
besprinkle
beeilllllrs
bell-siller
beeilllovw
boll-weevil
beeilllrsv
silver-bell
beeillmntu
minute-bell
beeillootw
wellie-boot
beeilloprw
pillow-bere
beeillorsu
rebellious
beeillossw
Boswellise
beeillrstt
belletrist
beeilmnnss
nimbleness

beeilmnrru
lime-burner
beeilnnssu
unsensible
beeilnosst
ostensible
beeilssssu
subsessile
beeimmnrtu
imbruement
beeimorrst
sombrerite
beeimorrtt
tribometer
beeimorrtv
vibrometer
beeimorssv
misobserve
beeimorstt
timber-toes
beeinnorrt
Norbertine
beeinorrtt
torbernite
beeinorstu
tenebrious
beeinrsstt
bitterness
beeinrsttu
burnettise
beeiprstuv
subreptive
beeiqrrsuu
brusquerie
beeirssuvv
subversive
beeklloors
bookseller
beekloorrv
love-broker
beekloortt
letter-book
beeknnoopt
poke-bonnet
beeknnopsu
unbespoken
beeknnorss
brokenness
beeknoorst
stone-broke
beellnoptu
pollen-tube
beelloosty
obsoletely
beellrrttu
bell-turret
beelmmmntu
mumblement
beelmmnsuw
mumble-news
beelmmorsu
lumbersome
beelmnrssu
numberless

beelnoostt
bottle-nose
beelnprtuu
puberulent
beelnssstu
subtleness
beeloqsttu
blottesque
beelorstuv
oversubtle
beemmnnott
entombment
beemmnosst
embossment
beemmoorrt
ombrometer
beemmrrssu
bressummer
beemnoorww
bowerwomen
beemnorsss
sombreness
beemnosttw
bestowment
beemorsttt
bettermost
beenoorrst
stone-borer
beenossstu
obtuseness
beenprsssu
superbness
beenqsstuu
subsequent
beenrrttuy
Tyburn-tree
beeprrstyy
presbytery
beffiimntu
minibuffet
beffijknru
buff-jerkin
beffillmnu
muffin-bell
beffnooruy
buffoonery
befghiilrt
fire-blight
befgiinnor
fibrinogen
befgilnorw
fingerbowl
befhhlorst
flesh-broth
befhhlrssu
flesh-brush
befhillmtu
thimbleful
befhilostt
bottle-fish
befhirsttu
butter-fish
befhlnorsw
fresh-blown

befiillnxy
inflexibly
befiillors
fibrillose
befiilrstu
filibuster
befillrsty
blister-fly
befilmortw
timber-wolf
befimorrtu
tuberiform
befinorsuu
nubiferous
befllmrsuu
slumberful
befllmrtuu
tumblerful
beflnostuy
self-bounty
befnoorrst
forest-born
begghiinnt
benighting
begghmruuy
humbuggery
beggiillny
negligibly
beggilnnos
belongings
beghhoopry
hygrophobe
beghiilmrt
thimble-rig
beghiilnrt
blithering
beghillnsu
bushelling
beghimorst
brightsome
beghinrsst
brightness
beghnostuu
unbesought
beghoortuv
overbought
begiiillny
ineligibly
begiiillty
legibility
begiiklrtz
blitzkrieg
begiiknrtt
bitter-king
begiillntt
belittling
begiilmrtu
limburgite
begiilnrst
blistering
begiilnrtt
bitterling
begiklnruy
rebukingly

begiknnosu
bousingken
begillnorw
well-boring
begilmnrsu
slumbering
begilnnnuy
unbenignly
begilnorst
bolstering
begilnrstu
blustering
begilnsttu
subletting
begiloooxy
exobiology
begimnnorw
embrowning
begimnorss
Bergsonism
beginnorwz
bronze-wing
beginnostx
nesting-box
beginnosuu
nubigenous
begionoott
gnotobiote
beglmooryy
embryology
begnorruyy
youngberry
begoorrttt
bogtrotter
behhikrssu
bush-shrike
behhiooppp
hippophobe
behhoooppt
photophobe
behiiiintv
inhibitive
behiiinotx
exhibition
behiioprrt
prohibiter
behiiortxy
exhibitory
behikoprrs
ship-broker
behillorww
willow-herb
behilmoopr
ombrophile
behilmossv
bolshevism
behilosstv
bolshevist
behilprstu
butlership
behilrsttu
bur-thistle
behimopruu
euphorbium

behinosssy
boyishness
behioprstt
hop-bitters
behknoortu
book-hunter
behlmoopty
phlebotomy
behlnoottu
button-hole
behmnorttu
burnet-moth
behmooorst
smooth-bore
behmprttuu
tub-thumper
behooprssu
Russophobe
beiiilmmos
immobilise
beiiilnqtu
biquintile
beiiimnost
ebionitism
beiiimnstu
bituminise
beiiioopss
biopoiesis
beiillnotu
ebullition
beiillossu
solubilise
beiilmopss
impossible
beiilmrtuy
muliebrity
beiilnnssy
insensibly
beiilnorst
strobiline
beiilprstu
spirit-blue
beiilrssty
resistibly
beiilrsttt
librettist
beiimsssuv
submissive
beiinorstu
inebritous
beiinorsty
insobriety
beijlrrtuy
jerry-built
beiklmrttu
butter-milk
beikmnootu
minute-book
beilllmmru
lumber-mill
beillmossw
Boswellism
beillmssuu
subsellium

beilloottu
bouillotte
beilloprst
billposter
beilmnoosw
snowmobile
beilmooost
lobotomise
beilmoosst
obsoletism
beilmoprst
problemist
beilmorssy
symboliser
beilmstuuv
vestibulum
beilnnopst
splint-bone
beilnnssuy
unsensibly
beilnooost
obsoletion
beilnoprsw
spin-bowler
beilnopssu
unpossible
beilnossty
ostensibly
beilnostuy
nebulosity
beilnprsuy
ruby-spinel
beilnssstu
subtilness
beilrrsuvy
ruby-silver
beilsstuuv
subsultive
beimnnoopt
embonpoint
beimnorssu
submersion
beimorrstu
Morris-tube
beinnostuv
subvention
beinoprstu
subreption
beinorssuv
subversion
beinorstuu
subroutine
beinosstwx
witness-box
beinsssttu
subsistent
beiooqssuu
obsequious
beioorrttt
bitter-root
beioorsstu
boisterous
beioqrstuu
soubriquet

beiorrrttu
retributor
beiorsttuy
tuberosity
beisstttuu
substitute
bejklnottu
junk-bottle
beklnnoruy
unbrokenly
bekmnorssu
mossbunker
bekmoorstu
muster-book
beknoorsty
stony-broke
bellmopstu
post-bellum
bellnosuuy
nebulously
belloossty
bootlessly
bellorstuy
trolley-bus
belmmoorru
lumber-room
belmoosstt
bottomless
belmorssuu
slumberous
belnoorsww
snow-blower
belnopprru
purple-born
belooprstt
lobster-pot
beloprsuuu
puberulous
belorsstuu
blusterous
belorsttuu
outbluster
bemmoortyy
embryotomy
bemnoprsuu
penumbrous
bennoorstw
brownstone
benoorrttw
torrent-bow
benorssstu
robustness
beorrtttuw
butterwort
bffgiijlnu
luffing-jib
bffnnorsuw
snuff-brown
bfghilntyy
fly-by-night
bfgiinrtuy
brutifying
bfgillmnuy
fumblingly

bfhimoostt
bottom-fish
bfiiilstuy
fusibility
bfiiiorsst
fibrositis
bfiillorsu
fibrillous
bfilllssuy
blissfully
bfillnssuu
unblissful
bfllmoottu
full-bottom
bggghimnuu
humbugging
bggiiinnnr
inbringing
bggiillnoy
obligingly
bggiinnpru
upbringing
bggillnnuy
bunglingly
bghhiinrtt
birthnight
bghhiirrtt
birthright
bghiinnrsu
burnishing
bghillmnuy
humblingly
bghillnsuy
blushingly
bghilnnsuu
unblushing
bghinnotux
hunting-box
bgiiilnoty
ignobility
bgiiilnstu
bilinguist
bgiiklnnnu
unblinking
bgiilnoopt
pot-boiling
bgiilnossu
subsoiling
bgiimnsttu
submitting
bgiinnorrv
virgin-born
bgiinorsuu
rubiginous
bgijllmnuy
jumblingly
bgillmmnuy
mumblingly
bgillmnruy
rumblingly
bgillmrsuu
mulligrubs
bgilmnooss
blossoming

bgilmoorty
timbrology
bgiloorsty
bryologist
bgilorsuuu
lugubrious
bgimnooorr
robing-room
bginprstuu
upbursting
bhhimorsty
biorhythms
bhhoorsttu
toothbrush
bhiiiinnot
inhibition
bhiiimrsst
Britishism
bhiiinorty
inhibitory
bhiikmnpsu
bumpkinish
bhiikmnstu
thumbikins
bhiillrstt
still-birth
bhiiooprrt
prohibitor
bhimnprttu
thumbprint
bhimoorsst
thrombosis
bhinorrstw
Brownshirt
bhinortwwy
whity-brown
bhknoootttu
button-hook
bhlloossuu
holus-bolus
bhllrruuyy
hurly-burly
bhnopsttuu
push-button
bhoooopsuz
zoophobous
biiiilrsty
risibility
biiiilstvy
visibility
biiilmmmos
immobilism
biiilmmoty
immobility
biilllsyy
silly-billy
biillnostu
bullionist
biillostuy
solubility
biillotuvy
volubility
biimnosssu
submission

biimnostuu
bituminous
biinossssy
byssinosis
biioqstuuu
ubiquitous
bikllorsst
stork's-bill
biklmnoosu
book-muslin
billmnoruu
rumbullion
billmoorsu
morbillous
billnoortu
tourbillon
bimnoorstt
trombonist
bimoopprru
opprobrium
binnoorsst
Sorbonnist
binopsssuu
subspinous
bioorsstuu
robustious
bkmoooopprt
prompt-book
blmmoorssu
rum-blossom
ccccginooo
gonococcic
cccciimoor
micrococci
cccdeilopy
cyclopedic
cccdeimruu
circumduce
cccdimrtuu
circumduct
ccceehkklr
check-clerk
ccceeinnos
conscience
ccceeinrst
crescentic
ccceeintuy
cecutiency
ccceelnsuu
succulence
ccceenorru
occurrence
ccceehiilmy
hemicyclic
ccceehiilno
colchicine
ccceehimoty
ecchymotic
ccceehkorss
cross-check
ccceiilpry
pericyclic
ccceiimrsu
circumcise

ccceilotuy
leucocytic
ccceinnort
concentric
ccceinoosu
coccineous
ccceinootv
concoctive
ccceiooprt
eccoprotic
ccceklnoor
corncockle
ccceelnsuuy
succulency
cccgnooosu
gonococcus
ccchikopst
spitchcock
ccchilmooy
homocyclic
cccillopyy
polycyclic
cccilmnooy
monocyclic
cccilnstuy
succinctly
cccinnooot
concoction
ccciooprsy
cryoscopic
cccloorssy
cyclo-cross
ccddeennos
condescend
ccddeikmno
midden-cock
ccdeeeenpr
precedence
ccdeeefiin
deficience
ccdeeehins
dehiscence
ccdeeeknrw
crew-necked
ccdeeenpry
precedency
ccdeeenrst
crescented
decrescent
ccdeeerrsu
recrudesce
ccdeefiiny
deficiency
ccdeefinno
confidence
ccdeeginsu
succeeding
ccdeehiort
ricocheted
ccdeehmosy
ecchymosed
ccdeehnosy
synecdoche

ccdeehortt
crotcheted
ccdeeiiipt
epideictic
ccdeeiilrt
dielectric
ccdeeiippr
precipiced
ccdeeilmoo
coomceiled
ccdeeimort
ectodermic
ccdeeinnor
cinder-cone
ccdeeinopr
procidence
ccdeelmopt
complected
ccdeelnnoo
condolence
ccdeennort
concentred
ccdeenrruy
decurrency
ccdefinnoy
confidency
ccdefkllou
full-cocked
ccdehillos
cold-chisel
ccdehnorsu
unscorched
ccdeiiilot
idiolectic
ccdeiiklss
dickcissel
ccdeiilopy
epicycloid
ccdeiinnor
endocrinic
ccdeiinnot
coincident
ccdeiinort
endocritic
ccdeiiostt
Docetistic
ccdeijkosy
disc-jockey
ccdeiklosu
cuckoldise
ccdeimooot
octodecimo
ccdeinnost
disconnect
ccdeinoops
endoscopic
ccdeinopuu
unoccupied
ccdeinorst
disconcert
ccdeinotuv
conductive
ccdekmnooy
cockneydom

ccdgilnnou
concluding
ccdgilooooy
codicology
ccdhiiiort
dichroitic
ccdhiinort
chondritic
ccdiloorsu
Crocodilus
ccdimnostu
misconduct
ccdinnootu
conduction
cceeeellnx
excellence
cceeeennss
senescence
cceeeffiin
efficience
cceeefnnor
conference
cceeehikps
pick-cheese
cceeeiinpr
recipience
cceeeinprs
prescience
cceeeinqsu
quiescence
cceeeinrsv
virescence
cceeeiopss
ecospecies
cceeeklnos
skene-occle
cceeellnxy
excellency
cceeemmnor
recommence
cceeemnopt
competence
cceeemnstu
tumescence
cceeenoprs
co-presence
cceeenrrru
recurrence
cceeenrstx
excrescent
cceeffiiny
efficiency
cceeffilno
off-licence
cceefiknrt
fen-cricket
cceefinttu
fettuccine
cceefklors
self-cocker
cceeflnnou
confluence
cceeginnor
congeneric

cceeginnot
congenetic
cceeginort
egocentric
geocentric
cceegnnoru
congruence
cceehhkopu
cheek-pouch
cceehinoss
choiceness
cceehioptu
touch-piece
cceehiostv
chest-voice
cceehlorsw
screech-owl
cceehnostu
escutcheon
cceeiiinnp
incipience
cceeiilmrs
semicircle
cceeiinpry
recipiency
cceeiiprtt
peritectic
cceeiipsst
scepticise
cceeiirrtu
circuiteer
cceeiklpuy
lucky-piece
cceeillotv
collective
cceeilmnny
inclemency
cceeilnorr
reconciler
cceeilnort
electronic
cceeilopst
telescopic
cceeilorvy
coercively
cceeinnnoo
cone-in-cone
cceeinnnot
continence
cceeinnnov
connivence
cceeinnotv
connective
cceeinnrru
incurrence
cceeinnrst
increscent
cceeinnrtu
encincture
cceeinoprt
preconceit
cceeinoprw
crown-piece
cceeinoptv
conceptive
cceeinortv
concretive
cceeinossv
concessive
cceeinotvv
convective
cceeinqsuy
quiescency
cceeioprss
crosspiece
cceeiopstt
copesettic
cceeiorrtv
corrective
cceeisssuv
successive
cceejnortu
conjecture
cceekkloyy
cockyleeky
cceelmorty
cyclometer
cceelnopru
corpulence
cceelnorty
concretely
cceelnrtuu
truculence
cceelprsuu
crepuscule
cceemnopty
competency
cceenoprrt
preconcert
cceenrrruy
recurrency
ccefhiimor
microfiche
ccefiiinst
scientific
ccefiinpsu
unspecific
ccefilllru
full-circle
ccefilmrux
circumflex
ccefilnotu
conceitful
ccefimrsuu
circumfuse
ccefinnoot
confection
cceflnotu
flocculent
cceflsssuu
successful
cceggilnoy
glycogenic
cceghhorru
church-goer
cceghiikmn
chemicking
cceghinort
crocheting
ccegiiknrt
cricketing
ccegiilnnr
encircling
ccegillnot
collecting
ccegilnoor
necrologic
cceginnnor
concerning
cceginorsy
cryogenics
ccegnnoruy
congruency
ccehhilotv
clove-hitch
ccehhlrssu
churchless
ccehhrttux
church-text
ccehiiimos
isocheimic
ccehiimoor
heroi-comic
ccehiinnno
cinchonine
ccehiinnos
cinchonise
ccehiinstt
technicist
ccehiirstu
ischuretic
ccehikmoor
mock-heroic
ccehiknnru
chicken-run
ccehiknopx
chickenpox
ccehiknosy
cockneyish
ccehilnorr
chronicler
ccehiloopr
pleochroic
ccehiloprr
perchloric
ccehilorru
hour-circle
ccehilorvw
cow-chervil
ccehimossy
ecchymosis
ccehinstty
synthectic
ccehioptty
ectophytic
ccehiorrst
orchestric
ccehiorsst
orchestics
ccehkloost
hot-cockles
ccehknoory
honey-crock
ccehknoost
chockstone
ccehkortuu
chucker-out
ccehlmotyy
cyclothyme
ccehmoorty
cytochrome
ccehnopruw
cowpuncher
ccehnossst
Scotchness
cceiiilnor
ricinoleic
cceiiinnpy
incipiency
cceiiinnrt
encrinitic
cceiilmnor
microcline
cceiilosst
solecistic
cceiimnost
misconceit
cceiimoors
seriocomic
cceiimpsst
scepticism
cceiinnopt
concipient
cceiinotvv
convictive
cceiinrtty
centricity
cceiioorst
crocoisite
cceiiopprs
periscopic
cceiiosstt
Scotticise
cceikkoppt
pick-pocket
cceikmnosy
cockneyism
cceiknosss
cocksiness
cceilllosu
cellulosic
cceillmtuy
multicycle
cceillnoot
collection
cceillsssu
ill-success
cceilnnosu
nucleonics
cceilnosuv
conclusive
vice-consul
cceilooqtu
coquelicot
cceimmrruu
circummure
cceimnnoou
uneconomic
cceimnorst
concretism
cceimnostt
concettism
cceimnrtuv
circumvent
cceimooprs
microscope
cceimoprsu
circumpose
cceimorrst
miscorrect
cceimorrty
cryometric
cceinnnoot
connection
cceinnnoty
continency
cceinnnovy
connivency
cceinnoopt
conception
cceinnoort
concertino
concretion
cceinnooss
concession
cceinnootv
convection
cceinooops
iconoscope
cceinoorrt
correction
cceinoorty
cryoconite
cceinorstt
concretist
cceinosssu
succession
cceinossuv
concussive
cceinosttt
concettist
cceinotuvy
vice-county
cceiooprsu
precocious
cceisssuuv
succussive
ccekkortuy
turkey-cock
ccekmoorst
comstocker
cceknnoory
cockernony
ccekorrttu
cork-cutter
ccellostyy
cyclostyle

ccelmoorty
motor-cycle
ccelmoosty
cyclostome
ccelnopruy
corpulency
ccelnosstu
occultness
ccelnrtuuy
truculency
ccelooopps
colposcope
cceloprsuu
corpuscule
ccelprstuu
cluster-cup
ccemnnoopy
componency
ccennorrtu
concurrent
ccenoopprt
pop-concert
ccenooprsy
necroscopy
ccenooprtu
contrecoup
ccenopsstu
conspectus
ccenorrttu
corn-cutter
cceoopssty
cystoscope
cceoorrrty
correctory
ccfgiinruy
crucifying
ccfhimnoor
conchiform
ccfiilmoru
culiciform
ccfimmoruu
cucumiform
ccfkkmoors
smock-frock
ccfkloooru
four-o-clock
ccghhikott
chock-tight
ccghlnoooy
conchology
ccgiiiknnp
picnicking
ccgiilmoor
micrologic
ccgiilnrty
tricycling
ccgiilooos
sociologic
ccgiinnnov
convincing
ccgilorsuu
glucosuric
ccgilorsuy
glycosuric

ccgimnooos
cosmogonic
ccginnorru
concurring
ccgiooprsy
gyroscopic
cchhhooptt
hotchpotch
cchhiiotty
ichthyotic
cchiiirstt
tristichic
cchiimnnos
cinchonism
cchiimnoor
chironomic
cchiimorrt
trichromic
cchiinorty
chronicity
cchiioprty
hypocritic
cchiklnquu
quick-lunch
cchiklostt
lockstitch
cchikopsst
chopsticks
cchiloopry
polychroic
cchilorstw
scritch-owl
cchimnooor
monochroic
cchimortyy
cymotrichy
cchinnorsy
synchronic
cchiooprs
horoscopic
cchiorsstu
trochiscus
cchkloorrs
schorl-rock
cchnoostuy
coconut-shy
cchoopssuu
hocus-pocus
cciiilmort
microlitic
cciiilosst
sciolistic
cciikkqrtu
quick-trick
cciikkqstu
quick-stick
cciillnopy
polyclinic
cciilmnnoo
monoclinic
cciilmopty
complicity
cciilooprt
coprolitic

cciilrstty
tricyclist
cciimmoort
microtomic
cciimnostv
convictism
cciimosstt
Scotticism
cciimostuv
Muscovitic
cciinnnoty
concinnity
cciinnootv
conviction
cciinooprs
scorpionic
cciiorstuu
circuitous
cciknooptu
cuckoo-pint
ccikoopstu
cuckoo-spit
ccillnooru
councillor
ccilmnoruu
corniculum
ccilmrruuu
curriculum
ccilnnoosu
conclusion
ccilnoootu
coconut-oil
cciloopry
polycrotic
ccimooprsy
microscopy
ccinnnoosu
concinnous
ccinnoossu
concussion
ccinosssuu
succussion
ccinostuvy
viscountcy
cciooopprs
poroscopic
cciopprrty
procryptic
cciorrssss
criss-cross
cciorssstu
scissor-cut
ccjlnnotuy
conjunctly
cclloooortu
collocutor
cclnoorsuy
conclusory
ccloooppsy
colposcopy
ccooossuuu
couscousou
ccoopsstyy
cystoscopy

cdddlrsuuy
sculduddry
cddeeeegkl
deckle-edge
cddeeeennp
dependence
cddeeeinuv
undeceived
cddeeejlty
dejectedly
cddeeelnor
needlecord
cddeeemntu
deducement
cddeeennpy
dependency
cddeeennst
descendent
cddeeenttu
undetected
cddeeffiin
diffidence
cddeeggklu
duck-legged
cddeeginns
descending
cddeeiinss
dissidence
cddeeijpru
prejudiced
cddeeimnor
endodermic
cddeeinrsu
undescried
cddeeinrtu
undirected
cddeellsuy
secludedly
cddeelmosu
cuddlesome
cddeelnuux
unexcluded
cddeennosu
unseconded
cddeenorru
unrecorded
cddefnnoou
confounded
cddegnoorr
corn-dodger
cddeikmmnu
muck-midden
cddeiloouv
loud-voiced
cddeimmnos
discommend
cddeimmoos
discommode
cddeinoruv
undivorced
cddelooors
closed-door
cddemnoopu
decompound

cddenoortu
undoctored
cddenoprtu
end-product
cddenopruu
unproduced
cddfilorsu
discordful
cddhilstuy
child-study
cddiilnory
cylindroid
cddikostty
toddy-stick
cddilnsuuu
Didunculus
cddiloopsu
Diplodocus
cddinnooty
dicynodont
cdeeeegnrt
detergence
cdeeeeinpx
expedience
cdeeeffinr
difference
cdeeeffist
side-effect
cdeeeffntu
uneffected
cdeeefhikr
kerchiefed
cdeeefiilp
fieldpiece
cdeeefilst
self-deceit
cdeeefiltv
deflective
cdeeegiipr
ridge-piece
cdeeeginrv
divergence
cdeeegnrty
detergency
cdeeehiprr
decipherer
cdeeehklor
cork-heeled
cdeeehlnsu
enschedule
cdeeehlrsu
reschedule
cdeeeiinps
desipience
cdeeeilopv
velocipede
cdeeeilqsu
deliquesce
cdeeeimnno
comédienne
cdeeeimnnp
impendence
cdeeeinnpz
pince-nezed

cdeeeinpxy
expediency
cdeeeinrrt
interceder
cdeeeinrsw
widescreen
cdeeeinruv
unreceived
cdeeeinsst
desistence
cdeeeknstw
'tween-decks
cdeeellnux
unexcelled
cdeeelmnot
dolcemente
cdeeeloprs
crêpe-soled
cdeeelptxy
expectedly
cdeeemnstu
seducement
cdeeennors
recondense
cdeeennrsu
unscreened
cdeeenptux
unexpected
cdeeentuux
unexecuted
cdeeffinry
differency
cdeefiinrt
dentifrice
cdeefilnot
deflection
cdeefilnrt
fernticled
cdeefinntu
uninfected
cdeefintuv
defunctive
cdeeflnort
centrefold
cdeeflnory
enforcedly
cdeefnorss
forcedness
cdeeghhikn
high-necked
cdeeghikqu
quick-hedge
cdeegiknnr
ring-necked
cdeegilnnu
indulgence
cdeeginopr
proceeding
cdeeginrvy
divergency
cdeegioops
piece-goods
cdeehiilop
ophicleide

cdeehiiltt
ditheletic
cdeehiiprr
cirrhipede
cdeehimnor
echinoderm
cdeehinnru
unenriched
cdeehlnosv
veldschoen
cdeehlrtwy
wretchedly
cdeehmnopr
comprehend
cdeehnnquu
unquenched
cdeehnnrtu
untrenched
cdeehnortu
untochered
cdeeiiilsv
decivilise
cdeeiiinsv
indecisive
cdeeiilsvy
decisively
cdeeiimnty
endemicity
cdeeiimprs
spermicide
cdeeiinopw
cowdie-pine
cdeeiinrst
cretinised
indiscreet
indiscrete
iridescent
cdeeiinsuv
undecisive
cdeeiiorrt
cordierite
Directoire
cdeeiiprtv
predictive
cdeeiirssv
disservice
cdeeiirstv
discretive
cdeeiisstv
dissective
cdeeijnoru
unrejoiced
cdeeiknnst
deck-tennis
cdeeiknpss
pickedness
cdeeiknssw
wickedness
cdeeillnst
stencilled
cdeeilmnou
undecimole
cdeeilnnos
declension

cdeeilnnsu
unlicensed
cdeeilnnty
indecently
cdeeilnoos
decolonise
cdeeilnoss
disenclose
cdeeilnotu
nucleotide
cdeeilnpsu
uneclipsed
cdeeilnrtu
interclude
cdeeiloors
decolorise
cdeeilorst
cloistered
cdeeilrsty
discreetly
discretely
cdeeimnnpy
impendency
cdeeimnntu
inducement
cdeeimnosu
eudemonics
cdeeimnpru
imprudence
cdeeimorrx
xerodermic
cdeeinnoss
descension
cdeeinnrsw
windscreen
cdeeinoprv
providence
cdeeinorrs
reconsider
cdeeinoruv
undervoice
cdeeinprsy
presidency
cdeeinrsst
directness
cdeeinrsty
dysenteric
cdeeiopstu
deceptious
cdeeiorrsv
discoverer
rediscover
cdeeiorstu
courtesied
cdeeiprrss
cider-press
cdeeiprsst
disrespect
cdeeirrsst
directress
cdeeirrstt
restricted
cdeekkknno
knock-kneed

cdeekknoor
crook-kneed
cdeeklnrru
under-clerk
cdeekltuvv
velvet-duck
cdeeknnoru
unreckoned
cdeeknpruu
unpuckered
cdeeknrtuu
untuckered
cdeekooprw
woodpecker
cdeellnosu
counselled
cdeelmnouw
unwelcomed
cdeelmorrs
scleroderm
cdeelnnosu
unenclosed
cdeelnovxy
convexedly
cdeemnnopr
precondemn
cdeemooprs
decomposer
cdeemoprss
compressed
decompress
cdeennnott
contendent
cdeennorsu
uncensored
cdeennorsy
condensery
cdeennortv
convertend
cdeennrsuu
uncensured
cdeenoootf
odontocete
cdeenoorrs
rood-screen
cdeenoostt
cottonseed
cdeenoottw
cotton-weed
cdeenorrsu
underscore
cdeenorruv
undercover
cdeenorstu
unescorted
cdeenostuu
consuetude
cdeenprstu
unsceptred
cdeenrrstu
undercrest
cdeenrsssu
cursedness

cdeensssu
cussedness
cdeeoprrru
reproducer
cdeerssstu
seductress
cdeffilnru
undercliff
cdeffinnou
uncoffined
cdefghiklt
flight-deck
cdefhinoru
four-inched
cdefhiorsy
cod-fishery
cdefiiiils
silicified
cdefiiinpr
principled
cdefiiostt
Scottified
cdefillouv
full-voiced
cdefilorst
disc-floret
cdefilorsw
disc-flower
cdefinnnou
unconfined
cdefinnotu
defunction
cdefinoorv
confervoid
cdeflnoruy
unforcedly
cdeflnosuy
confusedly
cdefnnosuu
unconfused
cdefnorrtu
undercroft
cdefnossuu
unfocussed
cdeggillnu
cudgelling
cdeghhiipr
high-priced
cdeghjotuu
touch-judge
cdeghooort
tocher-good
cdegiilnny
incedingly
cdegiinnrs
discerning
cdegiinotu
digoneutic
cdegiinsst
dissecting
cdegiiorty
ergodicity
cdegiknost
stockinged

cdegilmmno
commingled
cdegilnnuy
indulgency
cdegilnsuy
seducingly
cdegiloors
socdoliger
cdeginnnot
contending
cdeginorsw
scowdering
cdegioorrr
corregidor
cdegiortuu
court-guide
cdeglooors
socdologer
cdegmnoruu
curmudgeon
cdehhiiprt
diphtheric
cdehhoorry
hydrochore
cdehiiistt
ditheistic
cdehiilops
discophile
cdehiilors
chloridise
cdehiilpty
diphyletic
cdehiinost
hedonistic
cdehiinrty
enhydritic
cdehikmnot
kitchendom
cdehilnrsu
nurse-child
cdehiloost
school-tide
cdehilopry
polyhedric
cdehiloptw
low-pitched
cdehilrrwy
wild-cherry
cdehimnrsu
unsmirched
cdehimopry
hypodermic
cdehinooov
novicehood
cdehinoopr
princehood
cdehinopty
endophytic
cdehiooorw
hoodie-crow
cdehiooprt
orthopedic
cdehioorsu
orchideous

cdehlnoory
chlorodyne
cdehlnoosu
unschooled
cdehlooppr
clodhopper
cdehloopry
copyholder
cdehmnotuw
Dutchwomen
cdehnooort
octohedron
cdehooprsy
hydroscope
cdeiiillst
stillicide
cdeiiilnns
disincline
cdeiiilnps
discipline
cdeiiimrsv
recidivism
cdeiiinnos
indecision
cdeiiintvv
vindictive
cdeiiirstv
recidivist
cdeiijnost
disjection
cdeiiklsst
sick-listed
cdeiilnnor
crinolined
cdeiilnopu
unpolicied
cdeiilnoss
disinclose
cdeiilnppr
principled
cdeiilnrty
cylindrite
indirectly
cdeiilostu
solicitude
cdeiimnntt
indictment
cdeiimoort
iodometric
cdeiimorrs
misericord
cdeiimorty
iridectomy
mediocrity
cdeiimostt
demoticist
cdeiimprtu
impictured
cdeiinoprt
prediction
cdeiinorst
discretion
soricident

cdeiinosst
dissection
cdeiinsttu
discutient
cdeiiooptx
exopoditic
cdeiioorrs
sororicide
cdeiiorsuv
veridicous
cdeiiprstu
pedicurist
cdeiirssuv
discursive
cdeiisssuv
discussive
cdeiknrrtu
under-trick
cdeiknrsuw
wind-sucker
cdeikopptt
pockpitted
cdeikoqstu
deck-quoits
cdeikorrst
stock-rider
cdeikpttuy
picket-duty
cdeilllpuy
pellucidly
cdeillnoor
corn-dollie
cdeilmoppr
crippledom
cdeilnnosu
uninclosed
cdeilnossu
cloudiness
discounsel
cdeiloprtu
productile
cdeilopsuu
pediculous
cdeilorssu
disclosure
cdeimmnopu
compendium
cdeimnoops
incomposed
cdeimnoost
endosmotic
cdeimnoosy
diseconomy
cdeimnostu
undomestic
cdeimnosuu
mucedinous
cdeimoopss
discompose
cdeimosstu
customised
cdeimprstu
spermiduct

cdeinnosst
disconsent
cdeinnostt
discontent
cdeinnrtuu
under-tunic
cdeinoorsu
indecorous
cdeinoprty
decryption
cdeinorrtu
introducer
cdeinorstu
discounter
cdeinprstu
unscripted
cdeioprrtu
picture-rod
cdeioprtuv
productive
cdeiorrssu
discourser
cdeirrsttu
strictured
cdejnnossu
jocundness
cdekmmoost
mock-modest
cdeknorstu
understock
cdellnoort
controlled
cdelmnosuy
consumedly
cdelmoopsy
composedly
cdelmooptt
complotted
cdelnnoosu
unconsoled
cdelnooruu
uncoloured
cdelnooruy
Euroclydon
cdelnootuv
convoluted
cdelnprsuu
unscrupled
cdelnrtuuu
uncultured
cdeloooruv
dove-colour
cdeloorsuy
decorously
cdelorrssu
russel-cord
cdelprstuu
sculptured
cdemmnotuu
uncommuted
cdemmooors
cosmodrome
cdemnnosuu
unconsumed

cdemnoopru
compounder
cdemnostuu
uncustomed
cdennoopru
pronounced
cdenooprrs
correspond
cdeooopstu
scooped-out
cdeoorttuw
wood-cutter
cdeoprrstu
crop-duster
cdeorrsstu
court-dress
cdeorrsttu
destructor
cderrsttuu
structured
cdffiiltuy
difficulty
cdfghiinos
cod-fishing
cdfhiloopr
child-proof
cdfhioorst
doctor-fish
cdfimoorst
discomfort
cdghilnotu
night-cloud
cdghiloory
hydrologic
cdghilopsu
disc-plough
cdgiinoprr
riding-crop
cdgiklloos
goldilocks
cdgilmoooy
docimology
cdginnoopy
pycnogonid
cdginppruy
dry-cupping
cdhhiillsy
childishly
cdhhioorst
Christhood
cdhiiimstu
stichidium
cdhiiloost
Dolichotis
cdhiimmors
dichromism
cdhiimmoru
chromidium
cdhiimnoor
chironomid
cdhiioortt
diorthotic
cdhiiosstu
distichous

cdhillnrru
churn-drill
cdhilmnoot
codlin-moth
cdhilopryy
polyhydric
cdhilorsuu
dolichurus
cdhilortyy
hydrolytic
cdhimnoory
monohydric
cdhinooosu
cousinhood
cdhiooprst
doctorship
cdhioprsty
dystrophic
cdhknnpruu
punch-drunk
cdiiilnoty
indocility
cdiiimptuy
impudicity
cdiiinnstt
indistinct
cdiiinosss
discission
cdiikprstu
spirit-duck
cdiilnoosu
nidicolous
cdiilnpsuu
sipunculid
cdiilnstty
distinctly
cdiilorsuu
ridiculous
cdiinopsuu
cupidinous
cdiinorssu
discursion
cdiinosssu
discussion
cdiirssstu
discursist
cdijnorstu
disjunctor
cdikorsstw
sword-stick
cdillmoosu
molluscoid
cdilloquuy
dulciloquy
cdilmooorx
loxodromic
cdilmoopuy
Lycopodium
cdilooopty
octoploidy
cdimmooosu
commodious
cdinooprtu
production

cdiorrssuy
discursory
cdlmoorstu
storm-cloud
cdnoooottw
cotton-wood
cdoooopstu
octopodous
cdoorrstuw
court-sword
ceeeeffort
coffee-tree
ceeeeffrsv
effervesce
ceeeefllss
fleeceless
ceeeeflrst
free-select
ceeeefnprr
preference
ceeeegiips
siege-piece
ceeeegiptx
epexegetic
ceeeehimst
cheese-mite
ceeeehiprt
three-piece
ceeeehnprt
threepence
ceeeeinprx
experience
ceeeeirsvy
eye-service
ceeeellnpr
repellence
ceeeelnort
enterocele
ceeeelnrst
telescreen
ceeeennpsv
sevenpence
ceeeennrst
resentence
ceeeenrrrv
reverencer
ceeeffglnu
effulgence
ceeefflors
effloresce
ceeefflsst
effectless
ceeefglnru
refulgence
ceeefhiknt
kitchen-fee
ceeefhlmnt
fleechment
ceeefhlrtt
three-cleft
ceeefhnrtt
trench-feet
ceeefilrtv
reflective

ceeefinnns
Fescennine
ceeefinoru
nourice-fee
ceeefinrrs
fire-screen
ceeefinrss
fierceness
ceeefiprtv
perfective
ceeeflloow
fleece-wool
ceeefmnrst
fremescent
ceeefnrstv
fervescent
ceeefprrtu
prefecture
ceeeggilnn
negligence
ceeeghikln
ingle-cheek
ceeeghinpt
eightpence
ceeegiinpt
epigenetic
ceeegilntv
neglective
ceeeginnot
neogenetic
ceeeginotx
exogenetic
ceeeginrst
energetics
ceeeginrtv
viceregent
ceeeglnort
electrogen
ceeegnrrsu
resurgence
ceeehhlors
horse-leech
ceeehimstt
chemisette
ceeehinptt
epenthetic
ceeehinrss
cheeriness
ceeehinsss
cheesiness
ceeehinstt
teschenite
ceeehknpry
henpeckery
ceeehlpsss
speechless
ceeehmnosw
somewhence
ceeehmortt
hectometre
ceeehnorss
chersonese
ceeehorrst
threescore

ceeehorsst
score-sheet
ceeehorstt
hectostere
ceeeiilmpt
epimeletic
ceeeiilnrs
resilience
ceeeilltvy
electively
ceeeilmnnt
clementine
ceeeilmrtt
telemetric
ceeeilnort
re-election
ceeeilnprt
percentile
ceeeilnpst
pestilence
ceeeimnntt
enticement
ceeeimnntv
evincement
ceeeimnrst
mesenteric
ceeeimnrtt
centimeter
centimetre
ceeeimnttx
excitement
ceeeimopsu
mouse-piece
ceeeimrrrs
merceriser
ceeeinnppy
pennypiece
ceeeinnprt
pertinence
ceeeinorrt
re-erection
ceeeinprtt
penteteric
ceeeinttwy
winceyette
ceeeiorrst
corsetière
ceeeiortvx
overexcite
ceeeipprtv
perceptive
preceptive
ceeeiprstv
respective
ceeekklnps
kenspeckle
ceeekklopr
lock-keeper
ceeekoprrw
crowkeeper
ceeekrrssu
seersucker
ceeelllntt
nettle-cell

ceeellnnop
penoncelle
ceeellnpry
repellency
ceeellrrwy
crewellery
ceeelmorrt
electromer
ceeelnorrt
cornel-tree
ceeelnrssv
cleverness
ceeelnssst
selectness
ceeelorsst
electoress
ceeelorstt
corselette
ceeelrrssu
recureless
ceeemnnrst
secernment
ceeemnoprs
recompense
ceeemnrstu
securement
ceeemoprsu
creepmouse
ceeennrsst
recentness
ceeenopprt
prepotence
ceeenorssv
seven-score
ceeenrrstt
rest-centre
ceeenrssst
secretness
ceeenrsssu
secureness
ceeersstux
executress
ceefffiior
fire-office
ceeffhnoru
forfeuchen
ceeffillmo
coffee-mill
ceeffinpty
fifty-pence
ceeffioorv
overoffice
ceeffmooor
coffee-room
ceefghinnr
greenfinch
ceefgilnrt
reflecting
ceefginrtu
centrifuge
ceefgllntu
neglectful
ceefglnruy
refulgency

ceefhhnort
henceforth
ceefhklops
folk-speech
ceefhllruy
cheerfully
ceefhlnruu
uncheerful
ceefhloors
free-school
ceefhnoors
forechosen
ceefhorttu
fourchette
ceefiilntv
inflective
ceefiimnnu
munifience
ceefiinprt
perficient
ceefijloru
rejoiceful
ceefiklnrt
ferntickle
ceefiklnss
fickleness
ceefiklort
life-rocket
ceefilnort
reflection
ceefilrttu
file-cutter
ceefinoort
fore-notice
ceefinoprt
perfection
ceefinosuv
veneficous
ceefkllssy
fecklessly
ceefklortt
fetterlock
ceeflnopru
profluence
ceeflnorst
florescent
ceeflpprtu
pluperfect
ceeflprstu
respectful
ceefmnnort
conferment
ceefoorrsu
forecourse
ceeforrrss
cross-refer
ceeghiilmp
hemiplegic
ceeghiinpt
nightpiece
ceeghimort
geothermic
ceeghimost
geochemist

ceeghiorst
eightscore
ceeghlnort
greencloth
ceeghlopst
clothes-peg
ceegiinost
isogenetic
ceegiinprv
perceiving
ceegiinstt
geneticist
ceegilloot
teleologic
ceegilnnot
neglection
ceegilnpry
creepingly
ceeginnoor
coregonine
ceeginnoru
encoignure
neurogenic
ceeginnrss
screenings
ceeginnrst
nigrescent
ceeginnrsu
insurgence
ceeginnsty
syngenetic
ceeginoort
erotogenic
orogenetic
ceeginoost
osteogenic
ceeginorrs
recogniser
ceeginostv
congestive
ceeginprst
respecting
ceeginprtx
excerpting
ceeginrsty
synergetic
ceegmotyyz
zygomycete
ceegnnorrw
crown-green
ceegnnortv
convergent
ceegnoostu
ectogenous
ceegnprsuu
upsurgence
ceegnrsttu
turgescent
ceehhilnoy
honey-chile
ceehhilptw
pitch-wheel
ceehhimort
come-hither

ceehhkoott
cheek-tooth
ceehhnotty
theotechny
ceehiimrst
erethismic
ceehiinosv
incohesive
ceehiipprr
peripheric
ceehiirrst
heritrices
ceehiirstt
erethistic
ceehikpprs
schipperke
ceehilmnop
clomiphene
ceehilnopr
necrophile
ceehilnopt
telephonic
ceehilnoru
euchlorine
ceehiloops
helioscope
ceehiloprt
helicopter
ceehilortt
hectolitre
ceehilosvy
cohesively
ceehilssty
chessylite
ceehimmoor
homeomeric
ceehimnnrt
enrichment
ceehimnttu
technetium
ceehimoptu
mouthpiece
ceehimorry
cherimoyer
ceehimortx
exothermic
ceehinnort
incoherent
ceehinoppr
Hippocrene
ceehinopss
ecphonesis
ceehinorss
heroicness
ceehinpprw
pipe-wrench
ceehinrrst
rechristen
ceehinrstw
Winchester
ceehinsstt
tetchiness
ceehioprsx
exospheric

ceehirstty
hysteretic
ceehkloopt
pocket-hole
ceehllmort
mother-cell
ceehllnosw
well-chosen
ceehlmorty
emery-cloth
ceehlmoszz
schemozzle
ceehlnorty
coherently
ceehlnorww
crown-wheel
ceehlnotuw
count-wheel
ceehlnqssu
quenchless
ceehlorsst
tocherless
ceehnoopps
nephoscope
ceehnooprt
ctenophore
ceehnoortt
heterocont
ceehnoprty
hypocentre
ceehnpprtu
thruppence
ceehooprrs
horse-coper
ceeiiilnns
sicilienne
ceeiiinnps
insipience
ceeiiinstz
citizenise
ceeiijorst
jeistiecor
ceeiiklnpr
princelike
ceeiiklnpt
picket-line
ceeiillltv
vitellicle
ceeiillmrv
vermicelli
ceeiilnosu
isoleucine
ceeiilnrsy
resiliency
ceeiilnrtt
centilitre
ceeiilprsv
lip-service
ceeiilrtty
erectility
ceeiilttvy
electivity
ceeiimnntt
incitement

ceeiimortt
meteoritic
ceeiimosst
semeiotics
ceeiimprrt
perimetric
ceeiimpsss
speciesism
ceeiimpsst
epistemics
ceeiimqrsu
semicirque
ceeiinnsst
insistence
ceeiinoprw
cowrie-pine
ceeiinosst
sectionise
ceeiinpprt
percipient
ceeiinpstv
inspective
ceeiinrstt
interstice
ceeiinsstz
citizeness
ceeiinttvx
extinctive
ceeiioppss
episcopise
ceeiiorrst
escritoire
ceeijloprt
projectile
ceeijoprtv
projective
ceeiklnrss
silk-screen
ceeiknottz
zone-ticket
ceeiknprty
pernickety
ceeiknrsss
sickerness
ceeillnrst
stenciller
ceeillorss
recoilless
ceeillprtt
letter-clip
ceeilmnoot
teleonomic
ceeilmnopt
incomplete
ceeilmnort
clinometer
ceeilmnoss
comeliness
ceeilmnstu
semilucent
ceeilmoptv
completive
ceeilnnstu
inesculent

ceeilnoors
recolonise
ceeilnoorw
wine-cooler
ceeilnoprt
prelection
ceeilnorst
encloister
ceeilnortt
crinolette
ceeilnorvw
corn-weevil
ceeilnorvy
overnicely
ceeilnqstu
liquescent
ceeilnrsuy
insecurely
ceeilnrtuv
ventricule
ceeilorrst
cloisterer
ceeilossuv
vesiculose
ceeilprsuv
preclusive
ceeimmnosu
oecumenism
ceeimmoprt
emmetropic
ceeimmorrt
micrometer
micrometre
ceeimnnopr
prominence
ceeimnoors
economiser
ceeimnoort
iconometer
ceeimorstv
viscometer
ceeimosstv
vicomtesse
ceeinnnotv
convenient
ceeinnopst
post-Nicene
ceeinnortu
recontinue
ceeinnostt
co-sentient
ceeinnprty
pertinency
ceeinnpsst
spinescent
ceeinoopst
teinoscope
ceeinopprt
perception
ceeinoprss
precession
ceeinoprtu
pie-counter

ceeinoprtx
excerption
ceeinorrsw
cornerwise
ceeinorstv
ventricose
ceeinorttv
convertite
ceeinortty
co-eternity
ceeinosttx
co-existent
ceeinprrtx
precentrix
ceeinprstu
putrescine
ceeinprttu
percutient
ceeinrrstu
scrutineer
ceeinrssty
syncretise
ceeinrsttt
trecentist
ceeinrsttv
vitrescent
ceeinrttux
extincture
ceeioprttv
protective
ceeiopstux
exceptious
ceeiorrtuu
couturière
ceeiorsttu
tricoteuse
ceeiprrsuv
precursive
ceeiprssuv
percussive
ceeipsstuv
susceptive
ceejlnorww
crown-jewel
ceejnoosss
jocoseness
ceejoprrtu
projecture
ceekllrssy
recklessly
ceeklmoprt
rock-temple
ceeklopsst
pocketless
ceeklopstu
outspeckle
ceeklorrww
crewelwork
ceeknoorrv
overreckon
ceekoprstt
step-rocket
ceekopsttv
vest-pocket

ceellmopty
completely
ceelmmnopt
complement
ceelmnnoos
somnolence
ceelmnoptu
couplement
ceelmoortu
coulometer
ceelnorsvy
conversely
ceelnorvvy
revolvency
ceelooorsv
loose-cover
ceelorrsty
clerestory
ceelorsttu
locust-tree
ceemmotxyy
myxomycete
ceemnnstty
encystment
ceemnoorst
centrosome
ceemnooruv
unovercome
ceemnoprsu
preconsume
ceemnoprtu
recoupment
ceemnoprty
pycnometer
ceemnortuy
neurectomy
ceemnpsstu
spumescent
ceemoopprs
precompose
ceemoprrss
recompress
ceemorttuy
uterectomy
ceennoqstu
consequent
ceennorrtu
rencounter
ceennossvx
convexness
ceennprssy
pennycress
ceenooppr s
copper-nose
ceenoorttt
cotton-tree
ceenoppprr
peppercorn
ceenopprty
prepotency
ceenoprstt
torpescent
ceenoqrssu
conqueress

ceenoqrstu
reconquest
ceenorttux
contexture
ceenprrrtu
percurrent
ceenprsssu
spruceness
ceenprsttu
putrescent
ceeooprstv
Vertoscope®
ceeopprrty
preceptory
ceeoprrstt
retrospect
ceeoprrstu
persecutor
ceeprrsssw
screw-press
ceeprtttuy
type-cutter
ceersssuux
excursuses
cefffhiors
coffer-fish
ceffgiilor
office-girl
ceffhiinor
chiffonier
ceffhinssu
chuffiness
ceffiikkln
flick-knife
ceffiiltwy
Wycliffite
ceffiinstu
sufficient
ceffioopst
post-office
cefflloruy
forcefully
cefgiinpsy
specifying
cefgiinrty
certifying
rectifying
cefginnorr
conferring
cefgloorsu
golf-course
cefhilloos
life-school
cefhilprtu
pitcherful
cefhilsttu
cuttlefish
cefiiilntv
inflictive
cefiiilnty
infelicity
cefiiimnst
feministic

cefiiklrrt
rick-lifter
cefiikqrru
quick-firer
cefiilnnot
inflection
cefiilnoqu
cinque-foil
cefiilopry
fire-policy
cefiilostu
felicitous
cefiimnntu
munificent
cefiinoprt
proficient
cefiinopst
pontifices
cefiinostu
infectious
cefikloort
foot-licker
cefillmruy
mercifully
cefilmnruu
unmerciful
cefilmoors
frolicsome
cefilmopry
clypeiform
cefiloprrs
rifle-corps
cefilorsuu
luciferous
cefimorrsu
securiform
cefimorsuu
muciferous
cefinnooss
confession
cefinoorsu
coniferous
cefinorsuu
nuciferous
cefinrsssu
scurfiness
cefioorsuv
vociferous
cefklopstu
pocketfuls
cefllоorsu
self-colour
cefllsttuu
scuttleful
ceflnoorrw
cornflower
cefloorrww
crow-flower
ceflpsstuu
suspectful
cegghimnuw
chewing-gum
cegghiorst
ostrich-egg

ceggiilnnr
cringeling
ceggilnoss
clogginess
ceggimnttu
gem-cutting
cegginnorv
converging
cegginoost
geognostic
ceghiiilln
ice-hilling
ceghiiknnt
thickening
ceghiillns
chiselling
ceghiiloor
hierologic
ceghiinnuy
unhygienic
ceghiinorz
rhizogenic
ceghiinost
histogenic
ceghiinrtt
chittering
ceghilmnop
phlegmonic
ceghilnoop
nephologic
ceghilnqsu
squelching
ceghiloory
cheirology
ceghilopry
hypergolic
ceghimmnoo
home-coming
ceghinnopy
hypnogenic
ceghinoopt
photogenic
ceghinoorr
gonorrheic
ceghinoort
orthogenic
ceghinopty
phytogenic
pythogenic
ceghinorru
chirurgeon
ceghinorty
trichogyne
ceghiopssy
geophysics
ceghirrruy
chirurgery
ceghlnooty
technology
ceghlooory
choreology
ceghooprsy
hygroscope

cegiiinosv
visiogenic
cegiiinsst
gneissitic
cegiikllnn
nickelling
cegiikmnrs
smickering
cegiiknnqu
quickening
cegiikprst
pig-sticker
cegiillnnp
pencilling
cegiilnnpr
princeling
cegiilnnss
clinginess
cegiilnnty
enticingly
cegiilnpry
piercingly
cegiiloptt
epiglottic
cegiilostu
eulogistic
cegiinnrsv
scrivening
cegiinntux
unexciting
cegiinosst
Gnosticise
cegiinrrtu
recruiting
cegijnoprt
projecting
cegiknoopr
rock-pigeon
cegiknorst
stockinger
cegillmnop
compelling
cegillooxy
lexicology
cegilnnost
clingstone
cegilnorwy
coweringly
cegilnotvy
covetingly
cegilnrstu
clustering
cegilorsss
scissor-leg
cegimnnnot
contemning
cegimnoors
ergonomics
cegimnortu
tumorgenic
ceginnnott
contingent
ceginnoost
congestion

ceginnoqru
conquering
ceginnorst
constringe
ceginnostt
contesting
ceginnrruu
unrecuring
ceginnrsty
stringency
ceginnrsuy
insurgency
ceginoprtt
protecting
ceginoqttu
coquetting
ceginrttuv
curvetting
ceglmoooty
cometology
ceglmootyy
mycetology
ceglnoosyy
synecology
cegooprrty
gyrocopter
cehhhiikrt
hitch-hiker
cehhiilmnt
helminthic
cehhilorsw
shriche-owl
cehhimrtuy
eurhythmic
cehhiooprt
theophoric
cehhioopst
theosophic
cehhioprst
hectorship
cehhioptty
hypothetic
cehhklloss
shellshock
cehhloorst
horse-cloth
cehiijostv
Jehovistic
cehiiklrst
Christlike
cehiikrttw
whitterick
cehiillnss
chilliness
cehiilmost
homiletics
Mesolithic
cehiilnors
chlorinise
cehiilnpst
clientship
cehiilopty
heliotypic

cehiilorty
leiotrichy
cehiilpsst
ecthlipsis
cehiimnort
thermionic
cehiimnory
Hieronymic
cehiimoprt
hemitropic
cehiimrsty
mythiciser
cehiimsttw
time-switch
cehiinnoos
incohesion
cehiinopsv
noviceship
cehiinprss
chirpiness
cehiinpsst
pitchiness
cehiiprsty
sphericity
cehiipstuu
euphuistic
cehiirrttu
urethritic
cehiirrtty
erythritic
cehijkopsy
jockeyship
cehikopstw
whip-socket
cehikorrsw
crow-shrike
cehikrsttu
trekschuit
cehikrstyy
hystericky
cehillmssu
music-shell
cehilmoopr
lipochrome
cehilmoost
school-time
cehilmoppy
Polyphemic
cehilnopry
necrophily
cehilnopst
clothes-pin
cehilnrstt
slit-trench
cehiloorst
holosteric
cehiloprst
lectorship
cehiloprtu
Turcophile
cehilorsty
chrysolite
chrysotile

cehilrssst
Christless
cehimmoprs
morphemics
cehimnoopr
microphone
cehimnoorr
chironomer
cehimnoory
cheironomy
cehimnoott
nomothetic
cehimnopty
chimney-pot
chimney-top
cehimnopuy
eponychium
cehimnorry
microhenry
cehimooort
homoerotic
cehimoopty
mythopoeic
cehimootuz
zoothecium
cehimoprty
microphyte
cehimopsty
mesophytic
cehimorssu
semichorus
cehimorstt
thermotics
cehimortty
mother-city
cehimossuu
music-house
cehinnnppy
penny-pinch
pinchpenny
cehinnrstu
unchristen
cehinnrsty
strychnine
cehinooprs
rhinoscope
cehinoorrs
rhinoceros
cehinopprr
pronephric
cehinoppty
phenotypic
cehinoprss
censorship
cehinoprsy
hypersonic
cehinoprty
hypertonic
cehinopstt
open-stitch
pitchstone
cehinoptty
entophytic

cehinorstu
  urosthenic
cehinosssy
  coyishness
cehinosstu
  touchiness
cehinpsssu
  Spheniscus
cehiooprrt
  rheotropic
cehiooprry
  pyorrhoeic
cehiooprsy
  hieroscopy
cehioorrrt
  retrochoir
cehioprrst
  rectorship
cehioprstt
  prosthetic
  rope-stitch
cehioprtxy
  xerophytic
cehioqsttu
  coquettish
cehiorstvw
  switch-over
cehknorrsu
  cornhusker
cehkoopprr
  rock-hopper
cehkrssstu
  huckstress
cehlmoopry
  polychrome
cehlmoorst
  school-term
cehlmoorxy
  xylochrome
cehlmoptyy
  lymphocyte
cehlmprruy
  cherry-plum
cehloooprt
  tocopherol
cehloprsty
  polychrest
cehmmnooor
  monochrome
cehmmooors
  chromosome
cehmmottyy
  thymectomy
cehmnoottu
  touch-me-not
cehmooprty
  chromotype
  cormophyte
  ectomorphy
cehnoosttu
  touchstone
cehnoprsty
  phenocryst

cehnoprtyy
  pyrotechny
cehoorstuu
  court-house
cehorstttu
  outstretch
ceiiillnnp
  penicillin
ceiiilnptx
  inexplicit
ceiiilnsvy
  incisively
ceiiilopst
  politicise
ceiiimmprs
  empiricism
ceiiimosss
  isoseismic
ceiiimprst
  empiricist
ceiiimrstv
  victimiser
ceiiimssty
  seismicity
ceiiinpprt
  precipitin
ceiiiqsttu
  quietistic
ceiijnntuv
  injunctive
ceiiklnsss
  sickliness
ceiikmnort
  mini-rocket
ceiiknostt
  kenoticist
ceiiknrsst
  trickiness
ceiiknssst
  stickiness
ceiilllstu
  cellulitis
ceiillnnot
  centillion
ceiillossu
  siliculose
ceiillptxy
  explicitly
ceiilmnnou
  lenocinium
ceiilmopst
  polemicist
ceiilmortt
  tremolitic
ceiilnnost
  consilient
ceiilnopru
  rupicoline
ceiilnostu
  licentious
ceiilnostv
  novelistic
ceiilnqssu
  cliquiness

ceiilopstx
  post-exilic
ceiimmorss
  microseism
ceiimnnost
  omniscient
ceiimnrssu
  sinecurism
ceiimnrtuv
  centumviri
ceiimorsst
  isometrics
ceiimorstt
  cottierism
ceiinnopst
  cispontine
  inspection
ceiinnorsv
  environics
ceiinnottx
  extinction
ceiinnssty
  insistency
ceiinoprst
  isentropic
  triniscope
ceiinoprsu
  pernicious
ceiinoprtv
  voice-print
ceiinopstt
  nepotistic
ceiinorsss
  rescission
ceiinorstt
  trisection
ceiinpsstu
  suscipient
ceiinrsstu
  scrutinise
  sinecurist
ceiinrstuy
  insecurity
ceiioopstz
  epizootics
ceiioorstu
  trioecious
ceiioprsty
  preciosity
ceiiopssty
  speciosity
ceiiorsttu
  triticeous
ceiiorstvv
  vivisector
ceiipsstuy
  Puseyistic
ceiirrsttx
  trisectrix
ceijnooprt
  projection
ceikkorrww
  wickerwork

ceiklnnost
  clinkstone
ceiklnosst
  slickstone
ceiklnpssu
  pluckiness
ceiklooprw
  wool-picker
ceikloortv
  rock-violet
ceikloprsu
  prick-louse
ceiklopstt
  slit-pocket
ceikmoprtv
  mock-privet
ceiknopprs
  copperskin
ceiknorrst
  corn-kister
ceiknorrwz
  zinc-worker
ceiknossst
  stockiness
ceikopsttu
  soup-ticket
ceillmnorr
  corn-miller
ceillooqsu
  colloquise
ceillorssw
  scrollwise
ceilmmnopt
  compliment
ceilmnoopt
  completion
ceilmnoopx
  complexion
ceilmnoott
  melicotton
ceilmnorty
  clinometry
ceilmnossu
  miscounsel
ceilmnpssu
  clumpiness
ceilmnsssu
  clumsiness
ceilmoootv
  locomotive
ceilmoopst
  leptosomic
ceilmopsuv
  compulsive
ceilmoptxy
  complexity
ceilmorstu
  sclerotium
ceilmortuv
  volumetric
ceilmostuu
  meticulous
ceilnnnoty
  innocently

ceilnnosvy
  insolvency
ceilnnpruy
  unprincely
ceilnooprs
  necropolis
ceilnoorrs
  resorcinol
ceilnoprsu
  preclusion
ceilnorstu
  uncloister
ceilnortty
  contritely
ceilnossst
  costliness
ceilnosstt
  clottiness
ceilnostuv
  consultive
ceilnosuvv
  convulsive
ceilnprssy
  princessly
ceiloorttt
  troctolite
ceiloprsuu
  periculous
ceiloprsuy
  preciously
ceilopssuy
  speciously
ceilorrtuy
  courtierly
ceilorssst
  cloistress
ceimmmnott
  commitment
ceimmnoort
  metronomic
ceimmnoquu
  communique
ceimmnorty
  metronymic
ceimmooprs
  compromise
ceimmopstu
  miscompute
ceimmorrty
  micrometry
ceimmorssu
  commissure
ceimmortux
  commixture
ceimnnopry
  prominency
ceimnnostt
  miscontent
ceimnooosu
  monoecious
ceimnooprt
  pome-citron
ceimnoopss
  meconopsis

ceimnoorty
iconometry
ceimnoprsu
proscenium
ceimnorsuu
ceruminous
ceimnprsss
scrimpness
ceimnrssty
syncretism
ceimooprrs
microspore
ceimooprsy
myrioscope
ceimooprtt
competitor
ceimoorsty
sociometry
ceimoprrty
pyrometric
ceimorstvy
viscometry
ceinnnoott
contention
ceinnnootv
convention
ceinnoorsv
conversion
ceinnoosty
non-society
ceinnoprty
encryption
ceinnoptux
expunction
ceinnosstt
consistent
ceinooprrt
correption
porrection
ceinooprss
procession
ceinooprtt
protection
ceinooprtv
provection
ceinoorssu
censorious
ceinoorttv
contortive
ceinoossuy
synoecious
ceinoprssu
croupiness
percussion
supersonic
ceinoprstt
introspect
ceinoprstu
supertonic
ceinoqrrtu
quercitron
ceinorrsst
intercross

ceinorstuv
ventricous
ceinosstuu
incestuous
ceinostttu
constitute
ceinprstuu
sun-picture
ceinrssstt
strictness
ceinrssstu
crustiness
ceinrsssuv
scurviness
ceinrsstty
syncretist
ceiooprrst
proctorise
ceiooprrty
corporeity
ceiopprrtt
protreptic
ceioprrttx
protectrix
ceioprrtuv
corruptive
ceioprrtuz
prize-court
ceioprrtwy
copywriter
ceiorrsssy
rescissory
ceipprstty
typescript
ceklllssuy
lucklessly
ceklmooorr
locker-room
ceklmprsuu
lumpsucker
cekoopprrw
copper-work
cekopprstu
upper-stock
cekorrstuv
overstruck
celllntuuy
luculently
cellnoorrt
controller
cellnoorsu
counsellor
cellooosst
close-stool
celloorrsy
Rolls-Royce®
celloorssu
colourless
cellorsuuy
ulcerously
celmmoptuy
lumpectomy
celmnnoosy
somnolency

celmnoooot
melocotoon
celmooprty
completory
celmoorsty
sclerotomy
celmoortuy
coulometry
celnoprsuu
pronucleus
celnopstyy
pycnostyle
celoooprsu
procoelous
celooorrsu
rose-colour
celooorruv
overcolour
celooprrtu
colporteur
celoortuuz
zooculture
celoostuvy
covetously
celprssstu
sculptress
cemmnnooss
commonness
cemnooorsu
monocerous
cemoopprrw
copper-worm
cemooprrss
compressor
cennnnoott
non-content
cennnorrtu
non-current
cennooprru
pronouncer
cenooppprr
corn-popper
cenoopprsy
pycnospore
cenoorrttv
controvert
cenoorssst
cross-stone
cenoorstty
Notoryctes
cenoprstuy
counter-spy
ceoopprrst
prospector
ceooprrstu
prosecutor
ceooprrtty
protectory
ceopprsstu
prospectus
ceoprrrsuy
percursory
precursory

cepprrstuu
upper-crust
cffgiiiorr
frigorific
cffgiiknot
ticking-off
cffgilnooo
cooling-off
cffgilnosy
scoffingly
cffhiinops
coffin-ship
cfghiillny
filchingly
cfgiiklnor
frolicking
cfgiiknoss
fossicking
cfgiimnnor
confirming
cfgiinnoru
Finno-Ugric
Ugro-Finnic
cfgiinnosy
consignify
cfgiinoprt
forcing-pit
cfgiinosty
Scotifying
cfgilosuuu
lucifugous
cfhimoprsy
scyphiform
cfhkoooprs
shock-proof
cfhllooort
floorcloth
cfhlmooorr
chloroform
cfhoorrstu
fourscorth
cfiiilnnot
infliction
cfiiimnors
incisiform
cfiiinostt
fictionist
cfiiiosttu
fictitious
cfiilmoosu
fimicolous
music-folio
cfiilnopru
unprolific
cfiilorsst
floristics
cfiimorrst
cristiform
cfiinnnoot
non-fiction
cfiirsttuu
futuristic
cfilmmoruu
cumuliform

cfilmoopru
poculiform
cfilmoorty
cotyliform
cfilmorrtu
cultriform
cfilnostuu
fonticulus
cfimnoorst
conformist
cfimnoorty
conformity
cfllnorsuy
scornfully
cflloossuu
flosculous
cfloorssuu
scrofulous
cgghinnotu
hunting-cog
cgghinoopy
hypnogogic
cggiiknpsu
sucking-pig
cggiilnnry
cringingly
cgginnorsu
scrounging
cghhilortt
torchlight
cghhinrrtu
night-churr
cghiiiostv
Visigothic
cghiiklnop
holing-pick
cghiiknpsy
physicking
cghiiknstt
night-stick
cghiilloop
philologic
cghiilloot
lithologic
cghiilmort
microlight
cghiilnnpy
pinchingly
cghiilntwy
witchingly
cghiilooop
ophiologic
cghiiloost
histologic
cghiilopst
phlogistic
cghiilprty
triglyphic
cghiklnosy
shockingly
cghiknortw
thick-grown
cghilloors
schoolgirl

cghilmooty
mythologic
cghilnotuy
touchingly
cghilnrsuy
crushingly
cghiloorty
trichology
cghiloosty
stichology
cghilorrsu
chorus-girl
cghilorsst
crosslight
cghimnoory
chirognomy
cghinoosyz
schizogony
cghlnooory
chronology
cghlnoooss
song-school
cghloopsyy
psychology
cghnoopsyy
psychogony
cgiiijnost
jingoistic
cgiiiknnpt
nit-picking
cgiiilnnty
incitingly
cgiiilnost
soliciting
cgiiilnstu
linguistic
cgiiilpstu
pugilistic
cgiikllnor
rollicking
cgiiknnopr
corking-pin
cgiiknnopy
copying-ink
cgiilnpprs
spring-clip
cgiiloostt
isoglottic
cgiimmnott
committing
cgiimnosst
Gnosticism
cgiimnssuw
swing-music
cgiinnnotu
unnoticing
cgiinottuy
contiguity
cgiklnnotu
locking-nut
cgiklnoprs
spring-lock
cgiknosstw
swing-stock
cgillnoswy
scowlingly
cgilmoosty
mycologist
cgilmoosuy
musicology
cgilnnostu
consulting
cgilnooost
nostologic
oncologist
cgilooprt
tropologic
cgilootxy
toxicology
cgiloostty
cytologist
cgimnrrruu
curmurring
cginooprst
prognostic
cginoostuu
contiguous
cginopptyy
copy-typing
cglooortyy
oryctology
cglooprtyy
cryptology
cgnooostuy
octogynous
chhiikpsty
phthisicky
chhiiossty
ichthyosis
chhiipsttw
whip-stitch
chhillrsuy
churlishly
chhiloopss
school-ship
chhiloopty
holophytic
chhilorstw
shritch-owl
chhimnooop
homophonic
chhimopsss
schism-shop
chhiooppros
phosphoric
chhlloopry
chlorophyl
chhmmooory
homochromy
chiiiilnst
nihilistic
chiiilpsty
syphilitic
chiiinorst
histrionic
chiiinortt
trithionic
chiiipprtu
hippuritic
chiikllsty
ticklishly
chiilmnoot
monolithic
chiilmoott
lithotomic
chiilnoopt
phonolitic
chiilostty
histolytic
chiimooprs
isomorphic
chiimoprrt
trimorphic
chiimorrst
trichroism
chiimorsst
ostrichism
chiimorstu
humoristic
chiinnopsu
pincushion
chiinoprsx
crio-sphinx
chiinopssu
cousinship
chiinorstu
trichinous
unhistoric
chiiopssst
sophistics
chiiosssvy
vichyssois
chiiprrsty
pyrrhicist
chiirrstuu
Trichiurus
chikkllstu
thick-skull
chiknoqrtu
quickthorn
chiknorswy
corn-whisky
chikorsttw
stitchwork
throw-stick
chillnoswy
clownishly
chilmoosss
school-miss
chilnoopxy
xylophonic
chilnooqru
chloroquin
chilnopssu
consulship
chilooppsy
policy-shop
chilooptty
photolytic
chimmnoors
monorchism
chimnnooop
monophonic
chimnoorsu
Chironomus
chimnrssty
strychnism
chimoooprs
sophomoric
chimoooprz
zoomorphic
chimooprsy
hypocorism
chimoortty
trichotomy
chinooortt
orthotonic
chinooppty
phonotypic
chinooprsy
rhinoscopy
chinoprrst
corn-thrips
chioooprtz
zootrophic
chiooprry
pyrophoric
chioopptty
phototypic
chiooprstt
orthoptics
chiooptxy
phytotoxic
chiorstttw
stitchwort
chklooorsw
schoolwork
chlmmmotuy
mummy-cloth
chlmnosuuu
homunculus
chlmoooors
schoolroom
chlmoopryy
polychromy
chmmnooory
monochromy
chmnooptu
mutton-chop
chmoopppsy
psychopomp
chnnooorrt
chronotron
chnooorrtt
trochotron
choooorsuz
zoochorous
chooprrsuy
cryophorus
ciiiiklopt
poikilitic
ciiiilntvy
incivility
ciiiillmpty
implicitly
ciiilmnrtu
triclinium
ciiilmpsst
simplistic
ciiilmpsty
simplicity
ciiilnostt
tonsilitic
ciiilprtty
triplicity
ciiimnnost
nicotinism
ciiimnortu
tirocinium
ciiimnppru
principium
ciiimopstt
optimistic
ciiinnnott
intinction
ciijnnnotu
injunction
ciillmoosu
limicolous
ciillnootu
illocution
ciilmmntuu
nummulitic
ciilnossyz
zincolysis
ciiloosstu
solicitous
ciiloostuv
viticolous
ciiloprtvy
proclivity
ciilrrstuy
scurrility
ciilssstty
stylistics
ciimmnooss
commission
ciimmnootx
commixtion
ciimnnootz
monzonitic
ciimnoprrt
microprint
ciimorrstt
tricrotism
ciinnnoopt
conniption
ciinnoortt
contrition
ciinnottuy
continuity
ciinooprtx
picrotoxin
ciinoprrst
corn-spirit
ciioorstuv
victorious
ciiopsssuu
suspicious

ciipsttyy
stypticity
cijknoostt
joint-stock
cijlnnooty
conjointly
ciklloosstt
stockstill
ciklnoostt
silk-cotton
cikmnooppu
nickumpoop
cikorrstuw
rustic-work
cillmnoott
cotton-mill
cillmooquu
colloquium
cillooqstu
colloquist
cilloprstu
portcullis
cillossuuy
lusciously
cilmmopuuv
compluvium
cilmnoooot
locomotion
cilmnoopsu
compulsion
cilmnoopyy
polyonymic
cilmnoruuv
involucrum
cilmnostuu
monticulus
cilmooopss
cosmopolis
cilmoosstu
music-stool
cilnnoosuv
convulsion
cilooprsuu
rupicolous
cilorrssuu
scurrilous
cimnnooopp
nincompoop
cimnoopsty
toponymics
cimnoorsst
consortism
cimnoorstu
consortium
cimoooprst
compositor
cinnooortt
contortion
cinnoostuu
continuous
cinoooprsy
oniroscopy
cinoopprrs
prison-crop
cinooprrtu
corruption
cinooprsuy
urinoscopy
cinoorssty
consistory
cinoorsuuv
nucivorous
cinorrsttu
instructor
cinorsstuu
scrutinous
cinosttuuy
unctuosity
ciooprsttu
prosciutto
cioorrsttu
tricrotous
cioprrssy
procrypsis
cioprssttt
postscript
cioppsttyy
copy-typist
cipprrstuu
stirrup-cup
cklloorrsw
scrollwork
ckmnoorstu
moonstruck
cllmoopruu
plum-colour
cllmoossuu
molluscous
clmmnnoouy
uncommonly
clmnooosuu
monoculous
clmoooorty
locomotory
clmooprsuy
compulsory
clnooootw
cotton-wool
clnoooptty
polycotton
clnoorstuy
consultory
clnoortuwy
low-country
clnostuuuy
unctuously
cloooprrtu
prolocutor
clooopstuy
polytocous
clooorsstu
colostrous
cloostttuy
cutty-stool
cloprssuuu
scrupulous
cmnooostu
monotocous
cmnooorttw
cotton-worm
cmoopprty
prompt-copy
cooopprrrt
proproctor
cooorssttu
costus-root
dddddfuuyy
fuddy-duddy
dddddhooyy
hoddy-doddy
dddeeefnnu
undefended
dddeefiost
eisteddfod
dddeeinosw
disendowed
dddeeiorrs
disordered
dddefiloow
fiddlewood
dddegiioor
didgeridoo
dddoorwwyy
rowdy-dowdy
ddeeeeeltw
tweedledee
ddeeeemnru
unredeemed
ddeeefglnw
new-fledged
ddeeefimnr
free-minded
ddeeehirst
three-sided
ddeeehlnuy
unheededly
ddeeeimnnv
even-minded
ddeeeimnpt
pedimented
ddeeeimnru
unremedied
ddeeeinntx
inextended
ddeeeirssv
dissevered
ddeeelmmos
meddlesome
ddeeelmnty
dementedly
ddeeelmtuw
tweedledum
ddeeelntxy
extendedly
ddeeelrsvy
deservedly
ddeeennrru
unrendered
ddeeennrtu
untendered
ddeeenntux
unextended
ddeeenrrtu
undeterred
ddeeenrsuv
undeserved
ddeeenrsux
undersexed
ddeeeooprt
deep-rooted
ddeeffnnou
unoffended
ddeefgirru
red-figured
ddeefiiint
identified
ddeefiilln
ill-defined
ddeefiintu
definitude
ddeefinnru
unfriended
ddeeflmory
deformedly
ddeegghoop
hodgepodge
ddeeggnoss
doggedness
ddeeghnory
hodden-grey
ddeegiinst
indigested
ddeegilnsy
designedly
ddeegilsty
digestedly
ddeeginnsu
undesigned
ddeeginstu
undigested
ddeegjlluw
well-judged
ddeehiilnp
didelphine
ddeehilnsu
unshielded
ddeehinnru
unhindered
ddeehinnss
hiddenness
ddeehlorsu
shouldered
ddeehnrtuy
ythundered
ddeeiikllr
riddle-like
ddeeiiklmn
like-minded
ddeeiilmnv
evil-minded
ddeeiimnot
demi-ditone
ddeeiimopr
epidermoid
ddeeiimrsu
desiderium
ddeeiinrsw
sidewinder
ddeeiiopst
epidotised
ddeeiiorsx
deoxidiser
ddeeikmors
smoke-dried
ddeeillmnw
well-minded
ddeeillnrt
tendrilled
ddeeilnnty
intendedly
ddeeilnosy
one-sidedly
ddeeilsttu
lust-dieted
ddeeimmopr
demirepdom
ddeeimnnop
open-minded
ddeeimnnss
mindedness
ddeeimnors
endodermis
ddeeimnrtu
undertimed
ddeeinnntu
unintended
ddeeinoopt
endopodite
ddeeinoprs
perdendosi
ddeeinpruv
undeprived
ddeeinrruv
underdrive
ddeeinrsuz
undersized
ddeeinrtuv
undiverted
ddeeinstuv
undivested
ddeeioorrs
deodoriser
ddeeirssst
distressed
ddeelloorw
olde-worlde
ddeelnopru
undeplored
ddeelrrssu
rudderless
ddeennopst
despondent
ddeennortu
undernoted
undertoned
ddeennosss
soddenness
ddeennprsu
underspend

10 DDE

ddeennsssu
suddenness
ddeenoppst
end-stopped
ddeenopruw
unpowdered
ddeenrrssu
underdress
ddeffilsuy
diffusedly
ddefhiimuy
dehumidify
ddefhirrsu
rudder-fish
ddefhlnoru
fund-holder
ddefiiilos
solidified
ddefiimnou
unmodified
ddefiiorsx
dorsifixed
ddefillnou
ill-founded
ddefilnnsu
nun's-fiddle
ddefimnorr
dendriform
ddefknnruu
dunderfunk
ddefmnoruu
dumfounder
ddegggilor
gold-digger
ddeghhiimn
high-minded
ddeghinrsu
shuddering
ddeghmnouu
humdudgeon
ddeghnortu
thunder-god
ddegiilnnr
nidderling
ddegiilnry
deridingly
ddegiinppu
pudding-pie
ddegilnnow
long-winded
ddegilnuuv
undivulged
ddeginnops
desponding
ddeginnoru
redounding
ddegllnouu
loud-lunged
ddeglnoory
dendrology
ddeglnoruy
groundedly
ddegnnoruu
ungrounded

ddegnooruv
ground-dove
ddegoorsss
dress-goods
ddehhnoooy
hoydenhood
ddehiiimns
diminished
ddehiilnop
delphinoid
ddehiilnsw
windshield
ddehiilpsu
disulphide
ddehilopsu
didelphous
ddehimnost
hiddenmost
ddehinoprs
Dendrophis
ddehinosss
shoddiness
ddehiooopt
photodiode
ddeiiikknw
kiddiewink
ddeiiimpsy
epididymis
ddeiiiprst
dispirited
ddeiijnost
disjointed
ddeiimnnou
diminuendo
ddeiimoprv
improvided
ddeiinopss
indisposed
ddeiinostu
duodenitis
ddeiinosux
unoxidised
ddeiioprss
dispersoid
ddeiioprsv
disprovide
ddeiknnruw
wunderkind
ddeillnpsy
splendidly
ddeillttuw
dull-witted
ddeilmmost
middlemost
ddeilopssy
disposedly
ddeilorrsy
disorderly
ddeimnoorr
room-ridden
ddeinoorrw
iron-worded
ddeinopruv
unprovided

ddeinopssu
undisposed
ddeinopsuw
upside-down
ddeinorsss
sordidness
ddeinpstuu
undisputed
ddejrrruuy
jury-rudder
ddelnorruw
underworld
ddennoorsu
round-nosed
ddenooprww
powder-down
ddenoorstu
understood
ddenrstuuy
understudy
ddggilnruy
drudgingly
ddggoooyy
goody-goody
ddghiinoor
riding-hood
ddghiirryy
hirdy-girdy
ddghlnooru
ground-hold
ddghrruuyy
hurdy-gurdy
ddgiiilnow
wild-indigo
ddgiillnry
riddlingly
ddgiklnooo
odd-looking
ddgillnopy
ploddingly
ddhiiinoru
hirudinoid
ddhinoopty
diphyodont
ddhoooouwy
how-do-you-do
ddiiimnuuv
individuum
ddiiklntwy
tiddlywink
ddinnooott
notodontid
ddinoprswy
wind-dropsy
ddoooorrt
door-to-door
deeeeefprz
deep-freeze
deeeeenswz
sneezeweed
deeeefflrs
self-feeder
deeeeflrss
self-seeder

deeeefnrst
enfestered
deeeefnrtt
tenderfeet
deeeehlllw
well-heeled
deeeeilnnp
pine-needle
deeeelmrss
redeemless
deeeelnorw
ne'er-do-weel
deeeeloprv
redevelope
deeeelsssv
seed-vessel
deeeffoorr
free-fooder
deeeffoort
free-footed
deeefhilns
needle-fish
deeefhlorr
freeholder
deeefhorsw
foreshewed
deeefillsx
self-exiled
deeefilmnt
defilement
deeefimnnt
definement
deeeflnops
self-opened
deeeflorrw
deflowerer
deeefmnorw
freedwomen
deeefmnrru
referendum
deeefnrttu
unfettered
deeeforrst
deer-forest
deeeggglloy
goggle-eyed
deeeghhhil
high-heeled
deeeghisuy
hey-de-guise
deeeghsuyy
hey-de-guyes
deeegiknnw
week-ending
deeegillnr
ledger-line
deeegilmty
gimlet-eyed
deeegilnsy
single-eyed
deeeginrss
greediness
niger-seeds

deeegirrst
registered
deeegirssv
degressive
deeegllopr
poll-degree
deeeglnorv
glendoveer
deeeglorrs
gelder-rose
deeegnnrru
engendrure
deeegnnruv
unrevenged
deeegorrvy
overgreedy
deeehilott
diothelete
deeehilprt
three-piled
deeehimnrt
methedrine
deeehiprss
Hesperides
deeehjntuz
Judenhetze
deeehllssy
heedlessly
deeehlltww
well-thewed
deeehlmntu
unhelmeted
deeehlnors
lederhosen
deeehlotty
dyothelete
deeehlotww
two-wheeled
deeehlprsu
spur-heeled
deeehnorty
heterodyne
deeehnrrtu
thereunder
deeehnrruw
whereunder
deeehnrttu
untethered
deeeiiptvx
expeditive
deeeikllrw
weedkiller
deeeiknprs
deep-sinker
deeeillmos
demoiselle
deeeillmst
millet-seed
deeeilmrss
remediless
deeeilnrss
slenderise
deeeilnruv
unrelieved

deeeilnsvw
wind-sleeve
deeeilrrvy
redelivery
deeeilrsss
desireless
deeeilrsvw
silverweed
deeeimnost
demonetise
deeeimnrrt
determiner
deeeimnrst
densimeter
deeeimprtv
redemptive
deeeinnptv
pendentive
deeeinprst
predestine
deeeinpsss
speediness
deeeinrrst
residenter
tenderiser
deeeinrstt
interested
deeeiprssv
depressive
deeeirrssv
redressive
deeeirstwx
dexterwise
deeeklnorw
needlework
deeekooprr
door-keeper
deeellnorw
ne'er-do-well
deeellnpru
unrepelled
deeellnssy
needlessly
deeellowwy
yellow-weed
deeellowyy
yellow-eyed
deeelmprty
temperedly
deeelnrttu
unlettered
deeelopprv
predevelop
deeelopptt
pottle-deep
deeelrrsvy
reservedly
reversedly
deeelrssst
desertless
deeemnnott
denotement
deeemnnotu
dénouement

deeemnprtu
untempered
deeemnrssu
demureness
deeemnsttv
vestmented
deeennprtt
pretendent
deeennprtu
unrepented
deeennrruv
unreverend
deeennrsst
tenderness
deeennrssu
undersense
deeennrstu
unresented
deeenooswz
sneezewood
deeenopttt
tête-de-pont
deeenpppru
unpeppered
deeenprssu
superdense
deeenpsstt
pettedness
deeenrrstu
understeer
deeenrrsuv
undeserver
unreserved
unreversed
deeenrrtuv
unreverted
deeeopstty
eye-spotted
deeeorrrrt
reredorter
deeeorssty
seed-oyster
deeeprrssu
superseder
deeffloott
left-footed
deeffnorss
offendress
deefggilln
fledgeling
deefggloru
four-legged
deefghinrt
frightened
deefgiinrv
free-diving
deefginnrs
finger's-end
deefginsst
giftedness
deefglnnos
dog's-fennel
deefhilnrs
shield-fern

deefhmorrs
fresherdom
deefhoorsw
foreshowed
deefiiinnt
indefinite
deefiiintv
definitive
deefiiirvv
revivified
deefiillst
stellified
deefiilnty
definitely
deefiinruv
unverified
deefiinrvw
viewfinder
deefikllls
self-killed
deefilllsw
self-willed
deefillntu
unfilleted
deefillrsu
fleur-de-lis
deefilmmsu
misdeemful
deefilmosu
fieldmouse
deefilnost
fieldstone
deefilnrss
friendless
deefilnrsv
self-driven
deefilnrtu
unfiltered
deefilopss
self-poised
deefilortu
outfielder
deefilpstu
despiteful
deefinrssv
fervidness
deefknorss
forkedness
deefllmorw
well-formed
deefllnouw
unfellowed
deefllotvw
twelvefold
deefllpsuy
speedfully
deefllrsuy
fleur-de-lys
deefllssty
self-styled
deeflmnnot
enfoldment
deeflmrrsu
self-murder

deefloorvw
overflowed
deefmnnrtu
refundment
deefmnorru
unreformed
deefmnpruu
unperfumed
deefnnostu
unsoftened
deefnoortt
tenderfoot
deefnorstu
unforested
unfostered
deefooqrtu
fore-quoted
deefoorstu
surefooted
deeforruww
furrow-weed
deeggglino
long-legged
deeggiiprw
periwigged
deegginrss
dregginess
deeggnrssu
ruggedness
deeghhnort
thorn-hedge
deeghinouy
honey-guide
deeghinstt
night-steed
deeghinstu
Gesundheit
deeghlnoot
gentlehood
deeghnrruy
yerd-hunger
deegiiinns
indigenise
deegiilprv
privileged
deegiimmns
misdeeming
deegiinnrt
ingredient
deegiinstu
distinguée
deegiirssv
digressive
deegilnnrt
tenderling
deegilnopv
developing
deegilnrsy
resignedly
deegilnsss
designless
deegilrsst
stridelegs

deegimnnst
designment
deeginoopt
pigeon-toed
deeginorss
degression
deeginottu
tongue-tied
deeginprss
depressing
deeginrttw
dew-retting
deegnnoosu
endogenous
deegnnoruv
ungoverned
deegnoprst
serpent-god
deegnorruv
undergrove
deegorrtxy
dextrogyre
deehhiirst
hitherside
deehhimnor
hemihedron
deehhrrstu
reed-thrush
deehiilott
diothelite
deehillrsv
shrivelled
deehillsss
shieldless
deehillsww
well-wished
deehilmors
demolisher
deehilnrsu
unrelished
deehiloott
theodolite
deehiloprs
spider-hole
deehilortv
hot-livered
deehilotty
dyothelite
deehinoopv
videophone
deehinprsu
unperished
deehinrtuw
unwithered
deehiopprs
prophesied
deehiorrrs
horse-rider
deehiorstv
Shrovetide
deehirrttu
redruthite
deehknooss
hookedness

deehllmopr
phelloderm
deehlloowy
hollow-eyed
deehlnosuu
unhouseled
deehloprty
type-holder
deehlppruu
purple-hued
deehmorrty
hydrometer
deehnoortt
heterodont
deehnoprtu
three-pound
deehnorsuw
unshowered
deehnrsssw
shrewdness
deehoorsuw
dower-house
deehoortxy
heterodoxy
deeiiimnsv
semi-divine
deeiiimptv
impeditive
deeiiinppr
piperidine
deeiiioprt
epidiorite
deeiiklnrt
tinder-like
deeiiklprs
spider-like
deeiiillmpr
imperilled
deeiillnos
linseed-oil
deeiillopt
lepidolite
deeiilmnvw
vine-mildew
deeiilmpst
speed-limit
deeiilmstx
sex-limited
deeiilnnvy
vinylidene
deeiilnprs
spider-line
deeiilnsst
distensile
deeiilnssw
wieldiness
deeiilnstt
disentitle
deeiilorst
siderolite
deeiilprrv
pile-driver
deeiilrssv
silverside

deeiilrsvy
derisively
deeiimmnpt
impediment
deeiimnnrt
dinner-time
deeiimnntt
inditement
deeiinnrtt
Tridentine
deeiinnssv
divineness
deeiinnstw
disentwine
deeiinoptx
expedition
deeiinpttu
ineptitude
deeiinqstu
disquieten
deeiinqtuu
inquietude
deeiinrssv
divineress
deeiinrttw
winter-tide
deeiinssst
sensitised
deeiinsssy
syneidesis
deeiinsstv
distensive
deeiioprsx
peroxidise
deeiioprtt
peridotite
deeiiopstv
depositive
deeiiprssv
dispersive
deeijmnosw
jimson-weed
deeijnorru
rejoindure
deeikknpru
dukkeripen
deeikorsst
side-stroke
deeilllpuy
idle-pulley
deeillmpss
misspelled
deeillowww
willow-weed
deeillsuvy
delusively
deeilmmnpt
dimplement
deeilmnrtw
wilderment
deeilmopry
polymeride
deeilnnnru
underlinen

deeilnnort
tender-loin
deeilnnqtu
delinquent
deeilnnrss
dinnerless
deeilnnstu
unlistened
deeilnnttu
unentitled
deeilnopsv
disenvelop
deeilnorsu
sourdeline
deeilnpttu
plentitude
deeilnrssw
wilderness
deeilnrsuu
unleisured
deeilnrtvy
invertedly
deeilnsstu
diluteness
deeiloppprs
rose-lipped
deeilopprt
dopplerite
deeilorssv
redissolve
deeilosttt
stilettoed
deeimmmrtu
medium-term
deeimmrstu
summertide
deeimnnntt
intendment
deeimnnrru
underminer
deeimnnrtu
underntime
deeimnoops
empoisoned
deeimnoprt
redemption
deeimnoptt
idempotent
deeimnorrs
moderniser
deeimnrrsu
Mindererus
deeimnrstw
stemwinder
deeimnrsty
densimetry
deeimnrttu
unremitted
deeimnsttv
divestment
deeimoostu
tediousome
deeimoprry
pyromeride

deeinnnosu
innuendoes
deeinnoprs
prednisone
deeinnorrw
irrenowned
deeinnsstu
unitedness
deeinnstuv
uninvested
deeinoprss
depression
deeinprrst
rinderpest
deeinprruz
underprize
deeinprstu
unrespited
deeinprsty
predestiny
deeinqrruu
unrequired
deeinqrtuu
unrequited
deeinqstuy
squint-eyed
deeinrrtuw
underwrite
deeinrsssy
synderesis
deeinrsstu
unresisted
unsistered
deeinssttu
testudines
deeiopprrt
propertied
deeioppprss
predispose
deeiopsssu
disespouse
deeiopsstu
despiteous
deeiorrstv
overstride
deeipprrsu
purse-pride
deeiprrtuy
eurypterid
deejnprruu
unperjured
deeklmrttu
kettledrum
deellmnouw
unmellowed
deellmoosy
dolesomely
deellmpuvy
dumpy-level
deellnorty
redolently
deellnrtuw
well-turned

deellorsvy
resolvedly
deellortuw
out-dweller
deelmnopty
deployment
deelmnopuy
unemployed
deelmnosss
seldomness
deelmnostu
unmolested
deelnnoost
selenodont
deelnnossu
unlessoned
deelnnrtuy
untenderly
deelnoprux
unexplored
deelnorsuv
unresolved
deelnostuu
edentulous
deeloorttw
letter-wood
deeloovvyy
lovey-dovey
deeloprrtt
drop-letter
deeloprrty
reportedly
deeloprstw
spot-welder
deelorttuv
turtle-dove
deemmnrsuu
unsummered
deemnnoprt
ponderment
deemnnorss
modernness
deemnnortw
wonderment
deemnnrstu
sunderment
deemnoorry
money-order
deemnoprtt
deportment
deemnorstu
tremendous
deemnortuv
devourment
deemoorrst
drosometer
deemoprrty
redemptory
deennnoruw
unrenowned
deennoossw
woodenness
deennopprt
propendent

deennoprst
respondent
deennoprtu
ten-pounder
deennorsvw
news-vendor
deennosstw
wontedness
deennrrtuu
unreturned
deenooprtt
torpedo-net
deenoorsst
rootedness
deenoprrtu
unreported
deenoprruv
unreproved
deenoprruw
under-power
deenoqrtuu
underquote
deenorrstu
unrestored
deenorsuvz
rendezvous
deenosstuv
devoutness
deenpruuvy
unpurveyed
deenrssstu
unstressed
deenrsuuvy
unsurveyed
deeooprrsu
uredospore
deeoorrstt
street-door
deeopprssu
superposed
deeoprrrsu
superorder
deeoqrstuu
Tudoresque
deepprrsuu
super-duper
deepprsssu
suppressed
deffglortu
truffle-dog
deffhimors
sheriffdom
deffinnost
soft-finned
deffoortu
four-footed
deffooostt
soft-footed
deffoppruw
powder-puff
defggillru
full-rigged
defghilltu
delightful

defghilnor
fingerhold
defghinrtu
unfrighted
defgiilnrr
girlfriend
defgiilnyy
edifyingly
defgiinnuy
unedifying
defgiinrss
frigidness
defgillnsu
sdeignfull
defgillnuw
full-winged
defginootw
wing-footed
defgllooow
good-fellow
defgnoorru
foreground
defhiiiksw
whiskified
defhiiimru
humidifier
defhiinnsu
unfinished
defhiinprs
friendship
defhilorsu
flourished
defhlnosuw
flesh-wound
defhloprsu
proud-flesh
defhnooort
horn-footed
defhnoopru
unhoped-for
defhorrrtu
rutherford
defiiilmps
simplified
defiiilnty
infidelity
defiiinnot
definition
defiiinntu
infinitude
defiikllsu
dislikeful
defiillnry
friendlily
defiilorsu
fluoridise
defiilsttu
stultified
defiinossu
unossified
defiinpruu
unpurified
defiioprsu
perfidious

defiirrrtv
river-drift
defillorww
wild-fowler
defillpruy
pridefully
defilnnruy
unfriendly
defilnorss
floridness
defilnorww
wind-flower
defilnptuu
unuplifted
defiloorsu
florideous
defiloprsw
wolf-spider
defilprsuu
superfluid
defimmorsu
medusiform
defimnnoru
uninformed
definoprtu
unprofited
defioprsss
disprofess
defklmnouy
flunkeydom
defllmmsuu
full-summed
deflnoorru
underfloor
deflnoortu
unforetold
deflnoorvy
overfondly
deflnottwy
twentyfold
deflooopttt
polt-footed
deflooostw
slow-footed
defnnortuu
unfortuned
defnooprru
underproof
defnoorsuu
founderous
defnorruuw
unfurrowed
defooorsty
rosy-footed
degghiillr
hill-digger
degghiiprs
ship-rigged
deggijrruy
jury-rigged
deggiloors
sogdoliger
degginnoru
undergoing

deggllooors
sogdologer
deggmnooor
Demogorgon
deggnoostu
dog's-tongue
deghhiiklt
high-kilted
deghhilosu
high-souled
deghiillns
shieldling
deghiilnrt
right-lined
deghiilttw
twilighted
deghiimopp
pemphigoid
deghiinrrt
night-rider
deghiknntu
unknighted
deghilnnsu
unshingled
deghilnost
Odelsthing
deghinnort
dethroning
deghinnrtu
thundering
deghinossu
doughiness
deghinrruy
yird-hunger
deghinrsst
nightdress
deghiorrru
rough-rider
deghlnopuu
unploughed
deghmooort
good-mother
deghnnrtuu
dung-hunter
deghnrruyy
yerd-hungry
degiiiknns
die-sinking
degiillnnw
indwelling
degiillnps
dispelling
degiillnrv
drivelling
degiillnty
diligently
degiillnyy
yieldingly
degiilnnty
indigently
degiilnnuy
unyielding
degiilnors
soldiering

degiiloost
ideologist
degiimnrsy
semi-drying
degiinnosu
indigenous
degiinnrsu
undesiring
degiinnsst
dissenting
degiinorrv
overriding
degiinorss
digression
degiinprst
springtide
degiinptuu
pinguitude
degijlnstu
Jugendstil
degiklmoor
grimlooked
degillooty
deltiology
degilmnrsu
mud-slinger
degilnnnuy
unendingly
degilnnoru
loundering
degilnnruy
enduringly
underlying
degilnooss
goodliness
degilnosww
slow-winged
degilnrstu
disgruntle
degilooooz
zoogloeoid
degiloopst
pedologist
degimnortw
wrong-timed
degimnsssu
smudginess
deginnnorw
dinner-gown
deginnorst
grindstone
stringendo
deginnorsu
resounding
deginnrssu
undressing
deginnrstu
unstringed
deginooopw
wood-pigeon
deginorssu
gourdiness
deginorsty
destroying

deginossst
stodginess
deginprsuw
spur-winged
deginrsstu
turgidness
degioorsst
good-sister
degllnorsu
groundsell
deglmnoooy
demonology
deglnnrsuu
underslung
deglnoooty
deontology
deglnootuz
zeuglodont
deglnorssu
groundless
degloopsuy
pseudology
degloortty
troglodyte
degloortuw
towel-gourd
degnnoooty
odontogeny
degnnoopsw
sponge-down
degnnorrtu
ground-rent
degnnorruw
undergrown
degnooopsw
spongewood
degnoorruv
overground
degnoorruz
ground-zero
degooorsuw
wood-grouse
dehhilnotw
withholden
dehhilntuw
unwithheld
dehhiloprs
ship-holder
dehhilortw
withholder
dehhlnooor
holohedron
dehhlorrsu
rush-holder
dehhmooort
motherhood
dehhmoottu
hot-mouthed
dehhnoopry
hydrophone
dehhoprtyy
hydrophyte
dehiiinrst
disinherit

dehiiklloo
likelihood
dehiilloov
livelihood
dehiillsvy
devilishly
dehiilmnpu
delphinium
dehiilmost
diothelism
dehiilnnrs
hinderlins
dehiilnpss
displenish
dehiilnpsy
sylphidine
dehiimnpru
nephridium
dehiinopsy
hypnoidise
dehiinorss
disherison
dehiinrssw
widershins
dehiioprst
editorship
dehiiopsty
diophysite
dehiiorrst
disheritor
dehiirstvw
whist-drive
dehilmosty
dyothelism
dehilnopsu
unpolished
dehilnorsu
shroud-line
dehilnortu
unitholder
dehilnortv
thorn-devil
dehiloopss
shop-soiled
dehilorstv
short-lived
dehimmnorr
horn-rimmed
dehimmpssy
dysphemism
dehimnorst
hindermost
dehimnosss
modishness
dehimooppr
hippodrome
dehimoprsy
hypodermis
dehinnorru
dinner-hour
dehinnpsuu
unpunished
dehinorrss
horridness

dehinorstt
threnodist
dehinossty
dishonesty
dehinrrstu
undershirt
dehiooprst
priesthood
dehiooqrsu
squirehood
dehioorsst
sisterhood
dehiopprsw
worshipped
dehiopstyy
dyophysite
dehirrssst
dress-shirt
dehllmnosu
shell-mound
dehlloossu
doll's-house
dehlnoopry
polyhedron
dehlnouuzz
unhouzzled
dehloorrtw
otherworld
dehlorsssu
shroudless
dehmmnoory
monorhymed
dehmnoopry
endomorphy
dehmnoostu
unsmoothed
dehmoorssy
hydrosomes
dehmorrtyy
hydrometry
dehmortuwy
wry-mouthed
dehnnooruu
unhonoured
dehnnorsuu
nursehound
dehnooprrw
powder-horn
dehnooprtu
horned-pout
dehnoorrsu
horrendous
dehnoorstu
undershoot
dehnoorsuu
round-house
dehnoorttu
otter-hound
dehnorstuu
thunderous
dehooprrwy
hydropower
dehooprsuu
house-proud

deiiilmqsu
semi-liquid
deiiilmstu
similitude
deiiilnsst
dissilient
deiiiloprt
ripidolite
deiiilqrsu
liquidiser
deiiimnors
iridosmine
deiiimnpru
peridinium
deiiimnpry
pyrimidine
deiiimntuv
diminutive
deiiimsssv
dismissive
deiiinorsv
redivision
deiijmnors
misjoinder
deiikllnor
kirn-dollie
deiiklnnss
kindliness
deiillmptu
multiplied
deiillnops
spindle-oil
deiillnuwy
unwieldily
deiillopst
pistillode
deiillpsuv
pulvilised
deiillrsty
distillery
deiilmnoot
demolition
deiilmoost
dolomitise
deiilnosvv
disinvolve
deiilnprty
intrepidly
deiilnqssu
liquidness
deiilnstuu
unutilised
deiilprsty
spiritedly
deiilqstuy
disquietly
deiimnoprt
diremption
deiimoprsv
disimprove
deiinnoqru
inquirendo
deiinnorsv
disenviron

deiinnosss
dissension
deiinnosst
distension
deiinnostt
distention
deiinnprsu
uninspired
deiinnsstu
untidiness
deiinoopst
deposition
positioned
deiinoprss
dispersion
deiinoprxy
pyridoxine
deiinorttw
iron-witted
deiinpprst
pin-striped
deiinprstu
unspirited
deiiopsstu
dispiteous
deiiorsttv
distortive
deiiprstuv
disruptive
deiipssstu
spissitude
deijlnootw
dowel-joint
deijnnnoor
non-joinder
deikknnops
kind-spoken
deiklmnops
mild-spoken
deiklnnruw
unwrinkled
deiklnstuy
klendusity
deikmnnory
drink-money
deikmpprsu
mud-skipper
deiknnnssu
unkindness
deiknnrsuw
swine-drunk
deiknrrstu
underskirt
deikoprrsw
spider-work
deillmnssy
mindlessly
deillmoprw
powder-mill
deillnnoty
indolently
deillnopuw
unpillowed

deillnorss
lordliness
deilloprrw
power-drill
deillprrss
drill-press
deilmmosty
immodestly
deilmnnosu
unsmiled-on
deilmnopru
unimplored
deilmnossu
mouldiness
deilmnptuy
impudently
deilnnntuw
wind-tunnel
deilnnouvv
uninvolved
deilnooott
odontolite
deilnoorww
wool-winder
deilnootuv
devolution
deilnoqruu
unliquored
deilnossst
stolidness
deilnosstv
dissolvent
deilnossww
windowless
deilnppsuu
unsupplied
deilnrstty
stridently
deiloopssu
solipedous
deiloorrvw
wool-driver
deiloprsuu
preludious
deilopssty
stylopised
deilorssuy
desirously
deimmnntuu
indumentum
deimmopstu
impostumed
deimnnostw
disownment
deimnoosss
endosmosis
deimnoprsu
unpromised
deimnoprtu
minute-drop
deimnopruv
unimproved
deimnorstu
unmortised

deimnrssuu
unsurmised
deimoortuw
moudiewort
deimoortww
mowdiewort
deimopprst
prompt-side
deimoprssu
dispermous
deimrsstty
mistrysted
deinnnortu
trunnioned
deinnnouww
unwinnowed
deinnoopsu
unpoisoned
deinnoorst
tension-rod
deinnoprsu
unprisoned
deinnortuw
interwound
deinooprss
droopiness
deinooprst
desorption
deinoorsww
rose-window
deinoosssu
odiousness
deinoprsst
torpidness
deinopsssu
suspensoid
deinorrsst
torridness
deinorrttt
dirt-rotten
deinorssss
drossiness
deinorsssw
drowsiness
deinorssuu
undesirous
deinpprstu
unstripped
deinprsstu
putridness
deinpssstu
stupidness
deinrssstu
sturdiness
deiooprrtv
proveditor
deiooprstt
torpedoist
deiooprsty
depository
deioprrstw
spider-wort
deiopsssss
dispossess

dekknoorwy
donkey-work
dekllmnsuu
numskulled
dekmnoppuy
donkey-pump
deknoopruv
unprovoked
deknoopttt
top-knotted
deknoorrww
wonder-work
deknoorstw
downstroke
dellloptuy
pollutedly
dellnoptuu
unpolluted
dellooowwy
yellow-wood
dellossuuy
sedulously
delnnopssu
nonplussed
delnnotuwy
unwontedly
delnooortt
rondoletto
delnooprtu
pleurodont
delnoprsuu
plunderous
delooorrsw
wood-sorrel
delooorruv
louver-door
louvre-door
delooprtuu
trou-de-loup
deloppssuy
supposedly
delorstuxy
dextrously
demmnnosuu
unsummoned
demmoorrwy
word-memory
demnooopst
Podostemon
demnopprtu
unprompted
demnorstuu
surmounted
demoooprrw
powder-room
demooprrww
worm-powder
dennooprsu
pundonores
dennrrtuuu
unnurtured
denoopprru
propounder

denoopprsu
unproposed
denopprsuu
unpurposed
denoprrttu
protrudent
denoprssuu
supersound
denopsstuu
stupendous
denorrttuu
untortured
deoorrssuu
uredosorus
deopprrsuu
purse-proud
dffiimorty
difformity
dfggiiinny
dignifying
dfghiinors
fishing-rod
rodfishing
dfghilloot
floodlight
dfghiloosy
old-fogyish
dfgiiillnr
fringillid
dfgiiimort
digitiform
dfgiilorsy
disglorify
dfgiinosuu
nidifugous
dfgiinrrsu
surf-riding
dfgilsstuu
disgustful
dfhiinrssu
disfurnish
dfhillnopy
dolphin-fly
dfhilortty
thirtyfold
dfhinosstu
sound-shift
dfhloooopt
photoflood
dfhnooostu
hounds-foot
dfiiooorpt
idiot-proof
dfinooprst
spoondrift
dfinoprtuy
profundity
dflnoopruy
profoundly
dfnoooprsu
soundproof
dfooorstu
out-of-doors

dfoooprrsw
swordproof
dgggilnruy
grudgingly
dggginnruu
ungrudging
dgghinorru
rough-grind
dggiiilmno
ginglimoid
dggiiinssu
disguising
dggiiklnoo
good-liking
dggiinsstu
disgusting
dggilnnoru
groundling
dggilnootu
outlodging
dgginnoorw
wrong-doing
dghhiknoot
knighthood
dghhnooruu
rough-hound
dghiiinprw
riding-whip
dghiiklnoo
kinglihood
dghiilprty
ditriglyph
dghiinoorv
virginhood
dghinrruyy
yird-hungry
dghlnoorst
stronghold
dghmooorruu
good-humour
dghnoorsuw
showground
dgiiiknnsv
skin-diving
dgiiillnst
distilling
dgiiimortu
digitorium
dgiiinptuy
pinguidity
dgiiinrstu
riding-suit
dgiiinstuv
diving-suit
dgiilnossv
dissolving
dgiimmnnor
mid-morning
dgiimnnoor
dining-room
dgiimnorsw
miswording
dgiinnopru
pundigrion

dgiiooprsu
prodigious
dgillnorsu
groundsill
dgilnnosuy
soundingly
dgilnoopry
droopingly
dgilooopst
podologist
dginnoopru
undrooping
dginnooprw
roping-down
dginooprsw
springwood
dgknoorruw
groundwork
dglnooooty
odontology
dglnooprtu
groundplot
dglnooptty
glyptodont
dgmooorrw
good-morrow
dgnooprrux
groundprox
dhhilopryy
hydrophily
dhhmooosst
smooth-shod
dhhoorstuw
woodthrush
dhiiloopss
pholidosis
dhiimmoprs
dimorphism
dhiinorsuu
hirudinous
dhiioorsst
diorthosis
dhiioprssw
disworship
dhiiorsttu
struthioid
dhilmoostu
Lithodomus
dhilorssyy
hydrolysis
dhimooprsu
dimorphous
dhinoooprt
ornithopod
dhinoopsww
shop-window
dhinoostww
shot-window
dhioooptyz
zoophytoid
dhlooppryy
hydropolyp
dhmnoortuu
round-mouth

dhmooorrty
orthodromy
dhnooortux
unorthodox
dhoorrsstw
short-sword
diiiinpsty
insipidity
diiilnosty
insolidity
diiilsttuy
disutility
diiimmorsu
iridosmium
osmiridium
diiimnnotu
diminution
diiimnosss
dismission
diillnosww
window-sill
diilnoopss
displosion
diilnostuy
unsolidity
diimmoprru
primordium
diimoorsss
osmidrosis
diimorsssy
dismissory
diinoorstt
distortion
diinoprstu
disruption
diinrttuuy
diuturnity
diiooprsst
dispositor
diiooprstw
wood-spirit
dillooppyy
polyploidy
dilmooppuy
Polypodium
dilnoopstw
splintwood
dilorsstuu
stridulous
dilosstuuy
studiously
dimmnooopu
monopodium
dimoprssuy
dysprosium
dinoooprrs
prison-door
dinoorttuy
orotundity
dllooorsuy
dolorously
dlnoopssuy
spondylous

dlnoorsuwy
wondrously
eeeeelmsss
seemelesse
eeeeemprst
Peter-see-me
eeeeffnsst
effeteness
eeeefisssw
fesseewise
eeeefklrss
self-seeker
eeeeflmsst
self-esteem
eeeeflrssv
self-severe
eeeefrrrsv
free-verser
eeeegipssx
epexegesis
eeeegnrttv
genevrette
eeeehimrsu
euhemerise
eeeehirrsv
shire-reeve
eeeehlloty
eyelet-hole
eeeehlmrwy
emery-wheel
eeeehorrsw
wheresoe'er
eeeehrrvwy
everywhere
eeeeiipstw
sweetie-pie
eeeeikkppr
pike-keeper
eeeeikmprt
time-keeper
eeeeilrttv
televérité
eeeeilrtvw
televiewer
eeeeimrstt
semiterete
eeeeinpssw
sweep-seine
eeeekmrrsy
kerseymere
eeeellsssv
sleeveless
eeeelmnntv
enlevement
eeeelnrttt
nettle-tree
eeeelorsvv
oversleeve
eeeemnrsst
entremesse
eeeennrrvv
never-never
eeeennrsss
sereneness

eeeenntwyy
teeny-weeny
eeeenrsssv
severeness
eeeenrstvy
yestereven
eeeettttww
tweet-tweet
eeeffhirrs
free-fisher
eeeffiimns
effeminise
eeeffnoost
toffee-nose
eeefgiinnr
fire-engine
eeefgilnrr
rifle-green
eeefginors
foreseeing
eeefglnruv
revengeful
eeefhilssv
sleeve-fish
eeefhoorrt
heretofore
eeefillrss
reliefless
eeefillrtt
letter-file
eeefilnrrt
life-renter
eeefilorrs
free-soiler
eeefimnnrt
refinement
eeefimnrtv
fermentive
eeefinorrr
ferronière
eeefinorrv
over-refine
eeefinrrrt
interferer
eeefinrsvw
swine-fever
eeefknoprs
free-spoken
eeefllmstt
self-mettle
eeefllorrt
foreteller
eeeflorrvy
overfreely
eeeflrsstt
fetterless
eeefmnprrt
preferment
eeefnnorsu
unforeseen
eeefnorrtu
fourteener
eeefnqrrtu
frequenter

eeeforrstt
forest-tree
eeeghhintt
eighteenth
eeeghilnst
genteelish
eeeghimnot
eighteenmo
eeeghklnnt
knee-length
eeeghnorsu
greenhouse
eeeghnorty
heterogeny
eeeghrrtwy
grey-wether
eeegiinpss
epigenesis
eeegiinrss
greisenise
eeegiinrsu
seigneurie
eeegiiprss
periegesis
eeegilmnpw
weeping-elm
eeegilmnst
genteelism
eeegilnrst
singletree
eeegilnsst
gentilesse
eeegimnnrt
enregiment
eeegimorst
geometrise
eeeginnors
rose-engine
eeeginnoss
neogenesis
eeeginnrrt
re-entering
eeeginnstw
sweetening
eeeginopry
epeirogeny
eeeginrrst
enregister
interreges
eeegirrrst
reregister
eeegirrssv
regressive
eeeglmnrty
emergently
eeeglnnsst
gentleness
eeeglnostz
seltzogene
eeegmnnotu
engouement
eeegnnorst
greenstone

eeehhimprs
  hemisphere
eeehhlorsw
  wheel-horse
eeehhlosuw
  wheel-house
eeehhorrtw
  otherwhere
eeehiklprs
  sphere-like
eeehikpprs
  keepership
eeehilltww
  whewellite
eeehilmort
  heliometer
eeehilmrtw
  mitre-wheel
eeehilnprs
  prehensile
eeehilsttt
  title-sheet
eeehimmrsu
  euhemerism
eeehimprst
  ephemerist
eeehimrstu
  euhemerist
eeehinnntt
  nineteenth
eeehinprsv
  prehensive
eeehinpsst
  epenthesis
eeehinsswz
  wheeziness
eeehinsttv
  seventieth
eeehjlosuw
  jewel-house
eeehkopprs
  shopkeeper
eeehllntvy
  eleventhly
eeehlmnptt
  hemp-nettle
eeehlmntvy
  vehemently
eeehlmsstv
  themselves
eeehlnoprt
  telephoner
eeehlopssu
  sheep-louse
eeehlortww
  two-wheeler
eeehlprsss
  sphereless
eeehmnorrt
  nethermore
eeehmnortv
  veneer-moth
eeehmoprss
  mesosphere
eeehmoprsu
  ephemerous
eeehmortty
  hyetometer
eeehnnprty
  threepenny
eeehnorsvw
  whensoever
eeehnostwy
  honey-sweet
eeehnrsstt
  stern-sheet
eeeiiprttv
  repetitive
eeeijnrsuv
  rejuvenise
eeeikllnsv
  sleeve-link
eeeiklmswy
  semi-weekly
eeeiklnnpr
  pine-kernel
eeeillptvv
  velvet-pile
eeeilmmort
  mileometer
eeeilmnrtv
  revilement
eeeilmnsss
  seemliness
eeeilmprtv
  pelvimeter
eeeilmprtx
  pleximeter
eeeilmrsst
  missel-tree
eeeilnopps
  penelopise
eeeilnprrt
  terreplein
eeeilnpsss
  sleepiness
eeeilnrrst
  re-enlister
eeeilnssst
  sleetiness
  steeliness
eeeiloprrs
  leproserie
eeeilrrstv
  silver-tree
eeeilrrttw
  telewriter
eeeimmrrss
  mesmeriser
eeeimnnprt
  pre-eminent
  repinement
eeeimnorst
  remonetise
eeeimnprtx
  experiment
eeeimnrrtt
  retirement
eeeimnrtvv
  revivement
eeeimoprtz
  piezometer
eeeimpprtv
  pre-emptive
eeeimpsttv
  tempestive
eeeimrrstv
  time-server
eeeinnprst
  serpentine
eeeinnprtv
  prevenient
eeeinnrrtv
  intervener
eeeinnrsst
  entireness
eeeinpprsv
  prepensive
eeeinprrst
  enterprise
eeeinprsst
  serpentise
eeeinprssu
  purse-seine
eeeinprstv
  presentive
  vespertine
eeeinprtvv
  preventive
eeeinpssst
  steepiness
eeeinrrrtv
  irreverent
eeeinrsstw
  westernise
eeeinsstwy
  eye-witness
eeeioprrrt
  repertoire
eeeiprrssv
  repressive
eeeiprrsvv
  perversive
eeeiprrttu
  répétiteur
eeeiprssvx
  expressive
eeeirssttw
  streetwise
eeejjnnssu
  jejuneness
eeeklnosst
  sleekstone
eeekmnortv
  revokement
eeellnpsss
  spleenless
eeellnrsst
  relentless
eeellorttv
  love-letter
eeellprssy
  peerlessly
eeellrsstt
  letterless
eeelmmostt
  mettlesome
eeelmnnrtt
  relentment
eeelmnotvv
  evolvement
eeelmnsttt
  settlement
eeelmoostt
  teleostome
eeelnottvw
  twelve-note
  twelve-tone
eeelnpprsy
  prepensely
eeelnrrtvy
  reverently
eeelnrsttw
  newsletter
eeeloopprv
  overpeople
eeelprrsvy
  perversely
eeelprsstu
  reputeless
eeelrsssvw
  swerveless
eeelrstttu
  ulsterette
eeemmrrstu
  summer-tree
eeemnnorst
  mesenteron
eeemnnrstt
  resentment
eeemnnsstu
  unmeetness
eeemnorsst
  remoteness
eeemnorstt
  sermonette
eeemnprstt
  pesterment
eeennnpsvy
  sevenpenny
eeennnssuv
  unevenness
eeennrrtuv
  unreverent
eeenorstwz
  sneezewort
eeenosttuw
  outsweeten
eeenprsstx
  expertness
eeeooprsvx
  overexpose
eeeoprstty
  stereotype
eeeoprttuv
  éprouvette
eeepprrrsu
  rere-supper
eeeprrssux
  expressure
eeeprsttty
  typesetter
eeffffimou
  fee-fi-fo-fum
eeffgiinrv
  five-finger
eeffginorr
  forefinger
eeffgnrstu
  greenstuff
eeffhlrrsu
  refreshful
eeffilllrs
  self-filler
eeffilsuvy
  effusively
eeffimnntt
  infeftment
eeffiorrtu
  forfeiture
eefflorsst
  effortless
eeffnorrty
  effrontery
eeffssttuw
  sweetstuff
eefghilnor
  fingerhole
eefghinrrs
  refreshing
eefghlooss
  goose-flesh
eefgiillln
  ill-feeling
eefgillnry
  fleeringly
eefgillnty
  fleetingly
eefgilnrss
  fingerless
  fringeless
eefgilnrtw
  left-winger
eefginnrrt
  refringent
eefginprrr
  preferring
eefgkllnot
  gentlefolk
eefgllmnor
  fellmonger
eefgllnuvy
  vengefully
eefglmnntu
  engulfment
eefglnprtu
  prefulgent

eefgorrtty
forgettery
eefhhiorst
horse-thief
eefhhlorss
horseflesh
eefhiilnrs
line-fisher
eefhiklstt
fish-kettle
eefhillorw
fellow-heir
eefhilnsss
fleshiness
eefhilnstt
nettle-fish
eefhilorsv
fire-shovel
eefhilrsvy
feverishly
eefhinrsty
net-fishery
eefhlnorss
hornfelses
eefhmoorst
foster-home
eefhnorttu
fourteenth
eefhooprst
proof-sheet
eefhoopsst
sheep's-foot
eefhorrsuy
ferry-house
eefiikllnu
unlifelike
eefiiklnuw
unwifelike
eefiilmnny
femininely
eefiilmrsu
emulsifier
eefiilrrst
fertiliser
eefiimnnnu
unfeminine
eefiinnsst
finiteness
eefiklllrs
self-killer
eefikllruv
liver-fluke
eefikmnnoy
knife-money
eefiknnops
fine-spoken
eefilllssy
lifelessly
eefillnotu
feuilleton
eefilmrstu
muster-file
eefilnnort
florentine

eefilnrssu
irefulness
eefilnsszz
fizzenless
eefiloopr r
poor-relief
eefiloorsu
oleiferous
eefilprrsu
persifleur
eefilqrtuu
requiteful
eefilrssst
strifeless
eefimnostt
oftentimes
eefinnorrt
interferon
eefinnqrtu
infrequent
eefinopsst
fesse-point
eefinttvwy
twenty-five
eefiorrrtx
fox-terrier
eefiorstwy
oyster-wife
eefiprrtux
prefixture
eefirrsstu
fruiteress
eefklloowy
yoke-fellow
eefllnnrru
fell-runner
eefllorssw
flowerless
eeflmorrsu
remorseful
eeflnnsstu
fluentness
eeflnntuuv
uneventful
eeflnossuw
woefulness
eeflnqrtuy
frequently
eeflnrssuu
ruefulness
eeflnsssuu
usefulness
eeflorrttu
four-letter
eeflrsstuu
futureless
eefmoortzz
mezzo-forte
eefnnorrru
forerunner
eefnnqrtuu
unfrequent
eefnoorsty
festoonery

eefoprrruv
perfervour
eegggilmos
gigglesome
eegghmnnoo
hogen-mogen
eegginrrtt
regretting
eeggisstuv
suggestive
eeghhiosuw
weigh-house
eeghhorruw
rough-hewer
eeghhorstu
see-through
eeghiiltvw
live-weight
eeghiklrsu
kieselguhr
eeghilnoop
pigeonhole
eeghilnopr
negrophile
eeghilnrst
sheltering
eeghilnstw
lengthwise
eeghilnsww
swing-wheel
eeghiloost
theologise
eeghilsstw
weightless
eeghimmnos
hegemonism
eeghimnoos
homogenise
eeghimnost
hegemonist
eeghinnpty
eightpenny
eeghinprst
regentship
eeghinrtvy
everything
eeghiortvw
overweight
eeghiprrsv
vergership
eeghloooss
goloe-shoes
eeghloorty
heterology
eeghloprtu
plough-tree
eeghmorrty
hygrometer
eeghnnrstt
strengthen
eeghnoorty
heterogony
eeghnopsyz
zygosphene

eeghnorsuu
sure-enough
eeghorsstu
otherguess
eeghosstuu
guest-house
eegiiilmst
legitimise
eegiiklprs
kriegspiel
eegiilnnst
lentigines
eegiilnorr
religioner
eegiilnrvv
ever-living
eegiilntvy
genitively
eegiilopsu
epiloguise
eegiimmnss
misseeming
eegiinnqtu
quietening
eegiinnrrt
interreign
eegiinprss
serpigines
eegiinrrtv
retrieving
eegiinrssv
ingressive
eegiinrstv
vertigines
eegijnsttt
jet-setting
eegikllnnn
kennelling
eegikorssw
siege-works
eegillopss
gospellise
eegillopsw
Owlspiegel
eegilmmnnt
minglement
eegilmnnot
eloignment
eegilmnors
mongrelise
eegilmoosy
semeiology
eegilnnppu
pulp-engine
eegilnnprs
leg-spinner
eegilnnpsu
unsleeping
eegilnnrsy
sneeringly
eegilnnsss
singleness
eegilnosst
telegnosis

eegilnpprx
perplexing
eegilnpswy
sweepingly
eegilnrstw
sweltering
eegilorrst
sortileger
eegimnnoor
engine-room
eegimnnott
mignonette
eegimnnrst
resignment
eegimnnttu
integument
eegimnoort
goniometer
eegimorstt
geometrist
eeginnnopy
pony-engine
eeginnooss
noogenesis
eeginnorst
röntgenise
eeginnpruy
penguinery
eeginnsssy
syngenesis
eeginnssvx
vexingness
eeginoorss
orogenesis
eeginopssy
pyogenesis
eeginorrss
regression
eeginorrww
wine-grower
eeginorsty
generosity
eeginprrst
perstringe
eegiorsttu
urostegite
eegllnoosy
selenology
eegllnottw
well-gotten
eeglmmnooy
emmenology
eeglmnoorv
love-monger
eeglmnoovy
glove-money
eeglmnoprt
peltmonger
eeglnorsuy
generously
eeglnosstu
tongueless
eegloorrst
ergosterol

eeglorrstu
trouser-leg
eegmnnorsw
newsmonger
eegmnnortv
government
eegmnooprs
spermogone
eegmnooruy
rogue-money
eegmnosssu
ugsomeness
eegnnoosux
xenogenous
eegnnorsuu
ungenerous
eegnorssvy
governessy
eegnorsttu
tonguester
eegoprstuu
Portuguese
eegorrrsst
retrogress
eehhikmntt
methinketh
eehhilopty
heliophyte
eehhilortw
otherwhile
eehhilpssy
sheepishly
eehhimnost
henotheism
eehhinostt
henotheist
eehhinrttt
thirteenth
eehhiorrss
shire-horse
eehhiorstw
white-horse
eehhnrrrtu
Herrnhuter
eehhnrstuy
heresy-hunt
eehhooprst
theosopher
eehhoorrss
horseshoer
eehhoorsuw
whorehouse
eehhopssty
hypotheses
eehiilmptu
epithelium
eehiilnopr
perihelion
eehiirrstx
heritrixes
eehijnsssw
Jewishness
eehiklmnou
unhomelike

eehilllosv
olive-shell
eehillmrst
mitre-shell
eehillnsss
shelliness
eehillortz
lherzolite
eehillprst
tellership
eehillrsww
well-wisher
eehilmnoss
homeliness
eehilmoprt
thermopile
eehilnnrty
inherently
eehilnortt
enterolith
eehilnrtuw
whereuntil
eehilooprt
heliotrope
eehilosttu
silhouette
eehilprstt
ship-letter
eehilprstu
spherulite
eehilrsstv
thriveless
eehimnnrtu
mine-hunter
eehimnprst
reshipment
eehimoprsv
empoverish
eehimrrstw
Wertherism
eehimrsstv
verse-smith
eehinnoprs
prehension
eehinnoprt
interphone
eehinnorst
enthronise
rhinestone
eehinnosst
tennis-shoe
eehinooprs
ionosphere
eehinsssty
synthesise
eehinsstty
synthetise
eehiopprrs
prophesier
eehiopprst
epistrophe
eehiorrrsv
river-horse

eehiorsttu
stoutherie
eehirsssty
hysteresis
eehjnnooss
Johnsonese
eehkkoopyy
hokey-pokey
eehklnorrv
Herrenvolk
eehkmoossu
smoke-house
eehknoortt
heterokont
tenter-hook
eehlllpssy
helplessly
eehllmnosy
shell-money
eehllmoszz
shlemozzle
eehllnssuv
venus-shell
eehllopssy
hopelessly
eehllorstw
tower-shell
eehlmnooyz
holoenzyme
eehlmorsst
motherless
eehlnoossv
shovelnose
eehlnorsst
throneless
eehloorstw
towel-horse
eehlorsssw
showerless
eehmmooory
homoeomery
eehmmoprtu
Prometheum
eehmnnnoop
phenomenon
eehmnooprt
phonometer
eehmnoorty
heteronomy
eehmnoostt
nomothetes
eehmnoosuy
honey-mouse
eehmnorstt
nethermost
eehmooprtt
photometer
eehmoorrvw
hover-mower
eehmoorsvw
howsomever
whomsoever
eehmoprstt
stepmother

eehmoprsty
hypsometer
eehmoqrsuu
humoresque
eehmorssuw
shrew-mouse
eehnnoosty
honey-stone
eehnnoprty
Entryphone®
eehnnopssy
phoneyness
eehnnorrrt
northerner
eehnoooprr
orpheoreon
eehnoorsst
stonehorse
eehnopprxy
nephropexy
eehnoprrsy
prehensory
eehnoprsuy
Euphrosyne
eehnopsttu
theopneust
eehnopstuy
hypotenuse
eehnorrstu
southerner
eehooprrsw
horsepower
eehooprsuw
power-house
eehoopstty
osteophyte
eehoorrsvw
overshower
eehoorsstu
storehouse
eehopprsst
prophetess
eehorrsttw
otter-shrew
eeiikllmrt
time-killer
eeiikllnss
likeliness
eeiiklnprw
periwinkle
eeiiklprst
priest-like
eeiiklqrsu
squire-like
eeiiklrsst
sister-like
eeiillmnru
reillumine
eeiillnssv
liveliness
eeiilmnsst
timeliness
eeiilnnrst
listener-in

eeiilnostv
television
eeiilnottt
toilinette
eeiilopsst
epistolise
eeiiloptvx
exploitive
eeiilorstt
toiletries
eeiilossuz
Louis-Seize
eeiilrrsst
steriliser
eeiimnnptt
impenitent
pentimenti
eeiimnnttv
invitement
eeiimnrtzz
intermezzi
eeiimoprst
epitomiser
eeiimprssv
impressive
permissive
eeiimprstv
septemviri
eeiinnnstt
insentient
eeiinnrttw
intertwine
eeiinnsttx
inexistent
eeiinoprtt
petitioner
repetition
eeiinrsssst
sensitiser
eeiinrttvy
eviternity
eeiiopstvx
expositive
eeiiorrsst
rôtisserie
eeiipqrstu
perquisite
eeiiprsstv
persistive
eeiirrsttu
ureteritis
eeijknprty
perjinkety
eeijmnnnot
enjoinment
eeikklnnps
skip-kennel
eeikllnosv
slovenlike
eeikllnrsw
well-sinker
eeiklmmrsu
summerlike

eeiklnnssu
unlikeness
eeiklnpstt
kettle-pins
eeiklorrvw
evil-worker
eeikmnorrw
mine-worker
eeikorrrww
wireworker
eeikorrstv
overstrike
eeillllrww
well-willer
eeilllotvw
well-to-live
eeilllpstv
split-level
eeillmmort
immortelle
eeillmnsss
smelliness
eeillmpppr
peppermill
eeillmprtw
pewter-mill
eeillmssty
timelessly
eeillnnoss
loneliness
eeillnorrt
ritornelle
eeillnorvz
Zollverein
eeillnossv
loveliness
eeillnsstt
littleness
eeilloprrt
tiller-rope
eeillotwyy
yellow-yite
eeillprruw
wire-puller
eeillrsstu
Russellite
eeillrssty
tirelessly
eeillssvwy
viewlessly
eeilmnnott
entoilment
eeilmnnstt
enlistment
eeilmnorss
solemniser
eeilmnossu
mousseline
eeilmnpsss
simpleness
eeilmoostt
Teleostomi
eeilmoprsy
polymerise
eeilmorsty
tiresomely
eeilmortvy
overtimely
eeilmosstv
motiveless
eeilmprstu
pulsimeter
eeilmprtvy
pelvimetry
eeilmprtxy
pleximetry
eeilnnoqtu
ineloquent
eeilnnorty
Tyrolienne
eeilnnprsu
spinnerule
eeilnnptty
penitently
eeilnnssst
silentness
eeilnopptt
poplinette
eeilnoprrt
interloper
eeilnopsst
politeness
eeilnortvv
intervolve
eeilnosstw
stolenwise
eeilnprsst
tripleness
eeiloopsst
Osteolepis
eeilorrstu
irresolute
eeilorrttw
Rottweiler
eeilorrtxy
exteriorly
eeilorstuv
resolutive
eeilorsvwy
overwisely
eeilpprtxy
perplexity
eeilppstuv
suppletive
eeilprrsty
sperrylite
eeilprrsuv
pulveriser
eeilprssst
stripeless
eeilrsssst
resistless
sisterless
eeilrssttz
strelitzes
eeilrsstuv
virtueless
eeimmmnrtu
immurement
eeimmmorss
mesomerism
eeimmmrstu
summertime
eeimmorstu
osmeterium
eeimmrssty
symmetrise
eeimnnnrtt
internment
eeimnnoptt
pentimento
eeimnnorst
minestrone
eeimnnpstu
Pennisetum
septennium
eeimnnsstu
minuteness
eeimnnsttv
investment
eeimnopprt
pre-emption
eeimnoprtu
peritoneum
eeimnopryz
prize-money
eeimnorrss
sermoniser
eeimnorrtt
nitrometer
eeimnorrtu
urinometer
eeimnorttt
Tintometer®
eeimnortzz
intermezzo
eeimnppprt
peppermint
eeimnprssu
impureness
eeimnprstu
episternum
eeimnrssss
remissness
eeimnrsstw
westernism
eeimnrstuv
misventure
eeimooprst
opisometer
opsiometer
eeimoprrst
spirometer
temporiser
eeimoprstu
periosteum
eeimpprruu
puerperium
eeimpprstu
suppertime
eeimprrssu
impressure
presurmise
eeimprsstv
septemvirs
eeimprstuv
resumptive
eeimrssttu
sestertium
eeinnnsstt
intentness
eeinnopprt
porpentine
eeinnoprss
presension
eeinnoprst
pretension
eeinnoprtt
ten-pointer
eeinnoprtv
prevention
eeinnopsst
stone-snipe
eeinnorrtv
intervenor
eeinnosstw
swinestone
eeinnprssu
unripeness
eeinnprttu
turpentine
eeinnpsssu
supineness
eeinnqssuu
uniqueness
eeinnrsstv
inventress
eeinnsssuw
unwiseness
eeinopprsv
propensive
eeinopqttu
equipotent
eeinoprrss
repression
eeinoprrst
interposer
eeinoprrsv
perversion
eeinoprssv
responsive
eeinoprssx
expression
eeinoprstv
protensive
eeinoprtxy
pyroxenite
eeinoqrstu
questioner
eeinorrsuv
overinsure
eeinorrtvw
overwinter
eeinorssss
Insessores
eeinprsstt
persistent
prettiness
eeinpsssuv
suspensive
eeinqsstuy
squint-eyes
eeinrrstww
news-writer
eeinrsssty
synteresis
eeinssttuv
sustentive
eeiopprssv
oppressive
eeioprrstv
resorptive
eeioprrttu
pirouetter
eeioprssst
stereopsis
eeioprsttt
operettist
eeiopssssv
possessive
eeiorrrrst
terroriser
eeipprttuy
perpetuity
eeipqrrruu
perruquier
eeiprrsssu
pressurise
eeiprrstvy
perversity
eeiprrttwy
typewriter
eeiprssstt
stepsister
eeirrssstv
servitress
eejlmnostt
jostlement
eejlmrstwy
Jew's-myrtle
eekllnopsw
well-spoken
eeklooorrv
overlooker
eekloopprw
work-people
eeklorsstw
steelworks
eekmnnooty
token-money
eekmnoopry
monkey-rope
eekmnoprty
pyknometer
eekmrssttu
musket-rest

eellloprss
slop-seller
eellmnoosy
lonesomely
eellmnossw
mellowness
eellmnttuy
temulently
eellmossvy
movelessly
eellnnsssu
sullenness
eellnnssuw
unwellness
eellnopprt
prepollent
propellent
eellnoqtuy
eloquently
eellnossty
tonelessly
eellnosswy
yellowness
eellorstuy
resolutely
eellrssstu
lustreless
resultless
eellrsssty
restlessly
eelmmnopty
employment
eelmnnosss
solemnness
eelmnopprt
propelment
eelmnoppsu
pumple-nose
eelmnppstu
supplement
eelmnptuzz
puzzlement
eelmoprstu
pulsometer
eelmorrsst
tremorless
eelmorstty
metrostyle
eelmorstuy
temerously
eelmssssty
systemless
eelnopprsy
propensely
eelnoprstw
spleen-wort
eelnppsssu
suppleness
eelnrrsstu
returnless
eelooppsss
opposeless
eelooprstt
protostele
eelooprstu
petroleous
eelooprsty
proteolyse
eeloprsttt
post-letter
eelopssssu
spouseless
eelorrrsst
terrorless
eelorrrsty
retrorsely
eelorssuvy
yourselves
eelpprsssu
supperless
eelprrsttu
splutterer
eelrssssst
stressless
eemmoorrtt
tromometer
eemnnopstt
pentstemon
eemnnorrru
Rome-runner
eemnooprty
petromoney
eemnoorsss
moroseness
eemnoortty
enterotomy
eemnoprssy
press-money
eemnorrsty
yestermorn
eemnprrstu
presternum
eemoorrstt
street-room
eemoorstty
stereotomy
eemopprrty
peremptory
eemprssssst
sempstress
eennnnooss
no-nonsense
eennopsty
penny-stone
eennoqrstu
quernstone
eennorrruv
overrunner
eennorsstt
rottenness
eennrsstuu
untrueness
eenopprrss
properness
eenoprstty
stenotyper
eenoprstuu
soup-tureen
eenorrrtuv
overturner
eeoppprrtw
pepperwort
eeopppprssu
presuppose
eeopprrssw
power-press
eeopprrsuw
superpower
eeopprssss
prepossess
eeoprrsstu
streperous
superstore
eeoprsttyy
stereotypy
eeorrssstv
overstress
eeorrstttw
setterwort
eeprrstuuy
Eurypterus
efffhiprsu
pufferfish
efffilnssu
fluffiness
effghiinrs
fish-finger
effghnooru
forfoughen
effgiinnst
stiffening
effgillnot
telling-off
effgilprtu
truffle-pig
effginoprr
proffering
effgiorruu
four-figure
effiiknrtu
fruit-knife
effiinnsss
sniffiness
effillmntu
fulfilment
effilnsstu
fitfulness
effinnsssu
snuffiness
effinorttw
written-off
effinssstu
stuffiness
efgghilotv
glove-fight
efgghinrtu
gunfighter
efggiiilnv
life-giving
efggiilnnr
fingerling
efggiilnsv
self-giving
efggiinnnu
unfeigning
efggiinnrr
ring-finger
efgginortt
forgetting
efghiiknrs
kingfisher
efghiinnst
net-fishing
efghiiprtz
prize-fight
efghillsst
flightless
efghilnssw
swing-shelf
efghilopru
fire-plough
efghilortv
overflight
efghilsttt
test-flight
efghimnors
fishmonger
efghimorst
frightsome
efghirsttu
fish-gutter
efghlllntu
full-length
efghllnoru
flugelhorn
efghnnotuu
unfoughten
efghoopprr
frog-hopper
efgiiklnty
kite-flying
efgiilnquy
liquefying
efgiiltuvy
fugitively
efgiinnntu
fine-tuning
efgiinprst
firing-step
efgiinprsy
presignify
efgiinprty
petrifying
efgiinrrty
terrifying
efgiinrstu
surfeiting
efgiinrsvy
versifying
efgiinstty
testifying
efgillluuy
guilefully
efgillnosv
self-loving
efgillorrw
flower-girl
efgilnnotw
fowling-net
efgilnoost
single-foot
efgilnorst
fosterling
efgimnoprr
performing
efginnoruv
unforgiven
efginoprss
professing
efginoprst
fingerpost
efginorrty
torrefying
efginprtuy
putrefying
efginpstuy
stupefying
efglnoprtu
profulgent
efhiilnsst
filthiness
efhiilrssv
silver-fish
efhiinssst
shiftiness
efhiirsttt
thriftiest
efhiklnsuy
flunkeyish
efhiknorst
frithsoken
efhillopsw
fellowship
efhilooprt
hop-trefoil
efhiloprst
shop-lifter
efhilorstw
fish-trowel
efhilorsux
flexihours
efhilorsww
werwolfish
efhilrsstt
thriftless
efhinorsst
frothiness
efhiorsttu
stouthrief
efhlloopr s
shellproof
efhllossuv
shovelfuls
efhlmoortw
moth-flower
efhlmorsty
smother-fly
efhlmottuu
flute-mouth

efhloorsww
flower-show
efhnrtttuu
tuft-hunter
efhoooprsu
proof-house
efiiiinntv
infinitive
efiiillmor
millefiori
efiiilmnty
feminility
efiiilmprs
simplifier
efiiilnnty
infinitely
efiiimmnns
femininism
efiiimnnty
femininity
efiiknrsss
friskiness
efiillorsv
silver-foil
efiilmnsss
flimsiness
efiilnnsst
flintiness
efiilnorry
inferiorly
efiiloprsu
piliferous
efiilrsttu
stultifier
efiimnnrss
infirmness
efiimoprrv
viperiform
efiimorrsu
Fourierism
efiiorstuv
vitiferous
efiklmnsuy
flunkeyism
efiklnosss
folksiness
efiknpttuy
putty-knife
efillmorst
stelliform
efillnortu
ill-fortune
efillnssuw
wilfulness
efilloopr w
low-profile
efillpstuy
spitefully
efilmnoost
self-motion
efilmnosuu
fulmineous
efilmoprsu
promiseful

efilmorrty
elytriform
efilmorstw
mist-flower
efilmorsww
werwolfism
efilnnsssu
sinfulness
efilnoosss
foisonless
efilnoppss
floppiness
efilnortww
twinflower
efilnosssu
fusionless
efiloprsst
profitless
efimnoorrv
overinform
efimnoorsu
omniferous
efimnorstu
misfortune
efimooprrt
proteiform
efimooprsu
pomiferous
efinnorrty
forty-niner
efinooprss
profession
efinoprrrt
ferroprint
efinorrrtv
river-front
efinorssst
frostiness
efinorsttu
stone-fruit
efiooprrsu
poriferous
efioorrstu
rotiferous
efioorsssu
ossiferous
efjlloruwy
July-flower
efjlnossuy
joyfulness
efklloorww
work-fellow
efklmmoory
folk-memory
efklmnoosw
womenfolks
efklnoopsu
foul-spoken
efkmooopr s
smokeproof
efkmoorsst
frost-smoke
efknoopsst
soft-spoken

efkoorrstu
four-stroke
efllmooorw
room-fellow
efllmorssy
formlessly
efllnsuuuy
unusefully
efllopruwy
powerfully
eflmnooorw
moon-flower
eflmooorty
tomfoolery
eflooprtuy
fluorotype
eflopprsuu
purposeful
efmooprrtu
outperform
efnnoorrsu
non-ferrous
efnorttuwy
twenty-four
efoopprrss
press-proof
efooprrstu
four-poster
eggghilmsu
mishguggle
egggiilnnr
niggerling
egggiinnrs
sniggering
egggijjoty
jiggety-jog
eggginorss
grogginess
egghhimttu
hug-me-tight
egghhiprsu
hip-huggers
egghiilnnt
lightening
egghiinnuw
unweighing
egghinnotu
toughening
egghinoors
shore-going
egghinsttu
guest-night
eggiilmmnr
glimmering
eggiilnrst
glistering
eggiilnrtt
glittering
eggiilnrvy
grievingly
eggiinnopw
pigeon-wing
eggiinnrst
signet-ring

eggillllnpu
leg-pulling
eggillnorv
grovelling
eggilmoost
gemologist
eggilnnrsu
gunslinger
eggilnoort
toggle-iron
eggilnssuy
guessingly
egginnooor
gorgoneion
egginnorss
engrossing
egginosstu
suggestion
egglloopx
googolplex
egglnooosy
gnoseology
egglooptyy
Egyptology
eggloorsuy
gorgeously
eghhillorr
high-roller
eghhilopry
hieroglyph
eghhilorst
light-horse
eghhilostu
lighthouse
eghhimorst
highermost
eghhinnort
night-heron
eghhinostu
night-house
eghhoorsuu
rough-house
eghhoprtyy
hygrophyte
eghiijnnot
hinge-joint
eghiilmnss
Englishism
eghiilnnps
plenishing
eghiimmnrs
shimmering
eghiimnprw
whimpering
eghiimnsst
mightiness
eghiinnpss
ensignship
eghiinnsst
thinginess
eghiinpptw
whippeting
eghiinprsw
whispering

eghiinstux
extinguish
eghiklnsst
knightless
eghikmostt
smoketight
eghiknotuw
huntiegowk
eghillnost
hostelling
eghillnosu
houselling
eghillnosv
shovelling
eghillnpst
night-spell
eghilloopr
philologer
eghilloopu
philologue
eghillootv
light-o'-love
eghilmooos
homologise
eghilnorvy
hoveringly
eghilnssst
slightness
eghiloppt
phlogopite
eghiloopsu
geophilous
eghiloorst
rheologist
eghiloostt
ethologist
theologist
eghilopsuw
ploughwise
eghilorttw
light-tower
eghimnoprs
phorminges
eghimnorst
smothering
eghimnrrty
merry-night
eghimoppsu
pemphigous
eghimosstu
mouse-sight
eghinnorst
shortening
eghinoostt
theogonist
eghinorsst
shoestring
eghinorstu
southering
eghinrsttu
shuttering
eghiorsttw
ghost-write

eghlmoorty
mythologer
thermology
eghlnoopry
nephrology
phrenology
eghlooorty
heortology
eghlooppsy
psephology
eghlopprty
petroglyph
eghmnooosu
homogenous
eghmnoopry
morphogeny
eghmoootyz
homozygote
eghmorrtyy
hygrometry
eghoorrtuw
ore-wrought
eghoorrtvw
overgrowth
egiiilmprs
pilgrimise
egiiilmstt
legitimist
egiiilnorr
irreligion
egiiimnnst
meningitis
egiikklnnu
unkinglike
egiiklllnw
well-liking
egiiklltuy
guilty-like
egiiklnnrs
ink-slinger
egiiklnnss
kingliness
egiiklnprs
springlike
egiiknnrtt
trinketing
egiiknprst
priest-king
egiillnnst
tinselling
egiillnnsv
snivelling
egiillnotu
guillotine
egiillnrsv
silverling
egiillnrvy
revilingly
egiillrstv
silver-gilt
egiilnnpry
repiningly
egiilnprst
priestling

egiilnqrsu
squireling
egiilnrrty
retiringly
egiilnrsss
grisliness
egiilnrstu
linguister
egiilnrvvy
revivingly
egiilnsstu
guiltiness
egiilopstt
epiglottis
egiimnnrtu
unmeriting
egiimnoprt
primogenit
egiimnopru
perigonium
egiimnprst
springtime
egiimnprtt
permitting
egiinnnpru
unrepining
egiinnoptt
ignipotent
egiinnorss
ingression
egiinnssst
stinginess
egiinnstuu
unigenitus
egiinorrtt
intertrigo
egiinrrstw
sign-writer
egiinrsstt
grittiness
egiinrtttw
twittering
egiinstttv
vignettist
egijnnoruy
journeying
egijnotttu
outjetting
egiklorrsw
silk-grower
egiknnnost
Kensington
egiknooqsu
quink-goose
egilllnpsy
spellingly
egilllnswy
swellingly
egilllorwy
yellow-girl
egillmmnpu
pummelling
egillnnntu
tunnelling

egillnoppr
propelling
egillnoprt
petrolling
egillnortw
trowelling
egillnorwy
loweringly
egillnprsw
well-spring
egillntuxy
exultingly
egillooqsu
goose-quill
egillorssy
syllogiser
egilmmnors
mongrelism
egilmnooos
monologise
egilmnooss
gloominess
egilmnoprr
longprimer
egilmnopsy
polygenism
egilmnoptt
melting-pot
egilmnosuu
leguminous
egilmnptty
temptingly
egilmoossy
seismology
egilnnosst
slingstone
egilnnossv
lovingness
egilnnrruy
unerringly
egilnnsttu
unsettling
egilnooory
oneirology
egilnooost
oenologist
egilnoopst
penologist
egilnoprrv
ring-plover
egilnopsty
polygenist
egilnorrvw
liver-grown
egilnossss
glossiness
egilnossuy
lysigenous
egilnosttu
gluttonise
egilnostuu
lounge-suit
egilnprsss
springless

egilnprssy
pressingly
egilnqruyy
queryingly
egilnqstuy
questingly
egilnrssst
stringless
egilnrsttu
lutestring
egilooorst
oreologist
egiloopr su
prologuise
egiloorsst
serologist
egiloosstx
sexologist
egilorrsuu
irregulous
egilorsuvy
grievously
egimmnnoos
monogenism
egimmnnptu
impugnment
egimnnoorr
ironmonger
egimnnoors
Monsignore
egimnnoost
monogenist
egimnnoosu
omnigenous
egimnnortt
tormenting
egimnoorst
ergonomist
egimnoorty
goniometry
egimnprssu
grumpiness
egimnprttu
trumpeting
egimooprst
geotropism
egimoorrsu
morigerous
eginnoprsu
unreposing
eginnopsss
sponginess
eginnorrtw
intergrown
eginnrsuvw
unswerving
eginnssttu
sunsetting
eginooppst
pigeon-post
eginooprrt
progenitor
eginoprsuy
perigynous

eginorrstu
trousering
eginorrstw
songwriter
eginorstuw
outswinger
eginostttu
outsetting
eginprsttu
sputtering
eginrstttu
stuttering
egiopprsuu
pupigerous
egknoortuw
tongue-work
egllmorsuu
glomerulus
eglmnoooty
entomology
eglmnooruy
numerology
eglmnooyyz
enzymology
eglnooopry
ponerology
eglnoopsuy
polygenous
eglnoosuxy
xylogenous
eglooorrww
wool-grower
eglooprtyy
pyretology
egmmnoprsy
gymnosperm
egmnnooosu
monogenous
egnooprsuy
pyrogenous
egnoorrstv
overstrong
egnorrstuv
overstrung
egnorssst
songstress
egnpqrrsuu
quersprung
egoprsttuy
Pterygotus
ehhiiloppp
hippophile
ehhiilstvy
thievishly
ehhiimsttw
whitesmith
ehhillorst
thill-horse
ehhilmoprt
thermophil
ehhilmosty
hylotheism
ehhiloopps
philosophe

ehhilopsty
lithophyse
ehhiloptty
lithophyte
ehhilortww
worthwhile
ehhilostty
hylotheist
ehhilrsswy
shrewishly
ehhimoprst
mother-ship
ehhimorstt
hithermost
ehhinorttw
whitethorn
ehhiooprrz
rhizophore
ehhioppty
hippety-hop
ehhiopssty
hypothesis
ehhlloostt
tooth-shell
ehhlmrssty
rhythmless
ehhmmooopr
homeomorph
ehhmnnooty
honeymonth
ehhmnorttu
moth-hunter
ehhmorsttu
home-thrust
ehhnoooppr
phonophore
ehhnoooppt
photophone
ehhoooppprt
photophore
ehhoopprst
phosphoret
ehhooprrty
orthophyre
ehhopprstu
phosphuret
ehiiilnppp
philippine
ehiiilnpst
philistine
ehiiilppps
Philippise
ehiiinrrtx
inheritrix
ehiiiprsvz
viziership
ehiikmrrss
skirmisher
ehiikmstwy
tim-whiskey
ehiillopsy
lyophilise
ehiilmoprt
limitrophe
ehiilnoops
eosinophil
ehiilnqrsu
relinquish
ehiilorttt
lithotrite
ehiimnpsss
impishness
ehiimnsssw
whimsiness
ehiimoprsv
impoverish
ehiimpprsu
umpireship
ehiimppsty
epiphytism
ehiioprstv
Rh-positive
ehiipprrst
tripperish
ehiipprsst
priestship
ehiipqrssu
squireship
ehiiprrstw
writership
ehiiprstty
Triphysite
ehiirrsttu
urethritis
ehiirsstty
hysteritis
ehikloosvw
swivel-hook
ehikloprsy
pokerishly
ehikmnottt
kitten-moth
ehikoorsst
sister-hook
ehillmnpuy
phillumeny
ehillnrsss
shrillness
ehillosstu
still-house
ehilmnopst
polishment
ehilmnsssu
mulishness
ehilmopsty
polytheism
ehilnnortu
lion-hunter
ehilnnossu
unholiness
ehilnosssw
owlishness
ehilooprst
strophiole
ehiloprty
heliotropy
ehiloopstu
pilot-house
ehiloprssu
Russophile
ehilopstty
polytheist
ehilossttw
sow-thistle
ehilprssuu
sulphurise
ehilrssstt
thirstless
ehimmnoost
monotheism
ehimmoprtu
promethium
ehimmopstu
imposthume
ehimnnoors
moonshiner
ehimnnpstu
punishment
ehimnoorty
herniotomy
ehimnoostt
monotheist
ehimnopsss
mopishness
ehimooprru
eriophorum
ehimopprst
prophetism
ehimorrstt
thermistor
ehimorrtuv
river-mouth
ehimprrtuy
triumphery
ehimrsttu
time-thrust
ehinnorsst
thorniness
ehinnossst
tonishness
ehinoopsuu
euphonious
ehinopprty
periphyton
ehinoprrty
pyrrhotine
ehinoprsty
hypnotiser
ehinopsstx
sextonship
ehinorsstw
worthiness
ehinorstuu
ruthenious
ehinosssty
toyishness
ehinppsssu
uppishness
ehinssstty
synthesist
ehinssttty
synthetist
ehiooopprrs
spirophore
ehiooprssu
puir's-hoose
ehiooprstt
orthoepist
ehioorsstx
six-shooter
ehiopprrsw
worshipper
ehiopprrty
porphyrite
ehioprrsty
prehistory
ehioprrtty
pyrrhotite
ehioprssst
prosthesis
ehioprssuu
puir's-house
ehipprrssu
pursership
ehiprrsttu
turret-ship
ehiprsstuy
suretyship
ehjmoprsuw
showjumper
ehkmossttu
musket-shot
ehkoprsstu
push-stroke
ehllnoossw
hollowness
ehllrsstuy
hurtlessly
ruthlessly
ehlmnoppty
nympholept
ehlmnortuy
unmotherly
ehlmoopppry
pleomorphy
ehlmoppsuy
Polyphemus
ehlmorssuu
humourless
ehlnoorssu
honourless
ehlnorstuy
southernly
ehloopprry
plerophory
ehlooprstu
toolpusher
ehloortvwy
loveworthy
ehloprstuy
upholstery
ehmmooprsy
mesomorphy
ehmmoorrsu
mushroomer
ehmmoorsuu
humoursome
ehmnooorrt
throne-room
ehmnooostu
theonomous
ehmnooprty
nephrotomy
ehmnoossst
smoothness
ehmooprstt
mother-spot
ehmooprtty
photometry
ehmoorrttw
motherwort
ehmoprstyy
hypsometry
ehnnoprtwy
pennyworth
ehnnpprtuy
thruppenny
ehnoopprrs
pronephros
ehnoorsttw
stone-throw
ehnoorttwy
noteworthy
ehnorstwwy
newsworthy
ehoooopprrs
sporophore
ehooopprtt
phototrope
ehoooprrst
troop-horse
ehooooprssu
poor's-house
ehoopprsty
sporophyte
ehoopprtty
protophyte
tropophyte
ehopppstuw
puppet-show
ehorrsttuv
overthrust
ehorssttuu
trust-house
eiiilmnnop
epilimnion
eiiilorstv
vitriolise
eiiimnosss
missionise
eiiimprstt
time-spirit
eiiimsstvy
emissivity
eiiinprrst
reinspirit
eiijknprty
perjinkity

eiijlntuvy
juvenility
eiijmnortt
mitre-joint
eiiklnorst
triskelion
eiiklnpstt
kittle-pins
eiiklnrssv
silverskin
eiikmoprrs
morris-pike
eiiknnnsss
skinniness
eiiknqrssu
quirkiness
eiilllsuvy
illusively
eiillmmnnu
millennium
eiillmnoot
emollition
eiillmopty
impolitely
eiillmprtu
multiplier
eiillnnnop
pennillion
eiillnopst
septillion
eiillnorrt
ritornelli
eiillnortt
tortellini
eiillnostx
sextillion
eiillpprsy
slipperily
eiillpssty
pitilessly
eiilmmnnty
imminently
eiilmnnstt
instilment
eiilmnosst
lentissimo
eiilmnosty
mylonitise
eiilnnotuv
univoltine
eiilnoprst
prosilient
eiilnorrty
interiorly
eiilnosssv
visionless
eiilnppsss
slippiness
eiilnrssty
sinisterly
eiilnssstt
stiltiness
eiiloprstu
reptilious

eiilopsstt
epistolist
eiilopstvy
positively
eiilorstty
literosity
eiilprssst
spiritless
eiimmoprsv
misimprove
eiimmorstu
immeritous
eiimmprsuy
perimysium
eiimnnorsu
reunionism
eiimnoprss
impression
permission
eiimnrssst
ministress
eiimoprrsv
improviser
eiimoprssv
promissive
eiimoprsuv
impervious
eiimorrrsw
mirrorwise
eiimorsstu
moisturise
eiinnnortu
interunion
eiinnnrttu
innutrient
eiinnopssw
sops-in-wine
eiinnorstu
reunionist
eiinnrsstw
wintriness
eiinooprst
reposition
eiinoopstx
exposition
eiinoorsuv
Eurovision
eiinorsstv
versionist
eiinorttwz
zwitterion
eiinprssst
stripiness
eiinqssuzz
quizziness
eiinrssttw
twin-sister
eiinrstttu
instituter
eiinrstttw
intertwist
eiinrstuvy
university

eiiooppstv
oppositive
eiiooprssu
uropoiesis
eiioqrrstu
requisitor
eiiorsttvy
vitreosity
eijnorsstu
jointuress
eijoprrsuu
perjurious
eiklmnossy
Lysenkoism
eiklrssstu
tusser-silk
eikmnoorst
moonstrike
eikmnostuy
monkey-suit
eiknnosstt
knottiness
stinkstone
eiknoopsss
spookiness
eikorrsttu
striker-out
eikorsttty
Trotskyite
eillloortt
toilet-roll
eilllsssty
listlessly
eillmoosty
toilsomely
eillmpsssu
psellismus
eillnnosty
insolently
eillnoopss
pollenosis
eillnoorrt
ritornello
eillnoossw
woolliness
eillnoptuy
unpolitely
eillnorwww
willow-wren
eillnosstt
stone-still
eillnrtuvy
virulently
eilloprsuy
perilously
eillorrtuy
ulteriorly
eillortttu
litter-lout
eilmmnoopu
polemonium
eilmmoprsy
polymerism

eilmmssstu
summitless
eilmnnrtuu
unruliment
eilmnnsttu
insultment
eilmnooops
monopolise
eilmnoosst
motionless
eilmnossss
lissomness
eilmnrssty
minstrelsy
eilmooprst
metropolis
eilmopprry
improperly
eilmoprsst
importless
eilmopsuux
implexuous
eilmorsstt
moss-litter
eilmrsssty
mistressly
eilnnnootv
non-violent
eilnnoostw
low-tension
eilnnrssuu
unruliness
eilnoooptv
love-potion
eilnoorstu
resolution
eilnoortuv
revolution
eilnopprtw
nipplewort
eilnoppsss
sloppiness
eilnoppstu
suppletion
eilnoprsst
portliness
eilnoprssx
prolixness
eilnoprsuu
unperilous
eilnoprxyy
pyroxyline
eilnorrsty
introrsely
eilnorssuy
neurolysis
resinously
eilnostuuv
velutinous
eilnpqttuu
quintuplet
eilnprrtuy
pruriently

eilnprssty
spinsterly
eilnprstuy
unpriestly
eilnrssstu
sultriness
eilnrsstuy
unsisterly
eilooppsty
oppositely
eilopprsuv
propulsive
eiloprrstu
protrusile
eiloprrsuy
superiorly
eiloprssty
pterylosis
eiloprstuy
pyrolusite
eiloprstvy
sportively
eiloprsuvy
perviously
previously
viperously
eilrrstuvw
liverwurst
eimnnooptt
omnipotent
eimnnoprst
prisonment
eimnnorsuu
innumerous
eimnnrsttu
instrument
eimnooprrt
premonitor
eimnooprss
spoonerism
eimnoottzz
mezzotinto
eimnoprrtu
importuner
eimnoprstu
resumption
eimnorssst
storminess
eimnorstuy
numerosity
eimnpssstu
stumpiness
eimnsssttu
smuttiness
eimooqsstu
mosquitoes
eimoprrstu
romper-suit
eimoprrsty
spirometry
eimorsstuy
mysterious
eimqrrttuu
triquetrum

einnnooprt
pontonnier
einnoopprs
propension
einnooprst
protension
einnoopstu
out-pension
einnoortux
neurotoxin
einnopsssu
suspension
einnossstt
snottiness
einnosssty
syntenosis
einnosssuu
insensuous
einnossttu
sustention
einnprttuy
turpentiny
einoopprss
oppression
einoopprtw
power-point
einooprrst
resorption
einooprstu
proteinous
einoopssss
possession
einoopttttt
totipotent
einoorsstu
serotinous
einopprsty
propensity
einoprrrst
ripsnorter
einoprssst
sportiness
einoprstty
protensity
einopssstt
spottiness
einoqrttuu
tourniquet
einorrrtuu
nourriture
einprssst
spinstress
einrsssttu
trustiness
eiooooprstz
sporozoite
eiooopprrrt
proprietor
eioopprrst
prepositor
eiooprrsty
repository
eiooprsstt
strepitoso
eiooprsstu
isopterous
eiooprstxy
expository
eioorrsstu
roisterous
eioorsttuz
zootsuiter
eiopprrsty
prosperity
eiopprstuv
supportive
eioprrssuv
supervisor
eioprrsttu
tripterous
eioprrstuv
protrusive
eioprrttvy
protervity
eioprssttu
strepitous
eioprstttu
prostitute
eiorrstttu
restitutor
ejnnssstuu
unjustness
ejnoosssuy
joyousness
eklnoorstv
lover's-knot
ekloorrtuw
work-to-rule
ekmmnoppuy
monkey-pump
eknorrsstw
sternworks
ekooprsstt
spot-stroke
ekopprrsuw
upperworks
ekorrtttuy
turkey-trot
elllosssuy
soullessly
ellmmpssuu
mussel-plum
ellmorrstu
muster-roll
ellnooswwy
yellow-snow
ellnprtuuy
purulently
ellooortwy
yellow-root
elloopstwy
yellow-spot
elloortwwy
yellow-wort
elloppsstt
spell-stopt
ellopsssty
spotlessly
elmmooppsu
pompelmous
elmnoorsuy
enormously
elmnoosuvy
venomously
elmnorsuuy
numerously
elmnppstuy
supplyment
elmooprsuy
polymerous
elmooprtuy
pleurotomy
elmooprtxy
protoxylem
elnoorstuu
ultroneous
elnopprruy
unproperly
elnosssuuy
sensuously
elooorrstw
woolsorter
eloorrsssw
sorrowless
elopprstuy
Polypterus
suppletory
elopprsuvy
oversupply
eloprsttuu
turtle-soup
emmnrstuyy
unsymmetry
emmooprstt
post-mortem
emnnoooprt
monopteron
emnoooprst
monopteros
emnoopprtt
prompt-note
emnooqstuu
musquetoon
emnopprsst
promptness
emnorrstuu
surmounter
emnorsstuu
menstruous
emnostttuu
mutton-suet
emooorrstv
servo-motor
emoorrstvy
vestry-room
emoorsstty
root-system
enooprrssy
responsory
enooprsssu
porousness
enooprsttu
portentous
enoorstttu
troutstone
enoprsssuy
suspensory
eoooprssux
exosporous
eoopprrssu
prosperous
eooprrsstu
pro-oestrus
eooprssssy
possessory
eoorrssttu
stertorous
eoorrsstuy
roysterous
eopprrsssu
suppressor
eopprrstuu
supporture
ffffiittyy
fifty-fifty
ffghiiinrs
griffinish
ffghiilnsy
fly-fishing
ffghiioppr
hippogriff
ffghimnruu
humgruffin
ffghorstuu
rough-stuff
ffgiiimnrs
griffinism
ffgiilllnu
fulfilling
ffgiilnnsy
sniffingly
ffgiinorty
fortifying
ffginopttu
off-putting
ffiirrsttu
first-fruit
ffillrtuuy
fruitfully
ffilnrtuuu
unfruitful
ffiloorrst
first-floor
ffimprsttu
stiff-rumpt
ffnnoopssu
snuff-spoon
fgghhiilny
high-flying
fgghiiinnt
in-fighting
fgghinoort
forthgoing
fggiiilnny
lignifying
fggiiinnsy
signifying
fggiilnory
glorifying
fghhiinstt
night-shift
fghhiorrtt
forthright
fghhlottuu
thoughtful
fghiilnstu
insightful
fghiinnstu
unshifting
fghiinorry
horrifying
fghiinrstt
first-night
first-thing
fghillrtuy
rightfully
fghilnrtuu
unrightful
fghilooprt
lightproof
fghilprstu
sprightful
fghinnotux
fox-hunting
fghmoorstu
frog's-mouth
fgiiinnrty
nitrifying
fgiijnstuy
justifying
fgiiklnrsy
friskingly
fgiillmnoy
mollifying
fgiillnnuy
nullifying
fgiillnrty
flirtingly
triflingly
fgiillnsty
stiflingly
fgiilmnoru
linguiform
fgiilnosuu
fuliginous
fgiilnrstu
sling-fruit
fgiimmmnuy
mummifying
fgiimnorty
mortifying
fgiimnstyy
mystifying
fgiimorrst
strigiform
fgiinotttu
fitting-out
outfitting

fgiklnooor
looking-for
fgiknnortu
tuning-fork
fgillnotuy
floutingly
fgilnnorwy
frowningly
fgilnootuw
outflowing
fgilnopsty
flyposting
fgimnooprs
spongiform
fgllnoruwy
wrongfully
fgloortuuy
futurology
fgmnsstuuu
smut-fungus
fgnrsstuuu
rust-fungus
fhiillrrst
shirt-frill
fhillmrtuy
mirthfully
fhilmooost
tomfoolish
fhilnrttuy
unthriftly
fhiloorstt
frithstool
fhiloprsuw
worshipful
fhinorrstt
shirt-front
fhlllostuy
slothfully
fhllotuuyy
youthfully
fhllrttuuy
truthfully
fhlnrttuuu
untruthful
fiilmmnoor
moniliform
fiilmmorty
mytiliform
fiilmoprsy
ypsiliform
fiilnostux
fluxionist
fiimnortuy
uniformity
fiimoorsst
fortissimo
fiimorsttu
fortuitism
fiinorttuu
futurition
fiiorsttu
fortuitist
fiklloorst
folklorist

filnoorsuu
uniflorous
filoooprst
portfolios
fimnostttu
mutton-fist
fioorsttuu
fortuitous
fllmnoruuy
mournfully
fllmorstuy
stormfully
flloprstuy
sportfully
fllrsttuuy
trustfully
flnrsttuuu
untrustful
fmoooprrst
stormproof
gggijllnuy
jugglingly
gggilnrstu
struggling
gghhiilntt
night-light
gghhiilswy
Whiggishly
gghhiilttt
light-tight
gghhiinstt
night-sight
gghhinrstu
high-strung
gghiilnptu
lighting-up
gghiilprsy
priggishly
gghiiprryy
higry-pigry
gghillssuy
sluggishly
gghilnostu
oughtlings
ggiiiinstv
gingivitis
ggiiinnrtu
intriguing
ggiillmnny
minglingly
ggiilnnsty
stingingly
ggiilnnswy
swingingly
ggilllnoor
log-rolling
ggillnnouy
loungingly
ggillnorwy
growlingly
ggilnnrtuy
gruntingly
ggilnooosy
gnosiology

gginnnnruu
gunrunning
gglloooosy
glossology
gglloootty
glottology
gglnooopsy
spongology
ghhiilstty
tightishly
ghhiinrstt
nightshirt
ghhiiprstw
shipwright
ghhillopty
lithoglyph
ghhillosuy
ghoulishly
ghhimosttu
misthought
ghhinoprtt
triphthong
ghhiopppry
hippogryph
ghhlooppty
photoglyph
ghhloortuy
thoroughly
ghhnorsstu
song-thrush
ghhoorttuu
throughout
ghhoprttuu
through-put
ghiiklnnty
thinkingly
ghiiknnntu
unthinking
ghiillmrtw
millwright
ghiilmprrs
shrimp-girl
ghiilnopss
polishings
ghiilnrtvy
thrivingly
ghiilnrtwy
writhingly
ghiilnwyzz
whizzingly
ghiiloosty
histiology
ghiimnnost
nothingism
ghiimnprtu
triumphing
ghiinnorsu
nourishing
ghiklnntuy
unknightly
ghilmoooru
Horologium
horologium

ghilnoopru
plough-iron
ghilnoopst
phlogiston
ghilnoostt
night-stool
ghilnoosty
soothingly
ghilnorttt
throttling
ghilnosttu
gluttonish
ghilnostuy
shoutingly
ghilnrruyy
hurryingly
ghilooorst
horologist
ghiloopsyy
physiology
ghiloorstt
grith-stool
ghimmnoptu
humming-top
ghinnopttu
pot-hunting
ghinnrruuy
unhurrying
ghllooptyy
typhlology
ghlmoooosu
homologous
ghlmooopry
morphology
ghlnoopsuw
snow-plough
ghlooprty
trophology
ghmnoopsyy
gymnosophy
ghmooosuyz
homozygous
ghmoopryyz
zygomorphy
ghnoopsuyy
hypogynous
ghoorssty
ghost-story
ghoorttuuw
outwrought
giiiimmnns
minimising
giiiknnrtw
writing-ink
giiillnnst
instilling
giiilnnprt
tirling-pin
giiilnntvy
invitingly
giiimnnnor
iron-mining
giiimnnprt
imprinting

giiimnrsty
myringitis
giiinnntuv
uninviting
giiinrssty
syringitis
giijkknors
skikjöring
giijkmnpsu
ski-jumping
giiklllnoo
ill-looking
giikllnnty
tinklingly
giiklmmnsy
skimmingly
giiklmnpsy
skimpingly
giiklnnprs
sprinkling
giiklnnrst
strinkling
giiklnnsty
stinkingly
giiklnppsy
skippingly
giiklnrsty
strikingly
giiknnnrsu
ski-running
giiknrstwy
sky-writing
giilllnopu
louping-ill
giillnnopr
rolling-pin
giillnopry
pillorying
giillnopst
pistolling
giillnppry
ripplingly
giilmmnrty
trimmingly
giilmmnswy
swimmingly
giilmnoorv
living-room
giilmnopsy
imposingly
giilmoosst
misologist
giilnnnoty
intoningly
giilnnppsu
unslipping
giilnnrtuy
untiringly
giilnnstty
stintingly
giilnoopst
top-soiling
giilnoorsu
inglorious

giilnoosst
Sinologist
giilnoostv
vinologist
giilnpprty
trippingly
giilnprsst
slip-string
giilnrrsty
stirringly
giilnrstuy
linguistry
giilnrstvy
strivingly
giilntttwy
twittingly
giiloorstv
virologist
giimnnoors
Monsignori
giimnnopsu
unimposing
giimnoorrt
tiring-room
giimnossty
misogynist
giinnnsttu
unstinting
giinnsttuw
untwisting
giinotttuw
outwitting
giinpprsst
strippings
giinprrssu
surprising
gijkmnpsuy
sky-jumping
gijnnoorsu
sojourning
gijnotttuu
outjutting
gikkllnsuy
skulkingly
gikmnnnoos
non-smoking
giknnorstt
strong-knit
gillnnouvy
unlovingly
gillnooprt
trolloping
gillnoprwy
prowlingly
gillnoptty
plottingly
gillnpuyzz
puzzlingly
gillnrstuy
rustlingly
gilloorsuy
gloriously
gilmmnoouy
immunology

gilmnnoruy
mourningly
gilmnnuuzz
unmuzzling
gilmnooost
monologist
nomologist
gilmnoosvw
slow-moving
gilmooopst
pomologist
gilmoostyz
zymologist
gilnnnstuy
stunningly
gilnnooswy
swooningly
gilnnorsty
snortingly
gilnooopsy
oligopsony
gilnooosst
nosologist
gilnooostt
ontologist
gilnoopsty
stoopingly
gilnoprsty
sportingly
gilnorrwyy
worryingly
gilnprsuuy
pursuingly
usurpingly
gilnrsttuy
trustingly
gilooopstt
optologist
topologist
gilooopstu
goloptious
gilooorsty
storiology
gilooprstt
proglottis
giloopstty
typologist
giloopstuu
goluptious
giloorrsuy
rigorously
giloorsuvy
vigorously
gimnnnrruu
rum-running
gimnnoorss
Monsignors
gimnoossuy
misogynous
ginnoopstu
unstooping
ginnoprstu
unsporting

ginnrsstuu
untrussing
ginoopptu
topping-out
ginooprrsu
ring-porous
ginooprrtu
nitro-group
ginooprtuu
outpouring
ginopprstu
supporting
ginoprrstw
springwort
gkooorrttw
grotto-work
glnoopsuyy
polygynous
glnoorsuwy
wrongously
glnoosttuu
gluttonous
gmnnooosuy
monogynous
gmnoooopty
pogonotomy
gmnooorrst
strong-room
hhijknoswy
whisky-john
hhilooppsy
philosophy
hhilooppty
photophily
hhimnopstx
sphinx-moth
hhimoooppr
ophiomorph
hhimooprrz
rhizomorph
hhioppssyy
hypophysis
hhlloppsyy
hypsophyll
hhlmoprtyy
polyrhythm
hhnoooppty
photophony
hhoopprssu
phosphorus
hiiklssttty
skittishly
hiillnortt
trillionth
hiilmmpssy
symphilism
hiilmoopsz
zoophilism
hiilnoprtt
lithoprint
hiiloopstz
zoophilist
hiilopppsu
Pliohippus

hiiloppstw
pistol-whip
hiilortty
lithotrity
hiilosssty
histolysis
hiimmnoprs
morphinism
hiimoprssw
misworship
hiimssttyy
hitty-missy
hiinoorsst
ornithosis
hiinopprss
prison-ship
hiioooprst
oophoritis
hiioottyy
hoity-toity
hijmnnooss
Johnsonism
hiklnorstw
thrown-silk
hillooprst
trollopish
hillssttuy
sluttishly
hilmnortty
trimonthly
hilmopssuy
symphilous
hilnortuwy
unworthily
hilooopsuz
zoophilous
hilooprsty
polyhistor
hiloopsstt
pistol-shot
hiloopssty
photolysis
himmnootyy
homonymity
himnnoopsy
symphonion
himnoooopr
omophorion
himnoprrsy
pyrrhonism
himnopssty
symphonist
himooprrst
orthoprism
hinoopttxy
phytotoxin
hinoprrsty
pyrrhonist
hinoprssuw
sun-worship
hiooprsttt
orthoptist
hiooprttxy
thixotropy

hiorssttuu
struthious
hknooouwwy
you-know-who
hlloopprsy
sporophyll
hlmooostuy
hylotomous
hlmoorsuuy
humorously
hlmopssuyy
symphylous
hloprssuuu
sulphurous
hmmnooosuy
homonymous
hmnoooostu
homotonous
hmoopsstuu
posthumous
hnnorsstuy
synthronus
hooosssttt
hoots-toots
hoooprrtty
phototropy
hoooprrtty
orthotropy
hoopprrsuy
porphyrous
pyrophorus
hoosstttuu
houts-touts
iiikllnpss
spillikins
iiikllnpsw
pilliwinks
iiillmmnsu
illuminism
iiillmnstu
illuminist
iiillnopst
pillionist
iiilnosstt
tonsilitis
iiimnoopst
imposition
iiimnoprss
misprision
iiimopsstv
positivism
iiinnoopst
opinionist
iiinoqrstu
inquisitor
iiinoqstuu
iniquitous
iiiopssttv
positivist
iiiopsttvy
positivity
iiklmnnoot
link-motion

10 OPR

iikloopstt
Ostpolitik
iillllnwyy
willy-nilly
iilloppsw
pillowslip
iillmoostu
mollitious
iillnoopst
postillion
iilmmnoosu
moliminous
iilmnopsty
postliminy
iilmnostuy
luminosity
iilmostuuv
multivious
iilnnootuv
involution
iilnnottuy
non-utility
iilnooqrru
iron-liquor
iilooprsux
prolixious
iimmoortuv
vomitorium
iimnnoossu
insomnious
iimnnoqrtu
quint-minor
iimooprsst
isotropism

iinoooppst
opposition
iinooprstt
portionist
iinorssstu
sinistrous
iinorstttu
institutor
iinorsttuu
nutritious
iioooprstv
ovipositor
iiooppr stu
propitious
iioprsssuu
suspirious
iioprsstuu
spirituous
iioprsstuy
spuriosity
iiorsttuvy
virtuosity
ijlnooostt
joint-stool
ikmorsstty
Trotskyism
iknoprrstw
print-works
ikorssttty
Trotskyist
illmnosuuy
luminously
illmoqtuuy
multiloquy

illopppssy
slipsloppy
ilmnooopst
monopolist
ilmnooostw
slow-motion
ilmnooqsuy
somniloquy
ilmnoosuuv
voluminous
ilmnostuuy
mutinously
ilmoorstuy
timorously
ilmorsttuy
multistory
ilnoopprsu
propulsion
iloopprsst
spoil-sport
iloorsuuxy
uxoriously
iloprssuuy
spuriously
ilorssuuuy
usuriously
ilorstuuvy
virtuously
immooprstu
prostomium
imnnosstyy
synonymist
imnnostyyy
synonymity

imnooorsuv
omnivorous
imooprrssy
promissory
imtuuyzzzz
tuzzi-muzzy
inoooppr rt
proportion
inooprrstu
protrusion
inoossssty
synostosis
inoqrstuwy
quinsy-wort
inorstuuuv
unvirtuous
ioooprsssu
isosporous
ioooprsstu
isotropous
iooorsssuv
ossivorous
ioorstttuy
tortuosity
llooppsuuy
populously
llorsstuuy
lustrously
lmnooosuxy
monoxylous
lmooorrrty
motor-lorry
lmooostuxy
xylotomous

lmosttuuuu
tumultuous
lnooorssuy
sonorously
lnooppsuuu
unpopulous
loopprrsuy
propulsory
loopstuuuv
voluptuous
loorsttuuy
tortuously
mnnoooostu
monotonous
mnnoossuyy
synonymous
mnoooprrty
promontory
noooprsttu
trout-spoon
oooopr ssuz
zoosporous
oopppsswyy
popsy-wopsy
oprsttuvyy
topsyturvy

11 AAA

aaaaabbcdrr
abracadabra
aaaaabhhmrt
Mahabharata
aaaaanrrttt
taratantara
aaaabbcelnr
Calabar-bean
aaaabbinrst
Sabbatarian
aaaabcchiln
bacchanalia
aaaacccelmn
Malacca-cane
aaaacceehnt
Acanthaceae
aaaacdeennp
Pandanaceae
aaaaceelnpt
Platanaceae
aaaaceelnst
Santalaceae

aaaaceemnrt
Marantaceae
aaaacgilpss
passacaglia
aaaacnrrsvy
caravansary
aaaadehrtvv
Atharvaveda
aaaaeehnnpt
Panathenaea
aaaafinrrst
Rastafarian
aaaaghipprr
paragraphia
aaaahipprrx
paraphraxia
aaaahmnpstt
phantasmata
aaaamrtzzzz
razzamatazz
aaabbcceemo
Bombacaceae

aaabbceglmp
cabbage-palm
palm-cabbage
aaabccdlrry
Barclaycard
aaabcceeill
Bacillaceae
aaabcchnrss
chars-à-bancs
aaabcddirry
bradycardia
aaabcdeeinr
abecedarian
aaabcdeiors
scarabaeoid
aaabcdelnrs
candelabras
aaabcdemnru
maceranduba
aaabcdfiors
fascia-board

aaabcdklnnt
black-and-tan
aaabcdlllnw
claw-and-ball
aaabcegillr
algebraical
aaabcehinrt
abranchiate
aaabcehprsu
chapeau-bras
aaabceimprt
parabematic
aaabceirsst
scarabaeist
aaabcelrttt
attractable
aaabchilmnr
Brahmanical
aaabchllmps
paschal-lamb
aaabcillnty
abactinally

aaabcillopr
parabolical
aaabcilnott
ablactation
aaabdeggnov
vagabondage
aaabdeilnpt
inadaptable
aaabdelnptu
unadaptable
aaabeehlnpt
analphabete
aaabegilnpr
plea-bargain
aaabegkmnnr
bank-manager
aaabegopsst
passage-boat
aaabehimnps
amphisbaena
aaabeiilnrs
Rabelaisian

11 AAA

aaabeillnuv
unavailable
aaabeilpprs
appraisable
aaabellnptu
unpalatable
aaabelnrrtw
warrantable
aaabennoprt
Bonapartean
aaabfinnort
Fontarabian
aaabghioopr
agoraphobia
aaabhikrstv
svarabhakti
aaabhioprst
astraphobia
aaabiinorst
arabisation
aaabillnuvy
unavailably
aaabimpprst
parabaptism
aaabllnptuy
unpalatably
aaablnoprsu
parabolanus
aaablnrrtwy
warrantably
aaaccceiltt
acatalectic
aaaccceinpt
capacitance
aaacccilltt
catallactic
aaacccilmst
cataclasmic
aaacccilstt
cataclastic
aaacccisttu
catacaustic
aaaccdeeips
Dipsacaceae
aaaccdehrst
saccharated
aaaccdeiimn
academician
aaaccdhirty
tachycardia
aaacceeehty
Cyatheaceae
aaacceeelln
Canellaceae
aaacceehstt
attaché-case
aaacceenopy
Apocynaceae
aaacceersty
Styracaceae
aaaccehinpu
ipecacuanha
aaaccehnopr
achaenocarp

aaacceillor
calceolaria
aaacceilprt
Palaearctic
aaacceilptt
acataleptic
aaaccgllmno
clog-almanac
aaacchillry
archaically
aaacchilnrt
charlatanic
aaacchilrtt
cathartical
aaacchilrtu
autarchical
aaaccillnru
canalicular
aaaccillprt
parallactic
aaaccillstt
stalactical
aaaccilltty
catalytical
aaaccilmnot
acclamation
aaaccilrrtu
caricatural
aaaccilrsst
sarcastical
aaaccilstuv
accusatival
aaaccimnort
carcinomata
aaacclmoprt
caprolactam
aaacclmorty
acclamatory
aaacdeeeilp
Pedaliaceae
aaacdeeilox
Oxalidaceae
aaacdeeimrr
camaraderie
aaacdeeinps
Sapindaceae
aaacdeilmpr
paramedical
pre-adamical
aaacdeilnrt
cardinalate
aaacdeinrty
caryatidean
aaacdgilnrt
crag-and-tail
aaacdhilnor
arachnoidal
aaacdhilnrt
cantharidal
aaacdiimnrs
Arcadianism
aaacdiloprx
paradoxical

aaacdilqrtu
quadratical
aaaceeeginr
Geraniaceae
aaaceefimru
Fumariaceae
aaaceeflmns
malfeasance
aaaceeghnps
Sphagnaceae
aaaceegilno
Loganiaceae
aaaceegnnrr
carrageenan
aaaceenrttv
caravanette
aaaceghillp
cephalalgia
aaaceghilnw
caaing-whale
aaacegilmno
egomaniacal
aaacegirrwy
carriageway
aaaceglllrt
call-at-large
aaacehillpr
parheliacal
aaacehilptt
apathetical
aaacehinnpt
Panathenaic
aaacehinrrt
trachearian
aaaceiilnps
Caesalpinia
aaaceillmnr
all-American
aaaceillnpt
Placentalia
aaaceilnprs
Paracelsian
aaaceilnpsu
Aesculapian
aaaceilorsu
araliaceous
aaaceimmpru
paramaecium
aaaceimnnpr
Pan-American
aaacelmnptu
campanulate
aaacelmnrst
sacramental
aaacelmoprt
paracetamol
aaacfgilnpt
flag-captain
aaacfillnty
fanatically
aaacfilnstt
fantastical
aaacfimnnor
francomania

aaacfimnrrt
aircraftman
aaacfjlmnry
clanjamfray
aaacghipprr
paragraphic
aaacghlmoyz
chalazogamy
aaacghloprs
sarcophagal
aaacgiinnru
Aurignacian
aaacgillnty
agnatically
aaacgilmmrt
grammatical
aaacgilmnno
anglomaniac
aaacgilmprt
pragmatical
aaacgilnnnp
Pan-Anglican
aaacginnnrv
caravanning
aaacgnrrssy
canary-grass
aaachiilppr
paraphiliac
aaachiilprs
pharisaical
aaachikpprt
apparatchik
aaachilmrrt
matriarchal
aaachilmstt
asthmatical
aaachilnopr
anaphorical
aaachilnotu
anacoluthia
aaachilprrt
patriarchal
aaachilrswy
cash-railway
aaachimnnot
anthomaniac
aaachlnrrty
charlatanry
aaachnqtuuu
Chautauquan
aaaciilmotx
axiomatical
aaaciilnott
Taliacotian
aaaciilprst
parasitical
aaaciklrrwy
rack-railway
aaacillmnru
animalcular
aaacillmpst
plasmatical
aaacillnorv
Convallaria

aaacillnsty
satanically
aaacillrtuy
actuarially
aaacillsttt
stalactital
aaacilmorss
macassar-oil
aaacilmottu
automatical
aaacilmpsst
spasmatical
aaacilnnory
alcyonarian
aaacilnnrst
Lancastrian
aaacilopstt
apostatical
aaacimnnory
acronymania
aaacinprstt
pancratiast
aaacinpstuu
sapucaia-nut
aaacinqstuu
aquanautics
aaaddfhnrst
hard-and-fast
aaadeffnnor
fanfaronade
aaadefiosst
assafoetida
aaadegilmnn
Magdalenian
aaadegimruv
Marivaudage
aaadehimpst
Phasmatidae
aaadehmnowy
home-and-away
aaadehmnrrw
hardwareman
aaadehmopst
Phasmatodea
aaadehnrsww
wash-and-wear
aaadeilmptv
maladaptive
aaadeilmrrr
rear-admiral
aaadeilnnrx
Alexandrian
aaadeimnnns
Sandemanian
aaadeimnnrt
mandarinate
aaadennprst
transpadane
aaadffhhlln
half-and-half
aaadflnrrtu
auld-farrant
aaadgginort
aggradation

aaadghilmpr
diaphragmal
aaadgiilmnr
madrigalian
aaadgilnort
gradational
aaadiilnorr
radiolarian
aaadimoprst
paramastoid
aaadjmnnpru
panjandarum
aaaeeelnprs
paraselenae
aaaeeggmnst
stage-manage
aaaeeghmnop
Phaenogamae
aaaeeginprs
paragenesia
aaaeegmsstu
sausage-meat
aaaeegrttvx
extravagate
aaaeehinsst
anaesthesia
aaaeehmnttx
exanthemata
aaaeersttvx
extravasate
aaaefnrsswy
farawayness
aaaegginrst
staging-area
aaaeghilnrt
Argathelian
aaaeghpprrr
paragrapher
aaaegiilnrt
egalitarian
aaaegilmmno
megalomania
aaaegimrrtv
margraviate
aaaeglopress
paraglossae
aaaegnrttvx
extravagant
aaaehiilmpt
epithalamia
aaaehilmsst
thalassemia
aaaehilnprt
paranthelia
aaaehilnprx
hexaplarian
aaaehimnnrt
amaranthine
aaaehinpprt
Aphaniptera
aaaehmnnopp
panomphaean
aaaehpprrrs
paraphraser

aaaeilmnnot
emanational
aaaeilmnopt
petalomania
aaaeilpprrs
reappraisal
aaaeinssst
assassinate
aaaeklmnoot
malakatoone
aaaekmmnrtu
mantua-maker
aaaelmnprtt
apartmental
aaaemrsssty
assay-master
aaaepprsstu
apparatuses
aaafffilnst
Falstaffian
aaaffinprwx
paraffin-wax
aaaggginrtv
aggravating
aaagghhiopr
Hagiographa
aaagginortv
aggravation
aaagiilnprs
parasailing
aaagiimnrrs
agrarianism
aaagiinnrsu
Sanguinaria
aaagilnnpqu
aquaplaning
aaagilnprtv
travail-pang
aaagknoorrt
kangaroo-rat
rat-kangaroo
aaaglloprss
paraglossal
aaagmnnorst
manna-groats
aaagmpprsss
pampas-grass
aaahiilnntt
antithalian
aaahilmoprt
prothalamia
aaahilnpsxy
anaphylaxis
aaahimnnort
Marathonian
aaahinnortz
zoantharian
aaahinpsstt
phantasiast
aaahipprrsx
paraphraxis
aaahnnopsty
satanophany

aaaiilmprsu
Marsupialia
aaaiilnortv
variational
aaaiilnprtv
travail-pain
aaaiilnpstu
Saintpaulia
aaaiinnqrtu
antiquarian
aaaillmorty
amatorially
aaaillnotuv
valuational
aaaillorstt
saltatorial
aaailnnrstu
saturnalian
aaailoprrtt
raptatorial
aaaimnnoost
antonomasia
aaaimnooprs
paronomasia
aaaoprsstuu
Apatosaurus
aabbcciilst
cabbalistic
aabbceeegrt
cabbage-tree
aabbceegors
cabbage-rose
aabbceekkrr
backbreaker
aabbceghmot
cabbage-moth
aabbcegmorw
cabbage-worm
aabbceinort
bicarbonate
aabbckllnoo
balloon-back
aabbdeekrst
bread-basket
aabbdefflor
baffle-board
aabbdeglnrr
land-grabber
aabbdeillor
Della-Robbia
aabbeeirrtv
rebarbative
aabbeeklnru
unbreakable
aabbeeklrry
barley-brake
aabbeellmnu
unblameable
aabbeellrst
barbastelle
aabbeeqrrsu
barbaresque
aabbefglrst
flabbergast

aabbegiinrt
bear-baiting
aabbehiilnt
inhabitable
aabbehillos
abolishable
aabbehilntu
unhabitable
aabbehlssst
Sabbathless
aabbeiilnor
baron-bailie
aabbeiorrtv
abbreviator
aabbeirrttu
barbiturate
aabbellmnuy
unblameably
aabbhhioopt
bathophobia
aabbhikosuz
bashi-bazouk
aabbiiilmno
bibliomania
aabblorrsuy
barbarously
aabccchkrst
backscratch
scratch-back
aabccdeeklm
camel-backed
aabccdeklot
black-coated
aabcceellno
concealable
aabcceilprt
practicable
aabccekrstt
backscatter
aabccelmopt
accomptable
aabccelnotu
accountable
aabccelnsuu
unaccusable
aabccerruuy
bureaucracy
aabccgillnr
calling-crab
aabcciijlno
Jacobinical
aabcciijlot
Jacobitical
aabccilmost
saltimbocca
aabccilprty
practicably
aabcclnotuy
accountably
aabcclnrruu
carbuncular
aabcclnsuuy
unaccusably

aabcddeehkl
blackheaded
aabcddeorst
broadcasted
aabcdeeellr
leader-cable
aabcdeeflry
barefacedly
aabcdeefnrz
brazen-faced
aabcdeehrrt
acre-breadth
aabcdeeilmt
alembicated
aabcdeellnt
ballet-dance
aabcdeelnrt
tabernacled
aabcdeenort
decarbonate
aabcdefiiil
acidifiable
aabcdefnosu
bauson-faced
aabcdehimmr
chambermaid
aabcdehnpry
peach-brandy
aabcdeiklsv
black-a-vised
aabcdeilnry
clay-brained
aabcdeinoor
radio-beacon
aabcdeinort
debarcation
aabcdeinrru
unbarricade
aabcdelmnru
candelabrum
aabcdemossu
ambuscadoes
aabcdeorrst
broadcaster
rebroadcast
aabcdggioor
braggadocio
aabcdghkrtu
back-draught
aabcdhhortt
thatch-board
aabcdhioopr
Brachiopoda
aabcdhmnory
rhabdomancy
aabcdiiqrtu
biquadratic
aabcdilnosu
subdiaconal
aabcdinoorr
radiocarbon
aabceeeenrv
Verbenaceae

aabceeegino
Begoniaceae
aabceeehlst
escheatable
aabceeeiirs
Ribesiaceae
aabceeeillo
Lobeliaceae
aabceeellpr
replaceable
aabceeelnpu
unpeaceable
aabceeelrrt
retraceable
aabceeerrsu
Burseraceae
aabceeflrrt
refractable
aabceefnorr
forbearance
aabceegllno
congealable
aabceehilmp
impeachable
aabceehklrt
leather-back
aabceehlnru
unreachable
aabceehlntu
unteachable
aabceehlorx
Lochaber-axe
aabceehmmrr
hammer-brace
aabceehmnrt
antechamber
aabceehmrst
beach-master
aabceeiinrr
carabiniere
aabceeillmr
reclaimable
aabceeilmnv
ambivalence
aabceeilnps
inescapable
aabceeilnqu
equibalance
aabceeilnrs
increasable
aabceeilppr
appreciable
aabceelmnss
assemblance
aabceelnorv
overbalance
aabceelnpss
capableness
aabceelnpsu
unescapable
aabceelnrst
scarlet-bean
aabceelnrtu
untraceable

aabceelortt
bracteolate
aabceelrrtt
retractable
aabceelrttu
trabeculate
aabceelrttx
extractable
aabcefiirtv
fabricative
aabcefilnot
labefaction
aabcefinott
tabefaction
aabceflmnoy
flamboyance
aabceflnotu
confabulate
aabcehhpsty
bathyscaphe
aabcehiinnt
inhabitance
aabcehikrst
basket-chair
aabcehillry
Hebraically
aabcehilmnr
chamberlain
aabcehilnru
hibernacula
aabcehilsst
chastisable
aabcehimnrr
rain-chamber
aabcehlmntu
unmatchable
aabcehlprsu
purchasable
aabceiilnns
cannibalise
aabceiinnnr
cinnabarine
aabceikllmr
blackmailer
aabceillmry
reclaimably
aabceillory
aerobically
aabceillpru
burial-place
aabceillrtu
articulable
aabceilmnop
companiable
aabceilmnvy
ambivalency
aabceilnnot
containable
aabceilnort
baronetical
carbonalite
aabceilnrtt
intractable

aabceilpprt
parableptic
aabceilppry
appreciably
aabceimnort
embarcation
aabceimnprr
Pre-Cambrian
aabceirsttv
abstractive
aabcekklmrt
black-market
aabcekmruuv
vacuum-brake
aabcekqrrtu
quarter-back
aabcelllops
collapsable
aabcelloort
collaborate
aabcelmnotu
uncomatable
aabcelmopss
compassable
aabcelmrtuu
umbraculate
aabcelnorty
carbonylate
aabcelnrttu
untractable
aabceoorrsu
arboraceous
aabceoorttz
Azotobacter
aabcffjosst
Jacob's-staff
aabcfiinort
fabrication
aabcflmnoyy
flamboyancy
aabcgggiknn
back-ganging
aabcghioopr
agoraphobic
aabcgiillms
galliambics
aabcgilloot
batological
aabchiilmnr
Brahminical
aabchiinnty
inhabitancy
aabchiinort
brachiation
aabchnopprw
Cappah-brown
aabciiilmty
amicability
aabciijnnot
anti-Jacobin
antijacobin
aabciillpty
placability

aabciilmnns
cannibalism
aabciilnort
calibration
aabciilrsty
sybaritical
aabciimnnos
Baconianism
aabcillnoty
botanically
aabcillostv
Baltoslavic
aabcilmnost
saltimbanco
aabcilnnruu
incunabular
aabcilnrtty
intractably
aabcimnorrs
Carbonarism
aabcinnoort
carbonation
aabcinorrtu
carburation
aabcinorstt
abstraction
aabckmnsstu
subtacksman
aabclprssuu
subscapular
aabcmnnooty
botanomancy
aabcnoorsst
contrabasso
aabdddefmnu
deaf-and-dumb
aabdddelopr
paddle-board
aabddeglllr
gall-bladder
aabddehhnrt
hand-breadth
aabddehmory
hebdomadary
aabddeinost
bastinadoed
aabddelnnoy
abandonedly
aabddhlnnsu
husbandland
aabddnrsstu
substandard
aabdeegimrr
marriage-bed
aabdeehhrrs
haberdasher
aabdeehinrr
hare-brained
aabdeelmnnu
unamendable
aabdeelprsu
persuadable
aabdeelrstw
wastel-bread

aabdeemrrss
embarrassed
aabdeeqrsuu
arquebusade
aabdegilmnn
landing-beam
aabdegilnor
load-bearing
aabdeginosv
vagabondise
aabdegnortu
unabrogated
aabdehhirrt
hair-breadth
aabdehiinrr
hair-brained
aabdehrstwy
breadthways
aabdeiilnsv
inadvisable
aabdeiilrty
readability
aabdeiknort
debarkation
aabdeillnot
labiodental
aabdeillrvy
adverbially
aabdeilmntu
mandibulate
aabdeilnnru
undrainable
aabdeilnouv
unavoidable
aabdeilnsuv
unadvisable
aabdeilorrt
labradorite
aabdellnnry
blarney-land
aabdellnstu
unballasted
aabdelorruy
day-labourer
aabdemnnnot
abandonment
aabdghinosv
vagabondish
aabdgiinnst
bastinading
aabdgiinrsw
bias-drawing
aabdgimnosv
vagabondism
aabdginrstw
bastard-wing
aabdgklnouw
dak-bungalow
aabdglnrssy
brandy-glass
aabdhhooprr
Rhabdophora
aabdhiklnoy
bank-holiday

aabdhiosttv
Bodhisattva
aabdhloprss
splash-board
aabdhmmoory
rhabdomyoma
aabdiilmnty
damnability
aabdiilmqru
Liquidambar
aabdillmnoy
abdominally
aabdilnouvy
unavoidably
aabdilnsuvy
unadvisably
aabdimnooow
amboina-wood
aabdimnortu
adumbration
aabdmnooowy
amboyna-wood
aabdmoorrrt
mortar-board
aabdnrrrstu
surtarbrand
aabeeefkrrs
safe-breaker
aabeeeglnru
unagreeable
aabeeekstvw
basket-weave
aabeeelnrtt
entreatable
aabeeerrrtw
water-bearer
aabeeffllpt
baffle-plate
aabeefgirrr
barrage-fire
aabeeggiirr
argie-bargie
aabeeggllrr
argle-bargle
aabeegilnrt
tale-bearing
aabeeginnrt
annabergite
aabeeglmntu
augmentable
aabeeglnttu
ungetatable
aabeegmnotu
beaumontage
aabeegmrrst
barge-master
aabeehilntz
Elizabethan
aabeehilpst
alphabetise
aabeehklnsu
unshakeable
aabeehlrsty
breathalyse

aabeeiillnn
inalienable
aabeeiilrtw
water-bailie
aabeeilllqu
illaqueable
aabeeillnnu
unalienable
aabeeillnpx
explainable
aabeeillnrt
inalterable
aabeeilmnss
amiableness
aabeeilnnrr
inenarrable
aabeeilnort
inelaborate
aabeeilnprs
inseparable
aabeeilnruw
unweariable
aabeeilortv
elaborative
aabeeilprrr
irreparable
aabeeinrrrt
train-bearer
aabeeinrrst
brain-teaser
aabeekkmorr
make-or-break
aabeekkmrst
basket-maker
aabeeklnpsu
unspeakable
aabeeklpstt
plate-basket
aabeekssttw
waste-basket
aabeelllmnu
unmalleable
aabeellmnot
balletomane
aabeellnptt
battleplane
aabeellnrtu
unalterable
aabeellnsss
salableness
aabeellorty
elaborately
aabeellprry
pearl-barley
aabeellprsu
pleasurable
aabeelmpprr
marble-paper
aabeelmprtu
perambulate
preambulate
aabeelmptttt
attemptable

aabeelnorst
treasonable
aabeelnortu
unelaborate
aabeelnprsu
unseparable
aabeelnrttu
entablature
untreatable
aabeelnrtuv
unavertable
aabeelnsssv
savableness
aabeelprstt
breastplate
aabeelrrrtw
water-barrel
aabeelrrstt
sabre-rattle
aabeelrrstv
traversable
aabeelrrttu
terebratula
aabeelrrtwy
barley-water
aabeemmoprt
meprobamate
aabeemnrttt
rabattement
aabeffiills
falsifiable
aabefgiilmn
magnifiable
aabefhilnos
fashionable
aabefhilpst
half-baptise
aabefiillqu
qualifiable
aabefiilsst
satisfiable
aabefillmmn
inflammable
aabefllnppu
unflappable
aabeflmnoty
flamboyante
aabeflmntuu
funambulate
aabeggglry
gally-bagger
gally-beggar
aabeggilmnt
gaming-table
aabegginsst
staging-base
aabegiilnns
Albigensian
aabegiilnnv
innavigable
aabegiimnrt
time-bargain
aabegiklmnw
walking-beam

aabegilnnuv
unnavigable
aabegilnors
organisable
aabegirrrtu
arbitrageur
aabegjsstuu
assubjugate
aabegllmost
megaloblast
aabeglnorrr
barrel-organ
aabeglrrsuy
barley-sugar
aabehhioppt
taphephobia
aabehilnrst
tarnishable
aabehiloruv
behavioural
aabehklnsuy
unshakeably
aabehmprrss
bramah-press
aabeiiillmss
assimilable
aabeiillnny
inalienably
aabeiillsty
saleability
aabeiilmmor
memorabilia
aabeiilmnty
amenability
aabeiilmtty
tameability
aabeiilnrrt
libertarian
aabeiilrtty
rateability
aabeiilrtwy
wearability
aabeiklnnpt
table-napkin
aabeikmnort
embarkation
aabeilllrty
bilaterally
aabeillmnpu
manipulable
aabeillmrru
air-umbrella
aabeillnnuy
unalienably
aabeillrrtu
Turbellaria
aabeillrrtz
trail-blazer
aabeillrsuy
subaerially
aabeilmmost
ametabolism
aabeilmnrru
unmarriable

aabeilnnptu
unpaintable
aabeilnnstu
unstainable
aabeilnoort
elaboration
aabeilnortt
anteorbital
aabeilnprsy
inseparably
aabeilnrrtt
rattle-brain
aabeilnruwy
unweariably
aabeilnsstu
sustainable
aabeiloprsv
vaporisable
aabeilpprss
parablepsis
aabeilprrry
irreparably
aabeimnrrtt
arbitrament
aabeinnoort
anaerobiont
aabeiopprtv
approbative
aabeklnpsuy
unspeakably
aabelllnouw
unallowable
aabelllrrsy
sallal-berry
aabellmnrtu
umbrella-ant
aabellnrtuy
unalterably
aabelloprt
ballot-paper
aabellorsuv
slave-labour
aabellprsuy
pleasurably
aabelmmnssy
assemblyman
aabelmoostu
ametabolous
aabelmprruy
preambulary
aabelnorsty
treasonably
aabeloorrty
elaboratory
aabelprsssu
surpassable
aabfhilnosy
fashionably
aabfillmmny
inflammably
aabggimrrst
braggartism
aabghiilnty
hangability

aabghilloop
gallophobia
aabghilnoop
anglophobia
aabgiilnnvy
innavigably
aabgiilnost
sailing-boat
aabgilmnrsu
submarginal
aabginorssu
Sanguisorba
aabglnstuuu
Subungulata
aabhhimsttv
bathmitsvah
aabhhimttvz
bathmitzvah
aabhhiooppt
pathophobia
taphophobia
aabhiilortt
habilitator
aabhiinottu
habituation
aabhillnrty
labyrinthal
aabhimnpsst
batsmanship
aabhinooppt
pantophobia
aabhknoortt
katabothron
aabiiilrtvy
variability
aabiiilstty
satiability
aabiillnoot
abolitional
aabiillnort
librational
aabiillppty
palpability
aabiillstvy
salvability
aabiilmnruu
albuminuria
aabiilnortv
vibrational
aabiilorstu
atrabilious
aabiilosttu
ablatitious
aabiilrrrty
arbitrarily
aabiimmnort
timbromania
aabiimnnoot
abomination
aabiinorrtt
arbitration
aabiirrrttx
arbitratrix

aabillmorsy
ambrosially
aabillmorty
balmorality
aabillmpsty
baptismally
aabillmrsuy
syllabarium
aabillossww
wassail-bowl
aabillrsuxy
subaxillary
aabilmmnors
abnormalism
aabilmnorty
abnormality
aabilnooprt
probational
aabilnoorty
oblationary
aabilnortuy
ablutionary
aabilnssttu
substantial
aabilosstuw
wassail-bout
aabimnoprst
Bonapartism
aabinnopstu
subpanation
aabinoopprt
approbation
aabinoprstt
Bonapartist
aabinorrstu
saburration
subarration
aablmmnorsu
somnambular
aablnnorrtu
natural-born
aabmorrsttu
masturbator
aaboopprrty
approbatory
aacccehilt
cachectical
aaccdejnoy
coadjacency
aacccdeosuy
cycadaceous
aaccceilptt
cataplectic
aacccejkkrr
crackerjack
aacccghiopr
cacographic
aacccgiknrt
cat-cracking
aacccgiorst
cacogastric
aaccchhilrs
clairschach

aaccchnostu
cash-account
aaccchorstt
scratch-coat
aaccciillmt
climactical
aaccciilrtu
cicatricula
aacccilmsty
cataclysmic
aacccnnotuy
accountancy
aaccddeinor
endocardiac
aaccdeehior
Orchidaceae
aaccdeeilst
discalceate
aaccdeellnt
cancellated
aaccdeelnor
accelerando
aaccdehirtt
cathedratic
aaccdeiillt
dialectical
aaccdeiilps
Asclepiadic
aaccdeiimms
academicism
aaccdeiiprr
pericardiac
aaccdeilnot
anecdotical
aaccdeilopy
cyclopaedia
aaccdemmoot
accommodate
aaccdennort
contra-dance
aaccdgioryz
zygocardiac
aaccdhiinor
characinoid
aaccdhiinrt
cantharidic
aaccdhloort
octachordal
aaccdhlptyy
pachydactyl
aaccdiiilrt
diacritical
aaccdiilopt
apodictical
aaccdlmorty
macrodactyl
aaccdlnorty
accordantly
aaccdmoprss
compass-card
aacceefilnt
calefacient
aacceefiltv
calefactive

aacceefkrrs
safe-cracker
aacceeinrrt
incarcerate
aacceeinrtv
revaccinate
aacceellnot
collectanea
aacceellrtu
recalculate
aacceelnstu
acaulescent
aacceelorrt
accelerator
aacceelprtu
receptacula
aacceemnopr
compearance
aacceennott
concatenate
aaccefhstty
safety-catch
aaccefilnot
calefaction
aaccefilstu
fasciculate
aacceflorty
calefactory
aacceghillp
cephalalgic
aacceghilnr
archangelic
aacceghnrtt
gnatcatcher
aacceghoprr
cacographer
aaccegiknps
packing-case
aaccegilmor
acromegalic
aaccegilort
categorical
aaccegilott
geotactical
aaccegnorst
scant-o'-grace
aaccegorrty
ergatocracy
aaccehhmost
stomach-ache
aaccehhprst
catch-phrase
aaccehiimnn
mechanician
aaccehiimnr
air-mechanic
aaccehilmot
machicolate
aaccehilmrt
mail-catcher
aaccehilmst
catechismal
schematical

aaccehinopt
pinacotheca
aaccehirsst
catachresis
aaccehklrrt
crack-halter
aaccehlnnno
nonchalance
aaccehnrttw
want-catcher
aaccehorstu
chartaceous
aacceiilmst
acclimatise
aacceiimnot
amino-acetic
aacceiinprt
Capernaitic
aacceillsty
ascetically
aacceilltuu
cauliculate
aacceilltuv
calculative
aacceilmprt
malpractice
aacceilnors
anisocercal
aacceilorss
accessorial
aacceilossu
salicaceous
aacceilpprt
paraplectic
aacceimnopr
accompanier
aacceinnort
Anacreontic
canceration
aacceinoptt
acceptation
aacceinqttu
acquittance
aaccekktyyy
yackety-yack
aacceknrrtu
currant-cake
aaccellntuy
accentually
aaccellpprw
clapperclaw
aaccelmnuuv
vacuum-clean
aaccelnrtuu
caruncululate
aaccelprstu
spectacular
aaccelrttuu
acculturate
aaccenoprry
coparcenary
aaccenorsuy
sauce-crayon

aaccfiiilnr
carnificial
aaccfiiilrs
sacrificial
aaccfiillpy
pacifically
aaccfiilrty
farcicality
aaccfiimnor
acinaciform
aaccfiioprt
pacificator
aaccfilmorr
calcariform
aaccghiilrr
chiragrical
aaccghiknot
hacking-coat
aaccghimmos
chasmogamic
aaccghinrtt
rat-catching
aaccgillntu
calculating
aacchiimrst
charismatic
aacchiinrst
anarchistic
aacchiinrtt
anthracitic
aacchilloty
chaotically
aacchillpty
hypallactic
aacchilmnor
monarchical
aacchilmost
stomachical
aacchilorrv
vicar-choral
aacchinopst
cataphonics
aacchipprsy
parapsychic
aacchllottw
tallow-catch
aacchlnstuy
calycanthus
aacciilmnot
acclimation
aacciilmopt
apomictical
aacciilmprt
impractical
aacciilnnot
calcination
aacciilnorv
Clavicornia
aacciilnstt
Cisatlantic
aacciilsstu
casuistical
aacciilsttt
stalactitic

aacciinnotv
vaccination
aacciinopsu
incapacious
aacciinostu
acoustician
aaccilllnoy
laconically
aaccillssy
classically
aaccillnnoy
canonically
aaccillnotu
calculation
aaccillnssu
unclassical
aaccillnsuu
canaliculus
aaccilloopr
coprolaliac
aaccillprty
practically
aaccillstuy
caustically
aaccilnnnou
uncanonical
aaccilnostu
sacculation
aaccilnprtu
unpractical
aaccilnstty
syntactical
aaccilloppty
apocalyptic
aaccilopsuy
capaciously
aaccimnopst
accompanist
aaccinoortt
coarctation
aaccinortvy
vaccinatory
aaccioprrst
paracrostic
aacciorrsty
aristocracy
aacclmortuu
accumulator
aacclnoprty
plantocracy
aacclnorttu
contractual
aaccloorsst
sacrocostal
aaccmorstuy
accustomary
aaccorrstty
stratocracy
aacdddeinor
Dodecandria
aacddeeefns
defeasanced
aacddeeehlr
clear-headed

aacddeehnrt
dendrachate
aacddeeimps
aides-de-camp
aacddeginoy
Dodecagynia
aacddehinpp
handicapped
aacddehklns
slack-handed
aacddeilnor
endocardial
aacddeinrtu
candidature
aacddeintuu
nudicaudate
aacddiiinss
candidiasis
aacddijortu
adjudicator
aacdeeeflsw
weasel-faced
aacdeeeorrs
Droseraceae
aacdeeepprt
peace-parted
aacdeeghinp
phagedaenic
aacdeegkpss
deck-passage
aacdeehilnr
Heracleidan
aacdeehimmn
machine-made
aacdeehimnr
Archimedean
aacdeehlpst
sphacelated
aacdeeiilrs
deracialise
aacdeeiirtv
eradicative
aacdeeilrtv
declarative
aacdeeilstt
elasticated
aacdeeiprst
paederastic
aacdeellmos
Camaldolese
aacdeellnot
lanceolated
aacdeellrss
class-leader
aacdeellstt
castellated
aacdeelmopr
cameleopard
aacdeemnntv
advancement
aacdeemnosu
Osmundaceae
aacdeenoprr
opera-dancer

aacdeenqrsu
square-dance
aacdeentuvx
unexcavated
aacdeffglos
scaffoldage
aacdefilnot
defalcation
aacdefimnot
madefaction
aacdefinrux
fricandeaux
aacdefllotw
tallow-faced
aacdeggilmo
demagogical
aacdeggilop
pedagogical
aacdegiimnt
diamagnetic
aacdegimnns
damascening
aacdeglrstu
castle-guard
aacdegorstu
sugar-coated
aacdehhnrrt
charter-hand
aacdehiimrt
adiathermic
aacdehiinrt
Trachinidae
aacdehilors
icosahedral
aacdehimpry
pachydermia
aacdehimrty
diathermacy
aacdehinott
anticathode
aacdehinppr
handicapper
aacdehinrst
cantharides
aacdehipprt
crappit-head
aacdehirrtv
architraved
aacdehlltwy
what-d'ye-call
aacdehlmpry
pachydermal
aacdehlnrwx
wax-chandler
aacdehloopp
Cephalopoda
aacdehmorsu
Machaerodus
aacdehmrrtt
tetradrachm
aacdehprrrs
card-sharper
aacdeiilmrt
diametrical

aacdeiilmrv
vice-admiral
aacdeiilprr
pericardial
aacdeiimprt
pre-adamitic
aacdeiimstt
diastematic
aacdeiinnnr
incarnadine
aacdeiinnrt
incardinate
aacdeiinort
eradication
aacdeiinprr
pericardian
aacdeiiortv
radioactive
aacdeiiprst
paediatrics
aacdeiiprsu
parasuicide
aacdeillty
dialectally
aacdeillmot
Camaldolite
aacdeilmnot
declamation
aacdeilnopt
pedal-action
aacdeilnort
declaration
aacdeilnotu
educational
aacdeilnptu
paniculated
aacdeilnrru
ruridecanal
aacdeilnrss
radicalness
aacdeilnrst
calendarist
aacdeiloprr
praecordial
aacdeilorrt
redactorial
aacdeilrstt
strait-laced
aacdeilrttu
articulated
aacdeilrtuu
auriculated
aacdeilsttt
stalactited
aacdeimnnop
Pandemoniac
aacdeimnort
demarcation
aacdeimnory
aerodynamic
aacdeinnort
carnationed
aacdeinnott
decantation

aacdeinoprs
caparisoned
aacdeinotuv
coadunative
aacdeinrsst
incrassated
aacdeioprtt
parti-coated
aacdellnoty
anecdotally
aacdelmorst
closet-drama
aacdelmorty
declamatory
aacdelnptty
pentadactyl
aacdelooprt
proctodaeal
aacdelorrty
declaratory
aacdelrttty
tetradactyl
aacdemnostu
cat-and-mouse
aacdemorrru
armoured-car
aacdenoprtt
pedantocrat
aacdeoprrrs
road-scraper
aacdeoprtty
party-coated
aacdfiillty
fatidically
aacdfiilrrt
fratricidal
aacdgghiist
Haggadistic
aacdghioprr
cardiograph
aacdghoprsu
cardophagus
aacdgiilmnr
mailing-card
aacdgilnpry
playing-card
aacdgimrrtu
dramaturgic
aacdglmorty
dactylogram
aacdgnnooty
contango-day
aacdhiimrtt
Mithradatic
aacdhiioprs
aphrodisiac
aacdhiloprs
rhapsodical
aacdhimnnsw
sandwich-man
aacdhimorsu
Machairodus
aacdhmoprsy
psychodrama

aacdiiilmot
idiomatical
aacdiilmnru
adminicular
aacdiilmpry
pyramidical
aacdiilortt
dictatorial
aacdiimmrst
dramaticism
aacdiimnops
dipsomaniac
aacdiinnors
icosandrian
aacdillloor
coralloidal
aacdillmnoy
nomadically
aacdillmnyy
dynamically
aacdillnors
coral-island
aacdillrsty
drastically
aacdilmopss
spasmodical
aacdilnpsst
landscapist
aacdilortty
artiodactyl
aacdilosuuy
audaciously
aacdimmooty
mycodomatia
aacdimnnoor
monocardian
aacdimnnotu
manducation
aacdimnorst
nostradamic
aacdinnootu
coadunation
aacdklnoort
cool-tankard
aacdknorrtw
dock-warrant
aacdlmnooty
condylomata
aacdmnortuy
manducatory
aacdmoorstu
catadromous
aaceeehlmot
haematocele
aaceeehprst
space-heater
aaceeejmntt
ejectamenta
aaceefilltt
lattice-leaf
aaceefimnss
misfeasance
aaceefirrtv
rarefactive

aaceefnnnos
non-feasance
aaceefnorrt
confarreate
aaceeggnrsw
swagger-cane
aaceeghnopr
chaperonage
aaceeghnprr
crapehanger
aaceeghrrst
gatecrasher
aaceegikmnp
peacemaking
aaceegillnv
evangelical
aaceegilmns
seaming-lace
aaceegimnor
Moringaceae
aaceeginnrr
carrageenin
aaceeginprt
paragenetic
aaceegmmort
macrogamete
aaceehhltux
hexateuchal
aaceehilmnr
Amelanchier
aaceehilstt
aesthetical
aaceehimnpt
tape-machine
aaceehimppr
papier-mâché
aaceehinstt
anaesthetic
aaceehllnrt
chantarelle
aaceehlnnpy
anencephaly
aaceehlnnsv
clean-shaven
aaceehlortt
leather-coat
aaceehlprrt
arch-prelate
aaceehmnppt
appeachment
aaceehmprst
spermatheca
aaceehrrttt
tetrarchate
aaceeiimnrs
Americanise
aaceeiimnst
Scitamineae
aaceeiimpst
septicaemia
aaceeijltuv
ejaculative

aaceeillmns
mésalliance
miscellanea
aaceeilmpru
Primulaceae
aaceeilmtvx
exclamative
aaceeilnnrs
encarnalise
aaceeilnrtt
intercalate
aaceeilopst
Psilotaceae
aaceeilorst
aeroelastic
aaceeilrrst
secretarial
aaceeilrttv
altercative
aaceeimmnrt
amerciament
aaceeimnnnt
maintenance
aaceeimorrt
araeometric
aaceeimrssu
eremacausis
aaceeinnnrt
centenarian
aaceeinnrrt
reincarnate
aaceeinnrss
necessarian
renaissance
aaceeinrstt
tea-canister
aaceeiprrtv
prevaricate
aaceeirrstt
secretariat
aaceejkmstt
steam-jacket
aaceejkrttw
water-jacket
aaceekllnst
alkalescent
aaceeklmprt
market-place
aaceekmpstt
steam-packet
aaceeknprst
carpet-snake
aaceellltuv
valleculate
aaceelnpstu
encapsulate
aaceelnsstt
sclate-stane
aaceelntttu
tentaculate
aaceelprstv
space-travel
aaceemnorst
ocean-stream

aaceemnostu
amentaceous
aaceenrrssu
reassurance
aaceenrrtuv
averruncate
aaceffhinrs
affranchise
aaceffiirtv
affricative
aaceffilnot
affectional
aaceffinott
affectation
aaceffknors
saffron-cake
aacefgghinr
chafing-gear
aacefghinrr
far-reaching
aacefginprs
spacefaring
aacefglnort
conflagrate
aacefhirssw
sea-crawfish
aacefhirssy
sea-crayfish
aacefhmstty
safety-match
aacefiillns
fiançailles
aacefiilnrt
interfacial
aacefiilnrv
acriflavine
aacefilllmy
malefically
aacefilmnot
malefaction
aacefilmrsu
surface-mail
aacefilttuv
facultative
aacefinorrt
rarefaction
aacefinorrv
vicar-forane
aacefinorsu
farinaceous
aacefinortt
fractionate
aaceflmorty
malefactory
aaceflnsstu
factualness
aacefmnrtuu
manufacture
aaceggorstw
swagger-coat
aaceghillrt
lethargical
aaceghilnor
archegonial

aaceghiloot
Oligochaeta
aaceghilopr
archipelago
aaceghimnop
phaenogamic
aaceghllssv
cheval-glass
aaceghloory
archaeology
aaceghnortu
autochanger
aaceghprttu
gutta-percha
aacegiilmnt
enigmatical
aacegiimnnt
magnetician
aacegiimrrs
miscarriage
aacegiioprt
Areopagitic
aacegiklnnw
walking-cane
aacegiklnrw
race-walking
walking-race
aacegilllny
angelically
aacegilllor
allegorical
aacegillmmr
calligramme
aacegillmnn
name-calling
aacegillnpy
callipygean
aacegilloor
aerological
aacegillops
plagioclase
aacegilltuv
victuallage
aacegilnpry
panegyrical
aacegilostu
cataloguise
aacegilotuv
coagulative
aacegilrstt
strategical
aacegimmnrt
engrammatic
aacegimnnor
cinema-organ
aacegimnnpr
permanganic
aacegimnopt
compaginate
aaceginnrtw
watering-can
aaceginprtw
watering-cap

aaceginpstt
peat-casting
aaceglnrrtu
rectangular
aacegmnoorr
Graeco-Roman
aacegmnosty
gynaecomast
aacegnoorsu
onagraceous
aacehhilstx
hexastichal
aacehiillor
allocheiria
aacehiilmpt
epithalamic
aacehiilrsv
cavalierish
aacehiilstt
atheistical
aacehiimmns
Manichaeism
aacehillmno
melancholia
aacehillntu
hallucinate
aacehilmnnn
manna-lichen
aacehilmrsv
vice-marshal
aacehilmrtu
rheumatical
aacehilmsst
thalassemic
aacehilnpst
chain-plates
aacehilnrtt
intrathecal
aacehilnttu
authentical
aacehilppss
Cephalaspis
aacehilrrrt
trierarchal
aacehilrstt
theatricals
aacehimmstt
mathematics
aacehimnnoy
haemocyanin
aacehimorst
achromatise
aacehimortt
haematocrit
aacehimostt
haemostatic
aacehinotty
thiocyanate
aacehinpprr
paranephric
aacehinprrt
Petrarchian
aacehioprst
Spirochaeta

aacehiprstu
haruspicate
aacehknrsss
harness-cask
aacehlmnrtw
law-merchant
aacehlmnstu
steam-launch
aacehlooprr
Rhopalocera
aacehloptuy
autocephaly
aacehmmnnrt
merchantman
aacehmnorsu
rhamnaceous
aacehmnpsty
cash-payment
aacehnnorst
anthracnose
aacehnoprvy
anchovy-pear
aacehnopsww
weapon-schaw
aacehnppsww
wappenschaw
aacehoprstt
catastrophe
aacehopsstu
spathaceous
aacehpprrst
starch-paper
aacehprrsty
search-party
aaceiiklmnt
kinematical
aaceiillmns
misalliance
aaceiillnrt
lacertilian
aaceiillrtv
leviratical
aaceiilmrrr
mail-carrier
aaceiilmrsv
cavalierism
aaceiilnprr
pericranial
aaceiilnrrt
interracial
aaceiilpptv
applicative
aaceiimmnrs
Americanism
aaceiimnnpt
mine-captain
aaceiimnrst
Americanist
creatianism
aaceiimnrtv
carminative
aaceiinnrss
canariensis

aaceiinorst
societarian
aaceiinortt
ratiocinate
aaceiiosstv
associative
aaceiipprtt
participate
aaceijlnotu
ejaculation
aaceillllsty
elastically
aaceillmnpt
implacental
aaceillmnsu
animalcules
aaceillmpux
amplexicaul
aaceillntvy
venatically
aaceilloprr
Procellaria
aaceillprrt
caterpillar
aaceillrrty
erratically
aaceillrsst
rascalliest
aaceilmnopy
alycompaine
aaceilmnort
reclamation
aaceilmnotx
exclamation
aaceilmnptu
pneumatical
aaceilmorrt
crematorial
aaceilmossu
alismaceous
aaceilmprst
spermatical
aaceilmpstt
metaplastic
palmatisect
aaceilmrttu
matriculate
aaceilnnoss
ascensional
aaceilnnptt
pentactinal
aaceilnoprt
anaplerotic
aaceilnorst
ancestorial
aaceilnortt
altercation
aaceilnpstu
incapsulate
aaceilnrrtu
retinacular
aaceilnrrty
intercalary

aaceilnrttt
tetractinal
aaceiloppty
palaeotypic
aaceilprstu
spiraculate
aaceilprttu
catapultier
particulate
aaceilrrstt
strait-lacer
aaceilrssuv
vascularise
aaceilstuvy
causatively
aaceimmopru
paramoecium
aaceimmostt
metasomatic
aaceimnnott
contaminate
aaceimnoort
erotomaniac
aaceimnoprt
emancipator
aaceimnprst
campestrian
aaceimnprsu
parascenium
aaceimoprtv
comparative
aaceinnortt
recantation
aaceinnrstu
unsectarian
aaceinnrttt
interactant
aaceinorrty
reactionary
aaceinorstu
aeronautics
aaceinpqrtu
preacquaint
aaceinrsstu
sanctuarise
aaceinrstty
asynartetic
aaceiopprrt
appreciator
aaceiorsstt
aerostatics
aaceiorsttw
coast-waiter
aaceiprrstt
stair-carpet
aacejkqrrtu
quarter-jack
aacejlortuy
ejaculatory
aacekklrrtw
track-walker
aaceklqrsuv
quacksalver

aacelloprty
acropetally
aacelmnnnot
cannon-metal
aacelmorrsu
scale-armour
aacelmorstu
emasculator
aacelmortxy
exclamatory
aacelmrssst
master-class
aacelmrtttx
malt-extract
aacelnnrstt
transcalent
aacelnoossu
solanaceous
aacelnorstt
translocate
aaceloopprs
laparoscope
aacelprssty
play-actress
aacelqrtuuu
aquaculture
aacelrstuuv
vasculature
aacennnortw
water-cannon
aacenoopssu
saponaceous
aacenorrtvy
contrayerva
aaceoopsstu
sapotaceous
aaceopprsuy
papyraceous
aacffiinort
affrication
aacffiorrtt
trafficator
aacfgiinnst
fascinating
aacfglnnort
conflagrant
aacfhorrttu
authorcraft
aacfhpssttu
upcast-shaft
aacfiillnny
financially
aacfiilortt
facilitator
aacfiinnost
fascination
aacfillnotv
lactoflavin
aacfillnrty
frantically
aacfilmorrs
scalariform
aacfilnorst
infracostal
aacfilrrrtu
curtal-friar
aacfimmnopr
campaniform
aacfinorrty
fractionary
aacfklmsuuv
vacuum-flask
aacflnorrtu
currant-loaf
aacfmnortuy
manufactory
aacfnorstuu
anfractuous
aacggillloo
algological
aacggilloor
agrological
aacggilnosy
synagogical
aacggilopty
ptyalagogic
aacghhilnot
Chilognatha
aacghhprtyy
tachygraphy
aacghiipprs
pasigraphic
aacghikmmnt
matchmaking
aacghikmntw
watch-making
aacghillpry
calligraphy
graphically
aacghilnnot
gnathonical
aacghimnrsy
gymnasiarch
aacghinrrst
starch-grain
aacghioprtu
autographic
aacghlmooru
chaulmoogra
aacghlnoory
arachnology
aacghnooppr
coprophagan
aacghnooprr
coronagraph
aacghoprrty
cartography
aacghoprssu
sarcophagus
aacgiillmns
Gallicanism
aacgiillntv
vacillating
aacgiilloox
axiological
aacgiilmnns
Anglicanism
aacgiilmstt
stalagmitic
stigmatical
aacgiilnnnt
lancinating
aacgiilnnor
Carolingian
aacgiilnost
agonistical
aacgiimrstt
magistratic
aacgiinostt
castigation
aacgiinpttv
captivating
aacgijnnrtu
jaunting-car
aacgiklnrty
track-laying
aacgillnory
organically
aacgillopst
post-glacial
aacgilmnsty
gymnastical
aacgilnootu
coagulation
aacgiloorst
acarologist
aacgilossuy
sagaciously
aacgimmnorr
marconigram
aacgimmnrtu
ungrammatic
aacgimoprty
Cryptogamia
aacginnottv
noctivagant
aacgiorstty
castigatory
aacgllnooty
octagonally
aacglmnoopy
campanology
aacgloortuy
coagulatory
aacgmnorsty
gastromancy
aacgrsssstu
tussac-grass
aachhinorrw
chain-harrow
aachhlorttt
throat-latch
aachiiinrst
Christiania
aachiillnrv
arch-villain
aachiilorst
ahistorical
aachiimnnot
machination
aachiimnsst
shamanistic
aachiinppst
captainship
ship-captain
aachiinrssu
saurischian
aachillopry
parochially
aachilmnoos
monochasial
aachilmostu
moustachial
aachilnopps
pansophical
aachilnoprt
anthropical
aachilnopry
paronychial
aachilnorst
thrasonical
aachilqrrsu
squirarchal
aachimmnoty
mythomaniac
aachimmorst
achromatism
aachimnnors
anachronism
aachimnoptt
phantomatic
aachimnorru
chain-armour
aachimnotty
Titanomachy
aachimopprr
paramorphic
aachinnnoty
anthocyanin
aachinorsst
anthracosis
aachinorstw
waist-anchor
aachiorrrtt
arch-traitor
aachippssty
pataphysics
aachiprsttu
parachutist
aachlloostu
holocaustal
aachlmorrty
lachrymator
aachlnnootu
anacoluthon
aachmmrrsuu
harum-scarum
aachmnostwy
yachtswoman
aachnnoorsu
anachronous
aachorrstty
Thyrostraca
aaciiilnnot
laciniation
aaciiilnost
laicisation
aaciiilpprt
participial
aaciijnottt
jactitation
aaciillmrtu
multiracial
aaciillnoot
coalitional
aaciillnotv
cavillation
vacillation
aaciillprty
capillarity
piratically
aaciillrsty
satirically
aaciilmnnot
antinomical
aaciilmnost
anomalistic
aaciilmnstt
Atlanticism
aaciilmprst
prismatical
aaciilnnnot
lancination
aaciilnoppt
application
aaciilnprtu
puritanical
aaciilnprty
patricianly
aaciilnptty
antitypical
aaciilnrstu
unsatirical
aaciilnsttt
Atlanticist
aaciiloprst
piscatorial
aaciilprstt
patristical
aaciilprtuy
piacularity
aaciilrrtuu
Utricularia
aaciilssttt
statistical
aaciimnnopt
mancipation
aaciimnnotu
acumination
aaciimnootx
toxicomania
aaciimnostt
mastication
aaciinnnort
incarnation
aaciinnnott
incantation

aaciinoosst
association
aaciinoprtt
anticipator
aaciinorttv
vaticinator
aaciinosttv
vacationist
aaciinpprtt
participant
aaciinpsstt
antispastic
aacilllopst
alloplastic
aacillmosty
somatically
aacillnoprs
rapscallion
aacillnopty
polyactinal
aacilloopst
apostolical
aacilloprsy
prosaically
aacillortvy
vacillatory
aacillossuy
salaciously
aacillprtuy
capitularly
aacillpssty
spastically
aacillrruuy
auricularly
aacilmnnopt
complainant
aacilmnootu
autonomical
aacilmnootx
taxonomical
aacilmnoprt
proclaimant
aacilmnopst
complaisant
aacilmnortu
calumniator
aacilmorrty
lacrimatory
aacilnnopsv
Pan-Slavonic
aacilnootuv
vacuolation
aacilnortvy
clairvoyant
aacilopprty
applicatory
aaciloprsuy
rapaciously
aacilopsttu
autoplastic
aacilorrttu
articulator
aacilorrtuy
oracularity

aacilrstuvy
vascularity
aacimnnnott
contaminant
aacimnnottu
mountain-cat
aacimnoostt
anastomotic
aacimnoprty
mancipatory
aacimorstty
masticatory
aacinnnortu
annunciator
aacinnorstt
transaction
aacinnortty
incantatory
aacinnrrstu
transuranic
aacinoooppt
apocopation
aacinoppstt
post-captain
aacinoprstt
pantisocrat
aacinoprstu
carnaptious
aaclmorrtyy
lacrymatory
aaclnnnoost
consonantal
aaclnpsttuu
tantalus-cup
aacloopprsy
laparoscopy
aacloprsstu
supracostal
aaclorsttuu
auscultator
aacmnoprtuy
paramountcy
aacmoorsstu
sarcomatous
aacnooprrtt
Pantocrator
aadddeeehl
addle-headed
aadddeehhry
hydra-headed
aadddeiilpt
dilapidated
aadddeiiops
Dasipodidae
aadddeilrrt
tarradiddle
aaddeeehhvy
heavy-headed
aaddeeellrv
alder-leaved
aaddeeghlnr
large-handed
aaddeeghnnr
hand-grenade

aaddeehhnvy
heavy-handed
aaddeehhrrt
hard-hearted
aaddeehkmrt
death-marked
aaddeehlpry
paraldehyde
aaddeehorrw
arrow-headed
aaddeemmquz
queez-maddam
aaddefhlpst
paddle-shaft
aaddeghinrr
hard-grained
aaddeghirsv
hard-visaged
aaddeghnors
dragon's-head
aaddeghnrtu
dreadnaught
aaddeginort
degradation
gradationed
aaddegirtty
tardy-gaited
aaddegllooy
logodaedaly
aaddehinnpt
hand-painted
aaddeiilppp
Pedipalpida
aaddeinrsst
standardise
aaddeioprsx
Paradoxides
aaddejlmstu
maladjusted
aaddellnnsu
unsandalled
aaddelnrstw
land-steward
aaddelpqruu
quadrupedal
aaddenrssst
dastardness
aaddghinrry
daring-hardy
aaddgiilort
digladiator
aaddiiloprt
dilapidator
aaddilloopr
olla-podrida
aaddilmnruy
laundry-maid
aadeeefhhrt
feather-head
aadeeefhlln
halfendeale
aadeeefnrsy
free-and-easy

aadeeeglprs
spread-eagle
aadeeehhlrt
leather-head
aadeeehkrtw
weak-hearted
aadeeehlnnr
enneahedral
aadeeehlprt
pale-hearted
aadeeelnrsv
sea-lavender
aadeeepprtu
depauperate
aadeefglllt
flagellated
aadeefhhlrt
half-hearted
aadeefilnrt
anti-federal
aadeefllnrt
trade-fallen
aadeegilpsv
pale-visaged
aadeegilrrt
laterigrade
aadeeginpsu
spade-guinea
aadeeginrtu
aguardiente
aadeegllruy
leaguer-lady
aadeehhprst
heart-shaped
aadeehiinrt
Atherinidae
aadeehjnrrw
Wanderjahre
aadeehkmrrt
threadmaker
aadeehkqrtu
earthquaked
aadeehlnnrt
neanderthal
aadeehlnppt
pad-elephant
aadeehlnprt
pentahedral
aadeehlrrtt
tetrahedral
aadeehlrttt
death-rattle
aadeehmnsss
ashamedness
aadeehmrrtw
warm-hearted
aadeehnrsvw
heavenwards
aadeehpprrt
thread-paper
aadeeillmvy
mediaevally
aadeeillnpr
plain-dealer

aadeeilnnrx
alexandrine
aadeeilnrtx
alexandrite
aadeeinnnnr
enneandrian
aadeeinppsw
weasand-pipe
aadeeinrstt
tear-stained
aadeeirrttv
retardative
aadeeirstvv
adversative
aadeeisttvv
devastative
aadeejpprww
wapper-jawed
aadeeklmsst
damask-steel
aadeellnttu
landaulette
aadeellrrst
stall-reader
aadeelmnrsu
land-measure
aadeelnpttt
pantaletted
aadeelprttt
rattle-pated
aadeelrrstv
slave-trader
aadeemnnntu
antemundane
aadeemortww
water-meadow
aadeemqrrsu
masquerader
aadeenprstu
unseparated
aadeeorrrst
rear-roasted
aadeeorrtwy
ready-to-wear
aadefghnrrt
grandfather
aadefgiilnr
fair-dealing
aadefgiistt
fastigiated
aadefglorrt
deflagrator
aadefhlrstv
half-starved
aadefimnort
foraminated
aadefllmmtu
flammulated
aadeflmnntu
fundamental
aadeflsstty
steadfastly
aadefnrrsty
transfer-day

aadefnssttu
unsteadfast
aadeggiinrr
Gregarinida
aadeggillrt
draggle-tail
aadeggilnnr
landing-gear
aadegglnrss
garden-glass
aadeghinrrw
hard-wearing
aadegiillrs
galliardise
aadegiilntt
intagliated
aadegilmnpr
reading-lamp
aadegilnnrv
landgravine
aadegilnprt
plantigrade
aadegilnrvw
waldgravine
aadeginntuv
unnavigated
aadeginsttv
devastating
aadegllnrss
garlandless
aadegmnrrst
grandmaster
aadegmorssw
meadow-grass
aadegnnopru
unparagoned
aadegnnprrt
grandparent
aadegooprst
Gasteropoda
aadehiilopp
paedophilia
aadehiinpty
diaphaneity
aadehilmnop
Monadelphia
aadehilmnpy
Nymphalidae
aadehilnnst
lanthanides
aadehilprst
sharp-tailed
aadehinoppy
hypnopaedia
aadehinostt
head-station
aadehipstxy
asphyxiated
aadehjmnors
John-a-dreams
aadehlmnrrs
marshlander
aadehlmnsuy
unashamedly

aadehnptuwy
unpathwayed
aadehpprsst
strap-shaped
aadehprsstt
spatterdash
aadeiiirrtv
irradiative
aadeiilmnst
mediastinal
aadeiilmort
mediatorial
aadeiilnrrt
interradial
aadeiinnqru
quadriennia
aadeiinorrt
reradiation
aadeiiprstt
paediatrist
aadeikmnort
demarkation
aadeilllmot
metalloidal
aadeillmrty
diametrally
aadeillnnps
land-spaniel
aadeillnopt
planetoidal
aadeilmnrty
aldermanity
aadeilnorst
desalinator
aadeilnotuv
devaluation
aadeilnpsst
displeasant
aadeilnssuw
duniewassal
aadeiloprtz
trapezoidal
aadeilprsty
disparately
aadeimmnnoo
demonomania
aadeimmnrst
disarmament
aadeimnnnop
Pandemonian
aadeimnnosw
madonnawise
aadeimnrstv
maid-servant
servant-maid
aadeinnnprt
pentandrian
aadeinnnrst
transandine
aadeinnrrtt
tetrandrian
aadeinntttu
unattainted

aadeinoprtv
depravation
aadeinorrtt
retardation
aadeinorsst
diatessaron
aadeinosttv
devastation
aadeinpqrsu
pasquinader
aadeinprstu
unaspirated
aadeipsstww
wasp-waisted
aadeklnnrrt
dark-lantern
aadeknrssww
awkwardness
aadellmnsty
lady's-mantle
aadellnnort
rallentando
aadelnnoopt
pantalooned
aadelnprstu
pasture-land
aadelorrttu
adulterator
aademnoostu
adenomatous
aademnorstw
tradeswoman
aadennnottu
unannotated
aadennrrtuw
unwarranted
aadenprsttt
stand-patter
aadenrrsttu
understrata
aadenrsswwy
waywardness
aadenrsttuu
unsaturated
aadeoqrrrtu
quarter-road
aadeorrrtty
retardatory
aadffiinopr
paraffinoid
aadfghillnn
half-landing
aadfghinnst
handfasting
aadfhhilloy
half-holiday
aadfmnoorrs
mansard-roof
aadggiilnpr
paragliding
aadghhiknns
handshaking
aadghhilmnn
Highlandman

aadghhoprsw
shadowgraph
aadghinossw
washing-soda
aadghinrsww
wash-drawing
aadghioprry
radiography
aadghlrrryy
hydrargyral
aadghmnopry
dynamograph
aadghmnrstu
draughtsman
aadgiiimntw
waiting-maid
aadgiillnov
Gallovidian
aadgiilmrst
madrigalist
aadgiilnnno
Anglo-Indian
aadgikllnwy
walking-lady
aadgiklnotw
walking-toad
aadgilnnost
Gladstonian
aadginoprtu
upgradation
aadhhnooptw
wood-naphtha
aadhiiiknrs
kaisar-i-Hind
aadhiilmprs
admiralship
aadhiilnopr
dolphinaria
aadhiimoprs
adiaphorism
aadhiinoprs
Aphrodisian
aadhiioprst
adiaphorist
aadhinnostt
station-hand
aadhiooprsu
adiaphorous
aadhiopprty
paratyphoid
aadhioprrty
parathyroid
aadhlooprrt
arthropodal
aadhlorsuyz
hazardously
aadhmoorsty
hydrosomata
aadhnopqruy
quadraphony
aadhnorsuuz
unhazardous
aadiiinorrt
irradiation

aadiijnostu
Judaisation
aadiillnttu
altitudinal
latitudinal
aadiilnopss
anadiplosis
aadiilnortt
traditional
aadiilntttu
attitudinal
aadiilosuuv
audio-visual
aadiimnopst
adoptianism
aadiinopstt
adoptianist
aadillmnnoy
Madonna-lily
aadillmnoot
amontillado
aadillmorty
maladroitly
aadillmpryy
pyramidally
aadilmoprrt
port-admiral
aadilmoprru
parlour-maid
aadilnnoprt
Portlandian
aadiloorstv
vasodilator
aadilopprsv
disapproval
aadimnnssyy
syndyasmian
aadinoprssu
sauropsidan
aadirrsstuu
Straduarius
aadkmoorstu
katadromous
aadllmrstuw
wall-mustard
aadlmooprwy
palmyra-wood
aadmnorsstu
Nostradamus
aadmooopstt
Stomatopoda
aaeeefhprtt
feather-pate
aaeeegghrtw
weather-gage
aaeeegipqtu
tea-equipage
aaeeegrsstu
sausage-tree
aaeeegrstwy
steerage-way
aaeeehlnpst
sea-elephant

aaeeehnrrtw
earthenware
aaeeehnrtvw
weather-vane
aaeeehprttu
Therapeutae
aaeeelmnppr
paper-enamel
aaeeemnppst
appeasement
aaeeemprstu
tape-measure
aaeefhhilrt
faith-healer
aaeefhhllrt
half-leather
aaeefhilrtt
tail-feather
aaeefhirrtw
fair-weather
aaeefhlmprt
feather-palm
aaeefhlmrsu
half-measure
aaeefhrrstt
feather-star
aaeefiinnst
fainéantise
aaeeflstvvy
safety-valve
aaeegggirtv
aggregative
aaeeggglrty
aggregately
aaeegginnrw
wage-earning
aaeegglmort
agglomerate
aaeeggorrtx
exaggerator
aaeeghhmorr
haemorrhage
aaeeghinrst
heart-easing
aaeeghllrtw
weather-gall
aaeeghloops
oesophageal
aaeeghnpprr
paper-hanger
aaeeghrrttx
tax-gatherer
aaeegiklntv
leave-taking
aaeegiknnrw
reawakening
aaeegillins
selaginella
aaeegillltt
tagliatelle
aaeegillnnt
gentianella
aaeegilmssx
sexagesimal

aaeegilnppt
eating-apple
aaeegilnrvy
evangeliary
aaeegilprtt
tetraplegia
aaeeginnops
neopaganise
aaeeginprss
paragenesis
aaeeginrrtw
graniteware
aaeegknrrst
garter-snake
aaeeglllsvy
galley-slave
aaeegllrssu
leaguer-lass
aaeeglmnopt
planogamete
aaeeglnnorv
navel-orange
aaeeglnsstv
vantageless
aaeeglprsty
stage-player
aaeegmnnrrt
arrangement
aaeegmnoprt
pomegranate
aaeegmnsstu
assuagement
aaeegmrssss
sesame-grass
aaeegnpprrt
garnet-paper
aaeehhlnnpt
naphthalene
aaeehhlrstw
wash-leather
aaeehiilmns
leishmaniae
aaeehillmnw
wheel-animal
aaeehilmopr
hemeralopia
aaeehimmnpt
amphetamine
aaeehimmstt
mathematise
aaeehimnort
etheromania
aaeehinrstt
Anthesteria
aaeehinssst
anaesthesis
aaeehkmprrs
phrasemaker
aaeehllmnoy
hyalomelane
aaeehllsttu
haustellate
aaeehmmmrst
steam-hammer

aaeehmmrrtw
water-hammer
aaeehmnoorr
amenorrhoea
aaeehprsttt
shatter-pate
aaeeiilltvv
alleviative
aaeeiilmrst
materialise
aaeeiilrrst
arterialise
aaeeiilrttv
retaliative
aaeeiinrssv
sansevieria
aaeeiipttvx
expatiative
aaeeikllmrt
alkalimeter
aaeeilllprs
parallelise
aaeeillmprx
premaxillae
aaeeillpptv
appellative
aaeeillqrtu
equilateral
aaeeilmmpst
semipalmate
aaeeilnnprt
penetralian
aaeeilnoprt
peritonaeal
aaeeilnppss
epanalepsis
aaeeilnptvx
explanative
aaeeilnrttv
alternative
aaeeilpsttt
latiseptate
aaeeimnsstv
amativeness
aaeeimssstt
metastasise
aaeeioprtvv
evaporative
aaeeiorsttx
stereotaxia
aaeeipprrrs
reappraiser
aaeeipprrtv
preparative
aaeeisttttv
attestative
aaeeklmrtuv
market-value
aaeeklnrstt
rattlesnake
aaeelllmnos
salmonellae
aaeellnrtty
alternately

aaeellrrtuw
laurel-water
aaeelmnpprt
apparelment
aaeelmnsttt
testamental
aaeelmprrtw
plate-warmer
aaeelnnpttv
pentavalent
aaeelnopsvw
weapon-salve
aaeelnpqrru
quarrel-pane
aaeelnprssu
sea-purslane
aaeelnpsttt
pantalettes
aaeelnrrstt
retranslate
aaeelnrtttv
tetravalent
aaeeloprttx
extrapolate
aaeelqrrstu
quarter-seal
aaeelrrsttu
serratulate
aaeemmprrsu
map-measurer
aaeemmprtuy
empyreumata
aaeemnoprtt
treponemata
aaeemnorstz
estramazone
aaeemnortux
auxanometer
aaeemnrsttt
testamentar
aaeemorrssy
sea-rosemary
aaeemqrsstu
marquessate
aaeennrssuw
unawareness
aaeenprrttt
tetrapteran
aaeenprsttt
transeptate
aaeeoprrstx
exasperator
aaefffftttu
tufftaffeta
aaefffilrss
self-affairs
aaeffftttu
tufttaffeta
aaeffiimrtv
affirmative
aaefghilnrt
farthingale
aaefgikllnw
walking-leaf

aaefgillnrt
tear-falling
aaefgilprst
septifragal
aaefglllort
flagellator
aaefgmnrrty
fragmentary
aaefhillnt
hälleflinta
aaefhilmrrs
fire-marshal
aaefhilnrtw
father-in-law
aaefiiilmrs
familiarise
aaefiiorrsv
savoir-faire
aaefilmmnrt
firmamental
aaefilmnrty
filamentary
aaefiloprrt
prefatorial
aaefllnrrty
fraternally
aaefllorrtx
extra-floral
aaefmmnorst
foremastman
aaeggginort
aggregation
aaeggillnow
Gallowegian
aaeggilnttu
agglutinate
aaeggimmntu
gametangium
aaeggimnnuz
magazine-gun
aaegginrssu
guinea-grass
aaegglmmoru
grammalogue
aaeggloptuy
ptyalagogue
aaeggmmnrst
gammerstang
aaeggmnorst
steganogram
aaeggnorrss
orange-grass
aaeggnorruw
narrow-gauge
aaeghhippry
hyperphagia
aaeghimnorr
menorrhagia
aaeghimnprs
managership
aaeghinoort
Ornithogaea
aaeghllnoxy
hexagonally

aaeghlmooty
haematology
aaeghlnnopy
angelophany
aaeghlprstu
Tragelaphus
aaeghmoprrs
phraseogram
aaeghmrttuu
thaumaturge
aaeghnoprty
Pythagorean
aaeghnprrst
strap-hanger
aaegiiimntv
imaginative
aaegiilmnps
Pelagianism
aaegiilmnrs
marginalise
aaegiilmrst
magisterial
aaegiimmnrt
immarginate
aaegiimmrrs
mismarriage
aaegiinnotv
evagination
aaegiinortv
variegation
aaegiirttvv
gravitative
aaegikmnppr
paper-making
aaegiknnnuw
unawakening
aaegilllnpr
paralleling
aaegillnppr
apparelling
aaegillnppy
appealingly
aaegilmmnos
Maglemosian
aaegilmnnos
nonagesimal
aaegilmnrty
ligamentary
aaegilmnstu
glutaminase
aaegilnnrtt
alternating
aaegilnoprs
saprolegnia
aaegilnostt
gestational
aaegilnppsy
appeasingly
aaegilnprsv
palsgravine
aaegilnqruu
equiangular
aaegilnrttu
triangulate

aaegilnrtuv
granulative
aaegilorstt
gestatorial
aaegilprrsu
Spergularia
aaegimnnops
neopaganism
aaegimnnrrt
arraignment
aaegimprrst
pragmatiser
aaeginnnpty
pentagynian
aaeginnrtty
tetragynian
aaeginoprst
aspergation
aaegiopprtv
propagative
aaegiopstty
steatopygia
aaegkllmnos
maskallonge
aaegllnnsst
gallantness
aaegllnorty
angelolatry
aaegllorrst
Grallatores
aaegllorssu
sausage-roll
aaeglmnrtty
termagantly
aaeglnnprtu
pentangular
aaeglnrsttu
strangulate
aaeglorsstt
tessaraglot
aaegnnortwy
orange-tawny
aaegnoqrssu
squarsonage
aaegorrtuuv
autogravure
aaehhiilmop
haemophilia
aaehhilnpst
naphthalise
aaehiimnops
hemianopsia
aaehiimnsst
histaminase
aaehiknprss
Shaksperian
aaehillprrt
earth-pillar
aaehilnoopy
hypoaeolian
aaehilnpstw
Westphalian
aaehiloorrs
sialorrhoea

aaehilpprsy
hyperplasia
aaehimossst
haemostasis
aaehimprsst
metaphrasis
aaehimprstu
amateurship
aaehlnprsty
phalanstery
aaehlprsstw
water-splash
aaehmnorstu
athermanous
aaehmnorsww
washerwoman
aaehmoprttu
thaumatrope
aaehmpprsty
Spermaphyta
aaehnopprrs
paranephros
aaehoprsttw
potash-water
aaeiillmnnr
millenarian
aaeiillmnrt
matrilineal
aaeiillnnot
allineation
aaeiillnotv
alleviation
aaeiillnprt
patrilineal
aaeiillnrsv
Vallisneria
aaeiillprst
ipsilateral
aaeiilmmrst
materialism
aaeiilmnrrt
air-terminal
matrilinear
aaeiilmrstt
materialist
aaeiilmrtty
materiality
aaeiilnnntv
Valentinian
aaeiilnnost
nationalise
aaeiilnnpst
Palestinian
aaeiilnorst
rationalise
realisation
aaeiilnortt
retaliation
aaeiilnprrt
patrilinear
aaeiilnrttv
tire-valiant
aaeiilnstty
insatiately

aaeiilpprss
paraleipsis
aaeiilqttuv
qualitative
aaeiimnnort
reanimation
aaeiimnnott
antimoniate
aaeiimnnotx
examination
exanimation
aaeiimnrsst
Erastianism
aaeiinnpprt
paripinnate
aaeiinnsttt
instantiate
aaeiinopttx
expatiation
aaeiinosttv
aestivation
aaeikllmrty
alkalimetry
aaeikllttvy
talkatively
aaeiklmnopt
kleptomania
aaeiklmorrs
sailor-maker
aaeilllmprs
parallelism
aaeillllpptu
papillulate
aaeilllprst
parallelist
aaeillnoppt
appellation
aaeillorttu
ratatouille
aaeillortvy
alleviatory
aaeillpprst
epiplastral
aaeillqrstu
aquarellist
aaeilmnnott
lamentation
aaeilmnnrsu
semi-annular
aaeilmnorst
monasterial
aaeilmnprst
paternalism
aaeilmnprtu
planetarium
aaeilmnrrtu
ultramarine
aaeilnnopsx
expansional
aaeilnnoptx
explanation
aaeilnnortt
alternation

aaeilnnosst
sensational
aaeilnnprst
transalpine
aaeilnnpsst
plainstanes
aaeilnnpttu
antenuptial
aaeilnooprt
operational
aaeilnopppry
piano-player
player-piano
aaeilnoprrt
proletarian
aaeilnoprss
anaplerosis
aaeilnortuv
revaluation
aaeilnossty
seasonality
aaeilnrrstt
intertarsal
aaeilnrrstu
sertularian
aaeilnrrtvy
narratively
aaeilopprrs
paper-sailor
aaeiloprrtt
proletariat
aaeiloqrstu
quaestorial
aaeilorrtty
retaliatory
aaeilorssss
assessorial
aaeilqrrrtu
quarter-rail
aaeimnnottu
mountain-tea
aaeimnnrrst
transmarine
aaeimnntttt
attaintment
aaeimopprtx
approximate
aaeinnoprtt
trepanation
aaeinnosstt
assentation
aaeinnotttu
attenuation
aaeinnrrsvy
anniversary
aaeinooprtv
evaporation
aaeinoorstt
aerostation
aaeinopprrt
preparation
aaeinorrstt
arrestation

aaeinostttt
attestation
aaeioppprrt
appropriate
aaeioprrstu
Pterosauria
aaeioprttxy
expatiatory
aaeiorssttv
assortative
aaekmmnortw
market-woman
aaellmrsstt
stall-master
aaellopsstt
Elastoplast®
aaellrssttt
Tattersall's
aaelmnoorsv
vomeronasal
aaelmnoprss
salmon-spear
aaelmnsstty
statesmanly
aaelmoprrtu
armour-plate
plate-armour
aaelnnrsstu
naturalness
aaelnooppprs
aplanospore
aaelnoprtxy
explanatory
aaelnrrsstv
transversal
aaelnrssstv
servant-lass
aaelnrsstux
transsexual
aaeloopppt t
potato-apple
aaemmnoortt
Monotremata
aaemmnorsst
master-mason
aaemnnoostz
amazon-stone
aaemnoossst
anastomoses
aaemnoprttu
portmanteau
aaemnorsttu
atramentous
aaemnossttw
stateswoman
aaemnpprtty
part-payment
aaemooprstz
spermatozoa
aaemorssttt
toastmaster
aaennpprttu
appurtenant

aaennprrstt
transparent
aaennprsttu
supernatant
aaeoopprrrt
paratrooper
aaeopprrrty
preparatory
aaeoprssttu
stratopause
aaeoprssttw
potass-water
aaeqrrrtuwy
quarry-water
aaffghhiins
haaf-fishing
aaffgilopst
gaff-topsail
aaffiiilnot
affiliation
aaffiilnopr
paraffin-oil
aaffiimnort
affirmation
aaffimorrty
affirmatory
aafggggilnw
flag-wagging
aafgiilnott
flagitation
aafgikmnnrt
tank-farming
aafgillmruy
gallimaufry
aafgilnostt
stagflation
aafginorrsu
farraginous
aafhilllllsy
fallalishly
aafiiilmrty
familiarity
aafiiimnnrr
infirmarian
aafiilnrstu
fustilarian
aafiinnottu
infatuation
aafimnnnrty
infantryman
aafinnooprt
profanation
aafioqrsttu
aquafortist
aaflnnoorst
nasofrontal
aafnooprrty
profanatory
aagggh ilnsu
laughing-gas
aagggilnssz
glass-gazing
aagghhiinns
shanghaiing

aagghhiopry
hagiography
aagghinopry
angiography
aaggilnnttu
agglutinant
aaggimnrstu
Gargantuism
aagginrsttu
Gargantuist
aaggllllossw
gallowglass
aaggnnoortu
orang-outang
aaghhloppry
haplography
aaghhopprty
pathography
aaghiiinrrs
hair-raising
aaghiillnop
anglophilia
aaghiilnrtv
rival-hating
aaghillmnpy
lymphangial
aaghillmnrs
marshalling
aaghilnrssy
harassingly
aaghiloprsy
sialography
aaghimrrstt
straight-arm
aaghinopssv
shaving-soap
aaghiopprty
typographia
aaghirsttwy
straightway
aaghlnootty
thanatology
aaghmmmopry
mammography
aaghmmnoorr
harmonogram
aaghnopprty
pantography
aaghnoprruy
uranography
aaghoopstuu
autophagous
aagiiillnrs
sigillarian
aagiiimnnot
imagination
aagiiknnpst
painstaking
aagiilmnnty
animatingly
aagiilnnstt
tantalising
aagiimmnnty
magnanimity

aagiimmsstt
astigmatism
aagiinnorss
anagnorisis
aagiinnosst
assignation
aagiinnptwx
wax-painting
aagiinnsttu
unsatiating
aagiinnstuu
Augustinian
aagiinorttv
gravitation
aagiirssttu
Sagittarius
aagiklnprtw
walking-part
aagillnppy
appallingly
aagilllooss
glossolalia
aagillmnnty
malignantly
aagillmoory
malariology
aagilmmmost
mammalogist
aagilnnopss
Panglossian
aagilnnortu
granulation
aagilnorttu
gratulation
aagilnosuvy
Yugoslavian
aagilnrrtuy
granularity
aagiloprrtu
purgatorial
aagimmnnosu
magnanimous
aaginoopprt
propagation
aaginoprrtu
purgatorian
aaginorrtuu
inaugurator
aaglllnntuy
ungallantly
aagllmnrtuu
multangular
aagllnoosuy
analogously
aaglmnnnoor
Anglo-Norman
aaglmoopsuy
apogamously
aaglnooprtw
patrol-wagon
aaglorrttuy
gratulatory
aahhilmprss
marshalship

aahhlloptty
Thallophyta
aahhmoprsst
Rhamphastos
aahiilmnnot
Hamiltonian
aahiilmnsst
Stahlianism
aahiilnnort
annihilator
aahiilnnrsv
nail-varnish
aahiilnoort
hariolation
aahiilprswy
ship-railway
aahiinprsst
antiphrasis
aahiinpsttt
antipathist
aahijnnnoos
Johnsoniana
aahillloprt
prothallial
aahillmnopy
phyllomania
aahillopstt
allopathist
aahilloptxy
litholapaxy
aahilppssst
pissasphalt
aahimmnnopy
nymphomania
aahimnnostu
mountain-ash
aahimnoprss
oarsmanship
aahinnoprty
antiphonary
aahinopsstt
thanatopsis
aahioprstxy
asphyxiator
aahknoorttv
katavothron
aahkoprrsww
sparrow-hawk
aahllmmorsw
marshmallow
aahlloprsty
hyoplastral
aahmnnrsttu
transhumant
aahmnooprsu
anamorphous
aahnoopstuu
autophanous
aahnoprttuy
naturopathy
aahoprrsttt
throat-strap
aaiiilnrttu
utilitarian

aaiiimmnnrs
Arminianism
aaiiimnnnot
inanimation
aaiiimnnttv
anti-vitamin
aaiiinnrrtt
Trinitarian
aaiikmnoprt
imparkation
aaiilllnpsu
sinupallial
aaiilllpsuz
lapis-lazuli
aaiillmmnot
mamillation
aaiillmprty
impartially
aaiillnoprs
Apollinaris
aaiillnprst
pillar-saint
aaiilmmnort
matrimonial
aaiilmmnpss
panislamism
aaiilmnnost
nationalism
aaiilmnnotv
nominatival
aaiilmnoprt
patrimonial
aaiilmnopst
maintopsail
aaiilmnoptu
tulipomania
aaiilmnorst
rationalism
aaiilmnpsst
panislamist
aaiilnnostt
nationalist
aaiilnnotty
nationality
aaiilnoortv
variolation
aaiilnopptt
palpitation
aaiilnorstt
rationalist
aaiilnorttt
attritional
aaiilnortty
rationality
aaiilnosttu
situational
aaiilnotttu
attuitional
aaiimmnorsv
Moravianism
aaiimnnostv
Novatianism
aaiimnoostt
atomisation

aaiimnoprtt
impartation
aaiimnopstt
impastation
aaiimnorrst
Rotarianism
aaiimnprtvy
parvanimity
aaiinnoqttu
antiquation
aaiinnosttv
Novatianist
aaiioprssst
parasitosis
aailllostww
swallow-tail
aaillmnpruu
plumularian
aaillnruuvv
univalvular
aailloopryz
polyzoarial
aaillorrstt
latirostral
aaillorrsty
sartorially
aaillrrtuvv
trivalvular
aailmmnostu
summational
aailmmopprs
malapropism
aailmnoprtu
manipulator
aailmnrsttt
transmittal
aailmoprsst
pastoralism
aailnnorstt
translation
aailnoppssy
Passion-play
aailnoptuuv
upvaluation
aailoorsttt
totalisator
aailoprrsuv
larviparous
aailoprsstt
pastoralist
aaimmnnoory
monomyarian
aaimmnopstt
maintopmast
aaimnooostt
somatotonia
aaimnoossst
anastomosis
aainnnoprst
non-partisan
aainooprstt
asportation
aainoorrstz
Zoroastrian

aainorrsttu
instaurator
aaiopprsuvv
papovavirus
aallnnrtuuy
unnaturally
aalmmoopsst
somatoplasm
aalmnooprtw
patrolwoman
aalmnoprtuy
paramountly
aalmnprstuy
palmyra-nuts
aalnnrrstuy
translunary
aalnoprrstt
transportal
aalnoprstuy
uranoplasty
aalnorrstty
translatory
aamnooprsty
Trypanosoma
aamnprsstty
smartypants
aamooprrtuu
out-paramour
aannorrstuy
tyrannosaur
abbbbeelruy
abbey-lubber
abbbcellnuu
unclubbable
abbbcenoruy
baby-bouncer
abbbdeloorw
wobble-board
abbbeelmnrt
brabblement
abbbehlmrsu
bramble-bush
abbberrrssu
brass-rubber
abbccdehknu
bunch-backed
abbcceehknr
backbencher
abbcceehmor
beachcomber
abbcceeinor
bone-breccia
abbccekklor
back-blocker
abbcdeefiko
biofeedback
abbcdeeilrs
describable
abbcdeenrss
crabbedness
abbcdeensss
scabbedness
abbcdeiklrr
blackbirder

abbcdeklorw
black-browed
abbcdgiklno
black-boding
abbceeehrrs
bear's-breech
abbceeekllt
black-beetle
abbceeklort
beta-blocker
abbceellort
corbel-table
abbcehiikln
kibble-chain
abbcehiilot
bibliotheca
abbcehillmr
bill-chamber
abbceiilnrs
inscribable
abbcejkorwy
jabberwocky
abbcgiiillo
bibliogical
abbchhirttu
rabbit-hutch
abbchiilost
Hobbistical
abbchinprtu
rabbit-punch
abbciilmnoy
bibliomancy
abbddegiorr
bridgeboard
abbddeiinrr
bird-brained
abbdeeefinr
beef-brained
abbdeeilrst
bestridable
abbdeelortu
redoubtable
abbdeiilntu
indubitable
abbdeiinrru
india-rubber
abbdeilortu
boat-builder
abbdelnotuu
undoubtable
abbdelnsuuu
unsubduable
abbdemmnort
bombardment
abbdffiloru
buffalo-bird
abbdgginnor
Brobdingnag
abbdgiinrtt
bird-batting
abbdgijlnno
land-jobbing
abbdiilntuy
indubitably

abbeeeilnrt
beetlebrain
abbeeklrstu
stubble-rake
abbeelprrtu
perturbable
abbeemnsstu
subbasement
abbefflooru
buffalo-robe
abbegghlmuu
humbuggable
abbegijlnry
jabberingly
abbehhiprsu
rubbish-heap
abbehillpsu
publishable
abbehiorrty
bribery-oath
abbehlorrty
barley-broth
abbehnoortt
berthon-boat
abbeiillort
bibliolater
abbeijnortt
rabbet-joint
abbeilortty
liberty-boat
abbeinrssuu
suburbanise
abbeinrstuu
suburbanite
abbellmrsuu
subumbrella
abbelorrrtu
retrobulbar
abbemprrstu
rubber-stamp
abbgiillntu
bull-baiting
abbgiinstty
baby-sitting
abbgilnorsy
absorbingly
abbginorrss
ribbon-grass
abbgllorsuu
subglobular
abbiillorty
bibliolatry
abbiilmnoot
bombilation
abbiilmoprs
probabilism
abbiiloprst
probabilist
abbiiloprty
probability
abbiimnnoot
bombination
abbimnoortu
obumbration

abbimnrssuu
suburbanism
abbinrstuuy
suburbanity
abbllllooyy
loblolly-bay
abccccilory
carbocyclic
abccchkkloo
chock-a-block
abcccilmoox
coxcombical
abccddhiiky
chick-a-biddy
abccdeeiirt
bactericide
abccdeennos
abscondence
abccdefhikn
finch-backed
abccdehhknu
hunchbacked
abccdehirrt
bird-catcher
abccdehlstu
scutch-blade
abccdeiiill
bacillicide
abccdekkoor
crookbacked
abccdkllnou
cock-and-bull
abcceeehrsu
beach-rescue
abcceehklnu
uncheckable
abcceeilmrs
marcescible
abcceeilnoo
eccaleobion
abcceeilnov
conceivable
abcceeklopu
peacock-blue
abcceelllot
collectable
abcceelnnot
connectable
abcceelorrt
correctable
abcceemnnru
encumbrance
abcceemrsuu
sea-cucumber
abcceeprrst
spectre-crab
abccefilnos
confiscable
abccefiorsu
bacciferous
abcceginnou
concubinage
abccehiilmo
biochemical
abccehikmrs
sick-chamber
abccehilstt
cable-stitch
abccehinrtt
tectibranch
abccehoortt
boot-catcher
abcceiillno
conciliable
abcceiilpty
peccability
abcceikklpr
prickle-back
abcceikklst
stickleback
abcceiklmrt
balm-cricket
abcceilnovy
conceivably
abcceilnssu
cubicalness
abcceilortu
corbiculate
abcceilostt
ectoblastic
abcceinorrt
centrobaric
abcceinrrty
barycentric
abcceiooppt
tobacco-pipe
abccelorsuu
succourable
abcceoorttu
cocoa-butter
abcchklnost
snatch-block
abcciillnsu
subclinical
abcciilrstu
subcritical
abcciimoort
macrobiotic
abcciiorssu
scribacious
abcciklmnor
crambo-clink
abccikmmoru
cork-cambium
abccilorstu
scorbutical
subcortical
abccinnoruy
concubinary
abccinnottu
concubitant
abccinoostt
tobacconist
abccinortuy
buccinatory
abccioorsuv
baccivorous
abccknoootu
account-book
book-account
abccknortuy
back-country
abccnorsttu
subcontract
abcddeeelns
descendable
abcddeeflou
double-faced
abcddeehluy
debauchedly
abcddeehnuu
undebauched
abcddeeilnu
undecidable
abcddeelnos
close-banded
abcddefinor
forbiddance
abcddeflooy
bloody-faced
abcddeknoru
round-backed
abcddenorss
crossbanded
abcdeeeerrt
decerebrate
abcdeeehors
cheese-board
abcdeeekorr
code-breaker
abcdeefhill
bleach-field
abcdeehmntu
debauchment
abcdeeiilmm
immedicable
abcdeeiilmn
medicinable
abcdeeillmn
clean-limbed
abcdeeilorv
divorceable
abcdeeilprt
predictable
abcdeeinors
decarbonise
abcdeeirrsu
decarburise
abcdeellnry
belly-dancer
abcdeelmmno
commendable
abcdeelmnno
condemnable
abcdeelnnos
condensable
abcdeelnrry
candle-berry
abcdeelopsu
double-space
abcdeelorrs
close-barred
abcdeenorrt
centre-board
abcdeerrttu
carburetted
abcdefiinrr
bird-fancier
abcdeghiinr
chain-bridge
abcdegiklns
sling-backed
abcdehikprs
brickshaped
abcdehilstw
switchblade
abcdehirrtw
bird-watcher
abcdehlmoor
bachelordom
abcdeiilmru
Lumbricidae
abcdeiiloss
dissociable
abcdeiiltuy
educability
abcdeiinstu
subindicate
abcdeiipstu
bicuspidate
abcdeilorrs
soldier-crab
abcdeilsssu
discussable
abcdeinoort
notice-board
abcdeinrstu
disturbance
abcdeiooprs
Proboscidea
abcdeiorrsv
scrive-board
abcdeipprty
bradypeptic
abcdelloruy
boulder-clay
abcdelmmnoy
commendably
abcdenorsuy
subdeaconry
abcdeorrrss
crossbarred
abcdgiiklns
backsliding
abcdgiknnow
backing-down
abcdhiimrty
dithyrambic
abcdhiirstu
Hudibrastic
abcdhinoopr
branchiopod
abcdhiopstx
dispatch-box
abcdhiorstw
switchboard
abcdhlooors
board-school
school-board
abcdhnoorry
hydrocarbon
abcdiiilost
idioblastic
abcdiilossy
dissociably
abcdiimnosy
biodynamics
abcdmnorruu
Carborundum®
abceeefflot
coffee-table
abceeefiint
beneficiate
abceeeflnor
enforceable
abceeegllnt
neglectable
abceeehmnrt
beech-marten
abceeeilmpr
imperceable
abceeeilnrx
inexecrable
abceeeilprv
perceivable
abceeeilptt
battle-piece
abceeeilrsv
serviceable
abceeeilrsx
exercisable
abceeelmnrs
resemblance
abceeelorrv
recoverable
abceeelprru
recuperable
abceeelprst
respectable
abceeemmnrr
remembrance
abceeemmnrt
embracement
abceefghorr
herb-of-grace
abceefhmmru
fume-chamber
abceefiilps
specifiable
abceefiilrt
certifiable
rectifiable
abceefiinry
beneficiary
abceefillmr
leaf-climber
abceefinnot
benefaction

abceefinrtu
rubefacient
abceeflnorr
conferrable
abceefnorty
benefactory
abceeghllnt
cable-length
abceegiimpt
gambit-piece
abceegiinot
abiogenetic
abceeglopru
barge-couple
abceehiklpu
pickelhaube
abceehilmst
thimble-case
abceehinpst
spinach-beet
abceehklnos
shackle-bone
abceehorrrt
torch-bearer
abceeiilntx
inexcitable
abceeijottv
objectivate
abceeillmpt
Campbellite
abceeillntu
ineluctable
abceeilmrrs
cerebralism
abceeilnort
celebration
abceeilnsux
inexcusable
abceeilntux
unexcitable
abceeilorrv
irrevocable
abceeilprvy
perceivably
abceeilrrst
cerebralist
abceeilrrsu
irrecusable
abceeilrsvy
serviceably
abceeilrttx
extractible
abceeilssst
ecblastesis
abceeimrtuu
eubacterium
abceeinnost
incense-boat
abceeinnrty
bicentenary
abceeinorrt
cerebration
abceeinortx
exorbitance

abceeiorstt
stereobatic
abceekkorrr
rock-breaker
abceelllmop
compellable
abceellmopt
completable
abceellmrsu
mallee-scrub
abceelnoqru
conquerable
abceelnorsv
conservable
conversable
abceelnostt
contestable
abceelnrssu
curableness
abceeloprrr
procerebral
abceelprsty
respectably
abceelpsstu
suspectable
abceelrttuu
tuberculate
abceenorrst
arborescent
abceenorstu
counterbase
abceenprrtu
perturbance
abceeorrrss
crossbearer
abceeorstuu
tuberaceous
abceerrrttu
carburetter
abcefhiklrs
black-fisher
abcefhnoopr
francophobe
abcefiilrty
certifiably
abcefilmnor
confirmable
abcefinortu
rubefaction
abcefklllow
blackfellow
abceflmnoor
conformable
abceflmoort
comfortable
abcegiilnot
incogitable
abcegilmnry
embracingly
abcegilnnos
consignable
abcegilnost
blastogenic

abcegjlosst
object-glass
abcegklorsu
blackgrouse
abcegorstuy
subcategory
abcehhkrsuw
bushwhacker
abcehiimrst
Rechabitism
abcehiimrsw
Micawberish
abcehilmors
bachelorism
abcehimrtty
bathymetric
abcehinoopr
necrophobia
abcehioprrs
broach-spire
abcehkllost
shackle-bolt
abcehklnosu
unshockable
abcehlnnoru
luncheon-bar
abcehlnotuu
untouchable
abcehlnrsuu
uncrushable
abcehlorttt
bottle-chart
abcehnoorrw
bower-anchor
abceiiillsv
civilisable
abceiiiostv
bisociative
abceiijlstu
justiciable
abceiiklnrt
tickle-brain
abceiilmnru
Mulciberian
abceiilrtuv
lubricative
abceiimmrsw
Micawberism
abceiimnotv
combinative
abceiiorsst
bacteriosis
abceiklrrru
bulk-carrier
abceilllops
collapsible
abceillloqu
colliquable
abceillrtuv
carvel-built
abceilmoprs
comprisable
abceilmoprt
problematic

abceilmorst
meroblastic
abceilmosst
mesoblastic
abceilnnotu
continuable
abceilnortv
contrivable
abceilnrstu
inscrutable
abceilnsuxy
inexcusably
abceilorrsu
orbiculares
abceilorrvy
irrevocably
abceilorstt
obstetrical
abceilpstuu
usucaptible
abceilrrsuy
irrecusably
abceilrstuu
bursiculate
abceilrstuv
subvertical
abceimnnort
recombinant
abceimnoort
embrocation
abceinoorst
obsecration
abceinorrtu
carburetion
abceinortxy
exorbitancy
abceinrrrst
transcriber
abceiooprrt
bicorporate
abceirsttuv
subtractive
abcellmnoos
salmon-coble
abcelmortuu
tuberculoma
abcelnnortu
contubernal
abcelnnotuu
uncountable
abcelnorstu
construable
abcelnorsvy
conversably
abcelorssuu
scaberulous
abceooorrrt
corroborate
abceorrrttu
carburettor
abceorstuuy
butyraceous
abcfhinoost
sonofabitch

abcfiillmor
bacilliform
abcfiinortu
bifurcation
abcfinoostu
obfuscation
abcflmnoory
conformably
abcflmoorty
comfortably
abcghiknsuw
buck-washing
abcghilnoop
anglophobic
abcgiikkmnr
brickmaking
abcgiiklnry
bricklaying
abcgiiknouv
bivouacking
abcgiknpssu
buck-passing
abcgillmnsy
scamblingly
abcgilloory
bryological
abchhiilott
batholithic
abchhiilty
bathylithic
abchhilooop
ochlophobia
abchhlnoopr
lophobranch
abchiilnoot
halobiontic
abchiilnrty
labyrinthic
abchiiooptx
toxiphobiac
abchilloost
holoblastic
abchilmoost
homoblastic
abchilnoprt
branch-pilot
abchilopsty
hypoblastic
abchimprrsy
brachyprism
abchinoopty
nyctophobia
abchinorrsy
chrysarobin
abchiooopps
scopophobia
abchlmnopru
pulmobranch
abchorrsuuy
brachyurous
abciiilosty
sociability
abciiilrstt
tribalistic

abciiimnort
imbrication
abciiinoost
bisociation
abciiklnrsy
brainsickly
abciillmrsu
lumbricalis
abciillptuy
culpability
abciillrsty
trisyllabic
abciillstyy
syllabicity
abciilnoptu
publication
abciilnortu
lubrication
abciilorrsu
orbicularis
abciimnnoot
combination
abciinorrtu
rubrication
abciinorstt
abstriction
abciiooprst
saprobiotic
abciklmottu
buttock-mail
abcillnnouy
connubially
abcillnoruy
binocularly
abcillnoryy
Byronically
abcillorruy
orbicularly
abcilmmnosu
somnambulic
abcilmmoruu
columbarium
abcilmnnuuu
incunabulum
abcilmrstuu
rumbustical
abcilnnoors
Sorbonnical
abcilnortuu
lucubration
abcilnrstuy
inscrutably
abciloprstu
subtropical
abcimnoorty
combinatory
abcimnorsty
corybantism
abcinnoortu
conurbation
abcinoorstu
obscuration
abcinorsttu
subtraction

abcllrstuuu
subcultural
abcmnoorssw
crossbowman
abcnooorrrt
corroborant
abcnorrstuy
subcontrary
abcorrssttu
substractor
abdddeeefls
false-bedded
abdddeimnor
broad-minded
abddeeeglmr
marble-edged
abddeeeilty
baddeleyite
abddeeelrtt
treble-dated
abddeeensss
debasedness
abddeegglny
bandy-legged
abddeehills
shad-bellied
abddeehlosu
double-shade
abddeeiimnr
bridemaiden
abddeeprrry
drap-de-berry
abddefhlloo
half-blooded
abddeflnoru
fardel-bound
abddeginnst
standing-bed
abddehnnsuu
unhusbanded
abddeiiilnv
individable
abddeiilnuv
undividable
abddeillnru
dull-brained
abddeilmrsw
swim-bladder
abddeimnnst
disbandment
abddeinowwy
bay-windowed
abddelmoorw
warm-blooded
abddelmorrw
bladder-worm
abddelorrtw
bladderwort
abddgiinnrv
driving-band
abddgiinorv
diving-board
abddginoorr
dragoon-bird

abdeeegllou
double-eagle
abdeeeglnuw
unwedgeable
abdeeehilrt
hereditable
abdeeehllvw
well-behaved
abdeeehlrst
shard-beetle
abdeeeillrv
deliverable
abdeeeimntw
between-maid
abdeeellopv
developable
abdeeelmnru
denumerable
abdeeelnsst
belatedness
abdeeelorsv
sleeve-board
abdeeelrrrw
reed-warbler
abdeeenrrru
underbearer
abdeeeorrtt
teeter-board
abdeeeotttv
vedette-boat
abdeeerrttv
vertebrated
abdeefgiirr
fire-brigade
abdeefgnosu
sang-de-boeuf
abdeefiilnn
indefinable
abdeefiinrt
defibrinate
abdeefilltt
battlefield
abdeefilnnu
undefinable
abdeegginrr
gingerbread
abdeeghnory
honey-badger
abdeegillsw
swag-bellied
abdeegimnrt
abridgement
abdeeginprs
bespreading
abdeeglnotu
double-agent
abdeeglostu
about-sledge
abdeehilsst
established
abdeehirstw
breadthwise
abdeehnrrtu
underbreath

abdeeiiklls
dislikeable
abdeeiilnot
obediential
abdeeiilsst
destabilise
abdeeilmnno
denominable
abdeeilmnrs
simnel-bread
abdeeilmnst
disablement
abdeeilmsss
disassemble
abdeeilnnrt
dinner-table
abdeeilnpss
dispensable
abdeeilnrsu
undesirable
abdeeilnssu
audibleness
abdeeilorrt
deliberator
abdeeilortt
obliterated
abdeeinnrrw
breadwinner
abdeeiprstu
Buprestidae
abdeeklnoor
book-learned
abdeekmnory
monkey-bread
abdeelmnotu
demountable
abdeelmnruy
denumerably
abdeelnnruu
unendurable
abdeelnrssu
durableness
abdeelopptt
table-topped
abdeelorrtt
letter-board
abdeelorrtw
world-beater
abdeelorsty
destroyable
abdeelrsstt
battledress
abdeemnorty
embryonated
abdeeorrrsw
sword-bearer
abdeeqrrrtu
quarter-bred
abdefflorru
luffer-board
abdefginorr
fingerboard
abdefhoortt
footbreadth

abdefiillrt
fibrillated
abdefiilnny
indefinably
abdefllotuu
double-fault
abdeggilnot
gold-beating
abdegginorr
ragged-robin
abdeghhiltt
high-battled
abdeghhooru
headborough
abdeghloops
bog-asphodel
abdeghlorsu
shoulder-bag
abdegiilnnt
dining-table
abdegiinprt
paint-bridge
abdegiknoor
reading-book
abdegillnrv
gravel-blind
abdegilnoww
gable-window
abdeginnpsw
spawning-bed
abdeglmoott
bottom-glade
abdegnooruv
above-ground
abdehhmoorr
rhombohedra
abdehiinntu
uninhabited
abdehiklnsu
husbandlike
abdehilnosu
unabolished
abdehkmmrtu
thumb-marked
abdehllmoor
hall-bedroom
abdehlnsssu
husbandless
abdehloorst
heart's-blood
abdehloorsv
shovel-board
abdehloprsu
double-sharp
abdehnorruu
unharboured
abdehnosstu
basset-hound
abdehorrsuu
harbour-dues
abdeiiilllst
distillable
abdeiilltwy
weldability

abdeiilmnot
  indomitable
abdeiimnost
  demi-bastion
abdeiinrttu
  inturbidate
abdeiklnnru
  undrinkable
abdeillossv
  dissolvable
abdeilmnopu
  impoundable
abdeilmottu
  tolbutamide
abdeilmsssy
  disassembly
abdeilnnort
  bonnet-laird
abdeilnpssy
  dispensably
abdeilnrsuy
  undesirably
abdeilnssuy
  unbiassedly
abdeiloprsv
  disprovable
abdeinnorww
  window-barne
abdeinorstu
  subordinate
abdekmnoory
  monkey-board
abdelllnsuy
  unsyllabled
abdellmnrsu
  slumberland
abdellnoors
  ob-and-soller
abdelmoorst
  bloodstream
abdelnnosuu
  unsoundable
abdelnnouuw
  unwoundable
abdelnnruuy
  unendurably
abdeloorruv
  louver-board
  louvre-board
abdeloorrww
  wood-warbler
abdeloostwy
  bloody-sweat
abdeloprrtu
  protrudable
abdemnoorww
  meadow-brown
abdennorstv
  bondservant
abdenoprsuu
  superabound
abdenorstvy
  body-servant
abdeoooprtt
  torpedo-boat
abdfghiilnn
  half-binding
abdfiillsyy
  disyllabify
abdfilmoorr
  dolabriform
abdfllooorw
  follow-board
abdfnooruux
  fauxbourdon
abdghiiinrt
  riding-habit
abdghinnosw
  bond-washing
abdghinpssu
  spud-bashing
abdgiinnopr
  pair-bonding
abdgilloooy
  diabolology
abdgillorsw
  gallows-bird
abdgilmorru
  bur-marigold
abdgilnoptt
  blotting-pad
abdginoprrs
  springboard
abdginorrst
  string-board
abdgmoorrss
  smörgasbȯrd
abdhhiooprу
  hydrophobia
abdhimnnops
  bondmanship
abdhimooopr
  dromophobia
abdiillmssy
  disyllabism
abdiilmnoty
  indomitably
abdiinoorsy
  obsidionary
abdiinostuu
  subaudition
abdillorrrw
  drill-barrow
abdilnoopsv
  blood-spavin
abdilorsuzz
  blizzardous
abdimnnostu
  subdominant
abdimnoortt
  motor-bandit
abdinorrsuy
  subordinary
abdlmoorrsu
  dorsolumbar
abdlnooostt
  odontoblast
abdmoorruzz
  moor-buzzard
abdnrrrstuu
  surturbrand
abeeeeflors
  foreseeable
abeeeeglnrr
  regenerable
abeeeeiklmv
  make-believe
abeeeelrttw
  water-beetle
abeeeemnrtv
  bereavement
abeeeerrrtv
  reverberate
abeeefirrrr
  barrier-reef
abeeeflmnrt
  fermentable
abeeeflprrr
  preferrable
abeeeggilln
  negligeable
abeeegiksst
  siege-basket
abeeegirrtv
  verbigerate
abeeeglorsw
  elbow-grease
abeeeglrrtt
  regrettable
abeeehhinpr
  hebephrenia
abeeehhllrt
  bell-heather
abeeehlrstw
  breast-wheel
abeeehqrrsu
  queer-basher
abeeeiilnps
  plebeianise
abeeeillprv
  repleviable
abeeeilmmpr
  impermeable
abeeeilmmst
  emblematise
abeeeilnrsv
  inseverable
abeeeilrrtv
  retrievable
abeeeimnsst
  absenteeism
abeeejmmnnt
  enjambement
abeeelmnntt
  entablement
abeeelmnrru
  remunerable
abeeelnnruv
  unvenerable
abeeelnnsst
  tenableness
abeeelnprst
  presentable
abeeelnprtv
  preventable
abeeelnqssu
  equableness
abeeelpprrt
  perpetrable
abeeelpprtu
  perpetuable
abeeelprrsv
  preservable
abeeelpstuy
  beauty-sleep
abeeemoprtt
  obtemperate
abeeenrrrtv
  reverberant
abeeeprrrsu
  purse-bearer
abeeffhlrtu
  buff-leather
abeeffilort
  forfeitable
abeeffrsttu
  buffer-state
abeefgilnrr
  refrangible
abeefglortt
  forgettable
abeefiillqu
  liquefiable
abeefilnrss
  friableness
abeefilprtu
  putrefiable
abeefilrrtu
  irrefutable
abeefllnssu
  balefulness
abeeflmoprr
  performable
abeeflnnssu
  banefulness
abeeflorsuw
  sea-furbelow
abeefnrrrtu
  afterburner
abeeggilnps
  sleeping-bag
abeegiilnrt
  libertinage
abeegiilrrs
  bersaglieri
abeegiinoss
  abiogenesis
abeegilmnpr
  impregnable
abeegilnruz
  gaberlunzie
abeegilottt
  tattie-bogle
abeegilrrst
  registrable
abeeginorrv
  overbearing
abeeglrrtty
  regrettably
abeegnorsst
  barge-stones
abeegorttuw
  water-bouget
abeehhprsty
  bathysphere
abeehiilnrt
  inheritable
abeehikprrs
  ship-breaker
abeehilrsst
  establisher
  re-establish
abeehilstux
  exhaustible
abeehinrsss
  bearishness
abeehinrsst
  breathiness
abeehirrttt
  bitter-earth
abeehkoprrs
  shopbreaker
abeehlorrsu
  barrel-house
abeehlorrww
  wheelbarrow
abeehlosstu
  bastel-house
abeehnoprry
  hyperborean
abeehorrstt
  rother-beast
abeehorstuw
  whereabouts
abeeiilmnps
  plebeianism
abeeiilmnst
  inestimable
abeeiilmprv
  imperviable
abeeiilnqtu
  inequitable
abeeiilqrtu
  equilibrate
abeeikllrsv
  Baskerville
abeeillnort
  intolerable
abeeillnpss
  pliableness
abeeilloptx
  exploitable
abeeillottt
  toilet-table
abeeilmmosv
  immoveables
abeeilmmpry
  impermeably

abeeilmmstt
emblematist
abeeilmnnot
mentionable
abeeilmnnru
innumerable
abeeilmnoot
emotionable
abeeilmnrtu
unmeritable
abeeilmorrv
irremovable
abeeilmorst
steam-boiler
abeeilnnops
pensionable
abeeilnnstt
table-tennis
abeeilnprsu
insuperable
abeeilnqtuu
unequitable
abeeilnrttu
inutterable
abeeilnssst
beastliness
abeeilpprrs
perspirable
abeeilpprtt
bitter-apple
abeeilprssu
persuasible
abeeilprtuv
vituperable
abeeilrrtvy
retrievably
abeeimnnotu
aminobutene
abeeimnrrtt
arbitrement
abeeinnqrtu
barquentine
abeeinorrtt
terebration
abeeinorrtv
verberation
abeeinsssuv
abusiveness
abeeioprrtv
reprobative
abeeiorstvv
observative
abeeiqrrsuu
arquebusier
abeeklnortv
overblanket
abeekrrrsty
tarry-breeks
abeelllmssy
blamelessly
abeelllmtuy
umbellately
abeellrrtvy
vertebrally
abeelmmnoru
unmemorable
abeelmnoruv
unremovable
abeelmnossv
movableness
abeelmnsstu
mutableness
abeelnnosst
notableness
abeelnnsstu
tunableness
abeelnprsty
presentably
abeelnrttuu
unutterable
abeelnrtuxy
exuberantly
abeelortttw
water-bottle
abeelostuuy
beauteously
abeelprrsty
presbyteral
abeelprtttu
butter-plate
abeemmnorsu
membraneous
abeemnorstt
storm-beaten
abeemnrsstu
surbasement
abeemorrstt
strabometer
abeeoprrttu
protuberate
abeepprrttu
butter-paper
abeffiilort
fortifiable
abefgiiilns
signifiable
abefgiilnnr
infrangible
abefgilnosw
safe-blowing
abefhhlorrt
half-brother
abefhlnsssu
bashfulness
abefiiilrtv
vitrifiable
abefiiilsty
feasibility
abefiijlstu
justifiable
abefiilloot
bifoliolate
abefiilnoss
fissionable
abefillmrru
umbrella-fir
abefillnoor
fire-balloon
abefillnrtu
unfiltrable
abefilltuuy
beautifully
abefilntuuu
unbeautiful
abefilrrtuy
irrefutably
abefimorsst
asbestiform
abefirrttuy
fairy-butter
abeflmoortt
foot-lambert
abeflnnrssu
branfulness
abeggiilnor
globigerina
abeghillppt
apple-blight
abeghilmnoo
haemoglobin
abeghilnsuw
washing-blue
abeghinnrtu
unbreathing
abeghinoopr
negrophobia
abeghinrrsu
rush-bearing
abeghinrrtu
Antiburgher
abegiiilmmt
immitigable
abegiiklnnt
inking-table
abegiilmntu
unmitigable
abegiimnssu
subimagines
abegijmnnpu
jumping-bean
abegijortuv
objurgative
abegikmnorw
working-beam
abegillnpss
passing-bell
abegilmnpry
impregnably
abegilnnnty
benignantly
abegilnnrty
banteringly
abegilnoorw
wool-bearing
abegilnorsu
subregional
abegilnosuu
albugineous
abegilooory
aerobiology
abeginnnntu
unbenignant
abeginnortu
gubernation
abegllnoopr
prolongable
abegllorssw
glass-blower
abegllosstt
bottle-glass
abeglnstuuu
subungulate
abeglooqptt
potato-bogle
abegmorrstu
burgomaster
abehhhrrstu
hearth-brush
abehiiillps
baillieship
abehiilltvw
livable-with
abehiilmopt
amphibolite
abehiilprst
blepharitis
abehiimmnos
Bohemianism
abehiinnort
hibernation
abehiinrsst
inhabitress
abehiklnntu
unthinkable
abehilmnost
abolishment
abehilnorsu
nourishable
abehiloopru
ailurophobe
abehiloprsw
worshipable
abehinoortt
botheration
abehlmnosuw
bushel-woman
abehlmoortw
Bartholomew
abehlmopssu
blasphemous
abehlmortwy
blameworthy
abehlnnnsuu
unshunnable
abehlnorrty
abhorrently
abehlorrssu
harbourless
abehmnrstuu
subterhuman
abehnorstty
east-by-north
abehooorrtt
orthoborate
abehoorrrvw
hoverbarrow
abehossttuy
east-by-south
abeiiiilllmt
illimitable
abeiiiillnor
billionaire
abeiiillrty
reliability
abeiiilnntz
Leibnitzian
abeiiinnort
inebriation
abeiillllry
illiberally
abeiilllmnu
illuminable
abeiillmmst
bimetallism
abeiillmnry
bimillenary
abeiillmpsu
implausible
abeiillmstt
bimetallist
abeiillrstt
bristle-tail
abeiilmnnno
innominable
abeiilmnsty
inestimably
abeiilmotvy
moveability
abeiilnoprt
prelibation
abeiilnqtuy
inequitably
abeiilnrrtt
intertribal
abeiilnstuv
unvisitable
abeiiloopprt
propitiable
abeiilortxy
exorability
abeiilrstvy
versability
abeiimnorsv
ambiversion
abeiimoprtv
improbative
abeiinrrsst
bar-sinister
abeiirtttuv
attributive
abeiklllstt
skittle-ball
abeikllnoot
kite-balloon
abeiknnrrsu
brankursine
abeiknrrstw
winter's-bark
abeillllrsty
trisyllable

abeillmottu
multilobate
abeillnnoov
balloon-vine
abeillnorty
intolerably
abeillnpsuu
unplausible
abeilmnnruy
innumerably
abeilmnrstu
subterminal
abeilmorrvy
irremovably
abeilmosstw
misbestowal
abeilmrstuu
semi-tubular
abeilnnossu
non-issuable
abeilnnprtu
unprintable
abeilnnstty
abstinently
abeilnoosss
obsessional
abeilnorssu
Belorussian
abeilnostty
obstinately
abeilnprrst
splinter-bar
abeilnprsuy
insuperably
abeiloprtuu
Politbureau
abeilorsstw
belowstairs
abeilqrstuu
square-built
abeilrrsttt
brittle-star
abeimnnsssu
businessman
abeimnorstw
tribeswoman
abeinnnoqtu
tonquin-bean
abeinnnrstu
burnt-sienna
abeinnorstv
inobservant
abeinooprrt
probationer
reprobation
abeinoorstv
observation
abeinoosttt
obtestation
abeinosstuu
subitaneous
abeinssttuv
substantive

abeirssttuv
substrative
abejmorrttu
turbo-ram-jet
abekoostttu
statute-book
abekorstttu
trout-basket
abelmnorrsy
salmon-berry
abelnoppstu
unstoppable
abelnoprttu
pearl-button
abelnorstvy
observantly
abelnrttuuy
unutterably
abelopprstu
supportable
abeloprttty
bottle-party
abelrrsttuu
surrebuttal
abemnorrrst
barnstormer
abemnorttuw
butter-woman
abennorstuv
unobservant
abennosstuy
buoyantness
abenoprrttu
protuberant
abeooprrrty
reprobatory
abeoorrstvy
observatory
abeoprrrttu
perturbator
aberrsstuuy
subtreasury
abffillmstu
bull-mastiff
abfghinrstu
surf-bathing
abfiiillty
fallibility
abfiiimnort
fimbriation
abfiijlstuy
justifiably
abfilloostt
footballist
abfilmnstuu
funambulist
abggginnoot
tobogganing
abggilooory
agrobiology
abggiloorst
garbologist
abgginoostt
tobogganist

abghhoorrtu
tharborough
abghiinrstt
brattishing
abghiinsttu
bathing-suit
abghikllnoo
booking-hall
abghilmoopy
amphibology
abghnooprsy
snobography
abgiiilmmty
immitigably
abgiiilntty
tangibility
abgiilmntuy
unmitigably
abgiilnoops
soap-boiling
abgiilnrtuv
rib-vaulting
abgiinnoost
obsignation
abgiinorrst
rib-roasting
abgijnoortu
objurgation
abgijnostuu
subjugation
abgiknrrsty
stringy-bark
abgillortuy
globularity
abgilmnoost
gonimoblast
abgilmnosuu
lumbaginous
abgilmosuuy
ambiguously
abgilnnoruu
unlabouring
abgilorrsuu
burglarious
abgimnosuuu
unambiguous
abginoorstu
subrogation
abginoorsty
obsignatory
abgjoorrtuy
objurgatory
abglloopryy
pyroballogy
abgmoorsstt
bottom-grass
abhhimnpssu
bushmanship
abhhinooopp
phonophobia
abhhioooppt
photophobia
abhhiooppsy
hypsophobia

abhiiioopst
sitiophobia
abhilmoopsu
amphibolous
abhiooprssu
Russophobia
abhlooprstt
trophoblast
abiiiilmtty
imitability
abiiiilntvy
inviability
abiiiillmty
illimitably
abiiillosty
isolability
abiiilnostu
antibilious
abiiilnrttu
tribunitial
abiiilnstty
instability
abiiilprtty
partibility
abiiilpssty
passibility
abiiilrttvy
vibratility
abiiilsttuy
suitability
abiiinnrttu
tribunitian
abiiinoprtt
bipartition
abiiklortwy
workability
abiilllnrty
brilliantly
abiillostvy
solvability
abiilmnostu
sublimation
abiilmostuy
ambitiously
abiilnooqtu
obliquation
abiilnorttu
tribulation
abiilnrstuy
insalubrity
abiiloprtty
portability
abiiloqttuy
quotability
abiilrrttuy
tributarily
abiimnnstyz
Byzantinism
abiimnooprt
improbation
abiimnostuu
unambitious
abiinnsttyz
Byzantinist

abiinoopstt
obstipation
abiinoorstt
abortionist
abiinortttu
attribution
abiiorssttu
tibiotarsus
abillnpsuuy
unplausibly
abilloorsuy
laboriously
abilloprrsw
sparrow-bill
abillorsttu
sublittoral
abilmoortuu
taurobolium
abilmorstuu
umbratilous
abilnoorsuu
unlaborious
abilnostuux
subluxation
abimooprrty
improbatory
abinnoorstu
subornation
abinrrssttu
brains-trust
ablnoppstuy
unstoppably
ablopprstuy
supportably
acccceeenrs
accrescence
accccilmoor
micrococcal
acccdeeenns
candescence
acccdehilno
chalcedonic
acccdeilopy
cyclopaedic
acccdennoor
concordance
acccdennotu
conductance
accceeelnos
coalescence
accceeelnst
lactescence
accceefnort
café-concert
accceehilrs
ecclesiarch
accceehistt
catechetics
accceehmnor
chance-comer
accceehosuu
accoucheuse
accceeilnrt
eccentrical

accceelmnop
complacence
accceelnopt
conceptacle
accceennnos
connascence
accceffhioo
coach-office
accceehiistt
catechistic
acccehiknot
check-action
acccehimott
chemotactic
acccehnorty
cony-catcher
technocracy
accceiilmrt
climacteric
accceilnpty
pentacyclic
accceilrtty
tetracyclic
accceknorrr
corn-cracker
acccelmnopy
complacency
acccennnory
concernancy
acccennnosy
connascency
accchhiinno
Cochin-China
accchiillot
laccolithic
accchiloort
ochlocratic
accchooprty
ptochocracy
accchorrsyy
chrysocracy
accciilltyy
cyclicality
accciiooprs
capriccioso
acccilloosu
calcicolous
acccimmoors
macrocosmic
acccimooprs
macroscopic
acccimoorst
cosmocratic
accclooooprt
protococcal
acccnoosttu
cost-account
accddeinors
discordance
accddeklooo
cock-a-doodle
accddiiimst
didacticism
accddinorsy
discordancy
accdeeeennt
antecedence
accdeeeknnr
crane-necked
accdeeelnos
adolescence
accdeeenrst
crescentade
accdeefhhkl
half-checked
accdeefhlnt
fetch-candle
accdeefnory
confederacy
accdeefoppr
copper-faced
accdeehhklu
chuckle-head
accdeehiors
archdiocese
accdeeiirsu
race-suicide
accdeeiistv
desiccative
accdeeilnpr
pencil-cedar
accdeeimnor
decameronic
accdeeinprs
discrepance
accdeeiortt
decorticate
accdeelnnou
unconcealed
accdeemnsuu
succedaneum
accdefhitty
chitty-faced
accdefilnss
flaccidness
accdefnostu
safe-conduct
accdehhrssu
archduchess
accdehilnos
closed-chain
accdehilpry
diphycercal
accdehimpry
pachydermic
accdehinorw
choice-drawn
accdehlmorw
clam-chowder
accdehlnoxy
chalcedonyx
accdehnrstu
unscratched
accdeiillty
deictically
accdeiinost
desiccation
accdeiklnst
candle-stick
accdeiknrrt
cinder-track
accdeillops
peccadillos
accdeilmopt
complicated
accdeinnoor
co-ordinance
coordinance
accdeinoost
consociated
accdeinootu
coeducation
accdeinprsy
discrepancy
accdeiprrtu
picture-card
accdellostu
cloud-castle
accdelmopty
compactedly
accdelnosss
second-class
accdemnoory
demonocracy
accdemnoptu
uncompacted
accdennotuu
unaccounted
accdgilnory
accordingly
accdgilnost
cold-casting
accdginorrs
scoring-card
accdhhnssuu
such-and-such
accdhhrrsuw
churchwards
accdhiimort
dichromatic
accdhinoryy
hydrocyanic
accdhiortty
hydrotactic
accdiiinnos
scincoidian
accdiikknpp
pick-and-pick
accdiillllou
loculicidal
accdiillnry
cylindrical
accdiillory
codicillary
accdiilnoor
crocodilian
accdiiosstu
diacoustics
accdimosstu
disaccustom
accdlnrsuuu
dracunculus
acceeeehmrs
cream-cheese
acceeeennsv
evanescence
acceeefilmn
maleficence
acceeeflnrt
reflectance
acceeeikklo
cockaleekie
acceeellnps
pallescence
acceeelnops
opalescence
acceeelnrst
recalescent
acceefhprst
speechcraft
acceefiipst
specificate
acceefiirtt
certificate
acceefikrrr
fire-cracker
acceefinorv
vociferance
acceefnrrst
screencraft
acceeghikmn
game-chicken
acceeghilmo
geochemical
acceeghinty
eye-catching
acceeglnstu
glaucescent
acceehhiirs
Escherichia
acceehhirrt
arch-heretic
acceehhkrsw
screech-hawk
acceehhnttt
catch-the-ten
acceehilmno
chameleonic
acceehilnrt
chanticleer
acceehilrst
telearchics
acceehiprrt
Pherecratic
acceehirrtu
charcuterie
acceehirstv
cesarevitch
acceehirstw
cesarewitch
acceehkortw
weathercock
acceehllnry
chancellery
acceehlmort
molecatcher
acceehlnoxy
cyclohexane
acceehmnnoy
coenenchyma
acceehmnrsy
sarcenchyme
acceehnprrt
trencher-cap
acceeiilnrt
electrician
acceeiistvx
exsiccative
acceeikklop
peacock-like
acceeillllrt
all-electric
acceeilmnou
oecumenical
acceeilnnst
incalescent
acceeilnrux
Clarencieux
acceeilnsst
scale-insect
acceeilrrtu
recirculate
acceeimnops
CinemaScope®
acceeimnrtt
metacentric
acceeinnorv
cracovienne
acceeinprtt
net-practice
acceeinqstu
acquiescent
acceeioprrt
reciprocate
acceeiorttx
excorticate
acceelloprt
leptocercal
acceelmnnot
concealment
acceemnnorr
necromancer
acceemnoppu
come-uppance
comeuppance
acceemossty
ascomycetes
acceennnotu
countenance
acceennorsv
conversance
acceennortt
concentrate
concertante
acceennorvy
conveyancer
acceenoprry
coparcenery

acceenoprtu
counter-pace
acceenorrrt
catercorner
acceenpsstu
susceptance
acceeopprtu
preoccupate
acceeoprsuy
cyperaceous
acceffhrttu
chaff-cutter
acceffiiosu
efficacious
accefhiinty
chieftaincy
accefhikops
peacock-fish
accefilorsu
calciferous
acceghiinst
catechising
acceghiknqu
quick-change
acceghilmru
chemurgical
acceghioprr
cerographic
acceghllrtu
gull-catcher
accegikmrry
gimcrackery
accegilootu
autecologic
accegilorsu
calcigerous
accegklnops
spang-cockle
accehhrstuv
stave-church
accehiillrt
Callitriche
accehiilnst
calisthenic
accehiilopt
ophicalcite
accehiilost
catholicise
accehiimnst
mechanistic
accehiiorrt
hierocratic
accehiirstu
eucharistic
accehillmno
melancholic
accehillnty
technically
accehilmooz
zoochemical
accehilmopr
microcephal
accehilnntu
untechnical

accehilnoot
Neo-Catholic
accehiloppr
procephalic
accehilprty
phylacteric
accehimnnor
chrominance
accehimnory
cheiromancy
accehimpsty
metapsychic
accehimrtty
McCarthyite
accehklnost
schecklaton
accehkopptt
patch-pocket
accehkopttw
watch-pocket
accehllmnoy
collenchyma
accehllnort
concert-hall
accehllnory
chancellory
accehlrssst
scratchless
acceiiilmst
metasilicic
acceiiinprt
accipitrine
acceiillmrs
clericalism
acceiillrst
clericalist
acceiilnorr
cornice-rail
acceiilnstv
clavecinist
acceiilntuv
inculcative
acceiilrrsu
circularise
acceiilrtuv
circulative
acceiimnost
cosmetician
encomiastic
acceiinnosu
insouciance
acceiinostx
exsiccation
acceiiprtvy
pervicacity
acceiipttvy
acceptivity
acceiirrstt
criticaster
acceikknnry
nick-nackery
acceikkottt
tick-tack-toe

acceillnrty
centrically
acceillpsty
sceptically
acceilmnoss
comicalness
acceilmopst
ectoplasmic
acceilnnoty
anticyclone
acceilnnssy
cynicalness
acceilnortt
contractile
acceilnortu
corniculate
acceilnstty
syntectical
acceiloprst
ceroplastic
acceilopstt
ectoplastic
acceilopttu
octuplicate
acceilorssy
accessorily
acceimmnotu
communicate
acceimnnort
necromantic
acceimnorty
craniectomy
acceimnosty
Actinomyces
acceimorrty
meritocracy
acceinnnotu
continuance
acceinnorsu
co-insurance
acceinnortv
contrivance
acceinoprrt
reciprocant
acceinopsuu
punicaceous
acceinorstu
cater-cousin
acceinorttv
contractive
acceioorssu
scoriaceous
acceiorssss
scissor-case
acceiorstuu
urticaceous
accejlnortu
conjectural
acceklmorst
master-clock
acceklssttu
scuttle-cask
accekorrttu
racket-court

accellorsuy
sclerocauly
accellosttu
coal-scuttle
accelmmnoop
commonplace
accelnooort
concolorate
accelprrsuu
crepuscular
accemnopsst
compactness
accennorsvy
conservancy
conversancy
accenooprtu
pococurante
accenoorrst
consecrator
accenopprtu
preoccupant
accenoprrtt
precontract
accenorrttu
contracture
accenorsttu
counter-cast
accenprtuuu
acupuncture
acceorsstuu
crustaceous
accfgilosuu
calcifugous
accfhirsttt
stitchcraft
accfhloorst
schoolcraft
accfiilopry
prolificacy
accfinoorst
confiscator
accflnortuy
calf-country
accghiilrru
chirurgical
accghiinprv
chip-carving
accghiioops
hagioscopic
accghiooppr
coprophagic
accgiilnotu
glauconitic
accgiilnrtu
circulating
accgiinnnot
canting-coin
accgiinnoty
incogitancy
accgillmooy
mycological
accgillooty
cytological

accgilnoory
carcinology
accgimoprty
cryptogamic
acchhiinstt
chain-stitch
acchhmnoruw
churchwoman
acchiiimmpt
amphimictic
acchiiirstt
citharistic
acchiilmost
catholicism
acchiiloprt
cartophilic
acchiilosst
scholiastic
acchiilotty
catholicity
acchiimnort
chiromantic
acchiimosst
masochistic
acchiinpsyy
physiciancy
acchiioopst
sociopathic
acchiiopprt
Hippocratic
acchiioprrz
rhizocarpic
acchiiprsty
psychiatric
acchillnory
chronically
acchillpsyy
psychically
acchilmotyy
cyclothymia
acchiloostu
holocaustic
acchimmrsty
McCarthyism
acchimnorty
crithomancy
acchinnopyy
phycocyanin
acchinoostt
octastichon
acchinopsty
sycophantic
acchiooprrt
prothoracic
acchioopttt
phototactic
acchioorrsu
chiaroscuro
acchioprsyy
physiocracy
acchknoorst
anchor-stock
acchkorrstw
scratch-work

acchlloorsy
chrysocolla
acchmnnooyy
onychomancy
acchmnoostw
Scotchwoman
acchnooopsu
cacophonous
acciiikknpw
Pickwickian
acciiilmnrt
matriclinic
acciiilnprt
patriclinic
acciiilnstv
Calvinistic
acciiilosst
socialistic
acciiilrstu
curialistic
acciiilrtty
criticality
acciillopty
occipitally
acciilmnort
matroclinic
acciilnnotu
inculcation
acciilnnquu
quincuncial
acciilnoort
conciliator
acciilnoprt
patroclinic
acciilnortu
circulation
acciilnotvy
volcanicity
acciilntuvy
vulcanicity
acciilostuv
acclivitous
acciilrrtuy
circularity
acciinnstty
nyctinastic
acciinorrsu
Rosicrucian
accijnnotuv
conjunctiva
accikkkknny
knick-knacky
acciknprstu
panic-struck
accillnooot
collocation
accilloosuu
caulicolous
accillprtyy
cryptically
accilmnrruu
circumlunar
accilmoprru
circumpolar

accilmorrsu
circumsolar
accilnoottu
occultation
accilnortuy
inculcatory
acciloprsty
pyroclastic
acciloprttu
plutocratic
accilorrtuy
circulatory
accimmnnotu
communicant
accimnnoott
concomitant
accimnottuy
contumacity
accinnnosty
inconstancy
accinnoootv
convocation
accinnoopru
cornucopian
accinnoortt
contraction
accinooppst
pantoscopic
accinooprsy
cranioscopy
accinoorrrw
carrion-crow
accinoorstu
coruscation
accinosttuu
cunctatious
acciooprrty
procaryotic
acciorsssty
sarcocystis
accklorrsty
rock-crystal
acckooprrsw
cock-sparrow
acclmnooptu
coconut-palm
acclnnostuy
consultancy
acclnooortu
octonocular
acclnorsuuu
carunculous
accloprrsuu
corpuscular
acddeeeeprs
predeceased
acddeeffist
disaffected
acddeegiknw
wedding-cake
acddeehhikt
thick-headed
acddeehhkos
shock-headed

acddeehippw
wide-chapped
acddeehlnos
close-handed
acddeehlort
cold-hearted
acddeehlost
dead-clothes
acddeehlruy
curly-headed
acddeeiintu
indeciduate
acddeeilptu
pediculated
acddeeimssu
Sadduceeism
acddeeinnnr
dinner-dance
acddeelosty
dodecastyle
acddehinsss
caddishness
acddehkmoru
archdukedom
acddehllost
saddle-cloth
acddehnnoss
seconds-hand
acddehnoopy
dodecaphony
acddehnorru
round-arched
acddeiilnrt
dendritical
acddeijnnuu
unjaundiced
acddeillmss
middle-class
acddeimnoru
endocardium
acddeimnrst
discardment
acddeinoopt
paedodontic
acddeklosst
stock-saddle
acddellmnou
mould-candle
acddeloorsu
sad-coloured
acddgijknpu
Jack-pudding
acddhinoors
doch-an-doris
acddiimorsu
diascordium
acddilostuy
didactylous
acdeeeehlrr
cheer-leader
acdeeeflnrt
needlecraft
acdeeeflrst
self-created

acdeeefnort
confederate
acdeeegllot
décolletage
acdeeehorrv
overreached
acdeeeiklns
linseed-cake
acdeeeillpt
pedicellate
acdeeeilnrv
deliverance
acdeeeimprt
premedicate
acdeeeimrtv
decemvirate
acdeeeinpru
preaudience
acdeeeinrtv
revendicate
acdeeeiprtt
decrepitate
acdeeeiprtv
deprecative
acdeeellnrt
crenellated
acdeeellrvw
cave-dweller
acdeeelorrt
decelerator
acdeeffillt
ill-affected
acdeeffinot
affectioned
acdeefginru
figure-dance
acdeefilnrz
fence-lizard
acdeeflmott
mottle-faced
acdeeflnruu
fraudulence
acdeefnrrtu
unrefracted
acdeeggnort
congregated
acdeeggnrss
craggedness
acdeeghhprt
depth-charge
acdeeghilrs
sledge-chair
acdeeghnrru
undercharge
acdeegillmo
medico-legal
acdeegilnnr
calendering
acdeegilntu
geniculated
acdeeginrtu
nectar-guide
acdeegklnow
acknowledge

acdeehilnop
encephaloid
acdeehilnpp
Chippendale
acdeehilpsy
psychedelia
acdeehimnor
Echinoderma
acdeehimnpu
unimpeached
acdeehimnrs
merchandise
acdeehinrtw
windcheater
acdeehiortt
octahedrite
acdeehkklnu
knuckle-head
acdeehknnuy
unhackneyed
acdeehllosu
close-hauled
acdeehlnprr
randle-perch
acdeehlrrru
hurdle-racer
acdeehmnorw
reach-me-down
acdeehnnntu
unenchanted
acdeehnnstu
unchastened
acdeehnprss
parchedness
acdeehnrrtu
unchartered
acdeehrrstw
screw-thread
acdeeiilltv
divellicate
acdeeiillty
eidetically
acdeeiilmtv
maledictive
acdeeiiltuv
elucidative
acdeeiimmnn
medicine-man
acdeeiimrst
mediatrices
acdeeiinpst
pedanticise
acdeeiinrtv
revindicate
acdeeiiopps
epidiascope
acdeeiiprtv
predicative
acdeeijltvy
adjectively
acdeeijprtu
prejudicate
acdeeiklrst
stickleader

acdeeillmny
endemically
acdeeillors
radicellose
acdeeilmnru
unreclaimed
acdeeilnnst
clandestine
acdeeilnott
delectation
acdeeilnpst
lapidescent
acdeeilnrtu
declinature
acdeeilnttu
denticulate
acdeeilprtu
reduplicate
acdeeilrttu
reticulated
acdeeilstuv
vesiculated
acdeeimnosu
eudaemonics
acdeeimnprt
predicament
acdeeimnrty
determinacy
acdeeimorst
democratise
acdeeimostt
domesticate
acdeeinnrry
yince-errand
acdeeinnrst
disentrance
acdeeinoprt
capernoited
deprecation
acdeeinorst
considerate
desecration
acdeeinortu
decurionate
re-education
acdeeinortv
verde-antico
acdeeioprrt
depreciator
acdeeiopttt
petticoated
acdeeiorrtt
directorate
acdeeipprrt
paper-credit
acdeekllstw
well-stacked
acdeeknrrsw
sneck-drawer
acdeekqrrtu
quarter-deck
acdeellnotu
nucleolated

acdeelmnprs
sperm-candle
acdeelmorrs
scleroderma
acdeelnoprw
candle-power
acdeelnptuu
pedunculate
acdeeloortw
water-cooled
acdeeloprtu
operculated
acdeelorssv
cross-leaved
acdeelrstty
scatteredly
acdeelsstuy
decussately
acdeemnrttu
traducement
acdeenorrst
second-rater
acdeeoprrty
deprecatory
acdeerrsstt
detractress
acdeffiirtv
diffractive
acdefghllru
full-charged
acdefgilrsu
disgraceful
acdefhilpst
feldspathic
acdefhmoost
smooth-faced
acdefiiinnt
infanticide
acdefiiinot
deification
edification
acdefiiorty
edificatory
acdefinnotu
fecundation
acdefinnruw
wind-furnace
acdefirrttu
trifurcated
acdefllnoru
full-acorned
uncalled-for
acdeflmmnos
self-command
acdeflnruuy
fraudulency
acdeggiiint
giganticide
acdeghiilnp
hiding-place
acdeghiiopr
ideographic
acdeghillnt
candle-light

acdeghilnnr
chandlering
acdeghilorr
cigar-holder
acdeghimopr
demographic
acdeghoortu
rough-coated
acdegiilloo
ideological
acdegiilmru
demiurgical
acdegiimnsu
misguidance
acdegiinnrw
wire-dancing
acdegikprtu
picket-guard
acdegilloop
pedological
acdegimnosy
geodynamics
acdegimorty
tragi-comedy
acdeginnpst
step-dancing
acdegkloors
sockdolager
acdegoorstt
scattergood
acdehiiiprr
Cirrhipedia
acdehiikmnt
kitchen-maid
acdehiilopp
paedophilic
acdehiilort
Trochilidae
acdehiinnrv
chain-driven
acdehiioprt
diaphoretic
acdehiipprt
crappit-heid
acdehilmpty
itchy-palmed
acdehilopsu
dicephalous
acdehilrssy
chrysalides
acdehimoprs
comradeship
acdehimostu
mustachioed
acdehinnost
stanchioned
acdehinoors
icosahedron
acdehinsstu
unchastised
acdehiooprt
orthopaedic
acdehipstty
dyspathetic

acdehklnnst
landsknecht
acdehkmrstu
Deutschmark
acdehlllopy
phylloclade
acdehlmosuy
chlamydeous
acdehlnprtu
thunder-clap
acdehlprtyy
hyperdactyl
acdehmnnoor
enchondroma
acdehmoopst
smooth-paced
acdehmoortw
doomwatcher
acdehnnstuu
unstaunched
acdehnooprs
sancho-pedro
acdehnoorst
octahedrons
acdehnprsuu
unpurchased
acdehoorrtu
urochordate
acdeiiilmot
domiciliate
acdeiiintvv
vindicative
acdeiijlpru
prejudicial
acdeiillmny
medicinally
acdeiillnty
identically
acdeiillorv
varicelloid
acdeiillrvy
veridically
acdeiillsty
deistically
acdeiilmnot
malediction
acdeiilmprs
spermicidal
acdeiilnnot
declination
acdeiilnort
directional
acdeiilnotu
elucidation
acdeiilnotv
valediction
acdeiilnptu
induplicate
acdeiilorrt
directorial
acdeiilprsu
Pedicularis
acdeiilptuv
duplicative

acdeiimmnos
demoniacism
acdeiimnpst
pedanticism
acdeiimorrt
radiometric
acdeiimortu
audiometric
acdeiimprru
pericardium
acdeiinnrty
tyrannicide
acdeiinoprt
predication
acdeiinorrt
doctrinaire
acdeiiorrtt
Tortricidae
acdeiirsttv
distractive
acdeijnprtu
prejudicant
acdeillnoot
decollation
acdeilmnops
endoplasmic
acdeilmnotu
columniated
acdeilmorty
maledictory
acdeilnoopy
Lycopodinae
acdeilnoost
consolidate
acdeilnopst
endoplastic
acdeilnorss
cordialness
acdeilnorsy
secondarily
acdeilnorty
declinatory
acdeilnosuv
unvocalised
acdeilnrtuu
uncurtailed
acdeilortuy
elucidatory
acdeilortvy
valedictory
acdeilppsty
dyspeptical
acdeilprtuu
duplicature
acdeimnnoop
companioned
acdeimnnopu
uncompanied
acdeimnorrs
morris-dance
acdeimorstt
democratist
acdeinnnosu
uncanonised

acdeinnoort
incoronated
acdeinnorst
constrained
acdeinnortu
denunciator
underaction
acdeinnrtuu
uncurtained
acdeinoopry
Procyonidae
acdeinoorrt
Corrodentia
recordation
acdeinoprty
trypanocide
acdeinopstt
constipated
acdeinorrwy
cordwainery
acdeinosstu
decussation
acdeinosttu
outdistance
acdeinosttw
wainscotted
acdeinprstu
unpractised
acdeinprsty
candy-stripe
acdeiopprrt
dipterocarp
acdeioprrty
predicatory
acdeioprstt
disceptator
acdeiorsuxy
xyridaceous
acdeirsttuy
daisy-cutter
acdejorsstu
coadjutress
acdekoprstt
spatter-dock
acdelloptty
leptodactyl
acdelnooprs
Scolopendra
acdelnoortu
tan-coloured
acdelnpttuu
punctulated
acdeloorrtu
edulcorator
acdeloprtty
pterodactyl
acdemmmnnot
commandment
acdemmnoort
commendator
acdemnnortu
countermand
acdemnortuy
documentary

acdemooprtu
proctodaeum
acdemoorrst
ostracoderm
acdemoprssu
mass-produce
acdennnnouu
unannounced
acdenorrtuw
counterdraw
acdeoorrttw
water-doctor
acdeorrssst
star-crossed
acdffgiinnt
fact-finding
acdffgilnos
scaffolding
acdffiilmoo
officialdom
acdffiinort
diffraction
acdfghhiins
chafing-dish
acdfgilmnou
mould-facing
acdfhilpstu
dispatchful
acdfhinorrt
drift-anchor
acdfkloorrw
lock-forward
acdggiilnnr
dancing-girl
acdggiknorv
graving-dock
acdghiiiopr
idiographic
acdghimoosu
dichogamous
acdghioprsy
discography
acdgiiilost
dialogistic
acdgiiklnor
riding-cloak
acdgiinosst
diagnostics
acdgiinrstt
distracting
acdgiiorssu
disgracious
acdgilnoorw
wool-carding
acdgilnrtuy
traducingly
acdgimnnopu
up-and-coming
acdginnoopy
Pycnogonida
acdginnpstu
standing-cup
acdginoorvw
wood-carving

acdgioprrtu
agriproduct
acdgllootyy
dactylology
acdhhiiloty
ichthyoidal
acdhhioprrs
harpsichord
acdhhioprty
hydropathic
acdhhiorrsy
Hydrocharis
acdhiiimrtt
Mithridatic
acdhiiloopr
chiropodial
acdhiimnors
diachronism
disharmonic
acdhiinoopr
radiophonic
acdhiioprst
diastrophic
acdhiloopsz
schizopodal
acdhimnoort
trichomonad
acdhimnorsy
dysharmonic
acdhimnorty
hydromantic
acdhimnrssy
scrimshandy
acdhinooprs
discophoran
acdhinoorsu
diachronous
acdhiorstty
hydrostatic
acdhlloooow
wood-alcohol
acdhlnooort
notochordal
acdhloorssw
schoolwards
acdhnoprsuy
Hydnocarpus
acdiiiillnps
disciplinal
acdiiilloty
idiotically
acdiiilmory
domiciliary
acdiiilorst
dioristical
acdiiimnotu
unidiomatic
acdiiinnotv
vindication
acdiijllruy
juridically
acdiiknoost
dockisation

acdiillorst
clostridial
acdiilmnopr
palindromic
acdiilmnssy
syndicalism
acdiilmoost
sodomitical
acdiilmsttu
Talmudistic
acdiilnnoot
conditional
acdiilnnotu
inductional
acdiilnoost
dislocation
acdiilnoptu
duplication
acdiilnssty
syndicalist
acdiimorsty
myocarditis
acdiinnosty
syndication
acdiinooprs
Scorpionida
acdiinoprst
adscription
acdiinorstt
distraction
acdiinortvy
vindicatory
acdiioorrrr
air-corridor
acdiioorsss
sarcoidosis
acdillnorty
doctrinally
acdillnosyy
synodically
acdillorsty
crystalloid
acdilnosuuu
nudicaulous
acdimnoopst
spodomantic
acdimnoostt
mastodontic
acdimooorrt
cardiomotor
acdinnnooot
condonation
acdinoorssu
icosandrous
acdinoprrtu
drop-curtain
acdkllnoorr
rock-and-roll
acdllnoortu
dual-control
acdlloptyyy
polydactyly
acdlnooorty
condolatory

acdmnooopuz
azocompound
acdnorrsttu
transductor
aceeeeekppr
peace-keeper
aceeeerstwz
tweezer-case
aceeefffrtt
after-effect
aceeeffgstt
stage-effect
aceeeghhrst
charge-sheet
aceeeghllnr
rechallenge
aceeeghnprr
crepehanger
aceeegilnrt
energetical
aceeegimnrt
race-meeting
aceeegimnst
miscegenate
aceeegimntt
metagenetic
aceeegmnopr
peace-monger
aceeegnorru
re-encourage
aceeehiimpr
epicheirema
aceeehilnnp
encephaline
aceeehimntv
achievement
aceeehinsst
cenesthesia
aceeehiorvv
overachieve
aceeehklnrt
leather-neck
aceeehkmprs
speech-maker
aceeehllnrt
chanterelle
aceeehmnnnt
enhancement
aceeehmnstt
escheatment
aceeehmortt
tacheometer
aceeehrsstw
cheese-straw
aceeeillmrr
crémaillère
aceeeilmnpt
mantelpiece
aceeeilnquv
equivalence
aceeeilnrrv
irrelevance
aceeeimprst
masterpiece

aceeeinnppt
inappetence
aceeeinsstt
necessitate
aceeeipttvx
expectative
aceeejklpst
steeplejack
aceeejorstt
ejector-seat
aceeellmnov
malevolence
aceeellsssy
ceaselessly
aceeelmmnpt
emplacement
aceeelmnprt
replacement
aceeelmnrrt
recremental
aceeelmnrtx
excremental
aceeelqrrtu
lacquer-tree
aceeemnnrtt
re-enactment
aceeemnrttw
cement-water
water-cement
aceeenpprtu
perpetuance
aceeeoprttx
expectorate
aceeffghinn
chaff-engine
aceeffiilos
officialese
aceeffilntu
ineffectual
aceeffiltvy
affectively
aceeffioppr
paper-office
aceeffllost
coffee-stall
aceefflltuy
effectually
aceeffmnort
afforcement
aceefhinnrs
enfranchise
aceefhinrvw
weaver-finch
aceefhirrtw
fire-watcher
aceefhklttw
Twelfth-cake
aceefhlrrsu
researchful
aceefhnrrtu
furtherance
aceefiisttt
testificate
aceefillort
refocillate
aceefilnrsu
increaseful
aceefilpruu
Cupuliferae
aceefilrstv
service-flat
aceefimnors
freemasonic
aceefimnttu
tumefacient
aceefinorrt
refectorian
aceefkmoprt
pomfret-cake
aceefllnrst
crestfallen
aceeflnrssu
carefulness
aceeflorruv
overcareful
aceeflorsuu
ferulaceous
aceeflottuv
octave-flute
aceeflprrtu
prefectural
aceefmnoprr
performance
aceeggimmno
emmenagogic
aceeggimnot
geomagnetic
aceeghhnosu
change-house
aceeghhorsu
charge-house
aceeghhprry
hypercharge
aceeghillnr
all-cheering
aceeghilmno
hegemonical
aceeghiloot
oligochaete
aceeghilprt
telegraphic
aceeghinnox
ion-exchange
aceeghinnrt
interchange
aceeghkrstu
hucksterage
aceeghmmort
hectogramme
aceeghnrrsu
charge-nurse
aceeghprrsu
supercharge
aceegiilnnt
geanticline
aceegiinprr
ear-piercing
aceegiknnpp
knee-capping
aceegillnor
collegianer
aceegillnry
generically
aceegillnty
genetically
aceegillnuy
eugenically
aceegilmmrt
telegrammic
aceegilmort
geometrical
aceegilnprs
sleeping-car
aceegilnrry
gyre-carline
aceegilsttu
gesticulate
aceegimmnpt
camp-meeting
aceegimmnrt
centigramme
aceegimmort
microgamete
aceeginortt
teratogenic
aceegirrrty
cerargyrite
aceegirsttt
strategetic
aceegklnoor
cook-general
aceegknorrt
rocket-range
aceegllrssy
gracelessly
aceeglmnnot
congealment
aceeglmnopr
place-monger
aceeglnnstu
languescent
aceegmnorrs
scaremonger
aceegnnorrs
organ-screen
aceegnnosst
cognateness
aceegpprrsu
caper-spurge
aceegrrsssu
rescue-grass
aceehhilptw
Whitechapel
aceehhiprst
teachership
aceehhitttt
hatchettite
aceehhlmrst
crash-helmet
aceehhlorst
hearse-cloth
aceehhlostt
shoe-latchet
aceehhnorst
sheet-anchor
aceehhoptty
hypothecate
aceehiilnot
Aeneolithic
aceehiilnst
antihelices
aceehiilprt
perithecial
aceehiimmnt
time-machine
aceehiimrst
hetaerismic
aceehiinnrt
inheritance
aceehiipprt
perihepatic
aceehiirstt
theatricise
aceehillnnp
panhellenic
aceehillrty
heretically
aceehilnprt
phrenetical
aceehilnrtt
chain-letter
threnetical
aceehilortt
theoretical
aceehimmnpt
impeachment
aceehimnnnt
enchainment
aceehimnnsu
unmechanise
aceehimnopr
rope-machine
aceehimnrst
cashierment
aceehimortt
theorematic
aceehimrrsw
schwärmerei
aceehimrstt
catheterism
aceehimrtty
erythematic
aceehimsttw
witches'-meat
aceehinnstz
Nietzschean
aceehinorst
heteroscian
aceehinortt
Theocritean
aceehinprss
preachiness
aceehinprtt
parenthetic
aceehioprrt
Cheiroptera
aceehioprst
spirochaete
aceehiprrst
Petrarchise
aceehiprttu
therapeutic
aceehiprtvy
hyperactive
aceehirsstv
tsesarevich
aceehjkllst
shell-jacket
aceehkllopt
placket-hole
aceehklorrt
rock-leather
aceehllrrst
shell-crater
aceehlmopsy
mesocephaly
aceehlnopsu
encephalous
aceehlnprtu
place-hunter
aceehloorru
leucorrhoea
aceehloprrt
perchlorate
aceehlorstt
earth-closet
aceehmmnnrt
merchantmen
aceehmnnntt
enchantment
aceehmnnrrt
trencher-man
aceehmnnstt
chastenment
aceehmoptty
hepatectomy
aceehmopxyy
Myxophyceae
aceehmortty
tacheometry
aceehnnorrt
archenteron
aceehnnostt
chansonette
aceehnnrsst
enchantress
aceehnrrsst
stern-chaser
aceehorrstt
orchestrate
Sachertorte
aceehorrstu
treacherous
aceehorrttu
treachetour
aceeiikrstt
rickettsiae

aceeiillnpt
 penicillate
aceeiillnrt
 rectilineal
aceeiillppt
 epileptical
aceeiilnrrt
 rectilinear
aceeiilprss
 specialiser
aceeiilprsu
 peculiarise
aceeiilprtt
 periclitate
aceeiilptvx
 explicative
aceeiilrrst
 rectiserial
aceeiimrstv
 miscreative
aceeiinntuv
 enunciative
aceeiinoprt
 capernoitie
aceeiinrsst
 canisterise
aceeiinrttv
 interactive
aceeiipprtt
 peripatetic
 precipitate
aceeiiprttv
 crepitative
aceeiirsstt
 cassiterite
aceeijnnrtt
 interjacent
aceeikmprrt
 market-price
aceeiknrstw
 awe-stricken
aceeiknssss
 seasickness
aceeilllsty
 celestially
aceeillnnss
 cleanliness
aceeillnpst
 slate-pencil
 splenetical
aceeillorst
 selectorial
aceeillrtvy
 cleverality
aceeilmnnrt
 incremental
aceeilmnopt
 Incompletae
aceeilmnrry
 mercenarily
aceeilmorrt
 calorimeter
aceeilmorst
 elastomeric

aceeilmpsst
 esemplastic
aceeilmrtuv
 vermiculate
aceeilnnort
 intolerance
aceeilnnotu
 enucleation
aceeilnnrst
 intercensal
aceeilnntuu
 uninucleate
aceeilnntuy
 lieutenancy
aceeilnoptx
 exceptional
aceeilnorss
 recessional
aceeilnorst
 secretional
aceeilnosss
 secessional
aceeilnosst
 co-essential
aceeilnprrt
 pericentral
aceeilnprtt
 centripetal
aceeilnptty
 pectinately
aceeilnquvy
 equivalency
aceeilnrrvy
 irrelevancy
aceeilnrsst
 treacliness
aceeilnrssy
 necessarily
aceeilnssst
 elasticness
aceeilntttu
 tentaculite
aceeilopstt
 police-state
aceeilorrtv
 correlative
aceeilortux
 executorial
aceeilprtty
 rectipetaly
aceeilpstuv
 speculative
aceeilstttu
 testiculate
aceeimmnort
 anemometric
aceeimmnrrs
 mercenarism
aceeimmoprr
 microampere
aceeimmorst
 commiserate
aceeimnnott
 cementation

aceeimnorrt
 craniometer
aceeimnortt
 actinometer
aceeimnprtt
 permittance
aceeimnqrtu
 acquirement
aceeinnnsst
 ancientness
aceeinnoptz
 pentazocine
aceeinnorss
 reascension
aceeinnppty
 inappetency
aceeinnpttx
 inexpectant
aceeinnrrsu
 reinsurance
aceeinnsstx
 inexactness
aceeinopttx
 expectation
aceeinprrst
 transpierce
aceeinrrstv
 transceiver
aceeiooprtv
 cooperative
 co-operative
aceeiopprsu
 piperaceous
aceeioprrtv
 procreative
aceeiorrttv
 retroactive
aceeiorsttx
 stereotaxic
aceeirssttu
 resuscitate
aceejnprstu
 superjacent
aceekklmrsy
 mackerel-sky
aceeklmnrtt
 tracklement
aceeklnoprt
 rocket-plane
aceekmrrstw
 wreck-master
aceekprrsst
 racket-press
aceellmnrss
 small-screen
aceellnorty
 co-eternally
aceellnostt
 constellate
aceellooprt
 coleopteral
aceelloptuy
 eucalyptole

aceellqrsuy
 Carlylesque
aceellrrstu
 Craterellus
aceellrssty
 tracelessly
aceellsssuy
 causelessly
aceelmnnoov
 monovalence
aceelmnoptt
 contemplate
aceelnnnssu
 uncleanness
aceelnnrssu
 unclearness
aceelnoprtu
 counterplea
aceelnopstt
 Pentecostal
aceelnorstu
 counterseal
aceelnpttxy
 expectantly
aceeloorrtw
 water-cooler
aceeloorstw
 sea-colewort
aceelopppprt
 copperplate
aceeloppprtt
 Plectoptera
aceelorsttt
 store-cattle
aceelorsttw
 water-closet
aceemmmoort
 commemorate
aceemnnnotu
 mountenance
aceemnnortu
 connumerate
aceemnnrruy
 unmercenary
aceemnortty
 cementatory
aceemorsttt
 stactometer
aceennnopru
 preannounce
aceennoprtu
 counterpane
aceennorstt
 consternate
aceennpprsy
 scrape-penny
aceennpttux
 unexpectant
aceennrssuy
 unnecessary
aceenoorstt
 cotoneaster
aceenoprttx
 expectorant

aceeooprstu
 proteaceous
aceeoorsstu
 ostreaceous
aceeoprrrtu
 recuperator
aceeoprstuv
 superoctave
aceeorrstuw
 watercourse
aceeorsstuu
 Ceteosaurus
aceepprrttu
 paper-cutter
aceeprrssuu
 acupressure
aceeprssstt
 spectatress
acefffgilor
 flag-officer
acefffimors
 farm-offices
aceffghilnr
 cliffhanger
aceffgiilnt
 face-lifting
aceffgilnty
 affectingly
aceffginntu
 unaffecting
aceffiilpst
 spifflicate
aceffiittvy
 affectivity
aceffikoprr
 park-officer
aceffilortu
 forficulate
aceffilrsst
 trafficless
aceffimopst
 stamp-office
aceffiostuv
 suffocative
acefghllnuy
 changefully
acefghlnnor
 Anglo-French
acefghooprr
 proof-charge
acefgiiinst
 significate
acefgiimnnt
 magnificent
acefgiinnrt
 interfacing
acefgiknorw
 working-face
acefgilnrtu
 centrifugal
acefgilnttu
 leaf-cutting
acefginortu
 configurate

acefhhinstt
snatch-thief
acefhiilnps
pelican-fish
acefhiinrty
chieftainry
acefhilnopr
francophile
acefhilnosu
leaf-cushion
acefhilrsty
self-charity
acefhloprru
reproachful
acefhmorrtt
mothercraft
acefhnnoopr
francophone
acefhoorstu
house-factor
acefiiimnrt
rifacimenti
acefiiinort
reification
acefiikllrt
flickertail
acefiilnnss
finicalness
acefiilprsu
superficial
acefiimnort
rifacimento
acefiinoptt
pontificate
acefiinorst
fractionise
acefiinorsu
facinerious
acefiinrrtu
curtain-fire
acefilloruw
cauliflower
acefilnortt
fractionlet
acefilorstu
lactiferous
acefilostuy
facetiously
acefimnottu
tumefaction
acefimorrrt
crateriform
acefinnottu
functionate
acefinnrsst
franticness
acefinottuv
confutative
acefinprsty
presanctify
acefinrrrtu
franc-tireur
acefioorrtv
vociferator
acefiprrstt
priestcraft
acefklmorst
flock-master
acefkmorrst
stock-farmer
acefkmrrrtu
truck-farmer
acefllloss w
class-fellow
aceflnnoost
stone-falcon
acegghillnn
challenging
acegghopsuy
psychagogue
aceggillmoo
gemological
aceggillnou
colleaguing
acegginnoru
encouraging
acegginrsss
scragginess
aceggl nooyy
gynaecology
aceghhilopr
helicograph
aceghhilrst
searchlight
aceghhlortu
leach-trough
aceghhnorst
shortchange
aceghhooprr
choreograph
aceghhoprry
choregraphy
aceghiilprx
lexigraphic
aceghiilrru
hierurgical
aceghiiprrs
serigraphic
aceghikllns
shellacking
aceghikmnop
epoch-making
aceghillnnn
channelling
aceghillnrt
night-cellar
aceghilloot
ethological
theological
aceghilnoot
theogonical
aceghilnrsy
searchingly
aceghilopsy
geophysical
aceghimnoru
archegonium
aceghinnpru
unpreaching
aceghinprss
graphicness
aceghiooprr
oreographic
aceghloosty
eschatology
aceghloptty
glyptotheca
aceghmoorsu
hercogamous
aceghnoprsy
scenography
aceghooprsu
creophagous
aceghoopsty
phagocytose
aceghoprrst
port-charges
acegiiklnrs
arse-licking
acegiillnnv
clean-living
acegiillotv
colligative
acegiilostt
egotistical
acegiilrsst
sacrilegist
acegiimnost
isomagnetic
acegiimnrst
Germanistic
acegiimrrtv
gravimetric
acegiinrrrr
ring-carrier
acegiinrstu
cauterising
acegiinrstw
writing-case
acegiiprrst
perigastric
acegijnotuv
conjugative
acegiknorst
orange-stick
acegillmrtu
metallurgic
acegillnnoy
congenially
acegillnnru
unrecalling
acegillnooo
oenological
acegillnoop
penological
acegillnoss
logicalness
acegillooor
oreological
acegilloors
serological
acegilmnrsy
screamingly
acegilmosty
cleistogamy
acegilnnnou
uncongenial
acegilnnoos
cloisonnage
acegilnnoot
congelation
acegilnnprs
spring-clean
acegilnnrtu
clearing-nut
acegilnnsuy
unceasingly
acegilnosuu
cauligenous
acegilnrssy
caressingly
acegilnrstt
scatterling
acegilntuuu
unguiculate
acegiloopst
apologetics
acegiloortt
teratologic
acegilorsuv
clavigerous
acegilrrtuu
agriculture
acegimnnoot
cognominate
acegimnnopr
panic-monger
acegimnoost
somatogenic
acegimnootz
zoomagnetic
aceginnnosu
consanguine
aceginnopry
panegyricon
aceginnorty
octingenary
aceginnrsty
astringency
aceginnsstw
newscasting
aceginoortv
overcoating
aceginorstv
overcasting
aceginosstu
sea-scouting
aceginosttv
casting-vote
aceginrtttu
rate-cutting
acegioprssu
scapigerous
acegklnnouw
luckengowan
acegklopsst
pocket-glass
acegkrssttu
stage-struck
aceglmnorwy
clergy-woman
aceglnoprty
calyptrogen
aceglnortuy
granulocyte
aceglorrssv
clover-grass
aceglrssttu
glass-cutter
acegmnnorss
congressman
acegmoprrst
spectrogram
acegmorstty
gastrectomy
acegnorrsst
cross-garnet
acegooprsst
gastroscope
acegrrssttu
grass-cutter
acehhiilmst
hemistichal
acehhiimrrs
hierarchism
acehhiinnty
hyacinthine
acehhimnops
machine-shop
acehhimostt
theomachist
acehhinoppy
phycophaein
acehhinoptt
Phaethontic
acehhinrrtu
heart-urchin
acehhiprstt
heptarchist
acehhklrtuy
hurly-hacket
acehhlmmort
hammercloth
acehhlnoort
anthochlore
acehhmnnsuu
Munchhausen
acehhoprtyy
hypothecary
acehiiimrst
hetairismic
acehiiinpss
hispanicise
acehiillmot
homiletical
acehiillnrt
tiller-chain
trichinella

acehiillost
isolecithal
acehiilmstt
athleticism
acehiilnopr
necrophilia
acehiilnprt
nephritical
acehiilostt
chiastolite
acehiilppty
epiphytical
acehiilrsvw
swivel-chair
acehiilstww
welwitschia
acehiimnopt
hemianoptic
acehiimrstt
theatricism
acehiimssst
schismatise
acehiinnopt
phonetician
acehiinorrt
rhetorician
acehiinprsy
physicianer
acehiinpstt
pantheistic
acehikllors
scholar-like
acehiklprty
prickly-heat
acehikmnors
chain-smoker
acehikmnorw
machine-work
acehikmrtuy
rheumaticky
acehikrrsss
sherris-sack
acehikrsstw
cat's-whisker
acehikrsttv
harvest-tick
acehillmrty
thermically
acehilloprt
plethorical
acehillortw
white-collar
acehillprsy
spherically
acehilmmnpy
lamp-chimney
acehilmnoor
Melanochroi
acehilmnoot
machine-tool
acehilmnost
slot-machine
acehilmoptu
plaice-mouth

acehilmortt
thermotical
acehilnprst
sphincteral
acehilnstty
synthetical
acehilooprt
orthoepical
acehiloorrz
coleorrhiza
acehiloottu
acolouthite
acehilopprt
prophetical
acehilopprw
coal-whipper
acehilrsssy
chrysalises
acehimmoprt
metamorphic
acehimnnstt
tennis-match
acehimnopss
championess
acehimnorss
marchioness
acehimnosyy
hyoscyamine
acehimnottu
humectation
acehimnttuw
minute-watch
acehimoostt
homeostatic
acehimoprst
atmospheric
acehimorrst
choir-master
acehimorsst
metachrosis
acehimorttx
thermotaxic
acehimprrst
Petrarchism
acehimpssty
metaphysics
acehimpstty
sympathetic
acehinnnors
chansonnier
acehinnnrtt
intrenchant
acehinnoptt
pantothenic
acehinnrssu
raunchiness
acehinnstty
synanthetic
acehinnttuu
unauthentic
acehinoprrs
chairperson
acehinoprrt
chiropteran

acehinoprtu
neuropathic
acehinorrst
orchestrina
acehinrssst
starchiness
acehioopstt
osteopathic
acehioopttv
photoactive
acehioorttv
cohortative
acehioprrst
creatorship
acehioprrtt
Trichoptera
acehiprrstt
Petrarchist
acehiprssuy
hyperacusis
acehiqrrsuy
squirearchy
acehkkllmsu
Muschelkalk
acehkrrsttu
heart-struck
acehllmrssy
charmlessly
acehllmssty
matchlessly
acehlloorrs
horse-collar
acehlmoopty
cephalotomy
acehlmossst
stomachless
acehlnnrtty
trenchantly
acehlnoprty
lycanthrope
acehlopsuxy
sceuophylax
acehmnoprsy
prosenchyma
acehmnoprty
tephromancy
acehmooppst
compost-heap
acehmoortty
tracheotomy
acehnnooprt
ctenophoran
acehnnssstu
staunchness
acehnoorttu
tautochrone
acehnprsstu
snatch-purse
acehooppsty
hepatoscopy
acehooprrst
prothoraces
acehoprrssy
chrysoprase

acehoprrtyy
cryotherapy
acehorssttt
scattershot
acehorssttv
torch-staves
acehorstuwy
water-souchy
aceiiiknrst
kinesiatric
aceiiilmnrs
criminalise
aceiiilmptv
implicative
aceiiilnott
elicitation
aceiiilpstt
pietistical
aceiiimnnrt
incriminate
aceiiimnrtv
criminative
aceiiimnstt
anti-Semitic
aceiiinnoss
Socinianise
aceiiiqstuv
acquisitive
aceiiklrstt
rickettsial
aceiiknottu
autokinetic
aceiilll tvy
levitically
aceiillmmty
mimetically
aceiillmnnu
illuminance
aceiillmpry
empirically
aceiillnotv
vellication
aceiillnrtv
intervallic
aceiillnruv
curvilineal
aceiillnstt
scintillate
aceiillopst
epistolical
aceiillostv
oscillative
aceiillprtu
pleuritical
aceiilmnprt
planimetric
aceiilmnssu
masculinise
aceiilmorst
isometrical
aceiilmottu
itacolumite
aceiilmprsu
Laserpicium

aceiilmrrtt
trimetrical
aceiilnnort
reclination
aceiilnoort
coalitioner
aceiilnoppr
pilocarpine
aceiilnoprt
replication
aceiilnoptx
explication
aceiilnoqtu
equinoctial
aceiilnossv
Slavonicise
aceiilnotuv
inoculative
aceiilnpruy
pecuniarily
aceiilnrruv
curvilinear
aceiilnrstu
unrealistic
aceiilnrstx
extrinsical
aceiilnrtty
intricately
aceiiloorvv
cavo-rilievo
aceiilorrst
escritorial
aceiilprrtu
picture-rail
aceiilprsst
plasticiser
aceiilprstt
peristaltic
aceiilprtuy
peculiarity
aceiilrttvy
verticality
aceiimmnotv
comminative
aceiimnnors
Micronesian
aceiimnnort
incremation
aceiimnnrst
manneristic
aceiimnoprt
imprecation
aceiimnorst
creationism
miscreation
romanticise
aceiimnortt
metrication
aceiimnprru
pericranium
aceiimnpssu
impuissance
aceiimnrstt
martensitic

aceiimnrstu
insectarium
aceiimnsstt
semanticist
aceiimopssu
cassiopeium
aceiinnnotu
enunciation
aceiinnoptt
pectination
aceiinnorrt
incinerator
aceiinnortt
interaction
aceiinnpstt
pinnatisect
aceiinoortx
excoriation
aceiinoprtt
crepitation
aceiinopstt
pectisation
aceiinopstx
expiscation
aceiinorstt
creationist
reactionist
aceiinorstv
Insectivora
aceiinorttx
extrication
aceiinpprtt
precipitant
aceiinprtty
antipyretic
pertinacity
aceijkloptt
pilot-jacket
aceijlmmpru
claim-jumper
aceijlntuuw
walnut-juice
aceijmnoqtu
Jacqueminot
aceikllprtt
lick-platter
aceiklorttw
lattice-work
aceiklpprry
prickly-pear
aceikmnorst
section-mark
aceikmrsttt
smart-ticket
aceilllmnor
lamellicorn
aceilllmopy
polemically
aceilllnruu
unicellular
aceilllpsty
sylleptical
aceillmnnot
non-metallic

aceillmnost
Callistemon
aceillmnruy
numerically
aceillmnsuy
masculinely
aceillmorsy
lacrimosely
aceillmrruy
mercurially
aceillnnoty
octennially
aceillnoptu
cupellation
aceillnorru
carilloneur
aceillnosty
sectionally
aceillnotty
tonetically
aceillnrsty
crystalline
aceillopprt
proleptical
aceilloppsy
episcopally
aceilloquvy
equivocally
aceillorsuv
varicellous
aceillrrtuy
reticularly
aceillrssty
crystallise
aceillrstty
crystallite
aceillrtuvy
lucratively
aceillsstuv
victualless
aceilmmnosu
communalise
aceilmmnoty
metonymical
aceilmmorrt
coal-trimmer
aceilmmortt
recommittal
aceilmmrsty
symmetrical
aceilmnnort
conterminal
aceilmnnsuu
unmasculine
aceilmnoops
scopolamine
aceilmnoopw
policewoman
aceilmnottu
monticulate
aceilmnrttu
curtailment
aceilmnrtuu
retinaculum

aceilmnsssu
musicalness
aceilmorrty
calorimetry
aceilmrrtuu
mariculture
aceilnnnoss
nonsensical
aceilnnnott
continental
aceilnnoopt
Neoplatonic
aceilnnrtuy
uncertainly
aceilnnssty
incessantly
aceilnooprr
incorporeal
aceilnooprt
Neotropical
percolation
aceilnoorrt
correlation
aceilnoorsu
arenicolous
aceilnoortu
unicolorate
aceilnoosty
loan-society
aceilnopstu
speculation
aceilnopstx
xenoplastic
aceilnoptux
exculpation
aceilnoquuv
unequivocal
aceilnorrtu
interocular
aceilnorstt
intercostal
aceilnorttu
reluctation
aceilnortuv
countervail
involucrate
aceilnossst
stoicalness
aceilnostuy
tenaciously
aceilnpssty
typicalness
aceilnrrrtu
intercrural
aceilnrrtuv
ventricular
aceiloooprt
aeolotropic
aceiloopprs
polariscope
aceiloossst
osteoclasis
aceiloprrtt
protractile

aceiloprtxy
explicatory
aceilorsuvy
veraciously
aceilortvyy
viceroyalty
aceilpprtuy
picture-play
aceilprsttu
curtail-step
aceilprstty
spectrality
aceilprstux
speculatrix
aceilpssttu
speculatist
aceilqrtuuu
aquiculture
aceilrrttuu
turriculate
aceimmoossu
mimosaceous
aceimmorrtu
crematorium
aceimmottuv
commutative
aceimmprssu
supremacism
aceimmrsstu
music-master
aceimnnnott
containment
aceimnnoory
oneiromancy
aceimnooprs
rose-campion
aceimnoortx
axonometric
aceimnorrty
craniometry
aceimoprrty
Cryptomeria
imprecatory
aceimopttuv
computative
aceimortttu
tautometric
aceimprsstu
supremacist
aceimssstty
systematics
aceinnnnssu
uncanniness
aceinnoortt
contorniate
aceinnoottv
connotative
aceinnortuy
enunciatory
aceinnostty
encystation
aceinnprstu
Pentacrinus

aceinnptuuv
nuncupative
aceinnrrtuw
currant-wine
aceinnrttuy
uncertainty
aceinoooprt
co-operation
cooperation
aceinooprrt
incorporate
procreation
aceinooprss
sea-scorpion
aceinooprtu
aponeurotic
aceinoorrtt
retroaction
aceinopprty
cappernoity
aceinoprsss
prosaicness
aceinorrttu
centuriator
aceinorrtty
contrariety
aceinorsttv
contrastive
aceinorsuuv
unveracious
aceinpprsss
scrappiness
aceinpttuuv
punctuative
aceinrrtuuv
incurvature
aceinrssssu
narcissuses
aceinrssttu
resuscitant
aceinrssttv
transvestic
aceiooprrtv
corporative
aceiooprtvv
provocative
aceiooqrtuv
equivocator
aceioprrstt
tetrasporic
triceratops
aceioprrttv
protractive
aceioprstuu
precautious
aceioprstxy
expiscatory
acekkmorstt
stock-market
acekllrssty
tracklessly
acekmnorrtu
countermark

acekmorrsst
market-cross
acellImoruy
molecularly
acellmmnosy
commensally
acellmorsyy
lacrymosely
acellmprttu
trumpet-call
acellmpsssu
mussel-scalp
acellnorsuy
larcenously
acellnosssu
callousness
acellnrttuy
reluctantly
acellooprry
corporeally
acelmnnoopt
componental
acelmnnoort
nomenclator
acelmnnooru
mononuclear
acelmnnoovy
monovalency
acelmnnoptt
contemplant
acelmnoooty
Monocotylae
acelmpsssuu
mussel-scaup
acelmrstuuu
musculature
acelnnoopvx
plano-convex
acelnnorrtw
crown-antler
acelnnrsttu
translucent
acelnnrttuu
unreluctant
acelnorrwwy
crown-lawyer
acelnorsuuv
cavernulous
acelnorsuvy
cavernously
acelnossttu
sansculotte
acelnpprtuu
prepunctual
acelooprrtt
protectoral
acelooprrty
corporately
aceloorrtuw
water-colour
aceloprstuy
speculatory
aceloprtuxy
exculpatory

acemmnoortt
commentator
acemmnoprtt
compartment
acemnooprst
compensator
acemorssttu
scout-master
acennoorrtt
contra-tenor
acennoprstu
span-counter
acennprttyy
Nancy-pretty
acenoorrstv
conservator
acenoostttw
cotton-waste
acenopprstu
supportance
acenoprrstu
Procrustean
acenoprrttu
counterpart
acenoprsttu
constuprate
acenorsssuu
raucousness
acenorsttuy
country-seat
acenosssuuv
vacuousness
aceoopprrss
carpospores
aceooprrtuv
provocateur
acerrstttuw
straw-cutter
acffgiiknrt
trafficking
acffginostu
suffocating
acffhillnow
fallow-finch
acffiiilmos
officialism
acffiiiloty
officiality
acffinoostu
suffocation
acfghiiknps
fish-packing
acfghinosuv
vouchsafing
acfgiiinnst
significant
acfgiilnssy
classifying
acfgiinnsty
sanctifying
acfgilnttuu
fluctuating
acfglloooty
olfactology

acfhiilnoor
honorifical
acfhimorrst
ostrich-farm
acfhioprsty
factory-ship
acfiiillmry
mirifically
acfiiilmsst
facsimilist
acfiiinnotu
unification
acfiiinortv
vinificator
acfiilmnoru
californium
acfiilnopst
pontificals
acfiimmorru
formicarium
acfiimnoort
formication
acfiimnorst
informatics
acfiinnoort
fornication
acfiinooprt
forcipation
acfiioprrtu
purificator
acfillmoorr
coralliform
acfillooptt
toploftical
acfillostuu
lactifluous
acfilmnnotu
malfunction
acfilmoprrs
scalpriform
acfilmorsuv
vasculiform
acfilnottuu
fluctuation
acfilorstuy
fractiously
acfimnoorrt
confirmator
acfinnoottu
confutation
acfinnortuy
functionary
acfinorttuu
fructuation
acfnnnooopr
cannon-proof
acgghiilntt
tight-lacing
acgghiloopr
graphologic
logographic
acggijnnotu
conjugating

acggiknostz
gazing-stock
acghhiloopr
holographic
acghhinopry
ichnography
acghhioppty
phytophagic
acghhioprry
chirography
acghhmnorsu
ramgunshoch
acghhnooprr
chronograph
acghhooprry
chorography
acghhopprsy
psychograph
acghiillnop
anglophilic
acghiillrtv
gillravitch
acghiilmort
algorithmic
logarithmic
acghiilnort
granolithic
acghiilrrty
charity-girl
acghiinprty
pharyngitic
acghiiprsst
sphragistic
acghikmopry
kymographic
acghillmooo
homological
acghillooor
horological
acghilmoopr
lagomorphic
acghilmoost
logomachist
acghilnnoop
anglophonic
acghilnnsty
snatchingly
acghilnrstt
latch-string
acghilnrstu
nautch-girls
acghiloppry
polygraphic
acghiloprxy
xylographic
acghimnoopr
gramophonic
monographic
acghimooprt
tomographic
acghimoprry
micrography

acghimopsty
mycophagist
phagocytism
acghinooprs
nosographic
acghinoopry
iconography
acghinoprry
granophyric
acghinopryz
zincography
acghinprstw
watch-spring
acghiooppr t
topographic
acghiopprty
pictography
typographic
acghioprsty
hypogastric
acghiqrsstu
quitch-grass
acghirsstw
twitch-grass
acghirstttu
straight-cut
acghmooprsy
cosmography
acghnoooprr
coronograph
acghopprrty
cryptograph
acgiiilnost
logistician
acgiiilnpst
salpingitic
acgiikllpry
pilgarlicky
acgiilllloy
illogically
acgiillnoos
Sinological
acgiillnoot
colligation
acgiillnost
oscillating
acgiillntuv
victualling
acgiilloorv
virological
acgiilmnnop
complaining
acgiilnnoot
cognitional
acgiiloprtt
graptolitic
acgiimnosst
agnosticism
acgiimrsttu
Targumistic
acgiinnnost
incognisant
acgiinnostw
wainscoting

acgijjkmnpu
jumping-jack
acgijlnotuy
conjugality
acgijnnootu
conjugation
acgikknnort
knock-rating
acgikknostt
stocktaking
acgillmnooo
monological
nomological
acgillmooop
pomological
acgillmoors
oscillogram
acgillmooty
climatology
acgillmooyz
zymological
acgillnooos
nosological
acgillnooot
ontological
acgillnosty
gnostically
acgillnrryy
rallying-cry
acgillnrswy
scrawlingly
acgillooops
posological
acgillooopt
topological
acgilloopty
typological
acgillopsuy
callipygous
acgilmooost
somatologic
acgilnnoort
gain-control
acgilnorsuy
carousingly
acgimnnoory
craniognomy
acgimnoopru
carpogonium
acgimnoorst
gastronomic
acginnopstw
townscaping
acginoorrtu
corrugation
acginoorsty
co-signatory
acginoostuv
noctivagous
acgiorsstty
gyrostatics
acgllnooovy
volcanology

acgllnoouvy
vulcanology
acgmooprrtu
compurgator
acgmooprssy
gyrocompass
acgnoorsstt
cotton-grass
acgrrsssuvy
scurvy-grass
achhiillpty
ithyphallic
achhiilmopt
philomathic
achhillmoot
homothallic
achhiloprss
scholarship
achhinoortx
Xanthochroi
achhinsstuz
Schizanthus
achhiopstyz
Schizophyta
achhiorstuy
ichthyosaur
achhnoosttu
autochthons
achhnoottuy
autochthony
achhoppstyy
psychopathy
achiiimmrst
Mithraicism
achiiimnpss
hispanicism
achiiipprst
hippiatrics
achiijknrsw
jinrickshaw
achiillmswy
whimsically
achiilmostt
Thomistical
achiilmpssy
physicalism
achiilnopst
canophilist
achiilnrsty
Christianly
achiilooppr
coprophilia
achiiloopps
scopophilia
achiiloprsv
co-rivalship
achiilopsst
sophistical
achiilpssty
physicalist
achiilpstyy
physicality
achiinnrstu
unchristian

achiinoortz
Zonotrichia
achiinssttt
satin-stitch
achillorsst
choir-stalls
achilmoopst
homoplastic
achilmorryz
mycorrhizal
achilnooops
piano-school
achilnpsttw
switch-plant
achilooptyz
zoophytical
achimmnoosu
monochasium
achimnnnoor
nonharmonic
achimnoorst
Trichomonas
achimnoptyy
Amphictyony
achimnosstt
Scottishman
achimnppssy
panpsychism
achimooprsy
hypocorisma
achimooprtu
automorphic
achimoossst
Schistosoma
achimopppsu
hippocampus
achimoprssy
symposiarch
achimopssty
scyphistoma
achimorrsty
chrismatory
achimrsssty
Christmassy
achinooprtz
zoanthropic
achinoopstt
photonastic
achinppssty
panpsychist
achiooppprst
apostrophic
achiooepprtt
haptotropic
protopathic
achiooppstt
potato-chips
achiooprttu
autotrophic
achioorsttt
orthostatic
achiopprsty
saprophytic

achioprrstu
curatorship
achllnorsuy
unscholarly
achlloopprst
chloroplast
achlmmooors
chromosomal
achlmnoortu
motor-launch
achlmooprst
chromoplast
achlnoprtyy
lycanthropy
achloooprty
Cotylophora
achmmnooort
monochromat
achmmoppstu
stomach-pump
achmnoopsuy
cymophanous
achnoprstyy
sycophantry
aciiiilmnty
inimicality
aciiillmopt
impolitical
aciiillmptu
capillitium
aciiillnotv
villication
aciiilmnopt
implication
aciiilmnrst
criminalist
aciiilmnrty
criminality
aciiilmopst
apoliticism
aciiilnnnot
inclination
aciiilnnrst
intrinsical
aciiilnpstu
Paulinistic
aciiilrsttu
ritualistic
aciiimnnort
crimination
aciiimnnoss
Socinianism
aciiimossvv
vivacissimo
aciiinnottt
nictitation
aciiinoqstu
acquisition
aciiinprsst
Priscianist
aciiiossttu
ascititious
aciiilllopty
politically

aciillmnoos
colonialism
aciillmnoot
collimation
aciillmnpuy
municipally
aciillmosuy
maliciously
aciillnnstt
scintillant
aciillnoost
colonialist
oscillation
aciillnoptu
unpolitical
aciillnorst
carillonist
aciillnovvy
convivially
aciillnppry
principally
aciilloprty
pictorially
aciillprstu
pluralistic
aciillquyzz
quizzically
aciilmnnopt
incompliant
aciilmnnosy
synonimical
aciilmnnotu
culmination
aciilmnoopt
compilation
aciilmnopst
Platonicism
aciilmnortu
latrocinium
aciilmnossu
unsocialism
aciilmnosuu
unmalicious
aciilmnsstu
masculinist
aciilmnstuy
masculinity
aciilnnootu
inoculation
aciilnnoptu
inculpation
aciilnnorty
inclinatory
aciilnnsttu
instinctual
aciilnostuy
unsociality
aciilnottuv
cultivation
aciiloopsst
isapostolic
aciiloprrst
scriptorial

aciilorsst
scissor-tail
aciilorsttu
staurolitic
aciilorsuvy
vicariously
aciilosuvvy
vivaciously
aciilppstuv
supplicavit
aciimmmnost
mammonistic
aciimmnnoot
commination
aciimmnorst
romanticism
aciimmnosst
monasticism
aciimmnsstu
numismatics
aciimmooprr
comprimario
aciimnnostt
Montanistic
aciimnoorsu
acrimonious
aciimnorrty
criminatory
aciimnorstt
romanticist
aciinnortuv
incurvation
aciinooprst
anisotropic
aciinoossst
iconostasis
aciinoosttt
tostication
aciinoprttu
unpatriotic
aciinorsttu
rustication
aciinossttu
suscitation
aciinrtttuy
taciturnity
aciiopssstt
psittacosis
aciiorrstuu
urticarious
aciirssstuu
saussuritic
acijnnoortu
conjuration
acillmnopty
compliantly
acillmnsuuy
unmusically
acillmoosty
osmotically
acillmopsty
plasmolytic
acillmotyyz
zymotically

acillnnooop
apollonicon
acillnnotuy
continually
acillnooprr
incorporall
acilloorsty
oscillatory
acilmmmnosu
communalism
acilmmnooot
commotional
acilmmnooty
commonality
acilmmnostu
communalist
acilmmorssu
commissural
acilmnnoptu
uncompliant
acilmnoopty
toponymical
acilmnortuy
columnarity
acilmnostuu
musculation
acilmooprty
compilatory
acilmorstuy
customarily
acilmrstuuy
muscularity
acilnnooost
consolation
acilnooortu
colouration
acilnoopstu
unapostolic
acilnoorrst
conirostral
acilnoorstx
consolatrix
acilnoortuy
inoculatory
locutionary
acilnoprtuy
inculpatory
acilnorsstu
ultrasonics
acilnpsttuu
punctualist
acilnpttuuy
punctuality
aciloopprrty
corporality
aciloorstuy
atrociously
aciloorsuvy
voraciously
aciloprstuy
crapulosity
acilosstuuy
astuciously

acimmnoorty
comminatory
acimmnoottu
commutation
acimmopstty
symptomatic
acimmorstuu
muscatorium
acimnnooost
onomasticon
acimnnoopry
Cypro-Minoan
acimnnostyy
synonymatic
acimnoooptt
compotation
acimnooostt
somatotonic
acimnoopssu
poison-sumac
acimnoopttu
computation
acimnoprtuy
importunacy
acimooprrst
corporatism
acinnnnoost
inconsonant
acinnnooott
connotation
acinnnoptuu
nuncupation
acinnooprtt
contraption
acinnoopsty
syncopation
acinnoorttu
continuator
acinnopttuu
punctuation
acinnorssst
transsonics
acinoooprrt
corporation
acinoooprtv
provocation
acinooprrst
conspirator
acinooprrtt
protraction
acinooprrtu
procuration
acinoorrstu
contrarious
acinoorrsuv
carnivorous
acinoprstuu
curnaptious
aciooprrstt
corporatist
aciorssssy
syssarcosis
ackooprrrsw
rock-sparrow

acllmoorsuy
clamorously
acllnnortuy
nocturnally
aclloorsuuy
oraculously
aclloprstyy
polycrystal
aclmnoorsty
monocrystal
aclnnnoosty
consonantly
aclnoopttt
cotton-plant
aclnooorsty
consolatory
aclnooprrsu
proconsular
aclnoorrsuy
rancorously
aclooprrsuy
polycarpous
aclooprsuxy
xylocarpous
acloorrstuw
straw-colour
acmmnoorstu
consummator
acmnoooprsu
monocarpous
acmoooprtty
compotatory
acmooossttu
scotomatous
acnnoprtuuy
nuncupatory
acnooprssuu
Uranoscopus
acoooprrtvy
provocatory
acooprrrtuy
procuratory
addddeeghiy
giddy-headed
addddeehmuy
muddy-headed
adddeehnnru
underhanded
adddeehnoru
round-headed
adddeeimmtu
medium-dated
adddeeimnst
middenstead
adddeelnoss
saddle-nosed
adddeenrssu
unaddressed
adddefgorrt
draft-dodger
adddegginry
dandy-rigged
adddegglopy
doggy-paddle

adddersstu
star-studded
adddhilmooo
old-maidhood
adddimnostu
diamond-dust
addeeeehkls
sleek-headed
addeeeehllv
level-headed
addeeeehlst
steel-headed
addeeefilsu
defeudalise
addeeeghpsw
wedge-shaped
addeeegiltw
wedge-tailed
addeeeglntu
undelegated
addeeehhitw
white-headed
addeeehhnrt
three-handed
addeeehikns
hide-and-seek
addeeehllpw
paddle-wheel
addeeehllsw
swell-headed
addeeehlmty
metalhedyde
addeeehmpty
empty-headed
addeeeirtww
wide-watered
addeeellpst
pedestalled
addeeeoprss
desperadoes
addeefghinn
hand-feeding
addeefghirt
dead-freight
addeefmnrtu
defraudment
addeefnorrw
forwandered
addeeghhilt
light-headed
addeeghilpy
pigheadedly
addeeghnorw
wrong-headed
addeegiistt
sedigitated
addeegikmnr
redding-kame
addeegiknrs
reading-desk
addeegilmnr
large-minded
addeegilrst
girdlestead

addeeginprw
deep-drawing
addeeginrrw
reed-drawing
addeegjmntu
adjudgement
addeegnrssu
guardedness
addeehhintw
white-handed
addeehiilnp
Delphinidae
addeehiknrt
kind-hearted
addeehilmrt
middle-earth
addeehisttu
death-duties
addeehlnnsu
unhandseled
addeehlnorv
overhandled
addeehlorss
saddle-horse
addeehmnpty
empty-handed
addeehnortw
down-hearted
addeehpppuy
puppy-headed
addeehprrss
hard-pressed
addeeillsvw
well-advised
addeeilrrvy
dare-devilry
addeeimnory
ready-monied
addeeimnttu
unmeditated
addeeimrstu
desideratum
addeeinoprt
depredation
addeeinsssv
advisedness
addeeirttwy
ready-witted
addeellrssy
dreadlessly
addeelnoruv
round-leaved
addeemnnnru
undermanned
addeemnrstu
undermasted
addeenortww
watered-down
addeenprsuu
unpersuaded
addeenrsttu
understated
addeeoprrty
depredatory

addeffhlnoy
offhandedly
addefhinsss
faddishness
addegghortu
goddaughter
addeggiiirt
digitigrade
addeghhilnt
light-handed
addeghhinrt
right-handed
addeghilrst
saddle-girth
addeghnortu
dreadnought
addegiimnnr
mind-reading
addegilmnny
maddeningly
addegimnnnu
undemanding
addegimnnor
road-mending
addeginnosu
undiagnosed
addeginnrst
angst-ridden
addegjmntuy
judgment-day
addeglnruuy
unguardedly
addegnoortu
good-natured
addehhiopry
Hydrophidae
addehhmortu
hard-mouthed
addehhnnory
horny-handed
addehhnoopr
rhododaphne
addehhnorst
short-handed
addehiilmot
thalidomide
addehiknntt
hand-knitted
addehilnnrs
hinderlands
addehilopsu
diadelphous
addehinorty
dehydration
addehlorstt
stadtholder
addehmorsuy
hydromedusa
addehnrrttu
thunder-dart
addehoprssw
sword-shaped
addeiiintuv
individuate

addeiinootx
deoxidation
addeiinorst
disordinate
addeikmnrrr
dram-drinker
addeillmmns
small-minded
addeilnsuvy
unadvisedly
addeimnoors
rose-diamond
addeiooppsu
pseudopodia
addelmnotuu
unmodulated
addelnnrtuy
redundantly
addelnntuuy
undauntedly
addelnorrty
dendrolatry
addelooprw
leopard-wood
addemnooort
rodomontade
addemnoopsu
pseudomonad
addenoorssw
sanderswood
addeoopsttt
toad-spotted
addghillnno
landholding
addghilnoor
roadholding
addghnortuw
down-draught
addgimnnopw
damping-down
addhiilnoov
invalidhood
addhnoossuw
sound-shadow
addiiiimnot
dimidiation
addiiiosttu
addititious
addiinorstu
suraddition
addijnosuww
Judas-window
addillmnors
landlordism
addlloorrsw
sword-dollar
adeeeefghrt
feather-edge
adeeeefhlrt
three-leafed
adeeeefhrrt
free-hearted
adeeeefpprr
paper-feeder

adeeeggrst
desegregate
adeeeehimpr
Ephemeridae
adeeeehlrtv
three-leaved
adeeeelnppr
needle-paper
adeeefhnrtu
unfeathered
adeeefhnrtw
weather-fend
adeeefilnrt
deferential
adeeefinstv
defensative
adeeefnrrry
referendary
adeeefnrstt
fenestrated
adeeegghhos
sea-hedgehog
adeeeggilnw
eagle-winged
adeeeghlmpt
dephlegmate
adeeegilmnr
legerdemain
adeeegimnrr
gendarmerie
adeeegimnst
demagnetise
adeeegimort
Geometridae
adeeeginnrt
tragedienne
adeeegklnnr
Kendal-green
adeeegmnnrt
derangement
adeeegnotxy
deoxygenate
adeeehiiprs
Hesperiidae
adeeehirstw
weather-side
wise-hearted
adeeehllors
leaseholder
adeeehlorrs
horse-dealer
adeeehmorst
homesteader
adeeehmrstt
three-masted
adeeehnnnor
enneahedron
adeeehnoprt
open-hearted
adeeehnrrsu
unrehearsed
adeeehnrtuw
unweathered

adeeehprrtt
three-parted
adeeehrrttu
true-hearted
adeeeiilntv
delineative
adeeeiimnrv
Vendémiaire
adeeeiinssv
vine-disease
adeeeillmns
linseed-meal
adeeeilnrrt
interdealer
adeeeilssux
desexualise
adeeeimnrtt
determinate
adeeeimnsst
mediateness
adeeeimpprr
pipe-dreamer
adeeeimprtt
premeditate
adeeeiorrtt
deteriorate
adeeeipprsu
depauperise
adeeeirrstv
readvertise
adeeeklllrw
lake-dweller
adeeeklrrst
deerstalker
adeeellnswy
Wensleydale
adeeellpstt
steel-plated
adeeellsstt
tessellated
adeeelmnnow
needlewoman
adeeelnnrss
learnedness
adeeelnrsst
relatedness
adeeelnrttu
launderette
adeeelnsstx
exaltedness
adeeelorstt
sea-dotterel
adeeelprsty
desperately
adeeemmnnrt
reamendment
adeeemnprtv
depravement
adeeemostww
meadow-sweet
adeeenoprtu
deuteranope
adeeenrsssv
adverseness

adeeeprsssu
supersedeas
adeeffiinrt
differentia
adeefgilnor
freeloading
adeefginnrr
rangefinder
adeefginnrv
never-fading
adeefginorr
forereading
adeefgklnpr
frank-pledge
adeefhllrtu
full-hearted
adeefhorstt
soft-hearted
adeefillnox
deflexional
adeefilnrst
self-trained
adeefilnsuu
unfeudalise
adeefilprss
self-despair
adeefimrstu
misfeatured
adeefinnrrt
after-dinner
adeefinnsst
defiantness
adeefinrrtw
water-finder
adeefiopsst
safe-deposit
adeefkloopr
poodle-faker
adeefllnpst
self-planted
adeefllorsv
severalfold
adeeflmsssu
self-assumed
adeeflopprr
paper-folder
adeeflrrssx
flax-dresser
adeeflrsssu
self-assured
adeefmoorrs
reformadoes
adeefnrrrst
transferred
adeefooprrr
proof-reader
adeefprsttu
superfatted
adeegggirrv
grave-digger
adeegghnsss
shaggedness
adeeggimrst
steam-digger

adeegglortw
waterlogged
adeeggmoruy
demagoguery
adeeggopruy
pedagoguery
adeeghhhirt
high-hearted
adeeghikstw
weak-sighted
adeeghinprs
grandeeship
adeeghinrst
near-sighted
adeeghirrst
sight-reader
adeeghmoprr
demographer
adeeghnnprw
grandnephew
adeeghnoprs
hedge-parson
adeeghnorsu
garden-house
adeeghnorty
hydrogenate
adeeghnrruy
yeard-hunger
adeegiinnst
indesignate
adeegiinstv
designative
adeegilnnry
endearingly
adeegilnnst
disentangle
adeegilnttu
deglutinate
adeegimorrt
gradiometer
adeeginnnsu
ensanguined
adeeginnsux
exsanguined
adeegirrstv
stage-driver
adeegllnosu
eglandulose
adeeglnrtuu
unregulated
adeegmnnrtu
ungarmented
adeegmnntuu
unaugmented
adeegmnrrry
gerrymander
adeegmortuy
deuterogamy
adeehhimsst
missheathed
adeehhlorrs
shareholder
adeehhmmnoo
home-and-home

adeehiikmnt
nikethamide
adeehilmtww
wheat-mildew
adeehilnopt
elephantoid
adeehilnort
lion-hearted
adeehilnprr
philanderer
adeehilnsst
deathliness
adeehinorrt
iron-hearted
adeehinrsst
threadiness
adeehinstux
inexhausted
adeehiorttv
dehortative
adeehirrrss
hairdresser
adeehkmnort
mother-naked
adeehkorstt
death-stroke
adeehllorsv
slave-holder
adeehlmnott
mentholated
adeehlnosst
loathedness
adeehlnprtu
thunder-peal
adeehmnoptu
pneumathode
adeehnnoprt
pentahedron
adeehnnprsu
undershapen
unsharpened
adeehnnrssu
unharnessed
adeehnooswww
shawnee-wood
adeehnorrtt
tetrahedron
adeehnrrstw
netherwards
adeehnrstuv
unharvested
adeehnstuux
unexhausted
adeeiiillmpx
maxillipede
adeeiillnrt
interallied
adeeiilmmsv
medievalism
adeeiilmmty
immediately
adeeiilmnrt
intermedial

adeeiilmstv
medievalist
adeeiilnnot
delineation
adeeiilnnst
desinential
adeeiilnrst
residential
adeeiimmnpt
impedimenta
adeeiimnort
remediation
adeeiimnsst
disseminate
adeeiimrstx
taxidermise
adeeiinoprs
sideropenia
adeeiinpstt
stipendiate
adeeiinrtvy
evidentiary
adeeiiprtuv
repudiative
adeeiiprtvv
deprivative
adeeillmnnr
ill-mannered
adeeillnrtt
trendle-tail
adeeilmnort
endometrial
adeeilmnrst
streamlined
adeeilmnrtt
detrimental
adeeilmnrvy
delivery-man
adeeilmopst
diplomatese
adeeilmostv
dame's-violet
adeeilnnprr
linen-draper
adeeilnnptt
pentlandite
adeeilnnpux
unexplained
adeeilnnrtt
interdental
adeeilnprsu
under-espial
adeeilnrstw
windlestrae
adeeilnrsty
sedentarily
adeeilnruwy
unweariedly
adeeilnrvvy
delivery-van
adeeilopprt
Lepidoptera
adeeilpqssu
sesquipedal

adeeilprssu
displeasure
adeeilrrstv
evil-starred
adeeilrrsvv
slave-driver
adeeilrrttu
literatured
adeeimmnors
misdemeanor
adeeimmnosu
eudaemonism
adeeimmorst
maisterdome
adeeimnnptu
antependium
adeeimnnrtt
determinant
detrainment
adeeimnoppr
Pompeian-red
adeeimnoprt
predominate
adeeimnostu
eudaemonist
adeeimnrstv
steam-driven
adeeimnrsty
sedimentary
adeeimoprrt
madreporite
adeeimprssu
mispersuade
adeeinnrssu
unreadiness
adeeinnrttv
inadvertent
adeeinoprst
desperation
adeeinorttu
deuteration
adeeinosttt
detestation
adeeinprrsu
underpraise
adeeinqrtuv
verd-antique
adeeinrstuv
disaventure
adeeiprrstw
water-spider
adeeiprrtuy
Eurypterida
adeejmnrrry
jerrymander
adeekloprsu
loudspeaker
adeellmrssy
dreamlessly
adeellnnruy
unlearnedly
adeellnrtuv
untravelled

adeelmnoort
demonolater
adeelmoorst
osteodermal
adeelnprstu
unplastered
adeelnrruuv
undervaluer
adeelnrttvy
advertently
adeelopprrw
pearl-powder
adeelopprtw
plate-powder
adeeloqsstu
soldatesque
adeemmnorty
dynamometer
adeemnnooow
wood-anemone
adeemnnsstu
untamedness
adeemnopprr
name-dropper
adeemnorstt
demonstrate
adeemnostvw
woman-vested
adeemnptttu
unattempted
adeemnrrrwy
merry-andrew
adeemrrsttu
mustard-tree
adeennnorsu
enneandrous
adeennnrttu
undertenant
adeennprttu
unpatterned
adeenrrstuv
untraversed
adeenrrsuwy
under-sawyer
adeenrssssu
assuredness
adeenrsstuv
adventuress
adeeoprrrsw
reed-sparrow
adeeoprstwy
yeast-powder
adeerrssttw
streetwards
adeffilnrtu
fault-finder
adeffiorsst
disafforest
adefgginrru
fingerguard
adefgiinrtu
ungratified
adefgillnos
self-loading

adefgilnrsw
self-drawing
adefgilnrsy
lady's-finger
adefgittuuy
fatigue-duty
adefgknoors
god-forsaken
adefgllnssu
gladfulness
adefgllrruy
regardfully
adefhilopst
felspathoid
adefhinnosu
unfashioned
adefhlmoptu
flap-mouthed
adefhlnopru
half-pounder
adefhlooppr
flapperhood
adefiiilnot
defiliation
adefiillquy
qualifiedly
adefiilnoot
defoliation
adefiilnquu
unqualified
adefiinnotu
infeudation
adefiinsstu
unsatisfied
adefilloruv
ill-favoured
adefillrsty
lady-trifles
adefilnoort
defloration
adefilssttu
distasteful
adefimnoort
deformation
adefimnorww
window-frame
adefiorrsuv
disfavourer
adefkloprsw
powder-flask
adeflnoruuv
unflavoured
adefloopsty
splay-footed
adefmnorrst
transformed
adefnorrssw
forwardness
frowardness
adefoorrrvw
overforward
adegghilnrt
right-angled

adegghiopsu
pedagoguish
adeggiinnrw
wide-ranging
adeggiinrrv
driving-gear
adeggilnnot
goal-tending
adeggilnosv
long-visaged
adeggilnruu
unguligrade
adeggilrssu
sluggardise
adeggimmosu
demagoguism
adeggimopsu
pedagoguism
adegginnrru
unregarding
adegginosty
steady-going
adeggmnortu
unmortgaged
adeghhinntu
headhunting
adeghhinrrt
right-hander
adeghiilmnn
mind-healing
adeghillnns
handselling
adeghilnnsw
swing-handle
swingle-hand
adeghimnrst
hamstringed
adeghinnrsu
ungarnished
adeghmnnort
gander-month
adeghmnorrt
grandmother
adeghmoprry
dermography
adeghnoopsu
endophagous
adeghnrruyy
yeard-hungry
adeghooprrx
doxographer
adeghopprsu
pseudograph
adeghorrtuv
overdraught
adegiiikmnr
Kimeridgian
adegiiillno
Loliginidae
adegiillmnt
metalliding
adegiilmnps
mispleading

adegiilnotv
dovetailing
adegiilnpss
displeasing
adegiiloprs
prodigalise
adegiimnort
demigration
adegiimnrst
mistreading
adegiimnttu
unmitigated
adegiinnors
inorganised
adegiinnort
denigration
adegiinnost
designation
adegiinntuv
undeviating
adegiinoprr
Perigordian
adegiinorss
disorganise
adegiinrrww
wire-drawing
adegiinrstt
giant-stride
adegiinrstv
advertising
adegiinrttu
ingratitude
adegiiprstv
tripe-visag'd
adegikmnrss
dressmaking
adegiknnrtu
undertaking
adegiknrrst
ring-straked
adegillossu
gladioluses
adegilnnrwy
wanderingly
adegilnnssu
languidness
adegilnorsy
grandiosely
adegilnostw
long-waisted
adegilnprsy
spreadingly
adegilnprvy
depravingly
adegilnstty
settling-day
adegiloopst
paedologist
adegimnoorr
reading-room
adegimnorrs
gormandiser
adegimnorsu
gourmandise

adeginnnorw
dinner-wagon
adeginnnruw
unwandering
adeginnnttu
unattending
adeginnorsu
unorganised
adeginnqrsu
squandering
adeginnrruw
unrewarding
adeginoorvw
wood-vinegar
adeginoprtw
giant-powder
adeginorrrv
river-dragon
adeginorrtv
overtrading
adeginorsty
designatory
adeginosttu
degustation
adeginprsst
tap-dressing
adegklmnnoy
monkey-gland
adeglmoorty
dermatology
adeglnorsuy
dangerously
adegmnnotuy
many-tongued
adegnnopuuz
ungazed-upon
adegnopstuw
wasp-tongued
adegnorrtuw
ground-water
adegnorsttu
ground-state
adegorsttuy
degustatory
adehhimoorr
haemorrhoid
adehhiorrss
horseradish
adehhirrstw
hitherwards
adehhirrttw
thitherward
adehhirrtww
whitherward
adehiimmpst
midshipmate
adehiimnopr
diamorphine
adehiimnrtu
antheridium
adehiimprsu
sphaeridium
adehiinnopt
Diophantine

adehiioopru
Ophiuroidea
adehiioprss
diaphoresis
adehiiopsvv
vaivodeship
adehiiopsvw
waivodeship
adehiiorstt
historiated
adehiiprssv
advisership
adehiknorsw
whiskerando
adehillmosw
mishallowed
adehillnrst
disenthrall
adehilmnoop
Monodelphia
adehilnpryy
hyperlydian
adehilorsty
hysteroidal
adehimmmmos
Mohammedism
adehimnoprs
hand-promise
preadmonish
adehimnpsss
dampishness
adehimorstu
diathermous
adehimrrstt
third-stream
adehinnnssu
unhandiness
adehinnrstu
untarnished
adehinnrsuv
unvarnished
adehinnrttw
handwritten
adehinoortt
dehortation
adehinoortz
antherozoid
adehinoprry
hyperdorian
adehinorrty
rehydration
adehinosssw
shadowiness
adehinrsttw
withstander
adehioppssy
diapophyses
adehioprrty
pyritohedra
adehiprsstw
stewardship
adehiprsttw
sharp-witted

adehistttwy
hasty-witted
adehjlooosu
jealoushood
adehlllmors
smallholder
adehlnorstu
southlander
adehlorstyy
hydrolysate
adehmnnorss
horn-madness
adehnnopstu
open-and-shut
adehnoorttw
down-to-earth
adehnoprstu
heptandrous
adehnorrstw
sand-thrower
adehoopprty
paedotrophy
adehoorrttw
tooth-drawer
adehoorrtty
dehortatory
adehoprsstw
shop-steward
adeiiilmsst
dissimilate
adeiiimmmst
immediatism
adeiiinnttu
uninitiated
adeiiiopstv
diapositive
adeiiipsstv
dissipative
adeiilllops
ellipsoidal
adeiillnrtt
trindle-tail
adeiillnrtu
interludial
adeiillorty
editorially
adeiilmnnos
dimensional
adeiilmnrsu
semi-diurnal
adeiilmopst
diplomatise
adeiilmsstu
dissimulate
adeiilnnort
internodial
adeiilnnssv
invalidness
adeiilnqtuu
unqualitied
adeiimmnnos
demonianism
adeiimmnstu
mediastinum

adeiimnopss
impassioned
adeiimnorss
readmission
adeiimrsttx
taxidermist
adeiinnnott
indentation
adeiinnoops
Poseidonian
adeiinnoopt
opinionated
adeiinnoory
oneirodynia
adeiinnortt
denitration
adeiinnostt
destination
adeiinnottv
venditation
adeiinooprt
periodontia
adeiinoprtt
trepidation
adeiinoprtu
repudiation
adeiinoprtv
deprivation
adeiinopsst
Passion-tide
adeiinorrtt
traditioner
adeiinorsty
seditionary
adeiinorttx
extradition
adeiinprsty
stipendiary
adeiinqsttu
equidistant
adeiinrrstu
interradius
adeiioprstx
ideopraxist
adeiipsttuv
disputative
adeiknpprss
sand-skipper
adeillmrrst
drill-master
adeillnnrsu
disannuller
adeillnrttu
trundle-tail
adeillorsst
ill-assorted
adeillosvww
swallow-dive
adeillrsttu
illustrated
adeilmnnory
molendinary
adeilmnoptu
deplumation

adeilmnorsu
unmoralised
adeilmnttuu
unmutilated
adeilnnttuy
untaintedly
adeilnooprt
deploration
periodontal
adeilnoppty
pentaploidy
adeilnoprsu
unpolarised
adeilnopruy
pleurodynia
adeilnqsssu
squalidness
adeilnrstww
windlestraw
adeilnsstuy
sustainedly
adeiloprrty
predatorily
adeiloprtty
tetraploidy
adeimmnnopu
pandemonium
adeimmnsstt
dismastment
adeimnnoort
denominator
adeimnnoprt
predominant
adeimnnorsu
unromanised
adeimnnotuw
mountain-dew
adeimnnqruu
quadrennium
adeimnopstu
despumation
adeimnottuv
unmotivated
adeimnrrsuy
nurserymaid
adeimnrrtuy
rudimentary
adeimnrsttt
transmitted
adeimnrstuv
adventurism
adeimoprtuy
apodyterium
adeinnooprt
ponderation
adeinnopptu
unappointed
adeinnopssu
unpassioned
adeinnoqrtu
quaternion'd
adeinnqstuu
unquantised

adeinnssstt
distantness
adeinnssstu
unstaidness
adeinnsstuu
unsustained
adeinooprtt
deportation
adeinoprrtu
perduration
adeinoprrtw
word-painter
adeinoprsst
dispensator
adeinprstuy
superdainty
adeinqrrtuw
quarter-wind
adeinrsttuv
adventurist
adeinrsttuy
testudinary
adeioprrtty
trepidatory
adeiorrsstt
dissertator
adejmnnortu
adjournment
adejmnorrty
Tom-and-Jerry
adellmmorty
troll-my-dame
adellnosuww
unswallowed
adellnsstuy
dauntlessly
adelloorrsu
eurodollars
adelmnoorty
demonolatry
adelmnorrtu
ultra-modern
adelnooprsw
snow-leopard
adelnopptuu
unpopulated
adeloopprtu
depopulator
adelopprsuu
dual-purpose
adeloprrswy
swordplayer
ademmnnooss
moon-madness
ademmnortyy
dynamometry
ademnnosttu
astoundment
ademnoopssu
pseudomonas
ademnoortty
attorneydom
ademnoprstu
pound-master

ademorsstty
storm-stayed
adennoppstt
pendant-post
adennoprrst
transponder
adennoprstu
pentandrous
adenoorttuu
out-and-outer
adenoppprsy
Podsnappery
adenoprrrty
proterandry
adenoprrstt
transported
adenorrsttu
tetrandrous
adenorsssuu
arduousness
adenorsstuw
outwardness
adenorstuuv
adventurous
adenprsssuu
unsurpassed
adenrsttuuy
nature-study
adeooprsttu
tetrapodous
adffhinosst
stand-offish
adfgiiilnpy
lapidifying
adfgiiimrru
frigidarium
adfgiilllnn
landfilling
adfgiinnrsu
fund-raising
adfiiillnnu
nullifidian
adfiilmntuu
latifundium
adfillmsuyy
dismayfully
adfimnoprru
panduriform
adfinnoorrz
rinforzando
adfoopprrrw
prop-forward
propforward
adggghiilnn
hang-gliding
adgghhioors
road-hoggish
adgghiilnsw
wash-gilding
adggiilnnow
wing-loading
adggiinnnww
wing-and-wing

adgglmoooty
dogmatology
adghhiinrtt
hard-hitting
adghhilnopt
diphthongal
adghhnortuw
handwrought
adghhoprryy
hydrography
adghiilnnps
landing-ship
adghiinnrtw
handwriting
adghiknorrw
hard-working
adghinnnnru
hand-running
running-hand
adghioprtty
dittography
adghmrrruyy
hydrargyrum
adghnoooprt
odontograph
adghnoprrsu
sharp-ground
adgiiilooss
idioglossia
adgiiinnnot
indignation
adgiiinoott
goniatitoid
adgiiinstvy
visiting-day
adgiillmosy
sigmoidally
adgiilnnnty
indignantly
adgiilnotuv
divulgation
adgiiloorst
radiologist
adgiiloostu
audiologist
adgiiloprty
prodigality
adgiinnpppr
dripping-pan
adgiinoptuy
audiotyping
adgiinorrss
disgarrison
adgiinorsty
grandiosity
adgilmnnnor
morning-land
adgilnnoops
poison-gland
adgilnoossy
glossodynia
adgilnosswω
window-glass

adgimmnorsu
gourmandism
adgimnoorrw
drawing-room
adginnnopru
unpardoning
adginnosttu
outstanding
adginrsttyy
trysting-day
adgnnnoqtuu
quandong-nut
adgnnoorsuy
androgynous
adhhmnoottu
hand-to-mouth
adhhoorrtxy
hydrothorax
adhiiimopru
ophidiarium
adhiimoppst
hippodamist
adhiioppssy
diapophysis
adhiioprstu
auditorship
adhiiorrsst
diarthrosis
adhillooprt
prothalloid
adhillorrrw
drill-harrow
adhilmnoosw
old-womanish
adhimooppsu
amphipodous
hippodamous
adhinoooprt
Ornithopoda
adhinooortt
orthodontia
adhinoorrsy
dishonorary
adhiooorrtt
traitorhood
adhlnorrtwy
northwardly
adhlorstuwy
southwardly
adhnoopqruy
quadrophony
adiiiinorst
iridisation
adiiillstuv
diluvialist
adiiilnoqtu
liquidation
adiiimosstt
mastoiditis
adiiinopsst
dissipation
adiiinorsvy
divisionary

adiiioprstt
parotiditis
adiiillnoqru
quadrillion
adiilmopstt
diplomatist
adiilnortuy
dilutionary
adiimmnnory
myrmidonian
adiimmnostu
staminodium
adiimnoopst
Adoptionism
adiimnosttu
dismutation
adiinnoorrt
Torridonian
adiinoopstt
adoptionist
adiinopsttu
disputation
adiiooprsuv
avoirdupois
adiiopsttuy
audio-typist
adillmopsyy
sympodially
adilnnossty
dissonantly
adilorrsttu
stridulator
adilosssuuy
assiduously
adimprrrstu
stirrup-dram
adinooprssw
Windsor-soap
adinrstttuy
transit-duty
adklnootuwy
talk-you-down
adllooswww
wood-swallow
adlnooprsuy
polyandrous
adnooprrstu
protandrous
adoooprssuu
sauropodous
aeeeefgilpr
life-peerage
aeeeeghlrss
grease-heels
aeeeeglmsst
telemessage
aeeeeglnsuv
seven-league
aeeeehhnsst
heathenesse
aeeeehilrst
etherealise
aeeeehlrttt
leatherette

aeeeehmrstu
rheumateese
aeeeellmnos
leesome-lane
aeeeelmnrst
releasement
aeeeelnppqu
queene-apple
aeeeemmprrt
permeameter
aeeeeprrstv
perseverate
aeeeffloppt
toffee-apple
aeeefgiknps
safe-keeping
aeeefgirrrt
refrigerate
aeeefhinrrt
hereinafter
aeeefhmprrs
sheep-farmer
aeeefilnrrt
referential
aeeefilprst
steeple-fair
aeeefllmpsx
self-example
aeeefllnntt
flannelette
aeeeflrsstu
featureless
aeeefnnrsst
Fastern's-e'en
aeeefprsttu
superfetate
aeeeggilnos
genealogise
aeeeggirstv
segregative
aeeeggmmnou
emmenagogue
aeeeghlprrt
telegrapher
aeeeghnprtw
great-nephew
aeeeghorrtt
theatre-goer
aeeegilmmrr
lammergeier
aeeegimnnst
steam-engine
aeeegimnsst
metagenesis
aeeeginnrtw
water-engine
aeeeginortt
renegotiate
aeeeginprrt
peregrinate
aeeeginrrtt
reintegrate
aeeeglmmrry
lammergeyer

aeeeglmnnrt
enlargement
aeeegmnnrss
germaneness
aeeegmnprst
presagement
aeeegmnqrsu
Germanesque
aeeegnorrrt
regenerator
aeeegnqrsuw
Wagneresque
aeeehhlmmrv
helve-hammer
aeeehhlmrtw
weather-helm
aeeehhlorst
shoe-leather
aeeehiklnnp
enkephaline
aeeehilnnpt
elephantine
aeeehilnrtu
eleutherian
aeeehilpstt
telepathise
aeeehilrtty
ethereality
aeeehilsstt
telesthesia
aeeehimprss
re-emphasise
aeeehimrstx
hexametrise
aeeehiprsst
aspheterise
aeeehirstww
weather-wise
aeeehlmmnrt
Emmenthaler
aeeehlmpprt
pamphleteer
aeeehlmrstw
master-wheel
aeeehlnpttt
pentathlete
aeeehlorrtv
overleather
aeeehlprrwy
prayer-wheel
aeeehmprsst
sheep-master
aeeehmrrstt
three-master
aeeehnosstu
senate-house
aeeehnprsst
parentheses
aeeehnrsttw
news-theatre
aeeehoprrtt
Heteroptera
aeeehorrtvw
overweather

aeeehprrstu
superheater
aeeehprssww
sweep-washer
aeeehqrrstu
three-square
aeeeiinpprt
peripeteian
aeeeiinqstu
Equisetinae
aeeeiirrttv
reiterative
aeeeilllpwy
peelie-wally
aeeeilmnrst
mesenterial
aeeeilmnrtt
melanterite
aeeeilmprst
time-pleaser
aeeeilnortv
re-elevation
aeeeilnrrtv
reverential
aeeeilnrstv
interleaves
aeeeilnrstx
externalise
aeeeilnstuv
eventualise
aeeeilqsstu
Equisetales
aeeeimnprtt
impenetrate
intemperate
aeeeimnrsuw
wine-measure
aeeeimnrttx
exterminate
aeeeimnrtuv
enumerative
aeeeimprttv
temperative
aeeeimqrrtu
marqueterie
aeeeinnrrtt
entertainer
aeeeinoprsu
europeanise
aeeeinorrtt
reorientate
aeeeinortvx
exonerative
aeeeinprttv
penetrative
aeeeinsssvv
evasiveness
aeeeinttuvx
extenuative
aeeejlmssty
lese-majesty
aeeejlmstyz
leze-majesty

aeeekllostx
exoskeletal
aeeekllprsw
sleep-walker
aeeekpssstw
sweepstakes
aeeelllmnty
elementally
aeeellorrsv
sallee-rover
aeeellorttt
teetotaller
aeeelmmnnpt
empanelment
aeeelmnnstv
enslavement
aeeelmprtty
temperately
aeeelmrsssu
measureless
aeeelmssstv
steam-vessel
aeeelnssssw
awelessness
aeeelpprtvv
velvet-paper
aeeelpqrstu
plateresque
aeeelrrssvx
sex-reversal
aeeemmnprtt
temperament
aeeemmnrstu
measurement
aeeemnnrttt
entreatment
aeeemnnrtty
tenementary
aeeemnosssw
awesomeness
aeeemnrsttt
restatement
aeeemorrsuv
overmeasure
aeeemprrttu
temperature
aeeennrssst
earnestness
aeeenorrstv
overearnest
aeeenprrstv
perseverant
aeeenrssstu
austereness
aeeeppprrtw
water-pepper
aeeeqrssttu
sequestrate
aeeffgrsttu
suffragette
aeeffilnnrs
snaffle-rein
aeefflnrssu
fearfulness

aeefflnsstu
fatefulness
aeefghillns
self-healing
aeefghorrtt
heterograft
aeefgiimnrs
fair-seeming
aeefgillnss
self-sealing
aeefgilnprt
fingerplate
aeefgilnrss
fragileness
aeefginrrrt
refrigerant
aeefgiprrtu
prefigurate
aeefgllorsw
gallows-free
aeefglorstw
stage-flower
aeefgmnnrtt
engraftment
aeefgooprrs
grease-proof
aeefhhiknst
sheath-knife
aeefhhilrsw
whale-fisher
aeefhhorstu
housefather
aeefhilnnps
halfpennies
aeefhilprrs
pearl-fisher
aeefhklmrst
flesh-market
aeefhllmnst
mantelshelf
aeefhlnsstu
hatefulness
aeefhmorrrt
farthermore
aeefhorrstu
frater-house
aeefiilnnrt
inferential
aeefiilotvx
exfoliative
aeefilnstty
festinately
aeefiloprrt
proliferate
aeefilpprrt
filter-paper
aeefimoprrt
imperforate
aeefimorrtv
reformative
aeefinprstz
zip-fastener
aeefinrrrst
fraterniser

aeefioprrtv
perforative
aeefklnssuw
wakefulness
aeefllorrst
forestaller
aeefllprsuu
pleasureful
aeeflmorrtu
reformulate
aeeflmrssty
self-mastery
aeeflnrsstu
tearfulness
aeefloprrs
proper-false
aeeflrrsstt
self-starter
aeefmnoprty
forepayment
aeefmnorrsy
freemasonry
aeefmorrrst
store-farmer
aeefnnoprss
profaneness
aeefnopprst
pop-fastener
aeefnrrrrst
transferrer
aeefpprrstu
aftersupper
aeegggnnrrz
Grenzgänger
aeegghhmnsu
meshuggenah
aeeggiinors
seigniorage
aeeggilmrss
message-girl
aeeggilnost
genealogist
aeeggimnoss
gamogenesis
aeegginorst
segregation
aeegginqstu
gigantesque
aeeggirrttu
regurgitate
aeeghhitvwy
heavyweight
aeeghhnrrtu
earth-hunger
aeeghiilmns
Hegelianism
aeeghikllnu
keelhauling
aeeghillmrt
hellgramite
aeeghilmrwy
whigmaleery
aeeghilnprs
generalship

11 AEE

aeeghilnpss
single-phase
aeeghimmrtu
Megatherium
aeeghinnrtt
threatening
aeeghinostu
eating-house
aeeghinrstw
weather-sign
aeeghipprtw
paper-weight
aeeghiprrrs
serigrapher
aeeghiqrstu
eight-square
aeeghlnoprs
selenograph
aeeghlnorst
estranghelo
aeeghlrrstu
slaughterer
aeeghmoptty
gametophyte
aeeghnprstv
Stevengraph
aeeghooprst
ostreophage
aeeghoprrst
stereograph
aeegiiklls
skilligalee
aeegiillstv
legislative
aeegiilltu
aiguillette
aeegiilmnpt
leaping-time
aeegiilnnor
legionnaire
aeegiilnors
regionalise
aeegiilnppr
appleringie
aeegiilnrst
gelatiniser
aeegiilnrsu
seigneurial
aeegiimnrtv
germinative
aeegiinrttv
integrative
vinaigrette
aeegiinsttv
investigate
aeegijknrrt
tear-jerking
aeegikmnrsv
verse-making
aeegillmnnp
empanelling
aeegillmnnw
well-meaning

aeegillnnty
inelegantly
aeegillorrs
allegoriser
aeegillrstu
legislature
aeegilmnnrt
engrailment
realignment
aeegilmnnss
meaningless
aeegilmnosu
Leguminosae
aeegilnnpsy
palingenesy
aeegilnnrtt
intertangle
aeegilnnruv
unrevealing
aeegilnrstv
everlasting
aeegilrrstw
sweater-girl
aeegimmnsst
mass-meeting
aeegimmnsty
May-meetings
aeegimnottw
witenagemot
aeegimssttu
guesstimate
aeeginnprtt
penetrating
aeeginnrstv
evening-star
aeeginnttux
extenuating
aeeginopprt
oppignerate
aeeginoprrs
opera-singer
aeeginorrrv
overgrainer
aeeginorrtt
interrogate
aeeginosstu
autogenesis
aeegioprrtv
prerogative
aeegllmnnty
gentlemanly
aeegllmnoty
metallogeny
aeegllmnsty
segmentally
aeegllmortu
glomerulate
aeegllnsstt
tassell-gent
aeeglloopsy
spelaeology
aeegllorstw
gallows-tree

aeeglmnnotw
gentlewoman
aeeglmnoopr
prolegomena
aeeglmnorsu
long-measure
aeeglmnorsw
wranglesome
aeeglmnrsst
garmentless
aeegmmoorrt
meteorogram
aeegmnnosst
magnesstone
aeegmnorrtv
overgarment
aeegmnorstt
state-monger
aeegmnrttuy
tegumentary
aeegnnortuv
gouvernante
aeegnnrssst
strangeness
aeegnossssu
gaseousness
aeegorrsstu
retroussage
aeegppprrss
pepper-grass
aeehhilnsst
healthiness
aeehhilrttw
therewithal
whitleather
aeehhilrtww
wherewithal
aeehhiprstw
weather-ship
aeehhirrttv
rivet-hearth
aeehhirstww
whitewasher
aeehhllmrst
Stahlhelmer
aeehhmnorty
hearth-money
aeehhmorstv
harvest-home
aeehhnnprty
hearth-penny
aeehhnorstt
hearth-stone
aeehhprrssu
share-pusher
aeehiilmopt
epithelioma
aeehiimprss
phariseeism
aeehiinnort
anti-heroine
aeehiinprst
traineeship

aeehikpprss
speakership
aeehikrrstt
heart-strike
aeehilmmnty
methylamine
aeehilnpprs
planisphere
aeehilnpsss
shapeliness
aeehilnrsst
earthliness
aeehilnsstw
wealthiness
aeehilpprst
prelateship
aeehilpsttt
telepathist
aeehilrssty
hysteresial
aeehimnnstv
evanishment
aeehimnstty
amethystine
aeehimprsst
aspheterism
aeehimrsttt
tetratheism
aeehimrsttv
harvest-mite
aeehimrsttx
hexametrist
aeehinorstu
heterousian
aeehinprsst
parenthesis
aeehinrrstv
varnish-tree
aeehiooprtt
heterotopia
aeehioopsst
apotheosise
aeehiorsttx
heterotaxis
aeehiorttvx
exhortative
aeehipprrss
periphrases
aeehippstux
exhaust-pipe
aeehkmorstu
market-house
aeehkmprrty
hypermarket
aeehkoprrty
keratophyre
aeehllmsssy
shamelessly
aeehllnorty
lonely-heart
aeehllorrtw
weather-roll
aeehllortwy
yellow-earth

aeehllrssty
heartlessly
aeehlmnnrtt
enthralment
aeehlmnoopr
melanophore
aeehlmosstv
steam-shovel
aeehlmrrtuy
eurythermal
aeehlnpssss
haplessness
aeehlnssst
hatlessness
aeehlopprty
pelotherapy
aeehlpprstu
persulphate
aeehlprrstu
spur-leather
aeehlssstux
exhaustless
aeehmmmortt
mammoth-tree
aeehmmnorst
stone-hammer
aeehmmnrtux
xeranthemum
aeehmnnnoop
phaenomenon
aeehmnooprt
nematophore
aeehmnoprty
Hymenoptera
aeehmnprrtu
preterhuman
aeehmoprstu
heptamerous
aeehmorrrtt
earth-tremor
aeehmorrstw
whoremaster
aeehmorrttw
mother-water
aeehmorsstu
housemaster
aeehmorsttw
weathermost
aeehmorstvw
whatsomever
aeehmpprsty
spermaphyte
aeehnoprstu
houseparent
aeehnorrstt
north-easter
aeehnorrtww
weather-worn
aeehoprrsty
serotherapy
aeehorrsstu
house-arrest
aeehorssttu
south-easter

aeeiiilmntv
eliminative
aeeiiilmprs
imperialise
aeeiikllnps
spaniel-like
aeeiillmmpr
milliampere
aeeiillrrst
literaliser
aeeiilmmors
memorialise
aeeiilmnrrs
mineraliser
aeeiilmortv
meliorative
aeeiilnnptt
penitential
aeeiilnnrrt
interlinear
aeeiilnnrst
internalise
aeeiilnnsst
inessential
aeeiilnorst
orientalise
aeeiilnsttx
existential
aeeiilnttvv
ventilative
aeeiilrsstw
saltierwise
aeeiilrttvy
iteratively
aeeiimmsstt
misestimate
aeeiimnnrtt
interminate
aeeiimnrttv
terminative
aeeiimprttv
impetrative
aeeiinnsttv
intensative
aeeiinntttv
inattentive
aeeiinoprtv
inoperative
aeeiinorrtt
reiteration
aeeiinqsttu
Titianesque
aeeiinstuvv
vesuvianite
aeeiioprsst
sepiostaire
aeeiiprttvx
extirpative
aeeiklnrssw
warlikeness
aeeiknopssw
Passion-week
aeeiknqsssu
squeakiness
aeeiknrssst
streakiness
aeeilllmprt
pearl-millet
aeeillmmnpt
implemental
aeeillmnops
psilomelane
aeeillmprxy
exemplarily
aeeillnnpry
perennially
aeeillnnsxy
sexennially
aeeillnostt
stellionate
aeeillnrsst
literalness
aeeillnrtvy
eviternally
aeeillnssty
essentially
aeeilloortv
alto-relievo
aeeillprstv
silver-plate
aeeillrstvy
versatilely
aeeilmnnstt
sentimental
aeeilmnorst
salinometer
aeeilmnprst
sempiternal
aeeilmnprtv
prevailment
aeeilmnpttu
penultimate
aeeilmnrstx
externalism
aeeilmnssss
aimlessness
aeeilmnsswy
Wesleyanism
aeeilmnsttv
vestimental
aeeilmoprrt
polarimeter
aeeilmorrst
solarimeter
aeeilmorswy
wearisomely
aeeilmosttt
teetotalism
aeeilmpprrs
perispermal
aeeilmprtxy
exemplarity
aeeilnnnpry
penny-a-liner
aeeilnnoopt
napoleonite
aeeilnnoptx
exponential
aeeilnnostx
extensional
aeeilnnpstu
peninsulate
aeeilnnpstw
twalpennies
aeeilnnrrtu
interneural
aeeilnnsstu
unessential
aeeilnnssty
insensately
aeeilnoprss
personalise
aeeilnoprtt
interpolate
aeeilnorrsv
reversional
aeeilnorsst
interosseal
aeeilnpprtw
winter-apple
aeeilnprstt
interseptal
aeeilnprstv
vespertinal
aeeilnpsvxy
expansively
aeeilnrrstt
intersertal
aeeilnrrstu
neutraliser
aeeilnrsttx
externalist
aeeilnrstux
intersexual
aeeilnrttxy
externality
aeeilnssstt
stateliness
aeeilntttvy
attentively
tentatively
aeeilnttuvy
eventuality
aeeilopprst
sapropelite
aeeiloppritt
toilet-paper
aeeiloppssu
episepalous
aeeiloppstu
epipetalous
aeeiloprtvx
explorative
aeeiloprtvy
operatively
aeeilorssty
areosystile
aeeilorttvw
water-violet
aeeilppppst
pipe-stapple
aeeilppqrsu
apple-squire
aeeilpprrsv
silver-paper
aeeilprstuv
superlative
aeeilprsvvy
pervasively
aeeilpsttux
exstipulate
aeeilqrrtuv
quarter-evil
aeeilqrsstu
sesquialter
aeeilrrrstt
terrestrial
aeeilrrsttw
slate-writer
aeeilrrtttu
littérateur
aeeilrsstvy
assertively
aeeilrsttuv
resultative
aeeimmnnprt
impermanent
aeeimmnprst
pentamerism
aeeimmrrstt
tetramerism
aeeimnnnrtt
entrainment
aeeimnnoprt
prenominate
aeeimnnortu
enumeration
mountaineer
aeeimnnostt
maisonnette
aeeimnnprtt
intemperant
aeeimnnsttt
instatement
aeeimnoprst
impersonate
aeeimnoprsu
Europeanism
aeeimnoprtu
peritonaeum
aeeimnrrstt
tin-streamer
aeeimnrssst
streaminess
aeeimnrstuv
mensurative
aeeimnssssv
massiveness
aeeimnsssuv
amusiveness
aeeimoprrtv
vaporimeter
aeeimorrstu
temerarious
aeeimqrsttu
marquisette
aeeimsssty
systematise
aeeinnnoprt
perennation
aeeinnoortx
exoneration
aeeinnoprsx
re-expansion
aeeinnoprtt
penetration
aeeinnorstv
anteversion
aeeinnorsvv
varsovienne
aeeinnorttv
eventration
aeeinnottux
extenuation
aeeinnpprtt
appertinent
aeeinnqsstu
antiqueness
aeeinntttuv
unattentive
aeeinoprstu
Europeanist
aeeinoprstv
personative
aeeinoprtuv
unoperative
aeeinoqsssu
Ossianesque
aeeinorrsst
reassertion
aeeinorrstv
reservation
aeeinortvxy
over-anxiety
aeeinprsstt
Esperantist
aeeinprsstu
septenarius
aeeinprsstv
privateness
aeeinpssssv
passiveness
aeeinrsstuv
unassertive
aeeinssssuv
suasiveness
aeeiopprrtx
expropriate
aeeiorrsttv
restorative
aeeiorssttx
stereotaxis
aeeipprrssu
superpraise
aeeipprrtuw
water-purpie
aeeipprsstu
tissue-paper

aeeiprrsstu
pasteuriser
aeeiprrsttw
water-sprite
aeeiprssstt
spessartite
aeejlnosssu
jealousness
aeejnorrtuv
rejuvenator
aeekllorrst
roller-skate
aeeklmorrtw
metal-worker
aeekloorrsy
seal-rookery
aeekmmnorty
money-market
aeekmmrssty
system-maker
aeekmnortwy
water-monkey
aeekmprrstu
supermarket
aeeknprrstu
supertanker
aeelllmotwy
yellow-metal
aeelllnprty
repellantly
aeellmmnotu
emolumental
aeellmmorwy
yellow-ammer
aeellmnortt
reallotment
aeellmorrst
steam-roller
aeellmprssu
pearl-mussel
aeellnorstw
stonewaller
aeellnprtvy
prevalently
aeellnssssw
lawlessness
aeelloprstu
pastourelle
aeelloprtuv
pole-vaulter
aeellpprruy
puerperally
aeellpprtuy
perpetually
aeellpsssuy
pauselessly
aeellssstty
tastelessly
aeelmmoopps
pampelmoose
aeelmmoppsu
pampelmouse
aeelmnnprty
permanently

aeelmnnrtuv
unravelment
aeelmnprttt
prattlement
aeelmoqrrsu
quarrelsome
aeelmprrtuy
prematurely
aeelmprsttt
letter-stamp
aeelnnprtty
repentantly
aeelnnrttuw
water-tunnel
aeelnnssssu
sensualness
aeelnoprsss
salesperson
aeelnoprsst
prolateness
aeelnosssuz
zealousness
aeelnpsssss
saplessness
aeelnrsssst
artlessness
aeelnrssstv
servantless
aeeloppptvv
poppet-valve
aeeloprrsty
pearl-oyster
aeelopsttux
expostulate
aeelorssttu
lotus-eaters
aeelorsstuu
Teleosaurus
aeelppptuvv
puppet-valve
aeelpprrsty
parsley-pert
aeelprrsstu
raptureless
aeelprrsttu
perlustrate
aeelprssstu
pastureless
aeemnnorstt
stone-marten
aeemnnrsstv
men-servants
aeemnoprstu
pentamerous
aeemnoprtvy
overpayment
aeemnoqrttu
quantometer
aeemnorrrtu
remunerator
aeemnorrstt
remonstrate
aeemnorsstt
easternmost

aeemnrssttt
stentmaster
aeemoprrtxy
extemporary
aeemorrsttu
tetramerous
aeemrssssty
seamstressy
aeennnprttu
unrepentant
aeennopprst
parpen-stone
aeennorssst
sarsen-stone
aeenoprrstt
paternoster
aeenoqrrttu
quarter-note
quarter-tone
aeenorttuxy
extenuatory
aeenprrsstt
serpent-star
aeenprrstuu
supernature
aeenqrssttu
sequestrant
aeeoopstttw
sweet-potato
aeeopprrrtt
perpetrator
prêt-à-porter
aeeopprrttu
perpetuator
aeeoqrrstuu
terraqueous
aeeorrrstvy
reservatory
aeerssttttu
trust-estate
aeffffttuy
tufftaffety
aeffftttuy
tufttaffety
aeffghiinnt
infangthief
aeffghilrtu
fire-flaught
aeffgimstuu
suffumigate
aeffhilrsty
sheriffalty
aeffhinrsss
raffishness
aeffiiklnru
ruffian-like
aeffiimnorr
foraminifer
aeffknrrrtu
frankfurter
aefflnruuy
unfearfully
aeffmsssty
staff-system

aefgghirstt
stage-fright
aefggilnrss
finger-glass
aefgginrrss
finger-grass
aefghhorrtu
throughfare
aefghiilnss
seal-fishing
aefghillort
fothergilla
aefghilmnrs
self-harming
aefghoprrry
ferrography
aefghorrttw
aftergrowth
aefghorrtuv
overfraught
aefgiiinrrs
fire-raising
aefgiiklnrw
fire-walking
aefgiinnprt
finger-paint
aefgiklllnw
fell-walking
aefgillmoru
Glumiflorae
aefgillnrst
fingerstall
aefgillnrty
falteringly
aefgillosty
galley-foist
aefgilnnoor
gonfalonier
aefgilnnrtu
unfaltering
aefgilnnssu
gainfulness
aefgilnorsu
soul-fearing
aefginnnssw
fawningness
aefginnorrw
forewarning
aefginorsuu
guaniferous
aefginrrstu
transfigure
aefglloopry
galley-proof
aefhhiirstt
hatti-sherif
aefhhllltuy
healthfully
aefhhllntuu
unhealthful
aefhiilmnps
lifemanship
aefhillssty
faithlessly

aefhlmnrssu
harmfulness
aefhmorrstt
farthermost
aefhoottuwy
out-of-the-way
aefiiklnnrt
franklinite
aefiillnnox
inflexional
aefiillnntu
influential
aefiilnnort
reinflation
aefiilnnrty
infernality
aefiilnntuy
life-annuity
aefiilnootx
exfoliation
aefiiloprrw
prairie-wolf
aefiimnortv
informative
aefiinnostt
festination
infestation
sinfonietta
aefiklrsttu
strike-fault
aefilllmmor
lamelliform
aefillmoprt
patelliform
aefillnoors
saloon-rifle
aefillnorsw
snail-flower
aefilmnostu
filamentous
aefilmorrsu
formularise
aefilmprsuy
superfamily
aefilnnpssu
painfulness
aefilnoopst
point-of-sale
aefilnorsuy
nefariously
aefiloppstv
pop-festival
aefiloprrty
prefatorily
aefimmmorsu
mammiferous
aefimnnnort
antenniform
aefimnnoott
fomentation
aefimnnorsu
manniferous
aefimnoorrt
reformation

aefinnnoptu
fountain-pen
aefinooprrt
perforation
aefinoorstt
forestation
aefinrsstuv
transfusive
aefklloorrw
floorwalker
aefkllorstw
flower-stalk
aefknnorrrt
front-ranker
aeflllnttuy
flatulently
aeflllopruw
all-powerful
aeflllsstuy
faultlessly
aefllmrstuy
masterfully
aefllnpssuy
playfulness
aefllorssuv
flavourless
aefllprruyy
prayerfully
aefllrstuwy
wastefully
aeflmoorsuv
flavoursome
aeflnoopstu
teaspoonful
aeflnorttuy
fortunately
aefmnorrrst
transformer
aefmooprstt
foretopmast
aefmoorrrty
reformatory
aefnnorttuu
unfortunate
aefnossstuu
fatuousness
aegghhilotv
high-voltage
aegghiiilnnt
nightingale
aegghiinnrt
ingathering
aegghiirrrt
hair-trigger
aegghimnosu
gaming-house
aegghinsssw
waggishness
aegghklnrsu
Enghalskrug
aegghlooprr
logographer
aegghnnoowy
honey-waggon
aeggiilmprr
pilgrimager
aeggiinrttu
ingurgitate
aeggilnnrss
glaringness
aeggimnooty
geitonogamy
aeggimnorrw
worm-gearing
aeggimnrsst
gangsterism
aegginnnrru
running-gear
aegginorrvz
overgrazing
aegginorrzz
zero-grazing
aegginprrsu
spur-gearing
aegginrrttu
regurgitant
aegglnnoost
loggan-stone
aeggloorrst
gastrologer
aeghhilopry
heliography
aeghhinsstu
haughtiness
aeghhioprry
hierography
aeghhloprsu
ploughshare
aeghhmoprrt
thermograph
aeghhnoprty
ethnography
aeghhooprrr
horographer
aeghhoopstu
theophagous
aeghhoprtyy
hyetography
aeghhottuvw
thought-wave
aeghiilnnsw
washing-line
aeghiimnrst
time-sharing
aeghiinptty
tithe-paying
aeghiinrttt
night-attire
aeghiipprst
epigraphist
aeghijmnpru
jumping-hare
aeghijrsttt
straight-jet
aeghiklnrtw
night-walker
aeghiknoopr
reaping-hook
aeghiknoprt
kinetograph
aeghiknrstv
thanksgiver
aeghillmprt
lamplighter
aeghillnnrt
enthralling
aeghilmnopr
Germanophil
aeghilmopsu
meliphagous
aeghilnoost
anthologise
aeghilnopsv
leaving-shop
aeghilnssst
ghastliness
aeghilprsty
sight-player
aeghimmoprr
mimographer
aeghimnnrst
garnishment
aeghimoprss
seismograph
aeghinnosst
night-season
aeghinnsstu
naughtiness
aeghinnsttu
hunting-seat
aeghinorsuw
warehousing
aeghinossst
goatishness
aeghinprstw
spring-wheat
aeghinprttt
patent-right
aeghinrrstt
heart-string
aeghlmopstu
steam-plough
aeghlnooorr
gonorrhoeal
aeghlnoopty
pantheology
aeghlooprsy
phraseology
aeghloppryy
pyelography
aeghloprrxy
xylographer
aeghmnooprr
monographer
nomographer
aeghmnoopsu
phenogamous
aeghmnoopty
entomophagy
aeghmooprrt
ergatomorph
aeghmoprsuy
hypergamous
aeghnooprrs
nosographer
aeghnoopstu
pathogenous
aeghnoprsty
stenography
aeghnopstuy
heptagynous
aeghnorsttu
hart's-tongue
aeghoopprrt
topographer
aeghooprsty
osteography
ostreophagy
aeghopprrry
reprography
aeghopprrss
grasshopper
aeghopprrty
petrography
typographer
aegiiillntt
gentilitial
aegiiilmnpr
primigenial
aegiiilnntt
gentilitian
aegiiilnors
seigniorial
aegiiimnprt
pairing-time
aegiiinortv
originative
aegiiinsttv
instigative
aegiikllnrt
giant-killer
aegiiklnsst
glaikitness
aegiiknrstw
water-skiing
aegiillnost
legislation
aegiillntvy
genitivally
aegiilmnors
regionalism
aegiilmntuv
lignum-vitae
aegiilmosst
legatissimo
aegiilnnrtu
interlingua
aegiilnorry
religionary
aegiilnorst
regionalist
aegiilnrrsv
silver-grain
aegiilnrssu
singularise
aegiilnrtty
integrality
aegiimmorrr
mirror-image
aegiimmrstu
magisterium
aegiimnnnru
unremaining
aegiimnnort
germination
aegiimnnorv
Merovingian
aegiimnnrst
instreaming
aegiimnoprt
impignorate
aegiimnorrt
remigration
aegiimprstu
epigastrium
aegiinnnort
Ignorantine
aegiinnoott
negotiation
aegiinnorrs
searing-iron
aegiinnorst
resignation
aegiinnortt
integration
aegiinnortu
unoriginate
aegiinnostt
negationist
aegiinnprst
sign-painter
aegiinnrrst
restraining
aegiinnrttu
intriguante
aegiinnsttw
wine-tasting
aegiinorttx
negotiatrix
aegijlmttuu
multijugate
aegikllnnst
stalling-ken
aegiklnqsuy
squeakingly
aegikmmnnoy
money-making
aegikmmnrry
merrymaking
aegiknprstu
purse-taking
aegillmmnrt
trammelling
aegillmnnty
lamentingly
aegillmoops
megalopolis
aegillmprsu
aspergillum

aegillmrsst
millet-grass
aegillnnopr
pollen-grain
aegillnnruv
unravelling
aegillnopry
role-playing
aegillnqrru
quarrelling
aegillnrsvy
slaveringly
aegilloprsw
gallows-ripe
aegillopstv
post-village
aegillosstt
toilet-glass
aegillprssu
aspergillus
aegillrrruy
irregularly
aegilmmnotu
gemmulation
aegilmnnnuy
unmeaningly
aegilmnoort
glomeration
aegilmnopru
pelargonium
aegilmnostu
ligamentous
aegilmnrsty
streamingly
aegilmnsstu
minute-glass
aegilmoopst
plagiostome
aegilmoossy
semasiology
aegilnnostu
langoustine
aegilnnosvw
slave-owning
aegilnnrstv
navel-string
aegilnnssst
lastingness
aegilnnssty
assentingly
aegilnooprs
sporangiole
aegilnoossx
xenoglossia
aegilnorsst
Interglossa
aegilnqruvy
quaveringly
aegilnrrstv
servant-girl
aegilnrsuuv
unvulgarise
aegilnrttyy
yatteringly

aegiloosttu
tautologise
aegilprtuvy
purgatively
aegilrsttuu
gutturalise
aegimmmnorx
maxim-monger
aegimmoprsu
gemmiparous
aegimnorssu
ignoramuses
aeginnnoprs
none-sparing
aeginnnorsu
unreasoning
aeginnootxy
oxygenation
aeginnoprst
personating
aeginnopsst
passing-note
aeginnopstv
pavingstone
aeginnoptux
expugnation
aeginnorrtt
interrogant
aeginnossuu
sanguineous
aeginnprsss
sparingness
aeginoopprt
oppignorate
aeginoprttw
watering-pot
aeginoprtux
expurgation
aeginorrtty
intergatory
aeginprrstw
spring-water
water-spring
aeginrsstvw
wring-staves
aegiprrrtyy
pyrargyrite
aegklorrssw
glassworker
aegkmnorssy
monkey-grass
aegllnoopty
planetology
aegllnosssw
gallowsness
aeglloprutz
zygopleural
aeglmnoorsw
sea-longworm
aegmnoooptt
potamogeton
aegmnoorrst
gastronomer

aegnnnprtuu
unrepugnant
aegnnopstuy
pentagynous
aegnooprssu
saprogenous
aegnoorsttu
tetragonous
aegnorsttuy
tetragynous
aegoorrrtuv
rotogravure
aegoprrruvy
pyrogravure
aegoprrtuxy
expurgatory
aegorssstuu
Stegosaurus
aehhiimpsss
Messiahship
aehhikmmssy
shimmy-shake
aehhillntuy
unhealthily
aehhilopsty
lithophysae
aehhimoprty
hypothermia
aehhinnopty
hyphenation
aehhinoorrr
rhinorrhoea
aehhiortttw
whitethroat
aehhlloptty
thallophyte
aehhlmmoort
homothermal
aehhlmoprty
hypothermal
aehhlooprtx
axerophthol
aehhmooopty
homoeopathy
aehhmooprrt
Theromorpha
aehhmorstwy
shameworthy
aehhnoprtty
theanthropy
aehhoopprst
phosphorate
aehhrrsttuw
water-thrush
aehiiilmtuv
humiliative
aehiiilrsst
Israelitish
aehiikmrstt
Mekhitarist
aehiiknpsty
kinesipathy
aehiillopru
ailurophile

aehiillpstt
philatelist
aehiiloprrt
horripilate
aehiilopsst
hospitalise
aehiilprstt
peristalith
aehiimnnory
Hieronymian
aehiimpprst
primateship
aehiimrstuv
Sivatherium
aehiinoprrs
parishioner
aehiinorttt
trithionate
aehiipprrss
periphrasis
aehiklmrsuw
lukewarmish
aehikmnnort
inkhorn-mate
aehikmnsssw
mawkishness
aehiknnssss
snakishness
aehiknnsssv
knavishness
aehillnosst
loathliness
aehilloppty
apophyllite
aehilloprst
hospitaller
aehillprstu
hill-pasture
aehilmmopps
psammophile
aehilmnoppy
Polyphemian
aehilmnortw
mother-in-law
aehilmnotty
methylation
aehilmnrstu
Lutheranism
aehilmqssuy
squeamishly
aehilnprrty
platyrrhine
aehilnprsst
shin-plaster
aehilnssst
saltishness
aehilnssssv
slavishness
aehiloopprr
plerophoria
aehiloppsst
apostleship
aehiloprsty
physiolater

aehilorrtty
theriolatry
aehilorstvy
overhastily
aehilprstwy
whist-player
aehilrssttt
star-thistle
aehimmnnnry
ninny-hammer
aehimnnnsss
mannishness
aehimnooppr
apomorphine
aehimnoprst
misanthrope
aehimoprstt
metaphorist
aehimopssty
haemoptysis
aehimorsttx
thermotaxis
aehimpprstu
hippeastrum
aehimprssty
sympathiser
aehinnppssu
unhappiness
aehinnsssty
synanthesis
aehinoorttx
exhortation
aehinoprsst
senatorship
aehinoprstt
antistrophe
aehinopsstt
stephanotis
aehinorrsst
enarthrosis
aehinorsstt
throatiness
aehinpprrst
partnership
transhipper
aehinprsstv
servantship
aehinpssssw
waspishness
aehinqssssu
squashiness
aehinrssstw
swarthiness
aehiooprrtt
Prototheria
aehiopprrst
praetorship
aehiopsssty
hypostasise
aehiopssttу
hypostatise
aehkllnssty
thanklessly

aehkmmorrst
mother's-mark
aehknoorrty
arrhenotoky
aehlllmoopr
allelomorph
aehllloosww
swallow-hole
aehllmoosty
loathsomely
aehllnosssw
shallowness
aehlloprrst
shell-parrot
aehlmopprry
lamprophyre
aehlnprsttu
thrust-plane
aehloprsstt
short-staple
aehmmoooprt
ommatophore
aehmmoppsty
psammophyte
aehmnoorrss
harness-room
aehmnorstty
thermonasty
aehmopprsty
Spermophyta
aehnooprrtt
orthopteran
aehnooprsst
snapshooter
aehnooprstu
Eoanthropus
aehnopprstt
pattern-shop
aehnopprtty
tryptophane
aehnorstuwy
unseaworthy
aehnprruxyy
Eurypharynx
aehooprrrst
arthrospore
aehoorrttxy
exhortatory
aeiiillmnor
millionaire
aeiiillmnst
sillimanite
aeiiilmmprs
imperialism
aeiiilmnnot
elimination
aeiiilmnrst
ministerial
aeiiilmprst
imperialist
aeiiilmprty
imperiality
aeiiilmrrsv
verisimilar

aeiiilmttvy
imitatively
aeiiilnnnrt
nitraniline
aeiiilnprst
plein-airist
aeiiimnrstu
miniaturise
aeiiinnstuv
insinuative
aeiiinprstv
inspirative
aeiiklloprt
realpolitik
aeiiklmnprs
marlinspike
aeiiknosstu
autokinesis
aeiilllmntu
multilineal
aeiillmmnnr
man-milliner
aeiillmmnrs
millenarism
aeiillmnrtu
multilinear
aeiillmrrtu
mitrailleur
aeiillmrstu
multiserial
aeiillnnrty
triennially
aeiillnopst
pillion-seat
aeiillnotvx
vexillation
aeiillnotvy
inviolately
aeiillnptvy
plaintively
aeiillnrsuy
uniserially
aeiillntuux
luxulianite
aeiilloortv
alto-rilievo
aeiillprrsu
pluriserial
aeiillrrstt
artillerist
aeiilmmorst
immortalise
memorialist
aeiilmnoort
melioration
aeiilmnorst
misrelation
Orientalism
relationism
aeiilmnorty
eliminatory
aeiilmnostt
testimonial

aeiilmnostv
love-in-a-mist
neovitalism
aeiilmnprry
preliminary
aeiilmnptty
impatiently
aeiilmoprst
peristomial
aeiilmprstu
Laserpitium
aeiilmpssvy
impassively
aeiilmrrstt
trimestrial
aeiilmrrsty
literaryism
aeiilmsttuv
stimulative
aeiilnnnott
intentional
aeiilnnorst
insertional
aeiilnnortv
inventorial
aeiilnnottv
ventilation
aeiilnnprst
interspinal
aeiilnnrstt
transilient
aeiilnnrtty
internality
itinerantly
aeiilnnssst
saintliness
aeiilnoprsv
previsional
aeiilnopstx
post-exilian
aeiilnorsss
insessorial
aeiilnorstt
Orientalist
relationist
aeiilnorttu
elutriation
aeiilnortty
orientality
aeiilnosttv
neovitalist
aeiilnpprzz
Lippizzaner
aeiilnprsst
spinsterial
aeiilnrsstv
silvestrian
trivialness
aeiilnrsstw
sister-in-law
aeiilorrrtt
territorial
aeiilorrstv
servitorial

aeiilorsttu
lateritious
aeiilprssst
peristalsis
aeiilprttvy
partitively
aeiilprtvvy
privatively
aeiilrsttvy
versatility
aeiilttttuvy
attuitively
aeiimmmnnst
immanentism
aeiimmnnssw
Weismannism
aeiimmnnstt
immanentist
aeiimmnrstt
martinetism
aeiimmrrttu
termitarium
aeiimnnoptt
omnipatient
aeiimnnorst
inseminator
nitrosamine
aeiimnnortt
termination
aeiimnnortv
vermination
aeiimnoprtt
impetration
aeiimnprrss
primariness
aeiimopprrt
impropriate
aeiimoprstv
improvisate
aeiimrrttuv
triumvirate
aeiinnnorst
Tironensian
aeiinnnortv
innervation
aeiinnnottt
inattention
aeiinnnqquu
quinquennia
aeiinnoortt
orientation
aeiinnoqrtu
enquiration
aeiinnorstt
reinstation
aeiinnprsst
spinsterian
aeiinoppstt
peptisation
aeiinoprrst
respiration
retinispora

aeiinoprrtt
partitioner
repartition
aeiinoprstu
utopianiser
aeiinoprttx
extirpation
aeiinoprtty
petitionary
aeiinorrsvy
revisionary
aeiinorrtty
anteriority
aeiinpprstt
Trappistine
aeiinprsssu
Prussianise
aeiinpstvxy
expansivity
aeiinssttuv
antitussive
aeiiooppsss
aposiopesis
aeiiorrsvvv
savoir-vivre
aeiiprrsttw
water-spirit
aeijmnorstt
master-joint
aeijnnnottt
joint-tenant
aeikklmnorw
workmanlike
aeikllrsttw
stilt-walker
aeiklmorstw
sea-milkwort
aeiklnnopps
plain-spoken
aeikmnnprtu
turnpike-man
aeillmnnstt
installment
aeillmnooty
emotionally
aeillmnrtuv
intervallum
aeillmnttuv
multivalent
aeillmprsst
spill-stream
aeillnootuv
evolutional
aeillnoptty
potentially
aeillnosssy
sessionally
aeillnrstuv
surveillant
aeillnrsuvy
universally
aeillnsssty
stainlessly

aeillnsstty
taintlessly
aeillnsuuxy
unisexually
aeillntuuxy
luxulyanite
aeillorttuv
ultraviolet
aeilmmnorty
momentarily
aeilmnnnssu
unmanliness
aeilmnnoops
Napoleonism
aeilmnnootu
unemotional
aeilmnnossw
womanliness
aeilmnnrttu
nutrimental
aeilmnoostt
molestation
aeilmnoppry
propylamine
aeilmnoprss
personalism
aeilmnpprsu
paper-muslin
aeilmoprrsu
leprosarium
aeilmoprrty
polarimetry
temporarily
aeilmoprtty
temporality
aeilmoprtxy
proximately
aeilnnoopst
Napoleonist
aeilnnoprsu
unipersonal
aeilnnopsst
plainstones
aeilnnortuv
vulneration
aeilnnrrtuy
interlunary
aeilnnrstty
transiently
aeilnooprtx
exploration
aeilnopprst
epiplastron
aeilnopptty
platinotype
aeilnoprrst
tripersonal
aeilnoprsst
personalist
aeilnoprsty
personality
aeilnoprtuv
pulveration

aeilnopssss
passionless
aeilnorrstu
serrulation
aeilnottuvv
voluntative
aeilnrsstvy
sylvestrian
aeiloopprrrt
reportorial
aeilopprrsu
populariser
aeiloprsttu
tripetalous
aeiloprsttw
water-pistol
aeilostuvxy
vexatiously
aeimmnpprss
panspermism
aeimmnrsssu
summariness
aeimmopsttu
impostumate
aeimmorsttu
tautomerism
aeimmprsstu
suprematism
aeimmsssty
systematism
aeimnnoorty
ration-money
aeimnnopptt
appointment
aeimnnorstt
ornamentist
aeimnnorstu
mensuration
aeimnnssttu
sustainment
aeimnoorsst
astronomise
aeimnoorssu
anisomerous
aeimnoprttu
importunate
permutation
aeimnorrtty
terminatory
aeimnorsstu
stramineous
aeimnorstty
attorneyism
aeimnortttu
mutteration
aeimnosssty
seismonasty
aeimnpprsst
panspermist
aeimnrrsttt
transmitter
aeimooprrst
aerotropism

aeimoorrtty
arteriotomy
aeimoorsttu
autoerotism
aeimoprrssu
aspersorium
aeimoprrtty
impetratory
aeimopstttu
temptatious
aeimprrttuy
prematurity
aeimprssttu
suprematist
aeimsssttty
systematist
aeinnnorsty
Tyronensian
aeinnnorttu
antineutron
aeinnooprst
personation
aeinnoosttt
ostentation
aeinnopstty
spontaneity
aeinnorrtuv
nervuration
aeinnorstuv
intravenous
aeinnosssux
anxiousness
aeinnrrsttu
unrestraint
aeinoopprrt
reapportion
aeinooprrst
retinospora
aeinooprssu
aponeurosis
aeinooprttx
exportation
aeinoorrstt
restoration
aeinoorsuvx
over-anxious
aeinopppqru
appropinque
aeinoprsssv
vasopressin
aeinoprsstt
state-prison
aeinoqrstuy
questionary
aeinorsssuv
savouriness
variousness
aeinqssstu
squattiness
aeiooopppors
prosopopeia
aeiopprrrty
proprietary

aeioprrrsty
respiratory
aeioprrrttu
portraiture
aeioprrttuv
vituperator
aeioprrttxy
extirpatory
aeipprstuuv
suppurative
aeirrrstttu
stair-turret
aekllprsssy
sparklessly
aeklmoprrsw
sampler-work
aekloprrstw
plaster-work
aeklpppruwy
puppy-walker
aekmnoopssw
spokeswoman
aekoprrsttw
spatter-work
aellmssttyy
tally-system
aellnooprtw
pot-walloner
aellnoprstt
patent-rolls
aelloopprtw
pot-walloper
aellooprstw
wool-stapler
aelloqrrsuu
quarrellous
aelmnoprrsu
supernormal
aelmopsstuy
sympetalous
aelmprstyyy
mystery-play
aelnnsssuuu
unusualness
aelnoprstty
oyster-plant
aelnprrsuuy
superlunary
aelooprrtxy
exploratory
aeloopsstty
osteoplasty
aelpprstuwy
water-supply
aemnnorrstt
remonstrant
aemnooprsty
trypanosome
aemnoorsssu
amorousness
aemnoorstwy
oyster-woman
aemnopprrty
property-man

aemoopprrru
amour-propre
aemorrstttu
trout-stream
aemprrsttuy
muster-party
aennoopsstu
spontaneous
aenoprrrstt
transporter
aenorrstttu
sternutator
aenorssttu
sustentator
aenpprsssstu
suppressant
aeooprrsssv
vasopressor
aeoprstttyy
oyster-patty
aeoqrrsttuu
outquarters
afffghilrtu
affrightful
affghiimnrs
fish-farming
affghimnruu
humgruffian
affghllrtuu
full-fraught
affghlopstu
plough-staff
affgiilmnry
affirmingly
affgiknnstu
snuff-taking
affilnorstu
insufflator
afflllnortu
full-frontal
afgghiinnrt
night-faring
afggiilntuy
fatiguingly
afggiinsstt
gas-fittings
afgginoortz
zoografting
afghhiilntu
high-falutin
afghiiklnsw
walking-fish
afghilmopry
filmography
afghlorttuu
trough-fault
afghnoosttu
Nothofagust
afgiillnnty
inflatingly
afgiillnnuy
unfailingly
afgiilmnntu
fulminating

afgiilnnotu
antifouling
afgiimnorrt
granitiform
afgiimorstt
sagittiform
afgiinnnoru
Finno-Ugrian
afgiinnopsy
saponifying
afgiinosttu
fustigation
afgiinrstty
stratifying
afgillnntuy
flauntingly
afgilmnoprt
platforming
afgilmnorru
granuliform
afgilnortuu
fulguration
afgllooostw
gallows-foot
afhhiorttwy
faithworthy
afhiiinnsst
satin-finish
afhllmnruuy
unharmfully
afhlopprss
splashproof
afhloossttty
soothfastly
afiiiilnntv
infinitival
afiiilmnnst
infantilism
afiiilnrstu
fustilirian
afiiimprsss
fissiparism
afiiiprssty
fissiparity
afiilllmopr
lapilliform
afiillmmmor
mamilliform
afiillmoppr
papilliform
afiillnostu
fusillation
afiilmnnotu
fulmination
afiilmnopru
naupliiform
afiilmnorty
informality
afiilnorrtt
infiltrator
afiilorsttu
flirtatious
afiimnnoort
information
afiimnoorsu
omnifarious
afiimorstuv
favouritism
afiinnorstx
transfixion
afiioprsssu
fissiparous
afillmnopru
planuliform
afilmnoortu
formulation
afilmnortuy
fulminatory
afilnorsttu
flustration
afimmnoprty
tympaniform
afimnoorrty
informatory
afinnorsstu
transfusion
afinorrsttu
frustration
afkklmprtuu
Kulturkampf
agggiijnnor
jagging-iron
agggilnooty
gigantology
agggilnsuzz
gas-guzzling
agghhiiknnr
high-ranking
agghhlloppry
glyphograph
agghhnortuu
through-gaun
agghiijmntu
thingumajig
agghiiknntw
night-waking
agghiilnnsu
languishing
agghiiloost
hagiologist
agghinortww
wagon-wright
agghlnoopsy
sphagnology
agghmmoprsy
sphygmogram
aggiiklntww
walking-twig
aggiilnnoss
sloganising
aggiilnnosy
agonisingly
aggiilnrsst
tiring-glass
aggiinnoprt
pig-ignorant
aggiinnprst
part-singing
aggiinorttu
gurgitation
aggillnnopy
long-playing
aggillnntwy
twanglingly
aggimmnoprr
programming
aggimmoortu
maggotorium
agginopsstt
staging-post
aggllnooryy
laryngology
agglooorsty
agrostology
aghhiimnrst
nightmarish
aghhiirsstt
straightish
aghhiloprty
lithography
aghhloopsuy
hylophagous
aghhlortuwy
laughworthy
aghhmnopryy
hymnography
aghhmoprtyy
mythography
aghhnoopprry
phonography
aghhoopprty
photography
aghhooprrty
orthography
aghhoortuwx
thoroughwax
aghhopprsyy
hypsography
aghhopprtyy
phytography
aghiiilmntu
humiliating
aghiiilnpss
sailing-ship
aghiillnoop
philologian
aghiilmnoos
hooliganism
aghiilnnsvy
vanishingly
aghiilnrsvy
ravishingly
aghiinnosst
astonishing
aghiinprsty
pharyngitis
aghilmnnory
gymnorhinal
aghilmnooty
mythologian
aghilnoostt
anthologist
aghilnoprtw
whaling-port
aghilnorrwy
harrowingly
aghilnrttwy
thwartingly
aghiloopstt
pathologist
aghimnnsstu
hunting-mass
aghimnoopsy
siphonogamy
aghimnoprst
prognathism
aghimoprsty
myographist
Pythagorism
aghinnoppsw
swan-hopping
aghinoossty
soothsaying
aghiooppsux
xiphopagous
aghiooprrst
torsiograph
aghiooprstz
zoographist
aghioopstux
toxiphagous
aghiorsttu
straight-out
aghlloopssy
hypoglossal
aghlooppsuy
polyphagous
aghloopsuxy
xylophagous
aghloprstyy
stylography
aghmnooopsu
monophagous
aghnnosstuy
syngnathous
aghnoopprry
pornography
aghnooprstu
prognathous
aghooprssty
gastrosophy
aghoorrsttw
groatsworth
agiiiillnnt
initialling
agiiillnost
sigillation
agiiillpstu
pugilistial
agiiilmnstv
vigilantism
agiiilnnopt
oil-painting
agiiilnortv
invigilator
agiiilnorty
originality
agiiilnpsst
salpingitis
agiiilnsttw
waiting-list
agiiimmnort
immigration
agiiinnnstu
insinuating
agiiinnoort
origination
agiiinnostt
instigation
agiikknnrst
skating-rink
agiiknprssy
sky-aspiring
agiilmnnoty
longanimity
agiilmnrssu
singularism
agiilmnsttu
stimulating
agiilmoopst
Plagiostomi
agiilmoorst
Mariologist
agiilmoosst
gliomatosis
agiilnrsstu
singularist
agiilnrstuy
singularity
agiimmnnttu
manumitting
agiimnnortw
tiring-woman
agiimnoortw
waiting-room
agiinnooprt
pignoration
agiinnoprst
patronising
agiinnssstu
unassisting
agiinoorrtv
invigorator
agiinorsttt
tritagonist
agiinprrttw
part-writing
agikllnprsy
sparklingly
agillmnnoou
monolingual
agillnrstty
startlingly
agilmmnpsuw
lignum-swamp
agilmnnoosu
longanimous
agilmnnsuuy
unamusingly

agilmnorsst
storm-signal
agilmnrssuy
laryngismus
agilmooprty
primatology
agilmoorsty
Maryologist
agilmoosttu
tautologism
agilnnprsuy
unsparingly
agilnopprvy
approvingly
agilnopruvy
vapouringly
agilnosssuu
salsuginous
agiloorssyy
Assyriology
agiloostttu
tautologist
agimmnoorst
mooring-mast
agimmooprst
gamotropism
agimnnnorry
non-marrying
agimnnorrst
morning-star
aginnoppruv
unapproving
aginnoprrst
apron-string
aginnoprsst
transposing
aginnoqrrtu
quarrington
aginoooprrt
prorogation
aginooprstt
protagonist
aginoorrstu
surrogation
aginoorrsuv
granivorous
aglllnoopyy
polygonally
aglllooptty
polyglottal
agllmoorsuy
glamorously
agllorrsuuy
garrulously
aglmnooptuy
polygonatum
aglmnoortyy
laryngotomy
aglmooostty
stomatology
aglmooprrtu
promulgator
aglmoorrtyy
martyrology

aglooosttuu
tautologous
agmoorsstty
gastrostomy
agnooprrssw
song-sparrow
ahhiiiprsst
phthiriasis
ahhilloopsu
halophilous
ahhillpstuy
ithyphallus
ahhilmopstt
ophthalmist
ahhilmopsty
hylopathism
ahhilnoortu
holothurian
ahhilopstty
hylopathist
ahhimnnoopr
harmoniphon
ahhimnopssw
showmanship
ahhinorstuz
rhizanthous
ahhiprssttw
thwartships
ahhknorttwy
thankworthy
ahhllnoptxy
xanthophyll
ahiiilmnotu
humiliation
ahiiipprstt
hippiatrist
ahiijnoprst
janitorship
ahiillorsuy
hilariously
ahiilmnopst
notaphilism
ahiilmortuy
humiliatory
ahiilnoprrt
horripilant
ahiilnopstt
notaphilist
ahiilopstty
hospitality
ahiilpsstty
staphylitis
ahiilrsstty
hairstylist
ahiimmnsstu
shunamitism
ahiimnnosst
Smithsonian
ahiimnnrrtu
antirrhinum
ahiimnooosu
homoiousian
ahiimoopppt
hippopotami

ahiioprrstt
traitorship
ahikkoorrsw
kwashiorkor
ahikmnoprsw
workmanship
ahillmoprtu
prothallium
ahillopstxy
phyllotaxis
ahilmmoopsu
ammophilous
ahilnoprsty
rhinoplasty
ahilopprsxy
prophylaxis
ahiloprstyy
physiolatry
ahimnoprsty
misanthropy
ahimoorstuz
rhizomatous
ahimoprssty
stasimorphy
ahinnoorrst
horrisonant
ahinoopprst
patroonship
ahinoopsstx
saxophonist
ahinoorrstu
ornithosaur
ahiooprrstx
orthopraxis
ahiooprsttx
trophotaxis
ahknootuwwy
you-know-what
ahllnoorstw
sallow-thorn
ahlmnotuxxy
Xanthoxylum
ahlmnotuxyz
Zanthoxylum
ahlmoopprst
trophoplasm
ahlnooprsty
hyoplastron
ahloprrstuu
sulphurator
ahnorsstuuy
thysanurous
ahoopprsstu
apostrophus
aiiiiilnotvx
lixiviation
aiiiklmnrrs
larrikinism
aiiilllnptu
lilliputian
aiiillnoqtu
illiquation
aiiillnottt
titillation

aiiillrsttv
vitraillist
aiiilnnottu
intuitional
aiiilnorstt
institorial
aiiilnosttu
utilisation
aiiimnrsttu
miniaturist
aiiimpprrty
primiparity
aiiimpsstvy
impassivity
aiiinnnoqtu
inquination
aiiinnnostu
insinuation
aiiinnoprst
inspiration
aiiinnoqrtu
inquiration
aiiinnosttu
inusitation
unitisation
aiiinotttv
tittivation
aiiknrssstt
Sanskritist
aiillmmnotu
multinomial
aiillmnortu
illuminator
aiillmnstuu
illuminatus
aiillmprstu
multispiral
aiillnnoopt
pollination
aiillnprtuy
nulliparity
aiillnrssty
sinistrally
aiillpprtuy
pupillarity
aiillprstuy
spiritually
aiilmmortty
immortality
aiilmnooprt
imploration
aiilmnoopst
malposition
aiilmnoosst
solmisation
aiilmnosttu
stimulation
aiilmoopsst
lipomatosis
aiilmprttuy
multiparity
aiilnnoostt
notionalist

aiilnnorttu
nutritional
aiilnooprsv
provisional
aiilnoortvy
volitionary
aiilnoprtuy
unipolarity
aiilnopsttu
stipulation
aiilnortuux
luxuriation
aiilnosstty
stylisation
aiilnprstuu
unspiritual
aiilprsttuy
spiritualty
aiimmnnossu
manumission
aiimmnopstt
pantomimist
aiimmnssttu
numismatist
aiimnnoostu
antimonious
aiimnooprtt
importation
aiimnooprtx
proximation
aiimnossttu
mussitation
aiimnostttu
mutationist
aiimnprsssu
Prussianism
aiimopprrsu
primiparous
aiinnooostz
ozonisation
aiinnoorstt
nitrosation
aiinnorstuy
insinuatory
aiinoprrsty
inspiratory
aiinoprrsuu
uriniparous
aiinoprrttu
parturition
aiinoprssst
inspissator
aiinoprsstu
suspiration
aiinorrtttu
trituration
aiiopprrtt
propitiator
aiioprrsttt
portraitist
aiioprssttt
prostatitis
aiipprrstty
party-spirit

aillnoptuu
pullulation
ailllnosuvy
villanously
aillmooprst
allotropism
aillmopsssy
plasmolysis
aillmopstuy
ampullosity
aillnoostty
litany-stool
aillnoprsuu
nulliparous
aillnortuvy
voluntarily
aillnppstuy
suppliantly
aillnrtuuxy
luxuriantly
aillooprstt
postillator
aillorrsttu
illustrator
ailmmnnotuu
nummulation
ailmmnostuu
multanimous
ailmmopssty
polymastism
ailmnnosttu
multisonant
ailmnnosuuy
unanimously
ailmnoprtty
importantly
ailmnorstuv
voluntarism
ailmooprrty
imploratory
ailmoopruyz
polyzoarium
ailmoprstuu
multiparous
ailnnortuvy
involuntary
ailnnrtuuux
unluxuriant
ailnooprstu
sporulation
ailnoopsttu
postulation
ailnoppsttu
post-nuptial
ailnopsttuu
pustulation
ailnorsttuv
voluntarist
ailnorsuuvy
unsavourily
ailnrsstuuu
laurustinus
ailooprsuvy
oviparously

ailoprsttuy
stipulatory
ailorsttuy
statutorily
aimmnorrtuu
murmuration
aimmoorrstu
moratoriums
aimmoosstxy
myxomatosis
aimnnoopttu
mountain-top
aimnnoostuu
mountainous
aimnnoprttu
unimportant
ainoooprrsw
arrow-poison
ainooprrstt
prostration
ainopprstuu
suppuration
ainorrsstuu
susurration
aklnnoooptz
zooplankton
allnoppruuy
unpopularly
alloooprstu
allotropous
alloorstwww
swallow-wort
almmnossuuw
Mussulwoman
almnnoosuyy
anonymously
almnooorstu
monolatrous
almnoorsttu
salmon-trout
alnnorstuyy
tyrannously
aloooprstuv
pot-valorous
alooprsttuy
postulatory
aloprrstuuy
rapturously
amnooprsstw
sportswoman
amnoosttuuy
tautonymous
amooprrrtty
protomartyr
amooprrsttu
stump-orator
anoooprrtty
protonotary
bbbbdeeelru
beblubbered
bbbeehlllsu
bubble-shell
bbbeelmmory
lobby-member

bbbegiiinnw
wine-bibbing
bbcdeeorrru
rubber-cored
bbcdehiikrt
thick-ribbed
bbcdehirrtu
butcher-bird
bbceegiillr
gibberellic
bbceehnnoou
bonne-bouche
bbceelnoost
cobblestone
bbcegiiilop
bibliopegic
bbceginnouv
nubbing-cove
bbceilmostu
combustible
bbcejkoorst
stock-jobber
bbceklorstu
blockbuster
bbcelmorstu
cluster-bomb
bbcgiinrssu
subscribing
bbcgimoorry
borborygmic
bbciiilloop
bibliopolic
bbddeelloou
blue-blooded
bbddeillnou
double-blind
bbddeiloruy
body-builder
bbdeehhlooy
hobbledehoy
bbdeehirrsu
shrubberied
bbdegiimnov
dive-bombing
bbdelnooosy
bloody-bones
bbdelnrssuu
blunderbuss
bbdghloootu
blood-bought
bbdgiiknnoo
bookbinding
bbeeehrrstu
sheet-rubber
bbeeelnopst
pebble-stone
bbeegiiillnr
gibberellin
bbeegilmrsu
submergible
bbeeillmrty
belly-timber
bbeeilmrssu
submersible

bbeeilnsssu
subsensible
bbeeinnnoor
bonbonnière
bbeelnorstu
rubble-stone
bbeenorrsyy
boysenberry
bbefilorsuu
bulbiferous
bbegggilnow
begging-bowl
bbegilmnosx
sembling-box
bbeginosssu
gibbousness
bbehiiiillop
bibliophile
bbehinrsssu
shrubbiness
bbehlorsttu
bottle-brush
bbeiilmsssu
submissible
bbellnottuy
belly-button
bbelmpppuuy
bumble-puppy
bbghilnoory
hobgoblinry
bbghilnorty
throbbingly
bbgiillnquy
quibblingly
bbgilmnotux
tumbling-box
bbginoprstu
rubbing-post
bbgmoorrsuy
borborygmus
bbhiiillopy
bibliophily
bbllllooyy
loblolly-boy
bcccehhhnru
church-bench
bccdeehklou
double-check
bccdeilnotu
conductible
bccdeiopsuu
pseudocubic
bcceeeefinn
beneficence
bcceeeenrsu
erubescence
bcceeehoppr
copper-beech
bcceeeikllt
click-beetle
bcceeenrsuy
erubescency
bcceeiilnor
incoercible

bcceeilllot
collectible
bcceeilnnot
connectible
bcceeilnoss
concessible
bcceeilorrt
correctible
bcceeinrsty
cybernetics
bcceffikloo
office-block
bccefiipssu
subspecific
bccegilnoos
cognoscible
bccehilpsuy
push-bicycle
bcceiiirstu
rice-biscuit
bcceiilnnov
convincible
bcceiilnoru
ribonucleic
bcceiinooot
biocoenotic
bcceiklmorr
rock-climber
bcceiklorss
brissel-cock
bcceimnoosu
subeconomic
bcdddellooo
cold-blooded
bcddeeeilns
descendible
bcddeeiloos
close-bodied
bcddeeinrsu
undescribed
bcddegimnor
redding-comb
bcddehlotuu
double-dutch
bcdeeeeirrs
decerebrise
bcdeeefinnu
unbeneficed
bcdeeehimrs
Decemberish
bcdeeeiinno
inobedience
bcdeeeiinnt
Benedictine
bcdeeeiintv
benedictive
bcdeehilnpt
pitchblende
bcdeehmnooy
honeycombed
bcdeehmnotu
debouchment
bcdeeiiilrt
liberticide

bcdeeiiimno
biomedicine
bcdeeiilnrs
discernible
bcdeeiilrru
irreducible
bcdeeiilsst
dissectible
bcdeeiinnot
benediction
bcdeeilnoss
docibleness
bcdeeilnruu
unreducible
bcdeeimnrsu
disencumber
bcdeeimrtuu
decumbiture
bcdeeinorsv
bond-service
bcdeeinorty
benedictory
bcdeejnstuu
unsubjected
bcdeelmntuy
decumbently
bcdeghnrrsu
bergschrund
bcdehinosww
widow's-bench
bcdeiiilrty
credibility
bcdeiilnrsy
discernibly
bcdeiilrruy
irreducibly
bcdeiilsssu
discussible
bcdeiinnrsu
uninscribed
bcdeikloquu
double-quick
bcdeiooprss
proboscides
bcdekloorsu
bloodsucker
bcdelmnosuu
muscle-bound
bcdeloorssu
double-cross
bcdennoortu
counter-bond
bcdgiikmnor
mockingbird
mocking-bird
bcdhhiiopry
hydrophobic
bcdhimoorry
hydrobromic
bcdiiloopty
body-politic
bcdiinrtuuy
rubicundity

bcdiirssttu
subdistrict
bcdillnooru
colour-blind
bceeeelnnov
benevolence
bceeefforry
coffee-berry
bceeefilprt
perfectible
bceeegmnrsu
submergence
bceeehhinpr
hebephrenic
bceeehkltuw
bucket-wheel
bceeeilpprt
perceptible
bceeeinnopt
bonnet-piece
bceeellorsu
cerebellous
bceeennosss
obsceneness
bceeenqssuu
subsequence
bceefiiknst
sick-benefit
bceefimorrr
cerebriform
bceegilnost
congestible
bceehhinprs
benchership
bceehiiinrs
hibernicise
bceehimnttw
bewitchment
bceehioorrs
seborrhoeic
bceehklrruy
huckleberry
bceehnoopst
benthoscope
bceeiijostv
objectivise
bceeiilrstv
vitrescible
bceeiinrrst
interscribe
bceeijlotvy
objectively
bceeikoorsv
service-book
bceeilllosy
bellicosely
bceeilnortv
convertible
bceeilpprty
perceptibly
bceeilprstu
putrescible
bceeilpsstu
susceptible

bceeilrstuu
tuberculise
bceeinssstu
subsistence
bceeioprsst
corbie-steps
bceeiprrssu
superscribe
bceeirrsstt
bitter-cress
bceekklnnou
knuckle-bone
bceelmnrtuy
recumbently
bceelnoosst
obsolescent
bceelnosttt
scent-bottle
bceelorstuu
tuberculose
bceelrrruwy
curlew-berry
bceemnorstu
obscurement
bceemnosttu
obmutescent
bceemoprrru
procerebrum
bceenorsssu
obscureness
bceffnortuu
counter-buff
bceghilnnnu
unblenching
bcegiilnooy
cine-biology
bcegiimmnos
misbecoming
bcegilmoory
embryologic
bcehhiiloop
heliophobic
bcehhiimrtt
timber-hitch
bcehiiimnrs
Hibernicism
bcehijpsstu
subjectship
bcehiklmoor
hook-climber
bcehilnosst
blotchiness
bcehimnrssu
Burschenism
bcehklnootu
luckenbooth
bcehkmmorsu
Kommersbuch
bcehkoprrtu
pork-butcher
bcehlorrsyy
chrysoberyl
bcehlortttu
butter-cloth

bcehmoortty
thrombocyte
bcehmorrsuu
rhumb-course
bceiiinstuw
wine-biscuit
bceiijmostv
objectivism
bceiijosttv
objectivist
bceiijottvy
objectivity
bceiikllrst
billsticker
bceiillosty
bellicosity
bceiimnoost
coenobitism
bceiinoooss
biocoenosis
bceiinoorss
necrobiosis
bceijnstuuv
subjunctive
bceikllmnoo
nickel-bloom
bceikllosvw
swivel-block
bceikooprtu
picture-book
bceikoottty
tickettyboo
bceillnosuv
convulsible
bceillorssu
brucellosis
bceilmnntuy
incumbently
bceilmoopss
compossible
bceilmoorrt
root-climber
bceilmortuu
microtubule
bceilnortvy
convertibly
bceiloprrtu
corruptible
bceilpsstuy
susceptibly
bceiooprsss
proboscises
bceiorsttuv
obstructive
bcekklmnooy
monkey-block
bcekkoooory
cookery-book
bcekkoorrst
stockbroker
bceklmossty
block-system
bcekrrstuuy
scrub-turkey

bcelnoortuw
counter-blow
bcelorstuuu
tuberculous
bcelsttttuu
scuttle-butt
bceooprsst
stroboscope
bcfiiilorty
forcibility
bcfilmoorru
colubriform
bcgiiklnoot
bootlicking
bcgiinooott
gnotobiotic
bcgiklnoppu
upping-block
bcgilmnooow
wool-combing
bcgilmnrsuu
lignum-scrub
bcgilnoopux
coupling-box
bcgilooryy
cryobiology
bchhiooppt
photophobic
bchiiipsstu
ship-biscuit
bchprsstuuy
scrub-typhus
bciiiilmsty
miscibility
bciiiilntvy
vincibility
bciiilloruu
cuir-bouilli
bciiinnossu
subincision
bciillorsss
scissor-bill
bciilloruuy
cuir-bouilly
bciilmossty
symbolistic
bciinoorstt
obstriction
bciioorsttu
biscuit-root
bcijnnootux
box-junction
bciklloopw
pillow-block
bcilmosttuu
custom-built
bciloprrtuy
corruptibly
bcimoosstuu
combustious
bcinoorrttu
contributor
bcinoorsttu
obstruction

bdddeeeglou
double-edged
bdddeeeinrt
interbedded
bdddeeiimos
disembodied
bdddeeinrru
underbidder
bddeeeimmrs
dismembered
bddeeelnoru
double-ender
bddeefillln
blind-felled
bddeefillns
self-blinded
bddeeflssuu
self-subdued
bddeegiirrv
bridge-drive
bddeeginrru
underbridge
bddeeiinost
disobedient
bddeeillosw
disbowelled
bddeeillouv
double-lived
bddeeilmnno
noble-minded
bddeeilmnou
double-mined
bddeeilooos
loose-bodied
bddeeimnors
sober-minded
bddeeimnrsu
disemburden
bddeeloopru
pure-blooded
bddeensssuu
subduedness
bddefilnory
forbiddenly
bddefinnoru
unforbidden
bddeflllou
full-blooded
bddeflmooru
double-form'd
bddefmnoruu
dumbfounder
bddegginorx
dredging-box
bddeghhiloo
high-blooded
bddegiilotu
double-digit
bddegiimnnn
mind-bending
bddegiinorv
overbidding
bddegmoorry
Dogberrydom
bddehinnouu
unhidebound
bddeiinrstu
distribuend
bddeinoowww
bow-windowed
bddeinrstuu
undisturbed
bddelnnouuy
unboundedly
bddelnotuuy
undoubtedly
bddfillnnou
unblindfold
bddiiknooss
od's-bodikins
bddiilnnoww
window-blind
bddiinptuuy
pudibundity
bdeeeehirst
therebeside
bdeeeeiimrr
Biedermeier
bdeeefginrw
web-fingered
bdeeefiloou
oeil-de-boeuf
bdeeefilrru
reef-builder
bdeeefinntu
unbenefited
bdeeeiilrsv
disbeliever
bdeeeillntu
belle-de-nuit
bdeeeilmntv
bedevilment
bdeeeilmprt
redemptible
bdeeeilprss
depressible
bdeeeimmrrs
disremember
bdeeeimnntz
bedizenment
bdeeeimorrr
embroiderer
bdeeelllovw
well-beloved
bdeeelnssss
blessedness
bdeefhiills
fish-bellied
bdeefiiinrs
defibrinise
bdeefllnoru
bell-founder
bdeegghiirw
weigh-bridge
bdeeghinntu
unbenighted
bdeeghiorsu
bridge-house
bdeegiillnr
ill-breeding
bdeegiillnv
bedevilling
bdeegiilnrw
bewildering
bdeeginnrtu
reed-bunting
bdeeginortu
outbreeding
bdeeglnorry
goldenberry
bdeegmnrsuu
unsubmerged
bdeehiilltw
white-billed
bdeehilmnsu
unblemished
bdeehllmtuw
well-thumbed
bdeehnnrtuu
unburthened
bdeeiilnnyz
benzylidine
bdeeiilnsst
distensible
bdeeiimrstt
disembitter
bdeeillmoos
loose-limbed
bdeeillnprs
spellbinder
bdeeilmnoty
molybdenite
bdeeilmrrtu
tumble-drier
bdeeilorrsw
bowdleriser
bdeeimmorrv
overbrimmed
bdeeinnrttu
underbitten
bdeeioorsxy
deoxyribose
bdeeiorsstu
sober-suited
bdeelloortt
bloodletter
bdeellooss v
blood-vessel
bdeelnoostt
bottle-nosed
bdeelnortuy
double-entry
bdeelprrtuy
perturbedly
bdeenorsttu
deobstruent
bdeenprrtuu
unperturbed
bdeeooprttu
torpedo-tube
bdefhnoooru
bed-of-honour
bdefllnortu
bullfronted
bdefllnoruy
bell-foundry
bdeflloorw
blood-flower
bdeflnooorz
blood-frozen
bdegghiilln
hedging-bill
bdeggiinrsw
swing-bridge
bdeghooorrt
good-brother
bdegiilmnss
dissembling
bdegiinnrst
bird-nesting
bdegiioprtv
pivot-bridge
bdegilnnnuy
unbendingly
bdegilnttuw
butt-welding
bdegimorrsy
Dogberryism
bdeginorstw
bowstringed
bdegloorttu
bottle-gourd
gutter-blood
bdehhooorrt
brotherhood
bdehiiinntu
uninhibited
bdehiilprsu
shipbuilder
bdehiklnotu
double-think
bdehilnpsuu
unpublished
bdehiloopry
hyperboloid
bdehinnrsuu
unburnished
bdehinnrtuw
burn-the-wind
bdehlnorttu
thunderbolt
bdehmooorst
smooth-bored
bdehnorrsuy
hounds-berry
bdeiiiilnsv
indivisible
bdeiiiilnty
inedibility
bdeiiilmsss
dismissible
bdeiiilntvy
vendibility
bdeiiissuvv
subdivisive
bdeiilmrsuu
subdelirium
bdeiirrsttu
distributer
bdeiknorstu
strike-bound
bdeillostux
billets-doux
bdeilnorsty
blind-storey
bdeilntttuw
blunt-witted
bdeinorsttu
Brotstudien
bdeinosssuu
dubiousness
bdeissttuu
substituted
bdellosstuy
doubtlessly
bdelnooprst
bloodsprent
bdeloorrtuw
trouble-word
bdeloosttuu
double-stout
bdemooooprt
torpedo-boom
bdemooorssy
rosy-bosomed
bdfilmostuu
misdoubtful
bdggiiilnos
disobliging
bdggiiinnrs
singing-bird
bdghiimmnru
humming-bird
bdgiilmnnow
mind-blowing
bdgiilnotuu
outbuilding
bdgillootuy
blood-guilty
bdginnoorru
ground-robin
bdgnorrstuu
groundburst
bdhkoorstuy
Dukhobortsy
bdhnnooruu
honour-bound
bdiiiilnsvy
indivisibly
bdiiinossuv
subdivision
bdiimnortuy
moribundity
bdiimoorrss
bromidrosis
bdiiorrsttu
distributor
beeeegilrtt
tiger-beetle

beeeegimnst
besiegement
beeeehllsvw
bevel-wheels
beeeeimnttw
betweentime
beeeelppprt
betel-pepper
beeeennsstw
betweenness
beeefoorrty
freebootery
beeegillnps
spelling-bee
beeegillnrt
belligerent
beeegillnss
legibleness
beeegilmnsy
beseemingly
beeegilmntu
beguilement
beeegimnnsu
unbeseeming
beeeginrrst
Steinberger
beeeglnortt
bottle-green
greenbottle
beeehillmrs
embellisher
beeehillnor
helleborine
beeehilnprs
prehensible
beeehlorttt
three-bottle
beeehlpsstu
steeple-bush
beeeiijlmsu
semi-jubilee
beeeiilmrsv
misbeliever
beeeiknrttu
knee-tribute
beeeillrtyz
leze-liberty
beeeilmpprt
pre-emptible
beeeilnprtv
preventible
beeeilprrss
repressible
beeeilprrtv
pervertible
beeeilprssx
expressible
beeeimmmrrs
misremember
beeeimmnott
emboîtement
beeeioqrtuu
bouquetière

beeeirstttw
bittersweet
beeelmmnotw
embowelment
beeelmmnrtt
tremblement
beeelmnnnot
ennoblement
beeelorsswy
eyebrowless
beeemmnortw
embowerment
beeenopprty
teeny-bopper
beeenorsssv
verboseness
beefginoort
freebooting
beefglloorw
globe-flower
beefhllrrsu
fuller's-herb
beefiknrttu
butter-knife
beefilnrrst
bristle-fern
beefilrsttu
butterflies
beefkllruuy
rebukefully
beeggiilnsy
besiegingly
beeggilsstu
suggestible
beeghiinpst
sheep-biting
beeghimnntt
benightment
beeghinnorr
herring-bone
beegiiillnvy
believingly
beegiilnnuv
unbelieving
beegiilnqtu
quilting-bee
beegiimnrtt
embittering
beegiioorsu
bourgeoisie
beegikknoop
bookkeeping
beegillmnow
embowelling
beegilnnoss
ignobleness
beegilnsssu
leg-business
beegimnostt
misbegotten
beeginoprry
pigeon-berry
beegnnoortu
bonnet-rouge

beegnorrtuu
bourtree-gun
beehiklorrt
brotherlike
beehilmmnst
blemishment
beehiloprsy
hyperbolise
beehilotttw
white-bottle
beehilprrsu
republisher
beehimnoort
theobromine
beehinnottw
white-bonnet
beehknoorsu
house-broken
beehlrrrtuy
hurtleberry
beehmnorttt
betrothment
beehnorrtuv
overburthen
beehoprrstt
stepbrother
beeiiilpstt
epistilbite
beeiilmprss
impressible
permissible
beeiilnsssv
visibleness
beeiirrttuv
retributive
beeillorrsu
irresoluble
beeillrrrtu
bull-terrier
beeillrsttt
bellettrist
beeilmmnort
embroilment
beeilmnsssu
sublimeness
beeilnoprss
responsible
beeilnoqssu
obliqueness
beeilnpsssu
suspensible
beeilnrsstt
brittleness
beeilnssstu
subtileness
beeilprrssy
repressibly
beeimprsstt
Septembrist
beeinnoortu
boutonnière
beeinorrstt
sternotribe

beeinorsstu
stone-bruise
beeinorstty
tenebrosity
beeinortttw
twitter-bone
beeinrrrtwy
winter-berry
beeinrsstuv
subservient
beekmnoorry
money-broker
beelllowyy
yellow-belly
beellmrsssu
slumberless
beellnossuv
volubleness
beelmmorssu
slumbersome
beelmoorstu
troublesome
beelprsstuu
supersubtle
beenqrsssuu
brusqueness
beerrrsttuu
surrebutter
befghillrtu
bullfighter
befgiilntty
befittingly
befgiinnttu
unbefitting
befgilmrruy
mulberry-fig
befhillossw
bellows-fish
befhlmortuu
rule-of-thumb
befhloorrtw
froth-blower
befiiiilltxy
flexibility
befilmnrssu
brimfulness
befimoorrsu
morbiferous
befimorrsuu
umbriferous
befinorsttt
frostbitten
befknooortu
fortune-book
beflloorptu
bullet-proof
begggilnoot
bootlegging
beggiiillnnr
bell-ringing
beggiillnuy
beguilingly
beggiinnnnu
unbeginning

beggilnoovx
boxing-glove
beghiinnosw
wishing-bone
beghilnoruy
neighbourly
beghinrrssu
herring-buss
begiiiillty
eligibility
begiilnostu
biting-louse
begikllnoos
bookselling
begillmnrty
tremblingly
begilmnnrtu
untrembling
begilnorsvy
observingly
beginnorsuv
unobserving
behhioopstt
theophobist
behiiioprtv
prohibitive
behiimnprrs
brine-shrimp
behiimostwy
whiteboyism
behiinprstu
tribuneship
behiinrrtty
herb-trinity
behiknoosss
bookishness
behillnsssu
bullishness
behilmoprsy
hyperbolism
behimnnrstu
burnishment
behinoorsss
boorishness
behinorrttw
twin-brother
behinrssstu
brutishness
behioorrsuv
herbivorous
behkrrstuuy
brush-turkey
behlllsssuy
blushlessly
behlnorrtuy
unbrotherly
behnorsttwy
west-by-north
behosstttuwy
west-by-south
beiiilmnrst
libertinism
beiiilmqruu
equilibrium

beiiilnssty
sensibility
beiiilnstty
tensibility
beiiilqrstu
equilibrist
beiiilqrtuy
equilibrity
beiiilrrtty
terribility
beiilmprssy
permissibly
beiilnosssu
biliousness
beiilnrssst
bristliness
beiilrrsstv
verslibrist
beiinorrttu
retribution
beiinorstuv
inobtrusive
beilllosuy
libellously
beillmpstuu
submultiple
beillorrsuy
irresolubly
beillorsstt
stilbestrol
beilmnoopss
monoblepsis
beilmnoortw
winter-bloom
beilmorrstw
bristle-worm
beilmorsstu
mossbluiter
beilmssttuy
system-built
beilnoprssy
responsibly
beiloprrstu
protrusible
beilorstuvy
obtrusively
beimnpprtuu
turbine-pump
beimnssssu
submissness
beimoorrttv
riverbottom
beimpsstuuv
subsumptive
beinoosssuv
obviousness
beinoprrstu
stirrup-bone
beinorstuuv
unobtrusive
beinprrtttu
butter-print
beinqrrsuyy
quinsy-berry

beinssttuu
substituent
beiorrrttuy
retributory
beiorsstuuv
subvitreous
beklmoprruw
plumber-work
beknnnostuw
unbeknownst
bellnrttuuy
turbulently
belnoorttuw
trouble-town
belnoostuuy
bounteously
benoprssttu
press-button
berrsstttuu
trust-buster
bffginostux
stuffing-box
bfillnotuuy
bountifully
bfiloorstuu
tubiflorous
bgghiillnty
blightingly
bggillmnruy
grumblingly
bgginoortttt
bogtrotting
bgglmooorss
grog-blossom
bghhiimorsw
highbrowism
bghhloorttu
through-bolt
bghiinoppwy
whipping-boy
bghimnpttuu
tub-thumping
bghinooostx
shooting-box
bgiiillltuy
gullibility
bgiiknoortw
writing-book
bgiillnnpru
pruning-bill
bgiilnnopsw
spin-bowling
bgiilnnorru
burling-iron
bgiiloorstt
tribologist
bgiinooosst
gnotobiosis
bgiinostttw
towing-bitts
bgillmnstuy
stumblingly
bginnnostuw
snow-bunting

bginooopptt
boot-topping
bgllmooosyy
symbolology
bhhmmooptuy
hop-o'-my-thumb
bhiiinooprt
prohibition
bhiiioprstu
triphibious
bhiilmoprty
timbrophily
bhiiooprrty
prohibitory
bhimnooprrt
prothrombin
bhinorstttu
shirt-button
biiilmopsss
possibilism
biiilopssst
possibilist
biiilopssty
possibility
biiilorstty
torsibility
biikllmorst
Bristol-milk
biillnoortu
tourbillion
biilloosuvy
obliviously
biilooqstuu
obliquitous
biimnoostux
moxibustion
bilmopstuuy
bumptiously
bilnooosuxy
obnoxiously
bimnopsstuu
subsumption
bimorsstuuu
rumbustious
binnooosuux
unobnoxious
bioooprrrsu
opprobrious
bllmmoopssu
plum-blossom
bllmorssuuy
slumbrously
blloorstuuy
troublously
blmnorssuuu
unslumbrous
bmmnottuuy
tummy-button
bnoorrstuww
burrowstown
ccccimoorsu
micrococcus
ccckklooou
cuckoo-clock

cccdeeiinno
coincidence
cccdehinosy
synecdochic
cccdeiinnoy
coincidency
cccdennootu
unconcocted
cccdginoooo
gonococcoid
cccdiiiooss
coccidiosis
ccceeeenrsx
excrescence
ccceeeenrsxy
excrescency
ccceefllnou
flocculence
ccceeiilmst
eclecticism
ccceennorru
concurrence
ccceennorst
concrescent
cccefiinops
conspecific
cccefilmrtu
circumflect
ccchhiklrs
schrecklich
ccceiimrrsu
circumciser
ccceiinnopy
concipiency
ccceimprstu
circumspect
ccceinooprs
necroscopic
ccceirsstuy
cysticercus
cccennorruy
concurrency
cccgiknoorw
cock-crowing
cchhorrtuu
church-court
cchiiinnno
cinchoninic
cchilmotyy
cyclothymic
ccciimmoors
microcosmic
ccciimooprs
microscopic
cccinooossu
coconscious
cccinorstuy
succinctory
ccoooprstu
Protococcus
ccddeeenors
decrescendo
ccddeeensuu
unsucceeded

ccddeklnouu
uncuckolded
ccdeeefhikn
chicken-feed
ccdeeeiinrs
iridescence
ccdeeellort
recollected
ccdeeennort
concentered
ccdeehilpsy
psychedelic
ccdeehiortt
ricochetted
ccdeeiiinst
insecticide
ccdeeiilmrs
semicircled
ccdeeiilrrr
circle-rider
ccdeeiirrst
directrices
ccdeeilnoty
conceitedly
ccdeeilrrss
dress-circle
ccdeeimosty
discomycete
ccdeeinnouv
unconceived
ccdeeioppru
preoccupied
ccdeellloty
collectedly
ccdeellnotu
uncollected
ccdeelnnory
concernedly
ccdeelnnoty
connectedly
ccdeemnnotu
conducement
ccdeennnoru
unconcerned
ccdeennnotu
unconnected
ccdeennortu
unconcerted
ccdeenorrtu
uncorrected
ccdefimrsuu
circumfused
ccdehilopsy
psychodelic
ccdehiooprs
dichroscope
ccdeiilnops
condisciple
ccdeiiloort
crocidolite
crocodilite
ccdeimnoors
microsecond

ccdeinnnouv
unconvinced
ccdeinnotuv
unconvicted
ccdeinorstt
constricted
ccdeioprrtu
picture-cord
ccdenorsstu
conductress
ccdenorsuuu
unsuccoured
ccdhhilloos
school-child
ccdhhioorry
hydrochoric
ccdhiloopyy
hypocycloid
ccdhioorttw
witch-doctor
ccdkmosuuvy
muscovy-duck
cceeeefmnrs
fremescence
cceeeeinprt
centre-piece
cceeefhiknr
neckerchief
cceeefiknpt
picket-fence
cceeeflnors
florescence
cceeeginnrs
nigrescence
cceeeginott
ectogenetic
cceeeginrvy
vicegerency
cceeegnnorv
convergence
cceeegnrstu
turgescence
cceeehhlost
cheesecloth
cceeehinnor
co-inherence
incoherence
cceeehiprrs
speech-crier
cceeehorrtt
crotcheteer
cceeehorrty
heterocercy
cceeeiinppr
percipience
cceeeikoppt
pocket-piece
cceeeilnqsu
liquescence
cceeeilstwy
sweet-cicely
cceeeinnnov
convenience
cceeeinnpss
spinescence
cceeeinoprv
preconceive
cceeeinostx
co-existence
cceeeinrstv
vitrescence
cceeeirstux
executrices
cceeelorttu
electrocute
cceeemnpssu
spumescence
cceeennoqsu
consequence
cceeenoprst
torpescence
cceeenprstu
putrescence
cceeffiinot
coefficient
cceeffiinsu
sufficience
cceefiimnnu
munificence
cceefiinopr
proficience
cceefilnost
self-conceit
cceefiloopr
police-force
cceeflnnors
self-concern
cceeflnopst
self-concept
cceeginnnot
contingence
cceeginoott
geotectonic
cceegnnoost
cognoscente
cceegnnorvy
convergency
cceegnooprs
precognosce
cceegnoorrt
concert-goer
cceegnrstuy
turgescency
cceehhinott
theotechnic
cceehhkorry
chokecherry
cceehiiknrw
chicken-wire
cceehiklnor
nickel-ochre
cceehilorst
cholesteric
cceehimortt
ectothermic
cceehinnory
incoherency
cceehinorrs
choir-screen
cceehklllos
cockleshell
cceehmoptyy
phycomycete
cceehnrrsww
screw-wrench
cceeiikrssv
sick-service
cceeiilnnos
consilience
cceeiilorst
isoelectric
cceeiilrtty
electricity
cceeiimmnsu
ecumenicism
cceeiimnnos
omniscience
cceeiimnosv
misconceive
cceeiimosst
cosmeticise
cceeiinppry
percipiency
cceeiinprrt
pericentric
cceeiklmort
mole-cricket
cceeilmorty
myoelectric
cceeilnnort
non-electric
cceeilnnotv
conventicle
cceeilnoopr
cornice-pole
cceeilnorst
electronics
cceeilnorsy
cycloserine
cceeilnosst
conceitless
cceeilnqsuy
liquescency
cceeimnoort
econometric
cceeinnnovy
conveniency
cceeinnoqtu
cinquecento
cceeinnosss
conciseness
cceeinnosst
consistence
cceeinorrtu
Eurocentric
cceeinostuv
consecutive
cceelssssu
successless
cceemnnnort
concernment
cceenorrsst
correctness
cceeooprstv
vectorscope
cceeoorrrtv
overcorrect
cceffiinsuy
sufficiency
ccefgiklnos
self-cocking
ccefhiiistt
fetichistic
ccefiiipsty
specificity
ccefiilnotv
conflictive
ccefiinnops
non-specific
ccefiinopry
proficiency
ccefilmoors
scoleciform
ccefiorrsuu
cruciferous
ccefklloorw
flower-clock
cceghiinort
ricocheting
cceghiinosz
schizogenic
cceghiknrst
check-string
cceghinopsy
psychogenic
ccegiinnorr
cornice-ring
ccegilnoory
eccrinology
ccegilnoosy
synecologic
cceginnnort
concentring
cceginnnoty
contingency
cceginnoost
cognoscenti
ccegiorrsuu
crucigerous
ccehhiosstt
schottische
ccehhlnoory
rhynchocoel
ccehhmorsuu
church-mouse
ccehiiknnov
kinchin-cove
ccehiilnopr
necrophilic
ccehiiloops
helioscopic
ccehiimnoor
cheironomic
ccehiinprst
sphincteric
ccehiiprrty
hypercritic
ccehiknooor
cornice-hook
ccehiknpttu
ticket-punch
ccehillnoor
clinochlore
ccehilnopty
polytechnic
ccehimnoort
homocentric
ccehimnotyz
zymotechnic
ccehimooprt
chemotropic
ectomorphic
ccehimoorty
orchiectomy
ccehimoostt
cosmothetic
ccehinnrssu
crunchiness
ccehinoostz
zootechnics
ccehinoprty
pyrotechnic
ccehiorrsuv
hircocervus
ccehklosttu
shuttlecock
ccehlnoopsy
lychnoscope
ccehmoooprs
chromoscope
ccehnoooprs
chronoscope
cceiiimprtu
empiricutic
cceiiinsstt
scientistic
cceiiklrsty
city-slicker
cceiiknsstt
stick-insect
cceiilmnort
clinometric
cceiilmorst
cliometrics
cceiimmorrt
micrometric
cceiimmosst
cosmeticism
cceiimoorst
sociometric
cceiimorstv
viscometric
cceiinnnost
inconscient
cceiinoorst
coercionist
cceiinoprtu
open-circuit

cceijnnotuv
conjunctive
cceiklmoort
mortice-lock
cceiklnopru
cupro-nickel
cceilmoortu
coulometric
cceilmoruvv
circumvolve
cceilnnottu
noctilucent
cceilnorrty
incorrectly
cceilooprtu
police-court
cceinnoostu
consecution
cceinnossty
consistency
cceinoopstu
conceptious
ccejnnortuu
conjuncture
cceklorrttu
turret-clock
ccekmoorsty
comstockery
ccellnstuuy
succulently
ccelnoopprw
copple-crown
ccelorsssuu
succourless
ccenorrsttu
constructer
reconstruct
cceooopprst
proctoscope
ccfgiilnnot
conflicting
ccfiiinorux
crucifixion
ccfiilnnoot
confliction
ccgghhinoru
church-going
ccghiiklnoo
choking-coil
ccghiikmnot
thick-coming
ccghilnooor
chronologic
ccghilnorsy
scorchingly
ccghiloopsy
psychologic
ccghiooprsy
hygroscopic
cchhiiorsst
Scotch-Irish
cchiiilmort
microlithic

cchiiinortt
trichinotic
cchiiloopps
scopophilic
cchiimnoopr
microphonic
cchiimooorv
Mohorovicic
cchiimoprty
microphytic
cchiinooprs
rhinoscopic
cchilmoopry
polychromic
cchimnoopsy
psychonomic
cchimooprty
cormophytic
mycotrophic
cchiooprst
orthoscopic
cchioprssyy
cryophysics
cchiorssstt
cross-stitch
cciiinnotvy
convicinity
cciiinoorrt
onirocritic
cciiloopssu
piscicolous
cciimmnostu
communistic
cciinnoossu
inconscious
cciinoprtty
nyctitropic
cciinopstuy
conspicuity
ccijnnnootu
conjunction
cciklmnootu
coconut-milk
ccikmmoosst
comstockism
ccilmooopsy
cosmopolicy
ccilnnootuw
town-council
ccilnoossuy
consciously
ccilnoostuu
noctilucous
ccimnnooptu
compunction
ccinnoossuu
unconscious
ccinoopssuu
conspicuous
ccinoorrstt
constrictor
ccinoorsssu
cross-cousin

ccioooprssty
sporocystic
ccknoorrtuy
country-rock
ccllooortuy
collocutory
cclnoooorsu
concolorous
ccnoorrsttu
constructor
ccoooopprsty
proctoscopy
cdddeeeegkl
deckle-edged
cdddeeennsu
undescended
cdddeeilnuy
undecidedly
cdddelrsuuy
sculduddery
cddeeeenprt
precedented
cddeeeffopr
pedder-coffe
cddeeeilprt
predilected
cddeeeinnuv
unevidenced
cddeeeiprtu
decrepitude
cddeeennops
despondence
cddeefilnsu
self-induced
cddeehlnsuu
unscheduled
cddeeiinort
rodenticide
cddeeiltuvy
deductively
cddeeinnrsu
undiscerned
unrescinded
cddeeinprru
underpriced
cddeemmnnou
uncommended
cddeennopsy
despondency
cddefiiklst
fiddlestick
cddefiimost
discomfited
cddegiinpru
rice-pudding
cddegillnow
cold-welding
cddehiilmnr
childminder
cddehiinrtw
witch-ridden
cddeiiilnns
disinclined

cddeiinnoot
conditioned
cddeiinosuu
indeciduous
cddeilnooty
dicotyledon
cddeilnossu
undisclosed
cddeiloorsu
discoloured
cddeinsssuu
undiscussed
cddelllmooy
mollycoddle
cddeloopptu
cloud-topped
cddgiknnopu
ducking-pond
cddgiknoppu
pock-pudding
cdeeeefflns
self-defence
cdeeeefhmno
home-defence
cdeeeefllst
self-elected
cdeeeeflnss
defenceless
cdeeeeflors
close-reefed
cdeeeeginrr
regredience
cdeeeehkors
rose-cheeked
cdeeeehkrrt
three-decker
cdeeeeinprx
experienced
cdeeefhnrrt
trencher-fed
cdeeefiilrt
electrified
cdeeefilstx
self-excited
cdeeefiltvy
defectively
cdeeefiorrt
fore-recited
cdeeefkorst
stock-feeder
cdeeeflnrst
self-centred
cdeeeflnrtu
unreflected
cdeeeflorsv
self-covered
cdeeefmnort
deforcement
cdeeegiimno
geomedicine
cdeeegilnxy
exceedingly
cdeeehkorsy
rosy-cheeked

cdeeeiinsst
necessitied
cdeeeillntt
intellected
cdeeeilmnor
microneedle
cdeeeilnstt
delitescent
cdeeeiloprv
velocipeder
cdeeeilptvy
deceptively
cdeeeinnrtt
intercedent
cdeeeinprtu
unreceipted
cdeeeinpruv
unperceived
cdeeeinrsux
unexercised
cdeeelnprty
precedently
cdeeemmnorr
recommender
cdeeennnstu
unsentenced
cdeeennoprs
respondence
cdeeenorrtt
retrocedent
cdeeenorruv
unrecovered
cdeeenprstu
unrespected
cdeeeoprrss
predecessor
cdeeffiknst
stiff-necked
cdeeffinoru
unofficered
cdeefhooruv
forevouched
cdeefiilnty
deficiently
cdeefiinpsu
unspecified
cdeefiinrtu
uncertified
unrectified
cdeefiklnrt
ferntickled
cdeefilltuy
deceitfully
cdeefilnntu
uninflected
cdeefilnort
field-cornet
cdeefilosst
close-fisted
cdeefimnort
comet-finder
cdeeflnossy
confessedly

cdeefnnorst
frondescent
cdeefnnossu
unconfessed
cdeefnorstt
soft-centred
cdeefoprrtw
word-perfect
cdeegglorss
cross-legged
cdeeghhloos
hedge-school
cdeegiinopt
doting-piece
cdeegijlopu
police-judge
cdeegnosssu
second-guess
cdeehhnorrs
horse-drench
cdeehiilott
diotheletic
cdeehiinnos
Indo-Chinese
cdeehiinnst
indehiscent
cdeehiknntu
unthickened
cdeehikntvy
kidney-vetch
cdeehilmnnr
men-children
cdeehilotty
dyotheletic
cdeehimnort
endothermic
cdeehimnost
Demosthenic
cdeehioprtv
overpitched
cdeehioqstu
discothèque
cdeehlnortu
underclothe
cdeehnnortu
truncheoned
cdeehnoorsu
echo-sounder
cdeehnortuu
unretouched
cdeeiiilnss
dissilience
cdeeiiklnss
slickenside
cdeeiilnort
dereliction
cdeeiimnrst
densimetric
cdeeiimorrs
misericorde
cdeeiimosst
domesticise
cdeeiinoptv
point-device

cdeeiinrstv
viridescent
cdeeiinrttu
incertitude
cdeeiiprstv
descriptive
discerptive
cdeeiistttv
detectivist
cdeeiklnnoo
nickelodeon
cdeeiknnquu
unquickened
cdeeikopstz
pocket-sized
cdeeillopps
close-lipped
cdeeilnnquy
delinquency
cdeeilnsstu
ductileness
cdeeiloorsu
decolourise
cdeeilrsuvy
decursively
cdeeilrtuvy
reductively
cdeeilstuvy
seductively
cdeeimnnors
encrimsoned
cdeeimnnrst
discernment
cdeeimnoprs
endospermic
cdeeimnopty
idempotency
cdeeimnortv
divorcement
cdeeimoopst
decomposite
cdeeimoorst
osteodermic
cdeeimoostx
sextodecimo
cdeeinnostu
tendencious
cdeeinnprst
prescindent
cdeeinoortt
condottiere
cdeeinorrtu
reintroduce
cdeeinprsuu
superinduce
cdeeiooopps
opeidoscope
cdeeiorrsvy
rediscovery
cdeeiorrtxy
ex-directory
cdeeirrrsvw
screw-driver

cdeeirsttuv
destructive
cdeejnoprtu
unprojected
cdeeknnrssu
druckenness
cdeeknoorss
crookedness
cdeekorrsty
dyer's-rocket
cdeelllopuw
well-coupled
cdeellmnopu
uncompelled
cdeelmnnoot
condolement
cdeelmnoptu
uncompleted
cdeelnnotty
contentedly
cdeelnrrtuy
decurrently
cdeelnrttuu
uncluttered
cdeelpsstuy
suspectedly
cdeemnnnotu
uncontemned
cdeemnoprtu
producement
cdeennoprsy
respondency
cdeennoqruu
unconquered
cdeennortuu
unrecounted
cdeennortuv
unconverted
cdeennosttu
uncontested
cdeenoprssu
unprocessed
cdeenoprttu
unprotected
cdeenorrtuv
undercovert
cdeenpsstuu
unsuspected
cdeeooppssu
pseudoscope
cdeeooprruv
overproduce
cdeffloooru
off-coloured
cdefgloopru
cudgel-proof
cdefhiinrtw
witch-finder
cdefhilorst
foster-child
cdefiinntuy
infecundity
cdefiinorst
disinfector

cdefiinortu
countrified
cdefilnnoty
confidently
cdefimnnoru
unconfirmed
cdefinortuy
countryfied
cdeflnooors
second-floor
cdefmnoortu
uncomforted
cdegglrsuuy
sculduggery
cdeghhhiipt
high-pitched
cdeghinosst
second-sight
cdegiilnnnu
undeclining
cdegiinnors
considering
cdegiinsttu
side-cutting
cdegikloors
sockdoliger
cdegilmnooo
demonologic
cdegimnorru
corrigendum
cdeginnnoss
condignness
cdeginnooot
odontogenic
cdegklooors
sockdologer
cdegmorrsuy
dog's-mercury
cdehhioorsu
orchid-house
cdehhnooopr
chordophone
cdehiiilott
diothelitic
cdehiiinnor
enchiridion
cdehiiinrst
trichinised
cdehiikllnu
unchildlike
cdehiiklppt
thick-lipped
cdehiiktttw
thick-witted
cdehiillnot
decillionth
cdehiilotty
dyothelitic
cdehiimoost
dichotomise
cdehiimostt
methodistic
cdehiinorst
trichinosed

cdehiiooprt
epitrochoid
cdehikoortw
whicket-door
cdehilmnoop
monodelphic
cdehilmorsu
music-holder
cdehiloorxy
oxy-chloride
cdehilprtuu
pulchritude
cdehimnoopr
endomorphic
cdehimnoopu
Chenopodium
cdehimnooux
xenodochium
cdehimnorst
Christendom
cdehimorrtu
thermoduric
cdehimorrty
hydrometric
cdehinooprt
endotrophic
cdehinoorst
Chondrostei
cdehiooprst
orthopedics
cdehioprrst
short-priced
cdehkloorst
stock-holder
cdehlnoorsu
under-school
cdehlnoosuy
endochylous
cdehooorrst
horse-doctor
cdeiiilnprs
discipliner
cdeiiilnsuv
uncivilised
cdeiiilstuv
civil-suited
cdeiiimmstu
mediumistic
cdeiiinnort
indirection
cdeiiinntvy
incendivity
cdeiiinsttv
distinctive
cdeiiioprty
periodicity
cdeiiirttvy
directivity
cdeiiisstuv
vicissitude
cdeiijnstuv
disjunctive
cdeiikqttuw
quick-witted

cdeiillosuy
deliciously
cdeiillptuy
pellucidity
cdeiilnostu
unsolicited
cdeiilnrtuy
incredulity
cdeiilntuvy
inductively
cdeiiloorst
sclerotioid
cdeiilopssu
pediculosis
cdeiilostuv
declivitous
cdeiimnorst
modernistic
cdeiimostty
domesticity
cdeiimppruy
cypripedium
cdeiinnoort
conditioner
recondition
cdeiinnostu
discontinue
cdeiinoortt
condottieri
cdeiinoprst
description
discerption
cdeiinorrtu
irreduction
cdeiinrsttu
distincture
cdeiiooprtx
dexiotropic
cdeiiorssuv
discoursive
cdeijnrstuu
disjuncture
cdeilnnotuy
continuedly
cdeilnooruu
unicoloured
cdeilnopsst
split-second
cdeilnorsuu
incredulous
cdeiloorrtu
tricoloured
cdeimmnopsu
compendiums
cdeimmnottu
uncommitted
cdeimnoopsu
compendious
cdeimnossty
syndesmotic
cdeinnoprst
nondescript
cdeinnortuv
uncontrived

cdeinnrttuu
untinctured
cdeinorsssu
unscissored
cdeinorsttu
destruction
cdeinorstuy
countryside
cdeinortuwy
countrywide
cdeioprrtuw
word-picture
cdeiorsstuy
discourtesy
cdekknooorr
door-knocker
cdekloorsuy
sky-coloured
cdekmmoosty
mock-modesty
cdelllossuy
cloudlessly
cdellnorsuy
scoundrelly
cdelloooprt
protocolled
cdellorsuuy
credulously
cdenoprrtuu
uncorrupted
cdeoprrruwy
curry-powder
cdffiilltuy
difficultly
cdfggilnoor
cold-forging
cdfgiilnnoy
confidingly
cdfillosuuu
dulcifluous
cdfinnostuy
dysfunction
cdghhiinopt
diphthongic
cdghilnoopp
clodhopping
cdghilooory
orchidology
cdgiilossty
dyslogistic
cdgilnnopru
curling-pond
cdgilnoooot
odontologic
cdgiloortty
troglodytic
cdginnooopy
pycnogonoid
cdginoottuw
wood-cutting
cdginoprstu
crop-dusting
cdhhiilopry
hydrophilic

cdhhiiopsty
ichthyopsid
cdhhioprtyy
hydrophytic
cdhhnnoorty
rhynchodont
cdhiiimoopr
idiomorphic
cdhiilprsuu
disulphuric
cdhiimooppr
hippodromic
cdhiimoostt
dichotomist
cdhiiooprst
chiropodist
cdhiloottuw
cold-without
cdhimooorrt
orthodromic
cdhimooostu
dichotomous
cdhinooortt
orthodontic
cdhinooprsy
hydroponics
cdhiooprrty
hydrotropic
cdiiijnosuu
injudicious
cdiiilnttuy
inductility
cdiiinnostt
distinction
cdiiinttuvy
inductivity
cdiijlosuuy
judiciously
cdiijnnostu
disjunction
cdiilmorstu
clostridium
cdiilmpstuu
multicuspid
cdiilnopsuu
sipunculoid
cdiilopstuu
duplicitous
cdiimmnnoou
condominium
cdiimmnooty
incommodity
cdiioooostv
voodooistic
cdiklnopssu
spondulicks
cdillorsuuy
ludicrously
cdilmooorsx
loxodromics
cdilooruuu
douroucouli
cdmnooopuxy
oxy-compound

ceeeeegmnrr
re-emergence
ceeeeeprrrt
tree-creeper
ceeeehnrvwy
everywhence
ceeeehprsss
cheese-press
ceeeeilnort
electioneer
ceeeeimmnpt
empiecement
ceeeeimnnpr
pre-eminence
ceeeeimnnss
mise-en-scène
ceeeeinnprv
prevenience
ceeeeinrrrv
irreverence
ceeeeinrstx
re-existence
ceeeeirrstv
service-tree
ceeeejnrsuv
rejuvenesce
ceeeennrrtv
nerve-centre
ceeefffInos
self-offence
ceeeffhoosu
coffee-house
ceeeffiintv
ineffective
ceeeffiltvy
effectively
ceeefflnoss
offenceless
ceeefgllnst
self-neglect
ceeefhiiprs
speechifier
ceeefhnrrtv
trench-fever
ceeefikqruz
quick-freeze
ceeefilrssv
self-service
ceeefinnqru
infrequence
ceeefinorrt
refectioner
ceeefmnnort
enforcement
ceeefnprsst
perfectness
ceeegghinns
gegenschein
ceeeggnorrr
greengrocer
ceeeghinrsw
cheese-wring
ceeegiinopr
epeirogenic

ceeegiinpst
epigenetics
ceeegiknort
greenockite
ceeegilmnno
meningocele
ceeegimnort
merogenetic
ceeeginnotx
xenogenetic
ceeeginosst
ectogenesis
ceeehhklnop
heckelphone
ceeehhmmrsy
rhyme-scheme
ceeehikntttt
kitchenette
ceeehilortt
heteroclite
ceeehilsttt
telesthetic
ceeehimnrtu
hermeneutic
ceeehimorst
heteroecism
ceeehimprty
hyperemetic
ceeehinssst
cenesthesis
ceeehiprrsu
supercherie
ceeehiqrsuw
chequerwise
ceeehlmorst
chrome-steel
ceeehlnprsu
ensepulchre
ceeehlrttuw
wheel-cutter
ceeehmoprss
moss-cheeper
ceeehnorrtt
corner-teeth
ceeehopprst
sheet-copper
ceeeiiklntt
telekinetic
ceeeiilnrsv
service-line
ceeeiimnnpt
impenitence
ceeeiimrstv
time-service
ceeeiinnnrt
internecine
ceeeiinnnst
insentience
ceeeiinnrtv
internecive
ceeeiinnstx
inexistence
ceeeiipprsv
service-pipe

ceeeiiprrtv
irreceptive
ceeeiirrsvw
service-wire
ceeeijmnort
rejoicement
ceeeikllnst
nickel-steel
ceeeiknnrss
snickersnee
ceeeiknqrtu
quicken-tree
ceeeillorrt
electrolier
ceeeillstvy
selectively
ceeeilnnoqu
ineloquence
ceeeilnnotv
non-elective
ceeeilnoprt
pre-election
ceeeilnopst
Pleistocene
ceeeilnorst
reselection
ceeeilnrruv
culverineer
ceeeilrsssv
serviceless
ceeeilrssvy
recessively
ceeeilrstvy
secretively
ceeeilssvxy
excessively
ceeeiltuvxy
executively
ceeeimmpsuu
museum-piece
ceeeimnnnst
incensement
ceeeinnoprv
provenience
ceeeinnostv
venesection
ceeeinnrsss
sincereness
ceeeinortux
executioner
ceeeinostvx
co-extensive
ceeeinprrsw
screen-wiper
ceeeinprrtt
intercepter
ceeeinprsss
preciseness
ceeeinprsst
persistence
ceeeinprtuv
unreceptive
ceeeinrstvv
revivescent

ceeeioprrsv
over-precise
ceeeipprstv
perspective
ceeeippssty
type-species
ceeeiprstuv
persecutive
ceeeirstuxx
executrixes
ceeejnnstuv
juvenescent
ceeekmnorss
smokescreen
ceeeknprssy
cypress-knee
ceeelllntxy
excellently
ceeellnnnop
pennoncelle
ceeellnoppr
prepollence
ceeellorsty
electrolyse
ceeellortty
electrolyte
ceeelmnossw
welcomeness
ceeelmorrst
sclerometer
ceeelnrsssu
recluseness
ceeeloprrst
preselector
ceeeloprtty
electrotype
ceeelprssst
respectless
sceptreless
ceeemmnrtux
excrementum
ceeemnnnott
contenement
ceeemnnostt
cement-stone
ceeemnortty
enterectomy
ceeennoprtt
penteconter
ceeenprrsst
precentress
ceeeooprsst
stereoscope
ceeepprrsst
preceptress
ceeffiiinnt
inefficient
ceeffiilnty
efficiently
ceefghhimrt
Fehmgericht
ceefgiinstu
insectifuge

ceefginnrry
refringency
ceefhhnortt
thenceforth
ceefhhnortw
whenceforth
ceefhilorsu
cheliferous
ceefhinnrss
Frenchiness
ceefhipprst
prefectship
ceefhmoorrt
home-crofter
ceefiiklnrt
fernitickle
ceefiinosuv
veneficious
ceefiiprssu
superficies
ceefikknopt
pocket-knife
ceefiklnorr
ferronickel
ceefiklnrty
fernytickle
ceefillorsu
celliferous
ceefilmprty
imperfectly
ceefilnnoss
confineless
ceefilnorsu
fluorescein
ceefimnnnot
confinement
ceefinnqruy
infrequency
ceefinorttu
counterfeit
ceefllrstuu
self-culture
ceeflnnostt
self-content
ceeflnorstu
fluorescent
ceeflnprtuy
unperfectly
ceefloorrsu
foreclosure
ceeflorrsuu
resourceful
ceefmnnottu
confutement
ceeghhimrtv
Vehmgericht
ceeghiknnrr
neck-herring
ceeghimnoot
homogenetic
ceeghimnort
thermogenic
ceeghinrsst
sight-screen

ceegiilnsty
lysigenetic
ceegiimnsst
miscegenist
ceegiinortv
recognitive
ceegiinprst
string-piece
ceegiknoprw
weeping-rock
ceegilmnorr
relic-monger
ceegilnnosy
geosyncline
ceegilnopty
polygenetic
ceegilnptxy
expectingly
ceegimnnoot
monogenetic
ceeginnoott
ontogenetic
ceeginoorst
oestrogenic
ceeginoprty
pyrogenetic
ceeginossty
cytogenesis
ceegioprrtu
picture-goer
ceeglloorty
electrology
ceeglnrrsuy
curly-greens
ceegmostyyz
Zygomycetes
ceegnnoorsu
congenerous
ceehhiilprs
helispheric
ceehhiimprs
hemispheric
ceehhilmoor
heliochrome
ceehhimnrst
cherishment
ceehhiorsvw
whichsoever
ceehhmorstt
home-stretch
ceehiiinors
chinoiserie
ceehiiknoos
cookie-shine
ceehiillnst
Hellenistic
ceehiillrss
schillerise
ceehiilmort
heliometric
ceehiimnops
phonemicise
ceehiimprtu
perithecium

ceehiimpstu
euphemistic
ceehiimptty
epithymetic
ceehiimrtty
hermeticity
ceehiinopst
phoneticise
ceehiinpprr
perinephric
ceehiknpsss
peckishness
ceehiknssst
sketchiness
ceehillnost
clothes-line
ceehilmnort
thermocline
ceehilmorrt
chlorimeter
ceehilnorst
cholesterin
ceehiloprst
electorship
ceehilprstu
lectureship
ceehimmooor
homoeomeric
ceehimnoorr
cheironomer
ceehimpttuy
emphyteutic
ceehimrrtuy
eurythermic
ceehinqsttu
queen-stitch
ceehiooprtt
heterotopic
ceehioprrst
Terpsichore
ceehioprtty
heterotypic
ceehklnosuy
honeysuckle
ceehknorstt
netherstock
ceehknorsuy
honey-sucker
ceehkoqrruw
chequer-work
ceehkrssstu
hucksteress
ceehllnottt
nettle-cloth
ceehlloopst
clothes-pole
ceehlloorst
cholesterol
ceehllorsuy
lecherously
ceehlmoorrt
chlorometer
ceehlnooprr
chloroprene

ceehlooprrs
preschooler
ceehloorrtu
three-colour
ceehlrssstt
stretchless
ceehmnoorrt
chronometer
ceehmnoorst
stenochrome
ceehmnoprty
nephrectomy
ceehmooprss
cosmosphere
ceehmooprst
thermoscope
ceehmoorrtt
trochometer
ceehmoprsty
psychometer
ceehmppsstu
stump-speech
ceehnnorrtu
truncheoner
ceehnoorrtt
orthocentre
ceehnorrsty
cherry-stone
ceehnorstwy
oyster-wench
ceehnosstty
scythe-stone
ceehooprrsu
horse-couper
ceehoopsstt
stethoscope
ceehorrsttv
overstretch
ceehorrttyy
erythrocyte
ceeiiistvvv
vivisective
ceeiiknrsst
ricketiness
ceeiilmprtx
pleximetric
ceeiilmrtuv
vermiculite
ceeiilnnrsy
insincerely
ceeiilnrstv
virilescent
ceeiilntvvy
invectively
ceeiilsttvy
selectivity
ceeiimnnpty
impenitency
ceeiimnnrst
reminiscent
ceeiimopttv
competitive
ceeiimorsst
esotericism

ceeiimorstt
meteoritics
ceeiimorstx
exotericism
ceeiimpprrs
perispermic
ceeiinnnsty
insentiency
ceeiinnotux
inexecution
ceeiinnprst
serpentinic
ceeiinorstv
insectivore
ceeiinprsst
resipiscent
ceeiinrstvv
reviviscent
ceeiippttuy
eupepticity
ceeiiprrtuw
picture-wire
ceeiiprttvy
receptivity
ceeiirrsttv
restrictive
ceeikllnrst
Skillcentre
ceeiknoopst
kinetoscope
ceeiknosttt
stockinette
ceeillmnnty
inclemently
ceeillmrssu
music-seller
ceeillmrssy
mercilessly
ceeillprssy
pricelessly
ceeillsuvxy
exclusively
ceeilmmnopt
compilement
ceeilmnnstu
luminescent
ceeilmoorrt
colorimeter
ceeilmopstu
Telescopium
ceeilnnnoot
non-election
ceeilnnnoov
non-violence
ceeilnnopst
pencil-stone
ceeilnooprs
necropoleis
ceeilnoprtu
neuroleptic
ceeilnorttt
electrotint
ceeilnprsst
split-screen

ceeilnprstu
cluster-pine
ceeilnprsty
presciently
ceeilnqstuy
quiescently
ceeilnsuuvx
unexclusive
ceeiloorstv
locorestive
ceeiloorttv
toilet-cover
ceeilopsstt
telescopist
ceeilpprsty
clyster-pipe
ceeilrrstuu
sericulture
ceeilrsuvxy
excursively
ceeimnnoopt
omnipotence
ceeimnnoptt
incompetent
ceeimnnortu
countermine
ceeimnnsttu
intumescent
ceeimnoorsu
ceremonious
ceeimnopstu
pumice-stone
ceeimnorttu
counter-time
ceeimnrrttu
recruitment
ceeimoopsss
seismoscope
ceeimoorrsv
service-room
ceeimoprssv
compressive
ceeimoprstu
computerise
ceeinnnostt
consentient
ceeinnoorrt
reconnoitre
ceeinnoostx
co-extension
ceeinoorsst
stereosonic
ceeinoprrtt
interceptor
ceeinoprstu
persecution
ceeinorrsst
intercessor
ceeinorrstu
intercourse
ceeinortuvw
counter-view
ceeinossstu
necessitous

ceeinossstv
costiveness
ceeinprssst
inspectress
ceeinprssty
persistency
ceeinrrsstw
winter-cress
ceeinrssssw
swine's-cress
ceeiopprstv
prospective
ceeioprrtuv
overpicture
ceeioprsstt
stereoptics
ceeioprstty
stereotypic
ceeiorrttty
yttro-cerite
ceeipqrstuu
picturesque
ceejmnnortu
conjurement
ceejmnoprtt
projectment
ceeklrrstvy
vestry-clerk
ceekmnoopty
pocket-money
ceekoorrrtt
retro-rocket
ceellmnouwy
unwelcomely
ceellnoortt
telecontrol
ceellnoppry
prepollency
ceellrsstuu
cultureless
ceelmnnoost
consolement
ceelmnopssx
complexness
ceelmnopsty
splenectomy
ceelmnoptty
competently
ceelnnosstt
contentless
ceelnooppst
copple-stone
ceelnorstuw
stone-curlew
ceelnrrrtuy
recurrently
ceeloprttyy
electrotypy
ceelpssstu
suspectless
ceemmnnooss
commonsense
ceemmooprtt
Comptometer®

ceemmostxyy
Myxomycetes
ceemnnnottt
contentment
ceemnnorttu
recountment
ceemnnrsttu
encrustment
ceemnoortuv
counter-move
ceemnoprrtu
procurement
ceemnoprstt
contretemps
ceemnorrstt
storm-centre
ceemnorrtuu
countermure
ceemoprrssu
compressure
ceennooppst
postponence
ceennoorrst
corner-stone
ceennrrsstu
currentness
ceenoorttuv
counter-vote
ceenoppprry
peppercorny
ceenopqrstu
pre-conquest
ceenorstttu
stone-cutter
ceeooprssty
stereoscopy
ceeoprrsstt
protectress
ceeoprrstuy
persecutory
ceeorrrrstu
resurrector
ceerrrsttuu
restructure
ceffhirsstt
festschrift
ceffinrsssu
scruffiness
ceffiorrsuu
furciferous
cefgiiinprx
price-fixing
cefgikllnos
self-locking
cefgillnoss
self-closing
cefhiiisstt
fetishistic
cefhiiknstw
knife-switch
cefhlloorsu
flesh-colour
cefiimnorst
insectiform

cefiinorsuz
zinciferous
cefiknoqruz
quick-frozen
cefillloosu
folliculose
cefilmorsuu
culmiferous
cefilnoorrt
fire-control
cefilnoortu
counterfoil
cefiloorsuy
ferociously
cefimorrruv
verruciform
cefinoorrsu
corniferous
cefioprrsuu
cupriferous
cefkooopttu
out-of-pocket
cefllnnotuy
confluently
cefllnoorst
self-control
ceflmoorsst
comfortless
ceflooorsu
fluoroscope
cefnoorrttu
counter-fort
cefnoprrtuy
perfunctory
ceghiilnrst
christingle
ceghiilnrtt
chitterling
ceghiinnrst
christening
ceghillnooy
lichenology
ceghilmooor
oligochrome
ceghilnooou
euchologion
ceghilnoopr
phrenologic
ceghimnoory
cheirognomy
ceghimooost
Moeso-gothic
ceghimorrty
hygrometric
ceghinooorr
gonorrhoeic
ceghinoorst
orthogenics
ceghinorrst
torch-singer
ceghinorssu
grouchiness
ceghinorstu
scouthering
ceghiooprst
geostrophic
ceghllnoost
long-clothes
ceghlnooorr
chronologer
ceghlnoopst
sponge-cloth
cegiiilopst
epilogistic
cegiiinorst
Origenistic
cegiijlnory
rejoicingly
cegiijnnoru
unrejoicing
cegiiklnnsy
sickeningly
cegiiklnsst
singlestick
cegiillnnst
stencilling
cegiilmnost
closing-time
cegiilmooss
seismologic
cegiilnoost
neologistic
cegiilnotvy
cognitively
cegiiloopst
geopolitics
cegiimnoort
goniometric
cegiimnortu
tumorigenic
cegiinnoort
recognition
cegiinorrsu
crinigerous
cegiinrssty
synergistic
cegillllnoo
colonelling
cegillnnosu
counselling
cegilnoorst
necrologist
cegilnoosty
insectology
Scientology
cegimnnnost
consignment
cegimooorrv
microgroove
ceginnnnssu
cunningness
ceginnnortu
incongruent
ceginnoopst
coping-stone
ceginnorstu
countersign
ceginoorrsu
cornigerous
ceginoorrty
recognitory
ceginopprst
prospecting
ceginorstuy
courtesying
ceglmmooryy
myrmecology
ceglmooosty
cosmetology
ceglmoossty
glossectomy
ceglnooosyy
synoecology
ceglnoortuw
counter-glow
ceglooprsty
spectrology
cegloorstuy
Etruscology
cegnnopprsu
scuppernong
cegorrrsuyy
cryosurgery
cehhiilotty
ichthyolite
cehhiimmopr
hemimorphic
cehhiinorrt
tichorrhine
cehhiinprtt
pinch-hitter
cehhilmoory
heliochromy
cehhilmrsuy
helichrysum
cehhiloostt
chisel-tooth
cehhilosttw
whole-stitch
cehhimmoort
homothermic
cehhimooprt
theomorphic
cehhimosssu
schism-house
cehhimrstuy
eurhythmics
cehhiopstyz
schizophyte
cehhiprstty
Pterichthys
cehhlmoostt
clothes-moth
cehhlooossu
schoolhouse
cehhmnorssy
synchromesh
cehhmooprty
phytochrome
cehiiinpstz
citizenship
cehiiiorsst
historicise
cehiiirsttt
tritheistic
cehiijpsstu
justiceship
cehiikknnst
kitchen-sink
cehiikllrsy
lickerishly
cehiiklorst
ostrich-like
cehiikmnnuy
chimney-nuik
cehiiknssss
sickishness
cehiilopprs
scripophile
cehiilprstu
spherulitic
cehiimnopst
phonemicist
phoneticism
cehiimnoqtu
monchiquite
cehiimnorst
thermionics
cehiimopprr
perimorphic
cehiimossuv
mischievous
cehiinooprs
ionospheric
cehiinoorrt
co-inheritor
cehiinoorss
isochronise
cehiinoprty
hyperinotic
cehiinopstt
phoneticist
cehiinorstu
cushion-tire
cehiioosttz
zootheistic
cehiioprrst
prehistoric
cehiioprsvy
viceroyship
cehiiosssvy
vichyssoise
cehikmnnooy
chimney-nook
cehiknopstu
soup-kitchen
cehikooprtt
tooth-picker
cehillnnopu
Punchinello
cehillnoops
colonelship
cehilloottt
toilet-cloth
cehilmooppr
pleomorphic
cehilmooprs
pleochroism
cehilmorrty
chlorimetry
cehilmortty
thermolytic
cehilnooqru
chloroquine
cehiloprsuy
perichylous
cehimmooprs
mesomorphic
cehimmoosst
cosmotheism
cehimnooprx
xenomorphic
cehimnorrss
scrimshoner
cehimooprrx
xeromorphic
cehimooprtt
photometric
cehimooptty
mythopoetic
cehimoossst
schistosome
cehimopprst
coppersmith
cehimoprsty
hypsometric
cehimorstty
stichometry
cehinnorssy
synchronise
cehinoorrst
orchestrion
cehinopprtu
unprophetic
cehinoprssy
hypersonics
cehinorsssy
synchoresis
cehinorstuy
cushion-tyre
cehinrrsssu
currishness
cehioooprrt
photocopier
cehioopstty
osteophytic
cehioprsstt
prosthetics
cehkrrsstuw
shrew-struck
cehllloprsy
sclerophyll
cehlmoorrty
chlorometry
cehlnoostuy
honey-locust
cehloopprst
clothes-prop

cehloprssuu
sepulchrous
cehmmnooors
common-shore
cehmmooorsx
X-chromosome
cehmmooorsy
Y-chromosome
cehmnooostu
monothecous
cehmnoorrty
chronometry
cehmnoorsty
stenochromy
cehmoosstuu
custom-house
cehmoprstyy
psychometry
cehnnorttuu
hunt-counter
cehnnosstuu
uncouthness
cehoopsstty
stethoscopy
ceiiillmnpu
Penicillium
ceiiillnsst
illicitness
ceiiillptty
ellipticity
ceiiilmprst
simpliciter
ceiiilnnpty
incipiently
ceiiimnoprs
imprecision
ceiiimnosst
misoneistic
ceiiimpssst
pessimistic
ceiiinnrstv
vincristine
ceiiinnrsty
insincerity
ceiiinnsttv
instinctive
ceiiinoprtt
peritonitic
ceiiinorstu
cineritious
ceiiinostvv
vivisection
ceiiinprstv
inscriptive
ceiiioprstt
periostitic
ceiiiorsttu
icteritious
ceiikkmqssu
kiss-me-quick
ceiikllpstt
lickspittle
ceiiklnoorv
olivine-rock

ceiiklnprss
prickliness
ceiikloopty
poikilocyte
ceiiklqrsuv
quicksilver
ceiiklrsstv
silver-stick
ceiiknrssst
tricksiness
ceiillnsuvy
inclusively
ceiilmssuvx
exclusivism
ceiilnoprsy
prosiliency
ceiilnrtuuv
viniculture
ceiiloopprt
pleiotropic
ceiilorsstt
sclerotitis
ceiilrttuuv
viticulture
ceiilsstuvx
exclusivist
ceiimnoopst
incomposite
ceiimnooptt
competition
ceiimnopsuu
impecunious
ceiimnorstu
neuroticism
ceiimnosttu
Teutonicism
ceiimnprsss
scrimpiness
ceiimoopstv
compositive
ceiimoprrst
spirometric
ceiimorrstu
courtierism
ceiinnnnott
incontinent
ceiinnnortu
internuncio
ceiinoosssy
synoeciosis
ceiinoprsss
prescission
ceiinorrstt
restriction
ceiinosssuv
viciousness
ceiinrrsstu
scrutiniser
ceiinrsttuv
instructive
ceiiopprstu
precipitous
ceiiorrrstt
terroristic

ceiiorssssw
scissorwise
ceiiorstuvy
voyeuristic
ceiipprstuy
perspicuity
ceijooorssu
jocoserious
ceikkmnorty
monkey-trick
ceiklmoorst
mortise-lock
ceiklnnssuu
unluckiness
ceiknnorstu
countersink
ceilllnnors
linen-scroll
ceilllnooov
violoncello
ceilllosuvy
collusively
ceilloorruv
liver-colour
ceilmmoorsu
Coulommiers
ceilmmopruy
promycelium
ceilmooopst
cosmopolite
ceilmoorrty
colorimetry
ceilmoprtuu
pomiculture
ceilmorsuuv
vermiculous
ceilnnnotty
continently
ceilnooprtu
perlocution
ceilnorsstu
courtliness
ceilnprstuu
insculpture
ceilnrstuuv
ventriculus
ceiloooprst
protocolise
ceilooprrtu
turcopolier
ceiloooprtty
proteolytic
ceiloorrstu
terricolous
ceiloorrsvy
corrosively
ceiloprrstu
trouser-clip
ceilorsstvy
victoryless
ceimmnnooux
excommunion
ceimmnorssu
consumerism

ceimmoorrtt
tromometric
ceimnnoopty
omnipotency
ceimnooprss
compression
ceimnopsstu
postscenium
ceimnopstuv
consumptive
ceimnorsstu
consumerist
misconstrue
ceinnoorssu
connoisseur
ceinnoosttu
contentious
ceinnorsttu
tennis-court
ceinnostttu
constituent
ceinoooprsy
oneiroscopy
ceinoopprst
prospection
ceinooprrtu
neurotropic
ceinooprstu
point-source
prosecution
ceinooprsty
retinoscopy
ceinoopsssu
copiousness
ceinorrsssu
cursoriness
ceinorsssuu
curiousness
ceinossssuv
viscousness
ceinossstuv
viscountess
ceiooopprrtz
proterozoic
ceiopprssuu
perspicuous
ceioprrstux
prosecutrix
ceipprrsstu
superscript
cejoprrssuy
jury-process
ceklImpptuu
plume-pluckt
cekmooorrtt
rocket-motor
ceknoorrtuw
counter-work
cekoopprrsw
copper-works
cellmooprrt
comptroller
cellnoorrtu
counter-roll

cellnoprtuy
corpulently
cellnrttuuy
truculently
celmnnoortt
controlment
celmnoortuu
monoculture
celmooorsuu
mouse-colour
celnooorstu
stone-colour
celnooprttu
counter-plot
celoooprrst
coprosterol
celoorstuuy
courteously
cemmnooprtt
comportment
cemoooppsty
metoposcopy
cennoosssuu
nocuousness
cennorrttuu
counter-turn
cenooprsstt
cotton-press
cenoorrstvy
controversy
cenoorstuuu
uncourteous
cenoprrsstu
corruptness
ceprrssttuu
superstruct
cffgiiioorr
frigorifico
cffginoorsu
off-scouring
cffiiinoosu
inofficious
cffiiloosuy
officiously
cffiinoosuu
unofficious
cfflnoorsuu
snuff-colour
cfghiiknssu
sucking-fish
cfghiillnny
flinchingly
cfghiilnnnu
unflinching
cfghimnoort
forthcoming
cfgiiiknqru
quick-firing
cfgiinostty
Scottifying
cfgikmnoorr
rock-forming
cfgimnoppru
forcing-pump

cfiiiloprty
prolificity
cfilllloosuu
folliculous
cfillmooorr
corolliform
cfilnooprsy
scorpion-fly
cfinorstuuu
infructuous
cfklnoortuy
country-folk
cflnorsuuuu
furunculous
cfloooprsuy
fluoroscopy
cfnorstuuuu
unfructuous
cgghilnooos
schoolgoing
cggiiiknpst
pig-sticking
cggiinoorst
Gongoristic
cghhikosttu
thought-sick
cghhilnoost
night-school
cghhilootyy
ichthyology
cghhioprtyy
hygrophytic
cghiiloopsy
physiologic
cghiiloorst
chirologist
cghiknnorsu
cornhusking
cghilmooopr
morphologic
cghilooorst
chorologist
cghiloopsty
phycologist
cghiloorsty
Christology
cghimnoorst
shortcoming
cghimoopryz
zygomorphic
cghinnoprtu
hunting-crop
cghiooorstt
Ostrogothic
cgiiiklnopt
politicking
cgiiilnsstu
linguistics
cgiiinnpprs
crisping-pin
cgiiinnprtu
unit-pricing
cgiiinottvy
cognitivity

cgiikknopst
poking-stick
cgiikllmntu
tucking-mill
cgiiklnopst
stockpiling
cgiiknnrssu
sick-nursing
cgiiknopstt
poting-stick
cgiiillossty
syllogistic
cgiilmnoory
criminology
cgiilmoooss
sociologism
cgiilmoorst
micrologist
cgiilmootvy
victimology
cgiilnnnsuu
cunnilingus
cgiilnooost
iconologist
cgiilooosst
sociologist
cgiinnnnouv
unconniving
cgiinnorsst
cross-tining
cgiinnortuy
incongruity
cgiklnooort
rocking-tool
cgiknoppstu
upping-stock
cgillnnoort
controlling
cgillooptty
polyglottic
cgilmnnopuy
uncomplying
cgilmnooptt
complotting
cgilmooosst
cosmologist
cgilnprstuu
sculpturing
cgimnooosst
cosmogonist
cgimnoootyz
monozygotic
cginnnoopru
pronouncing
cginnoorsuu
incongruous
cginnoottuu
counting-out
cginooprsty
pyrognostic
cginoorsstu
outcrossing
cglnoorsuuy
congruously

chhiiloopps
philosophic
chhiilooppt
photophilic
chhiiloptty
lithophytic
chhiimorsty
isorhythmic
chhiimrttyy
rhythmicity
chhiinorsty
Ichthyornis
chhilmoopry
hylomorphic
chhilmoorty
lithochromy
chhimmooopr
homomorphic
chhinoooppt
photophonic
chhinorssuw
urchin-shows
chhiooprrty
orthophyric
chhioorstty
orthostichy
chhllloopry
chlorophyll
chhmoooprty
photochromy
chhnorsuxyy
oxyrhynchus
chiiilorttt
lithotritic
chiiimmnrsu
Michurinism
chiiimorsst
historicism
chiiinorsst
histrionics
trichinosis
chiiiorsstt
historicist
chiiiorstty
historicity
chiikmnnort
kinchin-mort
chiiknsstty
shinty-stick
chiillnoott
octillionth
chiiloostyz
hylozoistic
chiilopprsy
scripophily
chiimnoorss
isochronism
chiimooprtx
mixotrophic
chiinopstty
hypnotistic
chiiooprttx
thixotropic

chiiopprrty
porphyritic
chiiorssttu
tristichous
chiiossstty
schistosity
chilmoopprу
polymorphic
chilmooprsy
polychroism
chilmoprtuy
Polytrichum
chilmopstuy
Polystichum
chilnooopst
school-point
chiloorstuu
ulotrichous
chimmnooopr
monomorphic
chimnnoortu
unicorn-moth
chimnnorssy
synchronism
chimnoopppy
hypnopompic
chimnooprrs
prochronism
chinooorssu
isochronous
chinoorrstu
trichronous
chiooopprrs
sporophoric
chioooppprtt
phototropic
chiooopprrtt
orthotropic
chiooooprsst
horoscopist
chiooppprrst
proctorship
chiooppprsty
sporophytic
chiooppprtty
protophytic
tropophytic
chiopstttuy
touch-typist
chkmoossttu
tussock-moth
chkoooprsst
shock-troops
chmnoootttu
cottonmouth
chmoooprsty
psychomotor
chnnoorrsty
synchrotron
chnnoorssuy
synchronous
chrrrrsuuyy
hurry-scurry

ciiiikkklln
killikinick
ciiiikkknnn
kinnikinick
ciiiiprsstt
spiritistic
ciiillmopty
impoliticly
ciiillnostt
tonsillitic
ciiilmnosty
consimility
ciiilopssst
solipsistic
ciiimnorttu
micturition
ciiinnoprst
inscription
ciiinoostty
isotonicity
ciiinopsstz
Spinozistic
ciiinorstuy
incuriosity
ciilloorstt
torticollis
ciilnopstuu
punctilious
ciilnorsuuy
incuriously
ciimmnnootu
comminution
ciimmoorstt
microtomist
ciimnooopst
composition
ciimnrsstu
misinstruct
ciimoprrstu
scriptorium
ciimoprstuy
promiscuity
ciimprrsstu
scripturism
ciinnopssuu
unsuspicion
ciinnorsttu
instruction
ciinopsstty
synoptistic
ciiooprssuv
piscivorous
ciiprrssttu
scripturist
cillmooqsuu
colloquiums
cillmoortuu
multicolour
cilmnnooosu
monoclinous
cilmnooortu
monticolour
cilmnoossuu
somniculous

cilmnoostuu
  monticulous
cilmooprstu
  compulsitor
cilmooprsty
  polycrotism
cilnnoootuv
  convolution
cilnnoosuuy
  innocuously
cilnooprtu
  prolocution
cilnooorsuu
  unicolorous
cilnoprrtuy
  incorruptly
cilooprstt
  protocolist
ciloprrtux
  prolocutrix
cimnnnoosyy
  synonymicon
cimnnoopstu
  consumption
cimooprssuu
  promiscuous
cimoprsstuu
  scrumptious
cinnooorttt
  nitrocotton
cllnoosuuvv
  Convolvulus
ddddeeeefil
  fiddle-de-dee
dddeegilorv
  devil-dodger
dddeegimoss
  demigoddess
dddeeiilmsz
  middle-sized
dddeeoprwxy
  proxy-wedded
dddefhlnoru
  hundredfold
dddeiilnuvy
  undividedly
dddeillmorw
  middle-world
dddeimnopru
  proud-minded
dddeklrsuuy
  skulduddery
dddennoortw
  downtrodden
ddeeeeeghlw
  wedge-heeled
ddeeeeilmrr
  riddle-me-ree
ddeeefillnw
  well-defined
ddeeeflnoru
  enfouldered
ddeeeflostv
  self-devoted
ddeeeginpru
  unpedigreed
ddeeehillsv
  dishevelled
ddeeehmoptu
  deep-mouthed
ddeeeiinprs
  deserpidine
ddeeeillrsw
  well-desired
ddeeeillrvw
  well-derived
ddeeeilmnrt
  intermeddle
ddeeeilnruv
  undelivered
ddeeeimprst
  distempered
ddeeeinnnpt
  independent
ddeeellorrw
  well-ordered
ddeeellrssw
  well-dressed
ddeeelnopuv
  undeveloped
ddeeelnprty
  pretendedly
ddeeemnorrt
  dendrometer
ddeeenosstv
  devotedness
ddeeenprssu
  undepressed
ddeeenrrssu
  unredressed
ddeeeorttuv
  true-devoted
ddeeffglllu
  full-fledged
ddeefiiimnn
  indemnified
ddeefiiirsv
  diversified
ddeefllnouw
  well-founded
ddeeghillty
  delightedly
ddeeghilntu
  undelighted
ddeegilnnpy
  dependingly
ddeegilnoww
  window-ledge
ddeeginnnpu
  undepending
ddeeginnrsu
  undersigned
ddeeginnrty
  tender-dying
ddeeglnorru
  ground-elder
ddeegnnoruu
  unguerdoned
ddeegnoprsu
  groundspeed
ddeehilrsss
  dress-shield
ddeehinrsss
  reddishness
ddeehmorssu
  shuddersome
ddeeiiklnnx
  index-linked
ddeeiilnpss
  spindle-side
ddeeiimnnos
  dimensioned
ddeeiiqstuu
  disquietude
ddeeiknnrss
  kindredness
ddeeilmnntw
  dwindlement
ddeeilmnpuy
  unimpededly
ddeeilmopsy
  disemployed
ddeeilnopsu
  undespoiled
ddeeilprssy
  dispersedly
ddeeinnoorr
  Eriodendron
ddeeinnpssu
  undispensed
ddeeinnrruv
  under-driven
ddeeinssstu
  studiedness
ddeellnortw
  well-trodden
ddeellnoruw
  well-rounded
ddeennorssu
  roundedness
ddeennpssuu
  unsuspended
ddeenorstuy
  undestroyed
ddeeoorrsvw
  overdrowsed
ddeffiilnty
  diffidently
ddefgiiinnu
  undignified
ddefhilooos
  solid-hoofed
ddeflnnouuy
  unfoundedly
ddeggiinnrw
  wedding-ring
ddeghiilmnt
  light-minded
ddeghiimnrt
  right-minded
ddeghillstu
  dull-sighted
ddeghimnotu
  tough-minded
ddeghiopsss
  goddess-ship
ddeghlnopry
  dendroglyph
ddegiilmsuy
  misguidedly
ddegiilssuy
  disguisedly
ddegiimnptu
  pudding-time
ddegiinpppu
  pudding-pipe
ddegiinrssv
  diving-dress
ddegiinssuu
  undisguised
ddegilmnost
  dislodgment
ddegilnrstu
  disgruntled
ddegilsstuy
  disgustedly
ddegimnnorw
  wrong-minded
ddeginnoruw
  round-winged
ddegmnoooss
  moon-goddess
ddegnnorruu
  underground
ddehhiioprt
  diphtheroid
ddehiiknprs
  kindredship
ddehiinrssw
  widdershins
ddehinorssu
  disenshroud
ddehinorstw
  short-winded
ddehiooorww
  widowerhood
ddehlmootuu
  loud-mouthed
ddeiiikknwy
  kiddywinkie
ddeiiillnstu
  undistilled
ddeiiillopss
  ill-disposed
ddeilnopssu
  splendidous
ddeilnossuv
  undissolved
ddeimnooruz
  zoodendrium
ddeinnooprv
  non-provided
ddeinorsttu
  undistorted
ddfgilnooor
  folding-door
ddggggiilno
  gold-digging
ddgiiinnorv
  divining-rod
ddgiiklmnpu
  milk-pudding
ddgilmnppuu
  plum-pudding
ddginnoorsu
  sounding-rod
ddhimoooruw
  rhodium-wood
ddiiimrttuy
  rumti-iddity
ddinoooprtt
  diprotodont
deeeeflnruz
  needle-furze
deeeegghlrt
  three-legged
deeeegklopr
  lodge-keeper
deeeehimprs
  ephemerides
deeeehlmosw
  wheedlesome
deeeehnprrr
  reprehender
deeeeilrrrv
  redeliverer
deeeeilsssy
  sessile-eyed
deeeeimnrrt
  redetermine
deeeeknprru
  under-keeper
deeeellnrtw
  well-entered
deeeelnrsuv
  undersleeve
deeeemoprst
  speedometer
deeeennrssw
  renewedness
deeeennstuw
  unsweetened
deeeenopstw
  steepe-downe
deeeenrrrsu
  surrenderee
deeeeprrssu
  supersedere
deeeeqrsstu
  sequestered
deeeffgilns
  self-feeding
deeeffnoost
  toffee-nosed
deeefginnss
  feignedness
deeefgnortu
  free-tongued
deeefhlnssu
  heedfulness

deeefhloruw
four-wheeled
deeefhnrrsu
unrefreshed
deeefiilmpx
exemplified
deeefilnstv
self-evident
deeefilnsvy
defensively
deeefinnrss
refinedness
deeefllorrw
elder-flower
deeefllosvv
self-evolved
deeeflmpstt
self-tempted
deeeflnnssu
needfulness
deeeflorrtx
retroflexed
deeefmnnrtu
unfermented
deeefmoorrv
overfreedom
deeefnprrru
unpreferred
deeeghhillt
light-heeled
deeeghiprst
hedge-priest
deeeghirrtw
hedge-writer
deeegimnrtv
divergement
deeeginnnrv
nerve-ending
never-ending
deeeginosxy
deoxygenise
deeeglorrss
gelders-rose
deeeglorrsu
guelder-rose
deeegmnnstu
unsegmented
deeehhprsss
shepherdess
deeehiiltwy
white-eyelid
deeehilnprs
replenished
deeehilprsw
spider-wheel
deeehimrrsu
Rüdesheimer
deeehirsttu
three-suited
deeehknoort
three-nooked
deeehlnnort
Heldentenor
deeehlnrstu
unsheltered
deeehmoprtt
hot-tempered
deeeiilrssv
desilverise
deeeiimprtx
time-expired
deeeiinnptx
inexpedient
deeeiinssst
desensitise
deeeillmprt
ill-tempered
deeeillnrss
elderliness
deeeilmmnuv
mendelevium
deeeilnnopt
needle-point
deeeilnprst
spindle-tree
deeeilnptxy
expediently
deeeilorstu
deleterious
deeeimmprst
mistempered
deeeimnprtv
deprivement
deeeinprruv
unreprieved
deeeinprtux
expenditure
deeeinrrsst
retiredness
deeeinrrssv
vine-dresser
deeeinrruvw
underviewer
deeeknoppru
pound-keeper
deeellnrrsu
underseller
deeellpprxy
perplexedly
deeellrtttu
telluretted
deeelmnnory
money-lender
deeelmnoptv
development
deeelmnotvv
devolvement
deeelnnprst
resplendent
deeelnnrsss
slenderness
deeelnnssss
endlessness
deeelnpprux
unperplexed
deeelnrrttu
underletter
deeelnssstt
settledness
deeeloooprst
rood-steeple
deeelooprvv
overdevelop
deeelrrssuv
verdureless
deeemnnorst
endorsement
deeemnnortw
re-endowment
deeemnorssv
removedness
deeemoprrwy
emery-powder
deeennprtuv
unprevented
deeennrrstu
nurse-tender
deeenoprsss
reposedness
deeenopsssx
exposedness
deeenopsttu
pedetentous
deeenprrtuv
unperverted
deeenprssux
unexpressed
deeenrrrrsu
surrenderer
deeenrrsttt
trend-setter
deeeoprstty
stereotyped
deeeprrssst
pre-stressed
deeeprrssuu
supersedure
deeffgilrsu
self-figured
deeffiinnrt
indifferent
deeffilnrty
differently
deeffinortu
unforfeited
deeffinsssu
diffuseness
deefforstuv
overstuffed
deefgghhiin
high-feeding
deefghhirst
freight-shed
deefghillst
self-delight
deefghiorst
foresighted
deefgiinnrx
index-finger
deefgiinsst
fidgetiness
deefgiknorw
weeding-fork
deefgilnnsy
self-denying
deefgilnnuy
unfeignedly
deefgioortt
tiger-footed
deefhhlooow
whole-hoofed
deefhiikswy
whiskeyfied
deefhilttw
Twelfth-tide
deefhioottw
white-footed
deefhllnuuy
unheedfully
deefhllosst
soft-shelled
deefhlootw
whole-footed
deefiiinnst
intensified
deefiillmst
self-limited
deefiilmrsu
demulsifier
deefiilnquu
unliquefied
deefiilnstv
self-invited
deefiinoprs
personified
deefiinrrtu
unterrified
deefiklorrw
fieldworker
deefillrssu
fleurs-de-lis
deefilmopss
self-imposed
deefilmsssu
self-misused
deefilnrssu
direfulness
deefilorsty
oyster-field
deefinnssux
unfixedness
deefllnnuuy
unneedfully
deefllnossu
dolefulness
deefllrssuy
fleurs-de-lys
deeflnoorst
fender-stool
deeflnrstuu
unflustered
deefloprssy
professedly
deefmnoprru
unperformed
deefmorrrss
dress-reform
deefnoprssu
unprofessed
deefnoprtuy
type-founder
deefoorrttw
wood-fretter
deeggghillt
light-legged
deeggghloru
rough-legged
deeggiknorw
working-edge
deegginnoos
goods-engine
deegginnoov
good-evening
deegginoosw
goose-winged
deeghhilmtt
high-mettled
deeghhilsxy
highly-sexed
deeghhioprw
high-powered
deeghhopssy
hedge-hyssop
deeghiintww
white-winged
deeghiknoow
weeding-hook
deeghillosv
glove-shield
deeghillsst
delightless
deeghilmost
delightsome
deeghilnnsu
un-Englished
deeghilnntu
unlightened
deeghilnnuy
unheedingly
deeghinrtuw
underweight
deeghlnrsst
dress-length
deeghnorstu
groundsheet
deegiiinstv
indigestive
deegiikllns
sliding-keel
deegiilstvy
digestively
deegiilttuv
deglutitive
deegiimnnor
domineering
deegijmnpru
jumping-deer
deegillnoss
single-soled

deegillnpss
spindle-legs
deegilmnooy
endemiology
deegilnoruv
overindulge
deegilnrsvy
deservingly
deegilnrtvy
divergently
deegimorsuu
demiurgeous
deeginnrsuv
undeserving
deeginnrtuu
ungenitured
deeginorstu
dentigerous
deegjmnprtu
prejudgment
deegllmoorw
well-groomed
deeglnossss
godlessness
deehhiimmrs
hemihedrism
deehhloorsu
householder
deehhoprrsy
hydrosphere
deehiilmstt
ditheletism
deehiilsttw
white-listed
deehiimprsu
hesperidium
deehiinnpsz
denizenship
deehiioprss
spheroidise
deehiklnrtu
thunder-like
deehillortt
title-holder
deehilnnotw
down-the-line
deehilnowww
wheel-window
deehimprtuw
white-rumped
deehinnorst
disenthrone
deehinosssu
hideousness
deehinrrssu
hurriedness
deehkloptuy
loup-the-dyke
deehlloosuw
whole-souled
deehlnrsstu
thunderless
deehmnooptu
open-mouthed

deehmoorrty
hydrometeor
deehmoorsvw
howsomdever
deehnnorstu
underhonest
deeiiiqstuv
disquietive
deeiikllmrv
milk-livered
deeiikllmss
semi-skilled
deeiikllors
soldierlike
deeiiklnprs
kinderspiel
deeiilllrvy
lily-livered
deeiilmnsst
limitedness
deeiilmnssu
disseminule
deeiilnoprs
Lepidosiren
deeiimmnrst
determinism
deeiimmnrtu
intermedium
deeiimmprsu
peridesmium
deeiimnnntt
intendiment
deeiimnpsst
dissepiment
deeiimnrrst
irredentism
deeiimnrstt
determinist
deeiimorrst
deteriorism
deeiinnnott
intentioned
deeiinnsstt
dissentient
deeiinopstv
point-devise
deeiinprsty
serendipity
deeiinrrstt
irredentist
deeiinrsstt
disinterest
deeiinrttxy
indexterity
deeiiopstux
expeditious
deeiioqssux
sesquioxide
deeiiorrrtt
territoried
deeiiorrtty
deteriority
deeiirrrrvv
river-driver

deeiirsttuv
divestiture
deeijmnopsw
jimpson-weed
deeiknnosty
kidney-stone
deeillnopru
perduellion
deeilmmosst
seldom-times
deeilmnopst
despoilment
deeilmnrtuy
unmeritedly
deeilnnorvy
non-delivery
deeilnorrss
orderliness
deeilnssstt
stiltedness
deeiloppptу
polypeptide
deeilopsstu
Lepidosteus
deeimmnortu
endometrium
deeimnnootu
unemotioned
deeimnnostu
unmoistened
deeimnoprsy
money-spider
deeimnprssu
unimpressed
deeinnnopsu
unpensioned
deeinnnorst
non-resident
deeinnopsst
pointedness
deeinnosttu
tendentious
deeinnprstu
superintend
deeinnssstt
stintedness
deeinnsstuw
unwitnessed
deeinoprrvw
power-driven
deeinorrrvw
owner-driver
deeinossstu
tediousness
deeinosssuv
deviousness
deeinprrttu
interrupted
deeinrrrtuw
underwriter
deeiooprrsu
urediospore
deeioorstuv
overtedious

deeioprrtuy
eurypteroid
deeklnoorru
underlooker
deeknnnrssu
drunkenness
deeknorrruw
underworker
deellnortww
town-dweller
deellnsttuy
unsettledly
deelmnortty
tormentedly
deelorstuxy
dexterously
deemnnorttu
untormented
deemnoortuy
Deuteronomy
deennsssttu
stuntedness
deenoprsttu
unprotested
deenopssssu
unpossessed
deenopssstt
spottedness
deenorrrrsu
surrenderor
deenossstuu
duteousness
deeoopprrst
doorstepper
deeoorsttwy
two-storeyed
deffginnnou
unoffending
deffiilsuvy
diffusively
deffiinortu
unfortified
deffilllnuu
unfulfilled
deffimprstu
stiff-rumped
deffinpprsu
snuff-dipper
deffioosttw
swift-footed
defghiisttt
tight-fisted
defghilootT
light-footed
defghinorsu
unsighed-for
defghooortu
rough-footed
defgiiinnty
identifying
defgiilnnsw
self-winding
defgiinstww
swift-winged

defgillnsuy
sdeignfully
defgilnrssy
fly-dressing
defhimnortu
mouth-friend
defhinnrsuu
unfurnished
defhinorsuw
unwished-for
defhinprstt
spendthrift
defhiooprst
fish-torpedo
defhllmotuu
full-mouthed
defhlmootuu
foul-mouthed
defiiinrtuv
unvitrified
defiijnstuu
unjustified
defiillmnor
ill-informed
defiilqstuu
disquietful
defiimnortu
unmortified
defilmnnssu
mindfulness
defilnsstuu
dutifulness
defilooorst
foot-soldier
defilooruxy
oxy-fluoride
defilrssstu
distressful
defimnorstu
misfortuned
definnoorru
iron-founder
defiooorrsu
odoriferous
defioorrssu
dorsiferous
defklnoooru
unlooked-for
defllnoruwy
wonderfully
deflnoosstw
twofoldness
deflooostt
footstooled
defnooprruu
four-pounder
defnoprtuyy
type-foundry
degghhhiist
high-sighted
degghiilntw
light-winged
degghilnost
long-sighted

degghinosss
doggishness
deggiilnorv
riding-glove
deggiilnrvy
divergingly
deggiinnnsu
undesigning
deggijllnuw
well-judging
deggklrsuuy
skulduggery
degglnnootu
long-tongued
deghhloorsu
hog-shoulder
deghiilnnrs
hinderlings
deghiilpptt
tight-lipped
deghiimnrry
riding-rhyme
deghiinnttu
hunting-tide
deghiinorrs
horse-riding
riding-horse
deghilmnoop
phlegmonoid
deghilnorsu
shouldering
deghilosstw
slow-sighted
deghinnoprr
herring-pond
deghinopstt
potting-shed
deghinoptuw
pound-weight
deghinosstu
doughtiness
deghlmoooty
methodology
deghnnooprr
prong-horned
deghnooostt
honest-to-God
deghnoorsuy
hydrogenous
deghnoorxyy
oxy-hydrogen
deghnorrtuw
undergrowth
degiiinnost
indigestion
degiiinqstu
disquieting
degiiknrstw
writing-desk
degiiillnptw
pit-dwelling
degiiillnrsu
sliding-rule

degiilnottu
deglutition
degiilnrtvy
divertingly
degiimnnnru
undermining
degiimnnort
morning-tide
degiinnrtuv
undiverting
degiinoprvw
power-diving
degiinrssst
distressing
degijmmnstu
misjudgment
degillnntuy
indulgently
degillnopry
deploringly
degilmnorsu
smouldering
degilnnopry
ponderingly
degilnnorwy
wonderingly
degilnnossu
ungodliness
degilnoruvy
devouringly
degiloprty
pteridology
degilorttuy
deglutitory
deginnnssuy
undyingness
deginnosttw
down-setting
deginoprsst
top-dressing
degloorstty
troglodytes
degnnoorstu
stoneground
degnoootuwy
woody-tongue
dehhiiilmnot
helminthoid
dehhilmoors
holohedrism
dehhlnostuu
sleuth-hound
dehhoooppprt
prophethood
dehiiiilmstt
dithelitism
dehiiknnnst
thin-skinned
dehiiloprss
soldiership
dehiimnortu
Dinotherium
dehiinsttuw
Whitsuntide

dehiioopsvv
voivodeship
dehiioprstt
hot-spirited
dehiknssssu
duskishness
dehillmoruu
ill-humoured
dehillnosss
dollishness
dehilnossst
doltishness
dehilnossty
dishonestly
dehilnosttw
thistle-down
dehilnrruuy
unhurriedly
dehilprstuu
disulphuret
dehimmopstu
imposthumed
dehimnpsssu
dumpishness
dehinnorsss
dronishness
dehinnorsuu
unnourished
dehinoorrsu
dishonourer
dehinorsssw
wordishness
dehinorsstu
drouthiness
dehinprsssu
prudishness
dehinpssttu
studentship
dehinrrsttu
underthirst
dehiooopprt
photoperiod
dehiooprstt
orthopedist
dehmoopprsu
pseudomorph
dehnorrsstu
undershorts
dehnrrsttuu
underthrust
dehoooprttw
tooth-powder
deiiiillssuv
disillusive
deiiinnpsss
insipidness
deiiinprtty
intrepidity
deiiiopsstv
dispositive
deiiillmnnuu
unillumined
deiiillmntuy
unlimitedly

deiillorsuy
deliriously
deiillqrruv
quill-driver
deiilnoorww
oriel-window
deiilnosstu
delusionist
deiiloprstw
low-spirited
deiilosstuv
dissolutive
deiilosstuy
seditiously
deiimnoostv
misdevotion
deiimnoprtv
improvident
deiimnorttt
intromitted
deiinoosttv
devotionist
deiinossstu
dissentious
deiinostttu
destitution
deiioqsstuu
disquietous
deiklnnprsu
unsprinkled
deillmoosuy
melodiously
deillmrstuy
dusty-miller
deillnorssw
worldliness
deillnorstu
tendrillous
deillnorsuy
unsoldierly
deillorstuy
desultorily
deillorswwy
worldly-wise
deillosstuy
dissolutely
deilmnoosuu
unmelodious
deilmnprtuy
imprudently
deilnoprtvy
providently
deilnopstuy
pendulosity
deiloooorsw
rosewood-oil
deilprrssuy
surprisedly
deimmnnoptu
impoundment
deimmrsstyy
dissymmetry
deimnnopswy
penny-wisdom

deimnooprsu
imponderous
deimnoorrtv
motor-driven
deimnoprsst
spinsterdom
deimnoprstt
disportment
deimnossssy
syndesmosis
deimopprttu
promptitude
deinnooprtu
unportioned
deinnoprtuv
unprovident
deinooprstu
torpedinous
deinooprsty
ponderosity
deinopsstuu
stupendious
deinprrssuu
unsurprised
deiopprrsty
disproperty
dekoorrstww
worsted-work
dellnopsuuy
pendulously
dellnosssuy
soundlessly
delmorrsuuy
murderously
delnooprssu
splendorous
delnooprsuy
ponderously
delooprstuu
trous-de-loup
delopprrtuy
purportedly
demooprttuw
trumpet-wood
demoorssstt
storm-tossed
dennnosssuu
unsoundness
dennoosstty
snotty-nosed
denooorsssu
odorousness
denoopprrsw
snow-dropper
denoopprstu
petropounds
denopprstuu
unsupported
deopprttuwy
putty-powder
dffiiistuvy
diffusivity
dfgginooprr
drop-forging

dfgiiilnosy
solidifying
dfgiiimnnrt
drift-mining
dfgiiknnnsu
sinking-fund
dfgiillnoww
wild-fowling
dfgiinnrsuw
windsurfing
dfhhiilnops
dolphin-fish
dfhmooortuw
word-of-mouth
dfiilllmnoo
millionfold
dfiilmostuu
multifidous
dfillmnnuuy
unmindfully
dfillntuuuy
undutifully
dfilrssttuu
distrustful
dfinnoorruy
iron-foundry
dgghiiilnrt
riding-light
dggiiinnnrw
ring-winding
dggiilmnnsu
mud-slinging
dggiklnoooo
good-looking
dggimnnooor
good-morning
dghiiiimnns
diminishing
dghiiinsstu
distinguish
dghilllopru
drill-plough
dghilmorsty
goldsmithry
dghiloorsty
hydrologist
dghiloprtyy
tyroglyphid
dghlnoorstu
ground-sloth
dgiiiinprst
dispiriting
dgiiiknrrst
riding-skirt
dgiilnnopru
lip-rounding
dgiilnopssy
disposingly
dgiimnooouz
zoogonidium
dgiinnosttw
down-sitting
dgilnnooosy
sindonology

dgilnoorsty
strongyloid
dginnorrsuu
surrounding
dhhiooprtyy
hypothyroid
dhhnooosttu
hound's-tooth
dhhnooprtyy
hydrophyton
dhiiimpssty
diphysitism
dhiiiorstty
thyroiditis
dhillnooppy
podophyllin
dhilmooostu
lithodomous
dhimooosttw
wisdom-tooth
dhinoosttuw
unwithstood
dhiooorttuw
without-door
dhllmooppuy
Podophyllum
dhnooortuxy
unorthodoxy
diiiillqtuy
illiquidity
diiiimnossv
divisionism
diiiknopsst
od's-pitikins
diiillnossu
disillusion
diiilnossuy
insidiously
diiilnosuvy
invidiously
diiimmnortu
tridominium
diiimnoprss
disimprison
diiinnosstu
disunionist
diiinnosuuv
uninvidious
diiinoopsst
disposition
diilnoosstu
dissolution
diilnopssty
spondylitis
diiloprrstw
spirit-world
diinorsstuu
industrious
dilmoopstuy
stylopodium
dilnooorsuy
inodorously
dimnoorstww
storm-window

eeeeegknprr
green-keeper
eeeefhnrrrs
refreshener
eeeefilprss
life-peeress
eeeefilqrtu
téléférique
eeeegiilprs
espièglerie
eeeeginprtw
weeping-tree
eeeeglnnsst
genteelness
eeeeglnrssv
revengeless
eeeegmnnrtv
revengement
eeeegnnqrtu
queen-regent
eeeehkloprt
hotel-keeper
eeeehkoprsu
housekeeper
eeeehnnsttv
seventeenth
eeeehorrsvw
wheresoever
eeeeiinrtvw
interviewee
eeeeimnprsw
mine-sweeper
eeeekoprrst
storekeeper
eeeelnprsst
repleteness
eeeelrrsssv
reverseless
eeeemnprstt
estrepement
eeeemorrstt
stereometer
eeeenprrrst
representer
eeefffmnnot
enfeoffment
eeeffgillns
self-feeling
eeeffhilrtw
whiffletree
eeeffillrst
self-fertile
eeefgiklnss
self-seeking
eeefhiknrrt
free-thinker
eeefhlorruw
four-wheeler
eeefhmnrrst
refreshment
eeefhoorrtt
theretofore
eeefillrsst
self-sterile

eeefillrvxy
reflexively
eeefinnorrr
ferronnière
eeefinrrttv
vine-fretter
eeeflmprssu
perfumeless
eeefmoorrrv
forevermore
eeegghhmnsu
meshuggeneh
eeegghorttt
get-together
eeeggiinnnr
engineering
eeeggjlnnru
jungle-green
eeeggmnnort
engorgement
eeeghiklprt
lightkeeper
eeeghikmnop
home-keeping
eeegiilmnns
gelseminine
eeegiinpprw
weeping-ripe
eeegiinprss
perigenesis
eeegiinpsst
epigenesist
eeegillnoru
genouillère
eeegilnrstw
swingletree
eeegimnnsss
seemingness
eeegimnorss
merogenesis
eeegimnrstu
true-seeming
eeeginnnssu
genuineness
eeeginnorvw
overweening
eeeginnossx
xenogenesis
eeeginnrrtw
wintergreen
eeeginprrsv
persevering
eeegllnntuy
ungenteelly
eeegllnssss
leglessness
eeeglmnnotw
gentlewomen
eeeglnoorvy
venereology
eeegmnorrsv
verse-monger
eeegnorrstu
tree-surgeon

eeegrrrstuy
tree-surgery
eeehhillllnp
philhellene
eeehhilpptw
Hepplewhite
eeehhilrstw
elsewhither
eeehhlllmst
helmet-shell
eeehhmosttt
thesmothete
eeehhnprsty
hypersthene
eeehiilnnpt
nephelinite
eeehiinnppr
epinephrine
eeehillnprt
telpher-line
eeehilnprrs
replenisher
eeehilpprtw
whippletree
eeehilprssv
sheep-silver
eeehilrsstv
shirt-sleeve
eeehimmnprt
penthemimer
eeehimnnops
phenomenise
eeehimnrsst
smithereens
eeehimprssy
hyperemesis
eeehinpsssv
peevishness
eeehklmmost
smoke-helmet
eeehklmnowy
monkey-wheel
eeehllnoptw
Pelton-wheel
eeehllrssst
shelterless
eeehlmnoott
monothelete
eeehlmrrtty
rhyme-letter
eeehlnnosst
nonetheless
eeehmmorrtt
thermometer
eeehmnoqrtu
queen-mother
eeehmoprrst
spherometer
eeehnrssstt
sternsheets
eeehoorssvw
whosesoever
eeeiiklnsst
telekinesis

eeeiillmpss
semi-ellipse
eeeiinnpsvx
inexpensive
eeeiinnrrst
Niersteiner
eeeiinrrttv
irretentive
eeeiinrrtvw
interviewer
eeeiiorrstx
exteriorise
eeeiiprrstt
peristerite
eeeiiprrttv
preteritive
eeeiklnnquu
unqueenlike
eeeiklnosst
skeletonise
eeeiklnprst
serpentlike
eeeilmnnntv
enlivenment
eeeilmnnttt
entitlement
eeeilmoortt
meteorolite
eeeilmprsst
plessimeter
eeeilnnpsss
pensileness
eeeilnnqssu
queenliness
eeeilnprrtt
teleprinter
eeeilnpsvxy
expensively
eeeilnrttvy
retentively
eeeilnsstvv
velvetiness
eeeilnstvxy
extensively
eeeilqrsstu
requiteless
eeeimmnnsss
immenseness
eeeimmorsst
seismometer
eeeimnnnort
mentonnière
eeeimnnrrtt
reinterment
eeeimnqqruu
quinquereme
eeeimnqrrtu
requirement
eeeimnqrttu
requitement
eeeimoprstx
extemporise
eeeimorrttv
terremotive
eeeinnnssst
intenseness
eeeinnprstt
presentient
spinnerette
eeeinnprtux
unexperient
eeeinnpsssv
pensiveness
eeeinnpsuvx
unexpensive
eeeinnrttuv
unretentive
eeeinorrrsv
reversioner
eeeinppprss
pepperiness
eeeinpqrstu
Pinteresque
eeeinprrrst
enterpriser
eeeinprrrtt
interpreter
reinterpret
eeeinprrsst
intersperse
eeeinprrssu
purse-seiner
eeeinprsttx
pre-existent
eeeinrssstv
restiveness
eeeinrsttww
winter-sweet
eeeklnoostx
exoskeleton
eeeklnrstuv
trunksleeve
eeeklorrstw
steelworker
eeelllnprty
repellently
eeelllpsssy
sleeplessly
eeellnssssy
senselessly
eeelloprssu
soul-sleeper
eeelmnnoptv
envelopment
eeelmorrsss
remorseless
eeelnnopsst
spleen-stone
eeelnnptvwy
twelve-penny
eeelnssssu
uselessness
eeelnssssx
sexlessness
eeelorrstvw
overwrestle
eeelprrsstt
letterpress
eeelrssttux
textureless
eeemmnoprtv
premovement
eeemnnprstt
presentment
eeemnorstuv
venturesome
eeemnprsssu
supremeness
eeemoqrrttu
torque-meter
eeemorrstty
stereometry
eeemprrtttu
trumpet-tree
eeennprssst
presentness
eeenooprsss
operoseness
eeenprssssx
expressness
eeenqrrstuu
Turneresque
eeeoprrstty
stereotyper
eeffghiirrt
fire-fighter
eeffgiinrsv
fivefingers
eeffgilnrsu
glue-sniffer
eeffgllntuy
effulgently
eeffiinnosv
inoffensive
eeffillpptu
fipple-flute
eeffilnosvy
offensively
eeffinnosuv
unoffensive
eeffiorrrsu
ferriferous
eefflnrsstu
fretfulness
eefggioprtt
pettifogger
eefghhorttu
free-thought
eefghiilrrt
firelighter
eefghinrrst
frighteners
eefghiorrtv
overfreight
eefghlmnors
flesh-monger
eefgiilnopr
pigeon-flier
eefgillnnuy
unfeelingly
eefgilnnoux
genuflexion
eefgilnopry
pigeon-flyer
eefgilnrssv
self-serving
eefgilorrtw
tiger-flower
eefgimmorsu
gemmiferous
eefginnorss
foreignness
eefginorssv
forgiveness
eefglloorxy
reflexology
eefgllrrtuy
regretfully
eefglooorsw
goose-flower
eefgmnoortt
forget-me-not
eefhiiknrst
Kentish-fire
eefhiknorrt
forethinker
eefhillnsss
fleshliness
eefhilnssss
selfishness
eefhilooprt
photo-relief
eefhilorstu
lethiferous
eefhilorsww
werewolfish
eefhilosuwy
housewifely
eefhiorsuwy
housewifery
eefhllnpssu
helpfulness
eefhlnopssu
hopefulness
eefhmorrrtu
furthermore
eefhmorrstu
furthersome
eefhnoorrst
foreshorten
eefhorrsttt
setter-forth
eefiiinnrst
intensifier
eefiilnorrx
irreflexion
eefiilnrrtx
life-rentrix
eefiinoprrs
personifier
eefiknorsty
oyster-knife
eefilllmntu
mellifluent
eefilllmrsu
millefleurs
eefillmorsu
melliferous
eefilmorrtu
fluorimeter
eefilmorsww
werewolfism
eefilnnrttu
interfluent
eefilnorssw
floweriness
eefilooprrt
profiterole
eefiloorsst
loose-strife
eefinrsstuv
furtiveness
eefioprsstu
pestiferous
septiferous
eefllnorttu
fortune-tell
eefllnrstuy
resentfully
eeflloprsuy
reposefully
eeflmnorstt
self-torment
eeflmnosssu
fulsomeness
eeflmnrsttu
flusterment
eeflmoorrtu
fluorometer
eeflnnrstuu
unresentful
eeflnnsstuu
tunefulness
eeflnoprsuu
unreposeful
eeflnorsstu
fortuneless
eeflnorssuv
overfulness
eeflnpsssuu
suspenseful
eeflnrssstu
restfulness
eeflnssstuz
zestfulness
eeflorrsttu
self-torture
eefnoprsssu
profuseness
eefnorrsstu
foster-nurse
eefoprrrrsu
forespurrer
eegggiinrrt
rigging-tree
eeggginnptt
tent-pegging
eegghhloorw
whole-hogger

eegghiinsst
sightseeing
eeggillnnty
negligently
eeggilnnrvy
revengingly
eeggilorsuy
egregiously
eeggimnoott
go-to-meeting
eeggnooprst
progestogen
eeghhilrtww
wheelwright
eeghhipprst
high-stepper
eeghhllnotw
whole-length
eeghhllopuw
wheel-plough
eeghhopprtu
peep-through
eeghiilpprt
pipe-lighter
eeghiinrstw
wishing-tree
eeghiinsstw
weightiness
eeghiknopps
shopkeeping
eeghilnnrst
netherlings
eeghilnnsst
lengthiness
eeghilnossy
hylogenesis
eeghiloorst
theologiser
eeghiloorsy
heresiology
eeghilrsttt
streetlight
eeghimnnntu
unhingement
eeghimnoors
homogeniser
eeghimnooss
homogenesis
eeghimnooty
homogeneity
eeghimoorst
isogeotherm
eeghinnptwy
pennyweight
eeghinoopsu
pigeon-house
eeghinrstty
yesternight
eeghlmmortu
grummet-hole
eeghlooprty
herpetology
eeghmnooosu
homogeneous

eeghmnoorrw
whoremonger
eeghnorstyy
hysterogeny
eeghnosssuu
hugeousness
eegiiilnors
religionise
eegiiimnpst
impetigines
eegiiklllos
skilligolee
eegiiklprss
kriegsspiel
eegiillnntt
intelligent
eegiilmnnrt
intermingle
eegiilnnost
lentiginose
eegiimmnnpt
impingement
eegiimnnnrs
minnesinger
eegiimnrstv
time-serving
eegiinnorst
nitrogenise
eegiinnrstt
interesting
eegiinnrttw
wire-netting
eegiinnrtuu
unigeniture
eegiinprrty
peregrinity
eegikmnoopr
keeping-room
eegilllnpry
repellingly
eegilllssuy
guilelessly
eegillmoost
teleologism
eegilloostt
teleologist
eegillorrru
guerrillero
eegilmnnsst
meltingness
eegilmoosty
etymologise
eegilnnnrtu
unrelenting
eegilnnprty
repentingly
eegilnnrsty
resentingly
single-entry
eegilnntuwy
unweetingly
eegilnopssy
polygenesis

eegilnorsvy
sovereignly
eegilnprsty
pesteringly
eegiloprstt
poltergeist
eegimnnooss
monogenesis
eegimnnorsu
Monseigneur
eegimnnottw
town-meeting
eegimnnprtu
untempering
eegimnnrrtu
interregnum
eegimnorstw
swingometer
eeginnnprtu
unrepenting
eeginnnrstu
unresenting
eeginnoosst
ontogenesis
eeginnrrstt
restringent
eeginoorrtu
rouge-et-noir
eeginoprrtu
progeniture
eeginorrstu
terrigenous
eeginorstvy
sovereignty
eeginprsttu
guttersnipe
eeginpsttty
type-setting
eegioprrssv
progressive
eegkllmnsuu
muskellunge
eeglmooorty
meteorology
eegloqrstuy
grotesquely
eegmnnorrst
morgenstern
eegmnnorsst
engrossment
eegnooorstu
erotogenous
eegnooosstu
osteogenous
eegoqrrstuy
grotesquery
eehhiinrttw
therewithin
eehhillnsss
hellishness
eehhilmoprt
thermophile
eehhiloprst
lithosphere

eehhilorstw
otherwhiles
eehhimorstw
somewhither
eehhinssswy
wheyishness
eehhioopsst
theosophise
eehhioprrsz
rhizosphere
eehhiopssty
hypothesise
eehhiopstty
hypothetise
eehhlorsuuy
hurley-house
eehhmoorstu
housemother
eehhnopstuy
hypothenuse
eehhoopprst
photosphere
eehhooprrtt
heterotroph
eehiilmntuw
minute-while
eehiilrstvw
silver-white
eehiimnorty
Hieronymite
eehiimpprrs
premiership
eehiinrrsst
inheritress
eehiiorsttt
historiette
eehikmnnosy
monkey-shine
eehiknstuww
Whitsun-week
eehilmnoott
monothelite
eehilmopprs
spermophile
eehilnoorst
line-shooter
eehilnoprrt
leptorrhine
eehilnopstt
telephonist
eehilnosttv
novelettish
eehilorrstt
horse-litter
eehilssttuw
shuttlewise
eehimmnnops
phenomenism
eehimnnopst
phenomenist
eehimnorrtw
mine-thrower
eehimopprrs
emperorship

eehimoprstu
hemipterous
eehimpsstuy
emphyteusis
eehinnooptt
thiopentone
eehinnorrst
northernise
eehinnosssu
heinousness
eehinopstvy
hypotensive
eehinorrttu
rinthereout
eehinorsssw
showeriness
eehinorsstu
southernise
eehinpssstt
pettishness
eehinrssstu
hirsuteness
eehinrsssty
synthesiser
eehioprrstw
tree-worship
eehiprssttu
trusteeship
eehlllmsssu
mussel-shell
eehlllrsttu
turtle-shell
eehllmooswy
wholesomely
eehllorssty
oyster-shell
eehllrrtttu
truth-teller
eehlmnoosuw
unwholesome
eehlmnottvw
twelvemonth
eehloprrstu
upholsterer
eehlorsttyy
heterostyly
eehmmooorsu
homeomerous
eehmmorrtty
thermometry
eehmmorssuu
summer-house
eehmnnooory
honeymooner
eehmopprsty
spermophyte
eehnoooprsz
ozonosphere
eehnooprsty
stereophony
eehnopsttuy
theopneusty
eehnorrsttw
north-wester

11 EEH

eehoopprrst
troposphere
eehooprrstu
porterhouse
porter-house
eehooprrsty
heterospory
eehoorrrtvw
overthrower
eehorssttuw
south-wester
eeiiimnnstu
einsteinium
eeiiimrrssv
irremissive
eeiiinnsstv
insensitive
eeiiinnsttv
intensitive
eeiiinsttvv
investitive
eeiiillpprst
pipistrelle
eeiiillprstu
spirituelle
eeiiillprstv
spirit-level
eeiiilmmnprt
imperilment
eeiiilmnossu
emulsionise
eeiiilmnrsss
miserliness
eeiiilnnprrt
line-printer
eeiiilnnrsst
listeners-in
eeiiilnnstvy
intensively
eeiiilnntvvy
inventively
eeiiilnrsssv
silveriness
eeiiilnsstvy
sensitively
eeiiilorstuz
Louis-Treize
eeiiilqstuxy
exquisitely
eeiiilrsstvy
resistively
eeiimnnortu
munitioneer
eeiimnnprtt
impertinent
eeiimnoprtv
premonitive
eeiimnprruu
perineurium
eeiinnnostx
inextension
eeiinnntuvv
uninventive

eeiinnorrst
reinsertion
eeiinnorrtt
irretention
eeiinnprrwz
prize-winner
eeiinnsstuv
unsensitive
eeiinoprrtt
preterition
eeiinqrstuu
unrequisite
eeiinrsttuv
investiture
eeiinrtttvy
retentivity
eeiiopprstv
prepositive
eeiioprsttu
repetitious
eeiiorrttxy
exteriority
eeiirstttuv
restitutive
eeikllnoruv
unloverlike
eeiklnnnpwy
pennywinkle
eeiklopprsu
purpose-like
eeikmnorsss
irksomeness
eeillmmstuv
summit-level
eeillmprtux
multiplexer
eeillnopqtu
equipollent
eeillnorrtu
ritournelle
eeillnosssy
noiselessly
eeillnprrst
print-seller
eeillnpsssy
spinelessly
eeillnpstty
pestilently
eeillnrsuuy
unleisurely
eeillopsvxy
explosively
eeillostwww
sweet-willow
eeillprsuvy
prelusively
repulsively
eeilmnnotvv
involvement
eeilmnoosst
emotionless
eeilmnossss
lissomeness

eeilmnrttty
remittently
eeilmooprsu
pleiomerous
eeilmoprsss
promiseless
eeilmoprtuv
pluviometer
eeilmprssty
plessimetry
eeilmrrssuv
river-mussel
eeilnnopptt
plenipotent
eeilnnprtty
pertinently
eeilnnsssss
sinlessness
eeilnoortvv
overviolent
eeilnorsssu
elusoriness
eeilnosstvy
ostensively
eeilnostttv
novelettist
eeilnssstw
witlessness
eeiloppppst
pipe-stopple
eeiloprssty
proselytise
eeilorstvxy
extorsively
eeimmmnprsu
menispermum
eeimmnoprtv
improvement
eeimmnprsst
impressment
eeimmnprstu
sempiternum
eeimmorssty
seismometry
eeimmorstyz
zymosimeter
eeimmprsuvv
sempervivum
eeimnnnortv
environment
eeimnnoosss
noisomeness
eeimnnoprst
omnipresent
eeimnnosssw
winsomeness
eeimnnrtttu
unremittent
eeimnorstty
tensiometry
eeimnrssttw
Westminster
eeimopprssu
superimpose

eeimpprstuv
presumptive
eeinnnosttx
non-existent
eeinnoorttx
enterotoxin
eeinnopprss
nose-nippers
eeinnoprstt
septentrion
eeinnorrttv
interventor
eeinnosssuv
enviousness
eeinnossttu
sententious
eeinnqsstuu
unquietness
eeinoorrttx
extortioner
eeinoprsttu
pretentious
eeinopssstu
piteousness
eeinorrstuv
enterovirus
eeinorssssu
seriousness
eeinprrrttu
interrupter
eeinprtttwy
typewritten
eeioprrrstw
prose-writer
eeioprrsssu
superioress
eeioprssstx
expositress
eeipprsssuv
suppressive
eejlnossssy
joylessness
eekkoorrrtv
voortrekker
eekllmosssy
smokelessly
eeklorrsttw
trestle-work
eekmnooprtv
provokement
eelllmnoowy
lemon-yellow
eellloorrtw
roller-towel
eellmpprstu
pullet-sperm
eellnopstuy
plenteously
eellnprtuuv
pulverulent
eelloprsswy
powerlessly
eellorrstty
story-teller

eelmmooopps
pompelmoose
eelmmooppsu
pompelmouse
eelmmoortuv
volumometer
eelmnosssuu
emulousness
eelmoprrstt
storm-petrel
eelnnsssssu
sunlessness
eelnooppstw
townspeople
eelnooprstv
stone-plover
eelnoorrsuy
erroneously
eelnoprstyy
polystyrene
eelnopsssst
toplessness
eelnorstttu
turtle-stone
eeloprrsssu
purposeless
eeloprrssuw
low-pressure
eeloprstuuv
supervolute
eemnnrstttu
entrustment
eemnoorstty
enterostomy
eemnoprtttu
trumpet-tone
eemnorssttw
westernmost
eemopsstttt
tempest-tost
eemopssttuu
tempestuous
eennoorsssu
onerousness
eennoorsttt
rottenstone
eennoqrsuuy
Runyonesque
eennorsssuv
nervousness
eennossstuu
tenuousness
eepprrrstuu
purpresture
effghnoortu
forfoughten
effgiinnors
sin-offering
effgiinorsy
foresignify
effgiorrsuu
frugiferous
effgllortuy
forgetfully

effhhiiprss
sheriffship
effhhinsssu
huffishness
effhinossst
toffishness
effhlorrsuu
four-flusher
effiloorrsu
floriferous
effioorrstt
first-footer
efgghiinnrt
frightening
efggloorst
footslogger
efghhoorttu
forethought
efghiiilnns
line-fishing
efghiilnsst
flightiness
efghilnortw
night-flower
efghinorssu
surgeon-fish
efghlnrsttu
strengthful
efgiiillnnr
fringilline
efgiiinrvvy
revivifying
efgiillmoru
florilegium
efgiillnpry
pilferingly
efgiillnsty
stellifying
efgiilmnstt
filmsetting
efgiinnprrt
fingerprint
efgiinopruw
rouping-wife
efgiklllnru
fell-lurking
efgiklnnosw
self-knowing
efgiknnoorw
foreknowing
efgilllorwy
gillyflower
efgillnnnru
fell-running
efgilmnoort
montgolfier
efgilmnssuu
slime-fungus
efgilmorsuu
glumiferous
efgilnnossw
flowingness
efgilnoorvw
overflowing

efgimmorsuu
gummiferous
efginnnostu
unsoftening
efginorrsuu
ferruginous
efgiorsttuu
guttiferous
efglmnoottu
leg-of-mutton
efglnnosssu
songfulness
efgnnoorttu
unforgotten
efhhiilsstw
whistle-fish
efhhoopprrt
froth-hopper
efhiilorsty
life-history
efhiinrsstt
thriftiness
efhiioprrsw
fire-worship
efhikorrstw
shift-worker
efhillnssuy
unselfishly
efhillostww
wolf-whistle
efhillsssty
shiftlessly
efhilnoosss
foolishness
efhilnosssu
fushionless
efhilnsssuw
wishfulness
efhiloprssw
self-worship
efhimnnrstu
furnishment
efhimprsttu
trumpet-fish
efhinoppsss
foppishness
efhiorrstuu
thuriferous
efhllnopuuy
unhopefully
efhlnoooprr
forlorn-hope
efhlnpsssuu
pushfulness
efhlnrsstuu
hurtfulness
efhlosttuuy
theftuously
efhmorrsttu
furthermost
efhoooprrsw
shower-proof
efiiilnrtty
infertility

efiiinorrty
inferiority
efiijlnostt
stifle-joint
efiiknorsuz
zinkiferous
efiilmoortz
zeolitiform
efiilnnoops
self-opinion
efiilnpsstu
pitifulness
efiimmnorrs
misinformer
efiinnorstu
interfusion
efiinoprssu
spiniferous
efiinorrsuu
uriniferous
efikllnsssu
skilfulness
efilllmosuu
mellifluous
efilllnptuy
plentifully
efillnoosuy
feloniously
efillrsstuy
fruitlessly
efilnorstuu
interfluous
efilnssstuw
wistfulness
efiloopṙrsu
proliferous
efiloorsuuv
ovuliferous
efilorsstuy
styliferous
efilprstuuy
superfluity
efimnnorssu
uniformness
efimnoorssu
somniferous
efimoorrstu
mortiferous
efinooorsuz
ozoniferous
efinoprssuu
superfusion
efinorssstw
frowstiness
efinorsssuu
furiousness
efiooprrtuv
virtue-proof
efiorrsttuy
yttriferous
efkmooprstu
musket-proof
efknnnooruw
unforeknown

efllnntuuuy
untunefully
efllnorssty
frontlessly
efllnosssuu
soulfulness
efllnssstuu
lustfulness
eflloopprru
proof-puller
eflnnoorrss
forlornness
eflopprsstu
self-support
efloprssuuu
superfluous
efnnnorrrtu
front-runner
efooprsstuy
pussyfooter
egggiiinprw
periwigging
eggglnoossw
snow-goggles
egghhiilttw
lightweight
egghhinosss
hoggishness
egghiinpsss
piggishness
egghiinrrtw
right-winger
egghiinrsst
sight-singer
egghillnrru
herring-gull
egghlnoorsw
hornswoggle
eggiiknnnpu
king-penguin
eggiillnnry
lingeringly
eggiilnnswy
swingeingly
eggiinnorww
wine-growing
eggiinnrtww
wringing-wet
eggijlnoott
toggle-joint
eggiklmmorw
glimmer-gowk
eggilmmoost
gemmologist
egglnooorty
gerontology
eghhiiknrst
night-shriek
eghhiinnost
high-tension
eghhimorrtt
mother-right
eghhinnoors
shoeing-horn

eghhinnrttu
night-hunter
eghhknottuw
hunt-the-gowk
eghhllorstu
trough-shell
eghhlossttu
thoughtless
eghiiimnttw
whiting-time
eghiiklnrsy
shriekingly
eghiillnrsv
shrivelling
eghiillnsww
well-wishing
wishing-well
eghiilnnsst
thingliness
eghiilnprsy
perishingly
eghiilnrsss
girlishness
eghiilnrsvy
shiveringly
eghiilnrtwy
witheringly
eghiilnssst
sightliness
eghiiloorst
hierologist
eghiinnnsss
shiningness
eghiinnprsu
unperishing
eghiinnrtuw
unwithering
eghiinorstu
tiring-house
eghiipprssw
pig's-whisper
eghiknorrtw
nightworker
eghillsssty
sightlessly
eghilmnoort
moonlighter
eghilmnostu
unlightsome
eghilmoosty
mythologise
eghilnooprt
gerontophil
eghilnoopst
nephologist
phenologist
eghilnoostt
ethnologist
eghilnoostu
lithogenous
eghilnossst
ghostliness
eghilorstuy
righteously

eghilprssst
sprightless
eghinnnosst
nothingness
eghinoorsuz
rhizogenous
eghinopprsy
prophesying
eghinoprrtt
night-porter
eghinoprssu
spring-house
surgeonship
eghinorrttw
intergrowth
eghinorsssu
roguishness
eghinorstuu
unrighteous
eghinprsstu
uprightness
eghinrrtuww
wither-wrung
eghiorrsttw
ghost-writer
eghknooprsu
rough-spoken
eghllnrtuuy
gully-hunter
eghlmnoopsu
phlegmonous
eghnnoopsuy
hypnogenous
eghoorrtuvw
overwrought
egiiikllmnt
time-killing
egiiiklmmnt
milking-time
egiiiknnprs
sinking-ripe
egiiilmnors
religionism
egiiilnnnrt
interlining
egiiilnnnst
listening-in
egiiilnorst
religionist
egiiilorrsu
irreligious
egiiilorsty
religiosity
egiiimnnrst
ministering
egiiimnprrw
priming-wire
egiiinnoprt
pre-ignition
egiiinnoptt
petitioning
egiikllnnsw
well-sinking

egiiklnoosy
kinesiology
egiiknorrww
wireworking
egiillmnpss
misspelling
egiillnnssw
willingness
egiillnorty
loiteringly
egiillnpruw
wire-pulling
egiillnrstw
ill-wresting
egiillorsuy
religiously
egiilmnnsss
smilingness
egiilmnprsy
simperingly
egiilnnnstu
unlistening
egiilnnnsuv
nun's-veiling
egiilnnostu
lentiginous
egiilnnosuy
ingeniously
egiilnnttuy
ungentility
egiilnorsuu
unreligious
egiilnosttt
stilettoing
egiilnqruvy
quiveringly
egiilnrssty
resistingly
egiimnnrttu
unremitting
egiimnoprst
temporising
egiinnnnssw
winningness
egiinnnqruu
unenquiring
egiinnoqstu
questioning
egiinnosttu
tentiginous
egiinnprsss
springiness
egiinnrssst
stringiness
egiinnrsstu
unresisting
egiinoprrtx
progenitrix
egiinoprssu
serpiginous
spinigerous
egiinorstuv
vertiginous

egiinprttwy
typewriting
egiioprsstu
prestigious
egiklllnoow
well-looking
egikllnnors
snorkelling
egikllnoswy
king's-yellow
egiklnrtuuv
king-vulture
egiknnnossw
knowingness
egiknoorrvw
working-over
egillloovxy
vexillology
egilllsstuy
guiltlessly
egillnnostw
wellingtons
egillnortvy
revoltingly
egilmnooosu
monologuise
egilmnoorty
terminology
egilmnprsuy
presumingly
egilmnrttuy
mutteringly
egilmooorsu
oligomerous
egilmoorstt
metrologist
egilmoosstu
museologist
egilmoostty
etymologist
egilmoprsuu
plumigerous
egilnnosuuy
ingenuously
egilnnrstty
stringently
egilnnrstuy
unrestingly
egilnnrtuvy
venturingly
egilnooopst
poenologist
stool-pigeon
egilnoorstu
neurologist
egilnoprrty
reportingly
egilnoprrvy
reprovingly
egilnoprtty
potteringly
egilnortty
totteringly

egilnprsttu
spluttering
egilooorsty
soteriology
egiloosstt
osteologist
egiloprssy
perissology
egiloprstt
petrologist
egiloopsstt
pestologist
egimmnostuy
gynostemium
egimnnoorry
ironmongery
egimnnprsuu
unpresuming
egimnoorrsv
misgovernor
egimoprrsss
progressism
eginnnorruv
overrunning
eginnnrrtuu
unreturning
eginnoorstu
nitrogenous
eginnoppstu
upping-stone
eginnoprruv
unreproving
eginooprrss
progression
eginopprrst
ring-stopper
egioorrsssu
gressorious
egioprrssst
progressist
egllnopprsu
long-purples
egnoooprssu
sporogenous
egnooprrtyy
proterogyny
egnoorssty
oyster-tongs
ehhiimpssty
physitheism
ehhiinrsstw
withershins
ehhiinssstw
whitishness
ehhilmnostu
helminthous
ehhilooprs
philosopher
ehhimooprrt
theriomorph
ehhimoopsst
theosophism
ehhinorsssw
whorishness

ehhiooprrss
phosphorise
ehhiooprrst
phosphorite
ehhiooprrsw
hero-worship
ehhioopsstt
theosophist
ehhiopprst
prophetship
ehhiopsssst
hostess-ship
ehhmmoooopr
homoeomorph
ehhmmooopry
homeomorphy
ehhoopprsty
hypostrophe
ehhopprrtyy
hypertrophy
ehiiillppst
phillipsite
ehiiilosstt
hostilities
ehiikllmstt
milk-thistle
ehiiklrsvwy
whisky-liver
ehiiknnpsss
pinkishness
ehiilmrsstv
silversmith
ehiilnooprt
heliotropin
ehiilnoopst
oenophilist
ehiilnprstu
trisulphine
ehiiloopttx
toxophilite
ehiimnosstt
smithsonite
ehiimnsssss
missishness
ehiinnssssw
swinishness
ehiinoprssy
hyperinosis
ehiinprssst
spinsterish
ehiinrssstt
thirstiness
ehiklmssttu
musk-thistle
ehiklnsssu
luskishness
ehiklorrstw
silk-thrower
ehillmrssty
mirthlessly
ehillnrsttu
still-hunter
ehilloppsuy
epiphyllous

ehillortttw
littleworth
ehilmmnoost
monothelism
ehilmmnosty
semi-monthly
ehilmnoopty
entomophily
ehilmnpsssu
lumpishness
ehilmopttuy
Plymouthite
ehilmorssty
thermolysis
ehilnossstu
loutishness
ehilnssssty
stylishness
ehilooprsux
xerophilous
ehiloprsssw
worshipless
ehilopssttw
whistle-stop
ehimmnpsssu
mumpishness
ehimmooorst
homoerotism
ehimnnorrst
northernism
ehimnnorstu
nourishment
ehimnoopsty
monophysite
ehimnoorttu
Nototherium
ehimnoprsss
rompishness
ehimnorsstu
southernism
ehimooprrst
rheotropism
ehimooprstu
hemitropous
ehimoopstty
mythopoeist
ehimprsstyy
mystery-ship
ehinnnnsssu
nunnishness
ehinnnossst
tonnishness
ehinnoopsty
hypotension
ehinooprrtt
ornithopter
ehinooprssu
prison-house
ehinorssttu
Struthiones
ehinosssstt
sottishness
ehioooprrsu
Eriophorous

ehioooprttz
trophozoite
ehiooprsstt
photo-resist
ehioprssttt
prosthetist
ehkloosttuy
thelytokous
ehknnooostt
nook-shotten
ehknooprsst
short-spoken
ehllorsstwy
worthlessly
ehlmnoppsyy
nympholepsy
ehlooprstty
phytosterol
ehloprssstu
upholstress
ehloprssuuu
sulphureous
ehmnnoorstu
hunter's-moon
ehmnoorrstt
northermost
ehmnoorstwy
money's-worth
ehmoooprstu
homopterous
ehmoorssttu
southermost
ehmoorsttyy
hysterotomy
ehnnooprttw
twopenn'orth
ehnoooprrtt
orthopteron
ehnoopsttuy
entophytous
ehnoorssttw
stone's-throw
ehoopprsstw
show-stopper
ehooqrttuwy
quoteworthy
eiiiinqstuv
inquisitive
eiiiklnnpsw
pilniewinks
eiiilmprtvy
primitively
eiiilnnpsty
insipiently
eiiilnttuvy
intuitively
eiiimmnrstu
ministerium
eiiimnorrss
irremission
eiiimnorssv
revisionism
eiiinoprstt
peritonitis

eiiinopsttt
petitionist
eiiinoqrstu
requisition
eiiinorrtty
interiority
eiiinorsstv
revisionist
eiiinrsstty
sinisterity
eiiinssttvy
sensitivity
eiiinstttuv
institutive
eiiioprsstt
periostitis
eiiirssttvy
resistivity
eiikknorsss
kirk-session
eiiklnnnpwy
pinnywinkle
eiilllmssty
limitlessly
eiillmpsuvy
impulsively
eiillooqssu
soliloquise
eiilmoprsuy
imperiously
eiilnnsstty
insistently
eiilnoopprt
lipoprotein
eiilnoprstv
silver-point
eiilnoqsuuz
Louis-Quinze
eiilnrstuvy
intrusively
eiilnrttuvy
nutritively
eiiloppirsty
propylitise
eiilprrtuvy
irruptively
eiimnnooprt
premonition
eiimnnopstu
pneumonitis
eiimnorrttt
intromitter
eiimoorrstu
meritorious
eiimopprrty
impropriety
eiimoprssst
prestissimo
eiimopsttuy
impetuosity
eiimorrsstu
moisturiser
eiinoopprst
preposition

eiinoprssuv
supervision
eiinoqssttu
questionist
eiinorrssst
sinistrorse
eiinorstttu
restitution
eiiopprrrtx
proprietrix
eiioppsstuv
suppositive
eiiopqrrstu
perquisitor
eiioprrsstx
xerotripsis
eiioprrstuy
superiority
eiioqrrstuy
requisitory
eikklrrstuu
Kulturkreis
eikllorrstw
trellis-work
eikmmooprsu
opium-smoker
eillllmnoow
woollen-mill
eillmoorsuv
mellivorous
eillnopssty
pointlessly
eilloprrsuy
prelusorily
eilloprsttv
stilt-plover
eilmnnoostv
somnivolent
eilmnnoprty
prominently
eilmnooprs
monopoliser
eilmnoprtuy
importunely
eilmnoptttu
multipotent
eilmnostuuy
untimeously
eilmoossstu
tous-les-mois
eilmoprssty
proselytism
eilmopstuuy
impetuously
eilmorsttuy
multistorey
eilnooprsst
portionless
eilnoprsuuy
penuriously
eilnoqrtuvy
ventriloquy
eilooprrsty
posteriorly

eilooprssty
proteolysis
eilopprrstw
slipperwort
eimmooprsuz
zoospermium
eimnnoosssu
ominousness
eimnooprrty
premonitory
eimnopprstu
presumption
eimooprrssx
expromissor
eimooprsttt
optometrist
eimoorrsuvv
vermivorous
einnoopprtu
inopportune
einnooprsss
responsions
einnoosssux
noxiousness
einnoqrstuu
non-sequitur
einnorsssuu
ruinousness
einnossssuu
sinuousness
einoorssstu
riotousness
einopprsssu
suppression
einoprrrttu
interruptor
einopssttty
stenotypist
einorssttuy
strenuosity
eioprrssuvy
supervisory
eioqrrsttuu
triquetrous
eiorrssttuu
trouser-suit
eiorrsttuy
restitutory
ejknoorruwy
journey-work
ejmnnoorstu
sojournment
ekmnnoostuy
teknonymous
eknnnnossuw
unknownness
ellmnoosty
somnolently
ellmorstuuy
tremulously
elloqrsuuuy
querulously
elmmnoostuy
momentously

elmnorstuuu
untremulous
elnoooprrty
poltroonery
elnoopprtuy
opportunely
elnorsstuuy
strenuously
elnorstuuvy
venturously
elopprrsstu
purportless
eloppressstu
supportless
emnooppsssu
pompousness
emnopprsttu
supportment
emoooprrsst
moss-trooper
emorrsttuyy
mystery-tour
enoorrsttuu
torrentuous
eopprrssstu
supportress
eoprrrttuuw
rupturewort
fffghiimntu
muffin-fight
ffgghiinors
fishing-frog
ffghillnsuy
shufflingly
ffghillrtuy
frightfully
ffiirrssttu
first-fruits
ffimnorruwy
muffin-worry
fgggiilnort
rigging-loft
fgghiilnnty
night-flying
fgghiinnott
nothing-gift
fgghiinsttu
fish-gutting
fggiimnnort
morning-gift
fggiinnoruv
unforgiving
fghhnoottuu
unthought-of
fghiiinnnsu
unfinishing
fghiilloptw
pillow-fight
fghiilnopst
shop-lifting
fghiilnorsu
flourishing
fghiinnpstu
punt-fishing
fghiinnrssu
furnishings
fghiinopstt
fitting-shop
fghilnortty
fortnightly
fghinntttuu
tuft-hunting
fgiiilmnpsy
simplifying
fgiillnptuy
upliftingly
fgiilnnttuy
unfittingly
fgiilnsttuy
stultifying
fgiimnnnoru
uninforming
fgiinnoprtu
unprofiting
fgiinnopstu
fusing-point
fgiinnorrtu
turfing-iron
fgioorrsuuv
frugivorous
fhhiinoopst
photo-finish
fhiknooprrs
shrink-proof
fhllnrtuuuy
unhurtfully
fiillnoosux
solifluxion
fiillnptuuy
unpitifully
fiimmnoorty
omniformity
fiiooppprrst
proof-spirit
fiirtttttuu
tutti-frutti
fiklllnsuuy
unskilfully
filloorsuvy
frivolously
filmrssttuu
mistrustful
flloorrsuwy
sorrowfully
gghhhiortuw
highwrought
gghhiillnor
high-rolling
gghiillnsty
slightingly
gghilnopsuw
swing-plough
gghinnnostu
hunting-song
gghinorrstu
rough-string
gghlmoopsyy
sphygmology
ggiiinnrstw
sign-writing
ggilnooorww
wool-growing
ggimnnnoorw
morning-gown
gglmnnoooy
gnomonology
ghhiinnptuw
hunting-whip
ghhiloprttt
troth-plight
ghhinnnortu
hunting-horn
ghhiorsttwy
sightworthy
ghhlloprtuu
pull-through
ghhloopptyy
photoglyphy
ghhmnnooopt
monophthong
ghiiikmnrss
skirmishing
ghiiklnnrsy
shrinkingly
ghiiklntty
tightly-knit
ghiiknnnrsu
unshrinking
ghiilllnrty
thrillingly
ghiillnstwy
whistlingly
ghiilloopst
philologist
ghiilloostt
lithologist
ghiilnoorst
rhinologist
ghiilnopsty
philogynist
ghiilooopst
ophiologist
ghiiloopppst
hippologist
ghiiloosstt
histologist
ghiinopppptw
whipping-top
ghiinopprsw
worshipping
ghiinopttuw
whiting-pout
ghijmnopsuw
show-jumping
ghiknnnootw
know-nothing
ghiknnoopru
pruning-hook
ghillooopst
hoplologist
ghilloopsyy
syphilology
ghillopsttu
plough-stilt
ghilmmnrtuy
thrummingly
ghilmnoosty
hymnologist
ghilmoostty
mythologist
ghilnooopst
phonologist
ghilnooorty
ornithology
ghilnoopsuy
philogynous
ghiloopssuy
physiologus
ghiloopstty
phytologist
ghimnnoorrs
morsing-horn
ghimnoopsyy
physiognomy
ghimooossyz
homozygosis
ghinoorrtuw
wrought-iron
ghllmopuyyz
Zygophyllum
ghloprstuyy
Tyroglyphus
giiiinnprst
inspiriting
giiiknnnopr
pinking-iron
giiillostuy
litigiously
giiilnnprsy
inspiringly
giiilnnqruy
inquiringly
giiimnnoosu
ignominious
giiimnnoprr
priming-iron
giiinnnprsu
uninspiring
giiinnnqruu
uninquiring
giiklllnosu
soul-killing
giiklnnnuwy
unwinkingly
giikmmnnost
skimmington
giilllllmnor
rolling-mill
giilllnnuwy
unwillingly
giillmnnsuy
unsmilingly
giillmnoost
limnologist
giillmnopry
imploringly
giillmnptuy
multiplying
giillnnstuy
insultingly
giilmnoprsy
promisingly
giilmnoprvy
improvingly
giilnnoqtuy
longinquity
giilnnptuyy
unpityingly
giilnnqstuy
squintingly
giilnnttuwy
unwittingly
giilnoorsuv
lignivorous
giimnnoprsu
unpromising
giimnnoprtu
importuning
giimnoorstt
sitting-room
giinnnopstw
winning-post
giinnoprrst
ripsnorting
giinooprrsu
porriginous
giinoorstuv
vortiginous
giinoprrsuu
pruriginous
giinrttttyy
nitty-gritty
gijlmostuuu
multijugous
giklmorstuw
silkworm-gut
giklnnnouwy
unknowingly
giklnooprvy
provokingly
giknnnnortu
running-knot
giknnoopruv
unprovoking
gillnostuuy
glutinously
gilloopsttu
plutologist
gilmmnrruuy
murmuringly
gilmnooostu
monologuist
gilnnnopssu
nonplussing
gilnorrttuy
torturingly
gilnrstttuy
struttingly
gimmnnooorr
morning-room

11 MOO

gimmnnrruuu
  unmurmuring
gimmnoortyy
  myringotomy
gimmnoprtuu
  rumgumption
gimnnorstuu
  surmounting
gimnoooprsu
  sporogonium
gimnoorstyy
  syringotomy
ginnooprrtu
  root-pruning
ginnooprstt
  strongpoint
ginooppsttu
  stopping-out
gnoooprstuy
  protogynous
hhiinosstww
  wishtonwish
hhilmoopsty
  holophytism
hhimnooppsu
  phosphonium
hhimoopprss
  phosphorism
hhmnoooopsu
  homophonous
hhmnooortuu
  mouth-honour
hhoooppRssu
  phosphorous
hiiikklmnps
  milk-kinship
hiiilmnopss
  Sinophilism
hiiimnorsst
  histrionism
hiillnnnoot
  nonillionth
hiilloprsww
  will-worship
hiilmnnoopy
  hypolimnion

hiilmoosttt
  lithotomist
hiiloorrttt
  lithotritor
hiiloprstty
  lithotripsy
hiimmooprss
  isomorphism
hiimmoprrst
  trimorphism
hiimnooprst
  monitorship
hiiooprsstu
  Istiophorus
hilloopsuxy
  xylophilous
hilloprstuy
  triphyllous
hilmmopstuy
  Plymouthism
hilmooosttu
  lithotomous
hilmopsttuy
  Plymouthist
hilnooppsty
  polyphonist
  Psilophyton
hilnoopstxy
  xylophonist
hilooprstyy
  polyhistory
hiloorttwww
  whitlow-wort
himmoooprsz
  zoomorphism
himnoopssuy
  symphonious
himoooprssu
  isomorphous
himooprrstu
  trimorphous
himoopsttty
  phytotomist
himoortttwy
  thirty-twomo

hinnoooprtu
  honour-point
hinooorrssu
  horrisonous
hinoopprsss
  sponsorship
hinooppstty
  phonotypist
hinooprrtty
  thyrotropin
hiooppRsstv
  provostship
hiooppsstyy
  hypotyposis
hkrrrrsuuyy
  hurry-skurry
hlooprrstuu
  sulphur-root
hloprrstuuw
  sulphurwort
hmooooprssu
  homosporous
hoooppRrsuy
  pyrophorous
horrstttuwy
  trustworthy
iiiilmnnqsu
  inquilinism
iiiilnnqtuy
  inquilinity
iiiimmprstv
  primitivism
iiiimnsttuv
  intuitivism
iiiimprsttv
  primitivist
iiiinnoqstu
  inquisition
iiillmnopst
  pointillism
iiillmnossu
  illusionism
iiillnnoqtu
  quintillion
iiillnopstt
  pointillist

iiillnosstt
  tonsillitis
iiillnosstu
  illusionist
iiilloprsss
  spirillosis
iiilmpstuvy
  impulsivity
iiilnnoqsuu
  inquilinous
iiinnorttu
  innutrition
iiinnostttu
  institution
iiinoooopstv
  oviposition
iiinsstttu
  institutist
iijlnorsuuy
  injuriously
iillorsstuu
  illustrious
iilnnoosuxy
  innoxiously
iilnoosttu
  solutionist
iilooprrsvy
  provisorily
iimnoprttuy
  importunity
iimooprsstt
  Soroptimist
iinnnnoostu
  non-unionist
iinnooprrty
  non-priority
iinoooopprst
  proposition
iinooppsstu
  supposition
iinoppqrtuy
  propinquity
iinoprrrstu
  stirrup-iron
iiooprrtty
  top-priority

illopssuwwy
  pussywillow
illoqsttuuy
  stultiloquy
illorsuuuxy
  luxuriously
ilmnooostty
  tonsilotomy
ilmnoopsttu
  plutonomist
ilnooopssuy
  poisonously
ilnooorstuy
  notoriously
ilnorsuuuux
  unluxurious
imnnooopsst
  monopsonist
imnoopprstu
  opportunism
imnoorsstty
  monstrosity
imopssttuuy
  sumptuosity
imppprrstuu
  stirrup-pump
inoopprsttu
  opportunist
inoopprttuy
  opportunity
iooppRsstuy
  suppository
iooprrstttu
  prostitutor
lmmorrsuuuy
  murmurously
lmnooopsuyy
  polyonymous
lmnoorsstuy
  monstrously
lmopsstuuuy
  sumptuously
moooprrsstt
  storm-troops

12 AAA

aaaaaalmrstt
  taramasalata
aaaaaceemnrt
  Amarantaceae
aaaaacinrrsv
  caravansarai
aaaabbeklmst
  Balaam-basket
aaaabccelnru
  baccalaurean

aaaabcchilnn
  bacchanalian
aaaabcdeeirs
  Scarabaeidae
aaaabciillmt
  Balaamitical
aaaabdmnrssu
  massaranduba
aaaaccccirtu
  acciaccatura

aaaacceeimrt
  Tamaricaceae
aaaacchinrtt
  anacathartic
aaaaccilmort
  acroamatical
aaaaccilprtt
  paratactical
aaaacclmorst
  Malacostraca

aaaacdiilprs
  paradisaical
  paradisiacal
aaaacdiimort
  acaridomatia
aaaacdimoort
  acarodomatia
aaaaceeepprv
  Papaveraceae

aaaaceeimrtt
Marattiaceae
aaaaceilnpst
anapaestical
aaaaceinrrsv
caravanserai
aaaacgimmnrt
anagrammatic
aaaachinrsst
anacatharsis
aaaachnnprtt
Panchatantra
aaaacilmnpru
Campanularia
aaaacimnrsst
antimacassar
aaaadepqrrtu
paraquadrate
aaaadilmnnrs
salamandrian
aaaaeehnnnpt
Panathenaean
aaaaegglnpru
paralanguage
aaaaegilmmtv
amalgamative
aaaaeginprss
asparaginase
aaaaegnrtvxz
extravaganza
aaaaehilmsst
thalassaemia
aaaagilmmnot
amalgamation
aaaaiillmnrt
antimalarial
aaaaillprrss
sarsaparilla
aaaailnrsstu
Australasian
aaabbinrrstu
antibarbarus
aaabcciillst
cabalistical
aaabcdeellnw
weal-balanced
aaabcdhiinrt
Dibranchiata
aaabceegilrr
carriageable
aaabceeginor
Boraginaceae
aaabceeimrsu
Simarubaceae
aaabcehillpt
alphabetical
aaabcehilnpt
analphabetic
aaabcehloppr
approachable
aaabceiilnrt
celibatarian
aaabceillrwy
cable-railway

aaabceilmnru
air-ambulance
aaabcelmrtwy
cable-tramway
aaabcelnrrtu
tabernacular
aaabcghilnop
Anglophabiac
aaabcgiinnrt
Cantabrigian
aaabcgillotv
Volga-Baltaic
aaabciinpstt
anabaptistic
aaabcilnoruv
vocabularian
aaabdeekkmnr
make-and-break
aaabdeilmrst
dramatisable
aaabdemnrssu
masseranduba
aaabdemrssss
ambassadress
aaabdghmnrss
smash-and-grab
aaabdiilptty
adaptability
aaabdilloopr
paraboloidal
aaabeegilmrr
marriageable
aaabeeglmnnu
unmanageable
aaabeeilnpps
inappeasable
aaabeellnppu
unappealable
aaabeelnppsu
unappeasable
aaabeggginrt
baggage-train
aaabeglmnnuy
unmanageably
aaabeglnssuu
unassuagable
aaabehlmostt
haematoblast
aaabeiilmnnt
maintainable
aaabeillmnot
balletomania
aaabeillnssu
unassailable
aaabeilnnttu
unattainable
aaabellnnsuy
unanalysable
aaabellnrssw
ballanwrasse
aaabellnrstt
translatable
aaabellrsttw
water-ballast

aaabelnoopty
palaeobotany
aaabelqsttuu
absquatulate
aaabemnorttw
water-boatman
aaabgiilnrrt
Gibraltarian
aaabhinoopst
satanophobia
aaabiiilltvy
availability
aaabiillptty
palatability
aaabilnnoott
labanotation
aaabilnnttuy
unattainably
aaabilnprssu
Sublapsarian
aaaccceeiinv
Vacciniaceae
aaaccchiprtt
cataphractic
aaacccillstt
catallactics
aaaccdeeeipr
Epacridaceae
aaaccdeeiort
Cordaitaceae
aaaccdehiinr
Characinidae
aaaccdeillmy
academically
aaaccdhilors
saccharoidal
aaaccdhnrrsy
cash-and-carry
aaaccdiinrrt
intracardiac
aaacceeehisz
Schizaeaceae
aaacceelrssu
Crassulaceae
aaaccefhnntt
café-chantant
aaaccegilmtt
metagalactic
aaaccehnostu
acanthaceous
aaacceiinptt
incapacitate
aaacceilllnr
cancellarial
aaacceillnnr
cancellarian
aaacceillntu
canaliculate
aaacceinnqtu
acquaintance
aaaccghilmoz
chalazogamic
aaacchillnry
anarchically

aaacchilnpty
anaphylactic
aaacchilpsty
cataphysical
aaacciinoptt
capacitation
aaaccilorstu
accusatorial
aaacddehiirr
Charadriidae
aaacdeegjlnu
Juglandaceae
aaacdeeilnps
Asclepiadean
aaacdegiiprr
carriage-paid
aaacdehmprty
Pachydermata
aaacdeinrstt
tradescantia
aaacdennopsu
pandanaceous
aaacdgiimmrt
diagrammatic
aaacdgiimprt
paradigmatic
aaacdhiinnrt
cantharidian
aaacdiinnnsv
Scandinavian
aaacdillmrty
dramatically
aaacdilortty
Artiodactyla
aaacdlmmnopy
lampadomancy
aaaceeeginnt
Gentianaceae
aaaceeehmnpy
Nymphaeaceae
aaaceeeikmrr
Krameriaceae
aaaceeeilmrs
Marsileaceae
aaaceeenpprr
reappearance
aaaceegilmno
Magnoliaceae
aaaceegllopy
Polygalaceae
aaaceegnrtvx
extravagance
aaaceehilnnp
anencephalia
aaaceeiilnsv
Salviniaceae
aaaceeilnprt
paraenetical
aaaceenprrtw
peace-warrant
aaacefimnorr
Afro-American
aaacefinsttt
fantasticate

aaaceggglotu
galactagogue
aaacegiilmrr
mail-carriage
aaacegilmmno
megalomaniac
aaacegimnprt
paramagnetic
aaacegnnopry
paracyanogen
aaacegnrtvxy
extravagancy
aaacehillmpr
alphamerical
aaacehilmmtt
mathematical
aaacehilmsst
thalassaemic
aaacehilprst
share-capital
aaacehimrrtt
matriarchate
aaacehiprrtt
patriarchate
aaaceillprst
palaestrical
aaaceilmoost
osteomalacia
aaaceilmprrt
parametrical
aaaceilnnrst
Lancasterian
aaaceilnortu
aeronautical
aaaceilopprt
pearl-tapioca
aaacejjkmpty
pyjama-jacket
aaacejklnnrt
Jack-a-lantern
aaacelnopstu
platanaceous
aaacelnosstu
santalaceous
aaacelosttuy
autocatalyse
aaacemnrrsty
sacramentary
aaacfiinrrtt
anti-aircraft
aaacfimnrrst
aircraftsman
aaacflmnrtuu
manufactural
aaacggillnoy
anagogically
aaacggillopy
apagogically
aaacgiillnnt
anti-Gallican
aaacgiilnott
Tagliacotian
aaacgiimnstt
anastigmatic

aaacgilllnoy
analogically
aaacgillmmmo
mammalogical
aaachilmnpst
phantasmical
aaachilmnrst
charlatanism
aaachimnsttt
antasthmatic
aaachipprrst
paraphrastic
aaachllprtyy
cataphyllary
aaachmnnoppr
panpharmacon
aaaciiilnnrt
catilinarian
aaaciillmnst
talismanical
aaaciilnnost
canalisation
aaaciilnnrrt
intracranial
aaacilllntyy
analytically
aaacillmnoty
anatomically
aaacillnntuy
unanalytical
aaacilmmnnoo
monomaniacal
aaacilmnopry
pyromaniacal
aaacilpprtty
party-capital
aaacimnnottu
catamountain
aaacllmnorsy
nasolacrymal
aaaclmmopsty
mycoplasmata
aaacnnnorttt
contranatant
aaadddeeilnv
dead-and-alive
aaaddeeiiprs
Paradiseidae
aaaddeginstv
disadvantage
aaaddgillmoy
amygdaloidal
aaaddglnnnow
Gondwanaland
aaaddiinoprx
paradoxidian
aaaddilmnors
salamandroid
aaaddlmnprst
lamp-standard
aaadegilnrtv
landgraviate
aaadegilpqru
quadraplegia

aaadegimqrsu
Quadragesima
aaadeginopst
Spatangoidea
aaadegnostuv
advantageous
aaadehilnprs
nail-head-spar
aaadehnrrttw
death-warrant
aaadeiimnnst
East-Indiaman
aaadeilmnnrs
salamandrine
aaadeilnnprt
anteprandial
aaadeimnrtty
tetradynamia
aaadeinoprtt
readaptation
aaadfiinorst
faradisation
aaadgiillort
gladiatorial
aaadgiilnort
gladiatorian
aaadgimnrstv
avant-gardism
aaadginrsttv
avant-gardist
aaadglnqrruu
quadrangular
aaadiillmnps
palladianism
aaadiinnoptt
inadaptation
aaaeegglmntu
metalanguage
aaaeeggmnrst
stage-manager
aaaeeghmnopr
Phanerogamae
aaaeeginnrsx
sexagenarian
aaaeeglmnopt
aplanogamete
aaaeegmnnprt
permanganate
aaaeehimnstt
anathematise
aaaeehinpsst
panaesthesia
aaaeehiprsst
paraesthesia
aaaeelmmnsst
meat-salesman
aaaeemmmopst
mammee-sapota
aaaeggpprstu
egg-apparatus
aaaeghimnopr
Phanerogamia
aaaeghllttww
wag-at-the-wall

aaaeghloppry
palaeography
aaaeghnorstu
Saurognathae
aaaegillmott
agalmatolite
aaaegilrttww
water-wagtail
aaaeginnnnor
nonagenarian
aaaeglóprsst
paraglossate
aaaehhkllnrs
hallan-shaker
aaaehiknprss
Shaksperiana
aaaehimnortt
theatromania
aaaehnprstty
parasyntheta
aaaeiilnqrtu
equalitarian
aaaeilllnprt
antiparallel
aaaeilmnoppr
paralipomena
aaaeilmrrttx
extra-marital
aaaelqqrsuuv
quaquaversal
aaaemmrrsstt
master-at-arms
aaaenoprsuyy
pay-as-you-earn
aaafmmnnorsw
man-of-war's-man
aaaggiopprtu
appoggiatura
aaaghiimprst
amphigastria
aaaghimnprst
paragnathism
aaaghipprrst
paragraphist
aaaghirsttwy
straightaway
aaaghnoprstu
paragnathous
aaagiilnnotv
navigational
aaagilllorrt
grallatorial
aaahiilnnott
antihalation
aaahiimnnrtu
humanitarian
aaahkmmnotuy
thank-you-ma'am
aaahllmnpsty
phantasmally
aaaiillnnopr
Apollinarian
aaaiilmprrty
paramilitary

aaaiilmnnott
anti-national
aaaiilnnosst
nasalisation
aaaiilnopprt
apparitional
aaaiilnorttt
totalitarian
aaaiimmnrsst
Samaritanism
aaaiinpprsst
Patripassian
aaaiklnorsuy
Ankylosauria
aaaillnosttu
salutational
aaailmnorttu
maturational
aaailnorsttu
salutatorian
aaainnnrrstu
transuranian
aaainorsssst
assassinator
aaallmmnpttu
tantalum-lamp
aabbbeerrtty
baby-batterer
aabbccemoosu
bombacaceous
aabbcdeeehrr
bare-breached
aabbcdekllnu
black-and-blue
aabbcdelrsss
scabbardless
aabbcdfhirss
scabbard-fish
aabbceeghitw
cabbage-white
aabbceehlnru
unbreachable
aabbcegikknr
backbreaking
aabbcegkknsu
skunk-cabbage
aabbcehnrsty
baby-snatcher
aabbcgikllln
blackballing
aabbciiilmno
bibliomaniac
aabbciillnry
rabbinically
aabbciimorrx
mixobarbaric
aabbdeimnrry
barmy-brained
aabbdggilnnr
land-grabbing
aabbdiillllr
billiard-ball
aabbdilmnosu
subabdominal
aabbeeehlqtu
bequeathable
aabbeeelnrss
bearableness
aabbeehlnrtu
unbreathable
aabbeeirrtuv
abbreviature
aabbeellmnss
blamableness
aabbegillnrs
ball-bearings
aabbeginrstw
rabbeting-saw
aabbeiinortv
abbreviation
aabbeilnnotu
unobtainable
aabbeilrtttu
attributable
aabbeimmnpsy
namby-pambies
aabbeinrrrtw
rabbit-warren
aabbeiorrtvy
abbreviatory
aabbhiiiltty
habitability
aabbiilnrrsu
sublibrarian
aabccdeiilrt
bactericidal
aabccdeiknrr
crackbrained
aabccdeillsy
decasyllabic
aabccdelmmoo
accommodable
aabccdhlrtyy
brachydactyl
aabcceeemort
Combretaceae
aabcceehlnrt
carte-blanche
aabcceelnptu
unacceptable
aabccehhlpry
brachycephal
aabccehoortt
tobacco-heart
aabcceilllnu
incalculable
aabcceillmov
clavicembalo
aabcceilmnor
microbalance
aabcceirrtuu
bureaucratic
aabccelnortt
contractable
aabccenoorsu
carbonaceous
aabccgikknrt
back-tracking
aabcchhiimpr
amphibrachic
aabcchiinstu
antibacchius
aabccillnuy
incalculably
aabccinrsttu
subantarctic
aabccklnrrtu
blackcurrant
aabcclnooptt
tobacco-plant
aabcdddeekls
saddlebacked
aabcddejlors
Jacob's-ladder
aabcddeklrrw
bladder-wrack
aabcddeklrst
straddle-back
aabcddiilnrr
cardinal-bird
aabcdeefllns
self-balanced
aabcdeehklrt
black-hearted
aabcdeehrrst
acre's-breadth
aabcdeeiilnr
ineradicable
aabcdeeillps
displaceable
aabcdeellllnw
well-balanced
aabcdeelllsy
decasyllable
aabcdeellnrt
ballet-dancer
aabcdeelnnsu
unascendable
aabcdeelrttu
trabeculated
aabcdegiklsv
black-visaged
aabcdehiinrt
dibranchiate
aabcdehnnrst
bandersnatch
aabcdehorrty
carbohydrate
aabcdeiilnry
ineradicably
aabcdeiloruv
vocabularied
aabcdeinostu
subdiaconate
aabcdeknrssw
backwardness
aabcdelopprr
clapperboard
aabcdelrstty
abstractedly
aabcdenrrrtu
currant-bread
aabcdeoprrrs
scraper-board
aabcdginnort
carbon-dating
aabcdginorst
broadcasting
aabcdgkllruy
blackguardly
aabcdhinoopr
Branchiopoda
aabcdhinorsu
subarachnoid
aabcdhiopstt
dispatch-boat
aabcdiiilloy
diabolically
aabcdkmnoosw
backwoodsman
aabcdkmnorsw
backswordman
aabceeeekprr
peace-breaker
aabceeeffiln
ineffaceable
aabceeeghlnx
exchangeable
aabceeehllnw
balance-wheel
aabceeehlnst
balance-sheet
aabceeeilmor
Bromeliaceae
aabceeelortt
ebracteolate
aabceeemqrsu
macaberesque
aabceeffilny
ineffaceably
aabceefiprrt
prefabricate
aabceeggprrt
carpetbagger
aabceeghlnnu
unchangeable
aabceegiinno
Bignoniaceae
aabceehilnuv
unachievable
aabceehlmnrt
merchantable
aabceehlnrsu
unsearchable
aabceehloprr
reproachable
aabceehmmrst
steam-chamber
aabceeikmnrt
cabinetmaker
aabceeillmmt
emblematical
aabceeilmnss
amicableness
aabceeimrrrr
barrier-cream

aabceeinortx
exacerbation
aabceekmnorr
marker-beacon
aabceeknnops
pease-bannock
aabceelllnru
unrecallable
aabceellnoot
oblanceolate
aabceellnpss
placableness
aabceellorrt
correlatable
aabceelmnotu
uncomeatable
aabcefiillss
classifiable
aabcefiillty
beatifically
aabceflnrstu
blast-furnace
aabceghilpty
bathypelagic
aabceghlnnuy
unchangeably
aabcegiklnnr
clearing-bank
aabcegillnou
incoagulable
aabcehiiltty
teachability
aabcehiimnps
amphisbaenic
aabcehilnrtu
uncharitable
aabcehkllopr
alpha-blocker
aabcehlmnors
elasmobranch
aabcehlnnstu
unstanchable
aabcehlnrsuy
unsearchably
aabcehnnrrtw
bench-warrant
aabcehoprssu
habeas-corpus
aabceiillnpp
inapplicable
aabceiilmrst
bicameralist
aabceiilpprt
participable
aabceiilrtty
traceability
aabceiinoort
anaerobiotic
aabceillllty
balletically
aabceillnppu
unapplicable
aabceillnsuv
vulcanisable

aabceillttuv
cultivatable
aabceilmnnot
contaminable
aabceilmnopr
incomparable
aabceilmorrt
barometrical
aabceilnpsuz
uncapsizable
aabceimnnnor
cinnamon-bear
aabceinrrstt
scatter-brain
aabceiorsttt
bacteriostat
aabceklqrrtu
black-quarter
aabcenrssstt
abstractness
aabcflnoortu
confabulator
aabcghhprryy
brachygraphy
aabcghiilopr
biographical
aabcghnopprw
Cappagh-brown
aabcgiknrstt
backstarting
aabcgilloott
battological
aabchiinoott
cohabitation
aabchilnrtuy
uncharitably
aabciiilnpty
incapability
aabciillprsy
parisyllabic
aabciilmrsst
strabismical
aabciilrttty
tractability
aabciimmnort
timbromaniac
aabcillllsyy
syllabically
aabcilmnopry
incomparably
aabcinorstuu
subarcuation
aabclloooorrt
collaborator
aabclnorstuy
constabulary
aabcmnnnoott
non-combatant
aabdddeeilnr
addle-brained
aabddeehmorr
hebdomadarer
aabddehhnrst
hand's-breadth

aabddehllmoy
hebdomadally
aabddeilmntu
mandibulated
aabddghorrtu
draughtboard
aabddginorrw
drawing-board
aabddlmnootz
zalambdodont
aabdeeegilrs
disagreeable
aabdeeelnrss
readableness
aabdeegilrsy
disagreeably
aabdeeginrtu
drainage-tube
aabdeehhrrsy
haberdashery
aabdeehorrtw
weather-board
aabdeeiilrsv
adverbialise
aabdeeilrttx
extraditable
aabdeeklnrtu
undertakable
aabdeekorrst
skateboarder
aabdeellnssu
laudableness
aabdeelmnnss
damnableness
aabdeelnoprs
leopard's-bane
aabdeelnorss
adorableness
aabdeelnortu
unelaborated
aabdeemorrsu
board-measure
aabdeennprwy
brandy-pawnee
aabdefllnnor
flannelboard
aabdegijmorr
brigade-major
aabdegilnrtw
drawing-table
aabdegllmnor
balladmonger
aabdehhirrst
hair's-breadth
aabdehiinstt
absinthiated
aabdehinttuu
unhabituated
aabdehlnosuw
unshadowable
aabdehrrsttw
straw-breadth
aabdeiilnrst
distrainable

aabdeilllosw
disallowable
aabdeilrsttt
bastard-title
aabdeimoppst
paedobaptism
aabdeimrrsss
disembarrass
aabdeioppstt
paedobaptist
aabdelmortuy
deambulatory
aabdelnnopru
unpardonable
aabdeloprrst
plasterboard
aabdghinorsw
washing-board
aabdgiilnors
sailboarding
aabdgiinnost
bastinadoing
aabdgilnnsst
sand-blasting
aabdiiilltty
dilatability
aabdiiilstvy
advisability
aabdlnnopruy
unpardonably
aabeeefkmrrr
frame-breaker
aabeeegikmrr
image-breaker
aabeeeglmrss
reassemblage
aabeeehhlrtt
heather-bleat
aabeeehkrrrt
heartbreaker
aabeeeillprr
irrepealable
aabeeellnpru
unrepealable
aabeeellnruv
unrevealable
aabeeellnsss
saleableness
aabeeelmnnss
amenableness
aabeeelnprtu
unrepeatable
aabeeelrrttu
terebratulae
aabeefflorst
afforestable
aabeefgiknrs
safe-breaking
aabeefgilrrr
irrefragable
aabeefhinrrt
feather-brain
aabeefilmnst
manifestable

aabeefkrsstt
breakfast-set
aabeefllrsty
self-betrayal
aabeeflnrrst
transferable
aabeegiilrty
agreeability
aabeegilmnst
magnetisable
aabeegimnorr
marriage-bone
aabeegirrstt
Gastarbeiter
aabeeglnouvy
unvoyageable
aabeegmnotuu
beaumontague
aabeehiilrtt
rehabilitate
aabeehlmqrsu
Alhambresque
aabeehlrrsty
breathalyser
aabeeiillrrs
irrealisable
aabeeiilprrr
irrepairable
aabeeilllnpp
inappellable
aabeeillprry
irrepealably
aabeeilmmrsu
immeasurable
aabeeilmnott
antimetabole
aabeeilnprru
unrepairable
aabeeilnrrst
restrainable
aabeeilnrssv
variableness
aabeeinrrttv
Invertebrata
aabeeklmnrru
unremarkable
aabeeklmnrtu
unmarketable
aabeellmrstt
ballet-master
aabeellnppss
palpableness
aabeellnssuv
valuableness
aabeelmnoruv
manoeuvrable
aabeelmnrsuu
unmeasurable
aabeelmpprrr
paper-marbler
aabeelnnnttu
untenantable
aabeelnnorsu
unreasonable

aabeelnnossu
unseasonable
aabeelnnrsuw
unanswerable
aabeelnossvw
avowableness
aabeelnpssss
passableness
aabeelnrsttu
subalternate
aabeeloprstu
pleasure-boat
aabeelrrrstt
sabre-rattler
aabeemorrrru
armour-bearer
aabeennrrstu
subterranean
aabeerrtttwy
water-battery
aabeffiilrtw
water-bailiff
aabefflortuw
water-buffalo
aabefgilrrry
irrefragably
aabefhlmnotu
unfathomable
aabefiilnops
saponifiable
aabefiilnqtu
quantifiable
aabefilllnot
flabellation
aabefllmmnno
non-flammable
aabeflmorrru
farm-labourer
aabeflnoruuv
unfavourable
aabeggillntu
agglutinable
aabeghiknort
oath-breaking
aabeghiknrtt
breathtaking
aabeghimnttw
bantam-weight
aabeghimoprr
iambographer
aabeghinnrsw
weaning-brash
aabeghlltwwy
wag-by-the-wall
aabegiilmnnu
unimaginable
aabegikkmnst
basket-making
aabegilnnssu
unassignable
aabegimnrrtt
battering-ram
aabeglmmoprr
programmable

aabehilnqsuv
vanquishable
aabehilorstu
authorisable
aabehinrrstt
shatter-brain
aabeiiillnty
alienability
aabeiilllmty
malleability
aabeiillmnss
Sabellianism
aabeiillmrst
bilateralism
aabeiillorst
isobilateral
aabeiillrtty
alterability
aabeiilprrty
reparability
aabeiilprsty
separability
aabeiilrrrst
barristerial
aabeiinoorss
anaerobiosis
aabeiklmnstu
unmistakable
aabeillnrrtu
turbellarian
aabeilmmrsuy
immeasurably
aabeilnprrst
transpirable
aabeinssttu
substantiate
aabelmmnostu
somnambulate
aabelmnrsttu
transmutable
aabelmnrsuuy
unmeasurably
aabelmoprrtu
perambulator
aabelnnorsuy
unreasonably
aabelnnossuy
unseasonably
aabelnnrsttu
subalternant
aabelnnrsuwy
unanswerably
aabelnoprsst
transposable
aabelnsttuu
unstatutable
aabffglorssu
buffalo-grass
aabfhlmnotuy
unfathomably
aabfiillmmty
flammability
aabfiilnorrt
infraorbital

aabfllmnotyy
flamboyantly
aabflmnortuu
funambulator
aabflnoruuvy
unfavourably
aabghiinnrsw
brainwashing
aabgiiilnouv
bougainvilia
aabgiiilntvy
navigability
aabgiillnory
aboriginally
aabgiillnrtz
trail-blazing
aabgiilmnnuy
unimaginably
aabgilnorsuv
labour-saving
aabgilnrsstt
star-blasting
aabhiiilnott
habilitation
aabhiiilrssz
bilharziasis
aabhiiinnott
inhabitation
aabhiilnnrty
labyrinthian
aabhiiloopru
ailurophobia
aabhinorrstu
subarrhation
aabhinossttu
subhastation
aabiiilmntuy
unamiability
aabiiilnosst
assibilation
aabiiinqrtuu
ubiquitarian
aabiillnstuy
unsalability
aabiilnnnttu
tintinnabula
aabiilnoorty
abolitionary
aabiilorsstt
stabilisator
aabiinnorstu
urbanisation
aabiinoorrst
arborisation
aabiklmnstuy
unmistakably
aabillmrsuxy
submaxillary
aabillnosttu
blastulation
aabilnsssttu
substantials
aabilnssttuv
substantival

aabiloprrstu
supra-orbital
aabimnorsttu
masturbation
aabinooprrty
probationary
aabllmmosuxy
xylobalsamum
aablmmnnostu
somnambulant
aablmmnorsuy
somnambulary
aablmnrsttuy
transmutably
aablnstttuuy
unstatutably
aablorrrstuy
barratrously
aabmnnoottuw
man-about-town
aaccceehiltt
catechetical
aaccceennptu
unacceptance
aacccegnoryy
gynaecocracy
aaccceehirstt
catachrestic
aacccchilnoop
cacophonical
aacccciossttu
catacoustics
aaccddehiirs
disaccharide
aaccddhhnoor
doch-an-dorach
aaccddiillty
didactically
aaccddiiottu
autodidactic
aaccddinorst
disaccordant
aaccdeefhhtt
hatchet-faced
aaccdeehhiks
sick-headache
aaccdeeiinov
Vaccinoideae
aaccdefilstu
fasciculated
aaccdehhprru
church-parade
aaccdehilmot
machicolated
aaccdehiltxy
hexadactylic
aaccdehnorry
archdeaconry
aaccdeiiilnt
dialectician
aaccdeiilopt
apodeictical
aaccdeillnty
accidentally

aaccdeilmort
democratical
aaccdeiloops
Scolopacidae
aaccdeinntuv
unvaccinated
aaccdeirtuuv
curvicaudate
aaccdekmpuuv
vacuum-packed
aaccdellnrsu
Della-Cruscan
aaccdellntuu
uncalculated
aaccdenoprty
pedantocracy
aaccdginrrry
card-carrying
aaccdhiopsuy
pachydacious
aaccdiilnotu
claudication
aaccdiioprtt
catadioptric
aaccdillltyy
dactylically
aaccdlloorry
dollarocracy
aaccdlmortyy
macrodactyly
aaccdmmooort
accommodator
aacceeehipry
Hypericaceae
aacceeeilrtv
accelerative
aacceeekllns
alkalescence
aacceehilnnp
anencephalic
aacceehirrst
characterise
aacceehmpprr
camp-preacher
aacceehnopyy
Cyanophyceae
aacceeiillpr
capercaillie
aacceeiilprz
capercailzie
aacceeilnort
acceleration
aacceeilpstt
space-lattice
aacceeilrrtt
recalcitrate
aacceekllnsy
alkalescency
aacceelmmntu
calceamentum
aacceelorrty
acceleratory
aacceelprrtu
receptacular

aacceenrsstu
accurateness
aacceffrrstu
surface-craft
aaccefgiknrs
safe-cracking
aaccefillory
Calyciflorae
aacceghiilpr
archipelagic
aacceghilmor
agrochemical
aaccehhiilrr
hierarchical
aaccehiimnrv
vice-chairman
aaccehillmno
melancholiac
aaccehillmny
mechanically
aaccehilmnnu
unmechanical
aaccehilnort
anchoretical
aaccehilortt
theocratical
aaccehilprty
archetypical
aaccehilrrtt
tetrarchical
aaccehimortt
metathoracic
aaccehimprtu
pharmaceutic
aaccehimrrst
characterism
aaccehlmnort
coal-merchant
aaccehlmntyy
calycanthemy
aaccehlmopry
macrocephaly
aacceiillnrt
anticlerical
aacceillmstu
miscalculate
aacceillnnot
cancellation
aacceillnoss
neoclassical
aacceilloppt
apoplectical
aacceillopsu
capillaceous
aacceillprss
preclassical
aacceillstty
ecstatically
aacceilmnops
complaisance
aacceilmtuuv
accumulative
aacceilnorvy
clairvoyance

aacceilnpsuu
Sipunculacea
aacceilnrrtt
recalcitrant
aacceilnrtuy
inaccurately
aacceilnttuy
accentuality
aacceinnorst
transoceanic
aacceinnottu
accentuation
aacceinoortv
coacervation
aaccelloorsu
corallaceous
aaccellrrsty
crystal-clear
aaccelnnoopv
plano-concave
aaccenoopsuy
apocynaceous
aaccfiiinopt
pacification
aaccfiioprty
pacificatory
aaccfiiorrst
scarificator
aaccghhiprty
tachygraphic
aaccghhlopry
chalcography
aaccghiillor
oligarchical
aaccghilopty
phagocytical
aaccghioprrt
cartographic
aaccgiilmort
tragi-comical
aaccgilloort
cartological
aaccgilloost
scatological
aacchhiilnor
Archilochian
aacchiiinrtt
antirachitic
aacchiilmsst
schismatical
aacchiilnort
anchoritical
aacchiilnott
anticatholic
aacchiinnnot
cachinnation
aacchiinrsty
saccharinity
aacchillosst
scholastical
aacchimnoprt
panchromatic
aacchimooprt
apochromatic

aacchinnorty
cachinnatory
aacchioprstt
catastrophic
aacchllnoryy
acronychally
aacchlrsttwy
watch-crystal
aacchopprsuy
pachycarpous
aacciiilpstt
capitalistic
aacciillssty
classicality
aacciilmortt
timocratical
aacciilmprst
practicalism
aacciilnrtuy
inarticulacy
aacciiloppr t
paroccipital
aacciilprstt
practicalist
aacciilprtty
practicality
aacciiorrstt
aristocratic
aacciirrsttu
caricaturist
aaccikkorsty
kakistocracy
aaccilllnovy
volcanically
aaccillnnoop
plano-conical
aaccillnoosy
occasionally
aaccillnorty
narcotically
aaccillorsty
Socratically
aaccillostuy
acoustically
aaccilmnnoot
conclamation
aaccilmnotuu
accumulation
aaccilmnpsuy
scapulimancy
aaccilmoprss
sarcoplasmic
aaccilnooptu
occupational
aaccimnopsty
accompanyist
aaccinoprsty
pantisocracy
aacciorrsttt
stratocratic
aacclmoostty
Cyclostomata
aaccoqrsttuy
squattocracy

aacdddeehlor
dodecahedral
aacddeeehlty
acetaldehyde
aacddeehklls
saddle-hackle
aacddegilloo
logodaedalic
aacddeginnoy
dodecagynian
aacddeiilnot
dedicational
aacddeiilort
dedicatorial
aacddeilmnnr
carnal-minded
aacddeiorrtx
dextrocardia
aacddiijnotu
adjudication
aacdeeeffint
decaffeinate
aacdeeehrrtt
earth-created
aacdeefhlmsy
shamefacedly
aacdeeghinrs
scare-heading
aacdeeghlnno
hendecagonal
aacdeehimstt
semi-attached
aacdeehinstz
Zantedeschia
aacdeeiiillpr
pedicellaria
aacdeeiilpst
decapitalise
aacdeeiklrtt
racket-tailed
aacdeeillnnr
calendar-line
aacdeeillprv
pedal-clavier
aacdeeilmmnt
medicamental
aacdeeilmrvy
devil-may-care
aacdeeilrttu
dearticulate
aacdeeimmssu
cuisse-madame
aacdeeimnrtt
readmittance
aacdeeinoprs
Scorpaenidae
aacdeelnptty
pentadactyle
aacdeelnrstw
candle-waster
aacdegghirss
gas-discharge
aacdegillnnp
landing-place

aacdegilloop
paedological
aacdegilmnoy
geodynamical
aacdegilnotu
longicaudate
aacdegilpqru
quadraplegic
aacdeginnprs
parascending
aacdeglnotuu
uncatalogued
aacdehhimort
Hemichordata
aacdehiilopp
paedophiliac
aacdehiinnrt
cantharidine
aacdehilllry
heraldically
aacdehimnrty
diathermancy
aacdehlmosuy
achlamydeous
aacdehloprrt
procathedral
aacdehlorrtt
tetrachordal
aacdehnoppru
unapproached
aacdeiiiprst
parasiticide
aacdeiilmnos
Laodiceanism
aacdeiilmntu
adminiculate
aacdeiilnort
dilaceration
aacdeiilnrtu
clairaudient
aacdeiinnort
deracination
aacdeiinoptt
decapitation
aacdeiinottv
deactivation
aacdeiiossst
disassociate
aacdeijlltvy
adjectivally
aacdeillmnoy
demoniacally
aacdeillnosw
disallowance
aacdeillnpty
pedantically
aacdeillprry
dicarpellary
aacdeilmmort
melodramatic
aacdeilnppru
appendicular
aacdeimnorsy
aerodynamics

aacdeimoostu
diatomaceous
aacdeinnossy
Ascension-day
aacdeinnqtuu
unacquainted
aacdeinopssu
sapindaceous
aacdeinosstu
unassociated
aacdelllnotw
tallow-candle
aacdellorsty
sacerdotally
aacdelnpttyy
pentadactyly
aacdelpprstu
custard-apple
aacdelrtttyy
tetradactyly
aacdfgilnnrt
landing-craft
aacdfiiilnnt
infanticidal
aacdghhooprt
cathodograph
aacdghiioprr
radiographic
aacdghilnnpu
launching-pad
aacdghilnnrs
crash-landing
aacdghilnnty
land-yachting
aacdghinnsty
sand-yachting
aacdghioprry
cardiography
aacdghorrrss
orchard-grass
aacdgiilloor
radiological
aacdgiilloou
audiological
aacdgillmoty
dogmatically
aacdhiilnprs
cardinalship
aacdhiimnoor
orchidomania
aacdhimnoort
machairodont
aacdhinopqru
quadraphonic
aacdiiinortv
divarication
aacdiillmopt
diplomatical
aacdiillnoty
diatonically
aacdiilmnost
disclamation
aacdiilnnrty
tyrannicidal

aacdiilnostt
donatistical
aacdiimnrstu
Traducianism
aacdiinnorrt
doctrinarian
aacdiinorsst
dracontiasis
aacdiinrsttu
Traducianist
aacdillnorsy
sardonically
aacdillnstyy
dynastically
aacdilloprsy
sporadically
aacdilnoprty
trypanocidal
aacdimmnoort
monodramatic
aacdimooprss
radio-compass
aacdjlmooqru
Jacquard-loom
aacdllnossuy
scandalously
aacdmnooppru
para-compound
aaceeeeginrs
Gesneriaceae
aaceeeehnnpt
Nepenthaceae
aaceeeeiqstu
Equisetaceae
aaceeefgirrr
carriage-free
aaceeegilnrt
angelica-tree
aaceeehhoppy
Phaeophyceae
aaceeeillovz
Velloziaceae
aaceeeirrstt
secretariate
aaceeelnortt
Coelenterata
aaceeffinott
affectionate
aaceefgiorrr
forecarriage
aaceefrrstuw
surface-water
aaceeggillno
genealogical
aaceeghillnt
genethliacal
aaceeghinnrr
carragheenin
aaceeghinort
archegoniate
aaceeghinpst
space-heating
aaceeghnprtx
part-exchange

aaceegilnrrv
vicar-general
aaceegllpttu
cattle-plague
aaceeglmortt
galactometer
aaceeglnoopy
Polygonaceae
aaceehhrrttw
weather-chart
aaceehiilprt
perichaetial
aaceehiinstt
aesthetician
aaceehilmttt
metathetical
aaceehiloprt
choripetalae
aaceehimnort
etheromaniac
aaceehimnttx
exanthematic
aaceehintttu
authenticate
aaceehkmnrrs
snake-charmer
aaceehlmprst
chapelmaster
spermathecal
aaceehlnnnst
channel-stane
aaceehlnpttu
pentateuchal
aaceehlppssw
cashew-apples
aaceehmnrttt
reattachment
aaceehnnppst
happenstance
aaceeiilmstt
metasilicate
aaceeiilprst
recapitalise
aaceeiinrsst
sectarianise
aaceeiipprtv
appreciative
aaceeillmptt
metaleptical
aaceeillmstt
telesmatical
aaceeilmpprs
pre-eclampsia
aaceeilnorrt
recreational
aaceeilprstx
extra-special
aaceeilprttu
recapitulate
aaceeimnorru
Euro-American
aaceeinprsst
paracentesis

aaceeioprstt
ectoparasite
aaceeiorsttw
waistcoateer
aaceeirrrrtw
water-carrier
aaceelllnoty
lanceolately
aaceelnrrtux
extranuclear
aaceennpprtu
appurtenance
aaceennprrst
transparence
aaceennprrtt
carpenter-ant
aaceenprrssu
preassurance
aaceeorrrttw
water-reactor
aaceffilrstv
slave-traffic
aaceffmorttt
matter-of-fact
aacefgmnnorr
Franco-German
aacefhinpssu
saucepan-fish
aacefiiilttv
facilitative
aacefinosstu
assuefaction
aacefiorrstu
surface-to-air
aacefmnrrtuu
manufacturer
aacefmrrsstt
craftsmaster
aacegghiinnr
chain-gearing
aacegghilopr
geographical
aaceghhimorr
haemorrhagic
aaceghhprrty
tachygrapher
aaceghilloot
atheological
aaceghillprr
calligrapher
aaceghimnopr
anemographic
phanerogamic
aaceghimoptt
apothegmatic
aaceghlnnstv
canvas-length
aaceghmmopry
Myrmecophaga
aaceghmoprry
ceramography
aaceghnoopry
oceanography

aaceghoprrrt
cartographer
aacegiiinrrt
geriatrician
aacegiillnnt
geanticlinal
aacegiillnrt
interglacial
aacegiilloot
aetiological
aacegiilprrs
slip-carriage
aacegiimmprt
epigrammatic
aacegiimmrst
grammaticise
aacegiklnppr
parking-place
aacegiknpppr
packing-paper
aacegillmnry
Germanically
aacegillmnty
magnetically
aacegillnosu
gallinaceous
aacegillnrtw
watering-call
aacegilloopt
apologetical
aacegillorsu
argillaceous
aacegillorty
categorially
aacegilmorst
gasometrical
aacegilnrsst
tragicalness
aacegilnrtuw
caterwauling
aacegimnorsu
graminaceous
aaceginnoort
octogenarian
aaceginoprry
pony-carriage
aaceginpprrt
tracing-paper
aacegllopssw
scapegallows
aaceglnoopsv
galvanoscope
aaceglnorttu
congratulate
aaceglrrstyz
crystal-gazer
aacegmnostyy
gynaecomasty
aacehhhmoprt
rhamphotheca
aacehhiilmop
haemophiliac
aacehhiloprz
Rhizocephala

aacehiillopt
palaeolithic
aacehiilmprx
alexipharmic
aacehiilmrtt
arithmetical
aacehiilnttt
antithetical
aacehiiloprs
parochialise
aacehiimmnns
Manicheanism
aacehiinpttt
antipathetic
aacehijlmmpr
clamjamphrie
aacehillltty
athletically
aacehillmpty
emphatically
aacehillmtty
thematically
aacehillprsy
seraphically
aacehillptty
pathetically
aacehillrtty
theatrically
aacehilmnnor
enharmonical
aacehilmnpru
alphanumeric
aacehilmoprt
metaphorical
aacehilmpsty
metaphysical
aacehilnopst
sphacelation
aacehilqrrsu
squirearchal
aacehilrsttt
tetrastichal
aacehimprstt
metaphrastic
aacehioprsst
cataphoresis
aacehllooprr
rhopaloceral
aacehmnnrstu
transhumance
aacehmnorrst
march-treason
stream-anchor
aacehmoprrsy
hypersarcoma
aacehmorrrty
charter-mayor
aacehnoprrty
narcotherapy
aacehprrrtty
charterparty
aaceiiinpttv
anticipative
aaceiillmmnt
Macmillanite
aaceiilnopps
episcopalian
aaceiilnprtt
antiparticle
aaceiilnrttu
inarticulate
aaceiimnnopt
emancipation
aaceiimnorst
racemisation
aaceiimnrsst
Cartesianism
sectarianism
aaceiinnnott
incatenation
aaceiinnntuv
annunciative
aaceiinopprt
appreciation
aaceiinorttv
reactivation
aaceiinprstt
pancreatitis
aaceiinrsstv
incrassative
aaceijkrsttt
strait-jacket
aaceijllmsty
majestically
aaceiklmnopt
kleptomaniac
aaceillllmty
metallically
aaceilllprty
prelatically
aaceillmmtuy
immaculately
aaceillmnoty
noematically
aaceillmnsty
semantically
aaceillnoort
reallocation
aaceillnoprr
procellarian
aaceillnopst
pleonastical
aaceillnprtu
unprelatical
aaceillnptuy
paniculately
aaceilloprty
operatically
aaceillrttuy
articulately
aaceilmmnort
manometrical
aaceilmmrsty
asymmetrical
aaceilmnostu
emasculation
aaceilmsstty
systematical
aaceilnnoptt
placentation
aaceilnoprtu
precautional
aaceilnosstv
vacationless
aaceilnrttuu
unarticulate
aaceiloprstt
spectatorial
aaceilrtttvy
attractively
aaceimnnoopt
companionate
aaceimnpprst
panspermatic
aaceinopsstt
space-station
aaceinrtttuv
unattractive
aaceiopprrty
appreciatory
aaceioprrrtv
prevaricator
aacejklnnort
Jack-o'-lantern
aacekllmnost
salmon-tackle
aaceknnorstu
cantankerous
aacellllorty
collaterally
aacellnrruvy
vernacularly
aacelloosssu
salsolaceous
aacellorrsst
cross-lateral
aacelmnoppss
compass-plane
aacelmorstuy
emasculatory
aacelnorrssu
oracularness
aacelnprrsuu
supernacular
aacelppprrty
claptrappery
aacemmnrsstu
crassamentum
aacemnoorstt
Entomostraca
aacennprrsty
transparency
aacenorrrtuv
averruncator
aacfgiiinost
gasification
aacfgiillmny
magnifically
aacfhimnprst
craftmanship
aacfiiiilnrt
inartificial
aacfiiillrty
artificially
aacfiiilnnst
financialist
aacfiiilnopt
palification
aacfiiilnost
salification
aacfiiilnott
facilitation
aacfiiilnrtu
unartificial
aacfiiimnort
ramification
aacfiiinnopt
panification
aacfiiinortt
ratification
aacfiilllsvy
salvifically
aacfiilmnost
factionalism
aacfiilnostt
factionalist
aacfiiloqrtu
qualificator
aacfiimnsstt
fantasticism
aacfiinosstt
satisfaction
aacfilllosuy
fallaciously
aacfillnorty
fractionally
aacfilmorstt
stalactiform
aacfinoorrtt
fractionator
aacfiorsstty
satisfactory
aacgghhiiopr
hagiographic
aacgghiiilloo
hagiological
aacgghimnoty
gigantomachy
aacggiillnty
gigantically
aacggilmosty
mystagogical
aacghhoprrty
chartography
aacghilloopt
pathological
aacghilmopry
myographical
aacghilooprr
orographical
aacghilooprz
zoographical
aacghimnoprr
marconigraph

aacghimrttuu
thaumaturgic
aacghinopprt
pantographic
aacghlmoopry
pharmacology
aacghmmoorrt
chromatogram
aacghoopprsu
carpophagous
aacghooprssu
sarcophagous
aacghoopsstu
scatophagous
aacgiiknnott
action-taking
aacgiilnnorv
Carlovingian
aacgiilnortt
coat-trailing
aacgiilnrstt
strait-lacing
aacgiimmmrst
grammaticism
aacgiimmrrtt
trigrammatic
aacgiinnostt
antagonistic
aacgiinosttw
waistcoating
aacgijknorst
roasting-jack
aacgiklnqsuv
quacksalving
aacgillmoost
malacologist
aacgilloorst
astrological
aacgilloottu
tautological
aacgillrrtuu
agricultural
aacgilnrttty
attractingly
aacgimmoprrt
programmatic
aacgimnoprty
cryptogamian
aacginooprsu
angiocarpous
aacginopprtu
group-captain
aacglmoostuu
glaucomatous
aacglnnorttu
congratulant
aachhiilnpps
chaplainship
aachhiimnprs
chairmanship
aachhilmopty
hypothalamic
aachhinoortx
xanthochroia

aachhoopprst
approach-shot
aachiillnpsy
Hispanically
aachiilmnnor
inharmonical
aachiilmoprs
parochialism
aachiilnnopt
antiphonical
aachiiloorst
Aristolochia
aachiiloprty
parochiality
aachiimnoopt
potichomania
aachiimprrst
patriarchism
aachiinoprst
Aristophanic
aachiinprstt
antiphrastic
aachiinrrttt
antarthritic
aachillmnory
harmonically
aachilmmnoot
monothalamic
aachilmnorty
lachrymation
aachiloprrsu
scrophularia
aachilopstty
hypostatical
aachimmnnopy
nymphomaniac
aachimnoprrs
parachronism
aachimooprst
chromatopsia
aachimpprssy
parapsychism
aachinoprttu
naturopathic
aachirrsttuz
Zarathustric
aachllnnnoty
nonchalantly
aachlmmnoopy
omphalomancy
aachlmoppryy
polypharmacy
aachlmorrtyy
lachrymatory
aachnooprstu
anthocarpous
aaciiilnrstt
inartistical
aaciiinnoptt
anticipation
aaciiinnottv
inactivation
vaticination

aaciiinssttt
statistician
aaciiillopty
apolitically
aaciillmnosy
simoniacally
aaciillmnstu
animalculist
aaciillmotty
amitotically
aaciillnnott
cantillation
aaciillnoost
localisation
aaciillnosty
antisocially
aaciillppsty
papistically
aaciillrstty
artistically
aaciillsttuy
autistically
aaciilmmnopt
pantomimical
aaciilmmorss
commissarial
aaciilmnnotu
calumniation
aaciilmoprst
porismatical
aaciilnoostv
vocalisation
aaciilnopttu
capitulation
aaciilnorttu
articulation
aaciilnrsttu
naturalistic
aaciilorsttu
tralaticious
aaciilorsuvy
avariciously
aaciilprrsuy
supraciliary
aaciimmorsst
commissariat
marcatissimo
aaciimnosstu
causationism
aaciimotttuy
automaticity
aaciinnnnotu
annunciation
aaciinnnoost
canonisation
aaciinnorsst
incrassation
aaciinoprtty
anticipatory
aaciinossttu
causationist
aaciioorsstx
toxocariasis

aaciiopprrtt
participator
aacilllnopty
platonically
aacillmnorty
romantically
aacillmnosty
monastically
aacillmostuy
calamitously
aacillnnrtyy
tyrannically
aacillnootvy
vocationally
aacillnortty
cantillatory
aacilloorrty
oratorically
aacillopttuy
autoptically
aacillprrtuy
particularly
aacilmnnoopt
complanation
aacilmnnortu
unromantical
aacilmnooprt
proclamation
aacilmnoorst
astronomical
aacilmnortuy
calumniatory
aacilmopstty
asymptotical
aacilmorrttu
court-martial
matriculator
aacilnorsttu
claustration
aacilnosttuu
auscultation
aaciloprttuy
capitulatory
aacilorrttuy
articulatory
aacimnnoopwy
companion-way
aacimnooprst
paronomastic
aacimoorssst
sarcomatosis
aacinnoosttt
constatation
aacinoorrttt
tractoration
aacinorssttu
astronautics
aacioprrrtty
pyrotartaric
aacllnnortuy
connaturally
aaclmnoppsst
compass-plant

aaclmooprrty
proclamatory
aaclnnoprttu
contrapuntal
aaclnprsttyy
cryptanalyst
aaclorsttuuy
auscultatory
aadddeehlpss
saddle-shaped
aaddeeehhmmr
hammer-headed
aaddeeehlrtt
rattle-headed
aaddeefhilnt
life-and-death
aaddeefhrrtu
hard-featured
aaddeeghilnt
death-dealing
aaddeeghlssy
glassy-headed
aaddefhorruv
hard-favoured
aaddefinortu
defraudation
aaddeglloosu
logodaedalus
aaddegnopru
parade-ground
aaddeiimnrsw
Edwardianism
aaddeiinprrv
Pre-Dravidian
aaddeilllprs
saddle-pillar
aaddeinrrsst
standardiser
aaddellmnors
salmon-ladder
aaddelmmopry
lampadedromy
aaddgiiilnot
digladiation
aaddgiinorst
disgradation
aaddginnrstw
standard-wing
aaddiiilnopt
dilapidation
aaddiillnoty
additionally
aadeeefhlrst
false-hearted
aadeeeghlrrt
large-hearted
aadeeeghrrtt
great-hearted
aadeeegiprss
seaside-grape
aadeeegmmnnt
endamagement
aadeeehhrtvy
heavy-hearted

aadeeehnprst
reed-pheasant
aadeeenqsstu
adequateness
aadeeffnorrt
fore-and-after
aadeefhinrtt
faint-hearted
aadeegglmort
agglomerated
aadeeginrtuv
unvariegated
aadeegkmnrrt
market-garden
aadeehiirsst
radiesthesia
aadeehilnprt
plain-hearted
aadeehilnqru
harlequinade
aadeehimmstt
mathematised
aadeehisssty
dysaesthesia
aadeehlprssv
salver-shaped
aadeehqrrstu
headquarters
aadeeiilmmsv
mediaevalism
aadeeiilmstv
mediaevalist
aadeeiimnnrt
antemeridian
aadeeikllmnr
aldermanlike
aadeeilnqtuy
inadequately
aadeeilnrstu
denaturalise
aadeeimmnnrr
remainder-man
aadeeimmnnst
misdemeanant
aadeeimnrrtv
animadverter
aadeeimqstuv
desquamative
aadeeinoprst
endoparasite
aadeeinoprtu
deuteranopia
aadeeinpsstv
adaptiveness
aadeejlnnrtw
lantern-jawed
aadeelllnpru
unparalleled
aadeellnppru
unapparelled
aadeellrzzzz
razzle-dazzle
aadeelmnprtt
departmental

aadeelnrttuu
unadulterate
aadeemnnrtux
extra-mundane
aadeffiiilst
disaffiliate
aadeffiinort
diffareation
aadefgginrsu
safeguarding
aadefgilnort
deflagration
aadefgimnrrw
drawing-frame
aadefhiiprss
paradise-fish
aadefhinnotu
fountain-head
aadefilmorty
defamatorily
aadefilnorty
deflationary
aadeflnoosst
fast-and-loose
aadeggilnnst
landing-stage
aadegglnnrst
gangsterland
aadeghinnsty
Syngnathidae
aadeghioprrr
radiographer
aadeghiprssv
sharp-visaged
aadeghmnnnru
under-hangman
aadegiillnnp
plain-dealing
aadegiilpqru
quadriplegia
aadegiimmnst
diamagnetism
aadegilllrwy
wallydraigle
aadeginopprs
propagandise
aadeginpprrw
drawing-paper
aadeglnprsst
star-spangled
aadeglnrsttu
strangulated
aadegoprsttu
post-graduate
aadegqrrrtuu
quarter-guard
aadehiklmory
holidaymaker
aadehilloppy
Polyadelphia
aadehilmnprs
aldermanship
aadehilnorrt
enarthrodial

aadehinopprs
parasphenoid
aadehioprrty
radiotherapy
aadehnorstuy
thousand-year
aadeiiilnopp
Papilionidae
aadeiiilnost
idealisation
aadeiillnoty
ideationally
aadeiillntuv
antediluvial
aadeiillnuvv
vaudevillian
aadeiilmnnot
delamination
aadeiilmnrty
Lymantriidae
aadeiilnnost
desalination
aadeiilnnqru
quadriennial
aadeiilnntuv
antediluvian
aadeiilnortv
derivational
aadeiimnnntu
unmaintained
aadeiimnoprt
pteridomania
aadeiimnorst
maderisation
aadeiimnrstt
administrate
aadeiinnorw
Neo-Darwinian
aadeiinnorst
Tardenoisian
aadeiinoprst
deaspiration
aadeiklmnrtw
milk-and-water
aadeilnnnorr
noradrenalin
aadeilnnssuw
dunniewassal
aadeilnorttu
adulteration
aadeilnqrtuv
quadrivalent
aadeilnrtuvy
valetudinary
aadeimmnnopu
pandaemonium
aadeimnnnrtu
intramundane
aadeimnoqstu
desquamation
aadeinoprrux
paradoxurine
aadeinrrsttt
transit-trade

aadelmmnptuu
paludamentum
aadelmnnrtuu
ultramundane
aadelmoprrtu
armour-plated
aadelnnnpstu
sun-and-planet
aadelnnrsttu
untranslated
aademmoosttu
stomatodaeum
aademnnprsuu
supramundane
aademoqrstuy
desquamatory
aadffhlorrsw
flash-forward
aadfghilnnrt
farthingland
aadfinnoostu
soda-fountain
aadghiinprsu
guardianship
aadgiiimprrv
primigravida
aadgiilnnort
Darlingtonia
aadgiinnnors
Grandisonian
aadgillnppuy
applaudingly
aadgimnopprs
propagandism
aadgimrrsttu
dramaturgist
aadginopprst
propagandist
aadglooOprxy
paradoxology
aadhiiloppsy
diapophysial
aadhilnooprt
anthropoidal
aadhilnopsuy
diaphanously
aadiiilnnotv
invalidation
aadiiilnortv
divinatorial
aadiimnnoost
nomadisation
aadiimnnrstt
administrant
aadiinorrtty
traditionary
aadiirrsstuv
Stradivarius
aadilnopprst
post-prandial
aadiloorstvy
vasodilatory
aadimnpssttt
stand-pattism

aadinnorsttu
transudation
aadlmnnoruwy
laundry-woman
aadmnoqrsuuu
quadrumanous
aadnorrsttuy
transudatory
aaeeeekklltt
talkee-talkee
aaeeefhllnnv
heaven-fallen
aaeeegghrtuw
weather-gauge
aaeeeggirtvx
exaggerative
aaeeegglnnrt
agent-general
aaeeeghlmrtw
weather-gleam
aaeeehilsstt
telaesthesia
aaeeehimmsst
haematemesis
aaeeehinsstt
anaesthetise
aaeeehllprtt
plate-leather
aaeeehlnprst
elephant's-ear
aaeeehnpssty
pheasant's-eye
aaeeeikrrsst
seraskierate
aaeeeilprstt
tapsalteerie
aaeeeiprstvx
exasperative
aaeeemprsssu
passemeasure
aaeeemrrstuw
water-measure
aaeeenprssst
separateness
aaeefghrrsst
feather-grass
aaeefhhlrrst
father-lasher
aaeefhilrrtu
heart-failure
aaeefhlorssv
half-seas-over
aaeefhnoprtu
herpetofauna
aaeefhrssttv
harvest-feast
aaeefiilrrss
laisser-faire
aaeefiilrssz
laissez-faire
aaeefllppssu
self-applause
aaeegggllrt
raggle-taggle

aaeeggimnoss
agamogenesis
aaeeggimnrtv
gram-negative
aaeegginnrtu
guaranteeing
aaeegginortx
exaggeration
aaeeggllnssu
languageless
aaeeggorrtxy
exaggeratory
aaeeghhrrsst
sage-thrasher
aaeeghilnprt
tragelaphine
aaeeghilprsy
hyperalgesia
aaeeghinrstt
thereagainst
aaeeghinrstw
whereagainst
aaeeghlrsstw
weather-glass
aaeegiilmnps
Semi-Pelagian
aaeegiilnnps
palingenesia
aaeegiilnprt
patrilineage
aaeegiilnstu
Ustilagineae
aaeegiimnnry
aye-remaining
aaeegiklmnrs
leasing-maker
aaeegilmnnot
antilegomena
aaeegimnoprs
Angiospermae
aaeegimnttuv
augmentative
aaeegimpsstu
Septuagesima
aaeegimrsstw
semiwater-gas
aaeeginnstux
exsanguinate
aaeeginprstx
exasperating
aaeeginrsstv
asseverating
aaeegjlmnorr
major-general
aaeegknoorrt
tree-kangaroo
aaeeglmnortv
galvanometer
aaeeglnnprwy
Penang-lawyer
aaeeglnooptt
goat-antelope
aaeegloprsss
opera-glasses

aaeeglrrrtux
extra-regular
aaeegmnopssy
passage-money
aaeegmrrrstt
garret-master
aaeegnprsswy
way-passenger
aaeegnprstuy
septuagenary
aaeehhimprtt
amphitheatre
aaeehhmnrstw
what's-her-name
aaeehhorrttt
heart-to-heart
aaeehiiknsst
kinaesthesia
aaeehiilrtvx
exhilarative
aaeehiimprst
hemiparasite
aaeehilmnnop
phaeomelanin
aaeehiloprst
heteroplasia
aaeehilprstu
laureateship
aaeehinnrstu
neurasthenia
aaeehinpprrt
heir-apparent
aaeehinrsttw
weather-stain
aaeehinsssty
synaesthesia
aaeehinssttt
anaesthetist
aaeehkmnrrss
harness-maker
aaeehlopptxy
heat-apoplexy
aaeehlstuuvx
exhaust-value
aaeehmnorsuw
warehouseman
aaeehmoorstt
Heterosomata
aaeehmssttux
exhaust-steam
aaeehprrsttw
sprat-weather
aaeeiikklltw
walkie-talkie
aaeeiillmrss
Marseillaise
aaeeiillrttv
alliterative
aaeeiilmnttv
alimentative
aaeeiilmortv
ameliorative
aaeeiimprsst
semiparasite

aaeeiinnrrtv
veterinarian
aaeeilllprsw
parallelwise
aaeeilllrrss
laisser-aller
aaeeilllrssz
laissez-aller
aaeeillmnpst
planetesimal
aaeeillnortv
revelational
aaeeillprstt
septilateral
aaeeilmnrsst
materialness
aaeeilmorrst
alstroemeria
aaeeilnorrtt
re-alteration
aaeeilnorstt
Aristotelean
aaeeilnorstu
teleosaurian
aaeeilnprsst
pleasantries
aaeeilnprstw
water-spaniel
aaeeilnsstvx
laxativeness
aaeeiloprrtt
proletariate
aaeeilqrsstu
sesquialtera
aaeeimnpprst
appraisement
aaeeinnnortx
re-annexation
aaeeinoprstx
exasperation
aaeeinorsstv
asseveration
aaeeinpprrst
paper-stainer
aaeejkmmnrtz
katzenjammer
aaeekmnprrtt
pattern-maker
aaeekmqrrstu
market-square
aaeellnprrty
parenterally
aaeelmmnrttt
maltreatment
aaeelmnprsst
malapertness
aaeelmnprstt
saltpetreman
aaeelnnpssst
pleasantness
aaeelorsstyy
araeosystyle
aaeelpqrrttu
quarter-plate

aaeemnnpprsw
newspaperman
aaeemnrsttty
testamentary
aaeemprsssuy
passy-measure
aaeennossstu
assentaneous
aaeennpprsst
apparentness
aaeennprstuu
superannuate
aaeerrrsttuu
restaurateur
aaeffiimnorr
Foraminifera
aaeffqrrsttu
quarter-staff
aaefghhiilnt
faith-healing
aaefghllnnpr
flannelgraph
aaefgilllnot
flagellation
aaefginnortt
engraftation
aaefginrrtuw
fugie-warrant
aaefgiprttuy
fatigue-party
aaefglllorty
flagellatory
aaefgnnrrsst
fragrantness
aaefhilmnsss
fish-salesman
aaefhilnopst
fashion-plate
aaefhilnrstw
fathers-in-law
aaefillnsssy
self-analysis
aaefilnorrty
reflationary
aaefilnprtvy
trypaflavine
aaefilnqrrtu
quarter-final
aaefimrssttu
mutessarifat
aaeflloprrsv
self-approval
aaeflnoqrrtu
quartern-loaf
aaegghhioprr
hagiographer
aaegghlnnrsw
slang-whanger
aaegghmnoprt
magnetograph
aaegghnoprst
steganograph
aaeggiimnrrr
marriage-ring

aaeggiimnrrs
gregarianism
aaeggiinoprt
arpeggiation
aaeggllnorry
organ-gallery
aaeghhopprrs
phraseograph
aaeghiilnrtx
exhilarating
aaeghiknqrtu
earthquaking
aaeghimmnpss
gamesmanship
aaeghimmorrt
hierogrammat
aaeghimnrrtw
heart-warming
aaeghimorrrt
metrorrhagia
aaeghinpprsw
paper-washing
aaeghknoprru
keraunograph
aaeghlmnrstu
manslaughter
slaughterman
aaeghlmoppry
ampelography
aaeghloprttu
Telautograph®
aaeghmnoopsu
phaenogamous
aaeghmnosttu
metagnathous
aaeghmnottuy
thaumatogeny
aaeghnopprrt
pantographer
aaeghoopprrv
evaporograph
aaegiillnost
legalisation
aaegiilmnort
emigrational
aaegiilnnott
gelatination
aaegiimnnort
emargination
aaegiimnnrsw
Wagnerianism
aaegiinnpprt
appertaining
aaegiinnpstv
vase-painting
aaegillnntty
tangentially
aaegilmnoprs
angiospermal
aaegilmnppuz
pulp-magazine
aaegilnnprtv
vinegar-plant

aaegilnpsttu
Septuagintal
aaegimmnnprs
Pan-Germanism
aaegimnnottu
augmentation
aaegimnrrrtu
ring-armature
aaegimnrrstt
transmigrate
aaegimnrsttx
taxing-master
aaegimnsttty
syntagmatite
aaegimrrsttu
magistrature
aaeginnopttv
vantage-point
aaeginorsstu
stegosaurian
aaeginprrttw
water-parting
aaegkllmorsw
gallows-maker
aaegllnnopty
pentagonally
aaegllnppprt
grapple-plant
aaeglmnortvy
galvanometry
aaeglmoopssu
gamosepalous
aaeglmoopstu
gamopetalous
aaeglmorssuu
megalosaurus
aaegmoppsstt
postage-stamp
aaehhilmoptx
exophthalmia
aaehhimnsstw
what's-his-name
aaehhimrrrrs
marsh-harrier
aaehhinnopst
phonasthenia
aaehiiilnntv
annihilative
aaehiilmmptu
epithalamium
aaehiilmnopt
epithalamion
aaehiilnortx
exhilaration
aaehiinopstt
hepatisation
aaehiknosttv
stakhanovite
aaehillnnnpy
phenylalanin
aaehilmmrstu
rheumatismal
aaehilmnotxy
haematoxylin

aaehilmnpsss
salesmanship
aaehilmossty
haematolysis
aaehilmrstuy
amateurishly
aaehilnnoprt
paranthelion
aaehilnnrstt
transleithan
aaehilorrtxy
exhilaratory
aaehimmrsstu
shamateurism
aaehimnnortu
mountain-hare
aaehimnnsssu
haussmannise
aaehimnorsty
hysteromania
aaehimnprstw
watermanship
aaehimnssttw
what's-its-name
aaehinnoptty
enantiopathy
aaehinopprst
Siphonaptera
aaehinopssty
enhypostasia
aaehlmnootxy
haematoxylon
aaehlnprsttw
shawl-pattern
aaehmmnooprt
Nematomorpha
aaehmoorsttu
atheromatous
aaehnoprstty
Thysanoptera
aaehoppprssy
parapophyses
aaeiiilmsstv
assimilative
aaeiiimmnrss
semi-Arianism
aaeiillmmrty
immaterially
aaeiillmnrtx
intermaxilla
aaeiillmrttx
extra-limital
aaeiillnoqtu
illaqueation
aaeiillnortt
alliteration
aaeiillnpstu
sinupalliate
aaeiilmnnott
alimentation
aaeiilmnnrrt
interlaminar
aaeiilmnoort
amelioration

aaeiilmnptuv
manipulative
aaeiilmoprrt
imperatorial
aaeiilmrttuv
multivariate
aaeiilnnopst
penalisation
aaeiilnoprst
epistolarian
aaeiilnoqstu
equalisation
aaeiilnorstt
Aristotelian
laterisation
aaeiilnorstv
velarisation
aaeiilnprstt
interspatial
aaeiimnopsst
impassionate
aaeiinnosttt
tetanisation
aaeiinoprrtt
repatriation
aaeiinoprttx
expatriation
aaeiinqtttuv
quantitative
aaeilllmrttu
multilateral
aaeilllnorty
relationally
aaeilllnrtuy
unilaterally
aaeillmnnsuy
semi-annually
aaeillmnrrty
artillery-man
aaeillmprrxy
premaxillary
aaeillnntttw
tenant-at-will
aaeillnorsty
senatorially
aaeilloqrtuy
equatorially
aaeillppsuvy
applausively
aaeillqrsstu
quasi-stellar
aaeilmmnnotu
mountain-meal
aaeilmnorstv
malversation
aaeilmnpssux
pansexualism
aaeilmnrsstt
mistranslate
aaeilnnopptt
pentapolitan
aaeilnnoprtt
replantation

aaeilnnopttx
explantation
aaeilnnqttuv
quantivalent
aaeilnnrstuu
unnaturalise
aaeilnoprttt
tetrapolitan
aaeilnopsstu
antisepalous
aaeilnopssty
passionately
aaeilnopsttu
antipetalous
aaeilnopstzz
Pestalozzian
aaeilnorsttw
law-stationer
aaeilnppsuuv
unapplausive
aaeilnpsstux
pansexualist
aaeilnrssstu
salutariness
aaeilorrsttt
latirostrate
aaeimmmosstt
metasomatism
aaeimnoooopt
onomatopoeia
aaeinnoprsxy
expansionary
aaeinnopsstu
unpassionate
aaeinnorsstu
Austronesian
aaeinoprrstu
pterosaurian
aaeinoqrstuy
quaestionary
aaeinpprrstw
water-parsnip
aaeiooprrstt
root-parasite
aaeklmorrtww
low-watermark
aaeklnnooprt
aeroplankton
aaekloprstty
keratoplasty
aaeknorrsttt
stratotanker
aaellmnnorty
ornamentally
aaellnnpstuy
unpleasantly
aaellnoprstt
entoplastral
aaellnrsstuu
ultrasensual
aaelmnnnortu
unornamental
aaelmnnorttu
ultramontane

aaelmnooprtt
protonematal
aaelmooprstz
spermatozoal
aaelnnooprty
pantaloonery
aaelnnprrstt
transplanter
aaelnnprstuy
unpleasantry
aaelnprrstuu
supernatural
aaelnrssstttw
stalwartness
aaelooprrttx
extrapolator
aaemnnnorstt
transmontane
aaemnnoortuy
neuroanatomy
aaemnooprstz
spermatozoan
aaemnoprsttu
portmanteaus
aaemnoprttux
portmanteaux
aaemoorstttu
teratomatous
aaemoossttu
steatomatous
aaemqrrrstuy
quarrymaster
aaeopprssttu
passe-partout
aaeoprrrsstw
parrot-wrasse
aaeoprrrttty
pyrotartrate
aaffgiklnstw
walking-staff
aaffgillnnsy
snaffling-lay
aafghinnprst
span-farthing
aafgiklmnnor
frankalmoign
aafiiilnrttu
futilitarian
aafiillmnruy
unfamiliarly
aafiilmmnnot
inflammation
aafiilnnorty
inflationary
aafillmmnotu
flammulation
aafilmmnoort
malformation
aafilmmnorty
inflammatory
aafilmnnotux
mountain-flax
aagghnoopprry
organography

aaggiiinnrtt
ingratiating
aaggiikllnss
galligaskins
aaggikllnrss
larking-glass
aaggiknqrssu
quaking-grass
aaggnnoortuu
ourang-outang
aaghhiinorrr
rhinorrhagia
aaghhmnooprr
harmonograph
aaghiinnnort
nothingarian
aaghiinnostw
washingtonia
aaghilmoorty
hamartiology
aaghimooprst
Mastigophora
aaghinoppstt
pantophagist
aaghiprrstty
stratigraphy
aaghirssttwy
straightways
aaghllmoopsu
mallophagous
aaghloopprry
polarography
aaghmrsttuuu
thaumaturgus
aaghnooppstu
pantophagous
aaghoopprssu
saprophagous
aagiiilnorrt
irrigational
aagiiinnnotv
invagination
aagiillnnptw
wall-painting
aagiilnnrsuy
sanguinarily
aagiimnnotww
waiting-woman
aagiinnoorst
organisation
aagiinnortuu
inauguration
aagiklnrstww
walking-straw
aagillmntuwy
mulligatawny
aagillnrrtuy
triangularly
aagilnnsstwy
slantingways
aagilnorsttu
gastrulation
aagilooprsty
parasitology

aagimnnrrstt
transmigrant
aaginnoosttw
station-wagon
aaginorrtuuy
inauguratory
aagllnoopstt
stoop-gallant
aaglmnoprssy
laryngospasm
aaglmoorttuy
traumatology
aagoprrrsssw
sparrow-grass
aahhiimrrstt
hamarthritis
aahhinnnottx
anthoxanthin
aahhiopprstu
phosphaturia
aahhlmopstuy
hypothalamus
aahiiiillopru
ailurophilia
aahiiilnnnot
annihilation
aahiilmnortu
inhalatorium
aahiimnnostu
humanisation
aahiimopprss
paraphimosis
aahiinopstxy
asphyxiation
aahiinpprsst
partisanship
aahiinprrstt
panarthritis
aahikmnosstv
Stakhanovism
aahillmoprsx
morphallaxis
aahillnnopty
antiphonally
aahilloprstx
trophallaxis
aahilmnooprt
prothalamion
aahimmopprrs
paramorphism
aahimnooprss
anamorphosis
aahioppprssy
parapophysis
aahlmnoprsuy
orphan-asylum
aahlnorrstuy
anarthrously
aahmnoosttux
xanthomatous
aahmoqrrssuw
marrow-squash

aaiiilmnosst
assimilation
Islamisation
aaiiilmprtty
impartiality
aaiiilnnostv
insalivation
aaiiilnosttv
visitational
vitalisation
aaiiilorsttv
visitatorial
aaiiimnnrstu
unitarianism
aaiiimnosstv
avitaminosis
aaiiinnnostt
insanitation
aaiiinnosstt
sanitisation
aaiiinorsttv
variationist
aaiillmosstt
altaltissimo
aaiillnnostt
installation
aaiillnoottv
volitational
aaiillnorrty
irrationally
aaiilmnnoptt
implantation
aaiilmnnoptu
manipulation
aaiilmnoorst
moralisation
aaiilmnoottv
motivational
aaiilmnosstv
salvationism
aaiilnnorstt
transitional
aaiilnooppst
appositional
aaiilnooprst
polarisation
aaiilnoorsst
solarisation
aaiilnoorstv
valorisation
aaiilnoosttt
totalisation
aaiilnorrstu
ruralisation
aaiilnossttv
salvationist
aaiilorstttu
tralatitious
aaiimnnoorst
Romanisation
aaiimnoorstt
amortisation
aaiinnnnostu
antoninianus

aaiinnoqsttu
quantisation
aaiinnorsttu
instauration
aaiinooprstv
vaporisation
aaillmnoprtt
all-important
aaillmoprtyy
morality-play
aaillorsttuy
salutatorily
aailmnoprtuy
manipulatory
aailmoorrstu
Mariolatrous
aailoorssttu
saltatorious
aaimnnoopstu
mountain-soap
aaimnnrrstuu
transuranium
aainorssttuu
Titanosaurus
aaiooppprrrt
appropriator
aaklnnnnoopt
nanoplankton
aaklnorssuuy
Ankylosaurus
aallmoopprst
protoplasmal
aalmoorrstuy
Maryolatrous
abbbbbbeeill
bibble-babble
abbbbeeggill
gibble-gabble
abbbbeeillrr
ribble-rabble
abbbceilrssu
subscribable
abbbcelnnory
bonny-clabber
abbbdeloryzz
bobby-dazzler
abbbeelmrrry
bramble-berry
abbbehlmortu
blabbermouth
abbbginrrssu
brass-rubbing
abbbhiiiloop
bibliophobia
abbcceghimno
beachcombing
abbcdeehimrr
bride-chamber
abbcdeekknor
broken-backed
abbcdgiiklnr
blackbirding
abbceeggklru
buckle-beggar

abbceeklnoss
backboneless
abbceenortuy
abbey-counter
abbcefhilmnr
bramble-finch
abbceghinntu
nubbing-cheat
abbceikrrstu
rabbit-sucker
abbcelooorrr
corroborable
abbddeeklnou
double-banked
abbdeeeginrt
bate-breeding
abbdeeflorss
self-absorbed
abbdehiilrsy
hybridisable
abbdeillmrru
umbrella-bird
abbdelllnruy
land-lubberly
abbdelnortty
brandy-bottle
abbdenorrssu
brass-bounder
abbdffiilnou
bound-bailiff
abbdhikoorty
birthday-book
abbdilmoopss
bomb-disposal
abbdiloorrst
Bristol-board
abbeeeelmmrr
rememberable
abbeeeillnuv
unbelievable
abbeeelmmrry
rememberably
abbeeelnrttu
unbetterable
abbeegmnorrr
barber-monger
abbeeillnuvy
unbelievably
abbeeilnorsv
inobservable
abbeeilopqru
equiprobable
abbeeilrrttu
irrebuttable
abbeelmnorst
stone-bramble
abbeelnorsuv
unobservable
abbeelorrrsu
rabble-rouser
abbeelrrstuv
subvertebral
abbefflorruy
buffalo-berry

abbegiinnott
babingtonite
abbehiimnoss
Hobbesianism
abbellmrrsuu
subumbrellar
abbghiilopry
bibliography
abbiilnnootu
obnubilation
abccceehmnoy
come-by-chance
abccchoooptu
tobacco-pouch
abcccinnotuy
concubitancy
abccdeeelpst
bespectacled
abccdeehilnn
blanc-de-Chine
abccdeehkklu
huckle-backed
abccdeehkorr
checker-board
abccdehiloru
coachbuilder
abccdehlmoru
cloud-chamber
abccdghiinrt
bird-catching
abccdilnooru
council-board
abccdkloruzz
buzzard-clock
abcceeelnort
concelebrate
abcceeenorrs
arborescence
abcceeginnru
buccaneering
abcceehinrsu
buccaneerish
abcceeiilnss
inaccessible
abcceeillnor
reconcilable
abcceelnnort
concelebrant
abcceelorrsu
clare-obscure
clear-obscure
abcceemnnrru
encumbrancer
abcceennostt
contabescent
abcceenorrtu
counter-brace
abccehiimnos
biomechanics
abccehillruy
cherubically
abccehloootx
chocolate-box

abccehmnrrtu
curb-merchant
abcceiiilrst
criticisable
abcceiilnoot
coenobitical
abcceiilnssy
inaccessibly
abcceillnory
reconcilably
abcceilmmnou
communicable
abcceilnnoos
conscionable
abcceilnortt
contractible
abcceilorrsu
clair-obscure
abcceilorstu
scrobiculate
abccenoorrry
raccoon-berry
abccgilnrruw
curb-crawling
abcchhrrsstu
scratch-brush
abcchiooorrt
orthoboracic
abcciilopstu
suboccipital
abcciimoorst
macrobiotics
abccilloosty
octosyllabic
abccilmmnouy
communicably
abccilnnoosy
conscionably
abcddehiilnr
Hildebrandic
abcddgiklnpu
blackpudding
abcdeeehilpr
decipherable
abcdeeehlorr
breech-loader
abcdeeeilntt
indetectable
abcdeeeilnuv
undeceivable
abcdeeellntu
undelectable
abcdeeelnrtu
uncelebrated
abcdeeghloru
double-charge
abcdeegiknor
code-breaking
abcdeehipprr
bread-chipper
abcdeeiillmn
medicine-ball
abcdeeiillnn
indeclinable

abcdeeilmnss
dissemblance
abcdeeilmost
domesticable
abcdeeilnnsu
unascendible
abcdeeilnors
considerable
abcdeeilnrtu
uncreditable
abcdeeilorsv
discoverable
abcdeekllowy
yellow-backed
abcdeelmoops
decomposable
abcdeelrttuu
tuberculated
abcdeemnoott
cane-bottomed
abcdefmopruu
fume-cupboard
abcdeghiilnr
childbearing
abcdeghorrtu
turbocharged
abcdegilnotu
double-acting
abcdehhlooor
bachelorhood
abcdehimnory
chimney-board
abcdehnorsty
body-snatcher
abcdeiiillnny
indeclinably
abcdeiiilrstt
distractible
abcdeilnorsy
considerably
abcdeilnostu
discountable
abcdeilorsss
scissor-blade
abcdeilpstuu
subduplicate
abcdeinooprs
proboscidean
abcdekloorru
dock-labourer
abcdeloopruv
cupboard-love
abcdghiinrtw
bird-watching
abcdgiknnouw
backwounding
abcdginnorss
crossbanding
abcdginoorrs
scoring-board
abcdhiirsstu
Hudibrastics
abcdiinooprs
proboscidian

abcdilossuuu
subacidulous
abcdinnorsuy
subordinancy
abceeeenprrt
carpenter-bee
abceeeffiorr
office-bearer
abceeefnrsst
benefactress
abceeehhinpr
hebephreniac
abceeeiilmpr
impierceable
abceeeilntux
inexecutable
abceeekrrrtu
truce-breaker
abceeemmnrrr
remembrancer
abceeenorsuv
verbenaceous
abceeffiinrt
febrifacient
abceefiillny
beneficially
abceefiilnnu
unbeneficial
abceefinorst
sorbefacient
abceeghllnst
cable's-length
abceeghmrstu
guest-chamber
abceegilnors
recognisable
abceehkmnrrt
kerb-merchant
abceehlnnquu
unquenchable
abceehmmnnrt
embranchment
abceeiiillnpx
inexplicable
abceeiilnnnt
bicentennial
abceeiilnrtx
inextricable
abceeiilpprt
precipitable
abceeiinnnst
inabstinence
abceeillsstu
subcelestial
abceeilmmors
commiserable
abceeilnnotu
unnoticeable
abceeilnorsu
ribonuclease
abceeilnosss
sociableness
abceeilrsstu
resuscitable

abceeinnorsv
inobservance
abceeinoorrt
cerebrotonia
abceejklmrtu
lumber-jacket
abceejnrsttu
subterjacent
abceeklorrtw
lower-bracket
abceekpprrtu
upper-bracket
abceelllnosu
counsellable
abceellmnopt
contemplable
abceellmsttu
lamb's-lettuce
abceellnoost
console-table
abceellnpssu
culpableness
abceelmmmoor
commemorable
abceelmrrttu
marble-cutter
abceeloprstu
prosecutable
abceennoorsx
resonance-box
abceennorsuv
unobservance
abceenoprrtu
protuberance
abceeorrssuu
burseraceous
abceffinoorr
baron-officer
abcefhorrrtt
craft-brother
abcefilnnnou
unconfinable
abceghillorr
bachelor-girl
abceghlnoost
hog-constable
abceghorrrtu
turbocharger
abcegiilnnos
incognisable
abcegijlmnor
crambo-jingle
abcegiklnrrw
kerb-crawling
abcegilnorsy
recognisably
abcegilnpruy
burying-place
abcegiloorty
bacteriology
abcegllnootu
conglobulate
abcehhiloprs
bachelorship

abcehhrtttuy
buttery-hatch
abcehiillnry
Hibernically
abcehijknotx
Jack-in-the-box
abcehiknrsss
brackishness
abcehiksstt
basket-stitch
abcehillopry
hyperbolical
abcehilmnruu
hibernaculum
abcehirrrrsu
crush-barrier
abcehklrssuw
swashbuckler
abcehknorstu
sea-buckthorn
abcehlmoopss
peach-blossom
abcehlnnquuy
unquenchably
abceiiillrst
liberalistic
abceiiilttxy
excitability
abceiiimnort
biometrician
abceiiillnpxy
inexplicably
abceiilmnopt
incompatible
abceiilnrtuv
vibratiuncle
abceiilnrtxy
inextricably
abceiilorstt
cristobalite
abceiilortvy
revocability
abceiilprsty
plebiscitary
abceiinorstt
obstetrician
abceiirsttuw
water-biscuit
abceillnnoos
inconsolable
abceillntuuv
uncultivable
abceilmmnotu
incommutable
abceilmnnosu
inconsumable
abceilmnoptu
incomputable
abceilmoprst
problematics
abceilnortuu
elucubration
abceiloprrtt
protractible

abceilopssst
speiss-cobalt
abcelllnoort
controllable
abcelllloosty
octosyllable
abcelmnoopsu
uncomposable
abcelnoprruu
unprocurable
abcelnorsttu
counter-blast
abceloprrsuu
subopercular
abcemnnorrru
Marcobrunner
abcemoopsssw
bow-compasses
abcenorssssu
scabrousness
abcenosstuuu
subcutaneous
abcfghiiklns
black-fishing
abcflnooorru
fluorocarbon
abcghhiknsuw
bushwhacking
abcgiiklnst
blacklisting
abcgiilllooy
biologically
abcgillmnrsy
scramblingly
abcgillnostu
sculling-boat
abcgilnnooot
conglobation
abchiioooptx
toxicophobia
abciiiilrsty
irascibility
abciiilnrtuy
incurability
abciillnrttu
brilliant-cut
abciilmnopty
incompatibly
abciilnnotuy
connubiality
abciilnnstuu
incunabulist
abciilnpprsu
subprincipal
abciimnnoost
combinations
abciinorstuu
turbinacious
abcilllmosyy
symbolically
abcilllopsyy
polysyllabic
abcillmnoosy
monosyllabic

abcillnnoosy
inconsolably
abcilmmnostu
noctambulism
abcilmmnotuy
incommutably
abcilmnnosuy
inconsumably
abcilmnosttu
noctambulist
abcilmorrtuu
microtubular
abciloopsstu
subapostolic
abcimnorsstu
obscurantism
abcimnorstuu
rambunctious
abcinorssttu
obscurantist
substraction
abcoooorrrrt
corroborator
abdddeeehlou
double-headed
abdddeehlnou
double-handed
abddeeeeehlt
beetle-headed
abddeeeggglr
badger-legged
abddeeehirtw
white-bearded
abddeeehlltu
bullet-headed
abddeeehlnyz
benzaldehyde
abddeeelloru
double-dealer
abddeeelnnpu
undependable
abddeeggloru
double-dagger
abddeegllouz
double-glazed
abddeeillnru
unriddleable
abddeeimnnst
absent-minded
abddeelmnnou
double-manned
abddegilnprs
spring-bladed
abddeilnnssy
day-blindness
abddeilnoost
bloodstained
abddekmooosy
Domesday-book
abddglnooors
dragon's-blood
abddhilmnnoo
hoodman-blind

abddkmoooosy
Doomsday-book
abddnoortuuw
outward-bound
abdeeeeilmrr
irredeemable
abdeeeelmnru
unredeemable
abdeeefiilns
indefeasible
abdeeeghlrrw
hedge-warbler
abdeeegillrt
great-bellied
abdeeeglrrsw
sedge-warbler
abdeeehilrrs
shield-bearer
abdeeehllrtw
well-breathed
abdeeeiilmrr
irremediable
abdeeeiilrtv
deliberative
abdeeeillrty
deliberately
abdeeeilmnrt
determinable
abdeeeilmrry
irredeemably
abdeeeilnrtu
undeliberate
abdeeeimsttw
time-bewasted
abdeeelmnttt
battlemented
abdeeelmntzz
bedazzlement
abdeeelnrtuv
burnet-leaved
abdeefhilmrt
half-timbered
abdeefiiilnt
identifiable
abdeefiilnsy
indefeasibly
abdeefinstuu
subinfeudate
abdeeghlnort
long-breathed
abdeegilmnrs
disembrangle
abdeegilrrst
breast-girdle
abdeeginnrru
underbearing
abdeeginopst
speed-boating
abdeeglnostu
obtuse-angled
abdeehhoprrs
rhabdosphere
abdeehilmrtw
marbled-white

abdeehlrsttu
lust-breathed
abdeehnnortu
unbreathed-on
abdeehnortuw
weather-bound
abdeeiiilttv
debilitative
abdeeiilmrry
irremediably
abdeeiilnort
deliberation
abdeeiinorty
obedientiary
abdeeiiprsst
base-spirited
abdeeillnorr
banderillero
abdeeilmnopr
imponderable
abdeeilmnrty
determinably
abdeeilorruv
boulevardier
abdeeilprstu
disreputable
abdeeinnorss
debonairness
abdeeinnsssu
unbiasedness
abdeejnortuy
journey-bated
abdeeklnnrtu
underblanket
abdeekorrrsw
sword-breaker
abdeellprstu
spurtle-blade
abdeelmnorst
demonstrable
abdeenorsstu
obdurateness
abdeffgiilnr
diffrangible
abdeffhlorsu
shuffle-board
abdefiiillos
solidifiable
abdefiiilnty
definability
abdefiilmnor
informidable
abdefiilmnou
unmodifiable
abdefiilmnrr
rifleman-bird
abdefilmnoru
unformidable
abdefinostuu
subfeudation
abdefnorrssu
brassfounder
abdeforstuuy
subfeudatory

abdeghinrsst
bathing-dress
abdegiiknopr
boarding-pike
abdegiknoprw
baking-powder
abdegilllnny
belly-landing
abdegilnorru
organ-builder
abdegilnortw
world-beating
abdeglnorttu
battleground
abdehhlmoorr
rhombohedral
abdehhnossuu
house-husband
abdehiiilmns
diminishable
abdehiilnsuv
devil-in-a-bush
abdehiilssst
disestablish
abdehilmnnst
blandishment
abdehimnrrst
Rembrandtish
abdehnoruyzz
honey-buzzard
abdehorrttuy
ruby-throated
abdeiiilmnss
inadmissible
abdeiiilmtxy
mixed-ability
abdeiiilnott
debilitation
abdeiiilrsty
desirability
abdeiilnpstu
indisputable
abdeiilorstu
subeditorial
abdeiilttuvy
dubitatively
abdeiioprss
basidiospore
abdeiirsttuv
disturbative
abdeilmnstuu
unsublimated
abdeilprstuy
disreputably
abdeimmnrrst
Rembrandtism
abdeimorstux
ambidextrous
abdelmnorsty
demonstrably
abdelooqrrtu
quarter-blood
abdenoorstwy
sword-bayonet

abdenoqrrtuu
quarter-bound
abdfginorrsu
surf-boarding
surfing-board
abdfiilnnruu
infundibular
abdfiilnooov
bioflavonoid
abdghinooswx
shadow-boxing
abdgiilooory
radiobiology
abdgiinnnorr
branding-iron
abdgiinnoorr
ironing-board
abdgilnnostw
standing-bowl
abdgilnorruu
burial-ground
abdgimnnnoru
mourning-band
abdginnnorru
running-board
abdhiimrstty
dithyrambist
abdhiirsttuy
birthday-suit
abdiiiilntuy
inaudibility
abdiiilmnssy
inadmissibly
abdiiilrssuy
subsidiarily
abdiilnpstuy
indisputably
abdiirrsttuy
distributary
abdlmnnorstu
burnt-almonds
abdlnoortuuy
roundaboutly
abeeefillmru
Umbelliferae
abeeefilnsss
feasibleness
abeeegilnort
renegotiable
abeeehklrstt
bletherskate
abeeehkorrrs
horse-breaker
abeeehkorrsu
house-breaker
abeeehmnqttu
bequeathment
abeeeijmnnrt
benjamin-tree
abeeeillnrss
reliableness
abeeeillnruv
unrelievable

abeeeillprsv
replevisable
abeeeilmnprt
impenetrable
abeeeilmnrtx
exterminable
abeeeilnnssv
enviableness
abeeeilrrstv
silver-beater
abeeeinnprtv
brevipennate
abeeeinnrttw
winter-beaten
abeeeinrrttv
invertebrate
abeeeknorrst
stone-breaker
abeeellmrrtu
umbrella-tree
abeeellrsttt
trestle-table
abeeelmmnttt
embattlement
abeeelmnossv
moveableness
abeeelnsssss
baselessness
abeeemmnqrtu
embarquement
abeeemprsttu
subtemperate
abeeeoprrstt
obstreperate
abeeeorrrrtv
reverberator
abeeeprrstty
presbyterate
abeeffilnrsu
insufferable
abeefflnrsuu
unsufferable
abeefiilmnst
manifestible
abeefiilnruv
unverifiable
abeefillnrtu
unfilterable
abeefilmoprr
imperforable
abeefilmorrr
irreformable
abeefllmnssu
blamefulness
abeeflmnorru
unreformable
abeeflrsttuy
sea-butterfly
abeeggiiilnor
globigerinae
abeeggilnrss
beggarliness
abeeghinqrsu
queer-bashing

abeeghmnoopr
Germanophobe
abeegiilnstv
investigable
abeegiknpstu
speaking-tube
abeegillnort
bertillonage
abeegilnnpux
inexpugnable
abeegilnnsss
singableness
abeegilnnsst
tangibleness
abeegilnorrt
interrogable
abeeglnnoruv
ungovernable
abeeglnnpuux
unexpugnable
abeehhiilopp
ephebophilia
abeehiilmprs
imperishable
abeehiklrstt
blatherskite
abeehillmort
thermolabile
abeehillortt
Bertholletia
abeehilnortt
bletheration
abeehilnprsu
unperishable
abeehilprsst
pre-establish
abeehllrssty
breathlessly
abeehlmorstt
thermostable
abeehlnnoorr
blennorrhoea
abeehloprsst
blastosphere
abeehlorsttw
bottle-washer
abeehlorstty
heteroblasty
abeeiiiilllrs
illiberalise
abeeiillostt
biosatellite
abeeiilmnnrt
interminable
abeeiilmprty
permeability
abeeiilnnpsx
inexpansible
abeeiilnprtx
inextirpable
abeeiilnpsst
pitiableness
abeeiilorttv
obliterative

abeeiilprrrs
irrespirable
abeeikmoprrs
break-promise
abeeillnnruv
invulnerable
abeeillnoprt
interpolable
abeeillorrsv
irresolvable
abeeillprsuv
pulverisable
abeeillrstvy
livery-stable
abeeilmmnrsu
immensurable
abeeilmmoors
aeroembolism
abeeilmnprty
impenetrably
abeeilnoqstu
questionable
abeeilnpssss
passibleness
abeeilnssstu
suitableness
abeeiloorssv
basso-relievo
abeeilopprrx
expropriable
abeeiloprrrv
irreprovable
abeeilprrsty
presbyterial
abeeilrrsttw
water-blister
abeeimnrsttu
steam-turbine
abeeinnorstv
Observantine
abeeinorrttv
vertebration
abeeinorsstv
abortiveness
abeeinprrsty
Presbyterian
abeeinrrttuw
water-turbine
abeeioprrtvx
exprobrative
abeeiprrttuv
perturbative
abeekllnopst
pollen-basket
abeeklmorrtu
troublemaker
abeeklnnossw
knowableness
abeeklnorssw
workableness
abeekorrsstt
breaststroke
abeelllortty
trolley-table

abeellmnopuy
unemployable
abeellnnruuv
unvulnerable
abeellnorstw
snowball-tree
abeellnorsuv
unresolvable
abeellnprsuu
unrepulsable
abeellorstww
water-bellows
abeelmmnnotz
emblazonment
abeelmoopsss
pease-blossom
abeelnnrrtuu
unreturnable
abeelnnssstu
unstableness
abeelnoprrtu
unreportable
abeelnoprruv
unreprovable
abeelnoqsstu
quotableness
abeelnossstu
absoluteness
abeeloprrssu
superposable
abeelorstttu
trouble-state
abeemmrrsstu
breastsummer
abeenrssstu
abstruseness
abeerrrsstuu
subtreasurer
abeffilllmor
flabelliform
abeffilnrsuy
insufferably
abefgilnorry
forbearingly
abefginnrrtu
afterburning
abefiimnnors
Febronianism
abefillortuu
Tubuliflorae
abefilnoprtu
unprofitable
abefilnrsstu
transfusible
abefknoorrst
transfer-book
abeflnossstu
boastfulness
abeflnosssuu
fabulousness
abegghillllmn
gambling-hell
abegghioopry
biogeography

abeggiillnst
billingsgate
abeghhkorrtu
breakthrough
abeghiknoprs
shopbreaking
abeghilnrrtw
night-brawler
abeghinnrrtu
heartburning
abeghloprstu
breastplough
abeghnooprrs
snobographer
abegiilnrttw
writing-table
abegiinrsssu
agribusiness
abegiklnnoor
book-learning
abegilllnowy
bowling-alley
abegillmorsu
semiglobular
abegillnoost
balneologist
abegilmnnpuu
unimpugnable
abegilnnpuxy
inexpugnably
abegilnnrttu
table-turning
abeginnosstu
seasoning-tub
abeginorsssu
agrobusiness
abeginprstuy
spring-beauty
abeglmorsuuy
umbrageously
abeglnnoruvy
ungovernably
abehiiilrtty
heritability
abehiiimnnrs
Hibernianism
abehiilmprsy
imperishably
abehiilnnrty
labyrinthine
abehiilnopst
inhospitable
abehiimorsuv
behaviourism
misbehaviour
abehiiorstuv
behaviourist
abehiklnnrsu
unshrinkable
abehillnopsu
unpolishable
abehilmnsstt
stablishment

abehilnnpsuu
unpunishable
abehilnopstu
unhospitable
abehilnopsty
hypnotisable
abehilnorrtw
brother-in-law
abehilooopru
ailourophobe
abehlorrstty
erythroblast
abeiiiilllrty
illiberality
abeiiillnnrt
brilliantine
abeiiilrtvvy
revivability
abeiiillmptu
multipliable
abeiillortty
tolerability
abeiilmmorty
memorability
abeiilmnnrty
interminably
abeiilmnosst
ambitionless
abeiilmnrtuy
numerability
abeiilmortvy
removability
abeiilmptty
temptability
abeiilnnostu
nebulisation
sublineation
abeiilnnttuy
untenability
abeiilnoortt
obliteration
abeiilnorrtt
interorbital
abeiiloorssv
basso-rilievo
abeiiloqrrtu
equilibrator
abeiimnrstuu
subminiature
abeiinorsstu
suberisation
abeillnnruvy
invulnerably
abeillnorrtu
interlobular
abeilloprrvy
proverbially
abeillorrsvy
irresolvably
abeilmnnotuu
mountain-blue
abeilmnosuux
exalbuminous

abeilmosstuy
abstemiously
abeilnoqstuy
questionably
abeilnorssuy
Byelorussian
abeilnorttxy
exorbitantly
abeiloprrrvy
irreprovably
abeinooprrst
reabsorption
abeinooprrtx
exprobration
abeinoprrttu
perturbation
abellllopsyy
polysyllable
abelllmnoosy
monosyllable
abellmmnossw
swell-mobsman
abellmooppss
apple-blossom
abelmnorstuu
surmountable
abelnoppssuu
unsupposable
abemoorsttwy
bottom-sawyer
abeooprrrtxy
exprobratory
abeoprrrttuy
perturbatory
abfghiimnort
habit-forming
abfgiiilnrty
frangibility
abfgiiilrtuy
figurability
abfiiillnort
fibrillation
abfiiillrtty
filtrability
abfiiilnnotu
infibulation
abfilllortuu
tubulifloral
abfilnoprtuy
unprofitably
abggillnossw
glass-blowing
abggilnnrssu
burning-glass
abghhilorrtu
harbour-light
abghhinrssuv
shaving-brush
abghhoorsstu
thorough-bass
abghiilmnrsu
rhumb-sailing
abghiimmnstw
swimming-bath

abghilnosstt
shot-blasting
abghilooptttt
potato-blight
abgiiiilntty
ignitability
abgiiillmnsu
bilingualism
abgiillnortt
trolling-bait
abgiilloorty
obligatorily
abgilmnopsuu
plumbaginous
abgilnoorstu
urbanologist
abhiiilorssz
bilharziosis
abhiikmnnprs
brinkmanship
abhiilnopsty
inhospitably
abhiimnnortt
antithrombin
abhiinoprstv
vibraphonist
abhilnnpsuuy
unpunishably
abhimnnorrtu
Northumbrian
abiiiilmssty
amissibility
abiiiilrrtty
irritability
abiiillpptuy
pupilability
abiiillpstuy
plausibility
abiiilmmotvy
immovability
abiiilmmttuy
immutability
abiiilmnoost
abolitionism
mobilisation
abiiilmpttuy
imputability
abiiilnnoott
nobilitation
abiiilnoostt
abolitionist
abiiilnrstuy
insurability
abiilmmoostu
automobilism
abiilmoosttu
automobilist
abiilnoorstt
strobilation
abiilnorssuu
insalubrious
abiilooppsty
opposability

abiiloprstty
sportability
abiioprsttvy
absorptivity
abilllmortuu
multilobular
abilllnooopt
pilot-balloon
abillorssuuy
salubriously
abilmmmnossu
somnambulism
abilmmnosstu
somnambulist
abilmnorstuy
subnormality
abimnorssttu
nimbostratus
abinoorrttuw
rainbow-trout
abioprrstttu
portrait-bust
abllmoorstyy
symbololatry
abnoorrsstuu
brontosaurus
accedeeeelns
decalescence
acccdiioostt
coccidiostat
accceeeelnrs
recalescence
accceeeglnsu
glaucescence
accceeeilnns
incalescence
accceeeinqsu
acquiescence
accceeelnors
calorescence
accceehmnotu
accouchement
accceeiilsst
ecclesiastic
accceeillty
eclectically
accceelnosty
nectocalyces
acccegiinnor
carcinogenic
acccehinortt
technocratic
acccehinostu
Echinocactus
acccehioorsu
cichoraceous
acccehklortw
clock-watcher
accceijmnrtu
circumjacent
accceilnnort
concentrical
accceimnnoot
concomitance

accceimnrstu
circumstance
acccenoppruy
preoccupancy
accchhiillot
chalcolithic
accchiioprrt
chiropractic
accchiioprsz
schizocarpic
accciilmnnou
councilmanic
accciilnnoty
anticyclonic
accciilnoost
iconoclastic
acccimnnoosy
coscinomancy
acccimnnooty
concomitancy
acccnooortty
cottonocracy
accdddehiikl
chick-a-diddle
accddeeiiiln
Cicindelidae
accddeeinrtu
unaccredited
accddehinoop
dodecaphonic
accdeeehlmny
chance-medley
accdeeeilnps
lapidescence
accdeeelorsu
cedrelaceous
accdeeenorst
deconsecrate
accdeefiirtt
certificated
accdeehlrsty
cradle-scythe
accdeeiiilpt
epideictical
accdeeiknopt
patience-dock
accdeeillops
peccadilloes
accdeeilnopy
encyclopedia
accdeeinnnst
incandescent
accdeelnoprs
corpse-candle
accdeelnpstu
unspectacled
accdeenossuu
succedaneous
accdegnnorrt
concert-grand
accdehhnrruw
church-warden
accdehilmops
accomplished

accdehioorsu
orchidaceous
accdehlnnorr
corn-chandler
accdeiiilmst
dialecticism
accdeiillopy
epicycloidal
accdeiilnnot
coincidental
accdeillnoty
occidentally
accdeilnooru
Cain-coloured
accdeilnoptu
conduplicate
accdeiloosuy
calycoideous
accdeimnortu
undemocratic
accdekklmoru
cuckold-maker
accdelnortty
contractedly
accdemnostuu
unaccustomed
accdennortuy
country-dance
accdeooprsty
despotocracy
accdfiiinoot
codification
accdgiinnnss
scanning-disc
accdgilotyyz
zygodactylic
accdiiloorsu
radicicolous
accdiimnnoou
incomunicado
accdiinoorst
accordionist
accdinoorrtt
contradictor
accdlnnoorty
concordantly
accdloopstyy
dactyloscopy
acceeeffiopr
peace-officer
acceeehilnpp
epencephalic
acceeehlorrt
heterocercal
acceeeilssst
Ecclesiastes
acceeennorvy
reconveyance
acceeenorrst
reconsecrate
acceefgiimnn
magnificence
acceefhhirtt
thief-catcher

acceeghnnorx
corn-exchange
acceegilnnor
congenerical
acceegilnort
geocentrical
acceeginnors
recognisance
acceeglnoppr
copper-glance
acceehhrrstt
charter-chest
acceehiilnpt
encephalitic
acceehiknstu
chuckie-stane
acceehilmops
mesocephalic
acceehimrstu
music-teacher
acceehiorsss
chassé-croisé
acceehiorttt
heterotactic
acceehirrttu
architecture
acceehlmnrsy
sclerenchyma
acceehmnnort
encroachment
acceeiinnort
interoceanic
acceeiinnrss
circassienne
acceeiinpprt
precipitance
acceeijnnrty
interjacency
acceeilllrty
electrically
acceeillmnuy
ecumenically
acceeillopst
telescopical
acceeilnpttu
centuplicate
acceeilnrtty
tetracycline
acceeinnptxy
inexpectancy
acceeinopstu
pectinaceous
acceeiorsttt
stereotactic
acceeknoopst
peacock-stone
acceelloortt
collectorate
acceelmprtuu
receptaculum
acceelnnostv
convalescent
acceelnnrstu
translucence

acceelprrwyy
creepy-crawly
acceemnorttu
accoutrement
acceennnortu
countenancer
acceennorstu
unconsecrate
acceenoprrsu
precancerous
acceffhiortw
watch-officer
acceffiijkno
Jack-in-office
accefgiiinns
significance
accefhilmnsu
mischanceful
accefhilmrtu
lucifer-match
accefiiilnst
scientifical
accefiillpsy
specifically
accefiillrst
self-critical
accefilloorw
calico-flower
acceghhioprt
hectographic
acceghiloost
eschatologic
acceghinoprs
scenographic
accegiiknrsw
wisecracking
accegiilmost
cleistogamic
accegiinnnos
incognisance
accegiinrtux
excruciating
accegilllooy
ecologically
accegillnoor
necrological
accegilnnnou
unconcealing
accegimrrtuy
circumgyrate
acceginnnovy
conveyancing
accegnoorrty
gerontocracy
accehiillmry
chimerically
accehiillnst
callisthenic
accehiilmoor
heroi-comical
accehiilnopr
necrophiliac
accehiilnorr
rhinocerical

accehiilnsst
calisthenics
accehiilntty
technicality
accehiimnort
cheiromantic
accehiimrstt
chrematistic
accehiirrttw
carriwitchet
accehiirsttt
tetrastichic
accehiklmoor
mock-heroical
accehikmnsty
chimney-stack
accehilllory
cholerically
accehilmnoor
melanochroic
accehilmoprs
accomplisher
accehilmopry
microcephaly
pyrochemical
accehiloorsu
orichalceous
accehiloprty
chalcopyrite
accehimoorst
mesothoracic
accehimorttt
thermotactic
accehimpssty
metapsychics
accehinnnopt
pantechnicon
accehinooprt
acrophonetic
accehinorrtt
trochanteric
accehinrssst
scratchiness
accehiopstvy
psychoactive
accehkloosvz
Czechoslovak
accehlnopsuy
Cynocephalus
accehloorssu
schorlaceous
accehmnnorrt
corn-merchant
accehmnorrtu
counter-charm
countermarch
accehmopstuu
moustache-cup
accehmorsttu
scattermouch
accehooprsty
tracheoscopy
acceiiilnotv
conciliative

acceiiilpsst
specialistic
acceiikkmnrs
camiknickers
acceiilllnty
enclitically
acceiillosst
solecistical
acceiilmmort
microclimate
acceiilmnnop
incompliance
acceiilmoors
seriocomical
acceiilmoptv
complicative
acceiilmrrsu
semicircular
acceiilnortv
intervocalic
acceiilnrsst
criticalness
acceiiloprrr
irreciprocal
acceiilosstv
viscoelastic
acceiilrsstu
secularistic
acceiimnoprr
picrocarmine
acceiimorrtt
meritocratic
acceiinortux
excruciation
acceiinpprty
precipitancy
acceiioprsuv
pervicacious
acceiipprsty
perspicacity
acceikkkknnt
knick-knacket
acceillmmory
commercially
acceillmnooy
economically
acceillmosty
cosmetically
acceillnnort
centroclinal
acceillnotty
tectonically
acceilloprry
reciprocally
acceilmmnoru
uncommercial
acceilmnnoou
uneconomical
acceilmnortu
counter-claim
acceilmoprsu
microcapsule
acceilnnootv
convectional

acceilnoorrt
correctional
acceilnosssu
successional
acceiloprsst
ceroplastics
acceimnnoort
concremation
acceimnrttuu
circumnutate
acceinnnnoos
inconsonance
acceinnoorst
consecration
acceinooprtu
reoccupation
acceiooprrrt
reciprocator
acceiorsttuv
curvicostate
acceknnorstu
snack-counter
accellmnopty
complacently
accellooorsu
corollaceous
accelloorttx
tax-collector
accelnnrstuy
translucency
accelnoopprу
cyclopropane
accelnsssttuy
successantly
acceloopssu
scolopaceous
accennoorrtt
concentrator
accenoooprrt
concorporate
accenoorrsty
consecratory
accenoprrstu
counterscarp
accfgiiinnsy
significancy
accfiimnnosu
Confucianism
accfiinnoost
confiscation
accfiinnostu
Confucianist
accfillnootu
flocculation
accfinoorsty
confiscatory
accghhiinopr
ichnographic
accghhiooprr
chorographic
accghhiorsty
hygrochastic
accghiiknorr
rocking-chair
accghiimoprr
micrographic
accghiinoprz
zincographic
accghiiopprt
pictographic
accghillooor
chorological
accghilloopy
phycological
accghilnrsty
scratchingly
accghimooprs
cosmographic
accgiillmoor
micrological
accgiillooos
sociological
accgillmooos
cosmological
accgilmnooos
cosmogonical
accgilnortuy
granulocytic
acchhiinrtuy
churchianity
acchhillooty
ichthyocolla
acchhinoortx
xanthochroic
acchhinoprsy
chrysophanic
acchhioppsty
psychopathic
acchhlmnoruw
Low-Churchman
acchiiinstuv
chauvinistic
acchiiloopps
scopophiliac
acchiiloprty
hypocritical
acchiimmorst
chromaticism
acchiimnoost
iconomachist
acchiimnopty
amphictyonic
acchiimnorst
monarchistic
acchiimoorst
isochromatic
acchiimorrtt
trichromatic
acchiimortty
chromaticity
acchiioprsty
physiocratic
acchillnnooo
non-alcoholic
acchilloptty
phyllotactic
acchilnnorsy
synchronical
acchilnoprty
lycanthropic
acchiloopssy
psychosocial
acchiloppray
prophylactic
acchimnooppt
phonocamptic
acchinooopsu
cacophonious
acchinoopstt
phonotactics
acchiooprrrt
chiropractor
acchiooprstt
octastrophic
acchiooprttt
trophotactic
acchioossttu
octastichous
acciiilnnoot
conciliation
acciiinrssst
narcissistic
acciillnrtuy
uncritically
acciilloprty
pictorically
acciilmmoort
microtomical
acciilmnoopt
complication
acciilnoorty
conciliatory
acciiloprsuy
capriciously
acciimooprtt
compatriotic
acciinnooost
consociation
acciinnooptu
inoccupation
accijlnnotuv
conjunctival
accillnoottu
colluctation
accillortuuv
vocicultural
accilmoopsst
cosmoplastic
accilnossttu
sansculottic
accimmnoortu
communicator
accimnoosstu
cosmonautics
accimnoostuu
contumacious
accinossstuu
succussation
acdddeehnoor
dodecahedron
acdddeeinsst
addictedness
acdddefginpu
pudding-faced
acdddeginrsw
wedding-cards
acdddenoorsu
dodecandrous
acddeeeflstu
self-educated
acddeeehimst
semi-detached
acddeeehnsst
detachedness
acddeeelltuw
well-educated
acddeehilnry
cylinder-head
acddeehllnor
candle-holder
acddeeiimnst
demi-distance
acddeeilnnou
duodecennial
acddeeilnttu
denticulated
acddeeimossu
Discomedusae
acddeeimostt
domesticated
acddeelnptuu
pedunculated
acddefnnnoor
cannon-fodder
acddeghimnps
camp-shedding
acddeghimnrw
wedding-march
acddeghinrsu
undischarged
acddegnoosuy
dodecagynous
acddehiklruy
hydraulicked
acddehinorsu
deuch-an-doris
acddehinpstu
undispatched
acddeiiiprsv
disprivacied
acddeiilnoru
radionuclide
acddeiinorst
endocarditis
acddeillosty
dislocatedly
acddeilnoost
consolidated
acddeilrstty
distractedly
acddeimnossu
discomedusan
acddeinnnssu
uncandidness
acddeinoopst
paedodontics

acddeinrsttu
undistracted
acddemoprssu
mass-produced
acddennnoopr
pro-and-conned
acddgiklnosu
sack-doudling
acddhhiimnot
diamond-hitch
acddhimnoryy
hydrodynamic
acddiiijnotu
dijudication
acddiiilnotu
dilucidation
acddilnorsty
discordantly
acddinnorstu
undiscordant
acddklooopst
paddock-stool
acdeeefffl st
self-affected
acdeeeffnsst
affectedness
acdeeeginopt
paedogenetic
acdeeeginrtt
cigarette-end
acdeeegkllrt
ledger-tackle
acdeeehinruv
underachieve
acdeeehklnrt
halter-necked
acdeeehlrrtu
cruel-hearted
acdeeeiiprtv
depreciative
acdeeeilnopv
velocipedean
acdeeeilnort
deceleration
acdeeeilnprt
precedential
acdeeeilnrst
decentralise
acdeeeilnsst
delicateness
delicatessen
acdeeeinnrtv
inadvertence
acdeeeinrssv
disseverance
acdeeeknnrss
cankeredness
acdeeelnntty
antecedently
acdeeeoprrrt
tape-recorder
acdeefflntuy
unaffectedly
acdeefhhiknr
handkerchief
acdeefhnorrw
henceforward
acdeefiinrry
ferricyanide
acdeefillnot
deflectional
acdeefilmttu
multifaceted
acdeefinorry
ferrocyanide
acdeeggnrsss
scraggedness
acdeeghilrst
clear-sighted
acdeeghllnnu
unchallenged
acdeegiinopt
doating-piece
acdeegilloty
geodetically
acdeegilnors
close-grained
acdeegilnrsy
decreasingly
acdeegilorvv
gravel-voiced
acdeeginrsss
dressing-case
acdeegknottu
tongue-tacked
acdeegnnorss
gas-condenser
acdeegnnostt
decongestant
acdeehhoopry
Rhodophyceae
acdeehiiilltt
ditheletical
acdeehiinnrs
Schneiderian
acdeehiklpss
sickle-shaped
acdeehillorw
orchilla-weed
acdeehilmnor
echinodermal
acdeehilnnop
diencephalon
acdeehilnnrt
Netherlandic
acdeehimnnsu
unmechanised
acdeehinnrst
disenchanter
acdeehisstty
dysaesthetic
acdeehlortty
heterodactyl
acdeehnnopru
unchaperoned
acdeehnoprru
unreproached
acdeehnrssst
starchedness
acdeeiiillmpy
epidemically
acdeeiillnty
indelicately
acdeeiilltty
dietetically
acdeeiilnopv
velocipedian
acdeeiimnrty
intermediacy
acdeeiinoprt
depreciation
acdeeiinqstu
equidistance
acdeeiinttux
inexactitude
acdeeiiooprs
aecidiospore
acdeeijknnrt
dinner-jacket
acdeeikloops
kaleidoscope
acdeeillnnos
declensional
acdeeillnrsy
cylinder-seal
seal-cylinder
acdeeillrtuv
culvertailed
revictualled
acdeeilmnpst
displacement
acdeeilmorrs
sclerodermia
acdeeilmrtuv
vermiculated
acdeeilnnnou
non-Euclidean
acdeeilnnoss
descensional
acdeeilnoopy
Lycopodineae
acdeeilnssst
distanceless
acdeeilortuv
edulcorative
acdeeilortvy
decoratively
acdeeilstttu
testiculated
acdeeimnnopr
predominance
acdeeimorrtx
xerodermatic
acdeeinnoott
Notonectidae
acdeeinnoprr
preordinance
acdeeinnrtvy
inadvertency
acdeeinooprv
overcanopied
acdeeinoprtu
deuteranopic
acdeeinosssu
edaciousness
acdeeiopprtu
propaedeutic
acdeeioprrty
depreciatory
acdeelmnnott
malcontented
acdeelnnnotu
non-nucleated
acdeelnoprtu
counter-paled
counterplead
acdeeloprtty
pterodactyle
acdeemnoppty
appendectomy
acdeemopstty
stapedectomy
acdeennnotuv
uncovenanted
acdeennnrstt
transcendent
acdeennnrtuy
undertenancy
acdeenoorstu
Neoceratodus
acdeeoorrssu
droseraceous
acdeffiinost
disaffection
acdefhiinrss
disfranchise
acdefhinnrsu
unfranchised
acdefiiimotv
modificative
acdefiilnnot
confidential
acdefiilnssu
unclassified
acdefiilnsty
sanctifiedly
acdefiinnstt
disinfectant
acdefiinnstu
unsanctified
acdefiinoort
deforciation
acdefilllotu
folliculated
acdefimmoopr
campodeiform
acdeghilnrru
hurdle-racing
acdeghioprrs
discographer
acdegiilpqru
quadriplegic
acdegiimnnor
Indo-Germanic

acdegiiooprt
diageotropic
acdegiknnrsw
sneck-drawing
acdegiknrsss
dressing-sack
acdegillooty
dialectology
acdegilnnost
long-distance
acdegilnrtty
detractingly
acdegilntuuu
unguiculated
acdeginorrss
cross-grained
acdegklloors
slockdolager
acdegknorrtu
racket-ground
acdegnorrtuu
counter-guard
acdehhiilnor
chiliahedron
acdehhilnprs
ship-chandler
acdehhlosttu
slouch-hatted
acdehhoorrsu
orchard-house
acdehiiilstt
ditheistical
acdehiiirrtu
Trichiuridae
acdehiilmmot
immethodical
acdehiimnoor
Chironomidae
acdehiiprtyy
hyperacidity
acdehillmoty
methodically
acdehilmnotu
unmethodical
acdehiloprt
orthopedical
acdehilorsty
hydroelastic
acdehimnrrss
scrimshander
acdehimooppr
paedomorphic
acdehiooprst
orthopaedics
acdehlprtyyy
hyperdactyly
acdehlpsttu
Platt-Deutsch
acdehmooostt
smooth-coated
acdehmoprsuy
pachydermous
acdeiiilnstu
unidealistic
acdeiiilntvy
indicatively
acdeiiilosss
dissocialise
acdeiiilrtvy
veridicality
acdeiiimnnot
nicotinamide
acdeiiimnnrs
incendiarism
acdeiiimnrst
discriminate
acdeiiimorst
isodiametric
acdeiiinoprt
antiperiodic
acdeiiinppst
appendicitis
acdeiiinrstt
disintricate
acdeiiioprty
aperiodicity
acdeiiiosstv
dissociative
acdeiiiprrst
pericarditis
acdeiillnnty
incidentally
acdeiillopry
periodically
acdeiillopsy
episodically
acdeiilnoptu
pediculation
acdeiilnorst
discretional
acdeiilnossu
unsocialised
acdeiilrrtuv
diverticular
acdeiimnostu
miseducation
acdeiinnnotu
denunciation
acdeiinnoort
incoordinate
acdeiinnoott
conditionate
acdeiinnoprt
pentacrinoid
acdeiinnortt
indoctrinate
acdeiinooprs
Scorpionidea
acdeiinoortv
coordinative
co-ordinative
acdeiinoottx
detoxication
acdeiinopstt
disceptation
acdeiinosttu
educationist
acdeiinrsstv
vindicatress
acdeijlntuvy
adjunctively
acdeiknorstt
stock-in-trade
acdeillmoosu
Molluscoidea
acdeillmosty
domestically
acdeillmrsuy
scullery-maid
acdeillnstyy
syndetically
acdeilloopsy
Lycopodiales
acdeillopstu
leucoplastid
acdeillopsty
despotically
acdeilmnopru
unproclaimed
acdeilmnosuy
mendaciously
acdeilmopstu
deutoplasmic
acdeilnooort
decoloration
acdeilnoortu
edulcoration
acdeilnoorty
coordinately
co-ordinately
acdeilnoosst
disconsolate
acdeilnoprss
cross-and-pile
acdeilnorssw
cowardliness
acdeilnttuuv
uncultivated
acdeiloorruv
varicoloured
acdeilrrttuu
turriculated
acdeimmnnoot
commendation
acdeimmnorty
dynamometric
acdeimmooorr
air-commodore
acdeimnnnoot
condemnation
acdeimnnopry
predominancy
acdeimnorrrs
morris-dancer
acdeimoorstt
domesticator
acdeimoprstu
promuscidate
acdeinnnoost
condensation
acdeinnnostu
unsanctioned
acdeinnorrtu
counter-drain
acdeinnorttu
detruncation
acdeinnortuy
denunciatory
acdeinoprttv
privat-docent
acdeinorrtuv
turacoverdin
acdeinorsttu
decrustation
acdeiooprrst
discorporate
acdeiprrttvy
party-verdict
acdelmnooruy
many-coloured
acdelnoortyy
cotyledonary
acdelnoprruu
unprocedural
acdeloprrtty
protractedly
acdemmnoorty
commendatory
acdemnnoorty
condemnatory
acdennorsttu
counter-stand
acdennpttuuu
unpunctuated
acdfiiiinnot
nidification
acdfiiimnoot
modification
acdfiimoorty
modificatory
acdgghiinnnw
wind-changing
acdggiinorsu
discouraging
acdghhioprry
hydrographic
acdghilloory
hydrological
acdghimnootw
doomwatching
acdgiiinrstv
visiting-card
acdgiiknnrst
skirt-dancing
acdgiiloorst
cardiologist
acdgillootyy
dactyliology
acdgilmmnnoy
commandingly
acdgilmnoorr
corn-marigold
acdginoooprt
gonadotropic

acdhhiiknntt
thick-and-thin
acdhhiiopsty
ichthyopsida
acdhhimnoorr
harmonichord
acdhhinoopry
hypochondria
acdhhinoortx
xanthochroid
acdhhinootwy
wood-hyacinth
acdhiimmorst
dichromatism
acdhiimnoort
mitochondria
acdhiinooprs
radiophonics
acdhiinorrsw
Windsor-chair
acdhiioprstt
dictatorship
acdhilnossuy
lady's-cushion
acdhinoopqru
quadrophonic
acdhinopsstt
pitch-and-toss
acdhiorsstty
hydrostatics
acdhknnoorst
stock-and-horn
acdhnrstttuu
cut-and-thrust
acdiiijllnuy
injudicially
acdiiilnnpst
disciplinant
acdiiilnprsy
disciplinary
acdiiilossty
dissociality
acdiiimnnrst
discriminant
acdiiimnortv
mid-Victorian
acdiiinnoort
air-condition
acdiiinoosst
dissociation
acdiiiossttu
adscititious
acdiillmnptu
multiplicand
acdiilloopsu
lapidicolous
acdiilmnoptu
undiplomatic
acdiilnooqtu
coloquintida
acdiinnooort
co-ordination
coordination

acdiinorssyy
idiosyncrasy
acdiioorrsuv
radicivorous
acdillmooorx
loxodromical
acdilloooprsy
prosodically
acdilloopsuu
paludicolous
acdilmnsstyy
syndactylism
acdilmoorsuy
mordaciously
acdilnooorst
consolidator
acdilnooprtu
productional
acdilnorsuuu
iracundulous
acdilorsttuy
tridactylous
acdimmmootuy
mycodomatium
acdimoorrrty
dormitory-car
acdinnorsttu
transduction
acdinooqrstu
conquistador
acdlnosstuyy
syndactylous
acdloooprstt
post-doctoral
aceeeegiknpp
peace-keeping
aceeeegilptx
epexegetical
aceeeehlpsst
steeplechase
aceeeehrsstt
cheese-taster
aceeeelnortt
coelenterate
aceeeelnprss
pearl-essence
aceeeenprrsv
perseverance
aceeeflnpssu
peacefulness
aceeefnnrrst
transference
aceeeghinprs
cheese-paring
aceeegiknrrt
racketeering
aceeegilltxy
exegetically
aceeeginrrst
generatrices
aceeegnnrruy
unregeneracy
aceeehhlrrtu
eleutherarch

aceeehhlrttw
ratchet-wheel
aceeehiisstt
aestheticise
aceeehilsttt
telaesthetic
aceeehimnqtu
cinemathèque
aceeehinosst
coenesthesia
aceeehirrstv
heart-service
aceeehlnnopp
epencephalon
aceeehmorrtt
trocheameter
aceeehmorttt
cathetometer
aceeehnoortt
Heterocontae
aceeeilllntt
lenticellate
aceeeilnnnsv
Valenciennes
aceeeilrtvxy
execratively
aceeeimmnnpr
impermanence
aceeeimnnprt
intemperance
aceeeimnrsvx
ex-serviceman
aceeeinnprst
scene-painter
aceeeinrsstv
creativeness
reactiveness
aceeeippprtv
apperceptive
aceeeiprrtuv
recuperative
aceeeirrrrtv
river-terrace
aceeelloprtt
electroplate
aceeelmoprst
spermatocele
aceeelnnstvy
evanescently
aceeelnotxyy
oxy-acetylene
aceeelnrssss
carelessness
aceeemnnnrtt
entrancement
aceeemrrsstw
screw-steamer
aceeennnprtu
unrepentance
aceeennrrtty
tercentenary
aceeennrstxy
sexcentenary

aceeeppprrst
pepper-caster
aceefffgilns
self-effacing
aceeffgllost
staff-college
aceeffilstux
exsufflicate
aceeffilttuy
effectuality
aceeffinottu
effecutation
aceefghimnst
Gemeinschaft
aceefghllsst
Gesellschaft
aceefgiinrss
fricasseeing
aceefgillnns
self-cleaning
aceefgilnrst
self-catering
aceefgirrstu
figure-caster
aceefgllnnot
falcon-gentle
aceefglnrssu
gracefulness
aceefhiinsst
chieftainess
aceefhmnnrtt
fent-merchant
aceefiilnqtu
liquefacient
aceefiiprttv
petrifactive
aceefiknnnrs
frankincense
aceefillnrty
frenetically
aceefillrttt
cattle-lifter
aceefilnnort
conferential
aceefilnorst
self-creation
aceefilnprst
clip-fastener
aceefiloprrt
prefectorial
aceefimprrtu
picture-frame
aceefinoprtt
perfectation
aceefinprttu
putrefacient
aceefinpsttu
stupefacient
aceefiprttuv
putrefactive
aceefipsttuv
stupefactive
aceefllnpuuy
unpeacefully

aceegghnprss
sprechgesang
aceegginnrsv
scavengering
aceeggnortuu
counter-gauge
aceeghikmnps
speech-making
aceeghiknnrt
kitchen-range
aceeghiknpst
packing-sheet
aceeghillmns
mischallenge
aceeghilnnot
genethliacon
aceeghilnntw
canting-wheel
aceeghilnosu
chaise-longue
aceeghilprsy
hyperalgesic
aceeghimnpst
camp-sheeting
aceeghinnrrt
interchanger
aceeghinoptt
pathogenetic
aceeghirrsst
cash-register
aceeghlnoort
Cologne-earth
aceeghlnrtuy
legacy-hunter
aceeghloprrt
electrograph
aceeghlorstv
grave-clothes
aceeghmnnory
money-changer
aceeghnoprrr
necrographer
aceeghprrrsu
supercharger
aceegiilmnsv
evangelicism
aceegiilnstv
evangelistic
aceegiimnort
geometrician
aceegiiottvx
excogitative
aceegikmssst
message-stick
aceegiknnrrv
nerve-racking
aceegillloot
teleological
aceegilllrty
telergically
aceegillnrsv
silver-glance
aceegilnnpst
nesting-place

aceegilnprst
resting-place
aceegilqrrsu
squirrel-cage
aceegimnorst
miscegenator
aceeginnrstv
ingravescent
aceegllmmoru
gram-molecule
aceeglmnoort
conglomerate
aceegmnoprrt
carpetmonger
aceegnnorttu
counter-agent
aceegoprrssu
supercargoes
aceehhiopstt
Theopaschite
aceehhiopttt
theopathetic
aceehhipprrs
preachership
aceehhiprrsu
hire-purchase
aceehhllortt
leather-cloth
aceehhlmnrty
nychthemeral
aceehhlnorsu
charnel-house
aceehhlorttw
weather-cloth
aceehhmoprty
chemotherapy
aceehhoprstu
chapter-house
aceehhorrstu
Charterhouse
aceehiiknstt
kinaesthetic
aceehiiillnrt
trichinellae
aceehiiilmnos
isocheimenal
aceehiiilnpst
encephalitis
aceehiiilpprr
peripherical
aceehiimprrt
epirrhematic
aceehiimprtu
perichaetium
aceehiimssttt
aestheticism
aceehiinortt
theoretician
aceehiisstttt
aestheticist
aceehikknntv
kitchen-knave
aceehiklmnrt
merchantlike

aceehillmors
Hemerocallis
aceehillmrty
hermetically
aceehilmnrru
machine-ruler
aceehilmorrt
rheometrical
aceehilnorss
heroicalness
aceehiloprsx
exospherical
aceehimnnrtw
wine-merchant
aceehimnprst
parchmentise
aceehimnsstt
chastisement
aceehinnrstu
neurasthenic
aceehinoprrt
cheiropteran
aceehinprrtt
interchapter
aceehinsstty
synaesthetic
aceehiooprst
aethrioscope
aceehiprrstu
creatureship
aceehiprrtuy
curietherapy
aceehiprsttu
therapeutics
aceehirssttv
tsesarevitch
aceehkknorrs
horse-knacker
aceehklmortw
water-hemlock
aceehlllorst
Rochelle-salt
aceehlloorsv
school-leaver
aceehllopswy
peach-yellows
aceehllrrruy
cherry-laurel
aceehlmnnotu
luncheon-meat
aceehlnnnost
channel-stone
aceehloprrss
reproachless
aceehnnssstu
unchasteness
aceehnorsttt
stone-chatter
aceehopprrrs
share-cropper
aceeiillrttv
verticillate
aceeiilmrrsu
mercurialise

aceeiilnoprs
porcelainise
aceeiimmrstt
meristematic
aceeiimnprsu
Epicureanism
aceeiinnorst
containerise
aceeiinnrtuv
renunciative
aceeiinorstv
evisceration
aceeiinorttx
exercitation
aceeiinppprt
appercipient
aceeiinrrsst
irresistance
aceeijmnssst
majesticness
aceeiknnrstt
tennis-racket
aceeilllnttu
intellectual
aceeillmnory
ceremonially
aceeillmnsty
centesimally
aceeillmntuv
multivalence
aceeillmoptv
compellative
aceeillmorty
meteorically
aceeillnnort
crenellation
aceeillnoprs
porcellanise
aceeillnoprt
porcellanite
aceeillnorty
neoterically
aceeillnpstt
stencil-plate
aceeillnrsuv
surveillance
aceeillorsty
esoterically
aceeillortxy
exoterically
aceeillrttuy
reticulately
aceeilmmnpst
misplacement
aceeilmnnotv
nomenclative
aceeilmnopru
police-manure
aceeilnopprt
perceptional
aceeilnoprss
precessional
aceeilnoprtu
inoperculate

aceeilnortux
exulceration
aceeilnrsstv
verticalness
aceeiloopprs
corporealise
aceeilopprrt
preceptorial
aceeilpprstv
perspectival
aceeilrrttvy
retractively
aceeimmnnpry
impermanency
aceeimmoosst
semicomatose
aceeimmprtuy
empyreumatic
aceeimnnoorr
oneiromancer
aceeimnnortt
conterminate
aceeimnorssx
cross-examine
aceeimnorsvw
servicewoman
aceeimnrttuv
centumvirate
aceeinoorrtv
overreaction
aceeinoppprt
apperception
aceeinopprsu
sea-porcupine
aceeinoprrrt
carton-pierre
aceeinoprrtu
recuperation
aceeinoprstt
inspectorate
aceeinorstvv
conservative
aceeirrsttuy
treasure-city
aceejkkmnoty
monkey-jacket
aceellmmnopt
complemental
aceellooprrt
electropolar
aceelmnnortu
nomenclature
aceelmnoostu
lomentaceous
aceelnsssstt
tactlessness
aceelpsstuuy
eucalyptuses
aceelrrttuuw
water-culture
aceemmnorstu
commensurate
aceemnnnnotu
announcement

aceemnnnotuu
mountenaunce
aceemnnorrst
remonstrance
aceemoprstty
spermatocyte
aceenoprstuu
percutaneous
aceeooprrttt
protectorate
aceeoppprrst
pepper-castor
aceeoprrrtuy
recuperatory
aceffffiorst
staff-officer
aceffiiilmos
semi-official
aceffiiknnps
Pecksniffian
aceffiinrrtt
intertraffic
aceffilnnssu
fancifulness
acefforrsuuu
furfuraceous
acefghiinrtw
fire-watching
acefgiiknnrv
carving-knife
acefgillnnot
falcon-gentil
acefgilorssu
self-gracious
acefgllnruuy
ungracefully
acefhhhirsty
fish-hatchery
acefhhimnsty
chimney-shaft
acefhiimnrtu
fruit-machine
acefhlnsstuw
watchfulness
acefhmnnnorr
Norman-French
acefhnorsttu
countershaft
acefiiiklnrt
fairnitickle
acefiiilnost
fictionalise
acefiiilnott
felicitation
acefiiinortv
verification
acefiiiprtuv
purificative
acefiiklnrty
fairnytickle
acefiillnnot
inflectional
acefiillrrty
terrifically

acefiilnoqtu
liquefaction
acefiilorstu
laticiferous
acefiilortuv
curvifoliate
acefiilsttvy
self-activity
acefiimnortv
confirmative
acefiinoortv
vociferation
acefiinoprtt
petrifaction
acefiiorrstv
versificator
acefiiorrtvy
verificatory
acefiiorsttt
testificator
acefiiossstt
fissicostate
acefiirrttuv
vitrifacture
acefiirrttvy
refractivity
acefilmnoprt
placentiform
acefilnnooss
confessional
acefilnoopst
pelican's-foot
acefilorrrty
refractorily
acefinoorrtt
torrefaction
acefinoprttu
putrefaction
acefinopsttu
stupefaction
acefinorrsst
fornicatress
acefinossstu
factiousness
acefkloptttu
futtock-plate
acefllmooprw
camp-follower
aceggghilmop
phlegmagogic
acegghhhiinr
high-reaching
acegghinrrty
gathering-cry
aceggiilnnst
single-acting
aceggiknnoor
cooking-range
aceggikrsstw
swagger-stick
aceggillloy
geologically
aceggillmmoo
gemmological

aceggilnoost
geognostical
aceggimnorty
gyromagnetic
acegginnoort
congregation
aceghhiilopr
heliographic
aceghhiioprr
hierographic
aceghhinoprt
ethnographic
aceghhioprrr
chirographer
aceghhioprry
cheirography
aceghhioprty
hyetographic
aceghhnorrst
shortchanger
aceghhooprry
choreography
aceghiillnyy
hygienically
aceghikmnopr
epoch-marking
aceghiknprtt
carpet-knight
aceghillnnou
hallucinogen
aceghillnoop
nephological
phenological
aceghillnoot
ethnological
aceghilmopyy
hypoglycemia
aceghilnnnty
enchantingly
aceghilnoptt
Plectognathi
aceghilnrrtw
night-crawler
aceghilooprs
phraseologic
aceghiloopty
hepaticology
aceghiloprxy
lexicography
aceghimoprrr
micrographer
aceghinoprrz
zincographer
aceghinoprst
stenographic
aceghiopprrr
reprographic
aceghiopprrt
petrographic
aceghioprrst
cerographist
aceghirrsttt
garter-stitch

aceghmooprrs
cosmographer
aceghmooprty
cometography
aceghnooprsu
necrophagous
aceghopprrst
spectrograph
aceghopprtyy
ectypography
acegiiillmty
illegitimacy
acegiiilnnov
vaginicoline
acegiiinottv
incogitative
acegiikkmnty
mickey-taking
acegiilllmos
collegialism
acegiillloty
collegiality
acegiilloopt
geopolitical
acegiillosty
egoistically
acegiilnnotu
geniculation
acegiilnnoty
congeniality
acegiilnnrsy
increasingly
acegiilorssu
sacrilegious
acegiimnorrt
microgranite
acegiimnorst
gastrocnemii
acegiinoottx
excogitation
acegikllnpru
lurking-place
acegikllnsss
gall-sickness
acegiklnoopp
cooking-apple
acegiknpprss
packing-press
acegilllnooy
neologically
acegillmooty
etymological
acegillnnosy
geosynclinal
acegillnnoty
congenitally
acegillnooop
poenological
acegillnooru
neurological
acegillnorvw
wallcovering
acegillnrtty
clatteringly
acegillooost
osteological
acegillooprt
petrological
acegilloopst
pestological
acegilnnottu
conglutinate
acegilnooost
oceanologist
acegilnooprt
organoleptic
acegilnoortw
water-cooling
acegilnrstty
scatteringly
acegiloopsst
escapologist
acegilorsttu
gesticulator
acegimnnorsu
cousin-german
aceginnorrtu
raconteuring
aceginoprrsu
superorganic
aceginorsssu
graciousness
acegiooopprt
apogeotropic
aceglmnortyy
laryngectomy
aceglnooprsy
laryngoscope
acegloorsuuy
courageously
acegooprsstu
stegocarpous
acehhiimrstt
Mechitharist
acehhiinoprt
hierophantic
acehhilmoptx
exophthalmic
acehhiloopst
theosophical
acehhiloptty
hypothetical
acehhimooopt
homoeopathic
acehhinnostt
antichthones
acehhinoprtt
theanthropic
acehhllnnory
Rhynchonella
acehhmorstty
chrestomathy
acehhnoosttu
autochthones
acehhooprtty
hypothecator
acehiiiknpst
kinesipathic
acehiiinrsst
christianise
acehiiinsttt
antitheistic
acehiilmnntt
anthelmintic
acehiilmopsu
pleiochasium
acehiilnpprs
planispheric
acehiilnprst
sphincterial
acehiilprsty
sphericality
acehiimorstt
iatrochemist
acehiinnorst
Neo-Christian
acehiinopppr
hippocrepian
acehiinprrst
prechristian
acehiinssttu
enthusiastic
acehiintttuy
authenticity
acehiiopprst
Hippocratise
acehiiopsstt
sophisticate
acehiipprrst
periphrastic
acehiipsstuv
Sivapithecus
acehiklmnsty
chimney-stalk
acehikrrsssw
kirschwasser
acehillmnopy
phonemically
acehillnopst
plain-clothes
acehillnopty
phonetically
acehillnoruy
unheroically
acehillorrty
rhetorically
acehillorstu
Ulotrichales
acehillprrss
schiller-spar
acehillrstyy
hysterically
acehilmnoott
nomothetical
acehilmoorrt
horometrical
acehilnnnsss
clannishness
acehilnnoruw
unicorn-whale
acehilnoppty
phenotypical
acehilnpprtt
pitcher-plant
acehiloopstt
photoelastic
acehiloprstu
tricephalous
acehilpprsty
hyperplastic
acehimmmnstt
mismatchment
acehimmnorst
metachronism
acehimnpssss
scampishness
acehimooostt
homoeostatic
acehimoprrtt
tetramorphic
acehimoprsst
atmospherics
acehimorsttt
thermostatic
acehimpprsty
spermaphytic
acehimrssttw
master-switch
acehinopprtu
hippocentaur
acehinopssty
sycophantise
acehinopstty
enhypostatic
acehinorsstt
canister-shot
acehllllopss
scallop-shell
acehlllmosst
small-clothes
acehllmorsyy
lachrymosely
acehlmmnootw
commonwealth
acehlmoorsst
schoolmaster
acehlopssuxy
psychosexual
acehmmnooort
monochromate
acehmnorrrtt
trench-mortar
acehmoorstty
tracheostomy
acehmoorttty
tetrachotomy
acehoorrrstt
orchestrator
acehprrsttuy
Trachypterus
aceiiilmnnss
inimicalness
aceiiilmnpsu
municipalise
aceiiilnstty
inelasticity

aceiiilrsttv
relativistic
aceiiilrstvv
revivalistic
aceiiimnprss
precisianism
aceiiinnnort
incineration
aceiiinnrstt
intrinsicate
aceiiinprsst
precisianist
aceiijllstuy
Jesuitically
aceiilllpty
elliptically
aceiillmnsst
miscellanist
aceiillmntuu
multicauline
aceiillmpttu
multiplicate
aceiillnorrt
Torricellian
aceiilloqtuv
colliquative
aceiilmmnrst
mercantilism
aceiilmmrrsu
mercurialism
aceiilmnosst
sectionalism
aceiilmnrstt
mercantilist
aceiilmoppss
episcopalism
aceiilmoprrt
polarimetric
aceiilmoprst
semitropical
aceiilmrrstu
mercurialist
aceiilnnnrtu
internuncial
aceiilnnopst
inspectional
aceiilnnrsty
transiliency
aceiilnoprst
inspectorial
aceiilnorttu
reticulation
aceiilnostuv
vesiculation
aceiilnrsstt
triticalness
aceiilnrsttt
clarinettist
aceiilnssstu
sensualistic
aceiiloprstt
politicaster
aceiilprrsuy
superciliary

aceiilpsstuy
Puseyistical
aceiilrrsstu
surrealistic
aceiilrrttty
retractility
aceiimmnnnot
antimnemonic
aceiimnorrrt
recriminator
aceiimnorstt
cremationist
aceiimnossst
seismonastic
aceiimnosstu
scitamineous
aceiimnpttuy
pneumaticity
aceiimoprstt
peristomatic
aceiinnnortu
renunciation
aceiinnorttu
centuriation
aceiinnottuv
continuative
aceiinooqtuv
equivocation
aceiinoorstv
viscerotonia
aceiinoprrtt
practitioner
aceiinoprstu
pertinacious
aceiinorrstw
contrariwise
aceiiopprrtt
precipitator
aceijlnooprt
projectional
aceijnnnotty
joint-tenancy
aceilllnrtuy
lenticularly
aceillmmnoot
monometallic
aceillmmnopt
complimental
aceillmnoopt
compellation
aceillmnoopx
complexional
aceillmnrttu
multicentral
aceillmnrtuu
multinuclear
aceillmntuvy
multivalency
aceillmortuv
volumetrical
aceillmortuy
molecularity
aceillmsttuu
multisulcate

aceillmtuuvy
cumulatively
aceillnnorru
carillonneur
aceillnoptuy
unpoetically
aceillnosttu
scutellation
aceilmmmnoss
commensalism
aceilmmnosty
commensality
aceilmnnoopt
componential
aceilmnsssty
mysticalness
aceilmooprrs
corporealism
aceilmoopstt
leptosomatic
aceilmoosttu
coal-titmouse
aceilmoprrty
pyrometrical
aceilmoprsuu
primulaceous
aceilmopstuv
compulsative
aceilmostttu
multicostate
aceilnnnootv
conventional
aceilnooprss
processional
aceilnooprsu
porcelainous
aceilnooprtt
lactoprotein
aceilnoortuy
elocutionary
aceilnoprssu
percussional
aceilnosttuv
consultative
aceilooprrst
corporealist
prosectorial
aceilooprrtt
protectorial
aceilooprrty
corporeality
aceiloopsstt
osteoplastic
aceilopprrtt
protreptical
aceiloprrsuy
precariously
aceilopsstuu
stipulaceous
aceilorrrstt
rectirostral
aceilpprsstu
superplastic

aceimmnnoott
commentation
aceimmnostuv
consummative
aceimmoorrst
commiserator
aceimnnnortt
conterminant
aceimnnoopst
compensation
aceimnnoprtu
unimportance
aceimnoooopt
onomatopoeic
aceimnoprsty
cryptomnesia
aceimnorrsst
stercoranism
aceimnorsstv
conservatism
aceimnpsttuu
mispunctuate
aceimnssttuy
unsystematic
aceimooprstz
spermatozoic
zoospermatic
aceimoprrstu
periostracum
aceimprrrstw
writer's-cramp
aceinnnorstv
inconversant
aceinnooprtt
pernoctation
aceinnoorstv
conservation
conversation
aceinnoosttt
contestation
aceinnorrsst
contrariness
aceinnorrtuy
renunciatory
aceinnorsttu
encrustation
aceinoopprsx
praxinoscope
aceinopssssu
spaciousness
aceinopssstu
captiousness
aceinorrsstt
stercoranist
aceinorrstvx
conservatrix
aceinorrtttu
contriturate
aceinorrtuuv
vaunt-courier
aceinossstuu
cautiousness
aceiooprrrrt
troop-carrier

aceiooprrrtt
tricorporate
aceiooqrtuvy
equivocatory
aceiorrssttu
resuscitator
acejllnrrtuy
currant-jelly
aceklnprsttu
planet-struck
acekloogrruu
Quaker-colour
acellmopsuuu
plumulaceous
acellnnossuy
consensually
acellnooprsu
porcellanous
acellnorttuy
counter-tally
acellnottuxy
contextually
acelmmnostuy
consummately
acelmnooprtt
contemplator
acelmnprsuuu
supernaculum
acelnnrssuuu
ranunculuses
acelnooprstu
proconsulate
acelooopsstu
octosepalous
acelooopsttu
octopetalous
aceloprrsttu
court-plaster
acemmmooorrt
commemorator
acemnooprrty
contemporary
acemnooprsty
compensatory
acemooprrstu
macropterous
acempprssswy
cypress-swamp
acennnorstuv
unconversant
acennoorsssu
canorousness
acenooqrtttu
quattrocento
acenoorrstvy
conservatory
acffgghiilnn
cliffhanging
acffiillnouy
unofficially
acfgiiilnotu
uglification
acfgiiinorst
significator
acfgilnpsttu
scalping-tuft
acfhhlnorssy
synchroflash
acfhiiimnotu
humification
acfhiillorry
horrifically
acfhllntuuwy
unwatchfully
acfiiiilnotv
vilification
acfiiiimnnot
minification
acfiiiinnotv
vinification
acfiiiinotvv
vivification
acfiiilnopst
spiflication
acfiiinnoott
notification
acfiiinnortt
antifriction
acfiiinoosst
ossification
acfiiinoprtu
purification
acfiiinoptty
typification
acfiiinorttv
vitrifaction
acfiijorsttu
justificator
acfiilllopry
prolifically
acfiillnopty
pontifically
acfiilnnnoot
non-fictional
acfiilosttuy
factitiously
acfiimnnoort
confirmation
acfiinorrttu
trifurcation
acfiioprrtuy
purificatory
acfillnnotuy
functionally
acfimnnooort
conformation
acfimnoorrty
confirmatory
acfrrstuuuy
usufructuary
acgghhioprry
hygrographic
acgghilnnnuy
unchangingly
acggiilloost
glaciologist
acggilnppssu
cupping-glass
acggilnssttu
glass-cutting
acghhhioptyy
ichthyophagy
acghhiiloprt
lithographic
acghhinooppr
phonographic
acghhinoortt
orthognathic
acghhiooppr t
photographic
acghhiooprrt
orthographic
acghhiopprty
phytographic
acghhloosttu
school-taught
acghhnooprry
chronography
acghhopprsyy
psychography
acghiiknsstv
shaving-stick
acghiillloop
philological
acghiillloot
lithological
acghiillnoor
rhinological
acghiillooop
ophiological
acghiilloost
histological
acghiinnrrsu
nursing-chair
acghiinprsty
scintigraphy
acghiiprssst
sphragistics
acghillmooty
mythological
acghillnooop
phonological
acghilloprs
oscillograph
acghilloopty
phytological
acghiloprsty
stylographic
acghimnnortw
morning-watch
acghinoopprr
pornographic
acghiooppr st
coprophagist
acghioopssty
phagocytosis
acghkloppuyy
happy-go-lucky
acghooopprsu
coprophagous
acghopprrtyy
cryptography
acgiiillnstu
linguistical
acgiiilnosty
caliginosity
acgiiinnottx
intoxicating
acgiikklnstw
walking-stick
acgiikknprst
kicking-strap
acgiiklnnoru
caulking-iron
acgiiknorsst
stock-raising
acgiilllmnoo
limnological
acgiilllrtuy
liturgically
acgiilmnosuu
mucilaginous
acgiilnoorst
craniologist
acgiilnoosuv
vaginicolous
acgiilnppstu
supplicating
acgiiloopprt
plagiotropic
acgiinnnoost
consignation
acgiinnnoott
contignation
acgiinnoostt
contagionist
acgiinnosttw
wainscotting
acgikkmnosst
stocking-mask
acgiklnorssw
working-class
acgillloooyz
zoologically
acgillmnnooy
gnomonically
acgillnooost
nostological
acgillooop rt
tropological
acgilnnnottu
conglutinant
acgilnoostuy
contagiously
acgilnopsuuy
pugnaciously
acgilnorsuuy
ungraciously
acgimnooprtu
compurgation
acgimoprstty
cryptogamist
acginnoorsty
consignatory
acgkorsssstu
tussock-grass

acgllnoorsuy
clangorously
acglnooprsyy
laryngoscopy
acgmooprrtuy
compurgatory
acgmooprstuy
cryptogamous
achhhnooprry
Rhynchophora
achhiiinorst
Ornithischia
achhiilmnopr
philharmonic
achhiimnopps
championship
achhiimostty
stichomythia
achhiimostyz
schizothymia
achhillmrtyy
rhythmically
achhilmnrtuy
unrhythmical
achhiloopprst
holophrastic
achhilorttyy
ichthyolatry
achhinnoptxy
phycoxanthin
achhinoprsty
christophany
achhinopssty
sycophantish
achiiiinrsst
trichiniasis
achiiilmstwy
whimsicality
achiiilnorst
histrionical
achiiimnpssu
musicianship
achiiimnrsst
Christianism
achiiinrstty
Christianity
achiiklmoptt
Machtpolitik
achiillmoott
lithotomical
achiillnossu
hallucinosis
achiillorsty
historically
achiilnnoort
chlorination
achiilnoprst
rhinoplastic
achiilnorstu
unhistorical
achiilooppst
scoptophilia
achiiloprstt
cartophilist

achiimnoprst
misanthropic
achiimoopppt
hippopotamic
achiimopprst
Hippocratism
achiinnnorst
non-Christian
achiinoprstt
antistrophic
achiiprsstty
psychiatrist
achiklloopst
lock-hospital
achikmortuuv
kurchatovium
achillnoorsy
isochronally
achillnoptyy
hypnotically
achillorsuvy
chivalrously
achilmopprry
lamprophyric
achilnnopstu
cushion-plant
achilnooppty
phonotypical
achilnorsuuv
unchivalrous
achiloooopttv
photovoltaic
achiloopprrs
corporalship
achilorrstty
Christolatry
achimmoppsty
psammophytic
achimnnoorty
ornithomancy
achimnnorssy
asynchronism
achimnoopssu
poison-sumach
achinoostttu
Southcottian
achiooprrsuz
rhizocarpous
achioprsssty
astrophysics
achiqrssttuz
quartz-schist
achmmnooorsy
monochromasy
achnnoorssuy
asynchronous
aciiiilmrstt
militaristic
aciiiilnostv
civilisation
aciiillmpttu
multicipital
aciiilmmnpsu
municipalism

aciiilmnnost
nominalistic
aciiilmnoost
coalitionism
aciiilmnptuy
municipality
aciiilnoostt
coalitionist
solicitation
aciiilnoprtt
triplication
aciiilnostvv
convivialist
aciiilnotvvy
conviviality
aciiilnpprty
principality
aciiilqtuyzz
quizzicality
aciiimmnorst
Marcionitism
aciiimnorstv
Victorianism
aciiimprsstt
patristicism
aciiinnoottx
intoxication
aciiinnosttu
cutinisation
aciiinopssuu
inauspicious
aciiinprrttu
antipruritic
aciiiprsssty
scissiparity
aciijllrstuy
juristically
aciijlnorstu
journalistic
aciillmnoost
collision-mat
aciillnooqtu
colliquation
aciillnoprvy
provincially
aciillnorstt
scintillator
aciillnrtuuv
vinicultural
aciilloqtuxy
quixotically
aciillossuvy
lasciviously
aciillrsstty
crystallitis
aciilmnnootu
columniation
aciilmnorstu
matriclinous
aciilmoopsst
apostolicism
aciilnnooost
colonisation

aciilnnoostu
inosculation
aciilnnostuy
insouciantly
aciilnoorsst
consistorial
aciilnoppstu
supplication
aciilnoprstu
patriclinous
aciilnorssss
nail-scissors
aciilnostuuy
incautiously
aciiloopstty
apostolicity
aciilopssuuy
auspiciously
aciilprsttuu
apiculturist
aciimnoprttu
protactinium
aciimnopsssu
passion-music
aciinnnooort
incoronation
aciinnnoottu
continuation
aciinnooprst
conspiration
aciinnoopstt
constipation
aciinnoorsst
consistorian
aciinnorsttu
incrustation
aciinopssuuu
unauspicious
acikmnnoortu
mountain-cork
acilllllooquy
colloquially
acilllmortuu
multilocular
acillloprruu
plurilocular
acillmnosuuy
calumniously
acillmoootyz
zootomically
acillmorsuuy
miraculously
acillnnoosuv
convulsional
acillnopstyy
synoptically
acilloprrty
proctorially
acillooqsuuy
loquaciously
acillprrstuy
scripturally
acilmmnnoott
non-committal

acilmnooopst
cosmopolitan
acilmnoorstu
matroclinous
acilmnorsuuu
unmiraculous
acilmoopprst
protoplasmic
acilnnnostty
inconstantly
acilnnooortt
contortional
acilnnoosttu
consultation
acilnnopttuu
punctulation
acilnooorstt
colostration
acilnooprstu
patroclinous
acilnprrstuu
unscriptural
aciloopprstt
protoplastic
acilooprtty
prototypical
aciloprstuy
supplicatory
acilorrrstuv
curvirostral
acimmmnopruu
cuprammonium
acimmnnoostu
consummation
acimnnoooppt
pot-companion
acinnnorsttu
unconstraint
acinnoprttuu
puncturation
acinoooprrrt
incorporator
acinoprsstuu
transpicuous
aciorrrssttu
cirro-stratus
aclllprstuuy
sculpturally
acllmnooorsu
salmon-colour
acllrrsttuuy
structurally
aclmooprstuy
compulsatory
aclnoorsttuy
consultatory
acmmnoorstuy
consummatory
acmnnoortuwy
countrywoman
acmooorrrttt
motor-tractor
acnoooppr stt
contrapposto

adddddeeehlmu
muddleheaded
addddeeehnru
dunderheaded
addddeeffill
fiddle-faddle
adddeeehnoow
wooden-headed
adddeeghknou
dough-kneaded
adddeeghnrtu
hundred-gated
adddeehiilpy
Didelphyidae
adddeennrstu
understanded
adddefiilmno
diamond-field
adddfgginort
draft-dodging
adddiillmnor
diamond-drill
addeeeeflnrs
self-endeared
addeeefilnrs
self-indeared
addeeeflprsv
self-depraved
addeeegghlor
loggerheaded
addeeegnnnru
unendangered
addeeehilprt
triple-headed
addeeehinrst
disheartened
addeeehllowy
yellow-headed
addeeehlpuzz
puzzle-headed
addeeeiirstv
desiderative
addeeeinssss
diseasedness
addeeeklnooy
yankee-doodle
addeeemnoryy
ready-moneyed
addeeenprssv
depravedness
addeeffnrstu
understaffed
addeefhllnty
left-handedly
addeefhlmory
formaldehyde
addeefilnors
self-ordained
addeeflnrssu
dreadfulness
addeeggillnn
dingle-dangle
addeeghhlouy
oughly-headed

addeeghilnns
single-handed
addeeghinprs
spring-headed
addeeghmrstu
hedge-mustard
addeegilnnps
landing-speed
addeeginppsu
pease-pudding
addeegnorstu
adder's-tongue
addeehhilpss
shield-shaped
addeehiilmns
shield-maiden
addeehilmnow
diamond-wheel
addeehlloowy
woolly-headed
addeehmnottu
mutton-headed
addeehmorsuy
Hydromedusae
addeehoprrtu
proud-hearted
addeeiimmnno
demi-mondaine
addeeiimnsst
disseminated
addeeiinoprt
Torpedinidae
addeeiinorst
desideration
addeeillpssy
displeasedly
addeeilorrww
world-wearied
addeeimnsssy
dismayedness
addeeinrstuv
disadventure
addeelnosstt
staddle-stone
addeelnrruwy
unrewardedly
addeennrrstu
understander
addefgiillnn
landing-field
addefgilrrsu
disregardful
addefhilnoos
old-fashioned
addefhilopst
feldspathoid
addefiiissst
dissatisfied
addeflnnnouw
Newfoundland
addegilnnosu
sounding-lead
addegilnoprs
spring-loaded

addegilnpptu
pudding-plate
addegilnprss
saddle-spring
addeginnrruw
underdrawing
addehiilpprz
lizard-hipped
addehimnnosu
unadmonished
addehinprrwy
whip-and-derry
addehmnooort
rhodomontade
addehmnorsuy
hydromedusan
addeiiiqttuv
quidditative
addeiilmssvy
misadvisedly
addeiilnqtuu
unliquidated
addeiilpssty
dissipatedly
addeiinoppst
disappointed
addeilmnnstu
undismantled
addeimnnorrw
narrow-minded
addeinnooott
Notodontidae
addemnooorrt
rodomontader
addennoortuw
down-and-outer
addennorssww
downwardness
addfhiimorty
hydatidiform
addfhlnoostu
thousandfold
addfiillnsuy
disdainfully
addgiilnsstu
studding-sail
addiiiinnopr
diprionidian
addiiillnuvy
individually
adeeeefhnprt
pen-feathered
adeeeeginrtv
degenerative
adeeeeglnrty
degenerately
adeeeffiinrt
differentiae
adeeefghintv
heaven-gifted
adeeefgilnrr
rifle-grenade
adeeefhilssv
self-adhesive

adeeefhinprt
pin-feathered
adeeefillrst
alder-liefest
adeeegghilst
eagle-sighted
adeeegginnrt
degenerating
adeeeggnrstu
unsegregated
adeeeghlmmrs
sledge-hammer
adeeeghlprsy
hedge-parsley
adeeegiloprs
grapeseed-oil
adeeegimnrst
demagnetiser
disagreement
adeeeginnort
degeneration
adeeeginopss
paedogenesis
adeeeginprst
predesignate
adeeeginrrtt
redintegrate
adeeeglnnrss
enlargedness
adeeeglnrstw
strangle-weed
adeeegmnnnrt
endangerment
adeeegnoqruw
queen-dowager
adeeehhilrst
heater-shield
adeeehhlortw
whole-hearted
adeeehiimnpr
ephemeridian
adeeehimnrtt
hereditament
adeeehinortx
exheredation
adeeehinsssv
adhesiveness
adeeehirrttt
tetrahedrite
adeeehlnnrrt
Netherlander
adeeehlrsttx
tax-sheltered
adeeehnnrttu
unthreatened
adeeeiilnptx
expediential
adeeeiimmrst
semi-diameter
adeeeiimnrtt
intermediate
adeeeiiorrst
aerosiderite

adeeeillmmos
mademoiselle
adeeeillmnop
lepidomelane
adeeeilmnort
radio-element
adeeeilnprrt
interpleader
adeeeilrrtty
reiteratedly
adeeeimprstt
distemperate
adeeeinprstt
predestinate
adeeekllnost
endoskeletal
adeeellmnnrw
well-mannered
adeeelnossst
desolateness
adeeelopprst
tradespeople
adeeemnorsst
moderateness
adeeemnpprss
pamperedness
adeeennttuux
unextenuated
adeeenopprrt
preponderate
adeeenpprrss
preparedness
adeeenprrtuv
peradventure
adeeenrssvyy
everydayness
adeeeopprrsv
eavesdropper
adeeeoprrsuv
overpersuade
adeeffghinrt
affrightened
adeeffhirstt
stiff-hearted
adeeffiilnrt
differential
adeefginnort
finger-and-toe
adeefginnrst
free-standing
adeefgirsstu
fatigue-dress
adeefgllnnwy
newfangledly
adeefglnorrw
flower-garden
adeefhilnrtt
flint-hearted
adeefhilrstv
harvest-field
adeefhinnosw
new-fashioned
adeefiillnps
field-spaniel

adeefilnnost
self-anointed
adeefilnptxy
fixed-penalty
adeefiloruvv
evil-favoured
adeefimoprrt
imperforated
adeefinnrstu
Frauendienst
adeefinorstv
arfvedsonite
adeeflloruvw
well-favoured
adeefllprstu
apfelstrudel
adeefnnorruw
unforewarned
adeefnoprrtu
unperforated
adeefnorssuv
favouredness
adeegggnnotu
egg-and-tongue
adeegghirstt
straight-edge
adeeggiqrrsu
square-rigged
adeegglnoppr
doppel-ganger
adeeghhilrtt
light-hearted
adeeghhinoss
high-seasoned
adeeghhinstw
sheath-winged
adeeghimnost
homesteading
adeeghinnrrt
heart-rending
adeeghlmoprt
dephlegmator
adeeghnrsttu
stage-thunder
adeeghoprrsw
hedge-sparrow
adeeghprsttu
stepdaughter
adeegiilnnou
Euglenoidina
adeegiinrstt
disintegrate
adeegiipprtw
periwig-pated
adeegikllllnw
lake-dwelling
adeegiklnrst
deerstalking
adeegiknnrrt
kindergarten
adeegiknrrst
ring-streaked
adeegillorvy
gaol-delivery

adeegilnnrsu
undersealing
adeegilortvy
derogatively
adeeginnrrtw
winter-garden
adeeginnrttu
unintegrated
adeegioprrtv
prerogatived
adeegjmnsttu
judgment-seat
adeegllrrssy
regardlessly
adeeglmnosss
gladsomeness
adeeglrstuvv
velvet-guards
adeegmnnoorr
gander-mooner
adeegmnnrrtu
undergarment
adeegnoopsst
Steganopodes
adeegnoorrvw
wood-engraver
adeegnprtuux
unexpurgated
adeegorrttxy
dextrogyrate
adeehhiknrrs
headshrinker
adeehhnnptuy
unhyphenated
adeehiilmnty
diethylamine
adeehiilrrty
hereditarily
adeehiklnoop
kaleidophone
adeehilnpsty
synadelphite
adeehimnpprs
misapprehend
adeehimrssst
headmistress
adeehinnoost
Hindoostanee
adeehinorstu
house-trained
adeehllnnrtu
unenthralled
adeehlmmotuy
mealy-mouthed
adeehlmoostv
smooth-leaved
adeehlpprssu
pedal-pushers
adeehlprstuu
desulphurate
adeehmnnosss
handsomeness
adeehmnorrsy
dysmenorrhea

adeehmoprtty
dermatophyte
adeehnorstty
stony-hearted
adeehorsstuw
house-steward
adeehorstttu
stout-hearted
adeeiiilmrst
demilitarise
adeeiiilmttv
delimitative
adeeiiilorst
editorialise
adeeiijllrvy
jail-delivery
adeeiikprstw
weak-spirited
adeeiillnntt
Little-endian
adeeiillntvy
evidentially
adeeiilmmnpt
impedimental
adeeiilmnnss
maidenliness
adeeiilmttvy
meditatively
adeeiilnnrst
internalised
adeeiilnprst
presidential
adeeiilopptv
deoppilative
adeeiilrtvvy
derivatively
adeeiimnnotv
denominative
adeeiimnnrsu
unseminaried
adeeiimnprst
mean-spirited
adeeiimnrrty
intermediary
adeeiinopttx
expeditation
adeeiinorstt
disorientate
adeeiinpsstv
dispensative
adeeiinrrsty
residentiary
adeeiinrrtvw
water-diviner
adeeiipprssu
dispauperise
adeeiirssttv
dissertative
adeeikllmppr
lappered-milk
adeeiklmpprr
ripple-marked
adeeiknrrrtw
water-drinker

adeeillorstv
travel-soiled
adeeillprstv
silver-plated
adeeilmmorty
immoderately
adeeilmntttu
multidentate
adeeilmprtty
timely-parted
adeeilnnttuv
unventilated
adeeilnottvy
denotatively
adeeilnrrsty
restrainedly
adeeilorrstw
water-soldier
adeeimmnorsu
misdemeanour
adeeimnnnrtu
intermundane
adeeimnnrttu
unterminated
adeeimnrstuv
misadventure
adeeinnoopru
Indo-European
adeeinnoprst
respondentia
adeeinnrrstu
unrestrained
adeeinnssstu
unsteadiness
adeeinoprsst
dispersonate
adeeinorrstv
overstrained
adeeirrrsttw
water-strider
adeejmnrsttu
readjustment
adeellmmnrtu
untrammelled
adeellmoruzz
muzzle-loader
adeelmoprstu
deuteroplasm
adeelnpprruy
unpreparedly
adeeloorrsw
solar-powered
adeemnnnortu
unornamented
adeemnnprsuu
supermundane
adeemnnprtuy
underpayment
adeemnopprsw
newspaperdom
adeennoorrst
androsterone
adeennopprrt
preponderant

adeenorsssst
assortedness
adeenorsstuw
sweet-and-sour
adeffghilrty
affrightedly
adeffikknnor
knife-and-fork
adefghilnrtt
right-and-left
adefghiorsuw
shadow-figure
adefgiiillnr
Fringillidae
adefgiiknnrw
drawing-knife
adefgiillnpy
playing-field
adefgilnorsu
glandiferous
adefgilnrssy
lady's-fingers
adefginnnssu
unfadingness
adefginooprr
proof-reading
adefhimnoors
fore-admonish
adefhinrsssw
dwarfishness
adefhllorttu
full-throated
adefiiilqrsu
disqualifier
adefiilnostt
deflationist
adefiinnqtuu
unquantified
adefiinrsttu
unstratified
adefilmnnoss
manifoldness
adefilmnorsu
unformalised
adefinnoortu
foundationer
refoundation
adefllnrtuuy
fraudulently
adeflmnortuu
unformulated
adegghiinrst
sight-reading
adegghilnrtu
daughterling
adegghinorru
rough-grained
adeggiilnrtw
water-gilding
adeggiinorst
disgregation
adegginnorrr
organ-grinder

adeghhilnors
shareholding
adeghhiprsst
sharp-sighted
adeghhoprrry
hydrographer
adeghhorrstu
draught-horse
adeghhorstuu
draught-house
adeghiinrrss
hairdressing
adeghillnosv
slave-holding
adeghinorrst
horse-trading
adeghinrsstu
draughtiness
adeghjllmntu
judgment-hall
adeghllnorst
stranglehold
adeghlnosstu
thousand-legs
adeghnoprstu
sharp-tongued
adeghopprsuy
pseudography
adegiiikmmnr
Kimmeridgian
adegiiilnrtt
interdigital
adegiillmnsy
misleadingly
adegiillnntu
dentilingual
adegiilmnors
demoralising
adegiilnorss
digressional
adegiilnprsy
despairingly
adegiimnrrst
riding-master
adegiinnortu
unoriginated
adegiinnprsu
undespairing
adegiinoorrt
granodiorite
adegiinrsstt
giant's-stride
adegillnoruz
lounge-lizard
adegilnnrssw
drawlingness
adegilnootuz
Zeuglodontia
adegiloorrty
derogatorily
adegimnnoppr
name-dropping
adegimnorrsu
measuring-rod

adeginoprstu
outspreading
adegiorrssww
grass-widower
adehhillppsu
philadelphus
adehhirrsttw
thitherwards
adehhirrstww
whitherwards
adehhlmorrty
hydrothermal
adehhooprstt
sharp-toothed
adehhoprrtyy
hydrotherapy
adehiilnsttt
dilettantish
adehiimnorrt
Thermidorian
adehiimnorss
disharmonise
adehiimoprst
mediatorship
adehiinoortt
Theriodontia
adehiiopprrt
Rhipidoptera
adehiiorsstu
disauthorise
adehilloorwy
woolly-haired
adehillsstty
lady's-thistle
adehilmnnoop
monodelphian
adehilmnopsu
sulphonamide
adehiloprrty
pyritohedral
adehiloprstu
triadelphous
adehimmnnost
admonishment
adehimnrttww
withdrawment
adehinnoopty
phytonadione
adehinnortty
one-and-thirty
adehinnqsuuv
unvanquished
adehinooortz
antherozooid
adehinopprst
sharp-pointed
adehinorstuu
unauthorised
adehinqrrstu
hindquarters
adehiooprstt
orthopaedist
adehiopprtty
Pteridophyta
adehklmorrsu
shoulder-mark
adehlmnnosuy
unhandsomely
adehlmnoopsu
monadelphous
adehlmopstuy
splay-mouthed
adeiiilmnott
delimitation
adeiiimnorst
dimerisation
adeiiimnostv
deviationism
adeiiinosttv
deviationist
adeiiinsttu
attitudinise
adeiillmnory
meridionally
adeiillnpruv
Liverpudlian
adeiillstuvv
vaudevillist
adeiilmnsttt
dilettantism
adeiilnnopuv
unpavilioned
adeiilnnorty
inordinately
adeiilnooppt
deoppilation
adeiilnoopst
despoliation
adeiilnoprtv
providential
adeiilnorsst
dilatoriness
adeiilsssuvy
dissuasively
adeiimmnoort
immoderation
adeiimnnnoot
denomination
adeiimnnorsw
Neo-Darwinism
adeiimnnqruu
quadriennium
adeiimnnrstt
distrainment
adeiimnoprst
post-meridian
adeiimnorsst
disseminator
adeiinnnqquu
quinquenniad
adeiinnoorrt
reordination
adeiinnopsst
dispensation
adeiinnorstw
Neo-Darwinist
adeiinooprst
disoperation
adeiinooprtx
peroxidation
adeiinoopstt
deposítation
adeiinorrsvy
diversionary
adeiinorsstt
dissertation
adeiinosttuv
adventitious
adeiiooprst
radio-isotope
adeiiopprrst
dispropriate
adeiknooptty
kidney-potato
adeiknoprrtu
turnpike-road
adeilllnoosy
solenoidally
adeilllnrtuy
ill-naturedly
adeillnootvy
devotionally
adeillnprtuy
prudentially
adeillpprssy
lady's-slipper
adeilmnnnstu
disannulment
adeilmnsttuu
unstimulated
adeilnoopptu
depopulation
adeilnoprrsu
superordinal
adeilnorrstt
dentirostral
adeilnorrstv
dorsiventral
adeilnorsstw
towardliness
adeilnssstuy
unassistedly
adeimmoprsuy
praseodymium
adeimooprstz
spermatozoid
adeinnoprssu
underpassion
adeinnoprstu
unpatronised
adeinoprssty
dispensatory
adeinoprttvz
privat-dozent
adeinorsstuv
disaventrous
adejlooprsuy
jeopardously
adejlorssstu
loss-adjuster
adekmnnorruw
underworkman
adellmmorsty
troll-my-dames
adellnnorssu
all-roundness
adellnorssuy
slanderously
adellooprrst
petrodollars
adellorstuuy
adulterously
adelnorrsuvy
land-surveyor
ademnnrsttuu
untransmuted
ademnoorrstt
demonstrator
ademnrrsttuu
understratum
ademoprrstuy
pseudomartyr
adennorsstuw
untowardness
adenoqrrrtuu
quarter-round
adeoorrrsuvy
road-surveyor
adffgiilnntu
fault-finding
adfghhilostw
shadow-flight
adfghiinrstv
driving-shaft
adfhmnooottu
foot-and-mouth
adfiiilnnost
disinflation
adfiiilnostu
fluidisation
adfiilnoortu
fluoridation
adfiilosstuy
fastidiously
adfiinosstuu
unfastidious
adggiimnnors
gormandising
adggilnnnost
long-standing
adgginnnorsu
sound-ranging
adghhkoorstu
draught-hooks
adghilllmnos
smallholding
adghimrrrsyy
hydrargyrism
adghinoorttw
tooth-drawing
adghnoooprty
odontography
adghoooprstt
dogtooth-spar
adgiiinnrstw
winding-stair

adgiillnnnsu
disannulling
adgiillnnotu
longitudinal
adgiilnnprst
landing-strip
adgiinnoprtw
word-painting
adgillnntuuy
undulatingly
adgilnnostuy
astoundingly
adgimnnoorst
standing-room
adginnoooprt
gonadotropin
adginorrstuy
agroindustry
adglnnoortuw
long-drawn-out
adgoooprsstu
gastropodous
adhhioprstty
hydropathist
adhhnooprsuy
hydrophanous
adhiiimmrstt
mithridatism
adhiilmnopru
dolphinarium
adhiilnopstt
Dantophilist
adhiimoorrtu
radio-thorium
adhiimoprsst
diastrophism
adhillnostuy
outlandishly
adhinnnoopsy
sindonophany
adhllopssuyy
dasyphyllous
adhlnoooopt
odontophoral
adhnnooooprt
odontophoran
adiiiimnnott
intimidation
adiiilllmsww
wild-williams
adiiillmrssy
dissimilarly
adiiillnostt
distillation
adiiimnortty
intimidatory
adiiinnnoort
inordination
adiiinoprttu
tripudiation
adiiinorrttv
vitro-di-trina
adiiinorsttt
traditionist

adiiillmoprry
primordially
adiiillnossuy
sinusoidally
adiiillnrstuy
industrially
adiiillopstuv
post-diluvial
adiiillorstty
distillatory
adiiilmmnruuu
duraluminium
adiiilmnoprst
palindromist
adiiilmorsstu
dissimulator
adiiilnopstuv
post-diluvian
adiiilnorsttu
stridulation
adiiilnosttuu
altitudinous
latitudinous
adiiimnnnooss
non-admission
adiiopssttuu
disputatious
adillmnooopy
monopodially
adillnrsttuy
stridulantly
adilloorstuy
idolatrously
adilorrsttuy
stridulatory
adilorssstuy
disastrously
adimnnoootuw
mountain-wood
adiooprrssuu
sudoriparous
admnoooosttu
odontomatous
aeeeeggmnnrt
re-engagement
aeeeeghlprst
telegraphese
aeeeeginrrtv
regenerative
aeeeegnnrrtu
unregenerate
aeeeehhprrss
sheep-shearer
aeeeehlprsst
sheep-stealer
aeeeeiiprstt
tapsieteerie
aeeeenprrstt
serpent-eater
aeeeffilmnty
effeminately
aeeefgikmnrt
feeing-market

aeeefhiklnrt
leather-knife
aeeefhilrstv
live-feathers
aeeefhinrrtt
thereinafter
aeeefhinrsst
featheriness
aeeefiklnptt
palette-knife
aeeefilnprrt
preferential
aeeefimnrttv
fermentative
aeeeflnrssss
fearlessness
aeeegginrrst
steering-gear
aeeeghiilmrw
whigmaleerie
aeeeghinosst
aesthesiogen
aeeeghirsttz
gazetteerish
aeeegilnnrrv
line-engraver
aeeegilnrsst
single-seater
aeeegilttvvy
vegetatively
aeeegimnnstv
envisagement
aeeeginnorrt
regeneration
aeeeginnsstv
negativeness
aeeeginorrtt
interrogatee
aeeeginrrttv
vinegarrette
aeeegirrsttv
tergiversate
aeeegkmnorsy
grease-monkey
aeeegllnsstt
tassel-gentle
aeeeglmnnntt
entanglement
aeeeglnopstt
espagnolette
aeeegmmnortt
magnetometer
aeeegmmnosss
gamesomeness
aeeegmnnrstt
estrangement
aeeegmnoprsu
pergameneous
aeeegnnnqrtu
queen-regnant
aeeegnorrrty
regeneratory
aeeegoprrstu
supererogate

aeeehhorstuw
weather-house
aeeehilmprty
ephemerality
aeeehilnnssv
heavenliness
aeeehimnnopp
epiphenomena
aeeehinpprsv
apprehensive
aeeehinprsst
parenthesise
aeeehinrrttw
interwreathe
aeeehirsstux
heterauxesis
aeeehknopprs
speakerphone
aeeehlllprrs
pearl-sheller
aeeehlnprttw
pattern-wheel
aeeehlnsssst
hatelessness
aeeehlorstux
heterosexual
aeeehmnnsttw
enswathement
aeeehqrrrttu
three-quarter
aeeeiilmprtt
temperalitie
aeeeiilnprtx
experiential
aeeeillmmnst
elementalism
aeeeillnprtt
interpellate
aeeeilmnprtx
experimental
aeeeilmnrtty
intemerately
aeeeilnrsstv
relativeness
aeeeilnrttvy
inveterately
aeeeimnppstt
appetisement
aeeeimnrrtuv
remunerative
aeeeimoprrtv
evaporimeter
aeeeimorsttv
overestimate
aeeeimprsttv
septemvirate
aeeeinnorttx
exenteration
aeeeinprrttt
interpretate
aeeeinprsttv
presentative
aeeeinprttvv
preventative

aeeeinrrttux
extra-uterine
aeeeiprrstvv
preservative
aeeeklnooprs
saloon-keeper
aeeeklrrsttw
street-walker
aeeeklrssttw
welter-stakes
aeeekmoprrrt
pro-marketeer
aeeellprsssu
pleasureless
aeeelmnnssss
namelessness
aeeelmnorsyy
eleemosynary
aeeelmnsssst
tamelessness
aeeemnnorsty
earnest-money
aeeemnrsssst
reassessment
aeeennnprsty
earnest-penny
aeeennprrstt
representant
aeeeoprrrstv
perseverator
aeeffghirrtu
father-figure
aeeffgimnort
meat-offering
aeeffginorvw
wave-offering
aeeffhorrstt
foster-father
aeeffijnnors
Jeffersonian
aeeffllrstty
self-flattery
aeefflnnsstu
affluentness
aeefghinrsst
sergeant-fish
aeefgiilnnrv
never-failing
aeefgillnpss
self-pleasing
aeefginrrrsu
sugar-refiner
aeefgiorrrrt
refrigerator
aeefglnoorrw
orange-flower
aeefglnrsstu
gratefulness
aeefhhilrswy
whale-fishery
aeefhiknrsss
freakishness
aeefhillqrtu
quill-feather

aeefhilnrsst
fatherliness
aeefhilprrsy
pearl-fishery
aeefhlmnsssu
shamefulness
aeefhlmorrtw
flame-thrower
aeefhooprrtw
weather-proof
aeefiilnortt
interfoliate
aeefiknnnrst
Frankenstein
aeefilmnorrt
interfemoral
aeefiloprstu
petaliferous
aeefilprrsst
filter-passer
aeefimnnortt
fermentation
aeefimnnssst
manifestness
aeefimnorstu
amentiferous
aeefimoprrtv
performative
preformative
aeefinnorstt
fenestration
aeefinnostux
soixante-neuf
aeefknnorsss
forsakenness
aeeflmnooptt
footplatemen
aeeflmnorstt
forestalment
aeeflnsssttu
tastefulness
aeeflnssstuw
wastefulness
aeeflopqrsuw
pasque-flower
aeeflorrstww
water-flowers
aeefnoprrstt
foster-parent
aeefooprrsst
professorate
aeeggghhill
higgle-haggle
aeeggggillww
wiggle-waggle
aeegghlmopu
phlegmagogue
aeegggimnnrv
gem-engraving
aeeggginnnss
engagingness
aeegghnorttu
gang-there-out

aeeggijjllnn
jingle-jangle
aeeggikklnss
keeking-glass
aeeggillmmnn
mingle-mangle
aeeggilrssvy
aggressively
aeeggimmnost
geomagnetism
aeegginrsstt
resting-stage
aeeggiqrrrsu
square-rigger
aeeghhiloprr
heliographer
aeeghhioprrr
hierographer
aeeghhnoprrt
ethnographer
aeeghiinnrrv
Rhinegravine
aeeghillmmrt
hellgrammite
aeeghilmnopr
Germanophile
aeeghilnopsu
leaping-house
aeeghilnortw
watering-hole
aeeghilorruv
heliogravure
aeeghilprstt
telegraphist
aeeghinopsst
pathogenesis
aeeghinprsst
sergeantship
aeeghinrrstt
straightener
aeeghiprsstw
stage-whisper
aeeghllorrtt
toll-gatherer
aeeghlnoprsy
selenography
aeeghloorstt
theologaster
aeeghmnoprrs
phrasemonger
aeeghmooprrt
meteorograph
aeeghnoprrst
stenographer
aeeghnorsstu
anotherguess
aeeghoorsstv
harvest-goose
aeeghopprrrr
reprographer
aeeghopprrrt
petrographer
aeeghoprrsty
stereography

aeegiiillmtt
illegitimate
aeegiiklnpsv
evil-speaking
aeegiillmtty
legitimately
aeegiilmnors
mineralogise
aeegiilnnpss
palingenesis
aeegiinnnrtt
entertaining
aeegiinorrtv
reinvigorate
aeegiinprrtv
privateering
aeegikllnpsw
sleep-walking
aeegiklnsttt
giant's-kettle
aeegiknrrstt
street-raking
aeegilllnpsw
well-pleasing
aeegillrssst
legislatress
aeegilnnnopt
longipennate
aeegilnnpsss
pleasingness
aeegilnnrtty
entreatingly
aeegilnnssss
gainlessness
aeegimnnostt
segmentation
aeegimnnrsst
reassignment
aeegimnrrsst
mastersinger
aeeginnnsssu
sanguineness
aeeginnrssvw
waveringness
aeeginoprrrt
peregrinator
aeeginoprstt
poetastering
aeeginorsstt
negotiatress
aeegknoorstu
keratogenous
aeegllmnopsy
splenomegaly
aeegllmnruwz
mangel-wurzel
aeegllprrssy
press-gallery
aeegllprrsuu
spurge-laurel
aeeglmnnortv
governmental
aeeglmnnrstt
stranglement

aeegmnoprrry
prayer-monger
aeegmnoprsty
spermatogeny
aeegnoprrstu
supererogant
aeehhhilnsty
heathenishly
aeehhhoprrtt
three-ha'porth
aeehhilmmntu
Helianthemum
aeehhiloprty
heliotherapy
aeehhimprrty
hyperthermia
aeehhinprsty
hypersthenia
aeehhllortty
heterothally
aeehhlmmoort
homeothermal
aeehhlmprrty
hyperthermal
aeehhnooprtt
theatrophone
aeehhnopprty
phanerophyte
aeehhopprtty
phreatophyte
aeehiiknssst
kinaesthesis
aeehiinorstt
etherisation
aeehiinprrst
retainership
aeehiinstuvx
inexhaustive
aeehijnprsst
serjeantship
aeehiknnssss
sneakishness
aeehillmnnps
Panhellenism
aeehillmnnpu
panhellenium
aeehillnnnop
panhellenion
aeehillnnpst
Panhellenist
aeehilmmnrst
Simmenthaler
aeehilmmoost
mesothelioma
aeehilmnstuy
lese-humanity
aeehilmssttw
steam-whistle
aeehilnoprrs
prehensorial
aeehilnssstt
stealthiness
aeehilprsstt
spear-thistle

aeehimmorrtt
arithmometer
aeehimnnortt
nitromethane
aeehimorsttt
theorematist
aeehinnopprs
apprehension
aeehinoorstu
heteroousian
aeehinorrrst
horse-trainer
aeehinrssstw
waterishness
aeehiorrrrst
hair-restorer
aeehipprrxyy
hyperpyrexia
aeehiprrsttw
weather-strip
aeehiprstttu
therapeutist
aeehkmmmnory
monkey-hammer
aeehknnoortt
heterokontan
aeehllmmorwy
yellow-hammer
aeehllmnnopy
phenomenally
aeehllmnoopt
metallophone
aeehlmnrssss
harmlessness
aeehlmprrsuu
superhumeral
aeehlnoprtuy
polyurethane
aeehlnprssuy
hypersensual
aeehloprstty
heteroplasty
aeehlorsstuv
harvest-louse
aeehmmnoorrt
harmonometer
aeehmmooprst
metamorphose
aeehmnnoprty
hymenopteran
aeehmnooprrt
Enteromorpha
aeehmorsstuv
harvest-mouse
aeehmorsttuy
erythematous
aeehmprrstuy
serum-therapy
aeehnnorrstt
north-eastern
aeehnorrsssv
overrashness
aeehnorssttu
south-eastern

aeehoprrrstw
spear-thrower
aeehoprrsstt
stratosphere
aeehoqrrrstu
quarter-horse
aeeiiimmttxx
mixtie-maxtie
aeeiiklmnprs
marlinespike
aeeiikmnnssy
Keynesianism
aeeiilllrtty
illiterately
aeeiillmrstu
mitrailleuse
aeeiillmstww
sweet-william
aeeiillnostv
televisional
aeeiillnpstt
pestilential
aeeiillrrtvy
irrelatively
aeeiilmnssst
essentialism
aeeiilmprtvy
imperatively
aeeiilmrsttu
multiseriate
aeeiilnnprty
perenniality
aeeiilnoprtt
repetitional
aeeiilnrrsst
literariness
aeeiilnrssuv
universalise
aeeiilnrstuy
uniseriately
aeeiilnssstt
essentialist
aeeiilnsstty
essentiality
aeeiiloprttvx
exploitative
aeeiilprrstu
pluriseriate
aeeiinnnortt
inteneration
aeeiinnprtty
penitentiary
aeeiinnrrttu
intra-uterine
aeeiinprrsst
instep-raiser
aeeiinssttvv
vitativeness
aeeiiprttuvv
vituperative
aeeiiqrssttu
sesquitertia
aeeijloprtvy
pejoratively

aeeijnnortuv
rejuvenation
aeeiklllstty
skittle-alley
aeeikmnnssst
mistakenness
aeeillllltvyy
tilley-valley
aeeillmnrttt
ill-treatment
aeeillnnprtt
interpellant
aeeillnnpsty
septennially
aeeillnnstty
sententially
aeeillnorsst
relationless
aeeillnosstt
tessellation
aeeillnosstv
volatileness
aeeillnprrtu
interpleural
aeeillnprsty
presentially
aeeillnqstuy
sequentially
aeeillnqtuvy
equivalently
aeeillnrrstt
interstellar
aeeillnrrtvy
irrelevantly
aeeillnsssuv
allusiveness
aeeillttttttt
tittle-tattle
aeeilmnnnrss
mannerliness
aeeilmnnrstt
reinstalment
aeeilmnrssst
masterliness
aeeilmpprstu
perpetualism
aeeilmprrssu
superrealism
aeeilmpsttu
multiseptate
aeeilmqrrrtu
quarter-miler
aeeilnnnosst
non-essential
aeeilnnprsty
tennis-player
aeeilnnpssss
painlessness
aeeilnnrttuy
lieutenantry
aeeilnnsssuu
unsensualise
aeeilnoprssx
expressional

aeeilnprrsst
interspersal
aeeilnprssst
plasteriness
aeeilpprrstu
pleasure-trip
aeeilpprrsty
parsley-piert
aeeilpprsttu
perpetualist
aeeilpprttuy
perpetuality
aeeilprrsstu
superrealist
aeeilprssuvy
persuasively
aeeilprttuvy
reputatively
aeeimmnrsstu
immatureness
aeeimmnrsttt
mistreatment
aeeimmnssttt
misstatement
aeeimmrrttxx
mixter-maxter
aeeimnnorrtu
remuneration
aeeimnorrttx
exterminator
aeeimnpprssw
newspaperism
aeeimnrsttvy
vestimentary
aeeimoqrstuu
mousquetaire
aeeimrsssty
systematiser
aeeinnoprstt
presentation
aeeinoorrssu
aeroneurosis
aeeinoortttx
extortionate
aeeinopprrtt
perpetration
aeeinopprttu
perpetuation
aeeinoppssst
appositeness
aeeinoprrstv
preservation
aeeinorrrsvy
reversionary
aeeinorrstvx
extraversion
aeeinprssuuv
unpersuasive
aeeinrssttv
transvestite
aeeinrsttuv
sternutative
aeeinssttuv
sustentative

aeeipprrsstt
Strepsiptera
aeeipprrtttt
pitter-patter
aeekllorrrst
roller-skater
aeekllorrsst
roller-skates
aeeklmnrssuw
lukewarmness
aeekmoprrstu
posture-maker
aeekmorrsstt
masterstroke
aeelllmnotvy
malevolently
aeelllnopswy
Naples-yellow
aeelllorttwy
yellow-rattle
aeellmnoqruw
woman-queller
aeellmnppstu
supplemental
aeellprrssyy
prayerlessly
aeelmmnortuy
emolumentary
aeelmnprrstu
premenstrual
aeelmooprstu
somatopleure
aeelnoprsstt
plasterstone
aeelnorstuxy
extraneously
aeelnprsssuu
supersensual
aeelnrrsstvy
transversely
aeeloopprtuv
overpopulate
aeelqssttuuy
statuesquely
aeemmnnoostu
momentaneous
aeemmrrssttu
muster-master
aeemnooprstu
temporaneous
aeemnoortuuv
outmanoeuvre
aeemnorrrtuy
remuneratory
aeennorsssuv
ravenousness
aeennosssuu
nauseousness
aeenoprrsttu
streptoneura
aeenorrsstxy
extra-sensory
aeeoprrrstvy
preservatory

aeeoprrstttu
tetrapterous
aeeoqrrssttu
sequestrator
aeffghimnrtt
affrightment
aeffghinottu
outfangthief
aeffgiinortu
effiguration
aeffgilllmor
flagelliform
aeffgnorsstu
staff-surgeon
aeffhilnsstu
faithfulness
aeffilmmorsu
flammiferous
aeffilnostux
exsufflation
aefgggilnopr
leap-frogging
aefghhiilnsw
whale-fishing
aefghhoorrtu
thoroughfare
aefghhoorttu
aforethought
aefghhortttu
afterthought
aefghiilnprs
pearl-fishing
aefghiinrrtt
freight-train
aefghilnrsst
farthingless
aefghnnorrst
staghorn-fern
aefgiiilloru
Liguliflorae
aefgiilrtuvy
figuratively
aefgiimnrstu
misfeaturing
aefgiinppsww
wife-swapping
aefgillnorst
forestalling
aefgillnrtty
flatteringly
aefgillnssuw
wine-glassful
aefgilloprty
profligately
aefgilnnrttu
unflattering
aefgilnortww
water-flowing
aefginnrrrst
transferring
aefginooprtt
potato-finger
aefginorssuu
sanguiferous

aefgllnrtuuy
ungratefully
aefhhimnprss
freshmanship
aefhiinnssst
faintishness
aefhilmnorss
salmon-fisher
aefhinossssu
fashiousness
aefhklnnsstu
thankfulness
aefhllnosstu
loathfulness
aefhlnrsstuw
wrathfulness
aefhooprrstt
shatter-proof
aefiiilmnsst
semifinalist
aefiillmortw
water-milfoil
aefiillmottu
multifoliate
aefiillnootu
unifoliolate
aefiilnooprt
perfoliation
prefoliation
aefiinorsttu
titaniferous
aefiklnnpprt
flint-knapper
aefilmmnnoot
monofilament
aefilnnorrtt
interfrontal
aefilnnosstu
fountainless
aefilnnppsst
flippantness
aefilnooprrt
preflоration
aefilnooprss
professional
aefilooprrss
professorial
aefilopprsuu
papuliferous
aefiloprrstt
self-portrait
aefilorsstuu
salutiferous
aefimnnorrst
frontiersman
aefimnnorttu
frumentation
aefimnooprrt
preformation
aefinnorsstu
stanniferous
aefllnnssuuw
unlawfulness

aeflnoprrstu
superfrontal
aegggilnnotu
agglutinogen
aegggilnrsty
staggeringly
aegggilnrswy
swaggeringly
aegghipprrty
trigger-happy
aegghooopryz
zoogeography
aeggilmnnotu
Muggletonian
aeggilorrsuy
gregariously
aeggimnnorrw
warmongering
aegginnprsss
graspingness
aeggloorsty
astrogeology
aeggmnnoorrt
röntgenogram
aeghhiillns
shealing-hill
aeghhiloprrt
lithographer
aeghhinossuw
washing-house
aeghhiprsuwy
superhighway
aeghhmnoprry
hymnographer
aeghhmoprrty
mythographer
thermography
aeghhnoopprr
phonographer
aeghhnorsttu
through-stane
aeghhoopprrt
photographer
aeghhooprrrt
orthographer
aeghhopprrty
phytographer
aeghiilltuww
williewaught
aeghiilnstty
hesitatingly
aeghiimoprsw
image-worship
aeghiinnsttu
unhesitating
aeghiinpprsw
sapphire-wing
aeghiknnrrtt
knight-errant
aeghillopprs
ellipsograph
aeghilmnnosw
Englishwoman

aeghilmnnstu
languishment
aeghilnnrttu
turning-lathe
aeghilnorstt
starting-hole
aeghilnprrsw
wranglership
aeghiloopstt
hepatologist
aeghimmnnrtu
tuning-hammer
aeghimmnopry
hemp-agrimony
aeghimnorsuw
house-warming
aeghimoprssy
seismography
aeghinrssstt
straightness
aeghlmmnooou
homologumena
aeghlmnnoors
longshoreman
aeghlmoortuy
rheumatology
aeghlorsstuu
slaughterous
aeghmnoooptt
photomontage
aeghnnooprty
anthropogeny
aeghnoopprrr
pornographer
aeghooprrsst
gastrosopher
aeghooprrtuv
photogravure
aeghoppssyyz
zygapophyses
aegiiilmnott
legitimation
aegiiimnnnot
ingemination
aegiiinnprsw
awe-inspiring
aegiillnnotw
Wellingtonia
aegiillnnrtu
interlingual
aegiillnprvy
prevailingly
aegiilmnoprt
primogenital
aegiilmnorst
mineralogist
aegiilnnnssu
ungainliness
aegiilnnortu
urinogenital
aegiilnnpruv
unprevailing
aegiilnorsty
seignioralty

aegiilnppsty
appetisingly
aegiilnprstt
ear-splitting
aegiilnrsttw
slate-writing
aegiilrrrtuy
irregularity
aegiimnnoprt
impregnation
aegiimnnoptt
pigmentation
aegiimnnrstt
tin-streaming
aegiimnoorrt
morigeration
aegiimoprstv
gram-positive
aegiinnnopst
nose-painting
aegiinnnrstt
intransigent
aegiinnppstu
unappetising
aegiinnprsss
aspiringness
aegiinnstuxy
exsanguinity
aegiinoprrsv
overpraising
aegiinorrstt
registration
aegiinorsttv
investigator
aegiinpprrtw
writing-paper
aegiioprrstt
prestigiator
aegiklmnortw
metal-working
aegillmrsttu
metallurgist
aegillnnostw
stonewalling
aegillnnpsuy
unpleasingly
aegillqrssuu
liqueur-glass
aegilmmnrsty
stammeringly
aegilmnnnnot
non-alignment
aegilmnnoqtu
magniloquent
aegilmnoostt
nematologist
aegilmnrstty
smatteringly
aegilmooopry
paroemiology
aegilnnnostu
sanguinolent
aegilnnrstty
astringently

aegilnnrstuy
saunteringly
aegilnnruvwy
unwaveringly
aegilnnruwyy
unwearyingly
aegilnooprst
antigropelos
aegilnrrssuy
reassuringly
aegiloorsttt
teratologist
aegilorrsstu
grossularite
aegimmnoostz
zoomagnetism
aegimnnrtuuu
unguentarium
aeginnnprrsu
spear-running
aeginnorsstu
nugatoriness
aeginnossuux
exsanguinous
aeginoorrrtt
interrogator
aeginoprsttu
pregustation
aeginoprstwy
staying-power
aegllmnttuuu
multungulate
aeglmnooptuy
pneumatology
aegloorstuuy
outrageously
aegnorrrssst
transgressor
aegoopssttuy
steatopygous
aehhiiilmsst
Ishmaelitish
aehhillmsstt
Stahlhelmist
aehhilnoorrr
rhinorrhoeal
aehhilnopprt
philanthrope
aehhimnnoopr
harmoniphone
aehhimnoprss
horsemanship
aehhimooprrt
Theriomorpha
aehhimooprst
Thesmophoria
aehhimooprty
rhythmopoeia
aehhimoopstt
homeopathist
aehhlmoopstx
exophthalmos
aehhlmopstux
exophthalmus

aehhloppstuy
hyposulphate
aehhnopprtyy
hypnotherapy
aehhoopprtty
phototherapy
aehhooprrsst
sharpshooter
aehiiilnopss
Hispaniolise
aehiiimnprty
pyrithiamine
aehiilloopru
ailourophile
aehiilnoprst
relationship
aehiilprrstt
hair-splitter
aehiimnrttuu
Uintatherium
aehiinnssssw
swainishness
aehiinoprrst
prehistorian
aehiirrssttw
shirtwaister
aehikkmnrrss
skrimshanker
aehillmorsty
isothermally
aehilloorstu
heliolatrous
aehillprsttt
lath-splitter
aehilmnoopsu
anemophilous
aehilmnorstw
mothers-in-law
aehilmnqsssu
qualmishness
aehiloopr stt
strophiolate
aehimmmoprst
metamorphism
aehimmoprstt
metamorphist
aehimmopsttu
imposthumate
aehimnnooprt
enantiomorph
aehimnnoossu
mansion-house
aehimnnoppsu
one-upmanship
aehimnnosssw
womanishness
aehimnnosstt
astonishment
aehimnnqstuv
vanquishment
aehinnoprttx
xanthopterin
aehinnppssss
snappishness

aehinooprrtt
prototherian
aehinooprsst
epanorthosis
aehinoosst tu
station-house
aehinoprsttu
neuropathist
aehinoprstty
attorneyship
aehinpprrsst
transshipper
aehiooppr sst
apostrophise
aehioopsst tt
osteopathist
aehiopqrsstu
quaestorship
aehioprrstwy
praiseworthy
aehioprsssss
assessorship
aehlmnprsuuy
superhumanly
aehlnopsstuy
polyanthuses
aehmnooprtux
pneumothorax
aehnnorsstuy
synantherous
aehnooprrssu
sarrusophone
aeiiillmntuv
illuminative
aeiiilnnnort
nitroaniline
aeiiilnrsttt
interstitial
aeiiilprsstu
spiritualise
aeiiilrstttv
relativitist
aeiiimmnsstt
anti-Semitism
aeiiimnnnost
insemination
aeiiimnorsss
missionarise
aeiiimnosstt
Semitisation
aeiiimnrsttv
ministrative
aeiiinnooptv
opinionative
aeiiinnrsttv
intransitive
aeiiinorsttv
revisitation
aeiiiopprttv
propitiative
aeiikknorssy
karyokinesis
aeiikllnorsu
unsailorlike

aeiiklnrsttu
unartistlike
aeiillllmmsy
millesimally
aeiilllntuux
luxullianite
aeiilllprrtu
pluriliteral
aeiillmmmory
immemorially
aeiillnqrstu
tranquillise
aeiillprrstt
rail-splitter
aeiillqrrstu
squirrel-tail
aeiillrsttuv
illustrative
aeiilmmnoost
emotionalism
aeiilmnnotvy
nominatively
aeiilmnootty
emotionality
aeiilmnrssuv
universalism
aeiilmnrtuvy
ruminatively
aeiilmnsttuy
simultaneity
aeiilmorsstt
Aristotelism
aeiilmprtttu
multipartite
aeiilmpttuvy
imputatively
aeiilnnnqquu
quinquennial
aeiilnnoopty
opinionately
aeiilnnoortt
intoleration
aeiilnnoostv
novelisation
aeiilnnopsst
splenisation
aeiilnoopttx
exploitation
aeiilnoppsty
inappositely
aeiilnoptt ty
potentiality
aeiilnorssst
solitariness
aeiilnrsstuv
universalist
aeiilnrsttvy
transitively
aeiilnrstuvy
universality
aeiilnstuuxy
unisexuality
aeiimmnnnoos
neonomianism

aeiimmnoorst
memorisation
aeiimnnoostt
monetisation
aeiimnnopssx
expansionism
aeiimnnorsst
Nestorianism
aeiimnnossst
sensationism
aeiimnrssstv
transmissive
aeiinnnorttu
antineutrino
aeiinnoprstu
resupination
aeiinnopsstx
expansionist
aeiinnorsttt
strontianite
aeiinnossstt
sensationist
aeiinopprrst
perspiration
aeiinoprsttt
strepitation
aeiinoprttuv
vituperation
aeiinprrsssu
Prussianiser
aeiippprrrst
spirit-rapper
aeikllnosttw
sallow-kitten
aeikmnoqrstu
question-mark
aeikmrsssstt
taskmistress
aeillllprrrt
Pralltriller
aeillmmnostt
misallotment
aeillmnoprsy
impersonally
aeillnnortty
intolerantly
aeillnoopsxy
polysiloxane
aeillnoortuv
revolutional
aeillnoosttw
wollastonite
aeillnorrtty
torrentially
aeilmnnoopst
Neoplatonism
aeilmnnrsttu
instrumental
aeilmnooprtt
metropolitan
aeilmnoqsuuy
equanimously
aeilmnosstuu
simultaneous

aeilnnoopstt
neoplatonist
aeilnnosttyy
enantiostyly
aeilnooprrss
responsorial
aeilnooprrtt
interpolator
aeilnoortuvy
evolutionary
aeilnoprsssu
suspensorial
aeilnorrsttu
tenuirostral
aeilnorrsuvy
revulsionary
aeiloooppprs
prosopopeial
aeilooprstty
epistolatory
aeiloprsssuu
Plesiosaurus
aeimmopsstty
symptomatise
aeimnnoorsst
Montessorian
aeimnnorsttu
menstruation
aeimnooppttt
tappet-motion
aeimnooprrst
impersonator
aeimnoprsstu
reassumption
aeimnprsttuv
transumptive
aeimnrsssttv
transvestism
aeinnnnoottt
non-attention
aeinnnoprstt
transpontine
aeinnnorsstt
non-resistant
aeinnooprtty
enantiotropy
aeinnorrsstv
transversion
aeinnorstttu
sternutation
aeinnosstttu
sustentation
aeinooprsttt
protestation
aeinooprsttw
power-station
aeinoorrttxy
extortionary
aeinoossttttu
ostentatious
aeinoprrsttt
train-spotter
aeinoprrsttv
transportive

aeioooopppprs
prosopopoeia
aeiopprrrsty
perspiratory
aeioprrsttty
Post-Tertiary
aeioprrttuvy
vituperatory
aejmmoprrttu
trumpet-major
aelllmorsuvy
marvellously
aellmmnnotuy
monumentally
aellmnooosss
Solomon's-seal
aellooppssuy
polysepalous
aellooppstuy
polypetalous
aelmnnorrstt
storm-lantern
aelmnooopssu
monosepalous
aelmnooopstu
monopetalous
aelnnooprstt
entoplastron
aelooorrttvy
levorotatory
aelooprsttux
expostulator
aemnnoprrstt
Premonstrant
aemnoooprstz
spermatozoon
aemnoooprszz
mezzo-soprano
aemnoorrrstt
remonstrator
aemooprsstuw
water-opossum
aemprrssttuu
superstratum
aenooprsssuv
vaporousness
aenorrsttuy
sternutatory
aeooprrssttu
tetrasporous
affgilnnorty
affrontingly
affhillntuuy
unfaithfully
affiilnnostu
insufflation
afgggillnnuy
unflaggingly
afgghhiilntu
high-faluting
afgghiinprtw
whip-grafting
afggiilnrtyy
gratifyingly

afghilmnnoru
half-mourning
afgiiillnssu
fissilingual
afgiillllloru
liguliforal
afgiillmnoru
anguilliform
afgiillostuy
flagitiously
afgiilnsstyy
satisfyingly
afgiinnnnoww
winnowing-fan
afgiinnsstuy
unsatisfying
afgiknoorstt
toasting-fork
afgimnnorrst
transforming
afgimnorrsty
transmogrify
afhkllnntuuy
unthankfully
afiiillnrstu
fustillirian
afiiilmnnost
inflationism
afiiilnnortt
infiltration
afiiilnnostt
inflationist
afiilmorstuu
multifarious
afiilnnoortu
fluorination
afiilnoooprv
pavilion-roof
afiilorrssst
fissirostral
afiimmnnorst
misinformant
afiimmnoorst
misformation
afiinoprsstu
passion-fruit
afillmnopstu
slumpflation
afimmnorrsst
transformism
afimnorrsstt
transformist
agggillnrsty
stragglingly
agghhloppryy
glyphography
agghhmopprsy
sphygmograph
agghiiknnstv
thanksgiving
agghiilnpsty
sight-playing
agghilooprst
graphologist

agghlnoopryy
pharyngology
agghlooprssy
glossography
agghlopprtyy
glyptography
aggiinnoprsw
growing-pains
aggikllnooss
looking-glass
aggiklnpprsu
sparking-plug
aghhiimnnotu
mountain-high
aghhiiopppst
hippophagist
aghhilnoprtt
triphthongal
aghhiloopstu
lithophagous
aghhimnopsty
hypognathism
aghhinoppryy
hypophrygian
aghhinorrttu
through-train
aghhiooopppsu
ophiophagous
aghhiooppsu
hippophagous
aghhiooprst
opisthograph
aghhiooprsuz
rhizophagous
aghhiopprsyy
physiography
aghhlmoppryy
lymphography
aghhmoopprry
morphography
aghhnoopstuy
hypognathous
aghhooppstuy
phytophagous
aghiiinnprst
training-ship
aghiikllmnrs
shilling-mark
aghiilmnpsty
lymphangitis
aghiinnpprst
transhipping
aghiklnooprs
sharp-looking
aghillnnoort
all-or-nothing
aghilmnoooot
homologation
aghilmnoortu
ornithogalum
aghilorsstww
whitlow-grass

aghimnooprst
gramophonist
monographist
aghimoprstuy
hypogastrium
aghimorsstty
timothy-grass
aghinnoopsst
snapshooting
aghinnoopsww
whooping-swan
aghinooprstt
trap-shooting
aghinoorsstt
shooting-star
aghiopprstty
typographist
aghioppssyyz
zygapophysis
aghllmoopsuy
gamophyllous
aghllnooorty
orthogonally
aghlmoooprsu
lagomorphous
aghlnoopryy
laryngophony
aghlnoooprty
anthropology
aghloooptyz
zoopathology
aghmnooprtyy
pharyngotomy
aghnnoooprty
anthropogony
agiiiilnnotv
invigilation
agiiilmnnswz
Zwinglianism
agiiilnnstwz
Zwinglianist
agiiimnorstt
migrationist
agiiinnoortv
invigoration
agiiklnnoptt
talking-point
agiilllmntuu
multilingual
agiillmmnpst
stamping-mill
agiilmnnorsu
unmoralising
agiilmnnrtuy
ruminatingly
agiilnnnorrs
snarling-iron
agiilnnprsuy
unaspiringly
agiilnoorsuv
vainglorious
agiilnosstuu
ustilaginous

agiimnnrsttt
transmitting
agiinnnsstuu
unsustaining
agiinnoorstt
toasting-iron
agillnnoorst
snarling-tool
agillnoopptw
pot-walloping
agillnoopsty
palynologist
agilmnnssuuy
unassumingly
agilmnooprsu
sporangiolum
agilmnooprtu
promulgation
agilmooopstt
potamologist
agilnnnnoptw
town-planning
agilnnoooprt
prolongation
agilnprsssuy
surpassingly
agiloopprsty
papyrologist
agilorsttuuy
gratuitously
agimmnoprsuy
progymnasium
agimnnorrstw
storm-warning
agimnooosstu
angiostomous
agimnoorsstt
gastronomist
aginnoopprtu
propugnation
aginnoprrsst
apron-strings
aginnoprrstt
transporting
aginoorssuuv
sanguivorous
aginoprssttt
starting-post
agllmoopsuyy
polygamously
ahhhhiipprru
hip-hip-hurrah
ahhiilmopstt
ophthalmitis
ahhiiloppsst
hospital-ship
ahhilllssyy
shilly-shally
ahhillmmoost
homothallism
ahhilnoopstu
anthophilous
ahhilnopprty
philanthropy

ahhimnnpsstu
huntsmanship
ahhinnoprstt
strophanthin
ahhinoooopprs
Siphonophora
ahhnoprssttu
strophanthus
ahiiilorsstu
urolithiasis
ahiimmnorstu
harmoniumist
ahiimnnoorsu
inharmonious
ahikloorttuw
kilowatt-hour
ahillnoortyz
horizontally
ahilloorsttu
litholatrous
ahilmnoorsuy
harmoniously
ahilmnprttuy
triumphantly
ahilmoooprty
homopolarity
ahilnopprsty
psilanthropy
ahilnoprstuu
sulphuration
ahilooprstu
ophiolatrous
ahimmooprstu
automorphism
ahimmoopsstu
amphistomous
ahimnnoorsuu
unharmonious
ahimnooprsst
misanthropos
ahimoopppstu
hippopotamus
ahimoopprstt
haptotropism
ahimoopprstu
amphitropous
ahimopprssty
saprophytism
ahinnooprstt
antistrophon
ahinnoprsstu
Sinanthropus
ahinoopsstuy
autohypnosis
ahinorrsssty
synarthrosis
ahmnoooprtty
anthropotomy
ahnoooprrtty
prothonotary
aiiiillmnott
illimitation
aiiiimmnnost
minimisation

aiiillmnnotu
illumination
aiiillnnostt
instillation
aiiilmmnorst
trinomialism
aiiilmnoosst
isolationism
aiiilmnorstt
trinomialist
aiiilmprsstu
spiritualism
aiiilnoorttv
vitriolation
aiiilnoosstt
isolationist
aiiilnrsstty
sinistrality
aiiilprssttu
spiritualist
aiiilprsttuy
spirituality
aiiimmnnorss
Rosminianism
aiiimmnnostu
immunisation
aiiimnnorstt
ministration
aiiimnoopstt
optimisation
aiiinnnoostu
unionisation
aiiinnopssst
inspissation
aiiinoopprtt
propitiation
aiiinoprrttt
tripartition
aiiinoprsttt
partitionist
aiikmnnoprss
Parkinsonism
aiilllnootvy
volitionally
aiilllnosuvy
villainously
aiillmmnnotu
mill-mountain
aiillmnoorty
monitorially
aiillnnootuv
involutional
aiillnoopstt
postillation
aiillnorsttu
illustration
aiillnqrttuy
tranquillity
aiilmnnnootu
mountain-lion
aiilmnnorttu
malnutrition
aiilmnoprstt
trampolinist

aiilmnoprsty
postliminary
aiilmorstuuv
multivarious
aiilnnooopst
Polonisation
aiilnnottuuv
invultuation
aiilnooppst
oppositional
aiilnorrssst
sinistrorsal
aiilnorrstty
transitorily
aiiloprsuvvy
viviparously
aiimmmnosstu
missummation
aiimmnoortwy
minimotorway
aiimmnottuuy
auto-immunity
aiimnnorssst
transmission
aiimnooorstt
motorisation
aiimnooprssu
parsimonious
aiimnooqsttu
misquotation
aiimooorsttv
ovariotomist
aiimoopprrrt
impropriator
aiimooprrstv
improvisator
aiinooprrsvy
provisionary
aiiopprrtty
propitiatory
aiiopprsttt
potato-spirit
aillmnnoopry
pronominally
aillnooopsst
saloon-pistol
aillnoopttyy
polytonality
aillorrsttuy
illustratory
ailmnoprrstu
splint-armour
ailmnorstuvy
voluntaryism
ailmnotttuuu
tumultuation
ailnooopprrt
proportional
ailnopprtuuy
unpopularity
ailnorsttuvy
voluntaryist
ailooprrsuuy
uproariously

ailoorrsttuy
traitorously
aimnnoprsttu
transumption
ainooorrsttt
rotor-station
aipprrrssttu
stirrup-strap
amooprrsttuy
stump-oratory
bbbbbeehlluu
hubble-bubble
bbcdeinrssuu
unsubscribed
bbceeehorsuy
breeches-buoy
bbceeilmnrst
scribblement
bbceekorrruy
roebuck-berry
bbcejkoorsty
stock-jobbery
bbcekllmopru
plumber-block
bbcelllooswy
collywobbles
bbcenoorrstu
bronco-buster
bbcgiillnrsy
scribblingly
bbcgijknoost
stock-jobbing
bbcgiklnostu
blockbusting
bbciiklorrst
Bristol-brick
bbddeelooors
sober-blooded
bbddgiilnouy
body-building
bbdeeeelortw
beetle-browed
bbdeeelopprw
pebble-powder
bbdeeemnnssu
benumbedness
bbdeefillstu
stubble-field
bbdeeggklooo
gobbledegook
bbdeeilnopru
Bible-pounder
bbdeellmoott
bell-bottomed
bbdeggklooooy
gobbledygook
bbdegiilnotu
double-biting
bbdehlooorrt
blood-brother
bbdeiiilssuv
subdivisible
bbdelmoootttu
double-bottom

bbdgiilnoovy
voiding-lobby
bbeeeeehijsy
heeby-jeebies
bbeeforrstuv
Berufsverbot
bbeeglloosstu
stubble-goose
bbeegmnorruy
money-grubber
bbeegnoprrsu
sponge-rubber
bbeehilmprtu
Bible-thumper
bbeellmmrtuu
rumble-tumble
bbefghllootu
bull-of-the-bog
bbeflorttuwy
butterfly-bow
bbegiiilopst
bibliopegist
bbegillnrsuy
slubberingly
bbeginnorstu
rubbing-stone
bbehinnossss
snobbishness
bbennorssstu
stubbornness
bbghiilmnoos
hobgoblinism
bbgiiilloost
bibliologist
bbginnopsstu
snubbing-post
bbhjnnooooss
Hobson-Jobson
bbhmoooooprsu
ombrophobous
bbiiilloopst
bibliopolist
bccceiimrrsu
circumscribe
bcceeehkrrry
checker-berry
bcceeelnooss
obsolescence
bcceeemnostu
obmutescence
bcceeemrrtuu
cucumber-tree
bcceehnorrss
crossbencher
bcceehnorruy
cherry-bounce
bcceeiilnosv
obliviscence
bcceeinoorrt
cerebrotonic
bccehnooooprs
bronchoscope
bccehorstttu
butterscotch

bcceikkllnor
clinker-block
bcceilmoorty
motor-bicycle
bcceklooprss
process-block
bccgiiklmnor
rock-climbing
bcchilloopsu
public-school
bcchnooooprsy
bronchoscopy
bccinoosssuu
subconscious
bcciooooprsst
stroboscopic
bcckoorssttu
cross-buttock
bcdddeeeklou
double-decked
bcddeeeiinos
disobedience
bcddeeekloru
double-decker
bcddeeklloou
double-locked
bcddeginorss
cross-bedding
bcddeiiiltuy
deducibility
bcdeeeeknstw
between-decks
bcdeeefiilnt
indefectible
bcdeeeiilntt
indetectible
bcdeeeilnrss
credibleness
bcdeeekorrst
stock-breeder
bcdeeemnnruu
unencumbered
bcdeefiiklrr
brickfielder
bcdeefijnort
object-finder
bcdeefijostu
bed-of-justice
bcdeegiiinpr
birding-piece
bcdeeiilprst
discerptible
bcdeeiiopprr
bodice-ripper
bcdeeiloprru
reproducible
bcdeeilrsttu
destructible
bcdeeimnnruu
unincumbered
bcdeeinprrsu
unprescribed
bcdeelorstuu
tuberculosed

bcdeemooprss
obcompressed
bcdegmnorruu
cumber-ground
bcdeiiilrtuy
reducibility
bcdeiilnoorr
incorrodible
bcdeiilnortu
introducible
bcdeinorstuu
subintroduce
bcdeloorruuy
ruby-coloured
bcdenorsttuu
unobstructed
bcdgiklnoosu
bloodsucking
bceeeeehknrs
knee-breeches
bceeeefnrrsu
subreference
bceeeeghrrsu
cheeseburger
bceeeegillnr
belligerence
bceeefilnnty
beneficently
bceeeghilnsy
beseechingly
bceeegillnry
belligerency
bceeeiiilmms
semi-imbecile
bceeeikoorsx
exercise-book
bceeeinrssuv
subservience
bceeeirrrsvy
service-berry
bceeemmnnrtu
encumberment
bceefhnnorrt
front-bencher
bceefilnorss
forcibleness
bceeghiinprw
weeping-birch
bceegillmnow
well-becoming
bceegimnnoss
becomingness
bceehllnosst
Stellenbosch
bceeiijsstuv
subjectivise
bceeiillrstt
belletristic
bceeijlstuvy
subjectively
bceeijnnootv
non-objective
bceeilloopsu
ebullioscope

bceeilmnoptt
contemptible
bceeilmoprss
compressible
bceeimmosttu
subcommittee
bceeinrssuvy
subserviency
bceejlnoosst
object-lesson
bceelmmoortu
coulombmeter
bceelnoortvy
conveyor-belt
bceeloorrttu
butter-cooler
root-tubercle
bceghiilntwy
bewitchingly
bcegiiilnorr
incorrigible
bcegikklnoor
booking-clerk
bcegiklnostu
bluestocking
bcegilmnnouy
unbecomingly
bcehhlorsstu
clothes-brush
bcehiiilosty
cohesibility
bcehiimorsty
biochemistry
bcehiinopprs
prince-bishop
bcehiinostty
biosynthetic
bcehiklnrstu
slink-butcher
bcehimoorstw
witches'-broom
bcehimorstuy
heir-by-custom
bceiiinosstt
bioscientist
bceiijmsstuv
subjectivism
bceiijnnostu
insubjection
bceiijssttuv
subjectivist
bceiijsttuvy
subjectivity
bceiikllnrtu
clinker-built
bceiilnoorrs
incorrosible
bceiilnrsttu
instructible
bceiinorttuv
contributive
bceiiprsstuv
subscriptive

bceiknrtttuy
Tyburn-ticket
bceilloopsuy
ebullioscopy
bceillorttuy
butty-collier
bceilmnoptty
contemptibly
bceiloprtuu
probouleutic
bceilorsstuu
tuberculosis
bceilrrttuuy
trituberculy
bceinnnosttu
subcontinent
bceinoprsstu
subinspector
bceklmmopru
plummer-block
bcekmoosttuu
mouse-buttock
bcelmoprsuuu
suboperculum
bcemnorsssuu
cumbrousness
bcemoooprtt
copper-bottom
bcerrssttuuu
substructure
bcfiilmmorru
lumbriciform
bcggiiknnor
brick-nogging
bcghhilnottu
bolting-hutch
bcgiiilnorry
incorrigibly
bcgiilmoory
microbiology
bcgiiloooosy
sociobiology
bcgiinooostt
gnotobiotics
bcgikknoorst
stockbroking
bchhiimorsty
biorhythmics
bchhilooossy
schoolboyish
bchhimooorrt
orthorhombic
bchiiooprtt
trophobiotic
bciinnoorttu
contribution
bciinoprsstu
subscription
bciknoooprs
book-scorpion
bcilmmnosuuu
cumulo-nimbus
bcinoorrttuy
contributory

bcinorssttuu
substruction
bdddeilmnooy
bloody-minded
bdddgilnoopu
blood-pudding
bddeeeefilmn
feeble-minded
bddeeefinnru
unbefriended
bddeeeinnsst
indebtedness
bddeegginoor
good-breeding
bddeegiinnrt
interbedding
bddeegjmnttu
judgment-debt
bddeeiknnorw
broken-winded
bddeeilmnssu
undissembled
bddeeilnrruu
underbuilder
bddeeilooptt
pottle-bodied
bddeiinsssuu
unsubsidised
bddeilmnoruu
mound-builder
bddfgiilnory
forbiddingly
bddgiilnoruw
word-building
bdeeeemmnrru
unremembered
bdeeefiilnns
indefensible
bdeeefiloosu
oeils-de-boeuf
bdeeefmnoort
forebodement
bdeeegilnnos
nose-bleeding
bdeeeglnortu
ground-beetle
bdeeehiilltw
white-bellied
bdeeehmorrtu
mouth-breeder
bdeeeillmrtw
well-timbered
bdeeeilmnrtw
bewilderment
bdeeeilnnssv
vendibleness
bdeeeilrtuvy
delivery-tube
bdeeeimmnort
re-embodiment
bdeeeimnrttu
unembittered
bdeeelmnortu
redoublement

bdeeenossstt
besottedness
bdeefgiloruu
double-figure
bdeefiilnnsy
indefensibly
bdeefilmnoot
nimble-footed
bdeegiiilnst
indigestible
bdeehiillmss
disembellish
bdeehinostuu
hebetudinous
bdeehlloortt
bottle-holder
bdeehllorstu
shoulder-belt
bdeehlnoorsu
shoulder-bone
bdeeiiilnrtv
indivertible
bdeeiilmnttw
nimble-witted
bdeeiilnnoty
inobediently
bdeeiinnrsst
bend-sinister
bdeeiirrsttu
redistribute
bdeeijlrrruy
jerry-builder
bdeeilllowy
yellow-billed
bdeeillorstt
bottle-slider
bdeeilmrrrtu
tumbler-drier
bdeeimnrsstu
disbursement
bdeeinortttw
twitterboned
bdeelnorsuvy
unobservedly
bdeeloorstuy
double-storey
bdefgilnoory
forebodingly
bdefginnooru
unforeboding
bdefilnnoost
festoon-blind
bdefllmoottu
full-bottomed
bdeflnosstuu
doubtfulness
bdeghhoorrtu
thoroughbred
bdeghilorrtu
guild-brother
bdegiiilnsty
indigestibly
bdegiillnosw
disbowelling

bdegiinnrsst
bird's-nesting
bdegillnnruy
blunderingly
bdegillnoott
bloodletting
bdegilnooops
pigeon's-blood
bdeginoprtuw
powdering-tub
bdehhlorsstu
subthreshold
bdehhmnooorr
rhombohedron
bdehiinoprtu
unprohibited
bdehmooorstw
smooth-browed
bdehmoorsttu
rush-bottomed
bdeiiiillnty
indelibility
bdeiiimrrttu
turbidimiter
bdeiiirsttuv
distributive
bdeiillnossu
indissoluble
bdeiilorssuu
subdelirious
bdeilnnprssu
purblindness
bdelloorrtuw
trouble-world
bdeooprtuwyy
woodburytype
bdgggiilmnno
mind-boggling
bdghhioorrtu
thirdborough
bdghiiilnpsu
shipbuilding
bdghilooryy
hydrobiology
bdgiiknnortu
drinking-bout
bdgiinnrstuu
undisturbing
bdgillmnoouw
blow-moulding
bdgilnnotuuy
undoubtingly
bdhhoooprsuy
hydrophobous
bdhiimoorrss
bromhidrosis
bdhiloorstty
bloodthirsty
bdiiiiilstvy
divisibility
bdiiiilnosty
libidinosity
bdiiillnosuy
libidinously

bdiiilnnosuu
unlibidinous
bdiiinorsttu
distribution
bdiiillnossuy
indissolubly
beeeeeflmnnt
enfeeblement
beeeefhinorr
hereinbefore
beeeeimnsttw
betweentimes
beeeelmmntzz
embezzlement
beeeelnosttx
sexton-beetle
beeefglnostt
self-begotten
beeefillnssx
flexibleness
beeefllmmorw
fellow-member
beeeghoorruv
borough-reeve
beeegiillmns
ill-beseeming
beeegilnprst
spring-beetle
beeegimoorsu
embourgeoise
beeegmmnrstu
submergement
beeehiinnrtt
terebinthine
beeehimprsst
Septemberish
beeehqrrstuu
Thurberesque
beeeiilnnstx
inextensible
beeeiilrrrsv
irreversible
beeeiirrttvz
Zeitvertreib
beeeillmnttt
belittlement
beeeillrsstt
blister-steel
beeeilnnssss
sensibleness
beeeilnrrsst
terribleness
beeeilopprst
tribespeople
beeeimmnrttt
embitterment
beeeimprrsst
Septembriser
beeeinnnortz
nitrobenzene
beeeirrssssw
Besserwisser
beeeknorrstu
bunko-steerer

beeellnnotvy
benevolently
beeelnooprtt
bottle-opener
beeelnoossst
obsoleteness
beeelnosttuv
sleeve-button
beefgiinnrrt
birefringent
beefiilrrstu
filibusterer
beefiorrstuu
tuberiferous
beeflloottuw
Woulfe-bottle
beegghiinnnt
benightening
beeggiioooow
boogie-woogie
beeggilnnorw
bowling-green
beeghillostt
globe-thistle
beeghinnrttu
hunger-bitten
beegiiilllnt
intelligible
beegiiilmnsv
misbelieving
beegiilnnpux
inexpungible
beeginnooprz
bronze-pigeon
beegloorrttt
globe-trotter
beehiiinortx
exhibitioner
beehillmosty
blithesomely
beehilmoopst
phlebotomise
beehilnorrss
horribleness
beehloorstuu
trouble-house
beehlorrrtwy
whortleberry
beeiiilmrrss
irremissible
beeiiilrrsst
irresistible
beeiiklnsssu
business-like
beeiilnrsstu
unresistible
beeiilrrrsvy
irreversibly
beeiinssssuw
business-wise
beeilllorsuy
rebelliously
beeilnnoprst
splinter-bone

beeilpprsssu
suppressible
beeilprsstuu
supersubtile
beeimnorttuy
tribute-money
beeinnorrtuw
winter-bourne
beekmnnnooty
bonnet-monkey
beeknnnorssu
unbrokenness
beellllloorty
loblolly-tree
beelnnosssuu
nebulousness
beelnoosssst
bootlessness
beelnqsstuuy
subsequently
beelorsttuvy
oversubtlety
beeooprrsstu
obstreperous
befgiilnortu
foreign-built
befiilrsttuy
subfertility
befillmnrssu
brimfullness
befillnssssu
blissfulness
befilmoprsuu
plumbiferous
befilooorssu
soboliferous
beflnrtttuuy
butterfly-nut
begghiinnoru
neighbouring
beggiilnnoss
obligingness
beghinnorsuu
burning-house
begiiiillllty
illegibility
begiiilllnty
intelligibly
begiillmmnsw
swimming-bell
begiilnnoost
stone-boiling
begiiloooostx
exobiologist
begiinorrsvw
virgin's-bower
begikllnoops
spelling-book
begillmnrsuy
slumberingly
begillnrstuy
blusteringly
begilmnnrsuu
unslumbering

begilmoorsty
embryologist
begilnoooruy
neurobiology
behhnoopstty
phytobenthos
behiinosssty
biosynthesis
behillmmrstu
miller's-thumb
behilmoopstt
phlebotomist
behilmorrttu
trouble-mirth
behinossssuw
show-business
beiiiillmmnnu
bimillennium
beiiillnossu
insolubilise
beiiilrrssty
irresistibly
beiiilllllloru
Lillibullero
beiiillllorru
Lilliburlero
beiilmsssuvy
submissively
beiimnsssuuv
unsubmissive
beiinoosssst
obsessionist
beiiooprsttu
obreptitious
beiissttuuv
substitutive
beilloorsstt
stilboestrol
beilmnrsttuu
butter-muslin
beilooqssuuy
obsequiously
beiloorsstuy
boisterously
beilopprstuu
purpose-built
beinpprtttuy
Tyburn-tippet
bellmorssuuy
slumberously
belmnoopryyy
polyembryony
beoorrsstttu
buttress-root
bfgghiillntu
bullfighting
bfiiiiilnstuy
infusibility
bfiiilnnorsy
fibrinolysin
bfiillmmoorr
morbilliform
bfiilmoorrst
strobiliform

bggghiilnntu
lightning-bug
bggiimnnoosw
swinging-boom
bggilnooooty
gnotobiology
bghillnnsuuy
unblushingly
bghillnooopt
polling-booth
bghilooopty
photobiology
bgiiiiilntty
ignitibility
bgiiiknoostv
visiting-book
bgiiilnnoopt
boiling-point
bgiikllnnnuy
unblinkingly
bgiilmoorstt
timbrologist
bgiimnnsttuu
unsubmitting
bgiinnnoprtu
burning-point
bgillorsuuuy
lugubriously
bgilnoorruww
burrowing-owl
bhiiooprsst
trophobiosis
bhilmooprsu
ombrophilous
bhiooprssstu
Russophobist
biiiiilnstvy
invisibility
biiillnostuy
insolubility
biiloqstuuuy
ubiquitously
biinossttttuu
substitution
billorsstuuy
subsultorily
biloorsstuuy
robustiously
cccceeennors
concrescence
ccccehinoosu
echinococcus
cccdhiiooprs
dichroscopic
ccceehilorty
heterocyclic
ccceehknortu
countercheck
ccceeiinrtty
eccentricity
ccceeilnnotu
noctilucence
ccceeimnrrtu
circumcentre

ccceilmortuu
circumlocute
ccceinnopstu
concupiscent
ccceinnssstu
succinctness
ccceiooprstt
streptococci
cccemnoopsuu
pneumococcus
ccciiimnorsu
circumcision
ccciiimorrtu
microcircuit
ccddeehiilnr
cliché-ridden
ccddeeinnost
disconnected
ccdeeeehinpr
crêpe-de-chine
ccdeeeeilnst
delitescence
ccdeeeemnstu
detumescence
ccdeeefnnors
frondescence
ccdeeehiinns
indehiscence
ccdeeehnostu
escutcheoned
ccdeeeiinrsv
viridescence
ccdeeeikills
sickle-celled
ccdeeenrrstu
recrudescent
ccdeefilopsu
self-occupied
ccdeehorstuv
overscutched
ccdeeiilnorr
irreconciled
ccdeeiknqstu
quick-scented
ccdeeilmorrs
sclerodermic
ccdeeilnnoru
unreconciled
ccdeeimossty
Discomycetes
ccdeeiorrttu
correctitude
ccdegiiilnrr
circle-riding
ccdehiilnsty
schindyletic
ccdehilnnoru
unchronicled
ccdehimnossy
synecdochism
ccdehimoorty
orchidectomy
ccdehiooprs
dichrooscope

ccdeiiirrrtu
circuit-rider
ccdeiillmosu
molluscicide
ccdeiilnnoty
coincidently
ccdghiilnorw
childcrowing
ccdgknooooru
drongo-cuckoo
ccdgknooooruu
ground-cuckoo
ccdhhiloorry
hydrochloric
ccdhhinooopr
chordophonic
ccdhloooorst
school-doctor
ccdiiilnrtyy
cylindricity
ccdiinottuvy
conductivity
ccdnnnooortu
non-conductor
cceeeehrsttu
cheese-cutter
cceeeeiikklo
cockieleekie
cceeeeinrsvv
revivescence
cceeeejnnsuv
juvenescence
cceeeellmnos
emollescence
cceeeflnorsu
fluorescence
cceeeghhikrw
check-weigher
cceeegilnort
electrogenic
cceeehiimnpy
chimney-piece
cceeehooprrt
porte-cochère
cceeeiilnrsv
virilescence
cceeeiimnnrs
reminiscence
cceeeiinnrst
inter-science
cceeeiinprss
resipiscence
cceeeiinrsvv
reviviscence
cceeeillortv
recollective
cceeeilmnnrt
encirclement
cceeeilmnnsu
luminescence
cceeeilmorrt
electromeric
cceeeimnnopt
incompetence

cceeeimnnstu
intumescence
cceeeinnnost
consentience
cceeeinorssv
coerciveness
cceeeinrsvvy
revivescency
cceeeloprst
electroscope
cceeemmmnnot
commencement
cceeemnopprt
cement-copper
cceeennorsst
concreteness
cceeffiiinny
inefficiency
cceeffiikott
ticket-office
cceeffiiloop
police-office
cceefhiijstu
chief-justice
cceefinnoort
confectioner
cceefnoorrtu
counter-force
cceegilloosy
ecclesiology
cceeginnnort
concentering
cceeginoostt
geotectonics
cceeginostty
cytogenetics
cceehhikn ntw
kitchen-wench
cceehhloppru
churchpeople
cceehiilnort
heliocentric
cceehiilortt
heteroclitic
cceehiklnpst
pencil-sketch
cceehiklnrrt
lick-trencher
cceehiknostu
chuckie-stone
cceehimmnnot
mnemotechnic
cceehimostyz
schizomycete
cceehinnortt
ethnocentric
cceehinnostu
inescutcheon
cceehkloorst
electroshock
cceehmopstyy
Phycomycetes
cceeiiiikkkw
kickie-wickie

cceeiillostv
collectivise
cceeiilmnstu
multiscience
cceeiimmnosu
oecumenicism
cceeiinnnnot
incontinence
cceeiinprssy
resipiscency
cceeiinrsvvy
reviviscency
cceeiklnoppr
copper-nickel
cceeilllotvy
collectively
cceeillnoort
recollection
cceeillortty
electrolytic
cceeilnnortv
conventicler
cceeilnnotvy
connectively
cceeilnoortt
electrotonic
cceeiloprrty
pyro-electric
cceeiloprtty
electrotypic
cceeilsssuvy
successively
cceeimnnnotv
convincement
cceeimnnopty
incompetency
cceeimnoorst
econometrics
cceeimoprstt
spectrometic
cceeinnnortt
interconnect
cceeinoorrrt
correctioner
cceeinprrrtu
price-current
cceeinsssuuv
unsuccessive
cceeiorrstuv
service-court
cceelmnnotuy
locum-tenency
cceenorrruuy
Eurocurrency
cceeoopprsst
spectroscope
ccefhinoorsu
conchiferous
ccefiiinnstu
unscientific
ccefiilmrsuu
circumfusile
ccefilmnrtuu
circumfluent

ccefklooooruw
cuckoo-flower
cceflls ssuuy
successfully
ccefln sssuuu
unsuccessful
ccefoooprrrt
proof-correct
cceghiikqrtu
get-rich-quick
cceghiinortt
ricochetting
cceghikmnoor
checking-room
ccegiinprttu
price-cutting
ccegilmmoory
myrmecologic
cceginnnnoru
unconcerning
ccehhhmorrtu
mother-church
ccehhiilmoor
heliochromic
ccehiilmorrt
chlorimetric
ccehiimorstt
stichometric
ccehiinoorrt
rhinocerotic
ccehiklnorrw
clincher-work
ccehilmoorrt
chlorometric
ccehilnoortu
technicolour
ccehilnoosuu
council-house
ccehimnoorrt
chronometric
ccehimnostyz
zymotechnics
ccehimooprst
thermoscopic
ccehimoprsty
psychometric
ccehinoprsty
pyrotechnics
ccehioopsstt
stethoscopic
ccehkloorstt
throstle-cock
ccehlooorsuu
ochroleucous
cceiiimmorss
microseismic
cceiiinoorrt
oneirocritic
cceiiillmostv
collectivism
cceiillosttv
collectivist
cceiillottvy
collectivity

cceiilnnosuv
inconclusive
cceiilprstuu
pisciculture
cceiimoopsss
seismoscopic
cceiinnnnoty
incontinency
cceiinoorstv
viscerotonic
cceiinorsttv
constrictive
cceiinrsstty
syncretistic
cceillnosuvy
conclusively
cceillooopss
oscilloscope
cceilnnosuuv
unconclusive
cceilooprsuy
precociously
cceiloosstuy
leucocytosis
cceimnoprsty
cryptomnesic
cceimooppst
metoposcopic
cceinnosttuy
constituency
cceinoorssst
cross-section
cceinopsttuy
conspectuity
cceinorsttuv
constructive
ccelnnorrtuy
concurrently
cceloprssuuu
crepusculous
ccenoprrsttu
preconstruct
ccenorrrsstu
cross-current
ccenorrsttuu
constructure
cceoopprssty
spectroscopy
ccfgghiiknot
cockfighting
ccfiimnorsuu
circumfusion
ccfilmorsuuu
circumfluous
ccghiknnorsu
corn-shucking
ccghiknoortw
cock-throwing
ccghilnooost
conchologist
ccgiilnnnovy
convincingly
ccgiimnoopry
microcopying

ccgiinnnnouv
unconvincing
ccgiklnoostu
cucking-stool
ccgilmnoorty
motor-cycling
ccginorssttu
crosscutting
cchhiiiiqquu
chiquichiqui
cchhiiilotty
ichthyolitic
cchhiimostty
stichomythic
cchhiimostyz
schizothymic
cchhiiopstyz
schizophytic
cchhilmoorst
chrisom-cloth
cchhilmorsuw
Low-Churchism
cchhimoooprt
photochromic
cchhnnoorsuy
oncorhynchus
cchiiiloorst
orthosilicic
cchiimoprssy
microphysics
cchiimopssty
psychoticism
cchiiooprsty
hypocoristic
cchiiorrsttu
short-circuit
cchimmnnoops
pinchcommons
cchimnoopssy
psychonomics
cchimoorstuy
cymotrichous
cchiooossttu
octostichous
cchiopprsty
psychotropic
cciiiilloossu
silicicolous
cciiinnnnoty
inconcinnity
cciikkksswyy
kicksy-wicksy
cciilmooopst
cosmopolitic
cciilnnnoosu
inconclusion
cciilorstuuy
circuitously
cciimooprsst
microscopist
cciinnnnoosu
inconcinnous
cciinnooprst
conscription

cciinnoorstt
constriction
cciiootttxyy
cytotoxicity
cciknoooprrs
rock-scorpion
ccilmoorstty
motor-cyclist
ccilmorrsuuu
cirro-cumulus
cumulo-cirrus
ccimnoopstuu
compunctious
ccimnorssttu
misconstruct
ccinnoorsttu
construction
cclmooosstuy
cyclostomous
ccnoorrsstuy
cross-country
cddeeeefilsv
self-deceived
cddeeeeinnnp
independence
cddeeeejnsst
dejectedness
cddeeefilrst
self-directed
cddeeeillrtw
well-directed
cddeeeinnnpy
independency
cddeefloprsu
self-produced
cddeegilnosu
cloud-seeding
cddeehlnnosu
non-scheduled
cddeehlnortu
underclothed
cddeehmoopru
home-produced
cddeeiiklnss
slickensided
cddeeiilmmno
middle-income
cddeeijnpruu
unprejudiced
cddeeinnorsu
unconsidered
cddeeinnostt
discontented
cddeeinorsuv
undiscovered
cddeemnnotuu
undocumented
cddeemnoopsu
undecomposed
cddeemnootuy
duodenectomy
cddeenoopprs
dropped-scone

cddeenoprruu
under-produce
cddefiiklsst
fiddlesticks
cddeflnnoouy
confoundedly
cddehilnosss
cloddishness
cddehlloorsu
cold-shoulder
cddehlnortuu
thunder-cloud
cddehmooorst
odd-come-short
cddeinnortuu
unintroduced
cddelmnoorsu
scoundreldom
cddemnnoopuu
uncompounded
cddgiinnorsu
undiscording
cddgillmnoou
cold-moulding
cddiimmoosty
discommodity
cdeeeeeghprr
hedge-creeper
cdeeeefilnsv
self-evidence
cdeeeefilrsv
self-deceiver
cdeeeehnrrtt
three-centred
cdeeeeiinnpx
inexpedience
cdeeeeiklprw
pickerel-weed
cdeeeelnnprs
resplendence
cdeeeenprssu
supersedence
cdeeeensst tw
sweet-scented
cdeeeffginor
force-feeding
cdeeeffiinnr
indifference
cdeeefgimnnn
fence-mending
cdeeefhilrst
chesterfield
cdeeefillorw
flower-delice
cdeeeflloruw
flower-deluce
cdeeeflorrtt
retroflected
cdeeegiklnrs
single-decker
cdeeeginostv
decongestive
cdeeehimnprt
decipherment

cdeeehirsttw
white-crested
cdeeehnooptt
detectophone
cdeeehnrsstw
wretchedness
cdeeeiiinstz
decitizenise
cdeeeiinnpxy
inexpediency
cdeeeiinsssv
decisiveness
cdeeeilmnort
declinometer
cdeeeilnqstu
deliquescent
cdeeeimnortt
mine-detector
cdeeeinnnors
non-residence
cdeeeinprsst
decrepitness
cdeeeinrssst
discreetness
discreteness
cdeeeiorrrsv
rediscoverer
cdeeekllnowy
yellow-necked
cdeeeklnpsss
speckledness
cdeeeklnrttu
turtle-necked
cdeeelnnprsy
resplendency
cdeeelnoorst
electrosonde
cdeeelnptuxy
unexpectedly
cdeeemnnnotu
denouncement
cdeeenprstuu
unpersecuted
cdeeffhiloor
office-holder
cdeeffiinnry
indifferency
cdeefhllooss
self-schooled
cdeefhlnooov
cloven-hoofed
cdeefiiklmno
folk-medicine
cdeefiinostt
defectionist
cdeefilnnnuu
uninfluenced
cdeefilorrst
self-director
cdeeflloorsu
self-coloured
cdeeflmnossu
self-consumed

cdeeflnoootv
cloven-footed
cdeeflrssttu
self-destruct
cdeefnnosssu
confusedness
cdeegiilrrty
triglyceride
cdeeginnoost
decongestion
cdeeginnorsu
unrecognised
cdeeglnoostu
close-tongued
cdeehhklloss
shellshocked
cdeehiiinnor
encheiridion
cdeehiirsttw
wire-stitched
cdeehiklortt
ticket-holder
cdeehinnrstu
unchristened
cdeehinortww
white-crowned
cdeehioprrrs
recordership
cdeehlmoostu
close-mouthed
cdeehlnorstu
underclothes
cdeehlnprsuu
unsepulchred
cdeeiiilnsvy
indecisively
cdeeiiilopst
depoliticise
cdeeiiinnstv
disincentive
cdeeiiinrttv
interdictive
cdeeiillmpsu
semipellucid
cdeeiilmnrsy
semicylinder
cdeeiilmnruv
demi-culverin
cdeeiilnoprt
predilection
cdeeiilnrsty
indiscreetly
indiscretely
iridescently
cdeeiilopstv
velocipedist
cdeeiilorsvv
silver-voiced
cdeeiilrstvy
discretively
cdeeiimnoprv
improvidence
cdeeiinnrsst
indirectness

cdeeiknorsst
second-strike
cdeeillnpssu
pellucidness
cdeeilmnoopx
complexioned
cdeeilnooruw
wine-coloured
cdeeilnorstu
uncloistered
cdeeilnprtyy
type-cylinder
cdeeilrrstty
restrictedly
cdeeimnnostt
miscontented
cdeeimnoortu
Deuteronomic
cdeeimprstuw
wide-spectrum
cdeeinnorsww
window-screen
cdeeinopprrt
intercropped
cdeeinoprstw
insect-powder
cdeeinrrsttu
unrestricted
cdeeioprrtuv
reproductive
cdeeiopsssuy
pseudocyesis
cdeeiorrstuv
discoverture
cdeellnnosuu
uncounselled
cdeelooorrsu
rose-coloured
cdeelooprstw
powder-closet
cdeemnoopsss
composedness
cdeemooprrss
decompressor
cdeennnooost
second-to-none
cdeennooprst
co-respondent
cdeennrrrtuu
undercurrent
cdeenoorsssu
decorousness
cdeeooprstuy
deuteroscopy
cdeeorrrsstu
court-dresser
cdefhilnoors
school-friend
cdefiiinnost
disinfection
cdefiimorstu
discomfiture
cdefiinosttu
unscottified

cdefilnnnouy
unconfinedly
cdeflnnosuuy
unconfusedly
cdeghhiikstt
thick-sighted
cdeghhilooru
high-coloured
cdeghiikqstu
quick-sighted
cdeghilorsst
cross-lighted
cdeghinnoosu
echo-sounding
cdeghioopstu
pseudo-Gothic
cdeghnorrruy
ground-cherry
cdegiimnoosy
gynodioecism
cdegiinnnrsu
undiscerning
cdegiklmnnou
neck-moulding
cdegiknnostu
unstockinged
cdeglmnoruuy
curmudgeonly
cdehhiiiprtt
diphtheritic
cdehhiilnsss
childishness
cdehiiilppss
discipleship
cdehiikknnst
thick-skinned
cdehiillorsv
shrill-voiced
cdehiilnoosv
school-divine
cdehiilnsssy
schindylesis
cdehiimnosuu
eunuchoidism
cdehiimpssty
dysphemistic
cdehiinnrstt
herd-instinct
cdehiinooopr
conidiophore
cdehiinortyz
hydrozincite
cdehiioprrst
directorship
cdehiiprsstt
spider-stitch
cdehikkllstu
thick-skulled
cdehilloopry
policy-holder
cdehimnooors
chondriosome
cdehimorttyy
rhytidectomy

cdehiorrttwy
creditworthy
cdeiiiilnnps
indiscipline
cdeiiijrstuv
jurisdictive
cdeiiillnosv
cell-division
cdeiiilnnpsu
undiscipline
cdeiiilntvvy
vindictively
cdeiiimnorst
misdirection
cdeiiinnorst
indiscretion
cdeiiinnortt
interdiction
cdeiilmrtuuv
diverticulum
cdeiilnnppru
unprincipled
cdeiilrssuvy
discursively
cdeiimmnooss
commissioned
cdeiimmrssty
dissymmetric
cdeiimnoprrt
microprinted
cdeiimnorstu
reductionism
cdeiinnnoosx
disconnexion
cdeiinnooprt
precondition
cdeiinnssstt
distinctness
cdeiinoooprs
conidiospore
cdeiinooprst
periodontics
cdeiinorrtty
interdictory
cdeiinorsttu
reductionist
cdeiinorttuv
introductive
cdeiknrsttuy
sky-tinctured
cdeilmnorssu
scoundrelism
cdeilnoorsuy
indecorously
cdeiloprtuvy
productively
cdeimooprssu
discomposure
cdeinnrsttuu
uninstructed
cdeinooprrtu
reproduction
cdeinoprtuuv
unproductive

cdeioorsstuu
discourteous
cdeknorrstuw
wonder-struck
cdellnnoortu
uncontrolled
cdelnnoopruy
pronouncedly
cdelnooostuy
cotyledonous
cdelnprstuuu
unsculptured
cdelooorrsuy
rosy-coloured
cdeloorrstuu
rust-coloured
cdennnoopruu
unpronounced
cdennoorrtuu
counter-round
cdenrrsttuuu
unstructured
cdfgiiimnost
discomfiting
cdfhiloorruy
hydrofluoric
cdfiilmnorry
cylindriform
cdghiiilprty
ditriglyphic
cdghiilnoors
riding-school
cdgiiinnnoot
conditioning
cdgiiklnossu
cloud-kissing
cdgiimmnnoor
common-riding
cdgiklnoostu
ducking-stool
cdgimnnoopru
ring-compound
cdhhiiimorty
idiorhythmic
cdhhiooprty
hypotrochoid
cdhiiimooprs
isodimorphic
cdhimooorrst
orthodromics
cdhinooorstt
orthodontics
cdhioooprssu
discophorous
cdhiooopssuz
schizopodous
cdiiijnorstu
jurisdiction
cdiiilnnstty
indistinctly
cdiillorsuuy
ridiculously
cdiimmnooosu
incommodious

cdiimmnostuy
discommunity
cdiinnoorttu
introduction
cdiioprttuvy
productivity
cdilmmooosuy
commodiously
cdinoorrttuy
introductory
cdmmnnoooopu
mono-compound
ceeeeehnnrst
cheese-rennet
ceeeeffikors
office-seeker
ceeeeffnrstv
effervescent
ceeeefillstv
self-elective
ceeeefinnrrt
interference
ceeeeflorrst
free-selector
ceeeeghmnors
cheese-monger
ceeeegllnrtt
tercel-gentle
ceeeehhopprs
cheese-hopper
ceeeehnorsvw
whencesoever
ceeeeiilmptt
etepimeletic
ceeeeiinnprx
inexperience
ceeeeikkprtw
wicket-keeper
ceeeeinprstx
pre-existence
ceeeeinrrrsv
sir-reverence
ceeeelmorrtt
electrometer
ceeeelnprsst
pretenceless
ceeeffinnotv
non-effective
ceeefflnorst
efflorescent
ceeefghhimrt
Fehmgerichte
ceeefgillnst
self-electing
ceeefhinrsst
scene-shifter
ceeefhlnrssu
cheerfulness
ceeefiilrrtv
irreflective
ceeefiimprtv
imperfective
ceeefilllmnu
mellifluence

ceeefillnost
self-election
ceeefillnosv
self-violence
ceeefillrtvy
reflectively
ceeefilnnrtu
interfluence
ceeefilnrtuv
unreflective
ceeefilprtvy
perfectively
ceeefklnssss
fecklessness
ceeeghhimrtv
Vehmgerichte
ceeegiillnnt
intelligence
ceeegiinrstv
receiving-set
ceeeginoostt
osteogenetic
ceeeginoprtt
petrogenetic
ceeehhinrsss
cheerishness
ceeehiimrstu
euhemeristic
ceeehikprrrt
three-pricker
ceeehimnpswy
chimney-sweep
ceeehimnrstu
hermeneutics
ceeehinosssv
cohesiveness
ceeehioorstu
heteroecious
ceeehllpsssy
speechlessly
ceeehlnortuw
counter-wheel
ceeehmnnnrtt
entrenchment
ceeehmnnrrtt
retrenchment
ceeehmoorrst
stereochrome
ceeehnoprrst
centrosphere
ceeehpppprry
cherry-pepper
ceeeiillnttv
intellective
ceeeiimnnprt
impertinence
ceeeiimpprtv
imperceptive
ceeeiinprttv
interceptive
ceeeiinrrstv
interservice
ceeeiiprrstv
irrespective

ceeeijklnrrt
tercel-jerkin
ceeeiknoprst
specktioneer
ceeeillnopqu
equipollence
ceeeilnnoppt
plenipotence
ceeeilnoprst
preselection
ceeeilprstvy
respectively
ceeeimnnoprs
omnipresence
ceeeimorrstt
stereometric
ceeeinnnostx
non-existence
ceeeinnorssv
overniceness
ceeeinnqsstu
quintessence
ceeeinosstvv
covetiveness
ceeeinpprtuv
unperceptive
ceeeinprstuv
unrespective
ceeeinrrrstw
screen-writer
ceeeiorrsstv
retrocessive
ceeeiprrssuv
repercussive
ceeeirrrstuv
resurrective
ceeeklnrssss
recklessness
ceeellnpruuv
pulverulence
ceeelmnopsst
completeness
ceeelmorrtty
electrometry
ceeelmprrstu
spectre-lemur
ceeelnoprstu
Pleuronectes
ceeelnoprstw
steeple-crown
ceeeloprrtty
electrotyper
ceeelorrsssu
resourceless
ceeelorsttvv
velvet-scoter
ceeemnnnortu
renouncement
ceeennorsstu
counter-sense
ceeennprtuuv
venepuncture
ceeeooprrttx
exteroceptor

ceeffhiklrrs
sheriff-clerk
ceeffhinortu
office-hunter
ceeffiinnnot
non-efficient
ceefghoprrtu
rough-perfect
ceefgiilnopw
fowling-piece
ceefgiilnrty
electrifying
ceefgiilnstx
self-exciting
ceefgillnrty
reflectingly
ceefgilnnotu
genuflection
ceefgilnnrtu
unreflecting
ceefglllntuy
neglectfully
ceefhkmorrtu
mother-fucker
ceefhllnruuy
uncheerfully
ceefiilnorrt
irreflection
ceefiilrttvy
reflectivity
ceefiimnoprt
imperfection
ceefiinoprst
frontispiece
ceefilmnrssu
mercifulness
ceefilnossuv
voicefulness
ceefinnoprtu
unperfection
ceefllprstuy
respectfully
ceeflmnopstt
self-contempt
ceeflnoqruwy
low-frequency
ceefmoorrrtu
recomforture
ceefnoorssss
confessoress
ceegghlnoouz
cough-lozenge
ceeggillnnty
neglectingly
ceeghiinortz
rhizogenetic
ceeghiinostt
histogenetic
ceeghilnopty
phylogenetic
ceeghiloprt
herpetologic
ceeghimorsty
geochemistry

ceeghinnopty
hypnogenetic
ceeghinoortt
orthogenetic
ceeghinoprss
sheep-scoring
ceeghinoptty
phytogenetic
ceeghinorsty
hysterogenic
ceeghinortuw
counter-weigh
ceeghkoopprt
pocket-gopher
ceegiiklnstw
single-wicket
ceegiillnprs
selling-price
ceegiinnortt
reciting-note
ceegiinnprss
piercingness
ceegiinoprtv
precognitive
ceegikknnoor
knee-crooking
ceegikllnops
glockenspiel
ceegiklnpttu
putting-cleek
ceegiknosttt
stockingette
ceegillnnnor
Lincoln-green
ceegilmooort
meteorologic
ceeginoorrvv
vice-governor
ceeginoprssw
weeping-cross
ceegmnoorrst
costermonger
ceehhiilllnp
philhellenic
ceehhiinostt
henotheistic
ceehhimmoort
homeothermic
ceehhinoprsz
schizophrene
ceehhinprsty
hypersthenic
ceehhloorsst
clothes-horse
ceehhmnnorty
nychthemeron
ceehhmooprrs
chromosphere
ceehhnoorrty
heterochrony
ceehhoopprss
phosphoresce
ceehiillnprs
spine-chiller

ceehiinpprst
prenticeship
ceehiipprrst
peristrephic
ceehikmnosss
homesickness
ceehilmmopry
myrmecophile
ceehilmnoott
monotheletic
ceehilmnoprs
chrome-spinel
ceehilnnorty
incoherently
ceehimmorrtt
thermometric
ceehimmprsst
sprechstimme
ceehimnnnrtt
intrenchment
ceehinooprst
stereophonic
ceehinoorrss
rhinoceroses
ceehinopprtu
Picturephone®
ceehinorsttz
zenith-sector
ceehinrrrtwy
winter-cherry
ceehiooprstu
Oreopithecus
ceehioprstuu
picture-house
ceehioprstux
executorship
ceehipprrtyy
hyperpyretic
ceehkmnnorwy
monkey-wrench
ceehllmoorwy
chrome-yellow
ceehllnqssuy
quenchlessly
ceehlmooprtu
thermo-couple
ceehloprssst
clothes-press
ceehmoorrsty
stereochromy
ceehmoprrsty
psychrometer
ceehmorsttyy
hysterectomy
ceehoorrrssu
horse-courser
ceeiiinnprtt
intercipient
ceeiiinnsssv
incisiveness
ceeiijnnortt
interjection
ceeiikkllrst
stickler-like

ceeiikllnrsv
nickel-silver
ceeiiklorrtu
courtierlike
ceeiikrrtttw
ticket-writer
ceeiillmnott
monticellite
ceeiillmnpsx
mill-sixpence
ceeiillnnort
intercolline
ceeiillnnott
intellection
ceeiillrruuw
curliewurlie
ceeiilmnnort
inclinometer
ceeiilmprsst
plessimetric
ceeiilnnprss
princeliness
ceeiilnpsstx
explicitness
ceeiimmorsst
seismometric
ceeiimnnprty
impertinency
ceeiimnossss
secessionism
ceeiimnosttu
cementitious
ceeiimopprtt
micropipette
ceeiimoprssu
semi-precious
ceeiimorrstu
meretricious
ceeiimorsstv
viscosimeter
ceeiinnnnotv
inconvenient
ceeiinnoprst
reinspection
ceeiinnoprtt
interception
ceeiinnorsst
intercession
ceeiinnorstt
intersection
ceeiinoprrst
peristeronic
ceeiinoprstt
receptionist
ceeiinorssux
excursionise
ceeiinosssst
secessionist
ceeiinpsstuv
insusceptive
ceeiipprrstv
prescriptive
ceeiipprttvy
perceptivity

ceeijnoorrtt
retrojection
ceeiklmnppru
pumpernickel
ceeiklnorsss
session-clerk
ceeikoprrttt
ticket-porter
ceeillmnopty
incompletely
ceeillnopquy
equipollency
ceeillorssty
electrolysis
ceeillprsuvy
preclusively
ceeilmmnoprt
complimenter
ceeilmnnnoos
insomnolence
ceeilmnnossu
uncomeliness
ceeilmooprsy
co-polymerise
ceeilmoosttu
cole-titmouse
ceeilnnnotvy
conveniently
ceeilnnoppty
plenipotency
ceeilnnpsstu
spinulescent
ceeilnooprss
necropolises
ceeilnorrtvw
winter-clover
ceeilooprstt
coleopterist
ceeiloprttvy
protectively
ceeilprssuvy
percussively
ceeimmmnortt
recommitment
ceeimmnnortu
intercommune
ceeimnnorttv
contrivement
ceeimnooprst
contemporise
ceeimnoorstt
econometrist
ceeimnorsuzz
mizzen-course
ceeinnnoortv
conventioner
ceeinnnoqstu
inconsequent
ceeinnoorrrt
reconnoitrer
ceeinnoorrsv
reconversion
ceeinnorsstt
contriteness

ceeinnorsttu
reconsituent
ceeinnprtuuv
venipuncture
ceeinnrrrttu
intercurrent
ceeinooprrss
processioner
ceeinooprrtt
interoceptor
ceeinooprstt
stereopticon
ceeinooprstu
counterpoise
ceeinoorrsst
retrocession
ceeinoprrssu
repercussion
ceeinoprsssu
preciousness
ceeinopssssu
speciousness
ceeinorrrstu
resurrection
ceeinorrssty
intercessory
ceeinorstttu
reconstitute
ceeiooprrstt
stereotropic
ceekllnssssu
lucklessness
ceekooprrssu
pressure-cook
ceellnoorttv
electron-volt
ceelmnnoosst
somnolescent
ceelmooorrtt
electromotor
ceelnnoqstuy
consequently
ceelnoorsttu
electrotonus
ceelnorsssuu
ulcerousness
ceeloooprstu
coleopterous
ceeloopprstu
plecopterous
ceelprrsstuu
supercluster
ceemoprrstty
spectrometry
ceennooqrstu
queen-consort
ceennoorrttu
counter-tenor
ceenoossstuv
covetousness
ceeopprssstu
prospectuses
ceffgiknnoor
off-reckoning

ceffgilnossu
self-focusing
ceffhiknsttu
kitchen-stuff
ceffhiorrstu
sheriff-court
ceffiiinnstu
insufficient
ceffiilnstuy
sufficiently
ceffiinnstuu
unsufficient
ceffiorrstuu
fructiferous
ceffiorsstuu
suffruticose
cefghimnoort
home-crofting
cefghinoorsu
forcing-house
cefgiikllnry
flickeringly
cefgiilnostt
close-fitting
cefhhilnoprs
French-polish
cefhilmnnouy
ichneumon-fly
cefhimoorssu
moschiferous
cefhlllooosw
schoolfellow
cefhlmooorrr
chloroformer
cefiiilnostu
infelicitous
cefiiilorssu
siliciferous
cefiiiorrstu
Fourieristic
cefiillostuy
felicitously
cefiilmnntuy
munificently
cefiilmorrtu
fluorimetric
cefiilnoprss
prolificness
cefiilnoprty
proficiently
cefiilnorsst
frictionless
cefiilnostuy
infectiously
cefiioorstvy
vociferosity
cefillmnruuy
unmercifully
cefillmoorsy
frolicsomely
cefillorrtuu
floriculture
cefilmoorrtu
fluorometric

cefilnnosstu
functionless
cefiloorsuvy
vociferously
cefiloprsuuu
cupuliferous
ceflnnorsssu
scornfulness
ceflnoorrtuy
counter-flory
cefmnnnoortt
confrontment
cefnoooprrtu
counterproof
cegggiiinprr
price-rigging
cegghilosttw
toggle-switch
ceggiimnotvy
gingivectomy
ceghhiilopry
hieroglyphic
ceghhiilotvy
high-velocity
ceghhilnostt
night-clothes
ceghhinooptt
photo-etching
ceghhlnoprtu
trench-plough
ceghiiloorst
cheirologist
ceghiiopssty
geophysicist
ceghiknnosss
shockingness
ceghiknoorrs
rocking-horse
ceghilnoostt
technologist
ceghilnorruy
chirurgeonly
ceghilnorttu
counterlight
ceghilooorst
choreologist
ceghilooosty
stoechiology
ceghilopprty
petroglyphic
ceghimortuux
cough-mixture
ceghinnoorsu
corning-house
ceghinnosstu
touchingness
ceghinoossuz
schizogenous
ceghmooppssy
sphygmoscope
cegiiiilnpst
still-piecing
cegiikllnqsu
quick-selling

cegiikmnnors
misreckoning
cegiiknrrstt
trickstering
cegiilloostx
lexicologist
cegiilnnpsty
inspectingly
cegiimnnoost
monogenistic
cegiinnooprt
precognition
cegiinopttyy
genotypicity
cegijknosstt
jesting-stock
cegiklnoosst
stocking-sole
cegiklnossst
stockingless
cegiknnoorst
rocking-stone
cegilmmootuy
etymologicum
cegilmnoooty
etymologicon
cegilnnnosty
consentingly
cegilnnnotty
contingently
cegilnnoqruy
conqueringly
cegilnnorstu
curling-stone
cegilnnostty
contestingly
cegilnooprtu
glucoprotein
cegilnooprty
glycoprotein
cegilnoprtty
protectingly
cegimnooprsy
myringoscope
cegimnoorrsu
microsurgeon
cegimorrrsuy
microsurgery
ceginnnnostu
unconsenting
ceginnnoortw
conning-tower
ceginnnorstt
constringent
ceginnostttu
stone-cutting
ceginnpsstuu
unsuspecting
ceginoorrssv
crossing-over
ceginopprssy
copying-press
ceginorrsstu
string-course

ceginprssttu
press-cutting
cegmoostuyyz
zygomycetous
cehhiilmoprt
thermophilic
cehhiiloprst
lithospheric
cehhilnrsssu
churlishness
cehhiloprty
hypochlorite
cehhilorsttt
torch-thistle
cehhimmooopr
homeomorphic
cehhioopprst
photospheric
cehhiopprrty
hypertrophic
cehhloorsstt
short-clothes
cehiiklnssst
ticklishness
cehiiknrssst
trickishness
cehiillnnott
centillionth
cehiilmnoprs
necrophilism
cehiilnqsssu
cliquishness
cehiilnrssst
Christliness
cehiiloorstu
leiotrichous
cehiilopstty
polytheistic
cehiimnoostt
monotheistic
cehiimnopruy
perionychium
cehiimnsstty
syntheticism
cehiimoorstt
trichotomise
cehiinnoprty
pericynthion
cehiknosssst
stockishness
cehillnnorsu
unicorn-shell
cehillopptyy
polyphyletic
cehilmmopryy
myrmecophily
cehilmnoopty
monophyletic
cehilmnoppty
nympholeptic
cehilnnosssw
clownishness
cehilnooprsu
necrophilous

cehiloqsttuy
coquettishly
cehilorrttuu
horticulture
cehilpprrsuu
persulphuric
cehimmooprst
chemotropism
cehimnorrtyy
erythromycin
cehimooprrtt
thermotropic
cehimoorstyz
zoochemistry
cehimopprsty
spermophytic
cehinnorrssy
synchroniser
cehinoprstty
pyrotechnist
cehinoqsttuu
uncoquettish
cehinosssstt
Scottishness
cehiooprrst
tropospheric
cehiooprrstu
chiropterous
cehiooprrttt
tithe-proctor
cehllloprsyy
sclerophylly
cehmooooprty
oophorectomy
cehmoprrstyy
psychrometry
cehnoooprrsu
necrophorous
cehnoorstuuy
country-house
cehoooprrsst
photo-process
ceiiiiilnstv
incivilities
ceiiilmnpsst
implicitness
ceiiinnorstu
reunionistic
ceiiinoprsst
precisionist
ceiijlnntuvy
injunctively
ceiijnnoortt
introjection
ceiijoprttvy
projectivity
ceiikllpstty
lickety-split
ceiiklqrsuvy
quicksilvery
ceiiklsstwzz
swizzle-stick
ceiillnostuy
licentiously

ceiillrstuuv
silviculture
ceiilmnnoopt
incompletion
ceiilmnnosty
omnisciently
ceiilmnossux
exclusionism
ceiilmoprtuv
pluviometric
ceiilnnorstu
interclusion
ceiilnoosttu
elocutionist
ceiilnoprsuy
perniciously
ceiilnossstu
seclusionist
ceiilnosstux
exclusionist
ceiiloprssuu
supercilious
ceiimmnoorss
commissioner
recommission
ceiimorsstvy
viscosimetry
ceiinnnosstt
inconsistent
ceiinnorrstu
insurrection
ceiinooprrty
incorporeity
ceiinopprrst
prescription
ceiinoprrstt
prestriction
ceiinoprrtuv
incorruptive
ceiinorsstux
excursionist
ceiinostttuv
constitutive
ceiiopprrstv
proscriptive
ceiiprrrsttw
script-writer
ceiipssttuvy
susceptivity
ceijkklnnotu
knuckle-joint
ceikllmnooru
cork-linoleum
ceikllorstuy
kill-courtesy
ceiklooppstt
pocket-pistol
ceikmnnoorst
moonstricken
ceillmopsuvy
compulsively
ceillmostuuy
meticulously
ceillnosuvvy
convulsively
ceillrstuuvy
sylviculture
ceilmnoostty
tonsilectomy
ceilmnoostuu
contumelious
ceilnnosstty
consistently
ceilnoorrttu
interlocutor
ceilnoorssuy
censoriously
ceilnossssuu
lusciousness
ceilnosstuuy
incestuously
ceilooorssst
otosclerosis
ceiloopqrtuy
pectoriloquy
ceiloossssuw
colossus-wise
ceimnnooprsu
mispronounce
ceimnnoorstu
conterminous
ceimnoprstty
streptomycin
ceimooprrstu
micropterous
ceinnooprttu
counterpoint
ceinnoorssuu
uncensorious
ceinpsssttuu
intussuscept
ceinrrsssttu
instructress
ceioprrsstuu
Sciuropterus
celmnoprtuuu
mucopurulent
celmnottttuu
mutton-cutlet
celnooorrstv
servo-control
cemmnnnoossu
uncommonness
cemnoopsttuu
contemptuous
cemoooorrstt
motor-scooter
cennossstuuu
unctuousness
ceoopprrsssu
cross-purpose
cfgiknooostt
stocking-foot
cfgimnnnooru
unconforming
cfhiinooprss
scorpion-fish
cfiiilosttuy
fictitiously
cfiillnoostu
solifluction
cfiimmnoorst
Cominformist
cfilnorssuuu
furunculosis
cfimnnoortuy
unconformity
cfioorrstuuv
fructivorous
cgghhinooopu
hooping-cough
cggilnnorstu
curling-tongs
cghhilooppty
photoglyphic
cghiiknnossu
king's-cushion
cghiilooopprt
oligotrophic
cghiilooosty
stoichiology
cghiiloorstt
trichologist
cghiimnoopsy
physiognomic
cghiimooprtt
thigmotropic
cghikknnoops
knocking-shop
cghillnoopst
slop-clothing
cghilmoopssy
psychologism
cghilnooorst
chronologist
cghiloopssty
psychologist
cghinooppty
photocopying
cghinooossuz
schizogonous
cghinorrssuu
scouring-rush
cgiiimnnoprr
crimping-iron
cgiiinnoprrs
crisping-iron
cgiiinnrsstu
scrutinising
cgiiknrssstu
kissing-crust
cgiilmoosstu
musicologist
cgiilnnoprsy
conspiringly
cgiilnnorrsu
curling-irons
cgiilooosttx
toxicologist
cgiinnoostuu
incontiguous
cgikllnoorst
rolling-stock
cgillnoooprt
protocolling
cgilmnnnoopy
non-complying
cgilnooopssu
spongicolous
cgilnoostuuy
contiguously
cgiloooprstty
cryptologist
cgimnnooortu
counting-room
chhiimoooppr
ophiomorphic
chhilmoprtyy
polyrhythmic
chhinooprtty
trichophyton
chhinorrsstt
Christ's-thorn
chhmmoooorsu
homochromous
chiiilmnoops
iconophilism
chiiilnoopst
iconophilist
chiiilooptttx
toxophilitic
chiiiloprttt
lithotriptic
chiilmoprstu
Turcophilism
chiiiooprsty
polyhistoric
chiimnnrssty
strychninism
chiimnoopsty
monophysitic
chiinooopstt
opisthotonic
chiinoopprsw
whip-scorpion
chiinoorsttz
chorizontist
chiinopsstuv
viscountship
chilooopprsu
coprophilous
chimmnooorst
monochromist
chimnoooprst
monostrophic
chimnoooosstu
monostichous
chimoooopprrt
morphotropic
protomorphic
chimooorsttu
trichotomous
chinoooprsty
ornithoscopy

chinooorsstu
orthocousins
chinooppstty
post-hypnotic
chiooopprrtt
trophotropic
chiooorssstt
scissor-tooth
chkmnorsstuu
custom-shrunk
chkoorrrrstu
horror-struck
chnnoorrttuy
north-country
chnoorsttuuy
south-country
ciiiiimnostu
inimicitious
ciiiiopssttv
positivistic
ciiillmpttuy
multiplicity
ciilloosstuy
solicitously
ciilmnnorsuy
synclinorium
ciilmnooopst
monopolistic
ciilmoootttvy
locomotivity
ciilnoosstuu
unsolicitous
ciiloorstuvy
victoriously
ciilopsssuuy
suspiciously
ciimnoprstty
nyctitropism
ciinnooprrtu
incorruption
ciinnoostttu
constitution
ciinoooprsst
oniroscopist
ciinoopprrst
proscription
ciinopsssuuu
unsuspicious
cijlnorsstuu
jurisconsult
cillmooprsuy
compulsorily
cillorrssuuy
scurrilously
cilnnoostuuy
continuously
cilnorsstuuy
scrutinously
ciloprsstuuy
scrupulosity
cimmnnnnooou
non-communion
clloprssuuuy
scrupulously
clnoprssuuuu
unscrupulous
cmnooprstuyy
cryptonymous
ddddeeillnno
niddle-noddle
dddeeenrrssu
underdressed
dddeeginorww
wedding-dower
dddeeginrssw
wedding-dress
dddeeiiimpsy
epididymides
dddeeinorrsu
undisordered
dddeeinosttw
sodden-witted
dddeelmmttuy
muddy-mettled
dddegghinopu
hodge-pudding
dddehnnooorr
rhododendron
ddeeeefhnrtt
tender-hefted
ddeeeemnnsst
dementedness
ddeeefgnorru
ground-feeder
ddeeefmnorss
deformedness
ddeeeggilprs
spider-legged
ddeeeggilrst
stridelegged
ddeeegmooprt
good-tempered
ddeeeiimnnrt
indetermined
ddeeeilmnrrt
intermeddler
ddeeeilmnrty
determinedly
ddeeeimnnrtu
undetermined
ddeeeinnosss
one-sidedness
ddeeeinpssss
despisedness
ddeeelnoppru
underpeopled
ddeeelnopruv
underdevelop
ddeeelnrsuvy
undeservedly
ddeeenoprruw
underpowered
ddeeffglllluy
fully-fledged
ddeeffinsssu
diffusedness
ddeefhiiimru
dehumidifier
ddeefiiinntu
unidentified
ddeefiikllss
self-disliked
ddeeghiilmtw
middleweight
ddeegiilmnns
single-minded
ddeegilmnost
dislodgement
ddeegilnnsuy
undesignedly
ddeeginnnpwy
penny-wedding
ddeegllnoruw
well-grounded
ddeehimnostu
unmethodised
ddeehinrrtuv
thunder-drive
ddeeiiiikknw
kiddiewinkie
ddeeiilmmnps
simple-minded
ddeeiinprrst
priest-ridden
ddeeillopssw
well-disposed
ddeeilmmnoty
motley-minded
ddeeilnnpsss
splendidness
ddeeilnstuvy
undivestedly
ddeeimnnorsu
unmodernised
ddeeimnnostw
disendowment
ddeeinossstw
two-sidedness
ddeeiopsssss
dispossessed
ddeelnnopsty
despondently
ddefghilloot
floodlighted
ddefgiilnrst
fiddle-string
ddefginnnruu
underfunding
ddeghiinptuw
white-pudding
ddeghilnrsuy
shudderingly
ddeghmooruu
good-humoured
ddegikmnnoru
underkingdom
ddegilnnopsy
despondingly
ddegilnoorst
dendrologist
ddegimnnorst
strong-minded
ddeginnopstu
pudding-stone
ddeginnorssw
dressing-down
ddeglnnoruuy
ungroundedly
ddeglnooorsu
dendrologous
ddehiiimnnsu
undiminished
ddehilnnoopr
philodendron
ddehmnoortuu
round-mouthed
ddeiiilprsty
dispiritedly
ddeiijlnosty
disjointedly
ddeiilnnoorr
liriodendron
ddeiilnopssu
splendidious
ddeilnopruvy
unprovidedly
ddeilnpstuuy
undisputedly
ddeimnoorrww
dormer-window
ddeimooppsuu
pseudopodium
ddghilmnooou
hood-moulding
ddiiimprttuy
rumpti-iddity
deeeeilmprtv
evil-tempered
deeeeimnprrt
predetermine
deeeeimnprtx
experimented
deeeellmprtw
well-tempered
deeeelnnssss
needlessness
deeeenrrsssv
reservedness
deeefginrryz
freeze-drying
deeefiinnsst
definiteness
deeefinrrttt
interfretted
deeefllmopsy
self-employed
deeeflmrrrsu
self-murderer
deeefnnqrtuu
unfrequented
deeeggllllowy
yellow-legged
deeeghilnprs
spring-heeled
deeeghiortvw
overweighted

deeegiinnrrv
engine-driver
deeegiknnnoy
donkey-engine
deeegimnnrtu
unregimented
deeeginnrsss
resignedness
deeeginnrssv
evening-dress
deeeginrrstu
unregistered
deeegjmnprtu
prejudgement
deeehhlprsss
shepherdless
deeehhnrsttu
thunder-sheet
deeehiilrtvw
white-livered
deeehilmnstv
dishevelment
deeehilnsstw
swindle-sheet
deeehinrsstw
witheredness
deeehkllortt
kettleholder
deeehlorstty
heterostyled
deeehmnnortt
dethronement
deeehnoprrtu
three-pounder
deeehoostttw
sweet-toothed
deeeiilpprvy
delivery-pipe
deeeiinrsssv
derisiveness
deeeillmrssy
remedilessly
deeeillnruvy
unrelievedly
deeeilnrstty
interestedly
deeeilnsssuv
delusiveness
deeeimnnopst
semideponent
deeeimnoprrt
redemptioner
deeeimnorstt
densitometer
deeeimnrsstv
disseverment
deeeimprrttt
pretermitted
deeeinnrsttu
uninterested
deeeinprssst
presidentess
deeeiprrsssu
depressurise

deeejllopprt
jet-propelled
deeeklnnoost
endoskeleton
deeelmnoprty
redeployment
deeelnorsssv
resolvedness
deeelnrrsuvy
unreservedly
deeemmnoorst
endosmometer
deeenorrssst
stone-dresser
deeeopprssss
prepossessed
deeffhinrrsu
under-sheriff
deefghinnrtu
unfrightened
deefgiiknnrr
knife-grinder
deefginnorwz
freezing-down
deefginorrsy
rosy-fingered
deefgjlmnstu
self-judgment
deefgjmnortu
forejudgment
deefhiinnsss
fiendishness
deefhinorttw
white-fronted
deefiiilnnty
indefinitely
deefiiilntvy
definitively
deefiilnnrss
friendliness
deefiilnrstu
unfertilised
deefiilnstty
self-identity
deefiiprrtvy
perfervidity
deefillmnorw
well-informed
deefillnossu
self-delusion
deefillnosvv
self-involved
deefillpstuy
despitefully
deefilnoostv
self-devotion
deefilnprssu
pridefulness
deefiloorstv
silver-footed
deefinnssttu
unfittedness
deeflloootwy
yellow-footed

deefloorstuy
sure-footedly
deefmnoprrru
underperform
deefnnoorssv
overfondness
deeggimnorst
disgorgement
deegginnortu
teeing-ground
deegginnostw
weeding-tongs
deeghhilnprs
shepherdling
deeghiillnsv
dishevelling
deeghiilnrvw
driving-wheel
deeghiinnstw
winding-sheet
deeghilllptw
well-plighted
deeghnnootuy
honey-tongued
deegiiilprsv
disprivilege
deegiilllnpw
pile-dwelling
deegiilmoopy
epidemiology
deegiilnnssy
yieldingness
deegiilnopss
diplogenesis
deegiilnpruv
unprivileged
deegiilrssvy
digressively
deegiilssssu
disguiseless
deegiimnsstu
disguisement
deegiinoprst
predigestion
deegiinprstw
Speedwriting®
deegiinrrstw
wire-stringed
deegijmmnstu
misjudgement
deegiklmnosw
misknowledge
deegillllnorv
levelling-rod
deegillnorwy
yellow-ringed
deegillnrssw
well-dressing
deegilmnnnoy
money-lending
deegilnnprty
pretendingly
deegilnnrttu
underletting

deegilnorrtt
ring-dotterel
deegilnprssy
depressingly
deeginnnnssu
unendingness
deeginnnprtu
unpretending
deeginnnrstu
nurse-tending
deeginnrsttt
trend-setting
deeglloostyy
dysteleology
deegmnnoorrw
wonder-monger
deegnnoootuw
wooden-tongue
deehhiimoprs
hemispheroid
deehhmnootuy
honey-mouthed
deehiikrsssw
side-whiskers
deehiillnpps
nipple-shield
deehiimnortu
Deinotherium
deehiinprsst
residentship
deehiinrssst
dissenterish
deehiklnnosw
whole-skinned
deehilllnpss
spindle-shell
deehilmmnost
demolishment
deehilmostty
dyotheletism
deehilprssuu
desulphurise
deehimnoortu
time-honoured
deehiopprtty
pteridophyte
deehllnoorwy
yellow-horned
deehlnoorstu
shoulder-note
deehlprsttuu
sulphuretted
deehnnorsttu
thunder-stone
deeiiinsssvv
divisiveness
deeiilnnssuw
unwieldiness
deeiilnrsstu
unsterilised
deeiilnrstuu
underutilise
deeiimnnrstt
disinterment

deeiimnorstt
endometritis
deeiimnorttv
divertimento
deeiimnrssst
dissenterism
deeiinnssstu
unsensitised
deeiinprssst
spiritedness
deeiinqssstu
disquietness
deeiinrssttu
intertissued
deeijnorrrsu
surrejoinder
deeikknnrrsu
underskinker
deeikmnoprsy
spider-monkey
deeiknnorssv
overkindness
deeikrstttuu
skutterudite
deeillnnqtuy
delinquently
deeilmnnssss
mindlessness
deeilmnrttuy
unremittedly
deeilnnosttu
unlistened-to
deeilnprrttu
triple-turned
deeilnqrtuuy
unrequitedly
deeimnnrsttu
instrumented
deeimnorstty
densitometry
deeimopprrst
pteridosperm
deeimopprssu
superimposed
deeimoprrstt
redemptorist
deeinnoqstuu
unquestioned
deeinoopssss
possessioned
deeinopprrtu
unpropertied
deeinorssssu
desirousness
deeinosttuu
testudineous
deeinprssuuv
unsupervised
deekmnooprwy
powder-monkey
deeknnrrtuuy
under-turnkey
deeknoorrrww
wonder-worker

deellmopruwy
yellow-rumped
deellnopsstu
pollutedness
deelmnorstuy
tremendously
deelnoossssw
woodlessness
deelnossssuu
sedulousness
deelpprsssuy
suppressedly
deemnnorstuu
untremendous
deemooorsstu
osteodermous
deennnosstuw
unwontedness
deenooprrstw
snowdrop-tree
deenooprssst
dessertspoon
deenorssstux
dextrousness
deenpprsssuu
unsuppressed
deffginooorw
wood-offering
deffinoorrsu
frondiferous
defflnoorssu
fourfoldness
defggnooortt
god-forgotten
defghhiiilty
high-fidelity
defghiilnntu
hunting-field
defghillltuy
delightfully
defghillntuu
undelightful
defghinrrsuy
rushy-fringed
defgiiimnnny
indemnifying
defgiiinrsvy
diversifying
defginnoptuy
type-founding
defhiinnprsu
unfriendship
defhimnoorst
hindforemost
defiilnoorsx
dorsiflexion
defiilnosssu
unfossilised
defiiloprsuy
perfidiously
defilooorrsu
doloriferous
defiloorstuy
do-it-yourself

defilrsssttu
self-distrust
defioorrssuu
sudoriferous
defnnooprssu
profoundness
degghillorrs
shrill-gorged
degghilnnotu
hunting-lodge
degghilnoosu
lodging-house
degghloooryy
hydrogeology
degginnoopru
ground-pigeon
degginnorssw
dressing-gown
deghhhilorsu
shoulder-high
deghhiiiprst
high-spirited
deghhiinopst
diphthongise
deghhiorsstt
short-sighted
deghhloottuw
low-thoughted
deghiiilnrss
disrelishing
deghiknoorrs
drongo-shrike
deghilnnrtuy
thunderingly
deghinorsstu
droughtiness
deghnnoostuu
hound's-tongue
deghnorrtuuw
underwrought
degiiiklnnnx
index-linking
degiiinnstuy
disingenuity
degiiklmoprr
milk-porridge
degiiillnnuyy
unyieldingly
degiiillnoprr
rope-drilling
degiiilloostt
deltiologist
degiiilnnnosu
sounding-line
degiiilnnosuy
indigenously
degiiilnnssty
dissentingly
degiiilnoprsu
ligniperdous
degiinnnnpru
underpinning
degiinnossuu
disingenuous

degiinnrrtuw
underwriting
degiinopprss
predisposing
degiklmnoorw
working-model
degillnopprw
dropping-well
degilmnooost
demonologist
degilmopprru
plum-porridge
degilnnorsuy
resoundingly
degilnooostt
deontologist
degiloprstt
proglottides
degimnnooruv
mourning-dove
degimnnorrss
morning-dress
degimnoorrss
dressing-room
deginnnnrruu
underrunning
deginnorrtuw
winter-ground
degllnorssuy
groundlessly
degmnoorrruy
merry-go-round
dehhiiiprstt
diphtheritis
dehhiiloprty
hydrophilite
dehhilmnottw
withholdment
dehhilnnotuw
unwithholden
dehiiimmnnst
diminishment
dehiiinnorss
disinherison
dehiikllnoou
unlikelihood
dehiiloprsvw
devil-worship
dehiimoorstu
idiothermous
dehiioprrssy
hyperidrosis
dehiklnrstuw
whistle-drunk
dehillnoprsw
spindle-whorl
dehilloprssu
shoulder-slip
dehilooprrsv
overlordship
dehinnooqruy
hydroquinone
dehinooprrty
pyritohedron

dehinooprsst
spinsterhood
dehinopprsuw
unworshipped
dehiooprrtt
orthopteroid
dehklnoorstu
shoulder-knot
dehllnoopsuy
endophyllous
dehlloorrtwy
otherworldly
dehlmnooopsu
monodelphous
dehlmnpprtuu
thunder-plump
dehlnoorrsuy
horrendously
dehlnorstuuy
thunderously
dehmnorrsttu
thunder-storm
dehnooorstuw
southernwood
deiiiiqsstuv
disquisitive
deiiillnoprr
pillion-rider
deiiilmntuvy
diminutively
deiiimnprstt
dispiritment
deiiinorsstv
diversionist
deiiklnnnssu
unkindliness
deiilopsstuy
dispiteously
deiilprstuvy
disruptively
deiimnnnotuu
unmunitioned
deiimnnoprsu
unimprisoned
deiinooprstt
periodontist
deiiopprrst
poor-spirited
deijnprrstuu
jurisprudent
deilnooruvww
louver-window
louvre-window
deiloprrrsu
lord-superior
deilrsssttu
distrustless
deimnnoprtuu
unimportuned
deimnopstuyy
pseudonymity
deinoooprrt
proportioned

deinosssstuu
studiousness
deiooprsssss
dispossessor
deioprsttuvy
topside-turvy
deklnoopruvy
unprovokedly
delnnoopstyy
polysyndeton
delnooorsssu
dolorousness
delnopsstuuy
stupendously
demnoopssuuy
pseudonymous
dennoorsssuw
wondrousness
dffgiinnppsu
snuff-dipping
dffiiimnossu
diffusionism
dffiiinosstu
diffusionist
dfgiikklnouy
kilfud-yoking
dfgillsstuuy
disgustfully
dfhilnooopsu
pound-foolish
dgggilnnruuy
ungrudgingly
dgghhiinnosu
high-sounding
dgghiilnnort
lightning-rod
dggiilnsstuy
disgustingly
dggiinnopprr
ring-dropping
dghiiknnnorr
drinking-horn
dghiimnnoost
do-nothingism
dghinnorstuw
hunting-sword
dghllnoooruw
hollow-ground
dgiiillnqruv
quill-driving
dgiiilnnoosv
long-division
dgiiiooprsty
prodigiosity
dgiilnnossuv
undissolving
dgiilooprsuy
prodigiously
dgiimmnnopsw
swimming-pond
dgilmoorstty
troglodytism
dgilnoooostt
odontologist

dhhilooprsuy
hydrophilous
dhhooprstuyy
hydrophytous
dhimoooopsst
opisthodomos
dhimooprrsty
hydrotropism
dhinooorsttt
orthodontist
dhlnooopptyy
polyphyodont
dhmmpptuuyy
Humpty-dumpty
dhmnnoooopty
monophyodont
diiiinoqsstu
disquisition
diiioqrsstuy
disquisitory
diilnoosstuu
solitudinous
diioooprrstu
proditorious
dinooorrttuy
ororotundity
eeeeekprrstt
street-keeper
eeeefghilnrw
free-wheeling
eeeeghhilnot
eighteen-hole
eeeegiilnpss
spiegeleisen
eeeehinprrsv
reprehensive
eeeehlmnoprt
nephelometer
eeeehlnrrstw
stern-wheeler
eeeehlnrsstv
nevertheless
eeeehlopsstu
steeple-house
eeeehmnorrtv
neverthemore
eeeeilpprsst
spire-steeple
eeeeimnprrtx
experimenter
eeeeimnrrttv
retrievement
eeeeimnrsttx
extensimeter
eeeeinnqrstu
equestrienne
eeeelmnrsttt
resettlement
eeeelnprssss
peerlessness
eeeemnorsttx
extensometer
eeeennprrrtu
entrepreneur

eeeenprrsssv
perverseness
eeeeorrttttt
teeter-totter
eeeffimorstu
effusiometer
eeeffinsssuv
effusiveness
eeefflnnorw
fennel-flower
eeefgiinnrtt
engine-fitter
eeefgilnorsy
foreseeingly
eeefginnorsu
unforeseeing
eeefgllnruvy
revengefully
eeefglnnruuv
unrevengeful
eeefglnnssuv
vengefulness
eeefgnnoorss
foregoneness
eeefhinrsssv
feverishness
eeefiilnrrtt
interfertile
eeefiilnrstt
life-interest
eeefiimnnnss
feminineness
eeefillnssss
lifelessness
eeefilnorstx
self-exertion
eeefilnrsstt
self-interest
eeefilnssttx
self-existent
eeefinnorssv
overfineness
eeefllnsssss
selflessness
eeefllorrsst
forset-seller
eeefllorssst
fosset-seller
eeefnnqrsstu
frequentness
eeegggillnpv
level-pegging
eeeghhilntty
eighteenthly
eeeghiknopsu
housekeeping
eeeghilrtttw
letter-weight
eeeghilrttww
welter-weight
eeeghimnostu
meeting-house
eeeghinnrsss
greenishness

eeeghinsttvy
seventy-eight
eeeghnnrrstt
strengthener
eeeghnorsstt
togetherness
eeeghoorttyz
heterozygote
eeegiiknnpsw
swine-keeping
eeegiilmnntv
inveiglement
eeegiinnorrt
orienteering
eeegikmnnnoy
monkey-engine
eeegiknpprrs
spring-keeper
eeegiloqrrsu
Grolieresque
eeegilrrssvy
regressively
eeegimnrsssu
messeigneurs
eeeginnnorst
sonneteering
eeeginnpsssw
sweepingness
eeeginoossst
osteogenesis
eeeginoprsst
petrogenesis
eeegioqrrstu
grotesquerie
eeeglnnnsstu
ungentleness
eeegmnorsssu
gruesomeness
eeegnnorsssu
generousness
eeegnooprrst
progesterone
eeehhhimmprt
hephthemimer
eeehhinpssss
sheepishness
eeehhirrtvwy
everywhither
eeehhlnortuv
eleventh-hour
eeehhmoprrst
thermosphere
eeehhnrrstuy
heresy-hunter
eeehillmnnos
Neohellenism
eeehilmnrtty
trimethylene
eeehilnnntty
nineteenthly
eeehimnoostt
etheostomine
eeehimnrsttu
hermeneutist

eeehinnoprrs
reprehension
eeehinprstvy
hypertensive
eeehinsssstw
sweetishness
eeehlllortwy
trolley-wheel
eeehllnoptyy
polyethylene
eeehllnpssss
helplessness
eeehlmnoprty
nephelometry
eeehlmnossss
homelessness
eeehlnopssss
hopelessness
eeehmnnnortt
enthronement
eeehmoorrstu
heteromerous
eeeiilprttvy
repetitively
eeeiimnpsttv
intempestive
eeeiimoprrst
isoperimeter
eeeiinnnrttv
intervenient
eeeiinnprsst
serpentinise
eeeiinprrttv
interpretive
eeeiinprssvx
inexpressive
eeeiipqrrstu
prerequisite
eeeijlnnssuv
juvenileness
eeeilmnnprty
pre-eminently
eeeilmnnrstt
re-enlistment
eeeilmnnsssu
unseemliness
eeeilmnsssst
timelessness
eeeilnnprsty
serpentinely
eeeilnprtvvy
preventively
eeeilnrrrtvy
irreverently
eeeilnrsssst
tirelessness
eeeilprrssvy
repressively
eeeilprssvxy
expressively
eeeilrrrtttw
letter-writer
eeeimnnprstt
presentiment

eeeimnnprstu
supereminent
eeeimnnrsttv
reinvestment
eeeimnorsssst
tiresomeness
eeeimnorsstt
sensitometer
eeeimnprrsst
misrepresent
eeeimoorrsst
stereoisomer
eeeimoprstux
time-exposure
eeeinnprsstx
inexpertness
eeeinnprstuv
supervenient
eeeinoorrtvx
overexertion
eeeinoprrssv
overripeness
eeeinprrsstt
interpretess
eeeinprsstuv
eruptiveness
eeeinprssuvx
unexpressive
eeeinrrtttux
intertexture
eeellnrssty
relentlessly
eeellmorrttu
tellurometer
eeelmnnoosss
lonesomeness
eeelmnnstttu
unsettlement
eeelmnossssv
movelessness
eeelmnpprstu
supplementer
eeelmopprrtt
teleprompter
eeelnnosssst
tonelessness
eeelnoprssss
responseless
eeelnorssstu
resoluteness
eeelnrsssst
restlessness
eeelooprsttu
teleutospore
eeennopprsss
propenseness
eeennoprsstt
serpent-stone
eeennoprsttu
enteropneust
eeenoorssttt
testosterone
eeeooprrsuvx
overexposure

eeeoprrrssuv
overpressure
eeffhllrrsuy
refreshfully
eefggiilnrsu
single-figure
eefgginnoprs
sponge-finger
eefggioprtty
pettifoggery
eefghiiinnss
seine-fishing
eefghiiknnrt
free-thinking
eefghiilnrrt
freight-liner
eefghiilrttw
weight-lifter
eefghiiprrtz
prize-fighter
eefghilnrrsy
refreshingly
eefghimorrtu
mother-figure
eefghinnrrsu
unrefreshing
eefghinoprss
sponge-fisher
eefgiilmnpxy
exemplifying
eefgiimmnrsw
free-swimming
eefgiimnnnrt
infringement
eefgiinoprrt
profiteering
eefgiinsstuv
fugitiveness
eefgiknnoort
foretokening
eefgillnssuu
guilefulness
eefginorrsuu
ferrugineous
eefhlnorttuy
fourteenthly
eefhloprstty
flesh-pottery
eefhmoorrstt
foster-mother
eefiiinnnsst
infiniteness
eefiimnorssu
seminiferous
eefiimoqrstu
equisetiform
eefiinorrssu
resiniferous
eefillorsstu
stelliferous
eefilmorsttu
flitter-mouse
eefilnnqrtuy
infrequently

eefilnoorrtx
retroflexion
eefilnpssstu
spitefulness
eefimnoprrst
serpentiform
eefiorrssstt
foster-sister
eefklmnoorwy
monkey-flower
eefllmorrsuy
remorsefully
eefllnntuuvy
uneventfully
eefllnorssuv
overfullness
eeflmnorrsuu
unremorseful
eeflmnorssss
formlessness
eeflnnqrtuuy
unfrequently
eeflnnsssuuu
unusefulness
eeflnoprssuw
powerfulness
eefooprrssss
professoress
eeggghmrruu
hugger-mugger
eeggilsstuvy
suggestively
eegginnprttu
putting-green
eeggnoorsssu
gorgeousness
eeghhhorrttu
therethrough
eeghhhorrtuw
wherethrough
eeghhiilllns
sheeling-hill
eeghhiinrrtw
white-herring
eeghhinoorss
horseshoeing
eeghhiprrssu
high-pressure
eeghiinossst
histogenesis
eeghiinrstux
extinguisher
eeghiinrttww
winter-weight
eeghiknnorst
north-seeking
eeghiknosstu
south-seeking
eeghiknrrstu
hunger-strike
eeghilmnorvw
overwhelming
eeghilnooprs
phrenologise

eeghilnooprt
gerontophile
eeghilnopssy
phylogenesis
eeghimmrstuw
summer-weight
eeghimnossty
mythogenesis
eeghinnopssy
hypnogenesis
eeghinoorsst
orthogenesis
eeghinopssty
phytogenesis
eeghlnrssstt
strengthless
eeghlooorstu
heterologous
eeghmmoprsty
sphygmometer
eeghmnoorttu
mother-tongue
eeghnooorstu
heterogonous
eeghnoorssuu
house-surgeon
eeghoorstuyz
heterozygous
eegiilllnpps
sleeping-pill
eegiillnorss
religionless
eegiillnprst
still-peering
eegiinnnprst
serpentining
eegiinnprrst
enterprising
eegiinnrrsst
retiringness
eegiinnrrtty
eternity-ring
eegiirrsstvy
regressivity
eegijmnpquuu
queue-jumping
eegillnnpsux
sun-expelling
eegillnoosst
selenologist
eegillnpprxy
perplexingly
eegilmnooost
entomologise
eegilmooppss
goose-pimples
eegilmoopsty
epistemology
eegilorrstuy
elytrigerous
eegimnnorrtt
retromingent
eegimnnpsstt
temptingness

eegimnoorrtt
trigonometer
eeginnnrrssu
unerringness
eeginnosssuy
syngenesious
eeginooprrvw
overpowering
eeginooprsss
sporogenesis
eeginoprrsst
progenitress
resting-spore
eeginoprstty
stereotyping
eeginorsssuv
greviousness
eeginosssuux
exiguousness
eeginrrsttty
trysting-tree
eeglmnnooopr
prolegomenon
eeglnnorsuuy
ungenerously
eegmmnorssty
system-monger
eegnnoorrsuu
neurosurgeon
eegnorrrsuuy
neurosurgery
eehhiimmoprt
hemimorphite
eehhiinssstv
thievishness
eehhillnopty
theophylline
eehhilnrttty
thirteenthly
eehhinrssssw
shrewishness
eehhlloprtyy
heterophylly
eehhlmnortty
three-monthly
eehhmmorrtty
rhythmometer
eehhmooprrty
heteromorphy
eehhooosstuu
house-to-house
eehhooprrtty
heterotrophy
eehhoossuuyy
housey-housey
eehiilnprsty
prehensility
eehiimnpprru
perinephrium
eehillmnnssu
sneeshin-mull
eehilmnorsst
motherliness

eehilnnpstwy
penny-whistle
eehilnoopsst
siphonostele
eehilopprttt
throttle-pipe
eehilopssttu
spittle-house
eehimnorssst
smotheriness
eehinnoprsty
hypertension
eehinoossssu
session-house
eehllmprsttu
trumpet-shell
eehlmoprstty
stepmotherly
eehlnrsssstu
hurtlessness
ruthlessness
eehmmoooorsu
homoeomerous
eehmnooorstu
heteronomous
eehmnrrrsuyy
nursery-rhyme
eehmoprrsstu
sumpter-horse
eehmorrstuuy
eurythermous
eehnnooprstt
stentorphone
eehnnorrsttw
north-western
eehnorssttuw
south-western
eeiiiillrrtw
tirlie-wirlie
eeiiiklnnnpw
pinniewinkle
eeiiimnrsstv
intermissive
eeiiinprrstu
perineuritis
eeiiinrssstw
sinisterwise
eeiikllmnrrv
vermin-killer
eeiikllnnssu
unlikeliness
eeiillmpqtuu
equimultiple
eeiillnnssuv
unliveliness
eeiillnsssuv
illusiveness
eeiilmnnptty
impenitently
eeiilmnnsstu
untimeliness
eeiilmnopsst
impoliteness

eeiilmoorvzz
mezzo-rilievo
eeiilmprssvy
impressively
permissively
eeiilnpprsss
slipperiness
eeiilnprssst
priestliness
eeiilnpsssst
pitilessness
eeiilnrsssst
sisterliness
eeiimnnotttu
munitionette
eeiimnnrtttt
intermittent
eeiimnprrstt
misinterpret
eeiimnprsstt
impersistent
eeiimnprssuv
unimpressive
eeiimnprstty
sempiternity
eeiimnrrttux
intermixture
eeiimoprrsty
isoperimetry
eeiinnnorttv
intervention
eeiinnorsstt
retensionist
eeiinnossttx
extensionist
eeiinnppssst
snippetiness
eeiinoprrssv
irresponsive
eeiinopssstv
positiveness
eeiinorrstvv
introversive
eeiinorrttvv
introvertive
eeiinprrttuv
interruptive
eeiiprsstvxy
expressivity
eeijnnnnprsy
Jenny-spinner
eeillnnosssv
slovenliness
eeillnnossuv
unloveliness
eeillnssssst
listlessness
eeillorrstuy
irresolutely
eeillrssssty
resistlessly
eeilmnoossst
toilsomeness
eeilmnprsttu
multipresent
eeilmooprsst
metropolises
eeilmopprrty
peremptorily
eeilmorssstu
moistureless
eeilmprstuvy
resumptively
eeilmrssssst
mistressless
eeilnnoorttu
nitrotoluene
eeilnnopsstu
unpoliteness
eeilnoopprsy
polyisoprene
eeilnoorrstu
resolutioner
eeilnoorrtuv
revolutioner
eeilnoprsssu
perilousness
eeilnoprssvy
responsively
eeilnoqssstu
questionless
eeilnortuuvv
vulvo-uterine
eeilnprsstty
persistently
eeilnpsssuvy
suspensively
eeiloprssvy
oppressively
eeiloprrssty
proselytiser
eeiloprrstuv
retropulsive
eeilopsssvy
possessively
eeimmnnoopst
empoisonment
eeimnnnoprsy
money-spinner
eeimnnoopprs
perispomenon
eeinnooprstu
out-pensioner
eeinnoprsstu
serpentinous
eeinnoprssuv
unresponsive
eeinnoprstuv
supervention
eeinnoprtttv
ventripotent
eeinnprssttu
unprettiness
eeinooppssst
oppositeness
eeinooprssss
repossession
eeinooprsstt
enteroptosis
eeinoorrstvx
extroversion
eeinoorssstu
interosseous
eeinopprssuv
unoppressive
eeinoprrsttu
neuropterist
eeinoprssssu
supersession
eeinoprssstv
sportiveness
eeinoprsssuv
perviousness
previousness
eeinorssstuv
vitreousness
eeiopprrrsst
proprietress
eeiprrssstuu
pressure-suit
eeklmnopuyzz
monkey-puzzle
puzzle-monkey
eeklnoorttuv
true-love-knot
eeknoopprsss
spokesperson
eeknopprstty
pretty-spoken
eellloowwyyy
yellow-yowley
eellnnoorssv
lovelornness
eellnosssssu
soullessness
eelmmnnoptuy
unemployment
eelmooossttu
teleostomous
eelmoprrstty
stormy-petrel
eelnopssssst
spotlessness
eemnnooppstt
postponement
eemnnoorsssu
enormousness
eemnnoosssuv
venomousness
eemnnorsssuu
numerousness
eennooprstty
none-so-pretty
eennosssssuu
sensuousness
eennttttwwyy
twenty-twenty
eenooprrstuu
neuropterous
eenoprrsssuy
supersensory
eeoopprrsstu
preposterous
eeooprrrsstu
root-pressure
eepprrttttyy
pretty-pretty
effgghiiinrt
fire-fighting
effggiilnnsu
glue-sniffing
effghilorstu
foresightful
effgiinooprr
fireproofing
effhioprssst
sheriff's-post
effhnooorstu
front-of-house
effilnrsstuu
fruitfulness
efgggiinoptt
pettifogging
efgghiillnst
self-lighting
efggiilnnopy
pigeon-flying
efggilnortty
forgettingly
efghhiinrsty
night-fishery
efghhilntttw
twelfth-night
efghiiklnnst
self-thinking
efghiiknnntu
hunting-knife
efghiinrrstt
first-nighter
efghilnrsstu
rightfulness
efgiiinnnsty
intensifying
efgiiknnnpru
pruning-knife
efgiilnnrsst
triflingness
efgiilnorsuv
griseofulvin
efgiimorrsst
Strigiformes
efgiinnoprsy
personifying
efgiinnrrtuy
unterrifying
efgiinorrttt
retrofitting
efgilloorssu
self-glorious
efgimnnopru
unperforming
efglnnorssuw
wrongfulness
efhillmnortu
run-of-the-mill

efhillrsstty
thriftlessly
efhilmnrsstu
mirthfulness
efhilnopsssy
self-hypnosis
efhiloorrsuv
overflourish
efhinnoorssu
sunshine-roof
efhllnossstu
slothfulness
efhlnosstuuy
youthfulness
efhlnrssttuu
truthfulness
efiiiilnntvy
infinitively
efiilmnorsuu
luminiferous
efiilmoprsvy
oversimplify
efiioprrstuy
pyritiferous
efillmnossuu
self-luminous
efilloprssty
profitlessly
efilnoopsstt
toploftiness
efioooprrssu
soporiferous
eflloprsuuy
purposefully
eflmnnorssuu
mournfulness
eflmnorssstu
stormfulness
eflnoprssstu
sportfulness
eflnrsssttuu
trustfulness
efmnoorttuwy
twenty-four-mo
efnnoorrsssw
forswornness
eggghjloopru
plough-jogger
egggiilnnrsy
sniggeringly
egggilnnoost
logging-stone
egghhiinppst
high-stepping
egghhiinsssw
Whiggishness
egghiilnostu
soughing-tile
egghiinprsss
priggishness
egghilnssssu
sluggishness
egghlooopty
photogeology
eggiillmmnry
glimmeringly
eggiillnrtty
glitteringly
eggiloopstty
Egyptologist
eggimnooprss
gossip-monger
egglnnooorty
röntgenology
eghhhoorrttu
through-other
eghhiiillns
shieling-hill
eghhiilprsty
high-priestly
eghhiimnosst
shoeing-smith
eghhilnosssu
ghoulishness
eghhmnooppsy
sphygmophone
eghhmorrttuy
merry-thought
eghhnoorsstu
thoroughness
eghhnoorsttu
through-stone
eghiiimnrstv
shriving-time
eghiiinoprss
seigniorship
eghiiklnnsst
knightliness
eghiilllnsss
shillingless
eghiilmnoprs
negrophilism
eghiilmnprwy
whimperingly
eghiilnoprst
negrophilist
eghiilnprswy
whisperingly
eghiilopsstt
stegophilist
eghiinnosstw
wishing-stone
eghiinnrsstv
thrivingness
eghiknoorsuw
working-house
eghillnrtttu
truth-telling
eghilmnorsty
smotheringly
eghilmoorsty
mythologiser
eghilnooprst
nephrologist
phrenologist
eghilooppsst
psephologist
eghimnooorsu
rooming-house
eghinnortttu
otter-hunting
eghinooprrsv
governorship
eghinoopsttt
photosetting
eghinorrrstt
night-terrors
eghinorrttuw
interwrought
egiiiilllnnps
spilling-line
egiiilnosttu
gentilitious
egiiimnopstu
impetiginous
egiiinnnrttw
intertwining
egiiinnnsstv
invitingness
egiijlnnortu
jointing-rule
egiikllnnorr
inking-roller
egiiklnpprrs
klipspringer
egiiknnrssst
strikingness
egiiknopppprs
skipping-rope
egiilmnnoptt
melting-point
egiilmoossst
seismologist
egiilnnnpruy
unrepiningly
egiilnprssty
persistingly
egiilnrtttwy
twitteringly
egiimmnnsssw
swimmingness
egiimnnopsss
imposingness
egiimnooprrt
primogenitor
egiimnoorrst
risorgimento
egiimrsssttu
Trismegistus
egiinnnorsst
non-resisting
egiinpssttuy
tissue-typing
egiioprrsstw
gossip-writer
egijmmnopsuu
jumping-mouse
egikknnoprty
pony-trekking
egikllmnoory
Kremlinology
egillnorstty
story-telling
egilloorsuww
willow-grouse
egilmnnortty
tormentingly
egilmnooostt
entomologist
egilmnoostyz
enzymologist
egilnnnossuv
unlovingness
egilnnrsuvwy
unswervingly
egilnooprsuy
pyroligneous
egilnoorsssu
gloriousness
egilnoprstty
protestingly
egilnprsttuy
sputteringly
egilnrstttuy
stutteringly
egimmnooprsu
spermogonium
egimnoorrtty
trigonometry
eginnoprsttu
unprotesting
eginnopssssu
unpossessing
eginnopstttu
putting-stone
eginooprrtuv
route-proving
eginoorrsssu
rigorousness
eginoorsssuv
vigorousness
eginprrssstu
purse-strings
eglnnoopruyy
neurypnology
ehhiilloopsu
heliophilous
ehhiilooppss
philosophise
ehhiimmmoprs
hemimorphism
ehhilmrssstu
missel-thrush
ehhilooppsss
philosophess
ehhiloppstuy
hyposulphite
ehhimmooprst
theomorphism
ehhimnpssssu
sumphishness
ehhinoooppprs
siphonophore
ehhmmoooopry
homoeomorphy

ehhmmooorstu
homothermous
ehiiiilnpsst
Philistinise
ehiiilorsttt
lithotritise
ehiiknoopsst
photokinesis
ehiiknsssstt
skittishness
ehiillmnpstu
phillumenist
ehiillopstww
will-o'-the-wisp
ehiilmooprst
heliotropism
ehiimnprstux
xiphisternum
ehiimprsssst
mistress-ship
ehiinoooprss
ionophoresis
ehiinpprssst
spinstership
ehiiopprrssu
superiorship
ehiioprrsstv
servitorship
ehillopprtyy
pyrophyllite
ehilmmooppprs
pleomorphism
ehilmmoprstu
Lithospermum
ehilmooqrrtu
mother-liquor
ehilnoopsuuy
euphoniously
ehilnssssttu
sluttishness
ehiloprssuwy
whisperously
ehimmooooorsu
homoiomerous
ehimoopprrsu
perimorphous
ehimoopprrty
pyromorphite
ehinnorsstuw
unworthiness
ehinooorsstt
orthotonesis
ehinoopprsst
nephroptosis
ehinoprrstty
phrontistery
ehiooprrsttt
orthopterist
ehioprrssuvy
surveyorship
ehkmnooopsst
smooth-spoken
ehlmoooopprsu
pleomorphous
ehmmoooprssu
mesomorphous
ehmnnoorrstt
northernmost
ehmnoorsssuu
humorousness
ehmnoorssttu
southernmost
ehmoooprrsux
xeromorphous
ehmorrssttu
storm-shutter
ehnnoorrtuvw
unoverthrown
ehoooprrsttu
orthopterous
eiiiilmrstvy
verisimility
eiiillmnopst
pointillisme
eiiillnopstt
pointilliste
eiiilmorssuv
verisimilous
eiiimmmnorss
immersionism
eiiimmnorsst
immersionist
eiiimnnorsst
intermission
eiiimnooprst
reimposition
eiiimnorsstv
intromissive
eiiimprtttvy
permittivity
eiiinopqrstu
perquisition
eiiinqrssstu
inquisitress
eiillmnottuv
multivoltine
eiillnoosstv
volitionless
eiillprsssty
spiritlessly
eiilmnooqssu
somniloquise
eiilmnoostuv
evolutionism
eiilmoopprst
pleiotropism
eiilmoprsuvy
imperviously
eiilmrsttuvy
multiversity
eiilnoorrstu
irresolution
eiilnoosttuv
evolutionist
eiilnoprstuy
polyneuritis
eiimmnnoprst
imprisonment
eiimnnnqquuu
quinquennium
eiimnnortttt
intromittent
eiimnooprssx
expromission
eiimnooqrsuu
querimonious
eiimorrrrtw
mirror-writer
eiinnoorrstv
introversion
eiinnoprrttu
interruption
eiinnoprsstu
interspinous
eiinoorstttx
extortionist
eiinoprssttu
superstition
eiiooppssttv
postpositive
eiiooprrstty
posteriority
eikmorrssstw
workmistress
eillmnoqttuu
multiloquent
eillmoprtuvy
overmultiply
eilmnnooptty
omnipotently
eilmnnosssuu
luminousness
eilmopprstuu
multipurpose
eilmorsstuyy
mysteriously
eilmrssssttu
mistrustless
eilnooprrstu
retropulsion
eilooprrstuy
pleurisy-root
eiloprrstuvy
protrusively
eimmnnorssuw
snow-in-summer
eimnnnosssuu
numinousness
eimnnossstuu
mutinousness
eimnooossstu
isostemonous
eimnoorssstu
timorousness
eimnoprsssuu
suspensorium
eimnorsstuuv
misventurous
eimoprsssstt
postmistress
einnrssttuu
untrustiness
einoorsssuux
uxoriousness
einoprssssuu
spuriousness
einorssssuuu
usuriousness
einorssstuuv
virtuousness
eiooooprssst
osteoporosis
ellnoorstuuy
ultroneously
elnooppsssuu
populousness
elnooprsttuy
portentously
eloopprrssuy
prosperously
eloorrssttuy
stertorously
emoooppprrty
property-room
emoooprrrstt
storm-trooper
emopprsstuuu
presumptuous
ennooorssssu
sonorousness
enoopprrssuu
unprosperous
enoorssstuu
tortuousness
ffillnrtuuuy
unfruitfully
fflloossttyy
softly-softly
fgggilnooost
footslogging
fghhilorrtty
forthrightly
fghhllottuuy
thoughtfully
fghhlnottuuu
unthoughtful
fghiiknorstw
shift-working
fghiillmnotu
mouth-filling
fghiilnorryy
horrifyingly
fghillnrtuuy
unrightfully
fghillprstuy
sprightfully
fghinoprtttu
forth-putting
fgiiilnostuy
fuliginosity
fgiillnosuuy
fuliginously
fgiloorsttuu
futurologist
fhiikkrsswyy
whisky-frisky

fhiiloosttwy
foolish-witty
fhiinooopsst
photo-fission
fhilloprsuwy
worshipfully
fhilnoprsuuw
unworshipful
fhllnrttuuuy
untruthfully
fiilllmopruv
pulvilliform
fiilmmorttuy
multiformity
fillmoorstuu
multiflorous
filoorsttuuy
fortuitously
ggghhinoortu
through-going
ggghiiinnsst
sight-singing
gggillnrstuy
strugglingly
gghhhiitttyy
highty-tighty
gghhilnrstuy
highly-strung
gghhiloprtuw
ploughwright
gghhoorrtuuw
rough-wrought
gghiiinnnnsy
singing-hinny
gghiilmnnoot
moonlighting
gghiinnoostw
wing-shooting
ggiiilnnrtuy
intriguingly
ggiilloortuy
liturgiology
ggiimnnnorru
mourning-ring
ggiinnooprtw
growing-point
ggiinnopsstw
swinging-post
ggillooossst
glossologist
ggilmnnoorry
morning-glory
ggilnooopsst
spongologist
ghhilooprsuy
hygrophilous
ghiiklnnntuy
unthinkingly
ghiillnnsttu
still-hunting
ghiilooorsty
historiology
ghiiloopssty
physiologist

ghiinnnorsuu
unnourishing
ghiinnooorst
shooting-iron
ghiinopppstw
whipping-post
ghilmoooprst
morphologist
ghilmooopssu
Ophioglossum
ghilnoopprry
lorry-hopping
ghimmooprsyz
zygomorphism
ghimnoopssty
gymnosophist
ghlmoooppsuy
pompholygous
ghloooptyyz
zoophytology
ghmoooprsuyz
zygomorphous
giiillmnnnps
spinning-mill
giiilnnorstv
violin-string
giiimnnorttt
intromitting
giikllmnoost
milking-stool
giillnoorsuy
ingloriously
giilmmnoopsw
swimming-pool
giilmmnoostu
immunologist
giilmnnoostu
monolinguist
giilnorrsstu
soul-stirring
giilnprrssuy
surprisingly
giilooorsstt
storiologist
giinnoprttu
turning-point
gillmooprssy
prosyllogism
gilnoorsssty
strongylosis
gilooooprstty
protistology
gimnoooprsst
moss-trooping
ginoooprrstu
nitroso-group
gllnoosttuuy
gluttonously
gllooopsttuy
polyglottous
glooooprtyz
protozoology
hhiiiilooppst
ophiophilist

hhiilloopstu
lithophilous
hhiilmooppss
philosophism
hhiilnooprty
ornithophily
hhiilooppsst
philosophist
hhiilooprsuz
rhizophilous
hhiiooprsstu
Histiophorus
hhilloppsuxy
xiphophyllus
hhilmmooprsy
hylomorphism
hhilooopppstu
photophilous
hhimmmoooprs
homomorphism
hhimnoooprrt
ornithomorph
hhinooprrtty
thyrotrophin
hhioottttuuww
tu-whit-tu-whoo
hhmmoooprsu
homomorphous
hhmmoootttuu
mouth-to-mouth
hhmnoooprty
pythonomorph
hiiiilmnpsst
philistinism
hiiilorstttt
lithotritist
hiillmnoopsu
limnophilous
hiilloopprww
whip-poor-will
hiilmoprsssu
Russophilism
hiilooprrttt
lithotriptor
hiiloprsssttu
Russophilist
hiiooprsstuv
virtuosoship
hiioprrssuvv
survivorship
hilmmoopprsy
polymorphism
hilooopprstu
tropophilous
himoooppprstt
phototropism
himoooprrstt
orthotropism
hinooopssttt
opisthotonos
hioooprrstty
proto-history
hlllooppsuyy
polyphyllous

hlmmnooosuyy
homonymously
hlmoooprrsuy
polymorphous
hlmoopsstuuy
posthumously
hmmnoooprsu
monomorphous
hooooprrssu
sporophorous
hooooprrsttu
orthotropous
iiiimmnnnpyy
niminy-piminy
iiimnnosttu
intuitionism
iiinnosttu
intuitionist
iiilnoqstuuy
iniquitously
iiimnnoorsst
intromission
iiimnoorttuv
vomiturition
iiinnorssttu
intrusionist
iiinnorstttu
nutritionist
iiinnorsttuu
innutritious
iiioprssttuy
spirituosity
iilmmnooqssu
somniloquism
iilmnoopsstu
postliminous
iilmnooqsstu
somniloquist
iilmnoostuvy
voluminosity
iilmooprrssy
promissorily
iilnorssstuy
sinistrously
iilnorsttuuy
nutritiously
iiloopprstuy
propitiously
iinnnnoorstu
non-intrusion
iinnoooppttt
point-to-point
iinooppssttt
postposition
iinoopprstuu
unpropitious
iinooprstttu
prostitution
iiooppssstuu
suppositious
illmnooostty
tonsillotomy
illmnoosuuvy
voluminously

12 ILL

illmooqstuuu
multiloquous
ilnorstuuuvy
unvirtuously
iloopsttuuvy
voluptuosity
iloprsttuvyy
topsyturvily
llmosttuuuuy
tumultuously
lloopstuuuvy
voluptuously
lmnnoooostuy
monotonously
lmnnoossuyyy
synonymously
lmnosttuuuuu
untumultuous
ooosssttwyy
tootsy-wootsy

13 AAA

aaaaaccdeeinr
Anacardiaceae
aaaaaceehmnrt
Amaranthaceae
aaaabcceelrtu
baccalaureate
aaaabccilnnot
tobaccanalian
aaaabcdiillty
adiabatically
aaaabceeilmns
Balsaminaceae
aaaabdeeglntv
advantageable
aaaabdilmorss
ambassadorial
aaaabegggilmn
baggage-animal
aaaabehilnprt
alphabetarian
aaaaccceeorry
Caryocaraceae
aaaaccdeeippr
Capparidaceae
aaaaccdiiklls
lackadaisical
aaaacceeinrsu
Casuarinaceae
aaaacceelmnpu
Campanulaceae
aaaacchillnrt
charlatanical
aaaaccilllprt
parallactical
aaaacclmnorst
malacostracan
aaaacdiillnrt
cardinalatial
aaaaceeeilnrv
Valerianaceae
aaaaceefgirsx
Saxifragaceae
aaaaceeginprs
Sparganiaceae
aaaacegilmost
galactosaemia
aaaacehilmntt
anathematical
aaaacemnorstu
amarantaceous
aaaacghilpprr
paragraphical
aaaaciopssstt
apocatastasis
aaaadilmnoptt
maladaptation
aaaaegimmnrst
anagrammatise
aaaaehilnpprr
paraphernalia
aaaaelnnsttvw
savanna-wattle
aaaagimmmnrst
anagrammatism
aaaagimmnrstt
anagrammatist
aaaahilmnnpst
phantasmalian
aaabbbcehhrst
Sabbath-breach
aaabbcciillst
cabbalistical
aaabbcilmmnpy
namby-pambical
aaabbeiimnrrs
semi-barbarian
aaabbiinorrst
barbarisation
aaabcceehnoor
Orobanchaceae
aaabcdeelnrrs
scandal-bearer
aaabcdehinrtu
Chateaubriand
aaabcdiknortw
backwardation
aaabceeilnrst
ascertainable
aaabceenpprsu
subappearance
aaabcefilnott
labefactation
aaabcegilllry
algebraically
aaabcehinrrtt
Tetrabranchia
aaabceillnory
anaerobically
aaabcilllopry
parabolically
aaabcilnorstt
abstractional
aaabddeginorr
drainage-board
aaabdegiinnrs
drainage-basin
aaabdegmnnnor
rag-and-bone-man
aaabdhhinnssw
washhand-basin
aaabeeekprrtz
zebra-parakeet
aaabeehllrstv
ballast-heaver
aaabeeillnssv
availableness
aaabeellnpsst
palatableness
aaabegiilmnty
manageability
aaabegilnnsuy
ungainsayable
aaabeillmnptu
manipulatable
aaabelnnrrtuw
unwarrantable
aaabhhinooptt
thanatophobia
aaabhiooprrst
astrapophobia
aaabiiilmqrsu
aqua-mirabilis
aaabiiilnttty
attainability
aaabiiklnnost
Balkanisation
aaablnnrrtuwy
unwarrantably
aaaccceehlnty
Cyclanthaceae
aaacccghilopr
cacographical
aaaccdeglortu
card-catalogue
aaaccdehllnps
paschal-candle
aaaccdeiilmms
academicalism
aaaccdeiipstt
discapacitate
aaaccdeillntu
canaliculated
aaaccdhiilnor
archidiaconal
aaacceeeiloru
Eriocaulaceae
aaacceeginnty
nyctaginaceae
aaacceeillnrt
cancellariate
aaacceelnnruu
Ranunculaceae
aaacceeloprtu
Portulacaceae
aaacceghmnost
stagecoachman
aaaccegilrttx
extra-galactic
aaaccgilllmoo
malacological
aaacchilpprsy
parapsychical
aaacchlorssty
thalassocracy
aaacchlorttty
thalattocracy
aaacciillsttt
stalactitical
aaacciilmnott
acclimatation
aaaccilllnotu
calculational
aaaccillltty
catalytically
aaaccillmnory
macaronically
aaaccilloppty
apocalyptical
aaaccillrssty
sarcastically
aaaccilotttuy
autocatalytic
aaacddeghhilt
Gaidhealtachd
aaacddeimmnsu
unmacadamised
aaacdeeinpprs
disappearance
aaacdeglmosuy
amygdalaceous

aaacdeiiilruv
Aviculariidae
aaacdeiiinprt
paediatrician
aaacdeiilmops
Lasiocampidae
aaacdeiilmprt
pre-adamitical
aaacdeilmnnop
pandemoniacal
aaacdeilmnory
aerodynamical
aaacdghiimprt
diaphragmatic
aaacdgilmnoor
macrodiagonal
aaacdgmnorstu
coastguardman
aaacdhiinoprs
anaphrodisiac
aaacdiiillnrt
cardinalitial
aaacdiimmortu
acaridomatium
aaacdilloprxy
paradoxically
aaacdimmoortu
acarodomatium
aaaceeeehlmty
Thymelaeaceae
aaaceeeffilrs
Rafflesiaceae
aaaceeefiknnr
Frankeniaceae
aaaceeehlpsty
Staphyleaceae
aaaceeehnprrt
Pherecrataean
aaaceeelmmost
Melastomaceae
aaaceeelooprt
Tropaeolaceae
aaaceefiiloqu
Aquifoliaceae
aaaceeghiilmp
Malpighiaceae
aaaceeghinort
Archegoniatae
aaaceegimrrst
steam-carriage
aaaceegirrrtw
water-carriage
aaaceegllostu
sale-catalogue
aaaceeiiilnopp
Papilionaceae
aaaceeilmorrt
araeometrical
aaaceeinnpprt
appertainance
aaaceennnoppr
non-appearance
aaaceeopprsuv
papaveraceous

aaaceffilnprs
paraffin-scale
aaaceghiloppr
palaeographic
aaaceghloorrt
galactorrhoea
aaacegilmnnor
Anglo-American
aaacegimnosty
gynaecomastia
aaaceglorsttu
star-catalogue
aaacehiillmnv
Machiavellian
aaacehiimmnns
Manichaeanism
aaacehiimmntt
mathematician
aaacehillmtty
athematically
aaacehillptty
apathetically
aaacehimooppr
pharmacopoeia
aaacehnrrrstw
search-warrant
aaaceiilmnnrt
Latin-American
aaaceijnoprrt
terra-japonica
aaaceiklmnnor
Neo-Lamarckian
aaaceilnnssst
satanicalness
aaaceimopprss
caesaropapism
aaacellmnrsty
sacramentally
aaacelrrstuvw
water-vascular
aaacelrrstuvx
extra-vascular
aaacenrrrsttu
restaurant-car
aaacfiimnnprs
Pan-Africanism
aaacfillnstty
fantastically
aaacgghiimnot
gigantomachia
aaacghiilpprs
pasigraphical
aaacgiillmstt
stalagmitical
aaacgiilmrstt
magistratical
aaacgillmmrty
grammatically
aaacgillmnsty
synallagmatic
aaacgillmprty
pragmatically
aaacgilmmnrtu
ungrammatical

aaacgilnnottu
anticoagulant
aaachiillprsy
pharisaically
aaachillmstty
asthmatically
aaachillnopry
anaphorically
aaachimooprst
achromatopsia
aaaciiklmmnrs
Lamarckianism
aaaciillmnost
anomalistical
aaaciillmotxy
axiomatically
aaaciillprsty
parasitically
aaaciilnosstu
casualisation
aaaciilnosttu
actualisation
aaaciimnrrstt
tractarianism
aaaciiorssttu
Austroasiatic
aaacillmottuy
automatically
aaacillmrttuy
traumatically
aaacilnnorssy
narco-analysis
aaacilnnrsttt
transatlantic
aaacilnprrstu
intracapsular
aaacilossttuy
autocatalysis
aaadddeginstv
disadvantaged
aaaddhhnnsstw
washhand-stand
aaadefinqrrsu
fair-and-square
aaadegilmqrsu
quadragesimal
aaadeginrsttv
avant-gardiste
aaadehhimnnrt
rhadamanthine
aaadehhnprssz
haphazardness
aaadehilmoppr
lampadephoria
aaadeillqrrtu
quadrilateral
aaadeimnnqrsu
squandermania
aaadeinopprtt
preadaptation
aaadelllmnrsy
small-and-early
aaadghilmnrtu
draught-animal

aaadiiilnorst
radialisation
aaadiimnorstt
dramatisation
aaaeeehknprss
Shakespearean
aaaeeghlopprr
palaeographer
aaaeehiknprss
Shakespearian
aaaeeilmnoppr
paraleipomena
aaaeeilnnprtt
plantain-eater
aaaeejlnrsttw
serjeant-at-law
aaaefhillmort
Thalamiflorae
aaaefiilmmrst
materfamilias
aaaefiilmprst
paterfamilias
aaaefnnorsstv
savanna-forest
aaaeggimnoprs
megasporangia
aaaegilmnorsu
megalosaurian
aaaegilnnprtu
Pantagruelian
aaaegimmnnorr
neogrammarian
aaaegimmnprst
paramagnetism
aaaegklnooppr
kangaroo-apple
aaaeglllmoprr
parallelogram
aaaeglnrttvxy
extravagantly
aaaehhilmprtt
amphitheatral
aaaehilnnprst
phalansterian
aaaeiilnprrtt
intraparietal
aaaeiilnrrrtt
intra-arterial
aaaeilllnoppt
appellational
aaaeillrrtxxy
extra-axillary
aaaeilmmnnprt
parliament-man
aaaeilmnprrty
parliamentary
aaaeilnnopttt
tea-plantation
aaaeilnnprttw
water-plantain
aaaeilpppprstt
papaprelatist
aaaeimmmnrrtu
armamentarium

aaaeinorsttvx
extravasation
aaafhilllmort
thalamifloral
aaagggilnrtvy
aggravatingly
aaaggknoorrss
kangaroo-grass
aaaghhnoprtty
thanatography
aaaghiinnnrty
anythingarian
aaagiilnnostv
galvanisation
aaagiilnorttv
gravitational
aaagiilnsstvw
waiting-vassal
aaagiimmnsstt
anastigmatism
aaagilmoopstt
plagiostomata
aaagimmnprstt
pangrammatist
aaagllnopstvy
galvanoplasty
aaahhilmnoppt
panophthalmia
aaahiinorrttu
authoritarian
aaahilmnpstty
phantasmality
aaahilopppr sy
parapophysial
aaahinrrsttuz
Zarathustrian
aaahllllmossw
All-hallowmass
aaahlmortttuy
thaumatolatry
aaaiiilmnnost
animalisation
aaaiiimnnrsst
sanitarianism
aaaiiinnqrttu
antiquitarian
aaaiilmnrsstu
Australianism
aaaiilnnosttt
tantalisation
aaaiimnnprsss
Parnassianism
aaaiinnorsttv
intravasation
aaaiinnosssst
assassination
aaaillnnorstt
translational
aaaillprrsuxy
supra-axillary
aaailnnnorstt
transnational
aaailnnoprstu
supranational

aaalnorssttuu
Atlantosaurus
aaamnorstttuy
traumatonasty
aabbbcdegiorr
cribbage-board
aabbbeginrtty
baby-battering
aabbbiilorsty
absorbability
aabbcdeeeeirr
Berberidaceae
aabbcghinnsty
baby-snatching
aabbciinrrsuu
suburbicarian
aabbcillmosty
bombastically
aabbddeegilor
biodegradable
aabbdeeinrtuv
unabbreviated
aabbdeggiinrt
badger-baiting
aabbdeiiilllrt
billiard-table
aabbdggiinnor
Brobdignagian
aabbdiinorstw
boatswain-bird
aabbeeeklnrss
breakableness
aabbeehilnsst
habitableness
aabbegilnrstt
sabre-battling
aabbehiilnntu
uninhabitable
aabbeiillossu
bouillabaisse
aabbeiimmrrss
semi-barbarism
aabbekkllnnty
blankety-blank
aabbenorrsssu
barbarousness
aabbhimmnpsyy
namby-pambyish
aabbimmmnpsyy
namby-pambyism
aabccceeirtuu
Cucurbitaceae
aabcccehkrrst
backscratcher
aabccdhlrtyyy
brachydactyly
aabcceeeeillr
Illecebraceae
aabcceeeekrru
rebecca-eureka
aabcceeklrrrr
cracker-barrel
aabcceellnnou
unconcealable

aabccegimmrsu
circumambages
aabccehhlpryy
brachycephaly
aabcceiilmprt
impracticable
aabcceiilptty
acceptability
aabcceilmnrsv
canvas-climber
aabcceilnprtu
unpracticable
aabccelnnotuu
unaccountable
aabcciiillnot
actinobacilli
aabcciiilnnst
cannibalistic
aabcciilmprty
impracticably
aabccilllostu
lactobacillus
aabccillrsuuv
subclavicular
aabcclnnotuuy
unaccountably
aabcdeeefnrss
barefacedness
aabcdeefiprrt
prefabricated
aabcdeeiimrsz
semicarbazide
aabcdeelrrstt
battle-scarred
aabcdeennoruv
overabundance
aabcdegikllnp
back-pedalling
aabcdegillnnt
ballet-dancing
aabcdegillrrt
ball-cartridge
aabcdehiklntw
black-and-white
aabcdeiilttuy
educatability
aabcdeinnoort
decarbonation
aabcdelopprrs
clapperboards
aabcdfhioprtu
cupboard-faith
aabcdghimnort
matchboarding
aabcdgiklmrsu
blackguardism
aabcdgilmnssy
scambling-days
aabcdhnnoorrt
root-and-branch
aabcdimnnorst
contrabandism
aabcdinnorstt
contrabandist

aabceeeelnpss
peaceableness
aabceeeghllln
challengeable
aabceeegiinrz
Zingiberaceae
aabceeehiopru
Euphorbiaceae
aabceeehlnsst
teachableness
aabceeeillprr
irreplaceable
aabceeeilrstu
Eubacteriales
aabceeellnpru
unreplaceable
aabceeellnssv
cleavableness
aabceeelnrsst
traceableness
aabceeghioprt
bacteriophage
aabceeginprtt
carpet-beating
aabceeglnoors
barnacle-goose
aabceehilmnpu
unimpeachable
aabceehlmnort
thermobalance
aabceeiillmrr
irreclaimable
aabceeiilnppr
inappreciable
aabceeillmnru
unreclaimable
aabceeillprry
irreplaceably
aabceeilmnrsv
vraisemblance
aabceeirrstuu
bureaucratise
aabceellnostu
sublanceolate
aabceelmmorsu
commeasurable
aabceelnrsstt
tractableness
aabceemmnorsu
membranaceous
aabcefiiinott
beatification
aabcefiinortt
abortifacient
aabcefioprrrt
prefabricator
aabceghiilnty
changeability
aabcegiikmnnt
cabinet-making
aabcegilnnprs
spring-balance
aabceginoorsu
boraginaceous

aabcegllnortu
congratulable
aabcehilllmnr
lamellibranch
aabcehillpsty
heptasyllabic
aabcehilmrtty
bathymetrical
aabcehilnsstu
unchastisable
aabcehinorrsw
rainbow-chaser
aabcehlnnstuu
unstaunchable
aabcehlnprsuu
unpurchasable
aabceiillmrry
irreclaimably
aabceiinorrtt
nitrobacteria
aabceillmnruy
unreclaimably
aabceillmoprt
problematical
aabceillnpsty
pentasyllabic
aabceilloortv
collaborative
aabceillrstty
tetrasyllabic
aabceilmnnoop
companionable
aabceilnnorst
constrainable
aabceinoorrst
Serbo-Croatian
aabceirrsttuu
bureaucratist
aabceknoorssv
book-canvasser
aabcelmmnnosu
somnambulance
aabcelnooprty
polycarbonate
aabcfiilortty
factorability
aabcfikmnoort
back-formation
aabcfilnnootu
confabulation
aabcfilorrsuv
fibrovascular
aabcflnoortuy
confabulatory
aabcgiillotuy
coagulability
aabchiillnrty
labyrinthical
aabchimnoprrs
marsipobranch
aabchiorrssuu
brachiosaurus
aabciiillmpty
implacability

aabciiillnstt
antiballistic
aabciiillppty
applicability
aabciiilossty
associability
aabciiilqrtuy
acquirability
aabciilllrsty
trisyllabical
aabciillnosty
syllabication
aabciilmnoort
combinatorial
aabciilmoprty
comparability
aabciilmrruuv
vibracularium
aabciinnoorst
carbonisation
aabciinorrstu
carburisation
aabcillnooort
collaboration
aabcillnoostv
Baltoslavonic
aabcilmnnoopy
companionably
aabcilnnoorty
carbonylation
aabcnnooorsst
contrabassoon
aabdddgilnnsw
swaddling-band
aabddeekllnst
saddle-blanket
aabddegginrrw
badger-drawing
aabddeiilnssu
indissuadable
aabddiilnssuy
indissuadably
aabdeeegilrss
disagreeables
aabdeeehlmrrt
marble-hearted
aabdeefgiilnt
indefatigable
aabdeegllnorr
roller-bandage
aabdeeilmnrss
admirableness
aabdeeilnrrtt
rattle-brained
aabdeeilnsssv
advisableness
aabdeellrrtuv
barrel-vaulted
aabdeelnprsuu
unpersuadable
aabdeemnrrssu
unembarrassed
aabdefgiilnty
indefatigably

aabdegiknorst
skateboarding
aabdehiiilstt
dishabilitate
aabdeiilmnrst
administrable
aabdeilmnprru
premandibular
aabdellmnrstu
umbrella-stand
aabdelnorruyy
boundary-layer
aabdennprstuu
superabundant
aabdhimnorstt
rhabdomantist
aabeeeeglnrss
agreeableness
aabeeeehnrttw
weather-beaten
aabeeeflmnsst
self-abasement
aabeeegillnrs
generalisable
aabeeehrrrttw
water-breather
aabeeeilprsvw
variable-sweep
aabeeelllmnss
malleableness
aabeeelnnsstu
uneatableness
aabeeelnorsst
elaborateness
aabeeelnprsss
separableness
aabeefgilnsst
fatigableness
aabeeflnrrrst
transferrable
aabeeghiknrrt
heartbreaking
aabeeghllnssu
laughableness
aabeegilmorst
metagrabolise
aabeegilnnssv
navigableness
aabeehlnoprty
balneotherapy
aabeeikmnorrt
re-embarkation
aabeeillnnpux
unexplainable
aabeeillnorty
inelaborately
aabeeilmnnssu
unamiableness
aabeelllnossw
allowableness
aabeelllrstty
tetrasyllable
aabeellnprsuu
unpleasurable

aabeelmnnsstu
untamableness
aabeelnnprsuu
superannuable
aabeelnrrstuv
untraversable
aabeemmnrrsst
embarrassment
aabefhilmoprt
alphabetiform
aabefhilnnosu
unfashionable
aabefiilnsstu
unsatisfiable
aabefillmmnnu
uninflammable
aabefilmorssu
balsamiferous
aabefkmoorrst
breakfast-room
aabeflmnorrst
transformable
aabeghinnrrtu
bargain-hunter
aabeghinqrssu
square-bashing
aabegiimnnrst
straining-beam
aabegilnorrtu
gubernatorial
aabegllopprss
palpable-gross
aabeglnorstuu
obtuse-angular
aabehmorrrstu
harbour-master
aabeiiklmrtty
marketability
aabeiilllostv
volatilisable
aabeiillmnssu
unassimilable
aabeiillnstuy
unsaleability
aabeiilmsttty
metastability
aabeiilnorstv
verbalisation
aabeiilnrstwy
answerability
aabeiinrrrsst
arbitrariness
aabeillnoprsu
unpolarisable
aabeilmnoprtu
perambulation
aabeilmnrsttt
transmittable
aabeilnnsstuu
unsustainable
aabeilnoorstv
observational
aabeiloqrstuu
subequatorial

aabellnprsuuy
unpleasurably
aabelmoprrtuy
perambulatory
preambulatory
aabelmoprsstt
spermatoblast
aabelnoprrstt
transportable
aabelnprsssuu
unsurpassable
aabelnrrsttuu
subternatural
aabelorstttuu
statute-labour
aabfhilnnosuy
unfashionably
aabfilmnnotuu
funambulation
aabflmnortuuy
funambulatory
aabghiooprtuy
autobiography
aabgiiilmnors
aboriginalism
aabgiiilnorty
aboriginality
aabgiillnoost
globalisation
aabgilnrrstuu
subtriangular
aabgllnoosssu
Balanoglossus
aabhiiilnprrs
librarianship
aabhiilooopru
ailourophobia
aabiiiilnrtvy
invariability
aabiiiilnstty
insatiability
aabiiillmppty
impalpability
aabiiilmpssty
impassability
aabiiilnosstt
stabilisation
aabiilnnnrttu
tintinnabular
aabiilnnssttu
insubstantial
aabiilnorsttu
brutalisation
aabillnssttuy
substantially
aabilnnssttuu
unsubstantial
aablmmnoorstu
somnambulator
aablnprsssuuy
unsurpassably
aacccdilmorty
macrodactylic

aaccceeilnrrt
recalcitrance
aaccceennnopt
non-acceptance
aaccceginorty
gynaecocratic
aacccehiilstt
catechistical
aacccehilmopr
macrocephalic
aacccehmorssy
Saccharomyces
aaccceiillmrt
climacterical
aacccfiiilnot
calcification
aaccchilloort
ochlocratical
aaccciiilmntt
anticlimactic
aaccciilllmty
climactically
aaccddeiorrtx
dextrocardiac
aaccdeeehilty
Lecythidaceae
aaccdeeeioors
Dioscoreaceae
aaccdeegirrtt
cigarette-card
aaccdeeiilnru
clairaudience
aaccdeeilnopy
encyclopaedia
aaccdeeiloopy
Lycopodiaceae
aaccdeennttuu
unaccentuated
aaccdehhiknrz
chicken-hazard
aaccdehhloopr
Cephalochorda
aaccdehiirrst
trisaccharide
aaccdehioprsu
pseudo-archaic
aaccdehmoopwy
campeachy-wood
aaccdeiiillty
dialectically
aaccdeiilmnst
accidentalism
aaccdeiilntty
accidentality
aaccdeiinortt
accreditation
aaccdeilnootu
coeducational
aaccdeilnptty
pentadactylic
aaccdeimmootv
accommodative
aaccdeimnnopu
unaccompanied

aaccdeinoprtt
pedantocratic
aaccdfiiinot
acidification
aaccdgimmnoot
accommodating
aaccdhiilnoot
diacatholicon
aaccdhiimnoor
orchidomaniac
aaccdiillopty
apodictically
aaccdilmnotyy
dactyliomancy
aaccdimmnooot
accommodation
aacceeehmnttu
catechumenate
aacceeeilmmno
Commelinaceae
aacceeeilrstu
Sterculiaceae
aacceeenprrry
canary-creeper
aacceefirstuv
surface-active
aacceegimortt
categorematic
aacceehilmpry
hypercalcemia
aacceehimrrst
saccharimeter
aacceehlrrrst
clear-starcher
aacceehlrrsst
characterless
aacceehmorrst
saccharometer
aacceeiillprz
capercaillzie
aacceeiilmrst
reacclimatise
aacceeiimrsty
Myristicaceae
aacceeilpprtu
picture-palace
aacceellpprrw
clapperclawer
aacceelmnruuv
vacuum-cleaner
aaccefiiinott
acetification
aacceghhinost
stagecoaching
aacceghhloprr
chalcographer
aacceghijkknt
hacking-jacket
aacceghiloprr
cerographical
aacceghinoopr
oceanographic
aaccegiilnrtt
intergalactic

aaccegillnooo
oceanological
aaccegillootu
autecological
aaccegillorty
categorically
aaccegillotty
geotactically
aaccehhloppsy
scaphocephaly
aaccehiilmort
iatrochemical
aaccehiilrstu
eucharistical
aaccehillmrsv
clishmaclaver
aaccehillmsty
schematically
aaccehillppty
platycephalic
aaccehillprty
phylacterical
aaccehilmortt
tachometrical
aaccehilmpsty
metapsychical
aaccehilmrtty
tachymetrical
aaccehilrrttu
architectural
aaccehimprstu
pharmaceutics
aaccehimrrsty
saccharimetry
aaccehmnprrst
scrap-merchant
aaccehmooprsu
camphoraceous
aacceiilmnost
encomiastical
aacceiilnoptt
acceptilation
aacceiinnorrt
incarceration
aacceiinnortv
revaccination
aacceillmrtuv
circumvallate
aacceillnopry
porcelain-clay
aacceillnssss
classicalness
aacceilmnnort
necromantical
aacceilnprsst
practicalness
aacceiloprsty
palaeocrystic
aacceimmnnopt
accompaniment
aacceinnnoott
concatenation
aacceinopprt
copper-captain

aacceinopsssu
capaciousness
aacceknortttu
counter-attack
aaccellnooprr
lance-corporal
aaccellprstuy
spectacularly
aaccelnprstuu
unspectacular
aaccfiiillrsy
sacrificially
aaccfiiilnort
clarification
aaccfiiinoprt
caprification
aaccfiiinorst
scarification
aaccggiillloo
glaciological
aaccghillnoot
Anglo-Catholic
aaccgiillnoor
craniological
aaccgillnntuu
uncalculating
aacchiilmnoot
machicolation
aacchiilmnort
chiromantical
aacchiilprsty
psychiatrical
aacchiilqrrsu
squirarchical
aacchiinnorst
anachronistic
aacchillmorty
chromatically
aacchilloprtt
trophallactic
aacchilnopsty
sycophantical
aacciiillnstv
Calvinistical
aacciiinnoost
cocainisation
aacciiinorstt
cicatrisation
aacciillmopty
apomictically
aacciillsstuy
casuistically
aacciilmnooss
occasionalism
aacciilmnpstu
scapulimantic
aacciilnoosst
occasionalist
aacciilnoosty
occasionality
aacciimossstt
staccatissimo
aacciinoprstt
pantisocratic

aaccikknnorty
nick-nackatory
aaccillnprtuy
unpractically
aaccillnsttyy
syntactically
aaccilnnoootv
convocational
aaccilnnoortt
contractional
aaccilnorttuu
acculturation
aaccimnoorstu
carcinomatous
aaccinorsstty
sacrosanctity
aacddeegjotuv
judge-advocate
aacddegillnrs
scaling-ladder
aacddehiinpst
candidateship
aacddelmnorsu
Dendrocalamus
aacddfhiknnno
finnan-haddock
aacddklnoorsw
cloak-and-sword
aacdeeeiillpr
Pedicellariae
aacdeeemoopst
Podostemaceae
aacdeeghinnrs
case-hardening
aacdeegiirrrv
carriage-drive
aacdeeginorrs
coarse-grained
aacdeeginrrru
undercarriage
aacdeegnnnorr
non-regardance
aacdeehimnort
Echinodermata
aacdeehiostuz
autoschediaze
aacdeehllmtwy
what-d'ye-call-'em
aacdeehnrssvz
ranz-des-vaches
aacdeeillrtvy
declaratively
aacdeeilmnprt
predicamental
aacdeeilnpptu
appendiculate
aacdeeilnqruv
quadrivalence
aacdeeilooppy
Polypodiaceae
aacdeeilorsst
sacerdotalise
aacdeeimmnrty
medicamentary

aacdeeimnnott
decontaminate
aacdeeinnrstu
unascertained
aacdeeinpprtu
unappreciated
aacdeennnott
non-attendance
aacdeffiimnrs
disaffirmance
aacdeggillopy
pedagogically
aacdeghiilopr
ideographical
aacdeghioprrr
cardiographer
aacdegilnnpst
standing-place
aacdegimnnrst
dancing-master
aacdeginnqrsu
square-dancing
aacdegjlnosuu
juglandaceous
aacdeglmnnors
scandalmonger
aacdehiimnrrt
archimandrite
aacdehillttwy
what-d'ye-call-it
aacdehilooprt
orthopaedical
aacdehimosstu
autoschediasm
aacdehiorrstt
trisoctahedra
aacdehlostuxy
hexadactylous
aacdehmnnoort
enchondromata
aacdeiijlrtux
extra-judicial
aacdeiiillmrty
diametrically
aacdeiilmrtvy
vice-admiralty
aacdeiilnortv
valedictorian
aacdeiilrsttu
disarticulate
aacdeiinnpttu
unanticipated
aacdeillmorty
declamatorily
aacdeillnotuy
educationally
aacdeillorrty
declaratorily
aacdeilmorsst
sacerdotalism
aacdeilnrttuu
unarticulated
aacdeiloortuw
caliature-wood

aacdeilorsstt
sacerdotalist
aacdeilpqrtuu
quadruplicate
aacdeimnnnott
decontaminant
aacdeimnoqrtu
quartodeciman
aacdeinnorsuu
arundinaceous
aacdeinosssuu
audaciousness
aacdeklnorsvy
sandy-laverock
aacdelmnnrssu
underclassman
aacdfhnossttw
downcast-shaft
aacdfiiimnnot
damnification
aacdfiillóprs
spadicifloral
aacdghhooprty
cathodography
aacdghinosstw
shadowcasting
aacdghloprtyy
dactylography
aacdgiiillost
dialogistical
aacdgiiinnost
diagnostician
aacdgiillnnoo
clinodiagonal
aacdgilmrrstu
garlic-mustard
aacdhhiloprty
hydropathical
aacdhiiloorsu
Dolichosauria
aacdhilllruyy
hydraulically
aacdhilloprsy
rhapsodically
aacdhilorstty
hydrostatical
aacdhimmoosss
sado-masochism
aacdhimoossst
sado-masochist
aacdhinopqrsu
quadraphonics
aacdhlmmnoosy
Chlamydomonas
aacdhoooprrtt
Protochordata
aacdiiillmoty
idiomatically
aacdiiilpqrtu
quadricipital
aacdiiimnortu
radio-actinium
aacdiiiorttvy
radioactivity

aacdiijllstuy
Judaistically
aacdiikmnoopr
macropinakoid
aacdiilllstuy
dualistically
aacdiillmnopr
palindromical
aacdiillmpryy
pyramidically
aacdiillortty
dictatorially
aacdiilnnoptu
pandiculation
aacdiilnooort
radiolocation
aacdiilnoootu
audio-location
aacdiimnopsst
antispasmodic
aacdillmopssy
spasmodically
aacdilloqrruu
quadrilocular
aacdimnorssty
astrodynamics
aaceeeghilrrw
wheel-carriage
aaceeeglnnrst
lance-sergeant
aaceeehjklrtt
leather-jacket
aaceeeilmnoop
Polemoniaceae
aaceefilnrssu
life-assurance
aaceeflnrsssu
self-assurance
aaceeghilopst
Stegocephalia
aaceeghlmnopr
encephalogram
aaceeghlmopsu
megacephalous
aaceeghnooprr
oceanographer
aaceegilllnvy
evangelically
aaceegillnnuv
unevangelical
aaceegilmmrtt
telegrammatic
aaceegilnprtw
watering-place
aaceegilrsttt
strategetical
aaceeginnostu
gentianaceous
aaceehhnorrtw
weather-anchor
aaceehiilrstt
theatricalise
aaceehiimmstt
mathematicise

aaceehillstty
aesthetically
aaceehilmortt
theorematical
aaceehilmpsty
mesaticephaly
aaceehilnprtt
parenthetical
aaceehinnrstu
neurastheniac
aaceehkklmrrs
mackerel-shark
aaceehllmrstv
velt-mareschal
aaceehlnnoppr
parencephalon
aaceehlnoprst
Encephalartos
aaceehmnoorrt
Rhaeto-Romance
aaceehmoprstt
spermatotheca
aaceehoprrtxy
archaeopteryx
aaceeiilnrttv
intercalative
aaceeiilpprtt
peripatetical
aaceeiimnnrsu
un-Americanise
aaceeiimpprst
misappreciate
aaceeiinnrsst
necessitarian
aaceeijlnrttu
interjaculate
aaceeilmmrttu
multicamerate
aaceeilmrrttx
extra-metrical
aaceeilnnqtuv
quantivalence
aaceeilnrrsuv
vernacularise
aaceeimmnnrtt
remittance-man
aaceeimnnrstt
ascertainment
aaceelllrrtux
extra-cellular
aaceemnorsstu
sarmentaceous
aaceennorssst
Saracen's-stone
aacefhlloprsw
paschal-flower
aacefiiiilrst
artificialise
aacefiiilqtuv
qualificative
aacefiilnorst
fractionalise
aacefillttuvy
facultatively

aacefinnoorrt
confarreation
aaceflmopprst
space-platform
aaceggh ilnort
gathering-coal
aaceghhimnpst
camp-sheathing
aaceghhinoprt
ethnographica
aaceghiillprx
lexigraphical
aaceghilllrty
lethargically
aaceghillmpry
graphemically
aaceghillnoop
phaenological
aaceghilmoppt
apophlegmatic
aaceghilmopyy
hypogylcaemia
aaceghiloprr
oreographical
aaceghiloorst
archaeologist
aaceghimnoprt
cinematograph
aaceghoprsssu
sarcophaguses
aacegiillmnor
mineralogical
aacegiillmnty
enigmatically
aacegiillnnty
antigenically
aacegiilmrrtv
gravimetrical
aacegilllory
allegorically
aacegilllmrtu
metallurgical
aacegillnpryy
panegyrically
aacegilloortt
teratological
aacegillrstty
strategically
aacegilmnoosu
magnoliaceous
aaceginossssu
sagaciousness
aaceglnrrtuy
rectangularly
aacegloopsuy
polygalaceous
aacehhinpssty
psychasthenia
aacehhinrttwy
water-hyacinth
aacehhlooprtx
cephalothorax
aacehiiimnrtt
arithmetician

aacehiiimprst
hemiparasitic
aacehiillmmsv
Machiavellism
aacehiillntuv
hallucinative
aacehiillstty
atheistically
aacehiilmrstt
theatricalism
aacehiilnpstt
pantheistical
aacehiilrttty
theatricality
aacehiimmmstt
mathematicism
aacehiimnnost
mechanisation
aacehiimnpsty
metaphysician
aacehiiopssst
associateship
aacehillmrtuy
rheumatically
aacehillnttuy
authentically
aacehilmnprru
hurricane-lamp
aacehilmoprst
atmospherical
aacehilmoptyy
polycythaemia
aacehilmpstty
sympathetical
aacehilnoprtu
neuropathical
aacehilprstxy
extra-physical
aacehimnoorrt
Rhaeto-Romanic
aacehimprsttu
pharmaceutist
aacehinoprtty
actinotherapy
aacehinorttu
authenticator
aacehinprstty
parasynthetic
aacehlnopssyy
psychoanalyse
aacehloopstuu
autocephalous
aacehnopprrty
parthenocarpy
aacehnoprsstt
phase-contrast
aaceiiilmrstt
materialistic
aaceiiimprsst
semiparasitic
aaceiiinorttv
ratiocinative
aaceiipprttv
participative

aaceiiillmnor
Lamellicornia
aaceiiillprst
parallelistic
aaceiiillrsty
realistically
aaceiiillmnprt
planimetrical
aaceiiillnpsty
epinastically
aaceiiillprsty
peirastically
aaceiilmmnrsu
unicameralism
aaceiilmnrstu
unicameralist
aaceiilmnssst
ismaticalness
aaceiilmptttu
multicapitate
aaceiilnnortt
intercalation
aaceiilnnostt
cat-o'-nine-tails
aaceiilnopprt
reapplication
aaceiilnorstt
cartelisation
aaceiilnossuv
salviniaceous
aaceiilnrssst
satiricalness
aaceiilprrstu
particularise
aaceiimmosttu
semi-automatic
aaceiimnnottv
contaminative
aaceiimnorrst
reactionarism
aaceiimnsstty
systematician
aaceiinnnorrt
reincarnation
aaceiinnorsst
scenarisation
aaceiinoprrtv
prevarication
aaceiinorrstt
reactionarist
aaceiinorsttu
cauterisation
aaceiinrrrstu
curtain-raiser
aaceiklmmnors
Neo-Lamarckism
aaceillllnrrtu
intracellular
aaceillmnnsuu
sun-animalcule
aaceillmnptuy
pneumatically
aaceillprrrty
tricarpellary

aaceilmnrrsuv
vernacularism
aaceilmoprtvy
comparatively
aaceilmortttu
tautometrical
aaceilnnopstu
encapsulation
aaceilnnorstu
connaturalise
aaceilnoprsss
prosaicalness
aaceilnossssu
salaciousness
aaceilnprrstu
interscapular
aaceilnrrstuv
vernacularist
aaceilnrrtuvy
vernacularity
aaceiloprrttx
extra-tropical
aaceimnoopsst
compassionate
aaceimnopssty
synaposematic
aaceimnorsstw
water-mocassin
aaceinnorrtuv
averruncation
aaceinoprrstt
procrastinate
aaceinoprrtuy
precautionary
aaceinoprsssu
rapaciousness
aacellmnnortu
nomenclatural
aacelnorrsuuv
neurovascular
aacelnrssttuu
sustentacular
aacemnnoorstt
entomostracan
aacennoprrstt
transportance
aacffiiilnost
falsification
aacfgiiimnnot
magnification
aacfgiiinortt
gratification
aacfgiilllouv
fluvioglacial
aacfgilnnoort
conflagration
aacfgimnnrtuu
manufacturing
aacfgnooorttt
contrafagotto
aacfhimnprsst
craftsmanship
aacfiiiilrtty
artificiality

aacfiiilmnopt
amplification
palmification
aacfiiilnoqtu
qualification
aacfiiimnnort
informatician
aacfiilmnorst
fractionalism
aacfiilmortty
matrifocality
aacfiilnorstt
fractionalist
aacfiiloprtty
patrifocality
aacfiiloqrtuy
qualificatory
aacfiinnoortt
fractionation
aacfiinoorstt
factorisation
aacfinnorrssu
Franco-Russian
aacfinorsttuy
anfractuosity
aacgghilloopr
graphological
logographical
aacggiiknnptu
unit-packaging
aacggilloorst
gastrological
aacggilnrstyz
crystal-gazing
aacghhimnnttw
night-watchman
aacghhiprstty
tachygraphist
aacghhmooprrt
chromatograph
aacghiillmort
logarithmical
aacghiillprst
calligraphist
aacghiiprrstt
stratigraphic
aacghilloprxy
xylographical
aacghilmnoopr
monographical
aacghilmoprty
climatography
aacghilnnsuwy
launching-ways
aacghilnoorst
arachnologist
aacghiloopprt
topographical
aacghiloppryt
typographical
aacghimrsttuu
thaumaturgics
aacghmnooprsy
pharmacognosy

aacgiiinpprtt
participating
aacgiilllntvy
vacillatingly
aacgiillmstty
stigmatically
aacgiillnnory
inorganically
aacgiillnosty
agonistically
aacgiilmmoprt
lipogrammatic
aacgiilnorstu
cartilaginous
aacgiilnorttu
graticulation
aacgiimnnoopt
compagination
aacgiinnoottv
noctivagation
aacgijlnnootu
conjugational
aacgilllnoopy
palynological
aacgilllnosty
nostalgically
aacgillmnstyy
gymnastically
aacgillmooopt
potamological
aacgillmooost
somatological
aacgilmnoopst
campanologist
aacgilmnopsss
compass-signal
aacgimmmnoort
monogrammatic
aacginnorrstw
narrowcasting
aacglnoorrttu
congratulator
aachhiillmopt
philomathical
aachhiiorstuy
Ichthyosauria
aachhilnnopty
phthalocyanin
aachhimnoortx
xanthochromia
aachhimnoprsy
physharmonica
aachhimnpssty
yachtsmanship
aachiiimnnost
antiochianism
aachiiinnrstt
antichristian
aachiillnnotu
hallucination
aachiilrsttwy
railway-stitch
aachiimmnnors
monarchianism

aachiimnnnotu
mountain-chain
aachiinoprstu
haruspication
aachilllmptyy
lymphatically
aachillmoopsu
malacophilous
aachillnorsty
thrasonically
aachillnortuy
hallucinatory
aachilnoopttu
tautophonical
aachiloprssty
astrophysical
aachimmnoprst
panchromatism
aachimmooprst
apochromatism
aachimnnnoopr
panharmonicon
aachimoprsstt
catastrophism
aachiopprsssy
parapsychosis
aachioprssttt
catastrophist
aachlnnoorsuy
anachronously
aachlnopsstyy
psychoanalyst
aaciiiilnostt
italicisation
aaciiillnnnot
inclinational
aaciiillnpsty
pianistically
aaciiillpprty
participially
aaciiilmnosst
antisocialism
aaciiilnnostt
nationalistic
aaciiilnoosst
socialisation
aaciiilnorstt
rationalistic
aaciiilnosstt
antisocialist
aaciiilnostty
antisociality
aaciiinnoortt
ratiocination
aaciiinopprtt
participation
aaciiiossttvy
associativity
aaciillmostty
atomistically
aaciillmprsty
prismatically
aaciiillnprtuy
puritanically

aaciilloprtty
patriotically
aaciillosstty
isostatically
aaciillssttty
statistically
aaciilmnoostv
vocationalism
aaciilmnorssy
microanalysis
aaciilmnorttu
matriculation
aaciilmnortty
romanticality
aaciilmprrstu
particularism
aaciilnnoostv
volcanisation
aaciilnnostuv
vulcanisation
aaciilnoostuv
vacuolisation
aaciilnoprrtt
intratropical
aaciilnpprtty
participantly
aaciilossttu
stalactitious
aaciilprrsttu
particularist
aaciilprrttuy
particularity
aaciimmnnortu
communitarian
aaciimnnnoott
contamination
aaciimorrsstt
aristocratism
aaciinnnnostt
Constantinian
aaciinoorrtty
ratiocinatory
aacillloopsty
apostolically
aacillmnootxy
taxonomically
aacillmnopsty
complaisantly
aacillnoopstu
unapostolical
aacilloprrttu
ultra-tropical
aacilmmopstty
symptomatical
aacilmnnopstu
uncomplaisant
aacilmnoopttu
computational
aacilmnrrstuu
intramuscular
aacilmorrsttu
courts-martial
aacilmorrttuy
matriculatory

aacilnnoorstt
translocation
aacilnnorttuy
connaturality
aacilnprsstyy
cryptanalysis
aaciloprrrtu
procuratorial
aaclqrrsttuyz
quartz-crystal
aaddeeeehhrtw
weather-headed
aaddeeefhlrst
saddle-feather
aaddeeehqrrtu
headquartered
aaddeeelmprst
paddle-steamer
aaddeeggillrt
draggle-tailed
aaddeegnrrtuu
undergraduate
aaddeehhipssw
waspish-headed
aaddeehhlrrty
hard-heartedly
aaddeelnrttuu
unadulterated
aaddegghnrrtu
granddaughter
aaddeghnorruy
rough-and-ready
aaddeghoprrss
Addressograph®
aaddehhnnorsu
hare-and-hounds
aaddeilnrssst
dastardliness
aadeeegghimrr
hedge-marriage
aadeeeggnrtux
unexaggerated
aadeeehlnnrrt
neanderthaler
aadeeeiilmrst
dematerialise
aadeeeiknssww
wide-awakeness
aadeeeimnnrrt
mediterranean
aadeeelnrrtvw
lavender-water
aadeeemmnrstu
admeasurement
aadeefhhllrty
half-heartedly
aadeefnsssstt
steadfastness
aadeegilmorrt
radiotelegram
aadeegimnprst
disparagement
aadeeginnnstu
ensanguinated

aadeehimmmnos
Mohammedanise
aadeehimnoprt
diaphanometer
aadeehlorrttt
tetartohedral
aadeeiilnnost
denationalise
aadeeiklmnrst
tradesmanlike
aadeeilmnosss
salmon-disease
aadeeilnnnorr
noradrenaline
aadeeilnrsttv
travel-stained
aadeeilnrtttv
travel-tainted
aadeeinprssst
disparateness
aadeeioopsstt
potato-disease
aadeeioprrsst
parrot-disease
aadeellnrrtww
well-warranted
aadeelnppprst
pepper-and-salt
aadeennprstuu
superannuated
aadeffmnoorsw
meadow-saffron
aadefghlnrrty
grandfatherly
aadefiilnostu
feudalisation
aadefiiloqrtu
quadrifoliate
aadefilmnoppr
manifold-paper
aadefklnoorrt
foot-land-raker
aadefllmnntuy
fundamentally
aadeflnssttuy
unsteadfastly
aadegglnrttuu
gauntlet-guard
aadeggnnorrst
great-grandson
aadeggnnortuv
vantage-ground
aadeghilnrtuw
daughter-in-law
aadeghmoprrty
dermatography
aadegiiimprrv
primigravidae
aadegiilmnqru
quadrigeminal
aadegillmnort
road-metalling
aadegilmnnrsu
land-measuring

aadegilnsttvy
devastatingly
aadegimnrrstw
drawing-master
aadeginnqrruy
quadringenary
aadeginnrsttw
water-standing
aadeginnrtuuu
uninaugurated
aadehhiiillnpp
Philadelphian
aadehhilmoorr
haemorrhoidal
aadehiilmossy
haemodialysis
aadehiilnpsty
Staphylindiae
aadehiilnpsuz
sulphadiazine
aadehilllotw
All-hallowtide
aadehilnoprry
hydro-airplane
aadehimmmnos
Mohammedanism
aadehimnorstu
diathermanous
aadehnorrsttw
north-eastward
aadehnorsssuz
hazardousness
aadehorssttuw
south-eastward
aadeiiilmssst
disassimilate
aadeiiimnostt
mediatisation
aadeiillmorty
mediatorially
aadeiillnrrty
interradially
aadeiillqrrtu
quadriliteral
aadeiilmmnrst
maladminister
aadeiilmnsstu
unassimilated
aadeiilnoppss
epanadiplosis
aadeiilnrsstu
disnaturalise
aadeiimnnoort
enantiodromia
aadeiimnnorsv
animadversion
aadeiinopssst
dispassionate
aadeiipqrrttu
quadripartite
aadeilllostww
swallow-tailed
aadeillnnqruy
quadrennially

aadeillopstuy
dialypetalous
aadeilmmorstt
melodramatist
aadeilmnorsst
maladroitness
aadeilnnrstuu
unnaturalised
aadeimnorrrtu
armoured-train
aadeimqrrtuuv
quadrumvirate
aadeinorrrtxy
extraordinary
aadejlmmnsttu
maladjustment
aadelnnrrtuwy
unwarrantedly
aademnorsttuy
tetradynamous
aadfhimnprsst
draftsmanship
aadfiioqrrsuu
quadrifarious
aadfikllmoorw
maid-of-all-work
aadggiiilnprsy
disparagingly
aadggilorssst
dog's-tail-grass
aadghiiloprst
gladiatorship
aadghiinnrsvy
varnishing-day
aadghilmmorrs
marsh-marigold
aadghilnooort
orthodiagonal
aadgiiilnntwy
lady-in-waiting
aadgiillnqruu
quadrilingual
aadgiilnnsstt
distant-signal
aadglmnnooosx
Anglo-Saxondom
aadhilnorrsty
synarthrodial
aadiiillnortty
traditionally
aadiilmnnoqru
quadrinominal
aadiilnnopstt
displantation
aadiimnnoorst
randomisation
aadiimnorrstt
administrator
aadinnopsssuy
Passion-Sunday
aaeeeegnrrstw
sea-water-green
aaeeeflnrsssw
self-awareness

aaeeefnpprrst
paper-fastener
aaeeeglnrsstt
states-general
aaeeegmnnrrrt
rearrangement
aaeeegnoorrrt
aerogenerator
aaeeehilpprrt
Pre-Raphaelite
aaeeehkllprst
shell-parakeet
aaeeehlnprsst
elephant's-ears
aaeeeikmnrrtt
anti-marketeer
aaeeeilmnnnos
Neo-Melanesian
aaeeelmmnprtt
temperamental
aaeeemqrrssuu
square-measure
aaeeffgnrsstt
staff-sergeant
aaeefgiilmnrz
magazine-rifle
aaeefgillnnns
self-annealing
aaeefginrrtwy
wayfaring-tree
aaeefhmnsssst
shamefastness
aaeefhorstttt
state-of-the-art
aaeefiimnsttv
manifestative
aaeefnpprrrst
transfer-paper
aaeegghinprtt
gathering-peat
aaeeggilmortv
agglomerative
aaeeggilnnrsv
seal-engraving
aaeeghimmorrt
hierogrammate
aaeeghimopstt
apothegmatise
aaeegiilmnrrs
marriage-lines
aaeegiilmnruv
evangeliarium
aaeegiilnnorv
evangeliarion
aaeegiimmprst
epigrammatise
aaeegiimnrrrt
intermarriage
aaeegiimnrstv
vegetarianism
aaeegiimsstttt
semi-sagittate
aaeegillmssxy
sexagesimally

aaeegilmnoorr
oleomargarine
aaeegilnnppss
appealingness
aaeegilnrstvy
evangelistary
aaeegimmmnnst
mismanagement
aaeegimnprstu
measuring-tape
aaeegimnrttuv
argumentative
aaeeginoprstu
eusporangiate
aaeegjmnorrst
sergeant-major
aaeeglmmorstt
stalagmometer
aaeegloopssuy
go-as-you-please
aaeehhlmmrsty
shammy-leather
aaeehhmoppstt
metaphosphate
aaeehiilnpsst
elephantiasis
aaeehiklmmrrv
Hammerklavier
aaeehillnnnpy
phenylalanine
aaeehilmnnost
ethanolamines
aaeehilmoprtu
Palaeotherium
aaeehilmpprrs
Pre-Raphaelism
aaeehimnpsstt
panaesthetism
aaeehinrssttt
heat-resistant
aaeehipprrstw
water-sapphire
aaeehmnosttux
exanthematous
aaeehnorssttt
east-north-east
aaeehossstttu
east-south-east
aaeeiiilmmrst
immaterialise
aaeeiilmnnrtt
interlaminate
aaeeiilnprrtt
interparietal
aaeeiimnnnsst
inanimateness
aaeeiimnnortx
re-examination
aaeeiinnssstt
insatiateness
aaeeiklmnsstt
statesmanlike
aaeeiklnssttv
talkativeness

aaeeilllpptvy
appellatively
aaeeillnrttvy
alternatively
aaeeilnrrsttt
transliterate
aaeeiloprttvx
extrapolative
aaeeilpprrtvy
preparatively
aaeeilprssssz
laissez-passer
aaeeilrrsttwy
street-railway
aaeeimmnrrrst
master-mariner
aaeeimnnpprtt
appertainment
aaeeimnprrstv
privateersman
aaeelnprrrttu
preternatural
aaeemqrrrsttu
quartermaster
aaeeprrssttuu
supersaturate
aaeffgmnorsuw
woman-suffrage
aaeffiilmnorr
foraminiferal
aaeffiilmrtvy
affirmatively
aaeffiimnorrt
reaffirmation
aaeffinoorstt
afforestation
aaefgilllmnst
flagellantism
aaefgilmnrrty
fragmentarily
aaefgimnnorsu
manganiferous
aaefgimnnortt
fragmentation
aaefiimnnostt
manifestation
aaefilloprrty
prefatorially
aaefilmmmorsu
mammaliferous
aaegghinnpprs
paper-hangings
aaegghnoprsty
steganography
aaeggiiklmnns
leasing-making
aaeggiiillrtuv
villeggiatura
aaeggiilnttuv
agglutinative
aaeggilmnoort
agglomeration
aaegglnooprtu
protolanguage

aaeghiilmnopr
Germanophilia
aaeghikmnoprt
kinematograph
aaeghilmnrstw
whaling-master
aaeghilmoostt
haematologist
aaeghimopsttt
apothegmatist
aaeghinnopsww
weaponshawing
aaeghinnppsww
wappenshawing
aaeghiprrrstt
stratigrapher
aaeghllmoprty
metallography
aaeghlmnnoors
alongshoreman
aaeghlnoqrtuz
quartz-halogen
aaeghloppsyyz
zygapophyseal
aaeghloprttuy
telautography
aaeghmnooprsu
phanerogamous
aaeghnooprrty
organotherapy
aaegiiimnntuv
unimaginative
aaegiiklnnpps
plain-speaking
aaegiiilllorst
legislatorial
aaegiillmrsty
magisterially
aaegiillnsstu
Ustilaginales
aaegiilmnnprt
parliamenting
aaegiilmnrsst
sailing-master
aaegiilnnttty
tangentiality
aaegiimmprstt
epigrammatist
aaegiimnnorst
Germanisation
aaegiimnnostt
magnetisation
aaegiimnqqsuu
Quinquagesima
aaegikllmmnor
mallemaroking
aaegiklnpprsw
walking-papers
aaegillnrttuy
triangulately
aaegilmnprstu
Pantagruelism
aaegilnnoprtu
Pantagruelion

aaegilnprsttu
Pantagruelist
aaegiloprrtux
expurgatorial
aaegimnnorttu
argumentation
aaeginoorstty
geostationary
aaeginpppprrw
wrapping-paper
aaegioprrstuy
Sauropterygia
aaegllnooopty
palaeontology
aaegllooopyz
palaeozoology
aaeglmmorstty
stalagmometry
aaeglnnoosssu
analogousness
aaehhilmnnpty
naphthylamine
aaehhilmoprtx
xerophthalmia
aaehhimmprrss
marsh-samphire
aaehiiilmnsss
leishmaniasis
aaehiiimnnstt
antihistamine
aaehiiortttuv
authoritative
aaehilmnprsst
phalansterism
aaehilnprsstt
phalansterist
aaehimnpssstt
statesmanship
aaehinopprstu
aphanipterous
aaehinprsssty
parasynthesis
aaehmopprstty
Spermatophyta
aaehnnoprstty
parasyntheton
aaeiiilmmmrst
immaterialism
aaeiiilmmrstt
immaterialist
aaeiiilmmrtty
immateriality
aaeiiilnorrst
irrationalise
aaeiiilnorsst
serialisation
aaeiiimnnpprt
imparipinnate
aaeiikmnnnost
Neo-Kantianism
aaeiilllmnrty
matrilineally
aaeiillmnostt
metallisation

aaeiillmnrstu
unilateralism
aaeiillnopstt
palletisation
aaeiillnrsttu
unilateralist
aaeiillnrttuy
unilaterality
aaeiillqttuvy
qualitatively
aaeiilmmnopst
semipalmation
aaeiilmnnortt
terminational
aaeiilmnorstv
Voltaireanism
aaeiilmnprsst
impartialness
aaeiilmrrttxy
extra-limitary
aaeiilnnnortt
international
aaeiilnnorstv
vernalisation
aaeiilnoprrtt
intrapetiolar
aaeiilnoprssu
plesiosaurian
aaeiilorstuuv
suovetaurilia
aaeiimopprtvx
approximative
aaeiinnnosttx
annexationist
aaeiinnnsttty
instantaneity
aaeiinoppprrt
inappropriate
aaeiinopprstu
pauperisation
aaeiinoprsstt
separationist
aaeiiopprrtv
appropriative
aaeillnnossty
sensationally
aaeillnoprtxy
explanatorily
aaeilmnnooppr
paralipomenon
aaeilmopprtxy
approximately
aaeilnnnosstu
unsensational
aaeilnnoprstu
supernational
aaeilnnorrstt
retranslation
aaeilnooorttv
laevorotation
aaeilnooprttx
extrapolation
aaeilnoortuvv
overvaluation

aaeiloopprrrt
propraetorial
aaeiloppprrty
appropriately
aaeilopprrrty
preparatorily
aaeimmnpprsst
panspermatism
aaeimnnnoortt
ornamentation
aaeimnoprssst
master-passion
aaeimnorssttt
station-master
aaeimnpprsstt
panspermatist
aaeimnrstttuv
transmutative
aaeinnnosstu
instantaneous
aaeinoopprrrt
propraetorian
aaeinopppqrtu
appropinquate
aaeinoppprrtu
unappropriate
aaeioopprrstt
protospataire
aaellnrrsstvy
transversally
aaelmopprrstu
supratemporal
aaelnnnrsstuu
unnaturalness
aaelnnprrstty
transparently
aaelooorrttvy
laevorotatory
aaeloopprrttxy
extrapolatory
aaennnprrsttu
untransparent
aaffghinprssu
suffraganship
aaffinnoosttt
staff-notation
aafhinooprrst
parrot-fashion
aafiiilmnrtuy
unfamiliarity
aafiilmnnoort
informational
aafiilmnoorst
formalisation
aagghhiioprst
hagiographist
aaggiilnnottu
agglutination
aaggiilnnpsst
glass-painting
aaghhiklmnrst
knight-marshal
aaghhinoopprt
anthropophagi

aaghhnoopprtu
phonautograph
aaghhnoopprty
anthropophagy
aaghhopprrryy
rhyparography
aaghiilmnortt
antilogarithm
aaghiimmprstu
amphigastrium
aaghiloppsyyz
zygapophysial
aaghimmrsttuu
thaumaturgism
aaghimnooprst
mastigophoran
aaghimrstttuu
thaumaturgist
aaghknnooorrt
kangaroo-thorn
aaghnoorsstuu
saurognathous
aagiiillnostv
villagisation
aagiiinnorstt
granitisation
aagiijnnoorst
jargonisation
aagiillmoorst
malariologist
aagiillnnstty
tantalisingly
aagiilmnoorst
glamorisation
aagiilnnorttu
triangulation
aagiilnorstuv
vulgarisation
aagiilnrrttuy
triangularity
aagilmmnnosuy
magnanimously
aagilmnorrstt
mortal-staring
aagilnnnprstt
transplanting
aagilnnorsttu
strangulation
aagimnorrrstt
transmigrator
aaglmnoorstuu
granulomatous
aahhnoopprtty
anthropopathy
aahiiiilloopru
ailourophilia
aahiiilnnosty
hyalinisation
aahiiillpprstx
xiphiplastral
aahiilmmnsstu
Malthusianism
aahiilmnoprsw
animal-worship

aahiilnnprrty
platyrrhinian
aahiimmnnoopr
morphinomania
aahiimnnoorst
harmonisation
aahiimnnrsstt
transisthmian
aahiimnoopppt
hippopotamian
aahiinoorsttu
authorisation
aahilnnopssyy
hypno-analysis
aahimrrssttuz
Zarathustrism
aahinopsssstt
shop-assistant
aahllmoopstuy
polythalamous
aahlmmnooostu
monothalamous
aahlnooprrtty
anthropolatry
aaiiilmnorrst
irrationalism
aaiiilmnorstv
Voltairianism
aaiiilnnoprst
inspirational
aaiiilnorrstt
irrationalist
aaiiilnorrtty
irrationality
aaiiilnorsttu
ritualisation
uralitisation
aaiiilnosstuv
visualisation
aaiiimmnnnost
antinomianism
aaiiimnnnosst
Saint-Simonian
aaiiinnnosttt
instantiation
aaiiinnossttt
sanitationist
aaiiinoprsttv
privatisation
aaiiillmmnorty
matrimonially
aaiiillmnnottu
multinational
aaiiillmnnotvy
nominatively
aaiiillmnoprty
patrimonially
aaiiillnoprstu
pluralisation
aaiiillnoprttw
partition-wall
aaiilmnnoorst
normalisation

aaiilmnosttuu
mutualisation
aaiimnoopprtx
approximation
aaiimnrssttv
Vansittartism
aaiinnoprrstt
transpiration
aaiinnorrstty
transitionary
aaiinoopppprrt
appropriation
aaikmnooqrttu
quotation-mark
aaillmooppstu
papillomatous
aaillnoopsttu
postulational
aailnnoppsttu
supplantation
aailnoooprrtt
protonotarial
aaimnnorstttu
transmutation
aainoooprrttt
protonotariat
aainoprrrstty
transpiratory
aalmoopssttty
stomatoplasty
aannorrsstuuy
tyrannosaurus
abbbbceehlmru
bubble-chamber
abbcdeeehmorr
robe-de-chambre
abbcdeeiilnrs
indescribable
abbcdeeilnrsu
undescribable
abbcdeiilnrsy
indescribably
abbcdgiilnprs
scribbling-pad
abbceeijlnoot
objectionable
abbceeklorrry
roe-blackberry
abbcegimnoprt
carpet-bombing
abbcehiilorty
bibliothecary
abbcehkoorrss
shock-absorber
abbceijlnooty
objectionably
abbceilnorttu
contributable
abbcghiiilopr
bibliographic
abbchhiloorsy
hobby-horsical
abbciiiilloop
bibliopolical

abbciiiloprst
probabilistic
abbddgiilnoru
building-board
abbdeeeeilnrt
beetlebrained
abbdefgioorst
bridge-of-boats
abbdeiilrsttu
distributable
abbdffilmnnsu
blindman's-buff
abbeeeghlnsty
shabby-genteel
abbeegnorrrsu
barber-surgeon
abbeeilmprrtu
imperturbable
abbeelmmnootz
bamboozlement
abbeghiiloprr
bibliographer
abbegilnorrsu
rabble-rousing
abbehprrrssuy
raspberry-bush
abbeiiiloprst
probabilities
abbeilmprrtuy
imperturbably
abbghiiilopst
bibliophagist
abbiiillorstt
bibliolatrist
abbiiilmoprty
improbability
abbiilloorstu
bibliolatrous
abcccceeennost
contabescence
abcccillmooxy
coxcombically
abccdeeiklnor
cockle-brained
abccdeelnoouv
double-concave
abccdghiilnou
coachbuilding
abccdhhiioprw
coachwhip-bird
abccdooprrtuu
court-cupboard
abcceeiilmmrs
immarcescible
abcceeiilnnov
inconceivable
abcceeilnnouv
unconceivable
abcceejlnortu
conjecturable
abcceffhinorr
branch-officer
abccehilorttt
brattice-cloth

abcceiiilmpty
impeccability
abcceiiilssty
accessibility
abcceiilnnovy
inconceivably
abcceiilortty
bacteriolytic
abcceiimmnrtu
circumambient
abcceiklnostw
constablewick
abcceilnnouvy
unconceivably
abccelnorsttu
constructable
abcchhiioprrs
archbishopric
abcchkoqtttuu
quatch-buttock
abcciinorsttu
antiscorbutic
abccnoorrsttu
subcontractor
abcddeeehnssu
debauchedness
abcddeeelnnsu
undescendable
abcddeeginprt
carpet-bedding
abcddeehlrrry
bladder-cherry
abcddeeiilrst
discreditable
abcddeeiklmrt
middle-bracket
abcddeeilttux
tax-deductible
abcddeiilrsty
discreditably
abcdeeehlrrst
barrel-chested
abcdeeeilmnrt
clean-timbered
abcdeeeinorrt
decerebration
abcdeeelmmnor
recommendable
abcdeeflmrruy
mulberry-faced
abcdeeghilnor
breechloading
abcdeeghirstu
discharge-tube
abcdeegiilrtt
lattice-bridge
abcdeegilrrtt
cartridge-belt
abcdeeiiiltvy
deceivability
abcdeeiilltty
delectability
abcdeeiilmnnu
unmedicinable

abcdeeiilnnot
benedictional
abcdeeilnnnos
incondensable
abcdeeilnprtu
unpredictable
abcdeeirrrsty
secretary-bird
abcdeelloorsu
sable-coloured
abcdeelmmnnou
uncommendable
abcdeelmmnory
recommendably
abcdeelmopprw
wamble-cropped
abcdegiillllnr
cable-drilling
abcdegillmnou
cable-moulding
abcdehimorsww
widow's-chamber
abcdehinopssu
subdeaconship
abcdeiiillnps
disciplinable
abcdeiiilnoss
indissociable
abcdeiiilntuy
ineducability
abcdeiiilprty
predicability
abcdeiiilpsty
despicability
abcdeiiinstuv
subindicative
abcdeiilloqtu
quodlibetical
abcdeilnsssuu
undiscussable
abcdelmmnnouy
uncommendably
abcdemoprrstu
broad-spectrum
abcdghinooppr
chopping-board
abcdhiillllort
billiard-cloth
abcdiiiilntvy
vindicability
abcdiiinnostu
subindication
abceeefiillrt
electrifiable
abceeefiilnnt
beneficential
abceeehmmrrrt
charter-member
abceeeilnoptx
exceptionable
abceeeilnpruv
unperceivable
abceeeilnrsuv
unserviceable

abceeeilnsstx
excitableness
abceeeilorrrv
irrecoverable
abceeeilortvx
overexcitable
abceeelnorruv
unrecoverable
abceeelnorssv
revocableness
abceeelnsssux
excusableness
abceeenrrrty
cranberry-tree
abceefhllmorw
chamber-fellow
abceefiiinnot
beneficiation
abceeghilmnrs
single-chamber
abceegilnorsw
bowling-crease
abceegimnnrss
embracingness
abceegirttttu
cigarette-butt
abceehilorstt
heteroblastic
abceehimnrsty
chimney-breast
abceehimoprrs
promise-breach
abceehinnnprr
perennibranch
abceehklosstt
clothes-basket
abceehlnosstu
touchableness
abceeiiilrtvy
receivability
abceeiilmmrss
immarcessible
abceeiilnprsu
republicanise
abceeilmoorsu
bromeliaceous
abceeilnnorsv
inconversable
abceeilnnostt
incontestable
abceeilnnrssu
incurableness
abceeilnoprrs
cerebrospinal
abceeilnoptxy
exceptionably
abceeilnpruvy
unperceivably
abceeilorrrvy
irrecoverably
abceeilrrsttu
battle-cruiser
abceeimnorssv
misobservance

abceeimnosstv
combativeness
abceeinorsstx
resistance-box
abceeinprrssu
pressure-cabin
abceejmrstttu
subject-matter
abceelmmnorsu
commensurable
abceelnnoopru
pronounceable
abceelnnoqruu
unconquerable
abceelnnorsuv
unconversable
abceelnnosttu
uncontestable
abceelnorruvy
unrecoverably
abceeloorsttt
bottle-coaster
abceennnoorsv
non-observance
abcefgiilmmnr
climbing-frame
abcefiiilnopt
plebification
abcefiloorstu
cobaltiferous
abcefinoorrsu
carboniferous
abceflmnnooru
unconformable
abceflmnoortu
uncomfortable
abceghhoorrtu
thoroughbrace
abceghiloprty
copyrightable
abceghimnnsuu
submachine-gun
abcegiinnoosu
bignoniaceous
abcegillmoory
embryological
abcegilnnnoos
non-cognisable
abcehiiiklmns
mashie-niblick
abcehiiklstty
sketchability
abcehiklnsttt
blanket-stitch
abcehillmooot
holometabolic
abcehilnopsst
constableship
abcehkllorstu
bullock's-heart
abcehoprrstuy
brachypterous
abceiijnoottv
objectivation

abceiiknnrsss
brainsickness
abceiiillmptu
multiplicable
abceiilmnprsu
republicanism
abceiilnoprtu
republication
abceiilnorsty
bacteriolysin
abceiilorssty
bacteriolysis
abceiilprsttu
subtriplicate
abceiimnnoort
recombination
abceiimoorrst
isobarometric
abceilnnostty
incontestably
abceilnorttuu
tuberculation
abceiloorsstu
strobilaceous
abceilorrrtuu
arboriculture
abceilrrrttuu
tritubercular
abceimmoprsst
compass-timber
abceiooorrrtv
corroborative
abcelmmnorsuy
commensurably
abcelnnoqruuy
unconquerably
abcfilmmorruu
umbraculiform
abcflmnnooruy
unconformably
abcflmnoortuy
uncomfortably
abcgghinorrtu
turbocharging
abcghiklnssuw
swashbuckling
abchhinooprst
opisthobranch
abchiillrstuy
hubristically
abchiloopsrstt
trophoblastic
abciiiilnosty
insociability
abciiiilnrttu
tribuniticial
abciiiinnrttu
tribunitician
abciiillnotuy
inoculability
abciiilmoptty
compatibility
abciiilnostuy
unsociability

abciillmossty
symbolistical
abciillmostyy
symbiotically
abciilmmottuy
commutability
abcinooorrrt
corroboration
abclrrssttuuu
substructural
abcoooorrrrty
corroboratory
abddeeehlortu
double-hearted
abddeeeilmnot
diamond-beetle
abddeegillnou
double-dealing
abddeehllorsu
shoulder-blade
abddeelnortuu
double-natured
abddegiinprry
bidding-prayer
abddehiilmnrs
Hildebrandism
abddehlnoorrs
no-holds-barred
abddehmnooruw
homeward-bound
abddeinorrruy
boundary-rider
abddgilmnooru
moulding-board
abddginnoorsu
sound-boarding
sounding-board
abdeeeeilmrrs
irredeemables
abdeeefginrst
breast-feeding
abdeeeghilnrt
bleeding-heart
abdeeegilnost
désobligeante
abdeeegkllnow
knowledgeable
abdeeehirsttw
white-breasted
abdeeehknorrt
broken-hearted
abdeeehnrrrtu
thunder-bearer
abdeeeiilmrty
redeemability
abdeeeiinnort
Tenebrionidae
abdeeeillnssy
yieldableness
abdeeeilnrsss
desirableness
abdeeelnnrssu
endurableness

abdeeelostttt
estate-bottled
abdeeffillnrs
snaffle-bridle
abdeefghinrrt
finger-breadth
abdeefiiilrsv
diversifiable
abdeefiiilsty
defeasibility
abdeegiilnrst
disintegrable
abdeegilnrsst
dressing-table
abdeeginnorsw
Swedenborgian
abdeegkllnowy
knowledgeably
abdeehilnsstu
unestablished
abdeeiilnnpss
indispensable
abdeeiilnnssu
inaudibleness
abdeeiilnoprt
perditionable
abdeeiilnptxy
expendability
abdeeiilnttxy
extendability
abdeeiilsttty
detestability
abdeeiimrttxy
ambidexterity
abdeeiklnnrss
drinkableness
abdeeikmmnrst
disembarkment
abdeeilmnoprs
imponderables
abdeeilmrrstu
master-builder
abdeeimorstux
ambidexterous
abdeeinnssssu
unbiassedness
abdefiiinnort
defibrination
abdefiillorrt
defibrillator
abdefiilmorty
deformability
abdefiilnntuu
infundibulate
abdegghnorsuy
horse-and-buggy
abdeggillnouz
double-glazing
abdeghinoorsu
boarding-house
abdegiilnssuu
undisguisable
abdegilmoosvy
viol-de-gamboys

abdeginnooruv
overabounding
abdehilnoorsu
dishonourable
abdeiiiilqrsu
disequilibria
abdeiillnossv
indissolvable
abdeiilloprty
deplorability
abdeiilnnpssy
indispensably
abdeiilnoprty
ponderability
abdeiilprrtuy
perdurability
abdeiinnorstu
insubordinate
abdeiinnorttw
rainbow-tinted
abdeiinorstuv
subordinative
abdeillnooort
blood-relation
abdeilnorstuy
subordinately
abdekrrtuuyzz
turkey-buzzard
abdelnnoptuuw
unputdownable
abdfginnorssu
brassfounding
abdfiiilmorty
formidability
abdghinooorst
shooting-board
abdgiiilnoost
disobligation
abdgiiknorrst
skirting-board
abdgiiloorsty
disobligatory
abdgilmnnorsu
Bildungsroman
abdhiiinorsty
hybridisation
abdhilnoorsuy
dishonourably
abdiiiilmssty
admissibility
abdiiilnossuv
subdivisional
abdiiilpsttuy
disputability
abdiinnoorstu
subordination
abdllmmnoooss
almond-blossom
abeeeeflnorsu
unforeseeable
abeeeeglmnrtu
beleaguerment
abeeeeilmmprs
semipermeable

abeeeeirrrtvv
reverberative
abeeeelnnrssv
venerableness
abeeeelnprrst
representable
abeeeemnpsttt
tempest-beaten
abeeeffilnnss
ineffableness
abeeefhnnortt
feather-bonnet
abeeefiillmpx
exemplifiable
abeeeghhimntv
might-have-been
abeeeglmmnnrt
embranglement
abeeegoorrssy
sea-gooseberry
abeeehilnpprs
apprehensible
abeeehinrtttw
weather-bitten
abeeeiiklmnrs
Berkeleianism
abeeeiilrrrtv
irretrievable
abeeeikkrrrst
strike-breaker
abeeeilmnrsss
miserableness
abeeeilnprrtt
interpretable
abeeeilnprruv
unreprievable
abeeeilnqsstu
equitableness
abeeeinorrrtv
reverberation
abeeejlnnossy
enjoyableness
abeeelmmnorss
memorableness
abeeelmnpsstt
temptableness
abeeelnnnsstu
untenableness
abeeelnnprstu
unpresentable
abeeelnnprtuv
unpreventable
abeeelnrssttu
utterableness
abeeenossstuu
beauteousness
abeeeorrrrtvy
reverberatory
abeefgiilnrrr
irrefrangible
abeefgilnoruv
unforgiveable
abeefglnorttu
unforgettable

abeefiilprrty
preferability
abeefilnrrrst
transferrible
abeegghiooprr
biogeographer
abeeghiimnrtt
breathing-time
abeeghiknorsu
house-breaking
abeeghmnorrrt
brother-german
abeegiinorrtv
verbigeration
abeegillnorrr
roller-bearing
abeegilmoorst
metagrobolise
abeegilnorrvy
overbearingly
abeegilnossst
blastogenesis
abeehhmorrttu
mouth-breather
abeehiilnstux
inexhaustible
abeehilmnsstt
establishment
abeehimoprstt
Hemerobaptist
abeehlmnorstu
unsmotherable
abeehlmorstwy
weather-symbol
abeeiilnprtty
penetrability
abeeiilnrrsst
irritableness
abeeiiloprrsv
proverbialise
abeeiilqstuyz
squeezability
abeeiilrrrtvy
irretrievably
abeeikllssttt
table-skittles
abeeiknoprrrs
prison-breaker
abeeillnpsssu
plausibleness
abeeilmmnossv
immovableness
abeeilmmnsstu
immutableness
abeeilmnnnotu
unmentionable
abeeilmnpsstu
imputableness
abeeilnnsttuu
sublieutenant
abeeilnprsssu
suprasensible
abeeilnqsstuu
subsequential

abeeinnossstt
obstinateness
abeeinoprrsss
prisoners'-base
abeekmnnortuy
mountebankery
abeelmpprrruy
paper-mulberry
abeelnnnorrtu
non-returnable
abeelnnnsstuu
untunableness
abeenorrsstuu
subterraneous
abefgiilnrrry
irrefrangibly
abefglnorttuy
unforgettably
abefiiiilnsty
infeasibility
abefiiiilrtvy
verifiability
abefiiillrtty
filterability
abefiiilnrtuv
unvitrifiable
abefiijlnstuu
unjustifiable
abefiilmorrty
reformability
abefllnoopstu
tablespoonful
abegghilmnosu
gambling-house
abeghiiimmnrs
Birminghamise
abeghiillnrtw
whirling-table
abeghiknoorst
shooting-brake
abeghilnorttw
throwing-table
abeghilnosttw
washing-bottle
abegiiilnotty
negotiability
abegiiknnoprt
breaking-point
abegikmnnnotu
mountebanking
abegilmnnortu
Grumbletonian
abegilnopprtt
blotting-paper
abegimnosssuu
ambiguousness
abeglmnooorss
orange-blossom
abehhinnoorst
Heath-Robinson
abehiiilprsty
perishability
abehiiinnorst
hibernisation

abehiilnstuxy
inexhaustibly
abehiinoorrst
herborisation
abehiiprrrsst
barristership
abehikmnoorst
thrombokinase
abehllmopssuy
blasphemously
abeiiiilmnnsz
Leibnizianism
abeiiiilnttvy
inevitability
abeiiillnrtuy
unreliability
abeiiilmnorst
liberationism
abeiiilmnrtty
terminability
abeiiilnoprty
inoperability
abeiiilnoqrtu
equilibration
abeiiilnorstt
liberationist
abeiiilnortxy
inexorability
abeiiilnpstxy
expansibility
abeiiimmnnrsu
minisubmarine
abeiillnnrsst
brilliantness
abeiillnrtuvy
vulnerability
abeiillorstvy
resolvability
abeiilmnrssst
transmissible
abeiilmnrstuy
mensurability
abeiilmoprrsv
proverbialism
abeiilmprttuy
permutability
abeiilnorsstv
vibrationless
abeiilnsssttu
subsistential
abeiiloprrstv
proverbialist
abeiilrtttuvy
attributively
abeiimnossstu
ambitiousness
abeiinnoorstv
inobservation
abeiinnorsstt
baton-sinister
abeiinrrssttu
tributariness
abeinssttuv
substantivise

abeikmmnnostu
mountebankism
abeilllmottuu
multilobulate
abeilllorrwww
willow-warbler
abeilnoorsssu
laboriousness
abeilnopprstu
insupportable
abeilnssttuvy
substantively
abeinnorstuvy
subventionary
abeinooprrttu
protuberation
abeinorrssuvy
subversionary
abeknoqrsttuu
Quaker-buttons
abelnopprstuu
unsupportable
abelnoprrttuy
protuberantly
abfiiiiilllmns
infallibilism
abfiiiiilllnst
infallibilist
abfiiiiilllnty
infallibility
abfiiiloprtty
profitability
abfiijlnstuuy
unjustifiably
abgghiilnnrtw
night-warbling
abggiilooorst
agrobiologist
abghlmooprsyy
symbolography
abgiiiilnntty
intangibility
abgiiinorrstu
subirrigation
abgillorrsuuy
burglariously
abgilmnosuuuy
unambiguously
abhhiilooppsy
syphilophobia
abhiiilnpstuy
punishability
abhiiilnrstty
labyrinthitis
abhiimnoorrst
Romano-British
abiiiiilmntty
inimitability
abiiiillnotvy
inviolability
abiiiilmprtty
impartibility
abiiiilmpssty
impassibility

abiiillnostvy
insolvability
abiiilmoprtvy
improvability
abiiilnossttu
subtilisation
abiiilnsttuuy
unsuitability
abiilmnnnttuu
tintinnabulum
abiilmnoossty
symbolisation
abiilmnostuuy
unambitiously
abiilmorrttuv
multivibrator
abiinsstttuvy
substantivity
abilllmopssyy
polysyllabism
abillmmnoossy
monosyllabism
abilnooppstuu
subpopulation
abilnopprstuy
insupportably
accccceijmnruy
circumjacency
acccceikkllty
clickety-clack
accccilllnoyy
concyclically
acccdeeeinnns
incandescence
acccdeeilnopy
encyclopaedic
acccdehilnosy
synecdochical
acccdgiillooo
codicological
accceeelnnosv
convalescence
accceeillnrty
eccentrically
accceekoopppr
peacock-copper
accceelnnosvy
convalescency
acccegilmnnoo
meningococcal
acccehiilmopr
microcephalic
acccehiinortt
architectonic
acccehinnoosu
cinchonaceous
accceiinopsuu
pucciniaceous
accceilnooprs
necroscopical
accceimmnooor
macroeconomic
accceloooprst
Protococcales

accceloo prstt
streptococcal
acccennooovvx
concavo-convex
acccghiklnotw
clock-watching
acccghillnooo
conchological
accciilmmoors
microcosmical
accciilmooprs
microscopical
accciillooopps
colposcopical
accddeehrrstu
starch-reduced
accddehkooosw
woodcock's-head
accdeeeghnort
hedge-accentor
accdeeennnrst
transcendence
accdeeenorrrt
catercornered
accdeehhiklpt
thick-pleached
accdeehiknrru
hurricane-deck
accdeehloopru
peach-coloured
accdeeiilnost
occidentalise
accdeeinnoprt
accident-prone
accdeeinortuu
outrecuidance
accdeelmoorru
cream-coloured
accdeemnopsst
compactedness
accdeennnrsty
transcendency
accdeennorstu
unconsecrated
accdehhilloop
dolichocephal
accdehhilopry
hydrocephalic
accdehkloppprt
cock-thrappled
accdeiikloops
kaleidoscopic
accdeiilmnost
Occidentalism
accdeiilnostt
Occidentalist
accdeiinoortt
decortication
accdeiinorttv
contradictive
accdeilmnoptu
uncomplicated
accdeilnorsuy
cylindraceous

accdffinorstu
custard-coffin
accdfiiilnotu
dulcification
accdghiknorry
hydrocracking
accdhhinoopry
hypochondriac
accdhiiinorst
diachronistic
accdhilloopyy
hypocycloidal
accdhimnopsyy
psychodynamic
accdiiilnnoop
clinopinacoid
accdiiilnssty
syndicalistic
accdiiinorsty
idiosyncratic
accdiilllmosu
molluscicidal
accdiilllnryy
cylindrically
accdiimmnnoou
incommunicado
accdiinnoortt
contradiction
accdinoorrtty
contradictory
accdmnoorrttu
tram-conductor
acceeeehllnop
encephalocele
acceeeelmorrt
accelerometer
acceeehilmnps
mesencephalic
acceeeillorst
ecclesiolater
acceeeilmmors
commercialese
acceeeilnrstx
excrescential
acceefklooprw
peacock-flower
acceegghiinnp
changing-piece
acceeghhikmnw
check-weighman
acceeghillmoy
geochemically
acceeghmnortv
Congreve-match
acceeghnnortu
counterchange
acceeghnorrtu
countercharge
acceehhiopsyz
Schizophyceae
acceehhloopry
Chlorophyceae
acceehhloorst
school-teacher
acceehiinnort
co-inheritance
acceehilloppt
leptocephalic
acceehilmoprt
petrochemical
acceehilnnsst
technicalness
acceehimmnstu
catechumenism
acceehimnrrst
screech-martin
acceehknooprt
peacock-throne
acceehllnnops
splanchnocele
acceehlmnostt
casement-cloth
acceehorrstty
oyster-catcher
acceeiilmmnsu
ecumenicalism
acceeiilmmors
commercialise
acceeiioprrtv
reciprocative
acceeillorsty
ecclesiolatry
acceeillorttv
volta-electric
acceeilnnrsst
centricalness
acceeilnopstu
conceptualise
acceeilnostuv
vice-consulate
acceeilnqstuy
acquiescently
acceeilorsttt
electrostatic
acceeimmnotux
excommunicate
acceeinnorttv
concentrative
acceeinoprttv
contraceptive
acceeinorttuv
counteractive
acceejkorrsst
jack-crosstree
acceellmmooru
macromolecule
acceemnorrstt
concert-master
acceennoortty
octocentenary
acceennoosstu
consectaneous
acceenorrsttu
counter-caster
acceeoorrsstu
stercoraceous
acceffiiinosu
inefficacious
acceffiilosuy
efficaciously
accefhilmoorr
cochleariform
accefiiinopst
specification
accefiiinortt
certification
rectification
accefiilmoors
scoleciformia
accefiiorrtty
certificatory
accefinnoorty
confectionary
acceghhiooprr
choreographic
acceghiiloprx
lexicographic
acceghillnoot
technological
acceghilnnory
encroachingly
acceghilnoptt
plectognathic
accegiiklnpst
sticking-place
accegiilnqsuy
acquiescingly
accegillnoosy
synecological
accegilmnoort
conglomeratic
acceginoorrtt
gerontocratic
accehhiiopstt
theopaschitic
accehhilmoopt
photochemical
accehhilosstz
eschscholtzia
accehhimorstt
chrestomathic
accehiillnsst
callisthenics
accehiilprrty
hypercritical
accehiimrsstt
chrematistics
accehillnopty
polytechnical
accehilmnotyz
zymotechnical
accehilmoostt
cosmothetical
accehilnoprty
pyrotechnical
accehiloopprs
chorepiscopal
accehioopsstt
tachistoscope
acceiiilnpprv
vice-principal
acceiiimnnors
Ciceronianism
acceiiklnostw
anticlockwise
acceiiknnprst
panic-stricken
acceiilmmmors
commercialism
acceiilmmorrt
micrometrical
acceiilmmorst
commercialist
acceiilmmorty
commerciality
acceiilmnosss
neoclassicism
acceiilmorstv
viscometrical
acceiilnoprrt
calico-printer
acceiilnossst
neoclassicist
acceiilnrrstt
transit-circle
acceiiloprrty
reciprocality
acceiilprrstu
supercritical
acceiimmnotuv
communicative
acceiinooprrt
reciprocation
acceiinoorttx
excortication
acceiiopprssu
perspicacious
acceikkkknnry
knick-knackery
acceilmnnnoop
non-compliance
acceilmnoppss
pencil-compass
acceilmnopstu
conceptualism
acceilnopsttu
conceptualist
acceinnnoortt
concentration
acceinnooprtt
contraception
acceinnoorrty
concretionary
acceinnoorssy
concessionary
acceinnoorttu
counteraction
acceinoopprtu
preoccupation
acceinopprssu
percussion-cap
accejllnortuy
conjecturally
accelloorssuu
sclerocaulous

accfghhiknrtu
chuck-farthing
accfhiiimnoty
chymification
accfiiiinnotz
zincification
accfiiinnoort
cornification
accfiiinoorst
scorification
accfiiinoostt
Scotification
accfiilllnoot
floccillation
accghhhhimnru
High-Churchman
accghhinorsst
cross-hatching
accghhiopprsy
psychographic
accghiilloort
trichological
accghillnooor
chronological
accghilloopsy
psychological
accghilooprsy
hygroscopical
accghimnnooru
mourning-coach
accghiopprrty
cryptographic
accgiiimnorrt
micrograhitic
accgiillmoosu
musicological
accgiilloootx
toxicological
accgiilnoorst
carcinologist
accgillooprty
cryptological
accgilnooprsy
laryngoscopic
acchhiloorsty
charity-school
acchiilmossst
scholasticism
acchiimnooprt
actinomorphic
acchiinppssty
panpsychistic
acchilmooprty
polychromatic
acchimmnooort
monochromatic
acchimnooppst
phonocamptics
acchimoopssty
psychosomatic
acchiooprssuz
schizocarpous
acciiilnoorrt
onirocritical
acciiimmnoost
iconomaticism
acciillnnquuy
quincuncially
acciillnrrtuu
criniicultural
acciillprstuu
piscicultural
acciilmnooprv
comprovincial
acciilnorttty
contractility
acciimmnnootu
communication
acciimnoossty
actinomycosis
acciinooprsst
cranioscopist
accijlnnnootu
conjunctional
accilmnnootty
concomitantly
accimmnoortuy
communicatory
accimnooprstu
pococurantism
accinnooprstu
conspurcation
accinooprsttu
pococurantist
acdddfhiknnoo
findon-haddock
acddeeefhnrsu
schadenfreude
acddeeeinorrs
coriander-seed
acddeeeinprtu
undepreciated
acddeeffilsty
disaffectedly
acddeegiknnor
dead-reckoning
acddeeimnooty
adenoidectomy
acddegiiilnnpp
candle-dipping
acddegillnoor
dendrological
acddegilnooru
dead-colouring
acddeginorsuu
undiscouraged
acddehiiprrst
dispatch-rider
acddehilmosuy
dichlamydeous
acddehinoopst
dodecaphonist
acddehinoorsu
deoch-an-doruis
acddeiimnoors
androdioecism
acddeinnoortu
uncoordinated
unco-ordinated
acddejloorsuu
Judas-coloured
acddhimnorsyy
hydrodynamics
acdeeeeffioss
coffee-disease
acdeeeeilnrrv
redeliverance
acdeeefhikrst
sick-feathered
acdeeefhilrsv
cheval-de-frise
acdeeefinortv
confederative
acdeeeghinprs
speech-reading
acdeeegiklmmr
mackerel-midge
acdeeegiklmru
mackerel-guide
acdeeegiklnnp
packing-needle
acdeeegknprss
deck-passenger
acdeeegnnrsuv
unscavengered
acdeeehinrruv
underachiever
acdeeeiirsttv
carte-de-visite
acdeeeimnrstv
misadvertence
acdeeeipqrrsu
square-pierced
acdeeekqrrrtu
quarter-decker
acdeeelmopprr
emerald-copper
acdeeelnprrsu
supercalender
acdeeennopprr
preponderance
acdeeennrsstu
uncreatedness
acdeefflnnrsu
candle-snuffer
acdeefhnorrtw
thenceforward
acdeefiiilnrt
delirifacient
acdeefiiinort
re-edification
acdeefilnnost
self-contained
acdeefinnoort
confederation
acdeefllmooru
flame-coloured
acdeefnorrrtw
centre-forward
acdeeghiknnrt
kitchen-garden
acdeeghillnrt
candle-lighter
acdeeghnrrstu
draught-screen
acdeegiilrrtt
lattice-girder
acdeegilllnpw
dwelling-place
acdeegilmnrsu
muscle-reading
acdeegilnprty
deprecatingly
acdeeginoprrt
tape-recording
acdeegorrrsst
cross-gartered
acdeehiillntx
hexactinellid
acdeehiillott
diotheletical
acdeehillotty
dyotheletical
acdeehilorrtt
tetrachloride
acdeehlnnoorr
hole-and-corner
acdeehlnnoors
scalenohedron
acdeehmopssuy
Scyphomedusae
acdeeiiilmnrs
decriminalise
acdeeiijprtuv
prejudicative
acdeeiillrttv
verticillated
acdeeiilnnsst
identicalness
acdeeiilnpssu
unspecialised
acdeeiilprtuv
reduplicative
acdeeiilprtvy
predicatively
acdeeiilrttuv
diverticulate
acdeeiimnnrty
indeterminacy
acdeeiimnoprt
premedication
acdeeiinnorst
inconsiderate
acdeeiinnortv
revendication
acdeeiinnosst
Ascensiontide
acdeeiinoprtt
decrepitation
acdeeiinorstv
considerative
acdeeiinrsstt
Testicardines

acdeeiknqrsuw
quick-answered
acdeeillnnsty
clandestinely
acdeeilnoorst
reconsolidate
acdeeilnorsty
considerately
acdeeilnpprru
perpendicular
acdeeimnosttu
undomesticate
acdeeinnorsss
secondariness
acdeeinprsuvy
dispurveyance
acdeelloorstu
slate-coloured
acdeemnnopstu
uncompensated
acdeennopprry
preponderancy
acdeenorrsttu
unstercorated
acdefgillrsuy
disgracefully
acdefiiiilnost
fictionalised
acdefiiimntuv
mundificative
acdeghhhimost
high-stomached
acdeghhooprtu
thorough-paced
acdeghiimnnrs
merchandising
acdeghimnorty
hydromagnetic
acdegiillmruy
demiurgically
acdegiilnnprw
drawing-pencil
acdegillmnooo
demonological
acdegillnooot
deontological
acdegimmnnorw
wing-commander
acdegmnoorrst
costardmonger
acdehhilnprsy
ship-chandlery
acdehhloprsuy
hydrocephalus
acdehiiiillott
diothelitical
acdehiillotty
dyothelitical
acdehiilmostt
methodistical
acdehiimrsstt
Christmas-tide
acdehiiopsstt
sophisticated

acdehikmooosu
cook-housemaid
acdehilmorrty
hydrometrical
acdehilnoorst
school-trained
acdehimmnoprs
commandership
acdehimmnorty
thermodynamic
acdehllmnoost
old-clothesman
acdehlmooprsy
chlamydospore
acdeiiiloprst
periodicalist
acdeiiinnortv
revindication
acdeiijllpruy
prejudicially
acdeiijnoprtu
prejudication
acdeiikmnprty
prick-me-dainty
acdeiilnnottu
denticulation
acdeiilnnstty
clandestinity
acdeiilnoostv
consolidative
acdeiilnoprtu
reduplication
acdeiilnopsuu
Sipunculoidea
acdeiilrsttvy
distractively
acdeiimnnoort
enantiodromic
acdeiimnoostt
domestication
acdeiinnoorst
consideration
acdeiinoqrstu
quadrisection
acdeiinorrsty
discretionary
acdeiiopssttu
disceptatious
acdeillppstyy
dyspeptically
acdeilmnosttu
documentalist
acdeilnnorsty
constrainedly
acdeilnorsttu
destructional
acdeiloopprrtu
parti-coloured
acdeiloprssty
perissodactyl
acdeimnnnoopu
uncompanioned
acdeimnnoottu
documentation

acdeinnnorstu
unconstrained
acdeiopprrstu
Dipterocarpus
acdelnooostuy
acotyledonous
acdeloopprrtuy
party-coloured
acdeloorrstuw
straw-coloured
acdemmnnostuu
unconsummated
acdfgiiiinnot
dignification
acdfiiimnnotu
mundification
acdfilnnostuy
dysfunctional
acdghiiklnruy
hydraulicking
acdghiilmnnou
chain-moulding
acdghinoooprt
gonadotrophic
acdgiilnrstty
distractingly
acdgiinnrsttu
undistracting
acdgiinoossty
cytodiagnosis
acdgillnoooot
odontological
acdgilloortty
troglodytical
acdgilmostyyz
zygodactylism
acdginnnnoopr
pro-and-conning
acdgloostuyyz
zygodactylous
acdhhiinopsty
ichthyopsidan
acdhiilmnoort
mitochondrial
acdhiinopsstu
custodianship
acdhijooprstu
coadjutorship
acdhiloorssuu
Dolichosaurus
acdhimnnoooop
companionhood
acdhinoopqrsu
quadrophonics
acdiiiilmnoot
domiciliation
acdiiiklnnoop
clinopinakoid
acdiiillorsty
dioristically
acdiiilnnoptu
induplication
acdiiilnortvy
vindicatorily

acdiiimnorrst
discriminator
doctrinairism
acdiillmoosty
sodomitically
acdiillnnooty
conditionally
acdiilnnnootu
unconditional
acdiilnnooost
consolidation
acdiilnooorst
discoloration
acdiilnrsttuy
translucidity
acdiilpqrtuuy
quadruplicity
acdiinnoorrtt
indoctrinator
acdiinnortuww
window-curtain
acdiinoorrrrt
corridor-train
acdillmopstyy
polydactylism
acdimnoopssww
compass-window
acdinooqrsstu
conquistadors
acdlloopstuyy
polydactylous
acdlmnooostuy
condylomatous
monodactylous
aceeeefkmnrrr
reference-mark
aceeeehlprsst
steeplechaser
aceeeelnpssss
peacelessness
aceeeennppry
cayenne-pepper
aceeeepprrstw
carpet-sweeper
aceeeffginopr
peace-offering
aceeefflnsstu
effectualness
aceeefgijknrt
reefing-jacket
aceeefhiklrst
sickle-feather
aceeefiklottv
ticket-of-leave
aceeefinoprtt
perfectionate
aceeeflrsssuv
surface-vessel
aceeefmorrrtt
refractometer
aceeegillnrty
energetically
aceeeglmnortt
electromagnet

aceeeglnrssss
gracelessness
aceeegmnnortu
encouragement
aceeehhlmorrt
chrome-leather
aceeehhoorttt
toothache-tree
aceeehikllmno
chameleonlike
aceeehilmnrtu
hermeneutical
aceeehinossst
coenaesthesis
aceeehlmnnops
mesencephalon
aceeehrrssttu
treasure-chest
aceeeillmprst
capellmeister
aceeeilmnnrtt
interlacement
aceeeilnnnrtt
tercentennial
aceeeilnnorrt
cornelian-tree
aceeeilrrrrtt
letter-carrier
aceeeinnrssss
necessariness
aceeeinosstvv
evocativeness
aceeeioprttvx
expectorative
aceeeioqsstuu
equisetaceous
aceeellnorttv
electrovalent
aceeelnssssssu
causelessness
aceeffhinnprs
affenpinscher
aceeffillntuy
ineffectually
aceefgginrstu
gas-centrifuge
aceefghlnnssu
changefulness
aceefgiinnopr
pigeon-fancier
aceefgimnnrst
fencing-master
aceefgimnorrt
ferromagnetic
aceefginnorry
ferricyanogen
aceefgjlnostu
self-conjugate
aceefgnnoorry
ferrocyanogen
aceefhhirsttt
feather-stitch
aceefhiikmmrs
mischief-maker
aceefhiinnntt
tenant-in-chief
aceefhimnnrst
franchisement
aceefhlnssstu
scathefulness
aceefhmnostuv
vouchsafement
aceefiilnnrsu
life-insurance
aceefiinnrrsu
fire-insurance
aceefillnoprw
pelican-flower
aceefilnnrssu
self-insurance
aceefinorrstu
nectariferous
aceefinossstu
facetiousness
aceefmnorstuu
frumentaceous
aceeghhioprrr
cheirographer
aceeghhirttww
weight-watcher
aceeghhmnrrru
hunger-marcher
aceeghhooprrr
choreographer
aceeghiillnos
collieshangie
aceeghiimnnsw
sewing-machine
aceeghillopsu
colleagueship
aceeghilmnoot
homogenetical
aceeghilmpryy
hyperglycemia
aceeghilnoprs
selenographic
aceeghilnorsu
clearing-house
aceeghiloprrx
lexicographer
aceeghilopstu
Galeopithecus
aceeghimnnnru
machine-gunner
aceeghinnprtt
tent-preaching
aceeghinnrsss
searchingness
aceeghioprrst
stereographic
aceeghloprrty
electrography
aceeghmnrrstu
surchargement
aceegiiknopsv
speaking-voice
aceegiimnnost
miscegenation
aceegiimnoptz
piezomagnetic
aceegiinnnrst
intransigence
aceegiinoprrr
carrier-pigeon
aceegiknnrrvw
nerve-wracking
aceegilllnoos
selenological
aceegillmorty
geometrically
aceegillnnoot
non-collegiate
aceegilmmnorr
miracle-monger
aceegilmnnoqu
magniloquence
aceegilnnprrs
spring-cleaner
aceegimnoprst
spermatogenic
aceeginopppprs
popping-crease
aceeginorrstt
gastroenteric
aceehhiillprs
helispherical
aceehhiilmprs
hemispherical
aceehhillortt
heterothallic
aceehhilnpsss
seneschalship
aceehiilllnst
Hellenistical
aceehiilnoprt
epitrachelion
aceehiinnrstv
even-Christian
aceehiknrrstt
heart-stricken
aceehiknrssst
heart-sickness
aceehillnprty
phrenetically
aceehillortty
theoretically
aceehilmmopss
mesocephalism
aceehilmprrty
hypermetrical
aceehilnprsss
sphericalness
aceehiloprstt
heteroplastic
aceehimrrsstt
Christmas-tree
aceehinoprrst
terpsichorean
aceehinpprrst
ship-carpenter
aceehiprrssty
secretaryship
aceehllmooort
alcoholometer
aceehlloppstu
leptocephalus
aceehlmnoopty
encephalotomy
aceehlmnorrtu
thermonuclear
aceehlmnsssst
matchlessness
aceehlmoopssu
mesocephalous
aceehlorrstuy
treacherously
aceehmnopprrt
rapprochement
aceehnprrsstu
purse-snatcher
aceehnrstttuw
water-chestnut
aceehooprrstu
heterocarpous
aceeiiimnrrtv
recriminative
aceeiiinpsstt
antisepticise
aceeiiipprttv
precipitative
aceeiiklrsstt
Rickettsiales
aceeiillnrrty
rectilinearly
aceeiilmmnors
ceremonialism
aceeiilmnoprs
semiporcelain
aceeiilnorstt
electrisation
aceeiilnprtuv
plantie-cruive
aceeiilpprtty
precipitately
aceeiilpqsstu
sesquiplicate
aceeiilprttty
rectipetality
aceeiimmorstv
commiserative
aceeiimnnosst
amniocentesis
aceeiimnnprss
Spencerianism
aceeiimnorrst
mercerisation
aceeiinnorttw
winter-aconite
aceeiinnosstt
necessitation
aceeiinnrsstt
intricateness
aceeiirssttuv
resuscitative
aceeijlnrrttu
interjectural

aceeilllnotuv
involucellate
aceeilllnpsty
splenetically
aceeilllnrrtu
intercellular
aceeillmnossu
miscellaneous
aceeillmnttuu
multinucleate
aceeillnnnssu
uncleanliness
aceeillnoptxy
exceptionally
aceeillorrtvy
correlatively
aceeillpstuvy
speculatively
aceeillrrssty
recrystallise
aceeilmnnsssu
masculineness
aceeilmnopttv
contemplative
aceeilnnoprtv
convertiplane
aceeilnnoptux
unexceptional
aceeilnnoqstu
consequential
aceeilnnrssuy
unnecessarily
aceeilnooprsu
porcelaineous
aceeilnoqssuv
equivocalness
aceeilnorsttu
interosculate
aceeilnosttux
contextualise
aceeilnpstuuv
unspeculative
aceeilorrttvy
retroactively
aceeilppprrst
carpet-slipper
aceeimmmoortv
commemorative
aceeinnnorsst
non-resistance
aceeinnnostty
consentaneity
aceeinnnqrtuy
quincentenary
aceeinnnrsstu
uncertainness
aceeinnoorsvz
conversazione
aceeinnorrrtt
contraterrine
aceeinnorrsuv
overinsurance
aceeinnossstu
tenaciousness

aceeinooprstu
proteinaceous
aceeinooprttx
expectoration
aceeinooprtuv
uncooperative
unco-operative
aceeinoorrstv
conservatoire
aceeklnrsssst
tracklessness
aceellnooprsu
porcellaneous
aceelloorrrst
roller-coaster
aceelloprsstu
supercollate
aceelmmnoprty
complementary
aceelnnrrrstu
scarlet-runner
aceelnooprrtu
counter-parole
aceelnooprstt
creosote-plant
aceemmnnopsst
encompassment
aceennnoortvy
novocentenary
aceennnoosstu
consentaneous
aceenooprrsst
corporateness
aceffgiilnnns
self-financing
aceffhlssttuz
schutzstaffel
acefggiinrstu
figure-casting
acefghiiklnst
fishing-tackle
acefgiiiinstv
significative
acefgiiklnnps
scalping-knife
acefgiillnttt
cattle-lifting
acefgiilmnnty
magnificently
acefgikmnorst
stocking-frame
acefgillnrtuy
centrifugally
acefginosssuu
fugaciousness
acefhhiiinpst
chieftainship
acefhlloprruy
reproachfully
acefhlnoprruu
unreproachful
acefiiijsttuv
justificative

acefiiillmnot
mellification
acefiiimnortt
metrification
acefiiinnortu
reunification
acefiiinoprtt
petrification
acefiiinorstv
versification
acefiiinosttt
testification
acefiillnoort
refocillation
acefiillprsuy
superficially
acefiiorsttty
testificatory
acefilllmoprs
scalpelliform
acefilllooorr
Corolliflorae
acefilloorrsu
coralliferous
acefilnoorrrw
carrion-flower
acefinnoorssy
confessionary
acefinnorrtty
confraternity
acefinorssstu
fractiousness
acefinorsssuu
furaciousness
aceggghiinnnr
change-ringing
acegghiinsttw
casting-weight
acegghillllnny
challengingly
acegghiooopr z
zoogeographic
aceggilloopty
Egyptological
aceggilnnoruy
encouragingly
aceggilnoosty
gynaecologist
aceghhimoprrt
thermographic
aceghhnooprrr
chronographer
aceghhooprrsy
orchesography
aceghiilnnstu
launching-site
aceghiilopstt
phlogisticate
aceghiimmnnow
mowing-machine
aceghiimnnosw
sowing-machine
aceghiimnpprw
whipping-cream

aceghiimoprss
seismographic
aceghiinoptty
pathogenicity
aceghilllooty
theologically
aceghillnoopr
nephrological
phrenological
aceghillnoosv
school-leaving
aceghillnootu
untheological
aceghilloopps
psephological
aceghilmnoprt
chrome-plating
aceghilmorrty
hygrometrical
aceghilnorssu
soul-searching
aceghiloosstt
eschatologist
aceghilorrrty
chlorargyrite
aceghilorrstt
cloister-garth
aceghimnnnort
chrome-tanning
aceghimooprrt
ergatomorphic
aceghinnooprt
anthropogenic
aceghinnoprru
unreproaching
aceghnoopprsy
pharyngoscope
aceghopprrrty
cryptographer
aceghopprrsty
spectrography
acegiiilnoopt
geopolitician
acegiiinortty
iatrogenicity
acegiikklnttw
walking-ticket
acegiikknprtt
parking-ticket
acegiikllnnpt
nickel-plating
acegiiilllnoss
illogicalness
acegiillmooss
seismological
acegiillnoost
neologistical
acegiillnrtuv
revictualling
acegiillostty
egotistically
acegiilmnoort
goniometrical

acegiilnosttu
gesticulation
acegiinnnrsty
intransigency
acegiinprrstt
starting-price
acegikkllnpsu
skulking-place
acegillloorsy
serologically
acegillmnooot
entomological
acegillnnooty
ontogenically
acegillnoorsu
coralligenous
acegillnoptyy
genotypically
acegillooprty
geotropically
acegilmnopsty
salpingectomy
acegilmoosstu
cleistogamous
acegilnnoorss
congressional
acegilnnorstu
counter-signal
acegilnopppst
stopping-place
acegilnprstty
trysting-place
acegilorsttuy
gesticulatory
acegimnoopstt
magneto-optics
acegimnoprstu
pneumogastric
acegimnorsstu
gastrocnemius
aceginooprstt
prognosticate
aceglnooopsuy
polygonaceous
acegloopprssst
prospect-glass
acegmnnoorssw
Congresswoman
acehhiilmnntt
anthelminthic
acehhiinoprsz
schizophrenia
acehhilpprsyy
hyperphysical
acehhinooptty
hypothecation
acehhiopprtty
phreatophytic
acehhmmnrstuy
chrysanthemum
acehhmoooprrt
chromatophore
acehhopprstyy
psychotherapy

acehiiiklnrst
Christianlike
acehiiilrsttt
tritheistical
acehiiinnorst
corinthianise
acehiiinnprtt
antinephritic
acehiiillrstuy
heuristically
acehiilmnsssw
whimsicalness
acehiiloopprt
apheliotropic
acehiiloorstt
orthosilicate
acehiiloprrst
prehistorical
acehiimmrsstt
Christmas-time
acehiinnrssst
Christianness
acehiinooprsy
Syrophoenicia
acehiiprttvyy
hyperactivity
acehikllnorsu
unscholarlike
acehilllmoopr
allelomorphic
acehillloppst
phelloplastic
acehillloprty
plethorically
acehillmnoosu
melancholious
acehillnorsss
scholarliness
acehillnsttyy
synthetically
acehilloppriy
prophetically
acehilmnoorrs
rhinoscleroma
acehilmoprstt
thermoplastic
acehilnopprtu
unprophetical
acehilorrsstt
orchestralist
acehilpprssuy
superphysical
acehilrstttww
wristlet-watch
acehimnpsttuy
unsympathetic
acehimoprstuy
musicotherapy
acehinoorrstt
orchestration
acehinopprrst
copartnership
acehinopssttu
pentastichous

acehiopprsstt
spectatorship
acehioprrsssy
hypersarcosis
acehioprrsstt
stratospheric
acehiorsstttu
tetrastichous
acehllmooorty
alcoholometry
acehlmnooorsu
melanochroous
acehloooprrsu
rhopalocerous
acehmmopsttyy
sympathectomy
aceiiiilmprst
imperialistic
aceiiillmptvy
implicatively
aceiiilmpssst
pessimistical
aceiiilnoprsv
provincialise
aceiiilnostvv
vivisectional
aceiiimnnorrt
recrimination
aceiiimnpsstt
antisepticism
aceiiinopprtt
precipitation
aceiiinorsttt
recitationist
aceiiilllnoort
citronella-oil
aceiiillmorsty
isometrically
aceiiillnnoort
intercolonial
aceiiillnoqtuy
equinoctially
aceiiillnorrty
acrylonitrile
aceiiillnrstxy
extrinsically
aceiiilmnoprrw
crown-imperial
aceiiilmnopsst
Neo-Plasticism
neoplasticism
aceiiilmnortuv
vermiculation
aceiiilmnosssu
maliciousness
aceiiilnnoortt
interlocation
aceiiilnnopsst
non-specialist
aceiiilnnpprss
principalness
aceiiilnoopstt
police-station

aceiilnoprrtt
intertropical
aceiilnpprtty
precipitantly
aceiilnpqttuu
quintuplicate
aceiilorrttvy
correlativity
aceiimmnoorst
commiseration
aceiimnnooost
economisation
aceiimnorrrty
recriminatory
aceiimoorsttu
autoeroticism
aceiinnooprst
preconisation
aceiinnooprtt
enantiotropic
aceiinnoorsvz
conversazioni
aceiinooprrtv
incorporative
aceiinorsssuv
vicariousness
aceiinorssttu
resuscitation
aceiinosssuvv
vivaciousness
aceiinprrsttv
transcriptive
aceiiorrtttvy
retroactivity
aceilllllmrtuu
multicellular
aceilllpstyy
sylleptically
aceilllmottuu
multiloculate
aceillopprty
proleptically
aceillmmnotyy
metonymically
aceillmmrstyy
symmetrically
aceillnnnossy
nonsensically
aceillnnoostt
constellation
aceillnooprry
incorporeally
aceillnoquuvy
unequivocally
aceilmmnnortu
intercommunal
aceilmmnoprty
complimentary
aceilmmnrstuy
unsymmetrical
aceilmmottuvy
commutatively
aceilmnnoopss
companionless

aceilmnnooptt
contemplation
aceilmnnorrtu
intercolumnar
aceilmnooprss
compressional
aceilmnoprvyy
livery-company
aceilmnopsttt
contemplatist
aceilmnopttuy
pneumatolytic
aceilnnoorsty
clay-ironstone
aceilnnorsttu
interosculant
aceilnoorrstv
controversial
aceilnoprrssy
princess-royal
aceiloorptvvy
provocatively
aceimmmnooort
commemoration
aceimnnnnoost
cinnamon-stone
aceimnnnoortu
connumeration
aceimnoooopt t
onomatopoetic
aceimnorssstu
customariness
aceimooprrrss
air-compressor
aceinnnoorstt
consternation
aceinnnoorttv
contravention
aceinnnoortvy
conventionary
aceinnooorttt
contortionate
aceinnooprstt
cornet-à-piston
aceinooprrssy
processionary
aceinooprtuvv
unprovocative
aceinoorssstu
atrociousness
aceinoorsssuv
voraciousness
aceinoprrssst
conspiratress
aceinoprrsttu
perscrutation
aceioorrrsstu
stercorarious
aceiorrrssttu
stratocruiser
acellnnrsttuy
translucently
acellnoorstty
constellatory

acelmnoorsssu
clamorousness
acelmnoprrsuu
supercolumnar
acelmnssttuuu
sustentaculum
acelnoorsssuu
oraculousness
acemmmooorrty
commemoratory
acemooprsttty
prostatectomy
aceoqrrrssstu
cross-quarters
acffghiilrstt
traffic-lights
acffgilnostuy
suffocatingly
acffhhimnorty
fifth-monarchy
acffiiilnopst
spifflication
acffiiinoortt
fortification
acfghhiinprtt
pitch-farthing
acfgiiiiilnnot
lignification
acfgiiiinnnst
insignificant
acfgiiiinnost
signification
acfgiiilnnsty
significantly
acfgiiilnoort
glorification
acfgiiinorsty
significatory
acfgiilnnstyy
sanctifyingly
acfgiinnoortu
configuration
acfgillooostt
olfactologist
acfgilloortuu
futurological
acfhiiinorttu
thurification
acfhiillnoory
honorifically
acfiiiiknnotz
zinkification
acfiiiinnortt
nitrification
acfiiiinorttv
vitrification
acfiiijllnoot
jollification
acfiiijnosttu
justification
acfiiillmnoot
mollification
acfiiillnnotu
nullification

acfiiilmoprst
simplificator
acfiiilnooprt
prolification
acfiiilnoptty
pontificality
acfiiimmmnotu
mummification
acfiiimnoortt
mortification
acfiiimnostty
mystification
acfiiinorsstu
Russification
acfiijorsttuy
justificatory
acfiiillorsty
floristically
acfiilmnnostu
functionalism
acfiilmorrstu
formularistic
acfiilnnosttu
functionalist
acfillllooorr
corollifloral
acfilllorrtuu
floricultural
acfinnnooortt
confrontation
acgghhiloppry
glyphographic
acgghiklnostu
laughing-stock
acgghilopprty
glyptographic
acggilllooss
glossological
acghhhioprtyy
ichthyography
acghhiiopprsy
physiographic
acghhiioprrst
chirographist
acghhinoopsty
onychophagist
acghiiilloopsy
physiological
acghiimooprst
mastigophoric
acghilllmoooy
homologically
acghillmooopr
morphological
acghilnoopssu
sphagnicolous
acghimnnooopt
pathognomonic
acghiooopstux
toxicophagous
acghnoopprsyy
pharyngoscopy
acgiiiilnnstu
linguistician

acgiiilllossty
syllogistical
acgiiillmmnoou
immunological
acgiiillmnnopy
complainingly
acgiiillmoostt
climatologist
acgiiilmnnnopu
uncomplaining
acgiiilrrsttuu
agriculturist
acgiimmnoorrs
micro-organism
acgiimnnnooot
cognomination
acgiinnnostuy
consanguinity
acgiinnooprrt
incorporating
acgiklmnnooru
mourning-cloak
acgilllnoooty
ontologically
acgillloopty
topologically
acgillnooostv
volcanologist
acgillnoostuv
vulcanologist
acgilnnoorttu
conglutinator
acgilnorsstuv
cross-vaulting
acginooprrsss
scorpion-grass
achhiiinnorst
ornithischian
achhiiinppssy
physicianship
achhiilloopps
philosophical
achhiilnopprt
philanthropic
achhiinnnostu
Hutchinsonian
achhilmmoorss
school-marmish
achhimnoorstx
xanthochroism
achhimnoosttu
autochthonism
achhioppsstty
psychopathist
achhiorsstuuy
Ichthyosaurus
achhllmoptuyy
Cyathophyllum
achhnooorstux
xanthochroous
achhnooosttuu
autochthonous
achiiilnppprs
principalship

achiillopssty
sophistically
achiilnnrstuy
unchristianly
achiilnopprst
psilanthropic
achiimmorrstt
trichromatism
achiimnnoopps
companionship
achiimnnoortt
ornithomantic
achiiooprsstt
sophisticator
achillorrttuu
horticultural
achilmopsttyy
sympatholytic
achilnoprstty
lycanthropist
achilooopsttv
photovoltaics
achimnoorsttu
tautochronism
achinnooprssy
narcohypnosis
achmmnoooorrt
monochromator
achnooorsttuu
tautochronous
aciiiimnosttv
victimisation
aciiiilllmopty
impolitically
aciiillnnostt
scintillation
aciiillnnrsty
intrinsically
aciiillnooptt
pollicitation
aciiilmnnortu
anticlinorium
inclinatorium
aciiilmnoprsv
provincialism
aciiilmnorsty
consimilarity
aciiilnnoprst
inscriptional
aciiilnoprtvy
provinciality
aciiimnnorrty
incriminatory
aciilllmooqsu
colloquialism
aciilllooqstu
colloquialist
aciiilllssttyy
stylistically
aciillmoprttu
multiplicator
aciillnnsttuy
instinctually

aciillnoortuy
illocutionary
aciillnrsttyy
crystallinity
aciilmnooopst
compositional
aciilmnoorsuy
acrimoniously
aciilmnoortty
microtonality
aciilmprrsstu
scripturalism
aciilnnorsttu
instructional
aciilnorsttuv
voluntaristic
aciilopprstty
party-politics
aciilprrssttu
scripturalist
aciimmooprstt
compatriotism
aciimnnoosstu
sanctimonious
aciimnooprttu
protoactinium
aciinnnooprtu
pronunciation
aciinnoooprrt
incorporation
aciinnoorsttt
contristation
aciinnoprrstt
transcription
acilmnosssttu
sansculottism
acilmrrssttuu
structuralism
acilnnnnoosty
inconsonantly
acilnnoorsuvy
convulsionary
acilnnpttuuuy
unpunctuality
acilnoorrstuy
contrariously
acilnoorrsuvy
carnivorously
acilnossstttu
sansculottist
acilrrsstttuu
structuralist
acimnooorrttt
motor-traction
acinnooprsttu
constupration
acinnoprstttu
contrapuntist
acinnoqrstuwy
squinancy-wort
aclmooooppsty
omoplatoscopy
aclmorsssttuuu
strato-cumulus

acnnnooopsstt
stop-consonant
addddeeffillr
fiddle-faddler
addddeeghinpu
pudding-headed
adddeeeehllsw
swelled-headed
adddeeeflrsss
self-addressed
adddeehimnrsu
dunderheadism
adddeehlnnruy
underhandedly
adddeeiimnoww
maiden-widowed
adddegglllnosy
daddy-long-legs
adddeimnooprw
diamond-powder
addeeeehnrrtt
tender-hearted
addeeeghiknos
hide-and-go-seek
addeeeghinpss
pigheadedness
addeeegilnnnr
darning-needle
addeeehllnosw
swollen-headed
addeeehnnppru
unapprehended
addeeeilmnrst
Middle-Eastern
addeeelnrssss
dreadlessness
addeeenpprrru
underprepared
addeeffhnnoss
offhandedness
addeefilnprtt
fiddle-pattern
addeeghlnorwy
wrong-headedly
addeegimnnotu
maiden-tongued
addeegmnoorrw
wood-germander
addeegnnrssuu
unguardedness
addeehiknorsw
whiskerandoed
addeehilmnrty
earthly-minded
addeehilnppss
spindle-shaped
addeehnrrrttu
thunder-darter
addeeilmopprr
pompier-ladder
addeeimnnprru
unreprimanded
addeeimnnsssy
many-sidedness

addeeimnrstuv
misadventured
addeeinnsssuv
unadvisedness
addeemnoopssu
pseudomonades
addeennnsstuu
undauntedness
addefginoruvw
wedding-favour
addegiiknrrst
redding-straik
addegiimmnnot
Maginot-minded
addeginnnrstu
understanding
addegiooprrtw
partridge-wood
addeglnoortuy
good-naturedly
addeiiiilnsuv
individualise
addeiiinoostx
deoxidisation
addeiilnorsty
disordinately
addeiinooorst
deodorisation
addeiinoprstu
superaddition
addeiklnnrtuy
kindly-natured
addeimnnrsstu
misunderstand
addeinoopprsw
wood-sandpiper
addggilnnnoru
landing-ground
addhnnoopstuu
thousand-pound
addiiiilmnsuv
individualism
addiiiilnstuv
individualist
addiiiilntuvy
individuality
addiiiinnotuv
individuation
addiinoooprtt
Diprotodontia
adeeeeehllrrw
wheeler-dealer
adeeeeghlnrtt
gentle-hearted
adeeeegnnrrtu
unregenerated
adeeeeilnpppw
pineapple-weed
adeeeenprssst
desperateness
adeeeffgilnst
self-defeating
adeeeffiinrtt
differentiate

adeeefgghillt
eagle-flighted
adeeefhrrsttu
feather-duster
adeeefillnrty
deferentially
adeeeggimnnst
disengagement
adeeegginorst
desegregation
adeeeghilnrst
single-hearted
adeeeghilnrtw
leather-winged
adeeeghinoprt
pigeon-hearted
adeeeghllnrtu
leather-lunged
adeeeghlnopsz
lozenge-shaped
adeeegiinnoru
audio-engineer
adeeeginnnrss
endearingness
adeeeginrrstx
sex-intergrade
adeeegiopprrs
pease-porridge
adeeegiorsssu
grouse-disease
adeeeglllrtuw
well-regulated
adeeegnnrssst
estrangedness
adeeegoprrtuy
daguerreotype
adeeehhlorsuv
heave-shoulder
adeeehilmprst
simple-hearted
adeeehinrrtvw
weather-driven
adeeehlnsssst
deathlessness
adeeeiilnrrst
intersidereal
adeeeiimmnsst
immediateness
adeeeiimnnrtt
indeterminate
adeeeiimnrttv
determinative
adeeeiimprttv
premeditative
adeeeiinprsst
pedestrianise
adeeeiiorrttv
deteriorative
adeeeiklnprsv
spike-lavender
adeeeilmnrtty
determinately
adeeeilnoprss
depersonalise
adeeeimnnrttu
undeterminate
adeeeimnrsttu
underestimate
adeeeimnrsttv
advertisement
adeeeinnnrttu
unentertained
adeeeinnrssst
sedentariness
adeeeinopqrtu
equiponderate
adeeejmnostww
Jamestown-weed
adeeellmnoptv
developmental
adeeelmnrssss
dreamlessness
adeeelnnnrssu
unlearnedness
adeeemnorstuv
adventuresome
adeeenpprrttu
unperpetrated
adeeeorsstuvw
sweet-savoured
adeeffiilssst
self-satisfied
adeefginrrrty
tarry-fingered
adeefglnrrssu
regardfulness
adeefhilnnsst
left-handiness
adeefhilrsstv
silver-shafted
adeefhiortuvw
white-favoured
adeefiilprsss
self-dispraise
adeefilnoppst
self-appointed
adeefilnssstu
self-sustained
adeefinoorstt
deforestation
adeefiopsstty
safety-deposit
adeegghinnrtu
draught-engine
adeeghhorrttu
thought-reader
adeeghiinnrst
disheartening
adeeghilmnopt
dephlegmation
adeeghinnrrtw
night-wanderer
adeeghlmnnoot
gentlemanhood
adeegiiinrttt
interdigitate
adeegiilnnnrx
index-learning
adeegiknnrrrt
kindergartner
adeegillnrrst
drill-sergeant
adeegilmmorsv
mermaid's-glove
adeegimnnossy
dynamogenesis
adeegimnnprtu
unimpregnated
adeegimorsttu
deuterogamist
adeeginnrrstw
Winter-gardens
adeeginopprsv
eavesdropping
adeegnnorsssu
dangerousness
adeegoprrtuyy
daguerreotypy
adeehhilnnrst
Netherlandish
adeehhilnoott
toad-in-the-hole
adeehhimoprrt
hermaphrodite
adeehiilmmnty
dimethylamine
adeehlmnorrsy
dysmenorrheal
adeehlnoppstu
pentadelphous
adeehmnoorrsy
dysmenorrhoea
adeehmnrrsttu
thunder-master
adeehmpprsttu
trumpet-shaped
adeehnooprrtz
trapezohedron
adeeiiilnosst
dieselisation
adeeiiimnsstv
disseminative
adeeiilmnpsst
dissepimental
adeeiilmnsttt
dilettanteism
adeeiimnnortt
determination
adeeiimnnostt
sedimentation
adeeiimnoprtt
premeditation
adeeiimnorrtt
intermediator
adeeiimnprsst
pedestrianism
adeeiinoorrtt
deterioration
adeeiinoprtxy
expeditionary
adeeiinorsstt
desertisation
adeeiinorsstv
disseveration
adeeillmnrtty
detrimentally
adeeillnnrtty
interdentally
adeeillnopptw
well-appointed
adeeilnnrttvy
inadvertently
adeeilnprrstz
serpent-lizard
adeeimmprrssu
mermaid's-purse
adeeimnnoprrt
preordainment
adeeimnorsttv
demonstrative
adeeimnrrstuv
misadventurer
adeeinnnssttu
untaintedness
adeeinnopqrtu
equiponderant
adeeinoprrsst
predatoriness
adeeinoprrstt
predestinator
adeeinoprrstu
superordinate
adeeinprsstuu
unpasteurised
adeeioprssstw
power-assisted
adeellnooprrw
woollen-draper
adeelnnnqstuu
Queensland-nut
adeelnnsssstu
dauntlessness
adeemoorrstux
xerodermatous
adeenpprrrstu
understrapper
adeffhillnosu
full-fashioned
adefghhilnost
sleight-of-hand
adefghinoorsw
foreshadowing
adefhilnoorss
foolhardiness
adefiiilmmrtu
multiramified
adefiillnquuy
unqualifiedly
adefiilmnosss
self-admission
adefillloruvy
ill-favouredly
adefillssttuy
distastefully
adefinnoottu
foundation-net

adefmnnorrstu
untransformed
adeggiilnnrss
niggardliness
adegginnoorvw
wood-engraving
adeghiilllnrt
drilling-lathe
adeghilnorssu
sea-shouldring
adeghinnoorty
hydrogenation
adeghinnopprs
pendragonship
adeghinoprsww
washing-powder
adeghlmnorrty
grandmotherly
adegiiilmtttu
multidigitate
adegiiinorstv
disinvigorate
adegiillnpssy
displeasingly
adegiilmnttuy
unmitigatedly
adegiilnnoops
lead-poisoning
adegiilnnottu
deglutination
adegiilnntuvy
undeviatingly
adegiimnssttu
unstigmatised
adegiimooprst
diageotropism
adegiinoosttu
autodigestion
adegiinorrstt
disintegrator
adegiklnorrsw
walking-orders
adegillmnouzz
muzzle-loading
adegillnostuu
solidungulate
adegilmoorstt
dermatologist
adegilnnoqrtu
grandiloquent
adegilnnqrsuy
squanderingly
adegilnnrsuvy
land-surveying
adeginnnosstt
standing-stone
adegllmnoruwz
mangold-wurzel
adegnooopsstu
steganopodous
adegoooprsstu
gasteropodous
adehhilooortu
Holothuroidea
adehiklnnpsss
spindle-shanks
adehilmnorxyy
hydroxylamine
adehilnnoprsw
land-ownership
adehiloooprstt
strophiolated
adehimmoopprs
paedomorphism
adehimooprrst
moderatorship
adehllooppsuy
polyadelphous
adehloprrsstu
shoulder-strap
adehnorrsttww
north-westward
adehorssttuww
south-westward
adeiiillmnstu
disilluminate
adeiiilmnorty
meridionality
adeiiilmsstuv
dissimulative
adeiiilnpsttu
platitudinise
adeiiilnrsstu
industrialise
adeiiimnnosst
dissemination
adeiiimnosstt
disestimation
adeiiinooprst
periodisation
adeiiinoopstt
epidotisation
adeiiinorsttv
derivationist
adeiiinrstttu
attitudiniser
adeiiillmnntuu
unilluminated
adeiilmnprstu
prudentialism
adeiilmnrrtuy
rudimentarily
adeiilnoosttv
devotionalist
adeiilnprsttu
prudentialist
adeiilnprttuy
prudentiality
adeiilnqsttuy
equidistantly
adeiilpsttuvy
disputatively
adeiimnnooprt
preadmonition
predomination
adeiimnnoorst
modernisation
adeiimnnopssu
unimpassioned
adeiimnnorstu
trade-unionism
adeiinnooprrt
preordination
adeiinnorsttu
trade-unionist
adeiinoprsttu
disreputation
adeiipprrstty
party-spirited
adeiirsssstuu
saussuritised
adeillnrsttuu
unillustrated
adeilmnnoprty
predominantly
adeilnoortuvy
devolutionary
adeimnnoorstt
demonstration
adeimnnoprstu
superdominant
adeimnnrstttu
untransmitted
adeinoprrrsuy
superordinary
adeinosssssuu
assiduousness
adelnoprrstty
transportedly
adelnorstuuvy
adventurously
ademnoorrstty
demonstratory
ademooorsstu
ostodermatous
adennorstuuuv
unadventurous
adenooprrrstu
proterandrous
adeooprrrttww
water-dropwort
adfgiiinorstu
disfiguration
adfiiiilmnoss
solifidianism
adgggiilnnrss
glass-grinding
adgggilnnnoru
ground-angling
adghhillnopty
diphthongally
adghiiilnnopps
island-hopping
adghiilnnortu
hound-trailing
adghiinnnnotu
Huntingdonian
adghiinnrtuww
unwithdrawing
adghinnoooprt
gonadotrophin
adghmnnooprry
gynandromorph
adgiiilnprssy
dispraisingly
adgiiinnoppst
disappointing
adgillmooopty
diplomatology
adgilnnosttuy
outstandingly
adgilnooqrsuu
grandiloquous
adhhlmooppstu
podophthalmus
adhiiknoooprt
orthopinakoid
adhiiillnoqrtu
quadrillionth
adhiimnoorssu
disharmonious
adhimnoprsssw
swordsmanship
adhinoooprstt
prosthodontia
adhinoorrstww
Wordsworthian
adhioooprrtty
diaphototropy
adhmooorsstuy
hydrosomatous
adiiiilmnosst
dissimilation
adiiiilmrssty
dissimilarity
adiiilmmoprrs
primordialism
adiiilmnosstu
dissimulation
adiiilmnrsstu
industrialism
adiiilmoprrty
primordiality
adiiilnoopsst
dispositional
adiiilnrssttu
industrialist
adiiillmmoorst
still-room-maid
adiilmnrttuuy
multitudinary
adiilnnosttuu
undulationist
adiilnopsttuu
platitudinous
aeeeefghlnrrv
half-evergreen
aeeeeggmnnprt
pre-engagement
aeeeehmopprrt
Ephemeroptera
aeeeehmorrttw
weatherometer
aeeeeilnrrsst
rensselaerite

aeeeeimnprsst
passementerie
aeeeemmnrrstu
remeasurement
aeeeemnnprrst
representamen
aeeeemnprsstt
temperateness
aeeeffghinorv
heave-offering
aeeefflmmnrrw
Flammenwerfer
aeeefghhirttw
feather-weight
aeeefgiirrrtv
refrigerative
aeeefgillnrsv
self-revealing
aeeefglnnnssw
newfangleness
aeeefillnrrty
referentially
aeeefillqrtuu
quatrefeuille
aeeefilrssstv
self-assertive
aeeefinqrttuv
frequentative
aeeefkmnnnrtt
frank-tenement
aeeeflmnrsttt
self-treatment
aeeefnorrsttw
water-softener
aeeefnprrssst
press-fastener
aeeeggimnosst
gametogenesis
aeeeghhinprss
sheep-shearing
aeeeghhirrttt
tithe-gatherer
aeeeghilnpsst
sheep-stealing
aeeeghilprrtw
telegraph-wire
aeeeghimnnrst
garnisheement
aeeeghllopprt
telegraph-pole
aeeeghlnoprrs
selenographer
aeeeghlnoprtu
rogue-elephant
aeeeghmnoprst
magnetosphere
aeeegikllmnnt
gentlemanlike
aeeegillnnprs
sleep-learning
aeeegilmnnort
noli-me-tangere
aeeegilmnprss
passenger-mile
aeeegilprrstt
register-plate
aeeegimnprrty
prayer-meeting
aeeeginorrrtt
reinterrogate
aeeehhhlrrstw
thresher-whale
aeeehhlmorrtt
heterothermal
aeeehhnoprsst
asthenosphere
aeeehilmmnprt
penthemimeral
aeeehilmnnops
phenomenalise
aeeehllmnossw
meals-on-wheels
aeeehlmnsssss
shamelessness
aeeehlnpsssss
shapelessness
aeeehlnrssst
heartlessness
aeeehloprssuu
pleasure-house
aeeehmmnorttv
earth-movement
aeeehorrsstuu
treasure-house
aeeeiilnrrrtv
irreverential
aeeeiimnrttvx
exterminative
aeeeikllmprst
kapellmeister
aeeeillnrrtvy
reverentially
aeeeilmnprssx
exemplariness
aeeeilmnprtty
intemperately
aeeeilnnsssst
essentialness
aeeeilnprttvy
penetratively
aeeeilnrssstv
versatileness
aeeeimmprstuy
empyreumatise
aeeeimnnnrttt
entertainment
aeeeimnnrsttt
reinstatement
aeeeimnorsssw
wearisomeness
aeeeimnprrstv
imperseverant
aeeeinnnsssst
insensateness
aeeeinnpsssvx
expansiveness
aeeeinnssstv
assentiveness
aeeeinnsstttv
attentiveness
aeeeinoprrstv
perseveration
aeeeinoprsstv
operativeness
aeeeinprsssvv
pervasiveness
aeeeinrsssstv
assertiveness
aeeelnprstttt
letters-patent
aeeelnssssstt
statelessness
tastelessness
aeeemmnoprttu
pneumatometer
aeeemnorstttv
overstatement
aeeemnprrsstu
prematureness
aeeennoprsttu
Enteropneusta
aeeeorrrsttuv
treasure-trove
aeeffghhilrtt
flight-feather
aeeffghimnrtt
affreightment
aeefflllnnorw
flannel-flower
aeefggiinruvw
figure-weaving
aeefghhinrrtt
three-farthing
aeefghilnorsv
half-sovereign
aeefghllrsstu
self-slaughter
aeefgiinorrrt
refrigeration
aeefgiiprrtuv
prefigurative
aeefgilnoprst
self-operating
aeefgilnrssst
self-asserting
aeefginorrstu
argentiferous
garnetiferous
aeefginrrrsuy
sugar-refinery
aeefgiorrrrty
refrigeratory
aeefgnooprsst
foot-passenger
aeefhhllnsstu
healthfulness
aeefhiilmnnrs
line-fisherman
aeefhilnsssst
faithlessness
aeefhimnnorst
refashionment
aeefhlmooprrt
mother-of-pearl
aeefhlnoopstt
elephant's-foot
aeefiillnnrty
inferentially
aeefiiloprrtv
proliferative
aeefiinrrsstt
fire-resistant
aeefillmorstu
metalliferous
aeefilnorssst
self-assertion
aeefimoprrsss
Passeriformes
aeefinnnorstu
antenniferous
aeefinnoqrttu
frequentation
aeefinnorsssu
nefariousness
aeefinoprsttu
superfetation
aeefiooprrsst
professoriate
aeefllnorstvw
fellow-servant
aeefllnsssstu
faultlessness
aeeflmnrssstu
masterfulness
aeeflnprrssuy
prayerfulness
aeeflnrssstuw
wasterfulness
aeefnnorssttu
fortunateness
aeegghillnoty
genethlialogy
aeegghoooprrz
zoogeographer
aeeggiilnnnrv
line-engraving
aeegginnoorss
organogenesis
aeeghhioprrsy
heresiography
aeeghiiknnssv
heaven-kissing
aeeghiinnsstt
satin-sheeting
aeeghillnprs
pearl-shelling
aeeghilmnnpst
gentlemanship
aeeghilmoorst
isogeothermal
aeeghilnnrtty
threateningly
aeeghimoprrss
seismographer
aeeghinorstuw
watering-house

aegiiinsttvv
investigative
aeegiiillstvy
legislatively
aeegiilmnorss
generalissimo
aeegiilnnpsst
palingenesist
aeegiilnorstt
state-religion
aeegiimnnorst
generationism
aeegiimnnortt
regimentation
aeegiimnrsttu
time-signature
aeegiinnoortt
renegotiation
aeegiinnoprrt
peregrination
aeegiinnorrtt
reintegration
aeegiinorrttv
interrogative
aeegiklnrsttw
street-walking
aeegillinprst
selling-plater
aeegillmnrstv
serving-mallet
aeegillnrstvy
everlastingly
aeegilloopsst
spelaeologist
aeegilnnprtty
penetratingly
aeegilnnttuxy
extenuatingly
aeegilnooprst
antigropeloes
aeegiloprrtvy
prerogatively
aeegimmnoottv
magnetomotive
aeegimnnnnssu
unmeaningness
aeegimnnrttuy
integumentary
aeeginnnqrtuy
quingentenary
aeeginnossuux
exsanguineous
aeeginnpprrsv
preserving-pan
aeeginnrsttuu
signature-tune
aeeginrrssstv
transgressive
aeegiorrrsttv
tergiversator
aeegllmnnntuy
ungentlemanly
aeegllmnnotwy
gentlewomanly

aeeglmnnpsstu
puss-gentleman
aeeglmnooprry
prolegomenary
aeegmnoorrstv
steam-governor
aeegnnqrrrtuu
quarter-gunner
aeehhhkrrrsst
thresher-shark
aeehhillnotw
hole-in-the-wall
aeehhilmmnntt
nemathelminth
aeehhilnnsstu
unhealthiness
aeehhlmmooort
homoeothermal
aeehiiipprstt
perihepatitis
aeehiiknprsty
kinesitherapy
aeehiilmnrtty
triethylamine
aeehiimmnprty
pyrimethamine
aeehilmmnnops
phenomenalism
aeehilmnnopst
phenomenalist
aeehilmnnopty
phenomenality
aeehilnnrsstu
unearthliness
aeehimnnopstu
mountain-sheep
aeehimnnpssss
misshapenness
aeehimnprssuu
superhumanise
aeehimnqssssu
squeamishness
aeehimopprrty
hypermetropia
aeehinnoprttx
xanthopterine
aeehinopsstty
enhypostatise
aeehinorssstv
overhastiness
aeehinorssstw
seaworthiness
aeehiprrrsstu
treasurership
aeehklnnsssst
thanklessness
aeehllmnnorst
shell-ornament
aeehllortttvv
throttle-valve
aeehlmnoossst
loathsomeness
aeehlmorrstwy
whoremasterly

aeehlnorrstty
north-easterly
aeehlorssttuy
south-easterly
aeehmmooprsst
metamorphoses
aeehmmopsstuy
emphysematous
aeehmnoopprtu
pneumatophore
aeehmoopprrst
spermatophore
aeehmopprstty
spermatophyte
aeehopprrttyy
pyretotherapy
aeeiiilmnprrs
preliminaries
aeeiiimnssttv
imitativeness
aeeiiilllmnnpr
premillennial
aeeiillnnptty
penitentially
aeeiillnopstt
pelletisation
aeeiilmnoprss
impersonalise
aeeiilmnrttvy
terminatively
aeeiilnnorrtt
interrelation
aeeiilnnosstv
inviolateness
aeeiilnnpsstv
plaintiveness
aeeiilnntttvy
inattentively
aeeiilnopqttu
equipotential
aeeiilnoprrtt
interpetiolar
aeeiilnoprttv
interpolative
aeeiilnorsttv
revelationist
aeeiilnorstvy
televisionary
aeeiilnprrstt
interpilaster
aeeiilnprstty
presentiality
aeeiilnqsttuy
sequentiality
aeeiilorrrttx
exterritorial
aeeiimmnorsst
mesmerisation
aeeiimnnoprtt
impenetration
aeeiimnnorttx
extermination
aeeiimnpssssv
impassiveness

aeeiimnqrsstu
equestrianism
aeeiinnoorrtt
reorientation
aeeiinnoqrstu
questionnaire
aeeiinoprrtty
repetitionary
aeeiioprrrsty
prairie-oyster
aeeiklnprrstw
water-sprinkle
aeeillmnnstty
sentimentally
aeeillmnorsst
salmon-leister
aeeillnnoptxy
exponentially
aeeillnnostxy
extensionally
aeeillnorrsvy
reversionally
aeeillnrrstty
interstellary
aeeillprstuvy
superlatively
aeeillrrrstty
terrestrially
aeeillrtttttt
tittle-tattler
aeeilmmnrsstu
semimenstrual
aeeilmnnnortv
environmental
aeeilmnnnsttu
unsentimental
aeeilmoprrtxy
extemporarily
aeeilmorrstuy
temerariously
aeeilnnnoopps
Peloponnesian
aeeilnnnoprst
anti-personnel
aeeilnnoprrst
interpersonal
aeeilnnoprstt
septentrional
aeeilnnqqtuuv
quinquevalent
aeeilnnssssst
stainlessness
aeeilnrrrsttu
unterrestrial
aeeilnrrstvvy
livery-servant
aeeiloprsstuy
erysipelatous
aeeilopsttuvx
expostulative
aeeilorrsttvy
restoratively
aeeimmnnorsst
momentariness

aeeimnnopprtt
reappointment
aeeimnoprrsst
temporariness
aeeimnorrsttv
remonstrative
aeeimnorrttxy
exterminatory
aeeinnnrssstt
transientness
aeeinooprrttx
re-exportation
aeeinoopsssst
possessionate
aeeinoprrssty
arseno-pyrites
aeeinoprssttt
Protestantise
aeeinoqrssttu
sequestration
aeeinosssstuvx
vexatiousness
aeeiooprsttv
post-operative
aeeipprrssstt
asset-stripper
aeejllorrstvy
traveller's-joy
aeellmoqrrsuy
quarrelsomely
aeelmnpprstuy
supplementary
aeemnprrrsuuy
supernumerary
aeemoprrssttu
posture-master
aeffghiknnort
thank-offering
aefggiiknrstu
figure-skating
aefggiinnrrsu
sugar-refining
aefghinnnprty
penny-farthing
aefghinnrrstu
nursing-father
aefgiiilntttt
tattie-lifting
aefgiilmnqrtu
quilting-frame
aefgiilnnstvv
snifting-valve
aefgiinoprrtu
prefiguration
aefgillnnrtuy
unfalteringly
aefgilnopprsv
self-approving
aefgilnorrsuu
granuliferous
aefginooprrtw
waterproofing
aefhhlllntuuy
unhealthfully

aefhilmnorssy
salmon-fishery
aefhnoosssstt
soothfastness
aefiiiilmnnst
infinitesimal
aefiiilnorstt
fertilisation
aefiilllnntuy
influentially
aefiillmmnttu
multifilament
aefiillnnntuu
uninfluential
aefiillopprsu
papilliferous
aefiilmnorsuu
aluminiferous
aefiilnooprrt
proliferation
aefiilnoprstu
platiniferous
aefiimnnortuv
uninformative
aefiimnooprrt
imperforation
aefiimnorsstu
staminiferous
aefiinrrsttty
interstratify
aefilmnoprstt
self-important
aefilnooprssw
passion-flower
aefilnrsstuvy
transfusively
aefimnorrstuu
frumentarious
aefioqrrstuuz
quartziferous
aeflnnorttuuy
unfortunately
aegghhlopprry
glyphographer
aegghilnnostu
tongue-lashing
aegghilnoortw
wool-gathering
aegghinnoorst
shooting-range
aegghlooprrss
glossographer
aeggiimnnrsst
singing-master
aeggiinorrttu
regurgitation
aeggimmnorsty
gyromagnetism
aeggimnooostu
geitonogamous
aegginnnoorss
non-aggression
aeghhilmnorst
light-horseman

aeghhilmnostu
lighthouseman
aeghhinpprryy
hyperphrygian
aeghhiopprrsy
physiographer
aeghhmoopprrr
morphographer
aeghiiknnprss
pinking-shears
aeghiilmmorst
semilogarithm
aeghiilnooprt
gerontophilia
aeghiinnsttux
extinguishant
aeghiinrrrstt
heart-stirring
aeghiiprrrsst
registrarship
aeghiklnorsst
stalking-horse
aeghiknnrrstt
knights-errant
aeghilloooorty
aerolithology
aeghilnoopstt
pantheologist
aeghilnorstuv
vaulting-horse
aeghilnostuuv
vaulting-house
aeghilooprsst
phraseologist
aeghimnorttuw
mouthwatering
aeghinnprrssu
pruning-shears
aeghinoprsstt
stenographist
aeghioprrsstu
surrogateship
aeghlmmnoooou
homologoumena
aeghlmmoortty
thremmatology
aeghlopprrtyy
pterylography
aeghmnooopstu
entomophagous
aeghoooprsstu
ostreophagous
aegiiimnorstt
emigrationist
aegiiinnosttv
investigation
aegiiiprrsstt
perigastritis
aegiiilloprsss
aspergillosis
aegiilmnorsyy
syringomyelia
aegiilnnpprru
purple-in-grain

aegiilnnpprtt
plate-printing
aegiilnooprrt
progenitorial
aegiilnosstuu
ustilagineous
aegiimnoprrty
primogenitary
aegiimnrrsttw
writing-master
aegiinnoorrtt
interrogation
aegiinnorrtuy
genito-urinary
aegiinorsttvy
investigatory
aegikllnorrst
roller-skating
aegilllmnssst
smelling-salts
aegillnoopstt
planetologist
aegilnnnorsuy
unreasoningly
aegilnooprrss
progressional
aegilnoppprtt
plotting-paper
aegilnorrtttw
otter-trawling
aegimmnorrsuw
measuring-worm
aegimnnoprrry
morning-prayer
aegimnooprssu
angiospermous
aegimoooopprst
apogeotropism
aeginnnprsssu
unsparingness
aeginnorrssst
transgression
aeginnprssstu
untrespassing
aeginoorrrtty
interrogatory
aeglmoossttyy
systematology
aeglnorrsssuu
garrulousness
aehhiiilmnsst
helminthiasis
aehhiinnopsty
hyphenisation
aehhillnoptty
anthophyllite
aehhilmmooort
homoiothermal
aehhimnoprstt
theanthropism
aehhimooopstt
homoeopathist
aehhinoprsttt
theanthropist

aehhiopprstyy
physiotherapy
aehhlooppressy
phosphorylase
aehhnorssttuy
hysteranthous
aehhoopprrsty
pyrophosphate
aehiiiknpsstt
kinesipathist
aehiiilmnosss
leishmaniosis
aehiiklnnprst
skirl-in-the-pan
aehiimnortttu
Titanotherium
aehiinorrsstw
airworthiness
aehilloppssty
Psilophytales
aehilmoosstux
homosexualist
aehilmoostuxy
homosexuality
aehimmnoprtuy
immunotherapy
aehimmooprsst
metamorphosis
aehimnnooprty
enantiomorphy
aehimnprstuuy
superhumanity
aehinoprrstuw
nature-worship
aehinoprsssuv
vapourishness
aehloqrrrtuuy
quarter-hourly
aehmnnooorttt
tooth-ornament
aehmnooprrtty
anthropometry
aeiiiilllmnnst
millennialist
aeiiiillmmnnns
millennianism
aeiiiillmmnnrs
millenniarism
aeiiiillmnorss
millionairess
aeiiiillmnprry
preliminarily
aeiiiillmnrsty
ministerially
aeiiiillmrrstt
triliteralism
aeiiiillmrrsvy
verisimilarly
aeiiiilmnnrstu
unministerial
aeiiiilnnosttu
luteinisation
aeiiiilnorsstt
sterilisation

aeiiilprrsstu
spiritualiser
aeiiimnoorsst
isomerisation
aeiiinnorsssv
visionariness
aeiiinnossstt
sensitisation
aeiiinpprrrtu
prairie-turnip
aeiiillnnnotty
intentionally
aeiiillnnortvy
inventorially
aeiiillnoqrtuv
ventriloquial
aeiiillnqrrstu
tranquilliser
aeiiillorrrtty
territorially
aeiiilmnnoosst
solemnisation
aeiiilmnoprsty
impersonality
aeiiilnnnnottu
unintentional
aeiiilnnnorttu
interlunation
aeiiilnnnssstu
unsaintliness
aeiiilnnooprtt
interpolation
aeiiilnnprstuy
peninsularity
aeiiilnoopprst
prepositional
aeiiilnoopsttx
sexploitation
aeiiilnoorsttt
tolerationist
aeiiilnoprstuv
pulverisation
aeiiilnorrttty
torrentiality
aeiiilnprssstu
spiritualness
aeiiiloopprrrt
proprietorial
aeiiimnnooprst
impersonation
aeiiimnnoprttt
partitionment
aeiiimnooprstt
temporisation
aeiiimnoprsssu
mispersuasion
aeiiimnossstty
systemisation
aeiiimooprssuv
semioviparous
aeiiinnooppstt
peptonisation
aeiiinnoostttu
Teutonisation

aeiinnoqrsttu
quaternionist
aeiinoopprrtx
expropriation
aeiinoorrrstt
terrorisation
aeiinoprssttv
transpositive
aeiinorrssstt
transistorise
aeikklmnnoruw
unworkmanlike
aeikllnnprrsw
lawn-sprinkler
aeiklmnoprsst
sportsmanlike
aeilllmnoosss
salmonellosis
aeillmmmnoost
monometallism
aeillmmnoostt
monometallist
aeillmnnootuy
unemotionally
aeilmnnnossuw
unwomanliness
aeilmnoprttuy
importunately
aeilmnopsstuy
pneumatolysis
aeilnnnprrttu
turnip-lantern
aeilnnorsstuv
voluntariness
aeilnooprsttt
tortoise-plant
aeilnoopsttux
expostulation
aeilnoorrtuvy
revolutionary
aeilnoorsuvxy
over-anxiously
aeilnoprrsttu
perlustration
aeiloooppprs
prosopopoeial
aeilooqrstuuz
Louis-Quatorze
aeimnnoopprtt
apportionment
aeimnnoorrstt
remonstration
aeimnooopsst
onomatopoesis
aeimnoprssttt
Protestantism
aeimorsssttt
toastmistress
aeinnorsssuuv
unsavouriness
aeinoooprrtt
proportionate
aeinooprssssy
possessionary

aeinrrsssttu
rust-resistant
aelmnnorrstty
remonstrantly
aelnnoopsstuy
spontaneously
aeloopprsttuxy
expostulatory
aemmnooorsttu
monotrematous
aemnoorrrstty
remonstratory
aenooopprrtxy
proparoxytone
affgiimnostuu
suffumigation
afghhiorrsttt
straightforth
afghiilmnnoss
salmon-fishing
afghiilnnrtty
light-infantry
afghiinoprrst
profit-sharing
afgiiklnnnppt
flint-knapping
afiiiilnoossst
fossilisation
afiiloprsssuy
fissiparously
agghhiiprsttt
straight-pight
agghhmopprsyy
sphygmography
agghiiillnnsuy
languishingly
agghiklnooppr
grappling-hook
agghilnoopsst
sphagnologist
aggiiiilnnostu
isoagglutinin
aggiiilnnstty
instigatingly
aggiiinnorttu
ingurgitation
aggiilnnopprr
grappling-iron
aggiilnqssuzz
quizzing-glass
aggillnoorsty
laryngologist
aggilooorsstt
agrostologist
aghhiillmnrst
thrashing-mill
aghhiimnnostu
mountains-high
aghhimnoorstt
orthognathism
aghhinoopprst
phonographist
aghhinooprsst
sharpshooting

aghhiooprstt
photographist
aghhiooprsty
opisthography
aghhiooprrstt
orthographist
aghhllmooopty
ophthalmology
aghhllooppsuy
phyllophagous
aghhlmnnooopt
monophthongal
aghhnooorsttu
orthognathous
aghiiilnprstt
hair-splitting
aghiilnnossty
astonishingly
aghiinnpprsst
transshipping
aghoooppprrsy
prosopography
agiiilnnnstuy
insinuatingly
agiiilnnortuy
unoriginality
agiiimnnooprt
impignoration
agiiinppprrst
spirit-rapping
agiillnnoprty
rallying-point
agiillnoossty
syllogisation
agiilmoopprst
plagiotropism
agiilmooprstt
primatologist
agiilnnoprsty
patronisingly
agiiloorsssty
Assyriologist
agiimnoorrsuv
graminivorous
agiinnoooppprt
oppignoration
agiinnoprsttt
starting-point
train-spotting
agilmmnoostuy
numismatology
agilmooopsstu
plagiostomous
agilmoorrstty
martyrologist
agilnnoppruvy
unapprovingly
agilooopprstu
plaigotropous
agimnoooprsuz
zoosporangium
agimnoprrstty
storming-party

ahhiklnorttwy
thankworthily
ahhllopprsyyy
hypsophyllary
ahhmnoooppprrt
anthropomorph
ahhnooopprsty
anthroposophy
ahiiiilnooprrt
horripilation
ahiiilnopssty
syphilisation
ahiiilnopstty
inhospitality
ahiiinprrsstv
spirit-varnish
ahiijmnnnooss
Johnsonianism
ahiilnooprsty
polyhistorian
ahiilnoorttyz
horizontality
ahiilnopprstx
xiphiplastron
ahiimnoprsstt
misanthropist
ahiinnoopstty
hypnotisation
ahijnnoprstuz
Zinjanthropus
ahillnoopssuy
anisophyllous
ahilmmooppssu
psammophilous
ahimnopprssst
sportsmanship
ahinopprrsstt
transport-ship
ahklnnoopptty
phytoplankton
ahmoooprrstuu
tauromorphous
aiiiilnnoqstu
inquisitional
aiiiilnoqrstu
inquisitorial
aiiillmnpstuy
pusillanimity
aiiilmnoprsty
postliminiary
aiiilnnostttu
institutional
aiiimmnnoorss
Morisonianism
aiiimmnnossst
Saint-Simonism
aiiimnnossstt
Saint-Simonist
aiiimnoopprrt
impropriation
aiiimnooprstv
improvisation
aiiimoprrstvx
improvisatrix

aiiinnnoosttv
innovationist
aiijnoopsttux
juxtaposition
aiillmmnoopsy
polynomialism
aiillmnopssuu
pusillanimous
aiillnnortuvy
involuntarily
aiillnooprsvy
provisionally
aiillnprstuuy
unspiritually
aiilnoooppprst
propositional
aiilnooppsstu
suppositional
aiimmnoopsttu
impostumation
aiimnopsssttu
assumptionist
aiimooprrstvy
improvisatory
aiinnooprsstt
transposition
aiinopppqrtuy
appropinquity
aiioooprsuvvv
ovoviviparous
ailmooopssstx
toxoplasmosis
ailorrsttuuuv
ultra-virtuous
bbcceejjosttu
subject-object
bbcdgiikllnou
building-block
bbceehlorrrsy
sherry-cobbler
bbceeiorrssuv
oversubscribe
bbcehmoorrstu
butcher's-broom
bbceiilmnostu
incombustible
bbceiirstttuu
butter-biscuit
bbciilmnostuy
incombustibly
bbddeegiilrru
bridge-builder
bbddeellooort
blood-boltered
bbdiiilnoosvy
division-lobby
bbeeeeeehiijs
heebie-jeebies
bbeeeeillrstt
blister-beetle
bbeeegilnrtuy
burying-beetle
bbeilmoorstuy
Bloomsburyite

bbhiiiillmops
bibliophilism
bbhiiiillopst
bibliophilist
bccceiilnopsu
concupiscible
bccceiimrrrsu
circumscriber
bccchinoooprs
bronchoscopic
bccdeikllnory
cylinder-block
bcceeiinrstty
cyberneticist
bcceeikkknorr
knickerbocker
bcceeilorrttu
turbo-electric
bccefiiiinost
bioscientific
bccegiilnnoos
incognoscible
bccegillnootx
collecting-box
bccehiillnrtu
clincher-built
bcceiiijosttv
objectivistic
bcceiiilmmnos
incommiscible
bcceiiilnnnov
inconvincible
bcceiilloopsu
ebullioscopic
bcceilnorsttu
constructible
bccenoortttuu
coconut-butter
bccghiklnoopp
chopping-block
bcdddelllooy
cold-bloodedly
bcddeeeilnnsu
undescendible
bcddeeeilnssu
deducibleness
bcddeiiiltuy
deductibility
bcddgillnooru
blood-curdling
bcdeeeilnrssu
reducibleness
bcdeefiiiltty
defectibility
bcdeegiknorst
stock-breeding
bcdeeginorrss
crossbreeding
bcdeehnorrstt
stretcher-bond
bcdeeiiilnnrs
indiscernible
bcdeeiiilptty
deceptibility

bcdeeiilnnrsu
undiscernible
bcdeeiklnrsty
tickly-benders
bcdeeloorrssu
double-crosser
bcdehilmooorr
chlorobromide
bcdeiiiilnrty
incredibility
bcdeiiilnnrsy
indiscernibly
bcdeiilnnrsuy
undiscernibly
bcdeiilnsssuu
undiscussible
bcdiiiloprtuy
producibility
bceeeeffilrsv
effervescible
bceeeehlrrstu
beetle-crusher
bceeefgiinnrr
birefringence
bceeefiilmprt
imperfectible
bceeefprrstuu
subprefecture
bceeegillnort
co-belligerent
bceeegilnoors
bernicle-goose
bceeehknrrstu
trunk-breeches
bceeeiilmpprt
imperceptible
bceeeijnosstv
objectiveness
bceeeinnnrrsu
incense-burner
bceegiklnrsuw
swingebuckler
bceehirsttuw
witches-butter
bceeiiilprtty
receptibility
bceeiilmpprty
imperceptibly
bceeiilnnortv
inconvertible
bceeiilnpsstu
insusceptible
bceeiilpprrst
prescriptible
bceeilnnortuv
unconvertible
bceeilnpsstuu
unsusceptible
bceffgiiknooo
booking-office
bceghilnoooty
biotechnology
bceghkoooprtu
pocket-borough

bcegiklnosttu
sucking-bottle
bcehhmmnoooty
honeycomb-moth
bcehilmrsttuw
tumbler-switch
bceiilmnoopss
incompossible
bceiilnnortvy
inconvertibly
bceiilnoprrtu
incorruptible
bceiilnpsstuy
insusceptibly
bceijlnstuuvy
subjunctively
bceilmnoopryy
polyembryonic
bceilorsttuvy
obstructively
bceinorsttuuv
unobstructive
bceiooprrssss
probe-scissors
bcggiiklnnosw
swinging-block
bcghhilnottuu
boulting-hutch
bcghilnoooory
chronobiology
bcghilooopsyy
psychobiology
bcgiiiilorrty
corrigibility
bcgiiloooorsty
cryobiologist
bcgiklmnnootu
mounting-block
bcginoosstuuu
subcontiguous
bchiilllooppsy
polyphloisbic
bciiiiilmmsty
immiscibility
bciiiiilnntvy
invincibility
bciiiloorrsty
corrosibility
bciilnoprrtuy
incorruptibly
bciimmnoosssu
subcommission
bcinnoosstuuu
subcontinuous
bddeeflnootuu
double-founted
bddeeglnootuu
double-tongued
bddeehloosttu
double-shotted
bddeeiilnosty
disobediently
bddeeiimmnost
disembodiment

bddeeijlnootu
double-jointed
bddeeilnnrssu
unbridledness
bddeennnossuu
unboundedness
bddeiinrsttuu
undistributed
bddeilnnorssw
word-blindness
bddeilnrstuuy
undisturbedly
bdeeefgilnott
feeding-bottle
bdeeeflrttuwy
butterfly-weed
bdeeefmmnorru
founder-member
bdeeegiinnrrt
interbreeding
bdeeegilrrstt
trestle-bridge
bdeeehillmnsu
unembellished
bdeeeiillnnss
indelibleness
bdeeeillllowy
yellow-bellied
bdeeeimmmnrst
dismemberment
bdeeelnnssssu
unblessedness
bdeeelnprsstu
suspender-belt
bdeeenopssstt
bespottedness
bdeeffhllosuu
double-shuffle
bdeefiiilnsty
defensibility
bdeeghinnoruu
unneighboured
bdeegiillnrwy
bewilderingly
bdeegiilmnost
disobligement
bdeeginnnnssu
unbendingness
bdeeginoottuu
tongue-doubtie
bdeehhlmmotuu
humble-mouthed
bdeeiiilnttxy
extendibility
bdeeiilsttuw
subtile-witted
bdeeiklnrstty
kittly-benders
bdeellnoossss
bloodlessness
bdeelnnossssu
boundlessness
bdeffiinostuu
diffusion-tube

bdefggiiilnrt
lifting-bridge
bdeghhinoooru
neighbourhood
bdegiiiilstty
digestibility
bdegiijlnrruy
jerry-building
bdegiillmnssy
dissemblingly
bdegiimnnorru
mourning-bride
bdegillnoorst
soldering-bolt
bdeginnoooprt
pontoon-bridge
bdehiioprsstu
subeditorship
bdehjnoorruuu
bonheur-du-jour
bdehnoooprstu
boustrophedon
bdeiiiilnntvy
invendibility
bdeiiiilrttvy
divertibility
bdeilnnnosssw
snow-blindness
bdeiloprsstu
Lepidostrobus
bdeilooqrstuu
double-or-quits
bdffiiiilstuy
diffusibility
bdggiiillnosy
disobligingly
bdgginnorruuy
burying-ground
bdhiiiiinnost
disinhibition
bdhiiiinorsty
disinhibitory
bdiiillosstuy
dissolubility
beeeefhinorrt
thereinbefore
beeeegillmnsw
well-beseeming
beeeegimnnsss
beseemingness
beeeehilnprrs
reprehensible
beeeehilnstww
betweenwhiles
beeeelllrsstt
belles-lettres
beeegggilnrtt
begging-letter
beeeghilnprst
sleeping-berth
beeegiilllnss
illegibleness
beeegiimnrttt
time-bettering

beeegilllnrty
belligerently
beeegilmnnsuy
unbeseemingly
beeegimmnnrru
unremembering
beeegimnorssy
embryogenesis
beeehillmmnst
embellishment
beeehilnprrsy
reprehensibly
beeeiilnprssx
inexpressible
beeeiilprrrss
irrepressible
beeeilnprsssu
supersensible
beeeilnprssux
unexpressible
beeeimmnrrstu
reimbursement
beefginorsttt
first-begotten
beefginrrsttu
butter-fingers
beefhoorrrstt
foster-brother
beefiiillrtxy
reflexibility
beefillmorsuu
umbelliferous
beegghiilmrrt
thimble-rigger
beeggiiilmntu
time-beguiling
beeggiilnnnss
beginningless
beegiiiillrty
re-eligibility
beegiillnnuvy
unbelievingly
beehiklnorrtu
unbrotherlike
beehillorstww
whistle-blower
beehilnorrsst
brotherliness
beehipprrssty
presbytership
beeiiilmmprss
impermissible
beeiiilnnsssv
invisibleness
beeiiilnsttxy
extensibility
beeiiilrrstvy
reversibility
beeiilmnprssu
unimpressible
beeiilnoprrss
irresponsible
beeiilnorrstv
introversible
beeiilnprssxy
inexpressibly
beeiilprrrssy
irrepressibly
beeiilrrttuvy
retributively
beeillnnosssu
insolubleness
beeilnprsssuy
supersensibly
beeilnrsstuvy
subserviently
beeiloqrstuuu
turquoise-blue
beeinooqrstuu
bone-turquoise
beeinorssstuv
obtrusiveness
beellmoorstuy
troublesomely
beennoossstuu
bounteousness
beffginnorrtu
burnt-offering
beffhilrsttuy
butterfly-fish
befgiiilnrstu
filibustering
befgilloorsuu
globuliferous
befiiiillntxy
inflexibility
befiiilmrsstu
filibusterism
befiilorsstuu
filibusterous
befilnnosstuu
bountifulness
begghiilnnttu
lightning-tube
begghmnooorru
borough-monger
beggiiiillnty
negligibility
beggilnoorttt
globe-trotting
beghilnnoruuy
unneighbourly
beghimnoprstw
bowstring-hemp
begiiiiillnty
ineligibility
begiillmoprtt
pilgrim-bottle
begillmnnrtuy
untremblingly
begillnnotuwy
yellow-bunting
behiiiimnostx
exhibitionism
behiiiinosttx
exhibitionist
behiiiloprtvy
prohibitively
beiiiilmrssty
remissibility
beiiiilnnssty
insensibility
beiiiilrsstty
resistibility
beiiilmmprssy
impermissibly
beiiilnosstty
ostensibility
beiilnoosssuv
obliviousness
beiilnoprrssy
irresponsibly
beiilnorstuvy
inobtrusively
beiioprssttuu
subreptitious
beillmnopstuv
plumbisolvent
beilnorstuuvy
unobtrusively
beimnopssstuu
bumptiousness
beinnoooosssux
obnoxiousness
bellmnoopstuv
plumbosolvent
belnoorssstuu
troublousness
benoorrstttuu
trouser-button
bfilloorstuuu
tubuliflorous
bfilmmoorrstu
strombuliform
bghhnoorttuu
button-through
bgiimnnorrrru
burning-mirror
bhhmoopprrryy
rhombporphyry
bhiiilmoprstt
timbrophilist
bhlmooprsttuu
sulphur-bottom
biiiilmmopsss
impossibilism
biiiilmopssst
impossibilist
biiiilmopssty
impossibility
bilooopprrsuy
opprobriously
cccceeinnopsu
concupiscence
ccccegiimnnoo
meningococcic
cccceiikkllty
clickety-click
cccceiooprstt
streptococcic
cccdeeeenrrsu
recrudescence
cccdeeenrrsuy
recrudescency
cccdeiimnrsuu
uncircumcised
cccdhiiooprs
dichrooscopic
cccdiimnortuu
circumduction
cccdimorrtuuy
circumductory
ccceeeennoss
consenescence
ccceeefimnrru
circumference
ccceeehilmort
electrochemic
ccceeennossy
consenescency
ccceefilmnruu
circumfluence
ccceehhirrsuv
church-service
ccceehioprstu
Cercopithecus
ccceeilooprst
electroscopic
ccceffhhiorru
church-officer
cccefhkkooort
cock-of-the-rock
cccegimnnoosu
meningococcus
ccceiimostyz
schizomycetic
ccceiimmnooor
microeconomic
ccceiinnortty
concentricity
ccceilmprstuy
circumspectly
ccceiooprrsst
spectroscopic
ccceooprssttu
streptococcus
ccciimnorstuu
succinctorium
ccddeeginnnos
condescending
ccddeellnotuw
well-conducted
ccdeeeeefnrsv
defervescence
ccdeeeefnrsvy
defervescency
ccdeeeeilnqsu
deliquescence
ccdeeefilnost
self-conceited
ccdeeefllost
self-collected
ccdeeehiimnst
medicine-chest
ccdeeeinnosst
conceitedness

ccdeeelllorty
recollectedly
ccdeeellnnotw
well-connected
ccdeeellnortu
unrecollected
ccdeeellnosst
collectedness
ccdeeennnorss
concernedness
ccdeefilnostv
self-convicted
ccdeehilorrty
hydroelectric
ccdeeimoorrtt
microdetector
ccdeeinnnooss
condescension
ccdeeinoopruw
owner-occupied
ccdeeinoppruu
unpreoccupied
ccdeeiooprstu
deuteroscopic
ccdeejnnortuu
unconjectured
ccdeelnnnoruy
unconcernedly
ccdeelnoopprw
copple-crowned
ccdeginnnoort
connecting-rod
ccdehklnoortu
round-the-clock
ccdehkloopprt
cock-throppled
ccdeiinnnoost
disconnection
ccdeiinnoorst
disconcertion
ccdeimnoorstu
semiconductor
ccdeimoosstuy
discomycetous
ccdelmnooopuu
leuco-compound
ccdginnnnootu
non-conducting
ccdhinooprstu
conductorship
ccdiimnnoopuy
pycnoconidium
cceeeeeffnrsv
effervescence
cceeeefflnors
efflorescence
cceeeeffnrsvy
effervescency
cceeeelmnortt
electrocement
cceeeffiosttv
cost-effective
cceeefginnrtu
centrifugence
cceeefilnnors
inflorescence
cceeefilorrrt
ferroelectric
cceeefnoorrrt
ferroconcrete
cceeehhiiknnr
chinkerinchee
cceeehlnorsst
clothes-screen
cceeehmooprrt
chemoreceptor
cceeeiiloprtz
piezoelectric
cceeeiinnnnov
inconvenience
cceeeilmnnort
reconcilement
cceeeilmorrtt
electrometric
cceeeinnnoqsu
inconsequence
cceeeinnrrrtu
intercurrence
cceeeinprsstt
spectre-insect
cceeffiiinnsu
insufficience
cceeffiiloopr
police-officer
cceefiiinprst
interspecific
prescientific
cceefinnoorty
confectionery
cceeghiinostz
schizogenetic
cceeghinopsty
psychogenetic
cceegiimnorst
geocentricism
cceegiinortty
egocentricity
cceehhhrrsstu
screech-thrush
cceehhinoorrt
heterochronic
cceehilooprtt
photoelectric
cceehimmnnost
mnemotechnics
cceehimnnorry
chimney-corner
cceehimosstyz
Schizomycetes
cceeiilnoorst
isoelectronic
cceeiilrrstuu
sericiculture
cceeiimnrtuvv
circumventive
cceeiinnnnovy
inconveniency
cceeiinnnosst
inconsistence
cceeiinnostuv
inconsecutive
cceeijmnorstu
misconjecture
cceeijnooprrt
cine-projector
cceeilnoorttu
electrocution
cceeilnostuvy
consecutively
cceeinnoopprt
preconception
cceeinnorrsst
incorrectness
cceeinooprrtu
Europocentric
cceeinooprruw
owner-occupier
cceeinorstttu
section-cutter
cceeinprrrstu
prices-current
cceeioprrsstu
prosecutrices
cceellnoorrtt
rent-collector
cceellsssssuy
successlessly
cceemnnnnortu
unconcernment
cceennooovvxx
convexo-convex
cceenoprrrtuy
petrocurrency
cceffiiinnsuy
insufficiency
ccefiiilmorst
microfelsitic
ccefiiilmrsst
self-criticism
ccefiilmnorux
circumflexion
ccefilnoosssu
self-conscious
cceghinnorsss
scorchingness
ccegiikknoppt
pocket-picking
ccegiiknnqstu
quick-scenting
ccegiilnnoppy
copying-pencil
cceginnnorsty
constringency
ccehhiinoprsz
schizophrenic
ccehiiknopsty
psychokinetic
ccehiilosstty
cholecystitis
ccehillooprst
collectorship
ccehilmnoorty
Chloromycetin®
ccehimoprrsty
psychrometric
ccehimoprssty
psychometrics
ccehioprssssu
successorship
cceiiimorsstv
viscosimetric
cceiiioprrrty
irreciprocity
cceiilnnnosty
inconsciently
cceiimnnoopst
misconception
cceiimnnortuv
circumvention
cceiimnoorrst
miscorrection
cceiimnoosssu
semiconscious
cceiinnnossty
inconsistency
cceiinnoopstt
conceptionist
cceiinnoossst
concessionist
cceiinnoosstu
conscientious
cceiinosssstu
successionist
cceijlnnotuvy
conjunctively
cceijnnnotuuv
unconjunctive
cceikloopsttu
cuckoo-spittle
cceimmooprrtu
microcomputer
cceinnooprrst
prince-consort
cceinnoossssu
consciousness
cceinorsssuwy
swine's-succory
ccelmooprssuy
cyclospermous
cceloorrsssst
cross-crosslet
ccenoorrrsttu
reconstructor
ccghhhiimrsu
High-Churchism
ccgiiilooosst
sociologistic
ccgiiknnooptt
cotton-picking
ccgiiknorsstu
scouring-stick
cchhiilopprsy
psychrophilic
cchhimoooprst
photochromics

cchhioppsssyy
psychophysics
cchiinnorssty
synchronistic
cchiinnorstyy
synchronicity
cchilnooorrru
chlorocruorin
cciilmooopsst
cosmopolitics
cciimooosstxy
mycotoxicosis
cciinnoopssuu
inconspicuous
ccilnnoossuuy
unconsciously
ccilnoopssuuy
conspicuously
ccioorrrssssw
criss-cross-row
cdddeeeglnnos
long-descended
cddeeeennprtu
unprecedented
cddeeeffinnru
undifferenced
cddeeeflmnnos
self-condemned
cddeeeglnorst
golden-crested
cddeeehirsttw
wide-stretched
cddeeemmnnoru
unrecommended
cddeehiikmnnt
kitchen-midden
cddeeiiillnors
ill-considered
cddeeiiloopps
dipleidoscope
cddeeilnnrsuy
undiscernedly
cddeeilnoosty
Dicotyledones
cddeeinosssuu
deciduousness
cddeelnnossuu
uncloudedness
cddefiimnostu
undiscomfited
cddehhiloorry
hydrochloride
cddeiiilnnpsu
undisciplined
cddeiinnnootu
unconditioned
cddiimmooossu
discommodious
cdeeeeelmorrt
decelerometer
cdeeeefinsstv
defectiveness
cdeeeefllnssy
defencelessly
cdeeeeglnnsst
neglectedness
cdeeeehnorrrt
three-cornered
cdeeeeiinnprx
inexperienced
cdeeeeinnprux
unexperienced
cdeeeeinpsstv
deceptiveness
cdeeeellprstw
well-respected
cdeeeffillstu
self-deceitful
cdeeefflnosss
self-confessed
cdeeefhklnrsw
Schwenkfelder
cdeeefiilnrtu
unelectrified
cdeeefiinnsst
deficientness
cdeeefilnopst
self-deception
cdeeefilnsstu
deceitfulness
cdeeeghiilnsw
weeding-chisel
cdeeeghinopst
pigeon-chested
cdeeegilnorrt
telerecording
cdeeeiimnnott
mine-detection
cdeeeiinnrrsv
dinner-service
cdeeeiinprstv
vice-president
cdeeeikmpqrtu
quick-tempered
cdeeeilmorrst
sclerodermite
cdeeeilnpruvy
unperceivedly
cdeeeimoprssv
decompressive
cdeeeinnnrssu
underniceness
cdeeeinssstuv
seductiveness
cdeeelloorvwy
yellow-covered
cdeeelmnopssx
complexedness
cdeeemnnoprsu
unrecompensed
cdeeennnosstt
contentedness
cdeeenpsssstu
suspectedness
cdeeffiillnst
self-inflicted
cdeeffilnnost
self-confident
cdeefgiilnrst
self-directing
cdeefiilnorst
self-direction
cdeefilprsstu
disrespectful
cdeefinnoortv
over-confident
cdeehilmnnorw
women-children
cdeehilnoortu
leucitohedron
cdeehimmnoprs
miscomprehend
cdeehimnorrsy
dysmenorrheic
cdeehllooooruw
whole-coloured
cdeehnnooopps
phonendoscope
cdeeiiimnrstt
deterministic
cdeeiiklqrsuv
quicksilvered
cdeeiilnosssu
deliciousness
cdeeiilprstvy
descriptively
cdeeiimnorstt
densitometric
cdeeijnprrsuu
jurisprudence
cdeeilloorruv
liver-coloured
cdeeilnnooprs
scolopendrine
cdeeilnoprrtw
triple-crowned
cdeeiloorrsuv
versicoloured
cdeeilorrtuvy
overcredulity
cdeeilrsttuvy
destructively
cdeeimmnoorst
endosmometric
cdeeimnooprss
decompression
cdeeinnnosstu
continuedness
cdeeinopqsttu
cinque-spotted
cdeeinprrssss
princess-dress
cdeekklnrstuu
knuckleduster
cdeeknoprsssu
sock-suspender
cdeellmnoooru
lemon-coloured
cdeellnoorwwy
yellow-crowned
cdeelmooorsuu
mouse-coloured
cdeelmoorrssu
sclerodermous
cdeelnooorstu
stone-coloured
cdeelnorsssuu
credulousness
cdeelnpsstuuy
unsuspectedly
cdeeloorrsuuv
overcredulous
cdeennooprrst
correspondent
cdeffgiilnnos
self-confiding
cdeffginoorru
ground-officer
cdefflnoorsuu
snuff-coloured
cdefgiinnnoss
confidingness
cdefiilnnostu
self-induction
cdefilnnosttu
discontentful
cdeghhikosttu
sick-thoughted
cdeghiilnorst
riding-clothes
cdeghilnnortu
underclothing
cdegiikoprrst
porridge-stick
cdegiilnnorsy
consideringly
cdegiimooopss
sigmoidoscope
cdegiinnnorsu
unconsidering
cdegiinnnostt
discontenting
cdegiinooosuy
gynodioecious
cdegilnnooory
endocrinology
cdeginnooprrs
corresponding
cdehhimnnoost
smooth-chinned
cdehhiooorrst
rhodochrosite
cdehiiioprsty
spheroidicity
cdehiikmnsttu
stick-in-the-mud
cdehiiknorsty
hydrokinetics
cdehiimnopru
perichondrium
cdehiioooprt
photoperiodic
cdehimoopprsu
pseudomorphic
cdehinnorstuu
urchin-snouted

cdehknrrsttuu
thunder-struck
cdeiiiinnsttv
indistinctive
cdeiiilmnostu
consimilitude
cdeiiilnsttvy
distinctively
cdeiiimprsstv
descriptivism
cdeiiinnsttuv
undistinctive
cdeiijlnstuvy
disjunctively
cdeiijnosssuu
judiciousness
cdeiimnooopst
decomposition
cdeiinnrsstuu
unscrutinised
cdeiinoopprsy
pycnidiospore
cdeiinoprtuww
picture-window
cdeiirsstttuv
destructivist
cdeiirstttuvy
destructivity
cdeillmoortuu
multicoloured
cdeillnorsuuy
incredulously
cdeilmnooprsu
Scolopendrium
cdeilmnoopsuy
compendiously
cdeilnorsssuu
ludicrousness
cdeiloortuuux
tic-douloureux
cdeinnooprtuv
non-productive
cdeinoooppruw
porcupine-wood
cdelmnnoooty
monocotyledon
cdelooorrttuu
trout-coloured
cdelooprttuuy
putty-coloured
cdeloorrstuuy
rusty-coloured
cdemnnnooopru
non-compounder
cdfgilnnnoouy
confoundingly
cdfiimnoorsty
disconformity
cdghiilooorst
orchidologist
cdglnnooorrtu
ground-control
cdhhiiimorrty
idiorrhythmic
cdhhimnoopruy
hypochondrium
cdhiimnnooort
mitochondrion
cdhilmooostuy
dichotomously
cdhinnoorsssy
synchondrosis
cdhmnooooprtu
ortho-compound
cdiiiinnnostt
indistinction
cdiiijlnosuuy
injudiciously
cdiiimmnoosss
discommission
cdiiinnosttuy
discontinuity
cdiiinoorsssv
cross-division
cdiinnoosstuu
discontinuous
cdimnnooooprtu
nitro-compound
cdinnnoooprtu
non-production
ceeeeeghinnpt
eighteen-pence
ceeeeeilnorrt
electioneerer
ceeeeffinsstv
effectiveness
ceeeefilnorst
free-selection
ceeeefilnsstx
self-existence
ceeeeflprrttt
letter-perfect
ceeeefmnnorrt
re-enforcement
ceeeefpprrrtt
preterperfect
ceeeeghinortt
heterogenetic
ceeeegiinoprt
epeirogenetic
ceeeehnprrstt
three-per-cents
ceeeeimnnprsu
supereminence
ceeeeinnnppty
tenpenny-piece
ceeeeinnprsuv
supervenience
ceeeeinprsstv
receptiveness
ceeeeinrssssv
recessiveness
ceeeeinrssstv
secretiveness
ceeeeinsssssvx
excessiveness
ceeeejnnrstuv
rejuvenescent
ceeeeklnoprsu
counsel-keeper
ceeeenrrttuuv
revenue-cutter
ceeeffiilntvy
ineffectively
ceeeffprrttuu
future-perfect
ceeefgilnstux
self-executing
ceeefhlnpsssu
speechfulness
ceeefiinnsstv
infectiveness
ceeefilorrsvw
flower-service
ceeefimnnorrt
reinforcement
ceeefimnprsst
imperfectness
ceeefinorrttu
counterfeiter
ceeefnnprsstu
unperfectness
ceeeghiknnotu
tongue-in-cheek
ceeeghillnopt
phellogenetic
ceeeghimnortt
thermogenetic
ceeeghirrsstt
chest-register
ceeegiiinpstt
epigeneticist
ceeegiillnnrt
intelligencer
ceeegimnoprss
species-monger
ceeehhklrsttu
Kletterschuhe
ceeehilmnoprt
nephelometric
ceeehimnoprsv
comprehensive
ceeehkloprstw
sprocket-wheel
ceeehlmorrtty
electrothermy
ceeehlnorsssu
lecherousness
ceeehmmnostyy
Hymenomycetes
ceeeiilorsttv
toilet-service
ceeeiimnnrttt
intermittence
ceeeiinoprttv
interoceptive
ceeeilmmorrst
electromerism
ceeeilmnprstu
multipresence
ceeeilmnrssss
mercilessness
ceeeilmoorttv
electromotive
ceeeilnossssv
voicelessness
ceeeilnpprrsu
pluripresence
ceeeilnprssss
pricelessness
ceeeilnsssuvx
exclusiveness
ceeeilpprstvy
perspectively
ceeeinopssttx
post-existence
ceeeinrsssuvx
excursiveness
ceeeioprrsttv
retrospective
ceeelmnnossuw
unwelcomeness
ceeemnoprstyy
Pyrenomycetes
ceeeoprrrsssv
process-server
ceeffiiilnnty
inefficiently
ceeffiilnnost
self-infection
ceeffioorrrs
ferrosoferric
ceefgiiknrrst
grief-stricken
ceefiijlnnost
self-injection
ceefiiklnorsu
nickeliferous
ceefiillnotwz
fellow-citizen
ceefiimnoprst
perfectionism
ceefiinoprstt
perfectionist
ceefilllorsuu
celluliferous
ceefilmooprst
telescopiform
ceefilnoorrtt
retroflection
ceefilnorttuy
counterfeitly
ceefinoorsssu
ferociousness
ceeflmoorrsst
recomfortless
ceeflnorrtuuy
counter-fleury
ceeghhiinpprw
whipping-cheer
ceeghhilnoptt
Phlegethontic
ceeghiiinprsv
receiving-ship
ceeghiiklmttu
Gemütlichkeit

ceeghiiklnprr
pickle-herring
ceeghiiknrstv
knight-service
ceeghiimoorst
isogeothermic
ceeghiinosssz
schizogenesis
ceeghiirrstuw
cruiser-weight
ceeghimnooprt
morphogenetic
ceeghinopsssy
psychogenesis
ceeghinorttuw
counter-weight
ceegiimnnopru
mourning-piece
ceegiimnoorrv
receiving-room
ceegillnorssv
level-crossing
ceegimnnorrty
retromingency
ceehhiimorrtu
Cheirotherium
ceehhimmooort
homoeothermic
ceehhimmorstt
thermochemist
ceehhimooprrt
heteromorphic
ceehhiooprrtt
heterotrophic
ceehhnorssttu
horse-chestnut
ceehiiklnrsss
lickerishness
ceehiimmopstt
committeeship
ceehiimorttxy
exothermicity
ceehiinprrssv
scrivenership
ceehikloprstu
prick-the-louse
ceehiknorssss
horse-sickness
ceehiloorsttu
heteroclitous
ceehiloprtvyy
hypervelocity
ceehimmnnostt
mnemotechnist
ceehimmrssstt
Messerschmitt
ceehimnnooprs
comprehension
ceehimnnorstt
ethnocentrism
ceehimnopsstu
Semnopithecus
ceehimoorstty
stoechiometry

ceehimopprrty
hypermetropic
ceehimpprrsst
spectre-shrimp
ceehinnopsssy
synecphonesis
ceehinopprrst
precentorship
ceehiooprrstu
cheiropterous
ceehlnoooprtt
photoelectron
ceehlooprrstu
electrophorus
ceehmmooorssx
sex-chromosome
ceehnooprttww
twopenceworth
ceehoooprrtt
photo-receptor
ceeiiimmmprst
metempiricism
ceeiiimmprstt
metempiricist
ceeiikklnprsw
winkle-pickers
ceeiilmnnrsty
reminiscently
ceeiilmnrsttu
lectisternium
ceeiilrrsttvy
restrictively
ceeiimnnrttty
intermittency
ceeiimnopttuv
uncompetitive
ceeiimpprsstv
perspectivism
ceeiinoprsttv
introspective
ceeillmnoqtuu
multiloquence
ceeillnsuuvxy
unexclusively
ceeilmnnooqsu
somniloquence
ceeilmnnoptty
incompetently
ceeilmnoorsuy
ceremoniously
ceeilnnooprtu
nucleo-protein
ceeilnooprrst
scleroprotein
ceeilnossstuy
necessitously
ceeilopprstvy
prospectively
ceeiloprsttty
electrotypist
ceeilorrsttuu
ostreiculture
ceeilpqrstuuy
picturesquely

ceeimmnnooptt
omnicompetent
ceeimnnoorsuu
unceremonious
ceeimnoooprrt
reception-room
ceeimnooprrss
recompression
ceeimnoopssst
compositeness
ceeinooprrssv
corresponsive
ceeinooprrstt
retrospection
ceeinoorrsssv
corrosiveness
ceeiooprssstt
stereoscopist
ceeiopprrsty
copper-pyrites
ceeioprrsstux
prosecutrixes
ceejmnoprrtuu
counter-jumper
ceekmmnoorssu
smoke-consumer
ceeknoorrsttu
counterstroke
ceekooprrsttu
trouser-pocket
ceeloopprsttu
plectopterous
ceelooprrsstt
protectorless
ceelpqrsstuuu
sculpturesque
ceelrrsssttuu
structureless
ceemmnnooptuy
pneumonectomy
ceemnnnooprtu
pronouncement
ceenoorssstuu
courteousness
cefffgiilnssu
self-sufficing
ceffgiinnsssu
sufficingness
ceffiinoosssu
officiousness
cefghiiknnopp
chopping-knife
cefgilmnnossu
self-consuming
cefhimmoorrru
ferrochromium
cefhinooprsss
confessorship
cefiiiillmnopr
penicilliform
cefiinnnooprt
non-proficient
cefiiooprsttu
profectitious

cefilmmnnoosu
self-communion
cefilnoprrtuy
perfunctorily
cegghlnoooory
geochronology
ceggiinnnorrt
groin-centring
ceggiinnnorsu
unrecognising
ceghhikortttu
through-ticket
ceghiiillnnps
spine-chilling
ceghiillnoost
lichenologist
ceghiilooosty
stoicheiology
ceghiinnnnppy
penny-pinching
ceghinnoostuu
counting-house
ceghoprrssuyy
psychosurgery
cegiiiknrtttw
ticket-writing
cegiiillnprst
still-piercing
cegiiilnoorst
co-religionist
cegiiinnoorrt
irrecognition
cegiilnoosstt
insectologist
cegiimmnnostu
time-consuming
cegiimnoorrtt
trigonometric
cegiimnorttuy
tumorgenicity
cegiinnooprss
processioning
cegiinnopprrt
intercropping
cegilmmoorsty
myrmecologist
cegiloorssttu
Etruscologist
cegimmnnooosy
gynomonoecism
ceginnoprstuy
counter-spying
ceginoprrrsss
cross-springer
cegnnoooprsty
röntgenoscopy
cegnnoorsssuu
congruousness
cehhiiinnortt
ornithichnite
cehhiiipsstty
physitheistic
cehhiiloprsty
chrysophilite

cehhiimmooort
homoiothermic
cehhiimooprrt
theriomorphic
cehhimmoooopr
homoeomorphic
cehhinoprrtyy
phycoerythrin
cehiiknopsssy
psychokinesis
cehiilmossuvy
mischievously
cehiimmooorst
homoeroticism
cehiimoorstty
stoichiometry
cehiinoooprtt
iontophoretic
cehiinopprsst
inspectorship
cehiioprrsttt
trichopterist
cehilnoostttt
cotton-thistle
cehilnopsttyy
polysynthetic
cehimoprsstty
psychometrist
cehiooprrsst
prosectorship
cehiooprrstt
protectorship
cehiooprrsttu
trichopterous
cehioopssstt
stethoscopist
cehmnoorrttuy
mother-country
ceiiilnnsttvy
instinctively
ceiiilnprstvy
inscriptively
ceiiimnopstuy
impecuniosity
ceiiimorstuvv
vivisectorium
ceiijnooprstt
projectionist
ceiiknprrssst
princess-skirt
ceiilllnoostv
violoncellist
ceiilnnnnotty
incontinently
ceiilnnoorttu
interlocution
ceiilnopssssu
suspicionless
ceiilnorrttux
interlocutrix
ceiilnrsttuvy
instructively
ceiilooprrstw
power-politics
ceiiloprrstuy
precipitously
ceiilprrsttuu
stirpiculture
ceiilrrssttuu
sericulturist
ceiimmrsssstu
music-mistress
ceiimnnorrttu
micronutrient
ceiimnnorsssu
criminousness
ceiimnoooprst
recomposition
ceiimnooprstt
protectionism
ceiimnooprttu
motion-picture
ceiinnnoosttv
conventionist
ceiinnoprttu
interpunction
ceiinnooprstt
introspection
ceiinnorsssuu
incuriousness
ceiinnrsttuuv
uninstructive
ceiinoooprsst
oneiroscopist
ceiinooprsstt
retinoscopist
ceiinooprsttt
protectionist
ceiinoorsstuv
insectivorous
ceiinoprsssstu
percussionist
ceiiooprssstv
visceroptosis
ceillmnoostty
tonsillectomy
ceilmnnooossu
mononucleosis
ceilmnopstuvy
consumptively
ceilnnoosttuy
contentiously
ceilnnorsstuu
uncourtliness
ceilnoorrttuy
interlocutory
ceiloprrssuuy
perspicuously
ceimmmnoorsty
monosymmetric
ceimmmnoorsuu
Eurocommunism
ceimmnoorstuu
Eurocommunist
ceimnnooorttu
counter-motion
ceimooppsstt
metoposcopist
ceinnnooprstt
cotton-spinner
ceinnnoosssuu
innocuousness
ceinnnoosttuu
uncontentious
ceinnoooprstu
counter-poison
ceinnoprrsstu
incorruptness
ceinooqrssstu
cross-question
ceinoorrstttv
controvertist
ceioooppprrrt
proprioceptor
cffiiilnoosuy
inofficiously
cfghiillnnnuy
unflinchingly
cfghimnnoortu
unforthcoming
cfgiiikmnosst
kissing-comfit
cfgiklnoosttu
floutingstock
cfgimnnnnooor
nonconforming
cfhilmooorrst
chloroformist
cfilnorstuuuy
infructuously
cfimnnnooorst
nonconformist
cfimnnnooorty
nonconformity
cgghhinooopuw
whooping-cough
cghhiilloorss
schoolgirlish
cghhiiloostty
ichthyologist
cghhikmnorstu
mocking-thrush
cghiiknoosstt
shooting-stick
cghiiknorsttw
throwing-stick
cghiilnoorstw
writing-school
cghiiloorsstt
Christologist
cghlnnooorsyy
synchronology
cghloooopsyyz
zoopsychology
cgiiiknnopstt
sticking-point
cgiiilloopst
oligopolistic
cgiiilmnoorst
criminologist
cgiiilmoosttv
victimologist
cgiiilnoosstu
sociolinguist
cgiimnnoprrt
microprinting
cgiijnnoorstu
coursing-joint
cgiiknnoopstt
pointing-stock
cgilnnoorsuuy
incongruously
chhiilnooppsu
unphilosophic
chhilopprsuuy
hyposulphuric
chhimmoooprst
photochromism
chhiooorssttu
orthostichous
chhiooprsstyy
psychohistory
chiiiimnorsst
histrionicism
chiiilnoprttt
lithontriptic
chiiiloooprsst
solicitorship
chiiiloopprsst
scripophilist
chiiloorssstu
lissotrichous
chiioooprrstt
proto-historic
chiiooptttxyy
phytotoxicity
chillmooprsuy
microphyllous
chilnooorssuy
isochronously
chilnoopprssu
proconsulship
chilopprrsuuy
pyrosulphuric
chimnoooprsst
monostrophics
chlnnoorssuyy
synchronously
ciiiinnstttvy
instinctivity
ciiilnrsttuuv
viniculturist
ciiilrsttuuv
viticulturist
ciillnopstuuy
punctiliously
ciilmmooopsst
cosmopolitism
ciilmnoopsstu
compulsionist
ciilnnoosstuv
convulsionist
ciimnnooopsst
monopsonistic
ciimnnooorstt
contortionism

ciimnopsttuvy
consumptivity
ciinnooorsttt
contortionist
ciinooprrsttu
corruptionist
cilmooprssuuy
promiscuously
cilmoprsstuuy
scrumptiously
cimmnnooopstu
post-communion
dddeeiinnssuv
undividedness
dddeeilnnoopr
Lepidodendron
dddeennooruww
wonder-wounded
dddehimoorsuy
hydromedusoid
dddeiiklnstwy
tiddledywinks
dddeillmnorwy
worldly-minded
ddeeeeflnnpst
self-dependent
ddeeeeilnnopt
needle-pointed
ddeeeelllopvw
well-developed
ddeeefillrtvv
velvet-fiddler
ddeeeggillnps
spindle-legged
ddeeeghilnsst
delightedness
ddeeegiilnnpp
dipping-needle
ddeeegilnpsuv
pudding-sleeve
ddeeehhnprrsu
under-shepherd
ddeeeiinrsstt
disinterested
ddeeeilnnnpty
independently
ddeeeimnprstu
undistempered
ddeeeinprssss
dispersedness
ddeefggiinnrw
wedding-finger
ddeefiiinrsuv
undiversified
ddeegginnrrru
gerund-grinder
ddeeghhinrtuw
hundredweight
ddeegiinssssu
disguisedness
ddeehilnootwy
dyed-in-the-wool
ddeeiikmnrrst
Kidderminster

ddefinooprruv
unprovided-for
ddeghiiinsstu
distinguished
ddegiiillnntw
twiddling-line
ddegiilnssuuy
undisguisedly
ddehhiloprsuy
hydrosulphide
ddehiimoosttt
smooth-dittied
ddehiklnrstuw
whistled-drunk
ddehinnoorsuu
undishonoured
ddeiiiilmsstu
dissimilitude
ddeiiillnossu
disillusioned
ddeiiinoopsst
dispositioned
ddeimnoorsstu
misunderstood
deeeeemprsttw
sweet-tempered
deeeegilnnntt
netting-needle
deeeellprrsvw
well-preserved
deeeelmnoprtv
redevelopment
deeeelnpprssx
perplexedness
deeeennprrstu
unrepresented
deeeffhiprstu
sheriff-depute
deeeffiinqrtu
equidifferent
deeeffloprsss
self-professed
deeefgiilnnrr
life-rendering
deeefginnnssu
unfeignedness
deeefgjmnortu
forejudgement
deeefgkllnosw
self-knowledge
deeefgklnoorw
foreknowledge
deeefhlnorsst
threefoldness
deeefiilmnpux
unexemplified
deeefimnnoort
forementioned
deeefinprrssv
perfervidness
deeeflllopprs
self-propelled
deeeflnorrttu
letter-founder

deeeflnrrrssu
self-surrender
deeeghilnnntu
unenlightened
deeegiiilnors
dereligionise
deeegiilnoprv
pigeon-livered
deeehilnnprsu
unreplenished
deeehinpprrst
pretendership
deeehmoprrstt
short-tempered
deeeiilnnptxy
inexpediently
deeeiimnrsttv
divertisement
deeeillorstuy
deleteriously
deeeklmmrrttu
kettledrummer
deeellnnprsty
resplendently
deeelnnsssttu
unsettledness
deeelorrrstty
street-orderly
deeemopsssttt
tempest-tossed
deeenoprrsuux
underexposure
deeenorssstux
dexterousness
deefffinorrst
first-offender
deeffiilnnrty
indifferently
deeffiinsssuv
diffusiveness
deefgghiilnrt
light-fingered
deefghiillnss
self-shielding
deefghilnoors
shingle-roofed
deefgiimnrstu
disfigurement
deefgillnnstu
self-indulgent
deefgillnnsyy
self-denyingly
deefgilmnrrsu
self-murdering
deefgilmopstu
gumple-foisted
deefiiinnoprt
predefinition
deefiilnnoops
self-opinioned
deefiknnnorsu
unforeskinned
deefilnoprssu
splendiferous

deefllnoortwy
yellow-fronted
deeflnnorssuw
wonderfulness
deefloppprsstu
self-supported
deeggiiinnnnw
winding-engine
deeghillnosuw
dwelling-house
deeghilmoosty
demythologise
deegiiklnoprw
dog-periwinkle
deegilmnoosty
sedimentology
deegilnnortuv
overindulgent
deegilnnrsuvy
undeservingly
deegilnorstuv
silver-tongued
deehhiopprrty
hypertrophied
deehhnorrstuw
thunder-shower
deehhoopprstt
phosphoretted
deehhopprsttu
phosphuretted
deehiinpprsst
presidentship
deehiknrrsttu
thunder-strike
deehilprrssuu
desulphuriser
deehknorrsttu
thunder-stroke
deeiiimmnnrst
indeterminism
deeiiimnnrstt
indeterminist
deeiikllnorsu
unsoldierlike
deeiillnorsss
soldierliness
deeiilmnnosss
dimensionless
deeiilmnnsstu
unlimitedness
deeiilnorsssu
deliriousness
deeiiloppprstt
lepidopterist
deeiilopstuxy
expeditiously
deeiimnnrtttu
unintermitted
deeiimnnssttv
disinvestment
deeiimnoorsst
endometriosis
deeiimnoprstt
redemptionist

deeiinooprrsu
uredíniospore
deeiinoprsstu
serendipitous
deeiinosssstu
seditiousness
deeilmmnopsty
disemployment
deeilmnoosssu
melodiousness
deeilmnorstuv
silver-mounted
deeilmorttuuv
overmultitude
deeilnnosttuy
tendentiously
deeilnorssstu
desultoriness
deeilnossstu
dissoluteness
deeilnprrttuy
interruptedly
deeiloopprstu
lepidopterous
deeimmnrsstuy
unsymmetrised
deeimnoorsttu
Deuteronomist
deeimoprrrssv
dress-improver
deeinnprrttuu
uninterrupted
deeioprsttuvy
topside-turvey
deeklloortuww
well-worked-out
deelloopsttwy
yellow-spotted
deelnnopsssuu
pendulousness
deennooprsssu
ponderousness
deennopssstu
unspottedness
deffgiiknnorr
drink-offering
defhiillopssw
disfellowship
defhimorrrtuu
rutherfordium
defiillnopsuu
filipendulous
defiilprstuuy
superfluidity
defillrssstuy
distressfully
defilmnnnssuu
unmindfulness
defilnnsstuuu
undutifulness
defilooorrsuy
odoriferously
degghiknnoory
good-King-Henry
degghilnooost
shooting-lodge
deggiillnopss
disgospelling
degginnooprww
powdering-gown
deghhiloprttt
troth-plighted
deghiiilprstt
light-spirited
deghiiinrsstu
distinguisher
deghillnorstu
shrill-tongued
deghinnnoosst
do-nothingness
deghinnorsstw
downrightness
deghmnooosttu
smooth-tongued
degiiilnpsstt
side-splitting
degiiilnqstuy
disquietingly
degiilnnoorrs
soldering-iron
degiilnrsssty
distressingly
degiilooprstt
pteridologist
degiimnopprrw
priming-powder
degiinoprsstu
true-disposing
degiklnorsttu
skittle-ground
degiknnoorrww
wonder-working
degimnoooprrw
powdering-room
dehhiioprrssy
hyperhidrosis
dehhiloorrstw
otherworldish
dehhiloprstuy
hydrosulphite
dehiinooppsst
deipnosophist
dehijlnoorstu
shoulder-joint
dehinnooorstt
odontornithes
deiiiklmnnott
milk-dentition
deiiilmnoostt
demolitionist
deiiilopsstvy
dispositively
deiiinnossssu
insidiousness
deiiinnosssuv
invidiousness
deiilmnoprtvy
improvidently
deiilnnopstuu
plenitudinous
deiilnoorsstu
redissolution
deiilnoosttuv
devolutionist
deiinnooprsuv
unprovisioned
deiinoopsssss
dispossession
deillnnorssuw
unworldliness
deimmmnosttuu
mutton-dummies
deinnooorsssu
inodorousness
delnopprstuuy
unsupportedly
dfgghiiillnoot
floodlighting
dfginnoooprsu
soundproofing
dfiinoorsttuu
fortitudinous
dfillrssttuuy
distrustfully
dgghinnnortuu
hunting-ground
dghhiiilnnotuw
unwithholding
dghiiiilmnnsy
diminishingly
dgiiiilnprsty
dispiritingly
dgiiimnorrrrv
driving-mirror
dgiilnnooosst
sindonologist
dgiilnoprsttw
word-splitting
dgiinnopprrtu
round-tripping
dgillnoossuuu
solidungulous
dglmnooosstu
odontoglossum
dhhiiiooprst
histiophoroid
dhiiimmooprss
isodimorphism
dhiiinoorsstv
short-division
dhiimoooprssu
isodimorphous
dhnooooprstu
odontophorous
diiiinnoopsst
indisposition
diilmnosttuuu
multitudinous
diilnorsstuuy
industriously
diinooopprrst
disproportion
dlnoooopprtty
polyprotodont
dmooprsttuvyy
topsyturvydom
eeeeeprrssttw
street-sweeper
eeeefilprrrsv
life-preserver
eeeeghilnrstw
steering-wheel
eeeeghinnnpty
eighteen-penny
eeeeghinorsst
heterogenesis
eeeeghinortty
heterogeneity
eeeeghnoorstu
heterogeneous
eeeegiinoprss
epeirogenesis
eeeegimnrrssw
messenger-wire
eeeeginnrstvy
yesterevening
eeeehinorrsvw
whereinsoever
eeeehkllrrstt
helter-skelter
eeeehlnnsttvy
seventeenthly
eeeeiimmprrst
semiperimeter
eeeeinnpsssvx
expensiveness
eeeeinnrssttv
retentiveness
eeeeinnsssstvx
extensiveness
eeeeinprrsstt
preteriteness
eeeellnpsssss
sleeplessness
eeeelnnrssssv
nervelessness
eeeelnnssssss
senselessness
eeeemnnprrstt
representment
eeeffgilllnow
fellow-feeling
eeeffgillnory
forefeelingly
eeeffinnosssv
offensiveness
eeefgillllnsv
self-levelling
eeefgilnnnssu
unfeelingness
eeefgimnprrtu
prefigurement
eeefhikopssuw
housewifeskep
eeefhknorrstu
seek-no-further

eeefiilllllmsu
millefeuilles
eeefinnprsssu
superfineness
eeefjlmnnosty
self-enjoyment
eeefllnorrttu
fortune-teller
eeegggillnpsv
level-peggings
eeegginorsssu
egregiousness
eeeghilmnnntt
enlightenment
eeeghimnorsst
thermogenesis
eeegiilmmnpss
seeming-simple
eeegiimnrrsst
Meistersinger
eeegillnssssu
guilelessness
eeegilnoorstv
venereologist
eeegilnprrsvy
perseveringly
eeegimmmnrssu
summer-seeming
eeeginnnnssuu
ungenuineness
eeegiorrrsstv
retrogressive
eeegklnoosstu
skeletogenous
eeegnoqrssstu
grotesqueness
eeehhinprstty
hypersthenite
eeehhiorrstvw
whithersoever
eeehhnnoprrtt
threepenn'orth
eeehikllmopty
keyhole-limpet
eeehilmnnprst
replenishment
eeehilmnossst
lithesomeness
eeehilmoprrty
pyrheliometer
eeehimnnnoopp
epiphenomenon
eeehllorrtttv
throttle-lever
eeehlmnnooopt
monotelephone
eeehlmnooottu
homeoteleuton
eeehlmnoosssw
wholesomeness
eeehooprrsttu
heteropterous
eeeiilnnpsvxy
inexpensively
eeeiimnprsttx
experimentist
eeeiinnnssstv
intensiveness
eeeiinnnsstvv
inventiveness
eeeiinnsssstv
sensitiveness
eeeiinqrssstu
requisiteness
eeeiinqssstux
exquisiteness
eeeiioqrstuvx
over-exquisite
eeeilnnnpssss
pennilessness
eeeilnnosssss
noiselessness
eeeilnnpsssss
spinelessness
eeeilnnpsuvxy
unexpensively
eeeilnopsssvx
explosiveness
eeeilnprsssuv
repulsiveness
eeeimmoprssty
sympiesometer
eeeimnooprttt
potentiometer
eeeinnoprsstt
septentriones
eeeinprrrsstt
interpretress
eeeklmnosssss
smokelessness
eeellmorrsssy
remorselessly
eeellnpssssu
pulselessness
eeelmmnoortuv
volumenometer
eeelmnorrsssu
unremorseless
eeelmnorstuvy
venturesomely
eeelmnostttu
out-settlement
eeelnnopssstu
plenteousness
eeelnoprssssw
powerlessness
eeennoorrsssu
erroneousness
eefffgllorstu
self-forgetful
eeffglnorsstu
forgetfulness
eeffiillrstty
self-fertility
eeffiilnnosvy
inoffensively
eefggilnnorsv
self-governing
eefghilorssst
foresightless
eefgiiinrrsst
fire-resisting
eefgiilloottw
gillie-wetfoot
eefgiilnnrrty
interferingly
eefgiinnoprrt
finger-pointer
eefgiinnoprtz
freezing-point
eefginnorssuv
unforgiveness
eefgnnoorsstt
forgottenness
eefhhiilnopst
ship-of-the-line
eefhhiiopssuw
housewifeship
eefhilnnssssu
unselfishness
eefhilnssssst
shiftlessness
eefhiorrsstyy
oyster-fishery
eefhnnorrttuu
fortune-hunter
eefiillmnostu
feuilletonism
eefiillnnossx
inflexionless
eefiillnosttu
feuilletonist
eefiillrsstty
self-sterility
eefiiloprrstu
reptiliferous
eefiimnorsttu
fermentitious
eefilllmntuy
mellifluently
eefillnnpsstu
plentifulness
eefilnnoosssu
feloniousness
eefilnrsssstu
fruitlessness
eefilooprrstu
petroliferous
eefiloprsstuy
pestiferously
eeflmnoorrstt
self-tormentor
eeflmoprrttuw
trumpet-flower
eeflnnnsstuuu
untunefulness
eeflnnrssstuu
unrestfulness
eefmnoorrsstt
stern-foremost
eegghinnnrstt
strengthening
eeggiinnnnrtu
engine-turning
eeggiinnpprsw
weeping-spring
eeggiinossstu
suggestionise
eeggijkoprryy
jiggery-pokery
eeggjllnnnosy
Jenny-long-legs
eeghhiilopsvx
high-explosive
eeghiilnnnpsw
spinning-wheel
eeghiiloorsst
heresiologist
eeghiimnnooty
inhomogeneity
eeghiinnoosst
seine-shooting
eeghijnortuwy
journey-weight
eeghiknrrrstu
hunger-striker
eeghilmnossst
lightsomeness
eeghilmnosstu
smelting-house
eeghilnssssst
sightlessness
eeghiloopr stt
herpetologist
eeghimnnooosu
inhomogeneous
eeghimnooprss
morphogenesis
eeghimnorsttt
thermosetting
eeghinorssstu
righteousness
eeghlmnnooopy
phenomenology
eegiiimnoprtv
primogenitive
eegiilllnntty
intelligently
eegiillnnnttu
unintelligent
eegiillnopwww
weeping-willow
eegiillnostuv
vitelligenous
eegiilnnrstty
interestingly
eegiilnorsssu
religiousness
eegiimnoprrtu
primogeniture
eegiimnprrttt
pretermitting
eegiinnnosssu
ingeniousness
eegiinnnrsttu
uninteresting

eegillnnnrtuy
unrelentingly
eegillnsssstu
guiltlessness
eegilmooorstt
meteorologist
eegilnnnprtuy
unrepentingly
eegiloprrssvy
progressively
eegimmnnorstv
misgovernment
eegimnnorrsty
yestermorning
eegimnprsssst
sempstressing
eeginnnosssuu
ingenuousness
eeginnnrssstt
stringentness
eeginnnrssstu
unrestingness
eeginnoppsstt
stepping-stone
eeginoorrrsst
retrogression
eeginopprssss
prepossessing
eeginoprrssuv
unprogressive
eeginorstttuw
tongue-twister
eeglmnoooprsu
prolegomenous
eegmmnorrstyy
mystery-monger
eehhiilllmnps
philhellenism
eehhiilllnpst
philhellenist
eehhmmnoooppr
morphophoneme
eehhmmooorstu
homeothermous
eehhooprrstty
heterostrophy
eehiiinpprrst
perinephritis
eehiinooprrrt
heir-portioner
eehiinoprrsst
spheristerion
eehillnossswy
yellowishness
eehilloorsstt
tortoise-shell
eehilmmnoostt
monotheletism
eehilmnrsssst
mirthlessness
eehilmorsstty
heterostylism
eehilnnorrsst
northerliness

eehilnorssstu
southerliness
eehilqrrrssuw
squirrel-shrew
eehimnoptttuu
up-to-the-minute
eehimorssssttu
housemistress
eehinoosssssu
sessions-house
eehllmnoosuwy
unwholesomely
eehlnorrsttwy
north-westerly
eehlnorssssttw
worthlessness
eehlnrssssttu
truthlessness
eehloorssttuy
heterostylous
eehlorssttuwy
south-westerly
eehmmnooptttu
up-to-the-moment
eehmnooosssttt
toothsomeness
eehmnooprstuy
hymenopterous
eehoooprrsstu
heterosporous
eeiiilnnsstvy
insensitively
eeiiimnprsstv
primitiveness
eeiillmnsssst
limitlessness
eeiilmnnprtty
impertinently
eeiilmnpsssuv
impulsiveness
eeiilmoosstty
osteomyelitis
eeiilnoorstuv
revolutionise
eeiilnoqrstuv
ventriloquise
eeiiloprsttuy
repetitiously
eeiilprstuuvv
vivisepulture
eeiimnoprrsst
pretermission
eeiimnoprsssu
imperiousness
eeiimnoprsssx
expressionism
eeiinnoprrsst
interspersion
eeiinnrssstuv
intrusiveness
eeiinoprssstx
expressionist
eeiinpprsssuv
insuppressive

eeillnoosswyy
linsey-woolsey
eeilmmmnopsty
misemployment
eeilmnnrtttuy
unremittently
eeilmpprstuvy
presumptively
eeilnnopsssst
pointlessness
eeilnnossttuy
sententiously
eeilnoprsttuy
pretentiously
eeimnopssstuu
impetuousness
eeimooprrsstt
stereotropism
eeinnoprsssuu
penuriousness
eeinnoprsttuu
unpretentious
eeinoopprssss
prepossession
eeinopprsssuv
purposiveness
eeknnoopssstu
outspokenness
eellnoopppryy
polypropylene
eelloprrsssuy
purposelessly
eelmnorssstuu
tremulousness
eelmopssttuuy
tempestuously
eelnoqrsssuuu
querulousness
eelnrssssttu
trustlessness
eemmnnoossstu
momentousness
eennoopprsstu
opportuneness
eennorsssstuu
strenuousness
eennorssstuuv
venturousness
effggilnnorsu
long-suffering
effghilnrsstu
frightfulness
effgiinnnoort
non-forfeiting
effiiloorsssu
fossiliferous
effillmnnnotu
non-fulfilment
efgghiiilnttw
weight-lifting
efgghiiinprtz
prize-fighting
efgghiilnnrty
frighteningly

efgghiinnopss
sponge-fishing
efghhllootttuw
well-thought-of
efghiiilnnstt
thing-in-itself
efgiilnrssuvv
self-surviving
efgiklnnoorwy
foreknowingly
efgillnoorvwy
overflowingly
efgkllmoootyy
folk-etymology
efhiinnrssttu
unthriftiness
efhilmnopssty
self-hypnotism
efhiooppr rsss
professorship
efhlnnrsstuuu
unhurtfulness
efiillnooprsu
polliniferous
efiilnnpsstuu
unpitifulness
efiilnoprssuu
spinuliferous
efikllnnsssuu
unskilfulness
efilllmosuuy
mellifluously
efilllnoopstu
self-pollution
efillooprrsuy
proliferously
efilnooorsstu
stoloniferous
efilnoopprrst
splinter-proof
efilnoorsssuv
frivolousness
eflloprssuuuy
superfluously
eflnoorrsssuw
sorrowfulness
eflnoprssuuuu
unsuperfluous
egghinnoopssu
sponging-house
egghinnopssuu
spunging-house
egghlmooopry
geomorphology
eggiimnossstu
suggestionism
eggiinossttu
suggestionist
eggilnooorstt
gerontologist
eghhiillmnrst
threshing-mill
eghhiiloprsty
hieroglyphist

13 EGH

eghhillmnooty
helminthology
eghhllossttuy
thoughtlessly
eghiiiknnrsst
kiss-in-the-ring
eghiillnnrsst
thrillingness
eghiilnnssstu
unsightliness
eghiilnoppstu
tippling-house
eghiilnprssst
sprightliness
eghiinnnopssu
spinning-house
eghiinnoprstu
printing-house
eghilnorstuuy
unrighteously
eghiloprstuuy
uprighteously
egiiiklnoosst
kinesiologist
egiiillorrsuy
irreligiously
egiiilnossstu
litigiousness
egiiimnoprrtx
primogenitrix
egiijnnnnnpsy
spinning-jenny
egiiilloostvx
vexillologist
egiillmnorstt
millstone-grit
egiillnnnssuw
unwillingness
egiilmnnrttuy
unremittingly
egiilmnoprsty
temporisingly
egiilnnopsstt
listening-post
egiilnnoqstuy
questioningly
egiilnnrsstuy
unresistingly
egiilnopsttv
vote-splitting
egiilnorstuvy
vertiginously
egiilnrsstty
trysting-stile
egiiloossttv
Sovietologist
egiimoprrsssv
progressivism
egiinnnoqstuu
unquestioning
egiinnssttuw
unwittingness
egiinnoorrsst
introgression

egiinnpprrsst
printing-press
egiioprrssstv
progressivist
egiklmnorsstw
smelting-works
egiknnnnossuw
unknowingness
egillllnoorwyy
yellow-yorling
egillnprsttuy
splutteringly
egilmmnoprtuu
rumelgumption
rumlegumption
egilnnnrrtuuy
unreturningly
egmmnooprssuy
gymnospermous
egnoooprrstuy
proterogynous
ehhhioopppsty
hypophosphite
ehhiiloopprss
philosophiser
ehhilmooprstu
thermophilous
ehhimmmooprs
homeomorphism
ehhioooppsst
photophoresis
ehhmmooooprsu
homeomorphous
ehhoopprrstuy
hypertrophous
ehiiilpprstty
perityphlitis
ehiiklmooprty
poikilothermy
ehiillopsstww
will-o'-the-wisps
wills-o'-the-wisp
ehiilmmnoostt
monothelitism
ehiimnooopsst
photo-emission
ehiinoooprsst
iontophoresis
ehiklorrssttw
silk-throwster
ehillnnoopquy
phylloquinone
ehilmnooopstu
entomophilous
ehilnopssstyy
polysynthesis
ehimmooprrstt
thermotropism
ehinopprrssuw
sun-worshipper
ehiooprrsssss
possessorship
ehllloopstuy
leptophyllous

ehllloprsuuwy
sulphur-yellow
ehlloprssuuuy
sulphureously
ehmmnoprtttuu
mutton-thumper
ehmmoopsstyyy
symphyseotomy
ehnnooprttwwy
twopennyworth
eiiiilnqstuvy
inquisitively
eiiiinnqstuuv
uninquisitive
eiiiinnssttvy
insensitivity
eiiillmoopsty
poliomyelitis
eiiilnstttuvy
institutively
eiiimmnoprsss
impressionism
eiiimnoprssst
impressionist
eiiinnooprstt
interposition
eiijnnorsssuu
injuriousness
eiilmnooprrty
premonitorily
eiilmnoorstuv
revolutionism
eiilmnoqrstuv
ventriloquism
eiilmoorrstuy
meritoriously
eiilnoorsttuv
revolutionist
eiilnoqrsttuv
ventriloquist
eiiloopprssst
leptospirosis
eiinnnoosssux
innoxiousness
eiinoopprsstu
superposition
eiinoprsssstu
spiritousness
eiioprrssttuu
surreptitious
eiioprsssttuu
superstitious
eijlnoopprstu
jet-propulsion
eillnoqstttuu
stultiloquent
eilnnoopprtuy
inopportunely
eilnooqrstuuv
ventriloquous
eilnorsssuuux
luxuriousness
eiloqrrsttuuy
triquetrously

einnooopssssu
poisonousness
einnooorssstu
notoriousness
emnnoorsssstu
monstrousness
emnopsssstuuu
sumptuousness
ffgiiiillmnorr
fringilliform
ffgimnnorstuu
mourning-stuff
fflllllnoooorr
roll-on-roll-off
fghhllooortuw
follow-through
fghiiillnorsuy
flourishingly
fiiimoorssst
fortississimo
fillmrssttuuy
mistrustfully
filmnrssttuuu
unmistrustful
ggghhinooortu
thorough-going
gghhiiiknnrtt
right-thinking
gghiiinnpprtt
night-tripping
ggiillnnprstu
string-pulling
ghhiilnopsstw
whistling-shop
ghiiklnnnrsuy
unshrinkingly
ghiilloopssty
syphilologist
ghiilnooorstt
ornithologist
ghiimmooprstt
thigmotropism
ghiimnoopssty
physiognomist
giiiilnnprsty
inspiritingly
giiilmnnoosuy
ignominiously
giiimnorrrrtw
mirror-writing
giilmnnoprsuy
unpromisingly
giilmnrssttuy
mistrustingly
giinnooopprrt
proportioning
gilllmoopssyy
polysyllogism
gillnnoooprst
trolling-spoon
gilmmnnrruuuy
unmurmuringly
hhimmoooprss
homomorphosis

13 IIN

hhimoooopprsu
ophiomorphous
hhimoooprrsuz
rhizomorphous
hiiillnnoqttu
quintillionth
hiiiloprstttt
lithotriptist

hiilnooprrttt
lithontriptor
hiimmnoopssty
monophysitism
hilorrstttuwy
trustworthily
himmoopsstyyy
symphysiotomy

himooopprrstt
trophotropism
hnorrstttuuwy
untrustworthy
iiinooppsstt
oppositionist
iilllorsstuuy
illustriously

iimnoooopprrst
misproportion
iinnoopprsttu
inopportunist
iinnoopprttuy
inopportunity

14 AAA

aaaaacgilmmnrt
anagrammatical
aaaabbiimnrsst
Sabbatarianism
aaaaccceehlnty
Calycanthaceae
aaaaccdeeeilps
Asclepiadaceae
aaaacdeinorsu
anacardiaceous
aaaacceeeinrrs
Sarraceniaceae
aaaacceegimrrv
Marcgraviaceae
aaaacceehimnrt
Marchantiaceae
aaaaccehhlnopt
Acanthocephala
aaaaccillprtty
paratactically
aaaacdeeehilmm
Hamamelidaceae
aaaacdeeghilor
Haloragidaceae
aaaacdeeillmry
Amaryllidaceae
aaaacdgiilmprt
paradigmatical
aaaacdiimmnost
macadamisation
aaaaceegilnnpt
Plantaginaceae
aaaacehmnorstu
amaranthaceous
aaaaceimnnrrst
sacramentarian
aaaachilpprrst
paraphrastical
aaaadeginnqrru
quadragenarian
aaaaeehiknprss
Shakespeariana
aaaaellloopprtv
palato-alveolar
aaaafiilnnprrs
infralapsarian
aaaaghimnoprst
phantasmagoria

aaaagimmprrstt
paragrammatist
aaaailnpprrssu
Supralapsarian
aaaannoprrssvw
savanna-sparrow
aaabbbeehkrrst
Sabbath-breaker
aaabbciiillmno
bibliomaniacal
aaabbeefklrstt
breakfast-table
aaabbegllnoorr
barrage-balloon
aaabccilmnnooy
cyanocobalamin
aaabcdghilnory
brachydiagonal
aaabcdhiinnrtu
Nudibranchiata
aaabceegilmnpu
Plumbaginaceae
aaabceeillmnru
bear-animalcule
aaabcehilllpty
alphabetically
aaabcehilnoppr
inapproachable
aaabcehlnoppru
unapproachable
aaabceilmnrrtu
interambulacra
aaabcghhilprty
bathygraphical
aaabcghinortyz
Zygobranchiata
aaabchilnoppry
inapproachably
aaabchlnoppruy
unapproachably
aaabddeenrrrst
standard-bearer
aaabdhimoprsss
ambassadorship
aaabdiilmnnort
intra-abdominal
aaabdiinorsstt
bastardisation

aaabeeeglmnnss
manageableness
aaabeeekprrrtz
zebra-parrakeet
aaabeegilmnrru
unmarriageable
aaabeeilnnsstt
attainableness
aaabeggiilnnpr
plea-bargaining
aaabegiillnouv
bougainvillaea
aaabegnoossssu
sausage-bassoon
aaabeiiilmnrss
Rabelaisianism
aaabeilnoopstt
palaeobotanist
aaabellnnprstt
transplantable
aaabellnnrsttu
untranslatable
aaabiilnorsttu
tabularisation
aaabllnnrsttuy
untranslatably
aaaccceehlopty
Phytolaccaceae
aaacccehilrstt
catachrestical
aaaccddeilnnor
cardinal-deacon
aaaccdefhinnnr
French-Canadian
aaaccdeiopprsu
capparidaceous
aaaccdiiloprtt
catadioptrical
aaaccdilorrsuv
cardiovascular
aaacceefiilopr
Caprifoliaceae
aaacceehilmpry
hypercalcaemia
aaacceeilrssst
scale-staircase
aaacceeinnqrtu
reacquaintance

aaacceghilloor
archaeological
aaaccehilmprtu
pharmaceutical
aaaccehlmmortw
claw-hammer-coat
aaacceilnnortx
extracanonical
aaacceinnnqtuu
unacquaintance
aaaccelmnopsuu
campanulaceous
aaaccghhilprty
tachygraphical
aaaccghiilllpr
calligraphical
aaaccghillnoor
arachnological
aaaccghiloprrt
cartographical
aaaccgillmnoop
campanological
aaacchillmorty
achromatically
aaacchillnnory
anachronically
aaacchinorrsst
narcocatharsis
aaacciiinnoptt
incapacitation
aaacciiloprstv
vicar-apostolic
aaacciilorrstt
aristocratical
aaaccillorttuy
autocratically
aaacclmoorsstu
malacostracous
aaacddeggklnor
cloak-and-dagger
aaacdefgnorruv
grace-and-favour
aaacdeiilnppru
Appendicularia
aaacdeillmoprs
Camelopardalis
aaacdfhimnnrst
handicraftsman

aaacdgmnorsstu
coastguardsman
aaacdhiinoprst
antaphrodisiac
aaacdhilnooprs
achondroplasia
aaacdiiilnorst
radicalisation
aaacdiilnnosst
scandalisation
aaaceefiloprss
Passifloraceae
aaaceegiiillrs
Sigillariaceae
aaaceegiilnstu
Ustilaginaceae
aaaceegilnnprt
captain-general
aaaceeiilnorst
aeroelastician
aaaceeiklmnprt
parliament-cake
aaaceeilnorsuv
valerianaceous
aaaceeimmnnnnt
maintenance-man
aaaceffgimnrrt
traffic-manager
aaacefgiorssux
saxifragaceous
aaaceghilmoptt
apothegmatical
aaacegiilmmprt
epigrammatical
aaacegilnoorrs
saloon-carriage
aaacegimmrrstt
grammaticaster
aaacehiilmrrsv
air-vice-marshal
aaacehiilnpttt
antipathetical
aaacehilllmpry
alphamerically
aaacehillmmtty
mathematically
aaacehillmnpru
alphanumerical
aaacehilmmnttu
unmathematical
aaacehilmooppr
pharmacopoeial
aaacehilnopprt
palaeanthropic
aaacehiloprrtx
extra-parochial
aaacehimnooppr
pharmacopoeian
aaacehooprrttt
Prototracheata
aaaceiillmnnrs
miscellanarian
aaaceiilmnorst
caramelisation

aaaceiimmnnprs
Pan-Americanism
aaaceillmnnsty
anamnestically
aaaceilmmnrsst
sacramentalism
aaaceilmnrsstt
sacramentalist
aaaceimnorsttt
castrametation
aaacfiiinnorst
Africanisation
aaacfiilnsttty
fantasticality
aaacfimnorrstw
aircraftswoman
aaacgghhiilopr
hagiographical
aaacghilmrttuu
thaumaturgical
aaacghilnopprt
pantographical
aaacghimnoprst
phantasmagoric
aaacgiillmstty
astigmatically
aaacgiilmprtty
pragmaticality
aaacgillmnorty
morganatically
aaacgillnopstv
galvanoplastic
aaacgimnooprrs
macrosporangia
aaacgimnopprtt
pantopragmatic
aaachiilmmrrst
matriarchalism
aaachiilmprrst
patriarchalism
aaachiilnopstt
chaptalisation
aaachiilnprstt
antiphrastical
aaachilossttww
shawl-waistcoat
aaaciiilnopstt
capitalisation
aaacilmnooprst
paronomastical
aaadddgnnorrst
dragon-standard
aaadeeikllmnrs
salamander-like
aaadeglnostuvy
advantageously
aaadeiilnnrtuv
valetudinarian
aaadghiooprrtu
autoradiograph
radioautograph
aaadgllnqrruuy
quadrangularly

aaadiiilnnrttu
altitudinarian
latitudinarian
aaadiiinnrtttu
attitudinarian
aaadiilnoosttv
vasodilatation
aaadiloorsttvy
vasodilatatory
aaaeeehilpprrt
Praeraphaelite
aaaeegghloppry
palaegeography
aaaeegilnpprrw
wearing-apparel
aaaeeginnprstu
septuagenarian
aaaeegmnrrsstt
sergeant-at-arms
aaaeehhiinrrtv
heavier-than-air
aaaeehimnprrty
hypernatraemia
aaaeejmnrrsstt
serjeant-at-arms
aaaefgimorrruv
marriage-favour
aaaefiilmprsst
patresfamilias
aaaeghilopprst
palaeographist
aaaegiiilmnrst
egalitarianism
aaaegimnnorstt
station-manager
aaaeginoprrstt
tetrasporangia
aaaegmmnorrttt
tetragrammaton
aaaegnoprssstu
asparagus-stone
aaaehiklmnoprx
alexipharmakon
aaaehlnopprstu
Palaeanthropus
aaaeiilmpprttt
palmatipartite
aaaeiilnnoprrs
pararosaniline
aaaeilmoppprrt
malappropriate
aaaellqqrsuuvy
quaquaversally
aaafiillmnrrxy
inframaxillary
aaaghhloprssty
thalassography
aaaghhmoprttuy
thaumatography
aaagiilnnoorst
organisational
aaagiinnnoostt
antagonisation

aaaiiiilnnostt
Italianisation
aaaiiilnoprstt
patrialisation
aaaiiimnnqrstu
antiquarianism
aaaiilnnorsttu
naturalisation
aaailnnorsttuv
transvaluation
aabbcceeegltu
cabbage-lettuce
aabbceefinorst
absorbefacient
aabbddeenrrttu
bread-and-butter
aabbdeeelmrrst
marble-breasted
aabbdggiinnnor
brobdingnagian
aabbeeelnnrssu
unbearableness
aabbeegilnnprt
rabbeting-plane
aabbeeilmnnoss
abominableness
aabbeellmnnssu
unblamableness
aabbehikorsuyz
bashi-bazoukery
aabbeimmnnpssy
namby-pambiness
aabcccdhilrtyy
brachydactylic
aabccchhilpry
brachycephalic
aabcccghiknrst
backscratching
aabccddeillosy
dodecasyllabic
aabccdeilnortt
contradictable
aabcceeelnpsst
acceptableness
aabcceelnnortu
counterbalance
aabccehiiorrtt
trichobacteria
aabccehillmops
accomplishable
aabccehnooorsu
orobanchaceous
aabcceiiorsttt
bacteriostatic
aabcceilmmrtuu
circumambulate
aabcciiilprtty
practicability
aabcciillnostu
actinobacillus
aabcciilnottuy
accountability
aabcddeelllosy
dodecasyllable

aabcddeilmnopr
bladder-campion
aabcddhinorssw
sandwich-boards
aabcdeehnnruzz
nebuchadnezzar
aabcdeeinrrstt
scatter-brained
aabcdeennprsuu
superabundance
aabcdeenrssstt
abstractedness
aabcdegiklnrrt
blank-cartridge
aabcdehiinnrtu
nudibranchiate
aabcdehoorrsst
across-the-board
aabcdhiiknopry
brachypinakoid
aabcdhiilnoprs
cardinal-bishop
aabcdiillqrsuy
quadrisyllabic
aabceeeghllprt
telegraph-cable
aabceeeghlnnss
changeableness
aabceeeghlnrss
chargeableness
aabceeekklmrrt
black-marketeer
aabceeghinprst
breathing-space
aabceehilnrsst
charitableness
aabceehiloprrr
irreproachable
aabceehlmnnrtu
unmerchantable
aabceehlnprsuu
unpurchaseable
aabceeillllmmty
emblematically
aabceeillmnpss
implacableness
aabceeimnorssz
semicarbazones
aabceeklnorrtw
tabernacle-work
aabceellnnnort
cannonball-tree
aabceelmnoprss
comparableness
aabceelnprrtuu
unrecapturable
aabcefgiilorrt
fibrocartilage
aabcefiiinottu
beautification
aabcefiinoprrt
prefabrication
aabceghhiimnnt
bathing-machine

aabceghinortyz
zygobranchiate
aabcegiillooor
aerobiological
aabceginnorrtu
bargain-counter
aabcehiillrsty
hebraistically
aabcehiilmnors
Elasmobranchii
aabcehiimmostt
biomathematics
aabcehillprtyy
hyperbatically
aabcehiloprrry
irreproachably
aabceiilloorty
aerobiotically
aabceiilrtttxy
extractability
aabceiiorssstt
bacteriostasis
aabceilllrssty
crystallisable
aabceillmorrty
barometrically
aabceilmnoopss
compassionable
aabceilnnoorst
torsion-balance
aabcelmnnorstt
marble-constant
aabcggiillooor
agrobiological
aabcghiillmoop
amphibological
aabcghiillopry
biographically
aabchilooprstu
claustrophobia
aabciiijmnnost
anti-Jacobinism
aabciiiillmprsy
imparisyllabic
aabciiilnrttty
intractability
aabciillopsty
collapsability
aabciinorssttt
abstractionist
aabcilllllopsyy
polysyllabical
aabcillorrtuu
arboricultural
aabcilmnnoottu
noctambulation
aabcilnnossttu
consubstantial
aabddeelnnrstu
understandable
aabddefiioprrs
bird-of-paradise
aabddeghillnot
Gnathobdellida

aabddegiinoort
biodegradation
aabddehnprssuy
spade-husbandry
aabdeeehnrrsst
threadbareness
aabdeeelnnrssu
unreadableness
aabdeeelnrrssw
rewardableness
aabdeeghloprrt
telegraph-board
aabdeehinrrstt
shatter-brained
aabdeelnnoprss
pardonableness
aabdefgiiillrty
deflagrability
aabdefiiiillqsu
disqualifiable
aabdeiiiilmnopr
imponderabilia
aabdeiikllmrrr
billiard-marker
aabdeiikmnorst
disembarkation
aabdeiiloorrst
solitaire-board
aabdeiiopprstv
disapprobative
aabdeilllqrsuy
quadrisyllable
aabdeloopprrrru
parlour-boarder
aabdeloprrsstw
sparrow-blasted
aabdiiiiilnstvy
inadvisability
aabdiiilnotuvy
unavoidability
aabdiinoopprst
disapprobation
aabdiooppprrsty
disapprobatory
aabeeeehhlrrtt
heather-bleater
aabeeehklnrstt
bletheranskate
aabeeeklmnrrss
remarkableness
aabeeeklmnrsst
marketableness
aabeeelmnnsstu
untameableness
aabeeelmnrsssu
measurableness
aabeeelnnorsss
reasonableness
aabeeelnnossss
seasonableness
aabeeemorrrttw
water-barometer
aabeefghilnprt
finger-alphabet

aabeefgilnnost
self-abnegation
aabeefgilnsstu
fatiguableness
aabeeflmnortty
flamboyant-tree
aabeeflnnrrstu
untransferable
aabeeflnorssuv
favourableness
aabeeflrrrstwy
strawberry-leaf
aabeeghinrrttw
water-breathing
aabeegiilmnnss
imaginableness
aabeegikmorrrr
marriage-broker
aabeehiiilrttv
rehabilitative
aabeehiilmnstz
Elizabethanism
aabeeiilnnrssv
invariableness
aabeeiilnnssst
insatiableness
aabeeiilnrrrst
irrestrainable
aabeeilmnpssss
impassableness
aabeeilnnrrstu
unrestrainable
aabeeimnnortuv
mountain-beaver
aabeelnnpssssu
unpassableness
aabeghillnnqtu
banqueting-hall
aabeghiooprrtu
autobiographer
aabegiiilmnnss
Albigensianism
aabehiiilnortt
rehabilitation
aabehilnnqsuuv
unvanquishable
aabeiiiiillnnty
inalienability
aabeiiiillnorst
liberalisation
aabeiiillnrtty
inalterability
aabeiiilmnrrst
libertarianism
aabeiiilnprsty
inseparability
aabeiiilprrrty
irreparability
aabeiillllmntuy
unmalleability
aabeiilmpttttty
attemptability
aabeiilnnntttu
tintinnabulate

aabeiilnsssttu
substantialise
aabeilmnnrsttu
intransmutable
aabeilnnorsttu
subalternation
aabeilnoprrttu
perturbational
aabekmrrrrstwy
strawberry-mark
aabelmnnrsttuu
untransmutable
aabffiiiillsty
falsifiability
aabfiiillmmnty
inflammability
aabfiillnpptuy
unflappability
aabgiiilnorsty
organisability
aabiilmnsssttu
substantialism
aabiilnnnntttu
tintinnabulant
aabiilnnnrttuy
tintinnabulary
aabiilnsssttu
substantialist
aabiilnsstttuy
substantiality
aabiinnossttu
substantiation
aabillnssttuvy
substantivally
aabilmmnnoostu
somnambulation
aacccccennooovv
concavo-concave
aacccillnorty
contracyclical
aaccceehilltty
catechetically
aaccceehilmntu
catechumenical
aaccceeiillsst
ecclesiastical
aaccehhilopps
scaphocephalic
aacccehiirrstt
characteristic
aaccehlnostuy
cyclanthaceous
aacccgiillnoor
carcinological
aaccchlloopsty
staphylococcal
aacccnnoostttu
cost-accountant
aaccddeimmoost
disaccommodate
aaccddemmnootu
unaccommodated
aaccdeeehinoop
Chenopodiaceae
aaccdeeiinrrst
disincarcerate
aaccdeeilnnopy
encyclopaedian
aaccdehiloprsy
polysaccharide
aaccdehimnoors
monosaccharide
aaccdeiillopty
apodeictically
aaccdeiinnortt
contraindicate
aaccdeillmorty
democratically
aaccdhiillnory
diachronically
aaccdhimoprsty
psychodramatic
aaccdiinnnortt
contraindicant
aaccdiinnooopr
piano-accordion
aaccdlmoorstuy
macrodactylous
aacceeeiikrstt
Rickettsiaceae
aacceefknoprtt
Pontefract-cake
aacceeghhilnrt
archgenethliac
aacceegiilnttt
telangiectatic
aacceehiilmpst
mesaticephalic
aacceehilmortt
tacheometrical
aacceehilmotuy
leucocythaemia
aacceeilorsttt
stereotactical
aacceeinnnorss
reconnaissance
aacceellnoouvv
Convolvulaceae
aacceemnnnoopr
non-compearance
aaccefhiorrssu
sacchariferous
aaccefilnosstu
self-accusation
aaccefimnnorru
circumforanean
aacceflorsstuy
self-accusatory
aacceggillnooy
gynaecological
aacceghillnopy
coelanaglyphic
aacceghilloost
eschatological
aacceghilnrrst
clear-starching
aaccegiilooptt
galactopoietic
aaccegiimnrtuv
circumnavigate
aacceginnostuy
nyctaginaceous
aaccehhiillrry
hierarchically
aaccehhloppssu
scaphocephalus
aaccehiilmnort
cheiromantical
aaccehiiloppr s
archiepiscopal
aaccehiilqrrsu
squirearchical
aaccehillortty
theocratically
aaccehinopprrt
parthenocarpic
aaccehlmooprsu
macrocephalous
aacceiilmnooss
semi-occasional
aacceiilnorrtt
recalcitration
aacceiimnopstt
misacceptation
aacceillloppty
apoplectically
aacceilprsttuy
spectacularity
aaccelnnorsuuu
ranunculaceous
aaccfiiilnoort
calorification
aaccfiiilnosst
classification
aaccfiiinnostt
sanctification
aaccfiilorssty
classificatory
aaccfnnortttuu
turf-accountant
aaccghhiilnopr
ichnographical
aaccghhiloorpr
chorographical
aaccghhiloprst
chalcographist
aaccghiilnoprz
zincographical
aaccghilmooprs
cosmographical
aaccgiilllmoot
climatological
aaccgiillmorty
tragi-comically
aaccgilllnooov
volcanological
aaccgilllnoouv
vulcanological
aacchhhinrstty
starch-hyacinth
aacchhimnnoopt
companion-hatch
aacchiillmssty
schismatically
aacchilllloptty
phyllotactical
aacchilnopstyy
psychoanalytic
aacchinnopsttu
accountantship
aacciiilmprtty
impracticality
aacciillmnostu
miscalculation
aacciilmnrsttu
circumstantial
aacciilnnooost
consociational
aacciilnprttuy
unpracticality
aacciimnoorsst
carcinomatosis
aaccilnoprrsuu
corpuscularian
aaccinnoorrtty
contractionary
aaccllmnorstyy
crystallomancy
aacddeehinoott
Chaetodontidae
aacddeehiprstt
death-practised
aacddeeiilmmnr
Middle-American
aacddhilmnoryy
hydrodynamical
aacdeeeeinoprt
Pontederiaceae
aacdeeefhmnsss
shamefacedness
aacdeeeglmnntt
gentleman-cadet
aacdeegipprrrt
cartridge-paper
aacdeehiiillntx
Hexactinellida
aacdeehiimmstt
mathematicised
aacdeehiprrtty
Trachypteridae
aacdeehlmmnooy
Monochlamydeae
aacdeeillmmnty
medicamentally
aacdeeillnqtuw
well-acquainted
aacdeeilopprtu
propaedeutical
aacdeeilprrttu
ultracrepidate
aacdeelmrrsttu
treacle-mustard
aacdeelnnnrstt
transcendental
aacdeenorsssuv
cadaverousness

aacdefillnorrw
cardinal-flower
aacdefmnnrtuuu
unmanufactured
aacdeghhooprrt
cathodographer
aacdegillmoort
dermatological
aacdehimoprssu
pseudo-archaism
aacdehlllnortw
tallow-chandler
aacdehllmotuwy
what-d'you-call-em
aacdehlnooprsu
androcephalous
aacdehmoprstuy
pachydermatous
aacdeiiiilllsty
idealistically
aacdeiiilmnost
decimalisation
aacdeiiilmorst
isodiametrical
aacdeiiimnortu
audiometrician
aacdeiilnosttu
educationalist
aacdeiilnprrst
cardinal-priest
aacdeiiloprstt
disceptatorial
aacdeiimnorsty
aerodynamicist
aacdeillnnrstu
slantendicular
aacdeilmmnorty
dynamometrical
aacdeilmnpstty
pentadactylism
aacdeilmnrttuu
unmatriculated
aacdeiloprssty
Perissodactyla
aacdeimnnnottu
uncontaminated
aacdeimnnoortt
decontaminator
aacdelnnossssu
scandalousness
aacdelnopsttuy
pentadactylous
aacdelorstttuy
tetradactylous
aacdfiiiilnopt
lapidification
aacdggilmnnnos
scandalmonging
aacdghhiloprry
hydrographical
aacdghiloprtyy
dactyliography
aacdgiilnnoott
antiodontalgic

aacdhiiillopty
idiopathically
aacdhillottuwy
what-d'you-call-it
aacdhimmnnopst
commandantship
aacdhimooprtyy
cardiomyopathy
myocardiopathy
aacdiiiilnnprs
disciplinarian
aacdiiilnoppst
disapplication
aacdiiinoossst
disassociation
aacdiilllmopty
diplomatically
aacdiillnnrstu
slantindicular
aacdilnoosstuy
anisodactylous
aaceeeeimmnprs
Menispermaceae
aaceeegipprrtt
cigarette-paper
aaceeegklrstwy
greywacke-slate
aaceeehlmostuy
thymelaeaceous
aaceeellprrstv
space-traveller
aaceeffilnotty
affectionately
aaceefghllostu
shelf-catalogue
aaceegggilrrru
luggage-carrier
aaceeggillnoy
genealogically
aaceeghhinrrst
heart-searching
aaceeghhlnoppr
encephalograph
aaceeghiimnnpr
reaping-machine
aaceeghilllnty
genethliacally
aaceeghilmpryy
hyperglycaemia
aaceeghilnopst
stegocephalian
aaceeghllopyyz
Zygophyllaceae
aaceegiillmnsv
evangelicalism
aaceegiillnnpt
palingenetical
aaceegiilnsstt
telangiectasis
aaceegillloops
spelaeological
aaceegjlmnorry
major-generalcy

aaceehhinorrst
Archaeornithes
aaceehhiooprrz
Rhizophoraceae
aaceehilllptty
telepathically
aaceehilmmntty
enthymematical
aaceehilmnpsst
emphaticalness
aaceehilnrsstt
theatricalness
aaceehilprstxy
hypercatalexis
aaceehilrrtuvx
extravehicular
aaceehiprsstty
cryptaesthesia
aaceehmnorsstu
sacrament-house
aaceehmnorstuy
aerenchymatous
aaceeiiinpprtv
inappreciative
aaceeiiloprstv
overcapitalise
aaceeiilpprtvy
appreciatively
aaceeiilprttuv
recapitulative
aaceeiimnnnrst
centenarianism
aaceeiimnnrsss
necessarianism
aaceeiinpprtuv
unappreciative
aaceeijlmnssst
majesticalness
aaceeilllmstty
telesmatically
aaceeilmmnsstu
immaculateness
aaceeilmmprtuy
empyreumatical
aaceeilnrssttu
articulateness
aaceeinrsstttv
attractiveness
aaceelmmoosstu
melastomaceous
aaceelnnopstuu
pennatulaceous
aaceelooprrrtx
extracorporeal
aaceemnnnooprt
contemporanean
aaceffinorrrtw
warrant-officer
aacefghiinprrr
preaching-friar
aacefiiilnrsst
artificialness
aacefiilooqsuu
aquifoliaceous

aacefillnosssu
fallaciousness
aacegghillopry
geographically
aacegghinoprst
steganographic
aaceggiinprrrs
spring-carriage
aaceggilnnoort
congregational
aaceghhiiloprr
hierographical
aaceghhiimnnsw
washing-machine
aaceghhiloprty
hyetographical
aaceghhimopptt
apophthegmatic
aaceghiiklmnnt
talking-machine
aaceghiilmnnnp
planing-machine
aaceghiilmooty
oligocythaemia
aaceghiimmorrt
hierogrammatic
aaceghilllmpty
phlegmatically
aaceghillmoprt
metallographic
aaceghilloprs
phraseological
aaceghilnoprst
stenographical
aaceghilopprrt
petrographical
aaceghiloprttu
telautographic
aaceghimnoprty
cinematography
aaceghinnopsww
weapon-schawing
aaceghinnppsww
wappenschawing
aacegiilllsty
legalistically
aacegiilmoprty
Malacopterygii
aacegilllopty
apologetically
aacegillmnoort
organometallic
aacegilnorttuv
congratulative
aacegilnrrttuy
rectangularity
aacehhilnnopty
phthalocyanine
aacehiillmrtty
arithmetically
aacehiillntty
antithetically
aacehiilnssttu
enthusiastical

aacehiilpprrst
periphrastical
aacehiimnosstt
schematisation
aacehiimnprrst
Petrarchianism
aacehiinnotttu
authentication
aacehiinprrstt
Petrarchianist
aacehillmnnory
enharmonically
aacehillmnopty
phonematically
aacehillmoprsy
semaphorically
aacehillmoprty
metaphorically
aacehillmpstyy
metaphysically
aacehilmnoprtu
unmetaphorical
aacehilmnpstuy
unmetaphysical
aacehkoopprrst
approach-stroke
aacehlloppstuy
platycephalous
aacehloprrssty
sphaerocrystal
aacehmnoprstuy
parenchymatous
aaceiiilnopsst
specialisation
aaceiiilnpttvy
anticipatively
aaceiiinnopprt
inappreciation
aaceiillnpstty
antiseptically
aaceiillnrttuy
inarticulately
aaceiilmnrrrtu
intramercurial
aaceiilnnorstt
centralisation
aaceiilnooppsu
papilionaceous
aaceiilnoprttu
recapitulation
aaceiilnorrtvy
early-Victorian
aaceiilnorsstu
secularisation
aaceiilopstttt
petticoat-tails
aaceiimnnrsstu
unsectarianism
aaceiinorsssuv
avariciousness
aaceilllnopsty
pleonastically
aaceillmmrstyy
asymmetrically
aaceillmnnoort
nomenclatorial
aaceillmnorrtu
intramolecular
aaceillmrtttuu
multarticulate
aaceillmssttyy
systematically
aaceilmmnoortt
commentatorial
aaceilmnnoopst
compensational
aaceilmnossstu
calamitousness
aaceilmnssttuy
unsystematical
aaceilnnnrssty
tyrannicalness
aaceilnnoorstv
conservational
conversational
aaceilnorsttux
exclaustration
aaceilnprrsstu
particularness
aaceilnrtttuvy
unattractively
aaceiloprrttuy
recapitulatory
aaceinoorrrstt
rostrocarinate
aaceklnnorstuy
cantankerously
aacellmnooprry
monocarpellary
aacelnnnorsstu
connaturalness
aacemmnoprsstu
Castanospermum
aacennoprssttu
counter-passant
aacffgiilnrsst
traffic-signals
aacfgiiinnostu
sanguification
aacfiiiiillnrty
inartificially
aacfiiillnrtuy
unartificially
aacfiiinnoopst
saponification
aacfiiinnoqttu
quantification
aacfiiinorsttt
stratification
aacfiilmorsttt
stalactitiform
aacfiilorsstty
satisfactorily
aacfiinnossttu
unsatisfaction
aacfinorssttuy
unsatisfactory
aacgghhiloprry
hygrographical
aacggilllnoory
laryngological
aacggillooorst
agrostological
aacghhiilloprt
lithographical
aacghhiloopprt
photographical
aacghhiloopprrt
orthographical
aacghhiopprrry
rhyparographic
aacghhmooprrty
chromatography
aacghillloopty
pathologically
aacghilmooprst
pharmacologist
aacghloooprstu
galactophorous
aacghloopprsyy
parapsychology
aacgiiilnprstu
paralinguistic
aacgiimnooprrs
microsporangia
aacgillloorsty
astrologically
aacgillloottuy
tautologically
aacgillmoorrty
martyrological
aacgilmooprrtu
compurgatorial
aacgilnnoorttu
congratulation
aacgimoorssttt
stomatogastric
aacginnoorrttt
contrarotating
aacglnoorrttuy
congratulatory
aachhiinorstuy
ichthyosaurian
aachhinoopprtt
anthropopathic
aachiiillnnopty
antiphonically
aachiillnooost
alcoholisation
aachiilloprsty
aphoristically
aachiilmnoprst
misanthropical
aachiimmnnoopr
morphinomaniac
aachiimnnorstt
antimonarchist
aachillopsttyy
hypostatically
aachilmoopprst
pharmacopolist
aachilnopsssyy
psychoanalysis
aachllooopppry
Polyplacophora
aachlmnoooppr
Monoplacophora
aachlooprsstty
Arctostaphylos
aaciiilllsttvy
vitalistically
aaciiillmmrstu
multiracialism
aaciiillnrstty
inartistically
aaciiilmnoppst
misapplication
aaciiilnnorttu
inarticulation
aaciiilnoprtty
anticipatorily
aaciilllrsttuy
altruistically
aaciillmmnopty
pantomimically
aaciilnooprrst
conspiratorial
aaciilnprrsttu
antiscriptural
aaciinnootttux
auto-intoxicant
aacillmnnortuy
unromantically
aacillmnoorsty
astronomically
aacillmopsttyy
asymptotically
aacilmoopprstt
protoplasmatic
aacilnnnoorstt
triconsonantal
aacilnnnosttuv
anticonvulsant
aacinooprrrstt
procrastinator
aadddffillnowy
daffadowndilly
aaddeehilnnort
neanderthaloid
aaddeelnoqrrsu
squadron-leader
aaddeinorsttuw
outward-sainted
aadeeegilmprss
spread-eagleism
aadeeegkmnrrrt
market-gardener
aadeeehiimnrrt
maidenhair-tree
aadeeehipssstu
pseudaesthesia
aadeeehlrrrsss
dress-rehearsal
aadeeeillllnprv
parallel-veined

aadeeeillllpppr
parallelepiped
aadeeeinnqsstu
inadequateness
aadeefgilllnot
dinoflagellate
aadeefhilnrtty
faint-heartedly
aadeefiilmnrst
anti-federalism
aadeefiilnorst
federalisation
aadeefiilnrstt
anti-federalist
aadeeggimnnrst
aggrandisement
aadeeghiloprrt
radiotelegraph
aadeeghippprsu
pseudepigrapha
aadeegiimnqrtu
quadrigeminate
aadeegimnnrrst
disarrangement
aadeegimnoprwz
powder-magazine
aadeegllooppy
palaeopedology
aadeehiimnrtty
diathermaneity
aadeehlnooprry
aerohydroplane
hydro-aeroplane
aadeeiilmnrstu
unmaterialised
aadeeiilnpqssu
sesquipedalian
aadeeiinnprrst
predestinarian
aadeeilllopppr
parallelopiped
aadeeillnopprs
plane-polarised
aadeeilmnorttt
tatterdemalion
aadeeilorrrstt
street-railroad
aadeeinnprsstt
antidepressant
aadeellmnprtty
departmentally
aadefiilmnorst
self-admiration
aadefiimnorstu
diamantiferous
aadefilmmnnstu
fundamentalism
aadefilmnnsttu
fundamentalist
aadefilmnnttuy
fundamentality
aadeghilnrstuw
daughters-in-law

aadegiilnnptzz
dazzle-painting
aadegiinnorrtt
intergradation
aadeginoorrrtt
retrogradation
aadehiillmnpsu
sulphanilamide
aadehinnopsssu
diaphanousness
aadehnorrsstttw
north-eastwards
aadehorssstttuw
south-eastwards
aadeiiilnosttv
devitalisation
aadeiiimnrsttv
administrative
aadeiiilllntuvy
antediluvially
aadeiillnnqruy
quadriennially
aadeiilmnnnoot
denominational
aadeiilmnoorst
demoralisation
aadeiilnnopsst
dispensational
aadeiilnooprst
depolarisation
aadeiilnoorstv
devalorisation
aadeiilnorsstt
dissertational
aadeiiopppprrst
disappropriate
aadeilnnortuuv
undervaluation
aadeinoppprrtu
unappropriated
aadelmprrssttu
mustard-plaster
aadffiiiilnost
disaffiliation
aadffiiimnorst
disaffirmation
aadfiiilnnnost
Finlandisation
aadgghiilnstvy
daylight-saving
aadgilnnoprsst
prostaglandins
aadiiilmnorstt
traditionalism
aadiiilnnorstu
solitudinarian
aadiiilnorrtty
traditionarily
aadiiilnorsttt
traditionalist
aadiiilnorttty
traditionality
aadiiimnnorstt
administration

aadiiimnrrsttx
administratrix
aadimnooorrsty
radioastronomy
aaeeefglmmnnst
self-management
aaeeefgmnnorrs
ferro-manganese
aaeeeghimnosst
haematogenesis
aaeeegmnnprrrt
prearrangement
aaeeehhinrsstv
heart-heaviness
aaeeehhiprssty
hyperaesthesia
aaeeehillmnprt
parliament-heel
aaeeeimnpprrst
reappraisement
aaeeelppprrstt
saltpetre-paper
aaeeennprrrstu
superterranean
aaeefghilnorsv
half-a-sovereign
aaeefgillnnttu
flag-lieutenant
aaeefgimnnorrs
ferromagnesian
aaeefhhorrsttt
star-of-the-earth
aaeefhilmnrttw
wreath-filament
aaeefnoorrstux
extraforaneous
aaeegghnoprrst
steganographer
aaeeghllmoprrt
metallographer
aaeeghllnoopty
palaeethnology
aaeeghllnpprtt
telegraph-plant
aaeeghnnooprty
Neopythagorean
aaeegiillnorst
Anglo-Israelite
aaeegiilnnorst
generalisation
aaeegiilnnostv
evangelisation
aaeegillmnqrtuv
gram-equivalent
aaeegilnrsstvy
asseveratingly
aaeegimmnnrrst
misarrangement
aaeegllqrrrtuy
quarter-gallery
aaeeglmnprsstu
suprasegmental
aaeegmnoprsssu
rampageousness

aaeehiimnssttt
antimetathesis
aaeehilmpprsss
plasmapheresis
aaeehimnrssstu
amateurishness
aaeehinorstttw
weather-station
aaeehmooprrrst
spermatorrhoea
aaeeiillmnnprr
premillenarian
aaeeiilnnnortt
Internationale
aaeeiilnoprrst
proletarianise
aaeeiinnprrstt
painter-stainer
aaeeilmnnooppr
paraleipomenon
aaeeilmnrsttty
testamentarily
aaeeilnnoprstt
presentational
aaeeilnnprrtty
interplanetary
aaeeinnopsssst
passionateness
aaeeinrrsstttw
water-resistant
aaeelnnnpssstu
unpleasantness
aaeemnnopprsww
newspaper-woman
aaeffgilnopttu
palagonite-tuff
aaeffiiilmorst
forisfamiliate
aaefgiilnosttu
angustifoliate
aaefiinnorrstt
fraternisation
aaefimnorrsttv
transformative
aaegghimnoprty
enigmatography
aaeggiinnorrst
grangerisation
aaeggimmnoprsu
megasporangium
aaeghhiilnrrtt
lighter-than-air
aaeghhopprrrry
rhyparographer
aaeghiiillnrtxy
exhilaratingly
aaeghikmmnnppr
knapping-hammer
aaeghimnoprsty
Pythagoreanism
aaeghimoopprry
paroemiography
aaegiiilnnostt
gelatinisation

aaegiillnoorst
allegorisation
aaegiilmnqqsuu
quinquagesimal
aaegiilnorrstu
regularisation
aaegiilnqrtuuy
equiangularity
aaegiimnrrsttv
transmigrative
aaegiinnnrsssu
sanguinariness
aaegiinnoorrst
reorganisation
aaeginoprrstuy
sauropterygian
aaegllnoopsttu
stoope-gallaunt
aaehhillopstuz
sulphathiazole
aaehilnoppsssy
psephoanalysis
aaehiopprrstt
Protospathaire
aaehippqrrstuz
sapphire-quartz
aaehlmnnoostux
xanthomelanous
aaeiiiilnrsttu
utilitarianise
aaeiiiknnorstt
keratinisation
aaeiiillmmnnrs
millenarianism
aaeiiilmnnnstv
Valentinianism
aaeiiilmnnorst
mineralisation
aaeiiilnorsttt
retaliationist
aaeiiinnnrssst
insanitariness
aaeiiinnpprttt
pinnatipartite
aaeiiinnrrstuv
universitarian
aaeiiinprssstt
antiperistasis
aaeiillmnrrtxy
intermaxillary
aaeiillnprstty
interspatially
aaeiilmnnossst
sensationalism
aaeiilmnoprrst
proletarianism
aaeiilnnorsttu
neutralisation
aaeiilnnosssstt
sensationalist
aaeiilnnossstu
sensualisation
aaeiilnoorrstv
revalorisation

aaeiilnqtttuvy
quantitatively
aaeiimoppprrst
misappropriate
aaeiinnorssstt
stationariness
aaeiinnpprrstt
antiperspirant
aaeiinoprssttu
pasteurisation
aaeillllmorrst
lamellirostral
aaeilllnprrtty
artillery-plant
aaeillmnnortuu
mountain-laurel
aaeilmnrssstux
transsexualism
aaeilmoopprstt
spatiotemporal
aaeilnnnoooprt
non-operational
aaeilnnnprttuu
ultra-Neptunian
aaeilnorrrsttt
transliterator
aaeilnorttttty
yttro-tantalite
aaeilnrrssttvy
transversality
aaeilorrrrsstt
serratirostral
aaeimmnopsssty
synaposematism
aaeimnnoorsttu
neuroanatomist
aaeinnnoprstuu
superannuation
aaejmoprrsstuy
pyjama-trousers
aaellnprrstuuy
supernaturally
aafiiimnnorrtu
uniformitarian
aafilmnnooprtt
plant-formation
aafimnnoorrstt
transformation
aaghhnoopprrty
anthropography
aaghiiinoprstt
graphitisation
aaghiiprrssttt
stratigraphist
aaghimmnnoorru
organ-harmonium
aaghoopprttuyy
autotypography
aagiiimnnsstuu
Augustinianism
aagiiimnosstttt
stigmatisation
aagiiinnnoorst
inorganisation

aagiilmmmoprst
lipogrammatism
aagiilmmoprstt
lipogrammatist
aagiiloooprsstt
parasitologist
aagiimnnorrstt
transmigration
aagimnooosssttu
angiostomatous
aagimnooprsstu
potassium-argon
aagimnorrrstty
transmigratory
aahilnoooprrtt
prothonotarial
aahinoooprrttt
prothonotariat
aahlmooprrsstv
provost-marshal
aaiiiilmnorstt
militarisation
aaiiiilmnrsttu
utilitarianism
aaiiiilnorsttv
trivialisation
aaiiiimnnrrstt
Trinitarianism
aaiiillnoosttv
volatilisation
aaiiilmnoopstt
optimalisation
aaiiinnorssstu
Russianisation
aaiilllnorsttu
illustrational
aaiillnnorstty
transitionally
aaiilmnnorssst
transmissional
aaiilmnnorsstt
mistranslation
aaiilnoopprstu
popularisation
aaiimnoorrsstz
Zoroastrianism
aaillmnnoottuw
mountain-tallow
aailmmnnorsttu
ultramontanism
aailmnnorstttu
ultramontanist
aaimmnnoorrtuw
mountain-marrow
aainnooprrsttt
transportation
abbbbeeillpprr
pribble-prabble
abbbcdginorrsu
scrubbing-board
abbcdeeeiorrsu
berberidaceous
abbcdeeiilnrss
indescribables

abbcdeeimoorst
discomboberate
abbcdeilmoostu
discombobulate
abbcdikkklnrsu
skunk-blackbird
abbceenorrsstu
subarborescent
abbddeeelorstu
double-breasted
abbdiiiilnttuy
indubitability
abbeeelnorsssv
observableness
abbeehinnooprt
phenobarbitone
abbeeikkllmmss
skimble-skamble
abbegillmnrrtu
tumbling-barrel
abbeiilqrrrstu
rabbit-squirrel
abbiiilmooprrs
probabiliorism
abbiiiloooprrst
probabiliorist
abccceeeeenrsx
exacerbescence
abccceeiimmnru
circumambience
abcccehilmnoru
council-chamber
abccceiimmnruy
circumambiency
abcccceiorstuuu
cucurbitaceous
abccciilmootxy
coxcombicality
abccdeeimnnrsu
disencumbrance
abccdeeimoorss
Scombresocidae
abccdefiiloors
blood-sacrifice
abcceeeilnnouv
unconceiveable
abcceehlmnorsu
chamber-counsel
abcceeiikrrrtu
circuit-breaker
abcceeiiillnorr
irreconcilable
abcceeillnnoru
unreconcilable
abcceeilmmnoux
excommunicable
abcceeilnnoort
concelebration
abccefhhnrsstu
Burschenschaft
abccehiinorsst
bronchiectasis
abcceiiiilnotvy
conceivability

abcceiillnorry
irreconcilably
abcceiilmmnnou
incommunicable
abcceiilnnnoos
inconscionable
abcceillnnoruy
unreconcilably
abcceilmmnnouu
uncommunicable
abcceilnnnoosu
unconscionable
abcceoooprstt
tobacco-stopper
abccgiilloory
cryobiological
abcchiloprstu
claustrophobic
abcciilmmnnouy
incommunicably
abccilnnnoosuy
unconscionably
abccinooorrstt
boa-constrictor
abcddeeilmmnos
discommendable
abcddeelmnoopu
decompoundable
abcddegiinnptu
cabinet-pudding
abcdeeeeilnssv
deceivableness
abcdeeeeknrstw
neck-sweetbread
abcdeeeellnsst
delectableness
abcdeeeghhjkty
Jack-by-the-hedge
abcdeeehiilnpr
indecipherable
abcdeeehilnpru
undecipherable
abcdeeeiilrssv
disserviceable
abcdeeeilnpsss
despicableness
abcdeeeilnrsst
creditableness
abcdeeeilprsst
disrespectable
abcdeeghijnstu
subject-heading
abcdeeiiinnott
cabinet-edition
abcdeeiilnnors
inconsiderable
abcdeeiilnorsv
indiscoverable
abcdeeiimossty
Basidiomycetes
abcdeeilmnoops
indecomposable
abcdeeilnorsuv
undiscoverable

abcdeeklnnorru
blockade-runner
abcdeelmnoopsu
undecomposable
abcdeelnnorstu
under-constable
abcdefilmnoors
disconformable
abcdefilmoorst
discomfortable
abcdegiillnstu
castle-building
abcdehklnorrtu
alder-buckthorn
abcdeiiilprtty
predictability
abcdeiilnnorsy
inconsiderably
abcdeiilnnosty
condensability
abcdeilnorsuvy
undiscoverably
abcdenooorrrtu
uncorroborated
abcdghilnooors
boarding-school
abcdhilnooorrt
broncho-dilator
abcdiiiilossty
dissociability
abceeeeeklmrrz
mackerel-breeze
abceeeeilnrssv
receivableness
abceeefiilnnss
beneficialness
abceeelnnrsssu
censurableness
abceefiiilnprt
perfectibilian
abceegiilnorrs
irrecognisable
abceegiinorsuz
zingiberaceous
abceegillnrsuy
subgenerically
abceegilnnorsu
unrecognisable
abceehiooprsuu
euphorbiaceous
abceehklnnostu
luncheon-basket
abceeiiilrstvy
serviceability
abceeiiillrstt
belletristical
abceeiillnnnss
inclinableness
abceeiilorrtvy
recoverability
abceeiilprstty
respectability
abceeiilrrsstu
irresuscitable

abceeiinorsuzz
zinziberaceous
abceeilmnopsst
compatibleness
abceeilnnosssu
unsociableness
abceeilrrtttuu
trituberculate
abceenorrtttuy
counter-battery
abcefiiinnortu
eburnification
abceghhiklnort
knight-bachelor
abceghiilmnnru
burling-machine
abceghimnosttu
bathing-costume
abcegiiloorstt
bacteriologist
abcegilnnorsuy
unrecognisably
abcehhiilmrtuu
Baluchitherium
abcehilllopryy
hyperbolically
abceiiilnstuxy
inexcusability
abceiiilorrtvy
irrevocability
abceiilrrsstuy
irresuscitably
abceiimosssty
biosystematics
abceilllnnoort
incontrollable
abceillmnosssy
symbolicalness
abceilnnnosttu
subcontinental
abceinorrsttuy
subcontrariety
abcelllnnoortu
uncontrollable
abcelnosstuuuy
subcutaneously
abcfiilmnoorty
conformability
abcgiiiilnotty
incogitability
abcgillnnoootu
conglobulation
abciiilllopsty
collapsibility
abciiilnrsttuy
inscrutability
abciilmmnosstu
somnambulistic
abciilnorsttuy
construability
abcilllnnoorty
incontrollably
abcilmnorstuuy
rambunctiously

abclllnnoortuy
uncontrollably
abddeeehllnssu
bull-headedness
abddeehillosst
old-established
abddeeilmnnsty
absent-mindedly
abddelnoortuuy
roundaboutedly
abddhillnrrsuy
drill-husbandry
abddiilmnoorst
Bristol-diamond
abdeeeefilnsss
defeasibleness
abdeeeeilnrsst
deliberateness
abdeeeelnssstt
detestableness
abdeeegilnrsst
single-breasted
abdeeeginoprst
pigeon-breasted
abdeeeiillrtvy
deliberatively
abdeeeiilmnnrt
indeterminable
abdeeeiinnopzz
benzodiazepine
abdeeeilmnnrtu
undeterminable
abdeeeilmnprtu
unpremeditable
abdeeeilnnnssu
undeniableness
abdeeeimnnootv
above-mentioned
abdeeellnoprss
deplorableness
abdeeellorstwy
yellow-breasted
abdeeemmnoprsu
pseudomembrane
abdeeemnqrrstu
Rembrandtesque
abdeefghinrrst
finger's-breadth
abdeefiiilnntu
unidentifiable
abdeefilmnorss
formidableness
abdeegiprrrrty
partridge-berry
abdeehiiilrtty
hereditability
abdeeiiillrtvy
deliverability
abdeeiilmnnrty
indeterminably
abdeeilmnnorst
indemonstrable
abdeeilnpssstu
disputableness

abdeelmnnorstu
undemonstrable
abdefiinnostuu
subinfeudation
abdefinorstuuy
subinfeudatory
abdeghlmnortuu
rough-and-tumble
abdehiiilmnnsu
undiminishable
abdeiiilmnoost
demobilisation
abdeiiilnpssty
dispensability
abdeiiilnrstuy
undesirability
abdeiilnoorstw
bowdlerisation
abdennoorsstuu
roundaboutness
abdfghiinorsst
shifting-boards
abdhilnnoortty
labyrinthodont
abdiiillosstvy
dissolvability
abdiiilnorsttu
distributional
abeeeelnnprsst
penetrableness
abeeefflnrsssu
sufferableness
abeeehhilrrttu
heather-bluiter
abeeehhlrrtttu
heather-blutter
abeeehilnprsss
perishableness
abeeehlnrsssst
breathlessness
abeeeiilnnpssx
inexpiableness
abeeeiilnnsstv
inevitableness
abeeeikmoprrrs
promise-breaker
abeeeillnnrssu
unreliableness
abeeeilmnnrsst
terminableness
abeeeilnnoprss
inoperableness
abeeeilnnorssx
inexorableness
abeeeimnrrsttu
turbine-steamer
abeeellnnrssuv
vulnerableness
abeeelnnoprsss
personableness
abeeelnorrssst
restorableness
abeeerrrrsttwy
strawberry-tree
abeefiilmnrtty
fermentability
abeefilnoprsst
profitableness
abeefklnnooruw
unforeknowable
abeefllorrsttu
self-torturable
abeeghhiilnrtw
breathing-while
abeeghiilnstux
extinguishable
abeeghijnnorrs
Johannisberger
abeeghiknnnrtt
knight-banneret
abeegiikknrrst
strike-breaking
abeegiilnnnsst
intangibleness
abeegmnorsssuu
umbrageousness
abeegnoorrrttu
turbo-generator
abeehiiinnsstv
inhabitiveness
abeehilnopssst
hospitableness
abeehlnnoorssu
honourableness
abeehlnnoptuyz
phenylbutazone
abeeiiilmmprty
impermeability
abeeiiilmnnsst
inimitableness
abeeiillnnossv
inviolableness
abeeiilmnoprss
impressionable
abeeiilmnpssss
impassibleness
abeeiilnprstty
presentability
abeeiilnprttvy
preventability
abeeiilprrstvy
preservability
abeeillmrssstt
ballet-mistress
abeeillnnprstu
unsplinterable
abeeillprrsstt
blister-plaster
abeeillprrstyy
presbyterially
abeeilmnnnostu
unmentionables
abeeilmnoprssv
improvableness
abeeilnnoqstuu
unquestionable
abeeilnnssstuu
unsuitableness
abeeilrrrssttu
subterrestrial
abeeimmorrsstt
strabismometer
abeeimnosssstu
abstemiousness
abeeimooprrstt
absorptiometer
abeeinoprssstv
absorptiveness
abeeklnnnossuw
unknowableness
abeelmnooprtyy
polyembryonate
abefgiiilnrrty
refrangibility
abefiiilrrttuy
irrefutability
abefilnooprsst
self-absorption
abeghilmnoooxy
oxy-haemoglobin
abeghlmnrrsstu
bremsstrahlung
abegiiilmnprty
impregnability
abegiiknnoprrs
prison-breaking
abegiilnoorsst
obligatoriness
abegiilorrssty
gyrostabiliser
abegilmnrsttuu
Sturmabteilung
abeginnnnqrtuu
running-banquet
abehillmmooost
holometabolism
abehimmooprsty
symmetrophobia
abeiiiilmnnstz
Leibnitzianism
abeiiiilmprtvy
imperviability
abeiiiillnortty
intolerability
abeiiiilmnnrtuy
innumerability
abeiiiilmorrtvy
irremovability
abeiiiilnprstuy
insuperability
abeiiiilprsstuy
persuasibility
abeiiimnrsstuu
subminiaturise
abeiimnoprrttu
imperturbation
abeilmnnorstuu
insurmountable
abeilnnoqstuuy
unquestionably
abeilnooopprrt
proportionable
abeilnorssssuu
salubriousness
abeinnorsstuyz
Russo-Byzantine
abelmnnorstuuu
unsurmountable
abfgiiiilnnrty
infrangibility
abfiilnooorttv
vibroflotation
abhiiiklnnttuy
unthinkability
abhiiinooprrty
prohibitionary
abhilmnooprstt
thromboplastin
abiiiillmpstuy
implausibility
abiiiilmmnoost
immobilisation
abiiiimnnosttu
bituminisation
abiiiillnoosstu
solubilisation
abiiilnoorsstt
strobilisation
abiiinnnosstuu
subinsinuation
abiiillnorssuuy
insalubriously
abiiilnnnosttuu
tintinnabulous
abiiilnossttttuu
substitutional
abilmnnorstuuy
insurmountably
abilnoooprrrty
proportionably
accceehillnorv
vice-chancellor
accceeiilssstu
Ecclesiasticus
accceennooovvx
convexo-concave
acccehhilmopsy
psychochemical
acccehiinoorss
onchocerciasis
accceillnnorty
concentrically
accceimmnooors
macroeconomics
acccginnoosttu
cost-accounting
accchiioopsstt
tachistoscopic
accchloopsstuy
Staphylococcus
acccilnoossssu
class-conscious
accdddeklooooo
cock-a-doodle-doo
accddeinnorttu
uncontradicted

accdeeehhiknrt
chicken-hearted
accdeefiinrttu
uncertificated
accdeefilnnstu
self-inductance
accdeeghnnortu
counter-changed
accdeehhiknnns
hen-and-chickens
accdeehilostuy
lecythidaceous
accdeeilmnopsy
encyclopaedism
accdeeilmnorty
dynamo-electric
accdeeilnopsty
encyclopaedist
accdeeimnoppty
appendicectomy
accdeeinnnostu
discountenance
accdeeinnoorst
deconsecration
accdeeinoprrtu
unreciprocated
accdeeiooorssu
dioscoreaceous
accdeemnossstu
accustomedness
accdeennorsstt
contractedness
accdefhiorrrsu
Crouched-friars
accdefhirrrstu
Crutched-friars
accdefnnoortuu
unaccounted-for
accdehhilloopy
dolichocephaly
accdehhimnorsy
hydromechanics
accdehilmnopsu
unaccomplished
accdeiillnnoty
coincidentally
accdeiinnnostu
discontinuance
accdeimmnnotuu
uncommunicated
accdelmooprtuy
plutodemocracy
accdginnnortuy
country-dancing
accdhimnnoorru
chondrocranium
accdhimnopssyy
psychodynamics
accdiinoorsttu
contradictious
acceeellnortvy
electrovalency
acceeeorrsstuw
worcester-sauce

acceefllmnopst
self-complacent
acceegiinnorss
carcinogenesis
acceegillnorty
geocentrically
acceehhiilnnpr
rhinencephalic
acceehhilmmort
thermochemical
acceehhilprrty
Charley-pitcher
acceehhimnpstu
catechumenship
acceehiiiknprr
prairie-chicken
acceehilnopprs
prosencephalic
acceehimmotttw
watch-committee
acceehiprsttty
cryptaesthetic
acceeiilmmnosu
oecumenicalism
acceeiilnorsst
resistance-coil
acceeiimnnoort
econometrician
acceeiinnoorss
concessionaire
acceeilllnorty
electronically
acceeilllopsty
telescopically
acceeillrrtttt
clitter-clatter
acceeilmoprstu
proceleusmatic
acceeilnooptuy
leucocytopenia
acceeiloooprsst
stereoscopical
acceeilorssttt
electrostatics
acceeinnoorrst
reconsecration
acceelnopssstw
snow-spectacles
accefgiiiinnns
insignificance
accefiiillnsty
scientifically
accefilmnoorsw
moccasin-flower
acceghhilnoost
school-teaching
acceghiillnnou
hallucinogenic
acceghinoprrss
preaching-cross
acceghiopprrst
spectrographic
accegiilnrtuxy
excruciatingly

accegillmmoory
myrmecological
accegilloprst
spectrological
accehhillnoprs
chancellorship
accehiilmorstt
stichometrical
accehiilmrtuvy
clavicytherium
accehikllmoory
mock-heroically
accehilmmnopst
accomplishment
accehilmnoorrt
chronometrical
accehilmooprsu
microcephalous
accehilmoprsty
psychometrical
accehilmopsuuy
sceuophylacium
accehiloopsstt
stethoscopical
acceiiilmmorss
microseismical
acceiiilnnoort
reconciliation
acceiiilnoorrt
oneirocritical
acceiiillossty
solecistically
acceiillmrrsuy
semicircularly
acceiilnnopttu
centuplication
acceiilnoorrty
reconciliatory
acceiinoprsssu
capriciousness
acceillnosssuy
successionally
acceilmmnnooss
commonsensical
acceilmoooppst
metoposcopical
acceilnoorssst
cross-sectional
acceimnooprstu
pococuranteism
accellmooprstt
stamp-collector
accffiiinorttu
fructification
accfgiiiinnnsy
insignificancy
accfiiiiilnost
silicification
accfiiiiknnotz
zinckification
accfiiinoosttt
Scottification
accghhiillooty
ichthyological

accghiilloorst
Christological
accgiiillmoory
micrologically
accgiimnorrtuy
circumgyration
accgimnnoottu
coconut-matting
accgimorrrtuyy
circumgyratory
acchhiilmoortt
lithochromatic
acchhiloppssyy
psychophysical
acchhimooorrtt
orthochromatic
acchiiimnooorv
Mohorovicician
acchiiinnnoost
cinchonisation
acchiilloprtyy
hypocritically
acchiilooprsty
hypocoristical
acchillnnorsyy
synchronically
acchimoopsssty
psychosomatics
acciiimnorrssu
Rosicrucianism
acciillmooopst
cosmopolitical
acciillmorrttu
circumlittoral
acciilnnooprst
conscriptional
acciilnnoortuy
unconciliatory
acciimnnorttuu
circumnutation
acciinnnoorstt
triconsonantic
acciinnooosttv
convocationist
accikkmmnnrruu
crinkum-crankum
accillopprrtyy
procryptically
accilmnoostuuy
contumaciously
accilnnoorsttu
constructional
accimmnnnnootu
non-communicant
accimnorrttuuy
circumnutatory
acdddeeiilmnst
middle-distance
acddeeeehinrtv
heaven-directed
acddeeefnnortu
unconfederated
acddeeennorstx
extra-condensed

acddeegiklnosw
disacknowledge
acddeegklnnouw
unacknowledged
acddeeiilrttuv
diverticulated
acddeeimnosttu
undomesticated
acddeeinrssstt
distractedness
acddehmooprstu
proud-stomached
acddeiiinnoort
air-conditioned
acddeiinooorsu
androdioecious
acddeilnnoostu
unconsolidated
acddeilnrsttuy
undistractedly
acddghillnostw
swaddling-cloth
acdeeeffnnsstu
unaffectedness
acdeeefhirsuvx
chevaux-de-frise
acdeeefnopprst
copper-fastened
acdeeehhiknrsv
handkerchieves
acdeeeilnoprtu
Pleuronectidae
acdeeeinnopqru
equiponderance
acdeeeinorsstv
decorativeness
acdeeelnoprruw
nuclear-powered
acdeeenrrrstuy
under-secretary
acdeeffimorrtt
diffractometer
acdeefhiinnrss
disenfranchise
acdeefhiklnnsw
Schwenkfeldian
acdeefillmoprs
self-proclaimed
acdeefinoqruuy
audio-frequency
acdeeghiiloopt
galeopithecoid
acdeeghnnooruy
ocean-greyhound
acdeegiinorstt
stage-direction
acdeegijknrsst
dressing-jacket
acdeegilnnoqru
grandiloquence
acdeegimnorstu
discouragement
acdeegklmnnotw
acknowledgment

acdeeglnooorru
orange-coloured
acdeehiiinnrst
disinheritance
acdeehiiinrsst
dechristianise
acdeehiinnsttz
zenith-distance
acdeehiinoorrt
Rhinocerotidae
acdeehilmnosst
methodicalness
acdeehimnnnstt
disenchantment
acdeehinnrssst
disenchantress
acdeehinoopprt
apprenticehood
acdeeiilnnnsst
incidentalness
acdeeillmnttuu
multinucleated
acdeeilmnoortu
Deuteronomical
acdeeilnopssst
despoticalness
acdeeimmmoprrs
promise-crammed
acdeeimmnnoort
recommendation
acdeeimnnostww
casement-window
acdeeinnnoorst
recondensation
acdeeinnoorsst
co-ordinateness
coordinateness
acdeeinoprsssu
predaciousness
acdeellmnnotty
malcontentedly
acdeelmnnopttu
uncontemplated
acdeelnnnrstty
transcendently
acdeelnnoorttv
lavender-cotton
acdeemmnoorrty
recommendatory
acdefghiilmnno
folding-machine
acdefiiiinnott
identification
acdefiiinoottx
detoxification
acdefiiinorrtt
denitrificator
acdefiillnnoty
confidentially
acdeghimnorsty
hydromagnetics
acdegiiilloostt
dialectologist

acdeginnorrttu
counter-trading
acdegmmnnooorr
common-or-garden
acdehhiilmoprt
edriophthalmic
acdehhiimoprrt
hermaphroditic
acdehhlooprsuy
hydrocephalous
acdehiiilooprt
diaheliotropic
acdehiillmmoty
immethodically
acdehiilnrsstt
child-resistant
acdehiimorrsty
radiochemistry
acdehillmopryy
hypodermically
acdehillnoorry
hydrocoralline
acdehimmnorsty
thermodynamics
acdehimnoprtuy
hydropneumatic
acdehinoorrstt
trisoctahedron
acdehoorrrttxy
hydroextractor
acdeiiiimnnrst
indiscriminate
acdeiiiimnrstv
discriminative
acdeiiilmnrsty
discriminately
acdeiiilnnortu
unidirectional
acdeiillnorsty
discretionally
acdeiilmmrssty
dissymmetrical
acdeiilmpsttuu
multicuspidate
acdeiilnnooost
decolonisation
acdeiilnooorst
decolorisation
acdeiinoopprrst
disincorporate
acdeiknoprrttv
davenport-trick
acdeillmnoosty
endosmotically
acdeillnoossty
disconsolately
acdeillnrsstuy
uncrystallised
acdeilnosssttu
sansculottides
acdeimmnnooors
andromonoecism
acdeimmnnopsuy
pneumodynamics

acdeinnooprrtu
unincorporated
acdeinnorstuuy
consuetudinary
acdeinooqrsstu
conquistadores
acdeioopprrstu
dipterocarpous
acdellmnooorsu
salmon-coloured
acdelloopsttuy
leptodactylous
acdfhiiiimnotu
humidification
acdfiiiilnoost
solidification
acdgghinoootttw
chittagong-wood
acdggiilnorsuy
discouragingly
acdgiiiimnnrst
discriminating
acdginnorrsstu
strand-scouring
acdhhimnooprsy
hypochondriasm
acdhhinooprsty
hypochondriast
acdhiiooopprtt
diaphototropic
acdiiiilmnprsu
disciplinarium
acdiiiilnnnost
disinclination
acdiiiimnnorst
discrimination
acdiiijlnorstu
jurisdictional
acdiiilnnootty
conditionality
acdiiimnorrsty
discriminatory
acdiiinnnooort
incoordination
acdiiinnnoortt
indoctrination
acdiilnnooosst
disconsolation
acdiilnooorstu
discolouration
acdimnooprsstu
mass-production
aceeeefff lmnst
self-effacement
aceeeefhhlnprt
three-halfpence
aceeeegillptxy
epexegetically
aceeeehhilnrtw
Catherine-wheel
aceeefhiiimnnx
examine-in-chief
aceeefllorrtuw
fellow-creature

aceeeflnnssstu
self-sustenance
aceeeghiilnopt
galeopithecine
aceeeghiinosst
aesthesiogenic
aceeeghijknnrt
Jack-in-the-green
aceeeghilnpsst
steeplechasing
aceeegimmnrrtt
centimetre-gram
aceeegmorsstty
Gasteromycetes
aceeehhiprssty
hyperaesthesic
aceeehhiprstty
hyperaesthetic
aceeehllmorrtt
electrothermal
aceeehloprrtty
electrotherapy
aceeehnprsstuy
hyperacuteness
aceeeiilmnnnst
semi-centennial
aceeeiilmnrttx
excrementitial
aceeeiiloprssv
overspecialise
aceeeillprsstu
supercelestial
aceeeilmorrstt
stereometrical
aceeeilnnqquuv
quinquevalence
aceeeimnnpprtt
apprenticement
aceeemnooprstv
overcompensate
aceeemnoprrttu
contemperature
aceeemnorrstuu
counter-measure
aceeennorssstu
nectareousness
aceeffiilnttuy
ineffectuality
aceefgiilnrstu
centrifugalise
aceefgillloorx
reflexological
aceefglnnrssuu
ungracefulness
aceefhhiorrstt
ostrich-feather
aceefhiiinortt
etherification
aceefiiilprssu
superficialise
aceefiiinorstt
esterification
aceefiknrrsttt
transfer-ticket

aceefilmnoprst
self-importance
aceefinorrrsst
refractoriness
aceefmnnnooprr
non-performance
aceegghiiilnot
genethlialogic
aceeggimnnorrs
scaremongering
aceeghhinoprsu
preaching-house
aceeghiinnprst
speech-training
aceeghikprrrtt
prick-the-garter
aceeghilloprt
herpetological
aceeghilnoptty
phytogenetical
aceeghloopsstu
stegocephalous
aceeghmnrrtttu
gutter-merchant
aceegiiinnprst
straining-piece
aceegiimmoprtt
micropegmatite
aceegiinnnortt
traction-engine
aceegiklnprstu
plague-stricken
aceegillllooty
teleologically
aceegillmooort
meteorological
aceegillnoprtt
electroplating
aceegillprrtuy
picture-gallery
aceeginnnortty
octingentenary
aceeglnoorrstu
colour-sergeant
aceegnoorsssuu
courageousness
aceehhilnnnopr
rhinencephalon
aceehhmooprrst
chromatosphere
aceehiimnnsstz
Nietzscheanism
aceehiinppprst
apprenticeship
aceehillnopty
telephonically
aceehillmnoott
monotheletical
aceehilmmorrtt
thermometrical
aceehimmnorssv
servo-mechanism
aceehinpprrsst
ship's-carpenter

aceehlnnoopprs
prosencephalon
aceeiiilllmpst
semi-elliptical
aceeiiilmnnrst
reminiscential
aceeiiilmnpprr
prince-imperial
aceeiiilnrrtty
rectilinearity
aceeiiimpprstt
peripateticism
aceeiijlnnortt
interjectional
aceeiillrrsttv
verticillaster
aceeiilmmorsst
seismometrical
aceeiilmnprstt
centripetalism
aceeiilnnorsst
intercessional
aceeiilnnorstt
intersectional
aceeiilnorrsst
intercessorial
aceeiilnosstty
co-essentiality
aceeiklnnprstt
planet-stricken
aceeilllllnttuy
intellectually
aceeilllnnttuu
unintellectual
aceeillmnorrtu
intermolecular
aceeilmnooopsu
polemoniaceous
aceeilnnopsstu
unpoeticalness
aceeilnnorsttu
counter-salient
aceeilnopssttt
Pentecostalist
aceeilnorrrstu
resurrectional
aceeilnorssttu
sansculotterie
aceeimmnnorstu
incommensurate
aceeimnnooprtt
contemperation
aceeinnoorsstt
contesseration
aceeinnoorssvz
conversaziones
aceeinnprtttuu
interpunctuate
aceeinoprrsssu
precariousness
aceeinoqqsttuu
quinquecostate
aceeinoqssssuu
sequaciousness

aceellnortuwyy
yellow-centaury
aceelmmnorstuy
commensurately
aceelnoprstuuy
percutaneously
aceennnopsstty
pennystone-cast
aceffiiillmosy
semi-officially
aceffinrrrsttu
traffic-returns
acefggiinnnopy
pigeon-fancying
acefghiiikmmns
mischief-making
acefgiiinnortt
gentrification
acefgiillnorsu
fringillaceous
acefgiinnorttu
centrifugation
acefhlmnossstu
stomachfulness
acefhlnnsstuuw
unwatchfulness
acefiiiilmpstv
simplificative
acefiiiinnorst
resinification
acefiiiinortvv
revivification
acefiiilmnostu
emulsification
acefiiilprstuy
superficiality
acefiiinoprttt
prettification
acefiinossttu
factitiousness
acefilmnooprss
self-comparison
acefinnoorsssu
facinorousness
acefinrrrsttuu
infrastructure
aceggiilnnnprs
spring-cleaning
aceggillnooort
gerontological
aceggillnoosty
geognostically
aceghhiillopry
hieroglyphical
aceghhiioprrst
cheirographist
aceghiillnosty
histogenically
aceghiiloopstt
hepaticologist
aceghiiloprstx
lexicographist
aceghijknoostt
shooting-jacket

aceghillInooty
ethnologically
aceghiloppprty
pterylographic
aceghinnprsstu
purse-snatching
aceghiopprrssu
supercargoship
aceghlmoopstyy
metapsychology
aceghlnoopsttu
plectognathous
aceghmmooprsuy
myrmecophagous
acegiiilmnsttu
metalinguistic
acegiillllostuy
eulogistically
acegiillmnoort
terminological
acegiillooorst
soteriological
acegiilloostv
Sovietological
acegiillorssuy
sacrilegiously
acegiilnnnotuy
uncongeniality
acegiilnnottuv
conglutinative
acegilllmootyy
etymologically
acegillloprty
petrologically
acegilmnnooort
conglomeration
acegimnnoorrst
cairngorm-stone
aceginnnoossuu
consanguineous
aceginnoossstu
contagiousness
aceginnopsssuu
pugnaciousness
aceginnorsssuu
ungraciousness
aceginopprrssu
porcupine-grass
acehhiiilllosst
cholelithiasis
acehhiimopsstt
Theopaschitism
acehhiinoprrtt
therianthropic
acehhiinopssuy
house-physician
acehhilloopsty
theosophically
acehhillopttyy
hypothetically
acehhiloopprrty
hypertrophical
acehhimoopprst
metaphosphoric

acehhlmoooppst
ophthalmoscope
acehiiinnrsstu
unchristianise
acehiillopstty
polytheistical
acehiillpstuuy
euphuistically
acehiilmnoostt
monotheistical
acehiilnooopst
opisthocoelian
acehiimnnooprt
enantiomorphic
acehiimorrstty
iatrochemistry
acehiinnooprsy
Syrophoenician
acehiinnssttuu
unenthusiastic
acehiinnttuuy
unauthenticity
acehiinooprttu
eutrophication
acehiinopprsst
spinthariscope
acehiinopssttu
unsophisticate
acehiiooprssst
spirochaetosis
acehilllloppsst
phelloplastics
acehillmnoswwy
chimney-swallow
acehilmnooprrz
chlorpromazine
acehilnorsssuv
chivalrousness
acehimnooprrtt
anthropometric
acehimopprstty
spermatophytic
acehinnorssty
narcosynthesis
acehllmoorssty
schoolmasterly
acehmooorsttu
tetrachotomous
aceiiiinorsstt
sericitisation
aceiiillmpttuv
multiplicative
aceiiilnrrtuvy
curvilinearity
aceiiilnrsstuv
universalistic
aceiiilnrsttxy
extrinsicality
aceiiimmnoorss
commissionaire
aceiiimmnorrtu
microminiature
aceiiimnnorstt
interactionism

aceiiinnorsttt
interactionist
aceiillmnnooos
neocolonialism
aceiillmooprtt
metropolitical
aceiillmoprtuv
pluviometrical
aceiilmnnnostt
continentalism
aceiilmnooprrs
incorporealism
aceiilnnnossty
nonsensicality
aceiilnnnosttt
continentalist
aceiilnnooorst
recolonisation
aceiilnnorrstu
insurrectional
aceiilnooprrsv
provincial-rose
aceiilnooprrty
incorporeality
aceiilnooprrvy
ivory-porcelain
aceiilnoprstuy
pertinaciously
aceiilnosssuv
lasciviousness
aceiimnooorrtt
recitation-room
aceiimooqrstuv
vicesimo-quarto
aceiinnosssstuu
incautiousness
aceiinooprsttv
contrapositive
aceiinopssssuu
auspiciousness
aceilllmortuvy
volumetrically
aceillnnnootvy
conventionally
aceilmmoorrttu
ultramicrotome
aceilmnorsssuu
miraculousness
aceilnnnnootuv
unconventional
aceilnooprrtuy
perlocutionary
aceilnooqsssuu
loquaciousness
aceiloorrsttuw
water-colourist
aceilorrrrstuv
recurvirostral
aceimmnnoorstu
commensuration
aceimnnnooprtu
pronunciamento
aceimnoorrstuv
conservatorium

aceimnoqrstttu
quattrocentism
aceinnnoooprt
non-cooperation
aceinnooprsstt
cornet-à-pistons
aceinoqrstttu
quattrocentist
acelrrrsttuuu
ultrastructure
acemnooorssttu
entomostracous
acffghhiorrttu
through-traffic
acfgiilmnnnotu
malfunctioning
acfiiiilmnopst
simplification
acfiiiinoqtuzz
quizzification
acfiiilnostttu
stultification
acfiiinoprsstu
Prussification
acfiimnorrsstt
transformistic
acgghhiiilnnnt
chain-lightning
acgghhimopprsy
sphygmographic
acghhhiiopstty
ichthyophagist
acghhhioopstuy
ichthyophagous
acghhiiooppsrt
opisthographic
acghhinoosstuz
schizognathous
acghiiilnopstt
antiphlogistic
acghiilllloopy
philologically
acghiillnooort
ornithological
acghiilmnoopsy
physiognomical
acghillmootyy
mythologically
acghilnossttuw
swathing-clouts
acghiopprrstty
cryptographist
acgiiijllnosty
jingoistically
acgiiilllnstuy
linguistically
acgiiilllpstuy
pugilistically
acgiiilmnossty
misogynistical
acgiiinnnottux
unintoxicating
acgiillnppstuy
supplicatingly

acgiilnnnoottu
conglutination
acgillloooprty
tropologically
acgilnooprssty
laryngoscopist
acginoooprrstt
prognosticator
achhillmnrtuyy
unrhythmically
achhilnopsstyy
sycophantishly
achhiloorsttuy
ichthyolatrous
achhlmoooppsty
ophthalmoscopy
achhmmnooorrsu
mushroom-anchor
achiiiinnorstt
trichinisation
achiiillnorsty
histrionically
achiiilnoorstt
chloritisation
achiiimnoorsst
trichomoniasis
achiiinoopsstt
sophistication
achiimmoprsssy
commissaryship
achiioprsssty
astrophysicist
achimmmnooorst
monochromatism
achiooprrrstu
procuratorship
aciiiilnnrstty
intrinsicality
aciiiilnoopstt
politicisation
aciiiilprsstu
spiritualistic
aciiilllmpssty
simplistically
aciiillmnopttu
multiplication
aciiillmopstty
optimistically
aciiilnopssuuy
inauspiciously
aciilnnoostttu
constitutional
aciimmnoopsttu
miscomputation
aciimnnopsttuu
mispunctuation
aciinnoooprstt
contraposition
acillnprrstuuy
unscripturally
acilmmoorrttuy
ultramicrotomy
aclmoooprrstuy
campylotropous

addddeeehllmuy
muddleheadedly
addddeffgiilln
fiddle-faddling
addddegiimnnow
diamond-wedding
adddeeeggllrst
straddle-legged
adddeeinnooors
endoradiosonde
addeeefhlnnsst
left-handedness
addeeefillpsss
self-displeased
addeeegginnsss
disengagedness
addeeeghlnnoss
long-headedness
addeeegnrrttuu
undergraduette
addeeehilmnnvy
heavenly-minded
addeeehioprrty
Hydropterideae
addeeehnnnopss
open-handedness
addeeeikmnnssw
weak-mindedness
addeeeilmprtty
premeditatedly
addeeeilnpssss
displeasedness
addeeeimnprttu
unpremeditated
addeeffhlrruuy
furfuraldehyde
addeeggimnnrtw
wedding-garment
addeeghhhinnss
high-handedness
addeehiklnnpss
spindle-shanked
addeeiimnssssv
misadvisedness
addeelnopprtuu
under-populated
addefgillrrsuy
disregardfully
addefiilnnsssu
disdainfulness
addefiimnoorsu
diamondiferous
addeghhinoostw
wood-nightshade
addeiiimnopsss
disimpassioned
addeimnnooortx
andromedotoxin
addeinorsstuuv
disadventurous
addgginnnorstu
standing-ground
adeeeeegnnrsst
degenerateness

adeeeeghillnrw
wheeler-dealing
adeeeeilmorrtt
radiotelemeter
adeeeeimnprrtt
predeterminate
adeeeelnnnrrvv
never-never-land
adeeefglnnnssw
newfangledness
adeeefilrrsstv
self-advertiser
adeeefimnnoort
aforementioned
adeeefinnorstt
defenestration
adeeegiknnrrrt
kindergartener
adeeegilnnppst
leaden-stepping
adeeeglnrrssss
regardlessness
adeeegoprrrtuy
daguerreotyper
adeeehhllortwy
whole-heartedly
adeeehhlmorttu
leather-mouthed
adeeehiinrrsst
hereditariness
adeeehilnooprt
radiotelephone
adeeeiilmnrtty
intermediately
adeeeiimmqrsuv
demi-semiquaver
adeeeiimnssttv
meditativeness
adeeeiinprsttv
predestinative
adeeeimmnorsst
immoderateness
adeeeimprrsttu
distemperature
adeeeinnrrssst
restrainedness
adeeeinooprrtu
Neuropteroidea
adeeemnnrsttttu
understatement
adeeennpprrssu
unpreparedness
adeeennstttwwy
sweet-and-twenty
adeefffghilrst
self-affrighted
adeeffiillnrty
differentially
adeeffiinorrtt
differentiator
adeefflnoosstt
flat-footedness
adeefghorrsttu
foster-daughter

adeefgllooprsu
gold-of-pleasure
adeeflllmoorwy
follow-my-leader
adeeghhillrtty
light-heartedly
adeeghhilnossy
highly-seasoned
adeeghiillnrtw
willing-hearted
adeeghilnrsstu
daughterliness
adeeghipppr suy
pseudepigraphy
adeegiiinrsttv
disintegrative
adeegiinnoprst
predesignation
adeegiinnorrtt
redintegration
adeegilooossst
osteoglossidae
adeeginoorrsst
derogatoriness
adeeginoprrsty
predesignatory
adeeglllmnnoty
old-gentlemanly
adeeglnoprrsuu
pleasure-ground
adeehhiilmoprs
hemispheroidal
adeehiiiprsttw
tide-waitership
adeehilmnnrstt
disenthralment
adeehilnooprty
radiotelephony
adeehlmnoorrsy
dysmenorrhoeal
adeehlorstttuy
stout-heartedly
adeehmnnnosssu
unhandsomeness
adeeiiimnnortt
intermediation
adeeiiinorssst
radiosensitise
adeeiiinorsstv
radiosensitive
adeeiilmnnotvy
denominatively
adeeiilnpsstvy
dispensatively
adeeiilpqsstuy
sesquipedality
adeeiimnnnrstt
disentrainment
adeeiimnorrtty
intermediatory
adeeiinnnorsst
inordinateness
adeeiinnoprstt
predestination

adeeillnnrsstu
ill-naturedness
adeeilnnrrstuy
unrestrainedly
adeeimnnorrsst
arrondissement
adeeimnsssttuy
unsystematised
adeellnooprrwy
woollen-drapery
adeelnnopprrty
preponderantly
adeelnnorssssu
slanderousness
adefghimoorrty
fairy-godmother
adefgiimnorrst
transmogrified
adefgillnorsuu
glanduliferous
adefiiinnosstt
disinfestation
adefiilmnorrtw
manifold-writer
adefiinnooorrt
foreordination
adefiinosssstu
fastidiousness
adegghhinorttu
thought-reading
adegghiinnnrtw
night-wandering
adegghiknnortu
kneading-trough
adeggiilnnrsst
leading-strings
adeghilnnoprtu
hunting-leopard
adeghimmoprrrt
third-programme
adegiiiinnnost
indigenisation
adegiiinnorstt
disintegration
adegiilnnprsuy
undespairingly
adegiimnoqrsuu
quadrigeminous
adegilnooorruy
neuroradiology
adeginnpprrstu
understrapping
adehhiilnooprt
Ornithodelphia
adehiilnpprsuy
sulphapyridine
adehilnnossstu
outlandishness
adehilnoprstuu
desulphuration
adehimoooppprss
paedomorphosis
adehinoorrsstw
road-worthiness

adehnorrssttww
north-westwards
adehorsssttuww
south-westwards
adeiiillnorstt
redistillation
adeiiilmnnorst
tridimensional
adeiiinnoorstt
disorientation
adeiiinoprsttu
repudiationist
adeiillnoprtvy
providentially
adeiilmnnoostw
two-dimensional
adeiilnoprssty
dispensatorily
adeiilnosttuvy
adventitiously
adeiimnnoppstt
disappointment
adeilnnorsstuw
untowardliness
adeimnorsstuuv
misadventurous
adeinooorrtttx
dextrorotation
adeinoprrrrstt
transport-rider
adelloorrsswww
sword-swallower
adelmnooorsssu
malodorousness
adeooorrrtttxy
dextrorotatory
adfgiklnooorrw
forward-looking
adfiiimnnoorst
disinformation
adfinnooopsttu
foundation-stop
adgghooorssstt
dog's-tooth-grass
adggiiknnorrww
working-drawing
adggimnnoprstu
stamping-ground
adgginnnoprsuw
spawning-ground
adghlnnoorssst
longs-and-shorts
adghmnnooprryy
gynandromorphy
adgiiiinnstttu
attitudinising
adgiiillnnotuy
longitudinally
adgiilnopprsvy
disapprovingly
adhiilmnoopxyy
hypomixolydian
adiiiilnoqsstu
disquisitional

adiiillnorssuy
disillusionary
adiiilmnooostt
dolomitisation
adiiimnnnooopr
monoprionidian
adiilopssttuuy
disputatiously
adiimnoorrsttu
radio-strontium
aeeeeeklprrssu
pleasure-seeker
aeeeeffimnnsst
effeminateness
aeeeegilnrrtvy
regeneratively
aeeeeginssttvv
vegetativeness
aeeeegnoqrrsuz
orange-squeezer
aeeeeinnprrttt
interpenetrate
aeeeeinnrssttv
inveterateness
aeeeeinprrsttv
representative
aeeeellnprrttw
water-repellent
aeeeellrrrsttv
traveller's-tree
aeeefggilnnrst
self-generating
aeeefhhlnnprty
three-halfpenny
aeeefhlnrsssst
fatherlessness
aeeefiilnnrrtt
interferential
aeeefillnorstv
self-revelation
aeeefillnprrty
preferentially
aeeeflmmnprttu
temperamentful
aeeegggimnnnrt
engagement-ring
aeeeggilnnrstv
steel-engraving
aeeegginrssssv
aggressiveness
aeeeghhioprrrs
heresiographer
aeeeghilmnpprt
pamphleteering
aeeegiillrrsty
siege-artillery
aeeegiilmnsstt
legitimateness
aeeegiilprrtvw
water-privilege
aeeegioprrstuv
supererogative
aeeeglnopprrsu
general-purpose

aeeehhhilmmprt
hephthemimeral
aeeehhhinnssst
heathenishness
aeeehhimrrttux
heather-mixture
aeeehhllnsssst
healthlessness
aeeehhopprrttw
weather-prophet
aeeehiinnpprsv
inapprehensive
aeeehilnpprsvy
apprehensively
aeeehinnpprsuv
unapprehensive
aeeeiillnrsstt
illiterateness
aeeeiilmnnsstt
sentimentalise
aeeeiilmnnsstv
alimentiveness
aeeeiilnrrsstv
irrelativeness
aeeeiinprrtttv
interpretative
aeeeillmnprtxy
experimentally
aeeeillorstttt
ottrelite-slate
aeeeilmnnprstt
presentimental
aeeeilnoprstuv
superelevation
aeeeilnprssstu
superessential
aeeeimmmnrsstu
mismeasurement
aeeeimnnrrtuuv
unremunerative
aeeeimnoprttxy
extemporaneity
aeeeinnnprrttt
interpenetrant
aeeeinnoprrstt
representation
aeeeinprssssuv
persuasiveness
aeeeiooprrrttv
retro-operative
aeeelnprrssssy
prayerlessness
aeeemnooprstux
extemporaneous
aeeennorssstux
extraneousness
aeeenqssssttuu
statuesqueness
aeefffimorrrrt
tariff-reformer
aeeffgilllnstv
levelling-staff
aeeffgilllorsu
flagelliferous

aeeffgillnrstt
self-flattering
aeefghhinrrstt
three-farthings
aeefgiilllorsw
sea-gilliflower
aeefgiillnnpsx
self-explaining
aeefgiinrsstuv
figurativeness
aeefgilllorswy
sea-gillyflower
aeefglnnrsstuu
ungratefulness
aeefhhlnnopsvy
shove-halfpenny
aeefhllopprrst
propeller-shaft
aeefiilnoqqtuu
quinquefoliate
aeefimnooprrrt
pre-Reformation
aeefinooprsttu
superfoetation
aeefioprrrsstu
ferroprussiate
aeeggiilnprsuv
pleasure-giving
aeeggiinorsstt
segregationist
aeegginorrsssu
gregariousness
aeeghhloopprtt
phototelegraph
telephotograph
aeeghhlorsstuu
slaughter-house
aeeghinrsstttw
watertightness
aeegiiilllmtty
illegitimately
aeegiiilllnntt
intelligential
aeegiiillnnstt
intelligentsia
aeegiiillnnttz
intelligentzia
aeegiiinnorsst
greisenisation
aeegiilnnnrtty
entertainingly
aeegiimmnopstz
piezomagnetism
aeegiimnnnortu
mountaineering
aeegiinnnnrttu
unentertaining
aeegiinorrsttv
tergiversation
aeegilmnoprtuv
Protevangelium
aeegilnnoosssu
oleaginousness

aeeginooprrstu
supererogation
aeeginoorstttu
uterogestation
aeegmnooprsstu
spermatogenous
aeegnoorsssstuu
outrageousness
aeegooprrrstuy
supererogatory
aeehhiiitttww
whittie-whattie
aeehhillmorstt
heterothallism
aeehhlmmooprtt
ophthalmometer
aeehhopppprsstu
superphosphate
aeehiilmmnrtty
trimethylamine
aeehiilmnnprty
triphenylamine
aeehiilnnpsttu
lieutenantship
aeehiinnnopprs
inapprehension
aeehillmrssstw
Wilhelmstrasse
aeehillnorsssv
all-overishness
aeehilprrrsttu
stirrup-leather
aeehinppprrsw
whippersnapper
aeehlopppprssuy
pleurapophyses
aeehmooorssttu
heterosomatous
aeeiiiilmnosstt
testimonialise
aeeiiilmnssttx
existentialism
aeeiiilnnnortt
interlineation
aeeiiilnsstttx
existentialist
aeeiiilorrrstt
territorialise
aeeiiilllnpstty
pestilentially
aeeiiillnnopptt
plenipotential
aeeiiillnnoprtt
interpellation
aeeiilmmnnoptt
implementation
aeeiilmmnnsstt
sentimentalism
aeeiilmnnnprsy
penny-a-linerism
aeeiilmnnosstx
extensionalism
aeeiilmnnssttt
sentimentalist

aeeiilmnnsttty
sentimentality
aeeiilnnosttxy
extensionality
aeeiilnnqssttu
quintessential
aeeiilnrsttuxy
intersexuality
aeeiilprttuvvy
vituperatively
aeeiimnnoorstt
remonetisation
aeeiimnoorsttv
overestimation
aeeiimorrrrrvw
rear-view-mirror
aeeiinnoppssst
inappositeness
aeeiinnoprrttt
interpretation
aeeiinnorssttw
westernisation
aeeiinnrssstttv
transitiveness
aeeikkloopsstw
swoopstake-like
aeeillnnrssstt
slatternliness
aeeillpprrtttt
prittle-prattle
aeeilmnnnnrssu
unmannerliness
aeeilnoorttxy
extortionately
aeeimnoqrsstu
question-master
aeeinnppprrss
snipper-snapper
aeejkkoprruwyy
joukery-pawkery
aeelllmnppstuy
supplementally
aeellmnorsssuv
marvellousness
aeemopprrrstty
property-master
aeffgiilnsssty
self-satisfying
aeffhilnnsstuu
unfaithfulness
aeffiimnoorrsu
foraminiferous
aefggiiinnnprt
finger-painting
aefghhinorsttt
star-of-the-night
aefgiilnnssstu
self-sustaining
aefgiilnossstu
flagitiousness
aefgiimorssttu
stigmatiferous
aefgillnnrttuy
unflatteringly

aefhhlnnoprtwy
half-pennyworth
aefhiilnnoprty
hyperinflation
aefhklnnnsstuu
unthankfulness
aefiilllmoottu
multifoliolate
aefiillmmnoost
self-immolation
aefiimnoorrstt
reformationist
aefiinoqqrsuuu
quinquefarious
aefillnooprssy
professionally
aefillooprrssy
professorially
aefilmnopssstu
self-assumption
aefilnnooprssu
unprofessional
aefllmnnoostww
fellow-townsman
aegggiillnnrsy
singing-gallery
aegghhoopprtyy
phytogeography
aegghinnooprtv
photo-engraving
aegghinorrttuw
watering-trough
aegghnnooprrty
röntgenography
aeggiilmnnprst
spring-ligament
aeggilooorsstt
astrogeologist
aegginoossttuu
auto-suggestion
aeghhlmopprsty
plethysmograph
aeghiillnopsst
polishing-slate
aeghiilloprsst
legislatorship
aeghiilnnsttuy
unhesitatingly
aeghiilnoppsst
polishing-paste
aeghiimnnooost
homogenisation
aeghiknnrrrtty
knight-errantry
aeghilmoorsttu
rheumatologist
aeghiloopprsty
epistolography
aeghimmmnortuu
omnium-gatherum
aeghinooopprrs
sporangiophore
aeghllmoopprsy
megasporophyll

aeghllorsstuuy
slaughterously
aeghlnoooprtuy
neuropathology
aeghmmooprrtty
photogrammetry
aegiiiillmnott
illegitimation
aegiiimnnorrtt
intermigration
aegiinnoorrtv
reinvigoration
aegiiinnorsttt
integrationist
aegiilllnnrtuy
interlingually
aegiillnttttt
tittle-tattling
aegiimooqrstuv
vigesimo-quarto
aegiinnnprrttu
nature-printing
aegiinnnprsssu
unaspiringness
aegiinpprssstt
asset-stripping
aegillmnnoqtuy
magniloquently
aegilmnoopsttu
pneumatologist
aegilnnnoopstu
louping-on-stane
aegilnnpprsttu
snapping-turtle
aegimmnooprstu
spermatogonium
aegimnnnssssuu
unassumingness
aegimnprrssstt
spring-mattress
aeginnprssssu
surpassingness
aeginoooprrss
sporangiospore
aeginooprrrssy
progressionary
aehhhilnoorttu
holier-than-thou
aehhhoooprrstt
orthophosphate
aehhiiilmprsux
xiphihumeralis
aehhiillllrssy
shilly-shallier
aehhilmopprstu
periophthalmus
aehhiloopprsst
philosophaster
aehhlmmooprtty
ophthalmometry
aehhnnoorrsttt
north-north-east
aehhoossstttuu
south-south-east

aehiikllmooprt
poikilothermal
aehiilmnoorsty
Hierosolymitan
aehiilmoopprst
apheliotropism
aehiiloprrstwy
praiseworthily
aehiinnnoorstt
enthronisation
aehiioorrssttt
osteo-arthritis
aehilllmmooprs
allelomorphism
aehilopprssuy
pleurapophysis
aehimnnoorsssu
harmoniousness
aehimoopppsstu
hippopotamuses
aehimopprssstt
postmastership
aehinoprrstuwy
unpraiseworthy
aehiooorrssstt
osteoarthrosis
aehlmnooopsstu
haplostemonous
aehnooprssttuy
thysanopterous
aeiiiilmnrsstt
ministerialist
aeiiilmorrrstt
territorialism
aeiiilnnnottty
intentionality
aeiiilnnooptvy
opinionatively
aeiiilnnrsttvy
intransitively
aeiiilnprsstuu
unspiritualise
aeiiilorrrsttt
territorialist
aeiiilorrrttty
territoriality
aeiiinoqrrstuy
requisitionary
aeiilllmnnopst
post-millennial
aeiilllrsttuvy
illustratively
aeiillnnnqquuy
quinquennially
aeiilmnooprsty
polymerisation
aeiilmnoprrsst
tripersonalism
aeiilnoprrsstt
tripersonalist
aeiilnoprrstty
tripersonality
aeiimmnorsstty
symmetrisation

aeiimnnorrssst
retransmission
aeiimnoooopsst
onomatopoiesis
aeiimnoorrsstt
restorationism
aeiimnrssstttv
transvestitism
aeiinnorrssstt
transitoriness
aeiinoorrssttt
restorationist
aeiinoprsssuvv
viviparousness
aeillmnnrsttuy
instrumentally
aeillmnosstuuy
simultaneously
aeilnnoosttuy
enantiostylous
aeilnoopprtuv
overpopulation
aeilnooprstuuv
superovulation
aeilnoossttuy
ostentatiously
aeinnoosstttuu
unostentatious
aeinooprrsssuu
uproariousness
aeinoorrssttu
traitorousness
affiilnnooprt
inflation-proof
afgghiimnnnoos
fashionmonging
afghhilnoorrst
thrashing-floor
afghhinorrsttw
farthingsworth
afiiimmnnoorst
misinformation
afiillmorstuuy
multifariously
afiinnorssttu
transfusionist
agggghhinnortu
through-ganging
agglnoooortyy
otolaryngology
aghhiiooprrsty
historiography
aghhilooopstty
histopathology
aghhlooopttyy
phytopathology
aghhoooppprrty
pyrophotograph
aghiimnnpsstuy
unsympathising
aghilllooopssst
opisthoglossal
aghilnoooprstt
anthropologist

aghimoooprsstu
mastigophorous
aghloopprrxyyy
xylopyrography
aghlooopprtxyyy
xylotypography
agiiiiilnotttv
vitilitigation
agiiillmnnntuu
unilluminating
agiikllmnoprru
milking-parlour
agiillmmnnoosu
monolingualism
agiillnoorsuvy
vaingloriously
agiinnoorssuuv
sanguinivorous
agilnnoprrstty
transportingly
aglmmooopsttyy
symptomatology
ahhiilnopprstt
philanthropist
ahhimnoopprstu
anthropophuism
ahiiillnoopsty
lyophilisation
ahiilmnnoorsuy
inharmoniously
ahiilmnopprsst
psilanthropism
ahiilnopprsstt
psilanthropist
ahiimmnoopsttu
imposthumation
ahillooooprsst
alloiostrophos
ahoppqrrrtuyyz
quartz-porphyry
aiiiilmnnosttu
intuitionalism
aiiiilnnostttu
intuitionalist
aiiiilnoorsttv
vitriolisation
aiiiimnnoprsst
inspirationism
aiiiinnoprssttt
inspirationist
aiiilmnnoostty
mylonitisation
aiiiloopprrtty
propitiatorily
aiiimnrssssttvy
transmissivity
aiiinnorstttuy
institutionary
aiillnorrssssty
sinistrorsally
aiilmnooprssuy
parsimoniously
aiilnoooppsstt
postpositional

aiinoopprsstuy
suppositionary
aikkmmnnrrttuu
trinkum-trankum
aillnoooprrrty
proportionally
aimnnnopprsssu
snip-snap-snorum
bbbcghinrrssuu
scrubbing-brush
bbbcgiiklnoors
scribbling-book
bbbdgiiilnnoru
ribbon-building
bbccdeiimnrsuu
circumbendibus
bbcgikllmnostu
stumbling-block
bbciiilmosttuy
combustibility
bbddeehhlmoooy
hobbledehoydom
bbddeelooopstt
blood-bespotted
bbdeehhhiloosy
hobbledehoyish
bbdeehhilmoosy
hobbledehoyism
bbeeghoorrssuy
gooseberry-bush
bbegiiilmrstuy
submergibility
bbeiiilmrsstuy
submersibility
bbeilnoorrstuu
rubber-solution
bccciimooprssu
submicroscopic
bccddeehllotuu
double-declutch
bccdiiilnottuy
conductibility
bcceeiiilortty
bioelectricity
bcceejnorsttuu
counter-subject
bcceiiijssttuv
subjectivistic
bccilnoosssuuy
subconsciously
bcddeeginnrrtu
current-bedding
bcddeehiiotwww
widow-bewitched
bcdeeeghiinrrs
riding-breeches
bcdeeeiilmnott
medicine-bottle
bcdeeeiilnnrss
incredibleness
bcdeegiklnrsuw
swindge-buckler
bcdeeiiilnprst
indiscerptible
bcdeeiilnrsttu
indestructible
bcdeeiiloprrru
irreproducible
bcdeeilnoprruu
unreproducible
bcdeemoooprtt
copper-bottomed
bcdeghinnorstt
stretching-bond
bcdehiinoorrrs
rhinoceros-bird
bcdeiiiilprsty
discerpibility
bcdeiiiilrrtuy
irreducibility
bcdeiiilpprstu
public-spirited
bcdeiillnorstu
bill-discounter
bcdeiilnrsttuy
indestructibly
bcdeiknoorrstu
discount-broker
bcdgilmnnooosu
blood-consuming
bcdiiiloprttuy
productibility
bceeeefilmnrst
fermentescible
bceeeeghinnsss
beseechingness
bceeehilmnoprs
comprehensible
bceeeijnssstuv
subjectiveness
bceeeorrrrstwy
worcesterberry
bceefiiilmprst
perfectibilism
bceefiiilprstt
perfectibilist
bceefiiilprtty
perfectibility
bceeflrrsttuwy
butterfly-screw
bceeghiklnrruy
huckleberrying
bceegillooorty
electrobiology
bceegimnnnossu
unbecomingness
bceehhiilmsttw
witches'-thimble
bceehilmnoprsy
comprehensibly
bceeiiilnnnssv
invincibleness
bceeiiilpprtty
perceptibility
bceeiilmnoprss
incompressible
bceeilnoorrttv
controvertible
bceeimnnprstuu
superincumbent
bceiiiilrsttvy
vitrescibility
bceiiilnorttvy
convertibility
bceiiilpssttuy
susceptibility
bceiilmrrsttuu
trituberculism
bceilmoortttuy
yttro-columbite
bceilnoorrttvy
controvertibly
bcgiiilmooorst
microbiologist
bcgiiilooosst
sociobiologist
bciiilmoopssty
compossibility
bciiiloprrttuy
corruptibility
bciinoorsstttu
obstructionist
bddeeeefillmny
feeble-mindedly
bddeeefllooruw
double-flowered
bddeegginnorru
breeding-ground
bddeeikmnnooss
book-mindedness
bddefgiinnorss
forbiddingness
bdeeeeillrsstt
blistered-steel
bdeeefgiilmnnr
nimble-fingered
bdeeefginrrttu
butter-fingered
bdeeegimmnostu
disemboguement
bdeeeiinnnortz
dinitrobenzene
bdeeeilmmnostw
disembowelment
bdeeemnoorrsuv
overburdensome
bdeegiiilmnpru
empire-building
bdeehiinosttuy
hebetudinosity
bdeeillnossssu
dissolubleness
bdeghiilnnnsst
night-blindness
bdegiimnoorstt
bed-sitting-room
bdegilnooppstu
double-stopping
bdegimnnoorrru
mourning-border
bdeiiiilmqrsuu
disequilibrium
bdeiiiilnsstty
distensibility
bdeiiilnnosssu
libidinousness
bdeiiilrsttuvy
distributively
bdeiiinorrsttu
redistribution
bdghiiloorsty
hydrobiologist
bdgiilnnoooops
blood-poisoning
bdiiiiiilnstvy
indivisibility
beeeelmnorstuv
bouleversement
beeefiillnnssx
inflexibleness
beeeggiiinnnor
bioengineering
beeeginoorrswy
gooseberry-wine
beeehilmnossst
blithesomeness
beeeiilnnnssss
insensibleness
beeeiilnprsssx
inexpressibles
beeeillnorsssu
rebelliousness
beeeilmnnnootv
omnibenevolent
beeelmmnorsssu
lumbersomeness
beefglooorrsy
gooseberry-fool
beeghiillllmnsy
embellishingly
beeghmooorrsty
gooseberry-moth
beegiiilllnntu
unintelligible
beegilllmnostt
smelling-bottle
beehlooorrsttu
troubleshooter
beeiiklnnsssuu
unbusinesslike
beeiilnpprsssu
insuppressible
beeiimnsssssuv
submissiveness
beeinooqsssuu
obsequiousness
beeinoorsssstu
boisterousness
beelooprrsstuy
obstreperously
beenorsssstuuu
subtersensuous
begghhiiilmnrt
thimble-rigging
begghhilnoorsu
borough-English

beggiiilssttuy
suggestibility
beghiillnostww
whistle-blowing
begiiilllnntuy
unintelligibly
begilmmnoprtuu
rumblegumption
begilmnnossttu
stumbling-stone
behhmnoopprrry
rhombenporphyr
behhnooopprrsz
phosphor-bronze
beiiiilmprssty
impressibility
permissibility
beiiillorrstuy
irresolubility
beiiilnoprssty
responsibility
beiiilnpsssty
suspensibility
beiilnpprsssuy
insuppressibly
beiilsstttuuvy
substitutively
beiinooprssttu
subterposition
beinoorsssstuu
robustiousness
bghiiloooopstt
photobiologist
bhiiiimnooprst
prohibitionism
bhiiiinooprstt
prohibitionist
cccddeeeennnos
condescendence
ccceeehhhiinnr
chincherinchee
ccceeeillnoqsu
colliquescence
ccceeiimprstuv
circumspective
ccceennnnoorru
non-concurrence
ccceiiilmrsssu
circumscissile
ccceiimmnooors
microeconomics
ccceiimnoprstu
circumspection
ccciiimnnorsuu
uncircumcision
ccciilmnoortuu
circumlocution
cccilmoorrtuuy
circumlocutory
ccddeeilnnosty
disconnectedly
ccdeeeeiiillrst
diesel-electric

ccdeeeffilnnos
self-confidence
ccdeeefinnoorv
over-confidence
ccdeeehiiklnrv
chicken-livered
ccdeeeiinprsvy
vice-presidency
ccdeeelnoprrty
preconcertedly
ccdeeennooprrs
correspondence
ccdeeiimnoortt
microdetection
ccdeeimnnorstt
disconcertment
ccdeennooprrsy
correspondency
ccdegiimnnostu
semiconducting
ccdeiiooorrstt
corticosteroid
ccdenooprrstuu
superconductor
ccdiiimoosssuv
mucoviscidosis
cceeeeejnnrsuv
rejuvenescence
cceeeefnorrrss
cross-reference
cceeeehimoprtv
chemoreceptive
cceeeemmmnnort
recommencement
cceeefiioprsst
stereospecific
cceeehilmorrtt
electrothermic
thermo-electric
cceeehilmorstt
electrochemist
cceeehimnooprt
chemoreception
cceeeimmnnoopt
omnicompetence
cceeeinssssuv
successiveness
cceeellorrttuu
electroculture
cceefgilnorrst
self-correcting
cceefhiillnnoo
colonel-in-chief
cceefimnorrrtu
circumferentor
cceeflnssssuu
successfulness
cceegiilloosst
ecclesiologist
cceehiiiprrsty
hypercriticise
cceehiikkprryy
hickery-pickery

cceehiillmoptu
multiple-choice
cceehiimoorstt
stoechiometric
cceehlnosstuuu
succulent-house
cceehooprrsttt
chest-protector
cceeiilnorrttu
interlocutrice
cceeilnnosssuv
conclusiveness
cceeilnoooprtt
optoelectronic
cceeilnossssu
successionless
cceeinooorrrtv
overcorrection
cceeinooprsssu
precociousness
cceeinorrsttuv
reconstructive
cceennorrrttuu
counter-current
ccefiilnnoostv
self-conviction
ccefiinnoorsst
cross-infection
cceflnsssuuuy
unsuccessfully
ccegiiiklnrrst
striking-circle
ccegikmnnoorst
smoking-concert
ccehhiilorsstt
chlorite-schist
ccehhioopssuyz
schizophyceous
ccehiiimoorstt
stoichiometric
ccehiiimprrsty
hypercriticism
ccehiilnopssuv
vice-consulship
ccehiimmorrsty
microchemistry
ccehimoosstuyz
schizomycetous
ccehinooprssuy
hyperconscious
ccehinooprstuy
psychoneurotic
ccehlmooosttyy
cholecystotomy
cceiiillnnosuvy
inconclusively
cceiillnoopsst
scintilloscope
cceiimnnoooptu
pneumoconiotic
cceiinorsssttuu
circuitousness
cceiklnooprssu
percussion-lock

cceilloosstuyy
leucocytolysis
cceilnorsttuvy
constructively
cceimmnnoooprt
microcomponent
cceimooprrrss
microprocessor
cceimorrrsttuu
microstructure
cceinnoorrsttu
reconstruction
cceiooprsssttt
spectroscopist
ccghiiknossttt
stocking-stitch
ccghiiooprstyy
hygroscopicity
ccgiikmnoopsst
composing-stick
cchioorrrssstw
Christ-cross-row
cciiiimnoorrst
onirocriticism
cciiijnnosttuv
conjunctivitis
cciiilprssttuu
pisciculturist
cciiimnooprstu
circumposition
cciilmnoortuuv
circumvolution
cciimnorssttuv
constructivism
ccillnnooortuw
town-councillor
ccilmnoopstuuy
compunctiously
cddeeeeeflnnps
self-dependence
cddeeehmnnopru
uncomprehended
cddeeehnnprrtu
hundred-per-cent
cddeeilnnostty
discontentedly
cddehlmooorsty
odd-come-shortly
cddeiiiillnnoot
ill-conditioned
cddeilnooostuy
dicotyledonous
cdeeeeirrssstv
dessert-service
cdeeeelnoprstw
steeple-crowned
cdeeeennpsstux
unexpectedness
cdeeefgillnnsu
self-indulgence
cdeeefginoprsw
weeding-forceps
cdeeefhinnrrrt
trencher-friend

cdeeegiimnprru
murdering-piece
cdeeegiinorrrv
receiving-order
cdeeegilnnoruv
overindulgence
cdeeehiklnnotv
devil-on-the-neck
cdeeehlloopprrw
Rochelle-powder
cdeeeiiinnsssv
indecisiveness
cdeeeiinnrssst
indiscreetness
indiscreteness
cdeeeiiopprstt
deposit-receipt
cdeeeinooprrrt
reception-order
cdeeeinprrssss
princesse-dress
cdeefghilorrrt
flight-recorder
cdeefgiiknrsty
sticky-fingered
cdeefgilmnnnos
self-condemning
cdeefiiiillnpss
self-discipline
cdeeflllnoorst
self-controlled
cdeegghinoorrs
schooner-rigged
cdeeggiillnort
electrogilding
cdeeghinnoorss
chondrogenesis
cdeehiklnprrsu
under-clerkship
cdeehimnoorrsy
dysmenorrhoeic
cdeehllloorsuy
hydrocellulose
cdeeiiinnsstvv
vindictiveness
cdeeiinrssssuv
discursiveness
cdeeiknnorrstw
wonder-stricken
cdeeilnrrsttuy
unrestrictedly
cdeeiloprrtuvy
reproductively
cdeeimnnnosttt
discontentment
cdeeinnoorsssu
indecorousness
cdeeinoprsstuv
productiveness
cdeeinpsssttuu
intussuscepted
cdeellooppruu
purple-coloured

cdeennoorrttuv
uncontroverted
cdefglnooosstu
slug-foot-second
cdefllnoooorrt
food-controller
cdeghhiiilnppr
high-principled
cdeghmnrrstuuu
Durchmusterung
cdehhiilnooprt
ornithodelphic
cdehhinooprrty
hydronephrotic
cdehinooorrsty
hydrocortisone
cdeiiiilrsttuv
diverticulitis
cdeiiilorsstuv
diverticulosis
cdeiiinnnssstt
indistinctness
cdeiilnorsssuu
ridiculousness
cdeiinnoorrttu
reintroduction
cdeiinnoprstuu
superinduction
cdeiinoopprrss
scorpion-spider
cdeiinorssttu
destructionist
cdeiioprrttuvy
reproductivity
cdeilnoprtuuvy
unproductively
cdeiloorsstuuy
discourteously
cdeimmnooosssu
commodiousness
cdeinoooprrtuv
overproduction
cdelllnnoortuy
uncontrolledly
cdfhkoorssttuu
futtock-shrouds
cdhhiloprrsuuy
hydrosulphuric
cdhiiilnoostvy
school-divinity
cdhikmnooprrtu
durchkomponirt
cdhinoooprsstt
prosthodontics
cdiilmmnooosuy
incommodiously
cdiilnoorrttuy
introductorily
cdiinoprttuuvy
unproductivity
ceeeeeilnprssx
experienceless
ceeeefginnqruy
eigen-frequency

ceeeefiinnppvy
fivepenny-piece
ceeeefilnrsstv
reflectiveness
ceeeegiilnnort
electioneering
ceeeegilnorsst
electrogenesis
ceeeehimnprswy
chimney-sweeper
ceeeehlnpsssss
speechlessness
ceeeeinnorsstt
enterocentesis
ceeeeinpprsstv
perceptiveness
ceeeellnprstux
superexcellent
ceeeennnoqsstu
sonnet-sequence
ceeeffgilnrsvy
effervescingly
ceeeffhikprrsu
Kupferschiefer
ceeefggillnnst
self-neglecting
ceeefgllnnsstu
neglectfulness
ceeefhilmnnrst
self-enrichment
ceeefhlnnrssuu
uncheerfulness
ceeefiilmprtvy
imperfectively
ceeefillnorsst
reflectionless
ceeefiloprsttv
self-protective
ceeeflnnoqsstu
self-consequent
ceeeflnprssstu
respectfulness
ceeeghiinorsuv
receiving-house
ceeeghlorrsttv
glove-stretcher
ceeegiklnnopsu
counsel-keeping
ceeegilnoprsst
teleprocessing
ceeehimorsstty
hysterectomise
ceeehmmopsssty
metempsychoses
ceeehnoorrttuv
over-the-counter
ceeeiiknnprsst
pernicketiness
ceeeiilprrstvy
irrespectively
ceeeiimmoorrtt
micro-meteorite
ceeeiimoorrsst
stereoisomeric

ceeeiklnpssssy
sleepy-sickness
ceeeiknnoprrst
serpentine-rock
ceeeilmnnopsst
incompleteness
ceeeimmnnoprtv
pincer-movement
ceeeimnnorrsvy
money-scrivener
ceeeinoprssttv
protectiveness
ceeeiooprrttvv
overprotective
ceeellnnoortty
non-electrolyte
ceeellopprrrsw
screw-propeller
ceeffffhiiorrs
sheriff-officer
ceefffiilnsstu
self-sufficient
ceefgillnnrtuy
unreflectingly
ceefgilnoprstt
self-protecting
ceefhhilnoprrs
French-polisher
ceefiillnnosst
inflectionless
ceefiinnossstu
infectiousness
ceefilmmmnostt
self-commitment
ceefilmnnrssuu
unmercifulness
ceefilmnoorsss
frolicsomeness
ceefilnnossstt
self-consistent
ceefinoorsssuv
vociferousness
ceefinoprsssuu
percussion-fuse
ceefllmmnooorw
fellow-commoner
ceeghhiknnrrtt
trencher-knight
ceeghlnooortty
terotechnology
ceegiilnnnortw
electrowinning
ceegiilnnorrty
nitroglycerine
ceeginnnooprtu
counter-opening
ceehhiilmoppst
Mephistophelic
ceehhiiloopsty
heliosciophyte
ceehhilmnorstt
Trochelminthes
ceehhimnoorrst
heterochronism

ceehhimnosssty
chemosynthesis
ceehhiooprrstt
heterostrophic
ceehhmooorrstu
heterochromous
ceehhnooorrstu
heterochronous
ceehhnoopprsst
phosphorescent
ceehiilmoprrty
pyrheliometric
ceehiilnopprty
pyelonephritic
ceehiimoorstty
stoicheiometry
ceehiimoprstyz
piezochemistry
ceehimmopsssty
metempsychosis
ceehinoqssttu
coquettishness
ceeiiknprrssst
princesse-skirt
ceeiillmnorstt
scintillometer
ceeiilmorrstuy
meretriciously
ceeiilnnnnotvy
inconveniently
ceeiilnnossstu
licentiousness
ceeiilnpsstuvy
insusceptively
ceeiilpprrstvy
prescriptively
ceeiimnooprttt
potentiometric
ceeiinnnnoortx
interconnexion
ceeiinnoprsssu
perniciousness
ceeiinnorrsttv
non-restrictive
ceeiioopppprrtv
proprioceptive
ceeiknopprrstu
counter-skipper
ceeiknorrrrstt
terror-stricken
ceeilllnoorstu
nitrocellulose
ceeillmnoopssx
complexionless
ceeillmotuvyzz
muzzle-velocity
ceeillnoqsttuu
stultiloquence
ceeilmnossstuu
meticulousness
ceeilnnnoqstuy
inconsequently
ceeilnnosssuvv
convulsiveness

ceeilnorrssttu
interlocutress
ceeimmnnnosttt
miscontentment
ceeinnnoprsttu
supercontinent
ceeinnoorssssu
censoriousness
ceeinnosssstuu
incestuousness
ceeiprrssttuuv
superstructive
ceemnooprstuyy
pyrenomycetous
ceeprrrssttuuu
superstructure
ceffgiiinnoprt
printing-office
ceffiiilnnstuy
insufficiently
cefghiiknorsst
night-fossicker
cefgiikllnorst
stocking-filler
cefiiiiilopstt
filiopietistic
cegghilmooooopr
geomorphologic
ceghhiillmnoot
helminthologic
ceghhooprssttu
thought-process
ceghiiilnoprss
rice-polishings
ceghiinnorrstt
stretching-iron
ceghnnooorssuy
geosynchronous
ceghnoorrttuuw
counter-wrought
cegiiiklnqrsuv
quicksilvering
cegiiimnorttuy
tumorigenicity
cegiiinprrttuw
picture-writing
cegiinnooorrtt
retrocognition
cegiiooprrssty
Crossopterygii
cegilnnpsstuuy
unsuspectingly
cegimnnoooosuy
gynomonoecious
ceginnoossstuu
contiguousness
cehhiimorsstty
histochemistry
cehhimmnoooppr
morphophonemic
cehhimooprstty
photochemistry
cehhinoopsttty
photosynthetic

cehiiiklmooprt
poikilothermic
cehiiiklqrssuv
quicksilverish
cehiknoorrrrst
horror-stricken
cehillnooprrst
controllership
cehillnooprssu
counsellorship
cehilmmooprsuy
myrmecophilous
cehilmoorsssst
schoolmistress
cehiloooopsstu
opisthocoelous
cehinnoooprstt
stentorophonic
cehinooprsssuy
psychoneurosis
cehllloooprssuy
sclerophyllous
ceiiiinossttvv
vivisectionist
ceiiinorrssttt
restrictionist
ceiilloprssuuy
superciliously
ceiilnnnosstty
inconsistently
ceiilnoossstu
solicitousness
ceiiloopprrstvy
proscriptively
ceiimmnnnoortu
intercommunion
ceiimmnnorttuy
intercommunity
ceiimnnooopssu
pneumoconiosis
ceiinnoorstttu
reconstitution
ceiinoorssstuv
victoriousness
ceiinopprrsstu
superscription
ceiinopssssssuu
suspiciousness
ceillmnoostuuy
contumeliously
ceilnoprrstuuv
proventriculus
ceilnorrssssuu
scurrilousness
ceinnnnooosttu
non-contentious
ceinnnoossstuu
continuousness
ceinoprrssttuu
superstruction
celmnoopsttuuy
contemptuously
celnoprssssuuu
scrupulousness

celooprrssuuuv
overscrupulous
cfgiilmnnoorsu
soul-confirming
cfiillorrsttuu
floriculturist
cfilllooorrsu
corolliflorous
cggiiklnnosstw
swingling-stock
cghiilnopsstuy
psycholinguist
cgiiilnnrsstuy
scrutinisingly
cgiiilnooopsst
oligopsonistic
cgiilnnooqtttu
quilting-cotton
cgiilnnoostuuy
incontiguously
cgiimmnnooprsu
uncompromising
cgilmnnooorstu
consulting-room
chhhnoooprrsuy
rhynchophorous
chhiiiloopppsst
philosophistic
chhiilnoprttty
lithonthryptic
chhiimnoooprrt
ornithomorphic
chhiiooprsstty
trichophytosis
chhiooppprrsy
pyrophosphoric
chiilorrsttuu
horticulturist
chiiooorssttxy
thyrotoxicosis
chilmooorsttuy
trichotomously
chiloooprrstu
prolocutorship
ciiimnnorssttu
misinstruction
ciilnopsssuuuy
unsuspiciously
cllnoprssuuuuy
unscrupulously
ddddeeiilnoopr
lepidodendroid
dddeeeelnopruv
underdeveloped
ddeeeeegnrrswy
dyer's-greenweed
ddeeeefilmnrst
self-determined
ddeeeeimnorrtv
over-determined
ddeeeeinnnprtt
interdependent
ddeeeelmmnosss
meddlesomeness

ddeeeennrsssuv
undeservedness
ddeeefinnnrssu
unfriendedness
ddeeeginnnsssu
undesignedness
ddeeegnoprssst
serpent-goddess
ddeeeimnnnopss
open-mindedness
ddeeeimnnnortu
undermentioned
ddeefghinnortu
night-foundered
ddeeggiiiinnnv
dividing-engine
ddeeghhiimnnss
high-mindedness
ddeeghiilnrssv
silver-shedding
ddeeghillorrsu
shoulder-girdle
ddeegilnnnossw
long-windedness
ddeegnnnorssuu
ungroundedness
ddeehinnorrsuu
undernourished
ddeeiiinprssst
dispiritedness
ddeeiijnnossst
disjointedness
ddeeiilnorrsss
disorderliness
ddeeiinnopssss
indisposedness
ddeghlmoooruuy
good-humouredly
ddegiinnorssww
window-dressing
deeeefhlnorsty
self-heterodyne
deeeefilnrsstt
self-interested
deeeehillosttt
stiletto-heeled
deeeehilnooptv
videotelephone
deeeeillmmosss
mesdemoiselles
deeeeilmnrssss
remedilessness
deeeeinnrssstt
interestedness
deeeelmnopprtv
predevelopment
deeeennrrsssuv
unreservedness
deeefiiinnnsst
indefiniteness
deeefiiinnsstv
definitiveness
deeefilnnrssss
friendlessness
deeefilnpssstu
despitefulness
deeefnoorssstu
sure-footedness
deeeghnnnrsttu
unstrengthened
deeegiiklnnntt
knitting-needle
deeehiiklnoott
kinetheodolite
deeeiillnnossv
love-in-idleness
deeeiimmnprrst
predeterminism
deeeiimnrssttv
divertissement
deeeimnnrrsttu
reed-instrument
deeeinnnprsttu
superintendent
deeelnnorsssuv
unresolvedness
deeemnnorssstu
tremendousness
deeenopprssssu
unprepossessed
deeffiiimnnrst
indifferentism
deeffiiinnrstt
indifferentist
deefghillnsstu
delightfulness
deefgilnorssty
self-destroying
deefiilnnnrssu
unfriendliness
deefiinoprsssu
perfidiousness
deefikllorrtwy
flowery-kirtled
deeghhhilorstu
shoulder-height
deeghhmooorrst
horse-godmother
deeghiimnoprsw
whispering-dome
deeghiinnstuux
unextinguished
deegiiilmoopst
epidemiologist
deegiiinnrrstt
riding-interest
deegiilnnnssuy
unyieldingness
deegilloosstty
dysteleologist
deegilnnnprtuy
unpretendingly
deeglnnorssssu
groundlessness
deegmnoprtttuu
trumpet-tongued
deehiilmnnpsst
displenishment
deehiilpqsssuu
sesquisulphide
deeiiiilmrstuv
verisimilitude
deeiiimnnsstuv
diminutiveness
deeiiinrssttuv
disinvestiture
deeiinopssstu
dispiteousness
deeimnoppprrt
peppermint-drop
deemmoprsstuyy
pseudosymmetry
deennopsssstuu
stupendousness
defghillooopsw
good-fellowship
defgilnsssstuu
disgustfulness
defhiimnnrsstu
disfurnishment
degghilooorsty
hydrogeologist
deggiinnsssstu
disgustingness
deghhhiiooprst
high-priesthood
deghhilorsstty
short-sightedly
deghiloooottv
dogtooth-violet
degiiklnnnossv
loving-kindness
degiilnnossuuy
disingenuously
degiinooprsssu
prodigiousness
degilllnoorwyy
yellow-yoldring
degilnoooprty
periodontology
degilnoorsstuy
soul-destroying
degilnoqrrrsuu
ground-squirrel
dehhinooprrssy
hydronephrosis
dehiiilopprstt
pteridophilist
dehiimooopprst
photoperiodism
dehimmoopprssu
pseudomorphism
dehmoooprssuu
pseudomorphous
deiiiillnosssu
disillusionise
deiiinoopprsst
predisposition
deiimnnnrsttuw
wind-instrument
deilmnooopsstu
diplostemonous
deilnooopsstuu
pseudosolution
deinnooopprrtu
unproportioned
delmnoopssuuyy
pseudonymously
dfgghinnoooort
good-for-nothing
dgghiiiinnsstu
distinguishing
dggimnnooprstu
stomping-ground
dghiinnooppsww
window-shopping
dhhiimooprstyy
hypothyroidism
dhinoooprssttt
prosthodontist
diiilmnoossstu
dissolutionism
diiilnoossttu
dissolutionist
eeeefglnnrssuv
revengefulness
eeeefimnnorrtv
over-refinement
eeeefimnorrtt
interferometer
eeeefknnoprsss
free-spokenness
eeeeghmmoorrtt
geothermometer
eeeeginrrssssv
regressiveness
eeeehilnprrsvy
reprehensively
eeeehlmprrsstu
pressure-helmet
eeeeiinprssttv
repetitiveness
eeeeilprrtttwy
teletypewriter
eeeeinnprrtttu
turpentine-tree
eeeeinnprsssv
presentiveness
eeeeinnprsstvv
preventiveness
eeeeinprssssvx
expressiveness
eeeellnnrsssst
relentlessness
eeeelmmnossstt
mettlesomeness
eeefglmnnorstv
self-government
eeefilnoprsssx
self-expression
eeefimnorrrtty
interferometry
eeefllmmnopsty
self-employment
eeeflmnorrsssu
remorsefulness

14 EEE

eeeggimnnorrsv
verse-mongering
eeegginsssstuv
suggestiveness
eeeghilnsssstw
weightlessness
eeegiikmnopprs
promise-keeping
eeeginoqrrstuu
turquoise-green
eeehhilmoppsst
Mephistopheles
eeehiinnnopprr
norepinephrine
eeehiinprsssty
hypersensitise
eeehiinprsstvy
hypersensitive
eeehilllmnosst
shell-limestone
eeehiopprrrstw
tree-worshipper
eeehlmnoooottu
homoeoteleuton
eeeiimnnnrttw
intertwinement
eeeiimnprrrstt
misinterpreter
eeeiimnprssssv
impressiveness
permissiveness
eeeiinprssstuv
supersensitive
eeeilmnnprstuy
supereminently
eeeilmnosssstv
motivelessness
eeeilnoprssssx
expressionless
eeeilnorrssstu
irresoluteness
eeeilnrssssst
resistlessness
eeeimnopprrsst
peremptoriness
eeeinnoprssssv
responsiveness
eeeinopprssssv
oppressiveness
eeeinopssssssv
possessiveness
eeellnrssssstu
resultlessness
eefffilllmnstu
self-fulfilment
eefggilnossstu
self-suggestion
eefghhiinrrrsy
herring-fishery
eefghinnoorrst
foreshortening
eefgillnnorttu
fortune-telling
eefgilmnnorstt
self-tormenting
eefhhiloorsstw
two-for-his-heels
eefhiiopprrrsw
fire-worshipper
eefhilmnnpsstu
self-punishment
eefhilnrsssstt
thriftlessness
eefllmnorrsuuy
unremorsefully
eeflnopprsssuu
purposefulness
eegghhiilnnstt
sheet-lightning
eeghhiilnpsstw
sheep-whistling
eeghiimnnsttux
extinguishment
eeghillmnorvwy
overwhelmingly
eeghinoopprrty
Porphyrogenite
eegiilmnorttuu
ultimogeniture
eegiilmoopsstt
epistemologist
eegiilnnnprsty
serpentiningly
eegiilnnprrsty
enterprisingly
eegiinnnprrstu
unenterprising
eegilnooprrvwy
overpoweringly
eehhilnpprsttu
hunt-the-slipper
eehhiloopprsss
philosopheress
eehhimmooprrst
heteromorphism
eehhiopppptyy
hippety-hoppety
eehhllooprstuy
heterophyllous
eehhmmoooorstu
homoeothermous
eehhmoooprrstu
heteromorphous
eehiilmnnqrstu
relinquishment
eehiilnopprsty
pyelonephritis
eehiimmnoprstv
impoverishment
eehiinoopssstt
photosensitise
eehiinoopssttv
photosensitive
eehiiooprrssty
erythropoiesis
eehiklmnoprsst
skeleton-shrimp
eehilnnnopstty
penny-in-the-slot
eehimpprssssst
sempstress-ship
eehinnoorssttw
noteworthiness
eehinnorssstww
newsworthiness
eehinopprrsstw
serpent-worship
eehmmnoorsssuu
humoursomeness
eeiiimnpstttvy
intempestivity
eeiilmnnrtttty
intermittently
eeiilnnrsssstu
unsisterliness
eeiilnoprrssvy
irresponsively
eeiilnprrttuvy
interruptively
eeiilnprssssst
spiritlessness
eeiimmmnoprstv
misimprovement
eeiimnoprsssuv
imperviousness
eeiklmnoqrrsuy
squirrel-monkey
eeilmnnnnootvv
non-involvement
eeilnnoprssuvy
unresponsively
eeimnorsssstuy
mysteriousness
eeinoprrssstuv
protrusiveness
eeiopprrsssttu
strepsipterous
eeklnoorrsttuv
true-lover's-knot
eelnnoorssstuu
ultroneousness
eeloopprrsstuy
preposterously
eennoooprrsst
person-to-person
eennooprssstu
portentousness
eenoopprrssssu
prosperousness
eenoorrssssttu
stertorousness
efffgiillllnsu
self-fulfilling
effghhloorttuu
forethoughtful
effgiijlnsstuy
self-justifying
effilnnrsstuuu
unfruitfulness
efgghiilnnortw
night-flowering
efggiiinnnoprt
finger-pointing
efggiiinnnprrt
fingerprinting
efghhilnoorrst
threshing-floor
efghhinorrsstt
forthrightness
efghhlnossttuu
thoughtfulness
efghiilnoorrtw
withering-floor
efghilnnrsstuu
unrightfulness
efghilnprssstu
sprightfulness
efgilnopprsstu
self-supporting
efhilnoprsssuw
worshipfulness
efhlnnrssttuuu
untruthfulness
efillnoopprssu
self-propulsion
efilooprrssuy
soporiferously
efinoorsssttuu
fortuitousness
eghhimnnooopst
monophthongise
eghhllootttuuw
well-thought-out
eghiiilmnrsstv
silversmithing
eghiiklnnnsstu
unknightliness
eghiiknnnnsstu
unthinkingness
eghiimooqsttuw
mosquito-weight
eghiinoopprrst
progenitorship
eghlnnooopruyy
neurohypnology
eghloooprrtty
orthopterology
egiiilmnnrttty
intermittingly
egiiilnnnrttwy
intertwiningly
egiiimnnnrtttu
unintermitting
egiikllmnoorst
Kremlinologist
egiilnnoorsssu
ingloriousness
egiimnooprrsss
progressionism
egiinnoprrrstu
interior-sprung
egiinnprrssssu
surprisingness
egiinooprrssst
progressionist

14 IIL

egilmmmnoprtuu
rummelgumption
rummlegumption
ehhiiilmoppsst
Mephistophilis
ehhiimmooprrst
theriomorphism
ehhilmooppsstu
Mephostophilus
ehhimmmoooprs
homoeomorphism
ehhimmoooorstu
homoiothermous
ehhimoooprrstu
theriomorphous
ehhinoooppprst
phosphoprotein
ehhinoopssstty
photosynthesis
ehhmmooooprsu
homoeomorphous
ehhnnoorrstttw
north-north-west
ehhoossstttuuw
south-south-west
ehiilmnoprstuw
multi-ownership
ehiilnnooprrtt
trinitrophenol
ehiiooppprrrst
proprietorship

ehiiopprrsssuv
supervisorship
ehilmnopssttyy
polysynthetism
ehinoooprrsstu
trophoneurosis
eiiiinnqrsttuu
inquisiturient
eiiiinoqrssttu
requisitionist
eiiimnorsstttu
restitutionism
eiiinnoqssstuu
iniquitousness
eiiinorsstttu
restitutionist
eiikmnnooopssu
pneumokoniosis
eiikmnnoorrtuw
munition-worker
eiilmnooqrsuuy
querimoniously
eiilooppssttvy
postpositively
eiinnorssstuu
nutritiousness
eiinoopprrsstu
presupposition
eiinooprrssstu
propitiousness

eiinoprssssttuu
spirituousness
eilmnnoosssuuv
voluminousness
eilnooopprrsst
proportionless
eimmnopprsssuu
immunosuppress
eimnnoooprrtt
proportionment
einoprssttuvy
topsyturviness
elmnossttuuuu
tumultuousness
elmopprsstuuuy
presumptuously
elnoopprrssuuy
unprosperously
elnoopssstuuuv
voluptuousness
emnnnoooossstu
monotonousness
emnnnoossssuyy
synonymousness
emnopprsstuuuu
unpresumptuous
fgghiiiillnoptw
pillow-fighting
fghhllnottuuuy
unthoughtfully

ggiiiknnrsssst
kissing-strings
ggiiilloorsttu
liturgiologist
ghhiiikllnrrss
shrill-shriking
ghhiillnorsstw
shillingsworth
ghiikmnnnoostw
know-nothingism
ghiloooopsttyz
zoophytologist
giiiinprrrsstt
spirit-stirring
giilooooprssttt
protistologist
gilooooprsttz
protozoologist
hhiilnoooprstu
ornithophilous
hhloopprssuuuy
hyposulphurous
hiiilnoprstttt
lithontriptist
iiiooppssttuu
supposititious
iillnooorrtttu
trinitrotoluol
iilnoopprstuuy
unpropitiously

15 AAA

aaaabcchiilmnns
bacchanalianism
aaaabcehinrrttt
Tetrabranchiata
aaaabceillnoopt
palaeobotanical
aaaacccchhnstt
catch-as-catch-can
aaaaccilllltty
catallactically
aaaacceeeiilnps
Caesalpiniaceae
aaaaceghilloppr
palaeographical
aaaacegiilrrrwy
railway-carriage
aaaacghillpprry
paragraphically
aaaaeiilmnnprrt
parliamentarian
aaaaelmorrssttt
tarsometatarsal
aaaaghilmnoprst
phantasmagorial

aaabbbeghiknrst
Sabbath-breaking
aaabbddeefknrst
bed-and-breakfast
aaabbeegimnnrst
bargain-basement
aaabcceehlmnrsu
ambulance-chaser
aaabccehiinrttt
Tectibranchiata
aaabcdeeehilmnr
machine-readable
aaabcdeellmnprs
landscape-marble
aaabceehinrrttt
tetrabranchiate
aaabceeilnnrstu
unascertainable
aaabceflmnnrstu
blast-furnaceman
aaabceilllrstty
tetrasyllabical
aaabceillmnrrtu
interambulacral

aaabchiiloppry
approachability
aaabeeillnnssuv
unavailableness
aaabeelnnrrsstw
warrantableness
aaabiilmnprsssu
sublapsarianism
aaaccceefilnpst
self-capacitance
aaaccceehiillrt
Callitrichaceae
aaacccehhkmnnoy
hackney-coachman
aaacccilllmstyy
cataclysmically
aaaccdeehhilmry
Archichlamydeae
aaaccdeeilopssu
asclepiadaceous
aaacceeeilnooru
Eriocaulonaceae
aaacceeghiknrry
hackney-carriage

aaacceehknoppst
peacock-pheasant
aaacceehllopryy
Caryophyllaceae
aaacceeinnpqrtu
preacquaintance
aaaccefiirrrrt
aircraft-carrier
aaacceghilnoopr
oceanographical
aaacceiillnprty
Capernaitically
aaacceillnnorty
anacreontically
aaaccemopprrstu
carpometacarpus
aaacchiilmnnort
antimonarchical
aaacciiilmnostt
acclimatisation
aaacciilllsttty
stalactitically
aaacciillmnorty
microanalytical
aaaccilllopptyy
apocalyptically
aaacdeeffghirrs
chargé-d'affaires
aaacdefgiorrrrw
carriage-forward
aaacdefjkllorst
Jack-of-all-trades
aaacdeggiilnnrr
landing-carriage
aaacdegiillmnty
diamagnetically
aaacdehiilmmssy
Michaelmas-daisy
aaacdeillmorsuy
amaryllidaceous
aaacdeilnoprssx
paradoxicalness
aaacdiinnnnotuy
Annunciation-day
aaaceeeegilllns
Selaginellaceae
aaaceeeilnprrrs
seaplane-carrier
aaaceehillnstty
anaesthetically
aaaceehimmmsttt
metamathematics
aaacefhhiilmrrs
air-chief-marshal
aaacefilnnssstt
fantasticalness
aaacegilmnoprty
malacopterygian
aaacegilmnprsst
pragmaticalness
aaacegilnnopstu
plantaginaceous
aaacehhiilmprtt
amphitheatrical

aaacehiilnprsss
pharisaicalness
aaacehimpprstty
parasympathetic
aaaceiiillmrstt
materialistical
aaaceiilnprssst
parasiticalness
aaacgghijklnssu
laughing-jackass
aaacghhiloprsst
thalassographic
aaacghiilprrstt
stratigraphical
aaacghilloprtuy
autographically
aaacgiiillmnnst
anti-Gallicanism
aaacgiilllmstty
stalagmitically
aaacgillmmnrtuy
ungrammatically
aaacgillmoorttu
traumatological
aaacgimnopprstt
pantopragmatics
aaaciiilllmnosty
anomalistically
aaaciilnorsstuv
vascularisation
aaaciiorsstttw
strait-waistcoat
aaacillnnoorttv
contravallation
aaaddefhnnrssst
hard-and-fastness
aaaddeginosstuv
disadvantageous
aaaddiinnorsstt
standardisation
aaadeefgimorswx
meadow-saxifrage
aaadeegjlnnrttu
adjutant-general
aaadghiiimprstt
diaphragmatitis
aaadghiooprrtuy
autoradiography
aaadiiilnnprttu
platitudinarian
aaaeegghloopry
palaeogeography
aaaeegilmmnopst
palaeomagnetism
aaaeeglmmnnrstt
gentleman-at-arms
aaaeghhloprrsst
thalassographer
aaaeghlnoopprty
palaeontography
aaaegiimnnosttv
steam-navigation
aaaegiinnnqqruu
quinquagenarian

aaaeiiilmnorstt
materialisation
aaaeiiilmnqrstu
equalitarianism
aaaeiiilnorrstt
arterialisation
aaaeiillmnprrty
parliamentarily
aaaeiilmmnprrst
parliamentarism
aaaeilmnnprrtuy
unparliamentary
aaaemorrsssttu
tarsometatarsus
aaagiillnorttvy
gravitationally
aaagiinnoorsttv
astronavigation
aaahiiimmnnrstu
humanitarianism
aaaiiiinnnrrttt
antitrinitarian
aaaiiillmmnosst
malassimilation
aaaiiillmnnoprs
Apollinarianism
aaaiiilmnorsttt
totalitarianism
aaaiiilnnnoostt
nationalisation
aaaiiilnnoorstt
rationalisation
aaaiiimnpprssst
Patripassianism
aaaiilmnnortuwy
mountain-railway
aaailnnnoprsttt
transplantation
aabbbdeeklnqsuu
bubble-and-squeak
aabbcghiiillopr
bibliographical
aabbeeellmnnssu
unblameableness
aabbeilmmnnortu
mountain-bramble
aabbiinnorsstuu
suburbanisation
aabccdeehillnsy
hendecasyllabic
aabccdhlorstuyy
brachydactylous
aabcceehiilmnrv
vice-chamberlain
aabcceehiinrttt
tectibranchiate
aabcceeilnprsst
practicableness
aabcceelnnosstu
accountableness
aabcceelorrrsuv
cerebrovascular
aabccegiilloort
bacteriological

aabccegiilmnruv
circumnavigable
aabccehhloprsuy
brachycephalous
aabccgiimmorsuu
circumambagious
aabcciiilllntuy
incalculability
aabcciilnorttty
contractability
aabcdeeegkllnow
acknowledgeable
aabcdeeehlllnsy
hendecasyllable
aabcdeefiilmort
democratifiable
aabcdeegkllnowy
acknowledgeably
aabcdeelmnnortu
countermandable
aabcdehiinorrst
dorsibranchiate
aabcdeiinnoorst
decarbonisation
aabcdeiinorrstu
decarburisation
aabcdhiillmrtyy
dithyrambically
aabceeeelnnpssu
unpeaceableness
aabceeeghilnnrt
interchangeable
aabceeeghlllnnu
unchallengeable
aabceeegllnnoss
congealableness
aabceeehlnnsstu
unteachableness
aabceeghiilntxy
exchangeability
aabceeghilnnrty
interchangeably
aabceeghlllnnuy
unchallengeably
aabceegiillnoty
abiogenetically
aabceeillnortuv
countervailable
aabceeilnnrsstt
intractableness
aabceelnnrssttu
untractableness
aabcegghhimnnrs
chamber-hangings
aabcegghiiloopr
biogeographical
aabceghiilnntuy
unchangeability
aabcegilmnopsuu
plumbaginaceous
aabcehhiilmnprs
chamberlainship
aabcehhilnooprt
lophobranchiate
aabcehilmnoprtu
pulmobranchiate
aabcehilprrstuu
sulphur-bacteria
aabceilllmoprty
problematically
aabceilllmorsty
meroblastically
aabceilmmnrrtuu
interambulacrum
aabceilmnnnoopu
uncompanionable
aabceilmoprsstt
spermatoblastic
aabceilnnnorstu
unconstrainable
aabceinnosstttu
consubstantiate
aabcfiiillnosty
syllabification
aabchhiinooprst
Opisthobranchia
aabchiiimnoprrs
Marsipobranchii
aabciiiillnppty
inapplicability
aabciiilmnoprty
incomparability
aabciillllrstyy
trisyllabically
aabciinoorssttu
bioastronautics
aabdeefghinorrt
feather-boarding
aabdeeflmnnnost
self-abandonment
aabdeeghinorrtw
weather-boarding
aabdeegiiilrsty
disagreeability
aabdeeiilnnsssv
inadvisableness
aabdeeilnnossuv
unavoidableness
aabdeeilnnsssuv
unadvisableness
aabdeinnsstttuu
unsubstantiated
aabdelnnprstuuy
superabundantly
aabdhiiiilnostt
dishabilitation
aabdinnooorttuu
roundaboutation
aabeeeflmnortty
flamboyante-tree
aabeeehillnnpst
nepheline-basalt
aabeeeilnprrrss
irreparableness
aabeeellnnrsstu
unalterableness
aabeeellnprsssu
pleasurableness
aabeeelnnorssst
treasonableness
aabeefhilnnosss
fashionableness
aabeefillmmnnss
inflammableness
aabeeiiillprrty
irrepealability
aabeeinnpprrsty
Pan-Presbyterian
aabefgiiilrrrty
irrefragability
aabefillnssstu
self-substantial
aabefilnoopprst
self-approbation
aabeiilmnortuvy
manoeuvrability
aabeillnoorstvy
observationally
aabeilnnsssstu
substantialness
aabgiilmmoprrty
programmability
aabiillnnssttuy
insubstantially
aabiilmnrsttuy
transmutability
aacccdeeillnopy
encyclopaedical
aacccdefiiilnot
decalcification
aaccceehilprtty
hypercatalectic
aacccehiilnortt
architectonical
aacccehiiopprsy
archiepiscopacy
aaccchilllooorty
ochlocratically
aacccillmmoorsy
macrocosmically
aacccillmooprsy
macroscopically
aaccddeeeillnnr
Cinderella-dance
aaccdeeehilttuv
vehicle-actuated
aaccdeeioprsssu
peasecod-cuirass
aaccdehiiossttu
autoschediastic
aaccdfiimmoorrr
micromicrofarad
aaccdgimmnnootu
unaccommodating
aaccdhhilnoopry
hypochondriacal
aaccdhiimoossst
sado-masochistic
aaccdhilnooprst
achondroplastic
aaccdiiilnorsty
idiosyncratical

aacceeegiilmnrr
marriage-licence
aacceegilnorsst
categoricalness
aacceehiiopprst
archiepiscopate
aacceehnrrssttv
canvas-stretcher
aacceeimnnrsttu
casement-curtain
aaccefiilnrrstu
interfascicular
aaccefiilooprsu
caprifoliaceous
aacceghiilloopt
hepaticological
aacceghiilloprx
lexicographical
aacceghiimnoprt
cinematographic
aaccehhhilnopry
Rhynchocephalia
aaccehhilmnoopt
photomechanical
aaccehhilmorstt
chrestomathical
aaccehhlooppssu
scaphocephalous
aaccehiillmnsty
mechanistically
aaccehiklnoosvz
Czechoslovakian
aaccehinnnnoptv
pantechnicon-van
aaccehmnorsstuy
sarcenchymatous
aaccehnoopprrtu
counter-approach
aacceiiiillmnrst
anticlericalism
aacceiillmnosty
encomiastically
aacceiillnrrtuv
interclavicular
aacceiilmnprsst
impracticalness
aacceiimnrstttu
circumstantiate
aacceiinnopsssu
incapaciousness
aacceillmnnorty
necromantically
aacceilnnnnossu
uncanonicalness
aacceilnnooorst
consolation-race
aacceilrrrtuux
extra-curricular
aaccghhilopprsy
psychographical
aaccghhimooprrt
chromatographic
aaccghimnooprst
pharmacognostic

aaccgiimnorrtuv
circumnavigator
aacchiiimnnorst
monarchianistic
aacchillnopstyy
sycophantically
aacciiiilllossty
socialistically
aacciiilprrsttu
particularistic
aacciillmnortuv
circumvallation
aacciilmnrssttu
circumstantials
aaccikkkknnorty
knick-knackatory
aacddegghilnrrt
great-grandchild
aacddeilmnnoopr
companion-ladder
aacddellooprrrs
saddler-corporal
aacdeeeflmnnstv
self-advancement
aacdeeffiinostt
disaffectionate
aacdeehiiorrstt
icositetrahedra
aacdeehinntttuu
unauthenticated
aacdeeiiillnrttt
Tetractinellida
aacdeeiimnnottv
decontaminative
aacdeghiillopry
ideographically
aacdehhiilnprst
Christadelphian
aacdehillnoorry
Hydrocorallinae
aacdeiijllrtuxy
extra-judicially
aacdeiimnnnoott
decontamination
aacdeiimnoorstt
democratisation
aacdfiiinossstt
dissatisfaction
aacdfiiorssstty
dissatisfactory
aacdgghillnnorw
all-changing-word
aacdgiillnnrstu
slantingdicular
aacdgiillnrtuvy
victualling-yard
aacdhhilloprtyy
hydropathically
aacdhillorsttyy
hydrostatically
aacdiiiillmnotuy
unidiomatically
aacdiiilnorsttu
disarticulation

aacdiiimnnorrst
doctrinarianism
aacdiilnopqrtuu
quadruplication
aacdiimnorsstty
astrodynamicist
aacdiinnnoottuy
continuation-day
aaceeeghimoprrt
Megacheiroptera
aaceeegillnnssv
evangelicalness
aaceeegmnoprstu
pergamentaceous
aaceeehilllmnuw
wheel-animalcule
aaceeeinrrssstt
crease-resistant
aaceeennqrrttuy
quatercentenary
aaceeffhimnnrst
affranchisement
aaceeffiklrrstv
slave-trafficker
aaceefimmnrstuu
semimanufacture
aaceeghhlnoppry
encephalography
aaceeghilllprty
telegraphically
aaceeghillnoprs
selenographical
aaceeghilooopss
Ophioglossaceae
aaceeghiloprrst
stereographical
aaceeghimnoprrt
cinematographer
aaceegillnprstv
space-travelling
aaceehhhlnooprx
hexachlorophane
aaceehiilpprrst
Pre-Raphaelistic
aaceehillmortty
theorematically
aaceehillnprtty
parenthetically
aaceehillprttuy
therapeutically
aaceehilmopsstu
mesaticephalous
aaceeiiimpprstv
misappreciative
aaceeillnorssty
electroanalysis
aaceeilnnrrtttu
intertentacular
aacefghiikmnnnr
franking-machine
aaceegghilooprz
zoogeographical
aaceghiilmnnpst
stapling-machine

aaceghiilmoprss
seismographical
aaceghiimmnnpst
stamping-machine
aaceghillmoortu
rheumatological
aacegiikllmoorr
kilogram-calorie
aacegiilllmnory
mineralogically
aacegiilnnorstt
clearing-station
aacegillmnooptu
pneumatological
aacegillnorrsst
citronella-grass
aacehhillmoopty
homeopathically
aacehiiloopprrt
paraheliotropic
aacehillmoprsty
atmospherically
aacehillmpsttyy
sympathetically
aaceiiilmnoppss
episcopalianism
aaceiiilnprsttt
antiperistaltic
aaceiiimnnopstt
emancipationist
aaceiiimnopprst
misappreciation
aaceiiinnorsstt
canisterisation
aaceiilllprstty
peristaltically
aaceiillmnnrsty
manneristically
aaceiillmrtttuu
multiarticulate
aaceiilmnoprrtt
malpractitioner
aaceiilnoprrtvx
extra-provincial
aaceiinnnostty
co-instantaneity
aaceiinoprrsttv
procrastinative
aaceijlnorrttuy
interjaculatory
aaceillorrsstty
cross-laterality
aaceilmnoopssty
compassionately
aaceimnnoopsstu
uncompassionate
aaceinnnoossttu
co-instantaneous
aacellmmnoprtty
compartmentally
aacfgiiiinnortt
granitification
aacfgiilnnoortu
configurational

aacfiiinnoorstt
fractionisation
aacfilmmnnooort
malconformation
aacfilnnnooortt
confrontational
aacgghhilnoopry
cholangiography
aacgghillloopry
logographically
aacgghilloorss
glossographical
aacghhiiloprsy
physiographical
aacghhinooprtu
phonautographic
aacghiilllmorty
logarithmically
aacghillmnoopry
gramophonically
aacghillnoooprt
anthropological
aacghilloopprty
topographically
aacghillopprtyy
typographically
aacghimnnnoootott
thanatognomonic
aacghimnooprsst
pharmacognosist
aacghlloprrstyy
crystallography
aacgiiilnprsstu
paralinguistics
aacgiillrrsttuu
agriculturalist
aacgiilnorrsswy
railway-crossing
aacgiinnoprrstt
procrastinating
aacgimmnooprrsu
macrosporangium
aachhiillnopprt
philanthropical
aachiiilnnrstty
antichristianly
aachiiiloqrsstu
quasihistorical
aachillmooprtuy
automorphically
aaciiiilmnnorst
criminalisation
aaciiiilnorrstt
irrationalistic
aaciiilllrsttuy
ritualistically
aaciiimnnoorstt
romanticisation
aaciillnoprttuy
unpatriotically
aaciillnorsstty
crystallisation
aaciilmmnnoostu
communalisation

aaciilnnoprrstt
transcriptional
aaciinnooprrstt
procrastination
aacilllnoopstuy
unapostolically
aacillmmopsttyy
symptomatically
aacillmnnopstuy
uncomplaisantly
aacinooprrrstty
procrastinatory
aadddeiinnrrtvw
dividend-warrant
aaddeeeglnrrsst
saddler-sergeant
aaddeeehhnrrsst
hard-heartedness
aaddeefgilnorst
self-degradation
aaddehknorrrtww
drawn-threadwork
aadeeeegilprssw
spread-eaglewise
aadeeefhhlnrsst
half-heartedness
aadeeehmnrrsstw
warm-heartedness
aadeeeilmnprstt
departmentalise
aadeeeimnstttv
testament-dative
aadeefnnssssttu
unsteadfastness
aadeeggikmnnrrt
market-gardening
aadeeghiloprrty
radiotelegraphy
aadeeghlnoopsux
pseudohexagonal
aadeegiimnnostt
demagnetisation
aadeehilmnprrsy
hyperadrenalism
aadeeiilnosstux
desexualisation
aadeeiinorrrstx
extraordinaries
aadeeilmmnprstt
departmentalism
aadeghiilnnpsuu
sulphaguanidine
aadeghimnoooprr
radiogramophone
aadeghiooprrrxy
xeroradiography
aadeghmnooprrrt
ergatandromorph
aadegimnnrrsttu
untransmigrated
aadehhiijnnnory
Johnny-head-in-air
aadehhiilmnoprt
edriophthalmian

aadehimmnoopstw
shadow-pantomime
aadehlnorrsttwy
north-eastwardly
aadehlorssttuwy
south-eastwardly
aadeiiiilmssstv
disassimilative
aadeiilnopsssty
dispassionately
aadeiilnorrrtxy
extraordinarily
aadelnoprsttuuy
polyunsaturated
aademnooprrttuw
portmanteau-word
aadfghiorrrsttw
straightforward
aadfiiilnnorsty
disinflationary
aadgiiinnoorsst
disorganisation
aadhillnorrstyy
synarthrodially
aadiiinopqrrttu
quadripartition
aaeeeglnnorrtty
attorney-general
aaeeegmmnrrssst
messenger-at-arms
aaeeehiilnorstt
etherealisation
aaeeehkmmorrttt
katathermometer
aaeeeilmnnptttu
antepenultimate
aaeeeilnqrttuvw
water-equivalent
aaeeellmmnprtty
temperamentally
aaeeffinoorrstt
reafforestation
aaeefgimnnrrsst
fragmentariness
aaeefhilrssttvv
harvest-festival
aaeefiilmnnostx
self-examination
aaeefllnoprstxy
self-explanatory
aaeeghhimoppstt
apophthegmatise
aaeeghiilmnnprt
parliament-hinge
aaeeghilnoossty
anaesthesiology
aaeeghimoopprrr
paroemiographer
aaeegiiilmmnpss
Semi-Pelagianism
aaeegiiimnnsstv
imaginativeness
aaeegiilmnrssst
magisterialness
aaeegiilnnorstv
evangelistarion
aaeegijlmnnnrsu
Jungermanniales
aaeegilmnrttuvy
argumentatively
aaeeglnnooprsss
saloon-passenger
aaeehhiilpprrst
Pre-Raphaelitish
aaeehiilmpprrst
Pre-Raphaelitism
aaeehilmnnorttu
mountain-leather
aaeehilmnoprstu
parliament-house
aaeehinnoortttw
weather-notation
aaeeiiilnnorsttx
externalisation
aaeeiklmnnssttu
unstatesmanlike
aaeeillrrstttux
extra-illustrate
aaeeilmnnoprstt
malpresentation
aaeeilmnooprttt
metropolitanate
aaeeilnoprsttux
superexaltation
aaeeilnprrsstuu
supernaturalise
aaeeimnnprrsstt
semitransparent
aaeeinoppprrsst
appropriateness
aaeellnprrrttuy
preternaturally
aaeennnprrssstt
transparentness
aaefffiilmnorst
self-affirmation
aaefgiimorrrstu
margaritiferous
aaegghinoprsstt
steganographist
aaeghhillmooppt
ophthalmoplegia
aaeghhimoppsttt
apophthegmatist
aaeghhinoopprtt
anthropophagite
aaeghiimmorrstt
hierogrammatist
aaeghllooopptyy
palaeophytology
aaegiiilmnntuvy
unimaginatively
aaegiiilnnoorst
regionalisation
aaegiimnooprrrt
marriage-portion
aaegilllmnooopy
palaeolimnology
aaegillnooopstt
palaeontologist
aaegilloooopstz
palaeozoologist
aaegilloprrrtty
portrait-gallery
aaegilnnorrssst
transgressional
aaegimnoprrsttu
tetrasporangium
aaeginorrssttu
angustirostrate
aaehiilortttuvy
authoritatively
aaehiinortttuuv
unauthoritative
aaeiiilmnnnortt
interlamination
aaeiiilmnorsstt
Aristotelianism
aaeiillmnnoprst
post-millenarian
aaeiillmnnrsttu
transilluminate
aaeiillnnnortty
internationally
aaeiilnnooprsst
personalisation
aaeiilnnorrsttt
transliteration
aaeiilnoppprrty
inappropriately
aaeiimnosssttty
systematisation
aaeiinopprrrttt
portrait-painter
aaeilmnprrsstuu
supernaturalism
aaeilnnnossttuy
instantaneously
aaeilnprrssttuu
supernaturalist
aaeinoprrssttuu
supersaturation
aaelnoprrstttu
ultra-Protestant
aafgiinnorrsttu
transfiguration
aafiilmnoorrstu
formularisation
aafiiooprrssttw
two-pair-of-stairs
aafillmnoprstuy
slumpflationary
aaghhnoooppr stu
anthropophagous
aaghiiimnnnorst
nothingarianism
aaghlnooprrstuy
ultrasonography
aagiiilnnorsstu
singularisation
aagiiilnnorsttu
granulitisation

aagilmooopssttu
plagiostomatous
aahhhlopprrstyy
staphylorrhaphy
aahhiilmnoppstt
panophthalmitis
aahhimnoopprstt
anthropopathism
aahiiiilmnnnost
annihilationism
aahiiilnoopsstt
hospitalisation
aahioopprrssttu
protospatharius
aaiiiimnnorsttu
miniaturisation
aaiiillnnoprsty
inspirationally
aaiiilmmnoorstt
immortalisation
aaiiilmooprrstv
improvisatorial
aaiijlnoopsttux
juxtapositional
aaiiklmnoosssty
ankylostomiasis
aaiilnnooprsstt
transpositional
aaiimnooprsssty
trypanosomiasis
aaiinnoopppqrtu
appropinquation
aaillnoopsttuy
postulationally
abbccceiilmrrsu
circumscribable
abbceeijlnnootu
unobjectionable
abbceeilmmoorrt
bomb-calorimeter
abbcegiilnpprrs
scribbling-paper
abbceijlnnootuy
unobjectionably
abbddeeelllorru
double-barrelled
abbdeeiilnnsstu
indubitableness
abbdeiiilnrsttu
indistributable
abbeghiilnsttyy
shabby-gentility
abbehrrrrsstuwy
strawberry-shrub
abbeiiilopqrtuy
equiprobability
abcchilnoooprs
bronchoscopical
abcceeeehmnprrs
presence-chamber
abcceeeilnnossv
conceivableness
abcceeiillnnoru
unreconciliable
abcceeillnoopst
police-constable
abccefiiijnoott
objectification
abccefiillpssuy
subspecifically
abccehhinoorrst
brachistochrone
abcceiiiilnssty
inaccessibility
abcceiiillnorty
reconcilability
abcceiilllopsu
ebullioscopical
abcceiinorssssu
scribaciousness
abccgiiillooos
sociobiological
abcciiilmmnotuy
communicability
abcciiilnorttty
contractibility
abcddeeeeillops
peasecod-bellied
abcddeeeflnossu
double-facedness
abcddehhillnory
Rhynchobdellida
abcddeklnorrsuw
sword-and-buckler
abcdeeeilnprsst
predictableness
abcdeeelmmnnoru
unrecommendable
abcdeeelmmnnoss
commendableness
abcdeehiiilprty
decipherability
abcdeeiilnossss
dissociableness
abcdeiiiillnnps
indisciplinable
abcdeiiiillnnpsu
undisciplinable
abcdeiilmoopsty
decomposability
abcdeiimoosstuy
basidiomycetous
abcdeilnooorruw
rainbow-coloured
abcdghiiilooory
hydrobiological
abcdiiiilrsttty
distractibility
abceeeehrrrrstt
stretcher-bearer
abceeeeilnrsssv
serviceableness
abceeeelnorrssv
recoverableness
abceeeelnprssst
respectableness
abceeeilnnoptux
unexceptionable
abceeeilnnsssux
inexcusableness
abceeeilnorrssv
irrevocableness
abceeelnnoqrssu
conquerableness
abceehhlmnnoopr
rhombencephalon
abceeilmmnnorsu
incommensurable
abceeilnnoptuxy
unexceptionably
abceeilnnrssstu
inscrutableness
abceelnnnoopruu
unpronounceable
abceiiiilnptxy
inexplicability
abceiiiilpprtty
precipitability
abceiilloprsssy
perissosyllabic
abceiilnorsttuu
tuberculisation
abceilmmnnorsuy
incommensurably
abcggiiillnoooot
gnotobiological
abcghhiiopprsyy
psychobiography
abcgiiilllllntuv
victualling-bill
abcgiillnoootty
gnotobiotically
abciiiilmnoptty
incompatibility
abciiilmmnottuy
incommutability
abciilllmopssyy
polysyllabicism
abciilllnoortty
controllability
abciilorrrsttuu
arboriculturist
abdddehlnnoortu
blood-and-thunder
abdeeeeilmnprrt
predeterminable
abdeeeiiilmrrty
irredeemability
abdeeeilnnpssss
dispensableness
abdeeeilnnrsssu
undesirableness
abdeefiiiilnsty
indefeasibility
abdeehilmoorttw
Bartholomew-tide
abdeeiiilmnrtty
determinability
abdeeillnossssv
dissolvableness
abdeeinnorssstu
subordinateness

abdegghhiillnrv
high-gravel-blind
abdeghiiilnsstu
distinguishable
abdeiiilmnoprty
imponderability
abdeiiilprsttuy
disreputability
abdeiilmnorstty
demonstrability
abdeiilnnorstuy
insubordinately
abdffgiiiilnrty
diffrangibility
abdghiiilnsstuy
distinguishably
abdiiiiilmnssty
inadmissibility
abdiiilmnorsttu
maldistribution
abdiiinnnoorstu
insubordination
abdiilnoorttuuy
roundaboutility
abeeeeilmmnprss
impermeableness
abeeeeilnnprrtt
interpenetrable
abeeeeilnnprsss
inseperableness
abeeeeilnrrsstv
retrievableness
abeeeelnnprssst
presentableness
abeeefgilnnrrss
refrangibleness
abeeefhhlmorstt
star-of-Bethlehem
abeeefilnrrsstu
irrefutableness
abeeeginnorrssv
overbearingness
abeeehiilnnpprs
inapprehensible
abeeehilmnrsstt
re-establishment
abeeehilnnpprsu
unapprehensible
abeeeiilmnprssv
imperviableness
abeeeiinprrssty
Presbyterianise
abeeeillnnorsst
intolerableness
abeeeilmnnnrssu
innumerableness
abeeeilmnorrssv
irremovableness
abeeeilnnprrttu
uninterpretable
abeeeilnnprsssu
insuperableness
abeefgiilnnnrss
infrangibleness

abeefiijlnssstu
justifiableness
abeefilnoorsstv
self-observation
abeeghinnoqstuu
banqueting-house
abeehllnoooppsy
polyphloesboean
abeehoprrsssttu
substratosphere
abeeiiiilllmnsst
illimitableness
abeeiiilmnprtty
impenetrability
abeeiimnprrssty
Presbyterianism
abeeinnsssstuv
substantiveness
abeelnopprsssttu
supportableness
abeelnorrsstuuy
subterraneously
abefiiiilnrtuvy
unverifiability
abefiilnrrrstty
transferribilty
abehiiiilmprsty
imperishability
abehiinoopprrst
probationership
abeiiillnnrtuvy
invulnerability
abeiiillorrstvy
irresolvability
abeiiilmmnrstuy
immensurability
abeiiilmnnrssst
intransmissible
abeiiilnoqsttuy
questionability
abeiilmnnrssstu
untransmissible
abghilnoooprty
anthropobiology
abhiiilnopsttyy
hypnotisability
abiinorssttuuy
substitutionary
accddkllnooouu
cloud-cuckoo-land
acccdehhiilloop
dolichocephalic
acccdehillnosyy
synecdochically
accceeeelnnorsv
reconvalescence
accceeefllmnops
self-complacence
accceeehillmort
electrochemical
accceegiillloos
ecclesiological
acccefiiknnooty
cockneyfication

acccehhiilmopsy
physicochemical
accceiilnopsttu
conceptualistic
accceiloopprsst
spectroscopical
accciillmooprsy
microscopically
acccilllooppsy
colposcopically
accddeimmnnnoos
second-in-command
accdeeennorssst
consecratedness
accdeehinooopsu
chenopodiaceous
accdeeilmnorsty
electrodynamics
accdeiilnorttvy
contradictively
accdeiiloprssty
perissodactylic
accdfhiiinnoort
chondrification
accdiilnoorrtty
contradictorily
acceeefinnorstu
counterfeisance
acceeegilmnortt
electromagnetic
magneto-electric
acceeehilorrtty
heterocercality
acceeeiilmnrsst
éclaircissement
acceeeillmorrtt
electrometrical
acceeeilmnnoprt
porcelain-cement
acceeffiinosssu
efficaciousness
acceefhiiinopst
speechification
acceefiiilnortt
electrification
acceefiilmnrrtu
circumferential
acceeghilnopsty
psychogenetical
acceeilnorttuvy
counteractively
acceffhiiinnort
Frenchification
acceffiiilnosuy
inefficaciously
accefgiiiinostv
co-significative
accefimnoorrsuu
circumforaneous
accegghhillnstu
Gleichschaltung
acceghiiilnnort
anticholinergic

acceghiiimmnnpr
crimping-machine
acceghiiknpsttw
packet-switching
acceghiilloost
stoechiological
acceghiimnoprry
cinemicrography
acceghiioprrsty
psychogeriatric
acceghilllnooty
technologically
accegiiimmoprtt
micropegmatitic
accegilllnoosyy
synecologically
accehhillmnoopr
chloramphenicol
accehhimoprstyy
chemopsychiatry
accehiillprrtyy
hypercritically
accehiilnorsstt
interscholastic
accehiimnoprsty
psychometrician
accehiimooprrrt
Microchiroptera
accehilllmopstw
well-accomplisht
accehillnoprtyy
pyrotechnically
accehilmoprrsty
psychrometrical
accehinnooprrtt
anthropocentric
accehllmnoostuy
collenchymatous
acceiiilmorsstv
viscosimetrical
acceiiimmnnotuv
incommunicative
acceiilmmnotuvy
communicatively
acceiiloppr ssuy
perspicaciously
acceiimmnnootux
excommunication
acceiimmnnotuuv
uncommunicative
acceilmooprrstu
ultramicroscope
acceimmnoortuxy
excommunicatory
acceinnoooprtuw
owner-occupation
accfiiinoooprrt
corporification
accghiiilloost
stoichiological
accghilllnooory
chronologically
acchhiilmoorstt
lithochromatics
acchhilmoooppst
ophthalmoscopic
acchhinoopprsty
anthropopsychic
acchiilnnorssty
synchronistical
acchiinoprrstty
crypto-Christian
accijllnnootuy
conjunctionally
accilmooprrstuy
ultramicroscopy
accinooorrssttv
vasoconstrictor
acddeeeelnprrsu
supercalendered
acddeeeffinssst
disaffectedness
acddeehiillrsuy
dieselhydraulic
acddeeinnossttv
Second-adventist
acddeiimmnnoost
discommendation
acddhiimnorstyy
hydrodynamicist
acddiiiiilnstuv
individualistic
acdeeeeffhinprs
phase-difference
acdeeeghiknnrrt
kitchen-gardener
acdeeeghilorrtt
cigarette-holder
acdeeegilnorrrt
director-general
acdeeegklmnnotw
acknowledgement
acdeeehllorttuy
eleutherodactyl
acdeeeiimnprssv
manic-depressive
acdeeeilnnnssst
clandestineness
acdeeeimnnnrstt
disentrancement
acdeeeinnorssst
considerateness
acdeeeiprrrrstu
scripture-reader
acdeefgilnrsssu
disgracefulness
acdeefiiinorstt
desertification
acdeeghiilopstt
dephlogisticate
acdeeghiippprsu
pseudepigraphic
acdeegiiillmoop
epidemiological
acdeegillloosty
dysteleological
acdeehilmnorrsy
dysmenorrhealic
acdeehimnoorstu
echinodermatous
acdeehllopprrsu
shoulder-clapper
acdeehloorsttuy
heterodactylous
acdeeiiinnsstvv
vindicativeness
acdeeiilnnorsty
inconsiderately
acdeeiilnorstvy
considerativel
acdeeiinnoorrst
reconsideration
acdeeillnpprruy
perpendicularly
acdeeimmnorstuy
semi-documentary
acdeeimorrrrsuu
armoured-cruiser
acdeeinnprssstu
unpractisedness
acdeelmoorrsstu
sclerodermatous
acdefiiiimnnnot
indemnification
acdefiiiinnortt
denitrification
acdefiiiinorstv
diversification
acdefiiiinorttv
devitrification
acdefiiilmnostu
demulsification
acdefiiilnnostv
self-vindication
acdefiiilnnotty
confidentiality
acdeghiiiillmnnr
drilling-machine
acdeghilmoprsty
dermatoglyphics
acdehhlmmooosuy
homochlamydeous
acdehiillmostty
methodistically
acdehiinopssttu
unsophisticated
acdehlmmnooosuy
monochlamydeous
acdeiiilmnnoort
omnidirectional
acdeiiilnorrsty
discretionarily
acdeiiinnnoorst
inconsideration
acdeiilnnooorst
reconsolidation
acdeiilnooorstu
decolourisation
acdeilnnnorstuy
unconstrainedly
acdeimnnoooorsu
andromonoecious

acdghimnnooprry
gynandromorphic
acdgiiinnnoort
air-conditioning
acdgiilllosstyy
dyslogistically
acdhhiinooprssy
hypochondriasis
acdiiinnnoosttu
discontinuation
acdiillnnnootuy
unconditionally
aceeeeegilnrrrv
receiver-general
aceeeegilnorttv
electronegative
aceeeffilnnsstu
ineffectualness
aceeefhimnnnrst
enfranchisement
aceeeghimnnnrtt
interchangement
aceeeghinnoprtt
parthenogenetic
aceeegiillnortt
intercollegiate
aceeegiinrrssst
crease-resisting
aceeegimnoprstt
spermatogenetic
aceeehhhlnooprx
hexachlorophene
aceeehillmnrtuy
hermeneutically
aceeehilnnpprrs
pencil-sharpener
aceeehnorrssstu
treacherousness
aceeeiilllnsttu
intellectualise
aceeeilnorrsstv
correlativeness
aceeeilnpssstuv
speculativeness
aceeeimmnoprssu
menispermaceous
aceeeinnnrssssu
unnecessariness
aceeeinnqrsstuy
sesquicentenary
aceeeinoprrsstv
procreativeness
aceefghimnrrstt
stretching-frame
aceefgilmnnrstu
smelting-furnace
aceefgilnrrttuu
ultracentrifuge
aceefhlnoprrssu
reproachfulness
aceefiiilmnoptx
exemplification
aceefiillnopstx
self-explication
aceefiilnprsssu
superficialness
aceefilnorsttuu
tentaculiferous
aceegghhiiimnnw
weighing-machine
aceeggiillnnort
training-college
aceeghlmooprrty
electromyograph
aceegiillmoopst
epistemological
aceegillnnootty
ontogenetically
aceehhiilmmnntt
nemathelminthic
aceehiilllllnsty
hellenistically
aceehiillmnrsty
hemicrystalline
aceehiillmpstuy
euphemistically
aceehiilmnnopst
phenomenalistic
aceehiinooprrrs
prairie-schooner
aceehiknooppsst
phenakistoscope
aceehillnopsssu
lissencephalous
aceehiloorrssst
atherosclerosis
aceehlmmnnootww
new-Commonwealth
aceeiiilmoprrst
isoperimetrical
aceeiiinqssstuv
acquisitiveness
aceeiijnnorrtty
interjectionary
aceeiilllmnsttu
intellectualism
aceeiilllnstttu
intellectualist
aceeiilllntttuy
intellectuality
aceeiilnnnoostv
conventionalise
aceeiilnnnoqstu
inconsequential
aceeilllmnossuy
miscellaneously
aceeilllmnottuu
multinucleolate
aceeillmmnoprty
complementarily
aceeillmnopttvy
contemplatively
aceeillnnoptuxy
unexceptionally
aceeillnnoqstuy
consequentially
aceeilmmnoprtty
complementarity
aceeilmmnrsssty
symmetricalness
aceeilnnnnossss
nonsensicalness
aceeilnooprtuvy
uncooperatively
unco-operatively
aceeimnnooprtty
contemporaneity
aceeimnnorrrstu
resurrection-man
aceeinooprsstvv
provocativeness
aceeinorrrrstuy
resurrectionary
aceellnoopprrrt
contrapropeller
aceelnnnoosstuy
consentaneously
aceemnnnoooprstu
contemporaneous
aceennnnoosstuu
unconsentaneous
aceffiiinoorrtt
refortification
acefgiiiiinnstv
insignificative
acefgiiiilnstvy
significatively
acefhiilmnoqrsu
marsh-cinquefoil
acefiiiinnnostt
intensification
acefiiinnooprst
personification
acefiilmnnoosss
confessionalism
acefiilnnoossst
confessionalist
acegghhioopprty
phytogeographic
acegghiiimnnnrw
wringing-machine
aceghhiiilmnnrw
whirling-machine
aceghhiioprttyy
Ichthyopterygia
aceghhilnossttw
swathing-clothes
aceghiiikmnnntt
knitting-machine
aceghiiimnnnprt
printing-machine
aceghiilmnnostt
slotting-machine
aceghilllnoopry
phrenologically
aceghilmnoorsst
schoolmastering
aceghimmooprrtt
photogrammetric
aceghlloopsuyyz
zygophyllaceous

acegiiilmnssttu
metalinguistics
acegiiklnprsstt
sticking-plaster
acegiillmnoorty
goniometrically
acegiilmnoorrtt
trigonometrical
acegiimmnnoosst
commission-agent
acegiinooprsttv
prognosticative
acegilllmnoooty
entomologically
acegilmoorstuvy
cytomegalovirus
aceginooprrssty
crossopterygian
acehhiiloopsstt
theosophistical
acehhilmoorssst
schoolmasterish
acehhinopprsttu
Pithecanthropus
acehhiopprsstty
psychotherapist
acehiiiklnnrstu
unchristianlike
acehiiillnorsst
schillerisation
acehiiimnnoopst
phonemicisation
acehiiinnorstty
Neo-Christianity
acehiijklnppttu
Jack-in-the-pulpit
acehiilllooprty
heliotropically
acehiilloprrsty
prehistorically
acehiiloopsttty
photoelasticity
acehiimmmopstty
sympathomimetic
acehilllnoorsty
holocrystalline
acehillnopsttyy
polysynthetical
acehinooprrsstv
conservatorship
acehinooprrsstw
ancestor-worship
acehinoprrstuyy
neuropsychiatry
acehmnooprsstuy
prosenchymatous
aceiiiinnosttvv
antivivisection
aceiiillmpsssty
pessimistically
aceiiilnnnrssst
intrinsicalness
aceiiilnnoprrtv
interprovincial
aceiilllnnoorty
intercolonially
aceiilmnnnoostv
conventionalism
aceiilnnnoosttv
conventionalist
aceiilnnnoottvy
conventionality
aceiilnnoorsttu
interosculation
aceiilnooprssst
processionalist
aceiilnprrsttvy
transcriptively
aceiilpprssttuy
superplasticity
aceiimnnoorsstv
conversationism
aceiimnooprsttu
computerisation
aceiinnoorssttv
conservationist
conversationist
aceiinnorrrstuy
insurrectionary
aceiinnorrrtttu
counter-irritant
aceilllnoprstyy
polycrystalline
aceillmmnrstuyy
unsymmetrically
aceillmnnoorsty
monocrystalline
aceillnoorrstvy
controversially
aceilmmmnoorsty
monosymmetrical
aceilmmnnoprtuy
uncomplimentary
aceilnnoorrstuv
uncontroversial
aceinnoorrsssuv
carnivorousness
acelnoooopprrstu
counter-proposal
acelprrrssttuuu
superstructural
acffhhiimmnorst
fifth-monarchism
acffhhiimnorstt
fifth-monarchist
acfgiiiilnnnsty
insignificantly
acghhiiiooprrst
historiographic
acghhimoooopprrt
microphotograph
photomicrograph
acghhinoooopprtz
photozincograph
acghhlmoooprrxy
chromoxylograph
acghhlooopppstyy
psychopathology
acghiiiillnpstuv
victualling-ship
acghiiilloopsyy
physiologically
acghilloooooptyz
zoophytological
acghiloopprtxyy
xylotypographic
acgiilllllosstyy
syllogistically
acgiillmnnnopuy
uncomplainingly
acgiimmnooprrsu
microsporangium
acgiinnoooprstt
prognostication
acgilloooooprtz
protozoological
achhhhmnoprrsuy
Rhamphorhynchus
achhiilllooppsy
philosophically
achhiillnooppsu
unphilosophical
achhiinooprssty
psychohistorian
achhimnoooopprrt
anthropomorphic
achhiooprrsttyy
orthopsychiatry
achiiimoosssssst
schistosomiasis
achiillmoooprrt
allotriomorphic
achiimnoooppstt
compotationship
achiinnnoorssty
synchronisation
achmnnnoorrttuy
north-countryman
aciiilnnopqttuu
quintuplication
aciilmmnooopsst
cosmopolitanism
aciilmnnoosstuy
sanctimoniously
adddeeehnnnrssu
underhandedness
adddeefhilmoort
middle-of-the-road
addeeeehlnrrtty
tender-heartedly
addeeeeilmnrrst
Middle-Easterner
addeeeghhilnsst
light-headedness
addeeeghnnorssw
wrong-headedness
addeeehiknnrsst
kind-heartedness
addeeghhinnrsst
right-handedness
addeegnnoorsstu
good-naturedness

addeeiiilnrsstu
deindustrialise
addeggiinnnorww
window-gardening
addeghhinoostwy
woody-nightshade
addegilnnnrstuy
understandingly
adeeeeefhnrrsst
free-heartedness
adeeeehnnoprsst
open-heartedness
adeeeehnrrssttu
true-heartedness
adeeeeimnrrsttv
readvertisement
adeeefghllrsstu
self-slaughtered
adeeefiillnqstu
field-sequential
adeeeghillnrsty
single-heartedly
adeeeghinnrssst
near-sightedness
adeeegiinnorstt
degenerationist
adeeegilmnnnstt
disentanglement
adeeegklnnortuw
nature-knowledge
adeeegmmnrrrstu
sergeant-drummer
adeeehiioprrsst
sphaerosiderite
adeeeiilmnnrtty
indeterminately
adeeeiimnnorrtt
redetermination
adeeelllmnoptvy
developmentally
adeeffiiinnortt
differentiation
adeeffimnorsstt
disafforestment
adeefiiinrrsttt
interstratified
adeefiilnnoopst
self-opinionated
adeefiilnnqssuu
unqualifiedness
adeefiinnsssstu
unsatisfiedness
adeefillnorssuv
ill-favouredness
adeefilnssssttu
distastefulness
adeefnoorrrssvw
overforwardness
adeegghilnprstu
sleeping-draught
adeegghinopsssu
pedagoguishness
adeeggmmnorrttu
Götterdämmerung

adeeghiilnnrsty
dishearteningly
adeegiilnnpssss
displeasingness
adeegiimnooorrt
radiogoniometer
adeegioprrsttuy
daguerreotypist
adeehiiillmnnty
dimethylaniline
adeeiiiilnorsstv
desilverisation
adeeiiimnnnortt
indetermination
adeeiiinorrttvv
nitro-derivative
adeeiimnnnorttu
undetermination
adeeiimnnoprttu
unpremeditation
adeeiimnnorsttu
underestimation
adeeiimnnrrsstu
rudimentariness
adeeiinpsssttuv
disputativeness
adeeilmnorsttvy
demonstratively
adeeimnnorsttuv
undemonstrative
adeennoprrssstt
transportedness
adeennorssstuuv
adventurousness
adeffhinnossst
stand-offishness
adefgiiillnqstu
self-liquidating
adefinnnoosttu
foundation-stone
adeggghinnorrtu
gathering-ground
adeghllmorrtuyy
hydrometallurgy
adegiiiinnorttt
interdigitation
adegiiioprrsttt
prestidigitator
adegiinnorssstt
dressing-station
adegillnnoqrtuy
grandiloquently
adehhiilnnooprt
ornithodelphian
adehhiimmoprrst
hermaphroditism
adehhilmooprstu
edriophthalmous
adehiiilmooprst
diaheliotropism
adehiiinooprsst
spheroidisation
adehlnorrsttwwy
north-westwardly

adehlorssttuwwy
south-westwardly
adeiijlnprrstuu
jurisprudential
adeiilnorrsttvy
dorsiventrality
adeiinnooprrstu
superordination
adenoprrrsstuwy
sandwort-spurrey
adggggiiinnnrst
standing-rigging
adghiimnoorrtww
withdrawing-room
adghiinnnostttw
notwithstanding
adhiilmnoorssuy
disharmoniously
adhiimooopprstt
diaphototropism
adiiiinoqrsstuy
disquisitionary
adiilnooopprrst
disproportional
adilnoooopprtty
Polyprotodontia
admnoooosssttu
odontostomatous
aeeeegiklnprssu
pleasure-seeking
aeeeegllnrrryyy
greenery-yallery
aeeeeiilmnprstx
experimentalise
aeeeeiimnprttvx
experimentative
aeeeeilnnprrrtu
entrepreneurial
aeeeeimnnprsstt
intemperateness
aeeeeinnprssttv
penetrativeness
aeeefiilmnprrst
preferentialism
aeeefiilnprrstt
preferentialist
aeeeflllorrtvw
fellow-traveller
aeeegginnopprss
passenger-pigeon
aeeegglnnoorrrv
governor-general
aeeeghinnoprsst
parthenogenesis
aeeegikllmnnntu
ungentlemanlike
aeeegillmnnnsst
gentlemanliness
aeeegilmnnnrttt
intertanglement
aeeegilnnpprrst
sleeping-partner
aeeegilnnrssstv
everlastingness

aeeegimnoprssst
spermatogenesis
aeeehhilmmnnstt
Nemathelminthes
aeeehhilmnoppst
Mephistophelean
aeeehiimnpprssv
misapprehensive
aeeehilorsttuxy
heterosexuality
aeeeiiilmnprstx
experientialism
aeeeiiilnprsttx
experientialist
aeeeiilmmnprstx
experimentalism
aeeeiilmnprsttx
experimentalist
aeeeiimnnoprttx
experimentation
aeeeiinnnsstttv
inattentiveness
aeeeiinnoprsstv
inoperativeness
aeeeilnprssstuv
superlativeness
aeeeimnoprrsstx
extemporariness
aeeelmnoqrrsssu
quarrelsomeness
aeefgimnnrrsttu
transfigurement
aeefhhllnnsstuu
unhealthfulness
aeefiilnooprsss
professionalise
aeefilmnnssstu
self-sustainment
aeefiloprrrsttu
self-portraiture
aeefnnnorssttuu
unfortunateness
aeegghhoopprrty
phytogeographer
aeeghhlooprtty
phototelegraphy
telephotography
aeeghhmooprrtty
hyetometrograph
aeeghimnnorrsuz
Erziehungsroman
aeeghinnooprsst
anthropogenesis
aeeghnnooprrtty
röntgenotherapy
aeegiilnorrttvy
interrogatively
aeegiinnoorrrtt
reinterrogation
aeegiinorrssttt
gastroenteritis
aeegikmnpprsttu
speaking-trumpet
aeegilnoorrrsst
retrogressional
aeegilnrrssstvy
transgressively
aeegimnnnoorsst
sensation-monger
aeegmnnoprrttvy
party-government
aeegnooprrssttv
provost-sergeant
aeehhhillnnoppt
phenolphthalein
aeehhiilmnoppst
Mephistophelian
aeehhillmnpstty
Platyhelminthes
aeehiilmoopsttu
epitheliomatous
aeehiimnnopprss
misapprehension
aeehiklnnoprtuy
phenylketonuria
aeehinnorssstuw
unseaworthiness
aeeiiinoorrsttx
exteriorisation
aeeiilnnopprtty
plenipotentiary
aeeiimnnoprsstt
presentationism
aeeiimnooprsttx
extemporisation
aeeiinnoprssttt
presentationist
aeeiinoprrssttv
preservationist
aeeillmnpprstuy
supplementarily
aeeillnnoprrsty
interpersonally
aeeillnnoprstty
septentrionally
aeeilmnnooppruu
pleuro-pneumonia
aeeilmnnoppsttu
supplementation
aeeimnnoopprrtt
reapportionment
aeeimnnoprssttu
importunateness
aeeimqrrrsssttu
quartermistress
aeeinnoprssttu
unprotestantise
aeeinoqrrsssstu
quarter-sessions
aeennnoopsssstu
spontaneousness
aefghillllnnostw
half-wellingtons
aefgillllllorwwy
wall-gillyflower
aefhhiinorssttw
faithworthiness
aefhiiillmnostu
self-humiliation
aefiiiillmnnsty
infinitesimally
aefiilllnnoopst
self-pollination
aefiilmnooprsss
professionalism
aefiimmnooprrst
preformationism
aefiimnooprrstt
preformationist
aefilnnnooprss
non-professional
aeflooprsttuuu
paulo-post-future
aegghillnoorsty
shooting-gallery
aeghhiiooprrrst
historiographer
aegiiimnnnrsstt
intransigentism
aegiiinnnrssttt
intransigentist
aegilmnnorrstty
remonstratingly
aehhiimnoprrstt
therianthropism
aehhiiopprsstty
physiotherapist
aehhiknnorssttw
thankworthiness
aehiiknnrrssstt
shrink-resistant
aehiimmnnooprst
enantiomorphism
aehimnnoooprstu
enantiomorphous
aeiilllnoqrtuvy
ventriloquially
aeiillnnnnottuy
unintentionally
aeiillnoopprsty
prepositionally
aeiilloopprrrty
proprietorially
aeiilmmnnrssttu
instrumentalism
aeiilmnnrsstttu
instrumentalist
aeiilmnnrstttuy
instrumentality
aeiilnnnorsstuv
involuntariness
aeiimnnnorstttu
instrumentation
aeiklmnnoprsstu
unsportsmanlike
aeilnoooopprrtty
proportionately
aeinnoooopprrttu
unproportionate
afggiimnnorrsty
transmogrifying

afgiikmnnnooprt
non-profit-making
aghhhilooopprtt
photolithograph
aghhillmooopstt
ophthalmologist
aghhinooopssttu
opisthognathous
aghhlooopprtxyy
photoxylography
aghhoooppprrtyy
pyrophotography
agiilmmnoossttu
numismatologist
ahhilnoooppprsty
phosphorylation
ahhinoooppprsstt
anthroposophist
aiiiillnoqrstuy
inquisitorially
aiiillnnostttuy
institutionally
aiiilnoopprstty
propylitisation
aiilllmnopssuuy
pusillanimously
aiillnooppsstuy
suppositionally
aiilnoooppprrtty
proportionality
bbbbeefgiiilrtt
flibbertigibbet
bbcdeeiilorsttu
biodestructible
bbceeilmnossstu
combustibleness
bbddeehhhloooy
hobbledehoyhood
bbeeefhiillorty
lob-lie-by-the-fire
bbehilmmmooorst
thrombo-embolism
bcccdeiimnrrsuu
uncircumscribed
bcceeeiilmnnosu
bioluminescence
bcceeeimnnprsuu
superincumbence
bcdddeellnoooss
cold-bloodedness
bcdeeeiilnrrssu
irreducibleness
bcdeiiiilrrttuy
irreductibility
bcdeiiilrstttuy
destructibility
bceeeeilmnnnoov
omnibenevolence
bceeegiillnnstu
subintelligence
bceeegilnnoopst
boning-telescope
bceeeiijnrsttuv
intersubjective
bceeeilnpsssstu
susceptibleness
bceeejlmmorrtuy
jerry-come-tumble
bceeghiimoorsty
biogeochemistry
bceegiimmnnosss
misbecomingness
bceehhhioprrrst
herb-Christopher
bceeiiilmpprrst
imprescriptible
bceeiiillnnosttu
subintellection
bceeijoprrsstuu
subject-superior
bceeilnoprrsstu
corruptibleness
bcefhilorrsttuy
butterfly-orchis
bcehiiiiinosttx
exhibitionistic
bceiiilmnoptty
contemptibility
bceiiilmoprssty
compressibility
bceiimmnoorsssu
subcommissioner
bcghiiloopssty
psychobiologist
bcgiiiiilnorrty
incorrigibility
bcinnnooorrttuy
non-contributory
bddeeeilmnnnoss
noble-mindedness
bddeeeimnnorsss
sober-mindedness
bdeeeefimnnoort
before-mentioned
bdeefiiiilnnsty
indefensibility
bdeeflmmnoorruy
ferro-molybdenum
bdeeiiiilnnsssv
indivisibleness
bdeggiiilnnosss
disobligingness
bdegiiiiilnstty
indigestibility
bdegiillnoosstu
blood-guiltiness
bdffiiilmnnoruu
infundibuliform
bdiiiiillnosstuy
indissolubility
beeeehiilnprrrs
irreprehensible
beeegnooorrssty
gooseberry-stone
beeehiilnprrrsy
irreprehensibly
beeeiinnnorrttz
trinitrobenzene
beeelmnoorssstu
troublesomeness
beefflorrttuwy
butterfly-flower
beegggiinnoqstu
question-begging
beeghiilnnorssu
neighbourliness
beehiiinoprsstv
prohibitiveness
beeiiiilnnsttxy
inextensibility
beeiiiilrrrstvy
irreversibility
beeiinnorssstuv
inobtrusiveness
beeinnorssstuuv
unobtrusiveness
befilmoorrsstuu
strombuliferous
beghilnooorsttu
troubleshooting
begiiiiilllntty
intelligibility
begiiillnrsttuu
subintelligitur
behhmnoopprrryy
rhombenporphyry
beiiiiilmrrssty
irremissibility
beiiiiilrrsstty
irresistibility
beinoooprrsssu
opprobriousness
cccdklnoooottuuw
cloud-cuckoo-town
ccceeehilnorstt
electrotechnics
ccceefinnooprs
conscience-proof
ccceehhiikklrst
Schrecklichkeit
ccceehlmoosttyy
cholecystectomy
ccceeiilmnoorrt
microelectronic
ccceeiklloorttt
ticket-collector
ccceeimnprssstu
circumspectness
cccegiiiknnoquv
quick-conceiving
ccceiiimmoorrru
micromicrocurie
ccceiiimnnorssu
circumincession
ccceiiimprrstuv
circumscriptive
ccceinnooossssu
coconsciousness
ccciiimnoprrstu
circumscription
ccddeegilnnnosy
condescendingly

ccdeeeeinnortuv
counter-evidence
ccdeeeellnorsst
recollectedness
ccdeeennnnorssu
unconcernedness
ccdeeinoprstuuv
superconductive
ccdeennorrsttuu
unreconstructed
ccdegilllmnoopu
cloud-compelling
ccdeginnoprstuu
superconducting
ccdehinooopttuv
photoconductive
ccdeiiimnoorsst
microdissection
ccdghinnoooptt u
photoconducting
cceeeeellnprsux
superexcellence
cceeeeflnnoqssu
self-consequence
cceeeffgiiinorv
receiving-office
cceeehhnoopprss
phosphorescence
cceeehilmorrstt
electrothermics
cceeehiloopprtt
electrophoretic
cceeeiiklnorstt
electrokinetics
cceeeiilmnnorrt
irreconcilement
cceeeillmnoorst
mole-electronics
cceeeinnossstuv
consecutiveness
cceeelnssssssu
successlessness
cceefffiilnssuy
self-sufficiency
cceefilnnosssty
self-consistency
cceehhiinoprstz
schizophrenetic
cceehiiimoorstt
stoicheiometric
cceeiilnoopprst
police-inspector
cceeiiloprrttyy
pyro-electricity
cceeiinnnnoortt
interconnection
cceeijnnnosstuv
conjunctiveness
cceeilnoooprstt
optoelectronics
cceeinorrsttuuy
counter-security
ccefginoooprrrt
proof-correcting
ccefilnnoosssuu
unselfconscious
ccefinoooprrrt
proof-correction
cceghilmnooorty
microtechnology
ccehhimoprsstyy
psychochemistry
ccehiimmoopssty
psychosomimetic
ccehiimmoopstty
psychotomimetic
ccehilnoooprsst
school-inspector
ccehlmooossttyy
cholecystostomy
cceiiiimnoorrst
oneirocriticism
cceiiilrrssttuu
sericiculturist
cceiiimnnorsssu
circuminsession
cceiilnnoosstuy
conscientiously
cceiinnnoosstuu
unconscientious
cceinnnoossssuu
unconsciousness
cceinnooprrsttu
preconstruction
cceinnoopssssuu
conspicuousness
ccgiiiilnoosstu
sociolinguistic
cchhiioppssstyy
psychophysicist
cchinoooprsstyy
onychocryptosis
cciiinnooprsstt
conscriptionist
cciilnnoopssuuy
inconspicuously
cciimnnoorssttu
constructionism
misconstruction
ccimmnooprsttuy
crypto-communist
cdddegiinnoooot
good-conditioned
cddeeeeeinnnprt
interdependence
cddeeeelnnprtuy
unprecedentedly
cddeeeiimnopprr
medicine-dropper
cddeefiiinnorrt
direction-finder
cddeehklooorrsu
crook-shouldered
cddeeiiillnnootw
well-conditioned
cddeelmnnopssuu
seconds-pendulum
cddeghiiilmnstt
middle-stitching
cddeinnooprrtuu
under-production
cddiilmmooossuy
discommodiously
cdeeeeeflnnssss
defencelessness
cdeeeeinnnprstu
superintendence
cdeeeffiknnssst
stiff-neckedness
cdeeefilrssttuv
self-destructive
cdeeeflnoorrtuw
counter-flowered
cdeeeginnorstuu
secundogeniture
cdeeehnnorrttuu
under-the-counter
cdeeeiinprssstv
descriptiveness
cdeeeimnnprstuu
superinducement
cdeeeinnnprstuy
superintendency
cdeeeinrsssttuv
destructiveness
cdeeennoprssttu
unprotectedness
cdeeennpssssttuu
unsuspectedness
cdeeffillnnosty
self-confidently
cdeefgiilnnorss
self-considering
cdeefillprsstuy
disrespectfully
cdeefilnorssttu
self-destruction
cdeefilnossttu
self-constituted
cdeeghimnnnopru
uncomprehending
cdeegiiimmnortt
riding-committee
cdeegilnooprstw
powdering-closet
cdeeiiinnssttv
distinctiveness
cdeeiiknqssttuw
quick-wittedness
cdeeilnnorsssuu
incredulousness
cdeeimnnoopsssu
compendiousness
cdeelmnnoooosty
Monocotyledones
cdeelnnooprrsty
correspondently
cdefilmnoooprrs
scolopendriform
cdeghiinooprrty
chondropterygii

cdegiilmnoprtuu
picture-moulding
cdegilnnooprrsy
correspondingly
cdehhiiloorttuy
ichthyodorulite
cdehhiiloorttyy
ichthyodorylite
cdehikmnooprrtu
durchkomponiert
cdeiiiilnnsttvy
indistinctively
cdeiiijnnosssuu
injudiciousness
cdeiimmnnnoooss
non-commissioned
cdhiilnoprstuuu
pulchritudinous
cdiiiinossstuuv
vicissitudinous
cdiilnnoosstuuy
discontinuously
ceeeeffiinnsstv
ineffectiveness
ceeeehhnoprrttw
threepenceworth
ceeeeinnopprsst
sense-perception
ceeefiimnorrrtt
interferometric
ceeeflnorrsssuu
resourcefulness
ceeegiiillmnnst
misintelligence
ceeeginoprrsssw
crossing-sweeper
ceeehiimnnoprsv
incomprehensive
ceeehiimnoprssv
comprehensivise
ceeehilmnoprsvy
comprehensively
ceeehiloprrsst
electrophoresis
ceeehimnnoprsuv
uncomprehensive
ceeehimorrsstty
stereochemistry
ceeeiiloprsttv
electropositive
ceeeiimnopssttv
competitiveness
ceeeiimnorrsttu
recrementitious
ceeeiimnorsttux
excrementitious
ceeeiinoprrrstu
resurrection-pie
ceeeiinorrrsstu
resurrectionise
ceeeiloprrsttvy
retrospectively
ceeeimnnoorsssu
ceremoniousness

ceeeinnossssstu
necessitousness
ceeeinopprssstv
prospectiveness
ceeeinpqrssstuu
picturesqueness
ceeeioprrrrsttu
picture-restorer
ceeemmnnoorttuv
counter-movement
ceeenooqrrrttuv
torque-converter
ceeenoprrrsstuu
counter-pressure
ceefhiimnoprsss
Sphenisciformes
ceefinnoprrsstu
perfunctoriness
ceeflmnoorsssst
comfortlessness
ceehhimmorrstty
thermochemistry
ceehiimnnnooprs
incomprehension
ceehiimnosssuv
mischievousness
ceehiklnnoprtuy
phenylketonuric
ceehllnoooppry
polychloroprene
ceeiiiillmmmorrt
micromillimetre
ceeiiinoprssstx
expressionistic
ceeiimnorrrsstu
resurrectionism
ceeiinnorrrsttt
rent-restriction
ceeiinnrssttuv
instructiveness
ceeiinopprssstu
precipitousness
ceeiinorrrsstu
resurrectionist
ceeiinpssttuuv
intussusceptive
ceeiknoprrsttvy
poverty-stricken
ceeilmnnoorsuuy
unceremoniously
ceeimnnopssstuv
consumptiveness
ceeinnnoosssttu
contentiousness
ceeinopprssssuu
perspicuousness
ceffiiinnoosssu
inofficiousness
cefghhiilnnoprs
French-polishing
cegghilnoooorst
geochronologist
ceghilmnooostuy
ethnomusicology

cegiikmnnnorsss
morning-sickness
ceginnnoorsssuu
incongruousness
cehhimmnoooppr s
morphophonemics
cehiilmnrrsstty
Christy-minstrel
cehiimmmnorstuy
immunochemistry
cehiinnooprsssu
connoisseurship
cehnnnoorssssuy
synchronousness
ceiiiimnoprssst
impressionistic
ceiiilnoqrsttuv
ventriloquistic
ceiiimnorrsstu
insurrectionism
ceiiinnorrssttu
insurrectionist
ceiilnnopssstuu
punctiliousness
ceiilorrssttuu
ostreiculturist
ceiinnooprssttu
introsusception
ceiinnopssttuu
intussusception
ceilloprrsttuuw
pillow-structure
chhhinnoorrstuy
ornithorhynchus
chhhiooooppr rst
orthophosphoric
chillmoooppr rsy
microsporophyll
ciiimoorrsstuvy
myristicivorous
ciiinnoosstttu
constitutionist
dddeehlnoorrsuu
round-shouldered
ddeeeeiimnnnpst
semi-independent
ddeeeellorswwyy
dyer's-yellowweed
ddeeegiilnprruv
under-privileged
ddeeeiilnrsstty
disinterestedly
ddeeghiilmnnsst
light-mindedness
ddeeghiimnnrsst
right-mindedness
ddeehillopprssu
shoulder-slipped
ddeghiiinnsstuu
undistinguished
ddehilnoorttuww
world-without-end
deeeeehnnnrstuv
seventeen-hunder

deeeehnoprrstuy
superheterodyne
deeeeilnorssstu
deleteriousness
deeeelmnooprtvv
overdevelopment
deeefgiilmnnrst
self-determining
deeehlllоprstuw
well-upholstered
deeeiillnnnottw
well-intentioned
deeeiinopssstux
expeditiousness
deeeinnnosssttu
tendentiousness
deeelmmnnoprtuy
under-employment
deefhlmnoosstuu
foul-mouthedness
deefilnrssssstu
distressfulness
deefinooorrsssu
odoriferousness
deeflnooprssstu
dessertspoonful
deegghilnnossst
long-sightedness
deeggimnnnoorrw
wonder-mongering
deegiilmnoosstt
sedimentologist
deegillooopprty
lepidopterology
deehhlnoorssttu
shoulder-shotten
deehiiknnnnssst
thin-skinnedness
deehiilopprrsvw
devil-worshipper
deeiiilnoprsstt
stilpnosiderite
deeiilmnnrtttuy
unintermittedly
deeiilnoprssstw
low-spiritedness
deeilnnprrttuuy
uninterruptedly
defghiloprsstty
softly-sprighted
defilnrsssstttuu
distrustfulness
deghhiiilnrrsvw
whirling-dervish
deghiiimnnsstu
distinguishment
deghiilnoopprsw
polishing-powder
dehhiimoprrstyy
hyperthyroidism
dehhilnooоprstu
ornithodelphous
deiiillmnnosstu
disillusionment
deiiimmnnoprsst
disimprisonment
deiimnoooopprrst
misproportioned
diillmnosttuuuy
multitudinously
eeeeghlnoorstuy
heterogeneously
eeeeiinnnpsssvx
inexpensiveness
eeeeiinnrrssttv
irretentiveness
eeeelmnorrsssss
remorselessness
eeeemnnorssstuv
venturesomeness
eeeffiinnnosssv
inoffensiveness
eeefgiimnrrtuxz
freezing-mixture
eeefgilnorsstvy
self-sovereignty
eeefhmmnoorrrst
refreshment-room
eeefilmmnoprstv
self-improvement
eeeghmnnooosssu
homogeneousness
eeegiimnnoprrsv
evening-primrose
eeegiinnnrssstt
interestingness
eeegilnnnnrsstu
unrelentingness
eeegilorrrsstvy
retrogressively
eeeginoprrssssv
progressiveness
eeehhnnoprrttwy
threepennyworth
eeehiimpprrstuv
heir-presumptive
eeehiinpprrrstt
interpretership
eeehlmnnoosssuw
unwholesomeness
eeeiiinnnssstv
insensitiveness
eeeiimmoorrssst
stereoisomerism
eeeiinoprsssttu
repetitiousness
eeeinnnosssttu
sententiousness
eeeinnoprssttu
pretentiousness
eeelnopprsssssu
purposelessness
eeemnopsssttuu
tempestuousness
eefffglllorstuy
self-forgetfully
eefghiiilloottw
gillie-whitefoot
eefimnoorrssstu
mortiferousness
eeflnoprssssuuu
superfluousness
eeghhlnossssttu
thoughtlessness
eeghilmnnooopst
phenomenologist
eeghinnorssstuu
unrighteousness
eegiiilnorrsssu
irreligiousness
eegiilnnnrsttuy
uninterestingly
eegiimnnnrssttu
unremittingness
eegiimnorsstuuv
seeming-virtuous
eegiinnorssstuv
vertiginousness
eegilnopprssssy
prepossessingly
eegilnoprrssuvy
unprogressively
eeginnopprssssu
unprepossessing
eehiinooprssstt
photosensitiser
eehlnoprssssuuu
sulphureousness
eeiiiinnqssstuv
inquisitiveness
eeiiimnnnorsttv
interventionism
eeiiinnnorstttv
interventionist
eeiilnnoorrtttu
trinitrotoluene
eeiimnoorrssstu
meritoriousness
eeiinnnnnoorttv
non-intervention
eeimnnoooppprrs
properispomenon
eeinnnoopprsstu
inopportuneness
effiilnoorsssuu
unfossiliferous
efggiinnnorssuv
unforgivingness
efggilnnortttuu
flutter-tonguing
efilmnrsssstuu
mistrustfulness
egghilmoooоprst
geomorphologist
eghhiillmnoostt
helminthologist
eghilnoooprsuyy
neurophysiology
egiiilnnrstttwy
intertwistingly
ehhiimoooprrsst
theriomorphosis

15 EHI

ehinorrssstttuw
  trustworthiness
eiiimnoopprsstu
  superimposition
eiillmmnnooortt
  montmorillonite
eiillnorssssstuu
  illustriousness
eiiloprrssttuuy
  surreptitiously
eiiloprssstuuy
  superstitiously
hhhoooopppprssuy
  hypophosphorous
hilnorrstttuuwy
  untrustworthily
iiinnnnoorssttu
  non-intrusionist